# Northern California High Technology Directory

## 31st Edition

*A prospecting database of high-technology companies in Northern California*

**Published by Rich's Business Information**

**Rich's Business Information**

Pearline Jaikumar, *Editor*

\* \* \*

Rich's Business Information is in business to provide the most comprehensive up-to-date information on the high technology industry. This directory is part of a larger database and directory group covering all of California.

While every effort has been made to ensure that the information published in this directory is accurate, Rich's Business Information cannot be held liable or responsible for any errors, omissions or inaccuracies, typographical or otherwise. The companies and information featured in this directory was chosen and researched based on the creative judgement of Rich's staff.

**Published Annually**

**ISBN 978-0-7808-1751-7
Rich's Business Information
615 Griswold St, Suite 520
Detroit, MI 48226
Tel: 800-207-4103**

***www.richsdata.com***

# Table of Contents

# Statistics for 2020

## 4,578 Listings

*76 New Listings*

### By Size (Number of employees)

| | |
|---|---|
| Between 1 and 10 | 1 |
| Between 11 and 25 | 7 |
| Between 26 and 50 | 5 |
| Between 51 and 100 | 17 |
| Between 101 and 250 | 23 |
| Between 251 and 500 | 19 |
| Between 501 and 1000 | 26 |
| 1000+ | 80 |

### By Size (Number of employees)

| | |
|---|---|
| 10 or more | 3 |
| 50 or more | 2 |
| 100 or more | 11 |
| 500 or more | 8 |

### Misc. Statistics:

| | |
|---|---|
| Fax Number Count | 2,941 |
| Email Count | 3,315 |
| Addressess Count | 4,578 |
| Web | 4,537 |
| New Listing | 76 |

### Companies by Product:

| | |
|---|---|
| Biotechnology | 185 |
| Components | 301 |
| Equipment | 1,526 |
| Materials | 54 |
| Services | 1,887 |

### Companies by Function:

| | |
|---|---|
| HQ-Headquarters | 3,950 |
| DH-Division Headquarters | 77 |
| BR-Branch | 455 |
| LH-Local Headquarters | 23 |
| RH-Regional Headquarters | 73 |

### Companies by Year Established:

| | |
|---|---|
| 2016 – 2019 | 7 |
| 2010 – 2015 | 390 |
| 2000 – 2009 | 1,070 |
| 1990 – 1999 | 973 |
| 1980 – 1989 | 667 |
| 1970 – 1979 | 345 |
| Before 1970 | 391 |

## By County (Alphabetically)

| | | | |
|---|---|---|---|
| Alameda | 856 | Nevada | 21 |
| Amador | 2 | Orange | 7 |
| Butte | 27 | Placer | 73 |
| Calaveras | 2 | Sacramento | 178 |
| Contra Costa | 230 | Salt Lake | 1 |
| El Dorado | 36 | San Benito | 8 |
| Fresno | 58 | San Diego | 5 |
| Glenn | 2 | San Francisco | 367 |
| Humboldt | 5 | San Joaquin | 55 |
| Inyo | 1 | San Mateo | 462 |
| King | 1 | Santa Barbara | 2 |
| Kings | 3 | Santa Clara | 1,640 |
| Lake | 3 | Santa Cruz | 72 |
| Los Angeles | 2 | Shasta | 17 |
| Madera | 7 | Siskiyou | 3 |
| Maricopa | 1 | Solano | 55 |
| Marin | 75 | Sonoma | 127 |
| Mariposa | 2 | Stanislaus | 32 |
| Maui | 1 | Sutter | 6 |
| Mendocino | 9 | Tehama | 2 |
| Merced | 6 | Tulare | 13 |
| Modoc | 1 | Tuolumne | 9 |
| Mono | 1 | Yolo | 48 |
| Monterey | 23 | Yuba | 2 |
| Napa | 19 | | |

## By Department Head:

| | |
|---|---|
| President | 756 |
| Vice President | 497 |
| General Manager | 137 |
| CEO | 771 |
| COO | 533 |
| CFO | 533 |
| CTO | 314 |
| Owner | 218 |
| Engineer | 90 |
| Marketing | 604 |
| Marketing/Sales | 174 |
| Sales | 1,194 |
| Purchasing | 74 |
| MIS | 5 |
| Director | 202 |
| Manager | 115 |
| Facility Manager | 16 |
| Board Member | 23 |
| Designer | 15 |
| Controller | 108 |

# Cities

| City | # | County | City | # | County | City | # | County |
|------|---|--------|------|---|--------|------|---|--------|
| Acampo | 1 | San Joaquin | Cotati | 1 | Sonoma | Gold River | 3 | Sacramento |
| Alameda | 30 | Alameda | Cottonwood | 1 | Tehama | Granite Bay | 3 | Placer |
| Alamo | 4 | Contra Costa | Crows Landing | 1 | Stanislaus | Grass Valley | 17 | Nevada |
| Albany | 3 | Alameda | Cupertino | 38 | Santa Clara | Graton | 1 | Sonoma |
| American Canyon | 2 | Napa | Daly City | 3 | San Mateo | Groveland | 1 | Tuolumne |
| Anderson | 1 | Shasta | Danville | 10 | Contra Costa | Half Moon Bay | 6 | San Mateo |
| Angels Camp | 2 | Calaveras | Davis | 24 | Yolo | Hanford | 3 | Kings |
| Antioch | 3 | Contra Costa | Diamond Springs | 5 | El Dorado | Hayward | 100 | Alameda |
| Aptos | 4 | Santa Cruz | Dinuba | 1 | Tulare | Healdsburg | 2 | Sonoma |
| Arcata | 3 | Humboldt | Dixon | 3 | Solano | Hercules | 6 | Contra Costa |
| Auburn | 22 | Placer | Dublin | 15 | Alameda | Hollister | 7 | San Benito |
| Belmont | 8 | San Mateo | East Palo Alto | 1 | Santa Clara | Hughson | 1 | Stanislaus |
| Ben Lomond | 1 | Santa Cruz | El Dorado Hills | 21 | El Dorado | Huntington Beach | 1 | Orange |
| Benicia | 21 | Solano | El Granada | 1 | San Mateo | Irvine | 3 | Orange |
| Berkeley | 62 | Alameda | El Macero | 1 | Yolo | June Lake | 1 | Mono |
| Biola | 1 | Fresno | El Sobrante | 1 | Contra Costa | Kerman | 1 | Fresno |
| Bishop | 1 | Inyo | Elk Grove | 6 | Sacramento | La Mesa | 1 | Placer |
| Brentwood | 4 | Contra Costa | Emerald Hills | 1 | San Mateo | Lafayette | 8 | Contra Costa |
| Brisbane | 13 | San Mateo | Emeryville | 35 | Alameda | Lake Forest | 1 | Lake |
| Browns Valley | 1 | Yuba | Escalon | 2 | San Joaquin | Lakeport | 2 | Lake |
| Burbank | 1 | Los Angeles | Escondido | 1 | Santa Clara | Lincoln | 5 | Placer |
| Burlingame | 30 | San Mateo | Eureka | 2 | Humboldt | Lindsay | 1 | Tulare |
| Byron | 1 | Contra Costa | Exeter | 2 | Tulare | Livermore | 75 | Alameda |
| Cameron Park | 4 | El Dorado | Fair Oaks | 3 | Sacramento | Lodi | 12 | San Joaquin |
| Campbell | 47 | Santa Clara | Fairfax | 1 | Marin | Lone | 1 | Amador |
| Carlsbad | 3 | San Diego | Fairfield | 12 | Solano | Loomis | 2 | Placer |
| Carmel | 1 | Monterey | Felton | 2 | Santa Cruz | Los Altos | 29 | Santa Clara |
| Carmichael | 1 | Sacramento | Folsom | 21 | Sacramento | Los Altos Hills | 5 | Santa Clara |
| Castro Valley | 2 | Alameda | Forestville | 1 | Sonoma | Los Gatos | 28 | Santa Clara |
| Ceres | 3 | Stanislaus | Fort Bragg | 3 | Mendocino | Madera | 6 | Madera |
| Chico | 21 | Butte | Foster City | 21 | San Mateo | Manteca | 3 | San Joaquin |
| Chowchilla | 1 | Madera | Fountain Valley | 1 | Orange | Marina | 3 | Monterey |
| Citrus Heights | 4 | Sacramento | Fowler | 1 | Fresno | Marinez | 1 | Contra Costa |
| Cloverdale | 1 | Sonoma | Freedom | 2 | Santa Cruz | Mariposa | 2 | Mariposa |
| Clovis | 3 | Fresno | Fremont | 269 | Alameda | Martinez | 12 | Contra Costa |
| Colfax | 1 | Placer | Fresno | 46 | Fresno | McClellan | 1 | Sacramento |
| Comptche | 1 | Mendocino | Georgetown | 1 | El Dorado | Menlo Park | 62 | San Mateo |
| Concord | 47 | Contra Costa | Gilroy | 8 | Santa Clara | Merced | 6 | Merced |
| Corte Madera | 3 | Marin | Glen Ellen | 1 | Sonoma | Mesa | 1 | Maricopa |

## Cities

| City | # | County | City | # | County | City | # | County |
|---|---|---|---|---|---|---|---|---|
| Mill Valley | 8 | Marin | Portola Valley | 1 | San Mateo | Seaside | 1 | Monterey |
| Millbrae | 2 | San Mateo | Rancho Cordova | 34 | Sacramento | Sebastopol | 3 | Sonoma |
| Milpitas | 106 | Santa Clara | | | | Selma | 2 | Fresno |
| Mission Viejo | 1 | Orange | Red Bluff | 1 | Tehama | Shingle Springs | 1 | El Dorado |
| Modesto | 17 | Stanislaus | Redding | 16 | Shasta | Sonoma | 5 | Sonoma |
| Moffett Field | 2 | Santa Clara | Redwood City | 90 | San Mateo | Sonora | 7 | Tuolumne |
| Monte Sereno | 1 | Santa Clara | Redwood Shores | 6 | San Mateo | Soquel | 4 | Santa Cruz |
| Monterey | 14 | Monterey | | | | Soulsbyville | 1 | Tuolumne |
| Moraga | 4 | Contra Costa | Redwood Valley | 2 | Mendocino | South Lake Tahoe | 2 | El Dorado |
| Morgan Hill | 48 | Santa Clara | Reedley | 1 | Fresno | | | |
| Moss Beach | 1 | San Mateo | Richmond | 24 | Contra Costa | South Sacramento | 1 | Sacramento |
| Moss Landing | 1 | Monterey | Rio Vista | 1 | Solano | | | |
| Mount Shasta | 1 | Siskiyou | Ripon | 4 | San Joaquin | South San Francisco | 88 | San Mateo |
| Mountain View | 110 | Santa Clara | Rocklin | 19 | Placer | | | |
| Napa | 13 | Napa | Rodeo | 2 | Contra Costa | St. Helena | 4 | Napa |
| Nevada City | 1 | Nevada | Rohnert Park | 13 | Sonoma | Stockton | 24 | San Joaquin |
| Newark | 39 | Alameda | Roseville | 19 | Placer | Suisun | 1 | Solano |
| Newcastle | 1 | Placer | Sacramento | 101 | Sacramento | Suisun City | 1 | Solano |
| Newport Beach | 1 | King | Salida | 3 | Stanislaus | Sunnyvale | 173 | Santa Clara |
| Novato | 19 | Marin | Salinas | 3 | Monterey | Sutter | 1 | Sutter |
| Oakdale | 3 | Stanislaus | San Anselmo | 5 | Marin | Tiburon | 3 | Marin |
| Oakland | 76 | Alameda | San Bruno | 7 | San Mateo | Tollhouse | 1 | Fresno |
| Oakley | 1 | Contra Costa | San Carlos | 45 | San Mateo | Torrance | 1 | Los Angeles |
| Orangevale | 3 | Sacramento | San Diego | 1 | San Diego | Tracy | 9 | San Joaquin |
| Oregon House | 1 | Yuba | San Francisco | 362 | San Francisco | Truckee | 3 | Nevada |
| Orinda | 5 | Contra Costa | San Jose | 584 | Santa Clara | Tulare | 1 | Tulare |
| Orland | 2 | Glenn | San Juan Bautista | 1 | San Benito | Turlock | 4 | Stanislaus |
| Oroville | 3 | Butte | | | | Ukiah | 2 | Mendocino |
| Pacheco | 1 | Contra Costa | San Leandro | 39 | Alameda | Union City | 26 | Alameda |
| Pacifica | 2 | San Mateo | San Martin | 1 | Santa Clara | Vacaville | 13 | Solano |
| Palo Alto | 107 | Santa Clara | San Mateo | 80 | San Mateo | Vallejo | 3 | Solano |
| Paradise | 2 | Butte | San Pablo | 1 | Contra Costa | Visalia | 7 | Tulare |
| Parlier | 1 | Fresno | San Rafael | 30 | Marin | Vista | 1 | San Diego |
| Petaluma | 34 | Sonoma | San Ramon | 45 | Contra Costa | Walnut Creek | 34 | Contra Costa |
| Piedmont | 1 | Alameda | Sanger | 1 | Fresno | Watsonville | 11 | Santa Cruz |
| Pine Grove | 1 | Amador | Santa Ana | 1 | Salt Lake | West Sacramento | 12 | Yolo |
| Pinole | 2 | Contra Costa | Santa Clara | 345 | Santa Clara | | | |
| Pittsburg | 9 | Contra Costa | Santa Cruz | 28 | Santa Cruz | Willits | 1 | Mendocino |
| Placerville | 3 | El Dorado | Santa Rosa | 60 | Sonoma | Windsor | 4 | Sonoma |
| Pleasant Grove | 1 | Sutter | Santra Clara | 1 | Santa Clara | Woodland | 11 | Yolo |
| Pleasant Hill | 4 | Contra Costa | Saratoga | 8 | Santa Clara | Yreka | 2 | Siskiyou |
| Pleasanton | 85 | Alameda | Sausalito | 7 | Marin | Yuba City | 4 | Sutter |
| Point Richmond | 1 | Contra Costa | Scotts Valley | 20 | Santa Cruz | | | |
| Porterville | 1 | Tulare | Seal Beach | 1 | Orange | | | |

# Sample Entry

*Listing data include the following, as applicable and available:*

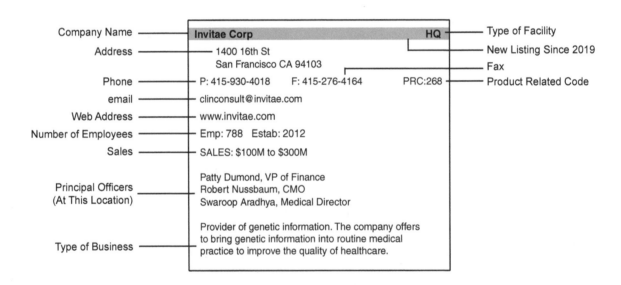

| Company Name | **Invitae Corp** | HQ | Type of Facility |
| Address | 1400 16th St | | New Listing Since 2019 |
| | San Francisco CA 94103 | | Fax |
| Phone | P: 415-930-4018    F: 415-276-4164    PRC:268 | | Product Related Code |
| email | clinconsult@invitae.com | | |
| Web Address | www.invitae.com | | |
| Number of Employees | Emp: 788   Estab: 2012 | | |
| Sales | SALES: $100M to $300M | | |
| Principal Officers (At This Location) | Patty Dumond, VP of Finance<br>Robert Nussbaum, CMO<br>Swaroop Aradhya, Medical Director | | |
| Type of Business | Provider of genetic information. The company offers to bring genetic information into routine medical practice to improve the quality of healthcare. | | |

## FACILITY CLASSIFICATION

**HQ = Headquarters**
**BR = Branch**
**RH = Regional Headquarters**
**DH = Division Headquarters**
**LH = Local Headquarters**

# MAIN INDEX

**10X Genomics Inc**   HQ
6230 Stoneridge Mall Rd
Pleasanton CA 94588-3260
P: 925-401-7300   PRC:34
www.10xgenomics.com
Email: info@10xgenomics.com
Estab: 2012

Ben Hindson, CSO
Serge Saxonov, CEO

Provider of gemcode, instruments, software, and
applications technology for RNA and DNA analysis.

**15five Inc**   HQ
12 Gallagher Lane Ste 279
San Francisco CA 94103
P: 415-967-3483   F: 601-510-3274   PRC:326
www.15five.com
Estab: 2011

David Hassell, CEO
Shane Metcalf, Chief Culture Officer
Bill Macaitis, Advisor
Jason Calacanis, Advisor
Mike Walsh, Advisor

Provider of services that allow you to question
and start conversations that matters to elevate
performance of employees, managers, and entire
organizations.

**1st Source Lighting**   HQ
1730 Industrial Dr
Auburn CA 95603
P: 530-887-1110   F: 530-887-0807   PRC:243
www.1stsourcelighting.com
Email: sales@1stsourcelight.com
Emp: 1-10   Estab: 1993

Robert Brown, Sales

Designer and manufacturer of energy efficient
lighting technologies. The company also focuses
on supply aspects.

**21Tech LLC**   BR
1330 Broadway Ste 1530
Oakland CA 94612
P: 415-355-9090   PRC:326
www.21tech.com
Email: contact@21tech.com
Estab: 1996

Brad Baker, Director of Sales
Linda Short, VP of Professional Services
Bill Carrick, Director of EAM Services
Dilraj Kahai, Managing Partner
Ali Nasiri, Corporate Architect

Provider of business and technology solutions such
as technology consultancy, strategic sourcing/place-
ment, and branding and creative services practice.

**23andme Inc**   HQ
1390 Shorebird Way
Mountain View CA 94043
P: 800-239-5230   PRC:34
www.23andme.com
Estab: 2006

Steve Lemon, VP of Engineering
Dennis Byrne, Senior Software Engineer
Kristen Widman, Software Engineer
Anne Wojcicki, CEO
Andy Page, President

Provider of genetic information. The company
specializes in DNA analysis technologies and
web-based interactive tools.

**M-2**

**2K Games Inc**   HQ
10 Hamilton Landing
Novato CA 94949
P: 415-479-3634   PRC:317
www.2k.com
Estab: 2005

Qiong Wang, Engineer
Adam Lupinacci, Lead Engineer
Jack Scalici, Director of Creative Production
Scott Sanford, Quality Assurance Director
Matt Gorman, VP of Marketing

Developer of interactive entertainment for console
systems. The company also focuses on handheld
gaming systems and personal computers.

**2ndEdison Inc**   HQ
11 El Gavilan Rd
Orinda CA 94563
P: 844-432-8466   PRC:316
www.2ndedison.com
Estab: 2000

Chris Bradley, Founder

Provider of e-Commerce applications. The company also offers business process consulting and
design services.

**314e Corp**   HQ
47102 Mission Falls Ct Ste 219
Fremont CA 94539
P: 510-371-6736   F: 510-255-4534   PRC:194
www.314e.com
Email: info@314e.com
Estab: 2004

Alok Sharma, COO
Kesav Kolla, CTO
Kat Mako, Regional VP of Sales
Gaurav Mundra, VP of Operations
Ryan Seratt, Director of Training

Provider of IT skills, methodologies, and cost-ef-
fective managed services for healthcare application and technical support services.

**37 Degrees Inc**   HQ
PO Box 411163
San Francisco CA 94141
P: 415-315-9380   F: 415-765-9201   PRC:322
37degrees.com
Email: info@37degrees.com
Estab: 1999

Jacob Pipe, Director

Provider of technology and management consulting services for publishing, media, software
technology, and beverage industries.

**3d Robotics Inc**   HQ
1608 Fourth St Ste 410
Berkeley CA 94710
P: 858-225-1414   PRC:311
3dr.com
Estab: 2009

Lauren Winter, VP of Engineering & Production
Mike Horn, Director of Web Engineering
Dmitry Malakhov, iOS Engineering Manager
Kevin Mehall, Engineer Manager
Anh Doan, Junior iOS Engineer

Manufacturer of drone systems for exploration
and business applications. The company offers
autopilot controllers and flight controllers.

**3dtl Inc**   HQ
1243 Reamwood Dr
Sunnyvale CA 94089
P: 408-541-8550   F: 408-541-8555   PRC:53
www.3dtl.com
Email: info@3dtl.com
Estab: 1996

Elizabeth Downing, President

Provider of authentication technology services.
The company develops 3D displays for medical,
industrial, and military applications.

**3Q Digital Inc**   HQ
301 Howard St 11th Fl
San Francisco CA 94105
P: 650-539-4124   PRC:45
3qdigital.com

David Rodnitzky, Founder
Rob Murray, President
Brian Grabowski, Chief Growth Officer
Laura Rodnitzky, Chief Human Resources Officer
Diego Rovira, SVP of Client Services

Performance and digital marketing agency that
provides digital media services.

**3rd Stone Design Inc**   HQ
30 Castro Ave
San Rafael CA 94901
P: 415-454-3005   PRC:13
www.3rdstonedesign.com
Email: info@3rdstonedesign.com
Estab: 2005

Jaquelyn Miyatake, Senior Mechanical Engineer
Brett Selvig, Engineer
Henry Warder, R&D Test Engineer
Jackie Miyatake, Mechanical Engineer
Jim Mccrea, Mechanical Engineer

Provider of design, product development, and
engineering services. The company serves the
consumer products and healthcare industries.

**3Scan**   HQ
2122 Bryant St
San Francisco CA 94110
P: 415-851-5376   PRC:34
www.3scan.com
Email: info@3scan.com
Estab: 2011

Cody Daniel, Master Chief Engineer
Ben Mossbarger, Optical Engineer
Squirrel Collins, Senior Engineer
Christopher Rhodes, Senior Engineer
Sara Brockmueller, Software Engineer

Provider of automated microscopy services and
supporting software for the 3D analysis of cells,
tissues, and organs.

**4d Inc**   DH
3031 Tisch Way Ste 900
San Jose CA 95128
P: 408-557-4600   F: 408-261-9879   PRC:323
www.4d.com
Email: info@4d.com
Estab: 1984

Asmae Benkirane, EVP
Laurent Esnault, VP of Research & Development

Developer of web and internet applications. The
company serves universities, corporations, governments, and individuals.

**4d Molecular Therapeutics LLC**    HQ
5980 Horton St Ste 460
Emeryville CA 94608
P: 510-505-2680    PRC:34
www.4dmoleculartherapeutics.com
Estab: 2013

Melissa Kotterman, VP of Discovery & Engineering
David Schaffer, Chief Scientific Advisor
Theresa Janke, COO
David Kirn, CEO
Fred Kamal, CTO

Provider of gene therapy product research & development for the treatment of genetic diseases such as diabetes, arthritis, and heart failure.

**500friends Inc**    HQ
49 Stevenson St 15th Fl
San Francisco CA 94105
P: 415-918-2990    PRC:319
www.merkleinc.com
Estab: 2010

Geoffrey Smalling, CTO
Justin Yoshimura, SVP of Loyalty Services

Provider of omnichannel loyalty solution. The company offers service and technology to deliver seamless and powerful customer retention solutions.

**6connect Inc**    HQ
548 Market St Ste 39313
San Francisco CA 94104-5401
P: 650-646-2206    PRC:324
www.6connect.com
Email: support@6connect.com
Estab: 2009

Aaron Hughes, CEO
Pete Sclafani, COO

Provider of network resource provisioning and automation products and services such as data normalizer, pro services, and provision jumpstart.

**6connex**    HQ
4900 Hopyard Rd Ste 100
Pleasanton CA 94588
P: 800-395-4702    PRC:326
6connex.com
Email: sales@6connex.com
Estab: 2008

Michael Nelson, CEO
Marc Goodell, EVP
Michael Chance, Director of Client Services

Provider of virtual environment space and powering virtual destinations for career fairs, corporate universities, product launches, and user conferences.

**6WIND USA Inc**    RH
2445 Augustine Dr Ste 150
Santa Clara CA 95054
P: 408-816-1366    PRC:97
www.6wind.com
Email: 6wind-contact@6wind.com
Estab: 2000

Eric Carmes, Founder
Jean-Mickael Guerin, CTO
Aymeric Pintaud, CFO
Rich Souza, VP of Sales for the Americas
Roland Rodriguez, VP of Sales for EMEA and APAC

Manufacturer of virtual accelerators, routers, and related accessories. The company offers network security and network appliance solutions.

**8minute Solar Energy**    HQ
4370 Town Center Blvd Ste 110
El Dorado Hills CA 95762
P: 916-608-9060    F: 916-608-9861    PRC:135
www.8minute.com
Email: info@8minutenergy.com
Emp: 11-50 Estab: 2010

Alexander Wong, Project Engineer
Mario Ricci, VP of Corporate Finance
Patrick Lynch, Finance Manager
Jiayin Li, Financial Analyst
Dennis Harper, VP

Developer of solar PV projects. The company specializes in project development, financing, utility engineering, and business development.

**8x8 Inc**    HQ
2125 O'Nel Dr
San Jose CA 95131
P: 408-727-1885    PRC:68
www.8x8.com
Estab: 1987
Sales: $300M to $1 Billion

John DeLozier, SVP
Dejan Deklich, Chief Product Officer
Kim Niederman, President
Bryan Martin, CTO
Vikram Verma, CEO

Provider of cloud communications and computing solutions. The company sells IP phones, IP conference, soft, video and analog phones and accessories.

**A A Networks**    HQ
111 Anza Blvd Ste 130
Burlingame CA 94010
P: 650-872-1998    F: 650-548-1999    PRC:59
www.aanetwork.com
Email: service@aanetworks.net
Estab: 1996

Bill Lui, Manager

Provider of internet, networks and cabling, computer hardware and software, remote and on-site technical support services.

**A J Edmond Co**    BR
1717 Solano Way
Concord CA 94520
P: 925-521-1555    F: 925-521-1556    PRC:51
ajedmondco.com
Estab: 1965

Jignesh Panchal, Director of Technology
Robert Llerena, Director of Field Operations
Douglas Schug, Field Operations Manager
Esther Iniguez, Lab Technician

Provider of sampling and analytical services to petroleum refineries. The company's service areas include petroleum coke, coal, and gypsum.

**A M Fitzgerald & Associates LLC**    HQ
700 Airport Blvd Ste 210
Burlingame CA 94010
P: 650-347-6367    F: 650-347-6366    PRC:87
www.amfitzgerald.com
Email: info@amfitzgerald.com
Estab: 2003

Carolyn White, Design of Analysis & Fabrication
Charles Chung, Design of Test & Integration

Provider of MEMS solutions. The company's products include piezoresistive cantilevers, ultrasound transducers, and infrared imagers.

**A Step Above**    HQ
1064 Horizon Dr Ste 5
Fairfield CA 94533
P: 707-421-2917    F: 855-787-5033    PRC:180
astepaboveelevator.com

Anthony Lewis II, Owner
Lindsey Lewis, Owner
Tatiana Lewis, Executive Administrative Assistant

Provider of elevator services. The company offers escalators, walks, manlifts, and traction cars and related troubleshooting, testing and service.

**A TEEM Electrical Engineering**    HQ
3841 N Freeway Blvd Ste 145
Sacramento CA 95834
P: 916-457-8144    F: 916-457-7876    PRC:144
www.ateem.com
Emp: 1-10   Estab: 1988

Erik Burns, Controls Engineer
Sharon Kimizuka, Owner

Provider of outreach safety training, electrical design and construction management, and control system programming services.

**A&D Engineering Inc**    RH
1756 Automation Pkwy
San Jose CA 95131
P: 408-263-5333    F: 408-263-0119    PRC:189
www.andonline.com
Email: info@andonline.com
Estab: 1982

Jerry Wang, Director of Engineering & QA
Terry Duesterhoeft, President
Fred Lau, Director of Finance & Information Technology

Supplier of electric scale balancers and blood pressure monitors. The company offers services to the business sector.

**A&D Precision Inc**    HQ
4155 Business Center Dr
Fremont CA 94538
P: 510-657-6781    PRC:80
www.adprecision.com
Estab: 1978

Andy Dreifort, CEO
Jimmy Ying, Quality Control Lead
Helen Tu, Senior Sales Representative
Caprice Dreifort, Marketing Manager
Taylor Kuryla, Buyer

Provider of contract manufacturing, program management, electro-mechanical assembly, and precision machining services.

**A&L Western Agricultural Lab**    HQ
1311 Woodland Ave Ste 1
Modesto CA 95351
P: 209-529-4080    F: 209-529-4736    PRC:139
www.al-labs-west.com
Emp: 11-50 Estab: 1971

Robert Butterfield, Owner
Kathryn Butterfield-Byrne, Operations Manager
Devan Vo, Lab Technician

Provider of analytical services to agricultural sector. The company's services include soil analysis, pathology, microbiology, and water analysis.

**A'n D Cable Products Inc** HQ
1460 Washington Blvd Ste A-102
Concord CA 94521
P: 925-672-3005  F: 925-672-0317  PRC:62
www.andcable.com
Email: sales@andcable.com
Estab: 1989

Louis Chompff, Owner

Manufacturer, installer, and reseller of cable accessories. The company focuses on cable management and labeling solutions.

**A-1 Jay's Machining Inc** HQ
2228 Oakland Rd
San Jose CA 95131
P: 408-262-1845  F: 408-262-4561  PRC:80
a1jays.com
Email: info@a1jays.com
Estab: 1991

Vasant Shetty, Tool Design Engineer
Shanmuga Ganesan, Senior Manager
Thomas Abraham, Manager

Provider of machining, product assembly, and finishing services. The company is engaged in vertical milling, laser Micro-machining and water-jet cutting.

**A-Laser** HQ
675 Trade Zone Blvd
Milpitas CA 95035
P: 408-954-8582  PRC:80
a-laser.com
Email: norcalorders@a-laser.com
Estab: 1994

Joe Azevedo, Sales Manager

Provider of precision parts manufacturing services. The company specializes in laser cutting and caters to a wide range of industries.

**A10 Networks Inc** HQ
3 W Plumeria Dr
San Jose CA 95134
P: 408-325-8668  F: 408-325-8666  PRC:97
www.a10networks.com
Email: sales@a10networks.com
Estab: 2004
Sales: $100M to $300M

Dhrupad Trivedi, President
Raj Jalan, CTO
Tom Constantino, EVP
Andrew Kim, VP of Worldwide Human Resources
Chris White, EVP of Worldwide Sales & Applications

Provider of networking and security solutions such as cloud computing and virtualization and bandwidth management.

**A3 Solutions Inc** HQ
1 Market Plz Spear Tower Fl 36
San Francisco CA 94105
P: 415-356-2300  PRC:325
a3solutions.com
Email: info@a3solutions.com
Estab: 1988

Rob Lautt, CEO
Stuart Ratner, COO
James Williamson, IT Administrator

Developer and marketer of enterprise modeling software. The company is also engaged in unified budgeting and consolidation services.

**A9 com Inc** HQ
101 Lytton Ave
Palo Alto CA 94301-1044
P: 650-331-2600  PRC:322
www.a9.com
Estab: 2003

Scott Siegler, Head of Engineering

Provider of product, visual, and cloud search services. The company also focuses on mobile apps, advertising, and technical operations.

**AA Portable Power Corp** HQ
825 S 19th St
Richmond CA 94804
P: 510-525-2328  F: 510-439-2808  PRC:288
www.batteryspace.com
Email: sales@batteryspace.com
Estab: 2000

Po-Feng Chen, Battery Engineer
Jing Chen, Manager

Manufacturer of lithium-ion batteries. The company serves the mobile, consumer electronics, energy storage, and light electric vehicle markets.

**Aat Bioquest Inc** HQ
520 Mercury Dr
Sunnyvale CA 94085
P: 408-733-1055  F: 408-733-1304  PRC:34
www.aatbio.com
Email: support@aatbio.com
Estab: 2006

Jack Diwu, President
George Yi, Organic Chemistry Manager
Jixiang Liu, Manager
Zhen Luo, Staff Scientist
Qinglin Meng, Research Chemist

Developer and manufacturer of bioanalytical research reagents and kits. The company focuses on photometric detections including absorption.

**Ab Medical Technologies Inc** HQ
20272 Skypark Dr
Redding CA 96002
P: 530-605-2522  PRC:189
www.abmedtech.com
Email: sales@abmedtech.com
Emp: 1-10  Estab: 2009

Dwight Abbott, President of Regulatory
Ken Brown, President of Operations

Manufacturer of electronic medical systems and powered surgical instruments such as surgical pumps, arthroscopy shavers and lab equipment.

**Ab&I Foundry** HQ
7825 San Leandro St
Oakland CA 94621
P: 510-632-3467  F: 510-632-8035  PRC:53
www.abifoundry.com
Email: info@mcwane.com
Estab: 1906

Al Chang, Controls Engineer
Rob Fraguglia, Project Engineer
Donald Wixson, Plant Engineer
Michael Lowe, General Manager
Matthew Maziarz, Regional Sales Manager

Provider of casting products and accessories. The company's products include pipes and fittings, custom castings, foundry, and recyclable materials.

**Abacus Solutions Inc** HQ
24704 Voorhees Dr
Los Altos Hills CA 94022
P: 650-941-1728  PRC:323
www.abacussolutionsinc.com
Email: info@abacussolutionsinc.com

Salim Jabbour, CEO
Vadim Nazaryants, Chief System Architect

Developer of SATURN, an integrated enterprise ETRM system and focuses on generation optimization, parameters estimation, and credit management.

**Abaxis Inc** HQ
3240 Whipple Rd
Union City CA 94587
P: 510-675-6500  F: 510-441-6150  PRC:303
www.abaxis.com
Email: abaxis@abaxis.com
Estab: 1989
Sales: $100M to $300M

Ross Taylor, CFO
Donald Wood, COO
Kenneth Aron, CTO
Craig Tockman, VP of Sales
Michelle Rodriguez, Marketing Communications Specialist

Provider of on-site patient testing, leading-edge point-of-care technologies for veterinary practices and laboratory services for medical professionals.

**Abbomax Inc** HQ
2528 Qume Dr Ste 8
San Jose CA 95131
P: 408-573-1898  F: 408-573-1858  PRC:249
abbomax.com
Email: info@abbomax.com
Estab: 2005

Yuan Zhou, CSO
Ma Li, Scientist

Provider of antibody, peptide, and assay products and services. The company offers antibody production, fragmentation, assay development, and other services.

**Abbott Diabetes Care** BR
1420 Harbor Bay Pkwy
Alameda CA 94502
P: 510-749-5400  F: 510-749-5401  PRC:34
www.abbott.com
Email: ruitservice@abbott.com

David Hua, Software Engineering Manager
Marco Medina, Process Engineer
Robert Ford, President
Kelly Duffy, DVP of Quality & Compliance
Aditya Ajwani, Marketing and Sales Director

Provider of healthcare solutions. The company specializes in diagnostics, diabetes care, vision technologies, nutrition, pharmaceuticals, and animal health.

**Abbott** BR
6035 Stoneridge Dr
Pleasanton CA 94588
P: 800-456-1477  F: 925-847-8571  PRC:195
www.cardiovascular.abbott/
Email: customer.service@thoratec.com
Estab: 1976
Sales: Over $3B

Steve Briana, Research & Development Manager
Judy Benenato, Senior Buyer

Provider of mechanical circulatory support products. The company offers a portfolio products to treat heart failure.

**Abbyy Usa** HQ
890 Hillview Ct Ste 300
Milpitas CA 95035
P: 408-457-9777   F: 408-457-9778   PRC:323
www.abbyy.com
Email: sales@abbyyusa.com
Estab: 1989

Peter Lang, Pre-sales Engineer
Anthony Macciola, Chief Innovation Officer
Konstantin Anisimovich, CTO
Vitaliy Tyshchenko, Chief Customer Officer
Jesse Ku, Director of Information Technology

Provider of optical character recognition solutions.
The company offers scanners, screen-shot readers, document converters, and linguistic solutions.

**ABCO Laboratories Inc** HQ
2450 S Watney Way
Fairfield CA 94533
P: 707-432-2200   F: 707-432-2240   PRC:268
www.abcolabs.com
Estab: 1964

David Baron, Owner
Adrian Cesana, CIO
Eric Whitaker, EVP
Rich Hale, Director of QA
Vanessa Montiel-Quiles, Accounts Receivable
Manager

Provider of turnkey solutions. The company also
offers contract manufacturing, product development and private labeling.

**ABCO Wire & Metal Products** BR
4061 E Castro Valley Blvd Unit 474
Castro Valley CA 94552-4840
P: 510-909-5626   F: 510-581-0889   PRC:88
www.abcowire.com
Email: sales@abcowire.com

Mike Hopper, General Manager

Designer and manufacturer of display racks. The
company focuses on roller grill, drying racks, and
POP displays.

**AbGenomics International Inc** HQ
555 Twin Dolphin Dr Ste 165
Redwood City CA 94065
P: 650-232-7634   PRC:249
www.abgenomics.com
Email: abg@abgenomics.com
Estab: 2000

Ron Lin, CEO
Patrick Yang, Executive Chairman of the Board
Hsiao-Wen Tuan, Associate VP of Finance
Leewen Lin, VP of Administration
Hazel Cheng, VP of Clinical and CMC Project
Management

Specializes in the development of drug candidates
for immune-mediated inflammation and cancer
therapies.

**Able Design Inc** HQ
2267 Old Middlefield Way
Mountain View CA 94043
P: 650-961-8245   F: 650-961-8246   PRC:159
www.abledesigninc.com
Email: sales@abledesigninc.com
Estab: 1978

John Meadows, Owner

Provider of design services that involves specialization in automated handling of small high
technology devices.

**Able Health Inc** HQ
1516 Folsom St Unit C
San Francisco CA 94103
P: 805-288-0240   PRC:194
ablehealth.com
Email: hello@ablehealth.com

Steve Daniels, Founder
Rachel Katz, CEO

Provider of value-based reimbursements under
MACRA, MIPS, PQRS, medicaids, and commercial programs.

**Ablesys Corp** HQ
20954 Corsair Blvd
Hayward CA 94545
P: 510-265-1883   F: 510-265-1993   PRC:322
www.wintick.com
Email: sales@ablesys.com
Estab: 1994

John Wang, CEO
Yi Fan, VP

Provider of financial trading software and web
applications. The company focuses on portfolio
and algorithmic trading solutions.

**ABM-USA Inc** HQ
305 Piercy Rd
San Jose CA 95138
P: 408-226-8722   F: 408-226-8775   PRC:124
www.abmusainc.com
Email: po@abmusainc.com
Estab: 1986

Anhvu Vu, VP
Jessica Do, Office Manager

Manufacturer and seller of mask aligner and exposure systems. The company also provides vacuum
chucks, intensity meters, and probes.

**Aborn Electronics Inc** HQ
2108 E Bering Dr
San Jose CA 95131
P: 408-436-5445   F: 408-436-0969   PRC:203
abornelectronicssanjose.com
Estab: 1978

Vijay Lumba, President

Manufacturer of fiber optic systems. The company
specializes in the design and manufacture of fiber
optic receivers and transmitters.

**ABT-TRAC** HQ
517 A Martin Ave
Rohnert Park CA 94928
P: 707-586-3155   F: 707-586-3159   PRC:155
abttrac.com
Email: info@abttrac.com
Estab: 1986

D'Milo Hallerberg, Founder
David Catterson, Product Manager

Provider of yacht & boat stabilizers and bow &
stern thrusters. The company also offers integrated hydraulic products.

**Abx Engineering Inc** HQ
875 Stanton Rd
Burlingame CA 94010-1503
P: 650-552-2300   F: 650-259-8750   PRC:86
www.abxengineering.com
Email: sales@abxengineering.com
Estab: 1982

Henry Deng, Engineer
John Turner, Sales Program Manager
Joe Gotisar, Sales Program Manager
Brian Helm, SVP

Manufacturer of printed circuit board assemblies
and electromechanical products for medical devices, agriculture, and military electronics industries.

**Ac Photonics Inc** HQ
2701 Northwestern Pkwy
Santa Clara CA 95051
P: 408-986-9838   F: 408-986-0188   PRC:170
www.acphotonics.com
Email: sales@acphotonics.com
Estab: 1995

Tony Cortez, Sales Manager
Henry Chang, Account Manager

Manufacturer of custom-made precision optical
components. The company also offers fiber optic
components and modules.

**Acadia Technology Inc** HQ
1021 Helena Dr
Sunnyvale CA 94087
P: 408-737-9528   PRC:101
www.globalwinusa.com
Email: sales@globalwinusa.com
Estab: 1996

Chung Bao, Manager

Dealer of power supplies, water cooling kits,
cases, fans and fan ducts, and digital temperature
displayers.

**Acc Environmental Consultants** HQ
7977 Capwell Dr Ste 100
Oakland CA 94621
P: 510-638-8400   F: 510-638-8404   PRC:139
www.accenv.com
Email: general@accenv.com
Estab: 1986

Mark Sanchez, President
Sarah Wilson, Marketing Coordinator
Chris Yama, Project Manager
Ian Sutherland, Project Manager
Gladys Gomez, Project & Training Coordinator

Provider of environmental consulting services. The
company's services include moisture testing, site
assessment, mold testing, and asbetos consulting.

**Accel North America Inc** HQ
4633 Old Ironsides Dr Ste 400
Santa Clara CA 95054
P: 408-514-5199   PRC:323
www.accelna.com
Email: info@accelna.com
Estab: 1991

Milind Kalurkar, President of Sales
John Rekesh, CTO

Provider of software development and technology
services for automotive, healthcare, life science,
networking, storage, and enterprise software
markets.

**Accel** HQ
500 University Ave
Palo Alto CA 94301
P: 650-614-4800 PRC:325
www.accel.com
Estab: 1983

Tracy Sedlock, Chief Operating Partner
Lauren Illovsky, Director of Talent
Kim Eisenstaedt, University Relations Manager
Arun Mathew, Principal
Sameer Gandhi, Partner

Provider of investment services specializing in the mobile, retail, energy, and security industries.

**Accela Inc** HQ
2633 Camino Ramon Ste 120
San Ramon CA 94583-2539
P: 925-659-3200 F: 925-659-3201 PRC:322
www.accela.com
Email: info@accela.com
Estab: 2002

Gary Kovacs, CEO
Jonathon Knight, Chief Customer Officer
Aaron Haggarty, Chief Legal Counsel
Bobby Wilson, CFO
Dennis Michalis, Chief Revenue Officer

Provider of licensing, asset and land management, and public health and safety solutions. The company offers technical support services.

**Accelerance Inc** HQ
303 Twin Dolphin Dr Ste 600
Redwood City CA 94065
P: 650-472-3785 F: 650-472-3785 PRC:325
www.accelerance.com
Email: info@accelerance.com
Estab: 2001

Rod McCowan, Founder
Steve Mezak, CEO
Scott Pollov, COO
Michael Kimball, Managing Director

Provider of software design, development, and deployment services. The company focuses on web hosting and programming solutions.

**Accelerate Mobile Apps Inc** HQ
1 Victor Sq Ste 8003
Scotts Valley CA 95066
P: 831-438-8500 PRC:322
www.accelerate-ld.com
Emp: 1-10

John Boring, CEO

Provider of design, live training, and performance support tools such as the influencer app that helps assess working style for managers.

**AccelerATE Solutions Inc** HQ
2033 Gateway Pl Ste 500
San Jose CA 95110
P: 408-573-6066 PRC:86
acceler-ate.com
Estab: 2006

Tom Nulsen, Founding Partner

Provider of test engineering services. The company offers device characterization, applications support, and test program development services.

**Accellion** HQ
1804 Embarcadero Rd Ste 200
Palo Alto CA 94303
P: 650-485-4300 F: 650-485-4308 PRC:325
www.accellion.com
Email: info@accellion.com
Estab: 1999

Vijay Rao, VP of Systems Engineering
Varun Verma, Senior Systems Integration Engineer
Andrew Maloata, Customer Success Engineer
Jonathan Yaron, Chairman
Glen Segal, CFO

Provider of web-based file transfer applications. The company also focuses on data management solutions.

**Accenture** BR
50 W San Fernando St Ste 1100
San Jose CA 95113
P: 408-817-2700 PRC:323
www.accenture.com
Estab: 1989

Julie Sweet, CEO
David Rowland, Executive Chairman
Debra Polishook, Group Chief Executive Accenture Operations
Bhaskar Ghosh, Group Chief Executive Accenture Technology Services
Dan London, Group Chief Executive Health & Public Service

Provider of management consulting, technology services and outsourcing services. The company serves a wide range of industries.

**Accenture** BR
415 Mission St Ste 3300
San Francisco CA 94105
P: 415-537-5000 F: 415-537-5042 PRC:45
www.accenture.com

Julie Sweet, CEO
David Rowland, Executive Chairman
Jo Deblaere, COO
Richard Lumb, Group Chief Executive
Adrian Lajtha, Chief Leadership Officer

Provider of management consulting and technology services. The company also offers application outsourcing and IT consulting services.

**Access Business Technologies LLC** HQ
850 Iron Point Rd
Folsom CA 95630
P: 888-636-5426 PRC:323
www.myabt.com
Email: info@myabt.com
Emp: 1-10 Estab: 1998

Chris Schwartz-Edmisten, VP of Sales & Marketing
Steven Tschoepe, EVP of Operations

Provider of cloud-based software and hosting solutions for government agencies, banks, credit unions, accounting firms, and servicing companies.

**Access Communications Inc** HQ
976 Rincon Cir
San Jose CA 95131-1313
P: 800-342-4439 F: 408-970-0941 PRC:62
www.access-comm.net
Estab: 1997

Allen Davis, Owner

Provider of telecommunications cabling and audio visual solutions. The company offers audio visual integration, installation, and design services.

**Access Softek Inc** HQ
727 Allston Way Ste C
Berkeley CA 94710-2229
P: 510-848-0606 F: 510-848-0608 PRC:323
www.accesssoftek.com
Email: sales@accesssoftek.com
Estab: 1986

Vladimir Vereschaka, Software Engineer
Chris Doner, CEO
Steve Siu, Quality Assurance Manager
Mark Barish, VP of Business Development
Evan Barale, Senior Product Manager

Developer of mobile banking software solutions. The company focuses on software and product development, QA testing, user interface, and graphic design.

**Access Video Productions** HQ
1442A Walnut St Ste 480
Berkeley CA 94709
P: 510-528-6044 PRC:60
www.accessvideoproductions.com
Email: accessvideo@hotmail.com
Estab: 1980

Dave Karp, Videographer

Provider of production, editing, and duplication services for small and large companies, and individuals.

**Acco Semiconductor Inc** HQ
1290 Oakmead Pkwy Ste 201
Sunnyvale CA 94085
P: 408-524-2600 F: 408-524-2626 PRC:68
www.acco-semi.com
Email: contact@acco-semi.com
Estab: 2008

Minh Dao, Manager of Test Development Engineering
Ron Das, Founder

Provider of outsourced operations and engineering services. The company serves fabless semiconductor companies.

**Accounting Micro Systems** HQ
1700 Montgomery St Ste 220
San Francisco CA 94111
P: 415-362-5100 F: 415-276-5875 PRC:322
www.accountingmicro.com
Email: sales@accountingmicro.com
Estab: 1988

John Kearns, President

Developer of accounting and business management software products. The company offers MAS500, MAS90 and MAS200, FAS Asset solutions, and SalesLogix.

**Accsys Technology Inc**    HQ
1177 A Quarry Ln
Pleasanton CA 94566
P: 925-462-6949   F: 925-462-6993    PRC:152
www.accsys.com
Email: info@linacs.com
Estab: 1985

Glenn James, Senior Electronics Engineer
Keenan Moore, Mechanical Engineer
Kazuko Omoto, Accounting Supervisor
May Lui, Supervisor
Bert Felix, Test Technician

Manufacturer of ion linear accelerator systems
used in medical imaging devices, industrial applications and in research.

**Accton Technology Corp**    DH
1200 Crossman Ave Ste 130
Sunnyvale CA 94089
P: 408-747-0994   F: 408-747-0982    PRC:97
www.accton.com
Estab: 1988

Joanne Hsu, Corporate Marketing Manager

Distributor of network connectivity products and
ethernet hubs. The company focuses on home security, cloud, data center switch, and other needs.

**Accu-Image Inc**    HQ
2360 Owen St
Santa Clara CA 95054-3210
P: 408-736-9066   F: 408-736-9065    PRC:324
www.accu-image.com
Email: support@accu-image.com
Estab: 1988

Nikki Lacey, iOS Engineer
Mai Chiem, Operations Manager
Greg Johnson, Senior Project Manager
Trang Le, Auditor

Supplier of transfer document image processing
equipment. The company is engaged in business
process consulting and document management.

**Accu-Swiss Inc**    HQ
544 Armstrong Way Hi-Tech Park
Oakdale CA 95361
P: 209-847-1016   F: 209-847-8362    PRC:80
www.accuswissinc.com
Email: info@accuswissinc.com
Emp: 1-10   Estab: 1977

Bill Bradford, Applications Engineer
Ali Gabajiwala, Manufacturing Engineer
Furqan Ahmed, Production Assistant
Millie Namowicz, Office Manager

Manufacturer of precision CNC and screw machined products. The company's services include
engineering, milling, and threading.

**Accurate Always Inc**    HQ
127 Ocean Ave
Half Moon Bay CA 94019
P: 650-728-9428   F: 650-331-3511    PRC:68
www.accuratealways.com
Email: sales@accuratealways.com
Estab: 2003

Yousef Shemisa, CTO
Alex Ford, Federal Account Manager
Elaine Frankovic, Service Delivery Manager
Sarah Layton, Software Developer

Provider of digital voice and video recording
services. The company also offers radio and telephone call monitoring service.

**Accuray Inc**    HQ
1310 Chesapeake Ter
Sunnyvale CA 94089
P: 408-716-4600   F: 408-716-4601    PRC:34
www.accuray.com
Estab: 1999
Sales: $300M to $1 Billion

Grant Weldon, Robotics Engineer
Philip Santos, Service Development Engineer
Dave Skowbo, Senior Electrical Engineer
Hadi Qassoudi, Software Engineer
Joshua Levine, President

Provider of oncology treatment solutions. The
company develops, manufactures and sells precise and innovative tumor treatment solutions.

**Accusilicon USA Inc**    HQ
2901 Tasman Dr Ste 107
Santa Clara CA 95054
P: 408-256-0858    PRC:200
www.accusilicon.com
Email: info@accusilicon.com
Estab: 2010

Yi Zhou, Founder
Jingjing Tong, Volunteer

Manufacturer of TCXO IC chips and designer and
developer of high frequency oscillators for the
industrial sector.

**Accusplit**    HQ
7901 Stoneridge Dr Ste 350
Pleasanton CA 94588
P: 800-935-1996    PRC:14
www.accusplit.com
Email: help@accusplit.com
Estab: 1972

W. Sutton, Founder
Barbara Jacobs, Sales
Joey Sutton, Sales

Provider of digital stopwatches and pedometer
products. The company is also engaged in technical support services.

**Ace Seal LLC**    HQ
23 Las Colinas Ln
San Jose CA 95119
P: 408-513-1070   F: 408-513-1074    PRC:163
www.aceseal.com
Estab: 1982

Barbara Gallaty, President
Cindy Graver, Sales & Marketing Manager
Gina Gallaty, Sales & Marketing Manager

Manufacturer of molded rubber, seals, and o-rings.
The company serves the aerospace, semiconductor, oil & gas, medical, and biotechnology sectors.

**Acelrx Pharmaceuticals Inc**    HQ
351 Galveston Dr
Redwood City CA 94063
P: 650-216-3500   F: 650-216-6500    PRC:268
www.acelrx.com
Email: info@acelrx.com
Estab: 2005
Sales: $1M to $3M

Badri Dasu, Chief Engineering Officer
Vincent Angotti, CEO
Raffi Asadorian, CFO
Larry Hamel, Chief Development Officer
Mark Curtiss, Quality Manager

Manufacturer of pharmaceuticals. The company
provides therapies for treatment of acute and
breakthrough pain.

**Acer America Corp**    HQ
333 W San Carlos St Ste 1500
San Jose CA 95110
P: 408-533-7700   F: 408-533-4555    PRC:93
www.acer.com
Email: ama.acercare@acer.com
Estab: 1976

Kevin Kuo, Director of Finance
Rich Black, Director of Marketing
Eric Ackerson, Senior Product Marketing & Brand
Manager
Chloe Tan, Marketing Program Specialist
Irene Chan, Director

Supplier of desktops, notebooks, tablets, monitors
and projectors. The company also offers application and support services.

**Acesis Inc**    HQ
2047 Old Middlefield Way
Mountain View CA 94043
P: 650-396-7540    PRC:319
www.acesis.com
Email: info@acesis.com
Estab: 2006

Kevin Chesney, CEO

Provider of web-based platform for overseeing
healthcare quality improvement and compliance
documentation, workflow, and analytics.

**Achaogen Inc**    HQ
1 Tower Pl Ste 300
S San Francisco CA 94080
P: 650-800-3636    PRC:34
www.achaogen.com
Email: info@achaogen.com
Estab: 2002

Kenneth Hillan, CEO
Derek Bertocci, CFO
Arthur Culang, Manager of Information Technol-
ogy
Dennis Hom, VP of Finance
Ian Friedland, CMO

Developers of antibacterials. The company discovers and develops antibacterial for the treatment of
serious bacterial infections.

**Achronix Semiconductor Corp**    HQ
2903 Bunker Hill Ln
Santa Clara CA 95054
P: 408-889-4100   F: 408-286-3645    PRC:212
www.achronix.com
Email: info@achronix.com
Estab: 2004

Chris Pelosi, VP of Hardware Engineering
Kamal Choudhary, SVP of Software Engineering
Ronak Mehta, Senior Hardware Engineer
Dhammika Kurumbalapitiya, Systems Engineer
Virantha Ekanayake, Founder

Manufacturer of semiconductor devices. The
company's products are used for networking,
edge networking, and test and measurement
applications.

**ACI Alloys Inc** HQ
1458 Seareel Pl
San Jose CA 95131
P: 408-259-7337  F: 408-729-0277    PRC:80
www.acialloys.com
Estab: 1985

Paul Albert, Founder
Larry Albert, Owner

Manufacturer of purity alloys for thin film applications. The company offers evaporation and thin film materials.

**Acies Engineering** HQ
3371 Olcott St
Santa Clara CA 95054
P: 408-522-5255  F: 408-522-5260    PRC:304
www.acies.net
Email: info@acies.net
Estab: 1999

Ivana Ljoljic, Plumbing Design Engineer
Jovan Cerovac, Senior Design Engineer
Tomislav Gajic, Owner
Rene Tanag, Project Manager
Roberto Simon, Project Manager

Provider of engineering and design development solutions. The company caters to retail, restaurant, residential and commercial sectors.

**Acionyx** HQ
PO Box 701013
San Jose CA 95170
P: 408-366-2908  F: 408-366-2909    PRC:322
www.acionyx.com
Email: opr@acionyx.com
Estab: 1997

Umesh Hiriyannaiah, President
Acionyx Recruiter, Recruiter

Provider of systems development and engineering consulting services. The company also deals with testing and quality assurance.

**Acm Machining Inc** HQ
3218 Luyung Dr
Rancho Cordova CA 95742
P: 916-852-8600  F: 916-852-8886    PRC:80
www.acmmachining.com
Email: acm@acmmachining.com
Emp: 11-50 Estab: 1974

Mariano Ispas, Senior CNC Engineer
Alfred Balbach, President
Pete Reynen, General Manager
Leo Martins, Sales & Production Manager
Daniel Goga, Production Expeditor

Manufacturer of machined products for pressure control products. The company serves oil, gas, and automotive industries.

**Acon Builders Construction Inc** HQ
2302 Tripaldi Way
Hayward CA 94545
P: 408-980-1388  F: 408-827-9559    PRC:304
www.aconbuilders.com
Email: info@aconbuilders.com
Estab: 1989

Jennifer Chan, Project Manager

Provider of scheduling, planning, change management, status reporting, zoning, and code compliance services.

**Acosta Sheet Metal Manufacturing Inc** HQ
930 Remillard Ct
San Jose CA 95122
P: 408-275-6370  F: 408-297-0130    PRC:154
www.acostamfg.com
Email: help@acostamfg.com

Michelle Acosta, Marketing Director

Manufacturer of HVAC and architectural products, and sheet metal building materials. The company provides gutter profile caps and conductor heads.

**Acoustic Emission Consulting Inc** HQ
5000 San Juan Ave Ste D
Fair Oaks CA 95628
P: 916-965-4827    PRC:87
Emp: 1-10  Estab: 1991

John Rodgers, President

Specializes in acoustic emission inspection services and testing, and acoustic emission instrumentation, sensors, and probes.

**Acree Technologies Inc** HQ
1980 Olivera Rd Ste D
Concord CA 94520
P: 925-798-5770  F: 510-588-4046    PRC:34
www.acreetech.com
Email: info@acreetech.com
Estab: 2004

Tanya Kavka, Research Scientist

Provider of PVD thin film coating services for medical, defense, and other sectors. The company also specializes in R&D and sell coating systems.

**Acro Associates Inc** HQ
1990 Olivera Rd Ste A
Concord CA 94520-5455
P: 925-676-8828  F: 925-680-8113    PRC:166
www.acroassociates.com
Email: sales@acroassociates.com
Estab: 1976

Blaik Musolf, Principal Engineer
Russell Ziegler, General Manager
James Hoelle, Production Manager
JoAnn Bernard, Manager of Quality Assurance & Document Control
Winston Wong, Director

Manufacturer and designer of pinch valves and fluid control components for the medical, bioprocessing and industrial markets.

**Acronics** HQ
2102 Commerce Dr
San Jose CA 95131
P: 408-432-0888  F: 408-884-2418    PRC:104
acronics.com
Email: sales@acronics.com
Estab: 1994

Long Nguyen, Principal Engineer
Kiem Vo, Product Manager

Provider of engineering services. The company is involved in systems and mechanical design services.

**Acrylic Art** HQ
1290 45th St
Emeryville CA 94608
P: 510-654-0953  F: 510-654-8003    PRC:80
www.acrylicart.com
Email: info@acrylicart.com
Estab: 1986

Jeff Schnur, President
Alice Vlachothanasi, Project Manager

Provider of fabrication and machining services. The company focuses on painting, product finishing, anodizing, and vapor polishing.

**Actagro LLC** HQ
4516 N Howard
Biola CA 93606
P: 559-369-2222  F: 559-843-2845    PRC:42
www.actagro.com
Email: info@actagro.com
Emp: 11-50 Estab: 1997

Nichole Cagle, Purchasing Agent
David Davis, National Sales Manager
Jeff Palmbach, Technical Sales Representative
Jeffrey Hunter, Director of Project Management
Jerel Kratt, Agronomist

Manufacturer of agricultural products for crops such as alfalfa, almonds, blueberries, corn, tomatoes, onions, rice, strawberries, and wine grapes.

**Actelis Networks Inc** HQ
47800 Westinghouse Dr
Fremont CA 94539
P: 510-545-1045  F: 510-657-8006    PRC:64
www.actelis.com
Email: info@actelis.com
Estab: 1999

Bruce Hammergren, EVP of Sales
Eric Vallone, VP of Marketing
Rob Shaeffer, Senior Manager of Technical Support

Provider of carrier Ethernet over copper networking equipment. The company serves government, service operators, and utilities.

**Actian Corp** HQ
2300 Geng Rd Ste 150
Palo Alto CA 94303
P: 650-587-5500  F: 650-587-5550    PRC:319
www.actian.com
Email: sales@actian.com
Estab: 2005

Volker John, VP of Engineering
Emma McGrattan, SVP of Engineering
Bikram Sarma, VP of Platform Engineering
Rohit De Souza, CEO
Robin Abrams, Chairman

Provider of on-premises applications and cloud data management solutions.

**Actinix** HQ
6060 Graham hill Rd
Felton CA 95018
P: 831-440-9388    PRC:34
www.actinix.com
Email: sales@actinix.com
Emp: 1-10  Estab: 1999

Jim Jacob, CEO

Developer of ultraviolet light generation, long-coherence-length pulsed fiber laser systems, high energy laser systems and optical tools/methods.

**Actiontec Electronics Inc**    HQ
760 N Mary Ave
Sunnyvale CA 94085
P: 408-752-7700   F: 408-541-9003    PRC:97
www.actiontec.com
Email: broadband-sales@actiontec.com
Estab: 1993

Xing Fang, System Software Engineer
Brian Paul, CFO
Brian Henrichs, Chief Business Development Officer
Bo Xiong, CTO
Chuang Li, VP of Engineering Quality Assurance

Provider of internet modems, networking adapters, and routers. The company offers fiber routers, powerline network kits and wireless display products.

**Active Video Networks**    HQ
333 W San Carlos St Ste 400
San Jose CA 95110
P: 408-931-9200   F: 408-931-9100    PRC:324
www.activevideo.com
Email: info@activevideo.com

Mike Baker, Software Engineering Manager of Server Infrastructure
Sneha Srinivasan, SQA Engineer
Jeff Miller, CEO
Brian Sereda, CFO
Ronald Brockmann, CTO

Designer and developer of advertising solutions. The company also provides mosaic, guide, and navigation enablement services.

**Acu Spec Inc**    HQ
990 Richard Ave Ste 103
Santa Clara CA 95050
P: 408-748-8600   F: 408-748-8605    PRC:80
www.acuspecinc.com

Amy Budde, CFO
Dominic Mathis, Operations Manager

Manufacturer of engineering products. The company offers horizontal & vertical machining, CNC turning, CAD software, and CMM inspection services.

**Acumen Pharmaceuticals Inc**    HQ
4435 N First St Ste 360
Livermore CA 94551
P: 925-368-8508   F: 925-605-3813    PRC:34
www.acumenpharm.com
Email: info@acumenpharm.com
Estab: 1996

Franz Hefti, President
William Goure, COO

Specializes in the discovery and development of therapeutics and diagnostics related to soluble A~oligomers.

**Acutherm**    HQ
6379 Clark Ave Ste 280
Hayward CA 94545
P: 510-785-0510   F: 510-785-2517    PRC:78
www.acutherm.com
Email: info@acutherm.com
Estab: 1978

Kurt Herzog, President
Mark Alan, Sheet Metal Worker

Manufacturer of components for heating and air conditioning systems. The company offers therma-fuser variable air volume diffusers.

**Acutrack Inc**    HQ
350 Sonic Ave
Livermore CA 94551
P: 925-579-5000   F: 925-579-5001    PRC:116
www.acutrack.com
Email: sales@acutrack.com
Estab: 1992

Brian Schmille, COO
Maureen Corrigan, Financial Controller
Scott Donovan, VP of Sales Operation
Chris Vogt, Business Development Manager
Stephen Sideris, Digital Media Manager

Provider of CD and DVD duplication and production services. The company is also engaged in kitting, assembly, and USB fulfillment.

**Acxiom LLC**    BR
100 Redwood Shores Pkwy
Redwood City CA 94065
P: 888-322-9466    PRC:324
www.acxiom.com
Estab: 1969

Chris Lanaux, CTO of Product and Engineering
Dennis Self, CEO
Janet Cinfio, Chief Information Officer of IT and Operations
Beth-Anne Bygum, Chief Security Officer
Brett Madison, CFO

Provider of e-mail marketing services for online marketers. The company is engaged in consulting and analytics services.

**Ad Art Inc**    HQ
150 Executive Park Blvd Ste 2100
San Francisco CA 94134
P: 800-675-6353   F: 415-239-7270    PRC:316
www.adart.com
Estab: 1958

Terry Long, Owner
Dana Long, VP
Neal Tibbs, EVP of Operations
Abigail Hall, Project Manager
Andrew Garabedian, Account Executive

Provider of digital signage solutions. The company also offers graphic designs, animation, commercial lighting, and maintenance services.

**Adamas Pharmaceuticals Inc**    HQ
1900 Powell St Ste 750
Emeryville CA 94608
P: 510-450-3500   F: 510-428-0519    PRC:268
www.adamaspharma.com
Email: info@adamaspharma.com
Estab: 2002
Sales: $30M to $100M

Greg Went, Founder
David Mahoney, Chairman
Jennifer Rhodes, Chief Business Officer
Vijay Shreedhar, CCO
Alfred Merriweather, CFO

Manufacturer of health care products. The company offer products for patients with chronic disorders of the central nervous system.

**Adapt Corp**    HQ
1733 Woodside Rd Ste 220
Redwood City CA 94061
P: 650-306-2400   F: 650-306-2401    PRC:322
adaptsoft.com
Email: info@adaptsoft.com
Estab: 1981

Carine Magalhaes, VP of Engineering Services
Bijan Aalami, Founder
Florian Aalami, President
Suranjan Bhanja, CEO
Spencer Lee, CTO

Provider of post-tensioning and reinforced concrete structural analysis software for building design.

**Adaptive Engineering**    HQ
PO Box 2330
San Ramon CA 94583
P: 415-518-7131   F: 925-828-3140    PRC:212
www.adaptiveengineering.com

Nitin Patel, Project Engineer
Pratik Patel, Mechanical Engineer

Provider of engineering products such as automatic mixture control, talking telemetry, and telephone-based microclimate monitors.

**Adaptive Insights**    HQ
2300 Geng Rd Ste 100
Palo Alto CA 94303
P: 650-528-7500    PRC:319
www.adaptiveinsights.com
Email: support@adaptiveinsights.com
Estab: 2003

Kshitij Dayal, VP of Engineering
Robert Hull, Founder
Tom Bogan, CEO
Bhaskar Himatsingka, Chief Product Officer
Scott LaFramboise, VP of Sales

Developers of a cloud business planning framework to enable seamless collaboration across the enterprise.

**Adaptive Insights**    HQ
2300 Geng Rd Ste 100
Palo Alto CA 94303
P: 650-528-7500    PRC:322
www.adaptiveinsights.com
Email: sales@adaptiveinsights.com
Estab: 2003

Kshitij Dayal, VP of Engineering
Robert Hull, Founder
Tom Bogan, CEO
Fred Gewant, Chief Revenue Officer
David Pefley, CFO

Provider of training, consulting, and related support services. The company serves the healthcare, insurance, and manufacturing industries.

**Adax Inc**    HQ
2900 Lakeshore Ave
Oakland CA 94610
P: 510-548-7047   F: 510-548-5526    PRC:68
www.adax.com
Email: sales@adax.com
Estab: 1982

Christopher Benson, Software Engineer
Javier Kim, Director of Integration

Provider of packet processing, security, and telecom network infrastructure components. The company's products include gateways and controllers.

**Adco Manufacturing** HQ
2170 Academy Ave
Sanger CA 93657
P: 559-875-5563   F: 559-875-7665   PRC:311
www.adcomfg.com
Email: info@adcomfg.com
Emp: 1-10   Estab: 1958

Darwin Rhodes, Field Service Engineer
Dan Egleston, Electrical Engineer
Nathan Shears, Mechanical Design Engineer
Ryan Poulsen, Engineering Engineering
Michael May, President

Provider of consumer packaged goods. The company's solutions include cartoners, top load systems, case packers, sleevers, and robotic packaging.

**Addepar Inc** HQ
303 Bryant St
Mountain View CA 94041
P: 855-464-6268   PRC:322
www.addepar.com
Email: inquiries@addepar.com
Estab: 2009

Nick Kochanski, Managing Director

Provider of investment management solutions and technology platform for data aggregation, powerful analytics, and empowering clients to excel.

**Addison Engineering Inc** HQ
150 Nortech Pkwy
San Jose CA 95134
P: 408-926-5000   F: 408-956-5111   PRC:86
www.addisonengineering.com

George McMaryion, Materials Manager

Supplier of silicon wafers and semiconductor process components. The company's products include ceramic packages and semiconductor equipment.

**Addonics Technologies Inc** HQ
1918 Junction Ave
San Jose CA 95131
P: 408-573-8580   F: 408-573-8588   PRC:95
www.addonics.com
Estab: 1998

Jacqueline Wong, Sales Administrator

Manufacturer of storage systems and products. The company's products include drive cartridge system, host controller, converter, and adapter.

**Adelphi Technology Inc** HQ
2003 E Bayshore Rd
Redwood City CA 94063
P: 650-474-2750   F: 650-474-2755   PRC:152
www.adelphitech.com
Email: info@adelphitech.com
Estab: 1984

Jack Harris, Senior Engineer
Eugene Guan, Engineer
Melvin Piestrup, President
J. Cremer, Chief Scientist
Charles Gary, VP of Operations

Developer and manufacturer of X-ray optics. The company serves the medical, industrial, and scientific sectors.

**Adem LLC** HQ
1040 Di Giulio Ave Ste 160
Santa Clara CA 95050
P: 408-727-8955   F: 408-727-2055   PRC:80
www.ademllc.com
Estab: 1997

Yury Nikolenko, Electrical Engineer
Val Sokolsky, Owner
Jacob Obolsky, Owner
Boris Kesil, President
Natallia Kushchanka, Senior Accountant

Designer and manufacturer of special and automated fixtures for assembly lines, and also provides turnkey production solutions.

**Adesto Technologies Corporation Inc** HQ
3600 Peterson Way
Santa Clara CA 95054
P: 408-400-0578   F: 408-400-0721   PRC:96
www.adestotech.com
Email: info@adestotech.com
Estab: 2007
Sales: $30M to $100M

Narbeh Derhacobian, President
Ron Shelton, CFO
Gideon Intrater, CTO
Sohrab Modi, CSO

Provider of power memory solutions. The company's portfolio comprises Fusion Serial Flash, DataFlas, and Mavriq serial memory.

**Adhesive Products Inc** HQ
520 Cleveland Ave
Albany CA 94710
P: 510-526-7616   F: 510-524-0573   PRC:47
www.adhesiveproductsinc.com
Email: sales@adhesiveproductsinc.com
Estab: 1878

Trish Shattuck, Owner
Mark Woodward, Technical Sales Manager
Cecilia Viera, Customer Service Manager
Kathleen Meyer, Senior Account Manager
Tim Shattuck, National Accounts Manager

Manufacturer of glues, adhesives, tapes, labels, and coatings. The company is engaged in sales and delivery services.

**Aditazz** HQ
2000 Sierra Point Pkwy
Brisbane CA 94005
P: 650-492-7000   F: 650-684-1145   PRC:304
www.aditazz.com
Email: info@aditazz.com
Estab: 2010

Deepak Aatresh, CEO
Agnessa Todorova, Architect
Anatoly Kaplan, Software Delivery Management
Pujuan Huang, Translator

Designer, manufacturer, and assembler of building components. The company is engaged in operational modeling.

**ADLINK Technology Inc** LH
5215 Hellyer Ave Ste 110
San Jose CA 95138
P: 408-360-0200   F: 408-360-0222   PRC:96
www.adlinktech.com
Email: info@adlinktech.com
Estab: 1995

Steve Marks, Director of Quality
Lawrence Shen, Hardware Manager
Brandon Chen, Software Developer

Designer and manufacturer of products for embedded computing, test & measurement, and automation applications. The company serves various sectors.

**Admecell Inc** HQ
980 Atlantic Ave Ste 110
Alameda CA 94501
P: 510-522-4200   F: 510-522-4203   PRC:34
www.admcell.com
Email: info@admcell.com
Estab: 2008

Sandy Koshkin, President
Matt Pourfarzaneh, CEO
Barbara Levin, CFO
Dokhi Nargessi, Chief Scientific Officer

Manufacturer of ready to use products such as cell based, TRANSIL, and ELISA based assays for in-vitro therapeutic modeling and re-profiling.

**Adobe Systems Inc** HQ
345 Park Ave
San Jose CA 95110-2704
P: 408-536-6000   F: 408-537-6000   PRC:319
www.adobe.com
Estab: 1982
Sales: Over $3B

David Welch, VP of Solution Leader Microsoft Solutions
Seth Reilly, Senior Engineering Manager
Peter Johnson, Senior Engineering Manager
Don Walling, Senior Manager of Engineering
Diana Helander, Engineer

Developer of software solutions for digital media creation and editing, multimedia authoring, and web development.

**ADPAC Corp** HQ
1996 Holmes St
Livermore CA 94550
P: 415-777-5400   F: 415-374-8505   PRC:319
www.adpac.com
Email: sales@adpac.com
Estab: 1963

Ed Severs, President

Provider of software to improve productivity and value of current application software focusing on business rule extraction, M&A, and documentation.

**Adr Environmental Group Inc** HQ
225 30th St Ste 202
Sacramento CA 95816
P: 916-921-0600   F: 916-648-6688   PRC:139
adreg.com
Emp: 1-10   Estab: 1995

Ron Kern, Account Manager
Kevin Gallagher, Account Manager

Provider of risk management services and due diligence services. The company's due diligence service includes engineering and structural services.

**Adtec Technology Inc**      HQ
  48625 Warm Springs Bvld
  Fremont CA 94539
P: 510-226-5766      PRC:292
www.adtecusa.com
Email: info@adtecusa.com
Estab: 1996

Shuitsu Fujii, President
Taras Bodrouk, VP

Manufacturer of RF plasma generators, matching units, and power measurement devices. The company serves semiconductor and solar processing tool needs.

**Aduro Biotech Inc**      HQ
  740 Heinz Ave
  Berkeley CA 94710-2224
P: 510-848-4400      PRC:28
www.aduro.com
Email: bd@adurobiotech.com
Estab: 2000
Sales: $10M to $30M

Stephen Isaacs, Chairman
Andrea van Elsas, CSO
Blaine Templeman, Corporate Development Head
Chief Legal Officer and Secretary
Dave Freund, Research Associate

Provider of engineered immunotherapy for the treatment of cancer. The company is engaged in clinical trials.

**Advan Int'l Corp**      BR
  47817 Fremont Blvd
  Fremont CA 94538
P: 510-490-1005      PRC:31
advancorp.com
Email: sales@advancorp.com
Estab: 1982

Kimiko Sudo, VP
Alan Yu, VP of R&D

Distributor of integrated circuits. The company's products include surgical and endoscopy imaging, diagnostic imaging, and touch screen.

**Advance Carbon Products Inc**      HQ
  2036 National Ave
  Hayward CA 94545
P: 510-293-5930    F: 510-293-5939    PRC:80
advancecarbon.com
Email: customerservice@advancecarbon.com
Estab: 1956

William Crader, Founder

Manufacturer of carbon. The company offers equipments such as CNC lathes, grinders, lappers, and diamond saws.

**Advance Research Associates**      HQ
  2350 Mission College Blvd Ste 825
  Santa Clara CA 95054
P: 650-810-1190    F: 650-810-1195    PRC:188
www.advanceresearch.com
Estab: 1996

Peter Shabe, Founder
Andria Wallace, Manager of Quality Systems
Lauren Intagliata, Senior Director of Clinical Data Management
Tami Crabtree, Director of Biostatistics
Michelle Stoddard, Senior Director of Clinical Data Management

Developer of human bio-therapeutic platform technology solutions, drug discovery, and related support services.

**Advanced Cell Diagnostics Inc**      HQ
  7707 Gateway Blvd
  Newark CA 94545
P: 510-576-8800    F: 510-576-8801    PRC:34
www.acdbio.com
Email: info@acdbio.com
Estab: 2007

Xiao-Jun Ma, CSO
Christopher Bunker, VP of Business Development

Developer of biotechnological diagnostic tests. The company specializes in the identification and validation of RNA biomarkers for cancer diagnosis.

**Advanced Component Labs**      HQ
  990 Richard Ave Ste 118
  Santa Clara CA 95050-2828
P: 408-327-0200    F: 408-327-0202    PRC:204
www.aclusa.com
Email: acl1@aclusa.com
Estab: 1994

Don Bentley, Engineering Manager
Mike Oswald, President
Winston Labucay, Purchasing Manager
Nerissa de Ramos, Sales Manager
Pat Smith, Operations Manager

Manufacturer of flip chips, thermal vias, build ups, and related supplies. The company's services include drilling, lamination, and engineering.

**Advanced Digital Solutions International Inc**      HQ
  4255 Business Center Dr
  Fremont CA 94538
P: 510-490-6667      PRC:93
www.adsii.com
Email: quote@adsii.com
Estab: 1989

Shahid H., CEO

Provider of information technology solutions. The company provides backup media tapes, bar-code labels, tape drives, and data center supplies.

**Advanced Fabrication Technology**      HQ
  31154 San Benito St
  Hayward CA 94544
P: 510-489-6218    F: 510-489-6686    PRC:80
www.aftmetal.com
Email: custser@aftmetal.com
Estab: 1983

Todd Morey, VP
Linda McKibbin, Customer Service Manager

Provider of metal fabricating services for the electronics, manufacturing, and semiconductor industries.

**Advanced Geoenvironmental Inc**      BR
  122 Calistoga Rd Ste 325
  Santa Rosa CA 95409
P: 800-511-9300      PRC:142
www.advgeoenv.com
Email: info@advgeoenv.com

Robert Marty, President
Dennis Delaney, Director of Air Quality Division
Arthur Deicke, Project Manager
Brian Millman, Professional Geologist
Rebecca Natal, Project Scientist

Provider of environmental consulting services. The company services include soil and groundwater remediation and water and wastewater services.

**Advanced Integrated Solutions Inc**      BR
  5072 Hillsdale Cir Ste 100
  El Dorado Hills CA 95762
P: 714-572-5600    F: 714-572-5655    PRC:301
www.aisconsulting.net
Email: info@aisconsulting.net
Emp: 11-50 Estab: 1994

Hagop Belekdanian, President

Provider of enterprise systems management, call center, and information technology infrastructure library based service management solutions.

**Advanced Laser & Waterjet Cutting Inc**      HQ
  820 Comstock St
  Santa Clara CA 95054
P: 408-486-0700    F: 408-486-0711    PRC:157
www.adv-laser.com
Email: info@adv-laser.com
Estab: 1996

Lester Gragg, President

Provider of precision cutting services for all types of materials. The company's services include electronic shielding, fabrivision, and overnight shipping.

**Advanced Linear Devices Inc**      HQ
  415 Tasman Dr
  Sunnyvale CA 94089
P: 408-747-1155    F: 408-747-1286    PRC:208
www.aldinc.com
Email: sales@aldinc.com
Estab: 1985

Robert Chao, President

Designer and manufacturer of precision CMOS analog integrated circuits. The company serves industrial control, computer, automotive, and other sectors.

**Advanced Micro Devices Inc**      HQ
  2485 Augustine Dr
  Santa Clara CA 95054
P: 408-749-4000      PRC:93
www.amd.com
Estab: 1969
Sales: Over $3B

Mark Papermaster, CTO
Lisa Su, President
Devinder Kumar, SVP
Forrest Norrod, SVP
Donna Lee, Senior Tax Manager of International

Provider of products such as desktops, notebooks, servers, workstations, and embedded systems. The company also offers a variety of software.

**Advanced Microwave Inc**      HQ
  333 Moffett Park Dr
  Sunnyvale CA 94089
P: 408-739-4214    F: 408-739-4148    PRC:206
www.advmic.com
Email: sales@advmic.com
Estab: 1995

Rene Magana, QA & Sales Engineer

Manufacturer of military electronic components and subsystems. The company offers amplifiers, mixers, threshold detectors, and converter products.

**Advanced Power Solutions**    HQ
5936 Las Positas Rd
Livermore CA 94551
P: 925-456-9890    F: 925-456-9050     PRC:290
www.advpower.com
Email: sales@advpower.com
Estab: 1982

Bob Vieira, President
Yvonne Marquez, Account Manager

Provider of power supplies. The company is involved in manufacturing, sales, and related support services.

**Advanced Radiation Corp**    HQ
2210 Walsh Ave
Santa Clara CA 95050
P: 408-727-9200    F: 408-727-9255     PRC:243
www.arc-lamps.com
Email: rcpaquette@arc-lamps.com
Estab: 1971

John Paquette, VP

Manufacturer of mercury-xenon, and capillary lamps. The company's services include design, installation, and delivery.

**Advanced Rotorcraft Technology Inc**    HQ
635 Vaqueros Ave
Sunnyvale CA 94085
P: 408-523-5100    F: 408-732-1206     PRC:3
www.flightlab.com
Email: info@flightlab.com
Estab: 1982

Dooyong Lee, Senior Aerospace Engineer
Ronald Val, President

Designer of fixed-wing and helicopter simulation productivity tools. The company services include avionics testing and simulator integration.

**Advanced Semiconductor Engineering US Inc**    DH
1255 E Arques Ave
Sunnyvale CA 94085
P: 408-636-9500     PRC:212
www.aseglobal.com

Elvira Rebano, Accounts Receivable Representative

Manufacturer of integrated circuits and semiconductor packaging products. The company is involved in delivery, installation, and sales.

**Advanced Software Design Inc**    HQ
1371 Oakland Blvd Ste 100
Walnut Creek CA 94596
P: 925-975-0694    F: 925-975-0696     PRC:326
www.asdglobal.com
Email: admin@asdintl.com
Estab: 1982

Sonali Singh, President
Salig Chada, VP of Business Development Alliances & Sales
Sharron Scott, Capture Manager
Kathleen Lonero, Accounting Associate

Provider of knowledge based engineering software and industry focused business solutions. The company offers services to the public sector.

**Advanced Witness Series Inc**    HQ
910 Bern Ct Ste 100
San Jose CA 95112
P: 408-453-5070    F: 408-453-5199     PRC:169
www.awitness.com
Email: sales@awitness.com

Craig Vossbrinck, President
Huy Huynh, Software Developer

Designer of electrical and mechanical components and tools. The company caters to various applications.

**Advancing Ideas LLC**    HQ
570 Hayes St Ste 4
San Francisco CA 94102
P: 415-625-3338     PRC:325
advancingideas.net
Email: hello@advancingideas.net
Estab: 2006

Samuel Ackerman, Co-Founder

Provider of market research and analysis, application branding, and user interface development services.

**Advansta Inc**    HQ
1505 Adams Dr Ste B
Menlo Park CA 94025
P: 650-325-1980    F: 650-325-1904     PRC:53
advansta.com
Estab: 2005

Rosar Vitug, Operations Manager
Tony Li, Product Specialist

Developer and manufacturer of bioresearch agents. The company focuses on protein staining, purification, and electrophoresis.

**Advantage Electric Supply Inc**    HQ
31857 Hayman St
Hayward CA 94544
P: 510-324-9070    F: 510-324-9073     PRC:124
www.advantageelectricsupply.com
Email: sales@advantageelectricsupply.com

Krystle Garrity, Office Manager
Sandra Sorce, VP

Distributor of electrical and electronic components for OEM's, industrial automation, solar, and renewable energy industries.

**Advantage for Analysts Inc**    HQ
184 Bulkley Ave
Sausalito CA 94965
P: 415-568-4800     PRC:322
www.advantageforanalysts.com
Email: info@advantageforanalysts.com
Estab: 2004

Richard Homich, CEO
Dennis Moritz, Principal

Developer of structuring and analysis software. The company finds application in originating, trading, and managing complex financial assets.

**Advantage Metal Products**    HQ
7855 Southfront Rd
Livermore CA 94551
P: 925-667-2009     PRC:88
www.advantagemetal.com
Email: customerservice@advantagemetal.com
Estab: 1988

Phil Segundo, Co-Owner

Provider of sheet metal and machining services. The company offers painting and silk screening, forming, welding, and machine shop services.

**Advantage Pharmaceutics Inc**    HQ
4351 Pacific St
Rocklin CA 95677
P: 916-630-4960    F: 916-624-2088     PRC:266
www.custom-meds.com
Emp: 1-10   Estab: 2004

Corey Whitney, Partner

Provider of pharmaceuticals specializing in compounding. The company provides compounded medicines in dosage forms for human and veterinary needs.

**Advantec MFS Inc**    HQ
6723 Sierra Ct Ste A
Dublin CA 94568
P: 925-479-0625    F: 925-479-0630     PRC:304
advantecmfs.com
Email: sales@advantecmfs.com
Estab: 1995

Koichi SHIODE, General Manager
Alex Rockwell, Assistant Logistics Manager
Katsuaki Tanaka, Manager
Debby Leglu, Senior Manager of Sales & Tech
Mitsuyo Bateman, Administrative Supervisor

Producer of filtration media and related scientific products. The company focuses on laboratory instruments and filtration products.

**Advantech Inc**    DH
380 Fairview Way
Milpitas CA 95035
P: 408-519-3898    F: 408-519-3899     PRC:91
www.advantech.com
Email: ags.usa@advantech.com
Estab: 1983

Kc Liu, Chairman
Chaney Ho, Founder
Eric Chen, Division President
Miller Chang, Division President
Linda Tsai, Division President

Provider of system integration, hardware, software, embedded systems, automation products, and logistics support.

**Advantek Inc**    BR
20969 Cabot Blvd
Hayward CA 94545
P: 510-623-1877    F: 510-623-1886     PRC:209
www.advantek.com
Email: sales@veridicon.com

Alex Lim, Director of Engineering
Arlene Tan, Materials Science Engineer

Provider of packaging products. The company offers carrier and cover tapes, and tape and reel packaging products.

**Advantest America Inc**    LH
3061 Zanker Rd
Santa Clara CA 95134
P: 408-456-3600    F: 408-987-0691     PRC:208
www.advantest.com
Email: support-americas@advantest.com

Jamal Saleh, Staff Field Service Engineer
Douglas Lefever, President
Keith Hardwick, Director
Kimiya Sakamoto, EVP of Sales Group
Sanjeev Mohan, EVP of Sales & Support

Provider of measurement systems and solutions. The company offers electronic measuring instruments, and optical sensing and imaging analysis systems.

**Advantiv Technologies Inc**    DH
46781 Fremont Blvd
Fremont CA 94538
P: 510-490-8260   F: 510-490-8264   PRC:212
www.advantivtech.com
Email: sales@advantivtech.com
Estab: 2002

Rich Furuya, COO

Manufacturer and supplier of semiconductor components. The company offers wafers, solar, materials, and vacuum components.

**Advantrics LLC**    HQ
1477 Drew Ave Ste 103
Davis CA 95618
P: 530-297-3660   F: 530-297-3661   PRC:324
www.advantrics.com
Emp: 1-10  Estab: 1998

Eric Overfield, Co-Founder
Greg Snow, Co-Founder
Jason Reckers, COO
Vic Bucher, CFO
Corrie Haffly, Senior Multimedia Developer

Designer and developer of internet technologies. The company also specializes in multimedia-based products.

**Advenira Enterprises Inc**    HQ
320 Soquel Way
Sunnyvale CA 94085
P: 408-732-3950   F: 408-732-3965   PRC:47
www.advenira.com
Email: info@advenira.com
Estab: 2010

Val Ryabov, Director of Engineering
Elmira Ryabova, CEO

Provider of equipment and provision of services for multi functional coating deposition using nanocomposite technology solution.

**Advent Software Inc**    HQ
600 Townsend St 4th Fl
San Francisco CA 94103
P: 415-645-1000   PRC:323
www.advent.com
Email: info@advent.com
Estab: 1983

Karen Geiger, Chief Development Officer
Robert Roley, General Manager
John Hayes, VP of Information Technology and Cloud Delivery
Jack Tsui, VP of Finance
Bob Conchiglia, VP of Advisory Sales and Channel Management

Provider of data services, portfolio, performance, research, client, margin and finance, and revenue management solutions.

**Advisor Software Inc**    HQ
2175 N California Blvd Ste 400
Walnut Creek CA 94596
P: 925-299-7782   PRC:323
www.advisorsoftware.com
Email: asi_sales@advisorsoftware.com
Estab: 1995

Steve Bradley, EVP of Operations and Client Implementation
Michael Granger, EVP of Product Development

Provider of planning, proposal generation, portfolio construction, rebalancing, and investment analytics services.

**Adynxx Inc**    HQ
100 Pine St Ste 500
San Francisco CA 94111
P: 415-512-7740   PRC:249
www.adynxx.com
Email: info@adynxx.com
Estab: 2007

Julien Mamet, Founder
Rick Orr, President
Dina Gonzalez, SVP of Finance
William Martin, EVP of Corporate Development and Operations
Kimberley Hebert, Senior Director of Clinical Operations

Developer of drugs to prevent acute post-surgical pain and the transition to persistent or chronic pain.

**Aechelon Technology Inc**    HQ
888 Brannan St Ste 210
San Francisco CA 94103
P: 415-255-0120   F: 415-255-0129   PRC:323
aechelon.com
Email: support@aechelon.com
Estab: 1998

Vishal Nayak, Senior Graphics Software Engineer
Lucas Fritz, Build
Ignacio Sanz-Pastor, President

Developer of real time computer graphics applications in the training, simulation, and entertainment markets.

**Aegea Medical Inc**    HQ
4055-A Campbell Ave
Menlo Park CA 94025
P: 650-701-1125   F: 650-701-1126   PRC:187
maratreatment.com
Email: info@aegeamedical.com
Estab: 2008

Maria Sainz, President
John Beck, Acting CFO
Don Gurskis, CTO
Thomas Kelly, VP of Operations & Quality Assurance
Natalie Shlafman, VP of Marketing

Developer of women healthcare solutions. The company develops a system for the treatment of excessive menstrual bleeding.

**Aehr Test Systems**    HQ
400 Kato Ter
Fremont CA 94539
P: 510-623-9400   F: 510-623-9450   PRC:15
www.aehr.com
Estab: 1977
Sales: $10M to $30M

Don Richmond, VP of Engineering
Larry Kells, Software Engineer
Azar Hanna, Senior Application Engineer
Jovan Jovanovic, Senior Mechanical Engineer
Jerry Naldo, Senior Applications Engineer

Designer and manufacturer of dynamic burn in and test systems. The company is engaged in troubleshooting and maintenance services.

**Aei Consultants**    BR
1900 Point West Way Ste 142
Sacramento CA 95815
P: 916-333-4568   F: 916-333-4655   PRC:139
aeiconsultants.com
Email: info@aeiconsultants.com
Emp: 11-50 Estab: 1992

Craig Hertz, Founder
Holly Neber, CEO
Paul Hinkston, COO
Mark Nobler, Chief Business Development Officer
Karen Flory, Human Resource Manager

Provider of environmental and engineering services. The company's services also include industrial hygiene and construction.

**Aelan Cell Technologies Inc**    HQ
655 Third St
San Francisco CA 94107
P: 415-488-6041   PRC:34
aelanct.com
Email: contact@aelanct.com
Estab: 2015

Victoria Lunyak, Founder
James Tollervey, Director
Meenakshi Gaur, Director

Provider of research, discovery, development, and commercialization of biomedical technologies for the advancement of human health.

**Aemetis Inc**    HQ
20400 Stevens Creek Blvd Ste 700
Cupertino CA 95014
P: 408-213-0940   F: 408-252-8044   PRC:34
www.aemetis.com
Emp: 53
Sales: $100M to $300M

Jerry Barlow, Mechanical Engineer
Andy Foster, EVP
Sanjeev Gupta, President
Eric McAfee, CEO
Todd Waltz, CFO

Producer of biochemicals, renewable fuels, food, and feed products. The company's products include Z-Microbe, Glycerin, and edible oils.

**AEMTEK Laboratories**    HQ
466 Kato Terrace
Fremont CA 94539
P: 510-979-1979   F: 510-668-1980   PRC:41
www.aemtek.com
Email: info@aemtek.com
Estab: 2002

Florence Wu, President
Feifei Han, Director of Food Testing

Provider of testing, research, training and consulting services and sampling products for the food, environmental and pharmaceutical industries.

**Aerin Medical Inc**    DH
232 E Caribbean Dr
Sunnyvale CA 94089
P: 833-484-8237   PRC:268
www.aerinmedical.com
Email: info@aerinmedical.com
Estab: 2011

Scott Wolf, CEO

Manufacturer of medical devices. The company is also engaged in the development of bionic devices for the mobility impaired.

**Aero Info Inc**      HQ
21115 Longeway Rd Ste A
Sonora CA 95370
P: 209-533-2868   F: 209-536-0497    PRC:8
www.aeroinfoinc.com
Email: sales@aeroinfoinc.com
Emp: 1-10   Estab: 1970

William Rieke, Owner

Designer and manufacturer of ground support equipment. The company caters to the aerospace industry.

**Aero Precision Industries**      HQ
201 Lindbergh Ave
Livermore CA 94551
P: 925-455-9900   F: 925-455-9901    PRC:219
www.aeroprecision.com
Estab: 1993

Evren Ergin, President
Rich Archer, President
Frank Cowle, President
Yuncuoglu Tayfur, Quality Assurance Director
Angel Flores, VP of Regional Sales

Supplier of military aircraft parts for the aerospace industry. The company's services include repair, replacement, and maintenance.

**Aero Turbine Inc**      HQ
6800 S Lindbergh St
Stockton CA 95206
P: 209-983-1112   F: 209-983-0544    PRC:150
www.aeroturbine.aero
Emp: 1-10   Estab: 1978

Douglas Clayton, President

Provider of overhaul, repair, and testing services for turbine engines and accessories. The company also sells engine components and accessories.

**Aero-Environmental Consulting**      HQ
1426 Via Isola
Monterey CA 93940
P: 831-394-1199   F: 831-394-1627    PRC:142
www.aero-enviro.com
Estab: 2002

Jorge Vizcaino, Certified Industrial Hygienist

Provider of environmental consulting solutions. The company's services include air quality assessment, regulatory compliance, and health planning.

**Aerohive Networks Inc**      HQ
1011 McCarthy Blvd
Milpitas CA 95035
P: 408-510-6100   F: 408-510-6199    PRC:67
www.aerohive.com
Email: info365@aerohive.com

Nabil Bukhari, Chief Product and Engineering Officer
E.D. Meyercord, President
John Shoemaker, Chairman
Katy Motiey, CAO
Eric Broockman, CTO

Provider of enterprise mobility solutions. The company offers access points, routers, switches, and VPN gateway solutions.

**Aerojet Rocketdyne**      RH
PO Box 13222
Sacramento CA 95813-6000
P: 916-355-4000   F: 916-351-8667    PRC:7
www.rocket.com
Emp: 11-50 Estab: 1942
Sales: $1B to $3B

Eileen Drake, CEO
Mark Tucker, COO
Paul Lundstrom, VP of Finance
Natalie Schilling, Chief Human Resources Officer
Arjun Kampani, VP

Provider of propulsion and energetic to its space, missile defense, strategic, tactical missile. and armaments customers.

**Aerojet Rocketdyne**      HQ
2001 Aerojet Rd
Sacramento CA 95813-6418
P: 916-355-4000   F: 916-351-8667    PRC:5
www.rocket.com
Email: comments@rocket.com
Emp: 11-50 Estab: 1942

Eileen Drake, CEO
Mark Tucker, COO
Paul Lundstrom, VP of Finance
Natalie Schilling, Chief Human Resources Officer
Tyler Evans, SVP of Defense

Manufacturer of missile and space propulsion components. The company also offers defense weapons and armaments.

**Aerometals**      HQ
3920 Sandstone Dr
El Dorado Hills CA 95762
P: 916-939-6888   F: 916-939-6555    PRC:5
www.aerometals.aero
Emp: 1-10   Estab: 1998

Ingo Cyliax, Electronics Engineer
Chris Campbell, Project Engineer
Jason Haldane, Project Engineer
Mathew Marucci, Engineer
Lorie Symon, President

Manufacturer of heater control valve assembly, gear shafts, and fuel filler caps. The company offers water jet cutting, milling, and lathe services.

**AerospaceComputing Inc**      HQ
465 Fairchild Dr Ste 224
Mountain View CA 94043
P: 650-988-0388   F: 650-988-0389    PRC:36
www.aerospacecomputing.com
Email: acihq@aerospacecomputing.com
Estab: 1989

Nathanial Smith, Research Engineer

Provider of computer technology application services to aerospace sciences. The company also focuses on business development services.

**Aethlabs**      HQ
1640 Valencia St Ste 1C
San Francisco CA 94110
P: 415-529-2355    PRC:138
aethlabs.com
Estab: 2011

Jeff Blair, Founder
Steven Blair, Founder

Provider of black carbon monitoring equipment. The company also deals in manufacturing and assembly services.

**Afc Finishing Systems**      HQ
250 Airport Pkwy
Oroville CA 95965
P: 800-331-7744   F: 530-533-0179    PRC:159
www.afc-ca.com
Email: sales@afc-ca.com
Emp: 1-10   Estab: 1967

Joshua Freeman, Sales Engineer
Carl Hagan, President
Nicky Trevino, VP
Scott Nail, Production Manager
Jeremy Hagan, Sales

Developer of air filter and spray booth products. The company offers auto and truck spray booths, air make-up units, and powder coating products.

**Ag Microsystems Inc**      HQ
3194 De La Cruz Blvd Ste 14
Santa Clara CA 95054
P: 408-834-4888    PRC:170
www.agmicrosystems.com
Email: info@agmicrosystems.com
Estab: 2005

Asif Godil, CEO
Francis Ho, AGM Director
Bushra Godil, AGM Director

Provider of testing and development in the areas of micro electro mechanical systems and micro optics.

**Agari Data Inc**      HQ
950 Tower Ln Ste 2000
Foster City CA 94404
P: 650-627-7667   F: 650-242-4999    PRC:325
www.agari.com
Email: sales@agari.com
Estab: 2009

Patrick Peterson, Founder
Raymond Lim, CFO
John Wilson, CTO
Doug Jones, Chief Business Development and Strategy Officer
John Giacomini, Chief Revenue Officer

Provider of email security and social engineering solutions. The company serves the healthcare, financial services, and government industries.

**Agiga Tech Inc**      BR
198 Champion Ct
San Jose CA 95134
P: 408-943-2600    PRC:126
www.agigatech.com
Email: info@agigatech.com
Estab: 2007

Mark Ross, Co-Founder
John Matze, Founder
Ron Sartore, President
Thad Trent, EVP
Pamela Tondreau, Chief Legal Officer & Human Resource Officer

Designer and manufacturer of memory solutions. The company's portfolio includes AGIGARAM, SDRAM, and PowerGEM.

**Agile Global Solutions Inc**  HQ
13405 Folsom Blvd Ste 507
Folsom CA 95630
P: 916-655-7745   F: 916-848-3659   PRC:323
www.agileglobalsolutions.com
Email: info@agileglobal.com
Emp: 11-50 Estab: 2003

Nathan Stewart, Business Development Manager
Jaswinder Singh, Talent Acquisition Specialist
Evan Privett, Geologist

Provider of business and IT solutions such as
custom and enterprise application management
and mobile business solutions.

**Agile Thermal Technologies Inc**  HQ
3663 N Laughlin Rd Ste 101
Santa Rosa CA 95403-9067
P: 707-570-0304   PRC:159
www.atsquared.com
Email: procurement@atsquared.com

Mark Mahone, President

Designer of industrial vacuum and atmosphere
systems. The company also provides procurement, program management, and prime contractor
capabilities.

**Agilis Software LLC**  HQ
548 Market St Ste 95777
San Francisco CA 94104
P: 415-458-2614   F: 408-404-8480   PRC:326
agilis-sw.com
Estab: 2002

Vinay Sabharwal, CEO
Matt Teter, VP of Customer Experience

Developer of software licensing and software
license management solution for enterprise
software, embedded systems, and cloud software
industries.

**Agiloft Inc**  HQ
460 Seaport Ct Ste 200
Redwood City CA 94063
P: 650-587-8615   F: 650-745-1209   PRC:319
www.agiloft.com
Email: sales@agiloft.com
Estab: 1991

Colin Earl, CEO
Patricia Pritts, VP of Sales

Provider of contract, work flow, change, and asset
management services. The company offers services to armed forces and universities.

**Agnitus**  HQ
120 Hawthorne Ave
Palo Alto CA 94301
P: 877-565-1460   PRC:322
www.agnitus.com
Estab: 2011

Azhar Khan, CEO
Haris Khan, Chief Product Officer & Co-Founder
Lance Vikaros, Executive Director of Education
Jillian OrRico, Director of Educational Partner-
ships
Heather Browning, STEM Game Designer

Developer of touch enabled learning applications
for iPad. The company specializes in educational
games such as little bo peep and ABC hide n
seek.

**Agra Tech Inc**  HQ
2131 Piedmont Way
Pittsburg CA 94565
P: 925-432-3399   F: 925-432-3521   PRC:137
agratech.com
Email: agratech@agratech.com
Estab: 1973

John Pound, CEO
Anita Pound, COO
Adam Pound, Sales Manager
James Roberts, Technical Support
Erik Klug, Order Coordinator

Manufacturer of greenhouses and accessories
for commercial, horticultural, and agricultural
growers. The company offers heating and cooling
equipment.

**Agri-Analysis LLC**  BR
950 W Chiles Rd
Davis CA 95616
P: 800-506-9852   F: 530-757-4655   PRC:43
agri-analysis.com
Email: info@agri-analysis.com
Emp: 11-50 Estab: 1981

Alan Wei, Owner
Andrew Zinkl, Lab Technician

Provider of agricultural diagnostic laboratory services. The company specializes in grapevine virus
testing services.

**Agrian Inc**  HQ
2665 N Air-Fresno Dr Ste 101
Fresno CA 93727
P: 559-437-5700   PRC:324
www.agrian.com
Email: support@agrian.com
Emp: 1-10   Estab: 2004

Peter Brandt, VP of Engineering
Trevor Stone, Software Engineer
Troy Lonie, Test Engineer
Richard Machado, President
Nishan Majarian, CEO

Provider of agridata tracking and information sharing system for applicator, retail outlets, grower, and
crop consultant via computer and mobile devices.

**Agricultural Manufacturing Company
Inc**  HQ
4106 S Cedar Ave
Fresno CA 93725
P: 559-485-1662   PRC:159
agmanco.com
Emp: 1-10

John Cabrera, Manager
Sabino Mendez, Manager

Manufacturer of sprayers. The company specializes in engineering agricultural spraying equipment
and other products such as pumps and tanks.

**Ags Inc**  HQ
5 Freelon St
San Francisco CA 94107
P: 415-777-2166   F: 415-777-2167   PRC:41
www.agsinc.com
Estab: 1983

Ken Litle, Senior Principal Civil Engineer
Kamran Ghiassi, Principal Engineer
Erik Scheller, Principal Civil Engineer
Keyvan Fotoohi, Principal Geotechnical Engineer
Jake Horwath, Staff Engineer

Provider of civil, structural, and geotechnical engineering services. The company serves the water
and transportation infrastructure markets.

**Ags Plasma Systems Inc**  HQ
3064 Kenneth St
Santa Clara CA 95054
P: 408-855-8686   PRC:165
www.agsplasma.com
Email: info@agsplasma.com
Estab: 1991

Allen Guastavino, President

Manufacturer and distributor of vacuum plasma
systems. The company serves microelectronics
and optoelectronics industries.

**AGTEK Development Company Inc**  HQ
396 Earhart Way
Livermore CA 94551
P: 925-606-8197   F: 925-606-9320   PRC:323
www.agtek.com
Email: sales@agtek.com

Michael Clapp, CTO
Victoria Swingle, CFO
Bill Cope, VP of Marketing
Theresa Clarke, Order Processing Renewals
Manager

Developer of high tech surveying, analysis, and
control solutions for residential, commercial, transportation, water, energy, and government.

**Aheadtek**  HQ
6410 Via Del Oro
San Jose CA 95119
P: 408-226-9800   F: 408-226-9195   PRC:60
www.aheadtek.com

Hui Xiao, Engineering Manager
Daisy Nguyen, Marketing Coordinator
Patrick Johnston, VP
Leslie Mesa, Manager
Anthony Rodriguez, Maintenance Technician

Supplier of magnetic head solutions. The company
specializes in television broadcast, video production, and computer and data storage.

**Ahram Biosystems Inc**  HQ
1549 Ilikai Ave
San Jose CA 95118-1943
P: 408-645-7300   PRC:31
www.ahrambio.com
Email: info@ahrambio-us.com
Estab: 2001

William Lee, Manager

Developer of new life science tools. The company
provides battery-powered, palm-size portable
PCR machine.

**Aimer Corp**  HQ
3250 McKinley Dr
Santa Clara CA 95051
P: 408-260-8588   F: 408-260-9539   PRC:80
aimercorp.com
Estab: 1994

John Tchiang, CEO

Provider of thermal management products. The
company also offers connectors, PCB boards,
cables, and mechanical parts.

**Aimmune Therapeutics** RH
8000 Marina Blvd Ste 200
Brisbane CA 94005-1884
P: 650-614-5220   F: 650-616-0075   PRC:34
www.aimmune.com
Email: info@aimmune.com
Estab: 2011
Sales: $100M to $300M

Stephen Dilly, CEO
Jeffrey Knapp, COO
Warren DeSouza, CFO
Kristin Bennett, Senior Director of Marketing
Jerome Pinkett, Senior Director of Clinical Operations

Developer of desensitization treatments. The company is engaged in clinical trials and it serves the healthcare sector.

**Air Exchange Inc** HQ
495 Edison Ct Ste A
Fairfield CA 94534
P: 800-300-2945   F: 707-864-2705   PRC:125
www.airexchange.com
Email: info@airexchange.com
Estab: 1982

Leif Neuman, Sales Engineer
James Fox, Sales Engineer
Dick Bertani, President

Supplier of air purification and clean air machines, and fans. The company serves commercial facilities and public institutions.

**Air Monitor Corp** HQ
1050 Hopper Ave
Santa Rosa CA 95403
P: 707-544-2706   F: 707-526-9970   PRC:233
www.airmonitor.com
Email: amcsales@airmonitor.com
Estab: 1967

Joseph Cox, Electronics Engineering Technician
Dean DeBaun, President
Andrew Chew, Project Manager of Engineering
Paresh Dave, Manager of Applications Engineering
Gordon Ayers, Service Supervisor

Manufacturer of airflow and space pressurization control systems and offers airflow traverse probes, pressure sensors, and electronic transmitters.

**Air Worldwide Corp** BR
388 Market St Ste 750
San Francisco CA 94111
P: 415-912-3111   F: 415-912-3112   PRC:322
www.air-worldwide.com
Email: info@air-worldwide.com

Bill Churney, President
Jayanta Guin, EVP
Boris Davidson, SVP
Peter Lewis, SVP of Information Technologies and Services
David Lalonde, SVP of Consulting & Client Services

Provider of software development and consulting services. The company focuses on risk modeling software and risk assessment and management consulting.

M-16

**Air-O-Fan Products** HQ
507 E Dinuba Ave
Reedley CA 93654
P: 559-638-6546   F: 559-638-9262   PRC:159
airofan.com
Email: info@airofan.com
Emp: 1-10   Estab: 1987

Brent Davis, Sales & Marketing Manager
Paul Mariscal, Welder

Developer of spray application machinery solutions. The company manufactures engine and PTO drives for orchard, vineyard, and herbicide sprayers.

**Aire Sheet Metal** HQ
1973 E Bayshore Rd
Redwood City CA 94063
P: 650-364-8081   PRC:88
www.airesm.com
Email: pm@airesm.com
Estab: 1971

Marie Madden, Sales Engineer
Arsalan Khan, Project Engineer
Eugene Bramlett, Founder
Bob Bramlett, President
Marlo Bramlett, VP

Provider of mechanical and architectural sheet metal services. The company is involved in the design and construction of commercial projects.

**Airgard Inc** HQ
2190 Paragon Dr
San Jose CA 95131
P: 408-573-0701   PRC:133
www.airgard.net
Email: info@airgard.net
Estab: 1988

Dan White, Chairman
Mark Johnsgard, CTO
Martin Johnson, CFO
Richard Dabu, Manufacturing Lead
Kevin McGinnis, VP of sales and Marketing

Manufacturer of gas scrubbers servicing epitaxial, metal etch, poly etch, and CVD process abatement applications.

**Airnex Communications Inc** HQ
PO Box 11357
Pleasanton CA 94588-1357
P: 800-708-4884   PRC:64
www.airnex.com
Email: info@airnex.com
Estab: 1995

Dennis Duran, Head of Network Operations
Zara Arev, Bilingual CSR

Provider of digital wireless telecommunications and internet access services. The company also focuses on web hosting.

**Airpoint Precision Inc** HQ
6221 D Enterprise Dr
Diamond Springs CA 95619
P: 530-622-0510   F: 530-621-0510   PRC:80
www.airpointinc.com
Email: customerservice@airpointinc.com
Emp: 1-10

Clem Fanning, Quality Control

Provider of precision machining services. The company serves the industrial needs of the community in a cost efficient and timely manner.

**Airtronics Metal Products Inc** HQ
140 San Pedro Ave
Morgan Hill CA 95037
P: 408-977-7800   F: 408-977-7810   PRC:88
www.airtronics.com
Email: info@airtronics.com
Estab: 1960

Jim Ellis, VP of Engineering & Production
Aaron Lahann, Customer Engineering Manager
Jeffrey Burke, President
Fermin Rodriguez, VP of Manufacturing
Mike Nevin, Director of Sales & Marketing

Manufacturer of sheet metal fabrication and machining. The company provides custom sheets for the electronics, telecommunications and other markets.

**Airxpanders Inc** HQ
3047 Orchard Pkwy
San Jose CA 95134
P: 650-390-9000   PRC:11
www.airxpanders.com
Estab: 2006

Thavy Dy, Production Supervisor
Nelida Vazquez, Quality Assurance Technician
Belinda Pinedo, Director of Regulatory Affairs

Provider of controlled tissue expander and small handheld wireless controller of breast cancer reconstructive surgery.

**Aitech International Corp** HQ
1288 Kifer Rd
Sunnyvale CA 94086
P: 408-991-9699   F: 408-991-9691   PRC:208
aitech.com
Email: aitech-sales@aitech.com
Estab: 1987

Michael Chen, Founder

Provider of video conversion technology solutions. The company provides scan converters, wireless products, HDTV tuners, HDMI switches, and cables.

**Aja Video Systems Inc** HQ
180 Litton Dr
Grass Valley CA 95945
P: 530-274-2048   F: 530-274-9442   PRC:60
www.aja.com
Email: sales@aja.com
Emp: 1-10   Estab: 1993

Eric Gysen, Director of Engineering
Ujval Lodha, Engineering Department Manager
Jim Schroeder, QA Engineer
Bonnie Galvin, Senior Software Engineer II
Nick Rashby, President

Provider of video systems and routers. The company also offers broadcast and mini converters and recording equipment.

**AKM Semiconductor Inc** HQ
226 Airport Pkwy Ste 470
San Jose CA 95110
P: 408-436-8580   PRC:208
www.akm.com
Estab: 1995

Masao Awatsu, RF Application Engineering Manager
Paul Werner, VP of Sales
Jun Tokunaga, Reference Design Manager
Alice Yen, Senior Accountant

Designer and manufacturer of mixed signal integrated circuits. The company serves consumer electronics, industrial, and automotive sectors.

**Akmi Corp** HQ
19240 Cabot Blvd
Hayward CA 94545
P: 510-670-9550   F: 510-670-9540   PRC:150
www.akmicorp.com
Email: inquiry@akmicorp.com
Estab: 1981

Mitra Ashraf, President
Charles Harvey, Purchasing Manager
Pat Johnson, Sales Manager
Kenneth Kling, Sales Representative

Distributor of aftermarket diesel engine parts. The company provides accessory drive units, camshafts, flywheels, and exhaust manifolds.

**Akon Inc** HQ
2135 Ringwood Ave
San Jose CA 95131
P: 408-432-8039   F: 408-432-1089   PRC:209
www.akoninc.com
Estab: 1980

Steven Pekarthy, CFO
Richard Sanders, Senior Program Manager
Lynette Ovalle, Accounting Assistant

Supplier of microwave products. The company focuses on airborne, ground, shipboard, and space applications.

**Akribis Systems Inc USA** RH
780 Montague Expy Ste 508
San Jose CA 95131
P: 408-913-1300   PRC:150
www.akribis-sys.com
Estab: 2004

Joseph Blake, Application Engineer
Wenhan Tang, Application Engineer
Thomas Barrett, Applications Engineer

Designer and manufacturer of motors, stages, and precision systems. The company's products are used in inspection and testing applications.

**Akros Silicon Inc** HQ
6399 San Ignacio Ave Ste 250
San Jose CA 95119
P: 408-746-9000   F: 408-746-9391   PRC:130
www.akrossilicon.com
Email: info@akrossilicon.com
Estab: 2005

John Camagna, VP of Engineering
J. Crepin, President
Dan Olson, VP of Sales
Danny Gur, VP
Sunil Vora, Director of Operations

Provider of power management ICs. The company offers digital DC-DC controllers and Ethernet protection dual channel active EMI suppressors.

**Aktana Inc** HQ
207 Powell St 8th Fl
San Francisco CA 94102
P: 888-707-3125   PRC:323
www.aktana.com
Estab: 2008

Jin Huang, CTO
Derek Choy, Co-Founder
David Ehrlich, President
Pini Ben or, Chief Science Officer
Richard Van Hoesen, CFO

Provider of decision support engine that pores through multiple data services and delivers insights and suggestions right in the rep's workflow.

**Al & L Crop Solutions** HQ
7769 N Meridian Rd
Vacaville CA 95688
P: 707-693-3050   F: 530-387-3270   PRC:41
www.allcropsolutions.com
Email: info@allcropsolutions.com

Anna-Liisa Fabritius, Plant Pathologist

Provider of solutions for crops. The company specializes in disease testing services for grapevine diseases and soil pathogens.

**Alacrinet Consulting Services Inc** HQ
530 Lytton Ave 2nd Fl
Palo Alto CA 94301
P: 650-646-2670   PRC:324
www.alacrinet.com
Email: info@alacrinet.com
Estab: 2002

Brian Bouchard, President
Daniel Duhaime, VP of Sales
Marykay Michaels, Director of Professional Services

Developer of software solutions. The company offers enterprise search, web content management, business intelligence, and analytics services.

**Alchemic Solutions Group Inc** HQ
1720 S Amphlett Blvd Ste 168
San Mateo CA 94030-2710
P: 510-919-8105   PRC:323
www.alchemicsolutions.com
Email: info@alchemicsolutions.com

Jane Chen, Partner
Mark Trinh, Partner
Peter Trinh, Partner
Ray Taylor, Partner

Provider of technology marketing solutions for wireless sectors. The company focuses on product management, software development, and consultation.

**Aldelo LP** HQ
6800 Koll Center Pkwy Ste 310
Pleasanton CA 94566
P: 925-621-2410   PRC:323
www.aldelo.com
Email: sales@aldelo.com

Jeff Moore, VP of Operations
Jerry Wilson, VP of Merchant Services
Brenden Carney, Information Technology Support Manager

Provider of software solutions. The company offers solutions for the hospitality, retail, and payment processing industries.

**Aldetec Inc** HQ
3560 Business Dr Ste 100
Sacramento CA 95820
P: 916-453-3382   F: 916-453-3384   PRC:60
www.aldetec.com
Email: aldetec@aldetec.com
Emp: 1-10   Estab: 1999

Dan Almond, Engineering Technician
Teresa Robertson, Office Manager

Manufacturer of microwave amplifier products. The company provides low noise amplifiers, down converters, and octave band amplifiers.

**Aldo Ventures Inc** HQ
7370 Viewpoint Rd
Aptos CA 95003
P: 831-662-2536   PRC:324
www.aldo.com
Email: info@aldo.com
Emp: 1-10

Avron Barr, Principal
Shirley Tessler, Principal

Provider of studies such as software technology, markets, companies, platforms, products, and investment strategies of the software industry.

**Alector LLC** HQ
151 Oyster Point Blvd Ste 300
S San Francisco CA 94080
P: 415-231-5660   PRC:268
www.alector.com
Email: info@alector.com
Estab: 2013
Sales: $10M to $30M

Sun Jeonghoon, Head of Antibody Discovery and Protein Engineering
Arnon Rosenthal, Co-Founder
Tillman Gerngross, Chairman
Robert King, Chief Development Officer
Sabah Oney, Chief Business Officer

Developer of therapeutics. The company specializes in cutting edge antibody technologies for treating alzheimers disease.

**Alert Technologies Corp** HQ
4847 Hopyard Rd
Pleasanton CA 94588
P: 925-461-5934   F: 925-461-5938   PRC:323
www.alerttech.com
Estab: 1996

Jim Paulson, Manager

Developer of emergency management software. The company offers professional services to assist customers in solving their information management challenges.

**Alertenterprise Inc** HQ
4350 Starboard Dr
Fremont CA 94538
P: 510-440-0840   F: 510-440-0841   PRC:327
www.alertenterprise.com
Email: info@alertenterprise.com
Estab: 2007

Jasvir Gill, CEO
Kaval Kaur, CFO
Ruby Deol, COO
Azizur Rahman, VP of Global Business Development & Sales
Willem Ryan, VP of Marketing and Communications

Developer of information and operational technology solutions such as identity intelligence, and enterprise access, and incident management.

**Algo-Logic Systems** HQ
172 Component Dr
San Jose CA 95131-1132
P: 408-707-3740   F: 408-618-8953   PRC:322
algo-logic.com
Email: solutions@algo-logic.com
Estab: 2009

John Lockwood, CEO
John Hagerman, VP of Marketing & Business Development
John Horn, Legal Counsel

Specializes in building networking solutions. The company also offers technological and data handling services to firms.

**AlgoMedica Inc** HQ
440 N Wolfe Rd
Sunnyvale CA 94085
P: 516-448-3124 PRC:194
www.algomedica.com
Email: info@algomedica.com

Ramesh Neelmegh, President
Jagdish Vij, CEO

Developer of medical imaging software based on artificial neural networks for abdomen/pelvis, head, and liver and pediatrics CT scans.

**Alien Technology Corp** HQ
845 Embedded Way
San Jose CA 95138-1030
P: 408-782-3900   F: 408-782-3908 PRC:61
www.alientechnology.com
Estab: 1994

Mark McDonald, VP of Engineering & Solutions
Leiping Lai, President
Zhongrui Xia, Chairman
Glenn Haegele, CFO
David Aaron, Chief Legal Officer

Provider of UHF radio frequency identification products and services to customers in retail, consumer goods, logistics, and pharmaceutical industries.

**Align Technology Inc** HQ
2560 Orchard Pkwy
San Jose CA 95131
P: 408-470-1000   F: 408-470-1010 PRC:189
www.aligntech.com
Estab: 1997
Sales: $1B to $3B

Geen George, Senior Software Engineer
Joseph Hogan, President
John Morici, CFO
Stuart Hockridge, SVP of Global Human Resources
Raphael Pascaud, Chief Marketing Portfolio & Business Development Officer

Provider of medical devices such as invisalign clear aligners, itero intraoral scanners and ortho-CAD digital services for orthodontic industry.

**Alisto Engineering Group Inc** HQ
2737 N Main St Ste 200
Walnut Creek CA 94597
P: 925-279-5000   F: 925-279-5001 PRC:142
www.alisto.com
Email: subcontracts@alisto.com
Estab: 1992

Stanley Hill, Senior Project Manager
James Ramos, Staff Engineer
Nancy Valero, CFO
Ray Valdez, Construction Manager
Clem Holst, Program Manager

Provider of engineering and environmental consulting services. The company serves the private industry and government agencies.

M-18

**All Fab Precision Sheetmetal Inc** HQ
1015 Timothy Dr
San Jose CA 95133
P: 408-279-1099   F: 408-297-3803 PRC:80
www.allfabprecision.com
Estab: 1999

Son Ho, President

Provider of contract manufacturing services for metal formed products. The company is involved in laser cutting, deburring, bending, and welding activities.

**All PCB Solutions Inc** HQ
1370 H Industrial Ave
Petaluma CA 94952
P: 707-778-2330 PRC:211
Estab: 1982

Janice Wistner, Manager

Provider of PCB solutions. The company is engaged in fabrication, solder masking, and finishing services.

**All Power Labs** HQ
1010 Murray St
Berkeley CA 94710
P: 510-845-1500   F: 510-550-2837 PRC:142
www.allpowerlabs.com
Estab: 2008

Brendan Quinlan, Mechanical Engineer
Jim Mason, Founder
Jay Hasty, Senior Technical Advisor
Herman Vinoya, Assembler
Dan Kammen, Manager

Manufacturer of biomass fueled power generators. The company is a global leader in small scale gasification.

**All Sensors Corp** HQ
16035 Vineyard Blvd
Morgan Hill CA 95037
P: 408-225-4314   F: 408-225-2079 PRC:236
www.allsensors.com
Email: info@allsensors.com
Estab: 1999

Joe Curren, Senior Development Engineer
Katie Dauenhauer, Production Control Manager
Jim Brownell, Sales Manager
Dale Dauenhauer, VP of Operations
Jason Paiva, QMS Specialist

Manufacturer of MEMS piezoresitive pressure sensors and pressure transducers. The company serves the medical, industrial, and HVAC markets.

**All Systems Broadband** HQ
50 Contractors St Ste 200
Livermore CA 94551
P: 877-272-4984 PRC:298
www.allsystemsbroadband.com
Email: info@allsystemsbroadband.com
Estab: 2006

Jason Skeoch, CEO
Sean Fernandez, COO
Janis Deroche, Director of Global Supplier Management & Quality
Carrie Powell, National Sales Coordinator
Gary Choy, Operations Manager

Provider of intelligent connectivity and engineering solutions and a supplier of fiber connectivity products.

**All Weather Inc** HQ
1165 National Dr
Sacramento CA 95834
P: 800-824-5873   F: 916-928-1165 PRC:13
www.allweatherinc.com
Email: marketing@allweatherinc.com
Emp: 1-10   Estab: 1977

Neal Dillman, CTO
Steve Glander, Sales Manager
Barbara Baca, Sales Manager
Bob Perrin, EVP of Engineering & Customer Service
Maria Gustafson, Office Manager

Manufacturer of meteorological instruments and systems. The company is also engaged in the development of air traffic management solutions.

**Allaccem Inc** HQ
1300 Industrial Rd Ste 16
San Carlos CA 94070
P: 650-593-8700 PRC:252
www.allaccem.com
Estab: 2005

Jeffery Whiteford, President

Manufacturer of pharmaceutical products such as dermatology, optic, and dental products for goats, dogs, and cats.

**Allakos Inc** HQ
975 Island Dr Ste 201
Redwood City CA 94070
P: 650-597-5002 PRC:30
www.allakos.com
Estab: 2012

Adam Tomasi, President
Robert Alexander, CEO
Simon Greenwood, Chief Business Officer
Tim Varacek, CCO
Leo Redmond, CFO

Developer of therapeutic antibodies for the treatment of inflammatory and proliferative diseases such as asthma, nasal polyposis, and fibrosis.

**ALLCells LLC** HQ
1301 Harbor Bay Pkwy Ste 200
Alameda CA 94502
P: 510-726-2700   F: 510-521-7600 PRC:36
allcells.com
Email: orders@allcells.com
Estab: 1998

Laurie Ho, Purchasing Associate
Eric Lau, Bioservices Scientist
Erin Kelly, Scientist

Provider of medical services for human primary cells. The company focuses on fields such as cell biology, oncology, and virology.

**Allegro Consultants Inc** HQ
PO Box 4049
Menlo Park CA 94026-4049
P: 408-252-2330   F: 408-200-4488 PRC:323
www.allegro.com
Email: info@allegro.com
Estab: 1984

Donna Hofmeister, Senior Support Specialist

Provider of operating system technical support for third party maintenance and multi-vendor service community.

**Allergy Research Group LLC** HQ
2300 N Loop Rd
Alameda CA 94502
P: 510-263-2000  F: 510-263-2100  PRC:250
www.allergyresearchgroup.com
Email: info@allergyresearchgroup.com
Estab: 1979

Stephen Levine, Founder
Fred Salomon, President
Jason Lui, Senior Financial Analyst

Provider of nutritional products for blood sugar,
brain, cardiovascular, metabolic, hormone, liver,
and immune support.

**Alliacense** HQ
20883 Stevens Creek Blvd Ste 100
Cupertino CA 95014
P: 408-446-4222  PRC:304
www.alliacense.com
Email: customerservice@alliacense.com

Mac Leckrone, President
Mike Davis, SVP of Licensing
Dung Nguyen, Technology Analyst
Parag Desai, Microprocessor Systems Analyst

Provider of intellectual property solutions. The
company's services include broad spectrum,
reverse engineering, and product reports.

**Alliance Memory Inc** BR
511 Taylor Way
San Carlos CA 94070
P: 650-610-6800  F: 650-620-9211  PRC:126
www.alliancememory.com

David Bagby, President
Mitch Labbie, Director of Sales

Manufacturer of memory semiconductor products.
The company's products include SRAM, DRAM,
SDRAM ICS, and DDR SDRAM.

**Alliance Support Partners Inc** HQ
5036 Commercial Cir Unit C
Concord CA 94520
P: 925-363-5382  F: 925-363-7882  PRC:316
www.asp-support.com
Email: sales@asp-support.com
Estab: 2004

Chuck Eyerly, President
Harold Ng, CEO

Provider of test solutions, instrumentation
engineering, test system design, and turn-key
outsourcing support services.

**Allied Crane Inc** HQ
855 N Parkside Dr
Pittsburg CA 94565
P: 925-427-9200  PRC:179
alliedcrane.us
Email: mail@alliedcrane.us
Estab: 1976

Dave Costa, President
Richard deNijs, Projects
Sandy Cariel, Accounting Analyst

Provider of crane services. The company offers
crane repair, installation and removal, and preventive maintenance programs.

**Allied Environmental Inc** HQ
26291 Production Ave Ste 1
Hayward CA 94545
P: 510-732-1300  PRC:139
alliedenv.com
Estab: 1995

Allen Wellborn, CEO
Alan Salmen, VP
Jamie Falgoust, Office Manager
Jason Standley, Project Manager
Ora Buckley, Estimator

Provider of asbestos and lead abatement services. The company specializes in commercial,
residential, and industrial contracting services.

**Allied Fire Protection** HQ
555 High St
Oakland CA 94601
P: 510-533-5516  F: 510-533-0913  PRC:159
www.alliedfire.com
Email: sales@alliedfire.com

Bill Milligan, Design Engineer
Tina Tiller, CAO
Kevin Thomas, Chief Estimator
Linda Lequieu, Office Manager
Tim Jausoro, Estimator

Designer and manufacturer of fire protection sprinkler systems. The company also offers installation
services.

**Allied Security Alarms** HQ
130 Produce Ave Ste D
S San Francisco CA 94080
P: 650-871-8959  F: 650-871-8973  PRC:59
www.allied24.com
Email: contactus@allied24.com
Estab: 1971

Rudy Alva, Owner
Patricia Alva, Manager

Provider of security products such as fire and bur-
glar alarms, video surveillance systems, motion
detectors, and access controls.

**Allied Telesis Inc** BR
3041 Orchard Pkwy
San Jose CA 95134
P: 408-519-8700  PRC:67
www.alliedtelesis.com
Estab: 1987

Dennis Duchmann, Manager of Components
Engineering
Carl Go, Senior Manufacturing Test Engineer
Roger Tong, Senior Mechanical Design Engineer
Satinder Singh, DVT Engineer
Tuan Ha, Quality Manager

Developer of network solutions for internet protocol surveillance. The company focuses on web
hosting and programming solutions.

**Allmotion Inc** HQ
30097 Ahern Ave
Union City CA 94587
P: 510-471-4000  F: 510-400-8001  PRC:292
www.allmotion.com
Email: support@allmotion.com

Brad Douglas, Engineer
David Goodin, Owner

Manufacturer and distributor of stepper drives,
stepper controllers, servo drives, and servo
controllers.

**Alloy Metal Products** HQ
7801 Las Positas Rd
Livermore CA 94551
P: 925-371-1234  F: 925-371-2367  PRC:80
www.alloymp.com
Estab: 1977

Fred Matter, Founder
Gary Pardini, Operations Manager

Provider of precision CNC machining, tumbling,
annealing, cutting, and packaging services. The
company serves aerospace and medical device
fields.

**Alltech** BR
4041 N Fresno Ste 104
Fresno CA 93726
P: 559-226-0405  F: 559-226-0409  PRC:23
www.alltech.com
Email: info@alltech.com
Emp: 11-50 Estab: 1980

Deirdre Lyons, Co-Founder
Mark Lyons, President
Nathan Hohman, VP
Ronan Power, VP
Alric Blake, COO

Provider of nutritional innovation in animal feed.
The company adds nutrition to food through yeast
fermentation, enzyme technology, algae and
nutrigenomics.

**Allteq Industries Inc** HQ
115 Pullman St
Livermore CA 94551
P: 925-243-6400  F: 925-243-6419  PRC:86
www.allteq.com
Email: info@allteq.com
Estab: 1983

William Miller, CEO

Manufacturer of microscopes, lighting, optics,
and semiconductor products. The company also
provides die coating, dispensing, and adhesion
promotion.

**Allterra Environmental Inc** HQ
207 McPherson St Ste B
Santa Cruz CA 95060
P: 831-425-2608  F: 831-425-2609  PRC:142
www.allterraenv.com
Email: info@allterraenv.com
Emp: 1-10

Samantha Willis, Staff Engineer
James Allen, President
Nathaniel Allen, COO
Micah Breeden, CFO
Joe Mangine, Environmental Division Director

Provider of environmental site remediation and
compliance services. The company offerings
include permitting, geologic hazards, and sustainable solutions.

**Allvia Inc** HQ
657 N Pastoria Ave
Sunnyvale CA 94085
P: 408-212-3200   F: 408-720-3334   PRC:79
www.allvia.com
Email: info@allvia.com
Estab: 1997

Sergey Savastiouk, CEO
Biswajit Sur, Director of Technology & Mfg
Jim Hewlett, Test & Equipment Manager

Provider of silicon interposer and through-silicon via foundry services to the semiconductor and optoelectronics industries.

**Allwin21 Corp** HQ
220 Cochrane Cir
Morgan Hill CA 95037
P: 408-778-7788   F: 408-904-7168   PRC:212
www.allwin21.com
Email: sales@allwin21.com
Estab: 2000

Qing Zhou, Engineer
Jian Xu, Staff Engineer
Han Yingjun, Engineer
Hunter Liu, System Engineer
Peter Chen, Market Manager

Provider of high-tech equipment, related services, and technical support for the semiconductor and biomedical industries.

**Allwire Inc** HQ
16395 Ave 24 1/2
Chowchilla CA 93610
P: 559-665-4893   F: 559-665-7389   PRC:202
allwire.com
Email: info@allwire.com
Emp: 1-10   Estab: 1967

Dana Oyler, VP of Sales

Provider of design, analysis, and programming services for businesses. The company is also involved in web hosting and technical support.

**Alpha & Omega Semiconductor** HQ
475 Oakmead Pkwy
Sunnyvale CA 94085
P: 408-830-9742   F: 408-830-9749   PRC:212
www.aosmd.com
Email: inquiries@aosmd.com
Estab: 2000
Sales: $300M to $1 Billion

James Yang, Product Engineering Manager
Jun Hu, Staff Engineer
Aaron Chou, Staff Product Engineer
Yi Su, Senior Staff Device Design Engineer
Yueh-Se Ho, Co-Founder

Designer, developer, and supplier of power semiconductors. The company's applications include notebook PCs and power supplies.

**Alpha Networks Inc** HQ
1551 McCarthy Blvd Ste. 201
Milpitas CA 95035
P: 408-844-8850   F: 408-844-8841   PRC:97
www.alphanetworks.com

Jerry Chang, Senior Hardware Engineer
Yuchin Lin, President
John Lee, CEO
Claire Yu, Manager of Investor Relations
Vanessa Lan, Associate Project Manager of Investor Relations

Designer and manufacturer of networking products. The company also focuses on computers and computer peripherals.

**Alpha Omega Wireless Inc** BR
5710 Auburn Blvd Ste 2
Sacramento CA 95841
P: 800-997-9250   F: 512-298-1646   PRC:63
www.aowireless.com
Email: info@aowireless.com
Emp: 11-50 Estab: 2003

Joe Wargo, President

Provider of broadband wireless network technology integration solutions. The company also focuses on wireless backhaul solutions.

**Alpha Orthotics Corp** HQ
PO Box 1107
Tiburon CA 94920
P: 415-389-8980   F: 415-389-1063   PRC:190
www.alphaorthotics.com
Email: info@alphaorthotics.com
Estab: 1998

Donna Egeberg, Office Manager

Distributor of non-invasive orthotic products. The company provides products for catalogs, specialty foot retailers, and medical distributors.

**Alpha Research & Technology Inc** HQ
5175 Hillsdale Cir
El Dorado Hills CA 95762-5708
P: 916-431-9340   F: 916-431-9360   PRC:327
www.artruggedsystems.com
Email: busdev@artruggedsystems.com
Emp: 1-10   Estab: 1993

Steve Totah, Systems Engineer
Donne Smith, CTO
Deann Kerr, Co-Founder
Sherrie Zeitler, Buyer

Designer and manufacturer of airborne systems for command, communications, intelligence, surveillance, and other needs and focuses on installation.

**Alpha Scientific Electronics** HQ
1868 National Ave
Hayward CA 94545
P: 510-782-4747   F: 510-782-5474   PRC:15
www.alphascientific.com
Email: sales@alphascientific.com
Estab: 1988

Bill Sherman, Engineer
Ron Rumrill, President
Osvaldo Alencar, CEO
Lita Clapper, Office Manager

Designer, manufacturer, and seller of precision power supplies and electronic products. The company's products are used in medical instrumentation.

**Alphaems Corp** HQ
44193 S Grimmer Blvd
Fremont CA 94538
P: 510-498-8788   F: 510-498-4484   PRC:91
www.alphaemscorp.com

Ben Wang, VP of Engineering
Micol Hung, Engineering Manager
Randy Nguyen, Manufacturing Engineer
Eric Chang, President
Shulin Chen, Co-Founder

Provider of printed circuit board prototyping and PCB assembly production services. The company also involves in material purchasing and warehousing.

**Alphalyse Inc** HQ
200 Page Mill Rd Ste 100
Palo Alto CA 94306
P: 650-543-3193   F: 650-543-3193   PRC:36
alphalyse.com
Email: info@alphalyse.com

Thomas Kofoed, CEO

Provider of protein analysis services. The company focuses on support research, manufacturing, and clinical development activities.

**AlphaSense Inc** HQ
1 Sansome St Ste 3500
San Francisco CA 94104
P: 415-738-8090   PRC:325
www.alpha-sense.com
Emp: 11-50 Estab: 2008

Raj Neervannan, CTO
Daniel Riccio, Marketing Manager
Lori Goodwin, VP
Gina Clinton, Senior Accountant

Provider of financial search engine. The company offers natural language processing algorithms with advanced semantic indexing and search technology.

**Alstem Inc** HQ
2600 Hilltop Dr Bldg B Ste C328
Richmond CA 94806
P: 510-708-0096   PRC:36
www.alstembio.com
Email: info@alstembio.com
Estab: 2012

Gang Li, Founder
Patrick Hop, Director of AI Research
Scott Ezell, Senior Data Scientist

Provider of virus concentration and transduction solutions. The company's offerings include assay kits, antibodies etc.

**Alta Design & Manufacturing Inc** HQ
885 Auzerais Ave
San Jose CA 95126
P: 408-450-5394   F: 408-450-5395   PRC:80
alta-eng.com
Estab: 1999

Steven Hernandez, President

Manufacturer of precision-machined components. The company is engaged in production manufacturing, prototype services, and electromechanical assembly.

**Alta Devices** HQ
545 Oakmead Pkwy
Sunnyvale CA 94085
P: 408-988-8600   PRC:212
www.altadevices.com
Email: info@altadevices.com
Estab: 2008

Khurshed Sorabji, Systems Engineering Manager
Kirsten Hessler, Development Engineer
Ryan Crowe, Technical Marketing Engineer
Linlin Yang, Solar Interconnect Engineer
Chris Norris, President

Provider of mobile power technology services. The company offers unmanned systems, consumer devices, and internet technology services.

**Alta Manufacturing Inc**     HQ
47650 Westinghouse Dr
Fremont CA 94539
P: 510-668-1870   F: 510-668-1877    PRC:211
www.altamfg.com
Email: info@altamfg.com
Estab: 1998

Billy Thach, Production Manager
Sean Chandler, National Sales Manager
Will Ziakas, Account Manager

Manufacturer of printed circuit board assemblies
and offers program management, testing, material
procurement, and optical inspection solutions.

**Altaflex**     HQ
336 Martin Ave
Santa Clara CA 95050
P: 408-727-6614     PRC:211
altaflex.com
Email: sales@altaflex.com
Estab: 2000

Rose Chang, Engineer
Renney Doser, Manufacturing Engineer
Wita Kawi, Finance Manager
James Cao, Program Manager
Francisco Duarte, Manager

Developer and fabricator of touch panels and
component assemblies, and circuits. The company
serves the electronic sector.

**Altair Technologies Inc**     HQ
41970 Christy St
Fremont CA 94538
P: 650-508-8700   F: 650-508-0307    PRC:157
www.altairusa.com
Email: sales@altairusa.com
Estab: 1991

Chris Wallace, Co-CEO
Chris Ferrari, Co-CEO
Greg Shouse, Production Manager
A. L. Luna, VP of Sales

Provider of precision furnace brazing services.
The company serves the medical, defense, and
semiconductor industries.

**Altamont Manufacturing Inc**     HQ
241 Rickenbacker Cir
Livermore CA 94551
P: 925-371-5401   F: 925-371-5434    PRC:80
www.altamontmfg.com
Email: rick.stivers@altamontmfg.com

Rick Stivers, Manager

Provider of precision CNC machining, welding,
and fabrication services. The company offers
semiconductor, aerospace, medical, and robotics
components.

**Alten Calsoft Labs**     HQ
2903 Bunker Hill Ln Ste 107
Santa Clara CA 95054
P: 408-755-3000   F: 925-249-3031    PRC:324
www.altencalsoftlabs.com
Email: salesinquiry@calsoftlabs.com
Estab: 1992

Ramandeep Singh, CEO
Sai Satyam, CFO
Narendra Dhara, CTO
Vinod Kumar, Lead of Talent Acquisition

Provider of breed consulting, enterprise IT, and
product engineering services for enterprises
in healthcare, telecom, and high-tech & retail
industries.

**Alterflex Corporation**     HQ
1717 Oakland Rd
San Jose CA 95131
P: 408-441-8688     PRC:80
www.alterflex.com
Estab: 1983

Kennth Wong, President

Designer and manufacturer of printed circuit
boards. The company also provides engineering
support services.

**Alterg Inc**     HQ
48438 Milmont Dr
Fremont CA 94538
P: 510-270-5900   F: 510-225-9399    PRC:189
www.alterg.com
Email: marketing@alter-g.com
Estab: 2005

Michael McGirr, VP of Engineering
Charles Remsberg, CEO
Kevin Davidge, COO
Fran Hackett, VP of Global Sales
Bea Tran, Accounts Payable Manager

Provider of new technologies and products such
as anti-gravity treadmills and bionic leg for physical therapy and athletic training.

**Altergy Systems**     HQ
140 Blue Ravine Rd
Folsom CA 95630
P: 916-458-8590   F: 916-200-0488    PRC:129
www.altergy.com
Email: info@altergy.com
Emp: 1-10   Estab: 2001

Matthew Ellington, Engineering Manager
Eric S. Mettler, President
Eric Strayer, VP of Sales & Business Development
James Oros, SVP of Deployment & Field Opera-
tions
Eric Veith, VP of Product Line Management

Designer and manufacturer of fuel cell power
systems. The company serves telecommunication, emergency response, data center, and other
fields.

**Altest Corporation**     HQ
898 Faulstich Ct
San Jose CA 95112
P: 408-436-9900     PRC:207
www.altestcorp.com
Email: info@altestcorp.com

Joe Corcoran, Director of Business Relations

Provider of PCB assembly and engineering
solutions. The company offers services to the
aerospace and commercial industries.

**Altierre Corp**     HQ
1980 Concourse Dr
San Jose CA 95131
P: 408-435-7343   F: 408-544-2323    PRC:324
www.altierre.com
Estab: 2003

Maneesh Dhagat, Director of Engineering
David Hodgkins, Test Engineering Manager
Dien Vu, Senior Manufacturing & RF Engineer
Jeremy Avenier, CFO
Ken Cioffi, VP RF Systems & RFIC Development

Provider of digital retail services. The company
offers retail integration, software support, and
consulting services.

**Altigen Communications Inc**     HQ
679 River Oaks Pkwy
San Jose CA 95134
P: 408-597-9000   F: 408-597-9020    PRC:68
www.altigen.com
Email: info@altigen.com
Estab: 1994
Sales: $10M to $30M

Hsi-Chieh Huang, Quality Assurance Engineer
Mike Plumer, COO
Wendy Lin, Web Developer

Manufacturer of voice and data telecommunication
equipment. The company specializes in hosted
business communication solutions.

**Alumawall Inc**     HQ
1701 S Seventh St Ste 9
San Jose CA 95112
P: 408-292-6353   F: 408-275-6225    PRC:80
www.alumawall.com
Estab: 1984

Jason Askins, Architectural Design Engineer
Ken Matarazzo, Chief Estimator
Maureen Sullivan, Project Manager
Reena Naidu, Architectural Designer

Manufacturer of metal panel and fabricator and
erector of aluminum and metal composite panel
systems.

**Alzeta Corp**     HQ
2343 Calle Del Mundo
Santa Clara CA 95054
P: 408-727-8282   F: 408-727-9740    PRC:154
www.alzeta.com
Estab: 1982

Angela Kendall, Owner
John Sullivan, President
John Kendall, Chairman
Stephen Egli, CFO
Gregory Shouse, Production Manager

Provider of clean air solutions and related research and development services. The company
offers services to the industrial and commercial
sectors.

**Amaranth Medical Inc**     HQ
1145 Terra Bella Ave Ste A
Mountain View CA 94043
P: 650-965-3830     PRC:251
Estab: 2006

Eveleen Tang, Principal Engineer
Kamal Ramzipoor, President
Sandy Liu, Controller

Specializes in proprietary polymer structure and
processing technology. The company's products
are used in vascular and nonvascular applications.

**Amasco**     HQ
6017 Snell Ave Ste 319
San Jose CA 95123
P: 408-360-1300     PRC:68
amasco.com
Email: sales@amasco.com
Estab: 1974

Alex Cordero, Sales Engineer
Jan Fichera, Office Manager

Distributor of products for the telecommunications, commercial, industrial, medical, and military
electronics markets.

**Amax Information Technologies Inc**    HQ
1565 Reliance Way
Fremont CA 94539
P: 510-651-8886   F: 510-651-4119    PRC:97
www.amax.com
Email: customer_service@amax.com
Estab: 1979

Edgardo Evangelista, Senior Solution Engineer
Jean Shih, President
Julia Shih, VP of Business Development

Manufacturer and seller of custom servers and storage solutions. The company focuses on platform design, custom branding, and supply chain management.

**Ambarella Inc**    HQ
3101 Jay St
Santa Clara CA 95054
P: 408-734-8888   F: 408-734-0788    PRC:86
www.ambarella.com
Emp: 165   Estab: 2004
Sales: $100M to $300M

Guy Rapaport, Principal Engineer of Algorithms
Malhar Palkar, Principal Software Engineer
Melvyn Lim, Principal Engineer
Shiyan Pan, Senior Staff Engineer
Howard Wang, Senior Physical Design Engineer

Developer of high-definition video compression and image processing solutions. The company's products are used in security IP cameras and sports cameras.

**Amber Precision Instruments Inc**    HQ
101 Bonaventura Dr
San Jose CA 95134
P: 408-752-0199   F: 408-752-0335    PRC:110
www.amberpi.com
Estab: 2006

Harris Park, Director

Provider of scanner products. The company specializes in electromagnetic immunity scanners and near field scanners.

**AmbiCom Holdings Inc**    HQ
877 Cedar St Ste 150
Santa Cruz CA 95060
P: 408-321-0822    PRC:64
Emp: 1-10   Estab: 1997

Suzy Guo, Controller

Manufacturer of networking hardware for mobile computers. The company offers wireless solutions and OEM modules.

**Amdocs Ltd**    BR
1100 Investment Blvd Ste 250
El Dorado Hills CA 95762
P: 916-934-7000   F: 916-934-7221    PRC:68
www.amdocs.com
Emp: 11-50   Estab: 1982

Velmurugan Sankaranarayanan, Principal Software Engineer
Michal Zuk, Global Travel Manager
Omri Yaniv, Head of Tax

Provider of customer management and billing solutions software. The company offers services to the industrial sector.

**Amerex Instruments Inc**    HQ
3951C Industrial Way
Concord CA 94520
P: 925-299-0743   F: 925-299-0745    PRC:195
www.amerexinst.com
Email: marketing@amerexinst.com

Saw Lee, Secretary

Provider of lab equipment. The company provides shakers, top-loading autoclaves, incubators, hybridization and convection ovens and water baths.

**America Aopen Inc**    HQ
2150 N First St
San Jose CA 95131
P: 888-972-6736    PRC:105
www.aopen.com
Estab: 1996

Dale Tsai, President

Specializes in the manufacture and marketing of personal computer (PC) components and peripherals. The company also offers speakers and bare systems.

**American Broadband Services**    HQ
5718 E Shields Ave
Fresno CA 93727
P: 866-827-4638   F: 559-272-5266    PRC:68
www.americanbroadbandservices.com
Emp: 1-10   Estab: 1999

Jeremy Hall, President
Daryl Plummer, Managing VP

Provider of web, internet connectivity, VoIP, spam & virus filtering, and technical support services.

**American Cylinder Head**    HQ
499 Lesser St
Oakland CA 94601
P: 800-356-4889   F: 510-536-6620    PRC:159
www.americancylinderheads.com
Email: sales@americancylinderheads.com

Arvid Elbeck, President

Provider of diesel and gas cylinder head repair and remanufacturing services. The company focuses on automotive, heavy duty, and CNG cylinder heads.

**American Die & Rollforming Inc**    HQ
3495 Swetzer Rd
Loomis CA 95650
P: 916-652-7667   F: 916-517-1437    PRC:80
www.americandieandrollforming.com
Emp: 1-10   Estab: 2008

Chris Tatasciore, Manager

Manufacturer of metal roofing, siding, and structural products. The company also specializes in canopies and decking.

**American International Group Inc**    RH
121 Spear St Ste 2
San Francisco CA 94105
P: 415-836-2700    PRC:325
www.aig.com
Estab: 1919

Peter Zaffino, EVP
Kevin Hogan, EVP
Siddhartha Sankaran, EVP
Douglas Dachille, EVP
Martha Gallo, EVP

Provider of international insurance solutions and financial services. The company serves individuals, group, and businesses.

**American Micro Detection Systems Inc**    HQ
2800 W March Ln
Stockton CA 95219
P: 209-985-1705    PRC:230
www.amdsinc.com
Emp: 11-50   Estab: 2003

Robert Keville, CEO
Lynn Essman, COO
Daniel Dietrich, Chief Science Officer

Provider of water analysis treatments. The company deals with research, development, and monitoring services.

**American Portable Welding**    HQ
3329 Baumberg Ave
Hayward CA 94545-4411
P: 510-887-4279   F: 510-887-0505    PRC:80
www.americanportablewelding.com
Email: apweld@sbcglobal.net
Estab: 1974

Lew Larimer, Owner
Alan Klepatsky, Office Manager

Provider of welding, fabrication, and engineering services. The company offers services to the industrial sector.

**American Portwell Technology Inc**    DH
44200 Christy St
Fremont CA 94538
P: 510-403-3399   F: 510-403-3184    PRC:91
www.portwell.com
Email: info@portwell.com
Estab: 1993

Zong Li, Senior Engineer
Mitch Lok, Senior Mechanical Design Engineer
Danny Chuang, Design Engineer
Frank Yeh, Technical Support Engineer
Allen Lee, CEO

Designer and manufacturer of industrial PC products. The company also offers embedded computing, network appliances, and human machine interfaces.

**American Power Systems**    BR
1627 Industrial Dr Ste C
Stockton CA 95206
P: 209-467-8999    PRC:68
ampowersys.com
Emp: 11-50   Estab: 1994

Gary Hughes, President
Tom Treacy, Power Systems of Sales
Deborah Thornton, Service Coordinator

Provider of power management products and services. The company's offerings include UPS, DC power, and battery testing.

**American Precision Spring Corp**    HQ
1513 Arbuckle Ct
Santa Clara CA 95054
P: 408-986-1020   F: 408-986-1012    PRC:80
www.americanprecspring.com
Email: sales@americanprecspring.com
Estab: 1979

Kathy Chu, CEO

Designer of electronic circuits. The company specializes in the design and fabrication of printed circuit boards.

**American Probe & Technologies Inc**　　HQ
　　1795 Grogan Ave
　　Merced CA 95341
P: 408-263-3356　F: 408-263-3797　　PRC:189
www.americanprobe.com
Email: sales@americanprobe.com
Emp: 1-10　Estab: 1984

Kenneth Chabraya, President
Dawn Fleming, Production Coordinator
Kim Merrill, VP
Kim Chabraya, VP
David Chabraya, Designer

Manufacturer of analytical probes and accessories for the semiconductor test and measurement industry.

**American Prototype And Production Inc**　　HQ
　　555 Bragato Rd
　　San Carlos CA 94070
P: 650-595-4994　F: 650-595-4282　　PRC:80
www.americanprototype.com
Email: quote@americanprototype.com

Blaine Bolich, President
Cheri Perez, Operations Manager

Manufacturer of industrial laser cutting machines. The company focuses on industries such as CNC milling, CNC turning, and laser engraving.

**American Telesource Inc**　　HQ
　　1350 Ocean Ave
　　Emeryville CA 94608
P: 800-333-8394　　PRC:325
www.ati-cti.com
Estab: 1983

Fred Schwartz, Field Service Engineer
Tenzin Passang, Accountant

Provider of voice and data communication applications. The company offers unified communications, wireless, and process automation solutions.

**Amerimade Technology Inc**　　HQ
　　449 Mountain Vista Pkwy
　　Livermore CA 94551
P: 925-243-9090　F: 925-243-9266　　PRC:86
amerimade.com
Estab: 1994

Armando Garil, Field Service Engineer
Greg Rondeau, Manager
Jay Patel, Senior Account Executive

Manufacturer of wet processing equipment. The company's equipment include fully and semi automated benches, chemical handling equipment, and process tanks.

**Ameritech Industries Inc**　　HQ
　　20208 Charlanne Dr
　　Redding CA 96002-9223
P: 530-221-4470　F: 530-221-5201　　PRC:8
www.americanpropeller.com
Email: info@ameritech-aviation.com
Emp: 1-10　Estab: 1976

James Bridgeman, General Manager
Robert Honig, Corporate Sales Manager

Provider of aircraft engines and certified and experimental engines and propellers and also offers overhaul and exchange services.

**Ameritechnology Group**　　HQ
　　PO Box 60155
　　Sacramento CA 95860
P: 916-395-6776　　PRC:323
www.ameritechnologygroup.com
Email: info@amtgi.com
Emp: 1-10　Estab: 1999

Tom McNabb, Owner
Matt Macbride, Technician

Provider of IT consulting, asset tracking, auditing, telecom connectivity logistics, relocation, and data recovery solutions for businesses.

**Amgen Inc**　　BR
　　1120 Veterans Blvd
　　S San Francisco CA 94080
P: 650-244-2000　F: 650-837-9421　　PRC:34
www.amgen.com
Estab: 1980

Bradway Robert, CEO
David Meline, EVP
Laura Hamill, SVP of Regional General Manager
Manjari Jain, Senior Manager of Information System
Paul McKenzie, Executive Director of Global Facilities Operations

Provider of scientific applications services. The company's services include clinical trials, ethical research, biosimilars, and web resources.

**AmigoCloud Inc**　　HQ
　　300 Third St Ste 724
　　San Francisco CA 94107
P: 415-935-1447　　PRC:322
www.amigocloud.com
Estab: 2011

Victor Chernetsky, Co-Founder
Daniel Caldwell, Director of GIS

Provider of geospatial platform that helps to collect, manage, analyze, visualize, and publish the location data using smartphone, camera, and sensors.

**Amimon Inc**　　HQ
　　2025 Gateway Pl Ste 450
　　San Jose CA 95110
P: 408-490-4686　　PRC:212
www.amimon.com
Email: contact@amimon.com
Estab: 2004

Ram Ofir, President
Efrat Birav, Director of Human Resources

Developer and manufacturer of HD wireless video modules. The company's products include Studio Link, Live Link, and View Link.

**Amind Solutions LLC**　　HQ
　　3201 Danville Blvd Ste 155
　　Alamo CA 94507
P: 925-804-6139　　PRC:322
www.amindsolutions.com
Email: marketing@amindsolutions.com
Estab: 2005

Billy Hunt, President
Robert Wing, CTO
Sharad Mitra, COO

Provider of technology and services. The company offers enterprise mobility, quoting and ordering, product configuration, and e-Commerce services.

**Amobee Inc**　　HQ
　　901 Marshall St Ste 200
　　Redwood City CA 94063
P: 650-353-4399　F: 650-802-8951　　PRC:322
www.amobee.com
Estab: 2005

Kim Perell, President
Mark Strecker, CEO

Provider of marketing intelligence and cross channel, cross device advertiser, and publisher solutions for marketers, publishers, and operators.

**AMPAC Fine Chemicals**　　DH
　　PO Box 1718
　　Rancho Cordova CA 95741-1718
P: 916-357-6880　F: 916-353-3523　　PRC:53
www.ampacfinechemicals.com
Email: afcbusdev@apfc.com
Emp: 1-10

Brent Kelson, Senior Process Engineer
Christopher Romero-Espitia, Associate Chemical Engineer
Eric Peprah, Senior Process Engineer
Jason Hand, PCB Design Engineer
Nandor Laszik, Process

Manufacturer of active pharmaceutical ingredients (APIs) and registered intermediates. The company's services include product development and scale-up.

**Ampex Data Systems Corporation**　　HQ
　　26460 Corporate Ave
　　Hayward CA 94545
P: 650-367-2011　　PRC:95
ampex.com
Email: info@ampex.com
Estab: 1944

Phat Ly, Senior Technician

Manufacturer of digital storage systems. The company also offers airborne and ground systems and related video solutions.

**Amprius Inc**　　HQ
　　1180 Page Ave
　　Fremont CA 94538
P: 800-425-8803　　PRC:140
www.amprius.com
Email: info@amprius.com
Estab: 2008

Yi-Lei Chow, Engineering Operations Manager
Chentao Yu, Director of Technology
Weijie Wang, Senior Director of Technology Development
Marquis Bernardo, Battery Technician

Developer and manufacturer of lithium-ion batteries. The company offers services to the industrial sectors.

**Ampro Systems Inc**　　RH
　　1000 Page Ave
　　Fremont CA 94538
P: 510-624-9000　F: 510-624-9002　　PRC:207
www.amprosystems.com
Email: sales@amprosystems.com
Estab: 1997

Ting Wang, CEO

Manufacturer of printed circuit board assemblies. The company deals with procurement services and serves the government and military industries.

**Ampteks Inc** HQ
265 Rickenbacker Cir
Livermore CA 94551-7216
P: 925-493-7150   F: 925-493-7151   PRC:85
tripunit.com
Email: mclark@ampteks.com

Mike Clark, CEO

Provider of engineering solutions. The company provides alternatives for dichromate plating and electro silver plating.

**Amtec Industries Inc** BR
7079 Commerce Cir
Pleasanton CA 94588
P: 510-887-2289   F: 510-887-0494   PRC:290
www.amtec1.com
Email: sales1@amtec1.com

Bryan Bidwell, Project Engineer
Robert Bradley, President
Tom Willis, Director of Sales

Manufacturer of industrial custom control panels. The company is engaged in design, fabrication, and installation services.

**AmTECH Microelectronics Inc** HQ
485 Cochrane Cir
Morgan Hill CA 95037
P: 408-612-8888   PRC:207
www.amtechmicro.com
Email: info@amtechmicro.com
Estab: 1993

Walter Chavez, President
Clifford Mihalyfi, Senior Executive

Provider of manufacturing solutions. The company deals with PCB fabrication, machining, and assembly services.

**Amulet Technologies LLC** HQ
1475 S Bascom Ave Ste 111
Campbell CA 95008
P: 408-374-4956   F: 408-374-4941   PRC:204
www.amulettechnologies.com
Email: info@amulettechnologies.com
Estab: 1998

Paul Indaco, President
Kimberly Cope, Marketing Communications

Provider of embedded graphical user interface solutions. The company also specializes in modules and chips.

**Amunix Pharmaceuticals Inc** HQ
500 Ellis St
Mountain View CA 94043
P: 650-428-1800   PRC:252
www.amunix.com
Email: bd@amunix.com
Estab: 2006

Volker Schellenberger, President
Angie You, CEO
Bryan Irving, CSO
Darcy Mootz, Chief Business Officer
Maninder Hora, CTO

Developer of biomolecular therapy. The company specializes in the development of protein and peptide based therapeutic products.

**Amyris Inc** HQ
5885 Hollis St Ste 100
Emeryville CA 94608
P: 510-450-0761   F: 510-225-2645   PRC:52
www.amyris.com
Email: info@amyris.com
Estab: 2003
Sales: $30M to $100M

Jonathan Wolter, Interim CFO
Gale Wichmann, Senior Scientist
Isabel Ribeiro, Associate Scientist
Chi-Li Liu, Principle Scientist

Provider of renewable products. The company delivers cosmetic emollients and fragrances, fuels and lubricants, and even biopharmaceuticals.

**Analatom Inc** HQ
4655 Old Ironsides Dr Ste 130
Santa Clara CA 95054
P: 408-980-9516   F: 408-980-9518   PRC:87
www.analatom.com
Email: info@analatom.com
Estab: 1997

Bernard Laskowski, President
Jeffrey Morse, Director of Advanced Research
Peter Steiniger, Accounting Manager
Stella Zhu, Accountant

Provider of materials science research services focusing on product development in the field of micro electrical mechanical systems.

**Analog Bits Inc** HQ
945 Stewart Dr Ste 250
Sunnyvale CA 94085
P: 650-314-0200   F: 650-618-1976   PRC:212
www.analogbits.com
Email: sales@analogbits.com
Estab: 1995

Amit Kumar, Circuit Design Engineer
Jimmy Lam, Engineer
Mahesh Tirupattur, EVP
Will Wong, Director of Customer Support
Mary Lee, IC Mask Layout Designer

Supplier of low-power, customizable analog IP for modern CMOS digital chips. The company also offers interfaces and converters.

**Analogix Semiconductor Inc** HQ
3211 Scott Blvd Ste 103
Santa Clara CA 95054
P: 408-988-8848   F: 408-988-8686   PRC:86
www.analogix.com
Email: info@analogixsemi.com
Estab: 2002

Richard Wang, Senior Application Engineer
Kewei Yang, CEO
Ning Zhu, CTO
Mike Seifert, CFO
Diana Zhang, VP

Designer of mixed-signal semiconductors. The company offers input-output display translators, timing controllers, and accessory display converters.

**Analytical Sciences LLC** HQ
110 Liberty St
Petaluma CA 94952
P: 707-769-3128   PRC:303
analyticalsciences.net
Estab: 1995

Joe Furlong, General & Sales Manager

Provider of laboratory services. The company specializes in environmental testing and analytical chemistry.

**Anamet Inc** HQ
26102 Eden Landing Rd Ste 3
Hayward CA 94545
P: 510-887-8811   F: 510-887-8427   PRC:139
www.anametinc.com
Email: info@anametinc.com
Estab: 1958

Kenneth Pytlewski, Director of Engineering
Ryan Wood, Materials Engineer
Audrey Fasching, Senior Material Engineer
Dilip Bhandarkar, Test Engineer
James Bellino, Materials Engineer

Provider of materials engineering analysis & lab testing services. The company focuses on product testing, failure analysis, and forensic engineering.

**Anand Systems Inc** HQ
35 E Tenth St Ste F
Tracy CA 95376
P: 209-830-1484   F: 209-830-0593   PRC:323
www.anandsystems.com
Email: info@anandsystems.com
Emp: 1-10   Estab: 1998

Pratik Vakil, Project Manager
Pratic Patel, Manager

Designer of custom software solutions for the hotel industry. The company also offers related hardware, website design, and surveillance systems.

**Anaspec Inc** HQ
34801 Campus Dr
Fremont CA 94555
P: 510-791-9560   F: 510-791-9572   PRC:50
www.anaspec.com
Email: service@anaspec.com
Estab: 1993

Lieven Janssens, President
Masatoshi Yoshimatsu, CFO
Alice Wen, QC Analyst
Xiaowei Zhang, Manager of Supply Chain Management

Provider of integrated proteomics solutions for life science research. The company offers peptides, detection reagents, and combinatorial chemistry.

**Anatech Usa** HQ
2947 Whipple Rd
Union City CA 94587
P: 510-401-5990   F: 510-401-5994   PRC:165
www.anatechusa.com
Email: info@anatechusa.com
Estab: 2006

Tracy Watts, President
Jason wright, Manufacturing Technician
Robert Misata, Sales & Marketing Manager
Melissa Watts, Administrator

Provider of high vacuum systems with plasma technology. The company's applications include flip chips, multichip modules, and photoresist strips.

**Anatomage Inc** HQ
303 Almaden Blvd Ste 700
San Jose CA 95110
P: 408-885-1474   F: 408-295-9786   PRC:185
www.anatomage.com
Email: info@anatomage.com
Estab: 2004

Samantha Chester, Application Engineer

Manufacturer of surgical devices, surgical instruments, radiology software, imaging equipment, and display equipment for medical and dental industries.

**Anchor Orthotics & Prosthetics**    HQ
1800 Tribute Rd Ste 150
Sacramento CA 95821
P: 877-977-0448    F: 916-484-0682     PRC:190
www.anchorot.com
Emp: 1-10

Jennifer Kelly, Office Manager

Provider of orthotics and prosthetics. The company offers personal ankle bionic systems, braces and support and artificial limbs for amputees.

**Anchor Semiconductor Inc**    HQ
3235 Kifer Rd Ste 200
Santa Clara CA 95051
P: 408-986-8969    F: 408-986-8999     PRC:126
www.anchorsemi.com
Email: info@anchorsemi.com
Estab: 2000

Zhijin Chen, Research

Developer of software to improve IC manufacturing efficiency and chip yield. The company specializes in semiconductor hotspot pattern management.

**Anderson Pacific Engineering Construction Inc**    HQ
1390 Norman Ave
Santa Clara CA 95054
P: 408-970-9900    F: 408-970-9975     PRC:304
www.andpac.com
Estab: 1960

Karen Thayer, Director of Finance
Sean McBurney, Senior Estimator
Michael Gossett, Project Manager
Ryan Mullen, Manager
Andrew Sullivan, Project Manager

Provider of constructing and retrofitting pump stations, lift stations, bridges, reservoirs, treatment plants, and seismic retrofit projects.

**Andes Technology USA Corporation**    RH
2860 Zanker Rd Ste 104
San Jose CA 95134
P: 408-809-2929     PRC:110
www.andestech.com
Email: america@andestech.com
Estab: 2002

Emerson Hsiao, SVP of Sales & Support

Provider of infrastructural solutions for embedded system applications. The company serves the semiconductor industry.

**Andover Consulting Group Inc**    HQ
1029 S Claremont St
S San Francisco CA 94402
P: 415-537-6950     PRC:97
www.andovercg.com
Email: sales@networktigers.com
Estab: 1996

Michael Syiek, President

Supplier of network components. The company offers data center liquidation, network security, and network equipment services.

**Andrew Ndt Engineering Corp**    HQ
1253 Fleming Ave
San Jose CA 95127
P: 408-710-0342     PRC:87
www.andrewndt.com

Cuong Le, President

Manufacturer of probes, ultrasonic transducers, diamond cutting tools, proximity sensors, cables, and offers calibration services.

**Angels Sheet Metal Inc**    HQ
2502 Gun Club Rd
Angels Camp CA 95222
P: 209-736-4541     PRC:88
www.angelssheetmetalinc.com
Emp: 1-10    Estab: 1968

Ron Dwelley, Sales Manager

Provider of sheet metal fabrication services. The company focuses on heating and air conditioning systems.

**Angular Machining Inc**    HQ
2040 Hartog Dr
San Jose CA 95131
P: 408-954-8326    F: 408-954-0440     PRC:157
angularmachining.com
Email: sales@angularmachining.com
Estab: 1999

Yen Nguyen, Senior Production Planner
Phi Nguyen, Set Up

Provider of product manufacturing services for aerospace, telecom, and biomedical sectors and focuses on mechanical assembly and quality control.

**Anki Inc**    HQ
55 Second St 15th Fl
San Francisco CA 94105
P: 415-670-9488     PRC:322
anki.com
Email: info@anki.com
Estab: 2010

Tom Eliaz, Director of Software Engineering
Boris Sofman, Co-Founder
Hanns Tappeiner, Co-Founder
Mark Palatucci, Co-Founder
Craig Rechenmacher, CMO

Provider of robotic racing products such as drive and expansion cars, starter, bottleneck and cross-road tracks, and accessories for consumers.

**Annexon Inc**    HQ
180 Kimball Way Fl 2 Ste 200
S San Francisco CA 94080
P: 650-822-5500    F: 650-636-9773     PRC:268
www.annexonbio.com
Email: info@annexonbio.com

Ted Yednock, President
Jennifer Lew, EVP
Sanjay Keswani, EVP

Focuses on the development of therapeutic products. The company serves patients with complement-mediated neurodegenerative disorders.

**Anomali**    RH
808 Winslow St
Redwood City CA 94063
P: 844-484-7328     PRC:325
www.anomali.com
Email: info@anomali.com
Estab: 2013

Greg Martin, Founder
Greg Oslan, Founder
Hugh Njemanze, CEO
Wei Huang, CTO
Jon Skoglund, CFO

Specializes in the delivery of cyber security solutions. The company services to big and small organizations.

**Anova Microsystems Inc**    HQ
173 Santa Rita Ct
Los Altos CA 94022
P: 408-941-1888     PRC:209
www.anova.com
Estab: 1990

Raymond Chuang, President

Provider of rack mount server cabinets and system components. The company deals with storage and GPU solutions.

**Anresco Inc**    HQ
1375 Van Dyke Ave
San Francisco CA 94124
P: 415-822-1100    F: 415-822-6615     PRC:47
www.anresco.com
Email: info@anresco.com
Estab: 1943

David Eisenberg, President
Zachary Eisenberg, VP
Vu Lam, Co-Laboratory Director
Cynthia Kushi, Co-Laboratory Director
Hingman Mang, Section Supervisor of Gas Chromatography

Provider of analysis and research to food and food-related industries. The company also offers solutions to support the business and analytical specifications.

**Anritsu Co**    DH
490 Jarvis Dr
Morgan Hill CA 95037-2809
P: 408-778-2000     PRC:18
www.anritsu.com
Email: marketing-communications@anritsu.com
Estab: 1895

Calvin Carter, Manufacturing Engineering Manager
Hirokazu Hamada, Representative Director
Masumi Niimi, Director
Yasunobu Hashimoto, VP
Akifumi Kubota, Director

Provider of test solutions for telecommunication applications. The company also caters to microwave applications.

**Ansari Structural Engineers Inc** HQ
300 Montgomery St Ste 860
San Francisco CA 94104
P: 415-348-8948 PRC:304
www.ansariinc.com
Email: info@ansariinc.com
Estab: 1999

Mehri Ansari, Founder

Provider of structural consulting services. The company focuses on remodeling, due diligence studies, equipment anchorage, and structural peer review.

**Ansync Labs Inc** HQ
5090 Robert J Mathews Pkwy Ste 1
El Dorado Hills CA 95762
P: 916-933-2850 PRC:159
www.ansync.com
Emp: 1-10

Sam Miller, CEO

Provider of engineering and design services. The company specializes in electrical engineering, mechanical engineering, and industrial design.

**Ansys Inc** BR
2855 Telegraph Ave Ste 501
Berkeley CA 94705
P: 844-462-6797 F: 510-841-8523 PRC:326
www.ansys.com
Email: info@ansys.com
Estab: 1970

Ajei Gopal, President
Maria Shields, CFO
Shane Emswiler, VP
Dipankar Choudhury, VP of Research

Provider of engineering solutions. The company serves the aerospace, defense, and construction industries.

**Antagene Inc** HQ
3350 Scott Blvd Bldg 46 Ste 4602
Santa Clara CA 95054
P: 408-588-1998 PRC:23
www.antageneinc.com
Email: info@antageneinc.com

Ming Mao, CEO

Provider of custom antibody and peptide synthesis. The company is engaged in animal and histology services.

**Antec Inc** HQ
47681 Lakeview Blvd
Fremont CA 94538
P: 510-770-1200 F: 510-770-1288 PRC:110
www.antec.com
Email: customersupport@antec.com
Estab: 1986

Chen Mingyong, Deputy General Manager
Jack Chiu, Sales Account Manager
Katie Chang, Supply Chain

Supplier of computer components and accessories. The company provides enclosures, power supplies, accessories, and mobile products.

**Antech Diagnostics** HQ
17620 Mt Herrmann St
Fountain Valley CA 92708
P: 800-872-1001 PRC:23
www.antechdiagnostics.com
Email: support@antechdiagnostics.com
Emp: 11-50 Estab: 1994

Robert Allen, Manufacturing Engineering Technician
Frank Shearer, Senior Network Engineer
Drake Josh, President
Scott Moroff, VP
Ann Maglio, Human Resource Manager

Provider of diagnostic and laboratory testing services for chemistry, pathology, endocrinology, serology, hematology, and microbiology.

**Antedo Inc** HQ
21952 Lindy Ln
Cupertino CA 95014
P: 408-253-1870 PRC:45
www.antedo.com
Email: ctaysi@antedo.com

Candan Taysi, Financial Officer

Provider of consulting services. The company offers international engineering and management consulting services.

**Anthera Pharmaceuticals Inc** HQ
25801 Industrial Blvd Ste B
Hayward CA 94545
P: 510-856-5600 F: 510-856-5597 PRC:257
www.anthera.com
Email: info@anthera.com
Estab: 2004
Sales: $10M to $30M

John Thompson, CEO
James Pennington, Chief Medical Officer
May Liu, SVP of Finance
Philip Sager, Group VP
Paul Adams, SVP of Global Regulatory Affairs & Compliance

Manufacturer of biopharmaceuticals that treat serious diseases like lupus, lupus with glomerulonephritis, IgA nephropathy and cystic fibrosis.

**Antibodies Inc** HQ
PO Box 1560
Davis CA 95617-1560
P: 530-758-4400 F: 530-758-6307 PRC:249
www.antibodiesinc.com
Email: info@antibodiesinc.com
Emp: 1-10 Estab: 1960

Will Fry, President
Ricardo Rodarte, Manager of OEM Manufacturing
Rick Gould, Manager of Biochemistry
Bjorn Kjellsson, Scientist

Manufacturer of monoclonal and polyclonal antibodies, diagnostic reagents, diagnostic kits, and developer of immunoassays.

**Antibody Solutions** HQ
1130 Mountain View Alviso Rd
Sunnyvale CA 94089-2221
P: 650-938-4300 F: 408-734-0400 PRC:26
www.antibody.com
Email: solutions@antibody.com
Estab: 1995

Judith Lynch-Kenney, CFO
John Kenney, Co-Founder
Joshua Lowitz, Project Manager
Michael Trang, Project Manager
John Nichols, Project Manager

Provider of antibody products and services. The company serves biotechnology, diagnostic and pharmaceutical companies.

**Anvato Inc** HQ
1600 Amphitheatre Pkwy
Mountain View CA 94043
P: 866-246-6942 PRC:61
www.anvato.com
Email: info@anvato.com
Estab: 2007

Alper Turgut, Manager

Provider of video software platform to television broadcasters and offers live and on-demand video management, analytics, and tracking features.

**Anybots 20 Inc** BR
6341 San Ignacio Ave
San Jose CA 95119-1202
P: 877-594-1836 F: 650-745-2487 PRC:68
anybots.com
Email: support@anybots.com
Estab: 2001

April Buchheit, Office Assistant

Provider of robotic device that acts as a personal remote avatar which can be operated remotely thus creating a virtual presence.

**Apex Envirotech Inc** HQ
11244 Pyrites Way
Gold River CA 95670
P: 800-242-5249 F: 916-851-0177 PRC:142
www.apexenvirotech.com
Emp: 11-50 Estab: 1993

Brandon Poteet, Field Services Department Manager
Tom Landwehr, Manager
Lisa Nicodemus, Manager

Provider of environmental management and remediation technology. The company also offers engineering services.

**Apex Technology Management Inc** HQ
310 Hemsted Dr. Suite 300
Redding CA 96001
P: 800-310-2739 F: 530-243-9184 PRC:326
www.apex.com
Email: info@apex.com
Emp: 1-10 Estab: 1991

Scott Putnam, President
George Passidakis, Director of Sales and Marketing
Daniel Langenberg, Project Manager
Tiffany Chipley, Finance Clerk II
Tom Grisell, Virtual CIO

Provider of information technology services such as business continuity planning, virtualization, and email protection.

**Apex Testing Labs** HQ
1790 Yosemite Ave
San Francisco CA 94124
P: 415-550-9800   F: 415-550-9880   PRC:306
www.apextestinglabs.com
Email: info@apextestinglabs.com

Norbu Dhonyo, Marketing Manager
Weimin Jiang, Manager
Josh Sircy, Construction Inspector

Provider of testing and inspection services. The
company engages in the geotechnical engineering
and inspection of construction materials.

**Apexigen** HQ
75 Shoreway Rd Ste C
San Carlos CA 94070
P: 650-931-6236   F: 650-931-6235   PRC:34
www.apexigen.com
Email: info@apexigen.com

Xiaodong Yang, President
Mark Nevins, VP of Business Development

Specializes in document management and
managed print solutions. The company serves the
business sector.

**Apixio Inc** HQ
1850 Gateway Dr 3rd Fl
San Mateo CA 94404
P: 877-424-4946   PRC:194
www.apixio.com
Estab: 2009

John Schneider, CTO
Meg Holland, COO
Tom McNamara, Chief Growth Officer
Mark Scott, CMO

Provider of cognitive computing platform that
enables the analysis of unstructured healthcare
data at individual level, providing groundbreaking
insights.

**Aplena Inc** HQ
819 Striker Ave Ste 4
Sacramento CA 95834
P: 408-256-0030   F: 408-273-6993   PRC:40
aplena.com

Norm Shockley, CEO
Larkin Ryder, Director of Process and Compliance

Provider of technology solutions for data center
services. The company offers relocation, installation, and managed services.

**APLEX Technology Inc** BR
2065 Martin Ave Ste 107
Santa Clara CA 95050
P: 669-999-2500   F: 669-999-2499   PRC:110
www.aplextec.com
Email: sales@aplextec.com
Estab: 2004

Siddhartha Khadka, Production Engineer

Manufacturer of industrial displays, heavy-duty
expandables, industrial panels, and related accessories. The company serves the healthcare sector.

**Apneos Corp** HQ
2033 Ralston Ave Ste 41
Belmont CA 94002
P: 650-591-2895   F: 501-694-9807   PRC:268
apneos.com
Email: info@apneos.com
Estab: 2001

William Taft, President

Developer of services for healthcare professionals. The company detects and manages sleep
breathing disorders.

**Apogee Software Inc** HQ
19039 Overlook Rd
Campbell CA 95030
P: 408-369-9001   F: 408-369-9018   PRC:319
www.apogee.com
Email: info@apogee.com
Estab: 1988

Yuko Malek, CFO
George Malek, Manager

Provider of integrated development environment
for Java and C. The company offers industrial
monitors and controllers.

**Apolent Corp** HQ
2570 N First St Ste 200
San Jose CA 95131
P: 408-203-6828   F: 408-262-4783   PRC:325
www.apolent.com
Email: info@apolent.com
Estab: 2006

Gary Winblad, Staff Engineer
Dinesh Kumar, VP
Chetan Sharma, Business Development Manager
Ed Chang, System Architect

Provider of business process and software
technology outsourcing services focusing on niche
market segments.

**Apollomics Inc** HQ
989 East Hillsdale Blvd Ste 220
Foster City CA 94404
P: 650-209-4055   F: 650-288-1674   PRC:196
www.apollomicsinc.com
Estab: 2016

Sanjeev Redkar, President
Tillman Pearce, Chief Medical Officer
Gavin Choy, EVP

Developer of oncology therapeutics. The company
focusses on discovering therapeutics for the
immune system and molecular pathways to treat
cancer.

**AppEnsure Inc** HQ
111 N Market St Ste 300
San Jose CA 95113
P: 408-418-4602   F: 408-418-4603   PRC:40
www.appensure.com
Email: info@appensure.com
Estab: 2012

Sri Chaganty, COO
Colin Macnab, CEO
Subha Chaganty, Director of Offshore Operations

Provider of cloud application performance and
infrastructure management such as applica-
tion-aware infrastructure performance management solution.

**Apple Inc** HQ
One Apple Pkwy
Cupertino CA 95014
P: 408-996-1010   PRC:209
www.apple.com
Estab: 1976
Sales: Over $3B

Thomas Lau, Environmental Program Manager
Ray Chang, Senior System Hardware Engineering
Manager
Owen O'Leary, Senior Software Engineer
Dan Kelly, Computer Architecture Engineer
Tomlinson Holman, Distinguished Engineer

Designer and marketer of consumer electronics.
The company also focuses on computer software
and personal computers.

**Apple Inc** HQ
908 N Temperance Ave
Clovis CA 93611
P: 559-275-2175   F: 559-275-4422   PRC:306
www.applinc.com
Emp: 1-10   Estab: 1982

BJ Watrous, VP

Provider of analytical testing services. The
company specializes in analysis of environmental
samples for chemical pollutants.

**Applian Technologies Inc** HQ
20 Vineyard Ave
San Anselmo CA 94960
P: 415-480-1748   F: 415-373-0558   PRC:318
www.applian.com
Estab: 1997

Bill Dettering, CEO
Tom Mayes, COO
Leslie Bee, Director of Marketing
Michael Christensen, Lead Software Developer

Provider of solutions for the capture and conversion of web video, streaming audio, and song and
radio program software for Windows users.

**Applied Aerospace Structures Corp** HQ
3437 S Airport Way
Stockton CA 95206
P: 209-983-3314   F: 209-983-3375   PRC:8
www.aascworld.com
Email: marketing@aascworld.com
Emp: 1-10   Estab: 1956

Robert Tiedeman, Laboratory Manager
Elliott Lampkin, Manufacturing Engineer
Phillip Calvin, Manufacturing Engineer
Cesar Fernandez, Senior Quality Assurance
Engineer
Dan Smith, Manufacturing Engineer

Designer of space and aircraft metal structures.
The company also specializes in fabrication and
other services.

**Applied Ceramics Inc** HQ
48630 Milmont Dr
Fremont CA 94538
P: 510-249-9700   F: 510-249-9797   PRC:212
www.appliedceramics.net
Email: info@appliedceramics.net
Estab: 1994

David Kolaric, General Manager
Rick Le, Chemical Manager

Manufacturer of custom ceramics, quartz silicon,
stainless steel, and sapphire for the semiconductor industries.

**Applied Chemical Laboratories Inc**     HQ
777 Aviation Blvd
Santa Rosa CA 95403
P: 408-737-8880        PRC:47
www.appchem.com
Email: info@appchem.com
Estab: 2006

Javad Sahbari, CEO
Gloria Weir, VP of Marketing

Developer and manufacturer of electronic chemicals and specialty materials. The company offers services like consultation and chemical purification.

**Applied Computer Solutions**     BR
3825 Hopyard Rd Ste 220
Pleasanton CA 94588
P: 925-251-1000   F: 925-467-1937    PRC:324
www.acsacs.com
Estab: 1989

Cyril Wilson, Senior Sales Engineer
Dennis DiPietro, Manager of Sales Operations
Cheryl Heslington, Inside Sales Manager
Paisley Sisson, Sales Manager
Brooke Gilfillan, Inside Sales Representative

Provider of information technology solutions. The company offers solutions for virtualization, storage, security, and networking.

**Applied Earthworks Inc**     HQ
1391 W Shaw Ave Ste C
Fresno CA 93711-3600
P: 559-229-1856        PRC:142
www.appliedearthworks.com
Email: info@appliedearthworks.com
Emp: 11-50 Estab: 1995

Jennifer Barbee, CAO
Barry Price, VP
Ann Munns, Regional Manager
Mary Baloian, Regional Manager
Susan Rapp, Publications Manager

Provider of history, archaeology, paleontology, and cultural resources management and related services.

**Applied Engineering**     HQ
6341 San Ignacio Ave Ste 10
San Jose CA 95119
P: 408-286-2134   F: 408-971-0776    PRC:209
www.appliedengineering.com
Email: sales@appliedengineering.com
Estab: 1979

Jack Yao, President
Jerry Cutini, Chairman
John Villadsen, COO
Colleen Sweeney, VP of Operations
Mark Danna, VP of sales and Marketing

Provider of contract electronics manufacturing services. The company also specializes in clean room assembly services.

**Applied Engineering**     HQ
991 Montague Expy Ste 207
Milpitas CA 95035
P: 408-263-5900   F: 408-263-5915    PRC:304
www.appliedse.com
Email: info@appliedse.com
Estab: 1991

Jinken Cho, Structural Design Engineer
Sasson Rajabi, Owner

Provider of structural analysis and seismic evaluation services. The company is involved in specialty engineering and project management.

**Applied Expert Systems Inc**     HQ
PO Box 50927
Palo Alto CA 94303
P: 650-617-2400   F: 650-617-2420    PRC:322
www.aesclever.com
Email: info@aesclever.com
Estab: 1991

David Cheng, VP of Engineering
Candy Tyner, Business Development Manager

Developer of networking solutions for business service management. The company provides virtualization and cloud computing services.

**Applied Fusion Inc**     HQ
1915 Republic Ave
San Leandro CA 94577
P: 510-351-8314   F: 510-351-0692    PRC:80
www.appliedfusioninc.com
Email: sales@appliedfusioninc.com
Estab: 1972

Jim Warner, Project Engineering Manager
George Silva, VP of Manufacturing
Steve Lockert, Safety Manager

Provider of precision metal fabrication, electron beam and laser welding, and CNC machining services.

**Applied Interconnect**     HQ
1262 Lawrence Station Rd
Sunnyvale CA 94089-2218
P: 408-749-9900   F: 408-734-9770    PRC:62
www.onlinecables.com
Email: sales@onlinecables.com

John Claras, CEO

Supplier of cables and electro mechanical assemblies. The company also specializes in microwave sub-assemblies.

**Applied Materials Inc**     HQ
3050 Bowers Ave
Santa Clara CA 95054-3299
P: 408-727-5555   F: 760-436-4774    PRC:212
www.appliedmaterials.com
Estab: 1967
Sales: Over $3B

Gino Addiego, Engineering Operations and Quality
Gary Dickerson, President
Jay Kerley, Chief Information Officer
Dan Durn, CFO
Susan Schmitt, Head of Human Resources

Provider of equipment, services, and software for the manufacture of semiconductor, flat panel display, and solar photovoltaic products.

**Applied Materials-Engineering**     HQ
980 41st St
Oakland CA 94608
P: 510-420-8190        PRC:304
www.appmateng.com

Tae Won, Director of Engineering
Nadine Alexis, Application Engineer
Mohammed Faiyaz, Senior Engineer
Dushyant Manmohan, Principal
Mark Murphy, Total Product Support Senior Manager

Provider of construction materials consulting services. The company focuses on petrographic and laboratory testing services.

**Applied Motion Products Inc**     HQ
404 Westridge Dr
Watsonville CA 95076
P: 831-761-6555   F: 831-761-6544    PRC:98
www.applied-motion.com
Email: customerservice@applied-motion.com
Emp: 1-10   Estab: 1978

Jim Amos, Applications Engineer
Glenn Johnson, Design Engineer
Jeff Kordik, CTO
Julie Georgiana, Director of Manufacturing
Dennis Joyce, East Regional Sales Manager

Manufacturer of stepper drives and motors, gearheads, power supplies, and related accessories. The company offers technical support services.

**Applied Optics Inc**     HQ
3349 Vincent Rd
Pleasant Hill CA 94523
P: 925-932-5686   F: 925-932-2502    PRC:173
www.applied-optics.com
Email: service@applied-optics.com
Estab: 1973

James Lee, Optical Engineer
Milton Biagas, Optic Polisher
Annette hurst, CNC Operator

Provider of precision optical components and custom optics. The company is engaged in delivery and installation services.

**Applied Photon Technology Inc**     HQ
3346 Arden Rd
Hayward CA 94545
P: 510-780-9500   F: 510-780-1798    PRC:243
www.appliedphoton.com
Email: info@appliedphoton.com
Estab: 2002

Rodney Romero, VP of Engineering
Len Goldfine, President
Rafael Olano, VP of Manufacturing
Barry Smith, VP of Sales & Marketing
Tian Liu, Business Development Manager

Provider of precision flash lamps. The company's products include Krypton arc lamps, OEM's and APT's laser flash lamps, and specialty lamps.

**Applied Physics Systems Inc**     HQ
425 Clyde Ave
Mountain View CA 94043
P: 650-965-0500   F: 650-965-0404    PRC:87
www.appliedphysics.com
Email: info@appliedphysics.com
Estab: 1976

Tim Pletschet, Senior Mechanical Engineer

Supplier of magnetic measure and other electronic equipment. The company specializes in measurement while drilling systems and magnetometers.

**Applied Poleramic Inc**     HQ
6166 Egret Ct
Benicia CA 94510
P: 707-747-6738   F: 707-747-6774    PRC:281
www.appliedpoleramic.com
Email: service@poleramic.com
Estab: 1991

Brian Hayes, President

Developer and manufacturer of composite materials for the aerospace, marine, and industrial markets. The company offers resins, pastes, and adhesives.

**Applied Process Cooling Corp** HQ
4812 Enterprise Way
Modesto CA 95356
P: 209-578-1000  F: 209-578-1021  PRC:159
apcco.net
Emp: 11-50 Estab: 1981

Jim Helsel, Project Engineer
Jodi Smith, Service Engineer
Gary Dunn, President
Nyssa Mirani, Human Resource Assistant
Dave Hill, North Coat Division Manager

Provider of refrigeration solutions. The company's services include laser alignment, control panel retrofits, valve exercising, and condenser cleaning.

**Applied Simulation Technology Inc** HQ
6475 Camden Ave Ste 102A
San Jose CA 95120
P: 408-436-9070  F: 408-436-9078  PRC:325
www.apsimtech.com
Estab: 1989

Fred Balistreri, Company Secretary

Developer of stimulators and molders in signal integrity, power integrity, and circuit simulation tools.

**Applied Spectra Inc** HQ
46665 Fremont Blvd
Fremont CA 94538
P: 510-657-7679  PRC:172
www.appliedspectra.com
Email: contact@appliedspectra.com
Estab: 2004

Jong Yoo, President
Richard Russo, Executive Chairman
Steve Shuttleworth, VP of Global Sales Management
Chunyi Liu, SVP
Diep Trieu, Manager of Global Product Support

Manufacturer of analytical instrumentation. The company's products include J200 Tandem, J200 Femtosecond, Laser Ablation System, and Aurora LIBS Spectrometer.

**Applied Stemcell Inc** HQ
521 Cottonwood Dr Ste 111
Milpitas CA 95035
P: 408-773-8007  F: 650-800-7179  PRC:23
www.appliedstemcell.com
Email: info@appliedstemcell.com
Estab: 2008

Ruhong Jiang, Co-founder
Ruby Chen-Tsai, Co-founder
Michael Cleary, Co-founder
Guo-Liang Yu, Executive Chairman
Alexander Wu, Team Leader

Provider of stem cell characterization, gene targeting, teratoma formation, and embryoid body (EB) formation services.

**Applied Systems Engineering Inc** HQ
1671 Dell Ave Ste 200
Campbell CA 95008
P: 408-364-0500  F: 408-364-0550  PRC:5
www.ase-systems.com
Email: products@ase-systems.com
Estab: 1980

Prasanth Gopalakrishnan, President

Provider of consulting, software, design, and testing services. The company's products cater to communication applications.

**Applied Wireless Identifications Group Inc** HQ
18300 Sutter Blvd
Morgan Hill CA 95037
P: 408-825-1100  F: 408-782-7402  PRC:68
www.awid.com
Email: support@awid.com
Estab: 1997

Young Carpenter, Office Manager

Provider of communication systems for engineering applications. The company also offers modules, antennas, and accessories.

**Applozic Inc** HQ
Stanford Financial Sq 2600 El Camino Real Ste 415
Palo Alto CA 94306
P: 310-909-7458  PRC:319
www.applozic.com
Email: contact@applozic.com
Estab: 2015

Devashish Mamgain, Co-Founder
Adarsh Kumar, Co-Founder
Vigil Vishwanathan, Director of Sales

Empowers businesses with in-app messaging solutions and all-in-one customer support solution.

**Appro Technology Inc** BR
1180 Miraloma Way Ste E
Sunnyvale CA 94085
P: 408-720-0018  F: 408-720-0019  PRC:59
appro-us.com
Email: info@appro-us.com

Spencer Tsai, President
Charlie Liu, Sales Manager
Wang Luo, VP
Jeffrey Yang, Hardware Manager

Manufacturer of network surveillance systems. The company's products include dome cameras, LCD monitors, and cables.

**Appsec Consulting** HQ
6110 Hellyer Ave Ste 100
San Jose CA 95138
P: 408-224-1110  PRC:39
www.appsecconsulting.com
Estab: 2005

Brian Bertacini, President
Melissa Sasaki, Office Manager
Scott Simmons, Senior Application Security Specialist
Josh Brashars, Team Leader

Provider of services to identify vulnerabilities in applications. The company focuses on penetration testing and PCI compliance.

**Apptimize Inc** HQ
330 Townsend St Ste 234
San Francisco CA 94107
P: 415-926-5398  PRC:319
apptimize.com
Email: contact@apptimize.com
Estab: 2013

Craig Gering, VP of Engineering
Scott Ings, VP of Product

Providers of robust mobile experimentation and optimization solution to improve an user's mobile experience through A/B testing.

**Apptology** HQ
2260 E Bidwell St
Folsom CA 95630
P: 877-990-2777  PRC:322
www.apptology.com
Email: information@apptology.com
Emp: 11-50 Estab: 2009

Rich Foreman, Founder
Dana Smith, Co-Founder
Gary Dalal, CTO
Christina Hollingsworth, Sales Manager
Robin Foreman, Account Manager

Provider of mobile application development, training, marketing, iPhone application development, and Android application development services.

**Apsalar Inc** HQ
480 Second St Ste 100
San Francisco CA 94107
P: 877-590-1854  PRC:323
www.apsalar.com
Email: info@apsalar.com
Estab: 2010

Michael Oiknine, CEO

Provider of data-powered mobile advertising solutions. The company offers marketing attribution and in-app analytics services.

**Aptible Inc** HQ
548 Market St Ste 75826
San Francisco CA 94104
P: 866-296-5003  PRC:68
www.aptible.com
Email: hello@aptible.com
Estab: 2013

Alex Kubacki, Customer Reliability Engineering Manager
Ashley Mathew, Software Engineering Lead
Bob Fairhead, Senior Software Engineer
David Wen, Senior Software Engineer
Albert Wong, Senior Software Engineer

Developer of secure, private cloud deployment platform built to automate HIPAA compliance for digital health.

**Apttus Corp** HQ
1400 Fashion Island Blvd Ste 100
San Mateo CA 94404
P: 650-445-7700  PRC:319
apttus.com
Estab: 2006

Neehar Giri, Co-Founder
Kent Perkocha, Co-Founder
Frank Holland, CEO
Gregg Hampton, CFO
Praniti Lakhwara, CIO

Developers of AI revenue intelligence software.

**Apx Power Markets Inc** BR
2001 Gateway Pl Ste 315W
San Jose CA 95110
P: 408-517-2100  PRC:142
www.apx.com
Email: intellectualproperty@apx.com
Estab: 1996

Jason Brome, CTO
Carl Schlemmer, Demand Response product Manager
Lars Kvale, Head of Business Development
Nino Mijares, Supervisor
Crystal Baird-Martowski, Research Analyst

Provider of e-commerce services for the electrical sector. The company serves residential, commercial, and industrial properties.

**Aqs Inc**     DH
401 Kato Ter
Fremont CA 94539
P: 510-249-5800   F: 510-249-5810    PRC:189
www.aqs-inc.com
Email: info@aqs-inc.com
Estab: 1991

Amir Nosrati, Quality Engineer

Provider of electronic manufacturing solutions. The company offers electronic assembly, test engineering, system integration and final test services.

**Aqua Metrology Systems Ltd**     HQ
1225 E Arques Ave
Sunnyvale CA 94085
P: 408-523-1900    PRC:11
www.aquametrologysystems.com
Email: info@aquametrologysystems.com
Estab: 2007

Jim Garvey, Director of Engineering & Customer Service
Rick Bacon, CEO

Developer of online and offline analytical instrumentation for determination of water contaminants and trace metals for municipal and industrial markets.

**Aqua Sierra Controls Inc**     HQ
1650 Industrial Dr
Auburn CA 95603
P: 530-823-3241   F: 530-823-3475    PRC:159
www.aquasierra.com
Email: service@aquasierra.com
Emp: 1-10   Estab: 1979

Les Watson, President
Josh Lane, SCADA Manager

Provider of instrumentation and electrical contract services. The company specializes in process control automation for industrial installations.

**Aqua Terra Consultants**     HQ
2685 Marine Way Ste 1314
Mountain View CA 94043
P: 650-962-1864   F: 650-962-0706    PRC:142
aquaterra.com
Estab: 1985

Tony Donigian, President
Anurag Mishra, Senior Environmental Engineer

Provider of environmental consulting and water resource engineering services. The company also offers software development and consulting services.

**Aquantia Corp**     HQ
91 E Tasman Dr Ste 100
San Jose CA 95134
P: 408-228-8300    PRC:208
www.aquantia.com
Email: info@aquantia.com
Estab: 2004

Narayana Kodeti, Principal Engineer
Ha Dinh, Senior Product Engineer
Anand Patil, Senior PD Engineer
Phil Delansay, Co-Founder
Nick Shamlou, VP of Sales

Provider of software solutions such as signal processing, agile management, and technical support. The company serves the IT sector.

**Aquifer Sciences Inc**     HQ
3520 Golden Gate Way
Lafayette CA 94549
P: 925-283-9098    PRC:139
www.aquifer.com
Estab: 1988

Becky Sterbentz, President
Duncan Knudsen, Senior Staff Geologist

Provider of environmental assessment and remediation services. The company is also engaged in remedial design and implementation.

**Aquifi Inc**     HQ
2225 E Bayshore Rd Ste 110
Palo Alto CA 94303
P: 650-213-8535    PRC:316
www.aquifi.com
Email: info@Aquifi.com
Estab: 2011

Gergely Tcth, Founder
Thomas Sawyer, CFO

Developer of fluid technology solutions. The company is involved in computer vision and machine learning algorithms.

**Arable Corporation**     HQ
10061 Bubb Rd Ste 200
Cupertino CA 95014
P: 408-825-4755   F: 408-659-3732    PRC:268
www.arablecorp.com
Email: info@arablecorp.com
Estab: 2010

Richard Williams, President
Ary Sarkar, CEO
Brian Fahle, EVP
Daniel Schell, Scientist

Provider of products and services to health care, pharmaceutical, biotechnology and medical device companies.

**Aradigm Corp**     HQ
3929 Point Eden Way
Hayward CA 94545
P: 510-265-9000   F: 510-265-8878    PRC:34
www.aradigm.com
Email: bd@aradigm.com
Estab: 1991

Rita Mateo, Executive Chairman Assistant
John Siebert, Interim Principal Executive Officer
Virgil Thompson, Chairman
Juergen Froehlich, CMO
Adrienne Ste. Marie, Clinical Project Director

Manufacturer of pharmaceuticals delivered by inhalation for the treatment of respiratory diseases such as bronchiectasis, cystic fibrosis, and biodefense.

**Aragen Bioscience**     HQ
380 Woodview Ave
Morgan Hill CA 95037
P: 408-779-1700   F: 408-779-1711    PRC:34
www.aragenbio.com
Email: info@aragenbio.com
Estab: 1993

Oren Beske, President
Rick Srigley, President
Axel Schleyer, CEO
Elizabeth Garcia, Associate Director Human Resources
Wade Simonsen, Facilities Manager

Provider of services such as protein expression and purification, molecular biology, immunology, and in vivo services to the biotech and pharma industries.

**Aragon Consulting Group Inc**     HQ
19925 Stevens Creek Blvd Ste 100
Cupertino CA 95014
P: 415-869-8818    PRC:45
www.krugle.com
Email: enterprise-support@krugle.com

Mel Badgett, VP of Product Marketing

Provider of software development services. The company also offers authoring, coding, consulting, and technical support solutions.

**Aras Power Technologies**     HQ
371 Fairview Way
Milpitas CA 95035
P: 408-935-8877   F: 408-935-9177    PRC:76
araspower.com
Email: sales@arastech.com

David Greenfield, Application Engineer

Provider of power delivery solutions. The company offers conventional, alternating current solutions, and custom power supply design services.

**Arasan Chip Systems Inc**     RH
2010 N First St Ste 510
San Jose CA 95131
P: 408-282-1600   F: 408-282-7800    PRC:212
arasan.com
Estab: 1996

Chari Santhanam, VP of Engineering
Ron Nikel, Director of Analog Engineering
Srinivasulu Pola, Design Engineer
A.K. Ganesan, President
Padamunnur Rao, CFO

Provider of total IP solutions such as digital IP cores, protocol analyzers, and traffic generators for mobile storage and connectivity applications.

**Aravo Solutions Inc**     HQ
88 Kearny St Ste 1200
San Francisco CA 94108
P: 415-835-7600   F: 415-835-7610    PRC:45
www.aravo.com
Email: info@aravo.com
Estab: 2000

Tim Albinson, Founder
Michael Saracini, CEO
Eric Hensley, CTO
David Rusher, Chief Customer Officer
Caroline Philippon, VP of Finance

Provider of risk and performance management, Supplier Information Management (SIM), and related services.

**Arbor Solution Inc** HQ
46539 Fremont Blvd
Fremont CA 94538
P: 408-452-8900   F: 408-452-8909   PRC:68
us.arborsolution.com
Email: info1@arborsolution.com
Estab: 1993

Long Hoang, Director of Engineering
Eric Lee, President
Steven Fong, Operations Manager

Provider of embedded computing and networking
solutions for the transportation, medical, automation, and military segments.

**Arbor Vita Corp** HQ
48371 Fremont Blvd Ste 101
Fremont CA 94538
P: 408-585-3900   F: 408-585-3901   PRC:28
www.arborvita.com
Email: info@arborvita.com
Estab: 1998

Peter Lu, Founder
Charles Trimble, Chairman
Pedro Caceres, Facilities Manager
Thuymy Phan, QA
Thuy Tran-Lam, Human Resources Assistant

Provider of protein-based molecular diagnostics
that is used for the management of infectious
diseases and cancer.

**Arc** HQ
12657 Alcosta Blvd Ste 200
San Ramon CA 94583
P: 925-949-5100   PRC:67
www.e-arc.com
Email: info@e-arc.com
Estab: 1988
Sales: $300M to $1 Billion

Srinivas Mukkamala, Director of Engineering &
R&D
Suriyakumar Kumarakulasingam, CEO
Jorge Avalos, CFO
Rahul Roy, CTO
Dilo Wijesuriya, COO

Provider of document management services to
the architectural, engineering, and construction
industries.

**Arcadia Biosciences Inc** HQ
202 Cousteau Pl Ste 105
Davis CA 95618
P: 530-756-7077   F: 530-756-7027   PRC:34
www.arcadiabio.com
Email: info@arcadiabio.com
Emp: 1-10   Estab: 2002
Sales: $1M to $3M

Matthew Plavan, President
Pam Haley, CFO
Sarah Reiter, CCO
Grant Aldridge, VP of Commercial Operations
Randall Shultz, VP of Research & Development

Developer of agricultural products with enhanced
traits. The company uses technological tools,
genetic screening and genetic engineering to
achieve this.

**Architectural Lighting Works** HQ
1035 22nd Ave Unit 1
Oakland CA 94606
P: 510-489-2530   F: 650-249-0412   PRC:243
www.alwusa.com
Email: talktous@alwusa.com
Estab: 2005

Jim Prior, President
Shira Steinbeck, CEO
Ricardo Vargas, General Manager
Marco Zarate, Purchasing Manager
Dale Patterson, Finance Manager

Manufacturer of suspended, wall, and ceiling
lighting products and related accessories. The
company also deals with installation services.

**Arcscale LLC** HQ
PO Box 20621
San Jose CA 95160
P: 408-476-0554   F: 408-267-7980   PRC:68
arcscale.com
Email: info@arcscale.com
Estab: 2005

Sheri Fliss, CFO
Shane Stewart, Inside Sales Manager

Provider of colocation, technology integration,
hosting, implementation, and telecommunication
services. The company also deals with procurement.

**Arcsoft Inc** HQ
46601 Fremont Blvd
Fremont CA 94538
P: 510-440-9901   F: 510-440-1270   PRC:323
www.arcsoft.com
Estab: 1994

Michael Deng, CEO
Lisa Zulueta-Rapo, Senior Sales Manager

Developer of multimedia technologies and applications. The company serves both desktop and
embedded platforms.

**Arcus Technology Inc** HQ
3159 Independence Dr
Livermore CA 94551
P: 925-373-8800   F: 925-373-8809   PRC:94
www.arcus-technology.com
Email: info@arcus-technology.com
Estab: 2002

Thomas Judge, Engineering Manager

Provider of motor controllers, stepper motors, and
related accessories such as cables, encoders,
and gearboxes.

**Ardelyx Inc** HQ
34175 Ardenwood Blvd Ste 200
Fremont CA 94555
P: 510-745-1700   F: 510-745-0493   PRC:268
www.ardelyx.com
Email: info@ardelyx.com
Estab: 2007
Sales: $1M to $3M

Mike Raab, CEO
David Mott, Chairman
Mark Kaufmann, CFO
David Rosenbaum, Chief Development Officer
James Davidson, Associate Director of CMC

Developer of non-systemic and small molecule
therapeutics that work in the GI tract to treat car-
dio-renal, GI, and metabolic diseases.

**Ardent Systems Inc** HQ
2040 Ringwood Ave
San Jose CA 95131
P: 408-526-0100   PRC:211
ardentsi.com
Email: info@ardentsi.com
Estab: 1989

Seonae Lee, Software Engineer
Thomas Han, President

Provider of electronics manufacturing services
and storage device test solutions. The company is
engaged in material management services.

**Ardica Technologies** HQ
2325 Third St Ste 424
San Francisco CA 94107
P: 415-568-9270   PRC:288
www.ardica.com
Email: info@ardica.com
Estab: 2004

Nathan Martin, Embedded Systems Engineer
Daniel Braithwaite, Chief Product Officer
Tibor Fabian, CTO
Kris Lichter, CEO
John Hardman, CFO

Provider of integrated power and fuel cell
technology solutions for commercial and military
applications.

**Area West Environmental Inc** HQ
7006 Anice St
Orangevale CA 95662
P: 916-987-3362   F: 916-988-2677   PRC:142
areawest.net
Email: areawest@pacbell.net
Emp: 1-10   Estab: 2000

Becky Rozumowicz, President
Aimee Dour-Smith, Senior Environmental Planner
Cay Goude, Senior Conservation Specialist

Provider of environmental assessment services.
The company is also engaged in planning, permitting, and regulatory compliance management
services.

**Areias Systems Inc** HQ
5900 Butler Ln Ste 280
Scotts Valley CA 95066
P: 831-440-9800   F: 831-439-9295   PRC:78
www.areiasys.com
Email: sales@areiasys.com
Emp: 1-10   Estab: 2000

Jonathan Lee, Controls Engineer
Clemm Noernberg, CEO
Michael Nunns, NPI Manager
George Scott, Supervisor

Provider of services to the technology sector. The
company focuses on design, engineering, manufacturing, and prototyping.

**Ares Corp**  HQ
1440 Chapin Ave Ste 390
Burlingame CA 94010
P: 650-401-7100  F: 650-401-7101  PRC:304
www.arescorporation.com
Email: areshq@arescorporation.com
Estab: 1992

Doug Schmidt, CFO
Stanley Lynch, SVP
Joyce Grant, Controller

Provider of engineering, risk assessment, project
management, and other services and focuses on
nuclear, clean technology, space, and defense
fields.

**Aria Technologies Inc**  HQ
102 Wright Brothers Ave
Livermore CA 94551
P: 925-447-7500  F: 925-447-7511  PRC:62
www.ariatech.com
Email: sales@ariatech.com
Estab: 1991

Ryan Gilbert, Engineer
Joe McGuinness, President
Paula McGuinness, CEO
David Dickens, VP of Manufacturing
Justin Tidd, Manufacturing Manager

Provider of fiber optic cable assemblies and
connectivity products to the data, telecom, and
operator market places.

**Aridis Pharmaceuticals LLC**  HQ
5941 Optical Ct
San Jose CA 95138
P: 408-385-1742  F: 408-960-3822  PRC:34
www.aridispharma.com
Email: info@aridispharma.com
Estab: 2003
Sales: $1M to $3M

L. Truong, Founder
Vu Truong, Founder
Eric Patzer, Founder
V.U. Truong, CEO
Paul Mendelman, Interim Chief Medical Officer

Focuses on anti-infective alternatives to conventional antibiotics. The company offers services to
the pharmaceutical sector.

**Arista Corp**  HQ
40675 Encyclopedia Cir
Fremont CA 94538
P: 510-226-1800  F: 510-226-1890  PRC:93
www.goarista.com
Estab: 1994

Bill Dong, Software Engineer
Arlinda Nguyen, Western Regional Sales Manager
Wei Wang, Accounting Manager
Dean Kirk, Business Development Manager
Zhichen Zhao, Product Material Controller

Manufacturer of industrial computer products such
as industrial rack mounts, touch screen displays,
and fanless, embedded, and wallmount computers.

**Arista Networks Inc**  HQ
5453 Great America Pkwy
Santa Clara CA 95054
P: 408-547-5500  F: 408-538-8920  PRC:68
www.arista.com
Email: sales@aristanetworks.com
Estab: 2004
Sales: $1B to $3B

John McCool, Chief Platform Officer
Adam Sweeney, VP of Software Engineering
Ashwin Kohli, Group VP of Customer Engineering
Christophe Metivier, VP of Manufacturing and
Platform Engineering
Hugh Holbrook, VP of Software Engineering

Provider of cloud networking, network virtualization, high frequency trading, and government
solutions for data center needs.

**Ark Diagnostics Inc**  HQ
48089 Fremont Blvd
Fremont CA 94538
P: 877-869-2320  F: 510-270-6298  PRC:186
www.ark-tdm.com
Email: info@ark-tdm.com
Estab: 2003

Byung Moon, VP of Operations
Melody Chao, Controller
Mitchell Low, Research
Leopoldo Guerrero, Scientist

Manufacturer of in vitro diagnostic products for
the treatment of cancer, veterinary, HIV/AIDS,
anti-fungal drugs, and epilepsy and pain management.

**Arkian**  RH
650 Nuttman St
Santa Clara CA 95054
P: 408-991-9800  PRC:212
arkian.com

Esmond Kim, CEO
HO PARK, General Manager

Provider of research and development services.
The company focuses on marketing logistics with
semiconductor manufacturers.

**Arm Ltd**  RH
150 Rose Orchard Way
San Jose CA 95134-1358
P: 408-576-1500  F: 408-576-1501  PRC:212
www.arm.com
Estab: 1990

Graham Budd, President
Rene Haas, President of IP Products Group
Simon Segars, CEO
Inder Singh, CFO
Jason Zajac, CSO

Manufacturer of digital products and offers wireless, networking, and consumer entertainment
solutions to imaging, automotive, and storage
devices.

**Armageddon Energy Inc**  HQ
949 Hamilton Ave
Menlo Park CA 94025
P: 650-641-2899  PRC:135
www.armageddonenergy.com
Email: info@armageddonenergy.com
Estab: 2008

Mark Goldman, CEO

Designer and manufacturer of rooftop solar
systems. The company is engaged in installation
services and serves homeowners.

**Armorstruxx LLC**  HQ
850 Thurman St
Lodi CA 95240-3131
P: 209-365-9400  F: 209-224-0959  PRC:80
www.armorstruxx.com
Email: info@armorstruxx.com
Emp: 1-10  Estab: 2006

Frank Koukis, Facilities Manager
Leah Arnold, Purchasing Agent
Ray Harper, Shipping Receiving Manager

Provider of ballistic and blast protection solutions.
The company offers armor systems design and
integration services.

**Array Networks Inc**  HQ
1371 McCarthy Blvd
Milpitas CA 95035
P: 408-240-8700  F: 408-240-8754  PRC:63
www.arraynetworks.com
Email: info@arraynetworks.com
Estab: 2000

Vinod Pisharody, CTO
Fara Zarrabi, VP of HW Engineering & Operations
Toan Than, Network Support Engineer
Michael Zhao, President
Robert Shen, Board Chairman

Developer of integrated web traffic management
technology. The company focuses on load balancing and application acceleration solutions.

**Arrayit Corp**  HQ
927 Thompson Pl
Sunnyvale CA 94085
P: 408-744-1331  F: 408-744-1711  PRC:31
www.arrayit.com
Email: arrayit@arrayit.com
Estab: 1999

Arrayit Arrayit, President
Mark Schena, President
William Sklar, Financial Consultant
Todd Martinsky, SVP

Focuses on the discovery, development and manufacture of proprietary life science technologies
and consumables for disease prevention.

**Arrgh!! Manufacturing Company Inc**  HQ
831 Vallejo Ave
Novato CA 94945-2430
P: 415-897-0220  F: 415-898-0831  PRC:13
www.arrgh.com
Email: sales@arrgh.com
Estab: 1972

Alan Dedier, Chief Engineer
Tom Graham, President
Marc Wilson, General Manager
Allen Coddington, VP

Manufacturer of battery chargers, controls, battery
discharge alarms, microcomputer charger controls, and gas detectors.

**Arrive Technologies Inc**  HQ
3693 Westchester Dr
Roseville CA 95747
P: 888-864-6959  PRC:67
www.arrivetechnologies.com
Email: sales@arrivetechnologies.com
Emp: 1-10  Estab: 2001

Ngoc Bui, VP of Engineering
Murat Uraz, CEO
Pete Keeler, Executive Chairman
John Schell, CFO
Tu Cao, VP of Systems Architecture

Provider of broadband and packet network semi-conductor solutions for the telecommunication companies.

**Art's Sheet Metal Manufacturing Inc**    HQ
16075 Caputo Dr
Morgan Hill CA 95037
P: 408-778-0606   F: 408-778-0879    PRC:88
www.artssheetmetal.com
Email: sales@artssheetmetal.com

Shawn Chizanskos, Owner

Manufacturer of flashings, vents, drainage products, tie plates, and hangers. The company also focuses on distribution aspects.

**Artcraft Welding Inc**    HQ
781 E McGlincy Ln
Campbell CA 95008
P: 408-377-2725    PRC:121
www.artcraftwelding.com

Dan Ammon, CFO

Designer and manufacturer of ultrasonic cleaning equipment. The company specializes in precision cleaning fixtures.

**Artec Group Inc**    BR
2880 Lakeside Dr Ste 135
Santa Clara CA 95054
P: 669-292-5611    PRC:159
www.artec3d.com
Email: info@artec-group.com
Estab: 2007

Anna Galdina, Sales Channel Director

Developer and distributor of 3D scanners and 3D cameras. The company's products include Artec iD, Artec 3D, Viewshape, and Shapify.

**Arteris Inc**    HQ
591 W Hamilton Ave Ste 250
Campbell CA 95008
P: 408-470-7300    PRC:86
www.arteris.com
Estab: 2003

Charles Janac, Chairman
Nick Hawkins, CFO
Benoit de Lescure, CTO
Don Werner, Senior Director of Sales for the Americas

Provider of interconnect semiconductor IP solutions to system-on-chip makers and serves networking, automotive, video and mobile-phone processors.

**Arterys Inc**    DH
51 Federal St Ste 305
San Francisco CA 94107
P: 650-319-7230    PRC:194
arterys.com
Email: info@arterys.com
Estab: 2007

Fabien Beckers, Co-Founder
John Cilies, Co-Founder

Developer of medical imaging cloud platform. The company specializes in diagnostic platform to make healthcare more accurate and data driven.

**Articulate Solutions Inc**    HQ
65 Fifth St Ste 100
Gilroy CA 95020
P: 408-842-2275   F: 408-852-0384    PRC:323
www.articulate-solutions.com
Email: info@articulate-solutions.com
Estab: 1991

Katherine Filice, CEO
Jenny Arellano, Marketing Communication Manager
Whitney Pintello, Marketing Coordinator
Jason Raby, Director of Communications
Dakota Filice, Head of Security

Provider of branding services such as website development, identity design, social media marketing, and search engine optimization.

**Artielle Immunotherapeutics Inc**    HQ
400 S El Camino Real
San Mateo CA 94402
P: 650-401-2000   F: 650-375-7077    PRC:268
www.artielle.com
Estab: 2004

Gilbert Miller, EVP

Provider of pharmaceuticals. The company develops therapeutics to treat a wide range of autoimmune inflammatory diseases.

**Artifex Software Inc**    HQ
1305 Grant Ave Ste 200
Novato CA 94903
P: 415-492-9861   F: 415-492-9862    PRC:322
www.artifex.com
Email: info@artifex.com
Estab: 1993

Miles Jones, President
Scott Sackett, VP of Sales & Licensing

Provider of software solutions for host based applications. The company also focuses on embedded printer markets.

**Artium Technologies Inc**    HQ
470 Lakeside Dr Unit C
Sunnyvale CA 94085
P: 408-737-2364   F: 408-737-2374    PRC:172
www.artium.com
Email: info@artium.com
Estab: 1998

Khalid Ibrahim, Senior Design Engineer
William Bachalo, CEO

Developer of products for spray diagnostics, particulate monitoring, and cloud research applications.

**ArtNet Pro Inc**    HQ
2315 Paragon Dr
San Jose CA 95131
P: 408-954-8383   F: 408-954-8380    PRC:172
www.artnetpro.com
Email: sales@artnetpro.com

Meir Polack, President

Provider of reused equipment. The company offers direct imaging systems, laser photo plotters, and scanners.

**Artwork Conversion Software Inc**    HQ
417 Ingalls St
Santa Cruz CA 95060
P: 831-426-6163   F: 831-426-2824    PRC:316
www.artwork.com
Email: info@artwork.com
Emp: 1-10   Estab: 1987

Steve Dibartolomeo, President
Hagai Pettel, Sales Manager
Felix Lev, Senior Scientist

Developer of CAD translation programs and CAD viewers software. The company also offers plotting software and IC packaging software.

**Aruba Networks Inc**    HQ
3333 Scott Blvd
Santa Clara CA 95054
P: 408-227-4500   F: 408-752-0626    PRC:63
www.arubanetworks.com
Email: corporate.compliance.hpe@hpe.com
Estab: 2002

Majid Saee, Systems Engineer
Keerti Melkote, President
Jim Bergkamp, CFO
Partha Narasimhan, CTO
Pradeep Iyer, Chief Architect

Manufacturer of enterprise network infrastructure equipment. The company serves healthcare, government, education, and other sectors.

**ARX Networks Corp**    HQ
37100 Central Ct
Newark CA 94560
P: 650-403-4000    PRC:325
www.arxnetworks.com
Email: info@arxnetworks.com
Estab: 1998

Ray Marmash, Founder

Provider of IT support and maintenance and cloud services. The company also focuses on unified communications and procurement.

**Arx Pax Labs Inc**    HQ
105 Cooper Ct
Los Gatos CA 95032
P: 408-335-7630    PRC:304
arxpax.com
Estab: 2014

Greg Henderson, Founder
Jill Henderson, Co-Founder

Developer of magnetic field architecture technology for structural isolation, recreation and entertainment, industrial automation, and transportation.

**Aryaka Networks Inc**    HQ
691 S Milpitas Blvd Ste 206
Milpitas CA 95035
P: 877-727-9252   F: 408-273-8430    PRC:325
aryaka.com
Email: info@aryaka.com
Estab: 2008

Vikas Garg, SVP of Engineering and Operations
Ashwath Nagaraj, Co-Founder
Matt Carter, CEO
Ram Gupta, Non-Executive Chairman
Kelly Hicks, CFO

Provider of cloud-based WAN optimization services. The company focuses on application performance, data protection, and bandwidth reduction.

**Asa Computers Inc** HQ
645 National Ave
Mountain View CA 94043
P: 650-230-8000 PRC:92
www.asacomputers.com
Email: sales@asacomputers.com
Estab: 1989

Ruchir Kute, Software Engineer
Satyam Sharma, Sales Engineer & Purchaser
Anu Bhargava, Co-Founder
Arvind Bhargava, Founder
Joel Wineland, CTO

Manufacturer of full service custom servers and storage systems. The company also focuses on integration.

**Asani Solutions LLC** HQ
2060 Walsh Ave Ste 115
Santa Clara CA 95050
P: 408-330-0821 F: 408-330-0822 PRC:324
www.asani.com
Email: info2@asani.com
Estab: 1999

Ryan Nelson, Senior Systems Administrator

Provider of networking solutions and system integration services. The company also focuses on internet and corporate consulting.

**Asap Systems** HQ
355 Piercy Rd
San Jose CA 95138
P: 408-227-2720 F: 408-227-2721 PRC:325
www.asapsystems.com
Email: sales@asapsystems.com
Estab: 1990

Timothy Laurin, Technical Engineer
Eric Fombona, Owner
Elie Touma, President
Megan Swanson, Support & Sales Manager
Joel Segovia, Channel Accounts Manager

Developer of inventory management and asset tracking software. The company also offers barcode scanners & printers and RFID tags.

**Asbestech Laboratory** HQ
6825 Fair Oaks Blvd Ste 103
Carmichael CA 95608
P: 916-481-8902 F: 916-481-3975 PRC:306
asbestechlab.com
Email: asbestech@sbcglobal.net
Emp: 1-10 Estab: 1987

Tommy Conlon, Laboratory Director

Provider of asbestos and lead testing services. The company also offers transmission electron microscopes.

**Asbestos Tem Laboratories Inc** HQ
600 Bancroft Way Ste A
Berkeley CA 94710
P: 510-704-8930 F: 510-704-8429 PRC:138
www.asbestostemlabs.com
Estab: 1989

Mark Bailey, President
Tom Suess, Quality Manager
Chase Aquino, Lab Operations Manager
Dorothea Rastegar, Accounting Manager
Gabriela Mondar, Administrative Assistant

Provider of laboratory services including asbestos and lead testing. The company serves geologists, contractors, and homeowners.

**Asbury Graphite Incorporated of CA** BR
2855 Franklin Canyon Rd
Rodeo CA 94572
P: 510-799-3636 F: 510-799-7460 PRC:278
asbury.com
Email: asburyinfo@asbury.com
Estab: 1895

Noah Nichelson, President
Stephen Riddle, CEO
Sue Rish, VP
Marc Stassen, General Manager Asbury Graphite and Carbons
David Soares, Director of Quality

Supplier of carbon and graphite products for the chemicals, cement, rubber, and metal industries. The company's products include coals, cokes, and carbon fiber.

**Asc Profiles Inc** HQ
2110 Enterprise Blvd
West Sacramento CA 95691-3428
P: 916-372-0933 F: 253-896-8471 PRC:82
www.ascprofiles.com
Email: ar@ascprofiles.com
Emp: 1-10 Estab: 1971

John Fitch, Outside Sales Representative
Susan Nahlen, Senior Accountant

Supplier of building products such as panels, roofing products, and standing seams. The company serves the commercial and residential markets.

**Ascendance Wireless LLC** HQ
11760 Atwood Rd Ste 6
Auburn CA 95603
P: 530-887-8300 F: 530-889-1255 PRC:61
www.ascendancewireless.com
Email: sales@ascendancewireless.com
Emp: 1-10 Estab: 2004

Mark Cederloff, President

Designer and manufacturer of fixed wireless networks. The company finds application in security and surveillance needs.

**Ascendis Pharma A/S** BR
500 Emerson St
Palo Alto CA 94301
P: 650-352-8389 F: 650-618-1592 PRC:34
www.ascendispharma.com
Email: info@ascendispharma.com
Estab: 2006

Jan Mikkelsen, President
Michael Jensen, Chairman
Thomas Larson, SVP
Scott Smith, SVP
Juha Punnonen, SVP

Focuses on the creation of drug candidates, proteins, peptides and small molecules, suitable for either local or systemic treatment.

**Ascentool** HQ
3711 Yale Way
Fremont CA 94538
P: 510-683-9332 PRC:165
www.ascentool.net/home.html
Estab: 2005

Efrain Velazquez, Electrical Engineer
Miya Yang, Finance Manager
George Guo, Manager

Designer, manufacturer, and marketer of vacuum thin-film deposition systems for making solar photovoltaic devices.

**ASCENX Technologies Inc** HQ
41900 Christy St
Fremont CA 94538
P: 408-945-1997 F: 408-945-1999 PRC:202
www.ascenx.com
Email: info@ascenx.com
Estab: 2003

Tung Bach, President

Provider of engineering services to the semiconductor industry. The company is also engaged in contract manufacturing and repair services.

**Asepco Corp** HQ
1161 Cadillac Ct
Milpitas CA 95035
P: 650-691-9500 F: 650-691-9600 PRC:78
www.watson-marlow.com
Email: info.asepco@wmftg.com
Estab: 1989

Barry Hoffman, Sales
Mark Embury, EVP
Terry Flanders, Designer

Manufacturer of valves and magnetic mixers. The company also offers diaphragms, connectors, and actuators.

**Asf Electric Inc** HQ
76 Hill St
Daly City CA 94014-2504
P: 650-755-9032 F: 650-755-2975 PRC:245
www.asfelectric.net
Email: info@asfelectric.com
Estab: 1971

Cathy Lagomarsino, President
Caren Ferrari, Director of Human Resource and Payroll
Nicole Lagomarsino, Marketing Communication Manager
John Ferrari, Senior Estimator and Project Manager
Damien LeClerc, Bid Coordinator

Provider of electrical contracting services. The company installs fire safety systems for the retail, health care and public entities.

**Ashby Communications** HQ
10642 Industrial Ave Ste 120
Roseville CA 95678
P: 916-960-0701 PRC:71
www.ashbycommunications.com
Email: sales@ashbycommunications.com
Emp: 1-10 Estab: 1991

Michael Bird, Network Engineer
Brian Ashby, Owner
Ron Reeder, Sales Manager
Abigail Joy, Office Manager

Provider of voice and data cabling solutions. The company's services include network installation, support, spam blocking, and cloud computing.

**Ashlock Co** HQ
855 Montague Ave
San Leandro CA 94577
P: 510-351-0560 F: 510-357-0329 PRC:153
www.ashlockco.com
Email: info@ashlockco.com

Karen Hallett, Office Manager

Provider of pitting equipment. The company offers equipment such as cherry pitting, date pitting, and olive pitting machines.

**Asi Controls** HQ
  2202 Camino Ramon
  San Ramon CA 94583-1339
P: 925-866-8808  F: 925-866-1369    PRC:147
www.asicontrols.com
Email: info@asicontrols.com
Estab: 1986

David Oest, Application Engineer
Christina Jones, Technical
Paul Chapman, President
Francis Chapman, CEO
Mashuri Warren, Director of Product Development

Manufacturer of direct digital controls for HVAC
and light industrial marketplace. The company also
offers networking products and unitary controls.

**Asian Pacific Environmental Network** HQ
  426 17th St Ste 500
  Oakland CA 94612
P: 510-834-8920    PRC:142
apen4ej.org

Miya Yoshitani, Executive Director
Parin Shah, Senior Strategist
Shina Robinson, Executive Assistant
Jing He, Community Organizer
Chiravann Uch, Operations Coordinator

Provider of environmental services. The company
engages in membership of low income immigrant
and refugee communities.

**ASM America Inc** BR
  97 E Brokaw Rd Ste 100
  San Jose CA 95112
P: 408-451-0830    PRC:86
www.asm.com
Estab: 1968

Charles del Prado, President
Peter Van Bommel, CFO

Provider of technology and consulting services
to semiconductor manufacturers. The company's
products include EPSILON 3200, ADVANCE
A400, and EMERALD XP.

**Asmeix Corp** HQ
  PO Box 5188
  Concord CA 94524
P: 877-977-7999  F: 925-930-8223    PRC:320
www.cspec.com
Email: software@cspec.com
Estab: 1985

Mike Bernasek, CEO
Fredrik Nilsson, Sales Manager

Provider of welding procedure software services
such as technical support, installation, maintenance, and demo services.

**Asml San Jose** BR
  399 W Trimble Rd
  San Jose CA 95131
P: 669-265-3200    PRC:159
www.asml.com

Martin van den Brink, President
Peter Wennink, President
Roger Dassen, EVP
Frederic Schneider-Maunoury, EVP
Frits van Hout, CSO

Manufacturer of lithography systems for semiconductor industries. The company also offers
customized imaging solutions.

**Aspen Environmental Group** BR
  235 Montgomery St Ste 640
  San Francisco CA 94104
P: 415-955-4775  F: 415-955-4776    PRC:139
www.aspeneg.com
Email: humanresources@aspeneg.com
Estab: 1991

Will Walters, Senior Engineer
Hamid Rastegar, Founder
Jon Davidson, VP
Tom Murphy, VP
Susan Lee, VP

Provider of environmental compliance, impact
assessment, and mitigation services. The company's services include construction monitoring and
project management.

**Aspera Inc** HQ
  5900 Hollis St Ste E
  Emeryville CA 94608
P: 510-849-2386  F: 510-868-8392    PRC:323
www.asperasoft.com
Email: info@asperasoft.com
Estab: 2004

Charles Shiflett, Software Engineer
David Mostardi, Senior Sales Engineer
Richard Heitmann, VP of Marketing
Scott Burger, Demand Generation Manager

Developer of file transport technologies. The
company provides client and server software,
consoles, and mobile uploaders.

**Aspire Systems Inc** BR
  1735 Technology Dr Ste 260
  San Jose CA 95110
P: 408-260-2076  F: 408-904-4591    PRC:325
www.aspiresys.com
Email: info@aspiresys.com
Estab: 1996

Gowri Subramanian, CEO
Sridhar Ps, SVP of Finance & Administration
Prathap Achuthan, VP of US Operations
Sunil N V, EVP of Delivery
Andy Chadha, Director

Provider of product engineering, infrastructure
and application support, and testing services. The
company serves healthcare and education fields.

**Assay Technology Inc** HQ
  1382 Stealth St
  Livermore CA 94551
P: 925-461-8880  F: 925-461-7149    PRC:233
www.assaytech.com
Email: custservice@assaytech.com
Estab: 1981

Steve Green, Director of Laboratories
Veronica Liebowitz, Quality Assurance
Rena Kirkpatrick, Chief Marketing Advisor
Beth Green, Marketing Manager of Product
Specialist

Provider of personal monitoring badges to monitor chemicals in worker's breathing zone. The
company also analyzes the contents of returned
samplers.

**Assembly Biosciences Inc** RH
  331 Oyster Point Blvd 4th Fl
  South San Francisco CA 94080
P: 833-509-4583    PRC:34
www.assemblybio.com
Email: info@assemblybio.com
Estab: 2014

Derek Small, Co-Founder
Uri Lopatin, CO-Founder
David Barrett, COO
Richard Colonno, CSO
Qi Huang, VP

Developer of therapeutics for the treatment of
hepatitis B virus (HBV) infection. The company
specializes in clinical trials.

**Assembly Tek** HQ
  175 El Pueblo Rd Ste 27
  Scotts Valley CA 95066
P: 831-439-0800    PRC:62
assemblytek.com
Email: info@assemblytek.com
Emp: 1-10  Estab: 1987

Glenn Smith, Manager

Manufacturer of custom cables. The company
offers services like design, laminating, JIT programs, and wire preparation.

**Assia Inc** HQ
  203 Redwood Shores Pkwy Ste 100
  Redwood City CA 94065
P: 650-654-3400  F: 650-654-3404    PRC:326
www.assia-inc.com
Email: info@assia-inc.com
Estab: 2003

Sina Zahedi, Director of System Engineering
John Cioffi, CEO
Kevin Mukai, Director of Product Marketing
Jarrett Miller, VP
Tuncay Cil, SVP of Product Management

Provider of broadband solution such as cloud-
check, technology licensing, DSL expresse, and
expresse products and solution.

**Associated Lighting Reps Inc** HQ
  7777 Pardee Ln
  Oakland CA 94621
P: 510-638-3800  F: 510-638-2908    PRC:245
www.alrinc.com
Estab: 1961

Dave Ruth, Principal of Information Technology
Margaret Porpora, Manager
Dennis Davis, Contractor
Jonathan Bredenkamp, Manager

Provider of lighting services. The company offers
controls, emergency, indoor, LED, outdoor and
pole lighting from several manufacturers.

**Associated Pathology Medical Group
Inc** HQ
  105A Cooper Ct
  Los Gatos CA 95032
P: 408-399-5050    PRC:303
apmglab.com
Email: services@apmglab.com
Estab: 1956

Julia Chan, President
Jeffrey Young, Director of Quality Assurance
Werner Stamm, Director of Cytopathology
Carlene Hawksley, Clinical Laboratory Director
Leonard Valentino, Pathologist

Provider of medical care services. The company focuses on women's health, dermatopathology, family practice, and urology areas.

**Assurx Inc**                                     HQ
   18525 Sutter Blvd Ste 150
   Morgan Hill CA 95037
P: 408-778-1376   F: 408-776-1267      PRC:326
www.assurx.com
Email: info@assurx.com
Estab: 1993

John Kielty, VP of Sales

Provider of quality management and regulatory compliance software solutions for biotechnology, medical devices, pharmaceutical, and energy industries.

**Asteelflash**                                    BR
   4211 Starboard Dr
   Fremont CA 94538-6427
P: 510-440-2840                        PRC:200
asteelflash.com
Email: sales@asteelflash.com

Peter Wang, Director of Information Technology
Johnson Wu, Information Technology Manager
Mathieu Kury, Business Development & Marketing Manager
Albert Yanez, EVP
Veronique Danciu, Director

Provider of electronic manufacturing services. The company offers engineering design, contract manufacturing, and delivery services.

**Astex Pharmaceuticals**                          HQ
   4420 Rosewood Dr Ste 200
   Pleasanton CA 94588
P: 925-560-0100   F: 925-560-0101      PRC:257
www.astx.com
Estab: 1991

Mohammad Azab, President
Harren Jhoti, President
David Rees, CSO
Martin Buckland, Chief Corporate Officer
Nancy Worrell, VP of Human Resources

Developer of small-molecule therapeutics. The company focuses on products for treatment of cancer and central nervous system disorders.

**Astreya**                                        HQ
   2099 Gateway Pl Ste 140
   San Jose CA 95110
P: 800-224-1117                        PRC:324
www.astreya.com
Email: sales@astreya.com
Estab: 2001

Jeffrey Freeland, Founder
Andrea Bendzick, CFO
Darrell Bradshaw, Director of Financial Program
Anita Nunes, SVP of Strategic Sales
Brandon Curry, SVP of Solution Sales

Provider of staffing services. The company specializes in recruitment of systems administrators, network engineers, system, and network architects.

**ASUSTeK Computer Inc**                           HQ
   800 Corporate Way
   Fremont CA 94539
P: 510-739-3777   F: 510-608-4555      PRC:105
www.asus.com.tw
Estab: 1989

Isaac Ho, Senior Hardware Engineer
Lillian Lin, Marketing Director
L. Chen, Senior Director

Manufacturer of computer systems and hardware components such as desktops, notebooks, peripherals, motherboards, and graphic cards.

**At&T Inc**                                       BR
   1040 Grant Rd
   Mountain View CA 94040
P: 650-938-9479                        PRC:68
www.att.com
Estab: 1876

Juan Contreras, Director of Content

Provider of smartphones, TV services, business solutions, wireless networks, and broadband services.

**At&T Inc**                                       BR
   1410 E Hatch Rd
   Modesto CA 95351
P: 209-556-9042                        PRC:64
www.att.com
Emp: 11-50 Estab: 1876

Sorabh Saxena, President

Provider of IP based communication solutions. The company offers services in the areas of broadband, Wi-Fi, wireless networks, and mobile phones.

**Atac Corp**                                      HQ
   2770 De La Cruz Blvd
   Santa Clara CA 95050-2624
P: 408-736-2822   F: 408-736-8447      PRC:6
www.atac.com
Estab: 1979

Scott Simcox, President

Developer of products and services like decision aids, analysis tools, and expert consulting for aviation modeling and simulation.

**Atara Biotherapeutics Inc**                      HQ
   611 Gateway Blvd Ste 900
   S San Francisco CA 94080
P: 650-278-8930                        PRC:254
atarabio.com
Email: office@atarabio.com
Estab: 2012

Christopher Haqq, Chief Medical Officer
John McGrath, CFO

Provider of biotherapeutic services. The company focuses on the treatment of cancer, kidney disease, and other illnesses.

**Atech Flash Technology Inc**                     HQ
   46045 Warm Springs Blvd
   Fremont CA 94539
P: 510-824-6868   F: 510-824-6869      PRC:110
www.atechflash.com
Email: sales@atechflash.com
Estab: 2001

Hsien-Rong Liang, CEO

Provider of commercial and consumer products that include drive bay multiple flash card reader, portable card readers, and iPod accessories.

**Atheer Inc**                                     HQ
   2350 Mission College Blvd Ste 1200
   Santa Clara CA 95054
P: 650-933-5004                        PRC:319
www.atheerair.com
Estab: 2011

Soulaiman Itani, Founder
Alka Patel, Accounting Manager

Developer of 3D smart glasses and productivity application for aerospace, insurance, field maintenance, oil & gas, and healthcare.

**Atlas Engineering Services Inc**                 HQ
   135 Spring St P O Box 1260
   Santa Cruz CA 95060
P: 831-426-1440                        PRC:142
atlasengineeringservices.com
Email: atlasengr@calcentral.com
Emp: 1-10

Frederick Yukic, President
Joshua East, Associate Geologist

Provider of environmental consulting services. The company offers services for aquifer testing, onsite wastewater disposal, and ground water sanitary surveys.

**Atlassian**                                      BR
   1098 Harrison St
   San Francisco CA 94103
P: 415-701-1110   F: 415-449-6222      PRC:323
atlassian.com

David Nicholson, Cloud Support Engineer
Daniel Rohan, Development Tools Support Engineer
David Chan, Support Engineer
Jay Simons, President
Cameron Deatsch, Head of Growth & Online Sales

Provider of software development and collaboration tools. The company offers software for chats, tracking, repository management, and code hosting.

**Atlona Inc**                                     HQ
   70 Daggett Dr
   San Jose CA 95134
P: 877-536-3976   F: 408-743-5622      PRC:61
www.atlona.com
Email: support@atlona.com
Estab: 2003

Michael Khain, Co-Founder
Ilya Khayn, Co-Founder
Mark Ramos, Customer Support Supervisor

Provider of technology products for classrooms, large corporations and small businesses, hospitality venues, and residences.

**Atn Corp**     HQ
  1341 San Mateo Ave
  S San Francisco CA 94080
P: 650-989-5100    F: 650-875-0129    PRC:168
www.atncorp.com
Email: info@atncorp.com
Estab: 1995

James Munn, CEO

Developer and manufacturer of precision night optics and thermal imaging solutions. The company serves law enforcement and military clients.

**Atomwise Inc**     HQ
  717 Market St Ste 800
  San Francisco CA 94103
P: 650-449-7925    PRC:268
www.atomwise.com
Email: hello@atomwise.com

Abraham Heifets, CEO
Izhar Wallach, CTO

Developer of artificial intelligence systems for the discovery of drugs. The company serves the healthcare sector.

**Atp Electronics Inc**     RH
  2590 N First St Ste 150
  San Jose CA 95131
P: 408-732-5000    F: 408-732-5055    PRC:96
www.atpinc.com
Email: sales@atpinc.com

Mike McClimans, VP of Sales
Eunice Chen, Sales & Marketing Manager
Jeff Hsieh, SVP
Liwei Liao, Operations Manager

Provider of NAND flash and DRAM memory modules. The company specializes in telecom, medical, automotive, and enterprise computing.

**Ats Inc**     HQ
  2785 Goodrick Ave
  Richmond CA 94801
P: 510-234-3173    F: 510-234-3185    PRC:166
www.atsduct.com
Estab: 1978

Lou Flores, Engineer
Jeff Shea, CEO
Doug Williams, Sales Manager
Kathleen Passalacqua, Accounting Analyst

Manufacturer of fiberglass duct work for fume exhaust systems. The company offers installation and other related services.

**Attention Control Systems Inc**     HQ
  650 Castro St Ste 120-197
  Mountain View CA 94041
P: 888-224-7328    PRC:323
www.brainaid.com
Email: info@brainaid.com
Estab: 1996

David Halper, VP

Manufacturer of cognitive aids. The company also offers technical assistance solutions and serves the healthcare sector.

**Atypon Systems LLC**     HQ
  5201 Great America Pkwy Ste 215
  Santa Clara CA 95054
P: 408-988-1240    F: 408-988-1070    PRC:320
www.atypon.com
Email: info@atypon.com
Estab: 1996

Kendall Shaw, Software Engineer
Mayank Varia, Software Engineer
Georgios Papadopoulos, CEO
Gordon Tibbitts, EVP of Corporate Development
Marty Picco, VP of Product Management

Provider of service content delivery software for publishers. The company serves information discovery, e-commerce, and business intelligence needs.

**Aubin Industries Inc**     HQ
  23833 S Chrisman Rd
  Tracy CA 95304
P: 209-833-7592    F: 209-833-7594    PRC:159
www.aubinindustries.com
Email: info@aubinindustries.com
Emp: 1-10

Philip Aubin, Owner
Dee Silveira, Office Administrator
Stefanie Price, Operations Officer
Shanda O'Donnell, Marketing Manager

Designer and manufacturer of mobile wheel systems. The company serves the material handling industry.

**Audible Magic Corp**     HQ
  985 University Ave Ste 35
  Los Gatos CA 95032
P: 408-399-6405    F: 408-399-6406    PRC:60
www.audiblemagic.com
Email: info@audiblemagic.com
Estab: 1999

Doug Keislar, Senior Engineer
Michael Perkins, Senior Software Engineer
Vance Ikezoye, President
Carol Murphy, Marketing Consultant

Developer of media identification and synchronization, content registration, and copyright compliance solutions.

**Augmedix Inc**     HQ
  1161 Mission St Ste 210
  San Francisco CA 94103
P: 888-669-4885    PRC:194
www.augmedix.com
Email: info@augmedix.com
Estab: 2012

Manny Krakaris, CEO
Ian Shakil, Founding Chairman
Davin Lundquist, Chief Medical Officer
Sandra Breber, COO
Jonathan Hawkins, Chief Revenue Officer

Provider of technology enabled documentation services for health systems and doctors.

**Augmentum Inc**     HQ
  1065 E Hillsdale Blvd Ste 413
  Foster City CA 94404
P: 650-578-9221    PRC:319
augmentum.com
Email: info@augmentum.com
Estab: 2004

Leonard Liu, Chairman
Wayne Hom, CTO
Yuen Lee, EVP of Worldwide Sales & Applications

Provider of software development & solution implementation services. The company focuses on internet applications and product development outsourcing.

**Auriga Corp**     HQ
  890 Hillview Ct Ste 130
  Milpitas CA 95035
P: 408-946-5400    F: 408-941-6298    PRC:323
www.aurigacorp.com
Email: info@aurigacorp.com
Estab: 1990

Shyam Nathan, Software Engineer
Athar Taha, Electrical Engineer
Ramesh Daryani, CTO
Willy Dommen, Director of Technology Services
Soham Mookerjea, Project Manager

Provider of technology consulting services for electric power, telecommunications, transportation, and information technology systems.

**Aurionpro Solutions Inc**     DH
  4000 Executive Pkwy Ste 250
  San Ramon CA 94583
P: 925-242-0777    F: 925-242-0778    PRC:322
www.aurionpro.com
Email: info@aurionpro.com

Samir Shah, CEO
Paresh Zaveri, Chairman
Dusan Jovanovic, CFO
Niraj Shah, Financial Analyst
Raj Biyani, VP of Delivery Banking & Payments

Provider of solutions to streamline corporate banking, treasury, fraud prevention, risk management, governance and compliance needs.

**Aurostar Corp**     HQ
  46560 Fremont Blvd Ste 201
  Fremont CA 94538
P: 510-249-9422    PRC:85
www.aurostar.net
Email: sales@aurostar.net
Estab: 2002

Vasudeva Kamath, CEO

Provider of technology products and services focusing on home theater systems, consumer electronics, desktops and notebooks, and networking solutions.

**AuSIM Inc**     HQ
  1110 La Avenida Ste C
  Mountain View CA 94043-1424
P: 650-322-8746    PRC:207
ausim3d.com
Email: info@ausim3d.com
Estab: 1998

William Chapin, President

Developer of audio simulation technology and products for auditory displays for mission-critical applications.

**Austin Precision Inc** HQ
4382 Contractors Common
Livermore CA 94551
P: 925-449-1049  F: 925-449-5176  PRC:80
austinprecisioninc.com
Estab: 1991

Andy McCorkle, Supervisor

Provider of precision machined parts. The company offers parts made from aluminum, plastics, stainless steel, and other metals.

**AutoCell Electronics Inc** HQ
9370 Studio Ct Ste 188
Elk Grove CA 95758
P: 888-393-6668  F: 916-393-6871  PRC:243
www.autocell.net
Email: info@autocell.net
Emp: 1-10

Richard Ng, CEO

Manufacturer and distributor of energy efficient lighting products. The company offers compact fluorescent lamps, LED flashlights, and showerheads.

**Autodesk Inc** BR
1 Market Ste 500
San Francisco CA 94105
P: 415-356-0700  F: 415-547-2222  PRC:316
www.autodesk.com
Email: na_mfg@autodesk.com
Estab: 1982

Minette Norman, VP of Global Engineering
Andrew Anagnost, President
Pascal Di Fronzo, SVP of Corporate Affairs
Richard Herren, Principal Accounting Officer
Jeff Brzycki, Chief Information Officer

Provider of 3D design, engineering, and entertainment software solutions. The company also offers technical support services.

**Autoflow Products Inc** HQ
3860 Cincinnati Ave
Rocklin CA 95765
P: 916-626-3058  F: 916-626-3068  PRC:230
autoflowproducts.com
Emp: 1-10  Estab: 1982

Peggy Stevens, Co-Owner
Miranda King, Manager

Manufacturer of flow switches. The company specializes in designing switches for chemical analyzers, chemical injectors, and chromatographic systems.

**AutoGrid Systems Inc** HQ
255 Shoreline Dr Ste 350
Redwood City CA 94065
P: 650-461-9038  PRC:323
www.auto-grid.com
Estab: 2011

Peter Bloom, Senior Software Engineer
Tommer Wizansky, Principal Engineer of Data Science
Amit Narayan, CEO
Rajeev Singh, CTO
Om Moolchandani, CSO

Provider of grid-sensing technologies. The company focuses on energy data platform and optimized demand management services.

**Automate Scientific Inc** HQ
812 Page St
Berkeley CA 94710
P: 510-845-6283  F: 510-280-3795  PRC:122
autom8.com
Email: info@autom8.com
Estab: 1992

Joe Cordes, President
Gong Cheng, Senior Sales Application Scientist
Ryan Arant, Application Scientist

Manufacturer and distributor of biomedical equipment. The company offers amplifiers, manipulators, software, and accessories.

**Automated Inspection Systems** HQ
1870 Arnold Industrial Pl Ste 1055
Concord CA 94520
P: 925-335-9206  PRC:19
www.ais4ndt.com
Email: ais@slip.net
Estab: 1996

Steve Madera, Software Engineer
Randy Fong, President

Designer and builder of inspection equipment. The company caters to the oil and gas pipeline inspection needs.

**Automatic Bar Controls Inc** HQ
2060 Cessna Dr
Vacaville CA 95688
P: 707-448-5151  F: 707-448-1521  PRC:19
www.wunderbar.com
Estab: 1971

Bret Baker, VP

Provider of beverage and liquor dispensers. The company's products include beverage and food and sauce dispensers, and food preparation systems.

**Automation Partners Inc** HQ
6115 State Farm Dr Unit A2
Rohnert Park CA 94928
P: 707-665-3980  F: 707-665-3989  PRC:94
www.automationpartners.com
Email: info@automationpartners.com
Estab: 1990

Larry Tausch, President
Mihir Shukla, CEO

Manufacturer of controls for control systems and regulators. The company specializes in products for fabric density measurement.

**Automattic Inc** HQ
60 29th St
San Francisco CA 94110
P: 877-273-3049  PRC:325
www.automattic.com
Estab: 2005

George Ng, Director of Finance
Peter Slutsky, Director of Platform Services
Matt Mullenweg, Principal
Paul Sieminski, General Counsel
Holly Hogan, Associate General Counsel

Provider of blogging services. The company specializes in handling non-profit and open source projects.

**Autonet Mobile** HQ
3636 N Laughlin Rd Ste 150
Santa Rosa CA 95403
P: 415-223-0316  F: 707-284-4458  PRC:68
www.autonetmobile.com
Email: support@autonetmobile.com
Estab: 2005

Danny Gomez, Test Engineer
Krysteen Hopkins, Operations Analyst
Neena Bonetti, Controller

Provider of internet based telematics and applications service platform for the automotive transportation market.

**Autonomic Software Inc** HQ
4185 Blackhawk Plz Cir Ste 102
Danville CA 94526
P: 925-683-8351  PRC:325
autonomic-software.com
Email: info@autonomic-software.com
Estab: 2004

Harish Rao, Principal Software Engineer
Tony Gigliotti, President
Alexander Gigliotti, Director of Sales

Developer of software for endpoint & security management, imaging, and other needs. The company serves government, finance, and other sectors.

**Avalanche Technology** HQ
3450 W Warren Ave
Fremont CA 94538
P: 510-897-3300  F: 510-438-0143  PRC:95
www.avalanche-technology.com
Email: info@avalanche-technology.com
Estab: 2006

Ebrahim Abedifard, VP of Engineering
Petro Estakhri, CEO
Rajiv Ranjan, Founder
Bob Netter, CFO
Danny Sabour, VP of Marketing and Business Development

Provider of programmable storage solutions. The company offers services to the consumer electronics industry.

**Avalent Technologies Inc** HQ
920 Hillview Ct Ste 195
Milpitas CA 95035
P: 408-657-7621  F: 408-727-6940  PRC:126
www.avalent.com
Email: info@avalent.com
Estab: 1999

Mazin Khurshid, VP of Engineering
Mike Rhoades, Senior IC Design Engineer
DuenShun Wen, President
Kanoon Chalabi, Quality Control & Welding Inspector

Provider of fabless semiconductor devices. The company's services include platform development, processor development, and analog design services.

**Avantec Vascular Corp**   HQ
870 Hermosa Ave
Sunnyvale CA 94085
P: 408-329-5400   F: 408-329-5499   PRC:189
www.avantecvascular.com
Email: info@avantecvascular.com
Estab: 1999

Teresa Ruvalcaba, R&D Associate Engineer
Sandeep Kaur, Quality Engineer
Cisco Miranda, Process Engineer
Jack Hoshino, CEO
Vivian Chen, Senior Director of Finance

Manufacturer of therapeutic medical devices
such as cardio and peripheral vascular devices
for cardiovascular, neurovascular, and peripheral
disease.

**AvantPage**   HQ
132 E St Ste 370
Davis CA 95616
P: 530-750-2040   F: 530-750-2024   PRC:325
avantpage.com
Email: info@avantpage.com
Emp: 1-10   Estab: 1996

Luis Miguel, CEO
Joanna Oseman, Project Manager

Provider of foreign language translation services
for the medical, technical, healthcare, financial
industries.

**Avatier Corp**   HQ
4733 Chabot Dr Ste 201
Pleasanton CA 94588
P: 925-217-5170   F: 925-275-0853   PRC:323
www.avatier.com
Email: sales@avatier.com
Estab: 1995

Nelson Cicchitto, CEO
Corey Merchant, VP of Sales
Mary Marshall, Marketing Manager
Richard Darrell, VP of Strategic Alliances
Christopher Arnold, VP of Development

Provider of identity management consulting, software development, password management, and
user provisioning solutions.

**Avaya Inc**   HQ
4655 Great America Pkwy
Santa Clara CA 95054-1233
P: 908-953-6000   PRC:64
www.avaya.com
Estab: 2000
Sales: $1B to $3B

Kevin Kennedy, President
Jim Chirico, EVP of Business Operations

Provider of PBX solutions, IVR applications,
IP telephony solutions, voice messaging, and
consulting.

**AverLogic Technologies Inc**   RH
2635 N First St Ste 243
San Jose CA 95134
P: 408-526-0400   F: 408-526-0500   PRC:94
www.averlogic.com
Email: sales@averlogic.com
Estab: 1996

Bo Luo, Principal Engineer of ASIC Design &
Verification
Kyle Chang, Owner
Becker Sze, Director of IC Design

Designer and seller of integrated ICs. The company primarily caters to multimedia and video
applications.

**Avermedia Technologies Inc**   DH
47358 Fremont Blvd
Fremont CA 94538
P: 510-403-0006   F: 510-403-0022   PRC:110
www.avermedia.com
Email: avtsales.usa@avermedia.com
Estab: 1990

Michael Kuo, Chairman
Ted Dai, CTO
Jesse Lin, Financial

Designer and manufacturer of multimedia, internet TV, and electronic products. The company
provides USB, TV box, streaming server, and
accessories.

**Aviat Networks Inc**   HQ
860 N McCarthy Blvd Ste 200
Milpitas CA 95035
P: 408-941-7100   F: 408-941-7110   PRC:70
www.aviatnetworks.com
Email: aviatcareeducate@aviatnet.com
Estab: 2007
Sales: $100M to $300M

Stan Gallagher, Interim CEO
Ola Gustafsson, SVP
Raj Kumar, SVP of International
Bryan Tucker, SVP of North America
Shaun McFall, SVP of Corporate Development

Provider of microwave networking solutions. The
company's products are interactive 3D product
models, trunking microwaves, and dual hybrid/
packet microwaves.

**Aviation Design**   HQ
20166 Pine Mountain Dr
Groveland CA 95321
P: 209-962-0415   F: 209-962-0418   PRC:8
www.aviationdesign.com
Email: thallock@aviationdesign.com
Emp: 1-10   Estab: 1979

Tim Hallock, Owner

Designer of aircraft interiors for commercial and
private aircrafts. The company offers services to
the aviation industry.

**Avid Technology Inc**   BR
2903 Bunker Hill Ln
Santa Clara CA 95054
P: 800-955-0960   PRC:60
www.avid.com
Email: info@euphonix.com
Estab: 1987

Jeff Rosica, CEO
Dana Ruzicka, Chief Product Officer
Jason Duva, Chief Legal and Administrative
Officer
Tom Cordiner, Chief Revenue Officer
Diana Brunelle, Chief Human Resources Officer

Manufacturer of computer automated audio mixing
consoles. The company offers audio product registration and software activation services.

**Avinger Inc**   HQ
400 Chesapeake Dr
Redwood City CA 94063
P: 800-208-2988   PRC:187
www.avinger.com
Estab: 2007

Jay Sundaram, Principal Quality Engineer
Jeff Soinski, President
Himanshu Patel, CTO
Wendy Lam, Senior R&D Technician
Xuanmin He, Senior Research Scientist

Designer and developer of precision medical
device technology solutions. The company is
engaged in manufacturing services.

**Aviram Networks Inc**   HQ
1175 Saratoga Ave Ste 11
San Jose CA 95129
P: 408-624-1234   PRC:59
www.nevisnetworks.com
Estab: 2002

Raghu Iyer, CTO

Provider of wire-speed IPS for recognition & visualization, access control, and other needs. The
company offers consulting and training services.

**Avision Labs Inc**   DH
6815 Mowry Ave
Newark CA 94560
P: 510-739-2369   F: 510-739-6060   PRC:176
www.avision.com
Email: sales@avision-labs.com
Estab: 1991

Jun Huang, OEM Manager

Designer and manufacturer of network and document scanners. The company specializes in sales
and installation services.

**Aviso Inc**   HQ
805 Veterans Blvd Ste 300
Redwood City CA 94063
P: 650-567-5470   PRC:322
www.aviso.com
Email: sales@aviso.com
Estab: 2012

Roxanna Farshchi, Director of Solution Engineer-
ing & Customer Experience
K. V. Rao, Co-Founder
Michael Lock, CEO
Ravi Suryanarayan, VP

Creator of software to change how enterprises
make critical revenue decisions and automate
sales forecasting process with data science for
enterprises.

**Avistar Communications Corp**   HQ
1855 S Grant St 4th Fl
San Mateo CA 94402
P: 650-525-3300   F: 650-525-1360   PRC:68
www.avistar.com
Email: info@avistar.com
Estab: 1994

Bob Kirk, CEO
Elias MurrayMetzger, CFO
Vladimir Vysotsky, CTO
Steve Westmoreland, COO
Bryan Kennedy, SVP of Business Development

Provider of communication solutions. The company provides call controls, conference tools,
internet gateway tools, and accessories.

**Avocet Sales & Marketing Inc** HQ
737 Second St Ste 305
Oakland CA 94607
P: 510-891-0093 PRC:80
www.avocetsales.com
Email: avocet@avocetsales.com
Estab: 1989

Jeff Briggs, Manufacturers Sales Representative
Zachary Makowsky, Outside Sales Executive
Anthony Esposo, Accounting

Provider of custom engineered mechanical component parts and sub assemblies. The company offers contract manufacturing and automation services.

**Avontus Software Corp** DH
2150 Shattuck Ste 750
Berkeley CA 94704
P: 800-848-1860 PRC:323
www.avontus.com
Email: sales@avontus.com
Estab: 1998

Brian Webb, CEO
Susie Sargent, Manager of Operations
Ali Hajighafouri, Director of Sales
Latoya Brown, Sales Manager
Emma Newman, Sales Manager

Creator of software for formwork, scaffolding, and shoring industries, both custom development for enterprises and packaged software for public.

**Avp Technology LLC** HQ
4140 Business Center Dr
Fremont CA 94538-6354
P: 510-683-0157 F: 510-683-0176 PRC:159
avptechnologyllc.com
Estab: 2005

Zhicheng Wang, Skills For Engineers
Son Tran, Director of Operations
Paul Nguyen, Systems Test Technician

Provider of thin film equipment services. The company provides custom designing, remanufacturing, and field services.

**Axcient Inc** HQ
1161 San Antonio Rd
Mountain View CA 94043
P: 800-715-2339 PRC:326
axcient.com
Estab: 2006

David Bennett, CEO
Angus Robertson, Chief Revenue Officer
Ben Nowacky, SVP of Products
Gary Su, Software Developer

Provider of single integrated cloud platform that makes it simple to restore data, failover applications, and virtualize servers or an entire office.

**Axelsys LLC** HQ
177 Park Ave Ste 200
San Jose CA 95113
P: 408-600-0871 PRC:2
www.axelsys.com
Email: sales@axelsys.com
Estab: 2009

Jay Aggarwal, CEO

Provider of electronic design and manufacturing services. The company's offerings include LED and AC to DC industrial power supplies.

**Axsen LLC** HQ
5472 Black Ave
Pleasanton CA 94566
P: 866-462-9736 F: 866-380-2189 PRC:325
www.axsen.com
Email: sales@axsen.com
Estab: 2002

Shane Workman, Owner
Michael Vincent, Member

Developer of web designs and provider of online marketing solutions. The company serves the industrial sector.

**Axt Inc** HQ
4281 Technology Dr
Fremont CA 94538
P: 510-438-4700 F: 510-353-0668 PRC:86
www.axt.com
Email: sales@axt.com
Estab: 1986
Sales: $100M to $300M

Morris Young, CEO
Gary Fischer, VP
Shun Sit, Director of Information Technology
Liming Zhu, VP of Sales
Michelle Chen, Inside Sales Manager

Designer, developer, manufacturer, and distributor of high performance compound semiconductor substrates.

**Ayala Research Corporation** HQ
337 Stealth Ct
Livermore CA 94551
P: 800-294-9050 F: 925-447-3558 PRC:189
www.ayalaresearch.com
Email: sales@ayalaresearch.com

John Bower, Owner

Provider of product development and manufacturing services. The company offers solutions for medical, scientific and industrial products.

**Ayantra Inc** HQ
47873 Fremont Blvd
Fremont CA 94538
P: 510-623-7526 F: 510-623-7839 PRC:17
www.ayantra.com
Email: info@ayantra.com

Ravi Koppula, VP of Engineering
Ashok Teckchandani, Chairman
Andy Rogers, VP of Sales
Ram Charan, VP of Operations

Provider of wireless communication technology services. The company is engaged in monitoring and asset tracking.

**Ayasdi Inc** HQ
4400 Bohannon Dr Ste 200
Menlo Park CA 94025
P: 650-704-3395 PRC:322
www.ayasdi.com
Estab: 2008

Ajith Warrier, SVP of Engineering
Ishan Manaktala, CEO
Peter Downs, CFO
Jennifer Kloke, CTO
Gurjeet Singh, Chief AI Officer

Provider of software applications that discovers critical intelligence in company data for right operational decisions quickly.

**Ayla Networks Inc** HQ
4250 Burton Dr
Santa Clara CA 95054
P: 408-830-9844 F: 408-716-2621 PRC:40
www.aylanetworks.com
Estab: 2010

Jonathan Cobb, CEO
Craig Payne, Security Privacy Officer

Provider of Ayla's IoT cloud platform that brings connected products to market quickly and securely for manufacturers and service providers.

**Azbil North America Inc** BR
3323 Kifer Rd
Santa Clara CA 95051
P: 408-245-3121 F: 408-245-3151 PRC:87
azbil.com
Estab: 1996

Gary Johnson, President
Fumitaka Nozawa, VP of Sales & Marketing

Designer, manufacturer, and supplier of medical devices. The company offers automation products, control products, and industrial automation systems.

**Azimuth Industrial Company Inc** HQ
30593 Union City Blvd Ste 110
Union City CA 94587
P: 510-441-6000 F: 510-441-6008 PRC:208
www.azimuthsemi.com
Email: questions@azimuthsemi.com
Estab: 1972

David Lee, General Manager

Provider of integrated circuit assembly and packaging services. The company specializes in prototyping and production.

**Aziyo Biologics Inc** BR
880 Harbour Way S Ste 100
Richmond CA 94804
P: 855-416-0596 F: 510-307-9896 PRC:34
aziyo.com
Email: orders@aziyo.com
Estab: 2015

Ron Lloyd, President
Kevin Rakin, Executive Chairman
Tom Englese, CCO
Angelica Khan, Human Resource Manager
Jeff Hamet, VP of Finance

Manufacturer of allograft tissue products for use in orthopedic, spinal, sports medicine, and dermal applications.

**Azul Systems Inc** HQ
1173 Borregas Ave
Sunnyvale CA 94089-1306
P: 650-230-6500 F: 650-230-6600 PRC:317
www.azul.com
Email: info@azulsystems.com
Estab: 2002

Anya Barski, VP of Engineering
Elias Atmeh, VP of Systems Engineering
Philip Reames, Principal Software Engineer
Gil Tene, Co-Founder
Scott Sellers, Co-Founder

Provider of Java applications for real time businesses. The company's Zing is a JVM enterprise application.

**B & J Specialties Inc**    HQ
321 Ingalls St
Santa Cruz CA 95060
P: 831-454-0713   F: 831-454-0743    PRC:212
bandjspecialties.com
Email: bjamrus@bandjspecialties.com
Emp: 1-10   Estab: 1989

Brian Jamrus, Owner

Manufacturer of nanometrics film thickness and CD measurement equipment. The company offers nanometrics equipment, Nanoline, and Nanospec.

**B&H Engineering**    HQ
1725 Old County Rd
San Carlos CA 94070
P: 650-594-2861   F: 650-594-0278    PRC:80
www.bhengineering.com
Email: info@bhengineering.com
Estab: 1972

Bakir Begovic, CEO
Hamida Begovic, CFO
Martin Villegas, Quality Manager
Jurica Jurkic, Purchasing Manager
Robert Gizatullin, Accounting Manager

Supplier of assemblies, process kits, and individual parts. The company caters to the semiconductor equipment industry.

**B&Z Manufacturing Company Inc**    HQ
1478 Seareel Ln
San Jose CA 95131
P: 408-943-1117   F: 408-943-1067    PRC:80
bzmfg.com
Email: info@bzmfg.com
Estab: 1960

Dennis Kimball, Owner

Provider of multi-axis milling and turning services. The company offers ultra precision components for electronic, aerospace, and computer fields.

**B-K Lighting Inc**    HQ
40429 Brickyard Dr
Madera CA 93636
P: 559-438-5800   F: 559-438-5900    PRC:243
www.bklighting.com
Email: info@bklighting.com
Emp: 1-10   Estab: 1984

Douglas Hagen, CEO
Nathan Sloan, Manufacturing Manager
Justin Perez, Manufacturing Manager
Ryan Berrios, National Sales Manager
Becky Carlson, Marketing Manager

Provider of architectural outdoor landscape lighting products. The company serves residential and commercial properties.

**B-Metal Fabrication**    HQ
318 S Maple Ave
S San Francisco CA 94080
P: 650-615-7705    PRC:80
www.bmetalfabrication.com
Email: bmfab@bmetalfabrication.com

Robert Steinebel, CEO

Provider of metal fabrication services. The company offers services for the commercial, residential, retail, and bio pharmaceutical industries.

**Babbitt Bearing Company Inc**    HQ
1170 N Fifth St
San Jose CA 95112
P: 408-298-1101   F: 408-998-4134    PRC:80
www.bbcmachine.com
Email: info@bbcmachine.com
Estab: 1945

Rick Valencia, Manager of Flame Spray Department

Provider of repair and manufacturing services. The company deals in hard chrome plating, non-destructive testing, and machinery repair.

**Backproject Corp**    HQ
170 N Wolfe Rd
Sunnyvale CA 94086
P: 408-730-1111   F: 408-404-8100    PRC:196
www.backproject.com
Email: info@backproject.com
Estab: 2001

Steve Hoffman, CEO

Manufacturer of physical therapy equipment. The company specializes in vertical physical therapy equipment for musculoskeletal pain relief.

**Backshop Inc**    HQ
85 Liberty Ship Way Ste 201
Sausalito CA 94965
P: 415-332-1110   F: 415-289-3802    PRC:323
www.backshop.com
Email: info@backshop.com
Estab: 2000

Jim Flaherty, President
Michelle Link, CTO
Jack Gao, VP
Katherine Geis, VP of Client Services
Jeff Holder, VP of Client Services

Provider of commercial real estate software for full deal-stack modeling, loan origination, asset management, and data library for customers.

**Bactrack**    HQ
300 Broadway Ste 26
San Francisco CA 94133
P: 415-693-9756   F: 415-358-8030    PRC:124
www.bactrack.com
Email: info@bactrack.com
Estab: 2001

Keith Nothacker, CEO
Tyson Henry, Manager of Foreign
Charly Mejia, Accounting Manager

Provider of breathalyzers. The company provides products for a wide range of personal, professional and smartphone use.

**Badger Maps Inc**    HQ
539 Broadway
San Francisco CA 94111
P: 415-592-5909    PRC:322
www.badgermapping.com

Gady Pitaru, CTO
Steve Benson, CEO
Jayne Head, Marketing Analyst
Jane Yu, Senior Marketing Associate
Sophie Lhoutellier, Operations Manager

Provider of easy to use interface to manage our daily call routes, track visits, and update records.

**Balance Hydrologics Inc**    HQ
800 Bancroft Way Ste 101
Berkeley CA 94710-2227
P: 510-704-1000   F: 510-704-1001    PRC:139
www.balancehydro.com
Email: office@balancehydro.com
Estab: 1988

Edward Ballman, Principal
Anna Nazarov, Hydrologist
Peter Kulchawik, Engineer
Denis Ruttenberg, Engineer
Colleen Haraden, Marketing Manager

Provider of hydrologic services. The company offers geomorphology, restoration design, watershed management, and wetland inspection services.

**Balance Therapeutics Inc**    HQ
1250 Bayhill Dr Ste 125
San Bruno CA 94066
P: 650-741-9100    PRC:268
www.balance-therapeutics.com
Email: info@balance-therapeutics.com

Lyndon Lien, Co-Founder

Developer of pharmaceuticals. The company develops therapeutics to address neurological disabilities resulting from excess inhibition of the brain.

**Baldor Electric Co**    BR
21056 Forbes St
Hayward CA 94545
P: 510-785-9900   F: 510-785-9910    PRC:245
www.baldor.com

Ronald Tucker, CEO
Jason Green, VP
Jeff Hines, VP
Scott Fullbright, VP
Randy Colip, EVP

Manufacturer of electric drives. The company also offers bearings, electric motors, drives, gear assemblies, and transmission systems.

**Baltimore Air Coil**    BR
15341 Rd 28 1/2
Madera CA 93638
P: 559-673-9231   F: 559-673-5095    PRC:154
www.baltimoreaircoil.com
Email: info@baltimoreaircoil.com
Emp: 11-50   Estab: 1938

Mark Giltmier, Plant Engineering Manager

Provider of assembled evaporative heat rejection and thermal storage equipment. The company also offers circuit cooling towers.

**Bandai Namco Entertainment America Inc**    HQ
2051 Mission College Blvd
Santa Clara CA 95054
P: 408-235-2000    PRC:317
www.bandainamcoent.com
Email: support@bandainamcoent.com

Micah Geary, Associate Tools Software Engineer
Sunao Uehara, Platform Engineer
Hide Irie, EVP
Lisa Le, Human Resource Representative
Bob Johnson, Senior Manager of Channel Marketing

Provider of gaming solutions. The company is engaged in technical support and it serves the entertainment industry.

**Bandwidth10 Inc**     BR
2150 Kittredge St Ste 250
Berkeley CA 94704
P: 203-561-0769     PRC:213
www.bandwidth10.com
Email: rlucas@bandwidth10.com
Estab: 2011

Phil Worland, Founder

Developer of tunable, singlemode, 1550 nm
long-wavelength VCSELs, and transceivers for
datacom applications.

**Banks Integration Group**     HQ
600 E Main St Ste 100
Vacaville CA 95688
P: 707-451-1100     PRC:159
banksintegration.com
Estab: 1994

Tom Crowl, Principal Engineer
Cassy Gardner, Group Engineering Manager
Bessida Taonda, Automation Engineer
Matthew Steben, Automation Engineer
Quyen Dinh, Automation Engineer

Developer and provider of control systems and
plant automation software. The company serves
biotech, food, brewery, oil & gas, and other
sectors.

**Banpil Photonics Inc**     HQ
4800 Patrick Henry Dr Ste 120
Santa Clara CA 95054
P: 408-282-3628     PRC:87
www.banpil.com
Email: info@banpil.com

Rabi Sengupta, Research & Development Manager

Developer and manufacturer of image sensors for
automotive & medical imaging systems, security &
surveillance, and machine vision applications.

**Barco Inc**     RH
3078 Prospect Park Dr
Rancho Cordova CA 95670
P: 888-414-7226     PRC:323
www.barco.com
Emp: 11-50 Estab: 1979
Sales: $30M to $100M

April Luong, Software Engineer
Kent Vogel, Quality Manager
Neil Wittering, Director of Strategic Marketing
Andreas Yerocostas, R&D Director of Projection &
Image Processing
Scott Nipper, Training Manager

Manufacturer of digital scan conversion equipment
and radars. The company serves healthcare,
defense, media, simulation, and other needs.

**Barracuda Networks Inc**     HQ
3175 Winchester Blvd
Campbell CA 95008
P: 408-342-5400   F: 408-342-1061   PRC:322
www.barracuda.com
Email: sales@barracuda.com
Estab: 2002

Zachary Levow, EVP
B.J. Jenkins, President
Diane Honda, CAO
Dustin Driggs, CFO
Hatem Naguib, SVP

Developer of solutions for IT problems primarily focusing on security and storage. The company also
focuses on application delivery and productivity.

**Barrington Consultants Inc**     HQ
2239 Valdes Ct
Santa Rosa CA 95403
P: 707-527-8254   F: 707-542-9730   PRC:289
www.barringtoninc.com
Email: ghb@barringtoninc.com
Estab: 1995

Gary Barrington, President

Manufacturer of transformer monitors and temperature monitors for testing high voltage circuit
breakers and offers circuit breaker simulators.

**Baseline Environmental Consulting**     HQ
5900 Hollis St Ste D
Emeryville CA 94608
P: 510-420-8686   F: 510-420-1707   PRC:139
www.baseline-env.com
Estab: 1985

Patrick Sutton, Environmental Engineer III
Mengzhu Luo, Environmental Engineer
Bruce Abelli-Amen, Principal
Cheri Page, Senior Geologist
Monika Krupa, Environmental Scientist

Provider of environmental consulting services
including remediation, investigations, data management, and surveys.

**BASF Venture Capital America Inc**     RH
46820 Fremont Blvd
Fremont CA 94538
P: 510-445-6140     PRC:42
www.basf.com

Teressa Szelest, President
Wayne Smith, CEO

Manufacturer of basic chemicals and intermediates such as solvents, plasticizers, and mono-
mers. The company serves the agriculture market.

**Basics Environmental Inc**     HQ
655 12th St Ste 126
Oakland CA 94607
P: 510-834-9099   F: 510-834-9098   PRC:142
www.basicsenvironmentalinc.com
Email: basicsenvironmental@gmail.com
Estab: 1994

Donavan Tom, Principal

Provider of environmental engineering consulting
services. The company focuses on environmental
site assessments for real estate transactions.

**Bat Gundrilling Services Inc**     HQ
2730 Scott Blvd
Santa Clara CA 95050
P: 408-727-1220   F: 408-727-1217   PRC:157
www.batgundrilling.com
Email: batgundrilling@gmail.com
Estab: 1993

Max Gomez, President

Provider of manufacturing services. The company
specializes in engineering, tap extraction, gun drill
tool sharpening, and deburring services.

**Batchtest Corporation**     HQ
2118 Walsh Ave Ste 150
Santa Clara CA 95050
P: 408-454-8378     PRC:207
www.batchtest.com
Estab: 2005

Dinesh Patel, President
Silvia Castellini, Business Development Manager

Provider of embedded solutions. The company
specializes in the design and manufacturing of
industrial PC products.

**Bauer Engraving Company Inc**     HQ
11290 Sunrise Gold Cir Ste G
Rancho Cordova CA 95742
P: 916-631-9800     PRC:157
www.bauerengraving.com
Email: artwork@bauerengraving.com
Emp: 1-10 Estab: 1900

Bauer Engraving, Owner
William Bratt, President

Provider of engraving services. The company
offers foil stamping dies, embossing dies, wood
branding dies, and letterpress printing plates.

**Baumbach & Piazza Inc**     HQ
323 W Elm St
Lodi CA 95240
P: 209-368-6618   F: 209-368-6610   PRC:304
www.bpengineers.net
Email: contact@bpengineers.net
Emp: 1-10 Estab: 1961

Kelly Sao, Assistant Engineer
Jonathan Martin, Senior Development Engineer
Josh Elson, Principal

Provider of design, engineering, and boundary
and topography surveying, and construction
staking services.

**Bay Advanced Technologies**     HQ
8100 Central Ave
Newark CA 94560
P: 510-857-0900   F: 510-857-1400   PRC:189
www.bayat.com
Email: sps-docs@bayat.com
Estab: 1961

Terri Au, System Engineer
John Herne, Corporate Quality Manager
Bob Rogers, Account Manager

Provider of solutions for automation and control
applications. The company offers precision automation, fluid controls and fabricated materials.

**Bay Area Circuits Inc**     HQ
44358 Old Warm Springs Blvd
Fremont CA 94538
P: 510-933-9000   F: 510-933-9001   PRC:76
bayareacircuits.com
Email: support@bacircuits.com
Estab: 1975

Stephen Garcia, President
Brian Paper, COO
Ron Charfauros, Sales Account Manager
Ron Franco, Business Development Manager

Provider of engineering services that include fabrication, layout, and design services to the original
equipment manufacturers.

**Bay Associates Wire Technologies**  HQ
46840 Lakeview Blvd
Fremont CA 94538
P: 510-933-3800  F: 510-933-3870  PRC:62
www.baycable.com
Email: bayinfo@baycable.com
Estab: 1962

Strato Han, Manufacturing Engineer
Mitzy Butte, Purchasing Manager
Barbara Scott, Inside Sales

Provider of cable and cable assembly solutions.
The company serves the medical, navigation,
audio, and automotive markets.

**Bay Dynamics Inc**  HQ
595 Market St Ste 920
San Francisco CA 94105
P: 415-912-3130  PRC:99
www.baydynamics.com
Email: info@baydynamics.com
Emp: 11-50 Estab: 2001

Humphrey Christian, VP of Engineering
Norman Stout, Senior Software Engineer
Rob Reyes, Senior Engineer
Feris Rifai, Founder
Ryan Stolte, Founder

Provider of IT analytics solutions. The company
offers data loss prevention, system management,
and security tool implementation services.

**Bay Materials LLC**  HQ
48450 Lakeview Blvd
Fremont CA 94538
P: 650-566-0800  PRC:306
baymaterials.com
Email: info@baymaterials.com
Estab: 1999

Ray Stewart, President
Chris Vogdes, Laboratory Manager
Klaus Dahl, Principal Scientist
John Lahlouh, Senior Polymer Scientist

Manufacturer of polymer products. The company
offers services for spectroscopy, osmometry,
viscosity, and surface measurement.

**Bay Microsystems Inc**  HQ
2055 Gateway Pl Ste 650
San Jose CA 95110
P: 408-841-4700  F: 408-437-0410  PRC:326
www.baymicrosystems.com
Email: info@baymicrosystems.com

Robert Smedley, SVP of System Engineering
Harry Carr, CEO
Michael McDonald, CFO
Russel Davis, COO
Stephen Wallo, CTO

Provider of secure networking solution for commercial market such as life sciences/healthcare,
oil and gas, digital media, and financial services.

**Bay Standard Manufacturing Inc**  HQ
24485 Marsh Creek Rd
Brentwood CA 94513
P: 800-228-8640  F: 925-634-1925  PRC:80
www.baystandard.com
Email: sales@baystandard.com
Estab: 1959

Michael Davis, Sales Manager
Wally Gross, Regional Sales Manager
E. Chow, Special Projects Manager

Manufacturer of machinery components. The
company offers thread, foundation bolts, u-bolts,
and specialty fasteners.

**BayFab Metals Inc**  HQ
870 Doolittle Dr
San Leandro CA 94577
P: 510-568-8950  PRC:80
bayfabmetals.com
Estab: 1968

Jim Bava, Sales Manager
Marcella Witt, Project Manager
Paul Tavares, Project Manager

Manufacturer of custom and production parts.
The company's products include Trumpf TruLaser,
Trumpf Laser Cutter, and AMADA.

**BayNODE LLC**  HQ
4 Embarcadero Ctr Ste 3350
San Francisco CA 94111
P: 415-274-3100  F: 415-274-3119  PRC:326
baynode.com
Estab: 1998

Sener Akyol, Senior Systems Architect

Provider of data network solutions, outsourcing,
and network security services. The company
caters to the IT sector.

**Bayometric**  HQ
1743 Park Ave
San Jose CA 95126
P: 408-940-3955  PRC:320
www.bayometric.com
Email: sales@bayometric.com
Estab: 2007

Danny Thakkar, Senior Product Manager

Supplier of fingerprint scanners, single sign-on
solution and access control systems. The company serves the business and industrial markets.

**BaySand Incorporated**  BR
6203 San Ignacio Ave Ste 110
San Jose CA 95119
P: 408-669-4992  PRC:86
www.baysand.com
Email: info@baysand.com
Estab: 2009

Salah Werfelli, President
Jonathan Park, EVP
Avi Zakai, SVP of Sales and Business Develop-
ment Worldwide
George Alexy, Marketing Research Analyst
Advisor
Sam Appleton, Board Member

Developer of metal only configurable ASIC. The
company uses disruptive metal configurable standard cell technology for its products.

**Bayspec Inc**  HQ
1101 McKay Dr
San Jose CA 95131
P: 408-512-5928  F: 408-512-5929  PRC:176
www.bayspec.com
Email: sales@bayspec.com

Jeff MacCubbin, Sales Manager

Manufacturer of mass spectrometers, microscopes, hyperspectral imagers, and OEM spectral
engines for biomedical, pharmaceuticals, and food
industries.

**Baystar Electrument Inc**  HQ
1903 Concourse Dr
San Jose CA 95131
P: 408-272-3669  PRC:87
baystar-inc.com
Email: info@baystar-inc.com

Meiyin Wu, Sales Administrator
John Bai, Manager

Manufacturer of pressure sensors, pressure transducers and transmitters. The company deals with
digital signal processing services.

**Bazell Technologies Corp**  HQ
5066 Commercial Cir
Concord CA 94520
P: 925-603-0900  F: 925-603-0901  PRC:156
www.bazell.com
Email: info@bazell.com
Estab: 1983

Helen Bazell, Office Administrator

Manufacturer of solid wall basket centrifuges.
The company also focuses on centrifugal fluid
processing systems.

**BBI Engineering Inc**  HQ
241 Quint St
San Francisco CA 94124
P: 415-695-9555  F: 415-695-9276  PRC:60
bbinet.com
Email: sales@bbinet.com
Estab: 1984

Steven Ramsey, Engineer
Sarah Roos, CFO
Jim Sallee, Project Manager
Kristian Collier, Technician
Tony Paredes, Administrator

Designer and installer of audiovisual, multimedia,
teleconferencing and data systems for museums,
aquariums, zoos, schools, and universities.

**Bcg Management Resources Inc**  HQ
1320 Willow Pass Rd Ste 600
Concord CA 94520
P: 800-456-8474  F: 510-747-1977  PRC:326
www.beckconsulting.com
Estab: 1986

Dirk Manders, President
Cheryl Irons, Account Executive

Provider of enterprise software solutions and professional services such as dynamics NAV and bc
solutions for food and manufacturing industry.

**Bcl Technologies** HQ
3031 Tisch Way Ste 1000
San Jose CA 95128
P: 408-557-2080  F: 408-249-4046  PRC:322
www.bcltechnologies.com
Email: info1@bcltechnologies.com
Estab: 1993

Tamas Demjen, Senior Software Engineer
Manan Vyas, Software Engineer
Hassan Alam, Founder
Aman Kumar, Senior Computational Linguist

Developer of document creation, conversion, and extraction solutions. The company offers BCL easyPDF Cloud, a cloud-based PDF conversion platform.

**Bct Consulting Inc** HQ
7910 N. Ingram Ave Suite #101
Fresno CA 93711
P: 559-579-1400  F: 559-472-7300  PRC:325
www.bctconsulting.com
Email: info@bctconsulting.com
Emp: 11-50 Estab: 1996

Mike Rosa, Business Development Engineer
Matthew Wagner, System Administrator
Matt Sotomayor, Senior Systems Administrator
Kevin Hawkins, PBX Server Administrator
Grant Robison, Senior Network Administrator

Provider of computer network support, web design, application programming, and other technology services.

**BD Biosciences** BR
2350 Qume Dr
San Jose CA 95131
P: 877-232-8995  PRC:186
www.bdbiosciences.com
Email: bdbcustomerservice@bd.com

Vishal Lokhande, Staff Mechanical Engineer
Robert Balderas, VP of Research & Development

Manufacturer of medical devices. The company provides a broad range of medical supplies, devices, laboratory equipment and diagnostic products.

**Beachhead Solutions Inc** HQ
1150 S Bascom Ave Ste 7
San Jose CA 95128
P: 408-496-6936  F: 408-246-3026  PRC:327
www.beachheadsolutions.com
Email: info@beachheadsolutions.com
Estab: 2003

Jim Obot, CEO
Tim Lavelle, VP of Sales
Cam Roberson, Director of Marketing
Rob Weber, Director of Product and Support

Provider of web-based console to enforce encryption, manage security, and give providers the ability to change policy on iPhones and android devices.

**Beahm Designs Inc** HQ
1502 Gladding Ct
Milpitas CA 95035
P: 408-395-5360  F: 408-871-8295  PRC:159
www.beahmdesigns.com
Email: sales@beahmdesigns.com
Estab: 1990

Anita Beahm, CEO

Provider of tailor made manufacturing equipment. The company focuses on tube processing machines for catheter manufacturing.

M-44

**Bear River Associates Inc** HQ
436 14th St Ste 300
Oakland CA 94612
P: 510-834-5300  F: 510-834-5396  PRC:325
www.bearriver.com
Email: info@bearriver.com
Estab: 1985

Val Perry, QA Lead Engineer
Anthony Meadow, President
Randall Matamoros, Co-CEO
Revital Gilad, Co-CEO

Provider of enterprise mobile computing products and services. The company serves business services, government, high-tech, and life science sectors.

**Beganto Inc** HQ
4800 Patrick Henry Dr
Santa Clara CA 95054
P: 510-280-0554  F: 408-492-1772  PRC:323
www.beganto.com
Email: sales@beganto.com
Estab: 2002

Yamamoto Masami, CEO
Ryan Saunders, Financial Analyst

Provider of web-based applications and support services. The company specializes in application, component, design, and sales engineering.

**Bell Biosystems Inc** HQ
626 Bancroft Way Ste A
Berkeley CA 94710
P: 877-420-3621  PRC:22
www.bellbiosystems.com

Daniel Bell, Agent

Provider of biotechnology services. The company develops proteins targeted to kill specific bacteria but cause minimal collateral damage.

**Bema Electronics Inc** HQ
4545 Cushing Pkwy
Fremont CA 94538
P: 510-490-7770  F: 510-490-6598  PRC:211
www.bemaelectronics.com
Email: info@bemaelectronics.com
Estab: 2000

Helen Kwong, President
Suju Kwong, VP of Finance
Wayne Yu, General Manager
Bud Kwan, Procurement Manager
Luis Medina, Program Manager

Provider of manufacturing, supply chain management, material procurement, prototyping, and surface mount technology of electronic appliances.

**Benchling Inc** HQ
555 Montgomery St Ste 1100
San Francisco CA 94111
P: 415-980-9932  F: 732-858-1337  PRC:34
benchling.com
Email: contact@benchling.com
Estab: 2012

Sajith Wickramasekara, Founder

Developer of integrated software solution for experiment design, note-taking, and molecular biology for industry and academia.

**Benchmark Electronics Inc** BR
4041 Pike Ln
Concord CA 94520
P: 925-363-4917  PRC:211
www.bench.com
Estab: 1986

Jan Janick, VP of Global Engineering
Jeff Benck, President
Kenneth Lamneck, President
Gayla Delly, President
Robert Gifford, COO

Provider of electronic manufacturing services to OEMs of telecommunication, computers, and related products.

**Benchmark Home Elevator** HQ
145 Berna Ave
Napa CA 94559
P: 707-255-4687  F: 707-254-7859  PRC:180
benchmarklift.com
Estab: 1997

Brian Hofacre, General Partner
Scott Britton, General Partner

Provider of elevator products. The company's products include curved rail stairlifts, straight rail stairlifts, home elevators, and wheelchair lifts.

**Benchmark Thermal Corp** HQ
13185 Nevada City Ave
Grass Valley CA 95945
P: 530-477-5011  F: 530-477-6507  PRC:153
www.benchmarkthermal.com
Email: thermal@benchmarkthermal.com
Emp: 1-10  Estab: 1984

Jim Gaines, Project Coordinator

Manufacturer of custom semiconductor products, drum and cartridge heaters, controls, and related accessories.

**Benevity Inc** BR
32 W 25th Ave Ste 203
San Mateo CA 94403-2266
P: 855-237-7875  PRC:319
www.benevity.com
Email: support@benevity.com

Bryan de Lottinville, Founder
Ryan Courtnage, Co-Founder
Jason Becker, Co-Founder
Kelly Schmitt, CFO
Vivian Farris, VP of Human Resources

Specializes in corporate social responsibility employee engagement software.

**Benicia Fabrication & Machine Inc** HQ
101 E Channel Rd
Benicia CA 94510
P: 707-745-8111  F: 707-745-8102  PRC:80
beniciafab.com
Email: info@beniciafab.com
Estab: 1983

Tom Cepernich, President
Randy Reffner, Manufacturing Manager
James Taylor, Fabrication Shop Manager
Janet Saladino, Controller

Manufacturer of industrial equipment and provider of repair and maintenance services. The company develops pressure vessels and heat exchangers.

**Bentek Corp** HQ
1991 Senter Rd
San Jose CA 95131
P: 408-954-9600   F: 408-954-9688   PRC:135
www.bentek.com
Email: info@bentek.com
Estab: 1985

Hrishikesh Marathe, Mechanical Engineer
Mitchell Schoch, President
Michal Hoppner, CFO
Wayne Erickson, VP of Sales Manufacturing
Services
John Buckley, Executive Sales

Provider of manufacturing and engineering
services. The company's offerings include power
distribution system design and mechanical manufacturing.

**Benvenue Medical Inc** HQ
4590 Patrick Henry Dr
Santa Clara CA 95054
P: 408-454-9300   F: 408-982-9023   PRC:195
www.benvenuemedical.com
Email: info@benvenuemedical.com
Estab: 2004

Jeff Stibling, Manufacturing Application Engineer
Laurent Schaller, Founder
Robert Weigle, CEO
Doug Lorang, Director of Program
Ophie Myint, Customer Service Manager

Developer of expandable implant systems for the
spine. The company focuses on cylindrical implant
design.

**Berkeley Analytical Associates LLC** HQ
815 Harbour Way S Ste 6
Richmond CA 94804-3614
P: 510-236-2325   F: 510-236-2335   PRC:47
www.berkeleyanalytical.com
Email: info@berkeleyanalytical.com
Estab: 1989

Raja Tannous, Agent

Provider of specialized chemical & flame retardant
analysis and formaldehyde testing services. The
company serves the flooring and textile industries.

**Berkeley Design Technology Inc** HQ
1646 N California Blvd Ste 220
Walnut Creek CA 94596
P: 925-954-1411   PRC:322
www.bdti.com
Email: info@bdti.com
Estab: 1991

Jeremy Giddings, Director of Business Development

Provider of analysis, advice, and engineering
solutions for embedded processing technology
and applications.

**Berkeley Forge & Tool Inc** HQ
1331 E shore Hwy
Berkeley CA 94710
P: 510-526-5034   F: 510-525-9014   PRC:158
www.berkforge.com
Email: sales@berkforge.com

Paul Bierwith, Owner

The company is engaged in the design, engineering, manufacture, and marketing of mining and
commercial forging products.

**Berkeley Nucleonics Corp** HQ
2955 Kerner Blvd
San Rafael CA 94901
P: 415-453-9955   F: 415-453-9956   PRC:293
www.berkeleynucleonics.com
Email: info@berkeleynucleonics.com
Estab: 1963

Mel Brown, CEO
Allan Gonzalez, Director of Sales and Marketing
John Monks, Manager
Mark Slattery, Applications Manager
Bernadette Jamieson, Customer Service Manager

Designer and manufacturer of precision test,
measurement, and nuclear instrumentation. The
company mainly offers generators and analyzers.

**Bess Mti Inc** BR
991 George St
Santa Clara CA 95054
P: 408-988-0101   F: 408-988-0103   PRC:304
besstestlab.com
Email: info@besstestlab.com
Emp: 11-50 Estab: 1964

Jose Bohorquez, President

Provider of subsurface utility engineering services.
The company engages in utility locating and structural concrete scanning services.

**BESST Inc** HQ
50 Tiburon St Ste 7
San Rafael CA 94901-4762
P: 415-453-2501   PRC:160
www.besstinc.com
Estab: 1999

Noah Heller, President
Ansel McClelland, Project Geologist

Provider of groundwater sampling technology
solutions. The company also offers customized
packages for specialized applications.

**Bestek Manufacturing Inc** HQ
2150 Del Franco St
San Jose CA 95131
P: 408-321-8834   F: 408-321-8670   PRC:306
www.bestekmfg.com

Tyler Dang, Director of Materials

Provider of supply chain services. The company
engages focuses on systems manufacturing, materials management, and prototype support areas.

**Bestronics** HQ
2090 Fortune Dr
San Jose CA 95131
P: 408-385-7777   F: 408-432-3455   PRC:207
www.bestronicsinc.com
Email: sales@bestronicsinc.com

Nat Mani, President
Ron Menigoz, CTO
Chuck Hong, Director of Manufacturing
Steve Yetso, VP of Operations and Supply Chain
Myung Yun, Director of Commercial Operations

Provider of electronics manufacturing services.
The company deals with product development,
system integration, and prototyping services.

**Beta Breakers Software Quality** HQ
7665 Redwood Blvd Ste 100
Novato CA 94945
P: 415-878-2990   F: 415-878-2989   PRC:306
betabreakers.com
Email: info@betabreakers.com

Evan Domingo, President
Robert Chrum, VP
Greg Masada, IT Manager
Jeremy Spear, Project Manager
Damon Perdue, Project Manager

Provider of software and application testing services. The company offers functionality, compatibility, website, and mobile device testing services.

**Beta Circuits Inc** HQ
1200 Norman Ave
Santa Clara CA 95054
P: 408-980-9938   F: 408-980-9920   PRC:211
www.betacircuits.com
Email: betacircuits@betacircuits.com
Estab: 1989

John Huang, Sales Manager

Manufacturer of printed circuit board. The
company offers all solutions from designing to
prototyping.

**Betatron Inc** HQ
1722 Ringwood Dr
San Jose CA 95131
P: 408-453-1880   PRC:209
www.betatron.net/home.html
Estab: 1999

Mike Young, CEO

Designer and manufacturer of PC board assemblies for the medical, telecommunication, industrial, commercial, and semiconductor markets.

**Better World Group Inc** BR
980 Ninth St 16th Fl
Sacramento CA 95814
P: 916-498-9411   PRC:142
www.betterworldgroup.com
Emp: 11-50 Estab: 1999

Wendy James, Founder
Sharon Wrathall, CFO

Provider of environmental strategy consulting
services. The company offers political strategy, co-
alition management, media, and communications.

**BetterDoctor Inc** HQ
945 Bryant St Ste 350
San Francisco CA 94103
P: 844-668-2543   PRC:322
betterdoctor.com
Email: support@betterdoctor.com
Estab: 2011

Ari Tulla, CEO
Tapio Tolvanen, CTO
Paul Whitaker, VP of Business Development
Joel Enquist, Director of Operations
Andrew Kobylinski, Head of Business Develop-
ment

Provider of mobile apps for iPhone to find primary
care, OBGYN, pediatricians, dentist, eye, and all
specialties doctors.

**Betts Spring Inc** HQ
2843 S Maple Ave
Fresno CA 93725
P: 559-498-3304 F: 559-445-9129 PRC:159
www.bettsspring.com
Emp: 1-10 Estab: 1868

Bill Betts, President
Mike Betts, CEO
Jonathan Lee, CTO
Dan Flores, CFO
John Devany, General Manager

Manufacturer of custom precision spring products.
The company offers coil and leaf springs and
serves the mining, military, and trucking industries.

**Beyond Lucid Technologies Inc** HQ
1220 Diamond Way Ste 240
Concord CA 94520
P: 650-648-3727 PRC:194
www.beyondlucid.com
Estab: 2009

David Saylor, Meng Chief Engineer
Christian Witt, CTO
Jonathon Feit, Co-Founder
Bruce Graham, Director of Operations
Michael Onkst, Director of Training & Process
Improvement

Developer of cloud-based software platform.
The company offers services to the emergency
medical, disaster management, and first response
industries.

**Beyond Oil Solar** HQ
49 Morning Sun Ave
Mill Valley CA 94941
P: 415-388-0838 PRC:129
beyondoilsolar.com
Email: sales@beyondoilsolar.com
Estab: 1998

Daniel Rivest, Owner
Alex Leason, Manager

Provider of energy equipment products. The
company offers solar panels, inverters, charge
controllers, mounting systems, and water pumps.

**Bhatia Associates Inc** HQ
595 Market St Ste 2170
San Francisco CA 94105
P: 415-646-0050 F: 415-646-0063 PRC:304
www.bhatiaassociates.com
Email: sat@bhatiaassociates.com
Estab: 1984

Sat Bhatia, President

Provider of design and electrical engineering consulting services to the institutional, commercial,
residential, and light industrial buildings.

**Bibbero Systems Inc** HQ
1300 N McDowell Blvd
Petaluma CA 94954
P: 800-242-2376 PRC:189
www.bibbero.com
Email: info@bibbero.com
Estab: 1953

Michael Buckley, President
Buz Buckley, VP
Sharon Hamernick, Manager of Accounts Receiv-
able

Manufacturer of filing and office supplies including
custom chart and index tab dividers, and color
coded and pressboard classification file folders.

**Big Joe Handling Systems** HQ
25932 Eden Landing Rd
Hayward CA 94545
P: 510-785-6900 PRC:181
www.bigjoelift.com
Estab: 2003

Rod Kiefus, VP of Sales
David Forseth, Motive Power Manager
Juan Reyes, Supervisor

Supplier of warehouse storage and material
handling equipment. The company specializes in
pallet and product storage systems.

**Big Switch Networks Inc** HQ
3111 Coronado Dr Bldg A
Santa Clara CA 95054
P: 650-322-6510 PRC:323
bigswitch.com
Email: info@bigswitch.com
Estab: 2010

Kyle Forster, Co-Founder
Douglas Murray, CEO
Gregg Holzrichter, VP of Marketing
Prashant Gandhi, VP of Product Management &
Strategy

Provider of hyperscale networking design princi-
ples and applying them to fit-for-purpose products
for enterprises, cloud, and service providers.

**Bigfoot Biomedical Inc** HQ
1561 Buckeye Dr
Milpitas CA 95035
P: 408-716-5600 PRC:194
www.bigfootbiomedical.com
Email: info@bigfootbiomedical.com
Estab: 2014

Jeffrey Brewer, Founder
Brett Hale, CFO
Ian Hanson, CTO
Jyoti Palaniappan, CCO

Developer of biomedical solution to improve the
lives of people with diabetes through the application of smart technology.

**Billington Welding & Manufacturing
Inc** HQ
1442 N Emerald Ave
Modesto CA 95352
P: 209-526-9312 F: 209-521-4759 PRC:82
www.billington-mfg.com
Email: info@billington-mfg.com
Emp: 1-10 Estab: 1969

Chris Hendryk, Manufacturing Engineer

Manufacturer of food process equipment and custom products. The company serves the construction, automotive, and food processing industries.

**Bio Plas Inc** HQ
4380 Redwood Hwy Ste C-16
San Rafael CA 94903
P: 415-472-3777 F: 415-472-3758 PRC:189
www.bioplas.com
Email: info@bioplas.com
Estab: 1977

Bill Slattery, National Marketing Manager

Manufacturer of laboratory disposables such as
foam tube racks, biopsy bags, bacti cell spreaders, and siliconized products.

**Bio Rad Laboratories Inc** BR
2000 Alfred Nobel Dr
Hercules CA 94547
P: 510-741-1000 F: 510-741-5800 PRC:28
www.bio-rad.com
Email: support@bio-rad.com
Estab: 1952

Norman Schwartz, Chairman
Annette Tumolo, EVP of President of Life Science
Group
John Hertia, EVP of President of Clinical Diagnos-
tics Group
Andrew Last, EVP
Giovanni Magni, EVP

Provider of life science research and clinical diagnostics products and services for pharmaceutical
manufacturers and biotechnology researchers.

**Bio Rad Laboratories** HQ
1000 Alfred Nobel Dr
Hercules CA 94547
P: 510-724-7000 F: 510-741-5817 PRC:28
www.bio-rad.com
Estab: 1952
Sales: $1B to $3B

Christine Tsingos, VP
Giovanni Magni, CSO
Catherine Hartman, Human Resource Business
Partner
Yann Jouvenot, Marketing Manager
Donna Chapman, VP

Provider of medical products and services that advance scientific discovery and improve healthcare
for life science research and clinical diagnostic.

**Bioassay Systems** HQ
3191 Corporate Pl
Hayward CA 94545
P: 510-782-9988 F: 510-782-1588 PRC:261
bioassaysys.com
Email: info@bioassaysys.com

Frank Huang, CEO

Developer and marketer of assay solutions. The
company focuses on solutions for research and
drug discovery.

**Biocardia Inc** HQ
125 Shoreway Rd Ste B
San Carlos CA 94070
P: 650-226-0120 F: 650-631-3731 PRC:187
www.biocardia.com
Email: info@biocardia.com
Estab: 2002
Sales: Under $1 Million

Bhavin Nasit, Senior Research & Development
Engineer
Peter Altman, President
David McClung, CFO
Ian McNiece, CSO
Eric Duckers, CMO

Developer of clinical stage regenerative therapeutic products for the treatment of cardiovascular
diseases.

**Biocare Medical LLC**      HQ
60 Berry Dr
Pacheco CA 94553
P: 925-603-8000    F: 925-603-8080     PRC:41
www.biocare.net
Estab: 1997

Gene Castagnini, CFO
Carla Cayson, Human Resource Manager
Mark Castagnini, Inside Sales Manager
Leah Smith, Payroll Coordinator

Developer of automated immunohistochemistry
instrumentation, reagents for IHC lab testing. The
company also offer tissue diagnostic products for
cancer.

**Biochain Institute Inc**      HQ
39600 Eureka Dr
Newark CA 94560
P: 510-783-8588    F: 510-783-5386     PRC:24
www.biochain.com
Email: info@biochain.com
Estab: 1994

Grace Tian, CEO
Jenny Weng, Production Manager
Zhongdong Liu, VP
Mathew Jimenez, Lead Administrator

Provider of bio-sample preparation, analysis, and
application assays accelerating the development
of personalized diagnostics, therapeutics, and
medicine.

**Biocheck Inc**      HQ
425 Eccles Ave
S San Francisco CA 94080
P: 650-573-1968    F: 650-573-1969     PRC:44
www.biocheckinc.com
Email: info@biocheckinc.com
Estab: 1997

Christine Kuo, Director of RA & Quality Assurance
David Herbert, Client Service Director
Anna Pao, Director of Administration
Cathleen Wong, Research

Provider of custom immunoassay development,
antibody conjugation and purification, and contract
manufacturing services.

**Biocision LLC**      HQ
101 Glacier Point Rd Ste E
San Rafael CA 94901
P: 800-367-4887     PRC:31
www.biocision.com
Email: sales@biocision.com
Estab: 2007

Rolf Ehrhardt, CEO
Casey DeCesari, Sales Representative

Provider of cell freezing and cell thawing systems,
and related supplies. The company's products are
used in research applications.

**BioClin Therapeutics Inc**      HQ
1040 Davis St Ste 202
San Leandro CA 94577
P: 925-413-6140     PRC:38
www.bioclintherapeutics.com
Email: info@bioclintherapeutics.com
Estab: 2010

Stephen Lau, CEO
Robert Shaffer, Quality Assurance Tester

Developer of biologic products for the treatment of
metastatic bladder cancer (urothelial cell carcinoma) and achondroplasia (dwarfism).

**Bioclinica Inc**      HQ
7707 Gateway Blvd Fl 3
Newark CA 94560
P: 415-817-8900    F: 415-817-8999     PRC:188
www.bioclinica.com
Estab: 1990

David Herron, President
Humaira Qureshi, President
Thomas Fuerst, Chief Science Officer
William Hogan, EVP
Michael O'Neal, Chief Medical Officer

Developer of medical therapies. The company
specializes in medical imaging services, cardiac
safety, and enterprise eClinical platforms.

**BioConsortia Inc**      HQ
1940 Research Park Dr Ste 200
Davis CA 95618
P: 530-564-5570     PRC:24
www.bioconsortia.com
Email: info@bioconsortia.com
Emp: 11-50 Estab: 2014

Marcus Meadows-Smith, CEO
Christina Huben, SVP of Operations & Adminis-
tration
Hong Zhu, SVP of Research & Development
Jorge Santiago Ortiz, Director of Process Devel-
opment
Graham Hymus, Director of Plant Physiology

Focuses on the discovery, development, and
commercialization of microbial consortia seed
treatment and soil additive products.

**Biodesy Inc**      HQ
170 Harbor Way Ste 100
S San Francisco CA 94080
P: 650-871-8716     PRC:42
www.biodesy.com
Email: info@biodesy.com
Estab: 2013

Gayle Kuokka, CFO
Ariel Notcovich, VP
Heather Meeks, Senior Office Manager
Laureen Asato, Contract Senior Technical Writer
David Shaya, Scientist

Developer of proteins and biological molecules for
the treatment of cancer, cardiovascular, Alzheimer's, and Parkinson's diseases.

**Biofuel Oasis**      HQ
1441 Ashby Ave
Berkeley CA 94702
P: 510-665-5509     PRC:134
biofueloasis.com
Estab: 2003

Sarahope Smith, Owner

Producer of biodiesel and seller of urban farm
supplies, poultry feed and equipment. The company specializes in biodiesel made from waste oil.

**Biogenex Laboratories Inc**      HQ
49026 Milmont Dr
Fremont CA 94538
P: 510-824-1400    F: 510-824-1490     PRC:187
www.biogenex.com
Email: customer.service@biogenex.com
Estab: 1981

Krishan Kalra, CEO

Manufacturer of automated slide-based staining
instruments and histology products for cancer
diagnosis, prognosis, and therapy selection.

**Biokey Inc**      HQ
44370 Old Warm Springs Blvd
Fremont CA 94538
P: 510-668-0881    F: 510-252-0188     PRC:41
www.biokeyinc.com
Email: info@biokeyinc.com

Christina Mi, Regulatory Affairs & Quality Assurance Associate
George Lee, VP

Provider of API characterization, pre-formulation
studies, formulation development, and analytical
method development services.

**Bioluminate Inc**      HQ
3371 Melendy Dr
San Carlos CA 94070
P: 650-743-0240     PRC:41
www.bioluminate.com
Estab: 2000

Richard Hular, CEO

Developer of probes that provide breast cancer
detection data to physicians. The company serves
the medical sector.

**Biolytic Lab Performance Inc**      HQ
5680 Stewart Ave
Fremont CA 94538
P: 510-795-1142    F: 510-795-1149     PRC:31
www.biolytic.com
Email: sales@biolytic.com
Estab: 1993

Nicole Parnala, Technical Support Engineer
Thomas Demmitt, President
Jeffery Demmitt, Manufacturing Supervisor
Kim Edmonds, Director of Finance

Provider of instrumentation and accessories
for oligonucleotide, dna synthesis and oligo
purification. The company specializes in rebuilt
instruments.

**Biomagnetics Diagnostics Corp**   HQ
8864 Greenback Ln Ste E
Orangevale CA 95662
P: 916-987-7078  F: 916-987-7922   PRC:34
www.biomagneticsbmgp.com
Email: info@biomagneticsbmgp.com
Emp: 1-10  Estab: 1997

Clayton Hardman, Founder
Gustavo Angular, Director of Strategic Alliances &
Government Affairs Mexico
Sanjay Mishra, Physics Advisor

Provider of medical device and biotechnology. The
company specializes in magnetic testing platform
and immunoassays products.

**Biomarin Pharmaceutical Inc**   HQ
770 Lindaro St
San Rafael CA 94901
P: 415-506-6700  F: 415-382-7889   PRC:249
www.biomarin.com
Email: support@biomarin-rareconnections.com
Estab: 1997
Sales: $1B to $3B

Eric Davis, President of Global Manufacturing and
Technical Operations
Robert Baffi, President of Global Manufacturing
and Technical Operations
Elizabeth McKee Anderson, Chairman
Jean-Jacques Bienaime, Chairman
Philip Scalzo, Chairman

Developer of biopharmaceutical products for
treatment of morquio A, phenylketonuria, mu-
copolysaccharidosis VI & I, and lambert-eaton
myasthenic syndrome.

**Biomarker Pharmaceuticals Inc**   HQ
5941 Optical Ct
San Jose CA 95138
P: 408-257-2000  F: 408-356-6661   PRC:254
www.biomarkerinc.com
Email: contactus@biomarkerinc.com
Estab: 2002

Xi Zhao-Wilson, Chairman
Saul Kent, Director
Charles Garvin, CEO
Mike Kope, VP of Corporate Development
Paul Watkins, VP of Business Development

Developer of scientifically-based aging intervention products for slowing the process of aging and
delaying the onset of age-related diseases.

**Biomarker Technologies Inc**   HQ
638 Martin Ave
Rohnert Park CA 94928
P: 707-829-5551  F: 707-586-9618   PRC:24
biomarker-inc.com
Email: info@biomarker-inc.com
Estab: 1993

John Moldowan, President
Jaime Moldowan, CFO
Shaun Moldowan, COO
Fred Fago, Technical Consultant

Provider of geochemical technology services. The
company offers asphaltene analysis, diamondoids,
and gas chromatography analysis services.

**Biomax Environmental LLC**   HQ
775 San Pablo Ave
Pinole CA 94564-2631
P: 510-724-3100   PRC:142
biomaxenvironmental.com
Estab: 1996

Michael Polkabla, Owner

Provider of indoor air quality assessment, sampling, industrial hygiene monitoring, auditing, and
assessment services.

**Biomedecon LLC**   HQ
PO Box 129
Moss Beach CA 94038
P: 650-563-9475  F: 650-563-9485   PRC:34
www.biomedecon.com
Email: media@biomedecon.com
Estab: 1904

Amy Bronstone, Director of Medical Writing

Provider of health economics and outcomes
research. The company caters to pharmaceutical
and medical industries.

**Biomedical Forensics**   HQ
1660 School St Ste 103
Moraga CA 94556
P: 925-376-1240   PRC:304
biomedicalforensics.com

Laura Liptai, Manager
Adrianne Lee, Bookkeeper

Provider of engineering and applied science. The
company specializes in mechanism and causation
of trauma and impact biomechanics.

**Biomertech**   HQ
1047 Serpentine Ln Ste 200
Pleasanton CA 94566
P: 925-931-0007  F: 925-931-0300   PRC:24
www.biomertechnology.com
Email: info@biomertech.com

Jerry Chou, Manager

Provider of tailor-made peptide and anti-body
solutions such as pepdyes and polyclonal antibody advantage for the scientific community.

**Biometrix Inc**   HQ
2419 Ocean Ave
San Francisco CA 94127
P: 415-333-0522  F: 415-333-0532   PRC:306
www.biometrixinc.com
Email: info@biometrixinc.com
Estab: 1998

John Ademola, President
Shilpa Goel, Clinical Research Manager

Manufacturer of pathway analysis and variant
analysis products. The company specializes in
web-analysis.

**Biomicrolab**   HQ
2500 Dean Lesher Dr Ste A
Concord CA 94520
P: 925-689-1200   PRC:160
www.biomicrolab.com
Email: info@biomicrolab.com
Estab: 2004

Katie Guillaume, Sales Representative
Jaime Maldonado, Manager
Cristina Perez, Manager

Manufacturer of robotics based sorting and weighing systems sample management automation. The
company serves bio-lab purposes.

**Bioneer Inc**   BR
155 Filbert St Ste 216
Oakland CA 94607
P: 877-264-4300  F: 510-865-0350   PRC:38
us.bioneer.com
Email: order.usa@bioneer.us.com

Edgar Elenes, Sales Representative

Developer of molecular biology products and technologies for life science researchers in academia,
biotech, and pharmaceutical companies.

**Bionexus Inc**   HQ
222 Madison St
Oakland CA 94607
P: 510-625-8400  F: 510-625-8419   PRC:191
www.bionexus.net
Email: info@bionexus.net
Estab: 1996

Thomas Quinto, Engineering Manager
Arman Berloui, Director of Operations
Azita Berloui, Director of Technology
Athena Berloui, Customer Relations

Provider of biomedical products and services for
research areas such as genomics, proteomics,
immunology, protein expression, and cell biology.

**Biopharmx Inc**   HQ
1505 Adams Dr Ste D
Menlo Park CA 94025
P: 650-889-5020   PRC:268
biopharmx.com
Email: info@biopharmx.com

David Tierney, CEO
Jim Pekarsky, CEO
Steven Bosacki, COO
Joyce Goto, CAO

Provider of healthcare products. The company
offers products for the dermatology, therapeutics,
aesthetics, and cosmetics industries.

**BioQ Pharma Inc**   HQ
1325 Howard St
San Francisco CA 94103
P: 415-336-6496   PRC:267
www.bioqpharma.com
Email: admin@bioqpharma.com

Ralph McNall, VP of Engineering
Josh Kriesel, CEO
Ronald Pauli, CFO
Walter Cleymans, CCO
Greg Meyer, VP of Quality & Regulatory

Manufacturer of proprietary products. The company is involved in the sale of infusion pharmaceuticals.

**Bioscience Advisors**   HQ
2855 Mitchell Dr Ste 103
Walnut Creek CA 94598
P: 925-954-1397   PRC:40
www.biosciadvisors.com
Estab: 2011

Mark Edwards, Managing Director

Provider of consulting services. The company
serves the pharmaceutical and biotechnology
industries concerning commercialization agree-
ments.

**Biosearch Technologies Inc**  RH
2199 S McDowell Blvd
Petaluma CA 94954-6904
P: 415-883-8400   F: 415-883-8488   PRC:34
www.biosearchtech.com
Email: info@biosearchtech.com
Estab: 1993

Ron Cook, President
Mikey Songster, Director of Information Technology
Chad Gerber, Director of IVD Oligonucleotide Manufacturing
Jason Erickson, Director of Quality
Luan Le, Research & Development Scientist

Manufacturer of nucleic acid based products that accelerate the discovery and application of genomic information.

**Biotium Inc**  HQ
46117 Landing Pkwy
Fremont CA 94538
P: 510-265-1027   F: 510-265-1352   PRC:268
biotium.com
Email: btinfo@biotium.com
Estab: 2001

Vivien Chen, VP of Business Development & Marketing
Fei Mao, CEO
Patrick McGarraugh, Director of Manufacturing
Wai-Yee Leung, VP of R&D
Lori Roberts, Director of Bioscience

Supplier of glowing products. The company offers enzyme substrates and kits for labeling proteins and antibodies.

**BioTrace Medical Inc**  HQ
3925 Bohannon Dr Ste 200
Menlo Park CA 94025
P: 650-779-4999   F: 650-779-4746   PRC:198
www.biotracemedical.com
Email: info@biotracemedical.com
Estab: 2013

Kevin Tausend, Head of Marketing

Manufacturer of medical devices. The company specializes in cardiac pacing device which can treat reversible symptomatic bradycardia.

**Bioved Pharmaceuticals Inc**  HQ
1929 O'Toole Way
San Jose CA 95131
P: 408-432-4020   F: 408-432-4027   PRC:261
www.bioved.com
Email: sales@bioved.com

Deepa Chitre, Chairman
Deben Dey, CSO
Alfred Grigsby, VP of Sales
Sadanand Bajekal, SVP of BIO-VED India
Prema Rao, VP of Preclinical Research

Manufacturer of health care products. The company specializes in ayurvedic pharmaceutical, neutraceutical and OTC drugs from plant extracts.

**Bioventrix Inc**  HQ
12647 Alcosta Blvd Ste 400
San Ramon CA 94583
P: 925-830-1000   F: 925-830-1002   PRC:189
bioventrix.com

Kenneth Miller, President
Lon Annest, Chief Medical Officer
Noel Messenger, VP of Quality
David Schickling, VP of Sales & Marketing
Kevin Van Bladel, SVP of Product & Therapeutic Development

Provider of medical devices. The company offers treatment for congestive heart failure by catheter based approaches.

**Biovir Laboratories Inc**  HQ
685 Stone Rd Unit 6
Benicia CA 94510-1126
P: 707-747-5906   F: 707-747-1751   PRC:306
www.biovir.com
Email: admin@biovir.com
Estab: 1988

Richard Danielson, Director of Laboratories

Provider of environmental testing needs, technology, and methodology for quality water, wastewater, and biosolids testing and research services.

**Biovision Inc**  RH
155 S Milpitas Blvd
Milpitas CA 95035
P: 408-493-1800   F: 408-493-1801   PRC:189
www.biovision.com
Email: support@biovision.com

Grigoriy Tchaga, Director of Research & Business Development
Nick Chacos, Director of Operations

Developer of medical products such as assay kits, antibodies, and research tools for studying apoptosis, metabolism, diabetes, and gene regulation.

**Bioxiness Pharmaceuticals Inc**  HQ
750 Alfred Nobel Dr Ste 106
Hercules CA 94547
P: 510-724-1548   PRC:268
www.bioxiness.com
Estab: 2007

Mansour Bassiri, President

Developer of small molecule antibiotic medicines. The company focuses on infectious disease treatments.

**Biozone Laboratories Inc**  HQ
580 Garcia Ave
Pittsburg CA 94565
P: 925-473-1000   F: 925-473-1001   PRC:261
www.biozonelabs.com
Email: info@biozonelabs.com
Estab: 1987

Bob Stoddard, Manager of Engineering

Manufacturer of over the counter drugs, cosmetics, personal care, and nutritional supplements such as creams, gels, drops, syrups, and sun protection.

**Birst Inc**  HQ
45 Fermont St 18th Fl
San Francisco CA 94105
P: 415-766-4800   PRC:322
birst.com
Email: birstteam@infor.com
Estab: 2005

Rick Spickelmier, CTO
Paul Staelin, Co-Founder
Brad Peters, Chief Product Officer

Provider of supply chain, marketing, human resources, financial, and sales analytics solutions for businesses.

**Bishop-Wisecarver Corp**  HQ
2104 Martin Way
Pittsburg CA 94565-5027
P: 925-439-8272   F: 925-439-5931   PRC:159
www.bwc.com
Email: info@bwc.com
Estab: 1950

Benjamin Domingo, Applications Engineer
Leslie Lui, Mechanical Design Engineer
Pamela Kan, President
Kelly Walden, VP of Manufacturing
Renee Halog, Sales & Marketing Administrative Assistant

Manufacturer of guide wheels and guided motion products for the medical, aerospace, electronic, and packaging industries.

**Bitglass**  HQ
675 Campbell Technology Pkwy Ste 225
Campbell CA 95008
P: 408-337-0190   PRC:319
www.bitglass.com
Email: sales@bitglass.com
Estab: 2013

Chris Chan, SVP of Engineering
Nat Kausik, CEO
Anurag Kahol, CTO
Anoop Bhattacharjya, Chief Scientist
Andrew Urushima, SVP of Finance

Provider of data protection solutions. The company focuses on cloud encryption, mobile security, and discovery solutions.

**BiTMICRO Networks Inc**  HQ
47929 Fremont Blvd
Fremont CA 94538
P: 888-723-0123   F: 510-623-2342   PRC:95
www.bitmicro.com
Email: sales@bitmicro.com
Estab: 1995

Hazel Tolosa, Account Executive

Developer and manufacturer of flash-based SSD technology, products, and solutions. The company focuses on cloud computing and gaming applications.

**BitPusher LLC** HQ
100 Pine St Ste 460
San Francisco CA 94111
P: 415-751-1055 PRC:325
www.bitpusher.com
Email: info@bitpusher.com
Estab: 1999

Ilya Gershov, Business Developer
Amy Squires, Office Administrator

Provider of IT infrastructure management services. The company also focuses on consulting and hosted IT services.

**Bitscopic** HQ
255 Constitution Dr Ste 106
Menlo Park CA 94025
P: 650-503-3120 PRC:40
bitscopic.com
Email: ca@bitscopic.com
Estab: 2012

Payam Etminani, Co-Founder
Farshid Sedghi, COO
Joel Mewton, CTO
Russell Ryono, Clinical Application Director
Steven Phelps, Director of Data Science

Provider of consulting and computer-related services. The company serves businesses and industrial customers.

**Bitsculptor** HQ
901 S Main St
Lakeport CA 95453
P: 707-263-5241 F: 480-436-5233 PRC:325
www.bitsculptor.com
Email: support@bitsculptor.com
Emp: 1-10

Eric Schlange, Owner
Sloan Reynolds, Web Developer

Provider of web design, hosting, branding and search engine positioning solutions. The company also offers SEO, photography, and consulting services.

**BitTorrent Inc** HQ
301 Howard St Ste 2000
San Francisco CA 94105
P: 415-568-9000 PRC:322
www.bittorrent.com
Email: adsales@bittorrent.com
Estab: 2004

Bram Cohen, Founder
Dipak Joshi, CFO
Kim Edwards, Senior Accountant

Provider of download software solutions. The company offers design, data and content management, and installation services.

**Bivio Networks Inc** HQ
4457 Willow Rd Ste 200
Pleasanton CA 94588
P: 925-924-8600 F: 925-924-8650 PRC:62
www.bivio.net
Email: info@bivio.net
Estab: 2000

Ronak Shukla, Engineering Manager
Keith Glover, President

Provider of cyber security and network control solutions. The company offers cyber defense systems, surveillance, flow analysis, and monitoring tools.

**Biw Connector Systems LLC** HQ
500 Tesconi Cir
Santa Rosa CA 95401
P: 707-523-2300 F: 707-523-3567 PRC:159
www.ittbiw.com

Pedro Andrade, Operations Director
Cal Wahhab, System Administrator

Supplier of connector systems and electrical feedthru products. The company's products include wellhead feedthrus and power interconnect products.

**BizeeBee Inc** HQ
661 Channing Ave
Palo Alto CA 94301
P: 650-489-6233 PRC:325
bizeebee.com
Email: support@bizeebee.com
Estab: 2010

Poornima Vijayashanker, CEO
Samihah Azim, Product Manager

Provider of lightweight software solution designed to help fitness studios and other membership based businesses.

**Bizlink Technology Inc** HQ
3400 Gateway Blvd
Fremont CA 94538
P: 510-252-0786 F: 510-252-1178 PRC:62
www.bizlinktech.com
Email: sales@bizlinktech.com
Estab: 1996

Felix Teng, CEO
Roger Liang, Chairman
Rita Chen, Chief Finance Officer
Hanibal Bitheydari, Director of Sales
Ted Hsiao, VP of Product Development

Manufacturer and assembler of cables and harnesses. The company serves the medical devices, solar energy, and fiber optics industries.

**Bkf Engineers** BR
1730 N First St Ste 600
San Jose CA 95112
P: 408-467-9100 F: 408-467-9199 PRC:304
www.bkf.com
Estab: 1915

Lessandro DeSousa, Water Resources Design Engineer
Nellie Moussa, Project Engineer
Dave LaVelle, President
Alex Cabezon, Human Resource
Chris Rideout, VP

Provider of civil engineering, design, surveying, design, transportation, and entitlement support services.

**Bkf Engineers** BR
1646 N California Blvd Ste 400
Walnut Creek CA 94596
P: 925-940-2200 F: 925-940-2299 PRC:304
www.bkf.com
Estab: 1915

David Lavelle, President
Natalina Bernardi, VP
David Richwood, VP

Provider of civil engineering consulting, and land surveying services. The company serves business organizations.

**BlackBag Technologies Inc** HQ
300 Piercy Rd
San Jose CA 95138
P: 408-844-8890 F: 408-844-8891 PRC:323
www.blackbagtech.com
Email: sales@blackbagtech.com
Estab: 2001

Derrick Donnelly, Co-Founder
Ben Charnota, Co-Founder
Ken Basore, CEO
Cari Graham, Director of Human Resources
Sheldon Feinland, VP of Global Sales

Provider of Mac-based data forensic and eDiscovery solutions. The company is involved in data processing and related services.

**Blackburn Consulting** HQ
11521 Blocker Dr Ste 110
Auburn CA 95603
P: 530-887-1494 F: 530-887-1495 PRC:139
blackburnconsulting.com
Emp: 11-50 Estab: 1998

Robert Lokteff, Principal Geotechnical Engineer
Nicole Hart, Senior Engineer
Laura Long, Environmental Engineer
Kristy Chapman, Project Engineer
Thomas Blackburn, President

Provider of geotechnical engineering, geo environmental engineering, design materials engineering, forensic, and construction services.

**Blackhawk Network Inc** HQ
6220 Stoneridge Mall Rd
Pleasanton CA 94588
P: 925-226-9990 F: 925-226-9083 PRC:45
blackhawknetwork.com
Email: sales@bhnetwork.com
Estab: 2001

Talbott Roche, CEO

Provider of employee engagement and customer engagement services such as gift cards, reloadable prepaid debit cards, and cash-based payment products.

**Blacksquare LLC** HQ
501 Greenwich St
San Francisco CA 94133
P: 415-640-6339 PRC:325
www.blacksquare.com
Email: hello@blacksquare.com
Estab: 1997

Julia Ogrydziak, Founding Partner
Alejandro Nunez, Investment Advisor

Provider of location-based, social, m-commerce, game, and video applications. The company serves Fortune 500 companies.

**Blackstone Technology Group Inc** HQ
455 Market St Ste 620
San Francisco CA 94105
P: 415-837-1400 F: 415-837-1474 PRC:322
www.bstonetech.com
Estab: 1998

Casey Courneen, Co-Founder
David Mysona, Co-Founder
Rakesh Agrawal, Co-Founder
Korrie Courneen, Director of Human Resources
Ken Hans, Partner

Provider of IT solutions, commercial, and government consulting, staffing services, and trellis natural gas transaction management web solution.

**Blade Therapeutics Inc**    HQ
442 Littlefield Ave S
South San Francisco CA 94080
P: 650-278-4291    PRC:25
www.blademed.com
Estab: 2015

Wendye Robbins, President
Brad Buckman, SVP of Drug Discovery & Medicinal Chemistry

Developer of biopharmaceutical products. The company specializes anti-fibrotic drug discovery and development for treatment of fibrotic disease.

**Blair Electric Services Inc**    HQ
1829 Thunderbolt Dr
Porterville CA 93257
P: 559-784-8658    F: 559-784-8657    PRC:94
blair-electric.com
Emp: 1-10

Bruce Blair, Owner
Greg Covarrubias, Parts Manager

Provider of electrical contracting services. The company offers pump and well controls, PLC controls, and surveillance systems.

**Blankinship & Associates Inc**    HQ
1615 Fifth St Ste A
Davis CA 95618
P: 530-757-0941    PRC:304
www.h2osci.com
Email: info@h2osci.com
Emp: 1-10   Estab: 2000

Kenneth Tanaka, Project Engineer
Mike Blankinship, President
Lindsey Curley, Staff Scientist
David Bonnar, Environmental Scientist
Stephen Burkholder, Project Biologist

Provider of environmental science and engineering services focusing on biological resources, stormwater & nitrogen management, and other needs.

**Blast Analytics & Marketing**    HQ
6020 W Oaks Blvd Ste 260
Rocklin CA 95765
P: 916-724-6701    F: 916-724-6714    PRC:325
www.blastam.com
Email: solutions@blastam.com
Emp: 11-50 Estab: 1999

Kayden Kelly, CEO
Sarah Katinger, Marketing Manager
David McCormick, Senior Marketing Strategist
Brian Correia, Marketing Strategist
Tod Hirsch, Marketing Strategist

Provider of web design, e-commerce, and brand design services. The company is involved in hosting and technical support.

**Blentech Corp**    HQ
2899 Dowd Dr
Santa Rosa CA 95407
P: 707-523-5949    F: 707-523-5939    PRC:159
www.blentech.com
Email: info@blentech.com
Estab: 1986

Neeraj Nagpal, Application Engineer
Krista Drechsler, Process Applications Engineer
Erin Whelan, Application Engineer
Drew Moug, Service Engineer
Zhengjun Xue, Application Engineer

Manufacturer of custom processing systems. The company serves the food production, pharmaceuticals, chemical, and biochemical industries.

**Bloom Energy Corp**    HQ
4353 N First St
San Jose CA 95134
P: 408-543-1500    F: 408-543-1501    PRC:293
bloomenergy.com

Venkat Venkataraman, EVP of Engineering
KR Sridhar, Founder
Randy Furr, EVP
Chris White, EVP
Susan Brennan, COO

Provider of power generation systems. The company focuses on solid oxide fuel cells and mission critical systems.

**Blue Chip Tek Inc**    HQ
3030 Olcott St
Santa Clara CA 95054
P: 408-731-7700    F: 408-731-7701    PRC:326
www.bluechiptek.com
Email: bct-sales@bluechiptek.com
Estab: 2002

Cindy Kennedy, President
Jessica Geis, CEO
Jason Geis, Principal
Marc Farmer, Account Executive

Provider of data management and protection, information life cycle management, networking, security, and data center solutions.

**Blue Danube Systems Inc**    BR
3131 Jay St Ste 201
Santa Clara CA 95054
P: 650-316-5010    PRC:71
www.bluedanube.com
Email: info@bluedanube.com
Estab: 2006

Mihai Banu, CTO
Mark Pinto, CEO
John Shelnutt, VP of Sales
David Poticny, VP of Business Development
Adam Grosser, Group Head

Designer and developer of mobile wireless access solutions that increase network capacity. The company serves the industrial sector.

**Blue Harbors**    HQ
167 Belvedere St
San Francisco CA 94117
P: 415-799-7769    PRC:328
blueharbors.com
Estab: 2001

Josh Riff, Project Manager
Carl Edwards, SAP Logistics Consultant

Provider of warehouse and transportation management, and shipping solutions. The company serves the industrial sector.

**Blue Jeans Network Inc**    HQ
516 Clyde Ave
Mountain View CA 94043
P: 408-550-2828    F: 408-550-2829    PRC:322
bluejeans.com
Estab: 2009

Brian Ashford, Senior Engineer of Media Protocols
Prasad Mohire, Software Engineer
Quentin Gallivan, CEO
Debbie Murray, Chief People Officer
Matt Collier, VP of Strategic Alliances and Business Development

Provider of cloud-based video conferencing solutions. The company also offers mobile video collaboration and cloud video bridging solutions.

**Blue Oak Energy**    HQ
1560 Drew Ave
Davis CA 95618
P: 530-747-2026    F: 530-747-0311    PRC:135
www.blueoakenergy.com
Email: information@blueoakenergy.com
Emp: 1-10   Estab: 2003

Dan Noren, Director of Engineering
Jayme Garcia, Engineering Project Manager
Lukas Klavins, Project Engineer
Mario Carreon, Senior Civil Engineer
Tobin Booth, Founder

Designer of photovoltaic solar energy systems. The company is engaged in designing, building, and maintenance of solar energy systems.

**Blue Sky Environmental Inc**    HQ
624 San Gabriel Ave
Albany CA 94706
P: 510-525-1261    PRC:306
blueskyenvironmental.com
Email: info@blueskyenvironmental.com
Estab: 1999

Guy Worthington, Owner
Jeramie Richardson, Project Manager
Adam Ashlin, Project Manager
Chuck Arrivas, Project Manager

Provider of air emissions source testing services. The company's services include alternative monitoring and validation testing.

**Blue Sky Research Inc**    HQ
510 Alder Dr
Milpitas CA 95035
P: 408-941-6068    F: 408-941-0406    PRC:83
www.blueskyresearch.com
Email: sales@blueskyresearch.com
Estab: 1989

Joe Kulakofsky, VP of Applications & Product Engineering
Bill Chang, Principal Optic Engineer
Chris Gladding, CEO
Sandip Basu, VP
Bin Li, Director of Manufacturing

Manufacturer of laser products and micro optics. The company designs and fabricates semiconductor based lasers and fiber optic cables.

**Blue Source LLC** BR
528 Market St Ste 1505
San Francisco CA 94104
P: 415-399-9101 PRC:142
www.bluesourcecan.com
Email: info@bluesource.com

Tooraj Moulai, Director of Engineering and Technical Services
Yvan Champagne, President of Bluesource Methane
Roger Williams, President
Eric Townsend, CEO
Bill Townsend, Chairman

Provider of services for the mining industry. The company offers project development, offset sales and marketing, consulting, and other related services.

**Blue Star Electronics** HQ
6748 Preston Ave Ste G
Livermore CA 94513
P: 925-420-5593 PRC:140
www.bluestarco.com
Email: recycle@bluestarco.com

Louis Sarkis, Manager

Focuses on the resale, recycling and end of life programs for electronic equipment and components. The company offers e-waste solutions.

**Blue Turtle Bio Technologies Inc** HQ
479 Jessie St
San Francisco CA 94103
P: 313-806-2774 PRC:34
blueturtlebio.com
Email: info@blueturtlebio.com
Estab: 2014

Nilesh Joshi, Co-Founder

Creator of therapeutic products. The company specializes in microbiome to recruit genetically malleable and easily replenishable organ in the human body.

**Blueplanet** HQ
1383 N McDowell Blvd Ste 300
Petaluma CA 94954
P: 707-735-2300 PRC:67
www.packetdesign.com
Estab: 2003

Sophia Litz, Owner
Aboo T.A, Owner
John Morrell, President
Madan Verma, Sales Executive
Saya Moon, Managing Director

Developer and supplier of network solutions for distributed intelligence of internet protocol and enhancement of the efficiency of IP networks.

**Blunk Microsystems LLC** HQ
8880 Cal Ctr Dr Ste 400
Sacramento CA 95826
P: 408-323-1758 F: 408-323-1757 PRC:322
www.blunkmicro.com
Email: sales@blunkmicro.com
Emp: 1-10 Estab: 1995

Tim Stoutamore, Principal Engineer

Provider of turnkey packages for embedded development to customers around the world. The company also offers development tools.

**Blymyer Engineers Inc** HQ
1101 Marina Village Pkwy Ste 100
Alameda CA 94501
P: 510-521-3773 F: 510-865-2594 PRC:129
www.blymyerengineers.com
Email: info@blymyer.com
Estab: 1961

Mike Rantz, Manager

Provider of solar engineering, facility design, and related services. The company serves the food and beverage and glass manufacturing industries.

**BMC Software Inc** BR
2755 Great America Way Ste 501
Santa Clara CA 95054-1170
P: 800-793-4262 F: 408-965-0353 PRC:324
www.bmc.com

Bill Miller, President of ZSolutions
Ayman Sayed, CEO
Bob Beauchamp, Chairman
Cory Bleuer, SVP
Scott Crowder, SVP

Provider of cloud management, workforce automation, and IT service management solutions. The company serves business enterprises and service providers.

**BMI Imaging Systems Inc** BR
749 W Stadium Ln
Sacramento CA 95834
P: 800-359-3456 F: 408-736-4397 PRC:171
bmiimaging.com
Email: info@bmiimaging.com
Emp: 11-50 Estab: 1958

Bill Whitney, President
Michael Aufranc, Direct Sales Manager
Brad Penfold, VP of National Accounts
Jim Modrall, VP
Brad Gilbert, VP of Software Development

Provider of document management services. The company offers document scanning and hosting, system integration, and microfilm conversion services.

**Boardwalktech Inc** HQ
10050 N Wolfe Rd
Cupertino CA 95014
P: 650-618-6200 PRC:325
www.boardwalktech.com
Email: info@boardwalktech.com
Estab: 2004
Sales: $3M to $10M

Andrew Duncan, CEO
Charlie Glavin, CFO
Ravi Krishnan, CTO
Glenn Cordingley, SVP of Sales
James Kuppe, SVP of Marketing

Provider of enterprise collaboration software specializing in tax planning, cash management, and revenue forecasting solutions.

**Bodhtree Solutions Inc** BR
210 Hammond Ave
Fremont CA 94539
P: 408-954-8700 PRC:320
bodhtree.com
Emp: 11-50 Estab: 1999

Sathish Kumar, Director of Human Resources
Rama Krishna, Sales Manager
Chandana Reddy, Accounts Manager

Provider of information technology consulting services. The company deals with product engineering, application development, and training.

**Bold Data Technology Inc** HQ
48363 Fremont Blvd
Fremont CA 94538
P: 510-490-8296 F: 510-490-7981 PRC:120
www.boldata.com
Estab: 1984

Andrew Kretzer, Director
Jamie Jin, Accounts Payable Manager

Provider of computer components and services. The company offers desktop computers, servers, notebooks, and workstations.

**Boldfocus Inc** HQ
1900 S Norfolk St Ste 350
San Mateo CA 94403
P: 650-212-2653 F: 650-212-2654 PRC:325
boldfocus.com
Estab: 1995

Caly Lam, Art Director
Eddy Mejia, Application Developer

Provider of digital communications and technology services focusing on development, content management, and search engine optimization.

**Bolsa Analytical** HQ
6950 Santa Teresa Blvd Ste C
San Jose CA 95119
P: 831-637-4590 F: 831-634-1854 PRC:306
www.bolsalab.com
Estab: 1993

Tomas Moreno, Director of Laboratories

Provider of reliable chemical and microbiological analysis and testing of water, soil, plants and food.

**Boly Media Communications Inc** HQ
3235 Kifer Rd Ste 260
Santa Clara CA 95051
P: 408-533-0207 PRC:168
www.bolymedia.com
Email: us_sales@bolymedia.com
Estab: 2000

Xiaoping Hu, CEO
David Tsang, Co-Founder
Michelle Lin, Account & HRD Manager
Jie Shen, Stockholder

Supplier of trail cameras and security cameras. The company also specializes in ultrasonic motors and optical zooms.

**Boracchia + Associates** HQ
3920 Cypress Dr
Petaluma CA 94954
P: 800-826-1690 F: 707-765-3113 PRC:189
bormed.com
Estab: 1978

Edward Boracchia, Founder
Brianna Frey, Finance Manager
Christopher Bettini, Director of Operations
Helene Tienda, Accounting Manager

Provider of consultant services and products to surgeons and medical facilities. The company offers operating room products, post-operative, and castroom products.

**Borden Lighting** HQ
460 Roland Way
Oakland CA 94621
P: 510-357-0171   F: 510-357-3832   PRC:243
www.bordenlighting.com

Min Yin, Design Engineer
Randy Borden, Owner
Barry Gould, Production Manager
David Berks, National Sales Manager
Karla Paredes-Perez, Office

Provider of lighting solutions. The company provides table and floor lamps, architectural lighting, and louvers.

**Border Collie Solutions Inc** HQ
433 Airport Blvd Ste 316
Burlingame CA 94010
P: 650-343-2400   F: 650-343-9707   PRC:322
www.bcsii.net
Email: support@bcsii.com

Howard Neckowitz, Founder

Provider of security surveillance software products. The company focuses on security panel, energy management, and medical monitoring.

**Borsting Laboratories Inc** HQ
14 Commercial Blvd Ste 105
Novato CA 94949
P: 415-883-1337   F: 415-883-3842   PRC:303
www.borstinglabs.com
Email: info@borstinglabs.com
Estab: 1961

Chris Oatman, General Manager
Jeff Morris, Quality Assurance Manager

Provider of histology services. The company specialize in processing skin biopsies and expert second-opinion dermatopathological interpretation.

**Boster Biological Technology** HQ
3942 B Valley Ave
Pleasanton CA 94566
P: 888-466-3604   F: 925-215-2184   PRC:24
www.bosterbio.com
Email: support@bosterbio.com
Estab: 1993

Steven Xia, Owner
CJ Xia, VP of Marketing and Sales

Provider of antibodies and ELISA kits. The company serves customers in the biochemicals and molecular biology areas.

**Boston Scientific Corporation** BR
150 Baytech Dr
San Jose CA 95134
P: 408-935-3400   PRC:195
www.bostonscientific.com

Kevin Ballinger, EVP
Art Butcher, SVP
Eric Th'paut, SVP
Michael Mahoney, CEO
Daniel Brennan, EVP

Manufacturer of baskets, forceps, imaging systems, needles, pacemakers, CTO and direct visualization systems.

**Boston Scientific** BR
47215 Lakeview Blvd
Fremont CA 94538-6530
P: 510-440-7700   PRC:189
www.bostonscientific.com

Michael Mahoney, President
Dan Brennan, EVP

Provider of forceps, imaging systems, needles, pacemakers, snares, probes, and other related accessories.

**Bowsmith Inc** HQ
131 Second St
Exeter CA 93221
P: 559-592-9485   F: 559-592-2314   PRC:166
www.bowsmith.com
Email: info@bowsmith.com
Emp: 11-50 Estab: 1974

Victor Gonzalez, Manufacturing Manager
Lee Gipson, Sales Manager
Kari Grove, Inside Sales Manager
Ken Berg, VP

Provider of micro-irrigation equipment for agriculture, landscape, greenhouse, and heap leach mining. The company offers drip emitters and sprinklers.

**Boyd Lighting** HQ
30 Liberty Ship Way Ste 3150
Sausalito CA 94965
P: 415-778-4300   F: 415-778-4319   PRC:243
www.boydlighting.com
Estab: 1921

Jay Sweet, Owner
Lincoln Lee, Credit Manager

Manufacturer of lighting devices. The company offers its products in white glass, clear ribbed glass, and gloss ivory acrylic product finishes.

**Bracesox The Original** HQ
5161 Soquel Dr Ste E
Soquel CA 95073
P: 831-479-7628   F: 831-479-3621   PRC:190
www.bracesox.com
Email: info@bracesox.com
Emp: 1-10   Estab: 1980

Anne Adams, President

Manufacturer of bracesox, a brace cover with undersleeves and oversleeves to give brace comfort for patients.

**Bradford Technologies Inc** HQ
302 Piercy Rd
San Jose CA 95138
P: 408-360-8520   F: 408-360-8529   PRC:323
www.bradfordsoftware.com
Email: support@bradfordsoftware.com
Estab: 1987

Ladonna Batterson, Product Manager

Developer of appraising software solutions for the real estate sector. The company offers backup and storage and digital signature scanning services.

**Braigo Labs Inc** HQ
3260 Hillview Ave
Palo Alto CA 94304
P: 408-850-0614   PRC:115
www.braigolabs.com
Email: info@braigolabs.com
Estab: 2014

Shubham Banerjee, Founder
Malini Banerjee, President

Developer of humanely optimized technologies such as research, design, and creation of technology-based innovations and services for marketplace.

**Bramasol Inc** BR
3979 Freedom Cir Ste 620
Santa Clara CA 95054
P: 408-831-0046   F: 408-831-0047   PRC:322
www.bramasol.com
Estab: 1996

Patrick Kelliher, SVP
Elizabeth Fisher, Human Resources Manager
Christine Molinaro, VP of Finance
Laxman Apte, Senior Consultant
Jitendra Dhande, Senior Consultant

Provider of SAP-based solution for high tech software, life science, industrial machinery & components, and Telco, wireless, and internet services.

**Branch Metrics** HQ
1400 Seaport Blvd Blgd B 2nd Fl
Redwood City CA 94063
P: 650-209-6461   PRC:319
branch.io/
Email: info@branch.io
Estab: 2014

Ian Chan, Director of Engineering
Brian Springer, Director of Engineering
Mike Molinet, Co-Founder
Alex Austin, CEO
Eric Stein, EVP

Provides deep link solutions that unify user measurement across different devices, platforms, and channels.

**Brandt Electronics Inc** HQ
1971 Tarob Ct
Milpitas CA 95035
P: 408-240-0004   F: 408-240-0014   PRC:209
www.brandtelectronics.com
Email: info@brandtelectronics.com
Estab: 1979

Kevin Berg, Senior Design Engineer
Phil Duvall, CEO
Shawn Tran, Operations Manager

Manufacturer of power supplies. The company specializes in the design and maintenance of power equipment used in military applications.

**Branesky Sheet Metal Inc**    HQ
636 N Franklin St
Fort Bragg CA 95437
P: 707-964-0691   F: 707-964-0410    PRC:151
braneskysheetmetal.com
Emp: 1-10

Norma Cleary, Owner
Sean Cleary, General Manager
Tim Harris, Sheet Metal Manager
Andy Barvitz, Service Manager
Marcie Lazarus, Office Manager

Provider of hydronic and forced air systems. The company also offers heating systems, stoves, and sheet metals.

**Bravo Communications Inc**    HQ
3463 Meadowlands Ln
San Jose CA 95135
P: 408-270-1547   F: 408-270-4500    PRC:62
www.bravobravo.us
Email: sales@bravobravo.us
Estab: 1985

Dennis Mozingo, President

Supplier of network surge and lightening protection products. The company also offers data line extenders and related accessories.

**Brechtel Manufacturing Inc**    HQ
1789 Addison Way
Hayward CA 94544
P: 510-732-9723   F: 510-732-9153    PRC:165
www.brechtel.com
Email: bmi_info@brechtel.com
Estab: 1986

Andy Corless, Senior Design Engineer
Fred Brechtel, CEO
Gloria Tabarez, Office Manager
Lorenzo Gamero, Senior Welding Specialist
Chhuauy Tan, Electro-Mechanical Technician

Provider of aerosol solutions to the government, academic, and corporate sectors. The company also supplies vacuum brazing furnaces and leak valves.

**Brekeke Software Inc**    HQ
1730 S El Camino Real Ste 400
San Mateo CA 94402
P: 650-401-6633    PRC:325
brekeke.com
Estab: 2002

Mitu Mitsumata, CTO
Dane Turner, Account Executive

Developer of session initiation protocol software products for internet protocol network communication needs.

**Brelje & Race Laboratories Inc**    HQ
425 S East St
Santa Rosa CA 95404
P: 707-544-8807   F: 707-544-5736    PRC:142
www.brlabsinc.com
Estab: 1967

Hal Race, General Manager
Jill Brodt, Laboratory Director
Linda Adams, Project Manager
Jaime Lynch, Principal Analyst
Lisa Surber, Principal Analyst

Provider of water and wastewater testing services. The company analyses process include nitrate, arsenic, and volatile organics compounds.

**Bridgepoint Systems Inc**    HQ
2607 Seventh St Ste C
Berkeley CA 94710
P: 510-346-1510   F: 510-346-2410    PRC:209
www.bridgepointsystems.com
Email: customerservice@bridgepointsystems.com
Estab: 1995

Jim Mullin, VP of Engineering
Tom Corder, President

Provider of security solutions such as CAC card readers, PIV card readers, and access control experts for government contractors and security integrators.

**Bright Computing Inc**    HQ
2880 Zanker Rd Ste 203
San Jose CA 95134
P: 408-300-9448   F: 408-715-0102    PRC:323
www.brightcomputing.com
Email: info@brightcomputing.com
Estab: 2009

Brian Cassidy, Independent Investor

Provider of software solutions for provisioning and managing HPC clusters, Hadoop clusters, and openstack private clouds.

**Bright Pattern Inc**    HQ
1250 Bayhill Dr Ste 101
San Bruno CA 94066
P: 650-529-4099   F: 415-480-1782    PRC:326
www.brightpattern.com
Email: sales@brightpattern.com
Estab: 2010

Alexei Vovenko, VP of Engineering
Aleksandr Lobastov, Director of Engineering
Plamen Nedkov, Senior Engineer
Shelby Faris, Marketing Manager
Ivan Malyshkin, Director of Business Development

Provider of enterprise contact center application for blended multi-channel interactions. The company offers products based on modern technology.

**BrightEdge Technologies Inc**    HQ
989 E Hillsdale Blvd Ste 300
Foster City CA 94404
P: 800-578-8023    PRC:325
www.brightedge.com
Estab: 2007

Jim Yu, CEO
Lemuel Park, CTO
Sammy Yu, Chief Architect
Joseph Russell, CFO
Krish Kumar, Chief Revenue

Developer of mobile web applications, websites, and publishing platforms. The company specializes in SmartPath technology.

**Brighterion Inc**    HQ
150 Spear St Fl 10
San Francisco CA 94105
P: 415-986-5600   F: 415-986-5694    PRC:325
www.brighterion.com
Email: info@brighterion.com
Estab: 2000

Remi Coursimault, Network Security Engineer
David Wang, Software QA Engineer
Jason Revelle, VP
Kurt Schwabe, Director of Marketing
Jeff Muschick, VP of Business Development

Provider of products for fraud prevention, predictive intelligence, risk management, and homeland security. The company focuses on adaptive analytics.

**Brightidea Inc**    HQ
25 Pacific Ave
San Francisco CA 94111
P: 415-692-1912    PRC:323
www.brightidea.com
Email: support@brightidea.com
Estab: 1999

Matthew Greeley, CEO
Vincent Carbone, COO
David Carter, VP of Finance
Brian Wright, Director of Sales
Brian Brown, Director of Sales

Provider of innovative management software solutions. The company's products include WebStorm, Switchboard, and Pipeline modules.

**Brightsign LLC**    HQ
983-A University Ave
Los Gatos CA 95032
P: 408-852-9263    PRC:323
brightsign.biz
Email: sales@brightsign.biz
Estab: 2002

Julian Sinai, Software Engineering Manager
Lee Dydo, Senior QA Engineer
Anthony Wood, Founder
Jeff Hastings, CEO
Sarah Dryden, CFO

Provider of digital sign media players, software, and networking solutions for the commercial digital signage industry.

**Brightsource Energy Inc**    HQ
1999 Harrison St Ste 2150
Oakland CA 94612
P: 510-550-8161   F: 510-550-8165    PRC:129
www.brightsourceenergy.com
Estab: 2006

Danny Eytani, SVP of Project Engineering
David Ramm, Chairman
Eitan Abramovitch, CFO
Tom Wray, VP of Business Development
Alan Salzman, Director

Developer of solar thermal technology for electric power, petroleum, and industrial-process markets.

**Brittmore Group LLC**    HQ
749 E Brokaw Rd
San Jose CA 95112
P: 408-912-2163    PRC:209
Estab: 2010

Jeff Moore, Co-Founder
John Samuels, Head of Marketing & Business Development

Developer of solar farms. The company offers design, optimization, and fabrication services of photo-voltaic cells and panels.

**Broadcom Inc**     HQ
1320 Ridder Park Dr
San Jose CA 95131
P: 408-433-8000     PRC:61
www.broadcom.com
Estab: 1991

Hock Tan, President
Tom Krause, CFO
Charlie Kawwas, SVP
Mark Brazeal, CLO
Kirsten Spears, VP

Developer of digital and analog semiconductors.
The company also specializes in optical communication semiconductors.

**Broadway Sheet Metal & Mfg**     HQ
133 Starlite St
S San Francisco CA 94080-6313
P: 650-873-4585   F: 650-873-4582     PRC:157
www.broadwaysheetmetal.com
Email: orders@broadwaysheetmetal.com

Alex Merzel, President

Manufacturer of sheet metals. The company's
products include hoods cartridge, sinks, tables,
and mixer stands.

**Bromium Inc**     HQ
20883 Stevens Creek Blvd Ste 100
Cupertino CA 95014
P: 408-213-5668     PRC:323
www.bromium.com
Email: info@bromium.com
Estab: 2010

Ian Pratt, Co-Founder
Simon Crosby, Co-Founder
Gregory Webb, CEO
Earl Charles, CFO
Kevin Mosher, Chief Revenue Officer

Provider of enterprise security solutions. The company focuses on security software development,
technical support, and task introspection.

**Broncus Medical Inc**     HQ
125 Nicholson Ln
San Jose CA 95134
P: 650-428-1600   F: 650-428-1542     PRC:28
www.broncus.com
Email: info@broncus.com

Todd Cornell, President
Henky Wibowo, Consulting CTO
Tom Keast, VP of Product Development & Oper-
ations

Provider of navigation, diagnostic and therapeutic
technology solutions for treating patients with lung
disease.

**Brooks Automation Inc**     BR
46702 Bayside Pkwy
Fremont CA 94538
P: 510-661-5000   F: 510-661-5166     PRC:121
www.brooks.com
Email: sales@brooks.com
Estab: 1978

Samson Kuang, Electrical Engineer
Stephen Schwartz, President
Lindon Robertson, EVP
William Montone, SVP of Human Resources
Barbara Culhane, Corporate Marketing Manager

Provider of automation, vacuum, and instrumentation solutions for the semiconductor manufacturing, life sciences, and clean energy industries.

**Brown and Caldwell**     BR
75 E Santa Clara Ste 375
San Jose CA 95113
P: 408-703-2528     PRC:142
www.brownandcaldwell.com
Email: info@brwncald.com
Estab: 1947

Susy Pepper, VP
Jay Patil, SVP

Provider of engineering consulting services. The
company specializes in contracting, pumping
station design, project management, and odor
control.

**Brs Media Inc**     HQ
350 Townsend St Ste 321
San Francisco CA 94107-1696
P: 415-677-4027   F: 415-677-4025     PRC:318
brsmedia.com
Estab: 1995

George Bundy, Founder
Junaid Siddiqui, Operations & Business Development Manager

Provider of multimedia e-commerce services.
The company specializes in radio and internet
applications.

**Bryza Wind Lab Inc**     HQ
1885 Concourse Dr
San Jose CA 95131
P: 408-605-8964     PRC:235
www.bryzawindlab.com
Estab: 2011

Rachael Ishaya, President
Viral Rathod, Manager

Provider of wind tunnel testing, anemometer calibration consulting services. The company offers
electricity producing wind turbines.

**Bsk Associates**     BR
3140 Gold Camp Dr Ste 160
Rancho Cordova CA 95670
P: 916-853-9293   F: 916-853-9297     PRC:140
www.bskassociates.com
Email: olau@bskassociates.com
Emp: 11-50 Estab: 1966

Hugo Kevorkian, Principal Geotechnical Engineer
Martin Cline, Senior Engineering Geologist
Corinne Goodwin, Staff Engineer
Carrie Foulk, Senior Geotechnical Engineer
Richard Johnson, President

Provider of geotechnical and environmental testing services. The company also offers materials
testing services.

**BT Laser & Manufacturing Inc**     HQ
425 Reed St
Santa Clara CA 95050
P: 408-566-0135   F: 408-562-3999     PRC:80
btlaser.com
Estab: 1995

Kirk Rossman, Founder

Provider of custom design, laser and water jet
cutting, fabrication, and welding services for solar,
semiconductor, and communication sectors.

**Buckles-Smith**     BR
540 Martin Ave
Santa Clara CA 95050
P: 408-280-7777     PRC:245
www.buckles-smith.com
Email: info@buckles-smith.com

Kevin Slattery, Engineering Manager
Art Cook, CEO
Kevin Machi, Director of Industrial Sales
Dennis Curley, Sales Manager
Mike Collier, Sales Manager

Supplier of industrial automation equipment.
The company offers signaling devices, wires and
cables, enclosures, and fasteners.

**Bugcrowd**     HQ
921 Front St 1st Fl
San Francisco CA 94111
P: 888-361-9734     PRC:326
bugcrowd.com
Email: hello@bugcrowd.com
Estab: 2012

Daniel Trauner, Staff Engineer
Casey Ellis, Founder
Jason Pitzen, Director of Sales
Sam Houston, Senior Community Manager

Provider of security solutions. The company is
engaged in pre-launch consulting, research, and
testing services.

**Buglab LLC**     HQ
3600 Clayton Rd Ste B
Concord CA 94521
P: 925-208-1952     PRC:187
www.buglab.com
Email: info@buglab.com
Estab: 2003

John Gwynn, Manufacturing Engineer
Martin Debreczeny, Co-Founder

Developer of biomass measuring equipment
such as sensors, biomass monitor, and biomass
multiplier involved in fermentation and microbial
cultures.

**Buildera**     HQ
570 El Camino Real Ste 150 PMB 415
Redwood City CA 94063-1262
P: 650-587-6738     PRC:319
www.buildera.com
Estab: 1999

Greg Lowitz, CEO

Focuses on structural crack monitoring solutions.
The company deals with installation services and
serves the industrial sector.

**BuildingIQ Inc**     HQ
2121 S El Camino Real Ste 200
San Mateo CA 94403
P: 888-260-4080     PRC:326
www.buildingiq.com
Estab: 2009

Steve Nguyen, VP
Scott McCormick, VP

Provider of software-as-a-service solution to optimize energy use in commercial buildings such as
hospitality, healthcare facilities, and utilities.

**Bullet Guard Co**  HQ
3963 Commerce Dr
West Sacramento CA 95691
P: 916-373-0402   F: 916-373-0208   PRC:137
www.bulletguard.com
Email: sheila@bulletguardmail.com
Emp: 1-10   Estab: 1976

Karlin Lynch, President

Designer and manufacturer of bullet resistant
and bullet proof products. The company serves
the banking, government, and law enforcement
sectors.

**Bulling Metal Works Inc**  HQ
459 Hester St
San Leandro CA 94577
P: 510-351-2073   F: 510-357-5718   PRC:82
www.bullingmetalworks.com
Estab: 1977

Walter Bulling, President
James Knoll, Design & Programming Manager

Manufacturer of pressure vessels and laser
cutting machinery. The company also offers other
custom fabrication products.

**Bunchball Inc**  HQ
2200 Bridge Pkwy Ste 201
Redwood City CA 94065
P: 408-985-2034   PRC:324
www.bunchball.com
Email: salesinfo@bunchball.com
Estab: 2005

Caroline Japic, SVP of Marketing
Vivian Lin, Customer Success Manager

Provider of cloud-based software as a service
gamification products. The company's products include Nitro, Nitro for Salesforce, and Nitro for Jive.

**Bureau Veritas Laboratories**  BR
735 Industrial Rd Ste 212
San Carlos CA 94070
P: 650-576-7765   PRC:304
www.bvlabs.com

Brenda Arseneault, CFO
Hons. Sc., VP
Shawn Heier, VP
Waylon Sharp, VP
Sara Leslie, Director of Human Resources

Provider of analytical products and services. The
company services customers in the energy, environmental, food, and DNA industries.

**Burleson Consulting Inc**  HQ
950 Glenn Dr Ste 245
Folsom CA 95630
P: 916-984-4651   F: 916-984-8261   PRC:142
www.burlesonconsulting.com
Email: info@burlesonconsulting.com
Emp: 11-50 Estab: 1985

Nadia Burleson, Principal Engineer
Alex Henson, Environmental Engineer
Jacque Thompson, CFO
Allison Nunes, Greenhouse Manager
Gregory Reller, Principal Geologist

Provider of environmental compliance and
engineering services for the clients in Southern
Oregon, Northern California, and Nevada.

**Burlington Safety Laboratory Inc**  BR
7087 Commerce Cir Ste B
Pleasanton CA 94588
P: 925-251-1412   F: 925-251-9554   PRC:306
www.burlingtonsafety.com
Email: info@burlingtonsafety.com
Estab: 1971

Michael Senin, General Manager
Justin White, Regional Manager
Bill Sherwood, Laboratory Manager

Designer and manufacturer of laboratory and electrical safety equipment. The company's customers
include electric utilities and contractors.

**Burstorm Inc**  HQ
355 Hartz Ave Ste D
Danville CA 94526
P: 650-610-1480   PRC:323
www.burstorm.com
Email: info@burstorm.com
Estab: 2009

Brandon Abbey, CEO

Provider of cloud design tools application. The
company specializes in design, collaborate, quote,
and implement of cloud architecture.

**Busse Design Usa Inc**  HQ
5857 Chabot Ct
Oakland CA 94618
P: 415-689-8090   PRC:323
www.bussedesign.com
Estab: 1997

Joy Busse, CEO

Provider of interface design services. The
company's services include website design and
application user interface.

**Butterfly Sciences**  HQ
PO Box 2363
Davis CA 95617
P: 415-518-8153   PRC:24
bf-sci.com
Email: info@bf-sci.com
Emp: 1-10   Estab: 2009

Brian Hanley, Founder

Developer of gene therapies for HIV and aging.
The company also provides consulting services
for biotech investment evaluations.

**BuyerLeverage**  HQ
2225 E Bayshore Ave Ste 200
Palo Alto CA 94303
P: 650-320-1608   PRC:320
www.buyerleverage.com
Email: corp-info@buyerleverage.com

Mark Landesmann, Developer

Provider of technologies and services that allow
consumers and businesses to profit and control
their communications and information.

**Bv Thermal Systems LLC**  BR
1064 Woodland Ave Ste K
Modesto CA 95351
P: 209-522-3701   F: 209-522-3733   PRC:131
www.bvthermal.com
Emp: 11-50 Estab: 1980

Frank Abagnale, CEO

Manufacturer of recirculating chillers and heat
exchangers for laboratory, semiconductor, laser,
medical, and research industries and institutions.

**C Sys Labs Inc**  HQ
3030 Thorntree Dr Ste 6
Chico CA 95973
P: 530-894-7954   F: 530-894-7496   PRC:211
www.csyslabs.com
Emp: 1-10   Estab: 1987

Thomas Mroz, President

Designer and manufacturer of test printed circuit
boards. The company is engaged in cable fabrication and failure analysis services.

**C&C Machining Inc**  HQ
28424 Century St
Hayward CA 94545
P: 510-876-8139   F: 510-876-8913   PRC:80
candcmachininginc.com

Steve Claesson, Owner

Provider of machining services. The company
specializes in magnetic alloys, expansion alloys,
and shielding alloys.

**C&D Semiconductor Services Inc**  HQ
2031 Concourse Dr
San Jose CA 95131
P: 408-383-1888   F: 408-383-1889   PRC:126
www.cdsemi.com
Email: info@cdsemi.com
Estab: 1989

Rick Acaba, Global Sales Manager

Manufacturer of cleaner systems, wafer sorters,
and wafer inspection systems. The company deals
with inspection and processing.

**C&M Biolabs**  HQ
2600 Hilltop Dr Ste B-C147
Richmond CA 94806
P: 510-691-7166   PRC:272
cmbiolabs.com
Email: info@cmbiolabs.com
Estab: 2011

Dao-Yao He, Founder

Provider of products and services to scientists.
The company offers cloning and sequencing and
antibody services.

**C&P Microsystems LLC**  HQ
1260 Holm Rd Ste C
Petaluma CA 94954
P: 707-776-4500   F: 707-776-4555   PRC:159
microcutsystems.com
Estab: 2003

Wayne Smith, VP

Manufacturer and seller of paper cutter control
systems. The company offers microcip, cutternet,
and microfacts.

**C&S Telecommunications Inc** — HQ
3105 Fite Cir Ste 104
Sacramento CA 95827
P: 916-364-8636   F: 916-363-6280   PRC:68
www.cstelecommunications.com
Emp: 1-10   Estab: 1994

Chuck Smith, Owner

Supplier of telephone systems and data networks.
The company offers installation, training, and
other services.

**C-Scan Corp** — HQ
14125 Capri Dr Ste 8A
Los Gatos CA 95032
P: 800-953-7888   PRC:12
www.cscan.com
Email: customersupport@cscan.com
Estab: 1988

Ata Khojasteh, CEO
Karen Mattson, Sales Administrator

Manufacturer and designer of thermal recorders
and printers for medical applications and the
healthcare sector.

**C3Nano Inc** — HQ
3988 Trust Way
Hayward CA 94545
P: 510-259-9650   PRC:87
c3nano.com
Email: info@c3nano.com
Estab: 2010

Yadong Cao, Research
Vicki Luo, Process Engineer
Ajay Virkar, Co-Founder
Cliff Morris, CEO

Developer of transparent conductive ink and film
such as touch sensors, OLED lighting and displays, EMI shielding for touch sensor and display
industry.

**Ca Technologies** — BR
1353 Redwood Way
Petaluma CA 94954
P: 800-225-5224   F: 707-793-8318   PRC:323
www.ca.com
Estab: 1976

Ayman Sayed, President
Mike Gregoire, CEO
Michael Madden, General Manager
Jeff Scheaffer, SVP
Lauren Flaherty, EVP

Focuses on technology leadership and cate-
gory-leading semiconductor and infrastructure
software solutions.

**Cable Connection Inc** — HQ
1035 Mission Ct
Fremont CA 94539
P: 510-249-9000   F: 510-354-8000   PRC:211
cable-connection.com
Email: sales@cable-connection.com

William Parrette, VP
Patrick McQuade, Director
Vince Truong, Manager

Provider of premium PCB assemblies and turnkey
OEM/ODM product. The company also specializes
in cable and wire harness services.

**Cable Labs** — BR
400 W California Ave
Sunnyvale CA 94086
P: 669-777-9020   PRC:62
www.cablelabs.com

Christopher Lammers, COO
Belal Hamzeh, CTO
Rachel Beisel, CMO

Provider of cable services. The company is
engaged in virtualization and network evaluation
services.

**Cable Moore Inc** — HQ
4700 Coliseum Way
Oakland CA 94601
P: 510-436-8000   F: 510-436.8010   PRC:159
www.cablemoore.com
Estab: 1986

Tino Faaumu, Purchasing Agent

Manufacturer and distributor of safety & construction equipment and guy & bridge strands. The
company offers wire ropes, cables, railings, and
slings.

**CAD Masters Inc** — HQ
201 N Civic Dr Ste 182
Walnut Creek CA 94596
P: 925-939-1378   F: 925-939-1380   PRC:316
cadmasters.com
Estab: 1994

Evelyn Corlett, Application Engineer
Mike Self, COO
Rita Self, Account Manager
Dwayne Tindall, Account Manager
Eloise Mondfrans, Account Manager

Designer and developer of software and hardware
solutions. The company focuses on drafting, engineering, plotting, and on-site project assistance.

**CAD PROS PCB Design Inc** — HQ
PO Box 54289
San Jose CA 95154
P: 408-734-9600   PRC:124
www.cadpros.com
Estab: 1997

John Koehne, Owner

Designer and manufacturer of printed circuit
boards. The company offers services to the residential and commercial sectors.

**Cadence Design Systems Inc** — HQ
2655 Seely Ave
San Jose CA 95134
P: 408-943-1234   F: 408-428-5001   PRC:155
www.cadence.com
Estab: 1988
Sales: $1B to $3B

Noosha Nayeri, Principal Product Validation
Engineer
Anirudh Devgan, President
Lip-Bu Tan, CEO
Neil Kole, SVP
John Wall, SVP

Provider of semiconductor IP and electronic
design automation services. The company offers
tools for logic & RF design, IC packaging, and
other needs.

**Cairn Biosciences** — HQ
455 Mission Bay Blvd S
San Francisco CA 94158
P: 415-503-1185   PRC:34
www.cairnbio.com
Email: info@cairnbio.com
Estab: 2013

Mary Ludlam, Founder
Duncan Parsons-Karavassilis, VP of Finance &
Operations

Provider of therapeutic solutions for treating
cancer. The company is involved in biotechnical
research and commercial business.

**Cal Semi LLC** — HQ
175 Bernal Rd Ste 100
San Jose CA 95119
P: 510-687-9960   PRC:212
www.calsemi.com

Mark Martin, President

Provider of semiconductor equipment remanufacturing services. The company specializes in products such as furnaces, cantilever, and wet sinks.

**Cal-Tron Corp** — HQ
2290 Dixon Ln
Bishop CA 93514
P: 760-873-8491   F: 760-873-8431   PRC:84
www.caltroncorp.com
Email: info@caltroncorp.com
Emp: 1-10   Estab: 1939

Scott Lasley, Operations Supervisor

Developer and manufacturer of cell reagent tools.
The company's products find application in pro-
teomic research.

**Cal-West Specialty Coatings Inc** — HQ
1058 W Evelyn Ave
Sunnyvale CA 94086
P: 408-720-7440   F: 408-720-7450   PRC:47
www.cal-west.net
Email: info@cal-west.net
Estab: 1988

Brian Wong, VP

Supplier of liquid masking and surface preparation
products. The company also offers temporary
protective coatings.

**Cala Health Inc** — HQ
875 Mahler Rd Ste 168
Burlingame CA 94010
P: 415-890-3961   PRC:196
www.calahealth.com
Email: info@calahealth.com

Kate Rosenbluth, Founder
Renee Ryan, CEO
Scott Wilson, VP of Quality Assurance & Regula-
tory Affairs
Kristie Burns, CMO
Manish Gupta, VP of Clinical & Regulatory Affairs

Provider of therapeutic solutions. The company
focusses on the development of neuroperipheral
therapy to treating chronic diseases.

**Calabazas Creek Research Inc** HQ
690 Port Dr
San Mateo CA 94404-1010
P: 650-312-9575   F: 650-312-9536   PRC:2
calcreek.com
Email: rlives@calcreek.com
Estab: 1994

Julie Givens, CFO
George Collins, Operations Manager

Specializes in the research and development of high power RF sources, and components. The company offers software development services.

**Calchemist** HQ
220 South Linden Ave Ste L
South San Francisco CA 94080
P: 650-551-1495   F: 650-551-1495   PRC:80
www.calchemist.com
Estab: 2007

Marc Schrier, Owner

Provider of contract research services. The company specializes in chemical, material science and laboratory equipment testing.

**Calcoast-Itl** HQ
683 Thornton St
San Leandro CA 94577
P: 510-924-7100   F: 510-878-9251   PRC:306
www.calcoast-itl.com
Email: sales@calcoast-itl.com
Estab: 1949

Mark Evans, Laboratory Director

Provider of testing services for automotive and roadway lightings. The company offers consultation, assistance, and laboratory installation services.

**Calcon Systems Inc** HQ
12919 Alcosta Blvd Ste 9
San Ramon CA 94583
P: 925-277-0665   F: 925-277-9647   PRC:228
www.calconsystems.com
Email: sales@calcon.com
Estab: 1987

Shawn Ferron, Project Engineer
Sean Ferguson, System Engineer
Pete Schratz, President
Ryan Smith, General Manager
Frank Ortega, Manager

Provider of process control, instrumentation, and automation solutions specializing in turnkey design-build system integration and support.

**Calcula Technologies** HQ
959 Peralta Ave
San Francisco CA 94110
P: 650-724-8696   PRC:189
www.calculatech.com
Estab: 2012

Buzz Bonneau, CEO

Developer of medical devices for the treatment of kidney stones. The company serves the healthcare sector.

**Calex Manufacturing Company Inc** HQ
2401 Stanwell Dr
Concord CA 94520-4841
P: 925-687-4411   F: 925-687-3333   PRC:209
www.calex.com
Email: sales@calex.com
Estab: 1962

Steve Cuff, Founder
Loren Goble, Manufacturing Manager
Susan Benker, Quality Assurance Manager
Robert Zorovic, Senior Buyer

Supplier of electrical instrument modules. The company also specializes in power supplies and converters.

**California Brazing & Nevada Heat Treating** HQ
37955 Central Ct
Newark CA 94560
P: 510-790-2300   F: 510-791-9300   PRC:159
www.californiabrazing.com
Email: info@californiabrazing.com

Jeff Ager, General Manager

Provider of brazing services. The company specializes in machining and heat treatment of components for the aviation industry.

**California Clinical Laboratory Association** HQ
1127 11th St Ste 820
Sacramento CA 95814
P: 916-446-2646   F: 916-446-6095   PRC:191
www.ccla.info
Emp: 1-10   Estab: 1976

Christine Sabol, President
Julie Ramage, President
Michael Arnold, Legislative Advocate
Traci Hundley, Executive Legislative Secretary
Kristian Foy, Legislative Advocate

Provider of an Association for small and large laboratories in California. The company files suits to prevent medicare from denying coverage for lab tests.

**California Contract Company** HQ
1900 Seventh St Unit D
Richmond CA 94801
P: 510-654-9375   F: 510-631-4669   PRC:82
californiacontractco.com
Email: railings@prodigy.net
Estab: 1973

Micheal Stang, Owner

Provider of metal fabrication and installation services. The company focuses on aluminum, stainless steel and glass, and bronze.

**California Eastern Laboratories** HQ
4590 Patrick Henry Dr
Santa Clara CA 95054-1817
P: 408-919-2500   F: 408-988-0279   PRC:61
www.cel.com
Estab: 1959

Gretchen King, Director of Human Resources
Sam Yacoub, Senior Product Marketing Manager
Mouqun Dong, QA Manager

Provider of RF, microwave, and optoelectronic semiconductors. The company also offers lasers, detectors, and other products.

**California Environmental Associates** HQ
423 Washington St Fourth Fl
San Francisco CA 94111
P: 415-421-4213   F: 866-496-7098   PRC:139
www.ceaconsulting.com
Estab: 1984

Kirk Marckwald, Founder
Kelly Solari, CFO
Laura Viggiano, Director
Max Levine, Director
Mark Michelin, Director

Provider of environmental consulting services. The company's services include recruiting and organizational design services.

**California Integration Coordinators Inc** HQ
6048 Enterprise Dr
Diamond Springs CA 95667
P: 530-626-6168   F: 530-626-7740   PRC:211
www.cic-inc.com
Email: customerservice@cic-inc.com
Emp: 1-10   Estab: 1988

Cherie Snyder-Myers, President
William Yu, Director
Debby Verry, Lab Manager
Harry Rehder, Project Coordinator
Justin Cary, Project Coordinator

Manufacturer of custom turnkey printed circuit boards. The company's services include repairs, component sourcing, fabrication, and assembly.

**California Laboratory Services** HQ
3249 Fitzgerald Rd
Rancho Cordova CA 95742
P: 800-638-7301   PRC:306
www.californialab.com
Emp: 1-10

Scott Furnas, President
Janet Massingill, Quality Control Chemist
Zhonqwen Liang, Laboratory Director
Mark Smith, Operations Manager
Janelle Sutphen, Project Manager

Provider of analytical testing services. The company offers a comprehensive range of soil and water testing for government and private agencies.

**California Motor Controls Inc** HQ
3070 Bay Vista Ct
Benicia CA 94510
P: 707-746-6255   F: 707-746-6165   PRC:228
www.cmcontrols.com
Email: sales@cmcontrols.com
Estab: 2004

Jarrod Slate, Manager

Manufacturer of electrical control panels. The company offers pump controls and communication systems for municipal and commercial applications.

**California Seed & Plant Lab** HQ
3556 Sankey Rd
Pleasant Grove CA 95668
P: 916-655-1581   F: 916-655-1582   PRC:34
calspl.com
Emp: 1-10   Estab: 1992

Sukhi Pannu, Director of Research & Business Development
Ashlee Bednorski, Testing Coordinator

Provider of pathological and genetic testing services. The company provides services for the vegetable seed, grapevine, and strawberry industries.

**California Software Systems** HQ
1791 San Juan Canyon Rd
San Juan Bautista CA 95045
P: 831-477-6843   F: 831-265-4553   PRC:322
californiasoftwaresystems.com
Email: sales@californiasoftwaresystems.com
Emp: 1-10

Russell Walton, Founder

Provider of graphics software solutions. The company products include DNC file server for windows and graphics software.

**California Solar Systems** BR
2780 N Miami Ave Ste 102
Fresno CA 93727
P: 855-227-6527   PRC:135
www.855casolar.com
Email: info@855casolar.com
Emp: 11-50

Barry Wardak, President
Ryan Lien, Regional Sales Manager
Derek Patterson, Marketing Manager
Nancy McLaughlin, Marketing Manager
Patti Pueschel, Operations Manager

Provider of grid-tied turn key solar electric systems. The company caters to both residential and commercial sectors.

**Calithera Biosciences Inc** HQ
343 Oyster Point Blvd Ste 200
S San Francisco CA 94080
P: 650-870-1000   PRC:191
www.calithera.com
Estab: 2010

Susan Molineaux, President
Curtis Hecht, Chief Business Officer
Keith Orford, Chief Medical Officer
Sumita Ray, SVP
Stephanie Wong, SVP of Finance and Secretary

Developer of small molecule drugs directed against tumor metabolism and tumor immunology targets for the treatment of cancer.

**Calix Inc** HQ
1035 N McDowell Blvd
Petaluma CA 94954
P: 707-766-3000   F: 707-283-3100   PRC:68
www.calix.com
Email: info@calix.com
Estab: 1999
Sales: $300M to $1 Billion

Carl Russo, CEO
Cory Sindelar, CFO
Michel Langlois, Chief Development Officer
Jill Von Berg, Information Technology
Michael Weening, EVP of Sales & Marketing

Provider of broadband communications access systems and software. The company offers business, fiber access, and mobile backhaul solutions.

**Callidus Software Inc** HQ
6200 Stoneridge Mall Rd Ste 500
Pleasanton CA 94588
P: 925-251-2200   F: 925-251-0525   PRC:322
www.calliduscloud.com
Email: info@callidussoftware.com
Estab: 1996
Sales: Over $3B

Steve Cheang, Senior Architect

Provider of sales performance management software. The company also offers incentive compensation management software and services.

**Callouette Fabricators Inc** HQ
320 W Channel Rd Unit E
Benicia CA 94510
P: 707-746-0962   F: 707-746-6429   PRC:80
callouettefabricators.com

Barry Callouette, President

Developer of machining components for automotive, process control, biotech, plasma, instrumentation, and aviation industries.

**Calmar Laser** HQ
951 Commercial St
Palo Alto CA 94303
P: 650-272-6980   F: 650-272-6988   PRC:170
www.calmarlaser.com
Email: contacts@calmarlaser.com
Estab: 1996

Kai You, Electronic Engineer
Shenghong Huang, Senior Optical Engineer
William Shao, Operations Manager

Manufacturer of ultrafast fiber laser and fiber amplifier solutions for the needs of industry, research institutions, and universities.

**Calmax Technology Inc** HQ
526 Laurelwood Rd
Santa Clara CA 95054
P: 408-748-8660   F: 408-513-1025   PRC:80
www.calmaxtechnology.com
Email: customerservice@calmaxtechnology.com
Estab: 1987

Scott Shimada, Director of Operations
Gary Keppers, Account Manager
Linda Walters, Manager Finance & Administration
Manny Adame, Business Development Manager

Provider of precision machined components and electro-mechanical assemblies. The company serves semi-conductor and medical industries.

**Calogic LLC** HQ
237 Whitney Pl
Fremont CA 94539
P: 510-656-2900   F: 510-651-1076   PRC:82
www.calogic.net
Estab: 2001

Wayne Tallant, Equipment Engineer Supervisor
Jonathan Kaye, President
Mark Sylva, Director of Sales and Operations
Kathryn Kaye, VP
Eric Prinz, Test

Designer and manufacturer of integrated circuits. The company caters to computer, telecom, and medical applications.

**Calsoft Inc** HQ
1762 Technology Dr Ste 229
San Jose CA 95110-1385
P: 408-834-7086   PRC:323
www.calsoftinc.com
Email: marcom@calsoftinc.com
Estab: 1998

Anupam Bhide, CEO
Bo Shao, VP

Designer and developer of storage, networking, and operating systems. The company deals with design, delivery, and installation.

**Caltest Analytical Lab** HQ
1885 N Kelly Rd
Napa CA 94558
P: 707-258-4000   F: 707-226-1001   PRC:306
www.caltestlabs.com
Estab: 1974

Todd Albertson, VP
Shawna Rees, Director of Technology
Sonya Allahyari, Project Manager
Mike Hamilton, Project Manager
Tiffiny Smith, Analyst

Provider of analyses services of wastewater, groundwater, non-radioactive water, and hazardous waste samples.

**Caltron Components Corp** HQ
3350 Scott Blvd Bldg 31
Santa Clara CA 95054
P: 408-748-2140   PRC:84
www.caltroncomponents.com
Email: sales@caltroncomponents.com
Estab: 1964

Brian Maguire, Director of Engineering
Kevin Kilpatrick, Sales Engineer
Bob Roumimper, President
Sue Mihalus, Inside Sales Manager
Kristy Reyes, Inside Sales

Distributor of electronic capacitors and resistors. The company also focuses on semiconductor products.

**Caltron Industries Inc** HQ
4120 Clipper Ct
Fremont CA 94538
P: 510-440-1800   PRC:110
www.caltronind.com
Estab: 1997

Jim Wang, General Manager
Andrew Leung, Account Executive

Manufacturer of digital signage products and touch screen monitors. The company specializes in digital video signage and media advertising services.

**Calypso Systems Inc** HQ
2255 O'Toole Ave Ste 60
San Jose CA 95131
P: 408-982-9955   PRC:15
www.calypsotesters.com
Email: info@calypsotesters.com
Estab: 1991

Eden Kim, CEO

Developer of solid state storage test and measurement. The company specializes in test results automatically stored in the CTS MySQL database.

**Calypso Technology Inc** HQ
595 Market St Ste 1800
San Francisco CA 94105
P: 415-530-4000  F: 415-284-1222  PRC:323
www.calypso.com
Estab: 1997

Richard Bentley, Chief Product and Engineering
Officer
Suhas Daivajna, Principal Software Engineer
Didier Bouillard, CEO
Laurent Jacquemin, Chief Customer Officer
Jonathan Walsh, CAO

Provider of front-to-back technology solutions
for the financial markets. The company offers
technology platform for cross asset trading risk
management.

**Calysta** HQ
1140 O'Brien Dr
Menlo Park CA 94025
P: 650-492-6880  PRC:268
www.calysta.com
Email: info@calysta.com
Estab: 2011

Alan Shaw, President
Lynsey Wenger, CFO
Tomas Belloso, VP of Regulatory Affairs
Blake Campbell, VP of Administration
Dennis Leong, VP of Business Development

Focuses on the development and manufacture of
protein for commercial aquaculture and livestock
feed.

**Calyx Technology Inc** HQ
6475 Camden Ave Ste 207
San Jose CA 95120
P: 408-997-5525  F: 214-252-5650  PRC:320
www.calyxsoftware.com
Email: sales@calyxsoftware.com
Estab: 1991

Gang Qin, SW Engineer
Doug Chang, President
Javier Mendez, Quality Assurance Technician
Max Youm, Director of Systems & QA Group
Mitra Eslami, Director of Program

Provider of mortgage solutions for banks and
credit unions. The company also serves mortgage
bankers and brokers.

**Cambrios Technologies Corp** HQ
930 E Arques Ave
Sunnyvale CA 94085
P: 408-738-7400  PRC:47
www.cambrios.com
Email: pr@cambrios.com
Estab: 2002

Debbie Finney, Materials Engineer
CC Hsiao Ph.D, President
Michael Spaid Ph.D, CTO
Pierre-Marc Allemand, Chemistry Manager

Manufacturer of electronic materials for the display
industry. The company mainly provides ClearOhm
films.

**Campbell/Harris Security Equipment
Company** HQ
875-A Island Dr Ste 356
Alameda CA 94502-6768
P: 510-864-8010  F: 510-864-8013  PRC:58
www.cseco.com
Email: info@cseco.com
Estab: 1984

Tony Harris, President

Manufacturer of busters, fiberscopes, probe kits,
and personal radiation detectors. The company
also focuses on distribution.

**Canary Instruments** HQ
1385 Eighth St Ste 205
Arcata CA 95521
P: 707-506-6611  PRC:131
www.canaryinstruments.com
Email: info@canaryinstruments.com
Emp: 1-10  Estab: 2013

Kimberli Hudson, CEO
Lonny Grafman, CPO
Gabriel Krause, CTO

Provider of home energy monitor with colorful
LED lights that provide instant feedback on the
electricity use.

**Cannon Water Technology Inc** HQ
233 Technology Way Ste 9
Rocklin CA 95765
P: 916-315-2691  PRC:50
cannonwater.com
Email: csd@cannonwater.com
Emp: 11-50  Estab: 1985

Richard Cannon, Owner
Paula Gallegos, Inside Sales Manager
David Cannon, Sales Manager
Janis Cannon, VP

Manufacturer of chemical pumps, water treatment
chemicals, and water treatment equipment. The
company offers services to the industrial sector.

**Cantabio Pharmaceuticals Inc** HQ
2225 E Bayshore Rd
Palo Alto CA 94303
P: 844-200-2826  PRC:34
www.cantabio.com
Email: info@cantabio.com
Estab: 2009

Gergely Toth, CEO
Simon Peace, CFO
Thomas Sawyer, CFO

Provider of therapeutic solutions. The company
specializes in developing therapeutic proteins to
prevent degenerative brain diseases.

**Cantaloupe Systems Inc** HQ
612 Howard St Ste 600
San Francisco CA 94105
P: 415-525-8100  F: 415-680-2368  PRC:325
www.cantaloupesys.com
Email: info@cantaloupesys.com
Estab: 2002

Tammy Baker, VP of Engineering
Anant Agrawal, CRO
Mandeep Arora, Co-Founder
Foster Geng, CFO
Elyssa Allahyar-Steiner, Director of Marketing

Developer of SQL based encryption solutions
for wireless vending services. The company
also focuses on dynamic scheduling and remote
monitoring.

**Capcom Usa** LH
185 Berry St Ste 1200
San Francisco CA 94107
P: 650-350-6500  PRC:317
www.capcom.com
Email: privacy@capcom.com
Estab: 1985

Kazuhiko Abe, President
Kiichiro Urata, CEO
Ikuo Hirano, Director of Corporate Planning

Manufacturer and distributor of electronic game
machines. The company specializes in resident
evil, monster hunter, lost planet, and devroom
games.

**Capella Microsystems Inc** HQ
2201 Laurelwood Rd
Santa Clara CA 95054
P: 408-988-8000  F: 408-969-0894  PRC:87
www.capellamicro.com.tw
Email: mycapella@vishay.com
Estab: 2002

Jim Kung, VP of Sales
Peter Henrici, SVP of Corporate Communications

Developer of integrated technology solutions for
IC design. The company is involved in installation
and technical support.

**Capital Asset Exchange & Trading
LLC** HQ
5201 Great America Pkwy Ste 272
Santa Clara CA 95054
P: 650-326-3313  PRC:86
www.caeonline.com
Email: info@caeonline.com
Estab: 1982

Jeff Robbins, President
Ryan Jacob, CEO
Andrew Hung, Associate Director
Ricky Vij, Director

Provider of secondary capital equipment. The
company offers evaporators, spectometers,
residual gas analyzers, and electronic testing
equipment.

**Capital Engineering Consultants Inc** HQ
11020 Sun Center Dr Ste 100
Rancho Cordova CA 95670
P: 916-851-3500  F: 916-631-4424  PRC:142
www.capital-engineering.com
Email: office@capital-engineering.com
Emp: 11-50  Estab: 1947

Emil Balceta, Engineer
John Say, Mechanical Engineer
Matthew Hamilton, Engineer
Joseph Carbonel, Senior Engineer
Lowell Shields, CEO

Provider of mechanical engineering, sustainable
design and green engineering, building commissioning, energy modeling, and other related
services.

**Capital Machine Corporation**  HQ
83 N 17th St
Sacramento CA 95814
P: 916-443-6671  F: 916-443-6675  PRC:290
www.capmachine.com
Emp: 1-10  Estab: 1936

John Collier, President
Eugene Spyksma, VP

Provider of machining, welding, fabrication, and
design services. The company also distributes
steel & power transmission products.

**Capital Network Solutions Inc**  HQ
8950 Cal Center Dr Ste 341
Sacramento CA 95826
P: 916-366-6566  PRC:326
www.cns-service.com
Email: help@cns-service.com
Emp: 1-10  Estab: 1989

Thom Scott, Service Engineer I
Don Thompson, CEO
John Guarienti, VP of Sales
Shareef Huddle, Senior Systems Architect

Provider of internet security systems, phone systems, and off-site encrypted backup for small and
medium sized businesses.

**Capital Sheet Metal**  HQ
500 N 16th St
Sacramento CA 95811
P: 916-443-3761  F: 916-443-3610  PRC:80
www.capitalsheetmetal.net
Email: info@capitalsheetmetal.net
Emp: 1-10  Estab: 1945

Ken Hammill, President
Scott Johnson, Project Manager
Marcus Pantoja, Estimator
Justin Shaffer, Estimator

Manufacturer of custom countertops. The company deals with shearing, welding, laser cutting, and
polishing services.

**Capitol Communications Inc**  HQ
480 Ninth St
San Francisco CA 94103
P: 415-861-1727  PRC:63
Estab: 1994

Ronald Burgess, President
Freddie Little, Project Manager

Provider of infrastructure communication solutions
for business operations. The company caters to
electronics, media, and manufacturing industries.

**Capitol Digital Document Solutions**  HQ
555 Capitol Mall Ste 235
Sacramento CA 95814
P: 916-449-2820  F: 916-449-2821  PRC:322
www.capitol-digital.com
Emp: 1-10  Estab: 1997

Tristan Hopkins, President
Karl Rozak, Production Manager
Thon Kong, Production Manager
Vang Lor, Production Coordinator
Sandi Scott, Executive Business Manager

Provider of litigation support services. The company offers forensic data collection, online document
review, and e-discovery processing services.

**Capnia**  HQ
1235 Radio Rd Ste 110
Redwood City CA 94065
P: 650-213-8444  F: 650-213-8383  PRC:186
www.capnia.com
Email: info@capnia.com

David O'Toole, CFO
Tony Wondka, SVP

Focuses on the development and commercialization of therapeutic and diagnostic products to
address significant unmet healthcare needs.

**Capriza Inc**  HQ
3000 El Camino Real Ste 5-800
Palo Alto CA 94306
P: 650-600-3661  PRC:326
www.capriza.com
Email: support@capriza.com
Estab: 2011

Oren Ariel, Co-Founder
Yuval Scarlat, Chairman

Provider of codeless enterprise mobility platform.
The company offers mobile-enabling business
applications such as design, zaaps, manage, and
security.

**CapsoVision**  HQ
18805 Cox Ave Ste 250
Saratoga CA 95070-6615
P: 408-624-1488  F: 408-370-4795  PRC:186
www.capsovision.com
Email: info@capsovision.com
Estab: 2006

Srini Muthuswamy, Manager
Susan Smith, Senior Marketing Manager

Specializes in the diagnostic imaging of the gastrointestinal systems. The company offers services
to hospitals and patients.

**Carando Technologies Inc**  HQ
345 N Harrison St
Stockton CA 95203
P: 209-948-6500  F: 209-948-6757  PRC:159
carando.net
Email: sales@carando.net
Emp: 1-10  Estab: 2003

Shannon Crawford, Office Manager

Manufacturer of container closing tools and dies.
The company fabricates drums, water heater
tanks, sapre parts, appliances, and container
closing tools.

**Carbon Five Inc**  HQ
585 Howard St Fl 2
San Francisco CA 94105
P: 415-546-0500  PRC:323
www.carbonfive.com
Email: info@carbonfive.com
Estab: 2000

Christian Nelson, Partner
Clark Cutler, Software Engineer
Jon Rogers, Senior Engineer
Don Thompson, Co-Owner
David Hendee, Partner

Provider of software development services such
as lean design and agile development for the web
and mobile sectors.

**Carbon3d Inc**  HQ
1089 Mills Way
Redwood City CA 94063
P: 650-285-6307  PRC:275
carbon3d.com
Email: info@carbon3d.com
Estab: 2013

Craig Carlson, VP of Engineering
Dave Scheinman, Hardware Engineer
Brenda Cucci, Electrical Engineer
Hardik Kabaria, Software Engineer
Joseph DeSimone, CEO

Provider of hardware and software engineering
and molecular science. The company specializes
in continuous liquid interface production technology.

**Cardinal Health**  HQ
5452 Betsy Ross Dr
Santa Clara CA 95054
P: 408-610-6500  F: 408-610-6701  PRC:187
www.accessclosure.com
Estab: 2002

Scott Barnhart, President of Global Manufacturing
and Supply Chain
Joseph DePinto, President
Patrick Holt, President
Tiffany Olson, President of Nuclear & Precision
Health Solutions
Robert Rajalingam, President

Provider of solutions in the cardiovascular and peripheral vascular markets. The company provides
advanced vascular closure devices for patients.

**Cardiodx Inc**  HQ
600 Saginaw Dr
Redwood City CA 94063
P: 650-475-2788  F: 650-475-2799  PRC:191
www.cardiodx.com
Email: info@cardiodx.com
Estab: 2004

David Levison, CEO
Mark Monane, Chief Medical Officer

Provider of corus cad blood test to assess ob-
structive cad. The company specializes in cardiovascular genomics and developing validated tests.

**Cardiva Medical Inc**  HQ
1615 Wyatt Drive
Santa Clara CA 95054
P: 408-470-7170  F: 408-470-7134  PRC:189
www.cardivamedical.com
Email: customerservice@cardivamedical.com
Estab: 2002

Jennifer Lee, Engineering Manager
John Russell, President
Lisa Garrett, CFO
Justin Ballotta, COO
Zia Yassinzadeh, CTO

Developer of vascular access management
products such as vascade and catalyst to facilitate
rapid hemostasis following diagnostic procedures.

**Caredx Inc** HQ
3260 Bayshore Blvd
Brisbane CA 94005
P: 415-287-2300  F: 415-287-2450  PRC:34
www.caredx.com
Email: customercare@caredx.com
Estab: 2000
Sales: $30M to $100M

Reginald Seeto, President
Peter Maag, CEO
Michael Bell, CFO
John Sninsky, CSO
Theresa Yu, Director of Finance

Provider of genomics technologies for the development of molecular diagnostic assays. The company specializes in molecular diagnostics.

**Carefree Computing Inc** HQ
268 Bush St Ste 3945
San Francisco CA 94104
P: 866-377-6275  F: 415-651-1905  PRC:67
www.carefreecomputing.com
Email: info@carefreecomputing.com
Estab: 1993

David Arrants, Owner

Provider of web hosting, software design, programming, technical support, and network design services.

**Caribou Biosciences Inc** HQ
2929 Seventh St Ste 105
Berkeley CA 94710
P: 510-982-6030  PRC:34
cariboubio.com
Email: info@cariboubio.com
Estab: 2011

Rachel Haurwitz, President
J.D Barbara McClung, Chief Legal Officer
Steven Kanner, CSO

Developer of cellular engineering and analysis solutions. The company is involved in applied biological research.

**Carlson Wireless Technologies Inc** HQ
3134 Jacobs Ave Suite C
Eureka CA 95501
P: 707-443-0100  F: 707-822-7010  PRC:61
www.carlsonwireless.com
Email: sales@carlsonwireless.com
Emp: 11-50 Estab: 1999

Robert Escher, Sales Engineer
Jim Carlson, Founder
James Carlson, CEO
John Zott, CFO
Sebastien Amiot, CTO

Manufacturer of wireless communication products. The company also provides broadband and related services.

**Carmot Therapeutics Inc** BR
409 Illinois St
San Francisco CA 94158
P: 510-828-0102  PRC:268
carmot-therapeutics.us
Email: info@carmot.us
Estab: 2008

Stig Hansen, Co-Founder
Roman Dvorak, VP of Clinical Development

Provider of drug discovery to address unmet chemical needs for the treatment of oncology, inflammation, and metabolic disease.

**Carroll Engineering Inc** HQ
1101 S Winchester Blvd Ste H 184
San Jose CA 95128-3903
P: 408-261-9800  PRC:304
www.carroll-engineering.com

Kim Murray, Engineer
Drew Spencer, Assistant Engineer
Milan KC, Assistant Engineer
Bryce Carroll, Founder
Robert Henry, President

Provider of civil engineering and surveying services focusing on boundary and topographic surveys, civil engineering design, and construction support.

**Carter Contact Lens Inc** HQ
105 W Dakota Ave Ste 109
Clovis CA 93612
P: 559-294-7063  F: 559-294-8851  PRC:173
cartercl.com
Emp: 1-10 Estab: 1997

Bill Carter, Founder
John Carter, Co-Founder

Manufacturer of contact lenses. The company product range include crescent bifocal, target bifocal, front bifocal, and keratoconic designs.

**Casahl Technology Inc** HQ
2400 Camino Ramon Bldg K Ste 355
San Ramon CA 94583
P: 925-328-2828  F: 925-328-1188  PRC:326
www.casahl.com
Email: info@casahl.com
Estab: 1993

Wesley Wong, VP of Engineering
Karim Senussi, Technical Sales Support Engineer

Provider of collaboration and content environment optimization services. The company focuses on cloud integration and content management.

**Cascadia Labs** HQ
1140 Bel Arbres Rd
Redwood Valley CA 95470
P: 855-800-6890  PRC:34
www.cascadia-labs.com
Emp: 1-10  Estab: 2011

Jeremy Sackett, Co-Founder

Provider of analytical services. The company specializes in analytical, pharmaceutical, horticulture, and food science.

**Casella Lighting** HQ
10183 Croydon Way Ste C
Sacramento CA 95827
P: 888-252-7874  PRC:243
www.casellalighting.com
Email: info@casellalighting.com
Emp: 1-10  Estab: 1930

Chuck Bird, Manager
Darrell Currie, Fabricator

Retailer of lamps and chandeliers. The company also sells floor lamps, wall lamps, picture lights, and ceiling fixtures.

**Casetrakker** HQ
990 Reserve Dr Ste 200
Roseville CA 95678
P: 916-757-1444  F: 916-781-0168  PRC:323
www.casetrakker.com
Email: sales@casetrakker.com
Emp: 1-10  Estab: 1989

Melissa Ruddick, Business Systems Analyst
Joseph Donovan, Business Systems Analyst

Developer of Windows-based case management software. The company is engaged in programming and hosting solutions.

**Casetronic Engineering Group** HQ
1126 Yosemite Dr
Milpitas CA 95035
P: 408-262-8588  PRC:79
www.casetronic.com
Email: sales@casetronic.com
Estab: 2000

Ed Huang, VP
Stella Zhou, Accountant

Designer and manufacturer of electronic enclosures, DC converters, AC adapters, flash readers, and IPC rack mount solutions.

**Caseware International Inc** DH
2425B Channing Way Ste 590
Berkeley CA 94704
P: 416-867-9504  F: 416-867-1906  PRC:319
www.caseware.com
Email: info@caseware.com
Estab: 1998

Dwight Wainman, CEO

Supplier of software solutions to accountants and auditors worldwide. The company offers working papers to accounting firms.

**Caspio** HQ
2953 Bunker Hill Ln Ste 201
Santa Clara CA 95054
P: 650-691-0900  PRC:315
www.caspio.com
Estab: 2000

Ioannis Kritikopoulos, VP of Engineering
Frank Zamani, Founder
Napoleon Valdez, Director of Sales
Brian Metzger, VP of Global Marketing
Valaine Anderson, Director of Product Marketing

Builds online database applications without coding.

**Castagnolo Dental Laboratory Inc** HQ
10055 Miller Ave Ste 102
Cupertino CA 95014
P: 408-446-1466  F: 408-446-9571  PRC:302
www.castagnolo-lab.com
Estab: 1977

David Castagnolo, President

Provider of custom packed columns, empty synthesis columns, empty synthesis plates, and related supports.

**Castle Rock Computing Inc**    HQ
12930 Saratoga Ave
Saratoga CA 95070
P: 408-366-6540    PRC:322
www.castlerock.com
Email: sales@castlerock.com
Estab: 1987

John Maytum, VP of Sales

Designer and manufacturer of SNMPC network management software. The company's product caters to a wide range of sectors.

**Catalia Health Inc**    HQ
629A Bryant
San Francisco CA 94107
P: 415-660-9264    PRC:194
www.cataliahealth.com
Email: info@cataliahealth.com

Cory Kidd, Founder
Gary Arnold, CTO

Provider of medical solutions for pharmaceuticals, healthcare systems, and home care. The company specializes in robotic aides for an aging population.

**Catalyst Biosciences**    HQ
611 Gateway Blvd Ste 710
S San Francisco CA 94080
P: 650-871-0761    PRC:34
www.catalystbiosciences.com
Email: info@catbio.com
Estab: 2002
Sales: Under $1 Million

Nassim Usman, President
Daniel Tsai, Scientist I

Developer of catalytic biopharmaceutical products based on engineering human proteases for hemostasis, age-related macular degeneration, and inflammation.

**Catalyst Business Solutions**    HQ
6203 San Ignacio Ave Ste 100
San Jose CA 95119
P: 408-281-7100    F: 408-281-7101    PRC:323
www.catalyst-us.com
Estab: 2002

Amol Awasthi, Co-Founder
Anupam Awasthi, Co-Founder
Jay Kalra, EVP of Technology

Provider of technology consulting services in business applications, data center, and machine-to-machine/internet of things.

**Catalyst Environmental Inc**    HQ
170 Glenn Way Ste 7
San Carlos CA 94070
P: 650-642-6583    F: 650-622-9881    PRC:142
www.catenv.com
Email: info@catenv.com

Ray Villanueva, Project Manager
Joseph Berkshire, Principal
Kurt Soto-Gambini, Principal

Provider of environmental services. The company's services comprise tank cleaning and hydro blasting services and soil and groundwater sampling.

**Cavendish Kinetics Inc**    HQ
2960 N First St
San Jose CA 95134
P: 408-457-1940    PRC:86
www.cavendish-kinetics.com
Email: info@cavendish-kinetics.com
Estab: 1994

Richard Knipe, VP of Engineering
Paul Santo, President
Luis Arzubi, Chairman
Patrick Murray, CFO
Dan Smith, CMO

Supplier of tunable components for RF circuit applications. The company offers antennas, power amps, filters, and other products.

**Cavium Inc**    HQ
2315 N First St
San Jose CA 95131
P: 408-943-7100    F: 408-577-1992    PRC:212
www.cavium.com
Email: info@cavium.com

Ananth Jasty, Senior Software Engineer
Anup Ramesh, Senior Engineer
Chad Reese, Senior Staff Engineer
Srikanth Pidugu, Senior Systems Applications Engineer
Syed Ali, President

Manufacturer of hardware components. The company products include processors, switches, and adapters, wireless displays and security software.

**Ccintegration Inc**    HQ
2060 Corporate Ct
San Jose CA 95131
P: 408-228-1314    F: 408-228-1315    PRC:325
www.ccintegration.com
Email: sales@ccintegration.com
Estab: 1985

Kevin Schoonover, VP of Engineering
Hank Ta, Founder
Anna Hung, CEO
Kelly Styskal, CFO
Keith Wood, VP of Sales & Marketing

Provider of business engagement models such as OEM and virtual OEM. The company services include design, integration, and logistics.

**Ccs Associates Inc**    HQ
2001 Gateway Pl Ste 350W
Mountain View CA 95110
P: 650-691-4400    F: 650-691-4410    PRC:268
www.ccsainc.com
Email: info@ccsainc.com
Estab: 1985

Caroline Sigman, President
Daniel Milgram, Chief of Technology and Bioinformatics
Linda Doody, Executive Director
Beverly Smolich, Senior Director of Clinical Research and Regulatory Affairs
Meena Navidi, Senior Director of Preclinical Research and Development Projects

Provider of scientific services in product discovery and development for government agencies, pharmaceutical, and biotech industries.

**CCS Inc**    HQ
400 China Rose Ct
Lincoln CA 95648
P: 949-855-9020    PRC:323
ideaweb.com
Emp: 1-10    Estab: 1970

Rudy Camacho, President
Michael O'Brien, CEO
Casey O'Brien, CTO
Jean-Pierre Jardin, VP of Marketing

Provider of business accounting software solutions. The company is also engaged in web integration and custom software development.

**Cdnetworks Inc**    RH
1919 S Bascom Ave Ste 600
Campbell CA 95008-2220
P: 408-228-3700    F: 408-228-3701    PRC:323
www.cdnetworks.com
Email: info@cdnetworks.com
Estab: 2000

Kyle Lee, Service Delivery Engineer
Max Kim, Senior Network Engineer

Developer of web and network acceleration solutions. The company serves the travel, tourism, gaming, and technology industries.

**Cedaron Medical Inc**    HQ
PO Box 2100
Davis CA 95617
P: 800-424-1007    F: 530-759-1699    PRC:194
www.cedaron.com
Email: cedaron@cedaron.com
Emp: 1-10    Estab: 1990

Vikram Singh, Software Engineer
Malcolm Bond, Chief Scientist and Founder
Loran Kelley, Customer Support Manager
Susan Fletcher, Controller

Provider of entrepreneurial, medical, technological, marketing, and documentation software solutions for healthcare providers.

**Ceecon Testing Inc**    HQ
434 N Canal St Ste 6
S San Francisco CA 94080
P: 650-827-7474    F: 650-827-7476    PRC:129
www.ceecon.com
Email: info@ceecon.com

Michael Hodges, Chief Adventure Officer

Provider of soil and groundwater remediation services. The company services also include regulatory compliance and remediation equipment.

**Celadon Inc**    HQ
58 Paul Dr Ste D
San Rafael CA 94903
P: 415-472-1177    F: 415-472-1179    PRC:61
www.celadon.com
Email: sales@celadon.com
Estab: 1990

Michael Griswold, VP of Sales

Provider of OEM products and services. The company's products include OEM remote controls, infrared receivers, and backlighting systems.

**Celestix Networks Inc** HQ
215 Fourier Ave Ste 140
Fremont CA 94539
P: 510-668-0700 PRC:322
www.celestix.com
Email: info@celestix.com
Estab: 1999

Bobby Chen, Director of Finance & Operation

Provider of security appliances and solutions for healthcare, legal & financial, education, commercial, small business, and public sector industries.

**Celigo Inc** HQ
1820 Gateway Dr
San Mateo CA 94404
P: 650-579-0210 F: 650-240-0143 PRC:323
www.celigo.com
Email: info@celigo.com
Estab: 2005

Yang Jiang, Engineering Manager
Jan Arendtsz, Founder
Scott Henderson, CTO
Chris Corcoran, General Manager of Productivity
Dev Chidipi, General Manager of India

Provider of cloud computing products and solutions. The company offers NetSuite consulting services that include implementation and optimization.

**Cell Marque Corp** HQ
6600 Sierra College Blvd
Rocklin CA 95677
P: 916-746-8900 F: 916-746-8989 PRC:249
www.cellmarque.com
Email: service@cellmarque.com
Emp: 1-10 Estab: 1994

Nora Lacey, President
David Zembo, CFO
Kathi Longobardi, Human Resources Manager
Annie Hext, Biologist
Jeff Gordon, Director of Sales

Producer of primary antibodies, buffers and pre-treatment, ancillary reagents, and lab equipment for pathology laboratories and research facilities.

**Cell Technology** HQ
48820 Kato Rd Ste 400B
Fremont CA 94538
P: 650-960-2170 F: 650-960-0367 PRC:36
www.celltechnology.com
Email: info@celltechnology.com
Estab: 1998

Sumant Dhawan, CSO

Developer of assays to study cellular functions by researchers using cell preamble agents for academic, biotechnology, and pharmaceutical industries.

**CellarStone Inc** HQ
80 Cabrillo Hwy Ste Q216
Half Moon Bay CA 94019
P: 650-242-0008 PRC:326
www.cellarstone.com
Email: info@cellarstone.com
Estab: 2000

Gopi Mattel, CEO
Ajoop Kalavath, VP of Customer Success
Sanal Sankar, Director of Technology
Srinivasa Rekapalli, Director of Operations
Mohamed Basha, Senior Project Manager

Provider of sales commissions and incentive compensation software and solutions. The company offers version upgrades and re-engineering services.

**Cellecta Inc** HQ
320 Logue Ave
Mountain View CA 94043
P: 650-938-3910 F: 650-938-3911 PRC:26
www.cellecta.com
Email: info@cellecta.com
Estab: 2006

Alex Chenchik, President
Donato Tedesco, Lead Research Scientist
Mikhail Makhanov, Scientist
Andrei Komarov, Senior Research Scientist
Marina Budnitskaya, Research Associate

Provider of custom and contract solutions for high-throughput genetic screening needs and also develops therapeutic targets and drugs.

**Cellerant Therapeutics Inc** HQ
1561 Industrial Rd
San Carlos CA 94070
P: 650-232-2122 F: 650-232-5495 PRC:34
www.cellerant.com
Email: info@cellerant.com
Estab: 2003

Ram Mandalam, President
Rodney Young, CFO
Joseph Chao, Quality Control Manager
William Reed, VP of Clinical Development
Steve Greenberg, Managing Director

Developer of novel innate and adaptive immunotherapies for oncology and blood-related disorders, including cell-based and antibody therapeutics.

**Cellmax Life** HQ
1271 Oakmead Pkwy
Sunnyvale CA 94085
P: 650-564-3905 PRC:41
cellmaxlife.in
Email: support@cellmaxlife.com
Estab: 2013

Atul Sharan, CEO
Rui Mei, CSO
Prabhat Goyal, CFO
Padma Sundar, VP of Marketing & Business Development
Mana Javey, Medical Director

Provider of personalized multi-biomarker technologies for non-invasive saliva and blood tests. The company is also involved in drug discovery.

**CellSight Technologies Inc** HQ
185 Berry St Ste 350
San Francisco CA 94107
P: 650-799-1589 F: 650-267-6023 PRC:194
www.cellsighttech.com
Email: contact@cellsighttechnologies.com
Estab: 2009

Aruna Gambhir, CEO
Sam Quezada, COO
Jelena Levi, Research & Development Director

Provider of imaging tools to assess immunotherapy for the clinicians. The company focusses on the development of polyethylene terephthalat tracers.

**Celltheon** HQ
32980 Alvarado Niles Rd Ste 826
Union City CA 94587
P: 510-306-2355 PRC:36
www.celltheon.com
Email: info@celltheon.com
Estab: 2012

Amita Goel, Founder

Developer of customized solutions for preclinical studies of the biotechnology and pharmaceutical industries.

**Cellular Biomedicine Group Inc** HQ
19925 Stevens Creek Blvd Ste 100
Cupertino CA 95014
P: 408-973-7884 F: 408-973-7846 PRC:24
www.cellbiomedgroup.com
Estab: 2009

Bizuo Liu, CFO
Andrew Chan, SVP of Business Development
Sarah Kelly, Director of Corporate Communications
Xia Meng, General Manger of Early Diagnosis & Intervention

Developer of technologies and products for the treatment of KOA, Asthma, COPD and other indications.

**Celsia Inc** HQ
3287 Kifer Rd
Santa Clara CA 95051
P: 650-667-1920 PRC:154
celsiainc.com
Email: engineering@celsiainc.com
Estab: 2001

George Meyer, CEO
Erin Chen, QC Director
Emily Liu, Purchasing Director
Zoe Ho, Customer Service Director

Designer and manufacturer of heat sinks. The company provides thermal solutions using vapor chamber, heat pipe, and hybrid designs.

**Cemex USA** BR
5180 Golden Foothills Pkwy
El Dorado Hills CA 95762
P: 916-941-2800 PRC:47
www.cemexusa.com
Emp: 11-50

Jaime Muguiro, President
Jeff Bobolts, Regional President of Florida Region
Scott Ducoff, Regional President of Texas Region
Marc Tyson, Regional President of Mid-South Region
Eric Wittmann, Regional President of West Region

Supplier of bulk cement, sand, aggregates, ready mix materials, and architectural products. The company serves the construction industry.

**Cenergy Power** HQ
1520 W Main St
Merced CA 95340
P: 209-233-9777 F: 209-668-5726 PRC:135
www.cenergypower.com
Email: info@cenergypower.com
Emp: 11-50 Estab: 2006

Doan Vo, VP of O&M & Quality
Nader Yarpezeshkan, Senior Director of Sales
Andrew Goldin, VP of EPC Operations
Ryan Kretschmer, Project Manager
Eilroma Sarkis, Project Manager

Developer and installer of solar for the agricultural, commercial, industrial, and utility scale markets.

**Ceniom Inc**                                          HQ
  333 University Ave Ste 200
  Sacramento CA 95825
P: 800-403-3204                                        PRC:67
www.ceniom.com
Email: info@ceniom.com
Emp: 1-10 Estab: 2004

Yan Chan, Director

Provider of security, network design, and data recovery services. The company is engaged in web design, hosting, and technical support.

**CenterVue Inc**                                        BR
  979 Corporate Way
  Fremont CA 94539
P: 408-988-8404   F: 408-716-3271      PRC:11
www.centervue.com
Email: infous@centervue.com
Estab: 2008

Stefano Gallucci, CEO

Designer and manufacturer of medical devices for the diagnosis and management of ocular pathologies.

**Centric Software Inc**                                 HQ
  485 Alberto Way Ste 200
  Los Gatos CA 95032
P: 408-574-7802   F: 408-884-8551      PRC:322
centricsoftware.com
Email: centric@centricsoftware.com
Estab: 1998

Chris Groves, CEO
Ravi Rangan, CTO
Fabrice Canonge, VP
Alice Gerbel, VP of Finance & Administration
James Horne, VP of Marketing

Provider of product lifecycle management solution to apparel, consumer goods, luxury good, and footwear industries.

**Centrify**                                             HQ
  3300 Tannery Way
  Santa Clara CA 95054
P: 669-444-5200                                        PRC:319
www.centrify.com
Email: support@centrify.com
Estab: 2004

Mark Oldemeyer, CFO
Bill Johnston, Director of SMB Sales
Phil Austin, Manager

Provider of identity and access management solutions. The company offers services to pharma companies and financial institutions.

**Centrillion Biosciences Inc**                          HQ
  2500 Faber Pl
  Palo Alto CA 94303
P: 650-618-0111   F: 650-318-3383      PRC:34
www.centrilliontech.com
Email: info@centrillionbio.com
Estab: 2009

Uzair Sikora, Instrument Engineer
Bolan Li, Mechanical Engineer of Research
Wei Zhou, President
James Zhang, CSO
Michael Henry, SVP

Provider of genomic and bioinformatics solution. The company offers genomic technology to improve sequencing performance.

**Centrillion Technology Holdings Ltd**      HQ
  2500 Faber Pl
  Palo Alto CA 94303
P: 650-618-0111   F: 650-618-0121      PRC:38
www.centrilliontech.com
Email: info@centrilliontech.com
Estab: 2009

Wei Zhou, President
James Zhang, CSO
Michael Henry, SVP
Suzanne Dee, VP of Product Science
Janet Warrington, SVP of Research and Development

Developer of genomics solutions for the researchers, physicians, and consumers. The company also offers clinical testing and consumer genomics services.

**Century Technology Inc**                               HQ
  225 Harris Ct
  S San Francisco CA 94080
P: 650-583-8908                                        PRC:207
century-technology.com
Email: info@century-technology.com

Henry Ho, Owner

Provider of PCB assembly services. The company also offers distribution, testing, and wire harness services.

**Cephasonics**                                          HQ
  160 Saratoga Ave Ste 180
  Santa Clara CA 95051
P: 800-510-4561                                        PRC:198
www.cephasonics.com
Email: info@cephasonics.com
Estab: 2012

Kiman Han, Senior Hardware Engineer
Richard Tobias, CEO

Developer of ultrasound-based measurement products. The company deals with research and clinical trials.

**Cepheid**                                              HQ
  904 Caribbean Dr
  Sunnyvale CA 94089
P: 408-541-4191   F: 408-541-4192      PRC:186
www.cepheid.com
Email: info@cepheidbenelux.com
Estab: 1996

Jonathan Siegrist, Director of Engineering Programs
Jennifer Glass, Executive Director of Engineering
Peter Woo, Equipment Automation Engineering Manager
Iqbal Khan, Electrical Test Engineer
Larisa Krasnovskaya, Software Quality Engineer

Provider of molecular diagnostic testing of patient specimen on a centralized basis enabling medical providers identify and treat disease early.

**Ceras Health Inc**                                     BR
  995 Market St 2nd Fl
  San Francisco CA 94103
P: 415-477-9908                                        PRC:40
cerashealth.com
Email: info@cerashealth.com

Anita Waxman, Co-Founder
Kevin Murphy, CEO

Focuses on mobile application development. The company serves patients, hospitals, and related healthcare organizations.

**Cermetek Microelectronics**                            HQ
  374 Turquoise St
  Milpitas CA 95035
P: 408-942-2200   F: 408-942-1346      PRC:97
www.cermetek.com
Email: info@cermetek.com
Estab: 1968

Frank Stempski, Sales Manager
Steven Clary, Marketing Manager

Manufacturer of communication modules for embedded systems. The company caters to power generation, irrigation control, and medical monitoring fields.

**Cernex Inc**                                           HQ
  1710 Zanker Rd Ste 103
  San Jose CA 95112-4219
P: 408-541-9226   F: 408-541-9229      PRC:209
www.cernex.com
Email: cernex@cernex.com
Estab: 1988

Bill Yu, VP of Engineering
Michael Nguyen, Support Engineer
Anh Nguyen, Production Manager
Lam Huynh, Business Development Manager
Duc Nguyen, RF Microwave

Manufacturer of microwave & millimeter-wave components and sub-assemblies. The company's products include amplifiers, converters, detectors, and cables.

**CERONIX Inc**                                          HQ
  13350 New Airport Rd
  Auburn CA 95602-2055
P: 530-886-6400   F: 530-888-1065      PRC:112
www.ceronix.com
Emp: 1-10 Estab: 1984

Brian Looper, Electronic Engineer
Don Whitaker, Founder
Sheri Bomhoff, Sales & Service Manager
Lisa Teal, Manager
Nathan Jay, Warehouse Manager

Manufacturer of color video touch display monitors and printed circuit boards. The company offers LCD and CRT monitor assemblies and spare parts.

**Certain Inc**                                          DH
  75 Hawthorne St Ste 550
  San Francisco CA 94105
P: 415-353-5330   F: 415-614-9192      PRC:320
www.certain.com
Email: help@certain.com
Estab: 1994

Jasvinder Matharu, VP of Engineering
Peter Micciche, CEO
Aleks Rabrenovich, CFO
Gerard Larios, VP of Development Operations & Information Technology
Marc Thornton, Director of Sales & Strategic Accounts

Provider of enterprise event management solutions that include e-mail marketing, event reporting, registration, and consulting services.

**Certent Inc**  HQ
4683 Chabot Dr Ste 260
Pleasanton CA 94588
P: 925-730-4300  F: 925-730-4045  PRC:322
certent.com
Estab: 2002

Vinay Krishna, Software Engineer
Michael Boese, CEO
Joanie Creger, VP of Human Resources
Tina Herron, Human Resource Business Partner
Don Gillotti, SVP of Sales

Provider of equity compensation management, equity compensation reporting, and disclosure management solutions.

**Certified Medical Testing**  HQ
7600 N Ingram Ave Ste 234
Fresno CA 93711
P: 800-243-5427  F: 559-435-8827  PRC:189
www.pipegas.com
Email: certifiedtesting@sbcglobal.net
Emp: 1-10

Jake Granger, Owner
Roland Lamer, Owner

Provider of engineering services. The company provides services for healthcare organizations related to piped medical gas and vacuum systems.

**Cerus Corp**  HQ
2550 Stanwell Dr
Concord CA 94520
P: 925-288-6000  F: 925-288-6001  PRC:36
www.cerus.com
Email: customer_services@cerus.com
Estab: 1991
Sales: $30M to $100M

William Greenman, President
Dan Swisher, Chairman
Kevin Green, VP of Finance
Chrystal Menard, Chief Legal Officer
Laurence Corash, CSO

Manufacturer of biomedical products such as the intercept blood system and pathogen reduction system, focused in the field of blood safety.

**Cesco Magnetics Inc**  HQ
PO Box 6359
Santa Rosa CA 95406
P: 877-624-8727  PRC:159
cescomagnetics.com
Estab: 1946

Steve Blackwell, Engineer
James Heinmiller, Staff Scientist

Provider of magnetic separators. The company offers magnetic filters, magnetic plates, and sanitary valves.

**Cetecom**  BR
411 Dixon Landing Rd
Milpitas CA 95035
P: 408-586-6200  F: 408-586-6299  PRC:68
www.cetecom.com
Email: info@cetecom.com
Estab: 1993

Rami Saman, Senior Engineering Project Manager
Donovan Lo, Lab Conformance Engineer
Ali Taba, Test Engineer
Issa Ghanma, EMC Engineer
Yuchan Lu, Associate Test Engineer

Provider of consulting and testing services. The company focuses on the telecommunications and information technology industries.

**Ceterix Orthopaedics Inc**  HQ
959 Hamilton Ave
Menlo Park CA 94025
P: 650-241-1748  PRC:195
www.ceterix.com
Email: info@ceterix.com
Estab: 2010

John McCutcheon, President
Michael Hendricksen, VP of Research & Development

Developer of medical devices such as suture passer is indicated for passing suture through soft tissue in orthopedic surgery.

**Ceva Inc**  HQ
1174 Castro St Ste 210
Mountain View CA 94040
P: 650-417-7900  F: 650-417-7995  PRC:61
www.ceva-dsp.com
Email: sales@ceva-dsp.com
Estab: 2000
Sales: $30M to $100M

Boris Shpitser, Field Application Engineer
Gideon Wertheizer, CEO
Michael Boukaya, COO
Erez Bar-Niv, CTO
Yaniv Arieli, CFO

Provider of digital signal processor technology. The company also specializes in offering consulting services.

**CGI Technical Services Inc**  HQ
1612 Insight Pl
Redding CA 96003
P: 530-244-6277  F: 530-244-6276  PRC:142
www.cgitechnical.com
Email: sales@currygroup.com
Emp: 1-10  Estab: 1999

Azeddine Bahloul, VP
Clifford Curry, President
Tanner Jones, QC Supervisor
Theodore Kinsey, Laboratory Manager
Vikram Kyatham, Operations Manager

Provider of technical services. The company offerings include geotechnical engineering, engineering geology, and pavement design services.

**Cha Corp**  HQ
1170 National Dr Ste 70
Sacramento CA 95834
P: 916-550-5380  F: 916-550-5342  PRC:139
chacorporation.com
Email: ccha@chacorporation.com
Emp: 1-10

Chang Cha, President
Chang Yul Cha, President

Developer and marketer of microwave technologies. The company offers carbon regeneration, hypergolic destruction, and emission control solutions.

**Chai**  HQ
990 Richard Ave Ste 110
Santa Clara CA 95050
P: 650-779-5577  F: 650-779-5606  PRC:34
www.chaibio.com
Estab: 2013

Josh Perfetto, Founder

Specializes in DNA diagnostics. The company offers services to clinics, patients, and the medical sector.

**Champ Systems Inc**  HQ
6060 Freeport Blvd
Sacramento CA 95822
P: 916-424-4066  F: 916-424-3844  PRC:319
champsystems.com
Emp: 1-10  Estab: 1979

Norm Champ, President
Rob Zarzana, Programming & Support Manager
Denise Maglinte, Senior System Analyst
Diana Reiff, Senior System Analyst
Kyle Kumasaki, Systems Analyst

Provider of business management and accounting software. The company offers ERP programming, training, software, and hardware services.

**Champion Microelectronic Corp**  RH
960 Saratoga Ave Ste 125
San Jose CA 95129
P: 408-985-1898  F: 408-985-1683  PRC:212
www.championmicro.com.tw

Jeffrey Hwang, CTO

Designer and manufacturer of semiconductor devices. The company's products include battery management IC, fan controller, and interface products.

**Channel Medsystems Inc**  HQ
5858 Horton St Ste 200
Emeryville CA 94608
P: 510-338-9301  PRC:188
www.channelmedsystems.com
Email: info@channelmedsystems.com
Estab: 2006

Ric Cote, President
Bill Malecki, COO
Rhonda Bracey, VP of Finance
Witney McKiernan, VP

Developer of cryothermic technology and streamlined delivery system for women with heavy menstrual bleeding.

**ChannelNet**  BR
1 Harbor Dr Ste 106
Sausalito CA 94965
P: 415-332-4704  PRC:319
www.channelnet.com
Estab: 1985

Nelson Johnson, Senior Software Engineer
Paula Tompkins, CEO
ERIC PETERSEN, CFO
CHRIS SIMS, CTO
JOE KARLE, VP of Sales & Account Management

Provider of digital solutions to connect brands and customers. The company specializes in strategy development, design, and content optimization.

**Chartware Inc** HQ
PO Box 3137
Rohnert Park CA 94927
P: 800-642-4278   F: 707-544-2712   PRC:189
www.chartware.com
Estab: 1995

David Tully-Smith, President
Reg Green, VP
Dana Tully-Smith, VP

Manufacturer of scheduler and practice management interfaces and systems. The company serves the medical sector.

**Check Point Software Technologies Inc** HQ
959 Skyway Rd Ste 300
San Carlos CA 94070
P: 800-429-4391   PRC:322
www.checkpoint.com
Estab: 1993
Sales: $1B to $3B

Marius Nacht, Founder
Gil Shwed, Founder
Ray Rothrock, Chairman
Jerry Ungerman, Vice Chairman
Tal Payne, CFO

Developer of software technology solutions such as mobile security and next generation firewalls for retail/point of sale and financial services.

**CHECKPOiNT Technologies** HQ
66 Bonaventura Dr
San Jose CA 95134
P: 408-321-9780   PRC:172
www.checkpointtechnologies.com
Email: sales@checkpointtechnologies.com
Estab: 1995

Kee Yang, Product Engineer
Hai Tran, Engineering Technician
Audrey Laurin, Recruiting Human Resources
Robert Hand, Manager of Sales

Manufacturer of optical failure analysis tools such as laser scanning microscopy, photon emission, infrascan, and solid immersion lens objectives.

**Chelsio Communications** HQ
209 N Fair Oaks Ave
Sunnyvale CA 94085
P: 408-962-3600   F: 408-962-3661   PRC:95
www.chelsio.com
Email: sales@chelsio.com
Estab: 1997

Bob Dugan, Director of Engineering
Mingmei Xu, Software Engineer
Kianoosh Naghshineh, CEO
Asgeir Eiriksson, CTO
William Delaney, CFO

Provider of Ethernet adapters. The company offers storage routers, wire adapters, virtualization and management software, and accessories.

**Chemical Safety Technology Inc** HQ
2461 Autumnvale Dr
San Jose CA 95131
P: 408-263-0984   F: 408-263-2640   PRC:53
www.kemsafe.com
Email: info@kemsafe.com
Estab: 1987

Lincoln Bejan, President
Jackie Bejan, EVP
Lee Stevens, VP of Operations
Curtis Galvan, Senior Product Manager

Supplier of chemical processing machines. The company also offers design, manufacturing, and sheet metal fabrication services.

**Chemocentryx Inc** HQ
850 Maude Ave
Mountain View CA 94043
P: 650-210-2900   F: 650-210-2910   PRC:268
www.chemocentryx.com
Email: info@chemocentryx.com
Estab: 1997
Sales: $30M to $100M

Thomas Schall, President
Markus Cappel, Chief Business Officer
Susan Kanaya, CFO
Rajinder Singh, SVP of Research
Dalia Rayes, SVP

Manufacturer of biopharmaceutical products and orally-administered therapeutics to treat autoimmune diseases, inflammatory disorders, and cancer.

**ChemSoft** HQ
1101 S Winchester Blvd Ste P299
San Jose CA 95128
P: 408-615-1001   F: 408-615-1073   PRC:319
www.chemsoft.com
Email: sales@chemsoft.com

John Rather, VP of IS
Lorrie Conklin, Software Developer

Provider of software consulting services. The company specializes in custom business solutions, access, excel, PowerPoint, word, and visual basic.

**Chesapeake Technology Inc** HQ
4906 El Camino Real Ste 206
Los Altos CA 94022
P: 650-967-2045   F: 650-903-4500   PRC:322
chesapeaketech.com
Email: info@chesapeaketech.com
Estab: 1995

David Finlayson, VP of Engineering
Eileen Gann, President
Ashley Chan, Marketing and Sales Manager
John Gann, VP of Software Development
Stephen D'Andrea, Business Manager

Provider of sonar mapping software as well as consulting services to the marine, geophysical, and geological survey industries.

**Chess com** HQ
PO Box 60400
Palo Alto CA 94306
P: 800-318-2827   PRC:317
www.chess.com
Email: support@chess.com
Estab: 2005

Erik Allebest, CEO

Provider of unlimited chess games and free tournaments that can be played by challenging friends and meet new players.

**Chevron Corp** HQ
6001 Bollinger Canyon Rd
San Ramon CA 94583
P: 925-842-1000   PRC:133
www.chevron.com
Email: chvcips@chevron.com
Estab: 1879
Sales: Over $3B

Pierre Breber, VP
Huma Abbasi, General Manager
Sheree Lomax, Human Resource Manager
Steven Howard, Manager of SBU Financial Support
James Johnson, EVP of Upstream

Provider of mobile asset tracking and management solutions. The company serves the marine, chemicals, and aviation industries.

**Chiapas Edi Technologies Inc** HQ
1405 Birch Ln
Davis CA 95618
P: 415-298-8166   PRC:322
chiapas-edi.org
Email: support@chiapas-edi.org
Emp: 1-10   Estab: 2010

Alden Temps, Founder

Developer of electronic data interchange software for health insurance exchange brokers, MSOs, HMOs, and healthcare business data analytics services.

**Chico Environmental Science & Planning** HQ
333 Main St Ste 260
Chico CA 95928
P: 530-899-2900   PRC:142
chicoenvironmental.com
Email: info@chicoenvironmental.com
Emp: 1-10

John Lane, Principal Scientist
Jess Kolstad, Staff Environmental Scientist

Provider of environmental consulting services. The company offers site assessments, storm water pollution prevention plans, and environmental forensics.

**China Custom Manufacturing Ltd** HQ
44843 Fremont Blvd
Fremont CA 94538
P: 510-979-1920   F: 510-979-1930   PRC:280
www.pacificbusinessco.com
Email: info@ccmfg.com
Estab: 1993

Bonnie Chen, Account Manager

Provider of tooling, plastic injection molding, and sheet metal stamping services. The company focuses on the aerospace and electronics industries.

**Chip-Tech Ltd** BR
PO Box 460
Fremont CA 94537
P: 510-505-9030   F: 510-505-9268   PRC:209
www.chiptech.com
Estab: 1989

Barbara Vanni, Quality Assurance Manager
Robin Cohen, Purchaser
Ali D'Onofrio, Purchaser
Traci Hyland, Purchaser
Lorrine Lindner, Sales Manager

Distributor of film capacitors, relay racks, oscillators, ferrite beads, grommets, clips, battery holders, lamps, displays, and accessories.

**Chouinard & Myhre Inc** HQ
655 Redwood Hwy Ste 102
Mill Valley CA 94941
P: 415-480-3636   F: 415-461-1253   PRC:325
www.cm-inc.com
Email: info@cm-inc.com
Estab: 1976

Steve Giondomenica, President
John Wondolowski, CTO
Peter Bussi, COO

Provider of IT solutions such as data management, enterprise security management, and private, public, and hybrid cloud solutions and services.

**Chris French Metal Inc** HQ
2500 Union St
Oakland CA 94607
P: 510-238-9339   F: 510-238-9373   PRC:82
cfrenchmetal.com
Estab: 2007

Richard Lovato, Project manager
David Hinman, Lead Fabricator

Provider of fabrication services. The company offers design, installation, prototyping, and repair services.

**Chrometa LLC** HQ
1029 H St Ste 103
Sacramento CA 95814
P: 916-546-9974   PRC:322
www.chrometa.com
Email: sales@chrometa.com
Emp: 1-10   Estab: 2008

Brett Owens, CEO

Provider of time keeping management software and services. The company offers products for PC, Mac, iPhone, and Android platforms.

**Chromeworks Inc** HQ
252 Lockheed Ave
Chico CA 95973
P: 530-343-2278   F: 530-343-2287   PRC:185
chromeworksinc.com
Email: info@chromeworksinc.com
Emp: 1-10   Estab: 1985

Jerry Robinson, Owner
Kathy Robinson, Co-Founder
Debbie Garcia, General Manager

Manufacturer of chrome frames for the dental lab industry. The company's services include shipping and delivery.

**Chronix Biomedical Inc** HQ
5941 Optical Ct Ste 201
San Jose CA 95138
P: 408-960-2306   F: 408-960-2305   PRC:187
www.chronixbiomedical.com
Email: info@chronixbiomedical.com
Estab: 1997

Bill Boeger, Co-Founder
John DiPietro, CFO
Julia Beck, VP of Research
Michael Jerstad, Non Executive Director
Paul Freiman, Non Executive Director

Provider of molecular diagnostics laboratory services such as second opinion tests and delta dot test for screening and monitoring cancer.

**Chrontel Inc** HQ
2210 O'toole Ave Ste 100
San Jose CA 95131
P: 408-383-9328   F: 408-383-9338   PRC:208
www.chrontel.com
Email: sales@chrontel.com
Estab: 1986

Joseph Wong, Design Engineer
Tin Hua, Senior Software Engineer
Yuan Xu, Digital IC Engineer
James Lin, CFO
Sidney Yen, Director of Applications

Designer of mixed-signal IC products. The company's products find application in personal computer and telecom sectors.

**Chs Consulting Group** HQ
220 Montgomery St Ste 346
San Francisco CA 94104
P: 415-392-9688   F: 415-392-9788   PRC:304
www.chsconsulting.net
Estab: 2000

Chi-Hsin Shao, President
William Lieberman, Transportation Planning Coordinator

Provider of transportation planning and traffic signal design services. The company also focuses on traffic safety.

**Cibiem Inc** HQ
5150 El Camino Real Ste E30
Los Altos CA 94022
P: 650-397-6685   F: 650-386-6125   PRC:189
www.cibiem.com
Email: info@cibiem.com

Xian Wei, Research
Ken Martin, President
Mark Gelfand, CTO
Howard Levin, Chief Scientific Officer

Manufacturer of medical devices. The company provides solutions to treat sympathetic nervous system-mediated diseases.

**Ciena Corp** BR
3939 N First St
San Jose CA 95134
P: 408-904-2100   F: 408-944-9290   PRC:97
www.ciena.com

Chanh Cao, Lead Test Engineer
Prasad Kotta, Lead Engineer
Joseph Forsythe, Lead Engineer
John Marson, VP of Product & Industry Marketing
Rob Meier, VP

Provider of cloud networking, network transformation, and packet network solutions for multi-data center environments.

**Cinematico Inc** HQ
1504 Bryant St Ste 333
San Francisco CA 94103
P: 415-896-5776   PRC:318
www.cinematico.com
Estab: 2002

Gustavo Manriquez, Founder

Provider of 3D design, animation, and motion capture services. The company is involved in product design and motion graphics.

**Cinnabar Bridge Communications** HQ
41 Sutter St Ste 1368
San Francisco CA 94104
P: 415-975-0950   F: 415-704-3212   PRC:45
www.cinnabarbridge.com

Paula Hendricks, Founder

Provider of writing, book publishing, book design, consulting, and project and process management services.

**Ciphercloud Inc** DH
2581 Junction Ave Ste 200
San Jose CA 95134
P: 855-524-7437   PRC:323
www.ciphercloud.com
Email: info@ciphercloud.com
Estab: 2010

Varun Badhwar, VP of Product Strategy & Solution Engineering
Sreekar Nagubadi, Software Engineer
Pravin Kothari, Founder

Provider of comprehensive cloud application discovery and risk assessment, data protection, data loss management, key management, and malware detection.

**Circle Pharma** HQ
280 Utah Ave Ste 100
South San Francisco CA 94080-6883
P: 650-392-0363   PRC:25
www.circlepharma.com
Email: info@circlepharma.com
Estab: 2012

Matthew Jacobson, Co-Founder
Scott Lokey, Co-Founder
David Earp, President
Walter Moos, Board Chairman
David Spellmeyer, Interim Chief Scientific Officer

Focuses on the development of cell permeable macrocyclic peptide therapeutics. The company serves the pharmaceutical sector.

**Circle Video Productions** HQ
630 N San Mateo Dr
San Mateo CA 94401
P: 650-619-7367   F: 650-340-7391   PRC:318
www.circlevideo.com
Email: support@circlevideo.com
Estab: 1984

Rob Delantoni, Owner

Provider of video production and multimedia solutions. The company offers video dispositions, editing, and duplication services.

**Circleci**　　　　　　　　　　　　　　HQ
201 Spear St
San Francisco CA 94105
P: 800-585-7075　　　　　　　　　　PRC:322
circleci.com
Email: sayhi@circleci.com
Estab: 2011

Jeffrey Palmer, VP of Engineering
Rose Kaplan-Bomberg, Community & Partner
Engineer
Hannah Henderson, Engineering Manager
Ryan Arlan, Senior Support Engineer
Ryan O'Hara, Success Engineer

Provider of continuous integration and delivery
solution. The company offers apps for docker,
enterprise, and mobiles.

**Circuit Therapeutics Inc**　　　　　　HQ
1505 O'Brien Dr
Menlo Park CA 94025
P: 650-324-9400　F: 650-324-9403　PRC:191
www.circuittx.com
Email: info@circuittx.com
Estab: 2011

Dan Andersen, VP of Engineering
Karoly Nikolich, Founder
Fred Moll, CEO
Michael Kaplitt, CSO
Chris Towne, Director of Gene Therapy

Focuses on drug discovery and development as
well as forging direct therapeutic applications of
optogenetics.

**Cirexx International Inc**　　　　　　HQ
791 Nuttman St
Santa Clara CA 95054
P: 408-988-3980　F: 408-988-4534　PRC:211
www.cirexx.com
Email: info@cirexx.com
Estab: 1980

Duane Cockcroft, Senior Technical Sales and Flex
Pre-Engineering Manager
Enrique Sanchez, Senior Process Engineering
Manager
Philipp Menges, President
Kurt Menges, VP
Don Angulo, Quality Systems Manager

Provider of PCB design layout, fabrication, and
assembly services. The company serves customers in the aerospace, military, semiconductor, and
medical sectors.

**Cirius Group Inc**　　　　　　　　　　HQ
2300 Contra Costa Blvd Ste 250
Pleasant Hill CA 94523
P: 925-685-9300　F: 925-685-6526　PRC:320
www.ciriusgroup.com
Email: sales@ciriusgroup.com
Estab: 1984

Paul Bartlett, President
Mark Ehnen, Senior Director of Sales and Mar-
keting
Denise Munoz, Marketing Manager
Erin Fernandez, Director of Compliance
Kristin Fodrini, Consulting Services Manager

Designer and marketer of financial and medical
software. The company serves hospitals and
healthcare providers.

**Cirrus Digital Systems**　　　　　　　HQ
2077 Centro E
Tiburon CA 94920
P: 415-608-9420　　　　　　　　　　PRC:168
cirrus-designs.com
Email: sales@cirrus-designs.com

John Arvesen, Principal Engineer

Developer of single and multi-camera mapping
systems for NASA applications and high altitude
manned and unmanned aircraft needs.

**Cirrus Systems Inc**　　　　　　　　　HQ
1997 S McDovell Blvd
Petaluma CA 94954
P: 877-636-2331　　　　　　　　　　PRC:169
cirrusled.com
Email: contact@cirrusled.com
Emp: 11-50　Estab: 2012

David Rycyna, CEO

Provider of display solutions for restaurants, education, church, financial, medical, automotive, and
professional services.

**Cirtec Medical**　　　　　　　　　　　HQ
101 B Cooper Ct
Los Gatos CA 95032
P: 408-395-0443　　　　　　　　　　PRC:187
www.cirtecmed.com
Estab: 1986

Brian Highley, CEO
Erik Morgan, Director of Information Technology

Manufacturer of complex implantable device manufacturing, medical device solutions, and smart
solutions for highly complex miniaturization.

**Cisco Systems Inc**　　　　　　　　　HQ
170 W Tasman Dr
San Jose CA 95134
P: 408-526-4000　　　　　　　　　　PRC:64
www.cisco.com
Estab: 1984
Sales: Over $3B

Plamen Nedeltchev, Distinguished Engineer
Kelly Kramer, EVP
Amy Chang, EVP
Jeanne Beliveau-Dunn, VP
Francine Katsoudas, EVP

Designer and manufacturer of IP-based networking products. The company also offers security
solutions and architectures.

**Cisco Systems Inc**　　　　　　　　　BR
201 Third St Ste 620
San Francisco CA 94103
P: 800-553-6387　　　　　　　　　　PRC:68
www.cisco.com
Estab: 1984

Manas Pati, Principal Engineer
Karl Benson, Project Manager
Dee Seesurat, Program Manager
Ashish Dey, Technical Leader
Ashish Verma, IT Lead

Provider of networking products and services
such as routers, switches, and optical and wireless networking devices.

**Citilabs Inc**　　　　　　　　　　　　HQ
2005 N St
Sacramento CA 95811
P: 888-770-2823　　　　　　　　　　PRC:40
citilabs.com
Emp: 11-50

Jacob Asplund, Director of Streetlytics Engineer-
ing & Support
Michael Clarke, President
Austen Duffy, CTO
Chris Simons, Director of Solutions
Alex Fox, Director of Mobility Analytics Solutions

Provider of software development services. The
company designs and develops products for transportation planning.

**Citrix Systems Inc**　　　　　　　　　BR
4988 Great America Pkwy
Santa Clara CA 95054
P: 408-790-8000　　　　　　　　　　PRC:322
www.citrix.com
Estab: 1989

David Henshall, CEO
Mark Ferrer, EVP
Donna Kimmel, EVP
Carlos Sartorius, SVP of Worldwide Sales and
Services
Mark Coyle, Manager of Product Design

Provider of transition to software-defining the
workplace, uniting virtualization, mobility management, networking, and SaaS solutions.

**CitrusBits**　　　　　　　　　　　　　HQ
5994 W Las Positas Blvd Ste 219
Pleasanton CA 94588
P: 925-452-6012　　　　　　　　　　PRC:315
citrusbits.com
Email: sales@citrusbits.com
Estab: 2005

Malik Mustafa, Head of Engineering
Harry Lee, CEO
James Hsu, VP of Growth
Chandler Faye, Art Director

Designs and develops impactful mobile apps for
businesses of all sizes by using augmented/virtual
reality, artificial intelligence, blockchain, and The
Internet of Things (IoT).

**Cityspan Technologies Inc**　　　　　HQ
2054 University Ave Ste 5F
Berkeley CA 94704
P: 510-665-1700　　　　　　　　　　PRC:323
cityspan.com
Email: info@cityspan.com
Estab: 1996

Mark Chuang, CTO
Kara Johnson, Director of Business Development
Hayley Cole, Project Manager
Ariel Hollie, Project Manager
Navdeep Sheena, Project Associate

Developer of software for social services. The
company offers software to manage grants, track
clients, and evaluate outcomes.

**Civil Maps**     HQ
2720 Taylor St Ste 320
San Francisco CA 94133
P: 415-287-9977     PRC:227
www.civilmaps.com
Email: info@civilmaps.com
Estab: 2013

Jian Wu, Engineer
Melody Li, Product Manager

Developer of autonomous vehicles and cognitive perception systems. The company specializes in localization technology and artificial intelligence.

**Cjs Labs**     HQ
57 States St
San Francisco CA 94114-1401
P: 415-923-9535     PRC:304
cjs-labs.com
Email: cjs@cjs-labs.com
Estab: 2006

Christopher Struck, CEO

Provider of electronic design, consulting, engineering, and test automation programming assistance services.

**CKC Engineering LLC**     HQ
6617 San Leandro St
Oakland CA 94621
P: 415-494-8225     PRC:81
www.ckcengineering.com
Email: info@ckcengineering.com
Estab: 2005

Chris Duggan, President
Carl Dipietro, VP
Kenji Sytz, Co-Founder

Provider of custom equipment solutions for clinical, manufacturing, pharmaceutical, medical device, and drug delivery industries.

**Ckc Laboratories Inc**     HQ
5046 Sierra Pines Dr
Mariposa CA 95338
P: 209-966-5240   F: 858-300-5341   PRC:306
www.ckc.com
Emp: 11-50 Estab: 1973

Steve Behm, Director of Engineering
Bonnie Robinson, President
William Brandle, Information Technology Manager
Christine Nicklas, Principal Consultant

Provider of electomagnetic compatibility testing, safety testing, design development and agency certification services for industries.

**Ckc Laboratories Inc**     BR
1120 Fulton Pl
Fremont CA 94539
P: 510-249-1170     PRC:159
www.ckc.com
Estab: 1973

Steve Behm, Director of Engineering Services
Bonnie Robinson, President
Todd Robinson, Director of Administration and Marketing
Dawniele Oliphant, Project Manager

Provider of design and testing consultation services. The company offers design consultation, testing, training, and support services.

**CI Hann Industries Inc**     HQ
1020 Timothy Dr
San Jose CA 95133
P: 408-293-4800   F: 408-293-5858   PRC:80
www.clhann.com
Email: info@clhann.com
Estab: 1971

Pete Hann, President
Cheyne Hann, CFO
Arthur Korp, VP
Jack Freitas, Manager of Weld Department
Georgette Hann, Office Manager

Provider of contract manufacturing services including CNC machining, welding, assembly and testing, and conditioning.

**Clare Computer Solutions**     HQ
2400 Camino Ramon Ste 195
San Ramon CA 94583
P: 925-277-0690   F: 925-277-0694   PRC:325
www.clarecomputer.com
Email: info@clarecomputer.com
Estab: 1990

Corey Moldes, Senior Field Service Engineer
Hadi Torab, Senior System Engineer
James Cizek, Systems Engineer
Ken Holloway, Senior Network Engineer
Russ Swindell, Network Engineer

Provider of information technology services. The company offers computer network, software consultation, visualization, and cloud computing solutions.

**Claresco Corp**     HQ
2342 Shattuck Ave Ste 504
Berkeley CA 94704
P: 510-528-0238   F: 510-549-2298   PRC:322
www.claresco.com

Brett D'Ambrosio, CEO
Daniel Pearson, Quality Assurance Manager
John Moore, Project Manager
Loren D'Ambrosio, Lead Programmer
Matthew Allen-Goebel, Linux System Administrator

Provider of design and implementation services for customized business software. The company serves multi-national firms.

**Claret Medical Inc**     HQ
1745 Copperhill Pkwy Ste 1
Santa Rosa CA 95403-9062
P: 707-528-9300   F: 707-528-9302   PRC:189
www.claretmedical.com
Email: info@claretmedical.com
Estab: 2009

Dan Fifer, VP of Research

Manufacturer of catheters to protect the patient's brain during Transcatheter Aortic Valve Implantation (TAVI) and other endovascular procedures.

**Clari Inc**     HQ
1154 Sonora Ct
Sunnyvale CA 94086
P: 650-265-2111     PRC:319
www.clari.com
Email: hello@clari.com
Estab: 2012

Malay Desai, VP of Engineering
Andy Byrne, CEO
Venkat Rangan, CTO
Alyssa Filter, CFO
Cornelius Willis, CMO

Developers of an AI-based data capturing software that helps the marketing, sales, and customer success teams.

**Clarizen**     HQ
2755 Campus Dr Ste 300
San Mateo CA 94403
P: 866-502-9813   F: 650-227-0308   PRC:325
www.clarizen.com
Email: info@clarizen.com
Estab: 2006

Boaz Chalamish, CEO
Viken Eldemir, CFO
Alon Rozenshein, CFO
Erin Codelli, Sales Development Representative
Cisco Villalta, CMO

Provider of collaborative online project management software. The company offers work management, time tracking, and project scheduling solutions.

**Clayborn Lab**     HQ
40173 Truckee Tahoe Airport Rd
Truckee CA 96161-4110
P: 530-587-4700   F: 530-587-5255   PRC:151
www.claybornlab.com
Email: info@claybornlab.com
Emp: 1-10 Estab: 1963

Nick O'neill, Sales Engineer
Maureen Horvath, Owner
Justin Horvath, President
David Millholen, Production Manager

Developer of heat tapes, hot tubes, and custom tape heaters. The company serves the medical, transportation, and pharmaceutical sectors.

**Clean Earth**     BR
30677 Huntwood Ave
Hayward CA 94544
P: 510-429-1129   F: 510-429-1498   PRC:139
aerc.com
Estab: 1990

Chris Dods, President
Sandra Coelho, Inside Sales Manager
Rick Rudd, Outside Sales Representative

Provider of recycling solutions. The company acts as regulated and permitted electronics and universal waste recycler.

**Clean Energy Systems Inc**     HQ
3035 Prospect Park Dr Ste 120
Rancho Cordova CA 95670-6071
P: 916-638-7967   F: 916-244-0709   PRC:152
www.cleanenergysystems.com
Email: info@cleanenergysystems.com
Emp: 1-10 Estab: 1993

Patrick Skutley, Project Engineer
Keith Pronske, President
Bill Hayes, Director of Manufacturing
Joshua Perron, Business Development Manager
Heath Evenson, Plant Manager

Developer and manufacturer of steam and drive gas generator units. The company is engaged in design, delivery, and installation services.

**Clean Power Research**  HQ
  1541 Third St
  Napa CA 94559
  P: 707-258-2765  PRC:319
  www.cleanpower.com
  Email: privacy@cleanpower.com
  Estab: 1998

  Alan Saunders, Director of Business Development
  Teresa Schmid, Manager
  Skip Dise, Product Manager
  William Molinari, Controller

  Provider of program automation, customer
  engagement, and solar data and intelligence
  solutions. The company offers services to the
  solar industry.

**CleanAir Solutions Inc**  HQ
  826 Bayridge Pl
  Fairfield CA 94534
  P: 707-864-9499  F: 707-864-9399  PRC:125
  www.cleanroomspecialists.com
  Email: info@cleanroomspecialists.com
  Estab: 1998

  Kathie Kalafatis, President

  Provider of stainless steel furniture and ESD cur-
  tain systems. The company serves pharmaceutical and medical device manufacturing companies.

**Cleangrow**  DH
  3734 Bradview Dr Ste A
  Sacramento CA 95827
  P: 415-460-7295  PRC:87
  www.cleangrow.com
  Email: info@cleangrow.com
  Emp: 1-10  Estab: 2009

  Donald Ormandy, Managing Director
  Lacey Macri, Director of Business Development
  Breeanna Ford, Operations Manager
  Louis Schink, Supply Chain Technician
  Iain Aspley, Electrochemist

  Manufacturer of sensors for the measurement of
  calcium, potassium, ammonium, magnesium, and
  fluoride ions.

**Cleantec**  HQ
  4120 Douglas Blvd
  Granite Bay CA 95746
  P: 916-791-8478  PRC:56
  www.gocleantec.com
  Email: info@gocleantec.com
  Emp: 1-10

  Aaron Tartakovsky, Co-Founder
  Bob Nelson, Manager

  Provider of solutions for greenhouse gas emissions, air pollution, water conservation, and waste
  management.

**Clear-Com LLC**  HQ
  1301 Marina Village Pkwy Ste 105
  Alameda CA 94501
  P: 510-337-6600  F: 510-337-6699  PRC:61
  www.clearcom.com
  Email: customerservicesus@clearcom.com
  Estab: 1968

  Robert Cruz, Director of Finance
  Albert Weber, Accountant

  Manufacturer of wireless and digital matrix
  intercom products and related accessories. The
  company serves the broadcasting and commercial
  markets.

**ClearCare Inc**  HQ
  150 Spear St Ste 1550
  San Francisco CA 94105
  P: 800-449-0645  PRC:323
  clearcareonline.com
  Estab: 2010

  Balki Nakshatrala, VP of Engineering
  Geoff Nudd, CEO
  David Cristman, COO
  Michael Cavan, VP of Sales
  Ed Chuang, Manager

  Provider of front and back office software solution
  such as billing, payroll, and marketing management for private duty home care agencies.

**CLEARink Displays Inc**  RH
  4020 Clipper Ct
  Fremont CA 94538
  P: 510-624-9305  PRC:124
  www.clearinkdisplays.com
  Estab: 2012

  Scott Ferguson, VP of Engineering & Operations
  Robert Fleming, VP of Research & Development

  Developer of reflective display modules for
  wearables, smart phones/tablets, electronic shelf
  labels, and outdoor signage.

**Clearstory Data Inc**  HQ
  4300 Bohannon Dr Ste 200
  Menlo Park CA 94025
  P: 650-322-2408  PRC:325
  www.clearstorydata.com
  Email: info@clearstorydata.com
  Estab: 2011

  Carol Kimura, Director of Corporate Marketing &
  Marketing Operations

  Provider of data analysis and collaboration
  solutions for food & beverage, healthcare & life
  services, media and entertainment, and financial
  services.

**Cleasby**  HQ
  1414 Bancroft Ave
  San Francisco CA 94124
  P: 415-822-6565  F: 415-822-1843  PRC:159
  www.cleasby.com
  Email: info@cleasby.com
  Estab: 1949

  John Cleasby, Founder

  Provider of roofing services. The company also
  offers single ply, cold process, and built up roofing
  services.

**Clickatell (pty) Ltd**  HQ
  900 Island Dr Ste 202
  Redwood City CA 94065
  P: 650-641-0011  F: 650-440-4961  PRC:323
  www.clickatell.com
  Estab: 2000

  Peter Villiers, CEO
  Casper Villiers, Founder
  Patrick Lawson, Founder
  Michael Jordan, Chairman
  Hannes Rensburg, Chief Commercial Officer

  Provider of SMS solutions such as SMS alerts,
  reminders, call centers, reservations and book-
  ings for healthcare, marketing, and IT/software
  industries.

**Clicktime Com Inc**  HQ
  282 Second St Fl 4
  San Francisco CA 94105
  P: 415-684-1180  F: 415-684-1099  PRC:325
  www.clicktime.com
  Email: info@clicktime.com
  Estab: 1997

  Alex Mann, CEO
  Anthony Severo, Customer Education and Senior
  Support Manager
  Allen Liu, Application Development Lead

  Provider of web-based tools, software, and IT
  consulting services. The company serves the
  aerospace, defense, automotive, and construction
  industries.

**Climate Earth**  HQ
  2150 Allston Way Ste 320
  Berkeley CA 94704-1381
  P: 415-391-2725  PRC:324
  www.climateearth.com
  Email: support@climateearth.com
  Estab: 2008

  Chris Erickson, CEO

  Provider of environmental product declarations
  and supply chain solutions such as supply chain,
  climate change risk, and natural capital management .

**Climax Laboratories Inc**  HQ
  1939 Monterey Rd Ste 10
  San Jose CA 95112
  P: 408-298-8630  F: 408-799-8222  PRC:303
  www.climaxlabs.com
  Email: info@climaxlabs.com
  Estab: 2009

  Yeping Zhao, President

  Provider of contract research services. The
  company offers bioanalytical and analytical testing
  services.

**Clinisense Corp**  HQ
  15466 Los Gatos Blvd Ste 109-355
  Los Gatos CA 95032
  P: 408-348-1495  F: 408-399-9705  PRC:189
  clinisense.com
  Email: admin@clinisense.com
  Estab: 2001

  Stephen Zweig, Founder

  Developer of technology for shelf-life monitoring.
  The company offers applications such as diagnostics, medical supplies, and RFID tags.

**Clinovo Inc**  HQ
  4010 Moorpark Ave Ste 226
  San Jose CA 95117
  P: 866-994-3121  PRC:194
  www.clinovo.com
  Estab: 2013

  Vamsi Maddipatla, President
  Ritesh Patel, CEO

  Provider of resourcing solutions for pharmaceutical, biotechnology, diagnostic, medical device, and
  CRO customers.

**Cloudera Inc** HQ
395 Page Mill Rd Bldg 2
Palo Alto CA 94306
P: 650-362-0488   F: 888-789-1488   PRC:323
www.cloudera.com
Email: info@cloudera.com
Estab: 2008
Sales: $300M to $1 Billion

Martin Cole, Chairman
Scott Aronson, Chief Revenue Officer
Anupam Singh, Chief Customer Officer
Arun Murthy, Chief Product Officer
Jim Frankola, CFO

Provider of professional services that include
cluster certification, descriptive analytics pilot, and
security integration pilot.

**CloudFlare Inc** RH
101 Townsend St
San Francisco CA 94107
P: 650-319-8930   PRC:325
www.cloudflare.com
Estab: 2009

Darth SriBear, Systems Reliability Engineer
Wanda Lee, Customer Success Manager
Greg Cohn, Customer Success Manager
Talea Seyed, Customer Success Manager
Daniella Vallurupalli, Head of Communications

Provider of load balancers, traffic controllers,
and web optimization products. The company is
engaged in analytics services.

**Cloudian** LH
950 Tower Ln Ste 300
Foster City CA 94404
P: 650-227-2380   F: 650-227-0299   PRC:323
www.cloudian.com
Estab: 2010

Gary Ogasawara, VP of Engineering
Bharatendra Boddu, Principal Software Engineer
Eddo Jansen, Senior Systems Engineer
Ka Chung, Software Engineer
Hiroshi Ohta, President

Provider of cloud storage platform and unstructured data storage. The company offers cloud
object storage software and appliances.

**Cloudmark Inc** HQ
128 King St Fl 2
San Francisco CA 94107
P: 415-946-3800   F: 415-543-1233   PRC:323
www.cloudmark.com
Email: info@cloudmark.com
Estab: 2001

Murray Kucherawy, Principal Engineer
Vipul Prakash, Owner
Hugh McCartney, CEO
Neil Cook, CTO
Kevin San Diego, VP of Product Management

Provider of messaging infrastructure and security
solutions. The company delivers scalable messaging platform, security intelligence, and filtering.

**Cloudpassage Inc** HQ
180 Townsend St
San Francisco CA 94107
P: 415-886-3020   F: 415-354-3417   PRC:324
www.cloudpassage.com
Estab: 2010

Vitaliy Geraymovych, Co-Founder
Carson Sweet, Co-Founder
Sami Laine, Principal Technologist

Developer of software solutions. The company
also offers account management, configuration
security monitoring, and alerting services.

**Cloudshare Inc** HQ
351 California St Ste 1600
San Francisco CA 94104
P: 888-609-4440   F: 800-848-2854   PRC:326
www.cloudshare.com
Email: info@cloudshare.com
Estab: 2007

Zvi Guterman, Co-Founder
Ariel Fattal, VP of Finance
Sheila Aharoni, Global VP of Sales
Annie Reiss, VP of Marketing
Muly Gottlieb, VP of R&D

Provider of flexible and cloud-computing platform
for developing and testing IT applications, software, and systems.

**Cloudtc** HQ
555 Bryant St Ste 337
Palo Alto CA 94301
P: 650-238-5203   PRC:71
cloudtc.com
Email: info@cloudtc.com
Estab: 2007

Anthony Gioeli, President

Designer and developer of voice communications
platform. The company specializes in business
applications.

**Cloudwords Inc** HQ
201 California St Ste 1350
San Francisco CA 94111
P: 415-394-8000   PRC:325
www.cloudwords.com
Email: sales@cloudwords.com
Estab: 2010

Michael Meinhardt, Founder
Steve Baggerly, CTO
Kevin Benson, Head of Sales
Steven Sakadales, Head of Global Customer
Success

Provider of translation management systems and
content localization solutions to manage translation process, vendors, and content systems.

**Clover Machine & Manufacturing** HQ
800 Mathew St Ste 101
Santa Clara CA 95050
P: 408-727-3380   F: 408-727-7015   PRC:80
www.clovermachine.com
Email: quotes@clovermachine.com
Estab: 1978

Bill Traill, Co-Owner

Provider of contract manufacturing and machining services. The company supplies tooling and
fixtures to its customers.

**Cloverleaf Solutions Inc** HQ
333 University Ave Ste 200
Sacramento CA 95825
P: 916-484-4141   PRC:324
www.cloverleafsolutions.com
Email: info@cloverleafsolutions.com
Emp: 1-10

Christopher Bodine, President
Carlos Hinojosa, Maintenance Manager

Provider of data validation and information processing computer solutions. The company caters
to businesses.

**Clovis Oncology** BR
499 Illinois St Ste 230
San Francisco CA 94158
P: 415-409-5440   F: 415-552-3427   PRC:254
clovisoncology.com
Email: medinfo@clovisoncology.com
Estab: 2009

Patrick Mahaffy, President
Daniel Muehl, EVP
Gillian Ivers-Read, EVP
Lindsey Rolfe, EVP of Clinical Preclinical Develop-
ment and Pharmacovigilance
Paul Gross, EVP

Developer of targeted therapies for the treatment
of patients with cancer. The company is involved
in clinical trials.

**Clustered Systems Company Inc** HQ
3350 Scott Blvd Bldg 30-01
Santa Clara CA 95054
P: 408-327-8100   F: 408-327-8101   PRC:209
www.clusteredsystems.com

Phillip Hughes, CEO
Robert Lipp, COO

Provider of cooling technology services. The company's resources include data sheets, technology,
deployment, and white papers.

**Clustrix Inc** HQ
201 Mission St Ste 1400
San Francisco CA 94105
P: 415-501-9560   PRC:326
mariadb.com
Estab: 2006

Andrew Redman, Build & Tools Engineer
Michael Howard, CEO
Michael Monty Widenius, CTO
Jon Bakke, Chief Revenue Officer
Kenneth Paqvalen, CFO

Provider of a SQL database with no limits to
database size, table size, query complexity, and
performance.

**CMD Products** HQ
1410 Flightline Dr Ste D
Lincoln CA 95648
P: 916-434-0228   F: 916-434-0214   PRC:159
www.cmdproducts.com
Email: info@cmdproducts.com
Emp: 11-50 Estab: 2003

David Harris, President
Monique Harris, President
Thamara Z. Quintero, Operations Manager
Mary Powers, Warehouse Manager

Manufacturer of replacement heads and accessories. It's products find application in gas and
electric weed trimmers.

**CMI Manufacutring Inc**     HQ
414 Umbarger Rd
San Jose CA 95111
P: 408-982-9580   F: 408-982-9583    PRC:157
www.cmi-mfg.com
Estab: 2011

Maria Baez-Moreno, President

Provider of prototype machining services. The company also focuses on 3D surfacing, production, and manufacturing engineering support.

**CMOS Sensor Inc**     HQ
20045 Stevens Creek Blvd Ste 1A
Cupertino CA 95014
P: 408-366-2898   F: 408-366-2841    PRC:87
www.csensor.com
Email: sales@csensor.com
Estab: 1997

Simon Lin, Engineer
Bill Wang, Founder

Designer and manufacturer of electro-optical image acquisition and also surveillance solutions for the medical market.

**Coadna Photonics Inc**     HQ
733 Palomar Ave
Sunnyvale CA 94085
P: 408-736-1100   F: 408-736-1106    PRC:124
www.coadna.com
Email: sales@coadna.com
Estab: 2000

Oliver Chan, QA Engineer
David Liu, IT Support Engineer
Jim Yuan, President
Jack Kelly, VP
Oliver Lu, Chief Commercial Officer

Provider of tunable fiber optic solutions for optical networks. The company's products are used in high broadband applications.

**Coast Metal Cutting**     HQ
2500 Bay Rd
Redwood City CA 94063
P: 650-369-9837   F: 650-369-1488    PRC:80
coastmetal.com
Email: sales@coastmetal.com
Estab: 1967

Brian Kottmeier, President

Provider of machining and metal cutting services. The company's services include production, turning, drilling, and tapping.

**Coastside Net**     HQ
525-B Obispo Rd
El Granada CA 94018
P: 650-712-5900    PRC:323
www.coastside.net
Email: info@coastside.net
Estab: 1994

Rob Genovesi, Owner
Steve Dennis, Senior Technician

Provider of internet access and technology solutions. The company also offers website services including website hosting, design, and development.

**Cobalt Polymers Inc**     HQ
PO Box 579
Cloverdale CA 95425
P: 800-337-0901   F: 707-894-9083    PRC:281
www.cobaltpolymers.com
Email: sales@cobaltpolymers.com

Robert Foley, President

Manufacturer of polymer tubing for medical device and high technology applications, with polymer chemistry, radiation science, and process engineering.

**Cobham Defence Electronics**     BR
5300 Hellyer Ave
San Jose CA 95138
P: 888-310-0010   F: 408-624-3913    PRC:5
www.cobham.com
Estab: 1994

Roger Smith, Senior Engineering Manager
John Ries, Program Manager

Manufacturer and designer of electrical components. The company caters to the military and commercial sectors.

**Codar Ocean Sensors Ltd**     HQ
1914 Plymouth St
Mountain View CA 94043
P: 408-773-8240   F: 408-773-0514    PRC:68
www.codar.com
Email: info@codar.com
Estab: 1960

Mason Kwiat, Support & Software Engineer
Don Barrick, President
Chad Whelan, CTO
Pederson Laura, Director of Marketing
Allison Mendes, Assistant Operations Manager

Designer and manufacturer of radar systems for ocean current and wave monitoring. The company specializes in sea state monitoring.

**Code-N Technology Inc**     HQ
1370 Willow Rd
Menlo Park CA 94025
P: 650-234-8400    PRC:315
www.code-n.com
Email: info1@code-n.com
Estab: 2012

Marketta Silvera, Founder
Randy Haldeman, CEO

Leverages advanced semantic web technology to provide software solutions to businesses.

**Codeobjects Inc**     HQ
490 N McCarthy Blvd
Milpitas CA 95035
P: 408-432-1180    PRC:322
www.codeobjects.com
Email: info@codeobjects.com
Estab: 2006

Sanjin Tulac, Lead Software Engineer
Jay Hsu, Software Engineer
Anil Annadata, CEO
Cathy Takahashi, Director of Business Analysis
Navnika Wason, Product Manager

Developer of insurance process management and business intelligence solutions. The company also offers claims management services.

**Codexis Inc**     HQ
200 Penobscot Dr
Redwood City CA 94063
P: 650-421-8100    PRC:34
www.codexis.com
Email: info@codexis.com
Emp: 132    Estab: 2002
Sales: $30M to $100M

John Nicols, President
Ross Taylor, SVP
Rossana Carillo, Automation Manager
Stefania Attard, Senior Human Resource Manager
Santhosh Sivaramakrishnan, Scientist

Provider of biocatalysts products such as screening kits and other accessories. The company serves the food and nutrition industries.

**Cofan Usa Inc**     HQ
48664 Milmont Dr
Fremont CA 94538
P: 510-490-7533   F: 510-490-7931    PRC:88
www.cofan-usa.com
Email: info@cofan-usa.com
Estab: 1994

Allen Ong, VP
Valerie Ramos, People Operations Manager
Joe Cabe, Head of Global Talent

Developer and manufacturer of products for thermal engineering. The company specializes in fans, heat sinks, and custom products.

**Coffer GroupLLC**     HQ
268 Bush St
San Francisco CA 94104
P: 415-963-4382    PRC:40
coffergroup.com
Estab: 2007

Brian Valadez, Information Technology Support Engineer
Ehsan Alahdad, Network Engineer
Jason Coffer, Founder

Provider of information technology solutions. The company specializes in private equity, venture capital, and hedge funds.

**Cogco Inc**     HQ
PO Box 1310
Woodland CA 95776-1310
P: 530-666-1716   F: 530-666-1942    PRC:133
www.cogcowireline.com
Email: info@cogcowireline.com
Emp: 1-10    Estab: 1977

James Cogbill, President
Nancy Goyet, Office Manager

Provider of gas and oil well services such as perforating, thru tubing, case logging, and jet cutting.

**Cognex Corp**     BR
20380 Town Ctr Ln Ste 195 and 250
Cupertino CA 95014
P: 858-481-2469   F: 858-792-0470    PRC:159
www.cognex.com
Estab: 1981

Matt Remnek, Senior Sales Engineer
Robert Shillman, Chairman
Robert Willett, President
John McGarry, SVP of Research
Sheila DiPalma, SVP of Corporate Employee Services

Supplier of barcode readers and sensor products. The company offers vision sensors, fixed mount readers, handheld readers, and mobile computers.

**Cognizant Technology Solutions**　　BR
　5000 Executive Pkwy Ste 295
　San Ramon CA 94583
P: 925-790-2000　　　　　　　　　PRC:323
cognizant.com
Email: inquiry@cognizant.com

Dharmendra Kumar Sinha, President
Ganesh Ayyar, President of Cognizant Digital
Operations
Gregory Hyttenrauch Greg, President of Cognizant Digital Systems & Technology
Santosh Thomas, President
Malcolm Frank, President of Cognizant Digital Business

Provider of business consulting, enterprise application development, IT infrastructure, and outsourcing services.

**CohBar Inc**　　HQ
　1455 Adams Dr
　Menlo Park CA 94025
P: 650-446-7888　　F: 650-446-7888　　PRC:303
www.cohbar.com
Email: info@cohbar.com
Estab: 2007

Simon Allen, CEO
Steven Engle, CEO
Albion Fitzgerald, Chairman
Jeffrey Biunno, CFO
Jon Stern, COO

Developer of treatments for metabolic dysfunction that includes NASH, obesity, cancer, neurodegenerative diseases, and more.

**Cohere Technologies Inc**　　HQ
　2550 Walsh Ave Ste 150
　Santa Clara CA 95051
P: 408-246-1277　　　　　　　　　PRC:68
cohere-technologies.com
Estab: 2013

Ronny Hadani, Founder
Shlomo Rakib, Founder
Raymond Dolan, Chairman
Ram Prasad, COO
Ronny Haraldsvik, CMO

Developers of wireless technology solutions. The company offers solutions for orthogonal time frequency space.

**Coherent Inc**　　HQ
　5100 Patrick Henry Dr
　Santa Clara CA 95054
P: 408-764-4000　　F: 408-764-4800　　PRC:172
www.coherent.com
Email: coherent.europe@coherent.com
Estab: 1966
Sales: $1B to $3B

John Ambroseo, President
Kevin Palatnik, EVP
Bret DiMarco, EVP
Sushil Shah, VP
Virginia Tong, Director of Global Taxes

Manufacturer of optics and laser instruments. The company serves the medical and research industries.

**Coherus Biosciences**　　HQ
　333 Twin Dolphin Dr Ste 600
　Redwood City CA 94065
P: 800-794-5434　　　　　　　　　PRC:34
www.coherus.com
Estab: 2010

Dennis Lanfear, President
Jean-Frederic Viret, CFO
Vincent Anicetti, COO
Vladimir Vexler, CSO
Peter Watler, CTO

Developer of biosimilars and it serves the global marketplace. The company is engaged in delivery services.

**Cohesion Inc**　　BR
　751 Laurel St Ste 319
　San Carlos CA 94070
P: 650-591-9122　　F: 650-590-7156　　PRC:325
www.cohesion.biz
Email: sales@cohesion.biz
Estab: 2001

Eric Crow, System Administrator
Joel Katz, SAP Developer

Provider of software and services. The company offers SAP quality management, batch management, business warehousing, and other services.

**Colabo Inc**　　HQ
　751 Laurel St Ste 840
　San Carlos CA 94070
P: 650-288-6649　　F: 650-240-0281　　PRC:322
colabo.com
Email: info@colabo.com
Estab: 2010

Asaf Wexler, Co-Founder
Naama Halperin, Co-Founder
Yoav Dembak, Co-Founder

Provider of multi-functional software that enables professionals across all industries to achieve a number of business objectives.

**Cold Ice Inc**　　HQ
　9999 San Leandro St
　Oakland CA 94603
P: 510-568-8129　　F: 510-568-2355　　PRC:159
www.coldice.com
Email: info@coldice.com
Estab: 1982

Ray Wilhelm, President
Melissa Malana, Office Supervisor

Manufacturer of refrigerants, insulated shipping containers and temperature monitors. The company serves the agricultural and gourmet food industries.

**Cold Room Solutions Inc**　　HQ
　1040 Serpentine Ln Ste L
　Pleasanton CA 94566
P: 925-462-2500　　F: 925-462-2502　　PRC:228
www.coldroomsolutions.com
Email: sales@coldroomsolutions.com
Estab: 2001

Brad Bidwell, President

Provider of walk-in cold rooms, freezers, and warm rooms. The company focuses on preventive maintenance programs.

**Colema Boards Of California Inc**　　HQ
　PO Box 1879
　Cottonwood CA 96022
P: 530-347-5700　　F: 530-347-2336　　PRC:189
colema.com
Email: info@colema.com
Emp: 1-10　Estab: 1975

Victor Irons, Founder

Manufacturer of home enema board kits. The company's products include colema boards and cleansing kits.

**Colfax International**　　HQ
　750 Palomar Ave
　Sunnyvale CA 94085
P: 408-730-2275　　F: 408-730-2274　　PRC:323
www.colfax-intl.com
Email: sales@colfax-intl.com
Estab: 1987

Thomas Lee, Senior Systems Engineer
Gautam Shah, CEO
Michael Fay, VP of Sales
Manish Shah, Manager of Marketing Communications
Richard Jackson, Director of Technical

Provider of workstations, servers, clusters, storage, and personal supercomputing solutions to accelerate business and research outcomes.

**Collaborative Drug Discovery Inc**　　HQ
　1633 Bayshore Hwy Ste 342
　Burlingame CA 94010
P: 650-242-5259　　　　　　　　　PRC:324
www.collaborativedrug.com
Email: info@collaborativedrug.com
Estab: 2004

Barry Bunin, CEO
Krishna Dole, CTO
Sean Ekins, CSO
Sylvia Ernst, Head of Sales and Sales Operations
Kellan Gregory, Director of Product Excellence

Provider of drug discovery research informatics. The company offers hosted biological and chemical database that securely manages private and external data.

**Collidion Inc**　　HQ
　1770 Corporate Cir
　Petaluma CA 94954
P: 707-668-7600　　　　　　　　　PRC:189
www.collidion.com
Email: info@collidion.com
Estab: 2015

Hoji Alimi, CEO

Provider of healthcare products. The company specializes in antibiotic resistance, specific drugs to eradicate biofilms, and delivery systems.

**Collimated Holes Inc**　　HQ
　460 Division St
　Campbell CA 95008
P: 408-374-5080　　F: 408-374-0670　　PRC:84
www.collimatedholes.com
Email: contact@collimatedholes.com
Estab: 1975

Richard Mead, President
Matt Fate, Director of Sales and Manufacturing

Designer and manufacturer of fiber optic components, sub-assemblies, and imaging systems. The company also provides design and manufacturing services.

**Columbia Machine Works**  HQ
934 75th Ave
Oakland CA 94621
P: 510-568-0808   F: 510-568-0810   PRC:80
www.columbiamachine.net
Email: jsol@columbiamachine.net
Estab: 1955

John Sol, General Manager

Provider of coining equipment and contracting services. The company offers coining presses, rimming machines, and consumable tooling.

**Comit Systems Inc**  HQ
1246 Gainsborough Dr
Sunnyvale CA 94087
P: 408-988-2988   PRC:212
www.comit.com/
Email: info@comit.com
Estab: 1992

Venkat Iyer, President

Provider of full service contract engineering for wireless & cleantech, methodology consulting , Soc design and verification, board design, and software.

**CommerceNet**  HQ
5050 El Camino Real Ste 215
Los Altos CA 94022
P: 650-289-4040   PRC:325
www.commerce.net
Email: info@commerce.net
Estab: 1994

Jay Tenenbaum, Founder
Allan Schiffman, Executive Director
Anne Ferris, Director of Operations
Jeff Shrager, Consulting Professor

Provider of internet based research and piloting services such as internet business, open trading networks, and internet-user demographic surveys.

**Commodity Resource & Environmental Inc**  BR
493 Reynolds Cir
San Jose CA 95112
P: 408-501-0691   F: 408-436-5578   PRC:142
www.creweb.com
Email: info@creweb.com
Estab: 1980

Stacy Aesoph, President
Charles Yohn, VP of Sales

Producer of silver. The company engages in silver recovery, photo solution waste disposal, and other activities.

**Common Interest Management Services**  BR
1720 S Amphlett Blvd Ste 130
San Mateo CA 94402
P: 650-286-0292   F: 650-286-0296   PRC:45
www.commoninterest.com
Estab: 1990

Mike Archer, CEO
Leonard Ataide, Property Manager
Lisa Marrone, Community Association Manager
Ann Naviaux, Community Association Manager
Adrianne Bretao, Association Manager

Provider of homeowner association management solutions such as escrow and disclosure, maintenance, online and community services.

**Communications & Power Industries LLC**  HQ
607 Hansen Way
Palo Alto CA 94304
P: 650-846-2900   F: 650-846-3276   PRC:61
www.cpii.com
Email: mppmarketing@cpii.com
Estab: 1948

Robert Fickett, President
Mike Bayless, Operations Manager
Marina Remmel, Senior Human Resources Representative

Developer and manufacturer of microwave, radio frequency, power, and control solutions. The company serves medical and critical defense fields.

**CommWorld of San Francisco**  HQ
4336 Jessica Cir
Fremont CA 94555
P: 650-358-8700   F: 650-585-2174   PRC:45
www.commworldsf.com
Email: sales@commworldsf.com
Estab: 1979

Carmelo Vazquez, Operations Manager
Terri Nubla, Manager
Mark Mandrik, National Accounts Manager

Provider of telecommunication services such as computer networking, structured cabling, project management and repair.

**Comp Pro Med Inc**  HQ
3418 Mendocino Ave
Santa Rosa CA 95403
P: 707-578-0239   PRC:41
www.comppromed.com
Email: info@comppromed.com
Estab: 1983

Hal Petersen, Operations Manager
Daniel Best, Senior Developer

Provider of laboratory information systems for clinical laboratories. The company offers services to the healthcare sector.

**Compact Imaging Inc**  HQ
897 Independence Ave Ste 5B
Mountain View CA 94043
P: 650-694-7801   F: 650-694-4972   PRC:187
compactimaging.com
Email: info@compactimaging.com

Carol Wilson, Founder
Josh Hogan, Founder
Don Bogue, CEO
Michael Hee, CMO

Developer of miniature optical sensor technology. The company specializes in mobile health applications.

**Compandent Inc**  HQ
26666 Birch Hill Way
Los Altos Hills CA 94022
P: 650-241-9231   F: 425-790-0949   PRC:62
www.compandent.com
Email: sales@compandent.com
Estab: 2001

Oded Gottesman, CEO

Developer of customized algorithms. The company offers digital sign processing services to telecommunications and semiconductor companies.

**Comparative Biosciences Inc**  HQ
786 Lucerne Dr
Sunnyvale CA 94085
P: 408-738-9260   F: 408-738-9278   PRC:34
www.compbio.com
Estab: 1996

Carol Meschter, CEO
James Christenson, SVP
Hongqing Du, Pharmacology & Study Director
Corey Eggers, Executive Assistant

Provider of research and development support services. The company serves the biotechnology and pharmaceutical industries.

**Compass & Anvil**  HQ
118 El Olivar
Los Gatos CA 95032
P: 408-205-1319   F: 408-866-5150   PRC:159
www.compass-anvil.com
Estab: 2005

Charlie Lawton, Owner

Provider of engineering services. The company focuses on metal prototypes, forgings, castings, and metal stampings.

**Compass Components Inc**  HQ
48133 Warm Springs Blvd
Fremont CA 94539-7498
P: 510-656-4700   F: 510-656-4682   PRC:202
www.ccicms.com
Email: compass@ccicms.com
Estab: 1979

Thomas Maurer, VP
Bill Turner, Director of Strategic Projects

Manufacturer of custom cables & harnesses and distributor of electronic components. The company also manufactures electromechanical products.

**Compatible Cable Inc**  HQ
5046 Commercial Cir Ste B
Concord CA 94520
P: 888-415-1115   PRC:62
www.compatiblecable.com
Email: sales@compatiblecable.com
Estab: 2009

Bill Calkins, Sales Manager
Angela Trantham, Office Manager

Manufacturer of custom cable assemblies and off-the shelf cables. The company offers services to the automotive, broadcast, and electronics industries.

**Competitive Power Ventures LLC**  BR
505 Sansome St Ste 475
San Francisco CA 94111
P: 415-293-1455   PRC:130
www.cpv.com
Email: info@cpv.com
Emp: 1-10

Jon Moorman, Graphics Engineer
Mark Turner, VP of Development
Mark McDaniels, VP
Michael Lynch, Associate Producer
Carter Carlton, Senior Associate

Provider of power generation services. The company focuses on natural gas and renewable energy generation and asset management.

**Complete Genomics Inc** HQ
2904 Orchard Pkwy
San Jose CA 95134
P: 408-648-2560 PRC:25
www.completegenomics.com
Email: info@completegenomics.com
Estab: 2006

Radoje Drmanac, CSO
Avanindra Chaturvedi, CFO
Jody Beecher, Director of Biochip Development &
Production
Yuan Jiang, Director of Research
Adam Borcherding, Senior Process Manager

Developer of human genome sequencing technology, research and development, clinical and
consumer applications.

**ComplianceEase** HQ
111 Anza Blvd Ste 200
Burlingame CA 94010-1823
P: 650-373-1111 F: 650-373-7844 PRC:326
www.complianceease.com
Estab: 2001

Anita Kwan, CEO
Al Ogrodski, SVP of Solution Strategy
Peter Phan, Associate Product Manager
Luke Chen, Channel Partner Manager

Provider of intelligent business solutions to
financial service institutions. The company offers
automated compliance and risk management
solutions.

**Comprehend Systems Inc** HQ
2010 Broadway St Ste 200
Redwood City CA 94063
P: 650-521-5449 PRC:323
www.comprehend.com
Email: support@comprehend.com
Estab: 2010

Rick Morrison, CEO
Lee Black, VP of Sales

Provider of invaluable clinical data insights enabling us to do better science and optimize clinical
operations.

**Comptech Usa** HQ
5437 Stationers Way
Sacramento CA 95842
P: 916-338-3434 F: 916-338-3432 PRC:80
www.comptechusa.com
Emp: 1-10 Estab: 1979

Fred Penney, President

Manufacturer and fabricator of race engines. The
company also offers R&D and road racing track
maintenance services.

**Compton Enterprises** HQ
2434 Dayton Rd
Chico CA 95928
P: 530-895-1942 F: 530-895-0760 PRC:179
www.comptonenterprises.com
Emp: 1-10

Laura Compton, CEO

Manufacturer of moving equipment. The company
specializes in rail-cars, conveyors, and truck
loaders.

**Compudata Inc** HQ
855 Folsom St Apt 122
San Francisco CA 94107
P: 415-495-3422 F: 415-495-1962 PRC:97
www.compu-data.net
Email: sales@compu-data.net

Roula Daniel, Sales Manager
Ed Guarrieri, VP of Technology
Bessie Lee-Cham, VP of Operations

Provider of sales, accounting, and manufacturing software. The company especially caters to
businesses.

**Compugraphics Usa Inc** BR
43455 Osgood Rd
Fremont CA 94539
P: 510-249-2600 PRC:77
www.compugraphics-photomasks.com
Email: us@compugraphics.com

Craig Durgy, Eastern Regional Sales Manager
Laurie Sullivan, Account Manager
Farzan Hakami, Engineering Section Head

Designer and developer of photomasks for
semiconductor, optoelectronic devices, MEMs,
nanotechnology, and renewable energy sectors.

**Computer Deductions Inc** HQ
8680 Greenback Ln Ste 210
Orangevale CA 95662
P: 916-987-3600 F: 916-987-3606 PRC:323
www.cdi-hq.com
Email: info@cdi-hq.com
Emp: 11-50 Estab: 1971

Tom Calabro, VP
Christopher Hadtrath, Senior Application Devel-
oper
Matthew Iskra, Senior Technical Analyst

Provider of software development services as a
subcontractor to corporations. The company also
offers management consulting services.

**Computer Logistics Corp** HQ
2001 Market St
Redding CA 96001
P: 530-241-3131 PRC:159
compulog.com
Emp: 1-10 Estab: 1986

Bob Andrews, CEO
Rafe Spaulding, Chief Information Officer
Damien Owen, Service Manager
Staphanie Marain, Support Manager
Mindy Stephens, Controller

Provider of system and internet integration,
system design, custom programming, web design,
and hosting services.

**Computer Methods** HQ
1660 W Linne Rd Ste H
Tracy CA 95377
P: 510-824-0252 F: 510-824-0254 PRC:324
computer-methods.com
Emp: 1-10 Estab: 1986

David Lieberman, Owner

Manufacturer of physical therapy testing equipment. The company's products include WebExam,
PP004, WinHand, and ActivitySuite.

**Computer Plastics Inc** HQ
1914 National Ave
Hayward CA 94545
P: 510-785-3600 F: 510-785-3229 PRC:163
www.computerplastics.com
Email: cpi-sales@computerplastics.com
Estab: 1969

Timalex Gina, Manager

Provider of molding services. The company offers
custom plastic injection molding, engineering,
assembly, and tooling services.

**Computer Presentation Systems Inc** HQ
3035 Prospect Park Dr Ste 90
Rancho Cordova CA 95670
P: 916-635-3487 F: 916-635-1809 PRC:323
www.cpsusa.com
Email: sales@cpsusa.com
Emp: 1-10 Estab: 1985

Zoe Miller, Owner
Robert Musa, President
Lisa Meylor, Marketing Manager

Designer and developer of hardware and software
solutions for home builders ranging from local
entrepreneurs to regional builders.

**Computer Software For Professionals
Inc** HQ
5346 College Ave
Oakland CA 94618
P: 510-547-8085 F: 510-547-8159 PRC:319
www.legalmaster.com
Email: csp@legalmaster.com
Estab: 1977

Phillip Rubin, Director of Design

Provider of law office management software and
related tools. The company offers services to the
legal industry.

**Computerland Of Silicon Valley** HQ
482 W San Carlos St
San Jose CA 95110
P: 408-519-3200 F: 408-519-3260 PRC:68
www.cland.com
Email: info@cland.com
Estab: 1991

Ken Chang, IT Technician

Provider of hardware, software, and networking
services. The company serves government and
educational institutions.

**Computers & Structures Inc** HQ
1646 N California Blvd Ste 600
Walnut Creek CA 94596
P: 510-649-2200 PRC:322
www.csiamerica.com
Email: feedback@csiamerica.com
Estab: 1975

Umer Haroon, Software Engineer
Ashraf Habibullah, President
Syed Hasanain, EVP
Faisal Habib, Software Support Manager

Provider of integrated design, analysis, assessment, drafting of building systems, and related
support services.

**CompuTrust Software** HQ
18625 Sutter Blvd Ste 500
Morgan Hill CA 95037
P: 800-222-7947 PRC:323
www.computrustcorp.com
Email: sales@computrustcorp.com
Estab: 1982

Paula Lomanto, Sales
Val Hollars, Manager of Software Development
Lily Yee, Technical Support

Developer and seller of software for public administrators. The company offers services to businesses and enterprises.

**Concentric Analgesics Inc** HQ
101 California St Ste 1210
San Francisco CA 94111
P: 415-484-7921 F: 707-313-7200 PRC:303
www.concentricanalgesics.com
Email: medinfo@concentricanalgesics.com
Estab: 2014

John Donovan, Founder
Frank Bellizzi, CEO
Mike Royal, Chief Medical Officer
Craig Husfeld, Chief Scientific Officer

Developer of therapeutic solutions. The company focusses on discovery and development of novel, non opioid therapeutics for treating acute and chronic pain.

**Concept Models Inc** HQ
2127 Research Dr Ste 9
Livermore CA 94550
P: 925-606-6743 PRC:80
www.cmodelz.com

Bob Hallock, Manager

Provider of prototyping devices. The company specializes in surgical devices, CNC programming, tap burning, and rubber molding.

**Concepts 2 Industries** HQ
2829 S Rodeo Gulch Rd Ste 6
Soquel CA 95073
P: 831-464-1111 F: 831-464-1100 PRC:163
www.concepts2.com
Email: molding@concepts2.com
Emp: 1-10 Estab: 1990

Michael Lodico, VP of Sales & Administration
Kayla Gammino, Customer Service Manager

Manufacturer of custom injection molded plastic parts. The company serves computer, medical, telecom, and other sectors.

**Concord Sheet Metal** HQ
1666 Willow Pass Rd
Pittsburg CA 94565
P: 800-799-1900 F: 925-680-6569 PRC:80
concordsheetmetal.com

Ron Wessels, President
Sean Murphy, Production Manager
Marcia Wessels, Office Manager
Randy Smith, Estimator

Provider of architectural metal products. The company focuses on fasteners, copper gutters, and decorative chimney tops.

**Condor Country Consulting** HQ
815 Estudillo St
Martinez CA 94553-1617
P: 925-335-9308 F: 925-231-0571 PRC:142
condorcountry.com
Email: info@condorcountry.com
Estab: 2001

Wendy Dexter, President
Christian Knowlton, Biological Technician
Denise Wight, Biological Technician
Samantha Weber, Senior Biologist
Ted Robertson, Staff Biologist

Provider of natural and cultural resource supporting services. The company also provides ecological, natural resource, and cartographic services.

**Configure Inc** HQ
1800 Hamilton Ave Ste 200
San Jose CA 95125
P: 877-408-2636 PRC:67
www.configureinc.com
Email: sales@configureinc.com
Estab: 1996

RUDAIN ARAFEH, Founder
A.J. VERDECCHIA, COO
Dina Fernandes, Project Manager
Debby McLaurin, Project Manager

Provider of communication consulting services. The company specializes in network design, transport service implementation, and project management.

**Confometrx** HQ
3070 Kenneth St
Santa Clara CA 95054
P: 408-496-6276 PRC:34
confometrx.com

Brian Kobilka, Founder
Tong Kobilka, CEO
Xichen Li, Lab Manager
Victoria Ahn, Scientist

Developer of a platform of drug development tools. The company specializes in drug discovery technologies.

**Conformiq Inc** HQ
14435 C Big Basin Way Ste 271
Saratoga CA 95070
P: 408-898-2140 PRC:322
www.conformiq.com
Email: conformiq@conformiq.com
Estab: 1998

Kimmo Nupponen, VP of Engineering
Mark Creamer, CEO
Stephan Schulz, CTO
Clark Cochran, VP of Field Operations Americas
Yuval Helfman, Solution Architect

Provider of automated test designing services. The company focuses on training, project implementation, change management, and executive consulting.

**Connectance Inc** HQ
38 Miller Ave Ste 315
Mill Valley CA 94941
P: 415-891-8872 PRC:194
www.connectance.com
Email: sales@connectance.com

Nabil Moukheibir, CEO
Rick Beberman, COO

Provider of software for diagnosis in health care industry. The company offer online access too to detect a disease and offer treatment suggestion.

**Connected Io Inc** HQ
573 University Ave
Los Gatos CA 95032
P: 669-221-6100 PRC:63
www.connectedio.com
Email: info@connectedio.com
Estab: 2013

Nishima Mohan, Lead Software Quality Assurance Engineer
Barakha Shah, Software Quality Assurance Engineer
Yakov Temov, CEO

Developer of altair-based cellular module for Internet of Things applications. The company provides hardware design & development services.

**Connected Marketing** HQ
1340 S De Anza Blvd Ste 201
San Jose CA 95129
P: 408-647-2198 PRC:324
connectedmarketing.com
Email: info@connectedmarketing.com

Carol Francavilla, Principal
Rebecca Seggel, Project Manager
Tammy Brooks, Project Manager

Provider of marketing services. The company also offers web development, branding, and lead generation services.

**Connekt LLC** HQ
15844 Norlene Way
Grass Valley CA 95949
P: 530-604-5821 PRC:78
connektllc.com
Email: scott@connektllc.com
Emp: 1-10 Estab: 1992

Scott Raitt, Head of Operations

Developer and manufacturer of mechanical engineering design solutions. The company's services include CAD, reverse engineering, and sheet metal design.

**Connor Manufacturing Services Inc** HQ
1710 S Amphlett Blvd Ste 318
San Mateo CA 94402
P: 800-968-7078 PRC:157
www.connorms.com
Email: sales@connorms.com
Estab: 1913

Robert Sloss, CEO

Provider of customized solutions for precision metal stamping, wire forms, springs, and integrated assembly needs.

**Connora Technologies Inc**    HQ
1488 Zephyr Ave
Hayward CA 94544
P: 415-315-9524    PRC:284
www.connoratech.com
Email: info@connoratech.com
Estab: 2011

Stefan Pastine, Founder
Rey Banatao, CEO

Manufacturer of electronic and composites
re-imagined. The company specializes in recycla-
mine thermoset technology.

**Conquip Inc**    HQ
11255 Pyrites Way
Rancho Cordova CA 95670
P: 916-379-8200   F: 916-379-8201    PRC:20
www.conquipinc.com
Email: sales@conquipinc.com
Emp: 1-10   Estab: 1994

John Dill, Controls Engineer
Bob Wenning, President
Bruce Ballard, CEO
Steve Imai, Project Manager
John Penman, Lead

Manufacturer of converting equipment. The
company specializes in volume manufacturing
solutions, and also offers repair and upgrade
services.

**Consensus Orthopedics Inc**    HQ
1115 Windfield Way Ste 100
El Dorado Hills CA 95762
P: 916-355-7100   F: 916-355-7190    PRC:190
consensusortho.com
Email: info@consensusortho.com
Emp: 11-50

Colleen Gray, President
Dan Lubeck, Senior Quality Systems Specialist
Curt Wiedenhoefer, VP of Global Sales & Mar-
keting
Michael Droege, Senior Director of Global Busi-
ness & Market Development
Kathy Toy, Accounting Manager

Manufacturer of orthopedic medical devices. The
company's products include consensus hip systems, revision knee systems, mobile bearing knee
systems, and others.

**ConSol Consulting & Solutions Corp**    HQ
201 Spear St Ste 1100
San Francisco CA 94105
P: 925-479-1370   F: 925-479-1371    PRC:325
www.consol.com
Email: info@consol.com

Ulrich Schwanengel, Founder
Michael Beutner, CEO
Markus Mayer, COO

Provider of information technology services. The
company offers software, networking, outsourcing,
and monitoring solutions.

**Construction Electrical Products**    HQ
7800 Las Positas Rd
Livermore CA 94551
P: 925-828-9420   F: 925-828-3416    PRC:243
www.cepnow.com
Email: sales@cepnow.com
Estab: 1976

Rob Larrabee, CEO
Emily Thompson, Manager

Provider of electrical products for the construction
sector. The company offers temporary power products, extension cords, and portable lighting.

**Contract Room Inc**    HQ
1670 S Amphlett Blvd Ste 140
San Mateo CA 94402
P: 800-950-9101    PRC:319
www.contractroom.com
Email: sales@contractroom.com
Estab: 2012

Cesar Soto, Head of Engineering
Emil Stefanutti, Co-Founder
Peter Thomson, Co-Founder
Charlene Dickey, VP of Enterprise Sales
Lloyd Alexander, VP of Customer Success

Provides contract management software.

**Contrast Media Labs**    HQ
388 Market St Ste 1300
San Francisco CA 94111
P: 415-471-1323    PRC:319
contrastmedialabs.com
Email: info@contrastmedialabs.com
Estab: 2010

Arvin Tehrani, Co-Founder

Provider of graphic design and software development services. The company services include
android applications and digital and print media
design.

**Contrast Security**    HQ
240 Third St 2nd Fl
Los Altos CA 94022
P: 888-371-1333   F: 650-397-4133    PRC:325
www.contrastsecurity.com
Email: support@contrastsecurity.com
Estab: 2014

Michelle Chen, Technical Support Engineer
Sourabh Katti, Technical Support Engineer
Jeff Williams, Co-Founder
Alan Naumann, Chairman
Surag Patel, CSO

Designer and developer of self-protection software. The company is also engaged in operations
support services.

**Control Laboratories Inc**    HQ
42 Hangar Way
Watsonville CA 95076
P: 831-724-5422   F: 831-724-3188    PRC:41
www.controllabs.com
Emp: 1-10

Mike Galloway, Manager

Provider of agricultural analytical services such
as compost, water, soil, plant, remediation and
bio-fuel testing.

**Control Systems West Inc**    HQ
1150 Industrial Ave Ste F
Petaluma CA 94952
P: 707-763-1108   F: 707-763-9324    PRC:143
www.controlwest.com
Email: info@controlwest.com
Estab: 1970

Richard Borders, VP
Joseph Perry, Engineering Manager
Bruce Borders, President

Designer and fabricator of a broad variety of custom electrical controls for industrial applications.

**Controlco**    HQ
3451 Vincent Rd Ste C
Pleasant Hill CA 94523
P: 855-371-9511   F: 925-948-8760    PRC:304
www.controlco.com
Email: sales@controlco.com
Estab: 1958

Brian Turner, President

Provider of automation and solutions to address
the Internet of Things for commercial buildings,
(BIoT).

**Conval Inc**    BR
6006 Kibler Rd
Paradise CA 95969
P: 530-877-5172    PRC:166
conval.com
Email: convalwest@sbcglobal.net
Emp: 11-50

Scott Hilke, US Western Regional Manager

Manufacturer of pressure forged steel valves.
The company products include globe valves, ball
valves, and strainers.

**Convergent Laser Technologies**    HQ
1660 S Loop Rd
Alameda CA 94502
P: 510-832-2130    PRC:189
www.convergentlaser.com
Email: sales@convergentlaser.com
Estab: 1984

Sarah Weld, Product Manager & Junior Executive

Provider of medical laser systems and fiber optic
devices. The company deals with training and
product support services.

**Cooling Source Inc**    HQ
3111 Independence Dr
Livermore CA 94551
P: 925-292-1293   F: 925-292-5061    PRC:129
www.coolingsource.com
Email: info@coolingsource.com
Estab: 2009

Michel Gelinas, President

Provider of thermal design solution for LED
lighting, medical, military/aero, and test equipment
industries.

**Coolsystems Inc** HQ
1800 Sutter St Ste 500
Concord CA 94520
P: 510-868-2100   F: 510-559-9402   PRC:196
www.gameready.com
Email: info@gameready.com
Estab: 1997

Emil Chavarria, Manufacturing Engineer
Arlene Alvarez, SVP of Regulatory Affairs and
Quality Assurance
Cindy Kumar, VP of Finance
Lindsay Romero, Associate Product Manager
Keith Price, Senior Buyer

Manufacturer of medical devices. The company
specializes in injury treatment and accelerated
recovery systems.

**Cooper** HQ
450 Sansome 9th Fl
San Francisco CA 94111
P: 415-267-3500   PRC:189
www.cooper.com
Email: hello@cooper.com
Estab: 1992

Alan Cooper, Founder
Doug Lemoine, Managing Director

Designer of kiosks, medical devices and software,
smartphone, IT tools, websites, irrigation, supply
chain management, and financial services system.

**Copypro Inc** HQ
2500-A Dean Lesher Dr
Concord CA 94520
P: 925-689-1200   F: 925-689-1263   PRC:95
www.copypro.com
Email: copypro@copypro.com
Estab: 1993

Bob Klein, General Manager

Manufacturer and seller of heavy-duty desktop
duplication systems such as duplicators, printers,
and analyzers.

**Corad Technology Inc** BR
3080 Olcott St Ste 202B
Santa Clara CA 95054
P: 408-496-5511   F: 408-496-1211   PRC:126
www.corad.com
Estab: 1987

Michael Lugay, Senior Applications Engineer

Manufacturer of load boards, probe cards, instrumentation systems, and related components. The
company deals with installation services.

**Corcept Therapeutics Inc** HQ
149 Commonwealth Dr
Menlo Park CA 94025
P: 650-327-3270   F: 650-327-3218   PRC:261
www.corcept.com
Email: info@corcept.com
Estab: 1998
Sales: $100M to $300M

Joseph Belanoff, Co-Founder
Charlie Robb, CFO
Carl Wilson, Director of Quality Assurance
Sean Maduck, SVP of Commercial
Juli Rombuck, Executive Assistant

Focuses on the discovery of drugs. The company
offers services to patients, physicians, and also
hospitals.

**Cordis A Cardinal Health Co** DH
1820 McCarthy Blvd
Milpitas CA 95035
P: 408-273-3700   F: 844-279-2752   PRC:189
www.cordis.com
Email: gmb-cordis-customer-support@cardinal-
health.com

Ramesh Marrey, Engineering Fellow
Gerry Prather, Area Sales Director
Ernest Estrada, National Sales Manager
Esteban Peralta, Chemist

Provider of diagnostic and interventional products
for healthcare devices such as catheters, balloons, stents, wires and vascular closure.

**Cordova Printed Circuits Inc** HQ
1648 Watson Ct
Milpitas CA 95035
P: 408-942-1100   F: 408-946-3252   PRC:207
cordovaprintedcircuits.com
Estab: 1978

Lisa Luna, Executive

Provider of flex circuits and printed circuit boards.
The company focuses on sculptured flex circuits
and multilayer flex circuits.

**Corecess Global Inc** BR
3080 Olcott St Ste 125-A
Santa Clara CA 95054
P: 408-567-5300   PRC:61
www.corecess.com
Email: sales@corecess.com
Estab: 1997

Lee Khang, Team Leader

Designer, developer, and manufacturer of
telecommunication equipment for the broadband
access network.

**Coretest Systems Inc** HQ
400 Woodview Av
Morgan Hill CA 95037
P: 408-778-3771   F: 408-779-9418   PRC:19
www.coretest.com
Email: sales@coretest.com
Estab: 1984

David Lynch, President
Scelina Guel, Administrative Assistant

Designer and manufacturer of core analysis
equipment for the oil and gas, hydrothermal, and
environmental segments.

**Corium International Inc** HQ
235 Constitution Dr
Menlo Park CA 94025
P: 650-298-8255   F: 650-298-8012   PRC:24
www.coriumintl.com
Estab: 1995

Benton Wong, Associate Engineer
Perry Sternberg, President
Adrian Faasse, CEO
Sophie Kornowski, Chairman
Bobby Singh, CTO

Provider of transdermal delivery systems and
related technology solutions. The company is also
engaged in therapeutic product development.

**Corman Technologies Inc** HQ
1060A Fourth St
Santa Rosa CA 95404
P: 707-575-7800   PRC:322
cormtech.com

Joseph Chenoweth, Software Engineer
Frances Corman, CFO

Provider of software development and consulting
services for a variety of clients in the software
industry.

**Cornerstone Environmental Group
LLC** BR
7600 Dublin Blvd Ste 200
Dublin CA 94568
P: 877-633-5520   F: 925-560-9879   PRC:142
cornerstoneeg.com

Jessica Bernardini, Project Manager
Maura Dougherty, Senior Project Manager
Paul Stout, Area Manager
Maria Bowen, Environmental Scientist II
Jessica Sees, Administrative Assistant

Provider of engineering consulting and field services. The company offers services for the solid
waste water industry and agricultural clients.

**Corning Technology Center** BR
680 W Maude Ave
Sunnyvale CA 94085
P: 650-846-6000   F: 650-846-6000   PRC:86
www.corning.com
Estab: 1851

Wendell Weeks, Chairman
David Morse, EVP
Donnell Walton, Research Director

Provider of specialty glass and ceramics services
and sells keystone components to electronics,
mobile emissions control, and life science industries.

**Corona Labs Inc** HQ
611 Mission St 7th Fl
San Francisco CA 94105
P: 415-996-6877   PRC:319
www.coronalabs.com
Email: info@coronalabs.com
Estab: 2008

Vlad Shcherban, Engineering Lead

Developer of games, e-books, and other interactive content. The company offers services to the
educational sector.

**Corona Labs Inc** HQ
611 Mission St 7th Fl
San Francisco CA 94105
P: 415-996-6877   PRC:319
coronalabs.com
Email: info@coronalabs.com
Estab: 2008

Rob Miracle, Developer Relations Manager

A cross-platform framework for creating apps and
games for mobile devices and desktop systems.

**Corrigo Inc** BR
1900 S Norfolk St Ste 100
San Mateo CA 94403
P: 877-267-7440 PRC:324
www.corrigo.com
Email: info@corrigo.com
Estab: 1999

Rick Michaux, Founder
Lyle Newkirk, EVP of Finance and Administration
David Rainton, EVP of Technology

Developer of facilities management platforms. The company offers services to business organizations.

**Corsair Inc** HQ
47100 Bayside Pkwy
Fremont CA 94538
P: 510-657-8747 F: 510-657-8748 PRC:91
www.corsair.com
Email: support@corsair.com
Estab: 1994

Andrew Paul, CEO
Thi La, COO
Michael Potter, CFO
Terri Stynes, Chief Human Resources Officer
Bertrand Chevalier, SVP of Worldwide Sales

Designer of high-speed modules for mission-critical servers. The company also caters to high-end workstations.

**Corvus Pharmaceuticals Inc** HQ
863 Mitten Rd Ste 102
Burlingame CA 94010
P: 650-900-4520 PRC:268
www.corvuspharma.com
Estab: 2014

Joseph Buggy, Co-Founder
J.D Daniel Hunt, SVP
Leiv Lea, CFO
Long Kwei, VP of Biometrics & Clinical Operations
William Ben Jones, SVP of pharmaceutical development

Focuses on the development of first-in-class agents that target the immune system. The company serves the healthcare industry.

**Cosmed Usa** HQ
1850 Bates Ave
Concord CA 94520
P: 925-676-6002 F: 925-676-6005 PRC:189
www.cosmed.com
Email: info@cosmed.com
Estab: 1980

Orla May, Owner
Steve Roberts, Director of Finance
Becky Keehn, Sales Manager of Health
Nathan Miller, Customer Service Manager
Michael Bryazki, Service Manager

Developer and manufacturer of medical devices for accurate body composition assessments for infants, children, and adults.

**Couchbase Inc** HQ
3250 Olcott St
Santa Clara CA 95054
P: 650-417-7500 PRC:323
www.couchbase.com
Email: info@couchbase.com
Estab: 2009

Ravi Mayuram, Engineering
Matt Cain, President
Denis Murphy, Chief Revenue Officer
Greg Henry, CFO
Chris Galy, Chief People Officer

Developer of products and technology to meet the elastic scalability, always-on availability, and data mobility requirements of critical applications.

**Countis Laboratories** HQ
12295 Charles Dr
Grass Valley CA 95945
P: 530-272-8334 F: 530-272-6702 PRC:70
www.countis.com
Email: tcountis@countis.com
Emp: 1-10 Estab: 1964

Michelle Baker, Manager

Manufacturer of microwave components. The company also offers custom machined components for space, defense, medical and telecommunication industries.

**Countryman Associates Inc** HQ
195 Constitution Dr
Menlo Park CA 94025
P: 650-364-9988 F: 650-364-2794 PRC:60
www.countryman.com
Email: support@countryman.com
Estab: 1978

Preston Countryman, CEO
Gabriela Sucher, Office Administrator

Manufacturer of direct boxes and ultra-miniature microphones. The company's products include ear sets, hanging, and podium microphones.

**Coupa Software Inc** HQ
1855 S Grant St
San Mateo CA 94402
P: 650-931-3200 PRC:319
www.coupa.com
Emp: 728 Estab: 2006
Sales: $1M to $3M

Jp Krishnamoorthy, EVP of Engineering
Sanket Naik, SVP of Cloud Engineering Operations
Rob Bernshteyn, CEO
Todd Ford, CFO
Mark Riggs, Chief Customer Officer

Global technology platform for Business Spend Management (BSM) to deliver measurable value.

**Cozad! Trailers** HQ
4907 Waterloo Rd
Stockton CA 95215
P: 209-931-3000 F: 209-931-0239 PRC:179
www.cozadtrailers.com
Email: sales@cozadtrailers.com
Emp: 1-10 Estab: 1955

Delores Pistacchio, President
Mark Westcott, Corporate Controller

Manufacturer of trailers. The company serves small and large construction companies and the military and aerospace industries.

**Cp Lab Safety** HQ
14 Commercial Blvd Ste 113
Novato CA 94949
P: 415-883-2600 F: 415-532-1662 PRC:20
www.calpaclab.com
Email: info@cplabsafety.com
Estab: 1996

Kelly Farhangi, President

Manufacturer of laboratory safety equipment to prevent fire, reduce waste emission and exposure to toxic fumes.

**CP Media Group Inc** HQ
2010 Crow Canyon Pl Ste 100
San Ramon CA 94583
P: 951-694-4830 PRC:324
www.cpcom.com

Robb Capielo, President

Provider of audio visual production, website development and hosting, social media marketing, and related services.

**Cp Software Group Inc** HQ
716 Figueroa St
Folsom CA 95630
P: 916-985-4445 F: 916-985-3557 PRC:326
www.cpsoftwaregroup.com
Emp: 1-10

David Saykally, President

Provider of capital formation, fund raising, management consulting, technical and marketing, and incubator services for startup and established companies.

**Cpacket Networks** HQ
2130 Gold St Ste 200
San Jose CA 94043
P: 650-969-9500 PRC:97
www.cpacket.com

Hari Miriyala, VP of Software Engineering
Paola Moretto, VP of System Engineering
Juneed Ahamed, Senior Software Engineer
Sarah Bravo, Software Engineer
Georgios Charitos, Engineer

Provider of solutions for network traffic monitoring and data center performance management. The company specializes in traffic monitoring switches.

**Cpc Scientific Inc** HQ
160 E Tasman Dr Ste 200
San Jose CA 95134
P: 408-734-3800 F: 408-734-3810 PRC:34
www.cpcscientific.com
Email: sales@cpcscientific.com
Estab: 2001

Shawn Lee, CEO
Theresa Cheng, President
Irvine Skeoch, COO
Xiaohe Tong, CTO
Baosheng Liu, General Manager

Provider of amino acids, cGMP, generic, catalog, modified, FRET & TR- FRET, and custom peptides to researchers and pharmaceutical companies.

**Cpi International** HQ
  5580 Skylane Blvd
  Santa Rosa CA 95403
P: 707-525-5788   F: 707-545-7901    PRC:31
www.cpiinternational.com
Email: sales@cpiinternational.com
Estab: 1986

Tommy Mitchell, President
Alissa Morse, Sales Manager
Christy Messina, Account Manager
Alexis Chappell, Customer Service
Bob Kemp, Corporate Controller

Manufacturer of microbiological testing products
and analytical instrument supplies. The company
serves the semi-conductor industry.

**Crcdj LLC** HQ
  1462 Seareel Pl Ste F
  San Jose CA 95131
P: 408-855-8909    PRC:163
www.crcdj.com
Email: dj@crcdj.com

Didier deGery, President

Provider of shaped bags and pouches. The company's services include rotary die cutting, steel
rule die cutting, and micro-form and fill.

**Creagri Inc** HQ
  25565 Whitesell St
  Hayward CA 94545
P: 510-732-6478   F: 510-732-6493    PRC:268
www.creagri.com
Email: info@creagri.com
Estab: 2002

Roberto Crea, President
Jessica Burkhard, Executive Assistant

Manufacturer of nutraceutical products. The
company also offers polyphenol and innovative
products related to olives for foods, health and
dietary supplements.

**Credence MedSystems Inc** HQ
  1430 O'Brien Dr Ste D
  Menlo Park CA 94025
P: 844-263-3797    PRC:248
www.credencemed.com
Email: info@credencemed.com
Estab: 2011

John Merhige, CCO

Provider of pharmaceutical products. The company specializes in single-dose injectable medications in pre-filled syringes.

**Creganna Medical** BR
  1353 Dell Ave
  Campbell CA 95008
P: 408-364-7100    PRC:188
www.creganna.com

Susan Engelking, Manager
Alex Elliott, Manager

Provider of medical devices. The company offers
services that ranges from clinical and regulatory
support to design and manufacturing services.

**Crescendo Bioscience Inc** HQ
  341 Oyster Point Blvd
  S San Francisco CA 94080
P: 650-351-1354   F: 650-871-7155    PRC:251
myriad.com

Bernie Tobin, President
David Chernoff, Chief Medical Officer
Eric Sasso, VP of Medical & Scientific Affairs
Alexander Voinov, Associate Director of Software
Viviane Chen, Senior Clinical Data Manager

Developer of diagnostic tools to provide diagnostics and treatment for autoimmune and inflammatory diseases.

**Crestpoint Solutions Inc** HQ
  4900 Hopyard Rd Ste 100
  Pleasanton CA 94588
P: 925-828-6005   F: 925-828-6022    PRC:322
www.crestpt.com
Email: info@crestpt.com
Estab: 2000

Jose Medina, ASP.Net Engineer
Erick Domingo, VP of Operations & Technology

Provider of project planning, programming, web
hosting, and wireless and records management
services.

**Cri Design Inc** HQ
  48834 Kato Rd Ste 101A
  Fremont CA 94538
P: 510-770-4925   F: 510-770-4930    PRC:211
www.cridesign.com
Email: sales@cridesign.com
Estab: 1996

Shenglei Yang, Senior PCB Design Engineer
Leo Jiang, Director of System Design Ario Data
Christine Yeh, Supply Chain Buyer

Provider of PCB layout design, fabrication, assembly and turnkey services. The company offers
services to the industrial sector.

**Crime Alert** HQ
  690 Lenfest Rd
  San Jose CA 95133
P: 800-367-1094   F: 408-254-9813    PRC:63
www.crimealert.com
Email: info@crimealert.com

Julie Buller, CEO
Jim Maruca, General Manager
Walter Cote, IT Network Administrator

Provider of residential, industrial, and commercial
security monitoring solutions. The company focuses on IP monitoring and disaster recovery.

**Criterion Network Services Inc** HQ
  763 Parma Way
  Los Altos CA 94024
P: 650-947-7755    PRC:67
www.criter.com
Email: info@criter.com

Srinivas Vegesna, Founder

Provider of network design, system integration,
configuration, and remote network management
services.

**Crmantra Inc** HQ
  2200 Powell St Ste 1070
  Emeryville CA 94608
P: 415-839-9672   F: 415-738-6345    PRC:322
www.crmantra.com
Email: info@crmantra.com
Estab: 2005

Amit Garg, Founder

Developer of software for customer relationship
management needs. The company also focuses
on business intelligence and analysis.

**CRMIT Solutions Pvt Ltd** HQ
  1525 McCarthy Blvd Ste 1000
  Milpitas CA 95035
P: 408-722-0634    PRC:326
www.crmit.com
Estab: 2003

Vinod Reddy, Founder

Provider of customer experience cloud solutions
for banking, insurance education, retail, life science, energy, telecom, and financial services.

**Crocus Technology** HQ
  2380 Walsh Ave
  Santa Clara CA 95051
P: 408-380-8300   F: 408-732-8250    PRC:86
www.crocus-technology.com
Email: info@crocus-technology.com

Jeff Childress, VP of Magnetic Devices
Lucas Pannell, Corporate Accounting Manager

Manufacturer of magnetic switches, current
sensors, and embedded memory products. The
company serves the automotive and industrial
sectors.

**Cross-Circuit Networks Inc** HQ
  6300 San Ignacio Ave Ste E
  San Jose CA 95119
P: 408-654-9637   F: 408-654-9657    PRC:326
www.cross-circuit.com
Email: sales@cross-circuit.com
Estab: 1997

Arthur Xu, CEO

Provider of networking solutions specializing in
information technology infrastructure design, systems virtual environment and consolidation.

**Crossbar Inc** HQ
  3200 Patrick Henry Dr Ste 110
  Santa Clara CA 95054
P: 408-884-0281   F: 408-884-0283    PRC:212
www.crossbar-inc.com
Email: info@crossbar-inc.com
Estab: 2010

Amit Prakash, Staff Device Engineer
John Nguyen, Design Engineer
Cheng Pan, Senior Process Engineer
Cung Vu, Engineer
Majid Milani, Device Characterization Engineer

Provider of 3D resistive RAM technology. The
company serves customers in the automotive,
connected devices, consumer, and enterprise
segments.

**CrowdANALYTIX** HQ

440 N Wolfe Rd Ste 170
Sunnyvale CA 94085
P: 866-333-4515 PRC:315
www.crowdanalytix.com
Email: connect@crowdanalytix.com
Estab: 2012

Divyabh Mishra, CEO
Amit Nagpal, COO
Aravind Venugopalan, VP of Solutions

Develops and deploys AI and Data Science
solutions.

**Crown Bioscience Inc** HQ

3375 Scott Blvd Ste 108
Santa Clara CA 95054
P: 855-827-6968 PRC:268
www.crownbio.com
Email: busdev@crownbio.com
Estab: 2006

Irene Chang, Operating Engineer
Jean-Pierre Wery, CEO
Henry Li, CSO
Eva Ho, CFO

Specializes in drug discovery, clinical trials, and
cardiovascular and metabolic disease research
programs.

**Crown Lift Trucks** BR

1420 Enterprise Blvd
West Sacramento CA 95691
P: 916-373-8980 PRC:179
crown.com
Emp: 11-50

Sam Dixon, Sales Manager
Jim Mozer, SVP
Tim Quellhorst, SVP
Kevin McCarthy, Branch Manager
Corey Sheehan, Allied Products Designer

Manufacturer of industrial lift trucks. The company
offerings include C-5 Series IC Trucks, Hand Pallet Trucks, Tow Tractors, and Walkie Stackers.

**Crown Manufacturing Company Inc** HQ

37625 Sycamore St
Newark CA 94560
P: 510-742-8800 F: 510-742-8500 PRC:157
www.crown-plastics.com
Email: cmc@crown-plastics.com
Estab: 1959

Aziz Shariat, President
John Coffman, Plant Manager

Provider of plastic and injection molded products.
The company offers insert and over molding,
drilling, tapping, and heat stamping services.

**Crypto Forensics Technologies Inc** HQ

14895 E 14th St Ste 320
San Leandro CA 94578
P: 510-483-1955 F: 510-483-1933 PRC:26
www.cryptoforensics.com
Email: enquiries@cryptoforensics.com

Austine Ohwobete, Cyberstrategist

Provider of cybersecurity solutions to businesses,
organizations, and the government. The company
focuses on cyberforensics and compliance
services.

**Crystal Dynamics Inc** HQ

1400A Seaport Blvd Ste 300
Redwood City CA 94063
P: 650-421-7600 PRC:317
crystald.com
Estab: 1992

Gary Snethen, CTO
Chad Queen, Director of Production
Noah Hughes, Studio Creative Director
Chris Hudson, Director of Operations
James Loe, Technical Director

Designer and developer of animated videos.
The company also specializes in mobile gaming
software products.

**Crystal River Optics** HQ

2111 Research Dr Ste 8
Livermore CA 94550
P: 925-371-1309 F: 925-454-0875 PRC:173
www.crystalriveroptics.com
Email: krystalriv@aol.com
Estab: 1994

Ted Judd, Owner

Provider of custom fabrication services of optical
components. The company is engaged in prototyping and offers technical support.

**Crystal Solar Inc** HQ

3050 Coronado Dr
Santa Clara CA 95054
P: 408-490-1340 F: 408-727-1705 PRC:135
www.xtalsolar.com
Email: info@xtalsolar.com
Estab: 2008

V. Siva, EVP of Engineering
T.S Ravi, Founder
David Bostwick, CFO
Somnath Nag, SVP of Product Development
Jean Vatus, Technology Director

Developer of solar cells and modules. The company focuses on the conversion of feedstock gas to
mono-crystalline silicon wafers.

**Crystallume Pvd** HQ

3300 Nicolaus Rd
Lincoln CA 95648
P: 916-645-3560 F: 916-645-0146 PRC:47
www.crystallumepvd.com
Email: sales@crystallumepvd.com
Emp: 1-10 Estab: 1984

David Baker, President

Provider of PVD coatings for functional applications. The company also specializes in infinium
coatings.

**CS Bio Company Inc** HQ

20 Kelly Ct
Menlo Park CA 94025
P: 650-322-1111 PRC:15
www.csbio.com
Estab: 1993

Jason Chang, CEO
Zoe Liang, Director of Operations
Hanson Chang, Senior Director of Instrumentation

Provider of automated peptide synthesis instrumentation, peptide synthesizers, and custom
peptides to the life science community.

**Csi Forensic Supply** HQ

PO Box 16
Martinez CA 94553
P: 925-686-6667 F: 925-686-6696 PRC:233
www.csiforensic.com
Email: sales@csiforensic.com
Estab: 1978

Bob Cellucci, President

Manufacturer and supplier of products for law
enforcement for crime scene and crime laboratory
applications.

**Csrware Inc** HQ

100 Shoreline Hwy Ste 100B
Mill Valley CA 94941
P: 855-277-9273 PRC:323
www.csrware.com
Email: info@csrware.com
Estab: 2006

Karen Alonardo, CEO
Adam Escobar, Environmental Sustainability
Manager

Developer of sustainability resource management
software. The company specializes in supply
chain, enterprise ERP solutions, and consulting
services.

**Css Corp** HQ

1900 McCarthy Blvd Ste 210
Milpitas CA 95035
P: 650-385-3820 F: 408-429-9232 PRC:67
www.csscorp.com
Email: info@csscorp.com
Estab: 1996

Brijesh Balakrishnan, SVP
Manish Tandon, CEO
Nishikant Nigam, EVP
Sundararajan Sampath, EVP
Satyanarayanan Visvanathan, SVP

Provider of enterprise level support solutions for
IT products. The company is involved in virtualization, storage, and archiving solutions.

**Cti Controltech** HQ

22 Beta Ct
San Ramon CA 94583
P: 925-208-4250 F: 925-208-4251 PRC:148
www.cti-ct.com
Email: contactus@cti-ct.com
Estab: 1976

Rency Ignacio, Control Systems Engineer
Adam Pennell, Sales Manager
Jeff Podesto, Technical Sales Manager
Steve Briggs, Inside Sales Manager
John Constas, Inside Sales Specialist

Provider of industrial process control and emission solutions. The company's services include
engineering, sales, and support.

**Ctt Inc** HQ

5870 Hellyer Ave Ste 70
San Jose CA 95138
P: 408-541-0596 F: 408-541-0794 PRC:209
www.cttinc.com
Email: sales@cttinc.com
Estab: 1981

Michael Roden, Quality Assurance Manager
Gordon Graham, Regional Sales Manager
Thanh Thai, VP of Operations
Russell Wong, Controller

Manufacturer and supplier of power amplifiers, frequency converters & multipliers, and transmitters & receivers. The company serves military purposes.

**Cubus Solutions Inc**    HQ
3049 Independence Dr Ste A
Livermore CA 94551
P: 925-606-8708    PRC:326
www.cubussolutions.com
Email: info@cubussolutions.com
Estab: 2006

John-Ashley Paul, President

Provider of online banking solutions to seamlessly integrate with core system while delivering real-time, and secure, banking services to members.

**Cultivate Systems**    HQ
1040 Main St Ste 301
Napa CA 94559
P: 707-690-9425   F: 707-944-1733   PRC:326
www.cultivatesystems.com
Email: sales@cultivatesystems.com
Estab: 1998

Eric Binau, Founder

Provider of construction services. The company offers civil site work, construction, demolition, and general contracting services.

**Cumulus Networks LLC**    HQ
185 E Dana St
Mountain View CA 94041
P: 650-383-6700    PRC:325
cumulusnetworks.com
Email: info@cumulusnetworks.com
Estab: 2010

JR Rivers, Co-Founder
Nolan Leake, CTO

Provider of Linux operating system hardware and software solution that offers flexibility for modern data networking designs and operations.

**CUneXus Solutions Inc**    HQ
50 Old Courthouse Sq Ste 300
Santa Rosa CA 95404
P: 877-509-2089    PRC:323
cunexusonline.com
Email: info@cunexus.com
Estab: 2008

Haans Galassi, VP of Product Development

Provider of pre-screening lending strategy that pre-approves entire loan product portfolio for customers.

**Cupertino Signal Processing**    HQ
PO Box 631
Cupertino CA 95015-0631
P: 408-725-0846    PRC:207
www.cupertinosignal.com
Email: info@cupertinosignal.com

John Wincn, Owner

Specializes in analog circuit analysis and evaluation services. The company offers technical documentation.

**Cureline Biopathology LLC**    HQ
150 N Hill Dr Ste 24
Brisbane CA 94005
P: 415-468-6400   F: 415-468-2248   PRC:306
curelinebiopathology.com
Estab: 2003

Olga Potapova, President
Kathleen Talmadge, VP of Finance and Operations
Lita DeLeon, Director of Histology Laboratory

Provider of human and animal tissue processing services. The company also focuses on preservation and biospecimen management.

**Curiox Biosystems Inc**    HQ
735 Industrial Rd Ste 109
San Carlos CA 94070
P: 650-226-8420   F: 650-590-5406   PRC:34
www.curiox.com
Email: sales@curiox.com
Emp: 11-50

Namyong Kim, CEO

Developer of assay platforms. The company specializes in surface chemistry and engineering. It focusses on automation of bioassays.

**Current Controls Inc**    HQ
4110 Citrus Ave Ste 5
Rocklin CA 95677
P: 916-630-5507   F: 916-630-5570   PRC:323
www.currentcontrols.net
Email: gcook@currentcontrols.net
Emp: 1-10

Gary Cook, Partner

Designer and manufacturer of control panels for OEMs in many sectors. The company also offers PLC programming, system integration, and other services.

**Curtis & Tompkins Laboratories**    HQ
2323 Fifth St
Berkeley CA 94710
P: 510-486-0900   F: 510-486-0532   PRC:138
www.curtisandtompkins.com
Estab: 1878

Matt Carroll, Programmer
Kurt Buss, Administrative Assistant
Jason Miller, GC & MS Analyst
Maichi Tu, Chemist
Faith Nichols, Sample Control Technician

Provider of environmental analytical testing services. The company is also engaged in operational management.

**Curtis Instruments Inc**    BR
235 E Airway Blvd
Livermore CA 94551
P: 925-961-1088   F: 925-961-1099   PRC:94
www.curtisinstruments.com
Estab: 1960

Mike Bachman, Special Project Staff Engineer
Anders Hultman, Manager
Gilbert Mink, Senior Technician

Manufacturer of hydraulic pump controllers. The company also specializes in electric steering controllers.

**Custom Alloy Corp**    BR
2337 California Ave
South Lake Tahoe CA 96150
P: 530-544-2836   F: 530-544-2888   PRC:81
www.customalloy.us
Emp: 11-50 Estab: 1968

Adam Ambielli, President

Manufacturer of metals for seamless and welded pipe fittings & forgings. The company's products are in alloy steels, nickel alloys, and carbon steels.

**Custom Coils Inc**    HQ
4000 Industrial Way
Benicia CA 94510
P: 707-752-8633   F: 707-752-8637   PRC:214
www.ccoils.com
Email: info@ccoils.com
Estab: 1978

Thomas Quinn, President
Deanna Larson, Human Resource Coordinator

Manufacturer of coils, coil assemblies, and solenoids. The company also offers other electro-magnetic devices.

**Custom Gear & Machine**    HQ
6459 Brisa St
Livermore CA 94550
P: 925-455-9985   F: 925-455-9925   PRC:80
www.cgmgear.com
Email: info@cgmgear.com
Estab: 1983

Anthony Castruccio, President
Jane Castruccio, VP
Tony Castruccio, Manager

Manufacturer of custom gears. The company also offers overhaul services for gearboxes and caters to industries like food and steel processing.

**Custom Micro Machining Inc**    HQ
707 Brown Rd
Fremont CA 94539
P: 510-651-9434   F: 510-351-9437   PRC:80
www.cmmusa.com
Estab: 1990

Victor Nguyen, Founder

Manufacturer of precision housing carriers and microwave assemblies. The company is involved in design, installation, and delivery services.

**Custom Microwave Components Inc**    HQ
44249 Old Warm Springs Blvd
Fremont CA 94538
P: 510-651-3434   F: 510-651-1054   PRC:86
www.customwave.com
Estab: 1982

Greg Mau, President
Nam Nguyen, Microwave Technician

Manufacturer of microwave components. The company also specializes in providing attenuators with control devices.

**Custom Product Development Co** HQ
4603A Las Positas Rd
Livermore CA 94551
P: 925-960-0577 PRC:80
www.cpd-corp.com
Estab: 1974

Gerald Ammirato, President

Developer and manufacturer of mechanical components and turn-key assembly solutions. The company specializes in developing customized products.

**Customweather Inc** HQ
230 California St Ste 420
San Francisco CA 94111
P: 415-777-3303 F: 415-777-3003 PRC:325
www.customweather.com
Email: sales@customweather.com
Estab: 2000

Geoff Flint, President
Agustin Diaz, Chief Meteorologist
Kevin Levey, VP of Operations
Susan Flint, Business Manager
Jared Lovell, Systems Administrator

Provider of industry solutions. The company offers hurricane tracking, developer tools, and marine forecasts.

**Cutera Inc** HQ
3240 Bayshore Blvd
Brisbane CA 94005
P: 415-657-5500 F: 415-330-2444 PRC:13
www.cutera.com
Email: info@cutera.com
Estab: 1998
Sales: $300M to $1 Billion

David Mowry, CEO
Fuad Ahmad, Interim CFO
Michael Karavitis, EVP
Jin Ho, Information Technology Manager
TJ Huffman, Regional Sales Manager

Manufacturer of aesthetic solutions such as face and body laser, light, and other energy-based aesthetic systems for hair removal and pigmented lesions.

**Cutting Edge Machining Inc** HQ
100 San Lucar Ct
Sunnyvale CA 94086
P: 408-738-8677 F: 408-738-3684 PRC:5
www.cemachining.com
Email: info@cemachining.com
Estab: 1922

Ron Gokan, Owner

Provider of contract manufacturing solutions for the medical, aerospace, and telecommunication sectors.

**Cvm Inc** HQ
7066-D Commerce Cir
Pleasanton CA 94588
P: 925-847-8808 F: 925-847-9635 PRC:80
www.cvmcvm.com
Estab: 1980

Glen Garrettson, VP of Engineering
James Blackburn, Engineering Technician
Garrett Gersten, Senior Mechanical Engineer
Paul Crothers, Senior Mechanical Engineer
Bob Switek, Founder

Provider of custom machine tools. The company also offers electrical fabrication, machining, and robotic services.

**Cyagen Biosciences Inc** HQ
2255 Martin Ave Ste E
Santa Clara CA 95050
P: 800-921-8930 F: 408-969-0336 PRC:34
www.cyagen.com
Email: service@cyagen.com
Estab: 2005

Xiao Xu, Manager

Manufacturer of cell culture products. The company also focuses on animal models and molecular biology tools.

**Cyberdata Corp** HQ
3 Justin Ct
Monterey CA 93940
P: 831-373-2601 F: 831-373-4193 PRC:62
www.cyberdata.net
Email: sales@cyberdata.net
Estab: 1974

Phil Lembo, President
Ken Chitpanich, Purchasing Manager
Allyn Donigian, Sales Manager
Paul Towber, RMA Manager

Designer and manufacturer of USB cables. The company also offers VoIP and printed circuit board design services.

**Cyberglove Systems LLC** HQ
2157 O'Toole Ave Ste L
San Jose CA 95131
P: 408-943-8114 F: 408-943-8119 PRC:316
www.cyberglovesystems.com
Estab: 1990

Faisal Yazadi, CEO

Provider of data glove technology. The company offers system installation and integration and custom software and hardware services.

**Cybermanor** HQ
610 University
Los Gatos CA 95032-4416
P: 408-399-3331 F: 408-399-3341 PRC:329
www.cybermanor.com
Email: info@cybermanor.com
Estab: 1999

Gordon Zuiden, Founder
PATRICK ROSENGARTEN, COO
Jim Kohl, Director of Operations
ED LALOSH, Senior Installer

Designer of internet connected home electronic and networking solutions. The company also offers installation services.

**Cybersoft** BR
165 Glenview Dr
San Francisco CA 94131
P: 415-449-7998 PRC:322
www.cybersoftbpo.com
Email: info@cyberconversion.com

Pawan Chalasani, CEO

Provider of offshore business and knowledge process outsourcing services. The company specializes in title, financial, and document processing services.

**Cybosoft General Cybernation Group Inc** HQ
2868 Prospect Park Dr Fl 3
Rancho Cordova CA 95670
P: 916-631-6313 F: 916-631-6312 PRC:99
www.cybosoft.com
Email: info@cybosoft.com
Emp: 1-10 Estab: 1994

George Cheng, ISA President

Provider of control technology solutions for the process control, building control, and equipment control markets.

**Cyclos Semiconductor** HQ
1995 University Ave Ste 375
Berkeley CA 94704
P: 510-649-3741 F: 510-665-1331 PRC:86
www.cyclos-semi.com
Estab: 2004

Alexander Ishii, VP of Engineering
Marios Papaefthymiou, President

Provider of resonant mesh semiconductor IP, design automation tools, and design consulting services to mobile, wireless, and medical sectors.

**Cygna Energy Services Inc** HQ
1600 S Main St
Walnut Creek CA 94596
P: 925-930-8377 F: 925-930-8375 PRC:322
cygna.net
Estab: 2003

Glenn Smith, President

Provider of application development, data integration, systems integration, consulting, and web services.

**Cymabay Therapeutics Inc** HQ
7575 Gateway Blvd Ste 110
Newark CA 94560
P: 510-293-8800 F: 510-293-9090 PRC:249
www.cymabay.com
Email: info@cymabay.com

Harold Wart, President
Sujal Shah, CFO
Charles McWherter, SVP
Janet Dorling, CCO
Klara Dickinson, Chief Regulatory

Developer of therapies for the treatment of metabolic diseases. The company serves the healthcare industry.

**Cymed** HQ
1123 N Market Blvd Ste 5
Sacramento CA 95834
P: 800-582-0707 F: 800-582-0707 PRC:187
cymed.us
Email: customerservice@cymed.us
Emp: 1-10

Nicholas Gritzai, Marketing Manager

Provider of ostomy pouching systems. The company specializes in skin care products and serves individuals and hospitals.

**Cypress Digital Media** HQ
650 Castro St Ste 120-500
Mountain View CA 94041
P: 650-257-0741   F: 650-268-8636   PRC:324
www.cypressdigitalmedia.com
Email: info@cypressdigitalmedia.com
Estab: 2010

John Ghashghai, Founder
James Yokota, Director of Client Operations

Provider of web design, mobile development,
and online marketing for interactive agencies and
marketing campaigns.

**Cypress Envirosystems Inc** HQ
5883 Rue Ferrari Ste 100
San Jose CA 95138
P: 800-544-5411   F: 888-681-8319   PRC:124
www.cypressenvirosystems.com
Email: info@cypressenvirosystems.com
Estab: 2006

Harry Sim, CEO

Provider of solutions to retrofit existing commercial buildings and industrial facilities for improved
asset utilization and lower maintenance costs.

**Cypress Semiconductor Corp** HQ
198 Champion Ct
San Jose CA 95134
P: 408-943-2600   F: 408-943-4730   PRC:212
www.cypress.com
Email: customercare@cypress.com
Estab: 1982
Sales: Under $1 Million

Brad Buss, CFO
J. de Oliveira, EVP
Thomas Surrette, EVP of Human Resources
Michael Balow, EVP of Worldwide Sales & Appli-
cations
Adrian Woolley, VP of Strategic Marketing

Provider of IC solutions to the data and telecommunication markets. The company is engaged in
training and technical support services.

**Cypress Systems Inc** HQ
40365 Brickyard Dr Ste 101
Madera CA 93636
P: 559-229-7850   F: 559-225-9007   PRC:272
www.cypressingredients.com
Email: info@cypressingredients.com
Emp: 1-10

Paul Willis, CEO
Mark Whitacre, Chief Science Officer
Roland Geiger, QI Business Operation & Custom-
er Support

Provider of natural food forms of organically
bound minerals and nutritional yeast products and
related supplies.

**Cyrun Corp** HQ
2125 Delaware Ave Ste C
Santa Cruz CA 95060
P: 831-458-0949   F: 831-459-9406   PRC:319
www.cyrun.com
Emp: 1-10   Estab: 1993

John Roevekamp, Founder
Glen Haimovitz, Founder
Darrell Luera, VP of Client Services
Gary Powell, Director of Business Development
Gaming

Developer of windows-based integrated software
system. The company caters to public safety
organizations.

**Cyterix Pharmaceuticals Inc** HQ
1700 Owens St Ste 500
San Francisco CA 94158
P: 415-865-2059   PRC:259
www.cyterix.com
Email: info@cyterix.com
Estab: 2010

Steven Everett, Founder
Luis Bayol, CFO
Lutz Giebel, SV Life Sciences
Tim Kutzkey, The Column Group

Engaged in the discovery and development of
small molecule oncology prodrugs. The company
is also involved in the development of cancer
therapeutics.

**Cytoculture International Inc** HQ
249 Tewksbury Ave
Point Richmond CA 94801
P: 510-233-0102   F: 510-233-3777   PRC:34
www.cytoculture.com
Email: cytoculture@gmail.com
Estab: 1986

Randall von Wedel, Founder
Alexa Davis, Administrative Assistant

Provider of technical consulting and microbiological laboratory services. The company specializes
in biofuel project.

**Cytokinetics Inc** HQ
280 E Grand Ave
S San Francisco CA 94080
P: 650-624-3000   F: 650-624-3010   PRC:34
www.cytokinetics.com
Estab: 1997
Sales: $30M to $100M

Robert Blum, President
David Cragg, CHRO
Ching Jaw, SVP
Andrew Wolff, SVP
Elisabeth Schnieders, SVP of Business Develop-
ment

Developer of cancer treatment programs for
cancer and also cardiovascular patients. The company specializes in therapeutic programs.

**Cytomx Therapeutics Inc** HQ
151 Oyster Point Blvd Ste 400
S San Francisco CA 94080-1913
P: 650-515-3185   F: 650-351-0353   PRC:249
www.cytomx.com
Estab: 2008

Sean McCarthy, CEO
Michael Kavanaugh, Chief Scientific Officer
Danielle Olander, VP of Human Resources
Bryan Irving, Senior Director of Cancer Immunol-
ogy
Marc Besman, Director of Program

Developer of biomolecular therapeutics. The company specializes in antibody drug development,
cancer study, clinical and translational medicine.

**Cytosport Inc** HQ
1340 Treat Blvd Ste 350
Walnut Creek CA 94597
P: 888-298-6629   PRC:272
www.musclemilk.com
Estab: 1998

Robin Sinni, Human Resource Manager
Frank Povich, Sales Manager
Brandon Hagy, Sports Marketing Manager
Laura Kight, Trade Marketing Manager
Ralph Knights, Director of Innovation

Manufacturer of health care supplements. The
company specializes in fitness supplements for
athletes, to strengthen muscles and bones.

**D & T Fiberglass Inc** HQ
8900 Osage Ave Ste D
Sacramento CA 95828
P: 916-383-9012   F: 916-383-1851   PRC:280
www.dtfiberglass.com
Email: info@dtfiberglass.com
Emp: 1-10   Estab: 1987

Donny Stommel, Manager

Manufacturer of fiberglass reinforced plastic bulk
containers. The company's products are used for
water and chemical treatment applications.

**D A M Good Engineering & Manufac-
turing Inc** HQ
2720 Aiello Dr Ste A
San Jose CA 95111
P: 408-224-6494   F: 408-224-5394   PRC:80
www.damgood.com
Email: contact@damgood.com
Estab: 1988

Adan Giron, Mechanical

Manufacturer of parts for microwave, telecom, and
industrial sectors. The company offers gaming
devices, model engine parts, and other products.

**D Danz & Sons Inc** HQ
6741 N Willow Ave Ste 101
Fresno CA 93710
P: 559-252-1770   F: 559-252-1781   PRC:190
www.ddanzandsons.com
Email: customerservice@ddanzandsons.com
Emp: 11-50   Estab: 1927

Antonio Alcorta, President
Angie Burke, CFO

Specializes in the custom fitting, designing, and
manufacturing of ophthalmic prosthetics. The company deals with patient care.

**D-EYE** HQ
6097 Rocky Point Cir
Truckee CA 96161
P: 401-473-6323   PRC:186
www.d-eyecare.com
Email: info@d-eyecare.com
Emp: 1-10   Estab: 2014

Alberto Scarpa, CEO

Designer and manufacturer of diagnostic instruments. The company offers smart phone based
retinal imaging systems for clinical assessments.

**D-Tools Inc** HQ
1850 Gateway Blvd Ste 1060
Concord CA 94520
P: 925-681-2326   F: 925-681-2900   PRC:318
www.d-tools.com
Email: sales@d-tools.com
Estab: 1998

Adam Stone, President
Steve Collard, COO
Corey Krehel, CTO
Tim Bigoness, VP of Sales
Josh Carlson, Senior Marketing Communications Manager

Developer and marketer of software to streamline processes which accompany the integration and installation of low-voltage systems.

**d2m Interactive** HQ
309 Westhill Dr
Los Gatos CA 95032
P: 408-315-6802   PRC:325
www.d2m.com
Email: d2m@d2m.com
Emp: 1-10   Estab: 1996

David Rose, Owner

Provider of web development, management, and e-commerce services. The company also focuses on marketing.

**D2s Inc** HQ
4040 Moorpark Ave Ste 250
San Jose CA 95117
P: 408-781-9017   PRC:323
www.design2silicon.com
Email: contact@design2silicon.com
Estab: 2007

Shone Lee, Director of Application Engineering
Tam Nguyen, Senior Engineer
Michael Pomerantsev, Software Engineer
Abhishek Shendre, Staff Engineer
Mariusz Niewczas, Senior Consulting Engineer

Supplier of a computational design platform to maximize eBeam technology. The company's products include TrueMask MDP and DS.

**Dac Semiconductor** HQ
2051 Junction Ave Ste 232
San Jose CA 95131
P: 408-435-7930   F: 408-435-7935   PRC:208
www.dacsemi.com

Chen Feng, Network Engineer

Manufacturer of semiconductor devices. The company specializes in quad-band switch modules and RF power amplifier ICs for mobile phones.

**Daihen Advanced Component Inc** RH
1223 E Arques Ave
Sunnyvale CA 94085
P: 408-736-2000   F: 408-736-2010   PRC:209
www.daihen-ac.com
Email: sales@daihen-ac.com
Estab: 1996

William Brown, VP of Business Operations
Brian Haines, VP

Supplier of vacuum environment material handling and RF transmission products to semiconductor, flat panel display and solar, and equipment manufacturers.

**Dakota Ultrasonics Corp** HQ
1500 Green Hills Rd Ste 107
Scotts Valley CA 95066
P: 831-431-9722   F: 831-431-9723   PRC:19
www.dakotaultrasonics.com
Email: info@dakotaultrasonics.com
Emp: 1-10

Russ Vogel, Software Engineer

Manufacturer of industrial ultrasonic testing equipment. The company serves the aerospace, power generation, and petrochemical industries.

**DalCor Pharmaceuticals** HQ
400 S El Camino Real Ste 1200
San Mateo CA 94402
P: 650-401-2000   PRC:268
www.dalcorpharma.com
Email: info@dalcorpharma.com
Emp: 1-10   Estab: 2015

Fouzia Thode, CEO
Louise Proulx, Chief Development Officer
Michael Dixon, CFO
Donald Black, Chief Medical Officer

Provider of precision medicines. The company is involved in the development of treatments for the cardiovascular events.

**Dali Wireless Inc** RH
535 Middlefield Rd Ste 280
Menlo Park CA 94025
P: 408-481-9400   F: 408-481-9420   PRC:63
daliwireless.com
Email: information@daliwireless.com
Estab: 2006

Sasa Trajkovic, VP of Engineering
Albert Lee, CEO
Shawn Stapleton, CTO
Basem Anshasi, COO
Andrew Leung, VP of Operations

Provider of RF router platform for healthcare, airport, education, hospitality, stadium, residential and MDU, and metros and train industries.

**Dance BioPharm Inc** HQ
2 Mint Plz Ste 804
San Francisco CA 94103
P: 415-769-4200   PRC:268
www.dancebiopharm.com
Email: info@dancebiopharm.com
Estab: 2010

John Patton, CEO
Michael Kaseta, CFO
Melissa Rhodes, Chief Development Officer
Truc Le, Chief Technical Operations & Manufacturing
Lisa Porter, CMO

Developer of pharmaceutical drugs. The company specializes in inhaled insulin products for the treatment of diabetes.

**Danco Machine** HQ
950 George St
Santa Clara CA 95054
P: 408-988-5235   PRC:80
dancomachine.com
Email: info@dancomachine.com
Estab: 1979

Jim Herget, Chief Engineer
Jesse Kuhn, Engineering, Estimating & Planning Manager
Juan Sanchez, Customer Service
Carlos Ocana, Manager

Developer of machined components and assemblies. The company is involved in EDM, welding, sheet metal, and precision grinding.

**Daniel B Stephens & Associates Inc** BR
1300 Clay St Ste 600
Oakland CA 94612
P: 800-933-3105   F: 510-645-1532   PRC:140
www.dbstephens.com

Nicole Sweetland, President
Stephen Cullen, SVP of California Operations
Eric Hendrix, VP
Gregory Schnaar, Senior Environmental Scientist
John Dodge, Associate

Provider of services in hydrology, environmental engineering, and science. The company services include water resources and soil testing.

**Dantel Inc** HQ
2991 N Argyle Ave
Fresno CA 93727
P: 559-292-1111   F: 559-292-9355   PRC:59
www.dantel.com
Email: info@dantel.com
Emp: 1-10   Estab: 1971

Al Hutcheson, CEO
Mary Papadopoulos, CFO
Frank Martinez, SVP of National Accounts
Ifty Husain, Director of Product Development
John Guerrant, Senior Customer Support

Manufacturer of telecommunications instrumentation equipment. The company offers documentation support and upgrading services.

**Darcoid Nor-Cal Seal** HQ
950 Third St
Oakland CA 94607
P: 510-836-2449   F: 510-836-2675   PRC:162
www.darcoid.com
Estab: 1947

Jason Hainer, Application Engineer
Yamita Anderson, Inside Sales Manager
Diane Deguzman, Inside Sales

Provider of rubber based products. The company offers gaskets, composite and dynamic seals, molded shapes, and thermal products.

**Data Distributing LLC** HQ
107 Dakota Ave
Santa Cruz CA 95060
P: 831-457-3537   F: 831-425-1186   PRC:95
www.datadistributing.com
Email: info@datadistributing.com
Emp: 11-50   Estab: 1984

Nancy Buell, COO
Robert Medina, National Sales Account Manager
Jason Smith, Shipping Manager
Jennifer King, Regional Account Manager

Provider of solutions such as mass storage, peripheral, storage management software, import, archive, and images and data distribution.

**Data ID Systems** HQ
286 E Hamilton Ave Ste F
Campbell CA 95008
P: 408-371-5764   F: 408-626-7066   PRC:103
www.dataid.com
Email: sales@dataid.com
Estab: 1982

Mark Fitchjian, Director of Sales

Provider of identification management solutions.
The company offers passport readers, bar code
scanners, and fixed asset tracking products.

**Data Path Inc** HQ
318 McHenry Ave
Modesto CA 95354
P: 209-521-0055   PRC:323
www.mydatapath.com
Email: info@mydatapath.com
Emp: 1-10   Estab: 2005

James Bates, VP of Operations

Provider of IT services such as IT management,
web design, software development, and education
related data services.

**Data Physics Corp** HQ
2480 N First St Ste 100
San Jose CA 95131
P: 408-437-0100   F: 408-456-0100   PRC:209
www.dataphysics.com
Email: sales@dataphysics.com
Estab: 1984

Kalyan Vitta, Applications Engineer
Leonard Kandt, Product Development Engineer
Raman Sridharan, Applications Engineer
Wes Christner, Service Engineer
Sabine Castagnet, COO

Provider of high performance test and measurement solutions for noise and vibration applications.
The company offers drop testing services.

**Data Scale** HQ
42430 Blacow Rd
Fremont CA 94539
P: 510-651-7350   PRC:159
www.datascale.com
Email: sales@datascale.com
Estab: 1973

Terry Lowe, Business Owner

Manufacturer of liquid net weight filling equipment.
The company offers services to the food and
chemical industries.

**Data Tech** HQ
1911 N Fine
Fresno CA 93727
P: 800-833-8824   F: 559-226-5418   PRC:322
www.datatechag.com
Email: sales@datatechag.com
Emp: 1-10   Estab: 1980

Isaac Davidian, President
Matthew Davidian, VP
Hannah Tarrats, Customer Service

Developer of specialized accounting software.
The company primarily caters to the agricultural
industry.

**Data-Com Solutions** HQ
8413 Washington Blvd Ste 140
Roseville CA 95678
P: 916-331-2377   F: 916-344-0104   PRC:64
www.data-comsolutions.com
Emp: 1-10

Rick Gewerth, President

Designer of data communication networks, national equipment roll outs, and network hardware
installation services.

**Database International** HQ
1301 McKenzie Ave
Los Altos CA 94024
P: 650-965-9102   PRC:325
www.databaseinternational.com
Estab: 1998

Vladimir Rubashevsky, Database Administration

Provider of database application development
and database administration services and also
offers project management and event coordination
services.

**Database Republic** HQ
8712 Marysville Rd
Oregon House CA 95962
P: 530-692-2500   PRC:324
databaserepublic.com
Emp: 1-10   Estab: 2002

Anthony Williams, Programmer

Provider of enterprise analysis and strategy modeling services. The company also focuses on DB
design and implementation.

**Databricks Inc** HQ
160 Spear St 13th Floor
San Francisco CA 94105
P: 866-330-0121   PRC:326
databricks.com
Email: info@databricks.com

Vijay Gill, SVP of Engineering
Ion Stoica, Co-Founder
Matei Zaharia, Co-Founder
Ali Ghodsi, Co-Founder
Matt Fryer, VP of Chief Data Science Officer

Provider of platform for big data processing
solutions. The company offers exploration and
visualization, production pipelines, and third party
apps.

**DataDirect Networks Inc** BR
2929 Patrick Henry Dr
Santa Clara CA 95054
P: 408-419-2800   PRC:95
www.ddn.com
Email: info@ddn.com
Estab: 1998

Randy Kreiser, Chief Architect

Provider of storage array, file system, and object
storage appliances to broadcast, biopharma,
supercomputing, and financial service sectors.

**Dataglance Inc** HQ
42840 Christy St Ste 106
Fremont CA 94538-3154
P: 510-656-0500   F: 510-656-0552   PRC:322
dataglance.com
Email: sales@dataglance.com

Martin Pyne, Software Engineer
Ashok Shetty, President

Provider of data management software that support LIVE data conversion/migration, electronic
document generation & processing, and web
services.

**Dataguise** HQ
39650 Liberty St Ste 400
Fremont CA 94538
P: 877-632-0522   PRC:324
www.dataguise.com
Estab: 2007

Jan Peters, Senior Technical Support Engineer
Manmeet Bhasin, Co-Founder
Ashish Gupta, CEO
Jim Emmons, VP of Sales
JT Sison, VP

Provider of cloud migration, auditing, and monitoring solutions. The company serves the healthcare,
consumer, and retail industries.

**Datalab** HQ
1893 Concourse Dr
San Jose CA 95131
P: 408-943-1888   PRC:53
datalabsj.com

Helen Ham, Director

Provider of analysis and certification of process
tanks and printed circuit board sections. The
company also offers chemical process control
software.

**Datameer Inc** BR
577 Second St Ste 200
San Francisco CA 94107
P: 800-874-0569   PRC:323
www.datameer.com
Email: info@datameer.com
Estab: 2009

Stefan Groschupf, CEO
Peter Voss, CTO
John Morrell, Senior Director of Product Marketing
Alex Malbet, Senior Product Manager of Cloud
Solutions
Shirley Liu, Senior Manager

Provider of data analytics solution for business
users. The company also focuses on integration,
business analytics consulting, and training.

**Dataray Inc** HQ
1675 Market St
Redding CA 96008
P: 866-946-2263   F: 530-255-9062   PRC:172
www.dataray.com
Email: corporate@dataray.com
Emp: 1-10   Estab: 1988

Rocco Dragone, VP of Engineering
Kevin Garvey, COO
Natalia Tjandra, Operations Manager

Supplier of performance beam profiling products
to the photonics community. The company provides BladeCam, Beam Scope, Phase Pro, and
UV converters.

**Datasafe** HQ
574 Eccles Ave
S San Francisco CA 94080
P: 650-875-3800 PRC:324
www.datasafe.com
Email: info@datasafe.com
Estab: 1946

Thomas Reis, President
Rob Reis, President
Tom Reis, CEO
Jose Moreno, Director of Information Technology
Scott Reis, Director of Sales

Provider of digital solutions. The company's services include records storage, document shredding and imaging, and rotation.

**Datastax Inc** RH
3975 Freedom Cir
Santa Clara CA 95054
P: 408-933-3120 PRC:324
www.datastax.com
Email: info@datastax.com
Estab: 2010

Martin Ryswyk, EVP of Engineering
Jonathan Ellis, CTO
Billy Bosworth, CEO
Robin Schumacher, VP of Products
Charlotte Crouch, Accounts Payable Manager

Distributor of database management system for internet enterprise. The company offers training & certification, expert support, and consulting services.

**Datavision Inc** HQ
3018 Knollwood Dr
Cameron Park CA 95682
P: 530-387-3575 F: 530-387-3587 PRC:319
www.datvsn.com
Email: support@datvsn.com
Emp: 1-10 Estab: 1978

Teri Christiansen, Software Design & Development

Provider of software solutions for accounting, supply chain, and water and utility applications. The company also offers hosting and support.

**Datest Corp** HQ
47810 Westinghouse Dr
Fremont CA 94539
P: 510-490-4600 F: 510-490-4111 PRC:189
www.datest.com
Email: info@datest.com
Estab: 1984

Robert Boguski, President

Provider of testing and inspection services. The company specializes in engineering testing and counterfeit inspection for industrial products.

**Datrium Inc** HQ
385 Moffett Park Dr
Sunnyvale CA 94089
P: 669-721-9444 F: 650-427-5001 PRC:116
www.datrium.com
Email: info@datrium.com
Estab: 2012

Brian Biles, Chief Product Officer
Hugo Patterson, Chief Scientist
Sazzala Reddy, CTO
Ganesh Venkitachalam, Co-Founder
Boris Weissman, Chief Architect

Provider of VM infrastructure convergence for elastic, on-demand, and VM-centric primary storage.

**Datum Technologies Inc** HQ
327 Ohair Ct Ste D
Santa Rosa CA 95407
P: 707-738-3914 PRC:80
www.datumtech-cnc.com
Email: info@datumtechnologiesinc.com
Estab: 2003

Richard Hunt, President
Analisa Hunt, CFO

Manufacturer of precision machining services. The company serves customers in the aerospace, medical device, and energy industries.

**David J Powers & Associates Inc** HQ
1871 The Alameda Ste 200
San Jose CA 95126
P: 408-248-3500 F: 408-248-9641 PRC:142
davidjpowers.com
Email: info@davidjpowers.com
Estab: 1972

Akoni Danielsen, President
Martha Silveira, CFO
Judy Shanley, VP
Zachary Dill, Creative Director
Amie Ashton, Senior Project Manager

Provider of environmental consulting services. The company focuses on transportation, parks, and recreation projects.

**Davlin Coatings** HQ
700 Allston Way
Berkeley CA 94710
P: 510-848-2863 F: 510-848-1464 PRC:47
www.davlincoatings.com
Estab: 1968

Jim Hofmeister, CEO
Janie Hofmeister, Director of Sales and Marketing
Matthew Jeffries, Sales Manager
Jonathan Baker, Operations Manager

Manufacturer of coatings for architectural and industrial purposes. The company offers elastomeric waterproof coatings.

**Davtron Inc** HQ
427 Hillcrest Way
Emerald Hills CA 94062
P: 866-369-5588 F: 650-369-9988 PRC:5
davtron.com

Rod Walker, Engineer
Kevin Torresdal, President

Designer and manufacturer of avionic instruments. The company's portfolio comprises volt meters, clocks, probes, and more.

**Dawn Reis Ecological Studies** HQ
38 Lower Cutter Dr
Watsonville CA 95076
P: 831-588-7550 F: 831-761-9496 PRC:34
ecologicalstudies.com
Email: moreinfo@ecologicalstudies.com
Emp: 1-10

Dawn Reis, Senior Wildlife & Aquatic Ecologist
Eric Scott, Wildlife Ecologist
Jessica Wheeler, Assistant Ecologist & GIS Specialist
Kaia Colestock, Wildlife Ecologist
Kim Glinka, Wildlife Ecologist

Provider of wildlife research and biological consulting services. The company is specialized in aquatic systems and endangered species population.

**Dawn VME Products** HQ
47915 Westinghouse Dr
Fremont CA 94539
P: 510-657-4444 F: 510-657-3274 PRC:79
www.dawnvme.com
Email: sales@dawnvme.com
Estab: 1985

Jorge Hernandez, Senior Mechanical Engineer
Barry Burnsides, CEO
Sharnjit Sekhon, Quality Manager
Eddie Chin, Regional Sales Manager
Nelson Carney, SVP of Corporate Development

Designer and manufacturer of enclosures, backplanes, chassis and card cage. The company also offers design services and power supplies.

**Day Wireless Systems** BR
4728 E Second St Ste 10
Benicia CA 94510
P: 707-746-5920 F: 707-746-5924 PRC:60
www.daywireless.com
Email: support@daywireless.com
Estab: 1969

Gordon Day, President
Mike Ishida, VP of Sales
Brent McGraw, EVP
Marty Gant, VP of Rentals

Supplier of RF, wireless, and radio communication equipment. The company's services include rentals, system integration, and marketing.

**Db Control Corp** HQ
1120 Auburn St
Fremont CA 94538-7328
P: 510-656-2325 F: 510-656-3214 PRC:70
www.dbcontrol.com
Email: marketing@dbcontrol.com
Estab: 1990

Jacob Thampan, VP of Engineering
Steven Olson, Marketing Manager
Steve Walley, VP of Business Development

Provider of high-power solutions for mission-critical applications. The company's services include repairs and contract manufacturing.

**DB Design Group** HQ
48507 Milmont Dr
Fremont CA 94538
P: 408-834-1400 PRC:19
www.dbdesign.com
Email: info@dbdesign.com
Estab: 1989

Mark Stenholm, President
Rennie Bowers, CEO
John Love, Sales Account Manager

Supplier of technology solutions. The company caters to the semiconductor, solar, and medical industries.

**Dc Electronics** HQ
1870 Little Orchard St
San Jose CA 95125
P: 408-947-4500  F: 408-947-4510  PRC:202
www.dcelectronics.com
Email: info@dcelectronics.com
Estab: 1979

Quy Vu, NPI & Manufacturing Engineering Manager
Vu Nguyen, Manufacturing Engineer
Ruben Macias, General Manager
Dharma Funder, Human Resource Manager
Liza Gampon, Quality Manager

Manufacturer of electronic cable assemblies. The company also offers distribution and other services.

**Dc Precision Machining** HQ
885 Jarvis Dr
Morgan Hill CA 95037
P: 408-928-2510  PRC:80
www.tecanannualreport.com
Estab: 1999

Cuu Banh, President
Achim von Leoprechting, CEO
Rudolf Eugster, CFO
Ulrich Kanter, CFO
Wael Yared, CTO

Manufacturer of engineered plastics and metals for many industries. The company offers CNC precision machining and turn-key assembly services.

**Dcl** HQ
48641 Milmont Dr
Fremont CA 94538
P: 510-330-1938  F: 510-651-1806  PRC:326
www.dclcorp.com
Email: info@dclcorp.com
Estab: 1982

Dave Tu, President
Norman Tu, CEO
Brian Tu, Chief Revenue Officer
Alan Nakasato, Director of Quality Management and Regulatory Compliance
Victoria Maddux, VP of Sales

Provider of fulfillment and supply chain management services. The company offers e-Commerce, retail fulfillment, and reverse logistics services.

**Dcm Datasystems** RH
39159 Paseo Padre Pkwy Ste 303
Fremont CA 94538
P: 510-494-2321  PRC:322
www.dcmds.com
Email: sales@dcmusa.com
Estab: 1972

Ashok Choudhury, President
A. Biji, Specialist

Provider of managed IT services. The company focuses on system administration, storage, enterprise management, and staffing services.

**DDRdrive LLC** HQ
384 Madeline Ct
Palo Alto CA 94306
P: 650-804-8227  PRC:126
www.ddrdrive.com
Email: sales@ddrdrive.com
Estab: 2007

Christopher George, Founder

Provider of solid-state storage system. The company specializes in ZFS and ZIL acceleration.

**De Anza Manufacturing Services Inc** HQ
1271 Reamwood Ave
Sunnyvale CA 94089
P: 408-734-2020  F: 408-734-2580  PRC:62
www.deanzamfg.com
Estab: 1978

Art Takahara, President
Mike Takahara, VP of marketing & Sales

Provider of manufacturing services. The company specializes in cable, harness, wiring, and mechanical assemblies.

**Delmar Pharmaceuticals Inc** DH
3475 Edison Way Ste R
Menlo Park CA 94025
P: 604-629-5989  PRC:254
www.delmarpharma.com
Email: info@delmarpharma.com

Saiid Zarrabian, President
Robert Hoffman, Chairman
Scott Praill, CFO

Developer of pharmaceutical products. The company specializes in treatment of various cancer such as lung, brain, cervical, ovarian tumors and leukemia.

**Delong Manufacturing Co** HQ
967 Parker Ct
Santa Clara CA 95050
P: 408-727-3348  F: 408-727-7615  PRC:80
www.delongmfg.com
Estab: 1966

Dave Delong, CEO

Provider of machining services. The company focuses on prototype development, production, engineering design, and kitting and assembly.

**Delphix** HQ
1400A Seaport Blvd Ste 200
Redwood City CA 94063
P: 650-494-1645  PRC:323
www.delphix.com
Email: sales@delphix.com
Estab: 2008

Marc Aronson, SVP of Engineering
Sumedh Bala, Engineering Manager
Roma Mehta, Engineering Manager
Kevin Greene, QA Engineer
Kyle Cackett, Staff Engineer

Developer of software, database, and database virtualization. The company focuses on website design and hosting and software application development.

**Delphon Industries LLC** HQ
31398 Huntwood Ave
Hayward CA 94544
P: 510-576-2220  F: 510-576-2282  PRC:86
delphon.com
Email: info@delphon.com
Estab: 2004

Jeanne Beacham, CEO
Raj Varma, CTO
Diana Morgan, CFO
Steven Chan, CFO
Philip Haseltine, VP of Manufacturing Operations

Provider of materials and services to the semiconductor, medical, photonics, telecommunications, and military markets.

**Delpor Inc** HQ
1 Tower Pl
S San Francisco CA 94080-1832
P: 415-480-6870  F: 415-480-6871  PRC:257
www.delpor.com
Email: info@delpor.com
Estab: 2009

Tassos Nicolaou, President
Frank Martin, CSO
Carl Spetzler, Director
Lana Ho, Associate Scientist

Developer of next generation drug delivery systems which improve the clinical and commercial value of new and existing drugs and biopharmaceuticals.

**Delta Machine** HQ
2180 Oakland Rd
San Jose CA 95131
P: 408-955-9140  PRC:80
www.deltamachine.com
Estab: 1989

Hugo Jungers, Quality Assurance Manager

Provider of precision machine components and custom parts. The company specializes in CNC milling, CNC turning, and turn key mechanical assemblies.

**Delta Pacific Products Inc** HQ
33170 Central Ave
Union City CA 94587
P: 510-487-4411  F: 510-487-5511  PRC:84
www.deltapacificinc.com
Estab: 1988

Ajeya Singh, Senior Manufacturing Engineer
Fred Betke, President
Pat Dooley, Manager
Yi Wang, Project Manager
Louie Cabrera, Shipping Supervisor

Provider of plastics injection molding and mold making services. The company serves the automotive, agriculture, aerospace, and recreational sectors.

**Delta Star Inc** BR
270 Industrial Rd
San Carlos CA 94070
P: 800-892-8673 PRC:296
www.deltastar.com
Estab: 1908

Ben Magana, General Manager
Bryan Noble, Production Supervisor

Manufacturer of devices for the electrical sector. The company offers devices for the generation, transmission, and distribution of electrical energy.

**Delta Tao Software** HQ
8032 Twin Oaks Ave
Citrus Heights CA 95610
P: 408-730-9336 PRC:319
www.deltatao.com
Email: help@deltatao.com
Emp: 1-10

Joe Williams, President
Tim Cotter, VP

Provider of Macintosh and Windows products and solutions. The company is engaged in installation and technical support.

**Delta Turnstiles LLC** HQ
1011 Detroit Ave Ste C
Concord CA 94518
P: 925-969-1498 PRC:82
www.deltaturnstile.com
Email: sales@deltaturnstile.com
Estab: 2005

Vanessa Howell, Project Manager

Manufacturer of optical turnstiles. The company mainly caters to the corporate sector and the government.

**Deltatrak Inc** HQ
PO Box 398
Pleasanton CA 94566
P: 925-249-2250 F: 925-249-2251 PRC:233
www.deltatrak.com
Email: salesinfo@deltatrak.com
Estab: 1989

Frederick Wu, President
Ray Caron, COO
Brian Edwards, VP of Sales of Cold Chain Solutions
Dave Nathan, VP of Corporate Sales
Dan Hurd, Director of Business Development and Marketing

Manufacturer of cold chain management systems. The company provides data loggers, chart recorders, thermometers, and timers and pH meters.

**Demtech Services Inc** HQ
PO Box 2165
Placerville CA 95667
P: 530-621-3200 F: 530-621-0150 PRC:157
www.demtech.com
Emp: 11-50 Estab: 1999

Dave McLaury, CEO
Gus Fauci, Production

Manufacturer of welding machines. The company also specializes in the manufacture of testing instruments for geo-synthetic installers.

**Denali Therapeutics Inc** HQ
151 Oyster Point Blvd
S San Francisco CA 94080
P: 650-866-8548 PRC:268
www.denalitherapeutics.com
Email: contact@dnli.com
Estab: 2015
Sales: $100M to $300M

Robert Nelsen, Managing Director
Ryan Watts, CEO
Vicki Sato, Chairman
Zach Sweeney, CSO
Carole Ho, Chief Medical Officer

Provider of therapeutic solutions for the treatment of neurodegenerative diseases. The company also specializes in blood brain barrier programs.

**Dendreon Pharmaceuticals LLC** HQ
1700 Saturn Way
Seal Beach CA 90740
P: 877-256-4545 PRC:188
www.dendreon.com
Emp: 11-50 Estab: 1992

Nadeem Sheikh, Senior Director
Ngoc Vu, Accounts payable supervisor
Bryan Boyd, Supervisor
Randall Chu, Senior Scientist
Lisa Lin, Statistician

Provider of biotechnology services. The company provides therapeutics for the treatment of cancer employing active cellular immunotherapy.

**Denele Analytical Inc** HQ
1232 South Ave
Turlock CA 95380
P: 209-634-9055 F: 209-634-9057 PRC:139
www.denelelabs.com
Email: info@denelelabs.com
Emp: 11-50 Estab: 1978

Brando Gonzalez, Laboratory Manager

Provider of agriculture and environmental support services. The company offers analytical services for plant tissue, manure, and wastewater needs.

**Denise Duffy & Associates Inc** HQ
947 Cass St Ste 5
Monterey CA 93940
P: 831-373-4341 F: 831-373-1417 PRC:37
ddaplanning.com
Estab: 1984

Denise Duffy, Owner
Josh Harwayne, Senior Project Manager

Provider of environmental sciences, planning, and biological consulting services. The company is also focused on land use and contract planning.

**Denodo Technologies Inc** HQ
525 University Ave Ste 31
Palo Alto CA 94301
P: 650-566-8833 F: 650-566-8836 PRC:67
www.denodo.com
Email: info.us@denodo.com
Estab: 1999

Juan Lozano, Director of Sales Engineering
Phoebe Bakanas, Service Sales Engineer
Angel Vi, CEO
Paul Moxon, SVP of Data Architectures & Chief Evangelist
Ravi Shankar, SVP

Provider of enterprise data virtualization, data federation, and cloud data integration middleware solutions.

**Dentoni's** HQ
801 S Airport Way
Stockton CA 95205
P: 209-464-4930 PRC:80
www.dentoni.com
Emp: 11-50 Estab: 1980

David Dentoni, President
Daniel Dentoni, Manager

Provider of services for trucks and trailers. The company specializes in welding, machining, ornamental iron, and springs.

**Dependable Plastics** HQ
4900 Fulton Dr
Fairfield CA 94534
P: 707-863-4900 PRC:280
www.dependableplastics.com
Email: info@dependableplastics.com
Estab: 1983

Harry Marquez, Owner
Emil Eger, Owner
Kathy Nunan, CFO

Provider of vacuum and pressure forming, plastic fabrication, and turnkey operations that involve assembly, conductive coating, and painting.

**Dependable Precision Manufacturing Inc** HQ
1111 S Stockton St
Lodi CA 95240
P: 209-369-1055 PRC:80
www.dependableprecision.com
Emp: 1-10 Estab: 1978

Cliff Bride, President

Provider of precision sheet metal fabrication services. The company serves the government and high tech sectors.

**Deplabs Inc** HQ
755 Baywood Dr Ste 165
Petaluma CA 94954
P: 855-445-6560 PRC:323
www.deplabs.com
Estab: 2004

Huw Roberts, Founder
Merrell Maschino, Senior Project Manager

Provider of eCommerce projects. The company involves in eCommerce co-development, application development, third party integration, and back-end integration.

**Depomed Inc** HQ
100 South Saunders Road Ste 300
Lake Forest IL 60045
P: 224-419-7106 F: 510-744-8001 PRC:257
www.assertiotx.com/
Email: investor@assertiotx.com
Estab: 1995
Sales: $100M to $300M

Arthur Higgins, CEO
Dan Peisert, CFO
Stan Bukofzer, SVP
Mark Booth, SVP
Jenny Truong, Human Resource Representative

Developer of therapies for the treatment of pain and other central nervous (CNS) system conditions. The company deals with drug development.

**Deposition Sciences Inc** HQ
3300 Coffey Ln
Santa Rosa CA 95403
P: 707-573-6700 PRC:175
www.depsci.com
Email: solutions@depsci.com
Estab: 1985

Stephanie Ferguson, Human Resource Business Partner
Robert Crase, Assistant Director of Manufacturing
Evan Craves, Program Manager
Allen Christensen, Tech Manager
Jarrod Lewis, Coating Technician

Manufacturer of heat resistant, optical thin film coatings, including color control, metal, optical mirror, and beam splitter coatings.

**DermDx Inc** HQ
2684 E Shea Dr
Fresno CA 93720
P: 559-577-2542 PRC:189
Emp: 1-10   Estab: 2008

Sampath Srikanth, Manager

Developer of solutions for skin cancer detection and diagnosis. The company offers services to the medical industry.

**Dermira Inc** HQ
275 Middlefield Rd Ste 150
Menlo Park CA 94025
P: 650-421-7200 PRC:34
www.dermira.com
Email: info@dermira.com
Estab: 2010

Luis Pena, Co-Founder
Eugene Bauer, Chief Medical Officer
Thomas Wiggans, CEO
Andrew Guggenhime, COO
Ian Clements, VP of Investor Relations

Developer of biopharmaceutical products for the treatment of dermatology diseases such as acne, plaque psoriasis, and hyperhidrosis.

**Desaware Inc** HQ
4750 Almaden Expy Ste 124-390
San Jose CA 95118
P: 408-404-4760   F: 408-404-4780 PRC:323
www.desaware.com
Email: info@desaware.com
Estab: 1991

Dan Appleman, Owner
Marian Kicklighter, Manager
Franky Wong, VP

Developer of tools and components for visual studio programmers. The company offers documentation and professional services.

**Designerx Pharmaceuticals Inc** HQ
4941 Allison Pkwy Ste B
Vacaville CA 95688
P: 707-451-0441   F: 707-451-0499 PRC:254
www.drxpharma.com
Estab: 2002

Robert Randolph, Information Technology Manager
Kunal Patel, Production Scientist
Jonathan Ngai, Assistant Production Scientist
Larry Dunham, Staff Accountant

Provider of pharmaceutical products for treatment of cancer cells from tumors such as melanoma, hepatocellular carcinoma, pancreatic, and mesothelioma.

**DesignMap** HQ
700 Alabama St
San Francisco CA 94110
P: 415-357-1875 PRC:323
www.designmap.com
Email: info@designmap.com
Estab: 2006

Ryan Cornwell, VP of UX Design
Kana Knaak, Design Director
Mike Aurelio, Principal Designer
Chuck Moore, Partner
Nathan Kendrick, Partner

Provider of web site and application design services. The company also specializes in research, usability studies, and visual design.

**Destiny Tool** HQ
3233 De La Cruz Blvd Ste C
Santa Clara CA 95054
P: 408-988-8898   F: 408-988-8927 PRC:157
www.destinytool.com
Email: sales@destinytool.com
Estab: 1982

Guy Calamia, Owner
Daniel Wagner, Outside Sales Manager
Brandon Latzke, Inside Sales Manager
Anabel Duarte, Inside Sales Manager
Nettie Calamia, Office Manager

Developer of end mills. The company offers technical support to customers in Philadelphia, Akron, Dayton, and Iowa regions.

**Detention Device Systems** HQ
25545 Seaboard Ln
Hayward CA 94545
P: 510-783-0771   F: 510-783-5409 PRC:159
www.detentiondevicesystems.com
Email: sales@dds-group.com
Estab: 1985

Dan Breuner, Quality Assurance Manager
Ron Blair, Plant Superintendent

Provider of design and manufacturing services for detention equipment metal fabrications. The company offers sliding door locking and other devices.

**Device Authority Ltd** RH
39300 Civic Ctr Dr Ste 230
Fremont CA 94538
P: 650-603-0997 PRC:324
www.deviceauthority.com
Email: info@deviceauthority.com
Estab: 2014

Darron Antill, CEO
Talbot Harty, CTO
James Penney, CTO
Rao Cherukuri, CSO

Provider of IoT security solutions for industrial, automotive, transportation, healthcare, utilities, and smart cities.

**Devicelock Inc** HQ
3130 Crow Canyon Pl Ste 215
San Ramon CA 94583
P: 925-231-4400   F: 925-886-2629 PRC:317
devicelock.com
Email: us.sales@devicelock.com
Estab: 1996

Ashot Oganesyan, Founder
Vitaly Shipitsin, CEO
Vladimir Chernavsky, EVP
David Matthiesen, Director of Strategic Accounts
Alexei Lesnykh, Executive Advisor

Developer of device control software solutions. The company offers contextual and content-based control for data leak prevention.

**Devonway** HQ
601 California St Ste 210
San Francisco CA 94108
P: 415-904-4000   F: 415-904-0440 PRC:322
www.devonway.com
Email: info@devonway.com
Estab: 2005

Tim Sherburne, Director of Mobile Engineering
Phillip Yin, IT Support Engineer
Chris Moustakas, President
Steve Johnson, CTO
Laurel Timothy, Director of Finance and Human Resources

Provider of enterprise software solutions for utilities and process industries. The company specializes in enterprise asset management solutions.

**Deweyl Tool Inc** HQ
959 Transport Way
Petaluma CA 94954
P: 707-765-5779   F: 707-765-0327 PRC:80
www.deweyl.com
Email: info@deweyl.com
Estab: 1969

William Cline, President

Manufacturer of bonding, large and double flat wire, and small wire bonding wedges. The company's products are used in ultrasonic applications.

**Dhap Digital Inc** HQ
1501 Mariposa St Ste 317
San Francisco CA 94107
P: 415-962-4900 PRC:323
www.dhapdigital.com
Email: hello@dhapdigital.com
Estab: 1998

Tim Irvin, Consultant

Provider of interface that translates a desktop experience to a smartphone and go through Scion vehicle configurations without app download.

**Diablo Analytical Inc** HQ
5141 Lone Tree Way
Antioch CA 94531
P: 925-755-1005   F: 925-755-1007 PRC:19
www.diabloanalytical.com
Email: info@diabloanalytical.com
Estab: 1993

Scott Hein, Co-Founder

Provider of system integration for analytical measuring instruments. The company is engaged in custom software development and laboratory analysis.

**Diablo Clinical Research Inc**　HQ
2255 Ygnacio Vly Rd Ste M
Walnut Creek CA 94598
P: 925-930-7267　F: 925-930-7392　PRC:268
www.diabloclinical.com
Estab: 1995

Emily Galdes, VP
Lori Vitti, Director of Finance
Leonard Chuck, Co-Medical Director
Mark Christiansen, Co-Medical Director
Charlette Vargas, Director of Regulatory Compliance

Provider of clinical research services specializing in endocrinology, internal medicine, cardiology, and neurology.

**Diablo Green Consulting Inc**　HQ
696 San Ramon Valley Blvd Ste 208
Danville CA 94526
P: 925-365-0730　F: 925-365-0729　PRC:142
diablogreen.com
Email: contact@diablogreen.com
Estab: 2005

Chad Simmons, Account Manager
Anindya Kar, Environmental Consultant

Provider of environmental consulting services. The company specializes in site assessments, geophysical survey, and cultural resource management.

**Diablo Precision Inc**　HQ
500 Park Center DR Ste 8
Hollister CA 95023
P: 831-634-0136　F: 831-634-0103　PRC:80
www.diabloprecision.com
Email: info@diabloprecision.com
Emp: 1-10　Estab: 2004

Conor Kelly, President
Michael David, Account Manager

Manufacturer of metal and plastic parts. The company also provides machining, milling, turning, and contract inspection services.

**Diablo Solar Services**　HQ
5021 Blum Rd Ste 2
Martinez CA 94553
P: 925-313-0600　PRC:135
www.diablosolar.com
Email: info@diablosolar.com
Estab: 1984

Phil Deatsch, Owner
Bryan Raymond, President
Dave Hampton, System Design
John Snyder, Manager
Linda Monroe, Bookkeeping

Provider of solar pool heating and solar power photo voltaic systems. The company also offers installation services.

**DiaCarta Inc**　HQ
2600 Hilltop Dr
Richmond CA 94806
P: 800-246-8878　F: 510-735-8636　PRC:34
www.diacarta.com
Email: information@diacarta.com
Estab: 2012

Aiguo Zhang, President
Michael Powell, CSO
Michael Sha, SVP of R&D
Nitin Udar, SVP of Diagnostics and Regulatory

Provider of molecular diagnostics tools such as genotyping tests, colon cancer tests, DNA sample card, and gene mutation detection kits.

**Diagnostic Biosystems Inc**　HQ
6616 Owens Dr
Pleasanton CA 94588
P: 925-484-3350　F: 925-484-3390　PRC:34
www.dbiosys.com
Email: customersupport@dbiosys.com
Estab: 1994

Bipin Gupta, Founder

Developer of primary and monoclonal antibodies, ancillaries, chromogens, and multiplex kits. The company serves the healthcare sector.

**Diagnostic Pathology Medical Group Inc**　HQ
3301 C St Ste 200E
Sacramento CA 95816
P: 916-446-0424　F: 916-446-9330　PRC:303
www.dpmginc.com
Emp: 1-10

Carol Smalley, Director of Operations
Cynthia Gasper, Pathologist
Ryan Kenery, Histotechnician
David Guillen, Manager

Specializes in identifying enzymes extracted from extremophiles for molecular biology, diagnostics, and industrial applications.

**Dialog Semiconductor Inc**　BR
2560 Mission College Blvd
Santa Clara CA 95054
P: 408-845-8500　F: 408-727-3205　PRC:207
dialog-semiconductor.com
Email: na_sales_enquiries@diasemi.com
Estab: 1986

Vivek Bhan, SVP of Engineering
Jalal Bagherli, CEO
Andrew Austin, Sr VP of Sales

Creator of mixed-signal integrated circuits. The company offers products such as audio, backlight LED, wireless audio, and home automation.

**Dialog Semiconductor**　RH
675 Campbell Technology Pkwy Ste 150
Campbell CA 95008
P: 408-374-4200　F: 408-341-0455　PRC:208
www.dialog-semiconductor.com

Jun Ruan, Principal Process Engineer
Thanh Nguyen, Senior QA Engineer
Jalal Bagherli, CEO
Wissam Jabre, CFO
Davin Lee, SVP

Manufacturer of AC/DC and LED SSL products. The company's products include home appliances, smart meters, power adapters, and backlighting devices.

**Dialogic Inc**　HQ
1504 McCarthy Blvd
Milpitas CA 95035-7405
P: 408-750-9400　F: 408-750-9450　PRC:64
www.dialogic.com
Email: insidesales@dialogic.com
Emp: 51-200　Estab: 1984
Sales: $100M to $300M

Kevin Cook, President
Bill Crank, President
Dean Schorno, CFO
Tracey Condra, VP
Norman St.Pierre, VP of Information Technology

Provider of communications products and media server software. The company serves business enterprises and organizations.

**Diamond Systems Corp**　HQ
158 Commercial St
Sunnyvale CA 94086
P: 650-810-2500　F: 650-810-2520　PRC:329
www.diamondsystems.com
Email: sales@diamondsystems.com
Estab: 1989

Joshil O., Senior Hardware Engineer
Jonathan Miller, President

Supplier of SBCs, embedded-ready subsystems, and system expansion modules targeting real-world applications.

**Diamond Tech Inc**　HQ
4347 Pacific St
Rocklin CA 95677
P: 916-624-1118　F: 916-624-1285　PRC:159
www.dtiinnovations.com
Emp: 1-10

Sean Ward, General Manager of Sales
Ingo Pfeiffer, Manufacturing Manager

Provider of drilling equipment and services. The company specializes in electric, core drills, hydraulic, and drill stands.

**Diamond Tool & Die Inc**　HQ
508 29th Ave
Oakland CA 94601
P: 510-534-7050　F: 510-534-0454　PRC:80
www.dtdjobshop.com
Email: rfq@dtdjobshop.com
Estab: 1968

Darrell Holt, President
Dan Welter, VP
Naya Pillazar, Accounting Assistant

Provider of general machine services for the high tech industry. The company serves the aerospace, construction, and food processing industries.

**Dice Molecules Inc**　HQ
220 Penobscot Dr
Redwood City CA 94063
P: 650-566-1402　F: 650-566-1429　PRC:34
www.dicemolecules.com
Email: info@dicemolecules.com
Estab: 2013

J. Judice, Founder
Pehr Harbury, Founder and member of the Board
Phil Patten, Founder
John Bedbrook, Founder
Kevin Judice, Founder

Developer of transformative platforms for the discovery of small molecules. The company translates DNA encoded information into organic compounds.

**Dicom Systems**  HQ
 1999 S Bascom Ave Ste 700
 Campbell CA 95008
P: 415-684-8790  F: 415-684-8790  PRC:189
www.dcmsys.com
Email: sales@dcmsys.com
Estab: 2008

Dmitriy Tochilnik, President
Josh Baker, Technical Project Manager

Provider of enterprise imaging, interoperability,
and teleradiology solutions. The company offers
services to patients.

**Dicon Fiberoptics Inc**  HQ
 1689 Regatta Blvd
 Richmond CA 94804
P: 510-620-5000  F: 510-620-4100  PRC:19
www.diconfiberoptics.com
Email: sales@diconfiber.com
Estab: 1986

Hoffman Cheung, Quality Assurance Director

Supplier of optical components, integrated
modules, and test equipment for the fiber optics
industry.

**Diener Precision Pumps Lp**  DH
 935 E Turner Rd
 Lodi CA 95240
P: 209-365-0405  F: 209-365-0667  PRC:160
dpp.swiss
Email: usa@dpp.swiss
Emp: 1-10  Estab: 1993

Audrey Roberts, USA Sales

Developer of gear and piston pumps, and valves
for cooling and flshing, refrigeration, medical,
biotech, and pharmaceutical industries.

**Dieselcraft Fluid Engineering**  HQ
 PO Box 4625
 Auburn CA 95604
P: 530-613-2150  PRC:159
www.dieselcraft.com
Email: sales@dieselcraft.com
Emp: 11-50

John Nightingale, Chief Engineer

Provider of oil and fuel cleaning technology. The
company offers services for pickup trucks, loaders,
boats, and gen sets.

**DIGICOM Electronics Inc**  HQ
 7799 Pardee Ln
 Oakland CA 94621
P: 510-639-7003  F: 510-639-7090  PRC:91
www.digicom.org
Email: info@digicom.org
Estab: 1982

Mo Ohady, General Manager
Norma Criglar, Controller

Provider of electronics manufacturing services.
The company also deals with packing, shipping,
and labeling services.

**DigiLens Inc**  HQ
 1288 Hammerwood Ave
 Sunnyvale CA 94089
P: 408-734-0219  PRC:176
www.digilens.com
Email: information@digilens.com
Estab: 2003

Thanh Le, Senior Material Engineer
Jonathan Waldern, Founder

Provider of optical design, software development,
electrical engineering, and illumination design
services.

**Digipede Technologies LLC**  HQ
 3527 Mt Diablo Blvd Ste 343
 Lafayette CA 94549
P: 510-834-3645  F: 510-834-8632  PRC:323
www.digipede.net

Robert Anderson, CTO
Daniel Ciruli, Director of Products

Provider of distributed computing solutions for
academic research, entertainment, financial services, and manufacturing business applications.

**Digital Anarchy**  HQ
 226 Tulare St
 Brisbane CA 94005
P: 415-287-6069  PRC:316
www.digitalanarchy.com
Email: sales@digitalanarchy.com

Garrick Meeker, Head Engineer
Jim Tierney, President
Maggie Percell, Customer Support

Provider of photography and video plugins for
Photoshop, elements, after effects, and final cut
pro.

**Digital Artforms Inc**  HQ
 264 Los Gatos-Saratoga Rd
 Los Gatos CA 95030
P: 408-356-6169  F: 408-395-3444  PRC:198
digitalartforms.com
Email: info@dartforms.com
Estab: 1998

Paul Mlyniec, President
Jason Jerald, Chief Scientist
Arun Yoganandan, Lead Architect

Provider of immersive 3D interaction for specialized markets and applications including medicine,
security, and military/command & control.

**Digital Canvas**  HQ
 3731 Sunset Ln Ste 210
 Antioch CA 94509
P: 925-706-1700  F: 925-405-0950  PRC:325
www.digitalcanvas.com
Email: support@digitalcanvas.com
Estab: 1997

Jeff Shaikh, CEO
Jonathan Bernardi, Programmer
Tina Shaikh, Accounting Analyst

Provider of web design and web application development services. The company also offers web
hosting, security solutions, and services.

**Digital Dynamics Inc**  HQ
 5 Victor Sq
 Scotts Valley CA 95066
P: 831-438-4444  F: 831-438-6825  PRC:207
digitaldynamics.com
Email: info@digitaldynamics.com
Emp: 1-10  Estab: 1974

Daryl Gault, President
Bill Murvihill, SVP
Steve Grube, Quality Assurance Manager
Ray Gorski, Director of Sales
Steve Richardson, Network Administrator

Supplier of embedded process control products.
The company is also engaged in manufacturing
OEM control system products.

**Digital Keystone Inc**  HQ
 21631 Stevens Creek Blvd Ste A
 Cupertino CA 95014
P: 650-938-7300  PRC:60
www.digitalkeystone.com
Email: sales@dkeystone.com
Estab: 2001

Mike Jones, Release Engineer
Paolo Siccardo, President
Luc Vantalon, CTO

Provider of solutions enabling content distribution
to tablets, connected TVs, and other entertainment platforms with suite of software and tools.

**Digital Loggers Inc**  HQ
 2695 Walsh Ave
 Santa Clara CA 95051
P: 408-330-5599  F: 408-970-3491  PRC:295
www.digital-loggers.com
Email: sales@digital-loggers.com
Estab: 1980

Rick Lebherz, Sales Engineer

Manufacturer of recording systems and power switches. The company offers call center
recorders, radio logging systems, and recording
accessories.

**Digital Mountain Inc**  HQ
 4633 Old Ironsides Dr Ste 401
 Santa Clara CA 95054
P: 866-344-3627  F: 408-845-9455  PRC:323
www.digitalmountain.com
Email: info@digitalmountain.com
Estab: 2003

Julie Lewis, President
Valerie Karty, Accounting Manager
David Dang, Senior Manager
Wansin Ounkeo, Computer Forensics Examiner

Provider of electronic discovery and computer
forensic services focusing on reduplication, data
management, ESI planning, and cybersecurity.

**Digital Power Corp**  HQ
 48430 Lakeview Blvd
 Fremont CA 94538
P: 510-657-2635  F: 510-657-6634  PRC:98
www.digipwr.com
Email: sales@digipwr.com
Estab: 1969

Amos Kohn, President
Fernando Sandoval, Director of Sales

Designer and manufacturer of switching power
supplies. The company serves the industrial,
military, and medical markets.

**Digital Products Co**     HQ
134 Windstar Cir
Folsom CA 95630-4929
P: 916-985-7219   F: 916-985-8460    PRC:68
www.digitalproductsco.com
Email: info2009@digitalproductsco.com
Emp: 1-10

T. Black, Owner

Provider of telephone line simulators. The company offers two-line telco and party-line simulators and real phone line products.

**Digital View Inc**     HQ
18440 Technology Dr Bldg 130
Morgan Hill CA 95037
P: 408-782-7773   F: 408-782-7883    PRC:94
www.digitalview.com
Estab: 1998

Thomas Saueressig, SAP Product Engineering
DJ Paoni, President
Neil Wood, President
James Henry, CEO
Steve Shander, Chief Customer Officer

Developer and manufacturer of flat panel-related products. The company's offerings include media players, video flyers, and accessories.

**Digite Inc**     HQ
21060 Homestead Rd Ste 220
Cupertino CA 95014
P: 408-418-3834    PRC:325
www.digite.com
Email: support@digite.com

Sudipta Lahiri, Head of Products & Engineering
A. Sridhar, Founder
Ram Subramanian, Co-Founder
Mahesh Singh, Co-Founder
V. Sridhar, Co-Founder

Provider of collaborative enterprise application software. The company's product finds application in process and portfolio management.

**Dinucci Corp**     HQ
1057 Shary Cir
Concord CA 94518
P: 925-798-3946   F: 925-798-3896    PRC:80
www.dinuccicorp.com
Estab: 1978

Sarah Hecker, Contracts Manager Planning & Procurement
Kitten Nash, Manager Shipping & Receiving

Provider of computerized manufacturing and prototyping services. The company offers services to the business sector.

**Diodes Inc**     BR
1545 Barber Ln
Milpitas CA 95035
P: 408-232-9100   F: 408-434-1040    PRC:212
www.diodes.com
Email: inquiries@diodes.com

Keh-Shew Lu, CEO
Brett Whitmire, CFO
Matthew Covert, Global Account Manager
Quynhnhu Ngo, Business System Analyst

Provider of electronic components for communications, lighting, motor control, and audio applications.

**Direct Mail Center**     HQ
1099 Mariposa St
San Francisco CA 94107
P: 415-252-1600   F: 415-252-9100    PRC:324
www.directmailctr.com
Email: dmc@directmailctr.com

Pierre Smit, General Manager
Ray Leung, Account Manager

Provider of data processing, fulfillment, digital and offset printing, mail production, and logistics services.

**Direct Technology**     HQ
3009 Douglas Blvd Ste 300
Roseville CA 95661
P: 916-787-2200    PRC:323
directtechnology.com
Email: info@directtechnology.com
Emp: 11-50 Estab: 1996

Daniel Konieczny, CEO
Damion Walkup, CTO
Kristen Long, VP of Human Resources
Hailey Sharpe, Human Resource Generalist
Davood Ghods, VP of Government Solutions

Provider of software application design and hosting services. The company is engaged in software application development.

**Directed Light Inc**     HQ
74 Bonaventura Dr
San Jose CA 95134
P: 408-321-8500   F: 408-321-8466    PRC:171
www.directedlight.com
Email: info@directedlight.com
Estab: 1983

Neil Ball, President
Michael McCourt, CEO
Pia Concepcion, Financial Controller
Karen Croom, Customer Service Manager

Manufacturer of industrial and scientific laser components. The company offers laser welding, cutting, drilling, ablation, and marking services.

**DirectGov Source Inc**     HQ
39 Bellarmine Ct
Chico CA 95928
P: 530-899-3327   F: 530-809-0372    PRC:188
www.directgovsource.com
Emp: 1-10   Estab: 2007

Jonathan Johnson, President

Manufacturer of personal protection kits. The company offers disposable clothing, biohazard disposal, antimicrobial sanitizers, and hand protection gloves.

**Directnu Energy Corp**     HQ
189 W Santa Clara St
San Jose CA 95113
P: 408-657-3314   F: 408-790-2038    PRC:135
www.directnuenergy.com
Email: info@directnuenergy.com
Estab: 2009

Stefano Falomi, Senior Design Engineer
Keegan Wada, Engineer
David Curtin, President
Hamid Saadat, VP of Operations
Randal Abraham, Business Development Manager

Provider of wind-solar energy solutions with integrated storage and control systems for businesses and government entities.

**Discoverx Corp**     HQ
42501 Albrae St Ste 100
Fremont CA 94538
P: 510-979-1415   F: 510-979-1650    PRC:24
www.discoverx.com
Email: info@discoverx.com
Estab: 2000

Jagdish Saini, VP of Operations
Neil Charter, VP of Cell-Based Assay Operations
Stephanie Fong, Associate Project Manager
Philip Achacoso, Scientist

Developer and marketer of innovative solutions to study major drug target classes such as GPCRs and kinases.

**DisplayLink Corp**     HQ
480 S California Ave Ste 305
Palo Alto CA 94306
P: 650-838-0481   F: 650-838-0482    PRC:95
www.displaylink.com
Email: sales@displaylink.com
Estab: 2003

John Cummins, SVP of Sales & Marketing

Provider of solutions for virtual graphics connectivity between computers and displays. The company makes use of USB, wireless USB, and ethernet.

**Distribution Technologies Inc**     HQ
19 Juno Rd
Tiburon CA 94920
P: 415-999-1191    PRC:179
Estab: 2003

Scott Sims, Founder

Provider of design, analysis, simulation, automation, and project implementation solutions. The company also deals with technical support.

**Ditom Microwave Inc**     HQ
7592 N Maroa Ave
Fresno CA 93711
P: 559-255-7045   F: 559-255-1667    PRC:70
www.ditom.com
Email: sales@ditom.com
Emp: 1-10   Estab: 1987

Mark Weisz, President
Aram Cooper, Manufacturing Manager
John Molina, Inside Sales Manager
Doug Waggoner, Inside Sales Manager

Provider of microwave components for both military and commercial applications. The company offers products such as isolators and circulators.

**Dkw Precision Machining Inc**     HQ
17731 Ideal Pkwy
Manteca CA 95336
P: 209-456-5709   F: 209-824-7889    PRC:80
dkwmachine.com
Emp: 1-10   Estab: 1984

Kurt Franklin, Owner

Manufacturer of precision machined parts and components. The company offers CNC miling and turning, prototype, and production services.

**Dna Bridges Inc**  HQ
55 New Montgomery St Ste 605
San Francisco CA 94105
P: 415-362-0442   F: 415-536-2871   PRC:268
dnabridges.com

L. Burton, Protein Chemistry and Process Development
Cori Gorman, Principal
Eileen Gorman, Registered Patent Agent

Provider of corporate development services. The company offers market analysis, business plan development, patent research, and other services.

**Dnamito Inc**  HQ
2225 E Bayshore Rd Ste 200
Palo Alto CA 94303
P: 650-687-0899   PRC:34
dnamito.com
Email: info@dnamito.com
Estab: 2015

Syed Hamdani, CEO

Provider of DNA technology and cloud platform to enable cancer treatment and early prediction of chronic disease thus vastly improving patient care.

**Dnanexus Inc**  HQ
1975 W El Camino Real Ste 204
Mountain View CA 94040
P: 415-857-0158   PRC:40
www.dnanexus.com
Email: info@dnanexus.com
Estab: 2009

Richard Daly, CEO
Omar Serang, Chief Cloud Officer
Tim O'Brien, VP of Sales

Provider of genome informatics and data management platform. The company provides a global network to share and manage genomic data.

**Dnn Corp**  HQ
155 Bovet Rd Ste 201
San Mateo CA 94402
P: 650-288-3150   PRC:319
www.dnnsoftware.com
Email: sales@dnnsoftware.com
Estab: 2006

Lee McGrath, CFO
Dennis Shiao, Director of Content Marketing
Will Morgenweck, VP of Product Management
John Kelly, Product Manager

Provider of software solutions for content management. The company also offers marketing & eCommerce and product development services.

**Docker Inc**  HQ
144 Townsend St
San Francisco CA 94107
P: 415-941-0376   F: 800-764-4847   PRC:325
www.docker.com
Email: info@docker.com
Estab: 2013

Scott Johnston, CEO
Graham Carroll, Corporate Finance Manager
Jesse Turcotte, Account Executive

Provider of docker platform and docker ecosystem of contributors, partners, and adopters the way distributed applications are built, shipped, and run.

**DOCOMO Innovations Inc**  HQ
3301 Hillview Ave
Palo Alto CA 94304
P: 650-493-9600   PRC:71
www.docomoinnovations.com
Email: inquiries@docomoinnovations.com
Estab: 2011

Hongfeng Yin, Principal Engineer
Hyungsik Shin, Research Engineer
Chenwei Wang, Research Engineer
Yuichi Kakishima, Senior Research Engineer
Lin Du, Software Engineer

Provider of products and services for businesses. The company focuses on business development, network solutions, and mobile network technology.

**Docsend Inc**  HQ
351 California St Ste 1200
San Francisco CA 94104
P: 888-258-5951   PRC:319
docsend.com
Email: sales@docsend.com
Estab: 2013

Frances Le, Software Engineer
Justine DiPrete, Software Engineer
Russ Heddleston, Co-Founder
Tony Cassanego, Co-Founder

Provider of service that makes documents more effective communication tool with intelligence to track, optimize, and control the business documents sent.

**Doctor on Demand**  HQ
275 Battery St Ste 650
San Francisco CA 94111
P: 800-997-6196   PRC:188
www.doctorondemand.com
Email: support@doctorondemand.com
Estab: 2013

Hill Ferguson, CEO

Provider of urgent care doctors. The company offers lab screens for the treatment of mental health and chronic conditions.

**Document Capture Technologies Inc**  HQ
41332 Christy St
Fremont CA 94538
P: 630-530-5400   F: 408-436-6151   PRC:108
www.docucap.com
Email: sales@docucap.com
Estab: 1998

Jim Hewes, Senior Software Engineer
Vien La, Quality Assurance Manager

Manufacturer of mobile document capture solutions such as scanners, copiers, and cloud and printing software.

**Docusign Inc**  HQ
221 Main St Ste 1000
San Francisco CA 94105
P: 877-720-2040   PRC:323
www.docusign.com
Estab: 2003
Sales: $300M to $1 Billion

Tom Casey, SVP of Engineering
Dan Springer, CEO
Emily Heath, Chief Trust and Security Officer
Kirsten Wolberg, CTO
Cynthia Gaylor, SVP

Provider of digital transaction management platform helps to accelerate transactions, reduce costs, and delight customers, suppliers, and employees.

**Doering Machines Inc**  HQ
1000 N Burke St Ste D
San Francisco CA 94124
P: 415-526-2131   F: 415-526-2136   PRC:159
www.doeringmachines.com
Email: sales@doeringmachines.com
Estab: 1884

Richard Doering, President

Manufacturer of food processing equipment. The company also offers pumping systems, extruders, and conveyors.

**Dogpatch Technology Inc**  HQ
548 Market St Ste 66918
San Francisco CA 94104
P: 415-663-6488   PRC:322
Estab: 2011

Jean Truelson, Co-Founder
Palmer Truelson, Co-Founder

Provider of digital strategy and mobile development solutions for game design and research, global media and communications, and grant writing projects.

**Dolby Laboratories Inc**  BR
432 Lakeside Dr
Sunnyvale CA 94085
P: 408-330-3300   F: 408-330-3200   PRC:60
www.dolby.com
Estab: 1965

Parvin Beekharry, Staff SQA Engineer
Kevin Yeaman, President
Lewis Chew, EVP
Dean Drougas, CIO
Linda Rogers, SVP of Human Resources

Provider of speech recognition and voice identification products. The company also offers voice control services.

**Dolcera Corp**  BR
155 Bovet Rd Ste 302
San Mateo CA 94402
P: 650-425-6772   PRC:323
www.dolcera.com
Email: info@dolcera.com
Estab: 2004

Samir Raiyani, CEO
Ed Rozenberg, Co-Founder
Lakshmikant Goenka, Co-Founder
Anil Sharma, Lead of Biomedical Practice
Sateesh Thipirisetti, Lead of High tech practice

Provider of business research, analytics, collaboration, IP patent licensing, and related support services.

**Dolphin Corp** HQ
17485 Monterey Rd Ste 201
Morgan Hill CA 95037
P: 610-725-9125 PRC:322
www.dolphin-corp.com
Email: contact@dolphin-corp.com
Estab: 1995

Kahki Perrine, Account Executive
Werner Hopf, Principal

Provider of information life cycle and business
process management services for organizations
using SAP solutions.

**Dolphin Graphics** HQ
17200 Foothill Blvd
Castro Valley CA 94546
P: 510-881-0154 F: 510-481-8286 PRC:115
www.dolphingraphics.com
Estab: 1986

Dolphin Andre, President
Heidi Heckman, Sales Associate
Linda Luis, Director of Marketing
Tim Treister, Project Manager
Ken Carbone, Principal

Provider of branding and marketing solutions. The
company also offers graphics design and web
design services.

**Dolphin Technology Inc** DH
2025 Gateway Pl Ste 270
San Jose CA 95110
P: 408-392-0012 F: 408-392-0090 PRC:126
www.dolphin-ic.com
Email: corp@dolphin-ic.com
Estab: 1996

Ta-Ke Tien, Senior Technical Staff Engineer
Mo Tamjidi, Founder

Provider of silicon-proven internet protocol for
memory, standard cells, input and output, memory
controllers, and memory test and repair.

**Domico Software** HQ
1220 Oakland Blvd Ste 300
Walnut Creek CA 94596
P: 510-841-4155 F: 510-644-3156 PRC:319
www.domico.com
Email: sales@domico.com
Estab: 1984

Rosie Austin, Office Coordinator

Supplier of management and accounting software
for managing self storage units, tenants, and
accounts.

**Dominar Inc** HQ
734 Aldo Ave
Santa Clara CA 95054
P: 408-496-0508 F: 408-496-0910 PRC:175
www.dominar-inc.com
Email: sales@dominar-inc.com
Estab: 1987

John Ellis, President

Provider of optical and semiconductor thin-film
coating services. The company serves customers
in Europe, Asia, and Australia.

**Domino Data Lab Inc** HQ
548 Fourth St
San Francisco CA 94107
P: 415-570-2425 PRC:191
www.dominodatalab.com
Email: support@dominodatalab.com
Estab: 2013

Madhavan Thirumalai, VP of Engineering
Chris Yang, Co-Founder
Matthew Granade, Co-Founder
Nick Elprin, Co-Founder

Provider of premise and cloud-based enterprise
data science platform for analysis applications.
The company serves the business sector.

**Donal Machine Inc** HQ
591 N McDowell Blvd
Petaluma CA 94954
P: 707-763-6625 PRC:80
www.donalmachine.com
Estab: 1969

Chris Bergstedt, President
Donna Bergstedt, CFO
Robert Alleman, Machinist

Provider of precision machining and sheet
metal services. The company focuses on CNC
machining, precision laser cutting, and welding &
fabrication.

**Donald P Dick Air Conditioning** HQ
1444 N Whitney Ave
Fresno CA 93703
P: 559-255-1644 PRC:147
mrcool4ac.com
Emp: 11-50 Estab: 1970

John Calandri, Sales Manager
Bill Hanner, Sales Manager
Nick Scott, VP
David Dick, VP
Doug Galvani, Estimator

Provider of air conditioning services. The company's offerings include sheet metal fabrication,
ductless heating, energy recovery ventilators, and
solar water heaters.

**Dorado Software Inc** HQ
4805 Golden Foothill Pkwy
El Dorado Hills CA 95762
P: 916-673-1100 PRC:329
www.doradosoftware.com
Email: sales@doradosoftware.com
Emp: 1-10 Estab: 1999

Tim Sebring, CEO
Chris Simon, CSO
Vicki Crozier, Manager
Erika Davis, Operations Manager

Provider of inventory, monitoring, storage management, network configuration, and mobile back
hauling solutions.

**Douglas Electronics Inc** HQ
2777 Alvarado St
San Leandro CA 94577
P: 510-483-8770 F: 510-995-7897 PRC:209
www.douglas.com
Email: info@douglas.com
Estab: 1953

Steve Vierra, Production Manager

Provider of CAD/CAM tools for personal computers.
The company specializes in custom board manufacturing and electronic design software products.

**Dowd & Guild Inc** HQ
14 Crow Canyon Ct Ste 200
San Ramon CA 94583
P: 925-820-7222 F: 925-820-7225 PRC:47
www.dowdandguild.com
Email: info@dowdandguild.com
Estab: 1986

Patrick Kelly, President
Tim Fetters, CEO
Laurie Morones, Manager of Information Systems
Dick Wildman, Manager of Marketing
Marcia Bellovary, Inside Sales

Distributor of chemicals and containers. The
company supplies resins, grinding media, oils and
maxes, rheological products, and pigments.

**Dps Telecom** HQ
4955 E Yale Ave
Fresno CA 93727
P: 559-454-1600 F: 559-454-1688 PRC:59
www.dpstele.com
Email: info@dpstele.com
Emp: 1-10 Estab: 1986

Sergey Dub, Director of Engineering
Marshall DenHartog, Sales Engineer
Richard Howell, Technical Support & Design
Engineer
Eric Storm, President
Bob Berry, CEO

Developer of network alarm monitoring solutions.
The company also focuses on publishing the
SNMP Tutorial.

**Dpss Lasers Inc** HQ
2525 Walsh Ave
Santa Clara CA 95051
P: 408-988-4300 F: 408-988-4305 PRC:159
www.dpss-lasers.com
Email: sales@dpss-lasers.com
Estab: 1998

Oscar Varela, Director of Engineering
Alex Laymon, President
Karen Wheeler, Human Resource Manager
Allie Constantino, Marketing Manager
Randy Kimball, VP of Business Development

Manufacturer of high power, short wavelength
solid state lasers for industrial, scientific, and
research applications.

**Drawbridge Health** HQ
2882 Sand Hill Rd Ste 240
Menlo Park CA 94025
P: 650-714-6791 PRC:24
drawbridgehealth.com
Email: info@dbhealth.com
Estab: 2015

Lee McCracken, CEO
Greg Nagy, CMO

Provider of diagnostic testing solutions. The
company offers blood testing solutions for a range
of biomarker.

**Drc Computer Corp**   HQ
  3375 Scott Blvd Ste 206
  Santa Clara CA 95054
P: 408-562-0000   PRC:209
www.drccomputer.com
Estab: 2004

Steve Sample, Director of HW Design

Provider of engineering and technology solutions.
The company designs and markets reconfigurable
coprocessors.

**Drchrono Inc**   HQ
  1001 N Rengstorff Ave Ste 200
  Mountain View CA 94043-1748
P: 844-569-8628   PRC:40
www.drchrono.com
Email: sales@drchrono.com
Estab: 2009

Daniel Kivatinos, Co-Founder
Michael Nusimow, CEO
Craig Silverman, VP of Sales

Provider of electronic health record and practice
management solution which includes scheduling
and clinical documentation.

**DreamFactory Software Inc**   HQ
  1999 S Bascom Ave Ste 928
  Campbell CA 95008
P: 415-993-5877   PRC:320
www.dreamfactory.com
Email: info@dreamfactory.com
Estab: 2005

Eric Rubin, Co-Founder
Bill Appleton, CEO

Provider of software development services. The
company offers hosting, external integration, SQL,
and user management services.

**Dripless Inc**   HQ
  527 Mendocino Ave Ste E
  Santa Rosa CA 95401
P: 707-568-5081   F: 707-568-5085   PRC:148
www.dripless.com
Email: dripless@sonic.net

Tom Allen, Director

Manufacturer of utility spatulas, caulking guns,
holsters, and related accessories. The company
serves the painting industry.

**Drivesavers Inc**   HQ
  400 Bel Marin Keys Blvd
  Novato CA 94949-5650
P: 415-382-2000   F: 415-883-0780   PRC:325
www.drivesaversdatarecovery.com
Estab: 1985

Mike Cobb, Director of Engineering
Jay Hagan, CEO

Provider of data recovery services for financial institutions, healthcare providers, major film studios,
government agencies, and small businesses.

**Drobo Inc**   HQ
  1289 Anvilwood Ave
  Sunnyvale CA 94089
P: 408-454-4200   F: 408-276-8401   PRC:95
www.drobo.com
Email: sales@drobo.com
Estab: 2004

Phat Ta, Senior Manufacturing Manager
Mihir Shah, CEO
Tom Wong, VP of Sales
Samina Subedar, Director of Marketing
John Apps, VP of Operations

Provider of virtualization and backup & archiving
services. The company also offers disaster recovery and cloud storage solutions.

**Droisys Inc**   HQ
  4800 Patrick Henry Dr
  Santa Clara CA 95054
P: 408-874-8333   F: 408-493-4533   PRC:322
www.droisys.com
Email: sales@droisys.com
Estab: 2003

Rahul Agarwal, VP of Engineering
Amit Kumar, CEO
Shum Mukherjee, CFO
Preeti Agrawal, Product Manager
Amish Srivastava,, Manager

Provider of business solutions and offers services
such as content management, enterprise resource
planning, and business efficiency consulting.

**Dropbox Inc**   HQ
  1800 Owens St
  San Francisco CA 94158
P: 415-857-6800   PRC:325
www.dropbox.com
Estab: 2007

Sergei Tsarev, Engineering Manager
Arash Ferdowsi, Co-Founder
Drew Houston, Founder
Ajay Vashee, CFO
Yamini Rangan, Chief Customer Officer

Provider of data transfer and sharing services that
involves sharing of files, documents, and pictures
from anywhere.

**Druva**   RH
  150 Mathilda Pl Ste 450
  Sunnyvale CA 94086
P: 650-238-6200   PRC:319
www.druva.com
Estab: 2008

Abhay Ghaisas, VP of Engineering
Jaspreet Singh, Founder
Milind Borate, Co-Founder
Mahesh Patel, CFO
Dave Packer, VP of Corporate & Product Market-
ing

Provider of cloud based data protection products.
The company offers services to the manufacturing, healthcare, and education industries.

**Dsp Concepts Inc**   HQ
  3235 Kifer Rd Ste 100
  Santa Clara CA 95051
P: 408-747-5200   F: 408-716-2496   PRC:322
www.dspconcepts.com
Email: info@dspconcepts.com
Estab: 2003

Steven Isabelle, VP of Engineering
Cole Li, DSP Engineer
Chin Beckmann, Co-Founder
Paul Beckmann, Founder
Tim Eun, CFO

Provider of embedded audio processing tools
and services. The company offers system design,
embedded software development, and optimization services.

**Dst Controls**   HQ
  651 Stone Rd
  Benicia CA 94510
P: 800-251-0773   PRC:228
www.dstcontrols.com
Email: info@dstcontrols.com
Estab: 1975

Andrew Pong, Software Engineer
Anu Mahinkanda, Project Engineer
Jerry Vin, Project Engineer
William Southard, President
Daniel Shneyer, Technical Sales Support Manager

Provider of control systems integration, industrial
data management, and related enterprise solutions. The company serves the industrial sector.

**Dt Research Inc**   HQ
  2000 Concourse Dr
  San Jose CA 95131
P: 408-934-6220   F: 408-934-6222   PRC:323
www.dtresearch.com
Email: sales@dtri.com
Estab: 1995

Hoan Ho, Technical Support Engineer
Jeffrey Johnston, Director of Channel Sales West
Mario Gosalvez, Business Development Manager

Developer and manufacturer of embedded computing systems. The company serves hospitality,
healthcare, and digital signage needs.

**Du Pont EKC Technology Inc**   BR
  2520 Barrington Ct
  Hayward CA 94545
P: 501-784-9105   PRC:53
www.dupont.com

Elaine Masser, Quality Manager
Charles Chen, Project Engineering Consultant

Provider of science and technology solutions. The
company engages in product line such as food,
personal care and industrial biotechnology.

**Dualsonic Inc**   HQ
  2294 Walsh Ave
  Santa Clara CA 95050
P: 408-457-8585   F: 408-748-1567   PRC:79
www.dual-sonic.com
Email: info@dual-sonic.com

Michael Chao, President

Provider of technology solutions for electronic and
precision CNC machining. The company designs
and manufactures PCMCIA cards and RFID
housings.

**Dubberly Design Office** HQ
2501 Harrison St Ste 7
San Francisco CA 94110
P: 415-648-9799   F: 415-648-9899   PRC:325
www.dubberly.com
Email: hello@dubberly.com
Estab: 2000

Knut Synstad, Visual Designer

Developer of software related solutions. The company offers user interface and visual design, brand development, and usability testing services.

**Duda** HQ
577 College Ave
Palo Alto CA 94306
P: 866-776-1550   PRC:325
www.duda.co/
Email: support@duda.co
Estab: 2009

Amir Glatt, Co-Founder
Itai Sadan, Co-Founder
Oded Ouaknine, Chief Customer Officer
Stephanie Hsiung, CFO
Alan Keller, CRO

A web design platform offering web design services to small businesses.

**Duke Empirical** HQ
2829 Mission St
Santa Cruz CA 95060
P: 831-420-1104   F: 831-420-1196   PRC:189
www.dukeempirical.com
Email: info@dukeempirical.com
Emp: 1-10   Estab: 2000

Albert Alavar, R&D Engineer
Robert LaDuca, CEO
Tony Lu, Quality Assurance Inspector
Michael Stramowski, VP of Operations

Provider of product development, catheter design, and manufacturing services to medical manufacturers.

**Duniway Stockroom Corp** HQ
48501 Milmont Dr
Fremont CA 94538
P: 650-969-8811   F: 650-965-0764   PRC:165
www.duniway.com
Email: info@duniway.com
Estab: 1976

Robert Reid, Operations Manager

Supplier of vacuum equipment. The company offers ion, diffusion, and mechanical pumps, and valves to the industrial sector.

**Dunlop Manufacturing Inc** HQ
150 Industrial Way
Benicia CA 94510
P: 707-745-2722   F: 707-745-2658   PRC:209
www.jimdunlop.com
Email: customerservice@jimdunlop.com
Estab: 1965

Spencer Silvestre, Mechanical Process Engineer
Ernie Ware, Production Manager
Joe Lam, Electronic Manufacturing Manager
Stephen Goodrich, Director of Sales
Nathan Becker, Sales Manager

Manufacturer of musical instruments and accessories. The company also designs amplifiers, guitar pedals, picks, capos, and strings.

**Durabook Americas Inc** BR
48329 Fremont Blvd
Fremont CA 94538
P: 510-492-0828   F: 510-492-0820   PRC:93
www.durabook.com
Email: sales@durabookamericas.com
Estab: 1987

Steven Gau, President
Julie Meng, Purchasing Manager
Kuo Claire, Inside Sales Manager
Emily Tang, Sales Assistant

Manufacturer of portable notebook computers. The company offers rugged notebook and tablet PC, parts, and accessories.

**Durabrake Co** HQ
2311 Calle Del Mundo
Santa Clara CA 95054
P: 408-748-0400   F: 408-748-0410   PRC:81
www.durabrake.com
Email: info@durabrake.com
Estab: 1998

Rita Shroff, CFO

Manufacturer of automotive products. The company's products include brake drums, rotors, and hubs for the aftermarket and OEMs.

**Duravent Inc** HQ
877 Cotting Ct
Vacaville CA 95688
P: 800-835-4429   PRC:134
www.duravent.com
Email: customerservice@duravent.com
Estab: 1958

Ron Weissmann, Human Resource Manager
Linda Hanson, Senior Human Resource Administrator
Pat Woods, Information Technology Manager
Mark Palmatier, Operations Manager
Cheryl Curnow, Senior Accountant

Manufacturer of pellets, pressure stacks, and special gas vents. The company is involved in condensing application installation.

**Durect Corp** HQ
10260 Bubb Rd
Cupertino CA 95014-4166
P: 408-777-1417   F: 408-777-3577   PRC:196
www.durect.com
Email: busdev@durect.com
Estab: 1998
Sales: $10M to $30M

Jim Filice, Engineering Fellow
James Brown, CEO
J.D Steve Helmer, VP
Charlie Claycomb, Director of Information Technology
Judy Joice, SVP of Operations

Developer of products for the treatment of chronic debilitating disease. The company specializes in biotechnology products.

**Dvk Integrated Services Inc** HQ
1570 The Alameda Ste 216
San Jose CA 95126
P: 408-436-0100   F: 408-436-0321   PRC:207
www.dvk.com
Estab: 1984

Richard Nadeau, Designer
Deb Albert, Partner

Provider of turnkey services that include prototyping services, printed circuit board design, and engineering services.

**DyAnsys Inc** HQ
300 N Bayshore Blvd
San Mateo CA 94401
P: 888-950-4321   PRC:186
www.dyansys.com
Email: customer.contact@dyansys.com
Estab: 2001

Srini Nageshwar, CEO

Provider of medical diagnostic and monitoring systems to clinicians and hospitals for patients. The company deals with research services.

**Dynamic Graphics Inc** HQ
1015 Atlantic Ave
Alameda CA 94501
P: 510-522-0700   F: 510-522-5670   PRC:319
www.dgi.com
Email: sales@dgi.com
Estab: 1969

Ronald Levine, Senior Engineer
Agnis Kaugars, Senior Software Engineer
Tamara Paradis, Owner
Arthur Paradis, President
Susan Brooks, Human Resource Manager

Provider of geospatial software solutions such as earth modeling, well planning, and visualization for the petroleum industries.

**Dynamic Test Solutions** BR
1762 Technology Dr Ste 201
San Jose CA 95110
P: 408-264-8880   PRC:211
www.dynamic-test.com
Email: saleusa@dynamic-test.com
Estab: 2003

Chandra Quibilan, Application Engineer
Kevin Hesse, CFO

Provider of design services. The company deals with gold and nickel plating, stub drilling and mixed dielectric fabrication.

**Dynamic Ventures Inc** HQ
10366 Avenida Ln
Cupertino CA 95014
P: 408-343-0234   PRC:323
www.dyve.com
Email: info@dyve.com
Estab: 1993

Yitzchak Ehrlich, CTO
Quang Nguyen, Project Manager

Provider of onsite and offsite custom software development services. The company also focuses on maintenance.

**Dynatex International** HQ
5577 Skylane Blvd
Santa Rosa CA 95403-1048
P: 707-542-4227   F: 707-579-8590   PRC:47
www.dynatex.com
Email: customerservice@dynatex.com
Estab: 1958

Richard Gaona, Software Engineer
Dale Humphrey, Mechanical Engineer
John Tyler, VP of Sales
Matt Acker, Manager of DP Product Group

Manufacturer of semiconductor, dicing equipment, and supplies. The company also offers dicing and wafer bonding services.

**Dynavax Technologies Corp**  HQ
2929 Seventh St Ste 100
Berkeley CA 94710-2753
P: 510-848-5100   F: 510-848-1327   PRC:268
www.dynavax.com
Email: contact@dynavax.com
Emp: 169   Estab: 1996
Sales: $3M to $10M

David Novack, President
Ryan Spencer, CEO
Michael Ostrach, CFO
Robert Janssen, Chief Medical Officer
Steven Gersten, SVP

Developer of clinical-stage biopharmaceutical company committed to discovering and developing products to prevent and treat infectious diseases.

**Dynaweb Inc**  HQ
1257 Sanguinetti Rd Ste 160
Sonora CA 95370
P: 925-373-9013   F: 925-373-1588   PRC:13
www.dynawebinc.com
Email: leo@dynawebinc.com
Emp: 1-10

Leo Willis, President

Manufacturer and marketer of web handling and tension control systems. The company's product finds use in packaging, printing, and textile needs.

**DynEd International Inc**  HQ
1350 Bayshore Hwy One Bay Plz Ste 850
Burlingame CA 94010
P: 650-375-7011   PRC:323
www.dyned.com
Email: info@dyned.com
Estab: 1987

Douglas Crane, SVP of Engineering
Lance Knowles, Founder
Hoa Tran, CFO

Provider of computer-based English language teaching solutions. The company offers mobile solutions, analytics, testing, and monitoring tools.

**Dysert Environmental Inc**  HQ
1206 S Amphlett Blvd Ste 2
San Mateo CA 94402
P: 650-799-9204   PRC:142
dysertenvironmental.com
Estab: 2005

Mark Dysert, President

Provider of environmental solutions. The company's services include wastewater sampling, project management, soil sampling, and decontamination confirmation.

**E Enterprise Tech**  HQ
3010 N First St
San Jose CA 95134
P: 408-844-8176   F: 408-844-8269   PRC:80
www.e-enterprisetech.com

Phan Pham, Owner
Abraham Najar, Purchaser
Edwin Escobar, Machinist
Rhonda Botros, Administrative Assistant

Manufacturer of machined components. The company offers CNC machining, sheetmetal, cabling, electrical, and mechanical assembly services.

**E la Carte Inc**  HQ
810 Hamilton St
Redwood City CA 94063
P: 650-468-0680   PRC:326
www.elacarte.com
Email: info@elacarte.com
Estab: 2008

Haaris Abbasi, Director of Engineering
Rajat Suri, CEO
Daniel Dreymann, Chief Product Officer
Bill Healey, CTO
Ashish Gupta, CFO

Provider of digital restaurant services. The company specializes in operations, engineering, business development, and marketing.

**E&F Plastics Inc**  HQ
2742 Aiello Dr
San Jose CA 95111
P: 408-226-6672   F: 408-226-6673   PRC:80
enfplastics.com
Email: sales@enfplastics.com

Eddie Seijas, Owner

Provider of plastic fabricated products. The company offers bonded PVC, vapor polished polycarbonates, and vacuum formed Kydex.

**E*Healthlinecom Inc**  HQ
2450 Venture Oaks Way Ste 100
Sacramento CA 95833
P: 916-924-8092   F: 916-924-8209   PRC:194
www.ehealthline.com
Email: contactus@ehealthline.com
Emp: 1-10   Estab: 1999

Georgette Smart, CEO

Provider of integrated health care information management software such as administration discharge transfer, bed management, and patient billing.

**E-3 Systems Inc**  HQ
1220 Whipple Rd
Union City CA 94587
P: 510-487-7393   F: 510-487-7794   PRC:63
www.e3systems.com
Estab: 1989

Andres Carrasco, Transport Division Manager

Provider of data center design and installation services. The company focuses on engineering, cable plant analysis and documentation, and maintenance.

**E-Fab Inc**  HQ
1075 Richard Ave
Santa Clara CA 95050
P: 408-727-5218   F: 408-988-3342   PRC:68
www.e-fab.com
Email: eng@e-fab.com
Estab: 1981

Rick Espino, President
Carol Spicker, Accounting Manager
Ed Hinson, Manager

Provider of precision manufacturing and fabrication solutions. The company offers mesh screens, etched antennas, encoder strips, and PCB jumpers.

**E-Health Records International Inc**  HQ
6800 Palm Ave Ste D
Sebastopol CA 95472
P: 707-284-4300   F: 707-284-4302   PRC:194
www.harmonimd.com
Email: sales@harmonimd.com
Estab: 2014

Nick Smith, CTO

Provider of electronic medical record system that can manage all aspects of clinical care in a busy hospital environment.

**E-M Manufacturing Inc**  HQ
1290 Dupont Ct
Manteca CA 95336
P: 209-825-1800   F: 209-825-1855   PRC:80
www.emmanufacturing.com
Email: sales@emmanufacturing.com
Emp: 1-10

Scott Hicken, VP

Provider of prototyping and short run production machining services. The company is engaged in sheet metal design.

**E-N-G Mobile Systems Inc**  HQ
2245 Via De Mercados
Concord CA 94520
P: 925-798-4060   F: 925-798-0152   PRC:61
www.e-n-g.com
Email: info@e-n-g.com
Estab: 1977

Joseph Arvizu, System Engineer
Dick Glass, President
Mary O'Hern, Inside Sales Manager
Claudia Cannata, Office Manager
Jason Ramos, Construction Technician

Manufacturer of specialty vehicles. The company focuses on TV vans and trucks, emergency respone trailers, mobile labs, and other vehicles.

**E-Scape Bio**  HQ
4000 Shoreline Ct Ste 400
S San Francisco CA 94080
P: 650-431-0100   PRC:34
www.e-scapebio.com
Email: info@e-scapebio.com
Estab: 2015

Julie Smith, President
Leon Chen, CEO
Anthony Rimac, CFO
Ann Kapoun, SVP of Research and Development
Jacob Schwarz, Head of Chemistry

Provider of therapeutic solutions. The company focusses on discovery and development of small molecule drugs for the treatment of neurodegenerative diseases.

**E-Z Tel Inc**  HQ
510 N L St
Livermore CA 94551-2808
P: 925-449-1504   PRC:61
www.e-ztel.com
Email: sales1@e-ztel.com
Estab: 1973

Brenda Leavy, Sales Manager

Provider of basic and unified communication solutions. The company serves small and medium-sized organizations and enterprises.

**E2c Remediation** HQ
1020 Winding Creek Rd Ste 110
Roseville CA 95678
P: 916-782-8700 PRC:140
e2cr.net
Email: atyourservice@e2cr.net
Emp: 1-10

Aiguo Xu, Principal Engineer
Philip Goalwin, President
Michael George, General Counsel

Provider of environmental remediation services.
The company services also include soil and
groundwater remediation and civil and geological
engineering.

**Ea Machining Inc** HQ
3390 De La Cruz Blvd Unit W
Santa Clara CA 95054-2631
P: 408-727-4962 F: 408-727-4970 PRC:8
eamachining.com
Email: aamaro@eamachining.com

Ann Amaro, CEO

Provider of CNC turning and milling services. The
company offers services to the semiconductor
manufacturing equipment industry.

**Eagle Shield** HQ
4115 Blackhawk Plaza Cir Ste 100
Danville CA 94506
P: 925-648-2017 F: 925-648-2016 PRC:129
eagleshield.com
Estab: 2003

Garrett Harwood, CEO

Provider of energy conservation and renewable
energy solutions. The company offers services to
homes and businesses.

**Eargo Inc** HQ
1600 Technology Dr 6th Fl
San Jose CA 95110
P: 650-351-7700 PRC:188
eargo.com
Email: sales@eargo.com
Estab: 2010

Wilson On, Senior Staff Design Engineer
Raphael Michel, Founder
Christian Gormsen, CEO
Ron Gill, Specialist

Creator of medical device. The company specializes in virtually invisible in-ear hearing device that is
comfortable, natural sounding, and rechargeable.

**Earlens Corp** HQ
4045-A Campbell Ave
Menlo Park CA 94025-4745
P: 650-366-9000 PRC:189
earlens.com
Email: customercare@earlens.com
Estab: 2005

Kyu-Hwa Jeong, Senior Firmware Engineer
Kyle Imatani, Senior Engineer
Priyanka Kapoor, Quality Engineer
Patricia Ho, Senior Research
Xavier Chabot, Senior Engineer

Manufacturer of medical devices such as contact
hearing devices and sensorineural and conductive
hearing impairment.

**Earthquake Protection Systems** HQ
451 Azuar Ave Bldg 759
Vallejo CA 94592
P: 707-644-5993 F: 707-644-5995 PRC:159
www.earthquakeprotection.com
Email: eps@earthquakeprotection.com
Estab: 1985

Victor Zayas, President
Julie Robinson, CFO
Anoop Mokha, VP

Supplier of seismic isolators for earthquake
bearings. The company offers single and triple
pendulum bearings and related supplies.

**Earthquake Sound Corp** HQ
2727 McCone Ave
Hayward CA 94545
P: 510-732-1000 F: 510-732-1095 PRC:60
www.earthquakesound.com
Email: us-sales@earthquakesound.com
Estab: 1984

Joseph Sahyoun, President
Abraham Sahyoun, Export Manager

Manufacturer and seller of sound equipment for
mobile audio, marine audio, gaming, and home
audio sectors.

**East Bay Machine** HQ
1030 Shary Ct
Concord CA 94518
P: 925-689-2421 F: 925-689-2837 PRC:80
www.eastbaymachine.com
Email: info@eastbaymachine.com

Sean McLellan, President

Provider of machining services including welding
and fabrication. The company offers services to
the business sector.

**Eastar Chemical Corp** HQ
1215 K St Ste 1700
Sacramento CA 95814
P: 800-898-2436 PRC:50
www.eastarchem.com
Email: info@eastarchem.com
Emp: 1-10 Estab: 1984

Tony Chu, President
George Chu, CEO
Charles Chu, Chairman
Howard Brainard, VP of Eastar Specialty Chem-
icals

Manufacturer of chemicals and pharmaceuticals.
The company offers Venlafaxine, Usnic acid,
Pentaerythritol, and Octanedinitrile.

**Eastern Research Group Inc** BR
8950 Cal Center Dr Ste 230
Sacramento CA 95826
P: 916-635-6592 PRC:142
www.erg.com
Emp: 11-50 Estab: 1984

John Koupal, Principal Engineer

Provider of performance measurement, risk
assessment, event planning and facilitation, and
training services.

**EB Stone & Son Inc** HQ
PO Box 550
Suisun CA 94585
P: 707-426-2500 F: 707-429-8960 PRC:48
www.ebstone.org
Estab: 1979

Lisa Scott, Sales Representative
Larry Byers, Territory Manager

Supplier of garden fertilizers. The company also
offers lawn maintenance, composite maker, soil,
and plant aid services.

**Ebara Technologies Inc** HQ
51 Main Ave
Sacramento CA 95838
P: 916-920-5451 F: 916-830-1900 PRC:212
www.ebaratech.com
Email: info@ebaratech.com
Emp: 11-50 Estab: 1912

Rich Ward, Engineering Manager
Stan Mok, Sales Support Engineer
Alex Reyes, Senior Process Engineer
Rob Hudson, Engineering Associate
Naoki Ando, President

Manufacturer of vacuum pumps for the semiconductor industry. The company offers repair,
training, and field & system services.

**Ebr Systems Inc** HQ
480 Oakmead Pkwy
Sunnyvale CA 94085
P: 408-720-1906 F: 408-720-1996 PRC:186
www.ebrsystemsinc.com

Tor Anderson, Principal Mechanical Engineer
Tom Huljev, Senior Mechanical Engineer
Daryl Jamgotchian, Senior Software Engineer
Rick Riley, COO
Allan Will, President

Designer and developer of implantable systems
for wireless tissue stimulation. The company
focuses on the treatment of heart failure.

**Ebusinessdesign** HQ
900 E Hamilton Ave Ste 100
Campbell CA 95008
P: 408-654-7900 F: 408-654-7907 PRC:323
www.ebusinessdesign.com
Email: info@ebusinessdesign.com
Estab: 1995

Amardeep Misha, Co-Founder
Pardeep Boparai, Co-Founder

Provider of technology consulting services, specializing in business analysis, architecture design,
and open source development.

**Echelon Corp** HQ
2901 Patrick Henry Dr
Santa Clara CA 95054
P: 408-938-5200 F: 408-790-3800 PRC:92
www.echelon.com
Email: info@echelon.com
Estab: 1988
Sales: $30M to $100M

Mingyu Wang, Senior Software Engineer
Jonathan Lloyd, Embedded Software Engineer
Darron Fick, Senior Software Engineer
Michael Milsner, Senior Software Engineer
Narbeh Derhacobian, President

Developer of open-standard control networking platforms. The company serves outdoor lighting, building automation, transportation, and other needs.

**Echopixel Inc** HQ
4677 Old Ironsides Dr Ste 445
Santa Clara CA 95054
P: 844-273-7766 PRC:187
www.echopixeltech.com
Email: info@echopixeltech.com
Estab: 2012

Sergio Aguirre, Founder
Ron Schilling, CEO

Provider of 3D medical visualization software for radiologists, cardiologists, pediatric cardiologists, and interventional neuroradiologists.

**Eckhart Corp** HQ
7110 Redwood Blvd Ste A
Novato CA 94945
P: 415-898-9528 PRC:268
www.eckhartcorp.com
Email: info@eckhartcorp.com
Estab: 1989

Deepak Chopra, CEO
Sandeep Chopra, CFO
Andrey Prokofiev, Director
Lynne Kimbell, Materials Manager
Kenny Reibel, Shipping Specialist

Manufacturer of nutritional supplements. The company is engaged in product development and packaging services.

**eClincher Inc** HQ
1121 San Antonio Rd
Palo Alto CA 94303
P: 408-718-6203 PRC:325
eclincher.com
Estab: 2012

Gilad Salamander, Co-Founder
Tal Mikaelovich, Co-Founder
Donna Lev, Product Operations Manager

Develops social media management platform that helps businesses to manage and organize their social media presence.

**Eclipse Metal Fabrication** HQ
2901 Spring St
Redwood City CA 94063
P: 650-298-8731    F: 650-298-8747    PRC:80
www.eclipsemf.com
Estab: 1999

Joe Anaya, Owner

Provider of metal fabrication services. The company provides CNC machining, laser, and waterjet cutting services in the San Francisco Bay area.

**Eco Sound Medical Services** HQ
1865 N Macarthur Dr
Tracy CA 95376
P: 800-494-6868    F: 209-835-7554    PRC:189
e-ecosound.com
Email: cs@e-ecosound.com
Emp: 1-10

Don Huhn, Owners and founders of Eco Sound
Mark Hineser, owners and founders of Eco Sound Medical Services
Patrick Meadows, COO
Paula Stinyard, Medi-Cal Department Director

Distributor of healthcare products and medical supplies. The company is focused on incontinence products, medical nutrients, and nursing supplies.

**Eco-Snow Systems** HQ
4935 Southfront Rd Ste A
Livermore CA 94551
P: 925-606-2000 PRC:153
www.ecosnow.com
Estab: 1980

Stephen Porter, Senior Engineer
Scott Swanson, General Manager

Provider of $CO2$ precision surface process equipment for cleaning applications. The company's products include VersaClean 1200 and Mask-Clean 150 systems.

**Ecodomus Inc** HQ
1203 Union St
San Francisco CA 94109
P: 571-277-6617 PRC:323
www.ecodomus.com
Email: info@ecodomus.com
Estab: 2008

Igor Starkov, President

Provider of information technology software for improved design & construction data collection, facility management, operation, and maintenance.

**Ecology & Environment Inc** BR
505 Sansome St Ste 300
San Francisco CA 94111
P: 415-398-5326 PRC:140
ene.com
Estab: 1970

Silvia Yanez, Environmental Specialist
Todd Musterait, President
Peter Sorci, Acting CFO
Colleen Mullaney-Westfall, VP of Corporate Secretary
Cheryl Karpowicz, SVP

Provider of environmental management services. The company's services also include planning, engineering, and emergency planning.

**Ecomicron Inc** HQ
2161 O'Toole Ave Ste 30
San Jose CA 95131
P: 408-526-1020    F: 408-526-1040    PRC:86
www.ecomicron.com
Email: info@ecomicron.com
Estab: 2008

Patrick Wilson, Software Engineer
Uladzislau Lekhtsikau, Software Quality Assurance Engineer
Junghoon Sun, Technical Support Manager

Manufacturer of semiconductor equipment. The company caters to semiconductor, photovoltaic, and hybrid industries.

**Econugenics Inc** HQ
396 Tesconi Ct
Santa Rosa CA 95401-4653
P: 800-521-0160    F: 707-526-7689    PRC:272
www.econugenics.com
Email: sales@econugenics.com
Estab: 1995

Isaac Eliaz, Founder
Barry Wilk, Director of Quality Assurance
Bonnie Frese, Sales Manager
Elaine Weil, Medical Research Specialist
Kristina Young, Accounting & Sales Analyst

Manufacturer and distributor of dietary supplements and healthcare products. The company serves the medical sector.

**Ecoshift Consulting LLC** HQ
126 Bonifacio Pl Ste G
Monterey CA 93940
P: 831-277-0167 PRC:142
www.ecoshiftconsulting.com

Kristin Cushman, CEO
Chris Sentieri, Manager of Climate Division
Alexander Gershenson, Advisor
Dustin Mulvaney, Manager
James Barsimantov, Advisor

Provider of consulting services. The company offers consulting for alternative fuels, climate change, carbon reduction strategies, and carbon trading.

**Ecrio Inc** HQ
19925 Stevens Creek Blvd Ste 100
Cupertino CA 95014
P: 408-973-7290    F: 408-973-7292    PRC:326
www.ecrio.com
Email: info@ecrio.com
Estab: 1998

Krishnakumar Narayanan, VP of Engineering
Alekhya Hari, Software Quality Assurance Engineer
Michel Gannage, Founder
Lina Martin, VP of Finance
Vikram Karmarkar, VP of Product Marketing and Business Development

Provider of wireless messaging applications. The company offers video telephony, content sharing, social communications, and enterprise solutions.

**Eda Direct Inc** HQ
4701 Patrick Henry Dr Ste 1301
Santa Clara CA 95054
P: 408-496-5890    F: 408-684-8854    PRC:319
edadirect.com
Email: sales@edadirect.com
Estab: 1997

Kate Vu, Sales Account Manager
Jack Lee, Inside Sales
Heather Cox, Office Manager
David Wagner, Senior FAE

Provider of EDA software products and services. The company's products include Cliosoft, MunE-DA, and Mentor Graphics.

**Edc Biosystems Inc** HQ
49090 Milmont Dr
Fremont CA 94538
P: 510-257-1500    F: 510-257-1186    PRC:159
www.edcbiosystems.com
Email: info@edcbiosystems.com

Charles Reichel, VP of Engineering
Greg Stephens, President
Linna Lee, Purchasing Manager
Michael Forbush, Physicist

Provider of technology solutions for biotech liquid transfer applications. The company serves the electronics, precision mechanics, and other sectors.

**Edeniq Inc**                                    HQ
2505 N Shirk Rd
Visalia CA 93291
P: 559-302-1777                                  PRC:24
www.edeniq.com
Email: info@edeniq.com
Emp: 1-10   Estab: 2007

Aubrey Zigler, Human Resource Generalist
Randy Asher, Section Head of Analytical Chemistry

Focuses on the production of ethanol, other biofuels, and/or biochemicals. The company combines mechanical and biological processes.

**Edgewater Networks Inc**                        HQ
5225 Hellyer Ave Ste 100
San Jose CA 95138
P: 408-351-7200   F: 408-727-6430               PRC:97
edgewaternetworks.com
Email: info@edgewaternetworks.com
Estab: 2002

Mohan Kannekanti, Software Engineer
Ben Pons, Senior Systems Engineer
Yun-Fong Loh, Senior Engineer
John Macario, VP of Marketing
Gernot Scheichl, VP of Support & Services

Provider of enterprise session controllers for business purposes. The company also offers security and policy management services.

**Edmar Engineering Inc**                         HQ
340 Industrial Way Ste H & I
Dixon CA 95620
P: 707-693-0390   F: 707-693-0395               PRC:80
www.edmarengineering.net
Estab: 1978

Ed Martinelli, VP

Manufacturer of precision machined products. The company's products include CNC mills and lathes, inspection equipment, and lathe and mill software.

**Edwards Lifesciences Corp**                     HQ
1 Edwards Way
Irvine CA 92614
P: 949-250-5070   F: 949-250-2625               PRC:184
www.edwards.com
Email: tech_support@edwards.com
Emp: 11-50 Estab: 2010
Sales: Over $3B

Shreyas Hoskere, Principal Engineer of Quality
Cory Fackiner, Quality Engineering Manager
Quinn Lavender, Quality Manager Internal Audit

Manufacturer of medical devices. The company specializes in technologies for structural heart diseases and critical care monitoring.

**Eeonyx Corp**                                   HQ
750 Belmont Way
Pinole CA 94564
P: 510-741-3632                                  PRC:129
eeonyx.com
Email: info@eeonyx.com

Jimmy Holliman, President
Mahemuti Abula, CTO
Chase Holliman, Market Analyst
Kanwar Ali, Product Developer

Manufacturer and provider of knitting services. The company focuses on textiles, foams, felts, and powders.

**Eezer Products Inc**                            HQ
4734 E Home Ave
Fresno CA 93703
P: 559-255-4140   F: 559-255-4907               PRC:53
www.eezer.com
Email: sales@eezer.com
Emp: 1-10   Estab: 1964

Leighton Sjostrand, President

Designer and manufacturer of sanding tools. The company also offers handles and various finishing tools.

**Efa Technologies Inc**                          HQ
2701 Del Paso Rd Ste 130-385
Sacramento CA 95835
P: 916-443-8842   F: 916-443-3759               PRC:13
www.efatech.com
Email: info@efatech.com
Emp: 1-10   Estab: 1975

Stacey Daniels, General Manager

Manufacturer of equipment for leak detection in pipelines. The company specializes in electrical and control systems projects.

**Efficient Drivetrains Inc**                     HQ
1181 Cadillac Ct
Milpitas CA 95035
P: 408-624-1231                                  PRC:150
www.efficientdrivetrains.com
Email: info@efficientdrivetrains.com

Andy Frank, CTO

Provider of vehicle developer equipment. The company also offers PHEV and CVT solutions, and hybrid vehicles.

**Effone Software Inc**                           HQ
4701 Patrick Henry Dr Bldg 16
Santa Clara CA 95054
P: 408-830-1010                                  PRC:325
www.effone.com
Email: info@effone.net
Estab: 1996

Hemanth Kumar, President

Provider of IT consulting services including software development, application integration, and staff augmentation.

**Efinix Inc**                                    HQ
900 Lafayette St Ste 406
Santa Clara CA 95050
P: 408-789-6917                                  PRC:110
www.efinixinc.com
Email: sales-na@efinixinc.com
Estab: 2012

Tony Ngai, Founder
Jay Schleicher, SVP of Software Engineering
Sammy Cheung, CEO
Ming Ng, SVP of Operations and Applications

Focuses on the building of programmable devices. The company serves the industrial, medical, and automotive markets.

**EG Systems LLC**                                HQ
6200 Village Pkwy
Dublin CA 94568
P: 408-528-3000   F: 408-528-3500               PRC:86
www.electroglas.com
Email: sales@electroglas.com

Richard J. Casler, VP of Engineering
Tom Rohrs, Chairman
Thomas E. Brunton, VP of Finance
Wes Highfill, VP of Global Sales & Marketing
Wayne E. Woodard, VP of Service and Operations

Provider of test equipment such as wafer probers, prober-based test handlers, and test floor management solutions.

**Egain**                                         HQ
1252 Borregas Ave
Sunnyvale CA 94089
P: 408-636-4500   F: 408-636-4400               PRC:323
www.egain.com
Estab: 1997
Sales: $30M to $100M

Ashutosh Roy, CEO
Eric Smit, CFO
Rex Dorricott, VP
Todd Woodstra, SVP of Sales
Anand Subramaniam, SVP of Marketing

Provider of custom engagement software solutions. The company offers co-browsing, email management, web self-service, and analytics services.

**Egeen Inc**                                     HQ
490 N McCarthy Blvd
Milpitas CA 95035
P: 650-967-5010   F: 650-967-5014               PRC:257
www.egeeninc.com
Email: info@egeeninc.com
Estab: 2001

Kalev Kask, CEO

Provider of drug development for biotech and pharmaceutical clients. The company serves clinics, hospitals, and the healthcare sector.

**Egnyte Inc**                                    HQ
1350 W Middlefield Rd
Mountain View CA 94043
P: 650-968-4018   F: 610-968-4012               PRC:325
www.egnyte.com
Estab: 2006

Tal Broner, VP of Software Engineering
Vineet Jain, CEO
Steve Sutter, CFO
Amrit Jassal, CTO
Eric Cross, Chief Revenue Officer

Provider of online storage, cloud computing, and file sharing services. The company serves the financial, banking, and pharmaceutical industries.

**Egs Inc**                                       HQ
2777 Yulupa Ave Ste 604
Santa Rosa CA 95405
P: 707-595-8760   F: 707-544-4127               PRC:139
www.envgeo.com
Estab: 1995

Paul Brophy, President
Gene Suemnicht, CEO

Provider of geothermal exploration development services. The company's services include remote sensing, geologic mapping, and subsurface visualization.

**Eigen**  HQ
13366 Grass Vly Ave
Grass Valley CA 95945
P: 530-274-1240  PRC:196
www.eigen.com
Email: sales@eigen.com
Emp: 1-10  Estab: 1975

Mahtab Damda, President
Syed Zaidi, CFO
William Mandel, VP of Regulatory Affairs
Michael Ahmadi, EVP of Global Marketing & Sales
Rajesh Venkataraman, R&D Manager

Manufacturer of cardiology and radiology imaging products. The company serves urologists and radiation oncologists.

**Eiger Biopharmaceuticals Inc**  HQ
2155 Park Blvd
Palo Alto CA 94306
P: 877-899-2051  F: 650-618-1621  PRC:249
www.eigerbio.com
Email: info@eigerbio.com
Estab: 2008

David Cory, CEO
Joanne Quan, Chief Medical Officer
James Shaffer, Chief Business Officer
Sri Ryali, CFO
Stephana Patton, General Counsel

Developer of anti viral therapy and treatments for rare disease therapeutics. The company specializes in treatment for Hepatitis Delta.

**Einfochips**  HQ
2025 Gateway Pl Ste 270
San Jose CA 95110
P: 408-496-1882  F: 801-650-1480  PRC:86
www.einfochips.com
Estab: 1994

Pratul Shroff, Founder
Shashank Waman Khare, CTO
Sumit Sethi, COO
Parag Mehta, Chief Business Development Officer
Rakesh Patel, Assistant Manager of Finance

Provider of product design services and solutions. The company offers product engineering and semiconductor services.

**Eiq Energy Inc**  HQ
294 Brokaw Rd
Santa Clara CA 95050
P: 408-643-0020  PRC:124
eiqenergy.com
Email: info@eiqenergy.com
Estab: 2007

William Reed, Director of Engineering
James Allen, Chief Power Designer

Designer and manufacturer of power electronics. The company provides solar cells, panels, and monitoring systems.

**Ekm Metering Inc**  HQ
122 Benito Ave
Santa Cruz CA 95062
P: 831-425-7371  PRC:233
ekmmetering.com
Email: info@ekmmetering.com
Emp: 1-10  Estab: 2007

Jonathan Park, CTO
Seth B., VP of Customer Support

Provider of submetering hardware and services. The company's solutions include revenue metering and data monitoring.

**Eko Devices Inc**  HQ
2600 Tenth St Ste 260
Berkeley CA 94710
P: 844-356-3384  PRC:186
ekodevices.com

Connor Landgraf, Co-Founder
Jason Bellet, Co-Founder
Tyler Crouch, Co-Founder

Developer of digital stethoscope/electronic stethoscope to help confidently and quickly assess patient's heart, lung, and body sounds.

**Ekso Bionics Holdings Inc**  HQ
1414 Harbour Way S Ste 1201
Richmond CA 94804
P: 510-984-1761  PRC:25
eksobionics.com
Email: customerrelations@eksobionics.com
Estab: 2005

Tom Looby, President
Darrell Musick, VP of Clinical Research

Developer and manufacturer of powered exoskeleton bionic devices. The company is engaged in distribution services.

**El Dorado Molds Inc**  HQ
2691 Mercantile Dr
Rancho Cordova CA 95742
P: 916-635-4558  F: 916-635-1125  PRC:159
www.eldoradomolds.com
Emp: 11-50 Estab: 1989

Terry Rheault, Design Engineer
Bob Brewer, President
Bob Kulp, Purchasing Agent
Tony Graham, Shop Supervisor

Provider of molding services. The company provides injection molds and related tooling for the plastics industry.

**El Portal Imaging Center**  HQ
3365 G St Ste 100
Merced CA 95340
P: 209-384-4250  F: 209-384-4269  PRC:198
www.elportalimaging.com
Emp: 1-10

Brian Amfahr, COO

Specializes in diagnostic imaging solutions. The company serves hospitals, clinics, and the healthcare sector.

**Elasticsearch Inc**  HQ
800 W El Camino Real Ste 350
Mountain View CA 94040
P: 650-458-2620  PRC:319
www.elastic.co/
Email: info@elastic.co
Estab: 2012
Sales: $1M to $3M

Kevin Kluge, SVP of Engineering
Steven Schuurman, Founder
Uri Boness, Founder
Simon Willnauer, Founder
Shay Banon, Founder

A software company that builds self-managed and SaaS offerings that make data usable in real time.

**Eldex Laboratories Inc**  HQ
30 Executive Ct
Napa CA 94558
P: 707-224-8800  F: 707-224-0688  PRC:20
www.eldex.com
Email: sales@eldex.com
Estab: 1972

Stephen Amendola, President
Robert Larsen, Manufacturing Manager

Manufacturer of instruments for analytical chemistry laboratories and chemical process control. The company also creates customized products.

**Eldridge Products Inc**  HQ
465 Reservation Rd
Marina CA 93933
P: 831-648-7777  F: 831-648-7780  PRC:14
www.epiflow.com
Email: sales@epiflow.com
Estab: 1988

Mark Eldridge, President
Ryan Eldridge, Purchasing Manager

Manufacturer of thermal mass flow meters and flow switches. The company focuses on sales, installation, and inspection.

**Elecraft Inc**  HQ
125 Westridge Dr
Aptos CA 95076
P: 831-763-4211  F: 831-763-4218  PRC:71
www.elecraft.com
Email: info@elecraft.com
Emp: 1-10  Estab: 1998

Wayne Burdick, CTO
Paul Giannini, Materials Manager
Michael Mistor, Production Control Bench Tech
Ed Muns, Field Tester

Provider of transceivers and accessories. The company also offers auto antenna tuners, antenna systems, microphones, wattmeter, and other products.

**Electric Cloud Inc**  BR
125 S Market St Ste 400
San Jose CA 95113
P: 408-419-4300  PRC:323
www.cloudbees.com
Email: info@cloudbees.com
Estab: 2002

Atanu Majumdar, Senior Director of Engineering
Sandeep Tamhankar, Principal Engineer
Nikhil Vaze, Software Engineer
Rohit Jainendra, Chief Product Officer
Carmine Napolitano, CFO

Provider of software development, information technology consulting, test automation, virtualization, and cloud computing solutions.

**Electric Power Research Institute Inc**  HQ
3420 Hillview Ave
Palo Alto CA 94304
P: 650-855-2000  PRC:131
www.epri.com
Email: askepri@epri.com
Estab: 1973

Michael Howard, President
Manuel Morales, Software Quality Assurance
Lead
Arshad Mansoor, SVP of Research & Development Group
Naresh Kumar, Senior Program Manager
Sunil Chhaya, Senior Technical Executive

Provider of research and development services related to the generation, delivery, and use of electricity for the benefit of the public.

**Electro Coatings Of California**          BR
893 Carleton St
Berkeley CA 94710
P: 510-849-4075    F: 510-849-1817    PRC:47
www.electro-coatings.com

Aaron Plechaty, Production Manager

Provider of electroless nickel coating services. The company also offers industrial hard chrome and nickel metal finishing services.

**Electro Diagnostic Imaging Inc**          HQ
200F Twin Dolphin Dr
Redwood City CA 94065-1402
P: 650-631-0120    F: 650-631-0122    PRC:78
www.veris-edi.com
Email: sales@veris-edi.com
Estab: 1989

Susan Martin, Operations Manager
Kenny Noble, Assistant Office Manager

Developer and manufacturer of products for electrophysiology. The company's services include research, sales, and marketing.

**Electro Magnetic Test Inc**          HQ
1547 Plymouth St
Mountain View CA 94043
P: 650-965-4000    F: 650-965-3000    PRC:142
emtlabs.com
Email: info@emtlabs.com

Jay Gandhi, Manager

Provider of testing and consulting services. The company focuses on engineering services in wireless, wireline telecom, and safety certifications.

**Electro Plating Specialties Inc**          HQ
2436 American Ave
Hayward CA 94545
P: 510-786-1881    F: 510-786-1060    PRC:159
www.eps-plating.com
Email: eps@eps-plating.com

Mary Hall, President
Robert Hall, General Manager

Provider of electroplating services. The company offers parts cleaning, anodizing, electropolishing, and rust removal services.

**Electro-Prep Corp**          HQ
2034 Abbey Ln
Campbell CA 95008
P: 408-370-7470    F: 408-370-7470    PRC:86
www.electro-prep.com
Email: elprep5@aol.com
Estab: 1972

George Morones, Sales Manager

Manufacturer of products for the assembly of PCBs in the electronic industry. The company offers board stiffeners, fixtures, and edge masks.

**Electrochem Solutions Inc**          HQ
32500 Central Ave
Union City CA 94587
P: 510-476-1840    F: 510-323-7200    PRC:80
www.electro-chem.com
Estab: 1982

Onur Bakirman, Process Engineer
David Rossiter, President
Francisco Ruiz, General Manager
Janet Nielsen, Sales Manager
S. Dean Novy, Senior Technician

Provider of plating, anodizing, parts cleaning services. The company caters to high technology industries.

**Electromax Inc**          HQ
1960 Concourse Dr
San Jose CA 95131
P: 408-428-9474    F: 408-428-9475    PRC:211
www.electromaxinc.com
Estab: 1991

Ken Wong, Director of Engineering
Aaron Wong, President
Linda Yue, Senior Manager of Human Resources
Keith McDavit, Quality Manager
Benny Lee, Director of Marketing

Manufacturer of heavy machinery. The company offers engineering support, materials management, prototyping and testing services.

**Electronic Arts Inc**          HQ
209 Redwood Shores Pkwy
Redwood City CA 94065
P: 650-628-1393    F: 650-628-1422    PRC:317
www.ea.com
Email: info@ea.com
Estab: 1982
Sales: Over $3B

Andrew Wilson, CEO
Ken Moss, CTO
Mala Singh, Chief People Officer
Chris Bruzzo, CMO
Matt Bilbey, EVP of Strategic Growth

Developer, publisher, and distributor of software for video game systems, personal computers, wireless devices, and internet.

**Electronic Carbide Inc**          HQ
13005 Loma Rica Dr
Grass Valley CA 95945
P: 530-272-6154    F: 530-272-3179    PRC:80
www.electroniccarbide.com
Email: ecpmichelle@sbcglobal.net
Emp: 1-10   Estab: 1978

Joseph Perry, Mechanical Manufacturing Engineer
Michelle Harris, CFO
Gordon C. Mulay, VP of Operations

Provider of CNC precision machining, fabrication, and wire EDM services. The company serves the industrial sector.

**Electronics Cooling Solutions Inc**          HQ
2344B Walsh Ave Bldg F
Santa Clara CA 95051
P: 408-738-8331    F: 408-738-8337    PRC:124
ecooling.com
Email: info@ecooling.com
Estab: 1998

Ceferino Sanchez, Consulting Engineer

Provider of thermal management consulting services. The company serves customers in the avionics, medical, and telecommunications industries.

**Elegrity Inc**          HQ
160 Pine St Ste 720
San Francisco CA 94111
P: 415-821-0900    F: 415-826-7758    PRC:325
www.elegrity.com
Email: info@elegrity.com
Estab: 1998

Joy Spicer, President
Craig Mason, Chief Architect
Kandace Donovan, VP of sales and Marketing
Timothy Conlon, Secretary of the Board
Jeffrey Wolk, Treasurer of the Board

Provider of law business management software, SharePoint, virtualization, and unified communication solutions.

**Element Science Inc**          HQ
200 Kansas St Ste 210
San Francisco CA 94103
P: 415-872-6500    PRC:189
www.elementscience.com
Estab: 2011

Uday Kumar, Founder
Sidney Negus, Senior Director of Manufacturing & Operations
Tim Bahney, Senior Director of Research & Development

Developer of wearable platform solution. The company offers wearable cardioverter defibrillator for monitoring the heart of the patient.

**Elemental LED Inc**          HQ
1195 Park Ave Ste 211
Emeryville CA 94608
P: 877-564-5051    PRC:209
www.elementalled.com
Email: answers@elementalled.com
Estab: 2007

Randy Holleschau, President
Jeff Johnson, CAO
Matt John, CSO
Preet Khangura, CFO
Andrew Yanev, VP of Sales

Provider LED lighting accessories and products. The company's products include LED strip lights, kits, light fixtures, and dimmable lighting products.

**Elementum Scm Inc**          HQ
1300 Terra Bella Ave Ste 200
Mountain View CA 94043
P: 650-318-1491    PRC:322
www.elementum.com
Estab: 2012

Nader Mikhail, CEO
David Blonski, Head of Operations

Provider of apps to manage your global supply chain. The company offers manufacturing operations, mission control, supplier, and logistics management.

**Elevator Controls Corp** HQ
6150 Warehouse Way
Sacramento CA 95826
P: 916-428-1708   F: 916-428-1728   PRC:86
www.elevatorcontrols.com
Email: sales@elevatorcontrols.com
Emp: 1-10   Estab: 1986

Francisco Ortiz, VP of Product Engineering and Support
Jorge Vidalon, Sales Engineer
Fernando Ortiz, President
Diane Ellis, Human Resource Manager
Orencio Reantazo, Production Manager

Manufacturer of non-proprietary microprocessor based elevator controllers. The company offers technical support and field services.

**Elevator Technology Inc** HQ
2050 Arroyo Vista Way
El Dorado Hills CA 95762
P: 916-939-4323   F: 916-933-6424   PRC:180
www.elevatortechnologyinc.com
Email: elevatortec@att.net
Emp: 1-10   Estab: 1991

Leonard Bates, Founder

Provider of elevator repair and installation services. The company specializes both in residential and commercial elevators.

**Elite E/M Inc** HQ
340 Martin Ave
Santa Clara CA 95050
P: 408-988-3505   F: 408-988-3540   PRC:80
eliteem.com

Igor Brovarny, Co-Owner

Provider of precision machining services. The company offers prototyping, tooling, shearing, and cutting services.

**Elixir Medical Corp** HQ
920 N. McCarthy Blvd Ste 100
Milpitas CA 95035-4104
P: 408-636-2000   PRC:189
www.elixirmedical.com
Email: info@elixirmedical.com
Estab: 2005

Motasim Sirhan, CEO
Erin Mazzone, Senior Director of Regulatory Affairs

Provider of pharmaceuticals for drug-device treatment solutions to patients. The company is engaged in drug delivery.

**Elk Antennas** HQ
2308 Lomond Ln
Walnut Creek CA 94598-3705
P: 925-330-0049   PRC:61
www.elkantennas.com
Estab: 1995

Jim Siemons, Owner

Provider of log periodic antennas made of aluminum elements and stainless steel hardware and with gain, directivity, and front-to-back ratio.

**Ellex iScience Inc** BR
41316 Christy St
Fremont CA 94538
P: 510-291-1300   PRC:172
ellex.com
Estab: 1985

Maria Maieli, Interim CEO
Victor Previn, Chairman
Cynthia Kendall, VP of Clinical Applications
Mike Mangano, Non Executive Director
Alex Sundich, Non Executive Director

Developer and provider of technology solutions for the treatment of eye conditions. The company products include tango, eye one, eye cubed, tango reflex, and more.

**Ellie Mae Inc** HQ
4420 Rosewood Dr Ste 500
Pleasanton CA 94588
P: 925-227-7000   F: 925-227-9030   PRC:322
www.elliemae.com
Email: info@elliemae.com
Estab: 1997
Sales: $300M to $1 Billion

Satheesh Ravala, SVP of Engineering
Jonathan Corr, President
Joe Tyrrell, COO
Selim Aissi, Chief Security Officer
Dan Madden, EVP

Focuses on mortgage compliance services. The company offers services to banks and other financial institutions.

**Elliott Manufacturing Company Inc** HQ
2664 S Cherry Ave
Fresno CA 93706
P: 559-233-6235   F: 559-233-9833   PRC:159
www.elliott-mfg.com
Email: elliottmfg@elliott-mfg.com
Emp: 1-10   Estab: 1929

Mike Tilly, Sales Manager

Manufacturer of case erectors, case sealers, cartoners, and case packers. The company is engaged in sales and delivery services.

**Ellison Fluid Systems Inc** HQ
23052H Alicia Pkwy Ste 395
Mission Viejo CA 92692
P: 877-339-3412   F: 909-906-1473   PRC:8
www.ellison-tbi.com
Email: info@ellison-fluid-systems.com
Emp: 1-10

Ben Ellison, President

Provider of fluid systems that includes throttle body injector. The company offers fuel metering for aircrafts engines and throttle response.

**Elma Electronic Inc** LH
44350 Grimmer Blvd
Fremont CA 94538
P: 510-656-3400   F: 510-656-3783   PRC:93
www.elma.com
Email: sales@elma.com
Estab: 1962

Manish Nasta, Manufacturing Engineer
Dragos Micodin, Senior Applications Engineer
Jonas Smith-Strawn, Storage Engineer
Urs Hess, VP of Information Technology
Peter Brunner, EVP of Finance & Administration

Designer and manufacturer of electronic components and enclosures. The company is involved in design, installation, and delivery services.

**Elo Touch Solutions Inc** HQ
670 N McCarthy Blvd
Milpitas CA 95035-7920
P: 408-597-8000   F: 408-597-8001   PRC:93
www.elotouch.com
Email: elosales.na@elotouch.com
Estab: 1971

Kenneth North, VP of Engineering
Craig Witsoe, CEO
Jay Delatte, CFO
John Lamb, CMO
Corbett Wood, VP

Designer, developer, and manufacturer of touch products and technologies. The company's products include tablets, touchscreens, and touchmonitors.

**Elucit** HQ
31575 Misty Ln
Fort Bragg CA 95437-6214
P: 707-961-1016   PRC:323
www.elucit.com
Email: info@elucit.com
Emp: 1-10   Estab: 2000

Karthikeyan V, Assistant Manager

Provider of hardware & software development services. The company also offers data recorders and calibratrion services.

**Em Lab P&K** BR
880 Riverside Pkwy
West Sacramento CA 95605
P: 916-374-4483   F: 650-742-8191   PRC:139
www.emlab.com
Emp: 11-50

Kamash Ramanathan, Regional Director

Provider of indoor air quality testing services. The company offers culturable air fungi, spore trap analysis, and yeast identification services.

**Emagined Security Inc** HQ
2816 San Simeon Wy
San Carlos CA 94070
P: 415-944-2977   PRC:67
www.emagined.com
Email: info@emagined.com
Estab: 2002

David Sockol, CEO
Paul Underwood, COO
David Zuckerman, SVP of Sales & Marketing

Provider of professional services for information security solutions. The company also focuses on compliance.

**Emanio Inc** HQ
832 Bancroft Way
Berkeley CA 94710
P: 510-849-9300   F: 510-849-9302   PRC:323
www.emanio.com
Email: info@emanio.com
Estab: 1994

Knut Oygardslia, Chief Scientist

Developer of products for data management, dashboarding, and reporting & predictive analysis needs. The company focuses on consulting and training.

**Embedur Systems Inc**  HQ
42808 Christy St Ste 102
Fremont CA 94538
P: 510-353-9111   F: 510-353-9986   PRC:71
embedur.com
Estab: 2004

Abhishek Sharma, VP of Development Engineering
Pervez Mohta, Director of Engineering
Balaji Gnanasekaran, Software Engineer
Rajas Mohile, Software Engineer
Rajesh Subramaniam, CEO

Developer of software solutions. The company also offers technical and management services for the embedded market.

**Emboline Inc**  HQ
2811 Mission St
Santa Cruz CA 95060
P: 831-900-5020   F: 831-900-5019   PRC:189
emboline.com
Email: info@emboline.com
Emp: 1-10   Estab: 2011

Scott Russell, CEO
Stephen Kleshinski, VP of Research & Development

Developer of cardiovascular embolic protection devices for transcatheter and surgical cardiac procedures.

**Eme Systems**  HQ
2229 Fifth St
Berkeley CA 94710
P: 510-848-5725   F: 510-848-5748   PRC:11
www.emesystems.com
Email: info@emesystems.com
Estab: 1985

Teri Piccolo, Co-Owner
Thomas Tracy Allen, Founder

Designer and manufacturer of instruments for environmental science. The company also offers signal conditioners, sensors, enclosures, and batteries.

**EMED**  HQ
1264 Hawks Flight Ct Ste 200
El Dorado Hills CA 95762
P: 916-932-0071   PRC:189
www.emedtc.com
Email: info@mysite.com
Emp: 1-10   Estab: 1990

Hoda Aref, Owner
Duane Boise, President
Peter Kollings, Manager of Quality Assurance
Joseph Barbrie, VP of Sales
Valeria Pershyna, Sales Manager

Manufacturer of safety medical products and specialty medical devices with a focus on infusion therapy.

**Emkay Manufacturing Inc**  HQ
815 Sweeney Ave Unit D
Redwood City CA 94063
P: 650-365-3010   F: 650-365-9135   PRC:80
www.emkaymfg.com
Email: emkaymfg@aol.com
Estab: 1978

Anne Feher, Owner

Provider of precision milling and turning services. The company serves the medical, electrical, aerospace, and defense sectors.

**Emlinux**  HQ
1240 McKendrie St
San Jose CA 95126-1408
P: 408-249-5574   PRC:224
www.emlinux.com
Email: sales@emlinux.com
Estab: 1999

Joel Williams, Principal Owner

Developer of embedded Linux designs. The company provides marketing level definition and system architecture services.

**Emotiv**  DH
490 Post St Ste 824
San Francisco CA 94102
P: 415-525-3149   PRC:209
emotiv.com
Estab: 2011

Tan Le, Founder

Provider of neuroengineering products and services. The company offers algorithms to detect subconscious emotional states and facial expressions.

**Emotive Brand**  HQ
580 Second St Ste 245
Oakland CA 94607
P: 510-496-8888   PRC:45
www.emotivebrand.com
Estab: 2009

Tracy Lloyd, Co-Founder
Bella Banbury, Co-Founder
Jonathan Fisher, Director of Production
Robert Saywitz, Design Director
Thomas Hutchings, Creative Director

Brand strategy and design firm that helps to transform the businesses.

**Empire Magnetics Inc**  HQ
5830 Commerce Blvd
Rohnert Park CA 94928
P: 707-584-2801   F: 707-584-3418   PRC:292
www.empiremagnetics.com
Email: sales@empiremagnetics.com
Estab: 1987

Rick Halstead, President

Manufacturer of specialty, cryogenic, dust proof, high temperature, water proof, and radiation hardened motors.

**Empire West Inc**  HQ
PO Box 511
Graton CA 95444
P: 707-823-1190   F: 707-823-8531   PRC:284
www.empirewest.com
Email: info@empirewest.com
Estab: 1968

Ed Davis, President
Rich Yonash, CEO
Susan Skocypec, Web Developer
Sonya Yonash, Controller

Designer and developer of envelope handling trays, custom thermoformed ceiling tiles and panels, and optic packaging solutions.

**Empower Micro Systems Inc**  HQ
3020 Kenneth St
Santa Clara CA 95054
P: 408-620-6458   PRC:126
www.empowermicro.com
Email: info@empowermicro.com
Estab: 2012

Jon Bonanno, CCO
Milan Ilic, CTO
Mika Nuotio, CEO
Tim Cowart, CFO

Provider of semiconductor technology for PV module and inverter manufacturers, solar distributors, solar finance companies, developers, and installers.

**Emsl Analytical Inc**  BR
464 McCormick St
San Leandro CA 94577
P: 510-895-3675   F: 510-895-3680   PRC:18
www.emsl.com
Email: info@emsl.com
Estab: 1981

Peter Frasca, President
Ron Smith, VP of Sales

Provider of laboratory analytical testing services. The company specializes in a wide range of environmental, material and forensic testing.

**Emtec Engineering**  HQ
16840 Joleen Way Bldg F1
Morgan Hill CA 95037
P: 408-779-5800   F: 408-778-2850   PRC:80
www.emtec.cc
Email: info@emtec.cc

Chris Fontaine, President

Provider of precision machining and precision sheet metal fabrication services to the computer, telecommunication, and medical industries.

**Emtrain**  HQ
2 Embarcadero 8th Fl
San Francisco CA 94111
P: 800-242-6099   F: 866-513-7171   PRC:326
emtrain.com
Estab: 2000

Janine Yancey, CEO
Ty Yancey, COO
Robert Todd, Chief Product Officer
Sophia Rodriguez, Customer Service Executive

Provider of learning management system such as online training platform for all levels of HR professionals, trainers, and administrators.

**Enablence Technologies Inc**  DH
2933 Bayview Dr
Fremont CA 94538
P: 510-226-8900   F: 510-226-8333   PRC:64
www.enablence.com
Email: info@enablence.com
Sales: $3M to $10M

Tao Zhang, CFO

Manufacturer of silicon products for communication needs. The company's offerings include optical splitters and channel filters.

**Encore Industries Inc**　　　　HQ
　597 Brennan St
　San Jose CA 95131-1202
P: 408-416-0501　F: 408-416-0511　　PRC:80
www.encoreindustries.com
Estab: 1997

Mark Hacker, President

Provider of technical services to engineering and procurement. The company's domain includes medical and science, consumer products, and structural.

**Endicia**　　　　HQ
　278 Castro St
　Mountain View CA 94041-1204
P: 650-321-2640　F: 650-321-0356　　PRC:323
www.endicia.com
Estab: 1989

Benjamin Preston, Implementations Engineer
Jaemin Ma, Server Software Engineer
Harry Whitehouse, CTO
Amine Khechfe, General Manager
Emma Johnson, Director of Marketing

Provider of electronic postage software solutions and offers shipping and mailing services to online sellers, warehouse shippers, and office mailers.

**Endo Gastric Solutions Inc**　　　　HQ
　1900 Ofarrell St Ste 235
　San Mateo CA 94403
P: 650-578-5100　F: 650-578-5101　　PRC:188
endogastricsolutions.com
Email: info@endogastricsolutions.com
Estab: 2003

Skip Baldino, President
Michael Burke, CFO
Adrian Lobontiu, Chief Medical Officer
Martin Reid, VP of Sales
Ted Stephens, VP of Marketing and Professional Education

Provider of treatment services for gastroesophageal reflux disease. The company also focuses on training and education.

**Endologix Inc**　　　　HQ
　3910 Brickway Blvd
　Santa Rosa CA 95403
P: 707-543-8800　F: 855-569-7763　　PRC:189
www.trivascular.com
Email: customerservice@trivascular.com
Estab: 1999

John Onopchenko, CEO
Dan Lemaitre, Chairman
Vaseem Mahboob, CFO
Jeff Brown, COO
Jeffry Fecho, CQO

Developer of endovascular grafts for the treatment of aneurysmal disease in the abdominal aorta and the thoracic aorta.

**Endpoint Clinical inc**　　　　HQ
　55 Francisco St Ste 200
　San Francisco CA 94133
P: 415-229-1600　　PRC:194
www.endpointclinical.com
Email: support@endpointclinical.com
Estab: 2009

Christine Oliver, VP of Operations
Ryan Harrison, Director of Business Development

Designer of response technology platforms to access data through phones, the web, and mobile devices. The company is engaged in engineering services.

**Enel X e-Mobility**　　　　HQ
　846 Bransten Rd
　San Carlos CA 94070
P: 844-584-2329　　PRC:209
emotorwerks.com
Estab: 2010

Surya Panditi, President
Alexander Gurzhi, Chief Software Architect of Cloud
Preston Roper, General Manager
Alan White, Head of Global Sales
Elise Benoit, VP of Marketing

Developer of electric vehicle charging technologies such as smart grid EV charging networks for residential, workplace, and commercial installation.

**Enerfin Resources Co**　　　　BR
　12242 Business Park Dr Ste 33
　Truckee CA 96161
P: 530-550-8419　F: 530-550-9681　　PRC:131
enerfin.com
Emp: 11-50

Jeff Williams, Manager of Gas Supply & Business Development

Producer of natural gas. The company is also engaged in the exploration of crude oil and natural gas.

**Energous Corp**　　　　HQ
　3590 N First St Ste 210
　San Jose CA 95134
P: 408-963-0200　　PRC:288
www.energous.com
Sales: Under $1 Million

Sreeni Aruru, Senior Director of Engineering
Mark Elliott, Senior Systems Engineer
Stephen Rizzone, President
Cesar Johnston, COO
Brian Sereda, SVP

Provider of energy solutions. The company offers a wire-free charging system for portable electronic devices.

**Energy Recovery Inc**　　　　HQ
　1717 Doolittle Dr
　San Leandro CA 94577
P: 510-483-7370　F: 510-483-7371　　PRC:134
www.energyrecovery.com
Email: support@energyrecovery.com
Estab: 1992
Sales: $30M to $100M

Robert Mao, Chairman
Farshad Ghasripoor, CTO
Joshua Ballard, CFO
Sean Sultani, Manager of Information Technology
Linda Yu, Accountant

Manufacturer of energy recovery devices. The company offers pressure exchangers, chargers, pumps for desalination processes, oil and gas applications.

**energyOrbit Inc**　　　　HQ
　1 Market St Spear Twr Ste 3600
　San Francisco CA 94105
P: 866-628-8744　　PRC:322
energy-orbit.com
Estab: 2007

Udi Merhav, CEO
Alex Zeltser, CTO
John Fruin, CFO
Jim Murray, VP of Professional Services
Jason Adge, VP of Business Development

Provider of cloud based platform and solution for streamline demand side management programs, projects, and relationship management for customers.

**Enerparc Inc**　　　　DH
　1999 Harrison St Ste 830
　Oakland CA 94612
P: 844-367-7272　　PRC:135
www.enerparc.de
Email: info@enerparc.us
Estab: 2008

Thomas Houghton, Director of Engineering & Construction
Florent Abadie, CEO
Donald Miller, General Counsel of Americas
Nikolaus Mainka, Associate Director of Finance
Patrick Schaufelberger, Associate Director of Project Finance

Developer and designer of photovoltaic systems. The company services include EPC work, EPC management, operation, and maintenance.

**EnerVault**　　　　HQ
　1244 Reamwood Ave
　Sunnyvale CA 94089
P: 408-934-6840　　PRC:288
www.enervault.com
Email: info@enervault.com
Estab: 2008

Peter Corr-Barberis, Mechanical Engineer

Designer and manufacturer of megawatt-hour scale energy storage systems based on iron-chromium redox flow battery technology.

**Eneura Therapeutics LLC**　　　　HQ
　715 N Pastoria Ave
　Sunnyvale CA 94085
P: 408-245-6400　　PRC:186
www.eneura.com
Estab: 2000

Terese Baker, President
Jacob Vogelstein, Partner
Michaun Auzenne, Corporate Controller
Sherrie Perkins, Medical Device Professional
Tom Brooks, Venture Partner at Camden Partners Nexus

Provider of medical technology solutions. The company offers transcranial magnetic stimulation devices for the treatment of migraine.

**Enfos Inc**  HQ
2929 Campus Dr Ste 415
San Mateo CA 94403
P: 650-357-0007  PRC:325
www.enfos.com
Email: sales@enfos.com
Estab: 2000

Craig Modesitt, CEO
Roger Well, COO
Sandeep Digra, CTO

Provider of business software solutions for environmental management. The company specializes in financial, compliance, and GIS data management.

**Engage Communication Inc**  HQ
9565 Soquel Dr
Aptos CA 95003
P: 831-688-1021  F: 831-688-1421  PRC:97
www.engageinc.com
Email: sales@engageinc.com
Emp: 11-50 Estab: 1989

Steve Corriveau, Technical Sales Engineer
Mark Doyle, CEO

Developer and manufacturer of telecommunications equipment. The company focuses on encryption, mobile, and cellular backhauling solutions.

**Engagio Inc**  HQ
181 Second Ave Ste 200
San Mateo CA 94401
P: 650-487-2050  PRC:319
www.engagio.com
Email: sales@engagio.com
Estab: 2015

Raj Lenin, Senior Director of Engineering
Mark Whitehouse, Director of Engineering
Jon Miller, Co-Founder
Brian Babcock, Co-Founder
Cheryl Chavez, Chief Product Officer

B2B Marketing Engagement Software that enables marketers and sellers to work as a team.

**Engineering By Design**  HQ
2157-G O'Toole Ave Ste 40
San Jose CA 95131
P: 408-324-1500  F: 408-324-1501  PRC:159
www.ebdesign.com
Email: info@ebdesign.com
Estab: 1985

Dale Henson, President
Judy Henson, CFO

Provider of engineering and support services. The company's products include laminators, coil and fiber winders, motors, and extrusion pullers.

**Enlighta**  HQ
111 Deerwood Rd Ste 200
San Ramon CA 94583
P: 510-279-5820  F: 510-279-5820  PRC:326
www.enlighta.com
Email: info@enlighta.com
Estab: 2002

Callistus Chui, Principle Engineer

Provider of software solutions to service organizations grappling with governance and management of global services delivery.

**Enlighted Inc**  HQ
930 Benecia Ave
Sunnyvale CA 94085
P: 650-964-1094  PRC:130
www.enlightedinc.com
Email: sales@enlightedinc.com
Estab: 2009

Tyler Ball, Field Engineer
Andre Quiazon, Field Engineer
Tanuj Mohan, Founder
Stefan Schwab, CEO
Dirk Rauber, CFO

Provider of lighting control systems to commercial buildings, office workspaces, and garages. The company serves facilities and development companies.

**Enocean Alliance Inc**  HQ
2400 Camino Ramon Ste 375
San Ramon CA 94583
P: 925-275-6601  F: 925-275-6691  PRC:227
www.enocean-alliance.org
Email: info@enocean-alliance.org
Estab: 2008

Graham Martin, CEO

Manufacturer of wireless switches, sensors, and controls for building automation and residential property needs.

**Enphase Energy Inc**  HQ
1420 N McDowell Blvd
Petaluma CA 94954
P: 877-797-4743  PRC:135
enphase.com
Estab: 2006
Sales: $300M to $1 Billion

Martin Fornage, Co-Founder
Raghu Belur, Co-Founder
Badri Kothandaraman, CEO
Dave Ranhoff, CCO
Eric Branderiz, CFO

Distributor of electronic products. The company offers services to the solar, telecom, networking, and software industries.

**Enplan**  HQ
3179 Bechelli Ln Ste 100
Redding CA 96002
P: 530-221-0440  F: 530-221-6963  PRC:142
www.enplan.com
Emp: 1-10

Randall Hauser, CEO

Provider of environmental and geospatial technology services. The company focuses on wetland delineation and permit processing activities.

**Enplas Tech Solutions Inc**  RH
3211 Scott Blvd Ste 103
Santa Clara CA 95054
P: 669-243-3600  F: 669-243-3696  PRC:86
enplas.co.jp
Email: info@enplas-ets.com
Estab: 1993

Jaime Bernal, Coordinator of Sales Administration

Distributor of engineering plastic products. The company also offers optical devices, semiconductor peripherals, and related supplies.

**Enpro Solutions Inc**  HQ
6500 Dublin Blvd Ste 215
Dublin CA 94568-3152
P: 925-803-8045  PRC:142
www.enprosolutionsinc.com
Estab: 1998

R. Qadir, Principal

Provider of environmental remediation, management, permitting, and construction services. The company also deals with process safety consulting.

**Ens Technology LLC**  HQ
3145 & 3165 Molinaro St
Santa Clara CA 95054
P: 408-496-0740  PRC:280
www.enstechnology.com
Email: estimating@enstechnology.com

Brett Dawson, President

Provider of plating services. The company plates materials such as common metals, alloys, and refractory metals.

**Ensemble Designs Inc**  HQ
PO Box 993
Grass Valley CA 95945
P: 530-478-1830  F: 530-478-1832  PRC:60
www.ensembledesigns.com
Email: info@ensembledesigns.com
Emp: 1-10  Estab: 1989

Jason Job, Hardware Design Engineer
David Wood, President
Mondae Hott, Director of Sales
Robert Nunez, Sales Manager
Cindy Zuelsdorf, Marketing Manager

Manufacturer of audio embedders, video converters, routers, and related products. The company serves post production, education, and other sectors.

**Ensenta Corp**  HQ
303 Twin Dolphin Dr Ste 201
Redwood Shores CA 94065
P: 866-219-4321  PRC:323
www.ensenta.com
Email: support@ensenta.com
Estab: 2001

Morgan Wilson, System Administrator

Developer of software solutions. The company is involved in development of cloud-based imaging and self-service technology.

**enSilo**  HQ
182 Second St Ste 210
San Francisco CA 94105
P: 800-413-1782  PRC:319
www.ensilo.com
Email: contact@ensilo.com
Estab: 2014

Roy Katmor, Co-Founder
Udi Yavo, Co-Founder
Aaron Sramek, Regional Sales Manager
Elad Horn, VP of Products
Noam Harel, Director of Demand Generation

Developer of data protection platforms and provider of exfiltration prevention solutions. The company offers services to the network industry.

**Ent Networks Inc** HQ
240 Spring St Ste A
Pleasanton CA 94566
P: 925-462-7125 PRC:93
www.entnetworks.com
Email: info@entnetworks.com
Estab: 1985

Emilio Martin, Network Engineer
Billy Buckley, CEO
Theresa Buckley, Sales Manager

Provider of custom system manufacturing, database management, hardware sales, business consulting, and repair services.

**Entech Electronics Inc** BR
5201 Great America Pkwy Ste 320
Santa Clara CA 95054
P: 408-730-2650 F: 408-562-5745 PRC:91
www.entechelectronics.us
Email: service@entechelectronics.us

Wayne Hoffman, CEO
Jason Reeves, Global Sales & Marketing Manager

Supplier of electronic equipment. The company also offers laser cut stencils, graphic decals, LCD screens, and engineering services.

**Envestnet** BR
160 W Santa Clara Ste 850
San Jose CA 95113
P: 866-924-8912 F: 408-962-7850 PRC:322
www.envestnet.com
Email: marketing@envestnet.com
Estab: 1999

Thomas Hempel, SVP of Engineering
James Lumberg, Co-Founder
Jim Patrick, Group President
Babu Sivadasan, Group President
Frank Coates, Executive Managing Director Co-Group President Envestnet Analytics

Provider of application software for financial service firms. The company is involved in practice and portfolio management.

**Enview Inc** HQ
164 Townsend St Unit 11
San Francisco CA 94107
P: 415-483-5680 PRC:323
enview.com
Estab: 2015

Eleanor Crane, Principal Software Engineer
Krassimir Piperkov, Co-Founder
San Gunawardana, Co-Founder

Specializes in threat prevention systems. The company deals with data analytics and remote sensing services.

**Enviro Safetech Inc** HQ
2160 B Oakland Rd
San Jose CA 95131
P: 408-943-9090 F: 408-943-9292 PRC:136
www.envirosafetech.com
Email: info@envirosafetech.com
Estab: 1990

Jay Jamali, Environmental Health & Safety Director

Provider of environmental, health, and safety consulting services. The company deals with auditing and inspections.

**Enviro Tech Chemicals Inc** HQ
500 Winmoore Way
Modesto CA 95358-5750
P: 209-581-9576 F: 209-581-9653 PRC:51
www.envirotech.com
Email: customerservice@envirotech.com
Emp: 1-10 Estab: 1991

Mike Harvey, President
Brent Bankosky, COO
Jesus Aceves, General Manager
Steve Jacobs, VP of Sales
Todd Wiseman, Corporate Sales Manager

Manufacturer of peracetic acid. The company focuses on the development of EPA and FDA regulated chemistries and novel solutions.

**Enviro-Tech Services Co** HQ
4851 Sunrise Dr Ste 101
Martinez CA 94553
P: 800-468-8921 F: 925-370-8037 PRC:138
envirotechonline.com
Estab: 1987

Charles Lawton, President
Steve Jacobs, VP of Sales
Sue Koepp-Baker, Principal

Designer and manufacturer of environmental products. The company offers water sampling equipment, air monitoring equipment, and general field supplies.

**Envirocare International** HQ
507 Green Island Rd
American Canyon CA 94503
P: 707-638-6800 PRC:151
www.envirocare.com
Email: info@envirocare.com
Estab: 1980

Jim Whitten, Project Engineer
John Fosgate, Project Engineer
John Tate, Owner
Reid Thomas, Manager Parts & Service

Designer of pollution control appliances. The company also specializes in manufacturing gas cooling and gas conditioning systems.

**Environmental Incentives** HQ
3351 Lake Tahoe Blvd Ste 2
South Lake Tahoe CA 96150
P: 530-541-2980 PRC:142
enviroincentives.com
Emp: 11-50 Estab: 2004

Jeremy Sokulsky, CEO
Andrew Alexandrovich, Director of Finance and Operations
Chad Praul, Partner
Eoin Doherty, Senior Associate
Katie Riley, Senior Associate

Provider of environmental conservation services. The company projects include Nevada conservation credit system and Colorado habitat exchange.

**Environmental Micro Analysis Inc** HQ
460 N East St
Woodland CA 95776
P: 530-666-6890 F: 530-666-2987 PRC:306
www.emalab.com
Email: customerservice@emalab.com
Emp: 1-10

Hardik Amin, Senior Chemist

Provider of food safety consulting services. The company specializes in pesticide residue analysis in agricultural products, processed foods and other matrices.

**Environmental Products & Technologies Corp** HQ
4216 S Mooney Blvd Ste 131
Visalia CA 93277
P: 559-201-6484 PRC:140
www.eptcorp.com
Emp: 1-10 Estab: 1983

Flint Parker, Director of Engineering
Marvin Mears, President
Terry Turner, CEO
John Graham, Chief Knowledge Officer
Scott Mears, VP of Marketing

Developer of closed-loop, short hydraulic retention time anaerobic digesters. The company specializes in biogas technology solutions.

**Environmental Remedies Inc** HQ
1999 Alpine Way
Hayward CA 94545
P: 888-710-2414 PRC:142
environmentalremediesinc.com

Jaime Tamayo, Owner
Scott Tamayo, General Manager
Melisa Christensen, Project Coordinator

Provider of asbestos abatement services. The company engages in mold remediation, lead removal, and biological containment rediation service.

**Environmental Risk Communications Inc** BR
2121 Tunnel Rd
Oakland CA 94611
P: 510-548-5570 PRC:139
erci.com
Email: info@erci.com
Estab: 1994

John Rosengard, President

Provider of consulting services in environmental liabilities management. The company's services include site strategic planning and project controls.

**Environmental Sampling Services LLC** HQ
6680 Alhambra Ave Ste 102
Martinez CA 94553
P: 925-372-8108 PRC:139
www.envsampling.com

Stephen Penman, Manager

Provider of technical services for environmental assessments needs. The company also focuses on investigation and remediation.

**Environmental Science Associates** HQ
550 Kearny St Ste 800
San Francisco CA 94108
P: 415-896-5900 PRC:139
www.esassoc.com
Estab: 1969

Albert Cuisinot, CFO
Mike Arnold, CFO
Ari Frink, Senior Associate

Provider of restoration and mitigation, regulatory permitting, compliance monitoring, and community planning services.

**Environmental Stress Systems Inc** HQ
21089 Longeway Rd
Sonora CA 95370
P: 209-588-1993  F: 209-588-1997  PRC:153
www.essproducts.com
Email: ess@essproducts.com
Emp: 1-10  Estab: 1989

Neil Johnson, Machinist

Manufacturer of mechanically refrigerated, cryogenically cooled, and liquid cooled thermal platforms.

**Envirosurvey Inc** HQ
82 Mary St
San Francisco CA 94103
P: 415-882-4549  F: 415-882-1685  PRC:142
envirosurvey.net
Estab: 1991

Mahsa Hakimi, Manager

Provider of environmental consulting and technical services. The company provides soil and groundwater remediation and environmental safety services.

**Eon Technologies Inc** HQ
1226 Lincoln Ave
Alameda CA 94501
P: 510-523-3832  PRC:40
eontech.com
Estab: 1990

Robert Cullmann, CEO

Provider of IT and computer support services. The company's services include malware and virus removal tools and printer repair services.

**Eonite Perception Inc** HQ
171 Main St Ste 212
Los Altos CA 94022
P: 650-681-9257  PRC:326
Estab: 2015

James Munch, Software Engineer
Peter Varvak, CTO
Anna Petrovskaya, Founder

Focuses on building 3D mapping and ego-tracking systems. The company serves the entertainment, robotics, and construction industries.

**EoPlex Inc** BR
1925 Zanker Rd
San Jose CA 95112
P: 408-638-5100  F: 408-638-5101  PRC:203
www.eoplex.com
Email: info@eoplex.com
Estab: 2001

Ali Modjtahedi, Engineer

Creator of HVAM technology and process for advanced 3D-printed components for mobile devices, IoT, automotive, medical, and wearable applications.

**Epiphotonics Corp** HQ
832 Jury Ct Unit 3
San Jose CA 95112
P: 408-920-7019  F: 408-920-7021  PRC:124
www.epiphotonics.com
Email: info@epiphotonics.com
Estab: 2007

Keiichi Nashimoto, President

Manufacturer of photonic components and subsystems. The company is engaged in design, delivery, and installation services.

**EPIX Orthopaedics Inc** HQ
445 Lambert Ave
Palo Alto CA 94306
P: 844-710-9105  PRC:190
epixortho.com
Email: info@epixortho.com

Amir Matityahu, Founder
Ben Clawson, Consultant
Debra Matityahu, Director

Developer of orthopaedic devices that improve patient outcomes, surgeon accuracy & efficiency, and reduce costs to patients and health care system.

**Epsilon Strategic Systems** HQ
PO Box 552 Saint Mathew Sta
San Mateo CA 94401
P: 650-579-5515  PRC:45
www.epsilon-systems.com
Email: sales@epsilon-systems.com
Estab: 1988

Roy Erickson, President

Provider of management consulting and information technology services. The company offers customization, advisory, and staff development services.

**Epylon Corp** HQ
630 San Ramon Valley Blvd Ste 210
Danville CA 94526
P: 925-407-1020  F: 925-407-1021  PRC:323
www.epylon.com
Email: service@epylon.com
Estab: 1999

Tim Blanton, CEO
Kelly Blanton, Chairman
Ted Witt, VP of Strategic Sourcing

Developer of e-procurement software and services. The company serves the government and education sectors.

**Equilar Inc** HQ
1100 Marshall St
Redwood City CA 94063
P: 877-441-6090  PRC:319
www.equilar.com
Email: info@equilar.com
Estab: 2001

David Chun, CEO
Steven Borden, Founder
Julie Fletcher, Chief Talent Officer
Lanny Baker, CFO
Michele Lau, SVP of Corporate Secretary & Associate GC

Developer of industry-leading data and tools for public and private companies, compensation consultants, attorneys, and corporate governance leaders.

**Equinix** HQ
1 Lagoon Dr Fl 4
Redwood City CA 94065
P: 866-378-4649  F: 650-598-6900  PRC:324
www.equinix.com
Email: info@equinix.com
Estab: 1998
Sales: Over $3B

Charles Meyers, President
Peter Van Camp, Executive Chairman
Eric Schwartz, Chief Strategy and Development Officer
Keith Taylor, CFO
Sara Baack, Chief Product Officer

Provider of interconnection data center and global colocation services focusing on cloud, business continuity, financial, and digital media.

**Equipment Solutions Inc** HQ
1098 W Evelyn Ave Ste 102
Sunnyvale CA 94086
P: 408-245-7162  F: 408-245-7160  PRC:176
equipsolutions.com
Email: info@equipsolutions.com
Estab: 1990

Jeff Knirck, CEO

Manufacturer and provider of actuators and motion control systems. The company offers optical scanners, servo amplifiers, and digital autocollimators.

**Ergo Direct Com** HQ
1601 Old County Rd
San Carlos CA 94070
P: 650-654-4300  PRC:60
ergodirect.com
Email: customerservice@ergodirect.com

Nick Moshiri, Founder

Provider of adjustable desks, arms, and mounts. The company offers ergonomic keyboards, monitor arms, and mounting adapters.

**Errigal Inc** HQ
3 Embarcadero Ctr Ste 1440
San Francisco CA 94111
P: 415-523-9245  PRC:322
errigal.com
Email: sales@errigal.com
Estab: 1996

Shea Lawrence, Software Engineer
Padraig Tobin, Founder
Patrick Gary, Technical Associate

Designer and developer of software products and services. The company also deals with configuration management and ticketing.

**Escalera Inc** HQ
PO Box 1359
Yuba City CA 95992
P: 530-673-6318  F: 530-673-6376  PRC:180
www.escalera.com
Email: info@escalera.com
Emp: 1-10  Estab: 1968

Bryan Miller, Manager

Manufacturer of stair climbing trucks. The company's products include forklifts, handtrucks, and load movers.

**Escend Pharmaceuticals Inc**      HQ
3475 Edison Way Ste R
Menlo Park CA 94025
P: 650-241-9128      PRC:268
www.escendpharma.com
Email: info@escendpharma.com
Estab: 1997

Dennis Brown, Co-Founder
Saira Bates, Co-Founder

Provider of therapeutic solutions. The company focusses on cancer stem cells in acute myelogenous leukemia and hematologic malignancies for drug development.

**Ese Consulting Engineers Inc**      HQ
1060 Grant St Ste 3D
Benicia CA 94510
P: 707-747-1755    F: 707-747-6538      PRC:304
eseweb.com
Email: mail@eseweb.com
Estab: 1988

Hadieh Elias, President
Amir Firouz, VP

Provider of structural engineering design, seismic analysis and retrofitting, and peer review services.

**eShares Inc**      HQ
333 Bush St 23rd Fl Ste 2300
San Francisco CA 94104
P: 650-669-8381      PRC:325
carta.com
Email: support@carta.com
Estab: 2012

David Goudreau, VP of Engineering
Preeti Kaur, VP of Software Engineering
Ron Pragides, VP of Engineering
Luis Miguel Gomez, Director of Engineering
Jerry Talton, Senior Director of Engineering Data

Specializes in capitalization table management and valuation software.

**ESI Bio**      HQ
1010 Atlantic Ave Ste 102
Alameda CA 94501
P: 510-521-3390    F: 510-648-3255      PRC:34
www.esibio.com
Email: orders@esibio.com
Estab: 2000

Jeffrey Janus, CEO

Provider of stem cell solutions. The company's products are used in bio printing, stem cell analysis, and stem cell reprogramming.

**Esilicon Corp**      HQ
2130 Gold St Ste 100
San Jose CA 95002
P: 408-635-6300    F: 408-635-6499      PRC:204
www.esilicon.com
Email: info@esilicon.com
Estab: 2000

Deepak Sabharwal, VP of IP Engineering
Hao Nham, SVP of Engineering
Jack Harding, President
Philippe Morali, CFO
Bruce Newton, VP of Worldwide Human Resources

Provider of design, product design, and manufacturing services for the production of integrated circuits.

**Esp Interactive Solutions Inc**      HQ
1223 Solano Ave Ste 8
Albany CA 94706
P: 510-526-2592    F: 510-526-2692      PRC:325
www.espinteractivesolutions.com
Email: info@espis.com
Estab: 2001

Tariq Khan, President
Salman Sethi, Business Development Manager

Provider of web design and development services such as web video creation, content management system, and social networks marketing.

**Esp Safety Inc**      HQ
555 N First St
San Jose CA 95112
P: 408-886-9746      PRC:13
www.espsafetyinc.com
Email: info@espsafetyinc.com
Estab: 1973

Fabian Martinez, Applications Engineer
Frank Paulsen, Sales Manager

Manufacturer of combustible gas and flame detectors, test lamps, and multi-channel controllers for custom applications.

**Ess Technology Inc**      HQ
237 South Hillview Dr
Milpitas CA 95035
P: 408-643-8800    F: 510-492-1511      PRC:60
www.esstech.com
Estab: 1984

Bob Blair, CEO
John Marsh, CFO
Connie Wong, Senior Production Planner
Duat Tran, Senior Design Manager
Edgar Mendoza, Senior Manager of Quality Assurance & Research Engineering

Designer and marketer of video and audio semiconductors for the home, automotive, and entertainment markets.

**Essai Inc**      HQ
48580 Kato Rd
Fremont CA 94538
P: 510-580-1700    F: 510-580-1810      PRC:209
essai.com

Kurt Sanfilippo, Manufacturing Manager
Linh Nguyen, Purchasing Manager
Kristina Ngo, Junior Buyer

Provider of engineering services. The company provides solutions for the semiconductors, telecom, computer components, and automotive sectors.

**Et Solar Inc**      DH
4900 Hopyard Rd Ste 290
Pleasanton CA 94588
P: 925-460-9898    F: 925-460-9929      PRC:135
www.etsolar.com
Email: sales@etsolar.com
Estab: 2005

May Khasem, Director of Operations

Provider of solar inverters and modules. The company offers design, installation, maintenance, and repair services.

**Eta-Usa**      HQ
16170 Vineyard Blvd Ste 180
Morgan Hill CA 95037
P: 408-778-2793    F: 408-779-2753      PRC:98
www.eta-usa.com
Email: sales@eta-usa.com

Phil Silverstein, Chief Engineer
Reza Sarzaeim, Mechanical Engineer
Bryan Frias, Manufacturing Associate
Sousan Manteghi-Safakish, Manager of Procurement
Adel B., Test & Assembly Tech

Provider of power supplies and manufacturer of battery chargers. The company serves the communication, gaming, and computing industries.

**Ethylene Control Inc**      HQ
8232 E Dinuba Ave
Selma CA 93662
P: 559-896-1909    F: 559-896-3232      PRC:53
www.ethylenecontrol.com
Email: info@ethylenecontrol.com
Emp: 1-10    Estab: 1986

Dave Biswell, General Manager of Sales
Norma Hollnagel, Production Manager

Manufacturer of ethylene and gas removal products. The company's products include filters, filtration systems, and sachets.

**ETM Electromatic Inc**      BR
35451 Dumbarton Ct
Newark CA 94560
P: 510-797-1100    F: 510-797-4358      PRC:120
www.etm-inc.com
Email: salesetm@etm-inc.com
Estab: 1973

Kayte Mariani, VP of Engineering and Program Management
Ken Lillis, Senior Engineer of Microwave Tube Test Products
Maarten Korringa, Senior Design Engineer
Mark McPherson, Service Engineer
Tom Hayse, CEO

Manufacturer of electronic products. The company offers microwaves, testing and measuring tools, and thermal management devices.

**Etm Electromatic Inc**      HQ
35451 Dumbarton Ct
Newark CA 94560
P: 510-797-1100    F: 510-797-4358      PRC:138
www.etm-inc.com
Email: supportetm@etm-inc.com
Estab: 1973

Kayte Mariani, VP of Engineering and Program Management
John Madigan, Mechanical Engineer
Tom Hayse, CEO
John Capovilla, Vice-Chairman & Executive Advisor
Richard Marquez, VP of Worldwide Sales

Manufacturer of custom high voltage power supplies and amplifiers. The company is engaged in troubleshooting, repairs, and maintenance services.

**Eton Corp** HQ
1015 Corporation Way
Palo Alto CA 94303
P: 650-903-3866   F: 650-903-3867   PRC:209
www.etoncorp.com
Email: info@etoncorp.com
Estab: 1986

John Smith, SVP

Manufacturer of solar energy products. The
company offers products for weather alert radios,
backup battery packs, and sound systems.

**Etouch Systems Corp** BR
6627 Dumbarton Cir
Fremont CA 94555
P: 510-795-4800   F: 510-795-4803   PRC:323
www.virtusa.com
Estab: 1998

Chandika Mendis, Global Head of Engineering
Samir Dhir, President
Kris Canekeratne, Chairman
Madu Ratnayake, EVP
Ranjan Kalia, EVP

Provider of design web engineering services. The
company focuses on business process management and enterprise application integration
services.

**Etrigue Corp** HQ
6399 San Ignacio Ave Second Fl
San Jose CA 95119
P: 408-490-2900   F: 408-490-2901   PRC:326
www.etrigue.com
Estab: 2005

Ewing Parton, Software Engineer
Jim Meyer, VP
Tony Tissot, Senior Director of Marketing
David Drach, IT SaaS Operations Manager

Provider of marketing automation solutions such
as email marketing, event management, derived
data, 3-D leading scoring, and marketing database management.

**Etron Technology America Inc** RH
3375 Scott Blvd Ste 128
Santa Clara CA 95054
P: 408-987-2255   F: 408-987-2250   PRC:212
www.etron.com
Estab: 1991

Nicky Lu, CEO

Provider of integrated circuits for applications,
such as storage device, display, handset, PDA,
and multimedia device.

**Ets Laboratories** HQ
899 Adams St Ste A
St. Helena CA 94574
P: 707-963-4806   F: 707-963-1054   PRC:305
www.etslabs.com
Email: info@etslabs.com
Estab: 1978

Gordon Burns, Co-Founder
Jim Welsh, Director of Information Technology
John Masyczek, Logistics Manager
Eric Herve, Research Scientist
Sedonia Yoshida, Microbiology Group Member

Specializes in analytical tools. The company
focuses on export analysis, harvest, and fuel
ethanol services.

**Ettus Research LLC** DH
4600 Patrick Henry Dr
Santa Clara CA 95054
P: 408-610-6399   PRC:63
www.ettus.com
Estab: 2004

Ashish Chaudhari, Senior R&D Software Engineer
Michael West, Senior Software Design Engineer
Nick Foster, Senior Electrical Engineer

Provider of software defined radio systems for
research, academic, industrial, and defense
applications.

**Eureka Chemical Co** HQ
234 Lawrence Ave
S San Francisco CA 94080
P: 650-761-3536   F: 650-589-1943   PRC:52
www.fluid-film.com
Email: info@fluid-film.com
Estab: 1953

Gen Hess, President

Provider of corrosion control services. The company is involved in creating products that offers
corrosion protection and lubrication for all metals.

**Evergreen (cp) USA Inc** HQ
338 N Canal St Ste 8
S San Francisco CA 94080
P: 650-952-8091   F: 650-952-3629   PRC:288
www.evergreencpusa.com
Email: sales@evergreencpusa.com
Estab: 1986

Stacy Li, Account Executive

Manufacturer of batteries. The company offers
lithium coin cells, nickel cadmium batteries, man-
ganese button cells, and silver oxide button cells.

**Evernote Corp** HQ
305 Walnut St
Redwood City CA 94063
P: 650-257-0885   F: 650-386-1571   PRC:319
www.evernote.com

Phil Libin, CEO
Dave Engberg, CTO
Andrew Sinkov, VP of Marketing
Philip Constantinou, VP of Products
Alex Pachikov, VP of Partnerships

Provider of note management and digital link
services. The company also offers handwriting
recognition services.

**EverString Ltd** HQ
1850 Gateway Dr Ste 400
San Mateo CA 94404
P: 650-425-3937   PRC:319
www.everstring.com
Email: contact@everstring.com
Estab: 2012

J.J. Kardwell, Co-Founder
Vincent Yang, Co-Founder
Jeff Stephens, CFO
Amit Rai, COO
Rakesh Gowda, CTO

Provider of AI SaaS solution for B2B sales and
marketing professionals.

**Evidation Health Inc** HQ
167 Second Ave
San Mateo CA 94401
P: 650-727-5557   PRC:191
www.evidation.com
Email: contact@evidation.com
Estab: 2012

Christine Lemke, Co-Founder
Luca Foschini, CDS
Mikki Nasch, Co-Founder
Deborah Kilpatrick, CEO

Provider of digital health solutions for healthcare
providers, payers, pharma/biotech, and digital
health companies.

**Evolphin Software Inc** HQ
2410 Camino Ramon Ste 228
San Ramon CA 94583
P: 888-386-4114   PRC:322
www.evolphin.com
Email: info@evolphin.com
Estab: 2007

Brian Ahearn, CEO
Rahul Bhargava, CTO
Silvia C., Director of Marketing

Provider of digital and media asset management
software for video production, game developers,
media, television broadcasters, and eLearning
groups.

**Evolve Biosystems** HQ
2121 Second St Ste C108
Davis CA 95618
P: 530-747-2012   PRC:42
www.evolvebiosystems.com
Email: info@evolvebiosystems.com
Emp: 1-10   Estab: 2012

Timothy Brown, CEO
David Kyle, Chairman
Sandy Argabrite, CFO
Michael Russell, Director of Product Development
& Quality
Christie Fleming, SVP of Sales & Marketing

Focuses on the development and marketing of
probiotic-based biotherapeutics. The company
serves the pharmaceutical industry.

**Evolve Manufacturing Technologies
Inc** HQ
47300 Bayside Pkwy
Fremont CA 94538
P: 510-690-8959   PRC:159
www.evolvemfg.com
Email: services@evolvemfg.com
Estab: 1999

Sarvar Samia, Human Resource Manager
Trang Tran, Production Manager
James Han, Customer Relations Manager

Designer and manufacturer of electro-mechanical,
optical, and prototyping products. The company offers testing, logistics, and documentation
services.

**Evolveware Inc** HQ
3375 Scott Blvd Bldg 224
Santa Clara CA 95054
P: 408-748-8301  F: 408-746-2850     PRC:322
www.evolveware.com
Email: infous@evolveware.com
Estab: 2001

Miten Marfatia, CEO

Developer of products to automate and modernize IT infrastructure focusing on assessment, documentation, impact analysis, and other solutions.

**Exabeam Inc** HQ
1 Waters Park Dr Ste 200
San Mateo CA 94403
P: 844-392-2326     PRC:326
www.exabeam.com
Email: info@exabeam.com
Estab: 2013

Domingo Mihovilovic, CTO
Nir Polak, CEO
Sylvain Gil, VP of Products
Ralph Pisani, EVP of Field Operations

Provider of software to discover attackers impersonating users and to protect against cyber attacks.

**Exacta Tech Inc** HQ
378 Wright Brothers Ave
Livermore CA 94551
P: 925-443-8963  F: 925-443-6296     PRC:21
www.exacta-tech.com
Email: exacta@exacta-tech.com
Estab: 1961

Carlos Manrique, President
Stacey Lopez, COO
Elena Chirimele, Administrative Assistant

Manufacturer of custom machine components and parts and provider of design, inspection and engineering services for industries.

**Exadel Inc** HQ
1340 Treat Blvd Ste 375
Walnut Creek CA 94597
P: 925-363-9510     PRC:319
exadel.com
Estab: 1998

Fima Katz, Founder
Lev Shur, President of Exadel Solutions
Igor Landes, CTO
Lynne Walter, CFO
Gregory Katzman, VP of Operations

Custom software agency that produces software and mobile solutions.

**Exadel Inc** HQ
1340 Treat Blvd Ste 375
Walnut Creek CA 94597
P: 925-363-9510     PRC:322
exadel.com
Email: info@exadel.com
Estab: 1998

Lev Shur, President Exadel Solutions
Igor Landes, CTO
Lynne Walter, CFO
Gregory Katzman, VP of Global Operations
Donna Burke, VP of Technology Solutions

Provider of software using technologies including mobile, cloud, and web user interfaces. The company also delivers tools and products for users.

**Exagen Inc** HQ
1261 Liberty Way Ste C
Vista CA 92081
P: 888-452-1522     PRC:41
www.exagen.com
Email: info@exagen.com
Emp: 11-50 Estab: 2002

Ron Rocca, President
Kamal Adawi, CFO
Dale Olson, VP
Brian Littlefield, SVP of Information Services
Mark Hazeltine, SVP of Finance & Corporate Development

Developer of laboratory technology solutions. The company offers services to hospitals, clinics, and the healthcare sector.

**Exatron Inc** HQ
2842 Aiello Dr
San Jose CA 95111-2154
P: 408-629-7600  F: 408-629-2832     PRC:171
www.exatron.com
Email: info@exatron.com
Estab: 1974

Adam Nomura, System Engineer
Robert Howell, President
Bob Garcia, Sales Manager
Robert garcia, Sales Manager
Kenny Nguyen, Manager

Manufacturer of automatic test equipment and IC handlers. The company also specializes in open short testers.

**Excel Precision Corp** HQ
3255 Scott Blvd Ste 1-101
Santa Clara CA 95054
P: 408-727-4260  F: 408-727-1026     PRC:87
www.excelprecision.com
Email: info@excelprecisionusa.com
Estab: 1986

Andrew Shu, Electrical Engineer

Designer and manufacturer of laser interferometer systems for measurement and calibration. The company's products include level sensors and angular sensors.

**Excelchem Laboratories Inc** HQ
1135 W Sunset Blvd Ste A
Rocklin CA 95765
P: 916-543-4445  F: 916-543-4449     PRC:142
www.ssalabs.com
Emp: 1-10  Estab: 1991

Brian Garcia, Lab Technician
Ajay Virk, Laboratory Technician

Provider of analytical consultation, on-site analysis, custom reporting, and mobile laboratory services.

**Excelfore Corp** HQ
3155 Kearney St
Fremont CA 94538
P: 510-868-2500     PRC:323
excelfore.com
Email: sales@excelfore.com
Estab: 2008

C. Anand, VP of Hardware Engineering
Pawel Veselov, Development Engineer
Danielle McCown, Technical Support Engineer
Shrinath Acharya, CEO
Beatrice Thella, Finance

Provider of cloud applications. The company offers infotainment and telematics products for insurance, financing, and logistics sectors.

**Excelitas Technologies Corp** HQ
44370 Christy St
Fremont CA 94538
P: 510-979-6500     PRC:124
www.excelitas.com
Estab: 1947

David Nislick, CEO
Jim Rao, EVP
Joel Falcone, EVP
Paul Igoe, EVP
Marc Reuss, EVP

Provider of opto-electronics solutions. The company serves the medical, industrial, aerospace, and defense markets.

**Exclara Inc** HQ
4701 Patrick Henry Dr Bldg 17
Santa Clara CA 95054
P: 408-492-1009  F: 408-492-1009     PRC:212
www.exclara.com
Email: sales@exclara.com
Estab: 2004

Joseph Cassio, SMPS Applications Engineer
Anwar Aslam, Senior Applications Engineer
Anatoly Shteynberg, CTO

Designer and manufacturer of high-voltage LED drivers which provide integrated-circuit and module-based solutions.

**Exelixis Inc** HQ
1851 Harbor Bay Pkwy
Alameda CA 94502
P: 650-837-7000  F: 650-837-8300     PRC:34
www.exelixis.com
Email: druginfo@exelixis.com
Estab: 1994
Sales: $300M to $1 Billion

Stelios Papadopoulos, Co-Founder
Michael Morrissey, President
Gisela Schwab, EVP
Peter Lamb, EVP of Discovery Research
Christopher Senner, EVP

Focuses on the development and commercialization of small molecule therapies. The company is also engaged in clinical trials.

**Exit445 Group** HQ
817 Marin Dr
Mill Valley CA 94941
P: 415-381-1852     PRC:325
www.exit445.com

Jonathan Schwartz, Owner

Provider of information architecture, e-Commerce, email marketing, search engine optimization, website hosting, and other services.

**Expandable Software Inc** HQ
900 Lafayette St Ste 400
Santa Clara CA 95050
P: 408-261-7880  F: 408-247-2160     PRC:323
www.expandable.com
Email: sales@expandable.com
Estab: 1983

John Buller, Principal Solutions Engineer
Jerry Lass, VP of R&D
David Kearney, CFO
Bob Swedroe, President
Patti Hales, VP of Finance

Developer of enterprise software for manufacturers. The company is engaged in medical technology and general manufacturing solutions.

**Expedite Precision Works Inc** HQ
931 Berryessa Rd
San Jose CA 95133
P: 408-573-9600  F: 408-573-9700  PRC:80
www.expediteprecision.com
Email: epwi@expediteprecision.com
Estab: 1995

Orlando Teixeira, Owner
Huy Nguyen, Quality Assurance Manager
Chiho Choi, Scientist

Manufacturer of diverse products involving micro & custom machining and fabrication of metal & plastic. The company also manufactures vessels and tanks.

**Experexchange Inc** HQ
46751 Fremont Blvd
Fremont CA 94538
P: 510-623-7071  F: 510-623-9290  PRC:326
www.experexchange.com
Email: it_consulting_team@experexchange.com
Estab: 1989

Bo Yan, VP

Provider of software and professional IT solutions such as web based applications, software life cycle service, embedded systems, and software testing.

**Expertech** HQ
10 Victor Sq Ste 100
Scotts Valley CA 95066
P: 831-439-9300  F: 831-439-8139  PRC:124
www.exper-tech.com
Email: service@exper-tech.com
Emp: 1-10  Estab: 1992

Jonathan George, Owner
Mark Cooper, President

Provider of custom, new and re-manufactured thermal processing solutions. The company offers diffusion furnaces for semiconductor and solar devices.

**Exploramed** HQ
2570 W El Camino Real Ste 310
Mountain View CA 94040
P: 650-472-0300  F: 650-472-0330  PRC:187
www.exploramed.com
Email: info@exploramed.com
Estab: 1995

Joshua Makower, Founder
Karen Nguyen, Director of Finance & HR
Jonathan Podmore, Project Architect

Developer of novel medical devices with cutting edge medical technology for use by major medical device manufacturing companies.

**Exponent Partners** HQ
720 Market St Ste 600
San Francisco CA 94102
P: 800-918-2917  PRC:323
www.exponentpartners.com
Email: info@exponentpartners.com
Estab: 2004

Anita Maldonado, CEO
Mary Antush, Assistant Director
Michelle Reiss-Top, Technology and Data Systems Manager
Peter Bender, Senior Consultant

Provider of performance and outcomes management solutions. The company's services include systems integration and custom application development.

**Extend Inc** HQ
4847 Hopyard Rd  Ste 4
Pleasanton CA 94588
P: 925-484-0395  F: 925-397-6722  PRC:323
www.extendinc.com
Email: info@extendinc.com
Estab: 1993

Joe Ciolek, Owner

Developer of business software. The company also provides internet and marketing consulting services.

**ExThera Medical Corp** HQ
757 Arnold Dr Ste B
Martinez CA 94553
P: 925-839-2060  F: 925-839-2075  PRC:187
www.extheramedical.com
Email: info@extheramedical.com
Estab: 2007

Keith Mccrea, VP of Research & Development
Vidur Sahney, COO
Polly Ascano, Production Manager

Developer of medical devices that address unmet clinical needs in the treatment of bloodstream infections and pathogen-reduction in blood banking.

**Extractable Inc** HQ
612 Howard St fourth fl
San Francisco CA 94105
P: 415-426-3600  PRC:322
www.extractable.com
Email: sales@extractable.com
Estab: 1999

Craig McLaughlin, CEO
Mark Ryan, Chief Analytics Officer
Alex Jimenez, CSO
Joel Oxman, VP of Business Development
Anthony Stack, Director of Project Management

Provider of websites, applications, social and mobile experiences for transactional, educational, lead generation, and entertainment purposes.

**Exxact Corp** HQ
46221 Landing Pkwy
Fremont CA 94538
P: 510-226-7366  F: 510-226-7367  PRC:91
www.exxactcorp.com
Email: sales@exxactcorp.com
Estab: 1992

Andrew Nelson, Director of Engineering
Kevin Wong, Senior Systems Engineer
Tito Nisperos, Systems Engineer
Julie Hsieh, Digital Marketing & Web Design
Jason Chen, VP

Supplier of workstation graphic cards and solutions. The company also offers servers, HPC clusters, and computing software.

**EXXIM Computing Corp** HQ
5165 Johnson Dr Ste 100
Pleasanton CA 94588
P: 925-416-1900  F: 925-369-0385  PRC:318
www.exxim-cc.com
Email: info@exxim-cc.com
Estab: 2002

Horst Bruning, President
Irene Bruning, VP
Sergei Gouzeev, VP
Larry Israel, General Counsel

Manufacturer of cutting-edge radiological imaging technology and equipment designed for dental, medical, and scientific and industrial industries.

**Eyefinity Inc** HQ
10875 International Dr Ste 200
Rancho Cordova CA 95670
P: 877-448-0707  F: 877-790-8162  PRC:323
www.eyefinity.com
Email: customercare@eyefinity.com
Emp: 1-10  Estab: 2000

Troy Eberlein, SVP of Product Management
Lara Cone, Account Manager of Strategic Services

Provider of software solutions for the eyecare industry. The company focuses on practice & revenue cycle management and electronic health records.

**Ezb Solutions** HQ
1400 Coleman Ave Ste E27
Santa Clara CA 95050
P: 408-988-8760  PRC:325
www.ezbsolutions.com
Email: info@ezbsolutions.com
Estab: 2003

Ruben Fernandes, Managing Partner

Provider of software, hardware, and installation services. The company also deals with training, consulting, and technical support.

**eze System** HQ
785 Orchard Dr Ste 100
Folsom CA 95630
P: 716-393-9330  PRC:87
ezesys.com
Email: contact@ezesys.com
Emp: 11-50  Estab: 2009

John Parman, Technical Support Specialist

Provider or monitoring and measuring solutions. The company's products include controllers, controller expansions, and sensors.

**F5 Networks Inc** BR
3545 N First St
San Jose CA 95134
P: 408-273-4800  F: 408-273-4925  PRC:319
www.f5.com
Email: info@f5.com
Estab: 1996

Francois Locoh-Donou, President
Frank Pelzer, EVP
Geng Lin, EVP
Tom Fountain, CSO
Ana White, EVP

Provider of strategic points of control throughout the IT infrastructure for organizations to scale, adapt, and align with changing business demands.

**Fab 7 Designs**                    HQ
2748 Ross Rd
Palo Alto CA 94303
P: 650-462-9745                      PRC:325
www.fab7.com
Email: business@fab7.com
Estab: 1993

Peter Lonsky, Owner

Provider of graphic designing services. The company offers website, multimedia, editorial, and package designing services.

**FAB-9 Corp**                       BR
5400 Hellyer Ave
San Jose CA 95138
P: 408-791-6462   F: 408-791-6757    PRC:211
www.fab-9.com
Estab: 2003

Quin Vo, Sales Manager

Provider of printed circuit board fabrication, design, assembly, and manufacturing services. The company serves the business sector.

**Facebook Inc**                     HQ
1 Hacker Way
Menlo Park CA 94025
P: 650-543-4800                      PRC:322
www.facebook.com
Email: facebookinc@usa.com
Estab: 2004
Sales: Over $3B

Eduardo Saverin, Co-Founder
Mark Zuckerburg, Founder
Dustin Moskovitz, Co-Founder
Chris Hughes, Co-Founder

Designer and developer of technologies to communicate with their family, friends, and also coworkers.

**Fafco Inc**                        HQ
435 Otterson Dr
Chico CA 95928-8207
P: 530-332-2100   F: 530-332-2109    PRC:135
www.fafco.com
Email: sales@fafco.com
Emp: 1-10   Estab: 1969

Alex Ward, Director of Engineering and Operations
Bob Leckinger, President
Freeman Ford, Chairman

Manufacturer of polymer heat exchangers. The company also specializes in thermal energy storage systems.

**Fair Isaac Corp**                  HQ
181 Metro Dr
San Jose CA 95110
P: 408-817-9100   F: 408-535-1776    PRC:319
www.fico.com
Email: info@fico.com
Emp: 177   Estab: 1956
Sales: $1B to $3B

Michael Leonard, VP
Stuart Wells, EVP
Wayne Huyard, EVP of Sales Marketing & Services
James Wehmann, EVP of Scores
Michael Pung, EVP

Provider of analytical, software installation, and integration services. The company serves business enterprises.

**Fair Isaac Corp**                  BR
200 Smith Ranch Rd
San Rafael CA 94903
P: 415-472-2211                      PRC:319
www.fico.com
Estab: 1956

William Lansing, President
Scott Zoldi, Chief Analytics Officer
Richard Deal, EVP
Michael Pung, EVP
Chirag Mandaviya, Lead Analytic Scientist

Provider of credit scoring, decision management, fraud detection, and credit risk score services offering global business consulting.

**Fairbanks Scales**                 BR
8240 Belvedere Ave Ste D
Sacramento CA 95826
P: 916-384-1394                      PRC:233
www.fairbanks.com
Emp: 11-50 Estab: 1830

Richard Norden, President
Nick Cillino, Manager
Kevin Oliver, Manager

Provider of scales and weighing systems. The company serves the agriculture, parcel shipping, transport, and waste management industries.

**Fairchild Imaging Inc**            DH
1841 Zanker Rd Ste 50
San Jose CA 95112
P: 650-479-5749   F: 408-433-2604    PRC:87
www.fairchildimaging.com
Email: cams.sales@baesystems.com
Estab: 2001

Carol Zhao, Senior Engineer
Bliss Ron, Financial Analyst

Developer and manufacturer of solid-state electronic imaging components, cameras, and systems. The company's products include image sensors and cameras.

**Fall Creek Engineering Inc**       HQ
1525 Seabright Ave
Santa Cruz CA 95062
P: 831-426-9054                      PRC:304
www.fallcreekengineering.com
Email: info@fallcreekengineering.com
Emp: 1-10   Estab: 1994

Peter Haase, Principal Engineer
Robyn Cooper, Senior Engineer
Carina Chen, Senior Associate Engineer
Samantha Sharp, Senior Associate Engineer
Vicki Miller, Office Manager

Provider of civil, environmental, and water resources engineering and consulting services. The company engages in site planning and design services.

**Famsoft**                          HQ
1762 Technology Dr Ste 108
San Jose CA 95110
P: 408-452-1550                      PRC:326
www.famsoft.com
Estab: 1997

Fahad Rahman, Sales & Marketing Assistant
Mohammed Ilyas, Office Manager
Gaurav Bahal, Analyst

Provider of ERP consulting and infrastructure management services such as managed support, IBM products, enterprise solution, and migration services.

**Farallon Geographics Inc**         HQ
601 Montgomery St Ste 1095
San Francisco CA 94111
P: 415-227-1140   F: 415-227-1148    PRC:325
fargeo.com
Email: info@fargeo.com
Estab: 1997

Dennis Wuthrich, CEO
Alexei Peters, Director of Web Development
Adam Lodge, Operations Manager

Provider of strategic planning, spatial data processing, training, and web application development services.

**Farasis Energy Inc**              HQ
21363 Cabot Blvd
Hayward CA 94545
P: 510-732-6600   F: 510-887-1211    PRC:288
www.farasis.com
Email: sales@farasis.com
Estab: 2002

Anita Pai, Software Engineer
Tanner DeVoe, Mechanical Engineering Manager
Gurjit Sohota, Engineer
Andrew Larson, Design Engineer
Kelly Flaherty, Test

Designer and developer of energy storage solutions. The company serves the transportation, consumer electronics, and power distribution markets.

**Farlow's Scientific Glassblowing Inc**  HQ
962 Golden Gate Ter Ste B
Grass Valley CA 95945
P: 530-477-5513   F: 530-477-9241    PRC:189
www.farlowsci.com
Email: carol@farlowsci.com
Emp: 1-10   Estab: 1981

Charlotte Farlow, CEO

Provider of precision drilling, boring, cutting, grinding, salvage and repair, custom tooling, metal-to-glass bonding, and related services.

**Farpointe Data Inc**               HQ
2195 Zanker Rd
San Jose CA 95131
P: 408-731-8700   F: 408-731-8705    PRC:63
www.farpointedata.com
Email: support@farpointedata.com
Estab: 2003

Kirk Bierach, Director of Engineering
Scott Lindley, President
Stephen Sheppard, Key Accounts Sales Manager
Tom Piston, Sales Manager
Francisco Alcala, Regional Sales Manager

Provider of RFID electronic access control technologies for electronic access control professionals around the world.

**Fast Trak Fabrication LP**  HQ
3011 W Dakota Ave
Fresno CA 93722
P: 559-222-4450  F: 559-222-4453  PRC:80
www.fasttrakfab.com
Email: info@fasttrakfab.com
Emp: 1-10  Estab: 2008

Ferol Garcia, Partner

Provider of metal fabrication services. The company's services include laser cutting, machining, forming, and welding.

**Fastening Systems International Inc**  HQ
1206 E Mac Arthur St
Sonoma CA 95476
P: 707-935-1170  F: 707-935-1828  PRC:157
www.fsirivet.com
Email: sales@fsirivet.com
Estab: 1983

Roger Nikkel, President
Kathryn Nikkel, CFO
Mark Herand, VP
Nolund Kowalski, Operations Manager

Supplier of blind fasteners and blind rivet installation tools. The company offers rivet guns, rivet nuts, pop rivets, and more.

**FCS Software Solutions**  HQ
2375 Zanker Rd Ste 250
San Jose CA 95131
P: 408-324-1203  PRC:326
www.fcsltd.com
Email: info@fcsltd.com
Estab: 1993

Anil Sharma, CFO

Provider of consulting, product development, e-learning, digital content, and product support services.

**Feeney Inc**  HQ
2603 Union St
Oakland CA 94607-2423
P: 510-893-9473  F: 510-893-9484  PRC:157
www.feeneyinc.com
Email: sales@feeneyinc.com
Estab: 1948

Katrina Ralston, President
Steve Imbrenda, CFO
Andrew Penny, VP of Marketing
George Shevchuk, Operations Specialist

Provider of architectural and garden products. The company specializes in products such as rail kits, lighting, and accessories.

**Femtochrome Research Inc**  HQ
2123 Fourth St
Berkeley CA 94710
P: 510-644-1869  F: 510-644-0118  PRC:172
www.femtochrome.com
Email: sales@femtochrome.com

Zafer Yasa, Research Director

Manufacturer of instruments for characterization of ultrafast laser pulses focusing on nonlinear crystal and two-photon conductivity autocorrelators.

**Fenix International**  HQ
30 Cleveland St
San Francisco CA 94103
P: 415-754-9222  PRC:135
www.fenixintl.com
Email: press@fenixintl.com
Estab: 2009

Emma Frederick, Mechanical Engineer
Allegra Fisher, Director of Strategic Projects

Provider of affordable power generation, smart-storage, and distribution solutions for the 1.6 billion people living off the electricity grid.

**Ferreira Service Inc**  HQ
2600 Old Crow Canyon Rd Ste 100
San Ramon CA 94583
P: 800-522-6064  F: 800-784-6727  PRC:151
www.ferreira.com

Susan Ferreira, CEO

Provider of energy engineering services. The company offers heating, ventilation, and air conditioning maintenance and repair services.

**Ferrotec Usa Corp**  RH
3945 Freedom Cir Ste 450
Santa Clara CA 95054
P: 408-964-7700  F: 408-961-5119  PRC:80
www.ferrotec.com
Email: info@ferrotec.com
Estab: 1968

Bob Otey, Chief of Technology of Thermal Solutions
Debbie McReynolds, Senior Director of Corporate Quality
Maria Ho, International Sales Administrator
Susan Hwang, Customer Service Coordinator

Manufacturer and distributor of quartz solutions and fluid sealants. The company serves business organizations and enterprises.

**FET Test Inc**  HQ
6292 San Ignacio Ave Ste G
San Jose CA 95119
P: 408-778-0234  F: 408-778-0822  PRC:212
www.fettest.com
Email: info@fettest.com
Estab: 1976

Helge Krystad, CTO
Wayne Pearson, Operations Manager

Manufacturer of automated test equipment. The company also offers modular analog/mixed-signal testers and test system controller software.

**Fiber Optic Cable Shop**  HQ
136 S Second St
Richmond CA 94804
P: 510-234-9090  PRC:62
www.fiberopticcableshop.com
Estab: 1976

Mark Wieber, Sales Manager

Provider of fiber optic cable products. The company's products include fiber optic media invertors, adapters, aerial cables, and fiber optic switches.

**Fibera Inc**  HQ
3255 Scott Blvd 1-101
Santa Clara CA 95054
P: 408-492-9555  F: 408-492-9559  PRC:170
fiberausa.com
Email: info@fiberausa.com
Estab: 2001

John Tsai, CEO

Manufacturer and designer of wavelength management products. The company also specializes in fiber optic products.

**Fibrogen Inc**  HQ
409 Illinois St
San Francisco CA 94158
P: 415-978-1200  F: 415-978-1902  PRC:34
www.fibrogen.com
Email: info@fibrogen.com
Estab: 1993

Pat Cotroneo, CFO
Carl Drinkwater, Executive Director of Information Technology
Roland Lee, QC Specialist
R. Frost, VP of Regulatory Affairs
Mike Martinelli, VP of Technical Development

Developer of therapeutic products. The company is engaged in commercialization and clinical trial programs.

**Fictiv Inc**  HQ
1221 Mission St
San Francisco CA 94103
P: 415-580-2509  PRC:280
www.fictiv.com
Email: info@fictiv.com

Andrew Hudak, Manufacturing Engineer
Sunny Sahota, Prototyping Engineer
Dave Evans, Co-Founder
Andy Sherman, Director of Production
Christine Evans, Marketing Associate

Provider of tooling services for hardware engineers. The company specializes in distributed manufacturing of idle 3D printers from single platform.

**Fiduciary Management Technologies Inc**  HQ
1 Capitol Mall Ste 200
Sacramento CA 95814
P: 916-930-9900  F: 916-930-9902  PRC:322
www.efmt.com
Emp: 1-10  Estab: 1990

Scott Sackett, President
Marilyn Bessey, Founder

Provider of insolvency case, fiduciary case, and estate management solutions. The company offers SEC distribution fund administration services.

**Fidus Systems Inc**  BR
927 Corporate Way
Fremont CA 94539-6118
P: 408-217-1928  PRC:326
fidus.com

Michael Wakim, CEO

Specializes in electronic product development and consulting services. The company also deals with hardware design.

**Fil-Tech West Inc**   BR
   5673 W Las Positas Blvd
   Pleasanton CA 94588
P: 925-251-8200   F: 925-251-8205    PRC:159
www.filtech.com
Email: paula@filtech.com
Estab: 1969

Douglas Becker, President

Distributor of semiconductor parts and vacuum components. The company is engaged in troubleshooting and maintenance services.

**Filemaker Inc**   DH
   5201 Patrick Henry Dr
   Santa Clara CA 95054
P: 408-987-7000   F: 408-987-7447    PRC:323
www.filemaker.com
Email: filemaker_pr@filemaker.com
Estab: 1998

Simon Thornhill, VP of Engineering
Brad Freitag, CEO
Sam Fong, Channel Sales Representative
Jon Sigler, VP of Product Management
Rick Kalman, Director of Product Management

Provider of database software which assists organizations in the management, analysis, and sharing of information.

**Fileopen Systems Inc**   HQ
   1010 Fair Ave Ste A
   Santa Cruz CA 95060
P: 831-706-2170    PRC:323
www.fileopen.com
Email: info@fileopen.com
Emp: 1-10   Estab: 1997

Michel Coste, Chief Engineer
Austin Neff, Senior Software Engineer
Nicholas Kalscheuer, Software Engineer
Diana Holm, Co-Founder
Sanford Bingham, President

Provider of digital rights management and document security solutions for corporations and governments.

**Filetrail Inc**   HQ
   111 N Market St
   San Jose CA 95113
P: 408-289-1300   F: 408-293-5357    PRC:326
www.filetrail.com
Email: sales@filetrail.com
Estab: 2001

Sean Snow, Senior Engineer

Provider of digital and physical management software and it serves the energy, pharmaceutical, and other industries.

**Filtration Group LLC**   BR
   498 Aviation Blvd
   Santa Rosa CA 95403
P: 707-525-8633    PRC:156
www.filtrationgroup.com
Estab: 1942

Tom Gebhardt, President
Matt Huser, CMO
Estela Prado, Manager

Provider of filtration solutions. The company supplies filtration products for the HVAC, turbine, cleanroom, and filter media markets.

**Filtration Solutions Inc**   HQ
   6372 Lower Wyandotte Rd
   Oroville CA 95966
P: 530-534-1000    PRC:143
www.filtrationsolutions.us
Emp: 1-10

Klaus Franz, Owner

Provider of water treatment systems. The company focuses on engineering, manufacturing, installation, and more.

**Financial Oxygen Inc**   HQ
   4620 Fortran Dr Ste 101
   San Jose CA 95134
P: 925-465-1225   F: 408-945-9533    PRC:319
www.financialoxygen.com
Email: info@financialoxygen.com
Estab: 1999

Pssmurthy Kruthiventi, Java Technical Lead
Satya Pati, Senior Systems Analyst

Provider of cash management and fixed income products and it serves individual banks and broker-dealers.

**FinancialContent Services Inc**   HQ
   195 Glenn Way Ste 250
   San Carlos CA 94070
P: 888-688-9880    PRC:325
www.financialcontent.com
Estab: 2000

Mark Dierolf, Founder

Provider of stock market information. The company deals with advertising, newspaper, and consulting services.

**Financialforce Com**   HQ
   595 Market St Ste 2700
   San Francisco CA 94105
P: 866-743-2220    PRC:325
www.financialforce.com
Email: info@financialforce.com
Estab: 2009

Jeremy Roche, President
Andrew Fawcett, CTO
Jim Carney, VP of Finance
Beach Dickey, Inside Sales Representative
Tom Brennan, VP of Marketing

Developer of automation software solutions. The company also deals with cloud accounting and resource planning solutions.

**Fine-Line Circuits Ltd**   BR
   11501 Dublin Blvd Ste 328
   Dublin CA 94568
P: 877-876-3660    PRC:211
www.finelineindia.com
Email: finelineus@aol.com

Abhay Doshi, Managing Director

Manufacturer of printed circuit boards. The company specializes in models such as single sided, double sided, and standard multilayer.

**Finelite Inc**   HQ
   30500 Whipple Rd
   Union City CA 94587-1530
P: 510-441-1100   F: 510-441-1510    PRC:243
www.finelite.com
Estab: 1991

Jimmy Deng, Electrical Engineering Manager
Terry Clark, Founder
Jerry Mix, CEO
Thai Quach, Information Technology Operations Manager
Marc Domingo, Production Supervisor

Manufacturer of lighting products. The company's services include design, installation, repairs and replacement, and maintenance.

**Finesse Solutions LLC**   HQ
   3501 Leonard Ct
   Santa Clara CA 95054
P: 408-570-9000   F: 888-235-6086    PRC:31
www.finesse.com
Email: sales@finesse.com
Estab: 2005

Jack Giese, Director of Quality

Manufacturer of bioreactor controllers and related supplies. The company offers technical support services.

**Fingerprint Digital Inc**   HQ
   240 Stockton St 6th Fl
   San Francisco CA 94108
P: 855-543-4263    PRC:317
www.fingerprintplay.com
Estab: 2010

Nancy MacIntyre, CEO

Designer and developer of mobile kids network solutions. The company offers services to kids of all ages.

**Finisar Corp**   HQ
   1389 Moffett Park Dr
   Sunnyvale CA 94089
P: 408-548-1000   F: 408-541-6138    PRC:60
www.finisar.com
Estab: 1988

Maziar Amirkiai, Engineering Manager
Tao Li, Senior Design Engineer
Brandon Wong, Hardware Design Engineer
Bob Bashaw, President
Giovanni Barbarossa, CSO

Developer of optical communications components and subsystems such as optical modules, active cables and components, passives and optical amplifiers.

**Finishline Advanced Composites**   HQ
   3820 Industrial Way Ste H
   Benicia CA 94510
P: 707-747-0788   F: 707-747-0780    PRC:157
www.finishlinecomposites.com
Email: info@finishlinecomposites.com

James Porreco, President

Provider of composite repair services for production projects. The company is involved in design, development, prototyping, testing, and production.

**Finjan Holdings Inc** HQ
2000 University Ave Ste 600
East Palo Alto CA 94303
P: 650-282-3228 PRC:304
www.finjan.com
Email: info@finjan.com
Estab: 1997
Sales: $30M to $100M

Phil Hartstein, President
Michael Noonan, CFO
Jevan Anderson, CFO
Julie Mar-Spinola, Chief Intellectual Property
Officer
Rebecca Galdos, Office & Human Resources
Manager

Specializes in the research and development of
transformative technologies for the securing of
information.

**Fire2wire** HQ
5462 Pirrone Rd
Salida CA 95368
P: 209-543-1800 F: 209-545-1469 PRC:67
www.fire2wire.com
Email: info@fire2wire.com
Emp: 1-10 Estab: 2000

Kristian Hoffmann, President
Duane Severson, CEO
William Moreno, VP of Sales
Marlene Sosa, Sales Manager
Chuck Profito, Outside Sales Representative

Provider of network consulting, server colocation,
website hosting and design, wireless internet, and
content management services.

**FireEye Inc** HQ
601 McCarthy Blvd
Milpitas CA 95035
P: 408-321-6300 F: 408-321-9818 PRC:323
www.fireeye.com
Email: info@fireeye.com
Estab: 2004
Sales: $300M to $1 Billion

Jason Martin, EVP of Research and Engineering
Travis Reese, President
Kevin Mandia, CEO
Frank Verdecanna, EVP
John Watters, EVP of Chief Corporate Strategy
Officer

Focuses on cyber security solutions. The company
serves the utilities and pharmaceutical industries.

**First Class Plus LLC** HQ
214 Ryan Way
S San Francisco CA 94080-1140
P: 650-589-8346 F: 415-824-6790 PRC:324
www.firstclassplus.com
Estab: 1986

Fernando Balazs, Founder

Provider of fundraising and marketing solutions.
The company deals with print production, design
assistance, and pre-press services.

**First Databank Inc** HQ
701 Gateway Blvd Ste 600
S San Francisco CA 94080
P: 650-588-5454 PRC:40
www.fdbhealth.com
Email: cs@fdbhealth.com
Estab: 1977

Bob Katter, EVP
Tracy Lofland, VP of Quality Management
Cynthia MacAskill, VP of Finance
Steve Fisher, Director of Sales
David Manin, Senior Director of Marketing

Provider of healthcare solutions to hospitals, retail
pharmacies, payers, drug manufacturers, and
healthcare providers.

**Fisher Manufacturing** HQ
1900 S O St
Tulare CA 93274
P: 800-421-6162 F: 800-832-8238 PRC:159
www.fisher-mfg.com
Emp: 11-50 Estab: 1936

Ray Fisher, President

Manufacturer of advanced plumbing systems.
The company's products include faucets, valves,
sprays, and fillers.

**Fit Bearings** HQ
47881 Fremont Blvd
Fremont CA 94538-6506
P: 510-623-1688 F: 510-226-6104 PRC:158
www.fitbearings.com
Estab: 1988

Will Horng, VP

Designer and manufacturer of bearings. The company's products include seals, drive components,
and agricultural & industrial wheel hubs.

**Five Prime Therapeutics Inc** HQ
111 Oyster Point Blvd
S San Francisco CA 94080
P: 415-365-5600 F: 415-365-5601 PRC:34
www.fiveprime.com
Email: pr@fiveprime.com
Estab: 2001
Sales: $30M to $100M

William Ringo, CEO
David Smith, EVP
Francis Sarena, CSO
Amy Collins, VP of Legal Affairs
Nallakkan Arvindan, SVP of Strategic Technology
Operations

Developer and discovery of therapeutics products
for the enhancement of lives of patients with
serious diseases.

**Five9 Inc** HQ
4000 Executive Pkwy Ste 400
San Ramon CA 94583
P: 925-201-2000 F: 925-480-6202 PRC:322
www.five9.com
Email: info@five9.com
Estab: 2001
Sales: $100M to $300M

David Pickering, EVP of Engineering
Bob Hillery, Provisioning Engineer
Dan Burkland, President
Rowan Trollope, CEO
Barry Zwarenstein, CFO

Seller of call center software focusing on IVR
System, an interactive voice response software,
Outbound Call Center software, and Auto Dialer.

**Five9 Network Systems LLC** HQ
3600 W Bayshore Rd Ste 105
Palo Alto CA 94303
P: 650-494-2220 PRC:97
www.five9network.com
Estab: 2008

Souheil Saliba, Founder
Annie Lin-Johnson, VP of Business and Corporate
Operations

Provider of server and storage solutions. The
company serves the government, printing, cloud
infrastructure, and energy markets.

**Flamort Company Inc** HQ
2368 Alvarado St
San Leandro CA 94577
P: 510-357-9494 PRC:47
www.flamort.com
Email: info@flamort.com
Estab: 1965

Dean Narahara, General Manager

Provider of fire retardant coatings. The company's
products are used in restaurants, trade shows,
amusement parks, and theaters.

**Flashline Electronics Inc** HQ
2151-B O'Toole Ave
San Jose CA 95131
P: 408-988-4722 F: 408-988-4724 PRC:211
flashlineelectronics.com
Email: sales@flashlineelectronics.com

Tom Hanighen, VP of Sales & Marketing

Manufacturer of printed circuit boards. The company develops blind and buried vias, rigid flex, and
flex PCB.

**Flashpoint Machining** HQ
517 Aldo Ave
Santa Clara CA 95054-2205
P: 408-213-0071 F: 408-213-0073 PRC:157
www.flashpointmachining.com
Email: info@flashpointmachining.com

Eric David, Owner
Karen Mesa, Office Manager

Provider of precision prototype, R&D, and detail &
production machining services. The company also
offers industrial machined parts.

**Flashtalking** BR
110 Sutter St Floor 7
San Francisco CA 94104
P: 628-207-8080 PRC:325
www.flashtalking.com
Estab: 2001

Betsy Adelstein, SVP of Midwest Sales
Chris Winburn, VP Of Sales
Adam Smith, VP Of Sales
Joe Sabol, CRO

Provider of online advertising technologies. The
company is also engaged in analytics and reporting services.

**Flex Interconnect Technologies Inc**          HQ
   1603 Watson Ct
   Milpitas CA 95035
P: 408-635-3540   F: 408-956-8278          PRC:211
www.fit4flex.com
Email: sales@fit4flex.com
Estab: 1998

Dean Matsuo, VP
Meet Shah, Solutions Provider

Developer of printed circuit technologies which
provide solutions to organizational inter connectivity problems.

**Flex Logix Technologies Inc**          HQ
   2465 Latham St
   Mountain View CA 94040
P: 650-851-1411          PRC:212
www.flex-logix.com
Email: info@flex-logix.com
Estab: 2014

Cheng Wang, SVP of Engineering
Geoffrey Tate, CEO
Andy Jaros, VP of Sales
Abhijit Abhyankar, VP
Tony Kozaczuk, Director of Solutions Architecture

Developer of reconfigurable RTL IP cores and
software.

**Flexline LLC**          HQ
   1394 Tully Rd Ste 201
   San Jose CA 95122
P: 408-295-3901   F: 408-295-7341          PRC:235
flexlinellc.com

Florence Usita, Principal Engineer
Hong Li, Software
John Oldham, President

Provider of custom solutions for manufacturing
and test problems. The company also deals with
automation, engineering, and production tooling.

**Flexstar Technology**          HQ
   1965 Concourse Dr
   San Jose CA 95131
P: 408-643-7000   F: 408-643-7090          PRC:19
flexstar.com
Email: sales@flexstar.com
Estab: 1981

Kevin Vo, System Engineer
Andrew Warner, CEO
Canh Phan, Manufacturing Manager
Luong Diep, Buyer

Provider of testing and measurement solutions.
The company's systems are used to test quality
and reliability of storage related devices.

**Flickerbox Inc**          HQ
   246 Shipley St
   San Francisco CA 94107
P: 415-436-9383          PRC:319
flickerbox.com
Email: hello@flickerbox.com
Estab: 1999

Paul Martinez, CEO
Kathy Stewart, Office Manager
Amber Turner, Associate Producer
Todd Collins, Senior Designer
Ben Bridge, Web Developer

Provider of marketing, design, and technology
support services. The company also deals with
lead generation campaigns.

**Flight Light Inc**          HQ
   2708 47th Ave
   Sacramento CA 95822-3806
P: 916-394-2800   F: 916-394-2809          PRC:243
www.flightlight.com
Email: sales@flightlight.com
Emp: 1-10   Estab: 1993

Kyle Owens, Founder
Isabel Martin, President

Supplier of airport lighting products. The company
is a manufacturer of runway lights, taxiway lights,
wind cones, and approach systems.

**FloStor Engineering**          HQ
   21371 Cabot Blvd
   Hayward CA 94545
P: 800-500-8256   F: 510-785-7463          PRC:159
www.flostor.com
Email: information@flostor.com
Estab: 1983

David Almquist, Manager of Engineering
Eric Landtbom, Senior Systems Engineer
Chuck Ireland, VP of System Sales

Developer of automation solutions for inventto-
ry, distribution, fulfillment, and manufacturing
systems.

**Fluid Inc**          HQ
   1611 Telegraph Ave Floor 4
   Oakland CA 94612
P: 877-343-3240   F: 415-263-7701          PRC:326
www.fluid.com
Email: sales@www.fluid.com
Estab: 1998

Bermi Ferrer, Software Engineer
Hernan Cussi, Software Engineer
Pedro Fern ndez, Software Engineer
David Street, Software Engineer
Edison Zuluaga, QA Engineer

Provider of software solutions. The company's
services include automated retail planning and
content strategy.

**Fluidigm Corp**          HQ
   7000 Shoreline Ct Ste 100
   S San Francisco CA 94080
P: 650-266-6000   F: 650-871-7152          PRC:36
fluidigm.com
Sales: $100M to $300M

Rudy Yeung, Staff Software Engineer
Dexter Mendiola, Field Service Engineer
Stephen Linthwaite, President
Fred Walder, COO
Vikram Jog, CFO

Manufacturer of life-science tools. The company's
technologies are focused on microfluidics and
mass cytometry.

**Fluidigm Sciences Inc**          HQ
   7000 Shoreline Ct Ste 100
   South San Francisco CA 94080
P: 650-871-7152          PRC:34
www.dvssciences.com
Estab: 1999

Chris Linthwaite, President
Vikram Jog, CFO
Colin McCracken, Chief Commercial Officer
Sudhakar Chilukuri, SVP
Angela Peters, VP of Global Human Resources

Developer and creator of technologies for life science tools designed to revolutionize biology. The
company is involved in research programs.

**FLYTECH Technology Company Ltd**          BR
   271 E Brokaw Rd
   San Jose CA 95112
P: 510-257-5180   F: 510-257-5181          PRC:91
www.flytech.com
Email: sales@flytech.com

Thomas Lam, Founder

Developer and manufacturer of touch screen,
LCD, and other peripherals. The company also
designs motherboard.

**Fm Industries Inc**          HQ
   221 Warren Ave
   Fremont CA 94539
P: 510-668-1900   F: 510-668-1920          PRC:80
www.fmindustries.com
Email: solutions@fmindustries.com
Estab: 1989

Musaud Yawar, RMA
Leslie Busch-Wilson, Planner

Designer and manufacturer of precision machined
components. The company also offers electro
mechanical assemblies.

**Foamlinx LLC**          HQ
   1248 Birchwood Dr
   Sunnyvale CA 94089
P: 408-454-6163   F: 408-212-8348          PRC:157
www.foamlinx.com
Email: info@foamlinx.com
Estab: 2002

Tal Barnea, Owner

Provider of foam cutting computer numerical
control machines. The company offers cutters,
shredders, compactors, and cutting services.

**Fochon Pharmaceuticals Ltd**          DH
   1933 Davis St Ste 270
   San Leandro CA 94577
P: 510-638-8080          PRC:268
fochon.com
Estab: 2009

Jacob Plattner, Co-Founder
Jiemin Fu, Co-Founder
Weibo Wang, Co-Founder

Provider of therapeutic solutions. The company
focusses on research and development of small
molecule drugs for health care.

**Force Flow Inc**          HQ
   2430 Stanwell Dr
   Concord CA 94520
P: 925-686-6700   F: 925-686-6713          PRC:159
www.forceflowscales.com
Email: info@forceflow.com
Estab: 1967

Kimball Vaughan, Information Technology Manager
Michael Donn, Manager of Product Development

Provider of chemical monitoring scales. The
company exclusively caters to the water and
wastewater industry.

**Foreal Spectrum Inc** HQ
2370 Qume Dr Ste A
San Jose CA 95131
P: 408-436-5558  F: 408-436-5557  PRC:175
forealspectrum.com
Email: salesteam@forealspectrum.com
Estab: 2003

Ronggui Shen, Engineer
Dan Cifelli, Manager

Provider of coating services for laser, biotech, and
medical industries. The company also offers LED
illumination and optical components.

**Forecross Corp** HQ
505 Montgomery St Fl 11
San Francisco CA 94111
P: 415-543-1515  F: 415-543-6701  PRC:325
www.forecross.com
Email: info@forecross.com
Estab: 1982

Bonnie Castello, SVP

Provider of automated migration of legacy systems. The company specializes in XML solutions,
migration solutions, and integrity solutions.

**Forell/Elsesser Engineers Inc** HQ
160 Pine St Ste 600
San Francisco CA 94111
P: 415-837-0700  F: 415-837-0800  PRC:304
www.forell.com
Email: marketing1@forell.com
Estab: 1960

Allen Nudel, Principal
Mei Liu, Senior Engineer
Andrew Salber, Engineer
Casey Li, Engineer
Hayley Dickson, Engineer

Provider of structural engineering, design build,
earthquake engineering, research and development, and seismic design services.

**Forensic Analytical Consulting Ser-
vices Inc** HQ
3777 Depot Rd Ste 413
Hayward CA 94545
P: 866-637-9924  PRC:306
forensicanalytical.com
Email: sales@forensicanalytical.com
Estab: 1986

Gustavo Delgado, CEO
Lily Yee, Program Manager of LIMS & Data
Solutions

Provider of analytical testing services. The company specializes in a wide array of material testing,
forensic and environmental testing.

**Forensic Logic Inc** HQ
712 Bancroft Rd Ste 423
Walnut Creek CA 94598
P: 833-267-5465  PRC:326
www.forensiclogic.com
Email: info@forensiclogic.com
Estab: 2003

Bob Batty, Executive Chairman
Ron Mayer, CTO
BRAD Davis, President
Dave Dunlap, COO
Mike Romano, SVP of Sales

Provider of software-as-a-service information
technology to local, state and federal government
workers and private sector organizations.

**Forescout Technologies Inc** HQ
900 E Hamilton Ave Ste 300
Campbell CA 95014
P: 408-213-3191  F: 408-371-2284  PRC:325
www.forescout.com
Email: info@forescout.com
Estab: 2000

Mike DeCesare, CEO
T. Elliott, Interim CEO
Christopher Harms, CFO
Nitin Yenigalla, Product Marketing Manager
Ori Naishtein, VP of Research & Development

Provider of network access control and policy
compliance management solutions. The company
serves the business sector.

**ForgeRock** HQ
201 Mission St Ste 2900
San Francisco CA 94105
P: 415-599-1100  PRC:319
www.forgerock.com
Estab: 2010

Greg Kalinsky, SVP
Dave Fletcher, CTO
Jeroen Tas, Chief Innovation & Strategy Officer
Philips
Grant Fengstad, Director of Information Technol-
ogy
Alex Fiddes, Programme Delivery Executive DVSA

Provider of identity solutions. The company serves
the digital health, financial services, communication, and media industries.

**Forio Corp** HQ
2601 Mission St Ste 800
San Francisco CA 94110
P: 415-440-7500  F: 415-529-5984  PRC:323
www.forio.com
Email: info@forio.com
Estab: 2001

Michael Bean, Co-Founder
Federico Pasumbal, Quality Assurance Manager
Andrew Northrop, VP of Operations
Andrew Natt, Manager
David Rosen, Senior Software Developer

Provider of software products for simulations, data
explorations, and predictive analysis needs. The
company caters to universities and corporations.

**Form & Fusion Mfg Inc** HQ
11261 Trade Center Dr
Rancho Cordova CA 95742
P: 916-638-8576  F: 916-638-2205  PRC:47
www.form-fusion.com
Email: info@form-fusion.com
Emp: 1-10

Dave Lewis, Founder

Provider of metal fabrication services. The company mainly focuses on powder coating, metal
fabrication, and assembly & packaging.

**Formfactor Inc** HQ
7005 Southfront Rd
Livermore CA 94551
P: 925-290-4000  F: 925-290-4010  PRC:86
www.formfactor.com
Email: info_usa@formfactor.com
Emp: 1188  Estab: 1993
Sales: $300M to $1 Billion

Susumu Kaneko, Design Engineer
Mike Slessor, President
Shai Shahar, CFO
Colleen Cremerius, Senior Director of Human
Resources
Stacey Barnes, Director of Information Technology

Provider of product and professional services to
semiconductor manufacturers. The company also
offers sales and support services.

**Formulation Technology Inc** HQ
571 Armstrong Way
Oakdale CA 95361
P: 209-847-0331  F: 209-847-1975  PRC:272
formulationtech.com
Email: info@formulationtech.com
Emp: 1-10  Estab: 1982

Keith Hensley, President
Ron Bahadur, Production Manager

Manufacturer of custom dietary supplements
and OTC medications. The company focuses on
contract manufacturing services.

**FormuMax Scientific Inc** HQ
1230 Bordeaux Dr
Sunnyvale CA 94089
P: 408-400-0108  F: 408-465-5338  PRC:34
formumax.com
Email: service@formumax.com

Bing Luo, Senior Scientist
Robert Abra, Principal Scientist

Provider of contract drug delivery to pharmaceutical and biotech industries. The company specializes in injectables, liposomes and microemulsions.

**Formurex Inc** HQ
2470 Wilcox Rd
Stockton CA 95215
P: 209-931-2040  F: 209-931-2177  PRC:268
www.formurex.com
Emp: 1-10

Bhaskara Jasti, Founder
Xiaoling Liang, CSO

Provider of services to the biotech industry in
preformulation, formulation development, stability
and clinical trial materials manufacturing.

**Forsgren Associate Inc** DH
3110 Gold Canal Dr
Rancho Cordova CA 95670
P: 916-638-1119  F: 916-638-1129  PRC:137
forsgren.com
Emp: 11-50  Estab: 1962

Richard Noll, President
Alan Driscoll, VP

Provider of civil and environmental engineering
consulting services. The company specializes
in planning, design, survey, and construction
management.

**ForteBio** BR
47661 Fremont Blvd
Fremont CA 94538
P: 650-322-1360   F: 650-322-1370   PRC:34
www.moleculardevices.com
Email: intlom@moldev.com

Susan Murphy, President
Steven Qian, CFO
Laurent Claisse, VP
Poonam Taneja, VP
Jennifer Marasco, VP of Human Resources

Provider of dip and read assay kits. The company's products are used in the application of kinetic characterization.

**Fortemedia Inc** HQ
4051 Burton Dr
Santa Clara CA 95054
P: 408-861-8088   F: 408-861-8089   PRC:204
www.fortemedia.com
Email: info@fortemedia.com
Estab: 1996

Quintin Liu, VP of Engineering
Xiao Lin, Senior Director
Yan-Chen Lu, Senior Manager of SW Engineering
Paul Huang, CEO

Provider of voice processing integrated circuits. The company also offers related hardware and software components.

**Fortinet Inc** HQ
899 Kifer Rd
Sunnyvale CA 94086
P: 408-235-7700   F: 408-235-7737   PRC:323
www.fortinet.com
Email: communications@fortinet.com
Estab: 2000
Sales: $1B to $3B

Charlih Chen, IT Engineer
Ken Xie, Founder
Michael Xie, Founder
Keith Jensen, CFO
Laurie Buzzell, SVP of Global Human Resources

Provider of network security appliances and threat management solutions such as network security platform and reporting and authentication.

**Fortrend Engineering Corp** HQ
2220 O'Toole Ave
San Jose CA 95131
P: 408-734-9311   F: 408-734-4299   PRC:138
www.fortrend.com
Email: sales@fortrend.com
Estab: 1979

Chris Wu, CEO
Harriet West, Materials Manager
Ruihan Zhao, Account Manager
Donna Cheng, Controller

Designer and manufacturer of mechanical handling equipment. The company also specializes in distribution services.

**Forty Seven Inc** HQ
1490 O'Brien Dr Ste A
Menlo Park CA 94025
P: 650-352-4150   F: 650-618-2308   PRC:44
www.fortyseveninc.com
Email: info@fortyseveninc.com
Estab: 2015

Mark Chao, Co-Founder
Craig Gibbs, Chief Business Officer
Norman Kruse, Chief Patent Counsel
Chris Takimoto, CMO
Kyle Elrod, VP

Provider of medical solutions to advancement of immuno-oncology through the engagement of new and complementary phagocytic pathways.

**Foster Brothers Security Systems Inc** HQ
555 S Murphy Ave
Sunnyvale CA 94086
P: 408-736-4500   F: 408-736-0468   PRC:59
fosterbrothers.com
Estab: 1955

Jeff Sanchez, Sales Manager

Provider of security systems. The company offers locks and keys, access control systems, and tools and accessories.

**Foundation Constructors Inc** HQ
81 Big Break Rd
Oakley CA 94561
P: 925-754-6633   PRC:304
www.foundationpiledriving.com
Email: info@foundationpiledriving.com
Estab: 1971

Wyatt Gregory, Project Engineer
Dermot Fallon, President
Nikki Sjoblom, CFO
Chris Kinley, Safety Director
Chris Jalowiec, Project Manager

Provider of pile solutions and shoring systems. The company also offers pile, H-beams, sheets, and concrete pile types.

**Four Dimensions Inc** HQ
3140 Diablo Ave
Hayward CA 94545
P: 510-782-1843   F: 510-786-9321   PRC:212
www.4dimensions.com
Email: info@4dimensions.com
Estab: 1978

Chen-Fan Huang, Electrical Engineer
James Chen, President

Manufacturer of semiconductor probing systems. The company offers Four Point Probe, Mercury Probe CV maps, and Mercury Four Imaging systems.

**Foveon Inc** HQ
2249 Zanker Rd
San Jose CA 95131
P: 408-855-6800   PRC:168
www.foveon.com
Estab: 1997

Federico Faggin, CEO
Rudy Guttosch, VP

Innovator of design and development of image sensors and image capture systems for a wide range of digital capture products.

**Foxit Corp** HQ
41841 Albrae St
Fremont CA 94538
P: 510-438-9090   F: 510-405-9288   PRC:322
foxitsoftware.com
Email: sales@foxitsoftware.com
Estab: 2001

Eugene Xiong, Founder
Susana De Abrew, President of Foxit SDK BU
Shinichi Mori, CEO
George Gao, CEO
Phil Lee, Chief Revenue Officer

Developer of software. The company offers software such as Foxit Reader, Enterprise, and Mobile Reader.

**Franz Inc** HQ
2201 Broadway Ste 715
Oakland CA 94612
P: 510-452-2000   F: 510-452-0182   PRC:323
www.franz.com
Email: info@franz.com
Estab: 1984

Kevin Layer, COO
Craig Norvell, VP of Global Sales & Marketing
Alexandra Demidova, Sales Representative
Sheng-Chuan Wu, VP of Asia & Corporate Development
David Margolies, Manager

Provider of information technology solutions. The company offers web technology and enterprise development tools, and professional services.

**Free Hot Water** HQ
2023 O'Toole Ave
San Jose CA 95131
P: 408-432-9900   F: 408-872-4142   PRC:135
www.freehotwater.com
Email: info@freehotwater.com
Estab: 1998

Gal Moyal, Founder

Manufacturer and distributor of solar thermal products. The company serves engineers, architects, developers, and business owners.

**Freetech Plastics Inc** HQ
2211 Warm Springs Ct
Fremont CA 94539
P: 510-651-9996   F: 510-651-9917   PRC:84
www.freetechplastics.com
Email: sales@freetechplastics.com
Estab: 1976

Richard Freeman, CEO
Judy Nguyen, Materials Manager

Manufacturer of pressure thermoforming products. The company's products include medical, scientific, and telecommunication enclosures.

**FreeWire Technologies Inc** HQ
1933 Davis St Ste 301A
San Leandro CA 94577
P: 415-779-5515   PRC:288
www.freewiretech.com

Arcady Sosinov, CEO

Provider of mobile distributed power solutions. The company serves the business and industrial sectors.

**Frequentis California Inc**     DH
2511 Garden Rd Ste A-165
Monterey CA 93940
P: 831-392-0430     PRC:66
www.frequentis.com
Estab: 1978

Norbert Haslacher, CEO
Dieter Eier, VP

Provider of air traffic management and other e-services. The company serves the defense and public transport sectors.

**Frequentz LLC**     HQ
12667 Alcosta Blvd
San Ramon CA 94583
P: 925-824-0300     PRC:326
frequentz.com
Email: hello@rfxcel.com
Estab: 2008

Byron Lee, CTO

Designer and developer of product tracking software. The company serves the life sciences and industrial sectors.

**Fresenius Medical Care**     BR
365 Lennon Ln Ste 160
Walnut Creek CA 94598
P: 925-947-4545    F: 925-947-4547     PRC:186
www.freseniuskidneycare.com

Janet Voss, Manufacturing Engineer
Thomas Merics, Senior Software Engineer

Focuses on the treatment of patients with renal and other chronic conditions. The company serves the healthcare industry.

**Freshwater Environmental Svc**     HQ
78 Sunnybrae Ctr
Arcata CA 95521
P: 707-839-0091     PRC:139
www.freshwaterenvironmentalservices.com
Emp: 1-10    Estab: 2007

Orrin Plocher, Geologist

Provider of environmental services. The company's services include soil investigation workplans, soil sampling reporting, sediment sampling, and monitoring.

**Freshworks Inc**     HQ
1250 Bayhill Dr Ste 315
San Bruno CA 94066
P: 650-513-0514     PRC:323
freshdesk.com
Estab: 2010

Girish Mathrubootham, CEO
Shan Krishnasamy, Co-Founder
Bobby Jaffari, President
Prakash Ramamurthy, Chief Product Officer
Sidharth Malik, Chief Revenue Officer

Provider of multi-channel support and asset management services. The company serves business organizations.

**Fresno Valves & Castings Inc**     HQ
7736 E Springfield Ave
Selma CA 93662
P: 559-834-2511    F: 559-834-2017     PRC:147
www.fresnovalves.com
Email: info@fresnovalves.com
Emp: 11-50 Estab: 1952

Leonor Lopez, Human Resource Manager
Rich Korbe, Fabricated Gates Sales Manager
Renee Moore, Territory Sales Manager
Kelvin Kerst, Regional Manager
Sergio Hernandez, Foundry Representative

Provider of water control devices used in irrigation applications. The company's products include valves, filters, air vents, fittings, gates, and lifts.

**Frey Environmental Inc**     BR
1336 Brommer St
Santa Cruz CA 95062
P: 831-464-1634    F: 831-464-1644     PRC:139
freyinc.com
Emp: 11-50 Estab: 1989

Joe Frey, Owner
Walter Bell, Engineer
Ed Rands, Senior Project Engineer
Brian Finkelstein, Staff Engineer
Uyen Le, Accounts Manager

Provider of geological and engineering consulting services. The company offers stormwater management, methane assessments/mitigation, and asbestos-related services.

**Frontier Analytical Laboratory**     HQ
5172 Hillsdale Cir
El Dorado Hills CA 95762
P: 916-934-0900    F: 916-934-0999     PRC:303
www.frontieranalytical.com
Email: info@frontieranalytical.com
Emp: 1-10    Estab: 2001

Dan Vickers, Director Of Air Toxics
Tom Crabtree, Director of Mass Spectrometry
Brad Silverbush, Director of Operations

Provider of testing services for analysis of polychlorinated dibenzo dioxins and furans polychlorinated biphenyls and polyaromatic hydrocarbons.

**Fruit Growers Laboratory Inc**     BR
2500 Stagecoach Rd
Stockton CA 95215
P: 209-942-0182    F: 209-942-0423     PRC:140
fglinc.com
Emp: 11-50 Estab: 1925

Kelly Dunnahoo, President
David Terz, Quality Assurance Director
Glenn Olsen, Marketing Director
Ellie Hengehold-Blackshear, Customer Service Manager
Richard Hawkins, Lab Manager

Provider of testing & analytical services. The company performs drinking and waste water analysis, agriculture testing, and hazardous waste analysis.

**FUEL Creative Group**     HQ
5001 24th St
Sacramento CA 95816
P: 916-669-1591     PRC:325
www.fuelcreativegroup.com
Emp: 1-10

Steve Worth, Owner
Brent Rector, Owner
Brittany Baledio, Production Designer
Nicolette Countryman, Project Manager
Megan Daly, Graphic Designer

Provider of graphic design, branding, and signage services. The company also focuses on packaging and printing.

**Fuji Electric Corporation of America**     BR
47520 Westinghouse Dr
Fremont CA 94539
P: 510-440-1060    F: 510-440-1063     PRC:86
americas.fujielectric.com
Estab: 1970

Steve Snyder, Western Regional Sales Manager

Provider of electric technology services. The company offers solutions for disk media, power supply, industrial systems, and radiation.

**Fujikin of America Inc**     RH
454 Kato Ter
Fremont CA 94539
P: 408-980-8269    F: 408-980-0572     PRC:166
www.fujikin.com
Email: sales@fujikin.com
Estab: 1930

Masayo Miyauchi, Human Resource Coordinator
Ayami Botkin, Senior Manager

Manufacturer of fluid and gas flow valves and fittings. The company also offers process equipment control systems.

**Fujikura America Inc**     BR
920 Stewart Dr Ste 150
Santa Clara CA 94085
P: 408-748-6991    F: 408-727-3415     PRC:81
www.fujikura.com

Vijit Wuttijumnong, Thermal Engineering Manager
Tetsuya Noda, General Manager
Danny Kobayashi, Sales Manager
Yasunori Okamoto, Regional Sales Manager
Ash Ooe, Regional Sales Manager

Manufacturer of fiber optics flexible printed circuits and cables. The company also offers membrane switches and printed circuit board assemblies.

**Fujitsu Components America Inc**     HQ
2290 N First St Ste 212
San Jose CA 95131
P: 408-745-4900    F: 408-745-4970     PRC:78
www.fujitsu.com
Email: components@us.fujitsu.com

Bob Thornton, President
Mark Madden, Senior Sales Manager
Ning Li, Product Marketing Manager
Ronald Norfleet, General Ledger Accountant

Provider of computing products and services. The company's products include servers, storage, scanners, and displays.

**Full Circle Crm Inc** HQ
3 Waters Park Dr Ste 120
San Mateo CA 94403
P: 650-641-2766 PRC:326
fullcircleinsights.com
Estab: 2011

Dan Appleman, Co-Founder
Bonnie Crater, President
Rochelle Richelieu, VP of Customer Success

Specializes in response management and it offers
management products. The company serves
businesses.

**Full Circle Insights Inc** HQ
1800 Gateway Dr Ste 130
San Mateo CA 94404
P: 650-641-2766 PRC:319
fullcircleinsights.com
Email: success@fullcircleinsights.com
Estab: 2011

Bob Teplitsky, VP of Engineering
Bonnie Crater, Co-Founder
Dan Appleman, Co-Founder
Rochelle Richelieu, VP of Customer Success

Delivers marketing and sales performance
measurement solutions to optimize a company's
marketing automation solutions.

**Funambol Inc** HQ
1065 E Hillsdale Blvd Ste 400
Foster City CA 94404
P: 650-701-1450 F: 650-701-1484 PRC:324
www.funambol.com
Email: info@funambol.com
Estab: 2002

Amit Chawla, CEO
Steve Tomasini, VP of Sales of Americas & APAC
Ata Rasekhi, VP of Marketing and Product Man-
agement

Provider of open source mobile application server
software. The company offers training and technical support services.

**Function Engineering** HQ
163 Everett Ave
Palo Alto CA 94301
P: 650-326-8834 PRC:304
www.function.com
Email: info@function.com
Estab: 1987

Joel Jensen, Principal Engineer
Stan Brigham, Senior Managing Engineer
Michelle Deng, Mechanical Engineer
Diane Elia, Human Resource Generalist
Sonya Fagan, Information Technology Manager

Provider of mechanical design and engineering
services for product development. The company
serves the consumer electronics and robotics
industries.

**Funmobility Inc** HQ
2430 Camino Ramon
San Ramon CA 94583
P: 925-598-9700 F: 925-244-0200 PRC:316
www.funmobility.com
Email: press@funmobility.com
Estab: 1999

Kai Yung, VP of Engineering
Adam Lavine, CEO
Bala Talkad, Quality Assurance Manager
Ken Nowak, VP of Content and Operations
Brian Dana, VP of Development Operations

Provider of solutions for mobile engagement and
mobile marketing. The company also offers content marketing, digital strategy, and other services.

**Furaxa Inc** HQ
808 Gilman St
Berkeley CA 94710
P: 925-253-2969 F: 925-253-4894 PRC:15
www.furaxa.com
Email: support@furaxa.com
Estab: 2001

Mike Ingle, VP of Engineering
Joel Libove, CEO
Steve Chacko, VP

Designer and supplier of signal synthesis,
sampling, and pulse generating technologies and
products.

**Furukawa Sangyo North America Inc** LH
1922 The Alameda Ste 205
San Jose CA 95126
P: 408-496-0051 F: 408-496-0052 PRC:212
www.furukawa.co.jp

Mitsuyoshi Shibata, President

Provider of electric products for telecommunications and automotive needs. The company also
serves energy, construction, and other sectors.

**Fusionstorm** BR
2 Bryant St Ste 150
San Francisco CA 94105
P: 800-228-8324 PRC:325
www.computacenter.com
Estab: 1995

Richard Bailey, Regional Engineering Director
James Richter, Engineering Operations Assistant
Matthew Harris, Director of Channel
Taylor Stinebaugh, Inside Account Manager

Provider of information technology services. The
company specializes in IT consulting, data center,
networking, and enterprise content management.

**Futronix Inc** HQ
855 Mathew St
Santa Clara CA 95050
P: 408-735-1122 PRC:94
www.futronix-inc.com
Email: admin@futronix-inc.com
Estab: 1974

Tony Erlund, Administrator

Designer and developer of energy management
systems. The company provides computer line
clocks, electronic cam systems, and energy
control systems.

**Future Facilities Inc** BR
2055 Gateway Pl Ste 110
San Jose CA 95110
P: 408-436-7701 F: 408-436-7705 PRC:322
www.futurefacilities.com
Email: info@futurefacilities.com
Estab: 2004

Sherman Ikemoto, Director

Developer of engineering simulation software for
the design and operation of electronics products.
The company serves the industrial sector.

**Future Fibre Technologies (US) Inc** HQ
800 W El Camino Real Ste 180
Mountain View CA 94040
P: 877-650-8900 F: 435-417-6671 PRC:59
www.fftsecurity.com
Estab: 1994

Rob Broomfield, COO

Provider of fiber optic based intrusion detection
systems for perimeter protection and pipeline
security.

**Futuredial Inc** HQ
392 Potrero Ave
Sunnyvale CA 94085
P: 408-245-8880 F: 408-245-8885 PRC:64
www.futuredial.com
Email: sales@futuredial.com
Estab: 1999

Jason Li, VP of Engineering
Rina Mehta, QA Engineer
Nicholas Consola, Sales Engineer
George Huang, CEO
Dan Kikinis, CTO

Developer of carrier-grade solutions and tools for
mobile device recyclers, wireless operators, and
mobile device manufacturers.

**FutureWei Technologies Inc** BR
2330 Central Expy
Santa Clara CA 95050
P: 408-330-5000 PRC:63
huawei.com
Estab: 1987

Chen Lifang, Director
L.I. Yingtao, Director
Tao Jingwen, Director
Yao Fuhai, Director
Yi Xiang Steven Yi, President of Middle East and
Africa

Provider of information and communications
technology solutions. The company focuses on
products such as transport network and data
communication.

**G Fred Lee & Associates** HQ
27298 E El Macero Dr
El Macero CA 95618-1005
P: 530-753-9630 PRC:142
www.gfredlee.com
Email: gfredlee@aol.com
Emp: 1-10

G. Lee, Owner

Provider of surface and groundwater evaluation services. The company focuses on landfill
impacts, eutrophication, watershed studies, and
other needs.

**G&R Labs** HQ
2395 De La Cruz Blvd
Santa Clara CA 95050
P: 408-986-0377  F: 408-986-0416  PRC:13
www.grlabs.com
Estab: 1995

George Richardson, Founder

Manufacturer, seller, and calibrator of light measurement equipment. The company is engaged in design, delivery, and installation services.

**g2 Engineering** BR
16991 McGill Rd
Saratoga CA 95070
P: 650-605-4500  F: 650-887-2332  PRC:159
www.g2-engineering.com
Email: inbox@g2-engineering.com
Estab: 2005

Dave Reeder, VP of Marketing

Manufacturer of engineering products such as bead mounts and related accessories. The company's applications include industrial automation and controls.

**G4s Secure Solutions (usa) Inc** BR
100 Century Center Ct Ste 200
San Jose CA 95112
P: 408-453-4133  F: 408-453-6440  PRC:322
www.g4s.com
Email: sfr_info@usa.g4s.com
Estab: 1901

Mel Brooks, Regional President
Sanjay Verma, Regional CEO
Ashley Almanza, CEO
John Kenning, Regional CEO
John Connolly, Non Executive Director

Provider of security management solutions such as compliance and investigations, disaster and emergency, and fraud abatement.

**Galaxy Biotech LLC** HQ
1230 Bordeaux Dr
Sunnyvale CA 94089
P: 408-400-8020  PRC:34
www.galaxybiotech.com
Estab: 2002

Cary Queen, President
Jin Kim, CSO

Provider of biotechnology services. The company develops monoclonal antibodies against growth factors and their receptors for treatment of cancer.

**Galil Motion Control** HQ
270 Technology Way
Rocklin CA 95765
P: 916-626-0101  F: 916-626-0102  PRC:94
www.galilmc.com
Email: galil@galilmc.com
Emp: 1-10  Estab: 1983

DJ Roberts, Applications Engineer
Jacob Tal, Co-Founder
Wayne Baron, Co-Founder
Mark Middleton, Manager of Worldwide Sales
John Thompson, VP of Operations

Manufacturer and supplier of motion controllers and software tools. The company also offers drives and power supplies.

**Gallery Systems Inc** BR
3200 College Ave Ste 6
Berkeley CA 94705
P: 510-652-8950  PRC:323
www.gallerysystems.com

Armen Baghdasaryan, Engineer
Heather Lake, Manager of EmbARK Client Services

Provider of collection management systems. The company offers procedures consulting, project management, and strategic planning services.

**Gambit Corp** HQ
586 Martin Ave Ste 7
Rohnert Park CA 94928-2095
P: 707-588-2797  F: 707-588-2799  PRC:163
www.gambitcorp.com
Email: sales@gambitcorp.com
Estab: 1962

George Weise, President

Provider of engineering parts and services. The company specializes in designing and building tools and dies.

**Game Your Game Inc** HQ
653 Bryant St
San Francisco CA 94107
P: 888-245-3433  PRC:322
www.gamegolf.com
Email: support@gameyourgame.com
Estab: 2011

John McGuire, CEO

Developer of digital tracking system such as automatic shot tracking and hands-free game tracking device to get the insights to improve the game.

**GangaGen Inc** HQ
3279 Emerson
Palo Alto CA 94306
P: 650-856-9642  PRC:34
www.gangagen.com
Email: info@gangagen.com
Estab: 2000

Amy Percy, President
Janakiraman Ramachandran, Chairman

Provider of proprietary recombinant protein for the topical prevention and treatment of Staplylococcal infections.

**Garcia And Associates** HQ
2601 Mission St Ste 600
San Francisco CA 94110
P: 415-642-8969  F: 415-642-8967  PRC:133
garciaandassociates.com

Gus Garcia, Owner
Pat Moyer, CFO
Joe Drennan, VP of Wildlife Ecologist and Wetlands Specialist
David Kelly, VP of Environmental Compliance Specialist
John McCarthy, VP of Environmental Compliance Specialist

Provider of natural and cultural resource consultant services. The company's services include permit acquisition, agency consultation, and ecological research.

**Garratt-Callahan Co** HQ
50 Ingold Rd
Burlingame CA 94010
P: 650-697-5811  F: 650-692-6098  PRC:233
garrattcallahan.com
Estab: 1904

Jeffrey Garratt, President
Manny Chargualaf, Marketing Manager
Matthew Garratt, EVP
Charles Burkland, Territory Manager
Cesar Zabala, Territory Manager

Provider of water treatment services. The company's solutions include cooling water treatment and safer chemical cleaning.

**Gasket Specialties Inc** HQ
6200 Hollis St
Emeryville CA 94608
P: 510-547-7955  F: 510-547-8242  PRC:162
www.gasketspecialties.com
Estab: 1925

Erna Cariaso, Sales Manager
Louise Barbee, Branch Manager

Manufacturer of gaskets. The company engages in adhesives, assembly, and bar coding services.

**Gatan Inc** HQ
5794 W Las Positas Blvd
Pleasanton CA 94588
P: 925-463-0200  F: 925-463-0204  PRC:20
www.gatan.com
Email: info@gatan.com
Estab: 1964

Steve Coyle, Engineering Manager
Gabriel Szantai, Mechanical Engineering Manager
Allen McGee, Field Service System Engineer
Kevin Scudder, General Manager
Paolo Longo, Global Analytical Sales Applications Manager

Manufacturer of instrumentation and software used to enhance and extend the operation and performance of electron microscopes.

**Gateway Precision Inc** HQ
2300 Calle De Luna
Santa Clara CA 95054
P: 408-855-8849  F: 408-855-9004  PRC:80
gatewayprecision.com
Email: sales@gatewayprecision.com
Estab: 1998

Chi To, Office Manager

Manufacturer of precision-machined components and assemblies for image equipment manufacturers, telecom, food processing, and semiconductor sectors.

**Gauss Surgical Inc** HQ
334 State St Ste 201
Los Altos CA 94022
P: 650-949-4153  PRC:189
www.gausssurgical.com
Email: info@gausssurgical.com
Estab: 2011

Andrew Hosford, VP of Engineering
Siddarth Satish, Founder
Griffeth Tully, Chief Medical Officer
Mac Farnsworth, CFO
Douglas Carroll, CCO

Manufacturer of mobile devices. The company is engaged in research and development services and it serves the healthcare sector.

**GC Micro Corp**      HQ
    3910 Cypress Dr
    Petaluma CA 94954
P: 707-789-0600   F: 707-789-0700    PRC:207
www.gcmicro.com
Email: info@gcmicro.com
Estab: 1986

Belinda Guadarrama, CEO
Eric Grumley, Account Manager
Joseph Whitson, Deputy Program Manager

Provider of IT hardware, software, and related
products to corporate and government accounts.
The company specializes in information technology.

**Gct Semiconductor Inc**      HQ
    2121 Ringwood Ave
    San Jose CA 95131
P: 408-434-6040   F: 408-434-6050    PRC:61
www.gctsemi.com
Email: contact_marketing@gctsemi.com
Estab: 1998

Jeongmin Jeemee Kim, CTO
Jiho Jang, VP of Engineering
John Schlaefer, CEO
Charles Chang, Director of Information Technol-
ogy
Gene Kulzer, Chief Financial & Administrative
Officer

Designer and supplier of 4G mobile semiconductor solutions. The company also offers wireless
solutions for its clients.

**Gcx Corp**      HQ
    3875 Cypress Dr
    Petaluma CA 94954-5635
P: 707-773-1100   F: 707-773-1180    PRC:94
www.gcx.com
Email: sales@gcx.com
Estab: 1971

Robert Glaser, Mechanical Engineer
John Kruger, President
Mark Ross, General Manager
Renee Crocker, Direct Segment Marketing
Manager
Maggie Coin, Internal Product Management

Provider of mounting solutions, application specific solutions, on-site services, and also technical
support.

**Gdca Inc**      HQ
    1799 Portola Ave
    Livermore CA 94551
P: 925-456-9900   F: 925-456-9901    PRC:211
www.gdca.com
Email: sales@gdca.com
Estab: 1987

James Brandt, Sales Engineering Manager
Ethan Plotkin, CEO
Christa Williams, Human Resource Manager
Anne Bennedsen, Director of Quality
Bill Spain, Director of Legacy Solutions

Manufacturer of legacy embedded computers and
single boards. The company also specializes in
assurance, planning, and engineering.

**Gdm Electronic Medical**      HQ
    2070 Ringwood Ave
    San Jose CA 95131
P: 408-945-4100   F: 408-945-4070    PRC:189
www.gdm1.com
Email: sales@gdm1.com
Estab: 1982

Grant Murphy, President
Karen Guerrero, Director of Operations
Diego Martinez, Customer Service Manager

Manufacturer of devices, electrical and electronics for medical, manufacturing and engineering
industries.

**GDR Engineering Inc**      HQ
    3525 Mitchell Rd
    Ceres CA 95307-9479
P: 209-538-3360    PRC:304
Emp: 1-10   Estab: 1978

Rick Ringler, Civil Engineer
Jason Andrews, Engineering Technician
Max Garcia, Principal

Provider of land development and infrastructure
engineering services. The company also focuses
on land planning and surveying.

**Gel-Pak**      DH
    31398 Huntwood Ave
    Hayward CA 94544
P: 510-576-2220   F: 510-576-2282    PRC:285
www.gelpak.com
Email: support@gelpak.com
Estab: 1980

Ginger DeMello, Production Manager
Raymund Abiera, National Sales Manager
Priya Anand, Administrative Assistant
Ted Villavicencio, Shipping Clerk
Holly Snider, Level Two Customer Service Repre-
sentative

Provider of safety transport and product handling
services from bare die to medical components,
and other fragile parts.

**Gemini Bio-Products**      HQ
    930 Riverside Pkwy
    West Sacramento CA 95605
P: 800-543-6464   F: 916-273-5222    PRC:24
www.gembio.com
Email: customerservice@gembio.com
Emp: 11-50 Estab: 1985

Dale Gordon, CEO
Don Neil, CCO
Rob Perry, COO
Scott Kantor, CFO
Pamela Brown, Sales Executive

Provider of supplements, reagents, and human
products. The company is involved in medical
research and development.

**Gen-9 Inc**      HQ
    800 W El Camino Real
    Mountain View CA 94040
P: 650-903-2235    PRC:325
www.gen-9.net
Email: info@gen-9.net
Estab: 2005

Mark Fauci, Founder

Provider of personal information management
services. The company offers services to the
industrial and commercial markets.

**Genapsys Inc**      HQ
    200 Cardinal Way 3rd Fl
    Redwood City CA 94063
P: 650-330-1096    PRC:34
genapsys.com
Email: info@genapsys.com
Estab: 2010

Hesaam Esfandyarpour, CEO

Developer of DNA sequencing to enable a paradigm shift in genomic diagnostics. The company
specializes in GENIUS system that has footprint
of Apple iPad.

**Genbook Inc**      HQ
    548 Market St
    San Francisco CA 94104
P: 415-227-9904    PRC:325
www.genbook.com
Email: bizdev@genbook.com
Estab: 2006

Rody Moore, Founder

Developer of online appointment scheduling
software. The company is engaged in social media
marketing services.

**Genemed Biotechnologies Inc**      HQ
    458 Carlton Ct
    S San Francisco CA 94080-2012
P: 650-952-0110   F: 650-952-1060    PRC:39
www.genemed.com
Email: order@genemed.com
Estab: 1987

Peter Luu, President
Dean Tsao, Chairman
Lynda Douglass, Quality Assurance Manager
Rina DeCamillis, VP of R&D and Operations
Erik Hasal, Technical Support Manager

Manufacturer of diagnostic reagents. The company caters to the pharmaceutical and diagnostic
sectors.

**Genentech Inc**      HQ
    1 DNA Way
    S San Francisco CA 94080-4990
P: 650-225-1000   F: 650-225-6000    PRC:34
www.gene.com
Email: busdev@gene.com
Estab: 1976

Roshni Varghese, Engineer
Paul Carter, Genentech Fellow of Antibody Engi-
neering
Bob Swanson, Founder
Julia Edwards, Chief of Staff
Lance Eck, Human Resource Talent Acquisition

Focuses on the treatment of breast cancer. The
company offers services to patients and medical
professionals.

**Genentech Inc**      BR
    1000 New Horizons Way
    Vacaville CA 95688-9431
P: 707-454-1000    PRC:34
www.gene.com
Email: supplierrelations@gene.com

Alexander Hardy, CEO
Ed Harrington, CFO
Sean Johnston, SVP
Cynthia Burks, SVP of Human Resources
Levi Garraway, EVP

Provider of biotechnology services. The company uses human genetic information to develop medicines for life-threatening medical conditions.

**Genepharm Inc** HQ
1237 Midas Way
Sunnyvale CA 94085
P: 408-773-1082   F: 408-773-1018   PRC:268
www.genepharminc.com
Email: info@genepharminc.com
Estab: 2000

Xinfan Huang, CEO
George Lee, Chairman
Hanafi Tanojo, VP of Research and Development

Developer and commercialization of therapeutics for skin-related problems. The company is engaged in pre-clinical research.

**General Foundry Service Corp** HQ
1390 Business Center Pl
San Leandro CA 94577
P: 510-297-5040   F: 510-614-2171   PRC:34
www.genfoundry.com
Email: sales@genfoundry.com
Estab: 1946

Rundong Zhu, Software Engineer
John Fehringer, Quality Manager
E. Ritelli, Project Manager
Dhivya Chandrasekaran, US IT Recruiter

Provider of foundry services. The company engages in pattern making, precision sand casting, and rubber plastic mold.

**General Grinding Inc** HQ
801 51st Ave
Oakland CA 94601
P: 510-261-5557   F: 510-261-5567   PRC:157
www.generalgrindinginc.com
Email: ggrind@aol.com
Estab: 1943

Michael Bardon, President
Lynne Fone, Office Manager

Provider of precision, centerless, and surface grinding services. The company serves the medical and military industries.

**General Hydroponics Inc** HQ
2877 Giffen Ave
Santa Rosa CA 95407
P: 707-824-9376   F: 707-824-9377   PRC:43
www.generalhydroponics.com
Estab: 1976

Keith Evans, Operations Manager

Providers of Hydroponics. The company offer solution for commercial producers especially in non arable areas.

**General Lasertronics Corp** HQ
1520 Montague Expy Ste 5
San Jose CA 95131-1408
P: 408-947-1181   PRC:159
www.lasertronics.com
Email: info@lasertronics.com
Estab: 1996

Haresh Patel, Electronics Engineer
Jan Orazem, Field Sales Engineer
Ron Erickson, Field Sales Engineer
Morley Huskinson, Field Sales Engineer
Ned Collins, Field Sales Engineer

Developer of scanning and control technologies that make laser ablation an alternative to traditional abrasives and solvents for removing coatings.

**General Vision** HQ
1150 Industrial Ave Ste A
Petaluma CA 94952
P: 707-765-6150   PRC:189
www.general-vision.com

Guy Paillet, CEO

Provider of hardware and software products. The company specializes in artificial intelligence and image analytics.

**Genesis Biofuel Inc** HQ
20151 Viva Cir
Huntington Beach CA 92646
P: 303-376-6221   PRC:137
www.genesis-biofuel.com
Emp: 1-10

Sonny Dorren, President
Harvey Dorren, President

Manufacturer of renewable energy products. The company offers green solutions to counter greenhouse gas emissions.

**Genesys Logic America Inc** BR
2860 Zanker Rd Ste 105
San Jose CA 95134
P: 408-435-8899   F: 408-435-8886   PRC:110
www.genesyslogic.com
Email: sales@genesysamerica.com
Estab: 2002

Simon Lou, Sales Manager

Developer of electric circuits, semiconductors, digital communications products, computer peripherals, and other related products.

**Genmark Automation Inc** HQ
46723 Lakeview Blvd
Fremont CA 94538
P: 510-897-3400   F: 510-897-3401   PRC:309
www.genmarkautomation.com
Email: mktg-sales@genmarkautomation.com
Estab: 1985

Carl McMahon, President
Victor Sales, President
Bill Harrell, VP of Operations
Brian Paiva, RMA Service Department Technician
inTest

Provider of robotics for automated manufacturing applications. The company offers services to the data storage and related industries.

**Genmega Inc** HQ
30587 Huntwood Ave
Hayward CA 94544
P: 510-344-6333   PRC:68
www.genmega.com
Email: sales@genmega.com
Estab: 2006

Tommy Park, Marketing Manager

Manufacturer and provider of ATM and transactional kiosk solutions. The company's products include GenLink, Onyx-P, Onyx-W, and G2500P ATM.

**Genomic Health Inc** HQ
301 Penobscot Dr
Redwood City CA 94063-4700
P: 650-556-9300   F: 650-556-1132   PRC:34
www.genomichealth.com
Email: customerservice@genomichealth.com
Estab: 2000
Sales: $300M to $1 Billion

Steven Shak, Founder
Jennifer Jones, Construction Coordinator

Specializes in the treatment of cancer. The company is engaged in patient management software development.

**Genstor Systems Inc** HQ
1501 Space Park Dr
Santa Clara CA 95054
P: 408-980-0121   F: 408-980-0127   PRC:91
www.genstor.com
Email: info@genstor.com

Michael Ko, Production Manager

Provider of customized hardware solutions for server, storage, clusters, personal computers, and workstations.

**Gentec Manufacturing Inc** HQ
2241 Ringwood Ave
San Jose CA 95131
P: 408-432-6220   F: 408-435-1757   PRC:80
gentecmfg.com
Email: sales@gentecmfg.com
Estab: 1976

Mark Diaz, President

Provider of machining services. The company also offers measuring, testing, turning, and engineering services.

**Geo M Martin Co** HQ
1250 67th St
Emeryville CA 94608-1121
P: 510-652-2200   F: 510-652-6447   PRC:80
www.geomartin.com
Email: info@geomartin.com
Estab: 1929

Jon Ames, Mechanical Engineering R&D Manager
Noah Horowitz, Mechanical Design Engineer
Greg Stevens, Electrical Engineer
Robert Morgan, President
George Martin, EVP

Developer of equipment for corrugated container industry. The company offers training, field support, and technical services.

**Geo Semiconductor Inc** HQ
101 Metro Dr Ste 620
San Jose CA 95110
P: 408-638-0400   F: 408-638-0443   PRC:86
www.geosemi.com
Email: sales@geosemi.com
Estab: 2009

Herve Brelay, VP of Software Engineering
Michael Yin, Principal Engineer
J. Hurtado, Imaging Engineer
Paul Russo, Founder
John Casey, VP

Provider of imaging solutions. The company specializes in the design and fabrication of image sensors and multimedia processing engines.

**Geo-Tech Information Solutions** HQ
PO Box 418150
Sacramento CA 95841
P: 916-941-8300  F: 916-941-6578  PRC:142
geo-techsolutions.com
Emp: 1-10

Keith Betchley, Principal

Provider of concierge services in the environmental and natural hazard disclosure risk management field.

**Geochemical Research Laboratory** HQ
20 Portola Green Cir
Portola Valley CA 94028-7833
P: 650-851-1410  PRC:131
www.geochemicalresearch.com
Estab: 1986

Richard Hughes, Director of Geochemical Research Laboratory

The company uses energy dispersive x-ray fluoresence spectrometry to determine the element composition of volcanic rocks. The company specializes in archaelogical geochemistry.

**Geofusion Inc** HQ
2830 Smith Grade
Santa Cruz CA 95060
P: 831-458-1418  PRC:316
www.geofusion.com
Email: sales@geofusion.com
Emp: 1-10  Estab: 2001

Alexander Matiyevsky, Founder

Specializes in virtual reality and 3D visualization services. The company offers software development kits.

**Geometrics Inc** HQ
2190 Fortune Dr
San Jose CA 95131
P: 408-954-0522  F: 408-954-0902  PRC:13
www.geometrics.com
Email: sales@geometrics.com
Estab: 1969

Tommy Ngo, Senior Engineer of Electronic Technology
Steve Rosen, Director of Marketing
Craig Lippus, VP of Seismic Division
Ron Royal, VP of Operations
Bart Hoekstra, Seismic Product Manager

Manufacturer of geo-physical instruments and equipment. The company also focuses on the sales and distribution.

**Geosyntec** BR
3043 Gold Canal Dr Ste 100
Rancho Cordova CA 95670
P: 916-637-8048  PRC:138
www.geosyntec.com
Emp: 11-50 Estab: 1983

Greg Corcoran, Principal Engineer
Jane Soule, Senior Engineer
Avery Blackwell, Senior Staff Engineer
Claire Wildman, Engineer
Eric Suchomel, Project Engineer

Provider of consulting and engineering services. The company serves customers in the oil and gas, refining, petrochemical, and waste management industries.

**Gerlinger Steel & Supply Co** HQ
1527 Sacramento St
Redding CA 96001
P: 530-243-1053  F: 530-246-4736  PRC:80
www.gerlinger.com
Email: sales@gerlinger.com
Emp: 1-10  Estab: 1929

Jo Gerlinger, CFO
Judy Waldear, Outside Sales Representative
Jason Bahr, Manager

Provider of metal products and industrial services. The company offers metalworking machinery and supplies.

**Geron Corp** HQ
149 Commonwealth Dr Ste 2070
Menlo Park CA 94025
P: 650-473-7700  F: 650-473-7750  PRC:268
www.geron.com
Email: info@geron.com
Estab: 1990
Sales: $1M to $3M

John Scarlett, President
Olivia Bloom, EVP
Andrew Grethlein, EVP
Melissa Kelly Behrs, EVP
Stephen Rosenfield, EVP

Developer of telomerase inhibitors, imetelstat, in hematologic myeloid malignancies. The company is engaged in clinical trials.

**GestureTek Inc** HQ
5255 Stevens Creek Blvd Ste 162
Santa Clara CA 95051
P: 408-506-2206  F: 408-732-3977  PRC:322
www.gesturetekmobile.com
Email: support@gesturetekmobile.com
Estab: 1986

Patti Jordan, Director of Marketing and Communications
Yoshitaro Kumagai, SVP

Provider of gesture-based user interfaces for mobile devices. The company offer services to the gaming and entertainment industries.

**Gevicam Inc** HQ
691 S Milpitas Blvd Ste 115
Milpitas CA 95035
P: 408-262-5772  F: 408-262-0962  PRC:68
gevicam.com
Email: info@gevicam.com
Estab: 2006

Toshi Hori, President

Developer and manufacturer of industrial cameras based on Gigabit Ethernet Technology for the industrial, scientific, and homeland security markets.

**GigaGen Inc** HQ
1 Tower Pl Ste 750
S San Francisco CA 94080
P: 415-978-2101  PRC:34
www.gigagen.com
Estab: 2010

Carter Keller, CEO
David Johnson, CEO
Adam Adler, CSO
David Bell, COO
Osborne Clarke, Senior Attorney

Provider of biotherapeutical solutions. The company offers recombinant polyclonal hyperimmune gammaglobulin.

**Gigamat Technologies** HQ
47269 Fremont Blvd
Fremont CA 94538-6502
P: 510-770-8008  PRC:159
www.gigamat.com
Email: sales@gigamat.com

Edmond Abrahamians, President

Provider of polishers, sorters, grinders, crystal pullers, and related accessories. The company offers services to the industrial sector.

**Gigamon** HQ
3300 Olcott St
Santa Clara CA 95054-5455
P: 408-831-4000  F: 408-831-4001  PRC:324
www.gigamon.com
Email: inside.sales@gigamon.com
Estab: 2004

Nathan Berg, Director of Hardware Engineering
Shane Buckley, President
Paul Hooper, CEO
Dave Arkley, CFO
Shehzad Merchant, CTO

Provider of traffic visibility solutions for enterprises, data centers, and the education, financial, and healthcare industries.

**Gigatest Labs** HQ
2324 Walsh Ave
Santa Clara CA 95051
P: 408-524-2700  F: 408-524-2777  PRC:209
www.gigatest.com
Estab: 1989

Harry Christie, VP of Sales

Provider of measurement and probing products for the electronics industry. The company offers test equipment and fixtures for modeling and simulation.

**Gigwalk Inc** HQ
535 Mission St Floor 14
San Francisco CA 94105
P: 888-237-5896  PRC:323
www.gigwalk.com
Email: sales@gigwalk.com
Estab: 2010

Sandeep Banisetti, Software Engineering Intern
Sriram Yadavalli, CEO
Molly Gallatin, VP of Marketing
Brian Niffen, Technical Account Manager
Carlos Ramirez, Quality Analyst

Provider of analytics and collaboration tools and they are used in the management of mobile work force.

**Gigya Inc** HQ
2513 E Charleston Rd
Mountain View CA 94043
P: 650-353-7230  PRC:322
www.sap.com

Christian Klein, Co-CEO
Jennifer Morgan, Co-CEO
Juergen Mueller, CTO
Luka Mucic, CFO
Anthony Coletta, CFO

Provider of widget distribution, content sharing, and advertising platform. The company caters to the needs of social web.

**Gilead Palo Alto Inc**                    BR
    7601 Dumbarton Cir
    Fremont CA 94555
P: 510-739-8400   F: 510-739-8401      PRC:258
www.gilead.com
Email: csafety@gilead.com

Daniel Day, Chairman
Johanna Mercier, CCO
Andrew Dickinson, CFO
Jyoti Mehra, EVP of Human Resources
Taiyin Yang, EVP of Pharmaceutical Development
and Manufacturing

Provider of biopharmaceutical research services.
The company discovers and develops medicines
to treat life-threatening diseases.

**Gilead Sciences Inc**                     HQ
    333 Lakeside Dr
    Foster City CA 94404
P: 650-574-3000   F: 650-578-9264      PRC:268
www.gilead.com
Email: corporate_development@gilead.com
Estab: 1987
Sales: Over $3B

Daniel Day, Chairman
Johanna Mercier, CCO
Andrew Dickinson, CFO
Jyoti Mehra, EVP of Human Resources
Taiyin Yang, EVP of Pharmaceutical Development
and Manufacturing

Provider of medicines for the treatment of liver
diseases, hematology, oncology, and other cardiovascular diseases.

**Gilmour Craves**                          HQ
    455 Irwin St Ste 201
    San Francisco CA 94107
P: 415-431-9955   F: 415-431-9905      PRC:323
gilmourcraves.com
Email: info@gilmourcraves.com
Estab: 1996

Joanne Walker, Production Manager
David Gilmour, Creative Director
Nathan Craves, Site Support Manager
Paul Lyons, Senior Web Developer
Matt Browne, Senior Designer

Provider of graphic design, advertising, media
planning, strategic marketing, and print management services.

**Gilsson Technologies**                    HQ
    2576 Barrington Ct
    Hayward CA 94545
P: 510-940-7777   F: 510-740-3459      PRC:68
www.gilsson.com
Estab: 2001

Ming Ho, President

Manufacturer of GPS systems and accessories.
The company offers external GPS antenna
mounts and GPS antenna network splitter kits.

**GiS Planning Inc**                        HQ
    1 Hallidie Plz Ste 760
    San Francisco CA 94102
P: 415-294-4775   F: 415-294-4770      PRC:325
gisplanning.com
Estab: 1998

Pablo Monzon, Managing Director
Jeff Suneson, Director of Client Services
David Battles, Regional Director

Provider of geographic information systems. The
company is engaged in the building of patent-pro-
tected site selection website.

**GitHub Inc**                              HQ
    88 Colin P Kelly Jr St
    San Francisco CA 94107
P: 877-448-4820                        PRC:315
github.com
Estab: 2007

Keith Ballinger, SVP of Engineering
Nat Friedman, CEO
Erica Brescia, COO
Mike Taylor, CFO
Jason Warner, CTO

Provider of an online platform that allows users to
learn, store and share codes with individuals.

**Glacier Microelectronics Inc**            HQ
    990 Richard Ave Ste 105
    Santa Clara CA 95050
P: 408-244-0778                        PRC:212
glaciermicroelectronics.com
Email: info@glaciermicroelectronics.com

Paul McCambridge, CEO
Dave Byrd, CTO

Developer of mixed signal semiconductor devices.
The company's products include synthesizers and
RFIC devices.

**Glaser & Associates Inc**                 HQ
    4808 Sunrise Dr
    Martinez CA 94553
P: 925-228-3200   F: 925-228-3220      PRC:80
www.glaserbolt.com
Email: customerservice@glaserbolt.com
Estab: 1964

William Glaser, Founder

Manufacturer and distributor of fastening solutions.
The company offers bolts, screws, rods & studs,
and anchors.

**Glassbeam Inc**                           HQ
    2350 Mission College Blvd Ste 777
    Santa Clara CA 95054
P: 408-740-4600   F: 408-740-4601      PRC:322
www.glassbeam.com
Email: info@glassbeam.com
Estab: 2009

Puneet Pandit, Co-Founder
Pramod Sridharamurthy, VP of Products and India
Operations
Mohammed Guller, Head of Machine Learning
Sashi Reddi, Strategic Advisor
Eric Milledge, Strategic Advisor

Provider of support solutions and it serves the
medical, storage, and wireless networking industries.

**Glasspoint Solar Inc**                    HQ
    47669 Fremont Blvd
    Fremont CA 94538
P: 415-778-2800   F: 415-762-1966      PRC:135
www.glasspoint.com
Email: info@glasspoint.com
Estab: 2009

Manish Chandra, Senior Mechanical Engineer
David Allsworth, CFO
Ali Zaabi, Information Technology Manager
Katie Struble, Marketing Communication Manager
John O'Donnell, VP of Business Development

Manufacturer of solar steam generators for the
oil and gas industry. The company is engaged in
design and installation services.

**Glenmount Global Solutions**              HQ
    630 Airpark Rd Ste G
    Napa CA 94558
P: 707-258-8400   F: 707-258-8465      PRC:304
www.glenmountglobal.com
Estab: 1978

Tom Nelson, EVP of Western Region of Glen-
mount Global Solutions
Brant Jorgenson, Senior Project Manager
Kristin Worrell, Scientist

Provider of industrial equipment control, energy
management, and other systems. The company
serves automotive, food, chemical, and other
sectors.

**GLF Integrated Power Inc**                HQ
    4500 Great America Pkwy Ste 210
    Santa Clara CA 95054
P: 408-239-4326                        PRC:126
glfipower.com
Email: info@glfipower.com
Estab: 2013

Stephen Bryson, VP of Engineering

Manufacturer of power switch devices for smart
phones, mobile health devices, laptops, remote
sensors, wearables, SSD modules, and off
batteries.

**Gliamed Inc**                             HQ
    1072 S De Anza Blvd Ste A107-538
    San Jose CA 95129
P: 408-457-8828                        PRC:257
www.gliamed.com
Email: info@gliamed.com
Estab: 2001

Barry Dickman, CEO
John McCartney, Senior Director of Project Management

Provider of drugs for the regeneration of skin,
cardiac muscle, cartilage, bone, brain and other
tissues.

**Global Cybersoft Inc**                    HQ
    5960 Inglewood Dr Ste 200
    Pleasanton CA 94588
P: 424-247-1226   F: 925-468-0408      PRC:322
www.globalcybersoft.com
Email: sales@globalcybersoft.com
Estab: 2000

Chris Nguyen, VP
Toan Ngo, Director

Provider of software development and IT outsourcing services, such as systems integration
and maintenance.

**Global Food Technologies**  HQ
802 N Douty St
Hanford CA 93230
P: 559-589-0100  F: 559-589-0111  PRC:43
www.globalfoodtech.com
Email: info@globalfoodtech.com
Emp: 1-10

Jan Statman, Director of Sales
Aaron Ormond, Director of Science

Focuses on the proprietary design, development, and production of commercial products and services to enhance food safety.

**Global Infotech Corp**  HQ
2890 Zanker Rd Ste 202
San Jose CA 95134
P: 408-567-0600  PRC:322
www.global-infotech.com
Email: info@global-infotech.com
Estab: 1996

Alka Singh, Account Manager
Praful Sharma, Staffing
Rhea Kapoor, Technical Recruiter
Manish Sharma, Recruiter

Provider of software services. The company's software solutions focuses on staff augmentation, telecom, systems integration, chip design, ERP, and CRM domains.

**Global Marketing Associates Inc**  HQ
751 N Canyon Pkwy
Livermore CA 94551
P: 510-887-2462  F: 510-887-1882  PRC:42
www.gmaherbs.com
Email: operation@gmaherbs.com

Jack Klein, Founder
Clement Yu, President
Kenneth Yeung, Chairman

Providers of nutrition supplements to health care industry. The company supply innovative and quality ingredients to health care industry.

**Global Presenter**  BR
728 Charcot Ave
San Jose CA 95131
P: 408-526-0221  F: 408-526-0212  PRC:316
www.globalpresenter.com
Email: sales@globalpresenter.com
Estab: 2000

Pat Kelley, Area Sales Manager
Murray Lewis, Sales Consultant

Designer and builder of meeting room communication systems. The company is a provider of design, delivery, and system integration solutions.

**Global Software Resources**  HQ
4447 Stoneridge Dr
Pleasanton CA 94588
P: 925-249-2200  F: 925-249-2203  PRC:323
www.gsr-inc.com
Email: corporate@gsr-inc.com
Estab: 1992

Fred Valdez, Information Technology Manager
Pallavi Mehta, Client Relationship Manager

Provider of application development, business intelligence, testing and mobile computing, and collaboration services.

**Global Touchpoints Inc**  DH
3005 Douglas Blvd Ste 108
Roseville CA 95661
P: 916-878-5940  F: 916-878-5951  PRC:326
touchpointsinc.com
Email: info@touchpointsinc.com
Emp: 11-50 Estab: 2004

Udayan Chanda, President
Seema Chanda, Director of Human Resources
Bhabani Panda, Senior Talent Manager
Harish Bhat, Principal
Amit Rout, Talent Acquisition Specialist

Provider of application development, big data engineering, and analytics solutions and it serves the public and commercial sectors.

**Global Unichip Corp**  HQ
2851 Junction Ave Ste 101
San Jose CA 95134
P: 408-382-8900  F: 408-321-8299  PRC:208
www.globalunichip.com
Email: sales@ip-semantics.com

Ken Chen, President
Daniel Chien, CFO
Louis Lin, SVP of Design Service
Chiang Fu, SVP
Chen-Yang Pan, Senior Director

Provider of technology and embedded CPU design services. The company's services include package engineering, test engineering, and supply chain management.

**Globalfoundries Inc**  BR
2600 Great America Way
Santa Clara CA 95054
P: 408-462-3900  PRC:86
www.globalfoundries.com
Estab: 2009

Thomas Caulfield, CEO
Cary Haggard, Chief Audit Executive
Doug Devine, SVP
Mike Hogan, SVP
Ron Sampson, SVP

Provider of semiconductor foundry services. The company deals with design tools, IP suppliers and ASIC partners.

**GlobalSoft Inc**  HQ
255 N Market St Ste 285
San Jose CA 95117
P: 408-564-0307  PRC:322
www.globalss.com
Email: info@globalss.com
Estab: 1998

Raj Lohia, CEO
Robert Caplan, COO

Provider of software consultancy services. The company offers application development, training program management, and engineering services.

**Globant**  BR
875 Howard St Fl 3 Ste 320
San Francisco CA 94103
P: 877-215-5230  PRC:323
www.globant.com
Email: info@globant.com

Andres Angelani, Chief Solutions Officer
Andrew Burgert, General Manager
Juan Pereyra, Solutions Partner

Provider of software products and solutions for cloud computing, mobile, gaming, enterprise consumerization, and data visualization.

**Globavir Biosciences Inc**  HQ
5150 El Camino Real Ste A-32
Los Altos CA 94022
P: 650-351-4495  PRC:34
www.globavir.com
Email: info@globavir.com
Estab: 2011

Shalabh Gupta, Founder

Developer of biotechnology products. The company specializes in small molecule drugs to treat cancer and infectious diseases.

**Glooko Inc**  HQ
303 Bryant St
Mountain View CA 94041
P: 650-720-5310  PRC:194
www.glooko.com
Email: support@glooko.com
Estab: 2010

Yogen Dalal, Founder
Rick Altinger, CEO
Vikram Singh, Marketing Manager
Sidhtara Tep, Marketing Manager
Sam Wynbrandt, Director of Product Management

Provider of diabetes management solution. The company offers platform to allow patients manage diabetes data and collaborate with their doctors.

**Glowlink Communications Technology Inc**  HQ
1215 Terra Bella Ave
Mountain View CA 94043
P: 650-237-0220  F: 650-237-0225  PRC:68
www.glowlink.com
Email: ushq@glowlink.com
Estab: 2000

Harry Zhu, Engineer
Chris Vo, Manager of Product Testing

Provider of emitters, global monitoring, and uplink power control devices. The company also offers alignment and commissioning services.

**Glycomine Inc**  HQ
733 Industrial Rd
San Carlos CA 94070
P: 650-401-2016  PRC:196
glycomine.com
Email: info@glycomine.com

Peter McWilliams, CEO
Kathlene Powell, Senior Director CMC & Quality Operations
Lisa Koch-Hulle, Senior Director of Regulatory Affairs
Mary Bagger, Senior Director of Clinical Operations
Teppei Shirakura, Scientific Director of Chemistry

Developer of therapy solutions for the treatment of orphan diseases of glycosylation. The company focusses on genetic disorders of lipid glycosylation and protein.

**Glyphic Technology**  HQ
156 E Dana St
Mountain View CA 94041-1508
P: 650-964-5311  F: 650-967-4379  PRC:323
www.glyphic.com
Email: frontdesk2@glyphic.com
Estab: 1992

Mark Lentczner, Chief Architect
Leslie Smith, COO
Regan Bauman, Director of Marketing

Provider of software design and architecture solutions. The company focuses on internet, server, desktop, mobile, and embedded systems.

**Gm Associates Inc**  HQ
9824 Kitty Ln
Oakland CA 94603
P: 510-430-0806  F: 510-562-9809  PRC:286
www.gmassoc.com
Email: info@gmassoc.com
Estab: 1974

Bryan Casiano, Materials Engineer
Karen Beato, VP
Deborah Camp, VP
Deacon French, Manager

Manufacturer of quartz fabricated products and etch chambers. The company offers machining, slicing, cutting, and other services.

**Gm Nameplate Inc**  BR
2095 O'Toole Ave
San Jose CA 95131
P: 408-435-1666  PRC:163
www.gmnameplate.com
Estab: 1954

David Fabris, General Manager

Manufacturer of die cut components. The company offers components for shielding, insulators, adhesives, and fabricated parts.

**Go Balto**  DH
500 Oracle Pkwy
Redwood Shores CA 94065
P: 650-506-7000  PRC:325
www.oracle.com
Estab: 2008

Zach Chen, Software Engineer
Dirk Shim, Director of Customer Support
Kim Mason, Senior Visual Designer

Provider of solutions for biotechnology and pharma. The company has products include Activate and Analyze.

**Go!Foton Corp**  BR
100 Century Center Ct Ste 203
San Jose CA 95112
P: 408-831-0131  F: 732-469-9654  PRC:63
gofoton.com
Estab: 1918

Simin Cai, President
Michael Zammit, VP

Supplier of optical materials and components. The company focuses on markets such as industrial, image and scanning, and biomedical research.

**GoEngineer**  BR
3350 Scott Blvd Bldg 44
Santa Clara CA 95054
P: 408-213-1580  F: 408-213-1581  PRC:224
www.goengineer.com
Email: info@goengineer.com
Estab: 1984

Phillip Hughes, CEO
Robert Lipp, COO
Ron Burleson, Inside Sales Coordinator
Bruce Gale, Sales Manager Southern Calif

Provider of solid works engineering and Oracle agile PLM products. The company offers services to the business sector.

**Gold Standard Diagnostics Corp**  HQ
2851 Spafford St
Davis CA 95618
P: 855-268-6940  F: 530-759-8012  PRC:20
www.gsdx.us
Emp: 1-10  Estab: 2006

John Griffiths, President
Jennifer Roth, VP of Product Development
Sarah Freligh, Buyer

Provider of laboratory diagnostic solutions. The company specializes in diagnosis of autoimmune diseases, bacterial and viral diseases.

**Gold Star Web**  HQ
2499 Bruce Rd
Chico CA 95928
P: 530-891-1841  F: 530-891-4025  PRC:67
www.gs-web.com
Email: design@gs-web.com
Emp: 1-10  Estab: 1995

Sherry Gillis, Owner

Provider of website design and hosting, development and web marketing, technical support, and programming services.

**Golden Altos Corp**  HQ
402 S Hillview Dr
Milpitas CA 95035
P: 408-956-1010  F: 408-956-1212  PRC:211
goldenaltos.com
Email: sales@goldenaltos.com
Estab: 1984

Roger Soroten, Equipment Engineer
Arlen Chou, President
Winston Kuok, Manager
Rosa Ho, Manager

Designer and manufacturer of burn-in boards. The company also provides post wafer fabrication services.

**Golden Pacific Laboratories LLC**  HQ
4720 W Jennifer Ave Ste 105
Fresno CA 93722
P: 559-275-9091  PRC:303
www.gplabs.com
Email: info@gplabs.com
Emp: 1-10

Sami Selim, President
Thomas Moate, General Manager

Provider of state of the art independent contract research services for agricultural, residential and occupational exposure assessments.

**Golden Plastics Corp**  HQ
8465 Baldwin St
Oakland CA 94621
P: 510-569-6465  F: 510-569-9741  PRC:280
goldenplasticscorp.com
Email: sales@goldenplasticscorp.com
Estab: 1953

Robert Pardee, Plastic Technician

Provider of thermoforming services. The company specializes in part trimming, part design, and tooling.

**Golden State Assembly LLC**  HQ
47823 Westinghouse Dr
Fremont CA 94539
P: 510-226-8155  PRC:62
gsassembly.com
Email: customerservice@gsassembly.com
Estab: 2006

Cesar Madrueno, President

Provider of turn-key engineered solutions for wiring, harnessing and custom cable assembly requirements. The company serves the industrial sector.

**Golden Valley Systems Inc**  HQ
1605 S Main St Ste 113
Milpitas CA 95035
P: 408-934-5898  F: 408-934-5896  PRC:325
www.gvsystems.com
Email: sales@gvsystems.com
Estab: 1989

Irene Lee, Accounting Manager

Provider of enterprise integration solutions. The company offers technical, IT consulting, and green energy services.

**Golder Associates Inc**  BR
425 Lakeside Dr
Sunnyvale CA 94085
P: 408-220-9223  F: 408-220-9224  PRC:142
www.golder.com
Estab: 1960

Bruce Downing, Principal Senior Geotechnical Engineer
David Sprott, Principal
Paul Bedell, Principal
Paul Dittrich, Principal
Scott Fidler, Principal

Provider of ground engineering and environmental services. The company serves business organizations and the industrial sector.

**Gongio**  HQ
814 Mission St 4th Fl
San Francisco CA 94103
P: 650-276-3068  PRC:319
www.gong.io/
Estab: 2015

Amit Bendov, Co-Founder
Eilon Reshef, Co-Founder
Eran Aloni, COO
Tim Riitters, CFO
Sandi Kochhar, Chief Human Resources Officer

Developers of revenue intelligence platform that delivers insights at scale.

**Gonsel'S Machine Shop**    HQ
8710 G St
Oakland CA 94621
P: 510-569-8086   F: 510-569-0433    PRC:80
www.gonsels.com
Email: gonsels@gmail.com
Estab: 1953

Jim Gonsalves, Owner
Ellen Gonsalves, Secretary

Provider of CNC and millwork, inspection, fabrication, and re-machining services. The company serves the food and beverage industry.

**Gooch & Housego**    BR
44247 Nobel Dr
Fremont CA 94538
P: 650-300-5744    PRC:74
www.goochandhousego.com
Estab: 1948

Mark Webster, CEO
Chris Jewell, CFO
Katherine Holiday, Human Resources Manager
Michael Bailey, Electronic Systems Engineering Manager

Manufacturer of precision optical components. The company also focuses on related sub-systems and systems.

**Good Dog Design**    HQ
21 Corte Madera Ave Ste 2
Mill Valley CA 94941
P: 415-383-0110    PRC:322
www.gooddogdesign.com
Email: info_us@gooddogdesign.com
Estab: 1992

Jerry Chai, Software Engineer
Laurie Chu, Project Manager
Tom Gooden, Principal
Wesley Huang, Front End Developer

Provider of digital designing services. The company offers web development & designing and mobile application services.

**Goodman Ball Inc**    HQ
3639 Haven Ave
Menlo Park CA 94025
P: 650-363-0113   F: 650-363-8294    PRC:152
www.goodmanball.com
Email: sales@goodmanball.com
Estab: 1983

Emmett Summers, Buyer
Tom Krpan, Controller

Manufacturer of spare military equipment for the U.S. Government. The company's in-house capabilities include CNC machining and structural welding.

**Google Inc**    HQ
1600 Amphitheatre Pkwy
Mountain View CA 94043
P: 650-253-0000    PRC:322
www.google.com
Estab: 1998

Peter Kiehtreiber, Staff Software Engineer
Sergey Brin, Co-Founder
Catherine Lacavera, VP of Legal
Iris Chen, VP of Legal
Ashish Pimplapure, Director of Strategic Partnerships

Provider of search engine to make world's information universally accessible. The company specializes in internet-related services and products.

**Gorilla Circuits Inc**    HQ
1445 Oakland Rd
San Jose CA 95112
P: 408-294-9897   F: 408-297-1540    PRC:211
www.gorillacircuits.com
Email: info@gorillacircuits.com

Crescencio Gutierrez, General Manager
Ted Nguyen, General Manager of Assembly Operations
Long Vu, Information Technology Manager
Karl Rauch, VP of Sales
Dave Williams, Military Program Manager

Provider of printed circuit engineering and fabrication solutions. The company caters to electronic companies.

**Grabber Construction Products Inc**    BR
205 Mason Cir
Concord CA 94520
P: 800-869-1375   F: 407-295-9305    PRC:80
www.grabberman.com
Email: deckmaster@deckmaster.com

Roland Snyder, President
Shawn Rogers, Outside Sales Representative
Tracy Yoder, Operations Manager
Terry Boswell, National Accounts Manager

Manufacturer of fasteners and machine tools. The company also specializes in distribution and other services.

**Grabit Inc**    HQ
751 Laurel St Ste 534
San Carlos CA 94070
P: 408-642-1830    PRC:311
www.grabitinc.com
Email: info@grabitinc.com
Estab: 2011

Dave Rocki, VP of Engineering
Harsha Prahlad, Co-Founder
Greg Miller, CEO
Ron Wilderink, CFO
Ken Lo, Director of Business Development

Inventor of electroadhesion technology. The company specializes in parts handling, package handling, and each pick applications.

**Gracenote Inc**    HQ
2000 Powell St Ste 1500
Emeryville CA 94608
P: 510-428-7200    PRC:323
www.gracenote.com
Estab: 1999

Jaysu Jeyachandran, Engineering Lead
Karthik Rao, President
Amilcar Perez, Chief Revenue Officer
Kay Johansson, CTO
Simon Adams, Chief Product Officer

Provider of music, video, and automotive solutions. The company focuses on television businesses and entertainment products.

**Graham Machining & Design**    HQ
1529 Addison St
Berkeley CA 94703
P: 510-848-2395    PRC:80
grahammachining.com
Estab: 1987

An Tran, Quality Engineer
Richard Graham, Owner

Provider of designing and fabrication services. The company develops inspection tools, fasteners, band saws, drill presses, and pedestal grinders.

**GRAIL Inc**    HQ
1525 O'Brien Dr
Menlo Park CA 94025
P: 650-542-0372    PRC:25
grail.com
Email: bd@grail.com
Estab: 2016

George Golumbeski, President
Jennifer Cook, CEO
Angela Lai, CTO
Fred Kohler, VP
Alex Aravanis, VP

Provider of research services and clinical study programs for the detection of cancer at an early stage.

**Granberg International**    HQ
1051 Los Medanos St
Pittsburg CA 94565
P: 925-380-9400    PRC:159
www.granberg.com
Email: info@granberg.com
Estab: 1954

Erik Granberg, President
John Mahley, General Manager
Ben Hawkins, Sales Manager
Lindsey Granberg, Marketing Manager
Sylvia Mahley, Office Manager

Manufacturer of saw chain maintenance tools to repair and sharpen saw chain & attachments. The company offers brush attachments and cutting bars.

**Grandflow Inc**    HQ
135 Lindberg Ave Ste D
Livermore CA 94551
P: 925-443-0855   F: 925-443-9428    PRC:323
www.grandflow.com
Email: support@grandflow.com
Estab: 1973

Matt Rusca, President
Tom Allen, COO
John Rusca, CFO
Jack Vallerga, Sales Manager
Jack Parker, Marketing Manager

Provider of e-cataloging and marketing automation solutions. The company offers print production, warehousing, and document management services.

**Grandt Line Products**    HQ
1040 Shary Ct Ste B
Concord CA 94518
P: 925-671-0143    PRC:84

Phyllis Nishimori, Secretary

Manufacturer and wholesaler of model railroad miniatures in plastics. The company's services include design and installation.

**Granite Digital** HQ
3101 Whipple Rd
Union City CA 94587
P: 510-471-6442   F: 510-471-6267      PRC:62
www.granitedigital.com
Email: info@granitedigital.com

Frank Gabrielli, Owner

Manufacturer of external diagnostic peripherals. The company is engaged in troubleshooting and maintenance services.

**Granite Horizon LLC** HQ
8153 Elk Grove Blvd  Ste 20
Elk Grove CA 95758-5965
P: 916-647-6350      PRC:320
www.granitehorizon.com
Emp: 1-10  Estab: 2007

Greg McAvoy-Jensen, CEO

Provider of content management solutions. The company offers design, development, project management, and user and developer training services.

**Graybug Vision Inc** HQ
275 Shoreline Dr Ste 450
Redwood City CA 94065
P: 650-487-2800      PRC:34
graybug.com
Email: info@graybug.com
Estab: 2011

Frederic Guerard, CEO
Christy Shaffer, Chairman
Dan Salain, CTO
Daniel Geffken, Interim CFO
Karl Trass, VP of Global Regulatory Affairs

Developer of pharmaceutical products for the treatment of blindness, including neovascular, glaucoma, and corneal graft rejection.

**Grayland Environmental** HQ
1807 Valdora St
Davis CA 95618-6315
P: 530-756-1441      PRC:139
graylandenvironmental.com
Email: grayland@prodigy.net
Emp: 1-10  Estab: 1993

Jeffrey Clayton, Principal Geologist

Provider of environmental and natural resources protections services. The company offers environmental engineering, geological and geophysical services.

**Greatlink International Inc** RH
44168 S Grimmer Blvd
Fremont CA 94538
P: 510-657-1667   F: 510-445-1588      PRC:97
www.greatlink.com
Email: ussales@greatlink.com
Estab: 1979

Herbert Hou, Operation Manager

Manufacturer of cable assemblies and related products for the medical, aerospace, and automotive industries.

**Green Plug** HQ
2694 Bishop Dr Bishop Ranch 2 Ste 209
San Ramon CA 94583
P: 925-867-2781      PRC:212
www.greenplug.us
Email: info@greenplug.us
Estab: 2006

Kathleen Harrison, Personal Assistant to CEO

Developer and provider of digital controller technology solutions and products to the consumer electronics markets.

**Green Source Automation LLC** HQ
3506 Moore Rd
Ceres CA 95307
P: 209-531-9163   F: 209-531-9171      PRC:311
www.greensourceautomation.com
Email: info@greensourceautomation.com
Emp: 1-10  Estab: 2009

Cliff Olson, Senior Service Engineer
Jim Frias, President

Provider of redefining solutions for diary industry. The company also offers technology for milking process.

**Greening Associates** HQ
PO Box 277
Ben Lomond CA 95005
P: 831-336-1745      PRC:34
www.greeningassociates.com
Email: info@greeningassociates.com
Emp: 1-10  Estab: 1992

Suzanne Schettler, Owner
Laurie Kiguchi, Botanist
Kevin Browning, Habitat Restorationist

Provider of biological consultants and landscape contracting services. The company specializes in revegetation plans, wildlife surveys, and coastal restoration.

**Greenliant Systems** HQ
3970 Freedom Cir Ste 100
Santa Clara CA 95054
P: 408-200-8000   F: 408-200-8099      PRC:212
www.greenliant.com
Email: media@greenliant.com
Estab: 2010

Kevin Zhang, Principal Engineer
Virgil Wright, Manager of QA Engineering
Bing Yeh, CEO
Arthur Kroyan, VP of Business Development & Marketing
Danny Ma, Senior Director

Developer of storage solutions for the embedded systems. The company offers solid-state storage, controllers, and specialty flash memory.

**Greenvity Communications Inc** HQ
2150 Trade Zone Blvd Ste 203
San Jose CA 95131
P: 408-935-9370   F: 408-273-6597      PRC:212
greenvity.com
Email: info@greenvity.com
Estab: 2011

John Tero, VP of Engineering
Hung Nguyen, President
Edward Cho, VP of Sales & Marketing
Jenny Lin, RF System Manager

Designer and developer of semiconductor solutions for home gateways, electric vehicles, and lighting products.

**Greenwood Machine & Fabrication Inc** HQ
2517 Railroad Ave
Ceres CA 95307-1099
P: 209-538-2277   F: 209-538-3065      PRC:80
www.greenwoodmachine.net
Email: info@greenwoodmachine.net
Emp: 1-10  Estab: 1976

Todd Greenwood, Owner
Kristin Willis, Office Manager

Provider of repair and fabrication services for commercial and industrial equipment. The company's customers include private companies and military contractors.

**Grey San Francisco** BR
1001 Front St
San Francisco CA 94111
P: 415-403-8000      PRC:63
www.grey.com

Owen Dougherty, Chief Communications Officer
Will Egan, SVP

Provider of advertising, planning, sports marketing solutions. The company also focuses on customer relationship management.

**Greytrix** RH
350 Rhode Is Ste 240
San Francisco CA 94103
P: 888-221-6661      PRC:323
www.greytrix.com
Email: us.sales@greytrix.com
Estab: 1997

Jiten Somani, COO
Amarjeet Prajapati, Developer
Krishna Shah, Senior Software Developer

Provider of integration and migration solutions. The company deals in analytics, cloud, mobility, and ERP/CRM consulting.

**Grid Net Inc** HQ
909 Montgomery St Ste 104
San Francisco CA 94133
P: 415-872-5097      PRC:323
www.grid-net.com
Estab: 2006

Ray Bell, CEO
Will Bell, CTO
Collin Breakstone, VP of Sales & Customer Solutions
Scott Maroney, VP of Engineering

Developer of products for applications such as advanced metering, distribution monitoring and control, and premise area networking.

**GridGain Systems Inc** HQ
1065 E Hillsdale Blvd Ste 220
Foster City CA 94404
P: 650-241-2281   F: 925-369-7193      PRC:325
www.gridgain.com
Email: info@gridgain.com
Estab: 2007

Nikita Ivanov, CTO
Abe Kleinfeld, President
Eoin Connor, CFO
Terry Erisman, VP of Marketing
Dane Christensen, Digital Marketing Manager

Developer of a Java and Scala-based cloud computing middleware for a wide range of multimedia applications.

## Grio HQ

201 Post St 11th Fl
San Francisco CA 94108
P: 415-395-9525 PRC:319
grio.com
Email: info@grio.com
Estab: 2008

Adam Keating, Director of Engineering
Chris Grelik, Manager of Engineering
Kristine Morinaka, Manager of Engineering
Meg McGinty, Director of Marketing
Brooks Mason, Managing Director

Specializes in web, iOS, and Android development.

## Groundwater & Environmental Services Inc BR

882 Dover Cir
Benicia CA 94510
P: 866-507-1411 PRC:142
gesonline.com
Estab: 1985

Rich Evans, SVP of Engineering
Ann Downey, President
Edward Van Woudenberg, CEO
Anthony Kull, Chairman
Michael Lemon, CFO

Provider of environmental consulting services.
The company serves customers in the oil and gas,
government, and petroleum markets.

## Group Manufacturing Services Inc HQ

1928 Hartog Dr
San Jose CA 95131
P: 408-436-1040 F: 408-436-7967 PRC:80
www.groupmanufacturing.com
Email: sales@groupmanufacturing.com
Estab: 1981

Don Bader, Quality Assurance Manager

Manufacturer of precision sheet metal fabrication,
precision machining, and design support services.

## Group Seven Corp HQ

2027 O'Toole Ave
San Jose CA 95131
P: 408-435-7477 F: 408-435-7478 PRC:209
www.group7.net
Email: info@group7.net
Estab: 1984

Jerry O'Connor, President

Producer of turnkey solutions to support high mix
and low volume needs. The company also offers
Vendor Managed Inventory (VMI) services.

## Growing Energy Labs Inc HQ

111 New Montgomery St Ste 500
San Francisco CA 94105
P: 415-857-4354 PRC:323
geli.net
Email: info@geli.net
Estab: 2010

Ryan Wartena, Co-Founder

Developer of software to integrate, network, and
economically operate energy storage systems.
The company is engaged in analysis services.

## Gs Cosmeceutical Usa Inc HQ

131 Pullman St
Livermore CA 94551-5128
P: 925-371-5000 F: 925-960-1400 PRC:251
www.gscos.com
Email: sales@gscos.com
Estab: 1998

Gogi Sangha, Founder
Gurkirpal Sandhu, COO
Sandhya Singh, Director of Research & Business
Development
Ronald Brooks, Associate Director of Operations
Norman Poon, IS Manager

Provider of custom contract manufacturing services. The company offers skin and personal care
products.

## Gsi Technology HQ

1213 Elko Dr
Sunnyvale CA 94089
P: 408-331-8800 F: 408-331-9795 PRC:96
www.gsitechnology.com
Email: apps@gsitechnology.com
Estab: 1995
Sales: Over $3B

Douglas Schirle, CFO
Hayden Ir, CFO
Jyn-Bang Shyu, Director of Analog Design
Alex Hsueh, Product Manager
Tai Um, Senior Manager of Product Engineering

Provider of telecommunication and networking
services. The company is also engaged in sales
and distribution.

## Gt Nexus Inc HQ

1111 Broadway 7th Fl
Oakland CA 94607
P: 510-808-2222 F: 510-808-2220 PRC:325
gtnexus.com
Email: information@gtnexus.com
Estab: 1998

Kurt Cavano, SVP

Provider of supply chain, transportation, and
investment management solutions. The company
serves retailers and manufacturers.

## Guardant Health Inc HQ

505 Penobscot Dr
Redwood City CA 94063
P: 855-698-8887 PRC:44
guardanthealth.com
Email: clientservices@guardanthealth.com
Emp: 454 Estab: 2012
Sales: $30M to $100M

AmirAli Talasaz, President
Helmy Eltoukhy, CEO
Derek Bertocci, CFO
Michael Wiley, Chief Legal Officer

Provider of sequencing and rare-cell diagnostics
services focusing on cancer. The company serves
the healthcare sector.

## Guardian Analytics HQ

2465 Latham St Ste 200
Mountain View CA 94040
P: 650-383-9200 PRC:325
guardiananalytics.com
Email: info@guardiananalytics.com
Estab: 2005

Terry Austin, President
Laurent Pacalin, CEO
Hue Harguindeguy, CFO
Stephen Walsh, VP of Global Sales
Lien McCarthy, Director of Sales

Provider of enterprise and community banking
solutions. The company is engaged in training and
applied fraud analysis services.

## Guerra Technologies Inc HQ

5205 Prospect Rd 135-157
San Jose CA 95129
P: 408-526-9386 PRC:61
Estab: 1993

Maria Guerra, Owner
Jorge Guerra, CFO

Designer and manufacturer of RF technology
related products. The company also offers consulting and evaluation services.

## Guided Wave Inc HQ

3033 Gold Canal Dr
Rancho Cordova CA 95670
P: 916-638-4944 F: 916-635-8458 PRC:11
www.guided-wave.com
Email: gwsales@guided-wave.com
Emp: 11-50 Estab: 1983

Ken Gruessing, Electronic Engineer
Roger Schirmer, Owner
Susan Foulk, President
Justin Stirrat, Manufacturing
Scott Shores, Senior Mechanical Designer

Provider of online optical measurements services.
The company caters to process analytical chemistry needs.

## Guidetech HQ

1300 Memorex Dr
Santa Clara CA 95050
P: 408-733-6555 PRC:19
www.guidetech.com
Email: sales@guidetech.com
Estab: 1988

Freddy Ben-Zeev, CTO

Developer of time measurement instruments. The
company mainly caters to the semiconductor test
industry.

## Guntert & Zimmerman Const Div Inc HQ

222 E Fourth St
Ripon CA 95366
P: 209-599-0066 F: 209-599-2021 PRC:159
www.guntert.com
Email: gz@guntert.com
Emp: 11-50 Estab: 1942

Ronald Guntert, CEO
R. K. Shaw, VP of International Sales & Service
Rolf Guntert, EVP of Sales
John Eisenhour, Sales Manager

Manufacturer of canal lining equipment, concrete
batch plants, and other special equipment. The
company serves the industrial sector.

**Guzik Technical Enterprises**    HQ
2443 Wyandotte St
Mountain View CA 94043
P: 650-625-8000   F: 650-625-9325    PRC:95
www.guzik.com
Email: sales@guzik.com
Estab: 1982

Sergey Melnik, Senior Hardware Engineer
Mikhail Konstantinov, Senior RF Engineer
Sergey Konshin, Senior Electronics Engineer
Boris Telitsyn, Hardware Design Engineer
Edward Vikutan, Production Engineer

Manufacturer of test equipment for the computer industry. The company is involved in sales, training, and software downloads.

**Gynesonics**    HQ
600 Chesapeake Dr
Redwood City CA 94063
P: 650-216-3860   F: 650-299-1566    PRC:187
gynesonics.com
Estab: 2005

Annabelle Presa, Associate Engineer
Hyeonsoo Chang, Senior Mechanical Engineer
Brian Placek, Senior Engineer
Tom Caballero, Engineer
Jordan Bajor, COO

Manufacturer and developer of therapeutic devices and related supplies for the treatment of uterine fibroids in women.

**H & M Precision Machining**    HQ
504 Robert Ave
Santa Clara CA 95050
P: 408-982-9184   F: 408-982-9186    PRC:80
h-mprecisionmachining.com
Estab: 1960

Bruce Harvey, President

Provider of precision manufacturing solutions. The company offers screw machines, CNC turning, CNC milling, and sawing services.

**H J Hirtzer & Associates Inc**    HQ
570 Valdry Ct Unit C-4
Brentwood CA 94513
P: 925-931-1450    PRC:179
www.hjhirtzer.com
Email: info@hjhirtzer.com

Jay Hirtzer, President

Manufacturer of steel links. The company specializes in the fabrication of insulated links for shipping and defense industries.

**H M Franklin Associates**    HQ
1860 Hollyview Dr
San Ramon CA 94582
P: 925-735-8848    PRC:324
www.hmfa.com
Email: info@hmfa.com
Estab: 1984

Hal Franklin, Principal

Provider of data processing consulting and related services. The company serves the government and corporate industries.

**H P Machine & Engineering Inc**    HQ
2150 Oakland Rd
San Jose CA 95131
P: 408-383-9075   F: 408-383-9027    PRC:80
www.hpmachine.com
Estab: 1974

Nicole Peisker, Office Manager

Provider of job shop, prototype machining, CNC, and wire EDM services. The company offers services to the industrial sector.

**H-Square Corp**    HQ
3100 Patrick Henry Dr
Santa Clara CA 95054-0701
P: 408-982-9108   F: 408-982-9183    PRC:209
www.h-square.com
Email: info@h-square.com
Estab: 1975

Myron Moreno, General Manager
Paul Vierhus, Production Manager
Caroline Montojo, Customer Service Manager

Designer and manufacturer of tools and equipment. The company caters to the wafer fabrication industry.

**H5**    HQ
595 Market St
San Francisco CA 94105
P: 415-625-6700    PRC:40
www.h5.com
Email: info@h5.com
Estab: 1999

Rajan VT, Director of Engineering
Josh Simms, Founder
Todd Barber, Owner
Nicolas Economou, Chairman
Katie Romweber, Executive Managing Director of Human Resources

Provider of investigation solutions. The company offers hosting, case preparation, and keyword consulting services.

**HackerRank**    HQ
700 E El Camino Real Ste 300
Mountain View CA 94041
P: 415-900-4023    PRC:319
www.hackerrank.com
Email: support@hackerrank.com
Estab: 2009

Jawahar Malhotra, SVP of Engineering
Vivek Ravisankar, Co-Founder
Harishankaran Karunanidhi, Co-Founder
Ramesh Sethuraman, CFO
Maria Chung, VP of Human Resources

Technology recruiting tool that helps tech recruiters and hiring managers to identify and hire talents.

**Hahnemann Labortories Inc**    HQ
1940 Fourth St
San Rafael CA 94901
P: 415-451-6978   F: 415-451-6981    PRC:268
www.hahnemannlabs.com
Email: info@hahnemannlabs.com
Estab: 1985

Michael Quinn, Founder

Manufacturer of homeopathic medicines. The company offers dispensing kits, first aid kits, and also professional kits.

**Haig Precision Manufacturing Corp**    HQ
3616 Snell Ave
San Jose CA 95136
P: 408-378-4920   F: 408-629-3459    PRC:2
www.haigprecision.com
Estab: 1960

Karl-Heinz Lachnit, Agent

Manufacturer of precision parts and assemblies. The company focuses on sheet metal, CNC milling and turning, stamping, welding, and power coating.

**Halo Electronics Inc**    HQ
2880 Lakeside Dr Ste 116
Santa Clara CA 95054
P: 650-903-3800   F: 650-903-9300    PRC:209
www.haloelectronics.com
Email: info@haloelectronics.com
Estab: 1991

Jeffrey Heaton, VP of Technical Marketing

Manufacturer of electromagnetic components. The company's products include DC/DC transformers, inductors, and RF transformers.

**Halo Neuro Inc**    HQ
735 Market 4th Fl
San Francisco CA 94103
P: 415-851-3338    PRC:189
www.haloneuro.com
Email: support@haloneuro.com
Estab: 2013

Brett Wingeier, CTO
Daniel Chao, CEO
Mark Mastalir, CMO

Developer of neurotech platform. The company offers services to athletes, elite teams, and organizations.

**Halus Power Systems**    HQ
2539 Grant Ave
San Leandro CA 94579
P: 510-278-2212   F: 510-278-2211    PRC:297
www.halus.com
Email: service@halus.com
Estab: 2000

Lindsey Kendall, Engineering Manager
Louis Rigaud, General Manager
Sean Scarlett, Production Manager
Kenneth Fries, Technical Services Manager

Manufacturer of renewable energy products specializing in wind turbines and controls. The company offers design and remanufacturing services.

**Hamamatsu Corp**    BR
2875 Moorpark Ave Ste 200
San Jose CA 95128
P: 408-261-2022    PRC:13
www.hamamatsu.com
Email: usa@hamamatsu.com

Connie Lazarus, Account Sales Manager
Reji Samuel, VP
Mai Idzkowski, Customer Service Representative

Manufacturer of devices for the generation and measurement of infrared, visible, and ultraviolet light.

**Hammett & Edison Inc** HQ
470 Third St W
Sonoma CA 95476-6509
P: 707-996-5200  F: 707-996-5280  PRC:304
h-e.com
Estab: 1952

Rajat Mathur, VP
Neil Olij, Staff Engineer
Andrea Bright, Staff Engineer
William Hammett, President
Kelly Aldana, Marketing Coordinator

Provider of engineering and related services to
the wireless telecommunications and broadcasting
industries.

**Hammon Plating Corp** HQ
890 Commercial St
Palo Alto CA 94303
P: 650-494-2691  PRC:53
www.hammonplating.com
Email: sales@hammonplating.com

Glenn Phinney, President
Dil Jeer, Quality Manager

Supplier of metal plating applications. The company also provides supply chain management
solutions.

**Hana Microelectronics Inc** BR
3100 De La Cruz Blvd Ste 204
Santa Clara CA 95054
P: 408-452-7474  F: 408-452-7488  PRC:212
www.hanagroup.com
Email: info-request@hanaus.com

Richard Han, CEO

Provider of electronic manufacturing services.
The company focuses on PCBs, circuit assembly,
RFID devices, LEDs, coil windings, and other
products.

**Hand Biomechanics Lab Inc** HQ
77 Scripps Dr Ste 104
Sacramento CA 95825
P: 916-923-5073  F: 916-920-2215  PRC:303
www.handbiolab.com
Email: info@handbiolab.com
Emp: 1-10  Estab: 1979

John Agee, President
Kim Sutton, Accountant

Provider of Biomechanics treatment devices. The
company offers products like Agee Turnkey FCS,
WristJack, and Digit Widget.

**Hanger Prosthetics & Orthotics Inc** BR
1248 32nd St
South Sacramento CA 95816
P: 916-452-5724  F: 916-452-2715  PRC:190
hangerclinic.com
Email: hanger@westwicke.com
Emp: 11-50 Estab: 1861

Vinit Asar, President

Provider of prosthetic and orthotic components
and services. The company serves hospitals,
patients, and the healthcare industry.

**Hanger Prosthetics & Orthotics Inc** BR
436 E Yosemite Ave Ste C
Merced CA 95340
P: 209-725-1295  F: 209-725-1769  PRC:189
hangerclinic.com
Email: hanger@westwicke.com
Emp: 11-50 Estab: 1861

Richard Mason, Area Practice Manager

Provider of orthotic and prosthetic services and
products. The company also offers clinically differentiated programs to its clients.

**Hantronix Inc** HQ
10080 Bubb Rd
Cupertino CA 95014-4132
P: 408-252-1100  F: 408-252-1123  PRC:169
www.hantronix.com
Estab: 1975

Andrew Kim, Sales Manager
Ali Mosiemi, Sales Manager
Max Mun, Sales Manager
Richard Choi, Sales Manager
Richard Kim, Regional Sales Manager

Producer of standard character and graphic
modules, notebook displays, and custom liquid
crystal displays.

**Harmon Ie** HQ
691 S Milpitas Blvd
Milpitas CA 95035
P: 408-907-1339  PRC:322
www.harmon.ie
Estab: 1993

Yaacov Cohen, Co-Founder
David Lavenda, VP of Product Strategy
Ashley Wilson, Business Development Executive

Provider of SharePoint applications for Outlook,
mobile, and desktop platforms. The company
offers records and knowledge management
services.

**Harmonic Inc** HQ
4300 N First St
San Jose CA 95134
P: 408-542-2500  F: 408-542-2511  PRC:60
www.harmonicinc.com
Email: support@harmonicinc.com
Emp: 375  Estab: 1988
Sales: $300M to $1 Billion

Dennis Mitchell, Engineering Manager
Patrick Harshman, President
Carolyn Aver, CFO
Sanjay Kalra, SVP
Nimrod Ben-Natan, SVP

Provider of production and delivery solutions. The
company serves the broadcast, media, service
providers, and post production markets.

**Harris & Bruno International** HQ
8555 Washington Blvd
Roseville CA 95678
P: 916-781-7676  F: 916-781-3645  PRC:159
www.harris-bruno.com
Email: info@harris-bruno.com
Emp: 1-10  Estab: 1948

Jim Riga, Director of Engineering & Service
Bryan Ball, Process Engineer
Larry Feuling, Product Development Engineer
Michael Sticlaru, Engineer
Nick Bruno, President

Provider of printing and coating solutions. The
company offers web coaters, chambers, offline
coaters, pumps, and other products.

**Harris & Lee Environmental Sciences
LLC** HQ
120 Ross Valley Dr
San Rafael CA 94901
P: 415-287-3007  PRC:142
hlenv.com
Email: request@hlenv.com

Elaine Everest, Manager
Robert Harris, Senior Scientist
Cathy Neumann, Senior Environmental Specialist

Provider of environmental consulting services.
The company's services include environmental
risk management, and preliminary environmental
assessment.

**Harris Industrial Gases** HQ
8475 Auburn Blvd
Citrus Heights CA 95610
P: 916-725-2168  F: 916-725-2117  PRC:51
www.harrisgas.com
Emp: 11-50

Aaron Haupt, COO
Tim Lettich, General Manager
Erron Ernst, Sales Manager
Steve Willis, Welding Sales
Scott Rosenberg, Account Manager

Provider of specialty gases welding equipment.
The company also offers services for welding
supplies and safety equipment.

**Hawk Ridge Systems** BR
4 Orinda Way Ste 100B
Orinda CA 94563
P: 510-482-6110  PRC:316
hawkridgesys.com
Email: info@hawkridgesys.com
Estab: 1996

Gabriel Rapisardo, VP of Sales
Sheree Carlson, Partner

Provider of 3D design software solutions. The
company offers CAD, analysis consulting, product
data management, and solid works services.

**Hawk Ridge Systems** BR
575 Clyde Ave Ste 420
Mountain View CA 94043
P: 877-266-4469  F: 650-428-1868  PRC:319
www.hawkridgesys.com
Email: info@hawkridgesys.com

Cameron Carson, VP of Engineering
Justin Ludwig, Senior Support Engineer
Mike Frey, Senior Support Engineer
Ricky Huynh, Senior Application Engineer
Dale Ford, President

Provider of parametric 3D product design and
analysis services. The company also offers data
management tools.

**Hayes Manufacturing Services Inc** HQ
1178 Sonora Ct
Sunnyvale CA 94086-2316
P: 408-730-5035   F: 408-730-5367      PRC:80
hayesms.com
Email: mail@hayesms.com
Estab: 1991

Brian Fanceour, President
Maria Villanueva, Purchasing Agent
James Rouse, Director of Operations

Provider of machining, fabrication, tooling, prototyping, reverse engineering, and design assistance services.

**Hayward Quartz Technology Inc** HQ
1700 Corporate Way
Fremont CA 94539
P: 510-657-9605   F: 510-657-6404      PRC:80
www.haywardquartz.com
Email: sales@haywardquartz.com
Estab: 1984

Hoang Nguyen, Quality Control Manager
Dean Gehrman, Sales Manager
Ken Jacoby, VP of Operations
Rafik Ayvazyan, Senior Research Developer

Manufacturer of machined and fabricated parts.
The company exclusively caters to the semiconductor industry.

**Hazelcast Inc** HQ
350 Cambridge Ave Ste 100
Palo Alto CA 94306
P: 650-521-5453   F: 650-521-5453      PRC:323
hazelcast.com
Email: sales@hazelcast.com
Estab: 2008

Enes Akar, Co-Founder
Kelly Herrell, CEO
Greg Luck, CTO
Marion Smith, CFO
Chris Wilson, VP of Worldwide Sales

Provider of training, consulting, and technical support services. The company serves the logistics
and healthcare industries.

**Hb Fuller** BR
10500 Industrial Ave
Roseville CA 95678
P: 916-787-6000                        PRC:47
www.hbfuller.com
Emp: 11-50 Estab: 1887

Zhiwei Cai, SVP of Engineering Adhesives
Jim Owens, President
Ted Clark, EVP
Abe Rezai, VP
John Corkrean, EVP

Manufacturer of adhesives and sealants. The company also specializes in paints and other specialty
chemical products.

**Hbr Industries** HQ
2261-B Fortune Dr
San Jose CA 95131
P: 408-988-0800   F: 408-432-0104      PRC:209
www.hbrindustries.com
Estab: 1979

Mike Ryssemus, President
Karl Steinkraus, Quality Control Manager
Karl Ryssemus, Director of Operations

Provider of electronics manufacturing services.
The company offers coil solutions and services for
the medical, military, and semiconductor industry.

**Hcl America Inc** LH
330 Potrero Ave
Sunnyvale CA 94085
P: 408-733-0480   F: 408-733-0482      PRC:323
www.hcltech.com
Estab: 1988

Sayantan Basu, General Manager
Ajay Dhankhar, General Manager
Vasant Shejwal, General Manager
Pankaj Gupta, General Manager
Satish Singh, General Manager

Provider of software and IT solutions, infrastructure, engineering, research and development, and
outsourcing services.

**Headsets Com Inc** HQ
211 Austin St
San Francisco CA 94109
P: 415-351-5897                        PRC:71
www.headsets.com
Email: info@headsets.com
Estab: 1997

Mike Faith, CEO
Chris Bentley, Marketing Coordinator

Provider of office telephone headsets. The company also offers cellphone, computer, and cordless
phone headsets.

**Headway Technologies Inc** HQ
682 S Hillview Dr
Milpitas CA 95035
P: 408-934-5300   F: 408-934-5353      PRC:95
www.headway.com
Email: info@headway.com
Estab: 1994

Jinsong Wang, Director of Product Engineering
Robert Gee, Project Engineering Manager
Qingjun Qin, Senior Process Development
Engineer
Wenjie Chen, President
Dan Burris, Senior Facilities Manager

Designer and manufacturer of hard-disk drives.
The company is engaged in installation and technical support services.

**Healfies** HQ
180 Sansome St 4th Fl
San Francisco CA 94104
P: 415-312-4525                        PRC:270
healfies.com
Estab: 2015

Helyson Velasco, Founder
Denis Avdic, Co-Founder
Alvin Yip, COO

Developer and provider of software platform to
manage health information. The company serves
the healthcare sector.

**Health Advances LLC** BR
601 Montgomery St Ste 1850
San Francisco CA 94111
P: 415-834-0800   F: 781-392-1484      PRC:191
healthadvances.com
Email: info@healthadvances.com
Estab: 1992

Balazs Felcsuti, VP
Carrie Jones, VP
Claudia Graeve, VP
Darcy Krzynowek, VP
Kate McLaughlin, VP

Provider of consulting services to the healthcare
industry. The company offers clinical development,
product positioning, lifecycle management, and
more.

**Health Fidelity Inc** HQ
4 W Fourth Ave Ste 501
San Mateo CA 94402
P: 650-727-3300                        PRC:324
healthfidelity.com
Email: info@healthfidelity.com
Estab: 2011

Kyle Patton, VP of Engineering
Nicole Keegan, Director of Engineering
Steve Whitehurst, CEO
Robin Lloyd, Chief Commercial Officer
Brian McDonald, CFO

Provider of natural language processing technology and inference platform to analyze vast amounts
of unstructured data for clinical and financial
insights.

**Health Gorilla Inc** DH
256 Gibraltar Dr Ste 101
Sunnyvale CA 94089
P: 844-446-7455   F: 844-446-7455      PRC:326
www.healthgorilla.com

Sergio Wagner, CSO
Andrei Zudin, CTO
Steve Yaskin, CEO
Ali Zaman, VP of Marketing
Vladimir Davydenko, VP of Technology

Focuses on diagnostic tests. The company offers
services to clinics, patients and healthcare organizations.

**Healthcare Systems & Technologies
LLC** HQ
3675 Mt Diablo Blvd Ste 100B
Lafayette CA 94549
P: 800-290-4078                        PRC:326
www.hstpathways.com
Email: hstsales@hstpathways.com
Estab: 2005

Tom Hui, President
Harry Yee, CTO
Karlene Ochoa, VP of Operations
Chris Beavor, SVP of Strategic Development

Designer and developer of AC surgery software.
The company offers services to corporate management companies.

**Healthline Networks** HQ
660 Third St
San Francisco CA 94107
P: 415-281-3100                        PRC:315
www.healthline.com
Estab: 2006

David Kopp, CEO
Cheryl Kim, CFO
Andy Atherton, SVP of Revenue Operations
Jeff Bernstein, SVP
Tracy Rosecrans, SVP of Marketing

Provider of health information.

## HealthLoop                                    HQ
605 Ellis St Ste 100
Mountain View CA 94043
P: 408-418-0998                              PRC:188
healthloop.com
Email: privacy@healthloop.com
Emp: 11-50 Estab: 2009

AdriaÃ°n Francke, Software Engineer
Jordan Shlain, Founder
Todd Johnson, CEO
Mayank Thanawala, CTO
Ben Rosner, Chief Medical Information Officer

Provider of healthcare solutions. The company
deals with the integration of doctors, patients and
care-givers.

## Healthstar Laser Services Inc                 HQ
PO Box 806
Lafayette CA 94549
P: 415-937-1942                              PRC:172
www.healthstarlaser.com
Estab: 1991

Allen Kent, Founder

Provider of web-based scheduling and mobile
laser services. The company serves the healthcare sector.

## HeartFlow Inc                                 RH
1400 Seaport Blvd Bldg B
Redwood City CA 94063
P: 650-241-1221                              PRC:270
www.heartflow.com
Email: info@heartflow.com
Estab: 2007

Jason Sarnoski, senior Field Engineer
Charles Taylor, Founder
Dana Mead, President
Baird Radford, EVP
Renata Naoumov, VP

Provider of analysis technology that creates a
personalized 3D model of the coronary arteries
and analyzes the impact that blockages have on
blood flow.

## HeartVista Inc                                HQ
4984 El Camino Real Ste 102
Los Altos CA 94022
P: 650-800-7937                              PRC:189
www.heartvista.com
Email: info@heartvista.com

William Overall, CTO
Juan Santos, President

Developer of magnetic resonance imaging (MRI)
applications and development tools to aid in the
diagnosis of cardiovascular disease.

## Heat & Control Inc                            HQ
21121 Cabot Blvd
Hayward CA 94545-1132
P: 510-259-0500   F: 510-259-0600    PRC:159
www.heatandcontrol.com
Email: info@heatandcontrol.com
Estab: 1950

Eric Brick, General Manager
Alex Caridis, Designer

Manufacturer of food processing and packaging
equipment systems. The company offers inspection system, product handling equipment, and
coating system.

## Heatscape Inc                                 HQ
318 Digital Dr
Morgan Hill CA 95037
P: 408-778-4615   F: 408-778-4616    PRC:159
heatscape.com
Estab: 1999

Ali Mira, President
Yashar Mira, Principal
Michael Mira, Global Manager

Designer and manufacturer of thermal solutions.
The company engages in thermal analysis, thermal testing, and finite element analysis.

## Heco Inc                                      HQ
2350 Del Monte St
West Sacramento CA 95691
P: 916-372-5411   F: 916-373-0952    PRC:163
www.hecogear.com
Email: info@hecogear.com
Emp: 1-10   Estab: 1974

Mike Jacobs, President
John Woodhouse, Director of Sales
Allen Rasmussen, VP

Manufacturer of planetary speed reducers. The
company's applications include swing drives,
wheel drives, conveyor drives, winch drives,
mixers, and augers.

## Heco Pacific Manufacturing Inc               HQ
1510 Pacific St
Union City CA 94587
P: 510-487-1155   F: 510-487-4466    PRC:183
www.hecopacific.com
Estab: 1961

German Morales, Project Engineer
Dwight Chew, Project Engineer
Allan Alarab, President
Rita Kachhia, Accounting Manager

Manufacturer and seller of industrial cranes and
overhead cranes. The company offers custom
engineering, maintenance, testing, and other
services.

## Heinzen Manufacturing International          HQ
405 Mayock Rd
Gilroy CA 95020
P: 408-842-7233   F: 408-842-6678    PRC:159
www.heinzen.com
Estab: 1978

Alan Heinzen, Founder
Jeffrey Goulding, Sales Manager

Designer and manufacturer of custom food
processing equipment. The company specializes
in shakers, bin dumpers, fruit equipment, and
trimlines.

## Heirloom Computing Inc                        HQ
3000 Danville Blvd
Alamo CA 94507
P: 510-573-3579                              PRC:322
heirloomcomputing.com
Estab: 2010

Gary Crook, President
Kevin Moultrup, COO
Mark Haynie, CTO

Focuses on the transformation of enterprise
applications. The company offers services to the
industrial sector.

## Heliodyne Inc                                 HQ
4910 Seaport Ave
Richmond CA 94804
P: 510-237-9614   F: 510-237-7018    PRC:151
heliodyne.com

Ole Pilgaard, President
David Stampfli, Sales Manager

Manufacturer of solar water heating systems
for the residential and commercial sectors. The
company focuses on installation, repair, and
replacement.

## Heliospectra                                  RH
1005 Northgate Dr
San Rafael CA 94903
P: 888-942-4769                              PRC:34
www.heliospectra.com
Email: sales@heliospectra.com
Estab: 2006

Lori Kunz, Director of Business Development

Focuses on lighting technology solutions. The
company is engaged in product development and
serves the environmental sector.

## HelioWorks Inc                                HQ
1275 Fourth St Ste 614
Santa Rosa CA 95404
P: 707-578-7200   F: 707-578-7200    PRC:243
www.helioworks.com
Email: info@helioworks.com
Estab: 2003

Don Wood, Owner

Manufacturer of infrared lamps. The company's
products are used in non-dispersive infrared gas
detectors for medical and industrial applications.

## Helium                                        HQ
1663 Mission St Ste 250
San Francisco CA 94103
P: 415-510-2110                              PRC:68
www.helium.com
Email: info@helium.com
Estab: 2013

Marc Nijdam, CTO

Provider of connectivity solutions for smart devices. The company offers services to individuals and
businesses.

**Helix Environmental Planning Inc**    HQ
7578 El Cajon Blvd
La Mesa CA 91942
P: 619-462-1515   F: 619-462-0552    PRC:142
www.helixepi.com
Emp: 11-50 Estab: 1995

Dianne Ransby, Human Resource & Accounting
Manager
Kelly Bayne, Senior Biologist
Michael Brewer, GIS Specialist

Provider of landscape architecture, planning, environmental consulting, restoration, and regulatory
permitting services.

**Hellwig Products Company Inc**    HQ
16237 Ave Ste 296
Visalia CA 93292
P: 559-734-7451   F: 559-734-7460    PRC:80
www.hellwigproducts.com
Email: customerservice@hellwigproducts.com
Emp: 1-10   Estab: 1946

Ben Knaus, Director of Engineering
Mark Hellwig, President
Nancy Souza, Director of Business

Provider of sway control and load control products
for trucks and SUV's. The company also offers
fleet solution services.

**Hemostat Laboratories**    HQ
PO Box 790
Dixon CA 95620
P: 800-572-6888   F: 707-678-1150    PRC:23
www.hemostat.com
Email: sales@hemostat.com
Estab: 1980

Jim McElligott, President

Provider of defibrinated sheep blood and other
animal blood products for cell culture, diagnostic
and veterinary applications.

**Hench Control Inc**    HQ
3701 Collins Ave Ste 8C
Richmond CA 94806
P: 510-741-8100   F: 510-307-9804    PRC:130
www.henchcontrol.com
Email: sales@henchcontrol.com
Estab: 1989

Alex Daneman, President
Tyler Winters, Software Developer

Manufacturer of modular energy management
systems. The company's products find application
in industrial refrigeration.

**Hepco Inc**    HQ
150 San Lazaro Ave
Sunnyvale CA 94086
P: 408-738-1880   F: 408-732-4456    PRC:159
www.hepcoblue.com
Email: info@hepcoblue.com
Estab: 1970

Tim Hoffman, President
Blair Kummer, Senior Recruiter

Manufacturer of electronic components. The
company offers design, fabrication, analysis, and
testing tools for semiconductor industries.

**Hera Systems Inc**    HQ
7013 Realm Dr
San Jose CA 95119
P: 844-437-2797    PRC:9
www.herasys.com
Email: info@herasys.com
Estab: 2013

Bobby Machinski, CEO
Dave Squires, VP
Jolyon Thurgood, VP
Jim Opfer, Senior Advisor

Provider of satellite information and analytics
that collects images of Earth, for commercial and
government organizations to monitor and make
decisions.

**Hermes Microvision Inc**    BR
1762 Automation Pkwy
San Jose CA 95131
P: 408-597-8600    PRC:86
www.asml.com

Ji Wang, System Integration Engineer
Liping Feng, Staff Software Engineer
Hao Hu, System Engineer
Derrick Lee, Network Dev Engineer II
Crystal Shen, Testing Engineer

Manufacturer of e-beam inspection and monitoring
solution. The company caters to the semiconductor manufacturing sector.

**Hero Digital**    HQ
55 Francisco st Ste 350
San Francisco CA 94133
P: 415-409-2400    PRC:325
herodigital.com
Estab: 2006

Patrick Frend, President
David Kilimnik, CEO
Tony Rems, CTO
Owen Frivold, General Manager
Kenneth Parks, CMO

Provider of website and mobile design and development services. The company specializes in
mobile marketing programs.

**Heroku Inc**    HQ
1 Market St Ste 300
San Francisco CA 94105
P: 866-278-1349    PRC:323
www.heroku.com
Email: pr@heroku.com
Estab: 2007

Mike Pyle, CTO

Designer and developer of cloud application platforms. The company offers services to software
developers.

**Heron Innovators**    HQ
1025 Nichols Dr
Rocklin CA 95765
P: 916-408-6601   F: 916-408-6991    PRC:144
www.heroninnovators.com
Email: info@heroninnovators.com
Emp: 1-10   Estab: 1975

John Barsotti, President
Boguslaw Marcinkowski, Owner

Provider of suspended air flotation systems. The
company offers products for processing tomato,
food, meat, and others.

**Hesco**    HQ
693 Whitney St
San Leandro CA 94577
P: 510-568-1380    PRC:198
www.hescoxray.com
Estab: 1990

Michael Depinna, President
Roger Owen, Director of Business

Provider of portable x-ray imaging services. The
company offer services for power plants, bridges,
dams, refineries, and more.

**Hesse Mechatronics Inc**    LH
225 Hammond Ave
Fremont CA 94539
P: 408-436-9300   F: 484-231-3232    PRC:126
www.hesse-mechatronics.com
Email: info@hesse-mechatronics.com
Estab: 1986

Kristian Oftebro, Senior Process Development
Engineer

Developer of equipment for heavy wire and thin
wire wedge bonders. The company also focuses
on the marketing aspects.

**Hexcel Corporation**    BR
11711 Dublin Blvd
Dublin CA 94568-2832
P: 800-444-3923    PRC:4
www.hexcel.com
Estab: 1948

Nick Stanage, Chairman
Tim Swords, President of Industrial
Patrick Winterlich, EVP
Paul Mackenzie, SVP
Kimberly Hendricks, SVP

Provider and manufacturer of advanced material
solutions. The company manufactures everything
from a carbon fiber to finished aircraft structures.

**HGST Inc**    HQ
5601 Great Oaks Pkwy
San Jose CA 95119
P: 408-717-6000    PRC:95
www.hgst.com
Estab: 2003

Siva Sivaram, President of Technology
Mike Cordano, President
Stephen Milligan, CEO
Martin Fink, CTO
Michael Ray, Chief Legal Officer

Provider of hard disk drives and external storage
products. The company is engaged in technical
support services.

**Hiebert Sculpture Works**    HQ
540 47th St
Oakland CA 94609
P: 510-654-7488   F: 510-654-2723    PRC:163
www.hieberts.com
Email: hsw@hieberts.com
Estab: 1966

Billy Hiebert, Owner

Provider of plastic injection molding products. The
company also offers composite epoxy tooling,
design assistance, and custom molds.

**Higgins Analytical Inc** HQ
950 N Rengstorff Ste C
Mountain View CA 94043
P: 650-988-8930  F: 650-988-8931  PRC:20
www.higanalyt.com
Email: hplc@higanalyt.com
Estab: 1994

Steve Jones, General Manager

Manufacturer and marketer of laboratory equipment and supplies. The company specializes in HPLC columns, catridges, and separations consumables.

**High Connection Density Inc** HQ
820A Kifer Rd
Sunnyvale CA 94086-5200
P: 408-743-9700  F: 408-743-9701  PRC:206
www.hcdcorp.com
Email: sales@hcdcorp.com
Estab: 1997

Shengjie Wang, Product Development Engineer
Charlie Stevenson, COO
Vishal Chetty, Web Marketing & Logistics

Supplier of electronic packaging solutions and connection technologies. The company serves communications, medical, military, and aerospace fields.

**Highfive** HQ
500 Arguello St Ste 300
Redwood City CA 94063
P: 844-464-4445  PRC:323
highfive.com
Email: sales@highfive.com
Estab: 2012

Jeremy Roy, Co-Founder

Focuses on video conferencing and re-imaging solutions. The company offers services to business organizations.

**Highland Technology Inc** HQ
18 Otis St
San Francisco CA 94103-1220
P: 415-551-1700  F: 415-551-5129  PRC:65
www.highlandtechnology.com
Email: info@highlandtechnology.com
Estab: 1984

Elizabeth Larkin, Project Coordinator
Rob Gaddi, Engineer
Karla Vega, Test Engineer Head of Test Department
Paul Bailey, Embedded Systems Engineer
Kevin Brown, Director of Business Development

Designer and manufacturer of precision analog instrumentation. The company serves laboratory research purposes.

**Highwired Inc** HQ
PO Box 420
Redwood Valley CA 95470
P: 516-785-6197  PRC:322
www.highwiredinc.com
Emp: 1-10  Estab: 1998

David Levine, Consultant
Michael Houston, District Manager

Developer of multimedia and supporting products and services. The company focuses on branding, billing, and delivery solutions.

**Hildy Licht Company Inc** HQ
897 Independence Ave Bldg 3B
Mountain View CA 94043
P: 650-962-9300  F: 650-254-1855  PRC:207
www.hildy.com
Email: keri@hildy.com

Keri Mackey, President
Cheryl Spears, Director of Operations

Provider of electric assembly and manufacturing services. The company is engaged in engineering and prototyping.

**Hill Brothers Chemical Co** BR
410 Charcot Ave
San Jose CA 95131
P: 408-599-5041  F: 408-435-1104  PRC:51
hillbrothers.com
Email: infomail@hillbrothers.com
Estab: 1923

Ron Hill, President
Tom James, CFO
Matt Thorne, EVP of Sales & Marketing
Adam Hill, Manager of Customer Service Administration
Darlene Harrison, Executive Secretary

Provider of industrial and construction chemicals. The company also offers decking systems and seaters.

**Hillstone Networks** RH
5201 Great America Pkwy Ste 420
Santa Clara CA 95054
P: 408-508-6750  PRC:325
www.hillstonenet.com
Email: inquiry@hillstonenet.com
Estab: 2006

Michael Lin, Senior Principal Engineer
Hao Dong, Senior Engineer
Tim Liu, CTO
Zhong Wang, VP

Provider of security solutions for enterprises and data center networks. The company serves Fortune 500 companies and educational institutions.

**Hilti Inc** BR
180 Pennsylvania
San Francisco CA 94107
P: 800-879-8000  F: 800-879-7000  PRC:157
www.hilti.com
Email: hnatechnicalservices@hilti.com

Christoph Loos, CEO

Developer and manufacturer of construction equipment. The company's services include trainings, engineering, administration, and tools.

**HiQ Solar Inc** HQ
1259 Reamwood Ave
Sunnyvale CA 94089
P: 408-970-9580  F: 408-753-2973  PRC:135
www.hiqsolar.com
Email: info@hiqsolar.com
Estab: 2009

Rob Howard, CEO
John Hoang, CFO
Sonia Isaac, Financial Controller

Manufacturer of solar power and renewable energy products and accessories such as communications gateway, AC splice, and inverter ballast mounting kit.

**Hirose Electric Usa Inc** BR
2841 Junction Ave Ste 200
San Jose CA 95134
P: 408-253-9640  F: 408-253-9641  PRC:76
www.hirose.com
Estab: 1937

Kazunori Ishii, President
Alicia Lalonde, Accounts Receivable Manager
Jeff Combs, Strategic Accounts Manager

Manufacturer of connectors. The company provides couplers, dividers, terminators, coaxial switches, and memory cards.

**Histo path** HQ
961 N Emerald Ave Ste D
Modesto CA 95351
P: 209-522-8240  F: 209-522-2486  PRC:36
www.histo-path.com
Email: kathy@histo-path.com
Emp: 1-10  Estab: 1974

Dan Garcia, President
Michael Garcia, VP of Business Relations and Operations
Kathy Cruz, Office Manager

Provider of histotechnology services. The company specializes in providing tissue culture slides for dermatologists.

**Hitachi America Ltd** BR
1000 Marina Blvd 5th Fl
Brisbane CA 94005-1835
P: 650-244-7400  F: 650-244-7935  PRC:60
www.hitachi-america.us
Email: vid.inquiries@hal.hitachi.com

Koji Takaichi, President
Levent Arabaci, EVP
Narayan Subramanian, Director
Jenny Bach, Procurement Manager

Manufacturer of electronic items specializing IT products. The company provides computers, home appliances, mobile phones, and supplies.

**Hitachi Chemical Diagnostics Inc** HQ
630 Clyde Ct
Mountain View CA 94043
P: 650-961-5501  F: 650-969-2745  PRC:41
www.hcdiagnostics.com
Email: info@hcdiagnostics.com
Estab: 1983

Hideki Itaya, VP of Business Development

Provider of in vitro allergy diagnostics products. The company offers alternative means of diagnosing allergy.

**Hitachi High Technologies America Inc** BR
5960 Inglewood Dr Ste 200
Pleasanton CA 94588-3355
P: 925-218-2800  PRC:11
www.hitachi-hightech.com
Email: iot.dg@hitachi-hightech.com
Estab: 2002

Masahiro Miyazaki, President
Dan Becker, Northwestern Sales Manager
Steve Joens, Nanotechnology Marketing Manager
Mary Tapia, Marketing Communications Specialist
Lorena Ferry, Director of Technology

Seller of semiconductor manufacturing equipment and analytical instrumentation and also offers electronic devices, bio-related, and other products.

**Hitachi Metals America Ltd**    BR
1920 Zanker Rd
San Jose CA 95112
P: 408-467-8900   F: 408-467-8901    PRC:157
www.hitachimetals.com
Estab: 1965

Joedel Dizon, Director of Sales

Manufacturer and marketer of metal products. The company offers cable systems, cutting tools, ceramics, sensors, and other materials.

**HMS Electronics Inc**    HQ
5711 Marsh Hawk Dr
Santa Rosa CA 95409
P: 707-584-8760    PRC:87
www.hms-electronics.com
Estab: 1985

Richard Harkey, Owner

Manufacturer of medical device components. The company offers custom made specialty component parts for x-ray machines.

**Hof Machining Inc**    HQ
2290 Ringwood Ave Unit B
San Jose CA 95131
P: 408-526-1155   F: 408-744-0443    PRC:80
www.hofmachining.com

Saju Kooplicat, Manager

Provider of exotic geometry and prototype machining services. The company's offerings include machine shop services and machining materials.

**Hogan Manufacturing Inc**    HQ
1704 First St
Escalon CA 95320
P: 209-838-2400   F: 209-838-8648    PRC:80
www.hoganmfg.com
Email: information@hoganmfg.com
Emp: 1-10   Estab: 1944

Joe DeBiasio, CFO

Provider of steel manufacturing fabrication services. The company's products include plate weldments, alloy specialties, and waste separation equipment.

**Hologic Inc**    BR
2520 Mission College Blvd Ste 202
Santa Clara CA 95054
P: 669-224-6420    PRC:186
www.hologic.com
Email: info@hologic.com

Sam London, Business Intelligence Engineer
Jay Stein, Co-founder
Peter Valenti, Division President of Breast and Skeletal Health Solutions
Stephen MacMillan, Chairman
Kevin Thornal, Division President of Diagnostics Solutions

Provider of healthcare and diagnostics. The company offers breast and skeletal healthcare and diagnostics, and GYN surgical solutions.

**Holz Rubber Co**    HQ
1129 S Sacramento St
Lodi CA 95240
P: 209-368-7171    PRC:57
www.holzrubber.com
Email: sales@holzrubber.com
Emp: 1-10   Estab: 1935

Dave Smith, President

Provider of custom molded services. The company's offerings include pump parts, slide-lag traction pads, and related supplies.

**Honda Research Institute Usa Inc**    HQ
375 Ravendale Dr Ste B
Mountain View CA 94043
P: 650-314-0400   F: 650-314-0405    PRC:150
www.honda-ri.com
Email: hri_contact@honda-ri.com
Estab: 2003

Joel Wormer, Senior Engineer
Miho Wise, Administrative Assistant
Yi-Ting Chen, Research Scientist

Manufacturer of engines. The company focuses on material science research, computer science research, and academic outreach activities.

**Hopelab**    HQ
100 California St Ste 1150
San Francisco CA 94111
P: 650-569-5900    PRC:268
www.hopelab.org
Email: communications@hopelab.org
Estab: 2001

Dan Cawley, COO
Fred Dillon, Director
Jana Haritatos, Director

Developer of technology to improve human health and well-being. The company provides online games to help young people fight cancer.

**Horiba Instruments Inc**    BR
3265 Scott Blvd
Santa Clara CA 95054
P: 408-730-4772   F: 408-730-8975    PRC:235
www.horiba.com

Atsushi Horiba, Chairman
Amy Hou, Applications Scientist

Provider of instruments and systems for automotive research and development, and process and environmental monitoring needs.

**Horizon Water & Environment**    BR
266 Grand Ave Ste 210
Oakland CA 94610
P: 510-986-1850   F: 510-350-3592    PRC:139
horizonh2o.com
Email: info@horizonh2o.com

Janis Offermann, Director
Laura Prickett, Director
Sandy Wieder, Business & Contracts Manager
Thomas Engels, Principal
Kenneth Schwarz, Founding Principal

Provider of environmental consulting services. The company specializes in watershed science, environmental compliance, and water resources management.

**Horn Machine Tools Inc**    HQ
40455 Brickyard Dr
Madera CA 93636
P: 559-431-4131   F: 559-431-4431    PRC:80
www.hornmachinetools.com
Email: info@hornmachinetools.com
Emp: 1-10   Estab: 1991

Lee Sanchez, Sales Service Engineer
Kent Horn, President
William Winn, Director of Sales
James Moffatt, Senior Service Technician

Supplier of CNC and semi-automatic tube benders. The company offers new tube benders, rebuilt tube benders, and bender rebuilding and retro-fitting.

**Hortonworks**    HQ
2550 Great America Way
Santa Clara CA 95054
P: 408-675-0983    PRC:322
hortonworks.com
Estab: 2011

Arun Murthy, Founder
Alan Gates, Co-Founder
Rob Bearden, CEO
Scott Davidson, CFO
Jean-Philippe Player, CTO

Specializes in open and connected data platforms. The company offers predictive analysis and data discovery solutions to the oil and gas industry.

**Hospital Systems Inc**    HQ
750 Garcia Ave
Pittsburg CA 94565
P: 925-427-7800   F: 925-427-0800    PRC:189
hsiheadwalls.com
Email: info@hsiheadwalls.com
Estab: 1970

David Miller, CEO
Cameron Ross, Draftsman

Manufacturer of lighting, electrical and architectural products, and related supplies. The company is engaged in installation services.

**HotLava Systems Inc**    HQ
1300 Clay St Ste 600
Oakland CA 94612
P: 510-531-1169   F: 855-468-4834    PRC:64
www.hotlavasystems.com
Email: hotinfo@hotlavasystems.com
Estab: 2003

Bill Young, President

Provider of board-level solutions for servers and appliances that operates in virtualized environments.

**Howard Wire Cloth Co**    HQ
28976 Hopkins St Ste A
Hayward CA 94545-5096
P: 510-887-8787   F: 510-786-4167    PRC:80
www.howardwire.com
Email: sales@howardwire.com
Estab: 1938

Tim Curren, Manager

Provider of screening & wire fabrication products. The company offers wire cloth, stainless steel netting, security screening, and perforated metals.

**Howlett Machine** HQ
746 Folger Ave
Berkeley CA 94710
P: 510-845-2759   F: 510-841-1018   PRC:80
www.howlettmachine.com
Email: howlettmachine@sbcglobal.net
Estab: 1921

Mike Young, Owner

Manufacturer of machine works and custom made tools. The company also offers custom test fixtures and test machines.

**HP Development Company LP** HQ
1501 Page Mill Rd
Palo Alto CA 94304
P: 650-857-1501   PRC:102
www.hp.com
Estab: 1939
Sales: Over $3B

Meg Whitman, CEO
Todd Bradley, EVP of Strategic Growth
Dion Weisler, EVP of Printing & Personal Systems
Tony Sumpster, VP

Provider of computer products that include desktops, monitors, printers and scanners, ink, toner and papers, and laptops.

**HP Inc** BR
1501 Page Mill Rd
Palo Alto CA 94304
P: 650-857-1501   PRC:108
www.hp.com

Dion Weisler, CEO
Enrique Lores, President of Imaging & Printing
Jon Flaxman, COO
Linh Ho, Senior Accountant

Provider of laptops, tablets, desktops, printers, and related accessories. The company specializes in business solutions.

**Hpm Systems Inc** HQ
70 Saratoga Ave Ste 200
Santa Clara CA 95051-7301
P: 408-615-6900   PRC:231
www.hpmsystems.com
Email: hpm@hpmsystems.com
Estab: 1997

Bert Buehler, President
Don Stevenson, Project Manager

Provider of gas monitoring control systems. The company's services include design, integration, installation, and maintenance.

**Hs&S Inc** HQ
2185 Ronald St
Santa Clara CA 95050-2838
P: 408-980-8909   F: 408-980-8894   PRC:80
www.hsands.com
Email: inquiry@hsands.com
Estab: 1979

John Servin, President

Designer and manufacturer of machine tool and custom machine manufacturing. The company offers services like CNC conversion and contract inspection.

**Hsq Technology** HQ
26227 Research Rd
Hayward CA 94545-3725
P: 510-259-1334   F: 510-259-1391   PRC:212
www.hsq.com
Email: sales@hsq.com
Estab: 1979

Igor Meyerovich, Engineer
Mike Robertson, Project Engineer
Walter Bosh, Control Systems Engineer
Harold Spence, President
Karen Santos, Administrative Supervisor

Provider of control system and energy management services, specializing in data and SCADA monitoring.

**Ht Harvey & Associates** HQ
983 University Ave Bldg D
Los Gatos CA 95032
P: 408-458-3200   F: 408-458-3210   PRC:142
www.harveyecology.com
Estab: 1970

Karin Hunsicker, CEO
Kim Kurtis, Human Resource
Michael Wong, Information Technology Service Desk Manager
Daniel Stephens, VP
Scott Terrill, VP

Provider of ecological consulting services that include ecological research, impact analysis, restoration design, and park planning.

**Ht Precision Inc** HQ
2284 Trade Zone Blvd
San Jose CA 95131
P: 408-719-1826   F: 408-719-1827   PRC:80
www.htprecision.com
Email: sales@htprecision.com

Steven Nguyen, General Manager

Provider of prototype, research, and production parts and equipment. The company serves electronics, medical, wireless, and semi-conductor industries.

**Hta Photomask** HQ
1605 Remuda Ln
San Jose CA 95112
P: 408-452-5500   F: 408-452-5505   PRC:86
www.htaphotomask.com
Email: sales@htaphotomask.com
Estab: 1984

Ken Caple, President
Mykola Kulishov, VP of Operations

Manufacturer of photo imaged products such as precision scales, resolution targets, and micro detectors.

**HTD Biosystems Inc** HQ
1061 Serpentine Ln Ste E
Pleasanton CA 94566-4800
P: 510-367-0528   F: 509-267-1491   PRC:29
www.htdcorp.com
Email: info@htdcorp.com
Estab: 2001

Rajiv Nayar, President

Focuses on the development of parenteral drugs. The company is engaged in design and product formulation services.

**Hub Strategy and Communication** BR
39 Mesa St Ste 212
San Francisco CA 94129
P: 415-561-4345   PRC:45
hubsanfrancisco.com
Email: get@hubsanfrancisco.com
Estab: 2002

Mike Reese, President
DJ O'Neil, CEO
Jason Rothman, Creative Director
Ryan Scheiber, Creative Director
Jess D'Elia, Brand Director

Provider of web design and digital advertising.

**Human Pheromone Sciences Inc** HQ
84 W Santa Clara St Ste 720
San Jose CA 95113
P: 408-938-3030   F: 408-938-3025   PRC:266
www.naturalattraction.com
Estab: 1989

Bernard Grosser, Scientist
Louis Monti, Scientist
Chloe Jennings-White, Scientist

Producer of natural attraction products and is engaged in research in the field of human pheromones in all areas of application.

**HumanAPI** HQ
1825 S Grant St Ste 450
San Mateo CA 94402
P: 650-241-8242   PRC:326
humanapi.co
Email: support@humanapi.co
Estab: 2014

George Chitouras, SVP of Engineering
Christopher Kruegel, CFO
Giovanni Vigna, CTO
Engin Kirda, Chief Architect
John DiLullo, CEO

Focuses on the integration of health data and it specializes in retrieval of health data and other healthcare applications.

**Hunter Micro Kitting & Turnkey** HQ
1840 Stone Ave
San Jose CA 95125
P: 408-977-7000   F: 408-977-7005   PRC:207
huntermicro.com
Email: sales@huntermicro.com
Estab: 2001

Scott Boyd, CEO
Bob Boyd, VP of Inside Sales

Provider of electronic solutions for emerging technology companies. The company offers design, distribution, and contract manufacturing services.

**Huntington Mechanical Laboratories Inc** HQ
13355 Nevada City Ave
Grass Valley CA 95945
P: 530-273-4135  F: 530-273-4165  PRC:209
www.huntvac.com
Email: vacman@huntvac.com
Emp: 1-10  Estab: 1969

Tami Isaacson, Accounting Controller

Manufacturer and designer of bellows, chambers, motion positioning products, and roughing accessories.

**Hurd & Associates Design** HQ
1343 Locust St Ste 209
Walnut Creek CA 94596
P: 925-930-8580  PRC:325
www.ihurd.com

Joan Hurd, Owner

Provider of print, logo, and web design, branding, marketing, advertising, and identity management services.

**Hybrid Circuits Inc** HQ
1391 Geneva Dr
Sunnyvale CA 94089
P: 408-744-9080  F: 408-744-0800  PRC:204
www.hybridcircuits.com
Email: info@hybridcircuits.com

Mike Loskutoff, Owner

Provider of contract manufacturing services. The company focuses on design, prototyping, contract manufacturing, and delivery.

**Hybrid Coating Technologies Inc** HQ
950 John Daly Blvd Ste 260
Daly City CA 94015
P: 650-491-3449  F: 650-755-3362  PRC:47
www.hybridcoatingtech.com
Email: info@hybridcoatingtech.com

Darin Nellis, Director of Sales and Marketing
Alex Trossman, VP of Israeli & European Operations
Elena Shenkar, Director of Operations
Oleg Figovsky, Director of Research & Business Development

Manufacturer of coatings and paint products including hybrid non-isocyanate polyurethane. The company serves chemical, food, and marine markets.

**Hydratech LLC** HQ
1331 S West Ave
Fresno CA 93706
P: 559-233-0876  F: 559-233-1754  PRC:159
www.hydratechcylinders.com
Emp: 1-10  Estab: 1977

Itamar Kandel, CEO
Robert Morgan, Quality Assurance Manager
Bob Hu, CMO
Dwight Nishimura, Manager
John Pauly, Manager

Manufacturer of cylinder component, hydraulic, and pneumatic cylinder with engineering capabilities needed to build superior cylinder solutions.

**Hydratight** BR
2070 Commerce Ave
Concord CA 94520
P: 925-691-4914  F: 925-691-4497  PRC:80
www.hydratight.com
Email: northamerica@hydratight.com

Clint Skala, Engineering Manager
Daniel Clayton, Field Service Engineer
Jimmy Linden, Senior Project Engineer
Avril Gray, Operations Engineer
Connie Duchan, Manufacturing Engineer

Manufacturer of flanges and mechanical connectors. The company focuses on the subsea, nuclear, wind, and mining industries.

**Hydraulic Controls Inc** HQ
4700 San Pablo Ave
Emeryville CA 94608
P: 510-658-8300  F: 510-658-3133  PRC:155
www.hydraulic-controls.com

Mark Bergh, Sales Engineer
Aaron Piper, President
Michael Murphy, Corporate Sales Manager
Pam Rodriguez, Sales Coordinator
Angela Figgs, Branch Manager

Distributor of fluid power systems. The company specializes in hydraulics, pneumatics, automation, and extrusion.

**Hydrofarm Inc** HQ
2249 S McDowell Ext
Petaluma CA 94954-5561
P: 800-634-9990  PRC:159
www.hydrofarm.com
Estab: 1977

Shanna Peterson, Staff Accountant
Sal Menicci, Sales Manager
Zoanne Kuhlman, National Director of Customer Service
Joe George, Director of Operations
Kelly Calapp, Director of Procurement

Manufacturer of hydroponics equipment. The company also supplies plant care products and garden accessories.

**Hydropoint Data Systems Inc** HQ
1720 Corporate Cir
Petaluma CA 94954
P: 800-362-8774  F: 707-769-9695  PRC:144
www.hydropoint.com
Estab: 2002

Tom McMillan, Senior Applications Engineer
Chris Spain, CEO
Peter Carlson, CTO
Chris Manchuck, SVP of Sales
Al Sonntag, VP of Operations

Provider of irrigation solutions. The company specializes in site evaluations, upgrade planning, deployment, and optimization services.

**Hygeia Laboratories Inc** HQ
1253 Commerce Ave
Woodland CA 95776
P: 530-661-1442  F: 530-661-1663  PRC:23
hygieialabs.com
Email: info@hygieialabs.com
Emp: 1-10  Estab: 1991

Jim Wallis, President

Developers of vaccines using novel technology for animals. The company offers animal pharmaceuticals for dairy cattle, sheep and poultry.

**Hynix Semiconductor America Inc** BR
3101 N First St
San Jose CA 95134
P: 408-232-8000  F: 408-232-8103  PRC:126
www.hynix.com

Seok-Hee Lee, President
Don Kim, Senior Strategic Marketing Manager
Junggeun Kim, Director

Manufacturer of DRAM products. The company focuses on consumer memory, graphics memory, mobile memory, and CMOS image sensors.

**Hyperarts Web Design Development & Maintenance** HQ
201 Fourth St Ste 404
Oakland CA 94607
P: 510-339-6084  PRC:323
www.hyperarts.com
Estab: 1998

Tim Ware, Owner
Bill Dailey, Project Manager

Provider of web design, development, and consulting services. The company performs SEO, SEM services, and web application development.

**Hypersurf Internet Services** HQ
1929 Concourse Dr
San Jose CA 95131
P: 408-325-0300  F: 408-325-0301  PRC:63
www.hypersurf.com
Estab: 1995

Don Carney, President
Richard Chen, Technical Support Manager

Provider of internet access and internet presence solutions such as dial-up, residential DSL, business DSL, fiber Ethernet, and web and email hosting.

**HyPower Hydraulics** HQ
1240 S First St
Turlock CA 95380
P: 209-632-2275  F: 209-634-6606  PRC:159
www.hypowerhydraulics.com
Email: sales@hypowerhydraulics.com
Emp: 1-10  Estab: 1911

Fick Perry, General Manager
Perry Fick, Manager

Manufacturer of hydraulic cylinders and related accessories. The company offers repair/rebuilding services.

**HyTrust Inc**  HQ
1975 W El Camino Real Ste 203
Mountain View CA 94040
P: 650-681-8100  F: 650-681-8101  PRC:317
www.hytrust.com
Email: sales@hytrust.com
Estab: 2007

Eric Chiu, Co-Founder

Provider of security, compliance, and control software for virtualization of information technology infrastructure.

**Hyve Solutions**  HQ
44201 Nobel Dr
Fremont CA 94538
P: 510-668-3877  PRC:95
hyvesolutions.com

Miguel Galaza, Prototype Engineer Manager
Roy Lee, Manager of Hardware Engineering
Bikram Singh, Platform Engineer
Anmol Jain, Server Hardware Engineer
Joseph Soares, Thermal Engineer

Designer of data center serve, storage, networking and appliance solutions. The company specializes in rack integration services.

**I-Tech Company LLC**  HQ
42978 Osgood Rd
Fremont CA 94539
P: 510-226-9226  F: 510-372-2736  PRC:169
www.i-techcompany.com
Email: info@itechlcd.com
Estab: 1998

Alan Chung, Owner

Manufacturer of panel mounts, server racks, industrial computers, touch screen displays, and related accessories.

**Iar Systems Software Inc**  RH
1065 E Hillsdale Blvd Century Plz
Foster City CA 94404
P: 650-287-4250  F: 650-287-4253  PRC:319
www.iar.com
Email: info@iar.com
Estab: 1983

Robert DeOliveira, Director of Global Strategic Sales
Anders Lundgren, Product Manager

Provider of software tools and embedded systems. The company's products include state machine tools, starter kits, and compiler and debugger tool suite.

**Ibase Technology (usa) Inc**  BR
1050 Stewart Dr
Sunnyvale CA 94085
P: 408-992-0888  F: 408-992-0808  PRC:91
www.ibase-usa.com
Email: sales@ibase-usa.com
Estab: 2000

Jeff Hsu, President
Jacky Chen, Business Development Manager

Developer of embedded products such as industrial motherboards, CPU modules, barebone systems, network appliances, and digital surveillance systems.

**Ibm Research - Almaden**  BR
650 Harry Rd
San Jose CA 95120-6099
P: 408-927-1080  PRC:300
www.research.ibm.com

Rama Akkiraju, Distinguished Engineer
C. Narayan, Director of Science & Technology
Heiko Ludwig, Manager of Cloud Management Services
Tanveer Syeda-Mahmood, Research Manager
Brent Hailpern, Head of Computer Science IBM Research

Provider of computer technology services. The company engages in cloud, mobility, and security services.

**Ibus Corp**  HQ
3350 Scott Blvd Bldg 54
Santa Clara CA 95054
P: 408-450-7880  F: 408-450-7881  PRC:92
www.ibus.com
Email: contact@ibus.com
Estab: 1982

Johni Chan, President

Manufacturer and provider of industrial computers. The company also specializes in prototyping and quality control.

**Ic Engineering Inc**  HQ
2603 Camino Ramon Ste 200
San Ramon CA 94583
P: 925-415-0074  PRC:304
www.ic-engineering.com
Email: info@ic-engineering.com
Estab: 2000

Ryan McCollum, Control Systems Engineer
Frederick Foote, President

Provider of design and engineering services to industrial & commercial clients. The company serves food, oil, parts manufacturing, and other sectors.

**iCharts Inc**  HQ
140 S Whisman Rd
Mountain View CA 94041
P: 650-472-0650  PRC:316
www.icharts.net
Estab: 2009

Fatima G., Senior Software Engineer

Provider of collaborative visual intelligence solutions. The company offers services to business and media companies.

**Ico Rally**  HQ
2575 E Bayshore Rd
Palo Alto CA 94303
P: 650-856-9900  F: 650-856-8378  PRC:285
www.icorally.com
Estab: 1950

Edwina Cioffi, President
Jason Cioffi, Quality Manager
Betty Klanda, Strategic Accounts Manager of Government Sales
Ico Rally, Inside Sales Manager
Rita David, Strategic Account Manager

Manufacturer and supplier of heat shrinkable materials, wiring accessories, and insulation products. The company serves automotive and marine sectors.

**ICON Aircraft Inc**  HQ
2141 ICON Way
Vacaville CA 95688
P: 707-564-4100  PRC:3
iconaircraft.com
Estab: 2004

Kirk Hawkins, Founder
Thomas Wieners, President
Tina Rulo, VP of Human Resources
Veronica Malo, VP of Supply Chain and Manufacturing
David Crook, EVP of Revenue

Manufacturer of consumer aircraft. The company specializes in giving the freedom, fun, and adventure of flying to all who have dreamed of flight.

**Iconic Therapeutics Inc**  HQ
701 Gateway Blvd Ste 100
S San Francisco CA 94080
P: 650-437-1000  F: 650-246-9011  PRC:251
iconictherapeutics.com
Email: info@iconictherapeutics.com

Brandon Smith, COO

Provider of tissue factor therapeutics. The company focusses on the solid tumors and wet age related macular degeneration.

**Iconix Inc**  HQ
255 W Julian St Ste 302
San Jose CA 95110
P: 408-727-6342  F: 408-727-6249  PRC:325
www.iconix.com
Estab: 2011

Scott Sachtjen, VP of Engineering
Jose Picazo, CEO
Robert Zager, CFO
Bill Ames, VP of Sales
Bob Zager, VP of Business Development

Provider of business solutions such as email identity software. The company caters to brand and customer security needs.

**Ics Electronics**  HQ
7034 Commerce Cir
Pleasanton CA 94588
P: 925-416-1000  F: 925-416-0105  PRC:94
www.icselect.com
Email: sales@icselect.com
Estab: 1978

Denise Romandia, Customer Service Manager

Provider of interfaces and controllers for assembling systems, interfacing devices, and legacy systems.

**ICU Eyewear**  HQ
1900 Shelton Dr
Hollister CA 95023
P: 800-435-5747  PRC:173
icueyewear.com
Email: info@icueyewear.com
Emp: 1-10  Estab: 1997

Patricia Kesten, Founder
Christine Roach, VP of Finance
Kelley Williams, Director of Distribution
Kaila Lango, Sales Planning Analyst
Raul Hurtado, Senior Accountant

Manufacturer of reading eye-wear and sunglasses. The company provides metal half rim, polarized oval, and metal full aviator sunglasses.

**Icube Information International**　　　HQ
200 Brown Rd Ste 114
Fremont CA 94539
P: 510-683-8928　F: 510-683-8607　　PRC:320
www.icubeinfo.com
Email: info@icubeinfo.com
Estab: 1993

Herman Li, President

Publisher of software work flow based management systems, documentation, inventory processing, and revision tracking services.

**Id Technology LLC**　　　BR
7447 N Palm Bluffs Ave
Fresno CA 93711
P: 559-436-8401　　PRC:79
www.idtechnology.com
Emp: 1-10　Estab: 1993

Joe Clear, National OEM Sales Manager
Wayne Moore, Regional Manager
Charles Shepherd, National Accounts Manager
Scott Pepin, National Accounts Manager

Designer and manufacturer of custom identification systems. The company offers labeling, coding, and marketing equipment services.

**Ideablade**　　　HQ
21C Orinda Way Ste 327
Orinda CA 94563-2534
P: 510-596-5100　F: 510-450-0379　　PRC:322
www.ideablade.com
Email: info@ideablade.com
Estab: 2001

Silvio Belini, Software Engineer
Jay Traband, Founder
Josh Otis, Information Technology Manager
Ward Bell, VP
Marcel Good, Senior Director of Professional Services

Provider of data base application services. The company's products include DevForce, Coctail, and Breeze.

**Ideal Aerosmith Inc**　　　BR
1301 Shoreway Rd Ste 185
Belmont CA 94002
P: 701-757-3400　F: 701-757-3459　　PRC:3
www.ideal-aerosmith.com
Email: sales@idealaero.com

John Mohn, President

Provider of precision motion simulation test systems. The company serves the aerospace, energy exploration, and automotive industries.

**IDEAYA Biosciences**　　　HQ
7000 Shoreline Ct Ste 350
S San Francisco CA 94080
P: 650-443-6209　　PRC:34
www.ideayabio.com
Email: info@ideayabio.com
Estab: 2015

Yujiro Hata, CEO
Jeffrey Hager, SVP
Michael Dillon, SVP
Julie Hambleton, SVP
Mark Lackner, VP

Provider of synthetic lethality medicines for the immuno oncology therapies. The company specializes in cancer biology, small molecule drug discovery, and immunology.

**Idec Corp**　　　BR
1175 Elko Dr
Sunnyvale CA 94089-2209
P: 408-747-0550　F: 408-744-9055　　PRC:310
www.idec.com
Email: opencontact@idec.com

John DeLand, Automation Sales Engineer
Toshiyuki Funaki, CEO
Ed Moran, Human Resource Manager
Roger Aubuchon, Regional Sales Manager
Madalene Kulich, Sales Assistant

Designer and manufacturer of automated machines for various sectors. The company also offers products for environment, safety, and other needs.

**Identiv Inc**　　　HQ
2201 Walnut Ave Ste 100
Fremont CA 94538
P: 888-809-8880　　PRC:110
www.identiv.com
Email: sales@identiv.com
Estab: 1996
Sales: $30M to $100M

Calaimany Bhoopathi, Senior Engineer of CTO Office
Steven Humphreys, CEO
Jim Ousley, Chairman
Manfred Mueller, COO
Sandra Wallach, CFO

Provider of security technology services. The company's products include desktop readers, terminals, modules, and development kits.

**IDEX Health & Science LLC**　　　BR
600 Park Ct
Rohnert Park CA 94928
P: 707-588-2000　F: 707-588-2020　　PRC:13
www.idex-hs.com
Email: info.rheodyne@idexcorp.com

Betsy Schaffer, Human Resource Manager
Audrey Schrock, Associate Product Manager

Provider of precision equipment for the health care industry. The company also offers detectors, fittings, and filters.

**Ieh JI Analytical Services**　　　HQ
217 Primo Way
Modesto CA 95358
P: 209-538-8111　F: 209-538-3966　　PRC:306
www.iehinc.com
Email: info@iehinc.com
Emp: 1-10　Estab: 1972

Mike Wolf, Laboratory Director

Provider of laboratory and consulting services for food microbiology, allergens, virology, and parasitology, forensics, and agricultural products.

**Ifos**　　　HQ
2363 Calle Del Mundo
Santa Clara CA 95054
P: 408-565-9000　F: 408-565-9003　　PRC:159
ifos.com
Estab: 2001

Behzad Moslehi, CEO
Richard Black, Chief Scientist

Developer of optical fiber sensing system level products. The company's products are used for monitoring and control of temperature and acoustic emission.

**iGenix Inc**　　　HQ
556 Gibraltar Dr
Milpitas CA 95035
P: 650-424-1191　F: 650-424-1196　　PRC:34
www.igenex.com
Email: customerservice@igenex.com
Estab: 1983

Akhila Poruri, Research Associate

Provider of immunology laboratory services. The company offers service to private practice physicians, hospitals, and clinical reference laboratories.

**iHEAR Medical Inc**　　　HQ
15250 Hesperian Blvd Ste 102
San Leandro CA 94578
P: 510-276-4437　F: 510-662-7900　　PRC:191
www.ihearmedical.com
Email: info@ihearmedical.com
Estab: 2010

Adnan Shennib, Founder
Michael Potter, Consulting CFO & Board Member
Marika Berkley, Director of Quality & Regulatory Affairs
Varun Bhardwaj, VP of Operations

Provider of hearing technology. The company specializes in web-enabled hearing device to fulfill the unmet needs of the hearing impaired.

**Iksanika LLC**　　　HQ
60 S Market St Ste 1200
San Jose CA 95113
P: 408-490-0777　F: 408-668-0858　　PRC:322
www.iksanika.com
Email: info@iksanika.com
Estab: 2000

Vital Volosiuk, EVP

Provider of custom software development, testing, quality assurance, porting, and re-engineering services.

**Illumina Inc**　　　BR
25861 Industrial Blvd
Hayward CA 94545
P: 510-670-9300　F: 510-670-9302　　PRC:31
www.illumina.com
Email: info@illumina.com
Estab: 1998

Francis deSouza, President
Mark Van Oene, SVP
Mostafa Ronaghi, SVP
Phil Febbo, Chief Medical Officer
Sam Samad, SVP

Developer, manufacturer, and marketer of integrated systems for the analysis of genetic variation and biological function.

**Illumio Inc**　　　HQ
920 De Guigne Dr
Sunnyvale CA 94085
P: 669-800-5000　　PRC:323
www.illumio.com
Estab: 2013

P.J. Kirner, CTO
Andrew Rubin, CEO
Anup Singh, CFO
Bobby Guhasarkar, CMO
Suresh Pottur, Member of Technical Staff

Developer of security platform and it is also involved in data encryption and technical support services.

**Illustris Pharmaceuticals Inc** HQ
131 Innovation Dr Ste 150
Irvine CA 92617
P: 650-334-2090 PRC:268
www.illustris.com
Email: info@illustris.com
Emp: 1-10 Estab: 2016

Jacob Waugh, Co-Founder
Mark Prygocki, CEO
Jonah Shacknai, Chairman

Developer and provider of technology solutions for
the delivery of large molecules through the tissue
structures.

**Ilm Tool Inc** HQ
23301 Clawiter Rd
Hayward CA 94545
P: 510-782-0100 F: 510-782-5475 PRC:80
www.ilmtool.com
Email: sales@ilmtool.com
Estab: 1981

Joe Ilmberger, Owner

Provider of engineering and CNC machining
services. The company offers precision machining services for the biotech and semiconductor
industries.

**Imageteq Technologies Inc** HQ
533 Airport Blvd Ste 400
Burlingame CA 94010
P: 650-403-4806 F: 650-403-0876 PRC:325
www.imageteq.com
Email: info@imageteq.com
Estab: 1999

Len Goldberg, Founder
Nancy Gaehwiler Goldberg, Founder
Rajan Jena, CTO
Jim Pavlovcak, Development Manager

Provider of IT consulting and services. The company focuses on consulting, enterprise application, and staff augmentation.

**Imagine That Inc** HQ
6830 Via Del Oro Ste 230
San Jose CA 95119
P: 408-365-0305 F: 408-629-1251 PRC:322
www.extendsim.com
Email: info@extendsim.com
Estab: 1987

Bob Diamond, Founder

Developer of simulation software. The company
offers services to the retail, healthcare, insurance,
and financial services industries.

**Imaging Visions** HQ
15850 Orange Blossom Ln
Los Gatos CA 95032
P: 408-358-6427 F: 408-348-2436 PRC:316
www.imagingvisions.com

Rod Juncker, Designer

Provider of design, prototyping, and visualization
services that include architectural and lighting,
exterior and landscape, and furnishing design.

**Imaja** HQ
1244 Hearst Ave Ste 7
Berkeley CA 94704
P: 510-526-4621 PRC:320
www.imaja.com
Email: support@imaja.com
Estab: 1985

Greg Jalbert, Owner
Margreet Hindriks, Owner
Sebastian Cuesta, Educator Social
Imanuel Widjaja, Construction Administrator

Developer of computer applications. The company
specializes in the development of educational
tools for Macs.

**iMaxsoft Corporation** HQ
PO Box 1222
Cupertino CA 95015
P: 408-253-1987 PRC:326
www.imaxsoft.com
Estab: 1984

Lee Tsai, Founder

Provider of database and application migration
services. The company offers services to government agencies.

**IMC Power Sources** HQ
1272 Alma Ct
San Jose CA 95112
P: 408-924-0800 F: 408-494-0804 PRC:288
www.imcpower.com

Ron Evans, Sales Manager
Kendra Latimore, Administrative Assistant

Supplier of SLA batteries, power test equipment,
and test loads. The company serves the industrial
market.

**iMiners Inc** HQ
6894 Brookview Ct
Livermore CA 94551
P: 925-447-6073 F: 925-447-6074 PRC:325
www.iminers.com
Email: info@iminers.com
Estab: 2005

Sandesh Prabhu, Chief Architect

Provider of investor relations management tools
& web-based communication platforms. The
company offers website plug-ins and shareholder
message boards.

**Immecor** HQ
1650 Northpoint Pkwy Ste C
Santa Rosa CA 95407
P: 707-636-2550 F: 707-636-2565 PRC:224
www.immecor.com
Estab: 1993

James Foley, National Sales Director
Nhon Tran, VP

Provider of industrial computers, custom cables,
and PCB assembly services. The company serves
entertainment, medical, and telecom sectors.

**Immersion Corp** HQ
50 Rio Robles
San Jose CA 95134
P: 408-467-1900 F: 408-467-1901 PRC:112
www.immersion.com
Estab: 1993
Sales: $100M to $300M

Jason Fleming, Applications Engineer
Vic Viegas, CEO
Christophe Ramstein, CTO
Nancy Erba, CFO
Sai Kim, Senior Manager of Information Technol-
ogy

Developer and marketer of haptic (touch feedback) technology. The company serves mobile
device, wearable, automotive, medical, and other
sectors.

**Immune Design Corp** HQ
601 Gateway Blvd Ste 250
S San Francisco CA 94080-7006
P: 650-887-6717 PRC:44
www.immunedesign.com
Email: info@immunedesign.com
Estab: 2008

Carlos Paya, CEO
Stephen Brady, Chief Business Officer
Wayne Gombotz, Chief Development Officer

Provider of clinical-stage immunotherapy services.
The company develops immuno-oncology drug
candidates.

**Immuno Concepts Na Ltd** HQ
9825 Goethe Rd Ste 350
Sacramento CA 95827
P: 916-363-2649 F: 916-363-2843 PRC:31
www.immunoconcepts.com
Email: technicalsupport@immunoconcepts.com
Emp: 1-10 Estab: 1979

Bert Williams, Owner
Natalie Zelenov, Quality Assurance Manager

Manufacturer and distributor of diagnostic assays.
The company's products are used for systemic
rheumatic diseases.

**Immunoscience Inc** HQ
6670 Owens Dr
Pleasanton CA 94588
P: 925-828-1000 F: 925-397-2114 PRC:34
www.immunoscience.com
Email: info@immunoscience.com
Estab: 1995

Sateesh Apte, President
Paul Oken, CFO
Victor Martin, VP of Manufacturing
Geeta Kalbag, Product Development Specialist

Provider of biotechnology research and development for diagnosis and treatment of AIDS and
HIV infection. The company also offers therapeutic
vaccines.

**Imosphere Inc**  BR
71 Forest View Dr
San Francisco CA 94132
P: 800-204-1852  PRC:194
imosphere.com
Email: info@imosphere.com
Estab: 1993

Paul Suart, Lead Software Engineer - Atmolytics
Aidan Morris, Co-Founder
Paul Clifford, CEO
Natalie Kenneison, COO
Paul Rawston, Head of Marketing

Developer of healthcare analytics platform. The
company offers services to healthcare professionals.

**Impax Laboratories Inc**  HQ
30831 Huntwood Ave
Hayward CA 94544
P: 510-240-6000  F: 510-471-3200  PRC:268
www.impaxlabs.com
Email: inquiries@impaxlabs.com

Nitha Jacob, Technical Services Engineer
Michael Yoon, Associate Director of Human
Resources
Linda Alt, Human Resource Manager
Josie Lake, Quality Operations Manager
Andrew Fox, Director of API Purchasing

Manufacturers and developer of technology-based
specialty pharmaceutical drug delivery system.
The company's serves physicians and patients.

**Impekable LLC**  HQ
465 S First St
San Jose CA 95113
P: 650-733-6006  PRC:319
impekable.com
Email: sales@impekable.com
Estab: 2012

Pek Pongpaet, CEO
Sara Gallagher, Director of Business Development

UI design and mobile development studio that
helps organizations to create human-centric
mobile experiences.

**Imperva Inc**  HQ
3400 Bridge Pkwy Ste 200
Redwood Shores CA 94065
P: 650-345-9000  F: 650-345-9004  PRC:322
imperva.com
Email: support@imperva.com
Estab: 2002
Sales: $300M to $1 Billion

Christopher Hylen, President
Kunal Anand, CTO
Jim Dildine, CFO
Dave Woodcock, SVP of Worldwide Sales
David Gee, CMO

Provider of application and data security solutions.
The company's products include database
firewalls, management server, and monitoring
software.

**Importio**  HQ
12980 Saratoga Ave Ste B Bldg 1
Saratoga CA 95070
P: 650-935-4336  PRC:315
import.io/
Email: hello@import.io
Estab: 2012

Masa Karahashi, VP of Engineering
Andrew Fogg, Founder
Matthew Painter, Founder
Gary Read, CEO
Carol Manchester, CFO

Enables organizations to gain intelligence,
abilities, and competing advantages from the vast
amount of data on the web.

**Impression Technology**  HQ
1777 N California Blvd Ste 240
Walnut Creek CA 94596
P: 925-280-0010  PRC:323
www.impression-technology.com
Email: sales@impression-technology.com
Estab: 1997

Charles Hou, VP of Engineering
Noel Ong, Senior Software Engineer
Michael Tokuyama, President
Bruce Lechner, VP of Business Development
Sohil Shah, Computer Programmer Analyst

Provider of automated data capture solutions
that meet the business objectives. The company
primarily offers scanners.

**Imprint Energy**  HQ
1320 Harbor Bay Pkwy Ste 110
Alameda CA 94502
P: 510-748-0233  PRC:288
www.imprintenergy.com

Christine Ho, CEO

Developer of zinc-based rechargeable batteries.
The company is engaged in energy management
solutions.

**Impulse Semiconductor Inc**  HQ
111 North Market St Ste 300
San Jose CA 95113
P: 408-355-5018  PRC:86
impulsesemi.com
Email: design@impulsesemi.com
Estab: 1994

Rosario Consiglio, Founder

Provider of electrostatic discharge and electrical
overstress products and services. The company
also provides virtual components and hardware.

**Imra America Inc**  BR
48834 Kato Rd Ste 106A
Fremont CA 94538
P: 510-623-3507  F: 510-656-2093  PRC:172
imra.com
Email: lasers@imra.com

Fumiyo Yoshino, Applications Research Engineer
Mariko Yamaguchi, Application Development
Scientist

Developer and manufacturer of fiber lasers. The
company's products are used in cutting, drilling,
welding, and thin-film removal applications.

**Imt Precision Inc**  HQ
31902 Hayman St
Hayward CA 94544
P: 510-324-8926  F: 510-324-8943  PRC:80
www.imtp.com
Email: rfq@imtp.com
Estab: 1994

Zack Lemley, Director of Production & Planning
Peter Kunze, Quality Assurance Manager
Jeff Nordloff, Business Development Manager
Tim Ilario, Shareholder

Provider of sheet metal machining, fabrication, inspection and assembly services to semiconductor,
aerospace, biotech, and education sectors.

**Imtec Acculine Inc**  HQ
49036 Milmont Dr
Fremont CA 94538
P: 510-770-1800  F: 510-770-1400  PRC:159
www.imtecacculine.com
Email: sales@imtecacculine.com
Estab: 1972

Paul Mendes, President
Mark West, Sales Manager
Rich Tapia, Marketing Communication Manager
Dick Grimsley, Mechanical Designer
Richard Faria, Controller

Provider of wet process modules and systems.
The company also supplies quartz constant temperature baths.

**Inabyte Inc**  HQ
5 Betty Ln
Novato CA 94947
P: 415-898-7905  F: 415-898-1652  PRC:324
www.inabyte.com
Email: information@inabyte.com
Estab: 1996

Myles Cagney, CEO

Manufacturer of developer tools. The company
also offers solutions and services for developers
and end users of PCs or workstations.

**Inbus Engineering**  HQ
4771 Arroyo Vista Ste C
Livermore CA 94551
P: 925-454-2500  F: 925-454-2501  PRC:91
www.inbus.com
Email: sales@inbus.com
Estab: 1978

Jim Wright, Project Coordinator

Manufacturer and supplier of obsolete Intel boards
emulators. The company offers repair & replacement and disk transfer services.

**Incal Technology Inc**  HQ
46420 Fremont Blvd
Fremont CA 94538
P: 510-657-8405  PRC:15
www.incal.com
Email: sales@incal.com
Estab: 1988

Hank Pedersen, Applications Engineer
Bruce Simikowski, VP
Stephen Tsun, Director of Sales
Don Bernier, Sales Manager
Dennis Puddester, Sales Manager

Designer and manufacturer of test and burn in
equipment and related hardware for board testing.
The company serves the semiconductor industry.

**InCarda Therapeutics Inc**　　　　HQ
　39899 Balentine Dr Ste 185
　Newark CA 94560
P: 510-422-5522　　　　　　　　　PRC:261
www.incardatherapeutics.com
Email: info@incardatherapeutics.com
Estab: 2009

Carlos Schuler, Chief Operating & Technology
Officer

Developer of drugs and inhaled therapy intended
to treat paroxysmal atrial fibrillation and other
cardiovascular diseases.

**Incelldx Inc**　　　　　　　　　　HQ
　1541 Industrial Rd
　San Carlos CA 94070
P: 650-777-7630　F: 650-587-1528　PRC:20
www.incelldx.com
Email: info@incelldx.com
Estab: 2010

Bruce Patterson, CEO
Brian Francisco, Field Application Specialist

Provider of molecular diagnostics to detect and
monitor cervical cancer, HIV/AIDS, hepatitis, and
organ transplant rejection diseases.

**Incentia Design Systems Inc**　　　HQ
　2620 Augustine Dr Ste 200
　Santa Clara CA 95054
P: 408-727-8988　F: 408-727-8008　PRC:319
www.incentia.com
Email: info@incentia.com
Estab: 1998

Shing-Chong Chang, VP of Engineering
Al Lipinski, VP of Sales

Provider of advanced timing and signal integrity
analysis, design closure, and logic synthesis
software for nanometer designs.

**Inclin Inc**　　　　　　　　　　　BR
　2655 Campus Dr Ste 100
　San Mateo CA 94403
P: 650-376-4000　　　　　　　　　PRC:189
www.inclin.com
Email: busdev@inclin.com
Estab: 1998

Arnold Wong, Co-Founder
Brian Horger, CEO
Rhonda Asis, Human Resource Manager
Deb Manuel, VP of Clinical Data Management
Mojtaba Noursalehi, SVP of Biometrics

Provider of clinical, regulatory, and quality assurance services to pharmaceutical, biotechnology,
and medical device companies.

**Incotec Inc**　　　　　　　　　　RH
　1293 Harkins Rd
　Salinas CA 93901-4408
P: 831-757-4367　F: 831-757-1512　PRC:39
www.incotec.com
Email: admin@incotec.com
Estab: 1968

Douwe Zijp, CEO
Brad Kortsen, Sales & Marketing Manager
Kathy Winn, Business Manager
Paul DeCarli, Account Manager
Kathy Townsend, Logistic Coordinator

Provider of solutions in the business areas such
as vegetables, field crops, ornamentals, and
analytical services.

**Increv Corp**　　　　　　　　　　HQ
　1877 Austin Ave
　Los Altos CA 94024
P: 408-689-2296　F: 650-625-9550　PRC:319
www.increvcorp.com
Email: info@increvcorp.com
Estab: 2006

Suthin Sadanandan, Senior Development Manager

Developer of business and information technology
solutions. The company is engaged in consulting
and product development services.

**InCube Labs**　　　　　　　　　　HQ
　2051 Ringwood Ave
　San Jose CA 95131
P: 408-457-3700　　　　　　　　　PRC:189
www.incubelabs.com
Estab: 1995

Mir Imran, CEO
Mir Hashim, CSO
Svai Sanford, CFO
Asif Mirza, Information Technology Manager
Betsy Gutierrez, Associate VP

Provider of laboratory services. The company
offers medical devices and pharmaceuticals to
various therapeutic areas.

**Indec Medical Systems**　　　　　HQ
　4701 Patrick Henry Dr Ste 2401 Bldg 24
　Santa Clara CA 95054
P: 408-986-1600　F: 408-986-1605　PRC:325
www.indecmedical.com
Email: info@indecmedical.com

Carol Hubler, VP

Provider of hardware and software solutions for
cardiovascular imaging applications such as intra-
vascular ultrasound and angiography.

**Individual Software Inc**　　　　　HQ
　2301 Armstrong St Ste 101
　Livermore CA 94551
P: 925-734-6767　F: 925-734-8337　PRC:319
www.individualsoftware.com
Email: customercare@individualsoftware.com
Estab: 1981

Dwayne Tatum, VP of Information Technology &
Technical Services
Paul Hendrickson, Materials Manager

Publisher and developer of education, business,
and personal productivity software for consumers,
schools, businesses, and government.

**Indtec Corp**　　　　　　　　　　HQ
　3348 Paul Davis Dr Ste 109
　Marina CA 93933
P: 831-582-9388　F: 831-582-9386　PRC:202
www.indtec.net
Email: sales@indtec.net
Estab: 1991

Pualani Visesio, Purchasing Manager

Manufacturer of printed circuit boards. The company specializes in assemblies, wires, cables, automated surface mounting, and harness services.

**Inductive Automation**　　　　　　HQ
　90 Blue Ravine
　Folsom CA 95630
P: 916-456-1045　F: 916-932-1194　PRC:319
inductiveautomation.com
Emp: 1-10

Kevin McClusky, Co-Director of Sales Engineering
Colby Clegg, Co-Director of Software Engineering
Mara Pillott, Design Services Engineer
Kent Melville, Sales Engineering Analyst
Jae Park, Software Engineer

Supplier of web-based industrial automation software. The company offers solutions for end-users
and integrators.

**Industrial Control Links Inc**　　　HQ
　12840 Earhart Ave
　Auburn CA 95602
P: 530-888-1800　F: 530-888-7017　PRC:64
www.iclinks.com
Email: info@iclinks.com
Emp: 1-10　Estab: 1986

Perry Spetz, Owner
Sarah Meyer, Account Manager

Designer and manufacturer of SCADA hardware
and software solutions. The company focuses on
monitoring, alarming, data collection, and other
needs.

**Industrial Electrical Co**　　　　　HQ
　1417 Coldwell Ave
　Modesto CA 95350
P: 209-527-2800　F: 209-527-4457　PRC:150
www.industrialelectricalco.com
Emp: 11-50　Estab: 1935

Michelle Howell, Owner
Paul Swanson, VP of Operations
Greg Heune, Estimator

Provider of electrical, manufacturing, and automation services for the commercial and industrial
sectors.

**Industrial Nuclear Co**　　　　　　HQ
　14320 Wicks Blvd
　San Leandro CA 94577
P: 510-352-6767　F: 510-352-6772　PRC:159
ir100.com
Email: sales@ir100.com

Charles Bollinger, Manager

Manufacturer of industrial gamma radiography
equipment and radioactive sources. The company's services include calibration and repair and
leak testing.

**Industrial Optics Unlimited**　　　HQ
　1680 S St
　Anderson CA 96007
P: 530-365-1972　　　　　　　　　PRC:173
www.iouoptics.com
Email: mail@iouoptics.com
Emp: 1-10　Estab: 1990

Kristie Fore, President

Provider of optical services. The company is
involved in fabricating optical components for both
commercial and laser applications.

**Ineda Systems Inc** RH

3400 Garrett Dr
Santa Clara CA 95054
P: 408-400-7375 PRC:323
www.inedasystems.com
Email: info@inedasystems.com
Estab: 2011

Gude Dasaradha, Founder

Provider of IoT and wearable applications with
multiple connectivity options, based on I/O virtualization and hierarchical computing technologies.

**Infineon Technologies North American
Corp** BR

18225 Serene Dr Ste 100
Morgan Hill CA 95037
P: 866-951-9519 PRC:208
www.infineon.com
Sales: $3M to $10M

Reinhard Ploss, CEO
Johann Dechant, Deputy Chairman of General
Works Council
Wolfgang Eder, Chairman
Sven Schneider, CFO
Rajeev Kumar, Director of Program Management

Provider of semiconductor and system solutions.
The company focuses on mobile security, sensors,
power management, and RF.

**Infinera Corp** HQ

140 Caspian Ct
Sunnyvale CA 94089
P: 408-572-5200 PRC:97
www.infinera.com
Email: info@infinera.com
Estab: 2001
Sales: $300M to $1 Billion

Andrew Phan, Principal Software Engineer
Shashikant Pople, Manufacturing Engineer
Jian Yao, Development Engineer
Huy Dinh, Test Engineer
Nhan Hoang, St., Mechanical Design Engineer

Provider of services and solutions in optical networks. The company serves cable operators and
internet content providers.

**InfinIT Consulting** HQ

55 N Third St Ste 201
Campbell CA 95008
P: 866-364-2007 PRC:319
www.infinitconsulting.com
Email: helpdesk@infinitconsulting.com
Estab: 2006

Alexis Nguyen, Support Engineer
Jerod Powell, Founder
Darrin Swan, CEO
Malu Milan, SVP of Strategy & Transformation
Daniel Schneiderman, Director of IT Services

Designer and developer of CNC machining and
billet products. The company's products include
fire extinguisher brackets, shift knobs, and boat
accessories.

**Infinite Technologies Inc** HQ

1264 Hawks Flight Ct Ste 210
El Dorado Hills CA 95762
P: 916-987-3261 F: 916-987-3264 PRC:323
www.infintech.com
Emp: 11-50 Estab: 1994

Michael Whittle, President
Eric Jonsson, Programmer
Don Petersen, Senior Lead Developer
Nicolas Bailey, Senior Application Architect
Derik Harris, System Architect

Provider of information technology, strategic consulting, and engineering services. The company
serves government and corporate entities.

**Infiniti Solutions Usa** BR

3910 N First St
San Jose CA 95134
P: 408-923-7300 F: 408-251-5431 PRC:124
www.infinitisolutions.com
Email: bi.sales@infinitisolutions.com

Vipul Panchal, Electronics Engineer
Selena Abebe, Purchasing & Administration
Manager

Provider of electronic manufacturing services. The
company specializes in burn-in board and system
design and manufacturing.

**Infinity Quick Turn** HQ

4063 Clipper Ct
Fremont CA 94538
P: 510-661-0555 F: 510-661-0655 PRC:211
www.infinityquickturn.com
Estab: 1994

Jeff Carr, President

Provider of manufacturing solutions and services.
The company deals with component distribution
and PCB fabrication.

**Inflection LLC** HQ

555 Twin Dolphin Dr Ste 630
Redwood City CA 94065
P: 650-618-9910 F: 650-593-2799 PRC:325
inflection.com
Email: company@inflection.com
Estab: 2006

Nachi Sendowski, CTO
Mike Grossman, CEO
Max Wesman, Chief Product
Peter Chantel, CFO
Joe Nagy, VP of Sales

Provider of technology solutions and software
products. The company develops search engines,
cloud management, and web server applications.

**Infobahn Softworld Inc** HQ

2010 N First St Ste 470
San Jose CA 95131
P: 408-855-9616 F: 408-855-9490 PRC:325
www.infobahnsw.com
Email: info@infobahnsw.com
Estab: 1996

Nitin Chandra, President
Nick Kapur, IT Sales Manager
Priti Sarma, Accounts Receivable Manager
Smitha Patanker, Senior Accounting Manager
Naveen Pole, Recruiter

Provider of consulting, enterprise application
integration, service oriented architecture, and
systems integration solutions to fortune 500
companies.

**Infoblox Inc** HQ

3111 Coronado Dr
Santa Clara CA 95054
P: 408-986-4000 F: 408-986-4001 PRC:97
www.infoblox.com
Email: info@infoblox.com
Estab: 1999

Jesper Andersen, President
Brad Bell, SVP
Hoke Horne, EVP
Sammie Walker, EVP
Liza Burns, VP of Business Operations

Provider of automated network control solutions. The company's services include training,
implementation, migration, upgrade, repair, and
maintenance.

**Infoimage Inc** HQ

141 Jefferson Dr
Menlo Park CA 94025
P: 650-473-6388 PRC:324
infoimageinc.com
Estab: 1984

Yi Liao, Software Engineer
Howard Lee, President
Rose Lee, COO
Lenora Lee, CFO
Guy Mason, Director of Account Management

Provider of technology solutions for job tracking
and business continuity needs. The company also
focuses on data integrity.

**Infolane Inc** HQ

2340 Powell St Ste 284
Emeryville CA 94608
P: 510-277-2399 PRC:323
www.infolane.com
Email: info@infolane.com
Estab: 1994

David Hillstrom, President

Provider of web design and development and
support services that includes web content management, application development, and technical
improvements.

**Informatica Corp** HQ

2100 Seaport Blvd
Redwood City CA 94063
P: 650-385-5000 F: 650-385-5500 PRC:315
www.informatica.com
Estab: 1993

Tracey Newell, President of Global Field Opera-
tions
AMIT Walia, President of Products
Anil Chakravarthy, CEO
Eric Brown, EVP
Ansa Sekharan, EVP

Provides data management software and services
to help a company to achieve a competitive edge.

**Informatica Corp** HQ
2100 Seaport Blvd
Redwood City CA 94063
P: 650-385-5000  F: 650-385-5500  PRC:324
www.informatica.com
Email: support@informatica.com
Estab: 1993

Anil Chakravarthy, CEO
Ansa Sekharan, EVP
Brad Lewis, SVP
Eric Brown, EVP
Graeme Thompson, SVP

Provider of enterprise data integration and
management solutions including data migration,
warehousing, identity resolution, and other needs.

**Informatix Inc** HQ
2485 Natomas Park Dr Ste 430
Sacramento CA 95833
P: 916-830-1400  PRC:323
www.informatixinc.com
Email: info@informatixinc.com
Emp: 1-10  Estab: 1999

Robert Crothers, Software Engineer
Raul Ocazionez, President
Michele Blanc, COO
Erica Batara, Finance Manager
Lisa Cruz, Director of BPO Services

Provider of information technology and business
solutions that include software development, document management, networking, and consulting
services.

**Infors USA Inc** BR
6711 Sierra Ct Ste B
Dublin CA 94568
P: 925-828-9800  PRC:25
www.infors-ht.us
Email: usla-sales@infors-ht.com
Emp: 1-10  Estab: 1965

Simon Egli, CEO
Christian Kocher, Senior Tech Sales Specialist
Brian LaPietra, Director
Chris Knese, Director
Andrew Magno, Product Manager

Manufacturer of bioreactors. The company offers
shakers, incubator shakers, and bioreactors.

**Infortrend Corp** LH
2200 Zanker Rd Ste 130
San Jose CA 95131
P: 408-988-5088  F: 408-988-6288  PRC:95
www.infortrend.com
Email: sales.us@infortrend.com
Estab: 1993

Tony Chu, President
Debbie Lin, Operations Supervisor

Provider of high performance storage networking
solutions. The company serves the energy, utilities, and healthcare industries.

**Infostat Systems Inc** HQ
1545 River Park Dr Ste 350
Sacramento CA 95815
P: 916-649-3244  PRC:326
www.infostatsystems.com
Email: sales@infostatsystems.com
Emp: 1-10  Estab: 1989

Joe Atkinson, CDO
Martyn Curragh, CFO
Gary Price, Partner Affairs Leader
Reggie Walker, CCO
Farhad Zaman, Chief Network Officer

Provider of reporting, database, and data distribution solutions. The company serves drilling
contractors and well operating companies.

**Infostretch Corp** HQ
3200 Patrick Henry Dr Ste 250
Santa Clara CA 95054
P: 408-727-1100  F: 408-716-2461  PRC:322
www.infostretch.com
Email: info@infostretch.com
Estab: 2004

Rutesh Shah, CEO
Pinakin Sheth, CFO
Avery Lyford, Chief Customer Officer
Leila Modarres, CMO

Provider of mobile application development,
quality assurance testing and automation, SaaS
solutions, and ERP testing solutions.

**InfoTech Spectrum Inc** HQ
2060 Walsh Ave Ste 120
Santa Clara CA 95050
P: 408-705-2237  F: 408-716-2625  PRC:224
www.infotechspectrum.com
Email: hr@infotechspectrum.com
Estab: 2003

Rajiv Pendyala, Director of Recruiting & Business
Development
Rajkumar Jangirala, Account Manager
Mahesh Aron, Account Manager
Arun Putluru, Technical Recruiter
Shaik Saleem, IT Technical Recruiter

Provider of integrated creative IT services including IT consulting, advanced technology deployment, and product development.

**Infoyogi LLC** HQ
2320 Walsh Ave Ste A
Santa Clara CA 95051
P: 408-850-1700  F: 408-516-8945  PRC:322
www.infoyogi.com
Email: info@infoyogi.com
Estab: 2004

Rao Tallapragada, President

Provider of information technology solutions for
software application development and systems
integration.

**Infrared Industries Inc** HQ
25590 Seaboard Ln
Hayward CA 94545
P: 510-782-8100  F: 510-782-8101  PRC:11
www.infraredindustries.com
Email: info@infraredindustries.com
Estab: 1959

Mark Russell, CEO
Martha Rykala, CFO

Developer of gas analyzer instrumentation for the
automotive, oil and gas, industrial, environmental,
and utility industries.

**Ingenuus Software Inc** HQ
43575 Mission Blvd Ste 151
Fremont CA 94539
P: 510-824-5653  PRC:326
www.ingenuus.com
Email: sales@ingennus.com

Vivek Prasad, President

Provider of enterprise process orchestration solutions. The company develops business process
management and process optimization software.

**Inikosoft Inc** HQ
15495 Los Gatos Blvd Ste 4
Los Gatos CA 95032
P: 408-402-9545  PRC:318
www.inikosoft.com
Email: info@inikosoft.com
Estab: 2003

Zach Crawford, Creative Director
Ryan Dedrick, Project Manager

Provider of web, graphic, and print design services. The company is also engaged in e-commerce development and social media marketing.

**Initio Corp** LH
2050 Ringwood Ave
San Jose CA 95131
P: 408-943-3189  F: 408-943-3100  PRC:208
www.initio.com
Estab: 1994

Jianjun Luo, Director

Provider of integrated circuits and solutions for
storage devices. The company is involved in
design, installation, and delivery services.

**Inland Metal Technologies** HQ
3245 Depot Rd
Hayward CA 94545
P: 510-785-8555  PRC:80
www.inlandmetal.com
Email: sales@inlandmetal.com
Estab: 1964

Moses Cardenas, Project Manager

Provider of sheet metal fabrication, manufacturing,
powder coating, silk-screening, and laser cutting
services.

**Inlite Corp**  HQ
939 Grayson St
Berkeley CA 94710
P: 800-346-5932  F: 510-849-3230  PRC:243
inlitelighting.com

Craig Belle, President

Manufacturer and distributor of directional lighting
equipment. The company offers tracks and lighting
components.

**Inmon Corp**  HQ
1 Sansome St Fl 35
San Francisco CA 94104
P: 415-946-8901  F: 415-946-8903  PRC:227
inmon.com
Email: info@inmon.com
Estab: 1999

Peter Phaal, President
Neil McKee, CTO

Developer of traffic management and monitoring
products such as sFlow Trend, sFlow-RT, Hyper-V
Agent, and others.

**Innerstep BSE**  HQ
4742 Scotts Valley Dr
Scotts Valley CA 95066
P: 831-461-5600  PRC:211
Emp: 11-50 Estab: 1992

Trung Vu, Manufacturing Test Supervisor
Dick Mason, Senior Program Manager
Elaine Canha, Buyer
Trisha Castaneda, Senior Buyer

Provider of manufacturing and design solutions
such as PCB and mechanical design for original
equipment manufacturers.

**Innodisk Corp**  BR
42996 Osgood Rd
Fremont CA 94539
P: 510-770-9421  F: 510-770-9424  PRC:95
www.innodisk.com
Email: usasales@innodisk.com
Estab: 2005

Johnny Vu, Field Application Engineer
Wang Licheng, Deputy General Manager
David Wang, VP of Embedded Flash BU
Fanyu Wang, Supply Chain Planner

Provider of embedded flash and dynamic random
access memory storage products and technology
solutions.

**InnoMedia Inc**  RH
1901 McCarthy Blvd
Milpitas CA 95035
P: 408-432-5400  F: 408-943-8604  PRC:61
www.innomedia.com
Email: sales_us@innomedia.com
Estab: 1995

Kai-Wa Ng, Chairman
Nan-Sheng Lin, Co-Founder
Harprit Chhatwal, CTO
Wymond Choy, Corporate VP of US
Shailesh Patel, Senior Director

Provider of broadband IP telephony products
and solutions including TDM-PRI SIP gateways,
enterprise SIP gatewayscable, and element management systems.

**Innominds Software Inc**  HQ
2055 Junction Ave Ste 122
San Jose CA 95131
P: 408-434-6463  F: 408-434-7061  PRC:322
www.innominds.com
Estab: 1998

Sai Chintala, President of Quality Engineering
Krishna Guda, President
Divakar Tantravahi, CEO
Rao Yendluri, CTO
Rajya Achanta, Chief People Officer

Provider of product incubation services for the
technology industries. The company focuses on
app development, analytics, mobility, and testing.

**Innosys Inc**  HQ
6400 Hollis St Ste 15
Emeryville CA 94608
P: 510-222-7717  F: 510-722-0311  PRC:319
www.innosys.com
Email: techsupport@innosys.com
Estab: 1973

Jennifer Hwu, CEO
Julius Simon, Technical Director
Risa Baumrind, Programmer

Provider of data communication solutions. The
company serves airlines, travel agencies, and
online travel services.

**Innovative Interfaces Inc**  HQ
1900 Powell St Ste 400
Emeryville CA 94608
P: 510-655-6200  F: 510-450-6350  PRC:322
www.iii.com
Email: info@iii.com
Estab: 1978

Kevin Mitchell, Support Engineer
Joe Wojtowicz, Senior Consultant

Provider of technology solutions and services.
The company deals with training and hosting, and
technical support.

**Innovion**  HQ
2121 Zanker Rd
San Jose CA 95131
P: 408-501-9100  F: 408-501-9110  PRC:211
www.innovioncorp.com
Email: sales@innovioncorp.com
Estab: 1981

Ray Pong, Applications Engineering Manager
Dave Buhs, Equipment Engineer
Gary Holyoak, CEO
John Schuur, CTO
Lisa Janello, Quality Manager

Provider of foundry and ion implantation services.
The company serves the microelectronics industry.

**Inovonics Inc**  HQ
5805 Highway 9
Felton CA 95018
P: 831-458-0552  F: 831-458-0554  PRC:61
www.inovonicsbroadcast.com
Email: info@inovon.com
Emp: 1-10  Estab: 1972

Joshua McAtee, Senior Development Engineer
Ben Barber, President

Manufacturer of a wide range of equipment for
radio broadcasters. The company also focuses on
the marketing aspects.

**Inoxpa Usa Inc**  HQ
3721 Santa Rosa Ave Ste B4
Santa Rosa CA 95407
P: 707-585-3900  PRC:160
www.inoxpausa.com
Email: inoxpa.us@inoxpa.com
Estab: 1972

Megan Hope, Technical Office Administrator

Manufacturer and trader of pumps and components. The company caters to industries like food
processing, dairy, wine-making, and cosmetics.

**Inphenix Inc**  HQ
250 N Mines Rd
Livermore CA 94551
P: 925-606-8809  F: 925-606-8810  PRC:83
www.inphenix.com
Email: info@inphenix.com
Estab: 1999

Rui Wang, Optical R&D Engineer
Miao Li, Engineer
Chunyang Hu, Opto-Electronics Engineer
Calin Moldovean, President of Business Assur-
ance
David Lin, Quality Assurance Assistant Manager

Designer and manufacturer of active optoelectronic chips and modules. The company serves telecom, defense, biomedical, and industrial markets.

**Inphi Corp**  HQ
2953 Bunker Hill Ln Ste 300
Santa Clara CA 95054
P: 408-217-7300  F: 408-217-7350  PRC:61
www.inphi.com
Email: sales@inphi.com
Estab: 2000
Sales: $100M to $300M

Vlad Shvydun, Principal ASIC Design Engineer
Loi Nguyen, Founder
Ford Tamer, President
Lawrence Tse, CTO
Radha Nagarajan, CTO of Optics

Provider of semiconductor solutions for the
computing and telecom markets. The company's
products include amplifiers, registers, buffers, and
modulator drivers.

**Inphora Inc**  HQ
1042 Country Club Dr Ste 1C
Moraga CA 94556
P: 925-322-5964  PRC:18
www.inphora.com
Email: info@inphora.com
Estab: 1989

Kathleen Muray, Founder
Murayk Kathleen, President
Lawrence Muray, CEO
Shelly Muray, Director of Operations
Ann Oeth, Controller

Supplier of high-precision photometric and
radiometric instruments. The company's products
include detectors, optical filters, and LED reference standards.

**Input Optics Inc**     HQ
914 N Rengstorff Ave
Mountain View CA 94043
P: 650-969-3108   F: 650-969-3186    PRC:323
www.inputoptics.com
Email: info@inputoptics.com
Estab: 1971

Gary Selig, President
Mike McGillis, CEO

Provider of integration solutions for dental practice. The company also offers complimentary assessments and web services.

**Inscopix Inc**     HQ
2462 Embarcadero Way
Palo Alto CA 94303
P: 650-600-3886     PRC:34
inscopix.com
Email: sales@inscopix.com
Estab: 2011

Michael Wycisk, Manufacturing Engineering Manager
Kunal Ghosh, Founder
Vikram Brar, Director of Manufacturing Operations
Pushkar Joshi, Director of Strategy & Business Development
Stephani Otte, Director of Application Development & Science

Provider of instrumentation and data analytics for next generation neuroscience. The company provides brain imaging solutions and data analysis suites.

**Insight Solutions Inc**     BR
19925 Stevens Creek Blvd Ste 136
Cupertino CA 95014
P: 877-776-0610     PRC:326
www.insight.com
Estab: 2011

Kenneth Lamneck, Insight President
Ken Lamneck, President
Michael Guggemos, CIO
Glynis Bryan, CFO
Helen Johnson, SVP

Provider of mobility, network, and security solutions. The company is engaged in design, integration, and implementation services.

**InsightRX Inc**     HQ
548 Market St Ste 88083
San Francisco CA 94104
P: 205-351-0574     PRC:40
insight-rx.com
Email: support@insight-rx.com
Estab: 2015

Ranvir Mangat, COO
Sirj Goswami, CEO

Developer of cloud-based platform for precision medicine and clinical analytics. The company serves individuals and healthcare organizations.

**InSilixa Inc**     HQ
1000 Hamlin Ct
Sunnyvale CA 94089-1400
P: 408-809-3000     PRC:34
www.insilixa.com
Email: info@insilixa.com
Estab: 2011

Arjang Hassibi, Founder
Nader Gamini, COO

Manufacturer of CMOS biosensor devices used to identify multiple targets including nucleic acids (DNA or RNA), peptides, or metabolites.

**Inspection Services Inc**     HQ
1798 University Ave
Berkeley CA 94703-1514
P: 510-900-2100   F: 510-900-2101    PRC:304
www.inspectionservices.net
Estab: 1995

Leslie Sakai, President
Ed King, Principal

Provider of structural steel and welding, wood framing, anchor and dowel installation, roofing, and waterproofing services.

**Inspironix Inc**     HQ
3400 Cottage Way Ste L
Sacramento CA 95825
P: 916-488-3222   F: 916-488-3210    PRC:323
www.inspironix.com
Email: info@inspironix.com
Emp: 1-10   Estab: 1987

Patrick Swayne, Senior Software Engineer
Cary Parkins, CEO
Erika Friedman, CFO
Matthew Grigas, CTO
Matt Yamamoto, Consultant

Provider of information technology solutions. The company offers software development, web application development, web design, and network services.

**Instant Systems Inc**     HQ
39199 Paseo Padre Pkwy Ste A-1
Fremont CA 94538
P: 415-682-6000     PRC:323
www.instantsys.com
Email: info@instantsys.com
Estab: 2004

Nishant Anand, Director of Engineering
Vipin Chawla, CEO
Uzay Takaoglu, VP of Product Development
David Esser, VP
Vikas Sood, Director of Product Development

Provider of internet based business software and services. The company's services include distribution and technical support.

**Instart Logic Inc**     HQ
450 Lambert Ave
Palo Alto CA 94306
P: 650-919-8856     PRC:322
www.instartlogic.com
Estab: 2010

Thirumalesh Reddy, SVP of Engineering
Hariharan Kolam, CTO
Sumit Dhawan, President
Jony Hartono, CFO
Mitch Parker, Chief Customer Officer

Provider of software-defined application delivery solutions. The company offers services to the travel and hospitality industries.

**InStyle Software Inc**     HQ
5249 Oak Meadow Dr
Santa Rosa CA 95401
P: 314-631-6982     PRC:323
www.instylesoft.com
Email: support@instylesoft.com
Estab: 1997

Sergio Prusky, CEO

Provider of Enterprise Resource Planning Software solutions. The company offers services to the apparel industry.

**Inszoom Inc**     HQ
2603 Camino Ramon Ste 375
San Ramon CA 94583
P: 925-244-0600   F: 925-244-1012    PRC:323
www.inszoom.com
Email: sales@inszoom.com
Estab: 1999

Sunil Kolkur, Product Owner
Umesh Vaidyamath, Founder
Raj Vaidyamath, VP
Lawrence Dsouza, Product Architect and Delivery Manager
Jeziel Eugenio, Executive Assistant

Focuses on immigration case management and compliance automation solutions. The company offers services to law firms.

**Inta Technologies**     HQ
2281 Calle De Luna
Santa Clara CA 95054
P: 408-748-9955   F: 408-727-3027    PRC:80
www.intatech.com
Email: sales@intatech.com
Estab: 1978

Francis Honey, Engineering Manager
Frank Kramer, CEO
Jim Lynch, General Manager
Pia Gronvaldt, Production Control
Roman Milter, Senior Member of Technical Staff

Manufacturer of components used in instruments for environmental analysis. The company also offers ceramic-to-metal assemblies connectors.

**Intake Screens Inc** HQ
8417 River Rd
Sacramento CA 95832
P: 916-665-2727  F: 916-665-2729  PRC:159
www.intakescreensinc.com
Email: screens@intakescreensinc.com
Emp: 1-10  Estab: 1996

Jacob Chapin, Mechanical Design Engineer
Russell Berry, President
Judy McAvoy, Office Manager
Dana Falvey, Operations Manager

Designer and manufacturer of intake screens for
fish protection and filtration. The company also
offers installation and maintenance services.

**Intapp Inc** HQ
200 Portage Ave
Palo Alto CA 94306
P: 650-852-0400  F: 650-852-0402  PRC:322
www.intapp.com
Email: info@intapp.com
Estab: 2000

John Hall, CEO
Thad Jampol, CTO
NgocLan Phan, Accounts Receivable Manager
Thomas Hadig, Company Security Officer
Victoria Onyenwe, Senior GL Accountant

Provider of software and services for risk manage-
ment, time management, and box management.
The company's products include Intapp Time and
Wall Builder.

**Intarcia Therapeutics Inc** BR
24650 Industrial Blvd
Hayward CA 94545
P: 510-782-7800  F: 510-782-7801  PRC:268
www.intarcia.com
Email: james.ahlers@intarcia.com
Estab: 1997

Kevin Galimba, Process Engineer
Kurt Graves, President
James Ahlers, CFO
Raymond Keane, CLO
Andrew Young, CSO

Provider of therapeutic products and related supplies. The company is engaged in research and
development services.

**Integenx Inc** HQ
5720 Stoneridge Dr Ste 300
Pleasanton CA 94588
P: 925-701-3400  PRC:24
www.thermofisher.com
Estab: 2003

Leto Farrales, Process Development Manager
Dean Tsou, Manager of Process Development
Sulatha Dwarakanath, Senior Scientist
Andrew McAllister, Senior Accountant
Yolanda Sanchez, ECO Change Analyst

Provider of rapid human DNA identification
technologies for forensics and law enforcement
applications.

**Integral Development Corp** HQ
850 Hansen Way Bldg 4
Palo Alto CA 94304
P: 650-424-4500  PRC:322
www.integral.com
Estab: 1993

Udyan Kumar, Director of Engineering
Tapan Nanawati, Technical Lead Engineer
Vishal Mahajan, Lead Quality Assurance Engineer
Raju Mishra, Senior Software Engineer
Suraj Shankar, Lead Systems Engineer

Provider of customer-branded trading solutions
for brokers, dealers, banks, and fund investment
managers.

**Integrated Archive Systems Inc** HQ
1121 N San Antonio Rd Ste D100
Palo Alto CA 94303
P: 650-390-9995  F: 650-390-9997  PRC:324
www.iarchive.com
Email: info@iarchive.com
Estab: 1994

John Woodall, VP of Engineering
Sally Rouses, Finance & AR Manager
Clifford Raynes, Account Manager
Tim Adams, Senior Technical Architect
Josh Viarreal, Service Representative

Provider of global data management services. The
company offers storage, data protection, microsoft
exchange, and virtualization services.

**Integrated Communication Systems** HQ
6680 Via Del Oro
San Jose CA 95119
P: 408-491-6000  PRC:59
www.ics-integration.com
Estab: 2002

Aaron Colton, President
Joe Semorad, Purchasing & Operations Manager
Michelle Mercado, Marketing Manager
Justin Gamble, Director of Audio Visual Division
Mark Berlo, AV Project Manager

Provider of communication and integration
services. The company offers installation, space
planning, project management, and maintenance
services.

**Integrated Device Technology Inc** HQ
6024 Silver Creek Valley Rd
San Jose CA 95138
P: 408-284-8200  F: 408-284-2775  PRC:86
www.idt.com
Email: ir@idt.com
Estab: 1980

Jianbin Hao, VP of Engineering
Upendra Kulkarni, Director of Applications Engi-
neering
Greg Waters, President
Brian White, SVP
Sailesh Chittipeddi, Global Operations VP

Manufacturer of semiconductor related products
for communications, computing, and consumer
industries.

**Integrated Engineering Services** HQ
70 Saratoga Ave Ste 200
Santa Clara CA 95051
P: 408-261-3500  F: 408-261-4176  PRC:209
www.iesengineering.net
Email: ies@intengr.com
Estab: 1995

Leanne Cossairt, Senior Mechanical Engineer
Tim Bancroft, Chemical Engineer
Jeff Tarter, Principal

Provider of designs for complex Hi-tech microelectronic needs. The company also serves the life
science facilities.

**Integrated Science Solutions Inc** HQ
1261 Locust St Ste 70
Walnut Creek CA 94596
P: 925-979-1535  PRC:304
issi-net.com
Email: info@issi-net.com
Estab: 1999

David Dobson, President
Cecelia McCloy, CEO
Carlin Gill, VP of Finance and Administration

Provider of professional services to federal and
state clients. The company offers earth and environmental science and engineering services.

**Integrated Silicon Solution Inc** HQ
1623 Buckeye Dr
Milpitas CA 95035-4216
P: 408-969-6600  F: 408-969-7800  PRC:208
www.issi.com
Email: sales@issi.com
Estab: 1988

Guo Zhang, Design Engineer
Eddie Wang, Technical Staff Design Engineer
Jong Park, Engineer
Jian-Yue Pan, Partner
Kong Han, CEO

Designer and developer of high performance
integrated circuits. The company also focuses on
the marketing aspects.

**Integrated Surface Technologies Inc** BR
3475-F Edison Way
Menlo Park CA 94025
P: 650-324-1824  PRC:209
www.insurftech.com
Email: info@insurftech.com
Estab: 2007

Jonathan Prindle, Senior Process Engineer
Jeff Chinn, Founder
Robert Ashurst, Chief Scientist of Auburn Univer-
sity Partnership
Zia Hassan, Manufacturing Manager
Ken Kotter, Manufacturing Lead

Provider of supermolecular ceramic coating for
watersafing electronics. The company offers stic-
tion control and surface modification services.

**Integrated Tooling Inc** HQ
1017 Pecten Ct
Milpitas CA 95035
P: 408-934-3862  F: 408-934-3863  PRC:80
www.integratedtoolinginc.com

Tony Silva, President

Developer and manufacturer of tools, dies, and
molds. The company specializes in fabricating
small intricate parts for machines.

**Integrated Wave Technologies**    HQ
4042 Clipper Ct
Fremont CA 94538
P: 510-353-0260    PRC:60
www.miltrans.com
Email: info@miltrans.com

Timothy McCune, President
Cindy Cook-Johnson, Business Manager

Provider of voice recognition technology services. The company offers printing calculators and electronic camera shutters.

**Intel Corp**    HQ
2200 Mission College Blvd
Santa Clara CA 95054-1549
P: 408-765-8080    PRC:91
www.intel.in
Sales: Over $3B

Andy Bryant, Chairman
George Davis, EVP
Claire Dixon, VP
Michael Mayberry, CTO
Ann Kelleher, SVP

Designer, developer, and marketer of processors and motherboards. The company also focuses on tablets, laptops, desktops, and other devices.

**IntelaMetrix Inc**    HQ
2145 Elkins Way Ste G
Brentwood CA 94513
P: 925-606-7044    PRC:194
intelametrix.com
Email: WebInfo@intelametrix.com
Estab: 2004

Luiz Da Silva, President
Heidi Stark, CFO
Daniel Watts, Accounts Manager
Patricia Bryan, Assembly Contractor

Specializes in ultrasound technology solutions. The company offers assessment tools for the health, fitness and wellness industries.

**Intelepeer Cloud Communications**    HQ
155 Bovet Rd Ste 405
San Mateo CA 94402
P: 650-525-9200    PRC:67
www.intelepeer.com
Email: info@intelepeer.com
Estab: 2003

Andre Simone, CFO
Jeremy Jones, CCO
John Ward, CTO
Kristin Manwarren, Chief Legal Officer
Matt Edic, Chief Experience Officer

Provider of on-demand cloud-based communication services. The company offers media peering, SIP trunking, and direct inward dialing services.

**Intelight ITS LLC**    HQ
5962 La Place Ct Ste 150
Carlsbad CA 92008
P: 520-795-8808    PRC:72
www.intelight-its.com
Email: info@intelight-its.com
Emp: 11-50 Estab: 2006

Mike Gallagher, Senior Systems Engineer
Craig Gardner, Founder

Provider of electrical engineering solutions. The company offers expertise on systems, traffic products and software.

**IntelinAir Inc**    HQ
75 E Santa Clara St 6th Fl
San Jose CA 95113
P: 818-445-2339    PRC:324
www.intelinair.com
Email: contact@intelinair.com
Estab: 2015

David Wilson, VP of Web & Cloud Engineering
Al Eisaian, CEO
Naira Hovakimyan, Chief Scientist
Harold Reetz, Chief Agronomist
Adrian Tudor, Chief of Product

Provider of aerial imagery analytics such as image analysis and change detection and deep learning and neural networks for farmers.

**Intellectsoft**    HQ
721 Colorado Ave Ste 101
Palo Alto CA 94303
P: 650-300-4335    PRC:315
www.intellectsoft.net/
Email: info@intellectsoft.net
Estab: 2007

Artem Kozel, Co-Founder
Alexander Skalabanov, Co-Founder
Vlad Vahromovs, CEO
Andrew Kashcheyev, CTO
Iurii Odnorogov, VP of Sales

Provider of impactful digital engineering solutions with latest technologies.

**Intelli-Touch Apps Inc**    HQ
2440 Camino Ramon Ste 155
San Ramon CA 94583
P: 925-884-1802    PRC:319
intelli-touch.com
Email: info@intelli-touch.com
Estab: 2011

William Westfall, CEO
Barry Ford, COO

Specializes in automating and simplifying the personal and business communications and it serves the legal industry.

**Intellicon Solutions**    HQ
7 Windeler Ct Ste 700
Moraga CA 94556
P: 925-377-7925    F: 925-377-5035    PRC:322
intelliconsol.com
Emp: 11-50

Doug Mosher, Co-Founder
Todd Parsons, Co-Founder

Provider of intelligent consulting solutions for learning and development, performance management systems, and related social media communication.

**Intelligent Inference Systems Corp**    HQ
566-108 Nasa Research Park
Moffett Field CA 94035
P: 408-390-1455    F: 408-730-1016    PRC:323
www.iiscorp.com
Estab: 1993

Prashant Sasatte, Founder
Hamid Berenji, CEO

Provider of computational intelligence services. The company primarily caters to high-tech companies.

**Intelliswift Software Inc**    HQ
2201 Walnut Ave Ste 180 1st Fl
Fremont CA 94538
P: 510-490-9240    F: 510-490-9246    PRC:323
www.intelliswift.com
Email: info@intelliswift.com
Estab: 2001

Pat Patel, Founder
Vinita Dujari, Human Resource Manager
Kristin Tran, Senior Marketing Executive
Michelle Rose, Account Manager
Shafiq Mohammed, Senior Manager

Provider of application development services for enterprises. The company also focuses on big data, cloud, web solutions, and staffing services.

**IntelliVision Technologies Corp**    HQ
6203 San Ignacio Ave Ste 112
San Jose CA 95119
P: 408-754-1690    PRC:318
intelli-vision.com
Email: info@intelli-vision.com
Estab: 2002

Krishna Khadloya, VP of Engineering
Whit Pritchett, President
Vaidhi Nathan, SVP of Cameras and Analytics
Sheri Becker, Controller

Provider of software and solutions for security, surveillance, traffic, automotive, robotics, drones, smart home, mobile, and retail analytics solutions.

**Intematix Corp**    HQ
46410 Fremont Blvd
Fremont CA 94538
P: 510-933-3300    F: 510-668-0793    PRC:243
www.intematix.com
Estab: 2000

Farid Tawfik, Senior Facilities Engineer
Yi-Qun Li, CEO
Xiongfei Shen, Manager
Shengfeng Liu, Director of R&D Nitride Phosphors
Mike Ko, Business Development Manager

Developer of microscopy metrology tools and electronic materials. The company offers services to commercial properties.

**Intercom Inc**    HQ
55 Second St 4th Fl
San Francisco CA 94105
P: 877-595-5175    PRC:323
www.intercom.com
Email: team@intercom.com
Estab: 2011

Darragh Curran, VP of Engineering
David Barrett, Co-Founder
Eoghan McCabe, CEO
Ciaran Lee, CTO
Paul Adams, VP of Products

Designer and developer of communication packages. The company also focuses on user intelligence solutions.

**Interface Masters Technologies Inc**   HQ
150 E Brokaw Rd
San Jose CA 95112
P: 408-441-9341   F: 815-364-0888   PRC:97
interfacemasters.com
Email: sales@interfacemasters.com
Estab: 1997

Ben Askarinam, Founder
Matthew Butrimovitz, Marketing Manager
Jennifer Tam, Director of Operations

Developer of technology and networking solutions.
The company's products include embedded
switches, adapters, and related accessories.

**Intergraphics**   HQ
667 Brighton Rd
Pacifica CA 94044
P: 650-359-3087   PRC:316
www.intergraphics.com
Email: kerstin@intergraphics.com
Estab: 1991

Kerstin Connelly, Owner

Developer of multi-lingual graphics. The company provides translation, typography, and other
services.

**Interhealth Nutraceuticals Inc**   HQ
5451 Industrial Way
Benicia CA 94510
P: 800-783-4636   F: 707-751-2801   PRC:272
www.interhealthusa.com
Email: info@interhealthusa.com
Estab: 1987

Paul Dijkstra, CEO
Maria Zimmer, Quality Manager
Patrick McCullough, Head of Sales & Marketing
- NAFTA
Jay Martin, Head of Sales & Marketing - APAC
Reto Renggli, Head of Sales & Marketing - EMEA

Developers and marketer of nutritional ingredients.
The company offers dietary supplement, food and
beverage, and animal healthcare products.

**Interloc Solutions**   HQ
340 Palladio Pkwy Ste 526
Folsom CA 95630
P: 916-817-4590   F: 916-817-4594   PRC:326
www.interlocsolutions.com
Email: info@interlocsolutions.com
Emp: 11-50 Estab: 2005

Mike Watson, President
Gretchen Gallagher, EVP of Business Develop-
ment & Marketing
Jason VenHuizen, EVP of Products & Technology
Joe Mendoza, VP of Technical Service
Brad Knowles, VP of Professional Services
Canada

Provider of consulting services and mobile solutions. The company serves the oil and gas and
transportation industries.

**Intermedia.net Inc**   HQ
825 E Middlefield Rd
Mountain View CA 94043
P: 800-379-7729   F: 650-965-7791   PRC:67
www.intermedia.net
Estab: 1995

Michael Gold, President
Jonathan McCormick, COO
Vincent Gullotta, Production System Administrator
Ryan Barrett, VP of Security & Privacy
Sarat Khilnani, VP of Product Management

Provider of cloud services including VoIP telephony, instant messaging, and file management to
small and mid-sized businesses.

**Intermedianet Inc**   HQ
100 Mathilda Pl Ste 600
Sunnyvale CA 94086
P: 650-641-4000   F: 646-225-7348   PRC:325
www.intermedia.net/
Email: sales@intermedia.net
Estab: 1995

Andrew Gachechiladze, SVP of Product Devel-
opment
Michael Gold, CEO
Jason Veldhuis, CFO
Jonathan McCormick, COO
Jonathan Levine, CTO

Provider of UCaaS, CCaaS, and cloud business
applications that helps businesses and partners
with secure solutions for communication and
collaboration.

**Intermems Inc**   HQ
7370 Basking Ridge Ave
San Jose CA 95138
P: 408-241-0007   PRC:87
intermems.com
Email: info@intermems.com
Estab: 2002

Wendell McCulley, President
Steven Repetto, Director of Sales
Abhijeet Sathe, SVP of Research

Provider of micromolding, plating, thin film
deposition, anodic and wafer bonding, and related
services.

**Intermolecular Inc**   HQ
3011 N First St
San Jose CA 95134
P: 408-582-5700   F: 408-582-5401   PRC:212
www.intermolecular.com
Email: inquiry@intermolecular.com
Estab: 2004
Sales: $30M to $100M

Minh Nguyen, Process Engineer
Bill Roeschlein, CFO
Karl Littau, CTO
Pat McGeachy, Accounts Payable Manager
Steve Kuhn, Equipment Service Group Manager

Provider of high productivity combinatorial
technologies. The company serves solar device
manufacturers.

**Internap Corp**   BR
2151 Mission College Blvd
Santa Clara CA 95054
P: 877-843-7627   PRC:67
www.internap.com
Estab: 1996

Michael Sicoli, President
Peter Aquino, Chairman
Andrew Day, COO
John Filipowicz, CAO
Richard Ramlall, Chief Communications Officer

Provider of internet network services, colocation, hosting, content delivery, and broadband
solutions.

**International Electronic Components
Inc**   RH
809 Aldo Ave Unit 104
Santa Clara CA 95054
P: 408-496-0474   F: 408-496-0478   PRC:202
www.ieccan.com
Email: tnarcelles@iecus.com
Estab: 1966

Geert Breesch, US Operations
Jennifer Lewis, Customer Service

Distributor of printed circuit boards, consumables,
and inspection and measuring equipment. The
company is engaged in installation services.

**International Manufacturing**   HQ
1745 Addison Way
Hayward CA 94544
P: 510-783-8872   F: 510-783-1430   PRC:80
www.international-mfg.com
Email: info@international-mfg.com
Estab: 1981

Clement Johnson, Owner

Manufacturer of precision components for use
in semiconductor equipment, medical devices,
aerospace vehicles, and defense systems.

**International Medcom Inc**   BR
103 Morris St Ste A-5
Sebastopol CA 95472
P: 707-823-0336   F: 707-823-7207   PRC:13
medcom.com
Estab: 1986

Steve Weiss, Chief Electronic Design Engineer
Dan Sythe, CEO
Ross Randrup, Special Projects

Provider of radiation detection instruments and
systems. The company provides technology for
nuclear medicine, health physics, and public
safety products.

**International Microsystems Inc**   HQ
48389 Fremont Blvd Ste 110
Fremont CA 94538
P: 408-942-1001   PRC:102
www.imi-test.com
Email: sales@imi-test.com

Tho Nguyen, Software Engineer
Wayne Chiu, Senior Software Engineer

Designer and manufacturer of flash memory duplication equipment. The company also offers related
test equipment.

**International Power Technology Inc**   HQ
  1042 W Hedding St Ste 100
  San Jose CA 95126
P: 408-246-9040   F: 408-246-9036   PRC:293
www.intpower.com
Estab: 1974

Robert Forgione, CFO

Provider of operation and maintenance services
for power plants. The company also focuses on
engineering and field service.

**International Process Solutions Inc**   HQ
  1300 Industrial Rd Ste 22
  San Carlos CA 94070
P: 650-595-7890   F: 650-595-7899   PRC:31
www.ips-us.com
Email: sales-support@ips-us.com
Estab: 1997

John Doe, President
Joseph Giacomo, Field Service Supervisor

Provider of calibration, maintenance, document
generation and validation services of pharmaceutical and biotech process equipment.

**Internet Software Sciences**   HQ
  13851 Fremont Pines Ln
  Los Altos Hills CA 94022
P: 650-949-0942   F: 650-917-0913   PRC:323
www.inet-sciences.com
Email: sales@inet-sciences.com
Estab: 1995

Scott Vanderlip, President

Developer of web based applications for IT help
desk, customer support, asset tracking, and facilities management needs.

**Internetspeech Inc**   HQ
  5942 Foligno Way
  San Jose CA 95138
P: 408-532-8460   F: 408-274-8151   PRC:67
www.internetspeech.com
Email: corporate@internetspeech.com
Estab: 1998

Emdad Khan, President
Jeff Griffin, VP of marketing & Sales
George Yan, Director of Applications

Provider of audio internet technology services.
The company offers world-wide web and enabled
services.

**Interphase Systems**   HQ
  3565 Victor St Ste C
  Santa Clara CA 95054
P: 408-315-8603   F: 408-516-9046   PRC:150
www.interphasesystems.us
Estab: 1995

Alex Cherkassky, VP of Engineering
Patty Gallagher, Team Leader
Bob Mullin, Consultant

Manufacturer of test equipment for the disc drive
industry. The company offers consulting and build-
to-print services.

**Interphasic LLC**   HQ
  1621 Plumas Ave
  Seaside CA 93955
P: 831-392-0708   F: 831-392-0710   PRC:211
www.interphasic.com
Email: sales@interphasic.com

Robert Engholm, President

Manufacturer of motion control systems. The company offers product support services and it serves
the industrial sector.

**Interra Systems Inc**   HQ
  1601 S De Anza Blvd Ste 212
  Cupertino CA 95014
P: 408-579-2000   F: 408-579-2050   PRC:323
www.interrasystems.com
Email: info@interrasystems.com
Estab: 2000

Mark Brown, CFO
Shelly Adhikari, Senior Manager

Provider of diversified software products and
services for digital media and semiconductor
industries.

**Intersect Ent Inc**   HQ
  1555 Adams Dr
  Menlo Park CA 94025
P: 650-641-2100   PRC:187
www.intersectent.com
Email: info@intersectent.com
Emp: 393
Sales: $100M to $300M

Susan Stimson, CSO
Amy Wolbeck, VP of Regulatory Affairs & Quality
Doug Rainforth, Senior Director of Finance
Michelle Jess, Principle Complaint Handling
Specialist

Provider of steroid-releasing implants that props
open the sinuses for the treatment of common
cold and sinusitis.

**Interson Corp**   HQ
  7150 Koll Ctr Pkwy
  Pleasanton CA 94566
P: 925-462-4948   F: 925-462-4833   PRC:198
www.interson.com
Estab: 1989

Dale Mowery, Manufacturing Engineer
Roman Solek, President
Monica Solek, Director of Human Resources

Manufacturer of ultrasound products. The company offers services to offices, hospitals, and clinics
around the world.

**Interstate Plastics Inc**   BR
  2065 Williams St
  San Leandro CA 94577
P: 510-483-4341   F: 510-483-4350   PRC:284
www.interstateplastics.com
Email: info@interstateplastics.com

Mike Feld, Medical Sales Development Manager
Gary Stelle, Sales Manager

Provider of plastic products. The company's
products include plastic sheets, rods, tubes, and
industrial accessories.

**Interstate Plastics Inc**   HQ
  330 Commerce Cir
  Sacramento CA 95815
P: 916-422-3110   F: 916-422-1608   PRC:284
www.interstateplastics.com
Email: info@interstateplastics.com
Emp: 11-50 Estab: 1980

Mike Feld, Medical Sales Development Manager

Manufacturer and distributor of industrial plastics.
The company offers plastic sheets, rods, tubing,
and profiles.

**Intertek Group PLC**   BR
  1365 Adams Ct
  Menlo Park CA 94025
P: 650-463-2900   F: 650-463-2910   PRC:269
www.intertek.com
Estab: 1885

Wolfhart Hauser, CEO
Andr' Lacroix, CEO
Patrick Lee, Joint CEO
Ross McCluskey, CFO
Diane Bitzel, Group Chief Information Officer

Provider of advisory, business consulting, risk
management, outsourcing, validation, and training
services.

**Intertrust Technologies Corp**   HQ
  920 Stewart Dr
  Sunnyvale CA 94085
P: 408-616-1600   F: 408-616-1626   PRC:325
www.intertrust.com
Estab: 1990

Talal Shamoon, CEO
David Maher, EVP
Jeff McDow, Chief Legal Officer
Tim Schaaff, EVP
Matthew Glotzer, CFO

Provider of security technology services such as
content protection, white label video distribution,
and software tamper resistance.

**InterVene Inc**   HQ
  415 Grand Ave Ste 302
  S San Francisco CA 94080
P: 650-351-6725   PRC:186
www.intervene-med.com
Email: info@intervene-med.com
Estab: 2011

Fletcher Wilson, Founder
Jeff Elkins, COO
Nancy Miceli, Quality Consultant
Michi Garrison, VP of Research
Tracy Roberts, VP of Clinical & Regulatory Affairs

Provider of medical devices such as blueleaf en-
dovenous valve formation system to treat severe
venous disease in the legs.

**Interworking Labs Inc** HQ
PO Box 66190
Scotts Valley CA 95067
P: 831-460-7010   F: 831-401-2320   PRC:97
www.iwl.com
Email: info@iwl.com
Emp: 1-10   Estab: 1993

Chris Wellens, President
Karl Auerbach, CTO
Judy Jones, Account Manager
Rico Sumarna, Accounts Executive

Provider of network related services. The company focuses on testing, emulation, and also offers network optimization products.

**Intest Ems Products** BR
47777 Warm Springs Blvd
Fremont CA 94539
P: 408-678-9167   F: 408-678-9101   PRC:208
www.intest.com
Email: info@intest.com

Leonard Torres, Operations Manager

Manufacturer of semiconductors to test integrated circuits. The company also focuses on testing wafer products.

**Intevac Inc** HQ
3560 Bassett St
Santa Clara CA 95054
P: 408-986-9888   F: 408-988-8145   PRC:95
www.intevac.com
Estab: 1991
Sales: $30M to $100M

Demetrius Scott, Research
Kevin Roderick, Process Engineer
Wendell Blonigan, President
Jeff Andreson, CFO
James Moniz, CFO

Supplier of magnetic media processing systems. The company offers advanced equipment to the hard disk drive, solar, and photonics industries.

**Intilop Inc** HQ
4800 Great America Pkwy Ste 231
Santa Clara CA 95054
P: 408-791-6700   F: 408-496-0444   PRC:200
www.intilop.com
Email: info@intilop.com
Estab: 2004

Kelly Masood, CTO

Provider of engineering design services. The company also develops and provides silicon IP products.

**Intool** HQ
807 Aldo Ave Ste 109
Santa Clara CA 95054
P: 408-727-7575   PRC:80
intoolmachineshop.com
Estab: 1989

Doug Mooney, Owner
Courtney Mooney, Regional Sales Manager

Manufacturer and designer of the machine components. The company is involved in machining, fabricating, casting and assembling services.

**Intraop Medical Corp** HQ
570 Del Rey Ave
Sunnyvale CA 94085
P: 408-636-1020   F: 408-636-0022   PRC:189
intraop.com
Email: info@intraopmedical.com
Estab: 1993

Derek DeScioli, VP of Global Sales
Rick Belford, VP of QA

Manufacturer of mobetron for the treatment of cancer. The company offers services to hospitals, clinics, and patients.

**Intresys Inc** BR
1301 Shoreway Rd Ste 190
Belmont CA 94002-4158
P: 888-372-1790   PRC:322
info.turbocourt.com
Estab: 1995

Alexander Zilberfayn, Co-Founder
Tania Wasser, Co-Founder
Diana Kardash, Solutions Technical Manager

Provider of child support and egovernment solutions. The company serves attorneys, public sector agencies, and governments.

**Intrinsic-Id Inc** HQ
710 Lakeway Dr Ste 150
Sunnyvale CA 94085
P: 408-933-9980   PRC:86
www.intrinsic-id.com
Email: info@intrinsic-id.com
Estab: 2008

Pim Tuyls, CEO

Designer of security solutions. The company offers services to semiconductor companies and device manufacturers.

**Intrinsyx Technologies Corp** BR
350 N Akron Rd Ste 2028 NASA Research Park MS 19-102
Moffett Field CA 94035
P: 650-210-9219   F: 650-210-9222   PRC:323
www.intrinsyx.com
Email: info@intrinsyx.com

Ghazala Mian, President
Ahsan Ali, CEO

Provider of information technology solutions. The company caters to federal, state, and commercial stakeholders.

**Intuit Inc** HQ
2700 Coast Ave
Mountain View CA 94043
P: 800-446-8848   PRC:324
www.intuit.com
Estab: 1983
Sales: Over $3B

Rajashree Pimpalkhare, Director of Engineering
Pavan Nutalapati, Software Engineer
Derek Tatman, Product Owner
Scott Cook, Founder
Sasan Goodarzi, CEO

Provider of financial management software solutions. The company offers services to small businesses and related organizations.

**Intuity Medical Inc** HQ
3500 W Warren Ave
Fremont CA 94538
P: 510-946-8800   F: 510-897-0603   PRC:187
www.presspogo.com
Estab: 2007

Edgar Ramirez, Senior Mechanical Engineer
Monica Joya, Senior Medical Device Engineer
Emory Anderson, President
Robb Hesley, COO
Tammy Cameron, CFO

Provider of medical products such as blood glucose monitoring system, meter, cartridge, and data management for diabetes management.

**Invensas Corp** HQ
3025 Orchard Pkwy
San Jose CA 95134
P: 408-321-6000   F: 408-321-8257   PRC:212
www.invensas.com
Email: info@invensas.com
Estab: 2011

Scott McGrath, Senior Process Engineer

Provider of software solutions for computer applications. The company also offers semiconductor technologies.

**Inventive Resources Inc** HQ
5038 Salida Blvd
Salida CA 95368
P: 209-545-1663   F: 209-545-3533   PRC:155
www.iriproducts.com
Email: info@iriproducts.com
Emp: 1-10   Estab: 1983

John Paoluccio, Engineer

Manufacturer of products for the environmental and contamination control industry. The company also focuses on distribution.

**Inverse Solutions Inc** HQ
3922 Valley Ave Ste A
Pleasanton CA 94566
P: 925) 931-9500   F: 925-931-9515   PRC:80
inversesolutionsinc.com
Email: info@inversesolutionsinc.com

David Jordan, Owner
Josh Jordan, VP of Manufacturing

Manufacturer of custom-made machines for commercial and government markets. The company serves semiconductor, medical devices, and aerospace fields.

**Invitae Corp** HQ
1400 16th St
San Francisco CA 94103
P: 415-930-4018   F: 415-276-4164   PRC:268
www.invitae.com
Email: clinconsult@invitae.com
Emp: 788   Estab: 2012
Sales: $100M to $300M

Patty Dumond, VP of Finance
Robert Nussbaum, CMO
Swaroop Aradhya, Medical Director

Provider of genetic information. The company offers to bring genetic information into routine medical practice to improve the quality of healthcare.

## Invoice2go Inc HQ

555 Bryant St Ste 263
Palo Alto CA 94301
P: 888-818-7110 PRC:319
invoice.2go.com
Email: support@invoice2go.com
Estab: 2002

Sebastian Urban, Senior Director of Engineering
Chris Strode, Founder
Greg Waldorf, CEO
Mark Bartels, CFO
Kyle Flowers, COO

A mobile and web app for micro and small business owners to create invoice, track expenses and track time.

## Invuity Inc HQ

444 De Haro St
San Francisco CA 94107
P: 415-655-2100 F: 877-711-7768 PRC:189
www.invuity.com
Estab: 2004

Gilbert Mata, Manufacturing Engineer
Nancy Hargreaves, Director of Finance
Sam McCue, Director of Sales
Craig Pritsky, Area Sales Manager
Susan Martin, VP of Marketing

Manufacturer of surgical devices with cutting edge photonics technology to view surgical cavities during open, minimally invasive procedures.

## Io Informatics Inc HQ

2550 Ninth St Ste 114
Berkeley CA 94710-2552
P: 510-705-8470 F: 510-705-8476 PRC:323
www.io-informatics.com
Email: info@io-informatics.com
Estab: 2003

Jason Eshleman, Director of Informatics
Larry Benbow, Director of Systems Engineering
Robert Martin, Director of Engineering and Senior Knowledge Engineer
Robert Stanley, President
Erich Gombocz, CSO

Provider of software and services for data integration applications in areas such as life science and medicine.

## Io Integration Inc HQ

20480 Pacifica Dr Ste 1C
Cupertino CA 95014
P: 408-996-3420 F: 408-996-3425 PRC:323
www.iointegration.com
Email: info@iointegration.com
Estab: 2001

Mike Holt, CEO
Bill Covington, CTO
Kevin Martorana, Chief Information Officer
Arlie Andrews, CFO
Damian Diaz, Director of Global Marketing

Provider of marketing technology and digital media workflow solutions. The company offers marketing automation and cross-media publishing services.

## Iometrix Inc HQ

2 Embarcadero Ctr Fl 8
San Francisco CA 94111
P: 650-872-4001 PRC:306
www.iometrix.com
Email: info@iometrix.com
Estab: 2003

Thomas Mandeville, Director of Operations

Developer of next generation packet networks and solutions for telecom service providers and equipment manufacturers.

## Ionix Internet HQ

266 Sutter St
San Francisco CA 94108
P: 888-884-6649 F: 415-840-0658 PRC:67
www.ionix.net
Email: info@ionix.net
Estab: 1997

Russ Richardson, Founder

Provider of web hosting solutions. The company offers network security, research, hi-speed access, and telecommuting services.

## Ios Optics HQ

3150 Molinaro St
Santa Clara CA 95054
P: 408-982-9510 F: 408-982-9513 PRC:175
www.iosoptics.com
Email: info@iosoptics.com
Estab: 1974

Derek Fitzpatrick, President
Douglas Fitzpatrick, Chairman
Keith Baldwin, Manufacturing Manager
Dino Valencia, VP of Sales & Marketing

Manufacturer of custom precision optical components. The company offers coating and filter glass services. It serves avionics and life sciences fields.

## Iosafe Inc HQ

12760 Earhart Ave
Auburn CA 95602
P: 530-820-3090 PRC:95
www.iosafe.com
Email: info@iosafe.com
Emp: 1-10 Estab: 2005

Robb Moore, CEO
Linda Miller, Senior National Sales Manager
Leif Watkins, Sales Manager
Adam Logan, Channel Sales Manager
Brigitte Bedell, Channel Sales Manager

Provider of disaster proof hardware. The company provides SoloPRO SSD External and ioSafe Rugged Portable.

## iota Computing Inc HQ

2275 E Bayshore Rd Ste 108
Palo Alto CA 94303-3222
P: 888-440-4004 PRC:323
www.iotacomputing.com
Email: info@iotacomputing.com
Estab: 2010

Jeremy Walker, Co-Founder

Specializes in turnkey architecture . The company is engaged in building core technology for tiny edge devices.

## Ip Infusion Inc HQ

1188 E Arques Ave
Sunnyvale CA 94085
P: 408-400-1900 F: 408-400-1863 PRC:323
www.ipinfusion.com
Email: info@ipinfusion.com
Estab: 1999

Atsushi Ogata, President
Manohar Radhakrishnan, Manager of Quality Assurance
Robert Kester, Director of Finance
Shaji Nathan, VP of Product Marketing

Developer of software for wireless internet products and offers data center networking, carrier ethernet transport, and mobile backhauling services.

## Ipass Inc HQ

3800 Bridge Pkwy
Redwood City CA 94065
P: 650-232-4100 F: 650-232-4111 PRC:68
www.ipass.com
Email: pr@ipass.com
Emp: 70 Estab: 1996
Sales: $30M to $100M

Anita Jerome, Release Engineer
Alex Chernyakhovsky, Lead SW Engineer
Gary Griffiths, President
Darin Vickery, CFO
Karen Willem, CFO

Provider of cloud-based mobility management and Wi-Fi connectivity services. The company serves global enterprises and telecommunication sectors.

## Ipdialog Inc HQ

542 Lakeside Dr Ste 7
Sunnyvale CA 94085
P: 408-830-0800 PRC:71
www.ipdialog.com
Email: info@ipdialog.com
Estab: 1999

Hardish Singh, President
Gerry Smith, Director of Hardware Development

Developer of hardware and software technology. The company creates SIP stack, user interface, and media stream handling for phones.

## Ipera Technology Inc HQ

20660 Stevens Creek Blvd Ste 269
Cupertino CA 95014
P: 650-286-0889 F: 650-286-0890 PRC:323
iperatech.com
Email: info@iperatech.com
Estab: 2005

Johnson Yan, President

Provider of multi-format video transcoder solutions for broadcast and IP multi-screen video production.

**Ipg Photonics**   BR
3930 Freedom Cir Ste 103
Santa Clara CA 95054
P: 408-492-8830   PRC:124
ipgphotonics.com
Email: salesus@ipgphotonics.com
Estab: 1990

Gregory Altshuler, President
Mike Klos, General Manager
Mike Mirov, General Manager
Bryce Samson, Director of Sales
Toby Strite, Sales & Marketing Director

Provider of high power fiber lasers and amplifiers.
The company's offerings include Q-switch lasers,
multi-mode diodes, pulsed and direct-diode lasers.

**Iridex Corp**   HQ
1212 Terra Bella Ave
Mountain View CA 94043
P: 650-940-4700   F: 650-940-4710   PRC:186
www.iridex.com
Email: info@iridex.com
Estab: 1989
Sales: $30M to $100M

William Moore, CEO
Bruce Hughes, Information Technology Manager
Cristina Quintos, Quality Assurance Supervisor
Ken Bice, VP of Aesthetic Sales
James Brumm, Area Sales Manager

Provider of therapeutic based laser consoles,
delivery devices, and consumable instrumentation.
The company serves the healthcare industry.

**Iris Ao Inc**   HQ
2930 Shattuck Ave Ste 304
Berkeley CA 94705-1883
P: 510-849-2375   F: 510-217-9646   PRC:200
www.irisao.com
Email: info@irisao.com
Estab: 2002

Pamela Caton, Microsystems Engineer

Manufacturer of microelectromechanical based
optical systems. The company's applications
include biomedical imaging and portable laser
communications.

**Iris Biotechnologies Inc**   HQ
5201 Great America Pkwy Ste 320
Santa Clara CA 95054
P: 408-867-2885   PRC:186
irisbiotechnologies.com
Email: simonchin@irisbiotech.com
Estab: 1999

Simon Chin, President
Ronald Gemberling, Chief Medical Officer
James LeBlanc, VP of Operations
Ralph Sinibaldi, VP of Product Development
Gayle Murray, Business Development Manager

Provider of medical informatics system. The company develops chips to precisely diagnose and
identify actionable treatment choices for breast
cancer.

**Irislogic Inc**   HQ
2354 Walsh Ave
Santa Clara CA 95051
P: 408-855-8741   PRC:323
www.irislogic.com
Estab: 1998

Nick Boswell, Manager
Lavita Dcruz, VP of Operations

Provider of global consulting services and
solutions. The company specializes in custom
software development, network security, cloud,
and testing.

**Iron Systems Inc**   HQ
980 Mission Ct
Fremont CA 94539
P: 408-943-8000   F: 408-943-8101   PRC:95
www.ironsystems.com
Email: info@ironsystems.com
Estab: 1996

Harpreet Dhillon, VP of Engineering
Anil Kumar, Senior Software Engineer
Billy Bath, President
Harvey Bath, COO
Bob Sidhu, VP of Worldwide Sales

Provider of network storage, hybrid cloud, and big
data infrastructure solutions. The company offers
OEM/ODM manufacturing services.

**Ironmind Enterprises Inc**   HQ
PO Box 1228
Nevada City CA 95959
P: 530-272-3579   F: 530-272-3095   PRC:82
www.ironmind.com
Email: sales@ironmind.com
Emp: 1-10   Estab: 1988

Chris Sheehan, Editor

Manufacturer of medical products with flower
essences. The company's offerings also include
gym equipment and training gears.

**Isa Corp**   HQ
3213 Whipple Rd
Union City CA 94587
P: 510-324-3755   F: 510-324-3701   PRC:135
www.isa-corporation.com
Email: info@isa-corporation.com
Estab: 1997

Tony Zante, Owner
Francisco Ferre, Owner
Juhi Verma, Project Manager
Gerald Zahn, Project Manager

Developer and manufacturer of solar mounting
systems for commercial applications. The company also offers solar thermal systems.

**iSchemaView Inc**   HQ
405 El Camino Real Ste 601
Menlo Park CA 94025
P: 650-388-9767   PRC:189
www.i-rapid.com
Estab: 2011

Matus Straka, Software Engineer
Don Listwin, President
Carolina Maier, VP of Research

Developer and provider of neuroimaging platform.
The company specializes in cerebrovascular
imaging analysis.

**Ise Labs Inc**   HQ
46800 Bayside Pkwy
Fremont CA 94538
P: 510-687-2500   F: 510-687-2513   PRC:208
www.iselabs.com
Estab: 1983

Ping Wong, Product Engineer
Mark Wang, Human Resources Manager
May Luo, Buyer

Provider of semiconductor services. The company
offers services such as production test, test interface, and mechanical testing.

**iSmart Alarm Inc**   HQ
120 San Lucar Ct
Sunnyvale CA 94086
P: 408-245-2551   PRC:59
www.ismartalarm.com
Email: customerservice@ismartalarm.com
Estab: 2012

Justin Chi, Product Manager
Joshua Proch, Customer Service Representative

Manufacturer of home security products. The company offers alarms, cameras, sirens, and related
accessories.

**iSOA Group Inc**   BR
1255 Treat Blvd Ste 100
Walnut Creek CA 94597
P: 925-465-7400   PRC:326
www.isoagroup.com
Email: commercesi@sisinc.com
Estab: 1997

Taylor Kataoka, DataPower Engineer
Peter Ling, Co-Founder
Bryon Kataoka, Founder
Cheryl Bertini, COO
Natalia Kataoka, Executive Administrative Assis-
tant

Provider of business process management,
service oriented architecture, and business analytics services to finance, energy, retail, and other
sectors.

**Isola Usa Corp**   BR
3233 Dwight Rd
Elk Grove CA 95758
P: 916-429-4462   F: 916-429-4464   PRC:211
www.isola-group.com
Email: info@isola-group.com
Emp: 11-50 Estab: 1912

Jeff Waters, President

Designer, developer, and manufacturer of laminate
materials used to fabricate multilayer PCBs. The
company serves the medical market.

**Isomorphic Software**   HQ
1 Sansome St Ste 3500
San Francisco CA 94104
P: 415-222-9902   F: 415-222-9912   PRC:322
www.smartclient.com
Estab: 1998

Charles Kendrick, CTO

Focuses on building web applications. The
company is engaged in training, consulting, and
technical support services.

**ISSE Services** HQ
9290 W Stockton Blvd Ste 100
Elk Grove CA 95758
P: 916-670-1082 PRC:323
isse-services.com
Emp: 1-10

Angela Spease, Owner
Kevin Spease, President

Provider of security solutions principally focusing
on supporting system implementation and security
testing.

**Issio Solutions Inc** HQ
1485 Civic Ct Ste 1338
Concord CA 94520
P: 888-994-7746 PRC:323
www.issio.com
Estab: 2011

Arne Utne, CEO
Yorick Phoenix, CTO

Provider of workforce management software for
surgical facilities. The company also serves ambu-
latory surgical centers.

**It Concepts LLC** BR
1244-B Quarry Ln
Pleasanton CA 94566
P: 925-401-0010 F: 925-401-0011 PRC:316
www.itconceptsworld.com
Email: sales@itcworld.com

Alla Balashov, Director of Operations

Manufacturer of borescopes, videoscopes, fiberscopes, documentation solutions, and accessories
for remote visual inspection needs.

**It Flux** HQ
135 Camino Dorado Ste 12 A
Napa CA 94558
P: 408-649-5642 PRC:323
www.itflux.com
Email: info@itflux.com
Estab: 2003

Ram Panikath, President
Krishnanath Venkataraman, COO

Provider of custom software development
services, outsourcing, and outsourced software
testing services.

**It Pro Source** HQ
2600 Kitty Hawk Rd Ste 115
Livermore CA 94551
P: 925-455-7701 PRC:325
www.itprosource.com
Email: sales@itprosource.com
Estab: 2001

Mark Becker, VP

Provider of on call plans, managed services, web
based monitoring, and communication cabling
services.

**IT Systemworks** HQ
7 Mt Lassen Dr Ste D-122
San Rafael CA 94903
P: 415-507-0123 F: 267-295-2542 PRC:325
www.itsystemworks.com

Keith Parker, Owner
Sean Maher, IT Consultant
Neicole Crepeau, Senior Technical Writer

Provider of networking and technological solutions. The company's services include installation,
implementation, repair, and maintenance.

**Italix Company Inc** HQ
120 Mast St Ste 1
Morgan Hill CA 95037
P: 408-988-2487 PRC:80
www.italix.com
Email: sales@italix.com
Estab: 1977

Frank Fantino, President
Alyssa DePalma, Controller

Provider of chemical machining, etching, and
metal finishing services. The company serves the
aerospace, defense, and transportation markets.

**Itc Service Group Inc** HQ
7777 Greenback Ln Ste 201
Citrus Heights CA 95610
P: 877-370-4482 F: 877-360-4482 PRC:63
www.callitc.com
Emp: 11-50 Estab: 1999

Tim Sauer, Founder
Jim Rush, President
Anca Hoiland, Chief of Staff
Jeremy Elmas, CFO
Patti Sanderson, Director of Human Resources
and Recruiting

Provider of personnel and managed services to
IT, telecom, and the CATV industry. The company
offers staffing and turnkey solutions.

**Itradenetwork Inc** HQ
4160 Dublin Blvd Ste 300
Dublin CA 94568
P: 925-660-1100 F: 925-660-1101 PRC:326
www.itradenetwork.com
Estab: 1999

Ryan Febus, Principal Engineer
Seema Shelar, Senior Quality Assurance Engi-
neer
Venkat Pininty, Engineer
Itje Tjokro, Senior Software Engineer
Rhonda Bassett-Spiers, CEO

Provider of supply chain management and intelligence solutions for procurement, order management, and data services.

**Itrenew Inc** HQ
8356 Central Ave
Newark CA 94560
P: 408-744-9600 F: 408-744-1963 PRC:142
www.itrenew.com
Estab: 2000

Mostafa Aghamiri, President
Aidin Aghamiri, VP of Corporate Strategy & Research & Development
Matthew Mickelson, Director of Product Management

Provider of information technology services. The
company focuses on data eradication, server
application, logistics management, and configuration.

**Itrezzo Inc** HQ
333 W San Carlos St Ste 600
San Jose CA 95110
P: 408-540-5020 PRC:319
www.itrezzo.com
Estab: 2001

Lakeshia Hardy, Head of Content
David Anderson, Principal
Nikki Phung, Lead UI & UX Designer

Provider of unified contact management solutions
and it serves schools, agencies, and healthcare
organizations.

**Ivalua Inc** HQ
702 Marshall St Ste 520
Redwood City CA 94063
P: 650-930-9710 F: 650-365-5267 PRC:323
ivalua.com
Email: info@ivalua.com
Estab: 2000

David Khuat-Duy, Corporate CEO
Dan Amzallag, CEO
Paul Noel, VP of Procurement Solutions
Laurence Mechali, Director of Customer Services
& Support
Clark Kent, Professional Services Manager

Designer and developer of spend management
solutions. The company offers services to medium
and large sized companies.

**Ixl Learning** HQ
777 Mariners Island Blvd Ste 600
San Mateo CA 94404
P: 650-372-4040 PRC:322
in.ixl.com
Email: info@ixl.com
Estab: 1998

Junjie Wang, Senior Software Engineer
Paul Mishkin, CEO
Joseph Kent, CTO
Jennifer Gu, COO
Diana Luhmann, VP of Human Resources

Specializes in online maths practice and related
lessons. The company serves educational institutions.

**Ixsystems Inc** HQ
2490 Kruse Dr
San Jose CA 95131
P: 408-943-4100  F: 408-943-4101  PRC:95
www.ixsystems.com
Email: info@ixsystems.com
Estab: 2002

Mike Lauth, CEO
Brett Davis, Director of Sales & Business Development
Denise Ebery, Director of Public Relations
Matt Finney, Director of Business Development
Thomas Pham, Account Manager

Provider of hardware, software, server, and storage solutions, and services such as software development and consultation.

**Ixys Corp** HQ
1590 Buckeye Dr
Milpitas CA 95035
P: 408-457-9000  F: 408-416-0223  PRC:208
www.ixys.com
Email: info@ixys.net
Estab: 1983

Moses Ho, Product Engineering Manager
Joe Roosma, R&D Product Development Engineer
Sherie Lyn, Product Marketing Engineer
David Heinzmann, President
Meenal Sethna, EVP

Manufacturer of power semiconductor products. The company specializes in power semiconductors, integrated circuits, and radio frequency power.

**J C Sales & MFG Co** HQ
414-C S Church St
Lone CA 95640
P: 800-527-6347  PRC:80
www.jcsalesmfg.com
Emp: 1-10  Estab: 1992

Bill Irmer, Owner

Manufacturer of CNC machining metal and plastic parts. The company offers products for the semiconductor, electronics, military, aircraft, and other industries.

**J P Aerospace** HQ
2530 Mercantile Dr Ste I
Rancho Cordova CA 95742
P: 916-858-0185  PRC:2
jpaerospace.com
Emp: 1-10

John Powell, President
Paul Turner, Manager

Developer of volunteer-based DIY space program. The company provides the PongSat, MiniCube and Airship to Orbit programs for space enthusiasts.

M-160

**J R Scientific Inc** HQ
1242 Commerce Ave
Woodland CA 95776
P: 530-666-9868  F: 530-666-1416  PRC:36
www.jrscientific.com
Email: info@jrscientific.com
Emp: 1-10  Estab: 1979

Ryan Mansfield, Production Manager

Provider of cell culture products and services. The company's offerings include antibiotics, reagents, and other supplies.

**J&C Consulting Services** HQ
5 Thomas Mellon Cir Ste 155
San Francisco CA 94134
P: 415-935-4313  PRC:318
jandcconsultingservices.mystrikingly.com
Estab: 2004

Jaime Jones, CFO

Developer of consulting services. The company offers strategic planning, executive coaching, and leadership and team development solutions.

**J&E Precision Machining Inc** HQ
2814 Aiello Dr Ste A
San Jose CA 95111
P: 408-281-1195  F: 408-281-1197  PRC:80
www.jandeprecision.com
Estab: 1988

Eva Sousa, President
Jorge Sousa, VP of Programmer
Cyrus Yousefi, CMM Programmer

Manufacturer of electromechanical turnkey fixtures, prototype tooling, and EDM services. The company serves computer, medical, and other sectors.

**J&M Manufacturing Inc** HQ
430 Aaron St
Cotati CA 94931
P: 707-795-8223  F: 707-795-6471  PRC:80
jmmfg.com
Estab: 2003

Jim Judd, Co-Owner
Maria Patchin, Quality Manager

Provider of TIG, MIG and spot welding, silk-screening, contract manufacturing, and assembly services.

**Jabil Circuit Inc** BR
30 Great Oaks Blvd
San Jose CA 95119
P: 408-361-3200  PRC:19
www.jabil.com

Michael Loparco, EVP
Steve Borges, EVP
Alessandro Parimbelli, EVP
Kenny Wilson, EVP
Mark Mondello, CEO

Provider of global manufacturing solutions. The company serves the defense, aerospace, and industrial markets.

**Jackrabbit Inc** HQ
471 Industrial Ave
Ripon CA 95366
P: 209-599-6118  F: 209-599-6119  PRC:159
jackrabbitequipment.com
Email: info@jackrabbit.bz
Emp: 1-10  Estab: 1981

Thomas Lenor, Senior Production Designer
Danny Thomas, VP of Sales

Provider of nut harvesting systems including runner, elevator, reservoir cart, conditioner and pruning tower.

**Jaguar Health** HQ
201 Mission St Ste 2375
San Francisco CA 94105
P: 415-371-8300  PRC:268
jaguar.health
Estab: 2013

Lisa Conte, Founder
Michael Guy, VP
Steven King, EVP of Sustainable Supply Ethnobotanical Research & IP

Provider of health solutions for the animals and humans. The company focusses on the development of gastrointestinal pharmaceuticals.

**James Cox & Sons Inc** HQ
1085 Alpine Way
Colfax CA 95713
P: 530-346-8322  F: 530-346-6854  PRC:159
jamescoxandsons.com
Email: info@jamescoxandsons.com
Emp: 1-10

Linda Sullivan, Financial Manager
Garrett Wren, Head of Operations
Wyatt Yates, Technician

Developer of products for asphalt, concrete, and soil testing. The company is also engaged in calibration and remote support services.

**JAMIS Software Corp** HQ
4909 Murphy Canyon Rd Ste 460
San Diego CA 92123
P: 800-655-2647  PRC:323
www.jamis.com
Email: info@jamis.com
Emp: 11-50  Estab: 1987

Jeffrey Noolas, President
Steve Brander, VP of Sales & Business Development
Dan Rusert, Director of Business Development & Marketing
Amanda Walenta, Marketing Manager
Naomi May, VP of Product Development & Support

Provider of job-cost, billing, and accounting systems and solutions. The company caters to the government contractors.

**Jampro Antennas Inc** HQ
6340 Sky Creek Dr
Sacramento CA 95828
P: 916-383-1177   F: 916-383-1182   PRC:61
www.jampro.com
Email: jampro@jampro.com
Emp: 1-10   Estab: 1954

Aaron Callahan, Engineering Manager
Jared Seese, Senior Field Engineer
David Houston, Production Manager
Val Munoz, Purchasing Manager
Greg Montano, Regional Sales Manager

Supplier of antennas, combiners and filters, and
radio frequency components for applications in the
broadcast industry.

**Jan Medical Inc** HQ
800 W El Camino Real Ste 180
Mountain View CA 94040
P: 650-316-8811   PRC:13
www.janmedical.com
Email: info@janmedical.com

Julie Aguas, Software Engineer
Stephan Mittermeyer, VP of Research

Manufacturer of portable brain sensing devices for
the detection of traumatic brain injuries, including
concussions.

**Jarvis Manufacturing** HQ
195 Lewis Rd Ste 36
San Jose CA 95111
P: 408-226-2600   F: 408-226-2650   PRC:80
www.jarvismfg.com
Email: info@jarvismfg.com
Estab: 1959

Harsimran Singh, Manufacturing Quality Engineer
Tony Grewal, President

Manufacturer of precision machinery. The company offers CNC turning and milling, programming,
and assembly and kitting services.

**Jasper Ridge Inc** HQ
PO Box 151
San Mateo CA 94401-9991
P: 650-804-5040   PRC:187
jasperridge.net
Email: info@jasperridge.net
Estab: 2011

Peter Borden, President
Michele Klein, CEO

Manufacturer of tint and lighting exam systems.
The company offers services to patients and
hospitals.

**Jasper Technologies Inc** HQ
3003 Bunker Hill Ln
Santa Clara CA 95054
P: 669-212-2340   PRC:323
www.jasper.com
Estab: 2004

Scott Barkley, VP of Products

Designer and developer of IoT Service Platform.
The company serves law enforcement agencies
and the security industry.

**Jatco Inc** HQ
725 Zwissig Way
Union City CA 94587
P: 510-487-0888   F: 510-487-1880   PRC:163
www.jatco.com
Estab: 1976

Steven Jones, President
Paul Appelblom, CEO
Eric Appelblom, VP of Sales and Marketing
Steve Gelphman, Program Manager
Cynthia Maldonado, Accounts Payable Manager

Manufactuer of plastic products. The company
offers molding, tooling, quality control, and warehousing and distribution services.

**Javad Electronic Manufacturing
Services** HQ
900 Rock Ave
San Jose CA 95131
P: 408-770-1700   F: 408-770-1799   PRC:209
www.javad.com
Email: ems@javad.com

Pam Walke, Manufacturing Operations Manager
Gary Walker, VP

Provider of electronic components. The company
specializes in products such as OEM, receivers,
antennas, and accessories.

**Jazz Pharmaceuticals** BR
3180 Porter Dr
Palo Alto CA 94304
P: 650-496-3777   PRC:261
www.jazzpharma.com
Email: corpgiving@jazzpharma.com
Estab: 2003

Russell Low, Systems Engineer
Daniel Swisher, President
Bruce Cozadd, Chairman
Elmar Schnee, Chairman
Heidi Manna, Chief Human Resources Officer

Developer and marketer of products for eurology
and psychiatry. The company is engaged in clinical trials and research and development.

**Jb Precision Inc** HQ
1640 Dell Ave
Campbell CA 95008
P: 408-866-1755   F: 408-866-2697   PRC:80
www.jesseebrothersinc.com
Estab: 1975

Kelley Mills, Office Manager

Manufacturer of precision machining services.
The company's services also include inspection,
production control, and management.

**Jeda Technologies Inc** HQ
2900 Gordon Ave Ste 100
Santa Clara CA 95051
P: 408-912-1856   F: 408-912-1855   PRC:319
www.jedatechnologies.net
Email: sales@jedatechnologies.net
Estab: 2003

Eugene Zhang, Founder
Teshager Tesfaye, Director of Product Development

Provider of chip based digital designs and
semiconductor services. The company focuses on
validation and automation solutions.

**Jei** HQ
3087 Alhambra Dr
Cameron Park CA 95682
P: 530-677-3210   F: 530-677-4714   PRC:68
www.jei-inc.com
Emp: 1-10   Estab: 1967

Jei Millbrae, Director

Provider of communication recorders, voice logging recorders, and audio and custom products for
public and military intelligence applications.

**Jelli Inc** HQ
703 S B St 2nd Fl
San Mateo CA 94401
P: 855-790-8275   PRC:325
www.jelli.com
Estab: 2009

Torsten Schulz, SVP of Product & Engineering
Em Huynh, Senior Software Engineer
Vinh Nguyen, Senior Software Engineer
Ryan Rishi, Software Engineer
Josh Newell, Software Engineer

Developer of user-controlled radio used in iPhone
and radio stations. The company's products are
used in the automation of radio advertising.

**Jem America Corp** RH
3000 Laurelview Ct
Fremont CA 94538
P: 510-683-9234   F: 510-683-9790   PRC:86
www.jemam.com
Email: sales@jemam.com
Estab: 1987

Eric Wu, Product Engineer
Patrick Mui, Engineer
Lynn Nguy, Human Resource Generalist
Karen Wong, Sales Manager

Manufacturer and supplier of probe cards and
tester interfaces. The company offers cantilever,
vertical, and special-applications probe cards.

**Jetronics Co** HQ
218 Roberts Ave
Santa Rosa CA 95401
P: 707-544-2436   PRC:298
www.jetronics.com
Estab: 1961

Frances Reilly, Service Manager

Manufacturer of custom cable assemblies and
harnesses, magnetics assemblies, sub-assembly
components, front and rear panels, and chassis
assemblies.

**Jetway Computer Corp** HQ
8058 Central Ave
Newark CA 94560
P: 510-857-0130   F: 510-857-0138   PRC:91
www.jetwaycomputer.com
Email: sales@jetwaycomputer.com
Estab: 1998

Alice Lo, Account Manager

Manufacturer of motherboards and LCD monitors.
The company also specializes in graphic cards
and barebones systems.

**Jitterbit Inc** HQ
1301 Marina Village Pkwy
Alameda CA 94501
P: 877-852-3500 PRC:322
www.jitterbit.com
Email: info@jitterbit.com
Estab: 2004

Manoj Chaudhary, CTO
Sharam Sasson, Chairman
George Gallegos, CEO
Allen Barr, CFO
Shekar Hariharan, VP of Marketing

Focuses on application integration solutions for
aerospace and defense, life sciences, pharmaceuticals, and financial services.

**Jiva Creative LLC** HQ
909 Marina Village Pkwy Ste 110
Alameda CA 94501
P: 510-864-8625 F: 510-864-8626 PRC:322
www.jivacreative.com
Estab: 1996

Eric Lee, Partner
Josh Carey, Interactive Developer
Stacie Kizziar, Partner

Provider of interactive design technology solutions. The company focuses on architecture,
website hosting, and enterprise application
development.

**JN Biosciences LLC** HQ
320 Logue Ave
Mountain View CA 94043
P: 650-967-9486 PRC:34
jn-bio.com
Email: info@jn-bio.com

J. Tso, Managing Partner
Naoya Tsurushita, Managing Partner

Developer of antibody-based therapeutics and
antibody engineered technologies. The company specializes in single homogenous molecular
species.

**Joe Kline Aviation Art** HQ
6420 Hastings Pl
Gilroy CA 95020
P: 408-842-6979 PRC:325
www.joeklineart.com
Estab: 1949

Joe Kline, Founder

Provider of military aircraft painting services. The
company offers customized prints, helicopter
paintings, fixed wing paintings, and other prints.

**Johansing Iron Works** HQ
849 Jackson St
Benicia CA 94510
P: 707-361-8190 F: 709-361-2349 PRC:153
www.johansing.com
Email: sales@johansing.com
Estab: 1990

Alicia Emerson, Office Manager

Manufacturer of heat exchangers and metal tanks.
The company also offers process equipment and
pressure vessels.

**Johnson Industrial Sheet Metal Inc** HQ
2131 Barstow St
Sacramento CA 95815
P: 916-927-8244 F: 916-927-3319 PRC:88
www.johnson-ind.com
Email: curtiss@jhonson-ind.com
Emp: 1-10 Estab: 1972

Donna Johnson, Owner

Designer, fabricator, and installer of blowpipe systems, custom fabricated products, and packaged
system projects.

**Johnson Manufacturing** HQ
38574 W Kentucky Ave
Woodland CA 95695
P: 530-662-1788 F: 530-666-5585 PRC:159
jfmco.com
Email: sales@jfmco.com
Emp: 1-10 Estab: 1943

Kirk Friedman, Owner
Alan Gickler, President
Morris Johnson, CEO
Carla Looper, Manager
Steve Benson, Director

Developer of farm machinery equipment and utility
vehicles. The company offers trailers, air compressors, electric cars and golf car parts.

**Jolly Technologies Inc** HQ
1510 Fashion Island Blvd Ste 102
San Mateo CA 94404
P: 650-594-5955 F: 650-989-2145 PRC:325
www.jollytech.com
Email: sales@jollytech.com
Estab: 2000

Ya-Lan Tsao, Junior Software Engineer

Provider of secure identification, visitor management, barcode and asset tracking software
services.

**JON BRODY Structural Engineers** HQ
235 Montgomery St Ste 1040
San Francisco CA 94104
P: 415-296-9494 PRC:304
www.jonbrody.com
Email: inquiries@jonbrody.com

David Ng, Project Manager
Jon Brody, Senior Personnel

Provider of structural engineering services. The
company focuses on construction documentation,
reports and studies, and seismic retrofitting.

**Josephson Engineering Inc** HQ
329A Ingalls St
Santa Cruz CA 95060
P: 831-420-0888 F: 831-420-0890 PRC:71
www.josephson.com
Email: info@josephson.com
Emp: 1-10 Estab: 1988

David Josephson, Engineer
Connie Winton, Assembler
David Gordon, Principal
Kelly Kay, Principal

Manufacturer of condenser microphones for
studio, stage, and field sound pickup, and audio
instrumentation.

**Jova Solutions Inc** HQ
1402 18th St
San Francisco CA 94107
P: 415-816-4482 PRC:322
www.jovasolutions.com
Email: info@jovasolutions.com
Estab: 2000

Martin Vasey, VP of ISL Business Unit

Developer of systems for distributed process
control and data management for science and
industrial sectors. The company offers USB
instruments.

**Joy Signal Technology LLC** HQ
1020 Marauder St
Chico CA 95973
P: 530-891-3551 F: 530-891-3599 PRC:206
www.joysignal.com
Email: customerservice@joysignal.com
Emp: 1-10 Estab: 1987

John Joy, President

Developer of PCB and differential terminators,
MMCX plug assemblies, single signal carrier systems, Z-Trace connectors, and custom solutions.

**Joyent Inc** HQ
655 Montgomery St Ste 1600
San Francisco CA 94111
P: 415-400-0600 PRC:325
www.joyent.com
Email: sales@joyent.com
Estab: 2004

Angela Fong, VP of Engineering
Seong-Kook Shin, Compute Product Owner
Eric Hahm, CFO
Winston Harrington, Director of IT
Sean Johnson, Head of the Commercial Group

Provider of cloud infrastructure services. The company's products include Compute service, Manta
storage, and Private Cloud.

**Jp Machine Manufacturing** HQ
1600 Norman Ave
Santa Clara CA 95054
P: 408-988-1400 F: 408-988-0223 PRC:80
www.jpmachinemfg.com
Email: sales@jpmachinemfg.com
Estab: 1984

Young Pak, Founder

Manufacturer of machine parts. The company
offers medical, semiconductor capital equipment,
robotics, lasers, fiber optics, and test equipment.

**Jr3 Inc** HQ
22 Harter Ave
Woodland CA 95776
P: 530-661-3677 F: 530-661-3701 PRC:87
www.jr3.com
Email: jr3@jr3.com
Emp: 1-10 Estab: 1983

John Ramming, President
Eric Applebaum, Quality Assurance Manager

Designer and manufacturer of multi-axis force-
torque sensors. The company caters to robotics
and other applications.

**JRP Historical Consulting LLC**　HQ
　2850 Spafford St
　Davis CA 95618
P: 530-757-2521　　　　　　　　　PRC:142
www.jrphistorical.com
Emp: 1-10　Estab: 1981

Christopher McMorris, Partner
Heather Norby, Staff Historian
Joseph Freeman, Staff Historian
Scott Miltenberger, Senior Historian

Provider of resources management services. The
company's services include water use studies,
flood control, public access history, and legislative
history research.

**JSK Associates**　HQ
　3561 Homestead Rd Ste 344
　Santa Clara CA 95051
P: 408-980-8575　F: 408-980-8576　PRC:188
www.jskrep.com
Estab: 1979

Jerry Karp, President

Provider of electronics, medical, and semiconductor manufacturing services. The company also
offers assembly and research services.

**Jsr Micro Inc**　HQ
　1280 N Mathilda Ave
　Sunnyvale CA 94089
P: 408-543-8800　　　　　　　　　PRC:79
jsrmicro.com
Estab: 1957

Jeffrey Kmiec, Development Engineer
Rama Ayothi, Senior Research Engineer
Victor Pham, Development Engineer
Zhong Xiang, Account Manager
Ray Hung, Assistant Plant Manager

Provider of semiconductor, life sciences, and energy material solutions. The company specializes in
lithography materials and CMP consumables.

**Judobaby Inc**　HQ
　955 Charter St Ste A
　Redwood City CA 94063
P: 650-368-3499　F: 586-408-6675　PRC:317
www.judobaby.com
Email: info@judobaby.com
Estab: 2008

Bill Gardner, Division President Publishing
Dan Mueller, CEO
Dan Mueller, CEO
Andrew Forthmann, Chairman
Stephen Pederson, CFO

Focuses on the establishment of software and
hardware products. The company offers services
to the gaming industry.

**Juki Americas**　BR
　412 Kato Terrace Ste 101
　Fremont CA 94539-7793
P: 510-249-6700　F: 510-249-6710　PRC:159
www.jukiamericas.com

Bob Black, President
Carlos Eijansantos, Sales Manager

Provider of SMT assembly machines. The company offers inline selective soldering systems, mini-
wave soldering machines, and stamp soldering
products.

**Junar Inc**　HQ
　111 N Market St Ste 300
　San Jose CA 95113
P: 844-695-8627　　　　　　　　　PRC:322
www.junar.com
Email: support@junar.com
Estab: 2010

Chris Sayre, VP

Provider of cloud-based open data platform. The
company offers collaboration services to business
organizations.

**Juniper Networks Inc**　HQ
　1133 Innovation Way
　Sunnyvale CA 94089
P: 408-745-2000　F: 408-745-2100　PRC:323
www.juniper.net/us/en
Estab: 1996
Sales: $300M to $1 Billion

Kireeti Kompella, CTO of Engineering
Pradeep Sindhu, CTO
Rami Rahim, CEO
Ken Miller, EVP
Gerry Gengyang, Director of Information Tech-
nology

Provider of network security solutions. The company serves the government, healthcare, utilities,
and manufacturing industries.

**Juvaris BioTherapeutics Inc**　HQ
　100 Monaco Ct
　Pleasanton CA 94566
P: 925-399-6200　　　　　　　　　PRC:34
Estab: 2003

Kimberlee Duval, CFO
Grant Pickering, Director

Developer of vaccines and immuno therapeutic
products. The company is engaged in the treatment of infectious diseases.

**Jvd Inc**　HQ
　2266 Trade Zone Blvd
　San Jose CA 95131
P: 408-263-7704　F: 408-263-9069　PRC:86
www.jvdinc.com
Email: contact@jvdinc.com
Estab: 1982

Brian Harlanmoff, Director of Engineering
Jerry van Dierendonck, Founder
Michael VanDierendonck, President
Gloria Reese, VP
Bob Frostholm, VP of sales and Marketing

Provider of custom integrated circuit design and
test services. The company is also involved in
wafer characterization.

**Jway Group Inc**　HQ
　4125 Blackford Ave Ste 128
　San Jose CA 95117
P: 408-247-5929　F: 408-247-5931　PRC:325
jway.com
Email: info@jway.com
Estab: 1994

Marvin Bituin, Web Applications Engineer
Jaryd Carino, Web Applications Engineer
Joey Concepcion, Web Applications Engineer
Lee Mendoza, Web Applications Engineer
John Roxas, Creative Developer

Retailer of web consulting and service solutions
such as web application development, web design, and mobile programming services.

**Jwp Manufacturing**　HQ
　3500 De La Cruz Blvd
　Santa Clara CA 95054-2111
P: 408-970-0641　F: 408-970-8612　PRC:80
www.jwpmfg.com
Email: info@jwpmfg.com

Chris Heider, Manufacturing Manager
Scott Harney, Quality Assurance Manager
Andrew Eden, Director of Sales
Carl Madau, Operations Manager
Joe Hurtado, Program Manager

Provider of manufacturing solutions. The company
offers CNC machining, engineering, and other
services.

**K&L Supply Co**　HQ
　2099 S Tenth St Unit 80
　San Jose CA 95112
P: 408-727-6767　　　　　　　　　PRC:159
www.klsupply.com
Estab: 1968

Joyce Perondi, Office & Sales Manager
Paul Martin, Sales Manager
Michael Salvador, Sales Manager

Manufacturer of specialty tools and shop equipment for motorcycle dealers. The company offers
shop lift & wheel equipment, jacks, and other
tools.

**K-Pax Pharmaceuticals Inc**　HQ
　655 Redwood Hwy Ste 346
　Mill Valley CA 94941
P: 415-381-7565　F: 415-381-7648　PRC:250
kpaxpharm.com
Email: ask@kpaxpharm.com

Jon Kaiser, Medical Director

Provider of pharmaceutical grade vitamins and
nutritional health supplements for kid's, women,
and men's health, joints & bones, and immune
support.

**Kaazing Corp**　HQ
　2107 North First St Ste 660
　San Jose CA 95131
P: 877-522-9464　F: 650-960-8145　PRC:322
kaazing.com
Email: press@kaazing.com
Estab: 2007

Jesse Selitham, Senior Support Engineer
John Fallows, CTO
Bob Miller, CEO
Sue Liu, VP of Professional Services
Sidda Eraiah, VP of Cloud Services & Customer
Support

Provider of software services. The company's IoT
gateway is used by mobile users, marketplaces,
and machines to connect and communicate in
real-time.

**Kahler Engineering Inc**     HQ
8 Elm Ct
San Anselmo CA 94960
P: 415-453-8836     PRC:304
www.ke-inc.com
Email: erkahler@comcast.net
Estab: 2009

Marjorie Widmeyer, President

Designer of instrumentation and power control systems. The company provides engineering services to power plant owners, operators, and constructors.

**Kaiam Corp**     HQ
39677 Eureka Dr
Newark CA 94560-4806
P: 510-226-8100   F: 510-474-3155     PRC:68
www.kaiam.com
Email: info@kaiamcorp.com
Estab: 2008

Tommy Le, Process Engineer
Mike Malave, Controller

Provider of single-mode solutions. The company develops transceivers, modules, and components for data centers.

**KaiserAir Inc**     BR
8735 Earhart Rd
Oakland CA 94621
P: 510-569-9622   F: 510-255-5017     PRC:2
www.kaiserair.com
Email: oak@kaiserair.com
Estab: 1954

Diane Hinds, Manager of Human Resources
Rob Guerra, SVP of Operations

Provider of aircraft management services. The company also offers business aircraft chartering services.

**Kal Machining Inc**     HQ
18450 Sutter Blvd
Morgan Hill CA 95037
P: 408-782-8989   F: 408-782-9696     PRC:80
kalmachining.com

David Luong, CEO

Manufacturer of medical, aeronautic, and military machine parts. The company offers CNC turning and milling services for plastic and metal parts.

**Kaliotek Inc**     HQ
19200 Stevens Creek Blvd Ste 210
Cupertino CA 95014
P: 408-550-8000   F: 408-550-8090     PRC:324
www.kaliotek.com
Email: sales@kaliotek.com
Estab: 1999

Mark Richards, CEO
Bill Kim, VP of Infrastructure and Security Services
Ben Fong, Director of Infrastructure Services
Eric Joyce, Director
Tom Lackovic, Director

Provider of enterprise applications. The company also specializes in technical infrastructure for companies.

**Kalman Manufacturing**     HQ
780 Jarvis Dr Ste 150
Morgan Hill CA 95037
P: 408-776-7664   F: 408-776-3345     PRC:80
www.kalman.com
Estab: 1985

Nick Franco, Process Engineer
John Drabek, Engineer
Alan Kalman, CEO
Jennifer Barbaglia, Human Resource Manager
Mark Alberti, Quality Manager

Provider of manufacturing and machining services. The company offers welding, shearing, cutting, and finishing services.

**Kalytera Therapeutics Inc**     HQ
4040 Civic Center Dr Ste 200
San Rafael CA 94903
P: 888-861-2008     PRC:268
kalytera.co
Email: info@kalytera.co
Estab: 2014

Robert Farrell, CEO
Sari Prutchi-Sagiv, Chief Scientific Officer
Victoria Rudman, CFO
Moshe Yeshurun, Chief Medical Officer
Ronen Raviv, Director of Finance

Developer of cannabidiol and cannabinoid therapeutics for the treatment of life threatening human disease.

**Kaman Industrial Technologies**     BR
30077 Ahern Ave
Union City CA 94587
P: 650-589-6800     PRC:163
kamandirect.com

Steven Smidler, President
Robert Goff, VP of Human Resources and Organization Development
Roger Jorgensen, SVP of Finance & Administration
David Mayer, VP of Marketing
Michael Pastore, VP of Operations

Provider of industrial technology solutions. The company's portfolio comprises bearings, gearing, linear motion, and power transmission products.

**Kamet Manufacturing Solutions**     HQ
171 Commercial St
Sunnyvale CA 94086
P: 408-522-8000   F: 408-524-7884     PRC:80
www.kamet.com
Email: info@kamet.com
Estab: 1986

Pedavalli Chowdary, Quality Engineer
Yolynar Boillet, Quality Management
Abel Nunez, Buyer
Jeff Hunter, Buyer

Provider of manufacturing solutions. The company offers engineering support, project management, and supply chain management solutions.

**Kan Herb Co**     HQ
380 Encinal St Ste 100
Santa Cruz CA 95060-2178
P: 831-438-9450   F: 831-438-9457     PRC:268
www.kanherb.com
Email: info@kanherb.com
Emp: 1-10   Estab: 1987

Robin Sigmann, Graphic Designer

Provider of Chinese herbal products and services.

**Kanopi Studios**     HQ
526 Elizabeth St
San Francisco CA 94114
P: 888-606-7339     PRC:319
kanopi.com
Estab: 2010

Matthew Luzitano, Director of Engineering
Anne Stefanyk, Founder
Katherine White, CTO
Jill Taiji, COO
Allison Manley, Director of Marketing

A web agency that designs and builds websites for clients.

**Karius Inc**     HQ
975 Island Dr Ste 101
Redwood City CA 94065
P: 866-452-7487   F: 866-246-6567     PRC:25
www.kariusdx.com
Email: help@kariusdx.com
Estab: 2014

Timothy Blauwkamp, Co-Founder
Brian Jung, CFO

Provider of microbial genomics diagnostics. The company focusses on transforming infectious disease diagnostics with genomics.

**Kaser Corp**     HQ
44240 Fremont Blvd
Fremont CA 94538
P: 510-894-6892     PRC:110
www.kasercorp.com
Estab: 1998

Steve Kaser, Manager
Rad Oyam, Emergency Medical Technician
Wu Dian, R&D Manager

Developer and marketer of internet and communication equipment. The company offers internet telephony, digital television, and accessories.

**Kaseya International Ltd**     BR
2033 Gateway Pl Ste 512
San Jose CA 95110
P: 415-694-5700     PRC:319
kaseya.com

Prakash Khot, CTO

Provider of software solutions. The company offers cloud and network monitoring, asset management, and backup recovery services.

**Kateeva Inc**                              HQ
  7015 Gateway Blvd
  Newark CA 94560
P: 800-385-7802                       PRC:169
www.kateeva.com
Email: info@kateeva.com
Estab: 2008

Manush Birang, VP of Engineering
Chris Cocca, Senior Software Engineer
Eli Martinez, Senior Process Engineer
Marc Le, Senior Mechanical Engineer
Ranjana Shah, Staff Process Engineer

Manufacturer of LED and other display products. The company specializes in the design and fabrication of OLED displays.

**Kaybus Inc**                               HQ
  148 Townsend St
  San Francisco CA 94107
P: 800-408-5161                       PRC:323
Estab: 2012

Dilip Angal, VP of Engineering
Seenu Banda, CEO
Uday Bellary, CFO
Vivek Goyal, VP

Focuses on reshaping content management, sales enablement and a top-down approach to enterprise collaboration.

**Kaz & Associates Environmental
Services**                                   HQ
  6600 Goodyear Rd
  Benicia CA 94510
P: 707-747-1126   F: 925-871-5172    PRC:139
www.kazandassoc.com

Sean Kazemi, Principal
Patrick Murphy, Principal
Alex Kazemi, Environmental Specialist

Provider of water management consulting services. The company's services include enforcement response, and groundwater contamination investigation.

**Kearney Pattern Works & Foundry**          HQ
  40 S Montgomery St
  San Jose CA 95110-2518
P: 408-293-7414                        PRC:82
Estab: 1919

Alan Wagner, Operations Manager

Provider of pattern works and foundry services. The company's services include heat treating, plating, machining, and casting finish.

**Kearneys Metals Inc**                      HQ
  2660 S Dearing Ave
  Fresno CA 93725
P: 559-233-2591   F: 559-441-8055    PRC:159
www.kearneysaluminumfoundry.com
Emp: 1-10

Michael Kearney, President
Bill Kearney, Sales Manager
Bobby Kearney, Operations Manager

Provider of foundry services. The company specializes in stainless steel and aluminium plates, sheets, structurals and bars.

**Keen Systems Inc**                         HQ
  1900 O'Farrell St Ste 145
  San Mateo CA 94403
P: 888-506-5336                       PRC:323
keenprint.com
Email: support@keenprint.com
Estab: 2008

Jim Dvorkin, Director

Provider of web-to print solutions. The company offers cloud-based services to small and medium sized printing companies.

**Keep IT Simple**                           HQ
  48383 Fremont Blvd Ste 122
  Fremont CA 94538
P: 510-403-7500   F: 510-403-7501    PRC:323
www.kiscc.com
Email: ContactUs@kiscc.com
Estab: 1988

Craig Miller, Director of Engineering
Sean Canevaro, CEO
John Marciano, COO
Allan Hurst, Director of Enterprise Strategy
David Powell, Partner

Provider of virtualization and information technology services. The company focuses on virtualization assessment, cloud computing, and networking.

**Keish Environmental PC**                   HQ
  6768 Crosby Ct
  San Jose CA 95129
P: 408-359-7248                       PRC:139
keishenv.com

Rachael Keish, CEO
Kristin Sideris, Manager

Provider of environmental and stormwater compliance services. The company also specializes in construction inspection services.

**Kelly-Moore Paint Company Inc**            HQ
  987 Commercial St
  San Carlos CA 94070
P: 650-592-8337   F: 650-592-1215     PRC:47
kellymoore.com
Estab: 1946

Greg Say, Controls Engineer
Steve Devoe, President
Dan Stritmatter, CFO
James Alberts, VP of Sales
Joseph Hoberg, Outside Sales Representative

Developer and manufacturer of interior and exterior paints. The company also offers painting tools and related accessories.

**Kelytech Corp**                            HQ
  1482 Gladding Ct
  Milpitas CA 95035
P: 408-935-0888   F: 408-935-0988    PRC:209
www.kelytech.com
Email: info@kelytech.com
Estab: 1990

Bo Sun, Manager

Provider of assembly solutions for PCBs, chassis, cables, and magnetic products. The company serves defense, medical, industrial, and other sectors.

**Kemet Electronics Corp**                   BR
  2350 Mission College Blvd Ste 972
  Santa Clara CA 95054
P: 877-695-3638   F: 408-986-1442    PRC:214
www.kemet.com
Email: capmaster@kemet.com

Monica Highfill, VP of Sales

Provider of relays, EMI filters, transformers, capacitors, and ferrite products. The company serves the aerospace, defense, and automotive industries.

**KEMPF Inc**                                HQ
  1245 Lakeside Dr Ste 3005
  Sunnyvale CA 94085
P: 408-773-0219   F: 408-773-0524    PRC:159
www.kempf-usa.com
Email: info@kempf-usa.com
Estab: 2007

Martine Kempf, Owner

Provider of driving solutions. The company offers digital hand controls and other handicap driving aids for paraplegic drivers.

**Kennerley-Spratling Inc**                  HQ
  2116 Farallon Dr
  San Leandro CA 94577
P: 510-351-8230   F: 510-352-9240     PRC:80
www.ksplastic.com
Email: email@ksplastic.com
Estab: 1955

Rob Lyneis, Engineering Manager
Dick Spratling, President
Jeff Krogh, IS Manager
Elvia Morales, Finishing Manager
Rachael Branas, Program Coordinator

Manufacturer of custom plastic injection and compression moldings. The company is involved in design, installation, and delivery services.

**Kensington Computer Products
Group**                                      DH
  1500 Fashion Island Blvd 3rd Fl
  San Mateo CA 94404
P: 650-572-2700                       PRC:108
Estab: 1981

Christine Coates, Director of Global Human Resources
Theresa Chavez, Financial Analyst

Provider of secure locking solution for laptops, portable laptop power, and mobile computing solutions.

**Kensington Laboratories LLC**              HQ
  6200 Village Pkwy
  Dublin CA 94568
P: 510-324-0126   F: 510-324-0130     PRC:86
www.kensingtonlabs.com
Email: sales@kensingtonlabs.com

Anatoli Pavlov, Field Service Engineer

Provider of automation products for the semiconductor industry. The company is engaged in precision machining, automation, and system integration.

**Kenzen Inc** HQ
1663 Mission St Ste 520
San Francisco CA 94103
P: 650-384-5140 PRC:194
www.kenzen.com
Estab: 2014

Heidi Lehmann, CCO

Focuses on the manufacture of personal health monitors. The company serves individuals and healthcare organizations.

**Keri Systems Inc** HQ
302 Enzo Dr Ste 190
San Jose CA 95138
P: 408-435-8400 F: 408-577-1792 PRC:314
www.kerisys.com
Email: info@kerisys.com
Estab: 1990

Dave Miller, Software Engineer
Russ Walker, Engineer
Maryann Gierke, Human Resource
Vickie Carr, Inside Sales Supervisor
Dennis Geiszler, VP

Provider of access control and integrated security systems. The company offers technology support and training solutions.

**Kespry Inc** HQ
4040 Campbell Ave Ste 200
Menlo Park CA 94025
P: 203-434-7988 PRC:309
kespry.com
Estab: 2013

John Laxson, Software Engineering Manager
Jordan Croom, Lead Mechanical Engineer
Jeff Palmer, President
Adam Rice, Business Development Director
Ilene Sempio, Office Manager

Developer of automated drone system and cloud that automatically uploads data in cloud for aggregates, insurance, and construction industries.

**Key Business Solutions Inc** HQ
4738 Duckhorn Dr
Sacramento CA 95834
P: 916-646-2080 F: 916-646-2081 PRC:328
www.keybusinessglobal.com
Email: info@keybusinessglobal.com
Emp: 11-50 Estab: 1999

Rajan Gutta, President

Provider of software development and database management services. The company also specializes in business intelligence.

**Key Performance Ideas Inc** HQ
268 Bush St Ste 2800
San Francisco CA 94104
P: 855-457-4462 PRC:322
www.keyperformanceideas.com
Email: info-web@keyperformanceideas.com
Estab: 2005

Chris Werle, Owner
Nate Coate, Owner
Selena Hira-Toth, Manager of Corporate Operations

Provider of enterprise performance management & business intelligence solutions. The company offers Oracle Hyperion and OBIEE software for this need.

**Key Solutions Inc** HQ
2803 Lakeview Ct
Fremont CA 94538
P: 510-456-4500 F: 510-456-4501 PRC:323
www.keyusa.com
Email: contact@keyusa.com

Srinivas Kudaravalli, Owner
Swarupa Mallipeddi, Operations Manager

Provider of software development and database management services. The company also specializes in business intelligence.

**Key Source International Inc** HQ
7711 Oakport St
Oakland CA 94621
P: 510-562-5000 F: 510-562-0689 PRC:108
www.ksikeyboards.com
Email: info@ksikeyboards.com
Estab: 1979

Phil Bruno, SVP of Sales & Marketing
Deanne VanKirk, National Sales Manager

Provider of disinfect and germicidal wipes for keyboards. The company focuses on infection control and cross contamination.

**Keysight Technologies Inc** HQ
1400 Fountaingrove Pkwy
Santa Rosa CA 95403
P: 800-829-4444 F: 800-829-4433 PRC:209
keysight.com
Sales: Over $3B

Stan Souza, Engineering Manager
John Flowers, Design Engineer
Kenneth Clark, Application Engineer
Matthew Chan, R&D Semiconductor Process Engineer
Raj Sodhi, R&D Hardware Development Engineer

Provider of electronic measurement services. The company products include oscilloscopes, network analyzers, and digital multimeters.

**Kezar Life Sciences Inc** HQ
4000 Shoreline Ct Ste 300
S San Francisco CA 94080
P: 650-822-5600 PRC:189
kezarlifesciences.com
Email: contact@kezarbio.com
Estab: 2015

Christopher Kirk, Co-Founder
John Fowler, CEO
Marc Belsky, CFO
Celia Economides, SVP of Strategy and External Affairs

Developer of small molecule therapeutics drugs targeting protein homeostasis for transformative treatments for autoimmune diseases.

**KG Technologies Inc** HQ
6028 State Farm Dr
Rohnert Park CA 94928
P: 888-513-1874 PRC:290
kgtechnologies.net
Email: info@kgtechnologies.net
Estab: 1999

Timothy Wells, VP of Engineering

Designer and developer of switching solutions. The company's applications include welding, brazing, and riveting.

**Kidaptive Inc** HQ
203 Redwood Shores Pkwy Ste 145
Redwood City CA 94065
P: 650-265-2485 PRC:326
www.kidaptive.com
Email: info@kidaptive.com
Estab: 2012

Dylan Arena, Co-Founder
P.J. Gunsagar, Co-Founder
Josine Verhagen, Director of Psychometrics
David Hatfield, Senior Director of Assessment
Naomi Lim, Office Manager

Provider of learning and integration solutions. The company offers services to learners and the educational sector.

**Kiefer Consulting Inc** HQ
13405 Folsom Blvd Ste 501
Folsom CA 95630
P: 916-932-7220 PRC:322
www.kieferconsulting.com
Email: info@kieferconsulting.com
Emp: 1-10 Estab: 1988

Gregory Kiefer, CEO
Amy Hoffman, VP
Brian Wallace, Director of Marketing & Sales
Ben Cox, Director of Operations
Doug Robbins, Senior Project Manager

Provider of mobile application software services. The company also offers SharePoint, Microsoft Dynamics, and Microsoft .Net application services.

**Kii Corp** HQ
1900 S Norfolk St Ste 350
San Mateo CA 94403
P: 650-577-2340 PRC:325
www.kii.com
Estab: 2010

Masanari Arai, Co-Founder
Naoshi Suzuki, Co-Founder
Phani Pandrangi, CPO

Provider of applications to device manufacturers and mobile network operators. The company serves enterprise, cross-platform games, and other needs.

**Kikusui America Inc** HQ
2975 Bowers Ave Ste 307
Santa Clara CA 95051
P: 408-980-9433 F: 408-980-9409 PRC:293
www.kikusuiamerica.com
Email: kikusui@kikusuiamerica.com
Estab: 2004

Sunao Yamamoto, President

Provider of electronic measuring instruments and power supplies. The company's products include electronic loads and power supply controllers.

**Kimberlite Corp** HQ
3621 W Beechwood Ave
Fresno CA 93711-0648
P: 559-264-9730 F: 559-233-5610 PRC:59
sonitrolsecurity.com
Emp: 11-50 Estab: 1996

Joey Rao-Russell, President
Susie O'Hara, Director of Human Resources
Mason Settlemoir, Regional Technical Manager
Andrew Smith, Security Systems Coordinator

Dealer of security verification systems. The company offers access control, video surveillance, fire detection, and intrusion detection systems.

**Kimia Corp** HQ
2102 Walsh Ave Ste B
Santa Clara CA 95050
P: 408-748-1046 PRC:306
kimiacorp.com
Estab: 1994

Farbi Aria, President

Manufacturer of chemicals and custom synthesis services. The company offers amino acids, vitamins, steroids, heptanes, and multifunctional heterocycles.

**Kindred Biosciences Inc** HQ
1555 Bayshore Hwy Ste 200
Burlingame CA 94010
P: 650-701-7901 PRC:273
www.kindredbio.com
Email: info@kindredbio.com
Estab: 2012
Sales: $3M to $10M

Denise Bevers, President
Wendy Wee, CFO
Hangjun Zhan, CSO
Karen Greenwood, VP of Project Management
Katja Buhrer, VP of Corporate Development and Investor Relations

Provider of pharmaceutical products for treatment of anemia, cancer, allergic, autoimmune, and gastrointestinal diseases in cats, dogs, and horses.

**Kinematic Automation Inc** HQ
21085 Longeway Rd
Sonora CA 95370
P: 209-532-3200 F: 209-532-0248 PRC:186
kinematic.mynetworksolutions.mobi
Emp: 1-10 Estab: 1980

Ted Meigs, Co-Founder
Lisa Hedges, Production Control Supervisor

Provider of manufacturing systems for the medical industry. The company also offers automation, strip cutting, rotatory slitting services.

**Kinetic Ceramics Inc** HQ
26240 Industrial Blvd
Hayward CA 94545
P: 510-264-2140 F: 510-264-2159 PRC:209
www.kineticceramics.com
Email: info@kineticceramics.com
Emp: 11-50 Estab: 1986

Dennis Creely, Designer

Manufacturer of performance products for motion control applications. The company's services include diamond turning and fabrication.

**Kinetic Technologies** RH
6399 San Ignacio Ave Ste 250
San Jose CA 95119
P: 512-694-6384 F: 408-351-0338 PRC:212
www.kinet-ic.com
Email: americasales@kinet-ic.com
Estab: 2006

Brian North, VP of Engineering
Lu Chen, IC Design Director

Designer and developer of analog and mixed-signal power management semiconductors. The company serves the consumer and communication markets.

**King Precision Inc** HQ
227 Technology Cir
Scotts Valley CA 95066
P: 831-426-2704 F: 831-426-2229 PRC:80
www.kingprecision.com
Email: info@kingprecision.com
Emp: 1-10 Estab: 1999

Richard King, Owner

Manufacturer and supplier of precision components. The company also offers semiconductor heater and magnet refurbish and repair services.

**King Sales & Engineering** HQ
9 Jules Dr
Novato CA 94947
P: 415-892-7961 PRC:159
www.kingpac.com
Estab: 1930

Craig Tabery, Representative
David Rossman, Manager

Designer and seller of rotary fillers, labelers, and case packers. The company offers products for the tomato and fruit canning industry.

**King Star Computer Inc** HQ
855 Kifer Rd
Sunnyvale CA 94086
P: 408-736-8590 F: 408-736-4151 PRC:94
www.kingstarusa.com
Email: sales@kingstarusa.com
Estab: 1989

John Wu, Senior Sales Engineer Intel Platinum Provider
Jessie Chen, Sales Engineer
Lucy Yin, Sales Engineer
Sandy Kuo, Sales & Marketing Coordinator
Chengnan Zhang, Server Technician

Provider of technology services to Fortune 500 companies, mid-size to small business, start-ups, and government and educational organizations.

**King-Solarman Inc** HQ
48900 Milmont Dr
Fremont CA 94538
P: 408-373-8800 PRC:130
king-solarman.com
Email: Info@King-Solarman.com
Estab: 2008

Michael Cung, CEO

Focuses on the sale of solar panels, power inverters, and related supplies. The company is involved in solar project financing services.

**Kings River Conservation District** HQ
4886 E Jensen Ave
Fresno CA 93725
P: 559-237-5567 F: 559-237-5560 PRC:139
www.krcd.org
Email: comments@krcd.org
Emp: 1-10 Estab: 1951

Randy Shilling, Deputy General Manager of Business Operations
David Merritt, Deputy General Manager of Power Operations
David Cone, Deputy General Manager
Paul Peschel, General Manager
Stacy Wright, Manager of Human Resources

Provider of resource management solutions. The company focuses on flood protection, water supply, power generation, and other needs.

**Kionix Inc** BR
2323 Owen St
Santa Clara CA 95054
P: 408-720-1900 PRC:87
www.kionix.com
Email: info.cal@kionix.com
Estab: 1993

Nader Sadrzadeh, President

Manufacturer of MEMS inertial sensors. The company offers accelerometers, gyroscopes, and combination sensors.

**Kirby Manufacturing Inc** HQ
484 S Hwy 59
Merced CA 95340
P: 209-723-0778 F: 209-723-3941 PRC:159
kirbymfg.com
Email: info@kirbymfg.com
Emp: 11-50 Estab: 1946

Ric Kirby, President
Richard Wallace, General Manager
Brett Baker, Sales Manager
Brachen Millikan, Manager
Stephannie Sandoval, Controller

Provider of cattle feeding equipment such as horizontal and vertical mixers, manure spreaders, freestall wagons, scale systems, and haybusters.

**KitApps Inc** HQ
75 E Santa Clara St 6th Fl
San Jose CA 95113
P: 866-944-8678 PRC:319
attendify.com
Email: support@attendify.com
Estab: 2012

Artyom Yaremchuk, Co-Founder
Michael Balyasny, CEO
Jacob Wiggins, Director of Global Sales
Anati Zubia, VP of Marketing
Jessica Waggoner, Director of Client Experience

Provider of networking and other information-based tools to event organizers and attendees (end-users).

**Kki Corp** HQ
5300 Claus Rd Ste 10
Modesto CA 95357
P: 209-863-8550 F: 209-863-8686 PRC:323
www.kkicorp.com
Email: support@kkicorp.com
Emp: 1-10 Estab: 1975

Justin Payne, Systems Engineer
Ken Iwahashi, President
Samantha Schonefeld, Operations Manager
Tom LaBarbera, Accounting Supervisor
James Buel, Systems Administrator

Provider of web and business services and software solutions. The company is also involved in design and technical support services.

**KLA-Tencor Corp** HQ
1 Technology Dr
Milpitas CA 95035
P: 408-875-3000  F: 408-875-4875  PRC:212
www.kla-tencor.com
Estab: 1976
Sales: Over $3B

Dan Pham, Associate Test Engineer
Rick Wallace, CEO
Bren Higgins, CFO
Ben Tsai, CTO
Bobby Bell, CSO

Provider of inspection and metrology tools. The company also specializes in process control and yield management products.

**Klc Enterprises** HQ
6 Woodside Ct
San Anselmo CA 94960
P: 415-485-0555  F: 415-485-0556  PRC:319
www.klcent.com
Email: info@klcent.com
Estab: 1988

Kit Christiansen, System Analyst

Provider of accounting software for the construction industry. The company offers services to the commercial and industrial sectors.

**Kleenrite Equipment** HQ
1122 Maple St
Madera CA 93637
P: 800-241-4865  F: 559-673-5725  PRC:159
www.kleenritemfg.com
Email: sales@kleenritemfg.com
Emp: 1-10  Estab: 1973

Jeremy Wheeler, Director of Operations

Developer and manufacturer of domestic & commercial cleaning devices. The company caters to commercial and constructional facilities.

**Klh Consulting Inc** HQ
2324 Bethards Dr
Santa Rosa CA 95405
P: 707-575-9986  F: 707-575-8758  PRC:325
www.klhconsulting.com
Email: info@klhconsulting.com
Estab: 1980

Casey Meister, Human Resource Manager
Aaron Sternad, Network Manager
Hub Lampert, Principal

Provider of IT consulting, cloud computing, and related business solutions. The company offers services to business executives and professionals.

**Klippenstein Corp** HQ
5399 S Villa Ave
Fresno CA 93725
P: 559-834-4258  F: 559-834-4263  PRC:159
klippenstein.com
Email: sales@klippenstein.com
Emp: 1-10  Estab: 1979

Dennis Schramm, Project Engineer
Justin Carroll, Project Engineer
Alec Weins, Project Engineer
Ken Klippenstein, President

Manufacturer of packaging equipment. The company's products also include case formers, erectors, and sealers.

**Kmic Technology Inc** HQ
2095 Ringwood Ave Ste 10
San Jose CA 95131
P: 408-240-3600  F: 408-240-3699  PRC:65
www.kmictech.com
Email: contact@kmictech.com
Estab: 1979

David Kim, President
Arthur Ignacio, Director of Sales

Provider of amplifier products and solutions to the radio frequency, microwave, and millimeter wave markets.

**Knightscope Inc** HQ
1070 Terra Bella Ave
Mountain View CA 94043
P: 650-924-1025  PRC:314
www.knightscope.com
Email: contact@knightscope.com
Estab: 2013

Mercedes Soria, VP of Software Engineering
William Li, CEO
Aaron Lehnhardt, VP

Provider of security technology. The company specializes in monotonous, computationally heavy, and sometimes dangerous work for security operations.

**Knowme Inc** HQ
25 Taylor St
San Francisco CA 94102
P: 800-713-9257  PRC:319
www.knowme.net
Email: info@knowme.net
Estab: 2005

Borris Medak, President
Austin Hills, Chairman
Dan Gregerson, Director
Dominic Johnson, Director
Fred Sakamoto, Project Manager

Provider of web based customer relationship management services. The company is also engaged in call routing and web and phone integration.

**Knurr Usa** BR
496 S Abbott Ave
Milpitas CA 95035
P: 510-353-0177  F: 510-257-1132  PRC:293
extroninc.com
Email: knurr@extroninc.com
Estab: 1931

Sandeep Duggal, CEO
Dinesh Chatkara, VP of Operations & Quality
Kien Nguyen, VP of Customer Integration
Richard Rogers, Business Development Manager
Joyce Cheng, Controller

Provider of custom enclosures, mobile equipment carriers and carts, outdoor cabinets, control room consoles, and technical furniture.

**Kodiak Precision Inc** HQ
444 S First St
Richmond CA 94804-2107
P: 510-234-4165  F: 510-232-5232  PRC:80
www.kodiakprecisioninc.com
Email: operations@kodiakprecisioninc.com
Estab: 2001

Neil Divers, VP
Kristy Divers, Operations Manager

Manufacturer of precision machine products. The company's products include milling and turning machines, fabricated parts, and machine support equipment.

**Kodiak Sciences Inc** HQ
2631 Hanover St
Palo Alto CA 94304
P: 650-281-0850  PRC:191
kodiak.com
Email: info@kodiak.com
Estab: 2009

Stephen Charles, Founder
Victor Perlroth, CEO
John Borgeson, SVP
Stephen Raillard, VP of Chemical Development and Manufacturing
Laurent Ducry, VP of Biologics Development and Manufacturing

Manufacturer of medicines for the treatment of patients with age-related macular degeneration and diabetic eye disease, two leading causes of blindness.

**Kokusai Semiconductor Equipment Corp** DH
2460 N First St Ste 290
San Jose CA 95131
P: 408-456-2750  F: 408-456-2760  PRC:212
www.ksec.com
Estab: 1992

Carl Lopez, Customer Support Engineer
Anne Panger, Human Resource Representative
Dinesh Patel, Controller

Provider of thermal processing solutions. The company also provides technical, installation, and retrofit services.

**Kone Inc** BR
15021 Wicks Blvd
San Leandro CA 94577
P: 510-351-5141  PRC:180
www.kone.us

Nicole Manzo, SVP of Human Resources
Jon Barr, Head of Information Technology
Ken Schmid, SVP of Finance
Dennis Viehweg, SVP of Modernization
Corey Ward, VP of Environment

Manufacturer of moving solutions. The company offers automatic building doors, elevators and escalators, and accessories.

**Konicom Inc** HQ
1819 J St
Sacramento CA 95811
P: 916-441-7373  F: 916-441-7577  PRC:325
www.konicom.com
Email: support@konicom.com
Emp: 1-10  Estab: 2001

Bryan Wu, Owner
Roy Zhao, Technician

Provider of computer services to businesses and individuals. The company offers internet related services such as wireless network and hot spot setup.

**Kopin Corp**     BR
225 Technology Cir
Scotts Valley CA 95066
P: 831-430-0688  F: 831-430-0689     PRC:86
www.kopin.com
Email: ruggedsolutions@kopin.com
Emp: 11-50

Bill Maffucci, VP
Mark Crane, Prototype Fabrication Manager

Developer of semi-conducting solutions. The
company develops cloud computing, hands-
free technology, and wireless usage in headset
computers.

**KOR-IT Inc**     HQ
1964 Auburn Blvd
Sacramento CA 95815
P: 916-372-6400  F: 877-767-3648     PRC:80
www.kor-it.com
Email: info@kor-it.com
Emp: 1-10  Estab: 1958

Jessica Sandler, CEO

Manufacturer of diamond tools and core drill
machines. The company caters to the concrete
cutting industry.

**Kortick Manufacturing**     HQ
2230 Davis Ct
Hayward CA 94545
P: 510-856-3600     PRC:68
www.kortick.com
Email: sales@kortick.com

Robert Frase, Owner
Gavin Frase, President
Jorge Yuikeng, Support Manager
Eugene Gaines, Assembly Supervisor
Tracy Shieh, Controller

Manufacturer and distributor of pole line hardware.
The company primarily caters to the telecom
industry.

**Kovair Software Inc**     HQ
2410 Camino Ramon Ste 230
San Ramon CA 94583
P: 408-262-0200     PRC:319
www.kovair.com
Email: sales@kovair.com
Estab: 2000

Bipin Shah, CEO

Provider of web-based document management
applications. The company offers product support
maintenance services.

**Kovarus Inc**     HQ
2000 Crow Canyon Pl Ste 250
San Ramon CA 94583
P: 650-392-7848  F: 650-952-2072     PRC:323
www.kovarus.com
Email: sales@kovarus.com
Estab: 2003

Chris Mills, Senior Implementation Engineer
Jeremy Brown, Sales Support Manager
Sabra Hill, Sales Support Representative
Alex Weeks, Regional Director of Consulting
Scott Wiele, Director of Public Sector

Provider of integrated business IT solutions. The
company also deals with leasing, financing, project management, and related services.

**KP LLC**     BR
13951 Washington Ave
San Leandro CA 94578
P: 510-351-5400  F: 510-351-2555     PRC:325
www.kpcorp.com
Email: info@kpcorp.com
Estab: 1929

Joe Atturio, CEO
Matthew Stupfel, CFO
Paul Braverman, COO
Thomas Middleton, CIO
Brett Olszewski, CMO

Provider of marketing and outsourcing solutions
offering digital and offset printing and mailing
services.

**Kraemer & Company Manufacturing
Inc**     HQ
3778 Road 99 W
Orland CA 95963
P: 530-865-7982  F: 530-865-5091     PRC:82
kcomfg.com
Emp: 1-10

Jerry Kraemer, Owner

Provider of industrial equipment. The company
specializes in dyers, sprayers, storage units, and
heaters.

**Kreck Design Solutions**     HQ
416 Aviation Blvd Ste E
Santa Rosa CA 95403
P: 707-433-6166  F: 707-433-6165     PRC:325
www.kreck.com
Email: info@kreck.com
Estab: 1997

Lydia Revelos, Manager
Brian Kreck, Partner

Provider of graphic design and internet-related
services. The company focuses on corporate
identity & marketing, web design, SEO, content
management.

**Krobach Manufacturing Corp**     HQ
3504 Arden Rd
Hayward CA 94544
P: 510-783-9480  F: 510-783-9727     PRC:80
www.krobach.com
Email: info@krobach.com
Estab: 1959

Nathan Moore, Quality Manager

Provider of precision machine shop and general
machining services. The company focuses on
turning, milling, and grinding.

**Krytar Inc**     HQ
1288 Anvilwood Ave
Sunnyvale CA 94089
P: 408-734-5999  F: 408-734-3017     PRC:13
www.krytar.com
Email: sales@krytar.com
Estab: 1975

Michael Romero, Engineering Manager
Doug Hagan, President
Hilda Clayton, Buyer

Provider of broadband microwave components
and test equipment. The company is engaged in
troubleshooting and maintenance services.

**Ksm Corp**     DH
1959 Concourse Dr
San Jose CA 95131-1708
P: 408-514-2400  F: 408-514-2499     PRC:82
www.ksm.co.kr
Email: solutions@ksmusa.com
Estab: 1979

Tony Singh, Owner

Manufacturer of welded metal bellows for transportation, solar, pharmaceutical, and other sectors
and provides build to print assembly services.

**Kucklick Design**     HQ
22700 Midpine Ct
Los Gatos CA 95033
P: 408-353-1508     PRC:191
kucklickdesign.com

Theodore Kucklick, CEO

Designer and developer of medical illustration
products. The company's portfolio includes Nova-
Som system, Starion devices, and Extravastat.

**Kumu Networks**     HQ
960 Hamlin Ct
Sunnyvale CA 94089
P: 408-786-9302     PRC:70
kumunetworks.com
Email: info@kumunetworks.com
Estab: 2011

Steffen Hahn, VP of Engineering
Jeff Mehlman, Director of Engineering
Mayank Jain, CTO
David Cutrer, CEO
Jung-Il Choi, Chief System Architect

Developer of wireless technology that cancels
self-interference, the unwanted energy that leaks
into a radio's receiver while transmitting.

**Kura MD Inc**     HQ
130 Diamond Creek Pl
Roseville CA 95747
P: 855-587-2220     PRC:194
www.kura.md
Email: info@kura.md
Emp: 1-10  Estab: 2013

Kevin Hamm, CEO

Provider of telemedicine platform enables con-
venient, secure, HIPAA compliant, and telehealth
appointments between physicians and patients
through tablet.

**Kurz Instruments Inc**     HQ
2411 Garden Rd
Monterey CA 93940
P: 831-646-5911  F: 831-646-8901     PRC:14
www.kurzinstruments.com
Email: sales@kurz-instruments.com
Estab: 1977

Scott Cooper, Engineering R&D
Ricardo Martinez, Design Engineer
Tom Setliff, International Sales Manager
Frederico Dias, Marketing Coordinator

Designer and manufacturer of thermal mass flow
transmitters. The company's products find application in industrial gases and liquids.

**Kwj Engineering Inc**      HQ
8430 Central Ave Ste C
Newark CA 94560
P: 510-794-4296    F: 510-574-8341     PRC:13
www.kwjengineering.com
Email: sales@kwjengineering.com
Estab: 1993

Bennett Meulendyk, Senior Engineer
David Peaslee, Senior Engineer
Joe Stetter, CTO
Larry Johnson, Production Manager
Tom Stetter, Marketing Director

Manufacturer of gas detection products. The company offers equipment to detect chlorine, carbon monoxide, ozone, and methane and propane.

**Kycon Inc**      HQ
305 Digital Dr
Morgan Hill CA 95037
P: 408-494-0330    F: 408-494-0325     PRC:159
www.kycon.com
Email: sales@kycon.com

Allen Chen, Test Engineer
Glen Pacheco, Regional Sales Manager
Kelli Huston, Sales Manager
Barbara Piper, Controller

Provider of interconnect solutions. The company offers products such as audio jacks, card edge, and modular jacks.

**Kyec Usa**      DH
101 Metro Dr Ste 540
San Jose CA 95110
P: 408-452-7680    F: 408-452-7689     PRC:86
www.kyec.com.tw
Estab: 1987

A. Liu, President
K. Lee, VP
Steven Chang, VP
Allen Tsai, Senior Director
Jason Wang, Senior Account Director

Provider of testing services. The company offers services for testing integrated circuit (IC) packaging.

**Kyosemi Opto America Corp**      BR
4655 Old Ironsides Dr Ste 230
Santa Clara CA 95054
P: 408-492-9361    F: 408-492-9843     PRC:62
www.kyosemi.co.jp/en/contact/world/#usa

Kurt Kawabuchi, President

Manufacturer of opto-semiconductor devices. The company focuses on optical communication devices and photo devices for sensors.

**L&T Precision Engineering Inc**      HQ
2395 Qume Dr
San Jose CA 95131
P: 408-441-1890    F: 408-441-1899     PRC:80
www.lt-engineering.com
Email: sales@lt-engineering.com
Estab: 1988

Steven Tran, Manager
Lan Pham, Quality Assurance Manager
My Truong, Sales Purchasing and Marketing
Joshua Sedillo, Sales Manager
Trung Nguyen, Technical Support

Provider of fabrication, precision engineering assistance, and assembly services. The company serves semiconductor, medical, and other sectors.

**L-3 Narda Microwave-West**      HQ
107 Woodmere Rd
Folsom CA 95630
P: 916-351-4500    F: 916-351-4550     PRC:70
www.nardamicrowavewest.com
Email: nmw.service@l-3com.com
Emp: 1-10   Estab: 1997

Brad Morris, Senior Program Manager
Jason Baggett, Manager
Theresa Moreno, Calibration Administrator

Designer and manufacturer of RF microwave components and subsystems. The company products include power dividers, filters, and linearizers.

**La Belle Inc**      BR
174 E Fourth St
Ripon CA 95366
P: 209-599-6605     PRC:251
www.labelleinc.com
Email: sales@labelleinc.com
Emp: 11-50   Estab: 1984

Mike Campbell, CSO
Mike Wiebe, COO
Gregg Whitley, VP of Sales & Marketing

Manufacturer of colostrum and chelated minerals. The company also specializes in spray drying.

**Lab Sensor Solutions Inc**      HQ
648 El Camino Real Ste P
Redwood City CA 94063
P: 650-275-3101     PRC:34
lsstracks.com
Email: forinfo@lsstracks.com
Estab: 2013

Daniel Paley, EVP of Engineering
Geoff Zawolkow, CEO
Jarie Bolander, COO

Provider of real-time sensor technology on healthcare assets so customers can monitor, report and act to assure items are in right place and condition.

**Labcon North America**      HQ
3700 Lakeville Hwy
Petaluma CA 94954
P: 707-766-2100    F: 707-766-2199     PRC:20
labcon.com
Email: info@labcon.com
Estab: 1959

Tom Sours, Senior Process Engineer
Steve Bumstead, Production Manager
Greg Kopple, Quality Control Supervisor
Gina Lachica, Lead Quality Control Technician
Amy Carson, Sales Representative

Manufacturer of disposable plastic products for laboratories. The company offers products for liquid handling, culture, and molecular biology.

**Labcyte Inc**      HQ
1190 Borregas Ave
Sunnyvale CA 94089
P: 408-747-2000    F: 408-747-2010     PRC:20
www.labcyte.com
Email: team@labcyte.com
Estab: 2000

Brent Browning, Director of Engineering
Brent Eaton, Staff Engineer
Willy Sagun, Senior Staff Electrical Engineer
Robert Walker, Staff Software Engineer
Alex Sakhanyuk, Senior SQA Engineer

Provider of cutting-edge solutions. The company is involved in the revolutionizing of liquid handling concepts.

**Labo America Inc**      HQ
920 Auburn Ct
Fremont CA 94538
P: 510-445-1257    F: 510-445-1317     PRC:174
www.laboamerica.com
Email: sales@laboamerica.com

Savita Aggarwal, Owner
Gautam Aggarwal, VP of Sales
Asif Mushtaq, Operation Manager

Manufacturer and distributor of stereo, compound, surgical and digital microscopes, digital cameras and measuring software.

**Laboratory Equipment Co**      HQ
2506 Technology Dr
Hayward CA 94545
P: 510-887-4040    F: 510-887-4112     PRC:159
www.labequipco.com
Email: info@labequipco.com
Estab: 1948

Britta Johnson, Technical Sales Representative

Manufacturer of laboratory equipment. The company's products include alarm monitor systems, bedding dispensers, dryers, and ovens.

**Lacroix Davis LLC**      BR
3685 Mt Diablo Blvd Ste 210
Lafayette CA 94549
P: 925-299-1140     PRC:140
lacroixdavis.com

Gordon Bizieff, Director of Architectural Services
Melinda Jones, Office Manager
James LaCroix, Principal

Provider of building and environmental forensics and consulting services. The company provides support for investigation, litigation, and education.

**Ladd Associates Inc**      HQ
3410 Geary Blvd Ste 216
San Francisco CA 94118
P: 415-921-1001    F: 415-921-2311     PRC:323
laddassociates.com
Email: info@laddassociates.com
Estab: 1975

Jim Jankowski, President
Jack Ladd, Advisor

Provider of decision support software systems for publishers, subscription businesses, and direct response marketing clients.

**LakePharma Inc**      BR
520 Harbor Blvd
Belmont CA 94002
P: 650-288-4891     PRC:34
lakepharma.com
Email: inquiries@lakepharma.com
Estab: 2009

Hoa Giang, Associate Director of Antibody Engineering
Hua Tu, CEO
Bill Hermans, Senior Director of Production Technology
Lisa Alexander, VP of Quality and Regulatory
Paula Criss, Director of Sales

Provider of contract research organization specializing in antibody and protein engineering, cell line development, and protein production.

**LAKOS Filtration Solutions** HQ
1365 N Clovis Ave
Fresno CA 93727-2282
P: 559-255-1601   F: 559-255-8093   PRC:156
www.lakos.com
Email: info@lakos.com
Emp: 1-10   Estab: 1972

Craig Malsam, VP of Engineering
Leonardo Zepeda, Production Scheduler
Ray Chatman, Welder
Matthew Navarro, Strategic Buyer

Manufacturer of centrifugal separators and other
filtration solutions to remove sand and other solids
from water and liquids.

**Lam Research Corp** HQ
4650 Cushing Pkwy
Fremont CA 94538
P: 510-572-0200   PRC:127
www.lamresearch.com
Email: training.fremont@lamresearch.com
Estab: 1980

Klay Kunkel, Director of Engineering
Butch Berney, Director of Engineering
Victor Wang, Director of Engineering
Griff O'Neill, Senior Director of Engineering
Glen Morisato, Engineer

Manufacturer and distributor of single wafer
systems. The company primarily serves the semiconductor industry.

**Lamar Tool & Die** HQ
4230 Technology Dr
Modesto CA 95356
P: 209-545-5525   F: 209-545-5527   PRC:80
www.lamartoolanddie.com
Emp: 1-10

Kelli Jones, Office Manager
Thomas Moore, Machine Operator
Shaheen Shamsavari, Senior Investment Manger

Manufacturer of die casting solutions. The company's offerings include machining and secondary
operations.

**Lamdagen Corp** BR
1455 Adams Dr Ste 1155
Menlo Park CA 94025
P: 650-571-5816   F: 650-571-5837   PRC:11
www.lamdagen.com
Email: info@lamdagen.com
Estab: 2005

Randy Storer, CEO

Developer of nano technology based biosensors
used in research and diagnostic equipment for
human and animal health testing.

**Lamek Industrial Corp** HQ
1254 Birchwood Dr
Sunnyvale CA 94089
P: 408-734-3363   PRC:80
www.lamekindustrial.com
Email: mail@lamekindustrial.com

Murat Yolcu, General Directorate Assistant

Manufacturer of machined parts for the semiconductor, medical, and aeronautic sectors. The
company focuses on bead blasting, tumbling and
packaging.

**Lamons** BR
189 Arthur Rd
Martinez CA 94553
P: 925-313-9080   F: 925-313-9348   PRC:162
www.lamons.com
Email: marketing@lamons.com

Bill Hinderman, District Manager
Thomas Lamons, Tax Counsel

Manufacturer of industrial gaskets. The company caters to the refinery and packing industrial
sectors.

**Lamphier-Gregory** HQ
1944 Embarcadero
Oakland CA 94606
P: 510-535-6690   F: 510-535-6699   PRC:139
lamphier-gregory.com
Estab: 1979

Scott Gregory, President
Britt Hallquist, Principal
Rebecca Gorton, Senior Planner
John Courtney, Senior Planner
Sharon Wright, Environmental Planner

Provider of urban planning services. The company
provides environmental analysis, project management, and coordination services.

**LAN-Power Inc** HQ
44240 Freemont Blvd
Fremont CA 94538-6000
P: 510-275-4572   PRC:59
www.lan-power.com
Email: sales@lan-power.com

Lance Rasmussen, VP of Marketing

Designer, developer, and manufacturer of break
through technology for implementing surveillance
and security systems.

**Landel** HQ
142 Martinvale Ln
San Jose CA 95119
P: 408-360-0490   PRC:66
landel.com
Email: sales@landel.com
Estab: 1998

Steve Landry, President

Provider of telecommunication products such as
MailBug, DataBug, and SurveyBug. The company
is engaged in technical support services.

**Langill's General Machine Inc** HQ
7850 14th Ave
Sacramento CA 95826-4302
P: 916-452-0167   F: 916-452-2812   PRC:80
www.langills.com
Email: langills@sbcglobal.net
Emp: 1-10   Estab: 1970

Benjamin Langill, Co-Owner

Manufacturer of precision machined components
with a full array of state-of-the-art machines, operated by a highly trained workforce.

**Langineers** HQ
1799 Bayshore Hwy Ste 230
Burlingame CA 94010
P: 650-692-2001   F: 650-692-2110   PRC:68
www.langineers.com
Email: sales@langineers.com
Estab: 1993

Lonnie Domnitz, President
Jason Baptista, Sales Manager
Pete Askar, Accounting Associate
Micah Levine, Technician

Provider of VoIP phone services, video conferencing, and hosting solutions. The company offers
cordless DECT phones and video conferencing
phones.

**Langtech** HQ
733 Front St Ste 110
San Francisco CA 94111
P: 415-364-9600   F: 415-364-9650   PRC:323
www.langtech.com
Email: contact@langtech.com
Estab: 1987

Eivind Sukkestad, Principal
Brian Mott, President
Chris Clothier, Technical Project Manager
Jason Madigan, IT Technical Manager

Provider of information technology services. The
company provides software solutions, cloud services, system integration, and consulting.

**Language Quest Traveler** HQ
309 N Mt Shasta Blvd
Mount Shasta CA 96067
P: 530-918-9540   F: 530-918-9541   PRC:323
www.languagequest.com
Email: info1@languagequest.com
Emp: 1-10

Jim Havlice, Owner

Retailer of foreign language bibles, software,
books, and dictionaries. The company also offers
video/audio supplies.

**Lanlogic** HQ
248 Rickenbacker Cir
Livermore CA 94551
P: 925-273-2300   PRC:326
www.lanlogic.com
Email: realpeople@lanlogic.com
Estab: 1995

Shane Deal, Senior Network Engineer
Ted Johnson, Field Engineer
Art Closson, Founder
Dan Ferguson, President
Wilma Smith, CFO

Provider of information technology services. The
company offers network management and support
services.

**Lansmont Corp** HQ
17 Mandeville Ct
Monterey CA 93940
P: 831-655-6600 F: 831-655-6606 PRC:235
www.lansmont.com
Estab: 1971

Doug Foss, Senior Electrical Design Engineer
Martin Suro, Hardware Controls Engineer
Jess Sumagang, Field Service Engineer
Peter Brown, Customer Service Manager
Rob Machado, Buyer

Provider of products such as field instruments,
shock machines, vibration systems, drop testers,
and package shakers.

**Lares Research** HQ
295 Lockheed Ave
Chico CA 95973
P: 530-345-1767 F: 530-345-1870 PRC:185
www.laresdental.com
Email: world-sales@laresdental.com
Emp: 1-10 Estab: 1956

Jason Orgain, Engineering Manager
Larry McCulloch, Manufacturing Engineer
Bruce Holderbein, Electrical Engineer
Craig Lares, President
Chuck Elton, Manufacturing Manager

Developer and manufacturer of dental hand piec-
es and dental lasers. The company offers services
to the healthcare industry.

**Larkin Precision Machining Inc** HQ
175 El Pueblo Rd
Scotts Valley CA 95066
P: 831-438-2700 F: 831-438-2704 PRC:80
lpmachining.com
Emp: 1-10 Estab: 1920

Henrik Ingesson, Quality Engineer
Richard Larkin, Senior Programming Engineer
Jon Larkin, Managing Partner
Rob Larkin, CEO
Seth Larkin, Managing Partner

Manufacturer of machined parts of precision CNC
milling and turning devices specializing in assemblies, fixtures, flanges, grinding, and sawing.

**Larry Walker Associates** HQ
1480 Drew Ave Ste 100
Davis CA 95618
P: 530-753-6400 F: 530-753-7030 PRC:142
lwa.com
Email: infolwa@lwa.com
Emp: 11-50 Estab: 1979

Larry Walker, Founder
Tom Grovhoug, President
Ashli Desai, VP
Brian Laurenson, VP
Karen Ashby, VP

Provider of environmental engineering and
consulting services. The company provides water
quality solutions.

**Larson Automation Inc** HQ
960 Rincon Cir
San Jose CA 95131
P: 408-432-4800 F: 408-432-4848 PRC:19
www.larsonautomation.com
Email: info@larsonautomation.com
Estab: 1993

Wayne Larson, Founder
Chris Reed, Production Manager
Cecilia Gold, Office Manager

Developer of automated test solutions for telecommunication companies. The company offers board
test stations and level shifters.

**Larson Electronic Glass** HQ
2840 Bay Rd
Redwood City CA 94063
P: 650-369-6734 F: 650-369-0728 PRC:82
www.larsonelectronicglass.com
Email: sales@larsonelectronicglass.com
Estab: 1954

Chuck Kraft, Manager

Manufacturer of glass to metal sealing products.
The company offers vacuum flanges, viewports,
bellows, and electrical & fiber optics feedthrus.

**Laru Technologies** HQ
400 Plaza Dr Ste 210
Folsom CA 95630
P: 916-458-6149 F: 916-404-7790 PRC:319
www.larutech.com
Email: sales@larutech.com
Emp: 1-10 Estab: 2004

Carl Daniel, VP

Provider of ACH and Wire transaction monitoring
and control tools. The company focuses on risk
management and compliance solutions.

**Laser Mark's Co** HQ
2109 O'Toole Ave Ste S
San Jose CA 95131
P: 408-433-9333 F: 408-433-9343 PRC:81
www.laser-marks.com
Email: lasermarks@gmail.com
Estab: 1988

Laser Mark, Manager

Provider of laser marking and engraving job shop
services. The company serves the agriculture,
food processing, automotive, and medical industries.

**Laser Reference Inc** HQ
151 Martinvale Ln
San Jose CA 95119
P: 408-361-0220 F: 408-361-3180 PRC:172
www.proshotlaser.com
Email: sales@proshotlaser.com
Estab: 1991

Lee Robson, President
David Kawano, Sales Manager

Supplier of laser level products for interior and
outdoor construction focusing on laser receivers
and accessories including telescopic laser tripods.

**Laserline Inc** BR
1800 Wyatt Dr Ste 9
Santa Clara CA 95054
P: 844-441-3691 PRC:171
www.laserline.com
Email: service-usa@laserline.com
Estab: 1997

Dave Matthews, Director of Customer Support

Manufacturer of diode lasers for welding metals
and plastics. The company also deals with cladding, hardening, and brazing.

**Lasertec USA Inc** HQ
2107 N First St Ste 210
San Jose CA 95131
P: 408-437-1441 F: 408-437-1430 PRC:68
www.lasertec.co.jp
Estab: 1960

Haruhiko Kusunose, EVP

Developer and manufacturer of systems for
semi-conductor applications. The company also
offers systems for flat panel displays.

**Lastline** HQ
1825 S Grant St Ste 635
San Mateo CA 94402
P: 877-671-3239 PRC:325
www.lastline.com
Email: sales@lastline.com
Estab: 2011

George Chitouras, VP of Engineering
Brian Laing, SVP
John Love, Director of Corporate Communications

Manufacturer of malware protection products. The
company serves schools, restaurants, and the
enterprise security industry.

**Lattice Engines** HQ
1825 S Grant St Ste 200
San Mateo CA 94402
P: 877-460-0010 PRC:322
www.lattice-engines.com
Estab: 2006

Brian Rackle, Engineering Manager
Shashi Upadhyay, Co-Founder
Chitrang Shah, Chief Product Officer
Gregory Haardt, CTO
Brett Dyer, CFO

Provider of business to business sales intelligence
software. The company is engaged in web design
and hosting and programming solutions.

**Lattice Semiconductor Corporation** BR
2115 O'Nel Dr
San Jose CA 95131
P: 408-826-6000 F: 408-826-6034 PRC:212
www.latticesemi.com
Estab: 1983

Jim Anderson, President
Jeff Richardson, Chairman
Sherri Luther, CFO
Sunil Mehta, Director of Technology
Fulong Zhang, Silicon Architect

Provider of design, development, and marketing
services for programmable logic devices. The
company also offers related software.

**Lattice Technology Inc**     BR
582 Market St Ste 1215
San Francisco CA 94104
P: 720-330-3197   F: 720-330-3198    PRC:319
www.lattice3d.com
Email: info@lattice3d.com
Estab: 1997

Masaru Hatakoshi, Solutions Engineer
Bill Barnes, General Manager
Erik Freeman, Sales Manager

Developer of 3D and 2D software for design review purposes. The company also focuses on 3D simulation and animation needs.

**Lavante Inc**     HQ
5285 Hellyer Ave Ste 200
San Jose CA 95138-1081
P: 408-754-1410    PRC:322
www.lavante.com
Estab: 2001

Vinay Ambekar, VP of Engineering
Sam Klepper, CEO
Nina Pozegija, VP of Operations

Provider of on-demand strategic profit recovery solutions. The company also offers vendor information management software.

**Lawson Mechanical Contractors**     HQ
6090 S Watt Ave
Sacramento CA 95829-1302
P: 916-381-5000   F: 916-381-5073    PRC:80
lawsonmechanical.com
Emp: 11-50 Estab: 1947

Bruce Edman, Mechanical Engineer
Kevin Smith, Project Engineer
Keith Velasquez, Project Engineer
Casey Whynoff, Project Engineer
Eric Fuchino Ii, Project Engineer

Provider of mechanical construction services. The company offers plumbing, HVAC, industrial, and process piping services.

**Lazar Machining Inc**     HQ
1001 Center St
San Carlos CA 94070
P: 650-591-6415   F: 650-593-8284    PRC:80
www.lazarmfg.com
Email: info@lazarmafg.com
Estab: 1978

Frank Lazar, Owner

Provider of precision machining services. The company serves the semiconductor, aerospace, and food processing industries.

**Lazestar Inc**     HQ
346 Earhart Way
Livermore CA 94551
P: 925-443-5293   F: 925-443-5262    PRC:80
www.lazestar.com

Gary Sickenger, Quality Manager
David Madrid, Laser Lab Manager

Provider of laser sealing, packing, precision fabrication, and welding services. The company serves the aerospace and commercial industries.

**LCS Technologies Inc**     HQ
11230 Gold Express Ste 310-140
Gold River CA 95670
P: 855-277-5527    PRC:326
www.lcs-technologies-inc.com
Email: sales@lcs-technologies-inc.com
Emp: 1-10 Estab: 2006

Stephane Come, Co-Founder
Steve Simonetto, Founder
Chris Wilson, COO
Ara Davis, Business Operations Manager

Provider of information services for customers with Oracle software and service needs using resources such as people, hardware, and software.

**Leadman Electronics USA Inc**     HQ
382 Laurelwood Rd
Santa Clara CA 95054
P: 408-380-4567   F: 408-738-2620    PRC:159
www.leadman.com
Email: sales@leadman.com
Estab: 1986

Jim Liang, VP
Eric Wang, Director of Power Supply

Provider of ODM/OEM, hardware engineering expertise, and custom solutions for a wide range of security, storage, server, and network applications.

**Leaf Healthcare Inc**     HQ
5994 W Las Positas Blvd Ste 217
Pleasanton CA 94588
P: 844-826-5323    PRC:189
leafhealthcare.com
Email: info@leafhealthcare.com
Estab: 2010

Mark Weckwerth, COO
Annemari Cooley, VP of Market Development
Mark Smith, VP of Marketing and Strategic Business Development

Specializes in wearable healthcare technologies. The company deals with patient mobility programs and serves the medical industry.

**LeapFILE Inc**     HQ
19989 Stevens Creek Blvd
Cupertino CA 95014
P: 650-701-7241    PRC:323
www.leapfile.com
Email: clientservices@leapfile.com
Estab: 2003

Alex Teu, VP

Provider of on-demand file transfer, delivery, and collaboration solutions for businesses. The company serves the healthcare and advertising sectors.

**Learning In Motion Inc**     HQ
113 Cooper St 2nd Fl
Santa Cruz CA 95060-4526
P: 831-600-6606    PRC:319
www.learninginmotion.com
Email: helpdesk@learninginmotion.com
Emp: 1-10 Estab: 1993

Marge Cappo, President

Provider of educational materials and services. The company offers content development, video production, and marketing collateral services.

**Ledger Systems Inc**     HQ
865 Laurel St
San Carlos CA 94070
P: 650-592-6211   F: 650-594-8453    PRC:224
www.ledgersys.com
Estab: 1983

Richard Wright, Founder
Stephen Kirby, Founder
Chris Monser, Director of Systems & Programming
Rick Hoelle, Director of Programming

Provider of network design and support services. The company also offers accounting and e-Commerce solutions.

**Lee & Ro Inc**     BR
1515 Oakland Blvd Ste 240
Walnut Creek CA 94596
P: 925-937-4050   F: 925-937-4052    PRC:304
www.lee-ro.com
Estab: 1979

Sam Lee, Civil Engineer
Murthy Kadiyala, Civil Engineer
James Pollock, Associate Engineer
Charles Ro, Civil Engineer
Jorge Anaya, Civil Engineer

Provider of environmental and infrastructure engineering solutions. The company is involved in design-build and construction management.

**Lee Mah Electronics Inc**     HQ
155 S Hill Dr
Brisbane CA 94005
P: 415-394-1288   F: 415-433-2560    PRC:209
leemah.com
Email: inquiry@leemah.com
Estab: 1971

Warren Gee, EVP

Provider of manufacturing solutions. The company serves customers in the medical, communications, and test and measurement industries.

**Legend Design Technology Inc**     HQ
2905 Stender Way Ste 50
Santa Clara CA 95054
P: 408-748-8888   F: 408-748-8988    PRC:126
www.legenddesign.com
Email: sales@legenddesign.com
Estab: 1996

You-Pang Wei, President

Provider of semiconductor IP characterization and verification tools and IC and PCB circuit simulators.

**Leica Geosystems HDS LLC**     RH
4550 Norris Canyon Rd
San Ramon CA 94583
P: 925-790-2300    PRC:172
hds.leica-geosystems.com
Estab: 1993

Tim Nolen, Southeast Regional Sales Manager

Manufacturer of surveying hardware and software solutions for measuring and modeling sites and structures with high accuracy, detail, speed, and safety.

**LekasMiller Design** HQ
1460 Maria Ln Ste 260
Walnut Creek CA 94596
P: 925-934-3971 PRC:325
www.lekasmiller.com
Estab: 1979

Tina Miller, Owner
Ali Gencarelle, Studio Manager

Provider of photography, printing, advertising,
graphic design, mailing, and project management
services.

**Lemo Usa Inc** HQ
635 Park Ct
Rohnert Park CA 94928
P: 707-578-8811 F: 707-578-0869 PRC:80
www.lemo.com
Email: info@lemousa.com

Trevor Lee, Applications & Materials Engineer
Steven Lassen, Applications Engineer
Julie Carlson, Marketing Manager
Bill Lee, Business Integration Manager
Chris Van Nuys, Operations Manager

Designer and manufacturer of precision custom
connectors, cable assemblies, and related accessories. The company serves the industrial sector.

**Lendingclub Corp** HQ
595 Market St Ste 200
San Francisco CA 94105
P: 415-632-5600 PRC:45
lendingclub.com
Email: info@lc-advisors.com
Emp: 1768 Estab: 2006
Sales: $300M to $1 Billion

Valerie Kay, Chief Capital Officer
John Steward, VP of Institutional Sales
Richard Loggins, VP of Institutional Sales
Jack Coogan, Senior Director of Institutional Sales
Doug Lambert, VP of Capital Markets Group

Provider of financial solutions. The company offers
home improvement, business, pool, and consoli-
dated debt loans.

**Lenos Software** HQ
142 Sansome St Fl 2
San Francisco CA 94104
P: 415-281-8828 PRC:323
www.lenos.com
Email: services@lenos.com
Estab: 1999

Debra Chong, Co-Founder and CEO
Patti Tackeff, President
Jacqueline Regalado, Professional Service
Manager
Matt Owens, QA Developer

Provider of enterprise resource management,
development of motion graphics, and value-added
management services.

**Lenthor Engineering** HQ
311 Turquoise St
Milpitas CA 95035
P: 408-945-8787 F: 408-956-1874 PRC:211
www.lenthor.com
Estab: 1985

Teresa Spada, Sales Engineer
Mark Lencioni, President
Rich Clemente, General Manager
Analyn Bringas, Production Support Manager
Rey Cervantes, Director of Quality

Designer and manufacturer of flexible and rigid
printed circuit boards. The company serves the
military, communications, medical, and other
markets.

**Lenz Precision Technology Inc** HQ
355 Pioneer St
Mountain View CA 94041
P: 650-966-1784 F: 650-966-1953 PRC:80
www.lenztech.com
Email: admin@lenztech.com
Estab: 1972

Eric Lenz, President
Steve Notti, Quality Assurance Manager
Shannon Lenz, Financial Manager

Manufacturer of precision machined components
and sub assemblies. The company also focuses
on the sales aspects.

**Leoco USA Corp** BR
4125 Business Center Dr
Fremont CA 94538
P: 510-429-3700 F: 510-429-3708 PRC:76
www.leoco.com.tw
Email: leocosales@leocousa.com
Estab: 1981

Alex Wang, VP

Manufacturer of interconnects. The company
offers wire to board, wire to wire, board to board,
and card and telecom connectors.

**Leotek Electronics USA LLC** HQ
1955 Lundy Ave
San Jose CA 95131
P: 408-380-1788 F: 408-518-8128 PRC:243
leotek.com
Estab: 1997

Frank Soltani, Engineering Assistant
Chen Wu, CEO

Manufacturer of light-emitting diodes and lights
for traffic and transit, street and area, commercial,
petroleum, and grocery and retail stores.

**Level 3 Communications LLC** BR
1741 Technology Dr
San Jose CA 95110
P: 877-453-8353 PRC:60
www.level3.com

Jeff Storey, President

Provider of voice data wireless and internet services. The company is also engaged in collaboration and security consulting.

**Lewiz Communications Inc** HQ
738 Charcot Ave
San Jose CA 95131
P: 408-432-6248 F: 408-452-9805 PRC:97
www.lewiz.com
Email: info@lewiz.com
Estab: 2000

Thanh Truong, Hardware Design Engineer
Chinh Le, CEO
John Floisand, VP
Steve Dowdell, VP of Sales
Ken Pope, VP of Marketing

Provider of computer networking solutions. The
company also offers data security, data management, and data streaming services.

**Lexar Media Inc** HQ
161 Baypointe Pkwy
San Jose CA 95134
P: 408-933-1088 F: 510-440-3499 PRC:96
www.lexar.com
Email: support@lexar.com
Estab: 1996

Donald Hills, Senior Pricing Manager

Provider of memory product lines such as USB
drives, memory cards, card readers, and dram
computer memory.

**Lexicon Branding Inc** HQ
30 Liberty Ship Way Ste 3360
Sausalito CA 94965
P: 415-332-1811 F: 415-332-2528 PRC:310
lexiconbranding.com
Email: info@lexiconbranding.com

David Placek, President
Alan Clark, Director of Trademark
Greg Alger, Director of Linguistics

Provider of services to develop, select and evaluate brand names. The company services include
trademark evaluation, name development, and
consumer research.

**Lfw Manufacturing** HQ
745 S Lincoln St
Stockton CA 95203
P: 209-465-0444 F: 209-465-6521 PRC:80
www.lfwmfg.com
Emp: 1-10

Leo Wickham, President
Rachelle Brown, Production Manager

Manufacturer of gearboxes and gear sets. The
company caters to a wide range of industrial
applications.

**LG Display America Inc** BR
2540 N First St Ste 400
San Jose CA 95131
P: 408-350-0190 PRC:168
www.lgdisplay.com
Estab: 1987

In-Byeong Kang, CTO
Rok Park, Senior Manager of Total Biz Operation

Manufacturer of thin-film transistor liquid crystal
display panels. The company is also focused on
OLEDs and flexible displays.

**Lge Electrical Sales Inc** HQ
650 University Ave Ste 218
Sacramento CA 95825
P: 916-563-2737 F: 916-563-2763 PRC:245
lgesales.com
Emp: 11-50 Estab: 1992

Daniel Iseman, Engineering Sales
Ray Landgraf, President
Terri Gierke, Outside Sales Manager
Dave Evans, VP

Provider of electrical distribution and transmission
products. The company's products include distran
packaged substation products, G&W, MGM, and
TIKA.

**Libby Labs**    HQ
1700 Sixth St
Berkeley CA 94710
P: 510-527-5400   F: 510-527-8687    PRC:261
www.libbylabs.com
Email: inquiries@libbylabs.com
Estab: 1959

Susan Libby, President

Manufacturer of cosmetics, OTC pharmaceuticals, drugs, and devices. The company offers skin & hair products, toiletries, natural & organic products.

**Liberty Labs Inc**    HQ
484 Vista Way
Milpitas CA 95035
P: 408-262-6633   F: 408-945-0826    PRC:41
www.libertylab.com
Email: sales@libertylab.com

Vijay Israni, CEO

Provider of testing services for the semiconductor industry. The company is engaged in custom programming and quality assurance services.

**Liberty Test Equipment**    HQ
1640 Lead Hill Blvd Ste 120
Roseville CA 95661
P: 916-625-4228   F: 916-782-0891    PRC:14
www.libertytest.com
Email: sales@libertytest.com
Emp: 1-10   Estab: 2002

Panayiotis Frantzis, CTO
Jennifer Allen, Inside Sales Associate
Patricia Phillimeano, Marketing Manager
Rumi Sakaya, Accounting Manager
Jennifer DuMond, Account Manager

Provider of refurbished and new test equipment and related accessories. The company deals with sales, lease, and rental services.

**LibraryWorld Inc**    HQ
PO Box 231
San Jose CA 95103
P: 408-993-2140   F: 408-993-2147    PRC:322
www.libraryworld.com
Email: sales@libraryworld.com
Estab: 1987

Norman Kline, CEO
John McIntyre, CTO
William Kline, Quality Assurance Manager
John Kline, Software Quality Assurance Manager

Provider of library automation software solutions. The company serves schools, healthcare, law firms, museum, and architectural firms.

**Life Sources Inc**    HQ
5006 Sunrise Blvd Ste 101
Fair Oaks CA 95628
P: 916-662-4580   F: 916-536-9934    PRC:272
www.life-sources.com
Email: info@life-sources.com
Emp: 1-10   Estab: 1999

Andrea McCreery, President

Developer of products to combat chronic illnesses. The company's services include targeted nutrition and vital hematology.

**Lifescience Plus Inc**    HQ
2520-A Wyandotte St
Mountain View CA 94043
P: 650-565-8172   F: 650-336-1130    PRC:195
www.lifescienceplus.com
Email: sales@lifescienceplus.com
Estab: 2005

Vicky Feng-Grubb, CEO
Shoba Viswanath, CSO
Cecilia Lin, Senior Accountant

Developer of wound care technology solutions and its applications include surgery, dentistry, and public safety.

**Ligandal Inc**    HQ
650 Fifth St
San Francisco CA 94107
P: 650-866-5212    PRC:191
www.ligandal.com
Estab: 2013

Andre Watson, Founder

Developer of nanotechnology for precise and high-efficiency delivery of nucleic acids to specific cells and organelles for genetic medicine.

**Light & Motion Industries**    HQ
711 Neeson Rd
Marina CA 93933
P: 831-645-1538    PRC:243
www.lightandmotion.com
Estab: 1989

Daniel Emerson, CEO

Provider of light and motion personal lighting system for mountain, bike, foot, camera, water, and underwater activities.

**Light Guard Systems Inc**    HQ
2292 Airport Blvd
Santa Rosa CA 95403
P: 707-542-4547   F: 707-525-6333    PRC:212
lightguardsystems.com
Email: office@lightguardsystems.com
Estab: 1994

Michael Harrison, President
Krista Kalemba, General Manager
Sher Paz, National Sales Manager
Jeannie Bartholdy, Executive Administrator

Provider of traffic safety products such as controllers, signal head and base plate modules, and LED signage products.

**Light Polymers Inc**    HQ
347 Littlefield Ave
S San Francisco CA 94080
P: 650-678-7733    PRC:53
www.lightpolymers.com
Email: info@lightpolymers.com
Estab: 2006

Sergey Fedotov, Director of US Marketing and Operations

Developer of polymers and materials. The company formulates and develops solutions for lyotropic liquid crystals.

**LightGuideOptics USA LLC**    RH
1101 S Winchester Blvd Ste L-238
San Jose CA 95128
P: 408-244-0686   F: 408-244-0714    PRC:62
lgoptics.com
Estab: 2008

Mick Speciale, CEO

Manufacturer of diameters, bundles and probes. The company's products are used in medical and hi-tech applications.

**Lighthouse Worldwide Solutions**    HQ
47300 Kato Rd
Fremont CA 94538
P: 510-438-0500   F: 510-438-3840    PRC:187
www.golighthouse.com
Email: info@golighthouse.com
Estab: 1982

Kevin Yu, Electrical Engineer
Holly Chamberlain, Senior Software Engineer
Tae Kim, CEO
Alvin Sojourner, Facilities Manager
Peter Maguire, Applications Sales Manager

Provider of dental supplies such as implants, dentures, partials, implant bars, and related accessories.

**Lightning Bolt Solutions Inc**    HQ
323 Allerton Ave
S San Francisco CA 94080
P: 866-678-3279   F: 650-651-1637    PRC:194
www.lightning-bolt.com
Email: info@lightning-bolt.com
Estab: 2002

Jo Bhullar, Software Engineer
Suvas Vajracharya, CEO
Kelly Challenger, Senior Director of Marketing
Alex Carson, Senior Application Consultant
Rahul Vaidya, Senior Software Architect

Provider of medical staff scheduling software and solutions. The company's services include scheduling, keeping backups, technical support, and training.

**Lightsand Communications**    BR
745 Emerson St
Palo Alto CA 94301
P: 619-865-6400    PRC:68
www.lightsand.com
Email: sales@lightsand.com
Estab: 1999

Victor Gissin, VP of Engineering
Richard Czech, CEO

Developer of SAN connectivity products. The company is engaged in troubleshooting and maintenance services.

**Lightwind Corp**    HQ
101 H St Ste E
Petaluma CA 94952
P: 707-981-4301   F: 925-820-2972    PRC:50
www.lightwindcorp.com
Email: info@lightwindcorp.com
Estab: 2001

Robin Halloran, Accounts Manager

Provider of semiconductor manufacturing solutions. The company also deals with chemical analysis, process assessment, and refurbishment services.

**Lilee Systems**  HQ
641 River Oaks Pkwy
San Jose CA 95134
P: 408-988-8672  F: 408-988-8813  PRC:61
lileesystems.com
Email: sales@lileesystems.com
Estab: 2009

Lele Nardin, VP of Engineering
Alan Opstedal, Systems Support Engineer
Jia-Ru Li, CEO
Jessica Sweeney, Senior Director of Market &
Product Strategy
Sam Kanakamedala, Director of Product Management & Market Development

Provider of integrated services that include
system prediction modeling, project management,
and training services for the railroad industry.

**LIM innovations Inc**  HQ
424 Ninth St
San Francisco CA 94103
P: 844-888-8546  F: 415-651-9444  PRC:190
www.liminnovations.com
Email: info@liminnovations.com
Estab: 2012

Andrew Pedtke, CEO
Sanjeev Sharma, COO

Designer and manufacturer of prosthetic sockets
for amputees. The company offers custom-molded, adjustable, and modular prosthetic sockets.

**LimFlow Inc**  BR
2934 Scott Blvd
Santa Clara CA 95054
P: 888-478-7705  F: 408-898-1459  PRC:189
www.limflow.com
Email: info@limflow.com
Estab: 2012

Tim Lenihan, Co-Founder
Dan Rose, CEO
Zachary Woodson, VP of Regulatory Affairs &
Quality
Paul Limmer, VP of Finance & Administration
Thomas Engels, VP of Clinical & Regulatory
Affairs

Designer and developer of LimFlow percutaneous
deep vein arterilization system to restore blood
flow to the ischemic foot.

**Lin Engineering**  HQ
16245 Vineyard Blvd
Morgan Hill CA 95037
P: 408-919-0200  F: 408-919-0201  PRC:150
www.linengineering.com
Email: sales@linengineering.com
Estab: 1987

Ted Lin, Founder
Belal Azim, Director of Marketing
Dave Solis, Materials Manager

Manufacturer of step motors. The company's
products include BLDC motors, optical encoders,
gearheads, and accessories.

**LinaTech USA**  HQ
1294 Kifer Rd Ste 705
Sunnyvale CA 94086
P: 408-733-2051  F: 408-733-2045  PRC:189
www.linatech.com
Estab: 1998

Terry Lane, Director of Sales and Marketing

Manufacturer of medical devices and software for
the treatment of cancer through radiotherapy. The
company also supplies informatics software for
managing cancer clinics.

**Linden Research Inc**  HQ
945 Battery St
San Francisco CA 94111
P: 415-243-9000  F: 415-243-9045  PRC:323
www.lindenlab.com
Email: business@lindenlab.com
Estab: 1999

Rod Humble, CEO

Designer and developer of digital entertainment
solutions. The company's products include Desura, Patterns, and Versu.

**Lindsley Lighting**  HQ
4871 Sunrise Dr Ste 101
Marinez CA 94553
P: 925-254-1860  F: 888-695-3699  PRC:243
www.lindsleylighting.com
Email: info@lindsleylighting.com
Estab: 1989

Karen Jess-Lindsley, CEO
Alan Lindsley, Chief Design Officer

Provider of lighting solutions focusing on design,
sales, installation, and delivery. The company
serves residential and commercial properties.

**Lineage Cell Therapeutics Inc**  HQ
2173 Salk Ave Ste 200
Carlsbad CA 92008
P: 510-871-4188  PRC:34
lineagecell.com
Email: contact@lineagecell.com
Emp: 11-50 Estab: 1990
Sales: $3M to $10M

Brian Culley, CEO
Rami Skaliter, CEO
Brandi Roberts, CFO
Tim Kang, Associate Director of Quality Assurance
Francois Binette, SVP of Global Head of R&D

Provider of cell-based technologies and regenerative medicine for the treatment of chronic and
degenerative diseases.

**Linear Integrated Systems**  HQ
4042 Clipper Ct
Fremont CA 94538-6540
P: 510-490-9160  F: 510-353-0261  PRC:208
www.linearsystems.com
Email: sales@linearsystems.com
Estab: 1987

Timothy McCune, President
Cindy Johnson, CEO
John Hall, Chairman
Will Hall, Shipping Manager

Manufacturer of semiconductor products. The
company offers bipolar transistors, input protection
diodes, resistors, and low leakage amplifiers.

**Linguastat Inc**  HQ
330 Townsend St Ste 108
San Francisco CA 94107
P: 415-814-2999  PRC:67
www.linguastat.com
Email: sales@linguastat.com
Estab: 2004

Jacob Portnoff, Senior Content Architect

Provider of web based services to corporations
and government agencies. The company offers
optimized product descriptions for millions of
landing pages.

**Linkbit Inc**  HQ
3180 De La Cruz Blvd Ste 200
Santa Clara CA 95054-2434
P: 408-969-9940  F: 408-273-6009  PRC:97
www.linkbit.com
Email: contactus@linkbit.com
Estab: 2000

Tanya Sukhar, Senior Software Engineer

Manufacturer of network equipment. The company
primarily caters to service providers and network
operators.

**Liqua-Tech Corp**  HQ
3501 N State St
Ukiah CA 95482
P: 707-462-3555  F: 707-462-3576  PRC:159
www.liqua-tech.com
Email: ltc@liqua-tech.com
Emp: 1-10 Estab: 1984

Ed Bruce, Director of Operations

Manufacturer of precision measurement systems.
The company offers flow meters, gear trains, and
measuring chambers.

**Litmos Ltd**  HQ
4140 Dublin Blvd Ste 500
Dublin CA 94568
P: 925-251-2220  PRC:324
www.litmos.com
Email: support@litmos.com
Estab: 2000

Dan Allen, VP of Engineering

Provider of learning management system
solutions. The company serves the energy and
engineering industries.

**Live Oak Associates Inc**  HQ
6840 Via Del Oro Ste 220
San Jose CA 95119
P: 408-224-8300  F: 408-224-1411  PRC:142
loainc.com

Davinna Ohlson, Director of Ecological Services
Tom Haney, Director of Cartography GIS
Pamela Peterson, Senior Project Manager
Katrina Krakow, Project Manager
Nathan Hale, Project Manager

Provider of ecological and biological consulting
services. The company is also focused on environmental permitting and planning activities.

**LiveAction** HQ
3500 West Bayshore Rd
Palo Alto CA 94303
P: 888-881-1116 PRC:319
www.liveaction.com
Email: info@savvius.com
Estab: 1990

John Smith, EVP
Stephen Stuut, CEO
Francine Geist, CFO
Pete Tyrrell, Chief Revenue Officer

Provider of network visibility and performance
diagnostics products. The company focuses on
network and security forensics.

**Livermore Software Technology Corp** HQ
7374 Las Positas Rd
Livermore CA 94551
P: 925-449-2500 F: 925-449-2507 PRC:323
www.lstc.com
Email: support@lstc.com
Estab: 1987

Todd Slavik, Engineer
John Hallquist, President
Wei Hu, Senior Scientist
Yun Huang, Senior Scientist of Software Devel-
oper
Ushnish Basu, Senior Scientist

Developer of software for automotive crashworthi-
ness, metal forming, aerospace, and other needs.
The company also offers training.

**Livevol Inc** BR
220 Montgomery St Ste 360
San Francisco CA 94104
P: 415-200-4536 F: 415-358-5818 PRC:322
livevol.com
Email: sales@livevol.com
Estab: 2009

Edward Tilly, Chairman
Alex Klein, Director of Information Technology

Designer and developer of customized data solutions. The company's services include consulting
and technical support.

**LiveVox Inc** HQ
655 Montgomery St Ste 1000
San Francisco CA 94111
P: 415-671-6000 PRC:326
www.livevox.com
Email: info@livevox.com
Estab: 2001

Raghuram Megharaj, Senior Development Engi-
neer
Larry Siegel, Co-Founder
Louis Summe, Co-Founder
OTIS SIEGEL, Chief Culture Officer
LINDA ESPERANCE, SVP of Human Capital

Specializes in business analytics and related
services. The company serves the telecom and
healthcare industries.

**Lloyd W Aubry Company Inc** HQ
2148 Dunn Rd
Hayward CA 94545
P: 510-732-9038 F: 510-732-3137 PRC:80
lloydaubry.com
Estab: 1961

Robert Butler, President
Stacey Henn, Accounts Receivable Specialist

Provider of mechanical contracting services specializing in fabrication, installation, relocation, and
maintenance of processing plant equipment.

**Lmi Net** HQ
1700 Martin Luther King Jr Way
Berkeley CA 94709
P: 510-843-6389 F: 510-843-6390 PRC:325
www.lmi.net
Email: info@lmi.net
Estab: 1992

Doran Mori, Systems Engineer
Gary Morrell, Owner
Julio Jefferson, Computer Technology Manager
Christopher Whitehorn, Computer Repair Tech-
nician

Provider of solar-assisted internet connections.
The company offers computer repair, IT services,
web site development, and virus removal services.

**Loadstar Sensors Inc** HQ
48501 Warm Springs Blvd Ste 308
Fremont CA 94539
P: 510-274-1872 F: 510-952-3700 PRC:76
www.loadstarsensors.com
Email: info@loadstarsensors.com
Estab: 2004

Div Harish, CEO
Jesus Salcedo, Sales Manager

Manufacturer of sensors and load cells with wireless output, used in medical device, automotive,
aerospace, consumer and other industries.

**Lobcom** HQ
185 Berry Ave Ste 1510
San Francisco CA 94108
P: 847-630-9275 PRC:315
lob.com
Estab: 2013

Harry Zhang, Co-Founder
Leore Avidar, Co-Founder

Builds an API toolkit that allows organizations
to innovate, move faster, and better differentiate
themselves.

**Locus Technologies** HQ
299 Fairchild Dr
Mountain View CA 94043
P: 650-960-1640 PRC:142
www.locustec.com
Email: info@locustec.com
Estab: 1997

Sandeep Khabiya, VP of Software Engineering
Luxy Martin, Assistant Project Engineer
Neno Duplan, Founder
Ben Afzal, Financial Controller
Amelia Anderson, Marketing Manager

Provider of web based environmental information
management systems. The company's services
include field installation, training, and technical
support.

**Lodi Iron Works Inc** HQ
820 S Sacramento St
Lodi CA 95240
P: 209-368-5395 F: 209-339-1453 PRC:80
www.lodiiron.com
Email: sales@lodiiron.com
Emp: 1-10 Estab: 1946

Kevin Van Steenberge, President
Lodi Paul, Quality Control Manager

Provider of machine shop services. The company
offers in-house pattern making, tooling, machining, and iron casting services.

**Logen Solutions USA** HQ
3003 N First St Ste 307
San Jose CA 95134
P: 408-519-5771 PRC:319
www.logensol.com

Andrew Chang, VP

Provider of truck, container, pallet and carton
loading and packaging software. The company
offers solutions for cargo load planning.

**Logosol Inc** BR
5041 Robert J Mathews Pkwy Ste 100
El Dorado Hills CA 95762
P: 408-744-0974 F: 408-744-0977 PRC:233
www.logosolinc.com
Email: info@logosolinc.com
Emp: 11-50

Stefan Nicov, Research
Kroum Mihaylov, Mechanical Engineer
George Georgiev, Software Engineer
Vladimir Mihaylov, Applications Engineer
Violin Zlatanov, Electronics Engineer

Manufacturer and designer of motion control
components. The company's products are used in
semiconductor material handling applications.

**Longevity Global Inc** HQ
23591 Foley St
Hayward CA 94545
P: 510-887-7090 F: 510-887-7091 PRC:152
www.longevity-inc.com
Email: help@longevity-inc.com
Estab: 2001

Simon Katz, President

Manufacturer of welding equipment. The company
also offers filler rods, generators, plasma cutters,
and related accessories.

**Loomis Industries Inc** HQ
1204 Church St
St. Helena CA 94574
P: 707-963-4111 F: 707-963-3753 PRC:127
www.loomisinc.com
Email: info@loomisinc.com
Estab: 1974

Rick Avidano, Mechanical Engineer
Diana Bustamante, COO
James Cook, Manager

Provider of fabrication services. The company
specializes in the design, print, and analysis of
semiconductor components.

**Loprest Water Treatment Co** HQ
2825 Franklin Canyon Rd
Rodeo CA 94572-2195
P: 510-799-3101   F: 510-799-7433   PRC:144
www.loprest.com
Email: sales@loprest.com
Estab: 1928

Randy Richey, President

Provider of water treatment systems design and
fabricating services. The company focuses on
media analysis and filter inspection.

**Lor-Van Manufacturing** HQ
3307 Edward Ave
Santa Clara CA 95054
P: 408-980-1045   F: 408-980-1047   PRC:80
www.lor-vanmfg.com
Estab: 2005

Ismelda Lopez, Manager of Engineering
James Hemphill, General Manager
Moriah Fernandez, Human Resource Manager
Jose Barajas, Manager of Quality Assurance
Lorena Lopez, Accounting Manager

Provider of precision sheet metal fabrication, laser
cutting, welding, and electronic chassis and card
cage assembly services.

**Lorentz Solution Inc** HQ
3375 Scott Blvd Ste 105
Santa Clara CA 95054
P: 408-922-0765   F: 408-716-4934   PRC:323
www.lorentzsolution.com
Email: sales@lorentzsolution.com
Estab: 2003

Hyungon Kim, Senior Research
Nick Karneyenka, Senior Software Engineer
Jinsong Zhao, Founder
Shun Lee, Administrative Manager

Developer of electronic design automation
software services. The company is engaged in
modeling and electromagnetic shielding.

**Lorom Industrial Co Ltd** BR
39650 Liberty St Ste 400
Fremont CA 94538
P: 919-535-5830   PRC:62
www.lorom.com
Email: info@lorom.com
Estab: 1988

YT. Yuan, President
Terry Tung, CFO

Designer and manufacturer of standard and be-
spoke cables and cable assemblies. The company
offers services to the industrial and commercial
sectors.

**Lorom West** HQ
1035 Mission Ct
Fremont CA 94539
P: 510-249-9000   F: 510-354-8000   PRC:19
www.loromwest.com
Email: sales@cable-connection.com
Estab: 1992

Greg Gaches, President

Manufacturer of PCB assemblies, turnkey OEM/
ODM products and custom cable and wire harnesses. The company offers industry solutions.

**Los Gatos Research Inc** HQ
3055 Orchard Dr
San Jose CA 95134
P: 650-965-7772   F: 650-965-7074   PRC:11
www.lgrinc.com
Email: icos.sales@ca.abb.com
Estab: 1993

Thomas Owano, VP of Engineering
Douglas Baer, President
Manish Gupta, CTO
Andrew Fahrland, Senior Scientist

Manufacturer of analyzers for the measurement
of trace gases and isotopes. The company serves
the industrial and environmental sectors.

**Lp Glass Blowing Inc** HQ
2322 Calle Del Mundo
Santa Clara CA 95054
P: 408-988-7561   F: 408-988-8981   PRC:286
www.lpglassblowing.com
Email: sales@lpglassblowing.com
Estab: 1974

Ivan Katalinic, Quartz Welder

Provider of high-precision quartz ware and glass
products. The company offers research and development assistance services.

**LS Biopath Inc** HQ
18809 Cox Ave Ste 140
Saratoga CA 95070
P: 408-464-4051   F: 408-963-6352   PRC:186
lsbiopath.com
Estab: 2007

Moshe Sarfaty, CEO

Developer of medical products and technologies
for the unmet need for real time imaging of ex-
cised tissue during breast cancer surgery.

**Lsa Associates Inc** BR
2215 Fifth St
Berkeley CA 94710
P: 510-540-7331   PRC:142
lsa.net
Estab: 1976

Les Card, Principal
Zhe Chen, Air Quality & Climate Change Manager
Ronald Brugger, Senior Air Quality Specialist
Heidi Roos, Financial Analyst
Erica Congelliere, Marketing Coordinator

Provider of consulting services. The company
focuses on environmental, transportation, and
planning services.

**LSI Design & Integration Corp** HQ
2081 Forest Ave
San Jose CA 95124
P: 408-283-8540   F: 408-283-8544   PRC:204
www.ldic.com
Email: sales@ldic.com
Estab: 1996

Mehdi Bathaee, Market Leader

Designer and manufacturer of custom chips. The
company offers storage, communication, imaging,
and memory components.

**Lsvp International Inc** HQ
12755 Alto Verde Ln
Los Altos CA 94022
P: 650-969-1000   F: 650-969-2300   PRC:189
www.lsvpusa.com
Email: info@lsvpusa.com
Estab: 1992

Sophia Pesotchinsky, Owner

Manufacturer of flexible and semi-rigid endoscopic instruments. The company's services include
engineering and distribution.

**Lucas Signatone Corp** HQ
393-J Tomkins Ct
Gilroy CA 95020
P: 408-848-2851   F: 408-848-5763   PRC:13
www.signatone.com
Email: sales@signatone.com
Estab: 1965

L. Dickson, VP of Engineering
Marc Pinard, Sales Manager
Richard Dickson, Sales Manager
Loren Dickson, Sales Manager
James Dickson, VP of Logistics

Manufacturer of micro-probe stations, holders,
and accessories. The company's products are
used in resistivity test equipment.

**Lucero Cables Inc** HQ
193 Stauffer Blvd
San Jose CA 95125
P: 408-298-6001   F: 408-298-6002   PRC:78
www.luceromfg.com
Email: sales@luceromfg.com
Estab: 1978

Serjik Avanes, VP

Manufacturer of electronic products. The company's products include cables, harnesses, and
electromechanical sub assemblies.

**Lucidport Technology Inc** HQ
150 W Iowa Ave Ste 101
Sunnyvale CA 94086
P: 408-720-8800   F: 408-720-8900   PRC:94
www.lucidport.com
Email: sales@lucidport.com
Estab: 2004

Weiti Liu, President
Angel Chien, Business Analyst

Provider of semiconductor solutions. The company
offers USB and wireless USB controllers for printers, scanners, digital cameras, and TV tuners.

**Lucidworks** HQ
717 Market St Ste 800
San Francisco CA 94103
P: 415-329-6515   F: 650-620-9540   PRC:325
lucidworks.com
Estab: 2008

Joel Westberg, Director of Engineering
Esther Quansah, Solutions Engineer Manager of
Customer Success
Varun Thacker, Engineer
Gitanjali Palwe, Search Engineer
Andy Tran, Senior Solutions Engineer

Provider of commercial foundation for architecture,
design, development, and deployment of search
solutions built with lucid works enterprise.

**Luhdorff & Scalmanini Consulting Engineers** HQ
500 First St
Woodland CA 95695
P: 530-661-0109  F: 530-661-6806  PRC:142
www.lsce.com
Emp: 1-10  Estab: 1980

Jason Coleman, Project Engineer
Gregory Garrison, Staff Engineer
Vicki Grabert, President
Scott Lewis, Principal Geologist
Jeevan Jayakody, Hydrogeologist

Provider of consulting and engineering services that include investigation, use, protection, development, and management of groundwater resources.

**Lumasense Technologies Inc** HQ
3301 Leonard Ct
Santa Clara CA 95054-2054
P: 408-727-1600  F: 408-727-1677  PRC:87
www.lumasenseinc.com
Email: info@lumasenseinc.com
Estab: 2005

Steve Chick, Systems Engineer
Adam Scott, Software Engineer
Yuval Wasserman, CEO
Neil Brinker, COO
Paul Oldham, CFO

Provider of temperature and gas sensing instruments for the energy, industrial, clean technology, and commercial markets.

**Lumedx Corp** HQ
555 Twelfth St Ste 2060
Oakland CA 94607
P: 800-966-0699  F: 510-419-3699  PRC:258
www.lumedx.com
Estab: 1990

Allyn McAuley, CEO
Chris Winquist, President

Provider of cardiovascular information and imaging systems. The company specializes in cloud-powered healthcare solutions.

**Lumen Therapeutics LLC** HQ
325 Sharon Park Dr Ste 753
Menlo Park CA 94025
P: 650-450-4439  PRC:34
www.lumentherapeutics.com

Garrison Fathman, Director
Paul McGrane, Director
Michael Danaher, Director

Provider of therapeutic solutions. The company focusses on the proprietary drugs based on oligo-L-arginine.

**Lumenetix Inc** HQ
4742 Scotts Valley Dr
Scotts Valley CA 95066
P: 877-805-7284  PRC:243
www.lumenetix.com
Email: info@lumenetix.com
Emp: 1-10  Estab: 2009

David Bowers, Senior Development Engineer
Yuko Nakazawa, Senior Optical Engineer
Linh Doan, QC Technician
Kellie Mages, Controller

Supplier of LED light engines, LED light modules, and LED components. The company also offers reflectors and surface mound LED light fixings.

**Lumenis Inc** DH
2033 Gateway Pl Ste 200
San Jose CA 95110
P: 877-586-3647  F: 408-764-3999  PRC:187
www.lumenis.com
Email: information@lumenis.com
Estab: 1973

Brad Oliver, VP
Karen Smith, VP of Regulatory Affairs & Quality
Roy Ramati, SVP of EMEA & Business Development
Hadas Padan, VP of Medical Business Group
Robert Garcia, Distribution Manager

Provider of minimally-invasive clinical solutions. The company develops and commercializes energy-based technologies.

**Lumens Integration Inc** RH
4116 Clipper Ct
Fremont CA 94538
P: 888-542-3235  F: 510-252-1389  PRC:60
www.lumens.com.tw
Estab: 1998

Rita Liu, Sales Operation Manager

Designer and developer of visual presentation solutions. The company offers document cameras, video conferencing cameras, and charging carts.

**Lumeras LLC** HQ
207 McPherson St Ste C
Santa Cruz CA 95060
P: 650-575-7448  F: 831-425-1845  PRC:172
www.lumeras-labs.com
Email: info@lumeras-labs.com
Emp: 1-10  Estab: 2006

Andrew Merriam, President

Developer and manufacturer of short-wavelength laser sources for materials characterization and chemical and biological analysis.

**Lumina Decision Systems Inc** HQ
26010 Highland Way
Los Gatos CA 95033-9758
P: 650-212-1212  F: 650-240-2230  PRC:316
www.lumina.com
Email: info@lumina.com
Estab: 1991

Max Henrion, CEO
Lonnie Chrisman, CTO
Kimberley Mullins, Senior Consulting Analyst

Provider of analytical training and consulting services. The company is engaged in technical support services.

**Lumiphore Inc** HQ
600 Bancroft Way Ste B
Berkeley CA 94710-2224
P: 510-898-1190  PRC:34
www.lumiphore.com
Email: info@lumiphore.com

Kenneth Raymond, President
Nathaniel Butlin, Chief Intellectual Property Officer
David Lund, CFO
Stephen Blose, Chief Business Development Officer
Darren Magda, VP of Research & Development

Developer of proprietary lanthanide technology. The company develops and markets biological detection reagents.

**Lumiquick Diagnostics Inc** HQ
2946 Scott Blvd
Santa Clara CA 95054
P: 408-855-0061  F: 408-855-0063  PRC:31
lumiquick.co
Email: info@lumiquick.com

Charles Yu, Founder
Jeff Wang, Quality Systems Manager
Rongrong Zhao, Office Manager

Manufacturer of diagnostic products and other raw materials. The company is engaged in distribution services.

**Lummen Lighting Inc** HQ
237 Talbot Ave
Santa Rosa CA 95405
P: 707-360-5428  PRC:83
lummenlighting.com
Email: info@lummenlighting.com

Henry Golobic, Lighting Manufacturer

Provider of lighting products like pendants, sconces, ballasts, and chandeliers. The company's services include design, installation, and delivery.

**Luna's Sheet Metal Inc** HQ
3125 Molinaro St
Santa Clara CA 95054
P: 408-492-1260  F: 408-492-1585  PRC:80
www.lunasheetmetal.com
Email: lunamtl@pacbell.net
Estab: 1989

Antonio Luna, President
Lupe Luna, CFO

Provider of metal fabrication and precision metal working services for the computer electronics, telecommunications, and automotive industries.

**Lunagraphica Inc** HQ
940 Stewart Dr Ste 256
Sunnyvale CA 94085
P: 408-962-1588  PRC:325
www.lunagraphica.com
Estab: 2004

Cindy Couling, President
Robert Nicholson, VP of Technology
Falline Danforth, Office Manager

Provider of internet marketing and consulting solutions. The company offers services in graphic design, website design, and web development.

**Luxience Technologies** HQ
2550 Zanker Rd
San Jose CA 95131
P: 669-235-5778  PRC:212
www.luxience.com
Email: info@luxience.com
Estab: 1988

Zoltan Albert, President

Provider of precision semiconductor equipment. The company specializes in design, fabrication, and supply of semiconductor equipment.

**Lynch Marks LLC** HQ
2105 Bancroft Way
Berkeley CA 94720
P: 510-559-7200 PRC:322
www.psship.com
Estab: 1982

Ryan Emery, Director of Development
Roger Gibby, Senior Application Architect
Jack Kern, Help Desk Lead

Provider of software development and technology
solutions focused on shipping applications. The
company focuses on consulting and package
tracking.

**Lynx Software Technologies** HQ
855 Embedded Way
San Jose CA 95138-1018
P: 408-979-3900 F: 408-979-3920 PRC:322
www.lynx.com
Email: inside@lynx.com
Estab: 1988

Arun Subbarao, VP of Engineering
Denis Mukhin, Senior Software Engineer
Gurjot Singh, CEO
Will Keegan, CTO
Keith Shea, Chief Revenue Officer

Developer of software technologies. The company
offers development tools, real-time monitoring
systems, and secure virtualization products.

**Lytrod Software Inc** HQ
2573 Claybank Rd Ste 4
Fairfield CA 94533
P: 707-422-9221 F: 707-429-5179 PRC:323
www.lytrod.com
Email: sales@lytrod.com
Estab: 1985

Michael Lytle, Sales Operations Manager
Karen Lytle, EVP

Provider of variable data print software prod-
ucts. The company's products include VisionDP
Production and Automate, Proform Designer, and
Office Designer.

**M & M Machine** HQ
10074 Streeter Rd
Auburn CA 95602
P: 530-268-2112 F: 530-268-6720 PRC:80
www.mandmmachine.com
Emp: 1-10 Estab: 1972

Chris Duckett, Machine Shop Owner

Designer and manufacturer of machined parts and
components for automotive, laser, audio and video
and body building equipment manufacturers.

**M A R's Engineering Company Inc** HQ
699 Montague Ave
San Leandro CA 94577
P: 510-483-0541 F: 510-483-1829 PRC:80
www.marseng.com
Email: info@marseng.com
Estab: 1964

Reine Ambrosio, Co-Founder

Manufacturer of screw machines. The company
also offers prototyping, fabrication, and assembly
services.

**M&L Precision Machining Inc** HQ
18665 Madrone Pkwy
Morgan Hill CA 95037
P: 408-224-2138 F: 408-224-2169 PRC:80
www.mlprecision.com
Email: sales@engbrecht.com
Estab: 1978

Karen Laisure, CFO
Mark Laisure, COO
Derek Frame, Production Manager
Dave Gonzales, Director of Quality
Ross Laisure, VP of Sales & Procurement

Provider of machine shop services. The company
offers precision fabricated components, semiconductors, and related devices.

**M-T Metal Fabrication Inc** HQ
536 Lewelling Blvd
San Leandro CA 94579
P: 510-357-5262 F: 510-351-5506 PRC:80
www.mtmetalfab.com
Estab: 1950

Ross Bigler, Owner
Justin Bigler, VP

Provider of sheet metal solutions. The company
offers CNC laser cutting, precision welding, gain-
ing, PEM fastening, and silk screen.

**M2 Antenna Systems Inc** HQ
4402 N Selland Ave
Fresno CA 93722
P: 559-432-8873 PRC:61
www.m2inc.com
Email: sales@m2inc.com
Emp: 1-10 Estab: 1995

Mike Staal, CEO
Mathew Staal, General Manager
Carrie Patton, Machinist

Manufacturer of antennas and systems. The
company specializes in computer aided antenna
design and simulation, and testing and prototyping
services.

**MabPlex USA Inc** BR
4059 Clipper Ct
Fremont CA 94538
P: 510-830-1065 PRC:34
mabplexinc.com
Email: info@mabplexinc.com
Estab: 2013

Wei Chen, CEO

Developer and manufacture of biopharmaceuticals. The company also offers contract services
from DNA to finished drug product.

**Mac Cal** HQ
1737 Junction Ave
San Jose CA 95112
P: 408-452-4809 PRC:80
www.maccal.com
Email: documents@maccal.com
Estab: 1964

Michael Hall, President
Jesus Contreras, Sales & Accounting Manager
Alexander Hall, Sales Representative
Katrina England, New Business Development
Manager

Provider of sheet metals, assembly, cables and
harnesses and engineering tools. The company
deals with engineering services.

**Machaon Diagnostics Inc** HQ
3023 Summit St
Oakland CA 94609-3408
P: 510-839-5600 F: 510-839-6153 PRC:303
www.machaondiagnostics.com
Email: lab@machaondiagnostics.com
Estab: 2003

Michael Ero, Founder
Brad Lewis, Director of Medical
Bjorn Stromsness, Director of Client Services
Tamara Mihailovski, Technical Supervisor
Sheila Flaherty, Technical Supervisor

Provider of laboratory services in diagnosis, treatment and monitoring of hemostatic and thrombotic
conditions.

**Machinist Group** HQ
7200 Alexander St
Gilroy CA 95020
P: 408-842-8437 F: 408-842-0246 PRC:80
www.machinistcoop.com
Email: info@machinistgroup.com
Estab: 1980

Lloyd Hennessy, Founder
Shawn Hennessy, VP

Manufacturer of precision machined parts. The
company serves defense, IR, laser components,
prototype, and production industries.

**Macken Instruments Inc** HQ
3196 Coffey Ln Ste 604
Santa Rosa CA 95403
P: 707-566-2110 F: 707-566-2119 PRC:171
www.macken.com
Email: info@macken.com

Michael Gibbs, Operations Manager

Manufacturer of devices for measuring and analyzing laser device power output. The company
offers laser power & beam probes and thermal
image plates.

**Macro Plastics Inc** HQ
2250 Huntington Dr
Fairfield CA 94533
P: 707-437-1200 PRC:280
macroplastics.com
Email: info@macroplastics.com

Warren MacDonald, CEO
Greg Sutton, CFO
Ann Mann, Human Resource Administrative
Assistant
Gabe Cota, Production Shift Supervisor
Peter Piccioli, VP of Sales & Services

Provider of agricultural, food processing, and
industrial bins. The company's services include
recycling, design, and business development.

**MacroGenics Inc** BR
3280 Bayshore Blvd Ste 200
Brisbane CA 94005
P: 650-624-2600 F: 650-624-2693 PRC:251
www.macrogenics.com
Email: info@macrogenics.com

Eric Risser, SVP of Business Development & Port-
folio Management
James Karrels, SVP
Tom Spitznagel, SVP of BioPharmaceutical Devel-
opment and Manufacturing
Lynn Cilinski, VP
Deryk Loo, Director

Developer, manufacturer, and marketer of innovative antibody-based therapeutics for the treatment of cancer and autoimmune disorders.

**Macronix America Inc** LH
680 N Mccarthy Blvd Ste 200
Milpitas CA 95035
P: 408-262-8887   F: 408-262-8810   PRC:96
www.macronix.com
Estab: 1989

Wilvin Lee, System Engineer
Mariano Bongulto, Quality Assurance Manager
Fazail Khan, Marketing & Business Development

Manufacturer of integrated device. The company offers application driven system solutions and non-volatile memory semiconductor solutions.

**Macrotron Systems Inc** HQ
44235 Nobel Dr
Fremont CA 94538
P: 510-683-9600   PRC:211
Estab: 1984

Anita Ting, CFO
Scott Blair, Business Developer
Vivian Lin, Accounting Analyst

Designer and manufacturer of memory modules. The company provides services such as electronics assembly and testing.

**Magee Scientific Corp** HQ
1916A ML King Jr Way
Berkeley CA 94704
P: 510-845-2801   F: 510-845-7137   PRC:235
www.mageesci.com
Email: mail@mageesci.com
Estab: 1986

Tony Hansen, Owner

Provider of measurement instruments such as aethalometers, transmissometers, and their accessories for monitoring air quality and source emissions.

**Maggiora Bros Drilling Inc** HQ
595 Airport Blvd
Watsonville CA 95076
P: 831-724-1338   F: 831-724-3228   PRC:144
www.maggiorabros.com
Emp: 11-50 Estab: 1962

Mark Maggiora, Owner

Provider of water well drilling and pump installation services. The company specializes in hydrologic cycle such as evaporation and condensation.

**Magnet Systems Inc** HQ
2300 Geng Rd Ste 100
Palo Alto CA 94303
P: 650-329-5904   PRC:322
www.magnet.com
Estab: 2008

Alfred Chuang, CEO
Nicole Laskowski, News Director
Susan Fogarty, Editorial Director
David Essex, Executive Editor
Tayla Holman, Site Editor

Provider of mobile apps with software, infrastructure and tools to build enterprise-grade mobile apps. The company serves enterprises.

**Magnetic Circuit Elements** HQ
1540 Moffett St
Salinas CA 93905
P: 831-757-8752   F: 831-757-5478   PRC:214
www.mcemagnetics.com
Email: sales@mcemagnetics.com

Jedediah Koch, Design Engineer
Abigail Bufil, Purchasing & Electronic Assembly Group Leader

Manufacturer of miniature transformers and inductors. The company's products include chokes, inductors, transformers, and sine wave invertors.

**Magnum Towers Inc** HQ
9370 Elder Creek Rd
Sacramento CA 95829
P: 916-381-5053   F: 916-381-2144   PRC:61
www.magnumtowers.com
Emp: 1-10   Estab: 1976

Jeff Styler, Project Manager

Provider of self-supporting and guy towers, and accessories such as safety climbs, ice bridges, antenna mounts, anti-climb devices, and insulators.

**Mailshell Inc** HQ
2336B Walsh Ave
Santa Clara CA 95051
P: 415-294-4242   F: 408-904-5079   PRC:323
www.mailshell.com
Email: info@mailshell.com
Estab: 1999

Senate Taka, Software Engineer
Tonny Yu, Founder
Manuel Mejia, CTO

Provider of traffic reputation software engines. The company also specializes in anti-spam and anti-phishing software engines.

**Maintenance Connection Inc** HQ
1477 Drew Ave Ste 103
Davis CA 95618
P: 888-567-3434   PRC:322
www.maintenanceconnection.com
Email: info@maintenanceconnection.com
Emp: 1-10   Estab: 1999

Andy Ruse, President
James Robb, CFO
Greg Rivera, Chief Product
Mark Van Daele, COO
Kevin Reichle, Chief of Staff

Provider of enterprise web based maintenance management software, work order software, and facility maintenance software.

**Makel Engineering Inc** HQ
1585 Marauder St
Chico CA 95973
P: 530-895-2770   F: 530-895-2777   PRC:86
www.makelengineering.com
Email: info@makelengineering.com
Emp: 1-10   Estab: 1995

Darby Makel, President

Developer and provider of products and services for aviation, space, military, and commercial applications.

**Mako Industries** HQ
831 N K St
Livermore CA 94551
P: 925-209-7985   F: 925-396-6084   PRC:142
makoindustries.com

Gunnar Bredek, VP
Robert Larsen, VP
Jack Decker, Service Technician

Manufacturer of remediation systems for the environmental industry. The company is focused on field and carbon change out services.

**Malaster Company Inc** HQ
3291 Edward Ave
Santa Clara CA 95054
P: 877-625-2783   F: 408-982-3295   PRC:157
www.malaster.com
Email: contact@malaster.com
Estab: 1988

Michael Cordingley, President
Melissa Hamro, Sales Manager

Provider of packing materials. The company specializes in offering package and shipping solutions for semiconductor industries.

**Malcolm Drilling Company Inc** HQ
92 Natoma St Ste 400
San Francisco CA 94105
P: 415-901-4400   F: 415-901-4421   PRC:159
www.malcolmdrilling.com
Estab: 1962

Rob Jameson, VP of Construction Engineering
CJ Stilger, Site Engineer
John Malcolm, President
Alan Rasband, President
Barry Kannon, EVP

Provider of specialty foundation industry services. The company is engaged in deep foundations, dewatering, and design build services.

**Marathon Products Inc** HQ
14500 Doolittle Dr
San Leandro CA 94577-1109
P: 510-562-6450   F: 510-562-6408   PRC:189
www.marathonproducts.com
Email: sales@marathonproducts.com
Estab: 1991

Greg Reel, Scientist
Martin Thang, Calibration Engineer
Jon Nakagawa, Founder
John Perry, VP of Sales
Mikkel Ridley, Wireless and Network Specialist

Manufacturer of equipment for collecting data on temperature for use in packaging and shipping industries.

**Marin Biologic Laboratories Inc** HQ
378 Bel Marin Keys Blvd
Novato CA 94949
P: 415-883-8000   F: 415-883-8011   PRC:34
www.marinbio.com
Email: marinbio378@marinbio.com
Estab: 1996

Tania Weiss, President
Peter Ralph, VP of Operations
Kevin Wilhelmsen, Senior Scientist

Provider of client research services. The company serves the pharmaceutical, biotechnology, diagnostic, agricultural, and legal markets.

**Marin Software** HQ
123 Mission St Fl 25
San Francisco CA 94105
P: 415-399-2580 PRC:319
www.marinsoftware.com
Email: info@marinsoftware.com
Estab: 2006
Sales: $30M to $100M

Doug Pan, SVP of Engineering
Chris Lien, CEO
Wister Walcott, Co-Founder
Bob Bertz, CFO
Wesley Maclaggan, SVP of Marketing

Developer of software products and provides software design and development for the architecture, engineering, and construction industries.

**Marketo Inc** HQ
901 Mariners Island Blvd Ste 500
San Mateo CA 94404
P: 650-581-8001 F: 650-376-2331 PRC:322
www.marketo.com
Email: support@marketo.com
Estab: 2007

Shantanu Narayen, CEO
Abhay Parasnis, CTO
John Murphy, CFO
Scott Belsky, Chief Product Officer
Donna Morris, Chief Human Resources Officer

Provider of marketing automation software services. The company offers email and social marketing, marketing software, and digital marketing services.

**Marki Microwave Inc** HQ
215 Vineyard Ct
Morgan Hill CA 95037
P: 408-778-4200 F: 408-778-4300 PRC:209
www.markimicrowave.com
Email: info@markimicrowave.com
Estab: 1991

Christopher Marki, CEO

Manufacturer of microwave mixers. The company offers adapters, amplifiers, couplers, diplexers, DC blocks, and other equipment.

**Marklogic Corp** HQ
999 Skyway Rd
San Carlos CA 94070
P: 650-655-2300 F: 650-655-2310 PRC:319
www.marklogic.com
Estab: 2001

Christopher Lindblad, Founder
Gary Bloom, CEO
Peter Norman, CFO
Daniel Jung, Senior Director of Finance
David Ponzini, EVP of Marketing

Provider of enterprise solutions. The company serves the healthcare, legal, and insurance industries.

**Markmonitor Inc** HQ
50 California St Ste 200
San Francisco CA 94111
P: 415-278-8400 F: 415-278-8444 PRC:325
www.markmonitor.com
Email: sales@markmonitor.com
Estab: 1999

Chandu K., Staff Engineer
Trina Schnapp, VP of Human Resources
Elizabeth Costa, Strategic Account Manager

Provider of brand protection, domain management, domain advisory, anti-piracy, and managed services.

**Marrone Bio Innovations Inc** HQ
1540 Drew Ave
Davis CA 95618
P: 530-750-2800 PRC:34
marronebio.com
Email: info@marronebio.com
Emp: 1-10 Estab: 2006

Jim Boyd, CFO
Keith Pitts, VP of Regulatory
Louis Boddy, Group Leader

Developer of naturally derived technologies of pest management and plant health products used in agricultural, ornamental, and water treatment.

**Marseille Inc** HQ
3211 Scott Blvd Ste 205
Santa Clara CA 95054
P: 408-855-9003 F: 408-855-9005 PRC:212
www.marseilleinc.com
Email: info@marseilleinc.com
Estab: 2005

Amine Chabane, Founder

Provider of video processing solutions. The company's applications include home theaters and audio and video receivers.

**Martin Sprocket & Gear Inc** BR
1199 Vine St
Sacramento CA 95811
P: 916-441-7172 F: 916-441-4600 PRC:78
www.martinsprocket.com
Emp: 11-50 Estab: 1951

Ryan Davie, Manager

Manufacturer of industrial hand tools, conveyor pulleys, and other products. The company offers power transmission and material handling products.

**Martin Testing Laboratories** HQ
4724 Arnold Ave
Mcclellan CA 95652
P: 916-920-4110 F: 916-920-4390 PRC:306
www.martintesting.com
Emp: 1-10 Estab: 2000

Perry Martin, Owner

Provider of product assurance, failure analysis, mechanical, metallurgical, electrical, and paint and coating testing services.

**Martin's Metal Fabrication & Welding Inc** HQ
7260 Lewis Rd
Vacaville CA 95687
P: 707-678-4117 F: 707-678-0251 PRC:159
www.martinsmetalfab.com
Email: info@martinsmetalfab.com
Estab: 1972

David Martin, President
Tom Graef, General Manager
Chantelle Martin, VP

Provider of structural steel fabrication services in Northern California. The company offers laser cutting, beam line drilling, and other servcies.

**Martinek Manufacturing** HQ
42650 Osgood Rd
Fremont CA 94539-5627
P: 510-438-0357 F: 510-438-0359 PRC:80
www.martinek.com
Email: support@martinek.com
Estab: 2000

Mark Martinek, Owner
Charles Martinek, Owner
Jim Rumsey, Operations Manager

Provider of painting, plating, silk screening, sheet metal fabrication, machining, and precision welding services.

**Martinelli Environmental Graphics** HQ
1829 Egbert Ave
San Francisco CA 94124
P: 415-468-4000 F: 415-468-4009 PRC:227
www.martinelli-graphics.com
Estab: 1989

Jack Martinelli, President
Jeff Osicka, VP
Kevin Hirst, Installation Manager
Jake Wyatt, Installer

Provide of environmental graphic designing services. The company offers fabrication, installation, and design build services.

**Marvac Scientific Manufacturing Co** HQ
3231 Monument Way
Concord CA 94518-2405
P: 925-825-4636 F: 925-825-4976 PRC:11
www.marvacscientific.com

Lori Stoos, Part Assembler

Provider of industrial grade belt drive vacuum pumps. The company also offers cooling system and other tools.

**Marymonte Systems** HQ
6630 Marymonte Ct
San Jose CA 95120
P: 408-927-0606 PRC:68
www.marymonte.com
Email: sales@marymonte.com

John Lee, Owner

Provider of bar coding, wireless, time data collection, and RFID technology. The company offers inventory control and material handling solutions.

**Maselli Measurements Inc** BR
7746 Lorraine Ave Ste 201
Stockton CA 95210
P: 209-474-9178  F: 209-474-9241  PRC:235
www.maselli.com
Email: infousa@maselli.com
Emp: 11-50 Estab: 1948

Giovanni Maselli, CEO

Provider of liquid measuring solutions. The company manufactures and distributes refractometers and liquid analyzers for several industries.

**Master Precision Machining** HQ
2199 Ronald St
Santa Clara CA 95050
P: 408-727-0185  F: 408-727-0396  PRC:80
www.master-precision.com
Email: support@master-precision.com
Estab: 1969

Richard Rossi, Founder

Provider of precision machining services. The company offers engineering, finishing, metrology, and milling services.

**Masterwork Electronics Inc** HQ
630 Martin Ave
Rohnert Park CA 94928
P: 707-588-9906  F: 707-588-9908  PRC:207
www.masterworkelectronics.com
Email: info@masterworkelectronics.com
Estab: 1994

L.J. Millick, Supply Chain Manager

Provider of printed circuit boards, cables, harness assemblies, and wiring products. The company is engaged in engineering and manufacturing services.

**Mateon Therapeutics Inc** HQ
701 Gateway Blvd Ste 210
S San Francisco CA 94080
P: 650-635-7000  F: 650-635-7001  PRC:254
www.mateon.com
Email: info@mateon.com
Estab: 1996

William Schwieterman, President
David Chaplin, CSO
Matthew Loar, CFO

Developer and provider of therapeutics. The company focusses on the treatment of acute myeloid leukemia.

**Materials Testing Inc** HQ
8798 Airport Rd
Redding CA 96002
P: 530-222-1116  F: 530-222-1611  PRC:140
mti-kcgeotech.com
Emp: 11-50 Estab: 1996

Andrew King, Principal Engineer
Douglas King, Founder
Lisa Peery, Office Manager
Genea Peery, Office Assistant
Brian Nichols, Managing Partner

Provider of geotechnical engineering and materials testing services. The company offers geotechnical, environment, special inspection, and material testing services.

**Materion Corporation** BR
44036 S Grimmer Blvd
Fremont CA 94538
P: 510-623-1500  PRC:47
materion.com
Estab: 1931

Dylan Johnson, Strip Process Engineer
John Grampa, SVP
William Carter, Human Resource Manager
Chelsea Rose, Human Resource Generalist
Shawn Dunton, Director of Finance

Provider of material solutions. The company deals with fabrication, analysis, research and development, and testing services.

**Matheson Tri-Gas Inc** BR
6775 Central Ave
Newark CA 94560
P: 510-793-2559  F: 510-790-6241  PRC:133
www.mathesongas.com
Email: mtgnewark@matheson-trigas.com
Estab: 1926

Melanie Damrel, Office Manager

Provider of industrial, electronic, medical, and specialty gases. The company also offers gas detection, purification, and control equipment.

**Matisse Software Inc** HQ
930 San Marcos Cir Ste 101
Mountain View CA 94043
P: 252-227-7013  F: 650-548-2581  PRC:319
www.matisse.com
Email: sales@matisse.com
Estab: 1998

Claude Ezran, VP of Marketing

Provider of database software and services. The company is also engaged in training, consulting, and technical support.

**Matriscope** BR
601 Bercut Dr
Sacramento CA 95811
P: 916-375-6700  F: 916-447-6702  PRC:142
matriscope.com
Email: info@matriscope.com
Emp: 11-50

Ying-Chi Liao, Senior Engineering Manager
Randall Leong, Geotechnical
Robert Tadlock, CEO
David Palermo, CFO
Ahmed Hamdy, Head of MatriScope Business Development

Provider of geotechnical and environmental engineering services. The company also provides materials testing and special inspection services.

**Matrix Computer Solutions Inc** HQ
3001 Bridgeway Ste K314
Sausalito CA 94965
P: 415-331-3600  F: 415-331-3655  PRC:323
www.matrixcomp.net

Peter Kambas, Owner
Jordan Gootnick, Founder
Tom Zinn, Technologist
Anthony Kritikos, Technologist
Aaron Powell, Technologist

Provider of computer and technology solutions for residential and business customers. The company also offers data backup, repair, and other services.

**Matrix Logic Corp** HQ
1380 East Ave Ste 124-240
Chico CA 95973
P: 415-893-9897  PRC:323
www.matrix-logic.com
Email: sales@matrix-logic.com
Emp: 11-50 Estab: 1994

Stephen Page, President
Jun Du, Accounting Manager

Provider of enterprise content management solutions for law firms, businesses, and government agencies.

**MatrixStream Technologies Inc** HQ
303 Twin Dolphin Dr Fl 6
Redwood Shores CA 94065
P: 650-292-4982  F: 650-292-4982  PRC:67
www.matrixstream.com
Estab: 1999

Kate King, CEO
Robert Liu, COO

Provider of end-to-end enterprise, hospitality, embedded, and wireless internet protocol television solutions.

**Matronics** HQ
PO Box 347
Livermore CA 94551-0347
P: 925-606-1001  F: 925-606-6281  PRC:5
www.matronics.com
Email: sales@matronics.com

Matt Dralle, President

Provider of aircraft products. The company's products include return flow controllers, pulsation dampers, and governor MK III.

**Mattermost Inc** HQ
530 Lytton Ave Ste 201
Palo Alto CA 94301
P: 650-866-5518  PRC:319
mattermost.com
Email: info@mattermost.com
Estab: 2015

Ian Tien, Co-Founder
Corey Hulen, Co-Founder
Aneal Vallurupalli, VP of Finance
Alexis Schmidt, VP of Worldwide Sales
Alison Holmlund, VP of Customer Success

Delivers open-source messaging tools for security-conscious enterprises and developers.

**MATTERNET** HQ
3511 Edison Way
Menlo Park CA 94025
P: 650-260-2727  PRC:309
mttr.net
Email: contact@matternet.us
Estab: 2011

Andreas Raptopoulos, Co-Founder

Specializes in the creation of integrated delivery solutions. The company's products are used in healthcare, on-campus, and humanitarian applications.

**Maverick Networks Inc**  HQ
7060 Koll Center Pkwy Ste 306
Pleasanton CA 94566
P: 925-931-1900   F: 925-931-1919   PRC:63
www.mavericknetworks.net
Estab: 1986

Darryl Pantonial, Convergence Engineer
David Ferris, Convergence Field Engineer
Aaron Lee, CEO
Lillian Maeda, Sales Account Manager
Andrew Williamson, Sales Executive

Provider of VoIP telephone and related communication services. The company also provides
design, implementation, and training solutions.

**Maverick Therapeutics**  HQ
3260 B Bayshore Blvd
Brisbane CA 94005
P: 650-338-1231   PRC:36
www.mavericktx.com
Email: info@mavericktx.com

James Scibetta, CEO
James Vasselli, VP
Robert DuBridge, EVP of Research
Chad May, VP

Provider of therapeutic solutions for the treatment
of cancer. The company focusses on the research
of cytotoxic T cells.

**Mawi DNA Technologies LLC**  HQ
26203 Production Ave Ste 3
Hayward CA 94545
P: 510-256-5186   F: 510-576-2948   PRC:36
www.mawidna.com
Email: sales@mawidna.com
Estab: 2013

Jerome David, VP of sales and Marketing

Provider of biosampling devices for non-invasive
sample collection with the main objective of simplifying genomics and proteomics workflows.

**Max Group Corp**  HQ
4841 Davenport Pl
Fremont CA 94538
P: 888-644-4629   F: 510-490-9942   PRC:91
maxgroup.com
Email: fremontsales@maxgroup.com
Estab: 1985

Michael Chan, Product Manager
Iris Wu, sales

Distributor for computing devices. The company
offers computer cases, fans and heatsinks, and
hard drives.

**Max Machinery Inc**  HQ
33A Healdsburg Ave
Healdsburg CA 95448
P: 707-433-2662   F: 707-433-1818   PRC:14
www.maxmachinery.com
Email: info@maxmachinery.com
Estab: 1967

Dan Turek, General Manager
Bobbie Denmon, Controller
Nancy Davis, Human Resource Manager
Craig Pust, Quality Manager
Paul Hock, Marketing Manager

Manufacturer of precision flow meters. The
company offers intermittent injection, low flow
metering, and bi-directional flow measurement
services.

**Maxeler Technologies Inc**  HQ
1928 Old Middlefield Way Ste B
Mountain View CA 94043
P: 650-938-8818   PRC:110
www.maxeler.com
Email: info@maxeler.com
Estab: 2003

Oliver Pell, VP of Engineering
Oskar Mencer, Founder
James Spooner, VP of Acceleration

Developer of computing solutions. The company
offers services to the oil and gas, analytical, and
financial sectors.

**Maxium Living Inc**  HQ
20071 Soulsbyville Rd
Soulsbyville CA 95372
P: 209-536-9300   F: 209-536-9375   PRC:272
www.maximumliving.com
Email: info@maximumliving.com
Emp: 1-10   Estab: 1992

John Canine, Owner

Supplier of nutritional supplement products. The
company offers liquid minerals, digestive supports,
healthy energy snacks, and children supports.

**MaxLinear**  BR
1060 Rincon Cir
San Jose CA 95131
P: 669-265-6100   PRC:209
maxlinear.com
Estab: 2003

Madhukar Reddy, VP of IC And RF Systems
Engineering
Yan Lu, Senior Staff Engineer
Kishore Seendripu, CEO
Steven Litchfield, CFO
Curtis Ling, CTO

Provider of integrated radio-frequency, analog,
and mixed signal semiconductor SoC solutions.
The company focuses on broadband communications applications.

**Maxon Precision Motors Inc**  BR
1065 E Hillsdale Blvd Ste 210
Foster City CA 94404
P: 650-524-8822   F: 650-372-9395   PRC:80
www.maxonmotorusa.com
Email: info.us@maxongroup.com
Estab: 1961

Biren Patel, Motion Control Engineering Manager
Scott Hamilton, Sales Engineer
Emmanuel Jimenez, Motion Control Applications
Engineer
Sam Robinson, Marketing Manager
Deborah Mitchell, Office Manager

Provider of high-precision drives and systems.
The company's products include brushed DC
motors, brushless DC motors, spindle drives, and
gearheads.

**Maxta Inc**  HQ
2350 Mission College Blvd Ste 703
Santa Clara CA 95054
P: 669-228-2800   PRC:326
www.maxta.com
Estab: 2009

Herb Schneider, VP of Engineering
Deepak Jagtap, Software Engineer
Yoram Novick, CEO
Kiran Sreenivasamurthy, Director of Product
Management

Provider of software-defined storage, disaster
recovery, and also testing and development
solutions.

**Mc Electronics**  HQ
1891 Airway Dr
Hollister CA 95023
P: 831-637-1651   F: 831-637-1309   PRC:202
www.mcelectronics.com
Email: info@mcelectronics.com
Emp: 1-10   Estab: 1981

Angie Trujillo, VP
Keith Parrish, Program Manager

Provider of turnkey solution for contract manufacturing. The company focuses on cable & harness
assembly and full system integration.

**Mc Microwave Inc**  HQ
1777 Saratoga Ave
San Jose CA 95129
P: 408-446-4100   F: 408-446-5430   PRC:159
www.mcmicrowave.com

Steve McCreddin, Sales & Engineering Support
Linda Eserini, Administrator

Provider of microwave and radio frequency
components. The company's products are used in
commercial and military applications.

**Mcafee Inc**  HQ
2821 Mission College Blvd
Santa Clara CA 95054
P: 800-937-2237   PRC:319
www.mcafee.com
Email: customer_service_emea@mcafee.com
Estab: 1987

John Giamatteo, President
Chris Young, CEO
Michael Berry, EVP
Ashutosh Kulkarni, EVP
Steve Grobman, SVP

Provider of computer security solutions. The
company specializes in database, web, email,
network, end-point, and mobile security services.

**Mccampbell Analytical Inc**  HQ
1534 Willow Pass Rd
Pittsburg CA 94565-1701
P: 925-252-9262   F: 925-252-9269   PRC:306
www.mccampbell.com
Email: main@mccampbell.com
Estab: 1991

Mike Allison, Service Engineer
Theresa Johnson, Quality Assurance & Control
Manager
Rosa Venegas, Sales Manager
Drew Gantner, Aquatic Toxicology Lab Director
Elisa Venegas, Accounting Manager

Provider of analytical tests on drinking water, efflu-
ent, soils, solids, hazardous waste, air, soil vapor,
and industrial materials.

**Mcintire Machine Inc**     HQ
22113 Hwy 33
Crows Landing CA 95313
P: 209-837-4409   F: 209-837-4413    PRC:80
www.mcintiremachineinc.com
Email: mcinmach@comcast.net
Emp: 1-10   Estab: 1993

Ken McIntire, Owner

Provider of precision machining, welding, and
fabrication services. The company offers services
to the industrial sector.

**Mckenzie Machining Inc**     HQ
481 Perry Ct
Santa Clara CA 95054
P: 408-748-8885   F: 408-748-8887    PRC:80
www.mckenziemachining.com
Email: smckenzie@mckenziemachining.com

Scott McKenzie, President

Provider of precision machining services of
pre-fabricated components. The company R&D,
manufacturing design, and other services.

**McKesson Corporation**     HQ
1 Post St Fl 33
San Francisco CA 94104
P: 415-983-8300      PRC:194
www.mckesson.com
Estab: 1833
Sales: Over $3B

Brian Tyler, CEO
Kathy McElligott, EVP
Britt Vitalone, EVP
Bansi Nagji, EVP
Lori Schechter, EVP

Provider of healthcare services. The company
offers revenue cycle management and managed
services for hospitals.

**Mclab**     HQ
320 Harbor Way
S San Francisco CA 94080
P: 650-871-8771   F: 650-871-8796    PRC:306
mclab.com
Email: mclab@mclab.com
Estab: 1998

Nelda Knight, CEO
Mikheil Kvirikashvili, Marketing Manager
Giorgi Kelaptrishvili, Bar Manager
Shaukat Ali, Programmer
Ning Zhu, Worker

Provider of DNA sequencing services. The company's products include enzymes and biochemical
reagents.

**Mclellan Industries Inc**     HQ
13221 Crown Ave
Hanford CA 93230
P: 559-582-8100   F: 650-589-7398    PRC:158
www.mclellanindustries.com
Email: mclellan@mclellan-ind.com
Emp: 11-50   Estab: 1965

Adithya Katakam, Mechanical Design Engineer
Dale McLellan, Founder
Molly Mausser, President
Jim Ulery, Quality Control Manager
Adrian Gonzalez, Inside Sales Representative

Manufacturer of stainless steel and mild steel
tanks, hook lifts, tank kits, and related accessories.

**Mcm Engineering Inc**     HQ
845 Hinckley Rd
Burlingame CA 94010-4953
P: 650-259-9100   F: 650-259-9344    PRC:74
www.mcmeng.com
Email: sales@mcmeng.com
Estab: 1991

Paul Bade, Director of Engineering
Patrick O'Brien, President
Julie Smith, Full Charge Bookkeeper

Provider of aircraft ground support systems. The
company offers products and services for airports
and aircraft manufacturers.

**Mcneal Enterprises Inc**     HQ
2031 Ringwood Ave
San Jose CA 95131-1703
P: 408-922-7290   F: 408-922-7299    PRC:80
www.mcnealplasticmachining.com
Email: sales@mcneal.com
Estab: 1976

Ibrahim Ozturk, Quality Assurance Manager
Paul Charland, CNC Programmer
Mike Rivera, Fabricator
Peter Smith, CNC Programmer

Provider of machined, fabricated, and thermoformed plastic components. The company serves
medical, semiconductor, solar, optics, and other
needs.

**McWong International Inc**     HQ
1921 Arena Blvd
Sacramento CA 95834
P: 916-371-8080   F: 916-371-6666    PRC:243
www.mcwonginc.com
Email: support@mcwonginc.com
Emp: 11-50   Estab: 1985

Blane Goettle, VP

Designer and manufacturer of lighting control
equipment and related electrical components. The
company offers sensors and LED drivers.

**Mda Precision**     HQ
360 Digital Dr
Morgan Hill CA 95037
P: 408-847-7796      PRC:80
www.mdaprecision.com
Email: info@mdaprecision.com
Estab: 2004

Daniel Menig, Mechanical Engineer
Markus Menig, Owner

Provider of benchtop milling machine and benchtop lathe systems. The company offers micro drilling machines, benchtop manual mills, and lathes.

**Meadows Manufacturing**     HQ
545 Parrott St
San Jose CA 95112
P: 408-988-1252   F: 408-988-1126    PRC:80
www.meadowsmfg.com
Email: sales@meadowsmfg.com
Estab: 1958

Adam Gregorczuk, VP of Operations

Provider of engineering, design, and manufacturing solutions. The company serves the commercial
and industrial sectors.

**Mean Well Usa Inc**     HQ
44030 Fremont Blvd
Fremont CA 94538
P: 510-683-8886   F: 510-683-8899    PRC:293
www.meanwellusa.com
Email: info@meanwellusa.com
Estab: 1999

Jerry Lin, Founder
Florence Wu, Inside Sales Manager
Leo Cheong, Product Manager
Joseph Taylor, Key Account Manager

Manufacturer of switching power supplies such as
AC to DC converters, DC to DC converters, DC to
AC inverters, and battery chargers.

**Mec Aerial Work Platforms**     HQ
1401 S Madera Ave
Kerman CA 93630
P: 559-842-1500   F: 559-842-1520    PRC:180
www.mecawp.com
Emp: 1-10

Mike Liberto, Regional Sales Manager
Jack Harwood, Manager

Manufacturer of aerial work platforms. The company specializes in the design and manufacture of
scissors and booms.

**Mechanical Air Service Inc**     HQ
2245-C Fortune Dr
San Jose CA 95131
P: 408-432-8282   F: 408-432-8992    PRC:153
www.mechanicalairservice.com
Email: info@mechanicalairservice.com
Estab: 1977

Russ Donnici, President
Scott Larson, VP of Service Manager
Matt Donnici, VP of Construction

Provider of air conditioning and heating services
to residential and commercial sectors. The company also offers indoor air quality and green energy
services.

**Mecoptron Inc**     HQ
3115 Osgood Ct
Fremont CA 94539
P: 510-226-9966   F: 510-226-6750    PRC:80
www.mecoptron.com
Estab: 1986

Andy Law, Founder
Christine Law, Finance Manager

Provider of precision machining services. The
company's services include protype machining,
production machining, and precision mechanical
assembly services.

**Medallia Inc**     HQ
450 Concar Dr
San Mateo CA 94402
P: 650-321-3000   F: 650-321-3156    PRC:324
www.medallia.com
Estab: 2001

Sabrina Rusi, Productivity and System Engineer-
ing Manager
Borge Hald, Co-Founder
Amy Pressman, President
John Abraham, General Manager
James Allworth, Director of Strategy

Provider of consulting, system configuration, user
training, and data warehouse integration services.

**MedAutonomic Inc** HQ
1235 Traud Dr
Concord CA 94518
P: 415-377-5653 PRC:34
medautonomic.com
Email: info@medautonomic.com

Valerio Cigaina, Co-Founder
John Gonzales, Co-Founder
Paolo Fabris, Co-Founder
Alfredo Saggioro, Chief Medical Advisor
Simone Cigaina, VP of Operations

Developer of Brain NeuroModulator. The company specializes in creating control action potentials in individual neurons and in functional groups.

**Meddev Corp** HQ
730 N Pastoria Ave
Sunnyvale CA 94085
P: 408-730-9702 F: 408-730-9732 PRC:189
www.meddev-corp.com
Email: info@meddev-corp.com
Estab: 1971

Suzanne Grey, President

Developer, manufacturer, and marketer of medical devices for niche market segments throughout the world.

**Medeanalytics Inc** HQ
5858 Horton St Ste 280
Emeryville CA 94608
P: 510-379-3300 F: 510-647-1325 PRC:194
medeanalytics.com
Estab: 1994

Andrea Sorensen, Associate VP of Solutions Engineering
Will Dong, Quality Engineer
Charles Zhang, Engineer
Leigh Crawford, Associate VP of Product Ownership
Scott Hampel, President

Provider of performance management, compliance, employer reporting, patient engagement, and satisfaction solutions.

**Medeor Therapeutics** HQ
611 Gateway Blvd Ste 120
S San Francisco CA 94080
P: 650-627-4531 PRC:34
www.medeortx.com
Email: inquiry@medeortx.com

Darin Weber, SVP
Scott Batty, Chief Medical Officer
Corinna Chen, VP of Corporate Development

Developer of personalized cellular immunotherapy for the organ transplant recipients. The company specializes in cellular immunotherapy, hematology, and transplantation product development.

**MedGenome Inc** HQ
348 Hatch Dr
Foster City CA 94404
P: 888-440-0954 PRC:34
www.medgenome.com
Email: research@medgenome.com
Estab: 2013

Sam Santhosh, Founder
Hiranjith GH, Senior Director
Amitabha Chaudhuri, VP of Research & Development

Provider of genomics based diagnostics and research services. The company specializes in bioinformatics, computing, genomics technologies, and big data analytics.

**Media Flint** HQ
800 W El Camino Real Ste 180
Mountain View CA 94040
P: 888-592-2921 PRC:325
www.mediaflint.com
Email: info@mediaflint.com

Amin Haq, CEO
Ali Ghaznavi, CTO
Tom Jagger, VP of Account Services

Provides internet marketing and advertising solutions to companies.

**Media Net Link Inc** HQ
6114 La Salle Ave Ste 415
Oakland CA 94611
P: 866-563-5152 PRC:322
www.mnl.com
Email: info@mnl.com
Estab: 1994

Richard Kitamura, Project Manager
Mike Keller, Lead Designer

Provider of web business solutions. The company focuses on application development, systems intergration, website design, and project management.

**Media Specialty Resources Inc** HQ
61 Galli Dr Ste A
Novato CA 94949
P: 415-883-8053 F: 415-883-8147 PRC:60
www.msr-inc.com
Email: info@msr-inc.com
Estab: 2003

Anthony Grimani, President

Provider of acoustic panels for recording studios and home theaters. The company also offers noise control and soundproofing services.

**Mediawave Pc Inc** HQ
46571 Fremont Blvd
Fremont CA 94538
P: 510-490-6768 F: 510-580-1171 PRC:93
www.mediawavepc.com
Email: info@mediawavepc.com
Estab: 1994

Charles Duncan, Director of Sales

Developer of rack optimized servers, digital signage, laptops, and desktop computer systems for resellers and end users.

**Medical Design Solutions** HQ
1525 McCarthy Blvd Ste 1089
Milpitas CA 95035
P: 408-393-5386 PRC:189
www.medicaldesignsolutions.com

Darius Przygoda, VP of Electrical Engineering
Robert Stone, CEO
Steve Sabram, Director of Wearable and Mobile Systems
Larry Czapla, Senior Executive

Provider of medical design solutions. The company develops miniaturized sensors and systems used in medical device applications.

**MedImmune LLC** BR
121 Oyster Point Blvd
S San Francisco CA 94080
P: 800-236-9933 PRC:268
www.astrazeneca.com

Pascal Soriot, Executive Director
Leif Johansson, Non-Executive Chairman of the Board
Marc Dunoyer, Executive Director
Katarina Ageborg, Chief Compliance Officer
Fiona Cicconi, EVP of Human Resources

Developer of biotechnology products and solutions. The company's products include Synagis, FluMist, and Trivalent FluMist.

**Meditab Software Inc** HQ
2233 Watt Ave Ste 360
Sacramento CA 95825
P: 510-201-0130 F: 510-259-9731 PRC:323
www.meditab.com
Email: info@meditab.com
Emp: 1-10 Estab: 1998

Paragi Patel, CEO
Darrin Luke, Project Manager

Developer of physical therapy, urology, cosmetic, and plastic surgery solutions. The company serves the healthcare industry.

**Medland & Associates Inc** BR
PO Box 1275
San Martin CA 95046
P: 408-686-0460 F: 408-686-0462 PRC:83
www.medlandandassociates.com
Email: sales@medlandandassociates.com
Estab: 1994

John Mason, Field Applications
David Medland, Owner
Susan Kline, Sales Representative
Sandy Medland, Sales & Accounting Manager

Manufacturer of OEM products. The company's products include AC and DC converters, power supplies, switching regulators, and cable assemblies.

**Medsoftware Inc** HQ
6415 Oak Hill Dr
Granite Bay CA 95746
P: 916-797-2363 F: 916-244-9888 PRC:323
www.medsoftware.com
Email: sales@medsoftware.com
Emp: 1-10 Estab: 1990

Will Williams, Technical Director
Laurie Waters, Director of Sales

Provider of practice management software solutions. The company's services include data conversion and repair, training, and implementation.

**MedStars Inc** HQ
12133 Foothill Ln
Los Altos Hills CA 94022
P: 650-917-9254 F: 650-917-9255 PRC:34
www.medstars.com
Email: info@medstars.com
Estab: 1986

Anne Degheest, Managing Partner

Provider of medical devices, healthcare information systems, health related consumer products, and biotechnology for medical and biotech companies.

**Medtronic CardioVascular inc**      BR
3576 Unocal Pl Fountaingrove A
Santa Rosa CA 95403
P: 707-525-0111   F: 707-525-0114     PRC:188
www.medtronic.com
Email: rs.meniettinformation@medtronic.com
Estab: 1949

Greg Dyer, Research
Michael Coyle, EVP
Sean Salmon, EVP
Brett Wall, EVP
Bob White, EVP

Provider of disease management services. The
company specializes in cardiovascular, diabetes,
surgical technologies, and spinal and biologics.

**Megaforce Corporation Inc**      HQ
2035 O'Toole Ave
San Jose CA 95131
P: 408-956-9989   F: 408-956-9989     PRC:207
www.megaforcecorp.com
Email: info@megaforcecorp.com
Estab: 1994

Jason Trenh, CEO
Ray Woodfin, Director of Sales

Provider of supply chain, materials management,
and test solutions. The company serves the industrial, commercial, and automotive sectors.

**Megapath**      HQ
6701 Koll Center Pkwy Ste 250
Pleasanton CA 94566
P: 866-300-0749     PRC:66
www.megapath.com
Estab: 1996

Kevin Brand, President
Brian George, CTO
Keith Soldan, CFO
Jim Smith, CIO
J. Mastin, VP of Finance

Provider of voice, data, networking, cloud, and
security services. The company serves healthcare,
finance, restaurant, and retail sectors.

**Meggitt Sensing Systems**      RH
355 N Pastoria Ave
Sunnyvale CA 94085
P: 949-493-8181     PRC:146
www.endevco.com
Estab: 1947

Jim Henderson, Principal Software Engineer
James Nelson, Mechanical Engineer
Andy Heckman, Director of Sales
George Markulis, VP of Health Safety
Arlene Griffin, Strategic Sourcing Manager

Provider of solutions for measurement applications. The company offers piezoelectric and
piezoresistive type transducers.

**Megmeet Usa Inc**      BR
4020 Moorpark Ave Ste 115
San Jose CA 95117
P: 408-260-7211     PRC:243
www.megmeetusa.com
Email: power@megmeet.com
Estab: 2003

Sandi Huang, Manager of Accounting & HR
Robert Staub, Business Development Executive

Manufacturer of electrical motors, general-used
converters, and optional devices. The company
offers industry automatic solutions.

**Meiji Techno America**      BR
5895 Rue Ferrari
San Jose CA 95138
P: 408-226-3454   F: 408-226-0900     PRC:174
www.meijitechno.com
Email: info@meijitechno.com
Estab: 1986

Anthony Rivero, Biologist
Rick McReynolds, Shipping

Manufacturer of optical microscope products.
The company offers gemological, biological, and
educational microscopes, and accessories.

**Meivac Inc**      HQ
5830 Hellyer Ave
San Jose CA 95138
P: 408-362-1000   F: 408-362-1010     PRC:83
www.meivac.com
Email: support@meivac.com
Estab: 1993

Aditya Walimbe, Applications Engineer
David Meidinger, President
Alan Schauer, VP of Operations
Todd Johnson, Components Product Manager
Rob Zvara, Customer Support Supervisor

Manufacturer of sputtering systems and components. The company offers throttle valves, integrators, OEM assemblies, and substrate heaters.

**Mektec International Corp**      HQ
1731 Technology Dr Ste 840
San Jose CA 95110
P: 408-392-4000   F: 408-392-4077     PRC:209
www.mektec.com

Steve Decia, President
Daniel Lien, Technical Sales Account Manager
Akio Yoshida, Director

Manufacturer of printed circuit boards. The
company deals with production, prototyping, and
application engineering services.

**Meline Engineering Corp**      HQ
PO Box 276665
Sacramento CA 95827
P: 916-366-3458     PRC:135
www.meline.com
Email: me_info@meline.com
Emp: 1-10   Estab: 1995

Lisa Meline, Principal Mechanical Engineer

Provider of energy efficient mechanical system
design services. The company also offers mechanical engineering services.

**Mellanox Technologies Inc**      RH
350 Oakmead Pkwy Ste 100
Sunnyvale CA 94085
P: 408-970-3400   F: 408-970-3403     PRC:212
www.mellanox.com
Email: info@mellanox.com
Estab: 1999

Eyal Waldman, President
Michael Kagan, CTO

Provider of Ethernet interconnect solutions and
services. The company offers virtualization and
Microsoft based solutions to its clients.

**Melrose Metal Products Inc**      HQ
44533 Grimmer Blvd
Fremont CA 94538
P: 510-657-8771   F: 510-657-7233     PRC:153
www.gomelrose.com
Email: mhoppe@gomelrose.com

Bob Lloyd, Sales Manager

Manufacturer of melrose metal products. The
company offers design and installation services
for food processing and emission control systems.

**Melrose Nameplate & Label Co**      HQ
26575 Corporate Ave
Hayward CA 94545
P: 510-732-3100   F: 510-732-3111     PRC:82
www.melrose-nl.com
Email: sales@melrose-nl.com
Estab: 1939

Jim Fritz, Purchasing
Shannon Looper, Customer Service Manager
Gabriella Cruz, Manager
Vanessa Hong, Manager

Developer and manufacturer of ID nameplates,
labels, and membrane switches. The company
offers touchscreen assembly and decorative
nameplates.

**Meltwater Group**      HQ
225 Bush St Ste 1000
San Francisco CA 94104
P: 415-236-3144   F: 415-848-9190     PRC:323
www.meltwater.com
Estab: 2001

Mike Ruggieri, Executive Director of Engineering
Jorn Lyseggen, CEO
Aditya Jami, CTO
Martin Hernandez, CFO
Kaveh Rostampor, Executive Director of Americas

Developer of software products such as Meltwater
BUZZ, Meltwater NEWS, and Meltwater DRIVE
to meet the specific needs of businesses around
the world.

**Membrane Technology & Research**  HQ
39630 Eureka Dr
Newark CA 94560
P: 650-328-2228  F: 650-328-6580  PRC:54
www.mtrinc.com
Estab: 1982

Priyanka Tiwari, Process Engineer
Sachin Joshi, Technical Sales Manager
Kaaeid Lokhandwala, VP of Commercial Operations
Doug Gottschlich, Director of Refining of Hydrogen & Syngas
Alicia Breen, Senior Project Manager of Petrochemical Group

Developer and manufacturer of membrane-based separation systems. The company serves the petrochemical, natural gas, and refining industries.

**Memsql Inc**  HQ
534 Fourth St
San Francisco CA 94107
P: 855-463-6775  PRC:323
www.memsql.com
Email: info@memsql.com
Estab: 2011

Robert Walzer, VP of Engineering
Nikita Shamgunov, Co-CEO
Raj Verma, Co-CEO
Aileen Casanave, Chief Legal Officer
Adam Prout, CTO

Provider of technology solutions and services. The company serves the finance and digital advertising industries.

**Menlo Security**  HQ
2300 Geng Rd Ste 200
Palo Alto CA 94303
P: 650-614-1705  PRC:325
www.menlosecurity.com
Email: info@menlosecurity.com
Estab: 2013

Lennart van den Ende, VP of Worldwide Sales Engineering
Todd Vender, VP of Engineering
Amir Ben Efraim, CEO
Kowsik Guruswamy, CTO
Gautam Altekar, Chief Architect

Provider of security solutions. The company's offerings include web isolation, document, and phishing isolation services.

**Menlo Therapeutics**  HQ
200 Cardinal Way 2nd Fl
Redwood City CA 94063
P: 650-486-1416  PRC:268
www.menlotherapeutics.com
Sales: $10M to $30M

Steve Basta, CEO
Kristine Ball, SVP of Corporate Strategy
Mary Spellman, Chief Medical Officer
Paul Kwon, Chief Scientific Officer
Ron Krasnow, General Counsel

Developer and manufacture of biopharmaceuticals. The company focusses on the commercialization and development of serlopitant for treating pruritus.

M-188

**Mentor Graphics**  RH
46871 Bayside Pkwy
Fremont CA 94538
P: 510-354-7400  F: 510-354-7467  PRC:209
www.mentor.com
Email: sales_info@mentor.com
Estab: 1981

Ping Yeung, Principal Engineer
Ajay Mishra, Senior Product Engineering Manager
Arvind Raghuraman, Staff Engineer
Geoffrey Ellis, Staff Engineer
Walden Rhines, CEO

Provider of electronic design automation software. The company focuses on mechanical analysis, system modeling, manufacturing, and verification.

**Meraki LLC**  BR
500 Terry A Francois Blvd
San Francisco CA 94158
P: 415-432-1000  F: 415-255-9629  PRC:68
meraki.cisco.com
Email: sales@meraki.com
Estab: 2006

Todd Nightingale, SVP
Paul Wolfe, Product Marketing Manager

Provider of branch networking solutions. The company offers services to the education, retail, and healthcare industries.

**Meran Technology**  HQ
8 Croydon Cir
Piedmont CA 94611-3601
P: 510-530-5119  F: 510-482-2802  PRC:125
www.meran.net
Email: info1@meran.net
Estab: 1989

Jerry Herrick, Owner

Provider of process equipment for memory disk manufacturers. The company offers material handling equipment for fiber optic manufacturers.

**Mercator Medsystems Inc**  HQ
1900 Powell St Ste 800
Emeryville CA 94608
P: 510-614-4550  F: 510-614-4560  PRC:196
www.mercatormed.com
Email: info@mercatormed.com

Kirk Seward, Co-Founder
Trent Reutiman, CEO
Steve Baker, CFO
Kevin Griego, Sales Operations Manager

Developer of therapeutics for vascular disease, oncology and regenerative medicine, and treatment of hypertension.

**Meridian Surveying Engineering Inc**  HQ
2958 Van Ness
San Francisco CA 94109
P: 415-440-4131  F: 415-233-9671  PRC:304
www.meridiansurvey.com
Estab: 1989

Emily Thomas, Project Manager of LSIT
Rick Mather, Senior Project Manager
Kurt Kvam, IT & Office Operations Manager
Stanley Gray, Principal

Provider or residential, commercial, and municipal surveys. The company also deals with claims litigation services.

**Merieux Nutrisciences Corp**  BR
5262 Pirrone Ct
Salida CA 95368
P: 209-549-7508  PRC:19
www.merieuxnutrisciences.com
Emp: 11-50 Estab: 1967

Jim Miller, President
Philippe Sans, CEO
John Marshall, General Manager

Provider of public health services. The company is focused on food and pharmaceutical products, cosmetics, and consumer goods.

**Meritronics Inc**  HQ
500 Yosemite Dr
Milpitas CA 95035
P: 408-969-0888  PRC:211
www.meritronics.com
Estab: 1995

Ramiro Equihua, Process Engineer
Race Wu, COO
FJ Rost, VP of Quality
Isabel Wang, Purchasing Agent
Francis Rost, VP

Provider of electronics assembly, and equipment assemblies. The company specializes in PCB assembly, cable assembly, and system assembly.

**Mesa/Boogie Ltd**  HQ
1317 Ross St
Petaluma CA 94954
P: 707-778-6565  F: 707-765-1503  PRC:60
www.mesaboogie.com
Estab: 1973

Tommy Waugh, Manufacturing Specialist
Randall Smith, President
Steve Mueller, Sales General Manager
Jim Aschow, EVP
Teri Bruce, Materials Manager

Provider of guitars, bass amplifiers, and cabinetry. The company provides pedals, speakers, guitars, and accessories.

**MeshDynamics Inc**  HQ
3555 Benton St
Santa Clara CA 95051
P: 408-373-7700  F: 408-516-8987  PRC:63
www.meshdynamics.com
Email: info@meshdynamics.com
Estab: 2002

Francis Da Costa, Founder

Provider of wireless mesh networking solutions focusing on wireless video surveillance, emergency response networks, and smart-grid multiuse products.

**Mesotech International Inc**  HQ
4531 Harlin Dr
Sacramento CA 95826
P: 916-368-2020  F: 916-368-2030  PRC:138
mesotech.com
Email: sales@mesotech.com
Emp: 1-10  Estab: 1993

Christopher Swinehart, Director of Operations

Provider of weather monitoring and reporting systems and software solutions. The company serves airport, defense, and agriculture industries.

**Messagesolution Inc** HQ
1851 McCarthy Blvd Ste 105
Milpitas CA 95035
P: 408-383-0100   F: 408-383-0222   PRC:326
www.messagesolution.com
Email: salesdesk@messagesolution.com
Estab: 2004

Alan Zheng, Software Engineer
Jeff Liang, CTO
Kevin McInerney, Sales & Marketing Manager
Josh Liang, VP of Marketing
Ilya Levin, Senior iOS Developer

Provider of enterprise archiving, e-discovery,
and migration solutions. The company deals with
storage management solutions.

**Met Labs Inc** BR
3162 Belick St
Santa Clara CA 95054
P: 408-748-3585   F: 510-489-6372   PRC:306
www.metlabs.com
Email: info@metlabs.com
Estab: 1959

Randy Hoopai, EMC Engineer
Lauren Foster, Project Engineer
Asad Bajwa, Director of EMC Lab
Camilo Obana, EMC Technical Manager

Provider of electrical testing services focusing on
product safety, RF testing, and others. The company serves medical, RFID, and other sectors.

**Meta Integration Technology Inc** HQ
700 E El Camino Real Ste 170
Mountain View CA 94040
P: 650-273-6382   F: 650-307-6382   PRC:322
www.metaintegration.net
Email: info@metaintegration.net
Estab: 1997

Volodymyr Vykhrushch, Senior Software Engineer
Christian Bremeau, CEO
John O'Byrne, UI Architect

Provider of metadata components to data modeling, data integration, business intelligence, and
metadata management tool vendors.

**Metabiota Inc** HQ
425 California St 2nd Fl
San Francisco CA 94104
P: 415-398-4712   F: 415-398-4716   PRC:328
metabiota.com
Email: info@metabiota.com

Nita Madhav, CEO
Mark Gallivan, Director of Data Science
Jaclyn Guerrero, Product Manager
Bri Maramonte, Corporate Controller
Jason Euren, Senior Scientist

Provider of risk analytics that help protect global
health for governments and multinationals, food
risk, and financial risk insights.

**Metabyte Inc** HQ
39350 Civic Center Dr Ste 200
Fremont CA 94538
P: 510-494-9700   F: 510-494-9100   PRC:323
www.metabyte.com
Email: info@metabyte.com
Estab: 1993

Manu Mehta, President

Provider of software solutions and related services to the government, healthcare, and retail
industries.

**MetaCert** HQ
585 Bryant St 2nd Fl
San Francisco CA 94107
P: 415-529-2571   PRC:322
metacert.com
Estab: 2012

Jim Swift, President
Liz Devine, Chief Information Officer
Greg Johnson, COO
Mike Landis, CFO

Provider of security API for mobile app developers. The company offers content-based filtering
services.

**Metacrylics** HQ
365 Obata Ct
Gilroy CA 95020
P: 408-280-7733   F: 408-280-6329   PRC:47
www.metacrylics.com
Email: sales@metacrylics.com
Estab: 1974

Mark Anthenien, Owner
David Vienna, Regional Sales Manager
Gary Anderson, Director of Operations
Steven Gruba, Office Manager
Pierce Sinclair, Roofing Consultant

Provider of coatings for commercial properties
including material safety data sheets, data sheets,
color chart, and test data.

**Metal Fusion Inc** HQ
425 Hurlingame Ave
Redwood City CA 94063-3407
P: 650-368-7692   F: 650-368-7691   PRC:80
www.metalfusioninc.com
Email: info@metalfusioninc.com
Estab: 1985

Michael Olivio, Management Consultant

Provider of thermal spray technology services.
The company's portfolio includes shaft repair, roll
repair, and mechanical seal.

**Metalfx Inc** HQ
200 N Lenore Ave
Willits CA 95490
P: 800-479-9451   F: 707-459-2046   PRC:82
www.metalfx.com
Email: info@metalfx.com
Emp: 1-10   Estab: 1976

Carol Bartow, Manager
Jill Porterfield, Controller

Provider of sheet metal fabrication services
for metal and wood products. The company is
engaged in engineering and quality assurance
services.

**Metaswitch Networks** DH
399 Main St
Los Altos CA 94022
P: 415-513-1500   F: 415-513-1501   PRC:64
www.metaswitch.com

Alastair Mitchell, EVP of Engineering
Martin Young, Commissioning Engineer
Alex Obradovic, Trials Engineer
Joseph Finnigan, Support Engineer
Martin Lund, CEO

Provider of service management solutions. The
company offers original equipment manufacturer, multimedia subsystem, and hosted business
services.

**Methode Electronics** BR
2025 Gateway Pl Ste 235
San Jose CA 95110
P: 408-453-9500   F: 408-943-6655   PRC:295
www.methode.com
Email: info@methode.com

Mehrdad Abtahi, Electronics HW Manager
Michael Hayward, VP
Timothy Glandon, VP of North American Automo-
tive Operations
Duane Campbell, Business Development Man-
ager

Manufacturer of power management electronic
products. The company is engaged in design,
engineering, and technical support services.

**Metis Technology Solutions Inc** HQ
333 Cobalt Way Ste 105
Sunnyvale CA 94085
P: 650-967-3051   PRC:326
www.metis-tech.com
Emp: 11-50 Estab: 2010

Laura Plice, Systems Engineer
Joy Colucci, President
Hadi Mahdavi, CEO
Charlie Beutter, Production Manager
Sara Hunter, Office Manager

Provider of technical services. The company
engages in engineering, IT, aviation, space, and
earth sciences fields.

**MetricStream Inc** HQ
2479 E Bayshore Rd
Palo Alto CA 94303
P: 650-620-2955   F: 650-565-8542   PRC:323
www.metricstream.com
Estab: 1999

Anindo Banerjea, SVP of Engineering
Gunjan Sinha, Executive Chairman
Jessica Zhou, Chief Legal Officer
Mike Strambi, CFO
Gaurav Kapoor, COO

Provider of enterprise risk, compliance, and internal audit management solutions. The company
offers training services.

**Mettler-Toledo Rainin LLC**    BR
  7500 Edgewater Dr
  Oakland CA 94621
P: 800-472-4646  F: 510-564-1617    PRC:20
www.mt.com
Email: cs@rainin.com
Estab: 1963

Henri Chahine, COO
Mark Richards, Head of Human Resources
Brett Demshar, Manager
Cynthia Saetre, Executive Assistant

Provider of laboratory weighing and process
analytics services. The company also focuses on
industrial weighing.

**Meyer Sound Laboratories Inc**    HQ
  2832 San Pablo Ave
  Berkeley CA 94702
P: 510-486-1166  F: 510-486-8356    PRC:31
www.meyersound.com
Email: sales@meyersound.com
Estab: 1979

Cliff Eldridge, CFO
Brad Friedman, VP
Kim Sandholdt, Director of Service Operations
Patricia Chu, Senior Buyer

Manufacturer of loud speakers, sub woofers, stage
monitors, and amplifiers. The company serves the
entertainment sector.

**Mg Technologies Inc**    HQ
  11680 Regnart Canyon Dr
  Cupertino CA 95014-4830
P: 408-255-8191    PRC:323
www.mgtech.com
Email: info@mgtech.com

Mario Guzman, President

Provider of software services. The company
offers conversion, training, installation, and tuning
services.

**Mge Engineering Inc**    HQ
  7415 Greenhaven Dr Ste 100
  Sacramento CA 95831
P: 916-421-1000  F: 916-421-1002    PRC:304
www.mgeeng.com
Emp: 11-50 Estab: 1990

Wesley Sennett, Project
Peter Zhao, Engineer
Robert Sennett, Principal
Kang Chen, Principal
Darrel Huckabay, Senior Project Manager

Provider of civil/structural engineering and
construction management services. The company
focuses on site development and construction
inspection.

**MiaSole Hi-Tech Corp**    HQ
  2590 Walsh Ave
  Santa Clara CA 95051
P: 404-843-1815    PRC:135
www.miasole.com
Email: info@miasole.com
Estab: 2004

Atiye Bayman, CTO
Suzy Berlant, Benefits Analyst
Yana Qian, Senior Research Scientist

Manufacturer of copper indium gallium selenide
thin-film photovoltaic solar panels. The company
offers solar power plants for industrial needs.

**Michael Patrick Partners**    HQ
  530 Howard St Ste 350
  San Francisco CA 94105
P: 650-327-3185    PRC:326
www.michaelpatrickpartners.com
Estab: 1979

Dan O'Brien, President
Duane Maidens, CSO
Robert Maidens, Creative Director

Provider of branding solutions. The company also
offers logo design, portfolio creation, web content,
and marketing services.

**Micro Dicing Services**    HQ
  780 Montague Expy Ste 303
  San Jose CA 95131
P: 408-321-8840  F: 408-321-8843    PRC:173
www.microdicingtechnology.com
Email: info@microdicingtechnology.com

Peter Chiang, CEO
Janet Huang, International Sales - Asia Pacific

Provider of sawing services. The company provides services to the microelectronic and optical
industries.

**Micro Lambda Wireless Inc**    HQ
  46515 Landing Pkwy
  Fremont CA 94538
P: 510-770-9221  F: 510-770-9213    PRC:15
www.microlambdawireless.com
Email: sales@microlambdawireless.com
Estab: 1990

David Suddarth, VP of Engineering
John Nguyen, CEO
Susan Sun, VP of Finance
Myra Verret, Marketing Administrator

Supplier of remote drivers, multipliers, bench test
filters, oscillators, synthesizers, and harmonic
generators.

**Micro Lithography Inc**    HQ
  1257 Elko Dr
  Sunnyvale CA 94089
P: 408-747-1769  F: 408-747-1978    PRC:34
www.mliusa.com
Estab: 1981

Kevin Duong, Customer Service Manager
Qoang Bih, Manager
David Wang, System Administrator

Manufacturer of pellicles using high end equipment for the production of frames and engineering
parts, automatic anodizing lines, and chemical
labs.

**Micro Machine Shop**    HQ
  743B Wakefield Ct
  Oakdale CA 95361
P: 209-848-8760  F: 209-848-8762    PRC:80
www.machining.us.com
Emp: 1-10  Estab: 1984

Diane Resz, VP of Sales & Finance
John Young, Operator

Manufacturer of micro machines for telecommunications, microwave, semiconductor equipment,
valve, laser, medical, and other industries.

**Micro Precision Calibration Inc**    HQ
  22835 Industrial Pl
  Grass Valley CA 95949
P: 530-268-1860  F: 530-268-1203    PRC:306
www.microprecision.com
Email: gv-contact@microprecision.com
Emp: 1-10  Estab: 1969

Jarrod Trammell, President
Enrique Hernandez, Quality Director
Danette Szymanski, Sales Manager
Steve Joos, MPC Global Director of Sales
Jeff Smith, Account Manager

Provider of electrical and mechanical calibration
services. The company also offers optical and
temperature calibration services.

**Micro Tech Systems**    HQ
  2037 W Bullard Ave Ste 101
  Fresno CA 93711
P: 559-438-7580  F: 559-438-7585    PRC:104
microtechsys.com
Email: sales@microtech.com
Emp: 1-10  Estab: 1980

Tino Sancetta, Manufacturing Manager
Joe Khoe, Principal

Provider of cabling solutions. The company involves in the installation and repair of voice, data,
and video network systems.

**Micro-Mechanics Inc**    DH
  465 Woodview Ave
  Morgan Hill CA 95037
P: 408-779-2927  F: 408-779-9189    PRC:157
www.micro-mechanics.com
Email: mmusa@micro-mechanics.com
Estab: 1983

Michael Maguire, Engineering Manager
Chris Borch, CEO
Thom Wojno, Human Resource Manager
Hau Nguyen, Quality Assurance Inspector
Andrew Eden, Director of Business Development

Manufacturer of precision tools, assemblies, and
consumable parts used to manufacture and test
semiconductors. The company offers mold pots
and trims.

**Micro-Vu**    HQ
  7909 Conde Ln
  Windsor CA 95492
P: 707-838-6272  F: 707-838-3985    PRC:13
www.microvu.com
Email: sales@microvu.com
Estab: 1959

Mervin Buenaflor, Software Engineer
Jordan Trout, Electrical Engineer
Ian Davison, Mechanical Engineer

Designer and manufacturer of measuring machines, including automated and manual video
systems, and optical comparators.

**MicroCamco**    HQ
  2597 Kerner Blvd
  San Rafael CA 94901
P: 415-729-9391    PRC:189
microcam.co

Larry Gerrans, Co-Founder

Provider of medical devices. The company focusses on commercializing the plug and play micro
imaging system.

**Microchek Inc**     HQ
922 Industrial Way Unit K
Lodi CA 95240
P: 209-333-5253   F: 209-339-1375     PRC:166
microchek.com
Email: sales@microchek.com
Emp: 11-50 Estab: 1988

Susan Sinclair, CEO
Kenneth McDole, CEO
Yoshiko McDole, Secretary

Manufacturer of check valves and self-activating
safety valves. The company's products include a
diverse variety of valves.

**Microchip Technology Inc**     BR
450 Holger Way
San Jose CA 95134
P: 408-961-6400      PRC:212
www.kleer.com

Milan Rai, Principal Electrical Design Engineer
Surjit Ghanta, Principal Engineer
Arpita Nigam, System Engineer
Roy Sasaki, Principal FAE

Provider of microcontroller and analog semiconductors. The company focuses on products such
as amplifiers, data converters, and embedded
controllers.

**Microcube**     HQ
47853 Warm Springs Blvd
Fremont CA 94539
P: 510-651-5000      PRC:189
www.microcube.org
Email: support@microcube.org

Mark Smith, Mechanical Engineer
Dinesh Mody, President
Grason Ott, Designer
Amrish Walke, Medical Device Innovator

Provider of concept development, design, rapid
prototyping and IP management, market mapping,
clinical trials, and regulatory submissions.

**Microdental Inc**     HQ
5601 Arnold Rd
Dublin CA 94568
P: 925-829-3611   F: 925-828-0153     PRC:185
www.microdental.com
Email: info@microdental.com
Estab: 1964

Dayna Montalvo, Human Resource Manager
Dazia Bosworth, Director of Service Operations
Karsten Klimmek, Director of Operations
Leonard Telesca, Dental Services Manager
Neil Rosa, Account Manager

Provider of laboratory-fabricated restorations
and related equipment. The company serves the
healthcare sector.

**Microelec Technical**     HQ
4633 Old Ironsides Dr Ste 110
Santa Clara CA 95054
P: 408-282-3508   F: 408-300-5780     PRC:126
www.microelecs.com
Email: sales@microelecs.com
Estab: 2006

K.Y Hwang, Engineering
Zafir Ahmad, Applications Engineer
Kevin Turner, Customer Analyst

Manufacturer of semiconductor, micro-electronics,
and mixed signal devices. The company specializes in switches, bridge rectifiers, and transistors.

**Microform Precision LLC**     HQ
4244 S Market Ct Ste A
Sacramento CA 95834
P: 916-419-0580   F: 916-419-0577     PRC:82
www.mform.com
Email: info@mform.com
Emp: 1-10   Estab: 1981

Bryan Wallace, Buyer
Manuel Buggs, Materials Handler

Provider of metal cutting, bending, fabrication, and
coating services. The company offers shearing,
punching, forming, and painting services.

**MicroMed Laboratories**     HQ
1129 N McDowell Blvd
Petaluma CA 94954
P: 707-782-0792      PRC:306
www.micromedlabs.com
Email: info@micromedlabs.com
Estab: 1999

Ann Hargens, Microscopy Engineer
Kerri Sturtevant, Client Account Manager

Provider of regulatory consulting, microbial identification, environmental monitoring, and steriliza-
tion validation services.

**Micromega Systems Inc**     HQ
2 Fifer Ave Ste 120
Corte Madera CA 94925
P: 415-924-4700   F: 415-945-3301     PRC:324
www.micromegasystems.com
Email: info@micromegasystems.com
Estab: 1979

Charles Bornheim, President

Provider of database systems and e-business
website design services. The company also focuses on training and installation.

**Micron Technology Inc**     BR
Tasman Technology Park 590 Alder Dr
Milpitas CA 95035
P: 408-855-4000   F: 408-855-4030     PRC:86
www.micron.com

Brian Shirley, SVP of DRAM & Emerging Memory
Engineering
Jeff VerHeul, SVP of Nonvolatile Engineering
Sanjay Mehrotra, President
Sumit Sadana, EVP
David Zinsner, SVP

Designer and manufacturer of semiconductor
systems for computing, networking, and communications applications.

**Micropoint Bioscience Inc**     HQ
3521 Leonard Ct
Santa Clara CA 95054
P: 408-588-1682   F: 408-588-1620     PRC:186
www.micropointbio.com
Email: info@micropointbio.com
Estab: 2006

Nan Zhang, CEO
William Sumida, Manufacturing Supervisor
Wilson Zhang, Research Associate

Developer of medical products and services for
treatment of vascular disease such as peripheral
artery disease and venous blood clots disorders.

**Microsemi**     DH
3000 Oakmead Village Dr Ste 100
Santa Clara CA 95051
P: 408-986-8031   F: 408-986-8120     PRC:212
www.microsemi.com
Estab: 1960

Tom Moore, Director of IP
Andrew Chang, Hardware Engineer
Jin Lee, Validation Engineer
Tom Parkinson, Staff Design Engineer
Mark Isham, Facilities Supervisor

Supplier of discrete military and aerospace
components. The company's applications include
embedded systems and power solutions.

**Microsonic Systems Inc**     HQ
76 Bonaventura Dr
San Jose CA 95134
P: 408-844-4980   F: 866-404-4898     PRC:31
www.microsonics.com
Email: jean.shieh@microsonics.com
Estab: 2004

Vibhu Vivek, President

Provider of ultrasonic fluid processing device built
with MEMS technology to biotech and pharmaceutical industries.

**Microvi Biotech Inc**     HQ
26229 Eden Landing Rd
Hayward CA 94545
P: 510-344-0668      PRC:24
www.microvi.com
Email: info@microvi.com

Fatemeh Shirazi, CEO
Karin Kidder, VP of Marketing
Norman Balme, SVP of IP & Legal
Ajay Nair, Global Director of Commercial & Techni-
cal Strategy
Ali Dorri, Director of Business Development

Designer and developer of biotechnology solutions. The company commercializes biocatalytic
solutions in the water, energy and chemical
industries.

**Microwave Technology Inc**     HQ
4268 Solar Way
Fremont CA 94538
P: 510-651-6700   F: 510-952-4000     PRC:70
www.mwtinc.com
Email: info@mwtinc.com
Estab: 1982

Greg Zhou, President
Hanh Nguyen, Quality Team
Don Apte, Director of Sales and Marketing
Alex Skuratov, Sales Manager
Tahrah Hunt, Inside Sales

Manufacturer of RF and microwave discrete
semiconductor products, GaAs and GaN RF
power amplifiers, low noise pHEMT devices, and
wireless amplifiers.

**MicuRx Pharmaceuticals Inc**    HQ
950 Tower Ln Ste 390
Foster City CA 94404
P: 510-782-2022    PRC:249
www.micurx.com
Email: info@micurx.com
Estab: 2007

Zhengyu Yuan, CEO
Mikhail Gordeev, EVP

Provider of pharmaceuticals. The company develops antibiotics to combat drug-resistant bacterial infections.

**Mid Labs Inc**    HQ
557 McCormick St
San Leandro CA 94577
P: 510-357-3952    F: 510-357-1582    PRC:186
www.midlabs.com
Email: info@midlabs.com
Estab: 1981

Michelle Francis, Human Resource Generalist
Sheila Mayo, Purchasing Agent
Angela Kent, Global Buyer

Manufacturer of ophthalmic products such as vitreous cutters, titanium forceps, and related accessories.

**Mikpower Technologies Inc**    HQ
800 Charcot Ave Ste 112
San Jose CA 95131
P: 408-493-5903    F: 408-680-0060    PRC:86
www.mikpowerinc.com
Email: info@mikpowerinc.com

Thomas Chao, President

Provider of lighting solutions. The company offers IC products for light bulbs, light tubes, and square lights.

**Mil-Ram Technology Inc**    HQ
48009 Fremont Blvd
Fremont CA 94538
P: 510-656-2001    F: 510-656-2004    PRC:87
www.mil-ram.com
Email: sls@mil-ram.com
Estab: 1990

Cecile Snow, Accounts Payable Manager

Manufacturer of industrial gas and detection systems. The company serves the oil and gas, pulp and paper, and chemical industries.

**Milagen Inc**    HQ
1255 Park Ave Ste B
Emeryville CA 94608-3679
P: 510-597-1244    PRC:43
www.milagen.com
Email: info@milagen.com
Estab: 1997

Moncef Jendoubi, Founder
Alfredo Quattrone, VP of Regulatory Affairs
Heinz Bodenmueller, VP of Business Development and Strategy
Rosaura Valle, VP of Operations & Strategic Alliances
Christine Chavany, Director of Immunoassay Development

Develops and manufactures healthcare products. The company offers immunohistochemistry and cytology products.

M-192

**Milestone Internet Marketing Inc**    HQ
3001 Oakmead Village Dr
Santa Clara CA 95051
P: 408-492-9055    F: 408-492-9053    PRC:325
www.milestoneinternet.com
Email: sales@milestoneinternet.com
Estab: 1998

Benu Aggarwal, Founder
Anil Aggarwal, CEO
Lauren Adams, Product Marketing Specialist
Mike Supple, Director of Products & Social Media
Zulema Romero, Director of Client Services

Provider of hotel internet marketing and website development services. The company focuses on website & social media marketing and ROI tracking.

**Millennia Music & Media Systems**    HQ
6411 Capitol Ave
Diamond Springs CA 95619
P: 530-647-0750    F: 530-647-9921    PRC:209
www.mil-media.com
Email: sales@mil-media.com
Emp: 1-10    Estab: 1989

John La Grou, Founder

Provider of music and media systems. The company also provides specialized tools for archival transfers and related applications.

**Millennium Consulting Associates**    HQ
401 Roland Way Ste 250
Oakland CA 94621
P: 925-808-6700    PRC:140
mecaenviro.com
Estab: 1986

Mike Noel, President

Provider of environmental and industrial hygiene services. The company offers environmental engineering, consulting, and compliance services.

**Millennium Lapping & Grind Engineering**    HQ
3760 Yale Way Unit 3 & Unit 2
Fremont CA 94538
P: 510-438-9908    F: 510-438-9918    PRC:80
www.millenniumlapping.com
Email: millenniumlap@comcast.net

Dave Naicker, President
Joseph Naicker, Manager

Provider of lapping and grinding for CNC machining. The company specializes in single and double side lapping diamond polishing of copper and silver.

**Milner's Anodizing**    HQ
3330 McMaude Pl
Santa Rosa CA 95407
P: 707-584-1188    F: 707-584-1180    PRC:79
www.milnersanodizing.com
Email: info@milnersanodizing.com
Estab: 1983

Mike Marian, QC Assistant
Vanessa Valentine, Manager

Provider of metal finishing solutions. The company's services include anodizing, anodizing, and passivation.

**Miltenyi Biotec Inc**    DH
2303 Lindbergh St
Auburn CA 95602
P: 530-888-8871    F: 530-888-8925    PRC:43
www.miltenyibiotec.com
Email: macs@miltenyibiotec.com
Emp: 11-50    Estab: 1990

Ira Marks, VP
Rebecca McHugh, Customer Training Manager
Noah Keefer, Service Specialist

Developer, manufacturer, and seller of products serving the fields of cell biology, immunology, regenerative medicine, and molecular biology.

**MiNDERA Corp**    HQ
329 Oyster Point Blvd 3rd Fl
S San Francisco CA 94080
P: 650-491-9643    PRC:191
www.minderadx.com
Email: info@minderadx.com
Estab: 2013

Tobin Dickerson, President
Tahir Mahmood, Secretary and Co-Founder

Provider of technology to extract skin biomarkers enabling non-invasive molecular testing for skin cancer and other skin diseases.

**Mindflash**    HQ
2825 El Camino Real Ste 200
Palo Alto CA 94306
P: 805-963-8417    F: 805-963-4020    PRC:319
www.mindflash.com
Emp: 11-50    Estab: 1999

Donna Wells, President
Jason MacMurray, VP of Sales & Operations
Grant King, VP

Provider of online training and related solutions. The company offers services to the software industry.

**Minerva Surgical Inc**    HQ
101 Saginaw Dr
Redwood City CA 94063
P: 855-646-7874    F: 866-465-2875    PRC:186
www.minervasurgical.com
Email: info@minervasurgical.com
Estab: 2008

Akos Toth, Principal Engineer
Ben Paulsen, Senior Manufacturing Engineer
Qiuyuan Liu, President
David Ferrito, VP of Sales & Customer Service

Manufacturer of medical devices. The company provides products for the treatment of abnormal uterine bleeding.

**Minimatics**    HQ
3445 De La Cruz Blvd
Santa Clara CA 95054-2110
P: 650-969-5630    F: 408-496-0111    PRC:74
www.minimatics.com
Email: sales@minimatics.com
Estab: 1961

Mark Lentz, General Manager
Larry Hutnick, Information Technology Manager

Provider of precision machining solutions. The company offers CNC milling, manual turning, lapping, and honing services.

**Minitool Inc**                    HQ
1610 Dell Ave Ste H
Campbell CA 95008
P: 408-395-1585   F: 408-395-1605      PRC:80
www.minitoolinc.com
Email: info@minitoolinc.com

Renate Schaller, Advertising Manager

Manufacturer of precision instruments and small
tools for microscopic investigation. The company
also specializes in under-microscope precision
tools.

**Minto Research & Development Inc**     HQ
20270 Charlanne Dr
Redding CA 96002
P: 530-222-2373   F: 530-222-0679      PRC:189
www.sagersplints.com
Email: mintord@aol.com
Emp: 1-10   Estab: 1979

Anne Borschneck, President

Supplier of emergency fracture response systems.

**MIODx Inc**                       HQ
5941 Optical Ct
San Jose CA 95138
P: 866-756-4639                        PRC:186
www.miodx.com
Estab: 2014

Sean Givens, Co-Founder
Graeme McLean, CEO
Nhi Nguyen, Scientist

Provider of diagnostics and biomarker expertise in
a variety of cancer treatments including immu-
no-therapies.

**Mirabilis Design Inc**               HQ
1159 Sonora Ct Ste 116
Sunnyvale CA 94086
P: 408-844-3234   F: 408-519-6719      PRC:323
www.mirabilisdesign.com
Email: info@mirabilisdesign.com
Estab: 2003

Deepak Shankar, Founder
Vaishnavi Shankar, CEO
Darryl Koivisto, CTO
S. Pradeep, Director of Sales

Provider of systems engineering solutions for
performance analysis and architecture exploration
of electronics and real-time software.

**Miramar Labs Inc**                  HQ
2790 Walsh Ave
Santa Clara CA 95051
P: 408-579-8700   F: 408-579-8795      PRC:186
www.miradry.com
Email: info@miramarlabs.com
Estab: 2006

Michael Vo, Senior Manufacturing Technician
Jason Rojas, Senior Manufacturing Technician
Melinda Kolar, Director of Customer Service
Shannon Holt, Business Manager
Suryakant Devangan, Senior Tech Lead

Provider of solutions for excessive sweat. The
company is engaged in clinical trials and research
programs.

**Mirantis Inc**                      HQ
900 E Hamilton Ave Ste 650
Campbell CA 95008
P: 650-963-9828   F: 650-968-2997      PRC:325
www.mirantis.com
Email: info@mirantis.com
Estab: 1999

Sergey Lukjanov, Director of Engineering
Ruslan Khanbikov, Senior Director of Engineering
Brian Donaldson, Senior Manager of Development
Engineering
Alex Freedland, Co-Founder
Adrian Ionel, Co-Founder

Specializes in the development and support of
Kubernetes and OpenStack.

**Mirion Technologies Inc**            DH
3000 Executive Pkwy Ste 222
San Ramon CA 94583
P: 925-543-0800                        PRC:189
www.mirion.com
Email: privacy@mirion.com
Estab: 2006

Scott Weires, System Engineer
Jani Rakkola, Manufacturing Engineer
Iain Wilson, President of Sensing Systems
Division
James Cocks, President of Detection & Measure-
ment Division
Loic Eloy, President of Radiation Monitoring
Systems Division

Provider of solutions in radiation detection. The
company serves the healthcare, nuclear power,
and other industries.

**Mission Bio**                       HQ
6000 Shoreline Ct Ste 104
S San Francisco CA 94080
P: 415-854-0058   F: 650-763-4483      PRC:186
missionbio.com
Email: info@missionbio.com
Estab: 2014

Adam Sciambi, Co-Founder
Charlie Silver, Co-Founder
Dennis Eastburn, Co-Founder
William Oldham, Director of Manufacturing
Pat Brooks, SVP of Sales & Sales Operations

Developer and deliverer of precision medicine.
The company offers instruments, fixed panels,
custom panels, and software for the researchers
and clinicians.

**Mission Peak Optics Inc**            HQ
46941 Rancho Higuera Rd
Fremont CA 94539
P: 510-438-0384   F: 510-438-9795      PRC:212
www.missionpeakoptics.com
Email: support@missionpeakoptics.com

Kent Lin, Operations Officer

Provider of measurement solutions for semiconductor industry. The company offers thin film
thickness measurement system.

**Mission Tool And Mfg Co Inc**        HQ
3440 Arden Rd
Hayward CA 94545
P: 510-782-8383   F: 510-785-0687      PRC:74
Estab: 1968

Carol Smith, VP
John Jackson, Director of Operations

Manufacturer of precision stamped and machined
components. The company serves aerospace,
automotive, medical, telecom, defense, and commercial sectors.

**Mistral Solutions Inc**             HQ
43092 Christy St
Fremont CA 94538
P: 408-705-2240   F: 408-987-9665      PRC:323
www.mistralsolutions.com
Email: usa@mistralsolutions.com
Estab: 1997

Ramanan V., VP of Engineering
Selvaraj Kaliyappan, VP of Engineering
Anees Ahmed, President
Mujahid Alam, CEO
Rajeev Ramachandra, Vice Chairman

Provider of technology design and systems
engineering solutions. The company's solutions
include hardware board design and embedded
software development.

**Mitsui High-tec Inc**               BR
2001 Gateway Pl E Tower Ste 325
San Jose CA 95110
P: 408-980-0782   F: 408-727-8160      PRC:80
www.mitsuihightec.com

Kensuke Gondai, Finance Manager
Emerson Erazo, Senior Sales Manager of New
Business Development

Provider of grinder parts, precision tools, and
stamping products. The company is involved in
design, installation, and delivery services.

**Mixbook**                           HQ
726 Main St
Redwood City CA 94063
P: 855-649-2665                        PRC:326
www.mixbook.com
Email: hello@mixbook.com
Estab: 2006

Andrew Laffoon, CEO
Tucker Taylor, Chief Marketing and Growth Officer
Brianna Yarber, Marketing Manager
Raffi Apelian, Community & Content Marketing
Manager
Allison Kreft, Art Director

Provider of customizable photo books, cards and
calendars, as well as creation of online scrap-
books on the web using design software.

**Mixed Signal Integration**          HQ
2157-50 O'Toole Ave
San Jose CA 95131
P: 408-434-6305   F: 408-434-6417      PRC:59
mix-sig.com
Email: info@mix-sig.com
Estab: 1997

Levent Ozcolak, President
Jeff Thompson, Director of Marketing & Sales

Specializes in the design, manufacture and sale
of turn-key analog and mixed-signal standard
products and custom ASICs.

**Mixel Inc** HQ
97 E Brokaw Rd Ste 250
San Jose CA 95112
P: 408-436-8500  F: 408-436-8400  PRC:204
www.mixel.com
Email: info@mixel.com
Estab: 1998

Jintao Zang, Mixed Signal Design Engineer
Scott Donnelly, Director of Process Development
Mandy Xu, Mixed-Signal IC Designer

Designer and developer of mixed-signal internet
protocol cores for the semiconductor and electronics industries.

**Mixonic** HQ
3749 Buchanan St Unit 487
San Francisco CA 94147
P: 866-838-5067  PRC:95
www.mixonic.com
Email: customercare@mixonic.com
Estab: 2001

Bob Jacobson, President
Daniel Weideman, Production Lead
Greg Rivera, Sales Associate
Shimeel Sajid, Systems Analyst
Marianne Jacobson, Product Concierge

Provider of design services. The company offers
custom CD and DVD duplication, disc packaging,
CD production, and printing services.

**Mizuho OSI** HQ
30031 Ahern Ave
Union City CA 94587-1234
P: 510-429-1500  F: 510-429-8500  PRC:189
www.mizuhosi.com
Email: custserv@mizuhosi.com
Estab: 1978

John Harris, New Product Introduction Engineering Manager
Donald Parker, Manufacturing Engineering Manager
Steve Lamb, President
Patrick Rimroth, General Manager
Yosup Kim, VP of Finance

Designs and manufactures medical components.
The company offers surgery tables, patient care
kits, trauma tables, and more.

**MJB Precision Machining Inc** HQ
715 E Mcglincy Ln
Campbell CA 95008
P: 408-559-3035  F: 408-559-3037  PRC:80
mjbprecisionmachining.com
Email: mjbprec@aol.com

Mark Bamberg, President
Robert Roe, Sales Manager

Manufacturer of precision and prototype machining parts and components for the defense,
telecom, medical, and semiconductor manufacturing industries.

**MLD Technologies LLC** HQ
2672 Bayshore Pkwy Ste 701
Mountain View CA 94043
P: 650-938-3780  F: 650-938-3113  PRC:173
www.mldtech.com
Email: info@mldtech.com
Estab: 1997

Linda Lingg, Senior Engineer
Gary DeBell, Co-Founder
Len Mott, Co-Founder
Tony Louderback, Co-Founder

Supplier of optical coatings and components. The
company specializes in the design, development,
and manufacture of ion beam sputtered thin-films.

**MMC AD Systems** HQ
PO Box 12287
Pleasanton CA 94588
P: 925-485-4949  PRC:325
www.mmcad.com
Estab: 1975

Judy Louie, Senior Project Manager
Bill Sumerlin, Senior Consultant

Provider of architectural and consulting services.
The company focuses on strategic planning, market research, and business and web development.

**MMR Technologies Inc** HQ
41 Daggett Dr
San Jose CA 94043-1346
P: 650-962-9620  F: 650-962-9647  PRC:154
www.mmr-tech.com
Email: sales@mmr-tech.com
Estab: 1980

Ted Sanchez, Engineer
William Little, CEO
Jessica Jordan, Accounting Administrator

Provider of micro-miniature refrigerator technology. The company offers hall measurement, optical
study systems, and temperature control services.

**mobiDEOS Inc** HQ
20 S Santa Cruz Ave Ste 300
Los Gatos CA 95030
P: 408-716-8347  PRC:322
www.mobideos.com
Email: info@mobideos.com
Estab: 2005

Palasamudram L., CEO
Ted Barron, Advisor
Stephen Cercone, Advisor
Naresh Shanker, Advisor

Manufacturer of video surveillance equipment. The
company offers services to government entities
and businesses.

**Mobileframe LLC** HQ
101 Blossom Hill Rd
Los Gatos CA 95032
P: 408-885-1200  F: 408-280-0555  PRC:320
www.mobileframe.com
Email: sales@mobileframe.com

Joseph Kliger, VP of Engineering
Lonny Oswalt, CEO
Glenn Wickman, CTO
Patricia Oswalt, EVP of Sales & Marketing
Bruce Redke, Business Development Manager

Provider of enterprise mobility solutions that
include mobile application development, device
management, GPS tracking, and integration
features.

**Mobileiron Inc** HQ
401 E Middlefield Rd
Mountain View CA 94043
P: 650-919-8100  F: 650-919-8006  PRC:322
www.mobileiron.com
Email: info@mobileiron.com
Estab: 2007
Sales: $100M to $300M

Suresh Batchu, Co-Founder
Ajay Mishra, Co-Founder
Simon Biddiscombe, President
Scott Hill, CFO
Jared Lucas, Chief People Officer

Provider of mobile security, device, and application management solutions. The company focuses
on technical support services.

**Mobitor Corp** HQ
1990 N California Blvd Ste 230
Walnut Creek CA 94596
P: 925-464-7700  PRC:319
Estab: 2001

Luke Hartsuyker, SQL Server Database Engineer
Ahrhan Kim, Product Manager

Provider of mobility software, connectivity, and
information solutions. The company serves the
aerospace, aviation, and manufacturing industries.

**Mobitv Inc** HQ
1900 Powell St 9th Fl
Emeryville CA 94608
P: 510-450-5000  F: 510-450-5001  PRC:68
www.mobitv.com
Estab: 1999

Ankur Sharma, VP of Engineering
Nitu Jain, Engineering Manager
Charlie Nooney, CEO
Bill Routt, COO
Casey Fann, Operations Program Manager

Provider of content delivery platforms. The
company's products find application in mobile and
broadband networks.

**Mobiveil Inc** HQ
890 Hillview Ct Ste 250
Milpitas CA 95035
P: 408-212-9512  F: 408-457-0406  PRC:323
www.mobiveil.com
Email: info@mobiveil.com
Estab: 2012

Amit Saxena, VP of Engineering
Ravi Thummarukudy, CEO
Gopa Periyadan, COO

Provider of technology solutions. The company's
products include Silicon IP and COTS Modules
and offers IC design and embedded software
services.

**Modern Ceramics Manufacturing Inc** HQ
2240 Lundy Ave
San Jose CA 95131
P: 408-383-0554  F: 408-383-0578  PRC:80
www.modernceramics.com
Estab: 1998

Julio Lung, Manufacturing Engineer

Supplier of ceramic materials and components.
The company serves the semi-conductor and
laser industries.

**Modern Linear Inc**     HQ
75 Pelican Way Unit A
San Rafael CA 94901
P: 415-924-7938  F: 415-927-2360   PRC:80
www.modernlinear.com
Email: info@modernlinear.com
Estab: 2004

Steve Fulton, Founder

Manufacturer of guide roller products. The company mainly focuses on linear motion industry and serves commercial, packaging, and medical fields.

**Modern Machine Co**     HQ
1633 Old Bayshore Hwy
San Jose CA 95112
P: 408-436-7670  F: 408-436-7674   PRC:159
www.modernmachine.com
Email: info@modernmachine.com

Ed Bauer, Owner
Brett Sherril, General Manager
Shelli Mazzone, Office Manager

Provider of machining services. The company focuses on robotic welding, automatic screw machines, and CNC machining centers.

**Modern Systems Research Inc**     HQ
PO Box 62
Los Altos CA 94022
P: 650-940-2000   PRC:63
www.msr.com
Estab: 1960

Sam Wood, President

Provider of telecom design and voice & data networking services. The company also focuses on power systems and systems architecture.

**Modius Inc**     HQ
71 Stevenson St Ste 400
San Francisco CA 94105
P: 415-655-6700  F: 415-655-6601   PRC:323
www.modius.com
Email: info@modius.com
Estab: 2004

Scott Brown, VP of Engineering
Craig Compiano, CEO
Mark Carberry, VP of Sales
Sean Gately, VP of Business Development

Provider of performance management software. The company serves infrastructure monitoring applications.

**Modular Process Technology Corp**     HQ
2233 Paragon Dr
San Jose CA 95131-1337
P: 408-325-8640  F: 408-325-8649   PRC:126
www.modularpro.com
Email: info@modularpro.com

Steven Shatas, Technical Director

Manufacturer of semiconductor equipment for thermal processing systems and stand-alone ultraviolet ozone cleaning systems.

**Modules Technology Inc**     HQ
2526 Qume Dr Unit 28
San Jose CA 95131
P: 408-392-0808 ext. 111   PRC:124
www.modulestech.com
Email: syeh@modulestech.com
Estab: 1993

Henry Faun, President
Kevin To, International Sales Executive
Eve Duchene, Sales Administrator

Provider of custom module design solutions. The company's offerings include grinders, etching systems, and thermal recorders.

**Modulus Data Systems**     HQ
386 Main St Ste 200
Redwood City CA 94063
P: 650-365-3111  F: 650-365-6111   PRC:41
www.modulusdatasystems.com
Email: info@modulusdatasystems.com
Estab: 1972

Kenji Tanaka, General Manager
Steve Waites, Production Manager

Provider digital clinical cell (tally) counters. The company's products include Diffcount III, Comp-U-Diff, and Uro-Comp.

**Modutek Corp**     HQ
6387 San Ignacio Ave
San Jose CA 95119
P: 408-362-2000  F: 408-362-2001   PRC:86
www.modutek.com
Email: sales@modutek.com
Estab: 1980

Joanne Turley, Director of Finance
Robert Brody, Director of Operations

Manufacturer of wet process equipment and environmental systems. The company serves the semiconductor sector and offers repair services.

**Mojo Mobility Inc**     HQ
3350 Scott Blvd Bldg 37A
Santa Clara CA 95054
P: 650-446-0004   PRC:288
www.mojomobility.com
Email: sales@mojomobility.com
Estab: 2005

Pouyan Shams, Hardware Systems Engineer
Afshin Partovi, CEO

Provider of mobile recharge devices such as batteries and pads for computer peripherals and headsets for medical and commercial sectors.

**Molecular Devices LLC**     HQ
3860 N First St
San Jose CA 95134-1136
P: 800-635-5577  F: 408-747-3601   PRC:31
www.moleculardevices.com
Email: service.eu@moleculardevices.com
Estab: 1983

Yuriy Roll, Senior Electronics Engineer
Susan Murphy, President
Steven Qian, CFO
Laurent Claisse, VP
Poonam Taneja, VP

Manufacturer of bioanalytical measurement systems. The company is engaged in life science research, pharma, and bio therapeutic development.

**Molecular Matrix Inc**     HQ
3410 Industrial Blvd Ste 103
West Sacramento CA 95691
P: 916-376-9404   PRC:24
molecularmatrix.com
Email: info@molecularmatrix.com
Emp: 1-10  Estab: 2011

Charles Lee, Founder
Christopher Wink, CFO
Steven Whitlock, CCO

Provider of research tools for cultivating and studying stem cells. The company products provide solutions for growing cells.

**Moller International Inc**     HQ
1855 N First St Ste C
Dixon CA 95620
P: 530-756-5086   PRC:4
www.moller.com
Email: dr.moller@moller.com
Estab: 1983

Paul Moller, President

Designer and developer of personal vertical take-off and landing aircraft. The company specializes in rotapower engines.

**Momentum Design Lab**     HQ
4 W Fourth Ave Ste 206
San Mateo CA 94402
P: 650-452-6290   PRC:323
momentumdesignlab.com
Email: hello@momentumdesignlab.com
Estab: 2002

David Thomson, CEO
Lydia Chang, Senior Product UX & UI Designer

Designer of enterprise-grade software products. The company focuses on design, discovery, and development of software.

**Mondee Inc**     HQ
951 Mariners Island Blvd Ste 130
San Mateo CA 94404
P: 650-646-3320   PRC:323
www.mondee.com
Estab: 2011

Jagmit Soni, President of Sales
William Gomes, President of Specialty and Global Sales
Prasad Gundumogula, CEO
Yuvraj Datta, Chief Commercial Officer
Venkat Pasupuleti, CTO

Developer of technology for the generation of private fare distribution. The company offers services to the travel industry.

**Mondo Media Inc**     HQ
550 15th St Ste 31
San Francisco CA 94103
P: 415-865-2700  F: 415-865-2645   PRC:317
www.mondomedia.com
Email: customerservice@mondomedia.com
Estab: 1997

Damian Nelson, Web Engineer
John Evershed, CEO
Douglas Kay, CFO
Stevie Levine, Animation Production Manager
Kris Fragomeni, Finance Manager

Provider of gaming solutions. The company's store features men's and women's T-shirts, smart phone cases, and related supplies.

**Monk & Associates Inc** HQ
1136 Saranap Ave Ste Q
Walnut Creek CA 94595
P: 925-947-4867  F: 925-947-1165  PRC:142
www.monkassociates.com
Email: monkadmin@monkassociates.com
Estab: 2003

Chris Milliken, Office Manager

Provider of environmental consulting services.
The company specializes in biological constraints
analyses and mitigation plans.

**Monogram Biosciences Inc** HQ
345 Oyster Point Blvd
S San Francisco CA 94080
P: 650-635-1100  PRC:257
www.monogrambio.com
Email: pharmainfo@monogrambio.com
Estab: 1995

Christos Petropoulos, CSO
Yolanda Lie, Clinical Research Program Manager
Jackie Reeves, Director of Virology R&D
Weidong Huang, Senior Director of Clinical
research
Carmeliza Santos, Account Manager

Develops and commercializes diagnostic products.
The company offers products for the treatment
of human immunodeficiency virus and other viral
illnesses.

**Monolith Materials Inc** BR
662 Laurel St Ste 201
San Carlos CA 94070
P: 650-933-4957  PRC:51
monolithmaterials.com
Estab: 2012

Chris Mesrobian, Lead Mechanical Engineer
Rob Hanson, Co-Founder
Bill Brady, Executive Chairman
Chris Cornille, Chief Commercial & Supply Chain
Officer
Tim Rens, CFO

Manufacturer of carbon black and hydrogen
for plastics, toner and printer ink, batteries and
conductive inks, and tires and industrial rubber
products.

**Monolithic Power Systems Inc** HQ
79 Great Oaks Blvd
San Jose CA 95119
P: 408-826-0600  F: 408-826-0601  PRC:126
www.monolithicpower.com
Email: usinfo@monolithicpower.com
Estab: 1997
Sales: $300M to $1 Billion

Bo Zhou, Application Engineer
D.A. Chen, Engineer
Ying Xiao, Senior IC Design Engineer
Simon Chambers, Senior Sales Engineer
Michael Hsing, CEO

Provider of analog semiconductor products. The
company offers battery chargers, linear regulators & analog switches, voltage supervisors, and
amplifiers.

**Montague** HQ
1830 Stearman Ave
Hayward CA 94545
P: 510-785-8822  PRC:159
montaguecompany.com
Email: domsales@montaguecompany.com
Estab: 1857

Tom Whalen, President
Joe Deckelman, VP of Sales & Marketing

Provider of commercial cooking equipment. The
company's products include boilers, ovens, and
refrigerated bases.

**Montavista Software LLC** HQ
5201 Great America Pkwy Ste 432
Santa Clara CA 95054
P: 408-520-1591  PRC:319
www.mvista.com
Email: info@mvista.com
Estab: 1999

Ravi Gupta, Head of Engineering & Services
Armin Kuster, Lead Software Engineer
Hiroshi Someya, Director of APAC Sales
Mark Baker, Director of Sales
Vahe Sarrafian, Legal Counsel

Developer of embedded Linux system software,
development tools, and related software products.
The company's products include CGE and Dev-
Rocket.

**Monterey Bay Analytical Services** HQ
4 Justin Ct Ste D
Monterey CA 93940
P: 831-375-6227  PRC:41
www.mbasinc.com
Email: MWeidner@MBASinc.com
Estab: 1999

David Holland, Principal Founder
Mollie Wooden, Laboratory Supervisor
Daniel Cook, Chemist
Hayden Maccagno, Lead Chemist
Linda Brown, Customer Relations Specialist

Provider of laboratory testing services. The company services include sample collection, bacteria
testing, and inorganic chemistry.

**Monterey Computer Corp** HQ
501 Webster St
Monterey CA 93940
P: 831-646-1147  F: 831-646-1118  PRC:328
www.mccnet.com
Email: mcc@mccnet.com
Estab: 1979

Tary McConnell, CTO
Roy Weischadle, Chief IT Analyst

Provider of technology and integrated network
services. The company offers networking, wireless
internet, server hosting, and surveillance services.

**Moog Animatics** BR
2581 Leghorn St
Mountain View CA 94043
P: 650-960-4215  PRC:68
www.animatics.com
Email: animatics_sales@moog.com
Estab: 1987

Joe Ruf, Software Engineer
Keith Webster, Software Engineer
Ester Hufana, Production Control Manager
David Torrez, Shop Manager
Sean Brennan, Operations Manager

Provider of motion control devices. The company
offers actuators, cables, power supplies, and
peripherals.

**Moog Csa Engineering** HQ
2581 Leghorn St
Mountain View CA 94043-1613
P: 650-210-9000  F: 650-210-9001  PRC:146
www.csaengineering.com
Email: infocsa@moog.com
Estab: 1982

Conor Johnson, Principal Engineer
Jackson Smith, Mechanical Engineer
Rainer Growitz, Business Manager
Christian Smith, Site Manager
David Kienholz, Principal Consultant

Designer and manufacturer of high precision
systems. The company offers positioning systems,
actuators, absorbers, and test systems.

**Moogsoft Inc** HQ
1265 Battery St
San Francisco CA 94111
P: 415-738-2299  PRC:323
www.moogsoft.com
Email: salesinfo@moogsoft.com
Estab: 2011

Phil Tee, Co-Founder
Rob Harper, CSO
David Casper, CTO
Dan Grigsby, SVP of Product
Mike Silvey, EVP

Provider of collaborative situation management
software solutions for Web-scale information
technology (IT) operations.

**Moon Valley Circuits** HQ
12350 Maple Glen Rd
Glen Ellen CA 95442
P: 707-996-4157  PRC:316
www.moonvalleycircuits.com
Estab: 1976

Mike Miller, Owner

Manufacturer of control systems for wineries. The
company specializes in tank temperature, bar-
rel-room, and refrigeration control systems.

**Moonstone Interactive Inc** HQ
2010 Crow Canyon Pl Ste 100
San Ramon CA 94583-1344
P: 866-246-9091  PRC:323
www.msinteractive.com
Email: info@msinteractive.com
Estab: 1996

Jason Herz, President
Stephen Herz, President

Provider of website design services. The company
offers web design and development, content management, and market visibility services.

**Moore Twining Associates Inc** HQ
2527 Fresno St
Fresno CA 93721
P: 559-268-7021  F: 559-268-7126  PRC:139
mooretwining.com
Emp: 11-50 Estab: 1898

Ken Clark, Engineering Geologist
Harry Moore, Owner
Allen Bushey, Manager
Read Andersen, Geotechnical Division Manager
Julio Morales, Client Services Supervisor

Provider of geotechnical engineering, environmental, construction inspection, materials testing, analytical chemistry, and drilling services.

**MORE Health Inc** HQ
999 Baker Way Ste 500
San Mateo CA 94404
P: 888-908-6673 PRC:186
morehealth.com
Email: hello@morehealth.com
Estab: 2013

Bo Hu, Co-Founder
Hope Lewis, CEO
Jeffrey Lasker, Chief Physician Officer
Marc Shuman, Chief Medical Officer
Robert Warren, Chief Medical Consultant

Specializes in collaborative diagnosis. The company serves patients, hospitals, and the medical industry.

**Morgan Manufacturing Inc** HQ
PO Box 737
Petaluma CA 94953
P: 707-763-6848 F: 707-763-4507 PRC:81
www.morganmfg.com
Email: customerservice@morganmfg.com
Estab: 1952

Carl Palmgren, Manager

Manufacturer of autobody tools and tie-down equipment. The company caters to the flat bed trucking industry.

**Morgan Royce Industries Inc** HQ
49050 Milmont Dr
Fremont CA 94538
P: 510-440-8500 F: 510-440-0886 PRC:179
www.morganroyce.com
Email: mri@morganroyce.com
Estab: 1991

Carl Paxton, CEO
Emily Alvarez, QC Analyst

Developer and manufacturer of custom cables, wire harness, and PCB assemblies. The company offers project management and quality control services.

**Morgan Technical Ceramics** BR
13079 Earhart Ave
Auburn CA 95602
P: 530-823-3401 PRC:53
www.morgantechnicalceramics.com
Emp: 11-50 Estab: 2003

Zack Waddle, Engineering Manager

Manufacturer of cast and powder metal stainless steels. The company also focuses on other specialty alloys.

**Morley Manufacturing Inc** HQ
14262 Meadow Dr
Grass Valley CA 95945
P: 530-477-6527 F: 530-477-0194 PRC:135
www.morleytanks.com
Email: morleymfg@att.net
Emp: 1-10 Estab: 1984

Bob Pelton, President

Designer and manufacturer of drainback water storage tanks for residential and commercial purposes. The company offers installation services.

**Morrill Industries Inc** HQ
24754 E River Rd
Escalon CA 95320
P: 209-838-2550 F: 209-838-3544 PRC:153
www.morrillinc.com
Emp: 1-10

Michael Morrill, Corporate Manager

Manufacturer and supplier of irrigation equipment. The company also offers custom built rotating suction screens and industrial pipes.

**MOS Plastics Inc** HQ
2308 Zanker Rd
San Jose CA 95131
P: 408-944-9407 F: 408-944-9439 PRC:163
mosinc.com
Email: sales@mosinc.com
Estab: 1974

Ernest Harper, Production Control Manager
Deanna Musil, Program Manager
Judy Louie, Executive Assistant

Provider of precision injection-molding, contract manufacturing, and assembly services for medical and electronics OEMs.

**Mosaic Industries Inc** HQ
5437 Central Ave Ste 1
Newark CA 94560
P: 510-790-8222 PRC:91
www.mosaic-industries.com
Email: info@mosaic-industries.com
Estab: 1985

Elena Belkine, Production Manager
Kelcey Hein, Office Assistant

Developer and manufacturer of embedded computers for instruments and automation. The company serves sensor calibration and PID control needs.

**Motion Analysis Corp** HQ
6085 State Farm Dr Ste 100
Rohnert Park CA 94928
P: 707-579-6500 PRC:168
www.motionanalysis.com
Email: info@motionanalysis.com
Estab: 1982

Shel Fung, SVP of Engineering
Emily Schaefer, Customer Support Engineer
Paul Taggart, Software Engineer
Tom Whitaker, CEO
Bill Van Haaften, Production Manager

Provider of motion analyzers. The company specializes in engineering, animation, design, reality augmentation, and simulation services.

**Motion Control Engineering Inc** HQ
11380 White Rock Rd
Rancho Cordova CA 95742
P: 916-463-9200 F: 916-463-9201 PRC:150
www.mceinc.com
Email: info@mceinc.com
Emp: 11-50 Estab: 1983

Lawrence Vo, Director of Engineering
Richard Wagner, Technical Writer

Manufacturer of elevator control products. The company's products include elevator and escalator controls, complete elevators, and components and peripherals.

**Motiondsp Inc** HQ
700 Airport Blvd Ste 270
Burlingame CA 94010
P: 650-288-1164 PRC:322
www.motiondsp.com
Email: sales@motiondsp.com
Estab: 2005

Sean Varah, CEO

Provider of software products. The company serves the defense & intelligence, law enforcement, energy, and transportation markets.

**Motive Medical Intelligence** HQ
580 California St Ste 1420
San Francisco CA 94104
P: 415-362-4007 F: 415-392-4067 PRC:188
motivemi.com
Email: info@motivemi.com
Estab: 1996

Jeanne Cohen, Founder
Leslie Kilgo, CFO
Nicholas Rains, Chief Solutions Officer
Julie Scherer, Chief Data Scientist
Jay Tyler, Chief Sales Officer

Developer of medical intelligence solutions. The company also offers care plans for population health management.

**Motor Guard Corp** HQ
580 Carnegie St
Manteca CA 95337
P: 209-239-9191 F: 209-239-5114 PRC:148
www.motorguard.com
Email: info@motorguard.com
Emp: 1-10

David Barleen, President
Brian Jacobson, National Sales Manager
Tim Keating, VP
Sandy Allen, Director

Designer and developer of spray equipment and tools for collision repairs. The company offers services to the automotive sector.

**Mountain View Pharmaceuticals Inc** HQ
3475 Edison Way Ste S
Menlo Park CA 94025-1821
P: 650-365-5515 F: 650-365-5525 PRC:257
www.mvpharm.com
Email: busdev@mvpharm.com
Estab: 1995

Merry Sherman, CEO
John French, Business Manager

Provider of pharmaceutical development, protein biochemistry, immunology and polymer chemistry solutions for delivery of therapeutic proteins.

**Mountford Group Inc** HQ
1486 Davis Ave
Concord CA 94518
P: 925-686-6613 F: 925-686-0226 PRC:323
www.mountfordgroup.com
Email: info@mountfordgroup.com

Gwaltney Mountford, Technical Communicator

Provider of system development and web application services. The company also focuses on technical communication.

**Mountz Inc**     HQ
1080 N 11th St
San Jose CA 95112
P: 408-850-9978   F: 408-292-2733    PRC:159
www.mountztorque.com
Email: sales@mountztorque.com
Estab: 1965

Alex Gregorios, Systems Specialist

Manufacturer of torque analyzers, sensors, bits, sockets, and adapters. The company is engaged in installation and technical support services.

**Moximed Inc**     BR
26460 Corporate Ave Ste 100
Hayward CA 94545
P: 510-887-3300     PRC:189
www.moximed.com

Anton Clifford, CEO
Nancy Isaac, Regulatory Counsel and VP Quality
Keith Fong, VP of Marketing and Business Development
Christine Barcelos, VP of Corporate Operations
Luigi Bivi, Managing Director

Developer of joint preserving option for patients with knee osteoarthritis. The company serves the medical industry.

**Mozilla Corp**     HQ
331 E Evelyn Ave
Mountain View CA 94041
P: 650-903-0800   F: 650-903-0875    PRC:323
www.mozilla.org/en-GB
Estab: 1998

Matthew Wobensmith, Senior Quality Assurance Engineer
Jeff Gilbert, Senior Software Engineer
Chris Beard, CEO
Amy Keating, Chief Legal Officer
Katharina Borchert, Chief Open Innovation Officer

Designer and developer of web application tools and browsers. The company serves individuals and businesses.

**Mphasis Corp**     BR
226 Airport Pkwy
San Jose CA 95110
P: 408-327-1240     PRC:322
www.mphasis.com
Estab: 1998

Sundar Subramanian, President Global Delivery
Dinesh Venugopal, President Mphasis Direct and Digital
Elango R., President DXC &HP SBU
Nitin Rakesh, CEO
Davinder Singh Brar, Chairman

Provider of applications, infrastructure, and business process outsourcing services to the banking and healthcare sectors.

**MSC Software**     BR
4675 MacArthur Ct
Newport Beach CA 92660
P: 714-540-8900     PRC:316
www.mscsoftware.com
Email: info-msc@mscsoftware.com
Emp: 11-50 Estab: 1963

Dominic Gallello, President
Doug Neill, VP

Developer of simulation software for acoustics, thermal analysis, and other needs. The company also offers software implementation and systems design services.

**mscripts LLC**     HQ
445 Bush St Ste 200
San Francisco CA 94108
P: 888-672-7478     PRC:194
www.mscripts.com
Email: info@mscripts.com
Estab: 2007

Mahesh Srivastava, VP of Engineering
Steve Brickman, VP of Engineering
Mark Cullen, CEO
Peter Towle, COO
Brian Davis, VP of Sales

Specializes in clinical and manufacturer programs. The company offers services to patients and pharmacies.

**MTI California Inc**     HQ
2890 N Main St Ste 300
Walnut Creek CA 94597
P: 925-937-1500   F: 925-937-8518    PRC:26
www.mti-ca.com
Email: sales@mti-ca.com
Estab: 1991

Scott McDonald, President

Specializes in designing and validating manufacturing controls. The company offers services to biotech companies.

**Multi Metrics Inc**     HQ
865 Lemon St
Menlo Park CA 94025
P: 650-328-0200   F: 650-328-3586    PRC:319
www.multimetrics.com
Estab: 1975

Bill Tandler, President

Provider of geometric dimensioning and tolerance technology products and services and offers training and corporate implementation services.

**Multibeam Corp**     HQ
3951 Burton Dr
Santa Clara CA 95054
P: 408-980-1800   F: 408-980-1808    PRC:212
www.multibeamcorp.com
Email: info@multibeamcorp.com

Thanh Cao, Electronics Engineer
Lynn Barringer, President
David Lam, Chairman

Producer of photomasks for optical lithography. The company's products are used in IC manufacturing and water defect inspection applications.

**MultiDimension Technology Company Ltd**     BR
6000 Hellyer Ave Ste 100
San Jose CA 95138
P: 650-275-2318   F: 408-705-4588    PRC:86
www.dowaytech.com
Email: sales@dowayusa.com
Estab: 2010

Song Xue, CEO

Supplier of TMR magnetic sensors. The company mainly offers switch, linear, angle, and gear tooth sensors.

**Multimedia Consulting Services Inc**     HQ
311 Grunion Ct
Foster City CA 94404
P: 650-578-8591   F: 650-649-2277    PRC:324
www.mmcs.net
Email: info@mmcs.net
Estab: 1991

Tony Bhanot, President

Provider of multimedia consulting services. The company offers design, implementation, and maintenance of the information technology infrastructure.

**Multispan Inc**     HQ
26219 Eden Landing Rd
Hayward CA 94545-3718
P: 510-887-0817     PRC:268
multispaninc.com
Email: info@multispaninc.com
Estab: 2004

Kishore HEMLANI, Chairman
Tiina Sepp, Director of Marketing
Jennifer Pham, Associate Scientist
Rebecca Wirth, Administrative Assistant

Provider of drug discovery services. The company also engages in compound profiling and antibody profiling services.

**Murdoc Technology LLC**     HQ
5683 E Fountain Way
Fresno CA 93727
P: 559-497-1580   F: 559-497-1587    PRC:91
www.murdoc.com
Email: sales@murdoc.com
Emp: 1-10 Estab: 1999

Yee Vang, Production Manager
Greg Miller, Administrator

Manufacturer of electronics. The company primarily offers precision and wire harnesses and cables to various sectors.

**Murigenics**     HQ
941 Railroad Ave
Vallejo CA 94592
P: 707-561-8900   F: 707-561-8943    PRC:24
murigenics.com

Henry Lopez, President
Steven Noonan, COO
Noy Vongphakham, Senior Research Associate

Provider of preclinical in-vivo and in-vitro contract drug discovery. The company is also focused on development services.

**Murray Trailers**     HQ
1754 E Mariposa Rd
Stockton CA 95205-7790
P: 209-466-0266   F: 209-466-0550    PRC:159
www.murraytrailer.com
Email: sales@murraytrailer.com
Emp: 11-50 Estab: 1946

Doug Murray, President
Sue Smith, Manager

Designer and manufacturer of trailers. The company also offers related accessories and hauling services.

## MusclePharm Corp     HQ
4400 Vanowen St
Burbank CA 91505
P: 800-292-3909     PRC:272
www.musclepharm.com
Email: customer.service@musclepharm.com
Emp: 1-10   Estab: 2006
Sales: $100M to $300M

Brian Casutto, EVP of Sales Operations & Director
David Garin, Controller

Provider of sports supplement and nutrition products such as fish oil, energy sport zero, and coco protein for weight loss, fitness, and athletes.

## Mvinix Systems Inc     HQ
2210 Lundy Ave
San Jose CA 95131-1816
P: 408-321-9109   F: 408-321-9110     PRC:211
www.mvinixsystems.com

Ronald Zuniga, Account Manager
Karma Dias, Account Executive

Provider of electronic and manufacturing service provider for printed circuit board assemblies. The company deals with design and testing services.

## MYCOM OSI Inc     BR
2365 Iron Point Rd Ste 170
Folsom CA 95630
P: 916-467-1500     PRC:323
www.mycom-osi.com
Email: info@mycom-osi.com
Emp: 11-50 Estab: 1989

Ian Meakin, Head of Marketing

Provider of performance management, compliance, employer reporting, patient engagement, and satisfaction solutions.

## Mydax Inc     HQ
12260 Shale Ridge Ln
Auburn CA 95602-8400
P: 530-888-6662   F: 530-888-0962     PRC:236
www.mydax.com
Email: sales@mydax.com
Emp: 1-10   Estab: 1986

Brandon Hall, Engineering Manager
Gary Kramer, VP of Engineering
Curtis Turley, Systems Design Engineer
Justin Clark, Quality Assurance Manager
Mark Mowrey, Builder Technician

Designer and manufacturer of temperature control systems. The company offers the elite chiller system.

## Myers Network Solutions     HQ
1101 S Winchester Blvd Ste P-298
San Jose CA 95128
P: 408-483-1881   F: 408-244-1881     PRC:327
myersnetsol.com
Estab: 2002

Rob Wallace, Network Engineer
Victoria Myers, Director of Operations & Marketing
Brad Myers, President
Patti Boor, Marketing Assistant

Provider of network solutions. The company focuses on IT consulting, disaster recovery, network assessment, and cloud computing.

## MyoKardia Inc     HQ
333 Allerton Ave
S San Francisco CA 94080
P: 650-741-0900     PRC:34
www.myokardia.com
Email: medinfo@myokardia.com
Estab: 2012
Sales: $30M to $100M

Tassos Gianakakos, CEO
Taylor Harris, CFO
Jake Bauer, Chief Business Officer
June Lee, EVP
Marc Semigran, Chief Medical Officer

Provider of precision medicine. The company focusses on developing and commercializing therapies for treating cardiovascular diseases.

## Myoscience Inc     HQ
46400 Fremont Blvd
Fremont CA 94538
P: 510-933-1500     PRC:189
iovera.com
Email: contact@myoscience.com
Estab: 2005

Bob Curtis, CEO
Erin Tiernan, Director of Human Resources
Ian Markle, Sales Account Manager
Gregg Bobis, Senior Accountant

Developer of medical technology. The company provides a therapy as the preeminent treatment for conditions involving nerves.

## Myvest Corp     HQ
500 Howard St Ste 425
San Francisco CA 94105
P: 415-369-9511     PRC:326
myvest.com
Email: info@myvest.com
Estab: 2001

Joanne Pons, VP of Engineering
Steve Warren, Co-Founder
Bill Harris, Co-Founder
Chuck Lewis, Co-Founder
Anton Honikman, CEO

Provider of enterprise wealth management solutions. The company offers services to business organizations.

## N&K Technology Inc     HQ
80 Las Colinas Ln
San Jose CA 95119
P: 408-513-3800   F: 408-513-3850     PRC:13
www.nandk.com
Email: inforequest@nandk.com
Estab: 1992

Iris Bloomer, Co-Founder
Rahim Forouhi, President

Manufacturer of metrology tools for the semiconductor, photomask, data storage, flat panel display, and solar cell industries.

## Nada Technologies Inc     HQ
4185 Blackhawk Plaza Cir Ste 220
Danville CA 94506
P: 650-678-4666   F: 650-401-7989     PRC:323
www.nadatechnologies.com

John Zuniga, Director of Global Customer Support

Provider of enterprise Oracle applications. The company also offers business intelligence solutions.

## Nady Systems Inc     HQ
870 Harbour Way S
Richmond CA 94804
P: 510-652-2411   F: 510-652-5075     PRC:68
www.nady.com
Email: support@nady.com
Estab: 1976

John Nady, CEO
Toby Nady, COO
Joy Ferrer, International Purchasing Manager

Designer and manufacturer of wireless microphones, and a full line of audio accessories. The company also focuses on marketing.

## Naehas Inc     HQ
3600 W Bayshore Rd Ste 205
Palo Alto CA 94303
P: 877-262-3427     PRC:323
naehas.com
Email: contact@naehas.com
Estab: 2006

Priti Mondol, Senior UI Engineer
Alka Jain, Board Member

Specializes in the automation of sales and marketing services. The company offers services to finance and insurance companies.

## Nano Precision Medical Inc     HQ
5858 Horton St Ste 280
Emeryville CA 94608
P: 415-506-8462     PRC:189
www.nanoprecisionmedical.com
Estab: 2007

Gregg Williams, Chairman

Developer of medical devices. The company specializes in rice-grain sized implant for the treatment of type II diabetes.

## Nanolab Technologies Inc     HQ
1708 McCarthy Blvd
Milpitas CA 95035
P: 408-433-3320   F: 408-433-3321     PRC:41
www.nanolabtechnologies.com
Estab: 2007

John Traub, President
Thomas Byrd, VP of Finance & Administration
Robert Hoelle, Senior FIB Analyst
Xinyu Zhao, Materials Analyst
Charlene Sun, Material Scientist

Provider of cutting edge technology and expertise for failure analysis, advanced microscopy and FIB circuit edit services.

## Nanometrics Inc     HQ
1550 Buckeye Dr
Milpitas CA 95035
P: 408-545-6000     PRC:86
www.nanometrics.com

Hemant Amin, Senior Applications Engineer
Arjun Dubbaka, Manager of Information Technology Applications
Greg Swyt, VP of Finance
Yudong Hao, Director of Strategic Accounts & AMC
Janet Taylor, General Counsel

Provider of process control metrology and inspection systems for data storage devices and solar photovoltaic applications.

**Nanomix Inc**      HQ
  5980 Horton St Ste 600
  Emeryville CA 94608
P: 510-428-5300  F: 510-658-0425    PRC:186
www.nano.com
Email: info@nano.com
Estab: 2000

Cris Padilla, Associate Manufacturing Engineer
Penny Hopkins, Finance Manager

Manufacturer of diagnostic systems and supplies.
The company is engaged in product development
services.

**Nanosyn**      HQ
  3100 Central Expy
  Santa Clara CA 95051
P: 408-987-2000    PRC:51
www.nanosyn.com
Email: info@nanosyn.com
Estab: 1998

Eric Humphreys, Production Manager
Yvonne Volz, Quality Assurance & Control
Chemist
Aaron Aquino, Chemical Purchasing Manager
Olga Issakova, EVP
Wen Yang, Director of Synthetic Chemistry

Provider of design, synthesis, and analysis of
small organic compounds for the pharmaceutical
and biotechnology industries.

**Nanosys Inc**      HQ
  233 S Hillview Dr
  Milpitas CA 95035
P: 408-240-6700  F: 408-240-6900    PRC:169
www.nanosysinc.com
Email: info@nanosysinc.com
Estab: 2001

Jason Hartlove, President
Nancy Raab, Director of Human Resources
Martin Devenney, SVP of Manufacturing
Andrew Filler, VP of Intellectual Property
Noland Granberry, EVP

Developer of nanotechnology products for the
LCD display and battery markets. The company focuses on display backlighting and energy
storage devices.

**Nanotech Biomachines Inc**      HQ
  2600 Hilltop Dr Bldg B Ste C110
  Richmond CA 94806
P: 855-900-6266    PRC:204
ntb2.zendentest.com
Email: info@nanotechbio.com

Krista Witte, Scientific Advisor

Developer of graphene. The company involves in
wafer scale graphene processing and photolithog-
raphy.

**Napajen Pharma Inc**      HQ
  533 Airport Blvd Ste 527
  Burlingame CA 94010
P: 650-685-2429  F: 650-401-2221    PRC:268
www.napajen.com
Email: info@napajen.com
Estab: 2004

Seiichi Okabe, CFO

Developer of novel drug delivery systems technologies for pharmaceutical and biotechnology
industries.

**Napo Pharmaceuticals Inc**      HQ
  201 Mission St Ste 2375
  San Francisco CA 94105
P: 415-963-9938    PRC:269
www.napopharma.com
Email: hello@napopharma.com
Estab: 2001

Lisa Conte, Interim CEO

Developer of pharmaceutical drugs. The company
specializes in the development of patent pharmaceutical products.

**Naprotek Inc**      HQ
  90 Rose Orchard Way
  San Jose CA 95134
P: 408-830-5000  F: 408-830-5050    PRC:209
naprotek.com
Email: info@naprotek.com
Estab: 1995

Paramajit Singh, Senior Director of Engineering
Najat Badriyeh, Founder
Amy Chen, Director of Production
Arlis Greco, Quality Manager
Larry Morrissey, VP of Operations

Provider of electronics manufacturing services.
The company serves customers in the satellites,
industrial, medical, military, and other sectors.

**Nasam Inc**      HQ
  601 Gateway Blvd Ste 1155
  South San Francisco CA 94080
P: 650-872-1155  F: 650-952-1205    PRC:2
www.nasam.com

William Zimmerman, CFO
Akira Yamamoto, VP
Hiro Egawa, Deputy Director

Distributor of electronics products. The company
offers military/defense equipment, aircraft support
equipment, and other products.

**Natera Inc**      HQ
  201 Industrial Rd Ste 410
  San Carlos CA 94070
P: 650-249-9090    PRC:34
natera.com
Email: info@natera.com
Emp: 975
Sales: $100M to $300M

Styrmir Sigurjonsson, SVP of R&D of Data Sci-
ence and Engineering
Steve Chapman, CEO
Matthew Rabinowitz, Executive Chairman
Jonathan Sheena, CTO
Robert Schueren, COO

Provider of prenatal testing services. The company specializes in non-invasive prenatal testing,
genetic carrier screening and paternity testing.

**Natero**      HQ
  2950 S Delaware St Ste 201
  San Mateo CA 94403
P: 650-727-0770    PRC:326
www.natero.com
Email: info@natero.com
Estab: 2012

Craig Soules, Founder
Garth Goodson, Founder
John Kelly, VP of EMEA
Vic Mahadevan, Advisor
Bob Garrow, Advisor

Developer of data science techniques for the
analysis and prediction of human behavior. The
company is also engaged in honing marketing
skills.

**National Analytical Laboratories Inc**      HQ
  10416 Investment Cir
  Rancho Cordova CA 95670
P: 916-361-0555  F: 916-361-0540    PRC:142
www.nal1.com
Email: nal1@nal1.com
Emp: 1-10  Estab: 1992

Paula Lee, President

Provider of environmental lab testing and consulting services. The company focuses on air monitoring, building inspection, and operations training.

**National Center For Appropriate
Technology**      BR
  36355 Russell Blvd
  Davis CA 95617
P: 530-792-7338    PRC:129
ncat.org
Email: rexd@ncat.org
Emp: 11-50 Estab: 1976

Jeff Amerman, CFO
Jacqueline Hutchinson, VP of Operations
Carol Werner, Executive Director

Provider of information and access services. The
company's offerings include weatherizing houses,
monitoring energy applications, and testing
products.

**National Fabtronix Inc**      HQ
  28800 Hesperian Blvd
  Hayward CA 94545-5038
P: 510-785-3135  F: 510-785-1253    PRC:80
www.natfab.com
Estab: 1971

Knute Ream, President

Provider of custom fabrication and precision sheet
metal services for the computer and medical
industries.

**National Vapor Industries Inc**      HQ
  1811 Park St
  Livermore CA 94551
P: 925-980-7341  F: 925-373-9692    PRC:152
www.nationalvapor.com
Email: davidjewell1@comcast.net
Estab: 2006

David Jewell, CEO
Terry Rice, Operations Director

Manufacturer of hydrogen generators. The company also offers marketing, installation, and other
services.

**Natron Resources Inc**      HQ
  1480 Moraga Rd Ste I 229
  Moraga CA 94556
P: 510-868-0701  F: 510-868-0701    PRC:135
www.natronresources.com
Email: info@natronresources.com
Estab: 2008

Jeff Ansley, Principal Solar Design Engineer

Provider of solar system, flat-plate photovoltaic, and solar thermal design and installations
services.

**Natural Logic** — HQ
PO Box 119
Berkeley CA 94701
P: 510-248-4940   F: 877-628-5644   PRC:325
natlogic.com
Email: info@natlogic.com
Estab: 1999

Jeremy Faludi, Director
Shana Gillis, Business Development

Provider of consulting, product development, e-learning, digital content, and product support services.

**Nature's Cure** — HQ
4096 Piedmont Ave Ste 171
Oakland CA 94611
P: 877-469-9487   PRC:43
www.naturescure.com
Estab: 1994

Amy Baker, President

Provider of health and beauty solutions. The company offers over-the-counter products featuring natural ingredients.

**Natus Medical Inc** — HQ
1501 Industrial Rd
San Carlos CA 94070
P: 650-802-0400   F: 650-802-0401   PRC:189
www.natus.com
Email: customer_service@natus.com
Estab: 1987
Sales: $300M to $1 Billion

Shawn Mosley, Senior Systems Engineer
Jonathan Kennedy, President
Drew Davies, EVP
Lisa Paul, VP
Ivan Pandiyan, VP of Global Research and Development

Provider of medical devices, software, and services. The company offers products for neurology, newborn care, hearing diagnostics, and more.

**Navire Pharma** — HQ
421 Kipling St
Palo Alto CA 94301
P: 650-391-9740   PRC:254
navirepharma.com
Email: info@navirepharma.com
Estab: 2017

Uma Sinha, CSO

Developer of novel therapies. The company focusses on developing SHP2 inhibitors for treating rare cancers.

**Navis LLC** — HQ
55 Harrison St Ste 600
Oakland CA 94607
P: 510-267-5000   F: 510-267-5100   PRC:323
www.navis.com
Email: partners@navis.com
Estab: 1988

Benoit de la Tour, President
Bruce Jacquemard, CCO
Andy Barrons, CSO
Rob Dillon, CFO
Scott Peoples, Chief Acquisitions Officer

Provider of terminal operating solutions. The company offers solutions for container terminal operations, expert decking, and process automation.

**Navlink** — LH
1001 Bayhill Dr Ste 200
San Bruno CA 94066
P: 650-616-4042   F: 650-616-4042   PRC:324
www.navlink.com
Estab: 1996

Richard Giugno, President
Bassel Dbaibo, CCO
Antoine El-Am, CIO
Bassem Soubra, VP of Global Market Development
Mansour Naufal, VP of Product Development and Service Enablement

Provider of managed data services, managed hosting services, and managed enterprise networking solutions.

**NB Corporation of America** — BR
46750 Lakeview Blvd
Fremont CA 94538
P: 510-490-1420   F: 510-490-1733   PRC:146
www.nbcorporation.com
Email: info@nbcorporation.com
Estab: 2000

Mark Shaffer, Field Sales Engineer
Larry Hansen, Director of Sales
Paul Morreale, Sales Manager
Melissa Lima, Inside Sales Leader
Edward Biegel, Inventory Controller

Manufacturer of linear motion bearings, slides, ball splines, and related products. The company's products include slide guides, spindle shafts, and actuators.

**NBA Engineering Inc** — HQ
897 Hyde St Fl 2
San Francisco CA 94109
P: 415-202-9840   F: 415-202-9838   PRC:154
www.nbaeng.com
Estab: 1994

Jan Groupp, Marketing Coordinator

Provider of mechanical and electrical engineering design, energy conversion, and construction management services.

**NComputing Co Ltd** — HQ
1875 S Grant St Ste 570
San Mateo CA 94402
P: 650-409-5959   F: 650-409-5958   PRC:110
www.ncomputing.com
Estab: 2003

Richard Sah, Co-Founder
Young Song, Co-Founder

Provider of desktop virtualization services. The company serves customers in the education, healthcare, enterprise, and enterprise sectors.

**NDK America Inc** — BR
1551 McCarthy Blvd Ste 107
Milpitas CA 95035
P: 408-428-0800   F: 408-428-0801   PRC:86
www.ndk.com
Email: sales@ndkxtal.com

Kory Stone, Technical Sales Manager

Manufacturer of crystal products for applications including gaming consoles, automotives, mobile phones, computers, and network equipment.

**NDS Inc** — HQ
851 N Harvard Ave
Lindsay CA 93247
P: 888-825-4716   F: 559-562-4488   PRC:144
www.ndspro.com
Email: nds@ndspro.com
Emp: 11-50

Ryan Larsen, Civil Engineer
Mike Gummeson, President
Mike Fallon, VP of Sales
Steve Kort, Western Region Sales Director
Shayna Burgess, Marketing Communication Manager

Provider of storm water management, efficient irrigation, and flow management solutions for residential and commercial applications.

**NDS Surgical Imaging** — HQ
5750 Hellyer Ave
San Jose CA 95138
P: 408-776-0085   F: 408-776-9878   PRC:169
www.ndssi.com
Email: info@ndssi.com
Estab: 1996

Rainer Scholl, VP of Engineering
Amir Baghdadi, Principal Engineer
Jim Leng, Regulatory Engineer
Kris Lothongkam, UWB Embedded System Engineering
Alan Ching, Junior Quality Engineer

Provider of medical imaging services. The company specializes in minimal invasive surgery viewing and diagnostic imaging.

**Nearsoft Inc** — HQ
1854 Anne Way Ste 110
San Jose CA 95124
P: 408-691-1034   PRC:327
www.nearsoft.com
Estab: 2007

Roberto Martinez, CEO
Matt Perez, COO

Provider of services to grow development team in companies. The company exclusively caters to software product sectors.

**Neato Robotics Inc** — HQ
8100 Jarvis Ave
Newark CA 94560
P: 510-795-1351   PRC:209
www.neatorobotics.com
Estab: 2006

Rachel Lucas, Mechanical Engineer
Bryant Pong, Robotics Software Engineer
Preetam Reddy, Software Engineer
Avril Murphy, General Manager
Aparna Aswani, Director of Global Communications

Manufacturer of robots. The company manufactures robots for cleaning and other activities.

**NEC Laboratories America Inc**  BR
10080 N Wolfe Rd Ste SW3-350
Cupertino CA 95014
P: 408-863-6007  PRC:306
www.nec-labs.com

Ali Hooshmand, Research Staff Member

Provider of technology research services. The company specializes in research departments such as integrated systems, machine learning, and media analytics.

**Nehanet Corp**  HQ
5001 Great America Pkwy Ste 250
Santa Clara CA 95054
P: 888-552-4470  PRC:323
www.nehanet.com
Email: info@nehanet.com
Estab: 2000

Ankur Sharma, CEO
Ryan W., Inside Sales Representative

Provider of corporate responsibility management and sales and operation planning solutions to semiconductor and electronics component manufacturers.

**Neil O Anderson & Associates Inc**  HQ
902 Industrial Way
Lodi CA 95240
P: 209-367-3701  F: 209-333-8303  PRC:131
noanderson.com
Email: info@noanderson.com
Emp: 11-50 Estab: 1991

Garret Hubbart, VP
Karen Vieyra, Office Manager
Troy Schiess, PE

Provider of engineering services including geotechnical engineering, foundation, and structural engineering services.

**Neilmed Pharmaceuticals Inc**  HQ
601 Aviation Blvd
Santa Rosa CA 95403
P: 707-525-3784  F: 707-525-3785  PRC:261
www.neilmed.com
Email: questions@neilmed.com
Estab: 2000

Ketan Mehta, CEO
Nina Mehta, President
Dinesh Patel, VP of QA & RA
Bharat Mehta, Director of European Operations
Srikanth Pai, Database Administrator

Manufacturer of large volume low pressure saline nasal irrigation systems for babies & children, first aid, dry noses, sterile saline spray, and ear care.

**Nektar Therapeutics**  HQ
455 Mission Bay Blvd S
San Francisco CA 94158
P: 415-482-5300  F: 415-339-5300  PRC:34
www.nektar.com
Email: nektarsf@nektar.com
Estab: 1990
Sales: $1B to $3B

Howard Robin, CEO
Robert Chess, Chairman
John Northcott, SVP
Stephen Doberstein, Chief Scientific Fellow
Gil Labrucherie, CFO

Provider of therapeutic products for the treatment of opioid-induced constipation in adult patients with chronic non-cancer pain.

**Nelson Biotechnologies Inc**  HQ
16080 Caputo Dr Ste 150
Morgan Hill CA 95037
P: 408-778-2020  F: 408-778-7207  PRC:34
www.nelsonbiotech.com
Email: custserv@nelsonbiotech.com
Estab: 2000

Paul Nelson, President

Provider of oligonucleotide labeling and modification services. The company also specializes in contract research and manufacturing.

**Neo Technology Inc**  HQ
111 E Fifth Ave
San Mateo CA 94401
P: 855-636-4532  PRC:326
neo4j.com
Email: info@neo4j.com
Estab: 2007

Emil Eifrem, CEO
Johan Svensson, CTO
Lars Nordwall, COO
Philip Rathle, VP of Products

Developer of enterprise applications. The company focuses on technical support and related services.

**Neo4j Inc**  HQ
111 E Fifth Ave
San Mateo CA 94401
P: 855-636-4532  PRC:325
neo4j.com
Email: info@neo4j.com
Estab: 2007

Ravi Ramanathan, VP of Sales Engineering
Magnus Vejlstrup, VP of Engineering
Michael Hunger, Director of Developer Relations Engineering
Viksit Puri, Director of Sales Engineering West
Ed Crowther, Director of Sales Engineering

Graph database platform that helps companies to access the business value of data connections.

**Neoconix Inc**  HQ
4020 Moorpark Ave Ste 108
San Jose CA 95117
P: 408-530-9393  F: 408-530-9383  PRC:206
www.neoconix.com
Email: info@neoconix.com
Estab: 2002

Todd Bridges, Human Resource Contractor Recruiter
Lisa Lloyd, Sales Manager

Provider of electrical interconnect solutions. The company offers LGA sockets, board-to-board interposers, and standard products.

**Neodyne Biosciences Inc**  HQ
7999 Gateway Blvd Ste 110
Newark CA 94560
P: 800-519-7127  PRC:34
www.embracescartherapy.com
Email: info@embracescartherapy.com
Estab: 2007

Henry de Leon, Research

Manufacturer of embrace devices and it helps in the concealment of scars. The company serves patients.

**Neomagic Corp**  HQ
830 Hillview Ct Ste 138
Milpitas CA 95035
P: 408-428-9725  F: 408-988-7036  PRC:86
www.neomagic.com
Email: sales@neomagic.com
Estab: 1993

Syed Zaidi, President
David Tomasello, VP of Strategic Planning
Roderick Peterson, VP of Administration And Information
Benjamin Bolinguit, Director of Operations
Jo Dietz, Executive Administrator

Developer of electronic device solutions. The company sells hardware, software, and microcontrollers for IP cameras and vehicle toll collection.

**Neopeutics Inc USA**  HQ
400 Oyster Point Blvd Ste 112
S San Francisco CA 94080
P: 650-624-4057  PRC:268
neopeutics.com
Email: info@neopeutics.com
Estab: 2009

Harlizawati Jahari, CEO
Anton Espira, COO

Provider of pre clinical contract research services and product development for the private and governmental regulatory agencies.

**Neophotonics Corp**  HQ
2911 Zanker Rd
San Jose CA 95134
P: 408-232-9200  F: 408-456-2971  PRC:208
www.neophotonics.com
Email: sales@neophotonics.com
Estab: 1996
Sales: $300M to $1 Billion

Xuan-Anh Nguyen, R&D Process Engineer
Marcello Sebastian, Engineer
Tim Jenks, CEO
Chi Cheung, COO
Elizabeth Eby, CFO

Designer and manufacturer of photonic integrated circuit based optoelectronic modules and subsystems for communications networks.

**Neospeech Inc**  HQ
4633 Old Ironsides Dr Ste 200
Santa Clara CA 95054
P: 408-914-2710  F: 408-890-4715  PRC:324
www.neospeech.com
Email: sales@neospeech.com
Estab: 2002

Brian Chiu, Sales & Marketing Project Specialist

Provider of text-to-speech software and applications for the mobile, enterprise, entertainment, and education markets.

**Neotract Inc**  HQ
4473 Willow Rd Ste 100
Pleasanton CA 94588
P: 925-401-0700  F: 925-401-0699  PRC:188
urolift.com
Email: info@neotract.com
Estab: 2004

Curtis Yarra, Research
Theodore Lamson, Founder
David Amerson, President
Sarah Cooley, Human Resource Director
Eric Pader, Manufacturing Manager

Provider of medical devices for the treatment of benign prostatic hyperplasia and its side effects such as loss of productivity and sleep and depression.

**Neova Tech Solutions Inc** BR
4701 Patrick Henry Dr, Bldg 16 Ste 106
Santa Clara CA 95054
P: 781-640-0588 PRC:323
www.neovasolutions.com
Email: sales@neovatechsolutions.com
Estab: 2007

Kalpesh Savla, Founder
Hemal Savla, Head of Finance
Sandip Chaudhari, Senior Software Architect

Provider of cloud solutions for web and mobile. The company offers mobile development and QA automation services.

**Neptec Optical Solutions Inc** HQ
48603 Warm Springs Blvd
Fremont CA 94539
P: 510-687-1101 F: 510-687-0599 PRC:62
www.neptecos.com
Email: info@neptecos.com
Estab: 2001

Orlando Basco, Production Engineer
David Cheng, CEO
Darlene Diaz, Customer Account Manager

Provider of quick-turn fiber optic connectivity solutions. The company also offers connector reconditioning, switches, and fiber arrays.

**Neptune Systems LLC** HQ
15750 Vineyard Blvd Ste 150
Morgan Hill CA 95037
P: 408-275-2205 F: 408-762-2042 PRC:159
www.neptunesystems.com
Email: support@neptunesystems.com

Terence Fugazzi, VP of Sales
Paul Jansen, Customer Support Manager

Provider of aquarium controllers. The company also offers expansion modules and accessories and offers support services.

**Net4site LLC** HQ
3350 Scott Blvd Bldg 34B
Santa Clara CA 95054
P: 408-427-3004 PRC:326
net4site.net
Email: info@net4site.net

Roger Diaz, Director

Provider of SAP solutions. The company serves customers in the enterprise mobility, business intelligence, and ERP arenas.

**Netafim Irrigation Inc** HQ
5470 E Home Ave
Fresno CA 93727
P: 559-453-6800 F: 559-453-1043 PRC:159
www.netafimusa.com
Emp: 1-10 Estab: 1965

Kathy Westerman, Production Planning Supervisor
Larry Munoz, Quality Assurance Manager
Michael Illia, Product Offering Manager
Dennis Hannaford, Product Manager
Jim McCarty, Technical Support Manager

Provider of drip and micro irrigation products for agriculture, greenhouse and nursery, landscape and turf, mining, and wastewater applications.

**NetApp Inc** HQ
1395 Crossman Ave
Sunnyvale CA 94089
P: 408-822-6000 F: 408-822-4501 PRC:324
www.netapp.com
Email: info@netapp.com
Estab: 1992
Sales: Over $3B

Rob Salmon, President
Jay Kidd, CTO
Scott Dawkins, CTO
Ronald Pasek, EVP
Julie Parrish, SVP

Provider of virtualization, mobile information management, and cloud storage solutions. The company serves the business sector.

**Netblaze Systems Inc** HQ
1299 Newell Hill Pl Ste 202
Walnut Creek CA 94596
P: 925-932-1765 PRC:63
www.netblaze.biz
Email: info@netblaze.biz
Estab: 2005

Alan Kaplan, Co-Founder
Igor Akkerman, President
Nicholas Dahlman, Senior Technician

Provider of IT, integration, and network consulting services. The company is also engaged in cloud computing, web hosting, and hosted exchange.

**Netease Inc** HQ
PO Box 1610
Forestville CA 95436
P: 800-580-0932 PRC:325
www.neteze.com
Email: support@neteze.com

William Perdue, Owner
Barbara Perdue, Owner

Provider of web hosting services. The company offers domain registration, hosting, and dial-up services.

**Netformx Inc** HQ
333 W Santa Clara St Ste 612
San Jose CA 95113
P: 408-423-6600 PRC:326
www.netformx.com
Email: support@netformx.com
Estab: 1994

Ittai Bareket, CEO
Mariquelle Lazaro, Executive Assistant

Designer and builder of solutions for the networking and service providers. The company specializes in desktop and cloud applications.

**NETGEAR Inc** HQ
350 E Plumeria Dr
San Jose CA 95134-1911
P: 408-907-8000 F: 408-907-8097 PRC:97
www.netgear.com
Email: sales@netgear.com
Estab: 1996
Sales: $1B to $3B

Patrick Lazar, VP of Engineering
Dennis Aldover, Director of Software Engineering
Bob Liu, Principal Software Engineer
Robert Whitaker, Senior Systems Administrator
Patrick Lo, CEO

Provider of network solutions for home and businesses. The company also offers home video monitoring systems and storage products.

**Netpace Inc** HQ
5000 Executive Pkwy Ste 530
San Ramon CA 94583
P: 925-543-7760 F: 925-558-4015 PRC:322
www.netpace.com
Email: support@netpace.com
Estab: 1997

Yasir Khan, Software Engineer
Hasnain Abidi, Software Engineer
Annie Sen, Senior Technical Recruiter

Provider of consulting, cloud computing, data base management, and proprietary development services.

**Netpulse Inc** HQ
50 Osgood Pl Ste 400
San Francisco CA 94133
P: 877-638-7857 PRC:322
www.netpulse.com
Email: sales@netpulse.com
Estab: 2009

Igor Ivashchenko, Director of Engineering
Alex Peacock, CEO
Brad Bean, VP of Digital Solutions
Charles Njoku, VP of Professional Services
Nadine Eichhorn, Head of Product Development

Provider of custom branded mobile apps. The company also offers technical support services to its customers.

**Netronome** HQ
2903 Bunker Hill Ln Ste 150
Santa Clara CA 95054
P: 408-496-0022 F: 408-586-0002 PRC:126
www.netronome.com
Email: support@netronome.com
Estab: 2003

Edwin Peer, Principal Software Engineer
Niel Viljoen, CEO
Jay Knowlton, Director of Finance
Brian Sparks, VP of Marketing Communications
Ron Renwick, Senior Director of Product Marketing

Provider of flow processing, server virtualization, cyber security, and software-defined networking solutions.

**Netscout** BR
178 E Tasman Dr Ste 101
San Jose CA 95134
P: 408-571-5000 PRC:322
www.netscout.com
Email: support@netscout.com
Estab: 2007

Anil Singhal, Co-founder
Richard Kenedi, President Core Markets business unit
Bruce Kelley, SVP
Jean Bua, CFO
Michael Szabados, COO

Developer of service assurance and applications, service delivery management, network performance management software, and hardware solutions.

**Netskope Inc**  HQ
270 Third St
Los Altos CA 94022
P: 800-979-6988  PRC:323
www.netskope.com
Email: contact@netskope.com
Estab: 2012

Joe DePalo, SVP of Platform Engineering
Sanjay Beri, CEO
Ravi Ithal, Chief Architect
Krishna Narayanaswamy, CTO
Drew Del Matto, CFO

Provider of cloud security brokering services. The company offers services to the healthcare sector.

**Network Design Associates Inc**  HQ
6060 Sunrise Vista Dr Ste 2440
Citrus Heights CA 95610
P: 916-853-1632  F: 916-853-0944  PRC:326
www.ndasacramento.com
Email: info@ndasacramento.com
Emp: 1-10  Estab: 1992

Gregory Nelson, VP of Engineering
Susan Gill, Engineer
Deborah Sackman, President

Provider of engineering services for computer systems. The company's services include network design, implementation, support, and maintenance.

**Network PCB Inc**  HQ
2360 Qume Dr Ste F
San Jose CA 95131
P: 408-943-8760  F: 408-943-8761  PRC:211
networkpcb.com
Email: sales@networkpcb.com
Estab: 2002

Charlie Nguyen, Production Manager
Pauline Vo, Marketing
Kevin Le, Director of Operations
Hieu Tran, Assistant Account Manager
Lan Do, Controller

Provider of printed circuit board solutions. The company's product line includes probe cards, high density board, and impedance control board.

**Netwoven Inc**  HQ
500 E Calaveras Blvd Ste 238
Milpitas CA 95035
P: 877-638-9683  F: 650-618-1541  PRC:323
www.netwoven.com
Email: info@netwoven.com
Estab: 2001

Asijit Giri, Principal Engineer
Niraj Tenany, CEO
Viraj Bais, Co-Founder
Angira Dey, Client Relationship Director
Vijender Singh, Recruiting Manager

Provider of enterprise content management and business intelligence solutions. The company also focuses on process management.

**Netxperts Inc**  HQ
1777 Botelho Dr Ste 102
Walnut Creek CA 94596
P: 925-806-0800  PRC:317
netxperts.com
Estab: 1996

Rondy Scippio, Network Operating Center Engineer
Gary Nordine, CEO
Kelly Nordine, Inside Sales Representative
Chris Hynes, WLAN Project Manager
Shawn Whitmore, Telecommunications Technician

Provider of unified communication solutions. The company offers services to the healthcare and transportation markets.

**Neudesic LLC**  BR
200 Spectrum Ctr Dr Ste 2000
Irvine CA 92618
P: 303-248-8300  F: 303-248-8400  PRC:326
www.neudesic.com
Email: info@neudesic.com
Emp: 11-50

Parsa Rohani, CEO
Tim Marshall, CTO
Howard Dinet, Senior Account Manager
Tim Corken, Director of Inside Sales

Provider of technology services. The company focuses on social software, integration platform, and CRM solutions and offers cloud computing services.

**Neuron Corp**  HQ
1777 Saratoga Ave Ste 104
San Jose CA 95129
P: 408-540-7959  PRC:323
www.neuroncorp.com

Ed Neubauer, President

Provider of computer and physical security products and services for the military, government, and corporate sectors.

**Neurona Therapeutics**  HQ
170 Harbor Way
S San Francisco CA 94080
P: 650-799-6465  PRC:34
www.neuronatherapeutics.com
Email: info@neuronatx.com
Estab: 2008

Cory Nicholas, Co-Founder
Gautam Banik, VP of Manufacturing and Process Sciences
Estela Alvarez, VP of Quality Assurance and Control
John Centanni, VP of Regulatory Affairs
Catherine Priest, VP of Preclinical Development

Developer of neuronal stem cells to transplant into the brain. The company offers services to the healthcare industry.

**Neuropace Inc**  HQ
455 N Bernardo Ave
Mountain View CA 94043
P: 650-237-2700  F: 650-237-2701  PRC:189
www.neuropace.com
Email: info@neuropace.com
Estab: 1999

Tygo Ebenhahn, Senior Design Engineer
Tom Taylor, Quality Engineer
Mike Kenzler, Associate Mechanical Engineer
Frank Fischer, CEO
Martha Morrell, Chief Medical Officer

Designer, developer, manufacturer, and marketer of implantable devices for the treatment of neurological disorders.

**Neurosky Inc**  HQ
125 S Market St Ste 900
San Jose CA 95113
P: 408-200-6675  PRC:87
www.neurosky.com
Email: sales@neurosky.com
Estab: 2004

Jongjin Lim, President
Stanley Yang, CEO
Rui Zou, Algorithm Development Scientist

Manufacturer of ECG biosensors and also EEG biosensors for mobile solutions, wearable devices, and service providers.

**Neurotrack Technologies Inc**  HQ
399 Bradford St Ste 101
Redwood City CA 94063
P: 650-549-8566  PRC:34
neurotrack.com
Email: support@neurotrack.com
Estab: 2012

Elli Kaplan, CEO

Provider of computer-based cognitive tests. The company offers services to Alzheimer's patients and the medical industry.

**Neutronix Inc**  HQ
385 Woodview Ave Ste 200
Morgan Hill CA 95037
P: 408-776-5190  F: 408-776-1039  PRC:212
www.neutronixinc.com
Email: sales@neutronixinc.com
Estab: 1989

Brett Arnold, CEO
Lenore Arnold, COO
David Geder, VP of Sales
Curt Gamm, Director of Customer Support

Manufacturer of contact or proximity and projection mask aligners. The company is involved in design, installation, and delivery services.

**Nevarez Machining Inc**  HQ
848 E Gish Rd
San Jose CA 95112
P: 408-279-1196  PRC:80

Jaime Nevarez, President
Janeth Enriquez, CFO
Gary Brusato, Programmer

Manufacturer of fabricated machined parts. The company offers welding, machining, inspection, and software machining services.

**Nevro Corp**     HQ
1800 Bridge Pkwy
Redwood City CA 94065
P: 650-251-0005     PRC:196
www.nevro.com
Email: legal@nevro.com
Estab: 2006
Sales: $300M to $1 Billion

David Marco, Senior Field Clinical Engineer
Frank Fischer, President
Keith Grossman, Chairman
Michael Demane, Lead Director
Tung Nguyen, Senior Information Technology
Support Specialist

Developer of new high-frequency stimulation
technology for improving the role of spinal cord
stimulation in the treatment of chronic pain.

**Nevtec Inc**     HQ
1150 S Bascom Ave Ste 12
San Jose CA 95128
P: 408-292-8600     PRC:224
www.nevtec.com
Email: sales@nevtec.com
Estab: 1996

Shawn Neverve, VP of Operations

Provider of networks implementation and maintenance services. The company also focuses on
workstations and the internet.

**New Faze Development Inc**     HQ
1825 Del Paso Blvd
Sacramento CA 95815
P: 916-929-6402    F: 916-929-0158    PRC:304
www.newfaze.com
Emp: 1-10    Estab: 1990

Allen Warren, Founder
Nick Pecha, CFO
Jeff Sigworth, Project Manager
Patty Poswall, Investment Fund Administrator

Provider of construction and management development services. The company also offers project
management and property management services.

**New Generation Software Inc**     HQ
3835 N Freeway Blvd Ste 200
Sacramento CA 95834
P: 916-920-2200    F: 916-920-1380    PRC:322
www.ngsi.com
Email: marketing@ngsi.com
Emp: 1-10    Estab: 1982

Bill Langston, Director of Marketing

Supplier of packaged data mart models with
analytical presentations and reports for wholesale
distribution, healthcare, and financial reporting.

**New Power Technologies**     HQ
25259 La Loma Dr
Los Altos Hills CA 94022
P: 650-948-4546     PRC:130
newpowertech.com
Estab: 2004

Peter Evans, President

Provider of energy solutions. The company's offerings include energynet platform and energynet
solutions.

**New Tech Solutions Inc**     HQ
4179 Business Center Dr
Fremont CA 94538
P: 510-353-4070    F: 510-353-4076    PRC:117
www.newtechsolutions.com
Email: info@ntsca.com
Estab: 1997

Himanshu Parikh, Computer Systems Engineer
Maulik Gandhi, Pre Sales Engineer
Rajesh Patel, President
Vijay Kumar, CEO
Satish Raina, Director of Sales

Provider of technology solutions. The company
caters to networking, security, and communication
manufacturers.

**New Vision Display Inc**     HQ
1430 Blue Oaks Blvd
Roseville CA 95747
P: 916-786-8111    F: 916-786-8121    PRC:169
www.newvisiondisplay.com
Emp: 1-10

Shahna Kothapally, VP of Product Engineering
Matthias Pfeiffer, CTO
Jeff Olyniec, CEO
Peter Jiang, CFO
Y.K. Hoo, COO

Provider of display products. The company's
products include LCD modules, TFT LCD and
touch products.

**New World Machining**     HQ
2799 Aiello Dr
San Jose CA 95111
P: 408-227-3810    F: 844-272-5214    PRC:80
newworldmachining.com
Email: contact@newworldmachining.com
Estab: 1973

Quang Le, Production Manager
Norma Gonzalez, Customer Service & Purchasing
Chris Elsten, VP of Operations
Janice Flores, Customer Service Manager
Mary Guilbert, Manager

Manufacturer of machined parts for the semiconductor, electronic, and security sectors specializing in prototype, production, and engineering
design.

**Newcomb Anderson Mccormick**     HQ
201 Mission St Ste 2000
San Francisco CA 94105
P: 415-896-0300     PRC:39
www.newcomb.cc
Estab: 1983

Jordan Crolly, Energy Engineer
Mary Leatherman, Accounting Manager
Matt Sullivan, Principal
John Newcomb, Principal
Michael Anderson, Principal

Provider of energy engineering and consulting services. The company also offers energy
program development and distributed generation
solutions.

**NewGen Surgical Inc**     HQ
41 Simms St Ste B
San Rafael CA 94901
P: 855-295-4500    F: 415-526-3742    PRC:195
newgensurgical.com
Email: info@newgensurgical.com
Estab: 2012

Peter Szyperski, Director of Engineering & Oper-
ations
Rob Chase, Founder
Kimberlee Luedee-Chase, VP of Business Opera-
tions & Marketing
Carol Summers, Senior Marketing Manager
Anne-Marie Regal, Medical Director

Designer of single use medical devices. The company offers skin staplers, needle counters, and
procedure kit packaging trays.

**NewGen Therapeutics Inc**     HQ
3475 Edison Way Ste R
Menlo Park CA 94025
P: 650-995-7508     PRC:268

Jeffrey Bacha, CEO

Provider of therapeutic solutions. The company
focusses on the development and discovery of
small molecule drugs for cancer treatment.

**Newland North America Inc**     HQ
46559 Fremont Blvd
Fremont CA 94538
P: 510-490-3888    F: 510-490-3887    PRC:59
www.newlandna.com
Email: info@newlandna.com
Estab: 2008

Wang Jing, President

Designer and developer of data collector and
scanning systems. The company also offers customer information terminals.

**Newnex Technology Corp**     HQ
3041 Olcott St
Santa Clara CA 95054
P: 408-986-9988    F: 408-986-8024    PRC:106
newnex.com
Email: information@newnex.com
Estab: 1993

Fuwen Xu, Senior Support Engineer

Developer of connecting cables, controllers, and
repeaters. The company's services include design,
installation, and technical support.

**Newport-West Data Services Inc**     HQ
18120 Bollinger Canyon Rd Bldg 2 Ste A
San Ramon CA 94583
P: 925-855-1131    F: 925-855-1161    PRC:322
www.nwds.com
Email: info@nwds.com
Estab: 1979

Scott Maclean, Director of Programming

Designer and developer of minicomputer based
business applications. The company specializes in
installation.

**Nexant Inc**    HQ
101 Second St Ste 1000
San Francisco CA 94105-3651
P: 415-369-1000   F: 415-369-9700    PRC:129
www.nexant.com
Email: sales@nexant.com
Estab: 2000

Basem Sarandah, Founder
John Gustafson, President
Arjun Gupta, Executive Chairman
Sunil Bhardwaj, CFO

Developer of software for utility, energy, chemical, and other sectors and also offers power grid consulting and energy advisory, and other services.

**Nexb Inc**    HQ
735 Industrial Rd Ste 101
San Carlos CA 94070
P: 650-592-2096    PRC:325
www.nexb.com
Email: info@nexb.com
Estab: 2003

Thomas Druez, Software Engineer
Michael Herzog, CEO
Dennis Clark, Product Manager
Pierre Lapointe, Customer Care Manager
Jono Yang, Software Analyst

Designer and developer of software tools and services. The company offers services to business enterprises and related organizations.

**Nexenta Systems Inc**    HQ
2025 Gateway Pl Ste 160
San Jose CA 95110
P: 408-791-3300   F: 408-791-3305    PRC:320
www.nexenta.com
Email: sales@nexenta.com
Estab: 2005

Bill Fuller, VP of Engineering
Dmitry Yusupov, CTO
Aditya Fotedar, CIO
Mavis Yee, CAO
Lisa Lee, Director of Quality Control

Provider of enterprise class storage software solutions. The company is engaged in virtualization and business continuity planning.

**Nexlogic**    HQ
2085 Zanker Rd
San Jose CA 95131
P: 408-436-8150   F: 408-436-8156    PRC:211
www.nexlogic.com
Email: support@nextlogic.com
Estab: 1899

Zulki Khan, Founder
Don Shell, Director of Business Development
Phillip Lerma, Fabrication Manager

Designer of electronic circuits. The company specializes in the design and fabrication of printed circuit boards.

**Nextaxiom Technology Inc**    HQ
600 Montgomery St Ste 2720
San Francisco CA 94111
P: 415-373-1890   F: 415-373-1899    PRC:322
www.nextaxiom.com
Email: info@nextaxiom.com
Estab: 2000

Ash Massoudi, CEO
Sandy Zylka, VP of Products & Technology
Dave Bakke, Principal

Provider of testing, certification, and other professional services. The company offers work management and scheduling solutions.

**Nextbus Inc**    BR
1800 Sutter St Ste 900
Concord CA 94520
P: 925-686-8200    PRC:319
www.cubic.com
Estab: 1997

Melanie Hagerty, VP of Corporate Engineering & Innovation
Matt Cole, SVP
Mike Knowles, SVP
Bradley Feldmann, CEO
Michael Twyman, SVP

Provider of transit management solutions. The company also provides real-time passenger information solutions to organizations.

**Nextec Microwave & Rf**    HQ
3010 Scott Blvd
Santa Clara CA 95054
P: 408-727-1189   F: 408-727-5915    PRC:70
www.nextec-rf.com
Email: sales@nextec-rf.com
Estab: 1996

Dongwook Lee, President

Provider of microwave amplifiers and integrated frequency multipliers. The company serves the aerospace, military, and defense sectors.

**Nextier Networks Inc**    HQ
2953 Bunker Hill Ln Ste 400
Santa Clara CA 95054
P: 408-282-3561   F: 408-282-3501    PRC:84
www.nextiernetworks.com
Email: info@nextiernetworks.com

Mark Calomeni, SVP of Systems Engineering
Tarique Mustafa, Founder
John Racioppi, VP of Business Development

Provider of data security services and solutions for vertical markets and original equipment manufacturers.

**NextInput Inc**    HQ
980 Linda Vista Ave
Mountain View CA 94043
P: 650-963-9310    PRC:322
nextinput.com
Email: sales@nextinput.com

Ali Foughi, CEO
Ryan Diestelhorst, CTO

Provider of MEMS-based force sensing solutions for touch enabled devices in markets such as wearable, automotive, industrial, and medical applications.

**NextLabs Inc**    HQ
2121 S El Camino Real Twr Plz Ste 600
San Mateo CA 94403
P: 650-577-9101   F: 650-577-9102    PRC:322
www.nextlabs.com
Email: info@nextlabs.com
Estab: 2004

Keng Lim, CEO
Jill Rubin, VP of Marketing
Andy Han, SVP of Products
Dennis Andrie, Director of Professional Services & Support
Phillip Annas, Desktop Support Specialist

Developer of software products. The company offers information risk management software products for enterprises.

**Nextracker Inc**    HQ
6200 Paseo Padre Pkwy
Fremont CA 94555
P: 510-270-2500   F: 510-793-8388    PRC:131
nextracker.com
Email: info@nextracker.com

Alex Roedel, Manager of Project Engineering
Stuart Upfill-Brown, Structural Engineer
Will Kirkland, IT Engineer
Colin Murphy, Software Engineer
Melissa Cooke, Project Engineer

Provider of horizontal tracking services. The company focuses on solar power plants and clean technology solutions.

**Nextrials Inc**    HQ
5000 Executive Pkwy Ste 540
San Ramon CA 94583
P: 925-355-3000   F: 925-355-3005    PRC:326
www.nextrials.com
Email: info@nextrials.com
Estab: 1999

Jim Rogers, CEO
Robert Barr, CTO
Karmen Ghobrial, Quality Assurance Analyst

Provider of e-clinical and electronic health record tools. The company is engaged in clinical research and related services.

**Nexusguard Ltd**    RH
548 Market St Ste 15269
San Francisco CA 94104
P: 415-299-8550    PRC:319
www.nexusguard.com
Email: media@nexusguard.com
Estab: 2008

Xenophon Giannis, VP of Sales

Provider of monitoring and DNA protection services. The company serves service providers and the entertainment sector.

**NGM Biopharmaceuticals Inc** HQ
333 Oyster Point Blvd
S San Francisco CA 94080
P: 650-243-5555 PRC:258
www.ngmbio.com
Email: info@ngmbio.com
Estab: 2008

Jeff Jonker, President
Alex DePaoli, Chief Medical Officer
Ruth Corbin, Director of Human Resources
Marc Learned, Director
Zhonghao Liu, Principal Scientist

Developer of novel and disease-altering biologics
such as protein, peptide, and antibody drug for
cancer, cardio-metabolic, and hepatic diseases.

**NIC Components Corp** BR
1732 N First St Ste 300
San Jose CA 95112
P: 669-342-3960 F: 669-342-3969 PRC:203
www.niccomp.com
Email: sales@niccomp.com
Estab: 1982

Mary Ly, Global Business Development Manager

Designer, manufacturer, and supplier of passive components. The company offers ceramic
capacitors, power inductors, and current sensing
resistors.

**Nice Touch Solutions Inc** HQ
PO Box 1149
Alamo CA 94507
P: 925-385-8321 PRC:323
www.ewbills.com
Email: info@nicetouch.com
Estab: 1996

Arnold Young, CEO

Developer of software for the heavy highway
construction industry. The company focuses on
products for generating extra work bills.

**Nichols Manufacturing Inc** HQ
913 Hanson Ct
Milpitas CA 95035
P: 408-945-0911 F: 408-945-8127 PRC:157
www.nicholsmfg.com
Email: nichols@nicholsmfg.com
Estab: 1979

Lettie Nichols, President

Provider of product engineering and design, prototyping, and manufacturing services. The company
serves the business sector.

**Nidek Inc** RH
47651 Westinghouse Dr
Fremont CA 94539
P: 800-223-9044 PRC:186
usa.nidek.com
Estab: 1971

Hisako Ueno, Quality Assurance Administrative
Support
Ron Kaiser, Director of Sales
Jay Wollack, Sales Manager
Naomi Nakayama, Controller

Manufacturer of ophthalmic devices. The company
also offers refractive systems and diagnostic
products to the medical industry.

**Nieco** HQ
7950 Cameron Dr
Windsor CA 95492
P: 707-284-7100 F: 707-284-7430 PRC:159
nieco.com
Email: sales@nieco.com
Estab: 1905

Korey Kohl, President
Ed Baker, President
Shari Kirichenko-Egan, Human Resource
Matt Baker, VP of Research
Tom Holmes, International VP

Manufacturer of automatic broilers. The company's
applications include restaurants, fast food centers,
and amusement parks.

**Nikon Precision Inc** HQ
1399 Shoreway Rd
Belmont CA 94002-4107
P: 650-508-4674 PRC:159
www.nikonprecision.com
Email: npicom@nikon.com
Estab: 1996

Mohamad Zarringhalam, SVP of Engineering
Services & Customer Support
Ikuo Ogawa, SVP of Engineering Services &
Customer Support
Yoshiyuki Takabatake, CEO
Gregory Sasaki, VP of Finance & Corporate
Services
Hamid Zarringhalam, EVP

Manufacturer of optical lenses and precision
equipment. The company is also the supplier of
step-and-repeat and step-and-scan lithography
systems.

**Nimbus Design** HQ
2363 Broadway
Redwood City CA 94063
P: 650-365-7568 F: 650-365-3025 PRC:67
www.nimbusdesign.com
Estab: 1991

Arturo Samayoa, Partner
Karen Sparks, CFO
Iikka Valli, Partner
John Novicki, Director of Quality Assurance
Felipe Salazar, Operations Manager

Provider of design services. The company specializes in website design, content management, and
e-commerce tools.

**Nisene Technology Group** HQ
384 Pine St
Watsonville CA 95076
P: 831-761-7980 F: 831-761-2992 PRC:212
www.nisene.com
Emp: 1-10

Lenna Wagner, President

Provider of automated decapsulator technology
and plastic etching services. The company offers
custom design services for nonstandard gaskets.

**Nitinol Devices & Components Inc** HQ
47533 Westinghouse Dr
Fremont CA 94539
P: 510-683-2000 PRC:235
www.nitinol.com
Email: sales@nitinol.com
Estab: 1991

Christine Trepanier, VP of Product Development &
Engineering
Colby James, Senior Engineer
Soane Eke, Process Development Engineer
Justin Owens, Process Development Engineer
Tom Duerig, CTO

Provider of rapid development and prototyping
services. The company is also engaged in commercialization.

**NK Technologies** HQ
3511 Charter Park Dr
San Jose CA 95136
P: 408-871-7510 F: 408-871-7515 PRC:87
www.nktechnologies.com
Email: sales@nktechnologies.com
Estab: 1982

Nitin Kelkar, Owner
Philip Gregory, President
Will Delsman, Technical Sales
Cuong Ngo, Manager
NY-Cuong Ngo, Manager

Manufacturer of current sensors and transducer
products for the factory and industrial automation
markets.

**Nobix Inc** HQ
PO Box 3592
San Ramon CA 94583
P: 925-659-3500 F: 925-659-3599 PRC:322
www.nobix.com
Email: sales@nobix.com
Estab: 1985

Pat Caster, Tech Manager

Provider IT management products for job scheduling, problem alerting, and notification as well as
provides software engineering services.

**Noble Image Inc** HQ
4141 Northgate Blvd Ste 1A
Sacramento CA 95834
P: 916-419-3570 F: 916-561-0542 PRC:318
www.nobleimage.com
Email: sales@nobleimage.com
Emp: 1-10

Mark Ruff, President
Elly Callison, Web Designer
Ryan Stora, Senior Web Designer

Provider of website and graphic design, website
development, hosting, programming, and technical support services.

**Noel Technologies Inc** HQ
1510-C Dell Ave
Campbell CA 95008
P: 408-374-9549 F: 408-374-4127 PRC:204
www.noeltech.com
Email: info@noeltech.com
Estab: 1996

Brenda Hill, VP

Provider of lithography, thin film deposition, and
water recycling solutions. The company serves
MEMS, defense, life science, and other sectors.

**Noise and Vibration Technologies LLC**    HQ
17 Mandeville Ct
Monterey CA 93940
P: 831-655-6600      PRC:31
www.nvtgroup.com
Estab: 2014

Patti Monahan, VP of Finance

Provider of measuring, simulating, and analyzing the effects of vibration, noise, shock, and other environmental variables for various industries.

**Nok Nok Labs Inc**    HQ
2100 Geng Rd Ste 105
Palo Alto CA 94303
P: 650-433-1300      PRC:325
www.noknok.com
Email: info@noknok.com
Estab: 2011

David Chao, Co-Founder
Terry Opdendyk, Founder
Rolf Lindemann, President
Phillip Dunkelberger, President
Richard Clarke, Chairman

Focuses on the development on online security solutions. The company is also involved in third party research services.

**Nokia Corp**    BR
200 S Mathilda Ave
Sunnyvale CA 94086
P: 408-737-0900      PRC:71
www.nokia.com

Basil Alwan, Co-president of IP
Bhaskar Gorti, President of Nokia Software
Federico Guillen, President of Customer Operations
Jenni Lukander, President of Nokia Technologies
Rajeev Suri, President

Specializes in mobile network infrastructure structure and services. The company is engaged in technology development.

**Nomis Solutions Inc**    HQ
8000 Marina Blvd Ste 700
Brisbane CA 94005
P: 650-588-9800      PRC:322
www.nomissolutions.com
Estab: 2004

Robert Phillips, Founder
Abhinav Mittal, CTO
Christopher Mondfrans, CFO
Michelle Scott, VP of Human Resources
Johnathan Bant, SVP of Sales

Provider of pricing and profitability management solutions. The company caters to the financial services.

**Nor-Cal Metal Fabricators**    HQ
1121 Third St
Oakland CA 94607
P: 510-833-7157    F: 510-893-2940      PRC:82
www.nc-mf.com
Email: telsales@nc-mf.com
Estab: 1953

Michael Tran, President
Rick Turner, Information Technology Manager
Troy Nickles, Manufacturing Superintendent
Martin Hooey, Estimator
Steve Vickers, Estimator

Provider of general industrial metal fabrication and parts. The company is engaged in contract manufacturing and structural rolling.

**Nor-Cal Perlite Inc**    HQ
2605 Goodrick Ave
Richmond CA 94801
P: 510-232-7337    F: 510-232-8127      PRC:53
www.norcalperlite.com
Email: info@norcalperlite.com
Estab: 1986

Justin Clarke, Manager

Manufacturer of perlite and perlite products. The company is involved in the development of specialty grades for individual customers.

**Nor-Cal Products Inc**    HQ
1967 S Oregon St
Yreka CA 96097
P: 530-842-4457    F: 530-842-9130      PRC:165
www.n-c.com
Email: ncsales@n-c.com
Emp: 11-50 Estab: 1962

Tom Deany, President
Ron Buracker, Production Manager
Jim Crowley, Product Manager

Provider of fabricating solutions for stainless steel flanges, fittings, and components. The company's services include welding, machining, and forming.

**Norden Millimeter Inc**    HQ
5441 Merchant Cir Ste C
Placerville CA 95667
P: 530-642-9123    F: 530-642-9420      PRC:70
www.nordengroup.com
Email: sales@nordengroup.com
Emp: 1-10   Estab: 2001

Duncan Smith, President
Clark Hickerson, Associated Technical Sales
Manny Olmedo, Associated Technical Sales
Lorrie Hartsough, Assembly supervisor
Stephen Sarver, Technician

Developer and manufacturer of amplifier products. The company specializes in millimeter wave amplifier products.

**Nordic Naturals Inc**    HQ
111 Jennings Dr
Watsonville CA 95076
P: 831-724-6200    F: 831-724-6600      PRC:272
www.nordicnaturals.com
Email: info@nordicnaturals.com
Emp: 11-50 Estab: 2002

Joar Opheim, CEO
Todd Murphy, Financial Analyst

Specializes in the delivery of omega oil to consumers, veterinary professionals, pharmacists, and healthcare professionals.

**Noron Precision Machining Inc**    HQ
1245 Mt View Alviso Rd
Sunnyvale CA 94089
P: 408-739-6486    F: 408-739-2734      PRC:80
www.noronprecision.com
Estab: 1977

Debbie Hanks, Owner
Debbie Williams, President
Jose Mendoza, Quality Assurance Manager
Trevor Hanks, Shop Assistant

Provider of machined parts for medical, microwave, aircraft, auto, computer peripheral, telecommunications, and biotech industries.

**North Coast Medical Inc**    HQ
780 Jarvis Dr Ste 100
Morgan Hill CA 95020
P: 408-776-5000    F: 877-213-9300      PRC:189
www.ncmedical.com
Email: custserv@ncmedical.com
Estab: 1974

Laura Langton, Sales Administration Manager
Preston Kincaid, Creative Marketing Director
Jeri Francis, Senior Graphic Designer
Sam Ramsey, Senior System Administrator
Becky Cohn, Product Labeling Coordinator

Manufacturer of medical and rehabilitation products such as castings, clinical supplies, and other wellness supplies.

**Northgate Environmental Management Inc**    HQ
428 13th St 4th fl
Oakland CA 94612
P: 510-839-0688    F: 510-839-4350      PRC:139
ngem.com
Email: contact@ngem.com
Estab: 1999

Alan Leavitt, Principal Engineer
Axel Rieke, Associate Engineer
Deni Chambers, President
Randa Bitar, Office Manager
Maile Smith, Principal Geologist

Provider of interdisciplinary technical solutions. The company focuses on results-oriented scientific and engineering investigation and analysis.

**Northstar Engineering**    HQ
111 Mission Ranch Blvd Ste 100
Chico CA 95926
P: 530-893-1600    F: 530-893-2113      PRC:142
northstareng.com
Email: info@northstareng.com
Emp: 11-50 Estab: 1983

Ross Simmons, Partner
Tony Melo, Director of Engineering
John Ellis, Civil Engineer Project Manager
Robin Kampmann, Assistant Engineer
Nicole Ledford, Associate Engineer

Provider of land development services, municipal infrastructure design, onsite waste water systems, and environmental consulting services.

**Nortra Cables Inc**    HQ
570 Gibraltar Dr
Milpitas CA 95035
P: 408-942-1106    F: 408-942-1109      PRC:62
www.nortra-cables.com
Estab: 1985

Khai Do, Engineer
Patrick Wilder, Quality Manager
Bill Clair, Sales Manager
Michelle Lateur, Sustainability Manager
Binhminh Le, Office Manager

Provider of discrete and flat mechanical assembly cables. The company offers design, prototyping, and manufacturing services.

**Nova Measuring Instruments Inc**  BR
3342 Gateway Blvd
Fremont CA 94538
P: 408-510-7400  PRC:159
www.novami.com
Email: info@novami.com

Eitan Oppenhaim, President
Gabriel Waisman, Chief Business Officer
Dror David, CFO
Shay Wolfling, CTO
Sharon Dayan, Chief Human Resources Officer

Provider of metrology solutions for semiconductor manufacturing industries. The company offers integrated and stand-alone metrology platforms.

**Novabay Pharmaceuticals Inc**  HQ
2000 Powell St Ste 1150
Emeryville CA 94608
P: 510-899-8800  F: 510-474-1577  PRC:34
novabay.com
Estab: 2000
Sales: $10M to $30M

Justin Hall, General Counsel
Mark Sieczkarek, CEO
Thomas Paulson, CFO
Lonnie Wong, Associate Director of Quality Assurance
David Stroman, SVP of Ophthalmic Product Development

Manufacturer of biopharmaceuticals. The company develops non-antibiotic anti-infective products to address the eye care market.

**Novalynx Corp**  HQ
431 Crown Point Cir Ste 120
Grass Valley CA 95945
P: 530-823-7185  F: 530-823-8997  PRC:233
www.novalynx.com
Email: nova@novalynx.com
Emp: 1-10  Estab: 1988

William Begg, Engineering Manager
Bill Begg, Technical Sales Engineer
Joseph Andre, President
Keith Andre, Sales Manager
Mary Sweetser, Sales Manager

Designer, manufacturer, and integrator of meteorological systems. The company's products are used in the industrial sector.

**Novani LLC**  HQ
900 Kearny St Ste 388
San Francisco CA 94133
P: 415-731-1111  F: 415-731-4270  PRC:324
www.novani.com
Email: sales@novani.com
Estab: 1989

Henry Dickinson, Systems Support Engineer
Francis Yiu, Founder
Nancy Perata, COO

Provider of disaster prevention and recovery solutions. The company also offers business continuity and virtualization solutions.

**Novartis Pharmaceuticals Corp**  BR
150 Industrial Rd
San Carlos CA 94070
P: 650-622-1500  F: 650-622-1699  PRC:268
www.novartis.com
Email: media.relations@novartis.com
Estab: 1996

Helen Lau, Director

Development of drugs and pharmaceutical products for complicated diseases. The company serves the healthcare sector.

**Novasentis Inc**  HQ
2560 Ninth St Ste 314
Berkeley CA 94710
P: 814-238-7400  PRC:209
www.novasentis.com
Estab: 2006

Francois Jeanneau, President
Linda Ara, CFO
Michael Vestel, CTO
Christine Kittinger, VP of Human Resources
John Jacobi, VP of Manufacturing

Creator of haptic actuator and sensor technology for the consumer electronics applications such as smart watches, jewelry, headbands, and smart glasses.

**Novici Biotech LLC**  HQ
3333 Vaca Valley Pkwy Ste 400
Vacaville CA 95688
P: 707-446-5502  F: 707-446-3917  PRC:269
www.novicibiotech.com
Email: info@novicibiotech.com

Hal Padgett, CEO

Focuses on product development as well as protein engineering. The company serves the agriculture, industrial and pharmaceutical sectors.

**Novozymes Inc**  BR
1445 Drew Ave
Davis CA 95616
P: 530-757-8100  F: 530-758-0317  PRC:25
www.novozymes.com
Email: info@novozymes.com
Emp: 11-50  Estab: 1992

Alan Berry, Managing Director
Debbie Yaver, Director
Eric Fechter, Patent Agent
Hanshu Ding, Senior Scientist
Kieu Le, Administrative Assistant

Provider of industrial biotechnology solutions for the food and beverage, agriculture, textile, and pulp and paper industries.

**NPI Solutions Inc**  HQ
685 Jarvis Dr
Morgan Hill CA 95037
P: 408-944-9178  F: 408-944-9644  PRC:202
www.npisolutions.com
Email: info@npisolutions.com
Estab: 2000

Kevin Andersen, President

Provider of design, engineering, and custom manufacturing solutions. The company offers on-site engineering services.

**Nq Engineering Inc**  HQ
7470 Carmelo Ave
Tracy CA 95304
P: 209-836-3255  F: 209-836-3255  PRC:80
www.nqengineering.com
Emp: 1-10  Estab: 1985

Mike Quigg, Machinist

Provider of engineering services. The company specializes in fabricating, materials, inspection, and quality control.

**NRC Environmental Services Inc**  BR
1605 Ferry Pt
Alameda CA 94501
P: 510-749-1390  F: 510-749-4150  PRC:140
nrcc.com
Estab: 1922

Joe Peterson, CFO
Lou O'Brien, SVP of Sales and Marketing
Robert George, SVP
Mike Reese, SVP
Neil Challis, SVP

Provider of environmental, industrial, and emergency solutions. The company offers oil spill response, industrial cleaning, sediment remediation, and other services.

**NRC Manufacturing**  HQ
47690 Westinghouse Dr
Fremont CA 94539
P: 510-438-9400  PRC:211
www.nrcmfg.com
Estab: 2008

Matt Davis, VP
Larry Wright, Account Manager
Nithys Nandini, General Admin Manager
David Sin, Technician

Provider of contract manufacturing and PCB assembly services. The company's services include cable assembly, box builds, and functional test.

**Nsymbio**  HQ
2330 Old Middlefield Way
Mountain View CA 94043
P: 650-968-2058  PRC:327
www.nsymbio.com
Email: service@nsymbio.com
Estab: 1969

Mahesh Tank, Owner
Adam Mason, Digital Solutions Specialist

Provider of printing services. The company is engaged in project management, graphic design, print, and online ordering system services.

**NTFB Combustion Equipment USA Inc**  HQ
950 Tower LN
Foster City CA 94404
P: 510-443-0066  F: 510-443-0069  PRC:151
www.ntfb.com
Email: info@ntfb.com

Edison Guerra, Director of Operations

Manufacturer of combustion equipment. The company offers mid to large size, single & multiple burner, water tube boiler, and furnace applications.

**Ntk Technologies Inc**                    HQ
  3979 Freedom Cir Ste 320
  Santa Clara CA 95054
  P: 408-727-5180   F: 408-727-5076      PRC:204
  www.ntktech.com
  Estab: 1936

Paul Furuya, President
Mariel Stoops, Senior Strategic Marketing Manager

Manufacturer of bio ceramics, oxygen sensors, ceramic heater, and transistor packages for the medical and telecommunication applications.

**Nuance Communications Inc**               BR
  1198 E Arques Ave
  Sunnyvale CA 94085
  P: 408-992-6100                        PRC:319
  www.nuance.com

Mark Benjamin, CEO
Daniel Tempesta, EVP
Robert Weideman, EVP
Lee Patch, VP

Provider of hosted application systems and mobile solutions. The company offers services to businesses and the healthcare sector.

**Nugen Technologies Inc**                  HQ
  201 Industrial Rd Ste 310
  San Carlos CA 94070
  P: 650-590-3600   F: 650-590-3630       PRC:28
  www.nugen.com
  Email: custserv@nugeninc.com
  Estab: 2000

Doug Amorese, CSO
Bin Li, Senior Scientist

Provider of solutions for genomic analysis. The company focuses on DNA analysis and RNA analysis applications.

**Nugentec**                                HQ
  1155 Park Ave
  Emeryville CA 94608
  P: 707-820-4080   F: 707-820-4079       PRC:56
  www.nugentec.com
  Email: salesteam@nugentec.com
  Estab: 1997

Dane Shannon, National Sales Manager

Provider of chemicals and polymers. The company offers oilfield chemicals, cleaners, and lubricants.

**NuMedii Inc**                             HQ
  66 Bovet Rd Ste 320
  San Mateo CA 94402
  P: 650-918-6363                        PRC:34
  numedii.com
  Email: info@numedii.com
  Estab: 2008

Gini Deshpande, Founder
Samuel Saks, Director
Atul Butte, Director

Provider of big data technology such as integrative genomics and chemoinformatics to discover and de-risk new indications for safe, existing drug.

**Numenta Inc**                             HQ
  791 Middlefield Rd
  Redwood City CA 94063
  P: 650-369-8282   F: 650-369-8283       PRC:67
  www.numenta.com
  Estab: 2005

Donna Dubinsky, CEO
Jeff Hawkins, Co-Founder
Christy Maver, VP of Marketing
Subutai Ahmad, VP of Research

Developer of biotechnology machine intelligence technologies for commercial and scientific applications.

**Numerate Inc**                            HQ
  1501 Mariposa St Ste 426
  San Francisco CA 94107
  P: 650-472-0632   F: 650-396-7574       PRC:257
  www.numerate.com
  Email: info@numerate.com
  Estab: 2007

Simon Wilkinson, Director of Engineering
Brandon Allgood, CTO
John Griffin, CSO
Uwe Klein, VP of Biology

Provider of data analytics and drug design technology services for the pharmaceutical and biotechnology industries.

**Numerify Inc**                            HQ
  1054 S De Anza Blvd Ste 203
  San Jose CA 95129
  P: 408-822-9611                        PRC:323
  numerify.com
  Email: info@numerify.com
  Estab: 2012

Gaurav Rewari, Co-Founder

Provider of business, service, and asset analytics services. The company offers services to information technology organizations.

**Nutanix Inc**                             HQ
  1740 Technology Dr Ste 150
  San Jose CA 95110
  P: 855-688-2649   F: 408-916-4039       PRC:322
  www.nutanix.com
  Estab: 2009
  Sales: $1B to $3B

Rajiv Mirani, SVP of Engineering
Dheeraj Pandey, Founder
Duston Williams, CFO
Howard Ting, SVP of Marketing
Julie O'Brien, VP of Corporate Marketing

Focuses on the simplification of datacenter infrastructure by integrating server and storage resources into a turnkey hyperconverged platform.

**Nute Engineering**                        HQ
  907 Mission Ave
  San Rafael CA 94901
  P: 415-453-4480   F: 415-453-0343       PRC:142
  www.nute.biz
  Email: info@nute-engr.com
  Estab: 1945

Adrian Bartshire, Engineer
David Stier, Engineer
Pippin Cavagnaro, Engineer
Edward Nute, Founder
Mark Wilson, President

Developer of technologies for the water, wastewater treatment, and environmental protection projects.

**Nutribiotic**                             HQ
  PO Box 238
  Lakeport CA 95453
  P: 707-263-0411   F: 707-263-7844       PRC:251
  www.nutribiotic.com
  Email: sales@nutribiotic.com
  Emp: 1-10   Estab: 1980

Carolyn Roberts, Administrative Assistant

Manufacturer of health, wellness, and fitness products. The company provides nutritional supplements and personal care products.

**Nutrition53 Inc**                         HQ
  3706 Mt Diablo Blvd Ste 200
  Lafayette CA 94549
  P: 925-900-3557                        PRC:272
  www.nutrition53.com
  Email: customerservice@nutrition53.com

Bill Romanowski, Founder
Aida Aragon, National Sales Manager

Manufacturer of nutritional supplements. The company manufactures health care products for staying lean, sleeping well and feeling energized.

**Nuvation Engineering**                    HQ
  151 Gibraltar Ct
  Sunnyvale CA 94089
  P: 408-228-5580                        PRC:327
  www.nuvation.com
  Email: info@nuvation.com
  Estab: 1997

Michael Worry, CEO

Provider of electronic engineering services. The company focuses on product design, embedded software development, and single integrity analysis.

**Nuvel Holdings Inc**                      HQ
  20 S Santa Cruz Ave
  Los Gatos CA 95030
  P: 408-884-8069                        PRC:322
  nuvelinc.com
  Estab: 2009

Jay Elliot, Founder
Rick Resnick, CEO

Provider of data acceleration solutions. The company focuses on data transfers and related communication services.

**Nuvolase Inc**                            HQ
  11 Ilahee Ln
  Chico CA 95973
  P: 530-809-1970                        PRC:172
  www.nuvolase.com
  Email: customercare@nuvolase.com
  Emp: 1-10   Estab: 2011

Steve Duddy, President
Maureen Brunner, Senior Marketing Consultant

Manufacturer of the pinpointe foot laser used for the treatment of nail fungus and in nail fungus procedures.

**Nuvora Inc** HQ
3350 Scott Blvd Ste 502
Santa Clara CA 95054
P: 877-530-9811  F: 408-727-1703  PRC:254
www.nuvorainc.com
Estab: 2007

Becky Jevons, Oral Health Care & Dental Manager

Focuses on dry mouth treatment and offers products for bad breath prevention. The company offers Dentiva and Sales.

**Nuvoton Technology Corporation
America** DH
2727 N First St
San Jose CA 95134
P: 408-544-1718  PRC:209
www.nuvoton.com
Estab: 2008

Aditya Raina, EVP of Engineering
Wei-Chan Hsu, VP of Engineering
Richard Jesse, Senior Field Applications Engineer
Sean Tai, President
Jou-Wei Fu, President

Manufacturer of semiconductor products and applications. The company's offerings include microcontrollers, microprocessors and cloud computing.

**NV5** BR
2525 Natomas Park Dr Ste 300
Sacramento CA 95833
P: 916-641-9100  F: 916-641-9222  PRC:304
www.nv5.com
Emp: 11-50

Alexander Hockman, President
Dickerson Wright, CEO
Edward Codispoti, CFO
Mary Jo Brien, EVP
Scott Kvandal, Chief Synergy Officer

Provider of technical consulting and certification services. The company serves the infrastructure, construction, and real estate markets.

**NVIDIA Corp** HQ
2788 San Tomas Expy
Santa Clara CA 95051
P: 408-486-2000  PRC:91
www.nvidia.com
Email: info@nvidia.com
Estab: 1993
Sales: Over $3B

Frank Fox, SVP of Consumer Electronics Engineering
Jensen Huang, Co-Founder
Colette Kress, EVP
Shanker Trivedi, VP of Enterprise Sales & Business Development
Kashi Anoosheh, VP of Mobile Sales

Provider of visual computing solutions that include video games, movie production, product design, medical diagnosis, and scientific research.

**Nvigen Inc** HQ
285 Sobrante Way Ste AB
Sunnyvale CA 94086
P: 650-209-0268  PRC:24
www.nvigen.com
Email: info@nvigen.com
Estab: 2011

Abdel Minalla, Senior Engineer
Aihua Fu, President
Weiwei Gu, Lab Manager

Developer of multifunctional and biodegradable nanoparticles. The company is engaged in research and development services.

**nVision Medical Corp** HQ
1192 Cherry Ave
San Bruno CA 94066
P: 408-655-3577  PRC:186
nvisionmedical.com
Email: info@nvisionmedical.com
Estab: 2011

Surbhi Sarna, CEO
David Snow, VP of Research & Development

Developer of women's health products. The company offers services to clinicians and the medical industry.

**nWay** HQ
301 Howard St Ste 1440
San Francisco CA 94105
P: 415-778-2866  PRC:317
nway.com
Email: info@nway.com
Estab: 2011

Liyue Shen, Software Engineer

Specializes in the development and publishing of free-to-play online multiplayer games. The company offers services to individuals.

**NXP Semiconductors** BR
411 E Plumeria Dr
San Jose CA 95134
P: 408-518-5500  PRC:86
www.nxp.com
Estab: 2006

Saurin Choksi, Principal Design Engineer
Ruediger Stroh, EVP
Janet Chou, VP

Manufacturer of amplifiers, diodes, data converters, microcontrollers, and bipolar transistors for the healthcare, automotive, and computing sectors.

**Nyad Inc** HQ
1647 Willow Pass Rd Ste 509
Concord CA 94520
P: 925-270-3971  PRC:11
www.nyad.com
Email: sales@nyad.com
Estab: 1987

Claire Parrott, President
Carissa Harrild, Executive Operations Manager

Supplier of gas analyzers. The company's product line includes analyzers for moisture, oxygen, carbon monoxide, carbon dioxide, hydrocarbon, transmitters.

**Nyden Corp** HQ
PO Box 640176
San Jose CA 95164
P: 510-894-3633  PRC:150
www.nydencorporation.com
Email: sales@nydencorporation.com

Clara Chien, VP of Sales

Supplier of stepper motors. The company deals with the design of semiconductor equipment, laser systems, and aerospace-related apparatus.

**O&M Industries Inc** HQ
5901 Ericson Way
Arcata CA 95521
P: 707-822-8800  F: 707-822-8995  PRC:80
www.omindustries.com
Email: info@omindustries.com
Emp: 11-50 Estab: 1946

Kevin Williams, Operations Manager

Provider of industrial, mechanical, structural contractors, and fabrication services. The company serves cement industries.

**O'hara Metal Products** HQ
4949 Fulton Ave
Fairfield CA 94534
P: 707-863-9090  F: 707-863-9006  PRC:80
www.oharamfg.com
Email: twives@oharamfg.com
Estab: 1964

Tim Ives, President

Manufacturer of metal products. The company's products include springs, stampings, sheet metals, and wires EDM's.

**O2micro USA** LH
3118 Patrick Henry Dr
Santa Clara CA 95054
P: 408-987-5920  F: 408-987-5929  PRC:64
www.o2micro.com
Email: ir@o2micro.com
Estab: 1998

Gary Abbott, Director of Investor Relations
Carl Durham, Senior Corporate Counsel

Provider of battery and power management products. The company also offers LED general lighting and backlighting products.

**Objectivity Inc** HQ
1980 Zanker Rd Ste 30
San Jose CA 95112
P: 408-992-7100  F: 408-992-7171  PRC:323
www.objectivity.com
Email: info@objectivity.com
Estab: 1988

Peiyi Mao, Software Engineer
Leon Guzenda, Founder
Gary Lewis, CFO
Stino Tapia, Manager of Information Systems
Brian Clark, VP of Product Management

Provider of distributed, real-time, SOA-enabled service and offers embedded database management solutions.

**Obscura Digital LLC**      HQ
14 Louisiana St Historic Pier 70
San Francisco CA 94107
P: 415-227-9979      PRC:67
www.msg.com
Estab: 2000

Melissa Hennessey, Senior Accountant
Ari Ali, Senior Media Producer

Provider of technology-driven creative solutions.
The company caters to advertising and marketing
needs.

**OCAMPO-ESTA Corp**      HQ
1419 Tennessee St
Vallejo CA 94590
P: 707-643-8072    F: 707-552-6047      PRC:68
www.ocampo-esta.com
Email: oec@ocampo-esta.com
Estab: 1986

Albert Palad, Substation Engineer
Bonifacio Rayala, Electrical Engineer
Tom Akin, Senior Design Engineer
Jake Mendoza, Senior Electrical Engineer
Oscar Ocampo, President

Provider of engineering, design, construction
management, instrumentation and controls, and
project management services.

**Occidental Power**      HQ
5982 Mission St
San Francisco CA 94112
P: 415-681-8861    F: 415-681-9911      PRC:135
www.oxypower.com
Email: sales@oxypower.com
Estab: 1989

Kimo Bailey, Owner
Greg Kennedy, Founder
Keith Burkland, Field Supervisor
Adam Diener, Estimator
Carmine Garofalo, Designer

Designer and installer of commercial and residential solar electric, solar thermal, and natural gas
cogeneration systems.

**Ocean Presence Technologies**      HQ
326 Pacheco Ave
Santa Cruz CA 95062
P: 831-426-4678      PRC:168
oceanpresence.com
Emp: 1-10

Robert Aston, President

Manufacturer of underwater video monitoring
camera systems and offers cable systems, power
systems, lighting, wireless networks, and accessories.

**Ocellus Inc**      HQ
450 Lindbergh Ave
Livermore CA 94551
P: 925-606-6540      PRC:191
www.ocellusinc.com
Email: information@ocellusinc.com
Estab: 1996

Shannan Downey, Manager of Laboratory Operations

Provider of multidisciplinary technology and services such as nanotechnology-based solutions for
aerospace, industrial, and medical applications.

**Oclaro Inc**      HQ
2560 Junction Ave
San Jose CA 95134
P: 408-383-1400    F: 408-919-1501      PRC:209
www.oclaro.com
Email: info@oclaro.com
Estab: 1988

Yuan Wo, Principal Software Engineer
Xianyun Meng, Senior Test Engineer
Richard Craig, President of Integrated Photonics
Tim Kattner, Senior Consultant

Provider of telecommunications and data communication products. The company offers lasers
& transmitters, receivers, transceivers, and other
products.

**OCSiAl**      BR
640 W California Ave Ste 210
Sunnyvale CA 94086
P: 415-906-5271      PRC:131
ocsial.com
Email: usa@ocsial.com

Oleg Kirillov, Co-Founder
Yuriy Zelvenskiy, Co-Founder
Yury Koropachinskiy, Co-Founder
Andrey Senyut, VP
Grigory Gurevich, CEO

Provider of technology and material solutions.
The company offers services to the nanomaterials
industry.

**Ocumetrics Inc**      HQ
2224-C Old Middlefield Way
Mountain View CA 94043-2421
P: 650-960-3955    F: 650-960-0611      PRC:187
www.ocumetrics.com
Email: info@ocumetrics.com
Estab: 1993

Bruce Ishimoto, Owner

Manufacturer of Fluorotron Master Ocular Fluoro-
photometers. The company deals with research
services.

**Odie Sheet Metal Shop**      HQ
375 Umbarger Rd
San Jose CA 95111
P: 408-281-2919    F: 408-281-2477      PRC:80
odiesheetmetal.com
Email: odiesheetmetal@sbcglobal.net
Estab: 1979

Michael Garcia, Shop Manager

Provider of sheet metal fabrication solutions. The
company also deals with manufacturing and prototype development.

**Oea International Inc**      HQ
155 E Main Ave Ste 110
Morgan Hill CA 95037
P: 408-778-6747    F: 408-778-6748      PRC:323
www.oea.com
Email: info@oea.com
Estab: 1988

Ersed Akcasu, President
Jerry Tallinger, VP of Sales & Marketing

Developer of signal integrity software. The company serves the electronic design automation
industry.

**Oepic Semiconductors Inc**      HQ
1231 Bordeaux Dr
Sunnyvale CA 94089
P: 408-747-0388    F: 408-747-5808      PRC:212
www.oepic.com
Email: sales@oepic.com
Estab: 2000

Minh-Tam Nguyen, Controller

Provider of semiconductor fabrication services.
The company's products include optical and optoelectronic components.

**Office Information Systems**      HQ
7730 Pardee Ln
Oakland CA 94621
P: 510-568-7900      PRC:329
www.ois-online.com
Estab: 1982

Richard Ozer, President

Provider of computer network design and consulting services. The company serves small and
medium sized organizations and law firms.

**Ogletree's Inc**      HQ
935 Vintage Ave
St. Helena CA 94574
P: 707-963-3537    F: 707-963-8217      PRC:80
www.ogletreecorp.com
Estab: 1946

Matt Cia, President
Dennis Souza, Estimator
Sam Peers, Systems Design Engineer

Provider of metal and equipment fabrication services. The company focuses on design, detailing,
fabrication, and installation services.

**Ohanae Inc**      HQ
16133 Hillvale Ave
Monte Sereno CA 95030
P: 888-617-7288    F: 413-691-1935      PRC:323
www.ohanae.com
Email: info@ohanae.com
Estab: 2007

Greg Hauw, Founder

Provider of data and password protection and
data compliance solutions. The company offers
services to businesses.

**OJO Technology Inc**      HQ
103 Hammond Ave
Fremont CA 94539
P: 877-306-4656      PRC:64
www.ojotech.com
Email: sales@ojotech.com
Estab: 2003

Derek Tokuda, Wireless Network Engineer
Angie Wong, CEO
Lai Wong, Project Manager
Bob Bisetti, Security Solutions Advisor

Manufacturer of video surveillance systems. The
company offers services to the education, transportation, and utility sectors.

**Okta Inc**　　　　　　　　　　　　HQ
301 Brannan St Fl 3
San Francisco CA 94107
P: 888-722-7871　　　　　　　　　PRC:322
okta.com
Email: info@okta.com
Estab: 2009
Sales: $300M to $1 Billion

Greg Salmon, VP of Software Engineering
Adam Landry, Principal Engineer
Hoa Nguyen, Staff Software Engineer
Frederic Kerrest, Executive Vice Chairperson
Todd McKinnon, CEO

Provider of identity and automated user management, administration, reporting, and application integration solutions.

**Olixir Technologies**　　　　　　　HQ
1525 McCarthy Blvd
Milpitas CA 95035
P: 408-719-0595　　　　　　　　　PRC:116
www.olixir.com
Email: sales@olixir.com
Estab: 2001

Andrae Browne, Web Developer

Provider of external hard drives and racks & towers. The company also offers video surveillance and backup solutions.

**Ologic**　　　　　　　　　　　　　HQ
3350 Scott Blvd Bldg 47
Santa Clara CA 95054
P: 408-663-6638　　　　　　　　　PRC:311
www.ologicinc.com
Email: info@ologicinc.com

Robert Garbanati, Robotics Engineer
Ted Larson, CEO
Brandon Blodget, VP of Technology Development

Manufacturer of consumer electronics and toy products. The company specializes in defense and educational projects.

**Omega Diamond Inc**　　　　　　　HQ
10125 Ophir Rd
Newcastle CA 95658-9504
P: 530-889-8977　F: 530-885-3785　PRC:80
omegadiamond.com
Emp: 1-10　Estab: 1985

Sam Devai, CEO
Roneily Devai, Office Manager

Developer and manufacturer of diamond tools for the ultra precise semiconductor and optics industry. The company also offers power tools.

**Oml Inc**　　　　　　　　　　　　HQ
300 Digital Dr
Morgan Hill CA 95037
P: 408-779-2698　F: 408-778-0491　PRC:65
www.omlinc.com
Email: info@omlinc.com
Estab: 1991

Yuenie Lau, President

Provider of millimeter wave test instruments, calibration equipment and systems for radio astronomy, communication, imaging, and other sectors.

**Omni Fab**　　　　　　　　　　　HQ
380 Martin Ave Ste 3
Santa Clara CA 95050
P: 408-492-1331　F: 408-492-1333　PRC:80
www.omnifab.com
Email: info@omnifab.com
Estab: 1977

Bruce Sunseri, Owner

Provider of precision sheet metal fabrication services. The company caters to the high technology industry.

**Omni Pro Systems**　　　　　　　HQ
50 Mendell St Ste 2
San Francisco CA 94124
P: 415-648-1121　F: 415-648-1174　PRC:92
www.omnipro.com
Email: info@omnipro.com

Edward Meyer, Sales Manager

Supplier and integrator of computer systems. The company offers custom logo engraving services and deployment ready solutions.

**Omnicia Inc**　　　　　　　　　　HQ
400 Oyster Point Blvd Ste 311
S San Francisco CA 94080-1904
P: 650-588-2188　F: 650-588-2488　PRC:320
www.omniciainc.com
Email: info@omniciainc.com
Estab: 2001

Peachy Dimanlig, COO

Provider of electronic submissions for the life science sector. The company offers electronics & desktop publishing and document management services.

**Omnicor**　　　　　　　　　　　HQ
1170 Foster City Blvd Ste 314
Foster City CA 94404
P: 650-572-0122　F: 650-572-0533　PRC:97
www.omnicor.com
Email: info@omnicor.com

Cathy Bianchi, Office Manager
Roman Porenta, Manager

Provider of network testing tools, vacuum capacitors, and interrupters and IP performance test systems.

**Omnivision Technologies Inc**　　　HQ
4275 Burton Dr
Santa Clara CA 95054
P: 408-567-3000　F: 408-567-3001　PRC:87
www.ovt.com
Email: info@ovt.com
Estab: 1995

Howard Rhodes, VP of Process Engineering
Kevin Wilkinson, Engineering Manager
Yuguo Ye, Senior Staff ASIC Design Engineer
He Li, Algorithm Engineer
Henry Yang, President

Developer of digital imaging solutions for consumer and commercial applications, and automotive, medical, and security imaging sectors.

**Omniyig Inc**　　　　　　　　　　HQ
3350 Scott Blvd Bldg 66
Santa Clara CA 95054
P: 408-988-0843　　　　　　　　　PRC:70
Estab: 1973

Tuan Ly, RF Design Engineer Manager
Elaine Capogeannis, Sales Manager
Michaela Nieblas, Contracts Manager

Manufacturer of microwave devices for the defense industry. The company also offers limiters, drivers, and oscillators.

**OMW Corp**　　　　　　　　　　HQ
354 Bel Marin Keys Blvd
Novato CA 94949
P: 415-382-1669　F: 415-382-9069　PRC:80
www.omwcorp.com
Email: rfq@omwcorp.com
Estab: 1996

Joe Osborn, Founder
Geno Adoline, General Manager
Matt Warr, Quality Assurance Manager

Manufacturer of CNC machined parts. The company also deals with production machining, prototyping, and support services.

**On Semiconductor**　　　　　　　BR
2975 Stender Way
Santa Clara CA 95054
P: 408-542-1104　　　　　　　　　PRC:212
www.onsemi.com
Email: quality@onsemi.com
Emp: 1001-5000
Sales: Under $1 Million

Douglas Lee, Applications Engineer

Supplier of semiconductor products and solutions. The company's products find application in green electronics.

**Onanon Inc**　　　　　　　　　　HQ
720 S Milpitas Blvd
Milpitas CA 95035
P: 408-262-8990　　　　　　　　　PRC:76
www.onanon.com
Estab: 1979

Billy Glass, Senior Sales Engineer
Dennis Johnson, CEO
Shiba Henderson, Product Development Manager

Manufacturer of connector components. The company offers pin connectors, cable assemblies, and machined plastics.

**Onchip Devices Inc**　　　　　　　HQ
3054 Scott Blvd
Santa Clara CA 95054
P: 408-654-9365　　　　　　　　　PRC:126
onchip.com
Email: sales@onchip.com
Estab: 2007

Ashok Chalaka, President
Swamy Venkidu, Chairman

Provider of silicon and ceramic solutions and integrated passive devices for the computing and consumer electronics industries.

**Oncomed Pharmaceuticals Inc** HQ
800 Chesapeake Dr
Redwood City CA 94063
P: 650-995-8200   F: 650-995-8600   PRC:252
www.oncomed.com
Email: info@oncomed.com
Emp: 22   Estab: 2004
Sales: $30M to $100M

John Lewicki, President
Yvonne Li, VP of Finance
Maria Houten, Finance Manager
Robert Stagg, SVP of Clinical Research & Development
Jonathan Root, General Partner

Focuses on the cancer treatment by discovering and developing monoclonal antibodies and other agents.

**Onda Corp** HQ
1290 Hammerwood Ave
Sunnyvale CA 94089
P: 408-745-0383   F: 408-745-0956   PRC:186
www.ondacorp.com
Email: info@ondacorp.com
Estab: 1990

Alfred Yue, Sales Engineer
Claudio Zanelli, Founder

Manufacturer of medical devices. The company offers ultrasound measurement instrumentation and services for scientific applications.

**Ondavia Inc** HQ
26102 Eden Landing Rd Ste 1
Hayward CA 94545
P: 510-576-0476   F: 510-887-3180   PRC:138
www.ondavia.com
Email: info@ondavia.com
Estab: 2009

Merwan Benhabib, VP of Engineering
Mark Peterman, CEO

Provider of water analysis solutions. The company offers OndaVia analysis system that enables laboratory-grade water testing.

**One Touch Systems** HQ
2528 Qume Dr Unit 14
San Jose CA 95131
P: 408-660-8435   PRC:326
www.onetouchsys.com
Email: info@onetouchsys.com
Estab: 1989

Gopinath Rebala, VP of Software Engineering
Larry Speckels, President
Bob Wilkinson, VP

Provider of virtual distance learning, training and communication systems. The company offers services to the educational sector.

**OneLogin** HQ
848 Battery St
San Francisco CA 94111
P: 415-645-6830   PRC:325
www.onelogin.com
Email: press@onelogin.com
Estab: 2009

Bob Dickinson, VP of Engineering
Ron Craswell, Senior Director of Engineering
Blake Ramsdell, Senior Director of Engineering
Thomas Pedersen, Founder
Christian Pedersen, Chief Architect

M-214

Provider of single sign-on and identity management for cloud-based applications. The company serves the industrial sector.

**Oneto Metal Products Corp** HQ
7485 Reese Rd
Sacramento CA 95828
P: 916-681-6555   F: 916-681-6565   PRC:88
www.onetometal.com
Emp: 1-10   Estab: 1988

Raymond Liberatore, President
Joe Liberatore, Controller
Paul Liberatore, Manager
Frank Yearsley, Manager
Catherine Liberatore, Controller

Manufacturer of fabricated sheet metal products. The company offers flashing, roof jacks, gravel stop and specialty architectural sheet metal.

**Onfulfillment Inc** HQ
8678 Thornton Ave
Newark CA 94560
P: 510-793-3009   PRC:325
www1.onfulfillment.com
Email: info@onfulfillment.com
Estab: 1999

Steve Friar, Founder
Dan Barnett, VP
Juan Rosales, Manufacturing Manager
Marvi Bajet, IT Program Manager
Carolyn Lajoie, Customer Service Manager

Provider of printing solutions. The company offers order fulfillment, online delivery, and print management services.

**Onque Technologies Inc** HQ
281 Second St E
Sonoma CA 95476
P: 707-569-3000   PRC:320
www.onque.com
Email: sales@onque.com
Estab: 1997

Bret Andrews, President

Provider of software tools used for the management of human resources. The company serves business organizations and enterprises.

**Onspec Electronic Inc** HQ
1111 Comstock St
Santa Clara CA 95054
P: 408-727-1819   F: 408-727-2219   PRC:94
www.onspecinc.com
Email: sales@onspecinc.com
Estab: 1990

Arockiyaswamy Venkidu, President

Provider of semiconductor and electronic devices. The company focuses on data transfer services using USB and also provides technical support.

**Onyx Optics Inc** HQ
6551 Sierra Ln
Dublin CA 94568
P: 925-833-1969   F: 925-833-1759   PRC:172
www.onyxoptics.com
Email: sales@onyxoptics.com
Estab: 1992

Huai-Chuan Lee, Senior Optical Engineer
Da Li, Electro-Optics Scientist
Stephanie Meissner, President
Helmuth Meissner, President
Dave Meissner, Production Supervisor

Manufacturer of laser and telecom composite crystals and glasses. The company also offers products for optical finishing and other needs.

**Oomnitza** HQ
393 Tehama St
San Francisco CA 94103
P: 650-417-3694   PRC:323
www.oomnitza.com
Email: team@oomnitza.com
Estab: 2012

Arthur Lozinski, Co-Founder

Provider of information technology asset management and related services. The company focuses on third party solutions.

**Opac Consulting Engineers Inc** HQ
315 Bay St Fl 2
San Francisco CA 94133
P: 415-989-4551   F: 415-989-4135   PRC:304
www.opacengineers.com
Estab: 1992

Kwong Cheng, President
Mark Ketchum, VP
Francis Drouillard, Principal
Vivian Chang, Principal

Provider of bridge and structural engineering services. The company's services are design, evaluation, and construction engineering.

**Opal Soft Inc** HQ
1288 Kifer Rd Ste 201
Sunnyvale CA 94086
P: 408-267-2211   F: 408-774-1451   PRC:68
www.opalsoft.com
Estab: 1997

Sharad Sharma, Director of Business Development
Kaarlo Heiskanen, Solution Architect

Provider of communications equipment installation and networking. The company's services include application development, network management, and maintenance.

**Open-Silicon Inc** HQ
490 N Mccarthy Blvd Ste 220
Milpitas CA 95035-5118
P: 408-240-5700   F: 408-240-5701   PRC:207
www.open-silicon.com
Estab: 2003

Yunsup Lee, Co-Founder
Stuart Ching, Chief Revenue Officer
Steve Wong, Senior Product Engineering Manager

Provider of IP, foundry, test, and packaging technologies. The company's services include system design, manufacturing, and program management.

**Openclovis** HQ
765 Baywood Dr Ste 336
Petaluma CA 94954-5507
P: 707-981-7120   PRC:322
www.openclovis.com
Email: sales@openclovis.com
Estab: 2002

V.K. Budhraja, CEO

Provider of system infrastructure software platform. The company mainly serves the communication industry.

**Opengov Inc** HQ
955 Charter St
Redwood City CA 94063
P: 650-336-7167 PRC:325
opengov.com
Estab: 2012

John Conley, Software Engineer
Nate Levine, Co-Founder
Joe Lonsdale, Co-Founder
Zac Bookman, Co-Founder
David Reeves, Chief Revenue Officer

Provider of financial transparency and business intelligence solutions. The company offers services to government agencies.

**OpensourceCM** HQ
1098 Foster City Blvd Ste 106-725
Foster City CA 94404
P: 650-200-0506 F: 650-345-2098 PRC:323
www.opensourceinc.com
Email: info@opensourceinc.com
Estab: 1995

Zvi Margalit, CEO
Nathan Brand, CTO

Designer and developer of contract management software. The company also offers technical support services.

**Openvpn Technologies Inc** HQ
7901 Stoneridge Dr Ste 540
Pleasanton CA 94588
P: 925-399-1481 PRC:323
openvpn.net
Email: info@openvpn.net
Estab: 2002

Elfredy Cadapan, Head of Engineering
Farhan Haq, Senior Software Engineer
Francis Dinha, Co-Founder
James Yonan, Co-Founder

Specializes in deploying VPN access solutions. The company is engaged in marketing and communication services.

**Openwave Mobility Inc** DH
400 Seaport Ct Ste 104
Redwood City CA 94063
P: 650-480-7200 PRC:322
owmobility.com
Email: info@owmobility.com

John Giere, President
Indranil Chatterjee, VP of Products Sales & Marketing

Provider of mobile media optimization solutions. The company is engaged in the mediation of encrypted traffic streams.

**Opinionmeter International** HQ
14727 Catalina St
San Leandro CA 94577
P: 510-352-4943 F: 510-352-4982 PRC:317
opinionmeter.com
Email: sales@opinionmeter.com
Estab: 1994

Russ Pow, Chief Support Engineer

Designer and developer of mobile research software. The company serves the healthcare, hospitality, and education sectors.

**Oplink Communications Inc** HQ
46335 Landing Pkwy
Fremont CA 94538
P: 510-933-7200 F: 510-933-7300 PRC:170
www.oplink.com
Email: info@oplink.com
Estab: 1995

Longzan Chen, Testing Engineer
Shawn Lin, VP of Marketing
Michael Cheng, Senior Manager of PLM
Li Chen, Pilot Line Manager

Provider of comprehensive networking components. The company offers products for amplification, interconnection, routing, and other needs.

**Oppo Digital Inc** HQ
162 Constitution Dr
Menlo Park CA 94025
P: 650-961-1118 F: 650-961-1119 PRC:110
www.oppodigital.com
Email: service@oppodigital.com

Nan Yang, Product Manager

Manufacturer of Blu-ray players and UP converting DVD players. The company's services include design, installation, and delivery.

**Opsol Integrators Inc** HQ
1566 La Pradera Dr
Campbell CA 95008
P: 408-364-9915 F: 408-364-9916 PRC:326
www.opsol.com
Email: support@omnipayments.com
Estab: 1995

Yash Kapadia, CEO
Tojo Vilson, Principal Consultant
Rahul Gorse, Software Developer

Provider of universal messaging, data integration, and encryption products. The company serves banks, retail, telecom, and other sectors.

**Opswat Inc** HQ
398 Kansas St
San Francisco CA 94103
P: 415-590-7300 F: 415-590-7399 PRC:323
www.opswat.com
Estab: 2002

Benny Czarny, President
Mike Spykerman, VP of Product Management
Tom Mullen, SVP of Business Development

Provider of end-point software management, compliance, URL filtering, network monitoring, and related solutions.

**Optical Structures Inc** HQ
11371 Pyrites Way Ste A
Rancho Cordova CA 95670
P: 916-638-2003 F: 916-671-5669 PRC:176
www.opticalstructures.com
Emp: 1-10 Estab: 2006

Cary Chleborad, President

Provider of optical systems and services. The company's products find application in research and education sectors.

**Optimal Synthesis Inc** HQ
95 First St Ste 240
Los Altos CA 94022
P: 650-559-8585 F: 650-559-8586 PRC:322
www.optisyn.com
Email: engineers@optisyn.com
Estab: 1992

Jason Kwan, Research Engineer
Vicky Lu, Director of Signal Processing Technologies
Parikshit Dutta, Research Scientist

Provider of research, algorithm development, and software design services. The company caters to a variety of engineering and science applications.

**Optimum Design Associates** HQ
1075 Serpentine Ln
Pleasanton CA 94566
P: 925-401-2004 F: 925-401-2010 PRC:211
www.optimumdesign.com
Email: sales@optimumdesign.com
Estab: 1990

J. Reed, Engineering Manager
Roger Hileman, CFO
Sherrie Hubbard, Director of Business Development
Brendon Parise, Senior Design Manager
Scott Nance, Senior PCB Designer

Provider of printed circuit board design and layout services. The company also focuses on engineering and manufacturing services.

**Optimum Processing Inc** HQ
55 Mitchell Blvd Ste 23
San Rafael CA 94903
P: 415-461-7033 PRC:268
opibioprocess.com
Email: info@opibioprocess.com
Estab: 1988

Peter Florez, Owner

Provider of filtration solutions and disposable bioprocess container systems. The company utilizes asymmetric morphology solutions.

**Optiscan Biomedical Corp** HQ
24590 Clawiter Rd
Hayward CA 94545
P: 510-342-5800 PRC:187
www.optiscancorp.com
Email: info@optiscancorp.com
Estab: 1994

Cary Vance, CEO
Patrick Nugent, CFO
Chip Zimliki, VP of Regulatory
Jim Causey, VP of Innovation
Mario Cervantes, VP of Operations

Provider of monitoring products for measuring glucose, plasma collection, and also detection of glucose among patients.

**Optiworks Inc** HQ
47211 Bayside Pkwy
Fremont CA 94538
P: 510-438-4560  F: 510-252-1178  PRC:170
www.optiworks.com
Email: sales@optiworks.com
Estab: 2000

Ma Yanyan, Sales Manager

Manufacturer of fiber optic components. The company's products include thin film filters, fused components, sub components, and accessories.

**Optoelectronix Inc** HQ
111 W Saint John St Ste 588
San Jose CA 95113
P: 408-241-1222  PRC:243
www.optoelectronix.com
Email: corp@optoelectronix.com
Estab: 2006

George Martin, VP of Engineering and IP Services
Chuck Berghoff, CEO
Nelda Pawan, Operations & Finance Manager
Jim Schenck, VP of Sales
Tom Thayer, SVP of Marketing and Business Development

Designer, developer, and manufacturer of plug-and-play and standardized LED-based landscape lighting and engines.

**Optoplex Corporation** HQ
48500 Kato Rd
Fremont CA 94538
P: 510-490-9930  F: 510-490-9330  PRC:62
www.optoplex.com
Email: info@optoplex.com
Estab: 2000

Vincent Chien, VP of Engineering
Tim Ngo, Optical Engineer
Carol Wu, Human Resource Manager
Lisa Cao, Accounting Manager
Nancy Guo, Document Control Specialist

Supplier of cutting-edge photonic components and modules for dynamic wavelength management and signal conditioning.

**Optovue Inc** HQ
2800 Bayview Dr
Fremont CA 94538
P: 510-743-0985  F: 510-623-8668  PRC:186
www.optovue.com
Email: info@optovue.com
Estab: 2003

David Chen, Senior Engineering Manager
Fang Guo, Senior Software Engineer
Jay Wei, CEO
David Voris, President
Marshall Coppage, VP of Supply Chain and Production

Manufacturer of ophthalmic devices. The company leads the commercialization of new imaging modalities to develop ophthalmic diagnosis.

**Optowaves Inc** HQ
6830 Via Del Oro Ste 200
San Jose CA 95119
P: 408-724-5888  F: 408-724-5889  PRC:170
www.optowaves.com
Estab: 2001

Jeffery Hsu, Project Manager

Manufacturer and supplier of passive fiber optic components, attenuator, coupler, and isolator for the medical and communication industries.

**Optumsoft Inc** HQ
200 Middlefield Rd Ste 112
Menlo Park CA 94025
P: 844-361-8222  PRC:319
optumsoft.com
Email: info@optumsoft.com

Xi Cheng, Software Engineer
David Cheriton, Founder
Fusun Ertemalp, President

Provider of distributed computing and technology based software development that includes maintenance of structured software systems.

**Oracle Corp** BR
475 Sansome St Fl 15
San Francisco CA 94111
P: 415-402-7200  F: 415-402-7250  PRC:322
www.oracle.com
Estab: 1977

Anil Gaur, VP of Engineering
Dave Stowell, VP of Engineering
Rohit Koul, Principal Engineer
Thomas Kurian, President of Product Development
Safra Catz, CEO

Developer of hardware and software systems. The company provides Oracle database, engineered systems, and enterprise manager solutions.

**Orange Enterprises Inc** HQ
2377 W Shaw
Fresno CA 93711
P: 559-229-2195  F: 559-229-9348  PRC:323
tigerjill.com
Email: support@orangesoftware.com
Emp: 1-10  Estab: 1984

Udi Sosnik, Owner
Shlomo Pleban, Research & Development Director

Provider of software solutions. The company mainly focuses on payroll tracking and agriculture management.

**Orbeon Inc** HQ
3941 Pasadena Dr
San Mateo CA 94403
P: 650-762-8184  PRC:322
www.orbeon.com
Email: info@orbeon.com
Estab: 1999

Erik Bruchez, Software Architect
Alessandro Vernet, Software Architect

Provider of web form deployment services. The company offers basic, gold, and platinum development support, and validation services.

**Orbex Group** HQ
46740 Lakeview Blvd
Fremont CA 94538
P: 408-945-8980  PRC:62
orbexgroup.com

Donna Sisk, Office Manager

Manufacturer of electronic rings. The company offers capsule slip rings, through-hole slip rings, and harsh environment slip rings.

**Orbotech LT Solar LLC** BR
5970 Optical Ct
San Jose CA 95138
P: 408-226-9900  F: 408-226-9910  PRC:209
www.orbotech.com
Estab: 1981

Tom Bailey, Director of Engineering
George Williams, Lead Software Quality Assurance Engineer
Eitan Judah, Corporate VP
Kevin Crofton, Corporate EVP
Yair Alcobi, Corporate VP

Manufacturer of electronic devices. The company offers printed circuit boards, flat panel displays, and touch screens.

**Orbus Therapeutics Inc** HQ
2479 E Bayshore Rd Ste 105
Palo Alto CA 94303
P: 650-656-9440  PRC:268
www.orbustherapeutics.com
Estab: 2012

Bob Myers, CEO
Jason Levin, COO
Noymi Yam, Head of Product Development

Developer of therapeutic products to treat rare disease such as anaplastic astrocytoma.

**Orchard Machinery Corp** HQ
2700 Colusa Hwy
Yuba City CA 95993
P: 530-673-2822  F: 530-673-0296  PRC:159
shakermaker.com
Emp: 1-10  Estab: 1961

Don Mayo, President
Denise Mayo, Human Resources Manager
Rodney Mayfield, Purchasing Manager
John Krum, Territory Sales Manager
Brian Andersen, VP of Research & Development

Manufacturer of tree shakers and material handling systems comprising shuttles, bin carriers, conveyor carts, and elevators.

**Ordinal Technology Corp** HQ
20 Crestview Dr
Orinda CA 94563
P: 925-253-9204  F: 925-253-8502  PRC:324
www.ordinal.com
Email: enquiries@ordinal.com
Estab: 1994

Chris Nyberg, Founder

Provider of sorting services of massive and production data sets such as web logs for high-traffic web sites, phone logs, and government agency data.

**Organic Inc**    HQ
600 California St 7th Fl
San Francisco CA 94108
P: 415-581-5300   F: 415-581-5400    PRC:322
organic.com

David Shulman, CEO

Provider of information technology services. The company develops websites, mobile applications, banner, and digital signage.

**ORIC Pharmaceuticals Inc**    HQ
240 E Grand Ave 2nd Fl
S San Francisco CA 94080
P: 650-388-5600    PRC:268
oricpharma.com
Email: info@oricpharma.com

Jacob Chacko, CEO
Lori Friedman, CSO
Dominic Piscitelli, CFO
Matthew Panuwat, Chief Business Officer
Valeria Fantin, CSO

Provider of pharmaceutical research. The company specializes in discovering and developing novel therapies for treatment-resistant cancers.

**Oriental Motor USA Corp**    DH
570 Alaska Ave
Torrance CA 90503
P: 408-392-9735    PRC:146
orientalmotor.com
Emp: 11-50

Kimberly Freisheim, Human Resource Manager

Provider of optimal motion systems. The company focuses on producing fractional horsepower products for motion control applications.

**Originate Inc**    DH
580 Market St
San Francisco CA 94104
P: 800-352-2292    PRC:322
www.originate.com
Email: hello@originate.com
Estab: 2007

Sasi Parthasarathy, Founder
Darrell Mervau, President
Rob Meadows, CEO
Shahar Hador, CIO

Developer of software to integrate, network, and economically operate energy storage systems. The company is engaged in analysis services.

**Orion Labs**    HQ
208 Utah St Ste 350
San Francisco CA 94103
P: 415-800-2035   F: 415-800-2035    PRC:64
www.orionlabs.io
Email: info@orionlabs.io
Estab: 2013

Bryan Kiechle, Quality Engineer
Jamirsen Ezell, Firmware Engineer
Greg Albrecht, Founder
Jesse Robbins, CEO
Jessie Sheng, Head of Supply Chain & Production Operations

Developer of wearable communication accessory for instant voice conversations with many people, across any distance.

**Orion Wine Software**    HQ
2455 Bennett Valley Rd Ste C208
Santa Rosa CA 95404
P: 877-632-3155   F: 707-545-5298    PRC:323
orionwinesoftware.com
Email: info@orionwinesw.com
Estab: 2007

Jason Curtis, Director of Product Development

Developer of winery management solutions. The company is also engaged in sales and inventory management.

**Ortho Group**    HQ
11431 Sunrise Gold Cir Ste B
Rancho Cordova CA 95742
P: 916-859-0881    PRC:190
www.orthogroup.com
Email: info@orthogroup.com
Emp: 1-10   Estab: 2003

Henry Fletcher, CEO

Designer of devices for the medical industry. The company specializes in orthopedic surgical devices.

**OrthoCyte Corp**    HQ
1010 Atlantic Ave Ste 102
Alameda CA 94501
P: 510-775-0451    PRC:36
orthocyte.com
Email: info@orthocyte.com
Estab: 2010

Michael West, CEO
Francois Binette, Head of Global Development

Developer of biotechnology products. The company specializes in cell-based therapies for bone and orthopedic soft tissue diseases and injuries.

**OrthoTrophix Inc**    HQ
303 Hegenberger Rd Ste 312
Oakland CA 94621
P: 510-488-3832   F: 510-567-8785    PRC:191
www.orthotrophix.com
Email: info@orthotrophix.com
Estab: 2011

Yoshi Kumagai, President
David Rosen, CSO
Dawn McGuire, CMO
Meghan Miller, Senior CRA Project Lead

Developer of therapies for medical needs of patients. The company specializes in regeneration of articular cartilage in knee and other joints.

**Oryx Advanced Materials Inc**    HQ
46458 Fremont Blvd
Fremont CA 94538
P: 510-249-1157   F: 510-249-2008    PRC:80
www.oryxadv.com
Email: info@oryxadv.com
Estab: 1976

Norman Mills, President

Provider of thin film materials for PV cells. The company also offers sputtering targets and bonding services to the magnetic data storage market.

**Oscar Larson & Associates**    HQ
317 Third St 2nd Fl
Eureka CA 95501
P: 707-445-2043   F: 707-445-8230    PRC:304
olarson.com
Email: larson@olarson.com
Emp: 11-50 Estab: 1945

Greg Hall, Project Engineer
Tyler Duncan, Engineering Technician

Provider of environmental planning, permitting, and related services and it specializes in residential and commercial projects.

**Osel Inc**    HQ
320 Logue Ave
Mountain View CA 94043
P: 650-964-1420   F: 650-964-4679    PRC:34
www.oselinc.com
Email: info@oselinc.com

Peter Lee, Founder
Laurel Lagenaur, Director of Research
Tom Parks, Director of Product Development
Michael Cannon, Board Member
Sandy Chau, Board Member

Developer of biotherapeutic products. The company focuses on treatment and prevention of conditions for women's health and infectious diseases.

**Osisoft LLC**    HQ
1600 Alvarado St
San Leandro CA 94577
P: 510-297-5800   F: 510-357-8136    PRC:323
www.osisoft.com
Email: customerservice@osisoft.com
Estab: 1980

Ray Hall, VP of Engineering
Ray Verhoeff, Director of Engineering
Brian Bostwick, Director of Engineering
J. Kennedy, Founder
Jenny Linton, President

Developer of PI system software. The company offers software such as PI Computing Engine, Batch, Data Access, and Clients.

**Otrs Inc**    BR
19925 Stevens Creek Blvd
Cupertino CA 95014-2358
P: 408-549-1717   F: 408-512-1748    PRC:323
www.otrs.com
Email: sales@otrs.com
Estab: 2003

Andr' Mindermann, CEO
Christopher Kuhn, COO

Focuses on business solutions. The company offers services to the hospitality, education, and financial sectors.

**Otsuka America Inc**    HQ
1 Embarcadero Ctr Ste 2020
San Francisco CA 94111
P: 415-986-5300   F: 415-986-5361    PRC:261
www.otsuka-america.com

Mike Gehrke, VP of Internal Audit & Administration

Developer of pharmaceutical products for the treatment of central nervous system, ophthalmology, cardiovascular, and skin conditions.

**Outformations Inc**  HQ
939 61st St Ste 13
Oakland CA 94608-1304
P: 510-655-7122
outformations.com  PRC:326
Email: info@outformations.com
Estab: 1989

David Chilcott, President
Jill Kaplan, Office Manager
Don Robins, Principal
Eric Babinet, Business Consultant

Provider of consulting, application development, programming, technical support, and design services.

**Outset Medical**  HQ
1830 Bering Dr
San Jose CA 95112
P: 669-231-8200  PRC:186
outsetmedical.com
Email: info@outsetmedical.com
Estab: 2010

Stuart Kao, Principal Quality Engineer
Chetna Priyadarshini, Mobile Software Engineer
Gopi Lingam, Staff Engineer
Leslie Trigg, CEO
Jeff Mack, CFO

Developer of hemodialysis systems. The company offers services to patients, families, providers and physicians.

**Outside Technology**  HQ
PO Box 685
San Anselmo CA 94979
P: 415-488-4909  PRC:322
www.outsidetech.com
Email: support@outsidetech.com

Dan Katz, Owner

Provider of automated reservation systems. The company mainly caters to the outdoor recreation industry.

**Overland Storage Inc**  BR
125 S Market St
San Jose CA 95113
P: 408-283-4700  F: 408-283-4701  PRC:324
www.overlandstorage.com
Email: sales@overlandstorage.com

Mark Grimes, Director of Software Engineering
Henry Norton, Senior Solutions Engineer
Eric Kelly, Chairman
Kurt Kalbfleisch, SVP
Craig Burney, Document Control Manager

Provider of data management and protection solutions. The company offers network attached storage, virtual tape libraries, LTO drives, and software.

**Owens Design**  HQ
47427 Fremont Blvd
Fremont CA 94538
P: 510-659-1800  F: 510-659-1896  PRC:86
www.owensdesign.com
Email: sales@owensdesign.com
Estab: 1982

Paul Shufflebotham, VP of Engineering
Stephen Chu, Electrical Engineer
Thomas Owens, Owner
Bob Fung, President
John Apgar, President

Developer of advanced technology systems for semiconductor, hard disk drive, solar, medical device, and other sectors.

**Owler Inc**  HQ
800 S Claremont St Ste 203
San Mateo CA 94402
P: 650-242-9253  PRC:325
owler.com
Email: support@owler.com
Estab: 2011

John Duffy, Head of Engineering
Tim Harsch, Co-Founder
Stephanie Vinella, CFO
Gretchen Vagharshakian, Head of Marketing
Dhruv Gupta, Head of Product Development

Provider of reliable and up-to-date business information.

**Oxigraf Inc**  HQ
238 E Caribbean Dr
Sunnyvale CA 94089
P: 650-237-0155  F: 650-237-0159  PRC:172
www.oxigraf.com
Email: sales@oxigraf.com
Estab: 1990

Jason Hoang, Test Engineer
Bruce McCaul, Owner
Xing Chao, Chief Scientist

Supplier of oxygen analyzers & oxygen gas concentration measurement products. The company offers laser diode oxygen analyzers and OEM oxygen sensors.

**Ozotech Inc**  HQ
2401 E Oberlin Rd
Yreka CA 96097
P: 530-842-4189  PRC:144
www.ozotech.com
Email: ozotech@ozotech.com
Emp: 1-10  Estab: 1986

Nick Rouhier, General Manager
Lance Vogel, Sales Tech

Provider of water purification solutions. The company offers products such as bolted water systems, oxygen concentrators, air dries, and generators.

**P&L Specialties**  HQ
1650 Almar Pkwy
Santa Rosa CA 95403
P: 707-573-3141  F: 707-573-3140  PRC:80
www.pnlspecialties.com
Email: sales@pnlspecialties.com
Estab: 1984

Ed Barr, President
Jeff Sommers, Production Manager
Lisa Hyde, VP
Monte Springer, Mechanical Designer

Provider of engineering and fabrication services. The company's services include waterjet cutting and harvest lug washing.

**Pac Integrations Inc**  HQ
PO Box 6008
Concord CA 94524-1008
P: 800-479-4722  F: 925-687-7662  PRC:59
www.pacintegrations.com
Email: sales@pacintegrations.com
Estab: 1982

Corey Alexander, Purchasing Manager
Mike Ganguet, Sales Manager
Jordan Scott, Sales Account Manager
Chad Custock, Service Manager
John Matthies, Customer Service Manager

Provider of security solutions. The company offers its solutions for residential, commercial, and fire and life safety applications.

**Paceco Corp**  HQ
25503 Whitesell St
Hayward CA 94545
P: 510-264-9288  F: 510-264-9280  PRC:183
pacecocorp.com
Estab: 1988

Vance Villanueva, R&D Engineer
Alan Liao, R&D Engineer
Sun Huang, General Manager

Manufacturer of equipment to handle port cargo. The company also offers terminal operating systems and crane modification services.

**Pacific Adhesives Company Inc**  HQ
8670 23rd Ave
Sacramento CA 95826
P: 916-383-1509  F: 916-383-0599  PRC:47
www.pacificadhesives.com
Email: info@pacificadhesives.com
Emp: 11-50  Estab: 1987

Snider Martinelli, President

Provider of adhesive solutions for industrial purposes. The company also offers labeling, packaging, and paper converting services.

**Pacific Biodevelopment LLC**  HQ
1900 Powell St Ste 600
Emeryville CA 94608
P: 510-858-5600  F: 510-858-5602  PRC:34
www.pacbiodev.com
Estab: 1997

Brian Rogers, Co-Founder
Jerome Moore, Co-Founder
Ira Wallis, VP of Regulatory Affairs

Provider of biotechnology services. The company offers drug development services to allow timely and cost efficient entry of drugs into the market.

**Pacific Biolabs**  HQ
551 Linus Pauling Dr
Hercules CA 94547
P: 510-964-9000  F: 510-964-0551  PRC:41
www.pacificbiolabs.com
Email: info@pacificbiolabs.com
Estab: 1982

Tom Spalding, President
Linda Guthrie, Purchasing Agent
Erik Foehr, VP
Steve Guthrie, Equipment Manager
Hilda Hernandez, Microbiologist

Provider of biological testing services. The company offers service to the pharmaceutical, biotechnology, and medical device industries.

**Pacific Biosciences Of California Inc**  HQ
1305 O'Brien Dr
Menlo Park CA 94025
P: 650-521-8000  PRC:34
www.pacb.com
Email: nasales@pacb.com
Sales: $30M to $100M

Michael Hunkapiller, President
Susan Barnes, CFO
Stephen Turner, CTO
Jonas Korlach, CSO
Michael Phillips, SVP of Research and Development

Provider of targeted sequencing, base modifications, microbiology, and isoform sequencing detection services.

**Pacific Capacitor Co**  HQ
288 Digital Dr
Morgan Hill CA 95037
P: 408-778-6670  F: 408-778-6680  PRC:203
www.pacific-capacitor.com
Email: info@pacific-capacitor.com
Estab: 1967

Mark Schiltz, Production Manager

Manufacturer of high voltage capacitors for the electronics industry. The company is engaged in sales and installation services.

**Pacific Ceramics Inc**  HQ
824 San Aleso Ave
Sunnyvale CA 94085
P: 408-747-4600  F: 408-745-6162  PRC:277
pceramics.com
Email: info@pceramics.com
Estab: 1969

Sehul Ahir, Quality Engineer
Dennis Fleming, President
Nicholas Forney, Manager Assistant
Wolfram Schmedding, Head

Manufacturer of microwave ceramic material. The company's products include earth iron garnets, calcium vanadium garnets, lithium, and titanate dielectrics.

**Pacific Coast Optics Inc**  HQ
10604 Industrial Ave Ste 100
Roseville CA 95678
P: 916-789-0111  F: 916-789-0121  PRC:159
pcoptics.com
Emp: 1-10

Shannon Rogers, President
Ignacio Ruvalcaba, Manager of Coatings

Provider of optical products, services and applications. The company offers prototype, polishing, grinding, and coating.

**Pacific Crest**  HQ
510 DeGuigne Dr
Sunnyvale CA 94085
P: 408-481-8070  F: 408-481-8984  PRC:64
www.pacificcrest.com
Email: info@pacificcrest.com
Estab: 1994

John Cameron, General Manager

Provider of communication solutions. The company specializes in the design and manufacture of radio controlled and spotlight data transfer systems.

**Pacific Die Cut Industries**  HQ
3399 Arden Rd
Hayward CA 94545-3924
P: 510-732-8103  F: 510-732-9073  PRC:163
www.pacificdiecut.com
Email: sales@pacificdiecut.com
Estab: 1989

Allen Yim, Tooling
Olatokunbo Aiyegbusi, Quality Engineer
Mike Behnam, President
Rosemarie Costa, Purchasing Assistant
Gin Chang, Business Development Manager

Provider of custom converting services that include die cutting, laminating, and slitting. The company also offers packaging solutions.

**Pacific Ethanol Inc**  HQ
400 Capitol Mall Ste 2060
Sacramento CA 95814
P: 916-403-2123  F: 916-446-3937  PRC:53
www.pacificethanol.com
Email: info@pacificethanol.com
Emp: 510  Estab: 2005
Sales: $1B to $3B

Neil Koehler, CEO
Bryon McGregor, CFO
Michael Kandris, COO
Ed Baker, Director of Human Resources
Rebecca Guaraglia, Finance Manager

Producer and marketer of carbonated fuel and corn oil. The company's services include ethanol sales and distribution.

**Pacific Gas & Electric Co**  BR
77 Beale St
San Francisco CA 94177
P: 800-743-5000  F: 415-973-3582  PRC:130
www.pge.com

Linda Rodriguez, Senior Project Manager
John Storm, Senior Business Analyst

Provider of natural gas and electric services. The company serves approximately 15 million people throughout northern and central California.

**Pacific Gas & Electric Co**  BR
PO Box 997300
Sacramento CA 95899-7300
P: 800-743-5000  PRC:134
www.pge.com
Emp: 11-50 Estab: 1905

Roland Trevino, VP of Gas Engineering and Design
Andrew Vesey, CEO
James Welsch, SVP of Generation
Stephen Cairns, VP of Internal Audit
David Thomason, VP

Provider of natural gas and electric services to the areas in northern and central California. The company specializes in promoting renewable energy.

**Pacific Instruments Inc**  HQ
4080 Pike Ln
Concord CA 94520
P: 925-827-9010  F: 925-827-9023  PRC:68
www.pacificinstruments.com
Email: sales@pacificinstruments.com
Estab: 1991

Moiz Balkhi, Owner
Patrick Rule, Sales Manager
Morgan Butay, Sales

Manufacturer of computer-automated physical measurement systems. The company specializes in signal conditioning & data acquisition equipment.

**Pacific Ozone Technology Inc**  HQ
6160 Egret Ct
Benicia CA 94510
P: 707-747-9600  F: 707-747-9209  PRC:152
pacificozone.com
Email: info@pacificozone.com
Estab: 1996

Brian Johnson, Director

Supplier of air-cooled, integrated ozone and oxygen systems and packaged controls for industrial ozone applications.

**Pacific Pneumatic Tools Inc**  HQ
71 Glenn Way Ste 3
San Carlos CA 94070-6274
P: 650-592-6116  F: 650-802-9334  PRC:157
www.pacificpneumatic.com
Email: ppt@pacificpneumatic.com

Bruce Wernick, President

Manufacturer of air tools for industrial and automotive customers. The company offers wrenches, grinders, sanders, and other tools.

**Pacific Powder Coating**  HQ
8637 23rd Ave
Sacramento CA 95826
P: 916-381-1154  F: 916-381-2811  PRC:80
www.pacpowder.com
Emp: 1-10  Estab: 1987

Jeff Rochester, President
Jolene Mark, Shipping

Provider of electrostatic powder coating and metal fabrication services. The company focuses on sandblasting & silkscreening services, and logistics.

**Pacific Precision Machine Inc**  HQ
21109 Longeway Rd Ste A
Sonora CA 95370
P: 209-588-9664  F: 209-588-9666  PRC:80
www.pacpre.com
Email: ppm@pacpre.com
Emp: 1-10  Estab: 1984

Thomas Pellarin, President
Linda Pellarin, Secretary

Provider of precision machining solutions. The company offers CNC turning and milling, procurement and assembly, and computer programming services.

**Pacific Roller Die Company Inc**     HQ
1321 W Winton Ave
Hayward CA 94545
P: 510-782-7242   F: 510-887-5639     PRC:159
www.prdcompany.com
Email: prdsales@prdcompany.com
Estab: 1961

Garrett Gersten, Senior Mechanical Engineer
June Miller, Project Manager

Designer and manufacturer of corrugated metal
pipes, coated and lined pipes, and duct products.
The company offers installation and delivery
services.

**Pacific Rubber & Packing Inc**     HQ
1160 Industrial Rd Ste 3
San Carlos CA 94070
P: 650-595-5888   F: 650-591-8002     PRC:84
www.pacificrubber.com
Estab: 1979

Ashley Burfield, Owner
John Farcich, VP

Provider of rubber seals, custom seals, rubber
gaskets and o-ring products for medical/phar-
macy, automotive, solar energy, and general
industries.

**Pacific Scientific Energetic Materials
Co (California) Inc**     HQ
3601 Union Rd
Hollister CA 95023
P: 831-637-3731     PRC:4
www.psemc.com
Emp: 1-10   Estab: 1975

Gary Churchman, Contracts Manager

Provider of energetic materials and services. The
company offers services to the aircraft, missiles,
space, and law enforcement industries.

**Pacific States Felt & MFG Company
Inc**     HQ
23850 Clawiter Rd Ste 20
Hayward CA 94545
P: 510-783-0277   F: 510-783-4725     PRC:162
www.pacificstatesfelt.net
Email: sales@pacificstatesfelt.net

Robert Perscheid, General Manager

Manufacturer of gaskets, seals, washers, pads,
and molded bumpers. The company is engaged in
lamination and fabrication.

**Packaging Aids Corp**     HQ
25 Tiburon St
San Rafael CA 94901
P: 415-454-4868   F: 415-454-6853     PRC:79
www.pacmachinery.com
Email: sales@pacaids.com

Johnny Pianka, Quality Assurance Lead

Manufacturer of heat sealing and packaging
equipment such as tube sealers, shrink wrap
systems, and skin packaging products.

**Pacmold**     HQ
19707 Cabot Blvd
Hayward CA 94545
P: 510-785-9882   F: 510-785-9885     PRC:163
www.pacmold.com
Estab: 1979

Rican Yu, Manager of Sales

Designer and manufacturer of plastic injection
molds. The company has production facilities in
Taiwan and China.

**Pactech Inc**     HQ
2260 Trade Zone Blvd
San Jose CA 95131
P: 408-526-9363   F: 408-526-1233     PRC:170
www.pactech-inc.com
Email: sales@pactech-inc.com
Estab: 1994

Aaron Chui, Founder

Provider of computer cables, cooling items, and
other components. The company also offers
networking products.

**Pactron/HJPC Corp**     HQ
3000 Patrick Henry Dr
Santa Clara CA 95054
P: 408-329-5500   F: 408-747-1239     PRC:211
www.pactroninc.com
Email: info@pactroninc.com
Estab: 1988

Sanjay Singh, VP of Sales

Provider of electronics design and design development services. The company is also involved in
engineering and contract manufacturing.

**Palantir Technologies Inc**     HQ
100 Hamilton Ave Ste 300
Palo Alto CA 94301
P: 650-815-0200   F: 650-618-2298     PRC:323
www.palantir.com
Estab: 2004

Shyam Sankar, Director of Forward Deployed
Engineering
Peter Wilczynski, Product Manager
Shilpa Balaji, Engineering Manager
Spencer Rivette, Product Quality Engineer
Eric Lin, Software Engineer

Provider of software for anti fraud, cyber security,
intelligence, and other needs. The company
serves government, commercial, and non-profit
sectors.

**Palo Alto Networks Inc**     HQ
3000 Tannery Way
Santa Clara CA 95054
P: 408-753-4000   F: 408-753-4001     PRC:323
www.paloaltonetworks.com
Email: contact_sales@paloaltonetworks.com
Estab: 2005
Sales: $1B to $3B

Patrick Xu, Software Engineering Manager
Jianmin Zhang, Staff Quality Assurance Engineer
Yuming Mao, Chief Architect
Nir Zuk, Founder
Rajiv Batra, Co-Founder

Provider of network and cyber security solutions.
The company offers consulting and support, and
solution assurance services.

**Palo Alto Research Center Inc**     DH
3333 Coyote Hill Rd
Palo Alto CA 94304
P: 650-812-4000   F: 650-812-4970     PRC:207
www.parc.com
Email: parcpr@parc.com
Estab: 1970

John Maxwell, Principal Engineer of Knowledge
Kyle Dent, Senior Research Engineer
David Phillips, Systems Engineer
Mark Bernstein, CEO
David Johnson, Area Manager

Provider of custom research services and intellectual property to global Fortune 500 companies
and government agency partners.

**PalPilot International Corp**     BR
500 Yosemite Dr
Milpitas CA 95035
P: 408-855-8866   F: 408-855-8868     PRC:211
www.palpilot.com
Estab: 1988

Leland Wang, Director of Engineering
Derrick Wagner, Director of Sales
Annie Teng, Inside Sales Manager
Fred Hillis, VP of Marketing
Jimmy Young, Director

Developer of interconnect solutions. The company
offers design, engineering, and manufacturing
support services.

**Pan-International**     LH
48008 Fremont Blvd
Fremont CA 94538
P: 510-623-3898   F: 510-623-3899     PRC:202
www.panintl.com
Email: sales@panintl.com
Estab: 1989

Gina Wong, Inside Sales

Supplier of computer cables, wiring, switch boxes,
and connectors. The company is involved in design, installation, and delivery services.

**Panasas Inc**     HQ
969 W Maude Ave
Sunnyvale CA 94085
P: 408-215-6800   F: 408-215-6801     PRC:140
www.panasas.com
Email: info@panasas.com
Estab: 1999

Jorge Titinger, CEO
Faye Pairman, President
Elliot Carpenter, CFO
Tom Shea, COO
Jim Donovan, Chief Sales & Marketing Officer

Provider of scale-out NAS storage system for
most demanding workloads in life sciences,
media and entertainment, energy, and education
environments.

**Pangea Environmental Services Inc**     HQ
1250 Addison St Ste 213
Berkeley CA 94702
P: 510-836-3700   F: 510-836-3709     PRC:142
pangeaenv.com
Email: inquiry@pangeaenv.com

Bob Clark-Riddell, President

Provider of environmental consulting services. The
company's services include site assessment and
remediation, litigation support, and soil testing.

**Panorama Environmental Inc** HQ
  717 Market St Ste 650
  San Francisco CA 94103
P: 650-373-1200  F: 650-373-1211    PRC:140
panoramaenv.com
Email: info@panoramaenv.com
Estab: 1983

Laurie Hietter, Principal
Tania Treis, Principal

Provider of environmental planning services. The
company engages in regulatory permitting and
geographic information systems.

**PanTerra Networks Inc** HQ
  4655 Old Ironsides Dr Ste 300
  Santa Clara CA 95054
P: 800-805-0558  F: 408-980-9877    PRC:323
www.panterranetworks.com
Email: info@panterranetworks.com
Estab: 2001

Jeff Boucher, CFO
Jerome Friesenhahn, VP of Customer Success
Joel Stalder, Operations Manager

Provider of cloud-based communications software
solutions. The company is engaged in unified
communication and technical support.

**Pantronix Corp** HQ
  2710 Lakeview Ct
  Fremont CA 94538
P: 510-656-5898  F: 510-656-7779    PRC:209
www.pantronix.com
Email: ptx@pantronix.com
Estab: 1974

Nay Soe, Electrical Engineer

Provider of fiber optic services including opto-
electronics component packaging, active module
assembly, alignment, and subsystem integration.

**Paradigm Strucural Engineers** HQ
  639 Front St Fl 4
  San Francisco CA 94111
P: 415-362-8944  F: 415-362-8945    PRC:304
www.paradigmse.com
Email: info@paradigmse.com
Estab: 1999

Jake Avella, Staff Engineer
Brandon Dashwood, Structural Engineer
Aaron Blum, Project Engineer
Sam Richardson, Staff Engineer
Kim Curry, Office Manager

Provider of structural engineering and consulting
services. The company offers schematic design,
planning, and construction documentation services.

**Paradromics Inc** HQ
  519 Parrott St
  San Jose CA 95112
P: 408-280-0500    PRC:322
www.paradromics.com
Email: info@paradromics.com
Estab: 2015

Chris LaReau, Senior Software Engineer
Matt Angle, CEO
Darrin Bomba, Director
Henry Johnson, Principal Scientist
Daniel Pouzzner, Principal

Developer of next generation brain-machine interfaces. The company specializes in CMOS sensor
technology with microwire bundles.

**Paragon Controls Inc** HQ
  2371 Circadian Way
  Santa Rosa CA 95407
P: 707-579-1424  F: 707-579-8480    PRC:236
www.paragoncontrols.com
Estab: 1984

Adam Havner, Sales Engineer
Michelle Foszcz, Manager

Designer and manufacturer of air flow and
pressure measurement & control systems. The
company also offers airflow sensing elements.

**Paragon Swiss Inc** HQ
  545 Aldo Ave Unit 1
  Santa Clara CA 95054
P: 408-748-1617  F: 408-748-0949    PRC:80
www.paragonswiss.com
Email: sales@paragonswiss.com
Estab: 1984

Kevin Beatty, President

Manufacturer of medical instruments, precision
shafts, optical bench fixtures, and related supplies.

**Parallax Inc** HQ
  599 Menlo Dr Ste 100
  Rocklin CA 95765
P: 916-624-8333  F: 916-624-8003    PRC:212
www.parallax.com
Email: info@parallax.com
Emp: 1-10  Estab: 1987

Andy Lindsay, Applications Engineer of Education
Department
Chip Gracey, Engineer
Kyle Montgomery, Mechanical Engineer
Jeff Martin, Senior Software Engineer
Ken Gracey, CEO

Manufacturer of electronic hardware and software
products. The company offers microcontrollers,
sensors, boards, and cables/converters.

**Paramit Corp** HQ
  18735 Madrone Pkwy
  Morgan Hill CA 95037
P: 408-782-5600  F: 408-782-9991    PRC:189
www.paramit.com
Email: support@paramit.com
Estab: 1990

Duc Lam, Test Development Engineer
Aniket Kaveri, Mechanical Process Engineer
Chuck Ketchu, Senior Supply Chain Engineer
Jason Ferrel, Industrial Engineer
Jeff Armato, Senior Process Engineer

Manufacturer of medical devices. The company is
engaged in the planning and also implementation
of strategies.

**Pariveda Solutions Inc** BR
  201 California St Ste 1250
  San Francisco CA 94111
P: 844-325-2729  F: 415-946-6101    PRC:322
www.parivedasolutions.com
Email: sanfrancisco@parivedasolutions.com
Estab: 2003

Bruce Ballengee, CEO
Kerry Stover, COO
Brian Orrell, CTO
James Kupferschmid, CFO
Hector Martinez, Chief Strategy and Process
Officer

Provider of IT consulting services and technology
solutions such as custom application development, portals and enterprise content management.

**Park Computer Systems Inc** HQ
  39899 Balentine Dr Ste 197
  Newark CA 94560
P: 510-353-1700  F: 510-353-1900    PRC:326
www.parkcom.com
Email: info@parkcom.com
Estab: 1995

Pinky Kundu, Senior Talent Acquisition Specialist

Provider of mobile products and services. The
company also offers sales content automation and
staff augmentation services.

**Parker Hannifin Corp** DH
  3400 Finch Rd
  Modesto CA 95354
P: 209-521-7860  F: 209-529-3278    PRC:74
www.parker.com
Emp: 1-10  Estab: 1969

Russ Sutherland, Research
Sheryle Knott, Administrator

Provider of fuel, air, oil, and coolant filtration
systems. The company serves the transportation,
marine, and oil and gas industries.

**Parmatech Corp** HQ
  2221 Pine View Way
  Petaluma CA 94954
P: 707-778-2266    PRC:163
www.atwcompanies.com
Email: sales@parmatech.com
Estab: 1973

Lourdes Galapate, Senior Material Engineer
Sean Rosenberg, Engineering Technician
Timur Gasanov, Engineering Technician
Jenette Huse, Quality Inspector
Nikola Janeski, Process Technician

Supplier of metal injection molding components.
The company serves the automotive, medical,
industrial, and electronics industries.

**Pasco Scientific** HQ
10101 Foothills Blvd
Roseville CA 95747-7100
P: 916-786-3800  F: 916-786-8905  PRC:87
www.pasco.com
Email: sales@pasco.com
Emp: 1-10  Estab: 1964

Donna Amado, VP of Engineering
Ann Hanks, Higher Ed Physics
Tom Reineking, Electronics Engineer
Matt Owens, Procurement Engineer
Christine Hanly, Engineering Specialist II

Provider of technology-based solutions for hands-on science services. The company is engaged in technical support.

**Pass Laboratories Inc** HQ
13395 New Airport Rd Ste G
Auburn CA 95602
P: 530-878-5350  F: 530-878-5358  PRC:318
www.passlabs.com
Email: info@passlabs.com
Emp: 1-10  Estab: 1991

Desmond Harrington, President
Kent English, North American Sales Director

Developer of prototypes for amplifier design. The company specializes in manufacturing amplifiers and speakers.

**Patriot Memory Inc** HQ
47027 Benicia St
Fremont CA 94538
P: 510-979-1021  F: 510-979-1586  PRC:92
patriotmemory.com
Email: sales@patriotmem.com
Estab: 1985

Mai Kosla, SVP of Sales Operations
Meng Choo, Flash Product Manager

Developer of flash memory solutions. The company offers memory modules, flash cards, USB drives, gaming memory cards, and accessories.

**Patz Materials & Technologies** HQ
4968 Industrial Way
Benicia CA 94510
P: 707-748-7577  F: 888-203-8791  PRC:34
patzmandt.com
Email: development@patzmandt.com
Estab: 2005

Gary Patz, Founder
Jez Talosig, Quality Assurance Manager
Tom Doolittle, Project Manager

Manufacturer of composite materials. The company portfolio includes unidirectional tapes, fabric prepregs, composite armor systems, and cellular developments.

**Paul Graham Drilling And Service Co** HQ
2500 Airport Rd
Rio Vista CA 94571
P: 707-374-5123  F: 707-374-6821  PRC:130
www.paulgrahamdrilling.com
Email: info@paulgrahamdrilling.com
Estab: 1968

Ted Coffey, Sales Manager
Kevin Graham, Manager

Provider of gas drilling services with over head cranes and computer operated plasma cutting machines for top notch drilling.

**Pauli Systems Inc** HQ
1820 Walters Ct
Fairfield CA 94533
P: 707-429-2434  F: 707-429-2424  PRC:8
paulisystems.com
Email: info@paulisystems.com
Estab: 1996

Robert Pauli, President

Manufacturer of custom finishing systems, abrasive booths, and equipment including blast rooms for aviation, automotive, and industrial applications.

**Pavilion Integration Corp** HQ
2528 Qume Dr Ste 1
San Jose CA 95131
P: 408-453-8801  PRC:172
www.pavilionintegration.com
Email: sales@pavilionintegration.com
Estab: 2004

Lindsay Austin, Co-Founder
Ningyi Luo, President

Designer and manufacturer of lasers, laser modules and subsystems for instrumentation. The company serves the industrial market.

**PAX Scientific Inc** HQ
999 Anderson Dr Ste 100
San Rafael CA 94901
P: 415-256-9900  F: 415-256-9901  PRC:159
www.paxscientific.com
Email: info@paxscientific.com
Estab: 1997

Francesca Bertone, COO
Leslie Miller, Administrative Manager
Robin Giguere, Principal Scientist

Provider of engineering research and product design services. The company is also involved in the design of industrial equipment.

**Paxata Inc** HQ
1800 Seaport Blvd 3rd Fl
Redwood City CA 94063
P: 650-542-7900  PRC:315
www.paxata.com
Email: info@paxata.com
Estab: 2012

Jayanta Bhowmik, SVP of Engineering
Prakash Nanduri, Co-Founder
Nenshad Bardoliwalla, Co-Founder
Dave Brewster, Co-Founder
Christopher Maddox, Co-Founder

Enables business analysts to easily absorb, analyze, and curate numerous raw data sets into consumable information in a self-service manner.

**Paxcell Group Inc** HQ
360 S Abbott Ave
Milpitas CA 95035
P: 408-945-8054  F: 408-945-8681  PRC:98
www.paxcell.com
Email: info@paxcell.com
Estab: 1993

Bill Cohune, Manager

Provider of electronic engineering and industrial design services. The company also offers contract manufacturing services.

**Paxvax Inc** HQ
555 Twin Dolphin Dr Ste 360
Redwood City CA 94065
P: 650-847-1075  PRC:34
paxvax.com
Email: info@paxvax.com
Estab: 2007

Tom Yonker, VP
Yi Zhang, Research Associate

Provider of vaccines to protect from infectious diseases. The company offers treatments to diseases such as typhoid, cholera, and anthrax.

**Pc Professional** HQ
1615 Webster St
Oakland CA 94612
P: 510-874-5871  F: 510-465-8327  PRC:323
pcprofessional.com
Email: sales@pcprofessional.com
Estab: 1981

Matthew Powers, VP of Sales

Provider of information technology solutions. The company focuses on cloud computing, application development, networking, and disaster recovery.

**PCC Structurals Inc** BR
414 Hester St
San Leandro CA 94577
P: 510-568-6400  PRC:163
www.pccstructurals.com
Estab: 1953

Simone Williams, Product Development Engineer
Brad Scott, Senior Project Engineer
Jim Collins, General Manager
Taylor Schaack, Operations Manager

Manufacturer of complex metal components and products. The company caters to industrial and aerospace applications.

**Pct Systems Inc** HQ
49000 Milmont Dr
Fremont CA 94538
P: 510-657-4412  F: 510-657-0112  PRC:86
www.pctsystems.com
Email: info@pctsystems.com
Estab: 1988

Sharyl Maraviov, President
Hank Miranda, CEO
Julie Garcia, Customer Service Manager
Nolan Harding, Manager

Manufacturer of semiconductor equipment and supplies. The company offers services to the semi-conductor industry.

**Pdf Solutions Inc** HQ
333 W San Carlos St Ste 700
San Jose CA 95110
P: 408-280-7900  F: 408-280-7915  PRC:207
www.pdf.com
Email: info@pdf.com
Estab: 1991
Sales: $30M to $100M

Kimon Michaels, VP of Products & Solutions
John Kibarian, Co-Founder
Andrzej Strojwas, CTO
Christine Russell, EVP
Gary Uyeda, Director of Information Technology

Provider of yield improvement technologies and services for the integrated circuit manufacturing process.

**Peak Laboratories LLC**  HQ
2330 Old Middlefield Way Ste 10
Mountain View CA 94043-2452
P: 650-691-1267   F: 650-691-1047   PRC:306
www.peaklaboratories.com
Email: sales_service@peaklaboratories.com
Estab: 2003

Heather Jones, Manager

Designer and manufacturer of process gas
chromatography systems. The company offers
mercuric oxide, pulse discharge, and thermal
conductivity detectors.

**Pearl Lemon**  HQ
3060 Fillmore St
San Francisco CA 94123
P: 628-214-1309   PRC:325
pearllemon.com

Deepak Shukla, Founder

Digital marketing agency that offers results-oriented SEO services.

**Pearson Electronics Inc**  HQ
4009 Transport St
Palo Alto CA 94303
P: 650-494-6444   F: 650-494-6716   PRC:209
www.pearsonelectronics.com
Email: sales@pearsonelectronics.com
Estab: 1955

David Ponce, Senior Engineer
Jeff Reed, President
Cathy Breton, Sales Assistant

Manufacturer of wide band current monitors. The
company also offers high voltage pulse transformers and voltage dividers.

**Peartech Inc**  HQ
1111 W El Camino Real Ste 109-354
Sunnyvale CA 94087
P: 408-542-9550   F: 408-716-2934   PRC:80
www.peartech.com
Estab: 1986

Bob Nordloff, President

Provider of solutions for electronic, computer, networking, and medical applications. The company
offers solutions for precision machining and sheet
metals.

**Pec Manufacturing**  HQ
2110 Ringwood Ave
San Jose CA 95131
P: 408-577-1839   F: 408-577-1829   PRC:80
www.pecmfg.com
Email: sales@pecmfg.com
Estab: 2003

Dung Dinh, QC Engineer

Provider of customized electromechanical, electronic, and mechanical solutions such as cable
and harness assemblies and electro-mechanical
assemblies.

**PeerNova inc**  HQ
2055 Gateway Pl Ste 750
San Jose CA 95110
P: 669-400-7800   PRC:327
peernova.com
Email: hello@peernova.com
Estab: 2013

Chris Mausler, CFO
Gangesh Ganesan, CTO

Provider of silicon valley-based technology such
as distributed systems, networking solutions, big
data, compiler technology, and financial services.

**Pega Precision Inc**  HQ
18800 Adams Ct
Morgan Hill CA 95037
P: 408-776-3700   F: 408-776-3707   PRC:88
www.pegaprecision.com
Estab: 1989

Aaron Fast, President
Dennis Mattish, QC Inspector
Manuel Gonzalez, Shipping Manager
Patricia Fast, Office Manager
James Hamilton, Manager

Manufacturer and marketer of precision sheet
metal and machining components. The company
serves the military, semiconductor, and solar
industries.

**Pegasus Design Inc**  HQ
3115 Independence Dr
Livermore CA 94551
P: 925-292-7567   PRC:159
www.pegasus-design.com
Estab: 1994

Steve Calderon, CEO

Provider of machine design and contract manufacturing services. The company serves the
pharmaceutical instrument industry.

**Pelco By Schneider Electric**  BR
625 W Alluvial Ave
Fresno CA 93711
P: 559-292-1981   PRC:209
www.pelco.com
Emp: 11-50

Sharad Shekhar, CEO

Developer of video surveillance and security solutions. The company also involves in camera and
video management.

**Pelco Inc**  HQ
3500 Pelco Way
Clovis CA 93612-5999
P: 559-292-1981   F: 559-348-1120   PRC:168
www.pelco.com
Email: sales@pelco.com
Emp: 11-50 Estab: 1957

Timothy Jackson, Owner

Manufacturer of closed circuit TV cameras and
accessories. The company's services include
training, engineering, and technical development.

**Peloton Technology**  HQ
1060 La Avenida St
Mountain View CA 94043
P: 650-395-7356   PRC:63
peloton-tech.com
Email: info@peloton-tech.com
Estab: 2013

Joe Bendor, Mechanical Design Engineer
Brian Silverman, Associate Software Engineer
Dave Lyons, Co-Founder
Oliver Bayley, VP
Esther Shon, Accounting Manager

Developer of truck platooning systems. The
company offers services to the transportation,
trucking, and railroad industries.

**Pelvalon Inc**  HQ
923 Thompson Pl
Sunnyvale CA 94085
P: 650-276-0130   F: 650-646-2213   PRC:196
eclipsesystem.com
Email: cs@pelvalon.com
Estab: 2010

Miles Rosen, Manager

Provider of non-surgical therapy such as unin-
flated and inflated devices that offers immediate
results for women experiencing loss of bowel
control.

**Pembroke Instruments LLC**  HQ
120 Stanford Heights Ave
San Francisco CA 94127
P: 415-860-4217   F: 415-585-0652   PRC:19
pembrokeinstruments.com
Email: sales@pembrokeinstruments.com
Estab: 2008

Leslie Tack, Founder

Manufacturer of products for scientific imaging
applications. The company also focuses on optical
spectroscopy needs.

**Pencom**  HQ
1300 Industrial Rd Ste 21
San Carlos CA 94070
P: 650-593-3288   F: 650-593-3299   PRC:80
www.pencomsf.com
Email: sales@pencomsf.com
Estab: 1982

Dan Hart, Sales Engineer
Nancy Rodgers, Sales Engineer
Michael Gray, CCO
Oscar Tsai, General Manager
Cleo Coronado, Sales Manager

Provider of component solutions to OEM design
engineers. The company focuses on supply chain
management, technical product support, and
logistics.

**Pendulum Therapeutics Inc**    HQ
933 20th St
San Francisco CA 94107
P: 415-855-0940    PRC:34
pendulum.co
Email: hello@pendulum.co
Estab: 2012

Connor Skennerton, Data Engineer of Engineering & Statistics
Michael Souza, Senior Software Engineer
William Chen, Senior Staff Engineer of Software Engineer
Yujie Zhu, Software Engineer
Colleen Cutcliffe, Co-Founder

Developer of microbiome interventions and diagnostics systems. The company is involved in research and development services.

**Penguin Computing Inc**    HQ
45800 Northport Loop W
Fremont CA 94538
P: 415-954-2800    PRC:40
www.penguincomputing.com
Email: sales@penguincomputing.com
Estab: 1998

Daniel Dowling, VP of Engineering Services
Akila Senevirathne, Application Engineer
Rajeswari Natarajan, Senior Research & Development Engineer
Lisa Cummins, CFO

Provider of Linux-based cloud and HPC solutions. The company's products include servers, network switches, and integrated rack solutions.

**Penhall Co**    BR
8416 Specialty Cir
Sacramento CA 95828
P: 916-386-1589    PRC:159
www.penhall.com
Emp: 11-50 Estab: 1957

Gregory Rice, CEO
Lee Barnett, CFO
Terry Cooley, VP of Human Resources
George Soriano, VP
Roger Raney, VP of HSE & Training

Provider of concrete cutting services. The company specializes in core drilling, diamond saw cutting, and pavement repair methods.

**Peninsula Engineering Solutions Inc**    HQ
PO Box 1095
Danville CA 94526
P: 925-837-2243    F: 925-837-2298    PRC:129
www.peninsulaengineering.com
Email: info@peninsulaengineering.com
Estab: 2001

Frank Martens, President

Manufacturer of microwave RF repeaters. The company also specializes in cellular & PCS repeaters and related products.

**Peninsula Laboratories Inc**    HQ
305 Old County Rd
San Carlos CA 94070
P: 650-801-6090    F: 650-595-4071    PRC:306
penlabs.com
Email: techsupport@penlabs.com

Damir Vidovic, CEO

Manufacturer of immunology products for biomedical research. The company is involved in technical support services.

**Peninsula Spring Corp**    HQ
6750 Silacci Way
Gilroy CA 95020
P: 408-848-3361    F: 408-848-4118    PRC:80
www.peninsulaspring.com
Estab: 1976

Laura Hampel, Manager

Provider of precision spring products. The company offers sheet metal stampings, electrical contacts, clips, and wire forms.

**Pentagon Technologies**    HQ
21031 Alexander Ct
Hayward CA 94545
P: 800-379-3361    F: 510-783-5055    PRC:86
www.pen-tec.com
Email: sales@pen-tec.com
Estab: 1998

Will Dizon, Mechanical Design Engineer
Camilo Martinez, Production Manager
Harley Mason, Quality Manager
Kathy Adams, Project Manager
Kenny Aguiar, Plant Manager

Distributor of electromechanical components. The company offers shaft couplings, seals, and cable assemblies.

**Penumbra Inc**    HQ
1321 Harbor Bay Pkwy 1 Penumbra Pl
Alameda CA 94502
P: 510-748-3200    F: 510-748-3232    PRC:189
www.penumbrainc.com
Email: info@penumbrainc.com
Estab: 2004
Sales: $300M to $1 Billion

Ben Sorci, VP of Manufacturing Engineering
Ian Sit, Manufacturing Engineering Manager
Don Vu, Quality Engineer
James Pray, President of International
Sri Kosaraju, President

Manufacturer of interventional therapy devices. The company develops products to treat challenging medical conditions.

**Perceptimed Inc**    HQ
365 San Antonio Rd
Mountain View CA 94040
P: 650-941-7000    PRC:189
www.perceptimed.com
Email: info@perceptimed.com
Estab: 2011

Sriram Kumar, Computer Vision Engineer
Jack Gratteau, Senior Electronic Engineer
Frank Starn, CEO
Tom Lavin, Partner
Frank Maione, Chief Business Officer

Provider of medical technologies for dispensing and administration of prescription drugs safer, reducing injuries, and death.

**Perfect World Co Ltd**    HQ
100 Redwood Shores Pkwy 4th Fl
Redwood City CA 94065
P: 650-590-7700    F: 650-591-1211    PRC:317
www.perfectworld.com
Email: dmca@perfectworld.com
Estab: 2008

Andrew Patrick, Quality Assurance Engineering Manager
Yoon Im, SVP of Platform Development & Publishing
Fen Qin, Data Analyst
Alec Obert, Graphic Designer
Ben Rico, Customer Service Representative

Provider of gaming solutions. The company is engaged in technical support and it serves the entertainment industry.

**Perforce Software Inc**    BR
2320 Blanding Ave
Alameda CA 94501
P: 510-864-7400    F: 510-864-5340    PRC:323
www.perforce.com
Email: info@perforce.com
Estab: 1995

Mike Goergen, CFO
Tim Russell, Chief Product Officer

Developer of software management tools and technology solutions. The company serves game development, banking, healthcare, and other sectors.

**Performance Polymer Technologies**    HQ
8801 Washington Blvd Ste 109
Roseville CA 95678
P: 916-677-1414    F: 916-677-1474    PRC:57
www.pptech.com
Email: pptinfo@pptech.com
Emp: 1-10 Estab: 1995

Donald Fenton, Applications Engineer
Bill Crawford, Quality Manager

Manufacturer of elastomeric components for material formulation, extruding, and stamping applications.

**Performex Machining Co**    HQ
963 Terminal Way
San Carlos CA 94070
P: 650-595-2228    F: 650-595-0169    PRC:209
www.performexmachining.com
Email: performex963@gmail.com
Estab: 1977

Joey Iffla, President

Provider of machining services. The company specializes in computer aided machining, designing, and fabrication.

**Peridot Corp**    HQ
1072 Serpentine Ln
Pleasanton CA 94566-4731
P: 925-461-8830    F: 925-461-8833    PRC:80
www.peridotcorp.com
Email: pat@peridotcorp.com
Estab: 1996

Patrick Pickerell, Owner
Anthony Cano, Production Manager
Ray Forbes, Quality Assurance Manager
Jojo Garcia, Purchasing Manager
Marisol Palomares, Sales Service Assistant

Provider of design for manufacturing and packaging. The company also manufacturers of medical components, miniature component and general product prototypes.

**PermaDri Inc**     HQ
4595 W Jacquelyn Ave
Fresno CA 93722
P: 559-275-9620     PRC:57
Emp: 1-10

Richard Rosman, Agent

Provider of eco-friendly waterproofing and corrosion protection products. The company serves the marine, landscape, and industrial markets.

**Perry Tool & Research Inc**     HQ
3415 Enterprise Ave
Hayward CA 94545
P: 510-782-9226   F: 510-782-0749    PRC:80
www.perrytool.com
Email: info@perrytool.com
Estab: 1962

Ken Fusselman, Owner

Designer and manufacturer of powder metal parts for OEMs. The company specializes in pulleys, bearings, cams, sprockets, and fasteners.

**Perryman Group Inc**     HQ
PO Box 6525
Folsom CA 95763
P: 916-630-7456     PRC:325
www.infostations.com
Email: support@infostations.com
Emp: 1-10   Estab: 1998

Ray Perryman, President
Greg Munsill, Business Analyst

Provider of website design and hosting, e-commerce solutions, and networking services. The company serves business and residential customers.

**Persistent Systems Inc**     BR
2055 Laurelwood Rd Ste 210
Santa Clara CA 95054
P: 408-216-7010   F: 408-451-9177    PRC:324
www.persistent.com
Estab: 1990

Pravin Tarde, General Manager of Human Resource
Sameer Bendre, Chief People Officer
Sunder Sarangan, CMO
Nitin Urdhwareshe, VP
Tom Klein, General Counsel

Developer of software & technology products for life science, banking, and other sectors. The company offers big data, security, and cloud solutions.

**Personal Tex Inc**     HQ
722 Lombard St Ste 201
San Francisco CA 94133
P: 415-296-7550   F: 415-296-7501    PRC:320
www.pctex.com
Email: sales@pctex.com
Estab: 1985

Lance Carnes, Software Developer

Publisher of PCTeX software that enables mathematicians to publish their formulas, equations, and thoughts.

**Personalis Inc**     HQ
1330 O'Brien Dr
Menlo Park CA 94025
P: 650-752-1300   F: 650-752-1301    PRC:39
www.personalis.com
Email: info@personalis.com

Lloyd Hsu, VP of Software Engineering
Jason Harris, Senior Director Bioinformatics Engineering
John West, CEO
Jonathan MacQuitty, Chairman
Richard Chen, CSO

Manufacturer of genome-guided medicine for the treatment of cancer. The company deals with research services.

**Persys Engineering Inc**     HQ
815 Swift St
Santa Cruz CA 95060-5851
P: 831-471-9300   F: 831-471-9818    PRC:86
www.persyseng.com
Email: office@persyseng.com
Emp: 1-10   Estab: 1988

Yitzhak Vanek, CEO

Provider of parts cleaning, refurbishing and manufacturing, decontamination, and maintenance of assemblies and machine parts.

**PFU America Inc**     BR
1250 E Arques Ave
Sunnyvale CA 94085
P: 408-992-2900   F: 408-992-2999    PRC:91
www.pfu.fujitsu.com
Email: inquire.pfu@us.fujitsu.com
Estab: 1997

Hasegawa Kiyoshi, President
Wilbur Tanaka, Project Coordinator

Provider of technology solutions. The company designs, develops, and sells computer hardware, peripheral products, and systems.

**Pgh Wong Engineering Inc**     HQ
182 Second St Ste 500
San Francisco CA 94105
P: 415-566-0800   F: 415-566-6030    PRC:304
www.pghwong.com
Email: info@pghwong.com
Estab: 1985

John Scott, Resident Engineer
Aaron Tirona, Field Engineer
Michael Holleran, Project Engineer
Matt Kyauk, Engineer
Shannon Gonzales, Office Engineer

Provider of engineering, program and construction management, and technology services for transit projects.

**Phage International Inc**     HQ
23 Railroad Ave Ste 355
Danville CA 94526
P: 925-984-9446   F: 925-937-6291    PRC:249
www.phageinternational.com
Estab: 2004

Christopher Smith, President
H. Fisher, Science Advisor

Provider of leverage bacteriophage therapy technologies. The company specializes in discovery and rediscovery of effective health care solutions.

**Pharmagenesis Inc**     HQ
303 Twin Dolphin Dr Ste 600
Redwood City CA 94065
P: 650-842-7060     PRC:257
Estab: 1991

John Musser, COO

Developer and manufacturer of prescription pharmaceuticals from plant extracts and other organic products sourced from Chinese medical practice.

**PharmaLogic Development Inc**     HQ
17 Bridgegate Dr
San Rafael CA 94903-1093
P: 415-472-2181     PRC:34
www.pharmalogic.com
Email: info@pharmalogic.com

Gary Novack, President

Focuses on planning, drug development, and marketing services. The company serves the pharmaceutical and biomedical industries.

**Pharmedix**     HQ
3281 Whipple Rd
Union City CA 94587-1218
P: 800-486-1811   F: 800-783-2038    PRC:268
www.pharmedixrx.com
Estab: 1984

Veronica Salazar, Pharmacy Technician
Jaime Di Fiore, Pharmacy Technician

Focuses on the repackaging of pharmaceutical products. The company offers dispensing systems and women's health products.

**Pharmout Laboratory Inc**     HQ
1151 Sonora Ct Ste 1
Sunnyvale CA 94086
P: 408-481-3090   F: 408-481-3091    PRC:268
www.pharmoutlabs.net
Email: chkiang@pharmoutlabs.net
Estab: 1993

Bih Hsu, President

Provider of analytical laboratory services. The company engages in protein precipitated plasma, liquid-liquid extraction, and solid phase extraction.

**Pharmtak Inc**     HQ
30 W Montague Expy Ste 80
San Jose CA 95134
P: 408-954-8223   F: 408-954-8203    PRC:268
pharmtak.com
Estab: 2009

J. C. Lee, President
Shirley Zhang, Manager of Analytical

Provider of pharmaceutical products and services. The company focuses on developing novel pharmaceuticals and cosmeceuticals utilizing technology.

**Phasespace Inc** HQ
1933 Davis St Ste 304
San Leandro CA 94577
P: 510-633-2865  F: 925-945-6718  PRC:77
www.phasespace.com
Email: inquiries@phasespace.com
Estab: 1994

Gregory D'Andrea, Senior Software Engineer
Lawrence Kwan, Software Engineer
Betty Ho, Creative Director
Sovann Neak, Electro Mechanical Technician

Developer of technologies for motion tracking markets. The company focuses on motion capture for industrial research and graphic community.

**Pherin Pharmaceuticals Inc** HQ
4962 El Camino Real Ste 223
Los Altos CA 94022
P: 650-961-2080  PRC:196
www.pherin.com
Email: lmonti@pherin.com
Estab: 1991

Louis Monti, President

Developer of novel compounds for intranasal spray delivery and also deals with the treatment of neuro-psychiatric and neuroendocrine conditions.

**Phihong Usa Corp** LH
47800 Fremont Blvd
Fremont CA 94538
P: 510-445-0100  F: 510-445-1678  PRC:200
phihong.com
Email: usasales@phihongusa.com
Estab: 1972

Raymond Liu, Power Supply Design Engineer
Sherwin Bi, PCB Layout Engineer Supervisor
Peter Lin, Chairman
Emily Tsai, Director of Finance
Jessica Fang, Director of Sales Operations

Provider of power solutions in the telecom sector. The company also offers data solutions in industrial and personal electronic markets.

**Phil Wood & Co** HQ
1125 North 7th St Ste A
San Jose CA 95112
P: 408-569-1860  F: 408-298-9016  PRC:80
www.philwood.com
Email: sales@philwood.com
Estab: 1971

Garrett Enright, General Manager

Manufacturer of cycling and related recreation oriented products. The company focuses to offer maintenance-free hubs for cyclists.

**Phoenix Pharmaceuticals Inc** DH
330 Beach Rd
Burlingame CA 94010
P: 650-558-8898  F: 650-558-1686  PRC:268
www.phoenixpeptide.com
Email: info@phoenixpeptide.com
Estab: 1995

Rong Lyu, Senior Manager

Provider of peptide related products to researchers. The company specializes in obesity, cardiovascular, and diabetes.

**Phoenix Technology Group LLC** HQ
6630 Owens Dr
Pleasanton CA 94588
P: 925-485-1100  F: 925-485-1155  PRC:187
phoenixtech.com
Email: info@phoenixtech.com
Estab: 2007

Kirk Sadler, Senior Manufacturing Engineer
Bert Massie, CEO

Provider of research laboratory services. The company offers anterior segment imaging and retinal imaging microscope services.

**Photo Etch Technology** BR
3014 Scott Blvd
Santa Clara CA 95054
P: 408-988-0220  F: 408-988-1422  PRC:88
www.stencil.com

Kevin Huynh, CAD & CAM Engineer
Dan Latessa, EVP
Maxey Lindsey, Contractor

Provider of stainless stell stencils. The company offers epoxy stencils, precision metal parts, fixture pallets, mesh screens, and artwork services.

**PhyNexus Inc** HQ
3670 Charter Park Dr Ste A
San Jose CA 95136
P: 408-267-7214  F: 408-267-7346  PRC:31
www.phynexus.com
Email: info@phynexus.com
Estab: 2002

Douglas Gjerde, CEO
Mannix Mendoza, Director of Manufacturing
Carrie Huynh, Head of Sales
Lee Hoang, Director of Research & Business Development
Jonathan Grambow, Product Manager

Provider of automated and scalable solutions for the low volume protein and nucleic acid purification.

**PhysioCue Inc** HQ
1798 Technology Dr Ste 258
San Jose CA 95110
P: 408-524-1595  PRC:189
physiocue.com
Email: info@physiocue.com
Estab: 2013

Simon Yi, CEO

Developer of therapies and focuses on the delivery of thermo-neuro-stimulation systems. The company serves patients.

**Pianodisc** HQ
4111 N Freeway Blvd
Sacramento CA 95834
P: 916-567-9999  F: 916-567-1941  PRC:209
www.pianodisc.com
Email: sales@pianodisc.com
Emp: 1-10  Estab: 1988

David Honeywell, Engineering Director
Yovi Peng, Recording Engineer
Irene Chu, CFO
Jerry Reiersen, Production Supervisor
Dave Huegel, Regional Sales Manager

Manufacturer of electronic reproducing systems for acoustic pianos. The company is engaged in design, delivery, and installation services.

**Pica8 Inc** HQ
1032 Elwell Ct Ste 105
Palo Alto CA 94303
P: 650-614-5838  PRC:97
www.pica8.com
Email: info@pica8.com
Estab: 2009

Lin Du, VP of Engineering
Nirmal Karia, Technical Support Engineer
James Liao, CEO
Niraj Jain, COO
Sharad Ahlawat, VP of Technology & Chief Architect

Manufacturer of white box switches. The company specializes in traditional switches and routing protocols.

**Picarro Inc** HQ
3105 Patrick Henry Dr
Santa Clara CA 95054
P: 408-962-3900  F: 408-962-3200  PRC:231
www.picarro.com
Email: info@picarro.com
Estab: 1998

Yousef Yacoub, VP of Software Engineering
James Lee, Systems Engineering Manager
Devanshi Shah, Senior Software Engineer
Tien-Hsiung Lee, Senior Software Engineer
Eugene Manalo, NPI Engineer

Provider of environmental transformation solutions. The company provides isotope analyzers, trace gas analyzers, accessories, and peripherals.

**Pickering Laboratories Inc** HQ
1280 Space Pkwy
Mountain View CA 94043-1434
P: 650-694-6700  F: 650-968-0749  PRC:189
www.pickeringlabs.com
Email: sales@pickeringlabs.com
Estab: 1984

Tony Mclsacc, Production Manager
Jay Abidog, Production Chemist
Anita Gribaldo, Production Technician
Saji George, Quality Assurance Manager
Wendy Rasmussen, Sales Manager

Developer of post-column derivatization technology. The company specializes in manufacturing of cation-exchange columns for amino acid analysis.

**Pictron Inc** HQ
1250 Oakmead Pkwy Ste 210
Sunnyvale CA 94085
P: 408-725-8888  F: 408-446-5552  PRC:320
www.pictron.com
Email: info@pictron.com
Estab: 1999

Sharon Huang, Senior Software Engineer

Provider of solutions for media applications in corporate communications, eLearning, broadcast production, and content based video search fields.

**Pierce Washington** HQ
Two Embarcadero Ctr
San Francisco CA 94111
P: 415-431-8300 PRC:325
piercewashington.com
Email: info@piercewashington.com
Estab: 2005

Faris Yamini, Partner
John Carey, Managing Partner
Rob Watters, Partner

Provider of systems integration and e-commerce solutions. The company also deals with the development of software tools.

**PinPointe** HQ
11 Ilahee Ln
Chico CA 95973
P: 530-809-1970 PRC:188
www.nuvolase.com
Emp: 1-10 Estab: 2011

Steve Duddy, President

Developer of laser light-based therapies for treating nail fungus. The company serves patients in patients in Australia and other countries.

**Pinterest** HQ
651 Brannan St
San Francisco CA 94107-1532
P: 415-762-7100 PRC:325
www.pinterest.com
Email: copyright@pinterest.com
Estab: 2010

Li Fan, Head of Engineering
Andrew Zhai, Software Engineer
Jared Wong, Software Engineer
Abby Maldonado, Human Resource Business Partner
John Egan, Manager

Specializes in mobile application tools. The company focuses on pinning items, creating boards, and interacting with other members.

**Pionetics Corporation** HQ
151H Old County Rd
San Carlos CA 94070
P: 866-611-8624 PRC:144
linxdrinkingwater.com
Email: info@linxwater.com
Estab: 1995

Olivia Hensley, Consultant

Provider of water treatment products. The company's products include LNX 160 water filters, bottless water coolers, and water treatment systems.

**Pipe Shields Inc** HQ
5199 Fulton Dr
Fairfield CA 94534
P: 800-538-7007 F: 707-447-4641 PRC:81
www.pipeshields.com
Email: info@pipeshields.com
Estab: 1971

Judith Betz, Sales Manager

Designer and manufacturer of pre-insulated pipe supports, slides, guides, and anchors. The company's products include hanger types, shoes, and riser clamps.

**Pipsqueak Productions LLC** HQ
120 El Camino Del Mar
San Francisco CA 94121
P: 415-668-4372 PRC:325
www.pipsqueak.com
Email: info@pipsqueak.com
Estab: 1994

Olga Werby, President
Christopher Werby, CEO

Provider of graphic design, photography, writing, editing, animation, and website development services.

**Pivot Bio Inc** HQ
2929 Seventh St Ste 120
Berkeley CA 94710
P: 877-451-1977 PRC:42
pivotbio.com

Karsten Temme, CEO
Alvin Tamsir, CSO

Provider of genome-scale programming of microbes. The company offers services to farmers and the agricultural sector.

**Pivot Systems Inc** HQ
4320 Stevens Creek Blvd Ste 174
San Jose CA 95129
P: 408-435-1000 F: 408-521-3322 PRC:322
www.pivotsys.com
Email: sales@pivotsys.com
Estab: 1997

Rajesh Nair, CEO

Provider of software development services and related solutions for small, large and mid-size companies.

**Pivotal Labs** HQ
875 Howard St FIFTH FL
San Francisco CA 94103
P: 415-777-4868 PRC:323
pivotal.io
Estab: 1999
Sales: $300M to $1 Billion

Bill Cook, President
Rob Mee, CEO
Paul Maritz, Chairman
Cynthia Gaylor, CFO
Joe Militello, Chief People Officer

Focuses on software development and related services. The company serves start-ups and Fortune 1000 companies.

**Pivotal Systems Corp** HQ
48389 Fremont Blvd Ste 100
Fremont CA 94538
P: 510-770-9125 PRC:226
pivotalsys.com
Email: info@pivotalsys.com

Joseph Monkowski, President
John Hoffman, CEO
Kevin Landis, Chief Investment Officer

Provider of monitoring and process control technology solutions for the semiconductor manufacturing industry.

**Pixami Inc** HQ
6754 Bernal Ave Ste 740-106
Pleasanton CA 94566
P: 925-465-5167 PRC:325
www.pixami.com
Email: info@pixami.com
Estab: 1999

Gary Wood, VP of Business Development

Provider of imaging technologies. The company caters to both photo-based and non-photo-based businesses.

**Pixelworks Inc** HQ
226 Airport Pkwy Ste 595
San Jose CA 95110
P: 408-200-9200 F: 408-200-9201 PRC:61
www.pixelworks.com
Email: info@pixelworks.com
Emp: 11-50 Estab: 1997
Sales: $30M to $100M

Tzoyao Chan, EVP of Engineering
Indra Laksono, President
Todd DeBonis, President
Hongmin Zhang, SVP
Elias Nader, CFO

Designer and developer of video and pixel processing semiconductors and software for digital video applications.

**Planet Biotechnology Inc** HQ
20980 Corsair Blvd
Hayward CA 94545
P: 510-887-1461 PRC:34
www.planetbiotechnology.com
Email: info@planetbiotechnology.com

Elliott Fineman, President
Jeffrey Price, Chairman
James Larrick, CSO
Keith Wycoff, VP of Research
Don Cheema, Maintenance & Facilities Manager

Provider of biotechnology services. The company develops antibody-based therapeutic and preventative products through plants to meet medical needs.

**Planetary Herbals** HQ
PO Box 1760
Soquel CA 95073
P: 831-438-1700 F: 831-438-7410 PRC:34
www.planetaryherbals.com
Emp: 1-10

Roy Upton, Herbalist

Provider of nutritional herbal healthcare products. The company's products include Acai, Full Spectrum, Bacopa Extract, and Digestive Comfort.

**Planeteria Media** HQ
110 Stony Point Rd Ste 225
Santa Rosa CA 95401
P: 707-843-3773 PRC:324
www.planeteria.com
Email: sales@planeteria.com
Estab: 1999

Renu Chadda, Managing Director
Sandeep Mehta, Director of Technical

Designer and developer of websites, applications, e-commerce, content management systems, video, and offers flash, and internet marketing services.

**PlanGrid**  HQ
2111 Mission St
San Francisco CA 94110
P: 800-646-0796  PRC:322
www.plangrid.com
Estab: 2011

Tracy Young, CEO
Ralph Gootee, CTO
Ryan Sutton-Gee, Co-Founder
Bill Smith, President
Michael Galvin, CFO

Developer of construction apps which automatically syncs notes, markups, and photos to all the users' devices.

**Planisware**  HQ
300 Montgomery St Ste 930
San Francisco CA 94104
P: 415-591-0941  PRC:323
planisware.com
Email: info@planisware.com
Estab: 1996

Nicolas Vilars, CMO
Theresa Hwang, Marketing Manager
Clare Grasset, Marketing Manager
David Gustafson, VP of Business Development
Loic Sautour, SVP of North America

Designer of portfolio management software solutions for product development and research and development organizations.

**Plant Sciences Inc**  HQ
342 Green Vly Rd
Watsonville CA 95076
P: 831-728-7771  F: 831-728-4967  PRC:41
www.plantsciences.com
Emp: 11-50 Estab: 1985

Eric Levesque, General Manager
George Graff, Facilities Manager
Kim Cronin, Intellectual Property Manager
Kendra Blaker, Manager
Rory Odegaard, Crop Manager

Provider of agricultural research services. The company develops new technology to yield good plant production.

**Plantronics Inc**  HQ
345 Encinal St
Santa Cruz CA 95060
P: 831-426-5858  F: 831-426-6098  PRC:60
www.plantronics.com
Emp: 11-50 Estab: 1961
Sales: $300M to $1 Billion

Gopal Anantharaman, Staff Software Engineer
Mary Huser, EVP
Chidambaram Ramaswamy, Senior Director of Information Technology
Jeff Loebbaka, EVP of Global Sales
Susanne Gomez, Channel Marketing Manager

Provider of audio technology systems that includes headsets, telephones, audio processors, and speakerphones.

M-228

**Plasma Ruggedized Solutions**  HQ
2284 Ringwood Ave Ste A
San Jose CA 95131
P: 408-954-8405  F: 408-954-8401  PRC:47
www.plasmarugged.com
Email: sales@plasmarugged.com
Estab: 1990

Justine Aguinaldo, Sales Engineer Representative
Jim Stameson, President
Evan Persky, CFO
George Forney, CTO
Erick Solis, Inside Sales Manager

Provider of coating and related specialty engineering services. The company specializes in plasma technologies and offers lab services.

**Plasma Technology Systems LLC**  HQ
30695 Huntwood Ave
Hayward CA 94544
P: 650-596-1606  F: 650-596-1180  PRC:159
www.plasmatechsystems.com
Estab: 1999

Jeff Leighty, Sales & Business Development Manager

Provider of equipment and process development services for plasma treatment of surfaces. The company specializes in modification of polymers.

**Plasmaterials Inc**  HQ
2268 Research Dr
Livermore CA 94550
P: 925-447-4030  F: 925-447-4031  PRC:79
www.plasmaterials.com
Email: info@plasmaterials.com
Estab: 1987

Don Sarrach, Owner

Provider of materials for thin film applications. The company offers base metal alloys, backing plates, and semiconductor alloys.

**Plastech**  HQ
3555A Haven Ave
Menlo Park CA 94025
P: 650-568-9206  F: 650-568-9230  PRC:80
www.pmiplastech.com
Estab: 1985

Paul Molnar, Owner

Provider of machined and fabricated plastic products for the semi conductor, biological, and medical industries.

**Plastikon Industries**  HQ
688 Sandoval Way
Hayward CA 94544
P: 510-400-1010  F: 510-400-1133  PRC:80
www.plastikon.com
Email: info@plastikon.com
Estab: 1974

Payal Doshi, Quality Engineer
Shirley Stapp, Corporate Senior Human Resource Manager
Angelica Lopez, Production Manager
Hany Botrous, Production Manager
Guiv Soofer, VP of Manufacturing

Provider of contract manufacturing services for custom designed plastic injection molding, for medical, pharmaceutical and other industries.

**Platina Systems Corp**  HQ
3180 De La Cruz Blvd Ste 110
Santa Clara CA 95054
P: 408-389-4268  PRC:97
www.platinasystems.com
Emp: 1-10  Estab: 2014

Raj Venkatesan, VP of Engineering
Frank Yang, Co-Founder
Mark Yin, Co-Founder
Sharad Mehrotra, Chief Product Officer
Meichi Lai, VP of Finance and Operations

Manufacturer of network equipment including switches. The company serves industrial and commercial customers.

**Platron**  HQ
26260 Eden Landing Rd
Hayward CA 94545
P: 510-781-5588  F: 510-781-5589  PRC:80
www.platron.com
Estab: 1985

James White, Operations Manager

Provider of selective plating services. The company caters to design engineering, electronics, mechanical, and field service applications.

**Plaxgen Inc**  HQ
1895 Mowry Ave Ste 101D
Fremont CA 94538
P: 510-894-0304  F: 510-894-3398  PRC:28
www.plaxgen.com
Email: info@plaxgen.com
Estab: 2007

Shanmugavel Madasamy, Founder

Developer of biodiagnostics solutions for clinical diagnostics and discovery of therapeutics to treat atherosclerosis and alzheimer's disease.

**Plethora**  HQ
1118 HARRISON ST
San Francisco CA 94103
P: 415-726-2256  PRC:316
www.plethora.com
Email: contact@plethora.com

Jeremy Herrman, Founder
Nick Pinkston, Founder
Michael Jeub, VP of Business Development
Mark Mnich, Head of Business Operations

Focuses on CNC milling with automatic manufacturing analysis. The company is also involved in prototyping services.

**Plexxikon Inc**  HQ
91 Bolivar Dr
Berkeley CA 94710
P: 510-647-4000  F: 510-548-8014  PRC:34
www.plexxikon.com
Email: info@plexxikon.com
Estab: 2001

Gideon Bollag, CEO
Chao Zhang, CSO
Joseph Young, VP of Finance
Marguerite Hutchinson, VP of Business Development and Legal Affairs
Wayne Spevak, VP of Chemistry

Developer of pharmaceuticals. The company utilizes its proprietary discovery platform to produce highly selective and targeted medicines.

**Pliant Therapeutics Inc**     HQ
260 Littlefield Ave
S San Francisco CA 94080
P: 650-481-6770     PRC:28
pliantrx.com
Email: info@pliantrx.com
Estab: 2016

J.D Hull, Chief Business Officer
Barbara Howes, Chief Human Resources Officer
Scott Turner, VP of Translational Sciences
Bill Greenlee, Principal
Brian Metcalf, Senior Consultant at Global Blood Therapeutics

Developer of therapeutics medicines for the treatment of fibrosis in organs and conditions, including liver, kidney, heart, and gastrointestinal tract.

**Plug-It Products**     HQ
940 E Pine St
Lodi CA 95240
P: 209-334-4904   F: 209-334-1671     PRC:166
www.plugitproducts.com
Emp: 11-50 Estab: 1986

Jon Smith, Internal Sales & Marketing
Steve Adolf, Shipping Receiving Manager

Provider of in-house products for the municipalities, maintenance contractors, underground contractors, and rental companies.

**PLX Devices Inc**     HQ
2526 Qume Dr Ste 23
San Jose CA 95131
P: 408-745-7591     PRC:209
www.plxdevices.com
Estab: 2003

Paul Lowchareonkul, Founder

Developer of high-tech measuring instruments. The company is engaged in manufacturing, product testing, and technical support services.

**Pneu Design LLC**     HQ
3164 N Shingle Rd
Shingle Springs CA 95682
P: 530-676-4702   F: 530-676-4434     PRC:159
www.pneudesign.com
Email: sales@pneudesign.com
Emp: 1-10

Mark Nagy, General Partner

Provider of electronic and pneumatic filling machines for the petroleum and food processing industry.

**Pni Sensor Corp**     BR
2331 Circadian Way
Santa Rosa CA 95407
P: 707-566-2260   F: 707-566-2261     PRC:87
www.pnicorp.com
Email: customerservice@pnicorp.com
Estab: 1987

Betty Zhang, Software Engineer
Becky Oh, President
George Hsu, CTO
Joe Zils, Chief Legal Counsel
Eric Walters, VP of Finance

Manufacturer of electronic sensors. The company designs and fabricates processors, three-axis controllers, and geomagnetic sensors.

**POC Medical Systems Inc**     HQ
4659 Las Positas Rd
Livermore CA 94551
P: 925-331-8010   F: 925-555-5555     PRC:186
www.pocmedicalsystems.com
Estab: 2013

Sanjeev Saxena, CEO
Andrea Cuppoletti, VP

Provider of diagnostic medical devices for the screening of life-threatening diseases like cancer, cardiovascular disorders, and infectious diseases.

**Poco Solar Energy Inc**     HQ
3345 Keller St
Santa Clara CA 95054
P: 408-970-0680   F: 408-987-0513     PRC:135
www.pocosolar.com
Email: info@pocosolar.com
Estab: 1984

Greg Cordero, Co-Founder
Paul Podesta, Co-Founder
Vern Johnson, Director of Sales
Jesse Cordero, Solar Technician
John McGuire, Solar Energy Consultant

Designer and installer of solar energy systems that provide electricity and heat for swimming pools.

**Polarity Inc**     HQ
11294 Sunrise Park Dr
Rancho Cordova CA 95742
P: 916-635-3050   F: 916-635-7866     PRC:290
www.polarity.net
Email: sales@polarity.net
Emp: 11-50 Estab: 1999

Bogdan Svityashchuk, Electrical Engineer
Robby Beard, Electrical Engineer
David Chuang, President
Wade Goins, President

Designer and manufacturer of power products for commercial and government entities. The company also offers supply solutions.

**Poly Seal Industries**     HQ
725 Channing Way
Berkeley CA 94710
P: 510-843-9722   F: 510-843-7316     PRC:284
www.polysealind.com
Email: info@polysealind.com
Estab: 1974

Daniel Baker, President

Manufacturer of molded rubber pipe gaskets for water and sewage treatment applications. The company serves the automotive and biomedical industries.

**Polycom Inc**     HQ
6001 America Center Dr Fl 1-6
San Jose CA 95002
P: 408-586-3837     PRC:68
www.polycom.com
Email: polycomcapital@polycom.com
Estab: 1990

Alex Bustamante, EVP of Global Operations and President of Plamex
Joe Burton, President
Phil Sherburne, SVP
Robert Hagerty, Director
Marv Tseu, Director

Manufacturer and seller of teleconferencing equipment and provider of all other communications solutions.

**Polymath Research Inc**     HQ
827 Bonde Ct
Pleasanton CA 94566
P: 925-417-0609   F: 925-417-0684     PRC:323
www.polymath-usa.com

Bedros Afeyan, President

Developer of wave propagation and interaction, and photonic devices. The company offers FEMLAB based photonics modeling package and wavelet tools.

**Polyphenolics Inc**     HQ
12667 Rd 24
Madera CA 93639
P: 559-661-5556   F: 559-661-5630     PRC:188
polyphenolics.com
Email: jessica.ornelas@cbrands.com
Emp: 1-10

James Kennedy, President
Steve Kupina, Director of Quality & Technology
Debra Cerda, Marketing Specialist
Jessica Ornelas, Customer Advocate

Supplier of grape seed, grape pomace, and whole grape extracts. The company offers MegaNatural-BP, MegaNatural Red Wine Grape Extract, and MegaNatural-GL.

**POLYSTAK Inc**     HQ
2372 D Qume Dr
San Jose CA 95131
P: 408-441-1400   F: 408-441-1420     PRC:96
www.polystak.com
Email: info@polystak.com
Estab: 1999

Terry Chung, General Manager

Provider of silicon based multi chip package products as well as package stacking solutions and repair services of components and modules.

**Polywell Computers Inc**     HQ
1461 San Mateo Ave
S San Francisco CA 94080
P: 650-583-7222   F: 650-583-1974     PRC:93
www.polywell.com
Email: info@polywell.com
Estab: 1987

Jack Chen, Storage Product Sales Manager
Chi Chi, System Administrator
Jiaying Zhao, Administrative Assistant

Manufacturer of computer systems. The company specializes in desktop PCs, workstations, and servers.

**PONTiS Orthopaedics LLC**     HQ
2299 Post St Ste 103
San Francisco CA 94115
P: 415-567-8935   F: 415-567-8934     PRC:189
www.pontisorthopaedics.com
Email: info@pontisorthopaedics.com
Estab: 2012

Jim Berman, VP of Sales & Marketing

Manufacturer of medical devices such as implants and instrumentation for use in upper & lower extremity bone and soft tissue repair.

**Portola Pharmaceuticals Inc**  HQ
270 E Grand Ave
S San Francisco CA 94080
P: 650-246-7000  F: 650-246-7376  PRC:268
www.portola.com
Email: contact@portola.com
Emp: 324  Estab: 2003
Sales: $30M to $100M

Scott Garland, President
Sheldon Koenig, EVP
Glenn Brame, EVP
Mardi Dier, EVP
Ernie Meyer, EVP

Focuses on the development and commercialization of therapeutic products for the treatment of hematologic disorders.

**Portola Systems**  HQ
7064 Corline Ct Ste B5
Sebastopol CA 95472
P: 707-824-8800  F: 707-824-8866  PRC:329
www.portolasystems.net
Email: info@portolasystems.net
Estab: 1994

James Brown, Information Technology Engineer
James Waters, Engineer
Juan Pulido, Senior Engineer
Rich Coibion, Senior Engineer
Grant Smoot, President

Provider of computer network engineering and integration services. The company also specializes in IT consultation.

**Portrait Displays Inc**  HQ
6663 Owens Dr
Pleasanton CA 94588
P: 925-227-2700  F: 925-227-2705  PRC:323
www.portrait.com
Email: sales@portrait.com
Estab: 1996

Albert Gomez, Principal Software Engineer
J. James, President
Eric Brumm, President
James Lund, Chief Software Architect
Derek Smith, CTO

Provider of extensible platforms supporting embedded control of all display technologies and monitors and operating system software.

**POS Specialists**  HQ
5051 Commercial Cir Ste F
Concord CA 94520
P: 925-626-3930  F: 925-626-3938  PRC:323
www.posspecialists.com
Email: sales@posspecialists.com
Estab: 1990

Doug Campbell, Owner
Bob Brockman, Owner
David Bowers, Sales Manager
Denver Gaasch, Project Manager
Marc Borge, Technology Consultant

Provider of digital dining solutions. The company is engaged in business consultation, on-site training, and cloud services.

**Posiflex Business Machines Inc**  LH
30689 Huntwood Ave
Hayward CA 94544
P: 510-429-7097  F: 510-475-0982  PRC:92
www.posiflexusa.com
Email: customer.service@posiflexusa.com
Estab: 1992

Kenneth Fang, Regional Sales Manager
Dora Young, VP of Operations

Provider of point of service hardware and platform technology. The company caters to diverse markets.

**Posiq Inc**  HQ
169 W Santa Clara St
San Jose CA 95113
P: 408-676-7470  F: 408-831-3300  PRC:322
posiq.net
Email: info@posiq.net
Estab: 2008

Rick Onyon, CEO
Jeremy Maselko, Director of Quality Assurance

Provider of customer relationship management and data solutions. The company offers services to the hospitality sector.

**PotBotics Inc**  HQ
2225 E Bayshore Rd Ste 200
Palo Alto CA 94303
P: 650-837-0420  PRC:34
www.potbotics.com
Estab: 2013

Rick Andersson, Sales Manager

Developer of medical marijuana products such as potbot, brainbot, and nanopot.

**Power Design Services**  HQ
121 E Brokaw Rd
San Jose CA 95112
P: 408-437-1931  PRC:211
www.powerdesignservices.com
Email: sales@powerdesignservices.com
Estab: 1988

Robert Valles, Quality Manager
Tuan Tran, Manager

Provider of power design services. The company involves in the design, fabrication, and assembly of printed circuit boards and flex circuits.

**Power Industries**  HQ
520 Barham Ave
Santa Rosa CA 95404
P: 707-545-7904  F: 707-541-2211  PRC:155
www.powerindustries.com
Estab: 1951

Rick Call, President

Supplier of ready-made solutions for industrial applications. The company's products include bearings and seals, hydraulics, and pneumatics.

**Power Integrations Inc**  HQ
5245 Hellyer Ave
San Jose CA 95138
P: 408-414-9200  F: 408-414-9201  PRC:208
www.power.com
Email: customerservice@power.com
Estab: 1998
Sales: $300M to $1 Billion

Kunal Patel, Senior Product Engineer
Balu Balakrishnan, President
Sandeep Nayyar, VP of Finance
Ben Sutherland, VP of Worldwide Sales
Douglas Bailey, VP of Marketing

Supplier of electronic components. The company's products include AC-DC converters and LED drivers.

**Power Standards Lab**  HQ
980 Atlantic Ave
Alameda CA 94501
P: 510-522-4400  F: 510-522-4455  PRC:293
www.powerstandards.com
Email: info@powerstandards.com
Estab: 2000

Robert Pompeani, VP of Engineering
Alex McEachern, Founder
Chris Hutter, Chairman
Barry Tangney, COO
Marco Mancilla, VP of Sales

Manufacturer of precision electronic power instruments. The company is involved in testing and calibration services.

**PowerBeam Research LLC**  RH
704 Calderon Ave
Mountain View CA 94041
P: 408-933-9373  PRC:209
www.powerbeaminc.com

David Graham, Agent

Provider of firmware, hardware, and software applications for video, optoelectronic systems (lasers, LEDs, photodiodes, waveguides), and robotics.

**Powerlift Dumbwaiters Inc**  HQ
2444 Georgia Slide Rd
Georgetown CA 95634
P: 530-333-1953  F: 530-333-1055  PRC:179
www.dumbwaiters.com
Email: info@dumbwaiters.com
Emp: 1-10  Estab: 1972

Larry Reite, Owner

Provider of dumbwaiters that includes residential powerlifts, commerical units, and mezzanine lifts.

**Powertest Inc**  HQ
3719 Callan Blvd Ste 200
S San Francisco CA 94080-2431
P: 415-778-0580  F: 415-778-0599  PRC:322
www.powertest.com
Email: info@powertest.com
Estab: 1995

Teresa Fontanilla, VP of Operations

Provider of software-related professional services. The company is also involved in load testing and application performance management.

**Powertronix Corp** HQ
1120 Chess Dr
Foster City CA 94404
P: 650-345-6800   F: 650-345-7240   PRC:290
www.powertronix.com
Email: sales@powertronix.com
Estab: 1991

Nettie Mah, Manager

Provider of in-house engineering and related
services. The company offers services to the
industrial sector.

**PPBC** HQ
2426 Sixth St Ste B
Berkeley CA 94710
P: 510-841-7242   PRC:288
polyplus.com
Email: info@polyplus.com
Estab: 1991

Steven Visco, CEO
Eugene Nimon, Director of Research & Business
Development

Engaged in the development of protected lithium
metal electrodes. The company's products include
lithium-sulfur batteries and protected lithium
aondes.

**Practice Fusion Inc** HQ
731 Market St Ste 400
San Francisco CA 94103
P: 415-346-7700   PRC:315
www.practicefusion.com
Estab: 2005

Ryan Howard, Founder
Matt Douglass, Co-Founder
Jonathan Malek, Co-Founder
Alan Wong, Co-Founder

Provider of cloud-based electronic health records
(EHR) platform in the U.S.

**Praesum Communications Inc** HQ
3558 Round Barn Blvd Ste 200
Santa Rosa CA 95403
P: 707-338-0946   PRC:97
www.praesum.com
Email: support@praesum.com
Estab: 2000

Kent Dahlgren, Owner

Provider of switching communication products.
The company offers IP cores, boards, and system
level products.

**Pragmatic Communications Systems
Inc** HQ
2340A Walsh Ave
Santa Clara CA 95051
P: 408-748-1100   F: 408-663-9783   PRC:60
www.wireless-experts.com
Email: sales@pragmatic1.com
Estab: 1994

Prasanna Shah, President
Karin Thompson, Senior Account Executive

Designer, developer, and manufacturer of pragmatic products. The company offers amplifiers, security cameras, speakers, and wireless products.

**Pragmatics Technologies Inc** HQ
100 Great Oaks Blvd Ste 140
San Jose CA 95119
P: 408-289-8202   F: 408-289-8109   PRC:200
www.pragmaticstech.com
Email: sales@pragmaticstech.com
Estab: 2000

Chris Mack, President

Provider of electromechanical interface solutions.
The company deals with the development of
custom and standard test interfaces.

**Praxair Technology Inc** BR
2430 Camino Ramon Ste 310
San Ramon CA 94583
P: 925-866-6800   F: 925-866-6899   PRC:49
www.praxair.com
Email: info@praxair.com
Estab: 1907

Eduardo Menezes, EVP

Provider of industrial gases. The company engages in gas supply and management, industrial, and
oil and gas services.

**Pre Plastics Inc** HQ
12600-100 Locksley Ln
Auburn CA 95602
P: 530-823-1820   F: 530-823-1866   PRC:84
www.preplastics.com
Emp: 1-10   Estab: 1986

Allen Grim, Production Manager
Sam Ivey, Quality Assurance Manager
Katie Kuhl, Sales Manager
Brian Miller, Director of Operations
Linda Nelson, Office Manager

Provider of engineering and precision tooling
services. The company also offers plastic injection
molding and assembly services.

**Precise Automation** HQ
47350 Fremont Blvd
Fremont CA 94538
P: 408-224-2838   PRC:80
www.preciseautomation.com
Email: sales@preciseautomation.com
Estab: 2004

Mike Ouren, Chief Sales Engineer
Rajesh Kulkarni, Director of Engineering
Carl Lee, Engineer
Betsy Lange, CFO

Provider of industrial automation solutions. The
company's products include robots, guidance
controllers, and kinematics.

**Precise Light Surgical** HQ
310 W Hamilton Ave Ste 210
Campbell CA 95008
P: 831-539-3323   PRC:189
www.preciselightsurgical.com
Email: info@preciselightsurgical.com

Gerald Mitchel, Co-Founder
Gerald Mitchel, Co-Founder
Ken Arnold, President

Provider of medical devices with vaporization
technology for the removal of delicate tissues,
reduce surgical risk, and down time in endoscopic
surgery.

**Precision Asphere Inc** HQ
48860 Milmont Dr Unit 105-C
Fremont CA 94538
P: 510-668-1508   F: 510-668-1595   PRC:173
precisionasphere.com
Email: sales@precisionasphere.com
Estab: 2002

John Kong, President

Provider of aspheric optical components fabrication services. The company offers optical surface
forming, polishing, and metrology services.

**Precision Contacts Inc** HQ
990 Suncast Ln
El Dorado Hills CA 95762
P: 916-939-4147   F: 916-939-4149   PRC:86
www.precisioncontacts.com
Email: sales@precisioncontacts.com
Emp: 1-10   Estab: 1974

Dean Wroblewski, President

Provider of replacement contacts for handler
manufacturer. The company's products include
sockets, contacts, elements, and custom products.

**Precision Identity Corp** HQ
804 Camden Ave
Campbell CA 95008
P: 408-374-2346   PRC:80
precisionidentity.com
Email: info@precisionidentity.com
Estab: 1970

Pierre Kamber, VP

Manufacturer of machined components for the
medical device manufacturing industries. The
company offers inspection, cleaning, and support
services.

**Precision Metal Tooling Inc** HQ
5101 San Leandro St
Oakland CA 94601
P: 510-436-0900   F: 510-436-3030   PRC:163
www.precisionmetaltooling.com
Email: info@precisionmetaltooling.com
Estab: 1983

Margaret Carter, VP

Manufacturer of production tool and die manufacturing products. The company also focuses on
prototype tooling, tool engineering, and custom
tooling.

**Precision Plastics Inc** HQ
8456 Carbide Ct
Sacramento CA 95828
P: 916-689-5284   F: 916-689-5424   PRC:284
www.precisionplasticsinc.com
Emp: 11-50 Estab: 1984

Justin Matisewski, Director of Sales
David Freriks, VP

Provider of plastic fabrication services. The
company is engaged in fabrication, countertops,
machining, and consumer services.

**Precision Swiss Products Inc**    HQ
1911 Tarob Ct
Milpitas CA 95035-6825
P: 408-433-5880   F: 408-434-0764   PRC:80
precisionswiss.com
Email: sales@precisionswiss.com

Norbert Kozar, CEO
Peter Pichler, Chief Quality Officer
Melissa Kozar, EVP

Manufacturer of precision machined components. The company serves medical, energy, and military industries.

**Precision Tool Distributors Inc**    HQ
46613 Fremont Blvd
Fremont CA 94538-6410
P: 408-774-1274   F: 408-774-1277   PRC:212
www.pretool.com
Email: mikeb@pretool.com
Estab: 1963

Frank Black, President
John Feuerhelm, Inspection Services Manager

Specializes in dimensional measurement products. The company offers inspection hand tools and related accessories.

**Precision Welding Technologies Inc**    HQ
6287 Viewridge Dr
Auburn CA 95602
P: 530-269-1826   F: 530-269-1827   PRC:82
www.pwt-online.com
Email: sales@pwt-online.com
Emp: 1-10   Estab: 1993

Gregg Martsching, President

Provider of welding systems and components. The company's service include equipment maintenance, planning and maintenance, and job shop.

**Preferred Products**    HQ
PO Box 150624
San Rafael CA 94915
P: 415-499-3544   F: 415-499-3551   PRC:186
www.preferredproduct.com

Michael Ryan, COO

Manufacturer of diagnostic instruments, headlights and mirrors, forceps, microscopes, office equipment, and ear instruments.

**Premier Biosoft International**    HQ
3786 Corina Way
Palo Alto CA 94303-4504
P: 650-856-2703   F: 650-618-1773   PRC:40
www.premierbiosoft.com
Email: support@premierbiosoft.com
Estab: 1994

Arun Apte, CEO

Specializes in software development, design, testing and maintenance services. The company serves life science companies and laboratories.

**Premier Finishing Inc**    HQ
7910 Longe St
Stockton CA 95206
P: 209-982-5585   F: 209-983-4050   PRC:47
www.premierfinishing.com
Emp: 1-10   Estab: 1996

Craig Walters, President
Ker Vang, Quality Assurance Manager
Thom Foulks, VP

Provider of precision services. The company focuses on powder coating, liquid coating, pad printing, and light mechanical assembly.

**Premier Wireless Solutions**    HQ
88 Bonaventura Dr
San Jose CA 95134
P: 650-230-1300   PRC:70
www.pws.bz

Chris Mabee, Director of Engineering
Andrew Spix, Principal Engineer
Vince Giacomini, CEO
John Shoemaker, CFO
Gregg Peterson, CTO

Provider of wireless products, design and test / certification services, network data plans, device portals, and device management middleware.

**Prescient Surgical**    HQ
1585 Industrial Rd
San Carlos CA 94070
P: 650-999-0263   PRC:186
www.prescientsurgical.com
Email: info@prescientsurgical.com

Insoo Suh, Co-Founder
Jonathan Coe, Co-Founder

Developer of medical devices and technologies to reduce the risk of surgical site infections in patients undergoing abdominal gastrointestinal surgery.

**Prescript Pharmaceuticals Inc**    HQ
39 California Ave Ste 104
Pleasanton CA 94566
P: 925-215-8608   F: 925-218-6973   PRC:270
www.prescript.net
Estab: 1992

William Hartig, President

Provider of repackaging services. The company offers its products in sealed and tamper evident containers.

**Presentek Inc**    HQ
987 University Ave Ste 11
Los Gatos CA 95032
P: 408-354-1264   F: 408-354-6261   PRC:224
www.presentek.com
Email: salessupport@presentek.com
Estab: 1987

Lee Mayfield, President

Designer of websites and web portals. The company also offers content management systems and e-commerce handlers.

**Presidio Inc**    BR
4900 Hopyard Rd Ste 282
Pleasanton CA 94588
P: 415-501-9020   PRC:323
presidio.com

Rudy Casasola, President of Sales
Bob Cagnazzi, CEO
Vinu Thomas, CTO
Dave Hart, COO
Neil Johnston, CFO

Provider of IP telephony and wireless networking services. The company also deals with deployment, integration, and hardware and software development.

**Presidio Pharmaceuticals Inc**    HQ
1700 Owens St Ste 184
San Francisco CA 94158
P: 415-655-7560   F: 415-986-2864   PRC:249
www.presidiopharma.com
Email: contact@presidiopharma.com
Estab: 2006

Leo Redmond, CFO
Thomas Plotts, CFO

Developers of small-molecule antiviral therapeutics. The company is a clinical-stage pharmaceutical company.

**Prestige Lens Lab**    HQ
338 N Canal St Ste 14
S San Francisco CA 94080
P: 650-588-5540   F: 650-588-3322   PRC:306
prestigesafetyrx.com
Email: info@prestigesafetyrx.com
Estab: 1994

Steve Mori-Prange, Manager
Richard Casey, Safety Rx Eyewear Specialist

Provider of optical laboratory services. The company specializes in prescription safety eyewear programs.

**Presto Engineering Inc**    HQ
109 Bonaventura Dr
San Jose CA 95134
P: 408-372-9500   PRC:304
www.presto-eng.com
Email: info@presto-eng.com
Estab: 2006

Alok Savadatti, RF Engineer
Michel Villemain, Founder
Tim Lillie, VP
Rick Vernor, Production Control Manager

Provider of semiconductor test and analysis solutions. The company also offers engineering services to the semiconductor market.

**Prezi Inc**    HQ
450 Bryant St
San Francisco CA 94107
P: 844-551-6941   PRC:322
prezi.com
Estab: 2008

Tyler Miller, VP of Engineering
Adam Somlai-Fischer, Principal Artist
Peter Arvai, Co-Founder
Jim Szafranski, COO
Narayan Menon, CFO

Provider of collaboration solutions. The company offers strategy and technical consulting services.

**Price Pump Co**      HQ
   21775 Eighth St E
   Sonoma CA 95476
P: 707-938-8441   F: 707-938-0764     PRC:160
www.pricepump.com
Email: sales@pricepump.com
Estab: 1932

Pawel Bankowski, VP of Engineering
John Armitage, Engineering
Rachel Brooks, Design Engineer
Karl Buder, CFO
Jestin Plowright, Sales & Marketing Manager

Manufacturer of centrifugal and air operated diaphragm pumps. The company offers engineering services and serves industrial and OEM users.

**Prima Environmental Inc**      HQ
   5070 Robert J Mathews Pkwy Ste 3
   El Dorado Hills CA 95762
P: 916-939-7300   F: 916-939-7398     PRC:140
primaenvironmental.com
Emp: 1-10

Cindy Schreier, President

Provider of laboratory testing services. The company specializes in treatability testing, technology evaluation, and scientific consulting services.

**PrimaryIo**      HQ
   716 Laurel St Ste 11
   San Carlos CA 94070
P: 415-601-0061     PRC:322
www.primaryio.com
Email: inquiry@primaryio.com
Estab: 2012

Vivek Pendharkar, COO
Vijay Karamcheti, CTO

Provider of business analytics and transaction processing solutions. The company offers storage acceleration data services for business applications.

**Prime Engineering**      HQ
   4202 W Sierra Madre Ave
   Fresno CA 93722
P: 559-276-0991   F: 559-276-3544     PRC:189
www.primeengineering.com
Email: info@primeengineering.com
Emp: 1-10   Estab: 1984

Mary Boegel, President
Bruce Boegel, CFO
Mark Allen, VP
Greg Boyer, Director of Transportation

Provider of standing systems products such as granstand, kidstand, symmetry mobile, uprite, cindylift, and the lift.

**Primepay LLC**      BR
   5600 Mowry School Rd Ste 230
   Newark CA 94560
P: 650-358-4555   F: 650-358-4559     PRC:45
primepay.com

William Pellicano, CEO
Ed Hughes, EVP
Todd Quarfot, EVP
Jamie Wilson, EVP
Karen Cimorelli-Moor, EVP

Provider of payroll processing services, HR solutions, and insurance and benefit management services.

**Primity Bio Inc**      HQ
   48383 Fremont Blvd Ste 118
   Fremont CA 94538
P: 510-210-0605     PRC:34
primitybio.com
Email: info@primitybio.com
Estab: 2010

Tom Wehrman, Department Head
Jason Tuig, Research Assistant

Provider of assay platforms for biological relevance. The company specializes in cell biology, flow cytometry, and molecular biology.

**Primus Power**      HQ
   3967 Trust Way
   Hayward CA 94545
P: 510-342-7600     PRC:288
www.primuspower.com
Email: sales@primuspower.com
Estab: 2009

Hossein Kazemi, Director of Systems Engineering
Jeffrey Bouchard, Electrical Engineer
Tom Stepien, CEO
Mark Collins, Senior Director NPI Operations
Paul Kreiner, Director of Mechanical Design

Provider of energy storage solutions. The company develops EnergyPod, energy storage batteries, and EnergyCell for industrial and consumer applications.

**Principia Biopharma Inc**      HQ
   220 E Grand Ave
   S San Francisco CA 94080
P: 650-416-7700     PRC:256
www.principiabio.com
Email: info@principiabio.com
Estab: 2008

Martin Babler, CEO
Christopher Chai, CFO
David Goldstein, VP of Drug Discovery
Betsy Santos, VP of People
Ken Brameld, Executive Director of Research Technologies

Provider of biopharmaceuticals. The company develops oral small molecule therapies to treat autoimmune and inflammatory diseases and cancer.

**Prism Inks Inc**      HQ
   824 W Ahwanee Ave
   Sunnyvale CA 94085
P: 408-744-6710     PRC:53
www.prisminks.com
Estab: 1999

Amir Ajanee, Business Development Department
Graham Dracup, Technical Support Department Manager
Rocky Road, Security Coordinator
Gul Kalal, Accounting Assistant
Griselda Quintero, Logistical Support Department

Manufacturer of inkjet printer inks to the proofing, signage, photography, arts and coding sectors. The company's products comprise UV curable and textile inks.

**Pro Lab Orthotics**      HQ
   575 Airpark Rd
   Napa CA 94558-7514
P: 707-257-4400     PRC:190
prolaborthotics.com

Paul Scherer, Founder
Todd Izuhara, General Manager
Dan DeMars, Human Resource Manager
Vicki Avila, Marketing Manager
Jose Tirado, VP

Manufacturer and supplier of orthoses products. The company's offerings include foot orthoses, pathology orthoses, and specialty orthoses.

**Pro-Form Laboratories**      HQ
   PO Box 626
   Orinda CA 94563
P: 707-752-9010   F: 707-752-9014     PRC:272
proformlabs.com
Email: info@proformlabs.com

Alex Gillespie, CEO
Ryan Gillespie, Direction of Operations
JoAnn Gillespie, Key Account Representative
Jeff Mitchell, CFO
Alex Gonzalez, Director of Human Resources

Developer and producer of nutritional powders. The company also specializes in contract manufacturing services.

**Pro-Tek Manufacturing Inc**      HQ
   4849 Southfront Rd
   Livermore CA 94551
P: 925-454-8100   F: 925-454-8101     PRC:80
www.protekmfg.com
Email: protek@protekmfg.com
Estab: 1981

Wade Menard, Production Manager
Bill Ness, Manager of Estimating
Ron Biela, Sales Account Manager

Provider of sheet metal fabrication and machining services. The company is involved in prototyping and manufacturing.

**Probe Logic**      HQ
   1885 Lundy Ave Ste 101
   San Jose CA 95131
P: 408-416-0777   F: 408-943-8117     PRC:211
www.probelogic.com
Email: sales@probelogic.com
Estab: 2003

Hon Cheng, CEO
Abi Pandey, Sales Representative
Steve Groden, Account Manager
Ken Chen, Manager
Neil Grinager, Account Manager

Developer and manufacturer of probe card for semiconductor industry. The company also offers printed circuit board design services.

**Procept Biorobotics** HQ
900 Island Dr Ste 101
Redwood City CA 94065
P: 650-232-7200   F: 650-232-5782   PRC:189
www.procept-biorobotics.com
Email: info@procept-biorobotics.com
Estab: 2009

Nishey Wanchoo, Senior R&D Engineer
Kevin Waters, SVP
Surag Mantri, SVP of Research and Development
Eric Steuben, VP of Operations

Provider of healthcare services. The company
primarily focuses on personalized image-guided
waterjet tissue resection services.

**Process Engineers Inc** HQ
26569 Corporate Ave
Hayward CA 94545
P: 510-782-5122   F: 510-785-8187   PRC:80
www.peiequipment.com
Email: peiequipment@sbcglobal.net

Gabriel Heredia, Production Manager
John Cortessis, Regional Sales Manager

Manufacturer of stainless steel equipment. The
company also specializes in installation and other
services.

**Process Metrix Corp** BR
6622 Owens Dr
Pleasanton CA 94588
P: 925-460-0385   F: 925-460-0728   PRC:171
www.processmetrix.com
Estab: 1987

Patrick Andre, Chief Executive
Guy Young, CFO
Hock Goh, Independent Non-executive Director
Holly Koeppel, Independent Non-executive
Director
Jane Hinkley, Independent Non-executive Director

Supplier of instruments for industrial measurement and control. The company's products are
used in molten metal applications.

**Process Solutions Inc** HQ
1077 Dell Ave Ste A
Campbell CA 95008
P: 408-370-6540   F: 408-866-4660   PRC:144
www.4psi.net
Estab: 2003

Gunnar Thordarson, VP

Provider of disinfection solutions. The company
is engaged in facility management services and
serves the commercial sector.

**ProcessWeaver Inc** BR
5201 Great America Pkwy Ste 300
Santa Clara CA 95054
P: 888-932-8373   PRC:323
www.processweaver.com
Email: sales@processweaver.com
Estab: 2005

Kumar Vidadala, President
Don Spatola, COO
Amit Patel, Revenue Growth Sales Operations
Prasad Chandra, Marketing Manager
Bhavana Musuluri, SVP

Developer of multi-carrier shipping software and a
provider of shipping solutions. The company also
offers inbound and desktop shipping solutions.

**Proco Products Inc** HQ
2431 N Wigwam Dr
Stockton CA 95205-0590
P: 209-943-6088   F: 209-943-0242   PRC:159
www.procoproducts.com
Emp: 1-10  Estab: 1980

Ed Marchese, President
Cal Hayes, General Manager

Manufacturer of expansion joints. The company
serves the oil and gas, power generation, chemical, and steel industries.

**Procurement Partners International
Inc** HQ
133 30th Ave
San Mateo CA 94403-2712
P: 650-345-6118   F: 650-574-1081   PRC:88
www.thesourcepros.com
Email: info@thesourcepros.com
Estab: 1998

James Landi, Account Sales Manager

Provider of procurement services. The company
offers mechanical components such as pins, rods,
rollers, and sheet metal.

**Prodigy Surface Tech Inc** HQ
807 Aldo Ave Ste 103
Santa Clara CA 95054
P: 408-492-9390   PRC:157
www.prodigysurfacetech.com
Estab: 2002

John Shaw, President

Provider of alternative to common electroplating
shop. The company focuses on chem lab for analysis, blaster, and clean room.

**Product Components Corporation** HQ
825 Arnold Dr Ste 7
Martinez CA 94553
P: 925-228-8930   F: 925-228-8933   PRC:84
www.product-components.com
Email: sales@product-components.com
Estab: 1962

Susan Lenz, Owner

Manufacturer of industrial plastic fasteners. The
company offers screws, washers, pipe plugs,
circuit board hardware, and other products.

**Production Robotics Inc** HQ
562 Whitney St
San Leandro CA 94577
P: 510-777-0375   F: 510-777-9033   PRC:80
www.productionrobotics.com
Email: info@productionrobotics.com
Estab: 1986

Leonard Ginsburg, President
Jayaram Bhattarai, Quality Systems Manager
Shaon Ghosh, Office Manager
Greg Majewski, Machine Shop Manager
Marco Ginsburg, Mechanical Designer

Designer and manufacturer of specialty engineered automation systems. The company serves
biotech, diagnostics, microsurgery, and other
sectors.

**Professional Finishing** HQ
770 Market Ave
Richmond CA 94801
P: 510-233-7629   F: 510-233-1359   PRC:47
www.professionalfinishing.com
Estab: 1979

Brian Ditman, Production Manager
Jing Li, Director of Design Verification
Delia Castro, Receptionist

Provider of liquid & powder coatings and finishing
to the scientific and aerospace industries. The
company focuses on sandblasting and silk
screening.

**Profusa Inc** HQ
5959 Horton St Ste 450
Emeryville CA 94608
P: 415-655-9861   PRC:187
profusa.com
Email: info@profusa.com
Estab: 2009

Karen Liu, Founder
Bill McMillan, Co-Founder
Natalie Wisniewski, Co-Founder
Ben Hwang, Chairman
Bruce Smith, Chief of Staff

Focuses on the development of biointegrated
sensors. The company offers services to the
environment sector.

**Progenitor Cell Therapy** BR
291 Bernardo Ave
Mountain View CA 94043
P: 650-964-6744   PRC:34
www.pctcelltherapy.com
Email: bdm@pctcaladrius.com
Estab: 1999

Robert Preti, CEO
J.O. Valentino, VP of Head of Global Quality
Brian Hanifin, VP of Technical Operations North
America
Thomas Heathman, Business Leader

Manufacturer of biotechnology products. The
company develops cell therapy products on a
contract basis.

**Progent Corporation** HQ
2570 N First St 2nd Fl
San Jose CA 95131
P: 408-240-9400   PRC:323
www.progent.com
Email: information@progent.com
Estab: 1999

Les Kent, Founder
Tom Anderson, VP of Consulting Services
Beverly Katz, Controller

Provider of online technical support for small networks, and specializes in remote diagnosis, repair,
and consulting services.

**Progressive Concepts Machining**   HQ
1236 Quarry Ln Ste 104
Pleasanton CA 94566-4730
P: 925-426-0400  F: 925-426-0709   PRC:80
www.proconmach.com
Email: sales@proconmach.com
Estab: 1987

Chris Studzinski, President

Provider of welding, assembly, and machining services. The company also deals with inspection solutions and serves businesses.

**Progressive Technology Inc**   HQ
4130 Citrus Ave Ste 17
Rocklin CA 95677
P: 916-632-6715  F: 916-632-9348   PRC:185
www.prgtech.com
Email: sales@prgtech.com
Emp: 1-10

Mike Fischer, Business Developer

Manufacturer of orthodontic braces. The company provides sapphire, alumina, zirconia, ceramic, and quartz braces.

**Project Partners LLC**   HQ
520 Purissima St
Half Moon Bay CA 94019
P: 650-712-6200  F: 650-726-7975   PRC:326
www.projectp.com
Email: info@projectp.com
Estab: 1997

Randy Egger, President
Tamim Kulaly, VP of Oracle Primavera Solutions
Neeraj Garg, VP of Product Development

Provider of business solutions and information technology systems. The company offers NetSuite, Oracle Fusion Applications, and Primavera.

**Prolific Interactive**   BR
535 Mission St Ste 2602
San Francisco CA 94105
P: 415-813-4199   PRC:319
www.prolificinteractive.com
Email: bd@prolificinteractive.com

Bobak Emamian, Co-Founder
Eric Weber, Co-Founder
Al Harnisch, VP of Growth
Dina Chaiffetz, Director of Product Strategy
Stefanie Rai, Managing Director

Mobile-focused product agency that engages in creating products and delivering mobile experiences for leading brands.

**Prolific Minds Inc**   HQ
20370 Town Center Ln Ste 166
Cupertino CA 95014
P: 408-777-1211  F: 408-317-4444   PRC:323
www.prolificminds.com

Sanjeev Malik, President
Bhargav G., Assistant Manager
Dylan C., Web Developer
Kelsey Brennan, Product Designer

Provider of software solutions. The company develops software architecture, and offers analysis, technical design, and development services.

**Prolynx LLC**   HQ
455 Mission Bay Blvd S Ste 145
San Francisco CA 94158
P: 415-552-5306   PRC:34
prolynxllc.com

Gary Ashley, Founder
Louise Robinson, Senior Scientist
Sam Pfaff, Scientist

Developer of technology solutions for releasable linkers. The company also specializes in injectable drugs.

**ProMab Biotechnologies Inc**   HQ
2600 Hilltop Dr Bldg B Ste C320
Richmond CA 94806
P: 510-860-4615  F: 510-740-3625   PRC:34
www.promab.com
Email: info@promab.com

John Wu, CEO

Provider of cell isolation kits, custom antibodies, cancer stem cells, and recombinant protein products.

**Promax Tools Lp**   HQ
11312 Sunrise Gold Cir
Rancho Cordova CA 95742
P: 916-638-0501  F: 916-638-0512   PRC:157
promaxtools.com
Emp: 1-10  Estab: 1967

Nancy Owens, President

Manufacturer of solid carbide round tools. The company offers finishing end mills, die & mold tools, and solid carbide end mills.

**ProMedia Audio & Video**   HQ
777 Arnold Dr Ste 100
Martinez CA 94553
P: 510-741-2925  F: 510-741-0790   PRC:209
www.promediaaudiovideo.com
Estab: 1978

Mike Trimble, Engineer
Zachary Calhoun, Audio Engineer
Mike Chase, Sales Design Engineer
Ted Leamy, SVP of Sales & Marketing

Focuses on the integration of audio/video and performance audio systems. The company serves educational facilities, concert halls, and auditoriums.

**Promex Industries Inc**   HQ
3075 Oakmead Village
Santa Clara CA 95051
P: 408-496-0222   PRC:209
www.promex-ind.com
Email: cpugh@promex-ind.com
Estab: 1975

Albert Gomes, Senior Manufacturing Engineer
Richard Otte, President
Annette Teng, CTO
Michael Lopez, COO
Hassan Sorkhabi, Director of Quality

Provider of packaging solutions. The company is engaged in onshore production process flows using process development.

**Promise Technology Inc**   HQ
580 Cottonwood Dr
Milpitas CA 95035
P: 408-228-1400  F: 408-228-1100   PRC:95
www.promise.com
Email: sales@promise.com
Estab: 1988

Nagendra Vadlakunta, Senior Firmware Engineer
James Lee, President
Heidi Tsui, Human Resource Manager
Thanh Ngo, Logistics & Warehouse Specialist

Provider of storage solutions such as cloud and surveillance storage and virtual tape library for digital home applications.

**Promptu**   HQ
333 Ravenswood Ave Bldg 201
Menlo Park CA 94025
P: 650-859-5800  F: 650-859-6985   PRC:67
www.promptu.com
Estab: 2000

Harry Printz, CTO
Liz McAuley, Senior Software Engineer
Giuseppe Staffaroni, President
Jason Simpson, VP of Product Marketing
Daniele Poggetta, VP of Business Development

Provider of voice-activated search and navigation services. The company is also engaged in engineering and product marketing.

**Proofpoint**   RH
892 Ross Dr
Sunnyvale CA 94089
P: 408-517-4710  F: 408-517-4711   PRC:324
www.proofpoint.com
Email: federalsales@proofpoint.com
Estab: 2002
Sales: $300M to $1 Billion

Ashan Willy, SVP of Systems Engineering and Customer Success
Gary Steele, CEO
Marcel DePaolis, CTO
Paul Auvil, CFO
Darren Lee, EVP

Manufacturer of threat, email, social media, and information protection products. The company offers security and compliance solutions.

**Proplus Design Solutions Inc**   HQ
2025 Gateway Pl Ste 130
San Jose CA 95110
P: 408-459-6128  F: 408-459-6111   PRC:326
proplussolutions.com
Email: info@proplussolution.com
Estab: 2006

Yutao Ma, VP of Engineering
Zhang Zhenzhong, Senior Engineer
James Ma, President
Zhihong Liu, Chairman
Lianfeng Yang, SVP of Marketing and Business Development

Provider of electronic design automation solutions. The company's products include NoisePro, Nano-Spice, and NanoYield.

**Prosoft Engineering Inc**   HQ
1599 Greenville Rd
Livermore CA 94550
P: 877-477-6763   F: 925-583-1750   PRC:322
www.prosofteng.com
Estab: 1985

Greg Brewer, CEO

Developer of data recovery software. The company provides Drive Genius, Data Rescue, and Data Backup software.

**Prosthetic Artists Inc**   HQ
1736 Professional Dr
Sacramento CA 95825
P: 916-485-4249   F: 916-485-4389   PRC:190
www.prostheticartists.com
Emp: 1-10   Estab: 1931

Eric Lindsey, President
Paul Martin, Account Manager

Provider of impression-fitted, hand-sculpted, hand-painted ocular prostheses. The company also fits thin shell prostheses over disfigured eyes.

**Prosthetic Solutions Inc**   HQ
191 San Felipe Rd Ste M1
Hollister CA 95023
P: 831-637-0491   F: 831-637-1977   PRC:190
www.prosthetic-solutions.com
Emp: 11-50   Estab: 2001

Steve Geib, Owner
Wade Skardoutos, President
Susan Stenman, Clinic Director
Linda Ornelas, Office Manager
Stephanie Eden, Office Manager

Manufacturer of medical devices. The company improves the lives of amputees by providing them prosthesis.

**Prosurg Inc**   HQ
2195 Trade Zone Blvd
San Jose CA 95131
P: 408-945-4044   F: 408-945-1390   PRC:189
www.prosurg.com
Email: mail@prosurg.com
Estab: 1989

Ashvin Desai, President
Twila Conner, Quality Assurance Manager

Manufacturer of medical devices. The company offers products for women's and men's healthcare, urological and gynecological disorders.

**Protection Plus Security Services Inc**   HQ
40543 Encyclopedia Cir
Fremont CA 94538
P: 510-770-9900   F: 510-770-9915   PRC:59
www.protectionplussecurity.com
Email: info@protectionplussecurity.com
Estab: 1990

Patrick Torpey, President

Provider of installation services to the electronic security industry. The company's products include access control, video surveillance, and fire alarm systems.

**Protein Research**   HQ
1852 Rutan Dr
Livermore CA 94551
P: 925-243-6300   F: 925-243-6308   PRC:268
www.proteinresearch.com
Estab: 1968

Ashley Matheson, President
Robert Matheson, CEO
Melissa Matheson, VP
Gary Troxel, VP of Business Development
Melissa Dethardt, VP

Manufacturer of nutritional products. The company develops and formulates supplements for human nutrition in capsules, tablets, powders and pre-mixes.

**ProteinSimple**   HQ
3001 Orchard Pkwy
San Jose CA 95134
P: 408-510-5500   F: 408-510-5599   PRC:31
www.proteinsimple.com
Email: info@proteinsimple.com
Estab: 2004

Tom Yang, Director of Engineering
Sarah Tiller, Senior Software Engineer
Andrew De La Rue, Consumables Production Manager
Mike Jandro, Director of Manufacturing
Rick Alfonso, IT & Facility Manager

Developer of proprietary systems, immunoassay system and consumables for protein analysis and purity of protein-based therapeutics.

**Protemp Mechanical Inc**   HQ
3350 Scott Blvd Bldg 3
Santa Clara CA 95054
P: 408-244-9821   F: 408-980-9358   PRC:138
protemp.net
Email: info@protemp.net

Marty Reich, President

Provider of environmental test equipment calibration services. The company's services include preventative maintenance, chamber modifications, and consulting.

**Proteus Digital Health Inc**   HQ
2600 Bridge Pkwy
Redwood City CA 94065
P: 650-632-4031   F: 650-632-4071   PRC:268
www.proteus.com
Email: press@proteus.com
Estab: 2001

Wesley Zink, Software Engineering Manager
Bill Weeks, Staff DSP Engineer
David O'Reilly, CPO
Oliver Salud, Head of Quality Assurance
Jeff Wiley, Associate Director of Marketing

Providers of health care service technology. The company offers health care products based on electronics technology.

**Proteus Industries Inc**   HQ
340 Pioneer Way
Mountain View CA 94041
P: 650-964-4163   F: 650-965-9355   PRC:14
www.proteusind.com
Email: sales@proteusind.com
Estab: 1978

Alex Gahrahmat, Senior Sales Engineer
Hamed Ershad, Automation Engineer
Jon Heiner, President
Mark Malfatti, Technical Sales Application Support
Grant Gower, Director of Marketing

Developer and manufacturer of rugged and sensitive flow sensing and control instruments. The company focuses on marketing.

**Prothena**   RH
650 Gateway Blvd
S San Francisco CA 94080
P: 650-837-8550   F: 650-837-8560   PRC:24
www.prothena.com
Email: info@prothena.com

Gene Kinney, President
Paula Cobb, President
Tara Nickerson, Chief Business Officer
Karin Walker, Chief Development Officer
Tran Nguyen, CFO

Focuses on the discovery, development and commercialization of protein immunotherapy programs for the treatment of diseases that involve amyloid.

**Proto Services Inc**   HQ
1991 Concourse Dr
San Jose CA 95131
P: 408-719-9088   F: 408-719-9091   PRC:211
protoservices.com
Estab: 1998

Lan Tran, Program Manager

Provider of process verification, yield analysis, testing design, program management, and functional debugging services.

**ProTrials Research Inc**   HQ
333 W San Carlos St Ste 800
San Jose CA 95110
P: 650-864-9180   F: 650-864-9190   PRC:34
www.protrials.com
Email: info@protrials.com
Estab: 1996

Inger Arum, Founder
Jodi Andrews, Founder
Matthew Smith, Chief Revenue Officer
Jackie Rauh, Director of Human Resources
Ellen Hellmoldt, Director of Quality Assurance

Provider of clinical research services. The company offers the ability to move a new drug or device from conception to FDA approval.

**Provectus IT Inc**   HQ
125 University Ave Ste 290
Palo Alto CA 94301
P: 800-679-8721   PRC:323
provectus.com
Email: info@provectus.com
Estab: 2010

Gene Galanter, CEO
Nick Antonov, COO
Maksim Galanter, Business Analyst

Provider of software development, wire framing, related design, and cloud and server development services.

**Provectus IT Inc**     HQ
125 University Ave Ste 290
Palo Alto CA 94301
P: 877-951-2224     PRC:319
reinvently.com
Email: hello@reinvently.com
Estab: 2010

Olga Korchmar, Business Development Manager

Accelerates digital transformation by using Artificial Intelligence.

**Provel Precision**     HQ
35263 Fircrest St Ste C
Newark CA 94560
P: 510-744-1885     PRC:80
www.provelprecision.com
Email: info@provelprecision.com

Phil Sage, General Manager

Provider of machining services. The company offers prototyping, precision machining, assembly, and outsourcing services.

**Providence Medical Technology Inc**     HQ
3875 Hopyard Rd Ste 300
Pleasanton CA 94588
P: 415-923-9376    F: 415-923-9377    PRC:188
www.providencemt.com
Email: providence@providencemt.com
Estab: 2008

Jeff Smith, CEO
Edward Liou, COO
Greg Curhan, CFO
Rebecca Chung, VP of Human Resources
Jeremy Laynor, VP of Sales

Developer of medical devices and technologies such as dtrax spinal systems, cavux cervical cages, and ally screw systems for cervical spine care.

**Provoltz Inc**     HQ
583 Division St Ste B
Campbell CA 95008
P: 408-796-4450     PRC:135
www.provoltz.com
Email: info@provoltz.com
Estab: 2010

Ash Wagner, Owner

Provider of solar, PV, photovoltaic, and solar power solutions. The company is involved in design and installation services.

**Prowess Inc**     HQ
1844 Clayton Rd
Concord CA 94520-7803
P: 925-356-0360    F: 925-356-0363    PRC:194
www.prowess.com

Tan Pham, Software Engineer
Thai Nguyen, Product Manager
Sharon Springorum, Support Manager

Focuses on Windows-based treatment planning systems for radiation therapy treatment and OIS software.

**Proxim Diagnostics Corp**     HQ
325 E Middlefield Rd
Mountain View CA 94043
P: 408-391-6090     PRC:186
www.proximdx.com
Email: hello@proximdx.com
Estab: 2009

Mikhail Briman, CEO
Vikram Joshi, Founder

Manufacturer of diagnostics products and related supplies. The company deals with testing and research related services.

**Proxim Wireless**     HQ
2114 Ringwood Ave
San Jose CA 95131
P: 408-383-7600    F: 408-383-7680    PRC:67
www.proxim.com

Fred Huey, CEO

Provider of Wi-Fi, point-to-point, and 4G wireless network technologies. The company's ORiNOCO product is used by service providers and enterprises.

**Proxio Inc**     HQ
3945 Freedom Cir Ste 940
Santa Clara CA 95054
P: 415-723-1691     PRC:326
proxio.com
Email: support@proxio.com
Estab: 2007

Janet Case, CEO
Peter Spicer, CTO

Provider of digital real estate marketing solutions for agents, brokers and developers. The company serves businesses.

**Prozyme Inc**     BR
3832 Bay Center Pl
Hayward CA 94545
P: 510-638-6900     PRC:31
Estab: 1990

Jo Wegstein, President
Olivia Guillen, Accounting
Antoinette Chavis, Production Scientist
Alexandria Orona, Production Associate
Liliya Boyko, Scientist production

Provider of biotechnology services. The company offers value-added reagents, kits and platforms for improved analytical results.

**Prunella Enterprises Inc**     HQ
986 Tower Pl
Santa Cruz CA 95062
P: 831-465-1818     PRC:80
www.prunellaenterprises.com
Emp: 1-10   Estab: 1983

Scott Prunella, President

Provider of custom machining and sub assembly services. The company serves the telecommunication and space sectors.

**Prysm Inc**     HQ
180 Baytech Dr Ste 200
San Jose CA 95134
P: 408-586-1100    F: 408-957-0364    PRC:169
www.prysm.com
Email: support@prysm.com
Estab: 2005

Amit Jain, President
Roger Hajjar, CTO
Jasbir Singh, CFO
Jeff Martinez, Manager

Provider of large format digital display solutions and software for real-time visual communication applications.

**Psc Electronics Inc**     HQ
2307 Calle Del Mundo
Santa Clara CA 95054
P: 408-737-1333    F: 408-330-0619    PRC:124
www.pscelex.com
Email: info@pscelex.com
Estab: 1985

Bob Gularte, VP of Sales & Engineering
Todd Derbique, Field Sales Engineer
Jena Craycroft, Sales Associate

Distributor of magnetic, interconnect, and electro-mechanical components. The company specializes in cable assembly and modification.

**Ptr Manufacturing Inc**     HQ
33390 Transit Ave
Union City CA 94587
P: 510-477-9654    F: 510-477-9653    PRC:82
www.ptrmanufacturing.com

Sai La, President
Phong La, General Manager

Manufacturer of machining and sheet metals. The company offers manufacturing and manufacturing presentation services.

**PubMatic Inc**     HQ
305 Main St 1st Fl
Redwood City CA 94063
P: 650-331-3485    F: 650-331-2810    PRC:325
www.pubmatic.com
Estab: 2006

Amar Goel, Founder
Rajeev Goel, Co-Founder
Cathie Black, President
Angela Pimentel, Senior Accounting Manager

Developer of marketing automation software. The company deals with the planning of media campaigns and offers services to publishers.

**Pulmonx Corp**     HQ
700 Chesapeake Dr
Redwood City CA 94063
P: 650-364-0400    F: 650-364-0403    PRC:186
www.pulmonx.com
Email: liberate@pulmonx.com
Estab: 1995

Sarah Guy, Manufacturing Engineer
Susan Ramirez, Quality Assurance Technician
Lauren Cristina, VP of Finance
Sri Radhakrishnan, VP of Research & Development
Lisa Simmonds, Director of Supply Chain

Manufacturer of medical devices. The company focuses on developing both diagnostic and therapeutic technologies for Interventional Pulmonology.

**Pulsar Vascular Inc**     HQ
4030 Moorpark Ave Ste 110
San Jose CA 95117
P: 408-260-9264   F: 408-260-9264    PRC:186

Viet Le, Quality Director
Kevin Costello, Manager

Manufacturer of endovascular diseases and it focuses on the treatment of complex aneurysms. The company is engaged in clinical trials.

**Pulse Secure LLC**     HQ
2700 Zanker Rd Ste 200
San Jose CA 95134
P: 408-372-9600    PRC:319
www.pulsesecure.net
Email: info@pulsesecure.net
Estab: 2014

Yvonne Sang, Director of Software Engineering
Dipti Desai, Senior DevOps Engineer
Karen Mayberry, Support Engineer
Felipe Acusa, Escalation Engineer
Sudhakar Ramakrishna, CEO

Provider of product, hardware, partner, and enterprise solutions. The company offers services to the financial services and healthcare industries.

**Pulver Labs Inc**     HQ
320 N Santa Cruz Ave
Los Gatos CA 95031-2353
P: 408-399-7000   F: 408-399-7001    PRC:41
www.pulverlabs.com
Email: information@pulverlabs.com
Estab: 1979

Lee Pulver, President

Provider of equipment evaluation and testing services. The company also offers services for information technology, industrial and medical equipment.

**Punchcut LLC**     HQ
150 California St 9th Fl
San Francisco CA 94111
P: 415-445-8855    PRC:325
www.punchcut.com
Email: business@punchcut.com
Estab: 2002

Jason Siu, Senior Engineer
Nate Cox, Senior Director of Solutions
Jared Benson, Principal
Ken Olewiler, Principal
Lonny Chu, Senior Director

Provider of interface designs. The company offers mid, small, large, micro, and medium screen solutions.

**Pure Storage Inc**     HQ
650 Castro St Ste 400
Mountain View CA 94041
P: 833-371-7873   F: 650-625-9667    PRC:95
www.purestorage.com
Email: info@purestorage.com
Estab: 2009
Sales: $1B to $3B

Brian Peterson, Engineering Manager
Feng Wang, Founding Engineer
Jianting Cao, Software Engineer
Charles Giancarlo, Chairman
Scott Dietzen, Vice Chairman

Provider of flash storage solutions. The company is focused on developing flash arrays for various enterprises.

**Purigen Biosystems Inc**     HQ
5700 Stoneridge Dr Ste 100
Pleasanton CA 94588
P: 925-264-1364    PRC:24
www.purigenbio.com
Email: info@purigenbio.com
Estab: 2012

Klint Rose, CEO
Peter Leigh, CEO
Pam Delucchi, SVP of Operations
Priyanka Agrawal, Analogs Manager
Gomathi Komanduru, Senior Analog

Provider of biotechnology such as isotachophoresis, an electric-field driven technique for extracting and quantifying DNA and RNA from biological samples.

**Puronics Inc**     HQ
5775 Las Positas Rd
Livermore CA 94551
P: 925-456-7000   F: 925-456-7010    PRC:144
puronics.com
Email: info@puronics.com
Estab: 2006

Scott Batiste, CEO
Colin Riggs, Assistant Manufacturing Manager
Heather Barbera, Marketing Program Manager
Joanne Wong, Operations Coordinator

Manufacturer of water treatment equipment. The company's products include drinking water systems, water softeners, and reverse osmosis systems.

**Purple Communications Inc**     HQ
595 Menlo Dr
Rocklin CA 95765
P: 877-885-3172    PRC:68
www.purplevrs.com
Email: government@purple.us
Emp: 11-50 Estab: 1982

Cliff Pearce, Sales Engineer
Laura Goeb, Human Resource Coordinator
Jacob White, Facilities Manager
James Parker, Strategic Sales Manager
Francine Cummings, VP

Provider of communication services to deaf or hard of hearing people. The company serves the medical sector and clinics.

**Pyramid Orthodontics**     HQ
4328 Redwood Hwy Ste 100
San Rafael CA 94903
P: 415-479-6400   F: 415-479-2745    PRC:190
www.pyramidorthodontics.com
Email: pyramid@pyramidorthodontics.com

Sacha Laskar, Manager

Provider of orthodontics products. The company's products include clear brackets, bands, buccal tubes, and wire accessories.

**Pyramid Semiconductor Corp**     HQ
1249 Reamwood Ave
Sunnyvale CA 94089
P: 408-734-8200   F: 408-734-0962    PRC:208
www.pyramidsemiconductor.com
Email: info@pyramidsemiconductor.com
Estab: 2003

Joe Rothstein, President
Jagtar Sandhu, VP of Quality Assurance
Doug Beaubien, VP of Operations
Rosevelyn Galban, Operations Assistant

Provider of assembly services. The company is focused in the assembly of monolithic ceramic products and multi-chip modules.

**Pyxis Laboratories Inc**     HQ
12499 Loma Rica Dr
Grass Valley CA 95945
P: 949-598-1978    PRC:41
www.pyxislabs.com
Email: orders@pyxislabs.com
Emp: 1-10 Estab: 1997

Ines Moretti, President
Francisco Rojas, VP
Carolina Rojas, Director of Operations and Sales

Specializes in the research, development and production of specialty reagents for the diagnostics, pharmaceutical, and environmental industries.

**Q Analysts LLC**     HQ
4320 Stevens Creek Blvd Ste 130
San Jose CA 95129
P: 408-907-8500   F: 408-907-8515    PRC:326
www.qanalysts.com
Email: info@qanalysts.com
Estab: 2003

Ross Fernandes, CEO
Haran Kosambi, Talent Acquisition Manager
Piper Berge, Senior Project Manager
Nitin Trivedi, Senior Technical Recruiter

Provider of consulting, strategic advisory, and related compliance services. The company is also involved in mobile testing.

**Qantel Technologies**     HQ
3506 Breakwater Ct
Hayward CA 94545-3611
P: 510-731-2080    PRC:322
www.qantel.com
Estab: 1996

Woody Smith, Software Engineer
Michael Galvin, President
Richard Morton, Director of Regional Sales
Jerry DeVries, VP of Application Development
Carroll Bowen, Director of Customer Relations

Manufacturer of software systems. The company provides network connectivity and business software solutions.

**Qarbon Inc**     HQ
111 N Market St Ste 830
San Jose CA 95113
P: 408-430-5560   F: 408-430-5570    PRC:322
www.qarbon.com
Email: sales@qarbon.com
Estab: 1997

Jay Lucke, President
Jim Lynch, Secretary
Dave Mosby, Director

Publisher of presentation software and the originator of patented Viewlet technology. The company serves business, government, and education markets.

**Qardio Inc**    HQ
115 Sansome St
San Francisco CA 94104
P: 855-240-7323    PRC:187
www.getqardio.com
Estab: 2012

Marco Peluso, Founder
Rosario Iannella, Founder
Alexis Zervoglos, Chief Business Officer
Betty Peng, Digital Marketing Manager

Creator of health monitoring devices such as blood pressure monitor, multiple-sensor EKG, and wireless scale and body analyzer.

**QB3**    HQ
1700 Fourth St Byers Hall Ste 214
San Francisco CA 94158
P: 415-514-9790    PRC:24
qb3.org
Estab: 2000

Agnes Buenaventura, Financial Analyst
Kaspar Mossman, Director of Communications & Marketing
Regis Kelly, Executive Director
Chris Jeans, Director
Nora Ke, Executive Assistant to the Director

Provider of life science services. The company focuses on research facilities, internships, mentoring, and seed-stage venture fund.

**Qct LLC**    HQ
1010 Rincon Cir
San Jose CA 95131
P: 510-270-6111    F: 510-270-6161    PRC:68
qct.io
Email: sales@quantaqct.com

Michael Quan, Director Sales Engineering

Provider of computer network services. The company also offers storage, database management, and data backup solutions.

**Qi Medical Inc**    HQ
1415 Whispering Pines Ln Ste 150
Grass Valley CA 95945
P: 530-272-8700    F: 530-272-8702    PRC:34
www.qimedical.com
Email: info@qimedical.com
Emp: 1-10    Estab: 1992

Jan Hedman, Owner
Brady Schwarz, Director of Marketing

Manufacturer of fingertip testing, syringe filters, rinse fluids, incubators, and vial adaptors for pharmacists and nurses who handle sterile solutions.

**Qool Therapeutics Inc**    HQ
453 Ravendale Dr Ste G
Mountain View CA 94043
P: 650-328-1426    PRC:269
qooltherapeutics.com
Email: bhuss@qooltherapeutics.com
Estab: 2005

Amir Belson, Founder
Beverly Huss, CEO
Kim Tompkins, VP of Regulatory Quality and Clinical Affairs
Mike Horzewski, SVP of Research and Development and Operations
Dalton Dietrich, Chair in Neurosurgery

Developer of therapeutic hypothermia/temperature management therapies to preserve cells and tissues. The company serves the medical industry.

**QSolv Inc**    HQ
440 N Wolfe Rd
Sunnyvale CA 94085
P: 408-962-3803    PRC:323
www.qsolv-inc.com
Estab: 1997

Son Nguyen, Software Engineer
Sujaya S, Director
Pradeep P, Resource Manager
Sandy V., Business Development Manager
Admin QSolv, Business Development Manager

Provider of cloud automation services. The company provides network management, gap analysis, tool evaluation, and framework implementation services.

**Qspec Technology Inc**    HQ
1190 Mountain View Alviso Rd Ste J
Sunnyvale CA 94089
P: 408-541-1398    PRC:41
qspec.us
Email: analysis@qspec.us

Jack Sheng, Co-Founder

Provider of surface analysis and materials characterization services. The company's applications include device processing for microelectronics.

**QT Ultrasound LLC**    HQ
3 Hamilton Landing Ste 160
Novato CA 94949
P: 415-842-7250    PRC:304
qtultrasound.com
Estab: 2011

John Klock, CEO
Mark Lenox, CTO
Ronald LoVetri, COO
Margaret Donigan, CSO
Nasser Pirshafiey, Chief Product Officer

Developer of ultrasound devices. The company is involved in software development and clinical testing services.

**Quadbase Systems Inc**    HQ
275 Saratoga Ave Ste 105
Santa Clara CA 95050
P: 408-982-0835    F: 408-982-0838    PRC:323
www.quadbase.com
Email: sales@quadbase.com
Estab: 1988

Fred Luk, President

Designer of web-delivered and mobile enabled business intelligence reporting, charting, and dashboard tools.

**Quail Electronics Inc**    HQ
2171 Research Dr
Livermore CA 94550
P: 925-373-6700    F: 925-373-7099    PRC:200
www.quail.com
Estab: 1988

Denise Ruppert, CFO
Larrie Pimentel, Inside Sales

Manufacturer of power cord supplies for the OEM market. The company offers solutions for power cords, current cords, and adapters, and traveler kits.

**Qualdeval International**    HQ
48837 Sauvignon Ct
Fremont CA 94539
P: 844-247-2523    PRC:80
www.qualdeval.com
Email: inquires@qualdeval.com

Ivy Lin, President
Gerry McFaull, CEO

Supplier of high-pressure fluid flow and special core analysis equipment. The company offers PCB fabrication & assembly, and other services.

**Qualitau Inc**    HQ
830 Maude Ave
Mountain View CA 94043
P: 650-282-6226    F: 650-230-9192    PRC:19
www.qualitau.com
Email: sales@qualitau.com
Estab: 1991

Toan Tran, Software Engineer
Sidney Chi, Hardware Engineer
Jacob Herschmann, President
Gadi Krieger, CEO
Nava Ben-Yehuda, VP of Finance and Control

Supplier of test equipment and services. The company is involved in the development of electronic equipment for semiconductor process reliability.

**Quality Circuit Assembly**    HQ
1709 Junction Ct Unit 380
San Jose CA 95112
P: 408-441-1001    PRC:209
www.qcamfg.com
Email: sales@qcamfg.com
Estab: 1988

Timmy Nguyen, President
Tim Garcia, Senior Business Development Manager

Manufacturer of printed circuit board and cable assemblies. The company is also involved in box build and turnkey solutions.

**Quality Machine Engineering Inc**    HQ
5600 Skylane Blvd
Santa Rosa CA 95403
P: 707-528-1900    F: 707-528-1999    PRC:80
www.qmeinc.com
Estab: 1991

Mark Hullinger, CFO

Provider of precision engineering solutions. The company serves the medical, semiconductor, aerospace, and other markets.

**Quality Metal Spinning & Machining Inc**    HQ
4047 Transport St
Palo Alto CA 94303
P: 650-858-2491    F: 650-858-2494    PRC:80
qualitymetalspinning.us

Xenia Czisch, VP of Operations

Provider of metal spinning, sputtering shielding, and purity coils. The company's services include packing, shipping, and handling.

**Quality Quartz Engineering Inc**    HQ
8484 Central Ave
Newark CA 94560
P: 510-745-9200   F: 510-745-7948    PRC:80
qqe.com
Email: info@qqe.com
Estab: 1995

Tim Youngdale, Sales & Marketing Manager
Kevin Cordia, EVP
Kim Phippen, Office Manager
Mezhgan Karim, Office Manager

Designer and manufacturer of solid quartz
products for solar, fiber optic, semiconductor, and
lighting industries.

**Quality Stainless Tanks**    HQ
510 Caletti Ave
Windsor CA 95492
P: 877-598-0672   F: 707-837-2733    PRC:153
www.qualitystainless.com

Justin George, Fabricator & Welder

Provider of ready-made tanks. The company
offers crafted tanks, stainless winery equipment,
and special application tanks.

**Quality Transformer & Electronics**    HQ
963 Ames Ave
Milpitas CA 95035
P: 408-263-8444   F: 408-263-8448    PRC:293
www.qte.com
Email: sales@qte.com
Estab: 1964

Tony Clift, Sales & Marketing Manager
Emilie Ho, Accounting Manager

Manufacturer and seller of transformers. The
company also specializes in power supplies and
other components.

**Qualtech Circuits Inc**    HQ
1101 Comstock St
Santa Clara CA 95054
P: 408-727-4125   F: 408-727-1411    PRC:211
qualtechcircuits.com
Email: info@qualtechcircuits.com

Jim Khosh, CEO

Producer of printed circuit boards. The company's
products include probe cards and edge plating.

**Qualys Inc**    HQ
919 E Hillsdale Blvd Fl 4
Foster City CA 94404
P: 650-801-6100   F: 650-801-6101    PRC:325
www.qualys.com
Email: info@qualys.com
Estab: 1999
Sales: $100M to $300M

Balaji Venkatesan, Principal Engineer
Chintan Shah, Engineering Manager
Sumedh Thakar, President
Philippe Courtot, CEO
Melissa Fisher, CFO

Provider of security and compliance solutions. The
company also offers asset discovery and threat
protection solutions.

**QuanDx Inc**    HQ
770 Charcot Ave
San Jose CA 95131
P: 650-262-4140   F: 866-928-7828    PRC:186
www.quandx.com
Email: info@quandx.com
Estab: 2012

Guo-Liang Yu, Co-Founder
Matthew Lei, Founder
Hao Yu, CEO
Graeme Duncan, VP of European Sales & Mar-
keting
Heather Kiefer, Marketing Specialist

Developer of molecular diagnostics for personalized cancer treatment. The company offers
detection kits and lung cancer assays.

**Quanergy Systems Inc**    HQ
482 Mercury Dr
Sunnyvale CA 94085-4706
P: 408-245-9500   F: 408-245-9503    PRC:326
www.quanergy.com

Ross Taylor, VP of Software Engineering
Tomoyuki Izuhara, VP of Engineering
Tianyue Yu, Co-Founder
Louay Eldada, CEO
Patrick Archambault, CFO

Developer of smart sensing solutions. The company offers solutions for real-time 3D mapping,
object detection, and tracking.

**Quanta Computer Usa Inc**    LH
45630 Northport Loop E
Fremont CA 94538
P: 510-226-1001   F: 510-226-1012    PRC:120
www.quantatw.com
Email: service@quantafremont.com
Estab: 1988

Lin Li, Process Engineer
Elton Yang, CFO
Paul Tsang, Facilities Manager
Angelina Chew, Purchasing Manager

Provider of design and manufacturing services for
technology products. The company specializes in
cloud computing solutions.

**Quanta Laboratories**    HQ
3199 De La Cruz Blvd
Santa Clara CA 95054
P: 408-988-0770    PRC:139
quantalabs.com
Email: quantalabs@quantalabs.com
Estab: 1985

Martin Nobre, Test Engineer
Hong-Sun Liu, President
Mike Hauf, General Manager
Terry Liu, Marketing Manager
Robin Gardiner, Customer Liaison & Quality
Analyst

Provider of environmental testing and consulting
services. The company offers vibration test, shock
test, and chambers test services.

**Quantapore Inc**    HQ
815 Dubuque Ave
S San Francisco CA 94080
P: 650-321-2032    PRC:34
www.quantapore.com
Email: info@quantapore.com
Estab: 2009

Martin Huber, CEO
Brett Anderson, Research Scientist

Developer of anopore based nucleic acid sequencing technology. The company's technology
is used to read human genomes.

**Quantenna Communications Inc**    HQ
1704 Automation Pkwy
San Jose CA 95131
P: 669-209-5500   F: 669-209-5501    PRC:212
www.quantenna.com
Email: info@quantenna.com
Estab: 2006

Kapil Gulati, Senior Manager of System Engi-
neering
Vivek Rathi, ASIC Verification Engineer
Sam Heidari, CEO
David Carroll, VP of Worldwide Sales
Lionel Bonnot, SVP of Marketing and Business
Development

Developer of semiconductor solutions for the
Wi-Fi networks. The company serves retail, home
networking, consumer electronics, and enterprise
needs.

**Quantitative Medical Systems Inc**    HQ
6001 Shellmound St Ste 875
Emeryville CA 94608
P: 510-654-9200   F: 510-654-1168    PRC:194
www.qms-us.com
Email: qms@qms-us.com
Estab: 1976

Jackie Wong, Senior Software Engineer
Melissa Gabriel, Quality Assurance Manager
Pat Parra, Business Development Specialist
Janice Lau, Database Administrator

Provider of medical systems and dialysis billing
software products. The company is engaged in
clinical support.

**Quantum Corporation**    HQ
224 Airport Pkwy Ste 550
San Jose CA 95110
P: 408-944-4000    PRC:319
www.quantum.com
Estab: 1980
Sales: Over $3B

Bruno Hald, VP of Engineering
Don Martella, SVP of Engineering
Greg Wade, VP of Advanced Engineering
Jim Kinder, Senior Director of Software Engineer-
ing
Neil Bannister, Head of StorNext Engineering

Provider of software for backup, recovery, and
archiving needs. The company serves the healthcare, media, and entertainment industries.

**Quantum Secure Inc**     HQ
100 Century Center Ct Ste 800
San Jose CA 95112
P: 408-453-1008     PRC:322
www.hidglobal.com
Estab: 2004

Stefan Widing, President
Laura Crumley, SVP
Ramesh Songukrishnasamy, SVP
Rodney Glass, SVP
Lisa Woodson, SVP of Human Resources

Provider of physical identity and access management solutions. The company focuses on compliance and risk management, and security intelligence.

**Quantum Semiconductor LLC**     HQ
4340 Stevens Creek Blvd Ste 284
San Jose CA 95129-1162
P: 408-243-2262    F: 408-243-2272    PRC:212
quantumsemi.com
Email: info@quantumsemi.com
Estab: 2000

Pedro Diniz, Co-Founder
Carlos Augusto, Co-Founder
Lynn Forester, Co-Founder

Manufacturer of semiconductor devices. The company specializes in silicon photonic receivers and solar cells.

**Quantum3D Inc**     HQ
1759 McCarthy Blvd
Milpitas CA 95035
P: 408-600-2500    F: 408-600-2608    PRC:319
quantum3d.com
Email: sales@quantum3d.com
Estab: 1997

Mark Matthews, President
Murat Kose, COO
Edith Talamantes, Human Resource Manager
Joe Silva, Test & Manufacturing Manager
Scott MacDougall, Marketing Manager

Developer and manufacturer of real-time visual simulation and computing systems for fast-jet, helicopter, refueling, and other needs.

**QuantumScape Corp**     HQ
1730 Technology Dr
San Jose CA 95110
P: 408-452-2007     PRC:242
www.quantumscape.com
Estab: 2010

Jagdeep Singh, CEO

Provider of energy storage, electronics, and related solutions. The company offers services to the environmental sector.

**Quark Pharmaceuticals Inc**     HQ
6501 Dumbarton Cir
Fremont CA 94555
P: 510-402-4020    F: 510-402-4021    PRC:268
www.quarkpharma.com
Email: qbi@quarkpharma.com
Estab: 1994

Daniel Zurr, CEO
Elena Feinstein, CSO
Juliana Friedmann, SVP of Strategy & Planning
Vidhya Gopalakrishnan, SVP of pharmaceutical development
Anna Muchnik, VP of Product Development & Pre-Clinical

Manufacturer of pharmaceuticals. The company focuses on the discovery and development of novel RNAi-based therapeutics.

**Quarterwave Corp**     HQ
1300 Valley House Dr Ste 130
Rohnert Park CA 94928
P: 707-793-9105    F: 707-793-9245    PRC:70
www.quarterwave.com
Email: sales@quarterwave.com
Estab: 1987

Steven Price, Owner
Paul Bradshaw, General Manager
Larry Kalder, Electronics Technician

Manufacturer of high power traveling wave-tube amplifiers, valves, and test equipment. The company deals with installation services.

**Quartet Mechanics Inc**     HQ
1040 Di Giulio Ave Ste 100
Santa Clara CA 95050
P: 408-564-8901    F: 510-490-1887    PRC:80
quartetmechanics.com
Email: inquiry@quartetmechanics.com

Elik Gershenzon, Senior Mechanical Engineer
Alex Kagan, Senior Optomechanical Engineer
J.D. Hawk, Sales Engineer

Provider of LED, MEMS, photovoltaics (PV) solar and medical/lab automation systems. The company also offers wafer sorting and packing products.

**Qubell Inc**     HQ
4600 Bohannon Dr Ste 220
Menlo Park CA 94025
P: 888-855-9440     PRC:323
qubell.com
Email: info@qubell.com
Estab: 2012

Stan Klimoff, Chief Product Officer
Eugene Horohorin, VP
Dmitry Ornatsky, Director

Specializes in autonomic management solutions. The company focuses on e-commerce and other cloud applications.

**Qubop Inc**     HQ
301 Folsom St Ste D
San Francisco CA 94105
P: 415-891-7788    F: 415-680-1721    PRC:322
www.qubop.com
Email: info@qubop.com
Estab: 2002

Chia Hwu, CEO

Developer of applications and games for mobile platforms. The company specializes in web applications, localization, IOS, and android development.

**Quesgen Systems Inc**     HQ
800 Airport Blvd Ste 410
Burlingame CA 94010
P: 415-738-8452     PRC:326
www.quesgen.com
Estab: 2004

Michael Jarrett, Founder
Martin Jorgensen, Director of Operations and Finance
Vibeke Brinck, Director of Client Services
Bianca Byrne, Client Services Manager

Provider of data management solutions. The company is involved in clinical research and related support services.

**Quest America Inc**     HQ
111 W Saint John St Ste 430
San Jose CA 95113
P: 408-492-1650    F: 408-492-1647    PRC:322
www.questam.com
Estab: 1995

Soundaran Natarajan, CEO
Melo Rajakumar, COO

Provider of information technology services. The company offers solutions through strategy, consulting, and outsourcing.

**Quest Business Systems Inc**     HQ
PO Box 715
Brentwood CA 94513
P: 925-634-2670     PRC:325
www.questbusinesssystems.com
Email: sales@questbizsystems.com
Estab: 1983

Tom Elliott, Owner

Provider of solutions in police equipment tracking systems. The company also focuses on purchasing management.

**Quest Diagnostics Inc**     BR
13847 E 14th St Ste 111
San Leandro CA 94578
P: 510-357-5438    F: 510-357-5413    PRC:303
www.questdiagnostics.com

Stephen Rusckowski, CEO

Provider of diagnostic laboratory testing services. The company offers a wide range of test menu for diagnosing medical conditions.

**Quest Diagnostics Inc**     BR
3714 Northgate Blvd
Sacramento CA 95834
P: 916-927-9900     PRC:186
www.questdiagnostics.com
Email: qualitysolutions@questdiagnostics.com
Emp: 11-50

Steve Rusckowski, President
Mark Guinan, EVP
Manuel M'ndez, SVP
Cecilia McKenney, SVP
Gabrielle Wolfson, SVP

Provider of diagnostic laboratory testing services. The company offers a wide range of test menu for diagnosing medical conditions.

**Quest Diagnostics Inc** BR
127 N San Mateo Dr
San Mateo CA 94401
P: 650-344-8143   F: 650-344-8208   PRC:186
www.questdiagnostics.com

Lawrence Munoz, Director of Scientific Affairs-US
Anna Lucien, Phlebotomist
Renee Ciletti, Phlebotomist

Provider of diagnostic laboratory testing services.
The company offers a wide range of test menu for
diagnosing medical conditions.

**Quest Inc** HQ
9000 Foothills Blvd Ste 100
Roseville CA 95747-4411
P: 800-326-4220   PRC:326
www.questsys.com
Email: presskit@questsys.com
Emp: 1-10   Estab: 1982

Tim Burke, CEO
Mike Dillon, CTO

Provider of technology and infrastructure management services. The company caters to a wide
range of businesses.

**Quest Microwave Inc** HQ
225 Vineyard Ct
Morgan Hill CA 95037-7121
P: 408-778-4949   F: 408-778-4950   PRC:200
www.questmw.com
Email: circulators@questmw.com
Estab: 1996

Nabeel Khayat, Founder

Provider of ferrite products for the microwave electronics industry. The company offers both standard
and custom designs.

**Questek Inc** BR
1916 O'Toole Way
San Jose CA 95131
P: 510-979-9311   PRC:211
questekinc.net
Estab: 2002

Joemarie Espanola, President

Provider of solutions for burn-in and test requirements. The company is engaged in PCB design
and testing services.

**Quicklogic Corp** HQ
2220 Lundy Ave
San Jose CA 95131
P: 408-990-4000   F: 408-990-4040   PRC:86
ir.quicklogic.com
Email: info@quicklogic.com
Estab: 1988
Sales: $10M to $30M

Brian Faith, President
Timothy Saxe, CTO
Sue Cheung, VP of Finance
Donald Alexander, VP of Worldwide Sales
Rajiv Jain, VP of Worldwide Operations

Provider of trading solutions for stock market
investors. The company offers online trading platforms for mobiles, smartphones, and tablets.

**Quicknet Technologies Inc** HQ
520 Townsend St Ste D
San Francisco CA 94103
P: 415-864-5225   PRC:67
www.quicknet.net
Estab: 1995

David Erhart, CTO
Iris Grable, VP of Worldwide Manufacturing

Developer of internet telephony technology
solutions. The company serves individuals, small
businesses and computer users.

**Quid Inc** HQ
1 California St 23rd Fl
San Francisco CA 94111
P: 415-813-5300   F: 415-400-5189   PRC:315
quid.com
Email: general@quid.com
Estab: 2010

Bob Goodson, Founder
Sinohe Terrero, CFO
Saravanan Subbiah, CTO
Shashi Reddy, Chief of Staff
Ryan Hilton, VP of Software Sales

Developers of artificial intelligence to help organizations make important decisions.

**Quiq Labs** HQ
8839 N Cedar Ave
Fresno CA 93720
P: 559-745-5511   PRC:322
www.quiqlabs.com
Email: team@quiqlabs.com
Emp: 1-10

Curlen Phipps, Software Developer

Developer of tools and solutions. The company
focuses on influencing consumer behavior and
engagement.

**Quisk Inc** HQ
1183 Bordeaux Dr
Sunnyvale CA 94089
P: 408-462-6800   PRC:322
www.quisk.co
Email: info@quisk.co
Estab: 2007

Steve Novak, CEO
Praveen Amancherla, CTO

Specializes in the development of payment
solutions. The company offers services to financial
institutions.

**Quizlet Inc** BR
501 Second St Ste 500
San Francisco CA 94107
P: 510-495-6550   PRC:322
quizlet.com
Email: support@quizlet.com
Estab: 2005

Tim Miller, VP of Engineering
Giancarlo D., Software Engineer
Josh Rai, Software Engineer
Daniel Cepeda, Infrastructure Engineer
Alan Vaughn, Engineer

Provider of learning tools for students and teach-
ers. The company offers services to the educational sector.

**Qulsar Inc** HQ
1798 Technology Dr Ste 292
San Jose CA 95119
P: 408-715-1098   F: 408-392-0865   PRC:97
qulsar.com
Email: info@qulsar.com
Estab: 2010

Kishan Shenoi, CTO
Minoo Mehta, VP of Business Development &
Marketing

Specializes in packaging, refinement, and distribution of precise time synchronization. The company
serves the telecom and networking industries.

**Qumu Inc** BR
1350 Old Bayshore Hwy Ste 470
San Bruno CA 94010
P: 650-396-8530   PRC:326
www.qumu.com
Estab: 2002

Vern Hanzlik, President
Sherman Black, CEO
Jim Stewart, CFO

Provider of web casting, marketing, event, and
other professional services. The company offers
enterprise video solutions.

**Quorum Technologies** HQ
2485 Natomas Park Dr  Ste 320
Sacramento CA 95833
P: 916-669-5577   PRC:322
quorumtech.net
Email: info@quorumtech.net
Emp: 1-10   Estab: 1998

Binda Mangat, President
Bethanne Ponci, Senior Account Executive
Mazhar Iqbal, Technical Support Analyst

Developer of recycling and waste disposal
solutions for the automotive, industrial, municipal,
hospitality, and food industries.

**Quovera** HQ
788 Stone Ln
Palo Alto CA 94303
P: 650-823-0903   F: 650-691-0373   PRC:301
www.quovera.com
Email: contactus@quovera.com
Estab: 1995

Nigel Jones, VP of Sales

Provider of business consulting and technology
integration services. The company serves the
high-tech and semiconductor industries.

**Qview Medical** HQ
4546 El Camino Real Ste 215
Los Altos CA 94022
P: 650-397-5174   PRC:186
www.qviewmedical.com
Email: info@qviewmedical.com
Estab: 2006

Bob Wang, CEO
Bob Foley, VP

Provider of assistance in the review of 3D automated breast ultrasound. The company offers
services to the radiologists.

**Qwilt Inc**   HQ
275 Shoreline Dr Ste 510
Redwood City CA 94065
P: 866-824-8009  F: 650-249-6521  PRC:318
qwilt.com
Email: hello@qwilt.com
Estab: 2010

Alon Maor, CEO
Greg Callanan, VP
Mark Fisher, VP
Nimrod Cohen, VP
Udi Lerner, VP

Developer of open caching, video intelligence, fixed, and mobile operators solutions. The company offers media analytics products.

**R F Circuits Inc**   HQ
2299 Ringwood Ave Ste C-4
San Jose CA 95131
P: 408-324-1670  F: 408-324-1770  PRC:211
rfcircuitsinc.com
Email: kenny@rfcircuitsinc.com

Kenny Lee, Sales
Song Lim, Engineer
Sun Young, Manager
Liz Villa, Manager

Manufacturer of printed circuit boards and assemblies. The company is engaged in engineering and electronics manufacturing services.

**R S Calibration Services**   HQ
1047 Serpentine Ln Ste 500
Pleasanton CA 94566
P: 925-462-4217  F: 925-426-0092  PRC:269
www.rscal.com
Email: info@rscalibration.com
Estab: 1995

Olivier Delrieu, Chairman

Provider of lab based calibration and validation services. The company offers dimensional, electronic, and pipette calibration services.

**R Systems Inc**   RH
5000 Windplay Dr Ste 5
El Dorado Hills CA 95762
P: 800-355-5159  F: 916-939-9697  PRC:322
www.rsystems.com
Email: rsi.marketing@rsystems.com
Emp: 1-10  Estab: 1993

Chan Ming, President ECNET & R Systems Singapore
Mandeep Sodhi, COO
Nand Sardana, CFO
Pankaj Dhall, Manager of Sales
Sidhartha Dubey, VP of Analytics & Knowledge Services

Provider of information technology services and solutions. The company offers application, testing, BPO, and packaged services.

**R&A Engineering Solutions Inc**   HQ
1111 Howe Ave Ste 655
Sacramento CA 95825
P: 916-920-5965  F: 916-920-9239  PRC:304
www.ra-solutions.com
Email: info@ra-solutions.com
Emp: 11-50  Estab: 1976

Scott Crosby, Mechanical Engineer
Wayne Watts, Mechanical Engineer
Amy Mountjoy, Office
Robert Thiele, Principal
Harold Hougham, Principal

Provider of engineering consulting services. The company offers design, analysis, verification, and planning of HVAC, and plumbing system services.

**R&D Logic Inc**   HQ
1611 Borel Pl Ste 2
San Mateo CA 94402
P: 650-356-9207  F: 650-571-1276  PRC:326
www.rdlogic.com
Estab: 2000

Wanda Ionescu, CEO
Joyce Bellomo, Chief Finance & Business Development Officer
Pierre Goldenstein, VP of Software Development

Developer of performance management software for R&D focused companies. The company offers implementation and training services.

**R&D Tech**   HQ
500 Yosemite Dr Ste 108
Milpitas CA 95035
P: 408-555-1234  F: 408-555-1234  PRC:211
www.rdtechpcb.com
Email: sales@rdtechpcb.com

Richard Hernadez, Director of Operations
Larry Pilbin, Representative

Provider of prototyping services. The company specializes in fabrication and assembly services.

**R&R Refrigeration And Air Conditioning Inc**   HQ
1775 Monterey Rd Ste 66A
San Jose CA 95112
P: 408-297-0383  F: 408-453-5853  PRC:85
getcooled.com
Email: service@getcooled.com

Cindy Fairfield, President

Provider of environmental technological solutions. The company also offers maintenance and repair services for process systems.

**R-Computer**   HQ
3953 Industrial Way Ste A
Concord CA 94520
P: 925-798-4884  F: 925-798-4894  PRC:323
www.r-computer.com
Email: info@r-computer.com
Estab: 1986

Matt Hart, Professional Service Engineer
Sean Earll, Professional Service Engineer
Ed Roth, Owner
Stephen Haitch, Sales & Production Manager
Ethan Ting, Director of Managed Services

Provider of computer solutions for small and medium-sized companies. The company also offers lifetime product guarantees and sales consultation.

**R-Hub Communications Inc**   HQ
4340 Stevens Creek Blvd Ste 282
San Jose CA 95129
P: 408-899-2830  F: 408-516-9612  PRC:95
www.rhubcom.com
Email: sales@rhubcom.com
Estab: 2005

John Mao, Co-Founder
Larry Dorie, CEO

Provider of web conferencing and remote support services. The company offers services for on-premise security, branding, and integration.

**RackWare Inc**   HQ
75 E Santa Clara St Unit 600
San Jose CA 95113
P: 408-430-5821  PRC:326
www.rackwareinc.com
Email: info@rackwareinc.com
Estab: 2009

Todd Matters, CTO
Bryan Gobbett, CEO
Ron Heinz, Chairman
Sunil Deo, Head India Operations

Provider of disaster prevention and recovery solutions. The company also offers business continuity and virtualization solutions.

**Raco Manufacturing & Engineering Company Inc**   HQ
1400 62nd St
Emeryville CA 94608
P: 510-658-6713  F: 510-658-3153  PRC:59
www.racoman.com
Email: sales@racoman.com
Estab: 1948

Sam Siggins, VP of Engineering
James Garnett, Quality Assurance Manager
Gene Cottom, Western Regional Sales Manager

Manufacturer of alarms and controllers. The company offers remote monitoring, reporting, datalogging, and control services.

**Radian Thermal Products Inc**   BR
2160 Walsh Ave
Santa Clara CA 95050-2512
P: 408-988-6200  F: 408-988-0683  PRC:124
www.radianheatsinks.com
Email: sales@radianheatsinks.com
Estab: 1974

Alejandro Valle, Manufacturing Engineer
Thierry Sin, President
Steve Johanson, Materials Manager
Phoebe Li, Controller

Manufacturer of custom and radiant heat sinks. The company's services include prototyping and engineering support.

**Radiant Logic Inc** HQ
75 Rowland Way Ste 300
Novato CA 94945
P: 415-209-6800  F: 415-798-5697  PRC:324
www.radiantlogic.com
Email: info@radiantlogic.com
Estab: 1995

Divya Kandi, Quality Assurance Engineer
Michel Prompt, Founder
Leah Mazurette, Project Manager
Prashanth Godey, Principal Architect
Elsy Alvarado, Accounting Assistant

Provider of identity and context virtualization solutions. The company caters to identity integration and management needs.

**RadioMate** HQ
2954 Treat Blvd Ste A
Concord CA 94518
P: 925-332-8991  PRC:60
www.radiomate.com
Email: sales@radiomate.com
Estab: 1989

Harry Servidio, CFO

Provider of radio accessories specializing in headsets. The company also offers headsets for surveillance and fire & rescue applications.

**Raditek Inc** HQ
1702L Meridian Ave Ste 127
San Jose CA 95125
P: 408-266-7404  F: 408-266-4483  PRC:68
www.raditek.com
Email: sales@raditek.com
Estab: 1993

Malcolm Lee, Founder

Provider of solutions for the wireless and microwave telecom sector. The company offers passive components, active assemblies, and telecom systems.

**RAF Electronics** HQ
10045 Nantucket Dr
San Ramon CA 94582
P: 925-551-5361  PRC:83
www.rafelectronics.com
Email: info@rafelectronics.com
Estab: 1989

Richard Flasck, Founder

Provider of optical system design and related services. The company deals with sales and delivery solutions.

**RagingWire Data Centers** HQ
PO Box 348060
Sacramento CA 95834
P: 916-286-3000  PRC:67
www.ragingwire.com
Emp: 1-10  Estab: 2000

Douglas Adams, President
Joe Goldsmith, SVP
Judi Lee, SVP of Human Resources
Jerry Gilreath, VP of Information Technology
Meghan Krafka, VP of Finance

Provider of information technology services such as storage, back up services, monitoring, migration planning, and disaster recovery.

M-244

**Rago & Son Inc** HQ
1029 51st Ave
Oakland CA 94601
P: 510-536-5700  F: 510-536-3460  PRC:80
www.rago-son.com
Email: info@rago-son.com
Estab: 1945

Eddie Rago, Quality Manager
Alfonso Munoz, Supervisor

Provider of metal stamping and machining services. The company's services include stamping, complete welding, and perforated tubing.

**Rainbow Electronics & Fasteners Corp** HQ
30095 Ahern Ave
Union City CA 94587
P: 510-475-9840  F: 510-475-9845  PRC:124
www.rainbowelectronics.com
Email: raincorp@sbcglobal.net
Estab: 1981

Hank Bombino, President

Distributor of electronic and mechanical hardware products. The company's products include fasteners, screws, standoffs, and spacers.

**Ralphs-Pugh Co** HQ
3931 Oregon St
Benicia CA 94510
P: 707-745-6222  PRC:159
ralphs-pugh.com
Email: sales@ralphs-pugh.com
Estab: 1912

Tom Anderson, VP
Larry Bauer, Plant Manager
Mary Anderson, Customer Service Manager

Manufacturer of conveyor rollers and related components. The company serves the agriculture, chemical, and food processing industries.

**Rambus** HQ
1050 Enterprise Way Ste 700
Sunnyvale CA 94089
P: 408-462-8000  F: 408-462-8001  PRC:64
www.rambus.com
Estab: 1990
Sales: $100M to $300M

Liji Gopalakrishnan, Senior Principal Engineer
Ron Black, President
Luc Seraphin, Interim CEO
Rahul Mathur, SVP of Finance
Martin Scott, SVP

Manufacturer of semiconductor, lighting, and IP products. The company serves the automotive and transportation markets.

**Randal Optimal Nutrients** HQ
PO Box 7328
Santa Rosa CA 95407
P: 707-528-1800  F: 707-528-0924  PRC:268
www.randaloptimal.com
Estab: 1947

Dan Brinker, President
Joseph Trejo, Production Specialist
Donna Coats, VP

Manufacturer of consumer goods. The company produces dietary supplements and nutraceuticals to the health food and profession health care markets.

**Range Networks Inc** HQ
2040 Martin Ave
Santa Clara CA 95050
P: 415-778-8700  PRC:325
rangenetworks.com
Email: info@rangenetworks.com
Estab: 2011

Brad Wurtz, CEO

Provider of mobile network solutions. The company is also engaged in software and hardware solutions and services.

**Rani Therapeutics** HQ
2051 Ringwood Ave
San Jose CA 95131
P: 408-457-3700  PRC:191
www.ranitherapeutics.com
Estab: 2012

Maulik Nanavaty, SVP
Svai Sanford, CFO
Mir Hashim, CSO
Betsy Gutierrez, Associate VP of Quality Assurance
Stephanie McGrory, VP of Business Development

Developer of drug molecules including peptides, proteins and antibodies. The company offers services to the pharmaceutical industry.

**Rapid Accu-Form Inc** HQ
3825 Sprig Dr
Benicia CA 94510
P: 707-745-1879  F: 707-745-6219  PRC:80
www.rapidaccuform.com
Estab: 1975

Larry Brown, Sales & Engineering
Linda Brown, Accounting Analyst

Provider of thermoforming and pressure forming services. The company specializes in tool and die and prototyping services.

**Rapid Precision Manufacturing Inc** HQ
1516 Montague Expy
San Jose CA 95131
P: 408-617-0771  F: 408-617-0772  PRC:80
www.rapidprecision.net
Email: rpm@rapidprecision.net
Estab: 1998

Paul Yi, CEO
Jane Yi, CFO

Provider of screw machining, surface grinding, sheet metal fabrication, tooling, and inspection services.

**Rapidwerks Inc** HQ
1257 Quarry Ln Ste 140
Pleasanton CA 94566
P: 925-417-0124  F: 925-417-0128  PRC:189
rapidwerks.com
Estab: 2004

Scott Herbert, President

Manufacturer of medical equipment and devices. The company also offers accessories and semiconductor products.

**RAPT Therapeutics** HQ
561 Eccles Ave
S San Francisco CA 94080
P: 650-489-9000 PRC:24
rapt.com
Email: inquiries@flxbio.com
Estab: 2015

Dirk Brockstedt, CSO
Rodney Young, CFO
Karen Lam, VP
David Wustrow, SVP
Paul Kassner, VP

Provider of immuno-oncologyoral medicines
designed to activate patients own immune system
to eradicate cancer.

**Rasilient Systems Inc** HQ
3281 Kifer Rd
Santa Clara CA 95051
P: 408-730-2568　F: 408-730-2568 PRC:60
rasilient.com
Estab: 2001

Sean Chang, CEO

Provider of technology products and services. The
company offers a range of video surveillance and
storage products.

**Rasteroids Design** HQ
195 Jackson St
San Jose CA 95112
P: 408-979-9138 PRC:325
www.rasteroids.com
Estab: 2000

Tamiko Rast, Co-Founder
Miles Rast, Owner

Provider of web designing, custom programming,
implementation, custom software development,
and hosting services.

**Rathbun Associates** HQ
48890 Milmont Dr Ste 111D
Fremont CA 94538
P: 510-661-0950　F: 510-668-0369 PRC:200
rathbun.com
Email: sales@rathbun.com
Estab: 1967

Maria Camara, Administrative Assistant
Pam Biagio, Administrative Assistant

Distributor and reseller of converters. The company offers thermal management solutions, specialty
tapes, and protective products.

**Ray Carlson & Associates Inc** HQ
411 Russell Ave
Santa Rosa CA 95403
P: 707-528-7649　F: 707-571-5541 PRC:301
www.rcmaps.com
Email: rca@rcmaps.com
Estab: 1976

Ray Carlson, President
Walter Moody, GIS Manager
Bob Muollo, Land Surveyor

Provider of consulting, research, surveying, mapping, video branding, and related services. The
company also offers data management products.

**Ray L Hellwig** HQ
1309 Laurelwood Rd
Santa Clara CA 95054
P: 408-727-5612　F: 408-727-5619 PRC:80
www.rlhellwig.com
Email: info@rlhellwig.com
Estab: 1992

Jim Hadley, Project Manager
Libby Sandoval, Construction Operations Manager
Roger Kruse, General Foreman Superintendent
Shari Bleeg, Controller
Chelsey Hadley, Project Administrator

Designer and manufacturer of tools. It's products
find application in mechanical, process piping, and
plumbing needs.

**Ray Morgan Co** BR
3131 Esplanade
Chico CA 95973
P: 530-343-6065　F: 530-343-9470 PRC:45
www.raymorgan.com
Email: info@raymorgan.com
Emp: 11-50 Estab: 1956

Ryan Dunn, Sales Engineer & Technical Consul-
tant
Chris Scarff, EVP
Sam Pulino, Co-Founder
Greg Martin, President
Bob Quadros, CFO

Provider of document technology solutions. The
company offers paperless, project management,
and imaging system solutions.

**Raymar Information Technology Inc** HQ
7325 Roseville Rd
Sacramento CA 95842
P: 916-783-1951　F: 916-783-1952 PRC:68
www.raymarinc.com
Email: sales@raymarinc.com
Emp: 11-50 Estab: 1982

David Figueroa, CFO
Gary Portellas, Managing Director
Don Breidenbach, Managing Director
Michael Ellsworth, Account Manager
Marcy Crawford, Accountant

Provider of hardware supplies, network infrastructure, virtualization, disaster recovery, and
managed services.

**Rayteq LLC** HQ
PO Box 1343
Healdsburg CA 95448
P: 510-638-2000 PRC:151
www.rayteq.com
Email: information@rayteq.com

Matthew Smith, EVP
Frank Smith, President

Manufacturer of energy-saving electric melting
furnaces for the metal casting industry and offers
electric heating systems and metal level sensors.

**Rcb Elevator Consulting LLC** HQ
684 Ellis St
San Francisco CA 94115-3103
P: 415-350-0402 PRC:304
www.blaska.com
Estab: 1984

Richard Blaska, Owner

Provider of elevator design and structural engineering services to building owners, architects,
and elevator companies and offers field surveys.

**RCH Associates Inc** HQ
4115 Business Center Dr
Fremont CA 94538-6355
P: 510-657-7846　F: 510-657-6138 PRC:86
www.rchassociates.com
Email: info@rchassociates.com
Estab: 1990

Matthew Furlo, Engineer Manager
Willie Nono, Project Engineer
Bob Hoelsch, President

Provider of engineering solutions. The company
specializes in equipment used in space, solar, and
semiconductor industries.

**Rcm Industries Inc** HQ
110 Mason Cir Ste D
Concord CA 94520
P: 925-687-8363　F: 925-671-9636 PRC:14
www.flo-gage.com
Email: info@flo-gage.com
Estab: 1972

Vernon Reizman, CFO

Manufacturer of direct reading flow meters for liquid and gases. The company's products are used
in chillers and satellite systems.

**RDM Industrial Products Inc** HQ
1652 Watson Ct
Milpitas CA 95035
P: 408-945-8400 PRC:32
www.rdm-ind.com
Estab: 1977

Michele Gomez, VP
Lynn Tweedie, Administrative Assistant

Provider of laboratory and industrial furniture
solutions. The company offers cabinets, counters,
carts, and mobile tables.

**Re Cyte Therapeutics Inc** HQ
1010 Atlantic Ave Ste 102
Alameda CA 94501
P: 510-521-3390 PRC:24
www.recyte.com
Estab: 2011

Michael West, CEO
David Larocca, VP of R&D

Provider of regenerative medicine. The company
focuses on repair of vascular disorders in both
age related diseases and injuries.

**Reach Analytics LLC** HQ
2055 Woodside Rd Ste 270
Redwood City CA 94061
P: 650-948-4993 PRC:326
reachanalytics.com

Dino Fire, President of Market Research and
Analytics
Mike Hail, CEO
David Schneider, EVP of Business Development
Marina Makarenko, VP of Customer Analytics

Provider of hosted training solutions. The company serves the healthcare, retail, and insurance industries.

**Reaction Technology Inc** HQ
3400 Bassett St
Santa Clara CA 95054
P: 408-970-9601 F: 408-970-9695 PRC:47
www.reactiontechnology.com
Email: sales@reactiontechnology.com
Estab: 1991

Kawika Cross, Manager
Janis Ammirato-Terwilliger, Office Manager

Supplier of silicon epitaxy and silicon coatings. The company caters to the semiconductor and industrial sectors.

**Readytech Corp** HQ
2201 Broadway Ste 725
Oakland CA 94612
P: 800-707-1009 PRC:319
readytech.com
Email: get-info@readytech.com
Estab: 1993

Miguel Palma, Marketing Manager

Provider of virtual labs for training, certification, and also sales demonstrations. The company deals with technology support.

**Real Environmental Products** HQ
1510 S State Hwy 49
Pine Grove CA 95665
P: 209-296-7900 F: 209-296-7944 PRC:134
www.realenvprod.com
Emp: 1-10 Estab: 2000

Rodney Peoples, Owner

Provider of landfill gas products. The company products include LFG well heads and 1200 series monitoring well monuments.

**Real Intent Inc** HQ
990 Almanor Ave Ste 220
Sunnyvale CA 94085
P: 408-830-0700 F: 408-737-1962 PRC:323
www.realintent.com
Email: info@realintent.com
Estab: 1999

Oren Katzir, VP of Applications Engineering
Ertai Cai, Applications Engineer
Prakash Narain, CEO
Pranav Ashar, CTO
Chris Morrison, Chief Architect

Provider of electronic design automation services. The company offers techniques for automatic design verification.

**Real Sensors Inc** HQ
20977 Cabot Blvd
Hayward CA 94545-1155
P: 510-785-4100 F: 510-785-4400 PRC:49
www.realsensors.com
Email: esales@realsensors.com

Ramesh Chand, Engineer

Manufacturer of chemical detection systems. The company also offers security solutions to government agencies and petrochemical industries.

**Real-Time Innovations Inc** HQ
232 E Java Dr
Sunnyvale CA 94089
P: 408-990-7400 F: 408-990-7402 PRC:325
rti.com
Email: info@rti.com
Estab: 1991

Stan Schneider, CEO
Gerardo Pardo-Castellote, CTO
David Barnett, VP of Products & Markets
Catherine Mekler, VP of Operations

Provider for real-time infrastructure software solutions. The company also offers engineering and product development services.

**ReaMetrix Inc** HQ
171 Main St Ste 670
Los Altos CA 94022
P: 650-226-4144 PRC:34
www.reametrix.com
Email: info@reametrix.com
Estab: 2003

Bala Manian, CEO

Provider of biotechnology services. The company develops innovative affordable diagnostic solutions.

**Rearden LLC** HQ
211 S Whisman Rd Ste D
Mountain View CA 94041
P: 415-947-5555 F: 415-947-5597 PRC:318
www.rearden.com
Email: rearden7@rearden.com
Estab: 2000

Steve Perlman, Founder

Provider of cloud computing, motion picture, video game, consumer electronics, wireless, imaging, communications, and alternative energy technologies.

**Recology Of The Coast** HQ
2305 Palmetto Ave
Pacifica CA 94044
P: 650-355-9000 F: 650-359-9580 PRC:141
www.recology.com
Estab: 1921

Michael Sangiacomo, President
Mark Arsenault, EVP
Catherine Langridge, SVP
Christine Porter, General Manager
Julie Bertani-Kiser, SVP

Provider of resource recovery services. The company's services include urban cleaning services, collection, sorting, transfer, recovery and landfill management.

**Recor Medical Inc** RH
1049 Elwell Ct
Palo Alto CA 94303
P: 650-542-7700 PRC:189
www.recormedical.com
Email: info@recormedical.com
Estab: 2009

Mano Iyer, Founder
Andrew Weiss, President
Matthew Franklin, CFO
Leslie Coleman, VP

Manufacturer of ultrasound denervation products. The company is involved in clinical trials and research solutions.

**Recortec Inc** HQ
2231-A Fortune Dr
San Jose CA 95131-1871
P: 408-928-1480 F: 408-928-1489 PRC:93
www.recortec.com
Email: info@recortec.com
Estab: 1969

Edward Lee, Business Development Manager
Toni Tung, Assembler

Manufacturer of LCD monitors, KVM, keyboards, speakers, and computers. The company also offers customization services.

**Red Hat Inc** BR
150 Mathilda Pl Ste 500
Sunnyvale CA 94041
P: 650-567-9039 F: 650-567-9041 PRC:319
www.redhat.com
Estab: 1993

James Whitehurst, President
Paul Cormier, EVP
Lee Congdon, Chief Information Officer
Eric Shander, EVP
Mark Enzweiler, SVP of Global Channel Sales and Alliances

Provider of training, certification, consulting, cloud, application, and other technical support services.

**Redbooth** HQ
95 Third St Ste 231
San Francisco CA 94103
P: 650-521-5459 PRC:319
redbooth.com
Email: info@redbooth.com
Estab: 2008

John Gabaix, CEO
Callie Strawn, Director of Operations

A task and project management platform for team collaboration tasks, discussions, and file sharing.

**Redis Labs Inc** HQ
700 E El Camino Real Ste 250
Mountain View CA 94040
P: 415-930-9666 PRC:326
redislabs.com
Email: info@redislabs.com
Estab: 2011

Ofer Bengal, Co-Founder
Yiftach Shoolman, Co-Founder
Alvin Richards, Chief Product Officer
David Golob, Chief Investment Officer
Rafael Torres, CFO

Provider of zero management, infinite scalability, and other solutions for start-ups and business enterprises.

**Redline Communications** BR
1800 Wyatt Dr Ste 5
Santa Clara CA 95054
P: 866-633-6669 PRC:61
rdlcom.com
Email: info@rdlcom.com
Estab: 1999

Robert Williams, CEO
Stephen Sorocky, CEO
Philip Jones, CFO
Reno Moccia, EVP of Global Sales & Marketing
Abdelsalam Aldwikat, VP of Operations and
Technology

Provider of networking and consulting solutions.
The company serves the government, telecommunication, and military sectors.

**Redline Solutions Inc** HQ
3350 Scott Blvd Ste 501 Bld 5
Santa Clara CA 95054
P: 408-562-1700   F: 408-562-1720 PRC:304
www.redlinesolutions.com
Estab: 1997

Todd Baggett, Founder

Provider of produce traceability and bar code solutions, and warehouse and inventory management
systems.

**Redolent Inc** HQ
4620 Fortran Dr Ste 201
San Jose CA 95134
P: 650-242-1195 PRC:323
www.redolentech.com
Email: contact@redolentech.com
Estab: 1999

Shubhada Ingole, Information Technology Man-
ager
Samir Vyas, Director
Rahul Thakkar, Technical Recruiter

Provider of software solution in web, open source,
e-commerce applications. The company also
focuses on enterprise wide applications.

**Redpark Product Development** HQ
1555 Third Ave
Walnut Creek CA 94597
P: 510-594-1034   F: 510-222-0325 PRC:202
www.redpark.com
Email: info@redpark.com
Estab: 1995

Mike Ridenhour, President

Manufacturer of connectivity accessories for
iPhone and iPad. The company's products include
lightning cables and 30-pin cables.

**Redpine Signals Inc** HQ
2107 N First St Ste 680
San Jose CA 95131-2019
P: 408-748-3385   F: 408-705-2019 PRC:68
www.redpinesignals.com
Email: info@redpinesignals.com
Estab: 2001

Prabhashankar Shastry, VP of Engineering
Venkat Mattela, Chairman
David Shefler, SVP of Sales and Business Devel-
opment
Dhiraj Sogani, SVP of Marketing
Narasimhan Venkatesh, VP of Advanced Technol-
ogies

Manufacturer of wireless systems. The company
offers chipset and system level products for wireless networks.

**Redwhale Software Corp** HQ
1755 E Bayshore Rd Ste 25B
Redwood City CA 94063
P: 650-312-1500   F: 650-285-6209 PRC:323
www.redwhale.com
Email: redwhale.info@redwhale.com
Estab: 1998

Jared Ho, Project Manager

Provider of software tools, technologies, and
professional services for the design, development,
and run-time management of user interfaces.

**Redwood Renewables** HQ
6 Endeavor Dr
Corte Madera CA 94925
P: 415-924-8140   F: 415-924-4041 PRC:135
www.redwoodrenewables.com
Email: tfaust@redwoodrenewables.com

Tom Faust, President

Developer and manufacturer of residential tiles
and solar roofing. The company also focuses on
the marketing aspects.

**Redwood Toxicology Laboratory** BR
3650 Westwind Blvd
Santa Rosa CA 95403
P: 707-577-7959 PRC:306
www.redwoodtoxicology.com
Email: info@redwoodtoxicology.com

Lisa Downing, Human Resource Manager
Janee Gully, Regulatory Affairs
Suman Rana, Director of Laboratory Operations
Marjetta Reed, Account Manager
Ellen Jones, Accounting Manager

Provider of drug and alcohol testing laboratories.
The company specializes in substance abuse
screening products to criminal justice and treatment markets.

**Reel Solar Power Inc** HQ
2219 Oakland Rd
San Jose CA 95131
P: 408-258-4714 PRC:135
reelsolar.com
Estab: 2009

Dori Gal, Founder
Scott Burton, CEO
Kuo-Jui Hsiao, Chief Scientist
Ariel Howard, Senior Process Technician

Provider of tools and materials to photovoltaic
manufacturing. The company also engages in the
manufacturing of cadmium telluride solar panels.

**Reflektion Inc** HQ
777 Mariners Island Blvd Ste 510
San Mateo CA 94404
P: 650-293-0800 PRC:326
reflektion.com
Email: sales@reflektion.com
Estab: 2012

Vivek Gupta, SVP of Product & Engineering
Steve Papa, Entrepreneur
Amar Chokhawala, Founder
Ray Villeneuve, President
Sanjay Jain, VP of Finance & Admin

Focuses on personalized site search, marketing,
analytics, and predictive product recommendation
solutions.

**Refresh Your Memory Inc** HQ
6920 Santa Teresa Blvd Ste 201
San Jose CA 95119
P: 408-224-9167 PRC:319
factorywiz.com
Estab: 1983

Richard Hefner, VP of Engineering
Karen Lattin, Office Manager

Provider of CNC Machine Tool monitoring and
data collection products. The company is also
involved in preventive maintenance services.

**Relay2 Inc** HQ
1525 McCarthy Blvd Ste 209
Milpitas CA 95035
P: 408-380-0031 PRC:68
www.relay2.com
Estab: 2011

Suryakant Devangan, Senior Technical Lead

Provider of cloud Wi-Fi Services platform which
allows service providers to monetize value added
Wi-Fi services.

**Relcomm Inc** HQ
4868 Hwy 4 Ste G
Angels Camp CA 95222
P: 301-924-7400   F: 301-924-7403 PRC:64
www.relcomm.com
Email: sales@relcomm.com
Emp: 1-10  Estab: 1989

Robert Henkel, Owner
Michael Shea, President
Paul Ungaro, Operations Manager

Manufacturer of computer and data communication devices. The company offers data switches,
inline buffers, and current loop products.

**Reliable Rubber Products** HQ
815 D St
Modesto CA 95354
P: 888-525-9750   F: 209-521-7123 PRC:157
www.reliablerubber.com
Email: sales@reliablerubber.com
Emp: 1-10

Marc Wilkins, President

Provider of rubber products. The company's products include dock bumpers, duty corner guards,
urethane wheel cocks, and street pads.

**Reliant Labs Inc** HQ
925 Thompson Pl
Sunnyvale CA 94085
P: 408-737-7500 PRC:306
www.reliantlabs.com
Email: info@reliantlabs.com
Estab: 2002

Roberto Carcamo, Lab Manager
Ken Duncan, Principal

Provider of environmental testing and reliability
services. The company is also engaged in power
supply evaluation.

**Relievant Medsystems Inc** HQ
385 Moffett Park Dr Ste 105
Sunnyvale CA 94089-1218
P: 650-368-1000 PRC:196
www.relievant.com

Michael Willink, Principal R&D Engineer
Kevin Hykes, President
Chris Green, CFO
Kirk Ellis, VP of Sales
Patrick Lyon, VP of Marketing

Provider of healthcare solutions . The company
develops a system that utilizes a small probe for
the treatment of chronic back pain.

**Reltek LLC** HQ
2345 Circadian Way
Santa Rosa CA 95407
P: 707-284-8808 F: 707-284-8812 PRC:47
www.reltekllc.com
Email: reltek@reltekllc.com
Estab: 1990

Robert Lindberg, Founder

Developer of analytical and empirical Accelerated
Life Testing technology for military, commercial,
and nuclear products.

**Relucent Solutions LLC** HQ
1415 N Dutton Ave Ste C
Santa Rosa CA 95401
P: 800-630-7704 PRC:188
www.relucent.com
Email: sales@relucent.com
Estab: 2007

Steve Parmelee, Founder
Tim Renaud, President
Becca Clover, Quality Manager
Stephen Endweiss, Director of Sales
Jennifer Griggs, Sales Manager

Manufacturer of medical devices. The company is
involved in laser cutting, precision manufacturing,
wire crimping, and related services.

**Relypsa Inc** HQ
700 Saginaw Dr
Redwood City CA 94063-4752
P: 650-421-9500 PRC:261
www.relypsa.com
Email: ir@relypsa.com
Estab: 2007

Scott Garland, SVP

Developer of polymer technology for the treatment
of patients with serious conditions. The company
is engaged in drug discovery.

**Remote Sensing Systems** HQ
444 Tenth St Ste 200
Santa Rosa CA 95401
P: 707-545-2904 F: 707-545-2906 PRC:304
www.remss.com
Email: support@remss.com
Estab: 1974

Deborah Smith, Research Scientist
Frank Wentz, Director
Lucrezia Ricciardulli, Scientist
Thomas Meissner, Scientist
Marty Brewer, Scientist

Processor of microwave data. The company
collects the data with the help of special satellite
microwave sensors.

**Renegade Labs** HQ
13342G Grass Valley Ave
Grass Valley CA 95945
P: 530-273-7047 F: 530-271-0757 PRC:60
renegadelabs.com
Emp: 1-10 Estab: 2004

Kirk Bradford, President

Manufacturer of tools for the broadcast, video, and
film industries. The company's products include
digital audio mixers, metering and input and
output systems.

**Renew Biocare Corp** BR
1001 Bayhill Dr
San Bruno CA 94066
P: 415-358-4110 F: 801-904-8451 PRC:31
renewbiocare.com

Vicky Wang, Group Managing Director

Provider of biomedical solutions. The company
offers treatment options for doctors specializing in
oral maxillofacial surgery.

**Renovorx Inc** HQ
4546 El Camino Real Ste 203
Los Altos CA 94022
P: 650-284-4433 F: 650-397-3344 PRC:189
www.renovorx.com
Estab: 2012

Kamran Najmabadi, CTO
Ramtin Agah, Co-Founder
Shaun Bagai, CEO
Paul Manners, CFO
Imtiaz Qureshi, Director of Imaging

Manufacturer of medical devices. The company
develops solutions for targeted delivery of therapeutic and diagnostic agents.

**Replicraft** HQ
1400 Gomes Rd
Fremont CA 94539
P: 510-656-6039 PRC:5
replicraft.us.fm
Email: sopwithace@comcast.net

Jim Kiger, Owner

Provider of World War I aircraft plan sets for mod-
elers. The company provides plans for the aircrafts
in one-fifth, one-sixth and one-tenth scales.

**Reprise Software Inc** HQ
1530 Meridian Ave Ste 290
San Jose CA 95125
P: 781-837-0884 F: 408-404-0890 PRC:320
www.reprisesoftware.com
Email: info@reprisesoftware.com
Estab: 2006

Bob Mearns, Lead Developer

Provider of license management software solutions. The company's products include Exa, Arxan,
LMS, and Pace.

**Res** HQ
2153 Martin Way
Pittsburg CA 94565
P: 925-432-1755 F: 925-432-1748 PRC:140
resenvironmentalservices.com
Estab: 1982

John Russo, President
Craig Joseph, General Manager

Provider of environmental services. The company
offers air-moving, contract safety, and vacuum
truck services.

**Resilient Networks Systems Inc** HQ
181 Second St
San Francisco CA 94105
P: 415-291-9600 PRC:323
www.resilient-networks.com
Email: info@resilient-networks.com
Estab: 2008

Ulagu Kumar, Principal Software QA Engineer
Ethan Ayer, CEO
Rochelle Gunn, CEO
Sandip Ghosh, CEO
Richard Spires, Chairman

Developer of internet software products. The company serves the healthcare, media, information
security, and government sectors.

**Resilinc Corp** HQ
890 Hillview Ct
Milpitas CA 95035
P: 408-883-8053 PRC:325
www.resilinc.com
Estab: 2010

Daniel Biran, CSO
Jon Bovit, Senior Director
Laurie Diekman, Regional Director of Sales
Nick Wildgoose, Principal Consultant

Provider of supply chain and risk management
solutions. The company serves the life science
and automotive industries.

**Responsible Metal Fab Inc** HQ
1256 Lawrence Station Rd
Sunnyvale CA 94089
P: 408-734-0713 F: 408-734-3006 PRC:80
www.responsiblemetal.com
Estab: 1985

Rafael Grimaldo, VP of Sales & Engineering
Denis Lemire, Estimating Engineer
Ron Perez, Estimating Engineer
Dan Martin, President
Cande Arreola, Production Manager

Provider of precision sheet metal fabrication
services. The company offers machining, electro-
mechanical assembly, packaging, and delivery
services.

**Responsive Communication Services
Inc** HQ
1771 Vineyard Dr Ste 6
Antioch CA 94509
P: 925-755-8000 F: 925-755-9000 PRC:68
www.responsivecomm.com
Email: rcs@responsivecomm.com
Estab: 1995

Kent Osborn, President

Provider of communication equipment. The company is involved in troubleshooting and maintenance services.

**Resq Manufacturing** HQ
 11365 Sunrise Park Dr Ste 200
 Rancho Cordova CA 95742
P: 916-638-6786  F: 916-914-2075  PRC:78
resqmfg.com
Emp: 1-10  Estab: 2012

Jim Chiodo, CEO
Kyle Varney, General Manager

Provider of contract manufacturing services. The
company offers cable assembly and electro-mechanical services.

**Retail Pro International** HQ
 400 Plaza Dr Ste 200
 Folsom CA 95630
P: 916-605-7200  PRC:322
www.retailpro.com
Email: moreinfo@retailpro.com
Emp: 1-10

Kerry Lemos, CEO
Mike Bishop, COO
Peter LaTona, VP of Channel Sales
Bevin Manian, VP of Channel Sales
William Colley, SVP of Client Services

Provider of software solutions. The company's
services include automated retail planning and
content strategy.

**RetailNext** HQ
 60 S Market St Ste 310
 San Jose CA 95113
P: 408-884-2162  PRC:325
retailnext.net
Email: info@retailnext.net
Estab: 2007

Andrew Golden, Head of Talent Acquisition Hu-
man Resources Manager
Dan Dixon, Mid Market Account Director
Bridget Johns, Head of Marketing & Customer
Experience
Lindsay Kelvie, Account Director
Mark Jamtgaard, Director of Technology

Provider of in-store analytics solutions. The
company offers services to retail labs, marketing
departments, and shopping centers.

**Retech Systems LLC** HQ
 100 Henry Station Rd
 Ukiah CA 95482
P: 707-462-6522  F: 707-462-4103  PRC:151
www.retechsystemsllc.com
Email: sales@retechsystemsllc.com
Emp: 1-10  Estab: 1963

John Wycoff, Mechanical Design Engineer
Thomas Wooley, Project Engineer
Dee Dix, Human Resource Manager
Terry Wickliffe, Information Technology Manager
Z. K., Purchasing Manager

Designer and manufacturer of consumable electrode and furnaces, powder production, and other
thermal processing equipment.

**RethinkDB** HQ
 156 E Dana St
 Mountain View CA 94041
P: 650-965-8308  PRC:319
rethinkdb.com
Email: info@rethinkdb.com
Estab: 2009

Paul Davenport, Executive Researcher

An open-source distributed document-oriented
database.

**Retrotope Inc** HQ
 4300 El Camino Real Ste 201
 Los Altos CA 94022
P: 650-917-9256  PRC:257
www.retrotope.com
Email: info@retrotope.com
Estab: 2006

Robert Molinari, Founder
Mikhail Shchepinov, Founder
Anil Kumar, CBO
Peter Milner, CMO
Frederic Heerinckx, VP of Clinical Operations

Focuses on the discovery of drugs and platforms
for the treatment of regenerative diseases. The
company offers services to the healthcare sector.

**Revance Therapeutics Inc** HQ
 7555 Gateway Blvd
 Newark CA 94560-0303
P: 510-742-3400  F: 510-742-3401  PRC:34
www.revance.com
Emp: 170  Estab: 2002
Sales: $3M to $10M

Dan Browne, President
Todd Zavodnick, CCO
Allen Li, Manufacturing Manager
Ashley Ma, Fermentation Manufacturing Associate
Tony Panaligan, Manufacturing Technician

Developers of botulinum toxin products. The company develops and manufactures botulinum toxin
products for aesthetic and therapeutic categories.

**Revel Systems Inc** BR
 575 Market St Ste 2200
 San Francisco CA 94105
P: 415-744-1433  PRC:209
revelsystems.com
Email: info@revelsystems.com
Estab: 2010

Mirza Asif, Architect & Lead Backend Engineer
Patrick Lee, Quality Assurance Engineer
Greg Dukat, CEO
Leslie Leaf, CCO
Arthur Beckman, CTO

Provider of POS systems and related services.
The company serves customers in the accounting,
security, reporting, and other industries.

**Reviva Pharmaceuticals Inc** HQ
 1250 Oakmead Pkwy Ste 210
 Sunnyvale CA 94085
P: 408-816-1470  F: 408-904-6270  PRC:257
www.revivapharma.com
Email: info.rp@revivapharma.com
Estab: 2006

Laxminarayan Bhat, President
Marc Cantillon, Chief Medical Officer
Partha Sarathy, CFO

Developer of therapy for CNS, cardiovascular,
metabolic and inflammatory diseases. The company is a clinical development pharmaceutical
company.

**REVOLUTION Medicines Inc** HQ
 700 Saginaw Dr
 Redwood City CA 94063
P: 650-481-6801  PRC:262
www.revolutionmedicines.com
Email: inquiries@revolutionmedicines.com
Estab: 2014

Kevan Shokat, Co-Founder
Michael Fischbach, Co-Founder
J.D Margaret Peg Horn, COO
Luan Wilfong, SVP of Human Resources
Walter Wally Reiher, VP of Information Sciences

Developer of medicines for the treatment of
serious diseases. The company is involved in the
synthesis of original compounds.

**Revstream Inc** HQ
 100 Marine Pkwy Ste 310
 Redwood Shores CA 94065
P: 888-738-0206  PRC:325
www.revstreamone.com
Email: sales@revstreamone.com
Estab: 2006

Rajiv Chopra, Founder
Kai Wong, Director of Pre-Sales Consulting

Provider of enterprise revenue and billing
management solutions. The company also offers
advisory and technical support services.

**Rex Key & Security** HQ
 1908 University Ave
 Berkeley CA 94704
P: 510-527-7000  F: 510-848-0126  PRC:59
www.rexkey.com
Email: sales@rexkey.com
Estab: 1910

Toni Moreland, Dispatcher

Designer of security systems for automotive,
institutional, commercial, industrial, and residential
purposes.

**Rgb Spectrum** HQ
 950 Marina Village Pkwy
 Alameda CA 94501
P: 510-814-7000  F: 510-814-7026  PRC:98
www.rgb.com
Email: sales@rgb.com
Estab: 1987

Timothy Lee, Applications Engineer
Bing-Yan Lee, Manufacturing Engineer
Bob Marcus, CEO
Iana Zemniakova, CFO
Steve Jaspar, Information Technology Manager

Manufacturer of video and computer signal display
processors. The company serves security, oil &
gas, corporate, and military sectors.

**RGS Industries** HQ
 445 Laurelwood Rd
 Santa Clara CA 95054
P: 669-238-0632  PRC:162
www.rgsindustries.com
Email: info@rgsind.com

Lisa Southard, CFO
Jane Morales, Marketing Manager

Manufacturer and supplier of gaskets. The company offers seals, shielding and related materials,
and die cutting services.

**Rheosense Inc**  HQ
2420 Camino Ramon Ste 240
San Ramon CA 94583
P: 925-866-3801  F: 925-866-3804  PRC:13
www.rheosense.com
Email: info@rheosense.com
Estab: 2001

Ryan Cohn, Support Engineer
Mahesh Gupta, Senior Staff Software Engineer
Angela Ng, Production Manager
Hua Han, Senior Production Manager
David Meissner, Production Supervisor

Designer and manufacturer of viscometers and
extensional viscometers. The company offers
calibration, sample testing, and maintenance
services.

**Ridge Communications Inc**  HQ
12919 Alcosta Blvd Ste 2
San Ramon CA 94583
P: 925-498-2340  F: 925-498-2341  PRC:63
www.ridgecommunicate.com

Rick Angkham, Field Engineering Manager
Wes Rigsby, General Manager
Sumita Ranganathan, Financial Analyst
Russ Patridge, Principal
Ron Roberts, Project Coordinator

Provider of network deployment and project
management services. The company serves the
wireless carrier industry.

**Ridge to River**  HQ
1050 Cedar St
Fort Bragg CA 95437
P: 707-357-0857  PRC:140
ridgetoriver.com
Emp: 1-10  Estab: 1995

Teri Jo Barber, Hydrologist

Provider of hydrologic analysis and modeling services. The company is also focused on ecological
restoration, erosion control, and water quality
analysis.

**Riga Analytical Lab Inc**  HQ
3375 Scott Blvd Ste 132
Santa Clara CA 95054
P: 408-496-6944  F: 408-496-0981  PRC:301
www.rigalab.com
Email: info@rigalab.com
Estab: 1982

Lydia Vorgias, Analyst

Provider of laboratory services specializing in
electrical failure analysis, circuit extraction, latch
up evaluation, and parallel and angel lapping.

**Rigel Pharmaceuticals Inc**  HQ
1180 Veterans Blvd
S San Francisco CA 94080
P: 650-624-1100  F: 650-624-1101  PRC:34
www.rigel.com
Email: communications@rigel.com
Estab: 1996
Sales: $30M to $100M

Raul Rodriguez, President
Eldon Mayer, EVP
Wolfgang Dummer, EVP
Tarek Sallam, Executive Director
Mike Sterba, Senior Director of Clinical Operations

Developer novel, small-molecule drugs for the
treatment of inflammatory and autoimmune
diseases, immuno-oncology related diseases, and
muscle disorders.

**RightITnow**  HQ
101A Clay St Ste 150
San Francisco CA 94111
P: 415-350-3581  PRC:323
www.rightitnow.com
Email: info@rightitnow.com
Estab: 2013

Marc Ferrie, Founder
Devi Menon, Java Developer

Provider of information technology operations
management software. The company offers
services to government agencies and business
organizations.

**Rightpoint**  BR
1611 Telegraph Ave Ste 1550
Oakland CA 94612
P: 415-935-3390  PRC:45
www.rightpoint.com
Email: oakland@rightpoint.com

Ross Freedman, Co-Founder
Brad Schneider, Co-Founder
Chris Locke, CFO
Julie Lewis, VP of Finance
John Herget, VP of Salesforce

A digital consultancy firm that designs and
engineers end-to-end digital experiences to help
clients succeed at the speed of innovation.

**Rightware Inc**  BR
470 Ramona St
Palo Alto CA 94301
P: 877-775-2694  PRC:322
www.rightware.com
Email: sales@rightware.com
Estab: 2009

Tero Sarkkinen, Founder
Ville Ilves, COO
Jussi Tammi, VP of Finance

Provider of user interface technologies serving
the mobile, automotive, and other embedded
industries.

**Riley Plastic Manufacturing Inc**  HQ
3551 Haven Ave Ste M
Menlo Park CA 94025
P: 650-366-5104  F: 650-366-2966  PRC:80
www.rileyplastic.com
Email: rileyplastic@yahoo.com

Richard Riley, President

Provider of vacuum forming, vapor polishing,
and assembly services. The company serves the
medical and bio-tech industries.

**Rimnetics Inc**  BR
3141 Swetzer Rd
Loomis CA 95650
P: 916-652-5555  PRC:187
www.rimnetics.com
Emp: 11-50  Estab: 1985

Siegfried Waaga, General Manager
Katilin Jones, Quality Control Inspector
Brena Winig, Office Manager
Suzanne Gonzales, Customer Service Manager
Vitaliy Khlystik, Finisher

Providers of RIM molded structural parts,
enclosures, cosmetic housings, encapsulation
and overmolding. The company makes molded
polyurethane parts.

**Rincon Consultants Inc**  BR
449 15th St Ste 303
Oakland CA 94612
P: 510-834-4455  F: 510-834-4433  PRC:139
rinconconsultants.com
Estab: 1994

Ed Morelan, Senior Engineering Geologist
Michael Gialketsis, President
Megan Jones, Senior Program Manager
Steve Hongola, Senior Ecologist
Ethan Ripperger, Biologist

Provider of environmental consulting services. The
company specializes in land use planning, site
assessment, remediation, and other services.

**Ripon Manufacturing Company Inc**  HQ
652 S Stockton Ave
Ripon CA 95366
P: 209-599-2148  F: 209-599-3114  PRC:80
www.riponmfgco.com
Email: sales@riponmfgco.com
Emp: 1-10  Estab: 1963

Ursula Navarro, Controller
Alana Navarro, Administrative Assistant

Fabricator of steel processing equipment. The
company manufactures and installs peelers,
sizers, hardshell crackers, hoppers, dryers, and
sorters.

**Rishang LED Inc**  LH
2320 Walsh Ave
Santa Clara CA 95051
P: 408-748-8889  PRC:169
rishang-led.com
Email: info@rishang-led.com
Estab: 2002

Lillian Guo, Regional Sales Director

Manufacturer of LED products for decorative and
green lighting solutions. The company's products are used in the residential and commercial
sectors.

**River Rock Software Inc**  BR
4120 Douglas Blvd Ste 306-336
Granite Bay CA 95746
P: 916-797-6746  PRC:323
www.riverrocksoftware.com
Email: sales@riverrocksoftware.com
Emp: 11-50  Estab: 1999

Javier Villanueva, Manager

Developer of software tools such as graphical user
interfaces, client server applications, spool file
viewers, and report formatters.

**Riverbed Technology**  HQ
680 Folsom St 6th Fl
San Francisco CA 94107
P: 415-247-8800  F: 415-247-8801  PRC:61
www.riverbed.com
Email: info@riverbed.com
Estab: 2002

Paul Hammer, Senior Software QA Engineer
Rich McBee, CEO
Alpna Doshi, Chief Digital Officer
Dante Malagrino, Chief Development Officer
Ian Halifax, CFO

Provider of WAN optimization, cloud, consolidation, disaster recovery, and network performance management solutions.

**Rix Industries** HQ
4900 Industrial Way
Benicia CA 94510
P: 707-747-5900   F: 707-747-9200   PRC:148
www.rixindustries.com
Email: info@rixindustries.com
Estab: 1878

Josh Trainor, Chief Engineer
Kelsey Waters, Senior R&D Engineer
Jason Thomas, Aerospace & GCV Staff Engineer
Keith Allen, Lead Engineer
Bert Otterson, President

Manufacturer of air and gas compressors. The company's products include industrial and commercial compressors, nitrogen generators, and AMS parts.

**Rki Instruments Inc** HQ
33248 Central Ave
Union City CA 94587
P: 510-441-5656   F: 510-441-5650   PRC:13
www.rkiinstruments.com
Email: mail4rki@rkiinstruments.com
Estab: 1994

Syed Hashim, Design Engineer
Erika Reyes, Applications Engineer
John Villalovos, Senior Applications Engineer
Michael Jeter, Applications Engineer
Bob Pellissier, President

Manufacturer of gas detectors and monitoring systems. The company caters to refineries, utilities, and oil tankers.

**Rm Machining Inc** HQ
950 Terminal Way
San Carlos CA 94070
P: 650-591-4178   F: 650-591-4412   PRC:80
www.rm-machining.com
Estab: 1983

Robert Myhre, VP

Provider of precision machining services. The company caters to the aerospace, defense, medical, and energy sectors.

**Rmc Engineering** HQ
255 Mayock Rd
Gilroy CA 95020
P: 408-842-2525   F: 408-842-0670   PRC:80
www.rmcengineering.com
Email: info@rmcengineering.com
Estab: 1978

Kevin McKenzie, CEO
Blake Rider, VP
Joe Miranda, Supervisor
Justin Wheeler, Truck Driver

Provider of automated safety systems, resurfacing tools, blowers, and related supplies. The company offers repair and replacement services.

**Robbjack Corp** HQ
3300 Nicolaus Rd
Lincoln CA 95648
P: 916-645-6045   F: 916-645-0146   PRC:157
www.robbjack.com
Email: sales@robbjack.com
Emp: 1-10   Estab: 1959

Mike MacArthur, VP of Engineering
Nick Molnar, Applications Engineer
Khadidja Norris, VP of Manufacturing
Meghan Gardner, Manager
Steve Handrop, EVP

Provider of tools for aerospace, aluminum tools, die mold and hard metal tools, custom end mills, and custom saws.

**Robertson Precision Inc** HQ
325 Sharon Park Dr Unit 444
Menlo Park CA 94025
P: 650-363-2212   PRC:80
www.robertsonprecision.com
Email: rfq@robertsonprecision.com
Estab: 1984

Bill Robertson, President

Manufacturer of precision metals and plastic products. The company's services include engineering support and process control.

**ROBLOX Corp** HQ
910 Park Pl
San Mateo CA 94403
P: 888-858-2569   PRC:317
www.roblox.com
Email: press@roblox.com
Estab: 2006

Toby Teel, Software Engineer
Shailendra Rathore, Engineer
David Baszucki, Founder

Specializes in game development, monetization, and publishing services. The company serves businesses.

**Robson Technologies Inc** HQ
135 E Main Ave Ste 130
Morgan Hill CA 95037
P: 408-779-8008   F: 408-782-7132   PRC:208
www.testfixtures.com
Email: rtisales@testfixtures.com
Estab: 1989

Trevor Johnson, Applications Engineer
Nicklaus Schmidt, Mechanical Design Engineer
Kulia Lemus, Inside Sales Manager
Aaron Petray, Product Marketing Specialist
John Widmeyer, VP

Provider of customizable hardware interfaces that bridge the gap between the test device and the measurement system.

**Rock Systems Inc** HQ
3250 Riverside Blvd
Sacramento CA 95818
P: 916-921-9000   F: 916-921-9070   PRC:80
www.rocksystems.com
Email: info@rocksystems.com
Emp: 1-10

John Bruce, Founder
Mike Bruce, President

Provider of material handling solutions. The company offers hoppers, feeders, conveyors, separators, and related accessories.

**Rocket Communications Inc** HQ
81 Langton St Ste 12
San Francisco CA 94103
P: 415-863-0101   PRC:323
www.rocketcom.com
Estab: 1992

Michal Rogondino, Founder
Kevin Hause, COO
Mandy Wallace, CFO
Pierre Granier, Program Director
Ty van Leuven, Visual Experience Director

Developer of user interface, visual, and icon design services for software and related applications.

**Rocket Ems Inc** HQ
2950 Patrick Henry Dr
Santa Clara CA 95054
P: 408-727-3700   PRC:207
www.rocketems.com
Email: sales@rocketems.com
Estab: 2011

Vinh Le, Process Engineer
Michael Kottke, President
Sandra Hebel, Human Resource
Peter Chipman, VP
Scott Schaetzle, Director of Service Operations

Provider of electronic manufacturing services. The company caters to high growth technology sectors.

**Rocket Software Inc** BR
2200 Powell St Ste 900
Emeryville CA 94608
P: 781-577-4323   PRC:323
www.rocketsoftware.com
Email: info@rocketsoftware.com
Estab: 1990

Kevin Norlin, SVP
Matt Deres, SVP
Rich Kraska, SVP
Tracey Leahy, SVP
Jeff Winter, SVP

Developer and designer of software and mobile solutions. The company offers services for the telecommunications industry.

**Rockliffe Systems Inc** HQ
1901 S Bascom Ave Ste 1190
Campbell CA 95008
P: 408-879-5600   F: 408-879-5610   PRC:322
www.rockliffe.com
Email: sales@rockliffe.com
Estab: 1995

John Davies, Founder

Provider of mobile communication software for service providers, enterprises, and consumers. The company offers design services.

**Rocklin Hydraulics** HQ
2304 Sierra Meadows Dr
Rocklin CA 95677
P: 916-624-8900   PRC:159
www.rocklinhydraulics.com
Emp: 1-10   Estab: 1995

Charlie Roberson, Manager

Manufacturer of hydraulic products. The company offers hydraulic hoses, caps & plugs, jaw couplers, and brass fittings.

**Rockwell Automation Inc**  BR
3000 Executive Pkwy Ste 210
San Ramon CA 94583
P: 925-242-5700  PRC:311
www.rockwellautomation.com
Estab: 1903

Hedwig Maes, President

Provider of control systems, sensing devices, security, and other products. The company offers asset management, network, and other services.

**Rockwell Automation Inc**  BR
111 N Market St
San Jose CA 95113
P: 408-271-3400  F: 408-271-3401  PRC:13
www.rockwellautomation.com

Kevin Chao, Director
Evan Forrest, Channel Accounts Manager

Provider of information and asset management solutions. The company serves the marine, metals, and pulp, and paper industries.

**Rockyou Inc**  HQ
642 Harrison St Ste 300
San Francisco CA 94107
P: 415-580-6400  PRC:317
Estab: 2005

Lisa Marino, CEO
Scott McClellan, VP of Ad Operations & Ad Product
Brent Allard, Senior Director of IT & Operations
Robin Molt, Assistant Secretary

Provider of gaming solutions. The company's games include Poker, Bingo, Zoo World, and others and serves the entertainment sector.

**Rod-L Electronics Inc**  HQ
935-F Sierra Vista
Mountain View CA 94043
P: 650-322-0711  F: 650-326-1993  PRC:209
www.rodl.com
Email: info@rodl.com
Estab: 1977

Roy Clay, Engineer

Provider of electrical safety testing equipment. The company also offers hipot test loads, test probes, bond testers, and ground testers.

**Roger K Sherman Co**  HQ
325 Los Altos Ave
Los Altos CA 94022
P: 650-941-8300  F: 650-949-3071  PRC:18
www.shermanstandards.com
Email: info@shermanstandards.com
Estab: 1962

Roger Sherman, President

Provider of microscope eyepiece reticules, calibration standards, and ruled master gages for the semiconductor and magnetic head industries.

**ROHM Semiconductor USA LLC**  BR
2323 Owen St
Santa Clara CA 95054
P: 408-720-1900  F: 408-720-1918  PRC:207
www.rohm.com
Estab: 1958

Desiree Doria, Human Resource Assistant
Zachary Hunter, Information Technology Manager
Go Ezaki, System Architect

Manufacturer of amplifiers, clocks, modules, passive components, remote control receivers, and timers.

**Rolepoint**  HQ
44 Tehama St Ste 306
San Francisco CA 94105
P: 888-571-2851  PRC:319
www.rolepoint.com
Email: inquiries@rolepoint.com
Estab: 2011

Kes Thygesen, Co-Founder
JP Bertram, Head of Marketing
Alessandra Williams, Marketing Development Lead

Focuses on talent acquisition services. The company serves small and medium businesses and Fortune 500 companies.

**Rollbar Inc**  HQ
51 Federal St Ste 401
San Francisco CA 94107
P: 888-568-3350  PRC:322
rollbar.com
Email: team@rollbar.com
Estab: 2012

Cory Virok, Co-Founder

Developer of error tracking software. The company is also engaged in coding and troubleshooting services.

**Rollin J Lobaugh Inc**  HQ
1331C Old County Rd
Belmont CA 94002-6308
P: 650-583-9682  F: 650-583-0445  PRC:80
www.rjlobaugh.com
Email: sales@rjlobaugh.com
Estab: 1922

Jack Corey, President

Manufacturer of machined components. The company mainly manufactures screws and offers supporting services.

**Rollinson Advertising Design**  HQ
45 Janin Pl
Pleasant Hill CA 94523
P: 925-518-6698  PRC:318
rollinsonadvertising.com
Estab: 1990

Martin Rollinson, Owner

Provider of graphic design, traditional marketing, strategic planning, and e-mail blasting services.

**Rolls-Royce Engine Services - Oakland Inc**  BR
7200 Earhart Rd
Oakland CA 94621
P: 510-613-1000  PRC:4
www.rolls-royce.com
Estab: 1960

John Rishton, CEO
Bilo Surdhar, VP of Customer Business
Anna Macias, Billing Analyst
Raul Palma, Aircraft Technician

Designer, manufacturer, and marketer of power systems. The company offers engines for airliners and military aircraft.

**Ron Witherspoon Inc**  HQ
1551 Dell Ave
Campbell CA 95008-6903
P: 408-370-6620  F: 408-370-9612  PRC:80
rwinc.com
Email: info@rwinc.com
Estab: 1977

Keshav Sharma, Quality Systems Manager
Miguel Saavedra, Quality Inspector
Dave Arterburn, EDM Department Manager
Ken Nelson, Manager
Courtney Guetschow, Coordinator

Manufacturer of high precision parts. The company offers milling, turning, electrical discharge machining, and grinding services.

**Roos Instruments Inc**  BR
2285 Martin Ave
Santa Clara CA 95050
P: 408-748-8589  F: 408-748-8595  PRC:212
www.roos.com
Email: info@alltekusa.com

Don Ferris, Engineer
Mark Brown, Software Engineer
Mark Roos, Founder
Catherine Roos, COO
Devin Morris, Product Marketing Manager

Manufacturer of automated test equipment. The company's products include MEMs devices, radars, amplifiers, and mixers.

**Rootdesign LLC**  HQ
946 Noe St
San Francisco CA 94114
P: 415-282-2484  PRC:322
www.rootdesign.com
Email: info@rootdesign.com
Estab: 1997

Kevin Rogers, Founder
Hien Phan, Programming Director

Provider of design solutions specializing in brand strategy, user interface design, and database development services.

**Roplast Industries Inc**  HQ
3155 S Fifth Ave
Oroville CA 95965
P: 530-532-9500  F: 530-532-9576  PRC:280
www.roplast.com
Emp: 1-10  Estab: 1990

Robert Berman, Owner
Michael Jobes, VP of Sales
Roxanne Vaughan, Director of Sales
Erik Johansen, Industrial Sales Manager
Ye Thao, Extrusion Manager

Manufacturer of bags. The company specializes in custom designed bags made out of polyethylene films.

**Rorze Automation Inc**  DH
48625 Warm Springs Blvd
Fremont CA 94539
P: 510-687-1340  PRC:153
rorzeautomation.com
Estab: 1985

Jeze Acosta, Field Service Engineer
Trey Cherry, Mechanical Engineer
Bill Fyall, President
Keith Miyamoto, Accounting Supervisor
Jeff Aihara, Operation Coordinator

Manufacturer of automation products. The company's applications include displays, semiconductors, and laboratories.

## Rose Electronics Distributing Company Inc HQ
2030 Ringwood Ave
San Jose CA 95131-1728
P: 408-943-0200   F: 408-943-0360   PRC:201
www.rosebatteries.com
Email: sales@rose-elec.com
Estab: 1963

Katherine Mack, VP of Sales & Marketing

Provider of batteries and power solutions. The company primarily serves original equipment manufacturers such as VRLA batteries and lithium ion batteries.

## Ross Engineering Corporation HQ
540 Westchester Dr
Campbell CA 95008
P: 408-377-4621   F: 408-377-5182   PRC:78
www.rossengineeringcorp.com
Email: info@rossengineeringcorp.com
Estab: 1964

Jim Ross, Sales Manager

Designer and manufacturer of high voltage electronic and electro-mechanical devices like relays, probes, voltmeters, switches, and breakers.

## Royal Circuit Solutions Inc HQ
21 Hamilton Ct
Hollister CA 95023
P: 831-636-7789   F: 831-636-4825   PRC:211
www.royalcircuits.com
Email: sales@royalcircuits.com
Emp: 1-10   Estab: 1988

Milan Shah, CEO

Manufacturer of printed circuit boards. The company's products are used in prototype and medium production runs and offers fabrication services.

## Royce Instruments Inc HQ
831 Latour Ct Ste C
Napa CA 94558
P: 707-255-9078   F: 707-255-9079   PRC:212
www.royceinstruments.com
Email: sales@royceinstruments.com
Estab: 1983

Markus Liebhard, Senior Mechanical Engineer
Sarah Parrish, Senior Sales Applications Engineer
Malcolm Cox, Founder
Ellen Souza, Purchaser
Scott Newell, Technical Sales Manager

Provider of bond testers and die sorters for the auto and medical electronics device manufacturers worldwide.

## RS Software Inc BR
1900 McCarthy Blvd Ste 103
Milpitas CA 95035
P: 408-382-1200   F: 408-382-0083   PRC:323
rssoftware.com
Email: sales@rssoftware.com
Estab: 1991

Raj Jain, Managing Director
Milind Kamat, COO
Vijendra Surana, CFO
Aniruddha Chaudhuri, General Manager
Francis Albin, SVP

Provider of business payment solutions for the risk prediction, residual management, payment gateway, and merchant boarding areas.

## Rucker Kolls Inc HQ
1064 Yosemite Dr
Milpitas CA 95035
P: 408-934-9875   F: 408-934-9720   PRC:211
ruckerkolls.com
Email: sales@ruckerkolls.com
Estab: 1968

Mark Waks, Regional Sales Manager
Jean Descanzo, Controller

Provider of solutions for ATE test interface products. The company's services include custom PCB design and card stiffeners and rings.

## Ruckus Networks HQ
350 W Java Dr
Sunnyvale CA 94089
P: 650-265-4200   F: 408-738-2065   PRC:63
www.ruckuswireless.com
Estab: 2004

Alexander Pease, EVP
Brooke Clark, SVP
Karen Renner, SVP
Morgan Kurk, EVP
Robyn Mingle, SVP

Designer and manufacturer of Wi-Fi products and wireless LAN systems. The company also focuses on the marketing aspects.

## Rudy's Commercial Refrigeration HQ
1660 Rumrill Blvd
San Pablo CA 94806-4305
P: 510-376-9163   F: 510-235-5556   PRC:154
rudysrefrigeration.com
Estab: 1947

Ben Plant, President

Provider of refrigeration products such as coolers and freezers, compressors, glass doors and strip curtains, and temperature alarms.

## Runscope Inc HQ
548 Market St Ste 14137
San Francisco CA 94108-5401
P: 888-812-6786   PRC:325
www.runscope.com
Email: dmca@runscope.com
Estab: 2013

Troy Miller, API Product Manager

Specializes in automated performance monitoring and testing solutions. The company serves developers.

## Runtime Design Automation HQ
2560 Mission College Blvd Ste 130
Santa Clara CA 95054-2904
P: 408-492-0940   F: 408-492-0941   PRC:322
runtimeinc.com
Email: info@rtda.com
Estab: 1995

Yohan Bouvron, Technical Support Engineer
Stuart Taylor, Senior Director

Provider of management system software for the IC design industry. The company is engaged in documentation and technical support.

## RUSH PCB Inc RH
2149-20 O'Toole Ave
San Jose CA 95131
P: 408-496-6013   F: 408-854-8094   PRC:211
www.rushpcb.com
Email: sales@rushpcb.com
Estab: 1997

Akber Roy, CEO
Padma Dantu, Manager

Manufacturer of printed circuit boards and assemblies. The company is engaged in engineering and electronics manufacturing services.

## Rutter Armey Inc HQ
2684 S Cherry Ave
Fresno CA 93706
P: 559-237-1866   F: 559-237-5806   PRC:80
www.rutterarmey.com
Email: rutterarmeyinc@yahoo.com
Emp: 1-10   Estab: 1941

Henry Lopez, Sales Manager
Kevin O'Neill, Service Department
David Fry, Shop Foreman
Al Smith, Shop Foreman

Provider of precision machining services. The company focuses on industrial hard chrome plating, welding, and metal spraying services.

## Ryss Lab Inc HQ
29540 Kohoutek Way
Union City CA 94587
P: 510-477-9570   F: 510-477-0534   PRC:34
www.ryss.com
Email: info@ryss.com
Estab: 1997

Ming Lee, President
Joyce Wang, Revenue Accounting Supervisor

Provider of biotechnology and pharmaceutical development services. The company offers services to the healthcare sector.

## S C Laboratories HQ
100 Pioneer St Ste E
Santa Cruz CA 95060
P: 866-435-0709   PRC:306
sclabs.com
Emp: 1-10

Alec Dixon, Co-Founder
Josh Wurzer, President
Joaquin Rodriguez, Sales Representative
Ian Rice, Director of Marketing
Jeff Dingman, Operations Manager

Provider of medical quality assurance and safety testing services. The company's services include potency testing, pesticide testing, and microbial screening.

## S T Johnson Co HQ
5160 Fulton Dr
Fairfield CA 94534
P: 510-652-6000   F: 510-652-4302   PRC:151
www.johnsonburners.com
Estab: 1903

Helen Friedland, Director of Engineering
Bob Nickeson, Engineer

Manufacturer of burners. The company specializes in the design and fabrication of gas and nitrous oxide burners for industries.

**S&C Electric Co** BR
1135 Atlantic Ave
Alameda CA 94501
P: 510-864-9300   F: 510-864-6860   PRC:245
www.sandc.com
Estab: 1911

David Koepp, Regional VP of US Sales

Provider of equipment and services for electric power systems. The company is involved in design and installation services.

**S2c Inc** HQ
1754 Technology Dr Ste 232
San Jose CA 95110
P: 408-213-8818   F: 408-549-9948   PRC:323
www.s2cinc.com
Estab: 2003

ChengLun Chang, VP of Engineering
ShiYi Ma, Sales Manager

Provider of prototyping solutions. The company's customers include chip design and system design companies.

**Sa Photonics Inc** HQ
120 Knowles Dr
Los Gatos CA 95032
P: 408-560-3500   F: 408-376-0950   PRC:159
www.saphotonics.com
Email: sales@saphotonics.com
Estab: 2002

Mark Koenig, Senior Software Engineer
Jim Coward, CEO
Dave Pechner, CTO
Toan Nguyen, Administrative Service Manager

Developer of photonic systems. The company offers solutions for head-mounted displays, micro-wave sensors, mirror sense, and control systems.

**Saba Software Inc** HQ
4120 Dublin Blvd Ste 200
Dublin CA 94568
P: 877-722-2101   PRC:323
saba.com
Estab: 1997

Srini Ogireddy, EVP of Products Engineering & Cloud
Phil Saunders, CEO
Pete Low, CFO
Mike Warren, General Manager
Debbie Shotwell, Chief People Officer

Provider of learning and talent management solutions such as social web meetings and trainings, onboarding, planning, and support services.

**Sabah International** HQ
5925 Stoneridge Dr
Pleasanton CA 94588
P: 925-463-0431   PRC:13
www.sabahinternationalinc.com
Email: nofires@sabah-intl.com
Estab: 1972

Rick Lewis, Senior Project Engineer
Brian Vierra, System Engineer
Matt Ramsey, President
Michele Sabah, CEO
Patrick Hallett, Director of Sales and Marketing

Provider of fire suppressors for the commercial and industrial sectors. The company also focuses on installation.

**SACC Inc** HQ
2903 Bunker Hill Lane Ste 107
Santa Clara CA 94054
P: 408-755-3000   F: 925-249-3031   PRC:324
www.saccinc.com
Email: salesinquiry@saccinc.com
Estab: 1998

Suhas Ahuja, Owner

Provider of enterprise resource planning, data warehousing, technology infrastructure, business process outsourcing, and staffing services.

**SAE Engineering Inc** HQ
365 Reed St
Santa Clara CA 95050
P: 408-987-9950   F: 408-987-9960   PRC:80
saeeng.com
Email: info@saeeng.com
Estab: 1963

James Millich, President
Alan Pats, CEO
Benjamin Rafferty, Sales Manager
Araceli Ramirez, Inside Sales Coordinator
Richard Lopez, Estimating Manager

Provider of integrated turnkey assembly, precision machining, and sheet metal fabrication services to many sectors. The company also offers software.

**Sae Magnetics (hk) Ltd** BR
100 S Milpitas Blvd
Milpitas CA 95035
P: 408-956-7100   PRC:95
www.saeus.com

Ellis Cha, VP

Manufacturer of magnetic recording heads, head gimbals assemblies, and head stack assemblies for computer disk drivers.

**Safe Hearing America Inc** HQ
130 Allison Ct Ste G-1
Vacaville CA 95688
P: 707-446-0880   F: 707-446-9632   PRC:189
www.safehearingamerica.com

Willena Beyer, President
Susanne Schwartz, Data Systems Manager

Provider of mobile hearing testing services and products. The company offerings include AQ Solid Plug, Sleep Plug, and Solid Plug.

**Safebridge Consultants Inc** HQ
1924 Old Middlefield Way
Mountain View CA 94043-2503
P: 650-961-4820   F: 650-623-0096   PRC:142
www.safebridge.com
Email: susan.custer@safebridge.com
Estab: 1998

Bob Ku, VP
Allan Ader, Managing Director
Robert Sussman, Managing Director
Gail Baer, Administrative Office Manager
Debbie Keys, Manager

Provider of consulting services and analytical support. The company provides safety, health and environmental services.

**Safeco Electric Supply Inc** HQ
201 Toland St
San Francisco CA 94124-1119
P: 415-206-0368   F: 415-946-3389   PRC:77
www.safecoelectric.com
Email: safecousa@gmail.com

Tony Leong, CEO
Ray Leong, General Manager

Distributor of electrical and lighting products. The company offers wires, cables, cords, fasteners, switch boxes, and accessories.

**Safety Equipment Corp** HQ
1141 Old County Rd
Belmont CA 94002
P: 650-595-5422   F: 650-595-0143   PRC:82
www.safetyequipmentcorp.com
Email: info@safetyequipmentcorp.com
Estab: 1979

Ken Hettman, Manager

Designer and manufacturer of gas cabinets, valve boxes, leaker cabinets, exhausted enclosures, and related products.

**SAGE Instruments Inc** RH
240 Airport Blvd
Freedom CA 95019
P: 831-761-1000   PRC:166
Emp: 11-50 Estab: 1984

Michael Groh, Engineering Director
Dave Morris, Senior Hardware Engineer

Provider of wireless base station test products. The company offers battery operated handhelds, portables, bench tops, and rackmount test platforms.

**Sage Metering Inc** HQ
8 Harris Ct Bldg D1
Monterey CA 93940
P: 831-242-2030   F: 831-655-4965   PRC:14
www.sagemetering.com
Email: info@sagemetering.com
Estab: 2002

Mark Crawford, Owner
Gary Russell, Product Manager
Myrna Thorson, Executive Assistant

Manufacturer of thermal mass flow meters. The company offers services to the environmental and industrial sectors.

**Sagimet Biosciences** HQ
155 Bovet Rd Ste 303
San Mateo CA 94402
P: 650-561-8600   PRC:249
sagimet.com
Email: businessdevelopment@sagimet.com
Estab: 2006

George Kemble, CEO
Dennis Hom, CFO

Focuses on the discovery and development of therapeutic products for the treatment of oncology and infectious diseases.

**Sai Technology Inc**     HQ
2376 Walsh Ave
Santa Clara CA 95051
P: 408-727-1560    F: 408-715-7514     PRC:64
saitechnology.com
Email: pr@saitechnology.com

Venkat Rayapati, President
Vijiyasri Rayapati, VP of Operations & HR
Xia Gao, Director of Technology

Designer and developer of wireless technology solutions. The company also deals with digital signage services.

**Sainergy Inc**     HQ
1999 S Bascom Ave Ste 700
Campbell CA 95008
P: 408-532-9800    F: 206-202-0750     PRC:326
www.sainergy.net
Email: admin@sainergy.net
Estab: 2001

Priyanka Gupta, President
Shyon Stuifzand, SAP Manager

Provider of SAP consulting services such as business intelligence to clients in the technical and functional areas.

**Salutron Inc**     HQ
8371 Central Ave Unit A
Newark CA 94560
P: 510-795-2876    F: 510-657-7334     PRC:187
www.salutron.com
Email: sales@salutron.com
Estab: 1995

Mike Tsai, Co-Founder
Thomas Lo, Co-Founder
Tom Lo, Founder
May Lee, Program Manager

Providers of health care solutions. The company offers on-demand ecg accurate heart rate monitoring solutions.

**Samax Precision Inc**     HQ
926 W Evelyn Ave
Sunnyvale CA 94086
P: 408-245-9555    F: 408-245-0123     PRC:80
www.samaxinc.com
Email: info@samaxinc.com
Estab: 1963

Vicki Murray, President
Michael Tampier, CNC Prototype Machinist

Manufacturer and supplier of precision machined products. The company offers services like grinding and honing. It serves military and aerospace fields.

**Samco Inc**     RH
2302 Walsh Ave
Santa Clara CA 95051
P: 408-734-0459    F: 408-734-0961     PRC:126
www.samcointl.com
Email: info@samcointl.com
Estab: 1979

Henry Chan, General Manager
Peter Wood, Director of US Operations

Manufacturer of deposition, etching, and surface treatment systems used in the manufacturing of LED, MEMS, power & RF device, and other products.

**Samsara Networks Inc**     HQ
444 De Haro St
San Francisco CA 94107
P: 415-985-2400     PRC:325
www.samsara.com
Email: sales@samsara.com
Estab: 2015

Ben Calderon, EVP of Hardware Engineering and Operations
John Bicket, Founder
Sanjit Biswas, Founder
Kiren Sekar, EVP of Marketing and Product Management

Manufacturer of flexible sensors. The company is engaged in fleet monitoring, industrial sensing, cold chain monitoring, and fleet telematics.

**Samsung Research America**     DH
665 Clyde Ave
Mountain View CA 94043
P: 650-210-1001     PRC:306
www.sra.samsung.com
Email: sra-careers@sisa.samsung.com
Estab: 1988

Pascal BRUNET, Principal DSP Engineer
Allan Devantier, VP of Audio Research & Development
Thomas George, Patent Director
Ken Brandt, Senior Technical Recruiter

Provider of commercial, physical, and biological research services. The company is involved in testing and identification solutions.

**Samsung Semiconductor Inc**     HQ
3655 N First St
San Jose CA 95134
P: 408-544-4000    F: 408-544-4980     PRC:86
samsungsemiconductor-us.com

Lifeng Zheng, Senior Engineer
Chris Goodhart, Director of Marketing Communications
Stephen Lum, Product Marketing Manager
Tony Jung, Senior Director

Provider of electronics manufacturing and digital media products. The company also offers mobile services and PC software.

**Samtec**     BR
2323 Owen St Ste 120
Santa Clara CA 95054
P: 800-726-8329     PRC:76
www.samtec.com
Email: info@samtec.com

John Shine, President
Danny Boesing, Director of Marketing

Manufacturer of high-speed assemblies, connectors, edge cards, and jumpers. The company serves the industrial sector.

**San Francisco Circuits**     HQ
1660 S Amphlett Blvd Ste 200
San Mateo CA 94402
P: 800-732-5143    F: 650-655-7206     PRC:211
www.sfcircuits.com
Email: info@sfcircuits.com
Estab: 2005

Alexander Danovich, President
Robert Boten, Director of Quality
Sam Danovich, VP of Sales

Provider and manufacturer of printed circuit boards. The company also offers services like PCB design & assembly and specializes in complex circuits.

**San Joaquin Chemicals Inc**     HQ
1236 N Sierra Vista
Fresno CA 93703
P: 559-725-1735     PRC:51
www.sjc-inc.com
Email: sales@sjc-inc.com
Emp: 1-10   Estab: 1955

James Scott, Chemist

Provider of chemicals and services for condensers, boilers, closed loops, potable water, and waste water. The company serves the healthcare industry.

**San-I-Pak Pacific Inc**     HQ
23535 S Bird Rd
Tracy CA 95378
P: 209-836-2310    F: 209-836-2336     PRC:159
www.sanipak.com
Email: info@sanipak.com
Emp: 1-10   Estab: 1978

Arthur McCoy, SVP
Mitch Alvillar, Director of Electronics & Technical Support

Manufacturer of compactors, shredders, and sterilizer supplies. The company serves the industrial sector and enterprises.

**Sanah Inc**     HQ
1104 Corporate Way Ste 127
Sacramento CA 95831
P: 888-306-1942     PRC:323
www.sanahinc.com
Email: info@sanahinc.com
Emp: 1-10   Estab: 2003

Monica Tahiliani, Co-Founder
Rajnish Tahiliani, Co-Founder
Maher Madhat, President
Maj Gen Tahiliani, Partner

Provider of IT services such as IT strategy consulting, systems integration, and custom application development.

**Sanbio Inc**     HQ
231 S Whisman Rd
Mountain View CA 94041-1522
P: 650-625-8965    F: 650-625-8969     PRC:34
www.san-bio.com
Email: info@san-bio.com
Estab: 2001

Keita Mori, Co-CEO

Developer of regenerative therapies for neurological disorders. The company offers services to the healthcare sector.

**Sancrosoft USA Inc** RH
4944 Sunrise Blvd Ste B4
Fair Oaks CA 95628
P: 916-671-5593 PRC:322
sankrosoft.com
Emp: 11-50 Estab: 2008

Sonal Khunger, Director of Tabmiles
Sam Hunt, Recruitment Manager
Jatinder Chauhan, Recruiter
Arvind Reddy, Recruiter
Rajeev Arora, Technical Recruiter

Provider of technology consulting, IT staffing, and recruiting services. The company offers systems integration and application development services.

**Sanctuary Stainless** HQ
7532 Sandholdt Rd Ste 1
Moss Landing CA 95039
P: 831-633-3867 PRC:82
www.sancsta.com
Email: sancsta@redshift.com

David Jablonski, Owner

Provider of metal fabrication services. The company specializes in stainless and aluminum tubing and pipe fabrication.

**Sandhu Products Inc** HQ
6052 Industrial Way
Livermore CA 94551
P: 510-996-7199 F: 510-996-7199 PRC:268
www.sandhuproducts.com
Email: info@sandhuproducts.com
Estab: 2004

Raman Sandhu, President
Bob Sandhu, CEO

Provider of ayurvedic herbal dietary supplements. The company offers products containing vitamins, amino acids, minerals and medicinal plant extracts.

**SanDisk Corp** HQ
951 SanDisk Dr
Milpitas CA 95035
P: 408-801-1000 F: 408-801-8657 PRC:116
www.sandisk.com
Email: support@sandisk.com
Estab: 1988

Sushant Sakhalkar, Verification Engineer - II
Sumit Sadana, CSO
Shuki Nir, SVP of Corporate Marketing
Tom Baker, SVP of Human Resources
Milo Azarmsa, SVP of Operations Finance

Manufacturer of flash memory cards. The company's products include card readers, solid state drives, USB flash drives, and microSD cards.

**Sandvik Thermal Process Inc** DH
19500 Nugget Blvd
Sonora CA 95370
P: 209-533-1990 F: 209-533-4079 PRC:159
www.mrlind.com
Emp: 1-10 Estab: 1979

Richard Rosenberger, Service Engineer
Tyke Johnson, General Manager of PC Components
Bjorn Larsson, Research & Development Manager

Provider of thermal processing equipment. The company offers solar cells, semiconductors, and industrial heaters.

**Sangamo Therapeutics** HQ
501 Canal Blvd
Richmond CA 94804
P: 510-970-6000 PRC:34
www.sangamo.com
Email: info@sangamo.com
Emp: 247 Estab: 1995
Sales: $30M to $100M

Alexander Macrae, CEO
Edward Conner, SVP
McDavid Stilwell, VP of Corporate Communications & Investor Relations
Shirley Clift, VP of Regulatory Affairs
Geoffrey Nichol, EVP of Research & Development

Developer of engineered DNA-binding proteins for the regulation of gene expression and for gene modification.

**Sanovas Inc** HQ
2597 Kerner Blvd Ste 3320
San Rafael CA 94901
P: 415-729-9391 F: 415-729-9389 PRC:195
www.sanovas.com
Email: info@sanovas.com
Estab: 2009

Jerry Katzman, Chairman
Steve Goldsmith, VP of Marketing
Marc Levinson, Marketing Director

Manufacturer of medical equipment. The company develops minimally invasive surgical tools and technologies.

**Santronics Inc** HQ
1240 Birchwood Dr Ste 2
Sunnyvale CA 94089
P: 408-734-1878 F: 408-734-3905 PRC:200
www.santronics-usa.com
Email: sales@santronics-usa.com
Estab: 1984

Grant Ahn, President

Designer and manufacturer magnetic components. The company offers transformers, inductors, and coils for data transmission and power conversion needs.

**SAP America Inc** BR
3110 Hillview Ave
Palo Alto CA 94304
P: 650-849-4000 F: 650-849-4200 PRC:319
www.sap.com

Christian Klein, Co-CEO
Jennifer Morgan, Co-CEO
Juergen Mueller, CTO
Luka Mucic, CFO
Anthony Coletta, CFO

Developer of software applications. The company provides data and technology, custom development, and implementation services.

**Sardee Industries Inc** BR
2731 E Myrtle St
Stockton CA 95205
P: 209-466-1526 F: 209-466-1046 PRC:165
sardee.com
Email: sales@sardee.com
Emp: 11-50 Estab: 1962

Thomas Hystad, Design Engineer
Bert Lum, Principal Scientist
Nancy Yu, Senior Research Associate

Provider of container manufacturing equipment. The company also offers engineering and repair services for packing and filling industries.

**Sasken Technologies Ltd** BR
710 Lakeway Dr Ste 265
Sunnyvale CA 94085
P: 408-730-0100 PRC:63
www.sasken.com
Estab: 1989

Anjan Lahiri, CEO
Rajiv Mody, Managing Director
Neeta Revankar, CFO

Provider of research and development consultation, wireless software products, and software services to automotive and health care sectors.

**Satellite AV LLC** HQ
4021 Alvis Ct Ste 5
Rocklin CA 95677
P: 916-677-0720 F: 916-644-6312 PRC:61
satelliteav.com
Email: support@satelliteav.com
Emp: 1-10 Estab: 2005

Eugene Zaikin, Manager

Provider of broadcaster support and call center services. The company also deals with repairs, distribution, and sales.

**Satori Labs Inc** HQ
1800 Green Hills Rd Ste 203
Scotts Valley CA 95066
P: 831-457-9100 PRC:303
satorilabs.com
Email: info@satorilabs.com
Emp: 1-10 Estab: 2003

Alan Copland, Director of Marketing

Provider of medical based software services. The company's offerings include FusionForm Desktop and FusionForm Mobile.

**SatPath Systems Inc** HQ
47971 Fremont Blvd
Fremont CA 94538
P: 510-979-1102 F: 510-979-1105 PRC:61
www.satpath.com

Herkea Jea, CEO
Cindy George, Office Manager

Provider of networking solutions. The company focuses on voice communication, video and video-conferencing, banking, and other applications.

**Savari Inc** HQ
2005 De La Cruz Blvd Ste 111
Santa Clara CA 95050
P: 408-833-6369 PRC:304
savari.net
Email: sales@savari.net
Estab: 2008

Ravi Puvvala, CEO
Paul Sakamoto, COO
Vibha Shrivastava, Human Resource Generalist

Provider of communications technology solutions. The company focuses on connecting cars to traffic lights, pedestrians, and smartphones.

**Sc Solutions Inc**                                HQ
   1261 Oakmead Pkwy
   Sunnyvale CA 94085
P: 408-617-4520   F: 408-617-4521        PRC:304
www.scsolutions.com
Email: sales@scsolutions.com
Estab: 1989

Eric Abrahamson, Principal Engineer
Vince Jacob, Principal Engineer
Harsh Nandan, Structural Engineer
Basilio Sumodobila, Structural Engineer
Jinquan Zhong, Senior Engineer

Provider of control design and implementation
services. The company also focuses on structural
design and software development.

**Sc-Mech Solution Inc**                          HQ
   2241 Paragon Dr
   San Jose CA 95131
P: 408-748-3380   F: 408-748-3381        PRC:80
www.sc-mechsolution.com
Estab: 2000

Edward Choi, Quality Assurance Manager
Jacqueline Nguyen, Coordinator

Manufacturer of electronic parts and components.
The company provides CNC milling, tooling, design, and contract manufacturing services.

**SCA Environmental Inc**                         HQ
   320 Justin Dr
   San Francisco CA 94112
P: 415-882-1675   F: 415-962-0736        PRC:139
www.sca-enviro.com
Email: info@scasah.com
Estab: 1992

Glenn Cass, VP
Chaowen Huang, Environmental Scientist
Chuck Siu, Senior Consultant

Provider of environmental science, occupational
health and safety, engineering, and laboratory
analyses services.

**Scales Unlimited Inc**                          HQ
   5401 Byron Hot Springs Rd
   Byron CA 94514
P: 925-634-8068                          PRC:13
www.scalesu.com
Email: sales@scalesu.com
Estab: 1981

Rory Ward, President
Jesse Wetherell, Regional Sales Manager
Courtney Ward, Operations Manager

Provider of mechanical and computer based
weighing systems. The company's services include repairs, replacement, and installation.

**Scandic Springs Inc**                           HQ
   700 Montague Ave
   San Leandro CA 94577
P: 510-352-3700                          PRC:82
www.scandic.com
Estab: 1969

Jason Hensel, Sales Engineering
Hale Foote, President

Provider of machine tools. The company offers
heat treatment, plating, engineering, and raw
material guidance services.

**Scepter Scientific Inc**                        HQ
   2021 Las Positas Ct Ste 129
   Livermore CA 94551
P: 925-373-4802   F: 925-373-4807        PRC:87
www.scepter.net
Email: sales@scepter.net

Steven Harbaugh, President
Grant Schleiger, VP

Provider of feasibility evaluations, electronic, optical, and mechanical engineering, and prototype
development services.

**Schindler Elevator Corp**                       BR
   555 Mccormick St
   San Leandro CA 94577-1107
P: 510-382-2075   F: 510-382-2250        PRC:180
www.schindler.com
Estab: 1874

Mike Relstab, Regional Field Engineer
Bradley Lay, General Manager

Provider of elevators, escalators, and related
services. The company creates and delivers urban
mobility solutions.

**Schmartboard Inc**                              HQ
   37423 Fremont Blvd
   Fremont CA 94536
P: 510-744-9900   F: 510-744-9909        PRC:200
schmartboard.com
Email: info@schmartboard.com
Estab: 1863

Andrew Yaung, Co-Founder
Neal Greenberg, Co-Founder
B. Schmart, CTO

Specializes in the production of hand soldering
components. The company's products are used in
sensor and USB technologies.

**Schurter Inc**                                  DH
   447 Aviation Blvd
   Santa Rosa CA 95403
P: 707-636-3000   F: 707-636-3033        PRC:209
www.schurterinc.com
Email: info@schurterinc.com

Bill Cardoza, Facilities Administrator
Gisela Babb, Senior Quality Operations Analyst
Diane Cupples, VP of Marketing
Rhiannon Schwartz, Receptionist

Manufacturer of fuses, connectors, and circuit
breakers. The company also offers input systems
and EMC products.

**Schutze & Assoc Inc**                           HQ
   44358 S Grimmer Blvd
   Fremont CA 94538
P: 510-226-9944   F: 510-226-9948        PRC:140
schutze-inc.com
Estab: 2000

Jan Schutze, Founder

Provider of environmental consulting services. The
company's services include groundwater monitoring and dry cleaning remediation.

**SciBac Inc**                                    HQ
   1828 El Camino Real Ste 704
   Burlingame CA 94010
P: 650-689-5343   F: 650-239-9160        PRC:34
www.scibac.com
Email: info@scibac.com
Estab: 2015

Derik Twomey, COO
Anthony Cann, CTO
Jeanette Mucha, CSO
Maya Kuttan, Chief Counsel
Gregory Govoni, Director of Pre-Clinical Research

Developer of bactoceuticals and medicinal
probiotics for the prevention and treatment of
clostridium difficile. The company serves the
medical sector.

**SciClone Pharmaceuticals Inc**                  HQ
   950 Tower Ln Ste 900
   Foster City CA 94404-2125
P: 650-358-3456                          PRC:254
www.sciclone.com
Email: bd@sciclone.com
Estab: 2003

Zhao Hong, President

Developer of therapeutics to treat life-threatening
diseases. The company serves hospitals and the
healthcare industry.

**Scientific Coating Labs**                       HQ
   350 Martin Ave
   Santa Clara CA 95050-3112
P: 408-727-3296   F: 408-727-8775        PRC:127
www.scientificcoatinglabs.com
Email: customerservice@scientificcoatinglabs.
com

Dick Rennolds, President
Tracie Rennolds, Front Office Manager

Provider of wafer coatings. The company specializes in coating components used in the semiconductor industry.

**Scientific Specialties Inc**                    HQ
   1310 Thurman St
   Lodi CA 95240
P: 209-333-2120   F: 209-333-8623        PRC:189
www.ssibio.com
Email: info@ssibio.com
Emp: 1-10   Estab: 1990

Robbie Hovatter, Co-Owner
Cindy Schock, Human Resource
Cory Vohs, Production Manager
Karen Ware, Director of Sales
Peter Cung, Business Development Manager

Manufacturer of injection molded plastic consumable and durable products such as tubes, pipette
tips, and racks for life science research industry.

**Scigene Corp** HQ
1287 Reamwood Ave
Sunnyvale CA 94089
P: 408-733-7337  F: 408-733-7336  PRC:31
www.scigene.com
Email: custserv@scigene.com
Estab: 2003

Terry Gill, Director of Manufacturing
Liz Robertson, Marketing Services Director
George Taylor, Director

Develops and commercializes solutions to automate sample workflows. The company offers reagents, microarray ovens, and arrays.

**Scimage Inc** HQ
4916 El Camino Real
Los Altos CA 94022
P: 866-724-6243  F: 650-694-4861  PRC:194
www.scimage.com
Email: corporate_sales@scimage.com
Estab: 1993

Vi Vo, UIUX Engineer
James Wong, Software Engineer
Sai Raya, Founder
Madvi Raya, CFO
Matthew Wolkenmuth, Product Manager

Provider of imaging solutions. The company also deals with clinical and cloud solutions and business intelligence support.

**Scimet LLC** HQ
2745 Deer Meadow Dr
Danville CA 94506
P: 925-736-2915  F: 925-736-2915  PRC:19
www.scimet.com
Estab: 2007

John Elmer, Founder

Provider of metallurgical consulting services. The company specializes in welding, brazing, soldering, bonding, and heat treating.

**Sciton Inc** HQ
925 Commercial St
Palo Alto CA 94303
P: 650-493-9155  F: 650-493-9146  PRC:188
www.sciton.com
Email: info@sciton.com
Estab: 1997

Kody Haaland, Research
James Hobart, President
Lars Isaacson, VP of Sales
Jamie Isenhart, Area Sales Manager
Carol Medlin, Accounts Payable Specialist

Provider of laser and light source solutions. The company's products include JOULE, BBL, ClearSense, Halo, and more.

**Screw Conveyor Corporation** BR
7807 Doe Ave
Visalia CA 93291-9220
P: 559-651-2131  F: 559-651-2135  PRC:179
www.screwconveyor.com
Email: sales@screwconveyor.com
Emp: 11-50  Estab: 1932

Adolfo De La Rosa, Sales Engineer
Randy Smith, General Manager Western Operations

Manufacturer of bulk material handling equipment including screw conveyors, drag conveyors, and bucket elevators.

**Scribner Plastics** HQ
11455 Hydraulic Dr
Rancho Cordova CA 95742
P: 916-638-1515  F: 916-638-2278  PRC:280
scribnerplastics.com
Email: info@scribnerplastics.com
Emp: 1-10  Estab: 197?

Scribner Plastics Rick, Scribner

Provider of shipping and packing solutions. The company also deals with custom plastics design and manufacturing services.

**SDL USA** BR
2550 N First St Ste 301
San Jose CA 95131
P: 408-743-3600  F: 408-743-3601  PRC:325
www.sdl.com
Estab: 1992

Tony White, Founder
Adolfo Hernandez, CEO
Azad Ootam, Chief Transformation Officer
Thomas Labarthe, Chief Revenue Officer
Xenia Walters, CFO

Provider of web content and structured content management, as well as e-commerce solutions, and language technologies.

**SE Ranking** BR
228 Hamilton Ave
Palo Alto CA 94301
P: 415-704-4387  PRC:325
seranking.com
Estab: 2012

Artem Kozel, Partner

SEO platform that allows individuals to optimize and promote a website on the web.

**Seagull Solutions Inc** HQ
15105 Concord Cir Ste 100
Morgan Hill CA 95037-5487
P: 408-778-1127  F: 408-779-2806  PRC:5
www.seagullsolutions.net
Email: info@seagullsolutions.net

Donald Ekhoff, Owner
Carol Lawless, Sales

Developer and manufacturer of air bearing spindles, clamps, and custom applications. The company mainly offers custom made services.

**Searchforce** HQ
3 Waters Park Dr Ste 211
San Mateo CA 94403
P: 650-235-8800  F: 650-312-8661  PRC:322
www.searchforce.com
Email: sales@searchforce.com
Estab: 2004

Zach Zelmar, Software Engineer
Sharath Goli, UI Engineer
Sergey Yakubov, Quality Assurance Engineer
Dhiren Dsouza, Co-Founder
Santhosh Nair, CTO

Developer of automation software. The company offers software for automation, optimization, campaign management, and tracking.

**Searchmetrics Inc** HQ
1100 Park Pl Ste 150
San Mateo CA 94403
P: 866-411 9494  PRC:319
www.searchmetrics.com
Estab: 2005

Jordan Koene, CEO
Doug Bell, CMO

A Search and Content Marketing Platform that uncovers the opportunities and pitfalls of online marketing.

**Seascape Lamps** HQ
PO Box 810
Freedom CA 95019
P: 831-728-5699  F: 831-728-0658  PRC:243
www.seascapelamps.com
Email: sales@seascapelamps.com
Emp: 1-10  Estab: 1980

Chris Brightman, Design Engineer
Mike Shenk, President

Provider of contemporary and retro home lighting solutions. The company also specializes in printed drum lamp shades.

**Seatec Lab Repair** HQ
520 Woodstock Way
Santa Clara CA 95054
P: 408-828-1815  PRC:306
www.seatec-lab.com

Rich O'Neil, Owner
Deb O'Neil, Office Manager

Provider of services to analytical, biotech, and industrial laboratories. The company also focuses on equipment validation.

**Sebastian** HQ
7600 N Palm Ave
Fresno CA 93711
P: 559-432-5800  F: 559-432-5858  PRC:304
www.sebastiancorp.com
Email: customerservicefresno@sebastiancorp.com
Emp: 11-50  Estab: 1946

Brandon Dukes, VP of Sales Marketing and Business Development

Provider of structured cabling and electrical contracting services. The company offers services to the residential and commercial sectors.

**Seco** HQ
4155 Oasis Rd
Redding CA 96003
P: 530-225-8155  F: 530-225-8162  PRC:19
www.surveying.com
Email: seco@surveying.com
Emp: 1-10  Estab: 1977

Daniel Moller, Mechanical Engineer

Manufacturer of surveying and positioning equipment and accessories. The company's products also finds application in site preparation.

**Second Genome Inc**    HQ
341 Allerton Ave Ste 215
S San Francisco CA 94080
P: 650-440-4606    PRC:25
www.secondgenome.com
Email: info@secondgenome.com
Estab: 2009

Todd DeSantis, Co-Founder
Corey Goodman, Co-Founder
Karim Dabbagh, President
Anu Hoey, Chief Business Officer
Bernat Raja, Scientist II

Focuses on the development of therapeutic products. The company serves pharmaceutical and nutritional companies.

**Secret Builders**    HQ
1900 S Norfolk St Ste 219
San Mateo CA 94403-1172
P: 650-204-9098    PRC:317
www.secretbuilders.com
Email: info@secretbuilders.com

Umair Khan, CEO
Vladimir Soskov, CTO
Georgi Marinoff, Chief Architect
Fawad Qadri, VP of Product Development
Bob Brattesani, VP of Creative Design

Provider of online games for children. The company also focuses on publishing writings, art, and videos.

**Secugen Corp**    HQ
2065 Martin Ave Ste 108
Santa Clara CA 95050
P: 408-727-7787    F: 408-834-7762    PRC:319
www.secugen.com
Email: sales@secugen.com
Estab: 1998

Dan Riley, VP of Engineering
Won Lee, CEO
Jeff Brown, VP of Sales

Manufacturer of fingerprint recognition devices. The company's products serve the purpose of integration into 3rd party hardware products.

**Securematics Inc**    HQ
1135 Walsh Ave
Santa Clara CA 95050
P: 888-746-6700    F: 408-731-9124    PRC:59
www.securematics.com
Email: sales@securematics.com
Estab: 2002

Anjum Khan, Senior Credit Financial Analyst
Ruby Ferguson, Marketing Assistant
Jon Bennett, Director
Keith H., Data Operations Manager

Provider of secure networking, security, storage products and solutions. The company focuses on demand generation and e-commerce.

**Seeo Inc**    HQ
3906 Trust Way
Hayward CA 94545
P: 510-782-7336    F: 510-782-7337    PRC:288
Estab: 2007

Jonathan Boylan, Senior Process Engineer
Albert Aumentado, Test Engineer
Jin Yang, Director of Polymer Manufacture
Xiao-Liang Wang, Research

Developer of rechargeable lithium batteries for the needs of electric vehicles and large-scale renewable energy storage.

**Seevider Inc**    HQ
4500 Great America Pkwy Ste 1054
Santa Clara CA 95054
P: 408-930-0852    PRC:87
www.seevider.com
Email: info@seevider.com
Estab: 2014

Hobin Kim, CEO

Manufacturer of smart vision devices. The company's products are used in light management, parking occupancy detection, and guiding.

**Seg Inc**    HQ
2550 Walsh Ave Ste 120
Santa Clara CA 95051
P: 408-260-8008    PRC:301
www.seg-corp.com
Estab: 2000

Jim Marsh, Senior Mechanical Engineer
James Maggard, President
Wayne Johnson, Managing Partner

Provider of consulting, design, engineering, project management, commissioning, and validation services.

**Seiwa Optical America Inc**    HQ
3042 Scott Blvd
Santa Clara CA 95054
P: 408-844-8008    F: 408-844-8944    PRC:168
www.seiwaamerica.com
Email: info@seiwaamerica.com
Estab: 1947

Megumi Morford, Sales & Marketing Manager

Manufacturer of optical components and photonic integrated circuits. The company offers network and access solutions.

**Sejin America Inc**    BR
46715 Fremont Blvd
Fremont CA 94538
P: 510-573-4852    F: 510-573-6565    PRC:109
www.sejin.com
Email: info@sejin.com

Jong Lee, Business Development Manager

Manufacturer of automobile parts, smart grid products, input devices, and convergence products. The company offers customer support services.

**Selectiva Systems Inc**    HQ
2051 Junction Ave Ste 225/215
San Jose CA 95131
P: 408-297-1336    F: 408-627-6484    PRC:325
www.selectiva.com
Email: info-sjc@selectiva.com

Ranjeet Jhala, Programmer Analyst
Vivek Sathe, Business Analyst

Provider of solutions for revenue reporting, customer service, and distributor management. The company serves hi-tech, pharma, and other sectors.

**Semi-Probes Inc**    HQ
2075 Bering Dr Ste D
San Jose CA 95131
P: 408-866-6535    F: 408-866-0437    PRC:196
www.semi-probes.com
Estab: 1979

Marisela Valdez, Customer Service Executive

Manufacturer and supplier of probe cards and tester interfaces. The company's services include design, installation, and delivery.

**Semicat Inc**    BR
47900 Fremont Blvd
Fremont CA 94538
P: 408-514-6900    F: 408-514-6901    PRC:126
www.semicat.com
Email: sales@semicat.com

Jin Kim, Marketing Director
Megan Park, Controller

Provider of refurbished equipments for semiconductors. The company deals in LED, and novel emerging applications.

**Semicore Equipment Inc**    HQ
470 Commerce Way
Livermore CA 94551
P: 925-373-8201    F: 925-373-8202    PRC:159
www.semicore.com
Email: sales@semicore.com
Estab: 1996

Trey Haight, Manufacturing
Jimmy Haight, Product Development Engineer
Matt Kuntz, Senior Mechanical Engineer
Alan Klaffke, Senior Electrical Engineer
Matthew Hughes, President

Manufacturer of vacuum systems and equipment. The company's products include PVD coating systems, thermal evaporation, and sputtering equipment.

**Semifab**    HQ
150 Great Oaks Blvd
San Jose CA 95119
P: 408-414-5928    F: 408-414-5926    PRC:230
www.semifab.com
Estab: 1970

Gerry Reynolds, Manager
Greg Krikorian, Manager
Showkot Hassan, Manager
John Tran, Manager

Supplier of process environment control systems for precise temperature, humidity, air flow, and airborne particulate management.

**Sempac Inc** HQ
PO Box 3217
Los Altos CA 94024
P: 408-400-9002   F: 408-400-9006   PRC:86
www.sempac.com
Email: sales@sempac.com
Estab: 2000

Deborah Benando-Morris, VP of Operations

Developer of pre-molded open-cavity plastic packages for optoelectronic, telecom, RF, MEMS, and sensor applications.

**Sendero Group LLC** HQ
PO Box 937
Rancho Cordova CA 95741
P: 888-757-6810   F: 888-757-6807   PRC:61
www.senderogroup.com
Email: info@senderogroup.com
Emp: 1-10   Estab: 1993

Mike May, CEO
Charles Lapierre, CTO
Kim Casey, Director

Provider of GPS systems and products to the visually impaired. The company focuses on documentation and technical support services.

**Sensifree Inc** HQ
21631 Stevens Creek Blvd Ste B
Cupertino CA 95014
P: 669-230-5116   PRC:87
www.sensifree.com
Email: info@sensifree.com
Estab: 2012

Eran Agmon, CEO
Llan Barak, CTO
Moshe Kamar, CMO
Asaf Bar, VP of Business Development & Marketing

Manufacturer of contactless sensors for wearables. The company offers heart rate sensors, including fitness trackers, and activity monitors.

**Sensing Electromagnetic Plus Corp** HQ
974 Commercial St Ste 200B
Palo Alto CA 94303
P: 415-954-0322   PRC:120
semplus.com
Estab: 2013

James Le, Software Engineer
Chinmay Tambat, FPGA Design Engineer

Developer of third touch dimension in human-machine interfaces. The company offers unobtrusive pressure sensitive solutions.

**Sensoplex Inc** HQ
1735 E Bayshore Rd Ste 29B
Redwood City CA 94063
P: 408-391-9019   PRC:189
sensoplex.com
Email: info@Rover.health
Estab: 2012

Hamid Najafi, CEO
Gabriel Griego, VP of Sales & Marketing
Adi Iyer, CMO

Developer and manufacturer of wearable sensors. The company offers rechargeable batteries, displays, interfaces, and related accessories.

**Sensor Concepts Inc** HQ
7950 National Dr
Livermore CA 94550
P: 925-443-9001   F: 925-443-9050   PRC:2
www.sensorconcepts.com
Email: sci@sensorconcepts.com
Estab: 1996

John Meehan, Design Engineer
Seitu Barron, Mechanical Engineer
Vince Dumaop, Product Support Engineer
Fiona Parken, Human Resource Manager
Matthew Bogdanov, Information Technology Manager

Developer of portable and integrated measurement systems. The company offers engineering, field measurement and software development services.

**Sensory Inc** HQ
4701 Patrick Henry Dr Bldg 7
Santa Clara CA 95054
P: 408-625-3300   F: 408-625-3350   PRC:325
www.sensoryinc.com
Email: sales@sensoryinc.com
Estab: 1994

Erich Adams, Senior Field Apps Engineer
Todd Mozer, CEO
Mina Wong, Director of Finance
Johnny Chan, Senior Operations Manager

Provider of speech recognition and voice biometric ICs. The company's products are used in toys and home electronic products.

**Sensys Networks Inc** HQ
1608 Fourth St Ste 200
Berkeley CA 94710
P: 510-548-4620   PRC:87
www.sensysnetworks.com
Estab: 2003

Brian Fuller, VP of Engineering
David Sheahen, Director of Field Engineering
Kian Kiani, Senior Mechanical Engineer
Daryl Potter, Systems Field Engineer
Amine Haoui, CEO

Manufacturer of wireless sensor cubes, repeaters, and related accessories. The company's services include training and technical support.

**Sentek Dynamics Inc** HQ
2370 Owen St
Santa Clara CA 95054
P: 408-200-3100   F: 408-659-8229   PRC:159
www.sentekdynamics.com
Email: sales@sentekdynamics.com
Estab: 2011

Sentek Dynamics, Vibration Test Equipment Manufacturer

Manufacturer of vibration test equipment, shakers, power amplifiers, and related instruments. The company offers customer support solutions.

**Sentient Energy Inc** HQ
880 Mitten Rd
Burlingame CA 94010
P: 650-523-6680   F: 650-239-9048   PRC:130
www.sentient-energy.com
Email: info@sentient-energy.com

Mark Sloan, EVP of Engineering and Manufacturing Technology Operations
Konda Ankireddyapalli, SVP of Engineering
Nace Reader, Software Engineer
Michael Bauer, CEO
James Keener, CEO

Provider of sensor devices for operational practices and engineering applications. The company also offers communication software.

**Sentieon Inc** HQ
465 Fairchild Dr Ste 135
Mountain View CA 94043
P: 650-282-5650   PRC:40
www.sentieon.com
Email: info@sentieon.com
Estab: 2014

Zhipan Li, Principal Engineer
Rafael Aldana, Product Application Director
Don Freed, Bioinformatics Scientist

Supplier and developer of bioinformatics secondary analysis tools. The company offers precision data for precision medicine.

**SentinelOne** HQ
605 Fairchild Dr
Mountain View CA 94043
P: 855-868-3733   PRC:63
sentinelone.com
Email: sales@sentinelone.com
Estab: 2013

Tomer Weingarten, CEO
Anthony Bates, Inside Sales Manager
Scott Gainey, CMO
Eran Ashkenazi, VP
Mark Danckert, Senior Director

Developer of end-point protection software. The company serves the healthcare, oil and gas, and financial services industries.

**Sentons Usa Inc** HQ
627 River Oaks Pkwy
San Jose CA 95134
P: 408-732-9000   PRC:212
www.sentons.com

Sam Sheng, President

Provider of touch solutions. The company offers flat panel display, retail point of sale, and factory/industry automation products.

**Sentreheart Inc** HQ
300 Saginaw Dr
Redwood City CA 94063
P: 650-354-1200   F: 650-354-1204   PRC:189
www.sentreheart.com
Email: info@sentreheart.com
Estab: 2005

Russell Seiber, President
Robert Strasser, VP
Pam Simons, VP of Clinical affairs
Greg Fung, Senior Director

Developer of catheter technology solutions. The company is engaged in suture delivery and related services.

**Sentry Products Inc**  HQ
2378 B Walsh Ave
Santa Clara CA 95051
P: 408-727-1866   F: 408-727-2129   PRC:59
www.sentryproducts.net
Email: sentryscan@earthlink.net
Estab: 1974

Sam Stone, Manager

Provider of duress alarm systems. The company
caters to judicial centers, emergency medical
facilities, and schools.

**Sepragen Corp**  HQ
1205 San Luis Obispo Ave
Hayward CA 94544
P: 510-475-0650   F: 510-475-0625   PRC:20
www.sepragen.com
Email: info@sepragen.com
Estab: 1985

Renu Chabra, VP of Manufacturing and Engineer-
ing
David Zuffi, Senior Systems Engineer
Vinit Saxena, CEO
Salah Ahmed, Director of Quality & Tech Support

Provider of equipment, systems, and materials for
the scale-up and purification of proteins, biopharmaceuticals, and nutraceuticals.

**Sequoia Analytical Labs**  HQ
1783 Tribute Rd Ste A
Sacramento CA 95815
P: 916-920-4009   PRC:41
www.sequoia-labs.com
Email: sales@sequoia-labs.com
Emp: 1-10

Jeffrey Hatley, President

Provider of laboratory testing services. The company specializes in testing of agro products for
components and microbe content.

**Sercomm Usa Inc**  BR
42808 Christy St Ste 231
Fremont CA 94538
P: 510-870-1598   F: 510-870-2320   PRC:323
www.sercomm.com
Email: market@sercomm.com
Estab: 1992

Ben Lin, CTO
Paul Wang, Co-Founder
James Wang, CEO
Arif Ahsan, Senior Director of Business Develop-
ment

Provider of software and firmware for the development of broadband networking. The company also
offers solutions for fixed mobile convergence.

**Serpa Packaging Solutions**  HQ
7020 W Sunnyview Ave
Visalia CA 93291
P: 559-651-2339   F: 559-651-2345   PRC:159
serpapackaging.com
Email: sales@serpapackaging.com
Emp: 1-10   Estab: 1985

Jon Gaiser, Engineering Manager
Justin Neece, Mechanical Engineering Manager
Andrew Nunez, Mechanical Engineer
Fernando Serpa, President
Debbie Nahial-Brown, Purchasing Manager

Provider of packaging solutions. The company's
applications include pharmaceutical industry and
bottles, vials, and ampules.

**Servicesource International Inc**  HQ
44 Montgomery St Ste 3450
San Francisco CA 94104
P: 720-889-8500   PRC:324
servicesource.com
Email: contactus@servicesource.com
Estab: 1999
Sales: $100M to $300M

Debbie Dunnam, COO
Denzil Samuels, CFO
James Boyce, SVP
Shaun Han, SVP

Provider of recurring revenue management solutions. The company focuses on process automation and managed services.

**Sessco Technologies Inc**  HQ
1701 Fortune Dr Ste A
San Jose CA 95131
P: 408-321-7437   PRC:19
www.sessco.com
Email: info@sessco.com
Estab: 1995

Ben Delavega, Founder
Vanessa Castro, Office Manager

Designer and manufacturer of tri-temperature test
handlers for the commercial, industrial, automotive, and military grade circuit test applications.

**Sfj Pharmaceuticals Group**  HQ
5000 Hopyard Rd Ste 330
Pleasanton CA 94588
P: 925-223-6233   F: 925-425-0986   PRC:268
www.sfj-pharma.com
Estab: 2008

Robert Debenedetto, President
Alexandra Dilis, EVP

Focuses on the clinical development and registration of pharmaceutical products. The company is
involved in clinical trials.

**Sgarlato Med LLC**  HQ
4135 S Power Rd Ste 110
Mesa CA 85212
P: 800-403-6876   PRC:189
www.sgarlatomed.com
Email: info@sgarlatomed.com
Emp: 1-10   Estab: 1989

Thomas Sgarlato, CEO

Manufacturer and distributor of foot and ankle
implants for surgical use. The company also
provides clinical, technical, and in-service training
services.

**Shape Security**  HQ
2755 Augustine Dr 8th Fl
Santra Clara CA 95054
P: 650-399-0400   PRC:326
www.shapesecurity.com
Email: info@shapesecurity.com
Estab: 2011

Jarrod Overson, Director of Engineering
Sergey Shekyan, Principal Engineer
Kenton Miller, Engineer
Michael Ficarra, Senior Software Engineer
Shilpi Jain, Automation Engineer

Provider of defense solutions against malicious
automated cyber-attacks on web and mobile
applications.

**ShareThis Inc**  HQ
3000 El Camino Real 5 Palo Alto Sq Ste
150
Palo Alto CA 94306
P: 650-323-1783   PRC:325
sharethis.com
Email: support@sharethis.com
Estab: 2007

Dana Hayes, CEO
Kurt Abrahamson, Executive Chairman
Chad Burns, CFO
Huanjin Chen, CTO
Myha Trieu, SVP of People

Developers of social sharing solutions for website
owners.

**Sharp Dimension Inc**  HQ
4240 Business Center Dr
Fremont CA 94538
P: 510-656-8938   F: 510-656-8940   PRC:80
www.sharpdimension.com
Email: contact@sharpdimension.com
Estab: 1993

Tracy Tran, Owner

Provider of production and prototype machining
services. The company serves semiconductor,
medical, robotics, solar, defense, and other
sectors.

**Sharp Microelectronics Of The Amer-
icas**  BR
1701 Junction Ct Ste 200
San Jose CA 95112
P: 408-452-6400   F: 408-436-0924   PRC:169
www.sharpsma.com
Emp: 11-50 Estab: 1912

Mary Holland, Director of Human Resources

Provider of LCD, optoelectronics, imagers, and RF
components. The company is involved in design
and installation services.

**Sharper Technology Inc**  HQ
1032 Elwell Ct Ste 110
Palo Alto CA 94303
P: 650-964-4600   F: 650-964-4650   PRC:323
www.sharpertechnology.com
Email: info@sharpertechnology.com
Estab: 2003

Ronald Steffen, President
Pat Glass, VP of Finance
Kevin McCarthy, VP of Operations

Provider of network security solutions and services. The company also offers design, implementation, and training services.

**Sharpesoft Inc**  HQ
925 Market St
Yuba City CA 95991
P: 530-671-6499   F: 530-671-5739   PRC:319
www.sharpesoft.com
Email: sales@sharpesoft.com
Emp: 1-10   Estab: 1986

Kristopher Wilkins, QA

Provider of cost accounting, dispatching, and
project management software. The company
exclusively serves the construction sector.

**Shasta Crystals Inc** HQ
1750 Cesar Chavez Unit J
San Francisco CA 94124
P: 415-426-7904  F: 415-697-3393  PRC:172
www.shastacrystals.com
Email: info@shastacrystals.com
Estab: 2006

Gisele Maxwell, President
Kevin McCarthy, EVP
Mark Selker, Director
Mike Farmwald, Director

Producer of nonlinear optical crystals for visible lasers. The company's services include research and evaluation.

**SHASTA Electronic Manufacturing Services Inc** HQ
525 E Brokaw Rd
San Jose CA 95112
P: 408-436-1267  PRC:124
www.shastaems.com
Email: contact@shasta-ems.com
Estab: 2005

Rang N., VP of Operations

Provider of electronic manufacturing services. The company's services include prototype manufacturing, testing, materials, and quality control.

**Shax Engineering Inc** HQ
44777 S Grimmer Blvd Ste C
Fremont CA 94538
P: 408-452-1500  F: 408-441-0634  PRC:124
www.shax-eng.com
Email: info@shax-eng.com
Estab: 1998

Isam Shakour, Founder

Provider of PCB fabrication and assembly services. The company serves original equipment manufacturers and technology companies.

**Shen Milsom Wilke LLC** BR
351 California St Ste 810
San Francisco CA 94104-2406
P: 415-391-7610  F: 415-391-0171  PRC:304
www.smwllc.com
Estab: 1986

Brian Takacs, Audiovisual Engineer
Bruce Manning, Audiovisual Engineer
Charles Danelutt, Audiovisual Engineer
Daniel Wright, Audiovisual Engineer
Thomas Edge, Audiovisual Engineer

Provider of technology design and consulting solutions such as acoustics, medical equipment planning, audiovisual, and building security.

**Shen Wei USA Inc** HQ
33278 Central Ave Ste 102
Union City CA 94587
P: 510-429-8692  F: 510-487-5347  PRC:195
shenweiusa.com
Email: info@shenweiusa.com
Estab: 1999

Belle Chou, Founder

Manufacturer of disposable gloves and customizable products. The company offers services to the healthcare industry.

**Shields Harper & Co** HQ
4591 Pacheco Blvd
Martinez CA 94553-2233
P: 510-653-9119  F: 510-658-8448  PRC:133
www.shieldsharper.com
Email: martinez@shieldsharper.com
Estab: 1917

Dave Sarginson, President
Doug DeLong, General Manager
Paul Chae, Information Technology Manager
Jennifer Nguyen, Purchasing Manager
Greg Matas, Sales Manager

Provider of design assistance, testing, monitoring, fleet fuel control, and underground solutions to contractors, engineers, and designers.

**Shifamed LLC** HQ
590 Division St
Campbell CA 95008
P: 408-560-2500  PRC:189
www.shifamed.com
Email: info@shifamed.com
Estab: 2008

Todor Jeliaskov, President
Amr Salahieh, President
Mike Dineen, President
Claudio Argento, CTO
Jean Orth, CSO

Manufacturer of medical technologies and products catheters, custom balloons, painted balloon electrodes, and diagnostic and therapeutic instrumentation.

**Shimon Systems Inc** HQ
4984 El Camino Real Ste 200
Los Altos CA 94022
P: 650-461-9104  F: 650-461-9105  PRC:71
www.shimonsystems.com
Email: info@shimonsystems.com
Estab: 2003

Ven Reddy, VP of Operations

Manufacturer of fingerprint authentication solutions. The company's services include research and development.

**Shin-Etsu Polymer America Inc** HQ
5600 Mowry School Rd Ste 320
Newark CA 94560
P: 510-623-1881  F: 510-623-1603  PRC:78
www.shinpoly.com
Estab: 1960

Yoshio Akinaga, President
Richard Villanueva, Production Manager
Linda Ishiguro, Inside Sales Coordinator
Akira Iwatsuki, Plant Manager

Manufacturer of electro-mechanical components such as custom made keypads and inter-connectors, decorative films, and switch devices.

**Shockwave Medical Inc** HQ
5403 Betsy Ross Dr
Santa Clara CA 95054
P: 877-775-4846  PRC:189
shockwavemedical.com
Email: info@shockwavemedical.com

Doug Godshall, CEO

Focuses on the production of highest performance personal submarines on the planet. The company is involved in research services.

**Shotspotter Inc** HQ
7979 Gateway Blvd Ste 210
Newark CA 94560
P: 510-794-3144  PRC:59
www.shotspotter.com
Email: info@shotspotter.com
Estab: 1996

Chris Belden, Technical Support Engineer
Robert Showen, Founder
Douglas McFarlin, VP
Joe Hawkins, VP
Paul Ames, VP

Provider of gunfire detection and location technology services. The company addresses gun violence in communities.

**Si-Bone Inc** RH
471 El Camino Real Ste 2200
San Jose CA 95128
P: 408-207-0700  F: 408-557-8312  PRC:187
si-bone.com
Email: info@si-bone.com
Estab: 2008
Sales: $30M to $100M

Michael Burke, Senior Engineer
Mark Reiley, CMO
Jeffrey Dunn, President
Scott Yerby, VP
Tony Recupero, Chief Commercial Officer

Developer of medical products and technologies such as implants and titanium implant technology for SI joint pain and sacroiliac joint fusion surgery.

**Sicon International Inc** HQ
568 Charcot Ave
San Jose CA 95131-2201
P: 408-954-9880  F: 408-954-9886  PRC:202
sicon.com
Estab: 1989

Louis Grijalva, Senior Sales Engineer
Alex He, Mechanical Engineer
Jack Wang, President

Manufacturer of electronic components. The company specializes in the fabrication of connectors, cables, circuit boards, and molded cables.

**Sienna Corporation** BR
41350 Christy St
Fremont CA 94538
P: 510-440-0200  F: 510-440-0201  PRC:70
siennagroup.com
Email: sales@siennagroup.com
Estab: 1995

Karuppiah Karuppiah, Industrial Engineer
Kenneth Horan, Manufacturing Engineer
Praveen A, Purchasing Engineer
Bruce Nimmer, Owner
Kunhamed Bicha, CEO

Provider of electronic manufacturing services including design and process engineering, prototyping, and electromechanical assembly services.

**Sierra Chemical Company**  HQ
788 Northport Dr
West Sacramento CA 95691
P: 916-371-5943  PRC:50
www.sierrachemicalcompany.com
Emp: 1-10  Estab: 1946

Steve Gould, President
Jerry Eykelbosh, Sales Manager
Tom Enos, Marketing Representative

Manufacturer of aquarium supplies, degreasers, descalers, glass cleaners, and growing products. The company deals with chemical consulting.

**Sierra Data Systems**  HQ
675 S Auburn St Ste 210
Grass Valley CA 95945
P: 916-242-4604  F: 916-290-0630  PRC:324
www.sierradata.com
Email: info@sierradata.com
Emp: 1-10

Keith Schneider, CEO
Steve Gallo, Account Manager
Scott French, Development Team Lead

Provider of data communication systems, internet related services, miscellaneous communications equipment, telephone, and voice equipment.

**Sierra Engineering Company Inc**  HQ
35111 Lodge Rd
Tollhouse CA 93667-9727
P: 559-855-2659  F: 559-855-8659  PRC:304
www.rvpartssierra.com
Email: sierraengineering@rvpartssierra.com
Emp: 1-10  Estab: 1969

Jesus Sierra, President
Jim Piluso, VP

Manufacturer of recreational vehicles. The company offers rebuilding, repair, and maintenance services.

**Sierra Instruments Inc**  HQ
5 Harris Ct Bldg L
Monterey CA 93940
P: 831-373-0200  F: 831-373-4402  PRC:14
www.sierrainstruments.com
Email: info@sierrainstruments.com
Estab: 1971

Morgan Zealear, Manufacturing Engineer
Fred Jesus, Application Engineer
John Olin, Founder
Daniel Durham, Purchasing Manager
Maryadine Washington, Marketing Communication Manager

Manufacturer of mass flow meters and mass flow controllers. The company serves gas, liquid, and steam applications.

**Sierra Monitor Corp**  HQ
1991 Tarob Ct
Milpitas CA 95035
P: 408-262-6611  F: 408-262-9042  PRC:13
www.sierramonitor.com
Email: info@sierramonitor.com
Estab: 1980
Sales: $10M to $30M

Clarke Ramilo, Technical Support Engineer
Neal Trias, Support Engineer
Tamara Allen, CFO
Quyen Truong, Purchasing Supervisor
Mike Nugent, Director of Sales and Marketing

Manufacturer and seller of safety and environmental instrumentation. The company offers hazardous gas detection systems and site management products.

**Sierra Precision Optics**  HQ
12830 Earhart Ave
Auburn CA 95602
P: 530-885-6979  F: 530-885-1037  PRC:173
www.sierraoptics.com
Email: sales@sierraoptics.com
Emp: 1-10

Stephen Bennion, Manufacturing Engineer
Russell Lowe, Sales
Karen Hartsfield, Senior Buyer

Manufacturer of optical products. The company's products include panels, mirrors, beam splitters, and cylindrical lenses.

**Sierra Proto Express**  HQ
1108 W Evelyn Ave
Sunnyvale CA 94086
P: 408-735-7137  F: 408-735-1408  PRC:211
www.protoexpress.com
Estab: 1986

Steve Carney, Senior Process Engineer
Bala Bahl, Co-Founder
Ken Bahl, CEO
Nilesh Parate, General Manager
Atar Mittal, General Manager of Design and Assembly

Designer and manufacturer of printed circuit boards. The company's manufacturing facilities are located in California and Kansas.

**Sierra Testing Service**  HQ
9450 E Collier Rd
Acampo CA 95220
P: 209-333-3337  F: 209-339-9691  PRC:306
www.sierratestingservice.com
Email: stshaytest@gmail.com
Emp: 1-10  Estab: 1983

Stan Seifert, Founder

Provider of laboratory testing services. The company offers services such as grain testing, silage, and grain samples.

**Siesta Medical Inc**  HQ
101 Church St Ste 3
Los Gatos CA 95030
P: 408-320-9424  F: 408-399-7600  PRC:189
www.siestamedical.com
Email: info@siestamedical.com
Estab: 2009

Peter Martin, President
Chris Feezor, VP of Research & Development
Erik Van Der Burg, Chairman
Jay Shukert, CFO
Tedd Hinton, VP of Operations

Providers of medical devices. The company offers surgical implants and tools for the treatment of osa.

**Sight Sciences Inc**  HQ
3000 Sand Hill Rd Bldg 3, Ste 105
Menlo Park CA 94025
P: 415-889-0550  PRC:176
www.sightsciences.com
Email: info@sightsciences.com
Estab: 2006

Joseph Anderson, Senior Manufacturing Engineer
David Badawi, Founder
Paul Badawi, Founder
Jesse Selnick, CFO
Shawn Neil, CCO

Manufacturer and developer of surgical instruments and ophthalmic medical devices. The company serves the medical sector.

**Sightech Vision Systems**  HQ
2953 Bunker Hill Ln Ste 400
Santa Clara CA 95054
P: 408-282-3770  F: 408-413-2600  PRC:168
www.sightech.com
Email: sales@sightech.com
Estab: 1983

Judy Gaffin, Owner
Art Gaffin, CEO
Judy Gaffom, Office Manager

Manufacturer of industrial vision systems. The company offers quality vision systems, hard disk inspection, and crimp verification services.

**Sigma Designs Inc**  HQ
47467 Fremont Blvd
Fremont CA 94538
P: 510-897-0200  F: 510-897-0350  PRC:212
www.sigmadesigns.com
Email: sales@sigmadesigns.com
Estab: 1982
Sales: $30M to $100M

Jianbo Zhang, VP of HW Engineering
Jin Park, Director of Platform Engineering
Jack Sheu, DFT Engineer
Elias Nader, Interim President
Jimmy Nguyen, Information Technology Manager

Provider of system-on-chip solutions for media processing, smart TV, video encoding, AV networking, video processing, and home control systems.

**Sigmatron International Inc**  BR
30000 Eigenbrodt Way
Union City CA 94587
P: 510-477-5000  PRC:211
www.sigmatronintl.com
Estab: 1994

Dennis McNamara, VP of Engineering
Yousef Heidari, VP of Engineering
Gary Fairhead, Chairman
Linda Frauendorfer, CFO
Curtis Campbell, VP of Sales

Provider of robust systems and program management support to track demand, material on order, inventory, finished goods, and shipments.

**Signosis Inc** HQ
1700 Wyatt Dr Ste 12
Santa Clara CA 95054
P: 408-747-0771   F: 408-470-7719   PRC:34
signosisinc.com
Email: info@signosisinc.com
Estab: 2007

Jason Li, Owner
Reza Keikhaee, Research Scientist

Provider of bioassays. The company focuses on
the development and commercialization of plate-
based analysis products.

**Siig Inc** HQ
6078 Stewart Ave
Fremont CA 94538-3152
P: 510-657-8688   F: 510-657-5962   PRC:95
www.siig.com
Email: siigsales@siig.com
Estab: 1985

Mike Woodmansee, Director of Sales
Edmund So, Material Planning Manager
Steve Nguyen, Product Manager

Manufacturer of computer connectivity products.
The company is involved in increasing the bandwidth between a computer system and external
devices.

**Silex Technology America Inc** HQ
201 East Sandpointe
Santa Ana CA 92707
P: 657-218-5199   F: 714-258-0730   PRC:104
www.silextechnology.com
Email: sales@silexamerica.com
Emp: 11-50 Estab: 1982

Keith Sugawara, CEO

Manufacturer of print servers for network printers
and fingerprint readers. The company serves
security applications.

**Silicon Dust** RH
2150 Portola Ave Ste D 143
Livermore CA 94551
P: 925-443-4388   F: 925-443-3243   PRC:245
www.silicondust.com
Email: info@silicondust.com
Estab: 2007

Theodore Head, President
Nick Kelsey, CTO

Provider of network connected TV tuners. The
company offers global solutions to Live TV
streaming in businesses, hotels, and education
facilities.

**Silicon Frontline Technology Inc** HQ
4030 Moorpark Ave Ste 249
San Jose CA 95117
P: 408-963-6916   F: 408-963-6906   PRC:126
www.siliconfrontline.com
Email: info@siliconfrontline.com
Estab: 2005

Yuri Feinberg, CEO
Dermott Lynch, COO

Provider of parasitic extraction and analysis
services for post layout verification. The company
specializes in electrostatic discharge analysis.

**Silicon Genesis Corp** HQ
145 Baytech Dr
San Jose CA 95134
P: 408-228-5858   F: 408-228-5859   PRC:126
sigen.net
Email: support@sigen.com
Estab: 1997

Theodore Fong, President
Marge Brandt, Executive Administrator

Manufacturer of semiconductor and solar fabrication tools . The company offers stand-alone
plasma tools and debond and cleave tools.

**Silicon Laboratories** BR
2708 Orchard Pkwy
San Jose CA 95134
P: 408-702-1400   PRC:326
www.silabs.com
Estab: 1996

Wentao Li, Principal Engineer
Keith Coffey, Engineer
Yang Gao, Design Engineer
Mark Haley, Test
Michael Hansen, Field Sales Engineer

Provider of silicon, software, and system solutions.
The company focuses on internet infrastructure,
industrial control, and consumer markets.

**Silicon Light Machines** DH
820 Kifer Rd
Sunnyvale CA 94086
P: 408-240-4700   F: 408-456-0708   PRC:212
www.siliconlight.com
Email: sales@siliconlight.com
Estab: 1994

Brad Patterson, Principal Engineer
Lars Eng, President
Cindy Lott, Director of Finance
Ken Fukui, SVP of Operations
Les Hawkins, IT Technician

Provider of optical micro-electro-mechanical systems. The company's applications include mask-
less lithography and large format digital displays.

**Silicon Microstructures Inc** HQ
1701 McCarthy Blvd
Milpitas CA 95035
P: 408-577-0100   F: 408-577-0123   PRC:163
www.si-micro.com
Email: sales@si-micro.com
Estab: 1991

J. Alfaro, Design Engineer
David Wong, R&D Engineering Technician
Omar Abed, President
Friedrich Holz, CFO
Holger Doering, COO

Developer and manufacturer of MEMS-based
pressure sensors. The company's products
are used in medical, industrial, and automotive
applications.

**Silicon Mitus** BR
20370 Town Center Ln Ste 211
Cupertino CA 95014
P: 408-446-3151   F: 408-446-3285   PRC:98
siliconmitus.com

Youngik Yoo, VP of Engineering
Alex Hanganu, Senior CAD & IT Engineer
Harold chang, CFO
Dong Kim, CSO
Kyunghwan Kim, VP of Operations

Manufacturer and distributor of smart power management integrated chips solutions. The company
focuses on power solutions.

**Silicon Motion Inc** DH
690 N McCarthy Blvd Ste 200
Milpitas CA 95035
P: 408-519-7289   F: 408-519-7101   PRC:212
www.siliconmotion.com
Estab: 1995

Jonjen Sern, Senior ASIC Design Engineer
Robert Abutan, Application Software
Wallace Kou, CEO
Riyadh Lai, CFO
Mike Jing, VP of Information Technology

Designer of low-power semiconductor solutions.
The company serves multimedia consumer electronic applications.

**Silicon Publishing Inc** HQ
100 Pine St Ste 1250
San Francisco CA 94111
P: 925-935-3899   PRC:320
www.siliconpublishing.com
Email: sales@siliconpublishing.com
Estab: 2000

Max Dunn, President
Aaron Hodges, COO

Provider of digital publishing solutions. The company deals with template designs and personalized communications.

**Silicon Storage Technology Inc** HQ
450 Holger Way
San Jose CA 95134
P: 408-735-9110   PRC:86
www.sst.com
Email: info@sst.com
Estab: 1989

Michael Doan, Senior Staff Engineer
Toan Ly, Manager

Designer and manufacturer of memory and
non-memory products. The company serves internet computing markets.

**Silicon Valley Mfg** HQ
6520 Central Ave
Newark CA 94560
P: 510-791-9450   PRC:80
www.svmfg.com
Email: sales@svmfg.com

Angie Ollendorf, Office Manager

Manufacturer and engineer of EDM prototype and
production machining. The company's services
include CNC milling, CNC turning, and manual
machining.

**Silicon Valley Precision Inc** HQ
5625 Brisa St Ste G
Livermore CA 94550
P: 925-373-8259   F: 925-373-6025   PRC:157
www.siliconvalleyprecision.com
Email: lara@siliconvalleyprecision.com
Estab: 1984

John Payne, Manager

Provider of custom vertical and horizontal CNC machining, fabrication and assembly of parts. The company offers powder coating, painting and grinding.

**Silicon Wafer Enterprises LLC** HQ
4741 Gresham Dr
El Dorado Hills CA 95762
P: 916-941-7728   F: 916-941-7529   PRC:212
siwaferenterprises.com
Emp: 1-10

Silicon Wafer Enterprises Llc Linda, Manager

Provider of silicon wafers and other raw materials. The company's offerings include silicon, plate glass, pyrex, and sapphire.

**Silicon360** HQ
1804 McCarthy Blvd
Milpitas CA 95035
P: 408-432-1790   F: 408-432-7350   PRC:212
www.silicon360.com
Email: sales@silicon360.com
Estab: 2009

Zef Malik, CEO

Supplier of semiconductors for the military, aerospace, industrial, medical, and commercial markets.

**Silk Road Medical Inc** HQ
735 N Pastoria Ave
Sunnyvale CA 94085
P: 408-720-9002   F: 408-720-9013   PRC:188
silkroadmed.com
Email: info@silkroadmed.com
Estab: 2007

Robert Nicholas, VP of Operations & Engineering
Erica Rogers, President
Lucas Buchanan, CFO
Alison Highlander, VP of Human Resources
Shari Rideout, VP of Regulatory & Quality

Specializes in the treatment of carotid artery diseases. The company is engaged in clinical trials and related services.

**Sillajen Inc** BR
450 Sansome St Fl 2
San Francisco CA 94111
P: 415-281-8886   PRC:34
www.sillajen.com
Estab: 2003

Eun Moon, CEO
Myung Song, CFO
Hyuk Kwon, CMO
Hyun Shin, Director
Terri Robertson, Director of Clinical Supply Chain

Developer of biotherapeutics specializing in cancer products. The company also focuses on marketing.

**Silpac** HQ
1850 Russell Ave
Santa Clara CA 95054
P: 408-492-0011   F: 408-492-0022   PRC:133
www.silpac.net
Email: sales@silpac.net
Estab: 2000

Joe McNulty, Field Service Engineer
Victor Strigelskiy, CAD Design Engineer
Tom Vass, Owner
Ray Mendoza, President
Rusty McCullar, General Manager

Distributor and manufacturer of specialty gas handling equipment. The company caters to markets like semiconductor, life science, and solar.

**Silvaco Inc** HQ
4701 Patrick Henry Dr Bldg 2
Santa Clara CA 95054
P: 408-567-1000   F: 408-496-6080   PRC:317
www.silvaco.com
Email: sales@silvaco.com
Estab: 1984

Andrei Pashkovich, Senior Engineering Manager
Misha Temkin, Engineering Manager
Slim Chourou, Software Engineer
Marek Turowski, Senior Engineer
David Lauderback, Software Engineer

Supplier of TCAD and EDA software for circuit simulation. The company also designs analog, mixed-signal, and RF integrated circuits.

**Silver Creek Pharmaceuticals Inc** HQ
409 Illinois St
San Francisco CA 94158
P: 415-978-2178   F: 415-978-1930   PRC:251
www.silvercreekpharma.com
Estab: 2010

Sam Pfaff, Associate Director
Yan Zhang, Medical Director
Kris Kuchenbecker, Lead scientist

Provider of pharmaceuticals. The company develops regenerative medicines with an initial focus on treating cardiovascular disease.

**Silver Peak Systems Inc** HQ
2860 De La Cruz Blvd
Santa Clara CA 95050
P: 408-935-1800   PRC:323
www.silver-peak.com
Email: info@silver-peak.com
Estab: 2004

David Hughes, Founder
Ian Whiting, President of Global Field Operations
Rick Valentine, Chief Customer Officer
Eric Yeaman, CFO
Julie Creasy, Human Resource Manager

Provider of miscellaneous communication equipment & services. The company focuses on WAN optimization, cloud networking, and replication acceleration.

**Silver Spring Networks Inc** HQ
230 W Tasman Dr
San Jose CA 95134
P: 669-770-4000   PRC:329
www.itron.com
Estab: 1977

Bob Luben, Senior Software Engineer
Bill Hespelt, Senior Product engineer
Tom Deitrich, President
Lynda Ziegler, Chairman
Joan Hooper, SVP

Provider of earthwork optimization solutions principally focusing on stress and property measurements for geotechnics.

**Silvestre Manufacturing** HQ
1745 Grant St Ste 5
Santa Clara CA 95050
P: 408-988-0937   PRC:80
silvestremfg.com

Julian Silvestre, Owner

Provider of custom fabrication services. The company specializes in machining and prototype production.

**Simco Electronics** HQ
3131 Jay St
Santa Clara CA 95054
P: 408-734-9750   F: 408-734-9780   PRC:40
www.simco.com
Email: sales@simco.com
Estab: 1962

Brian Kenna, CEO
Lee Kenna, CEO
John Connelly, Chief Commercial Officer
Marie-France Nelson, CFO
Laura S., Human Resources Manager

Providers of services and software to medical device manufacturers. The company specializes in biotechnology.

**Simco-Ion** BR
1601 Harbor Bay Pkwy Ste 150
Alameda CA 94502
P: 510-217-0600   F: 510-217-0484   PRC:159
www.simco-ion.com
Email: info@simco-ion.com

Ed Oldynski, Senior Electrical Engineer
Aleksey Klochkov, Senior Engineer
Echo Costanzo, Senior Sales Manager
Trevor Norman, Senior Director of Business Development
Steve Heymann, Senior Director of Technology Development

Manufacturer of static control and process control products. The company is engaged in design and installation services.

**Simonds Machinery Co** HQ
259 Harbor Way
S San Francisco CA 94080
P: 650-589-9900   F: 650-589-5900   PRC:160
www.simondsmachinery.com
Email: pumps@simondsmachinery.com
Estab: 1905

Stephen Hipp, President
Kurt Hipp, VP

Distributor of portable pump carts, custom control panels, pressure booster systems, and related accessories.

**Simplex Filler Co** HQ
640-A Airpark Rd Ste A
Napa CA 94558
P: 707-265-6801  F: 707-265-6868  PRC:159
www.simplexfiller.com
Email: simplex@simplexfiller.com
Estab: 1947

Dennis Bertolucci, Director of Engineering

Manufacturer of liquid filling machines. The company offers volumetric fillers, pressure fillers, and accessories.

**Simplicant Inc** HQ
950 Page Mill Rd
Palo Alto CA 94304
P: 650-285-2394  PRC:319
www.simplicant.com
Email: info@simplicant.com
Estab: 2012

Zartash Uzmi, Founder
Sajjad Masud, CEO

Producer of modern recruitment software that also helps to track applicants.

**Simplificare Inc** HQ
480 S California Ave
Palo Alto CA 94306
P: 800-464-5125  PRC:40
www2.simplee.com
Estab: 2010

Roberto Rabinovich, Co-Founder
Tomer Shoval, CEO

Provider of software solutions for patient financial care (PFC). The company odders services to patients and clinics.

**Simplion Technologies** HQ
1525 McCarthy Blvd Ste 228
Milpitas CA 95035
P: 408-935-8686  F: 408-935-8696  PRC:322
www.simplion.com
Email: info@simplion.com
Estab: 2004

Neha Bhatia, Account Manager
Sandeep Kumar, Practice Head
S. Swain, Senior Analyst
Satyam Jha, Senior Technical Recruiter

Provider of consulting solutions. The company offers strategy development, implementation, deployment, and technical support services.

**Single Cell Technology Inc** HQ
6280 San Ignacio Ave Ste E
San Jose CA 95119
P: 408-642-9740  PRC:23
www.single-cell-technology.com
Email: info@singlecelltechnology.com

Chun-Nan Chen, Founder
Jim Bowlby, COO

Developer of cell technology solutions and also proportionary therapeutic antibody process for its clients.

**Single Point Of Contact** HQ
992 San Antonio Rd
Palo Alto CA 94303
P: 800-791-4300  F: 650-213-8327  PRC:324
www.singlepointoc.com
Email: sales@singlepointoc.com
Estab: 1999

Fernando Leon, VP of Sales & Marketing

Provider of IT management, enterprise, and planning services. The company is also engaged in cloud computing, web hosting, and hosted exchange.

**Singulex Inc** HQ
1701 Harbor Bay Pkwy Ste 200
Alameda CA 94502
P: 510-995-9000  F: 510-995-9092  PRC:306
www.singulex.com
Email: clinicallabinfo@singulex.com

William Hammack, VP of Human Resources
Enrique Nevarez, Field Service Supervisor

Provider of life science products and cardiovascular monitoring products. The company deals with lab testing services.

**Sios Technology Corp** LH
155 Bovet Rd Ste 660
San Mateo CA 94402
P: 650-645-7000  F: 650-645-7030  PRC:324
us.sios.com
Email: info@us.sios.com

Tony Tomarchio, Director of Field Engineering
Jerry Melnick, COO
Sergey Razin, CTO

Provider of cloud virtualization protection solutions. The company also offers managed information technology services.

**Sitepen Inc** HQ
530 Lytton Ave Second Fl
Palo Alto CA 94301
P: 650-968-8787  PRC:323
sitepen.com
Estab: 2000

Martin Klosi, Engineering Team Lead
Carrie Rice, COO
Aimee Busch, Director of Operations
Joel Chacon, Supervisor

Developer and provider of software products and services. The company also offers web application development and java support services.

**Sitime Corp** HQ
990 Almanor Ave
Sunnyvale CA 94085
P: 408-328-4400  F: 408-328-4439  PRC:86
www.sitime.com
Email: america-west-sales@sitime.com
Estab: 2005

Sassan Tabatabaei, VP of Circuit Design Engineering
Vinod Menon, EVP of Engineering
Jonathan Poon, Systems Characterization Engineer
Markus Lutz, Founder
Aaron Partridge, Founder

Provider of programmable oscillators and clock generators. The company also offers embedded resonators.

**Situne Corp** HQ
2216 Ringwood Ave
San Jose CA 95131
P: 408-324-1711  F: 408-521-3340  PRC:208
www.situne-ic.com
Email: sales@situne-ic.com
Estab: 2007

Shokoufeh Arbabi, Design Engineer
Marzieh Veyseh, CTO
Vahid Toosi, Founder
Sam Heidari, Chairman
Ben Runyan, VP of Sales & Marketing

Provider of integrated circuits and systems. The company offers spectrum reception and concurrent tuners.

**Siva Power Inc** HQ
5102 Calle Del Sol
Santa Clara CA 95054
P: 408-834-7400  PRC:135
www.sivapower.com
Email: info@sivapower.com

Oswaldo Frausto, Equipment Engineer
Anthony Cook, Equipment & Facilities Engineer
Bruce Sohn, CEO
Mark Heising, Chairman
Chris McDonald, COO

Manufacturer of solar products. The company specializes in semiconductor, flat panel display, and solar devices.

**Sj Amoroso Construction** HQ
390 Bridge Pkwy
Redwood City CA 94065
P: 650-654-1900  F: 650-654-9002  PRC:304
www.sjamoroso.com
Estab: 1939

Cindy Quinteros, Project Engineer
Billy-Joel Celeste, Project Engineer
Dana Mcmanus, CEO
Jim Benson, Chief Estimator
Laura Heckenberg, CFO

Provider of construction contracting services. The company focuses on pre-construction consulting, design-build contracting and management.

**Sj Die Casting & Machining Corp** HQ
600 Business Park Dr
Lincoln CA 95648
P: 408-262-6500  PRC:80
www.sjdiecasting.com
Emp: 1-10

Mark Callaghan, President

Manufacturer of castings for computer, electronic, automotive, and military sectors specializing in sandblasting, deburring, and assembly services.

**Sjc Precision Inc** HQ
1811 Houret Ct
Milpitas CA 95035
P: 408-262-1680  F: 408-926-4311  PRC:157
www.sjcprecision.com
Email: jijo@sjcprecision.com
Estab: 1996

Jijo Chemmachel, CEO

Provider of precision machining and tool and die making services. The company designs and manufactures jigs, fixtures, and bookmolds.

**Skeletal Kinetics LLC**  HQ
10201 Bubb Rd
Cupertino CA 95014
P: 408-366-5000   F: 408-366-1077   PRC:53
www.skeletalkinetics.com
Email: cs@skeletalkinetics.com
Emp: 11-50 Estab: 2002
Sales: $3M to $10M

Ken Weissel, Production Supervisor
Christine Kuo, Director of RA
Ricky Luong, Material Handlers

Developer, manufacturer and marketer of bone
fixation cement designed for the treatment of
trauma fractures.

**Sks Diecasting & Machining**  HQ
1849 Oak St
Alameda CA 94501
P: 510-523-2541   F: 510-523-5619   PRC:163
www.sksdiecasting.com
Email: sales@sksdiecasting.com
Estab: 1946

Richard Wieckowski, Chief Engineer
Sean Keating, President
Jesusa JosonFusade, Controller

Manufacturer of aluminum die cast parts and
related supplies. The company offers services to
the high tech industry.

**Skybox Security Inc**  HQ
2077 Gateway Pl Ste 200
San Jose CA 95110
P: 408-441-8060   F: 408-441-8068   PRC:104
www.skyboxsecurity.com
Email: info@skyboxsecurity.com
Estab: 2002

Jessica Le, Research & Development Engineer
Gidi Cohen, CEO
Lior Barak, CFO
Stewart Fox, EVP of Worldwide Sales & Applications
Michelle Cobb, VP of Worldwide Marketing

Provider of risk analytics for cyber security. The
company offers threat management and network
security management solutions.

**Skyhigh Networks Inc**  RH
900 E Hamilton Ave Ste 400
Campbell CA 95008
P: 866-727-8383   PRC:325
Estab: 2011

Sam Herath, Senior Sales Engineer
Tim Harron, Regional Sales Manager

Developer of cloud security software. The company is engaged in compliance, threat protection,
and data security services.

**SL Corp**  HQ
240 Tamal Vista Blvd
Corte Madera CA 94925
P: 415-927-8400   F: 415-927-8401   PRC:319
sl.com
Email: info@sl.com
Estab: 1983

Tom Lubinski, CEO
Nina Cartee, CFO
Ted Wilson, COO
Gia Lombardi-Hodges, Marketing Manager
Ed Koo, VP of Technical Services

Provider of monitoring and analytics solutions for
middleware-powered applications. The company
serves the electrical commodity market.

**Sleepless Media**  HQ
2601 41st Ave Ste B
Soquel CA 95073
P: 831-427-1969   PRC:325
www.sleeplessmedia.com
Emp: 11-50 Estab: 2001

Jon Cattivera, Owner
Mark Serrano, Developer

Provider of website design and development
services. The company focuses on content management, e-commerce, SEO, hosting, and brand
identity.

**Small Precision Tools Inc**  BR
1330 Clegg St
Petaluma CA 94954
P: 707-765-4545   F: 707-559-2072   PRC:80
www.smallprecisiontools.com
Email: info-usa@spt.net

Juanita Flores, Electrical Engineer
Guangfu Wang, Mechanical Design Engineer
Michael Hutchison, Production Engineer
Joe Gracia, CFO
Mark Hamilton, General Manager

Manufacturer of chip bonding tools, fine ceramic,
and machining parts. The company offers neces-
sary technical support and services.

**Smart ERP Solutions Inc**  HQ
4683 Chabot Dr Ste 380
Pleasanton CA 94588
P: 925-271-0200   PRC:323
www.smarterp.com
Email: sales@smarterp.com
Estab: 2004

Raghu Yelluru, Co-Founder
Ramesh Panchagnula, Co-Founder
Sreeni Muniswamy, Co-Founder
Doris Wong, CEO
Hans Bukow, CSO

Developer of enterprise class software. The company provides vendor management software and
support services.

**Smart Modular Technologies**  HQ
39870 Eureka Dr
Newark CA 94560
P: 510-623-1231   F: 510-623-1434   PRC:96
www.smartm.com
Email: info@smartm.com
Estab: 1988
Sales: $1B to $3B

Mike Rubino, VP of Engineering
Kelvin Marino, Principal Design Engineer
Bob Pauley, Senior Staff Engineer
Kiet Le, Manufacturing Engineer
Ajay Shah, President

Manufacturer of add on memory boards, flash,
and storage products. The company serves defense, gaming, storage, and other sectors.

**Smart Monitor Corp**  HQ
6203 San Ignacio Ave Ste 112
San Jose CA 95119
P: 408-754-1695   F: 408-754-8629   PRC:187
www.smart-monitor.com
Email: support@smart-monitor.com
Estab: 2009

Anoo Nathan, CEO

Manufacturer of monitoring devices. The company
provides automated solution for detecting unusual
movements from chronic health conditions.

**Smart Products Inc**  HQ
675 Jarvis Dr
Morgan Hill CA 95037
P: 800-338-0404   PRC:160
www.smartproducts.com
Estab: 1984

Mark Whittington, Operations Manager

Supplier of engineering products. The company
offers valves, fittings, and pumps for the automotive, medical, and water treatment markets.

**Smart Tube Inc**  HQ
969 Industrial Rd Ste i
San Carlos CA 94070
P: 855-397-8467   F: 866-521-4037   PRC:20
www.smarttubeinc.com
Email: info@smarttubeinc.com

Matthew Hale, President

Manufacturer of reagents and one-touch automation systems. The company serves the healthcare
sector.

**Smart Wires Inc**  HQ
3292 Whipple Rd
Union City CA 94587
P: 415-800-5555   PRC:159
www.smartwires.com
Email: info@smartwires.com
Estab: 2010

Haroon Inam, CTO
Patricia Allen, Office Manager

Provider of grid optimization solutions. The company is involved in load and generation, alleviate
congestion, and network utilization services.

**SMC Corporation of America**  BR
2841 Junction Ave Ste 110
San Jose CA 95134
P: 408-943-9600   PRC:146
www.smcusa.com
Estab: 1959

Timothy Kuchta, Director of Sales
Chas Thomas, Sales Manager
Bob Fiscus, Sales Manager
Nick O'Riordan, Sales Manager
Mike Shillito, Western Regional Sales Manager

Provider of in pneumatic technology solutions
that are used in diverse range of industries from
automotive to lifescience.

**Smc Ltd**  BR
3250 Brickway Blvd
Santa Rosa CA 95403
P: 707-303-3000   PRC:189
www.smcltd.com
Email: inquiry@smcltd.com
Estab: 1988

Eric Myers, Operations Engineering Manager
Todd Sitzman, Senior Process Engineer
Rob Juul, New Product Development Engineer
Cory Lee, Project Manager

Provider of custom packing for product steriliza-
tion. The company is engaged in supply chain
management solutions.

**Smp Tech Inc**                                           HQ
   17500 Depot St Ste 210
   Morgan Hill CA 95037-5461
   P: 408-776-7776   F: 408-776-7772        PRC:186
   www.smptech.com
   Email: engineering@smptech.com
   Estab: 1990

Tom Roberts, CEO
Ann Roberts, CFO

Designer and builder of robotic DNA spotters, micro fluidic devices, medical equipment, automated machinery, and electro-mechanical products.

**SMTC Corp**                                              BR
   431 Kato Terr
   Fremont CA 94539
   P: 510-737-0700   F: 510-498-8525        PRC:86
   www.smtc.com
   Email: contact.us@smtc.com
   Estab: 1985

Edward Smith, President
Rich Fitzgerald, COO
Steven Waszak, CFO
Chris Xuan, VP of Global Operations
Kenny Lai, VP

Provider of electronics manufacturing services for the industrial, medical, computing, and communication markets.

**Sna Electronics Inc**                                    HQ
   3249 Laurelview Ct
   Fremont CA 94538
   P: 510-656-3903   F: 510-656-3907        PRC:68
   www.sna-electronic.com
   Email: sales@sna-electronic.com
   Estab: 1996

Chi Shin, CFO
Steve Hahn, Production Manager

Provider of electronic manufacturing services. The company offers services to OEMs in the networking, medical instruments, and aerospace industries.

**Snowline Engineering Inc**                               HQ
   4261 Business Dr
   Cameron Park CA 95682
   P: 530-677-2675   F: 530-677-9832        PRC:80
   www.snowlineengineering.com
   Email: sales@snowlineengineering.com
   Emp: 1-10

Cal Reynolds, President
Dave Greenacre, General Manager
Vern Holzer, Quality Assurance Supervisor
Lee Block, EVP

Provider of precision machining and fabrication services. The company also engages in sheet metal and assembly.

**Socionext Inc**                                          DH
   2811 Mission College Blvd 5th Fl
   Santa Clara CA 95054
   P: 408 550-6861                          PRC:63
   www.socionext.com
   Email: sna_inquiry@us.socionext.com
   Estab: 2015

Vaidehi Sudhakar, CFO
Matt Hall, Senior Sales Manager

Designer and developer of System-on-Chip products. The company's products are used in imaging, networking, and computing fields.

---

**Socket Mobile Inc**                                      HQ
   39700 Eureka Dr
   Newark CA 94560-4808
   P: 510-933-3000   F: 510-933-3030        PRC:71
   www.socketmobile.com
   Email: sales@socketmobile.com
   Estab: 1992
   Sales: $10M to $30M

Donnie Wong, Systems Engineer
Fahim Azimy, Vendor Quality Engineer
Gerald Herbel, Senior Software Engineer
Kevin Mills, CEO
Ana Valdez, Manager of Accounts Receivable

Developer of wireless handheld and hands-free barcode scanners and other products and serves retail, logistics, automotive, and other sectors.

**Softjourn Inc**                                          HQ
   39270 Paseo Padre Pkwy Ste 251
   Fremont CA 94538
   P: 510-744-1528   F: 815-301-2772        PRC:326
   www.softjourn.com
   Email: sales@softjourn.com
   Estab: 2000

Bogdan Mykhaylovych, Engineering Manager
Emmy Gengler, CEO
Jeff Kreuser, CTO
Sergiy Fitsak, Managing Director

Provider of outsource software development services and focuses on offshore assessments, application development, and quality assurance testing.

**Softnet Solutions Inc**                                  HQ
   940 Hamlin Ct
   Sunnyvale CA 94089
   P: 408-542-0888   F: 408-542-0848        PRC:326
   www.softnets.com
   Email: info@softnets.com
   Estab: 1994

Kush Hathi, President
Tehnaz Hathi, CFO

Provider of enterprise solutions for high performance computing and network security. The company specializes in IT consulting and cloud services.

**Softsol Inc**                                            HQ
   46755 Fremont Blvd
   Fremont CA 94538
   P: 510-824-2000   F: 510-824-2098        PRC:325
   www.softsol.com
   Email: info@softsol.net
   Estab: 1993

Srini Madala, Chairman
Robert Hersh, CFO
R. Ghanta, VP
Priya Softsol, Team Lead

Provider of software solutions. The company offers software such as Intellicourt Case Management, Corporate Investigations, STIC, and PB Migration.

---

**Software Ag**                                            BR
   2901 Tasman Dr Ste 219
   Santa Clara CA 95054
   P: 800-823-2212                          PRC:325
   www.softwareag.com
   Email: sales@softwareagusa.com
   Estab: 1969

Anneliese Schulz, President
Philippe La, President
Philippe La Fornara, President EMEA
Renato Morsch, President Latin America
Sanjay Brahmawar, CEO

Provider of enterprise management and business solutions that include process intelligence and automation, and enterprise architecture.

**Solano Archaeological Svc**                              HQ
   131 Sunset Ave Ste E120
   Suisun City CA 94585-2064
   P: 707-718-1416   F: 707-451-4775        PRC:135
   solanoarchaeology.com
   Email: admin@solanoarchaeology.com
   Estab: 2005

Jason Coleman, Founder

Provider of archaeological services. The company services also include cultural resource and artifact analysis and curation.

**Solar Components LLC**                                   HQ
   1725 S Bascom Ave Ste 216
   Campbell CA 95008
   P: 408-369-1727                          PRC:116
   solarjoos.com
   Email: support@solarcomponentsllc.com
   Estab: 2008

Warren Sattler, CEO
Hazel Keelan, Director of Sales Operations

Manufacturer of micro-processor controlled solar power electronic systems. The company provides solar power management and charge control solutions.

**Solar Design & Drafting**                                HQ
   149 Kentucky St Ste 5
   Petaluma CA 94952
   P: 415-305-3982                          PRC:304
   www.solardesignanddrafting.com

John Knueppel, Owner

Designer of solar devices. The company's services include design considerations, flat rate permit packages, and other services.

**Solar Junction**                                         HQ
   401 Charcot Ave
   San Jose CA 95131
   P: 408-503-7000                          PRC:135
   www.sj-solar.com
   Emp: 11-50 Estab: 2007
   Sales: Under $1 Million

Brian Bolander, Operations Engineer
Lan Zhang, VP of Manufacturing
Sabeur Siala, VP
Ferran Suarez, Director of Device Design
Ting Liu, Epitaxy Manager

Manufacturer of high-efficiency solar cells and receivers. The company's products find application in concentrated photovoltaic systems.

**Solar Sense PV Inc**     HQ
7083 Commerce Cir Ste C
Pleasanton CA 94588
P: 888-786-4339     PRC:129
solarsensepv.com
Email: info@solarsensepv.com
Estab: 2010

Richard Hurst, CEO

Provider of solar power system installation services. The company also focuses on design and serves residential, commercial, and utility applications.

**Solarbos Inc**     HQ
310 Stealth Ct
Livermore CA 94551
P: 925-456-7744    F: 925-456-7710     PRC:135
www.solarbos.com
Email: sales@solarbos.com
Estab: 2004

Anthony Parsons, Production Supervisor
Dustin Watson, VP of Sales
Jaimee Herschbach, Inside Sales Manager
Bryanna Monelo, Executive Assistant
Cole Snyder, CAD Designer

Designer and manufacturer of electrical products. The company exclusively caters to the solar industry.

**Solaria Corp**     HQ
6200 Paseo Padre Pkwy
Fremont CA 94555
P: 510-270-2500    F: 510-793-8388     PRC:135
www.solaria.com
Email: powerxt@solaria.com
Estab: 2006

Nadeem Haque, SVP of Engineering
Manny Castro, Engineering Technician
Norman Chan, Staff Engineer
Suvi Sharma, President
Kevin Gibson, CTO

Manufacturer of solar panels for residential and commercial use. The company also specializes in design services.

**Solarius Development Inc**     HQ
2390 Bering Dr
San Jose CA 95131
P: 408-435-2777    F: 408-435-2999     PRC:212
www.solarius-inc.com
Email: sales@solarius-inc.com
Estab: 1995

Kejul Patel, Application Engineer
Clarence Tamargo, System Engineer
Edgar Alvarez, Manager

Manufacturer of 3D metrology surface measurement systems. The company offers metrology services for surface form.

**Solaron Inc**     HQ
3480 Sunrise Blvd
Rancho Cordova CA 95742
P: 916-631-9293    F: 916-631-9244     PRC:135
www.solaron.net
Email: info@solaron.net
Emp: 11-50 Estab: 1989

Ron Harbeck, Owner
Megan DeGuerre, Manager

Manufacturer of swimming pool solar collectors and also provides the most efficient photovoltaic modules.

**Solid State Optronics**     HQ
15 Great Oaks Blvd
San Jose CA 95119
P: 408-293-4600    F: 408-293-4848     PRC:86
ssousa.com
Estab: 1982

Juan Kadah, General Manager
Hemant Koria, Sales Manager

Manufacturer of miniature Solid State Relays. The company offers MOSFET drivers, specialty products, and optocouplers.

**Soliton Systems Inc**     BR
2635 N First St Ste 213
San Jose CA 95134
P: 408-434-1923     PRC:325
www.soliton.co.jp
Email: sales@solitonsys.com

Nobuo Kamada, President

Provider of information technology solutions. The company offers IT security, network infrastructure, cloud computing, and IT management services.

**Solomon Systech Inc**     BR
2036 Avanti Ave
Dublin CA 94568
P: 330-256-3357    F: 408-320-1329     PRC:208
www.solomon-systech.com
Email: sales_usa@solomon-systech.com

Raymond Wang, Acting CEO

Provider of IC software application solutions. The company also offers mobile systems and mobile displays.

**Solonics Inc**     HQ
31072 San Antonio St
Hayward CA 94544
P: 510-471-7600    F: 510-471-2168     PRC:63
www.solonics.com
Email: info@solonics.com
Estab: 1985

Bill O'Neil, Co-Founder

Manufacturer of coded backboard systems and wire management products. The company focuses on design and delivery services.

**Solta Medical Inc**     HQ
25881 Industrial Blvd
Hayward CA 94545
P: 510-786-6946    F: 510-786-6895     PRC:186
www.solta.com
Email: info@solta.com
Estab: 1996

Craig Bockenstedt, Principal Mechanical Engineer
Karen Du, Director of Manufacturing
Peter Chang, Senior Director of Regulatory Affairs
Kristen Jenkins, Capital Equipment Manager

Designer, developer, manufacturer, and marketer of medical devices for the non-invasive treatment of wrinkles and other skin care devices.

**Soltac Inc**     HQ
1630 Castilleja Ave
Palo Alto CA 94306
P: 650-327-7090    F: 650-327-7095     PRC:131
Estab: 2000

Jonathan Stoumen, Manager
Linda Swett, Bookkeeper

Designer and provider of solar devices. It's products find application in warming batteries, signaling, and radar locating.

**Solution Architects Inc**     HQ
247 28th St
San Francisco CA 94131
P: 415-775-1656    F: 415-929-1118     PRC:322
www.solutionarchitects.com
Email: info@solutionarchitects.com
Estab: 1998

Asim Qadir, Founder

Provider of sophisticated IT solutions for complex systems. The company's services include analysis and product development.

**Solutions Cubed LLC**     HQ
3045 Esplanade
Chico CA 95973
P: 530-891-8045    F: 530-891-1643     PRC:64
www.solutions-cubed.com
Email: sales@solutions-cubed.com
Emp: 1-10 Estab: 1994

Lon Glazner, Partner

Provider of engineering solutions. The company is involved in early stage electronic prototyping to full production runs.

**Solutionware Corp**     HQ
467 Saratoga Ave Ste 474
San Jose CA 95129
P: 408-249-1529    F: 408-371-3712     PRC:316
www.solution-ware.com
Email: info@solution-ware.com
Estab: 1980

Joe Baumgardner, Sales Manager

Provider of design solutions. The company offers computer aided design and computer aided manufacturing services.

**SOMA Environmental Engineering Inc**   HQ
6620 Owens Dr Ste A
Pleasanton CA 94588
P: 925-734-6400  F: 925-734-6401   PRC:142
somaenv.com
Email: info@somaenv.com
Estab: 1992

Ruchi Mathur, Project Engineer
Mansour Sepehr, President

Provider of environmental engineering solutions.
The company offers services for remediation and
underground storage tanks.

**Somagenics Inc**   HQ
2161 Delaware Ave
Santa Cruz CA 95060
P: 831-426-7700  F: 831-420-0685   PRC:252
www.somagenics.com
Email: infor@somagenics.com
Emp: 1-10  Estab: 1997

Anne Scholz, VP of Administration
Sergei Kazakov, VP of Discovery Research
Anne Dallas, Principal Scientist
Sergio Barberan, Senior Scientist
Heini Ilves, Scientist

Developer of RNA-based therapeutics and diagnostics. The company's services include detection,
monitoring, testing, and analysis.

**Sonasoft Corp**   HQ
6920 Santa Teresa Blvd Ste 108
San Jose CA 95119
P: 408-708-4000  F: 408-946-5800   PRC:322
www.sonasoft.com
Estab: 2002

Vikas Agrawal, Chief Innovation Officer
Sen Jay, VP of Customer Success & Delivery

Provider of software based solutions to simplify
and automate replication, archiving, backup,
recovery, and data protection operations.

**Sonic Manufacturing Technologies**   HQ
47951 Westinghouse Dr
Fremont CA 94539
P: 510-580-8500  F: 510-492-0909   PRC:74
www.sonicmfg.com
Email: sales@sonicmfg.com
Estab: 1996

Henry Woo, Chief Process Engineer & Co-founder
Robert Pereyda, VP of Engineering & Co-founder
Harcharn Sokhi, Engineering Manager
Gerald Sobeck, Senior Quality Engineer
Kenneth Raab, President

Provider of contract manufacturing services. The
company engages in supply chain, quality assurance, and design and engineering services.

**Sonim Technologies Inc**   HQ
1825 S Grant St Ste 200
San Mateo CA 94402
P: 650-378-8100  F: 650-378-8109   PRC:71
www.sonimtech.com
Email: feedback@sonimtech.com
Estab: 2007

Bob Plaschke, CEO
Richard Long, CFO
Thomas Hornung, CTO
Peter Liu, SVP of Operations

Designer and manufacturer of water-submersible
mobile phones. The company's products are used
in construction, security guarding, and oil & gas
operations.

**Sono Group Inc**   HQ
696 San Ramon Valley Blvd Ste 401
Danville CA 94526
P: 925-855-8552  F: 925-886-4820   PRC:323
www.sonogroup.com
Email: info@sonogroup.com
Estab: 1992

Carla Adcock, Human Resource

Provider of custom software and application
development, training, social networking, and IT
staffing services.

**Sonoma Wire Works**   HQ
1049 El Monte Ave Ste C -73
Mountain View CA 94040
P: 650-948-2003  F: 650-948-0740   PRC:60
www.sonomawireworks.com
Email: info@sonomawireworks.com
Estab: 2003

Moses Abrego, Software Quality Assurance
Engineer
Douglas Wright, President
Michelle Wright, VP of Sales
Will Reichenthal, Software Developer

Provider of loop-based recording and collaboration software for musicians. It's products helps
musicians to play, record, and share music.

**Sootheze**   HQ
859 Washington St Ste 200
Red Bluff CA 96080
P: 844-576-6843  F: 530-727-6209   PRC:189
www.sootheze.com
Email: support@sootheze.com
Emp: 1-10  Estab: 1995

Paul Losch, President

Manufacturer of aromatherapy products and
other products that help relieve pain and provide
comfort.

**Soraa**   HQ
6500 Kaiser Dr
Fremont CA 94555
P: 510-456-2200   PRC:209
www.soraa.com
Email: info@soraa.com
Estab: 2008

Dane Sahlhoff, Senior Optical Engineer
Robert Harris, Engineer
Steve Denbaars, Co-Founder
Shuji Nakamura, Founder
Jeff Parker, CEO

Provider of lighting design and fixture lamp solutions. The company serves hotels, restaurants,
theaters, and private residences.

**Sotcher Measurement Inc**   HQ
115 Phelan Ave Ste 10
San Jose CA 95112
P: 800-922-2969  F: 408-574-0116   PRC:19
www.sotcher.com
Email: sales@sotcher.com
Estab: 1969

Marc Sotcher, President

Provider of test equipment. The company provides
test stations, service tags, generator test sets, and
automatic test stations.

**SoundHound Inc**   HQ
5400 Betsy Ross Dr
Santa Clara CA 95054
P: 408-441-3200   PRC:322
www.soundhound.com
Estab: 2005

Majid Emami, Co-Founder
Zili Li, Director of Machine Learning and Engi-
neering
Hsuan Yang, Senior Software Engineer
Qiaozhi Song, Software Engineer
Terry Kong, Senior Machine Learning Engineer

Developer of a sound and speech responsive
search engine. The company's product finds application in mobile and communication devices.

**Soundvision Inc**   HQ
27 Commercial Blvd Ste M
Novato CA 94949
P: 415-456-7000  F: 415-883-7199   PRC:243
www.svsf.com
Email: info@svsf.com
Estab: 1998

Scott Sullivan, President
Erik Kelzer, Purchasing Manager
Kellie King, Office Manager
Brian Stang, Operations Manager
Rodrigo Santamarina, Trainee Technician

Provider of home entertainment, home automation, house audio, lighting, and motorized window
shades.

**Source 1 X-Ray**   HQ
1610 Dell Ave Unit I
Campbell CA 95008
P: 408-866-6020  F: 408-866-6040   PRC:159
source1xray.com
Email: info@source1xray.com

Russ Toy, Product Designer

Manufacturer of X-Ray generators. The company
specializes in bone density measurement, radiography, and process control.

**Source Engineering Inc**   HQ
3283-H De La Cruz Blvd
Santa Clara CA 95054
P: 408-980-9822  F: 408-980-1860   PRC:150
www.sei-automation.com
Email: rick@sei-automation.com

Scott Zimmer, President
Jim Walls, VP of Sales & Customer Service

Manufacturer of motors, cables, harnesses, and
motion control products. The company also provides custom modification services on motors.

**Source Naturals Inc**   HQ
23 Janis Way
Scotts Valley CA 95066
P: 831-438-1144  F: 831-438-7410   PRC:272
www.sourcenaturals.com
Emp: 1-10  Estab: 1982

Ira Goldberg, CEO

Provider of vitamins, minerals, and nutritional
supplements. The company deals with sales and
delivery services.

**South Bay Solutions Inc**  HQ
37399 Centralmont Pl
Fremont CA 94536
P: 650-843-1800   F: 650-843-1803   PRC:74
southbaysolutions.com
Email: info@southbaysolutions.com
Estab: 1992

Adam Drewniany, Founder
Parveen Johal, Quality Assurance Manager
German Avalos, Quotation Specialist

Provider of manufacturing services for the semiconductor, medical, aerospace, solar, and petroleum industries.

**Southall Environmental Associates Inc**  HQ
9099 Soquel Dr Ste 8
Aptos CA 95003
P: 831-661-5177   F: 831-661-5178   PRC:23
sea-inc.net
Emp: 1-10

Brandon Southall, President
Joel Southall, Sustainability & Senior Scientist
Kristin Southall, Associate Scientist

Provider of science to support conservation management. The company specializes in marine and terrestrial ecosystems.

**Southwest Hazard Control Inc**  BR
712 Whitney St
San Leandro CA 94577
P: 510-352-5152   F: 510-352-5155   PRC:139
swhaz.com
Email: california@swhaz.com

David Bernal, Division Manager

Provider of environmental remediation services. The company's offerings include asbestos abatement and hazardous materials management services.

**Sp Controls Inc**  HQ
930 Linden Ave
S San Francisco CA 94080
P: 877-367-8444   F: 650-392-7881   PRC:60
www.spcontrols.com
Email: info@spcontrols.com
Estab: 1995

Diane Peter, Operations Manager

Designer and manufacturer of projector control systems. The company also offers audio systems, mounting, signal distribution, and other products.

**Sp3 Diamond Technologies**  HQ
1605 Wyatt Dr
Santa Clara CA 95054
P: 408-492-0630   F: 408-492-0633   PRC:80
www.sp3diamondtech.com
Email: info@sp3diamondtech.com
Estab: 1993

Todd Lindseth, Materials Manager

Provider of electronics thermal management, diamond-on-silicon applications, and enhanced cutting surface solutions.

**Space Machine Inc**  HQ
303 Twin Dolphin Dr Ste 600
Redwood Shores CA 94065
P: 650-669-8629   PRC:328
www.spacemachine.net
Email: quant@spacemachine.net
Estab: 1999

John Cheong, CEO
Scott Jenkins, Head of Sales & Growth
Akinori Honda, VP of Innovation & Technology

Specializes in academic research. The company focuses on the development of custom models and trading strategies.

**Space-Time Insight Inc**  HQ
1850 Gateway Dr Ste 125
San Mateo CA 94404
P: 650-513-8550   F: 650-349-3554   PRC:323
www.spacetimeinsight.com
Email: resources@spacetimeinsight.com

Rob Schilling, CEO
Paul Hofmann, CTO
Steve Zakar, Delivery Director

Developer of geospatial and information visualization software. The company also offers visual analytics solutions.

**Sparkle Power Inc**  HQ
48502 Kato Rd
Fremont CA 94538
P: 408-519-8888   F: 408-519-9999   PRC:290
www.sparklepower.com
Email: marketing@sparklepower.com
Estab: 1993

Melody Chen, Engineer
Su Lee, Senior Application Engineer
Wendy Su, Credit Manager
Mike Huang, Account Manager
David Hwang, Manager

Manufacturer of switching power supply devices. The company serves the PC, industrial PC, and telecommunication industries.

**Sparqtron Corp**  HQ
5079 Brandin Ct
Fremont CA 94538
P: 510-657-7198   F: 510-683-0892   PRC:208
www.sparqtron.com
Estab: 1999

Fred Huang, Senior Quality Engineer
Alex Lo, Manufacturing Engineer
Chen Yenhung, MIS Engineer
Callie Wang, PM of Business Development

Provider of electronic contract manufacturing services. The company focuses on prototyping, inspection, PCB assembly, and materials and logistics.

**Specialty Precision Machining**  HQ
1014 N Shaw Rd
Stockton CA 95215
P: 209-939-0546   F: 209-939-0617   PRC:80
www.specialtyprecisionmachining.com
Email: sales@specialtyprecisionmachining.com
Emp: 1-10   Estab: 1991

Victor Gorecki, Owner

Provider of machining services. The company also offers turning, contouring, milling, engraving, and drilling services.

**Specialty Products Design Inc**  HQ
11252 Sunco Dr
Rancho Cordova CA 95742
P: 916-635-8108   F: 916-635-2970   PRC:80
www.spdexhaust.com
Email: info@spdexhaust.com
Emp: 1-10

Clea Talley, Principal Engineer
Chris Hill, Owner

Provider of exhaust components. The company focuses on exhaust fabricators, CNC header flanges, stainless bellows, and sealing flanges.

**Spectra 7 Microsystems Ltd**  HQ
2550 N First St Ste 500
San Jose CA 95131
P: 408-770-2915   PRC:96
spectra7.com

Andrew Kim, VP of Engineering
Tony Stelliga, CEO
Robert Bosomworth, CFO

Manufacturer of analog semiconductor devices. The company focuses on micro-thin interconnects for consumer electronic products.

**Spectra Laboratories**  HQ
525 Sycamore Dr
Milpitas CA 95035
P: 800-433-3773   F: 888-621-1598   PRC:303
www.spectra-labs.com
Email: spectra.laboratories@fmc-na.com
Estab: 1982

Debra Shimada, Quality Systems Analyst
Charlene Horn, Financial Analyst
Alvin Queri, Senior Manager of Materials & Logistics
Joanne Ikeda, Billing & Collections Manager
Nicole Nomura, Billing & Collections Supervisor

Provider of testing services for a wide range of specialties. The company focuses on chemistry, serology, anemia testing, hematology, and others.

**Spectra Watermakers Inc**  HQ
20 Mariposa Rd
San Rafael CA 94901
P: 415-526-2780   F: 415-526-2787   PRC:53
www.spectrawatermakers.com
Email: sales@spectrawatermakers.com
Estab: 1997

Kelly Donahoe, Controller

Designer of energy recovery systems. The company specializes in manufacturing of reverse osmosis desalination systems for the ocean sailor.

**Spectra-Mat Inc**  HQ
100 Westgate Dr
Watsonville CA 95076
P: 831-722-4116   F: 831-722-4172   PRC:209
www.spectramat.com
Email: smicustomerservice@saes-group.com
Emp: 1-10   Estab: 1963

John Paff, Quality Assurance Manager

Manufacturer of products for electron emission and controlled expansion of thermal management materials for the microelectronics sector.

**Spectra-Physics**     RH
3635 Peterson Way
Santa Clara CA 95054
P: 408-980-4300   F: 408-980-6921   PRC:172
www.spectra-physics.com
Email: sales@spectra-physics.com

Curt Rettig, Principal Engineer
Inga Sirovsky, Product Development Engineer
Jerry Yang, Senior Reliability Engineer
Ramesh Prasad, Engineer
Vladimir Ivan, Manufacturing Engineer

Provider of precision laser technology services.
The company's products include ultrafast lasers,
fiber lasers, and tunable lasers.

**Spectralus Corp**     HQ
2953 Bunker Hill Ln Ste 205
Santa Clara CA 95054
P: 408-516-4870     PRC:172
www.spectralus.com
Email: info@spectralus.com
Estab: 2003

Stepan Essaian, CEO

Developer of green laser sources. The company
primarily caters to the need of mobile projection
applications.

**Spectrex Corp**     HQ
493 Seaport Ct Ste 105
Redwood City CA 94063
P: 650-365-6567   F: 650-365-5845   PRC:11
www.spectrex.com
Email: info@spectrex.com
Estab: 1966

John Hoyte, President
Stephen Figone, VP
Loan Tran, Corporate Secretary

Developer of environmental and analytical instruments. The company's offerings include detectors
and personal air samplers.

**Spectros Corp**     HQ
274 E Hamilton Ave Ste H
Campbell CA 95008
P: 650-851-4040   F: 866-677-5576   PRC:187
www.spectros.com
Email: info@spectros.com
Estab: 1995

David Benaron, Founder
John Bagnatori, Manager
Elizabeth van Thillo, Manager
William Curnan, Manager

Manufacturer of tissue perfusion monitors and
they are used in plastic surgery, critical care, and
vascular surgery.

**Spectrum Orthotics & Prosthetics**     BR
1844 South St
Redding CA 96001
P: 530-243-4500   F: 530-243-4554   PRC:190
www.spectrumoandp.com
Emp: 11-50 Estab: 1994

Tina Zeller, CFM
Jeff Zeller, Manager
Tyler Rowley, Prosthetist

Provider of orthotics and prosthetics products.
The company serves physicians and the medical
sector.

**Speedinfo**     HQ
100 W San Fernando St Ste 475
San Jose CA 95113
P: 408-446-7660   F: 408-289-9171   PRC:87
www.speedinfo.com
Email: info@speedinfo.com
Estab: 2002

Doug Finlay, Founder
Glenn Harter, Director of Business Development
George Whitehill, Director
Roger Higgins, Director
David Chang, Director

Developer of traffic measurement solutions for
broadcast media, government planning, and
mobile applications.

**Spence Engineering Services Inc**     HQ
1650 Borel Pl Ste 209
San Mateo CA 94402
P: 650-571-6500     PRC:323
www.spenceengr.com
Email: info@spenceengr.com

Ellen Spence, VP of Finance & Operations

Provider of solutions for hardware and software
engineering problems. The company offers services to the technical sector.

**Sperient Corporation Inc**     HQ
1813 Rutan Dr
Livermore CA 94550
P: 925-447-3333   F: 925-447-9999   PRC:87
www.sperient.com
Email: info@sperient.com
Estab: 2003

E. Rosenbury, President

Designer and developer of electronic systems.
The company's applications include telemedicine
and robotic sensing.

**SPI Lasers LLC**     BR
4000 Burton Dr
Santa Clara CA 95054
P: 408-454-1170   F: 408-454-1161   PRC:170
www.spilasers.com
Email: sales@spilasers.com
Estab: 2000

Gareth Lewis, Senior Process Development
Engineer
Mike Warner, Manufacturing Engineering Group
Leader
Mark Greenwood, CEO
Thomas Reinauer, CFO
Aaron Kentish, COO

Designer and manufacturer of fiber lasers for systems integrators, factory automation specialists,
job shops, OEMs, and other academic institutions.

**Spidercloud Wireless Inc**     HQ
475 Sycamore Dr
Milpitas CA 95035
P: 408-235-2900     PRC:68
www.corning.com
Estab: 2008

Kalle Ahmavaara, Principal Engineer
Vandana Chhabra, Staff Engineer
Wendell Weeks, Chairman
David Morse, EVP

Provider of wireless solutions for enterprise service delivery. The company offers services to the
industrial sector.

**Spinal Kinetics Inc**     HQ
501 Mercury Dr
Sunnyvale CA 94085
P: 408-636-2500   F: 408-636-2599   PRC:187
www.spinalkinetics.com
Estab: 2003

Mike Gandy, CFO
Larry Beeman, VP of RA, CA & Quality Assurance
Trudy Nichols, Director of Quality Assurance
Neal Defibaugh, VP of Clinical & Regulatory
Affairs
Nick Koske, Director of Research

Provider of preservation systems for treating
degenerative diseases of the spine. The company
serves the healthcare sector.

**Spineguard Inc**     DH
1388 Sutter St Ste 510
San Francisco CA 94109
P: 415-512-2500   F: 415-512-8004   PRC:189
www.spineguard.com
Email: contact@spineguard.com
Estab: 2009

Stephane Bette, Director

Specializes in spine surgery. The company offers
services to patients, hospitals, and healthcare
organizations.

**Spintrac Systems Inc**     HQ
690 Aldo Ave
Santa Clara CA 95054
P: 408-980-1155   F: 408-980-1267   PRC:159
www.spintrac.com
Email: info@spintrac.com
Estab: 1980

Alan Kukas, President

Manufacturer of automated resist coating equipment. The company is involved in repairs and
maintenance services.

**Spiralinks Corporation**     HQ
900 E Hamilton Ave Ste 100
Campbell CA 95008
P: 408-608-6900     PRC:325
www.spiralinks.com
Email: info@spiralinks.com
Estab: 1994

Diana Mecum, Software Test Engineer
Andrew Smith, Operations Director

Provider of compensation management software
products. The company offers compensation
management, HR analytics, and payroll integration services.

**Spire Manufacturing**     HQ
49016 Milmont Dr
Fremont CA 94538
P: 510-226-1070   F: 510-226-1069   PRC:211
www.spiremfg.com
Estab: 2008

Christine Bui, President

Designer and manufacturer of printed circuit
boards. The company offers vertical probe cards,
test sockets, and mother boards.

**Spirent Communications Inc**     LH

2708 Orchard Pkwy Ste 20
San Jose CA 95134
P: 408-752-7100  F: 408-752-7186    PRC:68
www.spirent.com
Email: support@spirent.com

Patrick Johnson, General Manager
Abhitesh Kastuar, General Manager of Cloud & IP
David DeSanto, Director of Products & Threat
Research
Philip Joung, Senior Manager of Knowledge
Services
Chris Chapman, Senior Methodologist at Spirent
Communications

Provider of performance analysis technology services. The company also offers network equipment and data center solutions.

**Splunk Inc**     HQ

270 Brannan St
San Francisco CA 94107
P: 415-848-8400  F: 415-568-4259    PRC:315
www.splunk.com
Email: info@splunk.com
Estab: 2003
Sales: $1B to $3B

Doug Merritt, President
Susan St. Ledger, President of Worldwide Field
Operations
Jason Child, SVP
Tim Tully, SVP
Scott Morgan, SVP

Develops software for monitoring, searching, and analyzing machine-generated big data through a web-style interface.

**Splunk Inc**     HQ

250 Brannan St
San Francisco CA 94107
P: 415-848-8400  F: 415-568-4259    PRC:322
www.splunk.com
Estab: 2004
Sales: $1B to $3B

Erik Swan, Co-Founder
Douglas Merritt, CEO
Susan Ledger, President of Worldwide Field
Operations
Doug Merritt, President
Susan St Ledger, President of Worldwide Field
Operations

Provider of search engine services specializing in IT data. The company serves the government, healthcare, and telecommunication industries.

**sPower**     BR

201 Mission St Ste 540
San Francisco CA 94105
P: 415-692-7740  F: 415-362-4001    PRC:135
www.silveradopower.com
Email: info@sPower.com
Estab: 2012

John Cheney, CEO

Provider of utility-scale solar generation and physical plant development services for landowners, utilities, and communities.

**Spracht**     HQ

974 Commercial St Ste 108
Palo Alto CA 94303
P: 650-215-7500  F: 650-318-8060    PRC:92
www.spracht.com
Email: sales@spracht.com
Estab: 1993

Spracht German, Electronics Manager
Margarita Kovats, Manager

Designer and manufacturer of consumer electronic products. The company offers digital imaging, acoustics, LCD image displays, and other products.

**Spraying Systems Co**     BR

PO Box 3678
Walnut Creek CA 94598
P: 800-957-7729    PRC:159
spray.com

Jason Boettcher, Senior Controls Engineer
Rudi Schick, VP

Provider of spray technology services. The company focuses on spray nozzles, automated spray systems, and coating.

**Spreadsheetworld Inc**     HQ

PO Box 200
June Lake CA 93529
P: 818-995-3931  F: 760-648-1096    PRC:328
Emp: 1-10  Estab: 1995

Janet Mincer, Director

Provider of services for application of MS Excel and VBA tools in various fields. The company focuses on science, engineering, and management.

**Springboard Biodiesel LLC**     HQ

2323 Park Ave
Chico CA 95928
P: 530-894-1793    PRC:133
www.springboardbiodiesel.com
Emp: 1-10  Estab: 2008

Mark Roberts, CEO

Manufacturer of automated bio-diesel processors. The company also offers fuel pumps, and tanks to consumers, small businesses, and municipalities.

**Sprint**     BR

4955 N Blackstone Ave
Fresno CA 93726
P: 559-244-3200    PRC:62
www.sprint.com
Emp: 11-50

Jan Geldmacher, President of Sprint Business
Michel Combes, President
Marcelo Claure, Executive Chairman
Nestor Cano, COO
Andrew Davies, CFO

Provider of telephone and voice equipment, data communication systems, and internet related services.

**Sprintcom**     BR

2920 N Main St
Walnut Creek CA 94597
P: 925-933-0142    PRC:68
www.sprint.com

Lavnya S, Java Developer

Provider of wireline and wireless communication services. The company serves consumers, businesses, and government entities.

**Sputnik Enterprises Inc**     HQ

1757 E Bayshore Rd Unit 16
Redwood City CA 94063
P: 650-363-7576    PRC:80
www.sputnikmodels.com
Estab: 2000

Val Kasvin, Founder

Provider of finishing, painting, casting, CNC machining, model making, and custom product development services.

**Sputtering Components Inc**     BR

5625 Brisa St Ste B
Livermore CA 94550
P: 925-606-7241  F: 925-606-7243    PRC:209
www.sputteringcomponents.com
Email: sales@sputteringcomponents.com
Estab: 2001

Barry Nudelman, President
Julie Magdefrau, Human Resource Manager
Joel Fiebiger, Assembly Manager

Provider of rotating cathodes and magnet assemblies. The company's products find application in industrial systems.

**SPYRUS**     HQ

103 Bonaventura Dr
San Jose CA 95134
P: 408-392-9131  F: 408-392-0319    PRC:325
www.spyrus.com
Email: info@spyrus.com
Estab: 1992

Grant Evans, Chairman
Simon Blake-Wilson, Chief Revenue Officer
Dan Turissini, CTO
Tom Hakel, CFO

Developer and marketer of hardware encryption, authentication, and digital content security products.

**Square Inc**     HQ

1455 Market St Ste 600
San Francisco CA 94103
P: 415-375-3176    PRC:89
www.squareup.com
Estab: 2009
Sales: Over $3B

Jack Dorsey, CEO
Amrita Ahuja, CFO
Sivan Whiteley, General Counsel

Builds tools to empower and enrich people and help sellers of all areas to start, run, and grow their businesses.

**SRI International** RH
333 Ravenswood Ave
Menlo Park CA 94025
P: 650-859-2000 PRC:34
www.sri.com
Email: hello@sri.com
Estab: 1946

Steve Ciesinski, President
Manish Kothari, President
William Mark, President
Diane Young, Managing Director
Dimitra Vergyri, Director of Speech Technology &
Research Lab

Provider of consulting, research, and development
services. The company offers services to the
defense, security, and energy sectors.

**SS Papadopulos & Associates Inc** BR
45 Belden Pl Fl 4
San Francisco CA 94104
P: 415-773-0400 F: 415-773-0401 PRC:142
www.sspa.com
Email: sanfrancisco@sspa.com
Estab: 1979

Kinsley Binard, Project Engineer
Michael Rafferty, VP
Mark Wit, Construction Manager

Provider of web-based applications for customized online communities. The company serves
business enterprises.

**SSL Industries Inc** HQ
PO Box 3113
Diamond Springs CA 95619-3113
P: 530-644-0233 PRC:62
www.sslinc.net
Email: ssl@sslinc.net
Emp: 1-10 Estab: 1975

John Russ, President

Designer and manufacturer of fiber optics and
networking products. The company is involved in
installation services.

**Ssp Data** HQ
1304 S 51st St
Richmond CA 94804
P: 510-215-3400 F: 510-412-4343 PRC:316
www.ssp.com
Email: info@ssp.com
Estab: 1982

Bill Guggemos, Systems Engineer
Anurag Jain, Senior Network Engineer
Jeff Westbrook, Program Account Manager
Donny Jackson, Account Representative
Sean Hawk, Account Representative

Developer of network solutions. The company also
offers design, deployment, and in-house management services.

**SST Group Inc** HQ
309 Laurelwood Rd Ste 20
Santa Clara CA 95054
P: 408-350-3450 F: 408-350-3100 PRC:189
www.sstgroup-inc.com
Email: sales@sstgroup-inc.com
Estab: 2004

Bob Huff, Sales & Support Manager
Lisa Riland, Sales Support Manager
Mike Sutherland, Director
Richard Murphy, Director
Robert Riland, Director

Provider of medical displays, recorders, film
digitizers, and related accessories. The company
offers optical library support services.

**Sst Systems Inc** HQ
1798 Technology Dr Ste 236
San Jose CA 95110
P: 408-452-8111 F: 408-452-8388 PRC:319
www.sstusa.com
Email: info@sstusa.com
Estab: 1983

P. B. Karthick, Chief Engineer of Engineering Auto-
mation & Products
G.V. Ranjan, Director of Engineering Analyses &
Software Development
Mark Sutton, Sales Manager
R.P. Sudarsan, VP of Civil & Steel Structures

Provider of solutions for piping design and analysis. The company's services include plant design
and engineering.

**Stack Plastics Inc** HQ
3525 Haven Ave
Menlo Park CA 94025
P: 650-361-8600 PRC:163
www.stackplastics.com
Estab: 1995

Mark Rackley, President
John Huynh, Production Manager
Carlene Duplan, Office Manager

Provider of plastic injection molding services. The
company offers thermoplastics, elastomers, and
resins.

**Stage 8** HQ
4318 Redwood Hwy Unit 200
San Rafael CA 94903
P: 415-485-5340 F: 415-485-0552 PRC:159
www.stage8.com
Email: info@stage8.com
Estab: 1986

Bruce Bennett, Founder

Designer and manufacturer of mechanical locking
systems. The company has more than 78 patents
and trademarks.

**Standard Metal Products** HQ
558 Bryant St
San Francisco CA 94107
P: 415-546-6784 F: 415-543-3472 PRC:156
www.smpmachine.com
Email: info@smpmachine.com
Estab: 1993

Kevin Binkert, President

Provider of prototype and production components
and assemblies for transportation, bicycle builders, and medical device companies.

**Stanfield Systems Inc** HQ
718 Sutter St Ste 108
Folsom CA 95630
P: 916-608-8006 F: 916-608-0657 PRC:323
www.stanfieldsystems.com
Emp: 1-10 Estab: 2000

Dave Doherty, CEO
Tim Jacobs, CTO
Bart Battaglia, VP of Technical Resources
Chris Nail, Business Manager
James Geary, Systems Administrator

Provider of system engineering and data management services. The company also focuses on web
development and technical services.

**Stanford Photonics Inc** HQ
1032 Elwell Ct Ste 104
Palo Alto CA 94303
P: 650-969-5991 F: 650-969-5993 PRC:210
www.stanfordphotonics.com
Email: info@stanfordphotonics.com
Estab: 1989

Michael Buchin, President
David Callard, President

Provider of electronic imaging, digital microscope
cameras, and photonics technology solutions for
the industrial and military markets.

**Stanford Research Systems** HQ
1290 Reamwood Ave Ste D
Sunnyvale CA 94089
P: 408-744-9040 F: 408-744-9049 PRC:15
www.thinksrs.com
Email: info@thinksrs.com
Estab: 1980

Greg Waters, Senior Mechanical Engineer
Judi Cushing, Software Engineer
Hoongsun Im, System Engineer
John Willison, Founder

Manufacturer of electronic instruments, optical
choppers, and temperature controllers for the
research industry.

**Stangenes Industries Inc** HQ
1052 E Meadow Cir
Palo Alto CA 94303
P: 650-493-0814 F: 650-855-9926 PRC:78
www.stangenes.com
Email: info@stangenes.com
Estab: 1974

Paul Holen, Associate Mechanical Engineer
Connie Cabrera, Quality Assurance Manager
Charles Ingebretsen, Quality Manager

Manufacturer of isolation transformers, current
monitors, charging inductors, and magnetic
components.

**Stantec Inc** BR
3875 Atherton Rd
Rocklin CA 95765-3716
P: 916-773-8100 PRC:142
www.stantec.com
Email: media@stantec.com
Emp: 11-50 Estab: 1954

Joe DiGiorgio, Supervising Engineer
Gord Johnston, President
Stuart Lerner, EVP
Scott Murray, EVP
Theresa Jang, EVP

Provider of civil construction services. The company also offers commercial program development
and infrastructure management services.

**Stantec** BR
5000 Bechelli Ln Ste 203
Redding CA 96002
P: 530-222-5347 F: 530-222-4958 PRC:139
www.stantec.com
Emp: 11-50 Estab: 1980

Gord Johnston, President
Theresa Jang, EVP
Tino DiManno, EVP
Stuart Lerner, EVP
Cath Schefer, EVP

Provider of environmental consulting services
specializing in GIS mapping, remote sensing,
permitting, and ecosystem restoration.

**Starch Medical Inc** HQ
2150 Ringwood Ave
San Jose CA 95131
P: 408-428-9818   F: 408-383-9189   PRC:195
starchmedical.com
Email: info@starchmedical.com
Estab: 2007

Stephen Heniges, President

Provider of hemostatic solutions. The company offers services to patients and serves the healthcare industry.

**StarNet Communications Corp** HQ
4677 Old Ironsides Dr Ste 210
Santa Clara CA 95054-1825
P: 408-739-0881   PRC:322
www.starnet.com
Email: sales@starnet.com
Estab: 1989

Steven Schoch, President

Developer of X Windows solutions for connecting computers to Unix and Linux desktops and applications.

**Statico** HQ
541 Taylor Way Ste 1
San Carlos CA 94070
P: 650-592-4733   F: 650-508-0761   PRC:212
statico.com
Email: sales2@statico.com

Fruhar Alavi, President
Elizabeth Paulsen, Office Manager
Micheal Byrd, Assembly Technician

Provider of ESD and static control products. The company offers test instruments, ionizers, and cleanroom products.

**Stats Chippac Inc** DH
46429 Landing Pkwy
Fremont CA 94538
P: 510-979-8000   F: 510-979-8001   PRC:86
www.statschippac.com
Email: salescontact@statschippac.com

Vincent Shek, Technical Program Manager

Provider of semiconductor packaging design, bump, probe, assembly, test, and distribution solutions.

**Stealth Network Communications Inc** HQ
100 Enterprise Way Ste C-109
Scotts Valley CA 95066
P: 925-846-7018   F: 925-426-8285   PRC:68
www.stealthnetwork.com
Emp: 1-10   Estab: 1994

Margaret Nyswonger, CEO
Brad Berlin, General Manager

Provider of voice, data, security, network, and wireless solutions. The company also deals with consulting, design, and maintenance services.

**Stella Technology Inc** HQ
6203 San Ignacio Ste 100
San Jose CA 95119
P: 844-278-3552   PRC:319
stellatechnology.com
Email: info@stellatechnology.com
Estab: 2012

Lalo Valdez, President
Lin Wan, CTO
Salim Kizaraly, SVP of Business Development
Jami Young, Senior Director of Client Services
Jeffrey Grant, Manager of Implementations

Provider of integration and collaboration solutions. The company deals with technology design, development, and consulting services.

**Stellar Solutions** HQ
250 Cambridge Ave Ste 204
Palo Alto CA 94306
P: 650-473-9866   F: 650-473-9867   PRC:5
www.stellarsolutions.com
Email: info@stellarsolutions.com
Estab: 1995

Celeste Ford, CEO
Michael Lencioni, President
Kevin Ford, CFO
Michael Abadjiev, Director of Information Technology
Will Fong, Controller

Provider of systems engineering, mission operations, and strategic planning services. The company focuses on commercial and government programs.

**Stellartech Research Corp** HQ
560 Cottonwood Dr
Milpitas CA 95035
P: 408-331-3000   F: 408-331-3101   PRC:186
www.stellartec.com
Email: info@stellartec.com
Estab: 1988

Dan Phan, Hardware Design Engineer
Larry Deter, Senior Service Quality Engineer
Tom Hussey, Senior Quality Engineer
Roger Stern, Founder
Mark Recob, Information Technology Manager

Designer, developer, and manufacturer of medical devices. The company specializes in surgical probes, balloon electrode catheters, and other products.

**Stellarvue** HQ
11802 Kemper Road
Auburn CA 95603
P: 530-823-7796   F: 530-823-8121   PRC:174
www.stellarvue.com
Email: mail@stellarvue.com
Emp: 1-10   Estab: 1998

C. Vic Maris, Owner

Designer and seller of refractor telescopes and telescope accessories. The company deals with design, delivery, and installation.

**Stem Inc** HQ
100 Rollins Rd
Millbrae CA 94030
P: 415-937-7836   PRC:288
www.stem.com
Email: info@stem.com
Estab: 2009

John Carrington, CEO
Karen Butterfield, Chief Commercial Officer
Mike Lasky, Director of Sales
Prakesh Patel, VP of Capital Markets & Strategy
Chris Zach, Product Marketing Manager

Provider of innovative solutions for efficient electricity grids. The company uses powerful learning software and advanced energy storage.

**Stemexpress** HQ
778 Pacific St
Placerville CA 95667
P: 530-626-7000   PRC:250
www.stemexpress.com
Email: info@stemexpress.com
Emp: 1-10   Estab: 2010

Cate Dyer, CEO
Regina King, Marketing Assistant
Tera Muir, Scientific Marketing Writer
Megan Barr, Director of Procurement
Pauliane Boyd, Administrative Assistant

Provider of immunophenotyping, DNA quantitation and viability, tissue transplant verification, and related services.

**Steven Engineering Inc** HQ
230 Ryan Way
S San Francisco CA 94080-6308
P: 800-258-9200   PRC:293
stevenengineering.com
Estab: 1975

Bonnie Walter, Chairman
Karen Mitts, Manager

Distributor of industrial controls and components. The company also provides contract manufacturing services.

**Steven R Young Ocularist Inc** HQ
411 - 30th St Ste 512
Oakland CA 94609
P: 510-836-2123   F: 510-836-0383   PRC:190
stevenryoungocularist.com
Estab: 1975

Steven Young, Owner

Provider of ocular prosthetic services. The company engages in scleral cover shells and maxillo-facial prosthetics.

**Stevens Creek Software** HQ
PO Box 2126
Cupertino CA 95015
P: 408-725-0424   F: 408-725-0424   PRC:322
www.stevenscreek.com
Email: sales@stevenscreek.com

Steven Patt, President
Joseph Wei, Sales Manager
Deborah Jamison, Director of Marketing
Eric Yeager, Assistant Service Manager

Provider of software solutions for the palm computing platform. The company is involved in custom development and technical support.

**Stewart Audio Inc**      HQ
14335 Cuesta Ct Ste C
Sonora CA 95370
P: 209-588-8111   F: 209-588-8113     PRC:60
www.stewartaudio.com
Email: sales@stewartaudio.com
Emp: 1-10   Estab: 1982

Debbie Ulrey, Engineer
Kevin Stone, General Manager

Provider of network amplifiers and sound systems.
The company's products include digital signal
processors, mixer amplifiers, and networked
accessories.

**Stewart Tool Company Inc**      HQ
3647 Omec Cir
Rancho Cordova CA 95742
P: 916-635-8321   F: 916-635-9487     PRC:80
www.stewarttool.com
Email: info@stewarttool.com
Emp: 1-10   Estab: 1972

Jeff Boyett, Engineering Manager
Amber Stewart, ISO Administrator
Stephen Shuman, Controller

Manufacturer of CNC precision machine components. The company specializes in manufacturing
pressure vessels and provides field and assembly
services.

**STMicroelectronics**      BR
2755 Great America Way 3rd Fl
Santa Clara CA 95054
P: 408-919-8400   F: 408-986-9644     PRC:208
www.st.com

Carlo Bozotti, President
Marco Cassis, President of Sales, Marketing,
Communications & Strategy Development
Orio Bellezza, President of Technology manufac-
turing and Quality
Steven Rose, President
Carlo Ferro, CFO

Provider of analog, mixed signal ICs, transistor,
and memories. The company also offers microcontroller products and services.

**Stockton Tri Industries Inc**      HQ
2141 E Anderson St
Stockton CA 95205
P: 209-948-9701   F: 209-948-2310     PRC:80
stocktontri.com
Email: info@stocktontri.com
Emp: 1-10   Estab: 1976

Fred Wells, Co-Owner
Ray Smith, Co-Owner
Denise Donahue, Sales Manager

Provider of custom rolling, bending, forming,
machining, metal fabrication, and field erection
services.

**Stokes Publishing Co**      HQ
1292 Reamwood Ave
Sunnyvale CA 94089
P: 408-541-9145   F: 408-541-9149     PRC:159
www.stokespublishing.com
Email: customerservice@stokespublishing.com
Estab: 1979

William Stokes, President

Manufacturer of overhead calculators. The company also offers timers, puzzles, manipulatives, and
posters.

**Stone Cobra**      HQ
201 Creekside Ridge Ct Ste 100
Roseville CA 95678
P: 916-797-6272     PRC:319
Emp: 1-10   Estab: 2001

Mark Sanders, Director of Operations
Ibrahim Lamdouar, Solution Architect

Provider of knowledge management solutions.
The company offers solutions for architecture,
system configuration, and data migration.

**Stonefly Inc**      HQ
26250 Eden Landing Rd
Hayward CA 94545
P: 510-265-1616     PRC:64
www.stonefly.com
Email: sales@stonefly.com
Estab: 2000

Viktor Nosov, Senior Software Engineer
John Harris, Director of Technical Sales
Sam Malik, Project Manager

Provider of storage optimization and disaster
recovery protection for software solutions. The
company also offers storage area networks.

**Stopware Inc**      HQ
5000 Pleasanton Ave Ste 210
Pleasanton CA 94566
P: 408-367-0220     PRC:323
www.stopware.com
Email: info@stopware.com
Estab: 1997

Bao Truong, Tech Support Engineer
Roberta Sosbee, Channel Sales Manager
John Izzo, Enterprise Sales Manager
Tito Cardoway, Director of Sales
Cha Yang, Development

Developer of visitor management security software. The company offers hardware, badge stock,
and training services.

**Storz & Bickel America Inc**      HQ
1078 60th St Ste A
Oakland CA 94608
P: 510-451-1553     PRC:159
www.storz-bickel.com
Estab: 2000

Markus Storz, Managing Director

Manufacturer of vaporizers. The company specializes in the design and fabrication of solid valve
and easy valve systems.

**Strataglass**      HQ
958 San Leandro Ave Ste 100
Mountain View CA 94043
P: 650-988-1700   F: 650-988-1739     PRC:86
strataglass.us
Email: info@strataglass.us
Estab: 1990

Dave Snow, President
Lisa Kerner, COO

Manufacturer of thin films. The company offers
research and development, pilot production, and
outsourced fabrication services.

**Stratamet Inc**      HQ
46009 Hotchkiss St
Fremont CA 94539
P: 510-651-7176   F: 510-315-3217     PRC:84
www.stratamet.com
Email: inquiry@stratamet.com

Mark Capalongan, CEO
Barbara Romero, Quality Control Technician

Provider of precision ceramic components. The
company offers engineering support, quick response, and customer support.

**Stratedigm Inc**      HQ
6541 Via Del Oro Ste A
San Jose CA 95119
P: 408-512-3901   F: 408-351-7700     PRC:245
www.stratedigm.com
Email: info@stratedigm.com
Estab: 2004

Shervin Javadi, CEO
Sirma Pandeva, Office Manager
Alex Gordon, Systems Specialist

Manufacturer of software products, consumables,
and related accessories. The company deals with
upgrades and installation.

**Stratogent Corp**      HQ
3 Waters Park Dr Ste 230
San Mateo CA 94403
P: 650-577-2332   F: 650-641-2645     PRC:326
www.stratogent.com
Email: info@stratogent.com
Estab: 2008

Ahmed Mohammed, Senior Network Engineer
Jishnu Mitra, President
Chetan Patwardhan, CEO
Sara Masic, Sales Associate
Susan Kwok, Controller

Provider of hosting and critical software systems
operations. The company is engaged in design
and programming solutions.

**Stratovan Corp**      HQ
202 Cousteau Pl Ste 115
Davis CA 95618
P: 530-746-7970   F: 530-746-7974     PRC:323
www.stratovan.com
Email: support@stratovan.com
Emp: 1-10   Estab: 2005

David Hinojosa, Senior Engineering Project
Manager
David Wiley, President
Jim Olson, CEO
Bernd Hamann, Director
Jamie Jones, Office Manager

Developer of visual analysis software. It's product
finds application in 3D imaging and surgical planning research.

**Streamline Circuits**      HQ
1410 Martin Ave
Santa Clara CA 95050
P: 408-727-1418   F: 408-727-1413     PRC:211
www.streamlinecircuits.com
Email: info@streamlinecircuits.com
Estab: 1982

David Aldape, Quality
Chuck Dimick, CEO
Tom Doslak, VP of Sales & Marketing
Greg Halvorson, President
Pamela Wilke, Production Manager

Designer and manufacturer of printed circuit boards. The company also offers engineering and other services.

**Streamline Electronics Manufacturing Inc** HQ
4285 Technology Dr
Fremont CA 94538
P: 408-263-3600   F: 408-508-5638   PRC:211
www.sem-inc.com
Email: info@sem-inc.com
Estab: 1994

Ali Jamal, Test Engineer
Shahab Jafri, President
Stephanie Broussard, Manager of Sales & Marketing
Syed Zaidi, Operational Control Manager

Provider of electronic manufacturing solutions and services. The company is engaged in product development and contract manufacturing.

**StrongKey** HQ
20045 Stevens Creek Blvd
Cupertino CA 95014
P: 408-331-2000   PRC:326
www.strongauth.com
Email: info@strongkey.com

Arshad Noor, CTO

Provider of enterprise key management solutions. The company serves the cloud computing, e-commerce, healthcare, finance, and other sectors.

**Structural Integrity Associates Inc** HQ
5215 Hellyer Ave Ste 210
San Jose CA 95138
P: 408-978-8200   F: 408-978-8964   PRC:13
www.structint.com
Email: info@structint.com
Estab: 1983

Laney Bisbee, CEO
Stager Dave, CFO
Afzal Ahmed, Staff Accountant
Ray Werner, Controller
Scott Chesworth, Senior Consultant

Provider of solutions for prevention and control of structural and mechanical failures and serves nuclear plants, oil and gas, and other sectors.

**Sts International Inc** HQ
4695 Chabot Dr Ste 102
Pleasanton CA 94588
P: 925-479-7800   F: 925-479-7810   PRC:323
www.stsii.com
Estab: 1992

Kristina Bennett, Human Resource Administrator
Kish Jha, VP of Operations
Tim Akers, Service Support Manager
STS Recruiter, Recruiter

Provider of information technology solutions that include infrastructure management, software application development, and systems integration.

**SubrosasoftCom Inc** HQ
5387 Diana Common
Fremont CA 94555
P: 510-870-7883   F: 510-868-3407   PRC:323
subrosasoft.com
Email: support@subrosasoft.com
Estab: 2002

Mark Hurlow, General Manager

Developer of software for Mac operating systems. The company offers software such as FileSalvage, CopyCat, and ParentRemote.

**SucceedNet** BR
970 Reserve Dr Ste 160
Roseville CA 95678
P: 530-674-4200   F: 530-674-4329   PRC:323
succeed.net
Email: sales@cwo.com
Emp: 11-50 Estab: 1994

Dale Karthauser, IT Manager
Robert Lavelock, CEO

Provider of internet services. The company specializes in metro Ethernet, wireless broadband, DSL service, national dial-up, and server co-location.

**Sumiden Wire Products Corp** BR
1412 El Pinal Dr
Stockton CA 95205
P: 209-466-8924   F: 209-941-2990   PRC:159
www.sumidenwire.com
Email: supportpcw@sumidenwire.com
Emp: 11-50 Estab: 1979

Jeff Feitler, VP of Sales & Marketing

Supplier of wire products. The company offers nickel plated wires, stainless spring wires, and industrial alloys.

**Sumitomo Electric Device Innovations Usa Inc** LH
2355 Zanker Rd
San Jose CA 95131-1138
P: 408-232-9500   F: 408-428-9111   PRC:62
www.sei-device.com
Estab: 2000

John Wyatt, President
Peggy Chang, Corporate Controller

Developer of electronic devices that includes wireless devices, optical data links, and optical devices.

**Summit Engineering Inc** HQ
463 Aviation Blvd Ste 200
Santa Rosa CA 95403
P: 707-527-0775   F: 707-527-0212   PRC:304
www.summit-sr.com
Email: info@summit-sr.com
Estab: 1978

Kevin Marx, Staff Engineer
Greg Swaffar, President
Paige Wray, Human Resource Manager
Jasper Lewis-Gehring, Principal
Katie Cornelius, Project Manager

Provider of facility planning, due diligence, design, project management, and other services to wineries, resorts, food, education, and other sectors.

**Summit Wireless Technologies Inc** HQ
6840 Via Del Oro Ste 280
San Jose CA 95119
P: 408-627-4716   PRC:208
www.summitwireless.com
Email: sales-americas-eu@summitsemi.com
Sales: $1M to $3M

Keith Greeney, VP of Engineering
Tony Ostrom, President WiSA
Brett Moyer, CEO
George Oliva, CFO
Gary Williams, VP of Finance

Developer of wireless audio integrated circuits. The company specializes in semiconductors, home entertainment, and pro-audio markets.

**Sumo Logic** RH
305 Main St
Redwood City CA 94063
P: 650-810-8700   PRC:324
www.sumologic.com
Email: info@sumologic.com
Estab: 2010

Xiaolei Li, Engineering Manager
Lei Huang, Senior Software Engineer
Christian Beedgen, CTO
B.J. Jenkins, President
Ramin Sayar, President

Provider of compliance, security, monitoring, troubleshooting, and delivery solutions. The company serves security, IT, and development teams.

**Sun Enterprise Inc** HQ
4010 Business Center Dr
Fremont CA 94538
P: 510-657-6507   PRC:80
www.sun-enterprise.com
Email: sales@sun-enterprise.com

Myles Ly, Owner

Provider of ceramic and quartz machining products. The company specializes in the semiconductor, solar, laser, and structural industries.

**Sun First! Solar** HQ
136 Mitchell Blvd
San Rafael CA 94903
P: 415-458-5870   F: 415-458-5871   PRC:135
www.sunfirstsolar.com
Email: info@sunfirstsolar.com
Estab: 1984

Aran Moore, Co-Owner
Kim Fink, CEO

Provider of renewable energy services. The company offers residential and commercial solar PV and swimming pool systems.

**Sun-Net Inc** HQ
2150 N First St Ste 550
San Jose CA 95131
P: 408-323-1318   F: 408-864-2064   PRC:323
www.sncsw.com
Email: info@sncsw.com
Estab: 1999

Han Zhang, Software Engineer
Sally Tan, Development Manager
Helen Hu, Manager
Razieh Shamsedin, Senior Software Developer

Provider of enterprise software solutions supporting outage scheduling, logging, and reporting for power, gas, and water utilities.

**SUNBURST Plant Disease Clinic Inc** HQ
677 E Olive Ave
Turlock CA 95380
P: 209-667-4442  F: 209-667-4443  PRC:306
www.sunburstpdcinc.com
Emp: 1-10  Estab: 1998

Thomas Yamashita, Founder
Kathleen Yamashita, Owner
Tim Yamashita, Owner
Susan Sallee, CEO
Theresa Borrelli, CFO

Provider of solutions for pathological & physiological problems in agriculture. The company focuses on soil & tissue examination and mineral analysis.

**Suni Medical Imaging Inc** HQ
6840 Via Del Oro Ste 160
San Jose CA 95119
P: 408-227-6698  F: 408-227-9949  PRC:198
www.suni.com
Email: sales@suni.com
Estab: 1995

Yongjie Gan, Senior Software Engineer
Marty Rudnick, Senior Support Engineer
Al Bettencourt, COO
Julie Meneses, Technical Support Representative

Manufacturer of digital radiography. The company designs, develops, manufactures and sell digital sensors for the medical field.

**Sunlink Corp** HQ
2 Belvedere Pl Ste 210
Mill Valley CA 94941
P: 415-925-9650  F: 415-276-8990  PRC:135
www.sunlink.com
Email: info@sunlink.com
Estab: 2004

Tracy Hsieh, Project Manager
Mark Ginalski, General Counsel

Designer and manufacturer of roof and ground mounted systems for commercial and utility-scale installations.

**Sunlink Corp** BR
2131 Williams St
San Leandro CA 94577
P: 510-483-4300  PRC:131
www.sunlink.com
Email: info@sunlink.com

Amena Baporia, Accounting Manager

Designer and manufacturer of roof and ground mounted systems for commercial and utility-scale installations.

**Sunmedica Inc** HQ
1661 Zachi Way
Redding CA 96003
P: 530-229-1600  F: 530-229-9457  PRC:189
www.sunmedica.com
Email: service@sunmedica.com
Emp: 1-10  Estab: 1988

Kimberly Mills, CFO

Specializes in surgical orthopaedics, wound management, cold therapy and sports medicine. The company also offers surgical positioning devices.

**Sunperfect Solar Inc** HQ
Silicon Valley Center 2570 N First St Ste 200
San Jose CA 95131
P: 408-273-4534  F: 408-273-4555  PRC:129
www.sunperfect.com
Email: info@sunperfect.com
Estab: 2009

Chung Wang, VP of Projects Engineering
Willy Chow, CEO
Kevin Chan, VP of Operations
Yoshi Hoashi, Accounts Manager
Caroline Chow, Controller

Provider of energy solutions. The company specializes in the design, manufacture, and installation of solar panels.

**Sunpreme Inc** HQ
615 Palomar Ave
Sunnyvale CA 94085-2913
P: 866-245-1110  F: 408-245-2760  PRC:135
www.sunpreme.com
Email: info@sunpreme.com
Estab: 2009

Joseph Bach, Co-Founder
Moris Kori, Advisor to CEO
Pawan Kapur, CSO
Farhad Moghadam, CTO
Rohini Raghunathan, SVP of Corporate Development

Developer of SmartSilicon based solar cells to satisfy growing global needs for abundant, low-cost, clean energy.

**Sunrise Medical (us) LLC** HQ
2842 Business Park Ave
Fresno CA 93727
P: 800-333-4000  F: 800-300-7502  PRC:190
www.sunrisemedical.com
Emp: 11-50  Estab: 1983

Thomas Babacan, President
Pete Coburn, President of Commercial Operations
Rohit Sathe, Chief Purchasing Officer
Adrian Platt, CFO
Bernd Krebs, CTO

Distributor of folding wheel chairs, seating and positioning systems, and other mobility products to its customers.

**Sunset Moulding Co** HQ
PO Box 326
Yuba City CA 95992
P: 530-790-2700  F: 530-695-2560  PRC:163
www.sunsetmoulding.com
Emp: 1-10  Estab: 1948

Mark Westlake, VP of Sales
Mike Morrison, Plant Manager

Provider of molding and millwork products. The company offers products such as interior jambs, board products, and shelving.

**Sunsil Inc** HQ
3174 Danville Blvd Ste 1
Alamo CA 94507
P: 925-648-7779  F: 925-648-7749  PRC:86
www.sunsil.com
Email: sales@sunsil.com
Estab: 1999

Seth Alavi, President

Provider of total electronics manufacturing solutions. The company offers wafer fabrication, component assembly, testing, and wafer probing services.

**Suntechnics Energy Systems Inc** HQ
660 J St Ste 270
Sacramento CA 95814
P: 888-786-8321  PRC:135
www.suntechnicsusa.com
Email: solarinfo@suntecnicusa.com
Emp: 11-50  Estab: 1996

Florian Edler, CEO

Provider of residential, commercial, and agricultural solar systems and solutions. The company offers custom installation services.

**Sunterra Solar Inc** HQ
285 Bel Marin Keys Blvd Ste J
Novato CA 94949
P: 415-883-6800  F: 415-883-6804  PRC:135
www.sunterrasolar.com
Email: info@sunterrasolar.com
Estab: 2009

Chris Bunas, CEO

Designer of turn-key grid-connected solar power systems for commercial, agricultural, and governmental customers.

**Suntrek Industries Inc** BR
4851 Sunrise Dr Ste 102
Martinez CA 94553-4302
P: 925-372-8983  F: 925-269-2374  PRC:135
www.suntreksolar.com
Email: info@suntreksolar.com

Roy Heine, Founder
Scott Miner, Area Manager

Manufacturer, designer, and installer of solar power systems for residential, commercial, and agricultural solar power applications.

**Sunverge Energy Inc** HQ
6665 Hardaway Rd
Stockton CA 95215
P: 209-931-5677  PRC:135
www.sunverge.com
Emp: 1-10  Estab: 2009

Liem Truong, Software Engineer
Clinton Davis, SVP
Trisha Grobeck, Controller

Provider of power and energy services. The company focuses on solar power and combines batteries and power electronics.

**Super Micro Computer Inc** HQ
980 Rock Ave
San Jose CA 95131
P: 408-503-8000  F: 408-503-8008  PRC:93
www.supermicro.com
Email: marketing@supermicro.com
Estab: 1993

Charles Liang, Founder
Sara Liu, Co-Founder
Perry Hayes, President
Kevin Bauer, SVP
Howard Hideshima, CFO

Provider of server technology and computing solutions. The company offers networking, gaming, micro cloud, and AMD services.

**Super Talent Technology**                    HQ
  2077 N Capitol Ave
  San Jose CA 95132
P: 408-934-2560   F: 408-719-5020          PRC:95
www.supertalent.com
Email: support@supertalent.com
Estab: 1991

Shimon Chen, VP of Engineering
James Lee, Director of Engineering
Frank Yu, Engineer Manager
Sharon Wu, VP of Finance
Jeffrey Vassallo, Sales Manager

Designer and manufacturer of flash based storage
solutions for enterprise servers, portable devices,
personal computers, and consumer electronics.

**Superior Automation**                        HQ
  48460 Lakeview Blvd
  Fremont CA 94538
P: 510-413-9790   F: 510-413-9984          PRC:311
www.superiorautomation.com
Email: sales@superiorautomation.com

Roger Kessinger, President

Provider of custom automation solutions. The
company primarily caters to the semiconductor
industry.

**SuperKlean**                                 HQ
  1 Edwards Ct Ste 101
  Burlingame CA 94010
P: 650-375-7001   F: 650-375-7010          PRC:160
www.superklean.com
Email: sales@superklean.com
Estab: 1985

Rajesh raajaa, Civil Engineer
Joel Alvarez, Division Manager
Adnan B., Accountant

Manufacturer of spray nozzles and swivel fittings.
The company also offers hot & cold water mixing
stations and hose racks.

**Supracor Inc**                               HQ
  2050 Corporate Ct
  San Jose CA 95131
P: 408-432-1616   F: 408-432-8985          PRC:189
www.supracor.com
Email: webmaster@supracor.com
Estab: 1982

Curtis Landi, Co-Founder
Steven Landi, Business Development Manager

Developer of honeycomb products. The company's offerings include sandals, saddle pads, and
related supplies.

**Surface Art Engineering**                    HQ
  81 Bonaventura Dr
  San Jose CA 95134
P: 408-433-4700   F: 408-433-9988          PRC:207
surfaceart.com
Email: sales@surface-art.com
Estab: 1994

Paul Edwards, Process Quality Engineer
Richard Diep, Manufacturing Engineer
Javier Guerrero, Quality Assurance Manager
Angela Choi, Program Manager
Minji Kang, Program Manager

Provider of Printed Circuit Board Assembly (PCA)
and mechanical assembly for prototype, pre-pro-
duction and production assemblies.

**Surplus Process Equipment Corp**             HQ
  1855 Norman Ave
  Santa Clara CA 95054-2029
P: 408-654-9500   F: 408-654-9400          PRC:212
specequipment.com
Email: sales@specequipment.com
Estab: 1998

John Sardi, President
Kyle Willis, Operations Manager
Lee Stevens, Operations Manager
John Oncay, Project Manager
Linda Sardi, Controller

Provider of new, used, and refurbished semiconductor equipment. The company offers ashing and
etching systems.

**Surtec Inc**                                 HQ
  1880 N MacArthur Dr
  Tracy CA 95376
P: 209-820-3700   F: 209-820-3793          PRC:53
surtecsystem.com
Email: orderdesk@surtecsystem.com
Emp: 1-10   Estab: 1975

Don Fromm, VP

Provider of technology solutions for maintenance
chemicals. The company is focused on services
for the commercial and industrial cleaning industry.

**Surveillance Systems Integration Inc**       HQ
  4465 Granite Dr Ste 700
  Rocklin CA 95677
P: 916-771-7272   F: 916-771-7297          PRC:159
www.ssicctv.com
Email: sales@ssicctv.com
Emp: 11-50 Estab: 2002

Todd Flowers, President
Candy Barry, Human Resource Manager
Melissa Mount, VP of Sales
Darren Young, Director of Field Operations
Ruben Gamboa, Director of Field Operations

Provider of security products. The company
serves customers in the gaming, retail, education,
and healthcare industries.

**SurveyMonkey**                               HQ
  1 Curiosity Way
  San Mateo CA 94403
P: 650-543-8400                            PRC:325
www.surveymonkey.com
Estab: 1999
Sales: $1M to $3M

Tom Hale, President
Zander Lurie, CEO
Ross Moser, Chief Product Officer
Eric Johnson, CIO
Debbie Clifford, CFO

Provider of a cloud-based people-powered data
platform.

**Sustainable Conservation**                   HQ
  98 Battery St Ste 302
  San Francisco CA 94111
P: 415-977-0380   F: 415-534-3480          PRC:142
www.suscon.org
Email: suscon@suscon.org
Estab: 1993

Bob Epstein, Co-Founder
Frank Boren, Co-Founder
Kristine Johnson, Founder
Laura Hattendorf, Head of Investments
Paula Daniels, Co-Founder

Provider of environmental protection services
and solutions. The company focuses on clean-air
farming and auto recycling projects.

**Sutro Biopharma Inc**                        HQ
  310 Utah Ave Ste 150
  S San Francisco CA 94080
P: 650-392-8412   F: 650-872-8924          PRC:268
www.sutrobio.com
Email: general@sutrobio.com
Emp: 147   Estab: 2003
Sales: $10M to $30M

William Newell, CEO
Jimmy Zawada, Associate Director of Process
Science
Jim Akins, Vivarium Manager
Nancy Taylor, Executive Assistant
Nathan Uter, Senior Scientist

Developer of therapeutics for cancer therapy. The
company shares with select pharmaceutical and
biotech companies to develop new therapeutics.

**Sutrovax Inc**                               HQ
  353 Hatch Dr
  Foster City CA 94404
P: 650-837-0111                            PRC:268
www.sutrovax.com
Email: info@sutrovax.com
Estab: 2003

Grant Pickering, CEO
Ash Khanna, Chief Business Officer
Elaine Sun, CFO
Jeff Fairman, VP of Research
Mark Iverson, Senior Scientist

Developer of vaccines for the treatment of infectious diseases. The company is also engaged in
the production of vaccine antigens.

**Sutter Instrument Co**                       HQ
  1 Digital Dr
  Novato CA 94949
P: 415-883-0128   F: 415-883-0572          PRC:209
www.sutter.com
Email: info@sutter.com
Estab: 1977

Adair Oesterle, Applications Engineer
Ali Mahloudji, Product Manager DG4
Dan Carte, Product Manager
Jan Dolzer, Product Development

Manufacturer of microprocessors and precision
electromechanical devices. The company offers
technical support services.

**Sv Tcl** BR
535 E Brokaw Rd
Santa Clara CA 95112
P: 408-727-6341   F: 408-492-1424   PRC:212
www.svprobe.com
Email: sales@svprobe.com
Estab: 1994

Kevin Kurtz, CEO
Chau Bui, Buyer

Manufacturer of probe cards. The company is
engaged in delivery and installation services and
serves the semiconductor industry.

**Swca Environmental Consultants** DH
60 Stone Pine Rd Ste 201
Half Moon Bay CA 94019
P: 650-440-4160   F: 650-440-4165   PRC:138
swca.com
Estab: 1981

Steven Carothers, Director
Rich Young, President
Joseph Fluder, CEO
Denis Henry, CFO
Deborah Owens, Chief People Officer

Provider of environmental consultant services.
The company focuses on environmental planning
and regulatory compliance activities.

**Sweco Products Inc** HQ
2455 Palm St
Sutter CA 95982
P: 530-673-8949   F: 530-671-0110   PRC:159
www.swecoproducts.com
Emp: 1-10   Estab: 1946

Michael Ziegenmeyer, VP of Sales
Tim Towne, Sales Manager

Manufacturer of agricultural & construction equipment and hydraulic cylinders, and related supplies.

**Swedcom Corp** HQ
1075 Old County Rd Ste C
Belmont CA 94002
P: 650-620-9420   F: 650-620-9281   PRC:68
www.swedcom.com
Email: info@swedcom.com
Estab: 1987

Hicham Chraibi, Senior Technician

Designer and manufacturer of log periodic antennas, channel banks, filters, and base stations for
the telecommunication sector.

**Swintek Enterprises Inc** HQ
5655 Silver Creed Valley Rd Ste 342
San Jose CA 95138
P: 408-727-4889   PRC:59
www.swintek.com
Email: sales@swintek.com

Bill Swintek, CEO

Provider of transceivers, tactical repeaters, and
surveillance solutions for the government agencies.

**Switchfly** HQ
601 Montgomery St Fl 17
San Francisco CA 94111
P: 415-541-9100   PRC:325
www.switchfly.com
Email: sales@switchfly.com
Estab: 2003

Craig Brennan, CEO
Bart Foster, Chairman
Ian Gillott, Chief Information Officer
Mark Kent, CFO
Alan Josephs, Chief Product Officer

Provider of software solutions such as travel
commerce platforms, payments engines, mobile
platforms, and social media solutions.

**SwitchGear Genomics Inc** HQ
1914 Palomar Oaks Way Ste 150
Carlsbad CA 92008
P: 760-431-1263   F: 760-431-1351   PRC:34
www.switchgeargenomics.com
Email: sales@activemotif.com
Emp: 11-50   Estab: 2006

Nathan Trinklein, Co-Founder

Focuses on custom cloning, pathway screening,
target validation, sequence variant assay, and
custom mutagenesis services.

**Swivl Inc** HQ
1450 El Camino Real
Menlo Park CA 94025
P: 888-837-6209   F: 650-362-1995   PRC:60
www.swivl.com
Email: info@swivl.com
Estab: 2010

Brian Lamb, Founder
Steve Clarence, VP of Sales

Provider of video tools for personalized teaching
and learning. The company offers services to
educators.

**Sycard Technology** HQ
1484 Pollard Rd Ste 151
Los Gatos CA 95032
P: 408-399-8073   F: 408-354-1649   PRC:102
www.sycard.com
Estab: 1989

Mike Mori, President

Provider of 16-bit PC card and CardBus devices.
The company also offers USB and smart media
development services.

**Symantec Corp** HQ
350 Ellis St
Mountain View CA 94043
P: 650-527-8000   PRC:325
www.symantec.com
Estab: 1982
Sales: Over $3B

Amit Mital, CTO
Paul Agbabian, VP
Stephen Trilling, VP
Scott Taylor, EVP
Biwen Xu, Director of Technology

Developer of storage management and disaster
recovery software. The company is engaged in
consulting, archiving, and clustering.

**Symic Bio Inc** BR
5980 Horton St Ste 600
Emeryville CA 94608
P: 415-805-9005   PRC:36
www.symic.bio
Email: info@symic.bio
Estab: 2012

Ken Horne, CEO
Jocelyn Jackson, CFO
Glenn Prestwich, CSO
Nathan Bachtell, CMO
Grace Wong-Sarad, VP

Developer of proprietary bioconjugates. The company offers therapeutics focused on extracellular
matrix biology.

**Symplectic Engineering Corp** HQ
2901 Benvenue Ave
Berkeley CA 94705
P: 510-528-1251   F: 510-528-7102   PRC:323
www.symplectic.com
Email: info@symplectic.com

Jerome Sackman, Research Engineer

Provider of custom computational mechanics
solutions. The company is involved in consulting
services and it serves the industrial sector.

**Symprotek Corp** HQ
950 Yosemite Dr
Milpitas CA 95035
P: 408-956-0700   F: 408-956-9400   PRC:211
www.symprotek.com
Email: sales@symprotek.com
Estab: 1994

Randy Hall, Engineering

Provider of electronics manufacturing and engineering services. The company also focuses on
procurement.

**Synack** HQ
1600 Seaport Blvd Ste 170
Redwood City CA 94063
P: 855-796-2251   PRC:325
www.synack.com
Email: info@synack.com
Estab: 2013

Jay Kaplan, CEO
Mark Kuhr, CTO
Amit Sirdeshpandey, VP of Finance
Tiffany Thielman, Southwest Sales Director
Ellie McCardwell, Marketing Manager

Provider of security intelligence solutions. The
company offers services to the commercial, industrial, and business sectors.

**Synapse Design** HQ
2200 Laurelwood Rd
Santa Clara CA 95054
P: 408-850-3640   F: 408-645-5850   PRC:90
www.synapse-da.com
Email: sales@synapse-da.com
Estab: 2003

Sundar Ramani, Associate VP of Engineering
Satish Bagalkotkar, President
Devesh Gautam, COO
Hem Hingarh, VP
Tom King, VP of Business Development

Provider of embedded software design services.
The company also offers test bench analysis and
block and chip level verification services.

**Synapsense Corp**   HQ
340 Palladio Pkwy Ste 540
Folsom CA 95630
P: 916-294-0110  F: 916-294-0270  PRC:322
www.synapsense.com
Email: info@synapsense.com
Emp: 1-10  Estab: 2006

Pat Weston, VP of Engineering
Jeff Boone, SVP of Engineering
Dave Lemoine, Engineering Technician
Raju Pandey, CTO
Jeff Fitch, Director of Product Management

Provider of wireless monitoring and cooling control solutions. The company also deals with data center infrastructure management.

**Synaptics Inc**   HQ
1251 McKay Dr
San Jose CA 95131
P: 408-904-1100  F: 408-904-1110  PRC:323
www.synaptics.com
Email: info@synaptics.com
Estab: 1986
Sales: $1B to $3B

Kin Cheung, VP of Quality & Product Engineering
John Reihl, Windows Software Engineer
Bertha Santoso, Firmware Engineer
Wenchang Chen, Firmware Engineer
John Zhao, Senior Software Engineer

Developer of human interface solutions. The company's products find application in mobile computing and entertainment devices.

**Synaptris Inc**   HQ
3031 Tisch Way Ste 300
San Jose CA 95128
P: 914-620-1614  F: 408-351-0199  PRC:322
www.synaptris.com
Email: info@synaptris.com
Estab: 1998

Madan Kumar, CEO

Provider of business reporting solutions. The company's products include IntelliVIEW, IntelliPRINT, and Synaptris Widget Viewer.

**Synchron Networks Inc**   HQ
100 Enterprise Way C230
Scotts Valley CA 95066
P: 831-461-9735  F: 831-401-2359  PRC:323
www.synchronnetworks.com
Email: info@synchronnetworks.com
Emp: 1-10  Estab: 1999

Carl Fravel, CEO

Developer of application and file distribution software. The company focuses on system management and digital asset delivery services.

**Syncplicity LLC**   HQ
2811 Mission College Blvd FL 7
Santa Clara CA 95054
P: 888-997-9627  PRC:325
www.syncplicity.com
Email: sales@syncplicity.com
Estab: 2007

Leonard Chung, Founder
Jeetu Patel, General Manager of Syncplicity Business Unit

Provider of cloud-based file management solutions such as access, sync, backup and share of files from anywhere for businesses and individuals.

**Synder Filtration**   HQ
4941 Allison Pkwy
Vacaville CA 95688
P: 707-451-6060  F: 707-451-6064  PRC:56
www.synderfiltration.com
Email: sales@synderfiltration.com
Estab: 1994

Charles Jao, VP of Engineering
Jeff Yeh, President
Carl Garcia, Manager

Manufacturer of membranes and systems. The company offers training and performance evaluation services. It serves mining, biotech, and food industries.

**Synergenics LLC**   HQ
1700 Owens St
San Francisco CA 94158
P: 415-554-8170  PRC:28
Estab: 2002

William Rutter, CEO
Bill Rutter, Chairman
Ella Zeltser, Accounting Manager

Provider of life science services. The company also provides financial support and shared laboratory services.

**Synergex**   HQ
2330 Gold Meadow Way
Gold River CA 95670
P: 916-635-7300  F: 916-635-6549  PRC:322
www.synergex.com
Email: information@synergex.com
Emp: 1-10  Estab: 1976

Kenneth Lidster, Synergex Co-Founder
Michele Wong, CEO
William Mooney, President
Roger Andrews, CTO
Daniela Calvitti, CFO

Provider of business application optimization solutions. The company serves the transportation, retail, and manufacturing sectors.

**Synergy Business Solutions**   HQ
582 Market St Ste 1204
San Francisco CA 94104
P: 415-263-1843  F: 415-263-1846  PRC:323
www.synergybiz.com
Email: synergy@synergybiz.com
Estab: 1993

Michael Bark, Director of Marketing
Bill Perrin, VP of Operations
Jim Bruckner, Administration Director
Sophie O'Neal, Principal

Provider of technology evaluation, business process improvement, and custom software development services to a wide range of sectors.

**Synopsys Corporate**   HQ
690 E Middlefield Rd
Mountain View CA 94043
P: 650-584-5000  PRC:322
www.synopsys.com
Sales: Over $3B

Tom De Schutter, VP of Engineering Embedded Software & Systems Solutions
Howard Ko, General Manager of Silicon Engineering Group
Yervant Zorian, Chief Architect Fellow
Chi-Foon Chan, Co-CEO
Aart de Geus, CEO

Developer of synthesis technology solutions. The company is also involved in design flow deployment, physical design assistance, and related services.

**Syntest Technologies Inc**   HQ
4320 Stevens Creek Blvd Ste 100
San Jose CA 95129
P: 408-720-9956  F: 408-720-9960  PRC:323
www.syntest.com
Email: info@syntest.com
Estab: 1990

Shianling Wu, VP of Engineering

Provider of test solutions for the electronics industry. The company is involved in fault simulation solutions and services.

**Syntonic Microwave Inc**   HQ
275 E Hacienda Ave
Campbell CA 95008
P: 408-866-5900  F: 408-866-5901  PRC:209
www.syntonicmicrowave.com
Email: sales@syntonicmicrowave.com

Jerry McCoy, VP of Engineering
Jay Goodfriend, President

Manufacturer of wire-band receivers, generators, translators, and related accessories. The company specializes in customization.

**Syrma Technology**   BR
4340 Stevens Creek Blvd Ste 275
San Jose CA 95129
P: 408-404-0500  PRC:77
www.syrmatech.com
Estab: 2006

Paul Dahl, Director of Business Development

Provider of entrepreneurial manufacturing services. The company's products include magnetics, memory, and RFID.

**System Biosciences Inc**   HQ
265 N Whisman Rd
Mountain View CA 94043-3911
P: 650-968-2200  F: 650-968-2277  PRC:32
www.systembio.com
Email: info@systembio.com

Jacob Lesnik, VP of Sales and Marketing and Commercial Development
Laurie Goldman, Sales Manager
Paul Kao, EVP

Provider of genome-wide analysis of the mechanisms that regulate cellular processes and biological responses.

**System General USA**   DH
6469 Almaden Expy Ste 80#377
San Jose CA 95035
P: 833-845-3900  PRC:212
www.sg.com.tw
Estab: 1983

Don Yang, Director of Finance

Designer and manufacturer of device programmers and offers consultancy services in device programming and power management.

**Systemacs**  HQ
616 Ramona St Ste 27
Palo Alto CA 94301
P: 650-329-9745  PRC:100
www.systemacs.com
Email: info@systemacs.com

Ken Easterby, Founder

Provider of solutions for upgrading or setting up
networks which include hardware, software, and
routers.

**Systems Studies Inc**  HQ
2-1340 E Cliff D
Santa Cruz CA 95062
P: 831-475-5777  F: 831-475-9207  PRC:62
www.airtalk.com
Email: support@airtalk.com
Emp: 11-50 Estab: 1979

Diane Bordoni, CEO
David Cook, HVAC Service Estimator

Supplier of cable pressurization products. The
company is involved in training services and it
serves the telephone industry.

**Systron Donner Inertial**  BR
2700 Systron Dr
Concord CA 94518
P: 925-979-4500  F: 925-349-1366  PRC:17
emcore.com
Email: sales@emcore.com
Estab: 2001

Michael Souza, Staff Software Engineer
Lonny Louie, Senior Quality Manager
David Hoyh, Director of Marketing
Ted Henry, International Marketing & Sales
Manager
Adrienne Warren, Marketing Coordinator

Manufacturer of high performance guidance and
motion systems. The company serves defense,
energy, transportation, and other sectors.

**SyTech Solutions Inc**  HQ
9362 Studio Ct
Elk Grove CA 95758
P: 916-381-3010  PRC:323
www.sytechsolutions.com
Emp: 1-10  Estab: 2000

Bryan Golden, President
Sam Velasquez, Director of Information Services
Jon Pritt, VP
Casey Morris, Account Manager

Provider of document management technology
services. The company offers archieve scanning,
web-based document management, and data
capture services.

**T & K Machine**  HQ
257 Wright Brothers Ave
Livermore CA 94551
P: 925-344-7091  F: 925-344-7093  PRC:80
www.tk-machine.com
Estab: 1994

Tony Gallien, Owner

Designer and manufacturer of precision machines.
The company also offers services like plating,
labeling, powdercoat, and silkscreen.

**T&D Communications**  BR
44830 Osgood Rd
Fremont CA 94539
P: 510-824-0010  F: 510-824-0027  PRC:63
tanddcomm.com
Email: info@tanddcomm.com
Estab: 1982

Anthony Alonzo, Data Installer

Supplier of telephones, and data and paging
equipment. The company also specializes in
installation.

**T&T Precision Inc**  HQ
1290 Pacific St
Union City CA 94587
P: 510-429-8088  F: 510-429-8488  PRC:80
www.ttprecision.com
Estab: 2003

Toan Tran, CEO
Thuan Nguyen, VP of Operations

Provider of precision machining services. The
company specializes in electronics, automotive,
and semiconductor equipment.

**T&T Valve & Instrument Inc**  HQ
1181 Quarry Ln Ste 150
Pleasanton CA 94566
P: 925-484-4898  F: 925-484-4727  PRC:166
www.tt-valve.com
Email: sales@tt-valve.com
Estab: 1987

Mike Harlan, Sales Engineer
Todd Wolfe, President
Javier Cendejas, General Manager

Provider of manual and automated valves to
industrial, municipal water, and wastewater industries. The company focuses on project assistance.

**T-Star Enterprises Inc**  HQ
966 77th Ave
Oakland CA 94621
P: 510-635-2736  F: 510-635-2738  PRC:280
thermalpoolcover.com
Estab: 1999

Han Tunggal, Owner

Manufacturer of deployers, manual storage reels,
and motorized re-winders. The company's services include repairs and parts replacement.

**Tactus Technology Inc**  HQ
47509 Seabridge Dr
Fremont CA 94538
P: 510-244-3968  F: 650-641-2348  PRC:68
www.tactustechnology.com
Email: support@tactustechnology.com
Estab: 2008

Justin Virgili, VP of Engineering
Ryosuke Isobe, Director of Process Engineering
Jonah Arines, Engineering Technician
Matthew Han, Materials Engineering Associate
Brian Flamm, Senior Material Engineer

Developer of tactile user interface for touchscreen
devices. The company serves the industrial and
technological sectors.

**Takex America Inc**  DH
151 San Zeno Way
Sunnyvale CA 94086
P: 408-747-0100  F: 408-734-1100  PRC:233
www.takex.com
Email: sales@takex.com
Estab: 1982

Rayman Ganap, Inside Sales
Gary Buth, Director of Technical Sales

Manufacturer of security and industrial sensor
products. The company's products include photo-
electric beams, outdoor and indoor PIR, and tower
enclosures.

**Talari Networks**  HQ
1 Almaden Blvd Ste 200
San Jose CA 95113
P: 408-689-0400  F: 408-864-2124  PRC:323
www.talari.com
Email: info@talari.com
Estab: 2006

Leo Ang, Software Engineer
Talari Sys, QA Engineer
Wei Huang, Staff Software Engineer
Sonia Rovner, Software Engineer
Rashmi Anand, Software Engineer

Provider of enterprise WANs. The company focuses on the banking, healthcare, manufacturing, and
mining industries.

**Talisman Systems Group Inc**  HQ
1111 Oak St
San Francisco CA 94117
P: 727-424-4261  PRC:323
www.talispoint.com
Estab: 1999

Monique Barkett, President
William Yu, Director of Technology
David Lovgren, Product Manager

Provider of document and panel management
tools. The company serves insurance companies
and managed care organizations.

**TalkCycle LLC**  HQ
63 Bovet Rd Ste 208
San Mateo CA 94402
P: 888-400-2220  PRC:319
www.frontspin.com
Email: info@frontspin.com
Estab: 2015

Mansour Salame, Founder
Randy Rubingh, Chief Customer Officer
Aaron Browning, VP of Sales
V. Kate, Product Manager

Providers of innovative sales communication
software.

**Tamalpais Group Inc**  HQ
PO Box 2564
San Anselmo CA 94979
P: 415-455-5770  F: 415-455-5771  PRC:326
www.tamgroup.com
Email: contact@tamgroup.com
Estab: 1995

Jyll Cassidy, CFO
Christian Franklin, Managing Partner

Provider of information technology solutions. The
company offers data-centric delivery, infrastructure assessment, and IT performance services.

**Tamura Corporation of America** BR
1040 S Andreasen Dr Ste 100
Escondido CA 92029
P: 760-871-2009   F: 760-740-0536    PRC:200
www.tamura-ss.co.jp

Jonathan Parker, COO

Manufacturer of DC power modules, current
sensor products, telecom transformers, and LED
products. The company is involved in distribution
services.

**Tangent Inc** HQ
191 Airport Blvd
Burlingame CA 94010
P: 650-342-9388   F: 650-342-9380    PRC:120
www.tangent.com
Email: support@tangent.com
Estab: 1989

Kevin Bradley, Director of Healthcare Solutions

Provider of computer solutions. The company
caters to healthcare, industrial, and military
applications.

**Tango Systems Inc** HQ
1980 Concourse Dr
San Jose CA 95131
P: 408-526-2330   F: 408-526-2336    PRC:124
www.tangosystemsinc.com
Email: info@tangosystemsinc.com

Lee LaBlanc, Senior Mechanical Engineer
Beverly Huss, President
Ravi Mullapudi, President
Harshal Vasa, Manufacturing Manager

Supplier of cluster tools for dielectric films. The
company's services include processing, thin film
deposition, and quality analysis.

**Tanium Inc** HQ
2100 Powell St Ste 300
Emeryville CA 94608
P: 510-704-0202    PRC:327
www.tanium.com
Email: info@tanium.com
Estab: 2007

Christian Hunt, SVP of Engineering
David Hindawi, Co-Founder
Orion Hindawi, Co-Founder
Thomas Stanley, Chief Revenue Officer
Charles Ross, Chief Customer Officer

Provider of IT operations management, asset visibility, and security hygiene solutions. The company
serves the healthcare and retail industries.

**Tapemation Machining Inc** HQ
13 Janis Way
Scotts Valley CA 95066
P: 831-438-3069   F: 831-438-2094    PRC:80
tapemation.com
Emp: 1-10

John Stepovich, General Manager

Manufacturer of machined parts and tools for
the aircraft, marine, electronic, solar, and space
communication industries.

**Tapjoy Inc** HQ
111 Sutter St Fl 13
San Francisco CA 94104
P: 415-766-6900    PRC:322
tapjoy.com
Estab: 2007

Steve Wadsworth, President
Jeff Drobick, Chief Product Officer
Paul Longhenry, VP
Peter Dille, CMO
Sarah Chafer, Senior Director of Strategic Ac-
counts & Planning

Provider of advertising and targeting solutions.
The company also deals with developer services
such as consulting and real-time reporting.

**Taracom Integrated Products** HQ
1220 Memorex Dr
Santa Clara CA 95050
P: 408-691-6655    PRC:212
taracom.net
Estab: 2000

Farhad Haghighi, CEO

Provider of multi-gigabit solutions for communications and storage applications. The company's
solutions include backplane and fiber channel.

**Tarana Wireless Inc** HQ
590 Alder Dr
Milpitas CA 95035
P: 408-351-4085    PRC:61
www.taranawireless.com
Email: info@taranawireless.com
Estab: 2009

Rabin Patra, Co-Founder

Provider of wireless performance solutions. The
company serves the residential and enterprise
markets.

**Taseon Inc** HQ
3099 N First St
San Jose CA 95134
P: 408-240-7800    PRC:97
Estab: 2007

Celeste Rogers, VP of Finance
Celeste Sim, VP of Finance
Sue Whitsett, Director of Finance

Developer of technology related solutions. The
company also offers system engineering and
software development services.

**Tavis Corp** HQ
3636 Hwy 49 S
Mariposa CA 95338
P: 209-966-2027   F: 209-966-3563    PRC:5
www.taviscorp.com
Email: applications@taviscorp.com
Emp: 1-10   Estab: 1969

Scott Carpenter, Staff Electrical Engineer
Carlo Sepe, Project Engineer
Dina Lambert, Information Technology Manager
Carrie Bonillas, Controller

Provider of custom pressure transducer sensor
designs. The company offers services to measurement environments.

**Tazmo Inc** BR
42840 Christy St Ste 103
Fremont CA 94538
P: 510-438-4890   F: 510-226-4871    PRC:159
www.tazmoinc.com
Email: sales@tazmoinc.com

Toshio Torigoe, President
Kelly McCulley, Service Manager

Manufacturer of SOG and LCD color filter coaters.
The company offers SOG, SOD, polyimide coaters
and developers and LCD Resist coaters.

**Tci International Inc** DH
3541 Gateway Blvd
Fremont CA 94538
P: 510-687-6100   F: 510-687-6101    PRC:61
www.spx.com
Estab: 1968
Sales: $1B to $3B

Christopher Dutrow, Electrical Engineer
Gene Lowe, President
Scott Sproule, CFO
Mary Alcon, CFO
Tausha White, VP

Provider of innovative radio frequency solutions.
The company caters to spectrum monitoring and
antenna applications.

**Tcs Healthcare Technologies** HQ
11641 Blocker Dr Ste 200
Auburn CA 95603
P: 530-886-1700    PRC:194
www.tcshealthcare.com
Email: info@tcshealthcare.com
Emp: 1-10   Estab: 1983

Robert Pock, CEO
Luis Luna, Director of Finance
Marissa L., Marketing Associate
Pat Stricker, SVP
Joshua Pock, Office Manager

Provider of care-management solutions. The company offers software implementation and training
and workflow design services.

**TDK Corporation of America** BR
1740 Technology Dr Ste 200
San Jose CA 95110
P: 408-467-5200   F: 408-437-9591    PRC:86
www.tdk.com
Estab: 1981

Christian Hoffman, Senior Chief Researcher
Mitch Oda, Regional Sales Manager
Rick Anderson, Account Manager
Youli Yao, Senior FAE

Distributor of electronic products including
capacitors, inductors, ferrites, factory automation
system, transformers, magnets, and anechoic
chambers.

**Tdn Electric Inc** HQ
1071 Wright Ave
Mountain View CA 94043
P: 650-968-8000   F: 650-968-8222    PRC:124
tdnelectric.com
Estab: 1997

Tim Daniels, President

Retailer of electrical construction services for
lighting, uninterruptible power supply, fire alarm,
and photovoltaic systems.

**Teamf1 Inc** HQ
39270 Paseo Padre Pkwy Ste 153
Fremont CA 94538
P: 510-505-9931  F: 510-505-9941  PRC:319
www.teamf1.com
Estab: 1998

Hitesh Patel, Business Operations Manager

Provider of networking and security software for embedded devices. The company also offers technical support services.

**Tecdia Inc** HQ
2255 S Bascom Ave Ste 120
Campbell CA 95008
P: 408-748-0100  F: 408-748-0111  PRC:80
us.tecdia.com
Email: sales@tecdia.com
Estab: 1985

Shinn Wolfe, VP

Manufacturer of precision machine tools and fixtures. The company also specializes in cutting and scribing tools.

**Tech Soft 3d** HQ
931 Ashby Ave
Berkeley CA 94710-2805
P: 510-883-2180  F: 510-883-2193  PRC:323
www.techsoft3d.com
Estab: 1996

Ryan Clark, Software Engineering Manager
Oren Radousky, Software Engineer
Amerigo Masini, Software Engineer
Peter Curtis, Software Engineer
Matthew LaRocca, Software Engineer

Provider of software solutions. The company offers software for desktop visualization, modeling, cloud and mobile solutions, and data exchange.

**Techbiz Inc** RH
48501 Warm Springs Blvd Ste 101
Fremont CA 94539
P: 510-249-6800  F: 510-249-6808  PRC:67
techbizinc.com
Email: sales@techbizinc.com
Estab: 1998

Anthony Thia, President
Kristine Kim, VP

Provider of custom network and server solutions. The company is involved in design and deployment services.

**TechExcel Inc** HQ
3675 Mt Diablo Blvd Ste 330
Lafayette CA 94549
P: 925-871-3900  F: 925-871-3991  PRC:322
techexcel.com
Email: sales@techexcel.com
Estab: 1995

Dan Randall, Inside Sales Manager
Prince Huang, Director of Operations & Marketing
Jason Hammon, Director of Product Management
Lin Pan, QA Manager
Hu Peng, Senior Development Manager

Provider of customer relationship management software applications. The company is involved in game development and hybrid agile management solutions.

**Technavibes Inc** HQ
6518 Commerce Way Ste 4
Diamond Springs CA 95619
P: 530-626-8093  F: 530-626-6901  PRC:159
technavibes.com
Email: dub@technavibes.com
Emp: 1-10  Estab: 1991

Dub Wilson, Owner

Manufacturer of feeder bowls. The company specializes in vibratory bowl feeders, vibratory feeder in-line tracks, and vibratory feeder hoppers.

**Techni-Glass Inc** HQ
7846 Bell Rd
Windsor CA 95492
P: 707-838-3325  F: 707-838-3326  PRC:286
www.techni-glass.com
Email: thassur@techni-glass.com
Estab: 1979

Thomas Hassur, Owner

Provider of glass blowing services. The company specializes in glass used for research, laser, oil, and medical services.

**Technic Inc** BR
1254 Alma Ct
San Jose CA 95112
P: 408-287-3732  F: 408-287-0763  PRC:53
www.technic.com
Email: info@technic.com
Estab: 1944

Rick Retzer, Information Technology Manager
George Federman, VP of Project Development

Manufacturer of specialty chemicals, analytical control tools, and surface finishing products. The company offers electroplating & engineered powders.

**TechniQuip Corp** HQ
530 Boulder Ct Ste 103
Pleasanton CA 94566
P: 925-251-9030  F: 925-251-0704  PRC:198
www.techniquip.com
Email: orders@techniquip.com
Estab: 1970

David Wensley, President
Charles Mathewson, Director of Sales
George Gauer, Director of Operations
Robin Steingraf, Materials Controller

Supplier of lighting products. The company's offerings include illuminators, fiber optics, and video equipment.

**Techvalidate Software Inc** HQ
5900 Hollis St Ste S
Emeryville CA 94608
P: 510-982-6640  PRC:322
www.surveymonkey.com
Estab: 2007

Adam Marszal, Account Executive

Provider of online content management services. The company handles content collection, validation, publishing, and utilization services.

**Tecma Co** HQ
1812 Silica Ave
Sacramento CA 95815-3431
P: 916-925-8206  F: 916-925-2135  PRC:80
www.tecmacompany.com
Email: tecma@tecmacompany.com
Emp: 1-10  Estab: 1957

Alfred Nohr, Co-Founder
Fred Schwarz, Co-Founder
Sonia Susac, President

Provider of CNC and conventional precision machining solutions. The company serves the aerospace, commercial, medical, and defense industries.

**Ted Pella Inc** HQ
PO Box 492477
Redding CA 96049-2477
P: 530-243-2200  F: 530-243-3761  PRC:31
www.tedpella.com
Email: sales@tedpella.com
Emp: 1-10  Estab: 1968

Bruce Blizzard, Engineering Manager
Christopher McNeill, Engineer
Tom Pella, President
Ken Cornyn, Director of Manufacturing
Bill Raab, Technology Sales Manager

Distributor of medical supplies and microscopy products such as inverted microscope for science and industry.

**Teikoku Pharma USA Inc** LH
1718 Ringwood Ave
San Jose CA 95131
P: 408-501-1800  F: 408-501-1900  PRC:268
teikokuusa.com
Email: info@teikokuusa.com
Estab: 1997

Ichiro Mori, President
Jutaro Shudo, SVP
Atsumu Matsushita, EVP
Junji Kachi, CFO
Jack Wen, Senior Director of Research & Development

Focuses on the drug development and delivery of treatments for CNS, pain management and oncology. The company serves the medical industry.

**TEKEVER Corp** DH
5201 Great America Pkwy
Santa Clara CA 95054
P: 408-730-2617  F: 408-562-5745  PRC:8
www.tekever.com

Pedro Sinogas, CEO

Developer of technologies for the enterprise, aerospace, defense, and security markets, with subsidiaries in Europe, Asia, and the Americas.

**Teknika Strapping Systems** HQ
761 Mabury Rd Ste 12
San Jose CA 95133
P: 408-441-9071  F: 408-441-9037  PRC:159
www.teknika.com
Email: teknika@teknika.com
Estab: 1988

Dmitry Kondratyev, CEO
Lev Girshfeld, Sales Manager

Provider of hand tools for plastic stripping. The company is engaged in repairs, replacement, and maintenance services.

**Teknova** HQ
2290 Bert Dr
Hollister CA 95023
P: 831-637-1100   F: 831-637-2355   PRC:271
www.teknova.com
Email: info@teknova.com
Emp: 1-10   Estab: 1996

Ted Davis, CEO
Irene Davis, COO
Ashley Holtz, Human Resource Manager

Provider of agar plates and broths for growth of bacterial, yeast, and microbiological applications such as cloning, DNA sequencing, and immunology.

**Tela Innovations Inc** HQ
475 Alberto Way Ste 120
Los Gatos CA 95032
P: 408-558-6300   PRC:208
www.tela-inc.com
Email: information@tela-inc.com
Estab: 2005

Scott Becker, CEO
Dhrumil Gandhi, COO
Peter Calverley, CFO
Neal Carney, VP of Marketing & Business Development
Liz Stewart, VP

Provider of lithography optimized solutions. The company's services include design, implementation, and technical support.

**Teledesign Systems Inc** HQ
1729 S Main St
Milpitas CA 95035
P: 408-941-1808   F: 408-941-1818   PRC:111
www.teledesignsystems.com
Email: productsales@teledesignsystems.com
Estab: 1991

Bruce Delevaux, VP

Provider of wireless data solutions. The company manufactures wireless industrial modems for commercial and industrial data collection applications.

**Teledyne Risi Inc** HQ
PO Box 359
Tracy CA 95378
P: 925-456-9700   PRC:47
www.teledynerisi.com
Email: risisales@teledyne.com
Emp: 1-10   Estab: 1984

Derek Hanton, Engineer
Jim Varosh, General Manager
Gary Grigsby, EHS Coordinator

Manufacturer of exploding bridge wire detonators. The company also manufactures electronic firing systems.

**Telemakus LLC** HQ
13405 Folsom Blvd Ste 502
Folsom CA 95630
P: 916-458-6346   F: 916-939-8713   PRC:87
www.telemakus.com
Email: mail@telemakus.com
Emp: 1-10   Estab: 2004

Craig Walsh, CEO
Paul Clark, Owner

Provider of USB controlled RF devices. The company devices include switches, vector modulators, and digital attenuators.

**Telemanagement Technologies Inc** HQ
2700 Ygnacio Valley Rd Ste 250
Walnut Creek CA 94598
P: 925-946-9800   F: 925-946-9801   PRC:319
www.telmantec.com
Email: sales@telmantec.com
Estab: 1987

Lou Sandler, Chief Software Architect
Charles Coakley, VP of Sales & Marketing
Tej Bloom, Accounting Manager
Pablo Sanchez, Project Manager

Provider of telemanagement software products and services. The company is engaged in troubleshooting and maintenance services.

**Teleresults Corp** HQ
870 Market St Ste 556
San Francisco CA 94102
P: 415-392-9670   F: 415-392-9674   PRC:322
teleresults.com
Email: info@teleresults.com
Estab: 1995

Tyler Charles, Support Engineer
James Jeha, Network Consultant
Darren Guan, Medical Software Developer

Provider of electronic medical record solutions and transplant software. The company's services include data conversion, interfaces, and training.

**TeleVital** HQ
1525 McCarthy Blvd Ste 1045
Milpitas CA 95035
P: 408-441-6732   PRC:194
www.televital.com
Email: info@televital.com
Estab: 2002

Kishore Rao, Founder

Provider of integrated electronic patient medical record and real-time telemedicine software modules.

**Telewave Inc** HQ
660 Giguere Ct
San Jose CA 95133
P: 408-929-4400   F: 408-929-4007   PRC:61
www.telewave.com
Email: sales@telewave.com
Estab: 1972

Jeff Cornehl, Associate Systems Engineer
Brad Senge, Senior International Sales Engineer
Robert Bagheri, CEO
Frank Amaral, Painter

Provider of wireless products such as transmitter couplers and receiver multi couplers. The company also offers antennas.

**Telosa Software Inc** HQ
610 Cowper St
Palo Alto CA 94301
P: 800-750-6418   F: 650-853-1677   PRC:323
www.telosa.com
Email: info@telosa.com
Estab: 1986

David Blyer, Co-Founder
Susan Packard Orr, Co-Founder
Gregg Davis, CEO
Sylvia Gastelbondo, CTO Online Fundraising
Frank Horkey, CFO

Provider of CRM and fundraising software for nonprofits. The company focuses on gift and grant tracking, donor and volunteer management.

**Tempo Automation** HQ
2460 Alameda St
San Francisco CA 94103
P: 415-320-1261   PRC:207
tempoautomation.com
Email: support@tempoautomation.com

Jeff McAlvay, Co-Founder
Jesse Koenig, Co-Founder
Daniel Radler, Operations Quality Manager
Christine Pearsall, VP of Marketing
Sophia Ouyang, Logistics Manager

Specializes in printed circuit board assemblies. The company is engaged in design and delivery services.

**Ten Pao International Inc** HQ
333 W El Camino Real Unit 380
Sunnyvale CA 94087
P: 408-389-3560   F: 408-389-3564   PRC:200
www.tenpaoinc.com
Email: request@tenpaoinc.com
Estab: 1979

Etienne Finet, VP of Business Development

Manufacturer of power supply systems such as switchings, displays, and traditional linear transformers.

**Tenera Environmental** HQ
971 Dewing Ave Ste 101
Lafayette CA 94549
P: 925-962-9769   F: 925-962-9758   PRC:142
tenera.com
Email: environmental@tenera.com

David Mayer, Owner
Doc Fish, President
Carol Raifsnider, VP
Eric Sommerauer, Biologist

Provider of environmental consulting, stream restoration, power generation support, and minerals management services.

**Tenergy Corp** HQ
436 Kato Ter
Fremont CA 94539
P: 510-687-0388   F: 510-687-0328   PRC:208
www.tenergybattery.com
Email: sales@tenergy.com
Estab: 2004

Jane Xie, Purchasing Manager
Lena Beppu, Sales Account Manager
Brian Qu, Warehouse Manager
Chi-An Chai, HR Manager
Alberto Lam, Graphic Designer

Designer and manufacturer of batteries and chargers. The company serves medical, consumer electronics, data management, military, and other sectors.

**Tennebaum-Manheim Engineers Inc** HQ
414 Mason St Ste 605
San Francisco CA 94102
P: 415-772-9891   PRC:304
tmesf.com
Email: info@tmesf.com
Estab: 1987

Nancy Tennebaum, Principal

Developer of engineering services. The company's projects include residential housing, commercial properties, and historical buildings.

**Ter Precision** HQ
306 Mathew St
Santa Clara CA 95050
P: 408-986-9920 PRC:80
Estab: 1984

Scott Jacobs, General Manager
Daryl Gillum, General Manager
Andrew Cech, Machinist
Douglas Cech, Programmer

Provider of CNC machining, metal fabrication, frame fabrication, and assembly services. The company focuses on prototype machining and milling.

**Terabit Radios Inc** HQ
1148 Cadillac Ct
Milpitas CA 95035
P: 408-431-6032 PRC:68
www.terabitradios.com
Email: info@terabitradios.com
Estab: 2012

Srinivas Sivaprakasam, Founder
S. Srinivas, CEO
Bruce Carpenter, VP of Global Sales

Manufacturer of wireless radios. The company offers IP-centric (Gigabit & Multi-Gigabit) LoS wireless IP transport technologies to its clients.

**Teradyne Inc** BR
875 Embedded Way
San Jose CA 95138
P: 480-777-7090 PRC:209
www.teradyne.com
Estab: 1960

Brad Robbins, President of LitePoint
Gregory Smith, President of Semiconductor Test Division
Jurgen von Hollen, President of Universal Robots
Mark Jagiela, CEO
Sanjay Mehta, VP

Supplier of automatic test equipment. The company caters to semiconductor, electronics, and automotive sectors.

**Teresonic LLC** HQ
1215 Fiddlers Green
San Jose CA 95125
P: 877-287-1649 PRC:60
www.teresonic.com
Email: info@teresonic.com

Mike Zivkovic, President
Miles Dabic, Chief Scientist

Designer and manufacturer of loudspeakers. The company also offers cables, amplifiers, and related products.

**Terminal Manufacturing Company LLC** HQ
707 Gilman St
Berkeley CA 94710
P: 510-526-3071 F: 510-526-3138 PRC:88
www.terminalmanufacturing.com
Email: tmci@terminalmanufacturing.com
Estab: 1918

Steve Mellinger, Owner

Designer and manufacturer of vacuum chambers, pressure vessels, truck tanks, and assorted fabrications.

**Terrace Consulting Inc** HQ
PO Box 597
San Francisco CA 94104
P: 415-848-7300 F: 415-848-7301 PRC:323
www.terrace.com
Estab: 1992

Samruddhi Suryaji, Software Engineer I
Shinya Ito, Software Engineer
Todd Ziesing, CEO
Tracy Leung, Director of Finance & Operations
Lisa Leung, VP of Project Management Office

Provider of custom software development services. The company focuses on eCommerce, back office, business intelligence, cloud, and other services.

**Terradex Inc** HQ
855 El Camino Real Ste 311
Palo Alto CA 94301
P: 650-227-3250 F: 650-227-3255 PRC:139
terradex.com
Email: sales@terradex.com
Estab: 2002

Bob Wenzlau, CEO
Peter Biffar, President
J. Sowinski, VP of Environmental Protection Services
Sara Strojwas, Project Manager

Provider of web and consulting services. The company offers dig clean, cleanupdeck, and web development services.

**Terrapass Inc** HQ
527 Howard St Fl 4
San Francisco CA 94105
P: 877-210-9581 PRC:139
www.terrapass.com
Email: info@terrapass.com
Estab: 2004

Erin Craig, CEO

Provider of carbon management solutions for farms, landfills, and wind power installations. The company specializes in project management and sales.

**Terraphase Engineering** HQ
1404 Franklin Ste 600
Oakland CA 94612
P: 510-645-1850 F: 510-380-6304 PRC:139
www.terraphase.com
Email: info@terraphase.com
Estab: 2010

William Carson, President
Doug Wolf, Principal Engineer
Hans Kramer, Associate Engineer
Nader Sherif, Associate Engineer
Alice Hale, Senior Project Engineer

Provider of environmental consulting services. The company offers environmental due diligence, and soil and groundwater remediation services.

**Terrasat Communications Inc** HQ
315 Digital Dr
Morgan Hill CA 95037
P: 408-782-5911 F: 408-782-5912 PRC:70
www.terrasatinc.com
Email: sales@terrasatinc.com
Estab: 1994

Jit Patel, President
Mary Convertino, Human Resource Administrator
Tony Morales, QC Inspector
Jason Saffell, Technical Sales Manager
Carl Hurst, VP of Operations

Manufacturer of RF solutions. The company caters to satellite communication and digital microwave systems.

**Tesco Controls Inc** HQ
8440 Florin Rd
Sacramento CA 95828
P: 916-395-8800 F: 916-429-2817 PRC:65
www.tescocontrols.com
Email: sales@tescocontrols.com
Emp: 11-50 Estab: 1972

Van Nguyen, Electrical Engineer
Menovue Lo, Instrumentation
Stephen Dicks, Engineer
Hoan Tran, Engineer
Dale Holler, Sales Engineer

Manufacturer of instrumentation, control systems, and service pedestals for water and traffic sectors. The company offers system integration services.

**Tesla** HQ
3500 Deer Creek Rd
Palo Alto CA 94304
P: 6500-681-5000 PRC:130
www.tesla.com
Email: press@tesla.com
Estab: 2003
Sales: Over $3B

Doug Field, SVP of Engineering
Elon Musk, CEO
Gilbert Passin, VP of Manufacturing
Brad Buss, Director
Josh Cohen, Trainer

Designer and manufacturer of electric sedans and electric SUVs. The company is engaged in the production of energy storage systems.

**Test O Pac Industries Inc** HQ
1188 Murphy Ave
San Jose CA 95131
P: 408-436-1117 F: 408-436-1255 PRC:139
www.testopac.com
Estab: 1977

Oscar Joya, Quality
Sam Sohal, President

Provider of environmental and package testing services. The company deals with component testing, product reliability, and medical package testing.

**Test21 Inc** HQ
48511 Warm Springs Blvd Ste 210
Fremont CA 94539
P: 510-438-0221   F: 510-438-0229   PRC:211
www.test21.com
Email: sales@test21.com

Tatang Putra, Software Engineer
Bon Ho, President

Designer and manufacturer of printed circuit
boards including probe cards for semiconductor,
ATE manufacturers, and silicon wafer foundries.

**Testamerica Laboratories Inc** BR
880 Riverside Pkwy
West Sacramento CA 95605
P: 916-373-5600   PRC:142
www.testamericainc.com
Email: webmaster@testamericainc.com
Emp: 11-50

Eric Redman, Director of Technical

Provider of environmental testing services. The
company offers indoor air quality, air testing and
emissions, and industrial hygiene services.

**Testmetrix Inc** HQ
426 S Hillview Dr
Milpitas CA 95035
P: 408-730-5511   PRC:19
www.testmetrix.com

Mike Bulat, VP of Engineering
Nick Balmez, Senior Hardware Engineer
Christian Cojocneanu, President

Manufacturer of high-throughput AVTE systems,
and offers official compliance certification test
services.

**Text Analysis International Inc** HQ
10146 Alpine Dr Unit 1
Cupertino CA 95014
P: 650-308-9323   PRC:325
www.textanalysis.com
Email: info@textanalysis.com
Estab: 1998

Avi Meyers, CEO
Amnon Meyers, CTO
Keith Woods-Holder, COO

Provider of software development services for
text analysis. The company focuses on project
management, testing and implementation, and
deployment.

**TextDigger Inc** HQ
12 S First St Ste 620
San Jose CA 95113
P: 408-416-3142   PRC:324
textdigger.com
Email: info@textdigger.com
Estab: 2005

Tim Musgrove, Founder

Developer of horizontal semantic solutions for
search engines. The company focuses on content
mining and analytics.

**TFD Group/Systems Exchange Inc** BR
80 Garden Court Ste 240
Monterey CA 93940
P: 831-649-3800   PRC:322
www.tfdg.com
Estab: 1976

Robert Nomelli, Director of Business Development

Developer of analytical methods and software
tools. The company caters to aerospace and
defense sectors.

**Tg Service Inc** HQ
PO Box 21225
El Sobrante CA 94820
P: 510-243-9931   PRC:326
genepilot.com
Email: sales@genepilot.com
Estab: 1998

Brett Miller, President

Producer of multimedia and internet solutions.
The company engages in microarray analysis on
machines.

**The Armada Group Inc** HQ
325 Soquel Ave
Santa Cruz CA 95062
P: 800-408-2120   F: 831-515-5111   PRC:323
www.thearmadagroup.com
Email: info@thearmadagroup.com
Emp: 11-50 Estab: 1995

Jeff Tavangar, Founder
Lisa Sullivan, COO
Tim Chapman, EVP
Jennifer Ireland, Business Development Manager

Provider of information technology and talent
consultation services. The company specializes in
software engineering and project management.

**The Best Electrical Company Inc** HQ
667 Walnut St
San Jose CA 95110
P: 408-287-2040   F: 408-287-0487   PRC:76
www.besteleco.com
Email: info@besteleco.com
Estab: 1954

Vic Giacalone, Owner

Provider of tenant improvement and maintenance
services for the retail, commercial, industrial, and
residential communities.

**THE BROACH MASTERS Inc** HQ
1605 Industrial Dr
Auburn CA 95603
P: 530-885-1939   F: 530-885-8157   PRC:80
www.broachmasters.com
Email: info@broachmasters.com
Emp: 1-10

Jim Shaneyfelt, Gear Shop Manager

Manufacturer of broaches, disc shapers, disc
shaper cutters, shank shapers, shank shaper
cutters, gear shaper cutters, and spline broaches.

**The Cohen Group** HQ
1660 S Amphlett Blvd Ste 110
San Mateo CA 94402
P: 650-349-9737   F: 650-349-3378   PRC:136
www.thecohengroup.com
Email: admin@thecohengroup.com
Estab: 1980

Joel Cohen, President
Timothy Bormann, VP
Deneen Barsi, Office Manager

Provider of health and safety training, litigation
support, indoor air quality, microbial contamination, and related services.

**The Cooper Companies Inc** HQ
6140 Stoneridge Mall Rd Ste 590
Pleasanton CA 94588
P: 925-460-3600   PRC:173
www.coopercos.com
Email: info@cooperco.com
Estab: 1980

Albert White, President
Daniel McBride, EVP
Paul Remmell, President
Nicholas Pichotta, CEO
Bob Weiss, CEO

Provider of healthcare solutions. The company
offers health and wellness programs for women,
individuals, and communities.

**The Detection Group Inc** HQ
440 N Wolfe Rd MS Ste 124
Sunnyvale CA 94085
P: 650-215-7300   PRC:230
www.thedetectiongroup.com
Email: info@thedetectiongroup.com
Estab: 2006

Jens Rasmussen, VP of Engineering & Architec-
ture
Matt Barth, Co-Founder
Laurie Conner, President
Mark Belinsky, COO
Cindy Anderson, VP of Marketing

Provider of monitoring and alarming solutions.
The company offers wireless water leak detection
systems for commercial buildings.

**The Foundry LLC** HQ
4040 Campbell Ave Ste 110
Menlo Park CA 94025
P: 650-326-2656   PRC:189
www.thefoundry.com
Email: info@thefoundry.com
Estab: 1998

Hanson Gifford, CEO

Focuses on product development, prototyping,
market analysis, development, and pre-clinical
and clinical support services.

**The Igneous Group Inc** HQ
PO Box 3702
Santa Cruz CA 95063
P: 831-469-7625   PRC:325
www.igneous.com
Emp: 1-10   Estab: 1991

Geoff Caras, General Manager

Provider of technology consulting services. The
company focuses on web content, application
development, and e-commerce.

**The Lincoln Electric Co**　BR
5030 Hillsdale Cir Ste 106
El Dorado Hills CA 95762
P: 916-939-8788　F: 916-939-8789　PRC:159
www.lincolnelectric.com
Emp: 11-50

Kevin Lowry, Senior Buyer

Provider of industrial control and automation solutions. The company's offerings also include torches, welding guns, and related accessories.

**The Okonite Co**　BR
2440 Camino Ramon Ste 315
San Ramon CA 94583
P: 925-830-0801　F: 925-830-0954　PRC:62
www.okonite.com
Email: info@okonite.com
Estab: 1878

Charlie Hagmaier, Plant Engineering Manager
Keith Weaver, Electrical Engineer
Luis Gonzalez, Manufacturing Engineer
Matt Sharp, Sales Engineer
Patrick Nash, District Manager

Manufacturer of electrical wire insulators. The company offers high and low voltage, instrumentation, and special purpose cables.

**The Olander Company Inc**　HQ
144 Commercial St
Sunnyvale CA 94086
P: 800-538-1500　F: 408-735-6515　PRC:5
www.olander.com
Email: rfq@olander.com
Estab: 1962

Annie Olander, CEO
Tony Desmond, Inside Sales Manager
Michelle Richards, Director of Operations
John Butler, Director of New Business Development
Carl Ericsson, Business Development Manager

Distributor of standard and metric fasteners and electromechanical components. The company offers tools, adhesives, and wire management products.

**The Wecker Group**　HQ
462 Webster St Ste 1
Monterey CA 93940
P: 831-372-8377　F: 831-372-1353　PRC:325
www.weckergroup.com
Email: wecker@weckergroup.com
Estab: 1974

Robert Wecker, Owner
Ruth Minerva, Senior Designer

Provider of design studio and ad agency services. The company specializes in corporate identity, collateral, TV advertising, and event promotion.

**The Wirebenders**　HQ
2075 Lincoln Ave Ste A
San Jose CA 95125
P: 408-265-5576　F: 408-265-5579　PRC:185
www.thewirebenders.com
Email: info@thewirebenders.com
Estab: 1974

Gary Hawke, Owner

Provider of clinical support, research, and development services. The company specializes in appliance designs.

**Themis Computer**　HQ
47200 Bayside Pkwy
Fremont CA 94538
P: 510-252-0870　F: 510-490-5529　PRC:95
www.mrcy.com
Estab: 1968

Mark Aslett, President
Michael Ruppert, EVP
Michelle Mccarthy, VP
William Conley, CTO
Didier Thibaud, EVP

Provider of embedded computing solutions for system integrators and OEMs. The company provides RES servers and HPCs, and rugged storage appliances.

**TheraBiol Inc**　HQ
185 Berry St (Lbby 6) China Basin Ste 350
San Francisco CA 94107
P: 415-608-3841　PRC:196
www.therabiol.com
Email: info@therabiol.com
Estab: 2012

Girish Vyas, Founder
Mel Kronick, Chief Business Advisor
Ramani Aiyer, EVP
Evelin Szakal, Director

Developer of therapies for the treatment of infectious diseases caused by agents such as Human Immunodeficiency Virus (HIV).

**Theraject Inc**　HQ
39270 Paseo Padre
Fremont CA 94536
P: 510-742-5832　F: 510-796-5732　PRC:261
www.theraject.com
Email: info@theraject.com

Sung-Yun Kwon, Founder

Developer of drug micro-needle technologies. The company is engaged in vaccine and also drug deliveries.

**Theralife Inc**　HQ
650 B Fremont Ave Ste 218
Los Altos CA 94022
P: 650-949-6080　PRC:251
www.theralife.com
Email: info@theralife.com
Estab: 2000

Yang Lily, CEO

Manufacturer of botanical drugs. The company offer botanicals that provide symptom relief for problems related to eyes.

**Theravance Biopharma Us Inc**　HQ
901 Gateway Blvd
S San Francisco CA 94080
P: 650-808-6000　PRC:268
www.theravance.com
Email: medicalaffairs@theravance.com
Sales: $30M to $100M

Ann Brady, President
Rick Winningham, Chairman
Brett Haumann, SVP of Clinical Development and Chief Medical Officer
Andrew Hindman, SVP
Frank Pasqualone, SVP

Provider of pharmaceuticals. The company develops new medicines with superior efficacy, convenience, tolerability and/or safety.

**TheraVida Inc**　HQ
177 Bovet Rd Ste 600
San Mateo CA 94402
P: 650-638-2335　PRC:257
www.theravida.com
Email: info@theravida.com
Estab: 2002

Ben McGraw, CEO

Developer of pharmaceutical products for the improved treatment of overactive bladder, urge urinary incontinence, and primary focal hyperhidrosis.

**Therm-X**　HQ
3200 Investment Blvd
Hayward CA 94545
P: 510 606-1012　F: 510-441-2414　PRC:157
www.therm-x.com
Email: info@therm-x.com
Estab: 1983

Dan Trujillo, CEO
Linda Trujillo, Controller

Provider of engineered solutions. The company serves the semiconductor, petrochemical, life sciences, and aerospace industries.

**Therma**　HQ
1601 Las Plumas Ave
San Jose CA 95133
P: 408-347-3400　PRC:80
www.therma.com
Email: info@therma.com
Estab: 1967

Clark Lowe, Senior Mechanical Engineer
Mike Fisher, COO
Mark Goupil, Service Director
Greg Conn, Project Manager
Mark Ross, Senior Project Manager

Provider of mechanical contracting services. The company also offers design and installation of environmental systems.

**Thermal Engineering Associates Inc**　HQ
3287 Kifer Rd
Santa Clara CA 95051-0826
P: 650-961-5900　F: 650-323-9237　PRC:212
www.thermengr.net
Email: info@thermengr.com
Estab: 1997

Bernie Siegal, Manager
Bill Ribble, Manager

Provider of semiconductor thermal measurement and modeling solutions. The company's products include thermal test systems, test fixtures, and test chips.

**Thermal Press International Inc**　HQ
341 Stealth Ct
Livermore CA 94551
P: 925-454-9800　F: 925-454-9810　PRC:153
www.thermalpress.com
Estab: 1976

Ian McLean, Owner
Lance Crawford, VP of Sales
Nathan Zimmerman, Designer

Manufacturer of thermal presses and heat staking machines. The company also offers heat sealing and degating machinery.

**Thermochem Inc** HQ
3414 Regional Pkwy Ste A
Santa Rosa CA 95403
P: 707-575-1310   F: 707-575-7932   PRC:14
www.thermochem.com
Estab: 1985

Mark Broaddus, Engineering Manager
Russell Kunzman, Senior Chemist
Matt Broaddus, Field Service Manager
Kaitlin Marie, Laboratory Project Coordinator
Lori Leigh, Office Administrator

Provider of chemical engineering, laboratory analysis, geochemistry and field testing services and products to a wide range of energy industries.

**ThermoGenesis Holdings Inc** HQ
2711 Citrus Rd
Rancho Cordova CA 95742
P: 916-858-5100   PRC:31
thermogenesis.com
Email: customerservice@thermogenesis.com
Emp: 11-50 Estab: 1986
Sales: $3M to $10M

Haihong Zhu, President
Chris Xu, CEO
Philip Coelho, CTO
Jeff Cauble, VP of Finance
James Xu, General Counsel

Manufacturer of therapeutic products and related supplies. The company is involved in cellular bioprocessing and bone marrow transplants.

**Theron Pharmaceuticals** HQ
365 San Aleso Ave
Sunnyvale CA 94085
P: 408-792-7424   F: 408-744-6773   PRC:261
www.theronpharma.com
Email: info@theronpharma.com
Estab: 2008

Xiaoming Zhang, Founder

Developer of long acting M3 muscarinic antagonist (LAMA) for the improved treatment of chronic respiratory diseases.

**Think Connected LLC** HQ
365 Main St
San Francisco CA 94105
P: 877-684-4654   F: 510-291-3076   PRC:323
www.thinkconnected.com
Email: info@thinkconnected.com
Estab: 2003

Tom Ivers, President
Joshua Demitro, Information Technology Service Manager
David Smart, System Administrator

Provider of data center, consulting, managed, and supplemental information technology services for small and medium-sized businesses.

**Thinkify** HQ
18450 Technology Dr Ste E1
Morgan Hill CA 95037
P: 408-782-7111   PRC:323
thinkifyit.com
Email: support@thinkifyit.com
Estab: 2008

Peter Soule, Founder

Provider of radio frequency identification technology application services. The company provides engineering services as well.

**Thinkoptics** HQ
5568 Del Oro Dr
San Jose CA 95124
P: 765-889-2848   PRC:97
thinkoptics.com
Email: sales@thinkoptics.com

Anders Jepsen, Founder

Provider of software solutions. The company's products include iWavit Blast, iWavit Premium, iWavit Basic, and Wavit 3D.

**Third Pillar Systems** HQ
577 Airport Blvd 8th Fl
Burlingame CA 94010
P: 650-372-1200   F: 650-240-0364   PRC:322
www.thirdpillar.com
Email: sales@thirdpillar.com
Estab: 1999

Anil Chalamalasetti, Software Engineer
Pankaj Chowdhry, President
Charles Stuard, Managing Director of Sales

Developer of networks and software for the commercial lending industry. The company offers implementation and integration services.

**Thor Electronics of California** HQ
420 W Market St
Salinas CA 93901
P: 831-758-6400   F: 831-758-0162   PRC:206
www.thorconnect.com
Email: info@thorconnect.com
Estab: 1966

Stephen Abrams, President
Don Cole, Quality Assurance Manager
Romeo Centeno, Facilities Manager

Manufacturer of special connectors, molded cable assemblies and covers, harness assemblies, and electro-mechanical devices.

**Thought Inc** HQ
5 Third St Ste 1030
San Francisco CA 94103
P: 415-836-9199   F: 415-836-9191   PRC:322
www.thoughtinc.com
Email: sales@thoughtinc.com
Estab: 1993

Greg Baker, Director of Sales and Marketing

Provider of data management solutions. The company uses dynamic mapping and related software for this purpose.

**Thoughtbot Inc** BR
795 Folsom St
San Francisco CA 94107
P: 877-976-2687   PRC:319
thoughtbot.com
Estab: 2012

Jessica Oceguera, Local Marketing Manager
Kane Baccigalupi, Director of Development
Skipper Warson, Director of Design
Kate Tsunoda, Managing Director
Camille Baclay, Office Manager

Provider of web and mobile app design and development.

**ThoughtSpot Inc** HQ
910 Hermosa Ct
Sunnyvale CA 94085
P: 800-508-7008   PRC:319
www.thoughtspot.com
Email: marketing@thoughtspot.com
Estab: 2012

Abhishek Rai, Co-Founder
Sanjay Agrawal, Co-Founder
Christos Mousouris, VP of Sales Engineering
Puneet Agarwal, VP of Engineering
Ajeet Singh, Co-Founder

A business intelligence platform that helps individuals to explore, analyze, and share real-time business analytics data.

**Thoughtworks Inc** BR
814 Mission St 5th FL
San Francisco CA 94103
P: 415-273-1389   F: 415-986-2964   PRC:323
www.thoughtworks.com
Email: info-us@thoughtworks.com
Estab: 1993

Roy Singham, Founder
Rebecca Parsons, CTO
Adam Monago, VP
David Rice, Managing Director
Tim Brown, Principal Consultant

Provider of system design and e-business consulting services. The company is also involved in software design and delivery and support.

**Thrasys Inc** HQ
250 Executive Park Blvd Ste 2000
San Francisco CA 94134
P: 650-449-1000   PRC:325
thrasys.com
Email: info@thrasys.com

Weimin Shen, Staff Engineer
Randy Belknap, CTO
George He, VP of Application Systems
Mark Knapp, Software Developer
Ranjani Ramakrishna, Corporate Counsel

Provider of health networking solutions. The company serves patients, service centers, payers, and public health administrators.

**ThreatMetrix** HQ
160 W Santa Clara St Ste 1400
San Jose CA 95113
P: 408-200-5755   F: 408-200-5799   PRC:319
www.threatmetrix.com
Estab: 2005

Srinivas Nayani, Senior Automation Engineer
Albert Nguyen, Product Support Engineer
Alisdair Faulkner, CPO
Andreas Baumhof, CTO
Frank Teruel, CFO

Provider of fraud prevention, threat detection, and authentication solutions. The company serves the gaming, media, and insurance industries.

**Three Palm Software**  HQ
16 Yankee Point Dr
Carmel CA 93923
P: 408-356-3240  PRC:322
threepalmsoft.com
Email: info@threepalmsoft.com
Estab: 2007

Patrick Heffernan, CTO
Daoxian Zhang, Chief Scientist Manager

Designer and developer of software products for
medical imaging and information. The company
also deals with data processing services.

**Threshold Enterprises Ltd**  HQ
23 Janis Wy
Scotts Valley CA 95066
P: 831-438-6851  F: 831-438-6430  PRC:268
www.thresholdenterprises.com
Emp: 1-10  Estab: 1978

Kevin Charries, Director of Quality Assurance

Distributor of nutritional supplements, healthcare,
and beauty care products.

**Thync Inc**  HQ
140 W Main St 2nd Fl
Los Gatos CA 95030
P: 408-484-4808  PRC:194
www.thync.com
Email: contact@thync.com
Estab: 2011

Isy Goldwasser, CEO
Sumon Pal, Co-Founder
Anil Thakur, CTO
Jwala Karnik, SVP of Clinical Development

Provider of wearable technology solutions. The
company is involved in testing and related support
services.

**Thyssenkrupp Elevator**  BR
14400 Catalina St
San Leandro CA 94577
P: 510-476-1900  PRC:180
thyssenkruppelevator.com

Josh Fosson, Branch Manager

Provider of elevators and elevator solutions. The
company offers MRL elevators, synergy elevators,
momentum elevators, and freight elevators.

**TIBCO Software Inc**  HQ
3307 Hillview Ave
Palo Alto CA 94304
P: 650-846-1000  F: 650-846-1005  PRC:319
www.tibco.com
Email: info@tibco.com
Estab: 1985

Scott Roza, President
Dan Streetman, CEO
Murray Rode, Vice Chairman
Matt Quinn, COO
Bill Hughes, EVP

Provider of enterprise application integration
software. The company serves the government,
healthcare, and insurance industries.

**Tintri Inc**  HQ
303 Ravendale Dr
Mountain View CA 94043
P: 650-810-8200  PRC:95
www.tintri.com
Email: info@tintri.com
Estab: 2008

Anand Ghatnekar, VP of Engineering
Alex Bouzari, CEO
Paul Bloch, President
Tom Ellery, General Manager
Mario Blandini, CMO

Developer of zero management storage systems.
The company focuses on building storage for
virtual environments.

**Titan Pharmaceuticals Inc**  HQ
400 Oyster Point Blvd Ste 505
S San Francisco CA 94080-1921
P: 650-244-4990  F: 650-244-4956  PRC:268
www.titanpharm.com
Email: busdev@titanpharm.com
Emp: 23  Estab: 1992
Sales: $3M to $10M

Sunil Bhonsle, President
Dane Hallberg, EVP
Kate DeVarney, EVP

Provider of biopharmaceuticals. The company
discovers proprietary therapeutics primarily for the
treatment of serious medical disorders.

**Tivix**  BR

600 California St
San Francisco CA 94108
P: 415-680-1299  PRC:319
www.tivix.com
Email: connect@tivix.com
Estab: 2008

Sumit Chachra, CEO
Bill Conneely, Senior Director of Finance
Katarzyna Szostak, Administrative Manager
Francis Cleary, Head of Technology
Anindya Roy, Head of Strategy

Focuses on the agile development of web, cloud,
and mobile applications.

**Tko Video Communications**  HQ
1665 Willow St
San Jose CA 95125
P: 408-252-4700  F: 408-557-6901  PRC:60
www.tkoworks.com
Email: info@tkoworks.com
Estab: 1995

John Roensch, President
Mary Roensch, CFO
Craig Ortiz, Program Manager
Manmei Lam, Web Specialist Corporate Marketing

Provider of video communication services. The
company focuses on audio and video conferencing, satellite broadcasting, and telecommunications training.

**Tmt Enterprises Inc**  HQ
1996 Oakland Rd
San Jose CA 95131
P: 408-432-9040  F: 408-432-9429  PRC:142
tmtenterprises.net
Email: info@tmtenterprises.net
Estab: 1961

Ted Moore, President
Colleen Moore, VP
Matt Moore, Operations Manager

Provider of baseball and softball playing surfaces
and supplier of agricultural mixes, construction
materials, organics, and aggregates.

**TOA Electronics Inc**  DH
400 Oyster Point Blvd Ste 301
S San Francisco CA 94080
P: 650-452-1200  PRC:60
www.toaelectronics.com
Email: support@toaelectronics.com
Emp: 51-200  Estab: 1974

Wynne Kwong, Account Manager
Robert McHale, Warehouse Coordinator

Developer and manufacturer of audio and security
products. The company is engaged in design,
delivery, and installation services.

**Tobar Industries**  HQ
912 Olinder Ct
San Jose CA 95122
P: 408-494-3530  F: 408-494-3540  PRC:82
www.tobar-ind.com
Estab: 1976

Ron Dias, Director of Engineering
Matthew Akiel, Engineering Intern
William Delaney, CFO
Marianne Ryan, Human Resource Manager
Kathleen Parsons, Human Resource

Provider of contract manufacturing services. The
company offers services for computer chassis,
card cages, and frames.

**TokBox Inc**  HQ
501 Second St Ste 310
San Francisco CA 94107
P: 415-284-4688  F: 415-284-4610  PRC:67
www.tokbox.com
Email: contact@tokbox.com
Estab: 2007

Scott Lomond, CEO
Lauren Slattery, Marketing Manager

Developer of free video chat tools and widgets.
The company offers services for the recreation
and entertainment industries.

**Tolerion Inc**  HQ
131 Oyster Point Blvd Ste 400
S San Francisco CA 94080
P: 415-795-5800  PRC:266
tolerion.bio
Email: info@tolerion.bio
Estab: 2013

John Donovan, President

Provider of medical treatment solutions for
autoimmune diseases. The company focuses on
restoring the patient's immune system.

**Tom Sawyer Software Corp**  HQ
1997 El Dorado Ave
Berkeley CA 94707
P: 510-208-4370  F: 510-208-4371  PRC:323
www.tomsawyer.com
Email: marketing@tomsawyer.com
Estab: 1992

Travis Cheng, Product Development Engineer
Liangrong Yi, Senior Product Development
Engineer
Brendan Madden, CEO
Jans Aasman, CEO

Developer of data relationship visualization and
analysis software for application developers. The
company offers training and consulting services.

**TOMA Biosciences Inc**  HQ
303 Vintage Park Dr
Foster City CA 94404
P: 650-691-8662  F: 800-923-8870  PRC:24
tomabio.com
Email: info@tomabio.com
Emp: 11-50 Estab: 2011

Wolfgang Daum, President

Provider of sequencing solutions. The company
serves laboratories and researchers to uncover
clinically meaningful genomic changes in tumors.

**Tomopal Inc**  HQ
1026 Florin Rd Ste 322
Sacramento CA 95831
P: 916-429-7240  F: 916-429-2701  PRC:156
www.tomopal.com
Email: sales@tomopal.com
Emp: 1-10

Pal Sandhu, CEO

Manufacturer and distributor of glass syringes,
scales & balances, gas filters, and other products
for the laboratory and industrial markets.

**Tooltek Engineering Corp**  HQ
4151 Business Center Dr
Fremont CA 94538
P: 510-683-9504  F: 510-683-9614  PRC:156
www.tooltek.com
Email: ttsales@tooltek.com
Estab: 1984

Roman Ruzhinsky, Systems Engineer
Jessie Zhu, Technician

Designer and fabricator of custom automated
equipment. The company is also engaged in material handling and robotics solutions.

**Toolwire Inc**  HQ
7031 Koll Center Pkwy Ste 200
Pleasanton CA 94566
P: 925-227-8500  F: 925-227-8501  PRC:323
toolwire.com
Estab: 1998

Joseph White, Manager of Technical Operations
Nancy Bissonnette, Office Manager

Designer and developer of experiential learning
solutions for higher education and corporate
training institutions.

**Top Microsystems Corp**  HQ
3261 Keller St
Santa Clara CA 95054
P: 408-980-9813  F: 408-980-8626  PRC:288
www.topmicro.com
Email: infor@topmicro.com
Estab: 1989

Kevin Rea, Sales Manager
Jared McCann, Account Manager

Provider of conversion solutions and integration
services. The company offers blade, storage,
and rack mount servers, medical equipment, and
others.

**Top Shelf**  BR
1851 E Paradise Rd Ste A
Tracy CA 95304
P: 866-592-0488  F: 209-834-8832  PRC:190
topshelforthopedics.com
Email: tsorders@topshelfmfg.com
Emp: 11-50

Scott Brougham, Founder

Manufacturer of orthopedic bracing and appliances. The company offers products for knee,
shoulder, foot & ankle, and spine.

**Toppan Printing Company Ltd**  BR
275 Battery St Ste 2600
San Francisco CA 94111
P: 415-393-9839  F: 415-393-9840  PRC:87
www.toppan.co.jp

Patrick Page, General Manager

Provider of printing solutions. The company serves
customers in the food, beverage, and high barrier
product industries.

**Tora Trading Services Ltd**  BR
1440 Chapin Ave Ste 205
Burlingame CA 94010
P: 650-513-6700  PRC:319
www.tora.com
Email: pr@tora.com

Robert Dykes, CEO
Keith Ducker, Chief Investment Officer
Paul Catuna, CFO
Mihai Iosivas, CTO
Chris Jenkins, Managing Director of Sales and
Operations

Provider of products such as Compass, Clearpool,
and Crosspoint for buy-side traders to specifically
address the trading challenges to Asia.

**Toray Advanced Composites USA**  BR
18255 Sutter Blvd
Morgan Hill CA 95037
P: 408-465-8500  F: 408-776-0107  PRC:57
www.toraytac.com

Joseph Morris, President
David Kapp, VP of Operations

Manufacturer of advanced composites like adhesives, prepregs, and liquid resin systems. The
company serves military, aerospace, and other
sectors.

**Toray International America Inc**  BR
411 Borel Ave Ste 520
San Mateo CA 94402
P: 650-341-7152  F: 650-341-0845  PRC:53
www.toray.com
Estab: 1988

Kentaro Hara, EVP
Ken Irokawa, Office Manager
Hiroyuki Niwa, Manager

Provider of chemicals, plastics, textiles, and IT-re-
lated products. The company offers environment,
engineering, life science, and other services.

**Torian Group Inc**  HQ
519 W Ctr Ave
Visalia CA 93291
P: 559-733-1940  F: 559-532-0207  PRC:323
www.toriangroup.com
Email: support@toriangroup.com
Emp: 1-10  Estab: 1983

Jose Lucatero, Senior Network Engineer
Tim Torian, President

Provider of computer, network, and web solutions
such as virus removal, home network setup, and
email.

**Toshiba America Inc**  BR
2590 Orchard Pkwy
San Jose CA 95131
P: 408-526-2400  F: 408-526-2410  PRC:93
www.toshiba.com

William Lam, VP of Engineering
David Marsac, Engineering Manager
Kaveh Baghaee, Network Engineer
John Miles, VP
Kenji Ito, VP

Manufacturer of LCD, laptop batteries, power
adapters, laptop cases, and other laptop related
accessories.

**Tosk Inc**  HQ
2672 Bayshore Pkwy Ste 507
Mountain View CA 94043
P: 408-245-6838  F: 408-245-6808  PRC:261
www.tosk.com
Email: info@tosk.com
Estab: 1998

Brian Frenzel, President
Stephen Yanofsky, VP of Research
Charles Garvin, Director
A. Moritz, Accounting Manager
Ravi Patel, Scientific Advisor

Manufacturer of drugs for the treatment of
debilitating and life-threatening diseases such as
cancer, arthritis, and psoriasis.

**Tosoh Bioscience Inc**  BR
6000 Shoreline Ct Ste 101
S San Francisco CA 94080
P: 650-615-4970  F: 650-615-0415  PRC:19
www.tosohbioscience.com
Email: info.diag.am@tosoh.com
Estab: 1989

Bill Christensen, Field Clinical Engineer
Joseph Troche, Quality Assurance Project Man-
ager
Randy Pietro, Regional Service Manager
Beth Sumpter, Clinical Support Specialist

Provider of monitoring services for life threatening diseases and cancers. The company focuses on preventing epidemics and purifying water.

**Total Environmental & Power Systems Inc**     HQ
  2500 Bisso Ln Ste 500
  Concord CA 94520
P: 925-681-2238  F: 510-217-2227   PRC:290
www.e-teps.net
Email: info@e-teps.net
Estab: 2002

Tom Masiewicz, President
Nicole Shipley, Senior Administrative Assistant

Provider of HVAC, electrical, and telecommunication services. The company's service areas include generators, radio frequency, and fabrication.

**Total Resolution LLC**     HQ
  20 Florida Ave
  Berkeley CA 94707
P: 510-527-6393  F: 510-527-9151   PRC:319
www.totalresolution.com
Email: roar@totalresolution.com

Roar Kilaas, Owner

Developer of software for electron microscopy needs. The company provides MacTempasX and CrystalKitX.

**Totango Inc**     HQ
  1200 Park Pl Ste 200
  San Mateo CA 94403
P: 800-634-1990   PRC:325
www.totango.com
Email: hi@totango.com
Estab: 2010

Yaron Avisror, SVP of Engineering
Omer Gotlieb, Co-Founder
Guy Nirpaz, Founder
Eric Benhamou, Chairman
Hamutal Anavi-Russo, CFO

A customer success software helps to connect customer data, monitor health changes, and proactively engage the customers by using an integrated platform.

**Totlcom Inc**     BR
  4610 Northgate Blvd Ste 150
  Sacramento CA 95834
P: 916-428-5000  F: 916-921-9767   PRC:64
www.totlcom.com
Email: info@totlcom.com
Emp: 11-50

Mason McNay, Sales Engineer
Bruce Guthrie, Network Engineer
Tristan Langstaff, Applications Engineer
Jerry Greer, President
Sam Bishop, CEO

Provider of IP voice and data services and products such as IP systems, VoIP systems, and mail systems for growing companies.

**Tps Aviation Inc**     HQ
  1515 Crocker Ave
  Hayward CA 94544-7038
P: 510-475-1010  F: 510-475-8817   PRC:5
www.tpsaviation.com
Email: admin@tpsaviation.com
Estab: 1961

Sue Bauer, Regional Sales Manager

Distributor of commercial and military aerospace fasteners and electric components. The company focuses on aerospace parts, components, and logistics.

**Trackdata Systems Corp**     HQ
  21684 Granada Ave
  Cupertino CA 95014
P: 408-446-5595   PRC:322
www.trackinfo.com
Email: help@trackdatasystems.com
Estab: 1980

Michael Exley, Director of Operations

Provider of greyhound, thoroughbred, and harness racing information. The company features up-to-date listing of racing schedules.

**Trane**     BR
  310 Soquel Way
  Sunnyvale CA 94085
P: 888-862-1619  F: 408-481-3666   PRC:154
www.trane.com
Estab: 1913

Chris Hsieh, Principal Systems Engineer
Alex Lindsey, Executive Engineering Account Manager
Beth Doyle, Sales Engineer
Andrew Mondell, Sales Engineer
Bill Barnhart, Sales Engineer

Provider of heating, ventilation & air conditioning (HVAC) systems, dehumidifying, and air cleaning products.

**Trans Bay Steel**     HQ
  2601 Giant Rd
  Richmond CA 94806
P: 510-809-8193  F: 510-525-8027   PRC:80
www.transbaysteel.com

William Kavicky, General Manager

Provider of structural steel construction services. The company offers heavy bridge piling and mechanical fabrication services.

**Transcriptic Inc**     HQ
  3565 Haven Ave Ste 3
  Menlo Park CA 94025
P: 650-763-8432   PRC:34
www.transcriptic.com
Email: team@transcriptic.com
Estab: 2012

Max Hodak, Founder
Scott Dillingham, Contract Administrator

Specializes in scientific research and the company also supports an array of vitro molecular biology and cell biology.

**Transend Corp**     HQ
  225 Emerson St
  Palo Alto CA 94301
P: 650-324-5370  F: 650-324-5377   PRC:322
www.transend.com
Email: sales.info@transend.com
Estab: 1978

Fred Krefetz, President
Jason Krefetz, VP of Sales
Joshua Krefetz, VP of Business Development

Provider of email migration and conversion solutions that support email systems. The company serves business, education, reselling, and other sectors.

**Transfer Engineering & Manufacturing Inc**     HQ
  47697 Westinghouse Dr Ste 100
  Fremont CA 94539
P: 510-651-3000  F: 510-651-3090   PRC:165
www.transferengineering.com
Email: info@transferengineering.com
Estab: 1999

Judy Ackeret, Manager

Manufacturer and marketer of loadlocks and transfer systems. The company offers precision magnetic manipulators and transporters, and other products.

**Transfer Flow Inc**     HQ
  1444 Fortress St
  Chico CA 95973
P: 530-893-5209  F: 530-893-0204   PRC:159
www.transferflow.com
Emp: 1-10  Estab: 1983

Bill Gaines, Senior Engineer
Mark Forwalter, Human Resource Manager of Government Regulations
Robert Green, Director of Sales
Warren Johnson, Advertising & Marketing Director
Ben Winter, Project Manager

Manufacturer of fuel tanks. The company offers axillary, replacement, and tanks with built-in toolboxes.

**Transgenomic Inc**     BR
  2032 Concourse Dr
  San Jose CA 95131
P: 408-432-3230  F: 408-894-0405   PRC:34
www.transgenomic.com
Email: info@transgenomic.com
Estab: 1997

Paul Kinnon, President
Katherine Richardson, VP

Provider of patient testing and biomarker identification services. The company specializes in high performance products.

**Transitional Systems Manufacturing Inc**     HQ
  PO Box 359
  Browns Valley CA 95918
P: 530-751-2610   PRC:166
www.transitionalsystems.com
Email: info@transitionalsystems.com
Emp: 1-10  Estab: 1985

Sean Siebern, CEO

Provider of products to repair landscape sprinkler systems. The company also focuses on installation needs.

**Translarity** HQ
46575 Fremont Blvd
Fremont CA 94538
P: 510-371-7900 PRC:212
translarity.com
Email: sales@translarity.com
Estab: 2003

Christopher Lane, VP of Engineering
Dominik Schmidt, President
Garry Crossland, VP of Sales & Marketing

Specializes in wafer translation technology. The company offers device design and testing solutions to the semiconductor industry.

**TRAXPayroll** HQ
740 Alfred Nobel Dr
Hercules CA 94547
P: 866-872-9123 PRC:323
www.traxpayroll.com
Estab: 1997

Kevin Kitani, Sales Executive
Darcy Peluso, Business Development Manager
Sonja Stuart, Tax Payroll Admin

Specializes in payroll management solutions. The company also offers wage garnishment, worker's compensation, and tax filing solutions.

**Trayer Engineering Corp** HQ
898 Pennsylvania Ave
San Francisco CA 94107
P: 415-285-7770   F: 415-285-0883 PRC:165
trayer.com
Email: sales@trayer.com
Estab: 1962

Adam Donoghue, Western Region Sales Manager
Ray Lemos, Press Operator
Brian Miller, Welder

Manufacturer of electronic distribution switchgears. The company's services include design, maintenance, and installation.

**Trc Companies Inc** BR
505 Sansome St Ste 1600
San Francisco CA 94111
P: 415-434-2600   F: 415-434-2321 PRC:68
trcsolutions.com
Estab: 1960

James Mayer, President of Power Sector
Ed Wiegele, President of Oil and Gas Sector
Parker Meeks, President of Infrastructure Sector
Mark Robbins, President of Environmental Sector
Christopher Vincze, CEO

Provider of scientific and engineering software services. The company offers hydropower licensing, power delivery, and telecommunications engineering services.

**Treasure Data Inc** HQ
2565 Leghorn St
Mountain View CA 94043
P: 866-899-5386 PRC:319
www.treasuredata.com
Estab: 2011

Hiro Yoshikawa, Founder
Rob Glickman, CMO

Empower enterprises by unifying data from multiple sources such as online, offline, IoT and device-generated data.

**Trellis Bioscience LLC** HQ
702 Marshall St Ste 614
Redwood City CA 94063
P: 650-838-1400 PRC:34
www.trellisbio.com
Estab: 1998

Stote Ellsworth, COO
Larry Kauvar, CSO-Co-Founder
Stefan Ryser, President
Bruce Keyt, CTO
Tony Leighton, CMO

Developer of human antibody therapeutics as treatment for infectious disease and oncology indications.

**Trench & Traffic Supply Inc** HQ
2175 Acoma St
Sacramento CA 95819
P: 916-920-3304   F: 916.920.3305 PRC:227
www.trenchandtraffic.com
Emp: 1-10   Estab: 2003

John Harrah, President

Provider of traffic control equipment for rent and sale. The company offers equipment for traffic control, shoring, and pipe testing.

**Trevi Systems** HQ
1415 N McDowell Blvd
Petaluma CA 94954
P: 707-792-2681   F: 707-792-2684 PRC:306
trevisystems.com
Email: info@trevisystems.com
Estab: 2010

John Webley, CEO
Gary Carmignani, Chief Science Officer
Michael Greene, Director of Manufacturing
Dave Zimkowski, Controller

Provider of desalination process services. The company focuses on osmosis system using proprietary membrane and draw solution using thermal heat.

**TRI MAP International Inc** HQ
119 Val Dervin Pkwy ste 5
Stockton CA 95206
P: 209-234-0100 PRC:92
www.trimapintl.com
Email: info@trimapintl.com
Emp: 1-10

Erika Jensen, Manager of Financial Services

Manufacturer of industrial grade rack mounts and desktop computers. The company is engaged in engineering and fabrication services.

**Tri Tool Inc** HQ
3041 Sunrise Blvd
Rancho Cordova CA 95742
P: 916-288-6100   F: 916-288-6160 PRC:80
tritool.com
Email: customer.service@tritool.com
Emp: 11-50 Estab: 1972

Aaron Curtis, Electrical & Software Engineering Manager
David Porter, Mechanical
Kevin Slattery, Mechanical Engineer
Clint Gabrielson, Senior Mechanical Engineer
Michael Silva, Software Engineer

Manufacturer of precision machine tools. The company also deals with products rentals, construction, and maintenance services.

**Trianni Inc** HQ
821 Irving St
San Francisco CA 94122
P: 866-374-9314 PRC:28
trianni.com
Email: info@trianni.com
Estab: 2010

Gloria Esposito, CTO
Maria Wabl, CFO
David Meininger, Chief Business Officer

Developer of humanized monoclonal antibody platform. The company offers services to pharmaceutical and biotechnology companies.

**Tric Tools Inc** HQ
1350 S Loop Rd Ste 104
Alameda CA 94502
P: 510-865-8742   F: 510-217-9493 PRC:142
www.trictools.com
Email: sales@trictrenchless.com
Estab: 1996

Max Darrow, R&D Engineer
Ward Carter, President
Michael Lien, CFO
Greg Lee, Head of Manufacturing
David Huff, National Sales Director

Provider of pipe-bursting systems. The company also offers installation, maintenance, and cleaning services for home-sewer systems.

**Tricida Inc** HQ
7000 Shoreline Ct Ste 201
S San Francisco CA 94080
P: 415-429-7800 PRC:34
www.tricida.com
Email: info@tricida.com
Estab: 2013

Claire Lockey, Chief Development Officer
David Skidmore, Director of Quality Assurance
Natasha Bassett, Senior Research Associate
Randi Gbur, Senior Scientist
Lillian Tsao, Senior Research Associate

Focuses on the discovery and clinical development of therapeutics to address renal, metabolic and cardiovascular diseases.

**Tricontinent Scientific Inc** BR
12740 Earhart Ave
Auburn CA 95602
P: 530-273-8888   F: 530-273-2586 PRC:186
www.gardnerdenver.com
Email: customerservice@tricontinent.com
Emp: 11-50 Estab: 1975

Mik Bajka, OEM Engineering & Business Development Manager
Randy Dismukes, COO
John McDaniel, Materials Manager

Provider of liquid-handling products and instrument components for the medical diagnostics and biotechnology industries.

**Tridecs Corp** HQ
3513 Arden Rd
Hayward CA 94545-3907
P: 510-785-2620  F: 510-785-3146  PRC:80
www.tridecs.com
Email: sales@tridecs.com
Estab: 1969

Frank Schenkhuizen, President
Branden Schenkhuizen, Production Manager
John Homa, Quality Control Manager
Tiffany Cavanaugh, Administrative Assistant
Steve Koski, Materials Planner

Manufacturer of machined metal and plastic parts. The company offers prototyping, product machining, engineering, and design and drafting services.

**Trimble Inc** HQ
935 Stewart Dr
Sunnyvale CA 94085
P: 408-481-8000  PRC:17
www.trimble.com
Email: mrmsales@trimble.com
Estab: 1978
Sales: Over $3B

Steven Berglund, President
Robert Painter, CFO
Rajat Bahri, CFO
Thomas Fansler, SVP
Michael Scarpa, SVP

Developer of positioning solutions for the agriculture, construction, mining, and surveying industries.

**Trina Solar US Inc** RH
100 Century Ctr Ste 501
San Jose CA 95112
P: 800-696-7114  PRC:135
www.trinasolar.com
Email: usa@trinasolar.com
Estab: 1997

Jim Day, Director of Sales and Marketing
Roy Shaw, Sales Manager
Chuck Rames, Inside Sales Leader

Manufacturer of mono and multicrystalline photovoltaic (PV) modules. The company serves residential, commercial, and utility purposes.

**Trinapco Inc** HQ
1101 57th Ave
Oakland CA 94621
P: 510-535-1082  F: 928-752-6271  PRC:51
www.trinapco.com
Email: sales@trinapco.com

Martin Johnson, President

Manufacturer of organic fine chemicals specializing in 1,8-naphthyridine compounds. The company offers custom synthesis services.

**Trinity Consultants Inc** BR
1901 Harrison St Ste 1590
Oakland CA 94612
P: 510-285-6351  PRC:138
trinityconsultants.com
Estab: 1974

Jay Hofmann, President
Dave Larsen, CFO
Chris Price, Director of Human Resources
Alan Chuang, Director of Information Technology
Paul Smith, Director of Quality Management

Provider of environmental consulting services. The company engages in environmental outsourcing and litigation support services.

**Trion Worlds Inc** HQ
350 Marine Pkwy
Redwood City CA 94065
P: 650-273-9618  PRC:317
trionworlds.com
Email: infoUS@gamigo.com
Estab: 2006

Deborah Davis, Community Coordinator
Len Williams, Lead Environment Artist

Publisher and developer of games. The company offers Defiance, RIFT, Archeage, and End of Nations games.

**Triple O Systems Inc** HQ
1550 Dell Ave Unit E
Campbell CA 95008
P: 408-378-3002  F: 408-378-7155  PRC:144
tripleo.com
Email: sales@tripleo.com
Estab: 1990

Larry Ramsauer, Founder

Designer and manufacturer of water treatment systems. The company also offers reverse osmosis product water tanks and water store water tanks.

**Triple Ring Technologies Inc** HQ
39655 Eureka Dr
Newark CA 94560-4806
P: 510-592-3000  PRC:189
www.tripleringtech.com
Email: info@tripleringtech.com
Estab: 2005

Phil Devlin, Chief Business Officer
Christina Goehrig, Director of Strategic Marketing

Manufacturer of in vitro diagnostics and life science tools. The company offer services to the medical devices, imaging, and industrial sectors.

**TriReme Medical LLC** RH
7060 Koll Ctr Pkwy Ste 300
Pleasanton CA 94566
P: 925-931-1300  F: 925-931-1361  PRC:196
qtvascular.com
Email: careers@qtvascular.com
Estab: 2005

Eitan Konstantino, CEO
Randal Farwell, CFO
Maria Pizarro, EVP
Tim Rooney, District Sales Manager

Developer of differentiated therapeutic solutions. The company manufactures and distributes the chocolate and glider families of angioplasty balloons.

**Trivad Inc** HQ
1350 Bayshore Hwy Ste 450
Burlingame CA 94010
P: 650-286-1086  F: 650-286-1686  PRC:64
www.trivad.com
Email: info@trivad.com

Jenna Lim, CEO
Zac Zuckerman, Senior Sales Consultant
Hans Lim, Solutions VP
Fil Gonzalez, Account Executive
Robert Brown, Senior Account Executive

Developer of IT solutions. The company also offers training, implementation, and infrastructure assessment services.

**Trofholz Technologies Inc** HQ
250 Technology Way Ste 100
Rocklin CA 95765
P: 916-577-1903  F: 916-577-1904  PRC:326
www.trofholz.com
Email: info@trofholz.com
Emp: 11-50 Estab: 2001

Yvonne Pire, CEO
Brenna Pedone, VP of Support
David Raymond, VP
Jesse Friedman, VP of Business Development
Brad Williams, Controller

Developer of IT information and security systems. The company also specializes in communication solutions.

**Tronex Technology Inc** HQ
2860 Cordelia Rd Ste 230
Fairfield CA 94534
P: 707-426-2550  F: 707-426-6462  PRC:157
tronex.descoindustries.com
Email: service@tronextools.com
Estab: 1982

Arne Salvesen, President

Manufacturer of precision cutting tools and pliers. The company offers hand cutters, hard wire cutters, and flat nose pliers.

**Tru Technical Partners Inc** HQ
286 E Hamilton Ave Ste D
Campbell CA 95008
P: 408-559-2800  F: 408-559-2813  PRC:63
trutechnical.com
Email: sales@trutechnical.com

Truman Roe, Manager

Provider of information technology services on a contract basis. The company's services include managed desktops, workstation, anti-virus, and others.

**True Circuits Inc** HQ
4300 El Camino Real Ste 200
Los Altos CA 94022
P: 650-949-3400  F: 650-949-3434  PRC:208
www.truecircuits.com
Email: sales@truecircuits.com
Estab: 1998

Aldo Bottelli, Principal Design Engineer
John Maneatis, President
Stephen Maneatis, CEO

Developer and marketer of phase-locked loops, delay-locked loops, and mixed-signal designs for integrated circuits.

**Trufocus Corp** HQ
468 Westridge Dr
Watsonville CA 95076
P: 831-761-9981  F: 831-761-9984  PRC:198
www.trufocus.com
Email: trufocus@trufocus.com
Emp: 1-10  Estab: 1987

Goerge Howard, CEO
James Price, Mechanical Designer

Supplier of x-ray products. The company's products are used in industrial, medical, aerospace, and analytical application.

**Tschida Engineering Inc** HQ
1812 Yajome St
Napa CA 94559
P: 707-224-4482   F: 707-224-2406   PRC:80
tschidaeng.com
Email: info@tschidaeng.com
Estab: 1977

Bruce Tschida, Owner

Provider of CNC turning & milling, machining, and fabrication services. The company serves semiconductor, defense, medical, and environmental sectors.

**Tsmc North America** HQ
2851 Junction Ave
San Jose CA 95134
P: 408-382-8000   F: 408-382-8008   PRC:126
www.tsmc.com
Email: west@tsmc.com
Estab: 1987
Sales: $300M to $1 Billion

David Keller, President
Roger Luo, President of TSMC Nanjing
C.C. Wei, CEO
Mark Liu, Chairman
Wendell Huang, VP of Finance

Manufacturer of products for the computer, communications, and consumer electronics market segments.

**Tss Consultants** HQ
5430 Carlson Dr Ste 100
Sacramento CA 95819-1720
P: 916-600-4174   PRC:142
tssconsultants.com
Emp: 1-10   Estab: 1986

Tad Mason, CEO
Frederick Tornatore, CTO
Andrea Stephenson, Energy and Solid Waste Consultant
David Augustine, Senior Environmental Consultant
Richard Harris, Senior Environmental Analyst

Provider of energy resources management, environmental permitting, and financial assessment services.

**Tti Inc** BR
6611 Folsom Auburn Rd
Folsom CA 95630
P: 916-987-4600   F: 916-987-4601   PRC:323
www.ttiinc.com
Email: information@ttiinc.com
Emp: 11-50

Paul Andrews, CEO
Don Akery, President
Mike Morton, COO
Chris Goodman, CFO
Michael Kennedy, VP of Global Strategic Accounts

Distributor of passive, connector, electromechanical, and discrete components for the industrial, military, and aerospace sectors.

**TTI Medical** HQ
220 Porter Dr Ste 120
San Ramon CA 94583
P: 925-553-7828   F: 925-718-8225   PRC:195
www.ttimedical.com
Email: info@ttimedical.com
Estab: 1984

Allen Howes, Owner
Andrea Wong, Finance Manager
Karole Schatzman, Customer Support

Designer and marketer of surgical instruments and medical devices. The company serves hospitals and the healthcare sector.

**TTM Technologies Inc** BR
407 Mathew St
Santa Clara CA 95050
P: 408-486-3100   PRC:209
www.ttmtech.com

Ron Meier, Quality Compliance Engineer
Douglas Soder, EVP
Phil Titterton, EVP
Thomas Edman, President
Todd Schull, EVP

Manufacturer of printed circuit boards and back plane assemblies. The company's services include design, installation, and delivery.

**Turbo-Doc Medical Record Systems Inc** HQ
6480 Pentz Rd Ste A
Paradise CA 95969
P: 530-877-8650   F: 530-877-8621   PRC:322
turbodoc.net
Email: turbodoc@turbodoc.com
Emp: 1-10   Estab: 2007

Lyle Hunt, Owner

Provider of electronic medical record systems. The company offers walkout statements, drug information handouts, and medication rewrites.

**Turley & Associates Mechanical Engineering Group I** HQ
2431 Capitol Ave
Sacramento CA 95816
P: 916-325-1065   PRC:304
turleymech.com
Email: office@turleymech.com
Emp: 1-10   Estab: 1975

Brian Provencal, President
John Thompson, Principal

Provider of engineering services to health care, education, industrial, public, and retail facilities.

**Turner Designs Inc** HQ
1995 N First St
San Jose CA 95112-4220
P: 408-749-0994   PRC:18
www.turnerdesigns.com
Email: sales@turnerdesigns.com
Estab: 1972

Karin Reed, Purchasing Manager
Jake Vandenberg, VP of Finance
Pam Mayerfeld, VP of Marketing

Provider of industrial fluorometers and rhodamine dyes. The company's applications include oil spill response and environmental monitoring.

**Tusker Medical Inc** HQ
155 Jefferson Dr Ste 200
Menlo Park CA 94025
P: 650-223-6900   PRC:189
www.tuskermed.com
Email: info@tuskermed.com
Estab: 2016

Elmer Yee, Senior Manufacturing Engineer
Ari Kermani, R&D Engineer
Jonathan Kurniawan, Manufacturing Engineer
Amir Abolfathi, CEO
Quang Vu, Manufacturing Technician

Developer of pediatric-focused technologies. The company specializes in the placement of tubes without general anesthetics.

**Tuv Rheinland Of North America Inc** DH
1279 Quarry Ln Ste A
Pleasanton CA 94566
P: 925-249-9123   F: 925-249-9124   PRC:211
www.tuv.com
Email: info@tuv.com
Estab: 1872

Keith Sinclair, Sales Executive Medical Division
Balazs Bozsik, Technical Manager of Medical Audit
Sean Warnock, Data Center operations Manager
Nikolaus Wahl, Technical Program Manager

Provider of product testing, market access, specialty services, and management systems certification services.

**Tuv Sud America Inc** BR
47460 Fremont Blvd
Fremont CA 94538
P: 510-257-7823   PRC:304
www.tuvsud.com
Email: info-us@tuvsud.com

Tiffany Long, Call & Research Manager
Nancy Knap, Lead Office Administrator
Johnny Wilson, Radiographer Technician

Provider of services for testing, certification, and engineering audits. The company is focused on medical devices and e-mobility.

**Tvu Networks Corp** HQ
857 Maude Ave
Mountain View CA 94043
P: 650-969-6732   F: 650-969-6747   PRC:324
www.tvunetworks.com
Email: info@tvunetworks.com
Estab: 2005

Paul Shen, CEO
Eric Chang, VP of Marketing
Dan Lofgren, SVP of Business Operations
Chris Bell, VP of Technical Operations
Matthew McEwen, VP of Product Management

Provider of wireless electronic news gathering services. The company offers TV broadcast, web streaming, and law enforcement services.

**Twilio Inc**                                          HQ
   375 Beale St Ste 300
   San Francisco CA 94105
P: 415-390-2337                                     PRC:325
www.twilio.com
Email: sales@twilio.com
Estab: 2008
Sales: $300M to $1 Billion

Ott Kaukver, VP of Engineering
Brian Tarricone, Principal Software Engineer
Kenneth Hoxworth, Engineering Manager
Thomas Wilsher, Lead Software Engineer
Kevin Burke, Software Engineer

Provider of infrastructure APIs for businesses to
build scalable, reliable voice, and text messaging
apps.

**Twist Bioscience**                                    HQ
   681 Gateway Blvd
   South San Francisco CA 94080
P: 800-719-0671                                     PRC:34
www.twistbioscience.com
Email: sales@twistbioscience.com
Estab: 2013
Sales: Under $1 Million

Emily Leproust, CEO
Bill Peck, CTO
Bill Banyai, COO
Jim Thorburn, CFO
Mark Daniels, Chief Legal Officer

Specializes in DNA synthesis programs. The
company is engaged in genome editing and drug
discovery services.

**twoXAR Inc**                                          HQ
   883 N Shoreline Blvd Ste A100
   Mountain View CA 94043
P: 650-382-2605                                     PRC:25
www.twoxar.com
Estab: 2014

Andrew Radin, CEO
Brian Moriarty, CFO
Aaron Daugherty, VP of Discovery
Mark Eller, SVP of Research and Development
Allen Poirson, SVP of Biopharmaceutical Busi-
ness Development

Developer of drug delivery platform. The company
is involved in biological data extraction, automated
model generation, and feature identification.

**Ty Lin International Group**                          HQ
   345 California St Ste 2300
   San Francisco CA 94104
P: 415-291-3700   F: 415-433-0807      PRC:304
www.tylin.com
Estab: 1954

Tony Peterson, President
Yang Jin, President
William Harnagel, VP
John Young, VP
Maribel Castillo, VP

Provider of engineering services such as construction management, inspection, design and
planning, and surveying.

**Tyan Computer Corp**                                  DH
   3288 Laurelview Ct
   Fremont CA 94538
P: 510-651-8868   F: 510-651-7688      PRC:93
www.tyan.com
Estab: 1989

George Koivun, VP of Sales
Jo Chang, Director of Sales

Designer and manufacturer of server/workstation
platforms. The company's products are sold to
OEMs, VARs, system integrators, and resellers.

**Tymphany HK Ltd**                                     HQ
   1 Thorndale Dr Ste 200
   San Rafael CA 94903
P: 415-887-9538                                     PRC:60
www.tymphany.com
Estab: 2004

Ed Boyd, CEO
Phil McPhee, Senior Director of Global Sales &
Marketing
Andrew Dielman, Director of Sales
Chris von Hellermann, Technology Research

Manufacturer of acoustic products. The company's
products include consumers and Pro audio, OEM
transducers, and peerless catalogs.

**Uc Components Inc**                                   HQ
   18700 Adams Ct
   Morgan Hill CA 95037
P: 408-782-1929   F: 408-782-7995      PRC:80
www.uccomponents.com
Email: sales@uccomponents.com
Estab: 1974

John Leetch, Purchasing

Manufacturer of RediVac coated and electro-pol-
ished vented screws. The company serves high
vacuum applications.

**Uhv Sputtering Inc**                                  HQ
   275 Digital Dr
   Morgan Hill CA 95037
P: 408-779-2826   F: 408-776-3407      PRC:47
www.uhvsputtering.com
Email: info@uhvsputtering.com
Estab: 1990

John Cavanaugh, Quality Manager

Manufacturer of semiconductor devices and
vacuum equipment. The company is involved in
sputtering and bonding services.

**Ulbrich Stainless Steels and Special
Metals Inc**                                            BR
   770 E Shaw Ave Ste 100
   Fresno CA 93710
P: 559-456-2310   F: 559-456-2321      PRC:298
www.ulbrich.com
Email: info@ulbrich.com
Emp: 11-50  Estab: 1924

Chris Ulbrich, CEO

The company manufactures and sells specialty
strip in stainless steel, and serves the industrial
sector.

**Ultimate Index Inc**                                  HQ
   12122 Dry Creek Rd Ste 104
   Auburn CA 95602
P: 530-878-0573   F: 530-878-0613      PRC:47
ultimateindexinc.com
Email: sales@ultimateindexinc.com
Emp: 1-10   Estab: 2003

Gordon King, Manager

Manufacturer of E-beam deposition cones. The
company specializes in prepared coating materials for the precision thin film coating industry.

**Ultra Clean Technology**                             HQ
   26462 Corporate Ave
   Hayward CA 94545
P: 510-576-4400   F: 510-576-4401      PRC:86
www.uct.com
Email: sales@uct.com
Estab: 1991
Sales: $1B to $3B

Mujeeb Mohammad, Senior Director of Engineer-
ing
Derrick Woo, Director of Engineering
Jim Scholhamer, CEO
Sheri Savage, CFO
Joan Sterling, SVP of Human Resources

Manufacturer of gas panel delivery systems. The
company primarily caters to the semiconductor
industry.

**Ultra Lift Corp**                                     HQ
   475 Stockton Ave Ste E
   San Jose CA 95126
P: 408-287-9400   F: 408-297-1199      PRC:179
www.ultralift.com
Email: info@ultralift.com

Dabb George, President

Manufacturer of hand trucks. The company specializes in the fabrication of trucks that combine
hand-power and electric drives.

**Ultra T Equipment Company Inc**                      HQ
   41980 Christy St
   Fremont CA 94538
P: 510-440-3909   F: 510-440-3920      PRC:86
www.ultrat.com
Email: sales@ultrat.com
Estab: 1991

Jack Williams, Associate Electrical Engineer

Manufacturer of spin coaters, developer stations,
reionizers, and microelectronics cleaning systems.

**Ultra-Flex Inc**                                      HQ
   169 Stanford Ave Ste 4
   Half Moon Bay CA 94019
P: 650-728-6060   F: 650-728-6063      PRC:202
www.ultraflexinc.com
Estab: 1982

Rocky Raynor, Principal

Designer of component manufacturing solutions.
The company offers springs, fasteners, castings,
machined parts, and hardware items.

**Ultra-X Inc**　　　　　　　　HQ
　2075 De La Cruz Blvd Ste 101
　Santa Clara CA 95050
P: 408-261-7090　F: 408-261-7077　　　PRC:68
www.uxd.com
Email: info@uxd.com
Estab: 1987

Cory Grand, Sales Representative
James Todd, International Sales Executive

Provider of personal computer diagnostic solutions
for developers, manufacturers, system engineers,
integrators, and computer professionals.

**Ultracor Inc**　　　　　　　　HQ
　2763 Boeing Way
　Stockton CA 95206
P: 209-983-3744　F: 925-454-3011　　　PRC:5
www.ultracorinc.com
Emp: 1-10　Estab: 1995

Asha Kai, CEO
Stan Wright, President
Thao Huynh, Quality Manager
Sovanda Sing, Operations Manager

Manufacturer of engineered specialty honeycomb
and related supplies. The company also deals with
custom designs.

**Ultragenyx Pharmaceutical Inc**　　　HQ
　60 Leveroni Ct
　Novato CA 94949
P: 415-483-8800　F: 415-483-8810　　　PRC:34
www.ultragenyx.com
Email: info@ultragenyx.com
Emp: 610　Estab: 2010
Sales: $30M to $100M

Michael Narachi, President
Dennis Huang, CTO
Erik Harris, CCO
Karah Parschauer, Chief Business Officer
Shalini Sharp, CFO

Developer of products for the treatment of rare
and ultra-rare diseases. The company is engaged
in commercialization of products.

**Ultrasolar Technology Inc**　　　　HQ
　1025 Comstock St
　Santa Clara CA 95054
P: 408-499-6227　F: 408-579-1985　　　PRC:135
www.ultrasolartech.com

Santosh Kumar, CEO

Manufacturer of solar panel devices. The company
specializes in residential, commercial, and utility
solar arrays.

**Ultrasound Laboratories Inc**　　　HQ
　305 South Dr Ste 7
　Mountain View CA 94040
P: 877-650-0650　　　　　　　　PRC:188
smarthealthscreening.com
Email: info@smarthealthscreening.com

Joseph Matthews, Technical Director
Nahid Kiani, Laboratory Technician

Provider of non-invasive ultrasound imaging
services. The company focuses on services such
as health screening, carotid artery, and kidney
screening.

**Ultratech - A Division Of Veeco**　　BR
　3050 Zanker Rd
　San Jose CA 95134
P: 408-321-8835　F: 510-413-9769　　　PRC:209
www.veeco.com
Estab: 1945

Peter Porshnev, SVP of Unified Engineering
William Miller, CEO
John Peeler, CEO
Shubham Maheshwari, EVP

Manufacturer of data storage, LED, and solar process equipment. The company serves solar, LED,
data storage, wireless, optical, and other sectors.

**Ultraview Corp**　　　　　　　BR
　808 Gilman St
　Berkeley CA 94710
P: 925-253-2960　F: 925-253-4894　　　PRC:91
www.ultraviewcorp.com
Email: sales@ultraviewcorp.com
Estab: 1987

Barbara Sacks, VP of Operations

Provider of data acquisition solutions, bus extenders, synthesizers, and direct digital synthesizers.

**Uni-Fab Industries Inc**　　　　HQ
　1461 N Milpitas Blvd
　Milpitas CA 95035
P: 408-945-9733　　　　　　　　PRC:80
www.uni-fab.com

Edwin Woo, Engineering Manager
Bud Rogers, President
Don Cook, Manager of Account

Provider of precision sheet metal fabrication
services. The company's equipment services
include laser, punching and cutting, machining,
and sawing.

**Uni-Flex Circuits Inc**　　　　HQ
　1782 Angela St
　San Jose CA 95125
P: 408-998-5500　F: 408-998-5505　　　PRC:211
www.uniflexcircuits.com
Email: sales@uniflexcircuits.com

Arnold Bulosan, Owner

Manufacturer of flexible circuits. The company
specializes in the design and fabrication of consumer electronic connectors.

**Unico Mechanical Corp**　　　　HQ
　1209 Polk St
　Benicia CA 94510
P: 707-745-9970　F: 707-745-9973　　　PRC:80
www.unicomechanical.com
Email: info@unicomechanical.com

Randall Flulk, Manufacturing Supervisor
Rick Lemos, Account Representative

Provider of replacement machine parts. The company's services include welding, repairs, onsite
machining, welding, and millwright.

**Uniform Industrial Corp**　　　　DH
　47341 Bayside Pkwy
　Fremont CA 94538
P: 510-438-6799　F: 510-438-6790　　　PRC:153
www.uicworld.com
Email: info@uicusa.com
Estab: 2007

Robin Tang, Director of Engineering
Kevin Chang, Software Engineering Manager
Cleo Chiang, Purchasing Manager
Edwin Young, Director of Product Management
Carlos Sedano, Territory Manager Latin America

Provider of systems and components for banking
and retail solutions. The company also offers technology solutions and customer services.

**Unigen Corp**　　　　　　　　HQ
　39730 Eureka Dr
　Newark CA 94560
P: 510-896-1818　F: 510-623-1242　　　PRC:86
www.unigen.com
Email: info@unigen.com
Estab: 1991

Steven Sun, Director
SY Chai, Director
Paul Heng, President
Demitry Pinski, Director
Henry Siller, Production Supervisor

Manufacturer and designer of custom enterprise-grade flash storage and DRAM and AR-
MOUR product applications serving the telecommunications industry.

**Unimicro Technologies Inc**　　　HQ
　440 Boulder Coulte 100-C
　Pleasanton CA 94566
P: 925-846-8638　F: 925-401-9548　　　PRC:13
www.unimicrotech.com
Email: info@unimicrotech.com
Estab: 1996

Chao Yan, President

Provider of chemical and biological separation
and analysis with micro separation technology
especially capillary electrochromatography.

**Uniq Vision Inc**　　　　　　　HQ
　2924 Scott Blvd
　Santa Clara CA 95054
P: 408-330-0818　F: 408-330-0886　　　PRC:168
www.uniqvision.com
Email: info@uniqvision.com

Rex Siu, VP of Sales

Designer and manufacturer of high resolution
CCD cameras for medical, scientific, industrial,
and military applications.

**Uniquify Inc**　　　　　　　　HQ
　2030 Fortune Dr Ste 200
　San Jose CA 95131
P: 408-235-8810　　　　　　　　PRC:126
www.uniquify.com
Email: sales@uniquify.com
Estab: 2005

Josh Lee, CEO
Sam Kim, COO
Graham Bell, VP of Marketing

Developer and manufacturer of SoC displays and
other semi-conductor products. The company
offers technical support services.

**Unisoft Corp** HQ
10 Rollins Rd Ste 118
Millbrae CA 94030-3128
P: 650-259-1290   F: 650-259-1299   PRC:325
www.unisoft.com
Email: info@unisoft.com
Estab: 1981

Audrey Ruelas, Director
Jose Rodriguez, Director

Provider of broadcast, development, and testing tools specific to interactive TV standards. The company focuses on US cable and broadcast industries.

**Unitech Tool & Machine Inc** HQ
3025 Stender Way
Santa Clara CA 95054
P: 408-566-0333   PRC:80
unitechtool.com
Email: sales@unitechtool.com

Jeanne Lak, Co-Owner
Ramin Lak, Owner

Manufacturer of custom finished parts, tooling, and fixtures. The company is specialized in milling and lathe fabrication, mechanical design consulting.

**United Mechanical Inc** HQ
548 Claire St
Hayward CA 94541
P: 510-537-4744   F: 510-537-9564   PRC:80
www.umec.net
Estab: 1982

Alex Polissky, Design Engineer
Linda Congdon, Assistant Project Manager
Mark Swan, Senior Account Manager
Samantha Suriano, Project Manager
Dirk Durham, Senior Account Manager

Provider of precision sheet metal fabrication services for semiconductor, disk drive, medical, pharmaceutical, and aerospace equipment.

**United Medical Instruments Inc** HQ
832 Jury Ct
San Jose CA 95112
P: 408-278-9300   F: 408-278-9797   PRC:189
www.umiultrasound.com
Email: info@umiultrasound.com
Estab: 1996

Mansoor Ghanavati, CEO
Paul Werp, VP of Business Development
Neil Walendy, National Director of Sales
Steven Kelley, Parts Sales Manager

Provider of ultra sound equipment. The company focuses on pain management, breast imaging, and pathology.

**United Pro-Fab Manufacturing Inc** HQ
45300 Industrial Pl Unit 5
Fremont CA 94538
P: 510-651-5570   F: 510-651-5761   PRC:80
www.pfmfg.com
Email: quotations@pfmfg.com
Estab: 1984

Rajesh Gupta, President

Provider of machining and fabrication services. The company offers services for the aircraft, semiconductors, telecommunications, and biotechnology sectors.

**United Sheetmetal Inc** BR
44153 S Grimmer Blvd
Fremont CA 94538
P: 510-257-1858   F: 510-257-1850   PRC:88
www.unitedsheetmetal.com
Estab: 1964

Jin Hu, Sales Engineer
Chay Mo, VP of Business Development
Paul Tsang, Business Development Manager

Manufacturer of precision metal products. The company specializes in tooling, die casting, plastic injection, and sheet metal fabrication services.

**United States Thermoelectric Consortium** HQ
13267 Contractors Dr
Chico CA 95973
P: 530-345-8000   F: 678-821-4337   PRC:233
www.ustechcon.com
Email: info@ustcmail.com
Emp: 1-10   Estab: 1997

James Kerner, President

Manufacturer of thermal management and control systems. The company's offerings also include controllers and air and liquid cooling systems.

**Unitedlayer LLC** HQ
200 Paul Ave Ste 110
San Francisco CA 94124
P: 415-349-2100   F: 415-520-5700   PRC:67
www.unitedlayer.com
Email: sales@unitedlayer.com
Estab: 2001

Abhijit Phanse, CEO
Aaron Hughes, Chief Network Architect
Edward Buck, VP of Services & Support
Anas Alousi, Global Head of Operations

Provider of cloud hosting solutions. The company offers server clusters and routers, disaster recovery, infrastructure, and colocation services.

**Unitek Inc** HQ
41350 Christy St
Fremont CA 94538
P: 510-623-8544   F: 510-623-8970   PRC:209
www.unitekinc.com
Estab: 1989

Anyi Emelogu, Engineering Specialist
Paul Hyun, President
Joseph McCutchen, Business Development Manager

Provider of electronic manufacturing services. The company provides PCB assembly, material management, testing, and system integration services.

**Universal Audio Inc** HQ
4585 Scotts Valley Dr
Scotts Valley CA 95066
P: 831-440-1176   F: 831-461-1550   PRC:148
www.uaudio.com
Email: info@uaudio.com
Emp: 1-10   Estab: 1958

Dan Freeman, Director of Hardware Engineering
Leif Ames, Software Engineer
Bill Putnam, Owner
Erik Hanson, Director of Marketing
Darrin Fox, Marketing Copywriter

Manufacturer of analog recording equipment. The company's products include audio interfaces, channel strips, plug-ins, and compressors.

**Universal Light Source Inc** HQ
1553 Folsom St
San Francisco CA 94103
P: 415-864-2880   F: 415-864-3207   PRC:243
ulsi.net
Email: sales@ulsi.net
Estab: 1975

Douglas Ascher, CEO
Bryan Ascher, Technical Sales Manager

Provider of technical lighting applications. The company specializes in flash lamps and strobes, glass and window manufacturing, and PCBs.

**Untangle** HQ
25 Metro Dr Ste 210
San Jose CA 95110
P: 408-598-4299   PRC:319
www.untangle.com
Email: info@untangle.com
Estab: 2003

Scott Devens, CEO
Lori Booroojian, CFO
Timur Kovalev, CTO
Abi Vickram, VP of Sales
Heather Paunet, VP of Product Management

Designer and developer of network management software. The company specializes in firewall and Internet management application.

**UpGuard Inc** HQ
723 N Shoreline Blvd
Mountain View CA 94043
P: 888-882-3223   PRC:325
www.upguard.com
Email: support@upguard.com
Estab: 2012

Alan Sharp-Paul, Co-Founder
Mike Baukes, Co-Founder
Jackie Ariston, Chief of Staff
Maripet Macabantad, Director of Finance
Hamish Hawthorn, VP of Corporate Development

Provider of integrity monitoring, vulnerability analysis, vendor risk assessment, and configuration differencing solutions.

**Upsolar America Inc** BR
268 Bush St Ste 2919
San Francisco CA 94104
P: 415-263-9920   PRC:135
upsolaramerica.com
Email: support@upsolar.com
Estab: 2009

Stephane Dufrenne, CTO
Sebastian Wykeham, Director of Investor Relations
Jessy Li, Office Manager

Developer and producer of solar photovoltaic modules. The company's services include installation and maintenance and offers packing solutions.

**Upwork Global Inc** HQ
2625 Augustine Dr Ste 601
Santa Clara CA 95054
P: 650-316-7500   PRC:325
www.upwork.com
Estab: 2015
Sales: $1M to $3M

Han Yuan, SVP of Engineering
Stephane Kasriel, CEO
Brian Kinion, CFO
Brian Levey, Chief Business Affairs
Zoe Harte, SVP of Human Resources

Web based platform for remote work.

**Us Hydrotech Environmental Solutions** HQ
1007 W College Ave Ste 461
Santa Rosa CA 95401
P: 707-793-4800   F: 888-473-3650   PRC:142
ushydrotech.com
Email: info@ushydrotech.com
Estab: 2007

Edward Bertain, President

Provider of hydro tech environmental solutions. The company offers wash pads, containments, pressure washers, and solar thermal products.

**Us Night Vision Corp** HQ
1420 E Roseville Pkwy Ste 140-321
Roseville CA 95661
P: 800-500-4020   F: 916-788-1113   PRC:176
www.usnightvision.com
Email: sales@usnightvision.com
Emp: 1-10   Estab: 2001

Chris Byrd, VP of Sales

Provider of night vision, thermal imaging, infrared and laser products. The company serves law enforcement agencies and US military.

**US Union Tool** BR
2962 Scott Blvd
Santa Clara CA 95054
P: 714-521-6242   F: 714-521-8642   PRC:157
www.usuniontool.com
Estab: 1981

John McCandlish, Regional Manager

Designer and manufacturer of micro cutting tools for the printed circuit industry. The company engages in mold and dies and medical and aerospace parts.

**USAPEX** HQ
933-G La Mesa Ter
Sunnyvale CA 94086
P: 408-730-9800   F: 408-730-9808   PRC:170
usapex.com
Email: info@usapex.com

David Liu, President

Manufacturer of fiber optic products, metal and plastic machined parts, lead free solder pastes, liquid flux, power adapters, cables, and connectors.

**USB Promos** HQ
268 Bush St Ste 4302
San Francisco CA 94104
P: 800-515-3990   PRC:68
www.usbpromos.com
Estab: 2006

Cassey Xu, Director
Alex Rice, Director of Sales

Provider of USB flash drives, power banks, web keys, video brochures and digital toys and promotional items.

**uSens Inc** HQ
226 Airport Pkwy Ste 550
San Jose CA 95110
P: 408-564-0227   PRC:319
www.usens.com
Email: info@usens.com
Estab: 2013

Yue Fei, CTO
Anli He, CEO
Chris Shi, COO
Yiwen Rong, VP of Product Development

Creator of 3D human computing interaction software and hardware solutions. The company focuses on artificial intelligence.

**UserTesting** HQ
690 Fifth St
San Francisco CA 94107
P: 888-877-1882   PRC:325
www.usertesting.com

Darrell Benatar, Executive Chairman
Dave Garr, SVP of Customer Experience
Andy MacMillan, CEO
Tien-Anh Nguyen, CFO
Kaj van de Loo, CTO

Deliver a human insight platform powered by customer experience for product teams, marketers, and advertising companies.

**Usk Manufacturing Inc** HQ
720 Zwissig Way
Union City CA 94587-3602
P: 510-471-7555   F: 510-471-7554   PRC:80
www.uskmfg.com
Email: sales@uskmfg.com
Estab: 1987

Kendrick Kim, Operations Manager

Provider of precision sheet metal and machining services. The company also focuses on mechanical assembly.

**USWired Inc** HQ
2107 N First St Ste 250
San Jose CA 95131
P: 408-669-3522   F: 408-432-8660   PRC:323
www.uswired.com
Email: info@uswired.com
Estab: 1996

Leonil Arce, Systems Engineer
Derek Wong, Desktop Support Engineer
Robin Hau, President
Jon Schwartz, Desktop Technician

Provider of computer networking solutions that include cloud hosting, network design and installation, and wireless networks.

**Utstarcom Inc** BR
1732 N First St Ste 220
San Jose CA 95112
P: 408-453-4557   F: 408-453-4046   PRC:63
www.utstar.com
Email: sales@utstar.com
Estab: 1991

Mickey Ming Yam, Senior Engineer
Matt Parker, Senior International Accountant

Manufacturer of IP based, end to end networking, and telecommunications solutions. The company also focuses on integration.

**Uvexs Inc** HQ
1287 Hammerwood Ave
Sunnyvale CA 94089-2205
P: 408-734-4402   F: 408-734-4502   PRC:209
www.uvexs.com
Email: customerservice@uvexs.com
Estab: 1977

Lonnie Tillett, Engineer
Brent Puder, Manager

Manufacturer of UV curing systems. The company's products find application in formulation of UV-curable inks, adhesives, and coatings.

**V&O Machine Inc** HQ
17591 County Rd 97
Woodland CA 95695
P: 530-662-0495   F: 530-309-0395   PRC:80
vomachine.com
Email: vomachine@vomachine.com
Emp: 1-10   Estab: 1974

Douglas Ostlind, Owner
Clifford Cooper, Manager

Manufacturer of machined parts for agri, hydraulics, food procesing, and veterinary applications. The company focuses on prototyping and CNC milling.

**V-Power Equipment Inc** HQ
4201 W Capitol Ave
West Sacramento CA 95691
P: 916-266-6743   F: 916-266-6744   PRC:160
www.vpowerequip.com
Email: sales@vpowerequip.com
Emp: 1-10   Estab: 2007

Melissa Reid, Director of Marketing
Chris Murray, Manager

Manufacturer and wholesaler of water well, wastewater, and construction dewatering pumps. The company provides pump repair and diagnostic services.

**V-Soft Inc** HQ
888 Saratoga Ave Ste 203
San Jose CA 95129
P: 408-342-1700   F: 408-342-1705   PRC:322
www.v-softinc.com
Email: info@v-softinc.com
Estab: 1995

Ashwin Vora, CEO

Provider of product development services. The company also specializes in mobile application development.

**V2plus Technology Inc** HQ
4030 Clipper Ct
Fremont CA 94538
P: 510-226-6006   PRC:67
www.v2-plus.com
Email: admin@v2-plus.com

Tom Lin, CTO

Provider of technology solutions. The company offers services for voice, data, and video over local wired and wireless communication networks.

**V5 Systems** HQ
3191 Laurelview Ct
Fremont CA 94538
P: 844-604-7350 PRC:77
v5systems.us
Email: info@v5systems.us
Estab: 2014

Alexander Motyashov, VP of Software Engineering
Saeed Arash Far, VP of Hardware Engineering
Mazin Bedwan, President
Steve Yung, CEO
Theodore Low, CFO

Provider of outdoor security and computing platforms. The company offers services to the government, military, and law enforcement industries.

**Vacuum Engineering & Materials Co** HQ
390 Reed St
Santa Clara CA 95050
P: 408-871-9900 F: 408-562-9125 PRC:212
www.vem-co.com
Email: info@vem-co.com
Estab: 1987

Bob Kavanaugh, President
Stephanie McConnell, CFO
Melvin Hirata, VP of Sales
Barry Henson, VP of Operations
Dennis Raney, Board Director

Manufacturer and supplier of PVD materials. The company also offers services like shield cleaning, material reclaim, and consignment programs.

**Vacuum Process Engineering Inc** HQ
110 Commerce Cir
Sacramento CA 95815-4208
P: 916-925-6100 F: 916-925-6111 PRC:86
www.vpei.com
Email: info@vpei.com
Emp: 1-10 Estab: 1976

Ryan Kim, Engineer Assistant
Brittany Wood, Project Engineer
Carl Schalansky, CEO
Tammy Volf, Purchasing Manager
Ben Irani, Technical Sales Manager

Provider of engineering services. The company focuses on precision brazing, diffusion bonding, heat treating, and production of precision assemblies.

**Valdor Fiber Optics Inc** RH
3116 Diablo Ave
Hayward CA 94545
P: 510-293-1212 F: 510-293-9996 PRC:170
www.valdor.com
Email: sales@valdor.com
Estab: 1985

Las Yabut, President
Elston Johnston, Chairman
Brian Findlay, CFO
Ron Boyce, VP of Sales & Marketing
Kandra Kalanick, Controller

Provider of product design and development services of fiber optic products such as connectors, attenuators, couplers, splitters, and multiplexers.

**Valent Usa Corp** HQ
PO Box 8025
Walnut Creek CA 94596-8025
P: 800-682-5368 PRC:48
www.valent.com
Estab: 1988

Bob Bryant, Manufacturing Engineer
Susan Morris, Purchasing
Michael Tagle, Director of Finance
Leanne Becker, Sales Representative
David Nothmann, VP of Marketing

Provider of agricultural products. The company also deals with pest management solutions and serves the commercial agricultural sector.

**Valiantica Inc** HQ
940 Saratoga Ave Ste 108
San Jose CA 95129
P: 408-725-2426 F: 408-580-8548 PRC:323
www.valiantica.com
Estab: 2007

Peiwei Mi, Co-Founder
Reena Sah, Human Resource & Accounting Manager
Archana Sinha, Human Resource & Accounts Administrator
Pratha Malhotra, Director of Sales
Monisha Mitra, Account Manager

Provider of global IT solutions. The company's services include consulting, outsourcing, and mobile, enterprise and business application development.

**Valimet Inc** HQ
431 Sperry Rd
Stockton CA 95206
P: 209-444-1600 F: 209-444-1636 PRC:50
www.valimet.com
Email: sales@valimet.com
Emp: 1-10 Estab: 1975

Sifan Zhu, Process Engineer
Larry Elam, Quality Control Manager
Valerie Waldon, Sales Manager

Manufacturer of spherical atomized metal powders. The company also offers aluminum silicon and aluminum bronze and special alloys.

**Valin** HQ
5225 Hellyer Ave Ste 250
San Jose CA 95138
P: 408-730-9850 F: 408-730-1363 PRC:319
www.valin.com
Email: customerservice@valin.com
Estab: 1974

Joseph Nettemeyer, President
David Hefler, VP
Robin Slater, Corporate VP of Sales
Brian Sullivan, Director of Sales & Technology
Chris Sullivan, Director of Sales

Provider of engineered solutions. The company serves the semiconductor, petrochemical, life sciences, and aerospace industries.

**Valitor Inc** HQ
East Bay Innovation Ctr 820 Heinz Ave
Berkeley CA 94710
P: 510-969-9246 F: 510-647-8429 PRC:34
www.valitorbio.com
Email: info@valitorbio.com
Estab: 2010

Wesley Jackson, CSO

Developer of therapeutic protein drugs. The company's drugs are used in dermatology, ophthalmology, orthopedics, and stem cell therapy.

**Valley Communications Inc** HQ
6921 Roseville Rd
Sacramento CA 95842
P: 916-349-7300 F: 916-349-7329 PRC:62
www.valley-com.com
Email: info@valley-com.com
Emp: 11-50 Estab: 1983

Kate DeWitt, VP of Finance
Jared Carpenter, Marketing Admin
Jami Walker, Project Manager
Bill Beban, Service Manager

Provider of services for network cabling infrastructure needs. The company focuses on designing and installation.

**Valley Tool & Manufacturing Co** HQ
2507 Tully Rd
Hughson CA 95326
P: 800-426-5615 PRC:159
valleytoolmfg.com
Email: info@valleytoolmfg.com
Emp: 1-10 Estab: 1969

Fred Brenda, President
Luann Klann, Controller

Manufacturer of agricultural equipment like flail mowers, sprayers, and shredders. The company also manufactures skid steer and excavator attachments.

**Valleytek Inc** HQ
930 Rincon Cir
San Jose CA 95131
P: 408-577-1218 F: 408-577-1299 PRC:209
valleytek.com
Email: info@valleytek.com
Estab: 2003

Thien Pham, Owner

Provider of expanded memory specification solutions, contract manufacturing services, and engineering services.

**Valmark Interface Solutions** HQ
7900 National Dr
Livermore CA 94550
P: 925-960-9900 F: 925-960-0900 PRC:87
nidec-vis.com
Email: vis@nidec-vis.com
Estab: 1976

Bill Canon, VP of Product Development & Engineering

Manufacturer of labels, panel overlays, and membrane switches. The company is engaged in engineering, assembly, and installation services.

**Valqua America Inc**      HQ
4655 Old Ironsides Dr Ste 380
Santa Clara CA 95054
P: 408-986-1425    F: 408-986-1426      PRC:86
www.valqua-america.com
Estab: 1998

Kaori Kawasaki, Sales Engineer
Noriko Ishikawa, Information Technology Manager
Takafumi Sakurai, Technical Project Manager

Seller and marketer of semiconductor related products. The company also offers R&D services for high performance elastomer seals.

**Value Products Inc**      HQ
2128 Industrial Dr
Stockton CA 95206
P: 209-983-4000    F: 209-983-4080      PRC:56
www.valueproductsinc.com
Emp: 1-10    Estab: 1970

Doug Hall, President
Silverio Fernandez, Production Manager
Erica Hall, Office Manager
June Guanzon, Lab Technician
Liz Maloney, Customer Service

Provider of chemical compounding and packaging solutions. The company services include silk screen printing and private labeling.

**ValueLabs Inc**      BR
1250 Oakmead Pkwy Ste 210
Sunnyvale CA 94085-4037
P: 408-475-2445    F: 408-716-2975      PRC:322
www.valuelabs.com

Venu Gangavarapu, Test Manager
Prakash Konakanchi, Module Lead
Amit Patel, Technical Lead
Nick Collins, Business Developer

Provider of technology solutions and services. The company's services include digital solutions, quality assurance, and application development.

**Vanderhulst Associates Inc**      HQ
3300 Victor Ct
Santa Clara CA 95054
P: 408-727-1313      PRC:80
vanderhulst.com
Estab: 1975

Hank Vanderhulst, Director of Human Resource
Chris Hernandez, Production Manager

Provider of precision machining and manufacturing services. The company serves the medical, analytical, and semiconductor industries.

**Vanderlans & Sons Inc**      HQ
1320 S Sacramento St
Lodi CA 95240
P: 209-334-4115    F: 209-339-8260      PRC:159
www.lansas.com
Email: information@lansas.com
Emp: 1-10    Estab: 1958

Eric Lans, VP

Manufacturer of pipe and high pressure plugs, test equipment, hoses, gauges, ventilators, and related accessories.

**Vandersteen**      HQ
116 W Fourth St
Hanford CA 93230
P: 559-582-0324    F: 559-582-0364      PRC:60
www.vandersteen.com
Email: international@vandersteen.com
Emp: 1-10

Richard Vandersteen, Founder

Manufacturer and distributor of loudspeakers. The company's products include VCC-5 Center, V2W Subwoofer, VLR, and 3a Signature.

**Vantage Data Center Services & Solutions**      HQ
2820 Northwestern Pkwy
Santa Clara CA 95051
P: 855-878-2682      PRC:290
www.vantagedatacenters.com
Email: info@vantage-dc.com
Estab: 2010

Alex O'Hearn, Project Engineer
Larry Scheierman, Critical Facilities Engineer
Sureel Choksi, CEO
Justin Thomas, CTO
Chris Yetman, COO

Provider of transformers, switches, generators, chillers, switch gears and security, and communication products.

**Vantage Robotics LLC**      HQ
1933 Davis St Ste 240
San Leandro CA 94577
P: 510-907-7012      PRC:311
vantagerobotics.com
Email: contact@vantagerobotics.com
Estab: 2013

Aaron Breen, Director of Mechanical Engineering
Joe Van Niekerk, Co-Founder
Tobin Fisher, Co-Founder
Assaf Stoler, VP of Software
Kaj Martin, Director of Operations

Developer and manufacturer of camera drones. The company serves the consumer electronics, automation, and robotics industries.

**Vanton Research Laboratory LLC**      HQ
1870 Arnold Industrial Pl Ste 1000-1010
Concord CA 94520
P: 925-687-7817    F: 925-687-7827      PRC:268
www.vantonlab.com
Email: info@vantonlab.com
Estab: 1993

Eric Sheu, Director

Specializes in the development of non-conventional drug delivery systems and integrated pharmaceutical services.

**Vapore LLC**      HQ
1130 Burnett Ave Ste P
Concord CA 94520
P: 925-998-6116      PRC:189
www.mypurmist.com
Email: care@mypurmist.com
Estab: 2011

Graham Booth, Data Engineer
Brett MacKinnon, President
Lars Barfod, CEO
Kasia Kirkbride, Sales

Manufacturer of personal steam inhalers. The company's products are used for relief from sinus congestion, allergies, and discomfort from sore throat.

**Varentec Inc**      HQ
3200 Patrick Henry Dr
Santa Clara CA 95054
P: 408-433-9900    F: 408-433-9919      PRC:290
www.varentec.com
Email: sales@varentec.com
Estab: 2009

Anish Prasai, Manager of Hardware Engineering
Curtis Rhymes, Senior Electronics Engineering Technician
Daniel White, Software Engineer
Deepak Divan, President
Guillaume Dufosse, CEO

Provider of grid control and monitoring solutions. The company also offers asset management and outage detection services.

**Varian Medical Systems Inc**      BR
660 N Mccarthy Blvd
Milpitas CA 95035
P: 408-321-9400      PRC:195
www.varian.com
Email: info.europe@varian.com
Estab: 1940

Chris Toth, President of Oncology Systems
Dow Wilson, President
Gary Bischoping, President of Interventional Oncology Solutions
Kolleen Kennedy, President of Proton Solutions and Chief Growth Officer
Magnus Momsen, SVP

Provider of radiation therapies for cancer. The company develops and markets different types of radiation technologies to cure various cancers.

**Varian Medical Systems Inc**      HQ
3100 Hansen Way
Palo Alto CA 94304-1038
P: 650-493-4000      PRC:189
www.varian.com
Email: info.europe@varian.com
Estab: 1948
Sales: $1B to $3B

Chris Toth, President of Oncology Systems
Kolleen Kennedy, President Proton Solutions and Chief Growth Officer
Dow Wilson, President
Gary Bischoping, President
Magnus Momsen, SVP

Provider of radiation therapies for cancer. The company develops and markets different types of radiation technologies to cure various cancers.

**Variant Microsystems** HQ
4128 Business Center Dr
Fremont CA 94538
P: 510-440-2870  F: 510-440-2873  PRC:120
www.variantusa.com
Email: sales@variantusa.com
Estab: 1994

Rajiv Chugh, President

Manufacturer and reseller of data collection
equipment such as bar code scanners, printers,
portables.

**Varite Inc** HQ
111 N Market St Ste 730
San Jose CA 95113
P: 408-977-0700  F: 408-977-0760  PRC:323
www.varite.com
Email: contact@varite.com
Estab: 2000

Adarsh Katyal, President
Amarjeet Singh, Associate Account Manager
Swetha Reddy, Business Development Manager
Anubhav Sood, Strategic Account Manager
Yogesh Sharma, Senior Resource Manager

Provider of custom software development, integration, deployment, and implementation services in
the domains of core networking and virtualization.

**vArmour Inc** HQ
270 third St
Los Altos CA 94022
P: 650-564-5100  F: 650-564-5101  PRC:325
www.varmour.com
Email: info@varmour.com
Estab: 2011

Roger Lian, Co-Founder
Michael Shieh, Co-Founder
Timothy Eades, CEO
Marc Woolward, CTO

Provider of cloud security, segmentation, monitoring, and deception solutions. The company serves
banks and healthcare organizations.

**Varna Products** HQ
4305 Business Dr
Cameron Park CA 95682
P: 530-676-7770  F: 530-676-7796  PRC:160
www.varnaproducts.com
Emp: 1-10  Estab: 2005

Thomas Martin, Engineering Manager
Jordan Uggla, Embedded Software Developer

Manufacturer of pump and valve solutions. The
company offers oil pumps, pump controls, pressure relief valves, and check valves.

**Vaxart Inc** HQ
395 Oyster Point Blvd Ste 405
S San Francisco CA 94080
P: 650-550-3500  F: 650-871-8580  PRC:268
www.vaxart.com
Email: info@vaxart.com
Estab: 2004

Sean Tucker, Founder
Wouter Latour, CEO
David Ingamells, VP of Manufacturing
David Taylor, CMO
Brant Biehn, SVP of Commercial Operations

Manufacturer and developer of oral vaccines. The
company is engaged in drug development and
related services.

**Vayusphere Inc** HQ
2685 Marine Way Ste 1305
Mountain View CA 94043
P: 650-960-2900  F: 650-960-2910  PRC:322
www.vayusphere.com
Email: sales@vayusphere.com
Estab: 2000

Pushpendra Mohta, CEO

Developer of instant messaging applications. The
company's customers include Morgan Stanley,
Deutsche Bank, and others.

**Vdx Veterinary Diagnostics** HQ
2019 Anderson Rd Ste C
Davis CA 95616
P: 530-753-4285  F: 530-753-4055  PRC:273
www.vdxpathology.com
Email: info@vdxpathology.com
Emp: 1-10  Estab: 2001

John Peauroi, Founder
Jeffrey Lewis, Clinical Operations Manager
Sonjia Shelly, Doctor of Veterinary Medicine
Robyn Mohr, Lab Assistant

Provider of histopathology and pathology support
to the medical device, biotech, pharmaceutical,
academic and veterinary communities.

**Vector Fabrication Inc** HQ
1629 Watson Ct
Milpitas CA 95035
P: 408-942-9800  F: 408-942-9896  PRC:211
www.vectorfab.com
Email: info@vectorfab.com
Estab: 1995

Quang Luong, President

Manufacturer of printed circuit boards. The company offers circuit board assembly, drilling, solder
mask, plating, and testing services.

**Vector Laboratories Inc** HQ
30 Ingold Rd
Burlingame CA 94010
P: 650-697-3600  F: 650-697-0339  PRC:34
www.vectorlabs.com
Email: vector@vectorlabs.com
Estab: 1976

Pam Williams, Business Manager
Darlene Ha, Production Scientist
Cherie Nolasco, Production Scientist
Jonathan Milbourne, Production Chemist
Erika Leonard, Director of Quality Control

Provider of labeling and detection services for
enzymes, antibodies and antigens, DNA and RNA
by using polymer reagents.

**Veeva Systems** HQ
4280 Hacienda Dr
Pleasanton CA 94588
P: 925-452-6500  F: 925-452-6504  PRC:323
www.veeva.com
Email: sales@veeva.com
Estab: 2007
Sales: $300M to $1 Billion

Derek Allwardt, Director of Engineering
Anna Liu, Associate Quality Assurance Engineer
Peter Gassner, Founder
Tom Schwenger, President
Tim Cabral, CFO

Provider of cloud-based business solutions such
as customer relationship management and content management for the life sciences industry.

**VeEX Inc** HQ
2827 Lakeview Ct
Fremont CA 94538
P: 510-651-0500  F: 510-651-0505  PRC:68
www.veexinc.com
Email: info@veexinc.com
Estab: 2006

Simon Sangwon, Senior SW Engineer
Ildefonso Polo, Director of Product Marketing
Terence Leong, Director of Customer Care
Hawkee NGU, Project Manager
Eve Danel, Senior Product Manager

Developer of test and measurement solutions
for next generation communication equipment
and networks. The company serves the industrial
sector.

**Velano Vascular Inc** HQ
221 Pine St Ste 200
San Francisco CA 94104
P: 844-835-2668  PRC:195
velanovascular.com
Email: support@velanovascular.com
Estab: 2012

Brian Funk, Research
Eric Ston, Co-Founder
Pitou Devgon, Co-Founder
Maura Flaherty, Marketing Associate

Manufacturer of needle-free devices for drawing
blood from hospitalized patients. The company
offers services to the medical industry.

**Velocity Pharmaceutical Development
LLC** HQ
400 Oyster Point Blvd Ste 202
S San Francisco CA 94080
P: 650-273-5748  F: 650-745-8179  PRC:268
www.vpd.net
Email: info@vpd.net
Estab: 2011

David Collier, CEO
Edward Schnipper, Managing Director
James Larrick, Managing Director
Andrew Perlman, Managing Director
Leslie Loven, Office Manager

Developer of drug candidates. The company
specializes in clinical development programs
and serves biotechnology and pharmaceutical
companies.

**Velos LLC** HQ
42840 Christy St Ste 201
Fremont CA 94538
P: 510-739-4010  F: 510-739-4018  PRC:304
velos.com
Email: info@velos.com
Estab: 1996

John McIlwain, CEO
Sonia Abrol, VP of Development and Operations
Madalynne Chapman, Director

Provider of clinical research solutions. The company offers services to hospitals, academic medical
centers, and also cancer centers.

**Vena Engineering Corp**    HQ
7 Hangar Way
Watsonville CA 95076
P: 831-724-5738    PRC:235
www.vena.com
Email: sales@vena.com
Emp: 1-10   Estab: 1995

Jeff Greatorex, VP
Disun Daas, Customer Support Manager

Manufacturer of hard drive test equipment and environmental chambers. The company also offers motors and power supplies.

**Ventek International**    HQ
1260 Holm Rd Ste A
Petaluma CA 94954
P: 707-773-3373   F: 707-773-3381    PRC:238
www.ventek-intl.com
Email: info@ventek-intl.com
Estab: 1950

Gary Catt, President
Craig Lewis, Chief of Production
Victoria Iacovetto, National Sales Manager
Erika Anderson, Sales Manager
Joan Barrie, Executive Assistant

Manufacturer of parking revenue control systems. The company offers recreation, commuter rail, and parking access control solutions.

**Ventex Corp**    HQ
2153 Otoole Ave Ste 10
San Jose CA 95131
P: 408-436-2929   F: 408-436-2928    PRC:159
www.ventexcorp.com
Email: info@ventexcorp.com

Joe Burke, Field Service Engineer
James Docherty, Owner
Eddie Ramirez, Engineering & Production Manager

Supplier of lithography equipment, spare parts, and services. The company also provides refurbishment and installation services.

**Venturi Wireless Inc**    HQ
152 N Third St Ste 510
San Jose CA 95112
P: 408-982-1130   F: 408-638-0314    PRC:67
www.venturiwireless.com
Email: sales@venturiwireless.com
Estab: 1993

Subappriya Muthuchamy, Senior Software Engineer
Uday Nagendran, President
Dan McEntee, VP of Finance & Administration
Ha Huynh, Senior Accountant

Provider of broadband optimization services. The company mainly caters to mobile and wireless operators.

**Veolia Water**    BR
601 Canal Blvd
Richmond CA 94804
P: 510-412-2001    PRC:100
www.richmond.veolianorthamerica.com

Aaron Winer, Project Manager

Provider of water and wastewater treatment solutions. The company offers services for public authorities and industrial companies.

**Veolia**    BR
8310 Umbria Ave
Sacramento CA 95828
P: 916-379-0872    PRC:142
www.veolianorthamerica.com
Emp: 11-50

John Gibson, EVP
Nisreen Bagasra, Chief Procurement Officer

Provider of complete environmental solutions. The company focuses on energy, water treatment, and waste management.

**Veracentra**    HQ
690 Airpark Rd
Napa CA 94558
P: 707-224-6161   F: 707-224-7518    PRC:326
www.veracentra.com
Estab: 1988

David Resnick, CIO of Technology & Client Solutions
Dan Plunkett, VP of Marketing Execution Services
Patti Arnold, Program Manager
Idalia Radillo, Supervisor
Kathleen Bradbury, Controller

Provider of data leveraging services to brands for marketing needs and also focuses on customer intelligence, marketing execution, and consultation.

**Veracyte Inc**    HQ
7000 Shoreline Ct Ste 250
S San Francisco CA 94080
P: 650-243-6300    PRC:268
www.veracyte.com
Email: info@veracyte.com
Estab: 2008
Sales: $30M to $100M

Bonnie Anderson, Chairman
Giulia Kennedy, CSO
John Hanna, Chief Commercial Officer
Keith Kennedy, CFO
Ashish Kheterpal, Chief Information Officer

Focuses on molecular analysis and diagnostic tests. The company serves patients and the healthcare sector.

**Verdafero Inc**    HQ
1012 Bent Oak Ln
San Jose CA 95129
P: 650-206-2441    PRC:315
www.verdafero.com
Estab: 2009

Alastair Hood, CEO
Terri Gilbert, Director of Information Technology
Christopher Hall, Director of Business Development

Offers a wide range of cloud-based software solutions that enable companies to manage their utility data and analytics.

**Verge Analytics Inc**    HQ
Two Tower Pl Ste 950
S San Francisco CA 94080
P: 415-355-4737    PRC:257
www.vergegenomics.com
Email: hello@vergegenomics.com
Estab: 2015

Alice Zhang, CEO

Provider of treatment for brain diseases. The company is involved in drug development and research services.

**Veridian Environmental Inc**    HQ
425 Merchant St Ste 101
Vacaville CA 95688
P: 707-449-4400    PRC:142
www.veridianenv.com
Estab: 1992

Charlotte Symms, President
Tracy Young, VP

Provider of environmental analysis and management consulting services. The company offers services to the industrial sector.

**Verient Inc**    HQ
1190 Saratoga Ave Ste 220
San Jose CA 95129
P: 408-521-1660   F: 408-521-1682    PRC:325
www.verient.com
Email: information@verient.com
Estab: 2006

Rajesh Shakkarwar, Founder
Ashley Holmes, System Administrator

Provider of cloud based financial products. The company's offerings convert non revenue producing payments to credit card transactions.

**Verific Design Automation Inc**    HQ
1516 Oak St Ste 115
Alameda CA 94501
P: 510-522-1555   F: 510-522-1553    PRC:212
www.verific.com
Email: info@verific.com
Estab: 1999

Michiel Ligthart, COO
Rick Carlson, VP of Sales
Lawrence Neukom, Senior Member Technical Staff

Specializes in electronic design automation solutions. The company offers services to the semiconductor industry.

**VeriSilicon Inc**    HQ
2150 Gold St Ste 200
San Jose CA 95002
P: 408-844-8560    PRC:208
www.verisilicon.com
Email: us-sales@verisilicon.com
Estab: 2002

Shuangbei Li, Data Processing Engineer
Wayne Dai, CEO
Sam Shieh, Corporate VP of Technology
Yanjun Zhang, VP of Software Development

Provider of IC design services specializing in custom silicon solutions. The company also offers SOC turnkey services.

**Veritas Technologies LLC**    HQ
2625 Augustine Dr
Santa Clara CA 95054
P: 866-837-4827    PRC:319
www.veritas.com
Estab: 2016

Greg Hughes, CEO
Mark Dentinger, EVP
John Abel, SVP
Sophie Ames, SVP
Todd Forsythe, SVP

Empowers business with a multi-cloud data management solution.

**Verix Inc** HQ
4340 Stevens Creek Blvd Ste 166
San Jose CA 95129
P: 650-949-2700  F: 650-949-2722  PRC:325
www.verix.com
Email: info@verix.com
Estab: 2007

Amir Ashiri, Co-Founder
Haggay Tsaban, Co-Founder
Doron Aspitz, CEO

Designer and developer of precision tooling and
equipment for performance engine builders and
mechanists.

**Versa Networks Inc** HQ
6001 America Center Dr Ste 400
Santa Clara CA 95002
P: 408-385-7660  PRC:63
versa-networks.com
Estab: 2012

Apurva Mehta, Founder
Kumar Mehta, Founder
Kelly Ahuja, CEO
Chris Kenny, VP of Sales
Rob Mustarde, SVP of Worldwide Sales

Provider of networking solutions. The company
specializes in virtualized network functions and
services.

**Versa Shore Inc** HQ
1999 S Bascom Ave Ste 700
Campbell CA 95008
P: 408-874-8330  PRC:323
www.versashore.com
Estab: 2003

Shawn Rao, CEO
Bruce Hobbs, Chief Architect
Donald Lightbody, CFO
Bruce Dunn, Sales Manager
Roni Wu, Office Manager

Provider of data warehouse implementation,
strategic blueprint creation, project management,
and testing consulting services.

**Versartis Inc** HQ
4200 Bohannon Dr Ste 250
Menlo Park CA 94025
P: 650-963-8580  PRC:42
www.versartis.co/index.htm
Email: info@versartis.com
Estab: 2008

Vinita Kumar, VP
Scott Gorcey, Compliance Manager

Manufacturer and developer of therapeutic proteins for the treatment of endocrine disorders. The
company develops recombinant human growth
hormone.

**Versatile Power** HQ
743 Camden Ave
Campbell CA 95008
P: 408-341-4600  F: 408-341-4601  PRC:98
www.versatilepower.com
Email: sales@versatilepower.com
Estab: 2002

Jerry Price, CEO
Shad Schidel, Quality Manager

Designer and manufacturer of electronic subsystems for manufacturers. The company focuses on
application of radio frequency, ultrasonics, and
lasers.

**Verseon Corp** HQ
47071 Bayside Pkwy
Fremont CA 94538
P: 510-225-9000  F: 510-225-9001  PRC:268
www.verseon.com
Email: info@verseon.com
Estab: 2007

Adityo Prakash, CEO
Eniko Fodor, COO
John Zhang, Senior Scientist

Focuses on the design of drug candidates. The
company offers services to the pharmaceutical
industry.

**Versonix Corp** HQ
1175 Saratoga Ave Ste 4
San Jose CA 95129
P: 408-873-3131  F: 408-873-3139  PRC:323
www.versonix.com
Email: info@versonix.com
Estab: 1986

Jacob Dreyband, Director of Software Engineering
Igor Vilenski, CTO
Yuri Polissky, COO
Kristen Kristich-Madar, Project Manager
Nadia Nurutdinov, Business Analyst

Provider of integrated and customized software
solutions. The company serves the travel and
leisure industries.

**VerTech Engineering Inc** HQ
383 Rio Lindo Ave Ste 200
Chico CA 95926
P: 530-899-8716  F: 805-421-5359  PRC:304
vertechengineering.com
Email: info@vertechengineering.com
Emp: 11-50 Estab: 1999

Mike Hubley, Principal Engineer

Provider of structural engineering services, geotechnical services, and civil engineering services
for architects, builders, and developers.

**Vertical Systems Inc** HQ
4320 Stevens Creek Blvd Ste 284
San Jose CA 95129
P: 408-752-8100  F: 408-752-8102  PRC:322
www.ver-sys.com
Email: info@ver-sys.com
Estab: 2001

Saeed Kazmi, Chairman
Idris Kothari, CTO
Charlotte Williams, Account Manager
Nighat Lotia, Financial Accountant Consultant
Saleem Kazmi, Controller

Provider of centric solutions for the hospitality
industry. The company is also engaged in mobile
application and custom solutions.

**Vetequip Inc** HQ
1452 N Vasco Rd Ste 303
Livermore CA 94551
P: 925-463-1828  F: 925-463-1943  PRC:23
www.vetequip.com
Email: info@vetequip.com
Estab: 1982

Bob Schrock, Co-Owner
Melinda Kolar, Director of Customer Service

Developer and manufacturer of drug delivery
systems. The company specializes in nasal anes-
thesia delivery systems.

**Via Licensing Corp** HQ
1275 Market St
San Francisco CA 94103
P: 415-645-4700  F: 415-645-4400  PRC:328
www.via-corp.com
Email: info@vialicensing.com
Estab: 2002

Joseph Siino, President
Zaynab Hararah, Senior Compliance Analyst
Cecilia Wong, Accountant
Khajal Cooper, Senior Analyst
Cindy Wong, Licensing Accountant

Provider of intellectual property programs and
business solutions. The company serves technology companies, entertainment companies, and
universities.

**Vian Enterprises Inc** HQ
1501 Industrial Dr
Auburn CA 95603
P: 530-885-1997  F: 530-885-1998  PRC:160
vianenterprises.com
Email: info@vianenterprises.com
Emp: 1-10  Estab: 1968

Brian Wargala, Manufacturing Engineer
Sokheng Chheng, Design Engineer

Manufacturer of gerotors, gears, and broached
hardware. The company also offers oil pump and
complete lubrication systems.

**Vicom Systems Inc** HQ
2336 Walsh Ave
Santa Clara CA 95051
P: 650-241-3302  F: 650-560-6441  PRC:91
www.vicom.com
Email: info@vicom.com
Estab: 1996

Harpreet Aulakh, Support Engineer
Samuel Tam, CEO
Mark Egerton, VP of Sales & Partner Manage-
ment
Horatio Lo, VP of Systems & Professional Ser-
vices
Noel Hernandez, Project Manager

Provider of migration data services. The company
is involved in offering transparent wire-speed data
services for systems and storage.

**Victorious** HQ
995 Market St
San Francisco CA 94301
P: 415-621-9830  PRC:325
victoriousseo.com
Email: sales@victoriousseo.com
Estab: 2012

Michael Transon, CEO
Dave Burton, VP of Finance
Pete Tkachuk, Director of Sales
Houston Barnett-Gearhart, VP of Product
Kyle Wade, Director of Customer Success

Search engine optimization agency that leverages a wealth of performance data and market
research to create scientifically-driven SEO
strategies.

**Vida Products Inc**   HQ
6167 State Farm Dr
Rohnert Park CA 94928
P: 707-541-7000   PRC:70
vidaproducts.com
Email: info@vidaproducts.com
Estab: 2003

Ronald Parrott, President

Supplier of radio frequency and microwave components and subsystems. The company provides magnetically tuned oscillators, filters, and synthesizers.

**Vidado Inc**   HQ
130 Webster St Ste 200
Oakland CA 94067
P: 415-237-3676   PRC:315
vidado.ai/
Estab: 2011

Nowell Outlaw, CEO
Bill Hoover, CFO
Elaine Zhou, CTO
Eng Lee, VP of Professional Services

Designed to help organizations collect and digitize inaccessible data.

**Video Clarity Inc**   HQ
1566 La Pradera Dr
Campbell CA 95008
P: 408-379-6952   PRC:60
videoclarity.com
Email: sales@videoclarity.com
Estab: 2005

Blake Homan, President
Adam Schadle, VP

Provider of real time and broadcast quality monitoring, perceptual analysis, recording, and automating services.

**Videofax**   HQ
1750 Cesar Chavez St Unit G
San Francisco CA 94124
P: 415-641-0100   PRC:168
www.videofax.com
Email: rentals@videofax.com
Estab: 1987

Mona Marks, Rental Manager
Nick Schrader, Shop Manager
Sophie Aissen, Business Manager

Manufacturer of cameras, recorders, players, and related accessories. The company offers technical support services.

**Viewics Inc**   HQ
2821 Scott Blvd
Santa Clara CA 95050
P: 415-439-0084   PRC:188
viewics.com
Email: info@viewics.com
Estab: 2009

Tim Kuruvilla, Co-Founder

Provider of consulting, custom development, and report authoring services. The company also offers packaged solutions.

**Viking Enterprise Solutions**   HQ
2700 N First St
San Jose CA 95134
P: 408-964-3730   PRC:95
www.vikingenterprisesolutions.com
Email: info@vikingenterprise.com
Estab: 2000

Nirmal Jain, Senior SI Engineer
Parker Boyce, Firmware Engineer

Provider of solutions for data enterpriser centers. The company also offers storage expansion product platform.

**Vindicia Inc**   HQ
303 Twin Dolphin Dr Ste 200
Redwood City CA 94065
P: 650-264-4700   F: 650-264-4701   PRC:325
www.vindicia.com
Estab: 2003

Mark Elrod, EVP of Engineering
Sharath Dorbala, CEO
Roy Barak, CFO
Jack Bullock, Chief Revenue Officer
Jesus Luzardo, VP

Developer of marketing and analytics solutions. The company offers customer acquisition and retention and customer relationship management services.

**VinSuite**   HQ
1700 Soscol Ave Ste 3
Napa CA 94559
P: 707-253-7400   PRC:326
www.vinsuite.com
Email: info@vinsuite.com
Estab: 2013

Carrie-Anne Wood, Enterprise Account Manager
Daniel Williams, Support Operations Manager
Erin Davis, Project Manager
Tom Gorton, Manager of Professional Services
Craig Blackmon, Technical Support Specialist

Developer of wine software and serves the consumer sector. The company offers support services to wineries and tasting rooms.

**Vintara Inc**   HQ
1714 Franklin St Ste 100303
Oakland CA 94612
P: 877-846-8272   PRC:325
www.vintara.com
Email: info@vintara.com
Estab: 1997

Rob Power, Director of Engineering
Glenn Kohner, CEO
Dawn Plaskon, Director of Consulting Services

Provider of web-based enterprise process management solutions and services. The company caters to a number of industries.

**ViOptix Inc**   HQ
39655 Eureka Dr
Newark CA 94560
P: 510-226-5860   F: 510-226-5864   PRC:186
www.vioptix.com
Email: info@vioptix.com
Estab: 1999

Derek Lee, Senior Engineer Technician
Scott Coleridge, CEO
Jack Lloyd, Executive Chairman
Mark Lonsinger, VP
Michael Glore, Account Manager

Manufacturer of medical support devices. The company specializes in devices used for respiratory support and oxygen supply.

**VipeCloud**   HQ
855 El Camino Real Ste 13A-302
Palo Alto CA 94301
P: 650-308-8473   PRC:325
vipecloud.com
Email: contact@vipecloud.com
Estab: 2011

Adam Peterson, CEO
Erica Lynne, COO
Joseph Macias, CRO

Developers of marketing CRM that helps small- and mid-sized businesses accelerate the growth.

**Virobay Inc**   HQ
200 Page Mill Rd Bldg A
Palo Alto CA 94304
P: 650-833-5700   F: 650-833-6892   PRC:249
Estab: 2006

David Karpf, Chief Medical Officer

Developer of clinical stage biopharmaceutical products for the treatment of neuropathic pain, autoimmune diseases, and fibrosis.

**Virovek**   HQ
22429 Hesperian Blvd.
Hayward CA 94541
P: 510-887-7121   F: 510-887-7178   PRC:36
www.virovek.com
Email: info@virovek.com

Haifeng Chen, CEO
Leslie Duprey, Senior Manager of Marketing
Courtney Jett, Buyer

Provider of adeno-associated virus production and purification services. The company involves in consulting and gene cloning services.

**Virtual Driver Interactive**   HQ
5137 Golden Foothill Pkwy Ste 150
El Dorado Hills CA 95762
P: 877-746-8332   PRC:329
www.driverinteractive.com
Email: support@driverinteractive.com
Emp: 1-10   Estab: 2009

Bob Davis, CEO
Van Burns, VP
Pam LeFevre, VP of Marketing
Andre Luongo, VP of Product Development

Manufacturer of virtual training simulators. The company serves schools, corporations, schools, and hospitals.

**Virtual Instruments** HQ
2331 Zanker Rd
San Jose CA 95131
P: 408-579-4000  F: 408-579-4001  PRC:329
www.virtualinstruments.com
Email: sales@virtualinstruments.com
Estab: 2008

Lisa Alger, SVP of Engineering
Susanta Pattanayak, Director of Engineering
Saranga Ashoka, Software Engineer
Juden Supapo, Staff Engineer of QE
Salini Pillai, Senior Engineer

Developer of storage area network and virtual
infrastructure solutions. The company serves
healthcare, federal, and outsourcing & hosting
sectors.

**Viscira LLC** HQ
200 Vallejo St
San Francisco CA 94111
P: 415-848-8010  PRC:322
www.viscira.com
Email: info@viscira.com
Estab: 2007

Dave Gulezian, Chairman
Rick Barker, President
Jeff Asada, Chief Revenue Officer
Shan Jaffar, COO
Kimberly Davis-Wells, VP of Client Services

Manufacturer of software products. The company
deals with the development of animation technology solutions.

**Vishay Intertechnology Inc** BR
3000 Bowers Ave
Santa Clara CA 95051
P: 408-727-2500  F: 408-727-5896  PRC:86
www.vishay.com
Estab: 1962

Gerald Paul, CEO
Marc Zandman, Chief Business Development
Officer
Johan Vandoorn, EVP
Lori Lipcaman, EVP
Robert Garcia, Facilities Manager

Manufacturer of electronic components. The company's products comprises of semiconductors and
passive components used across industries.

**Vision3 Lighting** HQ
2850 San Antonio Dr
Fowler CA 93625
P: 559-834-5749  F: 559-834-4779  PRC:243
www.vision3lighting.com
Email: info@vision3lighting.com
Emp: 1-10  Estab: 2001

Thomas Petrush, National Sales Manager

Manufacturer of landscape and exterior architectural lighting products. The company deals with
design and installation services.

**VisionCare Ophthalmic Technologies
Inc** HQ
14395 Saratoga Ave Ste 150
Saratoga CA 95070
P: 408-872-9393  F: 408-872-9395  PRC:189
www.visioncareinc.net
Estab: 1997

Wolfgang Tolle, CEO
Eli Aharoni, VP of Research & Development
Yona Katz, VP of Manufacturing
Doron Raz, VP of Finance and Administration
Richard Powers, EVP

Manufacturer and marketer of implantable ophthalmic devices and technologies for improving
vision of individuals with untreatable retinal
disorders.

**Visioneer Inc** HQ
5673 Gibraltar Dr
Pleasanton CA 94588
P: 925-251-6399  F: 925-416-8600  PRC:176
www.visioneer.com
Email: 2020@visioneer.com
Estab: 1992

Jon Harju, CTO
Dmitry Panich, Art Director

Marketer and distributor of digital imaging hardware devices. The company also offers related
tools & utilities and power tools.

**Vistagen Therapeutics Inc** HQ
343 Allerton Ave
S San Francisco CA 94080
P: 650-577-3600  F: 888-482-2602  PRC:191
www.vistagen.com
Estab: 1998

H.Ralph Snodgrass, Founder
Shawn Singh, CEO
Jon Saxe, Chairman
Jerrold Dotson, VP
Mark Mcpartland, VP of Corporate Development

Developer of medicine to treat depression, cancer
and diseases and disorders involving the central
nervous system.

**Vistrian Inc** HQ
562 Valey Way
Milpitas CA 95035
P: 408-719-0500  F: 408-719-0505  PRC:323
vistrian.com
Email: info@vistrian.com
Estab: 2003

Ronald Allen, CEO
Doug Pagel, VP of Sales & Business Development

Developer of software products. The company's
services include escalation management, problem
isolation, and remote access.

**VisualOn Inc** HQ
2590 N First St Ste 100
San Jose CA 95131
P: 408-645-6618  F: 408-596-5495  PRC:323
www.visualon.com
Email: sales@visualon.com
Estab: 2003

Yang Cai, CEO
Judy Li, Director of Finance
Jim Wang, Asia Sales VP

Provider of software applications for the mobile
handset market enabling customers to access
multimedia content without dedicated hardware.

**Visualware Inc** HQ
937 Sierra Dr
Turlock CA 95381-0668
P: 209-262-3491  F: 916-273-3099  PRC:325
www.visualware.com
Email: sales@visualware.com
Emp: 11-50 Estab: 2001

Kevin Hahn, Senior Software Engineer
Dan Palmer, Software Architect Engineer
Henry Harris, Founder
Julian Palmer, Founder

Provider of solutions to measure broadband
connection performance for enterprises, homes,
and offices. The company offers both hardware
and software.

**Vital Connect Inc** HQ
224 Airport Pkwy Ste 300
San Jose CA 95110
P: 408-963-4600  PRC:186
www.vitalconnect.com
Estab: 2011

Rod Moghadam, Senior Product Engineer
Thang Tran, Senior Firmware Engineer
Peter Haur, CEO
Nersi Nazari, Executive Chairman
Ian Felix, CPO

Provider of healthcare solutions. The company
focuses on biosensors, clinical-grade biometric
measurements.

**Vital Enterprises** HQ
1355 Market St Ste 488
San Francisco CA 94103
P: 650-394-6486  PRC:194
www.vital.enterprises
Email: info@vital.enterprises
Estab: 2013

Ash Eldritch, CEO
Aaron Vargas, CTO

Provider of field service and manufacturing solutions. The company offers services to hospitals
and R&D laboratories.

**Vitec Group Communications LLC** HQ
1301 Marina Village Pkwy Ste 105
Alameda CA 94501
P: 510-337-6600  F: 510-337-6699  PRC:60
www.clearcom.com
Email: salessupportus@clearcom.com
Estab: 1968

Judy Cheng, Director of Marketing

Designer, manufacturer, and marketer of voice
communications systems for live performance,
broadcast, houses of worship, and the commercial
markets.

**Vitec** BR

931 Benecia Ave
Sunnyvale CA 94085
P: 800-451-5101    F: 408-739-1706    PRC:60
www.vitec.com
Email: sunnyvale@vitec.com

Danielle Tal, Software Engineer
Kevin Mitchell, Senior IPTV Engineer
Chadi Farran, Process Engineering
Demetrius Perry, Human Resource Manager
Matt McKee, VP of Broadcast Sales

Provider of digital video products. The company offers software for video encoding, decoding, and conversion.

**Vitriflex Inc** HQ

2350 Zanker Rd
San Jose CA 95131-1115
P: 408-468-6700    PRC:209
www.vitriflex.com
Email: info@vitriflex.com

Martin Rosenblum, VP of Engineering
Rex Chang, Senior Process Development Engineer
Ravi Prasad, CTO
Dave Pearce, CEO
Mark George, Director

Manufacturer of ultra-barrier films for electronic applications. The company focuses on surface science and engineering.

**Vitron Electronic Services Inc** HQ

5400 Hellyer Ave
San Jose CA 95138
P: 408-251-1600    PRC:207
www.vitronmfg.com
Estab: 1985

Daniel Tran, Manager

Provider of electronics manufacturing services. The company deals with product development, system integration, and prototyping services.

**Vivante Corp** HQ

2150 Gold St Ste 200
San Jose CA 95002
P: 408-844-8560    F: 408-844-8563    PRC:325
www.giquila.com
Email: info@vivantecorp.com
Estab: 2004

James Kliegel, Verification Engineer
Ching-Hui Kao, Senior Application Engineer
Alan Huang, Senior Verification Engineer
Guoyu Zhu, Software Engineer
Mike Cai, CTO

Provider of semiconductors for graphics and multimedia. The company focuses on image and video processing services.

**Vivax-Metrotech Corp** HQ

3251 Olcott St
Santa Clara CA 95054
P: 408-734-1400    F: 408-734-1415    PRC:13
www.vivax-metrotech.com
Email: sales@vxmt.com
Estab: 1965

Matt Manning, Regional Sales Manager

Manufacturer of mapping tools. The company specializes in tools used for underground cabling and piping works.

**Vivid Vision Inc** HQ

424 Treat Ave Unit B
San Francisco CA 94110
P: 877-877-0310    PRC:317
www.seevividly.com
Email: contact@seevividly.com
Estab: 2013

James Blaha, Founder
Manish Gupta, Founder
Tuan Tran, Chief Optometrist
Ben Backus, Chief Science Officer
Sunao Miyoshi, VP of Asia

Provider of virtual reality solutions. The company offers services to eye clinics and also kids and adults.

**Vivotek Usa** BR

2050 Ringwood Ave
San Jose CA 95131
P: 408-773-8686    F: 408-773-8298    PRC:168
www.vivotek.com
Email: salesusa@vivotek.com
Estab: 2008

Roy Pangilinan, VP of Engineering
Kelly Lee, Finance & Administration Director
Stanley Chih, Regional Sales Manager
David Liu, National Sales Manager
Heinje Lleses, Inside Sales Representative

Provider of surveillance solutions. The company specializes in manufacturing network cameras for the network video surveillance industries.

**Vlsi Research Inc** HQ

2290 North First St Ste 202
San Jose CA 95131-2017
P: 408-453-8844    F: 408-437-0608    PRC:212
www.vlsiresearch.com
Email: sales@vlsiresearch.com
Estab: 1976

Risto Puhakka, President
Dan Hutcheson, CEO
Manjesh Singh, CTO
Andrea Lati, VP of Market Research
Lisa Steele, VP of Administration

Provider of chip market research, consultation, semiconductor analysis, and data spreadsheets and reports.

**VLSI Standards Inc** HQ

5 Technology Dr
Milpitas CA 95035-7916
P: 408-428-1800    F: 408-428-9555    PRC:209
www.vlsistandards.com
Email: sales.support@vlsistd.com
Estab: 1984

Lane Stump, Facilities Engineer
Yu Guan, Engineer

Manufacturer of electrical and solar energy products. The company offers calibration services to the semiconductor industry.

**VMware Inc** HQ

3401 Hillview Ave
Palo Alto CA 94304
P: 650-427-1000    F: 650-475-5001    PRC:322
www.vmware.com
Estab: 1998
Sales: Over $3B

Carl Eschenbach, President
Pat Gelsinger, CEO
Bask Iyer, SVP
Ben Fathi, CTO
Rajiv Ramaswami, COO of Products & Cloud Services

Provider of storage, data center, application virtualization, and enterprise mobility management products.

**Voce Communications** HQ

55 Union St
San Francisco CA 94111
P: 415-975-2200    F: 415-975-2201    PRC:67
vocecommunications.com
Email: info@vocecomm.com
Estab: 1999

Rich Cline, Owner

Provider of marketing and communication consultancy services. The company in engaged in public relation, media marketing, and web development.

**Vocera Communications Inc** HQ

525 Race St
San Jose CA 95126
P: 408-882-5600    PRC:68
www.vocera.com
Email: info@vocera.com
Estab: 2000
Sales: $100M to $300M

Benjamin Kanter, Chief Medical Information Officer
Dennis Tani, Facilities Manager
Dave George, Manager of Mobility and Integrations
Mauricio Cornejo, Sales Support Administrator of Global Sales Operations

Provider of mobile communication solutions. The company provides voice communication, messaging, wireless networking, and technical support.

**Voltage Multipliers Inc** HQ

8711 W Roosevelt Ave
Visalia CA 93291
P: 559-651-1402    F: 559-651-0740    PRC:209
www.voltagemultipliers.com
Email: sales@voltagemultipliers.com
Emp: 1-10   Estab: 1980

Jorge Mejia, Engineering Manager
Rob Hodgkins, Engineer
Matthew Gong, Engineer
Daniel Deschenes, Sales Engineer
Derek Onstott, Senior Engineer

Manufacturer of voltage multipliers, high voltage diodes, rectifiers, opto-couplers, and power supplies.

**Volume Precision Glass Inc**  HQ
150 Todd Rd Bldg 100
Santa Rosa CA 95407
P: 707-206-0100  F: 707-206-0105  PRC:175
www.vpglass.com
Email: info@vpglass.com
Estab: 1998

Croy Davis, President

Fabricator of optical components and thin-film coatings for photonics, military, industrial, and lighting applications.

**VORTRAN Medical Technology Inc**  HQ
21 Goldenland Ct Ste 100
Sacramento CA 95834
P: 800-434-4034  F: 916-648-9751  PRC:189
www.vortran.com
Email: info@vortran.com
Emp: 1-10  Estab: 1983

Reza Saied, VP of Engineering
James Lee, EVP

Developer of pulmonary modulation technology solutions. The company offers automatic disposable respiratory devices for treating pulmonary diseases.

**Vsi Voelker Sensors Inc**  HQ
3790 El Camino Real Ste 336
Palo Alto CA 94306
P: 650-618-8544  PRC:87
www.vsi-oil.com
Email: info@vsi-oil.com

Joe Hedges, President

Manufacturer of sensor products. The company offers in-line oil quality sensors for the industrial, transportation, and power generation markets.

**Vsp Optics Group**  HQ
3333 Quality Dr
Rancho Cordova CA 95670
P: 800-852-7600  PRC:170
vspglobal.com
Email: pathtopremier@vsp.com
Emp: 11-50  Estab: 1955

Jenn Fong, Ophthalmic Purchasing Analyst
Lee Plante, Channel Marketing Specialist
Jack Murphy, Maintenance Manager
Andy Kopitske, Product Manager
Brian Baxter, Lab Manager

Provider of eye care solutions. The company offers eye care insurance, eyewear, lenses, ophthalmic technology and retail solutions.

**VueMetrix Inc**  HQ
2149 O'Toole Ave
San Jose CA 95131
P: 408-770-3070  PRC:94
www.vuemetrix.com
Estab: 2000

Jim Chiu, CEO

Developer of laser diode-based systems. The company is focused on integrated laser diode control electronics.

**Vulcan Inc**  HQ
24803 Eichler St
Hayward CA 94545
P: 510-786-9181  PRC:78
www.vulcanwire.com
Estab: 1975

Michael Graffio, CEO

Focuses on the manufacture and fabrication of aluminum coiled sheets, aluminum sign blanks, and finished traffic control signs.

**VytronUS Inc**  HQ
658 N Pastoria Ave
Sunnyvale CA 94085
P: 408-730-1333  PRC:186
www.vytronus.com
Email: info@vytronus.com
Estab: 2006

Danielo Piazza, VP of Software Engineering
Patrick Phillips, SVP of Engineering & Manufacturing
Tony Pantages, Engineering Manager
John Pavlidis, CEO
Dave White, VP of Manufacturing

Developer of ablation systems for the treatment of atrial fibrillation and other cardiac arrhythmias. The company deals with customizable lesions.

**W E Plemons Machinery Services Inc**  HQ
13479 E Industrial Dr
Parlier CA 93648
P: 559-646-6630  F: 559-646-9630  PRC:80
www.weplemons.com
Email: pms@weplemons.com
Emp: 1-10

William Plemons, President
Jeff Winters, VP

Provider of flange seals and automatic lidding attachments. The company's services include box designs and rebuilding.

**W2 Systems**  HQ
304 Industrial Way
Brisbane CA 94005
P: 415-468-9858  F: 415-468-9854  PRC:143
www.w2systems.com
Email: info@w2systems.com
Estab: 1986

Kirk Howard, President

Provider of customized water treatment support and solutions. The company also offers services like design, technical support, and control services.

**Wachters' Organic Sea Products**  HQ
550 Sylvan St
Daly City CA 94014
P: 650-757-9851  PRC:272
wachters.com

Carrie Minucianni, CEO

Manufacturer and distributor of nutritional products. The company's products include pet products, personal care, and cleaning products.

**Wafab International**  HQ
6161 A Industrial Way
Livermore CA 94551
P: 925-455-5252  F: 925-455-5351  PRC:86
wafabintl.com
Email: sales@wafabintl.com
Estab: 1979

Evelyn Freitas, Human Resource Administrator
Frank Gavin, Sales Manager
Mathew Freitas, Electrician

Provider of wet processing and chemical handling tools. The company's products include solar cell processing equipment and stainless steel fume hoods.

**Wafer Process Systems Inc**  HQ
3641 Charter Park Dr
San Jose CA 95136
P: 408-445-3010  F: 408-445-3004  PRC:124
www.waferprocess.com
Estab: 1983

Christopher Schmitz, VP of Engineering
Douglas Caldwell, President
Barbara Caldwell, CFO
Stuart Lebherz, Customer Service Manager

Manufacturer of semiconductors, MEMS, and photonics. The company also focuses on RFID products, disc drives, and flat panel displays.

**WaferMasters Inc**  HQ
2251 Brandini Dr
Dublin CA 94568
P: 408-451-0850  PRC:86
www.wafermasters.com
Email: info@wafermasters.com
Estab: 1999

Shintaro Fujimoto, COO

Provider of thermal processing services. The company also focuses on diagnostic metrology and design and consulting services.

**WaferNet Inc**  HQ
2142 Paragon Dr
San Jose CA 95131
P: 866-749-2337  PRC:124
wafernet.com
Estab: 1988

Omar Ghosheh, VP of Sales

Supplier of silicon wafers. The company serves semiconductor equipment manufacturers and universities.

**WAGAN Corp**  HQ
31088 San Clemente St
Hayward CA 94544
P: 510-471-9221  F: 510-489-3451  PRC:135
wagan.com
Email: customerservice@wagan.com
Estab: 1983

Alex Hsu, President

Developer and marketer of automotive accessories to mobile professionals. The company's offerings include warmers, defrosters, and heated cushions.

**Walters & Wolf**     BR
41450 Boscell Rd
Fremont CA 94538
P: 510-490-1115   F: 510-651-7172    PRC:80
www.waltersandwolf.com
Email: infomain@waltersandwolf.com
Estab: 1977

Kent Marcuson, Project Engineer
Xiaxin Liang, Engineer
Rick Calhoun, President
Jeff Belzer, CFO
Elena Pichardo, Human Resource Generalist

Provider of cladding services. The company
specializes in design, engineering, fabrication, and
delivery and installation.

**Ward Systems Inc**     HQ
12912 Madrona Leaf Ct
Grass Valley CA 95945
P: 530-271-1800   F: 530-271-1801    PRC:180
www.wardventures.com
Email: sales@wardventures.com
Emp: 1-10

Glen Ward, President

Provider of custom automation services. The
company's services include valve installation,
maintenance, and reconfiguration.

**Warren & Baerg Manufacturing Inc**    HQ
39950 Rd 108
Dinuba CA 93618
P: 559-591-6790   F: 559-591-5728    PRC:159
warrenbaerg.com
Email: info@warrenbaerg.com
Emp: 11-50 Estab: 1966

Randy Baerg, Owner
Woody Randel, Technical Sales Manager
Wendell Spray, General Manager & Sales

Manufacturer of agricultural and industrial systems. The company's services include installation,
manufacturing, and technical support.

**Wasco Hardfacing Company Inc**    HQ
2660 S East Ave
Fresno CA 93745
P: 559-485-5860   F: 559-233-4436    PRC:158
www.ag1.net
Email: info@ag1.net
Emp: 1-10   Estab: 1952

Robin Messick, Owner

Manufacturer of hardfacing electrodes for steel,
cement, and mining applications. The company
also offers welding alloy solutions.

**Watchwith Inc**     HQ
301 Howard St 19th Fl
San Francisco CA 94105
P: 415-552-1552    PRC:324
www.watchwith.com
Estab: 2006

Mike Dalrymple, SVP of Engineering
Zane Vella, Founder
Susan Kalman, Corporate Controller

Provider of software and data solutions for the
film and television content creators and consumer
electronics manufacturers.

**Waterman Industries**     HQ
25500 Rd 204
Exeter CA 93221
P: 559-562-4000   F: 559-562-2277    PRC:144
watermanusa.com
Email: sales@watermanusa.com
Emp: 11-50 Estab: 1912

John Speidel, Engineering Manager of AG & Cast
Products & New Product Development
Darryl Pauls, Senior Mechanical Engineer
Mike Rudy, Estimating Manager
Francisco Soto, Project Manager

Designer and manufacturer of water-control
sluice gates, penstocks, valves, and water control
products.

**Wave 80 Biosciences Inc**     BR
2325 Third St Ste 215
San Francisco CA 94107
P: 415-487-7976   F: 415-487-7998    PRC:186
www.wave80.com
Estab: 2003

Amy Droitcour, SVP of Engineering
Richard Goozh, Senior Advisor

Developer of molecular diagnostics instruments
and consumables for hepatitis C, hepatitis B, HIV/
AIDS, and other human health conditions.

**Wave Systems Corp**     HQ
1159 Sonora Ct
Sunnyvale CA 94086
P: 408-524-8630    PRC:323
www.wavesystems.com
Email: info@wavesystems.com
Estab: 1988

Muhammad Umar, Senior Software Engineer
Joe Luong, Staff Engineer
Bhupinder Lehga, President

Provider of customized software development for
the law enforcement, casino, corporate security,
and hospitals segments.

**Wavesplitter Technologies Inc**    HQ
2080 Rancho Higuera Ct
Fremont CA 94539
P: 925-596-0414   F: 408-432-8111    PRC:61
www.wavesplitter.com
Email: info@wavesplitter.com
Estab: 1996

Sheau Chen, CEO

Manufacturer of passive devices and active optical
components for enterprise and residential broadband networks.

**Wcr Inc**     BR
4636 E Drummond Ave
Fresno CA 93725
P: 559-266-8374   F: 559-266-3354    PRC:153
www.wcrhx.com
Emp: 11-50

Greg Pinasco, VP of Western Operations

Developer and manufacturer of heat exchangers. The company's products include plate heat
exchangers, brazed heat exchangers, and welded
heat exchangers.

**Weatherflow Inc**     HQ
108 Whispering Pines Ste 245
Scotts Valley CA 95066
P: 800-946-3225    PRC:142
www.weatherflow.com
Email: info@weatherflow.com
Emp: 1-10

Buck Lyons, CEO

Provider of modeling and forecasting technologies
for the weather forecast industry. The company
also offers wind-based and coastal forecasting.

**Webenertia**     HQ
1570 The Alameda Ste 330
San Jose CA 95126
P: 408-246-0000   F: 408-275-0970    PRC:60
www.webenertia.com
Email: info@webenertia.com
Estab: 1999

Ian McGarvey, Engineering Manager
Steve Ohanians, Co-Founder
Michael Marcus, Lead Developer
David Scherbarth, Senior Designer
Naro Haig, Developer

Provider of web applications and e-commerce
services. The company also focuses on motion
graphics and internet marketing solutions.

**Weber Hayes & Assoc**     HQ
120 Westgate Dr
Watsonville CA 95076
P: 831-722-3580   F: 831-722-1159    PRC:142
weber-hayes.com
Email: info@weber-hayes.com
Emp: 1-10   Estab: 1974

Craig Drizin, Senior Engineer
Josh Hannaleck, Staff Civil and Environmental
Engineer
Shawn Mixan, Project Engineer
Pat Hoban, President
Laura Garcia, CFO

Provider of hydrogeologic and environmental
engineering consulting services. The company
offers cleanup of soil, groundwater, and stormwater services.

**Webvanta Inc**     HQ
One Harbor Dr Ste 300
Sausalito CA 94965
P: 888-670-6793    PRC:325
www.webvanta.com
Email: support@webvanta.com
Estab: 2007

Christopher Haupt, CTO

Provider of hosted content management and database system services. The company is involved in
website and mobile application development.

**Weichhart Stamping Co**     HQ
9131 San Leandro St Bldg 350
Oakland CA 94603-1208
P: 510-562-6886   F: 510-562-6856    PRC:82
www.weichhartstamping.com
Estab: 1933

John Weichhart, Owner

Manufacturer of tools and metal stampings in
the San Francisco area. The company's offerings
include flat springs, wire forms, spring washers,
and wave washers.

**Wellex Corp** HQ
551 Brown Rd
Fremont CA 94539-7003
P: 510-743-1818  F: 510-743-1899  PRC:211
www.wellex.com
Email: salesmarketing_web@wellex.com
Estab: 1983

Jim Hou, NPI Engineer
Jett Tsai, VP of Operations

Provider of printed circuit boards, cables, harness
assemblies, and wiring products. The company
is engaged in engineering and manufacturing
services.

**Wellmade Products** HQ
1715 Kibby Rd
Merced CA 95341
P: 209-723-9120  F: 209-723-9131  PRC:88
www.wlmd.com
Emp: 1-10

David Verstoppen, VP of Sales

Manufacturer of lighting, wheelbarrows, and sheet
metal products. The company also offers photometric sheets.

**WellnessFX Inc** HQ
1550 Bryant St Ste 590
San Francisco CA 94103
P: 415-796-3373  PRC:325
www.wellnessfx.com
Email: support@wellnessfx.com
Estab: 2010

Paul Jacobson, CEO
Jeremy Barth, CTO
Christine Keating, VP of Operations

Specializes in web-based services. The company
focuses on diagnostic testing and it serves medical practitioners.

**Wells Dental Inc** HQ
PO Box 106
Comptche CA 95427-0106
P: 707-937-0521  F: 707-937-2809  PRC:185
www.wellsdental.com
Emp: 1-10  Estab: 1975

Earl Wells, Founder

Supplier of dental laboratory equipment. The
company offers engine units, finishing machines,
quick chucks, and consumables.

**Wema Inc** HQ
1670 Zanker Rd
San Jose CA 95112
P: 408-453-5005  F: 408-453-5502  PRC:80
www.wemainc.com
Email: machining@wemainc.com
Estab: 1992

Max Ho, President

Provider of tank sensors, gauges, and smoke
detectors for automotive, marine, agricultural, and
construction equipment.

**Wenteq Inc** HQ
20550 E Kettleman Ln
Lodi CA 95240
P: 209-608-2374  PRC:80
www.wenteqmachine.com
Emp: 1-10

Shawn Wentzel, President

Manufacturer of print, precision, machined components, and assemblies. The company serves the
automotive, racing, and boat markets.

**Werlchem LLC** HQ
1660 Wayne Ave
San Leandro CA 94577
P: 510-918-1896  F: 510-352-1525  PRC:53
www.werlchem.net
Email: sales@werlchem.net
Estab: 2012

Wilson Wu, Co-Founder

Developer and manufacturer of specialty chemicals. The company's offerings include dyes,
pharmaceutical intermediates, and electronic
materials.

**Weslan Systems Inc** HQ
1244 Commerce Ave
Woodland CA 95776
P: 530-668-3304  F: 530-668-3414  PRC:159
www.weslan.com
Email: info@weslan.com
Emp: 1-10  Estab: 1978

Rick Weston, CEO
Jim Dittrich, Production Manager of Sales

Fabricator of custom plastic products for the semiconductor industry. The company offers contract
manufacturing services.

**Wessdel Inc** HQ
581 Dado St
San Jose CA 95131
P: 408-496-6822  F: 408-496-0569  PRC:80
www.wessdel.com
Email: info@wessdel.com
Estab: 1974

Bob Dorricott, President
Cindy Ketchum-Ewing, Office Manager

Provider of precision machining and engineering
services for the military, aerospace, defense, and
medical sectors.

**West Coast Fab Inc** HQ
700 S 32nd St
Richmond CA 94804
P: 510-529-0177  F: 510-233-2248  PRC:80
westcoastfabinc.com
Estab: 1973

Tom Nelson, President
Scott Shelby, Programmer
Diane Burnett, Office Manager

Provider of precision electronic sheet metal
fabrication services. The company specializes in
finished products.

**West Coast Magnetics** HQ
4848 Frontier Way  Ste 100
Stockton CA 95215
P: 800-628-1123  F: 209-941-1744  PRC:296
www.wcmagnetics.com
Email: sales@wcmagnetics.com
Emp: 1-10  Estab: 1974

David Harizal, Design Engineer
Weyman Lundquist, CEO
Lisa Reyes, Production Manager
Elizabeth Menchaca, Inside Sales Manager
Melissa Gonzales, Inside Sales Representative

Provider of electrical products. The company
specializes in inductor products, transformers,
chokes, and planar magnetic products.

**West Coast Pathology Laboratories** HQ
712 Alfred Nobel Dr
Hercules CA 94547-1805
P: 510-662-5200  F: 510-662-5240  PRC:306
www.wcpl.com
Email: contact@wcpl.com
Estab: 1985

Lisa Helfend, Laboratory Medical Director
Tracy Chang, Cytotechnologist
Nazila Hejazi, Associate Pathologist
Alfredo Asuncion, Associate Pathologist

Providers of anatomic pathology and cytology services. The company's expertise lies with molecular
genetics and diagnostics.

**West Coast Surgical** HQ
141 California Ave Ste 101
Half Moon Bay CA 94019
P: 650-728-8095  F: 650-728-8096  PRC:80
www.westcoastsurgical.com

Steve Petlansky, Principal

Manufacturer of surgical devices. The company
offers designing, assembling and finishing of
specialty surgical equipment.

**West Coast** HQ
2341 Stanwell Dr
Concord CA 94520
P: 925-270-3800  PRC:41
www.microqa.com
Email: info@analyticallabgroup.com
Estab: 2006

Alan Roth, CEO
Megan Cosgrove, Director of Marketing
Kelly Lauer, Director of Operations
Tony Ezell, Department Head
Katy Gainey, Controller

Provider of contract testing laboratory services.
The company offers testing laboratories, manufacturing services, and validation and calibration
services.

**West Yost Associates** HQ
2020 Research Park Dr Ste 100
Davis CA 95618
P: 530-756-5905  F: 530-756-5991  PRC:142
www.westyost.com
Email: info@westyost.com
Emp: 11-50  Estab: 1990

Polly Boissevain, Chief Engineer
David Anderson, Engineering Manager
Kambria Tiano, Associate Engineer
Jeffrey Wanlass, Senior Engineer
Amy Kwong, Senior Engineer

Provider of water, storm water, wastewater, and construction management project services. The company also offers recycling services.

**Westak** HQ
1116 Elko Dr
Sunnyvale CA 94089
P: 408-734-8686 PRC:211
westak.com
Email: info@westak.com
Estab: 1972

Louise Crisham, CEO
Lou George, COO
Donna Hill, Quality Assurance Manager
Debby Hall, Director of Business Services
Brian Alarid, Account Manager

Designer and manufacturer of printed circuit boards. The company offers rigid double-sided interconnects and rigid multi-layer interconnects.

**Westec Plastics Corp** HQ
6757-A Las Positas Rd
Livermore CA 94551
P: 925-454-3400 F: 925-454-3410 PRC:84
www.westecplastics.com
Email: westec@westecplastics.com
Estab: 1969

Julie Meeks, Project Manager
John Baker, Business Development Manager
Tina Scheck, Controller

Provider of plastics injection molding and mold making services. The company also offers customized services.

**Western Allied Mechanical Inc** HQ
1180 O'Brien Dr
Menlo Park CA 94025
P: 650-326-0750 F: 650-321-4946 PRC:159
www.westernallied.com
Email: info@westernallied.com
Estab: 1961

Zachary Russi, President
Angela Simon, CEO
Jeff Pierce, CFO
Bob Dills, VP
James Kastelic, VP

Designer and builder of heating and ventilation systems. The company serves the construction and energy automation industries.

**Western Digital Corp** HQ
5601 Great Oaks Pkwy
San Jose CA 95119
P: 408-717-6000 PRC:95
www.westerndigital.com
Estab: 1970
Sales: Over $3B

Li Yi, Director of Engineering
Mark Long, EVP of Strategy & Corporate Development
Roseann Schaefer, Global Mobility Programs Manager
David Nguyen, Credit Coordinator

Manufacturer of external storage devices. The company also focuses on network storage and backup solutions and offers technical support services.

**Western Digital Corporation** HQ
7999 Gateway Blvd Ste 120
Newark CA 94560
P: 510-791-7900 PRC:95
www.westerndigital.com
Estab: 2010

Siva Sivaram, President of Technology & Strategy
Michael Cordano, President
Stephen Milligan, CEO
Robert Eulau, EVP
Michael Ray, EVP

Provider of storage array solutions. The company focuses on desktop virtualization, server virtualization, database hosting, and file services.

**Western Stucco Co** HQ
1550 Pkwy Blvd
West Sacramento CA 95691
P: 916-372-7442 PRC:47
www.westernblended.com
Email: ssinfo@westernblended.com
Emp: 1-10 Estab: 1932

Jose Gomez, General Manager
Phill Hall, Plant Manager
Walter Rozewski, Office Manager

Developer and manufacturer of exterior products for the stucco industry. The company offers both cement color coats and resin based finishes.

**Western Truck Fab Inc** HQ
1923 W Winton Ave
Hayward CA 94545-1605
P: 510-785-9994 F: 510-785-9986 PRC:159
www.westerntruckfab.com
Estab: 1984

Julie Meyers, Owner
Ron Frost, Final QC Inspector
Brett Maury, Supervisor

Provider of custom truck body fabrication services. The company's products include lift gates, compressors, and cranes.

**Western Widgets CNC Inc** HQ
915 Commercial St
San Jose CA 95112
P: 408-436-1230 F: 408-436-7456 PRC:159
www.westernwidgets.com

Teresa Gale, Office Manager

Manufacturer of precision milled and turned components such as computers and optical assemblies. The company deals with milling and turning services.

**Westervelt Ecological Services** HQ
600 N Market Blvd Ste 3
Sacramento CA 95834
P: 916-646-3644 F: 916-646-3675 PRC:139
www.wesmitigation.com
Emp: 11-50 Estab: 2006

Steve Moore, Finance Manager
Greg DeYoung, VP
Greg Sutter, EVP
John Wigginton, Regional Manager
Travis Hemmen, Business Development Manager

Provider of ecological solutions. The company offers wetland mitigation and conservation banking, geographic information system analysis, and other services.

**Westfab Manufacturing Inc** HQ
3370 Keller St
Santa Clara CA 95054
P: 408-727-0550 F: 408-727-6776 PRC:88
www.westfab.com
Email: sale@westfab.com
Estab: 1986

Ashok Dadlani, Finance Manager
Rick Rey, Sales Manager
Nikita Shah, Accounting Manager

Manufacturer of simple brackets, multiple level frames, and enclosures. The company offers assembly services for power supplies, switches, and cables.

**Westland Technologies Inc** HQ
107 S Riverside Dr
Modesto CA 95354
P: 800-877-7734 F: 209-571-6411 PRC:57
westlandtech.com
Email: info@westlandtech.com
Emp: 1-10 Estab: 1996

Andy Jessup, VP of Operations & Engineering
John Grizzard, President
Tom Halyburton, President
Keryn Leger, CFO
Benjamin Banta, Director of Quality

Provider of injection and transfer molding, pressure testing, custom hand fabricating, and acid etching services.

**Westpak Inc** HQ
83 Great Oaks Blvd
San Jose CA 95119
P: 408-224-1300 F: 408-224-5113 PRC:306
www.westpak.com
Estab: 1986

Harmony Reynolds, General Manager
Aaron Suarez, Director of Engineering
Andrew Bevil, Engineering Services Manager
Alexea Kouris, Test Engineer
Jorge Campos, Test Engineer III

Provider of customized product and packaging testing services. The company also deals with packaging, material analysis, and supply chain management.

**Westport Machine Works Inc** HQ
700 Houston St
West Sacramento CA 95691
P: 916-371-4493 PRC:76
westportproducts.com
Email: westportproducts@att.net
Emp: 1-10 Estab: 1957

Cindi Taylor, Office Manager

Manufacturer of assembly and balancing equipment. The company's services include fixturing, installation, and technical support.

**Westside Research Inc** HQ
4293 County Rd 99 W
Orland CA 95963
P: 530-865-5587  F: 530-865-1474  PRC:179
www.westsideresearch.com
Email: info@westsideresearch.com
Emp: 1-10

Tim Dexter, President

Designer and manufacturer of interior and exterior
automotive cargo management products. The
company specializes in truck luggage product
lines.

**WHILL Inc** HQ
285 Old County Rd Ste 6
San Carlos CA 94070
P: 844-699-4455  PRC:189
whill.us
Email: info@whill.us
Estab: 2013

Satoshi Sugie, CEO

Manufacturer of personal electric vehicles, wheel
chairs, and mobility devices. The company serves
individuals and clinics.

**Whipple Industries Inc** HQ
3292 N Weber Ave
Fresno CA 93722
P: 559-442-1261  F: 559-442-4153  PRC:159
whipplesuperchargers.com
Email: sales@whipplesuperchargers.com
Emp: 1-10

Art Whipple, Founder

Provider of supercharger for vehicles. The company's products include twin-screw superchargers
and accessories.

**White Industries** HQ
1325 Ross St
Petaluma CA 94954
P: 707-769-5600  PRC:80
whiteind.com
Email: info@whiteind.com
Estab: 1978

Patrick Murphy, Engineer
Doug White, Owner

Manufacturer of bicycle components. The company's products include cranks, front hubs, brackets,
pedals, and related accessories.

**Whitehat Security** HQ
1741 Technology Dr Ste 300
San Jose CA 95110
P: 408-343-8300  F: 408-904-7142  PRC:325
www.whitehatsec.com
Email: whitehat.contact@whitehatsec.com
Estab: 2001

Kanthi Prasad, VP of Engineering
Ruth Iverson, Software Engineer
Matt Evans, Senior Application Security Engineer
& Manual Assessment Team Lead
Craig Hinkley, CEO
Eric Sheridan, Chief Scientist

Provider of web application security solutions
such as vulnerability management, threat modeling, and risk profiling.

**Whizz Systems** HQ
3240 Scott Blvd
Santa Clara CA 95054
P: 408-980-0400  PRC:209
www.whizzsystems.com
Email: info@whizzsystems.com
Estab: 1989

Asif Hassan, Senior Design Engineer
Fawad Munawar, Design Engineer
Shahbaz Mahmood, Electrical Engineer
Muhammad Irfan, President
Manny Karim, CFO

Provider of electronics design and manufacturing
services for the semiconductor, defense, computing, and industrial equipment markets.

**Whole You Inc** HQ
61 Metro Dr
San Jose CA 95110
P: 844-548-3385  PRC:189
www.wholeyou.com
Estab: 2014

Yasunori Nishiyama, CEO
Nid Sartnurak, Operations Manager

Provider of healthcare solutions. The company
specializes in sleep, dental, movement, and vision
solutions to its customers.

**Wi2wi Inc** HQ
1879 Lundy Ave Ste 218
San Jose CA 95131
P: 408-416-4200  F: 408-416-4201  PRC:63
www.wi2wi.com
Email: sales@wi2wi.com
Estab: 2005

Barry Arneson, VP of Engineering Frequency
Control and Timing Devices
Zachariah Mathews, President
Dawn Leeder, CFO
Don Good, National Sales Manager
Pierre Soulard, Company Secretary

Provider of wireless system-in-package, module,
and subsystems for embedded applications
including Wi-Fi, Bluetooth, and GPS.

**Wiegmann & Rose** HQ
263 S Vasco Rd
Livermore CA 94551
P: 510-632-8828  F: 510-632-8920  PRC:80
www.wiegmannandrose.com

Gary Keeler, Plant Superintendent Sales
Scott Logan, CEO
Jon Hammons, Quality Controller
Sam Flores, Purchasing Contact
Suzette Logan, Administration

Provider of custom heat exchangers, pressure
vessels, and weldments. The company offers
vacuum chambers and pipe spool products.

**Wiley X Inc** HQ
7800 Patterson Pass Rd
Livermore CA 94550
P: 925-243-9810  F: 925-455-8860  PRC:305
wileyx.com
Estab: 1987

Myles Freeman, President of Sales
Roseann Difu, Sales Manager
John Moore, Government Account Manager
Karen Stevens, IT Manager

Provider of high velocity protection services. The
company specializes in climate control frames,
light adjusting lenses, and polarized lenses.

**Willdan Energy Solutions** BR
9281 Office Park Cir Ste 135
Elk Grove CA 95758-8068
P: 916-585-7327  F: 916-478-6005  PRC:304
www.willdan.com
Email: info@willdan.com
Emp: 11-50 Estab: 2003

Candice Norton, Energy Engineer
Stacy McLaughlin, CFO
Joseph C., Marketing Associate
Mehdi Ganji, VP
Mike Teate, VP

Provider of energy efficiency, water conservation,
and renewable energy services. The company
serves education, utility, labs, and other sectors.

**William Stucky & Associates Inc** HQ
1 Embarcadero Ctr Ste 1220
San Francisco CA 94111
P: 415-788-2441  PRC:323
www.stuckynet.com
Email: bill.stucky@stuckynet.com
Estab: 1979

Rosanne Doyle, VP

Provider of software products and services. The
company mainly caters to the asset-based lending
industry.

**Willow Garage Inc** HQ
68 Willow Rd
Menlo Park CA 94025
P: 650-475-2700  F: 650-475-2828  PRC:314
www.willowgarage.com
Email: info@willowgarage.com
Estab: 2006

Steve Cousins, Founder

Developer of hardware and open source software
for personal robotics applications. The company
also offers robot design and machine learning
services.

**Wilson Research Group LLC** HQ
2116 Summer Dr
El Dorado Hills CA 95762
P: 530-350-8377  F: 530-350-7567  PRC:323
www.wilsonresearch.com
Emp: 1-10

Larry Wilson, President

Provider of market research products and services. The company serves publishing, embedded
systems, and high technology fields.

**Winbond Electronics Corporation
America** DH
2727 N First St
San Jose CA 95134
P: 408-943-6666  PRC:116
www.winbond.com
Estab: 1987

Omar Ma, Marketing Manager
Michael Stevenson, Founding Principal
Allison Chan, Senior Associate

Provider of memory solutions and services. The
company offers Pseudo SRAM, Serial NOR Flash,
Mobile DRAM, and KGD.

**Wind River** DH
500 Wind River Way
Alameda CA 94501
P: 510-748-4100  F: 510-749-2010  PRC:319
www.windriver.com
Email: license-ec@windriver.com
Estab: 1981

Jim Douglas, President
Michael Krutz, President
Gareth Noyes, CSO

Provider of automotive networking solutions. The
company's products include operating systems,
development tools, and middleware technologies.

**Window Solutions** HQ
186 Utah Ave
S San Francisco CA 94080
P: 800-400-7644  F: 650-349-2297  PRC:279
www.windowsolutions.com
Estab: 1969

Paul Murphy, Founder

Provider of 3M window film and tinting installation
services. The company offers services for residential, commercial, architects, and builders.

**WindSpring Inc** HQ
1735 N First St Ste 102
San Jose CA 95112
P: 408-452-7400  F: 408-452-7444  PRC:324
www.windspring.com
Email: info@windspring.com
Estab: 2004

Devanshi Patel, Software Quality Assurance
Engineer
Douglas Wadkins, CEO

Manufacturer of data management tools. The
company provides a framework for optimized
compressed data management in the storage and
embedded fields.

**Winedirect** HQ
450 Green Island Rd
American Canyon CA 94503
P: 800-819-0325  PRC:326
www.winedirect.com
Email: sales@winedirect.com
Estab: 2002

Yuan Yuan, Senior Engineer
Joe Waechter, CEO
Margie Rosewater, Director of Human Resources
Isidro Nunez, Planning & Production Manager
Jim Agger, VP of Sales

Provider of DTC services such as commerce,
compliance, fulfillment, marketing, and enterprise
services for wineries.

**Winnov Lp** HQ
3910 Freedom Cir Ste 102
Santa Clara CA 95054
P: 888-315-9460  F: 408-533-8808  PRC:60
www.winnov.com
Email: info@winnov.com
Estab: 1992

Olivier Garbe, Founder

Provider of video capture and streaming solutions.
The company serves education, enterprise,
healthcare, and live event sectors.

**Winslow Automation Inc** HQ
905 Montague Expy
Milpitas CA 95035
P: 408-262-9004  F: 408-956-0199  PRC:311
www.winslowautomation.com
Email: sales@solderquik.com
Estab: 1986

Russell Winslow, President
Tisha Wolf, Operations Manager
Alma Ebreo, Account Executive

Provider of lead tinning products and services.
The company caters to semiconductor and electrical companies.

**Wintec Industries Inc** HQ
8674 Thornton Ave
Newark CA 94560
P: 510-953-7421  F: 510-953-7414  PRC:96
www.wintecind.com
Email: sales@wintecind.com

Sue Jeng, President
Sanjay Bonde, CEO
David Jeng, CSO
Bhaskar Bhatt, Chief Information Officer
Brad Rawling, VP of SCM Pre-Sales & Client
Delivery

Manufacturer and distributor of memory modules
and components. The company serves consumer,
embedded OEM, e-commerce, and other needs.

**Wipro Technologies** BR
425 National Ave Ste 200
Mountain View CA 94043
P: 650-316-3555  F: 650-316-3468  PRC:325
www.wipro.com
Email: info@wipro.com
Estab: 1945

Srinivas Pallia, President of Consumer Business
Unit
N. Bala, President of Energy Natural Resources
Utilities & Construction
Partha Mukherjee, VP

Provider of analytics and information management, business process outsourcing, consulting,
and managed and cloud services.

**WNI Global Inc** HQ
1439 Graywood Dr
San Jose CA 95129
P: 408-307-2410  PRC:61
www.wnint.com
Email: info@wnint.com
Estab: 2001

Jim Bletas, President
Sam Lopez, Director of Sales

Provider of wireless communications solutions
for backhaul infrastructure and ethernet network
equipment for voice, data, and video applications.

**Wolfram Inc** HQ
1309 Doker Dr Ste B
Modesto CA 95351
P: 209-238-9610  F: 209-238-9615  PRC:159
wolframlights.com
Email: wolframlights@sbcglobal.net
Emp: 1-10

Steve Alexander, Founder
Kyle Alexander, Sales Manager

Designer and manufacturer of metal halide lamps
for the entertainment indent industry. The company's
lamps are used for filming motion pictures.

**Wolfs Precision Works Inc** HQ
3549 Haven Ave Unit F
Menlo Park CA 94025
P: 650-364-1341  F: 650-364-4386  PRC:80
www.wpw-inc.com
Email: info@wpw-inc.com
Estab: 1983

Bill Pursell, General Manager

Provider of precision machining solutions. The
company's services include milling, turning, and
surface gliding.

**Wonder Metals Corp** HQ
4351 Caterpillar Rd
Redding CA 96003
P: 800-366-5877  F: 530-241-1738  PRC:82
www.wondermetals.com
Email: info@wondermetals.com
Emp: 1-10  Estab: 1956

Viki Cubbage, Owner
Brandon Long, Project Manager

Provider of preventing environmental pollution
services. The company's products include louvers,
penthouses, and control dampers.

**Wong Electric Inc** HQ
4067 Transport St
Palo Alto CA 94303
P: 650-813-9999  F: 650-813-9664  PRC:304
www.wongelectric.com
Estab: 1978

Steven Wong, Owner
Dionisio Milo, Electrical Estimator

Provider of electrical contracting services. The
company is involved in industrial and multi-family
projects.

**Woodland Mdm** HQ
1229 E Kentucky Ave
Woodland CA 95776
P: 530-669-1400  F: 530-669-1413  PRC:159
www.woodlandmdm.com
Email: mail@woodlandmdm.com
Emp: 1-10  Estab: 1975

Rich Currie, Business Owner

Manufacturer and supplier of new and refurbished
machinery products. The company offers industrial
controls and automation & case handling equipment.

**Woodmack Products Inc** HQ
11430 White Rock Rd
Rancho Cordova CA 95742
P: 916-853-6150  F: 916-853-6473  PRC:82
www.woodmack.com
Email: sales@woodmack.com
Emp: 1-10  Estab: 1956

Nadine Grady, Controller

Manufacturer of tubes and pipes. The company
also specializes in customized designs and engineering solutions.

**Woodside Electronics Corp**    HQ
1311 Blue Grass Pl
Woodland CA 95776
P: 530-666-9190   F: 530-666-9428    PRC:159
wecotek.com
Emp: 1-10

Lisa B., VP of Marketing

Designer and manufacturer of electronic sorters. The company serves customers in the tomato harvesters and walnut industries.

**Workday Inc**    HQ
6110 Stoneridge Mall Rd
Pleasanton CA 94588
P: 925-951-9000    PRC:322
www.workday.com
Estab: 2005

Dave Duffield, Co-Founder
Chano Fernandez, Co-President
Aneel Bhusri, CEO
George Still, Vice Chairman
Mike Stankey, Vice Chairman

Provider of software solutions for human resources management and financial management. The company specializes in SaaS based enterprise solutions.

**World Products Inc**    HQ
19654 Eighth St E
Sonoma CA 95476
P: 707-996-5201   F: 707-996-3380    PRC:209
www.worldproducts.com
Email: sales@worldproducts.com
Estab: 1969

Leonard Drewes, Engineering Manager
David Redemer, Regional Sales Manager
Lyn Grosser, Operations Manager

Provider of electronic component solutions and services. The company offers sales, distribution, and technical support.

**Worldwide Energy & Manufacturing Usa Inc**    HQ
1675 Rollins Rd Unit F
Burlingame CA 94010
P: 650-692-7788   F: 650-692-7708    PRC:209
www.wwmusa.com
Email: sales@wwmusa.com
Estab: 1996

Philip Zhang, General Manager of Contract Manufacturing
Jane Xu, Senior Sales Manager

Provider of energy and manufacturing solutions. The company's products include cables, coils, PC boards, and electronic appliances.

**Worth Data Inc**    HQ
623 Swift St
Santa Cruz CA 95060
P: 831-458-9938   F: 831-458-9964    PRC:103
www.barcodehq.com
Email: wds@barcodehq.com
Emp: 1-10   Estab: 1985

Mike Luffman, Sales Engineer

Designer and manufacturer of bar code scanners and barcode software that includes bar code printing software and inventory tracking software.

**Wpg Americas Inc**    DH
5285 Hellyer Ave Ste 150
San Jose CA 95138
P: 408-392-8100   F: 408-436-9551    PRC:86
www.wpgamericas.com
Estab: 2007

Arthur Wang, CEO
Tonye Dreger, Program Operations Manager

Distributor of electronic products. The company's portfolio includes encoders, sensors, solid state batteries, and timing devices.

**WRA Inc**    HQ
2169 G E Francisco Blvd
San Rafael CA 94901
P: 415-454-8868   F: 415-454-0129    PRC:142
www.wra-ca.com
Estab: 1981

Allen Warren, President
Sherry Maloney, CFO
Timothy DeGraff, SVP
Joel Ruiz, Accountant
Daniel Chase, Associate Fisheries Biologist

Provider of environmental consulting, validation, mitigation and restoration, consultation, and wetland delineation services.

**Wra-Cal Industries Inc**    HQ
3515 Victor St
Santa Clara CA 95054
P: 408-988-4696    PRC:80
www.wra-cal.com
Email: support@wra-cal.com
Estab: 1973

Norman Wray, President

Manufacturer of precision machine products. The company's products include lathes, mills and grinders, drill press, and finishing equipment.

**Wrex Products Inc**    HQ
25 Wrex Ct
Chico CA 95928
P: 530-895-3838   F: 530-893-4426    PRC:80
www.wrexproducts.com
Email: info@wrexproducts.com
Emp: 1-10   Estab: 1960

Jim Barnett, President
Roger Cates, Sales Manager
Joe Vasquez, Sales Manager
Steve Overlock, Leadperson

Provider of plastic injection molding, CNC machining and finishing, coating, and tool design and engineering services.

**Wright Engineered Plastics**    HQ
3663 N Laughlin Rd Ste 201
Santa Rosa CA 95403
P: 707-575-1218    PRC:80
www.wepmolding.com
Email: info@wepmolding.com
Estab: 1970

Karrie Bertsch, Director of Engineering
Patrick Hall, Process Engineer
Barbara Roberts, President
Mike Nellis, EVP
Dale Lawler, Tooling Manager

Provider of medical components and devices. The company deals wtih custom plastic injection molding, tooling, and assembly related services.

**Wright Williams & Kelly Inc**    HQ
6200 Stoneridge Mall Rd Fl 3
Pleasanton CA 94588
P: 925-399-6246   F: 925-396-6174    PRC:323
www.wwk.com
Email: info@wwk.com
Estab: 1991

David Jimenez, Co-Founder
Daren Dance, VP of Technology
Alan Levine, Director

Provider of software products and consulting services. The company also offers decision tolls for cost management.

**WSI Smart Solutions**    HQ
4435 First St Ste 355
Livermore CA 94551
P: 925-245-0216    PRC:315
wsismartsolutions.com
Estab: 1995

Ryan Kelly, COO

Provider of search engine optimization services. The company also deals with internet marketing and web design solutions.

**Wso2 Inc**    HQ
4131 El Camino Real Ste 200
Palo Alto CA 94306
P: 408-754-7388   F: 408-689-4328    PRC:322
www.wso2.com
Email: bizdev@wso2.com
Estab: 2005

Vanjikumaran Sivajothy, Senior Lead Solution Engineer
Sanjiva Weerawarana, Founder
Paul Fremantle, President
Shevan Goonetilleke, President
Devaka Randeniya, VP of Sales

Provider of open source middleware platforms, security and identity gateway solutions, and enterprise integration solutions.

**Wunder Mold**    HQ
790 Eubanks Dr
Vacaville CA 95688
P: 707-448-2349   F: 707-448-6045    PRC:163
www.wundermold.com
Email: sales@wundermold.com
Estab: 1996

Calvin Swesey, General Manager

Provider of ceramic injection molding services. The company designs and produces art molded ceramics for appliances and electronics applications.

**X-Fab Texas Inc**    BR
275 Saratoga Ave
Santa Clara CA 95050
P: 408-844-0066    PRC:212
www.xfab.com
Estab: 1992

Rudi Winter, CEO
Alba Morganti, CFO
Manfred Riemer, COO

Provider of foundry services. The company focuses on analog and mixed signal semiconductor applications.

**X-Scan Imaging Corp**  HQ
   107 Bonaventura Dr
   San Jose CA 95134
P: 408-432-9888   F: 408-432-9889   PRC:91
www.x-scanimaging.com
Email: sales@x-scanimaging.com
Estab: 2006

Nguyen Luu, Principal Electrical Engineer
Andy Doan, Mechanical Engineer
Dongri Meng, Electrical Engineer

Supplier of x-ray imaging and inspection equipment. The company also offers array detectors and line-scan camera products.

**X-Z LAB Inc**  HQ
   231 Market Pl Ste 728
   San Ramon CA 94583
P: 925-355-5199   F: 925-380-6784   PRC:304
www.x-zlab.com
Email: contact@x-zlab.com
Estab: 2013

Ying Liu, CEO

Provider of digital radiation detection services. The company engages in detecting, measuring, and monitoring radiation activities.

**Xactly Corp**  HQ
   300 Park Ave Ste 1700
   San Jose CA 95110
P: 408-977-3132   F: 408-292-1153   PRC:322
www.xactlycorp.com
Estab: 2005

Kandarp Desai, Director of Engineering
Bernard Kassar, Chief Customer Officer
Ron Rasmussen, CTO
Arnab Mishra, Chief Product Officer
Elizabeth Salomon, CFO

Provider of web-based sales compensation applications. The company offers services to business organizations and enterprises.

**Xandex Inc**  DH
   1360 Redwood Way Ste A
   Petaluma CA 94954
P: 707-763-7799   F: 707-763-2631   PRC:86
www.xandexsemi.com
Email: info@xandex.com

Bill Simpson, Electrical Engineer
Sherri Hanson, Senior Human Resource Representative
Gregg Smith, Senior Quality Technician
Kiumars Kaveh, Purchasing Manager
Lori Nagayama, Sales Support Manager

Designer and manufacturer of products for the semiconductor test industry. The company's products include automated test equipment and interface products.

**Xantrex Technology Inc**  BR
   161 G S Vasco Rd
   Livermore CA 94551
P: 408-987-6030   F: 800-994-7828   PRC:288
www.xantrex.com
Email: customerservice@xantrex.com

Jing Wang, Deputy General Manager

Manufacturer of automotive batteries. The company offers power products for trucks, cars, and recreational vehicles.

**XC2 Software LLC**  HQ
   122 Taylor Dr
   Fairfax CA 94930
P: 800-761-4999   PRC:319
www.xc2software.com
Estab: 1989

Randy Engle, Owner
Sara Engle, Sales & Marketing
Bill Lease, Technical Support Manager

Provider of integrated software suite. The company's products find application in water and wastewater utilities.

**Xcell Biosciences Inc**  HQ
   455 Mission Bay Blvd S
   San Francisco CA 94158
P: 415-937-0321   PRC:36
www.xcellbio.com
Email: info@xcellbio.com
Estab: 2012

Brian Feth, CEO
James Lim, CSO

Provider of protocols and reagent kits for primary cell culture applications. The company specializes in cell-based assays.

**Xeltek Inc**  HQ
   1296 Kifer Rd Ste 605
   Sunnyvale CA 94086
P: 408-530-8080   F: 408-530-0096   PRC:212
www.xeltek.com
Email: sales@xeltek.com
Estab: 1985

Sam Kim, CEO

Manufacturer of automated, production, and in-system programmers, and socket adapters, and related supplies.

**XEODesign**  HQ
   5273 College Ave Ste 201
   Oakland CA 94618
P: 510-658-8077   PRC:317
www.xeodesign.com
Email: info@xeodesign.com
Estab: 1992

Nicole Lazzaro, President

Provider of computer multimedia software, website design hosting, programming, and technical support services.

**Xerox Corp**  BR
   1600 S Main St Ste 190
   Walnut Creek CA 94596
P: 510-460-4161   PRC:110
www.xerox.com

Steve Bandrowczak, President
Mike Feldman, EVP
John Visentin, Vice Chairman
William Osbourn, CFO
Suzan Morno-Wade, EVP

Provider of color printers and copiers. The company also specializes in document management solutions.

**Xetus Mortgage Corp**  HQ
   1325 Howard Ave Ste 527
   Burlingame CA 94010
P: 650-237-1225   PRC:319
www.xetusone.com
Email: support@xetus.com
Estab: 2002

Theo Meneau, Knowledge Manager
Terence Kent, Principal software Architect
Lu Han, Java Programmer

Provider of mortgage processing services such as documentation monitoring, data and image capture, and reporting and audit trail.

**Xia LLC**  HQ
   31057 Genstar Rd
   Hayward CA 94544
P: 510-401-5760   F: 510-401-5761   PRC:20
www.xia.com
Email: sales@xia.com

Peter Grudberg, President
William Warburton, President
Michael Sears, VP of Production
Jackson Harris, Senior Staff Scientist
Nicole Thomas, Administrative Assistant

Provider of x-ray and gamma-ray detector electronics, and related instruments for the research industry.

**Xicato Inc**  HQ
   4880 Stevens Creek Blvd Ste 204
   San Jose CA 95129
P: 866-223-8395   PRC:243
www.xicato.com
Email: info@xicato.com
Estab: 2007

Steve Workman, CFO
Mike Peanasky, Director of Manufacturing
Roger Sexton, VP of Specified Service
John Yriberri, VP of Worldwide Application Support
Ron Steen, VP of Business Development North America

Designer and manufacturer of lighting products. The company specializes in providing different types of LED modules.

**Xignite Inc**  HQ
   1825 S Grant St Ste 100
   San Mateo CA 94402
P: 650-655-3700   PRC:315
www.xignite.com
Email: info@xignite.com
Estab: 2006

Qin Yu, VP of Engineering
Stephane Dubois, Founder
Ryan Burdick, SVP
Kerry Langstaff, CMO
Vijay Choudhary, VP of Product Management

Provider of financial Data-as-a-Service (DaaS) solution to deliver market data from the AWS public cloud.

**Xmatters Inc** HQ
12647 Alcosta Blvd Ste 425
San Ramon CA 94583
P: 925-226-0300   F: 925-226-0310      PRC:323
www.xmatters.com
Email: sales@xmatters.com
Estab: 2000

Desi Dossantos, Co-Founder
Troy McAlpin, CEO
Doug Peete, CPO
Abbas Ali, CTO
Kendra Niedziejko, CFO

Provider of voice and text alerting system software. The company serves the healthcare, telecommunications, and manufacturing industries.

**Xms Corp** HQ
2351 Sunset Blvd Ste 170-101
Rocklin CA 95765-4306
P: 916-435-0267   F: 916-435-0268      PRC:196
www.x-icon.com
Email: theflin@x-icon.com
Emp: 1-10   Estab: 1987

Tom Marchione, President

Manufacturer and distributor of medical devices. The company specializes in cost effective, cutting edge radiation therapy equipment.

**Xo Communications LLC** BR
651 Brannan St Ste 310
San Francisco CA 94107
P: 408-817-2800                        PRC:67
www.xo.com
Estab: 1996

Chri Ancell, CEO

Provider of communication services including cloud security, collocation, email hosting, and conferencing for the healthcare and retail markets.

**Xoft Inc** HQ
101 Nicholson Ln
San Jose CA 95134
P: 408-493-1500                        PRC:186
www.xoftinc.com
Estab: 1998

Stacey Stevens, President
Michael Klein, Chairman
R. Areglado, CFO
Rob Neimeyer, Director of X-ray Technologies

Developer of electronic brachytherapy systems. The company's products include rigid shield, vacuum pumps, and physics kits.

**Xoma Corp** HQ
2910 Seventh St
Berkeley CA 94710
P: 510-204-7200                        PRC:34
www.xoma.com
Email: bizdevinfo@xoma.com
Emp: 11     Estab: 1981
Sales: $3M to $10M

Deepshikha Datta, Chief Business Officer
Kirk Johnson, VP of Development
Jim Neal, VP of Business Development

Developer and manufacturer of therapeutic antibodies and genetically-engineered protein products to treat immunological and inflammatory disorders.

**Xoriant Corp** HQ
1248 Reamwood Ave
Sunnyvale CA 94089
P: 408-743-4400   F: 408-743-4487      PRC:323
www.xoriant.com
Email: info@xoriant.com
Estab: 1990

Aniket Dorwat, Software Engineer
Hari Haran, President
Subu Subramanian, President
Sudhir Kulkarni, President of Digital Solutions
Mahesh Nalavade, CFO

Provider of enterprise applications. The company also offers mobile analytics and web application development services.

**Xperi Corp** HQ
3025 Orchard Pkwy
San Jose CA 95134
P: 408-321-6000                        PRC:79
www.xperi.com
Email: info@tessera.com
Estab: 1990
Sales: $300M to $1 Billion

Murali Dharan, President of Tessera
Craig Mitchell, President of Invensas
Jon Kirchner, CEO
Robert Andersen, CFO
Geir Skaaden, Chief Products and Services Officer

Provider of miniaturization technology services for electronic devices. The company offers micro-electronics, and imaging and optics services.

**XTAL Inc** HQ
97 E Brokaw Rd Ste 330
San Jose CA 95112
P: 408-642-5328                        PRC:212
www.xtalinc.com
Email: contact@xtalinc.com
Estab: 2014

Ke Zhao, Staff Software Engineer
Jinyu Zhang, Software Engineer
Zongchang Yu, CEO
Jihui Huang, CTO

Specializes in yield enhancement, software optimization and hardware implementation targeting semiconductor ecosystem.

**Xtelesis Corp** HQ
800 Airport Blvd Ste 417
Burlingame CA 94010
P: 650-239-1400   F: 650-239-1410      PRC:67
www.xtelesis.com
Email: support@xtelesis.co
Estab: 1997

Brandon Yang, Network Engineer
Christoph Pluchar, VP of Advanced Applications
Bill Russ, Account Manager
Lavonne Ubieta, Account Executive
Chun Wong, Accountant

Provider of voice and data solutions. The company is engaged in data networking, audio web conferencing, and managed IT services.

**Xtime Inc** HQ
1400 Bridge Pkwy Ste 200
Redwood City CA 94065
P: 650-508-4300   F: 650-508-8877      PRC:322
www.xtime.com
Email: salesweb@xtime.com
Estab: 2004

Adam Springer, VP of Engineering
Tracy Fred, VP
David Foutz, VP of Sales
Candy Lucey, Senior Director of Marketing
Darrel Ferguson, Director of Performance Management

Provider of CRM solutions for automotive service operations. The company offers scheduling and marketing solutions for automotive retailers.

**Y C Cable Usa Inc** LH
44061 Nobel Dr
Fremont CA 94538
P: 510-824-2788   F: 510-824-0339      PRC:62
www.yccable.com
Email: sales@yccable.com
Estab: 1985

Grand Fang, CEO
Yvonne Romero, Human Resource Manager
Bill Haas, Quality Manager

Manufacturer of cables. The company serves industrial, computer, telecommunications, consumer, medical and other sectors.

**Yamamoto Manufacturing USA Inc** HQ
2025 Gateway Pl Ste 370
San Jose CA 95110
P: 408-387-5250   F: 408-387-5248      PRC:211
www.yusa.com
Email: sales@yusa.com
Estab: 1945

Mike Ferem, Sales Manager North America

Manufacturer of printed circuit boards. The company has operations in regions of Japan, Korea, and China.

**Yamato Scientific America Inc** HQ
925 Walsh Ave
Santa Clara CA 95050
P: 408-235-7725   F: 408-235-7730      PRC:209
www.yamato-usa.com
Email: customerservice@yamato-usa.com

Marivic Lastimosa, Marketing Manager

Provider of ovens, incubators, evaporators, and stabilizers. The company deals with sales, distribution, and installation services.

**Yenzym Antibodies LLC** HQ
100 North Hill Dr
Brisbane CA 94005
P: 650-583-1031                        PRC:249
yenzym.com
Email: customerservice@yenzym.com

Glenn Ruiz, Manager of Operations

Provider of antigen design services. The company offers rabbit antibody and antigen specific affinity purification services.

## Yield Engineering Systems Inc   HQ
203-A Lawrence Dr
Livermore CA 94551-5152
P: 925-373-8353  F: 925-373-8354    PRC:86
www.yieldengineering.com
Email: sales@yieldengineering.com
Estab: 1980

Randy Hall, VP of Engineering
Michael Grave, Control Systems Engineer
William Moffat, Founder
Dan Dunkly, President
Ken MacWilliams, CEO

Manufacturer of process equipment for the semiconductor industry. The company offers products
for surface modification and photoresist treatment.

## Yola Inc   HQ
548 Market St Ste 38798
San Francisco CA 94104-5401
P: 866-764-0701  F: 415-227-0208    PRC:325
www.yola.com
Email: support@yola.com
Estab: 2007

Trevor Harries-Jones, CEO
David Saxton, SVP of Business Development &
Marketing

Provider of digital marketing services. The company offers mobile, facebook, and web publishing,
domain names, and reliable hosting services.

## York Machine Works   HQ
1401 Charter Oak Ave
St. Helena CA 94574
P: 707-963-4966  F: 707-963-8408    PRC:80
yorkmachineworks.com
Email: orders@yorkmachineworks.com
Estab: 1973

Alexander Mitchell, Owner

Provider of engineering services. The company's
services include machining, welding, pattern
burning, and engraving.

## Yosemite Pathology Medical Group
Inc   HQ
2625 Coffee Rd Ste S
Modesto CA 95355
P: 209-577-1200  F: 209-577-1012    PRC:306
www.ypmg.com
Email: billing@ypmg.com
Emp: 1-10

Jennifer Pinasco, CEO
Megan Dooley, CAO
Mike Murray, CIO
Toby Morley, Director of Finance
Emad Kaabipour, Director of Finance

Provider of anatomic pathology services such as
tissue pathology and gynecologic specimens of
oncologic and nononcologic diseases.

## Yotta Navigation Corp   HQ
3777 Stevens Creek Blvd
Santa Clara CA 95051-7364
P: 800-943-1220    PRC:217
www.yottanav.com
Email: support@yottanav.com

Andrew Zaydak, Senior Engineer

Manufacturer of sub-meter positioning systems
and underwater precision navigation platforms.
The company serves the homeland security
market.

## Yuhas Tooling & Machining Inc   HQ
1001 Pecten Ct
Milpitas CA 95035
P: 408-934-9196  F: 408-934-9197    PRC:80
yuhasmachining.com
Email: sales@yuhasmachining.com

Nick Buchko, CNC Programmer

Provider of tooling and machining products for the
semiconductor, medical, aerospace, telecommunications, and electronics industries.

## Yunsheng Usa   HQ
395 Oyster Point Blvd Ste 230
S San Francisco CA 94080
P: 650-827-7928  F: 650-827-7927    PRC:275
www.yunshengusa.com
Email: service@yunshengusa.com
Estab: 1996

John Ebert, Business Manager
Carlos Chou, Account Manager
Jonathan Huang, Account Manager

Manufacturer of permanent magnets. The company mainly offers Neodymium and rare earth
magnet products.

## Yy Labs Inc   HQ
PO Box 597
Fremont CA 94537
P: 510-739-6049  F: 510-405-9030    PRC:15
www.yylabs.com
Estab: 1997

Yan Yin, Researcher

Manufacturer and supplier of optical components.
The company provides LN modulators, bias controllers, generators, and accessories.

## Z-Plane Inc   HQ
1170 Hamilton Ave
Palo Alto CA 94301
P: 415-309-2647    PRC:68
www.z-planeinc.com
Estab: 2008

Timothy Lemke, CTO
Ralph Britton, Group VP

Provider of electronic packaging solutions for
high-speed telecommunications and computing equipment, including routers, servers, and
switches.

## Z-Source International   HQ
1181 Quarry Ln Ste 300
Pleasanton CA 94566
P: 925-401-0090  F: 925-401-0095    PRC:211
www.zsourceintl.com
Estab: 2003

Jeff Long, Owner

Manufacturer of printed circuit boards. The
company provides board procurement solutions
from prototypes to full production and stocking
programs.

## Zag Technical Services Inc   HQ
645 River Oaks Pkwy Ste 106
San Jose CA 95134
P: 408-383-2000  F: 408-383-2001    PRC:320
www.zagtech.com
Email: info@zagtech.com
Estab: 1998

David Dixon, Systems Engineer II
C.J. Morgan, Database Administrator
Dan King, Systems Engineer
Dat Tran, System Engineer
Greg Gatzke, President

Provider of services for server, email stability, reliability, migration, and security assessment needs.

## Zalda Technology   HQ
2488 Technology Dr
Hayward CA 94545
P: 510-783-4910  F: 510-783-1897    PRC:159
www.zaldatechnology.com
Email: zaldausa@zaldatechnology.com
Estab: 1991

Johnny Qiu, Manager

Fabricator of springs. The company also offers
spring design, testing, and prototype assembling
services.

## Zander Associates   HQ
4460 Redwood Hwy Ste 16-240
San Rafael CA 94903
P: 415-897-8781  F: 415-814-4125    PRC:142
zanderassociates.com
Email: mail@zanderassociates.com

Michael Zander, Principal Environmental scientist

Provider of environmental consulting and assessment services. The company service areas
include habitat conservation planning and wetland
delineation.

## Zapier Inc   HQ
548 Market St Ste 62411
San Francisco CA 94104-5401
P: 877-381-8743    PRC:325
zapier.com
Email: contact@zapier.com
Estab: 2011

Doug Gaff, VP of Engineering
Kristina Kemmer, Director of Engineering
Adam Serediuk, Director of Systems Engineering
Mike Knoop, Co-Founder
Bryan Helmig, Co-Founder

Developers of an integrated app that shares
information within a user's collective web app
automatically.

## Zapty Inc   HQ
2443 Fillmore St
San Francisco CA 94115
P: 415-830-4595    PRC:322

Teja Shah, Manager

Manufacturer of project monitoring tools. The company is engaged in design services and it serves
the business sector.

**Zaxel Systems Inc** HQ
1600 Wyatt Dr Ste 13
Santa Clara CA 95054
P: 408-727-6403 PRC:60
www.zaxel.com
Email: info@zaxel.com
Estab: 2004

Mark Marrin, Chief Engineer
Norihisa Suzuki, President

Manufacturer of 4k, 8k, and 16k video servers.
The company's products are used in post production facilities, museums, and planetariums.

**Zebra Technologies Corp** BR
2940 N First St
San Jose CA 95134-2021
P: 866-230-9494 PRC:115
www.zebra.com
Estab: 1969

Mark Zucherman, Senior Product Manager

Provider of business and printing solutions. The
company also offers printers such as desktop,
industrial, mobile, and card printers.

**Zeidman Technologies Inc** HQ
15565 Swiss Creek Ln
Cupertino CA 95014
P: 408-741-5809   F: 408-693-3727   PRC:224
www.zeidman.biz
Email: info@zeidman.biz
Estab: 1987

Bob Zeidman, President

Developer of hardware and software code design
tools. The company focuses on embedded system
development.

**Zeltiq Aesthetics Inc** HQ
4698 Willow Rd
Pleasanton CA 94588
P: 925-474-2500   F: 925-474-2599   PRC:34
www.coolsculpting.com
Estab: 2005

Patrick Williams, CFO
Brad Hauser, VP
Pan Ji, Researcher

Focuses on non-surgical fat reduction treatment
and it is involved in weight loss. The company
serves obese people.

**Zendesk Inc** HQ
1019 Market St Ste 300
San Francisco CA 94103
P: 415-418-7506   F: 415-778-9355   PRC:322
www.zendesk.com
Email: support@zendesk.com
Estab: 2007
Sales: $300M to $1 Billion

Alexander Aghassipour, Chief Product Officer
Mikkel Svane, CEO
Toke Nygaard, Chief Creative Officer
Matt Price, VP
Michael Hansen, VP

Designer and developer of cloud-based customer
service software. The company deals with reporting and analytics solutions.

**Zenflow Inc** HQ
395 Oyster Point Blvd Ste 501
S San Francisco CA 94080
P: 650-642-9658 PRC:187
www.zenflow.com
Estab: 2014

Austin Bly, Research
Nick Damiano, CEO
Ronald Jabba, COO
Shreya Mehta, CTO

Developer of products for the treatment of urinary
obstruction related to benign prostatic hyperplasia.
The company serves the medical sector.

**Zentner & Zentner** HQ
120 A Linden St Ste 3
Oakland CA 94607
P: 510-622-8110   F: 510-622-8116   PRC:142
www.zentner.com
Email: info@zentner.com
Estab: 1986

John Zentner, Senior Manager
Brian Davis, Partner

Provider of environmental planning and restoration services. The company is also involved in
permitting services.

**Zephyr Health Inc** HQ
450 Mission St Ste 201
San Francisco CA 94105
P: 415-529-7649 PRC:324
Estab: 2011

David Azaria, VP of Software Engineering
Lance Scott, CEO
Sandy Tang, Controller

Focuses on Service enterprise solutions. The
company deals with segment and referral analytics and serves physicians and hospitals.

**Zeptor Corp** HQ
3087 N First St
San Jose CA 95134
P: 408-432-6001   F: 408-432-6002   PRC:209
www.zeptoco.com
Email: info@zeptoco.com
Estab: 2009

Richard Fraga, Engineering Manager
Tatsunori Suzuki, CEO
Charles Consorte, CTO
Mikito Nagata, Director of Research & Business
Development
Dan Cameron, Senior Manager

Specializes in battery technologies. The company
develops and manufactures light-weight electrodes that are used in lithium batteries and fuel
cells.

**Zeta Instruments** HQ
2528 Qume Dr Ste 12
San Jose CA 95131
P: 408-818-9388   F: 408-573-7627   PRC:135
www.zeta-inst.com
Estab: 2009

Robert Lee, Software Engineer
Jeff Donnelly, COO
Ken Lee, VP of Special Projects
Vamsi Velidandla, VP

Provider of 3D optical profilers and its applications
include wafer quality analysis, texture characterization, and finger contact profiling.

**Zetta Inc** HQ
1362 Borregas Ave
Sunnyvale CA 94089
P: 650-590-0967 PRC:319
zetta.net
Email: sales@zetta.net
Estab: 1984

Oussama El-Hilali, CTO
Brent Skalicky, Chief Human Resources Officer
Rachel McClary, CMO
Tom Bollinger, VP of Operations
Jay Kleffman, EVP of Customer Experience

Provider of information technology solutions. The
company provides online backup, disaster recovery, and archiving solutions.

**ZigBee Alliance** HQ
508 Second St Ste 206
Davis CA 95616
P: 530-564-4565   F: 530-564-4721   PRC:64
www.zigbee.org
Emp: 11-50 Estab: 2002

Tobin Richardson, President

Provider of lighting solutions. The company offers
LED fixtures, light bulbs, remotes and switches and serves the residential and commercial
sectors.

**Zilog Inc** DH
1590 Buckeye Dr
Milpitas CA 95035-7418
P: 408-457-9000   F: 408-416-0223   PRC:208
www.zilog.com
Estab: 1974

Nathan Zommer, General Manager
Steve Darrough, VP of Sales & Marketing World-
wide
David Staab, VP of Research & Development
Alan Shaw, VP of Operations

Supplier of application-specific embedded system-
on-chip (SoC) solutions for the industrial and
consumer markets.

**Zip-Bit Inc** HQ
20640 Third St Ste 170
Saratoga CA 95070
P: 408-839-4252 PRC:304
www.zip-bit.com
Estab: 1984

John Morewood, Owner

Provider of engineering services. The company
specializes in 3D printing, 3D modeling, and 3D
scanning.

**Zip-Chem Products Inc** HQ
400 Jarvis Dr
Morgan Hill CA 95037
P: 408-782-2335   F: 408-782-6304   PRC:47
www.zipchem.com
Email: 4info@zipchem.com

Chuck Pottier, President
Charles Pottier, VP

Provider of airspace maintenance materials. The
company also offers metering equipment, spray
nozzle, and spray equipment.

**Zipline Medical Inc** HQ
747 Camden Ave Ste A
Campbell CA 95008
P: 408-412-7228   F: 888-265-0669   PRC:188
www.ziplinemedical.com
Email: info@ziplinemedical.com
Estab: 2009

Zachary Kimura, Senior R&D Engineer
John Tighe, President
Bauback Safa, Chief Medical Officer
Steve Lotz, Director of Sales
Eric Storne, VP of Marketing

Developer of zip surgical skin closure devices
for cardiology, orthopedics, dermatology, plastic
reconstructive surgery, and emergency medicine.

**Zircon Corp** HQ
1580 Dell Ave
Campbell CA 95008
P: 408-963-4550   F: 408-963-4597   PRC:13
www.zircon.com
Email: info@zircon.com
Estab: 1975

Jose Lara, Purchasing Manager
Abdul Hamid, Financial Controller
Jim Doull, Sales Manager
Ennis Pipe, VP of Global Channel Management
Barry Wingate, Design Director

Designer and manufacturer of stud finders. The
company offers electrical scanners, metal detectors, leveling tools, and accessories.

**ZI Technologies** HQ
860 N McCarthy Blvd
Milpitas CA 95035
P: 408-240-8989   F: 408-240-8990   PRC:322
www.zlti.com
Email: zl_info@zlti.com
Estab: 1999

Matthew Davis, VP of Client Operations
Zixuan Huang, Sales Engineer
Kon Leong, CEO
Arvind Srinivasan, Co-Founder
Ryan Splain, Account Management Executive

Provider of electronic content archiving software
solutions such as consulting and installation, product customization, and software upgrades.

**Zmanda - A Carbonite Co** HQ
756 N Pastoria Ave
Sunnyvale CA 94085
P: 408-732-3208   F: 408-830-9675   PRC:319
www.zmanda.com
Email: info@zmanda.com
Emp: 51-200

Paddy Sreenivasan, Co-Founder
Chander Kant, Founder

Provider of open source backup and recovery
software solutions. The company's applications
include centralized backup of file systems and
applications.

**Zoeticx** HQ
90 Great Oaks Blvd
San Jose CA 95119
P: 408-622-6119   PRC:189
zoeticx.com
Email: info@zoeticx.com
Estab: 2011

Thanh Tran, CEO
Alan Shoap, VP of Marketing
Terry Glenn, VP of Business Development
Layne Allred, VP of Business Development

Provider of healthcare solutions. The company
develops care applications and offers services to
inpatients, ICU, and outpatients.

**Zogenix Inc** BR
5959 Horton St 5th Fl
Emeryville CA 94608
P: 858-259-1165   PRC:257
www.zogenix.com
Email: info@zogenix.com
Estab: 2006

Steve Farr, President
Gail Farfel, Chief Development Officer
Mike Peterson, Director of Human Resources
AJ Acker, VP of Global Regulatory Affairs
Robin Ash, Director of Project Management

Developer of medicines to treat CNS disorders
and pain. The company serves clinics, physicians,
and the healthcare sector.

**Zoho Corp** HQ
4141 Hacienda Dr
Pleasanton CA 94588
P: 615-671-9025   F: 925-924-9600   PRC:319
www.zohocorp.com
Email: sales@zohocorp.com
Estab: 1996

Raj Sabhlok, President
Taylor Backman, Evangelist

Developer and provider of IT management software, business technology solutions, and network
management framework.

**Zone24x7 Inc** HQ
3150 Almaden Expressway Ste 234
San Jose CA 95118
P: 408-922-9887   PRC:322
www.zone24x7.com
Email: info@zone24x7.com
Estab: 2003

Llavan Fernando, CEO
Saw-Chin Fernando, CFO
Kevin Shea, Director of US Sales
Stefan Udumalagala, Innovation Manager

Provider of technology innovation, business consultation, software development, hardware design,
and system integration services.

**Zosano Pharma Inc** HQ
34790 Ardentech Ct
Fremont CA 94555
P: 510-745-1200   PRC:251
www.zosanopharma.com
Email: bd@zosanopharma.com

Steven Lo, President
Greg Kitchener, CFO
Hayley Lewis, SVP of Operations
Dushyant Pathak, SVP of Business Development
Donald Kellerman, VP of Clinical Development &
Medical Affairs

Manufacturer of biopharmaceutical products like
peptides, proteins, small molecules and vaccines
based on transdermal delivery technology.

**ZoZo Engineering** HQ
400 Spear St Ste 105
San Francisco CA 94105
P: 415-227-4450   PRC:19
www.zozoeng.com
Email: getinfo@zozoeng.com
Estab: 1997

Brian Greger, Co-Owner
Wendi Whitcomb, Principal

Manufacturer of RF surgical generators. The
company also offers gas analyzers and related
equipment.

**Zscaler Inc** HQ
110 Rose Orchard Way
San Jose CA 95134
P: 408-533-0288   PRC:325
www.zscaler.com
Email: info@zscaler.com
Estab: 2008
Sales: $300M to $1 Billion

Arun Bhallamudi, Software Engineer
John Chanak, Engineer
Ajit Singh, Senior Software Engineer
Abhinav Bansal, Software Engineer
Sushil Pangeni, Software Engineer

Provider of SaaS security solutions. The company
offers cloud security solutions for mobile enterprises.

**Zspace Inc** HQ
490 De Guigne Dr Ste 200
Sunnyvale CA 94085
P: 408-498-4050   PRC:110
www.zspace.com
Email: sales@zspace.com
Estab: 2007

Steve Yeung, Director of Engineering
Adam Magleby, Quality Assurance Engineer
Joe Powers, CFO
Amanda Austin, Marketing Manager
Mike Harper, EVP

Provider of solutions for viewing, manipulating,
and communicating complex ideas through direct
interaction with virtual-holographic simulations.

**Zultys Inc** HQ
785 Lucerne Dr
Sunnyvale CA 94085
P: 408-328-0450   F: 408-328-0451   PRC:68
www.zultys.com
Email: zultys@zultys.com
Estab: 2001

Ina Dzerushava, QA Engineer
Oleg Yefimov, Hardware Engineer
Alex Yefimov, Automation Test Engineer
Alexander Talalai, Senior Software Engineer
Ken Korpal, Senior Information Technology
Manager

Manufacturer of Voice-over-IP equipment. The
company mainly caters to small to medium sized
businesses.

**Zygo Corp** BR
3350 Scott Blvd Bldg 45 Ste 1
Santa Clara CA 95054
P: 408-434-1000   F: 408-434-0759   PRC:18
www.zygo.com
Email: inquire@zygo.com
Estab: 1970

Mackenzie Massey, Applications Engineer
Tony Allan, COO
Dan Bajuk, VP

Supplier of optical metrology instruments. The
company also specializes in high precision optical
components.

**Zymergen** HQ
5980 Horton St Ste 105
Emeryville CA 94608
P: 415-801-8073   PRC:24
www.zymergen.com
Email: info@zymergen.com
Estab: 2013

Dmitriy Ryaboy, VP of Software Engineering
Zach Serber, Chief Science Officer and Founder
Joshua Hoffman, CEO
Tom Stephenson, CCO
Aaron Kimball, CTO

Developer of engineering biology. The company
is engaged in new product development and it
serves the scientific market.

**Zynga Inc** HQ
699 Eighth St
San Francisco CA 94103
P: 800-762-2530   PRC:317
zynga.com
Emp: 1777  Estab: 2007
Sales: $300M to $1 Billion

William Wong, Lead Software Engineer
Jeff Ryan, Chief People Officer
Stuart Maynard, Manager

Provider of social game services with more than
240 million monthly active users. The company's
games include CityVille, Draw Something, and
Hidden Chronicles.

**Zypcom Inc** HQ
29400 Kohoutek Way Ste 170
Union City CA 94587-1212
P: 510-324-2501   F: 510-324-2414   PRC:97
www.zypcom.com
Estab: 1991

Karl Zorzi, President
Scott Porter, VP of sales and Marketing

Designer and manufacturer of analog modems.
The company mainly caters to the networking
professionals.

**Zypex Inc** HQ
2795 E Bidwell St Ste 100-405
Folsom CA 95630
P: 916-983-9450   F: 916-983-9448   PRC:68
www.zypex.com
Email: info@zypex.com
Emp: 1-10  Estab: 1992

Del Peck, President

Provider of solutions for product development. The
company specializes in industrial communication
products, modules, and drivers.

# PRODUCT INDEX

## PRODUCT CODE CATEGORIES

| COMPANY NAME | PRODUCT / SERVICE | PHONE | EMP | CITY |
|---|---|---|---|---|
| **2 = Aerospace R&D/Consulting** | | | | |
| Axelsys LLC (HQ) | Provider of electronic design and manufacturing services. The company's offerings include LED and AC to DC industrial power supplies. | 408-600-0871 | NA | San Jose |
| Calabazas Creek Research Inc (HQ) | Specializes in the research and development of high power RF sources, and components. The company offers software development services. | 650-312-9575 | NA | San Mateo |
| Haig Precision Manufacturing Corp (HQ) | Manufacturer of precision parts and assemblies. The company focuses on sheet metal, CNC milling and turning, stamping, welding, and power coating. | 408-378-4920 | NA | San Jose |
| J P Aerospace (HQ) | Developer of volunteer-based DIY space program. The company provides the PongSat, MiniCube and Airship to Orbit programs for space enthusiasts. | 916-858-0185 | 1-10 | Rancho Cordova |
| KaiserAir Inc (BR) | Provider of aircraft management services. The company also offers business aircraft chartering services. | 510-569-9622 | NA | Oakland |
| Nasam Inc (HQ) | Distributor of electronics products. The company offers military/defense equipment, aircraft support equipment, and other products. | 650-872-1155 | NA | San Francisco |
| Sensor Concepts Inc (HQ) | Developer of portable and integrated measurement systems. The company offers engineering, field measurement and software development services. | 925-443-9001 | NA | Livermore |
| **3 = Air Training/Simulation Equipment** | | | | |
| Advanced Rotorcraft Technology Inc (HQ) | Designer of fixed-wing and helicopter simulation productivity tools. The company services include avionics testing and simulator integration. | 408-523-5100 | NA | Sunnyvale |
| ICON Aircraft Inc (HQ) | Manufacturer of consumer aircraft. The company specializes in giving the freedom, fun, and adventure of flying to all who have dreamed of flight. | 707-564-4100 | NA | Vacaville |
| Ideal Aerosmith Inc (BR) | Provider of precision motion simulation test systems. The company serves the aerospace, energy exploration, and automotive industries. | 701-757-3400 | NA | Belmont |
| **4 = Aircraft** | | | | |
| Hexcel Corporation (BR) | Provider and manufacturer of advanced material solutions. The company manufactures everything from a carbon fiber to finished aircraft structures. | 800-444-3923 | NA | Dublin |
| ICON Aircraft Inc (HQ) | Manufacturer of consumer aircraft. The company specializes in giving the freedom, fun, and adventure of flying to all who have dreamed of flight. | 707-564-4100 | NA | Vacaville |
| J P Aerospace (HQ) | Developer of volunteer-based DIY space program. The company provides the PongSat, MiniCube and Airship to Orbit programs for space enthusiasts. | 916-858-0185 | 1-10 | Rancho Cordova |
| KaiserAir Inc (BR) | Provider of aircraft management services. The company also offers business aircraft chartering services. | 510-569-9622 | NA | Oakland |
| Moller International Inc (HQ) | Designer and developer of personal vertical takeoff and landing aircraft. The company specializes in rotapower engines. | 530-756-5086 | NA | Dixon |
| Pacific Scientific Energetic Materials Co (Califor (HQ) | Provider of energetic materials and services. The company offers services to the aircraft, missiles, space, and law enforcement industries. | 831-637-3731 | 1-10 | Hollister |
| Rolls-Royce Engine Services - Oakland Inc (BR) | Designer, manufacturer, and marketer of power systems. The company offers engines for airliners and military aircraft. | 510-613-1000 | NA | Oakland |
| **5 = Aircraft Parts & Auxiliary Equipment** | | | | |
| Aerojet Rocketdyne (HQ) | Manufacturer of missile and space propulsion components. The company also offers defense weapons and armaments. | 916-355-4000 | 11-50 | Sacramento |
| Aerometals (HQ) | Manufacturer of heater control valve assembly, gear shafts, and fuel filler caps. The company offers water jet cutting, milling, and lathe services. | 916-939-6888 | 1-10 | El Dorado Hills |
| Applied Systems Engineering Inc (HQ) | Provider of consulting, software, design, and testing services. The company's products cater to communication applications. | 408-364-0500 | NA | Campbell |
| Cobham Defence Electronics (BR) | Manufacturer and designer of electrical components. The company caters to the military and commercial sectors. | 888-310-0010 | NA | San Jose |
| Cutting Edge Machining Inc (HQ) | Provider of contract manufacturing solutions for the medical, aerospace, and telecommunication sectors. | 408-738-8677 | NA | Sunnyvale |
| Davtron Inc (HQ) | Designer and manufacturer of avionic instruments. The company's portfolio comprises volt meters, clocks, probes, and more. | 866-369-5588 | NA | Emerald Hills |
| ICON Aircraft Inc (HQ) | Manufacturer of consumer aircraft. The company specializes in giving the freedom, fun, and adventure of flying to all who have dreamed of flight. | 707-564-4100 | NA | Vacaville |
| Matronics (HQ) | Provider of aircraft products. The company's products include return flow controllers, pulsation dampers, and governor MK III. | 925-606-1001 | NA | Livermore |
| Replicraft (HQ) | Provider of World War I aircraft plan sets for modelers. The company provides plans for the aircrafts in one-fifth, one-sixth and one-tenth scales. | 510-656-6039 | NA | Fremont |
| Seagull Solutions Inc (HQ) | Developer and manufacturer of air bearing spindles, clamps, and custom applications. The company mainly offers custom made services. | 408-778-1127 | NA | Morgan Hill |
| Stellar Solutions (HQ) | Provider of systems engineering, mission operations, and strategic planning services. The company focuses on commercial and government programs. | 650-473-9866 | NA | Palo Alto |
| Tavis Corp (HQ) | Provider of custom pressure transducer sensor designs. The company offers services to measurement environments. | 209-966-2027 | 1-10 | Mariposa |

| COMPANY NAME | PRODUCT / SERVICE | PHONE | EMP | CITY |
|---|---|---|---|---|
| The Olander Company Inc (HQ) | Distributor of standard and metric fasteners and electromechanical components. The company offers tools, adhesives, and wire management products. | 800-538-1500 | NA | Sunnyvale |
| Tps Aviation Inc (HQ) | Distributor of commercial and military aerospace fasteners and electric components. The company focuses on aerospace parts, components, and logistics. | 510-475-1010 | NA | Hayward |
| Ultracor Inc (HQ) | Manufacturer of engineered specialty honeycomb and related supplies. The company also deals with custom designs. | 209-983-3744 | 1-10 | Stockton |

## 6 = Ground Support Equipment

| | | | | |
|---|---|---|---|---|
| Atac Corp (HQ) | Developer of products and services like decision aids, analysis tools, and expert consulting for aviation modeling and simulation. | 408-736-2822 | NA | Santa Clara |

## 7 = Missiles/Rockets

| | | | | |
|---|---|---|---|---|
| Aerojet Rocketdyne (RH) | Provider of propulsion and energetic to its space, missile defense, strategic, tactical missile. and armaments customers. | 916-355-4000 | 11-50 | Sacramento |
| Pacific Scientific Energetic Materials Co (Califor (HQ) | Provider of energetic materials and services. The company offers services to the aircraft, missiles, space, and law enforcement industries. | 831-637-3731 | 1-10 | Hollister |

## 8 = Other Aerospace/Aircraft Equipment

| | | | | |
|---|---|---|---|---|
| Aero Info Inc (HQ) | Designer and manufacturer of ground support equipment. The company caters to the aerospace industry. | 209-533-2868 | 1-10 | Sonora |
| Ameritech Industries Inc (HQ) | Provider of aircraft engines and certified and experimental engines and propellers and also offers overhaul and exchange services. | 530-221-4470 | 1-10 | Redding |
| Applied Aerospace Structures Corp (HQ) | Designer of space and aircraft metal structures. The company also specializes in fabrication and other services. | 209-983-3314 | 1-10 | Stockton |
| Atac Corp (HQ) | Developer of products and services like decision aids, analysis tools, and expert consulting for aviation modeling and simulation. | 408-736-2822 | NA | Santa Clara |
| Aviation Design (HQ) | Designer of aircraft interiors for commercial and private aircrafts. The company offers services to the aviation industry. | 209-962-0415 | 1-10 | Groveland |
| Cobham Defence Electronics (BR) | Manufacturer and designer of electrical components. The company caters to the military and commercial sectors. | 888-310-0010 | NA | San Jose |
| Davtron Inc (HQ) | Designer and manufacturer of avionic instruments. The company's portfolio comprises volt meters, clocks, probes, and more. | 866-369-5588 | NA | Emerald Hills |
| Ea Machining Inc (HQ) | Provider of CNC turning and milling services. The company offers services to the semiconductor manufacturing equipment industry. | 408-727-4962 | NA | Santa Clara |
| Ellison Fluid Systems Inc (HQ) | Provider of fluid systems that includes throttle body injector. The company offers fuel metering for aircrafts engines and throttle response. | 877-339-3412 | 1-10 | Mission Viejo |
| Hexcel Corporation (BR) | Provider and manufacturer of advanced material solutions. The company manufactures everything from a carbon fiber to finished aircraft structures. | 800-444-3923 | NA | Dublin |
| ICON Aircraft Inc (HQ) | Manufacturer of consumer aircraft. The company specializes in giving the freedom, fun, and adventure of flying to all who have dreamed of flight. | 707-564-4100 | NA | Vacaville |
| Moller International Inc (HQ) | Designer and developer of personal vertical takeoff and landing aircraft. The company specializes in rotapower engines. | 530-756-5086 | NA | Dixon |
| Nasam Inc (HQ) | Distributor of electronics products. The company offers military/defense equipment, aircraft support equipment, and other products. | 650-872-1155 | NA | San Francisco |
| Pauli Systems Inc (HQ) | Manufacturer of custom finishing systems, abrasive booths, and equipment including blast rooms for aviation, automotive, and industrial applications. | 707-429-2434 | NA | Fairfield |
| Rolls-Royce Engine Services - Oakland Inc (BR) | Designer, manufacturer, and marketer of power systems. The company offers engines for airliners and military aircraft. | 510-613-1000 | NA | Oakland |
| Seagull Solutions Inc (HQ) | Developer and manufacturer of air bearing spindles, clamps, and custom applications. The company mainly offers custom made services. | 408-778-1127 | NA | Morgan Hill |
| Stellar Solutions (HQ) | Provider of systems engineering, mission operations, and strategic planning services. The company focuses on commercial and government programs. | 650-473-9866 | NA | Palo Alto |
| Tavis Corp (HQ) | Provider of custom pressure transducer sensor designs. The company offers services to measurement environments. | 209-966-2027 | 1-10 | Mariposa |
| TEKEVER Corp (DH) | Developer of technologies for the enterprise, aerospace, defense, and security markets, with subsidiaries in Europe, Asia, and the Americas. | 408-730-2617 | NA | Santa Clara |
| Tps Aviation Inc (HQ) | Distributor of commercial and military aerospace fasteners and electric components. The company focuses on aerospace parts, components, and logistics. | 510-475-1010 | NA | Hayward |
| Ultracor Inc (HQ) | Manufacturer of engineered specialty honeycomb and related supplies. The company also deals with custom designs. | 209-983-3744 | 1-10 | Stockton |

## 9 = Spacecraft/Space Systems

| | | | | |
|---|---|---|---|---|
| Applied Systems Engineering Inc (HQ) | Provider of consulting, software, design, and testing services. The company's products cater to communication applications. | 408-364-0500 | NA | Campbell |

| COMPANY NAME | PRODUCT / SERVICE | PHONE | EMP | CITY |
|---|---|---|---|---|
| Hera Systems Inc (HQ) | Provider of satellite information and analytics that collects images of Earth, for commercial and government organizations to monitor and make decisions. | 844-437-2797 | NA | San Jose |
| KaiserAir Inc (BR) | Provider of aircraft management services. The company also offers business aircraft chartering services. | 510-569-9622 | NA | Oakland |
| Nasam Inc (HQ) | Distributor of electronics products. The company offers military/defense equipment, aircraft support equipment, and other products. | 650-872-1155 | NA | San Francisco |
| Pacific Scientific Energetic Materials Co (Califor (HQ) | Provider of energetic materials and services. The company offers services to the aircraft, missiles, space, and law enforcement industries. | 831-637-3731 | 1-10 | Hollister |

## 11 = Analytical Instruments

| COMPANY NAME | PRODUCT / SERVICE | PHONE | EMP | CITY |
|---|---|---|---|---|
| Airxpanders Inc (HQ) | Provider of controlled tissue expander and small handheld wireless controller of breast cancer reconstructive surgery. | 650-390-9000 | NA | San Jose |
| Aqua Metrology Systems Ltd (HQ) | Developer of online and offline analytical instrumentation for determination of water contaminants and trace metals for municipal and industrial markets. | 408-523-1900 | NA | Sunnyvale |
| CenterVue Inc (BR) | Designer and manufacturer of medical devices for the diagnosis and management of ocular pathologies. | 408-988-8404 | NA | Fremont |
| Eme Systems (HQ) | Designer and manufacturer of instruments for environmental science. The company also offers signal conditioners, sensors, enclosures, and batteries. | 510-848-5725 | NA | Berkeley |
| Guided Wave Inc (HQ) | Provider of online optical measurements services. The company caters to process analytical chemistry needs. | 916-638-4944 | 11-50 | Rancho Cordova |
| Hitachi High Technologies America Inc (BR) | Seller of semiconductor manufacturing equipment and analytical instrumentation and also offers electronic devices, bio-related, and other products. | 925-218-2800 | NA | Pleasanton |
| Infrared Industries Inc (HQ) | Developer of gas analyzer instrumentation for the automotive, oil and gas, industrial, environmental, and utility industries. | 510-782-8100 | NA | Hayward |
| Lamdagen Corp (BR) | Developer of nano technology based biosensors used in research and diagnostic equipment for human and animal health testing. | 650-571-5816 | NA | Menlo Park |
| Los Gatos Research Inc (HQ) | Manufacturer of analyzers for the measurement of trace gases and isotopes. The company serves the industrial and environmental sectors. | 650-965-7772 | NA | San Jose |
| Marvac Scientific Manufacturing Co (HQ) | Provider of industrial grade belt drive vacuum pumps. The company also offers cooling system and other tools. | 925-825-4636 | NA | Concord |
| Nyad Inc (HQ) | Supplier of gas analyzers. The company's product line includes analyzers for moisture, oxygen, carbon monoxide, carbon dioxide, hydrocarbon, transmitters. | 925-270-3971 | NA | Concord |
| Spectrex Corp (HQ) | Developer of environmental and analytical instruments. The company's offerings include detectors and personal air samplers. | 650-365-6567 | NA | Redwood City |

## 12 = Counting/Recording Devices

| COMPANY NAME | PRODUCT / SERVICE | PHONE | EMP | CITY |
|---|---|---|---|---|
| C-Scan Corp (HQ) | Manufacturer and designer of thermal recorders and printers for medical applications and the healthcare sector. | 800-953-7888 | NA | Los Gatos |

## 13 = Detection/Measuring Equipment

| COMPANY NAME | PRODUCT / SERVICE | PHONE | EMP | CITY |
|---|---|---|---|---|
| 3rd Stone Design Inc (HQ) | Provider of design, product development, and engineering services. The company serves the consumer products and healthcare industries. | 415-454-3005 | NA | San Rafael |
| All Weather Inc (HQ) | Manufacturer of meteorological instruments and systems. The company is also engaged in the development of air traffic management solutions. | 800-824-5873 | 1-10 | Sacramento |
| Arrgh!! Manufacturing Company Inc (HQ) | Manufacturer of battery chargers, controls, battery discharge alarms, microcomputer charger controls, and gas detectors. | 415-897-0220 | NA | Novato |
| Cutera Inc (HQ) | Manufacturer of aesthetic solutions such as face and body laser, light, and other energy-based aesthetic systems for hair removal and pigmented lesions. | 415-657-5500 | NA | Brisbane |
| Dynaweb Inc (HQ) | Manufacturer and marketer of web handling and tension control systems. The company's product finds use in packaging, printing, and textile needs. | 925-373-9013 | 1-10 | Sonora |
| Efa Technologies Inc (HQ) | Manufacturer of equipment for leak detection in pipelines. The company specializes in electrical and control systems projects. | 916-443-8842 | 1-10 | Sacramento |
| Esp Safety Inc (HQ) | Manufacturer of combustible gas and flame detectors, test lamps, and multi-channel controllers for custom applications. | 408-886-9746 | NA | San Jose |
| G&R Labs (HQ) | Manufacturer, seller, and calibrator of light measurement equipment. The company is engaged in design, delivery, and installation services. | 408-986-0377 | NA | Santa Clara |
| Geometrics Inc (HQ) | Manufacturer of geo-physical instruments and equipment. The company also focuses on the sales and distribution. | 408-954-0522 | NA | San Jose |
| Hamamatsu Corp (BR) | Manufacturer of devices for the generation and measurement of infrared, visible, and ultraviolet light. | 408-261-2022 | NA | San Jose |
| IDEX Health & Science LLC (BR) | Provider of precision equipment for the health care industry. The company also offers detectors, fittings, and filters. | 707-588-2000 | NA | Rohnert Park |
| International Medcom Inc (BR) | Provider of radiation detection instruments and systems. The company provides technology for nuclear medicine, health physics, and public safety products. | 707-823-0336 | NA | Sebastopol |

| COMPANY NAME | PRODUCT / SERVICE | PHONE | EMP | CITY |
|---|---|---|---|---|
| Jan Medical Inc (HQ) | Manufacturer of portable brain sensing devices for the detection of traumatic brain injuries, including concussions. | 650-316-8811 | NA | Mountain View |
| Krytar Inc (HQ) | Provider of broadband microwave components and test equipment. The company is engaged in troubleshooting and maintenance services. | 408-734-5999 | NA | Sunnyvale |
| Kwj Engineering Inc (HQ) | Manufacturer of gas detection products. The company offers equipment to detect chlorine, carbon monoxide, ozone, and methane and propane. | 510-794-4296 | NA | Newark |
| Lucas Signatone Corp (HQ) | Manufacturer of micro-probe stations, holders, and accessories. The company's products are used in resistivity test equipment. | 408-848-2851 | NA | Gilroy |
| Micro-Vu (HQ) | Designer and manufacturer of measuring machines, including automated and manual video systems, and optical comparators. | 707-838-6272 | NA | Windsor |
| N&K Technology Inc (HQ) | Manufacturer of metrology tools for the semiconductor, photomask, data storage, flat panel display, and solar cell industries. | 408-513-3800 | NA | San Jose |
| Rheosense Inc (HQ) | Designer and manufacturer of viscometers and extensional viscometers. The company offers calibration, sample testing, and maintenance services. | 925-866-3801 | NA | San Ramon |
| Rki Instruments Inc (HQ) | Manufacturer of gas detectors and monitoring systems. The company caters to refineries, utilities, and oil tankers. | 510-441-5656 | NA | Union City |
| Rockwell Automation Inc (BR) | Provider of information and asset management solutions. The company serves the marine, metals, and pulp, and paper industries. | 408-271-3400 | NA | San Jose |
| Sabah International (HQ) | Provider of fire suppressors for the commercial and industrial sectors. The company also focuses on installation. | 925-463-0431 | NA | Pleasanton |
| Scales Unlimited Inc (HQ) | Provider of mechanical and computer based weighing systems. The company's services include repairs, replacement, and installation. | 925-634-8068 | NA | Byron |
| Sierra Monitor Corp (HQ) | Manufacturer and seller of safety and environmental instrumentation. The company offers hazardous gas detection systems and site management products. | 408-262-6611 | NA | Milpitas |
| Spectrex Corp (HQ) | Developer of environmental and analytical instruments. The company's offerings include detectors and personal air samplers. | 650-365-6567 | NA | Redwood City |
| Structural Integrity Associates Inc (HQ) | Provider of solutions for prevention and control of structural and mechanical failures and serves nuclear plants, oil and gas, and other sectors. | 408-978-8200 | NA | San Jose |
| Unimicro Technologies Inc (HQ) | Provider of chemical and biological separation and analysis with micro separation technology especially capillary electrochromatography. | 925-846-8638 | NA | Pleasanton |
| Vivax-Metrotech Corp (HQ) | Manufacturer of mapping tools. The company specializes in tools used for underground cabling and piping works. | 408-734-1400 | NA | Santa Clara |
| Zircon Corp (HQ) | Designer and manufacturer of stud finders. The company offers electrical scanners, metal detectors, leveling tools, and accessories. | 408-963-4550 | NA | Campbell |

## 14 = Flowmeters & Counting Devices

| COMPANY NAME | PRODUCT / SERVICE | PHONE | EMP | CITY |
|---|---|---|---|---|
| Accusplit (HQ) | Provider of digital stopwatches and pedometer products. The company is also engaged in technical support services. | 800-935-1996 | NA | Pleasanton |
| Eldridge Products Inc (HQ) | Manufacturer of thermal mass flow meters and flow switches. The company focuses on sales, installation, and inspection. | 831-648-7777 | NA | Marina |
| Kurz Instruments Inc (HQ) | Designer and manufacturer of thermal mass flow transmitters. The company's products find application in industrial gases and liquids. | 831-646-5911 | NA | Monterey |
| Liberty Test Equipment (HQ) | Provider of refurbished and new test equipment and related accessories. The company deals with sales, lease, and rental services. | 916-625-4228 | 1-10 | Roseville |
| Max Machinery Inc (HQ) | Manufacturer of precision flow meters. The company offers intermittent injection, low flow metering, and bi-directional flow measurement services. | 707-433-2662 | NA | Healdsburg |
| Proteus Industries Inc (HQ) | Developer and manufacturer of rugged and sensitive flow sensing and control instruments. The company focuses on marketing. | 650-964-4163 | NA | Mountain View |
| Rcm Industries Inc (HQ) | Manufacturer of direct reading flow meters for liquid and gases. The company's products are used in chillers and satellite systems. | 925-687-8363 | NA | Concord |
| Sage Metering Inc (HQ) | Manufacturer of thermal mass flow meters. The company offers services to the environmental and industrial sectors. | 831-242-2030 | NA | Monterey |
| Sierra Instruments Inc (HQ) | Manufacturer of mass flow meters and mass flow controllers. The company serves gas, liquid, and steam applications. | 831-373-0200 | NA | Monterey |
| Thermochem Inc (HQ) | Provider of chemical engineering, laboratory analysis, geochemistry and field testing services and products to a wide range of energy industries. | 707-575-1310 | NA | Santa Rosa |

## 15 = Instruments for Measuring/Testing Electricity

| COMPANY NAME | PRODUCT / SERVICE | PHONE | EMP | CITY |
|---|---|---|---|---|
| Aehr Test Systems (HQ) | Designer and manufacturer of dynamic burn in and test systems. The company is engaged in troubleshooting and maintenance services. | 510-623-9400 | NA | Fremont |
| Alpha Scientific Electronics (HQ) | Designer, manufacturer, and seller of precision power supplies and electronic products. The company's products are used in medical instrumentation. | 510-782-4747 | NA | Hayward |
| Calypso Systems Inc (HQ) | Developer of solid state storage test and measurement. The company specializes in test results automatically stored in the CTS MySQL database. | 408-982-9955 | NA | San Jose |
| CS Bio Company Inc (HQ) | Provider of automated peptide synthesis instrumentation, peptide synthesizers, and custom peptides to the life science community. | 650-322-1111 | NA | Menlo Park |

| COMPANY NAME | PRODUCT / SERVICE | PHONE | EMP | CITY |
|---|---|---|---|---|
| Furaxa Inc (HQ) | Designer and supplier of signal synthesis, sampling, and pulse generating technologies and products. | 925-253-2969 | NA | Berkeley |
| Incal Technology Inc (HQ) | Designer and manufacturer of test and burn in equipment and related hardware for board testing. The company serves the semiconductor industry. | 510-657-8405 | NA | Fremont |
| Liberty Test Equipment (HQ) | Provider of refurbished and new test equipment and related accessories. The company deals with sales, lease, and rental services. | 916-625-4228 | 1-10 | Roseville |
| Micro Lambda Wireless Inc (HQ) | Supplier of remote drivers, multipliers, bench test filters, oscillators, synthesizers, and harmonic generators. | 510-770-9221 | NA | Fremont |
| Stanford Research Systems (HQ) | Manufacturer of electronic instruments, optical choppers, and temperature controllers for the research industry. | 408-744-9040 | NA | Sunnyvale |
| Yy Labs Inc (HQ) | Manufacturer and supplier of optical components. The company provides LN modulators, bias controllers, generators, and accessories. | 510-739-6049 | NA | Fremont |

## 17 = Navigational Equipment

| COMPANY NAME | PRODUCT / SERVICE | PHONE | EMP | CITY |
|---|---|---|---|---|
| Ayantra Inc (HQ) | Provider of wireless communication technology services. The company is engaged in monitoring and asset tracking. | 510-623-7526 | NA | Fremont |
| Systron Donner Inertial (BR) | Manufacturer of high performance guidance and motion systems. The company serves defense, energy, transportation, and other sectors. | 925-979-4500 | NA | Concord |
| Trimble Inc (HQ) | Developer of positioning solutions for the agriculture, construction, mining, and surveying industries. | 408-481-8000 | NA | Sunnyvale |
| Vivax-Metrotech Corp (HQ) | Manufacturer of mapping tools. The company specializes in tools used for underground cabling and piping works. | 408-734-1400 | NA | Santa Clara |

## 18 = Optical Measuring/Testing Devices

| COMPANY NAME | PRODUCT / SERVICE | PHONE | EMP | CITY |
|---|---|---|---|---|
| Anritsu Co (DH) | Provider of test solutions for telecommunication applications. The company also caters to microwave applications. | 408-778-2000 | NA | Morgan Hill |
| Emsl Analytical Inc (BR) | Provider of laboratory analytical testing services. The company specializes in a wide range of environmental, material and forensic testing. | 510-895-3675 | NA | San Leandro |
| Guided Wave Inc (HQ) | Provider of online optical measurements services. The company caters to process analytical chemistry needs. | 916-638-4944 | 11-50 | Rancho Cordova |
| Inphora Inc (HQ) | Supplier of high-precision photometric and radiometric instruments. The company's products include detectors, optical filters, and LED reference standards. | 925-322-5964 | NA | Moraga |
| Roger K Sherman Co (HQ) | Provider of microscope eyepiece reticules, calibration standards, and ruled master gages for the semiconductor and magnetic head industries. | 650-941-8300 | NA | Los Altos |
| Turner Designs Inc (HQ) | Provider of industrial fluorometers and rhodamine dyes. The company's applications include oil spill response and environmental monitoring. | 408-749-0994 | NA | San Jose |
| Yy Labs Inc (HQ) | Manufacturer and supplier of optical components. The company provides LN modulators, bias controllers, generators, and accessories. | 510-739-6049 | NA | Fremont |
| Zygo Corp (BR) | Supplier of optical metrology instruments. The company also specializes in high precision optical components. | 408-434-1000 | NA | Santa Clara |

## 19 = Other Analytical & Testing Equipment

| COMPANY NAME | PRODUCT / SERVICE | PHONE | EMP | CITY |
|---|---|---|---|---|
| Applied Systems Engineering Inc (HQ) | Provider of consulting, software, design, and testing services. The company's products cater to communication applications. | 408-364-0500 | NA | Campbell |
| Automated Inspection Systems (HQ) | Designer and builder of inspection equipment. The company caters to the oil and gas pipeline inspection needs. | 925-335-9206 | NA | Concord |
| Automatic Bar Controls Inc (HQ) | Provider of beverage and liquor dispensers. The company's products include beverage and food and sauce dispensers, and food preparation systems. | 707-448-5151 | NA | Vacaville |
| Calypso Systems Inc (HQ) | Developer of solid state storage test and measurement. The company specializes in test results automatically stored in the CTS MySQL database. | 408-982-9955 | NA | San Jose |
| Coretest Systems Inc (HQ) | Designer and manufacturer of core analysis equipment for the oil and gas, hydrothermal, and environmental segments. | 408-778-3771 | NA | Morgan Hill |
| Dakota Ultrasonics Corp (HQ) | Manufacturer of industrial ultrasonic testing equipment. The company serves the aerospace, power generation, and petrochemical industries. | 831-431-9722 | 1-10 | Scotts Valley |
| DB Design Group (HQ) | Supplier of technology solutions. The company caters to the semiconductor, solar, and medical industries. | 408-834-1400 | NA | Fremont |
| Diablo Analytical Inc (HQ) | Provider of system integration for analytical measuring instruments. The company is engaged in custom software development and laboratory analysis. | 925-755-1005 | NA | Antioch |
| Dicon Fiberoptics Inc (HQ) | Supplier of optical components, integrated modules, and test equipment for the fiber optics industry. | 510-620-5000 | NA | Richmond |
| Flexstar Technology (HQ) | Provider of testing and measurement solutions. The company's systems are used to test quality and reliability of storage related devices. | 408-643-7000 | NA | San Jose |
| Furaxa Inc (HQ) | Designer and supplier of signal synthesis, sampling, and pulse generating technologies and products. | 925-253-2969 | NA | Berkeley |
| Guidetech (HQ) | Developer of time measurement instruments. The company mainly caters to the semiconductor test industry. | 408-733-6555 | NA | Santa Clara |

| COMPANY NAME | PRODUCT / SERVICE | PHONE | EMP | CITY |
|---|---|---|---|---|
| Ideal Aerosmith Inc (BR) | Provider of precision motion simulation test systems. The company serves the aerospace, energy exploration, and automotive industries. | 701-757-3400 | NA | Belmont |
| Jabil Circuit Inc (BR) | Provider of global manufacturing solutions. The company serves the defense, aerospace, and industrial markets. | 408-361-3200 | NA | San Jose |
| Larson Automation Inc (HQ) | Developer of automated test solutions for telecommunication companies. The company offers board test stations and level shifters. | 408-432-4800 | NA | San Jose |
| Lorom West (HQ) | Manufacturer of PCB assemblies, turnkey OEM/ODM products and custom cable and wire harnesses. The company offers industry solutions. | 510-249-9000 | NA | Fremont |
| Merieux Nutrisciences Corp (BR) | Provider of public health services. The company is focused on food and pharmaceutical products, cosmetics, and consumer goods. | 209-549-7508 | 11-50 | Salida |
| Nyad Inc (HQ) | Supplier of gas analyzers. The company's product line includes analyzers for moisture, oxygen, carbon monoxide, carbon dioxide, hydrocarbon, transmitters. | 925-270-3971 | NA | Concord |
| Pembroke Instruments Llc (HQ) | Manufacturer of products for scientific imaging applications. The company also focuses on optical spectroscopy needs. | 415-860-4217 | NA | San Francisco |
| Qualitau Inc (HQ) | Supplier of test equipment and services. The company is involved in the development of electronic equipment for semiconductor process reliability. | 650-282-6226 | NA | Mountain View |
| Scimet Llc (HQ) | Provider of metallurgical consulting services. The company specializes in welding, brazing, soldering, bonding, and heat treating. | 925-736-2915 | NA | Danville |
| Seco (HQ) | Manufacturer of surveying and positioning equipment and accessories. The company's products also finds application in site preparation. | 530-225-8155 | 1-10 | Redding |
| Sessco Technologies Inc (HQ) | Designer and manufacturer of tri-temperature test handlers for the commercial, industrial, automotive, and military grade circuit test applications. | 408-321-7437 | NA | San Jose |
| Sotcher Measurement Inc (HQ) | Provider of test equipment. The company provides test stations, service tags, generator test sets, and automatic test stations. | 800-922-2969 | NA | San Jose |
| Testmetrix Inc (HQ) | Manufacturer of high-throughput AVTE systems, and offers official compliance certification test services. | 408-730-5511 | NA | Milpitas |
| Tosoh Bioscience Inc (BR) | Provider of monitoring services for life threatening diseases and cancers. The company focuses on preventing epidemics and purifying water. | 650-615-4970 | NA | S San Francisco |
| Turner Designs Inc (HQ) | Provider of industrial fluorometers and rhodamine dyes. The company's applications include oil spill response and environmental monitoring. | 408-749-0994 | NA | San Jose |
| Yy Labs Inc (HQ) | Manufacturer and supplier of optical components. The company provides LN modulators, bias controllers, generators, and accessories. | 510-739-6049 | NA | Fremont |
| Zircon Corp (HQ) | Designer and manufacturer of stud finders. The company offers electrical scanners, metal detectors, leveling tools, and accessories. | 408-963-4550 | NA | Campbell |
| ZoZo Engineering (HQ) | Manufacturer of RF surgical generators. The company also offers gas analyzers and related equipment. | 415-227-4450 | NA | San Francisco |

## 20 = Scientific/Laboratory Equipment

| COMPANY NAME | PRODUCT / SERVICE | PHONE | EMP | CITY |
|---|---|---|---|---|
| 3rd Stone Design Inc (HQ) | Provider of design, product development, and engineering services. The company serves the consumer products and healthcare industries. | 415-454-3005 | NA | San Rafael |
| Conquip Inc (HQ) | Manufacturer of converting equipment. The company specializes in volume manufacturing solutions, and also offers repair and upgrade services. | 916-379-8200 | 1-10 | Rancho Cordova |
| Cp Lab Safety (HQ) | Manufacturer of laboratory safety equipment to prevent fire, reduce waste emission and exposure to toxic fumes. | 415-883-2600 | NA | Novato |
| Diablo Analytical Inc (HQ) | Provider of system integration for analytical measuring instruments. The company is engaged in custom software development and laboratory analysis. | 925-755-1005 | NA | Antioch |
| Eldex Laboratories Inc (HQ) | Manufacturer of instruments for analytical chemistry laboratories and chemical process control. The company also creates customized products. | 707-224-8800 | NA | Napa |
| Gatan Inc (HQ) | Manufacturer of instrumentation and software used to enhance and extend the operation and performance of electron microscopes. | 925-463-0200 | NA | Pleasanton |
| Gold Standard Diagnostics Corp (HQ) | Provider of laboratory diagnostic solutions. The company specializes in diagnosis of autoimmune diseases, bacterial and viral diseases. | 855-268-6940 | 1-10 | Davis |
| Higgins Analytical Inc (HQ) | Manufacturer and marketer of laboratory equipment and supplies. The company specializes in HPLC columns, catridges, and separations consumables. | 650-988-8930 | NA | Mountain View |
| Incelldx Inc (HQ) | Provider of molecular diagnostics to detect and monitor cervical cancer, HIV/AIDS, hepatitis, and organ transplant rejection diseases. | 650-777-7630 | NA | San Carlos |
| Labcon North America (HQ) | Manufacturer of disposable plastic products for laboratories. The company offers products for liquid handling, culture, and molecular biology. | 707-766-2100 | NA | Petaluma |
| Labcyte Inc (HQ) | Provider of cutting-edge solutions. The company is involved in the revolutionizing of liquid handling concepts. | 408-747-2000 | NA | Sunnyvale |
| Mettler-Toledo Rainin Llc (BR) | Provider of laboratory weighing and process analytics services. The company also focuses on industrial weighing. | 800-472-4646 | NA | Oakland |
| Sepragen Corp (HQ) | Provider of equipment, systems, and materials for the scale-up and purification of proteins, biopharmaceuticals, and nutraceuticals. | 510-475-0650 | NA | Hayward |

| COMPANY NAME | PRODUCT / SERVICE | PHONE | EMP | CITY |
|---|---|---|---|---|
| Smart Tube Inc (HQ) | Manufacturer of reagents and one-touch automation systems. The company serves the healthcare sector. | 855-397-8467 | NA | San Carlos |
| Tosoh Bioscience Inc (BR) | Provider of monitoring services for life threatening diseases and cancers. The company focuses on preventing epidemics and purifying water. | 650-615-4970 | NA | S San Francisco |
| Unimicro Technologies Inc (HQ) | Provider of chemical and biological separation and analysis with micro separation technology especially capillary electrochromatography. | 925-846-8638 | NA | Pleasanton |
| Xia Llc (HQ) | Provider of x-ray and gamma-ray detector electronics, and related instruments for the research industry. | 510-401-5760 | NA | Hayward |

## 21 = Services, Distribution

| COMPANY NAME | PRODUCT / SERVICE | PHONE | EMP | CITY |
|---|---|---|---|---|
| Emsl Analytical Inc (BR) | Provider of laboratory analytical testing services. The company specializes in a wide range of environmental, material and forensic testing. | 510-895-3675 | NA | San Leandro |
| Exacta Tech Inc (HQ) | Manufacturer of custom machine components and parts and provider of design, inspection and engineering services for industries. | 925-443-8963 | NA | Livermore |

## 22 = Biotechnology

| COMPANY NAME | PRODUCT / SERVICE | PHONE | EMP | CITY |
|---|---|---|---|---|
| Bell Biosystems Inc (HQ) | Provider of biotechnology services. The company develops proteins targeted to kill specific bacteria but cause minimal collateral damage. | 877-420-3621 | NA | Berkeley |

## 23 = Animal Biotechnology

| COMPANY NAME | PRODUCT / SERVICE | PHONE | EMP | CITY |
|---|---|---|---|---|
| Alltech (BR) | Provider of nutritional innovation in animal feed. The company adds nutrition to food through yeast fermentation, enzyme technology, algae and nutrigenomics. | 559-226-0405 | 11-50 | Fresno |
| Antagene Inc (HQ) | Provider of custom antibody and peptide synthesis. The company is engaged in animal and histology services. | 408-588-1998 | NA | Santa Clara |
| Antech Diagnostics (HQ) | Provider of diagnostic and laboratory testing services for chemistry, pathology, endocrinology, serology, hematology, and microbiology. | 800-872-1001 | 11-50 | Fountain Valley |
| Applied Stemcell Inc (HQ) | Provider of stem cell characterization, gene targeting, teratoma formation, and embryoid body (EB) formation services. | 408-773-8007 | NA | Milpitas |
| Bell Biosystems Inc (HQ) | Provider of biotechnology services. The company develops proteins targeted to kill specific bacteria but cause minimal collateral damage. | 877-420-3621 | NA | Berkeley |
| Hemostat Laboratories (HQ) | Provider of defibrinated sheep blood and other animal blood products for cell culture, diagnostic and veterinary applications. | 800-572-6888 | NA | Dixon |
| Hygeia Laboratories Inc (HQ) | Developers of vaccines using novel technology for animals. The company offers animal pharmaceuticals for dairy cattle, sheep and poultry. | 530-661-1442 | 1-10 | Woodland |
| Single Cell Technology Inc (HQ) | Developer of cell technology solutions and also proportionary therapeutic antibody process for its clients. | 408-642-9740 | NA | San Jose |
| Southall Environmental Associates Inc (HQ) | Provider of science to support conservation management. The company specializes in marine and terrestrial ecosystems. | 831-661-5177 | 1-10 | Aptos |
| Vetequip Inc (HQ) | Developer and manufacturer of drug delivery systems. The company specializes in nasal anesthesia delivery systems. | 925-463-1828 | NA | Livermore |

## 24 = Biochemicals/Biomaterials

| COMPANY NAME | PRODUCT / SERVICE | PHONE | EMP | CITY |
|---|---|---|---|---|
| Bell Biosystems Inc (HQ) | Provider of biotechnology services. The company develops proteins targeted to kill specific bacteria but cause minimal collateral damage. | 877-420-3621 | NA | Berkeley |
| Biochain Institute Inc (HQ) | Provider of bio-sample preparation, analysis, and application assays accelerating the development of personalized diagnostics, therapeutics, and medicine. | 510-783-8588 | NA | Newark |
| BioConsortia Inc (HQ) | Focuses on the discovery, development, and commercialization of microbial consortia seed treatment and soil additive products. | 530-564-5570 | 11-50 | Davis |
| Biomarker Technologies Inc (HQ) | Provider of geochemical technology services. The company offers asphaltene analysis, diamondoids, and gas chromatography analysis services. | 707-829-5551 | NA | Rohnert Park |
| Biomertech (HQ) | Provider of tailor-made peptide and anti-body solutions such as pepdyes and polyclonal antibody advantage for the scientific community. | 925-931-0007 | NA | Pleasanton |
| Boster Biological Technology (HQ) | Provider of antibodies and ELISA kits. The company serves customers in the biochemicals and molecular biology areas. | 888-466-3604 | NA | Pleasanton |
| Butterfly Sciences (HQ) | Developer of gene therapies for HIV and aging. The company also provides consulting services for biotech investment evaluations. | 415-518-8153 | 1-10 | Davis |
| Cellular Biomedicine Group Inc (HQ) | Developer of technologies and products for the treatment of KOA, Asthma, COPD and other indications. | 408-973-7884 | NA | Cupertino |
| Corium International Inc (HQ) | Provider of transdermal delivery systems and related technology solutions. The company is also engaged in therapeutic product development. | 650-298-8255 | NA | Menlo Park |
| Discoverx Corp (HQ) | Developer and marketer of innovative solutions to study major drug target classes such as GPCRs and kinases. | 510-979-1415 | NA | Fremont |
| Drawbridge Health (HQ) | Provider of diagnostic testing solutions. The company offers blood testing solutions for a range of biomarker. | 650-714-6791 | NA | Menlo Park |
| Edeniq Inc (HQ) | Focuses on the production of ethanol, other biofuels, and/or biochemicals. The company combines mechanical and biological processes. | 559-302-1777 | 1-10 | Visalia |
| Gemini Bio-Products (HQ) | Provider of supplements, reagents, and human products. The company is involved in medical research and development. | 800-543-6464 | 11-50 | West Sacramento |

| COMPANY NAME | PRODUCT / SERVICE | PHONE | EMP | CITY |
|---|---|---|---|---|
| Integenx Inc (HQ) | Provider of rapid human DNA identification technologies for forensics and law enforcement applications. | 925-701-3400 | NA | Pleasanton |
| Microvi Biotech Inc (HQ) | Designer and developer of biotechnology solutions. The company commercializes biocatalytic solutions in the water, energy and chemical industries. | 510-344-0668 | NA | Hayward |
| Molecular Matrix Inc (HQ) | Provider of research tools for cultivating and studying stem cells. The company products provide solutions for growing cells. | 916-376-9404 | 1-10 | West Sacramento |
| Murigenics (HQ) | Provider of preclinical in-vivo and in-vitro contract drug discovery. The company is also focused on development services. | 707-561-8900 | NA | Vallejo |
| Nvigen Inc (HQ) | Developer of multifunctional and biodegradable nanoparticles. The company is engaged in research and development services. | 650-209-0268 | NA | Sunnyvale |
| Prothena (RH) | Focuses on the discovery, development and commercialization of protein immunotherapy programs for the treatment of diseases that involve amyloid. | 650-837-8550 | NA | S San Francisco |
| Purigen Biosystems Inc (HQ) | Provider of biotechnology such as isotachophoresis, an electric-field driven technique for extracting and quantifying DNA and RNA from biological samples. | 925-264-1364 | NA | Pleasanton |
| QB3 (HQ) | Provider of life science services. The company focuses on research facilities, internships, mentoring, and seed-stage venture fund. | 415-514-9790 | NA | San Francisco |
| RAPT Therapeutics (HQ) | Provider of immuno-oncologyoral medicines designed to activate patients own immune system to eradicate cancer. | 650-489-9000 | NA | S San Francisco |
| Re Cyte Therapeutics Inc (HQ) | Provider of regenerative medicine. The company focuses on repair of vascular disorders in both age related diseases and injuries. | 510-521-3390 | NA | Alameda |
| TOMA Biosciences Inc (HQ) | Provider of sequencing solutions. The company serves laboratories and researchers to uncover clinically meaningful genomic changes in tumors. | 650-691-8662 | 11-50 | Foster City |
| Zymergen (HQ) | Developer of engineering biology. The company is engaged in new product development and it serves the scientific market. | 415-801-8073 | NA | Emeryville |

## 25 = Bioinformatics

| COMPANY NAME | PRODUCT / SERVICE | PHONE | EMP | CITY |
|---|---|---|---|---|
| Bell Biosystems Inc (HQ) | Provider of biotechnology services. The company develops proteins targeted to kill specific bacteria but cause minimal collateral damage. | 877-420-3621 | NA | Berkeley |
| Blade Therapeutics Inc (HQ) | Developer of biopharmaceutical products. The company specializes anti-fibrotic drug discovery and development for treatment of fibrotic disease. | 650-278-4291 | NA | San Francisco |
| Circle Pharma (HQ) | Focuses on the development of cell permeable macrocyclic peptide therapeutics. The company serves the pharmaceutical sector. | 650-392-0363 | NA | San Francisco |
| Complete Genomics Inc (HQ) | Developer of human genome sequencing technology, research and development, clinical and consumer applications. | 408-648-2560 | NA | San Jose |
| Ekso Bionics Holdings Inc (HQ) | Developer and manufacturer of powered exoskeleton bionic devices. The company is engaged in distribution services. | 510-984-1761 | NA | Richmond |
| GRAIL Inc (HQ) | Provider of research services and clinical study programs for the detection of cancer at an early stage. | 650-542-0372 | NA | Menlo Park |
| Infors USA Inc (BR) | Manufacturer of bioreactors. The company offers shakers, incubator shakers, and bioreactors. | 925-828-9800 | 1-10 | Dublin |
| Integenx Inc (HQ) | Provider of rapid human DNA identification technologies for forensics and law enforcement applications. | 925-701-3400 | NA | Pleasanton |
| Karius Inc (HQ) | Provider of microbial genomics diagnostics. The company focusses on transforming infectious disease diagnostics with genomics. | 866-452-7487 | NA | Redwood City |
| Novozymes Inc (BR) | Provider of industrial biotechnology solutions for the food and beverage, agriculture, textile, and pulp and paper industries. | 530-757-8100 | 11-50 | Davis |
| Second Genome Inc (HQ) | Focuses on the development of therapeutic products. The company serves pharmaceutical and nutritional companies. | 650-440-4606 | NA | S San Francisco |
| twoXAR Inc (HQ) | Developer of drug delivery platform. The company is involved in biological data extraction, automated model generation, and feature identification. | 650-382-2605 | NA | Mountain View |

## 26 = Enzyme Systems

| COMPANY NAME | PRODUCT / SERVICE | PHONE | EMP | CITY |
|---|---|---|---|---|
| Antibody Solutions (HQ) | Provider of antibody products and services. The company serves biotechnology, diagnostic and pharmaceutical companies. | 650-938-4300 | NA | Sunnyvale |
| Bell Biosystems Inc (HQ) | Provider of biotechnology services. The company develops proteins targeted to kill specific bacteria but cause minimal collateral damage. | 877-420-3621 | NA | Berkeley |
| Cellecta Inc (HQ) | Provider of custom and contract solutions for high-throughput genetic screening needs and also develops therapeutic targets and drugs. | 650-938-3910 | NA | Mountain View |
| Crypto Forensics Technologies Inc (HQ) | Provider of cybersecurity solutions to businesses, organizations, and the government. The company focuses on cyberforensics and compliance services. | 510-483-1955 | NA | San Leandro |
| MTI California Inc (HQ) | Specializes in designing and validating manufacturing controls. The company offers services to biotech companies. | 925-937-1500 | NA | Walnut Creek |
| Novozymes Inc (BR) | Provider of industrial biotechnology solutions for the food and beverage, agriculture, textile, and pulp and paper industries. | 530-757-8100 | 11-50 | Davis |

| COMPANY NAME | PRODUCT / SERVICE | PHONE | EMP | CITY |
|---|---|---|---|---|
| **27 = Industrial** | | | | |
| Antibody Solutions (HQ) | Provider of antibody products and services. The company serves bio-technology, diagnostic and pharmaceutical companies. | 650-938-4300 | NA | Sunnyvale |
| Bell Biosystems Inc (HQ) | Provider of biotechnology services. The company develops proteins targeted to kill specific bacteria but cause minimal collateral damage. | 877-420-3621 | NA | Berkeley |
| MTI California Inc (HQ) | Specializes in designing and validating manufacturing controls. The company offers services to biotech companies. | 925-937-1500 | NA | Walnut Creek |
| Novozymes Inc (BR) | Provider of industrial biotechnology solutions for the food and beverage, agriculture, textile, and pulp and paper industries. | 530-757-8100 | 11-50 | Davis |
| **28 = Diagnostic** | | | | |
| Aduro Biotech Inc (HQ) | Provider of engineered immunotherapy for the treatment of cancer. The company is engaged in clinical trials. | 510-848-4400 | NA | Berkeley |
| Antibody Solutions (HQ) | Provider of antibody products and services. The company serves bio-technology, diagnostic and pharmaceutical companies. | 650-938-4300 | NA | Sunnyvale |
| Arbor Vita Corp (HQ) | Provider of protein-based molecular diagnostics that is used for the management of infectious diseases and cancer. | 408-585-3900 | NA | Fremont |
| Bell Biosystems Inc (HQ) | Provider of biotechnology services. The company develops proteins targeted to kill specific bacteria but cause minimal collateral damage. | 877-420-3621 | NA | Berkeley |
| Bio Rad Laboratories (HQ) | Provider of medical products and services that advance scientific discovery and improve healthcare for life science research and clinical diagnostic. | 510-724-7000 | NA | Hercules |
| Bio Rad Laboratories Inc (BR) | Provider of life science research and clinical diagnostics products and services for pharmaceutical manufacturers and biotechnology researchers. | 510-741-1000 | NA | Hercules |
| Broncus Medical Inc (HQ) | Provider of navigation, diagnostic and therapeutic technology solutions for treating patients with lung disease. | 650-428-1600 | NA | San Jose |
| MTI California Inc (HQ) | Specializes in designing and validating manufacturing controls. The company offers services to biotech companies. | 925-937-1500 | NA | Walnut Creek |
| Novozymes Inc (BR) | Provider of industrial biotechnology solutions for the food and beverage, agriculture, textile, and pulp and paper industries. | 530-757-8100 | 11-50 | Davis |
| Nugen Technologies Inc (HQ) | Provider of solutions for genomic analysis. The company focuses on DNA analysis and RNA analysis applications. | 650-590-3600 | NA | San Carlos |
| Plaxgen Inc (HQ) | Developer of biodiagnostics solutions for clinical diagnostics and discovery of therapeutics to treat atherosclerosis and alzheimer's disease. | 510-894-0304 | NA | Fremont |
| Pliant Therapeutics Inc (HQ) | Developer of therapeutics medicines for the treatment of fibrosis in organs and conditions, including liver, kidney, heart, and gastrointestinal tract. | 650-481-6770 | NA | S San Francisco |
| Synergenics Llc (HQ) | Provider of life science services. The company also provides financial support and shared laboratory services. | 415-554-8170 | NA | San Francisco |
| Trianni Inc (HQ) | Developer of humanized monoclonal antibody platform. The company offers services to pharmaceutical and biotechnology companies. | 866-374-9314 | NA | San Francisco |
| **29 = Instruments/Equipment** | | | | |
| Crypto Forensics Technologies Inc (HQ) | Provider of cybersecurity solutions to businesses, organizations, and the government. The company focuses on cyberforensics and compliance services. | 510-483-1955 | NA | San Leandro |
| HTD Biosystems Inc (HQ) | Focuses on the development of parenteral drugs. The company is engaged in design and product formulation services. | 510-367-0528 | NA | Pleasanton |
| Sepragen Corp (HQ) | Provider of equipment, systems, and materials for the scale-up and purification of proteins, biopharmaceuticals, and nutraceuticals. | 510-475-0650 | NA | Hayward |
| **30 = Bionics** | | | | |
| Allakos Inc (HQ) | Developer of therapeutic antibodies for the treatment of inflammatory and proliferative diseases such as asthma, nasal polyposis, and fibrosis. | 650-597-5002 | NA | Redwood City |
| Cellecta Inc (HQ) | Provider of custom and contract solutions for high-throughput genetic screening needs and also develops therapeutic targets and drugs. | 650-938-3910 | NA | Mountain View |
| MTI California Inc (HQ) | Specializes in designing and validating manufacturing controls. The company offers services to biotech companies. | 925-937-1500 | NA | Walnut Creek |
| **31 = Lab Instruments** | | | | |
| Advan Int'l Corp (BR) | Distributor of integrated circuits. The company's products include surgical and endoscopy imaging, diagnostic imaging, and touch screen. | 510-490-1005 | NA | Fremont |
| Ahram Biosystems Inc (HQ) | Developer of new life science tools. The company provides battery-powered, palm-size portable PCR machine. | 408-645-7300 | NA | San Jose |
| Arrayit Corp (HQ) | Focuses on the discovery, development and manufacture of proprietary life science technologies and consumables for disease prevention. | 408-744-1331 | NA | Sunnyvale |
| Bio Rad Laboratories Inc (BR) | Provider of life science research and clinical diagnostics products and services for pharmaceutical manufacturers and biotechnology researchers. | 510-741-1000 | NA | Hercules |
| Biocision Llc (HQ) | Provider of cell freezing and cell thawing systems, and related supplies. The company's products are used in research applications. | 800-367-4887 | NA | San Rafael |

| COMPANY NAME | PRODUCT / SERVICE | PHONE | EMP | CITY |
|---|---|---|---|---|
| Biolytic Lab Performance Inc (HQ) | Provider of instrumentation and accessories for oligonucleotide, dna synthesis and oligo purification. The company specializes in rebuilt instruments. | 510-795-1142 | NA | Fremont |
| Cellecta Inc (HQ) | Provider of custom and contract solutions for high-throughput genetic screening needs and also develops therapeutic targets and drugs. | 650-938-3910 | NA | Mountain View |
| Cp Lab Safety (HQ) | Manufacturer of laboratory safety equipment to prevent fire, reduce waste emission and exposure to toxic fumes. | 415-883-2600 | NA | Novato |
| Cpi International (HQ) | Manufacturer of microbiological testing products and analytical instrument supplies. The company serves the semi-conductor industry. | 707-525-5788 | NA | Santa Rosa |
| Exacta Tech Inc (HQ) | Manufacturer of custom machine components and parts and provider of design, inspection and engineering services for industries. | 925-443-8963 | NA | Livermore |
| Finesse Solutions Llc (HQ) | Manufacturer of bioreactor controllers and related supplies. The company offers technical support services. | 408-570-9000 | NA | Santa Clara |
| Illumina Inc (BR) | Developer, manufacturer, and marketer of integrated systems for the analysis of genetic variation and biological function. | 510-670-9300 | NA | Hayward |
| Immuno Concepts Na Ltd (HQ) | Manufacturer and distributor of diagnostic assays. The company's products are used for systemic rheumatic diseases. | 916-363-2649 | 1-10 | Sacramento |
| International Process Solutions Inc (HQ) | Provider of calibration, maintenance, document generation and validation services of pharmaceutical and biotech process equipment. | 650-595-7890 | NA | San Carlos |
| Lumiquick Diagnostics Inc (HQ) | Manufacturer of diagnostic products and other raw materials. The company is engaged in distribution services. | 408-855-0061 | NA | Santa Clara |
| Marvac Scientific Manufacturing Co (HQ) | Provider of industrial grade belt drive vacuum pumps. The company also offers cooling system and other tools. | 925-825-4636 | NA | Concord |
| Meyer Sound Laboratories Inc (HQ) | Manufacturer of loud speakers, sub woofers, stage monitors, and amplifiers. The company serves the entertainment sector. | 510-486-1166 | NA | Berkeley |
| Microsonic Systems Inc (HQ) | Provider of ultrasonic fluid processing device built with MEMS technology to biotech and pharmaceutical industries. | 408-844-4980 | NA | San Jose |
| Molecular Devices Llc (HQ) | Manufacturer of bioanalytical measurement systems. The company is engaged in life science research, pharma, and bio therapeutic development. | 800-635-5577 | NA | San Jose |
| MTI California Inc (HQ) | Specializes in designing and validating manufacturing controls. The company offers services to biotech companies. | 925-937-1500 | NA | Walnut Creek |
| Noise and Vibration Technologies LLC (HQ) | Provider of measuring, simulating, and analyzing the effects of vibration, noise, shock, and other environmental variables for various industries. | 831-655-6600 | NA | Monterey |
| PhyNexus Inc (HQ) | Provider of automated and scalable solutions for the low volume protein and nucleic acid purification. | 408-267-7214 | NA | San Jose |
| ProteinSimple (HQ) | Developer of proprietary systems, immunoassay system and consumables for protein analysis and purity of protein-based therapeutics. | 408-510-5500 | NA | San Jose |
| Prozyme Inc (BR) | Provider of biotechnology services. The company offers value-added reagents, kits and platforms for improved analytical results. | 510-638-6900 | NA | Hayward |
| Renew Biocare Corp (BR) | Provider of biomedical solutions. The company offers treatment options for doctors specializing in oral maxillofacial surgery. | 415-358-4110 | NA | San Bruno |
| Scigene Corp (HQ) | Develops and commercializes solutions to automate sample workflows. The company offers reagents, microarray ovens, and arrays. | 408-733-7337 | NA | Sunnyvale |
| Ted Pella Inc (HQ) | Distributor of medical supplies and microscopy products such as inverted microscope for science and industry. | 530-243-2200 | 1-10 | Redding |
| ThermoGenesis Holdings Inc (HQ) | Manufacturer of therapeutic products and related supplies. The company is involved in cellular bioprocessing and bone marrow transplants. | 916-858-5100 | 11-50 | Rancho Cordova |

**32 = Lab Accessories**

| COMPANY NAME | PRODUCT / SERVICE | PHONE | EMP | CITY |
|---|---|---|---|---|
| Advan Int'l Corp (BR) | Distributor of integrated circuits. The company's products include surgical and endoscopy imaging, diagnostic imaging, and touch screen. | 510-490-1005 | NA | Fremont |
| Biocision Llc (HQ) | Provider of cell freezing and cell thawing systems, and related supplies. The company's products are used in research applications. | 800-367-4887 | NA | San Rafael |
| Cellecta Inc (HQ) | Provider of custom and contract solutions for high-throughput genetic screening needs and also develops therapeutic targets and drugs. | 650-938-3910 | NA | Mountain View |
| MTI California Inc (HQ) | Specializes in designing and validating manufacturing controls. The company offers services to biotech companies. | 925-937-1500 | NA | Walnut Creek |
| RDM Industrial Products Inc (HQ) | Provider of laboratory and industrial furniture solutions. The company offers cabinets, counters, carts, and mobile tables. | 408-945-8400 | NA | Milpitas |
| System Biosciences Inc (HQ) | Provider of genome-wide analysis of the mechanisms that regulate cellular processes and biological responses. | 650-968-2200 | NA | Mountain View |

**33 = Lab Media**

| COMPANY NAME | PRODUCT / SERVICE | PHONE | EMP | CITY |
|---|---|---|---|---|
| Advan Int'l Corp (BR) | Distributor of integrated circuits. The company's products include surgical and endoscopy imaging, diagnostic imaging, and touch screen. | 510-490-1005 | NA | Fremont |
| Cellecta Inc (HQ) | Provider of custom and contract solutions for high-throughput genetic screening needs and also develops therapeutic targets and drugs. | 650-938-3910 | NA | Mountain View |
| MTI California Inc (HQ) | Specializes in designing and validating manufacturing controls. The company offers services to biotech companies. | 925-937-1500 | NA | Walnut Creek |

| COMPANY NAME | PRODUCT / SERVICE | PHONE | EMP | CITY |
|---|---|---|---|---|
| System Biosciences Inc (HQ) | Provider of genome-wide analysis of the mechanisms that regulate cellular processes and biological responses. | 650-968-2200 | NA | Mountain View |

## 34 = Biotechnology R&D

| COMPANY NAME | PRODUCT / SERVICE | PHONE | EMP | CITY |
|---|---|---|---|---|
| 10X Genomics Inc (HQ) | Provider of gemcode, instruments, software, and applications technology for RNA and DNA analysis. | 925-401-7300 | NA | Pleasanton |
| 23andme Inc (HQ) | Provider of genetic information. The company specializes in DNA analysis technologies and web-based interactive tools. | 800-239-5230 | NA | Mountain View |
| 3Scan (HQ) | Provider of automated microscopy services and supporting software for the 3D analysis of cells, tissues, and organs. | 415-851-5376 | NA | San Francisco |
| 4d Molecular Therapeutics Llc (HQ) | Provider of gene therapy product research & development for the treatment of genetic diseases such as diabetes, arthritis, and heart failure. | 510-505-2680 | NA | Emeryville |
| Aat Bioquest Inc (HQ) | Developer and manufacturer of bioanalytical research reagents and kits. The company focuses on photometric detections including absorption. | 408-733-1055 | NA | Sunnyvale |
| Abbott Diabetes Care (BR) | Provider of healthcare solutions. The company specializes in diagnostics, diabetes care, vision technologies, nutrition, pharmaceuticals, and animal health. | 510-749-5400 | NA | Alameda |
| Accuray Inc (HQ) | Provider of oncology treatment solutions. The company develops, manufactures and sells precise and innovative tumor treatment solutions. | 408-716-4600 | NA | Sunnyvale |
| Achaogen Inc (HQ) | Developers of antibacterials. The company discovers and develops antibacterial for the treatment of serious bacterial infections. | 650-800-3636 | NA | S San Francisco |
| Acree Technologies Inc (HQ) | Provider of PVD thin film coating services for medical, defense, and other sectors. The company also specializes in R&D and sell coating systems. | 925-798-5770 | NA | Concord |
| Actinix (HQ) | Developer of ultraviolet light generation, long-coherence-length pulsed fiber laser systems, high energy laser systems and optical tools/methods. | 831-440-9388 | 1-10 | Felton |
| Acumen Pharmaceuticals Inc (HQ) | Specializes in the discovery and development of therapeutics and diagnostics related to soluble AËœ oligomers. | 925-368-8508 | NA | Livermore |
| Admecell Inc (HQ) | Manufacturer of ready to use products such as cell based, TRANSIL, and ELISA based assays for in-vitro therapeutic modeling and re-profiling. | 510-522-4200 | NA | Alameda |
| Aduro Biotech Inc (HQ) | Provider of engineered immunotherapy for the treatment of cancer. The company is engaged in clinical trials. | 510-848-4400 | NA | Berkeley |
| Advan Int'l Corp (BR) | Distributor of integrated circuits. The company's products include surgical and endoscopy imaging, diagnostic imaging, and touch screen. | 510-490-1005 | NA | Fremont |
| Advanced Cell Diagnostics Inc (HQ) | Developer of biotechnological diagnostic tests. The company specializes in the identification and validation of RNA biomarkers for cancer diagnosis. | 510-576-8800 | NA | Newark |
| Aelan Cell Technologies Inc (HQ) | Provider of research, discovery, development, and commercialization of biomedical technologies for the advancement of human health. | 415-488-6041 | NA | San Francisco |
| Aemetis Inc (HQ) | Producer of biochemicals, renewable fuels, food, and feed products. The company's products include Z-Microbe, Glycerin, and edible oils. | 408-213-0940 | 51-200 | Cupertino |
| Ahram Biosystems Inc (HQ) | Developer of new life science tools. The company provides battery-powered, palm-size portable PCR machine. | 408-645-7300 | NA | San Jose |
| Aimmune Therapeutics (RH) | Developer of desensitization treatments. The company is engaged in clinical trials and it serves the healthcare sector. | 650-614-5220 | NA | Brisbane |
| Allakos Inc (HQ) | Developer of therapeutic antibodies for the treatment of inflammatory and proliferative diseases such as asthma, nasal polyposis, and fibrosis. | 650-597-5002 | NA | Redwood City |
| Amgen Inc (BR) | Provider of scientific applications services. The company's services include clinical trials, ethical research, biosimilars, and web resources. | 650-244-2000 | NA | S San Francisco |
| Antibody Solutions (HQ) | Provider of antibody products and services. The company serves biotechnology, diagnostic and pharmaceutical companies. | 650-938-4300 | NA | Sunnyvale |
| Apexigen (HQ) | Specializes in document management and managed print solutions. The company serves the business sector. | 650-931-6236 | NA | San Carlos |
| Applied Stemcell Inc (HQ) | Provider of stem cell characterization, gene targeting, teratoma formation, and embryoid body (EB) formation services. | 408-773-8007 | NA | Milpitas |
| Aradigm Corp (HQ) | Manufacturer of pharmaceuticals delivered by inhalation for the treatment of respiratory diseases such as bronchiectasis, cystic fibrosis, and biodefense. | 510-265-9000 | NA | Hayward |
| Aragen Bioscience (HQ) | Provider of services such as protein expression and purification, molecular biology, immunology, and in vivo services to the biotech and pharma industries. | 408-779-1700 | NA | Morgan Hill |
| Arcadia Biosciences Inc (HQ) | Developer of agricultural products with enhanced traits. The company uses technological tools, genetic screening and genetic engineering to achieve this. | 530-756-7077 | 1-10 | Davis |
| Aridis Pharmaceuticals Llc (HQ) | Focuses on anti-infective alternatives to conventional antibiotics. The company offers services to the pharmaceutical sector. | 408-385-1742 | NA | San Jose |
| Ascendis Pharma A/S (BR) | Focuses on the creation of drug candidates, proteins, peptides and small molecules, suitable for either local or systemic treatment. | 650-352-8389 | NA | Palo Alto |
| Assembly Biosciences Inc (RH) | Developer of therapeutics for the treatment of hepatitis B virus (HBV) infection. The company specializes in clinical trials. | 833-509-4583 | NA | San Francisco |

| COMPANY NAME | PRODUCT / SERVICE | PHONE | EMP | CITY |
|---|---|---|---|---|
| Aziyo Biologics Inc (BR) | Manufacturer of allograft tissue products for use in orthopedic, spinal, sports medicine, and dermal applications. | 855-416-0596 | NA | Richmond |
| Bell Biosystems Inc (HQ) | Provider of biotechnology services. The company develops proteins targeted to kill specific bacteria but cause minimal collateral damage. | 877-420-3621 | NA | Berkeley |
| Benchling Inc (HQ) | Developer of integrated software solution for experiment design, note-taking, and molecular biology for industry and academia. | 415-980-9932 | NA | San Francisco |
| Bio Rad Laboratories (HQ) | Provider of medical products and services that advance scientific discovery and improve healthcare for life science research and clinical diagnostic. | 510-724-7000 | NA | Hercules |
| Biocision Llc (HQ) | Provider of cell freezing and cell thawing systems, and related supplies. The company's products are used in research applications. | 800-367-4887 | NA | San Rafael |
| BioConsortia Inc (HQ) | Focuses on the discovery, development, and commercialization of microbial consortia seed treatment and soil additive products. | 530-564-5570 | 11-50 | Davis |
| Biomagnetics Diagnostics Corp (HQ) | Provider of medical device and biotechnology. The company specializes in magnetic testing platform and immunoassays products. | 916-987-7078 | 1-10 | Orangevale |
| Biomarker Technologies Inc (HQ) | Provider of geochemical technology services. The company offers asphaltene analysis, diamondoids, and gas chromatography analysis services. | 707-829-5551 | NA | Rohnert Park |
| Biomedecon Llc (HQ) | Provider of health economics and outcomes research. The company caters to pharmaceutical and medical industries. | 650-563-9475 | NA | Moss Beach |
| Biosearch Technologies Inc (RH) | Manufacturer of nucleic acid based products that accelerate the discovery and application of genomic information. | 415-883-8400 | NA | Petaluma |
| Blade Therapeutics Inc (HQ) | Developer of biopharmaceutical products. The company specializes anti-fibrotic drug discovery and development for treatment of fibrotic disease. | 650-278-4291 | NA | San Francisco |
| Blue Turtle Bio Technologies Inc (HQ) | Creator of therapeutic products. The company specializes in microbiome to recruit genetically malleable and easily replenishable organ in the human body. | 313-806-2774 | NA | San Francisco |
| Boster Biological Technology (HQ) | Provider of antibodies and ELISA kits. The company serves customers in the biochemicals and molecular biology areas. | 888-466-3604 | NA | Pleasanton |
| Butterfly Sciences (HQ) | Developer of gene therapies for HIV and aging. The company also provides consulting services for biotech investment evaluations. | 415-518-8153 | 1-10 | Davis |
| Cairn Biosciences (HQ) | Provider of therapeutic solutions for treating cancer. The company is involved in biotechnical research and commercial business. | 415-503-1185 | NA | San Francisco |
| California Seed & Plant Lab (HQ) | Provider of pathological and genetic testing services. The company provides services for the vegetable seed, grapevine, and strawberry industries. | 916-655-1581 | 1-10 | Pleasant Grove |
| Cantabio Pharmaceuticals Inc (HQ) | Provider of therapeutic solutions. The company specializes in developing therapeutic proteins to prevent degenerative brain diseases. | 844-200-2826 | NA | Palo Alto |
| Caredx Inc (HQ) | Provider of genomics technologies for the development of molecular diagnostic assays. The company specializes in molecular diagnostics. | 415-287-2300 | NA | Brisbane |
| Caribou Biosciences Inc (HQ) | Developer of cellular engineering and analysis solutions. The company is involved in applied biological research. | 510-982-6030 | NA | Berkeley |
| Cascadia Labs (HQ) | Provider of analytical services. The company specializes in analytical, pharmaceutical, horticulture, and food science. | 855-800-6890 | 1-10 | Redwood Valley |
| Catalyst Biosciences (HQ) | Developer of catalytic biopharmaceutical products based on engineering human proteases for hemostasis, age-related macular degeneration, and inflammation. | 650-871-0761 | NA | S San Francisco |
| Cellecta Inc (HQ) | Provider of custom and contract solutions for high-throughput genetic screening needs and also develops therapeutic targets and drugs. | 650-938-3910 | NA | Mountain View |
| Cellerant Therapeutics Inc (HQ) | Developer of novel innate and adaptive immunotherapies for oncology and blood-related disorders, including cell-based and antibody therapeutics. | 650-232-2122 | NA | San Carlos |
| Cellular Biomedicine Group Inc (HQ) | Developer of technologies and products for the treatment of KOA, Asthma, COPD and other indications. | 408-973-7884 | NA | Cupertino |
| Centrillion Biosciences Inc (HQ) | Provider of genomic and bioinformatics solution. The company offers genomic technology to improve sequencing performance. | 650-618-0111 | NA | Palo Alto |
| Chai (HQ) | Specializes in DNA diagnostics. The company offers services to clinics, patients, and the medical sector. | 650-779-5577 | NA | Santa Clara |
| Circle Pharma (HQ) | Focuses on the development of cell permeable macrocyclic peptide therapeutics. The company serves the pharmaceutical sector. | 650-392-0363 | NA | San Francisco |
| Codexis Inc (HQ) | Provider of biocatalysts products such as screening kits and other accessories. The company serves the food and nutrition industries. | 650-421-8100 | 51-200 | Redwood City |
| Coherus Biosciences (HQ) | Developer of biosimilars and it serves the global marketplace. The company is engaged in delivery services. | 800-794-5434 | NA | Redwood City |
| Comparative Biosciences Inc (HQ) | Provider of research and development support services. The company serves the biotechnology and pharmaceutical industries. | 408-738-9260 | NA | Sunnyvale |
| Confometrx (HQ) | Developer of a platform of drug development tools. The company specializes in drug discovery technologies. | 408-496-6276 | NA | Santa Clara |
| Cpc Scientific Inc (HQ) | Provider of amino acids, cGMP, generic, catalog, modified, FRET & TR- FRET, and custom peptides to researchers and pharmaceutical companies. | 408-734-3800 | NA | San Jose |

| COMPANY NAME | PRODUCT / SERVICE | PHONE | EMP | CITY |
|---|---|---|---|---|
| CS Bio Company Inc (HQ) | Provider of automated peptide synthesis instrumentation, peptide synthesizers, and custom peptides to the life science community. | 650-322-1111 | NA | Menlo Park |
| Curiox Biosystems Inc (HQ) | Developer of assay platforms. The company specializes in surface chemistry and engineering. It focusses on automation of bioassays. | 650-226-8420 | 11-50 | San Carlos |
| Cyagen Biosciences Inc (HQ) | Manufacturer of cell culture products. The company also focuses on animal models and molecular biology tools. | 800-921-8930 | NA | Santa Clara |
| Cytoculture International Inc (HQ) | Provider of technical consulting and microbiological laboratory services. The company specializes in biofuel project. | 510-233-0102 | NA | Point Richmond |
| Cytokinetics Inc (HQ) | Developer of cancer treatment programs for cancer and also cardiovascular patients. The company specializes in therapeutic programs. | 650-624-3000 | NA | S San Francisco |
| Dawn Reis Ecological Studies (HQ) | Provider of wildlife research and biological consulting services. The company is specialized in aquatic systems and endangered species population. | 831-588-7550 | 1-10 | Watsonville |
| Dermira Inc (HQ) | Developer of biopharmaceutical products for the treatment of dermatology diseases such as acne, plaque psoriasis, and hyperhidrosis. | 650-421-7200 | NA | Menlo Park |
| DiaCarta Inc (HQ) | Provider of molecular diagnostics tools such as genotyping tests, colon cancer tests, DNA sample card, and gene mutation detection kits. | 800-246-8878 | NA | Richmond |
| Diagnostic Biosystems Inc (HQ) | Developer of primary and monoclonal antibodies, ancillaries, chromogens, and multiplex kits. The company serves the healthcare sector. | 925-484-3350 | NA | Pleasanton |
| Dice Molecules Inc (HQ) | Developer of transformative platforms for the discovery of small molecules. The company translates DNA encoded information into organic compounds. | 650-566-1402 | NA | Redwood City |
| Discoverx Corp (HQ) | Developer and marketer of innovative solutions to study major drug target classes such as GPCRs and kinases. | 510-979-1415 | NA | Fremont |
| Dnamito Inc (HQ) | Provider of DNA technology and cloud platform to enable cancer treatment and early prediction of chronic disease thus vastly improving patient care. | 650-687-0899 | NA | Palo Alto |
| E-Scape Bio (HQ) | Provider of therapeutic solutions. The company focusses on discovery and development of small molecule drugs for the treatment of neurodegenerative diseases. | 650-431-0100 | NA | S San Francisco |
| Ekso Bionics Holdings Inc (HQ) | Developer and manufacturer of powered exoskeleton bionic devices. The company is engaged in distribution services. | 510-984-1761 | NA | Richmond |
| ESI Bio (HQ) | Provider of stem cell solutions. The company's products are used in bio printing, stem cell analysis, and stem cell reprogramming. | 510-521-3390 | NA | Alameda |
| Exelixis Inc (HQ) | Focuses on the development and commercialization of small molecule therapies. The company is also engaged in clinical trials. | 650-837-7000 | NA | Alameda |
| Fibrogen Inc (HQ) | Developer of therapeutic products. The company is engaged in commercialization and clinical trial programs. | 415-978-1200 | NA | San Francisco |
| Five Prime Therapeutics Inc (HQ) | Developer and discovery of therapeutics products for the enhancement of lives of patients with serious diseases. | 415-365-5600 | NA | S San Francisco |
| Fluidigm Sciences Inc (HQ) | Developer and creator of technologies for life science tools designed to revolutionize biology. The company is involved in research programs. | 650-871-7152 | NA | San Francisco |
| FormuMax Scientific Inc (HQ) | Provider of contract drug delivery to pharmaceutical and biotech industries. The company specializes in injectables, liposomes and microemulsions. | 408-400-0108 | NA | Sunnyvale |
| ForteBio (BR) | Provider of dip and read assay kits. The company's products are used in the application of kinetic characterization. | 650-322-1360 | NA | Fremont |
| Galaxy Biotech Llc (HQ) | Provider of biotechnology services. The company develops monoclonal antibodies against growth factors and their receptors for treatment of cancer. | 408-400-8020 | NA | Sunnyvale |
| GangaGen Inc (HQ) | Provider of proprietary recombinant protein for the topical prevention and treatment of Staplylococcal infections. | 650-856-9642 | NA | Palo Alto |
| Genapsys Inc (HQ) | Developer of DNA sequencing to enable a paradigm shift in genomic diagnostics. The company specializes in GENIUS system that has footprint of Apple iPad. | 650-330-1096 | NA | Redwood City |
| Genentech Inc (BR) | Provider of biotechnology services. The company uses human genetic information to develop medicines for life-threatening medical conditions. | 707-454-1000 | NA | Vacaville |
| Genentech Inc (HQ) | Focuses on the treatment of breast cancer. The company offers services to patients and medical professionals. | 650-225-1000 | NA | S San Francisco |
| General Foundry Service Corp (HQ) | Provider of foundry services. The company engages in pattern making, precision sand casting, and rubber plastic mold. | 510-297-5040 | NA | San Leandro |
| Genomic Health Inc (HQ) | Specializes in the treatment of cancer. The company is engaged in patient management software development. | 650-556-9300 | NA | Redwood City |
| GigaGen Inc (HQ) | Provider of biotherapeutical solutions. The company offers recombinant polyclonal hyperimmune gammaglobulin. | 415-978-2101 | NA | S San Francisco |
| Globavir Biosciences Inc (HQ) | Developer of biotechnology products. The company specializes in small molecule drugs to treat cancer and infectious diseases. | 650-351-4495 | NA | Los Altos |
| GRAIL Inc (HQ) | Provider of research services and clinical study programs for the detection of cancer at an early stage. | 650-542-0372 | NA | Menlo Park |

| COMPANY NAME | PRODUCT / SERVICE | PHONE | EMP | CITY |
|---|---|---|---|---|
| Graybug Vision Inc (HQ) | Developer of pharmaceutical products for the treatment of blindness, including neovascular, glaucoma, and corneal graft rejection. | 650-487-2800 | NA | Redwood City |
| Greening Associates (HQ) | Provider of biological consultants and landscape contracting services. The company specializes in revegetation plans, wildlife surveys, and coastal restoration. | 831-336-1745 | 1-10 | Ben Lomond |
| Heliospectra (RH) | Focuses on lighting technology solutions. The company is engaged in product development and serves the environmental sector. | 888-942-4769 | NA | San Rafael |
| HTD Biosystems Inc (HQ) | Focuses on the development of parenteral drugs. The company is engaged in design and product formulation services. | 510-367-0528 | NA | Pleasanton |
| IDEAYA Biosciences (HQ) | Provider of synthetic lethality medicines for the immuno oncology therapies. The company specializes in cancer biology, small molecule drug discovery, and immunology. | 650-443-6209 | NA | S San Francisco |
| iGenix Inc (HQ) | Provider of immunology laboratory services. The company offers service to private practice physicians, hospitals, and clinical reference laboratories. | 650-424-1191 | NA | Milpitas |
| Immunoscience Inc (HQ) | Provider of biotechnology research and development for diagnosis and treatment of AIDS and HIV infection. The company also offers therapeutic vaccines. | 925-828-1000 | NA | Pleasanton |
| Infors USA Inc (BR) | Manufacturer of bioreactors. The company offers shakers, incubator shakers, and bioreactors. | 925-828-9800 | 1-10 | Dublin |
| Inscopix Inc (HQ) | Provider of instrumentation and data analytics for next generation neuroscience. The company provides brain imaging solutions and data analysis suites. | 650-600-3886 | NA | Palo Alto |
| InSilixa Inc (HQ) | Manufacturer of CMOS biosensor devices used to identify multiple targets including nucleic acids (DNA or RNA), peptides, or metabolites. | 408-809-3000 | NA | Sunnyvale |
| JN Biosciences LLC (HQ) | Developer of antibody-based therapeutics and antibody engineered technologies. The company specializes in single homogenous molecular species. | 650-967-9486 | NA | Mountain View |
| Juvaris BioTherapeutics Inc (HQ) | Developer of vaccines and immuno therapeutic products. The company is engaged in the treatment of infectious diseases. | 925-399-6200 | NA | Pleasanton |
| Karius Inc (HQ) | Provider of microbial genomics diagnostics. The company focusses on transforming infectious disease diagnostics with genomics. | 866-452-7487 | NA | Redwood City |
| Lab Sensor Solutions Inc (HQ) | Provider of real-time sensor technology on healthcare assets so customers can monitor, report and act to assure items are in right place and condition. | 650-275-3101 | NA | Redwood City |
| LakePharma Inc (BR) | Provider of contract research organization specializing in antibody and protein engineering, cell line development, and protein production. | 650-288-4891 | NA | Belmont |
| Lineage Cell Therapeutics Inc (HQ) | Provider of cell-based technologies and regenerative medicine for the treatment of chronic and degenerative diseases. | 510-871-4188 | 11-50 | Carlsbad |
| Lumen Therapeutics LLC (HQ) | Provider of therapeutic solutions. The company focusses on the proprietary drugs based on oligo-L-arginine. | 650-450-4439 | NA | Menlo Park |
| Lumiphore Inc (HQ) | Developer of proprietary lanthanide technology. The company develops and markets biological detection reagents. | 510-898-1190 | NA | Berkeley |
| Lumiquick Diagnostics Inc (HQ) | Manufacturer of diagnostic products and other raw materials. The company is engaged in distribution services. | 408-855-0061 | NA | Santa Clara |
| MabPlex USA Inc (BR) | Developer and manufacture of biopharmaceuticals. The company also offers contract services from DNA to finished drug product. | 510-830-1065 | NA | Fremont |
| Marin Biologic Laboratories Inc (HQ) | Provider of client research services. The company serves the pharmaceutical, biotechnology, diagnostic, agricultural, and legal markets. | 415-883-8000 | NA | Novato |
| Marrone Bio Innovations Inc (HQ) | Developer of naturally derived technologies of pest management and plant health products used in agricultural, ornamental, and water treatment. | 530-750-2800 | 1-10 | Davis |
| MedAutonomic Inc (HQ) | Developer of Brain NeuroModulator. The company specializes in creating control action potentials in individual neurons and in functional groups. | 415-377-5653 | NA | Concord |
| Medeor Therapeutics (HQ) | Developer of personalized cellular immunotherapy for the organ transplant recipients. The company specializes in cellular immunotherapy, hematology, and transplantation product development. | 650-627-4531 | NA | S San Francisco |
| MedGenome Inc (HQ) | Provider of genomics based diagnostics and research services. The company specializes in bioinformatics, computing, genomics technologies, and big data analytics. | 888-440-0954 | NA | Foster City |
| MedStars Inc (HQ) | Provider of medical devices, healthcare information systems, health related consumer products, and biotechnology for medical and biotech companies. | 650-917-9254 | NA | Los Altos Hills |
| Micro Lithography Inc (HQ) | Manufacturer of pellicles using high end equipment for the production of frames and engineering parts, automatic anodizing lines, and chemical labs. | 408-747-1769 | NA | Sunnyvale |
| Microvi Biotech Inc (HQ) | Designer and developer of biotechnology solutions. The company commercializes biocatalytic solutions in the water, energy and chemical industries. | 510-344-0668 | NA | Hayward |
| Molecular Devices Llc (HQ) | Manufacturer of bioanalytical measurement systems. The company is engaged in life science research, pharma, and bio therapeutic development. | 800-635-5577 | NA | San Jose |

| COMPANY NAME | PRODUCT / SERVICE | PHONE | EMP | CITY |
|---|---|---|---|---|
| Molecular Matrix Inc (HQ) | Provider of research tools for cultivating and studying stem cells. The company products provide solutions for growing cells. | 916-376-9404 | 1-10 | West Sacramento |
| MTI California Inc (HQ) | Specializes in designing and validating manufacturing controls. The company offers services to biotech companies. | 925-937-1500 | NA | Walnut Creek |
| Murigenics (HQ) | Provider of preclinical in-vivo and in-vitro contract drug discovery. The company is also focused on development services. | 707-561-8900 | NA | Vallejo |
| MyoKardia Inc (HQ) | Provider of precision medicine. The company focusses on developing and commercializing therapies for treating cardiovascular diseases. | 650-741-0900 | NA | S San Francisco |
| Natera Inc (HQ) | Provider of prenatal testing services. The company specializes in non-invasive prenatal testing, genetic carrier screening and paternity testing. | 650-249-9090 | 501-1000 | San Carlos |
| Nektar Therapeutics (HQ) | Provider of therapeutic products for the treatment of opioid-induced constipation in adult patients with chronic non-cancer pain. | 415-482-5300 | NA | San Francisco |
| Nelson Biotechnologies Inc (HQ) | Provider of oligonucleotide labeling and modification services. The company also specializes in contract research and manufacturing. | 408-778-2020 | NA | Morgan Hill |
| Neodyne Biosciences Inc (HQ) | Manufacturer of embrace devices and it helps in the concealment of scars. The company serves patients. | 800-519-7127 | NA | Newark |
| Neurona Therapeutics (HQ) | Developer of neuronal stem cells to transplant into the brain. The company offers services to the healthcare industry. | 650-799-6465 | NA | S San Francisco |
| Neurotrack Technologies Inc (HQ) | Provider of computer-based cognitive tests. The company offers services to Alzheimer's patients and the medical industry. | 650-549-8566 | NA | Redwood City |
| Novabay Pharmaceuticals Inc (HQ) | Manufacturer of biopharmaceuticals. The company develops non-antibiotic anti-infective products to address the eye care market. | 510-899-8800 | NA | Emeryville |
| Novozymes Inc (BR) | Provider of industrial biotechnology solutions for the food and beverage, agriculture, textile, and pulp and paper industries. | 530-757-8100 | 11-50 | Davis |
| Nugen Technologies Inc (HQ) | Provider of solutions for genomic analysis. The company focuses on DNA analysis and RNA analysis applications. | 650-590-3600 | NA | San Carlos |
| NuMedii Inc (HQ) | Provider of big data technology such as integrative genomics and chemoinformatics to discover and de-risk new indications for safe, existing drug. | 650-918-6363 | NA | San Mateo |
| Osel Inc (HQ) | Developer of biotherapeutic products. The company focuses on treatment and prevention of conditions for women's health and infectious diseases. | 650-964-1420 | NA | Mountain View |
| Pacific Biodevelopment Llc (HQ) | Provider of biotechnology services. The company offers drug development services to allow timely and cost efficient entry of drugs into the market. | 510-858-5600 | NA | Emeryville |
| Pacific Biosciences Of California Inc (HQ) | Provider of targeted sequencing, base modifications, microbiology, and isoform sequencing detection services. | 650-521-8000 | NA | Menlo Park |
| Patz Materials & Technologies (HQ) | Manufacturer of composite materials. The company portfolio includes unidirectional tapes, fabric prepregs, composite armor systems, and cellular developments. | 707-748-7577 | NA | Benicia |
| Paxvax Inc (HQ) | Provider of vaccines to protect from infectious diseases. The company offers treatments to diseases such as typhoid, cholera, and anthrax. | 650-847-1075 | NA | Redwood City |
| Pendulum Therapeutics Inc (HQ) | Developer of microbiome interventions and diagnostics systems. The company is involved in research and development services. | 415-855-0940 | NA | San Francisco |
| PharmaLogic Development Inc (HQ) | Focuses on planning, drug development, and marketing services. The company serves the pharmaceutical and biomedical industries. | 415-472-2181 | NA | San Rafael |
| Planet Biotechnology Inc (HQ) | Provider of biotechnology services. The company develops antibody-based therapeutic and preventative products through plants to meet medical needs. | 510-887-1461 | NA | Hayward |
| Planetary Herbals (HQ) | Provider of nutritional herbal healthcare products. The company's products include Acai, Full Spectrum, Bacopa Extract, and Digestive Comfort. | 831-438-1700 | 1-10 | Soquel |
| Plexxikon Inc (HQ) | Developer of pharmaceuticals. The company utilizes its proprietary discovery platform to produce highly selective and targeted medicines. | 510-647-4000 | NA | Berkeley |
| PotBotics Inc (HQ) | Developer of medical marijuana products such as potbot, brainbot, and nanopot. | 650-837-0420 | NA | Palo Alto |
| Primity Bio Inc (HQ) | Provider of assay platforms for biological relevance. The company specializes in cell biology, flow cytometry, and molecular biology. | 510-210-0605 | NA | Fremont |
| Progenitor Cell Therapy (BR) | Manufacturer of biotechnology products. The company develops cell therapy products on a contract basis. | 650-964-6744 | NA | Mountain View |
| Prolynx Llc (HQ) | Developer of technology solutions for releasable linkers. The company also specializes in injectable drugs. | 415-552-5306 | NA | San Francisco |
| ProMab Biotechnologies Inc (HQ) | Provider of cell isolation kits, custom antibodies, cancer stem cells, and recombinant protein products. | 510-860-4615 | NA | Richmond |
| Prothena (RH) | Focuses on the discovery, development and commercialization of protein immunotherapy programs for the treatment of diseases that involve amyloid. | 650-837-8550 | NA | S San Francisco |
| ProTrials Research Inc (HQ) | Provider of clinical research services. The company offers the ability to move a new drug or device from conception to FDA approval. | 650-864-9180 | NA | San Jose |
| Purigen Biosystems Inc (HQ) | Provider of biotechnology such as isotachophoresis, an electric-field driven technique for extracting and quantifying DNA and RNA from biological samples. | 925-264-1364 | NA | Pleasanton |

| COMPANY NAME | PRODUCT / SERVICE | PHONE | EMP | CITY |
|---|---|---|---|---|
| Qi Medical Inc (HQ) | Manufacturer of fingertip testing, syringe filters, rinse fluids, incubators, and vial adaptors for pharmacists and nurses who handle sterile solutions. | 530-272-8700 | 1-10 | Grass Valley |
| Quantapore Inc (HQ) | Developer of anopore based nucleic acid sequencing technology. The company's technology is used to read human genomes. | 650-321-2032 | NA | S San Francisco |
| RAPT Therapeutics (HQ) | Provider of immuno-oncologyoral medicines designed to activate patients own immune system to eradicate cancer. | 650-489-9000 | NA | S San Francisco |
| Re Cyte Therapeutics Inc (HQ) | Provider of regenerative medicine. The company focuses on repair of vascular disorders in both age related diseases and injuries. | 510-521-3390 | NA | Alameda |
| ReaMetrix Inc (HQ) | Provider of biotechnology services. The company develops innovative affordable diagnostic solutions. | 650-226-4144 | NA | Los Altos |
| Renew Biocare Corp (BR) | Provider of biomedical solutions. The company offers treatment options for doctors specializing in oral maxillofacial surgery. | 415-358-4110 | NA | San Bruno |
| Revance Therapeutics Inc (HQ) | Developers of botulinum toxin products. The company develops and manufactures botulinum toxin products for aesthetic and therapeutic categories. | 510-742-3400 | 51-200 | Newark |
| Rigel Pharmaceuticals Inc (HQ) | Developer novel, small-molecule drugs for the treatment of inflammatory and autoimmune diseases, immuno-oncology related diseases, and muscle disorders. | 650-624-1100 | NA | S San Francisco |
| Ryss Lab Inc (HQ) | Provider of biotechnology and pharmaceutical development services. The company offers services to the healthcare sector. | 510-477-9570 | NA | Union City |
| Sanbio Inc (HQ) | Developer of regenerative therapies for neurological disorders. The company offers services to the healthcare sector.. | 650-625-8965 | NA | Mountain View |
| Sangamo Therapeutics (HQ) | Developer of engineered DNA-binding proteins for the regulation of gene expression and for gene modification. | 510-970-6000 | 201-500 | Richmond |
| SciBac Inc (HQ) | Developer of bactoceuticals and medicinal probiotics for the prevention and treatment of clostridium difficile. The company serves the medical sector. | 650-689-5343 | NA | Burlingame |
| Second Genome Inc (HQ) | Focuses on the development of therapeutic products. The company serves pharmaceutical and nutritional companies. | 650-440-4606 | NA | S San Francisco |
| Sepragen Corp (HQ) | Provider of equipment, systems, and materials for the scale-up and purification of proteins, biopharmaceuticals, and nutraceuticals. | 510-475-0650 | NA | Hayward |
| Signosis Inc (HQ) | Provider of bioassays. The company focuses on the development and commercialization of plate-based analysis products. | 408-747-0771 | NA | Santa Clara |
| Sillajen Inc (BR) | Developer of biotherapeutics specializing in cancer products. The company also focuses on marketing. | 415-281-8886 | NA | San Francisco |
| Single Cell Technology Inc (HQ) | Developer of cell technology solutions and also proportionary therapeutic antibody process for its clients. | 408-642-9740 | NA | San Jose |
| SRI International (RH) | Provider of consulting, research, and development services. The company offers services to the defense, security, and energy sectors. | 650-859-2000 | NA | Menlo Park |
| SwitchGear Genomics Inc (HQ) | Focuses on custom cloning, pathway screening, target validation, sequence variant assay, and custom mutagenesis services. | 760-431-1263 | 11-50 | Carlsbad |
| Synergenics Llc (HQ) | Provider of life science services. The company also provides financial support and shared laboratory services. | 415-554-8170 | NA | San Francisco |
| System Biosciences Inc (HQ) | Provider of genome-wide analysis of the mechanisms that regulate cellular processes and biological responses. | 650-968-2200 | NA | Mountain View |
| Transcriptic Inc (HQ) | Specializes in scientific research and the company also supports an array of vitro molecular biology and cell biology. | 650-763-8432 | NA | Menlo Park |
| Transgenomic Inc (BR) | Provider of patient testing and biomarker identification services. The company specializes in high performance products. | 408-432-3230 | NA | San Jose |
| Trellis Bioscience LLC (HQ) | Developer of human antibody therapeutics as treatment for infectious disease and oncology indications. | 650-838-1400 | NA | Redwood City |
| Trianni Inc (HQ) | Developer of humanized monoclonal antibody platform. The company offers services to pharmaceutical and biotechnology companies. | 866-374-9314 | NA | San Francisco |
| Tricida Inc (HQ) | Focuses on the discovery and clinical development of therapeutics to address renal, metabolic and cardiovascular diseases. | 415-429-7800 | NA | S San Francisco |
| Twist Bioscience (HQ) | Specializes in DNA synthesis programs. The company is engaged in genome editing and drug discovery services. | 800-719-0671 | NA | San Francisco |
| Ultragenyx Pharmaceutical Inc (HQ) | Developer of products for the treatment of rare and ultra-rare diseases. The company is engaged in commercialization of products. | 415-483-8800 | 501-1000 | Novato |
| Valitor Inc (HQ) | Developer of therapeutic protein drugs. The company's drugs are used in dermatology, ophthalmology, orthopedics, and stem cell therapy. | 510-969-9246 | NA | Berkeley |
| Vector Laboratories Inc (HQ) | Provider of labeling and detection services for enzymes, antibodies and antigens, DNA and RNA by using polymer reagents. | 650-697-3600 | NA | Burlingame |
| Xoma Corp (HQ) | Developer and manufacturer of therapeutic antibodies and genetically-engineered protein products to treat immunological and inflammatory disorders. | 510-204-7200 | 11-50 | Berkeley |
| Zeltiq Aesthetics Inc (HQ) | Focuses on non-surgical fat reduction treatment and it is involved in weight loss. The company serves obese people. | 925-474-2500 | NA | Pleasanton |

| COMPANY NAME | PRODUCT / SERVICE | PHONE | EMP | CITY |
|---|---|---|---|---|
| Zymergen (HQ) | Developer of engineering biology. The company is engaged in new product development and it serves the scientific market. | 415-801-8073 | NA | Emeryville |

## 35 = Catalysts

| | | | | |
|---|---|---|---|---|
| Catalyst Biosciences (HQ) | Developer of catalytic biopharmaceutical products based on engineering human proteases for hemostasis, age-related macular degeneration, and inflammation. | 650-871-0761 | NA | S San Francisco |

## 36 = Cell Culture Technology

| | | | | |
|---|---|---|---|---|
| 10X Genomics Inc (HQ) | Provider of gemcode, instruments, software, and applications technology for RNA and DNA analysis. | 925-401-7300 | NA | Pleasanton |
| 4d Molecular Therapeutics Llc (HQ) | Provider of gene therapy product research & development for the treatment of genetic diseases such as diabetes, arthritis, and heart failure. | 510-505-2680 | NA | Emeryville |
| Aduro Biotech Inc (HQ) | Provider of engineered immunotherapy for the treatment of cancer. The company is engaged in clinical trials. | 510-848-4400 | NA | Berkeley |
| Advanced Cell Diagnostics Inc (HQ) | Developer of biotechnological diagnostic tests. The company specializes in the identification and validation of RNA biomarkers for cancer diagnosis. | 510-576-8800 | NA | Newark |
| AerospaceComputing Inc (HQ) | Provider of computer technology application services to aerospace sciences. The company also focuses on business development services. | 650-988-0388 | NA | Mountain View |
| Allcells Llc (HQ) | Provider of medical services for human primary cells. The company focuses on fields such as cell biology, oncology, and virology. | 510-726-2700 | NA | Alameda |
| Alphalyse Inc (HQ) | Provider of protein analysis services. The company focuses on support research, manufacturing, and clinical development activities. | 650-543-3193 | NA | Palo Alto |
| Alstem Inc (HQ) | Provider of virus concentration and transduction solutions. The company's offerings include assay kits, antibodies etc. | 510-708-0096 | NA | Richmond |
| Applied Stemcell Inc (HQ) | Provider of stem cell characterization, gene targeting, teratoma formation, and embryoid body (EB) formation services. | 408-773-8007 | NA | Milpitas |
| Aziyo Biologics Inc (BR) | Manufacturer of allograft tissue products for use in orthopedic, spinal, sports medicine, and dermal applications. | 855-416-0596 | NA | Richmond |
| Biochain Institute Inc (HQ) | Provider of bio-sample preparation, analysis, and application assays accelerating the development of personalized diagnostics, therapeutics, and medicine. | 510-783-8588 | NA | Newark |
| Biolytic Lab Performance Inc (HQ) | Provider of instrumentation and accessories for oligonucleotide, dna synthesis and oligo purification. The company specializes in rebuilt instruments. | 510-795-1142 | NA | Fremont |
| Cell Technology (HQ) | Developer of assays to study cellular functions by researchers using cell preamble agents for academic, biotechnology, and pharmaceutical industries. | 650-960-2170 | NA | Mountain View |
| Celltheon (HQ) | Developer of customized solutions for preclinical studies of the biotechnology and pharmaceutical industries. | 510-306-2355 | NA | Union City |
| Cellular Biomedicine Group Inc (HQ) | Developer of technologies and products for the treatment of KOA, Asthma, COPD and other indications. | 408-973-7884 | NA | Cupertino |
| Cerus Corp (HQ) | Manufacturer of biomedical products such as the intercept blood system and pathogen reduction system, focused in the field of blood safety. | 925-288-6000 | NA | Concord |
| Curiox Biosystems Inc (HQ) | Developer of assay platforms. The company specializes in surface chemistry and engineering. It focusses on automation of bioassays. | 650-226-8420 | 11-50 | San Carlos |
| Cyagen Biosciences Inc (HQ) | Manufacturer of cell culture products. The company also focuses on animal models and molecular biology tools. | 800-921-8930 | NA | Santa Clara |
| Discoverx Corp (HQ) | Developer and marketer of innovative solutions to study major drug target classes such as GPCRs and kinases. | 510-979-1415 | NA | Fremont |
| Dnamito Inc (HQ) | Provider of DNA technology and cloud platform to enable cancer treatment and early prediction of chronic disease thus vastly improving patient care. | 650-687-0899 | NA | Palo Alto |
| ESI Bio (HQ) | Provider of stem cell solutions. The company's products are used in bio printing, stem cell analysis, and stem cell reprogramming. | 510-521-3390 | NA | Alameda |
| Finesse Solutions Llc (HQ) | Manufacturer of bioreactor controllers and related supplies. The company offers technical support services. | 408-570-9000 | NA | Santa Clara |
| Fluidigm Corp (HQ) | Manufacturer of life-science tools. The company's technologies are focused on microfluidics and mass cytometry. | 650-266-6000 | NA | S San Francisco |
| Galaxy Biotech Llc (HQ) | Provider of biotechnology services. The company develops monoclonal antibodies against growth factors and their receptors for treatment of cancer. | 408-400-8020 | NA | Sunnyvale |
| Gemini Bio-Products (HQ) | Provider of supplements, reagents, and human products. The company is involved in medical research and development. | 800-543-6464 | 11-50 | West Sacramento |
| Globavir Biosciences Inc (HQ) | Developer of biotechnology products. The company specializes in small molecule drugs to treat cancer and infectious diseases. | 650-351-4495 | NA | Los Altos |
| Graybug Vision Inc (HQ) | Developer of pharmaceutical products for the treatment of blindness, including neovascular, glaucoma, and corneal graft rejection. | 650-487-2800 | NA | Redwood City |
| Hemostat Laboratories (HQ) | Provider of defibrinated sheep blood and other animal blood products for cell culture, diagnostic and veterinary applications. | 800-572-6888 | NA | Dixon |

| COMPANY NAME | PRODUCT / SERVICE | PHONE | EMP | CITY |
|---|---|---|---|---|
| Histo path (HQ) | Provider of histotechnology services. The company specializes in providing tissue culture slides for dermatologists. | 209-522-8240 | 1-10 | Modesto |
| Infors USA Inc (BR) | Manufacturer of bioreactors. The company offers shakers, incubator shakers, and bioreactors. | 925-828-9800 | 1-10 | Dublin |
| InSilixa Inc (HQ) | Manufacturer of CMOS biosensor devices used to identify multiple targets including nucleic acids (DNA or RNA), peptides, or metabolites. | 408-809-3000 | NA | Sunnyvale |
| J R Scientific Inc (HQ) | Provider of cell culture products and services. The company's offerings include antibiotics, reagents, and other supplies. | 530-666-9868 | 1-10 | Woodland |
| Karius Inc (HQ) | Provider of microbial genomics diagnostics. The company focusses on transforming infectious disease diagnostics with genomics. | 866-452-7487 | NA | Redwood City |
| LakePharma Inc (BR) | Provider of contract research organization specializing in antibody and protein engineering, cell line development, and protein production. | 650-288-4891 | NA | Belmont |
| Lineage Cell Therapeutics Inc (HQ) | Provider of cell-based technologies and regenerative medicine for the treatment of chronic and degenerative diseases. | 510-871-4188 | 11-50 | Carlsbad |
| Maverick Therapeutics (HQ) | Provider of therapeutic solutions for the treatment of cancer. The company focusses on the research of cytotoxic T cells. | 650-338-1231 | NA | Brisbane |
| Mawi DNA Technologies LLC (HQ) | Provider of biosampling devices for non-invasive sample collection with the main objective of simplifying genomics and proteomics workflows. | 510-256-5186 | NA | Hayward |
| Micro Lithography Inc (HQ) | Manufacturer of pellicles using high end equipment for the production of frames and engineering parts, automatic anodizing lines, and chemical labs. | 408-747-1769 | NA | Sunnyvale |
| Molecular Matrix Inc (HQ) | Provider of research tools for cultivating and studying stem cells. The company products provide solutions for growing cells. | 916-376-9404 | 1-10 | West Sacramento |
| Neodyne Biosciences Inc (HQ) | Manufacturer of embrace devices and it helps in the concealment of scars. The company serves patients. | 800-519-7127 | NA | Newark |
| Neurona Therapeutics (HQ) | Developer of neuronal stem cells to transplant into the brain. The company offers services to the healthcare industry. | 650-799-6465 | NA | S San Francisco |
| Nugen Technologies Inc (HQ) | Provider of solutions for genomic analysis. The company focuses on DNA analysis and RNA analysis applications. | 650-590-3600 | NA | San Carlos |
| OrthoCyte Corp (HQ) | Developer of biotechnology products. The company specializes in cell-based therapies for bone and orthopedic soft tissue diseases and injuries. | 510-775-0451 | NA | Alameda |
| Patz Materials & Technologies (HQ) | Manufacturer of composite materials. The company portfolio includes unidirectional tapes, fabric prepregs, composite armor systems, and cellular developments. | 707-748-7577 | NA | Benicia |
| Primity Bio Inc (HQ) | Provider of assay platforms for biological relevance. The company specializes in cell biology, flow cytometry, and molecular biology. | 510-210-0605 | NA | Fremont |
| Progenitor Cell Therapy (BR) | Manufacturer of biotechnology products. The company develops cell therapy products on a contract basis. | 650-964-6744 | NA | Mountain View |
| Sanbio Inc (HQ) | Developer of regenerative therapies for neurological disorders. The company offers services to the healthcare sector.. | 650-625-8965 | NA | Mountain View |
| Single Cell Technology Inc (HQ) | Developer of cell technology solutions and also proportionary therapeutic antibody process for its clients. | 408-642-9740 | NA | San Jose |
| Symic Bio Inc (BR) | Developer of proprietary bioconjugates. The company offers therapeutics focused on extracellular matrix biology. | 415-805-9005 | NA | Emeryville |
| ThermoGenesis Holdings Inc (HQ) | Manufacturer of therapeutic products and related supplies. The company is involved in cellular bioprocessing and bone marrow transplants. | 916-858-5100 | 11-50 | Rancho Cordova |
| Trellis Bioscience LLC (HQ) | Developer of human antibody therapeutics as treatment for infectious disease and oncology indications. | 650-838-1400 | NA | Redwood City |
| Trianni Inc (HQ) | Developer of humanized monoclonal antibody platform. The company offers services to pharmaceutical and biotechnology companies. | 866-374-9314 | NA | San Francisco |
| Virovek (HQ) | Provider of adeno-associated virus production and purification services. The company involves in consulting and gene cloning services. | 510-887-7121 | NA | Hayward |
| Xcell Biosciences Inc (HQ) | Provider of protocols and reagent kits for primary cell culture applications. The company specializes in cell-based assays. | 415-937-0321 | NA | San Francisco |
| Zeltiq Aesthetics Inc (HQ) | Focuses on non-surgical fat reduction treatment and it is involved in weight loss. The company serves obese people. | 925-474-2500 | NA | Pleasanton |

## 37 = Consulting/Contracting Services

| COMPANY NAME | PRODUCT / SERVICE | PHONE | EMP | CITY |
|---|---|---|---|---|
| Dawn Reis Ecological Studies (HQ) | Provider of wildlife research and biological consulting services. The company is specialized in aquatic systems and endangered species population. | 831-588-7550 | 1-10 | Watsonville |
| Denise Duffy & Associates Inc (HQ) | Provider of environmental sciences, planning, and biological consulting services. The company is also focused on land use and contract planning. | 831-373-4341 | NA | Monterey |
| Inscopix Inc (HQ) | Provider of instrumentation and data analytics for next generation neuroscience. The company provides brain imaging solutions and data analysis suites. | 650-600-3886 | NA | Palo Alto |
| ProTrials Research Inc (HQ) | Provider of clinical research services. The company offers the ability to move a new drug or device from conception to FDA approval. | 650-864-9180 | NA | San Jose |

| COMPANY NAME | PRODUCT / SERVICE | PHONE | EMP | CITY |
|---|---|---|---|---|
| Ryss Lab Inc (HQ) | Provider of biotechnology and pharmaceutical development services. The company offers services to the healthcare sector. | 510-477-9570 | NA | Union City |

## 38 = Genetic Engineering/Research

| COMPANY NAME | PRODUCT / SERVICE | PHONE | EMP | CITY |
|---|---|---|---|---|
| 4d Molecular Therapeutics Llc (HQ) | Provider of gene therapy product research & development for the treatment of genetic diseases such as diabetes, arthritis, and heart failure. | 510-505-2680 | NA | Emeryville |
| Bell Biosystems Inc (HQ) | Provider of biotechnology services. The company develops proteins targeted to kill specific bacteria but cause minimal collateral damage. | 877-420-3621 | NA | Berkeley |
| BioClin Therapeutics Inc (HQ) | Developer of biologic products for the treatment of metastatic bladder cancer (urothelial cell carcinoma) and achondroplasia (dwarfism). | 925-413-6140 | NA | San Leandro |
| Bioneer Inc (BR) | Developer of molecular biology products and technologies for life science researchers in academia, biotech, and pharmaceutical companies. | 877-264-4300 | NA | Oakland |
| Cellecta Inc (HQ) | Provider of custom and contract solutions for high-throughput genetic screening needs and also develops therapeutic targets and drugs. | 650-938-3910 | NA | Mountain View |
| Centrillion Technology Holdings Ltd (HQ) | Developer of genomics solutions for the researchers, physicians, and consumers. The company also offers clinical testing and consumer genomics services. | 650-618-0111 | NA | Palo Alto |
| Crypto Forensics Technologies Inc (HQ) | Provider of cybersecurity solutions to businesses, organizations, and the government. The company focuses on cyberforensics and compliance services. | 510-483-1955 | NA | San Leandro |
| Genapsys Inc (HQ) | Developer of DNA sequencing to enable a paradigm shift in genomic diagnostics. The company specializes in GENIUS system that has footprint of Apple iPad. | 650-330-1096 | NA | Redwood City |
| Karius Inc (HQ) | Provider of microbial genomics diagnostics. The company focusses on transforming infectious disease diagnostics with genomics. | 866-452-7487 | NA | Redwood City |
| Natera Inc (HQ) | Provider of prenatal testing services. The company specializes in non-invasive prenatal testing, genetic carrier screening and paternity testing. | 650-249-9090 | 501-1000 | San Carlos |
| Transgenomic Inc (BR) | Provider of patient testing and biomarker identification services. The company specializes in high performance products. | 408-432-3230 | NA | San Jose |

## 39 = Diagnostic

| COMPANY NAME | PRODUCT / SERVICE | PHONE | EMP | CITY |
|---|---|---|---|---|
| 4d Molecular Therapeutics Llc (HQ) | Provider of gene therapy product research & development for the treatment of genetic diseases such as diabetes, arthritis, and heart failure. | 510-505-2680 | NA | Emeryville |
| Advanced Cell Diagnostics Inc (HQ) | Developer of biotechnological diagnostic tests. The company specializes in the identification and validation of RNA biomarkers for cancer diagnosis. | 510-576-8800 | NA | Newark |
| Aelan Cell Technologies Inc (HQ) | Provider of research, discovery, development, and commercialization of biomedical technologies for the advancement of human health. | 415-488-6041 | NA | San Francisco |
| Appsec Consulting (HQ) | Provider of services to identify vulnerabilities in applications. The company focuses on penetration testing and PCI compliance. | 408-224-1110 | NA | San Jose |
| Bell Biosystems Inc (HQ) | Provider of biotechnology services. The company develops proteins targeted to kill specific bacteria but cause minimal collateral damage. | 877-420-3621 | NA | Berkeley |
| Biochain Institute Inc (HQ) | Provider of bio-sample preparation, analysis, and application assays accelerating the development of personalized diagnostics, therapeutics, and medicine. | 510-783-8588 | NA | Newark |
| Bioneer Inc (BR) | Developer of molecular biology products and technologies for life science researchers in academia, biotech, and pharmaceutical companies. | 877-264-4300 | NA | Oakland |
| Centrillion Technology Holdings Ltd (HQ) | Developer of genomics solutions for the researchers, physicians, and consumers. The company also offers clinical testing and consumer genomics services. | 650-618-0111 | NA | Palo Alto |
| Genapsys Inc (HQ) | Developer of DNA sequencing to enable a paradigm shift in genomic diagnostics. The company specializes in GENIUS system that has footprint of Apple iPad. | 650-330-1096 | NA | Redwood City |
| Genemed Biotechnologies Inc (HQ) | Manufacturer of diagnostic reagents. The company caters to the pharmaceutical and diagnostic sectors. | 650-952-0110 | NA | S San Francisco |
| Immuno Concepts Na Ltd (HQ) | Manufacturer and distributor of diagnostic assays. The company's products are used for systemic rheumatic diseases. | 916-363-2649 | 1-10 | Sacramento |
| Incotec Inc (RH) | Provider of solutions in the business areas such as vegetables, field crops, ornamentals, and analytical services. | 831-757-4367 | NA | Salinas |
| Karius Inc (HQ) | Provider of microbial genomics diagnostics. The company focusses on transforming infectious disease diagnostics with genomics. | 866-452-7487 | NA | Redwood City |
| MTI California Inc (HQ) | Specializes in designing and validating manufacturing controls. The company offers services to biotech companies. | 925-937-1500 | NA | Walnut Creek |
| Natera Inc (HQ) | Provider of prenatal testing services. The company specializes in non-invasive prenatal testing, genetic carrier screening and paternity testing. | 650-249-9090 | 501-1000 | San Carlos |
| Newcomb Anderson Mccormick (HQ) | Provider of energy engineering and consulting services. The company also offers energy program development and distributed generation solutions. | 415-896-0300 | NA | San Francisco |
| Personalis Inc (HQ) | Manufacturer of genome-guided medicine for the treatment of cancer. The company deals with research services. | 650-752-1300 | NA | Menlo Park |

| COMPANY NAME | PRODUCT / SERVICE | PHONE | EMP | CITY |
|---|---|---|---|---|
| Transgenomic Inc (BR) | Provider of patient testing and biomarker identification services. The company specializes in high performance products. | 408-432-3230 | NA | San Jose |
| Trianni Inc (HQ) | Developer of humanized monoclonal antibody platform. The company offers services to pharmaceutical and biotechnology companies. | 866-374-9314 | NA | San Francisco |
| Twist Bioscience (HQ) | Specializes in DNA synthesis programs. The company is engaged in genome editing and drug discovery services. | 800-719-0671 | NA | San Francisco |

## 40 = Software & IT Services

| COMPANY NAME | PRODUCT / SERVICE | PHONE | EMP | CITY |
|---|---|---|---|---|
| Aplena Inc (HQ) | Provider of technology solutions for data center services. The company offers relocation, installation, and managed services. | 408-256-0030 | NA | Sacramento |
| AppEnsure Inc (HQ) | Provider of cloud application performance and infrastructure management such as application-aware infrastructure performance management solution. | 408-418-4602 | NA | San Jose |
| Ayla Networks Inc (HQ) | Provider of Ayla's IoT cloud platform that brings connected products to market quickly and securely for manufacturers and service providers. | 408-830-9844 | NA | Santa Clara |
| Benchling Inc (HQ) | Developer of integrated software solution for experiment design, note-taking, and molecular biology for industry and academia. | 415-980-9932 | NA | San Francisco |
| Bioscience Advisors (HQ) | Provider of consulting services. The company serves the pharmaceutical and biotechnology industries concerning commercialization agreements. | 925-954-1397 | NA | Walnut Creek |
| Bitscopic (HQ) | Provider of consulting and computer-related services. The company serves businesses and industrial customers. | 650-503-3120 | NA | Menlo Park |
| Ceras Health Inc (BR) | Focuses on mobile application development. The company serves patients, hospitals, and related healthcare organizations. | 415-477-9908 | NA | San Francisco |
| Citilabs Inc (HQ) | Provider of software development services. The company designs and develops products for transportation planning. | 888-770-2823 | 11-50 | Sacramento |
| Coffer Groupllc (HQ) | Provider of information technology solutions. The company specializes in private equity, venture capital, and hedge funds. | 415-963-4382 | NA | San Francisco |
| Complete Genomics Inc (HQ) | Developer of human genome sequencing technology, research and development, clinical and consumer applications. | 408-648-2560 | NA | San Jose |
| Dnanexus Inc (HQ) | Provider of genome informatics and data management platform. The company provides a global network to share and manage genomic data. | 415-857-0158 | NA | Mountain View |
| Drchrono Inc (HQ) | Provider of electronic health record and practice management solution which includes scheduling and clinical documentation. | 844-569-8628 | NA | Mountain View |
| Eon Technologies Inc (HQ) | Provider of IT and computer support services. The company's services include malware and virus removal tools and printer repair services. | 510-523-3832 | NA | Alameda |
| Finesse Solutions Llc (HQ) | Manufacturer of bioreactor controllers and related supplies. The company offers technical support services. | 408-570-9000 | NA | Santa Clara |
| First Databank Inc (HQ) | Provider of healthcare solutions to hospitals, retail pharmacies, payers, drug manufacturers, and healthcare providers. | 650-588-5454 | NA | S San Francisco |
| Fluidigm Sciences Inc (HQ) | Developer and creator of technologies for life science tools designed to revolutionize biology. The company is involved in research programs. | 650-871-7152 | NA | San Francisco |
| H5 (HQ) | Provider of investigation solutions. The company offers hosting, case preparation, and keyword consulting services. | 415-625-6700 | NA | San Francisco |
| Infors USA Inc (BR) | Manufacturer of bioreactors. The company offers shakers, incubator shakers, and bioreactors. | 925-828-9800 | 1-10 | Dublin |
| InsightRX Inc (HQ) | Developer of cloud-based platform for precision medicine and clinical analytics. The company serves individuals and healthcare organizations. | 205-351-0574 | NA | San Francisco |
| Molecular Devices Llc (HQ) | Manufacturer of bioanalytical measurement systems. The company is engaged in life science research, pharma, and bio therapeutic development. | 800-635-5577 | NA | San Jose |
| MTI California Inc (HQ) | Specializes in designing and validating manufacturing controls. The company offers services to biotech companies. | 925-937-1500 | NA | Walnut Creek |
| NuMedii Inc (HQ) | Provider of big data technology such as integrative genomics and chemoinformatics to discover and de-risk new indications for safe, existing drug. | 650-918-6363 | NA | San Mateo |
| Pacific Biosciences Of California Inc (HQ) | Provider of targeted sequencing, base modifications, microbiology, and isoform sequencing detection services. | 650-521-8000 | NA | Menlo Park |
| Penguin Computing Inc (HQ) | Provider of Linux-based cloud and HPC solutions. The company's products include servers, network switches, and integrated rack solutions. | 415-954-2800 | NA | Fremont |
| Premier Biosoft International (HQ) | Specializes in software development, design, testing and maintenance services. The company serves life science companies and laboratories. | 650-856-2703 | NA | Palo Alto |
| Sentieon Inc (HQ) | Supplier and developer of bioinformatics secondary analysis tools. The company offers precision data for precision medicine. | 650-282-5650 | NA | Mountain View |
| Simco Electronics (HQ) | Providers of services and software to medical device manufacturers. The company specializes in biotechnology. | 408-734-9750 | NA | Santa Clara |
| Simplificare Inc (HQ) | Provider of software solutions for patient financial care (PFC). The company odders services to patients and clinics. | 800-464-5125 | NA | Palo Alto |

## 41 = Lab Services (inc testing)

| COMPANY NAME | PRODUCT / SERVICE | PHONE | EMP | CITY |
|---|---|---|---|---|
| AEMTEK Laboratories (HQ) | Provider of testing, research, training and consulting services and sampling products for the food, environmental and pharmaceutical industries. | 510-979-1979 | NA | Fremont |

| | COMPANY NAME | PRODUCT / SERVICE | PHONE | EMP | CITY |
|---|---|---|---|---|---|
| | Ags Inc (HQ) | Provider of civil, structural, and geotechnical engineering services. The company serves the water and transportation infrastructure markets. | 415-777-2166 | NA | San Francisco |
| | Al & L Crop Solutions (HQ) | Provider of solutions for crops. The company specializes in disease testing services for grapevine diseases and soil pathogens. | 707-693-3050 | NA | Vacaville |
| | Allakos Inc (HQ) | Developer of therapeutic antibodies for the treatment of inflammatory and proliferative diseases such as asthma, nasal polyposis, and fibrosis. | 650-597-5002 | NA | Redwood City |
| | Alstem Inc (HQ) | Provider of virus concentration and transduction solutions. The company's offerings include assay kits, antibodies etc. | 510-708-0096 | NA | Richmond |
| | Antagene Inc (HQ) | Provider of custom antibody and peptide synthesis. The company is engaged in animal and histology services. | 408-588-1998 | NA | Santa Clara |
| | Antibody Solutions (HQ) | Provider of antibody products and services. The company serves biotechnology, diagnostic and pharmaceutical companies. | 650-938-4300 | NA | Sunnyvale |
| | Bio Rad Laboratories Inc (BR) | Provider of life science research and clinical diagnostics products and services for pharmaceutical manufacturers and biotechnology researchers. | 510-741-1000 | NA | Hercules |
| | Biocare Medical Llc (HQ) | Developer of automated immunohistochemistry instrumentation, reagents for IHC lab testing. The company also offer tissue diagnostic products for cancer. | 925-603-8000 | NA | Pacheco |
| | Biokey Inc (HQ) | Provider of API characterization, pre-formulation studies, formulation development, and analytical method development services. | 510-668-0881 | NA | Fremont |
| | Bioluminate Inc (HQ) | Developer of probes that provide breast cancer detection data to physicians. The company serves the medical sector. | 650-743-0240 | NA | San Carlos |
| | California Seed & Plant Lab (HQ) | Provider of pathological and genetic testing services. The company provides services for the vegetable seed, grapevine, and strawberry industries. | 916-655-1581 | 1-10 | Pleasant Grove |
| | Caredx Inc (HQ) | Provider of genomics technologies for the development of molecular diagnostic assays. The company specializes in molecular diagnostics. | 415-287-2300 | NA | Brisbane |
| N | Cascadia Labs (HQ) | Provider of analytical services. The company specializes in analytical, pharmaceutical, horticulture, and food science. | 855-800-6890 | 1-10 | Redwood Valley |
| | Cellmax Life (HQ) | Provider of personalized multi-biomarker technologies for non-invasive saliva and blood tests. The company is also involved in drug discovery. | 650-564-3905 | NA | Sunnyvale |
| | Comp Pro Med Inc (HQ) | Provider of laboratory information systems for clinical laboratories. The company offers services to the healthcare sector. | 707-578-0239 | NA | Santa Rosa |
| | Control Laboratories Inc (HQ) | Provider of agricultural analytical services such as compost, water, soil, plant, remediation and bio-fuel testing. | 831-724-5422 | 1-10 | Watsonville |
| | Cytoculture International Inc (HQ) | Provider of technical consulting and microbiological laboratory services. The company specializes in biofuel project. | 510-233-0102 | NA | Point Richmond |
| | Dnamito Inc (HQ) | Provider of DNA technology and cloud platform to enable cancer treatment and early prediction of chronic disease thus vastly improving patient care. | 650-687-0899 | NA | Palo Alto |
| | E-Scape Bio (HQ) | Provider of therapeutic solutions. The company focusses on discovery and development of small molecule drugs for the treatment of neurodegenerative diseases. | 650-431-0100 | NA | S San Francisco |
| N | Exagen Inc (HQ) | Developer of laboratory technology solutions. The company offers services to hospitals, clinics, and the healthcare sector. | 888-452-1522 | 11-50 | Vista |
| | Histo path (HQ) | Provider of histotechnology services. The company specializes in providing tissue culture slides for dermatologists. | 209-522-8240 | 1-10 | Modesto |
| | Hitachi Chemical Diagnostics Inc (HQ) | Provider of in vitro allergy diagnostics products. The company offers alternative means of diagnosing allergy. | 650-961-5501 | NA | Mountain View |
| | iGenix Inc (HQ) | Provider of immunology laboratory services. The company offers service to private practice physicians, hospitals, and clinical reference laboratories. | 650-424-1191 | NA | Milpitas |
| | Immuno Concepts Na Ltd (HQ) | Manufacturer and distributor of diagnostic assays. The company's products are used for systemic rheumatic diseases. | 916-363-2649 | 1-10 | Sacramento |
| | Liberty Labs Inc (HQ) | Provider of testing services for the semiconductor industry. The company is engaged in custom programming and quality assurance services. | 408-262-6633 | NA | Milpitas |
| | Merieux Nutrisciences Corp (BR) | Provider of public health services. The company is focused on food and pharmaceutical products, cosmetics, and consumer goods. | 209-549-7508 | 11-50 | Salida |
| | Microsonic Systems Inc (HQ) | Provider of ultrasonic fluid processing device built with MEMS technology to biotech and pharmaceutical industries. | 408-844-4980 | NA | San Jose |
| | Modulus Data Systems (HQ) | Provider digital clinical cell (tally) counters. The company's products include Diffcount III, Comp-U-Diff, and Uro-Comp. | 650-365-3111 | NA | Redwood City |
| | Monterey Bay Analytical Services (HQ) | Provider of laboratory testing services. The company services include sample collection, bacteria testing, and inorganic chemistry. | 831-375-6227 | NA | Monterey |
| | Nanolab Technologies Inc (HQ) | Provider of cutting edge technology and expertise for failure analysis, advanced microscopy and FIB circuit edit services. | 408-433-3320 | NA | Milpitas |
| | Pacific Biolabs (HQ) | Provider of biological testing services. The company offers service to the pharmaceutical, biotechnology, and medical device industries. | 510-964-9000 | NA | Hercules |
| | Personalis Inc (HQ) | Manufacturer of genome-guided medicine for the treatment of cancer. The company deals with research services. | 650-752-1300 | NA | Menlo Park |

| COMPANY NAME | PRODUCT / SERVICE | PHONE | EMP | CITY |
|---|---|---|---|---|
| Plant Sciences Inc (HQ) | Provider of agricultural research services. The company develops new technology to yield good plant production. | 831-728-7771 | 11-50 | Watsonville |
| Pulver Labs Inc (HQ) | Provider of equipment evaluation and testing services. The company also offers services for information technology, industrial and medical equipment. | 408-399-7000 | NA | Los Gatos |
| Purigen Biosystems Inc (HQ) | Provider of biotechnology such as isotachophoresis, an electric-field driven technique for extracting and quantifying DNA and RNA from biological samples. | 925-264-1364 | NA | Pleasanton |
| Pyxis Laboratories Inc (HQ) | Specializes in the research, development and production of specialty reagents for the diagnostics, pharmaceutical, and environmental industries. | 949-598-1978 | 1-10 | Grass Valley |
| Qspec Technology Inc (HQ) | Provider of surface analysis and materials characterization services. The company's applications include device processing for microelectronics. | 408-541-1398 | NA | Sunnyvale |
| Sequoia Analytical Labs (HQ) | Provider of laboratory testing services. The company specializes in testing of agro products for components and microbe content. | 916-920-4009 | 1-10 | Sacramento |
| Simco Electronics (HQ) | Providers of services and software to medical device manufacturers. The company specializes in biotechnology. | 408-734-9750 | NA | Santa Clara |
| Transcriptic Inc (HQ) | Specializes in scientific research and the company also supports an array of vitro molecular biology and cell biology. | 650-763-8432 | NA | Menlo Park |
| Transgenomic Inc (BR) | Provider of patient testing and biomarker identification services. The company specializes in high performance products. | 408-432-3230 | NA | San Jose |
| West Coast (HQ) | Provider of contract testing laboratory services. The company offers testing laboratories, manufacturing services, and validation and calibration services. | 925-270-3800 | NA | Concord |

## 42 = Protein Systems

| COMPANY NAME | PRODUCT / SERVICE | PHONE | EMP | CITY |
|---|---|---|---|---|
| Actagro Llc (HQ) | Manufacturer of agricultural products for crops such as alfalfa, almonds, blueberries, corn, tomatoes, onions, rice, strawberries, and wine grapes. | 559-369-2222 | 11-50 | Biola |
| Alstem Inc (HQ) | Provider of virus concentration and transduction solutions. The company's offerings include assay kits, antibodies etc. | 510-708-0096 | NA | Richmond |
| Applied Stemcell Inc (HQ) | Provider of stem cell characterization, gene targeting, teratoma formation, and embryoid body (EB) formation services. | 408-773-8007 | NA | Milpitas |
| BASF Venture Capital America Inc (RH) | Manufacturer of basic chemicals and intermediates such as solvents, plasticizers, and monomers. The company serves the agriculture market. | 510-445-6140 | NA | Fremont |
| Bell Biosystems Inc (HQ) | Provider of biotechnology services. The company develops proteins targeted to kill specific bacteria but cause minimal collateral damage. | 877-420-3621 | NA | Berkeley |
| Biochain Institute Inc (HQ) | Provider of bio-sample preparation, analysis, and application assays accelerating the development of personalized diagnostics, therapeutics, and medicine. | 510-783-8588 | NA | Newark |
| BioClin Therapeutics Inc (HQ) | Developer of biologic products for the treatment of metastatic bladder cancer (urothelial cell carcinoma) and achondroplasia (dwarfism). | 925-413-6140 | NA | San Leandro |
| Biodesy Inc (HQ) | Developer of proteins and biological molecules for the treatment of cancer, cardiovascular, Alzheimer's, and Parkinson's diseases. | 650-871-8716 | NA | S San Francisco |
| Confometrx (HQ) | Developer of a platform of drug development tools. The company specializes in drug discovery technologies. | 408-496-6276 | NA | Santa Clara |
| Cpc Scientific Inc (HQ) | Provider of amino acids, cGMP, generic, catalog, modified, FRET & TR- FRET, and custom peptides to researchers and pharmaceutical companies. | 408-734-3800 | NA | San Jose |
| Evolve Biosystems (HQ) | Focuses on the development and marketing of probiotic-based biotherapeutics. The company serves the pharmaceutical industry. | 530-747-2012 | 1-10 | Davis |
| Five Prime Therapeutics Inc (HQ) | Developer and discovery of therapeutics products for the enhancement of lives of patients with serious diseases. | 415-365-5600 | NA | S San Francisco |
| GangaGen Inc (HQ) | Provider of proprietary recombinant protein for the topical prevention and treatment of Staplylococcal infections. | 650-856-9642 | NA | Palo Alto |
| Global Marketing Associates Inc (HQ) | Providers of nutrition supplements to health care industry. The company supply innovative and quality ingredients to health care industry. | 510-887-2462 | NA | Livermore |
| Pivot Bio Inc (HQ) | Provider of genome-scale programming of microbes. The company offers services to farmers and the agricultural sector. | 877-451-1977 | NA | Berkeley |
| System Biosciences Inc (HQ) | Provider of genome-wide analysis of the mechanisms that regulate cellular processes and biological responses. | 650-968-2200 | NA | Mountain View |
| Versartis Inc (HQ) | Manufacturer and developer of therapeutic proteins for the treatment of endocrine disorders. The company develops recombinant human growth hormone. | 650-963-8580 | NA | Menlo Park |

## 43 = Plant Biotechnology

| COMPANY NAME | PRODUCT / SERVICE | PHONE | EMP | CITY |
|---|---|---|---|---|
| Agri-Analysis Llc (BR) | Provider of agricultural diagnostic laboratory services. The company specializes in grapevine virus testing services. | 800-506-9852 | 11-50 | Davis |
| Al & L Crop Solutions (HQ) | Provider of solutions for crops. The company specializes in disease testing services for grapevine diseases and soil pathogens. | 707-693-3050 | NA | Vacaville |
| California Seed & Plant Lab (HQ) | Provider of pathological and genetic testing services. The company provides services for the vegetable seed, grapevine, and strawberry industries. | 916-655-1581 | 1-10 | Pleasant Grove |

| COMPANY NAME | PRODUCT / SERVICE | PHONE | EMP | CITY |
|---|---|---|---|---|
| General Hydroponics Inc (HQ) | Providers of Hydroponics. The company offer solution for commercial producers especially in non arable areas. | 707-824-9376 | NA | Santa Rosa |
| Global Food Technologies (HQ) | Focuses on the proprietary design, development, and production of commercial products and services to enhance food safety. | 559-589-0100 | 1-10 | Hanford |
| Heliospectra (RH) | Focuses on lighting technology solutions. The company is engaged in product development and serves the environmental sector. | 888-942-4769 | NA | San Rafael |
| Incotec Inc (RH) | Provider of solutions in the business areas such as vegetables, field crops, ornamentals, and analytical services. | 831-757-4367 | NA | Salinas |
| Milagen Inc (HQ) | Develops and manufactures healthcare products. The company offers immunohistochemistry and cytology products. | 510-597-1244 | NA | Emeryville |
| Miltenyi Biotec Inc (DH) | Developer, manufacturer, and seller of products serving the fields of cell biology, immunology, regenerative medicine, and molecular biology. | 530-888-8871 | 11-50 | Auburn |
| Nature's Cure (HQ) | Provider of health and beauty solutions. The company offers over-the-counter products featuring natural ingredients. | 877-469-9487 | NA | Oakland |
| Pivot Bio Inc (HQ) | Provider of genome-scale programming of microbes. The company offers services to farmers and the agricultural sector. | 877-451-1977 | NA | Berkeley |
| Planet Biotechnology Inc (HQ) | Provider of biotechnology services. The company develops antibody-based therapeutic and preventative products through plants to meet medical needs. | 510-887-1461 | NA | Hayward |
| Plant Sciences Inc (HQ) | Provider of agricultural research services. The company develops new technology to yield good plant production. | 831-728-7771 | 11-50 | Watsonville |
| Synergenics Llc (HQ) | Provider of life science services. The company also provides financial support and shared laboratory services. | 415-554-8170 | NA | San Francisco |

## 44 = Immunological Substances/Research

| COMPANY NAME | PRODUCT / SERVICE | PHONE | EMP | CITY |
|---|---|---|---|---|
| Apexigen (HQ) | Specializes in document management and managed print solutions. The company serves the business sector. | 650-931-6236 | NA | San Carlos |
| Biochain Institute Inc (HQ) | Provider of bio-sample preparation, analysis, and application assays accelerating the development of personalized diagnostics, therapeutics, and medicine. | 510-783-8588 | NA | Newark |
| Biocheck Inc (HQ) | Provider of custom immunoassay development, antibody conjugation and purification, and contract manufacturing services. | 650-573-1968 | NA | S San Francisco |
| Biomertech (HQ) | Provider of tailor-made peptide and anti-body solutions such as pepdyes and polyclonal antibody advantage for the scientific community. | 925-931-0007 | NA | Pleasanton |
| Boster Biological Technology (HQ) | Provider of antibodies and ELISA kits. The company serves customers in the biochemicals and molecular biology areas. | 888-466-3604 | NA | Pleasanton |
| Butterfly Sciences (HQ) | Developer of gene therapies for HIV and aging. The company also provides consulting services for biotech investment evaluations. | 415-518-8153 | 1-10 | Davis |
| Forty Seven Inc (HQ) | Provider of medical solutions to advancement of immuno-oncology through the engagement of new and complementary phagocytic pathways. | 650-352-4150 | NA | Menlo Park |
| Guardant Health Inc (HQ) | Provider of sequencing and rare-cell diagnostics services focusing on cancer. The company serves the healthcare sector. | 855-698-8887 | 201-500 | Redwood City |
| Immune Design Corp (HQ) | Provider of clinical-stage immunotherapy services. The company develops immuno-oncology drug candidates. | 650-887-6717 | NA | S San Francisco |
| JN Biosciences LLC (HQ) | Developer of antibody-based therapeutics and antibody engineered technologies. The company specializes in single homogenous molecular species. | 650-967-9486 | NA | Mountain View |
| Maverick Therapeutics (HQ) | Provider of therapeutic solutions for the treatment of cancer. The company focusses on the research of cytotoxic T cells. | 650-338-1231 | NA | Brisbane |
| Medeor Therapeutics (HQ) | Developer of personalized cellular immunotherapy for the organ transplant recipients. The company specializes in cellular immunotherapy, hematology, and transplantation product development. | 650-627-4531 | NA | S San Francisco |
| Prothena (RH) | Focuses on the discovery, development and commercialization of protein immunotherapy programs for the treatment of diseases that involve amyloid. | 650-837-8550 | NA | S San Francisco |
| Rigel Pharmaceuticals Inc (HQ) | Developer novel, small-molecule drugs for the treatment of inflammatory and autoimmune diseases, immuno-oncology related diseases, and muscle disorders. | 650-624-1100 | NA | S San Francisco |
| Sangamo Therapeutics (HQ) | Developer of engineered DNA-binding proteins for the regulation of gene expression and for gene modification. | 510-970-6000 | 201-500 | Richmond |

## 45 = Business Management Services

| | COMPANY NAME | PRODUCT / SERVICE | PHONE | EMP | CITY |
|---|---|---|---|---|---|
| N | 3Q Digital Inc (HQ) | Performance and digital marketing agency that provides digital media services. | 650-539-4124 | NA | San Francisco |
| | Accenture (BR) | Provider of management consulting and technology services. The company also offers application outsourcing and IT consulting services. | 415-537-5000 | NA | San Francisco |
| | Antedo Inc (HQ) | Provider of consulting services. The company offers international engineering and management consulting services. | 408-253-1870 | NA | Cupertino |
| | Aragon Consulting Group Inc (HQ) | Provider of software development services. The company also offers authoring, coding, consulting, and technical support solutions. | 415-869-8818 | NA | Cupertino |

| COMPANY NAME | PRODUCT / SERVICE | PHONE | EMP | CITY |
|---|---|---|---|---|
| Aravo Solutions Inc (HQ) | Provider of risk and performance management, Supplier Information Management (SIM), and related services. | 415-835-7600 | NA | San Francisco |
| Blackhawk Network Inc (HQ) | Provider of employee engagement and customer engagement services such as gift cards, reloadable prepaid debit cards, and cash-based payment products. | 925-226-9990 | NA | Pleasanton |
| Cinnabar Bridge Communications (HQ) | Provider of writing, book publishing, book design, consulting, and project and process management services. | 415-975-0950 | NA | San Francisco |
| Common Interest Management Services (BR) | Provider of homeowner association management solutions such as escrow and disclosure, maintenance, online and community services. | 650-286-0292 | NA | San Mateo |
| CommWorld of San Francisco (HQ) | Provider of telecommunication services such as computer networking, structured cabling, project management and repair. | 650-358-8700 | NA | Fremont |
| Emotive Brand (HQ) | Brand strategy and design firm that helps to transform the businesses. | 510-496-8888 | NA | Oakland |
| Epsilon Strategic Systems (HQ) | Provider of management consulting and information technology services. The company offers customization, advisory, and staff development services. | 650-579-5515 | NA | San Mateo |
| Hub Strategy and Communication (BR) | Provider of web design and digital advertising. | 415-561-4345 | NA | San Francisco |
| iCatalysts (HQ) | A management consulting firm offers expert analysis on technology, industries, and markets and promotes training and software solutions. | | NA | San Anselmo |
| Lendingclub Corp (HQ) | Provider of financial solutions. The company offers home improvement, business, pool, and consolidated debt loans. | 415-632-5600 | 1001-5000 | San Francisco |
| Primepay Llc (BR) | Provider of payroll processing services, HR solutions, and insurance and benefit management services. | 650-358-4555 | NA | Newark |
| Ray Morgan Co (BR) | Provider of document technology solutions. The company offers paperless, project management, and imaging system solutions. | 530-343-6065 | 11-50 | Chico |
| Rightpoint (BR) | A digital consultancy firm that designs and engineers end-to-end digital experiences to help clients succeed at the speed of innovation. | 415-935-3390 | NA | Oakland |

## 47 = Adhesives/Coatings/Sealants

| COMPANY NAME | PRODUCT / SERVICE | PHONE | EMP | CITY |
|---|---|---|---|---|
| Acree Technologies Inc (HQ) | Provider of PVD thin film coating services for medical, defense, and other sectors. The company also specializes in R&D and sell coating systems. | 925-798-5770 | NA | Concord |
| Adhesive Products Inc (HQ) | Manufacturer of glues, adhesives, tapes, labels, and coatings. The company is engaged in sales and delivery services. | 510-526-7616 | NA | Albany |
| Advenira Enterprises Inc (HQ) | Provider of equipment and provision of services for multi functional coating deposition using nanocomposite technology solution. | 408-732-3950 | NA | Sunnyvale |
| Anresco Inc (HQ) | Provider of analysis and research to food and food-related industries. The company also offers solutions to support the business and analytical specifications. | 415-822-1100 | NA | San Francisco |
| Applied Chemical Laboratories Inc (HQ) | Developer and manufacturer of electronic chemicals and specialty materials. The company offers services like consultation and chemical purification. | 408-737-8880 | NA | Santa Rosa |
| Berkeley Analytical Associates Llc (HQ) | Provider of specialized chemical & flame retardant analysis and formaldehyde testing services. The company serves the flooring and textile industries. | 510-236-2325 | NA | Richmond |
| Cal-West Specialty Coatings Inc (HQ) | Supplier of liquid masking and surface preparation products. The company also offers temporary protective coatings. | 408-720-7440 | NA | Sunnyvale |
| Cambrios Technologies Corp (HQ) | Manufacturer of electronic materials for the display industry. The company mainly provides ClearOhm films. | 408-738-7400 | NA | Sunnyvale |
| Cemex USA (BR) | Supplier of bulk cement, sand, aggregates, ready mix materials, and architectural products. The company serves the construction industry. | 916-941-2800 | 11-50 | El Dorado Hills |
| Crystallume Pvd (HQ) | Provider of PVD coatings for functional applications. The company also specializes in infinium coatings. | 916-645-3560 | 1-10 | Lincoln |
| Davlin Coatings (HQ) | Manufacturer of coatings for architectural and industrial purposes. The company offers elastomeric waterproof coatings. | 510-848-2863 | NA | Berkeley |
| Dowd & Guild Inc (HQ) | Distributor of chemicals and containers. The company supplies resins, grinding media, oils and maxes, rheological products, and pigments. | 925-820-7222 | NA | San Ramon |
| Dynatex International (HQ) | Manufacturer of semiconductor, dicing equipment, and supplies. The company also offers dicing and wafer bonding services. | 707-542-4227 | NA | Santa Rosa |
| Electro Coatings Of California (BR) | Provider of electroless nickel coating services. The company also offers industrial hard chrome and nickel metal finishing services. | 510-849-4075 | NA | Berkeley |
| Flamort Company Inc (HQ) | Provider of fire retardant coatings. The company's products are used in restaurants, trade shows, amusement parks, and theaters. | 510-357-9494 | NA | San Leandro |
| Form & Fusion Mfg Inc (HQ) | Provider of metal fabrication services. The company mainly focuses on powder coating, metal fabrication, and assembly & packaging. | 916-638-8576 | 1-10 | Rancho Cordova |
| Hb Fuller (BR) | Manufacturer of adhesives and sealants. The company also specializes in paints and other specialty chemical products. | 916-787-6000 | 11-50 | Roseville |
| Hexcel Corporation (BR) | Provider and manufacturer of advanced material solutions. The company manufactures everything from a carbon fiber to finished aircraft structures. | 800-444-3923 | NA | Dublin |

| COMPANY NAME | PRODUCT / SERVICE | PHONE | EMP | CITY |
|---|---|---|---|---|
| Hybrid Coating Technologies Inc (HQ) | Manufacturer of coatings and paint products including hybrid non-iso-cyanate polyurethane. The company serves chemical, food, and marine markets. | 650-491-3449 | NA | Daly City |
| Kelly-Moore Paint Company Inc (HQ) | Developer and manufacturer of interior and exterior paints. The company also offers painting tools and related accessories. | 650-592-8337 | NA | San Carlos |
| Lohmann Precision Die Cutting LLC (DH) | Provider of non-metals precision die cutting services. The company caters to the bio medical sector. | | NA | San Jose |
| Materion Corporation (BR) | Provider of material solutions. The company deals with fabrication, analysis, research and development, and testing services. | 510-623-1500 | NA | Fremont |
| Metacrylics (HQ) | Provider of coatings for commercial properties including material safety data sheets, data sheets, color chart, and test data. | 408-280-7733 | NA | Gilroy |
| Pacific Adhesives Company Inc (HQ) | Provider of adhesive solutions for industrial purposes. The company also offers labeling, packaging, and paper converting services. | 916-383-1509 | 11-50 | Sacramento |
| Plasma Ruggedized Solutions (HQ) | Provider of coating and related specialty engineering services. The company specializes in plasma technologies and offers lab services. | 408-954-8405 | NA | San Jose |
| Premier Finishing Inc (HQ) | Provider of precision services. The company focuses on powder coating, liquid coating, pad printing, and light mechanical assembly. | 209-982-5585 | 1-10 | Stockton |
| Professional Finishing (HQ) | Provider of liquid & powder coatings and finishing to the scientific and aerospace industries. The company focuses on sandblasting and silk screening. | 510-233-7629 | NA | Richmond |
| Reaction Technology Inc (HQ) | Supplier of silicon epitaxy and silicon coatings. The company caters to the semiconductor and industrial sectors. | 408-970-9601 | NA | Santa Clara |
| Reltek Llc (HQ) | Developer of analytical and empirical Accelerated Life Testing technology for military, commercial, and nuclear products. | 707-284-8808 | NA | Santa Rosa |
| Teledyne Risi Inc (HQ) | Manufacturer of exploding bridge wire detonators. The company also manufactures electronic firing systems. | 925-456-9700 | 1-10 | Tracy |
| Uhv Sputtering Inc (HQ) | Manufacturer of semiconductor devices and vacuum equipment. The company is involved in sputtering and bonding services. | 408-779-2826 | NA | Morgan Hill |
| Ultimate Index Inc (HQ) | Manufacturer of E-beam deposition cones. The company specializes in prepared coating materials for the precision thin film coating industry. | 530-878-0573 | 1-10 | Auburn |
| Western Stucco Co (HQ) | Developer and manufacturer of exterior products for the stucco industry. The company offers both cement color coats and resin based finishes. | 916-372-7442 | 1-10 | West Sacramento |
| Zip-Chem Products Inc (HQ) | Provider of airspace maintenance materials. The company also offers metering equipment, spray nozzle, and spray equipment. | 408-782-2335 | NA | Morgan Hill |

## 48 = Agricultural Chemicals

| | | | | |
|---|---|---|---|---|
| EB Stone & Son Inc (HQ) | Supplier of garden fertilizers. The company also offers lawn maintenance, composite maker, soil, and plant aid services. | 707-426-2500 | NA | Suisun |
| Sound Agriculture Company (HQ) | Developer of crop protection and crop enhancement products to mitigate drought and increase agriculture yields and enhance farm revenues. | | NA | Emeryville |
| Valent Usa Corp (HQ) | Provider of agricultural products. The company also deals with pest management solutions and serves the commercial agricultural sector. | 800-682-5368 | NA | Walnut Creek |

## 49 = Explosives

| | | | | |
|---|---|---|---|---|
| Aerojet Rocketdyne (RH) | Provider of propulsion and energetic to its space, missile defense, strategic, tactical missile. and armaments customers. | 916-355-4000 | 11-50 | Sacramento |
| Praxair Technology Inc (BR) | Provider of industrial gases. The company engages in gas supply and management, industrial, and oil and gas services. | 925-866-6800 | NA | San Ramon |
| Real Sensors Inc (HQ) | Manufacturer of chemical detection systems. The company also offers security solutions to government agencies and petrochemical industries. | 510-785-4100 | NA | Hayward |
| Teledyne Risi Inc (HQ) | Manufacturer of exploding bridge wire detonators. The company also manufactures electronic firing systems. | 925-456-9700 | 1-10 | Tracy |

## 50 = Industrial Inorganic Chemicals/Gases

| | | | | |
|---|---|---|---|---|
| Anaspec Inc (HQ) | Provider of integrated proteomics solutions for life science research. The company offers peptides, detection reagents, and combinatorial chemistry. | 510-791-9560 | NA | Fremont |
| Cannon Water Technology Inc (HQ) | Manufacturer of chemical pumps, water treatment chemicals, and water treatment equipment. The company offers services to the industrial sector. | 916-315-2691 | 11-50 | Rocklin |
| Eastar Chemical Corp (HQ) | Manufacturer of chemicals and pharmaceuticals. The company offers Venlafaxine, Usnic acid, Pentaerythritol, and Octanedinitrile. | 800-898-2436 | 1-10 | Sacramento |
| Lightwind Corp (HQ) | Provider of semiconductor manufacturing solutions. The company also deals with chemical analysis, process assessment, and refurbishment services. | 707-981-4301 | NA | Petaluma |
| Sierra Chemical Company (HQ) | Manufacturer of aquarium supplies, degreasers, descalers, glass cleaners, and growing products. The company deals with chemical consulting. | 916-371-5943 | 1-10 | West Sacramento |
| Valent Usa Corp (HQ) | Provider of agricultural products. The company also deals with pest management solutions and serves the commercial agricultural sector. | 800-682-5368 | NA | Walnut Creek |
| Valimet Inc (HQ) | Manufacturer of spherical atomized metal powders. The company also offers aluminum silicon and aluminum bronze and special alloys. | 209-444-1600 | 1-10 | Stockton |

| COMPANY NAME | PRODUCT / SERVICE | PHONE | EMP | CITY |
|---|---|---|---|---|
| **51 = Industrial Organic Chemicals/Gases** | | | | |
| A J Edmond Co (BR) | Provider of sampling and analytical services to petroleum refineries. The company's service areas include petroleum coke, coal, and gypsum. | 925-521-1555 | NA | Concord |
| Actagro Llc (HQ) | Manufacturer of agricultural products for crops such as alfalfa, almonds, blueberries, corn, tomatoes, onions, rice, strawberries, and wine grapes. | 559-369-2222 | 11-50 | Biola |
| Enviro Tech Chemicals Inc (HQ) | Manufacturer of peracetic acid. The company focuses on the development of EPA and FDA regulated chemistries and novel solutions. | 209-581-9576 | 1-10 | Modesto |
| Harris Industrial Gases (HQ) | Provider of specialty gases welding equipment. The company also offers services for welding supplies and safety equipment. | 916-725-2168 | 11-50 | Citrus Heights |
| Hill Brothers Chemical Co (BR) | Provider of industrial and construction chemicals. The company also offers decking systems and seaters. | 408-599-5041 | NA | San Jose |
| Monolith Materials Inc (BR) | Manufacturer of carbon black and hydrogen for plastics, toner and printer ink, batteries and conductive inks, and tires and industrial rubber products. | 650-933-4957 | NA | San Carlos |
| Nanosyn (HQ) | Provider of design, synthesis, and analysis of small organic compounds for the pharmaceutical and biotechnology industries. | 408-987-2000 | NA | Santa Clara |
| San Joaquin Chemicals Inc (HQ) | Provider of chemicals and services for condensers, boilers, closed loops, potable water, and waste water. The company serves the healthcare industry. | 559-725-1735 | 1-10 | Fresno |
| Trinapco Inc (HQ) | Manufacturer of organic fine chemicals specializing in 1,8-naphthyridine compounds. The company offers custom synthesis services. | 510-535-1082 | NA | Oakland |
| **52 = Lubricants** | | | | |
| Amyris Inc (HQ) | Provider of renewable products. The company delivers cosmetic emollients and fragrances, fuels and lubricants, and even biopharmaceuticals. | 510-450-0761 | NA | Emeryville |
| Eureka Chemical Co (HQ) | Provider of corrosion control services. The company is involved in creating products that offers corrosion protection and lubrication for all metals. | 650-761-3536 | NA | S San Francisco |
| **53 = Miscellaneous Chemicals** | | | | |
| 3dtl Inc (HQ) | Provider of authentication technology services. The company develops 3D displays for medical, industrial, and military applications. | 408-541-8550 | NA | Sunnyvale |
| A J Edmond Co (BR) | Provider of sampling and analytical services to petroleum refineries. The company's service areas include petroleum coke, coal, and gypsum. | 925-521-1555 | NA | Concord |
| Ab&I Foundry (HQ) | Provider of casting products and accessories. The company's products include pipes and fittings, custom castings, foundry, and recyclable materials. | 510-632-3467 | NA | Oakland |
| Advansta Inc (HQ) | Developer and manufacturer of bioresearch agents. The company focuses on protein staining, purification, and electrophoresis. | 650-325-1980 | NA | Menlo Park |
| AMPAC Fine Chemicals (DH) | Manufacturer of active pharmaceutical ingredients (APIs) and registered intermediates. The company's services include product development and scale-up. | 916-357-6880 | 1-10 | Rancho Cordova |
| Applied Chemical Laboratories Inc (HQ) | Developer and manufacturer of electronic chemicals and specialty materials. The company offers services like consultation and chemical purification. | 408-737-8880 | NA | Santa Rosa |
| Berkeley Analytical Associates Llc (HQ) | Provider of specialized chemical & flame retardant analysis and formaldehyde testing services. The company serves the flooring and textile industries. | 510-236-2325 | NA | Richmond |
| Chemical Safety Technology Inc (HQ) | Supplier of chemical processing machines. The company also offers design, manufacturing, and sheet metal fabrication services. | 408-263-0984 | NA | San Jose |
| Datalab (HQ) | Provider of analysis and certification of process tanks and printed circuit board sections. The company also offers chemical process control software. | 408-943-1888 | NA | San Jose |
| Dowd & Guild Inc (HQ) | Distributor of chemicals and containers. The company supplies resins, grinding media, oils and maxes, rheological products, and pigments. | 925-820-7222 | NA | San Ramon |
| Du Pont EKC Technology Inc (BR) | Provider of science and technology solutions. The company engages in product line such as food, personal care and industrial biotechnology. | 501-784-9105 | NA | Hayward |
| Eezer Products Inc (HQ) | Designer and manufacturer of sanding tools. The company also offers handles and various finishing tools. | 559-255-4140 | 1-10 | Fresno |
| Electro Coatings Of California (BR) | Provider of electroless nickel coating services. The company also offers industrial hard chrome and nickel metal finishing services. | 510-849-4075 | NA | Berkeley |
| Ethylene Control Inc (HQ) | Manufacturer of ethylene and gas removal products. The company's products include filters, filtration systems, and sachets. | 559-896-1909 | 1-10 | Selma |
| Eureka Chemical Co (HQ) | Provider of corrosion control services. The company is involved in creating products that offers corrosion protection and lubrication for all metals. | 650-761-3536 | NA | S San Francisco |
| Gemini Bio-Products (HQ) | Provider of supplements, reagents, and human products. The company is involved in medical research and development. | 800-543-6464 | 11-50 | West Sacramento |
| Hammon Plating Corp (HQ) | Supplier of metal plating applications. The company also provides supply chain management solutions. | 650-494-2691 | NA | Palo Alto |
| Hybrid Coating Technologies Inc (HQ) | Manufacturer of coatings and paint products including hybrid non-isocyanate polyurethane. The company serves chemical, food, and marine markets. | 650-491-3449 | NA | Daly City |

| COMPANY NAME | PRODUCT / SERVICE | PHONE | EMP | CITY |
|---|---|---|---|---|
| Light Polymers Inc (HQ) | Developer of polymers and materials. The company formulates and develops solutions for lyotropic liquid crystals. | 650-678-7733 | NA | S San Francisco |
| Monolith Materials Inc (BR) | Manufacturer of carbon black and hydrogen for plastics, toner and printer ink, batteries and conductive inks, and tires and industrial rubber products. | 650-933-4957 | NA | San Carlos |
| Morgan Technical Ceramics (BR) | Manufacturer of cast and powder metal stainless steels. The company also focuses on other specialty alloys. | 530-823-3401 | 11-50 | Auburn |
| Nor-Cal Perlite Inc (HQ) | Manufacturer of perlite and perlite products. The company is involved in the development of specialty grades for individual customers. | 510-232-7337 | NA | Richmond |
| Pacific Ethanol Inc (HQ) | Producer and marketer of carbonated fuel and corn oil. The company's services include ethanol sales and distribution. | 916-403-2123 | 1-10 | Sacramento |
| Praxair Technology Inc (BR) | Provider of industrial gases. The company engages in gas supply and management, industrial, and oil and gas services. | 925-866-6800 | NA | San Ramon |
| Prism Inks Inc (HQ) | Manufacturer of inkjet printer inks to the proofing, signage, photography, arts and coding sectors. The company's products comprise UV curable and textile inks. | 408-744-6710 | NA | Sunnyvale |
| San Joaquin Chemicals Inc (HQ) | Provider of chemicals and services for condensers, boilers, closed loops, potable water, and waste water. The company serves the healthcare industry. | 559-725-1735 | 1-10 | Fresno |
| Sierra Chemical Company (HQ) | Manufacturer of aquarium supplies, degreasers, descalers, glass cleaners, and growing products. The company deals with chemical consulting. | 916-371-5943 | 1-10 | West Sacramento |
| Skeletal Kinetics LLC (HQ) | Developer, manufacturer and marketer of bone fixation cement designed for the treatment of trauma fractures. | 408-366-5000 | 11-50 | Cupertino |
| Spectra Watermakers Inc (HQ) | Designer of energy recovery systems. The company specializes in manufacturing of reverse osmosis desalination systems for the ocean sailor. | 415-526-2780 | NA | San Rafael |
| Surtec Inc (HQ) | Provider of technology solutions for maintenance chemicals. The company is focused on services for the commercial and industrial cleaning industry. | 209-820-3700 | 1-10 | Tracy |
| Technic Inc (BR) | Manufacturer of specialty chemicals, analytical control tools, and surface finishing products. The company offers electroplating & engineered powders. | 408-287-3732 | NA | San Jose |
| Toray International America Inc (BR) | Provider of chemicals, plastics, textiles, and IT-related products. The company offers environment, engineering, life science, and other services. | 650-341-7152 | NA | San Mateo |
| Werlchem Llc (HQ) | Developer and manufacturer of specialty chemicals. The company's offerings include dyes, pharmaceutical intermediates, and electronic materials. | 510-918-1896 | NA | San Leandro |

## 54 = Petrochemicals

| COMPANY NAME | PRODUCT / SERVICE | PHONE | EMP | CITY |
|---|---|---|---|---|
| A J Edmond Co (BR) | Provider of sampling and analytical services to petroleum refineries. The company's service areas include petroleum coke, coal, and gypsum. | 925-521-1555 | NA | Concord |
| Amyris Inc (HQ) | Provider of renewable products. The company delivers cosmetic emollients and fragrances, fuels and lubricants, and even biopharmaceuticals. | 510-450-0761 | NA | Emeryville |
| Membrane Technology & Research (HQ) | Developer and manufacturer of membrane-based separation systems. The company serves the petrochemical, natural gas, and refining industries. | 650-328-2228 | NA | Newark |
| Real Sensors Inc (HQ) | Manufacturer of chemical detection systems. The company also offers security solutions to government agencies and petrochemical industries. | 510-785-4100 | NA | Hayward |

## 55 = Plastic Materials

| COMPANY NAME | PRODUCT / SERVICE | PHONE | EMP | CITY |
|---|---|---|---|---|
| Amyris Inc (HQ) | Provider of renewable products. The company delivers cosmetic emollients and fragrances, fuels and lubricants, and even biopharmaceuticals. | 510-450-0761 | NA | Emeryville |

## 56 = Specialty Cleaning Preparations

| COMPANY NAME | PRODUCT / SERVICE | PHONE | EMP | CITY |
|---|---|---|---|---|
| Berkeley Analytical Associates Llc (HQ) | Provider of specialized chemical & flame retardant analysis and formaldehyde testing services. The company serves the flooring and textile industries. | 510-236-2325 | NA | Richmond |
| Cleantec (HQ) | Provider of solutions for greenhouse gas emissions, air pollution, water conservation, and waste management. | 916-791-8478 | 1-10 | Granite Bay |
| Nugentec (HQ) | Provider of chemicals and polymers. The company offers oilfield chemicals, cleaners, and lubricants. | 707-820-4080 | NA | Emeryville |
| Synder Filtration (HQ) | Manufacturer of membranes and systems. The company offers training and performance evaluation services. It serves mining, biotech, and food industries. | 707-451-6060 | NA | Vacaville |
| Value Products Inc (HQ) | Provider of chemical compounding and packaging solutions. The company services include silk screen printing and private labeling. | 209-983-4000 | 1-10 | Stockton |

## 57 = Synthetic Resins/Rubbers

| COMPANY NAME | PRODUCT / SERVICE | PHONE | EMP | CITY |
|---|---|---|---|---|
| Holz Rubber Co (HQ) | Provider of custom molded services. The company's offerings include pump parts, slide-lag traction pads, and related supplies. | 209-368-7171 | 1-10 | Lodi |
| Performance Polymer Technologies (HQ) | Manufacturer of elastomeric components for material formulation, extruding, and stamping applications. | 916-677-1414 | 1-10 | Roseville |

| COMPANY NAME | PRODUCT / SERVICE | PHONE | EMP | CITY |
|---|---|---|---|---|
| PermaDri Inc (HQ) | Provider of eco-friendly waterproofing and corrosion protection products. The company serves the marine, landscape, and industrial markets. | 559-275-9620 | 1-10 | Fresno |
| Ryss Lab Inc (HQ) | Provider of biotechnology and pharmaceutical development services. The company offers services to the healthcare sector. | 510-477-9570 | NA | Union City |
| Toray Advanced Composites USA (BR) | Manufacturer of advanced composites like adhesives, prepregs, and liquid resin systems. The company serves military, aerospace, and other sectors. | 408-465-8500 | NA | Morgan Hill |
| Westland Technologies Inc (HQ) | Provider of injection and transfer molding, pressure testing, custom hand fabricating, and acid etching services. | 800-877-7734 | 1-10 | Modesto |

## 58 = Communications Equipment/Services

| COMPANY NAME | PRODUCT / SERVICE | PHONE | EMP | CITY |
|---|---|---|---|---|
| Campbell/Harris Security Equipment Company (HQ) | Manufacturer of busters, fiberscopes, probe kits, and personal radiation detectors. The company also focuses on distribution. | 510-864-8010 | NA | Alameda |

## 59 = Alarms/Security Systems

| COMPANY NAME | PRODUCT / SERVICE | PHONE | EMP | CITY |
|---|---|---|---|---|
| A A Networks (HQ) | Provider of internet, networks and cabling, computer hardware and software, remote and on-site technical support services. | 650-872-1998 | NA | Burlingame |
| Allied Security Alarms (HQ) | Provider of security products such as fire and burglar alarms, video surveillance systems, motion detectors, and access controls. | 650-871-8959 | NA | S San Francisco |
| Appro Technology Inc (BR) | Manufacturer of network surveillance systems. The company's products include dome cameras, LCD monitors, and cables. | 408-720-0018 | NA | Sunnyvale |
| Aviram Networks Inc (HQ) | Provider of wire-speed IPS for recognition & visualization, access control, and other needs. The company offers consulting and training services. | 408-624-1234 | NA | San Jose |
| Campbell/Harris Security Equipment Company (HQ) | Manufacturer of busters, fiberscopes, probe kits, and personal radiation detectors. The company also focuses on distribution. | 510-864-8010 | NA | Alameda |
| Dantel Inc (HQ) | Manufacturer of telecommunications instrumentation equipment. The company offers documentation support and upgrading services. | 559-292-1111 | 1-10 | Fresno |
| Dps Telecom (HQ) | Developer of network alarm monitoring solutions. The company also focuses on publishing the SNMP Tutorial. | 559-454-1600 | 1-10 | Fresno |
| Foster Brothers Security Systems Inc (HQ) | Provider of security systems. The company offers locks and keys, access control systems, and tools and accessories. | 408-736-4500 | NA | Sunnyvale |
| Future Fibre Technologies (US) Inc (HQ) | Provider of fiber optic based intrusion detection systems for perimeter protection and pipeline security. | 877-650-8900 | NA | Mountain View |
| Integrated Communication Systems (HQ) | Provider of communication and integration services. The company offers installation, space planning, project management, and maintenance services. | 408-491-6000 | NA | San Jose |
| iSmart Alarm Inc (HQ) | Manufacturer of home security products. The company offers alarms, cameras, sirens, and related accessories. | 408-245-2551 | NA | Sunnyvale |
| Kimberlite Corp (HQ) | Dealer of security verification systems. The company offers access control, video surveillance, fire detection, and intrusion detection systems. | 559-264-9730 | 11-50 | Fresno |
| LAN-Power Inc (HQ) | Designer, developer, and manufacturer of break through technology for implementing surveillance and security systems. | 510-275-4572 | NA | Fremont |
| Mixed Signal Integration (HQ) | Specializes in the design, manufacture and sale of turn-key analog and mixed-signal standard products and custom ASICs. | 408-434-6305 | NA | San Jose |
| Newland North America Inc (HQ) | Designer and developer of data collector and scanning systems. The company also offers customer information terminals. | 510-490-3888 | NA | Fremont |
| Pac Integrations Inc (HQ) | Provider of security solutions. The company offers its solutions for residential, commercial, and fire and life safety applications. | 800-479-4722 | NA | Concord |
| Protection Plus Security Services Inc (HQ) | Provider of installation services to the electronic security industry. The company's products include access control, video surveillance, and fire alarm systems. | 510-770-9900 | NA | Fremont |
| Raco Manufacturing & Engineering Company Inc (HQ) | Manufacturer of alarms and controllers. The company offers remote monitoring, reporting, datalogging, and control services. | 510-658-6713 | NA | Emeryville |
| Rex Key & Security (HQ) | Designer of security systems for automotive, institutional, commercial, industrial, and residential purposes. | 510-527-7000 | NA | Berkeley |
| Sabah International (HQ) | Provider of fire suppressors for the commercial and industrial sectors. The company also focuses on installation. | 925-463-0431 | NA | Pleasanton |
| Securematics Inc (HQ) | Provider of secure networking, security, storage products and solutions. The company focuses on demand generation and e-commerce. | 888-746-6700 | NA | Santa Clara |
| Senstar Corp (BR) | Provider of perimeter intrusion detection and security solutions. The company's products include buried sensors, barrier sensors, and wall-mounted sensors. | | NA | San Jose |
| Sentry Products Inc (HQ) | Provider of duress alarm systems. The company caters to judicial centers, emergency medical facilities, and schools. | 408-727-1866 | NA | Santa Clara |
| Shotspotter Inc (HQ) | Provider of gunfire detection and location technology services. The company addresses gun violence in communities. | 510-794-3144 | NA | Newark |
| Swintek Enterprises Inc (HQ) | Provider of transceivers, tactical repeaters, and surveillance solutions for the government agencies. | 408-727-4889 | NA | San Jose |

## 60 = Audio/Video/Mulitmedia

| COMPANY NAME | PRODUCT / SERVICE | PHONE | EMP | CITY |
|---|---|---|---|---|
| Access Video Productions (HQ) | Provider of production, editing, and duplication services for small and large companies, and individuals. | 510-528-6044 | NA | Berkeley |
| Aheadtek (HQ) | Supplier of magnetic head solutions. The company specializes in television broadcast, video production, and computer and data storage. | 408-226-9800 | NA | San Jose |
| Aja Video Systems Inc (HQ) | Provider of video systems and routers. The company also offers broadcast and mini converters and recording equipment. | 530-274-2048 | 1-10 | Grass Valley |
| Aldetec Inc (HQ) | Manufacturer of microwave amplifier products. The company provides low noise amplifiers, down converters, and octave band amplifiers. | 916-453-3382 | 1-10 | Sacramento |
| Audible Magic Corp (HQ) | Developer of media identification and synchronization, content registration, and copyright compliance solutions. | 408-399-6405 | NA | Los Gatos |
| Avid Technology Inc (BR) | Manufacturer of computer automated audio mixing consoles. The company offers audio product registration and software activation services. | 800-955-0960 | NA | Santa Clara |
| BBI Engineering Inc (HQ) | Designer and installer of audiovisual, multimedia, teleconferencing and data systems for museums, aquariums, zoos, schools, and universities. | 415-695-9555 | NA | San Francisco |
| Countryman Associates Inc (HQ) | Manufacturer of direct boxes and ultra-miniature microphones. The company's products include ear sets, hanging, and podium microphones. | 650-364-9988 | NA | Menlo Park |
| Day Wireless Systems (BR) | Supplier of RF, wireless, and radio communication equipment. The company's services include rentals, system integration, and marketing. | 707-746-5920 | NA | Benicia |
| Digital Keystone Inc (HQ) | Provider of solutions enabling content distribution to tablets, connected TVs, and other entertainment platforms with suite of software and tools. | 650-938-7300 | NA | Cupertino |
| Dolby Laboratories Inc (BR) | Provider of speech recognition and voice identification products. The company also offers voice control services. | 408-330-3300 | NA | Sunnyvale |
| Earthquake Sound Corp (HQ) | Manufacturer and seller of sound equipment for mobile audio, marine audio, gaming, and home audio sectors. | 510-732-1000 | NA | Hayward |
| Ensemble Designs Inc (HQ) | Manufacturer of audio embedders, video converters, routers, and related products. The company serves post production, education, and other sectors. | 530-478-1830 | 1-10 | Grass Valley |
| Ergo Direct Com (HQ) | Provider of adjustable desks, arms, and mounts. The company offers ergonomic keyboards, monitor arms, and mounting adapters. | 650-654-4300 | NA | San Carlos |
| Ess Technology Inc (HQ) | Designer and marketer of video and audio semiconductors for the home, automotive, and entertainment markets. | 408-643-8800 | NA | Milpitas |
| Finisar Corp (HQ) | Developer of optical communications components and subsystems such as optical modules, active cables and components, passives and optical amplifiers. | 408-548-1000 | NA | Sunnyvale |
| Harmonic Inc (HQ) | Provider of production and delivery solutions. The company serves the broadcast, media, service providers, and post production markets. | 408-542-2500 | 201-500 | San Jose |
| Hitachi America Ltd (BR) | Manufacturer of electronic items specializing IT products. The company provides computers, home appliances, mobile phones, and supplies. | 650-244-7400 | NA | Brisbane |
| Integrated Communication Systems (HQ) | Provider of communication and integration services. The company offers installation, space planning, project management, and maintenance services. | 408-491-6000 | NA | San Jose |
| Integrated Wave Technologies (HQ) | Provider of voice recognition technology services. The company offers printing calculators and electronic camera shutters. | 510-353-0260 | NA | Fremont |
| Level 3 Communications Llc (BR) | Provider of voice data wireless and internet services. The company is also engaged in collaboration and security consulting. | 877-453-8353 | NA | San Jose |
| Lumens Integration Inc (RH) | Designer and developer of visual presentation solutions. The company offers document cameras, video conferencing cameras, and charging carts. | 888-542-3235 | NA | Fremont |
| Media Specialty Resources Inc (HQ) | Provider of acoustic panels for recording studios and home theaters. The company also offers noise control and soundproofing services. | 415-883-8053 | NA | Novato |
| Mesa/Boogie Ltd (HQ) | Provider of guitars, bass amplifiers, and cabinetry. The company provides pedals, speakers, guitars, and accessories. | 707-778-6565 | NA | Petaluma |
| Plantronics Inc (HQ) | Provider of audio technology systems that includes headsets, telephones, audio processors, and speakerphones. | 831-426-5858 | 11-50 | Santa Cruz |
| Pragmatic Communications Systems Inc (HQ) | Designer, developer, and manufacturer of pragmatic products. The company offers amplifiers, security cameras, speakers, and wireless products. | 408-748-1100 | NA | Santa Clara |
| RadioMate (HQ) | Provider of radio accessories specializing in headsets. The company also offers headsets for surveillance and fire & rescue applications. | 925-332-8991 | NA | Concord |
| Rasilient Systems Inc (HQ) | Provider of technology products and services. The company offers a range of video surveillance and storage products. | 408-730-2568 | NA | Santa Clara |
| Renegade Labs (HQ) | Manufacturer of tools for the broadcast, video, and film industries. The company's products include digital audio mixers, metering and input and output systems. | 530-273-7047 | 1-10 | Grass Valley |
| Sonoma Wire Works (HQ) | Provider of loop-based recording and collaboration software for musicians. It's products helps musicians to play, record, and share music. | 650-948-2003 | NA | Mountain View |
| Sp Controls Inc (HQ) | Designer and manufacturer of projector control systems. The company also offers audio systems, mounting, signal distribution, and other products. | 877-367-8444 | NA | S San Francisco |

| COMPANY NAME | PRODUCT / SERVICE | PHONE | EMP | CITY |
|---|---|---|---|---|
| Stewart Audio Inc (HQ) | Provider of network amplifiers and sound systems. The company's products include digital signal processors, mixer amplifiers, and networked accessories. | 209-588-8111 | 1-10 | Sonora |
| Swivl Inc (HQ) | Provider of video tools for personalized teaching and learning. The company offers services to educators. | 888-837-6209 | NA | Menlo Park |
| Teresonic Llc (HQ) | Designer and manufacturer of loudspeakers. The company also offers cables, amplifiers, and related products. | 877-287-1649 | NA | San Jose |
| Tko Video Communications (HQ) | Provider of video communication services. The company focuses on audio and video conferencing, satellite broadcasting, and telecommunications training. | 408-252-4700 | NA | San Jose |
| TOA Electronics Inc (DH) | Developer and manufacturer of audio and security products. The company is engaged in design, delivery, and installation services. | 650-452-1200 | 51-200 | S San Francisco |
| Tymphany HK Ltd (HQ) | Manufacturer of acoustic products. The company's products include consumers and Pro audio, OEM transducers, and peerless catalogs. | 415-887-9538 | NA | San Rafael |
| Vandersteen (HQ) | Manufacturer and distributor of loudspeakers. The company's products include VCC-5 Center, V2W Subwoofer, VLR, and 3a Signature. | 559-582-0324 | 1-10 | Hanford |
| Video Clarity Inc (HQ) | Provider of real time and broadcast quality monitoring, perceptual analysis, recording, and automating services. | 408-379-6952 | NA | Campbell |
| Vitec (BR) | Provider of digital video products. The company offers software for video encoding, decoding, and conversion. | 800-451-5101 | NA | Sunnyvale |
| Vitec Group Communications LLC (HQ) | Designer, manufacturer, and marketer of voice communications systems for live performance, broadcast, houses of worship, and the commercial markets. | 510-337-6600 | NA | Alameda |
| Webenertia (HQ) | Provider of web applications and e-commerce services. The company also focuses on motion graphics and internet marketing solutions. | 408-246-0000 | NA | San Jose |
| Winnov Lp (HQ) | Provider of video capture and streaming solutions. The company serves education, enterprise, healthcare, and live event sectors. | 888-315-9460 | NA | Santa Clara |
| Zaxel Systems Inc (HQ) | Manufacturer of 4k, 8k, and 16k video servers. The company's products are used in post production facilities, museums, and planetariums. | 408-727-6403 | NA | Santa Clara |

## 1 = Broadcasting/Receiving Equipment

| COMPANY NAME | PRODUCT / SERVICE | PHONE | EMP | CITY |
|---|---|---|---|---|
| Alien Technology Corp (HQ) | Provider of UHF radio frequency identification products and services to customers in retail, consumer goods, logistics, and pharmaceutical industries. | 408-782-3900 | NA | San Jose |
| Antedo Inc (HQ) | Provider of consulting services. The company offers international engineering and management consulting services. | 408-253-1870 | NA | Cupertino |
| Anvato Inc (HQ) | Provider of video software platform to television broadcasters and offers live and on-demand video management, analytics, and tracking features. | 866-246-6942 | NA | Mountain View |
| Ascendance Wireless Llc (HQ) | Designer and manufacturer of fixed wireless networks. The company finds application in security and surveillance needs. | 530-887-8300 | 1-10 | Auburn |
| Atlona Inc (HQ) | Provider of technology products for classrooms, large corporations and small businesses, hospitality venues, and residences. | 877-536-3976 | NA | San Jose |
| Broadcom Inc (HQ) | Developer of digital and analog semiconductors. The company also specializes in optical communication semiconductors. | 408-433-8000 | NA | San Jose |
| California Eastern Laboratories (HQ) | Provider of RF, microwave, and optoelectronic semiconductors. The company also offers lasers, detectors, and other products. | 408-919-2500 | NA | Santa Clara |
| Carlson Wireless Technologies Inc (HQ) | Manufacturer of wireless communication products. The company also provides broadband and related services. | 707-443-0100 | 11-50 | Eureka |
| Celadon Inc (HQ) | Provider of OEM products and services. The company's products include OEM remote controls, infrared receivers, and backlighting systems. | 415-472-1177 | NA | San Rafael |
| Ceva Inc (HQ) | Provider of digital signal processor technology. The company also specializes in offering consulting services. | 650-417-7900 | NA | Mountain View |
| Chaparral Communications Inc (HQ) | Designer, developer, and marketer of satellite components for the commercial and residential satellite reception systems. | | NA | Menlo Park |
| Clear-Com Llc (HQ) | Manufacturer of wireless and digital matrix intercom products and related accessories. The company serves the broadcasting and commercial markets. | 510-337-6600 | NA | Alameda |
| Communications & Power Industries Llc (HQ) | Developer and manufacturer of microwave, radio frequency, power, and control solutions. The company serves medical and critical defense fields. | 650-846-2900 | NA | Palo Alto |
| Corecess Global Inc (BR) | Designer, developer, and manufacturer of telecommunication equipment for the broadband access network. | 408-567-5300 | NA | Santa Clara |
| Day Wireless Systems (BR) | Supplier of RF, wireless, and radio communication equipment. The company's services include rentals, system integration, and marketing. | 707-746-5920 | NA | Benicia |
| E-N-G Mobile Systems Inc (HQ) | Manufacturer of specialty vehicles. The company focuses on TV vans and trucks, emergency respone trailers, mobile labs, and other vehicles. | 925-798-4060 | NA | Concord |
| E-Z Tel Inc (HQ) | Provider of basic and unified communication solutions. The company serves small and medium-sized organizations and enterprises. | 925-449-1504 | NA | Livermore |
| Elk Antennas (HQ) | Provider of log periodic antennas made of aluminum elements and stainless steel hardware and with gain, directivity, and front-to-back ratio. | 925-330-0049 | NA | Walnut Creek |

| COMPANY NAME | PRODUCT / SERVICE | PHONE | EMP | CITY |
|---|---|---|---|---|
| Ensemble Designs Inc (HQ) | Manufacturer of audio embedders, video converters, routers, and related products. The company serves post production, education, and other sectors. | 530-478-1830 | 1-10 | Grass Valley |
| Gct Semiconductor Inc (HQ) | Designer and supplier of 4G mobile semiconductor solutions. The company also offers wireless solutions for its clients. | 408-434-6040 | NA | San Jose |
| Guerra Technologies Inc (HQ) | Designer and manufacturer of RF technology related products. The company also offers consulting and evaluation services. | 408-526-9386 | NA | San Jose |
| InnoMedia Inc (RH) | Provider of broadband IP telephony products and solutions including TDM-PRI SIP gateways, enterprise SIP gatewayscable, and element management systems. | 408-432-5400 | NA | Milpitas |
| Inovonics Inc (HQ) | Manufacturer of a wide range of equipment for radio broadcasters. The company also focuses on the marketing aspects. | 831-458-0552 | 1-10 | Felton |
| Inphi Corp (HQ) | Provider of semiconductor solutions for the computing and telecom markets. The company's products include amplifiers, registers, buffers, and modulator drivers. | 408-217-7300 | NA | Santa Clara |
| Jampro Antennas Inc (HQ) | Supplier of antennas, combiners and filters, and radio frequency components for applications in the broadcast industry. | 916-383-1177 | 1-10 | Sacramento |
| Lilee Systems (HQ) | Provider of integrated services that include system prediction modeling, project management, and training services for the railroad industry. | 408-988-8672 | NA | San Jose |
| M2 Antenna Systems Inc (HQ) | Manufacturer of antennas and systems. The company specializes in computer aided antenna design and simulation, and testing and prototyping services. | 559-432-8873 | 1-10 | Fresno |
| Magnum Towers Inc (HQ) | Provider of self-supporting and guy towers, and accessories such as safety climbs, ice bridges, antenna mounts, anti-climb devices, and insulators. | 916-381-5053 | 1-10 | Sacramento |
| Pixelworks Inc (HQ) | Designer and developer of video and pixel processing semiconductors and software for digital video applications. | 408-200-9200 | 11-50 | San Jose |
| Redline Communications (BR) | Provider of networking and consulting solutions. The company serves the government, telecommunication, and military sectors. | 866-633-6669 | NA | Santa Clara |
| Renegade Labs (HQ) | Manufacturer of tools for the broadcast, video, and film industries. The company's products include digital audio mixers, metering and input and output systems. | 530-273-7047 | 1-10 | Grass Valley |
| Riverbed Technology (HQ) | Provider of WAN optimization, cloud, consolidation, disaster recovery, and network performance management solutions. | 415-247-8800 | NA | San Francisco |
| Satellite AV LLC (HQ) | Provider of broadcaster support and call center services. The company also deals with repairs, distribution, and sales. | 916-677-0720 | 1-10 | Rocklin |
| SatPath Systems Inc (HQ) | Provider of networking solutions. The company focuses on voice communication, video and videoconferencing, banking, and other applications. | 510-979-1102 | NA | Fremont |
| Sendero Group Llc (HQ) | Provider of GPS systems and products to the visually impaired. The company focuses on documentation and technical support services. | 888-757-6810 | 1-10 | Rancho Cordova |
| Tarana Wireless Inc (HQ) | Provider of wireless performance solutions. The company serves the residential and enterprise markets. | 408-351-4085 | NA | Milpitas |
| Tci International Inc (DH) | Provider of innovative radio frequency solutions. The company caters to spectrum monitoring and antenna applications. | 510-687-6100 | NA | Fremont |
| Telewave Inc (HQ) | Provider of wireless products such as transmitter couplers and receiver multi couplers. The company also offers antennas. | 408-929-4400 | NA | San Jose |
| Wavesplitter Technologies Inc (HQ) | Manufacturer of passive devices and active optical components for enterprise and residential broadband networks. | 925-596-0414 | NA | Fremont |
| WNI Global Inc (HQ) | Provider of wireless communications solutions for backhaul infrastructure and ethernet network equipment for voice, data, and video applications. | 408-307-2410 | NA | San Jose |

## 62 = Communications Cable & Wire (Including Fiber Optic)

| COMPANY NAME | PRODUCT / SERVICE | PHONE | EMP | CITY |
|---|---|---|---|---|
| A'nd Cable Products Inc (HQ) | Manufacturer, installer, and reseller of cable accessories. The company focuses on cable management and labeling solutions. | 925-672-3005 | NA | Concord |
| Access Communications Inc (HQ) | Provider of telecommunications cabling and audio visual solutions. The company offers audio visual integration, installation, and design services. | 800-342-4439 | NA | San Jose |
| Applied Interconnect (HQ) | Supplier of cables and electro mechanical assemblies. The company also specializes in microwave sub-assemblies. | 408-749-9900 | NA | Sunnyvale |
| Aria Technologies Inc (HQ) | Provider of fiber optic cable assemblies and connectivity products to the data, telecom, and operator market places. | 925-447-7500 | NA | Livermore |
| Assembly Tek (HQ) | Manufacturer of custom cables. The company offers services like design, laminating, JIT programs, and wire preparation. | 831-439-0800 | 1-10 | Scotts Valley |
| Bay Associates Wire Technologies (HQ) | Provider of cable and cable assembly solutions. The company serves the medical, navigation, audio, and automotive markets. | 510-933-3800 | NA | Fremont |
| Bivio Networks Inc (HQ) | Provider of cyber security and network control solutions. The company offers cyber defense systems, surveillance, flow analysis, and monitoring tools. | 925-924-8600 | NA | Pleasanton |
| Bizlink Technology Inc (HQ) | Manufacturer and assembler of cables and harnesses. The company serves the medical devices, solar energy, and fiber optics industries. | 510-252-0786 | NA | Fremont |
| Bravo Communications Inc (HQ) | Supplier of network surge and lightening protection products. The company also offers data line extenders and related accessories. | 408-270-1547 | NA | San Jose |

| COMPANY NAME | PRODUCT / SERVICE | PHONE | EMP | CITY |
|---|---|---|---|---|
| Cable Labs (BR) | Provider of cable services. The company is engaged in virtualization and network evaluation services. | 669-777-9020 | NA | Sunnyvale |
| Compandent Inc (HQ) | Developer of customized algorithms. The company offers digital sign processing services to telecommunications and semiconductor companies. | 650-241-9231 | NA | Los Altos Hills |
| Compatible Cable Inc (HQ) | Manufacturer of custom cable assemblies and off-the shelf cables. The company offers services to the automotive, broadcast, and electronics industries. | 888-415-1115 | NA | Concord |
| Cyberdata Corp (HQ) | Designer and manufacturer of USB cables. The company also offers VoIP and printed circuit board design services. | 831-373-2601 | NA | Monterey |
| De Anza Manufacturing Services Inc (HQ) | Provider of manufacturing services. The company specializes in cable, harness, wiring, and mechanical assemblies. | 408-734-2020 | NA | Sunnyvale |
| Fiber Optic Cable Shop (HQ) | Provider of fiber optic cable products. The company's products include fiber optic media invertors, adapters, aerial cables, and fiber optic switches. | 510-234-9090 | NA | Richmond |
| Golden State Assembly LLC (HQ) | Provider of turn-key engineered solutions for wiring, harnessing and custom cable assembly requirements. The company serves the industrial sector. | 510-226-8155 | NA | Fremont |
| Granite Digital (HQ) | Manufacturer of external diagnostic peripherals. The company is engaged in troubleshooting and maintenance services. | 510-471-6442 | NA | Union City |
| InnoMedia Inc (RH) | Provider of broadband IP telephony products and solutions including TDM-PRI SIP gateways, enterprise SIP gatewayscable, and element management systems. | 408-432-5400 | NA | Milpitas |
| Kyosemi Opto America Corp (BR) | Manufacturer of opto-semiconductor devices. The company focuses on optical communication devices and photo devices for sensors. | 408-492-9361 | NA | Santa Clara |
| LAN-Power Inc (HQ) | Designer, developer, and manufacturer of break through technology for implementing surveillance and security systems. | 510-275-4572 | NA | Fremont |
| LightGuideOptics USA LLC (RH) | Manufacturer of diameters, bundles and probes. The company's products are used in medical and hi-tech applications. | 408-244-0686 | NA | San Jose |
| Lorom Industrial Co Ltd (BR) | Designer and manufacturer of standard and bespoke cables and cable assemblies. The company offers services to the industrial and commercial sectors. | 919-535-5830 | NA | Fremont |
| Neptec Optical Solutions Inc (HQ) | Provider of quick-turn fiber optic connectivity solutions. The company also offers connector reconditioning, switches, and fiber arrays. | 510-687-1101 | NA | Fremont |
| Nortra Cables Inc (HQ) | Provider of discrete and flat mechanical assembly cables. The company offers design, prototyping, and manufacturing services. | 408-942-1106 | NA | Milpitas |
| Optoplex Corporation (HQ) | Supplier of cutting-edge photonic components and modules for dynamic wavelength management and signal conditioning. | 510-490-9930 | NA | Fremont |
| Orbex Group (HQ) | Manufacturer of electronic rings. The company offers capsule slip rings, through-hole slip rings, and harsh environment slip rings. | 408-945-8980 | NA | Fremont |
| Sprint (BR) | Provider of telephone and voice equipment, data communication systems, and internet related services. | 559-244-3200 | 11-50 | Fresno |
| SSL Industries Inc (HQ) | Designer and manufacturer of fiber optics and networking products. The company is involved in installation services. | 530-644-0233 | 1-10 | Diamond Springs |
| Sumitomo Electric Device Innovations Usa Inc (LH) | Developer of electronic devices that includes wireless devices, optical data links, and optical devices. | 408-232-9500 | NA | San Jose |
| Systems Studies Inc (HQ) | Supplier of cable pressurization products. The company is involved in training services and it serves the telephone industry. | 831-475-5777 | 11-50 | Santa Cruz |
| Teresonic Llc (HQ) | Designer and manufacturer of loudspeakers. The company also offers cables, amplifiers, and related products. | 877-287-1649 | NA | San Jose |
| The Okonite Co (BR) | Manufacturer of electrical wire insulators. The company offers high and low voltage, instrumentation, and special purpose cables. | 925-830-0801 | NA | San Ramon |
| Valley Communications Inc (HQ) | Provider of services for network cabling infrastructure needs. The company focuses on designing and installation. | 916-349-7300 | 11-50 | Sacramento |
| Y C Cable Usa Inc (LH) | Manufacturer of cables. The company serves industrial, computer, telecommunications, consumer, medical and other sectors. | 510-824-2788 | NA | Fremont |

## 63 = Communications Equipment Installation & Networking

| COMPANY NAME | PRODUCT / SERVICE | PHONE | EMP | CITY |
|---|---|---|---|---|
| A A Networks (HQ) | Provider of internet, networks and cabling, computer hardware and software, remote and on-site technical support services. | 650-872-1998 | NA | Burlingame |
| Access Communications Inc (HQ) | Provider of telecommunications cabling and audio visual solutions. The company offers audio visual integration, installation, and design services. | 800-342-4439 | NA | San Jose |
| Alpha Omega Wireless Inc (BR) | Provider of broadband wireless network technology integration solutions. The company also focuses on wireless backhaul solutions. | 800-997-9250 | 11-50 | Sacramento |
| Antedo Inc (HQ) | Provider of consulting services. The company offers international engineering and management consulting services. | 408-253-1870 | NA | Cupertino |
| Applied Systems Engineering Inc (HQ) | Provider of consulting, software, design, and testing services. The company's products cater to communication applications. | 408-364-0500 | NA | Campbell |
| Array Networks Inc (HQ) | Developer of integrated web traffic management technology. The company focuses on load balancing and application acceleration solutions. | 408-240-8700 | NA | Milpitas |
| Aruba Networks Inc (HQ) | Manufacturer of enterprise network infrastructure equipment. The company serves healthcare, government, eductaion, and other sectors. | 408-227-4500 | NA | Santa Clara |

| COMPANY NAME | PRODUCT / SERVICE | PHONE | EMP | CITY |
|---|---|---|---|---|
| Aviram Networks Inc (HQ) | Provider of wire-speed IPS for recognition & visualization, access control, and other needs. The company offers consulting and training services. | 408-624-1234 | NA | San Jose |
| Bivio Networks Inc (HQ) | Provider of cyber security and network control solutions. The company offers cyber defense systems, surveillance, flow analysis, and monitoring tools. | 925-924-8600 | NA | Pleasanton |
| Broadcom Inc (HQ) | Developer of digital and analog semiconductors. The company also specializes in optical communication semiconductors. | 408-433-8000 | NA | San Jose |
| Capitol Communications Inc (HQ) | Provider of infrastructure communication solutions for business operations. The company caters to electronics, media, and manufacturing industries. | 415-861-1727 | NA | San Francisco |
| Connected Io Inc (HQ) | Developer of altair-based cellular module for Internet of Things applications. The company provides hardware design & development services. | 669-221-6100 | NA | Los Gatos |
| Crime Alert (HQ) | Provider of residential, industrial, and commercial security monitoring solutions. The company focuses on IP monitoring and disaster recovery. | 800-367-1094 | NA | San Jose |
| Dali Wireless Inc (RH) | Provider of RF router platform for healthcare, airport, education, hospitality, stadium, residential and MDU, and metros and train industries. | 408-481-9400 | NA | Menlo Park |
| E-3 Systems Inc (HQ) | Provider of data center design and installation services. The company focuses on engineering, cable plant analysis and documentation, and maintenance. | 510-487-7393 | NA | Union City |
| Ettus Research Llc (DH) | Provider of software defined radio systems for research, academic, industrial, and defense applications. | 408-610-6399 | NA | Santa Clara |
| Farpointe Data Inc (HQ) | Provider of RFID electronic access control technologies for electronic access control professionals around the world. | 408-731-8700 | NA | San Jose |
| FutureWei Technologies Inc (BR) | Provider of information and communications technology solutions. The company focuses on products such as transport network and data communication. | 408-330-5000 | NA | Santa Clara |
| Go!Foton Corp (BR) | Supplier of optical materials and components. The company focuses on markets such as industrial, image and scanning, and biomedical research. | 408-831-0131 | NA | San Jose |
| Grey San Francisco (BR) | Provider of advertising, planning, sports marketing solutions. The company also focuses on customer relationship management. | 415-403-8000 | NA | San Francisco |
| Hypersurf Internet Services (HQ) | Provider of internet access and internet presence solutions such as dial-up, residential DSL, business DSL, fiber Ethernet, and web and email hosting. | 408-325-0300 | NA | San Jose |
| Integrated Communication Systems (HQ) | Provider of communication and integration services. The company offers installation, space planning, project management, and maintenance services. | 408-491-6000 | NA | San Jose |
| Itc Service Group Inc (HQ) | Provider of personnel and managed services to IT, telecom, and the CATV industry. The company offers staffing and turnkey solutions. | 877-370-4482 | 11-50 | Citrus Heights |
| Kyosemi Opto America Corp (BR) | Manufacturer of opto-semiconductor devices. The company focuses on optical communication devices and photo devices for sensors. | 408-492-9361 | NA | Santa Clara |
| LAN-Power Inc (HQ) | Designer, developer, and manufacturer of break through technology for implementing surveillance and security systems. | 510-275-4572 | NA | Fremont |
| Maverick Networks Inc (HQ) | Provider of VoIP telephone and related communication services. The company also provides design, implementation, and training solutions. | 925-931-1900 | NA | Pleasanton |
| MeshDynamics Inc (HQ) | Provider of wireless mesh networking solutions focusing on wireless video surveillance, emergency response networks, and smart-grid multiuse products. | 408-373-7700 | NA | Santa Clara |
| Modern Systems Research Inc (HQ) | Provider of telecom design and voice & data networking services. The company also focuses on power systems and systems architecture. | 650-940-2000 | NA | Los Altos |
| Netblaze Systems Inc (HQ) | Provider of IT, integration, and network consulting services. The company is also engaged in cloud computing, web hosting, and hosted exchange. | 925-932-1765 | NA | Walnut Creek |
| Peloton Technology (HQ) | Developer of truck platooning systems. The company offers services to the transportation, trucking, and railroad industries. | 650-395-7356 | NA | Mountain View |
| Ridge Communications Inc (HQ) | Provider of network deployment and project management services. The company serves the wireless carrier industry. | 925-498-2340 | NA | San Ramon |
| Riverbed Technology (HQ) | Provider of WAN optimization, cloud, consolidation, disaster recovery, and network performance management solutions. | 415-247-8800 | NA | San Francisco |
| Ruckus Networks (HQ) | Designer and manufacturer of Wi-Fi products and wireless LAN systems. The company also focuses on the marketing aspects. | 650-265-4200 | NA | Sunnyvale |
| Sasken Technologies Ltd (BR) | Provider of research and development consultation, wireless software products, and software services to automotive and health care sectors. | 408-730-0100 | NA | Sunnyvale |
| Securematics Inc (HQ) | Provider of secure networking, security, storage products and solutions. The company focuses on demand generation and e-commerce. | 888-746-6700 | NA | Santa Clara |
| SentinelOne (HQ) | Developer of end-point protection software. The company serves the healthcare, oil and gas, and financial services industries. | 855-868-3733 | NA | Mountain View |
| Socionext Inc (DH) | Designer and developer of System-on-Chip products. The company's products are used in imaging, networking, and computing fields. | 408 550-6861 | NA | Santa Clara |

| COMPANY NAME | PRODUCT / SERVICE | PHONE | EMP | CITY |
|---|---|---|---|---|
| Solonics Inc (HQ) | Manufacturer of coded backboard systems and wire management products. The company focuses on design and delivery services. | 510-471-7600 | NA | Hayward |
| Sumitomo Electric Device Innovations Usa Inc (LH) | Developer of electronic devices that includes wireless devices, optical data links, and optical devices. | 408-232-9500 | NA | San Jose |
| Systems Studies Inc (HQ) | Supplier of cable pressurization products. The company is involved in training services and it serves the telephone industry. | 831-475-5777 | 11-50 | Santa Cruz |
| T&D Communications (BR) | Supplier of telephones, and data and paging equipment. The company also specializes in installation. | 510-824-0010 | NA | Fremont |
| Tci International Inc (DH) | Provider of innovative radio frequency solutions. The company caters to spectrum monitoring and antenna applications. | 510-687-6100 | NA | Fremont |
| Tru Technical Partners Inc (HQ) | Provider of information technology services on a contract basis. The company's services include managed desktops, workstation, anti-virus, and others. | 408-559-2800 | NA | Campbell |
| Utstarcom Inc (BR) | Manufacturer of IP based, end to end networking, and telecommunications solutions. The company also focuses on integration. | 408-453-4557 | NA | San Jose |
| Versa Networks Inc (HQ) | Provider of networking solutions. The company specializes in virtualized network functions and services. | 408-385-7660 | NA | Santa Clara |
| Vivax-Metrotech Corp (HQ) | Manufacturer of mapping tools. The company specializes in tools used for underground cabling and piping works. | 408-734-1400 | NA | Santa Clara |
| Wi2wi Inc (HQ) | Provider of wireless system-in-package, module, and subsystems for embedded applications including Wi-Fi, Bluetooth, and GPS. | 408-416-4200 | NA | San Jose |

## 64 = Data Communication Systems

| COMPANY NAME | PRODUCT / SERVICE | PHONE | EMP | CITY |
|---|---|---|---|---|
| Actelis Networks Inc (HQ) | Provider of carrier Ethernet over copper networking equipment. The company serves government, service operators, and utilities. | 510-545-1045 | NA | Fremont |
| Airnex Communications Inc (HQ) | Provider of digital wireless telecommunications and internet access services. The company also focuses on web hosting. | 800-708-4884 | NA | Pleasanton |
| AmbiCom Holdings Inc (HQ) | Manufacturer of networking hardware for mobile computers. The company offers wireless solutions and OEM modules. | 408-321-0822 | 1-10 | Santa Cruz |
| At&T Inc (BR) | Provider of IP based communication solutions. The company offers services in the areas of broadband, Wi-Fi, wireless networks, and mobile phones. | 209-556-9042 | 11-50 | Modesto |
| Audible Magic Corp (HQ) | Developer of media identification and synchronization, content registration, and copyright compliance solutions. | 408-399-6405 | NA | Los Gatos |
| Avaya Inc (HQ) | Provider of PBX solutions, IVR applications, IP telephony solutions, voice messaging, and consulting. | 908-953-6000 | NA | Santa Clara |
| Cisco Systems Inc (HQ) | Designer and manufacturer of IP-based networking products. The company also offers security solutions and architectures. | 408-526-4000 | NA | San Jose |
| Data-Com Solutions (HQ) | Designer of data communication networks, national equipment roll outs, and network hardware installation services. | 916-331-2377 | 1-10 | Roseville |
| Dialogic Inc (HQ) | Provider of communications products and media server software. The company serves business enterprises and organizations. | 408-750-9400 | 51-200 | Milpitas |
| Enablence Technologies Inc (DH) | Manufacturer of silicon products for communication needs. The company's offerings include optical splitters and channel filters. | 510-226-8900 | NA | Fremont |
| Futuredial Inc (HQ) | Developer of carrier-grade solutions and tools for mobile device recyclers, wireless operators, and mobile device manufacturers. | 408-245-8880 | NA | Sunnyvale |
| FutureWei Technologies Inc (BR) | Provider of information and communications technology solutions. The company focuses on products such as transport network and data communication. | 408-330-5000 | NA | Santa Clara |
| HotLava Systems Inc (HQ) | Provider of board-level solutions for servers and appliances that operates in virtualized environments. | 510-531-1169 | NA | Oakland |
| Industrial Control Links Inc (HQ) | Designer and manufacturer of SCADA hardware and software solutions. The company focuses on monitoring, alarming, data collection, and other needs. | 530-888-1800 | 1-10 | Auburn |
| MeshDynamics Inc (HQ) | Provider of wireless mesh networking solutions focusing on wireless video surveillance, emergency response networks, and smart-grid multiuse products. | 408-373-7700 | NA | Santa Clara |
| Metaswitch Networks (DH) | Provider of service management solutions. The company offers original equipment manufacturer, multimedia subsystem, and hosted business services. | 415-513-1500 | NA | Los Altos |
| O2micro Usa (LH) | Provider of battery and power management products. The company also offers LED general lighting and backlighting products. | 408-987-5920 | NA | Santa Clara |
| OJO Technology Inc (HQ) | Manufacturer of video surveillance systems. The company offers services to the education, transportation, and utility sectors. | 877-306-4656 | NA | Fremont |
| Orion Labs (HQ) | Developer of wearable communication accessory for instant voice conversations with many people, across any distance. | 415-800-2035 | NA | San Francisco |
| Pacific Crest (HQ) | Provider of communication solutions. The company specializes in the design and manufacture of radio controlled and spotlight data transfer systems. | 408-481-8070 | NA | Sunnyvale |
| Peloton Technology (HQ) | Developer of truck platooning systems. The company offers services to the transportation, trucking, and railroad industries. | 650-395-7356 | NA | Mountain View |

| COMPANY NAME | PRODUCT / SERVICE | PHONE | EMP | CITY |
|---|---|---|---|---|
| Rambus (HQ) | Manufacturer of semiconductor, lighting, and IP products. The company serves the automotive and transportation markets. | 408-462-8000 | NA | Sunnyvale |
| Relcomm Inc (HQ) | Manufacturer of computer and data communication devices. The company offers data switches, inline buffers, and current loop products. | 301-924-7400 | 1-10 | Angels Camp |
| Sai Technology Inc (HQ) | Designer and developer of wireless technology solutions. The company also deals with digital signage services. | 408-727-1560 | NA | Santa Clara |
| Sentry Products Inc (HQ) | Provider of duress alarm systems. The company caters to judicial centers, emergency medical facilities, and schools. | 408-727-1866 | NA | Santa Clara |
| Solutions Cubed Llc (HQ) | Provider of engineering solutions. The company is involved in early stage electronic prototyping to full production runs. | 530-891-8045 | 1-10 | Chico |
| Sprint (BR) | Provider of telephone and voice equipment, data communication systems, and internet related services. | 559-244-3200 | 11-50 | Fresno |
| Stonefly Inc (HQ) | Provider of storage optimization and disaster recovery protection for software solutions. The company also offers storage area networks. | 510-265-1616 | NA | Hayward |
| Totlcom Inc (BR) | Provider of IP voice and data services and products such as IP systems, VoIP systems, and mail systems for growing companies. | 916-428-5000 | 11-50 | Sacramento |
| Trivad Inc (HQ) | Developer of IT solutions. The company also offers training, implementation, and infrastructure assessment services. | 650-286-1086 | NA | Burlingame |
| Wi2wi Inc (HQ) | Provider of wireless system-in-package, module, and subsystems for embedded applications including Wi-Fi, Bluetooth, and GPS. | 408-416-4200 | NA | San Jose |
| ZigBee Alliance (HQ) | Provider of lighting solutions. The company offers LED fixtures, light bulbs, remotes and switches and serves the residential and commercial sectors. | 530-564-4565 | 11-50 | Davis |

## 65 = Electric Signalling Equipment

| COMPANY NAME | PRODUCT / SERVICE | PHONE | EMP | CITY |
|---|---|---|---|---|
| Connected Io Inc (HQ) | Developer of altair-based cellular module for Internet of Things applications. The company provides hardware design & development services. | 669-221-6100 | NA | Los Gatos |
| Highland Technology Inc (HQ) | Designer and manufacturer of precision analog instrumentation. The company serves laboratory research purposes. | 415-551-1700 | NA | San Francisco |
| Kmic Technology Inc (HQ) | Provider of amplifier products and solutions to the radio frequency, microwave, and millimeter wave markets. | 408-240-3600 | NA | San Jose |
| Los Gatos Research Inc (HQ) | Manufacturer of analyzers for the measurement of trace gases and isotopes. The company serves the industrial and environmental sectors. | 650-965-7772 | NA | San Jose |
| Oml Inc (HQ) | Provider of millimeter wave test instruments, calibration equipment and systems for radio astronomy, communication, imaging, and other sectors. | 408-779-2698 | NA | Morgan Hill |
| Tesco Controls Inc (HQ) | Manufacturer of instrumentation, control systems, and service pedestals for water and traffic sectors. The company offers system integration services. | 916-395-8800 | 11-50 | Sacramento |

## 66 = Electronic Mail/Message Systems

| COMPANY NAME | PRODUCT / SERVICE | PHONE | EMP | CITY |
|---|---|---|---|---|
| Frequentis California Inc (DH) | Provider of air traffic management and other e-services. The company serves the defense and public transport sectors. | 831-392-0430 | NA | Monterey |
| Landel (HQ) | Provider of telecommunication products such as MailBug, DataBug, and SurveyBug. The company is engaged in technical support services. | 408-360-0490 | NA | San Jose |
| Megapath (HQ) | Provider of voice, data, networking, cloud, and security services. The company serves healthcare, finance, restaurant, and retail sectors. | 866-300-0749 | NA | Pleasanton |

## 67 = Internet Related Services

| COMPANY NAME | PRODUCT / SERVICE | PHONE | EMP | CITY |
|---|---|---|---|---|
| A A Networks (HQ) | Provider of internet, networks and cabling, computer hardware and software, remote and on-site technical support services. | 650-872-1998 | NA | Burlingame |
| Aerohive Networks Inc (HQ) | Provider of enterprise mobility solutions. The company offers access points, routers, switches, and VPN gateway solutions. | 408-510-6100 | NA | Milpitas |
| Allied Telesis Inc (BR) | Developer of network solutions for internet protocol surveillance. The company focuses on web hosting and programming solutions. | 408-519-8700 | NA | San Jose |
| Alpha Omega Wireless Inc (BR) | Provider of broadband wireless network technology integration solutions. The company also focuses on wireless backhaul solutions. | 800-997-9250 | 11-50 | Sacramento |
| Arc (HQ) | Provider of document management services to the architectural, engineering, and construction industries. | 925-949-5100 | NA | San Ramon |
| Arrive Technologies Inc (HQ) | Provider of broadband and packet network semiconductor solutions for the telecommunication companies. | 888-864-6959 | 1-10 | Roseville |
| Aruba Networks Inc (HQ) | Manufacturer of enterprise network infrastructure equipment. The company serves healthcare, government, eductaion, and other sectors. | 408-227-4500 | NA | Santa Clara |
| At&T Inc (BR) | Provider of IP based communication solutions. The company offers services in the areas of broadband, Wi-Fi, wireless networks, and mobile phones. | 209-556-9042 | 11-50 | Modesto |
| Aviram Networks Inc (HQ) | Provider of wire-speed IPS for recognition & visualization, access control, and other needs. The company offers consulting and training services. | 408-624-1234 | NA | San Jose |
| Bivio Networks Inc (HQ) | Provider of cyber security and network control solutions. The company offers cyber defense systems, surveillance, flow analysis, and monitoring tools. | 925-924-8600 | NA | Pleasanton |

| COMPANY NAME | PRODUCT / SERVICE | PHONE | EMP | CITY |
|---|---|---|---|---|
| Blueplanet (HQ) | Developer and supplier of network solutions for distributed intelligence of internet protocol and enhancement of the efficiency of IP networks. | 707-735-2300 | NA | Petaluma |
| Carefree Computing Inc (HQ) | Provider of web hosting, software design, programming, technical support, and network design services. | 866-377-6275 | NA | San Francisco |
| Ceniom Inc (HQ) | Provider of security, network design, and data recovery services. The company is engaged in web design, hosting, and technical support. | 800-403-3204 | 1-10 | Sacramento |
| Configure Inc (HQ) | Provider of communication consulting services. The company specializes in network design, transport service implementation, and project management. | 877-408-2636 | NA | San Jose |
| Connected Io Inc (HQ) | Developer of altair-based cellular module for Internet of Things applications. The company provides hardware design & development services. | 669-221-6100 | NA | Los Gatos |
| Criterion Network Services Inc (HQ) | Provider of network design, system integration, configuration, and remote network management services. | 650-947-7755 | NA | Los Altos |
| Css Corp (HQ) | Provider of enterprise level support solutions for IT products. The company is involved in virtualization, storage, and archiving solutions. | 650-385-3820 | NA | Milpitas |
| Denodo Technologies Inc (HQ) | Provider of enterprise data virtualization, data federation, and cloud data integration middleware solutions. | 650-566-8833 | NA | Palo Alto |
| Emagined Security Inc (HQ) | Provider of professional services for information security solutions. The company also focuses on compliance. | 415-944-2977 | NA | San Carlos |
| Farpointe Data Inc (HQ) | Provider of RFID electronic access control technologies for electronic access control professionals around the world. | 408-731-8700 | NA | San Jose |
| Fire2wire (HQ) | Provider of network consulting, server colocation, website hosting and design, wireless internet, and content management services. | 209-543-1800 | 1-10 | Salida |
| Gold Star Web (HQ) | Provider of website design and hosting, development and web marketing, technical support, and programming services. | 530-891-1841 | 1-10 | Chico |
| Hypersurf Internet Services (HQ) | Provider of internet access and internet presence solutions such as dial-up, residential DSL, business DSL, fiber Ethernet, and web and email hosting. | 408-325-0300 | NA | San Jose |
| InnoMedia Inc (RH) | Provider of broadband IP telephony products and solutions including TDM-PRI SIP gateways, enterprise SIP gatewayscable, and element management systems. | 408-432-5400 | NA | Milpitas |
| Intelepeer Cloud Communications (HQ) | Provider of on-demand cloud-based communication services. The company offers media peering, SIP trunking, and direct inward dialing services. | 650-525-9200 | NA | San Mateo |
| Intermedia Net Inc (HQ) | Provider of cloud services including VoIP telephony, instant messaging, and file management to small and mid-sized businesses. | 800-379-7729 | NA | Mountain View |
| Internap Corp (BR) | Provider of internet network services, colocation, hosting, content delivery, and broadband solutions. | 877-843-7627 | NA | Santa Clara |
| Internetspeech Inc (HQ) | Provider of audio internet technology services. The company offers world-wide web and enabled services. | 408-532-8460 | NA | San Jose |
| Ionix Internet (HQ) | Provider of web hosting solutions. The company offers network security, research, hi-speed access, and telecommuting services. | 888-884-6649 | NA | San Francisco |
| Itc Service Group Inc (HQ) | Provider of personnel and managed services to IT, telecom, and the CATV industry. The company offers staffing and turnkey solutions. | 877-370-4482 | 11-50 | Citrus Heights |
| Linguastat Inc (HQ) | Provider of web based services to corporations and government agencies. The company offers optimized product descriptions for millions of landing pages. | 415-814-2999 | NA | San Francisco |
| MatrixStream Technologies Inc (HQ) | Provider of end-to-end enterprise, hospitality, embedded, and wireless internet protocol television solutions. | 650-292-4982 | NA | Redwood Shores |
| Nimbus Design (HQ) | Provider of design services. The company specializes in website design, content management, and e-commerce tools. | 650-365-7568 | NA | Redwood City |
| Numenta Inc (HQ) | Developer of biotechnology machine intelligence technologies for commercial and scientific applications. | 650-369-8282 | NA | Redwood City |
| Obscura Digital Llc (HQ) | Provider of technology-driven creative solutions. The company caters to advertising and marketing needs. | 415-227-9979 | NA | San Francisco |
| Promptu (HQ) | Provider of voice-activated search and navigation services. The company is also engaged in engineering and product marketing. | 650-859-5800 | NA | Menlo Park |
| Proxim Wireless (HQ) | Provider of Wi-Fi, point-to-point, and 4G wireless network technologies. The company's ORiNOCO product is used by service providers and enterprises. | 408-383-7600 | NA | San Jose |
| Quicknet Technologies Inc (HQ) | Developer of internet telephony technology solutions. The company serves individuals, small businesses and computer users. | 415-864-5225 | NA | San Francisco |
| RagingWire Data Centers (HQ) | Provider of information technology services such as storage, back up services, monitoring, migration planning, and disaster recovery. | 916-286-3000 | 1-10 | Sacramento |
| SatPath Systems Inc (HQ) | Provider of networking solutions. The company focuses on voice communication, video and videoconferencing, banking, and other applications. | 510-979-1102 | NA | Fremont |
| SentinelOne (HQ) | Developer of end-point protection software. The company serves the healthcare, oil and gas, and financial services industries. | 855-868-3733 | NA | Mountain View |
| Socionext Inc (DH) | Designer and developer of System-on-Chip products. The company's products are used in imaging, networking, and computing fields. | 408 550-6861 | NA | Santa Clara |

| COMPANY NAME | PRODUCT / SERVICE | PHONE | EMP | CITY |
|---|---|---|---|---|
| SSL Industries Inc (HQ) | Designer and manufacturer of fiber optics and networking products. The company is involved in installation services. | 530-644-0233 | 1-10 | Diamond Springs |
| Tarana Wireless Inc (HQ) | Provider of wireless performance solutions. The company serves the residential and enterprise markets. | 408-351-4085 | NA | Milpitas |
| Techbiz Inc (RH) | Provider of custom network and server solutions. The company is involved in design and deployment services. | 510-249-6800 | NA | Fremont |
| TokBox Inc (HQ) | Developer of free video chat tools and widgets. The company offers services for the recreation and entertainment industries. | 415-284-4688 | NA | San Francisco |
| Tru Technical Partners Inc (HQ) | Provider of information technology services on a contract basis. The company's services include managed desktops, workstation, anti-virus, and others. | 408-559-2800 | NA | Campbell |
| Unitedlayer Llc (HQ) | Provider of cloud hosting solutions. The company offers server clusters and routers, disaster recovery, infrastructure, and colocation services. | 415-349-2100 | NA | San Francisco |
| V2plus Technology Inc (HQ) | Provider of technology solutions. The company offers services for voice, data, and video over local wired and wireless communication networks. | 510-226-6006 | NA | Fremont |
| Venturi Wireless Inc (HQ) | Provider of broadband optimization services. The company mainly caters to mobile and wireless operators. | 408-982-1130 | NA | San Jose |
| Voce Communications (HQ) | Provider of marketing and communication consultancy services. The company in engaged in public relation, media marketing, and web development. | 415-975-2200 | NA | San Francisco |
| Xo Communications Llc (BR) | Provider of communication services including cloud security, collocation, email hosting, and conferencing for the healthcare and retail markets. | 408-817-2800 | NA | San Francisco |
| Xtelesis Corp (HQ) | Provider of voice and data solutions. The company is engaged in data networking, audio web conferencing, and managed IT services. | 650-239-1400 | NA | Burlingame |

## 68 = Miscellaneous Communications Equipment/Services

| COMPANY NAME | PRODUCT / SERVICE | PHONE | EMP | CITY |
|---|---|---|---|---|
| 8x8 Inc (HQ) | Provider of cloud communications and computing solutions. The company sells IP phones, IP conference, soft, video and analog phones and accessories. | 408-727-1885 | NA | San Jose |
| Access Communications Inc (HQ) | Provider of telecommunications cabling and audio visual solutions. The company offers audio visual integration, installation, and design services. | 800-342-4439 | NA | San Jose |
| Acco Semiconductor Inc (HQ) | Provider of outsourced operations and engineering services. The company serves fabless semiconductor companies. | 408-524-2600 | NA | Sunnyvale |
| Accurate Always Inc (HQ) | Provider of digital voice and video recording services. The company also offers radio and telephone call monitoring service. | 650-728-9428 | NA | Half Moon Bay |
| Actelis Networks Inc (HQ) | Provider of carrier Ethernet over copper networking equipment. The company serves government, service operators, and utilities. | 510-545-1045 | NA | Fremont |
| Adax Inc (HQ) | Provider of packet processing, security, and telecom network infrastructure components. The company's products include gateways and controllers. | 510-548-7047 | NA | Oakland |
| Altigen Communications Inc (HQ) | Manufacturer of voice and data telecommunication equipment. The company specializes in hosted business communication solutions. | 408-597-9000 | NA | San Jose |
| Amasco (HQ) | Distributor of products for the telecommunications, commercial, industrial, medical, and military electronics markets. | 408-360-1300 | NA | San Jose |
| Amdocs Ltd (BR) | Provider of customer management and billing solutions software. The company offers services to the industrial sector. | 916-934-7000 | 11-50 | El Dorado Hills |
| American Broadband Services (HQ) | Provider of web, internet connectivity, VoIP, spam & virus filtering, and technical support services. | 866-827-4638 | 1-10 | Fresno |
| American Power Systems (BR) | Provider of power management products and services. The company's offerings include UPS, DC power, and battery testing. | 209-467-8999 | 11-50 | Stockton |
| Anritsu Co (DH) | Provider of test solutions for telecommunication applications. The company also caters to microwave applications. | 408-778-2000 | NA | Morgan Hill |
| Antedo Inc (HQ) | Provider of consulting services. The company offers international engineering and management consulting services. | 408-253-1870 | NA | Cupertino |
| Anybots 2.0 Inc (BR) | Provider of robotic device that acts as a personal remote avatar which can be operated remotely thus creating a virtual presence. | 877-594-1836 | NA | San Jose |
| Applied Systems Engineering Inc (HQ) | Provider of consulting, software, design, and testing services. The company's products cater to communication applications. | 408-364-0500 | NA | Campbell |
| Applied Wireless Identifications Group Inc (HQ) | Provider of communication systems for engineering applications. The company also offers modules, antennas, and accessories. | 408-825-1100 | NA | Morgan Hill |
| Appro Technology Inc (BR) | Manufacturer of network surveillance systems. The company's products include dome cameras, LCD monitors, and cables. | 408-720-0018 | NA | Sunnyvale |
| Aptible Inc (HQ) | Developer of secure, private cloud deployment platform built to automate HIPAA compliance for digital health. | 866-296-5003 | NA | San Francisco |
| Arbor Solution Inc (HQ) | Provider of embedded computing and networking solutions for the transportation, medical, automation, and military segments. | 408-452-8900 | NA | Fremont |
| Arcscale LLC (HQ) | Provider of colocation, technology integration, hosting, implementation, and telecommunication services. The company also deals with procurement. | 408-476-0554 | NA | San Jose |
| Arista Networks Inc (HQ) | Provider of cloud networking, network virtualization, high frequency trading, and government solutions for data center needs. | 408-547-5500 | NA | Santa Clara |

| COMPANY NAME | PRODUCT / SERVICE | PHONE | EMP | CITY |
|---|---|---|---|---|
| Array Networks Inc (HQ) | Developer of integrated web traffic management technology. The company focuses on load balancing and application acceleration solutions. | 408-240-8700 | NA | Milpitas |
| Aruba Networks Inc (HQ) | Manufacturer of enterprise network infrastructure equipment. The company serves healthcare, government, eductaion, and other sectors. | 408-227-4500 | NA | Santa Clara |
| At&T Inc (BR) | Provider of smartphones, TV services, business solutions, wireless networks, and broadband services. | 650-938-9479 | NA | Mountain View |
| At&T Inc (BR) | Provider of IP based communication solutions. The company offers services in the areas of broadband, Wi-Fi, wireless networks, and mobile phones. | 209-556-9042 | 11-50 | Modesto |
| Autonet Mobile (HQ) | Provider of internet based telematics and applications service platform for the automotive transportation market. | 415-223-0316 | NA | Santa Rosa |
| Avaya Inc (HQ) | Provider of PBX solutions, IVR applications, IP telephony solutions, voice messaging, and consulting. | 908-953-6000 | NA | Santa Clara |
| Aviram Networks Inc (HQ) | Provider of wire-speed IPS for recognition & visualization, access control, and other needs. The company offers consulting and training services. | 408-624-1234 | NA | San Jose |
| Avistar Communications Corp (HQ) | Provider of communication solutions. The company provides call controls, conference tools, internet gateway tools, and accessories. | 650-525-3300 | NA | San Mateo |
| Bivio Networks Inc (HQ) | Provider of cyber security and network control solutions. The company offers cyber defense systems, surveillance, flow analysis, and monitoring tools. | 925-924-8600 | NA | Pleasanton |
| Bravo Communications Inc (HQ) | Supplier of network surge and lightening protection products. The company also offers data line extenders and related accessories. | 408-270-1547 | NA | San Jose |
| C&S Telecommunications Inc (HQ) | Supplier of telephone systems and data networks. The company offers installation, training, and other services. | 916-364-8636 | 1-10 | Sacramento |
| Calix Inc (HQ) | Provider of broadband communications access systems and software. The company offers business, fiber access, and mobile backhaul solutions. | 707-766-3000 | NA | Petaluma |
| Campbell/Harris Security Equipment Company (HQ) | Manufacturer of busters, fiberscopes, probe kits, and personal radiation detectors. The company also focuses on distribution. | 510-864-8010 | NA | Alameda |
| Capitol Communications Inc (HQ) | Provider of infrastructure communication solutions for business operations. The company caters to electronics, media, and manufacturing industries. | 415-861-1727 | NA | San Francisco |
| Carlson Wireless Technologies Inc (HQ) | Manufacturer of wireless communication products. The company also provides broadband and related services. | 707-443-0100 | 11-50 | Eureka |
| Cetecom (BR) | Provider of consulting and testing services. The company focuses on the telecommunications and information technology industries. | 408-586-6200 | NA | Milpitas |
| Cisco Systems Inc (BR) | Provider of networking products and services such as routers, switches, and optical and wireless networking devices. | 800-553-6387 | NA | San Francisco |
| Clear-Com Llc (HQ) | Manufacturer of wireless and digital matrix intercom products and related accessories. The company serves the broadcasting and commercial markets. | 510-337-6600 | NA | Alameda |
| Cobham Defence Electronics (BR) | Manufacturer and designer of electrical components. The company caters to the military and commercial sectors. | 888-310-0010 | NA | San Jose |
| Codar Ocean Sensors Ltd (HQ) | Designer and manufacturer of radar systems for ocean current and wave monitoring. The company specializes in sea state monitoring. | 408-773-8240 | NA | Mountain View |
| Cohere Technologies Inc (HQ) | Developers of wireless technology solutions. The company offers solutions for orthogonal time frequency space. | 408-246-1277 | NA | Santa Clara |
| Computerland Of Silicon Valley (HQ) | Provider of hardware, software, and networking services. The company serves government and educational institutions. | 408-519-3200 | NA | San Jose |
| Cyberdata Corp (HQ) | Designer and manufacturer of USB cables. The company also offers VoIP and printed circuit board design services. | 831-373-2601 | NA | Monterey |
| Day Wireless Systems (BR) | Supplier of RF, wireless, and radio communication equipment. The company's services include rentals, system integration, and marketing. | 707-746-5920 | NA | Benicia |
| Digital Products Co (HQ) | Provider of telephone line simulators. The company offers two-line telco and party-line simulators and real phone line products. | 916-985-7219 | 1-10 | Folsom |
| Dolby Laboratories Inc (BR) | Provider of speech recognition and voice identification products. The company also offers voice control services. | 408-330-3300 | NA | Sunnyvale |
| E-3 Systems Inc (HQ) | Provider of data center design and installation services. The company focuses on engineering, cable plant analysis and documentation, and maintenance. | 510-487-7393 | NA | Union City |
| E-Fab Inc (HQ) | Provider of precision manufacturing and fabrication solutions. The company offers mesh screens, etched antennas, encoder strips, and PCB jumpers. | 408-727-5218 | NA | Santa Clara |
| E-N-G Mobile Systems Inc (HQ) | Manufacturer of specialty vehicles. The company focuses on TV vans and trucks, emergency respone trailers, mobile labs, and other vehicles. | 925-798-4060 | NA | Concord |
| E-Z Tel Inc (HQ) | Provider of basic and unified communication solutions. The company serves small and medium-sized organizations and enterprises. | 925-449-1504 | NA | Livermore |
| Ettus Research Llc (DH) | Provider of software defined radio systems for research, academic, industrial, and defense applications. | 408-610-6399 | NA | Santa Clara |

| COMPANY NAME | PRODUCT / SERVICE | PHONE | EMP | CITY |
|---|---|---|---|---|
| Finisar Corp (HQ) | Developer of optical communications components and subsystems such as optical modules, active cables and components, passives and optical amplifiers. | 408-548-1000 | NA | Sunnyvale |
| Genmega Inc (HQ) | Manufacturer and provider of ATM and transactional kiosk solutions. The company's products include GenLink, Onyx-P, Onyx-W, and G2500P ATM. | 510-344-6333 | NA | Hayward |
| Gevicam Inc (HQ) | Developer and manufacturer of industrial cameras based on Gigabit Ethernet Technology for the industrial, scientific, and homeland security markets. | 408-262-5772 | NA | Milpitas |
| Gilsson Technologies (HQ) | Manufacturer of GPS systems and accessories. The company offers external GPS antenna mounts and GPS antenna network splitter kits. | 510-940-7777 | NA | Hayward |
| Glowlink Communications Technology Inc (HQ) | Provider of emitters, global monitoring, and uplink power control devices. The company also offers alignment and commissioning services. | 650-237-0220 | NA | Mountain View |
| Guerra Technologies Inc (HQ) | Designer and manufacturer of RF technology related products. The company also offers consulting and evaluation services. | 408-526-9386 | NA | San Jose |
| Helium (HQ) | Provider of connectivity solutions for smart devices. The company offers services to individuals and businesses. | 415-510-2110 | NA | San Francisco |
| Integrated Communication Systems (HQ) | Provider of communication and integration services. The company offers installation, space planning, project management, and maintenance services. | 408-491-6000 | NA | San Jose |
| Intelepeer Cloud Communications (HQ) | Provider of on-demand cloud-based communication services. The company offers media peering, SIP trunking, and direct inward dialing services. | 650-525-9200 | NA | San Mateo |
| Ionix Internet (HQ) | Provider of web hosting solutions. The company offers network security, research, hi-speed access, and telecommuting services. | 888-884-6649 | NA | San Francisco |
| Ipass Inc (HQ) | Provider of cloud-based mobility management and Wi-Fi connectivity services. The company serves global enterprises and telecommunication sectors. | 650-232-4100 | 11-50 | Redwood City |
| Jei (HQ) | Provider of communication recorders, voice logging recorders, and audio and custom products for public and military intelligence applications. | 530-677-3210 | 1-10 | Cameron Park |
| Kaiam Corp (HQ) | Provider of single-mode solutions. The company develops transceivers, modules, and components for data centers. | 510-226-8100 | NA | Newark |
| Kimberlite Corp (HQ) | Dealer of security verification systems. The company offers access control, video surveillance, fire detection, and intrusion detection systems. | 559-264-9730 | 11-50 | Fresno |
| Kmic Technology Inc (HQ) | Provider of amplifier products and solutions to the radio frequency, microwave, and millimeter wave markets. | 408-240-3600 | NA | San Jose |
| Kortick Manufacturing (HQ) | Manufacturer and distributor of pole line hardware. The company primarily caters to the telecom industry. | 510-856-3600 | NA | Hayward |
| Krytar Inc (HQ) | Provider of broadband microwave components and test equipment. The company is engaged in troubleshooting and maintenance services. | 408-734-5999 | NA | Sunnyvale |
| Kyosemi Opto America Corp (BR) | Manufacturer of opto-semiconductor devices. The company focuses on optical communication devices and photo devices for sensors. | 408-492-9361 | NA | Santa Clara |
| Landel (HQ) | Provider of telecommunication products such as MailBug, DataBug, and SurveyBug. The company is engaged in technical support services. | 408-360-0490 | NA | San Jose |
| Langineers (HQ) | Provider of VoIP phone services, video conferencing, and hosting solutions. The company offers cordless DECT phones and video conferencing phones. | 650-692-2001 | NA | Burlingame |
| Lasertec USA Inc (HQ) | Developer and manufacturer of systems for semi-conductor applications. The company also offers systems for flat panel displays. | 408-437-1441 | NA | San Jose |
| Level 3 Communications Llc (BR) | Provider of voice data wireless and internet services. The company is also engaged in collaboration and security consulting. | 877-453-8353 | NA | San Jose |
| Lightsand Communications (BR) | Developer of SAN connectivity products. The company is engaged in troubleshooting and maintenance services. | 619-865-6400 | NA | Palo Alto |
| Lilee Systems (HQ) | Provider of integrated services that include system prediction modeling, project management, and training services for the railroad industry. | 408-988-8672 | NA | San Jose |
| Lorom Industrial Co Ltd (BR) | Designer and manufacturer of standard and bespoke cables and cable assemblies. The company offers services to the industrial and commercial sectors. | 919-535-5830 | NA | Fremont |
| Marymonte Systems (HQ) | Provider of bar coding, wireless, time data collection, and RFID technology. The company offers inventory control and material handling solutions. | 408-927-0606 | NA | San Jose |
| MatrixStream Technologies Inc (HQ) | Provider of end-to-end enterprise, hospitality, embedded, and wireless internet protocol television solutions. | 650-292-4982 | NA | Redwood Shores |
| Meraki LLC (BR) | Provider of branch networking solutions. The company offers services to the education, retail, and healthcare industries. | 415-432-1000 | NA | San Francisco |
| Mobitv Inc (HQ) | Provider of content delivery platforms. The company's products find application in mobile and broadband networks. | 510-450-5000 | NA | Emeryville |
| Modern Systems Research Inc (HQ) | Provider of telecom design and voice & data networking services. The company also focuses on power systems and systems architecture. | 650-940-2000 | NA | Los Altos |
| Moog Animatics (BR) | Provider of motion control devices. The company offers actuators, cables, power supplies, and peripherals. | 650-960-4215 | NA | Mountain View |

| COMPANY NAME | PRODUCT / SERVICE | PHONE | EMP | CITY |
|---|---|---|---|---|
| Nady Systems Inc (HQ) | Designer and manufacturer of wireless microphones, and a full line of audio accessories. The company also focuses on marketing. | 510-652-2411 | NA | Richmond |
| OCAMPO-ESTA Corp (HQ) | Provider of engineering, design, construction management, instrumentation and controls, and project management services. | 707-643-8072 | NA | Vallejo |
| Opal Soft Inc (HQ) | Provider of communications equipment installation and networking. The company's services include application development, network management, and maintenance. | 408-267-2211 | NA | Sunnyvale |
| Orion Labs (HQ) | Developer of wearable communication accessory for instant voice conversations with many people, across any distance. | 415-800-2035 | NA | San Francisco |
| Pacific Crest (HQ) | Provider of communication solutions. The company specializes in the design and manufacture of radio controlled and spotlight data transfer systems. | 408-481-8070 | NA | Sunnyvale |
| Pacific Instruments Inc (HQ) | Manufacturer of computer-automated physical measurement systems. The company specializes in signal conditioning & data acquisition equipment. | 925-827-9010 | NA | Concord |
| Plantronics Inc (HQ) | Provider of audio technology systems that includes headsets, telephones, audio processors, and speakerphones. | 831-426-5858 | 11-50 | Santa Cruz |
| Polycom Inc (HQ) | Manufacturer and seller of teleconferencing equipment and provider of all other communications solutions. | 408-586-3837 | NA | San Jose |
| Pragmatic Communications Systems Inc (HQ) | Designer, developer, and manufacturer of pragmatic products. The company offers amplifiers, security cameras, speakers, and wireless products. | 408-748-1100 | NA | Santa Clara |
| Proxim Wireless (HQ) | Provider of Wi-Fi, point-to-point, and 4G wireless network technologies. The company's ORiNOCO product is used by service providers and enterprises. | 408-383-7600 | NA | San Jose |
| Purple Communications Inc (HQ) | Provider of communication services to deaf or hard of hearing people. The company serves the medical sector and clinics. | 877-885-3172 | 11-50 | Rocklin |
| Qct Llc (HQ) | Provider of computer network services. The company also offers storage, database management, and data backup solutions. | 510-270-6111 | NA | San Jose |
| Raditek Inc (HQ) | Provider of solutions for the wireless and microwave telecom sector. The company offers passive components, active assemblies, and telecom systems. | 408-266-7404 | NA | San Jose |
| Raymar Information Technology Inc (HQ) | Provider of hardware supplies, network infrastructure, virtualization, disaster recovery, and managed services. | 916-783-1951 | 11-50 | Sacramento |
| Redpine Signals Inc (HQ) | Manufacturer of wireless systems. The company offers chipset and system level products for wireless networks. | 408-748-3385 | NA | San Jose |
| Relay2 Inc (HQ) | Provider of cloud Wi-Fi Services platform which allows service providers to monetize value added Wi-Fi services. | 408-380-0031 | NA | Milpitas |
| Responsive Communication Services Inc (HQ) | Provider of communication equipment. The company is involved in troubleshooting and maintenance services. | 925-755-8000 | NA | Antioch |
| Riverbed Technology (HQ) | Provider of WAN optimization, cloud, consolidation, disaster recovery, and network performance management solutions. | 415-247-8800 | NA | San Francisco |
| Ruckus Networks (HQ) | Designer and manufacturer of Wi-Fi products and wireless LAN systems. The company also focuses on the marketing aspects. | 650-265-4200 | NA | Sunnyvale |
| SatPath Systems Inc (HQ) | Provider of networking solutions. The company focuses on voice communication, video and videoconferencing, banking, and other applications. | 510-979-1102 | NA | Fremont |
| Sna Electronics Inc (HQ) | Provider of electronic manufacturing services. The company offers services to OEMs in the networking, medical instruments, and aerospace industries. | 510-656-3903 | NA | Fremont |
| Sonoma Wire Works (HQ) | Provider of loop-based recording and collaboration software for musicians. It's products helps musicians to play, record, and share music. | 650-948-2003 | NA | Mountain View |
| Spidercloud Wireless Inc (HQ) | Provider of wireless solutions for enterprise service delivery. The company offers services to the industrial sector. | 408-235-2900 | NA | Milpitas |
| Spirent Communications Inc (LH) | Provider of performance analysis technology services. The company also offers network equipment and data center solutions. | 408-752-7100 | NA | San Jose |
| Sprintcom (BR) | Provider of wireline and wireless communication services. The company serves consumers, businesses, and government entities. | 925-933-0142 | NA | Walnut Creek |
| SSL Industries Inc (HQ) | Designer and manufacturer of fiber optics and networking products. The company is involved in installation services. | 530-644-0233 | 1-10 | Diamond Springs |
| Stealth Network Communications Inc (HQ) | Provider of voice, data, security, network, and wireless solutions. The company also deals with consulting, design, and maintenance services. | 925-846-7018 | 1-10 | Scotts Valley |
| Sumitomo Electric Device Innovations Usa Inc (LH) | Developer of electronic devices that includes wireless devices, optical data links, and optical devices. | 408-232-9500 | NA | San Jose |
| Swedcom Corp (HQ) | Designer and manufacturer of log periodic antennas, channel banks, filters, and base stations for the telecommunication sector. | 650-620-9420 | NA | Belmont |
| Tactus Technology Inc (HQ) | Developer of tactile user interface for touchscreen devices. The company serves the industrial and technological sectors. | 510-244-3968 | NA | Fremont |
| Terabit Radios Inc (HQ) | Manufacturer of wireless radios. The company offers IP-centric (Gigabit & Multi-Gigabit) LoS wireless IP transport technologies to its clients. | 408-431-6032 | NA | Milpitas |

| COMPANY NAME | PRODUCT / SERVICE | PHONE | EMP | CITY |
| --- | --- | --- | --- | --- |
| Tko Video Communications (HQ) | Provider of video communication services. The company focuses on audio and video conferencing, satellite broadcasting, and telecommunications training. | 408-252-4700 | NA | San Jose |
| Totlcom Inc (BR) | Provider of IP voice and data services and products such as IP systems, VoIP systems, and mail systems for growing companies. | 916-428-5000 | 11-50 | Sacramento |
| Trc Companies Inc (BR) | Provider of scientific and engineering software services. The company offers hydropower licensing, power delivery, and telecommunications engineering services. | 415-434-2600 | NA | San Francisco |
| Ultra-X Inc (HQ) | Provider of personal computer diagnostic solutions for developers, manufacturers, system engineers, integrators, and computer professionals. | 408-261-7090 | NA | Santa Clara |
| USB Promos (HQ) | Provider of USB flash drives, power banks, web keys, video brochures and digital toys and promotional items. | 800-515-3990 | NA | San Francisco |
| Utstarcom Inc (BR) | Manufacturer of IP based, end to end networking, and telecommunications solutions. The company also focuses on integration. | 408-453-4557 | NA | San Jose |
| V2plus Technology Inc (HQ) | Provider of technology solutions. The company offers services for voice, data, and video over local wired and wireless communication networks. | 510-226-6006 | NA | Fremont |
| VeEX Inc (HQ) | Developer of test and measurement solutions for next generation communication equipment and networks. The company serves the industrial sector. | 510-651-0500 | NA | Fremont |
| Venturi Wireless Inc (HQ) | Provider of broadband optimization services. The company mainly caters to mobile and wireless operators. | 408-982-1130 | NA | San Jose |
| Versa Networks Inc (HQ) | Provider of networking solutions. The company specializes in virtualized network functions and services. | 408-385-7660 | NA | Santa Clara |
| Vitec Group Communications LLC (HQ) | Designer, manufacturer, and marketer of voice communications systems for live performance, broadcast, houses of worship, and the commercial markets. | 510-337-6600 | NA | Alameda |
| Vocera Communications Inc (HQ) | Provider of mobile communication solutions. The company provides voice communication, messaging, wireless networking, and technical support. | 408-882-5600 | NA | San Jose |
| Wi2wi Inc (HQ) | Provider of wireless system-in-package, module, and subsystems for embedded applications including Wi-Fi, Bluetooth, and GPS. | 408-416-4200 | NA | San Jose |
| WNI Global Inc (HQ) | Provider of wireless communications solutions for backhaul infrastructure and ethernet network equipment for voice, data, and video applications. | 408-307-2410 | NA | San Jose |
| Z-Plane Inc (HQ) | Provider of electronic packaging solutions for high-speed telecommunications and computing equipment, including routers, servers, and switches. | 415-309-2647 | NA | Palo Alto |
| Zultys Inc (HQ) | Manufacturer of Voice-over-IP equipment. The company mainly caters to small to medium sized businesses. | 408-328-0450 | NA | Sunnyvale |
| Zypex Inc (HQ) | Provider of solutions for product development. The company specializes in industrial communication products, modules, and drivers. | 916-983-9450 | 1-10 | Folsom |

## 70 = Satellite/Microwave Equipment

| COMPANY NAME | PRODUCT / SERVICE | PHONE | EMP | CITY |
| --- | --- | --- | --- | --- |
| Aldetec Inc (HQ) | Manufacturer of microwave amplifier products. The company provides low noise amplifiers, down converters, and octave band amplifiers. | 916-453-3382 | 1-10 | Sacramento |
| Anritsu Co (DH) | Provider of test solutions for telecommunication applications. The company also caters to microwave applications. | 408-778-2000 | NA | Morgan Hill |
| Aviat Networks Inc (HQ) | Provider of microwave networking solutions. The company's products are interactive 3D product models, trunking microwaves, and dual hybrid/packet microwaves. | 408-941-7100 | NA | Milpitas |
| Carlson Wireless Technologies Inc (HQ) | Manufacturer of wireless communication products. The company also provides broadband and related services. | 707-443-0100 | 11-50 | Eureka |
| Chaparral Communications Inc (HQ) | Designer, developer, and marketer of satellite components for the commercial and residential satellite reception systems. | | NA | Menlo Park |
| Codar Ocean Sensors Ltd (HQ) | Designer and manufacturer of radar systems for ocean current and wave monitoring. The company specializes in sea state monitoring. | 408-773-8240 | NA | Mountain View |
| Countis Laboratories (HQ) | Manufacturer of microwave components. The company also offers custom machined components for space, defense, medical and telecommunication industries. | 530-272-8334 | 1-10 | Grass Valley |
| Db Control Corp (HQ) | Provider of high-power solutions for mission-critical applications. The company's services include repairs and contract manufacturing. | 510-656-2325 | NA | Fremont |
| Ditom Microwave Inc (HQ) | Provider of microwave components for both military and commercial applications. The company offers products such as isolators and circulators. | 559-255-7045 | 1-10 | Fresno |
| Finisar Corp (HQ) | Developer of optical communications components and subsystems such as optical modules, active cables and components, passives and optical amplifiers. | 408-548-1000 | NA | Sunnyvale |
| Glowlink Communications Technology Inc (HQ) | Provider of emitters, global monitoring, and uplink power control devices. The company also offers alignment and commissioning services. | 650-237-0220 | NA | Mountain View |
| Harmonic Inc (HQ) | Provider of production and delivery solutions. The company serves the broadcast, media, service providers, and post production markets. | 408-542-2500 | 201-500 | San Jose |
| Krytar Inc (HQ) | Provider of broadband microwave components and test equipment. The company is engaged in troubleshooting and maintenance services. | 408-734-5999 | NA | Sunnyvale |

| COMPANY NAME | PRODUCT / SERVICE | PHONE | EMP | CITY |
|---|---|---|---|---|
| Kumu Networks (HQ) | Developer of wireless technology that cancels self-interference, the unwanted energy that leaks into a radio's receiver while transmitting. | 408-786-9302 | NA | Sunnyvale |
| L-3 Narda Microwave-West (HQ) | Designer and manufacturer of RF microwave components and subsystems. The company products include power dividers, filters, and linearizers. | 916-351-4500 | 1-10 | Folsom |
| Microwave Technology Inc (HQ) | Manufacturer of RF and microwave discrete semiconductor products, GaAs and GaN RF power amplifiers, low noise pHEMT devices, and wireless amplifiers. | 510-651-6700 | NA | Fremont |
| Nextec Microwave & Rf (HQ) | Provider of microwave amplifiers and integrated frequency multipliers. The company serves the aerospace, military, and defense sectors. | 408-727-1189 | NA | Santa Clara |
| Norden Millimeter Inc (HQ) | Developer and manufacturer of amplifier products. The company specializes in millimeter wave amplifier products. | 530-642-9123 | 1-10 | Placerville |
| Omniyig Inc (HQ) | Manufacturer of microwave devices for the defense industry. The company also offers limiters, drivers, and oscillators. | 408-988-0843 | NA | Santa Clara |
| Premier Wireless Solutions (HQ) | Provider of wireless products, design and test /certification services, network data plans, device portals, and device management middleware. | 650-230-1300 | NA | San JoseÃ¿ |
| Quarterwave Corp (HQ) | Manufacturer of high power traveling wave-tube amplifiers, valves, and test equipment. The company deals with installation services. | 707-793-9105 | NA | Rohnert Park |
| Satellite AV LLC (HQ) | Provider of broadcaster support and call center services. The company also deals with repairs, distribution, and sales. | 916-677-0720 | 1-10 | Rocklin |
| Sienna Corporation (BR) | Provider of electronic manufacturing services including design and process engineering, prototyping, and electromechanical assembly services. | 510-440-0200 | NA | Fremont |
| Swedcom Corp (HQ) | Designer and manufacturer of log periodic antennas, channel banks, filters, and base stations for the telecommunication sector. | 650-620-9420 | NA | Belmont |
| Terrasat Communications Inc (HQ) | Manufacturer of RF solutions. The company caters to satellite communication and digital microwave systems. | 408-782-5911 | NA | Morgan Hill |
| Vida Products Inc (HQ) | Supplier of radio frequency and microwave components and subsystems. The company provides magnetically tuned oscillators, filters, and synthesizers. | 707-541-7000 | NA | Rohnert Park |
| Wavesplitter Technologies Inc (HQ) | Manufacturer of passive devices and active optical components for enterprise and residential broadband networks. | 925-596-0414 | NA | Fremont |

## 71 = Telephone/Voice Equipment

| COMPANY NAME | PRODUCT / SERVICE | PHONE | EMP | CITY |
|---|---|---|---|---|
| 8x8 Inc (HQ) | Provider of cloud communications and computing solutions. The company sells IP phones, IP conference, soft, video and analog phones and accessories. | 408-727-1885 | NA | San Jose |
| A A Networks (HQ) | Provider of internet, networks and cabling, computer hardware and software, remote and on-site technical support services. | 650-872-1998 | NA | Burlingame |
| American Power Systems (BR) | Provider of power management products and services. The company's offerings include UPS, DC power, and battery testing. | 209-467-8999 | 11-50 | Stockton |
| Anybots 2.0 Inc (BR) | Provider of robotic device that acts as a personal remote avatar which can be operated remotely thus creating a virtual presence. | 877-594-1836 | NA | San Jose |
| Ashby Communications (HQ) | Provider of voice and data cabling solutions. The company's services include network installation, support, spam blocking, and cloud computing. | 916-960-0701 | 1-10 | Roseville |
| At&T Inc (BR) | Provider of IP based communication solutions. The company offers services in the areas of broadband, Wi-Fi, wireless networks, and mobile phones. | 209-556-9042 | 11-50 | Modesto |
| Blue Danube Systems Inc (BR) | Designer and developer of mobile wireless access solutions that increase network capacity. The company serves the industrial sector. | 650-316-5010 | NA | Santa Clara |
| C&S Telecommunications Inc (HQ) | Supplier of telephone systems and data networks. The company offers installation, training, and other services. | 916-364-8636 | 1-10 | Sacramento |
| Cetecom (BR) | Provider of consulting and testing services. The company focuses on the telecommunications and information technology industries. | 408-586-6200 | NA | Milpitas |
| Cloudtc (HQ) | Designer and developer of voice communications platform. The company specializes in business applications. | 650-238-5203 | NA | Palo Alto |
| Compandent Inc (HQ) | Developer of customized algorithms. The company offers digital sign processing services to telecommunications and semiconductor companies. | 650-241-9231 | NA | Los Altos Hills |
| DOCOMO Innovations Inc (HQ) | Provider of products and services for businesses. The company focuses on business development, network solutions, and mobile network technology. | 650-493-9600 | NA | Palo Alto |
| Elecraft Inc (HQ) | Provider of transceivers and accessories. The company also offers auto antenna tuners, antenna systems, microphones, wattmeter, and other products. | 831-763-4211 | 1-10 | Aptos |
| Embedur Systems Inc (HQ) | Developer of software solutions. The company also offers technical and management services for the embedded market. | 510-353-9111 | NA | Fremont |
| FutureWei Technologies Inc (BR) | Provider of information and communications technology solutions. The company focuses on products such as transport network and data communication. | 408-330-5000 | NA | Santa Clara |
| Headsets Com Inc (HQ) | Provider of office telephone headsets. The company also offers cellphone, computer, and cordless phone headsets. | 415-351-5897 | NA | San Francisco |

| COMPANY NAME | PRODUCT / SERVICE | PHONE | EMP | CITY |
|---|---|---|---|---|
| Ipdialog Inc (HQ) | Developer of hardware and software technology. The company creates SIP stack, user interface, and media stream handling for phones. | 408-830-0800 | NA | Sunnyvale |
| Josephson Engineering Inc (HQ) | Manufacturer of condenser microphones for studio, stage, and field sound pickup, and audio instrumentation. | 831-420-0888 | 1-10 | Santa Cruz |
| Langineers (HQ) | Provider of VoIP phone services, video conferencing, and hosting solutions. The company offers cordless DECT phones and video conferencing phones. | 650-692-2001 | NA | Burlingame |
| Megapath (HQ) | Provider of voice, data, networking, cloud, and security services. The company serves healthcare, finance, restaurant, and retail sectors. | 866-300-0749 | NA | Pleasanton |
| Nokia Corp (BR) | Specializes in mobile network infrastructure structure and services. The company is engaged in technology development. | 408-737-0900 | NA | Sunnyvale |
| Quicknet Technologies Inc (HQ) | Developer of internet telephony technology solutions. The company serves individuals, small businesses and computer users. | 415-864-5225 | NA | San Francisco |
| Shimon Systems Inc (HQ) | Manufacturer of fingerprint authentication solutions. The company's services include research and development. | 650-461-9104 | NA | Los Altos |
| Socket Mobile Inc (HQ) | Developer of wireless handheld and hands-free barcode scanners and other products and serves retail, logistics, automotive, and other sectors. | 510-933-3000 | NA | Newark |
| Sonim Technologies Inc (HQ) | Designer and manufacturer of water-submersible mobile phones. The company's products are used in construction, security guarding, and oil & gas operations. | 650-378-8100 | NA | San Mateo |
| Sprintcom (BR) | Provider of wireline and wireless communication services. The company serves consumers, businesses, and government entities. | 925-933-0142 | NA | Walnut Creek |
| T&D Communications (BR) | Supplier of telephones, and data and paging equipment. The company also specializes in installation. | 510-824-0010 | NA | Fremont |
| Techbiz Inc (RH) | Provider of custom network and server solutions. The company is involved in design and deployment services. | 510-249-6800 | NA | Fremont |

## 72 = Traffic Signals

| COMPANY NAME | PRODUCT / SERVICE | PHONE | EMP | CITY |
|---|---|---|---|---|
| N   Intelight ITS LLC (HQ) | Provider of electrical engineering solutions. The company offers expertise on systems, traffic products and software. | 520-795-8808 | 11-50 | Carlsbad |
| SatPath Systems Inc (HQ) | Provider of networking solutions. The company focuses on voice communication, video and videoconferencing, banking, and other applications. | 510-979-1102 | NA | Fremont |
| Tesco Controls Inc (HQ) | Manufacturer of instrumentation, control systems, and service pedestals for water and traffic sectors. The company offers system integration services. | 916-395-8800 | 11-50 | Sacramento |

## 74 = Aerospace

| COMPANY NAME | PRODUCT / SERVICE | PHONE | EMP | CITY |
|---|---|---|---|---|
| Cutting Edge Machining Inc (HQ) | Provider of contract manufacturing solutions for the medical, aerospace, and telecommunication sectors. | 408-738-8677 | NA | Sunnyvale |
| Ea Machining Inc (HQ) | Provider of CNC turning and milling services. The company offers services to the semiconductor manufacturing equipment industry. | 408-727-4962 | NA | Santa Clara |
| Gooch & Housego (BR) | Manufacturer of precision optical components. The company also focuses on related sub-systems and systems. | 650-300-5744 | NA | Fremont |
| Hammon Plating Corp (HQ) | Supplier of metal plating applications. The company also provides supply chain management solutions. | 650-494-2691 | NA | Palo Alto |
| Mcm Engineering Inc (HQ) | Provider of aircraft ground support systems. The company offers products and services for airports and aircraft manufacturers. | 650-259-9100 | NA | Burlingame |
| Minimatics (HQ) | Provider of precision machining solutions. The company offers CNC milling, manual turning, lapping, and honing services. | 650-969-5630 | NA | Santa Clara |
| Mission Tool And Mfg Co Inc (HQ) | Manufacturer of precision stamped and machined components. The company serves aerospace, automotive, medical, telecom, defense, and commercial sectors. | 510-782-8383 | NA | Hayward |
| Parker Hannifin Corp (DH) | Provider of fuel, air, oil, and coolant filtration systems. The company serves the transportation, marine, and oil and gas industries. | 209-521-7860 | 1-10 | Modesto |
| Sna Electronics Inc (HQ) | Provider of electronic manufacturing services. The company offers services to OEMs in the networking, medical instruments, and aerospace industries. | 510-656-3903 | NA | Fremont |
| Sonic Manufacturing Technologies (HQ) | Provider of contract manufacturing services. The company engages in supply chain, quality assurance, and design and engineering services. | 510-580-8500 | NA | Fremont |
| South Bay Solutions Inc (HQ) | Provider of manufacturing services for the semiconductor, medical, aerospace, solar, and petroleum industries. | 650-843-1800 | NA | Fremont |

## 76 = Electrical Connectors

| COMPANY NAME | PRODUCT / SERVICE | PHONE | EMP | CITY |
|---|---|---|---|---|
| Aras Power Technologies (HQ) | Provider of power delivery solutions. The company offers conventional, alternating current solutions, and custom power supply design services. | 408-935-8877 | NA | Milpitas |
| Assembly Tek (HQ) | Manufacturer of custom cables. The company offers services like design, laminating, JIT programs, and wire preparation. | 831-439-0800 | 1-10 | Scotts Valley |
| Bay Area Circuits Inc (HQ) | Provider of engineering services that include fabrication, layout, and design services to the original equipment manufacturers. | 510-933-9000 | NA | Fremont |
| Hirose Electric Usa Inc (BR) | Manufacturer of connectors. The company provides couplers, dividers, terminators, coaxial switches, and memory cards. | 408-253-9640 | NA | San Jose |

| COMPANY NAME | PRODUCT / SERVICE | PHONE | EMP | CITY |
|---|---|---|---|---|
| Leoco USA Corp (BR) | Manufacturer of interconnects. The company offers wire to board, wire to wire, board to board, and card and telecom connectors. | 510-429-3700 | NA | Fremont |
| Loadstar Sensors Inc (HQ) | Manufacturer of sensors and load cells with wireless output, used in medical device, automotive, aerospace, consumer and other industries. | 510-274-1872 | NA | Fremont |
| Onanon Inc (HQ) | Manufacturer of connector components. The company offers pin connectors, cable assemblies, and machined plastics. | 408-262-8990 | NA | Milpitas |
| Samtec (BR) | Manufacturer of high-speed assemblies, connectors, edge cards, and jumpers. The company serves the industrial sector. | 800-726-8329 | NA | Santa Clara |
| The Best Electrical Company Inc (HQ) | Provider of tenant improvement and maintenance services for the retail, commercial, industrial, and residential communities. | 408-287-2040 | NA | San Jose |
| Westport Machine Works Inc (HQ) | Manufacturer of assembly and balancing equipment. The company's services include fixturing, installation, and technical support. | 916-371-4493 | 1-10 | West Sacramento |

## 7 = Electrical Protection Equipment

| COMPANY NAME | PRODUCT / SERVICE | PHONE | EMP | CITY |
|---|---|---|---|---|
| Compugraphics Usa Inc (BR) | Designer and developer of photomasks for semiconductor, optoelectronic devices, MEMs, nanotechnology, and renewable energy sectors. | 510-249-2600 | NA | Fremont |
| Phasespace Inc (HQ) | Developer of technologies for motion tracking markets. The company focuses on motion capture for industrial research and graphic community. | 510-633-2865 | NA | San Leandro |
| Safeco Electric Supply Inc (HQ) | Distributor of electrical and lighting products. The company offers wires, cables, cords, fasteners, switch boxes, and accessories. | 415-206-0368 | NA | San Francisco |
| Syrma Technology (BR) | Provider of entrepreneurial manufacturing services. The company's products include magnetics, memory, and RFID. | 408-404-0500 | NA | San Jose |
| V5 Systems (HQ) | Provider of outdoor security and computing platforms. The company offers services to the government, military, and law enforcement industries. | 844-604-7350 | NA | Fremont |

## 8 = Electromechanical Devices

| COMPANY NAME | PRODUCT / SERVICE | PHONE | EMP | CITY |
|---|---|---|---|---|
| Acutherm (HQ) | Manufacturer of components for heating and air conditioning systems. The company offers therma-fuser variable air volume diffusers. | 510-785-0510 | NA | Hayward |
| Areias Systems Inc (HQ) | Provider of services to the technology sector. The company focuses on design, engineering, manufacturing, and prototyping. | 831-440-9800 | 1-10 | Scotts Valley |
| Asepco Corp (HQ) | Manufacturer of valves and magnetic mixers. The company also offers diaphragms, connnectors, and actuators. | 650-691-9500 | NA | Milpitas |
| Connekt Llc (HQ) | Developer and manufacturer of mechanical engineering design solutions. The company's services include CAD, reverse engineering, and sheet metal design. | 530-604-5821 | 1-10 | Grass Valley |
| Creative Labs Inc (RH) | Provider of digital entertainment products such as sound blaster, gaming headsets, speakers, headphones, MP3 players, software, and webcams. | | NA | Milpitas |
| Dicon Fiberoptics Inc (HQ) | Supplier of optical components, integrated modules, and test equipment for the fiber optics industry. | 510-620-5000 | NA | Richmond |
| Dynaweb Inc (HQ) | Manufacturer and marketer of web handling and tension control systems. The company's product finds use in packaging, printing, and textile needs. | 925-373-9013 | 1-10 | Sonora |
| Electro Diagnostic Imaging Inc (HQ) | Developer and manufacturer of products for electrophysiology. The company's services include research, sales, and marketing. | 650-631-0120 | NA | Redwood City |
| Fujitsu Components America Inc (HQ) | Provider of computing products and services. The company's products include servers, storage, scanners, and displays. | 408-745-4900 | NA | San Jose |
| Lucero Cables Inc (HQ) | Manufacturer of electronic products. The company's products include cables, harnesses, and electromechanical sub assemblies. | 408-298-6001 | NA | San Jose |
| Martin Sprocket & Gear Inc (BR) | Manufacturer of industrial hand tools, conveyor pulleys, and other products. The company offers power transmission and material handling products. | 916-441-7172 | 11-50 | Sacramento |
| Nortra Cables Inc (HQ) | Provider of discrete and flat mechanical assembly cables. The company offers design, prototyping, and manufacturing services. | 408-942-1106 | NA | Milpitas |
| Resq Manufacturing (HQ) | Provider of contract manufacturing services. The company offers cable assembly and electro-mechanical services. | 916-638-6786 | 1-10 | Rancho Cordova |
| Ross Engineering Corporation (HQ) | Designer and manufacturer of high voltage electronic and electro-mechanical devices like relays, probes, voltmeters, switches, and breakers. | 408-377-4621 | NA | Campbell |
| Shin-Etsu Polymer America Inc (HQ) | Manufacturer of electro-mechanical components such as custom made keypads and inter-connectors, decorative films, and switch devices. | 510-623-1881 | NA | Newark |
| Sna Electronics Inc (HQ) | Provider of electronic manufacturing services. The company offers services to OEMs in the networking, medical instruments, and aerospace industries. | 510-656-3903 | NA | Fremont |
| Solutions Cubed Llc (HQ) | Provider of engineering solutions. The company is involved in early stage electronic prototyping to full production runs. | 530-891-8045 | 1-10 | Chico |
| Sonic Manufacturing Technologies (HQ) | Provider of contract manufacturing services. The company engages in supply chain, quality assurance, and design and engineering services. | 510-580-8500 | NA | Fremont |
| Stangenes Industries Inc (HQ) | Manufacturer of isolation transformers, current monitors, charging inductors, and magnetic components. | 650-493-0814 | NA | Palo Alto |
| TOA Electronics Inc (DH) | Developer and manufacturer of audio and security products. The company is engaged in design, delivery, and installation services. | 650-452-1200 | 51-200 | S San Francisco |

| COMPANY NAME | PRODUCT / SERVICE | PHONE | EMP | CITY |
|---|---|---|---|---|
| Vulcan Inc (HQ) | Focuses on the manufacture and fabrication of aluminum coiled sheets, aluminum sign blanks, and finished traffic control signs. | 510-786-9181 | NA | Hayward |
| Westport Machine Works Inc (HQ) | Manufacturer of assembly and balancing equipment. The company's services include fixturing, installation, and technical support. | 916-371-4493 | 1-10 | West Sacramento |

## 79 = Electronic Enclosures/Packaging/Shielding

| COMPANY NAME | PRODUCT / SERVICE | PHONE | EMP | CITY |
|---|---|---|---|---|
| Allvia Inc (HQ) | Provider of silicon interposer and through-silicon via foundry services to the semiconductor and optoelectronics industries. | 408-212-3200 | NA | Sunnyvale |
| Bay Area Circuits Inc (HQ) | Provider of engineering services that include fabrication, layout, and design services to the original equipment manufacturers. | 510-933-9000 | NA | Fremont |
| Casetronic Engineering Group (HQ) | Designer and manufacturer of electronic enclosures, DC converters, AC adapters, flash readers, and IPC rack mount solutions. | 408-262-8588 | NA | Milpitas |
| Dawn VME Products (HQ) | Designer and manufacturer of enclosures, backplanes, chassis and card cage. The company also offers design services and power supplies. | 510-657-4444 | NA | Fremont |
| Dualsonic Inc (HQ) | Provider of technology solutions for electronic and precision CNC machining. The company designs and manufactures PCMCIA cards and RFID housings. | 408-457-8585 | NA | Santa Clara |
| Id Technology Llc (BR) | Designer and manufacturer of custom identification systems. The company offers labeling, coding, and marketing equipment services. | 559-436-8401 | 1-10 | Fresno |
| Jsr Micro Inc (HQ) | Provider of semiconductor, life sciences, and energy material solutions. The company specializes in lithography materials and CMP consumables. | 408-543-8800 | NA | Sunnyvale |
| Milner's Anodizing (HQ) | Provider of metal finishing solutions. The company's services include anodizing, anodizing, and passivation. | 707-584-1188 | NA | Santa Rosa |
| Packaging Aids Corp (HQ) | Manufacturer of heat sealing and packaging equipment such as tube sealers, shrink wrap systems, and skin packaging products. | 415-454-4868 | NA | San Rafael |
| Plasmaterials Inc (HQ) | Provider of materials for thin film applications. The company offers base metal alloys, backing plates, and semiconductor alloys. | 925-447-4030 | NA | Livermore |
| Syrma Technology (BR) | Provider of entrepreneurial manufacturing services. The company's products include magnetics, memory, and RFID. | 408-404-0500 | NA | San Jose |
| Tesco Controls Inc (HQ) | Manufacturer of instrumentation, control systems, and service pedestals for water and traffic sectors. The company offers system integration services. | 916-395-8800 | 11-50 | Sacramento |
| Xperi Corp (HQ) | Provider of miniaturization technology services for electronic devices. The company offers micro-electronics, and imaging and optics services. | 408-321-6000 | NA | San Jose |

## 80 = Machine Shop/Precision Fabricated Components

| COMPANY NAME | PRODUCT / SERVICE | PHONE | EMP | CITY |
|---|---|---|---|---|
| A&D Precision Inc (HQ) | Provider of contract manufacturing, program management, electro-mechanical assembly, and precision machining services. | 510-657-6781 | NA | Fremont |
| A-1 Jay's Machining Inc (HQ) | Provider of machining, product assembly, and finishing services. The company is engaged in vertical milling, laser Micro-machining and waterjet cutting. | 408-262-1845 | NA | San Jose |
| A-Laser (HQ) | Provider of precision parts manufacturing services. The company specializes in laser cutting and caters to a wide range of industries. | 408-954-8582 | NA | Milpitas |
| Accu-Swiss Inc (HQ) | Manufacturer of precision CNC and screw machined products. The company's services include engineering, milling, and threading. | 209-847-1016 | 1-10 | Oakdale |
| Aci Alloys Inc (HQ) | Manufacturer of purity alloys for thin film applications. The company offers evaporation and thin film materials. | 408-259-7337 | NA | San Jose |
| Acm Machining Inc (HQ) | Manufacturer of machined products for pressure control products. The company serves oil, gas, and automotive industries. | 916-852-8600 | 11-50 | Rancho Cordova |
| Acrylic Art (HQ) | Provider of fabrication and machining services. The company focuses on painting, product finishing, anodizing, and vapor polishing. | 510-654-0953 | NA | Emeryville |
| Acu Spec Inc (HQ) | Manufacturer of engineering products. The company offers horizontal & vertical machining, CNC turning, CAD software, and CMM inspection services. | 408-748-8600 | NA | Santa Clara |
| Adem Llc (HQ) | Designer and manufacturer of special and automated fixtures for assembly lines, and also provides turnkey production solutions. | 408-727-8955 | NA | Santa Clara |
| Advance Carbon Products Inc (HQ) | Manufacturer of carbon. The company offers equipments such as CNC lathes, grinders, lappers, and diamond saws. | 510-293-5930 | NA | Hayward |
| Advanced Fabrication Technology (HQ) | Provider of metal fabricating services for the electronics, manufacturing, and semiconductor industries. | 510-489-6218 | NA | Hayward |
| Aimer Corp (HQ) | Provider of thermal management products. The company also offers connectors, PCB boards, cables, and mechanical parts. | 408-260-8588 | NA | Santa Clara |
| Airpoint Precision Inc (HQ) | Provider of precision machining services. The company serves the industrial needs of the community in a cost efficient and timely manner. | 530-622-0510 | 1-10 | Diamond Springs |
| All Fab Precision Sheetmetal Inc (HQ) | Provider of contract manufacturing services for metal formed products. The company is involved in laser cutting, deburring, bending, and welding activities. | 408-279-1099 | NA | San Jose |
| Alloy Metal Products (HQ) | Provider of precision CNC machining, tumbling, annealing, cutting, and packaging services. The company serves aerospace and medical device fields. | 925-371-1234 | NA | Livermore |

| COMPANY NAME | PRODUCT / SERVICE | PHONE | EMP | CITY |
|---|---|---|---|---|
| Alta Design & Manufacturing Inc (HQ) | Manufacturer of precision-machined components. The company is engaged in production manufacturing, prototype services, and electromechanical assembly. | 408-450-5394 | NA | San Jose |
| Altamont Manufacturing Inc (HQ) | Provider of precision CNC machining, welding, and fabrication services. The company offers semiconductor, aerospace, medical, and robotics components. | 925-371-5401 | NA | Livermore |
| Alterflex Corporation (HQ) | Designer and manufacturer of printed circuit boards. The company also provides engineering support services. | 408-441-8688 | NA | San Jose |
| Alumawall Inc (HQ) | Manufacturer of metal panel and fabricator and erector of aluminum and metal composite panel systems. | 408-292-6353 | NA | San Jose |
| American Die & Rollforming Inc (HQ) | Manufacturer of metal roofing, siding, and structural products. The company also specializes in canopies and decking. | 916-652-7667 | 1-10 | Loomis |
| American Portable Welding (HQ) | Provider of welding, fabrication, and engineering services. The company offers services to the industrial sector. | 510-887-4279 | NA | Hayward |
| American Precision Gear Company Inc (HQ) | Distributor of precision gears. The company offers spur and ring gears, gear racks, miniature and helical gears, and segmented gears. | | NA | Foster City |
| American Precision Spring Corp (HQ) | Designer of electronic circuits. The company specializes in the design and fabrication of printed circuit boards. | 408-986-1020 | NA | Santa Clara |
| American Prototype And Production Inc (HQ) | Manufacturer of industrial laser cutting machines. The company focuses on industries such as CNC milling, CNC turning, and laser engraving. | 650-595-4994 | NA | San Carlos |
| Applied Fusion Inc (HQ) | Provider of precision metal fabrication, electron beam and laser welding, and CNC machining services. | 510-351-8314 | NA | San Leandro |
| Armorstruxx Llc (HQ) | Provider of ballistic and blast protection solutions. The company offers armor systems design and integration services. | 209-365-9400 | 1-10 | Lodi |
| Austin Precision Inc (HQ) | Provider of precision machined parts. The company offers parts made from aluminum, plastics, stainless steel, and other metals. | 925-449-1049 | NA | Livermore |
| Avocet Sales & Marketing Inc (HQ) | Provider of custom engineered mechanical component parts and sub assemblies. The company offers contract manufacturing and automation services. | 510-891-0093 | NA | Oakland |
| B&H Engineering (HQ) | Supplier of assemblies, process kits, and individual parts. The company caters to the semiconductor equipment industry. | 650-594-2861 | NA | San Carlos |
| B&Z Manufacturing Company Inc (HQ) | Provider of multi-axis milling and turning services. The company offers ultra precision components for electronic, aerospace, and computer fields. | 408-943-1117 | NA | San Jose |
| B-Metal Fabrication (HQ) | Provider of metal fabrication services. The company offers services for the commercial, residential, retail, and bio pharmaceutical industries. | 650-615-7705 | NA | S San Francisco |
| Babbitt Bearing Company Inc (HQ) | Provider of repair and manufacturing services. The company deals in hard chrome plating, non-destructive testing, and machinery repair. | 408-298-1101 | NA | San Jose |
| Bay Standard Manufacturing Inc (HQ) | Manufacturer of machinery components. The company offers thread, foundation bolts, u-bolts, and specialty fasteners. | 800-228-8640 | NA | Brentwood |
| BayFab Metals Inc (HQ) | Manufacturer of custom and production parts. The company's products include Trumpf TruLaser, Trumpf Laser Cutter, and AMADA. | 510-568-8950 | NA | San Leandro |
| Benicia Fabrication & Machine Inc (HQ) | Manufacturer of industrial equipment and provider of repair and maintenance services. The company develops pressure vessels and heat exchangers. | 707-745-8111 | NA | Benicia |
| BT Laser & Manufacturing Inc (HQ) | Provider of custom design, laser and water jet cutting, fabrication, and welding services for solar, semiconductor, and communication sectors. | 408-566-0135 | NA | Santa Clara |
| C&C Machining Inc (HQ) | Provider of machining services. The company specializes in magnetic alloys, expansion alloys, and shielding alloys. | 510-876-8139 | NA | Hayward |
| Calchemist (HQ) | Provider of contract research services. The company specializes in chemical, material science and laboratory equipment testing. | 650-551-1495 | NA | San Francisco |
| Callouette Fabricators Inc (HQ) | Developer of machining components for automotive, process control, biotech, plasma, instrumentation, and aviation industries. | 707-746-0962 | NA | Benicia |
| Calmax Technology Inc (HQ) | Provider of precision machined components and electro-mechanical assemblies. The company serves semi-conductor and medical industries. | 408-748-8660 | NA | Santa Clara |
| Capital Sheet Metal (HQ) | Manufacturer of custom countertops. The company deals with shearing, welding, laser cutting, and polishing services. | 916-443-3761 | 1-10 | Sacramento |
| CI Hann Industries Inc (HQ) | Provider of contract manufacturing services including CNC machining, welding, assembly and testing, and conditioning. | 408-293-4800 | NA | San Jose |
| Clover Machine & Manufacturing (HQ) | Provider of contract manufacturing and machining services. The company supplies tooling and fixtures to its customers. | 408-727-3380 | NA | Santa Clara |
| Coast Metal Cutting (HQ) | Provider of machining and metal cutting services. The company's services include production, turning, drilling, and tapping. | 650-369-9837 | NA | Redwood City |
| Columbia Machine Works (HQ) | Provider of coining equipment and contracting services. The company offers coining presses, rimming machines, and consumable tooling. | 510-568-0808 | NA | Oakland |
| Comptech Usa (HQ) | Manufacturer and fabricator of race engines. The company also offers R&D and road racing track maintenance services. | 916-338-3434 | 1-10 | Sacramento |
| Concept Models Inc (HQ) | Provider of prototyping devices. The company specializes in surgical devices, CNC programming, tap burning, and rubber molding. | 925-606-6743 | NA | Livermore |

| COMPANY NAME | PRODUCT / SERVICE | PHONE | EMP | CITY |
|---|---|---|---|---|
| Concord Sheet Metal (HQ) | Provider of architectural metal products. The company focuses on fasteners, copper gutters, and decorative chimney tops. | 800-799-1900 | NA | Pittsburg |
| Custom Gear & Machine (HQ) | Manufacturer of custom gears. The company also offers overhaul services for gearboxes and caters to industries like food and steel processing. | 925-455-9985 | NA | Livermore |
| Custom Micro Machining Inc (HQ) | Manufacturer of precision housing carriers and microwave assemblies. The company is involved in design, installation, and delivery services. | 510-651-9434 | NA | Fremont |
| Custom Product Development Co (HQ) | Developer and manufacturer of mechanical components and turn-key assembly solutions. The company specializes in developing customized products. | 925-960-0577 | NA | Livermore |
| Cutting Edge Machining Inc (HQ) | Provider of contract manufacturing solutions for the medical, aerospace, and telecommunication sectors. | 408-738-8677 | NA | Sunnyvale |
| Cvm Inc (HQ) | Provider of custom machine tools. The company also offers electrical fabrication, machining, and robotic services. | 925-847-8808 | NA | Pleasanton |
| D A M Good Engineering & Manufacturing Inc (HQ) | Manufacturer of parts for microwave, telecom, and industrial sectors. The company offers gaming devices, model engine parts, and other products. | 408-224-6494 | NA | San Jose |
| Danco Machine (HQ) | Developer of machined components and assemblies. The company is involved in EDM, welding, sheet metal, and precision grinding. | 408-988-5235 | NA | Santa Clara |
| Datum Technologies Inc (HQ) | Manufacturer of precision machining services. The company serves customers in the aerospace, medical device, and energy industries. | 707-738-3914 | NA | Santa Rosa |
| Dc Precision Machining (HQ) | Manufacturer of engineered plastics and metals for many industries. The company offers CNC precision machining and turn-key assembly services. | 408-928-2510 | NA | Morgan Hill |
| Delong Manufacturing Co (HQ) | Provider of machining services. The company focuses on prototype development, production, engineering design, and kitting and assembly. | 408-727-3348 | NA | Santa Clara |
| Delta Machine (HQ) | Provider of precision machine components and custom parts. The company specializes in CNC milling, CNC turning, and turn key mechanical assemblies. | 408-955-9140 | NA | San Jose |
| Dentoni's (HQ) | Provider of services for trucks and trailers. The company specializes in welding, machining, ornamental iron, and springs. | 209-464-4930 | 11-50 | Stockton |
| Dependable Precision Manufacturing Inc (HQ) | Provider of precision sheet metal fabrication services. The company serves the government and high tech sectors. | 209-369-1055 | 1-10 | Lodi |
| Deweyl Tool Inc (HQ) | Manufacturer of bonding, large and double flat wire, and small wire bonding wedges. The company's products are used in ultrasonic applications. | 707-765-5779 | NA | Petaluma |
| Diablo Precision Inc (HQ) | Manufacturer of metal and plastic parts. The company also provides machining, milling, turning, and contract inspection services. | 831-634-0136 | 1-10 | Hollister |
| Diamond Tool & Die Inc (HQ) | Provider of general machine services for the high tech industry. The company serves the aerospace, construction, and food processing industries. | 510-534-7050 | NA | Oakland |
| Dinucci Corp (HQ) | Provider of computerized manufacturing and prototyping services. The company offers services to the business sector. | 925-798-3946 | NA | Concord |
| Dkw Precision Machining Inc (HQ) | Manufacturer of precision machined parts and components. The company offers CNC miling and turning, prototype, and production services. | 209-456-5709 | 1-10 | Manteca |
| Donal Machine Inc (HQ) | Provider of precision machining and sheet metal services. The company focuses on CNC machining, precision laser cutting, and welding & fabrication. | 707-763-6625 | NA | Petaluma |
| Dynatex International (HQ) | Manufacturer of semiconductor, dicing equipment, and supplies. The company also offers dicing and wafer bonding services. | 707-542-4227 | NA | Santa Rosa |
| E Enterprise Tech (HQ) | Manufacturer of machined components. The company offers CNC machining, sheetmetal, cabling, electrical, and mechanical assembly services. | 408-844-8176 | NA | San Jose |
| E&F Plastics Inc (HQ) | Provider of plastic fabricated products. The company offers bonded PVC, vapor polished polycarbonates, and vacuum formed Kydex. | 408-226-6672 | NA | San Jose |
| E-Fab Inc (HQ) | Provider of precision manufacturing and fabrication solutions. The company offers mesh screens, etched antennas, encoder strips, and PCB jumpers. | 408-727-5218 | NA | Santa Clara |
| E-M Manufacturing Inc (HQ) | Provider of prototyping and short run production machining services. The company is engaged in sheet metal design. | 209-825-1800 | 1-10 | Manteca |
| Ea Machining Inc (HQ) | Provider of CNC turning and milling services. The company offers services to the semiconductor manufacturing equipment industry. | 408-727-4962 | NA | Santa Clara |
| East Bay Machine (HQ) | Provider of machining services including welding and fabrication. The company offers services to the business sector. | 925-689-2421 | NA | Concord |
| Eclipse Metal Fabrication (HQ) | Provider of metal fabrication services. The company provides CNC machining, laser, and waterjet cutting services in the San Francisco Bay area. | 650-298-8731 | NA | Redwood City |
| Edmar Engineering Inc (HQ) | Manufacturer of precision machined products. The company's products include CNC mills and lathes, inspection equipment, and lathe and mill software. | 707-693-0390 | NA | Dixon |
| Electro Coatings Of California (BR) | Provider of electroless nickel coating services. The company also offers industrial hard chrome and nickel metal finishing services. | 510-849-4075 | NA | Berkeley |

| COMPANY NAME | PRODUCT / SERVICE | PHONE | EMP | CITY |
|---|---|---|---|---|
| Electrochem Solutions Inc (HQ) | Provider of plating, anodizing, parts cleaning services. The company caters to high technology industries. | 510-476-1840 | NA | Union City |
| Electronic Carbide Inc (HQ) | Provider of CNC precision machining, fabrication, and wire EDM services. The company serves the industrial sector. | 530-272-6154 | 1-10 | Grass Valley |
| Elite E/M Inc (HQ) | Provider of precision machining services. The company offers prototyping, tooling, shearing, and cutting services. | 408-988-3505 | NA | Santa Clara |
| Emkay Manufacturing Inc (HQ) | Provider of precision milling and turning services. The company serves the medical, electrical, aerospace, and defense sectors. | 650-365-3010 | NA | Redwood City |
| Emtec Engineering (HQ) | Provider of precision machining and precision sheet metal fabrication services to the computer, telecommunication, and medical industries. | 408-779-5800 | NA | Morgan Hill |
| Encore Industries Inc (HQ) | Provider of technical services to engineering and procurement. The company's domain includes medical and science, consumer products, and structural. | 408-416-0501 | NA | San Jose |
| Expedite Precision Works Inc (HQ) | Manufacturer of diverse products involving micro & custom machining and fabrication of metal & plastic. The company also manufactures vessels and tanks. | 408-573-9600 | NA | San Jose |
| Fast Trak Fabrication LP (HQ) | Provider of metal fabrication services. The company's services include laser cutting, machining, forming, and welding. | 559-222-4450 | 1-10 | Fresno |
| Ferrotec Usa Corp (RH) | Manufacturer and distributor of quartz solutions and fluid sealants. The company serves business organizations and enterprises. | 408-964-7700 | NA | Santa Clara |
| Fm Industries Inc (HQ) | Designer and manufacturer of precision machined components. The company also offers electro mechanical assemblies. | 510-668-1900 | NA | Fremont |
| Form & Fusion Mfg Inc (HQ) | Provider of metal fabrication services. The company mainly focuses on powder coating, metal fabrication, and assembly & packaging. | 916-638-8576 | 1-10 | Rancho Cordova |
| Gateway Precision Inc (HQ) | Manufacturer of precision-machined components and assemblies for image equipment manufacturers, telecom, food processing, and semiconductor sectors. | 408-855-8849 | NA | Santa Clara |
| Gentec Manufacturing Inc (HQ) | Provider of machining services. The company also offers measuring, testing, turning, and engineering services. | 408-432-6220 | NA | San Jose |
| Geo M Martin Co (HQ) | Developer of equipment for corrugated container industry. The company offers training, field support, and technical services. | 510-652-2200 | NA | Emeryville |
| Gerlinger Steel & Supply Co (HQ) | Provider of metal products and industrial services. The company offers metalworking machinery and supplies. | 530-243-1053 | 1-10 | Redding |
| Glaser & Associates Inc (HQ) | Manufacturer and distributor of fastening solutions. The company offers bolts, screws, rods & studs, and anchors. | 925-228-3200 | NA | Martinez |
| Gonsel'S Machine Shop (HQ) | Provider of CNC and millwork, inspection, fabrication, and re-machining services. The company serves the food and beverage industry. | 510-569-8086 | NA | Oakland |
| Grabber Construction Products Inc (BR) | Manufacturer of fasteners and machine tools. The company also specializes in distribution and other services. | 800-869-1375 | NA | Concord |
| Graham Machining & Design (HQ) | Provider of designing and fabrication services. The company develops inspection tools, fasteners, band saws, drill presses, and pedestal grinders. | 510-848-2395 | NA | Berkeley |
| Greenwood Machine & Fabrication Inc (HQ) | Provider of repair and fabrication services for commercial and industrial equipment. The company's customers include private companies and military contractors. | 209-538-2277 | 1-10 | Ceres |
| Group Manufacturing Services Inc (HQ) | Manufacturer of precision sheet metal fabrication, precision machining, and design support services. | 408-436-1040 | NA | San Jose |
| H & M Precision Machining (HQ) | Provider of precision manufacturing solutions. The company offers screw machines, CNC turning, CNC milling, and sawing services. | 408-982-9184 | NA | Santa Clara |
| H P Machine & Engineering Inc (HQ) | Provider of job shop, prototype machining, CNC, and wire EDM services. The company offers services to the industrial sector. | 408-383-9075 | NA | San Jose |
| Haig Precision Manufacturing Corp (HQ) | Manufacturer of precision parts and assemblies. The company focuses on sheet metal, CNC milling and turning, stamping, welding, and power coating. | 408-378-4920 | NA | San Jose |
| Hayes Manufacturing Services Inc (HQ) | Provider of machining, fabrication, tooling, prototyping, reverse engineering, and design assistance services. | 408-730-5035 | NA | Sunnyvale |
| Hayward Quartz Technology Inc (HQ) | Manufacturer of machined and fabricated parts. The company exclusively caters to the semiconductor industry. | 510-657-9605 | NA | Fremont |
| Hellwig Products Company Inc (HQ) | Provider of sway control and load control products for trucks and SUV's. The company also offers fleet solution services. | 559-734-7451 | 1-10 | Visalia |
| Hof Machining Inc (HQ) | Provider of exotic geometry and prototype machining services. The company's offerings include machine shop services and machining materials. | 408-526-1155 | NA | San Jose |
| Hogan Manufacturing Inc (HQ) | Provider of steel manufacturing fabrication services. The company's products include plate weldments, alloy specialties, and waste separation equipment. | 209-838-2400 | 1-10 | Escalon |
| Horn Machine Tools Inc (HQ) | Supplier of CNC and semi-automatic tube benders. The company offers new tube benders, rebuilt tube benders, and bender rebuilding and retro-fitting. | 559-431-4131 | 1-10 | Madera |
| Howard Wire Cloth Co (HQ) | Provider of screening & wire fabrication products. The company offers wire cloth, stainless steel netting, security screening, and perforated metals. | 510-887-8787 | NA | Hayward |

| COMPANY NAME | PRODUCT / SERVICE | PHONE | EMP | CITY |
|---|---|---|---|---|
| Howlett Machine (HQ) | Manufacturer of machine works and custom made tools. The company also offers custom test fixtures and test machines. | 510-845-2759 | NA | Berkeley |
| Hs&S Inc (HQ) | Designer and manufacturer of machine tool and custom machine manufacturing. The company offers services like CNC conversion and contract inspection. | 408-980-8909 | NA | Santa Clara |
| Ht Precision Inc (HQ) | Provider of prototype, research, and production parts and equipment. The company serves electronics, medical, wireless, and semi-conductor industries. | 408-719-1826 | NA | San Jose |
| Hydratight (BR) | Manufacturer of flanges and mechanical connectors. The company focuses on the subsea, nuclear, wind, and mining industries. | 925-691-4914 | NA | Concord |
| IDEX Health & Science LLC (BR) | Provider of precision equipment for the health care industry. The company also offers detectors, fittings, and filters. | 707-588-2000 | NA | Rohnert Park |
| Ilm Tool Inc (HQ) | Provider of engineering and CNC machining services. The company offers precision machining services for the biotech and semiconductor industries. | 510-782-0100 | NA | Hayward |
| Imt Precision Inc (HQ) | Provider of sheet metal machining, fabrication, inspection and assembly services to semiconductor, aerospace, biotech, and education sectors. | 510-324-8926 | NA | Hayward |
| Inland Metal Technologies (HQ) | Provider of sheet metal fabrication, manufacturing, powder coating, silk-screening, and laser cutting services. | 510-785-8555 | NA | Hayward |
| Inta Technologies (HQ) | Manufacturer of components used in instruments for environmental analysis. The company also offers ceramic-to-metal assemblies connectors. | 408-748-9955 | NA | Santa Clara |
| Integrated Tooling Inc (HQ) | Developer and manufacturer of tools, dies, and molds. The company specializes in fabricating small intricate parts for machines. | 408-934-3862 | NA | Milpitas |
| International Manufacturing (HQ) | Manufacturer of precision components for use in semiconductor equipment, medical devices, aerospace vehicles, and defense systems. | 510-783-8872 | NA | Hayward |
| Intool (HQ) | Manufacturer and designer of the machine components. The company is involved in machining, fabricating, casting and assembling services. | 408-727-7575 | NA | Santa Clara |
| Inverse Solutions Inc (HQ) | Manufacturer of custom-made machines for commercial and government markets. The company serves semiconductor, medical devices, and aerospace fields. | 925) 931-9500 | NA | Pleasanton |
| Italix Company Inc (HQ) | Provider of chemical machining, etching, and metal finishing services. The company serves the aerospace, defense, and transportation markets. | 408-988-2487 | NA | Morgan Hill |
| J C Sales & MFG Co (HQ) | Manufacturer of CNC machining metal and plastic parts. The company offers products for the semiconductor, electronics, military, aircraft, and other industries. | 800-527-6347 | 1-10 | Lone |
| J&E Precision Machining Inc (HQ) | Manufacturer of electromechanical turnkey fixtures, prototype tooling, and EDM services. The company serves computer, medical, and other sectors. | 408-281-1195 | NA | San Jose |
| J&M Manufacturing Inc (HQ) | Provider of TIG, MIG and spot welding, silk-screening, contract manufacturing, and assembly services. | 707-795-8223 | NA | Cotati |
| Jarvis Manufacturing (HQ) | Manufacturer of precision machinery. The company offers CNC turning and milling, programming, and assembly and kitting services. | 408-226-2600 | NA | San Jose |
| Jb Precision Inc (HQ) | Manufacturer of precision machining services. The company's services also include inspection, production control, and management. | 408-866-1755 | NA | Campbell |
| Jp Machine Manufacturing (HQ) | Manufacturer of machine parts. The company offers medical, semiconductor capital equipment, robotics, lasers, fiber optics, and test equipment. | 408-988-1400 | NA | Santa Clara |
| Jwp Manufacturing (HQ) | Provider of manufacturing solutions. The company offers CNC machining, engineering, and other services. | 408-970-0641 | NA | Santa Clara |
| Kal Machining Inc (HQ) | Manufacturer of medical, aeronautic, and military machine parts. The company offers CNC turning and milling services for plastic and metal parts. | 408-782-8989 | NA | Morgan Hill |
| Kalman Manufacturing (HQ) | Provider of manufacturing and machining services. The company offers welding, shearing, cutting, and finishing services. | 408-776-7664 | NA | Morgan Hill |
| Kamet Manufacturing Solutions (HQ) | Provider of manufacturing solutions. The company offers engineering support, project management, and supply chain management solutions. | 408-522-8000 | NA | Sunnyvale |
| Kennerley-Spratling Inc (HQ) | Manufacturer of custom plastic injection and compression moldings. The company is involved in design, installation, and delivery services. | 510-351-8230 | NA | San Leandro |
| King Precision Inc (HQ) | Manufacturer and supplier of precision components. The company also offers semiconductor heater and magnet refurbish and repair services. | 831-426-2704 | 1-10 | Scotts Valley |
| Kodiak Precision Inc (HQ) | Manufacturer of precision machine products. The company's products include milling and turning machines, fabricated parts, and machine support equipment. | 510-234-4165 | NA | Richmond |
| KOR-IT Inc (HQ) | Manufacturer of diamond tools and core drill machines. The company caters to the concrete cutting industry. | 916-372-6400 | 1-10 | Sacramento |
| Krobach Manufacturing Corp (HQ) | Provider of precision machine shop and general machining services. The company focuses on turning, milling, and grinding. | 510-783-9480 | NA | Hayward |
| L&T Precision Engineering Inc (HQ) | Provider of fabrication, precision engineering assistance, and assembly services. The company serves semiconductor, medical, and other sectors. | 408-441-1890 | NA | San Jose |

| COMPANY NAME | PRODUCT / SERVICE | PHONE | EMP | CITY |
|---|---|---|---|---|
| Lamar Tool & Die (HQ) | Manufacturer of die casting solutions. The company's offerings include machining and secondary operations. | 209-545-5525 | 1-10 | Modesto |
| Lamek Industrial Corp (HQ) | Manufacturer of machined parts for the semiconductor, medical, and aeronautic sectors. The company focuses on bead blasting, tumbling and packaging. | 408-734-3363 | NA | Sunnyvale |
| Langill's General Machine Inc (HQ) | Manufacturer of precision machined components with a full array of state-of-the-art machines, operated by a highly trained workforce. | 916-452-0167 | 1-10 | Sacramento |
| Larkin Precision Machining Inc (HQ) | Manufacturer of machined parts of precision CNC milling and turning devices specializing in assemblies, fixtures, flanges, grinding, and sawing. | 831-438-2700 | 1-10 | Scotts Valley |
| Lawson Mechanical Contractors (HQ) | Provider of mechanical construction services. The company offers plumbing, HVAC, industrial, and process piping services. | 916-381-5000 | 11-50 | Sacramento |
| Lazar Machining Inc (HQ) | Provider of precision machining services. The company serves the semiconductor, aerospace, and food processing industries. | 650-591-6415 | NA | San Carlos |
| Lazestar Inc (HQ) | Provider of laser sealing, packing, precision fabrication, and welding services. The company serves the aerospace and commercial industries. | 925-443-5293 | NA | Livermore |
| Lemo Usa Inc (HQ) | Designer and manufacturer of precision custom connectors, cable assemblies, and related accessories. The company serves the industrial sector. | 707-578-8811 | NA | Rohnert Park |
| Lenz Precision Technology Inc (HQ) | Manufacturer of precision machined components and sub assemblies. The company also focuses on the sales aspects. | 650-966-1784 | NA | Mountain View |
| Lfw Manufacturing (HQ) | Manufacturer of gearboxes and gear sets. The company caters to a wide range of industrial applications. | 209-465-0444 | 1-10 | Stockton |
| Lloyd W Aubry Company Inc (HQ) | Provider of mechanical contracting services specializing in fabrication, installation, relocation, and maintenance of processing plant equipment. | 510-732-9038 | NA | Hayward |
| Lodi Iron Works Inc (HQ) | Provider of machine shop services. The company offers in-house pattern making, tooling, machining, and iron casting services. | 209-368-5395 | 1-10 | Lodi |
| Lor-Van Manufacturing (HQ) | Provider of precision sheet metal fabrication, laser cutting, welding, and electronic chassis and card cage assembly services. | 408-980-1045 | NA | Santa Clara |
| Luna's Sheet Metal Inc (HQ) | Provider of metal fabrication and precision metal working services for the computer electronics, telecommunications, and automotive industries. | 408-492-1260 | NA | Santa Clara |
| M & M Machine (HQ) | Designer and manufacturer of machined parts and components for automotive, laser, audio and video and body building equipment manufacturers. | 530-268-2112 | 1-10 | Auburn |
| M A R's Engineering Company Inc (HQ) | Manufacturer of screw machines. The company also offers prototyping, fabrication, and assembly services. | 510-483-0541 | NA | San Leandro |
| M&L Precision Machining Inc (HQ) | Provider of machine shop services. The company offers precision fabricated components, semiconductors, and related devices. | 408-224-2138 | NA | Morgan Hill |
| M-T Metal Fabrication Inc (HQ) | Provider of sheet metal solutions. The company offers CNC laser cutting, precision welding, gaining, PEM fastening, and silk screen. | 510-357-5262 | NA | San Leandro |
| Mac Cal (HQ) | Provider of sheet metals, assembly, cables and harnesses and engineering tools. The company deals with engineering services. | 408-452-4809 | NA | San Jose |
| Machinist Group (HQ) | Manufacturer of precision machined parts. The company serves defense, IR, laser components, prototype, and production industries. | 408-842-8437 | NA | Gilroy |
| Martinek Manufacturing (HQ) | Provider of painting, plating, silk screening, sheet metal fabrication, machining, and precision welding services. | 510-438-0357 | NA | Fremont |
| Master Precision Machining (HQ) | Provider of precision machining services. The company offers engineering, finishing, metrology, and milling services. | 408-727-0185 | NA | Santa Clara |
| Maxon Precision Motors Inc (BR) | Provider of high-precision drives and systems. The company's products include brushed DC motors, brushless DC motors, spindle drives, and gearheads. | 650-524-8822 | NA | Foster City |
| Mcintire Machine Inc (HQ) | Provider of precision machining, welding, and fabrication services. The company offers services to the industrial sector. | 209-837-4409 | 1-10 | Crows Landing |
| Mckenzie Machining Inc (HQ) | Provider of precision machining services of pre-fabricated components. The company R&D, manufacturing design, and other services. | 408-748-8885 | NA | Santa Clara |
| Mcneal Enterprises Inc (HQ) | Provider of machined, fabricated, and thermoformed plastic components. The company serves medical, semiconductor, solar, optics, and other needs. | 408-922-7290 | NA | San Jose |
| Mda Precision (HQ) | Provider of benchtop milling machine and benchtop lathe systems. The company offers micro drilling machines, benchtop manual mills, and lathes. | 408-847-7796 | NA | Morgan Hill |
| Meadows Manufacturing (HQ) | Provider of engineering, design, and manufacturing solutions. The company serves the commercial and industrial sectors. | 408-988-1252 | NA | San Jose |
| Mecoptron Inc (HQ) | Provider of precision machining services. The company's services include protype machining, production machining, and precision mechanical assembly services. | 510-226-9966 | NA | Fremont |
| Metal Fusion Inc (HQ) | Provider of thermal spray technology services. The company's portfolio includes shaft repair, roll repair, and mechanical seal. | 650-368-7692 | NA | Redwood City |
| Micro Machine Shop (HQ) | Manufacturer of micro machines for telecommunications, microwave, semiconductor equipment, valve, laser, medical, and other industries. | 209-848-8760 | 1-10 | Oakdale |

| COMPANY NAME | PRODUCT / SERVICE | PHONE | EMP | CITY |
|---|---|---|---|---|
| Millennium Lapping & Grind Engineering (HQ) | Provider of lapping and grinding for CNC machining. The company specializes in single and double side lapping diamond polishing of copper and silver. | 510-438-9908 | NA | Fremont |
| Minitool Inc (HQ) | Manufacturer of precision instruments and small tools for microscopic investigation. The company also specializes in under-microscope precision tools. | 408-395-1585 | NA | Campbell |
| Mission Tool And Mfg Co Inc (HQ) | Manufacturer of precision stamped and machined components. The company serves aerospace, automotive, medical, telecom, defense, and commercial sectors. | 510-782-8383 | NA | Hayward |
| Mitsui High-tec Inc (BR) | Provider of grinder parts, precision tools, and stamping products. The company is involved in design, installation, and delivery services. | 408-980-0782 | NA | San Jose |
| Mjb Precision Machining Inc (HQ) | Manufacturer of precision and prototype machining parts and components for the defense, telecom, medical, and semiconductor manufacturing industries. | 408-559-3035 | NA | Campbell |
| Modern Ceramics Manufacturing Inc (HQ) | Supplier of ceramic materials and components. The company serves the semi-conductor and laser industries. | 408-383-0554 | NA | San Jose |
| Modern Linear Inc (HQ) | Manufacturer of guide roller products. The company mainly focuses on linear motion industry and serves commercial, packaging, and medical fields. | 415-924-7938 | NA | San Rafael |
| National Fabtronix Inc (HQ) | Provider of custom fabrication and precision sheet metal services for the computer and medical industries. | 510-785-3135 | NA | Hayward |
| Nevarez Machining Inc (HQ) | Manufacturer of fabricated machined parts. The company offers welding, machining, inspection, and software machining services. | 408-279-1196 | NA | San Jose |
| New World Machining (HQ) | Manufacturer of machined parts for the semiconductor, electronic, and security sectors specializing in prototype, production, and engineering design. | 408-227-3810 | NA | San Jose |
| Noron Precision Machining Inc (HQ) | Provider of machined parts for medical, microwave, aircraft, auto, computer peripheral, telecommunications, and biotech industries. | 408-739-6486 | NA | Sunnyvale |
| Nq Engineering Inc (HQ) | Provider of engineering services. The company specializes in fabricating, materials, inspection, and quality control. | 209-836-3255 | 1-10 | Tracy |
| O&M Industries Inc (HQ) | Provider of industrial, mechanical, structural contractors, and fabrication services. The company serves cement industries. | 707-822-8800 | 11-50 | Arcata |
| O'hara Metal Products (HQ) | Manufacturer of metal products. The company's products include springs, stampings, sheet metals, and wires EDM's. | 707-863-9090 | NA | Fairfield |
| Odie Sheet Metal Shop (HQ) | Provider of sheet metal fabrication solutions. The company also deals with manufacturing and prototype development. | 408-281-2919 | NA | San Jose |
| Ogletree's Inc (HQ) | Provider of metal and equipment fabrication services. The company focuses on design, detailing, fabrication, and installation services. | 707-963-3537 | NA | St. Helena |
| Omega Diamond Inc (HQ) | Developer and manufacturer of diamond tools for the ultra precise semiconductor and optics industry. The company also offers power tools. | 530-889-8977 | 1-10 | Newcastle |
| Omni Fab (HQ) | Provider of precision sheet metal fabrication services. The company caters to the high technology industry. | 408-492-1331 | NA | Santa Clara |
| Omw Corp (HQ) | Manufacturer of CNC machined parts. The company also deals with production machining, prototyping, and support services. | 415-382-1669 | NA | Novato |
| Oryx Advanced Materials Inc (HQ) | Provider of thin film materials for PV cells. The company also offers sputtering targets and bonding services to the magnetic data storage market. | 510-249-1157 | NA | Fremont |
| P&L Specialties (HQ) | Provider of engineering and fabrication services. The company's services include waterjet cutting and harvest lug washing. | 707-573-3141 | NA | Santa Rosa |
| Pacific Powder Coating (HQ) | Provider of electrostatic powder coating and metal fabrication services. The company focuses on sandblasting & silkscreening services, and logistics. | 916-381-1154 | 1-10 | Sacramento |
| Pacific Precision Machine Inc (HQ) | Provider of precision machining solutions. The company offers CNC turning and milling, procurement and assembly, and computer programming services. | 209-588-9664 | 1-10 | Sonoma |
| Paragon Swiss Inc (HQ) | Manufacturer of medical instruments, precision shafts, optical bench fixtures, and related supplies. | 408-748-1617 | NA | Santa Clara |
| Peartech Inc (HQ) | Provider of solutions for electronic, computer, networking, and medical applications. The company offers solutions for precision machining and sheet metals. | 408-542-9550 | NA | Sunnyvale |
| Pec Manufacturing (HQ) | Provider of customized electromechanical, electronic, and mechanical solutions such as cable and harness assemblies and electro-mechanical assemblies. | 408-577-1839 | NA | San Jose |
| Pencom (HQ) | Provider of component solutions to OEM design engineers. The company focuses on supply chain management, technical product support, and logistics. | 650-593-3288 | NA | San Carlos |
| Peninsula Spring Corp (HQ) | Provider of precision spring products. The company offers sheet metal stampings, electrical contacts, clips, and wire forms. | 408-848-3361 | NA | Gilroy |
| Peridot Corp (HQ) | Provider of design for manufacturing and packaging. The company also manufacturers of medical components, miniature component and general product prototypes. | 925-461-8830 | NA | Pleasanton |

| COMPANY NAME | PRODUCT / SERVICE | PHONE | EMP | CITY |
|---|---|---|---|---|
| Perry Tool & Research Inc (HQ) | Designer and manufacturer of powder metal parts for OEMs. The company specializes in pulleys, bearings, cams, sprockets, and fasteners. | 510-782-9226 | NA | Hayward |
| Phil Wood & Co (HQ) | Manufacturer of cycling and related recreation oriented products. The company focuses to offer maintenance-free hubs for cyclists. | 408-569-1860 | NA | San Jose |
| Plastech (HQ) | Provider of machined and fabricated plastic products for the semi conductor, biological, and medical industries. | 650-568-9206 | NA | Menlo Park |
| Plastikon Industries (HQ) | Provider of contract manufacturing services for custom designed plastic injection molding, for medical, pharmaceutical and other industries. | 510-400-1010 | NA | Hayward |
| Platron (HQ) | Provider of selective plating services. The company caters to design engineering, electronics, mechanical, and field service applications. | 510-781-5588 | NA | Hayward |
| Precise Automation (HQ) | Provider of industrial automation solutions. The company's products include robots, guidance controllers, and kinematics. | 408-224-2838 | NA | Fremont |
| Precision Identity Corp (HQ) | Manufacturer of machined components for the medical device manufacturing industries. The company offers inspection, cleaning, and support services. | 408-374-2346 | NA | Campbell |
| Precision Swiss Products Inc (HQ) | Manufacturer of precision machined components. The company serves medical, energy, and military industries. | 408-433-5880 | NA | Milpitas |
| Pro-Tek Manufacturing Inc (HQ) | Provider of sheet metal fabrication and machining services. The company is involved in prototyping and manufacturing. | 925-454-8100 | NA | Livermore |
| Process Engineers Inc (HQ) | Manufacturer of stainless steel equipment. The company also specializes in installation and other services. | 510-782-5122 | NA | Hayward |
| Production Robotics Inc (HQ) | Designer and manufacturer of specialty engineered automation systems. The company serves biotech, diagnostics, microsurgery, and other sectors. | 510-777-0375 | NA | San Leandro |
| Progressive Concepts Machining (HQ) | Provider of welding, assembly, and machining services. The company also deals with inspection solutions and serves businesses. | 925-426-0400 | NA | Pleasanton |
| Provel Precision (HQ) | Provider of machining services. The company offers prototyping, precision machining, assembly, and outsourcing services. | 510-744-1885 | NA | Newark |
| Prunella Enterprises Inc (HQ) | Provider of custom machining and sub assembly services. The company serves the telecommunication and space sectors. | 831-465-1818 | 1-10 | Santa Cruz |
| Qualdeval International (HQ) | Supplier of high-pressure fluid flow and special core analysis equipment. The company offers PCB fabrication & assembly, and other services. | 844-247-2523 | NA | Fremont |
| Quality Machine Engineering Inc (HQ) | Provider of precision engineering solutions. The company serves the medical, semiconductor, aerospace, and other markets. | 707-528-1900 | NA | Santa Rosa |
| Quality Metal Spinning & Machining Inc (HQ) | Provider of metal spinning, sputtering shielding, and purity coils. The company's services include packing, shipping, and handling. | 650-858-2491 | NA | Palo Alto |
| Quality Quartz Engineering Inc (HQ) | Designer and manufacturer of solid quartz products for solar, fiber optic, semiconductor, and lighting industries. | 510-745-9200 | NA | Newark |
| Quartet Mechanics Inc (HQ) | Provider of LED, MEMS, photovoltaics (PV) solar and medical/lab automation systems. The company also offers wafer sorting and packing products. | 408-564-8901 | NA | Santa Clara |
| Rago & Son Inc (HQ) | Provider of metal stamping and machining services. The company's services include stamping, complete welding, and perforated tubing. | 510-536-5700 | NA | Oakland |
| Rapid Accu-Form Inc (HQ) | Provider of thermoforming and pressure forming services. The company specializes in tool and die and prototyping services. | 707-745-1879 | NA | Benicia |
| Rapid Precision Manufacturing Inc (HQ) | Provider of screw machining, surface grinding, sheet metal fabrication, tooling, and inspection services. | 408-617-0771 | NA | San Jose |
| Ray L Hellwig (HQ) | Designer and manufacturer of tools. It's products find application in mechanical, process piping, and plumbing needs. | 408-727-5612 | NA | Santa Clara |
| Responsible Metal Fab Inc (HQ) | Provider of precision sheet metal fabrication services. The company offers machining, electromechanical assembly, packaging, and delivery services. | 408-734-0713 | NA | Sunnyvale |
| Riley Plastic Manufacturing Inc (HQ) | Provider of vacuum forming, vapor polishing, and assembly services. The company serves the medical and bio-tech industries. | 650-366-5104 | NA | Menlo Park |
| Ripon Manufacturing Company Inc (HQ) | Fabricator of steel processing equipment. The company manufactures and installs peelers, sizers, hardshell crackers, hoppers, dryers, and sorters. | 209-599-2148 | 1-10 | Ripon |
| Rm Machining Inc (HQ) | Provider of precision machining services. The company caters to the aerospace, defense, medical, and energy sectors. | 650-591-4178 | NA | San Carlos |
| Rmc Engineering (HQ) | Provider of automated safety systems, resurfacing tools, blowers, and related supplies. The company offers repair and replacement services. | 408-842-2525 | NA | Gilroy |
| Robertson Precision Inc (HQ) | Manufacturer of precision metals and plastic products. The company's services include engineering support and process control. | 650-363-2212 | NA | Menlo Park |
| Rock Systems Inc (HQ) | Provider of material handling solutions. The company offers hoppers, feeders, conveyors, separators, and related accessories. | 916-921-9000 | 1-10 | Sacramento |
| Roger K Sherman Co (HQ) | Provider of microscope eyepiece reticules, calibration standards, and ruled master gages for the semiconductor and magnetic head industries. | 650-941-8300 | NA | Los Altos |
| Rollin J Lobaugh Inc (HQ) | Manufacturer of machined components. The company mainly manufactures screws and offers supporting services. | 650-583-9682 | NA | Belmont |

| COMPANY NAME | PRODUCT / SERVICE | PHONE | EMP | CITY |
|---|---|---|---|---|
| Ron Witherspoon Inc (HQ) | Manufacturer of high precision parts. The company offers milling, turning, electrical discharge machining, and grinding services. | 408-370-6620 | NA | Campbell |
| Rutter Armey Inc (HQ) | Provider of precision machining services. The company focuses on industrial hard chrome plating, welding, and metal spraying services. | 559-237-1866 | 1-10 | Fresno |
| SAE Engineering Inc (HQ) | Provider of integrated turnkey assembly, precision machining, and sheet metal fabrication services to many sectors. The company also offers software. | 408-987-9950 | NA | Santa Clara |
| Samax Precision Inc (HQ) | Manufacturer and supplier of precision machined products. The company offers services like grinding and honing. It serves military and aerospace fields. | 408-245-9555 | NA | Sunnyvale |
| Sc-Mech Solution Inc (HQ) | Manufacturer of electronic parts and components. The company provides CNC milling, tooling, design, and contract manufacturing services. | 408-748-3380 | NA | San Jose |
| Sharp Dimension Inc (HQ) | Provider of production and prototype machining services. The company serves semiconductor, medical, robotics, solar, defense, and other sectors. | 510-656-8938 | NA | Fremont |
| Silicon Valley Mfg (HQ) | Manufacturer and engineer of EDM prototype and production machining. The company's services include CNC milling, CNC turning, and manual machining. | 510-791-9450 | NA | Newark |
| Silvestre Manufacturing (HQ) | Provider of custom fabrication services. The company specializes in machining and prototype production. | 408-988-0937 | NA | Santa Clara |
| Sj Die Casting & Machining Corp (HQ) | Manufacturer of castings for computer, electronic, automotive, and military sectors specializing in sandblasting, deburring, and assembly services. | 408-262-6500 | 1-10 | Lincoln |
| Small Precision Tools Inc (BR) | Manufacturer of chip bonding tools, fine ceramic, and machining parts. The company offers necessary technical support and services. | 707-765-4545 | NA | Petaluma |
| Snowline Engineering Inc (HQ) | Provider of precision machining and fabrication services. The company also engages in sheet metal and assembly. | 530-677-2675 | 1-10 | Cameron Park |
| Solonics Inc (HQ) | Manufacturer of coded backboard systems and wire management products. The company focuses on design and delivery services. | 510-471-7600 | NA | Hayward |
| South Bay Solutions Inc (HQ) | Provider of manufacturing services for the semiconductor, medical, aerospace, solar, and petroleum industries. | 650-843-1800 | NA | Fremont |
| Sp3 Diamond Technologies (HQ) | Provider of electronics thermal management, diamond-on-silicon applications, and enhanced cutting surface solutions. | 408-492-0630 | NA | Santa Clara |
| Specialty Precision Machining (HQ) | Provider of machining services. The company also offers turning, contouring, milling, engraving, and drilling services. | 209-939-0546 | 1-10 | Stockton |
| Specialty Products Design Inc (HQ) | Provider of exhaust components. The company focuses on exhaust fabricators, CNC header flanges, stainless bellows, and sealing flanges. | 916-635-8108 | 1-10 | Rancho Cordova |
| Sputnik Enterprises Inc (HQ) | Provider of finishing, painting, casting, CNC machining, model making, and custom product development services. | 650-363-7576 | NA | Redwood City |
| Stewart Tool Company Inc (HQ) | Manufacturer of CNC precision machine components. The company specializes in manufacturing pressure vessels and provides field and assembly services. | 916-635-8321 | 1-10 | Rancho Cordova |
| Stockton Tri Industries Inc (HQ) | Provider of custom rolling, bending, forming, machining, metal fabrication, and field erection services. | 209-948-9701 | 1-10 | Stockton |
| Sun Enterprise Inc (HQ) | Provider of ceramic and quartz machining products. The company specializes in the semiconductor, solar, laser, and structural industries. | 510-657-6507 | NA | Fremont |
| T & K Machine (HQ) | Designer and manufacturer of precision machines. The company also offers services like plating, labeling, powdercoat, and silkscreen. | 925-344-7091 | NA | Livermore |
| T&T Precision Inc (HQ) | Provider of precision machining services. The company specializes in electronics, automotive, and semiconductor equipment. | 510-429-8088 | NA | Union City |
| Tapemation Machining Inc (HQ) | Manufacturer of machined parts and tools for the aircraft, marine, electronic, solar, and space communication industries. | 831-438-3069 | 1-10 | Scotts Valley |
| Tecdia Inc (HQ) | Manufacturer of precision machine tools and fixtures. The company also specializes in cutting and scribing tools. | 408-748-0100 | NA | Campbell |
| Technic Inc (BR) | Manufacturer of specialty chemicals, analytical control tools, and surface finishing products. The company offers electroplating & engineered powders. | 408-287-3732 | NA | San Jose |
| Tecma Co (HQ) | Provider of CNC and conventional precision machining solutions. The company serves the aerospace, commercial, medical, and defense industries. | 916-925-8206 | 1-10 | Sacramento |
| Ter Precision (HQ) | Provider of CNC machining, metal fabrication, frame fabrication, and assembly services. The company focuses on prototype machining and milling. | 408-986-9920 | NA | Santa Clara |
| THE BROACH MASTERS Inc (HQ) | Manufacturer of broaches, disc shapers, disc shaper cutters, shank shapers, shank shaper cutters, gear shaper cutters, and spline broaches. | 530-885-1939 | 1-10 | Auburn |
| Therma (HQ) | Provider of mechanical contracting services. The company also offers design and installation of environmental systems. | 408-347-3400 | NA | San Jose |
| Trans Bay Steel (HQ) | Provider of structural steel construction services. The company offers heavy bridge piling and mechanical fabrication services. | 510-809-8193 | NA | Richmond |
| Tri Tool Inc (HQ) | Manufacturer of precision machine tools. The company also deals with products rentals, construction, and maintenance services. | 916-288-6100 | 11-50 | Rancho Cordova |

| COMPANY NAME | PRODUCT / SERVICE | PHONE | EMP | CITY |
|---|---|---|---|---|
| Tridecs Corp (HQ) | Manufacturer of machined metal and plastic parts. The company offers prototyping, product machining, engineering, and design and drafting services. | 510-785-2620 | NA | Hayward |
| Tschida Engineering Inc (HQ) | Provider of CNC turning & milling, machining, and fabrication services. The company serves semiconductor, defense, medical, and environmental sectors. | 707-224-4482 | NA | Napa |
| Uc Components Inc (HQ) | Manufacturer of RediVac coated and electro-polished vented screws. The company serves high vacuum applications. | 408-782-1929 | NA | Morgan Hill |
| Uhv Sputtering Inc (HQ) | Manufacturer of semiconductor devices and vacuum equipment. The company is involved in sputtering and bonding services. | 408-779-2826 | NA | Morgan Hill |
| Uni-Fab Industries Inc (HQ) | Provider of precision sheet metal fabrication services. The company's equipment services include laser, punching and cutting, machining, and sawing. | 408-945-9733 | NA | Milpitas |
| Unico Mechanical Corp (HQ) | Provider of replacement machine parts. The company's services include welding, repairs, onsite machining, welding, and millwright. | 707-745-9970 | NA | Benicia |
| Unitech Tool & Machine Inc (HQ) | Manufacturer of custom finished parts, tooling, and fixtures. The company is specialized in milling and lathe fabrication, mechanical design consulting. | 408-566-0333 | NA | Santa Clara |
| United Mechanical Inc (HQ) | Provider of precision sheet metal fabrication services for semiconductor, disk drive, medical, pharmaceutical, and aerospace equipment. | 510-537-4744 | NA | Hayward |
| United Pro-Fab Manufacturing Inc (HQ) | Provider of machining and fabrication services. The company offers services for the aircraft, semiconductors, telecommunications, and biotechnology sectors. | 510-651-5570 | NA | Fremont |
| Usk Manufacturing Inc (HQ) | Provider of precision sheet metal and machining services. The company also focuses on mechanical assembly. | 510-471-7555 | NA | Union City |
| V&O Machine Inc (HQ) | Manufacturer of machined parts for agri, hydraulics, food procesing, and veterinary applications. The company focuses on prototyping and CNC milling. | 530-662-0495 | 1-10 | Woodland |
| Vanderhulst Associates Inc (HQ) | Provider of precision machining and manufacturing services. The company serves the medical, analytical, and semiconductor industries. | 408-727-1313 | NA | Santa Clara |
| W E Plemons Machinery Services Inc (HQ) | Provider of flange seals and automatic lidding attachments. The company's services include box designs and rebuilding. | 559-646-6630 | 1-10 | Parlier |
| Walters & Wolf (BR) | Provider of cladding services. The company specializes in design, engineering, fabrication, and delivery and installation. | 510-490-1115 | NA | Fremont |
| Wema Inc (HQ) | Provider of tank sensors, gauges, and smoke detectors for automotive, marine, agricultural, and construction equipment. | 408-453-5005 | NA | San Jose |
| Wenteq Inc (HQ) | Manufacturer of print, precision, machined components, and assemblies. The company serves the automotive, racing, and boat markets. | 209-608-2374 | 1-10 | Lodi |
| Wessdel Inc (HQ) | Provider of precision machining and engineering services for the military, aerospace, defense, and medical sectors. | 408-496-6822 | NA | San Jose |
| West Coast Fab Inc (HQ) | Provider of precision electronic sheet metal fabrication services. The company specializes in finished products. | 510-529-0177 | NA | Richmond |
| West Coast Surgical (HQ) | Manufacturer of surgical devices. The company offers designing, assembling and finishing of specialty surgical equipment. | 650-728-8095 | NA | Half Moon Bay |
| White Industries (HQ) | Manufacturer of bicycle components. The company's products include cranks, front hubs, brackets, pedals, and related accessories. | 707-769-5600 | NA | Petaluma |
| Wiegmann & Rose (HQ) | Provider of custom heat exchangers, pressure vessels, and weldments. The company offers vacuum chambers and pipe spool products. | 510-632-8828 | NA | Livermore |
| Wolfs Precision Works Inc (HQ) | Provider of precision machining solutions. The company's services include milling, turning, and surface gliding. | 650-364-1341 | NA | Menlo Park |
| Wra-Cal Industries Inc (HQ) | Manufacturer of precision machine products. The company's products include lathes, mills and grinders, drill press, and finishing equipment. | 408-988-4696 | NA | Santa Clara |
| Wrex Products Inc (HQ) | Provider of plastic injection molding, CNC machining and finishing, coating, and tool design and engineering services. | 530-895-3838 | 1-10 | Chico |
| Wright Engineered Plastics (HQ) | Provider of medical components and devices. The company deals wtih custom plastic injection molding, tooling, and assembly related services. | 707-575-1218 | NA | Santa Rosa |
| York Machine Works (HQ) | Provider of engineering services. The company's services include machining, welding, pattern burning, and engraving. | 707-963-4966 | NA | St. Helena |
| Yuhas Tooling & Machining Inc (HQ) | Provider of tooling and machining products for the semiconductor, medical, aerospace, telecommunications, and electronics industries. | 408-934-9196 | NA | Milpitas |

## 81 = Mechanical Connectors/Mounts

| COMPANY NAME | PRODUCT / SERVICE | PHONE | EMP | CITY |
|---|---|---|---|---|
| CKC Engineering LLC (HQ) | Provider of custom equipment solutions for clinical, manufacturing, pharmaceutical, medical device, and drug delivery industries. | 415-494-8225 | NA | Oakland |
| Custom Alloy Corp (BR) | Manufacturer of metals for seamless and welded pipe fittings & forgings. The company's products are in alloy steels, nickel alloys, and carbon steels. | 530-544-2836 | 11-50 | South Lake Tahoe |
| Durabrake Co (HQ) | Manufacturer of automotive products. The company's products include brake drums, rotors, and hubs for the aftermarket and OEMs. | 408-748-0400 | NA | Santa Clara |

| COMPANY NAME | PRODUCT / SERVICE | PHONE | EMP | CITY |
|---|---|---|---|---|
| Fujikura America Inc (BR) | Manufacturer of fiber optics flexible printed circuits and cables. The company also offers membrane switches and printed circuit board assemblies. | 408-748-6991 | NA | Santa Clara |
| Hydratight (BR) | Manufacturer of flanges and mechanical connectors. The company focuses on the subsea, nuclear, wind, and mining industries. | 925-691-4914 | NA | Concord |
| Laser Mark's Co (HQ) | Provider of laser marking and engraving job shop services. The company serves the agriculture, food processing, automotive, and medical industries. | 408-433-9333 | NA | San Jose |
| Morgan Manufacturing Inc (HQ) | Manufacturer of autobody tools and tie-down equipment. The company caters to the flat bed trucking industry. | 707-763-6848 | NA | Petaluma |
| Pipe Shields Inc (HQ) | Designer and manufacturer of pre-insulated pipe supports, slides, guides, and anchors. The company's products include hanger types, shoes, and riser clamps. | 800-538-7007 | NA | Fairfield |
| Wrex Products Inc (HQ) | Provider of plastic injection molding, CNC machining and finishing, coating, and tool design and engineering services. | 530-895-3838 | 1-10 | Chico |

## 82 = Miscellaneous Fabricated/Stamped Parts

| COMPANY NAME | PRODUCT / SERVICE | PHONE | EMP | CITY |
|---|---|---|---|---|
| Ab&I Foundry (HQ) | Provider of casting products and accessories. The company's products include pipes and fittings, custom castings, foundry, and recyclable materials. | 510-632-3467 | NA | Oakland |
| Accu-Swiss Inc (HQ) | Manufacturer of precision CNC and screw machined products. The company's services include engineering, milling, and threading. | 209-847-1016 | 1-10 | Oakdale |
| American Precision Spring Corp (HQ) | Designer of electronic circuits. The company specializes in the design and fabrication of printed circuit boards. | 408-986-1020 | NA | Santa Clara |
| Armorstruxx Llc (HQ) | Provider of ballistic and blast protection solutions. The company offers armor systems design and integration services. | 209-365-9400 | 1-10 | Lodi |
| Asc Profiles Inc (HQ) | Supplier of building products such as panels, roofing products, and standing seams. The company serves the commercial and residential markets. | 916-372-0933 | 1-10 | West Sacramento |
| Bay Area Circuits Inc (HQ) | Provider of engineering services that include fabrication, layout, and design services to the original equipment manufacturers. | 510-933-9000 | NA | Fremont |
| Billington Welding & Manufacturing Inc (HQ) | Manufacturer of food process equipment and custom products. The company serves the construction, automotive, and food processing industries. | 209-526-9312 | 1-10 | Modesto |
| Bulling Metal Works Inc (HQ) | Manufacturer of pressure vessels and laser cutting machinery. The company also offers other custom fabrication products. | 510-351-2073 | NA | San Leandro |
| California Contract Company (HQ) | Provider of metal fabrication and installation services. The company focuses on aluminum, stainless steel and glass, and bronze. | 510-654-9375 | NA | Richmond |
| Calogic LLC (HQ) | Designer and manufacturer of integrated circuits. The company caters to computer, telecom, and medical applications. | 510-656-2900 | NA | Fremont |
| Campbell/Harris Security Equipment Company (HQ) | Manufacturer of busters, fiberscopes, probe kits, and personal radiation detectors. The company also focuses on distribution. | 510-864-8010 | NA | Alameda |
| Capital Sheet Metal (HQ) | Manufacturer of custom countertops. The company deals with shearing, welding, laser cutting, and polishing services. | 916-443-3761 | 1-10 | Sacramento |
| Chris French Metal Inc (HQ) | Provider of fabrication services. The company offers design, installation, prototyping, and repair services. | 510-238-9339 | NA | Oakland |
| CKC Engineering LLC (HQ) | Provider of custom equipment solutions for clinical, manufacturing, pharmaceutical, medical device, and drug delivery industries. | 415-494-8225 | NA | Oakland |
| Columbia Machine Works (HQ) | Provider of coining equipment and contracting services. The company offers coining presses, rimming machines, and consumable tooling. | 510-568-0808 | NA | Oakland |
| Custom Product Development Co (HQ) | Developer and manufacturer of mechanical components and turn-key assembly solutions. The company specializes in developing customized products. | 925-960-0577 | NA | Livermore |
| Dawn VME Products (HQ) | Designer and manufacturer of enclosures, backplanes, chassis and card cage. The company also offers design services and power supplies. | 510-657-4444 | NA | Fremont |
| Delta Turnstiles Llc (HQ) | Manufacturer of optical turnstiles. The company mainly caters to the corporate sector and the government. | 925-969-1498 | NA | Concord |
| Expedite Precision Works Inc (HQ) | Manufacturer of diverse products involving micro & custom machining and fabrication of metal & plastic. The company also manufactures vessels and tanks. | 408-573-9600 | NA | San Jose |
| H P Machine & Engineering Inc (HQ) | Provider of job shop, prototype machining, CNC, and wire EDM services. The company serves services to the industrial sector. | 408-383-9075 | NA | San Jose |
| Howard Wire Cloth Co (HQ) | Provider of screening & wire fabrication products. The company offers wire cloth, stainless steel netting, security screening, and perforated metals. | 510-887-8787 | NA | Hayward |
| Ironmind Enterprises Inc (HQ) | Manufacturer of medical products with flower essences. The company's offerings also include gym equipment and training gears. | 530-272-3579 | 1-10 | Nevada City |
| J&M Manufacturing Inc (HQ) | Provider of TIG, MIG and spot welding, silk-screening, contract manufacturing, and assembly services. | 707-795-8223 | NA | Cotati |
| Kearney Pattern Works & Foundry (HQ) | Provider of pattern works and foundry services. The company's services include heat treating, plating, machining, and casting finish. | 408-293-7414 | NA | San Jose |

| COMPANY NAME | PRODUCT / SERVICE | PHONE | EMP | CITY |
|---|---|---|---|---|
| Kraemer & Company Manufacturing Inc (HQ) | Provider of industrial equipment. The company specializes in dyers, sprayers, storage units, and heaters. | 530-865-7982 | 1-10 | Orland |
| Ksm Corp (DH) | Manufacturer of welded metal bellows for transportation, solar, pharmaceutical, and other sectors and provides build to print assembly services. | 408-514-2400 | NA | San Jose |
| Larson Electronic Glass (HQ) | Manufacturer of glass to metal sealing products. The company offers vacuum flanges, viewports, bellows, and electrical & fiber optics feed-thrus. | 650-369-6734 | NA | Redwood City |
| Laser Mark's Co (HQ) | Provider of laser marking and engraving job shop services. The company serves the agriculture, food processing, automotive, and medical industries. | 408-433-9333 | NA | San Jose |
| Lloyd W Aubry Company Inc (HQ) | Provider of mechanical contracting services specializing in fabrication, installation, relocation, and maintenance of processing plant equipment. | 510-732-9038 | NA | Hayward |
| Mcm Engineering Inc (HQ) | Provider of aircraft ground support systems. The company offers products and services for airports and aircraft manufacturers. | 650-259-9100 | NA | Burlingame |
| Melrose Nameplate & Label Co (HQ) | Developer and manufacturer of ID nameplates, labels, and membrane switches. The company offers touchscreen assembly and decorative nameplates. | 510-732-3100 | NA | Hayward |
| Metalfx Inc (HQ) | Provider of sheet metal fabrication services for metal and wood products. The company is engaged in engineering and quality assurance services. | 800-479-9451 | 1-10 | Willits |
| Microform Precision Llc (HQ) | Provider of metal cutting, bending, fabrication, and coating services. The company offers shearing, punching, forming, and painting services. | 916-419-0580 | 1-10 | Sacramento |
| Minimatics (HQ) | Provider of precision machining solutions. The company offers CNC milling, manual turning, lapping, and honing services. | 650-969-5630 | NA | Santa Clara |
| Mitsui High-tec Inc (BR) | Provider of grinder parts, precision tools, and stamping products. The company is involved in design, installation, and delivery services. | 408-980-0782 | NA | San Jose |
| Modern Linear Inc (HQ) | Manufacturer of guide roller products. The company mainly focuses on linear motion industry and serves commercial, packaging, and medical fields. | 415-924-7938 | NA | San Rafael |
| Nor-Cal Metal Fabricators (HQ) | Provider of general industrial metal fabrication and parts. The company is engaged in contract manufacturing and structural rolling. | 510-833-7157 | NA | Oakland |
| Nq Engineering Inc (HQ) | Provider of engineering services. The company specializes in fabricating, materials, inspection, and quality control. | 209-836-3255 | 1-10 | Tracy |
| Omni Fab (HQ) | Provider of precision sheet metal fabrication services. The company caters to the high technology industry. | 408-492-1331 | NA | Santa Clara |
| Pacific Precision Machine Inc (HQ) | Provider of precision machining solutions. The company offers CNC turning and milling, procurement and assembly, and computer programming services. | 209-588-9664 | 1-10 | Sonoma |
| Precision Welding Technologies Inc (HQ) | Provider of welding systems and components. The company's service include equipment maintenance, planning and maintenance, and job shop. | 530-269-1826 | 1-10 | Auburn |
| Ptr Manufacturing Inc (HQ) | Manufacturer of machining and sheet metals. The company offers manufacturing and manufacturing presentation services. | 510-477-9654 | NA | Union City |
| Qualdeval International (HQ) | Supplier of high-pressure fluid flow and special core analysis equipment. The company offers PCB fabrication & assembly, and other services. | 844-247-2523 | NA | Fremont |
| Rapid Accu-Form Inc (HQ) | Provider of thermoforming and pressure forming services. The company specializes in tool and die and prototyping services. | 707-745-1879 | NA | Benicia |
| Safety Equipment Corp (HQ) | Designer and manufacturer of gas cabinets, valve boxes, leaker cabinets, exhausted enclosures, and related products. | 650-595-5422 | NA | Belmont |
| Sanctuary Stainless (HQ) | Provider of metal fabrication services. The company specializes in stainless and aluminum tubing and pipe fabrication. | 831-633-3867 | NA | Moss Landing |
| Scandic Springs Inc (HQ) | Provider of machine tools. The company offers heat treatment, plating, engineering, and raw material guidance services. | 510-352-3700 | NA | San Leandro |
| Synder Filtration (HQ) | Manufacturer of membranes and systems. The company offers training and performance evaluation services. It serves mining, biotech, and food industries. | 707-451-6060 | NA | Vacaville |
| Tobar Industries (HQ) | Provider of contract manufacturing services. The company offers services for computer chassis, card cages, and frames. | 408-494-3530 | NA | San Jose |
| Weichhart Stamping Co (HQ) | Manufacturer of tools and metal stampings in the San Francisco area. The company's offerings include flat springs, wire forms, spring washers, and wave washers. | 510-562-6886 | NA | Oakland |
| West Coast Fab Inc (HQ) | Provider of precision electronic sheet metal fabrication services. The company specializes in finished products. | 510-529-0177 | NA | Richmond |
| Wonder Metals Corp (HQ) | Provider of preventing environmental pollution services. The company's products include louvers, penthouses, and control dampers. | 800-366-5877 | 1-10 | Redding |
| Woodmack Products Inc (HQ) | Manufacturer of tubes and pipes. The company also specializes in customized designs and engineering solutions. | 916-853-6150 | 1-10 | Rancho Cordova |
| Wright Engineered Plastics (HQ) | Provider of medical components and devices. The company deals wtih custom plastic injection molding, tooling, and assembly related services. | 707-575-1218 | NA | Santa Rosa |

## 83 = Optoelectronics

| | | | | |
|---|---|---|---|---|
| Blue Sky Research Inc (HQ) | Manufacturer of laser products and micro optics. The company designs and fabricates semiconductor based lasers and fiber optic cables. | 408-941-6068 | NA | Milpitas |

| COMPANY NAME | PRODUCT / SERVICE | PHONE | EMP | CITY |
|---|---|---|---|---|
| Dicon Fiberoptics Inc (HQ) | Supplier of optical components, integrated modules, and test equipment for the fiber optics industry. | 510-620-5000 | NA | Richmond |
| Enablence Technologies Inc (DH) | Manufacturer of silicon products for communication needs. The company's offerings include optical splitters and channel filters. | 510-226-8900 | NA | Fremont |
| Inphenix Inc (HQ) | Designer and manufacturer of active optoelectronic chips and modules. The company serves telecom, defense, biomedical, and industrial markets. | 925-606-8809 | NA | Livermore |
| Lummen Lighting Inc (HQ) | Provider of lighting products like pendants, sconces, ballasts, and chandeliers. The company's services include design, installation, and delivery. | 707-360-5428 | NA | Santa Rosa |
| Medland & Associates Inc (BR) | Manufacturer of OEM products. The company's products include AC and DC converters, power supplies, switching regulators, and cable assemblies. | 408-686-0460 | NA | San Martin |
| Meivac Inc (HQ) | Manufacturer of sputtering systems and components. The company offers throttle valves, integrators, OEM assemblies, and substrate heaters. | 408-362-1000 | NA | San Jose |
| RAF Electronics (HQ) | Provider of optical system design and related services. The company deals with sales and delivery solutions. | 925-551-5361 | NA | San Ramon |
| Samtec (BR) | Manufacturer of high-speed assemblies, connectors, edge cards, and jumpers. The company serves the industrial sector. | 800-726-8329 | NA | Santa Clara |

## 84 = Plastic Parts/Components

| COMPANY NAME | PRODUCT / SERVICE | PHONE | EMP | CITY |
|---|---|---|---|---|
| Acrylic Art (HQ) | Provider of fabrication and machining services. The company focuses on painting, product finishing, anodizing, and vapor polishing. | 510-654-0953 | NA | Emeryville |
| Cal-Tron Corp (HQ) | Developer and manufacturer of cell reagent tools. The company's products find application in proteomic research. | 760-873-8491 | 1-10 | Bishop |
| Caltron Components Corp (HQ) | Distributor of electronic capacitors and resistors. The company also focuses on semiconductor products. | 408-748-2140 | NA | Santa Clara |
| Collimated Holes Inc (HQ) | Designer and manufacturer of fiber optic components, sub-assemblies, and imaging systems. The company also provides design and manufacturing services. | 408-374-5080 | NA | Campbell |
| Dc Precision Machining (HQ) | Manufacturer of engineered plastics and metals for many industries. The company offers CNC precision machining and turn-key assembly services. | 408-928-2510 | NA | Morgan Hill |
| Delta Pacific Products Inc (HQ) | Provider of plastics injection molding and mold making services. The company serves the automotive, agriculture, aerospace, and recreational sectors. | 510-487-4411 | NA | Union City |
| Expedite Precision Works Inc (HQ) | Manufacturer of diverse products involving micro & custom machining and fabrication of metal & plastic. The company also manufactures vessels and tanks. | 408-573-9600 | NA | San Jose |
| Freetech Plastics Inc (HQ) | Manufacturer of pressure thermoforming products. The company's products include medical, scientific, and telecommunication enclosures. | 510-651-9996 | NA | Fremont |
| Grandt Line Products (HQ) | Manufacturer and wholesaler of model railroad miniatures in plastics. The company's services include design and installation. | 925-671-0143 | NA | Concord |
| Kennerley-Spratling Inc (HQ) | Manufacturer of custom plastic injection and compression moldings. The company is involved in design, installation, and delivery services. | 510-351-8230 | NA | San Leandro |
| Mcneal Enterprises Inc (HQ) | Provider of machined, fabricated, and thermoformed plastic components. The company serves medical, semiconductor, solar, optics, and other needs. | 408-922-7290 | NA | San Jose |
| Nextier Networks Inc (HQ) | Provider of data security services and solutions for vertical markets and original equipment manufacturers. | 408-282-3561 | NA | Santa Clara |
| Pacific Rubber & Packing Inc (HQ) | Provider of rubber seals, custom seals, rubber gaskets and o-ring products for medical/pharmacy, automotive, solar energy, and general industries. | 650-595-5888 | NA | San Carlos |
| Plastikon Industries (HQ) | Provider of contract manufacturing services for custom designed plastic injection molding, for medical, pharmaceutical and other industries. | 510-400-1010 | NA | Hayward |
| Pre Plastics Inc (HQ) | Provider of engineering and precision tooling services. The company also offers plastic injection molding and assembly services. | 530-823-1820 | 1-10 | Auburn |
| Product Components Corporation (HQ) | Manufacturer of industrial plastic fasteners. The company offers screws, washers, pipe plugs, circuit board hardware, and other products. | 925-228-8930 | NA | Martinez |
| Solonics Inc (HQ) | Manufacturer of coded backboard systems and wire management products. The company focuses on design and delivery services. | 510-471-7600 | NA | Hayward |
| South Bay Solutions Inc (HQ) | Provider of manufacturing services for the semiconductor, medical, aerospace, solar, and petroleum industries. | 650-843-1800 | NA | Fremont |
| Stratamet Inc (HQ) | Provider of precision ceramic components. The company offers engineering support, quick response, and customer support. | 510-651-7176 | NA | Fremont |
| Westec Plastics Corp (HQ) | Provider of plastics injection molding and mold making services. The company also offers customized services. | 925-454-3400 | NA | Livermore |
| Wrex Products Inc (HQ) | Provider of plastic injection molding, CNC machining and finishing, coating, and tool design and engineering services. | 530-895-3838 | 1-10 | Chico |

## 85 = Sales, Distribution and/or Repair

| COMPANY NAME | PRODUCT / SERVICE | PHONE | EMP | CITY |
|---|---|---|---|---|
| Ampteks Inc (HQ) | Provider of engineering solutions. The company provides alternatives for dichromate plating and electro silver plating. | 925-493-7150 | NA | Livermore |
| Aurostar Corp (HQ) | Provider of technology products and services focusing on home theater systems, consumer electronics, desktops and notebooks, and networking solutions. | 510-249-9422 | NA | Fremont |
| R&R Refrigeration And Air Conditioning Inc (HQ) | Provider of environmental technological solutions. The company also offers maintenance and repair services for process systems. | 408-297-0383 | NA | San Jose |

## 6 = Semiconductors & Related Devices

| COMPANY NAME | PRODUCT / SERVICE | PHONE | EMP | CITY |
|---|---|---|---|---|
| Abx Engineering Inc (HQ) | Manufacturer of printed circuit board assemblies and electromechanical products for medical devices, agriculture, and military electronics industries. | 650-552-2300 | NA | Burlingame |
| AccelerATE Solutions Inc (HQ) | Provider of test engineering services. The company offers device characterization, applications support, and test program development services. | 408-573-6066 | NA | San Jose |
| Acu Spec Inc (HQ) | Manufacturer of engineering products. The company offers horizontal & vertical machining, CNC turning, CAD software, and CMM inspection services. | 408-748-8600 | NA | Santa Clara |
| Addison Engineering Inc (HQ) | Supplier of silicon wafers and semiconductor process components. The company's products include ceramic packages and semiconductor equipment. | 408-926-5000 | NA | San Jose |
| Allteq Industries Inc (HQ) | Manufacturer of microscopes, lighting, optics, and semiconductor products. The company also provides die coating, dispensing, and adhesion promotion. | 925-243-6400 | NA | Livermore |
| Allvia Inc (HQ) | Provider of silicon interposer and through-silicon via foundry services to the semiconductor and optoelectronics industries. | 408-212-3200 | NA | Sunnyvale |
| Altamont Manufacturing Inc (HQ) | Provider of precision CNC machining, welding, and fabrication services. The company offers semiconductor, aerospace, medical, and robotics components. | 925-371-5401 | NA | Livermore |
| Ambarella Inc (HQ) | Developer of high-definition video compression and image processing solutions. The company's products are used in security IP cameras and sports cameras. | 408-734-8888 | 51-200 | Santa Clara |
| Amerimade Technology Inc (HQ) | Manufacturer of wet processing equipment. The company's equipment include fully and semi automated benches, chemical handling equipment, and process tanks. | 925-243-9090 | NA | Livermore |
| Analogix Semiconductor Inc (HQ) | Designer of mixed-signal semiconductors. The company offers input-output display translators, timing controllers, and accessory display converters. | 408-988-8848 | NA | Santa Clara |
| Arrive Technologies Inc (HQ) | Provider of broadband and packet network semiconductor solutions for the telecommunication companies. | 888-864-6959 | 1-10 | Roseville |
| Arteris Inc (HQ) | Provider of interconnect semiconductor IP solutions to system-on-chip makers and serves networking, automotive, video and mobile-phone processors. | 408-470-7300 | NA | Campbell |
| ASM America Inc (BR) | Provider of technology and consulting services to semiconductor manufacturers. The company's products include EPSILON 3200, ADVANCE A400, and EMERALD XP. | 408-451-0830 | NA | San Jose |
| Axelsys LLC (HQ) | Provider of electronic design and manufacturing services. The company's offerings include LED and AC to DC industrial power supplies. | 408-600-0871 | NA | San Jose |
| Axt Inc (HQ) | Designer, developer, manufacturer, and distributor of high performance compound semiconductor substrates. | 510-438-4700 | NA | Fremont |
| B&H Engineering (HQ) | Supplier of assemblies, process kits, and individual parts. The company caters to the semiconductor equipment industry. | 650-594-2861 | NA | San Carlos |
| BaySand Incorporated (BR) | Developer of metal only configurable ASIC. The company uses disruptive metal configurable standard cell technology for its products. | 408-669-4992 | NA | San Jose |
| Blue Sky Research Inc (HQ) | Manufacturer of laser products and micro optics. The company designs and fabricates semiconductor based lasers and fiber optic cables. | 408-941-6068 | NA | Milpitas |
| Caltron Components Corp (HQ) | Distributor of electronic capacitors and resistors. The company also focuses on semiconductor products. | 408-748-2140 | NA | Santa Clara |
| Capital Asset Exchange & Trading LLC (HQ) | Provider of secondary capital equipment. The company offers evaporators, spectometers, residual gas analyzers, and electronic testing equipment. | 650-326-3313 | NA | Santa Clara |
| Cavendish Kinetics Inc (HQ) | Supplier of tunable components for RF circuit applications. The company offers antennas, power amps, filters, and other products. | 408-457-1940 | NA | San Jose |
| Clover Machine & Manufacturing (HQ) | Provider of contract manufacturing and machining services. The company supplies tooling and fixtures to its customers. | 408-727-3380 | NA | Santa Clara |
| Compugraphics Usa Inc (BR) | Designer and developer of photomasks for semiconductor, optoelectronic devices, MEMs, nanotechnology, and renewable energy sectors. | 510-249-2600 | NA | Fremont |
| Corning Technology Center (BR) | Provider of specialty glass and ceramics services and sells keystone components to electronics, mobile emissions control, and life science industries. | 650-846-6000 | NA | Sunnyvale |
| Crocus Technology (HQ) | Manufacturer of magnetic switches, current sensors, and embedded memory products. The company serves the automotive and industrial sectors. | 408-380-8300 | NA | Santa Clara |

| COMPANY NAME | PRODUCT / SERVICE | PHONE | EMP | CITY |
|---|---|---|---|---|
| Custom Microwave Components Inc (HQ) | Manufacturer of microwave components. The company also specializes in providing attenuators with control devices. | 510-651-3434 | NA | Fremont |
| Cyclos Semiconductor (HQ) | Provider of resonant mesh semiconductor IP, design automation tools, and design consulting services to mobile, wireless, and medical sectors. | 510-649-3741 | NA | Berkeley |
| Dawn VME Products (HQ) | Designer and manufacturer of enclosures, backplanes, chassis and card cage. The company also offers design services and power supplies. | 510-657-4444 | NA | Fremont |
| Delphon Industries Llc (HQ) | Provider of materials and services to the semiconductor, medical, photonics, telecommunications, and military markets. | 510-576-2220 | NA | Hayward |
| Ea Machining Inc (HQ) | Provider of CNC turning and milling services. The company offers services to the semiconductor manufacturing equipment industry. | 408-727-4962 | NA | Santa Clara |
| Ecomicron Inc (HQ) | Manufacturer of semiconductor equipment. The company caters to semiconductor, photovoltaic, and hybrid industries. | 408-526-1020 | NA | San Jose |
| EG Systems LLC (HQ) | Provider of test equipment such as wafer probers, prober-based test handlers, and test floor management solutions. | 408-528-3000 | NA | Dublin |
| Einfochips (HQ) | Provider of product design services and solutions. The company offers product engineering and semiconductor services. | 408-496-1882 | NA | San Jose |
| Electro-Prep Corp (HQ) | Manufacturer of products for the assembly of PCBs in the electronic industry. The company offers board stiffeners, fixtures, and edge masks. | 408-370-7470 | NA | Campbell |
| Elevator Controls Corp (HQ) | Manufacturer of non-proprietary microprocessor based elevator controllers. The company offers technical support and field services. | 916-428-1708 | 1-10 | Sacramento |
| Eme Systems (HQ) | Designer and manufacturer of instruments for environmental science. The company also offers signal conditioners, sensors, enclosures, and batteries. | 510-848-5725 | NA | Berkeley |
| Enplas Tech Solutions Inc (RH) | Distributor of engineering plastic products. The company also offers optical devices, semiconductor peripherals, and related supplies. | 669-243-3600 | NA | Santa Clara |
| Ess Technology Inc (HQ) | Designer and marketer of video and audio semiconductors for the home, automotive, and entertainment markets. | 408-643-8800 | NA | Milpitas |
| Finisar Corp (HQ) | Developer of optical communications components and subsystems such as optical modules, active cables and components, passives and optical amplifiers. | 408-548-1000 | NA | Sunnyvale |
| Formfactor Inc (HQ) | Provider of product and professional services to semiconductor manufacturers. The company also offers sales and support services. | 925-290-4000 | 1001-5000 | Livermore |
| Fuji Electric Corporation of America (BR) | Provider of electric technology services. The company offers solutions for disk media, power supply, industrial systems, and radiation. | 510-440-1060 | NA | Fremont |
| Geo Semiconductor Inc (HQ) | Provider of imaging solutions. The company specializes in the design and fabrication of image sensors and multimedia processing engines. | 408-638-0400 | NA | San Jose |
| Globalfoundries Inc (BR) | Provider of semiconductor foundry services. The company deals with design tools, IP suppliers and ASIC partners. | 408-462-3900 | NA | Santa Clara |
| Haig Precision Manufacturing Corp (HQ) | Manufacturer of precision parts and assemblies. The company focuses on sheet metal, CNC milling and turning, stamping, welding, and power coating. | 408-378-4920 | NA | San Jose |
| Hermes Microvision Inc (BR) | Manufacturer of e-beam inspection and monitoring solution. The company caters to the semiconductor manufacturing sector. | 408-597-8600 | NA | San Jose |
| Hta Photomask (HQ) | Manufacturer of photo imaged products such as precision scales, resolution targets, and micro detectors. | 408-452-5500 | NA | San Jose |
| Impulse Semiconductor Inc (HQ) | Provider of electrostatic discharge and electrical overstress products and services. The company also provides virtual components and hardware. | 408-355-5018 | NA | San Jose |
| Imt Precision Inc (HQ) | Provider of sheet metal machining, fabrication, inspection and assembly services to semiconductor, aerospace, biotech, and education sectors. | 510-324-8926 | NA | Hayward |
| Incal Technology Inc (HQ) | Designer and manufacturer of test and burn in equipment and related hardware for board testing. The company serves the semiconductor industry. | 510-657-8405 | NA | Fremont |
| Integrated Device Technology Inc (HQ) | Manufacturer of semiconductor related products for communications, computing, and consumer industries. | 408-284-8200 | NA | San Jose |
| Intrinsic-Id Inc (HQ) | Designer of security solutions. The company offers services to semiconductor companies and device manufacturers. | 408-933-9980 | NA | Sunnyvale |
| Jem America Corp (RH) | Manufacturer and supplier of probe cards and tester interfaces. The company offers cantilever, vertical, and special-applications probe cards. | 510-683-9234 | NA | Fremont |
| Jvd Inc (HQ) | Provider of custom integrated circuit design and test services. The company is also involved in wafer characterization. | 408-263-7704 | NA | San Jose |
| Kensington Laboratories Llc (HQ) | Provider of automation products for the semiconductor industry. The company is engaged in precision machining, automation, and system integration. | 510-324-0126 | NA | Dublin |
| Kopin Corp (BR) | Developer of semi-conducting solutions. The company develops cloud computing, hands-free technology, and wireless usage in headset computers. | 831-430-0688 | 11-50 | Scotts Valley |
| Kyec Usa (DH) | Provider of testing services. The company offers services for testing integrated circuit (IC) packaging. | 408-452-7680 | NA | San Jose |
| Lazar Machining Inc (HQ) | Provider of precision machining services. The company serves the semiconductor, aerospace, and food processing industries. | 650-591-6415 | NA | San Carlos |

| COMPANY NAME | PRODUCT / SERVICE | PHONE | EMP | CITY |
|---|---|---|---|---|
| Lightwind Corp (HQ) | Provider of semiconductor manufacturing solutions. The company also deals with chemical analysis, process assessment, and refurbishment services. | 707-981-4301 | NA | Petaluma |
| Makel Engineering Inc (HQ) | Developer and provider of products and services for aviation, space, military, and commercial applications. | 530-895-2770 | 1-10 | Chico |
| Micron Technology Inc (BR) | Designer and manufacturer of semiconductor systems for computing, networking, and communications applications. | 408-855-4000 | NA | Milpitas |
| Mikpower Technologies Inc (HQ) | Provider of lighting solutions. The company offers IC products for light bulbs, light tubes, and square lights. | 408-493-5903 | NA | San Jose |
| Mission Tool And Mfg Co Inc (HQ) | Manufacturer of precision stamped and machined components. The company serves aerospace, automotive, medical, telecom, defense, and commercial sectors. | 510-782-8383 | NA | Hayward |
| Modutek Corp (HQ) | Manufacturer of wet process equipment and environmental systems. The company serves the semiconductor sector and offers repair services. | 408-362-2000 | NA | San Jose |
| MultiDimension Technology Company Ltd (BR) | Supplier of TMR magnetic sensors. The company mainly offers switch, linear, angle, and gear tooth sensors. | 650-275-2318 | NA | San Jose |
| N&K Technology Inc (HQ) | Manufacturer of metrology tools for the semiconductor, photomask, data storage, flat panel display, and solar cell industries. | 408-513-3800 | NA | San Jose |
| Nanometrics Inc (HQ) | Provider of process control metrology and inspection systems for data storage devices and solar photovoltaic applications. | 408-545-6000 | NA | Milpitas |
| Ndk America Inc (BR) | Manufacturer of crystal products for applications including gaming consoles, automotives, mobile phones, computers, and network equipment. | 408-428-0800 | NA | Milpitas |
| Neomagic Corp (HQ) | Developer of electronic device solutions. The company sells hardware, software, and microcontrollers for IP cameras and vehicle toll collection. | 408-428-9725 | NA | Milpitas |
| Nor-Cal Metal Fabricators (HQ) | Provider of general industrial metal fabrication and parts. The company is engaged in contract manufacturing and structural rolling. | 510-833-7157 | NA | Oakland |
| Nugentec (HQ) | Provider of chemicals and polymers. The company offers oilfield chemicals, cleaners, and lubricants. | 707-820-4080 | NA | Emeryville |
| NXP Semiconductors (BR) | Manufacturer of amplifiers, diodes, data converters, microcontrollers, and bipolar transistors for the healthcare, automotive, and computing sectors. | 408-518-5500 | NA | San Jose |
| Owens Design (HQ) | Developer of advanced technology systems for semiconductor, hard disk drive, solar, medical device, and other sectors. | 510-659-1800 | NA | Fremont |
| Pct Systems Inc (HQ) | Manufacturer of semiconductor equipment and supplies. The company offers services to the semi-conductor industry. | 510-657-4412 | NA | Fremont |
| Pentagon Technologies (HQ) | Distributor of electromechanical components. The company offers shaft couplings, seals, and cable assemblies. | 800-379-3361 | NA | Hayward |
| Persys Engineering Inc (HQ) | Provider of parts cleaning, refurbishing and manufacturing, decontamination, and maintenance of assemblies and machine parts. | 831-471-9300 | 1-10 | Santa Cruz |
| Precision Contacts Inc (HQ) | Provider of replacement contacts for handler manufacturer. The company's products include sockets, contacts, elements, and custom products. | 916-939-4147 | 1-10 | El Dorado Hills |
| Qualitau Inc (HQ) | Supplier of test equipment and services. The company is involved in the development of electronic equipment for semiconductor process reliability. | 650-282-6226 | NA | Mountain View |
| Quality Quartz Engineering Inc (HQ) | Designer and manufacturer of solid quartz products for solar, fiber optic, semiconductor, and lighting industries. | 510-745-9200 | NA | Newark |
| Quicklogic Corp (HQ) | Provider of trading solutions for stock market investors. The company offers online trading platforms for mobiles, smartphones, and tablets. | 408-990-4000 | NA | San Jose |
| RCH Associates Inc (HQ) | Provider of engineering solutions. The company specializes in equipment used in space, solar, and semiconductor industries. | 510-657-7846 | NA | Fremont |
| Samsung Semiconductor Inc (HQ) | Provider of electronics manufacturing and digital media products. The company also offers mobile services and PC software. | 408-544-4000 | NA | San Jose |
| Sempac Inc (HQ) | Developer of pre-molded open-cavity plastic packages for optoelectronic, telecom, RF, MEMS, and sensor applications. | 408-400-9002 | NA | Los Altos |
| Silicon Storage Technology Inc (HQ) | Designer and manufacturer of memory and non-memory products. The company serves internet computing markets. | 408-735-9110 | NA | San Jose |
| Sitime Corp (HQ) | Provider of programmable oscillators and clock generators. The company also offers embedded resonators. | 408-328-4400 | NA | Sunnyvale |
| SMTC Corp (BR) | Provider of electronics manufacturing services for the industrial, medical, computing, and communication markets. | 510-737-0700 | NA | Fremont |
| Solid State Optronics (HQ) | Manufacturer of miniature Solid State Relays. The company offers MOSFET drivers, specialty products, and optocouplers. | 408-293-4600 | NA | San Jose |
| Solutions Cubed Llc (HQ) | Provider of engineering solutions. The company is involved in early stage electronic prototyping to full production runs. | 530-891-8045 | 1-10 | Chico |
| Stats Chippac Inc (DH) | Provider of semiconductor packaging design, bump, probe, assembly, test, and distribution solutions. | 510-979-8000 | NA | Fremont |
| Strataglass (HQ) | Manufacturer of thin films. The company offers research and development, pilot production, and outsourced fabrication services. | 650-988-1700 | NA | Mountain View |
| Sunsil Inc (HQ) | Provider of total electronics manufacturing solutions. The company offers wafer fabrication, component assembly, testing, and wafer probing services. | 925-648-7779 | NA | Alamo |

| COMPANY NAME | PRODUCT / SERVICE | PHONE | EMP | CITY |
|---|---|---|---|---|
| TDK Corporation of America (BR) | Distributor of electronic products including capacitors, inductors, ferrites, factory automation system, transformers, magnets, and anechoic chambers. | 408-467-5200 | NA | San Jose |
| Ultra Clean Technology (HQ) | Manufacturer of gas panel delivery systems. The company primarily caters to the semiconductor industry. | 510-576-4400 | NA | Hayward |
| Ultra T Equipment Company Inc (HQ) | Manufacturer of spin coaters, developer stations, reionizers, and microelectronics cleaning systems. | 510-440-3909 | NA | Fremont |
| Unigen Corp (HQ) | Manufacturer and designer of custom enterprise-grade flash storage and DRAM and ARMOUR product applications serving the telecommunications industry. | 510-896-1818 | NA | Newark |
| Vacuum Process Engineering Inc (HQ) | Provider of engineering services. The company focuses on precision brazing, diffusion bonding, heat treating, and production of precision assemblies. | 916-925-6100 | 1-10 | Sacramento |
| Valqua America Inc (HQ) | Seller and marketer of semiconductor related products. The company also offers R&D services for high performance elastomer seals. | 408-986-1425 | NA | Santa Clara |
| Vishay Intertechnology Inc (BR) | Manufacturer of electronic components. The company's products comprises of semiconductors and passive components used across industries. | 408-727-2500 | NA | Santa Clara |
| Wafab International (HQ) | Provider of wet processing and chemical handling tools. The company's products include solar cell processing equipment and stainless steel fume hoods. | 925-455-5252 | NA | Livermore |
| WaferMasters Inc (HQ) | Provider of thermal processing services. The company also focuses on diagnostic metrology and design and consulting services. | 408-451-0850 | NA | Dublin |
| Wpg Americas Inc (DH) | Distributor of electronic products. The company's portfolio includes encoders, sensors, solid state batteries, and timing devices. | 408-392-8100 | NA | San Jose |
| Xandex Inc (DH) | Designer and manufacturer of products for the semiconductor test industry. The company's products include automated test equipment and interface products. | 707-763-7799 | NA | Petaluma |
| Yield Engineering Systems Inc (HQ) | Manufacturer of process equipment for the semiconductor industry. The company offers products for surface modification and photoresist treatment. | 925-373-8353 | NA | Livermore |

## 87 = Sensors

| COMPANY NAME | PRODUCT / SERVICE | PHONE | EMP | CITY |
|---|---|---|---|---|
| A M Fitzgerald & Associates Llc (HQ) | Provider of MEMS solutions. The company's products include piezoresistive cantilevers, ultrasound transducers, and infrared imagers. | 650-347-6367 | NA | Burlingame |
| Acoustic Emission Consulting Inc (HQ) | Specializes in acoustic emission inspection services and testing, and acoustic emission instrumentation, sensors, and probes. | 916-965-4827 | 1-10 | Fair Oaks |
| Analatom Inc (HQ) | Provider of materials science research services focusing on product development in the field of micro electrical mechanical systems. | 408-980-9516 | NA | Santa Clara |
| Andrew Ndt Engineering Corp (HQ) | Manufacturer of probes, ultrasonic transducers, diamond cutting tools, proximity sensors, cables, and offers calibration services. | 408-710-0342 | NA | San Jose |
| Applied Physics Systems Inc (HQ) | Supplier of magnetic measure and other electronic equipment. The company specializes in measurement while drilling systems and magnetometers. | 650-965-0500 | NA | Mountain View |
| Azbil North America Inc (BR) | Designer, manufacturer, and supplier of medical devices. The company offers automation products, control products, and industrial automation systems. | 408-245-3121 | NA | Santa Clara |
| Banpil Photonics Inc (HQ) | Developer and manufacturer of image sensors for automotive & medical imaging systems, security & surveillance, and machine vision applications. | 408-282-3628 | NA | Santa Clara |
| Baystar Electrument Inc (HQ) | Manufacturer of pressure sensors, pressure transducers and transmitters. The company deals with digital signal processing services. | 408-272-3669 | NA | San Jose |
| C3Nano Inc (HQ) | Developer of transparent conductive ink and film such as touch sensors, OLED lighting and displays, EMI shielding for touch sensor and display industry. | 510-259-9650 | NA | Hayward |
| Cambrios Technologies Corp (HQ) | Manufacturer of electronic materials for the display industry. The company mainly provides ClearOhm films. | 408-738-7400 | NA | Sunnyvale |
| Capella Microsystems Inc (HQ) | Developer of integrated technology solutions for IC design. The company is involved in installation and technical support. | 408-988-8000 | NA | Santa Clara |
| Cleangrow (DH) | Manufacturer of sensors for the measurement of calcium, potassium, ammonium, magnesium, and fluoride ions. | 415-460-7295 | 1-10 | Sacramento |
| CMOS Sensor Inc (HQ) | Designer and manufacturer of electro-optical image acquisition and also surveillance solutions for the medical market. | 408-366-2898 | NA | Cupertino |
| Corning Technology Center (BR) | Provider of specialty glass and ceramics services and sells keystone components to electronics, mobile emissions control, and life science industries. | 650-846-6000 | NA | Sunnyvale |
| Eme Systems (HQ) | Designer and manufacturer of instruments for environmental science. The company also offers signal conditioners, sensors, enclosures, and batteries. | 510-848-5725 | NA | Berkeley |
| Excel Precision Corp (HQ) | Designer and manufacturer of laser interferometer systems for measurement and calibration. The company's products include level sensors and angular sensors. | 408-727-4260 | NA | Santa Clara |

| COMPANY NAME | PRODUCT / SERVICE | PHONE | EMP | CITY |
|---|---|---|---|---|
| eze System (HQ) | Provider or monitoring and measuring solutions. The company's products include controllers, controller expansions, and sensors. | 716-393-9330 | 11-50 | Folsom |
| Fairchild Imaging Inc (DH) | Developer and manufacturer of solid-state electronic imaging components, cameras, and systems. The company's products include image sensors and cameras. | 650-479-5749 | NA | San Jose |
| Finesse Solutions Llc (HQ) | Manufacturer of bioreactor controllers and related supplies. The company offers technical support services. | 408-570-9000 | NA | Santa Clara |
| Fujikura America Inc (BR) | Manufacturer of fiber optics flexible printed circuits and cables. The company also offers membrane switches and printed circuit board assemblies. | 408-748-6991 | NA | Santa Clara |
| Hamamatsu Corp (BR) | Manufacturer of devices for the generation and measurement of infrared, visible, and ultraviolet light. | 408-261-2022 | NA | San Jose |
| HMS Electronics Inc (HQ) | Manufacturer of medical device components. The company offers custom made specialty component parts for x-ray machines. | 707-584-8760 | NA | Santa Rosa |
| Intermems Inc (HQ) | Provider of micromolding, plating, thin film deposition, anodic and wafer bonding, and related services. | 408-241-0007 | NA | San Jose |
| Jan Medical Inc (HQ) | Manufacturer of portable brain sensing devices for the detection of traumatic brain injuries, including concussions. | 650-316-8811 | NA | Mountain View |
| Jr3 Inc (HQ) | Designer and manufacturer of multi-axis force-torque sensors. The company caters to robotics and other applications. | 530-661-3677 | 1-10 | Woodland |
| Kionix Inc (BR) | Manufacturer of MEMS inertial sensors. The company offers accelerometers, gyroscopes, and combination sensors. | 408-720-1900 | NA | Santa Clara |
| Lamdagen Corp (BR) | Developer of nano technology based biosensors used in research and diagnostic equipment for human and animal health testing. | 650-571-5816 | NA | Menlo Park |
| Lightwind Corp (HQ) | Provider of semiconductor manufacturing solutions. The company also deals with chemical analysis, process assessment, and refurbishment services. | 707-981-4301 | NA | Petaluma |
| Loadstar Sensors Inc (HQ) | Manufacturer of sensors and load cells with wireless output, used in medical device, automotive, aerospace, consumer and other industries. | 510-274-1872 | NA | Fremont |
| Lumasense Technologies Inc (HQ) | Provider of temperature and gas sensing instruments for the energy, industrial, clean technology, and commercial markets. | 408-727-1600 | NA | Santa Clara |
| Makel Engineering Inc (HQ) | Developer and provider of products and services for aviation, space, military, and commercial applications. | 530-895-2770 | 1-10 | Chico |
| Mil-Ram Technology Inc (HQ) | Manufacturer of industrial gas and detection systems. The company serves the oil and gas, pulp and paper, and chemical industries. | 510-656-2001 | NA | Fremont |
| MultiDimension Technology Company Ltd (BR) | Supplier of TMR magnetic sensors. The company mainly offers switch, linear, angle, and gear tooth sensors. | 650-275-2318 | NA | San Jose |
| Neurosky Inc (HQ) | Manufacturer of ECG biosensors and also EEG biosensors for mobile solutions, wearable devices, and service providers. | 408-200-6675 | NA | San Jose |
| Nk Technologies (HQ) | Manufacturer of current sensors and transducer products for the factory and industrial automation markets. | 408-871-7510 | NA | San Jose |
| Omnivision Technologies Inc (HQ) | Developer of digital imaging solutions for consumer and commercial applications, and automotive, medical, and security imaging sectors. | 408-567-3000 | NA | Santa Clara |
| Pasco Scientific (HQ) | Provider of technology-based solutions for hands-on science services. The company is engaged in technical support. | 916-786-3800 | 1-10 | Roseville |
| Peloton Technology (HQ) | Developer of truck platooning systems. The company offers services to the transportation, trucking, and railroad industries. | 650-395-7356 | NA | Mountain View |
| Pni Sensor Corp (BR) | Manufacturer of electronic sensors. The company designs and fabricates processors, three-axis controllers, and geomagnetic sensors. | 707-566-2260 | NA | Santa Rosa |
| Scepter Scientific Inc (HQ) | Provider of feasibility evaluations, electronic, optical, and mechanical engineering, and prototype development services. | 925-373-4802 | NA | Livermore |
| Seevider Inc (HQ) | Manufacturer of smart vision devices. The company's products are used in light management, parking occupancy detection, and guiding. | 408-930-0852 | NA | Santa Clara |
| Sensifree Inc (HQ) | Manufacturer of contactless sensors for wearables. The company offers heart rate sensors, including fitness trackers, and activity monitors. | 669-230-5116 | NA | Cupertino |
| Senstar Corp (BR) | Provider of perimeter intrusion detection and security solutions. The company's products include buried sensors, barrier sensors, and wall-mounted sensors. | | NA | San Jose |
| Sensys Networks Inc (HQ) | Manufacturer of wireless sensor cubes, repeaters, and related accessories. The company's services include training and technical support. | 510-548-4620 | NA | Berkeley |
| Sierra Instruments Inc (HQ) | Manufacturer of mass flow meters and mass flow controllers. The company serves gas, liquid, and steam applications. | 831-373-0200 | NA | Monterey |
| Solutions Cubed Llc (HQ) | Provider of engineering solutions. The company is involved in early stage electronic prototyping to full production runs. | 530-891-8045 | 1-10 | Chico |
| Speedinfo (HQ) | Developer of traffic measurement solutions for broadcast media, government planning, and mobile applications. | 408-446-7660 | NA | San Jose |
| Sperient Corporation Inc (HQ) | Designer and developer of electronic systems. The company's applications include telemedicine and robotic sensing. | 925-447-3333 | NA | Livermore |
| Telemakus Llc (HQ) | Provider of USB controlled RF devices. The company devices include switches, vector modulators, and digital attenuators. | 916-458-6346 | 1-10 | Folsom |

| COMPANY NAME | PRODUCT / SERVICE | PHONE | EMP | CITY |
|---|---|---|---|---|
| Toppan Printing Company Ltd (BR) | Provider of printing solutions. The company serves customers in the food, beverage, and high barrier product industries. | 415-393-9839 | NA | San Francisco |
| Valmark Interface Solutions (HQ) | Manufacturer of labels, panel overlays, and membrane switches. The company is engaged in engineering, assembly, and installation services. | 925-960-9900 | NA | Livermore |
| Vishay Intertechnology Inc (BR) | Manufacturer of electronic components. The company's products comprises of semiconductors and passive components used across industries. | 408-727-2500 | NA | Santa Clara |
| Vsi Voelker Sensors Inc (HQ) | Manufacturer of sensor products. The company offers in-line oil quality sensors for the industrial, transportation, and power generation markets. | 650-618-8544 | NA | Palo Alto |
| Westport Machine Works Inc (HQ) | Manufacturer of assembly and balancing equipment. The company's services include fixturing, installation, and technical support. | 916-371-4493 | 1-10 | West Sacramento |

## 88 = Sheet Metal Parts

| COMPANY NAME | PRODUCT / SERVICE | PHONE | EMP | CITY |
|---|---|---|---|---|
| ABCO Wire & Metal Products (BR) | Designer and manufacturer of display racks. The company focuses on roller grill, drying racks, and POP displays. | 510-909-5626 | NA | Castro Valley |
| Advantage Metal Products (HQ) | Provider of sheet metal and machining services. The company offers painting and silk screening, forming, welding, and machine shop services. | 925-667-2009 | NA | Livermore |
| Aire Sheet Metal (HQ) | Provider of mechanical and architectural sheet metal services. The company is involved in the design and construction of commercial projects. | 650-364-8081 | NA | Redwood City |
| Airtronics Metal Products Inc (HQ) | Manufacturer of sheet metal fabrication and machining. The company provides custom sheets for the electronics, telecommunications and other markets. | 408-977-7800 | NA | Morgan Hill |
| All Fab Precision Sheetmetal Inc (HQ) | Provider of contract manufacturing services for metal formed products. The company is involved in laser cutting, deburring, bending, and welding activities. | 408-279-1099 | NA | San Jose |
| Angels Sheet Metal Inc (HQ) | Provider of sheet metal fabrication services. The company focuses on heating and air conditioning systems. | 209-736-4541 | 1-10 | Angels Camp |
| Art's Sheet Metal Manufacturing Inc (HQ) | Manufacturer of flashings, vents, drainage products, tie plates, and hangers. The company also focuses on distribution aspects. | 408-778-0606 | NA | Morgan Hill |
| Asepco Corp (HQ) | Manufacturer of valves and magnetic mixers. The company also offers diaphragms, connnectors, and actuators. | 650-691-9500 | NA | Milpitas |
| Cofan Usa Inc (HQ) | Developer and manufacturer of products for thermal engineering. The company specializes in fans, heat sinks, and custom products. | 510-490-7533 | NA | Fremont |
| Concord Sheet Metal (HQ) | Provider of architectural metal products. The company focuses on fasteners, copper gutters, and decorative chimney tops. | 800-799-1900 | NA | Pittsburg |
| Custom Product Development Co (HQ) | Developer and manufacturer of mechanical components and turn-key assembly solutions. The company specializes in developing customized products. | 925-960-0577 | NA | Livermore |
| Group Manufacturing Services Inc (HQ) | Manufacturer of precision sheet metal fabrication, precision machining, and design support services. | 408-436-1040 | NA | San Jose |
| Inland Metal Technologies (HQ) | Provider of sheet metal fabrication, manufacturing, powder coating, silk-screening, and laser cutting services. | 510-785-8555 | NA | Hayward |
| Johnson Industrial Sheet Metal Inc (HQ) | Designer, fabricator, and installer of blowpipe systems, custom fabricated products, and packaged system projects. | 916-927-8244 | 1-10 | Sacramento |
| Lawson Mechanical Contractors (HQ) | Provider of mechanical construction services. The company offers plumbing, HVAC, industrial, and process piping services. | 916-381-5000 | 11-50 | Sacramento |
| Luna's Sheet Metal Inc (HQ) | Provider of metal fabrication and precision metal working services for the computer electronics, telecommunications, and automotive industries. | 408-492-1260 | NA | Santa Clara |
| M-T Metal Fabrication Inc (HQ) | Provider of sheet metal solutions. The company offers CNC laser cutting, precision welding, gaining, PEM fastening, and silk screen. | 510-357-5262 | NA | San Leandro |
| Melrose Nameplate & Label Co (HQ) | Developer and manufacturer of ID nameplates, labels, and membrane switches. The company offers touchscreen assembly and decorative nameplates. | 510-732-3100 | NA | Hayward |
| Micro Lithography Inc (HQ) | Manufacturer of pellicles using high end equipment for the production of frames and engineering parts, automatic anodizing lines, and chemical labs. | 408-747-1769 | NA | Sunnyvale |
| Odie Sheet Metal Shop (HQ) | Provider of sheet metal fabrication solutions. The company also deals with manufacturing and prototype development. | 408-281-2919 | NA | San Jose |
| Oneto Metal Products Corp (HQ) | Manufacturer of fabricated sheet metal products. The company offers flashing, roof jacks, gravel stop and specialty architectural sheet metal. | 916-681-6555 | 1-10 | Sacramento |
| Pec Manufacturing (HQ) | Provider of customized electromechanical, electronic, and mechanical solutions such as cable and harness assemblies and electro-mechanical assemblies. | 408-577-1839 | NA | San Jose |
| Pega Precision Inc (HQ) | Manufacturer and marketer of precision sheet metal and machining components. The company serves the military, semiconductor, and solar industries. | 408-776-3700 | NA | Morgan Hill |
| Peridot Corp (HQ) | Provider of design for manufacturing and packaging. The company also manufacturers of medical components, miniature component and general product prototypes. | 925-461-8830 | NA | Pleasanton |

| COMPANY NAME | PRODUCT / SERVICE | PHONE | EMP | CITY |
|---|---|---|---|---|
| Photo Etch Technology (BR) | Provider of stainless stell stencils. The company offers epoxy stencils, precision metal parts, fixture pallets, mesh screens, and artwork services. | 408-988-0220 | NA | Santa Clara |
| Procurement Partners International Inc (HQ) | Provider of procurement services. The company offers mechanical components such as pins, rods, rollers, and sheet metal. | 650-345-6118 | NA | San Mateo |
| Qualdeval International (HQ) | Supplier of high-pressure fluid flow and special core analysis equipment. The company offers PCB fabrication & assembly, and other services. | 844-247-2523 | NA | Fremont |
| Responsible Metal Fab Inc (HQ) | Provider of precision sheet metal fabrication services. The company offers machining, electromechanical assembly, packaging, and delivery services. | 408-734-0713 | NA | Sunnyvale |
| SAE Engineering Inc (HQ) | Provider of integrated turnkey assembly, precision machining, and sheet metal fabrication services to many sectors. The company also offers software. | 408-987-9950 | NA | Santa Clara |
| Sanctuary Stainless (HQ) | Provider of metal fabrication services. The company specializes in stainless and aluminum tubing and pipe fabrication. | 831-633-3867 | NA | Moss Landing |
| Terminal Manufacturing Company Llc (HQ) | Designer and manufacturer of vacuum chambers, pressure vessels, truck tanks, and assorted fabrications. | 510-526-3071 | NA | Berkeley |
| United Sheetmetal Inc (BR) | Manufacturer of precision metal products. The company specializes in tooling, die casting, plastic injection, and sheet metal fabrication services. | 510-257-1858 | NA | Fremont |
| Usk Manufacturing Inc (HQ) | Provider of precision sheet metal and machining services. The company also focuses on mechanical assembly. | 510-471-7555 | NA | Union City |
| Wellmade Products (HQ) | Manufacturer of lighting, wheelbarrows, and sheet metal products. The company also offers photometric sheets. | 209-723-9120 | 1-10 | Merced |
| West Coast Fab Inc (HQ) | Provider of precision electronic sheet metal fabrication services. The company specializes in finished products. | 510-529-0177 | NA | Richmond |
| Westfab Manufacturing Inc (HQ) | Manufacturer of simple brackets, multiple level frames, and enclosures. The company offers assembly services for power supplies, switches, and cables. | 408-727-0550 | NA | Santa Clara |

## 89 = Computer Systems (Hardware)

| | | | | |
|---|---|---|---|---|
| **N** Square Inc (HQ) | Builds tools to empower and enrich people and help sellers of all areas to start, run, and grow their businesses. | 415-375-3176 | NA | San Francisco |

## 90 = CAD/CAM/CAE Workstations

| | | | | |
|---|---|---|---|---|
| Synapse Design (HQ) | Provider of embedded software design services. The company also offers test bench analysis and block and chip level verification services. | 408-850-3640 | NA | Santa Clara |

## 91 = Computer Boards

| | | | | |
|---|---|---|---|---|
| Advantech Inc (DH) | Provider of system integration, hardware, software, embedded systems, automation products, and logistics support. | 408-519-3898 | NA | Milpitas |
| Alphaems Corp (HQ) | Provider of printed circuit board prototyping and PCB assembly production services. The company also involves in material purchasing and warehousing. | 510-498-8788 | NA | Fremont |
| American Portwell Technology Inc (DH) | Designer and manufacturer of industrial PC products. The company also offers embedded computing, network appliances, and human machine interfaces. | 510-403-3399 | NA | Fremont |
| Arbor Solution Inc (HQ) | Provider of embedded computing and networking solutions for the transportation, medical, automation, and military segments. | 408-452-8900 | NA | Fremont |
| Corsair Inc (HQ) | Designer of high-speed modules for mission-critical servers. The company also caters to high-end workstations. | 510-657-8747 | NA | Fremont |
| DIGICOM Electronics Inc (HQ) | Provider of electronics manufacturing services. The company also deals with packing, shipping, and labeling services. | 510-639-7003 | NA | Oakland |
| Entech Electronics Inc (BR) | Supplier of electronic equipment. The company also offers laser cut stencils, graphic decals, LCD screens, and engineering services. | 408-730-2650 | NA | Santa Clara |
| Exxact Corp (HQ) | Supplier of workstation graphic cards and solutions. The company also offers servers, HPC clusters, and computing software. | 510-226-7366 | NA | Fremont |
| FLYTECH Technology Company Ltd (BR) | Developer and manufacturer of touch screen, LCD, and other peripherals. The company also designs motherboard. | 510-257-5180 | NA | San Jose |
| Genstor Systems Inc (HQ) | Provider of customized hardware solutions for server, storage, clusters, personal computers, and workstations. | 408-980-0121 | NA | Santa Clara |
| Hotan Corp (HQ) | Distributor and manufacturer of batteries, chargers, flashlights and memory cards, and related media accessories. | | NA | Livermore |
| Ibase Technology (usa) Inc (BR) | Developer of embedded products such as industrial motherboards, CPU modules, barebone systems, network appliances, and digital surveillance systems. | 408-992-0888 | NA | Sunnyvale |
| Inbus Engineering (HQ) | Manufacturer and supplier of obsolete Intel boards emulators. The company offers repair & replacement and disk transfer services. | 925-454-2500 | NA | Livermore |
| Intel Corp (HQ) | Designer, developer, and marketer of processors and motherboards. The company also focuses on tablets, laptops, desktops, and other devices. | 408-765-8080 | NA | Santa Clara |
| Jetway Computer Corp (HQ) | Manufacturer of motherboards and LCD monitors. The company also specializes in graphic cards and barebones systems. | 510-857-0130 | NA | Newark |

| COMPANY NAME | PRODUCT / SERVICE | PHONE | EMP | CITY |
|---|---|---|---|---|
| Max Group Corp (HQ) | Distributor for computing devices. The company offers computer cases, fans and heatsinks, and hard drives. | 888-644-4629 | NA | Fremont |
| Mosaic Industries Inc (HQ) | Developer and manufacturer of embedded computers for instruments and automation. The company serves sensor calibration and PID control needs. | 510-790-8222 | NA | Newark |
| Murdoc Technology Llc (HQ) | Manufacturer of electronics. The company primarily offers precision and wire harnesses and cables to various sectors. | 559-497-1580 | 1-10 | Fresno |
| NVIDIA Corp (HQ) | Provider of visual computing solutions that include video games, movie production, product design, medical diagnosis, and scientific research. | 408-486-2000 | NA | Santa Clara |
| PFU America Inc (BR) | Provider of technology solutions. The company designs, develops, and sells computer hardware, peripheral products, and systems. | 408-992-2900 | NA | Sunnyvale |
| Synapse Design (HQ) | Provider of embedded software design services. The company also offers test bench analysis and block and chip level verification services. | 408-850-3640 | NA | Santa Clara |
| Ultraview Corp (BR) | Provider of data acquisition solutions, bus extenders, synthesizers, and direct digital synthesizers. | 925-253-2960 | NA | Berkeley |
| Vicom Systems Inc (HQ) | Provider of migration data services. The company is involved in offering transparent wire-speed data services for systems and storage. | 650-241-3302 | NA | Santa Clara |
| X-Scan Imaging Corp (HQ) | Supplier of x-ray imaging and inspection equipment. The company also offers array detectors and line-scan camera products. | 408-432-9888 | NA | San Jose |

## 92 = Computer Terminals

| COMPANY NAME | PRODUCT / SERVICE | PHONE | EMP | CITY |
|---|---|---|---|---|
| Asa Computers Inc (HQ) | Manufacturer of full service custom servers and storage systems. The company also focuses on integration. | 650-230-8000 | NA | Mountain View |
| Echelon Corp (HQ) | Developer of open-standard control networking platforms. The company serves outdoor lighting, building automation, transportation, and other needs. | 408-938-5200 | NA | Santa Clara |
| Exxact Corp (HQ) | Supplier of workstation graphic cards and solutions. The company also offers servers, HPC clusters, and computing software. | 510-226-7366 | NA | Fremont |
| Ibus Corp (HQ) | Manufacturer and provider of industrial computers. The company also specializes in prototyping and quality control. | 408-450-7880 | NA | Santa Clara |
| Max Group Corp (HQ) | Distributor for computing devices. The company offers computer cases, fans and heatsinks, and hard drives. | 888-644-4629 | NA | Fremont |
| Omni Pro Systems (HQ) | Supplier and integrator of computer systems. The company offers custom logo engraving services and deployment ready solutions. | 415-648-1121 | NA | San Francisco |
| Patriot Memory Inc (HQ) | Developer of flash memory solutions. The company offers memory modules, flash cards, USB drives, gaming memory cards, and accessories. | 510-979-1021 | NA | Fremont |
| Posiflex Business Machines Inc (LH) | Provider of point of service hardware and platform technology. The company caters to diverse markets. | 510-429-7097 | NA | Hayward |
| Spracht (HQ) | Designer and manufacturer of consumer electronic products. The company offers digital imaging, acoustics, LCD image displays, and other products. | 650-215-7500 | NA | Palo Alto |
| TRI MAP International Inc (HQ) | Manufacturer of industrial grade rack mounts and desktop computers. The company is engaged in engineering and fabrication services. | 209-234-0100 | 1-10 | Stockton |
| Ultraview Corp (BR) | Provider of data acquisition solutions, bus extenders, synthesizers, and direct digital synthesizers. | 925-253-2960 | NA | Berkeley |

## 93 = Computers (Mainframe, Micro, Mini & Personal)

| COMPANY NAME | PRODUCT / SERVICE | PHONE | EMP | CITY |
|---|---|---|---|---|
| Acer America Corp (HQ) | Supplier of desktops, notebooks, tablets, monitors and projectors. The company also offers application and support services. | 408-533-7700 | NA | San Jose |
| Advanced Digital Solutions International Inc (HQ) | Provider of information technology solutions. The company provides backup media tapes, bar-code labels, tape drives, and data center supplies. | 510-490-6667 | NA | Fremont |
| Advanced Micro Devices Inc (HQ) | Provider of products such as desktops, notebooks, servers, workstations, and embedded systems. The company also offers a variety of software. | 408-749-4000 | NA | Santa Clara |
| Alphaems Corp (HQ) | Provider of printed circuit board prototyping and PCB assembly production services. The company also involves in material purchasing and warehousing. | 510-498-8788 | NA | Fremont |
| Arista Corp (HQ) | Manufacturer of industrial computer products such as industrial rack mounts, touch screen displays, and fanless, embedded, and wallmount computers. | 510-226-1800 | NA | Fremont |
| Aurostar Corp (HQ) | Provider of technology products and services focusing on home theater systems, consumer electronics, desktops and notebooks, and networking solutions. | 510-249-9422 | NA | Fremont |
| Durabook Americas Inc (BR) | Manufacturer of portable notebook computers. The company offers rugged notebook and tablet PC, parts, and accessories. | 510-492-0828 | NA | Fremont |
| Elma Electronic Inc (LH) | Designer and manufacturer of electronic components and enclosures. The company is involved in design, installation, and delivery services. | 510-656-3400 | NA | Fremont |
| Elo Touch Solutions Inc (HQ) | Designer, developer, and manufacturer of touch products and technologies. The company's products include tablets, touchscreens, and touch-monitors. | 408-597-8000 | NA | Milpitas |

| COMPANY NAME | PRODUCT / SERVICE | PHONE | EMP | CITY |
|---|---|---|---|---|
| Ent Networks Inc (HQ) | Provider of custom system manufacturing, database management, hardware sales, business consulting, and repair services. | 925-462-7125 | NA | Pleasanton |
| Landel (HQ) | Provider of telecommunication products such as MailBug, DataBug, and SurveyBug. The company is engaged in technical support services. | 408-360-0490 | NA | San Jose |
| Max Group Corp (HQ) | Distributor for computing devices. The company offers computer cases, fans and heatsinks, and hard drives. | 888-644-4629 | NA | Fremont |
| Mediawave Pc Inc (HQ) | Developer of rack optimized servers, digital signage, laptops, and desktop computer systems for resellers and end users. | 510-490-6768 | NA | Fremont |
| MiTAC Holdings Corp (BR) | Manufacturer of precision navigation, positioning systems. The company's products are based on GPS and GNSS technology. | | NA | Newark |
| Mosaic Industries Inc (HQ) | Developer and manufacturer of embedded computers for instruments and automation. The company serves sensor calibration and PID control needs. | 510-790-8222 | NA | Newark |
| Omni Pro Systems (HQ) | Supplier and integrator of computer systems. The company offers custom logo engraving services and deployment ready solutions. | 415-648-1121 | NA | San Francisco |
| Polywell Computers Inc (HQ) | Manufacturer of computer systems. The company specializes in desktop PCs, workstations, and servers. | 650-583-7222 | NA | S San Francisco |
| Qct Llc (HQ) | Provider of computer network services. The company also offers storage, database management, and data backup solutions. | 510-270-6111 | NA | San Jose |
| Recortec Inc (HQ) | Manufacturer of LCD monitors, KVM, keyboards, speakers, and computers. The company also offers customization services. | 408-928-1480 | NA | San Jose |
| Super Micro Computer Inc (HQ) | Provider of server technology and computing solutions. The company offers networking, gaming, micro cloud, and AMD services. | 408-503-8000 | NA | San Jose |
| Toshiba America Inc (BR) | Manufacturer of LCD, laptop batteries, power adapters, laptop cases, and other laptop related accessories. | 408-526-2400 | NA | San Jose |
| Tyan Computer Corp (DH) | Designer and manufacturer of server/workstation platforms. The company's products are sold to OEMs, VARs, system integrators, and resellers. | 510-651-8868 | NA | Fremont |

## 4 = Controllers

| COMPANY NAME | PRODUCT / SERVICE | PHONE | EMP | CITY |
|---|---|---|---|---|
| Arcus Technology Inc (HQ) | Provider of motor controllers, stepper motors, and related accessories such as cables, encoders, and gearboxes. | 925-373-8800 | NA | Livermore |
| Automation Partners Inc (HQ) | Manufacturer of controls for control systems and regulators. The company specializes in products for fabric density measurement. | 707-665-3980 | NA | Rohnert Park |
| AverLogic Technologies Inc (RH) | Designer and seller of integrated ICs. The company primarily caters to multimedia and video applications. | 408-526-0400 | NA | San Jose |
| Blair Electric Services Inc (HQ) | Provider of electrical contracting services. The company offers pump and well controls, PLC controls, and surveillance systems. | 559-784-8658 | 1-10 | Porterville |
| Curtis Instruments Inc (BR) | Manufacturer of hydraulic pump controllers. The company also specializes in electric steering controllers. | 925-961-1088 | NA | Livermore |
| Digital View Inc (HQ) | Developer and manufacturer of flat panel-related products. The company's offerings include media players, video flyers, and accessories. | 408-782-7773 | NA | Morgan Hill |
| Futronix Inc (HQ) | Designer and developer of energy management systems. The company provides computer line clocks, electronic cam systems, and energy control systems. | 408-735-1122 | NA | Santa Clara |
| Galil Motion Control (HQ) | Manufacturer and supplier of motion controllers and software tools. The company also offers drives and power supplies. | 916-626-0101 | 1-10 | Rocklin |
| Gcx Corp (HQ) | Provider of mounting solutions, application specific solutions, on-site services, and also technical support. | 707-773-1100 | NA | Petaluma |
| Highland Technology Inc (HQ) | Designer and manufacturer of precision analog instrumentation. The company serves laboratory research purposes. | 415-551-1700 | NA | San Francisco |
| Ics Electronics (HQ) | Provider of interfaces and controllers for assembling systems, interfacing devices, and legacy systems. | 925-416-1000 | NA | Pleasanton |
| King Star Computer Inc (HQ) | Provider of technology services to Fortune 500 companies, mid-size to small business, start-ups, and government and educational organizations. | 408-736-8590 | NA | Sunnyvale |
| Lucidport Technology Inc (HQ) | Provider of semiconductor solutions. The company offers USB and wireless USB controllers for printers, scanners, digital cameras, and TV tuners. | 408-720-8800 | NA | Sunnyvale |
| Modutek Corp (HQ) | Manufacturer of wet process equipment and environmental systems. The company serves the semiconductor sector and offers repair services. | 408-362-2000 | NA | San Jose |
| O2micro Usa (LH) | Provider of battery and power management products. The company also offers LED general lighting and backlighting products. | 408-987-5920 | NA | Santa Clara |
| Onspec Electronic Inc (HQ) | Provider of semiconductor and electronic devices. The company focuses on data transfer services using USB and also provides technical support. | 408-727-1819 | NA | Santa Clara |
| VueMetrix Inc (HQ) | Developer of laser diode-based systems. The company is focused on integrated laser diode control electronics. | 408-770-3070 | NA | San Jose |

## 95 = Storage & Disk

| COMPANY NAME | PRODUCT / SERVICE | PHONE | EMP | CITY |
|---|---|---|---|---|
| Addonics Technologies Inc (HQ) | Manufacturer of storage systems and products. The company's products include drive cartridge system, host controller, converter, and adapter. | 408-573-8580 | NA | San Jose |

| COMPANY NAME | PRODUCT / SERVICE | PHONE | EMP | CITY |
|---|---|---|---|---|
| Ampex Data Systems Corporation (HQ) | Manufacturer of digital storage systems. The company also offers airborne and ground systems and related video solutions. | 650-367-2011 | NA | Hayward |
| Asa Computers Inc (HQ) | Manufacturer of full service custom servers and storage systems. The company also focuses on integration. | 650-230-8000 | NA | Mountain View |
| Avalanche Technology (HQ) | Provider of programmable storage solutions. The company offers services to the consumer electronics industry. | 510-897-3300 | NA | Fremont |
| BiTMICRO Networks Inc (HQ) | Developer and manufacturer of flash-based SSD technology, products, and solutions. The company focuses on cloud computing and gaming applications. | 888-723-0123 | NA | Fremont |
| Chelsio Communications (HQ) | Provider of Ethernet adapters. The company offers storage routers, wire adapters, virtualization and management software, and accessories. | 408-962-3600 | NA | Sunnyvale |
| Copypro Inc (HQ) | Manufacturer and seller of heavy-duty desktop duplication systems such as duplicators, printers, and analyzers. | 925-689-1200 | NA | Concord |
| Data Distributing Llc (HQ) | Provider of solutions such as mass storage, peripheral, storage management software, import, archive, and images and data distribution. | 831-457-3537 | 11-50 | Santa Cruz |
| DataDirect Networks Inc (BR) | Provider of storage array, file system, and object storage appliances to broadcast, biopharma, supercomputing, and financial service sectors. | 408-419-2800 | NA | Santa Clara |
| DisplayLink Corp (HQ) | Provider of solutions for virtual graphics connectivity between computers and displays. The company makes use of USB, wireless USB, and ethernet. | 650-838-0481 | NA | Palo Alto |
| Drobo Inc (HQ) | Provider of virtualization and backup & archiving services. The company also offers disaster recovery and cloud storage solutions. | 408-454-4200 | NA | Sunnyvale |
| Exxact Corp (HQ) | Supplier of workstation graphic cards and solutions. The company also offers servers, HPC clusters, and computing software. | 510-226-7366 | NA | Fremont |
| Genstor Systems Inc (HQ) | Provider of customized hardware solutions for server, storage, clusters, personal computers, and workstations. | 408-980-0121 | NA | Santa Clara |
| Guzik Technical Enterprises (HQ) | Manufacturer of test equipment for the computer industry. The company is involved in sales, training, and software downloads. | 650-625-8000 | NA | Mountain View |
| Headway Technologies Inc (HQ) | Designer and manufacturer of hard-disk drives. The company is engaged in installation and technical support services. | 408-934-5300 | NA | Milpitas |
| HGST Inc (HQ) | Provider of hard disk drives and external storage products. The company is engaged in technical support services. | 408-717-6000 | NA | San Jose |
| Hotan Corp (HQ) | Distributor and manufacturer of batteries, chargers, flashlights and memory cards, and related media accessories. | | NA | Livermore |
| Hyve Solutions (HQ) | Designer of data center serve, storage, networking and appliance solutions. The company specializes in rack integration services. | 510-668-3877 | NA | Fremont |
| Infortrend Corp (LH) | Provider of high performance storage networking solutions. The company serves the energy, utilities, and healthcare industries. | 408-988-5088 | NA | San Jose |
| Innodisk Corp (BR) | Provider of embedded flash and dynamic random access memory storage products and technology solutions. | 510-770-9421 | NA | Fremont |
| Intevac Inc (HQ) | Supplier of magnetic media processing systems. The company offers advanced equipment to the hard disk drive, solar, and photonics industries. | 408-986-9888 | NA | Santa Clara |
| Iosafe Inc (HQ) | Provider of disaster proof hardware. The company provides SoloPRO SSD External and ioSafe Rugged Portable. | 530-820-3090 | 1-10 | Auburn |
| Iron Systems Inc (HQ) | Provider of network storage, hybrid cloud, and big data infrastructure solutions. The company offers OEM/ODM manufacturing services. | 408-943-8000 | NA | Fremont |
| Ixsystems Inc (HQ) | Provider of hardware, software, server, and storage solutions, and services such as software development and consultation. | 408-943-4100 | NA | San Jose |
| Mixonic (HQ) | Provider of design services. The company offers custom CD and DVD duplication, disc packaging, CD production, and printing services. | 866-838-5067 | NA | San Francisco |
| Oryx Advanced Materials Inc (HQ) | Provider of thin film materials for PV cells. The company also offers sputtering targets and bonding services to the magnetic data storage market. | 510-249-1157 | NA | Fremont |
| Owens Design (HQ) | Developer of advanced technology systems for semiconductor, hard disk drive, solar, medical device, and other sectors. | 510-659-1800 | NA | Fremont |
| Patriot Memory Inc (HQ) | Developer of flash memory solutions. The company offers memory modules, flash cards, USB drives, gaming memory cards, and accessories. | 510-979-1021 | NA | Fremont |
| Promise Technology Inc (HQ) | Provider of storage solutions such as cloud and surveillance storage and virtual tape library for digital home applications. | 408-228-1400 | NA | Milpitas |
| Pure Storage Inc (HQ) | Provider of flash storage solutions.The company is focused on developing flash arrays for various enterprises. | 833-371-7873 | NA | Mountain View |
| Qct Llc (HQ) | Provider of computer network services. The company also offers storage, database management, and data backup solutions. | 510-270-6111 | NA | San Jose |
| R-Hub Communications Inc (HQ) | Provider of web conferencing and remote support services. The company offers services for on-premise security, branding, and integration. | 408-899-2830 | NA | San Jose |
| Rasilient Systems Inc (HQ) | Provider of technology products and services. The company offers a range of video surveillance and storage products. | 408-730-2568 | NA | Santa Clara |
| Sae Magnetics (hk) Ltd (BR) | Manufacturer of magnetic recording heads, head gimbals assemblies, and head stack assemblies for computer disk drivers. | 408-956-7100 | NA | Milpitas |

| COMPANY NAME | PRODUCT / SERVICE | PHONE | EMP | CITY |
|---|---|---|---|---|
| Siig Inc (HQ) | Manufacturer of computer connectivity products. The company is involved in increasing the bandwidth between a computer system and external devices. | 510-657-8688 | NA | Fremont |
| Super Talent Technology (HQ) | Designer and manufacturer of flash based storage solutions for enterprise servers, portable devices, personal computers, and consumer electronics. | 408-934-2560 | NA | San Jose |
| Themis Computer (HQ) | Provider of embedded computing solutions for system integrators and OEMs. The company provides RES servers and HPCs, and rugged storage appliances. | 510-252-0870 | NA | Fremont |
| Tintri Inc (HQ) | Developer of zero management storage systems. The company focuses on building storage for virtual environments. | 650-810-8200 | NA | Mountain View |
| Viking Enterprise Solutions (HQ) | Provider of solutions for data enterpriser centers. The company also offers storage expansion product platform. | 408-964-3730 | NA | San Jose |
| Western Digital Corp (HQ) | Manufacturer of external storage devices. The company also focuses on network storage and backup solutions and offers technical support services. | 408-717-6000 | NA | San Jose |
| Western Digital Corporation (HQ) | Provider of storage array solutions. The company focuses on desktop virtualization, server virtualization, database hosting, and file services. | 510-791-7900 | NA | Newark |
| Winnov Lp (HQ) | Provider of video capture and streaming solutions. The company serves education, enterprise, healthcare, and live event sectors. | 888-315-9460 | NA | Santa Clara |

## 6 = Memory Systems

| COMPANY NAME | PRODUCT / SERVICE | PHONE | EMP | CITY |
|---|---|---|---|---|
| Adesto Technologies Corporation Inc (HQ) | Provider of power memory solutions. The company's portfolio comprises Fusion Serial Flash, DataFlas, and Mavriq serial memory. | 408-400-0578 | NA | Santa Clara |
| ADLINK Technology Inc (LH) | Designer and manufacturer of products for embedded computing, test & measurement, and automation applications. The company serves various sectors. | 408-360-0200 | NA | San Jose |
| Atp Electronics Inc (RH) | Provider of NAND flash and DRAM memory modules. The company specializes in telecom, medical, automotive, and enterprise computing. | 408-732-5000 | NA | San Jose |
| Avalanche Technology (HQ) | Provider of programmable storage solutions. The company offers services to the consumer electronics industry. | 510-897-3300 | NA | Fremont |
| Corsair Inc (HQ) | Designer of high-speed modules for mission-critical servers. The company also caters to high-end workstations. | 510-657-8747 | NA | Fremont |
| Gsi Technology (HQ) | Provider of telecommunication and networking services. The company is also engaged in sales and distribution. | 408-331-8800 | NA | Sunnyvale |
| Innodisk Corp (BR) | Provider of embedded flash and dynamic random access memory storage products and technology solutions. | 510-770-9421 | NA | Fremont |
| Iron Systems Inc (HQ) | Provider of network storage, hybrid cloud, and big data infrastructure solutions. The company offers OEM/ODM manufacturing services. | 408-943-8000 | NA | Fremont |
| Lexar Media Inc (HQ) | Provider of memory product lines such as USB drives, memory cards, card readers, and dram computer memory. | 408-933-1088 | NA | San Jose |
| Macronix America Inc (LH) | Manufacturer of integrated device. The company offers application driven system solutions and non-volatile memory semiconductor solutions. | 408-262-8887 | NA | Milpitas |
| Max Group Corp (HQ) | Distributor for computing devices. The company offers computer cases, fans and heatsinks, and hard drives. | 888-644-4629 | NA | Fremont |
| Mixonic (HQ) | Provider of design services. The company offers custom CD and DVD duplication, disc packaging, CD production, and printing services. | 866-838-5067 | NA | San Francisco |
| POLYSTAK Inc (HQ) | Provider of silicon based multi chip package products as well as package stacking solutions and repair services of components and modules. | 408-441-1400 | NA | San Jose |
| Pure Storage Inc (HQ) | Provider of flash storage solutions. The company is focused on developing flash arrays for various enterprises. | 833-371-7873 | NA | Mountain View |
| Qct Llc (HQ) | Provider of computer network services. The company also offers storage, database management, and data backup solutions. | 510-270-6111 | NA | San Jose |
| Smart Modular Technologies (HQ) | Manufacturer of add on memory boards, flash, and storage products. The company serves defense, gaming, storage, and other sectors. | 510-623-1231 | NA | Newark |
| Spectra 7 Microsystems Ltd (HQ) | Manufacturer of analog semiconductor devices. The company focuses on micro-thin interconnects for consumer electronic products. | 408-770-2915 | NA | San Jose |
| Super Talent Technology (HQ) | Designer and manufacturer of flash based storage solutions for enterprise servers, portable devices, personal computers, and consumer electronics. | 408-934-2560 | NA | San Jose |
| Testmetrix Inc (HQ) | Manufacturer of high-throughput AVTE systems, and offers official compliance certification test services. | 408-730-5511 | NA | Milpitas |
| Wintec Industries Inc (HQ) | Manufacturer and distributor of memory modules and components. The company serves consumer, embedded OEM, e-commerce, and other needs. | 510-953-7421 | NA | Newark |

## 7 = Networking Equipment

| COMPANY NAME | PRODUCT / SERVICE | PHONE | EMP | CITY |
|---|---|---|---|---|
| 6WIND USA Inc (RH) | Manufacturer of virtual accelerators, routers, and related accessories. The company offers network security and network appliance solutions. | 408-816-1366 | NA | Santa Clara |
| A10 Networks Inc (HQ) | Provider of networking and security solutions such as cloud computing and virtualization and bandwidth management. | 408-325-8668 | NA | San Jose |

| COMPANY NAME | PRODUCT / SERVICE | PHONE | EMP | CITY |
|---|---|---|---|---|
| Accton Technology Corp (DH) | Distributor of network connectivity products and ethernet hubs. The company focuses on home security, cloud, data center switch, and other needs. | 408-747-0994 | NA | Sunnyvale |
| Actiontec Electronics Inc (HQ) | Provider of internet modems, networking adapters, and routers. The company offers fiber routers, powerline network kits and wireless display products. | 408-752-7700 | NA | Sunnyvale |
| Alpha Networks Inc (HQ) | Designer and manufacturer of networking products. The company also focuses on computers and computer peripherals. | 408-844-8850 | NA | Milpitas |
| Alphaems Corp (HQ) | Provider of printed circuit board prototyping and PCB assembly production services. The company also involves in material purchasing and warehousing. | 510-498-8788 | NA | Fremont |
| Amax Information Technologies Inc (HQ) | Manufacturer and seller of custom servers and storage solutions. The company focuses on platform design, custom branding, and supply chain management. | 510-651-8886 | NA | Fremont |
| Andover Consulting Group Inc (HQ) | Supplier of network components. The company offers data center liquidation, network security, and network equipment services. | 415-537-6950 | NA | S San Francisco |
| Appro Technology Inc (BR) | Manufacturer of network surveillance systems. The company's products include dome cameras, LCD monitors, and cables. | 408-720-0018 | NA | Sunnyvale |
| Arcus Technology Inc (HQ) | Provider of motor controllers, stepper motors, and related accessories such as cables, encoders, and gearboxes. | 925-373-8800 | NA | Livermore |
| Arista Networks Inc (HQ) | Provider of cloud networking, network virtualization, high frequency trading, and government solutions for data center needs. | 408-547-5500 | NA | Santa Clara |
| Avaya Inc (HQ) | Provider of PBX solutions, IVR applications, IP telephony solutions, voice messaging, and consulting. | 908-953-6000 | NA | Santa Clara |
| Aviram Networks Inc (HQ) | Provider of wire-speed IPS for recognition & visualization, access control, and other needs. The company offers consulting and training services. | 408-624-1234 | NA | San Jose |
| Bivio Networks Inc (HQ) | Provider of cyber security and network control solutions. The company offers cyber defense systems, surveillance, flow analysis, and monitoring tools. | 925-924-8600 | NA | Pleasanton |
| Cermetek Microelectronics (HQ) | Manufacturer of communication modules for embedded systems. The company caters to power generation, irrigation control, and medical monitoring fields. | 408-942-2200 | NA | Milpitas |
| Ciena Corp (BR) | Provider of cloud networking, network transformation, and packet network solutions for multi-data center environments. | 408-904-2100 | NA | San Jose |
| Cisco Systems Inc (BR) | Provider of networking products and services such as routers, switches, and optical and wireless networking devices. | 800-553-6387 | NA | San Francisco |
| Compudata Inc (HQ) | Provider of sales, accounting, and manufacturing software. The company especially caters to businesses. | 415-495-3422 | NA | San Francisco |
| Cpacket Networks (HQ) | Provider of solutions for network traffic monitoring and data center performance management. The company specializes in traffic monitoring switches. | 650-969-9500 | NA | San Jose |
| Edgewater Networks Inc (HQ) | Provider of enterprise session controllers for business purposes. The company also offers security and policy management services. | 408-351-7200 | NA | San Jose |
| Embedur Systems Inc (HQ) | Developer of software solutions. The company also offers technical and management services for the embedded market. | 510-353-9111 | NA | Fremont |
| Engage Communication Inc (HQ) | Developer and manufacturer of telecommunications equipment. The company focuses on encryption, mobile, and cellular backhauling solutions. | 831-688-1021 | 11-50 | Aptos |
| Ent Networks Inc (HQ) | Provider of custom system manufacturing, database management, hardware sales, business consulting, and repair services. | 925-462-7125 | NA | Pleasanton |
| Five9 Network Systems LLC (HQ) | Provider of server and storage solutions. The company serves the government, printing, cloud infrastructure, and energy markets. | 650-494-2220 | NA | Palo Alto |
| Genstor Systems Inc (HQ) | Provider of customized hardware solutions for server, storage, clusters, personal computers, and workstations. | 408-980-0121 | NA | Santa Clara |
| Greatlink International Inc (RH) | Manufacturer of cable assemblies and related products for the medical, aerospace, and automotive industries. | 510-657-1667 | NA | Fremont |
| HotLava Systems Inc (HQ) | Provider of board-level solutions for servers and appliances that operates in virtualized environments. | 510-531-1169 | NA | Oakland |
| Hyve Solutions (HQ) | Designer of data center serve, storage, networking and appliance solutions. The company specializes in rack integration services. | 510-668-3877 | NA | Fremont |
| Ibase Technology (usa) Inc (BR) | Developer of embedded products such as industrial motherboards, CPU modules, barebone systems, network appliances, and digital surveillance systems. | 408-992-0888 | NA | Sunnyvale |
| Infinera Corp (HQ) | Provider of services and solutions in optical networks. The company serves cable operators and internet content providers. | 408-572-5200 | NA | Sunnyvale |
| Infoblox Inc (HQ) | Provider of automated network control solutions. The company's services include training, implementation, migration, upgrade, repair, and maintenance. | 408-986-4000 | NA | Santa Clara |
| Infortrend Corp (LH) | Provider of high performance storage networking solutions. The company serves the energy, utilities, and healthcare industries. | 408-988-5088 | NA | San Jose |

| COMPANY NAME | PRODUCT / SERVICE | PHONE | EMP | CITY |
|---|---|---|---|---|
| Interface Masters Technologies Inc (HQ) | Developer of technology and networking solutions. The company's products include embedded switches, adapters, and related accessories. | 408-441-9341 | NA | San Jose |
| Interworking Labs Inc (HQ) | Provider of network related services. The company focuses on testing, emulation, and also offers network optimization products. | 831-460-7010 | 1-10 | Scotts Valley |
| Iosafe Inc (HQ) | Provider of disaster proof hardware. The company provides SoloPRO SSD External and ioSafe Rugged Portable. | 530-820-3090 | 1-10 | Auburn |
| King Star Computer Inc (HQ) | Provider of technology services to Fortune 500 companies, mid-size to small business, start-ups, and government and educational organizations. | 408-736-8590 | NA | Sunnyvale |
| Lewiz Communications Inc (HQ) | Provider of computer networking solutions. The company also offers data security, data management, and data streaming services. | 408-432-6248 | NA | San Jose |
| Linkbit Inc (HQ) | Manufacturer of network equipment. The company primarily caters to service providers and network operators. | 408-969-9940 | NA | Santa Clara |
| NETGEAR Inc (HQ) | Provider of network solutions for home and businesses. The company also offers home video monitoring systems and storage products. | 408-907-8000 | NA | San Jose |
| OJO Technology Inc (HQ) | Manufacturer of video surveillance systems. The company offers services to the education, transportation, and utility sectors. | 877-306-4656 | NA | Fremont |
| Omnicor (HQ) | Provider of network testing tools, vacuum capacitors, and interrupters and IP performance test systems. | 650-572-0122 | NA | Foster City |
| Pica8 Inc (HQ) | Manufacturer of white box switches. The company specializes in traditional switches and routing protocols. | 650-614-5838 | NA | Palo Alto |
| Platina Systems Corp (HQ) | Manufacturer of network equipment including switches. The company serves industrial and commercial customers. | 408-389-4268 | 1-10 | Santa Clara |
| POLYSTAK Inc (HQ) | Provider of silicon based multi chip package products as well as package stacking solutions and repair services of components and modules. | 408-441-1400 | NA | San Jose |
| Praesum Communications Inc (HQ) | Provider of switching communication products. The company offers IP cores, boards, and system level products. | 707-338-0946 | NA | Santa Rosa |
| Qct Llc (HQ) | Provider of computer network services. The company also offers storage, database management, and data backup solutions. | 510-270-6111 | NA | San Jose |
| Qulsar Inc (HQ) | Specializes in packaging, refinement, and distribution of precise time synchronization. The company serves the telecom and networking industries. | 408-715-1098 | NA | San Jose |
| R-Hub Communications Inc (HQ) | Provider of web conferencing and remote support services. The company offers services for on-premise security, branding, and integration. | 408-899-2830 | NA | San Jose |
| Raymar Information Technology Inc (HQ) | Provider of hardware supplies, network infrastructure, virtualization, disaster recovery, and managed services. | 916-783-1951 | 11-50 | Sacramento |
| Redline Communications (BR) | Provider of networking and consulting solutions. The company serves the government, telecommunication, and military sectors. | 866-633-6669 | NA | Santa Clara |
| Sai Technology Inc (HQ) | Designer and developer of wireless technology solutions. The company also deals with digital signage services. | 408-727-1560 | NA | Santa Clara |
| Siig Inc (HQ) | Manufacturer of computer connectivity products. The company is involved in increasing the bandwidth between a computer system and external devices. | 510-657-8688 | NA | Fremont |
| Stonefly Inc (HQ) | Provider of storage optimization and disaster recovery protection for software solutions. The company also offers storage area networks. | 510-265-1616 | NA | Hayward |
| Taseon Inc (HQ) | Developer of technology related solutions. The company also offers system engineering and software development services. | 408-240-7800 | NA | San Jose |
| Thinkoptics (HQ) | Provider of software solutions. The company's products include iWavit Blast, iWavit Premium, iWavit Basic, and Wavit 3D. | 765-889-2848 | NA | San Jose |
| Utstarcom Inc (BR) | Manufacturer of IP based, end to end networking, and telecommunications solutions. The company also focuses on integration. | 408-453-4557 | NA | San Jose |
| Zypcom Inc (HQ) | Designer and manufacturer of analog modems. The company mainly caters to the networking professionals. | 510-324-2501 | NA | Union City |

## 98 = Power Supplies

| COMPANY NAME | PRODUCT / SERVICE | PHONE | EMP | CITY |
|---|---|---|---|---|
| Aldetec Inc (HQ) | Manufacturer of microwave amplifier products. The company provides low noise amplifiers, down converters, and octave band amplifiers. | 916-453-3382 | 1-10 | Sacramento |
| Applied Motion Products Inc (HQ) | Manufacturer of stepper drives and motors, gearheads, power supplies, and related accessories. The company offers technical support services. | 831-761-6555 | 1-10 | Watsonville |
| Areias Systems Inc (HQ) | Provider of services to the technology sector. The company focuses on design, engineering, manufacturing, and prototyping. | 831-440-9800 | 1-10 | Scotts Valley |
| Corsair Inc (HQ) | Designer of high-speed modules for mission-critical servers. The company also caters to high-end workstations. | 510-657-8747 | NA | Fremont |
| Digital Power Corp (HQ) | Designer and manufacturer of switching power supplies. The company serves the industrial, military, and medical markets. | 510-657-2635 | NA | Fremont |
| Eta-Usa (HQ) | Provider of power supplies and manufacturer of battery chargers. The company serves the communication, gaming, and computing industries. | 408-778-2793 | NA | Morgan Hill |
| Go!Foton Corp (BR) | Supplier of optical materials and components. The company focuses on markets such as industrial, image and scanning, and biomedical research. | 408-831-0131 | NA | San Jose |

| COMPANY NAME | PRODUCT / SERVICE | PHONE | EMP | CITY |
|---|---|---|---|---|
| MiTAC Holdings Corp (BR) | Manufacturer of precision navigation, positioning systems. The company's products are based on GPS and GNSS technology. | | NA | Newark |
| Paxcell Group Inc (HQ) | Provider of electronic engineering and industrial design services. The company also offers contract manufacturing services. | 408-945-8054 | NA | Milpitas |
| Rgb Spectrum (HQ) | Manufacturer of video and computer signal display processors. The company serves security, oil & gas, corporate, and military sectors. | 510-814-7000 | NA | Alameda |
| Silicon Mitus (BR) | Manufacturer and distributor of smart power management integrated chips solutions. The company focuses on power solutions. | 408-446-3151 | NA | Cupertino |
| Stangenes Industries Inc (HQ) | Manufacturer of isolation transformers, current monitors, charging inductors, and magnetic components. | 650-493-0814 | NA | Palo Alto |
| Telemakus Llc (HQ) | Provider of USB controlled RF devices. The company devices include switches, vector modulators, and digital attenuators. | 916-458-6346 | 1-10 | Folsom |
| Versatile Power (HQ) | Designer and manufacturer of electronic subsystems for manufacturers. The company focuses on application of radio frequency, ultrasonics, and lasers. | 408-341-4600 | NA | Campbell |

## 99 = Process Control Computers

| COMPANY NAME | PRODUCT / SERVICE | PHONE | EMP | CITY |
|---|---|---|---|---|
| ADLINK Technology Inc (LH) | Designer and manufacturer of products for embedded computing, test & measurement, and automation applications. The company serves various sectors. | 408-360-0200 | NA | San Jose |
| Bay Dynamics Inc (HQ) | Provider of IT analytics solutions. The company offers data loss prevention, system management, and security tool implementation services. | 415-912-3130 | 11-50 | San Francisco |
| Cybosoft General Cybernation Group Inc (HQ) | Provider of control technology solutions for the process control, building control, and equipment control markets. | 916-631-6313 | 1-10 | Rancho Cordova |
| Omni Pro Systems (HQ) | Supplier and integrator of computer systems. The company offers custom logo engraving services and deployment ready solutions. | 415-648-1121 | NA | San Francisco |
| Siig Inc (HQ) | Manufacturer of computer connectivity products. The company is involved in increasing the bandwidth between a computer system and external devices. | 510-657-8688 | NA | Fremont |

## 100 = Repair & Maintenance

| COMPANY NAME | PRODUCT / SERVICE | PHONE | EMP | CITY |
|---|---|---|---|---|
| Ibus Corp (HQ) | Manufacturer and provider of industrial computers. The company also specializes in prototyping and quality control. | 408-450-7880 | NA | Santa Clara |
| Omni Pro Systems (HQ) | Supplier and integrator of computer systems. The company offers custom logo engraving services and deployment ready solutions. | 415-648-1121 | NA | San Francisco |
| Systemacs (HQ) | Provider of solutions for upgrading or setting up networks which include hardware, software, and routers. | 650-329-9745 | NA | Palo Alto |
| Veolia Water (BR) | Provider of water and wastewater treatment solutions. The company offers services for public authorities and industrial companies. | 510-412-2001 | NA | Richmond |

## 101 = Computer Peripherals/Accessories

| COMPANY NAME | PRODUCT / SERVICE | PHONE | EMP | CITY |
|---|---|---|---|---|
| Acadia Technology Inc (HQ) | Dealer of power supplies, water cooling kits, cases, fans and fan ducts, and digital temperature displayers. | 408-737-9528 | NA | Sunnyvale |

## 102 = ATMs

| COMPANY NAME | PRODUCT / SERVICE | PHONE | EMP | CITY |
|---|---|---|---|---|
| HP Development Company LP (HQ) | Provider of computer products that include desktops, monitors, printers and scanners, ink, toner and papers, and laptops. | 650-857-1501 | NA | Palo Alto |
| International Microsystems Inc (HQ) | Designer and manufacturer of flash memory duplication equipment. The company also offers related test equipment. | 408-942-1001 | NA | Fremont |
| Sycard Technology (HQ) | Provider of 16-bit PC card and CardBus devices. The company also offers USB and smart media development services. | 408-399-8073 | NA | Los Gatos |

## 103 = Bar Code Scanners

| COMPANY NAME | PRODUCT / SERVICE | PHONE | EMP | CITY |
|---|---|---|---|---|
| Data ID Systems (HQ) | Provider of identification management solutions. The company offers passport readers, bar code scanners, and fixed asset tracking products. | 408-371-5764 | NA | Campbell |
| LifeMed ID Inc (HQ) | Provider of patient identification technology solutions. The company offers services to healthcare organizations. | | 1-10 | Roseville |
| Worth Data Inc (HQ) | Designer and manufacturer of bar code scanners and barcode software that includes bar code printing software and inventory tracking software. | 831-458-9938 | 1-10 | Santa Cruz |

## 104 = Computer R&D & Other Services

| COMPANY NAME | PRODUCT / SERVICE | PHONE | EMP | CITY |
|---|---|---|---|---|
| Acronics (HQ) | Provider of engineering services. The company is involved in systems and mechanical design services. | 408-432-0888 | NA | San Jose |
| Micro Tech Systems (HQ) | Provider of cabling solutions. The company involves in the installation and repair of voice, data, and video network systems. | 559-438-7580 | 1-10 | Fresno |
| N Silex Technology America Inc (HQ) | Manufacturer of print servers for network printers and fingerprint readers. The company serves security applications. | 657-218-5199 | 11-50 | Santa Ana |
| Skybox Security Inc (HQ) | Provider of risk analytics for cyber security. The company offers threat management and network security management solutions. | 408-441-8060 | NA | San Jose |
| Tru Technical Partners Inc (HQ) | Provider of information technology services on a contract basis. The company's services include managed desktops, workstation, anti-virus, and others. | 408-559-2800 | NA | Campbell |

| COMPANY NAME | PRODUCT / SERVICE | PHONE | EMP | CITY |
|---|---|---|---|---|

## 05 = Computer Supplies

| COMPANY NAME | PRODUCT / SERVICE | PHONE | EMP | CITY |
|---|---|---|---|---|
| America Aopen Inc (HQ) | Specializes in the manufacture and marketing of personal computer (PC) components and peripherals. The company also offers speakers and bare systems. | 888-972-6736 | NA | San Jose |
| ASUSTeK Computer Inc (HQ) | Manufacturer of computer systems and hardware components such as desktops, notebooks, peripherals, motherboards, and graphic cards. | 510-739-3777 | NA | Fremont |
| Computerland Of Silicon Valley (HQ) | Provider of hardware, software, and networking services. The company serves government and educational institutions. | 408-519-3200 | NA | San Jose |
| Ergo Direct Com (HQ) | Provider of adjustable desks, arms, and mounts. The company offers ergonomic keyboards, monitor arms, and mounting adapters. | 650-654-4300 | NA | San Carlos |
| Landel (HQ) | Provider of telecommunication products such as MailBug, DataBug, and SurveyBug. The company is engaged in technical support services. | 408-360-0490 | NA | San Jose |

## 06 = Computer Wire & Harness Assemblies

| COMPANY NAME | PRODUCT / SERVICE | PHONE | EMP | CITY |
|---|---|---|---|---|
| America Aopen Inc (HQ) | Specializes in the manufacture and marketing of personal computer (PC) components and peripherals. The company also offers speakers and bare systems. | 888-972-6736 | NA | San Jose |
| Granite Digital (HQ) | Manufacturer of external diagnostic peripherals. The company is engaged in troubleshooting and maintenance services. | 510-471-6442 | NA | Union City |
| Lorom West (HQ) | Manufacturer of PCB assemblies, turnkey OEM/ODM products and custom cable and wire harnesses. The company offers industry solutions. | 510-249-9000 | NA | Fremont |
| Newnex Technology Corp (HQ) | Developer of connecting cables, controllers, and repeaters. The company's services include design, installation, and technical support. | 408-986-9988 | NA | Santa Clara |

## 08 = Input/Output Devices

| COMPANY NAME | PRODUCT / SERVICE | PHONE | EMP | CITY |
|---|---|---|---|---|
| Applied Systems Engineering Inc (HQ) | Provider of consulting, software, design, and testing services. The company's products cater to communication applications. | 408-364-0500 | NA | Campbell |
| Document Capture Technologies Inc (HQ) | Manufacturer of mobile document capture solutions such as scanners, copiers, and cloud and printing software. | 630-530-5400 | NA | Fremont |
| Ergo Direct Com (HQ) | Provider of adjustable desks, arms, and mounts. The company offers ergonomic keyboards, monitor arms, and mounting adapters. | 650-654-4300 | NA | San Carlos |
| HP Development Company LP (HQ) | Provider of computer products that include desktops, monitors, printers and scanners, ink, toner and papers, and laptops. | 650-857-1501 | NA | Palo Alto |
| HP Inc (BR) | Provider of laptops, tablets, desktops, printers, and related accessories. The company specializes in business solutions. | 650-857-1501 | NA | Palo Alto |
| Kensington Computer Products Group (DH) | Provider of secure locking solution for laptops, portable laptop power, and mobile computing solutions. | 650-572-2700 | NA | San Mateo |
| Key Source International Inc (HQ) | Provider of disinfect and germicidal wipes for keyboards. The company focuses on infection control and cross contamination. | 510-562-5000 | NA | Oakland |
| Max Group Corp (HQ) | Distributor for computing devices. The company offers computer cases, fans and heatsinks, and hard drives. | 888-644-4629 | NA | Fremont |
| Micro Tech Systems (HQ) | Provider of cabling solutions. The company involves in the installation and repair of voice, data, and video network systems. | 559-438-7580 | 1-10 | Fresno |

## 09 = Keyboards

| COMPANY NAME | PRODUCT / SERVICE | PHONE | EMP | CITY |
|---|---|---|---|---|
| Ergo Direct Com (HQ) | Provider of adjustable desks, arms, and mounts. The company offers ergonomic keyboards, monitor arms, and mounting adapters. | 650-654-4300 | NA | San Carlos |
| Kensington Computer Products Group (DH) | Provider of secure locking solution for laptops, portable laptop power, and mobile computing solutions. | 650-572-2700 | NA | San Mateo |
| Key Source International Inc (HQ) | Provider of disinfect and germicidal wipes for keyboards. The company focuses on infection control and cross contamination. | 510-562-5000 | NA | Oakland |
| Max Group Corp (HQ) | Distributor for computing devices. The company offers computer cases, fans and heatsinks, and hard drives. | 888-644-4629 | NA | Fremont |
| PFU America Inc (BR) | Provider of technology solutions. The company designs, develops, and sells computer hardware, peripheral products, and systems. | 408-992-2900 | NA | Sunnyvale |
| Sejin America Inc (BR) | Manufacturer of automobile parts, smart grid products, input devices, and convergence products. The company offers customer support services. | 510-573-4852 | NA | Fremont |

## 10 = Miscellaneous Computer Equipment

| COMPANY NAME | PRODUCT / SERVICE | PHONE | EMP | CITY |
|---|---|---|---|---|
| Acer America Corp (HQ) | Supplier of desktops, notebooks, tablets, monitors and projectors. The company also offers application and support services. | 408-533-7700 | NA | San Jose |
| Acronics (HQ) | Provider of engineering services. The company is involved in systems and mechanical design services. | 408-432-0888 | NA | San Jose |
| ADLINK Technology Inc (LH) | Designer and manufacturer of products for embedded computing, test & measurement, and automation applications. The company serves various sectors. | 408-360-0200 | NA | San Jose |
| Advantech Inc (DH) | Provider of system integration, hardware, software, embedded systems, automation products, and logistics support. | 408-519-3898 | NA | Milpitas |
| Alpha Networks Inc (HQ) | Designer and manufacturer of networking products. The company also focuses on computers and computer peripherals. | 408-844-8850 | NA | Milpitas |

| COMPANY NAME | PRODUCT / SERVICE | PHONE | EMP | CITY |
|---|---|---|---|---|
| Alphaems Corp (HQ) | Provider of printed circuit board prototyping and PCB assembly production services. The company also involves in material purchasing and warehousing. | 510-498-8788 | NA | Fremont |
| Amber Precision Instruments Inc (HQ) | Provider of scanner products. The company specializes in electromagnetic immunity scanners and near field scanners. | 408-752-0199 | NA | San Jose |
| America Aopen Inc (HQ) | Specializes in the manufacture and marketing of personal computer (PC) components and peripherals. The company also offers speakers and bare systems. | 888-972-6736 | NA | San Jose |
| Ampex Data Systems Corporation (HQ) | Manufacturer of digital storage systems. The company also offers airborne and ground systems and related video solutions. | 650-367-2011 | NA | Hayward |
| Andes Technology USA Corporation (RH) | Provider of infrastructural solutions for embedded system applications. The company serves the semiconductor industry. | 408-809-2929 | NA | San Jose |
| Antec Inc (HQ) | Supplier of computer components and accessories. The company provides enclosures, power supplies, accessories, and mobile products. | 510-770-1200 | NA | Fremont |
| APLEX Technology Inc (BR) | Manufacturer of industrial displays, heavy-duty expandables, industrial panels, and related accessories. The company serves the healthcare sector. | 669-999-2500 | NA | Santa Clara |
| ASUSTeK Computer Inc (HQ) | Manufacturer of computer systems and hardware components such as desktops, notebooks, peripherals, motherboards, and graphic cards. | 510-739-3777 | NA | Fremont |
| Atech Flash Technology Inc (HQ) | Provider of commercial and consumer products that include drive bay multiple flash card reader, portable card readers, and iPod accessories. | 510-824-6868 | NA | Fremont |
| Avermedia Technologies Inc (DH) | Designer and manufacturer of multimedia, internet TV, and electronic products. The company provides USB, TV box, streaming server, and accessories. | 510-403-0006 | NA | Fremont |
| Caltron Industries Inc (HQ) | Manufacturer of digital signage products and touch screen monitors. The company specializes in digital video signage and media advertising services. | 510-440-1800 | NA | Fremont |
| Echelon Corp (HQ) | Developer of open-standard control networking platforms. The company serves outdoor lighting, building automation, transportation, and other needs. | 408-938-5200 | NA | Santa Clara |
| Efinix Inc (HQ) | Focuses on the building of programmable devices. The company serves the industrial, medical, and automotive markets. | 408-789-6917 | NA | Santa Clara |
| Exxact Corp (HQ) | Supplier of workstation graphic cards and solutions. The company also offers servers, HPC clusters, and computing software. | 510-226-7366 | NA | Fremont |
| Genesys Logic America Inc (BR) | Developer of electric circuits, semiconductors, digital communications products, computer peripherals, and other related products. | 408-435-8899 | NA | San Jose |
| HP Inc (BR) | Provider of laptops, tablets, desktops, printers, and related accessories. The company specializes in business solutions. | 650-857-1501 | NA | Palo Alto |
| Ibus Corp (HQ) | Manufacturer and provider of industrial computers. The company also specializes in prototyping and quality control. | 408-450-7880 | NA | Santa Clara |
| Identiv Inc (HQ) | Provider of security technology services. The company's products include desktop readers, terminals, modules, and development kits. | 888-809-8880 | NA | Fremont |
| International Microsystems Inc (HQ) | Designer and manufacturer of flash memory duplication equipment. The company also offers related test equipment. | 408-942-1001 | NA | Fremont |
| Jetway Computer Corp (HQ) | Manufacturer of motherboards and LCD monitors. The company also specializes in graphic cards and barebones systems. | 510-857-0130 | NA | Newark |
| Kaser Corp (HQ) | Developer and marketer of internet and communication equipment. The company offers internet telephony, digital television, and accessories. | 510-894-6892 | NA | Fremont |
| Kensington Computer Products Group (DH) | Provider of secure locking solution for laptops, portable laptop power, and mobile computing solutions. | 650-572-2700 | NA | San Mateo |
| Maxeler Technologies Inc (HQ) | Developer of computing solutions. The company offers services to the oil and gas, analytical, and financial sectors. | 650-938-8818 | NA | Mountain View |
| Micro Tech Systems (HQ) | Provider of cabling solutions. The company involves in the installation and repair of voice, data, and video network systems. | 559-438-7580 | 1-10 | Fresno |
| NComputing Co Ltd (HQ) | Provider of desktop virtualization services. The company serves customers in the education, healthcare, enterprise, and enterprise sectors. | 650-409-5959 | NA | San Mateo |
| Oppo Digital Inc (HQ) | Manufacturer of Blu-ray players and UP converting DVD players. The company's services include design, installation, and delivery. | 650-961-1118 | NA | Menlo Park |
| Posiflex Business Machines Inc (LH) | Provider of point of service hardware and platform technology. The company caters to diverse markets. | 510-429-7097 | NA | Hayward |
| Recortec Inc (HQ) | Manufacturer of LCD monitors, KVM, keyboards, speakers, and computers. The company also offers customization services. | 408-928-1480 | NA | San Jose |
| Sejin America Inc (BR) | Manufacturer of automobile parts, smart grid products, input devices, and convergence products. The company offers customer support services. | 510-573-4852 | NA | Fremont |
| Shimon Systems Inc (HQ) | Manufacturer of fingerprint authentication solutions. The company's services include research and development. | 650-461-9104 | NA | Los Altos |
| Siig Inc (HQ) | Manufacturer of computer connectivity products. The company is involved in increasing the bandwidth between a computer system and external devices. | 510-657-8688 | NA | Fremont |

| COMPANY NAME | PRODUCT / SERVICE | PHONE | EMP | CITY |
|---|---|---|---|---|
| Sp Controls Inc (HQ) | Designer and manufacturer of projector control systems. The company also offers audio systems, mounting, signal distribution, and other products. | 877-367-8444 | NA | S San Francisco |
| Spectra 7 Microsystems Ltd (HQ) | Manufacturer of analog semiconductor devices. The company focuses on micro-thin interconnects for consumer electronic products. | 408-770-2915 | NA | San Jose |
| Sycard Technology (HQ) | Provider of 16-bit PC card and CardBus devices. The company also offers USB and smart media development services. | 408-399-8073 | NA | Los Gatos |
| Xerox Corp (BR) | Provider of color printers and copiers. The company also specializes in document management solutions. | 510-460-4161 | NA | Walnut Creek |
| Zspace Inc (HQ) | Provider of solutions for viewing, manipulating, and communicating complex ideas through direct interaction with virtual-holographic simulations. | 408-498-4050 | NA | Sunnyvale |

## 111 = Modems

| COMPANY NAME | PRODUCT / SERVICE | PHONE | EMP | CITY |
|---|---|---|---|---|
| Applied Systems Engineering Inc (HQ) | Provider of consulting, software, design, and testing services. The company's products cater to communication applications. | 408-364-0500 | NA | Campbell |
| Bivio Networks Inc (HQ) | Provider of cyber security and network control solutions. The company offers cyber defense systems, surveillance, flow analysis, and monitoring tools. | 925-924-8600 | NA | Pleasanton |
| Cermetek Microelectronics (HQ) | Manufacturer of communication modules for embedded systems. The company caters to power generation, irrigation control, and medical monitoring fields. | 408-942-2200 | NA | Milpitas |
| NComputing Co Ltd (HQ) | Provider of desktop virtualization services. The company serves customers in the education, healthcare, enterprise, and enterprise sectors. | 650-409-5959 | NA | San Mateo |
| Ruckus Networks (HQ) | Designer and manufacturer of Wi-Fi products and wireless LAN systems. The company also focuses on the marketing aspects. | 650-265-4200 | NA | Sunnyvale |
| Teledesign Systems Inc (HQ) | Provider of wireless data solutions. The company manufactures wireless industrial modems for commercial and industrial data collection applications. | 408-941-1808 | NA | Milpitas |
| Zypcom Inc (HQ) | Designer and manufacturer of analog modems. The company mainly caters to the networking professionals. | 510-324-2501 | NA | Union City |

## 112 = Monitors

| COMPANY NAME | PRODUCT / SERVICE | PHONE | EMP | CITY |
|---|---|---|---|---|
| Atech Flash Technology Inc (HQ) | Provider of commercial and consumer products that include drive bay multiple flash card reader, portable card readers, and iPod accessories. | 510-824-6868 | NA | Fremont |
| Caltron Industries Inc (HQ) | Manufacturer of digital signage products and touch screen monitors. The company specializes in digital video signage and media advertising services. | 510-440-1800 | NA | Fremont |
| Cambrios Technologies Corp (HQ) | Manufacturer of electronic materials for the display industry. The company mainly provides ClearOhm films. | 408-738-7400 | NA | Sunnyvale |
| CERONIX Inc (HQ) | Manufacturer of color video touch display monitors and printed circuit boards. The company offers LCD and CRT monitor assemblies and spare parts. | 530-886-6400 | 1-10 | Auburn |
| Elo Touch Solutions Inc (HQ) | Designer, developer, and manufacturer of touch products and technologies. The company's products include tablets, touchscreens, and touchmonitors. | 408-597-8000 | NA | Milpitas |
| HP Development Company LP (HQ) | Provider of computer products that include desktops, monitors, printers and scanners, ink, toner and papers, and laptops. | 650-857-1501 | NA | Palo Alto |
| HP Inc (BR) | Provider of laptops, tablets, desktops, printers, and related accessories. The company specializes in business solutions. | 650-857-1501 | NA | Palo Alto |
| Immersion Corp (HQ) | Developer and marketer of haptic (touch feedback) technology. The company serves mobile device, wearable, automotive, medical, and other sectors. | 408-467-1900 | NA | San Jose |
| Key Source International Inc (HQ) | Provider of disinfect and germicidal wipes for keyboards. The company focuses on infection control and cross contamination. | 510-562-5000 | NA | Oakland |
| NComputing Co Ltd (HQ) | Provider of desktop virtualization services. The company serves customers in the education, healthcare, enterprise, and enterprise sectors. | 650-409-5959 | NA | San Mateo |
| PFU America Inc (BR) | Provider of technology solutions. The company designs, develops, and sells computer hardware, peripheral products, and systems. | 408-992-2900 | NA | Sunnyvale |
| Tactus Technology Inc (HQ) | Developer of tactile user interface for touchscreen devices. The company serves the industrial and technological sectors. | 510-244-3968 | NA | Fremont |
| Valmark Interface Solutions (HQ) | Manufacturer of labels, panel overlays, and membrane switches. The company is engaged in engineering, assembly, and installation services. | 925-960-9900 | NA | Livermore |

## 114 = Optical Character Recognition Equipment

| COMPANY NAME | PRODUCT / SERVICE | PHONE | EMP | CITY |
|---|---|---|---|---|
| Cambrios Technologies Corp (HQ) | Manufacturer of electronic materials for the display industry. The company mainly provides ClearOhm films. | 408-738-7400 | NA | Sunnyvale |
| Data ID Systems (HQ) | Provider of identification management solutions. The company offers passport readers, bar code scanners, and fixed asset tracking products. | 408-371-5764 | NA | Campbell |
| Newland North America Inc (HQ) | Designer and developer of data collector and scanning systems. The company also offers customer information terminals. | 510-490-3888 | NA | Fremont |

## 115 = Printers

| COMPANY NAME | PRODUCT / SERVICE | PHONE | EMP | CITY |
|---|---|---|---|---|
| Braigo Labs Inc (HQ) | Developer of humanely optimized technologies such as research, design, and creation of technology-based innovations and services for marketplace. | 408-850-0614 | NA | Palo Alto |
| C-Scan Corp (HQ) | Manufacturer and designer of thermal recorders and printers for medical applications and the healthcare sector. | 800-953-7888 | NA | Los Gatos |
| Dolphin Graphics (HQ) | Provider of branding and marketing solutions. The company also offers graphics design and web design services. | 510-881-0154 | NA | Castro Valley |
| HP Development Company LP (HQ) | Provider of computer products that include desktops, monitors, printers and scanners, ink, toner and papers, and laptops. | 650-857-1501 | NA | Palo Alto |
| HP Inc (BR) | Provider of laptops, tablets, desktops, printers, and related accessories. The company specializes in business solutions. | 650-857-1501 | NA | Palo Alto |
| Max Group Corp (HQ) | Distributor for computing devices. The company offers computer cases, fans and heatsinks, and hard drives. | 888-644-4629 | NA | Fremont |
| Posiflex Business Machines Inc (LH) | Provider of point of service hardware and platform technology. The company caters to diverse markets. | 510-429-7097 | NA | Hayward |
| Prism Inks Inc (HQ) | Manufacturer of inkjet printer inks to the proofing, signage, photography, arts and coding sectors. The company's products comprise UV curable and textile inks. | 408-744-6710 | NA | Sunnyvale |
| Xerox Corp (BR) | Provider of color printers and copiers. The company also specializes in document management solutions. | 510-460-4161 | NA | Walnut Creek |
| Zebra Technologies Corp (BR) | Provider of business and printing solutions. The company also offers printers such as desktop, industrial, mobile, and card printers. | 866-230-9494 | NA | San Jose |

## 116 = Storage Devices

| COMPANY NAME | PRODUCT / SERVICE | PHONE | EMP | CITY |
|---|---|---|---|---|
| Acutrack Inc (HQ) | Provider of CD and DVD duplication and production services. The company is also engaged in kitting, assembly, and USB fulfillment. | 925-579-5000 | NA | Livermore |
| Addonics Technologies Inc (HQ) | Manufacturer of storage systems and products. The company's products include drive cartridge system, host controller, converter, and adapter. | 408-573-8580 | NA | San Jose |
| Amax Information Technologies Inc (HQ) | Manufacturer and seller of custom servers and storage solutions. The company focuses on platform design, custom branding, and supply chain management. | 510-651-8886 | NA | Fremont |
| Ampex Data Systems Corporation (HQ) | Manufacturer of digital storage systems. The company also offers airborne and ground systems and related video solutions. | 650-367-2011 | NA | Hayward |
| Arcscale LLC (HQ) | Provider of colocation, technology integration, hosting, implementation, and telecommunication services. The company also deals with procurement. | 408-476-0554 | NA | San Jose |
| Avalanche Technology (HQ) | Provider of programmable storage solutions. The company offers services to the consumer electronics industry. | 510-897-3300 | NA | Fremont |
| Datrium Inc (HQ) | Provider of VM infrastructure convergence for elastic, on-demand, and VM-centric primary storage. | 669-721-9444 | NA | Sunnyvale |
| Exxact Corp (HQ) | Supplier of workstation graphic cards and solutions. The company also offers servers, HPC clusters, and computing software. | 510-226-7366 | NA | Fremont |
| Granite Digital (HQ) | Manufacturer of external diagnostic peripherals. The company is engaged in troubleshooting and maintenance services. | 510-471-6442 | NA | Union City |
| HP Development Company LP (HQ) | Provider of computer products that include desktops, monitors, printers and scanners, ink, toner and papers, and laptops. | 650-857-1501 | NA | Palo Alto |
| Infortrend Corp (LH) | Provider of high performance storage networking solutions. The company serves the energy, utilities, and healthcare industries. | 408-988-5088 | NA | San Jose |
| Max Group Corp (HQ) | Distributor for computing devices. The company offers computer cases, fans and heatsinks, and hard drives. | 888-644-4629 | NA | Fremont |
| Mixonic (HQ) | Provider of design services. The company offers custom CD and DVD duplication, disc packaging, CD production, and printing services. | 866-838-5067 | NA | San Francisco |
| NComputing Co Ltd (HQ) | Provider of desktop virtualization services. The company serves customers in the education, healthcare, enterprise, and enterprise sectors. | 650-409-5959 | NA | San Mateo |
| Olixir Technologies (HQ) | Provider of external hard drives and racks & towers. The company also offers video surveillance and backup solutions. | 408-719-0595 | NA | Milpitas |
| Rambus (HQ) | Manufacturer of semiconductor, lighting, and IP products. The company serves the automotive and transportation markets. | 408-462-8000 | NA | Sunnyvale |
| Samsung Semiconductor Inc (HQ) | Provider of electronics manufacturing and digital media products. The company also offers mobile services and PC software. | 408-544-4000 | NA | San Jose |
| SanDisk Corp (HQ) | Manufacturer of flash memory cards. The company's products include card readers, solid state drives, USB flash drives, and microSD cards. | 408-801-1000 | NA | Milpitas |
| Solar Components Llc (HQ) | Manufacturer of micro-processor controlled solar power electronic systems. The company provides solar power management and charge control solutions. | 408-369-1727 | NA | Campbell |
| Spectra 7 Microsystems Ltd (HQ) | Manufacturer of analog semiconductor devices. The company focuses on micro-thin interconnects for consumer electronic products. | 408-770-2915 | NA | San Jose |
| Super Talent Technology (HQ) | Designer and manufacturer of flash based storage solutions for enterprise servers, portable devices, personal computers, and consumer electronics. | 408-934-2560 | NA | San Jose |

| COMPANY NAME | PRODUCT / SERVICE | PHONE | EMP | CITY |
|---|---|---|---|---|
| TDK Corporation of America (BR) | Distributor of electronic products including capacitors, inductors, ferrites, factory automation system, transformers, magnets, and anechoic chambers. | 408-467-5200 | NA | San Jose |
| Themis Computer (HQ) | Provider of embedded computing solutions for system integrators and OEMs. The company provides RES servers and HPCs, and rugged storage appliances. | 510-252-0870 | NA | Fremont |
| Unigen Corp (HQ) | Manufacturer and designer of custom enterprise-grade flash storage and DRAM and ARMOUR product applications serving the telecommunications industry. | 510-896-1818 | NA | Newark |
| Winbond Electronics Corporation America (DH) | Provider of memory solutions and services. The company offers Pseudo SRAM, Serial NOR Flash, Mobile DRAM, and KGD. | 408-943-6666 | NA | San Jose |

## 17 = Backup Equipment

| COMPANY NAME | PRODUCT / SERVICE | PHONE | EMP | CITY |
|---|---|---|---|---|
| Mixonic (HQ) | Provider of design services. The company offers custom CD and DVD duplication, disc packaging, CD production, and printing services. | 866-838-5067 | NA | San Francisco |
| New Tech Solutions Inc (HQ) | Provider of technology solutions. The company caters to networking, security, and communication manufacturers. | 510-353-4070 | NA | Fremont |

## 19 = Electronics Production Equipment

| COMPANY NAME | PRODUCT / SERVICE | PHONE | EMP | CITY |
|---|---|---|---|---|
| Ambarella Inc (HQ) | Developer of high-definition video compression and image processing solutions. The company's products are used in security IP cameras and sports cameras. | 408-734-8888 | 51-200 | Santa Clara |

## 20 = Computer Manufacturing Equipment

| COMPANY NAME | PRODUCT / SERVICE | PHONE | EMP | CITY |
|---|---|---|---|---|
| Ambarella Inc (HQ) | Developer of high-definition video compression and image processing solutions. The company's products are used in security IP cameras and sports cameras. | 408-734-8888 | 51-200 | Santa Clara |
| Aurostar Corp (HQ) | Provider of technology products and services focusing on home theater systems, consumer electronics, desktops and notebooks, and networking solutions. | 510-249-9422 | NA | Fremont |
| Bold Data Technology Inc (HQ) | Provider of computer components and services. The company offers desktop computers, servers, notebooks, and workstations. | 510-490-8296 | NA | Fremont |
| Bravo Communications Inc (HQ) | Supplier of network surge and lightening protection products. The company also offers data line extenders and related accessories. | 408-270-1547 | NA | San Jose |
| Chelsio Communications (HQ) | Provider of Ethernet adapters. The company offers storage routers, wire adapters, virtualization and management software, and accessories. | 408-962-3600 | NA | Sunnyvale |
| ETM Electromatic Inc (BR) | Manufacturer of electronic products. The company offers microwaves, testing and measuring tools, and thermal management devices. | 510-797-1100 | NA | Newark |
| Polywell Computers Inc (HQ) | Manufacturer of computer systems. The company specializes in desktop PCs, workstations, and servers. | 650-583-7222 | NA | S San Francisco |
| Quanta Computer Usa Inc (LH) | Provider of design and manufacturing services for technology products. The company specializes in cloud computing solutions. | 510-226-1001 | NA | Fremont |
| Sensing Electromagnetic Plus Corp (HQ) | Developer of third touch dimension in human-machine interfaces. The company offers unobtrusive pressure sensitive solutions. | 415-954-0322 | NA | Palo Alto |
| Tangent Inc (HQ) | Provider of computer solutions. The company caters to healthcare, industrial, and military applications. | 650-342-9388 | NA | Burlingame |
| Variant Microsystems (HQ) | Manufacturer and reseller of data collection equipment such as bar code scanners, printers, portables. | 510-440-2870 | NA | Fremont |

## 21 = Component Placement & Handling Systems

| COMPANY NAME | PRODUCT / SERVICE | PHONE | EMP | CITY |
|---|---|---|---|---|
| Artcraft Welding Inc (HQ) | Designer and manufacturer of ultrasonic cleaning equipment. The company specializes in precision cleaning fixtures. | 408-377-2725 | NA | Campbell |
| Brooks Automation Inc (BR) | Provider of automation, vacuum, and instrumentation solutions for the semiconductor manufacturing, life sciences, and clean energy industries. | 510-661-5000 | NA | Fremont |

## 22 = Diffusion/Ion Implant Equipment

| COMPANY NAME | PRODUCT / SERVICE | PHONE | EMP | CITY |
|---|---|---|---|---|
| Ambarella Inc (HQ) | Developer of high-definition video compression and image processing solutions. The company's products are used in security IP cameras and sports cameras. | 408-734-8888 | 51-200 | Santa Clara |
| Artcraft Welding Inc (HQ) | Designer and manufacturer of ultrasonic cleaning equipment. The company specializes in precision cleaning fixtures. | 408-377-2725 | NA | Campbell |
| Automate Scientific Inc (HQ) | Manufacturer and distributor of biomedical equipment. The company offers amplifiers, manipulators, software, and accessories. | 510-845-6283 | NA | Berkeley |
| Los Gatos Research Inc (HQ) | Manufacturer of analyzers for the measurement of trace gases and isotopes. The company serves the industrial and environmental sectors. | 650-965-7772 | NA | San Jose |

## 23 = Deposition Equipment

| COMPANY NAME | PRODUCT / SERVICE | PHONE | EMP | CITY |
|---|---|---|---|---|
| Ambarella Inc (HQ) | Developer of high-definition video compression and image processing solutions. The company's products are used in security IP cameras and sports cameras. | 408-734-8888 | 51-200 | Santa Clara |

## 24 = Electronic/Photonic Manufacturing Equipment

| COMPANY NAME | PRODUCT / SERVICE | PHONE | EMP | CITY |
|---|---|---|---|---|
| Abm-Usa Inc (HQ) | Manufacturer and seller of mask aligner and exposure systems. The company also provides vacuum chucks, intensity meters, and probes. | 408-226-8722 | NA | San Jose |
| Advantage Electric Supply Inc (HQ) | Distributor of electrical and electronic components for OEM's, industrial automation, solar, and renewable energy industries. | 510-324-9070 | NA | Hayward |
| Allvia Inc (HQ) | Provider of silicon interposer and through-silicon via foundry services to the semiconductor and optoelectronics industries. | 408-212-3200 | NA | Sunnyvale |
| Bactrack (HQ) | Provider of breathalyzers. The company provides products for a wide range of personal, professional and smartphone use. | 415-693-9756 | NA | San Francisco |
| BASF Venture Capital America Inc (RH) | Manufacturer of basic chemicals and intermediates such as solvents, plasticizers, and monomers. The company serves the agriculture market. | 510-445-6140 | NA | Fremont |
| Bay Area Circuits Inc (HQ) | Provider of engineering services that include fabrication, layout, and design services to the original equipment manufacturers. | 510-933-9000 | NA | Fremont |
| CAD PROS PCB Design Inc (HQ) | Designer and manufacturer of printed circuit boards. The company offers services to the residential and commercial sectors. | 408-734-9600 | NA | San Jose |
| CLEARink Displays Inc (RH) | Developer of reflective display modules for wearables, smart phones/ tablets, electronic shelf labels, and outdoor signage. | 510-624-9305 | NA | Fremont |
| Coadna Photonics Inc (HQ) | Provider of tunable fiber optic solutions for optical networks. The company's products are used in high broadband applications. | 408-736-1100 | NA | Sunnyvale |
| Creative Labs Inc (RH) | Provider of digital entertainment products such as sound blaster, gaming headsets, speakers, headphones, MP3 players, software, and webcams. | | NA | Milpitas |
| Cypress Envirosystems Inc (HQ) | Provider of solutions to retrofit existing commercial buildings and industrial facilities for improved asset utilization and lower maintenance costs. | 800-544-5411 | NA | San Jose |
| Eiq Energy Inc (HQ) | Designer and manufacturer of power electronics. The company provides solar cells, panels, and monitoring systems. | 408-643-0020 | NA | Santa Clara |
| Electronics Cooling Solutions Inc (HQ) | Provider of thermal management consulting services. The company serves customers in the avionics, medical, and telecommunications industries. | 408-738-8331 | NA | Santa Clara |
| Epiphotonics Corp (HQ) | Manufacturer of photonic components and subsystems. The company is engaged in design, delivery, and installation services. | 408-920-7019 | NA | San Jose |
| N ETM Electromatic Inc (BR) | Manufacturer of electronic products. The company offers microwaves, testing and measuring tools, and thermal management devices. | 510-797-1100 | NA | Newark |
| Excelitas Technologies Corp (HQ) | Provider of opto-electronics solutions. The company serves the medical, industrial, aerospace, and defense markets. | 510-979-6500 | NA | Fremont |
| Expertech (HQ) | Provider of custom, new and re-manufactured thermal processing solutions. The company offers diffusion furnaces for semiconductor and solar devices. | 831-439-9300 | 1-10 | Scotts Valley |
| Fairchild Imaging Inc (DH) | Developer and manufacturer of solid-state electronic imaging components, cameras, and systems. The company's products include image sensors and cameras. | 650-479-5749 | NA | San Jose |
| Farpointe Data Inc (HQ) | Provider of RFID electronic access control technologies for electronic access control professionals around the world. | 408-731-8700 | NA | San Jose |
| Hta Photomask (HQ) | Manufacturer of photo imaged products such as precision scales, resolution targets, and micro detectors. | 408-452-5500 | NA | San Jose |
| Infiniti Solutions Usa (BR) | Provider of electronic manufacturing services. The company specializes in burn-in board and system design and manufacturing. | 408-923-7300 | NA | San Jose |
| Ipg Photonics (BR) | Provider of high power fiber lasers and amplifiers. The company's offerings include Q-switch lasers, multi-mode diodes, pulsed and direct-diode lasers. | 408-492-8830 | NA | Santa Clara |
| iSmart Alarm Inc (HQ) | Manufacturer of home security products. The company offers alarms, cameras, sirens, and related accessories. | 408-245-2551 | NA | Sunnyvale |
| Jabil Circuit Inc (BR) | Provider of global manufacturing solutions. The company serves the defense, aerospace, and industrial markets. | 408-361-3200 | NA | San Jose |
| Meivac Inc (HQ) | Manufacturer of sputtering systems and components. The company offers throttle valves, integrators, OEM assemblies, and substrate heaters. | 408-362-1000 | NA | San Jose |
| Modules Technology Inc (HQ) | Provider of custom module design solutions. The company's offerings include grinders, etching systems, and thermal recorders. | 408-392-0808 ext. 111 | NA | San Jose |
| Psc Electronics Inc (HQ) | Distributor of magnetic, interconnect, and electro-mechanical components. The company specializes in cable assembly and modification. | 408-737-1333 | NA | Santa Clara |
| Quarterwave Corp (HQ) | Manufacturer of high power traveling wave-tube amplifiers, valves, and test equipment. The company deals with installation services. | 707-793-9105 | NA | Rohnert Park |
| Radian Thermal Products Inc (BR) | Manufacturer of custom and radiant heat sinks. The company's services include prototyping and engineering support. | 408-988-6200 | NA | Santa Clara |
| Rainbow Electronics & Fasteners Corp (HQ) | Distributor of electronic and mechanical hardware products. The company's products include fasteners, screws, standoffs, and spacers. | 510-475-9840 | NA | Union City |
| SHASTA Electronic Manufacturing Services Inc (HQ) | Provider of electronic manufacturing services. The company's services include prototype manufacturing, testing, materials, and quality control. | 408-436-1267 | NA | San Jose |
| Shax Engineering Inc (HQ) | Provider of PCB fabrication and assembly services. The company serves original equipment manufacturers and technology companies. | 408-452-1500 | NA | Fremont |
| Silicon Mitus (BR) | Manufacturer and distributor of smart power management integrated chips solutions. The company focuses on power solutions. | 408-446-3151 | NA | Cupertino |

| COMPANY NAME | PRODUCT / SERVICE | PHONE | EMP | CITY |
|---|---|---|---|---|
| Syrma Technology (BR) | Provider of entrepreneurial manufacturing services. The company's products include magnetics, memory, and RFID. | 408-404-0500 | NA | San Jose |
| Tango Systems Inc (HQ) | Supplier of cluster tools for dielectric films. The company's services include processing, thin film deposition, and quality analysis. | 408-526-2330 | NA | San Jose |
| Tdn Electric Inc (HQ) | Retailer of electrical construction services for lighting, uninterruptible power supply, fire alarm, and photovoltaic systems. | 650-968-8000 | NA | Mountain View |
| Tecdia Inc (HQ) | Manufacturer of precision machine tools and fixtures. The company also specializes in cutting and scribing tools. | 408-748-0100 | NA | Campbell |
| Wafer Process Systems Inc (HQ) | Manufacturer of semiconductors, MEMS, and photonics. The company also focuses on RFID products, disc drives, and flat panel displays. | 408-445-3010 | NA | San Jose |
| WaferNet Inc (HQ) | Supplier of silicon wafers. The company serves semiconductor equipment manufacturers and universities. | 866-749-2337 | NA | San Jose |

## 125 = Production Clean Rooms and Related Equipment

| COMPANY NAME | PRODUCT / SERVICE | PHONE | EMP | CITY |
|---|---|---|---|---|
| Air Exchange Inc (HQ) | Supplier of air purification and clean air machines, and fans. The company serves commercial facilities and public institutions. | 800-300-2945 | NA | Fairfield |
| Ambarella Inc (HQ) | Developer of high-definition video compression and image processing solutions. The company's products are used in security IP cameras and sports cameras. | 408-734-8888 | 51-200 | Santa Clara |
| CleanAir Solutions Inc (HQ) | Provider of stainless steel furniture and ESD curtain systems. The company serves pharmaceutical and medical device manufacturing companies. | 707-864-9499 | NA | Fairfield |
| Cleantec (HQ) | Provider of solutions for greenhouse gas emissions, air pollution, water conservation, and waste management. | 916-791-8478 | 1-10 | Granite Bay |
| Fairchild Imaging Inc (DH) | Developer and manufacturer of solid-state electronic imaging components, cameras, and systems. The company's products include image sensors and cameras. | 650-479-5749 | NA | San Jose |
| Farpointe Data Inc (HQ) | Provider of RFID electronic access control technologies for electronic access control professionals around the world. | 408-731-8700 | NA | San Jose |
| Meran Technology (HQ) | Provider of process equipment for memory disk manufacturers. The company offers material handling equipment for fiber optic manufacturers. | 510-530-5119 | NA | Piedmont |

## 126 = Semiconductor Manufacturing Equipment

| COMPANY NAME | PRODUCT / SERVICE | PHONE | EMP | CITY |
|---|---|---|---|---|
| Abm-Usa Inc (HQ) | Manufacturer and seller of mask aligner and exposure systems. The company also provides vacuum chucks, intensity meters, and probes. | 408-226-8722 | NA | San Jose |
| Addison Engineering Inc (HQ) | Supplier of silicon wafers and semiconductor process components. The company's products include ceramic packages and semiconductor equipment. | 408-926-5000 | NA | San Jose |
| Agiga Tech Inc (BR) | Designer and manufacturer of memory solutions. The company's portfolio includes AGIGARAM, SDRAM, and PowerGEM. | 408-943-2600 | NA | San Jose |
| Alliance Memory Inc (BR) | Manufacturer of memory semiconductor products. The company's products include SRAM, DRAM, SDRAM ICS, and DDR SDRAM. | 650-610-6800 | NA | San Carlos |
| Anchor Semiconductor Inc (HQ) | Developer of software to improve IC manufacturing efficiency and chip yield. The company specializes in semiconductor hotspot pattern management. | 408-986-8969 | NA | Santa Clara |
| Artcraft Welding Inc (HQ) | Designer and manufacturer of ultrasonic cleaning equipment. The company specializes in precision cleaning fixtures. | 408-377-2725 | NA | Campbell |
| Avalent Technologies Inc (HQ) | Provider of fabless semiconductor devices. The company's services include platform development, processor development, and analog design services. | 408-657-7621 | NA | Milpitas |
| Brooks Automation Inc (BR) | Provider of automation, vacuum, and instrumentation solutions for the semiconductor manufacturing, life sciences, and clean energy industries. | 510-661-5000 | NA | Fremont |
| C&D Semiconductor Services Inc (HQ) | Manufacturer of cleaner systems, wafer sorters, and wafer inspection systems. The company deals with inspection and processing. | 408-383-1888 | NA | San Jose |
| Cambrios Technologies Corp (HQ) | Manufacturer of electronic materials for the display industry. The company mainly provides ClearOhm films. | 408-738-7400 | NA | Sunnyvale |
| Capital Asset Exchange & Trading LLC (HQ) | Provider of secondary capital equipment. The company offers evaporators, spectometers, residual gas analyzers, and electronic testing equipment. | 650-326-3313 | NA | Santa Clara |
| Corad Technology Inc (BR) | Manufacturer of load boards, probe cards, instrumentation systems, and related components. The company deals with installation services. | 408-496-5511 | NA | Santa Clara |
| Corning Technology Center (BR) | Provider of specialty glass and ceramics services and sells keystone components to electronics, mobile emissions control, and life science industries. | 650-846-6000 | NA | Sunnyvale |
| Crocus Technology (HQ) | Manufacturer of magnetic switches, current sensors, and embedded memory products. The company serves the automotive and industrial sectors. | 408-380-8300 | NA | Santa Clara |
| DDRdrive LLC (HQ) | Provider of solid-state storage system. The company specializes in ZFS and ZIL acceleration. | 650-804-8227 | NA | Palo Alto |
| Dolphin Technology Inc (DH) | Provider of silicon-proven internet protocol for memory, standard cells, input and output, memory controllers, and memory test and repair. | 408-392-0012 | NA | San Jose |

| COMPANY NAME | PRODUCT / SERVICE | PHONE | EMP | CITY |
|---|---|---|---|---|
| Ecomicron Inc (HQ) | Manufacturer of semiconductor equipment. The company caters to semiconductor, photovoltaic, and hybrid industries. | 408-526-1020 | NA | San Jose |
| Empower Micro Systems Inc (HQ) | Provider of semiconductor technology for PV module and inverter manufacturers, solar distributors, solar finance companies, developers, and installers. | 408-620-6458 | NA | Santa Clara |
| GLF Integrated Power Inc (HQ) | Manufacturer of power switch devices for smart phones, mobile health devices, laptops, remote sensors, wearables, SSD modules, and off batteries. | 408-239-4326 | NA | Santa Clara |
| Globalfoundries Inc (BR) | Provider of semiconductor foundry services. The company deals with design tools, IP suppliers and ASIC partners. | 408-462-3900 | NA | Santa Clara |
| Hammon Plating Corp (HQ) | Supplier of metal plating applications. The company also provides supply chain management solutions. | 650-494-2691 | NA | Palo Alto |
| Hesse Mechatronics Inc (LH) | Developer of equipment for heavy wire and thin wire wedge bonders. The company also focuses on the marketing aspects. | 408-436-9300 | NA | Fremont |
| Hynix Semiconductor America Inc (BR) | Manufacturer of DRAM products. The company focuses on consumer memory, graphics memory, mobile memory, and CMOS image sensors. | 408-232-8000 | NA | San Jose |
| Jem America Corp (RH) | Manufacturer and supplier of probe cards and tester interfaces. The company offers cantilever, vertical, and special-applications probe cards. | 510-683-9234 | NA | Fremont |
| Jsr Micro Inc (HQ) | Provider of semiconductor, life sciences, and energy material solutions. The company specializes in lithography materials and CMP consumables. | 408-543-8800 | NA | Sunnyvale |
| Kaiam Corp (HQ) | Provider of single-mode solutions. The company develops transceivers, modules, and components for data centers. | 510-226-8100 | NA | Newark |
| Lasertec USA Inc (HQ) | Developer and manufacturer of systems for semi-conductor applications. The company also offers systems for flat panel displays. | 408-437-1441 | NA | San Jose |
| Legend Design Technology Inc (HQ) | Provider of semiconductor IP characterization and verification tools and IC and PCB circuit simulators. | 408-748-8888 | NA | Santa Clara |
| Microelec Technical (HQ) | Manufacturer of semiconductor, micro-electronics, and mixed signal devices. The company specializes in switches, bridge rectifiers, and transistors. | 408-282-3508 | NA | Santa Clara |
| Modular Process Technology Corp (HQ) | Manufacturer of semiconductor equipment for thermal processing systems and stand-alone ultraviolet ozone cleaning systems. | 408-325-8640 | NA | San Jose |
| Monolithic Power Systems Inc (HQ) | Provider of analog semiconductor products. The company offers battery chargers, linear regulators & analog switches, voltage supervisors, and amplifiers. | 408-826-0600 | NA | San Jose |
| Netronome (HQ) | Provider of flow processing, server virtualization, cyber security, and software-defined networking solutions. | 408-496-0022 | NA | Santa Clara |
| Onchip Devices Inc (HQ) | Provider of silicon and ceramic solutions and integrated passive devices for the computing and consumer electronics industries. | 408-654-9365 | NA | Santa Clara |
| Samco Inc (RH) | Manufacturer of deposition, etching, and surface treatment systems used in the manufacturing of LED, MEMS, power & RF device, and other products. | 408-734-0459 | NA | Santa Clara |
| Semicat Inc (BR) | Provider of refurbished equipments for semiconductors. The company deals in LED, and novel emerging applications. | 408-514-6900 | NA | Fremont |
| Silicon Frontline Technology Inc (HQ) | Provider of parasitic extraction and analysis services for post layout verification. The company specializes in electrostatic discharge analysis. | 408-963-6916 | NA | San Jose |
| Silicon Genesis Corp (HQ) | Manufacturer of semiconductor and solar fabrication tools . The company offers stand-alone plasma tools and debond and cleave tools. | 408-228-5858 | NA | San Jose |
| Solid State Optronics (HQ) | Manufacturer of miniature Solid State Relays. The company offers MOSFET drivers, specialty products, and optocouplers. | 408-293-4600 | NA | San Jose |
| Tsmc North America (HQ) | Manufacturer of products for the computer, communications, and consumer electronics market segments. | 408-382-8000 | NA | San Jose |
| Uniquify Inc (HQ) | Developer and manufacturer of SoC displays and other semi-conductor products. The company offers technical support services. | 408-235-8810 | NA | San Jose |
| Yield Engineering Systems Inc (HQ) | Manufacturer of process equipment for the semiconductor industry. The company offers products for surface modification and photoresist treatment. | 925-373-8353 | NA | Livermore |

## 127 = Wafer Fabrication/Crystal Finishing Equipment

| COMPANY NAME | PRODUCT / SERVICE | PHONE | EMP | CITY |
|---|---|---|---|---|
| Addison Engineering Inc (HQ) | Supplier of silicon wafers and semiconductor process components. The company's products include ceramic packages and semiconductor equipment. | 408-926-5000 | NA | San Jose |
| Artcraft Welding Inc (HQ) | Designer and manufacturer of ultrasonic cleaning equipment. The company specializes in precision cleaning fixtures. | 408-377-2725 | NA | Campbell |
| Intermems Inc (HQ) | Provider of micromolding, plating, thin film deposition, anodic and wafer bonding, and related services. | 408-241-0007 | NA | San Jose |
| Lam Research Corp (HQ) | Manufacturer and distributor of single wafer systems. The company primarily serves the semiconductor industry. | 510-572-0200 | NA | Fremont |
| Loomis Industries Inc (HQ) | Provider of fabrication services. The company specializes in the design, print, and analysis of semiconductor components. | 707-963-4111 | NA | St. Helena |

| COMPANY NAME | PRODUCT / SERVICE | PHONE | EMP | CITY |
|---|---|---|---|---|
| Qualitau Inc (HQ) | Supplier of test equipment and services. The company is involved in the development of electronic equipment for semiconductor process reliability. | 650-282-6226 | NA | Mountain View |
| Scientific Coating Labs (HQ) | Provider of wafer coatings. The company specializes in coating components used in the semiconductor industry. | 408-727-3296 | NA | Santa Clara |
| Semicat Inc (BR) | Provider of refurbished equipments for semiconductors. The company deals in LED, and novel emerging applications. | 408-514-6900 | NA | Fremont |

## 129 = Alternative Energy Systems

| COMPANY NAME | PRODUCT / SERVICE | PHONE | EMP | CITY |
|---|---|---|---|---|
| Altergy Systems (HQ) | Designer and manufacturer of fuel cell power systems. The company serves telecommunication, emergency response, data center, and other fields. | 916-458-8590 | 1-10 | Folsom |
| Beyond Oil Solar (HQ) | Provider of energy equipment products. The company offers solar panels, inverters, charge controllers, mounting systems, and water pumps. | 415-388-0838 | NA | Mill Valley |
| Blymyer Engineers Inc (HQ) | Provider of solar engineering, facility design, and related services. The company serves the food and beverage and glass manufacturing industries. | 510-521-3773 | NA | Alameda |
| Brightsource Energy Inc (HQ) | Developer of solar thermal technology for electric power, petroleum, and industrial-process markets. | 510-550-8161 | NA | Oakland |
| Ceecon Testing Inc (HQ) | Provider of soil and groundwater remediation services. The company services also include regulatory compliance and remediation equipment. | 650-827-7474 | NA | S San Francisco |
| Cooling Source Inc (HQ) | Provider of thermal design solution for LED lighting, medical, military/aero, and test equipment industries. | 925-292-1293 | NA | Livermore |
| Eagle Shield (HQ) | Provider of energy conservation and renewable energy solutions. The company offers services to homes and businesses. | 925-648-2017 | NA | Danville |
| Eeonyx Corp (HQ) | Manufacturer and provider of knitting services. The company focuses on textiles, foams, felts, and powders. | 510-741-3632 | NA | Pinole |
| National Center For Appropriate Technology (BR) | Provider of information and access services. The company's offerings include weatherizing houses, monitoring energy applications, and testing products. | 530-792-7338 | 11-50 | Davis |
| Nexant Inc (HQ) | Developer of software for utility, energy, chemical, and other sectors and also offers power grid consulting and energy advisory, and other services. | 415-369-1000 | NA | San Francisco |
| Peninsula Engineering Solutions Inc (HQ) | Manufacturer of microwave RF repeaters. The company also specializes in cellular & PCS repeaters and relateed products. | 925-837-2243 | NA | Danville |
| Solar Sense PV Inc (HQ) | Provider of solar power system installation services. The company also focuses on design and serves residential, commercial, and utility applications. | 888-786-4339 | NA | Pleasanton |
| Sunperfect Solar Inc (HQ) | Provider of energy solutions. The company specializes in the design, manufacture, and installation of solar panels. | 408-273-4534 | NA | San Jose |
| Versatile Power (HQ) | Designer and manufacturer of electronic subsystems for manufacturers. The company focuses on application of radio frequency, ultrasonics, and lasers. | 408-341-4600 | NA | Campbell |

## 130 = Energy Conservation/Management Systems

| COMPANY NAME | PRODUCT / SERVICE | PHONE | EMP | CITY |
|---|---|---|---|---|
| Akros Silicon Inc (HQ) | Provider of power management ICs. The company offers digital DC-DC controllers and Ethernet protection dual channel active EMI suppressors. | 408-746-9000 | NA | San Jose |
| Altergy Systems (HQ) | Designer and manufacturer of fuel cell power systems. The company serves telecommunication, emergency response, data center, and other fields. | 916-458-8590 | 1-10 | Folsom |
| Brightsource Energy Inc (HQ) | Developer of solar thermal technology for electric power, petroleum, and industrial-process markets. | 510-550-8161 | NA | Oakland |
| Ceecon Testing Inc (HQ) | Provider of soil and groundwater remediation services. The company services also include regulatory compliance and remediation equipment. | 650-827-7474 | NA | S San Francisco |
| Competitive Power Ventures LLC (BR) | Provider of power generation services. The company focuses on natural gas and renewable energy generation and asset management. | 415-293-1455 | 1-10 | San Francisco |
| Enlighted Inc (HQ) | Provider of lighting control systems to commercial buildings, office workspaces, and garages. The company serves facilities and development companies. | 650-964-1094 | NA | Sunnyvale |
| Hench Control Inc (HQ) | Manufacturer of modular energy management systems. The company's products find application in industrial refrigeration. | 510-741-8100 | NA | Richmond |
| King-Solarman Inc (HQ) | Focuses on the sale of solar panels, power inverters, and related supplies. The company is involved in solar project financing services. | 408-373-8800 | NA | Fremont |
| Makel Engineering Inc (HQ) | Developer and provider of products and services for aviation, space, military, and commercial applications. | 530-895-2770 | 1-10 | Chico |
| New Power Technologies (HQ) | Provider of energy solutions. The company's offerings include energynet platform and energynet solutions. | 650-948-4546 | NA | Los Altos Hills |
| Newcomb Anderson Mccormick (HQ) | Provider of energy engineering and consulting services. The company also offers energy program development and distributed generation solutions. | 415-896-0300 | NA | San Francisco |

| COMPANY NAME | PRODUCT / SERVICE | PHONE | EMP | CITY |
|---|---|---|---|---|
| Pacific Gas & Electric Co (BR) | Provider of natural gas and electric services. The company serves approximately 15 million people throughout northern and central California. | 800-743-5000 | NA | San Francisco |
| Paul Graham Drilling And Service Co (HQ) | Provider of gas drilling services with over head cranes and computer operated plasma cutting machines for top notch drilling. | 707-374-5123 | NA | Rio Vista |
| Peninsula Engineering Solutions Inc (HQ) | Manufacturer of microwave RF repeaters. The company also specializes in cellular & PCS repeaters and relateed products. | 925-837-2243 | NA | Danville |
| Sentient Energy Inc (HQ) | Provider of sensor devices for operational practices and engineering applications. The company also offers communication software. | 650-523-6680 | NA | Burlingame |
| Tesla (HQ) | Designer and manufacturer of electric sedans and electric SUVs. The company is engaged in the production of energy storage systems. | 6500-681-5000 | NA | Palo Alto |
| Visible Energy Inc (HQ) | Provider of products and interactive energy conservation services that take control of electricity consumption. | | NA | Palo Alto |

## 131 = Energy-Related R&D

| COMPANY NAME | PRODUCT / SERVICE | PHONE | EMP | CITY |
|---|---|---|---|---|
| Aemetis Inc (HQ) | Producer of biochemicals, renewable fuels, food, and feed products. The company's products include Z-Microbe, Glycerin, and edible oils. | 408-213-0940 | 51-200 | Cupertino |
| Akros Silicon Inc (HQ) | Provider of power management ICs. The company offers digital DC-DC controllers and Ethernet protection dual channel active EMI suppressors. | 408-746-9000 | NA | San Jose |
| Bv Thermal Systems Llc (BR) | Manufacturer of recirculating chillers and heat exchangers for laboratory, semiconductor, laser, medical, and research industries and institutions. | 209-522-3701 | 11-50 | Modesto |
| Canary Instruments (HQ) | Provider of home energy monitor with colorful LED lights that provide instant feedback on the electricity use. | 707-506-6611 | 1-10 | Arcata |
| Cooling Source Inc (HQ) | Provider of thermal design solution for LED lighting, medical, military/aero, and test equipment industries. | 925-292-1293 | NA | Livermore |
| Electric Power Research Institute Inc (HQ) | Provider of research and development services related to the generation, delivery, and use of electricity for the benefit of the public. | 650-855-2000 | NA | Palo Alto |
| Enerfin Resources Co (BR) | Producer of natural gas. The company is also engaged in the exploration of crude oil and natural gas. | 530-550-8419 | 11-50 | Truckee |
| Geochemical Research Laboratory (HQ) | The company uses energy dispersive x-ray fluoresence spectrometry to determine the element composition of volcanic rocks. The company specializes in archaelogical geochemistry. | 650-851-1410 | NA | Portola Valley |
| Neil O Anderson & Associates Inc (HQ) | Provider of engineering services including geotechnical engineering, foundation, and structural engineering services. | 209-367-3701 | 11-50 | Lodi |
| New Power Technologies (HQ) | Provider of energy solutions. The company's offerings include energynet platform and energynet solutions. | 650-948-4546 | NA | Los Altos Hills |
| Newcomb Anderson Mccormick (HQ) | Provider of energy engineering and consulting services. The company also offers energy program development and distributed generation solutions. | 415-896-0300 | NA | San Francisco |
| Nextracker Inc (HQ) | Provider of horizontal tracking services. The company focuses on solar power plants and clean technology solutions. | 510-270-2500 | NA | Fremont |
| OCSiAl (BR) | Provider of technology and material solutions. The company offers services to the nanomaterials industry. | 415-906-5271 | NA | Sunnyvale |
| Pacific Gas & Electric Co (BR) | Provider of natural gas and electric services. The company serves approximately 15 million people throughout northern and central California. | 800-743-5000 | NA | San Francisco |
| Praxair Technology Inc (BR) | Provider of industrial gases. The company engages in gas supply and management, industrial, and oil and gas services. | 925-866-6800 | NA | San Ramon |
| Radio Thermostat Company of America Inc (HQ) | Provider of home energy management solutions. The company offers wave and programmable communicating thermostats to its clients. | | 1-10 | Modesto |
| Soltac Inc (HQ) | Designer and provider of solar devices. It's products find application in warming batteries, signaling, and radar locating. | 650-327-7090 | NA | Palo Alto |
| Sunlink Corp (BR) | Designer and manufacturer of roof and ground mounted systems for commercial and utility-scale installations. | 510-483-4300 | NA | San Leandro |

## 132 = Nuclear Power Systems/Equipment

| COMPANY NAME | PRODUCT / SERVICE | PHONE | EMP | CITY |
|---|---|---|---|---|
| Praxair Technology Inc (BR) | Provider of industrial gases. The company engages in gas supply and management, industrial, and oil and gas services. | 925-866-6800 | NA | San Ramon |

## 133 = Oil & Gas Field Machinery & Equipment

| COMPANY NAME | PRODUCT / SERVICE | PHONE | EMP | CITY |
|---|---|---|---|---|
| A J Edmond Co (BR) | Provider of sampling and analytical services to petroleum refineries. The company's service areas include petroleum coke, coal, and gypsum. | 925-521-1555 | NA | Concord |
| Airgard Inc (HQ) | Manufacturer of gas scrubbers servicing epitaxial, metal etch, poly etch, and CVD process abatement applications. | 408-573-0701 | NA | San Jose |
| Altergy Systems (HQ) | Designer and manufacturer of fuel cell power systems. The company serves telecommunication, emergency response, data center, and other fields. | 916-458-8590 | 1-10 | Folsom |
| Chevron Corp (HQ) | Provider of mobile asset tracking and management solutions. The company serves the marine, chemicals, and aviation industries. | 925-842-1000 | NA | San Ramon |
| Cogco Inc (HQ) | Provider of gas and oil well services such as perforating, thru tubing, case logging, and jet cutting. | 530-666-1716 | 1-10 | Woodland |
| Coretest Systems Inc (HQ) | Designer and manufacturer of core analysis equipment for the oil and gas, hydrothermal, and environmental segments. | 408-778-3771 | NA | Morgan Hill |

| COMPANY NAME | PRODUCT / SERVICE | PHONE | EMP | CITY |
|---|---|---|---|---|
| Garcia And Associates (HQ) | Provider of natural and cultural resource consultant services. The company's services include permit acquisition, agency consultation, and ecological research. | 415-642-8969 | NA | San Francisco |
| Kwj Engineering Inc (HQ) | Manufacturer of gas detection products. The company offers equipment to detect chlorine, carbon monoxide, ozone, and methane and propane. | 510-794-4296 | NA | Newark |
| Los Gatos Research Inc (HQ) | Manufacturer of analyzers for the measurement of trace gases and isotopes. The company serves the industrial and environmental sectors. | 650-965-7772 | NA | San Jose |
| Matheson Tri-Gas Inc (BR) | Provider of industrial, electronic, medical, and specialty gases. The company also offers gas detection, purification, and control equipment. | 510-793-2559 | NA | Newark |
| Membrane Technology & Research (HQ) | Developer and manufacturer of membrane-based separation systems. The company serves the petrochemical, natural gas, and refining industries. | 650-328-2228 | NA | Newark |
| Paul Graham Drilling And Service Co (HQ) | Provider of gas drilling services with over head cranes and computer operated plasma cutting machines for top notch drilling. | 707-374-5123 | NA | Rio Vista |
| Praxair Technology Inc (BR) | Provider of industrial gases. The company engages in gas supply and management, industrial, and oil and gas services. | 925-866-6800 | NA | San Ramon |
| Shields Harper & Co (HQ) | Provider of design assistance, testing, monitoring, fleet fuel control, and underground solutions to contractors, engineers, and designers. | 510-653-9119 | NA | Martinez |
| Silpac (HQ) | Distributor and manufacturer of specialty gas handling equipment. The company caters to markets like semiconductor, life science, and solar. | 408-492-0011 | NA | Santa Clara |
| Springboard Biodiesel LLC (HQ) | Manufacturer of automated bio-diesel processors. The company also offers fuel pumps, and tanks to consumers, small businesses, and municipalities. | 530-894-1793 | 1-10 | Chico |

## 134 = Oil & Gas Recovery Equipment

| COMPANY NAME | PRODUCT / SERVICE | PHONE | EMP | CITY |
|---|---|---|---|---|
| Aemetis Inc (HQ) | Producer of biochemicals, renewable fuels, food, and feed products. The company's products include Z-Microbe, Glycerin, and edible oils. | 408-213-0940 | 51-200 | Cupertino |
| Biofuel Oasis (HQ) | Producer of biodiesel and seller of urban farm supplies, poultry feed and equipment. The company specializes in biodiesel made from waste oil. | 510-665-5509 | NA | Berkeley |
| Chevron Corp (HQ) | Provider of mobile asset tracking and management solutions. The company serves the marine, chemicals, and aviation industries. | 925-842-1000 | NA | San Ramon |
| Cogco Inc (HQ) | Provider of gas and oil well services such as perforating, thru tubing, case logging, and jet cutting. | 530-666-1716 | 1-10 | Woodland |
| Duravent Inc (HQ) | Manufacturer of pellets, pressure stacks, and special gas vents. The company is involved in condensing application installation. | 800-835-4429 | NA | Vacaville |
| Energy Recovery Inc (HQ) | Manufacturer of energy recovery devices. The company offers pressure exchangers, chargers, pumps for desalination processes, oil and gas applications. | 510-483-7370 | NA | San Leandro |
| Pacific Gas & Electric Co (BR) | Provider of natural gas and electric services to the areas in northern and central California. The company specializes in promoting renewable energy. | 800-743-5000 | 11-50 | Sacramento |
| Pacific Gas & Electric Co (BR) | Provider of natural gas and electric services. The company serves approximately 15 million people throughout northern and central California. | 800-743-5000 | NA | San Francisco |
| Praxair Technology Inc (BR) | Provider of industrial gases. The company engages in gas supply and management, industrial, and oil and gas services. | 925-866-6800 | NA | San Ramon |
| Real Environmental Products (HQ) | Provider of landfill gas products. The company products include LFG well heads and 1200 series monitoring well monuments. | 209-296-7900 | 1-10 | Pine Grove |

## 135 = Solar Energy Collectors/Systems

| COMPANY NAME | PRODUCT / SERVICE | PHONE | EMP | CITY |
|---|---|---|---|---|
| 3rd Stone Design Inc (HQ) | Provider of design, product development, and engineering services. The company serves the consumer products and healthcare industries. | 415-454-3005 | NA | San Rafael |
| 8minute Solar Energy (HQ) | Developer of solar PV projects. The company specializes in project development, financing, utility engineering, and business development. | 916-608-9060 | 11-50 | El Dorado Hills |
| Armageddon Energy Inc (HQ) | Designer and manufacturer of rooftop solar systems. The company is engaged in installation services and serves homeowners. | 650-641-2899 | NA | Menlo Park |
| Bentek Corp (HQ) | Provider of manufacturing and engineering services. The company's offerings include power distribution system design and mechanical manufacturing. | 408-954-9600 | NA | San Jose |
| Beyond Oil Solar (HQ) | Provider of energy equipment products. The company offers solar panels, inverters, charge controllers, mounting systems, and water pumps. | 415-388-0838 | NA | Mill Valley |
| Blue Oak Energy (HQ) | Designer of photovoltaic solar energy systems. The company is engaged in designing, building, and maintenance of solar energy systems. | 530-747-2026 | 1-10 | Davis |
| California Solar Systems (BR) | Provider of grid-tied turn key solar electric systems. The company caters to both residential and commercial sectors. | 855-227-6527 | 11-50 | Fresno |
| Cenergy Power (HQ) | Developer and installer of solar for the agricultural, commercial, industrial, and utility scale markets. | 209-233-9777 | 11-50 | Merced |
| Crystal Solar Inc (HQ) | Developer of solar cells and modules. The company focuses on the conversion of feedstock gas to mono-crystalline silicon wafers. | 408-490-1340 | NA | Santa Clara |
| Diablo Solar Services (HQ) | Provider of solar pool heating and solar power photo voltaic systems. The company also offers installation services. | 925-313-0600 | NA | Martinez |

| COMPANY NAME | PRODUCT / SERVICE | PHONE | EMP | CITY |
|---|---|---|---|---|
| Directnu Energy Corp (HQ) | Provider of wind-solar energy solutions with integrated storage and control systems for businesses and government entities. | 408-657-3314 | NA | San Jose |
| Eagle Shield (HQ) | Provider of energy conservation and renewable energy solutions. The company offers services to homes and businesses. | 925-648-2017 | NA | Danville |
| Eiq Energy Inc (HQ) | Designer and manufacturer of power electronics. The company provides solar cells, panels, and monitoring systems. | 408-643-0020 | NA | Santa Clara |
| Enerparc Inc (DH) | Developer and designer of photovoltaic systems. The company services include EPC work, EPC management, operation, and maintenance. | 844-367-7272 | NA | Oakland |
| Enphase Energy Inc (HQ) | Distributor of electronic products. The company offers services to the solar, telecom, networking, and software industries. | 877-797-4743 | NA | Petaluma |
| Et Solar Inc (DH) | Provider of solar inverters and modules. The company offers design, installation, maintenance, and repair services. | 925-460-9898 | NA | Pleasanton |
| Fafco Inc (HQ) | Manufacturer of polymer heat exchangers. The company also specializes in thermal energy storage systems. | 530-332-2100 | 1-10 | Chico |
| Fenix International (HQ) | Provider of affordable power generation, smart-storage, and distribution solutions for the 1.6 billion people living off the electricity grid. | 415-754-9222 | NA | San Francisco |
| Free Hot Water (HQ) | Manufacturer and distributor of solar thermal products. The company serves engineers, architects, developers, and business owners. | 408-432-9900 | NA | San Jose |
| Garcia And Associates (HQ) | Provider of natural and cultural resource consultant services. The company's services include permit acquisition, agency consultation, and ecological research. | 415-642-8969 | NA | San Francisco |
| Glasspoint Solar Inc (HQ) | Manufacturer of solar steam generators for the oil and gas industry. The company is engaged in design and installation services. | 415-778-2800 | NA | Fremont |
| HiQ Solar Inc (HQ) | Manufacturer of solar power and renewable energy products and accessories such as communications gateway, AC splice, and inverter ballast mounting kit. | 408-970-9580 | NA | Sunnyvale |
| Intevac Inc (HQ) | Supplier of magnetic media processing systems. The company offers advanced equipment to the hard disk drive, solar, and photonics industries. | 408-986-9888 | NA | Santa Clara |
| Isa Corp (HQ) | Developer and manufacturer of solar mounting systems for commercial applications. The company also offers solar thermal systems. | 510-324-3755 | NA | Union City |
| King-Solarman Inc (HQ) | Focuses on the sale of solar panels, power inverters, and related supplies. The company is involved in solar project financing services. | 408-373-8800 | NA | Fremont |
| Meline Engineering Corp (HQ) | Provider of energy efficient mechanical system design services. The company also offers mechanical engineering services. | 916-366-3458 | 1-10 | Sacramento |
| MiaSole Hi-Tech Corp (HQ) | Manufacturer of copper indium gallium selenide thin-film photovoltaic solar panels. The company offers solar power plants for industrial needs. | 404-843-1815 | NA | Santa Clara |
| Morley Manufacturing Inc (HQ) | Designer and manufacturer of drainback water storage tanks for residential and commercial purposes. The company offers installation services. | 530-477-6527 | 1-10 | Grass Valley |
| Natron Resources Inc (HQ) | Provider of solar system, flat-plate photovoltaic, and solar thermal design and installations services. | 510-868-0701 | NA | Moraga |
| Nextracker Inc (HQ) | Provider of horizontal tracking services. The company focuses on solar power plants and clean technology solutions. | 510-270-2500 | NA | Fremont |
| Occidental Power (HQ) | Designer and installer of commercial and residential solar electric, solar thermal, and natural gas cogeneration systems. | 415-681-8861 | NA | San Francisco |
| Peninsula Engineering Solutions Inc (HQ) | Manufacturer of microwave RF repeaters. The company also specializes in cellular & PCS repeaters and relateed products. | 925-837-2243 | NA | Danville |
| Poco Solar Energy Inc (HQ) | Designer and installer of solar energy systems that provide electricity and heat for swimming pools. | 408-970-0680 | NA | Santa Clara |
| Provoltz Inc (HQ) | Provider of solar, PV, photovoltaic, and solar power solutions. The company is involved in design and installation services. | 408-796-4450 | NA | Campbell |
| Redwood Renewables (HQ) | Developer and manufacturer of residential tiles and solar roofing. The company also focuses on the marketing aspects. | 415-924-8140 | NA | Corte Madera |
| Reel Solar Power Inc (HQ) | Provider of tools and materials to photovoltaic manufacturing. The company also engages in the manufacturing of cadmium telluride solar panels. | 408-258-4714 | NA | San Jose |
| Silicon Genesis Corp (HQ) | Manufacturer of semiconductor and solar fabrication tools . The company offers stand-alone plasma tools and debond and cleave tools. | 408-228-5858 | NA | San Jose |
| Siva Power Inc (HQ) | Manufacturer of solar products. The company specializes in semiconductor, flat panel display, and solar devices. | 408-834-7400 | NA | Santa Clara |
| Solano Archaeological Svc (HQ) | Provider of archaeological services. The company services also include cultural resource and artifact analysis and curation. | 707-718-1416 | NA | Suisun City |
| Solar Junction (HQ) | Manufacturer of high-efficiency solar cells and receivers. The company's products find application in concentrated photovoltaic systems. | 408-503-7000 | 11-50 | San Jose |
| Solar Sense PV Inc (HQ) | Provider of solar power system installation services. The company also focuses on design and serves residential, commercial, and utility applications. | 888-786-4339 | NA | Pleasanton |
| Solarbos Inc (HQ) | Designer and manufacturer of electrical products. The company exclusively caters to the solar industry. | 925-456-7744 | NA | Livermore |
| Solaria Corp (HQ) | Manufacturer of solar panels for residential and commercial use. The company also specializes in design services. | 510-270-2500 | NA | Fremont |

| COMPANY NAME | PRODUCT / SERVICE | PHONE | EMP | CITY |
|---|---|---|---|---|
| Solaron Inc (HQ) | Manufacturer of swimming pool solar collectors and also provides the most efficient photovoltaic modules. | 916-631-9293 | 11-50 | Rancho Cordova |
| Soltac Inc (HQ) | Designer and provider of solar devices. It's products find application in warming batteries, signaling, and radar locating. | 650-327-7090 | NA | Palo Alto |
| sPower (BR) | Provider of utility-scale solar generation and physical plant development services for landowners, utilities, and communities. | 415-692-7740 | NA | San Francisco |
| Sun First! Solar (HQ) | Provider of renewable energy services. The company offers residential and commercial solar PV and swimming pool systems. | 415-458-5870 | NA | San Rafael |
| Sunlink Corp (HQ) | Designer and manufacturer of roof and ground mounted systems for commercial and utility-scale installations. | 415-925-9650 | NA | Mill Valley |
| Sunlink Corp (BR) | Designer and manufacturer of roof and ground mounted systems for commercial and utility-scale installations. | 510-483-4300 | NA | San Leandro |
| Sunperfect Solar Inc (HQ) | Provider of energy solutions. The company specializes in the design, manufacture, and installation of solar panels. | 408-273-4534 | NA | San Jose |
| Sunpreme Inc (HQ) | Developer of SmartSilicon based solar cells to satisfy growing global needs for abundant, low-cost, clean energy. | 866-245-1110 | NA | Sunnyvale |
| Suntechnics Energy Systems Inc (HQ) | Provider of residential, commercial, and agricultural solar systems and solutions. The company offers custom installation services. | 888-786-8321 | 11-50 | Sacramento |
| Sunterra Solar Inc (HQ) | Designer of turn-key grid-connected solar power systems for commercial, agricultural, and governmental customers. | 415-883-6800 | NA | Novato |
| Suntrek Industries Inc (BR) | Manufacturer, designer, and installer of solar power systems for residential, commercial, and agricultural solar power applications. | 925-372-8983 | NA | Martinez |
| Sunverge Energy Inc (HQ) | Provider of power and energy services. The company focuses on solar power and combines batteries and power electronics. | 209-931-5677 | 1-10 | Stockton |
| Trina Solar US Inc (RH) | Manufacturer of mono and multicrystalline photovoltaic (PV) modules. The company serves residential, commercial, and utility purposes. | 800-696-7114 | NA | San Jose |
| Ultrasolar Technology Inc (HQ) | Manufacturer of solar panel devices. The company specializes in residential, commercial, and utility solar arrays. | 408-499-6227 | NA | Santa Clara |
| Upsolar America Inc (BR) | Developer and producer of solar photovoltaic modules. The company's services include installation and maintenance and offers packing solutions. | 415-263-9920 | NA | San Francisco |
| WAGAN Corp (HQ) | Developer and marketer of automotive accessories to mobile professionals. The company's offerings include warmers, defrosters, and heated cushions. | 510-471-9221 | NA | Hayward |
| Zeta Instruments (HQ) | Provider of 3D optical profilers and its applications include wafer quality analysis, texture characterization, and finger contact profiling. | 408-818-9388 | NA | San Jose |

## 136 = Environmental

| COMPANY NAME | PRODUCT / SERVICE | PHONE | EMP | CITY |
|---|---|---|---|---|
| Enviro Safetech Inc (HQ) | Provider of environmental, health, and safety consulting services. The company deals with auditing and inspections. | 408-943-9090 | NA | San Jose |
| The Cohen Group (HQ) | Provider of health and safety training, litigation support, indoor air quality, microbial contamination, and related services. | 650-349-9737 | NA | San Mateo |

## 137 = Bioremediation Equipment/Systems

| COMPANY NAME | PRODUCT / SERVICE | PHONE | EMP | CITY |
|---|---|---|---|---|
| Agra Tech Inc (HQ) | Manufacturer of greenhouses and accessories for commercial, horticultural, and agricultural growers. The company offers heating and cooling equipment. | 925-432-3399 | NA | Pittsburg |
| Bullet Guard Co (HQ) | Designer and manufacturer of bullet resistant and bullet proof products. The company serves the banking, government, and law enforcement sectors. | 916-373-0402 | 1-10 | West Sacramento |
| Forsgren Associate Inc (DH) | Provider of civil and environmental engineering consulting services. The company specializes in planning, design, survey, and construction management. | 916-638-1119 | 11-50 | Rancho Cordova |
| N Genesis Biofuel Inc (HQ) | Manufacturer of renewable energy products. The company offers green solutions to counter greenhouse gas emissions. | 303-376-6221 | 1-10 | Huntington Beach |
| Ultra T Equipment Company Inc (HQ) | Manufacturer of spin coaters, developer stations, reionizers, and microelectronics cleaning systems. | 510-440-3909 | NA | Fremont |

## 138 = Environmental Analysis Equipment

| COMPANY NAME | PRODUCT / SERVICE | PHONE | EMP | CITY |
|---|---|---|---|---|
| Aethlabs (HQ) | Provider of black carbon monitoring equipment. The company also deals in manufacturing and assembly services. | 415-529-2355 | NA | San Francisco |
| Asbestos Tem Laboratories Inc (HQ) | Provider of laboratory services including asbestos and lead testing. The company serves geologists, contractors, and homeowners. | 510-704-8930 | NA | Berkeley |
| Curtis & Tompkins Laboratories (HQ) | Provider of environmental analytical testing services. The company is also engaged in operational management. | 510-486-0900 | NA | Berkeley |
| Eme Systems (HQ) | Designer and manufacturer of instruments for environmental science. The company also offers signal conditioners, sensors, enclosures, and batteries. | 510-848-5725 | NA | Berkeley |
| Enviro-Tech Services Co (HQ) | Designer and manufacturer of environmental products. The company offers water sampling equipment, air monitoring equipment, and general field supplies. | 800-468-8921 | NA | Martinez |

| COMPANY NAME | PRODUCT / SERVICE | PHONE | EMP | CITY |
|---|---|---|---|---|
| Etm Electromatic Inc (HQ) | Manufacturer of custom high voltage power supplies and amplifiers. The company is engaged in troubleshooting, repairs, and maintenance services. | 510-797-1100 | NA | Newark |
| Fortrend Engineering Corp (HQ) | Designer and manufacturer of mechanical handling equipment. The company also specializes in distribution services. | 408-734-9311 | NA | San Jose |
| Geosyntec (BR) | Provider of consulting and engineering services. The company serves customers in the oil and gas, refining, petrochemical, and waste management industries. | 916-637-8048 | 11-50 | Rancho Cordova |
| Inta Technologies (HQ) | Manufacturer of components used in instruments for environmental analysis. The company also offers ceramic-to-metal assemblies connectors. | 408-748-9955 | NA | Santa Clara |
| Los Gatos Research Inc (HQ) | Manufacturer of analyzers for the measurement of trace gases and isotopes. The company serves the industrial and environmental sectors. | 650-965-7772 | NA | San Jose |
| Mesotech International Inc (HQ) | Provider of weather monitoring and reporting systems and software solutions. The company serves airport, defense, and agriculture industries. | 916-368-2020 | 1-10 | Sacramento |
| Ondavia Inc (HQ) | Provider of water analysis solutions. The company offers OndaVia analysis system that enables laboratory-grade water testing. | 510-576-0476 | NA | Hayward |
| Protemp Mechanical Inc (HQ) | Provider of environmental test equipment calibration services. The company's services include preventative maintenance, chamber modifications, and consulting. | 408-244-9821 | NA | Santa Clara |
| Sierra Monitor Corp (HQ) | Manufacturer and seller of safety and environmental instrumentation. The company offers hazardous gas detection systems and site management products. | 408-262-6611 | NA | Milpitas |
| Spectrex Corp (HQ) | Developer of environmental and analytical instruments. The company's offerings include detectors and personal air samplers. | 650-365-6567 | NA | Redwood City |
| Swca Environmental Consultants (DH) | Provider of environmental consultant services. The company focuses on environmental planning and regulatory compliance activities. | 650-440-4160 | NA | Half Moon Bay |
| Trinity Consultants Inc (BR) | Provider of environmental consulting services. The company engages in environmental outsourcing and litigation support services. | 510-285-6351 | NA | Oakland |
| Turner Designs Inc (HQ) | Provider of industrial fluorometers and rhodamine dyes. The company's applications include oil spill response and environmental monitoring. | 408-749-0994 | NA | San Jose |

## 139 = Environmental Analysis Services

| COMPANY NAME | PRODUCT / SERVICE | PHONE | EMP | CITY |
|---|---|---|---|---|
| 3rd Stone Design Inc (HQ) | Provider of design, product development, and engineering services. The company serves the consumer products and healthcare industries. | 415-454-3005 | NA | San Rafael |
| A&L Western Agricultural Lab (HQ) | Provider of analytical services to agricultural sector. The company's services include soil analysis, pathology, microbiology, and water analysis. | 209-529-4080 | 11-50 | Modesto |
| Acc Environmental Consultants (HQ) | Provider of environmental consulting services. The company's services include moisture testing, site assessment, mold testing, and asbetos consulting. | 510-638-8400 | NA | Oakland |
| Adr Environmental Group Inc (HQ) | Provider of risk management services and due diligence services. The company's due diligence service includes engineering and structural services. | 916-921-0600 | 1-10 | Sacramento |
| Aei Consultants (BR) | Provider of environmental and engineering services. The company's services also include industrial hygiene and construction. | 916-333-4568 | 11-50 | Sacramento |
| Allied Environmental Inc (HQ) | Provider of asbestos and lead abatement services. The company specializes in commercial, residential, and industrial contracting services. | 510-732-1300 | NA | Hayward |
| Anamet Inc (HQ) | Provider of materials engineering analysis & lab testing services. The company focuses on product testing, failure analysis, and forensic engineering. | 510-887-8811 | NA | Hayward |
| Aquifer Sciences Inc (HQ) | Provider of environmental assessment and remediation services. The company is also engaged in remedial design and implementation. | 925-283-9098 | NA | Lafayette |
| Aspen Environmental Group (BR) | Provider of environmental compliance, impact assessment, and mitigation services. The company's services include construction monitoring and project management. | 415-955-4775 | NA | San Francisco |
| Balance Hydrologics Inc (HQ) | Provider of hydrologic services. The company offers geomorphology, restoration design, watershed management, and wetland inspection services. | 510-704-1000 | NA | Berkeley |
| Baseline Environmental Consulting (HQ) | Provider of environmental consulting services including remediation, investigations, data management, and surveys. | 510-420-8686 | NA | Emeryville |
| Blackburn Consulting (HQ) | Provider of geotechnical engineering, geo environmental engineering, design materials engineering, forensic, and construction services. | 530-887-1494 | 11-50 | Auburn |
| California Environmental Associates (HQ) | Provider of environmental consulting services. The company's services include recruiting and organizational design services. | 415-421-4213 | NA | San Francisco |
| Cha Corp (HQ) | Developer and marketer of microwave technologies. The company offers carbon regeneration, hypergolic destruction, and emission control solutions. | 916-550-5380 | 1-10 | Sacramento |
| Clean Earth (BR) | Provider of recycling solutions. The company acts as regulated and permitted electronics and universal waste recycler. | 510-429-1129 | NA | Hayward |
| Curtis & Tompkins Laboratories (HQ) | Provider of environmental analytical testing services. The company is also engaged in operational management. | 510-486-0900 | NA | Berkeley |

| COMPANY NAME | PRODUCT / SERVICE | PHONE | EMP | CITY |
|---|---|---|---|---|
| Denele Analytical Inc (HQ) | Provider of agriculture and environmental support services. The company offers analytical services for plant tissue, manure, and wastewater needs. | 209-634-9055 | 11-50 | Turlock |
| Egs Inc (HQ) | Provider of geothermal exploration development services. The company's services include remote sensing, geologic mapping, and subsurface visualization. | 707-595-8760 | NA | Santa Rosa |
| Em Lab P&K (BR) | Provider of indoor air quality testing services. The company offers culturable air fungi, spore trap analysis, and yeast identification services. | 916-374-4483 | 11-50 | West Sacramento |
| Enviro Safetech Inc (HQ) | Provider of environmental, health, and safety consulting services. The company deals with auditing and inspections. | 408-943-9090 | NA | San Jose |
| Environmental Risk Communications Inc (BR) | Provider of consulting services in environmental liabilities management. The company's services include site strategic planning and project controls. | 510-548-5570 | NA | Oakland |
| Environmental Sampling Services Llc (HQ) | Provider of technical services for environmental assessments needs. The company also focuses on investigation and remediation. | 925-372-8108 | NA | Martinez |
| Environmental Science Associates (HQ) | Provider of restoration and mitigation, regulatory permitting, compliance monitoring, and community planning services. | 415-896-5900 | NA | San Francisco |
| Freshwater Environmental Svc (HQ) | Provider of environmental services. The company's services include soil investigation workplans, soil sampling reporting, sediment sampling, and monitoring. | 707-839-0091 | 1-10 | Arcata |
| Frey Environmental Inc (BR) | Provider of geological and engineering consulting services. The company offers stormwater management, methane assessments/mitigation, and asbestos-related services. | 831-464-1634 | 11-50 | Santa Cruz |
| Grayland Environmental (HQ) | Provider of environmental and natural resources protections services. The company offers environmental engineering, geological and geophysical services. | 530-756-1441 | 1-10 | Davis |
| Horizon Water & Environment (BR) | Provider of environmental consulting services. The company specializes in watershed science, environmental compliance, and water resources management. | 510-986-1850 | NA | Oakland |
| Kaz & Associates Environmental Services (HQ) | Provider of water management consulting services. The company's services include enforcement response, and groundwater contamination investigation. | 707-747-1126 | NA | Benicia |
| Keish Environmental PC (HQ) | Provider of environmental and stormwater compliance services. The company also specializes in construction inspection services. | 408-359-7248 | NA | San Jose |
| Kings River Conservation District (HQ) | Provider of resource management solutions. The company focuses on flood protection, water supply, power generation, and other needs. | 559-237-5567 | 1-10 | Fresno |
| Lamphier-Gregory (HQ) | Provider of urban planning services. The company provides environmental analysis, project management, and coordination services. | 510-535-6690 | NA | Oakland |
| Moore Twining Associates Inc (HQ) | Provider of geotechnical engineering, environmental, construction inspection, materials testing, analytical chemistry, and drilling services. | 559-268-7021 | 11-50 | Fresno |
| National Center For Appropriate Technology (BR) | Provider of information and access services. The company's offerings include weatherizing houses, monitoring energy applications, and testing products. | 530-792-7338 | 11-50 | Davis |
| Neil O Anderson & Associates Inc (HQ) | Provider of engineering services including geotechnical engineering, foundation, and structural engineering services. | 209-367-3701 | 11-50 | Lodi |
| Northgate Environmental Management Inc (HQ) | Provider of interdisciplinary technical solutions. The company focuses on results-oriented scientific and engineering investigation and analysis. | 510-839-0688 | NA | Oakland |
| Quanta Laboratories (HQ) | Provider of environmental testing and consulting services. The company offers vibration test, shock test, and chambers test services. | 408-988-0770 | NA | Santa Clara |
| Rincon Consultants Inc (BR) | Provider of environmental consulting services. The company specializes in land use planning, site assessment, remediation, and other services. | 510-834-4455 | NA | Oakland |
| SCA Environmental Inc (HQ) | Provider of environmental science, occupational health and safety, engineering, and laboratory analyses services. | 415-882-1675 | NA | San Francisco |
| Shields Harper & Co (HQ) | Provider of design assistance, testing, monitoring, fleet fuel control, and underground solutions to contractors, engineers, and designers. | 510-653-9119 | NA | Martinez |
| Southwest Hazard Control Inc (BR) | Provider of environmental remediation services. The company's offerings include asbestos abatement and hazardous materials management services. | 510-352-5152 | NA | San Leandro |
| Stantec (BR) | Provider of environmental consulting services specializing in GIS mapping, remote sensing, permitting, and ecosystem restoration. | 530-222-5347 | 11-50 | Redding |
| Swca Environmental Consultants (DH) | Provider of environmental consultant services. The company focuses on environmental planning and regulatory compliance activities. | 650-440-4160 | NA | Half Moon Bay |
| Terradex Inc (HQ) | Provider of web and consulting services. The company offers dig clean, cleanupdeck, and web development services. | 650-227-3250 | NA | Palo Alto |
| Terrapass Inc (HQ) | Provider of carbon management solutions for farms, landfills, and wind power installations. The company specializes in project management and sales. | 877-210-9581 | NA | San Francisco |
| Terraphase Engineering (HQ) | Provider of environmental consulting services. The company offers environmental due diligence, and soil and groundwater remediation services. | 510-645-1850 | NA | Oakland |

| COMPANY NAME | PRODUCT / SERVICE | PHONE | EMP | CITY |
|---|---|---|---|---|
| Test O Pac Industries Inc (HQ) | Provider of environmental and package testing services. The company deals with component testing, product reliability, and medical package testing. | 408-436-1117 | NA | San Jose |
| The Cohen Group (HQ) | Provider of health and safety training, litigation support, indoor air quality, microbial contamination, and related services. | 650-349-9737 | NA | San Mateo |
| Trc Companies Inc (BR) | Provider of scientific and engineering software services. The company offers hydropower licensing, power delivery, and telecommunications engineering services. | 415-434-2600 | NA | San Francisco |
| Westervelt Ecological Services (HQ) | Provider of ecological solutions. The company offers wetland mitigation and conservation banking, geographic information system analysis, and other services. | 916-646-3644 | 11-50 | Sacramento |

## 140 = Environmental R&D

| COMPANY NAME | PRODUCT / SERVICE | PHONE | EMP | CITY |
|---|---|---|---|---|
| Acc Environmental Consultants (HQ) | Provider of environmental consulting services. The company's services include moisture testing, site assessment, mold testing, and asbetos consulting. | 510-638-8400 | NA | Oakland |
| Adr Environmental Group Inc (HQ) | Provider of risk management services and due diligence services. The company's due diligence service includes engineering and structural services. | 916-921-0600 | 1-10 | Sacramento |
| Aei Consultants (BR) | Provider of environmental and engineering services. The company's services also include industrial hygiene and construction. | 916-333-4568 | 11-50 | Sacramento |
| Allied Environmental Inc (HQ) | Provider of asbestos and lead abatement services. The company specializes in commercial, residential, and industrial contracting services. | 510-732-1300 | NA | Hayward |
| Amprius Inc (HQ) | Developer and manufacturer of lithium-ion batteries. The company offers services to the industrial sectors. | 800-425-8803 | NA | Fremont |
| BASF Venture Capital America Inc (RH) | Manufacturer of basic chemicals and intermediates such as solvents, plasticizers, and monomers. The company serves the agriculture market. | 510-445-6140 | NA | Fremont |
| Blue Star Electronics (HQ) | Focuses on the resale, recycling and end of life programs for electronic equipment and components. The company offers e-waste solutions. | 925-420-5593 | NA | Livermore |
| Bsk Associates (BR) | Provider of geotechnical and environmental testing services. The company also offers materials testing services. | 916-853-9293 | 11-50 | Rancho Cordova |
| California Environmental Associates (HQ) | Provider of environmental consulting services. The company's services include recruiting and organizational design services. | 415-421-4213 | NA | San Francisco |
| Cytoculture International Inc (HQ) | Provider of technical consulting and microbiological laboratory services. The company specializes in biofuel project. | 510-233-0102 | NA | Point Richmond |
| Daniel B Stephens & Associates Inc (BR) | Provider of services in hydrology, environmental engineering, and science. The company services include water resources and soil testing. | 800-933-3105 | NA | Oakland |
| E2c Remediation (HQ) | Provider of environmental remediation services. The company services also include soil and groundwater remediation and civil and geological engineering. | 916-782-8700 | 1-10 | Roseville |
| Ecology & Environment Inc (BR) | Provider of environmental management services. The company's services also include planning, engineering, and emergency planning. | 415-398-5326 | NA | San Francisco |
| Eeonyx Corp (HQ) | Manufacturer and provider of knitting services. The company focuses on textiles, foams, felts, and powders. | 510-741-3632 | NA | Pinole |
| Enviro Safetech Inc (HQ) | Provider of asbestos, health, and safety consulting services. The company deals with auditing and inspections. | 408-943-9090 | NA | San Jose |
| Enviro-Tech Services Co (HQ) | Designer and manufacturer of environmental products. The company offers water sampling equipment, air monitoring equipment, and general field supplies. | 800-468-8921 | NA | Martinez |
| Environmental Products & Technologies Corp (HQ) | Developer of closed-loop, short hydraulic retention time anaerobic digesters. The company specializes in biogas technology solutions. | 559-201-6484 | 1-10 | Visalia |
| Environmental Risk Communications Inc (BR) | Provider of consulting services in environmental liabilities management. The company's services include site strategic planning and project controls. | 510-548-5570 | NA | Oakland |
| Fruit Growers Laboratory Inc (BR) | Provider of testing & analytical services. The company performs drinking and waste water analysis, agriculture testing, and hazardous waste analysis. | 209-942-0182 | 11-50 | Stockton |
| Grayland Environmental (HQ) | Provider of environmental and natural resources protections services. The company offers environmental engineering, geological and geophysical services. | 530-756-1441 | 1-10 | Davis |
| Greening Associates (HQ) | Provider of biological consultants and landscape contracting services. The company specializes in revegetation plans, wildlife surveys, and coastal restoration. | 831-336-1745 | 1-10 | Ben Lomond |
| Horizon Water & Environment (BR) | Provider of environmental consulting services. The company specializes in watershed science, environmental compliance, and water resources management. | 510-986-1850 | NA | Oakland |
| Kaz & Associates Environmental Services (HQ) | Provider of water management consulting services. The company's services include enforcement response, and groundwater contamination investigation. | 707-747-1126 | NA | Benicia |
| Lacroix Davis Llc (BR) | Provider of building and environmental forensics and consulting services. The company provides support for investigation, litigation, and education. | 925-299-1140 | NA | Lafayette |

| COMPANY NAME | PRODUCT / SERVICE | PHONE | EMP | CITY |
|---|---|---|---|---|
| Materials Testing Inc (HQ) | Provider of geotechnical engineering and materials testing services. The company offers geotechnical, environment, special inspection, and material testing services. | 530-222-1116 | 11-50 | Redding |
| Millennium Consulting Associates (HQ) | Provider of environmental and industrial hygiene services. The company offers environmental engineering, consulting, and compliance services. | 925-808-6700 | NA | Oakland |
| Neil O Anderson & Associates Inc (HQ) | Provider of engineering services including geotechnical engineering, foundation, and structural engineering services. | 209-367-3701 | 11-50 | Lodi |
| NRC Environmental Services Inc (BR) | Provider of environmental, industrial, and emergency solutions. The company offers oil spill response, industrial cleaning, sediment remediation, and other services. | 510-749-1390 | NA | Alameda |
| Panasas Inc (HQ) | Provider of scale-out NAS storage system for most demanding workloads in life sciences, media and entertainment, energy, and education environments. | 408-215-6800 | NA | Sunnyvale |
| Panorama Environmental Inc (HQ) | Provider of environmental planning services. The company engages in regulatory permitting and geographic information systems. | 650-373-1200 | NA | San Francisco |
| Prima Environmental Inc (HQ) | Provider of laboratory testing services. The company specializes in treatability testing, technology evaluation, and scientific consulting services. | 916-939-7300 | 1-10 | El Dorado Hills |
| Quanta Laboratories (HQ) | Provider of environmental testing and consulting services. The company offers vibration test, shock test, and chambers test services. | 408-988-0770 | NA | Santa Clara |
| Res (HQ) | Provider of environmental services. The company offers air-moving, contract safety, and vacuum truck services. | 925-432-1755 | NA | Pittsburg |
| Ridge to River (HQ) | Provider of hydrologic analysis and modeling services. The company is also focused on ecological restoration, erosion control, and water quality analysis. | 707-357-0857 | 1-10 | Fort Bragg |
| Schutze & Assoc Inc (HQ) | Provider of environmental consulting services. The company's services include groundwater monitoring and dry cleaning remediation. | 510-226-9944 | NA | Fremont |
| Southall Environmental Associates Inc (HQ) | Provider of science to support conservation management. The company specializes in marine and terrestrial ecosystems. | 831-661-5177 | 1-10 | Aptos |

## 41 = Hazardous & Other Waste Disposal or Management Services

| COMPANY NAME | PRODUCT / SERVICE | PHONE | EMP | CITY |
|---|---|---|---|---|
| Baseline Environmental Consulting (HQ) | Provider of environmental consulting services including remediation, investigations, data management, and surveys. | 510-420-8686 | NA | Emeryville |
| Blackburn Consulting (HQ) | Provider of geotechnical engineering, geo environmental engineering, design materials engineering, forensic, and construction services. | 530-887-1494 | 11-50 | Auburn |
| Recology Of The Coast (HQ) | Provider of resource recovery services. The company's services include urban cleaning services, collection, sorting, transfer, recovery and landfill management. | 650-355-9000 | NA | Pacifica |
| SCA Environmental Inc (HQ) | Provider of environmental science, occupational health and safety, engineering, and laboratory analyses services. | 415-882-1675 | NA | San Francisco |

## 42 = Other Environmental Services

| COMPANY NAME | PRODUCT / SERVICE | PHONE | EMP | CITY |
|---|---|---|---|---|
| Adr Environmental Group Inc (HQ) | Provider of risk management services and due diligence services. The company's due diligence service includes engineering and structural services. | 916-921-0600 | 1-10 | Sacramento |
| Advanced Geoenvironmental Inc (BR) | Provider of environmental consulting services. The company services include soil and groundwater remediation and water and wastewater services. | 800-511-9300 | NA | Santa Rosa |
| AEMTEK Laboratories (HQ) | Provider of testing, research, training and consulting services and sampling products for the food, environmental and pharmaceutical industries. | 510-979-1979 | NA | Fremont |
| Aero-Environmental Consulting (HQ) | Provider of environmental consulting solutions. The company's services include air quality assessment, regulatory compliance, and health planning. | 831-394-1199 | NA | Monterey |
| Agra Tech Inc (HQ) | Manufacturer of greenhouses and accessories for commercial, horticultural, and agricultural growers. The company offers heating and cooling equipment. | 925-432-3399 | NA | Pittsburg |
| Ags Inc (HQ) | Provider of civil, structural, and geotechnical engineering services. The company serves the water and transportation infrastructure markets. | 415-777-2166 | NA | San Francisco |
| Alisto Engineering Group Inc (HQ) | Provider of engineering and environmental consulting services. The company serves the private industry and government agencies. | 925-279-5000 | NA | Walnut Creek |
| All Power Labs (HQ) | Manufacturer of biomass fueled power generators. The company is a global leader in small scale gasification. | 510-845-1500 | NA | Berkeley |
| Allterra Environmental Inc (HQ) | Provider of environmental site remediation and compliance services. The company offerings include permitting, geologic hazards, and sustainable solutions. | 831-425-2608 | 1-10 | Santa Cruz |
| Anamet Inc (HQ) | Provider of materials engineering analysis & lab testing services. The company focuses on product testing, failure analysis, and forensic engineering. | 510-887-8811 | NA | Hayward |
| Apex Envirotech Inc (HQ) | Provider of environmental management and remediation technology. The company also offers engineering services. | 800-242-5249 | 11-50 | Gold River |
| Applied Earthworks Inc (HQ) | Provider of history, archaeology, paleontology, and cultural resources management and related services. | 559-229-1856 | 11-50 | Fresno |

| COMPANY NAME | PRODUCT / SERVICE | PHONE | EMP | CITY |
|---|---|---|---|---|
| Apx Power Markets Inc (BR) | Provider of e-commerce services for the electrical sector. The company serves residential, commercial, and industrial properties. | 408-517-2100 | NA | San Jose |
| Aqua Terra Consultants (HQ) | Provider of environmental consulting and water resource engineering services. The company also offers software development and consulting services. | 650-962-1864 | NA | Mountain View |
| Aquifer Sciences Inc (HQ) | Provider of environmental assessment and remediation services. The company is also engaged in remedial design and implementation. | 925-283-9098 | NA | Lafayette |
| Area West Environmental Inc (HQ) | Provider of environmental assessment services. The company is also engaged in planning, permitting, and regulatory compliance management services. | 916-987-3362 | 1-10 | Orangevale |
| Asian Pacific Environmental Network (HQ) | Provider of environmental services. The company engages in membership of low income immigrant and refugee communities. | 510-834-8920 | NA | Oakland |
| Atlas Engineering Services Inc (HQ) | Provider of environmental consulting services. The company offers services for aquifer testing, onsite wastewater disposal, and ground water sanitary surveys. | 831-426-1440 | 1-10 | Santa Cruz |
| Balance Hydrologics Inc (HQ) | Provider of hydrologic services. The company offers geomorphology, restoration design, watershed management, and wetland inspection services. | 510-704-1000 | NA | Berkeley |
| Basics Environmental Inc (HQ) | Provider of environmental engineering consulting services. The company focuses on environmental site assessments for real estate transactions. | 510-834-9099 | NA | Oakland |
| Better World Group Inc (BR) | Provider of environmental strategy consulting services. The company offers political strategy, coalition management, media, and communications. | 916-498-9411 | 11-50 | Sacramento |
| Biomax Environmental Llc (HQ) | Provider of indoor air quality assessment, sampling, industrial hygiene monitoring, auditing, and assessment services. | 510-724-3100 | NA | Pinole |
| Blackburn Consulting (HQ) | Provider of geotechnical engineering, geo environmental engineering, design materials engineering, forensic, and construction services. | 530-887-1494 | 11-50 | Auburn |
| Blue Source LLC (BR) | Provider of services for the mining industry. The company offers project development, offset sales and marketing, consulting, and other related services. | 415-399-9101 | NA | San Francisco |
| Blymyer Engineers Inc (HQ) | Provider of solar engineering, facility design, and related services. The company serves the food and beverage and glass manufacturing industries. | 510-521-3773 | NA | Alameda |
| Brelje & Race Laboratories Inc (HQ) | Provider of water and wastewater testing services. The company analyses process include nitrate, arsenic, and volatile organics compounds. | 707-544-8807 | NA | Santa Rosa |
| Brown and Caldwell (BR) | Provider of engineering consulting services. The company specializes in contracting, pumping station design, project management, and odor control. | 408-703-2528 | NA | San Jose |
| Burleson Consulting Inc (HQ) | Provider of environmental compliance and engineering services for the clients in Southern Oregon, Northern California, and Nevada. | 916-984-4651 | 11-50 | Folsom |
| Capital Engineering Consultants Inc (HQ) | Provider of mechanical engineering, sustainable design and green engineering, building commissioning, energy modeling, and other related services. | 916-851-3500 | 11-50 | Rancho Cordova |
| Catalyst Environmental Inc (HQ) | Provider of environmental services. The company's services comprise tank cleaning and hydro blasting services and soil and groundwater sampling. | 650-642-6583 | NA | San Carlos |
| CGI Technical Services Inc (HQ) | Provider of technical services. The company offerings include geotechnical engineering, engineering geology, and pavement design services. | 530-244-6277 | 1-10 | Redding |
| Cha Corp (HQ) | Developer and marketer of microwave technologies. The company offers carbon regeneration, hypergolic destruction, and emission control solutions. | 916-550-5380 | 1-10 | Sacramento |
| Chico Environmental Science & Planning (HQ) | Provider of environmental consulting services. The company offers site assessments, storm water pollution prevention plans, and environmental forensics. | 530-899-2900 | 1-10 | Chico |
| Clean Earth (BR) | Provider of recycling solutions. The company acts as regulated and permitted electronics and universal waste recycler. | 510-429-1129 | NA | Hayward |
| Commodity Resource & Environmental Inc (BR) | Producer of silver. The company engages in silver recovery, photo solution waste disposal, and other activities. | 408-501-0691 | NA | San Jose |
| Condor Country Consulting (HQ) | Provider of natural and cultural resource supporting services. The company also provides ecological, natural resource, and cartographic services. | 925-335-9308 | NA | Martinez |
| Cornerstone Environmental Group Llc (BR) | Provider of engineering consulting and field services. The company offers services for the solid waste water industry and agricultural clients. | 877-633-5520 | NA | Dublin |
| David J Powers & Associates Inc (HQ) | Provider of environmental consulting services. The company focuses on transportation, parks, and recreation projects. | 408-248-3500 | NA | San Jose |
| Dawn Reis Ecological Studies (HQ) | Provider of wildlife research and biological consulting services. The company is specialized in aquatic systems and endangered species population. | 831-588-7550 | 1-10 | Watsonville |
| Denise Duffy & Associates Inc (HQ) | Provider of environmental sciences, planning, and biological consulting services. The company is also focused on land use and contract planning. | 831-373-4341 | NA | Monterey |

| COMPANY NAME | PRODUCT / SERVICE | PHONE | EMP | CITY |
|---|---|---|---|---|
| Diablo Green Consulting Inc (HQ) | Provider of environmental consulting services. The company specializes in site assessments, geophysical survey, and cultural resource management. | 925-365-0730 | NA | Danville |
| Dysert Environmental Inc (HQ) | Provider of environmental solutions. The company's services include wastewater sampling, project management, soil sampling, and decontamination confirmation. | 650-799-9204 | NA | San Mateo |
| Eastern Research Group Inc (BR) | Provider of performance measurement, risk assessment, event planning and facilitation, and training services. | 916-635-6592 | 11-50 | Sacramento |
| Ecology & Environment Inc (BR) | Provider of environmental management services. The company's services also include planning, engineering, and emergency planning. | 415-398-5326 | NA | San Francisco |
| Ecoshift Consulting LLC (HQ) | Provider of consulting services. The company offers consulting for alternative fuels, climate change, carbon reduction strategies, and carbon trading. | 831-277-0167 | NA | Monterey |
| Egs Inc (HQ) | Provider of geothermal exploration development services. The company's services include remote sensing, geologic mapping, and subsurface visualization. | 707-595-8760 | NA | Santa Rosa |
| Electro Magnetic Test Inc (HQ) | Provider of testing and consulting services. The company focuses on engineering services in wireless, wireline telecom, and safety certifications. | 650-965-4000 | NA | Mountain View |
| Enplan (HQ) | Provider of environmental and geospatial technology services. The company focuses on wetland delineation and permit processing activities. | 530-221-0440 | 1-10 | Redding |
| Enpro Solutions Inc (HQ) | Provider of environmental remediation, management, permitting, and construction services. The company also deals with process safety consulting. | 925-803-8045 | NA | Dublin |
| Enviro-Tech Services Co (HQ) | Designer and manufacturer of environmental products. The company offers water sampling equipment, air monitoring equipment, and general field supplies. | 800-468-8921 | NA | Martinez |
| Environmental Incentives (HQ) | Provider of environmental conservation services. The company projects include Nevada conservation credit system and Colorado habitat exchange. | 530-541-2980 | 11-50 | South Lake Tahoe |
| Environmental Remedies Inc (HQ) | Provider of asbestos abatement services. The company engages in mold remediation, lead removal, and biological containment rediation service. | 888-710-2414 | NA | Hayward |
| Environmental Sampling Services Llc (HQ) | Provider of technical services for environmental assessments needs. The company also focuses on investigation and remediation. | 925-372-8108 | NA | Martinez |
| Envirosurvey Inc (HQ) | Provider of environmental consulting and technical services. The company provides soil and groundwater remediation and environmental safety services. | 415-882-4549 | NA | San Francisco |
| Excelchem Laboratories Inc (HQ) | Provider of analytical consultation, on-site analysis, custom reporting, and mobile laboratory services. | 916-543-4445 | 1-10 | Rocklin |
| Frey Environmental Inc (BR) | Provider of geological and engineering consulting services. The company offers stormwater management, methane assessments/mitigation, and asbestos-related services. | 831-464-1634 | 11-50 | Santa Cruz |
| Fruit Growers Laboratory Inc (BR) | Provider of testing & analytical services. The company performs drinking and waste water analysis, agriculture testing, and hazardous waste analysis. | 209-942-0182 | 11-50 | Stockton |
| G Fred Lee & Associates (HQ) | Provider of surface and groundwater evaluation services. The company focuses on landfill impacts, eutrophication, watershed studies, and other needs. | 530-753-9630 | 1-10 | El Macero |
| Geo-Tech Information Solutions (HQ) | Provider of concierge services in the environmental and natural hazard disclosure risk management field. | 916-941-8300 | 1-10 | Sacramento |
| Geosyntec (BR) | Provider of consulting and engineering services. The company serves customers in the oil and gas, refining, petrochemical, and waste management industries. | 916-637-8048 | 11-50 | Rancho Cordova |
| Golder Associates Inc (BR) | Provider of ground engineering and environmental services. The company serves business organizations and the industrial sector. | 408-220-9223 | NA | Sunnyvale |
| Groundwater & Environmental Services Inc (BR) | Provider of environmental consulting services. The company serves customers in the oil and gas, government, and petroleum markets. | 866-507-1411 | NA | Benicia |
| Harris & Lee Environmental Sciences Llc (HQ) | Provider of environmental consulting services. The company's services include environmental risk management, and preliminary environmental assessment. | 415-287-3007 | NA | San Rafael |
| Helix Environmental Planning Inc (HQ) | Provider of landscape architecture, planning, environmental consulting, restoration, and regulatory permitting services. | 619-462-1515 | 11-50 | La Mesa |
| Ht Harvey & Associates (HQ) | Provider of ecological consulting services that include ecological research, impact analysis, restoration design, and park planning. | 408-458-3200 | NA | Los Gatos |
| Itrenew Inc (HQ) | Provider of information technology services. The company focuses on data eradication, server application, logistics management, and configuration. | 408-744-9600 | NA | Newark |
| JRP Historical Consulting LLC (HQ) | Provider of resources management services. The company's services include water use studies, flood control, public access history, and legislative history research. | 530-757-2521 | 1-10 | Davis |

| COMPANY NAME | PRODUCT / SERVICE | PHONE | EMP | CITY |
|---|---|---|---|---|
| Kaz & Associates Environmental Services (HQ) | Provider of water management consulting services. The company's services include enforcement response, and groundwater contamination investigation. | 707-747-1126 | NA | Benicia |
| Lacroix Davis Llc (BR) | Provider of building and environmental forensics and consulting services. The company provides support for investigation, litigation, and education. | 925-299-1140 | NA | Lafayette |
| Larry Walker Associates (HQ) | Provider of environmental engineering and consulting services. The company provides water quality solutions. | 530-753-6400 | 11-50 | Davis |
| Live Oak Associates Inc (HQ) | Provider of ecological and biological consulting services. The company is also focused on environmental permitting and planning activities. | 408-224-8300 | NA | San Jose |
| Locus Technologies (HQ) | Provider of web based environmental information management systems. The company's services include field installation, training, and technical support. | 650-960-1640 | NA | Mountain View |
| Lsa Associates Inc (BR) | Provider of consulting services. The company focuses on environmental, transportation, and planning services. | 510-540-7331 | NA | Berkeley |
| Luhdorff & Scalmanini Consulting Engineers (HQ) | Provider of consulting and engineering services that include investigation, use, protection, development, and management of groundwater resources. | 530-661-0109 | 1-10 | Woodland |
| Mako Industries (HQ) | Manufacturer of remediation systems for the environmental industry. The company is focused on field and carbon change out services. | 925-209-7985 | NA | Livermore |
| Matriscope (BR) | Provider of geotechnical and environmental engineering services. The company also provides materials testing and special inspection services. | 916-375-6700 | 11-50 | Sacramento |
| Millennium Consulting Associates (HQ) | Provider of environmental and industrial hygiene services. The company offers environmental engineering, consulting, and compliance services. | 925-808-6700 | NA | Oakland |
| Monk & Associates Inc (HQ) | Provider of environmental consulting services. The company specializes in biological constraints analyses and mitigation plans. | 925-947-4867 | NA | Walnut Creek |
| Moore Twining Associates Inc (HQ) | Provider of geotechnical engineering, environmental, construction inspection, materials testing, analytical chemistry, and drilling services. | 559-268-7021 | 11-50 | Fresno |
| National Analytical Laboratories Inc (HQ) | Provider of environmental lab testing and consulting services. The company focuses on air monitoring, building inspection, and operations training. | 916-361-0555 | 1-10 | Rancho Cordova |
| National Center For Appropriate Technology (BR) | Provider of information and access services. The company's offerings include weatherizing houses, monitoring energy applications, and testing products. | 530-792-7338 | 11-50 | Davis |
| Northgate Environmental Management Inc (HQ) | Provider of interdisciplinary technical solutions. The company focuses on results-oriented scientific and engineering investigation and analysis. | 510-839-0688 | NA | Oakland |
| Northstar Engineering (HQ) | Provider of land development services, municipal infrastructure design, onsite waste water systems, and environmental consulting services. | 530-893-1600 | 11-50 | Chico |
| NRC Environmental Services Inc (BR) | Provider of environmental, industrial, and emergency solutions. The company offers oil spill response, industrial cleaning, sediment remediation, and other services. | 510-749-1390 | NA | Alameda |
| Nute Engineering (HQ) | Developer of technologies for the water, wastewater treatment, and environmental protection projects. | 415-453-4480 | NA | San Rafael |
| Pangea Environmental Services Inc (HQ) | Provider of environmental consulting services. The company's services include site assessment and remediation, litigation support, and soil testing. | 510-836-3700 | NA | Berkeley |
| Panorama Environmental Inc (HQ) | Provider of environmental planning services. The company engages in regulatory permitting and geographic information systems. | 650-373-1200 | NA | San Francisco |
| Pyxis Laboratories Inc (HQ) | Specializes in the research, development and production of specialty reagents for the diagnostics, pharmaceutical, and environmental industries. | 949-598-1978 | 1-10 | Grass Valley |
| Quanta Laboratories (HQ) | Provider of environmental testing and consulting services. The company offers vibration test, shock test, and chambers test services. | 408-988-0770 | NA | Santa Clara |
| Recology Of The Coast (HQ) | Provider of resource recovery services. The company's services include urban cleaning services, collection, sorting, transfer, recovery and landfill management. | 650-355-9000 | NA | Pacifica |
| Ridge to River (HQ) | Provider of hydrologic analysis and modeling services. The company is also focused on ecological restoration, erosion control, and water quality analysis. | 707-357-0857 | 1-10 | Fort Bragg |
| Rincon Consultants Inc (BR) | Provider of environmental consulting services. The company specializes in land use planning, site assessment, remediation, and other services. | 510-834-4455 | NA | Oakland |
| Safebridge Consultants Inc (HQ) | Provider of consulting services and analytical support. The company provides safety, health and environmental services. | 650-961-4820 | NA | Mountain View |
| SCA Environmental Inc (HQ) | Provider of environmental science, occupational health and safety, engineering, and laboratory analyses services. | 415-882-1675 | NA | San Francisco |
| SOMA Environmental Engineering Inc (HQ) | Provider of environmental engineering solutions. The company offers services for remediation and underground storage tanks. | 925-734-6400 | NA | Pleasanton |
| Southwest Hazard Control Inc (BR) | Provider of environmental remediation services. The company's offerings include asbestos abatement and hazardous materials management services. | 510-352-5152 | NA | San Leandro |
| SS Papadopulos & Associates Inc (BR) | Provider of web-based applications for customized online communities. The company serves business enterprises. | 415-773-0400 | NA | San Francisco |

| Stantec Inc (BR) | Provider of civil construction services. The company also offers commercial program development and infrastructure management services. | 916-773-8100 | 11-50 | Rocklin |
| Sustainable Conservation (HQ) | Provider of environmental protection services and solutions. The company focuses on clean-air farming and auto recycling projects. | 415-977-0380 | NA | San Francisco |
| Swca Environmental Consultants (DH) | Provider of environmental consultant services. The company focuses on environmental planning and regulatory compliance activities. | 650-440-4160 | NA | Half Moon Bay |
| Tenera Environmental (HQ) | Provider of environmental consulting, stream restoration, power generation support, and minerals management services. | 925-962-9769 | NA | Lafayette |
| Terradex Inc (HQ) | Provider of web and consulting services. The company offers dig clean, cleanupdeck, and web development services. | 650-227-3250 | NA | Palo Alto |
| Testamerica Laboratories Inc (BR) | Provider of environmental testing services. The company offers indoor air quality, air testing and emissions, and industrial hygiene services. | 916-373-5600 | 11-50 | West Sacramento |
| Tmt Enterprises Inc (HQ) | Provider of baseball and softball playing surfaces and supplier of agricultural mixes, construction materials, organics, and aggregates. | 408-432-9040 | NA | San Jose |
| Trc Companies Inc (BR) | Provider of scientific and engineering software services. The company offers hydropower licensing, power delivery, and telecommunications engineering services. | 415-434-2600 | NA | San Francisco |
| Tric Tools Inc (HQ) | Provider of pipe-bursting systems. The company also offers installation, maintenance, and cleaning services for home-sewer systems. | 510-865-8742 | NA | Alameda |
| Trinity Consultants Inc (BR) | Provider of environmental consulting services. The company engages in environmental outsourcing and litigation support services. | 510-285-6351 | NA | Oakland |
| Tss Consultants (HQ) | Provider of energy resources management, environmental permitting, and financial assessment services. | 916-600-4174 | 1-10 | Sacramento |
| Us Hydrotech Environmental Solutions (HQ) | Provider of hydro tech environmental solutions. The company offers wash pads, containments, pressure washers, and solar thermal products. | 707-793-4800 | NA | Santa Rosa |
| Veolia (BR) | Provider of complete environmental solutions. The company focuses on energy, water treatment, and waste management. | 916-379-0872 | 11-50 | Sacramento |
| Veridian Environmental Inc (HQ) | Provider of environmental analysis and management consulting services. The company offers services to the industrial sector. | 707-449-4400 | NA | Vacaville |
| Weatherflow Inc (HQ) | Provider of modeling and forecasting technologies for the weather forecast industry. The company also offers wind-based and coastal forecasting. | 800-946-3225 | 1-10 | Scotts Valley |
| Weber Hayes & Assoc (HQ) | Provider of hydrogeologic and environmental engineering consulting services. The company offers cleanup of soil, groundwater, and stormwater services. | 831-722-3580 | 1-10 | Watsonville |
| West Yost Associates (HQ) | Provider of water, storm water, wastewater, and construction management project services. The company also offers recycling services. | 530-756-5905 | 11-50 | Davis |
| Westervelt Ecological Services (HQ) | Provider of ecological solutions. The company offers wetland mitigation and conservation banking, geographic information system analysis, and other services. | 916-646-3644 | 11-50 | Sacramento |
| WRA Inc (HQ) | Provider of environmental consulting, validation, mitigation and restoration, consultation, and wetland delineation services. | 415-454-8868 | NA | San Rafael |
| Zander Associates (HQ) | Provider of environmental consulting and assessment services. The company service areas include habitat conservation planning and wetland delineation. | 415-897-8781 | NA | San Rafael |
| Zentner & Zentner (HQ) | Provider of environmental planning and restoration services. The company is also involved in permitting services. | 510-622-8110 | NA | Oakland |

## 143 = Waste Disposal Equipment

| COMPANY NAME | PRODUCT / SERVICE | PHONE | EMP | CITY |
|---|---|---|---|---|
| Chemical Safety Technology Inc (HQ) | Supplier of chemical processing machines. The company also offers design, manufacturing, and sheet metal fabrication services. | 408-263-0984 | NA | San Jose |
| Control Systems West Inc (HQ) | Designer and fabricator of a broad variety of custom electrical controls for industrial applications. | 707-763-1108 | NA | Petaluma |
| Cp Lab Safety (HQ) | Manufacturer of laboratory safety equipment to prevent fire, reduce waste emission and exposure to toxic fumes. | 415-883-2600 | NA | Novato |
| E2c Remediation (HQ) | Provider of environmental remediation services. The company services also include soil and groundwater remediation and civil and geological engineering. | 916-782-8700 | 1-10 | Roseville |
| Filtration Solutions Inc (HQ) | Provider of water treatment systems. The company focuses on engineering, manufacturing, installation, and more. | 530-534-1000 | 1-10 | Oroville |
| Forsgren Associate Inc (DH) | Provider of civil and environmental engineering consulting services. The company specializes in planning, design, survey, and construction management. | 916-638-1119 | 11-50 | Rancho Cordova |
| Grayland Environmental (HQ) | Provider of environmental and natural resources protections services. The company offers environmental engineering, geological and geophysical services. | 530-756-1441 | 1-10 | Davis |
| Neil O Anderson & Associates Inc (HQ) | Provider of engineering services including geotechnical engineering, foundation, and structural engineering services. | 209-367-3701 | 11-50 | Lodi |

| COMPANY NAME | PRODUCT / SERVICE | PHONE | EMP | CITY |
|---|---|---|---|---|
| Tesco Controls Inc (HQ) | Manufacturer of instrumentation, control systems, and service pedestals for water and traffic sectors. The company offers system integration services. | 916-395-8800 | 11-50 | Sacramento |
| W2 Systems (HQ) | Provider of customized water treatment support and solutions. The company also offers services like design, technical support, and control services. | 415-468-9858 | NA | Brisbane |

## 144 = Water/Air Treatment Equipment

| COMPANY NAME | PRODUCT / SERVICE | PHONE | EMP | CITY |
|---|---|---|---|---|
| A TEEM Electrical Engineering (HQ) | Provider of outreach safety training, electrical design and construction management, and control system programming services. | 916-457-8144 | 1-10 | Sacramento |
| Control Systems West Inc (HQ) | Designer and fabricator of a broad variety of custom electrical controls for industrial applications. | 707-763-1108 | NA | Petaluma |
| E2c Remediation (HQ) | Provider of environmental remediation services. The company services also include soil and groundwater remediation and civil and geological engineering. | 916-782-8700 | 1-10 | Roseville |
| Filtration Solutions Inc (HQ) | Provider of water treatment systems. The company focuses on engineering, manufacturing, installation, and more. | 530-534-1000 | 1-10 | Oroville |
| Forsgren Associate Inc (DH) | Provider of civil and environmental engineering consulting services. The company specializes in planning, design, survey, and construction management. | 916-638-1119 | 11-50 | Rancho Cordova |
| Freshwater Environmental Svc (HQ) | Provider of environmental services. The company's services include soil investigation workplans, soil sampling reporting, sediment sampling, and monitoring. | 707-839-0091 | 1-10 | Arcata |
| Frey Environmental Inc (BR) | Provider of geological and engineering consulting services. The company offers stormwater management, methane assessments/mitigation, and asbestos-related services. | 831-464-1634 | 11-50 | Santa Cruz |
| Heron Innovators (HQ) | Provider of suspended air flotation systems. The company offers products for processing tomato, food, meat, and others. | 916-408-6601 | 1-10 | Rocklin |
| Horizon Water & Environment (BR) | Provider of environmental consulting services. The company specializes in watershed science, environmental compliance, and water resources management. | 510-986-1850 | NA | Oakland |
| Hydropoint Data Systems Inc (HQ) | Provider of irrigation solutions. The company specializes in site evaluations, upgrade planning, deployment, and optimization services. | 800-362-8774 | NA | Petaluma |
| Loprest Water Treatment Co (HQ) | Provider of water treatment systems design and fabricating services. The company focuses on media analysis and filter inspection. | 510-799-3101 | NA | Rodeo |
| Maggiora Bros Drilling Inc (HQ) | Provider of water well drilling and pump installation services. The company specializes in hydrologic cycle such as evaporation and condensation. | 831-724-1338 | 11-50 | Watsonville |
| Nds Inc (HQ) | Provider of storm water management, efficient irrigation, and flow management solutions for residential and commercial applications. | 888-825-4716 | 11-50 | Lindsay |
| Ondavia Inc (HQ) | Provider of water analysis solutions. The company offers OndaVia analysis system that enables laboratory-grade water testing. | 510-576-0476 | NA | Hayward |
| Ozotech Inc (HQ) | Provider of water purification solutions. The company offers products such as bolted water systems, oxygen concentrators, air dries, and generators. | 530-842-4189 | 1-10 | Yreka |
| Pionetics Corporation (HQ) | Provider of water treatment products. The company's products include LNX 160 water filters, bottless water coolers, and water treatment systems. | 866-611-8624 | NA | San Carlos |
| Process Solutions Inc (HQ) | Provider of disinfection solutions. The company is engaged in facility management services and serves the commercial sector. | 408-370-6540 | NA | Campbell |
| Puronics Inc (HQ) | Manufacturer of water treatment equipment. The company's products include drinking water systems, water softeners, and reverse osmosis systems. | 925-456-7000 | NA | Livermore |
| Synder Filtration (HQ) | Manufacturer of membranes and systems. The company offers training and performance evaluation services. It serves mining, biotech, and food industries. | 707-451-6060 | NA | Vacaville |
| Tesco Controls Inc (HQ) | Manufacturer of instrumentation, control systems, and service pedestals for water and traffic sectors. The company offers system integration services. | 916-395-8800 | 11-50 | Sacramento |
| Triple O Systems Inc (HQ) | Designer and manufacturer of water treatment systems. The company also offers reverse osmosis product water tanks and water store water tanks. | 408-378-3002 | NA | Campbell |
| Veolia Water (BR) | Provider of water and wastewater treatment solutions. The company offers services for public authorities and industrial companies. | 510-412-2001 | NA | Richmond |
| W2 Systems (HQ) | Provider of customized water treatment support and solutions. The company also offers services like design, technical support, and control services. | 415-468-9858 | NA | Brisbane |
| Waterman Industries (HQ) | Designer and manufacturer of water-control sluice gates, penstocks, valves, and water control products. | 559-562-4000 | 11-50 | Exeter |

## 146 = Actuators

| COMPANY NAME | PRODUCT / SERVICE | PHONE | EMP | CITY |
|---|---|---|---|---|
| Meggitt Sensing Systems (RH) | Provider of solutions for measurement applications. The company offers piezoelectric and piezoresistive type transducers. | 949-493-8181 | NA | Sunnyvale |

| COMPANY NAME | PRODUCT / SERVICE | PHONE | EMP | CITY |
|---|---|---|---|---|
| Moog Animatics (BR) | Provider of motion control devices. The company offers actuators, cables, power supplies, and peripherals. | 650-960-4215 | NA | Mountain View |
| Moog Csa Engineering (HQ) | Designer and manufacturer of high precision systems. The company offers positioning systems, actuators, absorbers, and test systems. | 650-210-9000 | NA | Mountain View |
| Nb Corporation Of America (BR) | Manufacturer of linear motion bearings, slides, ball splines, and related products. The company's products include slide guides, spindle shafts, and actuators. | 510-490-1420 | NA | Fremont |
| Oriental Motor USA Corp (DH) | Provider of optimal motion systems. The company focuses on producing fractional horsepower products for motion control applications. | 408-392-9735 | 11-50 | Torrance |
| Precision Contacts Inc (HQ) | Provider of replacement contacts for handler manufacturer. The company's products include sockets, contacts, elements, and custom products. | 916-939-4147 | 1-10 | El Dorado Hills |
| SMC Corporation of America (BR) | Provider of in pneumatic technology solutions that are used in diverse range of industries from automotive to lifescience. | 408-943-9600 | NA | San Jose |

## 147 = Air Purification Equipment

| COMPANY NAME | PRODUCT / SERVICE | PHONE | EMP | CITY |
|---|---|---|---|---|
| Asi Controls (HQ) | Manufacturer of direct digital controls for HVAC and light industrial marketplace. The company also offers networking products and unitary controls. | 925-866-8808 | NA | San Ramon |
| Donald P. Dick Air Conditioning (HQ) | Provider of air conditioning services. The company's offerings include sheet metal fabrication, ductless heating, energy recovery ventilators, and solar water heaters. | 559-255-1644 | 11-50 | Fresno |
| Fresno Valves & Castings Inc (HQ) | Provider of water control devices used in irrigation applications. The company's products include valves, filters, air vents, fittings, gates, and lifts. | 559-834-2511 | 11-50 | Selma |
| SMC Corporation of America (BR) | Provider of in pneumatic technology solutions that are used in diverse range of industries from automotive to lifescience. | 408-943-9600 | NA | San Jose |

## 148 = Compressors

| COMPANY NAME | PRODUCT / SERVICE | PHONE | EMP | CITY |
|---|---|---|---|---|
| Brooks Automation Inc (BR) | Provider of automation, vacuum, and instrumentation solutions for the semiconductor manufacturing, life sciences, and clean energy industries. | 510-661-5000 | NA | Fremont |
| Cti Controltech (HQ) | Provider of industrial process control and emission solutions. The company's services include engineering, sales, and support. | 925-208-4250 | NA | San Ramon |
| Dripless Inc (HQ) | Manufacturer of utility spatulas, caulking guns, holsters, and related accessories. The company serves the painting industry. | 707-568-5081 | NA | Santa Rosa |
| Motor Guard Corp (HQ) | Designer and developer of spray equipment and tools for collision repairs. The company offers services to the automotive sector. | 209-239-9191 | 1-10 | Manteca |
| Precision Contacts Inc (HQ) | Provider of replacement contacts for handler manufacturer. The company's products include sockets, contacts, elements, and custom products. | 916-939-4147 | 1-10 | El Dorado Hills |
| Rix Industries (HQ) | Manufacturer of air and gas compressors. The company's products include industrial and commercial compressors, nitrogen generators, and AMS parts. | 707-747-5900 | NA | Benicia |
| Universal Audio Inc (HQ) | Manufacturer of analog recording equipment. The company's products include audio interfaces, channel strips, plug-ins, and compressors. | 831-440-1176 | 1-10 | Scotts Valley |
| WAGAN Corp (HQ) | Developer and marketer of automotive accessories to mobile professionals. The company's offerings include warmers, defrosters, and heated cushions. | 510-471-9221 | NA | Hayward |

## 149 = Cryogenic Tanks & Equipment

| COMPANY NAME | PRODUCT / SERVICE | PHONE | EMP | CITY |
|---|---|---|---|---|
| E-N-G Mobile Systems Inc (HQ) | Manufacturer of specialty vehicles. The company focuses on TV vans and trucks, emergency respone trailers, mobile labs, and other vehicles. | 925-798-4060 | NA | Concord |
| Morley Manufacturing Inc (HQ) | Designer and manufacturer of drainback water storage tanks for residential and commercial purposes. The company offers installation services. | 530-477-6527 | 1-10 | Grass Valley |

## 150 = Engines/Motors

| COMPANY NAME | PRODUCT / SERVICE | PHONE | EMP | CITY |
|---|---|---|---|---|
| Aero Turbine Inc (HQ) | Provider of overhaul, repair, and testing services for turbine engines and accessories. The company also sells engine components and accessories. | 209-983-1112 | 1-10 | Stockton |
| Akmi Corp (HQ) | Distributor of aftermarket diesel engine parts. The company provides accessory drive units, camshafts, flywheels, and exhaust manifolds. | 510-670-9550 | NA | Hayward |
| Akribis Systems Inc USA (RH) | Designer and manufacturer of motors, stages, and precision systems. The company's products are used in inspection and testing applications. | 408-913-1300 | NA | San Jose |
| Arcus Technology Inc (HQ) | Provider of motor controllers, stepper motors, and related accessories such as cables, encoders, and gearboxes. | 925-373-8800 | NA | Livermore |
| Comptech Usa (HQ) | Manufacturer and fabricator of race engines. The company also offers R&D and road racing track maintenance services. | 916-338-3434 | 1-10 | Sacramento |
| Efficient Drivetrains Inc (HQ) | Provider of vehicle developer equipment. The company also offers PHEV and CVT solutions, and hybrid vehicles. | 408-624-1231 | NA | Milpitas |
| Honda Research Institute Usa Inc (HQ) | Manufacturer of engines. The company focuses on material science research, computer science research, and academic outreach activities. | 650-314-0400 | NA | Mountain View |
| Industrial Electrical Co (HQ) | Provider of electrical, manufacturing, and automation services for the commercial and industrial sectors. | 209-527-2800 | 11-50 | Modesto |

| COMPANY NAME | PRODUCT / SERVICE | PHONE | EMP | CITY |
|---|---|---|---|---|
| Interphase Systems (HQ) | Manufacturer of test equipment for the disc drive industry. The company offers consulting and build-to-print services. | 408-315-8603 | NA | Santa Clara |
| Lin Engineering (HQ) | Manufacturer of step motors. The company's products include BLDC motors, optical encoders, gearheads, and accessories. | 408-919-0200 | NA | Morgan Hill |
| Motion Control Engineering Inc (HQ) | Manufacturer of elevator control products. The company's products include elevator and escalator controls, complete elevators, and components and peripherals. | 916-463-9200 | 11-50 | Rancho Cordova |
| Motor Guard Corp (HQ) | Designer and developer of spray equipment and tools for collision repairs. The company offers services to the automotive sector. | 209-239-9191 | 1-10 | Manteca |
| Nyden Corp (HQ) | Supplier of stepper motors. The company deals with the design of semiconductor equipment, laser systems, and aerospace-related apparatus. | 510-894-3633 | NA | San Jose |
| Oriental Motor USA Corp (DH) | Provider of optimal motion systems. The company focuses on producing fractional horsepower products for motion control applications. | 408-392-9735 | 11-50 | Torrance |
| Source Engineering Inc (HQ) | Manufacturer of motors, cables, harnesses, and motion control products. The company also provides custom modification services on motors. | 408-980-9822 | NA | Santa Clara |

## 151 = Furnaces, Heating Equipment

| COMPANY NAME | PRODUCT / SERVICE | PHONE | EMP | CITY |
|---|---|---|---|---|
| Branesky Sheet Metal Inc (HQ) | Provider of hydronic and forced air systems. The company also offers heating systems, stoves, and sheet metals. | 707-964-0691 | 1-10 | Fort Bragg |
| Clayborn Lab (HQ) | Developer of heat tapes, hot tubes, and custom tape heaters. The company serves the medical, transportation, and pharmaceutical sectors. | 530-587-4700 | 1-10 | Truckee |
| Enphase Energy Inc (HQ) | Distributor of electronic products. The company offers services to the solar, telecom, networking, and software industries. | 877-797-4743 | NA | Petaluma |
| Envirocare International (HQ) | Designer of pollution control appliances. The company also specializes in manufacturing gas cooling and gas conditioning systems. | 707-638-6800 | NA | American Canyon |
| Ferreira Service Inc (HQ) | Provider of energy engineering services. The company offers heating, ventilation, and air conditioning maintenance and repair services. | 800-522-6064 | NA | San Ramon |
| Heliodyne Inc (HQ) | Manufacturer of solar water heating systems for the residential and commercial sectors. The company focuses on installation, repair, and replacement. | 510-237-9614 | NA | Richmond |
| NTFB Combustion Equipment USA Inc (HQ) | Manufacturer of combustion equipment. The company offers mid to large size, single & multiple burner, water tube boiler, and furnace applications. | 510-443-0066 | NA | Foster City |
| Packaging Aids Corp (HQ) | Manufacturer of heat sealing and packaging equipment such as tube sealers, shrink wrap systems, and skin packaging products. | 415-454-4868 | NA | San Rafael |
| Rayteq Llc (HQ) | Manufacturer of energy-saving electric melting furnaces for the metal casting industry and offers electric heating systems and metal level sensors. | 510-638-2000 | NA | Healdsburg |
| Retech Systems Llc (HQ) | Designer and manufacturer of consumable electrode and furnaces, powder production, and other thermal processing equipment. | 707-462-6522 | 1-10 | Ukiah |
| S T Johnson Co (HQ) | Manufacturer of burners. The company specializes in the design and fabrication of gas and nitrous oxide burners for industries. | 510-652-6000 | NA | Fairfield |
| Safeco Electric Supply Inc (HQ) | Distributor of electrical and lighting products. The company offers wires, cables, cords, fasteners, switch boxes, and accessories. | 415-206-0368 | NA | San Francisco |

## 152 = Generators

| COMPANY NAME | PRODUCT / SERVICE | PHONE | EMP | CITY |
|---|---|---|---|---|
| Accsys Technology Inc (HQ) | Manufacturer of ion linear accelerator systems used in medical imaging devices, industrial applications and in research. | 925-462-6949 | NA | Pleasanton |
| Adelphi Technology Inc (HQ) | Developer and manufacturer of X-ray optics. The company serves the medical, industrial, and scientific sectors. | 650-474-2750 | NA | Redwood City |
| Clean Energy Systems Inc (HQ) | Developer and manufacturer of steam and drive gas generator units. The company is engaged in design, delivery, and installation services. | 916-638-7967 | 1-10 | Rancho Cordova |
| Glasspoint Solar Inc (HQ) | Manufacturer of solar steam generators for the oil and gas industry. The company is engaged in design and installation services. | 415-778-2800 | NA | Fremont |
| Goodman Ball Inc (HQ) | Manufacturer of spare military equipment for the U.S. Government. The company's in-house capabilities include CNC machining and structural welding. | 650-363-0113 | NA | Menlo Park |
| Industrial Electrical Co (HQ) | Provider of electrical, manufacturing, and automation services for the commercial and industrial sectors. | 209-527-2800 | 11-50 | Modesto |
| Longevity Global Inc (HQ) | Manufacturer of welding equipment. The company also offers filler rods, generators, plasma cutters, and related accessories. | 510-887-7090 | NA | Hayward |
| National Vapor Industries Inc (HQ) | Manufacturer of hydrogen generators. The company also offers marketing, installation, and other services. | 925-980-7341 | NA | Livermore |
| Pacific Ozone Technology Inc (HQ) | Supplier of air-cooled, integrated ozone and oxygen systems and packaged controls for industrial ozone applications. | 707-747-9600 | NA | Benicia |
| Telemakus Llc (HQ) | Provider of USB controlled RF devices. The company devices include switches, vector modulators, and digital attenuators. | 916-458-6346 | 1-10 | Folsom |

## 153 = Heat Exchangers/Pressure Vessels

| COMPANY NAME | PRODUCT / SERVICE | PHONE | EMP | CITY |
|---|---|---|---|---|
| Ashlock Co (HQ) | Provider of pitting equipment. The company offers equipment such as cherry pitting, date pitting, and olive pitting machines. | 510-351-0560 | NA | San Leandro |

| COMPANY NAME | PRODUCT / SERVICE | PHONE | EMP | CITY |
|---|---|---|---|---|
| ASM America Inc (BR) | Provider of technology and consulting services to semiconductor manufacturers. The company's products include EPSILON 3200, ADVANCE A400, and EMERALD XP. | 408-451-0830 | NA | San Jose |
| Benchmark Thermal Corp (HQ) | Manufacturer of custom semiconductor products, drum and cartridge heaters, controls, and related accessories. | 530-477-5011 | 1-10 | Grass Valley |
| Eco-Snow Systems (HQ) | Provider of CO2 precision surface process equipment for cleaning applications. The company's products include VersaClean 1200 and MaskClean 150 systems. | 925-606-2000 | NA | Livermore |
| Environmental Stress Systems Inc (HQ) | Manufacturer of mechanically refrigerated, cryogenically cooled, and liquid cooled thermal platforms. | 209-588-1993 | 1-10 | Sonora |
| Johansing Iron Works (HQ) | Manufacturer of heat exchangers and metal tanks. The company also offers process equipment and pressure vessels. | 707-361-8190 | NA | Benicia |
| Ksm Corp (DH) | Manufacturer of welded metal bellows for transportation, solar, pharmaceutical, and other sectors and provides build to print assembly services. | 408-514-2400 | NA | San Jose |
| Lloyd W Aubry Company Inc (HQ) | Provider of mechanical contracting services specializing in fabrication, installation, relocation, and maintenance of processing plant equipment. | 510-732-9038 | NA | Hayward |
| Mechanical Air Service Inc (HQ) | Provider of air conditioning and heating services to residential and commercial sectors. The company also offers indoor air quality and green energy services. | 408-432-8282 | NA | San Jose |
| Melrose Metal Products Inc (HQ) | Manufacturer of melrose metal products. The company offers design and installation services for food processing and emission control systems. | 510-657-8771 | NA | Fremont |
| Morrill Industries Inc (HQ) | Manufacturer and supplier of irrigation equipment. The company also offers custom built rotating suction screens and industrial pipes. | 209-838-2550 | 1-10 | Escalon |
| Quality Stainless Tanks (HQ) | Provider of ready-made tanks. The company offers crafted tanks, stainless winery equipment, and special application tanks. | 877-598-0672 | NA | Windsor |
| Rorze Automation Inc (DH) | Manufacturer of automation products. The company's applications include displays, semiconductors, and laboratories. | 510-687-1340 | NA | Fremont |
| Terminal Manufacturing Company Llc (HQ) | Designer and manufacturer of vacuum chambers, pressure vessels, truck tanks, and assorted fabrications. | 510-526-3071 | NA | Berkeley |
| Thermal Press International Inc (HQ) | Manufacturer of thermal presses and heat staking machines. The company also offers heat sealing and degating machinery. | 925-454-9800 | NA | Livermore |
| Uniform Industrial Corp (DH) | Provider of systems and components for banking and retail solutions. The company also offers technology solutions and customer services. | 510-438-6799 | NA | Fremont |
| Wcr Inc (BR) | Developer and manufacturer of heat exchangers. The company's products include plate heat exchangers, brazed heat exchangers, and welded heat exchangers. | 559-266-8374 | 11-50 | Fresno |
| Wiegmann & Rose (HQ) | Provider of custom heat exchangers, pressure vessels, and weldments. The company offers vacuum chambers and pipe spool products. | 510-632-8828 | NA | Livermore |

## 154 = HVAC Equipment

| COMPANY NAME | PRODUCT / SERVICE | PHONE | EMP | CITY |
|---|---|---|---|---|
| Acadia Technology Inc (HQ) | Dealer of power supplies, water cooling kits, cases, fans and fan ducts, and digital temperature displayers. | 408-737-9528 | NA | Sunnyvale |
| Acosta Sheet Metal Manufacturing Inc (HQ) | Manufacturer of HVAC and architectural products, and sheet metal building materials. The company provides gutter profile caps and conductor heads. | 408-275-6370 | NA | San Jose |
| Acutherm (HQ) | Manufacturer of components for heating and air conditioning systems. The company offers therma-fuser variable air volume diffusers. | 510-785-0510 | NA | Hayward |
| Alzeta Corp (HQ) | Provider of clean air solutions and related research and development services. The company offers services to the industrial and commercial sectors. | 408-727-8282 | NA | Santa Clara |
| Asi Controls (HQ) | Manufacturer of direct digital controls for HVAC and light industrial marketplace. The company also offers networking products and unitary controls. | 925-866-8808 | NA | San Ramon |
| Baltimore Air Coil (BR) | Provider of assembled evaporative heat rejection and thermal storage equipment. The company also offers circuit cooling towers. | 559-673-9231 | 11-50 | Madera |
| Branesky Sheet Metal Inc (HQ) | Provider of hydronic and forced air systems. The company also offers heating systems, stoves, and sheet metals. | 707-964-0691 | 1-10 | Fort Bragg |
| Celsia Inc (HQ) | Designer and manufacturer of heat sinks. The company provides thermal solutions using vapor chamber, heat pipe, and hybrid designs. | 650-667-1920 | NA | Santa Clara |
| Environmental Stress Systems Inc (HQ) | Manufacturer of mechanically refrigerated, cryogenically cooled, and liquid cooled thermal platforms. | 209-588-1993 | 1-10 | Sonora |
| Meline Engineering Corp (HQ) | Provider of energy efficient mechanical system design services. The company also offers mechanical engineering services. | 916-366-3458 | 1-10 | Sacramento |
| Melrose Metal Products Inc (HQ) | Manufacturer of melrose metal products. The company offers design and installation services for food processing and emission control systems. | 510-657-8771 | NA | Fremont |
| Mmr Technologies Inc (HQ) | Provider of micro-miniature refrigerator technology. The company offers hall measurement, optical study systems, and temperature control services. | 650-962-9620 | NA | San Jose |
| NBA Engineering Inc (HQ) | Provider of mechanical and electrical engineering design, energy conversion, and construction management services. | 415-202-9840 | NA | San Francisco |

| COMPANY NAME | PRODUCT / SERVICE | PHONE | EMP | CITY |
|---|---|---|---|---|
| R&R Refrigeration And Air Conditioning Inc (HQ) | Provider of environmental technological solutions. The company also offers maintenance and repair services for process systems. | 408-297-0383 | NA | San Jose |
| Rudy's Commercial Refrigeration (HQ) | Provider of refrigeration products such as coolers and freezers, compressors, glass doors and strip curtains, and temperature alarms. | 510-376-9163 | NA | San Pablo |
| Trane (BR) | Provider of heating, ventilation & air conditioning (HVAC) systems, dehumidifying, and air cleaning products. | 888-862-1619 | NA | Sunnyvale |

## 155 = Hydraulic/Pneumatic Equipment

| COMPANY NAME | PRODUCT / SERVICE | PHONE | EMP | CITY |
|---|---|---|---|---|
| ABT-TRAC (HQ) | Provider of yacht & boat stabilizers and bow & stern thrusters. The company also offers integrated hydraulic products. | 707-586-3155 | NA | Rohnert Park |
| Cadence Design Systems Inc (HQ) | Provider of semiconductor IP and electronic design automation services. The company offers tools for logic & RF design, IC packaging, and other needs. | 408-943-1234 | NA | San Jose |
| Ferreira Service Inc (HQ) | Provider of energy engineering services. The company offers heating, ventilation, and air conditioning maintenance and repair services. | 800-522-6064 | NA | San Ramon |
| Hydraulic Controls Inc (HQ) | Distributor of fluid power systems. The company specializes in hydraulics, pneumatics, automation, and extrusion. | 510-658-8300 | NA | Emeryville |
| Inventive Resources Inc (HQ) | Manufacturer of products for the environmental and contamination control industry. The company also focuses on distribution. | 209-545-1663 | 1-10 | Salida |
| Meggitt Sensing Systems (RH) | Provider of solutions for measurement applications. The company offers piezoelectric and piezoresistive type transducers. | 949-493-8181 | NA | Sunnyvale |
| Power Industries (HQ) | Supplier of ready-made solutions for industrial applications. The company's products include bearings and seals, hydraulics, and pneumatics. | 707-545-7904 | NA | Santa Rosa |
| V&O Machine Inc (HQ) | Manufacturer of machined parts for agri, hydraulics, food procesing, and veterinary applications. The company focuses on prototyping and CNC milling. | 530-662-0495 | 1-10 | Woodland |

## 156 = Industrial Filters/Centrifuges

| COMPANY NAME | PRODUCT / SERVICE | PHONE | EMP | CITY |
|---|---|---|---|---|
| Bazell Technologies Corp (HQ) | Manufacturer of solid wall basket centrifuges. The company also focuses on centrifugal fluid processing systems. | 925-603-0900 | NA | Concord |
| Filtration Group LLC (BR) | Provider of filtration solutions. The company supplies filtration products for the HVAC, turbine, cleanroom, and filter media markets. | 707-525-8633 | NA | Santa Rosa |
| Inventive Resources Inc (HQ) | Manufacturer of products for the environmental and contamination control industry. The company also focuses on distribution. | 209-545-1663 | 1-10 | Salida |
| LAKOS Filtration Solutions (HQ) | Manufacturer of centrifugal separators and other filtration solutions to remove sand and other solids from water and liquids. | 559-255-1601 | 1-10 | Fresno |
| Parker Hannifin Corp (DH) | Provider of fuel, air, oil, and coolant filtration systems. The company serves the transportation, marine, and oil and gas industries. | 209-521-7860 | 1-10 | Modesto |
| Standard Metal Products (HQ) | Provider of prototype and production components and assemblies for transportation, bicycle builders, and medical device companies. | 415-546-6784 | NA | San Francisco |
| Tomopal Inc (HQ) | Manufacturer and distributor of glass syringes, scales & balances, gas filters, and other products for the laboratory and industrial markets. | 916-429-7240 | 1-10 | Sacramento |
| Tooltek Engineering Corp (HQ) | Designer and fabricator of custom automated equipment. The company is also engaged in material handling and robotics solutions. | 510-683-9504 | NA | Fremont |

## 157 = Machine Tools - Metal Cutting or Forming

| COMPANY NAME | PRODUCT / SERVICE | PHONE | EMP | CITY |
|---|---|---|---|---|
| Adem Llc (HQ) | Designer and manufacturer of special and automated fixtures for assembly lines, and also provides turnkey production solutions. | 408-727-8955 | NA | Santa Clara |
| Advanced Laser & Waterjet Cutting Inc (HQ) | Provider of precision cutting services for all types of materials. The company's services include electronic shielding, fabrivision, and overnight shipping. | 408-486-0700 | NA | Santa Clara |
| Altair Technologies Inc (HQ) | Provider of precision furnace brazing services. The company serves the medical, defense, and semiconductor industries. | 650-508-8700 | NA | Fremont |
| Angular Machining Inc (HQ) | Provider of product manufacturing services for aerospace, telecom, and biomedical sectors and focuses on mechanical assembly and quality control. | 408-954-8326 | NA | San Jose |
| Bat Gundrilling Services Inc (HQ) | Provider of manufacturing services. The company specializes in engineering, tap extraction, gun drill tool sharpening, and deburring services. | 408-727-1220 | NA | Santa Clara |
| Bauer Engraving Company Inc (HQ) | Provider of engraving services. The company offers foil stamping dies, embossing dies, wood branding dies, and letterpress printing plates. | 916-631-9800 | 1-10 | Rancho Cordova |
| Billington Welding & Manufacturing Inc (HQ) | Manufacturer of food process equipment and custom products. The company serves the construction, automotive, and food processing industries. | 209-526-9312 | 1-10 | Modesto |
| Broadway Sheet Metal & Mfg (HQ) | Manufacturer of sheet metals. The company's products include hoods cartridge, sinks, tables, and mixer stands. | 650-873-4585 | NA | S San Francisco |
| BT Laser & Manufacturing Inc (HQ) | Provider of custom design, laser and water jet cutting, fabrication, and welding services for solar, semiconductor, and communication sectors. | 408-566-0135 | NA | Santa Clara |
| CMI Manufacutring Inc (HQ) | Provider of prototype machining services. The company also focuses on 3D surfacing, production, and manufacturing engineering support. | 408-982-9580 | NA | San Jose |
| Connor Manufacturing Services Inc (HQ) | Provider of customized solutions for precision metal stamping, wire forms, springs, and integrated assembly needs. | 800-968-7078 | NA | San Mateo |

| COMPANY NAME | PRODUCT / SERVICE | PHONE | EMP | CITY |
|---|---|---|---|---|
| Crown Manufacturing Company Inc (HQ) | Provider of plastic and injection molded products. The company offers insert and over molding, drilling, tapping, and heat stamping services. | 510-742-8800 | NA | Newark |
| Danco Machine (HQ) | Developer of machined components and assemblies. The company is involved in EDM, welding, sheet metal, and precision grinding. | 408-988-5235 | NA | Santa Clara |
| Demtech Services Inc (HQ) | Manufacturer of welding machines. The company also specializes in the manufacture of testing instruments for geo-synthetic installers. | 530-621-3200 | 11-50 | Placerville |
| Destiny Tool (HQ) | Developer of end mills. The company offers technical support to customers in Philadelphia, Akron, Dayton, and Iowa regions. | 408-988-8898 | NA | Santa Clara |
| Donald P. Dick Air Conditioning (HQ) | Provider of air conditioning services. The company's offerings include sheet metal fabrication, ductless heating, energy recovery ventilators, and solar water heaters. | 559-255-1644 | 11-50 | Fresno |
| Emkay Manufacturing Inc (HQ) | Provider of precision milling and turning services. The company serves the medical, electrical, aerospace, and defense sectors. | 650-365-3010 | NA | Redwood City |
| Fastening Systems International Inc (HQ) | Supplier of blind fasteners and blind rivet installation tools. The company offers rivet guns, rivet nuts, pop rivets, and more. | 707-935-1170 | NA | Sonoma |
| Feeney Inc (HQ) | Provider of architectural and garden products. The company specializes in products such as rail kits, lighting, and accessories. | 510-893-9473 | NA | Oakland |
| Finishline Advanced Composites (HQ) | Provider of composite repair services for production projects. The company is involved in design, development, prototyping, testing, and production. | 707-747-0788 | NA | Benicia |
| Flashpoint Machining (HQ) | Provider of precision prototype, R&D, and detail & production machining services. The company also offers industrial machined parts. | 408-213-0071 | NA | Santa Clara |
| Foamlinx Llc (HQ) | Provider of foam cutting computer numerical control machines. The company offers cutters, shredders, compactors, and cutting services. | 408-454-6163 | NA | Sunnyvale |
| Gateway Precision Inc (HQ) | Manufacturer of precision-machined components and assemblies for image equipment manufacturers, telecom, food processing, and semiconductor sectors. | 408-855-8849 | NA | Santa Clara |
| General Grinding Inc (HQ) | Provider of precision, centerless, and surface grinding services. The company serves the medical and military industries. | 510-261-5557 | NA | Oakland |
| Grabber Construction Products Inc (BR) | Manufacturer of fasteners and machine tools. The company also specializes in distribution and other services. | 800-869-1375 | NA | Concord |
| Hilti Inc (BR) | Developer and manufacturer of construction equipment. The company's services include trainings, engineering, administration, and tools. | 800-879-8000 | NA | San Francisco |
| Hitachi Metals America Ltd (BR) | Manufacturer and marketer of metal products. The company offers cable systems, cutting tools, ceramics, sensors, and other materials. | 408-467-8900 | NA | San Jose |
| Hs&S Inc (HQ) | Designer and manufacturer of machine tool and custom machine manufacturing. The company offers services like CNC conversion and contract inspection. | 408-980-8909 | NA | Santa Clara |
| Kearney Pattern Works & Foundry (HQ) | Provider of pattern works and foundry services. The company's services include heat treating, plating, machining, and casting finish. | 408-293-7414 | NA | San Jose |
| KOR-IT Inc (HQ) | Manufacturer of diamond tools and core drill machines. The company caters to the concrete cutting industry. | 916-372-6400 | 1-10 | Sacramento |
| Lfw Manufacturing (HQ) | Manufacturer of gearboxes and gear sets. The company caters to a wide range of industrial applications. | 209-465-0444 | 1-10 | Stockton |
| Longevity Global Inc (HQ) | Manufacturer of welding equipment. The company also offers filler rods, generators, plasma cutters, and related accessories. | 510-887-7090 | NA | Hayward |
| Malaster Company Inc (HQ) | Provider of packing materials. The company specializes in offering package and shipping solutions for semiconductor industries. | 877-625-2783 | NA | Santa Clara |
| Micro-Mechanics Inc (DH) | Manufacturer of precision tools, assemblies, and consumable parts used to manufacture and test semiconductors. The company offers mold pots and trims. | 408-779-2927 | NA | Morgan Hill |
| Mitsui High-tec Inc (BR) | Provider of grinder parts, precision tools, and stamping products. The company is involved in design, installation, and delivery services. | 408-980-0782 | NA | San Jose |
| Mjb Precision Machining Inc (HQ) | Manufacturer of precision and prototype machining parts and components for the defense, telecom, medical, and semiconductor manufacturing industries. | 408-559-3035 | NA | Campbell |
| Morrill Industries Inc (HQ) | Manufacturer and supplier of irrigation equipment. The company also offers custom built rotating suction screens and industrial pipes. | 209-838-2550 | 1-10 | Escalon |
| Nichols Manufacturing Inc (HQ) | Provider of product engineering and design, prototyping, and manufacturing services. The company serves the business sector. | 408-945-0911 | NA | Milpitas |
| Omega Diamond Inc (HQ) | Developer and manufacturer of diamond tools for the ultra precise semiconductor and optics industry. The company also offers power tools. | 530-889-8977 | 1-10 | Newcastle |
| Pacific Pneumatic Tools Inc (HQ) | Manufacturer of air tools for industrial and automotive customers. The company offers wrenches, grinders, sanders, and other tools. | 650-592-6116 | NA | San Carlos |
| Precision Identity Corp (HQ) | Manufacturer of machined components for the medical device manufacturing industries. The company offers inspection, cleaning, and support services. | 408-374-2346 | NA | Campbell |
| Procurement Partners International Inc (HQ) | Provider of procurement services. The company offers mechanical components such as pins, rods, rollers, and sheet metal. | 650-345-6118 | NA | San Mateo |

| COMPANY NAME | PRODUCT / SERVICE | PHONE | EMP | CITY |
|---|---|---|---|---|
| Prodigy Surface Tech Inc (HQ) | Provider of alternative to common electroplating shop. The company focuses on chem lab for analysis, blaster, and clean room. | 408-492-9390 | NA | Santa Clara |
| Promax Tools Lp (HQ) | Manufacturer of solid carbide round tools. The company offers finishing end mills, die & mold tools, and solid carbide end mills. | 916-638-0501 | 1-10 | Rancho Cordova |
| Reliable Rubber Products (HQ) | Provider of rubber products. The company's products include dock bumpers, duty corner guards, urethane wheel cocks, and street pads. | 888-525-9750 | 1-10 | Modesto |
| Robbjack Corp (HQ) | Provider of tools for aerospace, aluminum tools, die mold and hard metal tools, custom end mills, and custom saws. | 916-645-6045 | 1-10 | Lincoln |
| Saint Clare Global A California Corporation (HQ) | Manufacturer of slicing and stacking machines. The company is engaged in design and production services. | | 1-10 | Roseville |
| Silicon Valley Precision Inc (HQ) | Provider of custom vertical and horizontal CNC machining, fabrication and assembly of parts. The company offers powder coating, painting and grinding. | 925-373-8259 | NA | Livermore |
| Sjc Precision Inc (HQ) | Provider of precision machining and tool and die making services. The company designs and manufactures jigs, fixtures, and bookmolds. | 408-262-1680 | NA | Milpitas |
| T&T Precision Inc (HQ) | Provider of precision machining services. The company specializes in electronics, automotive, and semiconductor equipment. | 510-429-8088 | NA | Union City |
| Therm-X (HQ) | Provider of engineered solutions. The company serves the semiconductor, petrochemical, life sciences, and aerospace industries. | 510 606-1012 | NA | Hayward |
| Tri Tool Inc (HQ) | Manufacturer of precision machine tools. The company also deals with products rentals, construction, and maintenance services. | 916-288-6100 | 11-50 | Rancho Cordova |
| Tronex Technology Inc (HQ) | Manufacturer of precision cutting tools and pliers. The company offers hand cutters, hard wire cutters, and flat nose pliers. | 707-426-2550 | NA | Fairfield |
| US Union Tool (BR) | Designer and manufacturer of micro cutting tools for the printed circuit industry. The company engages in mold and dies and medical and aerospace parts. | 714-521-6242 | NA | Santa Clara |
| Westport Machine Works Inc (HQ) | Manufacturer of assembly and balancing equipment. The company's services include fixturing, installation, and technical support. | 916-371-4493 | 1-10 | West Sacramento |
| Wonder Metals Corp (HQ) | Provider of preventing environmental pollution services. The company's products include louvers, penthouses, and control dampers. | 800-366-5877 | 1-10 | Redding |

## 158 = Mining Machinery

| COMPANY NAME | PRODUCT / SERVICE | PHONE | EMP | CITY |
|---|---|---|---|---|
| Berkeley Forge & Tool Inc (HQ) | The company is engaged in the design, engineering, manufacture, and marketing of mining and commercial forging products. | 510-526-5034 | NA | Berkeley |
| Fit Bearings (HQ) | Designer and manufacturer of bearings. The company's products include seals, drive components, and agricultural & industrial wheel hubs. | 510-623-1688 | NA | Fremont |
| Materion Corporation (BR) | Provider of material solutions. The company deals with fabrication, analysis, research and development, and testing services. | 510-623-1500 | NA | Fremont |
| Mclellan Industries Inc (HQ) | Manufacturer of stainless steel and mild steel tanks, hook lifts, tank kits, and related accessories. | 559-582-8100 | 11-50 | Hanford |
| Wasco Hardfacing Company Inc (HQ) | Manufacturer of hardfacing electrodes for steel, cement, and mining applications. The company also offers welding alloy solutions. | 559-485-5860 | 1-10 | Fresno |

## 159 = Miscellaneous Special Industry Equipment

| COMPANY NAME | PRODUCT / SERVICE | PHONE | EMP | CITY |
|---|---|---|---|---|
| Able Design Inc (HQ) | Provider of design services that involves specialization in automated handling of small high technology devices. | 650-961-8245 | NA | Mountain View |
| ABT-TRAC (HQ) | Provider of yacht & boat stabilizers and bow & stern thrusters. The company also offers integrated hydraulic products. | 707-586-3155 | NA | Rohnert Park |
| Acosta Sheet Metal Manufacturing Inc (HQ) | Manufacturer of HVAC and architectural products, and sheet metal building materials. The company provides gutter profile caps and conductor heads. | 408-275-6370 | NA | San Jose |
| Afc Finishing Systems (HQ) | Developer of air filter and spray booth products. The company offers auto and truck spray booths, air make-up units, and powder coating products. | 800-331-7744 | 1-10 | Oroville |
| Agile Thermal Technologies Inc (HQ) | Designer of industrial vacuum and atmosphere systems. The company also provides procurement, program management, and prime contractor capabilities. | 707-570-0304 | NA | Santa Rosa |
| Agricultural Manufacturing Company Inc (HQ) | Manufacturer of sprayers. The company specializes in engineering agricultural spraying equipment and other products such as pumps and tanks. | 559-485-1662 | 1-10 | Fresno |
| Air-O-Fan Products (HQ) | Developer of spray application machinery solutions. The company manufactures engine and PTO drives for orchard, vineyard, and herbicide sprayers. | 559-638-6546 | 1-10 | Reedley |
| Allied Fire Protection (HQ) | Designer and manufacturer of fire protection sprinkler systems. The company also offers installation services. | 510-533-5516 | NA | Oakland |
| Altamont Manufacturing Inc (HQ) | Provider of precision CNC machining, welding, and fabrication services. The company offers semiconductor, aerospace, medical, and robotics components. | 925-371-5401 | NA | Livermore |
| American Cylinder Head (HQ) | Provider of diesel and gas cylinder head repair and remanufacturing services. The company focuses on automotive, heavy duty, and CNG cylinder heads. | 800-356-4889 | NA | Oakland |

| COMPANY NAME | PRODUCT / SERVICE | PHONE | EMP | CITY |
|---|---|---|---|---|
| American Prototype And Production Inc (HQ) | Manufacturer of industrial laser cutting machines. The company focuses on industries such as CNC milling, CNC turning, and laser engraving. | 650-595-4994 | NA | San Carlos |
| Amerimade Technology Inc (HQ) | Manufacturer of wet processing equipment. The company's equipment include fully and semi automated benches, chemical handling equipment, and process tanks. | 925-243-9090 | NA | Livermore |
| Ampteks Inc (HQ) | Provider of engineering solutions. The company provides alternatives for dichromate plating and electro silver plating. | 925-493-7150 | NA | Livermore |
| Ansync Labs Inc (HQ) | Provider of engineering and design services. The company specializes in electrical engineering, mechanical engineering, and industrial design. | 916-933-2850 | 1-10 | El Dorado Hills |
| Applied Process Cooling Corp (HQ) | Provider of refrigeration solutions. The company's services include laser alignment, control panel retrofits, valve exercising, and condenser cleaning. | 209-578-1000 | 11-50 | Modesto |
| Aqua Sierra Controls Inc (HQ) | Provider of instrumentation and electrical contract services. The company specializes in process control automation for industrial installations. | 530-823-3241 | 1-10 | Auburn |
| Artec Group Inc (BR) | Developer and distributor of 3D scanners and 3D cameras. The company's products include Artec iD, Artec 3D, Viewshape, and Shapify. | 669-292-5611 | NA | Santa Clara |
| Ashlock Co (HQ) | Provider of pitting equipment. The company offers equipment such as cherry pitting, date pitting, and olive pitting machines. | 510-351-0560 | NA | San Leandro |
| Asml San Jose (BR) | Manufacturer of lithography systems for semiconductor industries. The company also offers customized imaging solutions. | 669-265-3200 | NA | San Jose |
| Aubin Industries Inc (HQ) | Designer and manufacturer of mobile wheel systems. The company serves the material handling industry. | 209-833-7592 | 1-10 | Tracy |
| Automatic Bar Controls Inc (HQ) | Provider of beverage and liquor dispensers. The company's products include beverage and food and sauce dispensers, and food preparation systems. | 707-448-5151 | NA | Vacaville |
| Avp Technology Llc (HQ) | Provider of thin film equipment services. The company provides custom designing, remanufacturing, and field services. | 510-683-0157 | NA | Fremont |
| Banks Integration Group (HQ) | Developer and provider of control systems and plant automation software. The company serves biotech, food, brewery, oil & gas, and other sectors. | 707-451-1100 | NA | Vacaville |
| Bazell Technologies Corp (HQ) | Manufacturer of solid wall basket centrifuges. The company also focuses on centrifugal fluid processing systems. | 925-603-0900 | NA | Concord |
| Beahm Designs Inc (HQ) | Provider of tailor made manufacturing equipment. The company focuses on tube processing machines for catheter manufacturing. | 408-395-5360 | NA | Milpitas |
| Berkeley Forge & Tool Inc (HQ) | The company is engaged in the design, engineering, manufacture, and marketing of mining and commercial forging products. | 510-526-5034 | NA | Berkeley |
| Betts Spring Inc (HQ) | Manufacturer of custom precision spring products. The company offers coil and leaf springs and serves the mining, military, and trucking industries. | 559-498-3304 | 1-10 | Fresno |
| Billington Welding & Manufacturing Inc (HQ) | Manufacturer of food process equipment and custom products. The company serves the construction, automotive, and food processing industries. | 209-526-9312 | 1-10 | Modesto |
| Bishop-Wisecarver Corp (HQ) | Manufacturer of guide wheels and guided motion products for the medical, aerospace, electronic, and packaging industries. | 925-439-8272 | NA | Pittsburg |
| Biw Connector Systems Llc (HQ) | Supplier of connector systems and electrical feedthru products. The company's products include wellhead feedthrus and power interconnect products. | 707-523-2300 | NA | Santa Rosa |
| Blentech Corp (HQ) | Manufacturer of custom processing systems. The company serves the food production, pharmaceuticals, chemical, and biochemical industries. | 707-523-5949 | NA | Santa Rosa |
| C&P Microsystems Llc (HQ) | Manufacturer and seller of paper cutter control systems. The company offers microcip, cutternet, and microfacts. | 707-776-4500 | NA | Petaluma |
| Cable Moore Inc (HQ) | Manufacturer and distributor of safety & construction equipment and guy & bridge strands. The company offers wire ropes, cables, railings, and slings. | 510-436-8000 | NA | Oakland |
| California Brazing & Nevada Heat Treating (HQ) | Provider of brazing services. The company specializes in machining and heat treatment of components for the aviation industry. | 510-790-2300 | NA | Newark |
| Carando Technologies Inc (HQ) | Manufacturer of container closing tools and dies. The company fabricates drums, water heater tanks, sapre parts, appliances, and container closing tools. | 209-948-6500 | 1-10 | Stockton |
| Cesco Magnetics Inc (HQ) | Provider of magnetic separators. The company offers magnetic filters, magnetic plates, and sanitary valves. | 877-624-8727 | NA | Santa Rosa |
| Chemical Safety Technology Inc (HQ) | Supplier of chemical processing machines. The company also offers design, manufacturing, and sheet metal fabrication services. | 408-263-0984 | NA | San Jose |
| Ckc Laboratories Inc (BR) | Provider of design and testing consultation services. The company offers design consultation, testing, training, and support services. | 510-249-1170 | NA | Fremont |
| Clayborn Lab (HQ) | Developer of heat tapes, hot tubes, and custom tape heaters. The company serves the medical, transportation, and pharmaceutical sectors. | 530-587-4700 | 1-10 | Truckee |
| Cleasby (HQ) | Provider of roofing services. The company also offers single ply, cold process, and built up roofing services. | 415-822-6565 | NA | San Francisco |
| CMD Products (HQ) | Manufacturer of replacement heads and accessories. It's products find application in gas and electric weed trimmers. | 916-434-0228 | 11-50 | Lincoln |

| COMPANY NAME | PRODUCT / SERVICE | PHONE | EMP | CITY |
|---|---|---|---|---|
| Cognex Corp (BR) | Supplier of barcode readers and sensor products. The company offers vision sensors, fixed mount readers, handheld readers, and mobile computers. | 858-481-2469 | NA | Cupertino |
| Cold Ice Inc (HQ) | Manufacturer of refrigerants, insulated shipping containers and temperature monitors. The company serves the agricultural and gourmet food industries. | 510-568-8129 | NA | Oakland |
| Columbia Machine Works (HQ) | Provider of coining equipment and contracting services. The company offers coining presses, rimming machines, and consumable tooling. | 510-568-0808 | NA | Oakland |
| Compass & Anvil (HQ) | Provider of engineering services. The company focuses on metal prototypes, forgings, castings, and metal stampings. | 408-205-1319 | NA | Los Gatos |
| Computer Logistics Corp (HQ) | Provider of system and internet integration, system design, custom programming, web design, and hosting services. | 530-241-3131 | 1-10 | Redding |
| Conquip Inc (HQ) | Manufacturer of converting equipment. The company specializes in volume manufacturing solutions, and also offers repair and upgrade services. | 916-379-8200 | 1-10 | Rancho Cordova |
| Corium International Inc (HQ) | Provider of transdermal delivery systems and related technology solutions. The company is also engaged in therapeutic product development. | 650-298-8255 | NA | Menlo Park |
| Crown Manufacturing Company Inc (HQ) | Provider of plastic and injection molded products. The company offers insert and over molding, drilling, tapping, and heat stamping services. | 510-742-8800 | NA | Newark |
| Cti Controltech (HQ) | Provider of industrial process control and emission solutions. The company's services include engineering, sales, and support. | 925-208-4250 | NA | San Ramon |
| Custom Gear & Machine (HQ) | Manufacturer of custom gears. The company also offers overhaul services for gearboxes and caters to industries like food and steel processing. | 925-455-9985 | NA | Livermore |
| Data Scale (HQ) | Manufacturer of liquid net weight filling equipment. The company offers services to the food and chemical industries. | 510-651-7350 | NA | Fremont |
| Delta Pacific Products Inc (HQ) | Provider of plastics injection molding and mold making services. The company serves the automotive, agriculture, aerospace, and recreational sectors. | 510-487-4411 | NA | Union City |
| Detention Device Systems (HQ) | Provider of design and manufacturing services for detention equipment metal fabrications. The company offers sliding door locking and other devices. | 510-783-0771 | NA | Hayward |
| Diamond Tech Inc (HQ) | Provider of drilling equipment and services. The company specializes in electric, core drills, hydraulic, and drill stands. | 916-624-1118 | 1-10 | Rocklin |
| Dieselcraft Fluid Engineering (HQ) | Provider of oil and fuel cleaning technology. The company offers services for pickup trucks, loaders, boats, and gen sets. | 530-613-2150 | 11-50 | Auburn |
| Doering Machines Inc (HQ) | Manufacturer of food processing equipment. The company also offers pumping systems, extruders, and conveyors. | 415-526-2131 | NA | San Francisco |
| Dpss Lasers Inc (HQ) | Manufacturer of high power, short wavelength solid state lasers for industrial, scientific, and research applications. | 408-988-4300 | NA | Santa Clara |
| Dripless Inc (HQ) | Manufacturer of utility spatulas, caulking guns, holsters, and related accessories. The company serves the painting industry. | 707-568-5081 | NA | Santa Rosa |
| Dynatex International (HQ) | Manufacturer of semiconductor, dicing equipment, and supplies. The company also offers dicing and wafer bonding services. | 707-542-4227 | NA | Santa Rosa |
| Dynaweb Inc (HQ) | Manufacturer and marketer of web handling and tension control systems. The company's product finds use in packaging, printing, and textile needs. | 925-373-9013 | 1-10 | Sonora |
| Earthquake Protection Systems (HQ) | Supplier of seismic isolators for earthquake bearings. The company offers single and triple pendulum bearings and related supplies. | 707-644-5993 | NA | Vallejo |
| Eco-Snow Systems (HQ) | Provider of CO2 precision surface process equipment for cleaning applications. The company's products include VersaClean 1200 and MaskClean 150 systems. | 925-606-2000 | NA | Livermore |
| Edc Biosystems Inc (HQ) | Provider of technology solutions for biotech liquid transfer applications. The company serves the electronics, precision mechanics, and other sectors. | 510-257-1500 | NA | Fremont |
| El Dorado Molds Inc (HQ) | Provider of molding services. The company provides injection molds and related tooling for the plastics industry. | 916-635-4558 | 11-50 | Rancho Cordova |
| Electro Plating Specialties Inc (HQ) | Provider of electroplating services. The company offers parts cleaning, anodizing, electropolishing, and rust removal services. | 510-786-1881 | NA | Hayward |
| Elliott Manufacturing Company Inc (HQ) | Manufacturer of case erectors, case sealers, cartoners, and case packers. The company is engaged in sales and delivery services. | 559-233-6235 | 1-10 | Fresno |
| Engineering By Design (HQ) | Provider of engineering and support services. The company's products include laminators, coil and fiber winders, motors, and extrusion pullers. | 408-324-1500 | NA | San Jose |
| Ethylene Control Inc (HQ) | Manufacturer of ethylene and gas removal products. The company's products include filters, filtration systems, and sachets. | 559-896-1909 | 1-10 | Selma |
| Evolve Manufacturing Technologies Inc (HQ) | Designer and manufacturer of electro-mechanical, optical, and prototyping products. The company offers testing, logistics, andumendation services. | 510-690-8959 | NA | Fremont |
| Fil-Tech West Inc (BR) | Distributor of semiconductor parts and vacuum components. The company is engaged in troubleshooting and maintenance services. | 925-251-8200 | NA | Pleasanton |

| COMPANY NAME | PRODUCT / SERVICE | PHONE | EMP | CITY |
|---|---|---|---|---|
| Fisher Manufacturing (HQ) | Manufacturer of advanced plumbing systems. The company's products include faucets, valves, sprays, and fillers. | 800-421-6162 | 11-50 | Tulare |
| FloStor Engineering (HQ) | Developer of automation solutions for inventory, distribution, fulfillment, and manufacturing systems. | 800-500-8256 | NA | Hayward |
| Force Flow Inc (HQ) | Provider of chemical monitoring scales. The company exclusively caters to the water and wastewater industry. | 925-686-6700 | NA | Concord |
| Fortrend Engineering Corp (HQ) | Designer and manufacturer of mechanical handling equipment. The company also specializes in distribution services. | 408-734-9311 | NA | San Jose |
| g2 Engineering (BR) | Manufacturer of engineering products such as bead mounts and related accessories. The company's applications include industrial automation and controls. | 650-605-4500 | NA | Saratoga |
| General Foundry Service Corp (HQ) | Provider of foundry services. The company engages in pattern making, precision sand casting, and rubber plastic mold. | 510-297-5040 | NA | San Leandro |
| General Lasertronics Corp (HQ) | Developer of scanning and control technologies that make laser ablation an alternative to traditional abrasives and solvents for removing coatings. | 408-947-1181 | NA | San Jose |
| Geo M Martin Co (HQ) | Developer of equipment for corrugated container industry. The company offers training, field support, and technical services. | 510-652-2200 | NA | Emeryville |
| Gigamat Technologies (HQ) | Provider of polishers, sorters, grinders, crystal pullers, and related accessories. The company offers services to the industrial sector. | 510-770-8008 | NA | Fremont |
| Granberg International (HQ) | Manufacturer of saw chain maintenance tools to repair and sharpen saw chain & attachments. The company offers brush attachments and cutting bars. | 925-380-9400 | NA | Pittsburg |
| Guntert & Zimmerman Const Div Inc (HQ) | Manufacturer of canal lining equipment, concrete batch plants, and other special equipment. The company serves the industrial sector. | 209-599-0066 | 11-50 | Ripon |
| Harris & Bruno International (HQ) | Provider of printing and coating solutions. The company offers web coaters, chambers, offline coaters, pumps, and other products. | 916-781-7676 | 1-10 | Roseville |
| Heat & Control Inc (HQ) | Manufacturer of food processing and packaging equipment systems. The company offers inspection system, product handling equipment, and coating system. | 510-259-0500 | NA | Hayward |
| Heatscape Inc (HQ) | Designer and manufacturer of thermal solutions. The company engages in thermal analysis, thermal testing, and finite element analysis. | 408-778-4615 | NA | Morgan Hill |
| Heinzen Manufacturing International (HQ) | Designer and manufacturer of custom food processing equipment. The company specializes in shakers, bin dumpers, fruit equipment, and trimlines. | 408-842-7233 | NA | Gilroy |
| Hepco Inc (HQ) | Manufacturer of electronic components. The company offers design, fabrication, analysis, and testing tools for semiconductor industries. | 408-738-1880 | NA | Sunnyvale |
| Hesse Mechatronics Inc (LH) | Developer of equipment for heavy wire and thin wire wedge bonders. The company also focuses on the marketing aspects. | 408-436-9300 | NA | Fremont |
| Hitachi Metals America Ltd (BR) | Manufacturer and marketer of metal products. The company offers cable systems, cutting tools, ceramics, sensors, and other materials. | 408-467-8900 | NA | San Jose |
| Horn Machine Tools Inc (HQ) | Supplier of CNC and semi-automatic tube benders. The company offers new tube benders, rebuilt tube benders, and bender rebuilding and retro-fitting. | 559-431-4131 | 1-10 | Madera |
| Hydratech LLC (HQ) | Manufacturer of cylinder component, hydraulic, and pneumatic cylinder with engineering capabilities needed to build superior cylinder solutions. | 559-233-0876 | 1-10 | Fresno |
| Hydrofarm Inc (HQ) | Manufacturer of hydroponics equipment. The company also supplies plant care products and garden accessories. | 800-634-9990 | NA | Petaluma |
| Hydropoint Data Systems Inc (HQ) | Provider of irrigation solutions. The company specializes in site evaluations, upgrade planning, deployment, and optimization services. | 800-362-8774 | NA | Petaluma |
| HyPower Hydraulics (HQ) | Manufacturer of hydraulic cylinders and related accessories. The company offers repair/rebuilding services. | 209-632-2275 | 1-10 | Turlock |
| Ifos (HQ) | Developer of optical fiber sensing system level products. The company's products are used for monitoring and control of temperature and acoustic emission. | 408-565-9000 | NA | Santa Clara |
| Imtec Acculine Inc (HQ) | Provider of wet process modules and systems. The company also supplies quartz constant temperature baths. | 510-770-1800 | NA | Fremont |
| Industrial Electrical Co (HQ) | Provider of electrical, manufacturing, and automation services for the commercial and industrial sectors. | 209-527-2800 | 11-50 | Modesto |
| Industrial Nuclear Co (HQ) | Manufacturer of industrial gamma radiography equipment and radioactive sources. The company's services include calibration and repair and leak testing. | 510-352-6767 | NA | San Leandro |
| Intake Screens Inc (HQ) | Designer and manufacturer of intake screens for fish protection and filtration. The company also offers installation and maintenance services. | 916-665-2727 | 1-10 | Sacramento |
| Jackrabbit Inc (HQ) | Provider of nut harvesting systems including runner, elevator, reservoir cart, conditioner and pruning tower. | 209-599-6118 | 1-10 | Ripon |
| James Cox & Sons Inc (HQ) | Developer of products for asphalt, concrete, and soil testing. The company is also engaged in calibration and remote support services. | 530-346-8322 | 1-10 | Colfax |
| Johnson Manufacturing (HQ) | Developer of farm machinery equipment and utility vehicles. The company offers trailers, air compressors, electric cars and golf car parts. | 530-662-1788 | 1-10 | Woodland |

| COMPANY NAME | PRODUCT / SERVICE | PHONE | EMP | CITY |
|---|---|---|---|---|
| Juki Americas (BR) | Provider of SMT assembly machines. The company offers inline selective soldering systems, mini-wave soldering machines, and stamp soldering products. | 510-249-6700 | NA | Fremont |
| K&L Supply Co (HQ) | Manufacturer of specialty tools and shop equipment for motorcycle dealers. The company offers shop lift & wheel equipment, jacks, and other tools. | 408-727-6767 | NA | San Jose |
| Kearneys Metals Inc (HQ) | Provider of foundry services. The company specializes in stainless steel and aluminium plates, sheets, structurals and bars. | 559-233-2591 | 1-10 | Fresno |
| KEMPF Inc (HQ) | Provider of driving solutions. The company offers digital hand controls and other handicap driving aids for paraplegic drivers. | 408-773-0219 | NA | Sunnyvale |
| King Sales & Engineering (HQ) | Designer and seller of rotary fillers, labelers, and case packers. The company offers products for the tomato and fruit canning industry. | 415-892-7961 | NA | Novato |
| Kirby Manufacturing Inc (HQ) | Provider of cattle feeding equipment such as horizontal and vertical mixers, manure spreaders, freestall wagons, scale systems, and haybusters. | 209-723-0778 | 11-50 | Merced |
| Kleenrite Equipment (HQ) | Developer and manufacturer of domestic & commercial cleaning devices. The company caters to commercial and constructional facilities. | 800-241-4865 | 1-10 | Madera |
| Klippenstein Corp (HQ) | Manufacturer of packaging equipment. The company's products also include case formers, erectors, and sealers. | 559-834-4258 | 1-10 | Fresno |
| KOR-IT Inc (HQ) | Manufacturer of diamond tools and core drill machines. The company caters to the concrete cutting industry. | 916-372-6400 | 1-10 | Sacramento |
| Kycon Inc (HQ) | Provider of interconnect solutions. The company offers products such as audio jacks, card edge, and modular jacks. | 408-494-0330 | NA | Morgan Hill |
| Laboratory Equipment Co (HQ) | Manufacturer of laboratory equipment. The company's products include alarm monitor systems, bedding dispensers, dryers, and ovens. | 510-887-4040 | NA | Hayward |
| LAKOS Filtration Solutions (HQ) | Manufacturer of centrifugal separators and other filtration solutions to remove sand and other solids from water and liquids. | 559-255-1601 | 1-10 | Fresno |
| Lasertec USA Inc (HQ) | Developer and manufacturer of systems for semi-conductor applications. The company also offers systems for flat panel displays. | 408-437-1441 | NA | San Jose |
| Leadman Electronics USA Inc (HQ) | Provider of ODM/OEM, hardware engineering expertise, and custom solutions for a wide range of security, storage, server, and network applications. | 408-380-4567 | NA | Santa Clara |
| Liqua-Tech Corp (HQ) | Manufacturer of precision measurement systems. The company offers flow meters, gear trains, and measuring chambers. | 707-462-3555 | 1-10 | Ukiah |
| Longevity Global Inc (HQ) | Manufacturer of welding equipment. The company also offers filler rods, generators, plasma cutters, and related accessories. | 510-887-7090 | NA | Hayward |
| M&L Precision Machining Inc (HQ) | Provider of machine shop services. The company offers precision fabricated components, semiconductors, and related devices. | 408-224-2138 | NA | Morgan Hill |
| Malcolm Drilling Company Inc (HQ) | Provider of specialty foundation industry services. The company is engaged in deep foundations, dewatering, and design build services. | 415-901-4400 | NA | San Francisco |
| Martin Sprocket & Gear Inc (BR) | Manufacturer of industrial hand tools, conveyor pulleys, and other products. The company offers power transmission and material handling products. | 916-441-7172 | 11-50 | Sacramento |
| Martin's Metal Fabrication & Welding Inc (HQ) | Provider of structural steel fabrication services in Northern California. The company offers laser cutting, beam line drilling, and other servcies. | 707-678-4117 | NA | Vacaville |
| Mc Microwave Inc (HQ) | Provider of microwave and radio frequency components. The company's products are used in commercial and military applications. | 408-446-4100 | NA | San Jose |
| Mclellan Industries Inc (HQ) | Manufacturer of stainless steel and mild steel tanks, hook lifts, tank kits, and related accessories. | 559-582-8100 | 11-50 | Hanford |
| Meivac Inc (HQ) | Manufacturer of sputtering systems and components. The company offers throttle valves, integrators, OEM assemblies, and substrate heaters. | 408-362-1000 | NA | San Jose |
| Microelec Technical (HQ) | Manufacturer of semiconductor, micro-electronics, and mixed signal devices. The company specializes in switches, bridge rectifiers, and transistors. | 408-282-3508 | NA | Santa Clara |
| Modern Machine Co (HQ) | Provider of machining services. The company focuses on robotic welding, automatic screw machines, and CNC machining centers. | 408-436-7670 | NA | San Jose |
| Montague (HQ) | Provider of commercial cooking equipment. The company's products include boilers, ovens, and refrigerated bases. | 510-785-8822 | NA | Hayward |
| Motor Guard Corp (HQ) | Designer and developer of spray equipment and tools for collision repairs. The company offers services to the automotive sector. | 209-239-9191 | 1-10 | Manteca |
| Mountz Inc (HQ) | Manufacturer of torque analyzers, sensors, bits, sockets, and adapters. The company is engaged in installation and technical support services. | 408-850-9978 | NA | San Jose |
| Murray Trailers (HQ) | Designer and manufacturer of trailers. The company also offers related accessories and hauling services. | 209-466-0266 | 11-50 | Stockton |
| Nb Corporation Of America (BR) | Manufacturer of linear motion bearings, slides, ball splines, and related products. The company's products include slide guides, spindle shafts, and actuators. | 510-490-1420 | NA | Fremont |
| Neptune Systems Llc (HQ) | Provider of aquarium controllers. The company also offers expansion modules and accessories and offers support services. | 408-275-2205 | NA | Morgan Hill |
| Netafim Irrigation Inc (HQ) | Provider of drip and micro irrigation products for agriculture, greenhouse and nursery, landscape and turf, mining, and wastewater applications. | 559-453-6800 | 1-10 | Fresno |

| COMPANY NAME | PRODUCT / SERVICE | PHONE | EMP | CITY |
|---|---|---|---|---|
| Nichols Manufacturing Inc (HQ) | Provider of product engineering and design, prototyping, and manufacturing services. The company serves the business sector. | 408-945-0911 | NA | Milpitas |
| Nieco (HQ) | Manufacturer of automatic broilers. The company's applications include restaurants, fast food centers, and amusement parks. | 707-284-7100 | NA | Windsor |
| Nikon Precision Inc (HQ) | Manufacturer of optical lenses and precision equipment. The company is also the supplier of step-and-repeat and step-and-scan lithography systems. | 650-508-4674 | NA | Belmont |
| Nova Measuring Instruments Inc (BR) | Provider of metrology solutions for semiconductor manufacturing industries. The company offers integrated and stand-alone metrology platforms. | 408-510-7400 | NA | Fremont |
| NTFB Combustion Equipment USA Inc (HQ) | Manufacturer of combustion equipment. The company offers mid to large size, single & multiple burner, water tube boiler, and furnace applications. | 510-443-0066 | NA | Foster City |
| OCSiAl (BR) | Provider of technology and material solutions. The company offers services to the nanomaterials industry. | 415-906-5271 | NA | Sunnyvale |
| Onchip Devices Inc (HQ) | Provider of silicon and ceramic solutions and integrated passive devices for the computing and consumer electronics industries. | 408-654-9365 | NA | Santa Clara |
| Ondavia Inc (HQ) | Provider of water analysis solutions. The company offers OndaVia analysis system that enables laboratory-grade water testing. | 510-576-0476 | NA | Hayward |
| Orchard Machinery Corp (HQ) | Manufacturer of tree shakers and material handling systems comprising shuttles, bin carriers, conveyor carts, and elevators. | 530-673-2822 | 1-10 | Yuba City |
| Pacific Coast Optics Inc (HQ) | Provider of optical products, services and applications. The company offers prototype, polishing, grinding, and coating. | 916-789-0111 | 1-10 | Roseville |
| Pacific Ozone Technology Inc (HQ) | Supplier of air-cooled, integrated ozone and oxygen systems and packaged controls for industrial ozone applications. | 707-747-9600 | NA | Benicia |
| Pacific Roller Die Company Inc (HQ) | Designer and manufacturer of corrugated metal pipes, coated and lined pipes, and duct products. The company offers installation and delivery services. | 510-782-7242 | NA | Hayward |
| Pauli Systems Inc (HQ) | Manufacturer of custom finishing systems, abrasive booths, and equipment including blast rooms for aviation, automotive, and industrial applications. | 707-429-2434 | NA | Fairfield |
| PAX Scientific Inc (HQ) | Provider of engineering research and product design services. The company is also involved in the design of industrial equipment. | 415-256-9900 | NA | San Rafael |
| Pegasus Design Inc (HQ) | Provider of machine design and contract manufacturing services. The company serves the pharmaceutical instrument industry. | 925-292-7567 | NA | Livermore |
| Penhall Co (BR) | Provider of concrete cutting services. The company specializes in core drilling, diamond saw cutting, and pavement repair methods. | 916-386-1589 | 11-50 | Sacramento |
| Phil Wood & Co (HQ) | Manufacturer of cycling and related recreation oriented products. The company focuses to offer maintenance-free hubs for cyclists. | 408-569-1860 | NA | San Jose |
| Plasma Ruggedized Solutions (HQ) | Provider of coating and related specialty engineering services. The company specializes in plasma technologies and offers lab services. | 408-954-8405 | NA | San Jose |
| Plasma Technology Systems Llc (HQ) | Provider of equipment and process development services for plasma treatment of surfaces. The company specializes in modification of polymers. | 650-596-1606 | NA | Hayward |
| Plastech (HQ) | Provider of machined and fabricated plastic products for the semi conductor, biological, and medical industries. | 650-568-9206 | NA | Menlo Park |
| Pneu Design Llc (HQ) | Provider of electronic and pneumatic filling machines for the petroleum and food processing industry. | 530-676-4702 | 1-10 | Shingle Springs |
| Process Engineers Inc (HQ) | Manufacturer of stainless steel equipment. The company also specializes in installation and other services. | 510-782-5122 | NA | Hayward |
| Proco Products Inc (HQ) | Manufacturer of expansion joints. The company serves the oil and gas, power generation, chemical, and steel industries. | 209-943-6088 | 1-10 | Stockton |
| Prodigy Surface Tech Inc (HQ) | Provider of alternative to common electroplating shop. The company focuses on chem lab for analysis, blaster, and clean room. | 408-492-9390 | NA | Santa Clara |
| Progressive Concepts Machining (HQ) | Provider of welding, assembly, and machining services. The company also deals with inspection solutions and serves businesses. | 925-426-0400 | NA | Pleasanton |
| Quality Stainless Tanks (HQ) | Provider of ready-made tanks. The company offers crafted tanks, stainless winery equipment, and special application tanks. | 877-598-0672 | NA | Windsor |
| R&R Refrigeration And Air Conditioning Inc (HQ) | Provider of environmental technological solutions. The company also offers maintenance and repair services for process systems. | 408-297-0383 | NA | San Jose |
| Rainbow Electronics & Fasteners Corp (HQ) | Distributor of electronic and mechanical hardware products. The company's products include fasteners, screws, standoffs, and spacers. | 510-475-9840 | NA | Union City |
| Ralphs-Pugh Co (HQ) | Manufacturer of conveyor rollers and related components. The company serves the agriculture, chemical, and food processing industries. | 707-745-6222 | NA | Benicia |
| Ripon Manufacturing Company Inc (HQ) | Fabricator of steel processing equipment. The company manufactures and installs peelers, sizers, hardshell crackers, hoppers, dryers, and sorters. | 209-599-2148 | 1-10 | Ripon |
| Rocklin Hydraulics (HQ) | Manufacturer of hydraulic products. The company offers hydraulic hoses, caps & plugs, jaw couplers, and brass fittings. | 916-624-8900 | 1-10 | Rocklin |

| COMPANY NAME | PRODUCT / SERVICE | PHONE | EMP | CITY |
|---|---|---|---|---|
| Sa Photonics Inc (HQ) | Developer of photonic systems. The company offers solutions for head-mounted displays, microwave sensors, mirror sense, and control systems. | 408-560-3500 | NA | Los Gatos |
| Safety Equipment Corp (HQ) | Designer and manufacturer of gas cabinets, valve boxes, leaker cabinets, exhausted enclosures, and related products. | 650-595-5422 | NA | Belmont |
| Saint Clare Global A California Corporation (HQ) | Manufacturer of slicing and stacking machines. The company is engaged in design and production services. | | 1-10 | Roseville |
| San-I-Pak Pacific Inc (HQ) | Manufacturer of compactors, shredders, and sterilizer supplies. The company serves the industrial sector and enterprises. | 209-836-2310 | 1-10 | Tracy |
| Sandvik Thermal Process Inc (DH) | Provider of thermal processing equipment. The company offers solar cells, semiconductors, and industrial heaters. | 209-533-1990 | 1-10 | Sonora |
| Seagull Solutions Inc (HQ) | Developer and manufacturer of air bearing spindles, clamps, and custom applications. The company mainly offers custom made services. | 408-778-1127 | NA | Morgan Hill |
| Semicore Equipment Inc (HQ) | Manufacturer of vacuum systems and equipment. The company's products include PVD coating systems, thermal evaporation, and sputtering equipment. | 925-373-8201 | NA | Livermore |
| Sentek Dynamics Inc (HQ) | Manufacturer of vibration test equipment, shakers, power amplifiers, and related instruments. The company offers customer support solutions. | 408-200-3100 | NA | Santa Clara |
| Serpa Packaging Solutions (HQ) | Provider of packaging solutions. The company's applications include pharmaceutical industry and bottles, vials, and ampules. | 559-651-2339 | 1-10 | Visalia |
| Silicon Valley Mfg (HQ) | Manufacturer and engineer of EDM prototype and production machining. The company's services include CNC milling, CNC turning, and manual machining. | 510-791-9450 | NA | Newark |
| Simco-Ion (BR) | Manufacturer of static control and process control products. The company is engaged in design and installation services. | 510-217-0600 | NA | Alameda |
| Simplex Filler Co (HQ) | Manufacturer of liquid filling machines. The company offers volumetric fillers, pressure fillers, and accessories. | 707-265-6801 | NA | Napa |
| Sjc Precision Inc (HQ) | Provider of precision machining and tool and die making services. The company designs and manufactures jigs, fixtures, and bookmolds. | 408-262-1680 | NA | Milpitas |
| Smart Wires Inc (HQ) | Provider of grid optimization solutions. The company is involved in load and generation, alleviate congestion, and network utilization services. | 415-800-5555 | NA | Union City |
| Sonic Manufacturing Technologies (HQ) | Provider of contract manufacturing services. The company engages in supply chain, quality assurance, and design and engineering services. | 510-580-8500 | NA | Fremont |
| Source 1 X-Ray (HQ) | Manufacturer of X-Ray generators. The company specializes in bone density measurement, radiography, and process control. | 408-866-6020 | NA | Campbell |
| Source Engineering Inc (HQ) | Manufacturer of motors, cables, harnesses, and motion control products. The company also provides custom modification services on motors. | 408-980-9822 | NA | Santa Clara |
| Sp3 Diamond Technologies (HQ) | Provider of electronics thermal management, diamond-on-silicon applications, and enhanced cutting surface solutions. | 408-492-0630 | NA | Santa Clara |
| Spectra Watermakers Inc (HQ) | Designer of energy recovery systems. The company specializes in manufacturing of reverse osmosis desalination systems for the ocean sailor. | 415-526-2780 | NA | San Rafael |
| Spintrac Systems Inc (HQ) | Manufacturer of automated resist coating equipment. The company is involved in repairs and maintenance services. | 408-980-1155 | NA | Santa Clara |
| Spraying Systems Co (BR) | Provider of spray technology services. The company focuses on spray nozzles, automated spray systems, and coating. | 800-957-7729 | NA | Walnut Creek |
| Stage 8 (HQ) | Designer and manufacturer of mechanical locking systems. The company has more than 78 patents and trademarks. | 415-485-5340 | NA | San Rafael |
| Stokes Publishing Co (HQ) | Manufacturer of overhead calculators. The company also offers timers, puzzles, manipulatives, and posters. | 408-541-9145 | NA | Sunnyvale |
| Storz & Bickel America Inc (HQ) | Manufacturer of vaporizers. The company specializes in the design and fabrication of solid valve and easy valve systems. | 510-451-1553 | NA | Oakland |
| Sumiden Wire Products Corp (BR) | Supplier of wire products. The company offers nickel plated wires, stainless spring wires, and industrial alloys. | 209-466-8924 | 11-50 | Stockton |
| Surveillance Systems Integration Inc (HQ) | Provider of security products. The company serves customers in the gaming, retail, education, and healthcare industries. | 916-771-7272 | 11-50 | Rocklin |
| Sweco Products Inc (HQ) | Manufacturer of agricultural & construction equipment and hydraulic cylinders, and related supplies. | 530-673-8949 | 1-10 | Sutter |
| Tazmo Inc (BR) | Manufacturer of SOG and LCD color filter coaters. The company offers SOG, SOD, polyimide coaters and developers and LCD Resist coaters. | 510-438-4890 | NA | Fremont |
| Technavibes Inc (HQ) | Manufacturer of feeder bowls. The company specializes in vibratory bowl feeders, vibratory feeder in-line tracks, and vibratory feeder hoppers. | 530-626-8093 | 1-10 | Diamond Springs |
| Teknika Strapping Systems (HQ) | Provider of hand tools for plastic stripping. The company is engaged in repairs, replacement, and maintenance services. | 408-441-9071 | NA | San Jose |
| Tesla (HQ) | Designer and manufacturer of electric sedans and electric SUVs. The company is engaged in the production of energy storage systems. | 6500-681-5000 | NA | Palo Alto |
| The Lincoln Electric Co (BR) | Provider of industrial control and automation solutions. The company's offerings also include torches, welding guns, and related accessories. | 916-939-8788 | 11-50 | El Dorado Hills |
| Therm-X (HQ) | Provider of engineered solutions. The company serves the semiconductor, petrochemical, life sciences, and aerospace industries. | 510 606-1012 | NA | Hayward |

| COMPANY NAME | PRODUCT / SERVICE | PHONE | EMP | CITY |
|---|---|---|---|---|
| Thermal Press International Inc (HQ) | Manufacturer of thermal presses and heat staking machines. The company also offers heat sealing and degating machinery. | 925-454-9800 | NA | Livermore |
| Tooltek Engineering Corp (HQ) | Designer and fabricator of custom automated equipment. The company is also engaged in material handling and robotics solutions. | 510-683-9504 | NA | Fremont |
| Transfer Flow Inc (HQ) | Manufacturer of fuel tanks. The company offers axillary, replacement, and tanks with built-in toolboxes. | 530-893-5209 | 1-10 | Chico |
| Ultra T Equipment Company Inc (HQ) | Manufacturer of spin coaters, developer stations, reionizers, and microelectronics cleaning systems. | 510-440-3909 | NA | Fremont |
| Uniform Industrial Corp (DH) | Provider of systems and components for banking and retail solutions. The company also offers technology solutions and customer services. | 510-438-6799 | NA | Fremont |
| V&O Machine Inc (HQ) | Manufacturer of machined parts for agri, hydraulics, food proceing, and veterinary applications. The company focuses on prototyping and CNC milling. | 530-662-0495 | 1-10 | Woodland |
| Valley Tool & Manufacturing Co (HQ) | Manufacturer of agricultural equipment like flail mowers, sprayers, and shredders. The company also manufactures skid steer and excavator attachments. | 800-426-5615 | 1-10 | Hughson |
| Vanderlans & Sons Inc (HQ) | Manufacturer of pipe and high pressure plugs, test equipment, hoses, gauges, ventilators, and related accessories. | 209-334-4115 | 1-10 | Lodi |
| Ventex Corp (HQ) | Supplier of lithography equipment, spare parts, and services. The company also provides refurbishment and installation services. | 408-436-2929 | NA | San Jose |
| Warren & Baerg Manufacturing Inc (HQ) | Manufacturer of agricultural and industrial systems. The company's services include installation, manufacturing, and technical support. | 559-591-6790 | 11-50 | Dinuba |
| Wasco Hardfacing Company Inc (HQ) | Manufacturer of hardfacing electrodes for steel, cement, and mining applications. The company also offers welding alloy solutions. | 559-485-5860 | 1-10 | Fresno |
| Waterman Industries (HQ) | Designer and manufacturer of water-control sluice gates, penstocks, valves, and water control products. | 559-562-4000 | 11-50 | Exeter |
| Weslan Systems Inc (HQ) | Fabricator of custom plastic products for the semiconductor industry. The company offers contract manufacturing services. | 530-668-3304 | 1-10 | Woodland |
| Westec Plastics Corp (HQ) | Provider of plastics injection molding and mold making services. The company also offers customized services. | 925-454-3400 | NA | Livermore |
| Western Allied Mechanical Inc (HQ) | Designer and builder of heating and ventilation systems. The company serves the construction and energy automation industries. | 650-326-0750 | NA | Menlo Park |
| Western Truck Fab Inc (HQ) | Provider of custom truck body fabrication services. The company's products include lift gates, compressors, and cranes. | 510-785-9994 | NA | Hayward |
| Western Widgets CNC Inc (HQ) | Manufacturer of precision milled and turned components such as computers and optical assemblies. The company deals with milling and turning services. | 408-436-1230 | NA | San Jose |
| Westport Machine Works Inc (HQ) | Manufacturer of assembly and balancing equipment. The company's services include fixturing, installation, and technical support. | 916-371-4493 | 1-10 | West Sacramento |
| Whipple Industries Inc (HQ) | Provider of supercharger for vehicles. The company's products include twin-screw superchargers and accessories. | 559-442-1261 | 1-10 | Fresno |
| Wolfram Inc (HQ) | Designer and manufacturer of metal halide lamps for the entertainment industry. The company's lamps are used for filming motion pictures. | 209-238-9610 | 1-10 | Modesto |
| Woodland Mdm (HQ) | Manufacturer and supplier of new and refurbished machinery products. The company offers industrial controls and automation & case handling equipment. | 530-669-1400 | 1-10 | Woodland |
| Woodside Electronics Corp (HQ) | Designer and manufacturer of electronic sorters. The company serves customers in the tomato harvesters and walnut industries. | 530-666-9190 | 1-10 | Woodland |
| Wpg Americas Inc (DH) | Distributor of electronic products. The company's portfolio includes encoders, sensors, solid state batteries, and timing devices. | 408-392-8100 | NA | San Jose |
| Zalda Technology (HQ) | Fabricator of springs. The company also offers spring design, testing, and prototype assembling services. | 510-783-4910 | NA | Hayward |
| Zircon Corp (HQ) | Designer and manufacturer of stud finders. The company offers electrical scanners, metal detectors, leveling tools, and accessories. | 408-963-4550 | NA | Campbell |

## 160 = Pumps

| COMPANY NAME | PRODUCT / SERVICE | PHONE | EMP | CITY |
|---|---|---|---|---|
| Aqua Sierra Controls Inc (HQ) | Provider of instrumentation and electrical contract services. The company specializes in process control automation for industrial installations. | 530-823-3241 | 1-10 | Auburn |
| BESST Inc (HQ) | Provider of groundwater sampling technology solutions. The company also offers customized packages for specialized applications. | 415-453-2501 | NA | San Rafael |
| Biomicrolab (HQ) | Manufacturer of robotics based sorting and weighing systems sample management automation. The company serves bio-lab purposes. | 925-689-1200 | NA | Concord |
| Control Systems West Inc (HQ) | Designer and fabricator of a broad variety of custom electrical controls for industrial applications. | 707-763-1108 | NA | Petaluma |
| Diener Precision Pumps Lp (DH) | Developer of gear and piston pumps, and valves for cooling and flshing, refrigeration, medical, biotech, and pharmaceutical industries. | 209-365-0405 | 1-10 | Lodi |
| IDEX Health & Science LLC (BR) | Provider of precision equipment for the health care industry. The company also offers detectors, fittings, and filters. | 707-588-2000 | NA | Rohnert Park |
| Infrared Industries Inc (HQ) | Developer of gas analyzer instrumentation for the automotive, oil and gas, industrial, environmental, and utility industries. | 510-782-8100 | NA | Hayward |

| COMPANY NAME | PRODUCT / SERVICE | PHONE | EMP | CITY |
|---|---|---|---|---|
| Inoxpa Usa Inc (HQ) | Manufacturer and trader of pumps and components. The company caters to industries like food processing, dairy, wine-making, and cosmetics. | 707-585-3900 | NA | Santa Rosa |
| Mclellan Industries Inc (HQ) | Manufacturer of stainless steel and mild steel tanks, hook lifts, tank kits, and related accessories. | 559-582-8100 | 11-50 | Hanford |
| Morrill Industries Inc (HQ) | Manufacturer and supplier of irrigation equipment. The company also offers custom built rotating suction screens and industrial pipes. | 209-838-2550 | 1-10 | Escalon |
| Price Pump Co (HQ) | Manufacturer of centrifugal and air operated diaphragm pumps. The company offers engineering services and serves industrial and OEM users. | 707-938-8441 | NA | Sonoma |
| Process Engineers Inc (HQ) | Manufacturer of stainless steel equipment. The company also specializes in installation and other services. | 510-782-5122 | NA | Hayward |
| Simonds Machinery Co (HQ) | Distributor of portable pump carts, custom control panels, pressure booster systems, and related accessories. | 650-589-9900 | NA | S San Francisco |
| Smart Products Inc (HQ) | Supplier of engineering products. The company offers valves, fittings, and pumps for the automotive, medical, and water treatment markets. | 800-338-0404 | NA | Morgan Hill |
| SuperKlean (HQ) | Manufacturer of spray nozzles and swivel fittings. The company also offers hot & cold water mixing stations and hose racks. | 650-375-7001 | NA | Burlingame |
| V-Power Equipment Inc (HQ) | Manufacturer and wholesaler of water well, wastewater, and construction dewatering pumps. The company provides pump repair and diagnostic services. | 916-266-6743 | 1-10 | West Sacramento |
| Varna Products (HQ) | Manufacturer of pump and valve solutions. The company offers oil pumps, pump controls, pressure relief valves, and check valves. | 530-676-7770 | 1-10 | Cameron Park |
| Vian Enterprises Inc (HQ) | Manufacturer of gerotors, gears, and broached hardware. The company also offers oil pump and complete lubrication systems. | 530-885-1997 | 1-10 | Auburn |

## 162 = Seals/Gaskets

| COMPANY NAME | PRODUCT / SERVICE | PHONE | EMP | CITY |
|---|---|---|---|---|
| Campbell/Harris Security Equipment Company (HQ) | Manufacturer of busters, fiberscopes, probe kits, and personal radiation detectors. The company also focuses on distribution. | 510-864-8010 | NA | Alameda |
| Darcoid Nor-Cal Seal (HQ) | Provider of rubber based products. The company offers gaskets, composite and dynamic seals, molded shapes, and thermal products. | 510-836-2449 | NA | Oakland |
| Gasket Specialties Inc (HQ) | Manufacturer of gaskets. The company engages in adhesives, assembly, and bar coding services. | 510-547-7955 | NA | Emeryville |
| Lamons (BR) | Manufacturer of industrial gaskets. The company caters to the refinery and packing industrial sectors. | 925-313-9080 | NA | Martinez |
| Pacific States Felt & MFG Company Inc (HQ) | Manufacturer of gaskets, seals, washers, pads, and molded bumpers. The company is engaged in lamination and fabrication. | 510-783-0277 | NA | Hayward |
| Power Industries (HQ) | Supplier of ready-made solutions for industrial applications. The company's products include bearings and seals, hydraulics, and pneumatics. | 707-545-7904 | NA | Santa Rosa |
| Process Engineers Inc (HQ) | Manufacturer of stainless steel equipment. The company also specializes in installation and other services. | 510-782-5122 | NA | Hayward |
| RGS Industries (HQ) | Manufacturer and supplier of gaskets. The company offers seals, shielding and related materials, and die cutting services. | 669-238-0632 | NA | Santa Clara |

## 163 = Special Dies, Tools & Molds

| COMPANY NAME | PRODUCT / SERVICE | PHONE | EMP | CITY |
|---|---|---|---|---|
| Ace Seal Llc (HQ) | Manufacturer of molded rubber, seals, and o-rings. The company serves the aerospace, semiconductor, oil & gas, medical, and biotechnology sectors. | 408-513-1070 | NA | San Jose |
| American Die & Rollforming Inc (HQ) | Manufacturer of metal roofing, siding, and structural products. The company also specializes in canopies and decking. | 916-652-7667 | 1-10 | Loomis |
| Bulling Metal Works Inc (HQ) | Manufacturer of pressure vessels and laser cutting machinery. The company also offers other custom fabrication products. | 510-351-2073 | NA | San Leandro |
| Computer Plastics Inc (HQ) | Provider of molding services. The company offers custom plastic injection molding, engineering, assembly, and tooling services. | 510-785-3600 | NA | Hayward |
| Concepts 2 Industries (HQ) | Manufacturer of custom injection molded plastic parts. The company serves computer, medical, telecom, and other sectors. | 831-464-1111 | 1-10 | Soquel |
| Crcdj Llc (HQ) | Provider of shaped bags and pouches. The company's services include rotary die cutting, steel rule die cutting, and micro-form and fill. | 408-855-8909 | NA | San Jose |
| Crown Manufacturing Company Inc (HQ) | Provider of plastic and injection molded products. The company offers insert and over molding, drilling, tapping, and heat stamping services. | 510-742-8800 | NA | Newark |
| Diamond Tool & Die Inc (HQ) | Provider of general machine services for the high tech industry. The company serves the aerospace, construction, and food processing industries. | 510-534-7050 | NA | Oakland |
| Fastening Systems International Inc (HQ) | Supplier of blind fasteners and blind rivet installation tools. The company offers rivet guns, rivet nuts, pop rivets, and more. | 707-935-1170 | NA | Sonoma |
| Finishline Advanced Composites (HQ) | Provider of composite repair services for production projects. The company is involved in design, development, prototyping, testing, and production. | 707-747-0788 | NA | Benicia |
| Foamlinx Llc (HQ) | Provider of foam cutting computer numerical control machines. The company offers cutters, shredders, compactors, and cutting services. | 408-454-6163 | NA | Sunnyvale |
| Gambit Corp (HQ) | Provider of engineering parts and services. The company specializes in designing and building tools and dies. | 707-588-2797 | NA | Rohnert Park |

| COMPANY NAME | PRODUCT / SERVICE | PHONE | EMP | CITY |
|---|---|---|---|---|
| Gm Nameplate Inc (BR) | Manufacturer of die cut components. The company offers components for shielding, insulators, adhesives, and fabricated parts. | 408-435-1666 | NA | San Jose |
| Grandt Line Products (HQ) | Manufacturer and wholesaler of model railroad miniatures in plastics. The company's services include design and installation. | 925-671-0143 | NA | Concord |
| Heco Inc (HQ) | Manufacturer of planetary speed reducers. The company's applications include swing drives, wheel drives, conveyor drives, winch drives, mixers, and augers. | 916-372-5411 | 1-10 | West Sacramento |
| Hiebert Sculpture Works (HQ) | Provider of plastic injection molding products. The company also offers composite epoxy tooling, design assistance, and custom molds. | 510-654-7488 | NA | Oakland |
| Jatco Inc (HQ) | Manufactuer of plastic products. The company offers molding, tooling, quality control, and warehousing and distribution services. | 510-487-0888 | NA | Union City |
| Kaman Industrial Technologies (BR) | Provider of industrial technology solutions. The company's portfolio comprises bearings, gearing, linear motion, and power transmission products. | 650-589-6800 | NA | Union City |
| Kearney Pattern Works & Foundry (HQ) | Provider of pattern works and foundry services. The company's services include heat treating, plating, machining, and casting finish. | 408-293-7414 | NA | San Jose |
| Malaster Company Inc (HQ) | Provider of packing materials. The company specializes in offering package and shipping solutions for semiconductor industries. | 877-625-2783 | NA | Santa Clara |
| Minitool Inc (HQ) | Manufacturer of precision instruments and small tools for microscopic investigation. The company also specializes in under-microscope precision tools. | 408-395-1585 | NA | Campbell |
| Morgan Manufacturing Inc (HQ) | Manufacturer of autobody tools and tie-down equipment. The company caters to the flat bed trucking industry. | 707-763-6848 | NA | Petaluma |
| Mos Plastics Inc (HQ) | Provider of precision injection-molding, contract manufacturing, and assembly services for medical and electronics OEMs. | 408-944-9407 | NA | San Jose |
| Pacific Die Cut Industries (HQ) | Provider of custom converting services that include die cutting, laminating, and slitting. The company also offers packaging solutions. | 510-732-8103 | NA | Hayward |
| Pacmold (HQ) | Designer and manufacturer of plastic injection molds. The company has production facilities in Taiwan and China. | 510-785-9882 | NA | Hayward |
| Parmatech Corp (HQ) | Supplier of metal injection molding components. The company serves the automotive, medical, industrial, and electronics industries. | 707-778-2266 | NA | Petaluma |
| PCC Structurals Inc (BR) | Manufacturer of complex metal components and products. The company caters to industrial and aerospace applications. | 510-568-6400 | NA | San Leandro |
| Precision Metal Tooling Inc (HQ) | Manufacturer of production tool and die manufacturing products. The company also focuses on prototype tooling, tool engineering, and custom tooling. | 510-436-0900 | NA | Oakland |
| Silicon Microstructures Inc (HQ) | Developer and manufacturer of MEMS-based pressure sensors. The company's products are used in medical, industrial, and automotive applications. | 408-577-0100 | NA | Milpitas |
| Sjc Precision Inc (HQ) | Provider of precision machining and tool and die making services. The company designs and manufactures jigs, fixtures, and bookmolds. | 408-262-1680 | NA | Milpitas |
| Sks Diecasting & Machining (HQ) | Manufacturer of aluminum die cast parts and related supplies. The company offers services to the high tech industry. | 510-523-2541 | NA | Alameda |
| Solonics Inc (HQ) | Manufacturer of coded backboard systems and wire management products. The company focuses on design and delivery services. | 510-471-7600 | NA | Hayward |
| Sp3 Diamond Technologies (HQ) | Provider of electronics thermal management, diamond-on-silicon applications, and enhanced cutting surface solutions. | 408-492-0630 | NA | Santa Clara |
| Stack Plastics Inc (HQ) | Provider of plastic injection molding services. The company offers thermoplastics, elastomers, and resins. | 650-361-8600 | NA | Menlo Park |
| Sunset Moulding Co (HQ) | Provider of molding and millwork products. The company offers products such as interior jambs, board products, and shelving. | 530-790-2700 | 1-10 | Yuba City |
| Teknika Strapping Systems (HQ) | Provider of hand tools for plastic stripping. The company is engaged in repairs, replacement, and maintenance services. | 408-441-9071 | NA | San Jose |
| United Sheetmetal Inc (BR) | Manufacturer of precision metal products. The company specializes in tooling, die casting, plastic injection, and sheet metal fabrication services. | 510-257-1858 | NA | Fremont |
| Westec Plastics Corp (HQ) | Provider of plastics injection molding and mold making services. The company also offers customized services. | 925-454-3400 | NA | Livermore |
| Westport Machine Works Inc (HQ) | Manufacturer of assembly and balancing equipment. The company's services include fixturing, installation, and technical support. | 916-371-4493 | 1-10 | West Sacramento |
| Wunder Mold (HQ) | Provider of ceramic injection molding services. The company designs and produces art molded ceramics for appliances and electronics applications. | 707-448-2349 | NA | Vacaville |

## 64 = Speed Changers

| | | | | |
|---|---|---|---|---|
| Heco Inc (HQ) | Manufacturer of planetary speed reducers. The company's applications include swing drives, wheel drives, conveyor drives, winch drives, mixers, and augers. | 916-372-5411 | 1-10 | West Sacramento |

## 65 = Vacuum Products & Systems

| COMPANY NAME | PRODUCT / SERVICE | PHONE | EMP | CITY |
|---|---|---|---|---|
| Agile Thermal Technologies Inc (HQ) | Designer of industrial vacuum and atmosphere systems. The company also provides procurement, program management, and prime contractor capabilities. | 707-570-0304 | NA | Santa Rosa |
| Ags Plasma Systems Inc (HQ) | Manufacturer and distributor of vacuum plasma systems. The company serves microelectronics and optoelectronics industries. | 408-855-8686 | NA | Santa Clara |
| Anatech Usa (HQ) | Provider of high vacuum systems with plasma technology. The company's applications include flip chips, multichip modules, and photoresist strips. | 510-401-5990 | NA | Union City |
| Ascentool (HQ) | Designer, manufacturer, and marketer of vacuum thin-film deposition systems for making solar photovoltaic devices. | 510-683-9332 | NA | Fremont |
| Brechtel Manufacturing Inc (HQ) | Provider of aerosol solutions to the government, academic, and corporate sectors. The company also supplies vacuum brazing furnaces and leak valves. | 510-732-9723 | NA | Hayward |
| Brooks Automation Inc (BR) | Provider of automation, vacuum, and instrumentation solutions for the semiconductor manufacturing, life sciences, and clean energy industries. | 510-661-5000 | NA | Fremont |
| Duniway Stockroom Corp (HQ) | Supplier of vacuum equipment. The company offers ion, diffusion, and mechanical pumps, and valves to the industrial sector. | 650-969-8811 | NA | Fremont |
| Finishline Advanced Composites (HQ) | Provider of composite repair services for production projects. The company is involved in design, development, prototyping, testing, and production. | 707-747-0788 | NA | Benicia |
| Ksm Corp (DH) | Manufacturer of welded metal bellows for transportation, solar, pharmaceutical, and other sectors and provides build to print assembly services. | 408-514-2400 | NA | San Jose |
| Malaster Company Inc (HQ) | Provider of packing materials. The company specializes in offering package and shipping solutions for semiconductor industries. | 877-625-2783 | NA | Santa Clara |
| Marvac Scientific Manufacturing Co (HQ) | Provider of industrial grade belt drive vacuum pumps. The company also offers cooling system and other tools. | 925-825-4636 | NA | Concord |
| Mcintire Machine Inc (HQ) | Provider of precision machining, welding, and fabrication services. The company offers services to the industrial sector. | 209-837-4409 | 1-10 | Crows Landing |
| Nor-Cal Products Inc (HQ) | Provider of fabricating solutions for stainless steel flanges, fittings, and components. The company's services include welding, machining, and forming. | 530-842-4457 | 11-50 | Yreka |
| Plasma Technology Systems Llc (HQ) | Provider of equipment and process development services for plasma treatment of surfaces. The company specializes in modification of polymers. | 650-596-1606 | NA | Hayward |
| Sardee Industries Inc (BR) | Provider of container manufacturing equipment. The company also offers engineering and repair services for packing and filling industries. | 209-466-1526 | 11-50 | Stockton |
| SMC Corporation of America (BR) | Provider of in pneumatic technology solutions that are used in diverse range of industries from automotive to lifescience. | 408-943-9600 | NA | San Jose |
| SuperKlean (HQ) | Manufacturer of spray nozzles and swivel fittings. The company also offers hot & cold water mixing stations and hose racks. | 650-375-7001 | NA | Burlingame |
| Terminal Manufacturing Company Llc (HQ) | Designer and manufacturer of vacuum chambers, pressure vessels, truck tanks, and assorted fabrications. | 510-526-3071 | NA | Berkeley |
| Transfer Engineering & Manufacturing Inc (HQ) | Manufacturer and marketer of loadlocks and transfer systems. The company offers precision magnetic manipulators and transporters, and other products. | 510-651-3000 | NA | Fremont |
| Trayer Engineering Corp (HQ) | Manufacturer of electronic distribution switchgears. The company's services include design, maintenance, and installation. | 415-285-7770 | NA | San Francisco |
| Vacuum Process Engineering Inc (HQ) | Provider of engineering services. The company focuses on precision brazing, diffusion bonding, heat treating, and production of precision assemblies. | 916-925-6100 | 1-10 | Sacramento |

## 166 = Valves

| COMPANY NAME | PRODUCT / SERVICE | PHONE | EMP | CITY |
|---|---|---|---|---|
| Acro Associates Inc (HQ) | Manufacturer and designer of pinch valves and fluid control components for the medical, bioprocessing and industrial markets. | 925-676-8828 | NA | Concord |
| Ats Inc (HQ) | Manufacturer of fiberglass duct work for fume exhaust systems. The company offers installation and other related services. | 510-234-3173 | NA | Richmond |
| Bowsmith Inc (HQ) | Provider of micro-irrigation equipment for agriculture, landscape, greenhouse, and heap leach mining. The company offers drip emitters and sprinklers. | 559-592-9485 | 11-50 | Exeter |
| Campbell/Harris Security Equipment Company (HQ) | Manufacturer of busters, fiberscopes, probe kits, and personal radiation detectors. The company also focuses on distribution. | 510-864-8010 | NA | Alameda |
| Conval Inc (BR) | Manufacturer of pressure forged steel valves. The company products include globe valves, ball valves, and strainers. | 530-877-5172 | 11-50 | Paradise |
| Finishline Advanced Composites (HQ) | Provider of composite repair services for production projects. The company is involved in design, development, prototyping, testing, and production. | 707-747-0788 | NA | Benicia |
| Fresno Valves & Castings Inc (HQ) | Provider of water control devices used in irrigation applications. The company's products include valves, filters, air vents, fittings, gates, and lifts. | 559-834-2511 | 11-50 | Selma |
| Fujikin of America Inc (RH) | Manufacturer of fluid and gas flow valves and fittings. The company also offers process equipment control systems. | 408-980-8269 | NA | Fremont |

| COMPANY NAME | PRODUCT / SERVICE | PHONE | EMP | CITY |
|---|---|---|---|---|
| Gerlinger Steel & Supply Co (HQ) | Provider of metal products and industrial services. The company offers metalworking machinery and supplies. | 530-243-1053 | 1-10 | Redding |
| IDEX Health & Science LLC (BR) | Provider of precision equipment for the health care industry. The company also offers detectors, fittings, and filters. | 707-588-2000 | NA | Rohnert Park |
| Inoxpa Usa Inc (HQ) | Manufacturer and trader of pumps and components. The company caters to industries like food processing, dairy, wine-making, and cosmetics. | 707-585-3900 | NA | Santa Rosa |
| Mclellan Industries Inc (HQ) | Manufacturer of stainless steel and mild steel tanks, hook lifts, tank kits, and related accessories. | 559-582-8100 | 11-50 | Hanford |
| Microchek Inc (HQ) | Manufacturer of check valves and self-activating safety valves. The company's products include a diverse variety of valves. | 209-333-5253 | 11-50 | Lodi |
| Morrill Industries Inc (HQ) | Manufacturer and supplier of irrigation equipment. The company also offers custom built rotating suction screens and industrial pipes. | 209-838-2550 | 1-10 | Escalon |
| Nor-Cal Products Inc (HQ) | Provider of fabricating solutions for stainless steel flanges, fittings, and components. The company's services include welding, machining, and forming. | 530-842-4457 | 11-50 | Yreka |
| Plug-It Products (HQ) | Provider of in-house products for the municipalities, maintenance contractors, underground contractors, and rental companies. | 209-334-4904 | 11-50 | Lodi |
| Process Engineers Inc (HQ) | Manufacturer of stainless steel equipment. The company also specializes in installation and other services. | 510-782-5122 | NA | Hayward |
| Proco Products Inc (HQ) | Manufacturer of expansion joints. The company serves the oil and gas, power generation, chemical, and steel industries. | 209-943-6088 | 1-10 | Stockton |
| SAGE Instruments Inc (RH) | Provider of wireless base station test products. The company offers battery operated handhelds, portables, bench tops, and rackmount test platforms. | 831-761-1000 | 11-50 | Freedom |
| Smart Products Inc (HQ) | Supplier of engineering products. The company offers valves, fittings, and pumps for the automotive, medical, and water treatment markets. | 800-338-0404 | NA | Morgan Hill |
| SMC Corporation of America (BR) | Provider of in pneumatic technology solutions that are used in diverse range of industries from automotive to lifescience. | 408-943-9600 | NA | San Jose |
| SuperKlean (HQ) | Manufacturer of spray nozzles and swivel fittings. The company also offers hot & cold water mixing stations and hose racks. | 650-375-7001 | NA | Burlingame |
| T&T Valve & Instrument Inc (HQ) | Provider of manual and automated valves to industrial, municipal water, and wastewater industries. The company focuses on project assistance. | 925-484-4898 | NA | Pleasanton |
| Transitional Systems Manufacturing Inc (HQ) | Provider of products to repair landscape sprinkler systems. The company also focuses on installation needs. | 530-751-2610 | 1-10 | Browns Valley |
| Varna Products (HQ) | Manufacturer of pump and valve solutions. The company offers oil pumps, pump controls, pressure relief valves, and check valves. | 530-676-7770 | 1-10 | Cameron Park |
| Waterman Industries (HQ) | Designer and manufacturer of water-control sluice gates, penstocks, valves, and water control products. | 559-562-4000 | 11-50 | Exeter |

## 168 = Cameras & Related Equipment

| COMPANY NAME | PRODUCT / SERVICE | PHONE | EMP | CITY |
|---|---|---|---|---|
| Appro Technology Inc (BR) | Manufacturer of network surveillance systems. The company's products include dome cameras, LCD monitors, and cables. | 408-720-0018 | NA | Sunnyvale |
| Atn Corp (HQ) | Developer and manufacturer of precision night optics and thermal imaging solutions. The company serves law enforcement and military clients. | 650-989-5100 | NA | S San Francisco |
| Boly Media Communications Inc (HQ) | Supplier of trail cameras and security cameras. The company also specializes in ultrasonic motors and optical zooms. | 408-533-0207 | NA | Santa Clara |
| Cirrus Digital Systems (HQ) | Developer of single and multi-camera mapping systems for NASA applications and high altitude manned and unmanned aircraft needs. | 415-608-9420 | NA | Tiburon |
| Fairchild Imaging Inc (DH) | Developer and manufacturer of solid-state electronic imaging components, cameras, and systems. The company's products include image sensors and cameras. | 650-479-5749 | NA | San Jose |
| Foveon Inc (HQ) | Innovator of design and development of image sensors and image capture systems for a wide range of digital capture products. | 408-855-6800 | NA | San Jose |
| LG Display America Inc (BR) | Manufacturer of thin-film transistor liquid crystal display panels. The company is also focused on OLEDs and flexible displays. | 408-350-0190 | NA | San Jose |
| Meraki LLC (BR) | Provider of branch networking solutions. The company offers services to the education, retail, and healthcare industries. | 415-432-1000 | NA | San Francisco |
| Motion Analysis Corp (HQ) | Provider of motion analyzers. The company specializes in engineering, animation, design, reality augmentation, and simulation services. | 707-579-6500 | NA | Rohnert Park |
| Ocean Presence Technologies (HQ) | Manufacturer of underwater video monitoring camera systems and offers cable systems, power systems, lighting, wireless networks, and accessories. | 831-426-4678 | 1-10 | Santa Cruz |
| OJO Technology Inc (HQ) | Manufacturer of video surveillance systems. The company offers services to the education, transportation, and utility sectors. | 877-306-4656 | NA | Fremont |
| Pelco Inc (HQ) | Manufacturer of closed circuit TV cameras and accessories. The company's services include training, engineering, and technical development. | 559-292-1981 | 11-50 | Clovis |
| Pragmatic Communications Systems Inc (HQ) | Designer, developer, and manufacturer of pragmatic products. The company offers amplifiers, security cameras, speakers, and wireless products. | 408-748-1100 | NA | Santa Clara |
| Seiwa Optical America Inc (HQ) | Manufacturer of optical components and photonic integrated circuits. The company offers network and access solutions. | 408-844-8008 | NA | Santa Clara |

| COMPANY NAME | PRODUCT / SERVICE | PHONE | EMP | CITY |
|---|---|---|---|---|
| Sightech Vision Systems (HQ) | Manufacturer of industrial vision systems. The company offers quality vision systems, hard disk inspection, and crimp verification services. | 408-282-3770 | NA | Santa Clara |
| TOA Electronics Inc (DH) | Developer and manufacturer of audio and security products. The company is engaged in design, delivery, and installation services. | 650-452-1200 | 51-200 | S San Francisco |
| Uniq Vision Inc (HQ) | Designer and manufacturer of high resolution CCD cameras for medical, scientific, industrial, and military applications. | 408-330-0818 | NA | Santa Clara |
| Videofax (HQ) | Manufacturer of cameras, recorders, players, and related accessories. The company offers technical support services. | 415-641-0100 | NA | San Francisco |
| Vivotek Usa (BR) | Provider of surveillance solutions. The company specializes in manufacturing network cameras for the network video surveillance industries. | 408-773-8686 | NA | San Jose |
| X-Scan Imaging Corp (HQ) | Supplier of x-ray imaging and inspection equipment. The company also offers array detectors and line-scan camera products. | 408-432-9888 | NA | San Jose |

## 169 = Displays

| COMPANY NAME | PRODUCT / SERVICE | PHONE | EMP | CITY |
|---|---|---|---|---|
| Advanced Witness Series Inc (HQ) | Designer of electrical and mechanical components and tools. The company caters to various applications. | 408-453-5070 | NA | San Jose |
| Arista Corp (HQ) | Manufacturer of industrial computer products such as industrial rack mounts, touch screen displays, and fanless, embedded, and wallmount computers. | 510-226-1800 | NA | Fremont |
| Cirrus Systems Inc (HQ) | Provider of display solutions for restaurants, education, church, financial, medical, automotive, and professional services. | 877-636-2331 | 11-50 | Petaluma |
| CLEARink Displays Inc (RH) | Developer of reflective display modules for wearables, smart phones/tablets, electronic shelf labels, and outdoor signage. | 510-624-9305 | NA | Fremont |
| Digital View Inc (HQ) | Developer and manufacturer of flat panel-related products. The company's offerings include media players, video flyers, and accessories. | 408-782-7773 | NA | Morgan Hill |
| Hantronix Inc (HQ) | Producer of standard character and graphic modules, notebook displays, and custom liquid crystal displays. | 408-252-1100 | NA | Cupertino |
| I-Tech Company Llc (HQ) | Manufacturer of panel mounts, server racks, industrial computers, touch screen displays, and related accessories. | 510-226-9226 | NA | Fremont |
| Kateeva Inc (HQ) | Manufacturer of LED and other display products. The company specializes in the design and fabrication of OLED displays. | 800-385-7802 | NA | Newark |
| Kopin Corp (BR) | Developer of semi-conducting solutions. The company develops cloud computing, hands-free technology, and wireless usage in headset computers. | 831-430-0688 | 11-50 | Scotts Valley |
| LG Display America Inc (BR) | Manufacturer of thin-film transistor liquid crystal display panels. The company is also focused on OLEDs and flexible displays. | 408-350-0190 | NA | San Jose |
| Medland & Associates Inc (BR) | Manufacturer of OEM products. The company's products include AC and DC converters, power supplies, switching regulators, and cable assemblies. | 408-686-0460 | NA | San Martin |
| Nanosys Inc (HQ) | Developer of nanotechnology products for the LCD display and battery markets. The company focuses on display backlighting and energy storage devices. | 408-240-6700 | NA | Milpitas |
| Nds Surgical Imaging (HQ) | Provider of medical imaging services. The company specializes in minimal invasive surgery viewing and diagnostic imaging. | 408-776-0085 | NA | San Jose |
| New Vision Display Inc (HQ) | Provider of display products. The company's products include LCD modules, TFT LCD and touch products. | 916-786-8111 | 1-10 | Roseville |
| Pragmatic Communications Systems Inc (HQ) | Designer, developer, and manufacturer of pragmatic products. The company offers amplifiers, security cameras, speakers, and wireless products. | 408-748-1100 | NA | Santa Clara |
| Prysm Inc (HQ) | Provider of large format digital display solutions and software for real-time visual communication applications. | 408-586-1100 | NA | San Jose |
| RAF Electronics (HQ) | Provider of optical system design and related services. The company deals with sales and delivery solutions. | 925-551-5361 | NA | San Ramon |
| Rishang LED Inc (LH) | Manufacturer of LED products for decorative and green lighting solutions. The company's products are used in the residential and commercial sectors. | 408-748-8889 | NA | Santa Clara |
| Sensing Electromagnetic Plus Corp (HQ) | Developer of third touch dimension in human-machine interfaces. The company offers unobtrusive pressure sensitive solutions. | 415-954-0322 | NA | Palo Alto |
| Sharp Microelectronics Of The Americas (BR) | Provider of LCD, optoelectronics, imagers, and RF components. The company is involved in design and installation services. | 408-452-6400 | 11-50 | San Jose |
| Silicon Mitus (BR) | Manufacturer and distributor of smart power management integrated chips solutions. The company focuses on power solutions. | 408-446-3151 | NA | Cupertino |

## 170 = Fiber Optic Cables/Equipment

| COMPANY NAME | PRODUCT / SERVICE | PHONE | EMP | CITY |
|---|---|---|---|---|
| Ac Photonics Inc (HQ) | Manufacturer of custom-made precision optical components. The company also offers fiber optic components and modules. | 408-986-9838 | NA | Santa Clara |
| Ag Microsystems Inc (HQ) | Provider of testing and development in the areas of micro electro mechanical systems and micro optics. | 408-834-4888 | NA | Santa Clara |
| Aria Technologies Inc (HQ) | Provider of fiber optic cable assemblies and connectivity products to the data, telecom, and operator market places. | 925-447-7500 | NA | Livermore |

| COMPANY NAME | PRODUCT / SERVICE | PHONE | EMP | CITY |
|---|---|---|---|---|
| Calmar Laser (HQ) | Manufacturer of ultrafast fiber laser and fiber amplifier solutions for the needs of industry, research institutions, and universities. | 650-272-6980 | NA | Palo Alto |
| Dicon Fiberoptics Inc (HQ) | Supplier of optical components, integrated modules, and test equipment for the fiber optics industry. | 510-620-5000 | NA | Richmond |
| Fibera Inc (HQ) | Manufacturer and designer of wavelength management products. The company also specializes in fiber optic products. | 408-492-9555 | NA | Santa Clara |
| Ifos (HQ) | Developer of optical fiber sensing system level products. The company's products are used for monitoring and control of temperature and acoustic emission. | 408-565-9000 | NA | Santa Clara |
| Neptec Optical Solutions Inc (HQ) | Provider of quick-turn fiber optic connectivity solutions. The company also offers connector reconditioning, switches, and fiber arrays. | 510-687-1101 | NA | Fremont |
| Nortra Cables Inc (HQ) | Provider of discrete and flat mechanical assembly cables. The company offers design, prototyping, and manufacturing services. | 408-942-1106 | NA | Milpitas |
| Oplink Communications Inc (HQ) | Provider of comprehensive networking components. The company offers products for amplification, interconnection, routing, and other needs. | 510-933-7200 | NA | Fremont |
| Optiworks Inc (HQ) | Manufacturer of fiber optic components. The company's products include thin film filters, fused components, sub components, and accessories. | 510-438-4560 | NA | Fremont |
| Optowaves Inc (HQ) | Manufacturer and supplier of passive fiber optic components, attenuator, coupler, and isolator for the medical and communication industries. | 408-724-5888 | NA | San Jose |
| Pacific Coast Optics Inc (HQ) | Provider of optical products, services and applications. The company offers prototype, polishing, grinding, and coating. | 916-789-0111 | 1-10 | Roseville |
| Pactech Inc (HQ) | Provider of computer cables, cooling items, and other components. The company also offers networking products. | 408-526-9363 | NA | San Jose |
| SPI Lasers LLC (BR) | Designer and manufacturer of fiber lasers for systems integrators, factory automation specialists, job shops, OEMs, and other academic institutions. | 408-454-1170 | NA | Santa Clara |
| Sumitomo Electric Device Innovations Usa Inc (LH) | Developer of electronic devices that includes wireless devices, optical data links, and optical devices. | 408-232-9500 | NA | San Jose |
| Thinkoptics (HQ) | Provider of software solutions. The company's products include iWavit Blast, iWavit Premium, iWavit Basic, and Wavit 3D. | 765-889-2848 | NA | San Jose |
| USAPEX (HQ) | Manufacturer of fiber optic products, metal and plastic machined parts, lead free solder pastes, liquid flux, power adapters, cables, and connectors. | 408-730-9800 | NA | Sunnyvale |
| Valdor Fiber Optics Inc (RH) | Provider of product design and development services of fiber optic products such as connectors, attenuators, couplers, splitters, and multiplexers. | 510-293-1212 | NA | Hayward |
| Vsp Optics Group (HQ) | Provider of eye care solutions. The company offers eye care insurance, eyewear, lenses, ophthalmic technology and retail solutions. | 800-852-7600 | 11-50 | Rancho Cordova |

## 171 = Laser Measuring/Scanning/Aligning Equipment

| COMPANY NAME | PRODUCT / SERVICE | PHONE | EMP | CITY |
|---|---|---|---|---|
| BMI Imaging Systems Inc (BR) | Provider of document management services. The company offers document scanning and hosting, system integration, and microfilm conversion services. | 800-359-3456 | 11-50 | Sacramento |
| Cutera Inc (HQ) | Manufacturer of aesthetic solutions such as face and body laser, light, and other energy-based aesthetic systems for hair removal and pigmented lesions. | 415-657-5500 | NA | Brisbane |
| Directed Light Inc (HQ) | Manufacturer of industrial and scientific laser components. The company offers laser welding, cutting, drilling, ablation, and marking services. | 408-321-8500 | NA | San Jose |
| Exatron Inc (HQ) | Manufacturer of automatic test equipment and IC handlers. The company also specializes in open short testers. | 408-629-7600 | NA | San Jose |
| Laserline Inc (BR) | Manufacturer of diode lasers for welding metals and plastics. The company also deals with cladding, hardening, and brazing. | 844-441-3691 | NA | Santa Clara |
| Macken Instruments Inc (HQ) | Manufacturer of devices for measuring and analyzing laser device power output. The company offers laser power & beam probes and thermal image plates. | 707-566-2110 | NA | Santa Rosa |
| Process Metrix Corp (BR) | Supplier of instruments for industrial measurement and control. The company's products are used in molten metal applications. | 925-460-0385 | NA | Pleasanton |

## 172 = Lasers/Laser Related Equipment

| COMPANY NAME | PRODUCT / SERVICE | PHONE | EMP | CITY |
|---|---|---|---|---|
| Applied Spectra Inc (HQ) | Manufacturer of analytical instrumentation. The company's products include J200 Tandem, J200 Femtosecond, Laser Ablation System, and Aurora LIBS Spectrometer. | 510-657-7679 | NA | Fremont |
| Artium Technologies Inc (HQ) | Developer of products for spray diagnostics, particulate monitoring, and cloud research applications. | 408-737-2364 | NA | Sunnyvale |
| ArtNet Pro Inc (HQ) | Provider of reused equipment. The company offers direct imaging systems, laser photo plotters, and scanners. | 408-954-8383 | NA | San Jose |
| Blue Sky Research Inc (HQ) | Manufacturer of laser products and micro optics. The company designs and fabricates semiconductor based lasers and fiber optic cables. | 408-941-6068 | NA | Milpitas |
| Calmar Laser (HQ) | Manufacturer of ultrafast fiber laser and fiber amplifier solutions for the needs of industry, research institutions, and universities. | 650-272-6980 | NA | Palo Alto |

| COMPANY NAME | PRODUCT / SERVICE | PHONE | EMP | CITY |
|---|---|---|---|---|
| CHECKPOiNT Technologies (HQ) | Manufacturer of optical failure analysis tools such as laser scanning microscopy, photon emission, infrascan, and solid immersion lens objectives. | 408-321-9780 | NA | San Jose |
| Coherent Inc (HQ) | Manufacturer of optics and laser instruments. The company serves the medical and research industries. | 408-764-4000 | NA | Santa Clara |
| Cutera Inc (HQ) | Manufacturer of aesthetic solutions such as face and body laser, light, and other energy-based aesthetic systems for hair removal and pigmented lesions. | 415-657-5500 | NA | Brisbane |
| Dataray Inc (HQ) | Supplier of performance beam profiling products to the photonics community. The company provides BladeCam, Beam Scope, Phase Pro, and UV converters. | 866-946-2263 | 1-10 | Redding |
| Dpss Lasers Inc (HQ) | Manufacturer of high power, short wavelength solid state lasers for industrial, scientific, and research applications. | 408-988-4300 | NA | Santa Clara |
| Ellex iScience Inc (BR) | Developer and provider of technology solutions for the treatment of eye conditions. The company products include tango, eye one, eye cubed, tango reflex, and more. | 510-291-1300 | NA | Fremont |
| Femtochrome Research Inc (HQ) | Manufacturer of instruments for characterization of ultrafast laser pulses focusing on nonlinear crystal and two-photon conductivity autocorrelators. | 510-644-1869 | NA | Berkeley |
| General Lasertronics Corp (HQ) | Developer of scanning and control technologies that make laser ablation an alternative to traditional abrasives and solvents for removing coatings. | 408-947-1181 | NA | San Jose |
| Healthstar Laser Services Inc (HQ) | Provider of web-based scheduling and mobile laser services. The company serves the healthcare sector. | 415-937-1942 | NA | Lafayette |
| Imra America Inc (BR) | Developer and manufacturer of fiber lasers. The company's products are used in cutting, drilling, welding, and thin-film removal applications. | 510-623-3507 | NA | Fremont |
| Ipg Photonics (BR) | Provider of high power fiber lasers and amplifiers. The company's offerings include Q-switch lasers, multi-mode diodes, pulsed and direct-diode lasers. | 408-492-8830 | NA | Santa Clara |
| Laser Mark's Co (HQ) | Provider of laser marking and engraving job shop services. The company serves the agriculture, food processing, automotive, and medical industries. | 408-433-9333 | NA | San Jose |
| Laser Reference Inc (HQ) | Supplier of laser level products for interior and outdoor construction focusing on laser receivers and accessories including telescopic laser tripods. | 408-361-0220 | NA | San Jose |
| Laserline Inc (BR) | Manufacturer of diode lasers for welding metals and plastics. The company also deals with cladding, hardening, and brazing. | 844-441-3691 | NA | Santa Clara |
| Lazestar Inc (HQ) | Provider of laser sealing, packing, precision fabrication, and welding services. The company serves the aerospace and commercial industries. | 925-443-5293 | NA | Livermore |
| Leica Geosystems HDS LLC (RH) | Manufacturer of surveying hardware and software solutions for measuring and modeling sites and structures with high accuracy, detail, speed, and safety. | 925-790-2300 | NA | San Ramon |
| Lumeras LLC (HQ) | Developer and manufacturer of short-wavelength laser sources for materials characterization and chemical and biological analysis. | 650-575-7448 | 1-10 | Santa Cruz |
| Macken Instruments Inc (HQ) | Manufacturer of devices for measuring and analyzing laser device power output. The company offers laser power & beam probes and thermal image plates. | 707-566-2110 | NA | Santa Rosa |
| Microform Precision Llc (HQ) | Provider of metal cutting, bending, fabrication, and coating services. The company offers shearing, punching, forming, and painting services. | 916-419-0580 | 1-10 | Sacramento |
| Modern Ceramics Manufacturing Inc (HQ) | Supplier of ceramic materials and components. The company serves the semi-conductor and laser industries. | 408-383-0554 | NA | San Jose |
| Nuvolase Inc (HQ) | Manufacturer of the pinpointe foot laser used for the treatment of nail fungus and in nail fungus procedures. | 530-809-1970 | 1-10 | Chico |
| Onyx Optics Inc (HQ) | Manufacturer of laser and telecom composite crystals and glasses. The company also offers products for optical finishing and other needs. | 925-833-1969 | NA | Dublin |
| Oxigraf Inc (HQ) | Supplier of oxygen analyzers & oxygen gas concentration measurement products. The company offers laser diode oxygen analyzers and OEM oxygen sensors. | 650-237-0155 | NA | Sunnyvale |
| Pavilion Integration Corp (HQ) | Designer and manufacturer of lasers, laser modules and subsystems for instrumentation. The company serves the industrial market. | 408-453-8801 | NA | San Jose |
| Shasta Crystals Inc (HQ) | Producer of nonlinear optical crystals for visible lasers. The company's services include research and evaluation. | 415-426-7904 | NA | San Francisco |
| Spectra-Physics (RH) | Provider of precision laser technology services. The company's products include ultrafast lasers, fiber lasers, and tunable lasers. | 408-980-4300 | NA | Santa Clara |
| Spectralus Corp (HQ) | Developer of green laser sources. The company primarily caters to the need of mobile projection applications. | 408-516-4870 | NA | Santa Clara |
| SPI Lasers LLC (BR) | Designer and manufacturer of fiber lasers for systems integrators, factory automation specialists, job shops, OEMs, and other academic institutions. | 408-454-1170 | NA | Santa Clara |
| Stanford Research Systems (HQ) | Manufacturer of electronic instruments, optical choppers, and temperature controllers for the research industry. | 408-744-9040 | NA | Sunnyvale |

| COMPANY NAME | PRODUCT / SERVICE | PHONE | EMP | CITY |
|---|---|---|---|---|
| Sumitomo Electric Device Innovations Usa Inc (LH) | Developer of electronic devices that includes wireless devices, optical data links, and optical devices. | 408-232-9500 | NA | San Jose |

## 173 = Lenses

| COMPANY NAME | PRODUCT / SERVICE | PHONE | EMP | CITY |
|---|---|---|---|---|
| Applied Optics Inc (HQ) | Provider of precision optical components and custom optics. The company is engaged in delivery and installation services. | 925-932-5686 | NA | Pleasant Hill |
| Atn Corp (HQ) | Developer and manufacturer of precision night optics and thermal imaging solutions. The company serves law enforcement and military clients. | 650-989-5100 | NA | S San Francisco |
| Carter Contact Lens Inc (HQ) | Manufacturer of contact lenses. The company product range include crescent bifocal, target bifocal, front bifocal, and keratoconic designs. | 559-294-7063 | 1-10 | Clovis |
| Crystal River Optics (HQ) | Provider of custom fabrication services of optical components. The company is engaged in prototyping and offers technical support. | 925-371-1309 | NA | Livermore |
| ICU Eyewear (HQ) | Manufacturer of reading eye-wear and sunglasses. The company provides metal half rim, polarized oval, and metal full aviator sunglasses. | 800-435-5747 | 1-10 | Hollister |
| Industrial Optics Unlimited (HQ) | Provider of optical services. The company is involved in fabricating optical components for both commercial and laser applications. | 530-365-1972 | 1-10 | Anderson |
| Micro Dicing Services (HQ) | Provider of sawing services. The company provides services to the microelectronic and optical industries. | 408-321-8840 | NA | San Jose |
| Mld Technologies Llc (HQ) | Supplier of optical coatings and components. The company specializes in the design, development, and manufacture of ion beam sputtered thin-films. | 650-938-3780 | NA | Mountain View |
| Nikon Precision Inc (HQ) | Manufacturer of optical lenses and precision equipment. The company is also the supplier of step-and-repeat and step-and-scan lithography systems. | 650-508-4674 | NA | Belmont |
| Precision Asphere Inc (HQ) | Provider of aspheric optical components fabrication services. The company offers optical surface forming, polishing, and metrology services. | 510-668-1508 | NA | Fremont |
| Seiwa Optical America Inc (HQ) | Manufacturer of optical components and photonic integrated circuits. The company offers network and access solutions. | 408-844-8008 | NA | Santa Clara |
| Sierra Precision Optics (HQ) | Manufacturer of optical products. The company's products include panels, mirrors, beam splitters, and cylindrical lenses. | 530-885-6979 | 1-10 | Auburn |
| The Cooper Companies Inc (HQ) | Provider of healthcare solutions. The company offers health and wellness programs for women, individuals, and communities. | 925-460-3600 | NA | Pleasanton |
| Vsp Optics Group (HQ) | Provider of eye care solutions. The company offers eye care insurance, eyewear, lenses, ophthalmic technology and retail solutions. | 800-852-7600 | 11-50 | Rancho Cordova |

## 174 = Microscopes/Telescopes

| COMPANY NAME | PRODUCT / SERVICE | PHONE | EMP | CITY |
|---|---|---|---|---|
| 3Scan (HQ) | Provider of automated microscopy services and supporting software for the 3D analysis of cells, tissues, and organs. | 415-851-5376 | NA | San Francisco |
| CHECKPOiNT Technologies (HQ) | Manufacturer of optical failure analysis tools such as laser scanning microscopy, photon emission, infrascan, and solid immersion lens objectives. | 408-321-9780 | NA | San Jose |
| Ellex iScience Inc (BR) | Developer and provider of technology solutions for the treatment of eye conditions. The company products include tango, eye one, eye cubed, tango reflex, and more. | 510-291-1300 | NA | Fremont |
| Labo America Inc (HQ) | Manufacturer and distributor of stereo, compound, surgical and digital microscopes, digital cameras and measuring software. | 510-445-1257 | NA | Fremont |
| Meiji Techno America (BR) | Manufacturer of optical microscope products. The company offers gemological, biological, and educational microscopes, and accessories. | 408-226-3454 | NA | San Jose |
| Seiwa Optical America Inc (HQ) | Manufacturer of optical components and photonic integrated circuits. The company offers network and access solutions. | 408-844-8008 | NA | Santa Clara |
| Stellarvue (HQ) | Designer and seller of refractor telescopes and telescope accessories. The company deals with design, delivery, and installation. | 530-823-7796 | 1-10 | Auburn |

## 175 = Optical Coatings

| COMPANY NAME | PRODUCT / SERVICE | PHONE | EMP | CITY |
|---|---|---|---|---|
| Deposition Sciences Inc (HQ) | Manufacturer of heat resistant, optical thin film coatings, including color control, metal, optical mirror, and beam splitter coatings. | 707-573-6700 | NA | Santa Rosa |
| Dicon Fiberoptics Inc (HQ) | Supplier of optical components, integrated modules, and test equipment for the fiber optics industry. | 510-620-5000 | NA | Richmond |
| Dominar Inc (HQ) | Provider of optical and semiconductor thin-film coating services. The company serves customers in Europe, Asia, and Australia. | 408-496-0508 | NA | Santa Clara |
| Foreal Spectrum Inc (HQ) | Provider of coating services for laser, biotech, and medical industries. The company also offers LED illumination and optical components. | 408-436-5558 | NA | San Jose |
| Ios Optics (HQ) | Manufacturer of custom precision optical components. The company offers coating and filter glass services. It serves avionics and life sciences fields. | 408-982-9510 | NA | Santa Clara |
| Micro Dicing Services (HQ) | Provider of sawing services. The company provides services to the microelectronic and optical industries. | 408-321-8840 | NA | San Jose |
| Pacific Coast Optics Inc (HQ) | Provider of optical products, services and applications. The company offers prototype, polishing, grinding, and coating. | 916-789-0111 | 1-10 | Roseville |
| RAF Electronics (HQ) | Provider of optical system design and related services. The company deals with sales and delivery solutions. | 925-551-5361 | NA | San Ramon |

| COMPANY NAME | PRODUCT / SERVICE | PHONE | EMP | CITY |
|---|---|---|---|---|
| Volume Precision Glass Inc (HQ) | Fabricator of optical components and thin-film coatings for photonics, military, industrial, and lighting applications. | 707-206-0100 | NA | Santa Rosa |

## 176 = Optical Scanners & Other Optoelectronic Devices

| COMPANY NAME | PRODUCT / SERVICE | PHONE | EMP | CITY |
|---|---|---|---|---|
| Ac Photonics Inc (HQ) | Manufacturer of custom-made precision optical components. The company also offers fiber optic components and modules. | 408-986-9838 | NA | Santa Clara |
| Avision Labs Inc (DH) | Designer and manufacturer of network and document scanners. The company specializes in sales and installation services. | 510-739-2369 | NA | Newark |
| Bayspec Inc (HQ) | Manufacturer of mass spectrometers, microscopes, hyperspectral imagers, and OEM spectral engines for biomedical, pharmaceuticals, and food industries. | 408-512-5928 | NA | San Jose |
| BMI Imaging Systems Inc (BR) | Provider of document management services. The company offers document scanning and hosting, system integration, and microfilm conversion services. | 800-359-3456 | 11-50 | Sacramento |
| Corning Technology Center (BR) | Provider of specialty glass and ceramics services and sells keystone components to electronics, mobile emissions control, and life science industries. | 650-846-6000 | NA | Sunnyvale |
| Dicon Fiberoptics Inc (HQ) | Supplier of optical components, integrated modules, and test equipment for the fiber optics industry. | 510-620-5000 | NA | Richmond |
| DigiLens Inc (HQ) | Provider of optical design, software development, electrical engineering, and illumination design services. | 408-734-0219 | NA | Sunnyvale |
| Enplas Tech Solutions Inc (RH) | Distributor of engineering plastic products. The company also offers optical devices, semiconductor peripherals, and related supplies. | 669-243-3600 | NA | Santa Clara |
| Equipment Solutions Inc (HQ) | Manufacturer and provider of actuators and motion control systems. The company offers optical scanners, servo amplifiers, and digital autocollimators. | 408-245-7162 | NA | Sunnyvale |
| Industrial Optics Unlimited (HQ) | Provider of optical services. The company is involved in fabricating optical components for both commercial and laser applications. | 530-365-1972 | 1-10 | Anderson |
| Infinera Corp (HQ) | Provider of services and solutions in optical networks. The company serves cable operators and internet content providers. | 408-572-5200 | NA | Sunnyvale |
| Intevac Inc (HQ) | Supplier of magnetic media processing systems. The company offers advanced equipment to the hard disk drive, solar, and photonics industries. | 408-986-9888 | NA | Santa Clara |
| Ios Optics (HQ) | Manufacturer of custom precision optical components. The company offers coating and filter glass services. It serves avionics and life sciences fields. | 408-982-9510 | NA | Santa Clara |
| Leica Geosystems HDS LLC (RH) | Manufacturer of surveying hardware and software solutions for measuring and modeling sites and structures with high accuracy, detail, speed, and safety. | 925-790-2300 | NA | San Ramon |
| Optical Structures Inc (HQ) | Provider of optical systems and services. The company's products find application in research and education sectors. | 916-638-2003 | 1-10 | Rancho Cordova |
| Pacific Coast Optics Inc (HQ) | Provider of optical products, services and applications. The company offers prototype, polishing, grinding, and coating. | 916-789-0111 | 1-10 | Roseville |
| Seiwa Optical America Inc (HQ) | Manufacturer of optical components and photonic integrated circuits. The company offers network and access solutions. | 408-844-8008 | NA | Santa Clara |
| Sharp Microelectronics Of The Americas (BR) | Provider of LCD, optoelectronics, imagers, and RF components. The company is involved in design and installation services. | 408-452-6400 | 11-50 | San Jose |
| Sight Sciences Inc (HQ) | Manufacturer and developer of surgical instruments and ophthalmic medical devices. The company serves the medical sector. | 415-889-0550 | NA | Menlo Park |
| Socket Mobile Inc (HQ) | Developer of wireless handheld and hands-free barcode scanners and other products and serves retail, logistics, automotive, and other sectors. | 510-933-3000 | NA | Newark |
| Us Night Vision Corp (HQ) | Provider of night vision, thermal imaging, infrared and laser products. The company serves law enforcement agencies and US military. | 800-500-4020 | 1-10 | Roseville |
| Visioneer Inc (HQ) | Marketer and distributor of digital imaging hardware devices. The company also offers related tools & utilities and power tools. | 925-251-6399 | NA | Pleasanton |
| Wavesplitter Technologies Inc (HQ) | Manufacturer of passive devices and active optical components for enterprise and residential broadband networks. | 925-596-0414 | NA | Fremont |
| Zygo Corp (BR) | Supplier of optical metrology instruments. The company also specializes in high precision optical components. | 408-434-1000 | NA | Santa Clara |

## 177 = Photonics R&D and Services

| COMPANY NAME | PRODUCT / SERVICE | PHONE | EMP | CITY |
|---|---|---|---|---|
| Banpil Photonics Inc (HQ) | Developer and manufacturer of image sensors for automotive & medical imaging systems, security & surveillance, and machine vision applications. | 408-282-3628 | NA | Santa Clara |
| Intevac Inc (HQ) | Supplier of magnetic media processing systems. The company offers advanced equipment to the hard disk drive, solar, and photonics industries. | 408-986-9888 | NA | Santa Clara |
| Meivac Inc (HQ) | Manufacturer of sputtering systems and components. The company offers throttle valves, integrators, OEM assemblies, and substrate heaters. | 408-362-1000 | NA | San Jose |
| Sa Photonics Inc (HQ) | Developer of photonic systems. The company offers solutions for head-mounted displays, microwave sensors, mirror sense, and control systems. | 408-560-3500 | NA | Los Gatos |

| COMPANY NAME | PRODUCT / SERVICE | PHONE | EMP | CITY |
|---|---|---|---|---|
| Sight Sciences Inc (HQ) | Manufacturer and developer of surgical instruments and ophthalmic medical devices. The company serves the medical sector. | 415-889-0550 | NA | Menlo Park |

## 179 = Conveying Equipment

| COMPANY NAME | PRODUCT / SERVICE | PHONE | EMP | CITY |
|---|---|---|---|---|
| Allied Crane Inc (HQ) | Provider of crane services. The company offers crane repair, installation and removal, and preventive maintenance programs. | 925-427-9200 | NA | Pittsburg |
| Compton Enterprises (HQ) | Manufacturer of moving equipment. The company specializes in rail-cars, conveyors, and truck loaders. | 530-895-1942 | 1-10 | Chico |
| Cozad! Trailers (HQ) | Manufacturer of trailers. The company serves small and large construction companies and the military and aerospace industries. | 209-931-3000 | 1-10 | Stockton |
| Crown Lift Trucks (BR) | Manufacturer of industrial lift trucks. The company offerings include C-5 Series IC Trucks, Hand Pallet Trucks, Tow Tractors, and Walkie Stackers. | 916-373-8980 | 11-50 | West Sacramento |
| Distribution Technologies Inc (HQ) | Provider of design, analysis, simulation, automation, and project implementation solutions. The company also deals with technical support. | 415-999-1191 | NA | Tiburon |
| FloStor Engineering (HQ) | Developer of automation solutions for inventory, distribution, fulfillment, and manufacturing systems. | 800-500-8256 | NA | Hayward |
| H J Hirtzer & Associates Inc (HQ) | Manufacturer of steel links. The company specializes in the fabrication of insulated links for shipping and defense industries. | 925-931-1450 | NA | Brentwood |
| Lemo Usa Inc (HQ) | Designer and manufacturer of precision custom connectors, cable assemblies, and related accessories. The company serves the industrial sector. | 707-578-8811 | NA | Rohnert Park |
| Morgan Royce Industries Inc (HQ) | Developer and manufacturer of custom cables, wire harness, and PCB assemblies. The company offers project management and quality control services. | 510-440-8500 | NA | Fremont |
| Orchard Machinery Corp (HQ) | Manufacturer of tree shakers and material handling systems comprising shuttles, bin carriers, conveyor carts, and elevators. | 530-673-2822 | 1-10 | Yuba City |
| Powerlift Dumbwaiters Inc (HQ) | Provider of dumbwaiters that includes residential powerlifts, commerical units, and mezzanine lifts. | 530-333-1953 | 1-10 | Georgetown |
| Ralphs-Pugh Co (HQ) | Manufacturer of conveyor rollers and related components. The company serves the agriculture, chemical, and food processing industries. | 707-745-6222 | NA | Benicia |
| Rock Systems Inc (HQ) | Provider of material handling solutions. The company offers hoppers, feeders, conveyors, separators, and related accessories. | 916-921-9000 | 1-10 | Sacramento |
| Sardee Industries Inc (BR) | Provider of container manufacturing equipment. The company also offers engineering and repair services for packing and filling industries. | 209-466-1526 | 11-50 | Stockton |
| Screw Conveyor Corporation (BR) | Manufacturer of bulk material handling equipment including screw conveyors, drag conveyors, and bucket elevators. | 559-651-2131 | 11-50 | Visalia |
| Ultra Lift Corp (HQ) | Manufacturer of hand trucks. The company specializes in the fabrication of trucks that combine hand-power and electric drives. | 408-287-9400 | NA | San Jose |
| Westside Research Inc (HQ) | Designer and manufacturer of interior and exterior automotive cargo management products. The company specializes in truck luggage product lines. | 530-865-5587 | 1-10 | Orland |
| Woodland Mdm (HQ) | Manufacturer and supplier of new and refurbished machinery products. The company offers industrial controls and automation & case handling equipment. | 530-669-1400 | 1-10 | Woodland |

## 180 = Elevators/Moving Stairways

| COMPANY NAME | PRODUCT / SERVICE | PHONE | EMP | CITY |
|---|---|---|---|---|
| A Step Above (HQ) | Provider of elevator services. The company offers escalators, walks, manlifts, and traction cars and related troubleshooting, testing and service. | 707-421-2917 | NA | Fairfield |
| Benchmark Home Elevator (HQ) | Provider of elevator products. The company's products include curved rail stairlifts, straight rail stairlifts, home elevators, and wheelchair lifts. | 707-255-4687 | NA | Napa |
| Compton Enterprises (HQ) | Manufacturer of moving equipment. The company specializes in rail-cars, conveyors, and truck loaders. | 530-895-1942 | 1-10 | Chico |
| Crown Lift Trucks (BR) | Manufacturer of industrial lift trucks. The company offerings include C-5 Series IC Trucks, Hand Pallet Trucks, Tow Tractors, and Walkie Stackers. | 916-373-8980 | 11-50 | West Sacramento |
| Elevator Controls Corp (HQ) | Manufacturer of non-proprietary microprocessor based elevator controllers. The company offers technical support and field services. | 916-428-1708 | 1-10 | Sacramento |
| Elevator Technology Inc (HQ) | Provider of elevator repair and installation services. The company specializes both in residential and commercial elevators. | 916-939-4323 | 1-10 | El Dorado Hills |
| Escalera Inc (HQ) | Manufacturer of stair climbing trucks. The company's products include forklifts, handtrucks, and load movers. | 530-673-6318 | 1-10 | Yuba City |
| Kone Inc (BR) | Manufacturer of moving solutions. The company offers automatic building doors, elevators and escalators, and accessories. | 510-351-5141 | NA | San Leandro |
| Mec Aerial Work Platforms (HQ) | Manufacturer of aerial work platforms. The company specializes in the design and manufacture of scissors and booms. | 559-842-1500 | 1-10 | Kerman |
| Melrose Metal Products Inc (HQ) | Manufacturer of melrose metal products. The company offers design and installation services for food processing and emission control systems. | 510-657-8771 | NA | Fremont |
| Motion Control Engineering Inc (HQ) | Manufacturer of elevator control products. The company's products include elevator and escalator controls, complete elevators, and components and peripherals. | 916-463-9200 | 11-50 | Rancho Cordova |

| COMPANY NAME | PRODUCT / SERVICE | PHONE | EMP | CITY |
|---|---|---|---|---|
| Schindler Elevator Corp (BR) | Provider of elevators, escalators, and related services. The company creates and delivers urban mobility solutions. | 510-382-2075 | NA | San Leandro |
| Thyssenkrupp Elevator (BR) | Provider of elevators and elevator solutions. The company offers MRL elevators, synergy elevators, momentum elevators, and freight elevators. | 510-476-1900 | NA | San Leandro |
| Ward Systems Inc (HQ) | Provider of custom automation services. The company's services include valve installation, maintenance, and reconfiguration. | 530-271-1800 | 1-10 | Grass Valley |
| Woodland Mdm (HQ) | Manufacturer and supplier of new and refurbished machinery products. The company offers industrial controls and automation & case handling equipment. | 530-669-1400 | 1-10 | Woodland |

## 181 = Factory Assembly Line Equipment

| COMPANY NAME | PRODUCT / SERVICE | PHONE | EMP | CITY |
|---|---|---|---|---|
| Big Joe Handling Systems (HQ) | Supplier of warehouse storage and material handling equipment. The company specializes in pallet and product storage systems. | 510-785-6900 | NA | Hayward |
| Ward Systems Inc (HQ) | Provider of custom automation services. The company's services include valve installation, maintenance, and reconfiguration. | 530-271-1800 | 1-10 | Grass Valley |

## 183 = Overhead Cranes

| COMPANY NAME | PRODUCT / SERVICE | PHONE | EMP | CITY |
|---|---|---|---|---|
| Allied Crane Inc (HQ) | Provider of crane services. The company offers crane repair, installation and removal, and preventive maintenance programs. | 925-427-9200 | NA | Pittsburg |
| Heco Pacific Manufacturing Inc (HQ) | Manufacturer and seller of industrial cranes and overhead cranes. The company offers custom engineering, maintenance, testing, and other services. | 510-487-1155 | NA | Union City |
| Malcolm Drilling Company Inc (HQ) | Provider of specialty foundation industry services. The company is engaged in deep foundations, dewatering, and design build services. | 415-901-4400 | NA | San Francisco |
| Paceco Corp (HQ) | Manufacturer of equipment to handle port cargo. The company also offers terminal operating systems and crane modification services. | 510-264-9288 | NA | Hayward |
| Rock Systems Inc (HQ) | Provider of material handling solutions. The company offers hoppers, feeders, conveyors, separators, and related accessories. | 916-921-9000 | 1-10 | Sacramento |

## 184 = Medical Equipment/Devices & Services

| COMPANY NAME | PRODUCT / SERVICE | PHONE | EMP | CITY |
|---|---|---|---|---|
| N Edwards Lifesciences Corp (HQ) | Manufacturer of medical devices. The company specializes in technologies for structural heart diseases and critical care monitoring. | 949-250-5070 | 11-50 | Irvine |

## 185 = Dental Equipment, Supplies & Prosthetics

| COMPANY NAME | PRODUCT / SERVICE | PHONE | EMP | CITY |
|---|---|---|---|---|
| Anatomage Inc (HQ) | Manufacturer of surgical devices, surgical instruments, radiology software, imaging equipment, and display equipment for medical and dental industries. | 408-885-1474 | NA | San Jose |
| Chromeworks Inc (HQ) | Manufacturer of chrome frames for the dental lab industry. The company's services include shipping and delivery. | 530-343-2278 | 1-10 | Chico |
| Lares Research (HQ) | Developer and manufacturer of dental hand pieces and dental lasers. The company offers services to the healthcare industry. | 530-345-1767 | 1-10 | Chico |
| Microdental Inc (HQ) | Provider of laboratory-fabricated restorations and related equipment. The company serves the healthcare sector. | 925-829-3611 | NA | Dublin |
| Progressive Technology Inc (HQ) | Manufacturer of orthodontic braces. The company provides sapphire, alumina, zirconia, ceramic, and quartz braces. | 916-632-6715 | 1-10 | Rocklin |
| The Wirebenders (HQ) | Provider of clinical support, research, and development services. The company specializes in appliance designs. | 408-265-5576 | NA | San Jose |
| Wells Dental Inc (HQ) | Supplier of dental laboratory equipment. The company offers engine units, finishing machines, quick chucks, and consumables. | 707-937-0521 | 1-10 | Comptche |

## 186 = Medical Diagnostic/Analyzing Equipment

| COMPANY NAME | PRODUCT / SERVICE | PHONE | EMP | CITY |
|---|---|---|---|---|
| 3rd Stone Design Inc (HQ) | Provider of design, product development, and engineering services. The company serves the consumer products and healthcare industries. | 415-454-3005 | NA | San Rafael |
| Airxpanders Inc (HQ) | Provider of controlled tissue expander and small handheld wireless controller of breast cancer reconstructive surgery. | 650-390-9000 | NA | San Jose |
| Ark Diagnostics Inc (HQ) | Manufacturer of in vitro diagnostic products for the treatment of cancer, veterinary, HIV/AIDS, anti-fungal drugs, and epilepsy and pain management. | 877-869-2320 | NA | Fremont |
| BD Biosciences (BR) | Manufacturer of medical devices. The company provides a broad range of medical supplies, devices, laboratory equipment and diagnostic products. | 877-232-8995 | NA | San Jose |
| Biochain Institute Inc (HQ) | Provider of bio-sample preparation, analysis, and application assays accelerating the development of personalized diagnostics, therapeutics, and medicine. | 510-783-8588 | NA | Newark |
| Biocodex Usa (HQ) | Developer of pharmaceutical products for the treatment of gastroenterology, neuropsychiatry, and pain. | | NA | Redwood City |
| Bioluminate Inc (HQ) | Developer of probes that provide breast cancer detection data to physicians. The company serves the medical sector. | 650-743-0240 | NA | San Carlos |
| Capnia (HQ) | Focuses on the development and commercialization of therapeutic and diagnostic products to address significant unmet healthcare needs. | 650-213-8444 | NA | Redwood City |
| CapsoVision (HQ) | Specializes in the diagnostic imaging of the gastrointestinal systems. The company offers services to hospitals and patients. | 408-624-1488 | NA | Saratoga |

| COMPANY NAME | PRODUCT / SERVICE | PHONE | EMP | CITY |
|---|---|---|---|---|
| Cepheid (HQ) | Provider of molecular diagnostic testing of patient specimen on a centralized basis enabling medical providers identify and treat disease early. | 408-541-4191 | NA | Sunnyvale |
| D-EYE (HQ) | Designer and manufacturer of diagnostic instruments. The company offers smart phone based retinal imaging systems for clinical assessments. | 401-473-6323 | 1-10 | Truckee |
| Diagnostic Biosystems Inc (HQ) | Developer of primary and monoclonal antibodies, ancillaries, chromogens, and multiplex kits. The company serves the healthcare sector. | 925-484-3350 | NA | Pleasanton |
| Drawbridge Health (HQ) | Provider of diagnostic testing solutions. The company offers blood testing solutions for a range of biomarker. | 650-714-6791 | NA | Menlo Park |
| DyAnsys Inc (HQ) | Provider of medical diagnostic and monitoring systems to clinicians and hospitals for patients. The company deals with research services. | 888-950-4321 | NA | San Mateo |
| Ea Machining Inc (HQ) | Provider of CNC turning and milling services. The company offers services to the semiconductor manufacturing equipment industry. | 408-727-4962 | NA | Santa Clara |
| Ebr Systems Inc (HQ) | Designer and developer of implantable systems for wireless tissue stimulation. The company focuses on the treatment of heart failure. | 408-720-1906 | NA | Sunnyvale |
| Eko Devices Inc (HQ) | Developer of digital stethoscope/electronic stethoscope to help confidently and quickly assess patient's heart, lung, and body sounds. | 844-356-3384 | NA | Berkeley |
| Electro Diagnostic Imaging Inc (HQ) | Developer and manufacturer of products for electrophysiology. The company's services include research, sales, and marketing. | 650-631-0120 | NA | Redwood City |
| Eneura Therapeutics Llc (HQ) | Provider of medical technology solutions. The company offers transcranial magnetic stimulation devices for the treatment of migraine. | 408-245-6400 | NA | Sunnyvale |
| Evena Medical Inc (HQ) | Developer of medical smart glasses and wearables. The company specializes in portable vein finder device for IV access procedures. | | 1-10 | Roseville |
| Fresenius Medical Care (BR) | Focuses on the treatment of patients with renal and other chronic conditions. The company serves the healthcare industry. | 925-947-4545 | NA | Walnut Creek |
| Gold Standard Diagnostics Corp (HQ) | Provider of laboratory diagnostic solutions. The company specializes in diagnosis of autoimmune diseases, bacterial and viral diseases. | 855-268-6940 | 1-10 | Davis |
| Hitachi Chemical Diagnostics Inc (HQ) | Provider of in vitro allergy diagnostics products. The company offers alternative means of diagnosing allergy. | 650-961-5501 | NA | Mountain View |
| Hologic Inc (BR) | Provider of healthcare and diagnostics. The company offers breast and skeletal healthcare and diagnostics, and GYN surgical solutions. | 669-224-6420 | NA | Santa Clara |
| Integenx Inc (HQ) | Provider of rapid human DNA identification technologies for forensics and law enforcement applications. | 925-701-3400 | NA | Pleasanton |
| InterVene Inc (HQ) | Provider of medical devices such as blueleaf endovenous valve formation system to treat severe venous disease in the legs. | 650-351-6725 | NA | S San Francisco |
| Invenio Imaging Inc (HQ) | Provider of technology for non-destructive microscopic analysis of the molecular make-up of tissues and other materials. | | NA | Santa Clara |
| Iridex Corp (HQ) | Provider of therapeutic based laser consoles, delivery devices, and consumable instrumentation. The company serves the healthcare industry. | 650-940-4700 | NA | Mountain View |
| Iris Biotechnologies Inc (HQ) | Provider of medical informatics system. The company develops chips to precisely diagnose and identify actionable treatment choices for breast cancer. | 408-867-2885 | NA | Santa Clara |
| Kinematic Automation Inc (HQ) | Provider of manufacturing systems for the medical industry. The company also offers automation, strip cutting, rotatory slitting services. | 209-532-3200 | 1-10 | Sonora |
| Los Gatos Research Inc (HQ) | Manufacturer of analyzers for the measurement of trace gases and isotopes. The company serves the industrial and environmental sectors. | 650-965-7772 | NA | San Jose |
| LS Biopath Inc (HQ) | Developer of medical products and technologies for the unmet need for real time imaging of excised tissue during breast cancer surgery. | 408-464-4051 | NA | Saratoga |
| Lumiquick Diagnostics Inc (HQ) | Manufacturer of diagnostic products and other raw materials. The company is engaged in distribution services. | 408-855-0061 | NA | Santa Clara |
| Micropoint Bioscience Inc (HQ) | Developer of medical products and services for treatment of vascular disease such as peripheral artery disease and venous blood clots disorders. | 408-588-1682 | NA | Santa Clara |
| Mid Labs Inc (HQ) | Manufacturer of ophthalmic products such as vitreous cutters, titanium forceps, and related accessories. | 510-357-3952 | NA | San Leandro |
| Minerva Surgical Inc (HQ) | Manufacturer of medical devices. The company provides products for the treatment of abnormal uterine bleeding. | 855-646-7874 | NA | Redwood City |
| MIODx Inc (HQ) | Provider of diagnostics and biomarker expertise in a variety of cancer treatments including immuno-therapies. | 866-756-4639 | NA | San Jose |
| Miramar Labs Inc (HQ) | Provider of solutions for excessive sweat. The company is engaged in clinical trials and research programs. | 408-579-8700 | NA | Santa Clara |
| Mission Bio (HQ) | Developer and deliverer of precision medicine. The company offers instruments, fixed panels, custom panels, and software for the researchers and clinicians. | 415-854-0058 | NA | S San Francisco |
| MORE Health Inc (HQ) | Specializes in collaborative diagnosis. The company serves patients, hospitals, and the medical industry. | 888-908-6673 | NA | San Mateo |
| Nanomix Inc (HQ) | Manufacturer of diagnostic systems and supplies. The company is engaged in product development services. | 510-428-5300 | NA | Emeryville |
| Nidek Inc (RH) | Manufacturer of ophthalmic devices. The company also offers refractive systems and diagnostic products to the medical industry. | 800-223-9044 | NA | Fremont |

| COMPANY NAME | PRODUCT / SERVICE | PHONE | EMP | CITY |
|---|---|---|---|---|
| nVision Medical Corp (HQ) | Developer of women's health products. The company offers services to clinicians and the medical industry. | 408-655-3577 | NA | San Bruno |
| Onda Corp (HQ) | Manufacturer of medical devices. The company offers ultrasound measurement instrumentation and services for scientific applications. | 408-745-0383 | NA | Sunnyvale |
| Optovue Inc (HQ) | Manufacturer of ophthalmic devices. The company leads the commercialization of new imaging modalities to develop ophthalmic diagnosis. | 510-743-0985 | NA | Fremont |
| Outset Medical (HQ) | Developer of hemodialysis systems. The company offers services to patients, families, providers and physicians. | 669-231-8200 | NA | San Jose |
| POC Medical Systems Inc (HQ) | Provider of diagnostic medical devices for the screening of life-threatening diseases like cancer, cardiovascular disorders, and infectious diseases. | 925-331-8010 | NA | Livermore |
| Preferred Products (HQ) | Manufacturer of diagnostic instruments, headlights and mirrors, forceps, microscopes, office equipment, and ear instruments. | 415-499-3544 | NA | San Rafael |
| Prescient Surgical (HQ) | Developer of medical devices and technologies to reduce the risk of surgical site infections in patients undergoing abdominal gastrointestinal surgery. | 650-999-0263 | NA | San Carlos |
| Proxim Diagnostics Corp (HQ) | Manufacturer of diagnostics products and related supplies. The company deals with testing and research related services. | 408-391-6090 | NA | Mountain View |
| Pulmonx Corp (HQ) | Manufacturer of medical devices. The company focuses on developing both diagnostic and therapeutic technologies for Interventional Pulmonology. | 650-364-0400 | NA | Redwood City |
| Pulsar Vascular Inc (HQ) | Manufacturer of endovascular diseases and it focuses on the treatment of complex aneurysms. The company is engaged in clinical trials. | 408-260-9264 | NA | San Jose |
| QuanDx Inc (HQ) | Developer of molecular diagnostics for personalized cancer treatment. The company offers detection kits and lung cancer assays. | 650-262-4140 | NA | San Jose |
| Quest Diagnostics Inc (BR) | Provider of diagnostic laboratory testing services. The company offers a wide range of test menu for diagnosing medical conditions. | 916-927-9900 | 11-50 | Sacramento |
| Quest Diagnostics Inc (BR) | Provider of diagnostic laboratory testing services. The company offers a wide range of test menu for diagnosing medical conditions. | 650-344-8143 | NA | San Mateo |
| Qview Medical (HQ) | Provider of assistance in the review of 3D automated breast ultrasound. The company offers services to the radiologists. | 650-397-5174 | NA | Los Altos |
| Smp Tech Inc (HQ) | Designer and builder of robotic DNA spotters, micro fluidic devices, medical equipment, automated machinery, and electro-mechanical products. | 408-776-7776 | NA | Morgan Hill |
| Solta Medical Inc (HQ) | Designer, developer, manufacturer, and marketer of medical devices for the non-invasive treatment of wrinkles and other skin care devices. | 510-786-6946 | NA | Hayward |
| Stellartech Research Corp (HQ) | Designer, developer, and manufacturer of medical devices. The company specializes in surgical probes, balloon electrode catheters, and other products. | 408-331-3000 | NA | Milpitas |
| Tricontinent Scientific Inc (BR) | Provider of liquid-handling products and instrument components for the medical diagnostics and biotechnology industries. | 530-273-8888 | 11-50 | Auburn |
| ViOptix Inc (HQ) | Manufacturer of medical support devices. The company specializes in devices used for respiratory support and oxygen supply. | 510-226-5860 | NA | Newark |
| Vital Connect Inc (HQ) | Provider of healthcare solutions. The company focuses on biosensors, clinical-grade biometric measurements. | 408-963-4600 | NA | San Jose |
| VytronUS Inc (HQ) | Developer of ablation systems for the treatment of atrial fibrillation and other cardiac arrhythmias. The company deals with customizable lesions. | 408-730-1333 | NA | Sunnyvale |
| Wave 80 Biosciences Inc (BR) | Developer of molecular diagnostics instruments and consumables for hepatitis C, hepatitis B, HIV/AIDS, and other human health conditions. | 415-487-7976 | NA | San Francisco |
| Xoft Inc (HQ) | Developer of electronic brachytherapy systems. The company's products include rigid shield, vacuum pumps, and physics kits. | 408-493-1500 | NA | San Jose |

## 187 = Medical Monitoring and Test Equipment

| COMPANY NAME | PRODUCT / SERVICE | PHONE | EMP | CITY |
|---|---|---|---|---|
| Aegea Medical Inc (HQ) | Developer of women healthcare solutions. The company develops a system for the treatment of excessive menstrual bleeding. | 650-701-1125 | NA | Menlo Park |
| Avinger Inc (HQ) | Designer and developer of precision medical device technology solutions. The company is engaged in manufacturing services. | 800-208-2988 | NA | Redwood City |
| Bactrack (HQ) | Provider of breathalyzers. The company provides products for a wide range of personal, professional and smartphone use. | 415-693-9756 | NA | San Francisco |
| Biocardia Inc (HQ) | Developer of clinical stage regenerative therapeutic products for the treatment of cardiovascular diseases. | 650-226-0120 | NA | San Carlos |
| Biocheck Inc (HQ) | Provider of custom immunoassay development, antibody conjugation and purification, and contract manufacturing services. | 650-573-1968 | NA | S San Francisco |
| Biogenex Laboratories Inc (HQ) | Manufacturer of automated slide-based staining instruments and histology products for cancer diagnosis, prognosis, and therapy selection. | 510-824-1400 | NA | Fremont |
| Bioluminate Inc (HQ) | Developer of probes that provide breast cancer detection data to physicians. The company serves the medical sector. | 650-743-0240 | NA | San Carlos |
| Buglab Llc (HQ) | Developer of biomass measuring equipment such as sensors, biomass monitor, and biomass multiplier involved in fermentation and microbial cultures. | 925-208-1952 | NA | Concord |

| COMPANY NAME | PRODUCT / SERVICE | PHONE | EMP | CITY |
|---|---|---|---|---|
| Cardinal Health (HQ) | Provider of solutions in the cardiovascular and peripheral vascular markets. The company provides advanced vascular closure devices for patients. | 408-610-6500 | NA | Santa Clara |
| Chai (HQ) | Specializes in DNA diagnostics. The company offers services to clinics, patients, and the medical sector. | 650-779-5577 | NA | Santa Clara |
| Chronix Biomedical Inc (HQ) | Provider of molecular diagnostics laboratory services such as second opinion tests and delta dot test for screening and monitoring cancer. | 408-960-2306 | NA | San Jose |
| Cirtec Medical (HQ) | Manufacturer of complex implantable device manufacturing, medical device solutions, and smart solutions for highly complex miniaturization. | 408-395-0443 | NA | Los Gatos |
| Communications & Power Industries Llc (HQ) | Developer and manufacturer of microwave, radio frequency, power, and control solutions. The company serves medical and critical defense fields. | 650-846-2900 | NA | Palo Alto |
| Compact Imaging Inc (HQ) | Developer of miniature optical sensor technology. The company specializes in mobile health applications. | 650-694-7801 | NA | Mountain View |
| Cutera Inc (HQ) | Manufacturer of aesthetic solutions such as face and body laser, light, and other energy-based aesthetic systems for hair removal and pigmented lesions. | 415-657-5500 | NA | Brisbane |
| Cymed (HQ) | Provider of ostomy pouching systems. The company specializes in skin care products and serves individuals and hospitals. | 800-582-0707 | 1-10 | Sacramento |
| DyAnsys Inc (HQ) | Provider of medical diagnostic and monitoring systems to clinicians and hospitals for patients. The company deals with research services. | 888-950-4321 | NA | San Mateo |
| Ea Machining Inc (HQ) | Provider of CNC turning and milling services. The company offers services to the semiconductor manufacturing equipment industry. | 408-727-4962 | NA | Santa Clara |
| Ebr Systems Inc (HQ) | Designer and developer of implantable systems for wireless tissue stimulation. The company focuses on the treatment of heart failure. | 408-720-1906 | NA | Sunnyvale |
| Echopixel Inc (HQ) | Provider of 3D medical visualization software for radiologists, cardiologists, pediatric cardiologists, and interventional neuroradiologists. | 844-273-7766 | NA | Santa Clara |
| Eneura Therapeutics Llc (HQ) | Provider of medical technology solutions. The company offers transcranial magnetic stimulation devices for the treatment of migraine. | 408-245-6400 | NA | Sunnyvale |
| Exploramed (HQ) | Developer of novel medical devices with cutting edge medical technology for use by major medical device manufacturing companies. | 650-472-0300 | NA | Mountain View |
| ExThera Medical Corp (HQ) | Developer of medical devices that address unmet clinical needs in the treatment of bloodstream infections and pathogen-reduction in blood banking. | 925-839-2060 | NA | Martinez |
| Fluidigm Sciences Inc (HQ) | Developer and creator of technologies for life science tools designed to revolutionize biology. The company is involved in research programs. | 650-871-7152 | NA | San Francisco |
| Gcx Corp (HQ) | Provider of mounting solutions, application specific solutions, on-site services, and also technical support. | 707-773-1100 | NA | Petaluma |
| Genapsys Inc (HQ) | Developer of DNA sequencing to enable a paradigm shift in genomic diagnostics. The company specializes in GENIUS system that has footprint of Apple iPad. | 650-330-1096 | NA | Redwood City |
| Gynesonics (HQ) | Manufacturer and developer of therapeutic devices and related supplies for the treatment of uterine fibroids in women. | 650-216-3860 | NA | Redwood City |
| Immuno Concepts Na Ltd (HQ) | Manufacturer and distributor of diagnostic assays. The company's products are used for systemic rheumatic diseases. | 916-363-2649 | 1-10 | Sacramento |
| Intersect Ent Inc (HQ) | Provider of steroid-releasing implants that props open the sinuses for the treatment of common cold and sinusitis. | 650-641-2100 | 201-500 | Menlo Park |
| Intuity Medical Inc (HQ) | Provider of medical products such as blood glucose monitoring system, meter, cartridge, and data management for diabetes management. | 510-946-8800 | NA | Fremont |
| Jasper Ridge Inc (HQ) | Manufacturer of tint and lighting exam systems. The company offers services to patients and hospitals. | 650-804-5040 | NA | San Mateo |
| Lighthouse Worldwide Solutions (HQ) | Provider of dental supplies such as implants, dentures, partials, implant bars, and related accessories. | 510-438-0500 | NA | Fremont |
| Lumenis Inc (DH) | Provider of minimally-invasive clinical solutions. The company develops and commercializes energy-based technologies. | 877-586-3647 | NA | San Jose |
| Micropoint Bioscience Inc (HQ) | Developer of medical products and services for treatment of vascular disease such as peripheral artery disease and venous blood clots disorders. | 408-588-1682 | NA | Santa Clara |
| Mission Bio (HQ) | Developer and deliverer of precision medicine. The company offers instruments, fixed panels, custom panels, and software for the researchers and clinicians. | 415-854-0058 | NA | S San Francisco |
| Modulus Data Systems (HQ) | Provider digital clinical cell (tally) counters. The company's products include Diffcount III, Comp-U-Diff, and Uro-Comp. | 650-365-3111 | NA | Redwood City |
| Neurosky Inc (HQ) | Manufacturer of ECG biosensors and also EEG biosensors for mobile solutions, wearable devices, and service providers. | 408-200-6675 | NA | San Jose |
| Ocumetrics Inc (HQ) | Manufacturer of Fluorotron(TM) Master Ocular Fluorophotometers. The company deals with research services. | 650-960-3955 | NA | Mountain View |
| Onda Corp (HQ) | Manufacturer of medical devices. The company offers ultrasound measurement instrumentation and services for scientific applications. | 408-745-0383 | NA | Sunnyvale |

| COMPANY NAME | PRODUCT / SERVICE | PHONE | EMP | CITY |
|---|---|---|---|---|
| Optiscan Biomedical Corp (HQ) | Provider of monitoring products for measuring glucose, plasma collection, and also detection of glucose among patients. | 510-342-5800 | NA | Hayward |
| Phoenix Technology Group LLC (HQ) | Provider of research laboratory services. The company offers anterior segment imaging and retinal imaging microscope services. | 925-485-1100 | NA | Pleasanton |
| Profusa Inc (HQ) | Focuses on the development of biointegrated sensors. The company offers services to the environment sector. | 415-655-9861 | NA | Emeryville |
| Qardio Inc (HQ) | Creator of health monitoring devices such as blood pressure monitor, multiple-sensor EKG, and wireless scale and body analyzer. | 855-240-7323 | NA | San Francisco |
| Rimnetics Inc (BR) | Providers of RIM molded structural parts, enclosures, cosmetic housings, encapsulation and overmolding. The company makes molded polyurethane parts. | 916-652-5555 | 11-50 | Loomis |
| Salutron Inc (HQ) | Providers of health care solutions. The company offers on-demand ecg accurate heart rate monitoring solutions. | 510-795-2876 | NA | Newark |
| Si-Bone Inc (RH) | Developer of medical products and technologies such as implants and titanium implant technology for SI joint pain and sacroiliac joint fusion surgery. | 408-207-0700 | NA | San Jose |
| Smart Monitor Corp (HQ) | Manufacturer of monitoring devices. The company provides automated solution for detecting unusual movements from chronic health conditions. | 408-754-1695 | NA | San Jose |
| Spectros Corp (HQ) | Manufacturer of tissue perfusion monitors and they are used in plastic surgery, critical care, and vascular surgery. | 650-851-4040 | NA | Campbell |
| Spinal Kinetics Inc (HQ) | Provider of preservation systems for treating degenerative diseases of the spine. The company serves the healthcare sector. | 408-636-2500 | NA | Sunnyvale |
| ViOptix Inc (HQ) | Manufacturer of medical support devices. The company specializes in devices used for respiratory support and oxygen supply. | 510-226-5860 | NA | Newark |
| Vital Connect Inc (HQ) | Provider of healthcare solutions. The company focuses on biosensors, clinical-grade biometric measurements. | 408-963-4600 | NA | San Jose |
| Zenflow Inc (HQ) | Developer of products for the treatment of urinary obstruction related to benign prostatic hyperplasia. The company serves the medical sector. | 650-642-9658 | NA | S San Francisco |

## 188 = Medical Services

| COMPANY NAME | PRODUCT / SERVICE | PHONE | EMP | CITY |
|---|---|---|---|---|
| Accuray Inc (HQ) | Provider of oncology treatment solutions. The company develops, manufactures and sells precise and innovative tumor treatment solutions. | 408-716-4600 | NA | Sunnyvale |
| Advance Research Associates (HQ) | Developer of human bio-therapeutic platform technology solutions, drug discovery, and related support services. | 650-810-1190 | NA | Santa Clara |
| Aegea Medical Inc (HQ) | Developer of women healthcare solutions. The company develops a system for the treatment of excessive menstrual bleeding. | 650-701-1125 | NA | Menlo Park |
| AmbiCom Holdings Inc (HQ) | Manufacturer of networking hardware for mobile computers. The company offers wireless solutions and OEM modules. | 408-321-0822 | 1-10 | Santa Cruz |
| Bell Biosystems Inc (HQ) | Provider of biotechnology services. The company develops proteins targeted to kill specific bacteria but cause minimal collateral damage. | 877-420-3621 | NA | Berkeley |
| Bioclinica Inc (HQ) | Developer of medical therapies. The company specializes in medical imaging services, cardiac safety, and enterprise eClinical platforms. | 415-817-8900 | NA | Newark |
| Channel Medsystems Inc (HQ) | Developer of cryothermic technology and streamlined delivery system for women with heavy menstrual bleeding. | 510-338-9301 | NA | Emeryville |
| Creganna Medical (BR) | Provider of medical devices. The company offers services that ranges from clinical and regulatory support to design and manufacturing services. | 408-364-7100 | NA | Campbell |
| Cutera Inc (HQ) | Manufacturer of aesthetic solutions such as face and body laser, light, and other energy-based aesthetic systems for hair removal and pigmented lesions. | 415-657-5500 | NA | Brisbane |
| N Dendreon Pharmaceuticals LLC (HQ) | Provider of biotechnology services. The company provides therapeutics for the treatment of cancer employing active cellular immunotherapy. | 877-256-4545 | 11-50 | Seal Beach |
| DirectGov Source Inc (HQ) | Manufacturer of personal protection kits. The company offers disposable clothing, biohazard disposal, antimicrobial sanitizers, and hand protection gloves. | 530-899-3327 | 1-10 | Chico |
| Doctor on Demand (HQ) | Provider of urgent care doctors. The company offers lab screens for the treatment of mental health and chronic conditions. | 800-997-6196 | NA | San Francisco |
| Eargo Inc (HQ) | Creator of medical device. The company specializes in virtually invisible in-ear hearing device that is comfortable, natural sounding, and rechargeable. | 650-351-7700 | NA | San Jose |
| Endo Gastric Solutions Inc (HQ) | Provider of treatment services for gastroesophageal reflux disease. The company also focuses on training and education. | 650-578-5100 | NA | San Mateo |
| Eneura Therapeutics Llc (HQ) | Provider of medical technology solutions. The company offers transcranial magnetic stimulation devices for the treatment of migraine. | 408-245-6400 | NA | Sunnyvale |
| Genapsys Inc (HQ) | Developer of DNA sequencing to enable a paradigm shift in genomic diagnostics. The company specializes in GENIUS system that has footprint of Apple iPad. | 650-330-1096 | NA | Redwood City |
| HealthLoop (HQ) | Provider of healthcare solutions. The company deals with the integration of doctors, patients and care-givers. | 408-418-0998 | 11-50 | Mountain View |
| JSK Associates (HQ) | Provider of electronics, medical, and semiconductor manufacturing services. The company also offers assembly and research services. | 408-980-8575 | NA | Santa Clara |

| COMPANY NAME | PRODUCT / SERVICE | PHONE | EMP | CITY |
|---|---|---|---|---|
| Lorom West (HQ) | Manufacturer of PCB assemblies, turnkey OEM/ODM products and custom cable and wire harnesses. The company offers industry solutions. | 510-249-9000 | NA | Fremont |
| Medtronic CardioVascular inc (BR) | Provider of disease management services. The company specializes in cardiovascular, diabetes, surgical technologies, and spinal and biologics. | 707-525-0111 | NA | Santa Rosa |
| Minerva Surgical Inc (HQ) | Manufacturer of medical devices. The company provides products for the treatment of abnormal uterine bleeding. | 855-646-7874 | NA | Redwood City |
| Motive Medical Intelligence (HQ) | Developer of medical intelligence solutions. The company also offers care plans for population health management. | 415-362-4007 | NA | San Francisco |
| Neotract Inc (HQ) | Provider of medical devices for the treatment of benign prostatic hyperplasia and its side effects such as loss of productivity and sleep and depression. | 925-401-0700 | NA | Pleasanton |
| PinPointe (HQ) | Developer of laser light-based therapies for treating nail fungus. The company serves patients in patients in Australia and other countries. | 530-809-1970 | 1-10 | Chico |
| Plastikon Industries (HQ) | Provider of contract manufacturing services for custom designed plastic injection molding, for medical, pharmaceutical and other industries. | 510-400-1010 | NA | Hayward |
| Polyphenolics Inc (HQ) | Supplier of grape seed, grape pomace, and whole grape extracts. The company offers MegaNatural-BP, MegaNatural Red Wine Grape Extract, and MegaNatural-GL. | 559-661-5556 | 1-10 | Madera |
| Providence Medical Technology Inc (HQ) | Developer of medical devices and technologies such as dtrax spinal systems, cavux cervical cages, and ally screw systems for cervical spine care. | 415-923-9376 | NA | Pleasanton |
| Qardio Inc (HQ) | Creator of health monitoring devices such as blood pressure monitor, multiple-sensor EKG, and wireless scale and body analyzer. | 855-240-7323 | NA | San Francisco |
| Relucent Solutions Llc (HQ) | Manufacturer of medical devices. The company is involved in laser cutting, precision manufacturing, wire crimping, and related services. | 800-630-7704 | NA | Santa Rosa |
| Sciton Inc (HQ) | Provider of laser and light source solutions. The company's products include JOULE, BBL, ClearSense, Halo, and more. | 650-493-9155 | NA | Palo Alto |
| Silk Road Medical Inc (HQ) | Specializes in the treatment of carotid artery diseases. The company is engaged in clinical trials and related services. | 408-720-9002 | NA | Sunnyvale |
| Smart Monitor Corp (HQ) | Manufacturer of monitoring devices. The company provides automated solution for detecting unusual movements from chronic health conditions. | 408-754-1695 | NA | San Jose |
| The Cooper Companies Inc (HQ) | Provider of healthcare solutions. The company offers health and wellness programs for women, individuals, and communities. | 925-460-3600 | NA | Pleasanton |
| Ultrasound Laboratories Inc (HQ) | Provider of non-invasive ultrasound imaging services. The company focuses on services such as health screening, carotid artery, and kidney screening. | 877-650-0650 | NA | Mountain View |
| Viewics Inc (HQ) | Provider of consulting, custom development, and report authoring services. The company also offers packaged solutions. | 415-439-0084 | NA | Santa Clara |
| Zipline Medical Inc (HQ) | Developer of zip surgical skin closure devices for cardiology, orthopedics, dermatology, plastic reconstructive surgery, and emergency medicine. | 408-412-7228 | NA | Campbell |

## 189 = Miscellaneous Medical/Hospital Equipment

| COMPANY NAME | PRODUCT / SERVICE | PHONE | EMP | CITY |
|---|---|---|---|---|
| 3rd Stone Design Inc (HQ) | Provider of design, product development, and engineering services. The company serves the consumer products and healthcare industries. | 415-454-3005 | NA | San Rafael |
| A&D Engineering Inc (RH) | Supplier of electric scale balancers and blood pressure monitors. The company offers services to the business sector. | 408-263-5333 | NA | San Jose |
| Ab Medical Technologies Inc (HQ) | Manufacturer of electronic medical systems and powered surgical instruments such as surgical pumps, arthroscopy shavers and lab equipment. | 530-605-2522 | 1-10 | Redding |
| Abx Engineering Inc (HQ) | Manufacturer of printed circuit board assemblies and electromechanical products for medical devices, agriculture, and military electronics industries. | 650-552-2300 | NA | Burlingame |
| Accsys Technology Inc (HQ) | Manufacturer of ion linear accelerator systems used in medical imaging devices, industrial applications and in research. | 925-462-6949 | NA | Pleasanton |
| Accuray Inc (HQ) | Provider of oncology treatment solutions. The company develops, manufactures and sells precise and innovative tumor treatment solutions. | 408-716-4600 | NA | Sunnyvale |
| Airxpanders Inc (HQ) | Provider of controlled tissue expander and small handheld wireless controller of breast cancer reconstructive surgery. | 650-390-9000 | NA | San Jose |
| Align Technology Inc (HQ) | Provider of medical devices such as invisalign clear aligners, itero intra-oral scanners and orthoCAD digital services for orthodontic industry. | 408-470-1000 | NA | San Jose |
| Alterg Inc (HQ) | Provider of new technologies and products such as anti-gravity treadmills and bionic leg for physical therapy and athletic training. | 510-270-5900 | NA | Fremont |
| American Probe & Technologies Inc (HQ) | Manufacturer of analytical probes and accessories for the semiconductor test and measurement industry. | 408-263-3356 | 1-10 | Merced |
| Amgen Inc (BR) | Provider of scientific applications services. The company's services include clinical trials, ethical research, biosimilars, and web resources. | 650-244-2000 | NA | S San Francisco |
| Aqs Inc (DH) | Provider of electronic manufacturing solutions. The company offers electronic assembly, test engineering, system integration and final test services. | 510-249-5800 | NA | Fremont |

| COMPANY NAME | PRODUCT / SERVICE | PHONE | EMP | CITY |
|---|---|---|---|---|
| Avantec Vascular Corp (HQ) | Manufacturer of therapeutic medical devices such as cardio and peripheral vascular devices for cardiovascular, neurovascular, and peripheral disease. | 408-329-5400 | NA | Sunnyvale |
| Ayala Research Corporation (HQ) | Provider of product development and manufacturing services. The company offers solutions for medical, scientific and industrial products. | 800-294-9050 | NA | Livermore |
| Bay Advanced Technologies (HQ) | Provider of solutions for automation and control applications. The company offers precision automation, fluid controls and fabricated materials. | 510-857-0900 | NA | Newark |
| BD Biosciences (BR) | Manufacturer of medical devices. The company provides a broad range of medical supplies, devices, laboratory equipment and diagnostic products. | 877-232-8995 | NA | San Jose |
| Bibbero Systems Inc (HQ) | Manufacturer of filing and office supplies including custom chart and index tab dividers, and color coded and pressboard classification file folders. | 800-242-2376 | NA | Petaluma |
| Bio Plas Inc (HQ) | Manufacturer of laboratory disposables such as foam tube racks, biopsy bags, bacti cell spreaders, and siliconized products. | 415-472-3777 | NA | San Rafael |
| Biocare Medical Llc (HQ) | Developer of automated immunohistochemistry instrumentation, reagents for IHC lab testing. The company also offer tissue diagnostic products for cancer. | 925-603-8000 | NA | Pacheco |
| Biocision Llc (HQ) | Provider of cell freezing and cell thawing systems, and related supplies. The company's products are used in research applications. | 800-367-4887 | NA | San Rafael |
| Bioventrix Inc (HQ) | Provider of medical devices. The company offers treatment for congestive heart failure by catheter based approaches. | 925-830-1000 | NA | San Ramon |
| Biovision Inc (RH) | Developer of medical products such as assay kits, antibodies, and research tools for studying apoptosis, metabolism, diabetes, and gene regulation. | 408-493-1800 | NA | Milpitas |
| Boracchia + Associates (HQ) | Provider of consultant services and products to surgeons and medical facilities. The company offers operating room products, post-operative, and castroom products. | 800-826-1690 | NA | Petaluma |
| Boston Scientific (BR) | Provider of forceps, imaging systems, needles, pacemakers, snares, probes, and other related accessories. | 510-440-7700 | NA | Fremont |
| C-Scan Corp (HQ) | Manufacturer and designer of thermal recorders and printers for medical applications and the healthcare sector. | 800-953-7888 | NA | Los Gatos |
| Calcula Technologies (HQ) | Developer of medical devices for the treatment of kidney stones. The company serves the healthcare sector. | 650-724-8696 | NA | San Francisco |
| CapsoVision (HQ) | Specializes in the diagnostic imaging of the gastrointestinal systems. The company offers services to hospitals and patients. | 408-624-1488 | NA | Saratoga |
| Cardiva Medical Inc (HQ) | Developer of vascular access management products such as vascade and catalyst to facilitate rapid hemostasis following diagnostic procedures. | 408-470-7170 | NA | Santa Clara |
| CenterVue Inc (BR) | Designer and manufacturer of medical devices for the diagnosis and management of ocular pathologies. | 408-988-8404 | NA | Fremont |
| Cerebrotech Medical Systems Inc (HQ) | Provider of clinical monitoring solutions. The company offers ICP monitors and volumetric integral spectroscopy. | | NA | Pleasanton |
| Certified Medical Testing (HQ) | Provider of engineering services. The company provides services for healthcare organizations related to piped medical gas and vacuum systems. | 800-243-5427 | 1-10 | Fresno |
| Chartware Inc (HQ) | Manufacturer of scheduler and practice management interfaces and systems. The company serves the medical sector. | 800-642-4278 | NA | Rohnert Park |
| Chemux Bioscience Inc (HQ) | Provider of clinical research and testing services. The company offers eye care, dental care, and personal care support programs. | | NA | San Francisco |
| Cibiem Inc (HQ) | Manufacturer of medical devices. The company provides solutions to treat sympathetic nervous system-mediated diseases. | 650-397-6685 | NA | Los Altos |
| Cirtec Medical (HQ) | Manufacturer of complex implantable device manufacturing, medical device solutions, and smart solutions for highly complex miniaturization. | 408-395-0443 | NA | Los Gatos |
| Claret Medical Inc (HQ) | Manufacturer of catheters to protect the patient's brain during Transcatheter Aortic Valve Implantation (TAVI) and other endovascular procedures. | 707-528-9300 | NA | Santa Rosa |
| Clinisense Corp (HQ) | Developer of technology for shelf-life monitoring. The company offers applications such as diagnostics, medical supplies, and RFID tags. | 408-348-1495 | NA | Los Gatos |
| CMOS Sensor Inc (HQ) | Designer and manufacturer of electro-optical image acquisition and also surveillance solutions for the medical market. | 408-366-2898 | NA | Cupertino |
| Colema Boards Of California Inc (HQ) | Manufacturer of home enema board kits. The company's products include colema boards and cleansing kits. | 530-347-5700 | 1-10 | Cottonwood |
| Collidion Inc (HQ) | Provider of healthcare products. The company specializes in antibiotic resistance, specific drugs to eradicate biofilms, and delivery systems. | 707-668-7600 | NA | Petaluma |
| Convergent Laser Technologies (HQ) | Provider of medical laser systems and fiber optic devices. The company deals with training and product support services. | 510-832-2130 | NA | Alameda |
| Cooper (HQ) | Designer of kiosks, medical devices and software, smartphone, IT tools, websites, irrigation, supply chain management, and financial services system. | 415-267-3500 | NA | San Francisco |
| Cordis A Cardinal Health Co (DH) | Provider of diagnostic and interventional products for healthcare devices such as catheters, balloons, stents, wires and vascular closure. | 408-273-3700 | NA | Milpitas |

| COMPANY NAME | PRODUCT / SERVICE | PHONE | EMP | CITY |
|---|---|---|---|---|
| Corium International Inc (HQ) | Provider of transdermal delivery systems and related technology solutions. The company is also engaged in therapeutic product development. | 650-298-8255 | NA | Menlo Park |
| Cortexyme Inc (HQ) | Developer of therapeutic products for the treatment of Alzheimer's and other degenerative disorders. | | NA | S San Francisco |
| Cosmed Usa (HQ) | Developer and manufacturer of medical devices for accurate body composition assessments for infants, children, and adults. | 925-676-6002 | NA | Concord |
| Cutera Inc (HQ) | Manufacturer of aesthetic solutions such as face and body laser, light, and other energy-based aesthetic systems for hair removal and pigmented lesions. | 415-657-5500 | NA | Brisbane |
| Cymed (HQ) | Provider of ostomy pouching systems. The company specializes in skin care products and serves individuals and hospitals. | 800-582-0707 | 1-10 | Sacramento |
| Datest Corp (HQ) | Provider of testing and inspection services. The company specializes in engineering testing and counterfeit inspection for industrial products. | 510-490-4600 | NA | Fremont |
| DermDx Inc (HQ) | Developer of solutions for skin cancer detection and diagnosis. The company offers services to the medical industry. | 559-577-2542 | 1-10 | Fresno |
| Dicom Systems (HQ) | Provider of enterprise imaging, interoperability, and teleradiology solutions. The company offers services to patients. | 415-684-8790 | NA | Campbell |
| DirectGov Source Inc (HQ) | Manufacturer of personal protection kits. The company offers disposable clothing, biohazard disposal, antimicrobial sanitizers, and hand protection gloves. | 530-899-3327 | 1-10 | Chico |
| Duke Empirical (HQ) | Provider of product development, catheter design, and manufacturing services to medical manufacturers. | 831-420-1104 | 1-10 | Santa Cruz |
| Earlens Corp (HQ) | Manufacturer of medical devices such as contact hearing devices and sensorineural and conductive hearing impairment. | 650-366-9000 | NA | Menlo Park |
| Ebr Systems Inc (HQ) | Designer and developer of implantable systems for wireless tissue stimulation. The company focuses on the treatment of heart failure. | 408-720-1906 | NA | Sunnyvale |
| Echopixel Inc (HQ) | Provider of 3D medical visualization software for radiologists, cardiologists, pediatric cardiologists, and interventional neuroradiologists. | 844-273-7766 | NA | Santa Clara |
| Eco Sound Medical Services (HQ) | Distributor of healthcare products and medical supplies. The company is focused on incontinence products, medical nutrients, and nursing supplies. | 800-494-6868 | 1-10 | Tracy |
| Element Science Inc (HQ) | Developer of wearable platform solution. The company offers wearable cardioverter defibrillator for monitoring the heart of the patient. | 415-872-6500 | NA | San Francisco |
| Elixir Medical Corp (HQ) | Provider of pharmaceuticals for drug-device treatment solutions to patients. The company is engaged in drug delivery. | 408-636-2000 | NA | Milpitas |
| Emboline Inc (HQ) | Developer of cardiovascular embolic protection devices for transcatheter and surgical cardiac procedures. | 831-900-5020 | 1-10 | Santa Cruz |
| EMED (HQ) | Manufacturer of safety medical products and specialty medical devices with a focus on infusion therapy. | 916-932-0071 | 1-10 | El Dorado Hills |
| Endologix Inc. (HQ) | Developer of endovascular grafts for the treatment of aneurysmal disease in the abdominal aorta and the thoracic aorta. | 707-543-8800 | NA | Santa Rosa |
| Exploramed (HQ) | Developer of novel medical devices with cutting edge medical technology for use by major medical device manufacturing companies. | 650-472-0300 | NA | Mountain View |
| Farlow's Scientific Glassblowing Inc (HQ) | Provider of precision drilling, boring, cutting, grinding, salvage and repair, custom tooling, metal-to-glass bonding, and related services. | 530-477-5513 | 1-10 | Grass Valley |
| ForteBio (BR) | Provider of dip and read assay kits. The company's products are used in the application of kinetic characterization. | 650-322-1360 | NA | Fremont |
| Gauss Surgical Inc (HQ) | Manufacturer of mobile devices. The company is engaged in research and development services and it serves the healthcare sector. | 650-949-4153 | NA | Los Altos |
| Gcx Corp (HQ) | Provider of mounting solutions, application specific solutions, on-site services, and also technical support. | 707-773-1100 | NA | Petaluma |
| Gdm Electronic Medical (HQ) | Manufacturer of devices, electrical and electronics for medical, manufacturing and engineering industries. | 408-945-4100 | NA | San Jose |
| Genapsys Inc (HQ) | Developer of DNA sequencing to enable a paradigm shift in genomic diagnostics. The company specializes in GENIUS system that has footprint of Apple iPad. | 650-330-1096 | NA | Redwood City |
| General Foundry Service Corp (HQ) | Provider of foundry services. The company engages in pattern making, precision sand casting, and rubber plastic mold. | 510-297-5040 | NA | San Leandro |
| General Vision (HQ) | Provider of hardware and software products. The company specializes in artificial intelligence and image analytics. | 707-765-6150 | NA | Petaluma |
| Gynesonics (HQ) | Manufacturer and developer of therapeutic devices and related supplies for the treatment of uterine fibroids in women. | 650-216-3860 | NA | Redwood City |
| Halo Neuro Inc (HQ) | Developer of neurotech platform. The company offers services to athletes, elite teams, and organizations. | 415-851-3338 | NA | San Francisco |
| Hanger Prosthetics & Orthotics Inc (BR) | Provider of orthotic and prosthetic services and products. The company also offers clinically differentiated programs to its clients. | 209-725-1295 | 11-50 | Merced |
| HeartVista Inc (HQ) | Developer of magnetic resonance imaging (MRI) applications and development tools to aid in the diagnosis of cardiovascular disease. | 650-800-7937 | NA | Los Altos |
| Hitachi Chemical Diagnostics Inc (HQ) | Provider of in vitro allergy diagnostics products. The company offers alternative means of diagnosing allergy. | 650-961-5501 | NA | Mountain View |

| COMPANY NAME | PRODUCT / SERVICE | PHONE | EMP | CITY |
|---|---|---|---|---|
| HMS Electronics Inc (HQ) | Manufacturer of medical device components. The company offers custom made specialty component parts for x-ray machines. | 707-584-8760 | NA | Santa Rosa |
| Hologic Inc (BR) | Provider of healthcare and diagnostics. The company offers breast and skeletal healthcare and diagnostics, and GYN surgical solutions. | 669-224-6420 | NA | Santa Clara |
| Hospital Systems Inc (HQ) | Manufacturer of lighting, electrical and architectural products, and related supplies. The company is engaged in installation services. | 925-427-7800 | NA | Pittsburg |
| Illumina Inc (BR) | Developer, manufacturer, and marketer of integrated systems for the analysis of genetic variation and biological function. | 510-670-9300 | NA | Hayward |
| Inclin Inc (BR) | Provider of clinical, regulatory, and quality assurance services to pharmaceutical, biotechnology, and medical device companies. | 650-376-4000 | NA | San Mateo |
| InCube Labs (HQ) | Provider of laboratory services. The company offers medical devices and pharmaceuticals to various therapeutic areas. | 408-457-3700 | NA | San Jose |
| Intersect Ent Inc (HQ) | Provider of steroid-releasing implants that props open the sinuses for the treatment of common cold and sinusitis. | 650-641-2100 | 201-500 | Menlo Park |
| Intraop Medical Corp (HQ) | Manufacturer of mobetron for the treatment of cancer. The company offers services to hospitals, clinics, and patients. | 408-636-1020 | NA | Sunnyvale |
| Invuity Inc (HQ) | Manufacturer of surgical devices with cutting edge photonics technology to view surgical cavities during open, minimally invasive procedures. | 415-655-2100 | NA | San Francisco |
| Iridex Corp (HQ) | Provider of therapeutic based laser consoles, delivery devices, and consumable instrumentation. The company serves the healthcare industry. | 650-940-4700 | NA | Mountain View |
| iSchemaView Inc (HQ) | Developer and provider of neuroimaging platform. The company specializes in cerebrovascular imaging analysis. | 650-388-9767 | NA | Menlo Park |
| J R Scientific Inc (HQ) | Provider of cell culture products and services. The company's offerings include antibiotics, reagents, and other supplies. | 530-666-9868 | 1-10 | Woodland |
| Jasper Ridge Inc (HQ) | Manufacturer of tint and lighting exam systems. The company offers services to patients and hospitals. | 650-804-5040 | NA | San Mateo |
| Kezar Life Sciences Inc (HQ) | Developer of small molecule therapeutics drugs targeting protein homeostasis for transformative treatments for autoimmune diseases. | 650-822-5600 | NA | S San Francisco |
| Kinematic Automation Inc (HQ) | Provider of manufacturing systems for the medical industry. The company also offers automation, strip cutting, rotatory slitting services. | 209-532-3200 | 1-10 | Sonora |
| Lamdagen Corp (BR) | Developer of nano technology based biosensors used in research and diagnostic equipment for human and animal health testing. | 650-571-5816 | NA | Menlo Park |
| Leaf Healthcare Inc (HQ) | Specializes in wearable healthcare technologies. The company deals with patient mobility programs and serves the medical industry. | 844-826-5323 | NA | Pleasanton |
| LimFlow Inc (BR) | Designer and developer of LimFlow percutaneous deep vein arterilization system to restore blood flow to the ischemic foot. | 888-478-7705 | NA | Santa Clara |
| LinaTech USA (HQ) | Manufacturer of medical devices and software for the treatment of cancer through radiotherapy. The company also supplies informatics software for managing cancer clinics. | 408-733-2051 | NA | Sunnyvale |
| Loadstar Sensors Inc (HQ) | Manufacturer of sensors and load cells with wireless output, used in medical device, automotive, aerospace, consumer and other industries. | 510-274-1872 | NA | Fremont |
| Lsvp International Inc (HQ) | Manufacturer of flexible and semi-rigid endoscopic instruments. The company's services include engineering and distribution. | 650-969-1000 | NA | Los Altos |
| Marathon Products Inc (HQ) | Manufacturer of equipment for collecting data on temperature for use in packaging and shipping industries. | 510-562-6450 | NA | San Leandro |
| Meddev Corp (HQ) | Developer, manufacturer, and marketer of medical devices for niche market segments throughout the world. | 408-730-9702 | NA | Sunnyvale |
| Medical Design Solutions (HQ) | Provider of medical design solutions. The company develops miniaturized sensors and systems used in medical device applications. | 408-393-5386 | NA | Milpitas |
| Merieux Nutrisciences Corp (BR) | Provider of public health services. The company is focused on food and pharmaceutical products, cosmetics, and consumer goods. | 209-549-7508 | 11-50 | Salida |
| MicroCam.co (HQ) | Provider of medical devices. The company focusses on commercializing the plug and play micro imaging system. | 415-729-9391 | NA | San Rafael |
| Microcube (HQ) | Provider of concept development, design, rapid prototyping and IP management, market mapping, clinical trials, and regulatory submissions. | 510-651-5000 | NA | Fremont |
| Microdental Inc (HQ) | Provider of laboratory-fabricated restorations and related equipment. The company serves the healthcare sector. | 925-829-3611 | NA | Dublin |
| Micropoint Bioscience Inc (HQ) | Developer of medical products and services for treatment of vascular disease such as peripheral artery disease and venous blood clots disorders. | 408-588-1682 | NA | Santa Clara |
| Mid Labs Inc (HQ) | Manufacturer of ophthalmic products such as vitreous cutters, titanium forceps, and related accessories. | 510-357-3952 | NA | San Leandro |
| Minerva Surgical Inc (HQ) | Manufacturer of medical devices. The company provides products for the treatment of abnormal uterine bleeding. | 855-646-7874 | NA | Redwood City |
| Minto Research & Development Inc (HQ) | Supplier of emergency fracture response systems. | 530-222-2373 | 1-10 | Redding |
| Mirion Technologies Inc (DH) | Provider of solutions in radiation detection. The company serves the healthcare, nuclear power, and other industries. | 925-543-0800 | NA | San Ramon |
| Mizuho Osi (HQ) | Designs and manufactures medical components. The company offers surgery tables, patient care kits, trauma tables, and more. | 510-429-1500 | NA | Union City |

| COMPANY NAME | PRODUCT / SERVICE | PHONE | EMP | CITY |
|---|---|---|---|---|
| Motive Medical Intelligence (HQ) | Developer of medical intelligence solutions. The company also offers care plans for population health management. | 415-362-4007 | NA | San Francisco |
| Moximed Inc (BR) | Developer of joint preserving option for patients with knee osteoarthritis. The company serves the medical industry. | 510-887-3300 | NA | Hayward |
| Myoscience Inc (HQ) | Developer of medical technology. The company provides a therapy as the preeminent treatment for conditions involving nerves. | 510-933-1500 | NA | Fremont |
| Nano Precision Medical Inc (HQ) | Developer of medical devices. The company specializes in rice-grain sized implant for the treatment of type II diabetes. | 415-506-8462 | NA | Emeryville |
| Nanomix Inc (HQ) | Manufacturer of diagnostic systems and supplies. The company is engaged in product development services. | 510-428-5300 | NA | Emeryville |
| Natus Medical Inc (HQ) | Provider of medical devices, software, and services. The company offers products for neurology, newborn care, hearing diagnostics, and more. | 650-802-0400 | NA | San Carlos |
| Neotract Inc (HQ) | Provider of medical devices for the treatment of benign prostatic hyperplasia and its side effects such as loss of productivity and sleep and depression. | 925-401-0700 | NA | Pleasanton |
| Neuropace Inc (HQ) | Designer, developer, manufacturer, and marketer of implantable devices for the treatment of neurological disorders. | 650-237-2700 | NA | Mountain View |
| Neurosky Inc (HQ) | Manufacturer of ECG biosensors and also EEG biosensors for mobile solutions, wearable devices, and service providers. | 408-200-6675 | NA | San Jose |
| North Coast Medical Inc (HQ) | Manufacturer of medical and rehabilitation products such as castings, clinical supplies, and other wellness supplies. | 408-776-5000 | NA | Morgan Hill |
| Ocumetrics Inc (HQ) | Manufacturer of Fluorotron(TM) Master Ocular Fluorophotometers. The company deals with research services. | 650-960-3955 | NA | Mountain View |
| Onda Corp (HQ) | Manufacturer of medical devices. The company offers ultrasound measurement instrumentation and services for scientific applications. | 408-745-0383 | NA | Sunnyvale |
| Optovue Inc (HQ) | Manufacturer of ophthalmic devices. The company leads the commercialization of new imaging modalities to develop ophthalmic diagnosis. | 510-743-0985 | NA | Fremont |
| Paramit Corp (HQ) | Manufacturer of medical devices. The company is engaged in the planning and also implementation of strategies. | 408-782-5600 | NA | Morgan Hill |
| Pegasus Design Inc (HQ) | Provider of machine design and contract manufacturing services. The company serves the pharmaceutical instrument industry. | 925-292-7567 | NA | Livermore |
| Penumbra Inc (HQ) | Manufacturer of interventional therapy devices. The company develops products to treat challenging medical conditions. | 510-748-3200 | NA | Alameda |
| Perceptimed Inc (HQ) | Provider of medical technologies for dispensing and administration of prescription drugs safer, reducing injuries, and death. | 650-941-7000 | NA | Mountain View |
| Peridot Corp (HQ) | Provider of design for manufacturing and packaging. The company also manufacturers of medical components, miniature component and general product prototypes. | 925-461-8830 | NA | Pleasanton |
| PhysioCue Inc (HQ) | Developer of therapies and focuses on the delivery of thermo-neuro-stimulation systems. The company serves patients. | 408-524-1595 | NA | San Jose |
| Pickering Laboratories Inc (HQ) | Developer of post-column derivatization technology. The company specializes in manufacturing of cation-exchange columns for amino acid analysis. | 650-694-6700 | NA | Mountain View |
| Plastikon Industries (HQ) | Provider of contract manufacturing services for custom designed plastic injection molding, for medical, pharmaceutical and other industries. | 510-400-1010 | NA | Hayward |
| POC Medical Systems Inc (HQ) | Provider of diagnostic medical devices for the screening of life-threatening diseases like cancer, cardiovascular disorders, and infectious diseases. | 925-331-8010 | NA | Livermore |
| PONTiS Orthopaedics LLC (HQ) | Manufacturer of medical devices such as implants and instrumentation for use in upper & lower extremity bone and soft tissue repair. | 415-567-8935 | NA | San Francisco |
| Precise Light Surgical (HQ) | Provider of medical devices with vaporization technology for the removal of delicate tissues, reduce surgical risk, and down time in endoscopic surgery. | 831-539-3323 | NA | Campbell |
| Prime Engineering (HQ) | Provider of standing systems products such as granstand, kidstand, symmetry mobile, uprite, cindylift, and the lift. | 559-276-0991 | 1-10 | Fresno |
| Procept Biorobotics (HQ) | Provider of healthcare services. The company primarily focuses on personalized image-guided waterjet tissue resection services. | 650-232-7200 | NA | Redwood City |
| Prosurg Inc (HQ) | Manufacturer of medical devices. The company offers products for women's and men's healthcare, urological and gynecological disorders. | 408-945-4044 | NA | San Jose |
| Providence Medical Technology Inc (HQ) | Developer of medical devices and technologies such as dtrax spinal systems, cavux cervical cages, and ally screw systems for cervical spine care. | 415-923-9376 | NA | Pleasanton |
| Qi Medical Inc (HQ) | Manufacturer of fingertip testing, syringe filters, rinse fluids, incubators, and vial adaptors for pharmacists and nurses who handle sterile solutions. | 530-272-8700 | 1-10 | Grass Valley |
| Qview Medical (HQ) | Provider of assistance in the review of 3D automated breast ultrasound. The company offers services to the radiologists. | 650-397-5174 | NA | Los Altos |
| Rapidwerks Inc (HQ) | Manufacturer of medical equipment and devices. The company also offers accessories and semiconductor products. | 925-417-0124 | NA | Pleasanton |

| COMPANY NAME | PRODUCT / SERVICE | PHONE | EMP | CITY |
|---|---|---|---|---|
| RDM Industrial Products Inc (HQ) | Provider of laboratory and industrial furniture solutions. The company offers cabinets, counters, carts, and mobile tables. | 408-945-8400 | NA | Milpitas |
| Recor Medical Inc (RH) | Manufacturer of ultrasound denervation products. The company is involved in clinical trials and research solutions. | 650-542-7700 | NA | Palo Alto |
| Relucent Solutions Llc (HQ) | Manufacturer of medical devices. The company is involved in laser cutting, precision manufacturing, wire crimping, and related services. | 800-630-7704 | NA | Santa Rosa |
| Renovorx Inc (HQ) | Manufacturer of medical devices. The company develops solutions for targeted delivery of therapeutic and diagnostic agents. | 650-284-4433 | NA | Los Altos |
| Safe Hearing America Inc (HQ) | Provider of mobile hearing testing services and products. The company offerings include AQ Solid Plug, Sleep Plug, and Solid Plug. | 707-446-0880 | NA | Vacaville |
| Scientific Specialties Inc (HQ) | Manufacturer of injection molded plastic consumable and durable products such as tubes, pipette tips, and racks for life science research industry. | 209-333-2120 | 1-10 | Lodi |
| Sensoplex Inc (HQ) | Developer and manufacturer of wearable sensors. The company offers rechargeable batteries, displays, interfaces, and related accessories. | 408-391-9019 | NA | Redwood City |
| Sentreheart Inc (HQ) | Developer of catheter technology solutions. The company is engaged in suture delivery and related services. | 650-354-1200 | NA | Redwood City |
| Sgarlato Med Llc (HQ) | Manufacturer and distributor of foot and ankle implants for surgical use. The company also provides clinical, technical, and in-service training services. | 800-403-6876 | 1-10 | Mesa |
| Shifamed LLC (HQ) | Manufacturer of medical technologies and products catheters, custom balloons, painted balloon electrodes, and diagnostic and therapeutic instrumentation. | 408-560-2500 | NA | Campbell |
| Shockwave Medical Inc (HQ) | Focuses on the production of highest performance personal submarines on the planet. The company is involved in research services. | 877-775-4846 | NA | Santa Clara |
| Si-Bone Inc (RH) | Developer of medical products and technologies such as implants and titanium implant technology for SI joint pain and sacroiliac joint fusion surgery. | 408-207-0700 | NA | San Jose |
| Siesta Medical Inc (HQ) | Providers of medical devices. The company offers surgical implants and tools for the treatment of osa. | 408-320-9424 | NA | Los Gatos |
| Silicon Valley Precision Inc (HQ) | Provider of custom vertical and horizontal CNC machining, fabrication and assembly of parts. The company offers powder coating, painting and grinding. | 925-373-8259 | NA | Livermore |
| Skeletal Kinetics LLC (HQ) | Developer, manufacturer and marketer of bone fixation cement designed for the treatment of trauma fractures. | 408-366-5000 | 11-50 | Cupertino |
| Smc Ltd (BR) | Provider of custom packing for product sterilization. The company is engaged in supply chain management solutions. | 707-303-3000 | NA | Santa Rosa |
| Solta Medical Inc (HQ) | Designer, developer, manufacturer, and marketer of medical devices for the non-invasive treatment of wrinkles and other skin care devices. | 510-786-6946 | NA | Hayward |
| Sootheze (HQ) | Manufacturer of aromatherapy products and other products that help relieve pain and provide comfort. | 844-576-6843 | 1-10 | Red Bluff |
| Spineguard Inc (DH) | Specializes in spine surgery. The company offers services to patients, hospitals, and healthcare organizations. | 415-512-2500 | NA | San Francisco |
| SST Group Inc (HQ) | Provider of medical displays, recorders, film digitizers, and related accessories. The company offers optical library support services. | 408-350-3450 | NA | Santa Clara |
| Stellartech Research Corp (HQ) | Designer, developer, and manufacturer of medical devices. The company specializes in surgical probes, balloon electrode catheters, and other products. | 408-331-3000 | NA | Milpitas |
| Sunmedica Inc (HQ) | Specializes in surgical orthopaedics, wound management, cold therapy and sports medicine. The company also offers surgical positioning devices. | 530-229-1600 | 1-10 | Redding |
| Supracor Inc (HQ) | Developer of honeycomb products. The company's offerings include sandals, saddle pads, and related supplies. | 408-432-1616 | NA | San Jose |
| The Cooper Companies Inc (HQ) | Provider of healthcare solutions. The company offers health and wellness programs for women, individuals, and communities. | 925-460-3600 | NA | Pleasanton |
| The Foundry LLC (HQ) | Focuses on product development, prototyping, market analysis, development, and pre-clinical and clinical support services. | 650-326-2656 | NA | Menlo Park |
| Triple Ring Technologies Inc (HQ) | Manufacturer of in vitro diagnostics and life science tools. The company offer services to the medical devices, imaging, and industrial sectors. | 510-592-3000 | NA | Newark |
| Tusker Medical Inc (HQ) | Developer of pediatric-focused technologies. The company specializes in the placement of tubes without general anesthetics. | 650-223-6900 | NA | Menlo Park |
| United Medical Instruments Inc (HQ) | Provider of ultra sound equipment. The company focuses on pain management, breast imaging, and pathology. | 408-278-9300 | NA | San Jose |
| Vapore LLC (HQ) | Manufacturer of personal steam inhalers. The company's products are used for relief from sinus congestion, allergies, and discomfort from sore throat. | 925-998-6116 | NA | Concord |
| Varian Medical Systems Inc (HQ) | Provider of radiation therapies for cancer. The company develops and markets different types of radiation technologies to cure various cancers. | 650-493-4000 | NA | Palo Alto |
| VisionCare Ophthalmic Technologies Inc (HQ) | Manufacturer and marketer of implantable ophthalmic devices and technologies for improving vision of individuals with untreatable retinal disorders. | 408-872-9393 | NA | Saratoga |

| COMPANY NAME | PRODUCT / SERVICE | PHONE | EMP | CITY |
|---|---|---|---|---|
| VORTRAN Medical Technology Inc (HQ) | Developer of pulmonary modulation technology solutions. The company offers automatic disposable respiratory devices for treating pulmonary diseases. | 800-434-4034 | 1-10 | Sacramento |
| West Coast Surgical (HQ) | Manufacturer of surgical devices. The company offers designing, assembling and finishing of specialty surgical equipment. | 650-728-8095 | NA | Half Moon Bay |
| WHILL Inc (HQ) | Manufacturer of personal electric vehicles, wheel chairs, and mobility devices. The company serves individuals and clinics. | 844-699-4455 | NA | San Carlos |
| Whole You Inc (HQ) | Provider of healthcare solutions. The company specializes in sleep, dental, movement, and vision solutions to its customers. | 844-548-3385 | NA | San Jose |
| Zoeticx (HQ) | Provider of healthcare solutions. The company develops care applications and offers services to inpatients, ICU, and outpatients. | 408-622-6119 | NA | San Jose |

## 190 = Orthopedics & Prosthetics

| COMPANY NAME | PRODUCT / SERVICE | PHONE | EMP | CITY |
|---|---|---|---|---|
| Alpha Orthotics Corp (HQ) | Distributor of non-invasive orthotic products. The company provides products for catalogs, specialty foot retailers, and medical distributors. | 415-389-8980 | NA | Tiburon |
| Alterg Inc (HQ) | Provider of new technologies and products such as anti-gravity treadmills and bionic leg for physical therapy and athletic training. | 510-270-5900 | NA | Fremont |
| Anchor Orthotics & Prosthetics (HQ) | Provider of orthotics and prosthetics. The company offers personal ankle bionic systems, braces and support and artificial limbs for amputees. | 877-977-0448 | 1-10 | Sacramento |
| Bracesox The Original (HQ) | Manufacturer of bracesox, a brace cover with undersleeves and oversleeves to give brace comfort for patients. | 831-479-7628 | 1-10 | Soquel |
| Consensus Orthopedics Inc (HQ) | Manufacturer of orthopedic medical devices. The company's products include consensus hip systems, revision knee systems, mobile bearing knee systems, and others. | 916-355-7100 | 11-50 | El Dorado Hills |
| D Danz & Sons Inc (HQ) | Specializes in the custom fitting, designing, and manufacturing of ophthalmic prosthetics. The company deals with patient care. | 559-252-1770 | 11-50 | Fresno |
| EPIX Orthopaedics Inc (HQ) | Developer of orthopaedic devices that improve patient outcomes, surgeon accuracy & efficiency, and reduce costs to patients and health care system. | 844-710-9105 | NA | Palo Alto |
| Hanger Prosthetics & Orthotics Inc (BR) | Provider of orthotic and prosthetic services and products. The company also offers clinically differentiated programs to its clients. | 209-725-1295 | 11-50 | Merced |
| Hanger Prosthetics & Orthotics Inc (BR) | Provider of prosthetic and orthotic components and services. The company serves hospitals, patients, and the healthcare industry. | 916-452-5724 | 11-50 | South Sacramento |
| LIM innovations Inc (HQ) | Designer and manufacturer of prosthetic sockets for amputees. The company offers custom-molded, adjustable, and modular prosthetic sockets. | 844-888-8546 | NA | San Francisco |
| Moximed Inc (BR) | Developer of joint preserving option for patients with knee osteoarthritis. The company serves the medical industry. | 510-887-3300 | NA | Hayward |
| Ortho Group (HQ) | Designer of devices for the medical industry. The company specializes in orthopedic surgical devices. | 916-859-0881 | 1-10 | Rancho Cordova |
| Plastikon Industries (HQ) | Provider of contract manufacturing services for custom designed plastic injection molding, for medical, pharmaceutical and other industries. | 510-400-1010 | NA | Hayward |
| PONTiS Orthopaedics LLC (HQ) | Manufacturer of medical devices such as implants and instrumentation for use in upper & lower extremity bone and soft tissue repair. | 415-567-8935 | NA | San Francisco |
| Pro Lab Orthotics (HQ) | Manufacturer and supplier of orthoses products. The company's offerings include foot orthoses, pathology orthoses, and specialty orthoses. | 707-257-4400 | NA | Napa |
| Prosthetic Artists Inc (HQ) | Provider of impression-fitted, hand-sculpted, hand-painted ocular prostheses. The company also fits thin shell prostheses over disfigured eyes. | 916-485-4249 | 1-10 | Sacramento |
| Prosthetic Solutions Inc (HQ) | Manufacturer of medical devices. The company improves the lives of amputees by providing them prosthesis. | 831-637-0491 | 11-50 | Hollister |
| Pyramid Orthodontics (HQ) | Provider of orthodontics products. The company's products include clear brackets, bands, buccal tubes, and wire accessories. | 415-479-6400 | NA | San Rafael |
| Spectrum Orthotics & Prosthetics (BR) | Provider of orthotics and prosthetics products. The company serves physicians and the medical sector. | 530-243-4500 | 11-50 | Redding |
| Spinal Kinetics Inc (HQ) | Provider of preservation systems for treating degenerative diseases of the spine. The company serves the healthcare sector. | 408-636-2500 | NA | Sunnyvale |
| Steven R Young Ocularist Inc (HQ) | Provider of ocular prosthetic services. The company engages in scleral cover shells and maxillo-facial prosthetics. | 510-836-2123 | NA | Oakland |
| Sunrise Medical (us) Llc (HQ) | Distributor of folding wheel chairs, seating and positioning systems, and other mobility products to its customers. | 800-333-4000 | 11-50 | Fresno |
| Top Shelf (BR) | Manufacturer of orthopedic bracing and appliances. The company offers products for knee, shoulder, foot & ankle, and spine. | 866-592-0488 | 11-50 | Tracy |
| United Medical Instruments Inc (HQ) | Provider of ultra sound equipment. The company focuses on pain management, breast imaging, and pathology. | 408-278-9300 | NA | San Jose |

## 191 = R&D

| COMPANY NAME | PRODUCT / SERVICE | PHONE | EMP | CITY |
|---|---|---|---|---|
| Accuray Inc (HQ) | Provider of oncology treatment solutions. The company develops, manufactures and sells precise and innovative tumor treatment solutions. | 408-716-4600 | NA | Sunnyvale |
| Advance Research Associates (HQ) | Developer of human bio-therapeutic platform technology solutions, drug discovery, and related support services. | 650-810-1190 | NA | Santa Clara |
| Airxpanders Inc (HQ) | Provider of controlled tissue expander and small handheld wireless controller of breast cancer reconstructive surgery. | 650-390-9000 | NA | San Jose |

| COMPANY NAME | PRODUCT / SERVICE | PHONE | EMP | CITY |
|---|---|---|---|---|
| Arrayit Corp (HQ) | Focuses on the discovery, development and manufacture of proprietary life science technologies and consumables for disease prevention. | 408-744-1331 | NA | Sunnyvale |
| BD Biosciences (BR) | Manufacturer of medical devices. The company provides a broad range of medical supplies, devices, laboratory equipment and diagnostic products. | 877-232-8995 | NA | San Jose |
| Bionexus Inc (HQ) | Provider of biomedical products and services for research areas such as genomics, proteomics, immunology, protein expression, and cell biology. | 510-625-8400 | NA | Oakland |
| Broncus Medical Inc (HQ) | Provider of navigation, diagnostic and therapeutic technology solutions for treating patients with lung disease. | 650-428-1600 | NA | San Jose |
| Cairn Biosciences (HQ) | Provider of therapeutic solutions for treating cancer. The company is involved in biotechnical research and commercial business. | 415-503-1185 | NA | San Francisco |
| California Clinical Laboratory Association (HQ) | Provider of an Association for small and large laboratories in California. The company files suits to prevent medicare from denying coverage for lab tests. | 916-446-2646 | 1-10 | Sacramento |
| Calithera Biosciences Inc (HQ) | Developer of small molecule drugs directed against tumor metabolism and tumor immunology targets for the treatment of cancer. | 650-870-1000 | NA | S San Francisco |
| Cardiodx Inc (HQ) | Provider of corus cad blood test to assess obstructive cad. The company specializes in cardiovascular genomics and developing validated tests. | 650-475-2788 | NA | Redwood City |
| CenterVue Inc (BR) | Designer and manufacturer of medical devices for the diagnosis and management of ocular pathologies. | 408-988-8404 | NA | Fremont |
| Channel Medsystems Inc (HQ) | Developer of cryothermic technology and streamlined delivery system for women with heavy menstrual bleeding. | 510-338-9301 | NA | Emeryville |
| Circuit Therapeutics Inc (HQ) | Focuses on drug discovery and development as well as forging direct therapeutic applications of optogenetics. | 650-324-9400 | NA | Menlo Park |
| Cortexyme Inc (HQ) | Developer of therapeutic products for the treatment of Alzheimer's and other degenerative disorders. | | NA | S San Francisco |
| Domino Data Lab Inc (HQ) | Provider of premise and cloud-based enterprise data science platform for analysis applications. The company serves the business sector. | 415-570-2425 | NA | San Francisco |
| Eargo Inc (HQ) | Creator of medical device. The company specializes in virtually invisible in-ear hearing device that is comfortable, natural sounding, and rechargeable. | 650-351-7700 | NA | San Jose |
| Evena Medical Inc (HQ) | Developer of medical smart glasses and wearables. The company specializes in portable vein finder device for IV access procedures. | | 1-10 | Roseville |
| Evidation Health Inc (HQ) | Provider of digital health solutions for healthcare providers, payers, pharma/biotech, and digital health companies. | 650-727-5557 | NA | San Mateo |
| Fluidigm Sciences Inc (HQ) | Developer and creator of technologies for life science tools designed to revolutionize biology. The company is involved in research programs. | 650-871-7152 | NA | San Francisco |
| Halo Neuro Inc (HQ) | Developer of neurotech platform. The company offers services to athletes, elite teams, and organizations. | 415-851-3338 | NA | San Francisco |
| Health Advances LLC (BR) | Provider of consulting services to the healthcare industry. The company offers clinical development, product positioning, lifecycle management, and more. | 415-834-0800 | NA | San Francisco |
| iHEAR Medical Inc (HQ) | Provider of hearing technology. The company specializes in web-enabled hearing device to fulfill the unmet needs of the hearing impaired. | 510-276-4437 | NA | San Leandro |
| InCube Labs (HQ) | Provider of laboratory services. The company offers medical devices and pharmaceuticals to various therapeutic areas. | 408-457-3700 | NA | San Jose |
| InterVene Inc (HQ) | Provider of medical devices such as blueleaf endovenous valve formation system to treat severe venous disease in the legs. | 650-351-6725 | NA | S San Francisco |
| Kodiak Sciences Inc (HQ) | Manufacturer of medicines for the treatment of patients with age-related macular degeneration and diabetic eye disease, two leading causes of blindness. | 650-281-0850 | NA | Palo Alto |
| Kucklick Design (HQ) | Designer and developer of medical illustration products. The company's portfolio includes NovaSom system, Starion devices, and Extravastat. | 408-353-1508 | NA | Los Gatos |
| Ligandal Inc (HQ) | Developer of nanotechnology for precise and high-efficiency delivery of nucleic acids to specific cells and organelles for genetic medicine. | 650-866-5212 | NA | San Francisco |
| Lineage Cell Therapeutics Inc (HQ) | Provider of cell-based technologies and regenerative medicine for the treatment of chronic and degenerative diseases. | 510-871-4188 | 11-50 | Carlsbad |
| Medical Design Solutions (HQ) | Provider of medical design solutions. The company develops miniaturized sensors and systems used in medical device applications. | 408-393-5386 | NA | Milpitas |
| MiNDERA Corp (HQ) | Provider of technology to extract skin biomarkers enabling non-invasive molecular testing for skin cancer and other skin diseases. | 650-491-9643 | NA | S San Francisco |
| Minerva Surgical Inc (HQ) | Manufacturer of medical devices. The company provides products for the treatment of abnormal uterine bleeding. | 855-646-7874 | NA | Redwood City |
| Miramar Labs Inc (HQ) | Provider of solutions for excessive sweat. The company is engaged in clinical trials and research programs. | 408-579-8700 | NA | Santa Clara |
| Motive Medical Intelligence (HQ) | Developer of medical intelligence solutions. The company also offers care plans for population health management. | 415-362-4007 | NA | San Francisco |
| Nuvolase Inc (HQ) | Manufacturer of the pinpointe foot laser used for the treatment of nail fungus and in nail fungus procedures. | 530-809-1970 | 1-10 | Chico |

| COMPANY NAME | PRODUCT / SERVICE | PHONE | EMP | CITY |
|---|---|---|---|---|
| Ocellus Inc (HQ) | Provider of multidisciplinary technology and services such as nanotechnology-based solutions for aerospace, industrial, and medical applications. | 925-606-6540 | NA | Livermore |
| OrthoTrophix Inc (HQ) | Developer of therapies for medical needs of patients. The company specializes in regeneration of articular cartilage in knee and other joints. | 510-488-3832 | NA | Oakland |
| Penumbra Inc (HQ) | Manufacturer of interventional therapy devices. The company develops products to treat challenging medical conditions. | 510-748-3200 | NA | Alameda |
| Phoenix Technology Group LLC (HQ) | Provider of research laboratory services. The company offers anterior segment imaging and retinal imaging microscope services. | 925-485-1100 | NA | Pleasanton |
| PhysioCue Inc (HQ) | Developer of therapies and focuses on the delivery of thermo-neuro-stimulation systems. The company serves patients. | 408-524-1595 | NA | San Jose |
| Plaxgen Inc (HQ) | Developer of biodiagnostics solutions for clinical diagnostics and discovery of therapeutics to treat atherosclerosis and alzheimer's disease. | 510-894-0304 | NA | Fremont |
| Qi Medical Inc (HQ) | Manufacturer of fingertip testing, syringe filters, rinse fluids, incubators, and vial adaptors for pharmacists and nurses who handle sterile solutions. | 530-272-8700 | 1-10 | Grass Valley |
| Rani Therapeutics (HQ) | Developer of drug molecules including peptides, proteins and antibodies. The company offers services to the pharmaceutical industry. | 408-457-3700 | NA | San Jose |
| RDM Industrial Products Inc (HQ) | Provider of laboratory and industrial furniture solutions. The company offers cabinets, counters, carts, and mobile tables. | 408-945-8400 | NA | Milpitas |
| Renovorx Inc (HQ) | Manufacturer of medical devices. The company develops solutions for targeted delivery of therapeutic and diagnostic agents. | 650-284-4433 | NA | Los Altos |
| Sangamo Therapeutics (HQ) | Developer of engineered DNA-binding proteins for the regulation of gene expression and for gene modification. | 510-970-6000 | 201-500 | Richmond |
| Sensoplex Inc (HQ) | Developer and manufacturer of wearable sensors. The company offers rechargeable batteries, displays, interfaces, and related accessories. | 408-391-9019 | NA | Redwood City |
| Siesta Medical Inc (HQ) | Providers of medical devices. The company offers surgical implants and tools for the treatment of osa. | 408-320-9424 | NA | Los Gatos |
| Silk Road Medical Inc (HQ) | Specializes in the treatment of carotid artery diseases. The company is engaged in clinical trials and related services. | 408-720-9002 | NA | Sunnyvale |
| SwitchGear Genomics Inc (HQ) | Focuses on custom cloning, pathway screening, target validation, sequence variant assay, and custom mutagenesis services. | 760-431-1263 | 11-50 | Carlsbad |
| System Biosciences Inc (HQ) | Provider of genome-wide analysis of the mechanisms that regulate cellular processes and biological responses. | 650-968-2200 | NA | Mountain View |
| Triple Ring Technologies Inc (HQ) | Manufacturer of in vitro diagnostics and life science tools. The company offer services to the medical devices, imaging, and industrial sectors. | 510-592-3000 | NA | Newark |
| ViOptix Inc (HQ) | Manufacturer of medical support devices. The company specializes in devices used for respiratory support and oxygen supply. | 510-226-5860 | NA | Newark |
| Vistagen Therapeutics Inc (HQ) | Developer of medicine to treat depression, cancer and diseases and disorders involving the central nervous system. | 650-577-3600 | NA | S San Francisco |

## 192 = Reproduction-Related Equipment

| COMPANY NAME | PRODUCT / SERVICE | PHONE | EMP | CITY |
|---|---|---|---|---|
| Airxpanders Inc (HQ) | Provider of controlled tissue expander and small handheld wireless controller of breast cancer reconstructive surgery. | 650-390-9000 | NA | San Jose |
| Sentreheart Inc (HQ) | Developer of catheter technology solutions. The company is engaged in suture delivery and related services. | 650-354-1200 | NA | Redwood City |
| SST Group Inc (HQ) | Provider of medical displays, recorders, film digitizers, and related accessories. The company offers optical library support services. | 408-350-3450 | NA | Santa Clara |

## 193 = Rental/Repair

| COMPANY NAME | PRODUCT / SERVICE | PHONE | EMP | CITY |
|---|---|---|---|---|
| International Process Solutions Inc (HQ) | Provider of calibration, maintenance, document generation and validation services of pharmaceutical and biotech process equipment. | 650-595-7890 | NA | San Carlos |

## 194 = Software

| COMPANY NAME | PRODUCT / SERVICE | PHONE | EMP | CITY |
|---|---|---|---|---|
| 314e Corp (HQ) | Provider of IT skills, methodologies, and cost-effective managed services for healthcare application and technical support services. | 510-371-6736 | NA | Fremont |
| Able Health Inc (HQ) | Provider of value-based reimbursements under MACRA, MIPS, PQRS, medicaids, and commercial programs. | 805-288-0240 | NA | San Francisco |
| AlgoMedica Inc (HQ) | Developer of medical imaging software based on artificial neural networks for abdomen/pelvis, head, and liver and pediatrics CT scans. | 516-448-3124 | NA | Sunnyvale |
| Apixio Inc (HQ) | Provider of cognitive computing platform that enables the analysis of unstructured healthcare data at individual level, providing groundbreaking insights. | 877-424-4946 | NA | San Mateo |
| Arterys Inc (DH) | Developer of medical imaging cloud platform. The company specializes in diagnostic platform to make healthcare more accurate and data driven. | 650-319-7230 | NA | San Francisco |
| Augmedix Inc (HQ) | Provider of technology enabled documentation services for health systems and doctors. | 888-669-4885 | NA | San Francisco |
| Beyond Lucid Technologies Inc (HQ) | Developer of cloud-based software platform. The company offers services to the emergency medical, disaster management, and first response industries. | 650-648-3727 | NA | Concord |

| COMPANY NAME | PRODUCT / SERVICE | PHONE | EMP | CITY |
|---|---|---|---|---|
| Bigfoot Biomedical Inc (HQ) | Developer of biomedical solution to improve the lives of people with diabetes through the application of smart technology. | 408-716-5600 | NA | Milpitas |
| Biosearch Technologies Inc (RH) | Manufacturer of nucleic acid based products that accelerate the discovery and application of genomic information. | 415-883-8400 | NA | Petaluma |
| Catalia Health Inc (HQ) | Provider of medical solutions for pharmaceuticals, healthcare systems, and home care. The company specializes in robotic aides for an aging population. | 415-660-9264 | NA | San Francisco |
| Cedaron Medical Inc (HQ) | Provider of entrepreneurial, medical, technological, marketing, and documentation software solutions for healthcare providers. | 800-424-1007 | 1-10 | Davis |
| CellScope Inc (HQ) | Developer of smart mobile tools for the clinicians and families. The company focusses on the remote diagnosis of infectious diseases. | | NA | San Francisco |
| CellSight Technologies Inc (HQ) | Provider of imaging tools to assess immunotherapy for the clinicians. The company focusses on the development of polyethylene terephthalat tracers. | 650-799-1589 | NA | San Francisco |
| Chartware Inc (HQ) | Manufacturer of scheduler and practice management interfaces and systems. The company serves the medical sector. | 800-642-4278 | NA | Rohnert Park |
| Clinovo Inc (HQ) | Provider of resourcing solutions for pharmaceutical, biotechnology, diagnostic, medical device, and CRO customers. | 866-994-3121 | NA | San Jose |
| Compact Imaging Inc (HQ) | Developer of miniature optical sensor technology. The company specializes in mobile health applications. | 650-694-7801 | NA | Mountain View |
| Connectance Inc (HQ) | Provider of software for diagnosis in health care industry. The company offer online access too to detect a disease and offer treatment suggestion. | 415-891-8872 | NA | Mill Valley |
| Creganna Medical (BR) | Provider of medical devices. The company offers services that ranges from clinical and regulatory support to design and manufacturing services. | 408-364-7100 | NA | Campbell |
| D-EYE (HQ) | Designer and manufacturer of diagnostic instruments. The company offers smart phone based retinal imaging systems for clinical assessments. | 401-473-6323 | 1-10 | Truckee |
| Dicom Systems (HQ) | Provider of enterprise imaging, interoperability, and teleradiology solutions. The company offers services to patients. | 415-684-8790 | NA | Campbell |
| Digital Element Inc (HQ) | Developer of computer artwork, software, and tools for computer artists and developers. The company offers 3D animation, plug-ins, and art tools. | | NA | Fremont |
| Doctor on Demand (HQ) | Provider of urgent care doctors. The company offers lab screens for the treatment of mental health and chronic conditions. | 800-997-6196 | NA | San Francisco |
| E*Healthlinecom Inc (HQ) | Provider of integrated health care information management software such as administration discharge transfer, bed management, and patient billing. | 916-924-8092 | 1-10 | Sacramento |
| E-Health Records International Inc (HQ) | Provider of electronic medical record system that can manage all aspects of clinical care in a busy hospital environment. | 707-284-4300 | NA | Sebastopol |
| Eargo Inc (HQ) | Creator of medical device. The company specializes in virtually invisible in-ear hearing device that is comfortable, natural sounding, and rechargeable. | 650-351-7700 | NA | San Jose |
| Ebr Systems Inc (HQ) | Designer and developer of implantable systems for wireless tissue stimulation. The company focuses on the treatment of heart failure. | 408-720-1906 | NA | Sunnyvale |
| Endpoint Clinical inc (HQ) | Designer of response technology platforms to access data through phones, the web, and mobile devices. The company is engaged in engineering services. | 415-229-1600 | NA | San Francisco |
| Evena Medical Inc (HQ) | Developer of medical smart glasses and wearables. The company specializes in portable vein finder device for IV access procedures. | | 1-10 | Roseville |
| First Databank Inc (HQ) | Provider of healthcare solutions to hospitals, retail pharmacies, payers, drug manufacturers, and healthcare providers. | 650-588-5454 | NA | S San Francisco |
| Gauss Surgical Inc (HQ) | Manufacturer of mobile devices. The company is engaged in research and development services and it serves the healthcare sector. | 650-949-4153 | NA | Los Altos |
| Glooko Inc (HQ) | Provider of diabetes management solution. The company offers platform to allow patients manage diabetes data and collaborate with their doctors. | 650-720-5310 | NA | Mountain View |
| Halo Neuro Inc (HQ) | Developer of neurotech platform. The company offers services to athletes, elite teams, and organizations. | 415-851-3338 | NA | San Francisco |
| Health Advances LLC (BR) | Provider of consulting services to the healthcare industry. The company offers clinical development, product positioning, lifecycle management, and more. | 415-834-0800 | NA | San Francisco |
| HealthLoop (HQ) | Provider of healthcare solutions. The company deals with the integration of doctors, patients and care-givers. | 408-418-0998 | 11-50 | Mountain View |
| Imosphere Inc (BR) | Developer of healthcare analytics platform. The company offers services to healthcare professionals. | 800-204-1852 | NA | San Francisco |
| IntelaMetrix Inc (HQ) | Specializes in ultrasound technology solutions. The company offers assessment tools for the health, fitness and wellness industries. | 925-606-7044 | NA | Brentwood |
| Kenzen Inc (HQ) | Focuses on the manufacture of personal health monitors. The company serves individuals and healthcare organizations. | 650-384-5140 | NA | San Francisco |

| COMPANY NAME | PRODUCT / SERVICE | PHONE | EMP | CITY |
|---|---|---|---|---|
| Kura MD Inc (HQ) | Provider of telemedicine platform enables convenient, secure, HIPAA compliant, and telehealth appointments between physicians and patients through tablet. | 855-587-2220 | 1-10 | Roseville |
| Leaf Healthcare Inc (HQ) | Specializes in wearable healthcare technologies. The company deals with patient mobility programs and serves the medical industry. | 844-826-5323 | NA | Pleasanton |
| Lighthouse Worldwide Solutions (HQ) | Provider of dental supplies such as implants, dentures, partials, implant bars, and related accessories. | 510-438-0500 | NA | Fremont |
| Lightning Bolt Solutions Inc (HQ) | Provider of medical staff scheduling software and solutions. The company's services include scheduling, keeping backups, technical support, and training. | 866-678-3279 | NA | S San Francisco |
| LinaTech USA (HQ) | Manufacturer of medical devices and software for the treatment of cancer through radiotherapy. The company also supplies informatics software for managing cancer clinics. | 408-733-2051 | NA | Sunnyvale |
| McKesson Corporation (HQ) | Provider of healthcare services. The company offers revenue cycle management and managed services for hospitals. | 415-983-8300 | NA | San Francisco |
| Medeanalytics Inc (HQ) | Provider of performance management, compliance, employer reporting, patient engagement, and satisfaction solutions. | 510-379-3300 | NA | Emeryville |
| Modulus Data Systems (HQ) | Provider digital clinical cell (tally) counters. The company's products include Diffcount III, Comp-U-Diff, and Uro-Comp. | 650-365-3111 | NA | Redwood City |
| Motive Medical Intelligence (HQ) | Developer of medical intelligence solutions. The company also offers care plans for population health management. | 415-362-4007 | NA | San Francisco |
| mscripts LLC (HQ) | Specializes in clinical and manufacturer programs. The company offers services to patients and pharmacies. | 888-672-7478 | NA | San Francisco |
| Natus Medical Inc (HQ) | Provider of medical devices, software, and services. The company offers products for neurology, newborn care, hearing diagnostics, and more. | 650-802-0400 | NA | San Carlos |
| Nds Surgical Imaging (HQ) | Provider of medical imaging services. The company specializes in minimal invasive surgery viewing and diagnostic imaging. | 408-776-0085 | NA | San Jose |
| Prowess Inc (HQ) | Focuses on Windows-based treatment planning systems for radiation therapy treatment and OIS software. | 925-356-0360 | NA | Concord |
| Quantitative Medical Systems Inc (HQ) | Provider of medical systems and dialysis billing software products. The company is engaged in clinical support. | 510-654-9200 | NA | Emeryville |
| Qview Medical (HQ) | Provider of assistance in the review of 3D automated breast ultrasound. The company offers services to the radiologists. | 650-397-5174 | NA | Los Altos |
| Roam Analytics (HQ) | Developer of collaborative platform that collects and provides data. The company offers services to pharmaceutical and medical device companies. | | NA | San Mateo |
| Scimage Inc (HQ) | Provider of imaging solutions. The company also deals with clinical and cloud solutions and business intelligence support. | 866-724-6243 | NA | Los Altos |
| SST Group Inc (HQ) | Provider of medical displays, recorders, film digitizers, and related accessories. The company offers optical library support services. | 408-350-3450 | NA | Santa Clara |
| Tcs Healthcare Technologies (HQ) | Provider of care management solutions. The company offers software implementation and training and workflow design services. | 530-886-1700 | 1-10 | Auburn |
| TeleVital (HQ) | Provider of integrated electronic patient medical record and real-time telemedicine software modules. | 408-441-6732 | NA | Milpitas |
| Thync Inc (HQ) | Provider of wearable technology solutions. The company is involved in testing and related support services. | 408-484-4808 | NA | Los Gatos |
| Varian Medical Systems Inc (HQ) | Provider of radiation therapies for cancer. The company develops and markets different types of radiation technologies to cure various cancers. | 650-493-4000 | NA | Palo Alto |
| Viewics Inc (HQ) | Provider of consulting, custom development, and report authoring services. The company also offers packaged solutions. | 415-439-0084 | NA | Santa Clara |
| Vital Connect Inc (HQ) | Provider of healthcare solutions. The company focuses on biosensors, clinical-grade biometric measurements. | 408-963-4600 | NA | San Jose |
| Vital Enterprises (HQ) | Provider of field service and manufacturing solutions. The company offers services to hospitals and R&D laboratories. | 650-394-6486 | NA | San Francisco |
| Zoeticx (HQ) | Provider of healthcare solutions. The company develops care applications and offers services to inpatients, ICU, and outpatients. | 408-622-6119 | NA | San Jose |

## 95 = Surgical Instruments & Equipment

| COMPANY NAME | PRODUCT / SERVICE | PHONE | EMP | CITY |
|---|---|---|---|---|
| Ab Medical Technologies Inc (HQ) | Manufacturer of electronic medical systems and powered surgical instruments such as surgical pumps, arthroscopy shavers and lab equipment. | 530-605-2522 | 1-10 | Redding |
| Abbott (BR) | Provider of mechanical circulatory support products. The company offers a portfolio products to treat heart failure. | 800-456-1477 | NA | Pleasanton |
| Amerex Instruments Inc (HQ) | Provider of lab equipment. The company provides shakers, top-loading autoclaves, incubators, hybridization and convection ovens and water baths. | 925-299-0743 | NA | Concord |
| BD Biosciences (BR) | Manufacturer of medical devices. The company provides a broad range of medical supplies, devices, laboratory equipment and diagnostic products. | 877-232-8995 | NA | San Jose |
| Benvenue Medical Inc (HQ) | Developer of expandable implant systems for the spine. The company focuses on cylindrical implant design. | 408-454-9300 | NA | Santa Clara |

| COMPANY NAME | PRODUCT / SERVICE | PHONE | EMP | CITY |
|---|---|---|---|---|
| Bibbero Systems Inc (HQ) | Manufacturer of filing and office supplies including custom chart and index tab dividers, and color coded and pressboard classification file folders. | 800-242-2376 | NA | Petaluma |
| Bioluminate Inc (HQ) | Developer of probes that provide breast cancer detection data to physicians. The company serves the medical sector. | 650-743-0240 | NA | San Carlos |
| Boracchia + Associates (HQ) | Provider of consultant services and products to surgeons and medical facilities. The company offers operating room products, post-operative, and castroom products. | 800-826-1690 | NA | Petaluma |
| Boston Scientific (BR) | Provider of forceps, imaging systems, needles, pacemakers, snares, probes, and other related accessories. | 510-440-7700 | NA | Fremont |
| Boston Scientific Corporation (BR) | Manufacturer of baskets, forceps, imaging systems, needles, pacemakers, CTO and direct visualization systems. | 408-935-3400 | NA | San Jose |
| Cardiva Medical Inc (HQ) | Developer of vascular access management products such as vascade and catalyst to facilitate rapid hemostasis following diagnostic procedures. | 408-470-7170 | NA | Santa Clara |
| Ceterix Orthopaedics Inc (HQ) | Developer of medical devices such as suture passer is indicated for passing suture through soft tissue in orthopedic surgery. | 650-241-1748 | NA | Menlo Park |
| Cirtec Medical (HQ) | Manufacturer of complex implantable device manufacturing, medical device solutions, and smart solutions for highly complex miniaturization. | 408-395-0443 | NA | Los Gatos |
| Convergent Laser Technologies (HQ) | Provider of medical laser systems and fiber optic devices. The company deals with training and product support services. | 510-832-2130 | NA | Alameda |
| Earlens Corp (HQ) | Manufacturer of medical devices such as contact hearing devices and sensorineural and conductive hearing impairment. | 650-366-9000 | NA | Menlo Park |
| Emboline Inc (HQ) | Developer of cardiovascular embolic protection devices for transcatheter and surgical cardiac procedures. | 831-900-5020 | 1-10 | Santa Cruz |
| Hologic Inc (BR) | Provider of healthcare and diagnostics. The company offers breast and skeletal healthcare and diagnostics, and GYN surgical solutions. | 669-224-6420 | NA | Santa Clara |
| Hospital Systems Inc (HQ) | Manufacturer of lighting, electrical and architectural products, and related supplies. The company is engaged in installation services. | 925-427-7800 | NA | Pittsburg |
| InterVene Inc (HQ) | Provider of medical devices such as blueleaf endovenous valve formation system to treat severe venous disease in the legs. | 650-351-6725 | NA | S San Francisco |
| Iridex Corp (HQ) | Provider of therapeutic based laser consoles, delivery devices, and consumable instrumentation. The company serves the healthcare industry. | 650-940-4700 | NA | Mountain View |
| Lifescience Plus Inc (HQ) | Developer of wound care technology solutions and its applications include surgery, dentistry, and public safety. | 650-565-8172 | NA | Mountain View |
| LIM innovations Inc (HQ) | Designer and manufacturer of prosthetic sockets for amputees. The company offers custom-molded, adjustable, and modular prosthetic sockets. | 844-888-8546 | NA | San Francisco |
| Lorom West (HQ) | Manufacturer of PCB assemblies, turnkey OEM/ODM products and custom cable and wire harnesses. The company offers industry solutions. | 510-249-9000 | NA | Fremont |
| Lumenis Inc (DH) | Provider of minimally-invasive clinical solutions. The company develops and commercializes energy-based technologies. | 877-586-3647 | NA | San Jose |
| Mid Labs Inc (HQ) | Manufacturer of ophthalmic products such as vitreous cutters, titanium forceps, and related accessories. | 510-357-3952 | NA | San Leandro |
| Minerva Surgical Inc (HQ) | Manufacturer of medical devices. The company provides products for the treatment of abnormal uterine bleeding. | 855-646-7874 | NA | Redwood City |
| Neodyne Biosciences Inc (HQ) | Manufacturer of embrace devices and it helps in the concealment of scars. The company serves patients. | 800-519-7127 | NA | Newark |
| NewGen Surgical Inc (HQ) | Designer of single use medical devices. The company offers skin staplers, needle counters, and procedure kit packaging trays. | 855-295-4500 | NA | San Rafael |
| Nidek Inc (RH) | Manufacturer of ophthalmic devices. The company also offers refractive systems and diagnostic products to the medical industry. | 800-223-9044 | NA | Fremont |
| Penumbra Inc (HQ) | Manufacturer of interventional therapy devices. The company develops products to treat challenging medical conditions. | 510-748-3200 | NA | Alameda |
| Plastikon Industries (HQ) | Provider of contract manufacturing services for custom designed plastic injection molding, for medical, pharmaceutical and other industries. | 510-400-1010 | NA | Hayward |
| Preferred Products (HQ) | Manufacturer of diagnostic instruments, headlights and mirrors, forceps, microscopes, office equipment, and ear instruments. | 415-499-3544 | NA | San Rafael |
| Prosurg Inc (HQ) | Manufacturer of medical devices. The company offers products for women's and men's healthcare, urological and gynecological disorders. | 408-945-4044 | NA | San Jose |
| Providence Medical Technology Inc (HQ) | Developer of medical devices and technologies such as dtrax spinal systems, cavux cervical cages, and ally screw systems for cervical spine care. | 415-923-9376 | NA | Pleasanton |
| Pulsar Vascular Inc (HQ) | Manufacturer of endovascular diseases and it focuses on the treatment of complex aneurysms. The company is engaged in clinical trials. | 408-260-9264 | NA | San Jose |
| Qview Medical (HQ) | Provider of assistance in the review of 3D automated breast ultrasound. The company offers services to the radiologists. | 650-397-5174 | NA | Los Altos |
| Renovorx Inc (HQ) | Manufacturer of medical devices. The company develops solutions for targeted delivery of therapeutic and diagnostic agents. | 650-284-4433 | NA | Los Altos |
| Sanovas Inc (HQ) | Manufacturer of medical equipment. The company develops minimally invasive surgical tools and technologies. | 415-729-9391 | NA | San Rafael |

| COMPANY NAME | PRODUCT / SERVICE | PHONE | EMP | CITY |
|---|---|---|---|---|
| Shen Wei USA Inc (HQ) | Manufacturer of disposable gloves and customizable products. The company offers services to the healthcare industry. | 510-429-8692 | NA | Union City |
| Spinal Kinetics Inc (HQ) | Provider of preservation systems for treating degenerative diseases of the spine. The company serves the healthcare sector. | 408-636-2500 | NA | Sunnyvale |
| Spineguard Inc (DH) | Specializes in spine surgery. The company offers services to patients, hospitals, and healthcare organizations. | 415-512-2500 | NA | San Francisco |
| Starch Medical Inc (HQ) | Provider of hemostatic solutions. The company offers services to patients and serves the healthcare industry. | 408-428-9818 | NA | San Jose |
| Supracor Inc (HQ) | Developer of honeycomb products. The company's offerings include sandals, saddle pads, and related supplies. | 408-432-1616 | NA | San Jose |
| TTI Medical (HQ) | Designer and marketer of surgical instruments and medical devices. The company serves hospitals and the healthcare sector. | 925-553-7828 | NA | San Ramon |
| Tusker Medical Inc (HQ) | Developer of pediatric-focused technologies. The company specializes in the placement of tubes without general anesthetics. | 650-223-6900 | NA | Menlo Park |
| Varian Medical Systems Inc (HQ) | Provider of radiation therapies for cancer. The company develops and markets different types of radiation technologies to cure various cancers. | 650-493-4000 | NA | Palo Alto |
| Varian Medical Systems Inc (BR) | Provider of radiation therapies for cancer. The company develops and markets different types of radiation technologies to cure various cancers. | 408-321-9400 | NA | Milpitas |
| Velano Vascular Inc (HQ) | Manufacturer of needle-free devices for drawing blood from hospitalized patients. The company offers services to the medical industry. | 844-835-2668 | NA | San Francisco |
| VisionCare Ophthalmic Technologies Inc (HQ) | Manufacturer and marketer of implantable ophthalmic devices and technologies for improving vision of individuals with untreatable retinal disorders. | 408-872-9393 | NA | Saratoga |
| West Coast Surgical (HQ) | Manufacturer of surgical devices. The company offers designing, assembling and finishing of specialty surgical equipment. | 650-728-8095 | NA | Half Moon Bay |
| Zipline Medical Inc (HQ) | Developer of zip surgical skin closure devices for cardiology, orthopedics, dermatology, plastic reconstructive surgery, and emergency medicine. | 408-412-7228 | NA | Campbell |

## 196 = Therapeutic Equipment

| COMPANY NAME | PRODUCT / SERVICE | PHONE | EMP | CITY |
|---|---|---|---|---|
| Admecell Inc (HQ) | Manufacturer of ready to use products such as cell based, TRANSIL, and ELISA based assays for in-vitro therapeutic modeling and re-profiling. | 510-522-4200 | NA | Alameda |
| Airxpanders Inc (HQ) | Provider of controlled tissue expander and small handheld wireless controller of breast cancer reconstructive surgery. | 650-390-9000 | NA | San Jose |
| Alterg Inc (HQ) | Provider of new technologies and products such as anti-gravity treadmills and bionic leg for physical therapy and athletic training. | 510-270-5900 | NA | Fremont |
| Amgen Inc (BR) | Provider of scientific applications services. The company's services include clinical trials, ethical research, biosimilars, and web resources. | 650-244-2000 | NA | S San Francisco |
| Apollomics Inc (HQ) | Developer of oncology therapeutics. The company focusses on discovering therapeutics for the immune system and molecular pathways to treat cancer. | 650-209-4055 | NA | Foster City |
| Ark Diagnostics Inc (HQ) | Manufacturer of in vitro diagnostic products for the treatment of cancer, veterinary, HIV/AIDS, anti-fungal drugs, and epilepsy and pain management. | 877-869-2320 | NA | Fremont |
| Backproject Corp (HQ) | Manufacturer of physical therapy equipment. The company specializes in vertical physical therapy equipment for musculoskeletal pain relief. | 408-730-1111 | NA | Sunnyvale |
| Bactrack (HQ) | Provider of breathalyzers. The company provides products for a wide range of personal, professional and smartphone use. | 415-693-9756 | NA | San Francisco |
| Cairn Biosciences (HQ) | Provider of therapeutic solutions for treating cancer. The company is involved in biotechnical research and commercial business. | 415-503-1185 | NA | San Francisco |
| Cala Health Inc (HQ) | Provider of therapeutic solutions. The company focusses on the development of neuroperipheral therapy to treating chronic diseases. | 415-890-3961 | NA | Burlingame |
| Calithera Biosciences Inc (HQ) | Developer of small molecule drugs directed against tumor metabolism and tumor immunology targets for the treatment of cancer. | 650-870-1000 | NA | S San Francisco |
| Caribou Biosciences Inc (HQ) | Developer of cellular engineering and analysis solutions. The company is involved in applied biological research. | 510-982-6030 | NA | Berkeley |
| Circuit Therapeutics Inc (HQ) | Focuses on drug discovery and development as well as forging direct therapeutic applications of optogenetics. | 650-324-9400 | NA | Menlo Park |
| CoA Therapeutics (HQ) | Developer of novel therapies for treating genetic disorders. The company specializes in drug development in oncology, cardiology, and dermatology fields. | | NA | San Francisco |
| Coolsystems Inc (HQ) | Manufacturer of medical devices. The company specializes in injury treatment and accelerated recovery systems. | 510-868-2100 | NA | Concord |
| Dendreon Pharmaceuticals LLC (HQ) | Provider of biotechnology services. The company provides therapeutics for the treatment of cancer employing active cellular immunotherapy. | 877-256-4545 | 11-50 | Seal Beach |
| Directed Light Inc (HQ) | Manufacturer of industrial and scientific laser components. The company offers laser welding, cutting, drilling, ablation, and marking services. | 408-321-8500 | NA | San Jose |
| Durect Corp (HQ) | Developer of products for the treatment of chronic debilitating disease. The company specializes in biotechnology products. | 408-777-1417 | NA | Cupertino |

| COMPANY NAME | PRODUCT / SERVICE | PHONE | EMP | CITY |
|---|---|---|---|---|
| Eigen (HQ) | Manufacturer of cardiology and radiology imaging products. The company serves urologists and radiation oncologists. | 530-274-1240 | 1-10 | Grass Valley |
| Evidation Health Inc (HQ) | Provider of digital health solutions for healthcare providers, payers, pharma/biotech, and digital health companies. | 650-727-5557 | NA | San Mateo |
| Glycomine Inc (HQ) | Developer of therapy solutions for the treatment of orphan diseases of glycosylation. The company focusses on genetic disorders of lipid glycosylation and protein. | 650-401-2016 | NA | San Carlos |
| Gynesonics (HQ) | Manufacturer and developer of therapeutic devices and related supplies for the treatment of uterine fibroids in women. | 650-216-3860 | NA | Redwood City |
| Health Advances LLC (BR) | Provider of consulting services to the healthcare industry. The company offers clinical development, product positioning, lifecycle management, and more. | 415-834-0800 | NA | San Francisco |
| iSchemaView Inc (HQ) | Developer and provider of neuroimaging platform. The company specializes in cerebrovascular imaging analysis. | 650-388-9767 | NA | Menlo Park |
| Kucklick Design (HQ) | Designer and developer of medical illustration products. The company's portfolio includes NovaSom system, Starion devices, and Extravastat. | 408-353-1508 | NA | Los Gatos |
| Lamdagen Corp (BR) | Developer of nano technology based biosensors used in research and diagnostic equipment for human and animal health testing. | 650-571-5816 | NA | Menlo Park |
| LimFlow Inc (BR) | Designer and developer of LimFlow percutaneous deep vein arterilization system to restore blood flow to the ischemic foot. | 888-478-7705 | NA | Santa Clara |
| Lorom West (HQ) | Manufacturer of PCB assemblies, turnkey OEM/ODM products and custom cable and wire harnesses. The company offers industry solutions. | 510-249-9000 | NA | Fremont |
| Medtronic CardioVascular inc (BR) | Provider of disease management services. The company specializes in cardiovascular, diabetes, surgical technologies, and spinal and biologics. | 707-525-0111 | NA | Santa Rosa |
| Mercator Medsystems Inc (HQ) | Developer of therapeutics for vascular disease, oncology and regenerative medicine, and treatment of hypertension. | 510-614-4550 | NA | Emeryville |
| Modulus Data Systems (HQ) | Provider digital clinical cell (tally) counters. The company's products include Diffcount III, Comp-U-Diff, and Uro-Comp. | 650-365-3111 | NA | Redwood City |
| Myoscience Inc (HQ) | Developer of medical technology. The company provides a therapy as the preeminent treatment for conditions involving nerves. | 510-933-1500 | NA | Fremont |
| Nanomix Inc (HQ) | Manufacturer of diagnostic systems and supplies. The company is engaged in product development services. | 510-428-5300 | NA | Emeryville |
| Neuropace Inc (HQ) | Designer, developer, manufacturer, and marketer of implantable devices for the treatment of neurological disorders. | 650-237-2700 | NA | Mountain View |
| Nevro Corp (HQ) | Developer of new high-frequency stimulation technology for improving the role of spinal cord stimulation in the treatment of chronic pain. | 650-251-0005 | NA | Redwood City |
| OrthoTrophix Inc (HQ) | Developer of therapies for medical needs of patients. The company specializes in regeneration of articular cartilage in knee and other joints. | 510-488-3832 | NA | Oakland |
| Paramit Corp (HQ) | Manufacturer of medical devices. The company is engaged in the planning and also implementation of strategies. | 408-782-5600 | NA | Morgan Hill |
| Pelvalon Inc (HQ) | Provider of non-surgical therapy such as uninflated and inflated devices that offers immediate results for women experiencing loss of bowel control. | 650-276-0130 | NA | Sunnyvale |
| Penumbra Inc (HQ) | Manufacturer of interventional therapy devices. The company develops products to treat challenging medical conditions. | 510-748-3200 | NA | Alameda |
| Pherin Pharmaceuticals Inc (HQ) | Developer of novel compounds for intranasal spray delivery and also deals with the treatment of neuro-psychiatric and neuroendocrine conditions. | 650-961-2080 | NA | Los Altos |
| Profusa Inc (HQ) | Focuses on the development of biointegrated sensors. The company offers services to the environment sector. | 415-655-9861 | NA | Emeryville |
| Pulmonx Corp (HQ) | Manufacturer of medical devices. The company focuses on developing both diagnostic and therapeutic technologies for Interventional Pulmonology. | 650-364-0400 | NA | Redwood City |
| Relievant Medsystems Inc (HQ) | Provider of healthcare solutions . The company develops a system that utilizes a small probe for the treatment of chronic back pain. | 650-368-1000 | NA | Sunnyvale |
| Sanbio Inc (HQ) | Developer of regenerative therapies for neurological disorders. The company offers services to the healthcare sector.. | 650-625-8965 | NA | Mountain View |
| Semi-Probes Inc (HQ) | Manufacturer and supplier of probe cards and tester interfaces. The company's services include design, installation, and delivery. | 408-866-6535 | NA | San Jose |
| TheraBiol Inc (HQ) | Developer of therapies for the treatment of infectious diseases caused by agents such as Human Immunodeficiency Virus (HIV). | 415-608-3841 | NA | San Francisco |
| Trellis Bioscience LLC (HQ) | Developer of human antibody therapeutics as treatment for infectious disease and oncology indications. | 650-838-1400 | NA | Redwood City |
| TriReme Medical LLC (RH) | Developer of differentiated therapeutic solutions. The company manufactures and distributes the chocolate and glider families of angioplasty balloons. | 925-931-1300 | NA | Pleasanton |
| Vistagen Therapeutics Inc (HQ) | Developer of medicine to treat depression, cancer and diseases and disorders involving the central nervous system. | 650-577-3600 | NA | S San Francisco |
| Xms Corp (HQ) | Manufacturer and distributor of medical devices. The company specializes in cost effective, cutting edge radiation therapy equipment. | 916-435-0267 | 1-10 | Rocklin |

## 198 = Medical Imaging and X-Ray Apparatus

| COMPANY NAME | PRODUCT / SERVICE | PHONE | EMP | CITY |
|---|---|---|---|---|
| Accsys Technology Inc (HQ) | Manufacturer of ion linear accelerator systems used in medical imaging devices, industrial applications and in research. | 925-462-6949 | NA | Pleasanton |
| Bioclinica Inc (HQ) | Developer of medical therapies. The company specializes in medical imaging services, cardiac safety, and enterprise eClinical platforms. | 415-817-8900 | NA | Newark |
| BioTrace Medical Inc (HQ) | Manufacturer of medical devices. The company specializes in cardiac pacing device which can treat reversible symptomatic bradycardia. | 650-779-4999 | NA | Menlo Park |
| Boston Scientific Corporation (BR) | Manufacturer of baskets, forceps, imaging systems, needles, pacemakers, CTO and direct visualization systems. | 408-935-3400 | NA | San Jose |
| CapsoVision (HQ) | Specializes in the diagnostic imaging of the gastrointestinal systems. The company offers services to hospitals and patients. | 408-624-1488 | NA | Saratoga |
| CenterVue Inc (BR) | Designer and manufacturer of medical devices for the diagnosis and management of ocular pathologies. | 408-988-8404 | NA | Fremont |
| Cephasonics (HQ) | Developer of ultrasound-based measurement products. The company deals with research and clinical trials. | 800-510-4561 | NA | Santa Clara |
| D-EYE (HQ) | Designer and manufacturer of diagnostic instruments. The company offers smart phone based retinal imaging systems for clinical assessments. | 401-473-6323 | 1-10 | Truckee |
| Dicom Systems (HQ) | Provider of enterprise imaging, interoperability, and teleradiology solutions. The company offers services to patients. | 415-684-8790 | NA | Campbell |
| Digital Artforms Inc (HQ) | Provider of immersive 3D interaction for specialized markets and applications including medicine, security, and military/command & control. | 408-356-6169 | NA | Los Gatos |
| El Portal Imaging Center (HQ) | Specializes in diagnostic imaging solutions. The company serves hospitals, clinics, and the healthcare sector. | 209-384-4250 | 1-10 | Merced |
| Hesco (HQ) | Provider of portable x-ray imaging services. The company offer services for power plants, bridges, dams, refineries, and more. | 510-568-1380 | NA | San Leandro |
| HMS Electronics Inc (HQ) | Manufacturer of medical device components. The company offers custom made specialty component parts for x-ray machines. | 707-584-8760 | NA | Santa Rosa |
| Interson Corp (HQ) | Manufacturer of ultrasound products. The company offers services to offices, hospitals, and clinics around the world. | 925-462-4948 | NA | Pleasanton |
| iSchemaView Inc (HQ) | Developer and provider of neuroimaging platform. The company specializes in cerebrovascular imaging analysis. | 650-388-9767 | NA | Menlo Park |
| MicroCam.co (HQ) | Provider of medical devices. The company focusses on commercializing the plug and play micro imaging system. | 415-729-9391 | NA | San Rafael |
| Micropoint Bioscience Inc (HQ) | Developer of medical products and services for treatment of vascular disease such as peripheral artery disease and venous blood clots disorders. | 408-588-1682 | NA | Santa Clara |
| Nds Surgical Imaging (HQ) | Provider of medical imaging services. The company specializes in minimal invasive surgery viewing and diagnostic imaging. | 408-776-0085 | NA | San Jose |
| Onda Corp (HQ) | Manufacturer of medical devices. The company offers ultrasound measurement instrumentation and services for scientific applications. | 408-745-0383 | NA | Sunnyvale |
| Procept Biorobotics (HQ) | Provider of healthcare services. The company primarily focuses on personalized image-guided waterjet tissue resection services. | 650-232-7200 | NA | Redwood City |
| SST Group Inc (HQ) | Provider of medical displays, recorders, film digitizers, and related accessories. The company offers optical library support services. | 408-350-3450 | NA | Santa Clara |
| Suni Medical Imaging Inc (HQ) | Manufacturer of digital radiography. The company designs, develops, manufactures and sell digital sensors for the medical field. | 408-227-6698 | NA | San Jose |
| TechniQuip Corp (HQ) | Supplier of lighting products. The company's offerings include illuminators, fiber optics, and video equipment. | 925-251-9030 | NA | Pleasanton |
| Trufocus Corp (HQ) | Supplier of x-ray products. The company's products are used in industrial, medical, aerospace, and analytical application. | 831-761-9981 | 1-10 | Watsonville |
| Varian Medical Systems Inc (HQ) | Provider of radiation therapies for cancer. The company develops and markets different types of radiation technologies to cure various cancers. | 650-493-4000 | NA | Palo Alto |
| Xoft Inc (HQ) | Developer of electronic brachytherapy systems. The company's products include rigid shield, vacuum pumps, and physics kits. | 408-493-1500 | NA | San Jose |

## 200 = Adapters

| COMPANY NAME | PRODUCT / SERVICE | PHONE | EMP | CITY |
|---|---|---|---|---|
| Accusilicon USA Inc (HQ) | Manufacturer of TCXO IC chips and designer and developer of high frequency oscillators for the industrial sector. | 408-256-0858 | NA | Santa Clara |
| ADLINK Technology Inc (LH) | Designer and manufacturer of products for embedded computing, test & measurement, and automation applications. The company serves various sectors. | 408-360-0200 | NA | San Jose |
| Asteelflash (BR) | Provider of electronic manufacturing services. The company offers engineering design, contract manufacturing, and delivery services. | 510-440-2840 | NA | Fremont |
| Cooper (HQ) | Designer of kiosks, medical devices and software, smartphone, IT tools, websites, irrigation, supply chain management, and financial services system. | 415-267-3500 | NA | San Francisco |
| eze System (HQ) | Provider or monitoring and measuring solutions. The company's products include controllers, controller expansions, and sensors. | 716-393-9330 | 11-50 | Folsom |
| Intilop Inc (HQ) | Provider of engineering design services. The company also develops and provides silicon IP products. | 408-791-6700 | NA | Santa Clara |

| COMPANY NAME | PRODUCT / SERVICE | PHONE | EMP | CITY |
|---|---|---|---|---|
| Iris Ao Inc (HQ) | Manufacturer of microelectromechanical based optical systems. The company's applications include biomedical imaging and portable laser communications. | 510-849-2375 | NA | Berkeley |
| Phihong Usa Corp (LH) | Provider of power solutions in the telecom sector. The company also offers data solutions in industrial and personal electronic markets. | 510-445-0100 | NA | Fremont |
| Pragmatics Technologies Inc (HQ) | Provider of electromechanical interface solutions. The company deals with the development of custom and standard test interfaces. | 408-289-8202 | NA | San Jose |
| Quail Electronics Inc (HQ) | Manufacturer of power cord supplies for the OEM market. The company offers solutions for power cords, current cords, and adapters, and traveler kits. | 925-373-6700 | NA | Livermore |
| Quality Quartz Engineering Inc (HQ) | Designer and manufacturer of solid quartz products for solar, fiber optic, semiconductor, and lighting industries. | 510-745-9200 | NA | Newark |
| Quest Microwave Inc (HQ) | Provider of ferrite products for the microwave electronics industry. The company offers both standard and custom designs. | 408-778-4949 | NA | Morgan Hill |
| Rathbun Associates (HQ) | Distributor and reseller of converters. The company offers thermal management solutions, specialty tapes, and protective products. | 510-661-0950 | NA | Fremont |
| Santronics Inc (HQ) | Designer and manufacturer magnetic components. The company offers transformers, inductors, and coils for data transmission and power conversion needs. | 408-734-1878 | NA | Sunnyvale |
| Schmartboard Inc (HQ) | Specializes in the production of hand soldering components. The company's products are used in sensor and USB technologies. | 510-744-9900 | NA | Fremont |
| Shasta Crystals Inc (HQ) | Producer of nonlinear optical crystals for visible lasers. The company's services include research and evaluation. | 415-426-7904 | NA | San Francisco |
| Solar Components Llc (HQ) | Manufacturer of micro-processor controlled solar power electronic systems. The company provides solar power management and charge control solutions. | 408-369-1727 | NA | Campbell |
| Tamura Corporation of America (BR) | Manufacturer of DC power modules, current sensor products, telecom transformers, and LED products. The company is involved in distribution services. | 760-871-2009 | NA | Escondido |
| Ten Pao International Inc (HQ) | Manufacturer of power supply systems such as switchings, displays, and traditional linear transformers. | 408-389-3560 | NA | Sunnyvale |

## 201 = Anodes/Cathodes/Electrodes

| COMPANY NAME | PRODUCT / SERVICE | PHONE | EMP | CITY |
|---|---|---|---|---|
| Rose Electronics Distributing Company Inc (HQ) | Provider of batteries and power solutions. The company primarily serves original equipment manufacturers such as VRLA batteries and lithium ion batteries. | 408-943-0200 | NA | San Jose |

## 202 = Cable & Wiring Assemblies

| COMPANY NAME | PRODUCT / SERVICE | PHONE | EMP | CITY |
|---|---|---|---|---|
| Aimer Corp (HQ) | Provider of thermal management products. The company also offers connectors, PCB boards, cables, and mechanical parts. | 408-260-8588 | NA | Santa Clara |
| Allwire Inc (HQ) | Provider of design, analysis, and programming services for businesses. The company is also involved in web hosting and technical support. | 559-665-4893 | 1-10 | Chowchilla |
| ASCENX Technologies Inc (HQ) | Provider of engineering services to the semiconductor industry. The company is also engaged in contract manufacturing and repair services. | 408-945-1997 | NA | Fremont |
| Assembly Tek (HQ) | Manufacturer of custom cables. The company offers services like design, laminating, JIT programs, and wire preparation. | 831-439-0800 | 1-10 | Scotts Valley |
| Bay Associates Wire Technologies (HQ) | Provider of cable and cable assembly solutions. The company serves the medical, navigation, audio, and automotive markets. | 510-933-3800 | NA | Fremont |
| Blue Danube Systems Inc (BR) | Designer and developer of mobile wireless access solutions that increase network capacity. The company serves the industrial sector. | 650-316-5010 | NA | Santa Clara |
| Compass Components Inc (HQ) | Manufacturer of custom cables & harnesses and distributor of electronic components. The company also manufactures electromechanical products. | 510-656-4700 | NA | Fremont |
| Dc Electronics (HQ) | Manufacturer of electronic cable assemblies. The company also offers distribution and other services. | 408-947-4500 | NA | San Jose |
| Ettus Research Llc (DH) | Provider of software defined radio systems for research, academic, industrial, and defense applications. | 408-610-6399 | NA | Santa Clara |
| eze System (HQ) | Provider or monitoring and measuring solutions. The company's products include controllers, controller expansions, and sensors. | 716-393-9330 | 11-50 | Folsom |
| Gdm Electronic Medical (HQ) | Manufacturer of devices, electrical and electronics for medical, manufacturing and engineering industries. | 408-945-4100 | NA | San Jose |
| Greatlink International Inc (RH) | Manufacturer of cable assemblies and related products for the medical, aerospace, and automotive industries. | 510-657-1667 | NA | Fremont |
| Indtec Corp (HQ) | Manufacturer of printed circuit boards. The company specializes in assemblies, wires, cables, automated surface mounting, and harness services. | 831-582-9388 | NA | Marina |
| International Electronic Components Inc (RH) | Distributor of printed circuit boards, consumables, and inspection and measuring equipment. The company is engaged in installation services. | 408-496-0474 | NA | Santa Clara |
| Lorom West (HQ) | Manufacturer of PCB assemblies, turnkey OEM/ODM products and custom cable and wire harnesses. The company offers industry solutions. | 510-249-9000 | NA | Fremont |

| COMPANY NAME | PRODUCT / SERVICE | PHONE | EMP | CITY |
|---|---|---|---|---|
| Lucero Cables Inc (HQ) | Manufacturer of electronic products. The company's products include cables, harnesses, and electromechanical sub assemblies. | 408-298-6001 | NA | San Jose |
| Mac Cal (HQ) | Provider of sheet metals, assembly, cables and harnesses and engineering tools. The company deals with engineering services. | 408-452-4809 | NA | San Jose |
| Mc Electronics (HQ) | Provider of turnkey solution for contract manufacturing. The company focuses on cable & harness assembly and full system integration. | 831-637-1651 | 1-10 | Hollister |
| Morgan Royce Industries Inc (HQ) | Developer and manufacturer of custom cables, wire harness, and PCB assemblies. The company offers project management and quality control services. | 510-440-8500 | NA | Fremont |
| Murdoc Technology Llc (HQ) | Manufacturer of electronics. The company primarily offers precision and wire harnesses and cables to various sectors. | 559-497-1580 | 1-10 | Fresno |
| NPI Solutions Inc (HQ) | Provider of design, engineering, and custom manufacturing solutions. The company offers on-site engineering services. | 408-944-9178 | NA | Morgan Hill |
| Pactech Inc (HQ) | Provider of computer cables, cooling items, and other components. The company also offers networking products. | 408-526-9363 | NA | San Jose |
| Pan-International (LH) | Supplier of computer cables, wiring, switch boxes, and connectors. The company is involved in design, installation, and delivery services. | 510-623-3898 | NA | Fremont |
| Pec Manufacturing (HQ) | Provider of customized electromechanical, electronic, and mechanical solutions such as cable and harness assemblies and electro-mechanical assemblies. | 408-577-1839 | NA | San Jose |
| Quail Electronics Inc (HQ) | Manufacturer of power cord supplies for the OEM market. The company offers solutions for power cords, current cords, and adapters, and traveler kits. | 925-373-6700 | NA | Livermore |
| Qualdeval International (HQ) | Supplier of high-pressure fluid flow and special core analysis equipment. The company offers PCB fabrication & assembly, and other services. | 844-247-2523 | NA | Fremont |
| Redpark Product Development (HQ) | Manufacturer of connectivity accessories for iPhone and iPad. The company's products include lightning cables and 30-pin cables. | 510-594-1034 | NA | Walnut Creek |
| Safeco Electric Supply Inc (HQ) | Distributor of electrical and lighting products. The company offers wires, cables, cords, fasteners, switch boxes, and accessories. | 415-206-0368 | NA | San Francisco |
| Sicon International Inc (HQ) | Manufacturer of electronic components. The company specializes in the fabrication of connectors, cables, circuit boards, and molded cables. | 408-954-9880 | NA | San Jose |
| Ultra-Flex Inc (HQ) | Designer of component manufacturing solutions. The company offers springs, fasteners, castings, machined parts, and hardware items. | 650-728-6060 | NA | Half Moon Bay |

## 203 = Capacitors

| COMPANY NAME | PRODUCT / SERVICE | PHONE | EMP | CITY |
|---|---|---|---|---|
| Aborn Electronics Inc (HQ) | Manufacturer of fiber optic systems. The company specializes in the design and manufacture of fiber optic receivers and transmitters. | 408-436-5445 | NA | San Jose |
| Caltron Components Corp (HQ) | Distributor of electronic capacitors and resistors. The company also focuses on semiconductor products. | 408-748-2140 | NA | Santa Clara |
| EoPlex Inc (BR) | Creator of HVAM technology and process for advanced 3D-printed components for mobile devices, IoT, automotive, medical, and wearable applications. | 408-638-5100 | NA | San Jose |
| eze System (HQ) | Provider or monitoring and measuring solutions. The company's products include controllers, controller expansions, and sensors. | 716-393-9330 | 11-50 | Folsom |
| NIC Components Corp (BR) | Designer, manufacturer, and supplier of passive components. The company offers ceramic capacitors, power inductors, and current sensing resistors. | 669-342-3960 | NA | San Jose |
| Omnicor (HQ) | Provider of network testing tools, vacuum capacitors, and interrupters and IP performance test systems. | 650-572-0122 | NA | Foster City |
| Pacific Capacitor Co (HQ) | Manufacturer of high voltage capacitors for the electronics industry. The company is engaged in sales and installation services. | 408-778-6670 | NA | Morgan Hill |

## 204 = Chips/Substrates/Wafers

| COMPANY NAME | PRODUCT / SERVICE | PHONE | EMP | CITY |
|---|---|---|---|---|
| Aborn Electronics Inc (HQ) | Manufacturer of fiber optic systems. The company specializes in the design and manufacture of fiber optic receivers and transmitters. | 408-436-5445 | NA | San Jose |
| Advanced Component Labs (HQ) | Manufacturer of flip chips, thermal vias, build ups, and related supplies. The company's services include drilling, lamination, and engineering. | 408-327-0200 | NA | Santa Clara |
| Ag Microsystems Inc (HQ) | Provider of testing and development in the areas of micro electro mechanical systems and micro optics. | 408-834-4888 | NA | Santa Clara |
| Amulet Technologies Llc (HQ) | Provider of embedded graphical user interface solutions. The company also specializes in modules and chips. | 408-374-4956 | NA | Campbell |
| C&D Semiconductor Services Inc (HQ) | Manufacturer of cleaner systems, wafer sorters, and wafer inspection systems. The company deals with inspection and processing. | 408-383-1888 | NA | San Jose |
| C&P Microsystems Llc (HQ) | Manufacturer and seller of paper cutter control systems. The company offers microcip, cutternet, and microfacts. | 707-776-4500 | NA | Petaluma |
| Dolphin Technology Inc (DH) | Provider of silicon-proven internet protocol for memory, standard cells, input and output, memory controllers, and memory test and repair. | 408-392-0012 | NA | San Jose |
| Esilicon Corp (HQ) | Provider of design, product design, and manufacturing services for the production of integrated circuits. | 408-635-6300 | NA | San Jose |
| Fortemedia Inc (HQ) | Provider of voice processing integrated circuits. The company also offers related hardware and software components. | 408-861-8088 | NA | Santa Clara |

| COMPANY NAME | PRODUCT / SERVICE | PHONE | EMP | CITY |
|---|---|---|---|---|
| Hybrid Circuits Inc (HQ) | Provider of contract manufacturing services. The company focuses on design, prototyping, contract manufacturing, and delivery. | 408-744-9080 | NA | Sunnyvale |
| Intel Corp (HQ) | Designer, developer, and marketer of processors and motherboards. The company also focuses on tablets, laptops, desktops, and other devices. | 408-765-8080 | NA | Santa Clara |
| Intrinsic-Id Inc (HQ) | Designer of security solutions. The company offers services to semiconductor companies and device manufacturers. | 408-933-9980 | NA | Sunnyvale |
| Jvd Inc (HQ) | Provider of custom integrated circuit design and test services. The company is also involved in wafer characterization. | 408-263-7704 | NA | San Jose |
| LSI Design & Integration Corp (HQ) | Designer and manufacturer of custom chips. The company offers storage, communication, imaging, and memory components. | 408-283-8540 | NA | San Jose |
| Mixel Inc (HQ) | Designer and developer of mixed-signal internet protocol cores for the semiconductor and electronics industries. | 408-436-8500 | NA | San Jose |
| Nanotech Biomachines Inc (HQ) | Developer of graphene. The company involves in wafer scale graphene processing and photolithography. | 855-900-6266 | NA | Richmond |
| Noel Technologies Inc (HQ) | Provider of lithography, thin film deposition, and water recycling solutions. The company serves MEMS, defense, life science, and other sectors. | 408-374-9549 | NA | Campbell |
| Ntk Technologies Inc (HQ) | Manufacturer of bio ceramics, oxygen sensors, ceramic heater, and transistor packages for the medical and telecommunication applications. | 408-727-5180 | NA | Santa Clara |
| POLYSTAK Inc (HQ) | Provider of silicon based multi chip package products as well as package stacking solutions and repair services of components and modules. | 408-441-1400 | NA | San Jose |
| Qualitau Inc (HQ) | Supplier of test equipment and services. The company is involved in the development of electronic equipment for semiconductor process reliability. | 650-282-6226 | NA | Mountain View |
| Small Precision Tools Inc (BR) | Manufacturer of chip bonding tools, fine ceramic, and machining parts. The company offers necessary technical support and services. | 707-765-4545 | NA | Petaluma |
| Sperient Corporation Inc (HQ) | Designer and developer of electronic systems. The company's applications include telemedicine and robotic sensing. | 925-447-3333 | NA | Livermore |
| WaferMasters Inc (HQ) | Provider of thermal processing services. The company also focuses on diagnostic metrology and design and consulting services. | 408-451-0850 | NA | Dublin |
| Xperi Corp (HQ) | Provider of miniaturization technology services for electronic devices. The company offers micro-electronics, and imaging and optics services. | 408-321-6000 | NA | San Jose |

## 206 = Electronic Connectors & Subsystems

| COMPANY NAME | PRODUCT / SERVICE | PHONE | EMP | CITY |
|---|---|---|---|---|
| A'nd Cable Products Inc (HQ) | Manufacturer, installer, and reseller of cable accessories. The company focuses on cable management and labeling solutions. | 925-672-3005 | NA | Concord |
| Advanced Microwave Inc (HQ) | Manufacturer of military electronic components and subsystems. The company offers amplifiers, mixers, threshold detectors, and converter products. | 408-739-4214 | NA | Sunnyvale |
| Aimer Corp (HQ) | Provider of thermal management products. The company also offers connectors, PCB boards, cables, and mechanical parts. | 408-260-8588 | NA | Santa Clara |
| EoPlex Inc (BR) | Creator of HVAM technology and process for advanced 3D-printed components for mobile devices, IoT, automotive, medical, and wearable applications. | 408-638-5100 | NA | San Jose |
| High Connection Density Inc (HQ) | Supplier of electronic packaging solutions and connection technologies. The company serves communications, medical, military, and aerospace fields. | 408-743-9700 | NA | Sunnyvale |
| Joy Signal Technology Llc (HQ) | Developer of PCB and differential terminators, MMCX plug assemblies, single signal carrier systems, Z-Trace connectors, and custom solutions. | 530-891-3551 | 1-10 | Chico |
| Neoconix Inc (HQ) | Provider of electrical interconnect solutions. The company offers LGA sockets, board-to-board interposers, and standard products. | 408-530-9393 | NA | San Jose |
| Peridot Corp (HQ) | Provider of design for manufacturing and packaging. The company also manufacturers of medical components, miniature component and general product prototypes. | 925-461-8830 | NA | Pleasanton |
| Pragmatics Technologies Inc (HQ) | Provider of electromechanical interface solutions. The company deals with the development of custom and standard test interfaces. | 408-289-8202 | NA | San Jose |
| Ten Pao International Inc (HQ) | Manufacturer of power supply systems such as switchings, displays, and traditional linear transformers. | 408-389-3560 | NA | Sunnyvale |
| Thor Electronics of California (HQ) | Manufacturer of special connectors, molded cable assemblies and covers, harness assemblies, and electro-mechanical devices. | 831-758-6400 | NA | Salinas |
| USAPEX (HQ) | Manufacturer of fiber optic products, metal and plastic machined parts, lead free solder pastes, liquid flux, power adapters, cables, and connectors. | 408-730-9800 | NA | Sunnyvale |

## 207 = Electronic Design/R&D Services

| COMPANY NAME | PRODUCT / SERVICE | PHONE | EMP | CITY |
|---|---|---|---|---|
| Altest Corporation (HQ) | Provider of PCB assembly and engineering solutions. The company offers services to the aerospace and commercial industries. | 408-436-9900 | NA | San Jose |
| Ampro Systems Inc (RH) | Manufacturer of printed circuit board assemblies. The company deals with procurement services and serves the government and military industries. | 510-624-9000 | NA | Fremont |
| AmTECH Microelectronics Inc (HQ) | Provider of manufacturing solutions. The company deals with PCB fabrication, machining, and assembly services. | 408-612-8888 | NA | Morgan Hill |

| COMPANY NAME | PRODUCT / SERVICE | PHONE | EMP | CITY |
|---|---|---|---|---|
| AuSIM Inc (HQ) | Developer of audio simulation technology and products for auditory displays for mission-critical applications. | 650-322-8746 | NA | Mountain View |
| Avp Technology Llc (HQ) | Provider of thin film equipment services. The company provides custom designing, remanufacturing, and field services. | 510-683-0157 | NA | Fremont |
| Batchtest Corporation (HQ) | Provider of embedded solutions. The company specializes in the design and manufacturing of industrial PC products. | 408-454-8378 | NA | Santa Clara |
| Bay Area Circuits Inc (HQ) | Provider of engineering services that include fabrication, layout, and design services to the original equipment manufacturers. | 510-933-9000 | NA | Fremont |
| Bestronics (HQ) | Provider of electronics manufacturing services. The company deals with product development, system integration, and prototyping services. | 408-385-7777 | NA | San Jose |
| C&P Microsystems Llc (HQ) | Manufacturer and seller of paper cutter control systems. The company offers microcip, cutternet, and microfacts. | 707-776-4500 | NA | Petaluma |
| C3Nano Inc (HQ) | Developer of transparent conductive ink and film such as touch sensors, OLED lighting and displays, EMI shielding for touch sensor and display industry. | 510-259-9650 | NA | Hayward |
| Century Technology Inc (HQ) | Provider of PCB assembly services. The company also offers distribution, testing, and wire harness services. | 650-583-8908 | NA | S San Francisco |
| Ckc Laboratories Inc (BR) | Provider of design and testing consultation services. The company offers design consultation, testing, training, and support services. | 510-249-1170 | NA | Fremont |
| Cordova Printed Circuits Inc (HQ) | Provider of flex circuits and printed circuit boards. The company focuses on sculptured flex circuits and multilayer flex circuits. | 408-942-1100 | NA | Milpitas |
| Cupertino Signal Processing (HQ) | Specializes in analog circuit analysis and evaluation services. The company offers technical documentation. | 408-725-0846 | NA | Cupertino |
| Dawn VME Products (HQ) | Designer and manufacturer of enclosures, backplanes, chassis and card cage. The company also offers design services and power supplies. | 510-657-4444 | NA | Fremont |
| Dialog Semiconductor Inc (BR) | Creator of mixed-signal integrated circuits. The company offers products such as audio, backlight LED, wireless audio, and home automation. | 408-845-8500 | NA | Santa Clara |
| Digital Dynamics Inc (HQ) | Supplier of embedded process control products. The company is also engaged in manufacturing OEM control system products. | 831-438-4444 | 1-10 | Scotts Valley |
| Dolphin Technology Inc (DH) | Provider of silicon-proven internet protocol for memory, standard cells, input and output, memory controllers, and memory test and repair. | 408-392-0012 | NA | San Jose |
| Dvk Integrated Services Inc (HQ) | Provider of turnkey services that include prototyping services, printed circuit board design, and engineering services. | 408-436-0100 | NA | San Jose |
| Ettus Research Llc (DH) | Provider of software defined radio systems for research, academic, industrial, and defense applications. | 408-610-6399 | NA | Santa Clara |
| GC Micro Corp (HQ) | Provider of IT hardware, software, and related products to corporate and government accounts. The company specializes in information technology. | 707-789-0600 | NA | Petaluma |
| Hildy Licht Company Inc (HQ) | Provider of electric assembly and manufacturing services. The company is engaged in engineering and prototyping. | 650-962-9300 | NA | Mountain View |
| Hunter Micro Kitting & Turnkey (HQ) | Provider of electronic solutions for emerging technology companies. The company offers design, distribution, and contract manufacturing services. | 408-977-7000 | NA | San Jose |
| Masterwork Electronics Inc (HQ) | Provider of printed circuit boards, cables, harness assemblies, and wiring products. The company is engaged in engineering and manufacturing services. | 707-588-9906 | NA | Rohnert Park |
| Megaforce Corporation Inc (HQ) | Provider of supply chain, materials management, and test solutions. The company serves the industrial, commercial, and automotive sectors. | 408-956-9989 | NA | San Jose |
| Nortra Cables Inc (HQ) | Provider of discrete and flat mechanical assembly cables. The company offers design, prototyping, and manufacturing services. | 408-942-1106 | NA | Milpitas |
| Open-Silicon Inc (HQ) | Provider of IP, foundry, test, and packaging technologies. The company's services include system design, manufacturing, and program management. | 408-240-5700 | NA | Milpitas |
| Palo Alto Research Center Inc (DH) | Provider of custom research services and intellectual property to global Fortune 500 companies and government agency partners. | 650-812-4000 | NA | Palo Alto |
| Pdf Solutions Inc (HQ) | Provider of yield improvement technologies and services for the integrated circuit manufacturing process. | 408-280-7900 | NA | San Jose |
| Rocket Ems Inc (HQ) | Provider of electronic manufacturing services. The company caters to high growth technology sectors. | 408-727-3700 | NA | Santa Clara |
| ROHM Semiconductor USA LLC (BR) | Manufacturer of amplifiers, clocks, modules, passive components, remote control receivers, and timers. | 408-720-1900 | NA | Santa Clara |
| Scepter Scientific Inc (HQ) | Provider of feasibility evaluations, electronic, optical, and mechanical engineering, and prototype development services. | 925-373-4802 | NA | Livermore |
| Schmartboard Inc (HQ) | Specializes in the production of hand soldering components. The company's products are used in sensor and USB technologies. | 510-744-9900 | NA | Fremont |
| Surface Art Engineering (HQ) | Provider of Printed Circuit Board Assembly (PCA) and mechanical assembly for prototype, pre-production and production assemblies. | 408-433-4700 | NA | San Jose |
| Tempo Automation (HQ) | Specializes in printed circuit board assemblies. The company is engaged in design and delivery services. | 415-320-1261 | NA | San Francisco |
| Vitron Electronic Services Inc (HQ) | Provider of electronics manufacturing services. The company deals with product development, system integration, and prototyping services. | 408-251-1600 | NA | San Jose |

## 208 = Integrated Circuits

| COMPANY NAME | PRODUCT / SERVICE | PHONE | EMP | CITY |
|---|---|---|---|---|
| Accusilicon USA Inc (HQ) | Manufacturer of TCXO IC chips and designer and developer of high frequency oscillators for the industrial sector. | 408-256-0858 | NA | Santa Clara |
| Advanced Component Labs (HQ) | Manufacturer of flip chips, thermal vias, build ups, and related supplies. The company's services include drilling, lamination, and engineering. | 408-327-0200 | NA | Santa Clara |
| Advanced Linear Devices Inc (HQ) | Designer and manufacturer of precision CMOS analog integrated circuits. The company serves industrial control, computer, automotive, and other sectors. | 408-747-1155 | NA | Sunnyvale |
| Advantest America Inc (LH) | Provider of measurement systems and solutions. The company offers electronic measuring instruments, and optical sensing and imaging analysis systems. | 408-456-3600 | NA | Santa Clara |
| Aehr Test Systems (HQ) | Designer and manufacturer of dynamic burn in and test systems. The company is engaged in troubleshooting and maintenance services. | 510-623-9400 | NA | Fremont |
| Aitech International Corp (HQ) | Provider of video conversion technology solutions. The company provides scan converters, wireless products, HDTV tuners, HDMI switches, and cables. | 408-991-9699 | NA | Sunnyvale |
| AKM Semiconductor Inc (HQ) | Designer and manufacturer of mixed signal integrated circuits. The company serves consumer electronics, industrial, and automotive sectors. | 408-436-8580 | NA | San Jose |
| Akros Silicon Inc (HQ) | Provider of power management ICs. The company offers digital DC-DC controllers and Ethernet protection dual channel active EMI suppressors. | 408-746-9000 | NA | San Jose |
| AmTECH Microelectronics Inc (HQ) | Provider of manufacturing solutions. The company deals with PCB fabrication, machining, and assembly services. | 408-612-8888 | NA | Morgan Hill |
| Aquantia Corp (HQ) | Provider of software solutions such as signal processing, agile management, and technical support. The company serves the IT sector. | 408-228-8300 | NA | San Jose |
| Arteris Inc (HQ) | Provider of interconnect semiconductor IP solutions to system-on-chip makers and serves networking, automotive, video and mobile-phone processors. | 408-470-7300 | NA | Campbell |
| Azimuth Industrial Company Inc (HQ) | Provider of integrated circuit assembly and packaging services. The company specializes in prototyping and production. | 510-441-6000 | NA | Union City |
| Broadcom Inc (HQ) | Developer of digital and analog semiconductors. The company also specializes in optical communication semiconductors. | 408-433-8000 | NA | San Jose |
| C&P Microsystems Llc (HQ) | Manufacturer and seller of paper cutter control systems. The company offers microcip, cutternet, and microfacts. | 707-776-4500 | NA | Petaluma |
| CAD PROS PCB Design Inc (HQ) | Designer and manufacturer of printed circuit boards. The company offers services to the residential and commercial sectors. | 408-734-9600 | NA | San Jose |
| Caltron Components Corp (HQ) | Distributor of electronic capacitors and resistors. The company also focuses on semiconductor products. | 408-748-2140 | NA | Santa Clara |
| Capella Microsystems Inc (HQ) | Developer of integrated technology solutions for IC design. The company is involved in installation and technical support. | 408-988-8000 | NA | Santa Clara |
| Chrontel Inc (HQ) | Designer of mixed-signal IC products. The company's products find application in personal computer and telecom sectors. | 408-383-9328 | NA | San Jose |
| Dac Semiconductor (HQ) | Manufacturer of semiconductor devices. The company specializes in quad-band switch modules and RF power amplifier ICs for mobile phones. | 408-435-7930 | NA | San Jose |
| Dialog Semiconductor (RH) | Manufacturer of AC/DC and LED SSL products. The company's products include home appliances, smart meters, power adapters, and backlighting devices. | 408-374-4200 | NA | Campbell |
| Dvk Integrated Services Inc (HQ) | Provider of turnkey services that include prototyping services, printed circuit board design, and engineering services. | 408-436-0100 | NA | San Jose |
| Echelon Corp (HQ) | Developer of open-standard control networking platforms. The company serves outdoor lighting, building automation, transportation, and other needs. | 408-938-5200 | NA | Santa Clara |
| Enplas Tech Solutions Inc (RH) | Distributor of engineering plastic products. The company also offers optical devices, semiconductor peripherals, and related supplies. | 669-243-3600 | NA | Santa Clara |
| EoPlex Inc (BR) | Creator of HVAM technology and process for advanced 3D-printed components for mobile devices, IoT, automotive, medical, and wearable applications. | 408-638-5100 | NA | San Jose |
| Esilicon Corp (HQ) | Provider of design, product design, and manufacturing services for the production of integrated circuits. | 408-635-6300 | NA | San Jose |
| Exatron Inc (HQ) | Manufacturer of automatic test equipment and IC handlers. The company also specializes in open short testers. | 408-629-7600 | NA | San Jose |
| Fuji Electric Corporation of America (BR) | Provider of electric technology services. The company offers solutions for disk media, power supply, industrial systems, and radiation. | 510-440-1060 | NA | Fremont |
| Global Unichip Corp (HQ) | Provider of technology and embedded CPU design services. The company's services include package engineering, test engineering, and supply chain management. | 408-382-8900 | NA | San Jose |
| Hermes Microvision Inc (BR) | Manufacturer of e-beam inspection and monitoring solution. The company caters to the semiconductor manufacturing sector. | 408-597-8600 | NA | San Jose |
| Infineon Technologies North American Corp (BR) | Provider of semiconductor and system solutions. The company focuses on mobile security, sensors, power management, and RF. | 866-951-9519 | NA | Morgan Hill |

| COMPANY NAME | PRODUCT / SERVICE | PHONE | EMP | CITY |
|---|---|---|---|---|
| Initio Corp (LH) | Provider of integrated circuits and solutions for storage devices. The company is involved in design, installation, and delivery services. | 408-943-3189 | NA | San Jose |
| Integrated Silicon Solution Inc (HQ) | Designer and developer of high performance integrated circuits. The company also focuses on the marketing aspects. | 408-969-6600 | NA | Milpitas |
| Intel Corp (HQ) | Designer, developer, and marketer of processors and motherboards. The company also focuses on tablets, laptops, desktops, and other devices. | 408-765-8080 | NA | Santa Clara |
| Intest Ems Products (BR) | Manufacturer of semiconductors to test integrated circuits. The company also focuses on testing wafer products. | 408-678-9167 | NA | Fremont |
| Ise Labs Inc (HQ) | Provider of semiconductor services. The company offers services such as production test, test interface, and mechanical testing. | 510-687-2500 | NA | Fremont |
| Ixys Corp (HQ) | Manufacturer of power semiconductor products. The company specializes in power semiconductors, integrated circuits, and radio frequency power. | 408-457-9000 | NA | Milpitas |
| Jvd Inc (HQ) | Provider of custom integrated circuit design and test services. The company is also involved in wafer characterization. | 408-263-7704 | NA | San Jose |
| Lewiz Communications Inc (HQ) | Provider of computer networking solutions. The company also offers data security, data management, and data streaming services. | 408-432-6248 | NA | San Jose |
| Linear Integrated Systems (HQ) | Manufacturer of semiconductor products. The company offers bipolar transistors, input protection diodes, resistors, and low leakage amplifiers. | 510-490-9160 | NA | Fremont |
| Macronix America Inc (LH) | Manufacturer of integrated device. The company offers application driven system solutions and non-volatile memory semiconductor solutions. | 408-262-8887 | NA | Milpitas |
| Micro Lithography Inc (HQ) | Manufacturer of pellicles using high end equipment for the production of frames and engineering parts, automatic anodizing lines, and chemical labs. | 408-747-1769 | NA | Sunnyvale |
| Mixed Signal Integration (HQ) | Specializes in the design, manufacture and sale of turn-key analog and mixed-signal standard products and custom ASICs. | 408-434-6305 | NA | San Jose |
| Mixel Inc (HQ) | Designer and developer of mixed-signal internet protocol cores for the semiconductor and electronics industries. | 408-436-8500 | NA | San Jose |
| Mosaic Industries Inc (HQ) | Developer and manufacturer of embedded computers for instruments and automation. The company serves sensor calibration and PID control needs. | 510-790-8222 | NA | Newark |
| Neophotonics Corp (HQ) | Designer and manufacturer of photonic integrated circuit based optoelectronic modules and subsystems for communications networks. | 408-232-9200 | NA | San Jose |
| Nikon Precision Inc (HQ) | Manufacturer of optical lenses and precision equipment. The company is also the supplier of step-and-repeat and step-and-scan lithography systems. | 650-508-4674 | NA | Belmont |
| Noel Technologies Inc (HQ) | Provider of lithography, thin film deposition, and water recycling solutions. The company serves MEMS, defense, life science, and other sectors. | 408-374-9549 | NA | Campbell |
| Pdf Solutions Inc (HQ) | Provider of yield improvement technologies and services for the integrated circuit manufacturing process. | 408-280-7900 | NA | San Jose |
| Photo Etch Technology (BR) | Provider of stainless stell stencils. The company offers epoxy stencils, precision metal parts, fixture pallets, mesh screens, and artwork services. | 408-988-0220 | NA | Santa Clara |
| Power Integrations Inc (HQ) | Supplier of electronic components. The company's products include AC-DC converters and LED drivers. | 408-414-9200 | NA | San Jose |
| Pyramid Semiconductor Corp (HQ) | Provider of assembly services. The company is focused in the assembly of monolithic ceramic products and multi-chip modules. | 408-734-8200 | NA | Sunnyvale |
| Qualitau Inc (HQ) | Supplier of test equipment and services. The company is involved in the development of electronic equipment for semiconductor process reliability. | 650-282-6226 | NA | Mountain View |
| Qulsar Inc (HQ) | Specializes in packaging, refinement, and distribution of precise time synchronization. The company serves the telecom and networking industries. | 408-715-1098 | NA | San Jose |
| Robson Technologies Inc (HQ) | Provider of customizable hardware interfaces that bridge the gap between the test device and the measurement system. | 408-779-8008 | NA | Morgan Hill |
| Schmartboard Inc (HQ) | Specializes in the production of hand soldering components. The company's products are used in sensor and USB technologies. | 510-744-9900 | NA | Fremont |
| Situne Corp (HQ) | Provider of integrated circuits and systems. The company offers spectrum reception and concurrent tuners. | 408-324-1711 | NA | San Jose |
| Solomon Systech Inc (BR) | Provider of IC software application solutions. The company also offers mobile systems and mobile displays. | 330-256-3357 | NA | Dublin |
| Sonics Inc (HQ) | Provider of system-on-chip design solutions. The company's products include on-chip networks, memory subsystems, performance analysis, and development tools. | | NA | San Jose |
| Sparqtron Corp (HQ) | Provider of electronic contract manufacturing services. The company focuses on prototyping, inspection, PCB assembly, and materials and logistics. | 510-657-7198 | NA | Fremont |
| STMicroelectronics (BR) | Provider of analog, mixed signal ICs, transistor, and memories. The company also offers microcontroller products and services. | 408-919-8400 | NA | Santa Clara |

| COMPANY NAME | PRODUCT / SERVICE | PHONE | EMP | CITY |
|---|---|---|---|---|
| Summit Wireless Technologies Inc (HQ) | Developer of wireless audio integrated circuits. The company specializes in semiconductors, home entertainment, and pro-audio markets. | 408-627-4716 | NA | San Jose |
| Tela Innovations Inc (HQ) | Provider of lithography optimized solutions. The company's services include design, implementation, and technical support. | 408-558-6300 | NA | Los Gatos |
| Tenergy Corp (HQ) | Designer and manufacturer of batteries and chargers. The company serves medical, consumer electronics, data management, military, and other sectors. | 510-687-0388 | NA | Fremont |
| True Circuits Inc (HQ) | Developer and marketer of phase-locked loops, delay-locked loops, and mixed-signal designs for integrated circuits. | 650-949-3400 | NA | Los Altos |
| VeriSilicon Inc (HQ) | Provider of IC design services specializing in custom silicon solutions. The company also offers SOC turnkey services. | 408-844-8560 | NA | San Jose |
| Zilog Inc (DH) | Supplier of application-specific embedded system-on-chip (SoC) solutions for the industrial and consumer markets. | 408-457-9000 | NA | Milpitas |

## 209 = Miscellaneous Electronic Devices

| COMPANY NAME | PRODUCT / SERVICE | PHONE | EMP | CITY |
|---|---|---|---|---|
| A M Fitzgerald & Associates Llc (HQ) | Provider of MEMS solutions. The company's products include piezoresistive cantilevers, ultrasound transducers, and infrared imagers. | 650-347-6367 | NA | Burlingame |
| Advanced Microwave Inc (HQ) | Manufacturer of military electronic components and subsystems. The company offers amplifiers, mixers, threshold detectors, and converter products. | 408-739-4214 | NA | Sunnyvale |
| Advantek Inc (BR) | Provider of packaging products. The company offers carrier and cover tapes, and tape and reel packaging products. | 510-623-1877 | NA | Hayward |
| Aehr Test Systems (HQ) | Designer and manufacturer of dynamic burn in and test systems. The company is engaged in troubleshooting and maintenance services. | 510-623-9400 | NA | Fremont |
| Aitech International Corp (HQ) | Provider of video conversion technology solutions. The company provides scan converters, wireless products, HDTV tuners, HDMI switches, and cables. | 408-991-9699 | NA | Sunnyvale |
| Akon Inc (HQ) | Supplier of microwave products. The company focuses on airborne, ground, shipboard, and space applications. | 408-432-8039 | NA | San Jose |
| Alliance Memory Inc (BR) | Manufacturer of memory semiconductor products. The company's products include SRAM, DRAM, SDRAM ICS, and DDR SDRAM. | 650-610-6800 | NA | San Carlos |
| Ambarella Inc (HQ) | Developer of high-definition video compression and image processing solutions. The company's products are used in security IP cameras and sports cameras. | 408-734-8888 | 51-200 | Santa Clara |
| Ampex Data Systems Corporation (HQ) | Manufacturer of digital storage systems. The company also offers airborne and ground systems and related video solutions. | 650-367-2011 | NA | Hayward |
| AmTECH Microelectronics Inc (HQ) | Provider of manufacturing solutions. The company deals with PCB fabrication, machining, and assembly services. | 408-612-8888 | NA | Morgan Hill |
| Andrew Ndt Engineering Corp (HQ) | Manufacturer of probes, ultrasonic transducers, diamond cutting tools, proximity sensors, cables, and offers calibration services. | 408-710-0342 | NA | San Jose |
| Anova Microsystems Inc (HQ) | Provider of rack mount server cabinets and system components. The company deals with storage and GPU solutions. | 408-941-1888 | NA | Los Altos |
| Apple Inc (HQ) | Designer and marketer of consumer electronics. The company also focuses on computer software and personal computers. | 408-996-1010 | NA | Cupertino |
| Applied Engineering (HQ) | Provider of contract electronics manufacturing services. The company also specializes in clean room assembly services. | 408-286-2134 | NA | San Jose |
| Applied Motion Products Inc (HQ) | Manufacturer of stepper drives and motors, gearheads, power supplies, and related accessories. The company offers technical support services. | 831-761-6555 | 1-10 | Watsonville |
| Applied Physics Systems Inc (HQ) | Supplier of magnetic measure and other electronic equipment. The company specializes in measurement while drilling systems and magnetometers. | 650-965-0500 | NA | Mountain View |
| Arbor Solution Inc (HQ) | Provider of embedded computing and networking solutions for the transportation, medical, automation, and military segments. | 408-452-8900 | NA | Fremont |
| Azbil North America Inc (BR) | Designer, manufacturer, and supplier of medical devices. The company offers automation products, control products, and industrial automation systems. | 408-245-3121 | NA | Santa Clara |
| Bestronics (HQ) | Provider of electronics manufacturing services. The company deals with product development, system integration, and prototyping services. | 408-385-7777 | NA | San Jose |
| Betatron Inc (HQ) | Designer and manufacturer of PC board assemblies for the medical, telecommunication, industrial, commercial, and semiconductor markets. | 408-453-1880 | NA | San Jose |
| Brandt Electronics Inc (HQ) | Manufacturer of power supplies. The company specializes in the design and maintenance of power equipment used in military applications. | 408-240-0004 | NA | Milpitas |
| Bridgepoint Systems Inc (HQ) | Provider of security solutions such as CAC card readers, PIV card readers, and access control experts for government contractors and security integrators. | 510-346-1510 | NA | Berkeley |
| Brittmore Group Llc (HQ) | Developer of solar farms. The company offers design, optimization, and fabrication services of photo-voltaic cells and panels. | 408-912-2163 | NA | San Jose |
| CAD PROS PCB Design Inc (HQ) | Designer and manufacturer of printed circuit boards. The company offers services to the residential and commercial sectors. | 408-734-9600 | NA | San Jose |
| Calex Manufacturing Company Inc (HQ) | Supplier of electrical instrument modules. The company also specializes in power supplies and converters. | 925-687-4411 | NA | Concord |

| COMPANY NAME | PRODUCT / SERVICE | PHONE | EMP | CITY |
|---|---|---|---|---|
| Caltron Components Corp (HQ) | Distributor of electronic capacitors and resistors. The company also focuses on semiconductor products. | 408-748-2140 | NA | Santa Clara |
| Cambrios Technologies Corp (HQ) | Manufacturer of electronic materials for the display industry. The company mainly provides ClearOhm films. | 408-738-7400 | NA | Sunnyvale |
| Capella Microsystems Inc (HQ) | Developer of integrated technology solutions for IC design. The company is involved in installation and technical support. | 408-988-8000 | NA | Santa Clara |
| Century Technology Inc (HQ) | Provider of PCB assembly services. The company also offers distribution, testing, and wire harness services. | 650-583-8908 | NA | S San Francisco |
| Cernex Inc (HQ) | Manufacturer of microwave & millimeter-wave components and sub-assemblies. The company's products include amplifiers, converters, detectors, and cables. | 408-541-9226 | NA | San Jose |
| Chip-Tech Ltd (BR) | Distributor of film capacitors, relay racks, oscillators, ferrite beads, grommets, clips, battery holders, lamps, displays, and accessories. | 510-505-9030 | NA | Fremont |
| Clustered Systems Company Inc (HQ) | Provider of cooling technology services. The company's resources include data sheets, technology, deployment, and white papers. | 408-327-8100 | NA | Santa Clara |
| Cordova Printed Circuits Inc (HQ) | Provider of flex circuits and printed circuit boards. The company focuses on sculptured flex circuits and multilayer flex circuits. | 408-942-1100 | NA | Milpitas |
| Countryman Associates Inc (HQ) | Manufacturer of direct boxes and ultra-miniature microphones. The company's products include ear sets, hanging, and podium microphones. | 650-364-9988 | NA | Menlo Park |
| Ctt Inc (HQ) | Manufacturer and supplier of power amplifiers, frequency converters & multipliers, and transmitters & receivers. The company serves military purposes. | 408-541-0596 | NA | San Jose |
| Daihen Advanced Component Inc (RH) | Supplier of vacuum environment material handling and RF transmission products to semiconductor, flat panel display and solar, and equipment manufacturers. | 408-736-2000 | NA | Sunnyvale |
| Data Physics Corp (HQ) | Provider of high performance test and measurement solutions for noise and vibration applications. The company offers drop testing services. | 408-437-0100 | NA | San Jose |
| Dawn VME Products (HQ) | Designer and manufacturer of enclosures, backplanes, chassis and card cage. The company also offers design services and power supplies. | 510-657-4444 | NA | Fremont |
| Dicon Fiberoptics Inc (HQ) | Supplier of optical components, integrated modules, and test equipment for the fiber optics industry. | 510-620-5000 | NA | Richmond |
| DIGICOM Electronics Inc (HQ) | Provider of electronics manufacturing services. The company also deals with packing, shipping, and labeling services. | 510-639-7003 | NA | Oakland |
| Digital Dynamics Inc (HQ) | Supplier of embedded process control products. The company is also engaged in manufacturing OEM control system products. | 831-438-4444 | 1-10 | Scotts Valley |
| Dolphin Technology Inc (DH) | Provider of silicon-proven internet protocol for memory, standard cells, input and output, memory controllers, and memory test and repair. | 408-392-0012 | NA | San Jose |
| Douglas Electronics Inc (HQ) | Provider of CAD/CAM tools for personal computers. The company specializes in custom board manufacturing and electronic design software products. | 510-483-8770 | NA | San Leandro |
| Drc Computer Corp (HQ) | Provider of engineering and technology solutions. The company designs and markets reconfigurable coprocessors. | 408-562-0000 | NA | Santa Clara |
| Dunlop Manufacturing Inc (HQ) | Manufacturer of musical instruments and accessories. The company also designs amplifiers, guitar pedals, picks, capos, and strings. | 707-745-2722 | NA | Benicia |
| Dvk Integrated Services Inc (HQ) | Provider of turnkey services that include prototyping services, printed circuit board design, and engineering services. | 408-436-0100 | NA | San Jose |
| Eiq Energy Inc (HQ) | Designer and manufacturer of power electronics. The company provides solar cells, panels, and monitoring systems. | 408-643-0020 | NA | Santa Clara |
| Elemental LED Inc (HQ) | Provider LED lighting accessories and products. The company's products include LED strip lights, kits, light fixtures, and dimmable lighting products. | 877-564-5051 | NA | Emeryville |
| Elevator Controls Corp (HQ) | Manufacturer of non-proprietary microprocessor based elevator controllers. The company offers technical support and field services. | 916-428-1708 | 1-10 | Sacramento |
| Elma Electronic Inc (LH) | Designer and manufacturer of electronic components and enclosures. The company is involved in design, installation, and delivery services. | 510-656-3400 | NA | Fremont |
| Emotiv (DH) | Provider of neuroengineering products and services. The company offers algorithms to detect subconscious emotional states and facial expressions. | 415-525-3149 | NA | San Francisco |
| Enel X e-Mobility (HQ) | Developer of electric vehicle charging technologies such as smart grid EV charging networks for residential, workplace, and commercial installation. | 844-584-2329 | NA | San Carlos |
| Equipment Solutions Inc (HQ) | Manufacturer and provider of actuators and motion control systems. The company offers optical scanners, servo amplifiers, and digital autocollimators. | 408-245-7162 | NA | Sunnyvale |
| Ess Technology Inc (HQ) | Designer and marketer of video and audio semiconductors for the home, automotive, and entertainment markets. | 408-643-8800 | NA | Milpitas |
| Essai Inc (HQ) | Provider of engineering services. The company provides solutions for the semiconductors, telecom, computer components, and automotive sectors. | 510-580-1700 | NA | Fremont |
| ETM Electromatic Inc (BR) | Manufacturer of electronic products. The company offers microwaves, testing and measuring tools, and thermal management devices. | 510-797-1100 | NA | Newark |

| COMPANY NAME | PRODUCT / SERVICE | PHONE | EMP | CITY |
|---|---|---|---|---|
| Etm Electromatic Inc (HQ) | Manufacturer of custom high voltage power supplies and amplifiers. The company is engaged in troubleshooting, repairs, and maintenance services. | 510-797-1100 | NA | Newark |
| Eton Corp (HQ) | Manufacturer of solar energy products. The company offers products for weather alert radios, backup battery packs, and sound systems. | 650-903-3866 | NA | Palo Alto |
| Ettus Research Llc (DH) | Provider of software defined radio systems for research, academic, industrial, and defense applications. | 408-610-6399 | NA | Santa Clara |
| Fujikura America Inc (BR) | Manufacturer of fiber optics flexible printed circuits and cables. The company also offers membrane switches and printed circuit board assemblies. | 408-748-6991 | NA | Santa Clara |
| Gdm Electronic Medical (HQ) | Manufacturer of devices, electrical and electronics for medical, manufacturing and engineering industries. | 408-945-4100 | NA | San Jose |
| Gigatest Labs (HQ) | Provider of measurement and probing products for the electronics industry. The company offers test equipment and fixtures for modeling and simulation. | 408-524-2700 | NA | Santa Clara |
| Group Seven Corp (HQ) | Producer of turnkey solutions to support high mix and low volume needs. The company also offers Vendor Managed Inventory (VMI) services. | 408-435-7477 | NA | San Jose |
| H-Square Corp (HQ) | Designer and manufacturer of tools and equipment. The company caters to the wafer fabrication industry. | 408-982-9108 | NA | Santa Clara |
| Halo Electronics Inc (HQ) | Manufacturer of electromagnetic components. The company's products include DC/DC transformers, inductors, and RF transformers. | 650-903-3800 | NA | Santa Clara |
| Hbr Industries (HQ) | Provider of electronics manufacturing services. The company offers coil solutions and services for the medical, military, and semiconductor industry. | 408-988-0800 | NA | San Jose |
| Hermes Microvision Inc (BR) | Manufacturer of e-beam inspection and monitoring solution. The company caters to the semiconductor manufacturing sector. | 408-597-8600 | NA | San Jose |
| Highland Technology Inc (HQ) | Designer and manufacturer of precision analog instrumentation. The company serves laboratory research purposes. | 415-551-1700 | NA | San Francisco |
| Hildy Licht Company Inc (HQ) | Provider of electric assembly and manufacturing services. The company is engaged in engineering and prototyping. | 650-962-9300 | NA | Mountain View |
| Hitachi America Ltd (BR) | Manufacturer of electronic items specializing IT products. The company provides computers, home appliances, mobile phones, and supplies. | 650-244-7400 | NA | Brisbane |
| Howlett Machine (HQ) | Manufacturer of machine works and custom made tools. The company also offers custom test fixtures and test machines. | 510-845-2759 | NA | Berkeley |
| Hunter Micro Kitting & Turnkey (HQ) | Provider of electronic solutions for emerging technology companies. The company offers design, distribution, and contract manufacturing services. | 408-977-7000 | NA | San Jose |
| Huntington Mechanical Laboratories Inc (HQ) | Manufacturer and designer of bellows, chambers, motion positioning products, and roughing accessories. | 530-273-4135 | 1-10 | Grass Valley |
| Hybrid Circuits Inc (HQ) | Provider of contract manufacturing services. The company focuses on design, prototyping, contract manufacturing, and delivery. | 408-744-9080 | NA | Sunnyvale |
| Ibase Technology (usa) Inc (BR) | Developer of embedded products such as industrial motherboards, CPU modules, barebone systems, network appliances, and digital surveillance systems. | 408-992-0888 | NA | Sunnyvale |
| Infineon Technologies North American Corp (BR) | Provider of semiconductor and system solutions. The company focuses on mobile security, sensors, power management, and RF. | 866-951-9519 | NA | Morgan Hill |
| Integrated Engineering Services (HQ) | Provider of designs for complex Hi-tech microelectronic needs. The company also serves the life science facilities. | 408-261-3500 | NA | Santa Clara |
| Integrated Surface Technologies Inc (BR) | Provider of supermolecular ceramic coating for watersafing electronics. The company offers stiction control and surface modification services. | 650-324-1824 | NA | Menlo Park |
| Intilop Inc (HQ) | Provider of engineering design services. The company also develops and provides silicon IP products. | 408-791-6700 | NA | Santa Clara |
| Ipg Photonics (BR) | Provider of high power fiber lasers and amplifiers. The company's offerings include Q-switch lasers, multi-mode diodes, pulsed and direct-diode lasers. | 408-492-8830 | NA | Santa Clara |
| Iris Ao Inc (HQ) | Manufacturer of microelectromechanical based optical systems. The company's applications include biomedical imaging and portable laser communications. | 510-849-2375 | NA | Berkeley |
| Ixys Corp (HQ) | Manufacturer of power semiconductor products. The company specializes in power semiconductors, integrated circuits, and radio frequency power. | 408-457-9000 | NA | Milpitas |
| Javad Electronic Manufacturing Services (HQ) | Provider of electronic components. The company specializes in products such as OEM, receivers, antennas, and accessories. | 408-770-1700 | NA | San Jose |
| Josephson Engineering Inc (HQ) | Manufacturer of condenser microphones for studio, stage, and field sound pickup, and audio instrumentation. | 831-420-0888 | 1-10 | Santa Cruz |
| JSK Associates (HQ) | Provider of electronics, medical, and semiconductor manufacturing services. The company also offers assembly and research services. | 408-980-8575 | NA | Santa Clara |
| Juki Americas (BR) | Provider of SMT assembly machines. The company offers inline selective soldering systems, mini-wave soldering machines, and stamp soldering products. | 510-249-6700 | NA | Fremont |

| COMPANY NAME | PRODUCT / SERVICE | PHONE | EMP | CITY |
|---|---|---|---|---|
| Kelytech Corp (HQ) | Provider of assembly solutions for PCBs, chassis, cables, and magnetic products. The company serves defense, medical, industrial, and other sectors. | 408-935-0888 | NA | Milpitas |
| Kensington Computer Products Group (DH) | Provider of secure locking solution for laptops, portable laptop power, and mobile computing solutions. | 650-572-2700 | NA | San Mateo |
| Keysight Technologies Inc (HQ) | Provider of electronic measurement services. The company products include oscilloscopes, network analyzers, and digital multimeters. | 800-829-4444 | NA | Santa Rosa |
| Kinetic Ceramics Inc (HQ) | Manufacturer of performance products for motion control applications. The company's services include diamond turning and fabrication. | 510-264-2140 | 11-50 | Hayward |
| Kmic Technology Inc (HQ) | Provider of amplifier products and solutions to the radio frequency, microwave, and millimeter wave markets. | 408-240-3600 | NA | San Jose |
| Lee Mah Electronics Inc (HQ) | Provider of manufacturing solutions. The company serves customers in the medical, communications, and test and measurement industries. | 415-394-1288 | NA | Brisbane |
| Marki Microwave Inc (HQ) | Manufacturer of microwave mixers. The company offers adapters, amplifiers, couplers, diplexers, DC blocks, and other equipment. | 408-778-4200 | NA | Morgan Hill |
| Masterwork Electronics Inc (HQ) | Provider of printed circuit boards, cables, harness assemblies, and wiring products. The company is engaged in engineering and manufacturing services. | 707-588-9906 | NA | Rohnert Park |
| MaxLinear (BR) | Provider of integrated radio-frequency, analog, and mixed signal semiconductor SoC solutions. The company focuses on broadband communications applications. | 669-265-6100 | NA | San Jose |
| Media Specialty Resources Inc (HQ) | Provider of acoustic panels for recording studios and home theaters. The company also offers noise control and soundproofing services. | 415-883-8053 | NA | Novato |
| Mektec International Corp (HQ) | Manufacturer of printed circuit boards. The company deals with production, prototyping, and application engineering services. | 408-392-4000 | NA | San Jose |
| Melrose Nameplate & Label Co (HQ) | Developer and manufacturer of ID nameplates, labels, and membrane switches. The company offers touchscreen assembly and decorative nameplates. | 510-732-3100 | NA | Hayward |
| Mentor Graphics (RH) | Provider of electronic design automation software. The company focuses on mechanical analysis, system modeling, manufacturing, and verification. | 510-354-7400 | NA | Fremont |
| Mettler-Toledo Rainin Llc (BR) | Provider of laboratory weighing and process analytics services. The company also focuses on industrial weighing. | 800-472-4646 | NA | Oakland |
| Micro Lambda Wireless Inc (HQ) | Supplier of remote drivers, multipliers, bench test filters, oscillators, synthesizers, and harmonic generators. | 510-770-9221 | NA | Fremont |
| Millennia Music & Media Systems (HQ) | Provider of music and media systems. The company also provides specialized tools for archival transfers and related applications. | 530-647-0750 | 1-10 | Diamond Springs |
| Nady Systems Inc (HQ) | Designer and manufacturer of wireless microphones, and a full line of audio accessories. The company also focuses on marketing. | 510-652-2411 | NA | Richmond |
| Naprotek Inc (HQ) | Provider of electronics manufacturing services. The company serves customers in the satellites, industrial, medical, military, and other sectors. | 408-830-5000 | NA | San Jose |
| Neato Robotics Inc (HQ) | Manufacturer of robots. The company manufactures robots for cleaning and other activities. | 510-795-1351 | NA | Newark |
| Neophotonics Corp (HQ) | Designer and manufacturer of photonic integrated circuit based optoelectronic modules and subsystems for communications networks. | 408-232-9200 | NA | San Jose |
| Neurosky Inc (HQ) | Manufacturer of ECG biosensors and also EEG biosensors for mobile solutions, wearable devices, and service providers. | 408-200-6675 | NA | San Jose |
| Norden Millimeter Inc (HQ) | Developer and manufacturer of amplifier products. The company specializes in millimeter wave amplifier products. | 530-642-9123 | 1-10 | Placerville |
| Novasentis Inc (HQ) | Creator of haptic actuator and sensor technology for the consumer electronics applications such as smart watches, jewelry, headbands, and smart glasses. | 814-238-7400 | NA | Berkeley |
| Nuvoton Technology Corporation America (DH) | Manufacturer of semiconductor products and applications. The company's offerings include microcontrollers, microprocessors and cloud computing. | 408-544-1718 | NA | San Jose |
| Oclaro Inc (HQ) | Provider of telecommunications and data communication products. The company offers lasers & transmitters, receivers, transceivers, and other products. | 408-383-1400 | NA | San Jose |
| Oppo Digital Inc (HQ) | Manufacturer of Blu-ray players and UP converting DVD players. The company's services include design, installation, and delivery. | 650-961-1118 | NA | Menlo Park |
| Orbotech LT Solar LLC (BR) | Manufacturer of electronic devices. The company offers printed circuit boards, flat panel displays, and touch screens. | 408-226-9900 | NA | San Jose |
| Pantronix Corp (HQ) | Provider of fiber optic services including optoelectronics component packaging, active module assembly, alignment, and subsystem integration. | 510-656-5898 | NA | Fremont |
| Paxcell Group Inc (HQ) | Provider of electronic engineering and industrial design services. The company also offers contract manufacturing services. | 408-945-8054 | NA | Milpitas |
| Pearson Electronics Inc (HQ) | Manufacturer of wide band current monitors. The company also offers high voltage pulse transformers and voltage dividers. | 650-494-6444 | NA | Palo Alto |
| Pelco By Schneider Electric (BR) | Developer of video surveillance and security solutions. The company also involves in camera and video management. | 559-292-1981 | 11-50 | Fresno |

| COMPANY NAME | PRODUCT / SERVICE | PHONE | EMP | CITY |
|---|---|---|---|---|
| Performex Machining Co (HQ) | Provider of machining services. The company specializes in computer aided machining, designing, and fabrication. | 650-595-2228 | NA | San Carlos |
| Pianodisc (HQ) | Manufacturer of electronic reproducing systems for acoustic pianos. The company is engaged in design, delivery, and installation services. | 916-567-9999 | 1-10 | Sacramento |
| PLX Devices Inc (HQ) | Developer of high-tech measuring instruments. The company is engaged in manufacturing, product testing, and technical support services. | 408-745-7591 | NA | San Jose |
| PowerBeam Research LLC (RH) | Provider of firmware, hardware, and software applications for video, optoelectronic systems (lasers, LEDs, photodiodes, waveguides), and robotics. | 408-933-9373 | NA | Mountain View |
| ProMedia Audio & Video (HQ) | Focuses on the integration of audio/video and performance audio systems. The company serves educational facilities, concert halls, and auditoriums. | 510-741-2925 | NA | Martinez |
| Promex Industries Inc (HQ) | Provider of packaging solutions. The company is engaged in onshore production process flows using process development. | 408-496-0222 | NA | Santa Clara |
| Quail Electronics Inc (HQ) | Manufacturer of power cord supplies for the OEM market. The company offers solutions for power cords, current cords, and adapters, and traveler kits. | 925-373-6700 | NA | Livermore |
| Quality Circuit Assembly (HQ) | Manufacturer of printed circuit board and cable assemblies. The company is also involved in box build and turnkey solutions. | 408-441-1001 | NA | San Jose |
| Quest Microwave Inc (HQ) | Provider of ferrite products for the microwave electronics industry. The company offers both standard and custom designs. | 408-778-4949 | NA | Morgan Hill |
| Radian Thermal Products Inc (BR) | Manufacturer of custom and radiant heat sinks. The company's services include prototyping and engineering support. | 408-988-6200 | NA | Santa Clara |
| Raditek Inc (HQ) | Provider of solutions for the wireless and microwave telecom sector. The company offers passive components, active assemblies, and telecom systems. | 408-266-7404 | NA | San Jose |
| Revel Systems Inc (BR) | Provider of POS systems and related services. The company serves customers in the accounting, security, reporting, and other industries. | 415-744-1433 | NA | San Francisco |
| Rishang LED Inc (LH) | Manufacturer of LED products for decorative and green lighting solutions. The company's products are used in the residential and commercial sectors. | 408-748-8889 | NA | Santa Clara |
| Robson Technologies Inc (HQ) | Provider of customizable hardware interfaces that bridge the gap between the test device and the measurement system. | 408-779-8008 | NA | Morgan Hill |
| Rod-L Electronics Inc (HQ) | Provider of electrical safety testing equipment. The company also offers hipot test loads, test probes, bond testers, and ground testers. | 650-322-0711 | NA | Mountain View |
| Rose Electronics Distributing Company Inc (HQ) | Provider of batteries and power solutions. The company primarily serves original equipment manufacturers such as VRLA batteries and lithium ion batteries. | 408-943-0200 | NA | San Jose |
| Sae Magnetics (hk) Ltd (BR) | Manufacturer of magnetic recording heads, head gimbals assemblies, and head stack assemblies for computer disk drivers. | 408-956-7100 | NA | Milpitas |
| Sage Metering Inc (HQ) | Manufacturer of thermal mass flow meters. The company offers services to the environmental and industrial sectors. | 831-242-2030 | NA | Monterey |
| Schmartboard Inc (HQ) | Specializes in the production of hand soldering components. The company's products are used in sensor and USB technologies. | 510-744-9900 | NA | Fremont |
| Schurter Inc (DH) | Manufacturer of fuses, connectors, and circuit breakers. The company also offers input systems and EMC products. | 707-636-3000 | NA | Santa Rosa |
| Seco (HQ) | Manufacturer of surveying and positioning equipment and accessories. The company's products also finds application in site preparation. | 530-225-8155 | 1-10 | Redding |
| Semi-Probes Inc (HQ) | Manufacturer and supplier of probe cards and tester interfaces. The company's services include design, installation, and delivery. | 408-866-6535 | NA | San Jose |
| Sharp Microelectronics Of The Americas (BR) | Provider of LCD, optoelectronics, imagers, and RF components. The company is involved in design and installation services. | 408-452-6400 | 11-50 | San Jose |
| Sienna Corporation (BR) | Provider of electronic manufacturing services including design and process engineering, prototyping, and electromechanical assembly services. | 510-440-0200 | NA | Fremont |
| Sitime Corp (HQ) | Provider of programmable oscillators and clock generators. The company also offers embedded resonators. | 408-328-4400 | NA | Sunnyvale |
| SMTC Corp (BR) | Provider of electronics manufacturing services for the industrial, medical, computing, and communication markets. | 510-737-0700 | NA | Fremont |
| Soraa (HQ) | Provider of lighting design and fixture lamp solutions. The company serves hotels, restaurants, theaters, and private residences. | 510-456-2200 | NA | Fremont |
| Sparqtron Corp (HQ) | Provider of electronic contract manufacturing services. The company focuses on prototyping, inspection, PCB assembly, and materials and logistics. | 510-657-7198 | NA | Fremont |
| Spectra-Mat Inc (HQ) | Manufacturer of products for electron emission and controlled expansion of thermal management materials for the microelectronics sector. | 831-722-4116 | 1-10 | Watsonville |
| Sputtering Components Inc (BR) | Provider of rotating cathodes and magnet assemblies. The company's products find application in industrial systems. | 925-606-7241 | NA | Livermore |
| Sutter Instrument Co (HQ) | Manufacturer of microprocessors and precision electromechanical devices. The company offers technical support services. | 415-883-0128 | NA | Novato |

| COMPANY NAME | PRODUCT / SERVICE | PHONE | EMP | CITY |
|---|---|---|---|---|
| Syntonic Microwave Inc (HQ) | Manufacturer of wire-band receivers, generators, translators, and related accessories. The company specializes in customization. | 408-866-5900 | NA | Campbell |
| Tactus Technology Inc (HQ) | Developer of tactile user interface for touchscreen devices. The company serves the industrial and technological sectors. | 510-244-3968 | NA | Fremont |
| Tamura Corporation of America (BR) | Manufacturer of DC power modules, current sensor products, telecom transformers, and LED products. The company is involved in distribution services. | 760-871-2009 | NA | Escondido |
| Ten Pao International Inc (HQ) | Manufacturer of power supply systems such as switchings, displays, and traditional linear transformers. | 408-389-3560 | NA | Sunnyvale |
| Teradyne Inc (BR) | Supplier of automatic test equipment. The company caters to semiconductor, electronics, and automotive sectors. | 480-777-7090 | NA | San Jose |
| Therm-X (HQ) | Provider of engineered solutions. The company serves the semiconductor, petrochemical, life sciences, and aerospace industries. | 510 606-1012 | NA | Hayward |
| TTM Technologies Inc (BR) | Manufacturer of printed circuit boards and back plane assemblies. The company's services include design, installation, and delivery. | 408-486-3100 | NA | Santa Clara |
| Ultratech - A Division Of Veeco (BR) | Manufacturer of data storage, LED, and solar process equipment. The company serves solar, LED, data storage, wireless, optical, and other sectors. | 408-321-8835 | NA | San Jose |
| Ultraview Corp (BR) | Provider of data acquisition solutions, bus extenders, synthesizers, and direct digital synthesizers. | 925-253-2960 | NA | Berkeley |
| Unitek Inc (HQ) | Provider of electronic manufacturing services. The company provides PCB assembly, material management, testing, and system integration services. | 510-623-8544 | NA | Fremont |
| USB Promos (HQ) | Provider of USB flash drives, power banks, web keys, video brochures and digital toys and promotional items. | 800-515-3990 | NA | San Francisco |
| USCL Corp (HQ) | Provider of home energy management products. The company offers services to the residential, commercial, and industrial sectors. | | 1-10 | Sacramento |
| Uvexs Inc (HQ) | Manufacturer of UV curing systems. The company's products find application in formulation of UV-curable inks, adhesives, and coatings. | 408-734-4402 | NA | Sunnyvale |
| Valleytek Inc (HQ) | Provider of expanded memory specification solutions, contract manufacturing services, and engineering services. | 408-577-1218 | NA | San Jose |
| Valmark Interface Solutions (HQ) | Manufacturer of labels, panel overlays, and membrane switches. The company is engaged in engineering, assembly, and installation services. | 925-960-9900 | NA | Livermore |
| Vida Products Inc (HQ) | Supplier of radio frequency and microwave components and subsystems. The company provides magnetically tuned oscillators, filters, and synthesizers. | 707-541-7000 | NA | Rohnert Park |
| Vitec (BR) | Provider of digital video products. The company offers software for video encoding, decoding, and conversion. | 800-451-5101 | NA | Sunnyvale |
| Vitriflex Inc (HQ) | Manufacturer of ultra-barrier films for electronic applications. The company focuses on surface science and engineering. | 408-468-6700 | NA | San Jose |
| VLSI Standards Inc (HQ) | Manufacturer of electrical and solar energy products. The company offers calibration services to the semiconductor industry. | 408-428-1800 | NA | Milpitas |
| Voltage Multipliers Inc (HQ) | Manufacturer of voltage multipliers, high voltage diodes, rectifiers, opto-couplers, and power supplies. | 559-651-1402 | 1-10 | Visalia |
| Whizz Systems (HQ) | Provider of electronics design and manufacturing services for the semiconductor, defense, computing, and industrial equipment markets. | 408-980-0400 | NA | Santa Clara |
| World Products Inc (HQ) | Provider of electronic component solutions and services. The company offers sales, distribution, and technical support. | 707-996-5201 | NA | Sonoma |
| Worldwide Energy & Manufacturing Usa Inc (HQ) | Provider of energy and manufacturing solutions. The company's products include cables, coils, PC boards, and electronic appliances. | 650-692-7788 | NA | Burlingame |
| Yamato Scientific America Inc (HQ) | Provider of ovens, incubators, evaporators, and stabilizers. The company deals with sales, distribution, and installation services. | 408-235-7725 | NA | Santa Clara |
| Zeptor Corp (HQ) | Specializes in battery technologies. The company develops and manufactures light-weight electrodes that are used in lithium batteries and fuel cells. | 408-432-6001 | NA | San Jose |
| Zeta Instruments (HQ) | Provider of 3D optical profilers and its applications include wafer quality analysis, texture characterization, and finger contact profiling. | 408-818-9388 | NA | San Jose |
| ZoZo Engineering (HQ) | Manufacturer of RF surgical generators. The company also offers gas analyzers and related equipment. | 415-227-4450 | NA | San Francisco |

## 210 = Optoelectronics

| COMPANY NAME | PRODUCT / SERVICE | PHONE | EMP | CITY |
|---|---|---|---|---|
| Aborn Electronics Inc (HQ) | Manufacturer of fiber optic systems. The company specializes in the design and manufacture of fiber optic receivers and transmitters. | 408-436-5445 | NA | San Jose |
| Ess Technology Inc (HQ) | Designer and marketer of video and audio semiconductors for the home, automotive, and entertainment markets. | 408-643-8800 | NA | Milpitas |
| Foreal Spectrum Inc (HQ) | Provider of coating services for laser, biotech, and medical industries. The company also offers LED illumination and optical components. | 408-436-5558 | NA | San Jose |
| Meivac Inc (HQ) | Manufacturer of sputtering systems and components. The company offers throttle valves, integrators, OEM assemblies, and substrate heaters. | 408-362-1000 | NA | San Jose |
| Stanford Photonics Inc (HQ) | Provider of electronic imaging, digital microscope cameras, and photonics technology solutions for the industrial and military markets. | 650-969-5991 | NA | Palo Alto |

| COMPANY NAME | PRODUCT / SERVICE | PHONE | EMP | CITY |
|---|---|---|---|---|
| **211 = Printed Circuit Boards** | | | | |
| Aimer Corp (HQ) | Provider of thermal management products. The company also offers connectors, PCB boards, cables, and mechanical parts. | 408-260-8588 | NA | Santa Clara |
| All PCB Solutions Inc (HQ) | Provider of PCB solutions. The company is engaged in fabrication, solder masking, and finishing services. | 707-778-2330 | NA | Petaluma |
| Alta Manufacturing Inc (HQ) | Manufacturer of printed circuit board assemblies and offers program management, testing, material procurement, and optical inspection solutions. | 510-668-1870 | NA | Fremont |
| Altaflex (HQ) | Developer and fabricator of touch panels and component assemblies, and circuits. The company serves the electronic sector. | 408-727-6614 | NA | Santa Clara |
| Alterflex Corporation (HQ) | Designer and manufacturer of printed circuit boards. The company also provides engineering support services. | 408-441-8688 | NA | San Jose |
| Altest Corporation (HQ) | Provider of PCB assembly and engineering solutions. The company offers services to the aerospace and commercial industries. | 408-436-9900 | NA | San Jose |
| Anova Microsystems Inc (HQ) | Provider of rack mount server cabinets and system components. The company deals with storage and GPU solutions. | 408-941-1888 | NA | Los Altos |
| Arbor Solution Inc (HQ) | Provider of embedded computing and networking solutions for the transportation, medical, automation, and military segments. | 408-452-8900 | NA | Fremont |
| Ardent Systems Inc (HQ) | Provider of electronics manufacturing services and storage device test solutions. The company is engaged in material management services. | 408-526-0100 | NA | San Jose |
| ArtNet Pro Inc (HQ) | Provider of reused equipment. The company offers direct imaging systems, laser photo plotters, and scanners. | 408-954-8383 | NA | San Jose |
| Bay Area Circuits Inc (HQ) | Provider of engineering services that include fabrication, layout, and design services to the original equipment manufacturers. | 510-933-9000 | NA | Fremont |
| Bema Electronics Inc (HQ) | Provider of manufacturing, supply chain management, material procurement, prototyping, and surface mount technology of electronic appliances. | 510-490-7770 | NA | Fremont |
| Benchmark Electronics Inc (BR) | Provider of electronic manufacturing services to OEMs of telecommunication, computers, and related products. | 925-363-4917 | NA | Concord |
| Beta Circuits Inc (HQ) | Manufacturer of printed circuit board. The company offers all solutions from designing to prototyping. | 408-980-9938 | NA | Santa Clara |
| Blair Electric Services Inc (HQ) | Provider of electrical contracting services. The company offers pump and well controls, PLC controls, and surveillance systems. | 559-784-8658 | 1-10 | Porterville |
| C Sys Labs Inc (HQ) | Designer and manufacturer of test printed circuit boards. The company is engaged in cable fabrication and failure analysis services. | 530-894-7954 | 1-10 | Chico |
| Cable Connection Inc (HQ) | Provider of premium PCB assemblies and turnkey OEM/ODM product. The company also specializes in cable and wire harness services. | 510-249-9000 | NA | Fremont |
| Cadence Design Systems Inc (HQ) | Provider of semiconductor IP and electronic design automation services. The company offers tools for logic & RF design, IC packaging, and other needs. | 408-943-1234 | NA | San Jose |
| California Integration Coordinators Inc (HQ) | Manufacturer of custom turnkey printed circuit boards. The company's services include repairs, component sourcing, fabrication, and assembly. | 530-626-6168 | 1-10 | Diamond Springs |
| Century Technology Inc (HQ) | Provider of PCB assembly services. The company also offers distribution, testing, and wire harness services. | 650-583-8908 | NA | S San Francisco |
| Cirexx International Inc (HQ) | Provider of PCB design layout, fabrication, and assembly services. The company serves customers in the aerospace, military, semiconductor, and medical sectors. | 408-988-3980 | NA | Santa Clara |
| Cordova Printed Circuits Inc (HQ) | Provider of flex circuits and printed circuit boards. The company focuses on sculptured flex circuits and multilayer flex circuits. | 408-942-1100 | NA | Milpitas |
| Cri Design Inc (HQ) | Provider of PCB layout design, fabrication, assembly and turnkey services. The company offers services to the industrial sector. | 510-770-4925 | NA | Fremont |
| Cyberdata Corp (HQ) | Designer and manufacturer of USB cables. The company also offers VoIP and printed circuit board design services. | 831-373-2601 | NA | Monterey |
| Dawn VME Products (HQ) | Designer and manufacturer of enclosures, backplanes, chassis and card cage. The company also offers design services and power supplies. | 510-657-4444 | NA | Fremont |
| DIGICOM Electronics Inc (HQ) | Provider of electronics manufacturing services. The company also deals with packing, shipping, and labeling services. | 510-639-7003 | NA | Oakland |
| Douglas Electronics Inc (HQ) | Provider of CAD/CAM tools for personal computers. The company specializes in custom board manufacturing and electronic design software products. | 510-483-8770 | NA | San Leandro |
| Drc Computer Corp (HQ) | Provider of engineering and technology solutions. The company designs and markets reconfigurable coprocessors. | 408-562-0000 | NA | Santa Clara |
| Dvk Integrated Services Inc (HQ) | Provider of turnkey services that include prototyping services, printed circuit board design, and engineering services. | 408-436-0100 | NA | San Jose |
| **N** Dynamic Test Solutions (BR) | Provider of design services. The company deals with gold and nickel plating, stub drilling and mixed dielectric fabrication. | 408-264-8880 | NA | San Jose |
| Electromax Inc (HQ) | Manufacturer of heavy machinery. The company offers engineering support, materials management, prototyping and testing services. | 408-428-9474 | NA | San Jose |
| Entech Electronics Inc (BR) | Supplier of electronic equipment. The company also offers laser cut stencils, graphic decals, LCD screens, and engineering services. | 408-730-2650 | NA | Santa Clara |

| COMPANY NAME | PRODUCT / SERVICE | PHONE | EMP | CITY |
|---|---|---|---|---|
| EoPlex Inc (BR) | Creator of HVAM technology and process for advanced 3D-printed components for mobile devices, IoT, automotive, medical, and wearable applications. | 408-638-5100 | NA | San Jose |
| FAB-9 Corp (BR) | Provider of printed circuit board fabrication, design, assembly, and manufacturing services. The company serves the business sector. | 408-791-6462 | NA | San Jose |
| Fine-Line Circuits Ltd (BR) | Manufacturer of printed circuit boards. The company specializes in models such as single sided, double sided, and standard multilayer. | 877-876-3660 | NA | Dublin |
| Flashline Electronics Inc (HQ) | Manufacturer of printed circuit boards. The company develops blind and buried vias, rigid flex, and flex PCB. | 408-988-4722 | NA | San Jose |
| Flex Interconnect Technologies Inc (HQ) | Developer of printed circuit technologies which provide solutions to organizational inter connectivity problems. | 408-635-3540 | NA | Milpitas |
| FLYTECH Technology Company Ltd (BR) | Developer and manufacturer of touch screen, LCD, and other peripherals. The company also designs motherboard. | 510-257-5180 | NA | San Jose |
| Gdca Inc (HQ) | Manufacturer of legacy embedded computers and single boards. The company also specializes in assurance, planning, and engineering. | 925-456-9900 | NA | Livermore |
| Golden Altos Corp (HQ) | Designer and manufacturer of burn-in boards. The company also provides post wafer fabrication services. | 408-956-1010 | NA | Milpitas |
| Gorilla Circuits Inc (HQ) | Provider of printed circuit engineering and fabrication solutions. The company caters to electronic companies. | 408-294-9897 | NA | San Jose |
| Guerra Technologies Inc (HQ) | Designer and manufacturer of RF technology related products. The company also offers consulting and evaluation services. | 408-526-9386 | NA | San Jose |
| Hybrid Circuits Inc (HQ) | Provider of contract manufacturing services. The company focuses on design, prototyping, contract manufacturing, and delivery. | 408-744-9080 | NA | Sunnyvale |
| Ibase Technology (usa) Inc (BR) | Developer of embedded products such as industrial motherboards, CPU modules, barebone systems, network appliances, and digital surveillance systems. | 408-992-0888 | NA | Sunnyvale |
| Indtec Corp (HQ) | Manufacturer of printed circuit boards. The company specializes in assemblies, wires, cables, automated surface mounting, and harness services. | 831-582-9388 | NA | Marina |
| Infinity Quick Turn (HQ) | Provider of manufacturing solutions and services. The company deals with component distribution and PCB fabrication. | 510-661-0555 | NA | Fremont |
| Innerstep BSE (HQ) | Provider of manufacturing and design solutions such as PCB and mechanical design for original equipment manufacturers. | 831-461-5600 | 11-50 | Scotts Valley |
| Innovion (HQ) | Provider of foundry and ion implantation services. The company serves the microelectronics industry. | 408-501-9100 | NA | San Jose |
| International Electronic Components Inc (RH) | Distributor of printed circuit boards, consumables, and inspection and measuring equipment. The company is engaged in installation services. | 408-496-0474 | NA | Santa Clara |
| Interphasic LLC (HQ) | Manufacturer of motion control systems. The company offers product support services and it serves the industrial sector. | 831-392-0708 | NA | Seaside |
| Isola Usa Corp (BR) | Designer, developer, and manufacturer of laminate materials used to fabricate multilayer PCBs. The company serves the medical market. | 916-429-4462 | 11-50 | Elk Grove |
| Lee Mah Electronics Inc (HQ) | Provider of manufacturing solutions. The company serves customers in the medical, communications, and test and measurement industries. | 415-394-1288 | NA | Brisbane |
| Legend Design Technology Inc (HQ) | Provider of semiconductor IP characterization and verification tools and IC and PCB circuit simulators. | 408-748-8888 | NA | Santa Clara |
| Lenthor Engineering (HQ) | Designer and manufacturer of flexible and rigid printed circuit boards. The company serves the military, communications, medical, and other markets. | 408-945-8787 | NA | Milpitas |
| Macrotron Systems Inc (HQ) | Designer and manufacturer of memory modules. The company provides services such as electronics assembly and testing. | 510-683-9600 | NA | Fremont |
| Megaforce Corporation Inc (HQ) | Provider of supply chain, materials management, and test solutions. The company serves the industrial, commercial, and automotive sectors. | 408-956-9989 | NA | San Jose |
| Meritronics Inc (HQ) | Provider of electronics assembly, and equipment assemblies. The company specializes in PCB assembly, cable assembly, and system assembly. | 408-969-0888 | NA | Milpitas |
| Mvinix Systems Inc (HQ) | Provider of electronic and manufacturing service provider for printed circuit board assemblies. The company deals with design and testing services. | 408-321-9109 | NA | San Jose |
| Naprotek Inc (HQ) | Provider of electronics manufacturing services. The company serves customers in the satellites, industrial, medical, military, and other sectors. | 408-830-5000 | NA | San Jose |
| Neoconix Inc (HQ) | Provider of electrical interconnect solutions. The company offers LGA sockets, board-to-board interposers, and standard products. | 408-530-9393 | NA | San Jose |
| Network Pcb Inc (HQ) | Provider of printed circuit board solutions. The company's product line includes probe cards, high density board, and impedance control board. | 408-943-8760 | NA | San Jose |
| Nexlogic (HQ) | Designer of electronic circuits. The company specializes in the design and fabrication of printed circuit boards. | 408-436-8150 | NA | San Jose |
| NRC Manufacturing (HQ) | Provider of contract manufacturing and PCB assembly services. The company's services include cable assembly, box builds, and functional test. | 510-438-9400 | NA | Fremont |

| COMPANY NAME | PRODUCT / SERVICE | PHONE | EMP | CITY |
|---|---|---|---|---|
| Optimum Design Associates (HQ) | Provider of printed circuit board design and layout services. The company also focuses on engineering and manufacturing services. | 925-401-2004 | NA | Pleasanton |
| Pactron/Hjpc Corp (HQ) | Provider of electronics design and design development services. The company is also involved in engineering and contract manufacturing. | 408-329-5500 | NA | Santa Clara |
| PalPilot International Corp (BR) | Developer of interconnect solutions. The company offers design, engineering, and manufacturing support services. | 408-855-8866 | NA | Milpitas |
| Pan-International (LH) | Supplier of computer cables, wiring, switch boxes, and connectors. The company is involved in design, installation, and delivery services. | 510-623-3898 | NA | Fremont |
| Paxcell Group Inc (HQ) | Provider of electronic engineering and industrial design services. The company also offers contract manufacturing services. | 408-945-8054 | NA | Milpitas |
| Power Design Services (HQ) | Provider of power design services. The company involves in the design, fabrication, and assembly of printed circuit boards and flex circuits. | 408-437-1931 | NA | San Jose |
| Probe Logic (HQ) | Developer and manufacturer of probe card for semiconductor industry. The company also offers printed circuit board design services. | 408-416-0777 | NA | San Jose |
| Proto Services Inc (HQ) | Provider of process verification, yield analysis, testing design, program management, and functional debugging services. | 408-719-9088 | NA | San Jose |
| Qualdeval International (HQ) | Supplier of high-pressure fluid flow and special core analysis equipment. The company offers PCB fabrication & assembly, and other services. | 844-247-2523 | NA | Fremont |
| Quality Circuit Assembly (HQ) | Manufacturer of printed circuit board and cable assemblies. The company is also involved in box build and turnkey solutions. | 408-441-1001 | NA | San Jose |
| Qualtech Circuits Inc (HQ) | Producer of printed circuit boards. The company's products include probe cards and edge plating. | 408-727-4125 | NA | Santa Clara |
| Questek Inc (BR) | Provider of solutions for burn-in and test requirements. The company is engaged in PCB design and testing services. | 510-979-9311 | NA | San Jose |
| Qulsar Inc (HQ) | Specializes in packaging, refinement, and distribution of precise time synchronization. The company serves the telecom and networking industries. | 408-715-1098 | NA | San Jose |
| R F Circuits Inc (HQ) | Manufacturer of printed circuit boards and assemblies. The company is engaged in engineering and electronics manufacturing services. | 408-324-1670 | NA | San Jose |
| R&D Tech (HQ) | Provider of prototyping services. The company specializes in fabrication and assembly services. | 408-555-1234 | NA | Milpitas |
| Robson Technologies Inc (HQ) | Provider of customizable hardware interfaces that bridge the gap between the test device and the measurement system. | 408-779-8008 | NA | Morgan Hill |
| Royal Circuit Solutions Inc (HQ) | Manufacturer of printed circuit boards. The company's products are used in prototype and medium production runs and offers fabrication services. | 831-636-7789 | 1-10 | Hollister |
| Rucker Kolls Inc (HQ) | Provider of solutions for ATE test interface products. The company's services include custom PCB design and card stiffeners and rings. | 408-934-9875 | NA | Milpitas |
| RUSH PCB Inc (RH) | Manufacturer of printed circuit boards and assemblies. The company is engaged in engineering and electronics manufacturing services. | 408-496-6013 | NA | San Jose |
| San Francisco Circuits (HQ) | Provider and manufacturer of printed circuit boards. The company also offers services like PCB design & assembly and specializes in complex circuits. | 800-732-5143 | NA | San Mateo |
| Schurter Inc (DH) | Manufacturer of fuses, connectors, and circuit breakers. The company also offers input systems and EMC products. | 707-636-3000 | NA | Santa Rosa |
| Sicon International Inc (HQ) | Manufacturer of electronic components. The company specializes in the fabrication of connectors, cables, circuit boards, and molded cables. | 408-954-9880 | NA | San Jose |
| Sierra Proto Express (HQ) | Designer and manufacturer of printed circuit boards. The company's manufacturing facilities are located in California and Kansas. | 408-735-7137 | NA | Sunnyvale |
| Sigmatron International Inc (BR) | Provider of robust systems and program management support to track demand, material on order, inventory, finished goods, and shipments. | 510-477-5000 | NA | Union City |
| SMTC Corp (BR) | Provider of electronics manufacturing services for the industrial, medical, computing, and communication markets. | 510-737-0700 | NA | Fremont |
| Sparqtron Corp (HQ) | Provider of electronic contract manufacturing services. The company focuses on prototyping, inspection, PCB assembly, and materials and logistics. | 510-657-7198 | NA | Fremont |
| Spire Manufacturing (HQ) | Designer and manufacturer of printed circuit boards. The company offers vertical probe cards, test sockets, and mother boards. | 510-226-1070 | NA | Fremont |
| Streamline Circuits (HQ) | Designer and manufacturer of printed circuit boards. The company also offers engineering and other services. | 408-727-1418 | NA | Santa Clara |
| Streamline Electronics Manufacturing Inc (HQ) | Provider of electronic manufacturing solutions and services. The company is engaged in product development and contract manufacturing. | 408-263-3600 | NA | Fremont |
| Surface Art Engineering (HQ) | Provider of Printed Circuit Board Assembly (PCA) and mechanical assembly for prototype, pre-production and production assemblies. | 408-433-4700 | NA | San Jose |
| Symprotek Corp (HQ) | Provider of electronics manufacturing and engineering services. The company also focuses on procurement. | 408-956-0700 | NA | Milpitas |
| Tempo Automation (HQ) | Specializes in printed circuit board assemblies. The company is engaged in design and delivery services. | 415-320-1261 | NA | San Francisco |
| Test21 Inc (HQ) | Designer and manufacturer of printed circuit boards including probe cards for semiconductor, ATE manufacturers, and silicon wafer foundries. | 510-438-0221 | NA | Fremont |

| COMPANY NAME | PRODUCT / SERVICE | PHONE | EMP | CITY |
|---|---|---|---|---|
| TTM Technologies Inc (BR) | Manufacturer of printed circuit boards and back plane assemblies. The company's services include design, installation, and delivery. | 408-486-3100 | NA | Santa Clara |
| Tuv Rheinland Of North America Inc (DH) | Provider of product testing, market access, specialty services, and management systems certification services. | 925-249-9123 | NA | Pleasanton |
| Tyan Computer Corp (DH) | Designer and manufacturer of server/workstation platforms. The company's products are sold to OEMs, VARs, system integrators, and resellers. | 510-651-8868 | NA | Fremont |
| Uni-Flex Circuits Inc (HQ) | Manufacturer of flexible circuits. The company specializes in the design and fabrication of consumer electronic connectors. | 408-998-5500 | NA | San Jose |
| Unitek Inc (HQ) | Provider of electronic manufacturing services. The company provides PCB assembly, material management, testing, and system integration services. | 510-623-8544 | NA | Fremont |
| Vector Fabrication Inc (HQ) | Manufacturer of printed circuit boards. The company offers circuit board assembly, drilling, solder mask, plating, and testing services. | 408-942-9800 | NA | Milpitas |
| Wafer Process Systems Inc (HQ) | Manufacturer of semiconductors, MEMS, and photonics. The company also focuses on RFID products, disc drives, and flat panel displays. | 408-445-3010 | NA | San Jose |
| Wellex Corp (HQ) | Provider of printed circuit boards, cables, harness assemblies, and wiring products. The company is engaged in engineering and manufacturing services. | 510-743-1818 | NA | Fremont |
| Wenteq Inc (HQ) | Manufacturer of print, precision, machined components, and assemblies. The company serves the automotive, racing, and boat markets. | 209-608-2374 | 1-10 | Lodi |
| Westak (HQ) | Designer and manufacturer of printed circuit boards. The company offers rigid double-sided interconnects and rigid multi-layer interconnects. | 408-734-8686 | NA | Sunnyvale |
| Worldwide Energy & Manufacturing Usa Inc (HQ) | Provider of energy and manufacturing solutions. The company's products include cables, coils, PC boards, and electronic appliances. | 650-692-7788 | NA | Burlingame |
| X-Scan Imaging Corp (HQ) | Supplier of x-ray imaging and inspection equipment. The company also offers array detectors and line-scan camera products. | 408-432-9888 | NA | San Jose |
| Yamamoto Manufacturing USA Inc (HQ) | Manufacturer of printed circuit boards. The company has operations in regions of Japan, Korea, and China. | 408-387-5250 | NA | San Jose |
| Z-Plane Inc (HQ) | Provider of electronic packaging solutions for high-speed telecommunications and computing equipment, including routers, servers, and switches. | 415-309-2647 | NA | Palo Alto |
| Z-Source International (HQ) | Manufacturer of printed circuit boards. The company provides board procurement solutions from prototypes to full production and stocking programs. | 925-401-0090 | NA | Pleasanton |

## 212 = Semiconductors & Related Devices

| COMPANY NAME | PRODUCT / SERVICE | PHONE | EMP | CITY |
|---|---|---|---|---|
| Acco Semiconductor Inc (HQ) | Provider of outsourced operations and engineering services. The company serves fabless semiconductor companies. | 408-524-2600 | NA | Sunnyvale |
| Achronix Semiconductor Corp (HQ) | Manufacturer of semiconductor devices. The company's products are used for networking, edge networking, and test and measurement applications. | 408-889-4100 | NA | Santa Clara |
| Adaptive Engineering (HQ) | Provider of engineering products such as automatic mixture control, talking telemetry, and telephone-based microclimate monitors. | 415-518-7131 | NA | San Ramon |
| Advanced Component Labs (HQ) | Manufacturer of flip chips, thermal vias, build ups, and related supplies. The company's services include drilling, lamination, and engineering. | 408-327-0200 | NA | Santa Clara |
| Advanced Semiconductor Engineering US Inc (DH) | Manufacturer of integrated circuits and semiconductor packaging products. The company is involved in delivery, installation, and sales. | 408-636-9500 | NA | Sunnyvale |
| Advantek Inc (BR) | Provider of packaging products. The company offers carrier and cover tapes, and tape and reel packaging products. | 510-623-1877 | NA | Hayward |
| Advantest America Inc (LH) | Provider of measurement systems and solutions. The company offers electronic measuring instruments, and optical sensing and imaging analysis systems. | 408-456-3600 | NA | Santa Clara |
| Advantiv Technologies Inc (DH) | Manufacturer and supplier of semiconductor components. The company offers wafers, solar, materials, and vacuum components. | 510-490-8260 | NA | Fremont |
| Ag Microsystems Inc (HQ) | Provider of testing and development in the areas of micro electro mechanical systems and micro optics. | 408-834-4888 | NA | Santa Clara |
| Agiga Tech Inc (BR) | Designer and manufacturer of memory solutions. The company's portfolio includes AGIGARAM, SDRAM, and PowerGEM. | 408-943-2600 | NA | San Jose |
| AKM Semiconductor Inc (HQ) | Designer and manufacturer of mixed signal integrated circuits. The company serves consumer electronics, industrial, and automotive sectors. | 408-436-8580 | NA | San Jose |
| Alliance Memory Inc (BR) | Manufacturer of memory semiconductor products. The company's products include SRAM, DRAM, SDRAM ICS, and DDR SDRAM. | 650-610-6800 | NA | San Carlos |
| Allteq Industries Inc (HQ) | Manufacturer of microscopes, lighting, optics, and semiconductor products. The company also provides die coating, dispensing, and adhesion promotion. | 925-243-6400 | NA | Livermore |
| Allwin21 Corp (HQ) | Provider of high-tech equipment, related services, and technical support for the semiconductor and biomedical industries. | 408-778-7788 | NA | Morgan Hill |
| Alpha & Omega Semiconductor (HQ) | Designer, developer, and supplier of power semiconductors. The company's applications include notebook PCs and power supplies. | 408-830-9742 | NA | Sunnyvale |
| Alta Devices (HQ) | Provider of mobile power technology services. The company offers unmanned systems, consumer devices, and internet technology services. | 408-988-8600 | NA | Sunnyvale |

| COMPANY NAME | PRODUCT / SERVICE | PHONE | EMP | CITY |
|---|---|---|---|---|
| American Probe & Technologies Inc (HQ) | Manufacturer of analytical probes and accessories for the semiconductor test and measurement industry. | 408-263-3356 | 1-10 | Merced |
| Amimon Inc (HQ) | Developer and manufacturer of HD wireless video modules. The company's products include Studio Link, Live Link, and View Link. | 408-490-4686 | NA | San Jose |
| Analatom Inc (HQ) | Provider of materials science research services focusing on product development in the field of micro electrical mechanical systems. | 408-980-9516 | NA | Santa Clara |
| Analog Bits Inc (HQ) | Supplier of low-power, customizable analog IP for modern CMOS digital chips. The company also offers interfaces and converters. | 650-314-0200 | NA | Sunnyvale |
| Anchor Semiconductor Inc (HQ) | Developer of software to improve IC manufacturing efficiency and chip yield. The company specializes in semiconductor hotspot pattern management. | 408-986-8969 | NA | Santa Clara |
| Anova Microsystems Inc (HQ) | Provider of rack mount server cabinets and system components. The company deals with storage and GPU solutions. | 408-941-1888 | NA | Los Altos |
| Applied Ceramics Inc (HQ) | Manufacturer of custom ceramics, quartz silicon, stainless steel, and sapphire for the semiconductor industries. | 510-249-9700 | NA | Fremont |
| Applied Engineering (HQ) | Provider of contract electronics manufacturing services. The company also specializes in clean room assembly services. | 408-286-2134 | NA | San Jose |
| Applied Materials Inc (HQ) | Provider of equipment, services, and software for the manufacture of semiconductor, flat panel display, and solar photovoltaic products. | 408-727-5555 | NA | Santa Clara |
| Aquantia Corp (HQ) | Provider of software solutions such as signal processing, agile management, and technical support. The company serves the IT sector. | 408-228-8300 | NA | San Jose |
| Arasan Chip Systems Inc (RH) | Provider of total IP solutions such as digital IP cores, protocol analyzers, and traffic generators for mobile storage and connectivity applications. | 408-282-1600 | NA | San Jose |
| Arkian (RH) | Provider of research and development services. The company focuses on marketing logistics with semiconductor manufacturers. | 408-991-9800 | NA | Santa Clara |
| Arm Ltd (RH) | Manufacturer of digital products and offers wireless, networking, and consumer entertainment solutions to imaging, automotive, and storage devices. | 408-576-1500 | NA | San Jose |
| Arteris Inc (HQ) | Provider of interconnect semiconductor IP solutions to system-on-chip makers and serves networking, automotive, video and mobile-phone processors. | 408-470-7300 | NA | Campbell |
| Axelsys LLC (HQ) | Provider of electronic design and manufacturing services. The company's offerings include LED and AC to DC industrial power supplies. | 408-600-0871 | NA | San Jose |
| B & J Specialties Inc (HQ) | Manufacturer of nanometrics film thickness and CD measurement equipment. The company offers nanometrics equipment, Nanoline, and Nanospec. | 831-454-0713 | 1-10 | Santa Cruz |
| Benchmark Electronics Inc (BR) | Provider of electronic manufacturing services to OEMs of telecommunication, computers, and related products. | 925-363-4917 | NA | Concord |
| C&D Semiconductor Services Inc (HQ) | Manufacturer of cleaner systems, wafer sorters, and wafer inspection systems. The company deals with inspection and processing. | 408-383-1888 | NA | San Jose |
| Cadence Design Systems Inc (HQ) | Provider of semiconductor IP and electronic design automation services. The company offers tools for logic & RF design, IC packaging, and other needs. | 408-943-1234 | NA | San Jose |
| Cal Semi LLC (HQ) | Provider of semiconductor equipment remanufacturing services. The company specializes in products such as furnaces, cantilever, and wet sinks. | 510-687-9960 | NA | San Jose |
| Calogic LLC (HQ) | Designer and manufacturer of integrated circuits. The company caters to computer, telecom, and medical applications. | 510-656-2900 | NA | Fremont |
| Caltron Components Corp (HQ) | Distributor of electronic capacitors and resistors. The company also focuses on semiconductor products. | 408-748-2140 | NA | Santa Clara |
| Cavium Inc (HQ) | Manufacturer of hardware components. The company products include processors, switches, and adapters, wireless displays and security software. | 408-943-7100 | NA | San Jose |
| Century Technology Inc (HQ) | Provider of PCB assembly services. The company also offers distribution, testing, and wire harness services. | 650-583-8908 | NA | S San Francisco |
| Champion Microelectronic Corp (RH) | Designer and manufacturer of semiconductor devices. The company's products include battery management IC, fan controller, and interface products. | 408-985-1898 | NA | San Jose |
| CHECKPOiNT Technologies (HQ) | Manufacturer of optical failure analysis tools such as laser scanning microscopy, photon emission, infrascan, and solid immersion lens objectives. | 408-321-9780 | NA | San Jose |
| Comit Systems Inc (HQ) | Provider of full service contract engineering for wireless & cleantech, methodology consulting , Soc design and verification, board design, and software. | 408-988-2988 | NA | Sunnyvale |
| Crossbar Inc (HQ) | Provider of 3D resistive RAM technology. The company serves customers in the automotive, connected devices, consumer, and enterprise segments. | 408-884-0281 | NA | Santa Clara |
| Cyclos Semiconductor (HQ) | Provider of resonant mesh semiconductor IP, design automation tools, and design consulting services to mobile, wireless, and medical sectors. | 510-649-3741 | NA | Berkeley |
| Cypress Semiconductor Corp (HQ) | Provider of IC solutions to the data and telecommunication markets. The company is engaged in training and technical support services. | 408-943-2600 | NA | San Jose |

| COMPANY NAME | PRODUCT / SERVICE | PHONE | EMP | CITY |
|---|---|---|---|---|
| Delphon Industries Llc (HQ) | Provider of materials and services to the semiconductor, medical, photonics, telecommunications, and military markets. | 510-576-2220 | NA | Hayward |
| Dialog Semiconductor (RH) | Manufacturer of AC/DC and LED SSL products. The company's products include home appliances, smart meters, power adapters, and backlighting devices. | 408-374-4200 | NA | Campbell |
| Dialog Semiconductor Inc (BR) | Creator of mixed-signal integrated circuits. The company offers products such as audio, backlight LED, wireless audio, and home automation. | 408-845-8500 | NA | Santa Clara |
| Diodes Inc (BR) | Provider of electronic components for communications, lighting, motor control, and audio applications. | 408-232-9100 | NA | Milpitas |
| Dolphin Technology Inc (DH) | Provider of silicon-proven internet protocol for memory, standard cells, input and output, memory controllers, and memory test and repair. | 408-392-0012 | NA | San Jose |
| Dominar Inc (HQ) | Provider of optical and semiconductor thin-film coating services. The company serves customers in Europe, Asia, and Australia. | 408-496-0508 | NA | Santa Clara |
| DSG Technologies Inc (HQ) | Provider of microwave processing technology in the manufacturing of advanced semiconductors, LED, solar photovoltaic, and display markets. | | NA | San Jose |
| Dynamic Test Solutions (BR) | Provider of design services. The company deals with gold and nickel plating, stub drilling and mixed dielectric fabrication. | 408-264-8880 | NA | San Jose |
| eASIC Corp (HQ) | Developer of structured ASIC fabric for SoC and platform designs. The company focuses on programming and development services. | | NA | Santa Clara |
| Ebara Technologies Inc (HQ) | Manufacturer of vacuum pumps for the semiconductor industry. The company offers reapir, training, and field & system services. | 916-920-5451 | 11-50 | Sacramento |
| Embedur Systems Inc (HQ) | Developer of software solutions. The company also offers technical and management services for the embedded market. | 510-353-9111 | NA | Fremont |
| Eme Systems (HQ) | Designer and manufacturer of instruments for environmental science. The company also offers signal conditioners, sensors, enclosures, and batteries. | 510-848-5725 | NA | Berkeley |
| EoPlex Inc (BR) | Creator of HVAM technology and process for advanced 3D-printed components for mobile devices, IoT, automotive, medical, and wearable applications. | 408-638-5100 | NA | San Jose |
| Esilicon Corp (HQ) | Provider of design, product design, and manufacturing services for the production of integrated circuits. | 408-635-6300 | NA | San Jose |
| Etron Technology America Inc (RH) | Provider of integrated circuits for applications, such as storage device, display, handset, PDA, and multimedia device. | 408-987-2255 | NA | Santa Clara |
| Exclara Inc (HQ) | Designer and manufacturer of high-voltage LED drivers which provide integrated-circuit and module-based solutions. | 408-492-1009 | NA | Santa Clara |
| FET Test Inc (HQ) | Manufacturer of automated test equipment. The company also offers modular analog/mixed-signal testers and test system controller software. | 408-778-0234 | NA | San Jose |
| Flex Logix Technologies Inc (HQ) | Developer of reconfigurable RTL IP cores and software. | 650-851-1411 | NA | Mountain View |
| Fortrend Engineering Corp (HQ) | Designer and manufacturer of mechanical handling equipment. The company also specializes in distribution services. | 408-734-9311 | NA | San Jose |
| Four Dimensions Inc (HQ) | Manufacturer of semiconductor probing systems. The company offers Four Point Probe, Mercury Probe CV maps, and Mercury Four Imaging systems. | 510-782-1843 | NA | Hayward |
| Furukawa Sangyo North America Inc (LH) | Provider of electric products for telecommunications and automotive needs. The company also serves energy, construction, and other sectors. | 408-496-0051 | NA | San Jose |
| Gambit Corp (HQ) | Provider of engineering parts and services. The company specializes in designing and building tools and dies. | 707-588-2797 | NA | Rohnert Park |
| Gct Semiconductor Inc (HQ) | Designer and supplier of 4G mobile semiconductor solutions. The company also offers wireless solutions for its clients. | 408-434-6040 | NA | San Jose |
| Glacier Microelectronics Inc (HQ) | Developer of mixed signal semiconductor devices. The company's products include synthesizers and RFIC devices. | 408-244-0778 | NA | Santa Clara |
| Global Unichip Corp (HQ) | Provider of technology and embedded CPU design services. The company's services include package engineering, test engineering, and supply chain management. | 408-382-8900 | NA | San Jose |
| Gooch & Housego (BR) | Manufacturer of precision optical components. The company also focuses on related sub-systems and systems. | 650-300-5744 | NA | Fremont |
| Green Plug (HQ) | Developer and provider of digital controller technology solutions and products to the consumer electronics markets. | 925-867-2781 | NA | San Ramon |
| Greenliant Systems (HQ) | Developer of storage solutions for the embedded systems. The company offers solid-state storage, controllers, and specialty flash memory. | 408-200-8000 | NA | Santa Clara |
| Greenvity Communications Inc (HQ) | Designer and developer of semiconductor solutions for home gateways, electric vehicles, and lighting products. | 408-935-9370 | NA | San Jose |
| H-Square Corp (HQ) | Designer and manufacturer of tools and equipment. The company caters to the wafer fabrication industry. | 408-982-9108 | NA | Santa Clara |
| Hamamatsu Corp (BR) | Manufacturer of devices for the generation and measurement of infrared, visible, and ultraviolet light. | 408-261-2022 | NA | San Jose |
| Hana Microelectronics Inc (BR) | Provider of electronic manufacturing services. The company focuses on PCBs, circuit assembly, RFID devices, LEDs, coil windings, and other products. | 408-452-7474 | NA | Santa Clara |

| COMPANY NAME | PRODUCT / SERVICE | PHONE | EMP | CITY |
|---|---|---|---|---|
| High Connection Density Inc (HQ) | Supplier of electronic packaging solutions and connection technologies. The company serves communications, medical, military, and aerospace fields. | 408-743-9700 | NA | Sunnyvale |
| Hitachi America Ltd (BR) | Manufacturer of electronic items specializing IT products. The company provides computers, home appliances, mobile phones, and supplies. | 650-244-7400 | NA | Brisbane |
| Hitachi High Technologies America Inc (BR) | Seller of semiconductor manufacturing equipment and analytical instrumentation and also offers electronic devices, bio-related, and other products. | 925-218-2800 | NA | Pleasanton |
| Hsq Technology (HQ) | Provider of control system and energy management services, specializing in data and SCADA monitoring. | 510-259-1334 | NA | Hayward |
| Impulse Semiconductor Inc (HQ) | Provider of electrostatic discharge and electrical overstress products and services. The company also provides virtual components and hardware. | 408-355-5018 | NA | San Jose |
| Inphi Corp (HQ) | Provider of semiconductor solutions for the computing and telecom markets. The company's products include amplifiers, registers, buffers, and modulator drivers. | 408-217-7300 | NA | Santa Clara |
| Integrated Engineering Services (HQ) | Provider of designs for complex Hi-tech microelectronic needs. The company also serves the life science facilities. | 408-261-3500 | NA | Santa Clara |
| Integrated Silicon Solution Inc (HQ) | Designer and developer of high performance integrated circuits. The company also focuses on the marketing aspects. | 408-969-6600 | NA | Milpitas |
| Intel Corp (HQ) | Designer, developer, and marketer of processors and motherboards. The company also focuses on tablets, laptops, desktops, and other devices. | 408-765-8080 | NA | Santa Clara |
| Intermems Inc (HQ) | Provider of micromolding, plating, thin film deposition, anodic and wafer bonding, and related services. | 408-241-0007 | NA | San Jose |
| Intermolecular Inc (HQ) | Provider of high productivity combinatorial technologies. The company serves solar device manufacturers. | 408-582-5700 | NA | San Jose |
| International Electronic Components Inc (RH) | Distributor of printed circuit boards, consumables, and inspection and measuring equipment. The company is engaged in installation services. | 408-496-0474 | NA | Santa Clara |
| Interphase Systems (HQ) | Manufacturer of test equipment for the disc drive industry. The company offers consulting and build-to-print services. | 408-315-8603 | NA | Santa Clara |
| Intevac Inc (HQ) | Supplier of magnetic media processing systems. The company offers advanced equipment to the hard disk drive, solar, and photonics industries. | 408-986-9888 | NA | Santa Clara |
| Invensas Corp (HQ) | Provider of software solutions for computer applications. The company also offers semiconductor technologies. | 408-321-6000 | NA | San Jose |
| Ise Labs Inc (HQ) | Provider of semiconductor services. The company offers services such as production test, test interface, and mechanical testing. | 510-687-2500 | NA | Fremont |
| Ixys Corp (HQ) | Manufacturer of power semiconductor products. The company specializes in power semiconductors, integrated circuits, and radio frequency power. | 408-457-9000 | NA | Milpitas |
| JSK Associates (HQ) | Provider of electronics, medical, and semiconductor manufacturing services. The company also offers assembly and research services. | 408-980-8575 | NA | Santa Clara |
| Kinetic Technologies (RH) | Designer and developer of analog and mixed-signal power management semiconductors. The company serves the consumer and communication markets. | 512-694-6384 | NA | San Jose |
| KLA-Tencor Corp (HQ) | Provider of inspection and metrology tools. The company also specializes in process control and yield management products. | 408-875-3000 | NA | Milpitas |
| Kokusai Semiconductor Equipment Corp (DH) | Provider of thermal processing solutions. The company also provides technical, installation, and retrofit services. | 408-456-2750 | NA | San Jose |
| Lam Research Corp (HQ) | Manufacturer and distributor of single wafer systems. The company primarily serves the semiconductor industry. | 510-572-0200 | NA | Fremont |
| Lattice Semiconductor Corporation (BR) | Provider of design, development, and marketing services for programmable logic devices. The company also offers related software. | 408-826-6000 | NA | San Jose |
| Liberty Labs Inc (HQ) | Provider of testing services for the semiconductor industry. The company is engaged in custom programming and quality assurance services. | 408-262-6633 | NA | Milpitas |
| Light Guard Systems Inc (HQ) | Provider of traffic safety products such as controllers, signal head and base plate modules, and LED signage products. | 707-542-4547 | NA | Santa Rosa |
| Linear Integrated Systems (HQ) | Manufacturer of semiconductor products. The company offers bipolar transistors, input protection diodes, resistors, and low leakage amplifiers. | 510-490-9160 | NA | Fremont |
| Lumasense Technologies Inc (HQ) | Provider of temperature and gas sensing instruments for the energy, industrial, clean technology, and commercial markets. | 408-727-1600 | NA | Santa Clara |
| Luxience Technologies (HQ) | Provider of precision semiconductor equipment. The company specializes in design, fabrication, and supply of semiconductor equipment. | 669-235-5778 | NA | San Jose |
| Macrotron Systems Inc (HQ) | Designer and manufacturer of memory modules. The company provides services such as electronics assembly and testing. | 510-683-9600 | NA | Fremont |
| Malaster Company Inc (HQ) | Provider of packing materials. The company specializes in offering package and shipping solutions for semiconductor industries. | 877-625-2783 | NA | Santa Clara |
| Marseille Inc (HQ) | Provider of video processing solutions. The company's applications include home theaters and audio and video receivers. | 408-855-9003 | NA | Santa Clara |
| Mellanox Technologies Inc (RH) | Provider of Ethernet interconnect solutions and services. The company offers virtualization and Microsoft based solutions to its clients. | 408-970-3400 | NA | Sunnyvale |

| COMPANY NAME | PRODUCT / SERVICE | PHONE | EMP | CITY |
|---|---|---|---|---|
| Micro-Mechanics Inc (DH) | Manufacturer of precision tools, assemblies, and consumable parts used to manufacture and test semiconductors. The company offers mold pots and trims. | 408-779-2927 | NA | Morgan Hill |
| Microchip Technology Inc (BR) | Provider of microcontroller and analog semiconductors. The company focuses on products such as amplifiers, data converters, and embedded controllers. | 408-961-6400 | NA | San Jose |
| Microsemi (DH) | Supplier of discrete military and aerospace components. The company's applications include embedded systems and power solutions. | 408-986-8031 | NA | Santa Clara |
| Mission Peak Optics Inc (HQ) | Provider of measurement solutions for semiconductor industry. The company offers thin film thickness measurement system. | 510-438-0384 | NA | Fremont |
| Mixed Signal Integration (HQ) | Specializes in the design, manufacture and sale of turn-key analog and mixed-signal standard products and custom ASICs. | 408-434-6305 | NA | San Jose |
| Mixel Inc (HQ) | Designer and developer of mixed-signal internet protocol cores for the semiconductor and electronics industries. | 408-436-8500 | NA | San Jose |
| Modular Process Technology Corp (HQ) | Manufacturer of semiconductor equipment for thermal processing systems and stand-alone ultraviolet ozone cleaning systems. | 408-325-8640 | NA | San Jose |
| Modutek Corp (HQ) | Manufacturer of wet process equipment and environmental systems. The company serves the semiconductor sector and offers repair services. | 408-362-2000 | NA | San Jose |
| Monolithic Power Systems Inc (HQ) | Provider of analog semiconductor products. The company offers battery chargers, linear regulators & analog switches, voltage supervisors, and amplifiers. | 408-826-0600 | NA | San Jose |
| Multibeam Corp (HQ) | Producer of photomasks for optical lithography. The company's products are used in IC manufacturing and water defect inspection applications. | 408-980-1800 | NA | Santa Clara |
| Naprotek Inc (HQ) | Provider of electronics manufacturing services. The company serves customers in the satellites, industrial, medical, military, and other sectors. | 408-830-5000 | NA | San Jose |
| Neophotonics Corp (HQ) | Designer and manufacturer of photonic integrated circuit based optoelectronic modules and subsystems for communications networks. | 408-232-9200 | NA | San Jose |
| Netronome (HQ) | Provider of flow processing, server virtualization, cyber security, and software-defined networking solutions. | 408-496-0022 | NA | Santa Clara |
| Neutronix Inc (HQ) | Manufacturer of contact or proximity and projection mask aligners. The company is involved in design, installation, and delivery services. | 408-776-5190 | NA | Morgan Hill |
| Nisene Technology Group (HQ) | Provider of automated decapsulator technology and plastic etching services. The company offers custom design services for nonstandard gaskets. | 831-761-7980 | 1-10 | Watsonville |
| Noel Technologies Inc (HQ) | Provider of lithography, thin film deposition, and water recycling solutions. The company serves MEMS, defense, life science, and other sectors. | 408-374-9549 | NA | Campbell |
| Novasentis Inc (HQ) | Creator of haptic actuator and sensor technology for the consumer electronics applications such as smart watches, jewelry, headbands, and smart glasses. | 814-238-7400 | NA | Berkeley |
| Nuvoton Technology Corporation America (DH) | Manufacturer of semiconductor products and applications. The company's offerings include microcontrollers, microprocessors and cloud computing. | 408-544-1718 | NA | San Jose |
| Oepic Semiconductors Inc (HQ) | Provider of semiconductor fabrication services. The company's products include optical and optoelectronic components. | 408-747-0388 | NA | Sunnyvale |
| Omnivision Technologies Inc (HQ) | Developer of digital imaging solutions for consumer and commercial applications, and automotive, medical, and security imaging sectors. | 408-567-3000 | NA | Santa Clara |
| Omniyig Inc (HQ) | Manufacturer of microwave devices for the defense industry. The company also offers limiters, drivers, and oscillators. | 408-988-0843 | NA | Santa Clara |
| On Semiconductor (BR) | Supplier of semiconductor products and solutions. The company's products find application in green electronics. | 408-542-1104 | 1001-5000 | Santa Clara |
| Onspec Electronic Inc (HQ) | Provider of semiconductor and electronic devices. The company focuses on data transfer services using USB and also provides technical support. | 408-727-1819 | NA | Santa Clara |
| Open-Silicon Inc (HQ) | Provider of IP, foundry, test, and packaging technologies. The company's services include system design, manufacturing, and program management. | 408-240-5700 | NA | Milpitas |
| Optoplex Corporation (HQ) | Supplier of cutting-edge photonic components and modules for dynamic wavelength management and signal conditioning. | 510-490-9930 | NA | Fremont |
| Owens Design (HQ) | Developer of advanced technology systems for semiconductor, hard disk drive, solar, medical device, and other sectors. | 510-659-1800 | NA | Fremont |
| Pactech Inc (HQ) | Provider of computer cables, cooling items, and other components. The company also offers networking products. | 408-526-9363 | NA | San Jose |
| Pactron/Hjpc Corp (HQ) | Provider of electronics design and design development services. The company is also involved in engineering and contract manufacturing. | 408-329-5500 | NA | Santa Clara |
| Parallax Inc (HQ) | Manufacturer of electronic hardware and software products. The company offers microcontrollers, sensors, boards, and cables/converters. | 916-624-8333 | 1-10 | Rocklin |
| Peninsula Engineering Solutions Inc (HQ) | Manufacturer of microwave RF repeaters. The company also specializes in cellular & PCS repeaters and relateed products. | 925-837-2243 | NA | Danville |
| Peridot Corp (HQ) | Provider of design for manufacturing and packaging. The company also manufacturers of medical components, miniature component and general product prototypes. | 925-461-8830 | NA | Pleasanton |

| COMPANY NAME | PRODUCT / SERVICE | PHONE | EMP | CITY |
|---|---|---|---|---|
| Pragmatics Technologies Inc (HQ) | Provider of electromechanical interface solutions. The company deals with the development of custom and standard test interfaces. | 408-289-8202 | NA | San Jose |
| Precision Tool Distributors Inc (HQ) | Specializes in dimensional measurement products. The company offers inspection hand tools and related accessories. | 408-774-1274 | NA | Fremont |
| Probe Logic (HQ) | Developer and manufacturer of probe card for semiconductor industry. The company also offers printed circuit board design services. | 408-416-0777 | NA | San Jose |
| Pyramid Semiconductor Corp (HQ) | Provider of assembly services. The company is focused in the assembly of monolithic ceramic products and multi-chip modules. | 408-734-8200 | NA | Sunnyvale |
| Qualitau Inc (HQ) | Supplier of test equipment and services. The company is involved in the development of electronic equipment for semiconductor process reliability. | 650-282-6226 | NA | Mountain View |
| Quantenna Communications Inc (HQ) | Developer of semiconductor solutions for the Wi-Fi networks. The company serves retail, home networking, consumer electronics, and enterprise needs. | 669-209-5500 | NA | San Jose |
| Quantum Semiconductor Llc (HQ) | Manufacturer of semiconductor devices. The company specializes in silicon photonic receivers and solar cells. | 408-243-2262 | NA | San Jose |
| Rambus (HQ) | Manufacturer of semiconductor, lighting, and IP products. The company serves the automotive and transportation markets. | 408-462-8000 | NA | Sunnyvale |
| Rishang LED Inc (LH) | Manufacturer of LED products for decorative and green lighting solutions. The company's products are used in the residential and commercial sectors. | 408-748-8889 | NA | Santa Clara |
| ROHM Semiconductor USA LLC (BR) | Manufacturer of amplifiers, clocks, modules, passive components, remote control receivers, and timers. | 408-720-1900 | NA | Santa Clara |
| Roos Instruments Inc (BR) | Manufacturer of automated test equipment. The company's products include MEMs devices, radars, amplifiers, and mixers. | 408-748-8589 | NA | Santa Clara |
| Royce Instruments Inc (HQ) | Provider of bond testers and die sorters for the auto and medical electronics device manufacturers worldwide. | 707-255-9078 | NA | Napa |
| Rucker Kolls Inc (HQ) | Provider of solutions for ATE test interface products. The company's services include custom PCB design and card stiffeners and rings. | 408-934-9875 | NA | Milpitas |
| Schurter Inc (DH) | Manufacturer of fuses, connectors, and circuit breakers. The company also offers input systems and EMC products. | 707-636-3000 | NA | Santa Rosa |
| Semi-Probes Inc (HQ) | Manufacturer and supplier of probe cards and tester interfaces. The company's services include design, installation, and delivery. | 408-866-6535 | NA | San Jose |
| Sempac Inc (HQ) | Developer of pre-molded open-cavity plastic packages for optoelectronic, telecom, RF, MEMS, and sensor applications. | 408-400-9002 | NA | Los Altos |
| Sentons Usa Inc (HQ) | Provider of touch solutions. The company offers flat panel display, retail point of sale, and factory/industry automation products. | 408-732-9000 | NA | San Jose |
| Sigma Designs Inc (HQ) | Provider of system-on-chip solutions for media processing, smart TV, video encoding, AV networking, video processing, and home control systems. | 510-897-0200 | NA | Fremont |
| Silicon Frontline Technology Inc (HQ) | Provider of parasitic extraction and analysis services for post layout verification. The company specializes in electrostatic discharge analysis. | 408-963-6916 | NA | San Jose |
| Silicon Genesis Corp (HQ) | Manufacturer of semiconductor and solar fabrication tools . The company offers stand-alone plasma tools and debond and cleave tools. | 408-228-5858 | NA | San Jose |
| Silicon Light Machines (DH) | Provider of optical micro-electro-mechanical systems. The company's applications include maskless lithography and large format digital displays. | 408-240-4700 | NA | Sunnyvale |
| Silicon Motion Inc (DH) | Designer of low-power semiconductor solutions. The company serves multimedia consumer electronic applications. | 408-519-7289 | NA | Milpitas |
| Silicon Wafer Enterprises Llc (HQ) | Provider of silicon wafers and other raw materials. The company's offerings include silicon, plate glass, pyrex, and sapphire. | 916-941-7728 | 1-10 | El Dorado Hills |
| Silicon360 (HQ) | Supplier of semiconductors for the military, aerospace, industrial, medical, and commercial markets. | 408-432-1790 | NA | Milpitas |
| Sitime Corp (HQ) | Provider of programmable oscillators and clock generators. The company also offers embedded resonators. | 408-328-4400 | NA | Sunnyvale |
| Small Precision Tools Inc (BR) | Manufacturer of chip bonding tools, fine ceramic, and machining parts. The company offers necessary technical support and services. | 707-765-4545 | NA | Petaluma |
| Socionext Inc (DH) | Designer and developer of System-on-Chip products. The company's products are used in imaging, networking, and computing fields. | 408 550-6861 | NA | Santa Clara |
| Solarius Development Inc (HQ) | Manufacturer of 3D metrology surface measurement systems. The company offers metrology services for surface form. | 408-435-2777 | NA | San Jose |
| Sparqtron Corp (HQ) | Provider of electronic contract manufacturing services. The company focuses on prototyping, inspection, PCB assembly, and materials and logistics. | 510-657-7198 | NA | Fremont |
| Sperient Corporation Inc (HQ) | Designer and developer of electronic systems. The company's applications include telemedicine and robotic sensing. | 925-447-3333 | NA | Livermore |
| Statico (HQ) | Provider of ESD and static control products. The company offers test instruments, ionizers, and cleanroom products. | 650-592-4733 | NA | San Carlos |
| STMicroelectronics (BR) | Provider of analog, mixed signal ICs, transistor, and memories. The company also offers microcontroller products and services. | 408-919-8400 | NA | Santa Clara |

| COMPANY NAME | PRODUCT / SERVICE | PHONE | EMP | CITY |
|---|---|---|---|---|
| Surplus Process Equipment Corp (HQ) | Provider of new, used, and refurbished semiconductor equipment. The company offers ashing and etching systems. | 408-654-9500 | NA | Santa Clara |
| Sv Tcl (BR) | Manufacturer of probe cards. The company is engaged in delivery and installation services and serves the semiconductor industry. | 408-727-6341 | NA | Santa Clara |
| System General USA (DH) | Designer and manufacturer of device programmers and offers consultancy services in device programming and power management. | 833-845-3900 | NA | San Jose |
| Taracom Integrated Products (HQ) | Provider of multi-gigabit solutions for communications and storage applications. The company's solutions include backplane and fiber channel. | 408-691-6655 | NA | Santa Clara |
| Tazmo Inc (BR) | Manufacturer of SOG and LCD color filter coaters. The company offers SOG, SOD, polyimide coaters and developers and LCD Resist coaters. | 510-438-4890 | NA | Fremont |
| Tela Innovations Inc (HQ) | Provider of lithography optimized solutions. The company's services include design, implementation, and technical support. | 408-558-6300 | NA | Los Gatos |
| Teradyne Inc (BR) | Supplier of automatic test equipment. The company caters to semiconductor, electronics, and automotive sectors. | 480-777-7090 | NA | San Jose |
| Test21 Inc (HQ) | Designer and manufacturer of printed circuit boards including probe cards for semiconductor, ATE manufacturers, and silicon wafer foundries. | 510-438-0221 | NA | Fremont |
| Thermal Engineering Associates Inc (HQ) | Provider of semiconductor thermal measurement and modeling solutions. The company's products include thermal test systems, test fixtures, and test chips. | 650-961-5900 | NA | Santa Clara |
| Toppan Printing Company Ltd (BR) | Provider of printing solutions. The company serves customers in the food, beverage, and high barrier product industries. | 415-393-9839 | NA | San Francisco |
| Translarity (HQ) | Specializes in wafer translation technology. The company offers device design and testing solutions to the semiconductor industry. | 510-371-7900 | NA | Fremont |
| True Circuits Inc (HQ) | Developer and marketer of phase-locked loops, delay-locked loops, and mixed-signal designs for integrated circuits. | 650-949-3400 | NA | Los Altos |
| Tsmc North America (HQ) | Manufacturer of products for the computer, communications, and consumer electronics market segments. | 408-382-8000 | NA | San Jose |
| Vacuum Engineering & Materials Co (HQ) | Manufacturer and supplier of PVD materials. The company also offers services like shield cleaning, material reclaim, and consignment programs. | 408-871-9900 | NA | Santa Clara |
| Verific Design Automation Inc (HQ) | Specializes in electronic design automation solutions. The company offers services to the semiconductor industry. | 510-522-1555 | NA | Alameda |
| VeriSilicon Inc (HQ) | Provider of IC design services specializing in custom silicon solutions. The company also offers SOC turnkey services. | 408-844-8560 | NA | San Jose |
| Versatile Power (HQ) | Designer and manufacturer of electronic subsystems for manufacturers. The company focuses on application of radio frequency, ultrasonics, and lasers. | 408-341-4600 | NA | Campbell |
| Vlsi Research Inc (HQ) | Provider of chip market research, consultation, semiconductor analysis, and data spreadsheets and reports. | 408-453-8844 | NA | San Jose |
| VLSI Standards Inc (HQ) | Manufacturer of electrical and solar energy products. The company offers calibration services to the semiconductor industry. | 408-428-1800 | NA | Milpitas |
| VueMetrix Inc (HQ) | Developer of laser diode-based systems. The company is focused on integrated laser diode control electronics. | 408-770-3070 | NA | San Jose |
| Wafer Process Systems Inc (HQ) | Manufacturer of semiconductors, MEMS, and photonics. The company also focuses on RFID products, disc drives, and flat panel displays. | 408-445-3010 | NA | San Jose |
| Westfab Manufacturing Inc (HQ) | Manufacturer of simple brackets, multiple level frames, and enclosures. The company offers assembly services for power supplies, switches, and cables. | 408-727-0550 | NA | Santa Clara |
| World Products Inc (HQ) | Provider of electronic component solutions and services. The company offers sales, distribution, and technical support. | 707-996-5201 | NA | Sonoma |
| X-Fab Texas Inc (BR) | Provider of foundry services. The company focuses on analog and mixed signal semiconductor applications. | 408-844-0066 | NA | Santa Clara |
| X-Scan Imaging Corp (HQ) | Supplier of x-ray imaging and inspection equipment. The company also offers array detectors and line-scan camera products. | 408-432-9888 | NA | San Jose |
| Xeltek Inc (HQ) | Manufacturer of automated, production, and in-system programmers, and socket adapters, and related supplies. | 408-530-8080 | NA | Sunnyvale |
| XTAL Inc (HQ) | Specializes in yield enhancement, software optimization and hardware implementation targeting semiconductor ecosystem. | 408-642-5328 | NA | San Jose |
| Zeta Instruments (HQ) | Provider of 3D optical profilers and its applications include wafer quality analysis, texture characterization, and finger contact profiling. | 408-818-9388 | NA | San Jose |

## 213 = Transducers/Transistors/Resistors

| COMPANY NAME | PRODUCT / SERVICE | PHONE | EMP | CITY |
|---|---|---|---|---|
| Andrew Ndt Engineering Corp (HQ) | Manufacturer of probes, ultrasonic transducers, diamond cutting tools, proximity sensors, cables, and offers calibration services. | 408-710-0342 | NA | San Jose |
| Bandwidth10 Inc (BR) | Developer of tunable, singlemode, 1550 nm long-wavelength VCSELs, and transceivers for datacom applications. | 203-561-0769 | NA | Berkeley |
| Caltron Components Corp (HQ) | Distributor of electronic capacitors and resistors. The company also focuses on semiconductor products. | 408-748-2140 | NA | Santa Clara |
| Data Physics Corp (HQ) | Provider of high performance test and measurement solutions for noise and vibration applications. The company offers drop testing services. | 408-437-0100 | NA | San Jose |

| COMPANY NAME | PRODUCT / SERVICE | PHONE | EMP | CITY |
|---|---|---|---|---|
| Infineon Technologies North American Corp (BR) | Provider of semiconductor and system solutions. The company focuses on mobile security, sensors, power management, and RF. | 866-951-9519 | NA | Morgan Hill |
| Josephson Engineering Inc (HQ) | Manufacturer of condenser microphones for studio, stage, and field sound pickup, and audio instrumentation. | 831-420-0888 | 1-10 | Santa Cruz |
| Kinetic Ceramics Inc (HQ) | Manufacturer of performance products for motion control applications. The company's services include diamond turning and fabrication. | 510-264-2140 | 11-50 | Hayward |
| NIC Components Corp (BR) | Designer, manufacturer, and supplier of passive components. The company offers ceramic capacitors, power inductors, and current sensing resistors. | 669-342-3960 | NA | San Jose |
| Nk Technologies (HQ) | Manufacturer of current sensors and transducer products for the factory and industrial automation markets. | 408-871-7510 | NA | San Jose |
| Tavis Corp (HQ) | Provider of custom pressure transducer sensor designs. The company offers services to measurement environments. | 209-966-2027 | 1-10 | Mariposa |
| Voltage Multipliers Inc (HQ) | Manufacturer of voltage multipliers, high voltage diodes, rectifiers, op-to-couplers, and power supplies. | 559-651-1402 | 1-10 | Visalia |

## 214 = Transformers

| COMPANY NAME | PRODUCT / SERVICE | PHONE | EMP | CITY |
|---|---|---|---|---|
| Bandwidth10 Inc (BR) | Developer of tunable, singlemode, 1550 nm long-wavelength VCSELs, and transceivers for datacom applications. | 203-561-0769 | NA | Berkeley |
| Custom Coils Inc (HQ) | Manufacturer of coils, coil assemblies, and solenoids. The company also offers other electro-magnetic devices. | 707-752-8633 | NA | Benicia |
| Kemet Electronics Corp (BR) | Provider of relays, EMI filters, transformers, capacitors, and ferrite products. The company serves the aerospace, defense, and automotive industries. | 877-695-3638 | NA | Santa Clara |
| Magnetic Circuit Elements (HQ) | Manufacturer of miniature transformers and inductors. The company's products include chokes, inductors, transformers, and sine wave inverters. | 831-757-8752 | NA | Salinas |
| Pearson Electronics Inc (HQ) | Manufacturer of wide band current monitors. The company also offers high voltage pulse transformers and voltage dividers. | 650-494-6444 | NA | Palo Alto |
| Stangenes Industries Inc (HQ) | Manufacturer of isolation transformers, current monitors, charging inductors, and magnetic components. | 650-493-0814 | NA | Palo Alto |
| Tamura Corporation of America (BR) | Manufacturer of DC power modules, current sensor products, telecom transformers, and LED products. The company is involved in distribution services. | 760-871-2009 | NA | Escondido |
| Tecdia Inc (HQ) | Manufacturer of precision machine tools and fixtures. The company also specializes in cutting and scribing tools. | 408-748-0100 | NA | Campbell |

## 217 = Defense-Related R&D

| COMPANY NAME | PRODUCT / SERVICE | PHONE | EMP | CITY |
|---|---|---|---|---|
| Axelsys LLC (HQ) | Provider of electronic design and manufacturing services. The company's offerings include LED and AC to DC industrial power supplies. | 408-600-0871 | NA | San Jose |
| Ea Machining Inc (HQ) | Provider of CNC turning and milling services. The company offers services to the semiconductor manufacturing equipment industry. | 408-727-4962 | NA | Santa Clara |
| Yotta Navigation Corp (HQ) | Manufacturer of sub-meter positioning systems and underwater precision navigation platforms. The company serves the homeland security market. | 800-943-1220 | NA | Santa Clara |

## 218 = Electronic Warfare Equipment

| COMPANY NAME | PRODUCT / SERVICE | PHONE | EMP | CITY |
|---|---|---|---|---|
| Tps Aviation Inc (HQ) | Distributor of commercial and military aerospace fasteners and electric components. The company focuses on aerospace parts, components, and logistics. | 510-475-1010 | NA | Hayward |

## 219 = Military Aircraft & Related Equipment

| COMPANY NAME | PRODUCT / SERVICE | PHONE | EMP | CITY |
|---|---|---|---|---|
| Aero Precision Industries (HQ) | Supplier of military aircraft parts for the aerospace industry. The company's services include repair, replacement, and maintenance. | 925-455-9900 | NA | Livermore |
| Tps Aviation Inc (HQ) | Distributor of commercial and military aerospace fasteners and electric components. The company focuses on aerospace parts, components, and logistics. | 510-475-1010 | NA | Hayward |

## 220 = Military Search, Detection & Navigation Systems & Instruments

| COMPANY NAME | PRODUCT / SERVICE | PHONE | EMP | CITY |
|---|---|---|---|---|
| Bridgepoint Systems Inc (HQ) | Provider of security solutions such as CAC card readers, PIV card readers, and access control experts for government contractors and security integrators. | 510-346-1510 | NA | Berkeley |
| Sna Electronics Inc (HQ) | Provider of electronic manufacturing services. The company offers services to OEMs in the networking, medical instruments, and aerospace industries. | 510-656-3903 | NA | Fremont |

## 221 = Missiles & Related Equipment

| COMPANY NAME | PRODUCT / SERVICE | PHONE | EMP | CITY |
|---|---|---|---|---|
| Yotta Navigation Corp (HQ) | Manufacturer of sub-meter positioning systems and underwater precision navigation platforms. The company serves the homeland security market. | 800-943-1220 | NA | Santa Clara |

## 224 = Systems Analysis, Integration & Other Military Services

| COMPANY NAME | PRODUCT / SERVICE | PHONE | EMP | CITY |
|---|---|---|---|---|
| Compudata Inc (HQ) | Provider of sales, accounting, and manufacturing software. The company especially caters to businesses. | 415-495-3422 | NA | San Francisco |

| COMPANY NAME | PRODUCT / SERVICE | PHONE | EMP | CITY |
|---|---|---|---|---|
| Emlinux (HQ) | Developer of embedded Linux designs. The company provides marketing level definition and system architecture services. | 408-249-5574 | NA | San Jose |
| GoEngineer (BR) | Provider of solid works engineering and Oracle agile PLM products. The company offers services to the business sector. | 408-213-1580 | NA | Santa Clara |
| Immecor (HQ) | Provider of industrial computers, custom cables, and PCB assembly services. The company serves entertainment, medical, and telecom sectors. | 707-636-2550 | NA | Santa Rosa |
| InfoTech Spectrum Inc (HQ) | Provider of integrated creative IT services including IT consulting, advanced technology deployment, and product development. | 408-705-2237 | NA | Santa Clara |
| Ledger Systems Inc (HQ) | Provider of network design and support services. The company also offers accounting and e-Commerce solutions. | 650-592-6211 | NA | San Carlos |
| Nevtec Inc (HQ) | Provider of networks implementation and maintenance services. The company also focuses on workstations and the internet. | 408-292-8600 | NA | San Jose |
| Presentek Inc (HQ) | Designer of websites and web portals. The company also offers content management systems and e-commerce handlers. | 408-354-1264 | NA | Los Gatos |
| Zeidman Technologies Inc (HQ) | Developer of hardware and software code design tools. The company focuses on embedded system development. | 408-741-5809 | NA | Cupertino |

## 226 = Monitoring/Controlling Equipment

| COMPANY NAME | PRODUCT / SERVICE | PHONE | EMP | CITY |
|---|---|---|---|---|
| Pivotal Systems Corp (HQ) | Provider of monitoring and process control technology solutions for the semiconductor manufacturing industry. | 510-770-9125 | NA | Fremont |

## 227 = Automatic Regulating Controls

| COMPANY NAME | PRODUCT / SERVICE | PHONE | EMP | CITY |
|---|---|---|---|---|
| Civil Maps (HQ) | Developer of autonomous vehicles and cognitive perception systems. The company specializes in localization technology and artificial intelligence. | 415-287-9977 | NA | San Francisco |
| Enocean Alliance Inc (HQ) | Manufacturer of wireless switches, sensors, and controls for building automation and residential property needs. | 925-275-6601 | NA | San Ramon |
| Inmon Corp (HQ) | Developer of traffic management and monitoring products such as sFlow Trend, sFlow-RT, Hyper-V Agent, and others. | 415-946-8901 | NA | San Francisco |
| Lamphier-Gregory (HQ) | Provider of urban planning services. The company provides environmental analysis, project management, and coordination services. | 510-535-6690 | NA | Oakland |
| Martinelli Environmental Graphics (HQ) | Provide of environmental graphic designing services. The company offers fabrication, installation, and design build services. | 415-468-4000 | NA | San Francisco |
| Pivotal Systems Corp (HQ) | Provider of monitoring and process control technology solutions for the semiconductor manufacturing industry. | 510-770-9125 | NA | Fremont |
| Simco-Ion (BR) | Manufacturer of static control and process control products. The company is engaged in design and installation services. | 510-217-0600 | NA | Alameda |
| Trench & Traffic Supply Inc (HQ) | Provider of traffic control equipment for rent and sale. The company offers equipment for traffic control, shoring, and pipe testing. | 916-920-3304 | 1-10 | Sacramento |

## 228 = Control Panels

| COMPANY NAME | PRODUCT / SERVICE | PHONE | EMP | CITY |
|---|---|---|---|---|
| Calcon Systems Inc (HQ) | Provider of process control, instrumentation, and automation solutions specializing in turnkey design-build system integration and support. | 925-277-0665 | NA | San Ramon |
| California Motor Controls Inc (HQ) | Manufacturer of electrical control panels. The company offers pump controls and communication systems for municipal and commercial applications. | 707-746-6255 | NA | Benicia |
| Cold Room Solutions Inc (HQ) | Provider of walk-in cold rooms, freezers, and warm rooms. The company focuses on preventive maintenance programs. | 925-462-2500 | NA | Pleasanton |
| Control Systems West Inc (HQ) | Designer and fabricator of a broad variety of custom electrical controls for industrial applications. | 707-763-1108 | NA | Petaluma |
| Dst Controls (HQ) | Provider of control systems integration, industrial data management, and related enterprise solutions. The company serves the industrial sector. | 800-251-0773 | NA | Benicia |
| Interphasic LLC (HQ) | Manufacturer of motion control systems. The company offers product support services and it serves the industrial sector. | 831-392-0708 | NA | Seaside |
| Pivotal Systems Corp (HQ) | Provider of monitoring and process control technology solutions for the semiconductor manufacturing industry. | 510-770-9125 | NA | Fremont |

## 230 = Flow Control Instruments

| COMPANY NAME | PRODUCT / SERVICE | PHONE | EMP | CITY |
|---|---|---|---|---|
| American Micro Detection Systems Inc (HQ) | Provider of water analysis treatments. The company deals with research, development, and monitoring services. | 209-985-1705 | 11-50 | Stockton |
| Autoflow Products Inc (HQ) | Manufacturer of flow switches. The company specializes in designing switches for chemical analyzers, chemical injectors, and chromatographic systems. | 916-626-3058 | 1-10 | Rocklin |
| Pivotal Systems Corp (HQ) | Provider of monitoring and process control technology solutions for the semiconductor manufacturing industry. | 510-770-9125 | NA | Fremont |
| Semifab (HQ) | Supplier of process environment control systems for precise temperature, humidity, air flow, and airborne particulate management. | 408-414-5928 | NA | San Jose |
| SuperKlean (HQ) | Manufacturer of spray nozzles and swivel fittings. The company also offers hot & cold water mixing stations and hose racks. | 650-375-7001 | NA | Burlingame |
| The Detection Group Inc (HQ) | Provider of monitoring and alarming solutions. The company offers wireless water leak detection systems for commercial buildings. | 650-215-7300 | NA | Sunnyvale |

| COMPANY NAME | PRODUCT / SERVICE | PHONE | EMP | CITY |
|---|---|---|---|---|
| **231 = Gas & Liquid Control Instruments** | | | | |
| American Micro Detection Systems Inc (HQ) | Provider of water analysis treatments. The company deals with research, development, and monitoring services. | 209-985-1705 | 11-50 | Stockton |
| Autoflow Products Inc (HQ) | Manufacturer of flow switches. The company specializes in designing switches for chemical analyzers, chemical injectors, and chromatographic systems. | 916-626-3058 | 1-10 | Rocklin |
| Hpm Systems Inc (HQ) | Provider of gas monitoring control systems. The company's services include design, integration, installation, and maintenance. | 408-615-6900 | NA | Santa Clara |
| Lumasense Technologies Inc (HQ) | Provider of temperature and gas sensing instruments for the energy, industrial, clean technology, and commercial markets. | 408-727-1600 | NA | Santa Clara |
| Picarro Inc (HQ) | Provider of environmental transformation solutions. The company provides isotope analyzers, trace gas analyzers, accessories, and peripherals. | 408-962-3900 | NA | Santa Clara |
| Semifab (HQ) | Supplier of process environment control systems for precise temperature, humidity, air flow, and airborne particulate management. | 408-414-5928 | NA | San Jose |
| Sierra Monitor Corp (HQ) | Manufacturer and seller of safety and environmental instrumentation. The company offers hazardous gas detection systems and site management products. | 408-262-6611 | NA | Milpitas |
| **232 = Industrial Controllers & Relays** | | | | |
| California Motor Controls Inc (HQ) | Manufacturer of electrical control panels. The company offers pump controls and communication systems for municipal and commercial applications. | 707-746-6255 | NA | Benicia |
| Enphase Energy Inc (HQ) | Distributor of electronic products. The company offers services to the solar, telecom, networking, and software industries. | 877-797-4743 | NA | Petaluma |
| Green Plug (HQ) | Developer and provider of digital controller technology solutions and products to the consumer electronics markets. | 925-867-2781 | NA | San Ramon |
| Motion Control Engineering Inc (HQ) | Manufacturer of elevator control products. The company's products include elevator and escalator controls, complete elevators, and components and peripherals. | 916-463-9200 | 11-50 | Rancho Cordova |
| O2micro Usa (LH) | Provider of battery and power management products. The company also offers LED general lighting and backlighting products. | 408-987-5920 | NA | Santa Clara |
| Sierra Monitor Corp (HQ) | Manufacturer and seller of safety and environmental instrumentation. The company offers hazardous gas detection systems and site management products. | 408-262-6611 | NA | Milpitas |
| **233 = Industrial Instruments for Measurement, Display & Control** | | | | |
| Acosta Sheet Metal Manufacturing Inc (HQ) | Manufacturer of HVAC and architectural products, and sheet metal building materials. The company provides gutter profile caps and conductor heads. | 408-275-6370 | NA | San Jose |
| Advantest America Inc (LH) | Provider of measurement systems and solutions. The company offers electronic measuring instruments, and optical sensing and imaging analysis systems. | 408-456-3600 | NA | Santa Clara |
| Air Monitor Corp (HQ) | Manufacturer of airflow and space pressurization control systems and offers airflow traverse probes, pressure sensors, and electronic transmitters. | 707-544-2706 | NA | Santa Rosa |
| Arista Corp (HQ) | Manufacturer of industrial computer products such as industrial rack mounts, touch screen displays, and fanless, embedded, and wallmount computers. | 510-226-1800 | NA | Fremont |
| Assay Technology Inc (HQ) | Provider of personal monitoring badges to monitor chemicals in worker's breathing zone. The company also analyzes the contents of returned samplers. | 925-461-8880 | NA | Livermore |
| Automate Scientific Inc (HQ) | Manufacturer and distributor of biomedical equipment. The company offers amplifiers, manipulators, software, and accessories. | 510-845-6283 | NA | Berkeley |
| Celadon Inc (HQ) | Provider of OEM products and services. The company's products include OEM remote controls, infrared receivers, and backlighting systems. | 415-472-1177 | NA | San Rafael |
| Control Systems West Inc (HQ) | Designer and fabricator of a broad variety of custom electrical controls for industrial applications. | 707-763-1108 | NA | Petaluma |
| Csi Forensic Supply (HQ) | Manufacturer and supplier of products for law enforcement for crime scene and crime laboratory applications. | 925-686-6667 | NA | Martinez |
| Deltatrak Inc (HQ) | Manufacturer of cold chain management systems. The company provides data loggers, chart recorders, thermometers, and timers and pH meters. | 925-249-2250 | NA | Pleasanton |
| Dynaweb Inc (HQ) | Manufacturer and marketer of web handling and tension control systems. The company's product finds use in packaging, printing, and textile needs. | 925-373-9013 | 1-10 | Sonora |
| Ekm Metering Inc (HQ) | Provider of submetering hardware and services. The company's solutions include revenue metering and data monitoring. | 831-425-7371 | 1-10 | Santa Cruz |
| Enlighted Inc (HQ) | Provider of lighting control systems to commercial buildings, office workspaces, and garages. The company serves facilities and development companies. | 650-964-1094 | NA | Sunnyvale |

| COMPANY NAME | PRODUCT / SERVICE | PHONE | EMP | CITY |
|---|---|---|---|---|
| Enphase Energy Inc (HQ) | Distributor of electronic products. The company offers services to the solar, telecom, networking, and software industries. | 877-797-4743 | NA | Petaluma |
| Fairbanks Scales (BR) | Provider of scales and weighing systems. The company serves the agriculture, parcel shipping, transport, and waste management industries. | 916-384-1394 | 11-50 | Sacramento |
| Futronix Inc (HQ) | Designer and developer of energy management systems. The company provides computer line clocks, electronic cam systems, and energy control systems. | 408-735-1122 | NA | Santa Clara |
| Garratt-Callahan Co (HQ) | Provider of water treatment services. The company's solutions include cooling water treatment and safer chemical cleaning. | 650-697-5811 | NA | Burlingame |
| Gonsel'S Machine Shop (HQ) | Provider of CNC and millwork, inspection, fabrication, and re-machining services. The company serves the food and beverage industry. | 510-569-8086 | NA | Oakland |
| Hsq Technology (HQ) | Provider of control system and energy management services, specializing in data and SCADA monitoring. | 510-259-1334 | NA | Hayward |
| Logosol Inc (BR) | Manufacturer and designer of motion control components. The company's products are used in semiconductor material handling applications. | 408-744-0974 | 11-50 | El Dorado Hills |
| Los Gatos Research Inc (HQ) | Manufacturer of analyzers for the measurement of trace gases and isotopes. The company serves the industrial and environmental sectors. | 650-965-7772 | NA | San Jose |
| Mission Peak Optics Inc (HQ) | Provider of measurement solutions for semiconductor industry. The company offers thin film thickness measurement system. | 510-438-0384 | NA | Fremont |
| Neptune Systems Llc (HQ) | Provider of aquarium controllers. The company also offers expansion modules and accessories and offers support services. | 408-275-2205 | NA | Morgan Hill |
| Novalynx Corp (HQ) | Designer, manufacturer, and integrator of meteorological systems. The company's products are used in the industrial sector. | 530-823-7185 | 1-10 | Grass Valley |
| Pearson Electronics Inc (HQ) | Manufacturer of wide band current monitors. The company also offers high voltage pulse transformers and voltage dividers. | 650-494-6444 | NA | Palo Alto |
| Pivotal Systems Corp (HQ) | Provider of monitoring and process control technology solutions for the semiconductor manufacturing industry. | 510-770-9125 | NA | Fremont |
| SAGE Instruments Inc (RH) | Provider of wireless base station test products. The company offers battery operated handhelds, portables, bench tops, and rackmount test platforms. | 831-761-1000 | 11-50 | Freedom |
| Semifab (HQ) | Supplier of process environment control systems for precise temperature, humidity, air flow, and airborne particulate management. | 408-414-5928 | NA | San Jose |
| Takex America Inc (DH) | Manufacturer of security and industrial sensor products. The company's products include photoelectric beams, outdoor and indoor PIR, and tower enclosures. | 408-747-0100 | NA | Sunnyvale |
| United States Thermoelectric Consortium (HQ) | Manufacturer of thermal management and control systems. The company's offerings also include controllers and air and liquid cooling systems. | 530-345-8000 | 1-10 | Chico |
| Video Clarity Inc (HQ) | Provider of real time and broadcast quality monitoring, perceptual analysis, recording, and automating services. | 408-379-6952 | NA | Campbell |
| Zalda Technology (HQ) | Fabricator of springs. The company also offers spring design, testing, and prototype assembling services. | 510-783-4910 | NA | Hayward |

## 234 = Machine Vision/Inspection Systems

| COMPANY NAME | PRODUCT / SERVICE | PHONE | EMP | CITY |
|---|---|---|---|---|
| Advanced Witness Series Inc (HQ) | Designer of electrical and mechanical components and tools. The company caters to various applications. | 408-453-5070 | NA | San Jose |
| Csi Forensic Supply (HQ) | Manufacturer and supplier of products for law enforcement for crime scene and crime laboratory applications. | 925-686-6667 | NA | Martinez |

## 235 = Measurement & Test

| COMPANY NAME | PRODUCT / SERVICE | PHONE | EMP | CITY |
|---|---|---|---|---|
| Advanced Witness Series Inc (HQ) | Designer of electrical and mechanical components and tools. The company caters to various applications. | 408-453-5070 | NA | San Jose |
| Advantest America Inc (LH) | Provider of measurement systems and solutions. The company offers electronic measuring instruments, and optical sensing and imaging analysis systems. | 408-456-3600 | NA | Santa Clara |
| All Weather Inc (HQ) | Manufacturer of meteorological instruments and systems. The company is also engaged in the development of air traffic management solutions. | 800-824-5873 | 1-10 | Sacramento |
| Azbil North America Inc (BR) | Designer, manufacturer, and supplier of medical devices. The company offers automation products, control products, and industrial automation systems. | 408-245-3121 | NA | Santa Clara |
| Bryza Wind Lab Inc (HQ) | Provider of wind tunnel testing, anemometer calibration consulting services. The company offers electricity producing wind turbines. | 408-605-8964 | NA | San Jose |
| Buglab Llc (HQ) | Developer of biomass measuring equipment such as sensors, biomass monitor, and biomass multiplier involved in fermentation and microbial cultures. | 925-208-1952 | NA | Concord |
| Csi Forensic Supply (HQ) | Manufacturer and supplier of products for law enforcement for crime scene and crime laboratory applications. | 925-686-6667 | NA | Martinez |
| Dakota Ultrasonics Corp (HQ) | Manufacturer of industrial ultrasonic testing equipment. The company serves the aerospace, power generation, and petrochemical industries. | 831-431-9722 | 1-10 | Scotts Valley |
| Fibera Inc (HQ) | Manufacturer and designer of wavelength management products. The company also specializes in fiber optic products. | 408-492-9555 | NA | Santa Clara |

| COMPANY NAME | PRODUCT / SERVICE | PHONE | EMP | CITY |
|---|---|---|---|---|
| Finishline Advanced Composites (HQ) | Provider of composite repair services for production projects. The company is involved in design, development, prototyping, testing, and production. | 707-747-0788 | NA | Benicia |
| Flexline Llc (HQ) | Provider of custom solutions for manufacturing and test problems. The company also deals with automation, engineering, and production tooling. | 408-295-3901 | NA | San Jose |
| Horiba Instruments Inc (BR) | Provider of instruments and systems for automotive research and development, and process and environmental monitoring needs. | 408-730-4772 | NA | Santa Clara |
| Lansmont Corp (HQ) | Provider of products such as field instruments, shock machines, vibration systems, drop testers, and package shakers. | 831-655-6600 | NA | Monterey |
| Magee Scientific Corp (HQ) | Provider of measurement instruments such as aethalometers, transmissometers, and their accessories for monitoring air quality and source emissions. | 510-845-2801 | NA | Berkeley |
| Maselli Measurements Inc (BR) | Provider of liquid measuring solutions. The company manufactures and distributes refractometers and liquid analyzers for several industries. | 209-474-9178 | 11-50 | Stockton |
| Mirion Technologies Inc (DH) | Provider of solutions in radiation detection. The company serves the healthcare, nuclear power, and other industries. | 925-543-0800 | NA | San Ramon |
| Modutek Corp (HQ) | Manufacturer of wet process equipment and environmental systems. The company serves the semiconductor sector and offers repair services. | 408-362-2000 | NA | San Jose |
| Nitinol Devices & Components Inc (HQ) | Provider of rapid development and prototyping services. The company is also engaged in commercialization. | 510-683-2000 | NA | Fremont |
| Pacific Instruments Inc (HQ) | Manufacturer of computer-automated physical measurement systems. The company specializes in signal conditioning & data acquisition equipment. | 925-827-9010 | NA | Concord |
| Picarro Inc (HQ) | Provider of environmental transformation solutions. The company provides isotope analyzers, trace gas analyzers, accessories, and peripherals. | 408-962-3900 | NA | Santa Clara |
| Prysm Inc (HQ) | Provider of large format digital display solutions and software for real-time visual communication applications. | 408-586-1100 | NA | San Jose |
| Safe Hearing America Inc (HQ) | Provider of mobile hearing testing services and products. The company offerings include AQ Solid Plug, Sleep Plug, and Solid Plug. | 707-446-0880 | NA | Vacaville |
| Sentient Energy Inc (HQ) | Provider of sensor devices for operational practices and engineering applications. The company also offers communication software. | 650-523-6680 | NA | Burlingame |
| Solarius Development Inc (HQ) | Manufacturer of 3D metrology surface measurement systems. The company offers metrology services for surface form. | 408-435-2777 | NA | San Jose |
| Sotcher Measurement Inc (HQ) | Provider of test equipment. The company provides test stations, service tags, generator test sets, and automatic test stations. | 800-922-2969 | NA | San Jose |
| Telemakus Llc (HQ) | Provider of USB controlled RF devices. The company devices include switches, vector modulators, and digital attenuators. | 916-458-6346 | 1-10 | Folsom |
| Teradyne Inc (BR) | Supplier of automatic test equipment. The company caters to semiconductor, electronics, and automotive sectors. | 480-777-7090 | NA | San Jose |
| Vanderlans & Sons Inc (HQ) | Manufacturer of pipe and high pressure plugs, test equipment, hoses, gauges, ventilators, and related accessories. | 209-334-4115 | 1-10 | Lodi |
| Vena Engineering Corp (HQ) | Manufacturer of hard drive test equipment and environmental chambers. The company also offers motors and power supplies. | 831-724-5738 | 1-10 | Watsonville |

## 236 = Pressure Instruments

| COMPANY NAME | PRODUCT / SERVICE | PHONE | EMP | CITY |
|---|---|---|---|---|
| All Sensors Corp (HQ) | Manufacturer of MEMS piezoresitive pressure sensors and pressure transducers. The company serves the medical, industrial, and HVAC markets. | 408-225-4314 | NA | Morgan Hill |
| Altair Technologies Inc (HQ) | Provider of precision furnace brazing services. The company serves the medical, defense, and semiconductor industries. | 650-508-8700 | NA | Fremont |
| Mydax Inc (HQ) | Designer and manufacturer of temperature control systems. The company offers the elite chiller system. | 530-888-6662 | 1-10 | Auburn |
| Paragon Controls Inc (HQ) | Designer and manufacturer of air flow and pressure measurement & control systems. The company also offers airflow sensing elements. | 707-579-1424 | NA | Santa Rosa |
| Vanderlans & Sons Inc (HQ) | Manufacturer of pipe and high pressure plugs, test equipment, hoses, gauges, ventilators, and related accessories. | 209-334-4115 | 1-10 | Lodi |

## 238 = Automatic Vending Machines

| COMPANY NAME | PRODUCT / SERVICE | PHONE | EMP | CITY |
|---|---|---|---|---|
| Ventek International (HQ) | Manufacturer of parking revenue control systems. The company offers recreation, commuter rail, and parking access control solutions. | 707-773-3373 | NA | Petaluma |

## 239 = Calculating & Accounting Machines

| COMPANY NAME | PRODUCT / SERVICE | PHONE | EMP | CITY |
|---|---|---|---|---|
| Stokes Publishing Co (HQ) | Manufacturer of overhead calculators. The company also offers timers, puzzles, manipulatives, and posters. | 408-541-9145 | NA | Sunnyvale |

## 242 = Electric Security Systems

| COMPANY NAME | PRODUCT / SERVICE | PHONE | EMP | CITY |
|---|---|---|---|---|
| Mil-Ram Technology Inc (HQ) | Manufacturer of industrial gas and detection systems. The company serves the oil and gas, pulp and paper, and chemical industries. | 510-656-2001 | NA | Fremont |
| QuantumScape Corp (HQ) | Provider of energy storage, electronics, and related solutions. The company offers services to the environmental sector. | 408-452-2007 | NA | San Jose |

**243 = Lighting Systems**

| COMPANY NAME | PRODUCT / SERVICE | PHONE | EMP | CITY |
|---|---|---|---|---|
| 1st Source Lighting (HQ) | Designer and manufacturer of energy efficient lighting technologies. The company also focuses on supply aspects. | 530-887-1110 | 1-10 | Auburn |
| Advanced Radiation Corp (HQ) | Manufacturer of mercury-xenon, and capillary lamps. The company's services include design, installation, and delivery. | 408-727-9200 | NA | Santa Clara |
| Applied Photon Technology Inc (HQ) | Provider of precision flash lamps. The company's products include Krypton arc lamps, OEM's and APT's laser flash lamps, and specialty lamps. | 510-780-9500 | NA | Hayward |
| Architectural Lighting Works (HQ) | Manufacturer of suspended, wall, and ceiling lighting products and related accessories. The company also deals with installation services. | 510-489-2530 | NA | Oakland |
| AutoCell Electronics Inc (HQ) | Manufacturer and distributor of energy efficient lighting products. The company offers compact fluorescent lamps, LED flashlights, and showerheads. | 888-393-6668 | 1-10 | Elk Grove |
| B-K Lighting Inc (HQ) | Provider of architectural outdoor landscape lighting products. The company serves residential and commercial properties. | 559-438-5800 | 1-10 | Madera |
| BBI Engineering Inc (HQ) | Designer and installer of audiovisual, multimedia, teleconferencing and data systems for museums, aquariums, zoos, schools, and universities. | 415-695-9555 | NA | San Francisco |
| Blair Electric Services Inc (HQ) | Provider of electrical contracting services. The company offers pump and well controls, PLC controls, and surveillance systems. | 559-784-8658 | 1-10 | Porterville |
| Borden Lighting (HQ) | Provider of lighting solutions. The company provides table and floor lamps, architectural lighting, and louvers. | 510-357-0171 | NA | Oakland |
| Boyd Lighting (HQ) | Manufacturer of lighting devices. The company offers its products in white glass, clear ribbed glass, and gloss ivory acrylic product finishes. | 415-778-4300 | NA | Sausalito |
| Casella Lighting (HQ) | Retailer of lamps and chandeliers. The company also sells floor lamps, wall lamps, picture lights, and ceiling fixtures. | 888-252-7874 | 1-10 | Sacramento |
| Construction Electrical Products (HQ) | Provider of electrical products for the construction sector. The company offers temporary power products, extension cords, and portable lighting. | 925-828-9420 | NA | Livermore |
| Cooling Source Inc (HQ) | Provider of thermal design solution for LED lighting, medical, military/aero, and test equipment industries. | 925-292-1293 | NA | Livermore |
| Finelite Inc (HQ) | Manufacturer of lighting products. The company's services include design, installation, repairs and replacement, and maintenance. | 510-441-1100 | NA | Union City |
| Flight Light Inc (HQ) | Supplier of airport lighting products. The company is a manufacturer of runway lights, taxiway lights, wind cones, and approach systems. | 916-394-2800 | 1-10 | Sacramento |
| HelioWorks Inc (HQ) | Manufacturer of infrared lamps. The company's products are used in non-dispersive infrared gas detectors for medical and industrial applications. | 707-578-7200 | NA | Santa Rosa |
| Inlite Corp (HQ) | Manufacturer and distributor of directional lighting equipment. The company offers tracks and lighting components. | 800-346-5932 | NA | Berkeley |
| Intematix Corp (HQ) | Developer of microscopy metrology tools and electronic materials. The company offers services to commercial properties. | 510-933-3300 | NA | Fremont |
| Kateeva Inc (HQ) | Manufacturer of LED and other display products. The company specializes in the design and fabrication of OLED displays. | 800-385-7802 | NA | Newark |
| Leotek Electronics USA LLC (HQ) | Manufacturer of light-emitting diodes and lights for traffic and transit, street and area, commercial, petroleum, and grocery and retail stores. | 408-380-1788 | NA | San Jose |
| Light & Motion Industries (HQ) | Provider of light and motion personal lighting system for mountain, bike, foot, camera, water, and underwater activites. | 831-645-1538 | NA | Marina |
| Light Guard Systems Inc (HQ) | Provider of traffic safety products such as controllers, signal head and base plate modules, and LED signage products. | 707-542-4547 | NA | Santa Rosa |
| Light Polymers Inc (HQ) | Developer of polymers and materials. The company formulates and develops solutions for lyotropic liquid crystals. | 650-678-7733 | NA | S San Francisco |
| Lindsley Lighting (HQ) | Provider of lighting solutions focusing on design, sales, installation, and delivery. The company serves residential and commercial properties. | 925-254-1860 | NA | Marinez |
| Lumenetix Inc (HQ) | Supplier of LED light engines, LED light modules, and LED components. The company also offers reflectors and surface mound LED light fixings. | 877-805-7284 | 1-10 | Scotts Valley |
| Lummen Lighting Inc (HQ) | Provider of lighting products like pendants, sconces, ballasts, and chandeliers. The company's services include design, installation, and delivery. | 707-360-5428 | NA | Santa Rosa |
| McWong International Inc (HQ) | Designer and manufacturer of lighting control equipment and related electrical components. The company offers sensors and LED drivers. | 916-371-8080 | 11-50 | Sacramento |
| Megmeet Usa Inc (BR) | Manufacturer of electrical motors, general-used converters, and optional devices. The company offers industry automatic solutions. | 408-260-7211 | NA | San Jose |
| Ocean Presence Technologies (HQ) | Manufacturer of underwater video monitoring camera systems and offers cable systems, power systems, lighting, wireless networks, and accessories. | 831-426-4678 | 1-10 | Santa Cruz |
| Optoelectronix Inc (HQ) | Designer, developer, and manufacturer of plug-and-play and standardized LED-based landscape lighting and engines. | 408-241-1222 | NA | San Jose |
| Phihong Usa Corp (LH) | Provider of power solutions in the telecom sector. The company also offers data solutions in industrial and personal electronic markets. | 510-445-0100 | NA | Fremont |
| Rambus (HQ) | Manufacturer of semiconductor, lighting, and IP products. The company serves the automotive and transportation markets. | 408-462-8000 | NA | Sunnyvale |

| COMPANY NAME | PRODUCT / SERVICE | PHONE | EMP | CITY |
|---|---|---|---|---|
| Rishang LED Inc (LH) | Manufacturer of LED products for decorative and green lighting solutions. The company's products are used in the residential and commercial sectors. | 408-748-8889 | NA | Santa Clara |
| Safeco Electric Supply Inc (HQ) | Distributor of electrical and lighting products. The company offers wires, cables, cords, fasteners, switch boxes, and accessories. | 415-206-0368 | NA | San Francisco |
| Seascape Lamps (HQ) | Provider of contemporary and retro home lighting solutions. The company also specializes in printed drum lamp shades. | 831-728-5699 | 1-10 | Freedom |
| Soraa (HQ) | Provider of lighting design and fixture lamp solutions. The company serves hotels, restaurants, theaters, and private residences. | 510-456-2200 | NA | Fremont |
| Soundvision Inc (HQ) | Provider of home entertainment, home automation, house audio, lighting, and motorized window shades. | 415-456-7000 | NA | Novato |
| TechniQuip Corp (HQ) | Supplier of lighting products. The company's offerings include illuminators, fiber optics, and video equipment. | 925-251-9030 | NA | Pleasanton |
| Ultratech - A Division Of Veeco (BR) | Manufacturer of data storage, LED, and solar process equipment. The company serves solar, LED, data storage, wireless, optical, and other sectors. | 408-321-8835 | NA | San Jose |
| Universal Light Source Inc (HQ) | Provider of technical lighting applications. The company specializes in flash lamps and strobes, glass and window manufacturing, and PCBs. | 415-864-2880 | NA | San Francisco |
| Vision3 Lighting (HQ) | Manufacturer of landscape and exterior architectural lighting products. The company deals with design and installation services. | 559-834-5749 | 1-10 | Fowler |
| WAGAN Corp (HQ) | Developer and marketer of automotive accessories to mobile professionals. The company's offerings include warmers, defrosters, and heated cushions. | 510-471-9221 | NA | Hayward |
| Xicato Inc (HQ) | Designer and manufacturer of lighting products. The company specializes in providing different types of LED modules. | 866-223-8395 | NA | San Jose |
| Zeta Instruments (HQ) | Provider of 3D optical profilers and its applications include wafer quality analysis, texture characterization, and finger contact profiling. | 408-818-9388 | NA | San Jose |

## 244 = Magnetic Tape/Compact Disks, etc.

| COMPANY NAME | PRODUCT / SERVICE | PHONE | EMP | CITY |
|---|---|---|---|---|
| Hotan Corp (HQ) | Distributor and manufacturer of batteries, chargers, flashlights and memory cards, and related media accessories. | | NA | Livermore |
| Meran Technology (HQ) | Provider of process equipment for memory disk manufacturers. The company offers material handling equipment for fiber optic manufacturers. | 510-530-5119 | NA | Piedmont |
| Owens Design (HQ) | Developer of advanced technology systems for semiconductor, hard disk drive, solar, medical device, and other sectors. | 510-659-1800 | NA | Fremont |
| Ultratech - A Division Of Veeco (BR) | Manufacturer of data storage, LED, and solar process equipment. The company serves solar, LED, data storage, wireless, optical, and other sectors. | 408-321-8835 | NA | San Jose |

## 245 = Miscellaneous Electrical/Electronic Products

| COMPANY NAME | PRODUCT / SERVICE | PHONE | EMP | CITY |
|---|---|---|---|---|
| Applied Physics Systems Inc (HQ) | Supplier of magnetic measure and other electronic equipment. The company specializes in measurement while drilling systems and magnetometers. | 650-965-0500 | NA | Mountain View |
| Aqua Sierra Controls Inc (HQ) | Provider of instrumentation and electrical contract services. The company specializes in process control automation for industrial installations. | 530-823-3241 | 1-10 | Auburn |
| Asf Electric Inc (HQ) | Provider of electrical contracting services. The company installs fire safety systems for the retail, health care and public entities. | 650-755-9032 | NA | Daly City |
| Associated Lighting Reps Inc (HQ) | Provider of lighting services. The company offers controls, emergency, indoor, LED, outdoor and pole lighting from several manufacturers. | 510-638-3800 | NA | Oakland |
| Axelsys LLC (HQ) | Provider of electronic design and manufacturing services. The company's offerings include LED and AC to DC industrial power supplies. | 408-600-0871 | NA | San Jose |
| Baldor Electric Co (BR) | Manufacturer of electric drives. The company also offers bearings, electric motors, drives, gear assemblies, and transmission systems. | 510-785-9900 | NA | Hayward |
| Buckles-Smith (BR) | Supplier of industrial automation equipment. The company offers signaling devices, wires and cables, enclosures, and fasteners. | 408-280-7777 | NA | Santa Clara |
| Cable Connection Inc (HQ) | Provider of premium PCB assemblies and turnkey OEM/ODM product. The company also specializes in cable and wire harness services. | 510-249-9000 | NA | Fremont |
| California Motor Controls Inc (HQ) | Manufacturer of electrical control panels. The company offers pump controls and communication systems for municipal and commercial applications. | 707-746-6255 | NA | Benicia |
| Control Systems West Inc (HQ) | Designer and fabricator of a broad variety of custom electrical controls for industrial applications. | 707-763-1108 | NA | Petaluma |
| Cvm Inc (HQ) | Provider of custom machine tools. The company also offers electrical fabrication, machining, and robotic services. | 925-847-8808 | NA | Pleasanton |
| Dunlop Manufacturing Inc (HQ) | Manufacturer of musical instruments and accessories. The company also designs amplifiers, guitar pedals, picks, capos, and strings. | 707-745-2722 | NA | Benicia |
| Enel X e-Mobility (HQ) | Developer of electric vehicle charging technologies such as smart grid EV charging networks for residential, workplace, and commercial installation. | 844-584-2329 | NA | San Carlos |
| Headsets Com Inc (HQ) | Provider of office telephone headsets. The company also offers cellphone, computer, and cordless phone headsets. | 415-351-5897 | NA | San Francisco |

| COMPANY NAME | PRODUCT / SERVICE | PHONE | EMP | CITY |
|---|---|---|---|---|
| HelioWorks Inc (HQ) | Manufacturer of infrared lamps. The company's products are used in non-dispersive infrared gas detectors for medical and industrial applications. | 707-578-7200 | NA | Santa Rosa |
| iSmart Alarm Inc (HQ) | Manufacturer of home security products. The company offers alarms, cameras, sirens, and related accessories. | 408-245-2551 | NA | Sunnyvale |
| Lee Mah Electronics Inc (HQ) | Provider of manufacturing solutions. The company serves customers in the medical, communications, and test and measurement industries. | 415-394-1288 | NA | Brisbane |
| Lge Electrical Sales Inc (HQ) | Provider of electrical distribution and transmission products. The company's products include distran packaged substation products, G&W, MGM, and TIKA. | 916-563-2737 | 11-50 | Sacramento |
| Lumenetix Inc (HQ) | Supplier of LED light engines, LED light modules, and LED components. The company also offers reflectors and surface mound LED light fixings. | 877-805-7284 | 1-10 | Scotts Valley |
| Magnetic Circuit Elements (HQ) | Manufacturer of miniature transformers and inductors. The company's products include chokes, inductors, transformers, and sine wave invertors. | 831-757-8752 | NA | Salinas |
| Medland & Associates Inc (BR) | Manufacturer of OEM products. The company's products include AC and DC converters, power supplies, switching regulators, and cable assemblies. | 408-686-0460 | NA | San Martin |
| Meyer Sound Laboratories Inc (HQ) | Manufacturer of loud speakers, sub woofers, stage monitors, and amplifiers. The company serves the entertainment sector. | 510-486-1166 | NA | Berkeley |
| Modules Technology Inc (HQ) | Provider of custom module design solutions. The company's offerings include grinders, etching systems, and thermal recorders. | 408-392-0808 ext. 111 | NA | San Jose |
| Nady Systems Inc (HQ) | Designer and manufacturer of wireless microphones, and a full line of audio accessories. The company also focuses on marketing. | 510-652-2411 | NA | Richmond |
| Oml Inc (HQ) | Provider of millimeter wave test instruments, calibration equipment and systems for radio astronomy, communication, imaging, and other sectors. | 408-779-2698 | NA | Morgan Hill |
| Orbotech LT Solar LLC (BR) | Manufacturer of electronic devices. The company offers printed circuit boards, flat panel displays, and touch screens. | 408-226-9900 | NA | San Jose |
| Owens Design (HQ) | Developer of advanced technology systems for semiconductor, hard disk drive, solar, medical device, and other sectors. | 510-659-1800 | NA | Fremont |
| Pentagon Technologies (HQ) | Distributor of electromechanical components. The company offers shaft couplings, seals, and cable assemblies. | 800-379-3361 | NA | Hayward |
| Psc Electronics Inc (HQ) | Distributor of magnetic, interconnect, and electro-mechanical components. The company specializes in cable assembly and modification. | 408-737-1333 | NA | Santa Clara |
| Rod-L Electronics Inc (HQ) | Provider of electrical safety testing equipment. The company also offers hipot test loads, test probes, bond testers, and ground testers. | 650-322-0711 | NA | Mountain View |
| S&C Electric Co (BR) | Provider of equipment and services for electric power systems. The company is involved in design and installation services. | 510-864-9300 | NA | Alameda |
| Sensifree Inc (HQ) | Manufacturer of contactless sensors for wearables. The company offers heart rate sensors, including fitness trackers, and activity monitors. | 669-230-5116 | NA | Cupertino |
| Sensoplex Inc (HQ) | Developer and manufacturer of wearable sensors. The company offers rechargeable batteries, displays, interfaces, and related accessories. | 408-391-9019 | NA | Redwood City |
| Sienna Corporation (BR) | Provider of electronic manufacturing services including design and process engineering, prototyping, and electromechanical assembly services. | 510-440-0200 | NA | Fremont |
| Silicon Dust (RH) | Provider of network connected TV tuners. The company offers global solutions to Live TV streaming in businesses, hotels, and education facilities. | 925-443-4388 | NA | Livermore |
| Stratedigm Inc (HQ) | Manufacturer of software products, consumables, and related accessories. The company deals with upgrades and installation. | 408-512-3901 | NA | San Jose |
| Sumitomo Electric Device Innovations Usa Inc (LH) | Developer of electronic devices that includes wireless devices, optical data links, and optical devices. | 408-232-9500 | NA | San Jose |
| Tesla (HQ) | Designer and manufacturer of electric sedans and electric SUVs. The company is engaged in the production of energy storage systems. | 6500-681-5000 | NA | Palo Alto |
| The Best Electrical Company Inc (HQ) | Provider of tenant improvement and maintenance services for the retail, commercial, industrial, and residential communities. | 408-287-2040 | NA | San Jose |
| Thync Inc (HQ) | Provider of wearable technology solutions. The company is involved in testing and related support services. | 408-484-4808 | NA | Los Gatos |

### 246 = Timers

| | | | | |
|---|---|---|---|---|
| Sensoplex Inc (HQ) | Developer and manufacturer of wearable sensors. The company offers rechargeable batteries, displays, interfaces, and related accessories. | 408-391-9019 | NA | Redwood City |
| Stokes Publishing Co (HQ) | Manufacturer of overhead calculators. The company also offers timers, puzzles, manipulatives, and posters. | 408-541-9145 | NA | Sunnyvale |

### 248 = Anesthetics

| | | | | |
|---|---|---|---|---|
| Aridis Pharmaceuticals Llc (HQ) | Focuses on anti-infective alternatives to conventional antibiotics. The company offers services to the pharmaceutical sector. | 408-385-1742 | NA | San Jose |
| Credence MedSystems Inc (HQ) | Provider of pharmaceutical products. The company specializes in single-dose injectable medications in pre-filled syringes. | 844-263-3797 | NA | Menlo Park |

| COMPANY NAME | PRODUCT / SERVICE | PHONE | EMP | CITY |
|---|---|---|---|---|
| DyAnsys Inc (HQ) | Provider of medical diagnostic and monitoring systems to clinicians and hospitals for patients. The company deals with research services. | 888-950-4321 | NA | San Mateo |

## 249 = Anti Infective Agents

| COMPANY NAME | PRODUCT / SERVICE | PHONE | EMP | CITY |
|---|---|---|---|---|
| Abbomax Inc (HQ) | Provider of antibody, peptide, and assay products and services. The company offers antibody production, fragmentation, assay development, and other services. | 408-573-1898 | NA | San Jose |
| AbGenomics International Inc (HQ) | Specializes in the development of drug candidates for immune-mediated inflammation and cancer therapies. | 650-232-7634 | NA | Redwood City |
| Adynxx Inc (HQ) | Developer of drugs to prevent acute post-surgical pain and the transition to persistent or chronic pain. | 415-512-7740 | NA | San Francisco |
| Antibodies Inc (HQ) | Manufacturer of monoclonal and polyclonal antibodies, diagnostic reagents, diagnostic kits, and developer of immunoassays. | 530-758-4400 | 1-10 | Davis |
| Antibody Solutions (HQ) | Provider of antibody products and services. The company serves biotechnology, diagnostic and pharmaceutical companies. | 650-938-4300 | NA | Sunnyvale |
| Aridis Pharmaceuticals Llc (HQ) | Focuses on anti-infective alternatives to conventional antibiotics. The company offers services to the pharmaceutical sector. | 408-385-1742 | NA | San Jose |
| Biomarin Pharmaceutical Inc (HQ) | Developer of biopharmaceutical products for treatment of morquio A, phenylketonuria, mucopolysaccharidosis VI & I, and lambert-eaton myasthenic syndrome. | 415-506-6700 | NA | San Rafael |
| Cell Marque Corp (HQ) | Producer of primary antibodies, buffers and pretreatment, ancillary reagents, and lab equipment for pathology laboratories and research facilities. | 916-746-8900 | 1-10 | Rocklin |
| Cerus Corp (HQ) | Manufacturer of biomedical products such as the intercept blood system and pathogen reduction system, focused in the field of blood safety. | 925-288-6000 | NA | Concord |
| Cymabay Therapeutics Inc (HQ) | Developer of therapies for the treatment of metabolic diseases. The company serves the healthcare industry. | 510-293-8800 | NA | Newark |
| Cytomx Therapeutics Inc (HQ) | Developer of biomolecular therapeutics. The company specializes in antibody drug development, cancer study, clinical and translational medicine. | 650-515-3185 | NA | S San Francisco |
| DyAnsys Inc (HQ) | Provider of medical diagnostic and monitoring systems to clinicians and hospitals for patients. The company deals with research services. | 888-950-4321 | NA | San Mateo |
| Eiger Biopharmaceuticals Inc (HQ) | Developer of anti viral therapy and treatments for rare disease therapeutics. The company specializes in treatment for Hepatitis Delta. | 877-899-2051 | NA | Palo Alto |
| Exelixis Inc (HQ) | Focuses on the development and commercialization of small molecule therapies. The company is also engaged in clinical trials. | 650-837-7000 | NA | Alameda |
| Genentech Inc (HQ) | Focuses on the treatment of breast cancer. The company offers services to patients and medical professionals. | 650-225-1000 | NA | S San Francisco |
| MicuRx Pharmaceuticals Inc (HQ) | Provider of pharmaceuticals. The company develops antibiotics to combat drug-resistant bacterial infections. | 510-782-2022 | NA | Foster City |
| Perceptimed Inc (HQ) | Provider of medical technologies for dispensing and administration of prescription drugs safer, reducing injuries, and death. | 650-941-7000 | NA | Mountain View |
| Phage International Inc (HQ) | Provider of leverage bacteriophage therapy technologies. The company specializes in discovery and rediscovery of effective health care solutions. | 925-984-9446 | NA | Danville |
| Planet Biotechnology Inc (HQ) | Provider of biotechnology services. The company develops antibody-based therapeutic and preventative products through plants to meet medical needs. | 510-887-1461 | NA | Hayward |
| Presidio Pharmaceuticals Inc (HQ) | Developers of small-molecule antiviral therapeutics. The company is a clinical-stage pharmaceutical company. | 415-655-7560 | NA | San Francisco |
| Sagimet Biosciences (HQ) | Focuses on the discovery and development of therapeutic products for the treatment of oncology and infectious diseases. | 650-561-8600 | NA | San Mateo |
| Ultragenyx Pharmaceutical Inc (HQ) | Developer of products for the treatment of rare and ultra-rare diseases. The company is engaged in commercialization of products. | 415-483-8800 | 501-1000 | Novato |
| Virobay Inc (HQ) | Developer of clinical stage biopharmaceutical products for the treatment of neuropathic pain, autoimmune diseases, and fibrosis. | 650-833-5700 | NA | Palo Alto |
| Yenzym Antibodies Llc (HQ) | Provider of antigen design services. The company offers rabbit antibody and antigen specific affinity purification services. | 650-583-1031 | NA | Brisbane |

## 250 = Blood Products

| COMPANY NAME | PRODUCT / SERVICE | PHONE | EMP | CITY |
|---|---|---|---|---|
| Admecell Inc (HQ) | Manufacturer of ready to use products such as cell based, TRANSIL, and ELISA based assays for in-vitro therapeutic modeling and re-profiling. | 510-522-4200 | NA | Alameda |
| Allergy Research Group Llc (HQ) | Provider of nutritional products for blood sugar, brain, cardiovascular, metabolic, hormone, liver, and immune support. | 510-263-2000 | NA | Alameda |
| Cerus Corp (HQ) | Manufacturer of biomedical products such as the intercept blood system and pathogen reduction system, focused in the field of blood safety. | 925-288-6000 | NA | Concord |
| Drawbridge Health (HQ) | Provider of diagnostic testing solutions. The company offers blood testing solutions for a range of biomarker. | 650-714-6791 | NA | Menlo Park |
| DyAnsys Inc (HQ) | Provider of medical diagnostic and monitoring systems to clinicians and hospitals for patients. The company deals with research services. | 888-950-4321 | NA | San Mateo |

| COMPANY NAME | PRODUCT / SERVICE | PHONE | EMP | CITY |
|---|---|---|---|---|
| Hemostat Laboratories (HQ) | Provider of defibrinated sheep blood and other animal blood products for cell culture, diagnostic and veterinary applications. | 800-572-6888 | NA | Dixon |
| K-Pax Pharmaceuticals Inc (HQ) | Provider of pharmaceutical grade vitamins and nutritional health supplements for kid's, women, and men's health, joints & bones, and immune support. | 415-381-7565 | NA | Mill Valley |
| Stemexpress (HQ) | Provider of immunophenotyping, DNA quantitation and viability, tissue transplant verification, and related services. | 530-626-7000 | 1-10 | Placerville |

## 251 = Biological/Botanical Products

| COMPANY NAME | PRODUCT / SERVICE | PHONE | EMP | CITY |
|---|---|---|---|---|
| Amaranth Medical Inc (HQ) | Specializes in proprietary polymer structure and processing technology. The company's products are used in vascular and nonvascular applications. | 650-965-3830 | NA | Mountain View |
| Aridis Pharmaceuticals Llc (HQ) | Focuses on anti-infective alternatives to conventional antibiotics. The company offers services to the pharmaceutical sector. | 408-385-1742 | NA | San Jose |
| Cerus Corp (HQ) | Manufacturer of biomedical products such as the intercept blood system and pathogen reduction system, focused in the field of blood safety. | 925-288-6000 | NA | Concord |
| Crescendo Bioscience Inc (HQ) | Developer of diagnostic tools to provide diagnostics and treatment for autoimmune and inflammatory diseases. | 650-351-1354 | NA | S San Francisco |
| Exelixis Inc (HQ) | Focuses on the development and commercialization of small molecule therapies. The company is also engaged in clinical trials. | 650-837-7000 | NA | Alameda |
| Global Marketing Associates Inc (HQ) | Providers of nutrition supplements to health care industry. The company supply innovative and quality ingredients to health care industry. | 510-887-2462 | NA | Livermore |
| Gs Cosmeceutical Usa Inc (HQ) | Provider of custom contract manufacturing services. The company offers skin and personal care products. | 925-371-5000 | NA | Livermore |
| Iconic Therapeutics Inc (HQ) | Provider of tissue factor therapeutics. The company focusses on the solid tumors and wet age related macular degeneration. | 650-437-1000 | NA | S San Francisco |
| La Belle Inc (BR) | Manufacturer of colostrum and chelated minerals. The company also specializes in spray drying. | 209-599-6605 | 11-50 | Ripon |
| MacroGenics Inc (BR) | Developer, manufacturer, and marketer of innovative antibody-based therapeutics for the treatment of cancer and autoimmune disorders. | 650-624-2600 | NA | Brisbane |
| Marrone Bio Innovations Inc (HQ) | Developer of naturally derived technologies of pest management and plant health products used in agricultural, ornamental, and water treatment. | 530-750-2800 | 1-10 | Davis |
| Nutribiotic (HQ) | Manufacturer of health, wellness, and fitness products. The company provides nutritional supplements and personal care products. | 707-263-0411 | 1-10 | Lakeport |
| Sagimet Biosciences (HQ) | Focuses on the discovery and development of therapeutic products for the treatment of oncology and infectious diseases. | 650-561-8600 | NA | San Mateo |
| Silver Creek Pharmaceuticals Inc (HQ) | Provider of pharmaceuticals. The company develops regenerative medicines with an initial focus on treating cardiovascular disease. | 415-978-2178 | NA | San Francisco |
| Theralife Inc (HQ) | Manufacturer of botanical drugs. The company offer botanicals that provide symptom relief for problems related to eyes. | 650-949-6080 | NA | Los Altos |
| Zosano Pharma Inc (HQ) | Manufacturer of biopharmaceutical products like peptides, proteins, small molecules and vaccines based on transdermal delivery technology. | 510-745-1200 | NA | Fremont |

## 252 = Diagnostic Agents

| COMPANY NAME | PRODUCT / SERVICE | PHONE | EMP | CITY |
|---|---|---|---|---|
| Aat Bioquest Inc (HQ) | Developer and manufacturer of bioanalytical research reagents and kits. The company focuses on photometric detections including absorption. | 408-733-1055 | NA | Sunnyvale |
| Acumen Pharmaceuticals Inc (HQ) | Specializes in the discovery and development of therapeutics and diagnostics related to soluble AËœ oligomers. | 925-368-8508 | NA | Livermore |
| Allaccem Inc (HQ) | Manufacturer of pharmaceutical products such as dermatology, optic, and dental products for goats, dogs, and cats. | 650-593-8700 | NA | San Carlos |
| Amunix Pharmaceuticals Inc (HQ) | Developer of biomolecular therapy. The company specializes in the development of protein and peptide based therapeutic products. | 650-428-1800 | NA | Mountain View |
| Arbor Vita Corp (HQ) | Provider of protein-based molecular diagnostics that is used for the management of infectious diseases and cancer. | 408-585-3900 | NA | Fremont |
| Aridis Pharmaceuticals Llc (HQ) | Focuses on anti-infective alternatives to conventional antibiotics. The company offers services to the pharmaceutical sector. | 408-385-1742 | NA | San Jose |
| Ark Diagnostics Inc (HQ) | Manufacturer of in vitro diagnostic products for the treatment of cancer, veterinary, HIV/AIDS, anti-fungal drugs, and epilepsy and pain management. | 877-869-2320 | NA | Fremont |
| Assembly Biosciences Inc (RH) | Developer of therapeutics for the treatment of hepatitis B virus (HBV) infection. The company specializes in clinical trials. | 833-509-4583 | NA | San Francisco |
| Biochain Institute Inc (HQ) | Provider of bio-sample preparation, analysis, and application assays accelerating the development of personalized diagnostics, therapeutics, and medicine. | 510-783-8588 | NA | Newark |
| HTD Biosystems Inc (HQ) | Focuses on the development of parenteral drugs. The company is engaged in design and product formulation services. | 510-367-0528 | NA | Pleasanton |
| J R Scientific Inc (HQ) | Provider of cell culture products and services. The company's offerings include antibiotics, reagents, and other supplies. | 530-666-9868 | 1-10 | Woodland |
| Lumiquick Diagnostics Inc (HQ) | Manufacturer of diagnostic products and other raw materials. The company is engaged in distribution services. | 408-855-0061 | NA | Santa Clara |

| COMPANY NAME | PRODUCT / SERVICE | PHONE | EMP | CITY |
|---|---|---|---|---|
| Neurotrack Technologies Inc (HQ) | Provider of computer-based cognitive tests. The company offers services to Alzheimer's patients and the medical industry. | 650-549-8566 | NA | Redwood City |
| Oncomed Pharmaceuticals Inc (HQ) | Focuses on the cancer treatment by discovering and developing mono-clonal antibodies and other agents. | 650-995-8200 | 11-50 | Redwood City |
| Somagenics Inc (HQ) | Developer of RNA-based therapeutics and diagnostics. The company's services include detection, monitoring, testing, and analysis. | 831-426-7700 | 1-10 | Santa Cruz |

## 253 = Drugs

| COMPANY NAME | PRODUCT / SERVICE | PHONE | EMP | CITY |
|---|---|---|---|---|
| Aridis Pharmaceuticals Llc (HQ) | Focuses on anti-infective alternatives to conventional antibiotics. The company offers services to the pharmaceutical sector. | 408-385-1742 | NA | San Jose |
| Ascendis Pharma A/S (BR) | Focuses on the creation of drug candidates, proteins, peptides and small molecules, suitable for either local or systemic treatment. | 650-352-8389 | NA | Palo Alto |
| Coherus Biosciences (HQ) | Developer of biosimilars and it serves the global marketplace. The company is engaged in delivery services. | 800-794-5434 | NA | Redwood City |
| Credence MedSystems Inc (HQ) | Provider of pharmaceutical products. The company specializes in single-dose injectable medications in pre-filled syringes. | 844-263-3797 | NA | Menlo Park |

## 254 = Antineoplastic

| COMPANY NAME | PRODUCT / SERVICE | PHONE | EMP | CITY |
|---|---|---|---|---|
| Apexigen (HQ) | Specializes in document management and managed print solutions. The company serves the business sector. | 650-931-6236 | NA | San Carlos |
| Aridis Pharmaceuticals Llc (HQ) | Focuses on anti-infective alternatives to conventional antibiotics. The company offers services to the pharmaceutical sector. | 408-385-1742 | NA | San Jose |
| Atara Biotherapeutics Inc (HQ) | Provider of biotherapeutic services. The company focuses on the treatment of cancer, kidney disease, and other illnesses. | 650-278-8930 | NA | S San Francisco |
| Biomarin Pharmaceutical Inc (HQ) | Developer of biopharmaceutical products for treatment of morquio A, phenylketonuria, mucopolysaccharidosis VI & I, and lambert-eaton my-asthenic syndrome. | 415-506-6700 | NA | San Rafael |
| Biomarker Pharmaceuticals Inc (HQ) | Developer of scientifically-based aging intervention products for slowing the process of aging and delaying the onset of age-related diseases. | 408-257-2000 | NA | San Jose |
| Calithera Biosciences Inc (HQ) | Developer of small molecule drugs directed against tumor metabolism and tumor immunology targets for the treatment of cancer. | 650-870-1000 | NA | S San Francisco |
| Catalyst Biosciences (HQ) | Developer of catalytic biopharmaceutical products based on engineering human proteases for hemostasis, age-related macular degeneration, and inflammation. | 650-871-0761 | NA | S San Francisco |
| Cellular Biomedicine Group Inc (HQ) | Developer of technologies and products for the treatment of KOA, Asth-ma, COPD and other indications. | 408-973-7884 | NA | Cupertino |
| Clovis Oncology (BR) | Developer of targeted therapies for the treatment of patients with cancer. The company is involved in clinical trials. | 415-409-5440 | NA | San Francisco |
| Coherus Biosciences (HQ) | Developer of biosimilars and it serves the global marketplace. The company is engaged in delivery services. | 800-794-5434 | NA | Redwood City |
| Delmar Pharmaceuticals Inc (DH) | Developer of pharmaceutical products. The company specializes in treat-ment of various cancer such as lung, brain, cervical, ovarian tumors and leukemia. | 604-629-5989 | NA | Menlo Park |
| Designerx Pharmaceuticals Inc (HQ) | Provider of pharmaceutical products for treatment of cancer cells from tumors such as melanoma, hepatocellular carcinoma, pancreatic, and mesothelioma. | 707-451-0441 | NA | Vacaville |
| MacroGenics Inc (BR) | Developer, manufacturer, and marketer of innovative antibody-based therapeutics for the treatment of cancer and autoimmune disorders. | 650-624-2600 | NA | Brisbane |
| Mateon Therapeutics Inc (HQ) | Developer and provider of therapeutics. The company focusses on the treatment of acute myeloid leukemia. | 650-635-7000 | NA | S San Francisco |
| Milagen Inc (HQ) | Develops and manufactures healthcare products. The company offers immunohistochemistry and cytology products. | 510-597-1244 | NA | Emeryville |
| Navire Pharma (HQ) | Developer of novel therapies. The company focusses on developing SHP2 inhibitors for treating rare cancers. | 650-391-9740 | NA | Palo Alto |
| Nuvora Inc (HQ) | Focuses on dry mouth treatment and offers products for bad breath pre-vention. The company offers Dentiva and Sales. | 877-530-9811 | NA | Santa Clara |
| Oncomed Pharmaceuticals Inc (HQ) | Focuses on the cancer treatment by discovering and developing mono-clonal antibodies and other agents. | 650-995-8200 | 11-50 | Redwood City |
| Sangamo Therapeutics (HQ) | Developer of engineered DNA-binding proteins for the regulation of gene expression and for gene modification. | 510-970-6000 | 201-500 | Richmond |
| SciClone Pharmaceuticals Inc (HQ) | Developer of therapeutics to treat life-threatening diseases. The compa-ny serves hospitals and the healthcare industry. | 650-358-3456 | NA | Foster City |

## 255 = Antitussives

| COMPANY NAME | PRODUCT / SERVICE | PHONE | EMP | CITY |
|---|---|---|---|---|
| Aridis Pharmaceuticals Llc (HQ) | Focuses on anti-infective alternatives to conventional antibiotics. The company offers services to the pharmaceutical sector. | 408-385-1742 | NA | San Jose |
| Cairn Biosciences (HQ) | Provider of therapeutic solutions for treating cancer. The company is in-volved in biotechnical research and commercial business. | 415-503-1185 | NA | San Francisco |
| Coherus Biosciences (HQ) | Developer of biosimilars and it serves the global marketplace. The com-pany is engaged in delivery services. | 800-794-5434 | NA | Redwood City |

## 256 = Autonomic

| COMPANY NAME | PRODUCT / SERVICE | PHONE | EMP | CITY |
|---|---|---|---|---|
| Aridis Pharmaceuticals Llc (HQ) | Focuses on anti-infective alternatives to conventional antibiotics. The company offers services to the pharmaceutical sector. | 408-385-1742 | NA | San Jose |
| Coherus Biosciences (HQ) | Developer of biosimilars and it serves the global marketplace. The company is engaged in delivery services. | 800-794-5434 | NA | Redwood City |
| Crescendo Bioscience Inc (HQ) | Developer of diagnostic tools to provide diagnostics and treatment for autoimmune and inflammatory diseases. | 650-351-1354 | NA | S San Francisco |
| FormuMax Scientific Inc (HQ) | Provider of contract drug delivery to pharmaceutical and biotech industries. The company specializes in injectables, liposomes and microemulsions. | 408-400-0108 | NA | Sunnyvale |
| Principia Biopharma Inc (HQ) | Provider of biopharmaceuticals. The company develops oral small molecule therapies to treat autoimmune and inflammatory diseases and cancer. | 650-416-7700 | NA | S San Francisco |

## 257 = CNS Drugs

| COMPANY NAME | PRODUCT / SERVICE | PHONE | EMP | CITY |
|---|---|---|---|---|
| Antagene Inc (HQ) | Provider of custom antibody and peptide synthesis. The company is engaged in animal and histology services. | 408-588-1998 | NA | Santa Clara |
| Anthera Pharmaceuticals Inc (HQ) | Manufacturer of biopharmaceuticals that treat serious diseases like lupus, lupus with glomerulonephritis, IgA nephropathy and cystic fibrosis. | 510-856-5600 | NA | Hayward |
| Aridis Pharmaceuticals Llc (HQ) | Focuses on anti-infective alternatives to conventional antibiotics. The company offers services to the pharmaceutical sector. | 408-385-1742 | NA | San Jose |
| Astex Pharmaceuticals (HQ) | Developer of small-molecule therapeutics. The company focuses on products for treatment of cancer and central nervous system disorders. | 925-560-0100 | NA | Pleasanton |
| BASF Venture Capital America Inc (RH) | Manufacturer of basic chemicals and intermediates such as solvents, plasticizers, and monomers. The company serves the agriculture market. | 510-445-6140 | NA | Fremont |
| Biocodex Usa (HQ) | Developer of pharmaceutical products for the treatment of gastroenterology, neuropsychiatry, and pain. | | NA | Redwood City |
| Biomarker Pharmaceuticals Inc (HQ) | Developer of scientifically-based aging intervention products for slowing the process of aging and delaying the onset of age-related diseases. | 408-257-2000 | NA | San Jose |
| Codexis Inc (HQ) | Provider of biocatalysts products such as screening kits and other accessories. The company serves the food and nutrition industries. | 650-421-8100 | 51-200 | Redwood City |
| Coherus Biosciences (HQ) | Developer of biosimilars and it serves the global marketplace. The company is engaged in delivery services. | 800-794-5434 | NA | Redwood City |
| Crescendo Bioscience Inc (HQ) | Developer of diagnostic tools to provide diagnostics and treatment for autoimmune and inflammatory diseases. | 650-351-1354 | NA | S San Francisco |
| Delpor Inc (HQ) | Developer of next generation drug delivery systems which improve the clinical and commercial value of new and existing drugs and biopharmaceuticals. | 415-480-6870 | NA | S San Francisco |
| Depomed Inc (HQ) | Developer of therapies for the treatment of pain and other central nervous (CNS) system conditions. The company deals with drug development. | 510-744-8000 | NA | Newark |
| Discoverx Corp (HQ) | Developer and marketer of innovative solutions to study major drug target classes such as GPCRs and kinases. | 510-979-1415 | NA | Fremont |
| Egeen Inc (HQ) | Provider of drug development for biotech and pharmaceutical clients. The company serves clinics, hospitals, and the healthcare sector. | 650-967-5010 | NA | Milpitas |
| Gliamed Inc (HQ) | Provider of drugs for the regeneration of skin, cardiac muscle, cartilage, bone, brain and other tissues. | 408-457-8828 | NA | San Jose |
| Monogram Biosciences Inc (HQ) | Develops and commercializes diagnostic products. The company offers products for the treatment of human immunodeficiency virus and other viral illnesses. | 650-635-1100 | NA | S San Francisco |
| Mountain View Pharmaceuticals Inc (HQ) | Provider of pharmaceutical development, protein biochemistry, immunology and polymer chemistry solutions for delivery of therapeutic proteins. | 650-365-5515 | NA | Menlo Park |
| Numerate Inc (HQ) | Provider of data analytics and drug design technology services for the pharmaceutical and biotechnology industries. | 650-472-0632 | NA | San Francisco |
| Pharmagenesis Inc (HQ) | Developer and manufacturer of prescription pharmaceuticals from plant extracts and other organic products sourced from Chinese medical practice. | 650-842-7060 | NA | Redwood City |
| Retrotope Inc (HQ) | Focuses on the discovery of drugs and platforms for the treatment of regenerative diseases. The company offers services to the healthcare sector. | 650-917-9256 | NA | Los Altos |
| Reviva Pharmaceuticals Inc (HQ) | Developer of therapy for CNS, cardiovascular, metabolic and inflammatory diseases. The company is a clinical development pharmaceutical company. | 408-816-1470 | NA | Sunnyvale |
| Sangamo Therapeutics (HQ) | Developer of engineered DNA-binding proteins for the regulation of gene expression and for gene modification. | 510-970-6000 | 201-500 | Richmond |
| SciClone Pharmaceuticals Inc (HQ) | Developer of therapeutics to treat life-threatening diseases. The company serves hospitals and the healthcare industry. | 650-358-3456 | NA | Foster City |
| TheraVida Inc (HQ) | Developer of pharmaceutical products for the improved treatment of overactive bladder, urge urinary incontinence, and primary focal hyperhidrosis. | 650-638-2335 | NA | San Mateo |
| Verge Analytics Inc (HQ) | Provider of treatment for brain diseases. The company is involved in drug development and research services. | 415-355-4737 | NA | S San Francisco |

| COMPANY NAME | PRODUCT / SERVICE | PHONE | EMP | CITY |
|---|---|---|---|---|
| Zogenix Inc (BR) | Developer of medicines to treat CNS disorders and pain. The company serves clinics, physicians, and the healthcare sector. | 858-259-1165 | NA | Emeryville |

### 258 = Cardiovascular

| COMPANY NAME | PRODUCT / SERVICE | PHONE | EMP | CITY |
|---|---|---|---|---|
| Amaranth Medical Inc (HQ) | Specializes in proprietary polymer structure and processing technology. The company's products are used in vascular and nonvascular applications. | 650-965-3830 | NA | Mountain View |
| Antipodean Pharmaceuticals Inc (BR) | Provider of pharmaceutical research and development in the ophthalmological and organ transplant therapeutic areas. | | NA | Menlo Park |
| Aridis Pharmaceuticals Llc (HQ) | Focuses on anti-infective alternatives to conventional antibiotics. The company offers services to the pharmaceutical sector. | 408-385-1742 | NA | San Jose |
| Avantec Vascular Corp (HQ) | Manufacturer of therapeutic medical devices such as cardio and peripheral vascular devices for cardiovascular, neurovascular, and peripheral disease. | 408-329-5400 | NA | Sunnyvale |
| Cellular Biomedicine Group Inc (HQ) | Developer of technologies and products for the treatment of KOA, Asthma, COPD and other indications. | 408-973-7884 | NA | Cupertino |
| Coherus Biosciences (HQ) | Developer of biosimilars and it serves the global marketplace. The company is engaged in delivery services. | 800-794-5434 | NA | Redwood City |
| Gilead Palo Alto Inc (BR) | Provider of biopharmaceutical research services. The company discovers and develops medicines to treat life-threatening diseases. | 510-739-8400 | NA | Fremont |
| Lumedx Corp (HQ) | Provider of cardiovascular information and imaging systems. The company specializes in cloud-powered healthcare solutions. | 800-966-0699 | NA | Oakland |
| Lumiquick Diagnostics Inc (HQ) | Manufacturer of diagnostic products and other raw materials. The company is engaged in distribution services. | 408-855-0061 | NA | Santa Clara |
| Ngm Biopharmaceuticals Inc (HQ) | Developer of novel and disease-altering biologics such as protein, peptide, and antibody drug for cancer, cardio-metabolic, and hepatic diseases. | 650-243-5555 | NA | S San Francisco |
| Pliant Therapeutics Inc (HQ) | Developer of therapeutics medicines for the treatment of fibrosis in organs and conditions, including liver, kidney, heart, and gastrointestinal tract. | 650-481-6770 | NA | S San Francisco |
| Silver Creek Pharmaceuticals Inc (HQ) | Provider of pharmaceuticals. The company develops regenerative medicines with an initial focus on treating cardiovascular disease. | 415-978-2178 | NA | San Francisco |
| West Coast Surgical (HQ) | Manufacturer of surgical devices. The company offers designing, assembling and finishing of specialty surgical equipment. | 650-728-8095 | NA | Half Moon Bay |

### 259 = Gastrintestinal

| COMPANY NAME | PRODUCT / SERVICE | PHONE | EMP | CITY |
|---|---|---|---|---|
| Aridis Pharmaceuticals Llc (HQ) | Focuses on anti-infective alternatives to conventional antibiotics. The company offers services to the pharmaceutical sector. | 408-385-1742 | NA | San Jose |
| Biocodex Usa (HQ) | Developer of pharmaceutical products for the treatment of gastroenterology, neuropsychiatry, and pain. | | NA | Redwood City |
| Coherus Biosciences (HQ) | Developer of biosimilars and it serves the global marketplace. The company is engaged in delivery services. | 800-794-5434 | NA | Redwood City |
| Cyterix Pharmaceuticals Inc (HQ) | Engaged in the discovery and development of small molecule oncology prodrugs. The company is also involved in the development of cancer therapeutics. | 415-865-2059 | NA | San Francisco |
| Lyric Pharmaceuticals Inc (HQ) | Developer of pharmaceutical products. The company specializes in therapeutics for gastrointestinal diseases. | | NA | S San Francisco |
| Osel Inc (HQ) | Developer of biotherapeutic products. The company focuses on treatment and prevention of conditions for women's health and infectious diseases. | 650-964-1420 | NA | Mountain View |
| TheraVida Inc (HQ) | Developer of pharmaceutical products for the improved treatment of overactive bladder, urge urinary incontinence, and primary focal hyperhidrosis. | 650-638-2335 | NA | San Mateo |

### 260 = Metabolic

| COMPANY NAME | PRODUCT / SERVICE | PHONE | EMP | CITY |
|---|---|---|---|---|
| Aridis Pharmaceuticals Llc (HQ) | Focuses on anti-infective alternatives to conventional antibiotics. The company offers services to the pharmaceutical sector. | 408-385-1742 | NA | San Jose |
| Cellular Biomedicine Group Inc (HQ) | Developer of technologies and products for the treatment of KOA, Asthma, COPD and other indications. | 408-973-7884 | NA | Cupertino |
| Coherus Biosciences (HQ) | Developer of biosimilars and it serves the global marketplace. The company is engaged in delivery services. | 800-794-5434 | NA | Redwood City |
| Credence MedSystems Inc (HQ) | Provider of pharmaceutical products. The company specializes in single-dose injectable medications in pre-filled syringes. | 844-263-3797 | NA | Menlo Park |
| Second Genome Inc (HQ) | Focuses on the development of therapeutic products. The company serves pharmaceutical and nutritional companies. | 650-440-4606 | NA | S San Francisco |

### 261 = OTC Drugs

| COMPANY NAME | PRODUCT / SERVICE | PHONE | EMP | CITY |
|---|---|---|---|---|
| Aridis Pharmaceuticals Llc (HQ) | Focuses on anti-infective alternatives to conventional antibiotics. The company offers services to the pharmaceutical sector. | 408-385-1742 | NA | San Jose |
| Bioassay Systems (HQ) | Developer and marketer of assay solutions. The company focuses on solutions for research and drug discovery. | 510-782-9988 | NA | Hayward |

| COMPANY NAME | PRODUCT / SERVICE | PHONE | EMP | CITY |
|---|---|---|---|---|
| Bioved Pharmaceuticals Inc (HQ) | Manufacturer of health care products. The company specializes in ayurvedic pharmaceutical, neutraceutical and OTC drugs from plant extracts. | 408-432-4020 | NA | San Jose |
| Biozone Laboratories Inc (HQ) | Manufacturer of over the counter drugs, cosmetics, personal care, and nutritional supplements such as creams, gels, drops, syrups, and sun protection. | 925-473-1000 | NA | Pittsburg |
| Coherus Biosciences (HQ) | Developer of biosimilars and it serves the global marketplace. The company is engaged in delivery services. | 800-794-5434 | NA | Redwood City |
| Corcept Therapeutics Inc (HQ) | Focuses on the discovery of drugs. The company offers services to patients, physicians, and also hospitals. | 650-327-3270 | NA | Menlo Park |
| Cymed (HQ) | Provider of ostomy pouching systems. The company specializes in skin care products and serves individuals and hospitals. | 800-582-0707 | 1-10 | Sacramento |
| Emsl Analytical Inc (BR) | Provider of laboratory analytical testing services. The company specializes in a wide range of environmental, material and forensic testing. | 510-895-3675 | NA | San Leandro |
| InCarda Therapeutics Inc (HQ) | Developer of drugs and inhaled therapy intended to treat paroxysmal atrial fibrillation and other cardiovascular diseases. | 510-422-5522 | NA | Newark |
| Jazz Pharmaceuticals (BR) | Developer and marketer of products for eurology and psychiatry. The company is engaged in clinical trials and research and development. | 650-496-3777 | NA | Palo Alto |
| Libby Labs (HQ) | Manufacturer of cosmetics, OTC pharmaceuticals, drugs, and devices. The company offers skin & hair products, toiletries, natural & organic products. | 510-527-5400 | NA | Berkeley |
| Neilmed Pharmaceuticals Inc (HQ) | Manufacturer of large volume low pressure saline nasal irrigation systems for babies & children, first aid, dry noses, sterile saline spray, and ear care. | 707-525-3784 | NA | Santa Rosa |
| Novabay Pharmaceuticals Inc (HQ) | Manufacturer of biopharmaceuticals. The company develops non-antibiotic anti-infective products to address the eye care market. | 510-899-8800 | NA | Emeryville |
| Nuvora Inc (HQ) | Focuses on dry mouth treatment and offers products for bad breath prevention. The company offers Dentiva and Sales. | 877-530-9811 | NA | Santa Clara |
| Otsuka America Inc (HQ) | Developer of pharmaceutical products for the treatment of central nervous system, ophthalmology, cardiovascular, and skin conditions. | 415-986-5300 | NA | San Francisco |
| PharmaLogic Development Inc (HQ) | Focuses on planning, drug development, and marketing services. The company serves the pharmaceutical and biomedical industries. | 415-472-2181 | NA | San Rafael |
| Relypsa Inc (HQ) | Developer of polymer technology for the treatment of patients with serious conditions. The company is engaged in drug discovery. | 650-421-9500 | NA | Redwood City |
| Rigel Pharmaceuticals Inc (HQ) | Developer novel, small-molecule drugs for the treatment of inflammatory and autoimmune diseases, immuno-oncology related diseases, and muscle disorders. | 650-624-1100 | NA | S San Francisco |
| Theraject Inc (HQ) | Developer of drug micro-needle technologies. The company is engaged in vaccine and also drug deliveries. | 510-742-5832 | NA | Fremont |
| Theron Pharmaceuticals (HQ) | Developer of long acting M3 muscarinic antagonist (LAMA) for the improved treatment of chronic respiratory diseases. | 408-792-7424 | NA | Sunnyvale |
| Tosk Inc (HQ) | Manufacturer of drugs for the treatment of debilitating and life-threatening diseases such as cancer, arthritis, and psoriasis. | 408-245-6838 | NA | Mountain View |
| Valitor Inc (HQ) | Developer of therapeutic protein drugs. The company's drugs are used in dermatology, ophthalmology, orthopedics, and stem cell therapy. | 510-969-9246 | NA | Berkeley |
| Vistagen Therapeutics Inc (HQ) | Developer of medicine to treat depression, cancer and diseases and disorders involving the central nervous system. | 650-577-3600 | NA | S San Francisco |

## 262 = Plant-based

| COMPANY NAME | PRODUCT / SERVICE | PHONE | EMP | CITY |
|---|---|---|---|---|
| Aridis Pharmaceuticals Llc (HQ) | Focuses on anti-infective alternatives to conventional antibiotics. The company offers services to the pharmaceutical sector. | 408-385-1742 | NA | San Jose |
| Coherus Biosciences (HQ) | Developer of biosimilars and it serves the global marketplace. The company is engaged in delivery services. | 800-794-5434 | NA | Redwood City |
| REVOLUTION Medicines Inc (HQ) | Developer of medicines for the treatment of serious diseases. The company is involved in the synthesis of original compounds. | 650-481-6801 | NA | Redwood City |

## 263 = Pulmonary

| COMPANY NAME | PRODUCT / SERVICE | PHONE | EMP | CITY |
|---|---|---|---|---|
| Aradigm Corp (HQ) | Manufacturer of pharmaceuticals delivered by inhalation for the treatment of respiratory diseases such as bronchiectasis, cystic fibrosis, and biodefense. | 510-265-9000 | NA | Hayward |
| Aridis Pharmaceuticals Llc (HQ) | Focuses on anti-infective alternatives to conventional antibiotics. The company offers services to the pharmaceutical sector. | 408-385-1742 | NA | San Jose |
| Cellular Biomedicine Group Inc (HQ) | Developer of technologies and products for the treatment of KOA, Asthma, COPD and other indications. | 408-973-7884 | NA | Cupertino |
| Coherus Biosciences (HQ) | Developer of biosimilars and it serves the global marketplace. The company is engaged in delivery services. | 800-794-5434 | NA | Redwood City |
| Theron Pharmaceuticals (HQ) | Developer of long acting M3 muscarinic antagonist (LAMA) for the improved treatment of chronic respiratory diseases. | 408-792-7424 | NA | Sunnyvale |

## 264 = Skin/Mucous Membrane Drugs

| COMPANY NAME | PRODUCT / SERVICE | PHONE | EMP | CITY |
|---|---|---|---|---|
| Amyris Inc (HQ) | Provider of renewable products. The company delivers cosmetic emollients and fragrances, fuels and lubricants, and even biopharmaceuticals. | 510-450-0761 | NA | Emeryville |
| Aridis Pharmaceuticals Llc (HQ) | Focuses on anti-infective alternatives to conventional antibiotics. The company offers services to the pharmaceutical sector. | 408-385-1742 | NA | San Jose |
| Coherus Biosciences (HQ) | Developer of biosimilars and it serves the global marketplace. The company is engaged in delivery services. | 800-794-5434 | NA | Redwood City |
| Dermira Inc (HQ) | Developer of biopharmaceutical products for the treatment of dermatology diseases such as acne, plaque psoriasis, and hyperhidrosis. | 650-421-7200 | NA | Menlo Park |
| Gs Cosmeceutical Usa Inc (HQ) | Provider of custom contract manufacturing services. The company offers skin and personal care products. | 925-371-5000 | NA | Livermore |
| Hitachi Chemical Diagnostics Inc (HQ) | Provider of in vitro allergy diagnostics products. The company offers alternative means of diagnosing allergy. | 650-961-5501 | NA | Mountain View |
| Libby Labs (HQ) | Manufacturer of cosmetics, OTC pharmaceuticals, drugs, and devices. The company offers skin & hair products, toiletries, natural & organic products. | 510-527-5400 | NA | Berkeley |
| Retrotope Inc (HQ) | Focuses on the discovery of drugs and platforms for the treatment of regenerative diseases. The company offers services to the healthcare sector. | 650-917-9256 | NA | Los Altos |
| Revance Therapeutics Inc (HQ) | Developers of botulinum toxin products. The company develops and manufactures botulinum toxin products for aesthetic and therapeutic categories. | 510-742-3400 | 51-200 | Newark |

## 265 = Reproductive Organ

| COMPANY NAME | PRODUCT / SERVICE | PHONE | EMP | CITY |
|---|---|---|---|---|
| Aridis Pharmaceuticals Llc (HQ) | Focuses on anti-infective alternatives to conventional antibiotics. The company offers services to the pharmaceutical sector. | 408-385-1742 | NA | San Jose |
| Coherus Biosciences (HQ) | Developer of biosimilars and it serves the global marketplace. The company is engaged in delivery services. | 800-794-5434 | NA | Redwood City |

## 266 = Hormones/Synthetic Substitutes

| COMPANY NAME | PRODUCT / SERVICE | PHONE | EMP | CITY |
|---|---|---|---|---|
| Advantage Pharmaceutics Inc (HQ) | Provider of pharmaceuticals specializing in compounding. The company provides compounded medicines in dosage forms for human and veterinary needs. | 916-630-4960 | 1-10 | Rocklin |
| Cyterix Pharmaceuticals Inc (HQ) | Engaged in the discovery and development of small molecule oncology prodrugs. The company is also involved in the development of cancer therapeutics. | 415-865-2059 | NA | San Francisco |
| D Danz & Sons Inc (HQ) | Specializes in the custom fitting, designing, and manufacturing of ophthalmic prosthetics. The company deals with patient care. | 559-252-1770 | 11-50 | Fresno |
| Human Pheromone Sciences Inc (HQ) | Producer of natural attraction products and is engaged in research in the field of human pheromones in all areas of application. | 408-938-3030 | NA | San Jose |
| Tolerion Inc (HQ) | Provider of medical treatment solutions for autoimmune diseases. The company focuses on restoring the patient's immune system. | 415-795-5800 | NA | S San Francisco |

## 267 = Pharmaceutical Packaging

| COMPANY NAME | PRODUCT / SERVICE | PHONE | EMP | CITY |
|---|---|---|---|---|
| Aridis Pharmaceuticals Llc (HQ) | Focuses on anti-infective alternatives to conventional antibiotics. The company offers services to the pharmaceutical sector. | 408-385-1742 | NA | San Jose |
| BioQ Pharma Inc (HQ) | Manufacturer of proprietary products. The company is involved in the sale of infusion pharmaceuticals. | 415-336-6496 | NA | San Francisco |
| Corium International Inc (HQ) | Provider of transdermal delivery systems and related technology solutions. The company is also engaged in therapeutic product development. | 650-298-8255 | NA | Menlo Park |

## 268 = Pharmaceutical R&D

| COMPANY NAME | PRODUCT / SERVICE | PHONE | EMP | CITY |
|---|---|---|---|---|
| ABCO Laboratories Inc (HQ) | Provider of turnkey solutions. The company also offers contract manufacturing, product development and private labeling. | 707-432-2200 | NA | Fairfield |
| Acelrx Pharmaceuticals Inc (HQ) | Manufacturer of pharmaceuticals. The company provides therapies for treatment of acute and breakthrough pain. | 650-216-3500 | NA | Redwood City |
| Achaogen Inc (HQ) | Developers of antibacterials. The company discovers and develops antibacterial for the treatment of serious bacterial infections. | 650-800-3636 | NA | S San Francisco |
| Acumen Pharmaceuticals Inc (HQ) | Specializes in the discovery and development of therapeutics and diagnostics related to soluble AËœ oligomers. | 925-368-8508 | NA | Livermore |
| Adamas Pharmaceuticals Inc (HQ) | Manufacturer of health care products. The company offer products for patients with chronic disorders of the central nervous system. | 510-450-3500 | NA | Emeryville |
| Aerin Medical Inc (DH) | Manufacturer of medical devices. The company is also engaged in the development of bionic devices for the mobility impaired. | 833-484-8237 | NA | Sunnyvale |
| Alector Llc (HQ) | Developer of therapeutics. The company specializes in cutting edge antibody technologies for treating alzheimers disease. | 415-231-5660 | NA | S San Francisco |
| Allaccem Inc (HQ) | Manufacturer of pharmaceutical products such as dermatology, optic, and dental products for goats, dogs, and cats. | 650-593-8700 | NA | San Carlos |
| AMPAC Fine Chemicals (DH) | Manufacturer of active pharmaceutical ingredients (APIs) and registered intermediates. The company's services include product development and scale-up. | 916-357-6880 | 1-10 | Rancho Cordova |
| Annexon Inc (HQ) | Focuses on the development of therapeutic products. The company serves patients with complement-mediated neurodegenerative disorders. | 650-822-5500 | NA | S San Francisco |

| COMPANY NAME | PRODUCT / SERVICE | PHONE | EMP | CITY |
|---|---|---|---|---|
| Apneos Corp (HQ) | Developer of services for healthcare professionals. The company detects and manages sleep breathing disorders. | 650-591-2895 | NA | Belmont |
| Arable Corporation (HQ) | Provider of products and services to health care, pharmaceutical, bio-technology and medical device companies. | 408-825-4755 | NA | Cupertino |
| Ardelyx Inc (HQ) | Developer of non-systemic and small molecule therapeutics that work in the GI tract to treat cardio-renal, GI, and metabolic diseases. | 510-745-1700 | NA | Fremont |
| Aridis Pharmaceuticals Llc (HQ) | Focuses on anti-infective alternatives to conventional antibiotics. The company offers services to the pharmaceutical sector. | 408-385-1742 | NA | San Jose |
| Arrayit Corp (HQ) | Focuses on the discovery, development and manufacture of proprietary life science technologies and consumables for disease prevention. | 408-744-1331 | NA | Sunnyvale |
| Artielle Immunotherapeutics Inc (HQ) | Provider of pharmaceuticals. The company develops therapeutics to treat a wide range of autoimmune inflammatory diseases. | 650-401-2000 | NA | San Mateo |
| Ascendis Pharma A/S (BR) | Focuses on the creation of drug candidates, proteins, peptides and small molecules, suitable for either local or systemic treatment. | 650-352-8389 | NA | Palo Alto |
| Assembly Biosciences Inc (RH) | Developer of therapeutics for the treatment of hepatitis B virus (HBV) infection. The company specializes in clinical trials. | 833-509-4583 | NA | San Francisco |
| Atomwise Inc (HQ) | Developer of artificial intelligence systems for the discovery of drugs. The company serves the healthcare sector. | 650-449-7925 | NA | San Francisco |
| Balance Therapeutics Inc (HQ) | Developer of pharmaceuticals. The company develops therapeutics to address neurological disabilities resulting from excess inhibition of the brain. | 650-741-9100 | NA | San Bruno |
| Bioassay Systems (HQ) | Developer and marketer of assay solutions. The company focuses on solutions for research and drug discovery. | 510-782-9988 | NA | Hayward |
| Biochain Institute Inc (HQ) | Provider of bio-sample preparation, analysis, and application assays accelerating the development of personalized diagnostics, therapeutics, and medicine. | 510-783-8588 | NA | Newark |
| Biocodex Usa (HQ) | Developer of pharmaceutical products for the treatment of gastroenterol-ogy, neuropsychiatry, and pain. | | NA | Redwood City |
| Biodesy Inc (HQ) | Developer of proteins and biological molecules for the treatment of can-cer, cardiovascular, Alzheimer's, and Parkinson's diseases. | 650-871-8716 | NA | S San Francisco |
| Biokey Inc (HQ) | Provider of API characterization, pre-formulation studies, formulation de-velopment, and analytical method development services. | 510-668-0881 | NA | Fremont |
| Biomarin Pharmaceutical Inc (HQ) | Developer of biopharmaceutical products for treatment of morquio A, phenylketonuria, mucopolysaccharidosis VI & I, and lambert-eaton my-asthenic syndrome. | 415-506-6700 | NA | San Rafael |
| Biomarker Pharmaceuticals Inc (HQ) | Developer of scientifically-based aging intervention products for slowing the process of aging and delaying the onset of age-related diseases. | 408-257-2000 | NA | San Jose |
| Biopharmx Inc (HQ) | Provider of healthcare products. The company offers products for the dermatology, therapeutics, aesthetics, and cosmetics industries. | 650-889-5020 | NA | Menlo Park |
| Biotium Inc (HQ) | Supplier of glowing products. The company offers enzyme substrates and kits for labeling proteins and antibodies. | 510-265-1027 | NA | Fremont |
| Bioved Pharmaceuticals Inc (HQ) | Manufacturer of health care products. The company specializes in ayurvedic pharmaceutical, neutraceutical and OTC drugs from plant extracts. | 408-432-4020 | NA | San Jose |
| Bioxiness Pharmaceuticals Inc (HQ) | Developer of small molecule antibiotic medicines. The company focuses on infectious disease treatments. | 510-724-1548 | NA | Hercules |
| Calysta (HQ) | Focuses on the development and manufacture of protein for commercial aquaculture and livestock feed. | 650-492-6880 | NA | Menlo Park |
| Cantabio Pharmaceuticals Inc (HQ) | Provider of therapeutic solutions. The company specializes in developing therapeutic proteins to prevent degenerative brain diseases. | 844-200-2826 | NA | Palo Alto |
| Carmot Therapeutics Inc (BR) | Provider of drug discovery to address unmet chemical needs for the treatment of oncology, inflammation, and metabolic disease. | 510-828-0102 | NA | San Francisco |
| Ccs Associates Inc (HQ) | Provider of scientific services in product discovery and development for government agencies, pharmaceutical, and biotech industries. | 650-691-4400 | NA | Mountain View |
| Cellerant Therapeutics Inc (HQ) | Developer of novel innate and adaptive immunotherapies for oncology and blood-related disorders, including cell-based and antibody therapeu-tics. | 650-232-2122 | NA | San Carlos |
| Centrillion Biosciences Inc (HQ) | Provider of genomic and bioinformatics solution. The company offers ge-nomic technology to improve sequencing performance. | 650-618-0111 | NA | Palo Alto |
| Chemocentryx Inc (HQ) | Manufacturer of biopharmaceutical products and orally-administered therapeutics to treat autoimmune diseases, inflammatory disorders, and cancer. | 650-210-2900 | NA | Mountain View |
| Circuit Therapeutics Inc (HQ) | Focuses on drug discovery and development as well as forging direct therapeutic applications of optogenetics. | 650-324-9400 | NA | Menlo Park |
| Coherus Biosciences (HQ) | Developer of biosimilars and it serves the global marketplace. The com-pany is engaged in delivery services. | 800-794-5434 | NA | Redwood City |
| Comparative Biosciences Inc (HQ) | Provider of research and development support services. The company serves the biotechnology and pharmaceutical industries. | 408-738-9260 | NA | Sunnyvale |
| Corium International Inc (HQ) | Provider of transdermal delivery systems and related technology solu-tions. The company is also engaged in therapeutic product development. | 650-298-8255 | NA | Menlo Park |

| COMPANY NAME | PRODUCT / SERVICE | PHONE | EMP | CITY |
|---|---|---|---|---|
| Corvus Pharmaceuticals Inc (HQ) | Focuses on the development of first-in-class agents that target the immune system. The company serves the healthcare industry. | 650-900-4520 | NA | Burlingame |
| Creagri Inc (HQ) | Manufacturer of nutraceutical products. The company also offers polyphenol and innovative products related to olives for foods, health and dietary supplements. | 510-732-6478 | NA | Hayward |
| Crown Bioscience Inc (HQ) | Specializes in drug discovery, clinical trials, and cardiovascular and metabolic disease research programs. | 855-827-6968 | NA | Santa Clara |
| Cyterix Pharmaceuticals Inc (HQ) | Engaged in the discovery and development of small molecule oncology prodrugs. The company is also involved in the development of cancer therapeutics. | 415-865-2059 | NA | San Francisco |
| Cytoculture International Inc (HQ) | Provider of technical consulting and microbiological laboratory services. The company specializes in biofuel project. | 510-233-0102 | NA | Point Richmond |
| Cytokinetics Inc (HQ) | Developer of cancer treatment programs for cancer and also cardiovascular patients. The company specializes in therapeutic programs. | 650-624-3000 | NA | S San Francisco |
| DalCor Pharmaceuticals (HQ) | Provider of precision medicines. The company is involved in the development of treatments for the cardiovascular events. | 650-401-2000 | 1-10 | San Mateo |
| Dance BioPharm Inc (HQ) | Developer of pharmaceutical drugs. The company specializes in inhaled insulin products for the treatment of diabetes. | 415-769-4200 | NA | San Francisco |
| Denali Therapeutics Inc (HQ) | Provider of therapeutic solutions for the treatment of neurodegenerative diseases. The company also specializes in blood brain barrier programs. | 650-866-8548 | NA | S San Francisco |
| Depomed Inc (HQ) | Developer of therapies for the treatment of pain and other central nervous (CNS) system conditions. The company deals with drug development. | 510-744-8000 | NA | Newark |
| Dermira Inc (HQ) | Developer of biopharmaceutical products for the treatment of dermatology diseases such as acne, plaque psoriasis, and hyperhidrosis. | 650-421-7200 | NA | Menlo Park |
| Designerx Pharmaceuticals Inc (HQ) | Provider of pharmaceutical products for treatment of cancer cells from tumors such as melanoma, hepatocellular carcinoma, pancreatic, and mesothelioma. | 707-451-0441 | NA | Vacaville |
| Diablo Clinical Research Inc (HQ) | Provider of clinical research services specializing in endocrinology, internal medicine, cardiology, and neurology. | 925-930-7267 | NA | Walnut Creek |
| Dna Bridges Inc (HQ) | Provider of corporate development services. The company offers market analysis, business plan development, patent research, and other services. | 415-362-0442 | NA | San Francisco |
| Dynavax Technologies Corp (HQ) | Developer of clinical-stage biopharmaceutical company committed to discovering and developing products to prevent and treat infectious diseases. | 510-848-5100 | 51-200 | Berkeley |
| Eckhart Corp (HQ) | Manufacturer of nutritional supplements. The company is engaged in product development and packaging services. | 415-898-9528 | NA | Novato |
| Escend Pharmaceuticals Inc (HQ) | Provider of therapeutic solutions. The company focusses on cancer stem cells in acute myelogenous leukemia and hematologic malignancies for drug development. | 650-241-9128 | NA | Menlo Park |
| Exelixis Inc (HQ) | Focuses on the development and commercialization of small molecule therapies. The company is also engaged in clinical trials. | 650-837-7000 | NA | Alameda |
| Fochon Pharmaceuticals Ltd (DH) | Provider of therapeutic solutions. The company focusses on research and development of small molecule drugs for health care. | 510-638-8080 | NA | San Leandro |
| FormuMax Scientific Inc (HQ) | Provider of contract drug delivery to pharmaceutical and biotech industries. The company specializes in injectables, liposomes and microemulsions. | 408-400-0108 | NA | Sunnyvale |
| Formurex Inc (HQ) | Provider of services to the biotech industry in preformulation, formulation development, stability and clinical trial materials manufacturing. | 209-931-2040 | 1-10 | Stockton |
| Galaxy Biotech Llc (HQ) | Provider of biotechnology services. The company develops monoclonal antibodies against growth factors and their receptors for treatment of cancer. | 408-400-8020 | NA | Sunnyvale |
| Genepharm Inc (HQ) | Developer and commercialization of therapeutics for skin-related problems. The company is engaged in pre-clinical research. | 408-773-1082 | NA | Sunnyvale |
| Geron Corp (HQ) | Developer of telomerase inhibitors, imetelstat, in hematologic myeloid malignancies. The company is engaged in clinical trials. | 650-473-7700 | NA | Menlo Park |
| Gilead Palo Alto Inc (BR) | Provider of biopharmaceutical research services. The company discovers and develops medicines to treat life-threatening diseases. | 510-739-8400 | NA | Fremont |
| Gilead Sciences Inc (HQ) | Provider of medicines for the treatment of liver diseases, hematology, oncology, and other cardiovascular diseases. | 650-574-3000 | NA | Foster City |
| Gs Cosmeceutical Usa Inc (HQ) | Provider of custom contract manufacturing services. The company offers skin and personal care products. | 925-371-5000 | NA | Livermore |
| Hahnemann Labortories Inc (HQ) | Manufacturer of homeopathic medicines. The company offers dispensing kits, first aid kits, and also professional kits. | 415-451-6978 | NA | San Rafael |
| Hitachi Chemical Diagnostics Inc (HQ) | Provider of in vitro allergy diagnostics products. The company offers alternative means of diagnosing allergy. | 650-961-5501 | NA | Mountain View |
| Hopelab (HQ) | Developer of technology to improve human health and well-being. The company provides online games to help young people fight cancer. | 650-569-5900 | NA | San Francisco |
| Hygeia Laboratories Inc (HQ) | Developers of vaccines using novel technology for animals. The company offers animal pharmaceuticals for dairy cattle, sheep and poultry. | 530-661-1442 | 1-10 | Woodland |

| COMPANY NAME | PRODUCT / SERVICE | PHONE | EMP | CITY |
|---|---|---|---|---|
| Iconic Therapeutics Inc (HQ) | Provider of tissue factor therapeutics. The company focusses on the solid tumors and wet age related macular degeneration. | 650-437-1000 | NA | S San Francisco |
| Illustris Pharmaceuticals Inc (HQ) | Developer and provider of technology solutions for the delivery of large molecules through the tissue structures. | 650-334-2090 | 1-10 | Irvine |
| Impax Laboratories Inc (HQ) | Manufacturers and developer of technology-based specialty pharmaceutical drug delivery system. The company's serves physicians and patients. | 510-240-6000 | NA | Hayward |
| InCube Labs (HQ) | Provider of laboratory services. The company offers medical devices and pharmaceuticals to various therapeutic areas. | 408-457-3700 | NA | San Jose |
| Intarcia Therapeutics Inc (BR) | Provider of therapeutic products and related supplies. The company is engaged in research and development services. | 510-782-7800 | NA | Hayward |
| Intraop Medical Corp (HQ) | Manufacturer of mobetron for the treatment of cancer. The company offers services to hospitals, clinics, and patients. | 408-636-1020 | NA | Sunnyvale |
| Invitae Corp (HQ) | Provider of genetic information. The company offers to bring genetic information into routine medical practice to improve the quality of healthcare. | 415-930-4018 | 501-1000 | San Francisco |
| Jaguar Health (HQ) | Provider of health solutions for the animals and humans. The company focusses on the development of gastrointestinal pharmaceuticals. | 415-371-8300 | NA | San Francisco |
| Juvaris BioTherapeutics Inc (HQ) | Developer of vaccines and immuno therapeutic products. The company is engaged in the treatment of infectious diseases. | 925-399-6200 | NA | Pleasanton |
| Kalytera Therapeutics Inc (HQ) | Developer of cannabidiol and cannabinoid therapeutics for the treatment of life threatening human disease. | 888-861-2008 | NA | San Rafael |
| Kan Herb Co (HQ) | Provider of Chinese herbal products and services. | 831-438-9450 | 1-10 | Santa Cruz |
| Lamdagen Corp (BR) | Developer of nano technology based biosensors used in research and diagnostic equipment for human and animal health testing. | 650-571-5816 | NA | Menlo Park |
| Lumen Therapeutics LLC (HQ) | Provider of therapeutic solutions. The company focusses on the proprietary drugs based on oligo-L-arginine. | 650-450-4439 | NA | Menlo Park |
| Lumiphore Inc (HQ) | Developer of proprietary lanthanide technology. The company develops and markets biological detection reagents. | 510-898-1190 | NA | Berkeley |
| MabPlex USA Inc (BR) | Developer and manufacture of biopharmaceuticals. The company also offers contract services from DNA to finished drug product. | 510-830-1065 | NA | Fremont |
| Mateon Therapeutics Inc (HQ) | Developer and provider of therapeutics. The company focusses on the treatment of acute myeloid leukemia. | 650-635-7000 | NA | S San Francisco |
| MedAutonomic Inc (HQ) | Developer of Brain NeuroModulator. The company specializes in creating control action potentials in individual neurons and in functional groups. | 415-377-5653 | NA | Concord |
| MedGenome Inc (HQ) | Provider of genomics based diagnostics and research services. The company specializes in bioinformatics, computing, genomics technologies, and big data analytics. | 888-440-0954 | NA | Foster City |
| MedImmune LLC (BR) | Developer of biotechnology products and solutions. The company's products include Synagis, FluMist, and Trivalent FluMist. | 800-236-9933 | NA | S San Francisco |
| Menlo Therapeutics (HQ) | Developer and manufacture of biopharmaceuticals. The company focusses on the commercialization and development of serlopitant for treating pruritus. | 650-486-1416 | NA | Redwood City |
| MicuRx Pharmaceuticals Inc (HQ) | Provider of pharmaceuticals. The company develops antibiotics to combat drug-resistant bacterial infections. | 510-782-2022 | NA | Foster City |
| Minerva Surgical Inc (HQ) | Manufacturer of medical devices. The company provides products for the treatment of abnormal uterine bleeding. | 855-646-7874 | NA | Redwood City |
| Mountain View Pharmaceuticals Inc (HQ) | Provider of pharmaceutical development, protein biochemistry, immunology and polymer chemistry solutions for delivery of therapeutic proteins. | 650-365-5515 | NA | Menlo Park |
| Multispan Inc (HQ) | Provider of drug discovery services. The company also engages in compound profiling and antibody profiling services. | 510-887-0817 | NA | Hayward |
| Murigenics (HQ) | Provider of preclinical in-vivo and in-vitro contract drug discovery. The company is also focused on development services. | 707-561-8900 | NA | Vallejo |
| Napajen Pharma Inc (HQ) | Developer of novel drug delivery systems technologies for pharmaceutical and biotechnology industries. | 650-685-2429 | NA | Burlingame |
| Nature's Cure (HQ) | Provider of health and beauty solutions. The company offers over-the-counter products featuring natural ingredients. | 877-469-9487 | NA | Oakland |
| Navire Pharma (HQ) | Developer of novel therapies. The company focusses on developing SHP2 inhibitors for treating rare cancers. | 650-391-9740 | NA | Palo Alto |
| Neopeutics Inc USA (HQ) | Provider of pre clinical contract research services and product development for the private and governmental regulatory agencies. | 650-624-4057 | NA | S San Francisco |
| Neurotrack Technologies Inc (HQ) | Provider of computer-based cognitive tests. The company offers services to Alzheimer's patients and the medical industry. | 650-549-8566 | NA | Redwood City |
| NewGen Therapeutics Inc (HQ) | Provider of therapeutic solutions. The company focusses on the development and discovery of small molecule drugs for cancer treatment. | 650-995-7508 | NA | Menlo Park |
| Ngm Biopharmaceuticals Inc (HQ) | Developer of novel and disease-altering biologics such as protein, peptide, and antibody drug for cancer, cardio-metabolic, and hepatic diseases. | 650-243-5555 | NA | S San Francisco |
| Nitinol Devices & Components Inc (HQ) | Provider of rapid development and prototyping services. The company is also engaged in commercialization. | 510-683-2000 | NA | Fremont |

| COMPANY NAME | PRODUCT / SERVICE | PHONE | EMP | CITY |
|---|---|---|---|---|
| Novabay Pharmaceuticals Inc (HQ) | Manufacturer of biopharmaceuticals. The company develops non-antibiotic anti-infective products to address the eye care market. | 510-899-8800 | NA | Emeryville |
| Novartis Pharmaceuticals Corp (BR) | Development of drugs and pharmaceutical products for complicated diseases. The company serves the healthcare sector. | 650-622-1500 | NA | San Carlos |
| Numerate Inc (HQ) | Provider of data analytics and drug design technology services for the pharmaceutical and biotechnology industries. | 650-472-0632 | NA | San Francisco |
| Oncomed Pharmaceuticals Inc (HQ) | Focuses on the cancer treatment by discovering and developing monoclonal antibodies and other agents. | 650-995-8200 | 11-50 | Redwood City |
| Optimum Processing Inc (HQ) | Provider of filtration solutions and disposable bioprocess container systems. The company utilizes asymmetric morphology solutions. | 415-461-7033 | NA | San Rafael |
| Orbus Therapeutics Inc (HQ) | Developer of therapeutic products to treat rare disease such as anaplastic astrocytoma. | 650-656-9440 | NA | Palo Alto |
| ORIC Pharmaceuticals Inc (HQ) | Provider of pharmaceutical research. The company specializes in discovering and developing novel therapies for treatment-resistant cancers. | 650-388-5600 | NA | S San Francisco |
| OrthoTrophix Inc (HQ) | Developer of therapies for medical needs of patients. The company specializes in regeneration of articular cartilage in knee and other joints. | 510-488-3832 | NA | Oakland |
| Osel Inc (HQ) | Developer of biotherapeutic products. The company focuses on treatment and prevention of conditions for women's health and infectious diseases. | 650-964-1420 | NA | Mountain View |
| Pacific Biosciences Of California Inc (HQ) | Provider of targeted sequencing, base modifications, microbiology, and isoform sequencing detection services. | 650-521-8000 | NA | Menlo Park |
| Phage International Inc (HQ) | Provider of leverage bacteriophage therapy technologies. The company specializes in discovery and rediscovery of effective health care solutions. | 925-984-9446 | NA | Danville |
| Pharmagenesis Inc (HQ) | Developer and manufacturer of prescription pharmaceuticals from plant extracts and other organic products sourced from Chinese medical practice. | 650-842-7060 | NA | Redwood City |
| PharmaLogic Development Inc (HQ) | Focuses on planning, drug development, and marketing services. The company serves the pharmaceutical and biomedical industries. | 415-472-2181 | NA | San Rafael |
| Pharmedix (HQ) | Focuses on the repackaging of pharmaceutical products. The company offers dispensing systems and women's health products. | 800-486-1811 | NA | Union City |
| Pharmout Laboratory Inc (HQ) | Provider of analytical laboratory services. The company engages in protein precipitated plasma, liquid-liquid extraction, and solid phase extraction. | 408-481-3090 | NA | Sunnyvale |
| Pharmtak Inc (HQ) | Provider of pharmaceutical products and services. The company focuses on developing novel pharmaceuticals and cosmeceuticals utilizing technology. | 408-954-8223 | NA | San Jose |
| Pherin Pharmaceuticals Inc (HQ) | Developer of novel compounds for intranasal spray delivery and also deals with the treatment of neuro-psychiatric and neuroendocrine conditions. | 650-961-2080 | NA | Los Altos |
| Phoenix Pharmaceuticals Inc (DH) | Provider of peptide related products to researchers. The company specializes in obesity, cardiovascular, and diabetes. | 650-558-8898 | NA | Burlingame |
| Portola Pharmaceuticals Inc (HQ) | Focuses on the development and commercialization of therapeutic products for the treatment of hematologic disorders. | 650-246-7000 | 201-500 | S San Francisco |
| Presidio Pharmaceuticals Inc (HQ) | Developers of small-molecule antiviral therapeutics. The company is a clinical-stage pharmaceutical company. | 415-655-7560 | NA | San Francisco |
| Primity Bio Inc (HQ) | Provider of assay platforms for biological relevance. The company specializes in cell biology, flow cytometry, and molecular biology. | 510-210-0605 | NA | Fremont |
| Progenitor Cell Therapy (BR) | Manufacturer of biotechnology products. The company develops cell therapy products on a contract basis. | 650-964-6744 | NA | Mountain View |
| Prolynx Llc (HQ) | Developer of technology solutions for releasable linkers. The company also specializes in injectable drugs. | 415-552-5306 | NA | San Francisco |
| Protein Research (HQ) | Manufacturer of nutritional products. The company develops and formulates supplements for human nutrition in capsules, tablets, powders and premixes. | 925-243-6300 | NA | Livermore |
| Proteus Digital Health Inc (HQ) | Providers of health care service technology. The company offers health care products based on electronics technology. | 650-632-4031 | NA | Redwood City |
| ProTrials Research Inc (HQ) | Provider of clinical research services. The company offers the ability to move a new drug or device from conception to FDA approval. | 650-864-9180 | NA | San Jose |
| Prowess Inc (HQ) | Focuses on Windows-based treatment planning systems for radiation therapy treatment and OIS software. | 925-356-0360 | NA | Concord |
| Quark Pharmaceuticals Inc (HQ) | Manufacturer of pharmaceuticals. The company focuses on the discovery and development of novel RNAi-based therapeutics. | 510-402-4020 | NA | Fremont |
| Randal Optimal Nutrients (HQ) | Manufacturer of consumer goods. The company produces dietary supplements and nutraceuticals to the health food and profession health care markets. | 707-528-1800 | NA | Santa Rosa |
| ReaMetrix Inc (HQ) | Provider of biotechnology services. The company develops innovative affordable diagnostic solutions. | 650-226-4144 | NA | Los Altos |
| Relypsa Inc (HQ) | Developer of polymer technology for the treatment of patients with serious conditions. The company is engaged in drug discovery. | 650-421-9500 | NA | Redwood City |

| COMPANY NAME | PRODUCT / SERVICE | PHONE | EMP | CITY |
|---|---|---|---|---|
| Retrotope Inc (HQ) | Focuses on the discovery of drugs and platforms for the treatment of regenerative diseases. The company offers services to the healthcare sector. | 650-917-9256 | NA | Los Altos |
| Revance Therapeutics Inc (HQ) | Developers of botulinum toxin products. The company develops and manufactures botulinum toxin products for aesthetic and therapeutic categories. | 510-742-3400 | 51-200 | Newark |
| Reviva Pharmaceuticals Inc (HQ) | Developer of therapy for CNS, cardiovascular, metabolic and inflammatory diseases. The company is a clinical development pharmaceutical company. | 408-816-1470 | NA | Sunnyvale |
| Ryss Lab Inc (HQ) | Provider of biotechnology and pharmaceutical development services. The company offers services to the healthcare sector. | 510-477-9570 | NA | Union City |
| Sandhu Products Inc (HQ) | Provider of ayurvedic herbal dietary supplements. The company offers products containing vitamins, amino acids, minerals and medicinal plant extracts. | 510-996-7199 | NA | Livermore |
| Sangamo Therapeutics (HQ) | Developer of engineered DNA-binding proteins for the regulation of gene expression and for gene modification. | 510-970-6000 | 201-500 | Richmond |
| Sfj Pharmaceuticals Group (HQ) | Focuses on the clinical development and registration of pharmaceutical products. The company is involved in clinical trials. | 925-223-6233 | NA | Pleasanton |
| Silver Creek Pharmaceuticals Inc (HQ) | Provider of pharmaceuticals. The company develops regenerative medicines with an initial focus on treating cardiovascular disease. | 415-978-2178 | NA | San Francisco |
| Skeletal Kinetics LLC (HQ) | Developer, manufacturer and marketer of bone fixation cement designed for the treatment of trauma fractures. | 408-366-5000 | 11-50 | Cupertino |
| Stemexpress (HQ) | Provider of immunophenotyping, DNA quantitation and viability, tissue transplant verification, and related services. | 530-626-7000 | 1-10 | Placerville |
| Sutro Biopharma Inc (HQ) | Developer of therapeutics for cancer therapy. The company shares with select pharmaceutical and biotech companies to develop new therapeutics. | 650-392-8412 | 51-200 | S San Francisco |
| Sutrovax Inc (HQ) | Developer of vaccines for the treatment of infectious diseases. The company is also engaged in the production of vaccine antigens. | 650-837-0111 | NA | Foster City |
| Teikoku Pharma USA Inc (LH) | Focuses on the drug development and delivery of treatments for CNS, pain management and oncology. The company serves the medical industry. | 408-501-1800 | NA | San Jose |
| Theraject Inc (HQ) | Developer of drug micro-needle technologies. The company is engaged in vaccine and also drug deliveries. | 510-742-5832 | NA | Fremont |
| Theravance Biopharma Us Inc (HQ) | Provider of pharmaceuticals. The company develops new medicines with superior efficacy, convenience, tolerability and/or safety. | 650-808-6000 | NA | S San Francisco |
| TheraVida Inc (HQ) | Developer of pharmaceutical products for the improved treatment of overactive bladder, urge urinary incontinence, and primary focal hyperhidrosis. | 650-638-2335 | NA | San Mateo |
| Theron Pharmaceuticals (HQ) | Developer of long acting M3 muscarinic antagonist (LAMA) for the improved treatment of chronic respiratory diseases. | 408-792-7424 | NA | Sunnyvale |
| Threshold Enterprises Ltd (HQ) | Distributor of nutritional supplements, healthcare, and beauty care products. | 831-438-6851 | 1-10 | Scotts Valley |
| Titan Pharmaceuticals Inc (HQ) | Provider of biopharmaceuticals. The company discovers proprietary therapeutics primarily for the treatment of serious medical disorders. | 650-244-4990 | 11-50 | S San Francisco |
| Tolerion Inc (HQ) | Provider of medical treatment solutions for autoimmune diseases. The company focuses on restoring the patient's immune system. | 415-795-5800 | NA | S San Francisco |
| Tosk Inc (HQ) | Manufacturer of drugs for the treatment of debilitating and life-threatening diseases such as cancer, arthritis, and psoriasis. | 408-245-6838 | NA | Mountain View |
| Trellis Bioscience LLC (HQ) | Developer of human antibody therapeutics as treatment for infectious disease and oncology indications. | 650-838-1400 | NA | Redwood City |
| twoXAR Inc (HQ) | Developer of drug delivery platform. The company is involved in biological data extraction, automated model generation, and feature identification. | 650-382-2605 | NA | Mountain View |
| Ultragenyx Pharmaceutical Inc (HQ) | Developer of products for the treatment of rare and ultra-rare diseases. The company is engaged in commercialization of products. | 415-483-8800 | 501-1000 | Novato |
| Valitor Inc (HQ) | Developer of therapeutic protein drugs. The company's drugs are used in dermatology, ophthalmology, orthopedics, and stem cell therapy. | 510-969-9246 | NA | Berkeley |
| Vanton Research Laboratory Llc (HQ) | Specializes in the development of non-conventional drug delivery systems and integrated pharmaceutical services. | 925-687-7817 | NA | Concord |
| Vaxart Inc (HQ) | Manufacturer and developer of oral vaccines. The company is engaged in drug development and related services. | 650-550-3500 | NA | S San Francisco |
| Velocity Pharmaceutical Development LLC (HQ) | Developer of drug candidates. The company specializes in clinical development programs and serves biotechnology and pharmaceutical companies. | 650-273-5748 | NA | S San Francisco |
| Veracyte Inc (HQ) | Focuses on molecular analysis and diagnostic tests. The company serves patients and the healthcare sector. | 650-243-6300 | NA | S San Francisco |
| Verseon Corp (HQ) | Focuses on the design of drug candidates. The company offers services to the pharmaceutical industry. | 510-225-9000 | NA | Fremont |
| Virobay Inc (HQ) | Developer of clinical stage biopharmaceutical products for the treatment of neuropathic pain, autoimmune diseases, and fibrosis. | 650-833-5700 | NA | Palo Alto |

| COMPANY NAME | PRODUCT / SERVICE | PHONE | EMP | CITY |
|---|---|---|---|---|
| Vistagen Therapeutics Inc (HQ) | Developer of medicine to treat depression, cancer and diseases and disorders involving the central nervous system. | 650-577-3600 | NA | S San Francisco |
| Zogenix Inc (BR) | Developer of medicines to treat CNS disorders and pain. The company serves clinics, physicians, and the healthcare sector. | 858-259-1165 | NA | Emeryville |
| Zosano Pharma Inc (HQ) | Manufacturer of biopharmaceutical products like peptides, proteins, small molecules and vaccines based on transdermal delivery technology. | 510-745-1200 | NA | Fremont |

## 269 = Pharmaceutical Services

| COMPANY NAME | PRODUCT / SERVICE | PHONE | EMP | CITY |
|---|---|---|---|---|
| Acumen Pharmaceuticals Inc (HQ) | Specializes in the discovery and development of therapeutics and diagnostics related to soluble AËœ oligomers. | 925-368-8508 | NA | Livermore |
| Adamas Pharmaceuticals Inc (HQ) | Manufacturer of health care products. The company offer products for patients with chronic disorders of the central nervous system. | 510-450-3500 | NA | Emeryville |
| Adynxx Inc (HQ) | Developer of drugs to prevent acute post-surgical pain and the transition to persistent or chronic pain. | 415-512-7740 | NA | San Francisco |
| Aimmune Therapeutics (RH) | Developer of desensitization treatments. The company is engaged in clinical trials and it serves the healthcare sector. | 650-614-5220 | NA | Brisbane |
| Allaccem Inc (HQ) | Manufacturer of pharmaceutical products such as dermatology, optic, and dental products for goats, dogs, and cats. | 650-593-8700 | NA | San Carlos |
| Allergy Research Group Llc (HQ) | Provider of nutritional products for blood sugar, brain, cardiovascular, metabolic, hormone, liver, and immune support. | 510-263-2000 | NA | Alameda |
| Anthera Pharmaceuticals Inc (HQ) | Manufacturer of biopharmaceuticals that treat serious diseases like lupus, lupus with glomerulonephritis, IgA nephropathy and cystic fibrosis. | 510-856-5600 | NA | Hayward |
| Apollomics Inc (HQ) | Developer of oncology therapeutics. The company focusses on discovering therapeutics for the immune system and molecular pathways to treat cancer. | 650-209-4055 | NA | Foster City |
| Arable Corporation (HQ) | Provider of products and services to health care, pharmaceutical, biotechnology and medical device companies. | 408-825-4755 | NA | Cupertino |
| Ardelyx Inc (HQ) | Developer of non-systemic and small molecule therapeutics that work in the GI tract to treat cardio-renal, GI, and metabolic diseases. | 510-745-1700 | NA | Fremont |
| Aridis Pharmaceuticals Llc (HQ) | Focuses on anti-infective alternatives to conventional antibiotics. The company offers services to the pharmaceutical sector. | 408-385-1742 | NA | San Jose |
| Arrayit Corp (HQ) | Focuses on the discovery, development and manufacture of proprietary life science technologies and consumables for disease prevention. | 408-744-1331 | NA | Sunnyvale |
| Artielle Immunotherapeutics Inc (HQ) | Provider of pharmaceuticals. The company develops therapeutics to treat a wide range of autoimmune inflammatory diseases. | 650-401-2000 | NA | San Mateo |
| Biochain Institute Inc (HQ) | Provider of bio-sample preparation, analysis, and application assays accelerating the development of personalized diagnostics, therapeutics, and medicine. | 510-783-8588 | NA | Newark |
| Biokey Inc (HQ) | Provider of API characterization, pre-formulation studies, formulation development, and analytical method development services. | 510-668-0881 | NA | Fremont |
| Biomarin Pharmaceutical Inc (HQ) | Developer of biopharmaceutical products for treatment of morquio A, phenylketonuria, mucopolysaccharidosis VI & I, and lambert-eaton myasthenic syndrome. | 415-506-6700 | NA | San Rafael |
| Biopharmx Inc (HQ) | Provider of healthcare products. The company offers products for the dermatology, therapeutics, aesthetics, and cosmetics industries. | 650-889-5020 | NA | Menlo Park |
| Cantabio Pharmaceuticals Inc (HQ) | Provider of therapeutic solutions. The company specializes in developing therapeutic proteins to prevent degenerative brain diseases. | 844-200-2826 | NA | Palo Alto |
| Ccs Associates Inc (HQ) | Provider of scientific services in product discovery and development for government agencies, pharmaceutical, and biotech industries. | 650-691-4400 | NA | Mountain View |
| Centrillion Biosciences Inc (HQ) | Provider of genomic and bioinformatics solution. The company offers genomic technology to improve sequencing performance. | 650-618-0111 | NA | Palo Alto |
| Coherus Biosciences (HQ) | Developer of biosimilars and it serves the global marketplace. The company is engaged in delivery services. | 800-794-5434 | NA | Redwood City |
| Comparative Biosciences Inc (HQ) | Provider of research and development support services. The company serves the biotechnology and pharmaceutical industries. | 408-738-9260 | NA | Sunnyvale |
| Corium International Inc (HQ) | Provider of transdermal delivery systems and related technology solutions. The company is also engaged in therapeutic product development. | 650-298-8255 | NA | Menlo Park |
| Credence MedSystems Inc (HQ) | Provider of pharmaceutical products. The company specializes in single-dose injectable medications in pre-filled syringes. | 844-263-3797 | NA | Menlo Park |
| Crescendo Bioscience Inc (HQ) | Developer of diagnostic tools to provide diagnostics and treatment for autoimmune and inflammatory diseases. | 650-351-1354 | NA | S San Francisco |
| Denali Therapeutics Inc (HQ) | Provider of therapeutic solutions for the treatment of neurodegenerative diseases. The company also specializes in blood brain barrier programs. | 650-866-8548 | NA | S San Francisco |
| Depomed Inc (HQ) | Developer of therapies for the treatment of pain and other central nervous (CNS) system conditions. The company deals with drug development. | 510-744-8000 | NA | Newark |
| Durect Corp (HQ) | Developer of products for the treatment of chronic debilitating disease. The company specializes in biotechnology products. | 408-777-1417 | NA | Cupertino |
| Dynavax Technologies Corp (HQ) | Developer of clinical-stage biopharmaceutical company committed to discovering and developing products to prevent and treat infectious diseases. | 510-848-5100 | 51-200 | Berkeley |

| COMPANY NAME | PRODUCT / SERVICE | PHONE | EMP | CITY |
|---|---|---|---|---|
| Eckhart Corp (HQ) | Manufacturer of nutritional supplements. The company is engaged in product development and packaging services. | 415-898-9528 | NA | Novato |
| Egeen Inc (HQ) | Provider of drug development for biotech and pharmaceutical clients. The company serves clinics, hospitals, and the healthcare sector. | 650-967-5010 | NA | Milpitas |
| FormuMax Scientific Inc (HQ) | Provider of contract drug delivery to pharmaceutical and biotech industries. The company specializes in injectables, liposomes and microemulsions. | 408-400-0108 | NA | Sunnyvale |
| Gs Cosmeceutical Usa Inc (HQ) | Provider of custom contract manufacturing services. The company offers skin and personal care products. | 925-371-5000 | NA | Livermore |
| Hahnemann Labortories Inc (HQ) | Manufacturer of homeopathic medicines. The company offers dispensing kits, first aid kits, and also professional kits. | 415-451-6978 | NA | San Rafael |
| HTD Biosystems Inc (HQ) | Focuses on the development of parenteral drugs. The company is engaged in design and product formulation services. | 510-367-0528 | NA | Pleasanton |
| Human Pheromone Sciences Inc (HQ) | Producer of natural attraction products and is engaged in research in the field of human pheromones in all areas of application. | 408-938-3030 | NA | San Jose |
| Impax Laboratories Inc (HQ) | Manufacturers and developer of technology-based specialty pharmaceutical drug delivery system. The company's serves physicians and patients. | 510-240-6000 | NA | Hayward |
| Inclin Inc (BR) | Provider of clinical, regulatory, and quality assurance services to pharmaceutical, biotechnology, and medical device companies. | 650-376-4000 | NA | San Mateo |
| Intertek Group PLC (BR) | Provider of advisory, business consulting, risk management, outsourcing, validation, and training services. | 650-463-2900 | NA | Menlo Park |
| Jaguar Health (HQ) | Provider of health solutions for the animals and humans. The company focusses on the development of gastrointestinal pharmaceuticals. | 415-371-8300 | NA | San Francisco |
| K-Pax Pharmaceuticals Inc (HQ) | Provider of pharmaceutical grade vitamins and nutritional health supplements for kid's, women, and men's health, joints & bones, and immune support. | 415-381-7565 | NA | Mill Valley |
| Lamdagen Corp (BR) | Developer of nano technology based biosensors used in research and diagnostic equipment for human and animal health testing. | 650-571-5816 | NA | Menlo Park |
| Merieux Nutrisciences Corp (BR) | Provider of public health services. The company is focused on food and pharmaceutical products, cosmetics, and consumer goods. | 209-549-7508 | 11-50 | Salida |
| Minerva Surgical Inc (HQ) | Manufacturer of medical devices. The company provides products for the treatment of abnormal uterine bleeding. | 855-646-7874 | NA | Redwood City |
| Mission Bio (HQ) | Developer and deliverer of precision medicine. The company offers instruments, fixed panels, custom panels, and software for the researchers and clinicians. | 415-854-0058 | NA | S San Francisco |
| Molecular Devices Llc (HQ) | Manufacturer of bioanalytical measurement systems. The company is engaged in life science research, pharma, and bio therapeutic development. | 800-635-5577 | NA | San Jose |
| Napo Pharmaceuticals Inc (HQ) | Developer of pharmaceutical drugs. The company specializes in the development of patent pharmaceutical products. | 415-963-9938 | NA | San Francisco |
| Neilmed Pharmaceuticals Inc (HQ) | Manufacturer of large volume low pressure saline nasal irrigation systems for babies & children, first aid, dry noses, sterile saline spray, and ear care. | 707-525-3784 | NA | Santa Rosa |
| Neopeutics Inc USA (HQ) | Provider of pre clinical contract research services and product development for the private and governmental regulatory agencies. | 650-624-4057 | NA | S San Francisco |
| Novici Biotech Llc (HQ) | Focuses on product development as well as protein engineering. The company serves the agriculture, industrial and pharmaceutical sectors. | 707-446-5502 | NA | Vacaville |
| Optimum Processing Inc (HQ) | Provider of filtration solutions and disposable bioprocess container systems. The company utilizes asymmetric morphology solutions. | 415-461-7033 | NA | San Rafael |
| Perceptimed Inc (HQ) | Provider of medical technologies for dispensing and administration of prescription drugs safer, reducing injuries, and death. | 650-941-7000 | NA | Mountain View |
| Phage International Inc (HQ) | Provider of leverage bacteriophage therapy technologies. The company specializes in discovery and rediscovery of effective health care solutions. | 925-984-9446 | NA | Danville |
| Pharmedix (HQ) | Focuses on the repackaging of pharmaceutical products. The company offers dispensing systems and women's health products. | 800-486-1811 | NA | Union City |
| Pharmout Laboratory Inc (HQ) | Provider of analytical laboratory services. The company engages in protein precipitated plasma, liquid-liquid extraction, and solid phase extraction. | 408-481-3090 | NA | Sunnyvale |
| Pharmtak Inc (HQ) | Provider of pharmaceutical products and services. The company focuses on developing novel pharmaceuticals and cosmeceuticals utilizing technology. | 408-954-8223 | NA | San Jose |
| Pherin Pharmaceuticals Inc (HQ) | Developer of novel compounds for intranasal spray delivery and also deals with the treatment of neuro-psychiatric and neuroendocrine conditions. | 650-961-2080 | NA | Los Altos |
| Portola Pharmaceuticals Inc (HQ) | Focuses on the development and commercialization of therapeutic products for the treatment of hematologic disorders. | 650-246-7000 | 201-500 | S San Francisco |
| Principia Biopharma Inc (HQ) | Provider of biopharmaceuticals. The company develops oral small molecule therapies to treat autoimmune and inflammatory diseases and cancer. | 650-416-7700 | NA | S San Francisco |

| COMPANY NAME | PRODUCT / SERVICE | PHONE | EMP | CITY |
|---|---|---|---|---|
| Prolynx Llc (HQ) | Developer of technology solutions for releasable linkers. The company also specializes in injectable drugs. | 415-552-5306 | NA | San Francisco |
| Protein Research (HQ) | Manufacturer of nutritional products. The company develops and formulates supplements for human nutrition in capsules, tablets, powders and premixes. | 925-243-6300 | NA | Livermore |
| Proteus Digital Health Inc (HQ) | Providers of health care service technology. The company offers health care products based on electronics technology. | 650-632-4031 | NA | Redwood City |
| Qool Therapeutics Inc (HQ) | Developer of therapeutic hypothermia/temperature management therapies to preserve cells and tissues. The company serves the medical industry. | 650-328-1426 | NA | Mountain View |
| R S Calibration Services (HQ) | Provider of lab based calibration and validation services. The company offers dimensional, electronic, and pipette calibration services. | 925-462-4217 | NA | Pleasanton |
| Reviva Pharmaceuticals Inc (HQ) | Developer of therapy for CNS, cardiovascular, metabolic and inflammatory diseases. The company is a clinical development pharmaceutical company. | 408-816-1470 | NA | Sunnyvale |
| Ryss Lab Inc (HQ) | Provider of biotechnology and pharmaceutical development services. The company offers services to the healthcare sector. | 510-477-9570 | NA | Union City |
| Safebridge Consultants Inc (HQ) | Provider of consulting services and analytical support. The company provides safety, health and environmental services. | 650-961-4820 | NA | Mountain View |
| Sfj Pharmaceuticals Group (HQ) | Focuses on the clinical development and registration of pharmaceutical products. The company is involved in clinical trials. | 925-223-6233 | NA | Pleasanton |
| Somagenics Inc (HQ) | Developer of RNA-based therapeutics and diagnostics. The company's services include detection, monitoring, testing, and analysis. | 831-426-7700 | 1-10 | Santa Cruz |
| Stemexpress (HQ) | Provider of immunophenotyping, DNA quantitation and viability, tissue transplant verification, and related services. | 530-626-7000 | 1-10 | Placerville |
| Sutrovax Inc (HQ) | Developer of vaccines for the treatment of infectious diseases. The company is also engaged in the production of vaccine antigens. | 650-837-0111 | NA | Foster City |
| Theraject Inc (HQ) | Developer of drug micro-needle technologies. The company is engaged in vaccine and also drug deliveries. | 510-742-5832 | NA | Fremont |
| Theravance Biopharma Us Inc (HQ) | Provider of pharmaceuticals. The company develops new medicines with superior efficacy, convenience, tolerability and/or safety. | 650-808-6000 | NA | S San Francisco |
| TheraVida Inc (HQ) | Developer of pharmaceutical products for the improved treatment of overactive bladder, urge urinary incontinence, and primary focal hyperhidrosis. | 650-638-2335 | NA | San Mateo |
| Titan Pharmaceuticals Inc (HQ) | Provider of biopharmaceuticals. The company discovers proprietary therapeutics primarily for the treatment of serious medical disorders. | 650-244-4990 | 11-50 | S San Francisco |
| Tolerion Inc (HQ) | Provider of medical treatment solutions for autoimmune diseases. The company focuses on restoring the patient's immune system. | 415-795-5800 | NA | S San Francisco |
| Ultragenyx Pharmaceutical Inc (HQ) | Developer of products for the treatment of rare and ultra-rare diseases. The company is engaged in commercialization of products. | 415-483-8800 | 501-1000 | Novato |
| Verseon Corp (HQ) | Focuses on the design of drug candidates. The company offers services to the pharmaceutical industry. | 510-225-9000 | NA | Fremont |
| Vetequip Inc (HQ) | Developer and manufacturer of drug delivery systems. The company specializes in nasal anesthesia delivery systems. | 925-463-1828 | NA | Livermore |

## 270 = Pharmaceutical Software

| COMPANY NAME | PRODUCT / SERVICE | PHONE | EMP | CITY |
|---|---|---|---|---|
| Adynxx Inc (HQ) | Developer of drugs to prevent acute post-surgical pain and the transition to persistent or chronic pain. | 415-512-7740 | NA | San Francisco |
| Allaccem Inc (HQ) | Manufacturer of pharmaceutical products such as dermatology, optic, and dental products for goats, dogs, and cats. | 650-593-8700 | NA | San Carlos |
| Arable Corporation (HQ) | Provider of products and services to health care, pharmaceutical, biotechnology and medical device companies. | 408-825-4755 | NA | Cupertino |
| Atomwise Inc (HQ) | Developer of artificial intelligence systems for the discovery of drugs. The company serves the healthcare sector. | 650-449-7925 | NA | San Francisco |
| Healfies (HQ) | Developer and provider of software platform to manage health information. The company serves the healthcare sector. | 415-312-4525 | NA | San Francisco |
| HeartFlow Inc (RH) | Provider of analysis technology that creates a personalized 3D model of the coronary arteries and analyzes the impact that blockages have on blood flow. | 650-241-1221 | NA | Redwood City |
| Lumedx Corp (HQ) | Provider of cardiovascular information and imaging systems. The company specializes in cloud-powered healthcare solutions. | 800-966-0699 | NA | Oakland |
| Mission Bio (HQ) | Developer and deliverer of precision medicine. The company offers instruments, fixed panels, custom panels, and software for the researchers and clinicians. | 415-854-0058 | NA | S San Francisco |
| Molecular Devices Llc (HQ) | Manufacturer of bioanalytical measurement systems. The company is engaged in life science research, pharma, and bio therapeutic development. | 800-635-5577 | NA | San Jose |
| Perceptimed Inc (HQ) | Provider of medical technologies for dispensing and administration of prescription drugs safer, reducing injuries, and death. | 650-941-7000 | NA | Mountain View |
| Prescript Pharmaceuticals Inc (HQ) | Provider of repackaging services. The company offers its products in sealed and tamper evident containers. | 925-215-8608 | NA | Pleasanton |

| COMPANY NAME | PRODUCT / SERVICE | PHONE | EMP | CITY |
|---|---|---|---|---|
| Prowess Inc (HQ) | Focuses on Windows-based treatment planning systems for radiation therapy treatment and OIS software. | 925-356-0360 | NA | Concord |
| Veracyte Inc (HQ) | Focuses on molecular analysis and diagnostic tests. The company serves patients and the healthcare sector. | 650-243-6300 | NA | S San Francisco |

## 271 = Serum/Vaccines

| COMPANY NAME | PRODUCT / SERVICE | PHONE | EMP | CITY |
|---|---|---|---|---|
| Amunix Pharmaceuticals Inc (HQ) | Developer of biomolecular therapy. The company specializes in the development of protein and peptide based therapeutic products. | 650-428-1800 | NA | Mountain View |
| Aridis Pharmaceuticals Llc (HQ) | Focuses on anti-infective alternatives to conventional antibiotics. The company offers services to the pharmaceutical sector. | 408-385-1742 | NA | San Jose |
| Biocheck Inc (HQ) | Provider of custom immunoassay development, antibody conjugation and purification, and contract manufacturing services. | 650-573-1968 | NA | S San Francisco |
| Biomertech (HQ) | Provider of tailor-made peptide and anti-body solutions such as pepdyes and polyclonal antibody advantage for the scientific community. | 925-931-0007 | NA | Pleasanton |
| Corvus Pharmaceuticals Inc (HQ) | Focuses on the development of first-in-class agents that target the immune system. The company serves the healthcare industry. | 650-900-4520 | NA | Burlingame |
| Hygeia Laboratories Inc (HQ) | Developers of vaccines using novel technology for animals. The company offers animal pharmaceuticals for dairy cattle, sheep and poultry. | 530-661-1442 | 1-10 | Woodland |
| Teknova (HQ) | Provider of agar plates and broths for growth of bacterial, yeast, and microbiological applications such as cloning, DNA sequencing, and immunology. | 831-637-1100 | 1-10 | Hollister |
| Vaxart Inc (HQ) | Manufacturer and developer of oral vaccines. The company is engaged in drug development and related services. | 650-550-3500 | NA | S San Francisco |

## 272 = Vitamins

| COMPANY NAME | PRODUCT / SERVICE | PHONE | EMP | CITY |
|---|---|---|---|---|
| ABCO Laboratories Inc (HQ) | Provider of turnkey solutions. The company also offers contract manufacturing, product development and private labeling. | 707-432-2200 | NA | Fairfield |
| Allergy Research Group Llc (HQ) | Provider of nutritional products for blood sugar, brain, cardiovascular, metabolic, hormone, liver, and immune support. | 510-263-2000 | NA | Alameda |
| Alltech (BR) | Provider of nutritional innovation in animal feed. The company adds nutrition to food through yeast fermentation, enzyme technology, algae and nutrigenomics. | 559-226-0405 | 11-50 | Fresno |
| Aridis Pharmaceuticals Llc (HQ) | Focuses on anti-infective alternatives to conventional antibiotics. The company offers services to the pharmaceutical sector. | 408-385-1742 | NA | San Jose |
| Biozone Laboratories Inc (HQ) | Manufacturer of over the counter drugs, cosmetics, personal care, and nutritional supplements such as creams, gels, drops, syrups, and sun protection. | 925-473-1000 | NA | Pittsburg |
| C&M Biolabs (HQ) | Provider of products and services to scientists. The company offers cloning and sequencing and antibody services. | 510-691-7166 | NA | Richmond |
| Calysta (HQ) | Focuses on the development and manufacture of protein for commercial aquaculture and livestock feed. | 650-492-6880 | NA | Menlo Park |
| Cypress Systems Inc (HQ) | Provider of natural food forms of organically bound minerals and nutritional yeast products and related supplies. | 559-229-7850 | 1-10 | Madera |
| Cytosport Inc (HQ) | Manufacturer of health care supplements. The company specializes in fitness supplements for athletes, to strengthen muscles and bones. | 888-298-6629 | NA | Walnut Creek |
| Eckhart Corp (HQ) | Manufacturer of nutritional supplements. The company is engaged in product development and packaging services. | 415-898-9528 | NA | Novato |
| Econugenics Inc (HQ) | Manufacturer and distributor of dietary supplements and healthcare products. The company serves the medical sector. | 800-521-0160 | NA | Santa Rosa |
| Formulation Technology Inc (HQ) | Manufacturer of custom dietary supplements and OTC medications. The company focuses on contract manufacturing services. | 209-847-0331 | 1-10 | Oakdale |
| Global Marketing Associates Inc (HQ) | Providers of nutrition supplements to health care industry. The company supply innovative and quality ingredients to health care industry. | 510-887-2462 | NA | Livermore |
| Hitachi Chemical Diagnostics Inc (HQ) | Provider of in vitro allergy diagnostics products. The company offers alternative means of diagnosing allergy. | 650-961-5501 | NA | Mountain View |
| HTD Biosystems Inc (HQ) | Focuses on the development of parenteral drugs. The company is engaged in design and product formulation services. | 510-367-0528 | NA | Pleasanton |
| Interhealth Nutraceuticals Inc (HQ) | Developers and marketer of nutritional ingredients. The company offers dietary supplement, food and beverage, and animal healthcare products. | 800-783-4636 | NA | Benicia |
| K-Pax Pharmaceuticals Inc (HQ) | Provider of pharmaceutical grade vitamins and nutritional health supplements for kid's, women, and men's health, joints & bones, and immune support. | 415-381-7565 | NA | Mill Valley |
| Life Sources Inc (HQ) | Developer of products to combat chronic illnesses. The company's services include targeted nutrition and vital hematology. | 916-662-4580 | 1-10 | Fair Oaks |
| Maxium Living Inc (HQ) | Supplier of nutritional supplement products. The company offers liquid minerals, digestive supports, healthy energy snacks, and children supports. | 209-536-9300 | 1-10 | Soulsbyville |
| MusclePharm Corp (HQ) | Provider of sports supplement and nutrition products such as fish oil, energy sport zero, and coco protein for weight loss, fitness, and athletes. | 800-292-3909 | 1-10 | Burbank |
| Nordic Naturals Inc (HQ) | Specializes in the delivery of omega oil to consumers, veterinary professionals, pharmacists, and healthcare professionals. | 831-724-6200 | 11-50 | Watsonville |

| COMPANY NAME | PRODUCT / SERVICE | PHONE | EMP | CITY |
|---|---|---|---|---|
| Nutribiotic (HQ) | Manufacturer of health, wellness, and fitness products. The company provides nutritional supplements and personal care products. | 707-263-0411 | 1-10 | Lakeport |
| Nutrition53 Inc (HQ) | Manufacturer of nutritional supplements. The company manufactures health care products for staying lean, sleeping well and feeling energized. | 925-900-3557 | NA | Lafayette |
| Pharmedix (HQ) | Focuses on the repackaging of pharmaceutical products. The company offers dispensing systems and women's health products. | 800-486-1811 | NA | Union City |
| Planetary Herbals (HQ) | Provider of nutritional herbal healthcare products. The company's products include Acai, Full Spectrum, Bacopa Extract, and Digestive Comfort. | 831-438-1700 | 1-10 | Soquel |
| Pro-Form Laboratories (HQ) | Developer and producer of nutritional powders. The company also specializes in contract manufacturing services. | 707-752-9010 | NA | Orinda |
| Protein Research (HQ) | Manufacturer of nutritional products. The company develops and formulates supplements for human nutrition in capsules, tablets, powders and premixes. | 925-243-6300 | NA | Livermore |
| Randal Optimal Nutrients (HQ) | Manufacturer of consumer goods. The company produces dietary supplements and nutraceuticals to the health food and profession health care markets. | 707-528-1800 | NA | Santa Rosa |
| Sfj Pharmaceuticals Group (HQ) | Focuses on the clinical development and registration of pharmaceutical products. The company is involved in clinical trials. | 925-223-6233 | NA | Pleasanton |
| Source Naturals Inc (HQ) | Provider of vitamins, minerals, and nutritional supplements. The company deals with sales and delivery services. | 831-438-1144 | 1-10 | Scotts Valley |
| Threshold Enterprises Ltd (HQ) | Distributor of nutritional supplements, healthcare, and beauty care products. | 831-438-6851 | 1-10 | Scotts Valley |
| Wachters' Organic Sea Products (HQ) | Manufacturer and distributor of nutritional products. The company's products include pet products, personal care, and cleaning products. | 650-757-9851 | NA | Daly City |

## 273 = Veterinary Pharmaceuticals

| COMPANY NAME | PRODUCT / SERVICE | PHONE | EMP | CITY |
|---|---|---|---|---|
| Allaccem Inc (HQ) | Manufacturer of pharmaceutical products such as dermatology, optic, and dental products for goats, dogs, and cats. | 650-593-8700 | NA | San Carlos |
| Antech Diagnostics (HQ) | Provider of diagnostic and laboratory testing services for chemistry, pathology, endocrinology, serology, hematology, and microbiology. | 800-872-1001 | 11-50 | Fountain Valley |
| J R Scientific Inc (HQ) | Provider of cell culture products and services. The company's offerings include antibiotics, reagents, and other supplies. | 530-666-9868 | 1-10 | Woodland |
| Kindred Biosciences Inc (HQ) | Provider of pharmaceutical products for treatment of anemia, cancer, allergic, autoimmune, and gastrointestinal diseases in cats, dogs, and horses. | 650-701-7901 | NA | Burlingame |
| Vdx Veterinary Diagnostics (HQ) | Provider of histopathology and pathology support to the medical device, biotech, pharmaceutical, academic and veterinary communities. | 530-753-4285 | 1-10 | Davis |

## 275 = Advanced Materials R&D

| COMPANY NAME | PRODUCT / SERVICE | PHONE | EMP | CITY |
|---|---|---|---|---|
| Carbon3d Inc (HQ) | Provider of hardware and software engineering and molecular science. The company specializes in continuous liquid interface production technology. | 650-285-6307 | NA | Redwood City |
| Davlin Coatings (HQ) | Manufacturer of coatings for architectural and industrial purposes. The company offers elastomeric waterproof coatings. | 510-848-2863 | NA | Berkeley |
| Dowd & Guild Inc (HQ) | Distributor of chemicals and containers. The company supplies resins, grinding media, oils and maxes, rheological products, and pigments. | 925-820-7222 | NA | San Ramon |
| Yunsheng Usa (HQ) | Manufacturer of permanent magnets. The company mainly offers Neodymium and rare earth magnet products. | 650-827-7928 | NA | S San Francisco |

## 276 = Carbon & Graphite Products

| COMPANY NAME | PRODUCT / SERVICE | PHONE | EMP | CITY |
|---|---|---|---|---|
| Airxpanders Inc (HQ) | Provider of controlled tissue expander and small handheld wireless controller of breast cancer reconstructive surgery. | 650-390-9000 | NA | San Jose |

## 277 = Ceramics

| COMPANY NAME | PRODUCT / SERVICE | PHONE | EMP | CITY |
|---|---|---|---|---|
| Corning Technology Center (BR) | Provider of specialty glass and ceramics services and sells keystone components to electronics, mobile emissions control, and life science industries. | 650-846-6000 | NA | Sunnyvale |
| Morgan Technical Ceramics (BR) | Manufacturer of cast and powder metal stainless steels. The company also focuses on other specialty alloys. | 530-823-3401 | 11-50 | Auburn |
| Ntk Technologies Inc (HQ) | Manufacturer of bio ceramics, oxygen sensors, ceramic heater, and transistor packages for the medical and telecommunication applications. | 408-727-5180 | NA | Santa Clara |
| Pacific Ceramics Inc (HQ) | Manufacturer of microwave ceramic material. The company's products include earth iron garnets, calcium vanadium garnets, lithium, and titanate dielectrics. | 408-747-4600 | NA | Sunnyvale |
| Sun Enterprise Inc (HQ) | Provider of ceramic and quartz machining products. The company specializes in the semiconductor, solar, laser, and structural industries. | 510-657-6507 | NA | Fremont |
| Toray Advanced Composites USA (BR) | Manufacturer of advanced composites like adhesives, prepregs, and liquid resin systems. The company serves military, aerospace, and other sectors. | 408-465-8500 | NA | Morgan Hill |

## 278 = Composites

| COMPANY NAME | PRODUCT / SERVICE | PHONE | EMP | CITY |
|---|---|---|---|---|
| Asbury Graphite Incorporated of CA (BR) | Supplier of carbon and graphite products for the chemicals, cement, rubber, and metal industries. The company's products include coals, cokes, and carbon fiber. | 510-799-3636 | NA | Rodeo |
| Toray Advanced Composites USA (BR) | Manufacturer of advanced composites like adhesives, prepregs, and liquid resin systems. The company serves military, aerospace, and other sectors. | 408-465-8500 | NA | Morgan Hill |
| Toray International America Inc (BR) | Provider of chemicals, plastics, textiles, and IT-related products. The company offers environment, engineering, life science, and other services. | 650-341-7152 | NA | San Mateo |

## 279 = Laminates

| | | | | |
|---|---|---|---|---|
| Window Solutions (HQ) | Provider of 3M window film and tinting installation services. The company offers services for residential, commercial, architects, and builders. | 800-400-7644 | NA | S San Francisco |

## 280 = Miscellaneous Plastic Products

| | | | | |
|---|---|---|---|---|
| Acrylic Art (HQ) | Provider of fabrication and machining services. The company focuses on painting, product finishing, anodizing, and vapor polishing. | 510-654-0953 | NA | Emeryville |
| Airxpanders Inc (HQ) | Provider of controlled tissue expander and small handheld wireless controller of breast cancer reconstructive surgery. | 650-390-9000 | NA | San Jose |
| BASF Venture Capital America Inc (RH) | Manufacturer of basic chemicals and intermediates such as solvents, plasticizers, and monomers. The company serves the agriculture market. | 510-445-6140 | NA | Fremont |
| Bio Plas Inc (HQ) | Manufacturer of laboratory disposables such as foam tube racks, biopsy bags, bacti cell spreaders, and siliconized products. | 415-472-3777 | NA | San Rafael |
| Carbon3d Inc (HQ) | Provider of hardware and software engineering and molecular science. The company specializes in continuous liquid interface production technology. | 650-285-6307 | NA | Redwood City |
| China Custom Manufacturing Ltd (HQ) | Provider of tooling, plastic injection molding, and sheet metal stamping services. The company focuses on the aerospace and electronics industries. | 510-979-1920 | NA | Fremont |
| Computer Plastics Inc (HQ) | Provider of molding services. The company offers custom plastic injection molding, engineering, assembly, and tooling services. | 510-785-3600 | NA | Hayward |
| D & T Fiberglass Inc (HQ) | Manufacturer of fiberglass reinforced plastic bulk containers. The company's products are used for water and chemical treatment applications. | 916-383-9012 | 1-10 | Sacramento |
| Delta Pacific Products Inc (HQ) | Provider of plastics injection molding and mold making services. The company serves the automotive, agriculture, aerospace, and recreational sectors. | 510-487-4411 | NA | Union City |
| Dependable Plastics (HQ) | Provider of vacuum and pressure forming, plastic fabrication, and turn-key operations that involve assembly, conductive coating, and painting. | 707-863-4900 | NA | Fairfield |
| Ens Technology Llc (HQ) | Provider of plating services. The company plates materials such as common metals, alloys, and refractory metals. | 408-496-0740 | NA | Santa Clara |
| Fictiv Inc (HQ) | Provider of tooling services for hardware engineers. The company specializes in distributed manufacturing of idle 3D printers from single platform. | 415-580-2509 | NA | San Francisco |
| Freetech Plastics Inc (HQ) | Manufacturer of pressure thermoforming products. The company's products include medical, scientific, and telecommunication enclosures. | 510-651-9996 | NA | Fremont |
| Golden Plastics Corp (HQ) | Provider of thermoforming services. The company specializes in part trimming, part design, and tooling. | 510-569-6465 | NA | Oakland |
| Kennerley-Spratling Inc (HQ) | Manufacturer of custom plastic injection and compression moldings. The company is involved in design, installation, and delivery services. | 510-351-8230 | NA | San Leandro |
| Macro Plastics Inc (HQ) | Provider of agricultural, food processing, and industrial bins. The company's services include recycling, design, and business development. | 707-437-1200 | NA | Fairfield |
| Mos Plastics Inc (HQ) | Provider of precision injection-molding, contract manufacturing, and assembly services for medical and electronics OEMs. | 408-944-9407 | NA | San Jose |
| Pacific States Felt & MFG Company Inc (HQ) | Manufacturer of gaskets, seals, washers, pads, and molded bumpers. The company is engaged in lamination and fabrication. | 510-783-0277 | NA | Hayward |
| Plastikon Industries (HQ) | Provider of contract manufacturing services for custom designed plastic injection molding, for medical, pharmaceutical and other industries. | 510-400-1010 | NA | Hayward |
| Riley Plastic Manufacturing Inc (HQ) | Provider of vacuum forming, vapor polishing, and assembly services. The company serves the medical and bio-tech industries. | 650-366-5104 | NA | Menlo Park |
| Roplast Industries Inc (HQ) | Manufacturer of bags. The company specializes in custom designed bags made out of polyethylene films. | 530-532-9500 | 1-10 | Oroville |
| Scribner Plastics (HQ) | Provider of shipping and packing solutions. The company also deals with custom plastics design and manufacturing services. | 916-638-1515 | 1-10 | Rancho Cordova |
| Stack Plastics Inc (HQ) | Provider of plastic injection molding services. The company offers thermoplastics, elastomers, and resins. | 650-361-8600 | NA | Menlo Park |
| T-Star Enterprises Inc (HQ) | Manufacturer of deployers, manual storage reels, and motorized re-winders. The company's services include repairs and parts replacement. | 510-635-2736 | NA | Oakland |
| Toray International America Inc (BR) | Provider of chemicals, plastics, textiles, and IT-related products. The company offers environment, engineering, life science, and other services. | 650-341-7152 | NA | San Mateo |

| COMPANY NAME | PRODUCT / SERVICE | PHONE | EMP | CITY |
|---|---|---|---|---|
| Wafab International (HQ) | Provider of wet processing and chemical handling tools. The company's products include solar cell processing equipment and stainless steel fume hoods. | 925-455-5252 | NA | Livermore |

## 281 = Monomers/Polymers

| COMPANY NAME | PRODUCT / SERVICE | PHONE | EMP | CITY |
|---|---|---|---|---|
| Applied Poleramic Inc (HQ) | Developer and manufacturer of composite materials for the aerospace, marine, and industrial markets. The company offers resins, pastes, and adhesives. | 707-747-6738 | NA | Benicia |
| Carbon3d Inc (HQ) | Provider of hardware and software engineering and molecular science. The company specializes in continuous liquid interface production technology. | 650-285-6307 | NA | Redwood City |
| Cobalt Polymers Inc (HQ) | Manufacturer of polymer tubing for medical device and high technology applications, with polymer chemistry, radiation science, and process engineering. | 800-337-0901 | NA | Cloverdale |
| Pacific Rubber & Packing Inc (HQ) | Provider of rubber seals, custom seals, rubber gaskets and o-ring products for medical/pharmacy, automotive, solar energy, and general industries. | 650-595-5888 | NA | San Carlos |

## 283 = Plastic Film/Sheets

| COMPANY NAME | PRODUCT / SERVICE | PHONE | EMP | CITY |
|---|---|---|---|---|
| C3Nano Inc (HQ) | Developer of transparent conductive ink and film such as touch sensors, OLED lighting and displays, EMI shielding for touch sensor and display industry. | 510-259-9650 | NA | Hayward |
| Procurement Partners International Inc (HQ) | Provider of procurement services. The company offers mechanical components such as pins, rods, rollers, and sheet metal. | 650-345-6118 | NA | San Mateo |
| T-Star Enterprises Inc (HQ) | Manufacturer of deployers, manual storage reels, and motorized re-winders. The company's services include repairs and parts replacement. | 510-635-2736 | NA | Oakland |
| Window Solutions (HQ) | Provider of 3M window film and tinting installation services. The company offers services for residential, commercial, architects, and builders. | 800-400-7644 | NA | S San Francisco |

## 284 = Plastic Materials, Synthetic Resins & Elastomerss

| COMPANY NAME | PRODUCT / SERVICE | PHONE | EMP | CITY |
|---|---|---|---|---|
| Acrylic Art (HQ) | Provider of fabrication and machining services. The company focuses on painting, product finishing, anodizing, and vapor polishing. | 510-654-0953 | NA | Emeryville |
| Amyris Inc (HQ) | Provider of renewable products. The company delivers cosmetic emollients and fragrances, fuels and lubricants, and even biopharmaceuticals. | 510-450-0761 | NA | Emeryville |
| Ats Inc (HQ) | Manufacturer of fiberglass duct work for fume exhaust systems. The company offers installation and other related services. | 510-234-3173 | NA | Richmond |
| Aubin Industries Inc (HQ) | Designer and manufacturer of mobile wheel systems. The company serves the material handling industry. | 209-833-7592 | 1-10 | Tracy |
| Connora Technologies Inc (HQ) | Manufacturer of electronic and composites re-imagined. The company specializes in recyclamine thermoset technology. | 415-315-9524 | NA | Hayward |
| Dependable Plastics (HQ) | Provider of vacuum and pressure forming, plastic fabrication, and turn-key operations that involve assembly, conductive coating, and painting. | 707-863-4900 | NA | Fairfield |
| Dowd & Guild Inc (HQ) | Distributor of chemicals and containers. The company supplies resins, grinding media, oils and maxes, rheological products, and pigments. | 925-820-7222 | NA | San Ramon |
| Empire West Inc (HQ) | Designer and developer of envelope handling trays, custom thermo-formed ceiling tiles and panels, and optic packaging solutions. | 707-823-1190 | NA | Graton |
| Finishline Advanced Composites (HQ) | Provider of composite repair services for production projects. The company is involved in design, development, prototyping, testing, and production. | 707-747-0788 | NA | Benicia |
| Freetech Plastics Inc (HQ) | Manufacturer of pressure thermoforming products. The company's products include medical, scientific, and telecommunication enclosures. | 510-651-9996 | NA | Fremont |
| Interstate Plastics Inc (BR) | Provider of plastic products. The company's products include plastic sheets, rods, tubes, and industrial accessories. | 510-483-4341 | NA | San Leandro |
| Interstate Plastics Inc (HQ) | Manufacturer and distributor of industrial plastics. The company offers plastic sheets, rods, tubing, and profiles. | 916-422-3110 | 11-50 | Sacramento |
| Jatco Inc (HQ) | Manufactuer of plastic products. The company offers molding, tooling, quality control, and warehousing and distribution services. | 510-487-0888 | NA | Union City |
| Loprest Water Treatment Co (HQ) | Provider of water treatment systems design and fabricating services. The company focuses on media analysis and filter inspection. | 510-799-3101 | NA | Rodeo |
| Poly Seal Industries (HQ) | Manufacturer of molded rubber pipe gaskets for water and sewage treatment applications. The company serves the automotive and biomedical industries. | 510-843-9722 | NA | Berkeley |
| Precision Plastics Inc (HQ) | Provider of plastic fabrication services. The company is engaged in fabrication, countertops, machining, and consumer services. | 916-689-5284 | 11-50 | Sacramento |

## 285 = Polystyrene/Urethane Foams

| COMPANY NAME | PRODUCT / SERVICE | PHONE | EMP | CITY |
|---|---|---|---|---|
| Foamlinx Llc (HQ) | Provider of foam cutting computer numerical control machines. The company offers cutters, shredders, compactors, and cutting services. | 408-454-6163 | NA | Sunnyvale |
| Gel-Pak (DH) | Provider of safety transport and product handling services from bare die to medical components, and other fragile parts. | 510-576-2220 | NA | Hayward |

| COMPANY NAME | PRODUCT / SERVICE | PHONE | EMP | CITY |
|---|---|---|---|---|
| Ico Rally (HQ) | Manufacturer and supplier of heat shrinkable materials, wiring accessories, and insulation products. The company serves automotive and marine sectors. | 650-856-9900 | NA | Palo Alto |

## 286 = Quartz, Silicon & Other Electronic Materials

| COMPANY NAME | PRODUCT / SERVICE | PHONE | EMP | CITY |
|---|---|---|---|---|
| Gm Associates Inc (HQ) | Manufacturer of quartz fabricated products and etch chambers. The company offers machining, slicing, cutting, and other services. | 510-430-0806 | NA | Oakland |
| Hayward Quartz Technology Inc (HQ) | Manufacturer of machined and fabricated parts. The company exclusively caters to the semiconductor industry. | 510-657-9605 | NA | Fremont |
| Isola Usa Corp (BR) | Designer, developer, and manufacturer of laminate materials used to fabricate multilayer PCBs. The company serves the medical market. | 916-429-4462 | 11-50 | Elk Grove |
| Lp Glass Blowing Inc (HQ) | Provider of high-precision quartz ware and glass products. The company offers research and development assistance services. | 408-988-7561 | NA | Santa Clara |
| Quality Quartz Engineering Inc (HQ) | Designer and manufacturer of solid quartz products for solar, fiber optic, semiconductor, and lighting industries. | 510-745-9200 | NA | Newark |
| Sun Enterprise Inc (HQ) | Provider of ceramic and quartz machining products. The company specializes in the semiconductor, solar, laser, and structural industries. | 510-657-6507 | NA | Fremont |
| Techni-Glass Inc (HQ) | Provider of glass blowing services. The company specializes in glass used for research, laser, oil, and medical services. | 707-838-3325 | NA | Windsor |

## 288 = Batteries/Energy Storage Devices

| COMPANY NAME | PRODUCT / SERVICE | PHONE | EMP | CITY |
|---|---|---|---|---|
| AA Portable Power Corp (HQ) | Manufacturer of lithium-ion batteries. The company serves the mobile, consumer electronics, energy storage, and light electric vehicle markets. | 510-525-2328 | NA | Richmond |
| Amprius Inc (HQ) | Developer and manufacturer of lithium-ion batteries. The company offers services to the industrial sectors. | 800-425-8803 | NA | Fremont |
| Ardica Technologies (HQ) | Provider of integrated power and fuel cell technology solutions for commercial and military applications. | 415-568-9270 | NA | San Francisco |
| BASF Venture Capital America Inc (RH) | Manufacturer of basic chemicals and intermediates such as solvents, plasticizers, and monomers. The company serves the agriculture market. | 510-445-6140 | NA | Fremont |
| Energous Corp (HQ) | Provider of energy solutions. The company offers a wire-free charging system for portable electronic devices. | 408-963-0200 | NA | San Jose |
| EnerVault (HQ) | Designer and manufacturer of megawatt-hour scale energy storage systems based on iron-chromium redox flow battery technology. | 408-934-6840 | NA | Sunnyvale |
| Enovix Corp (HQ) | Developer and producer of 3D Wave Array energy storage cells for products such as Bluetooth, mobile phones, notebooks, and media players. | | NA | Fremont |
| Evergreen (cp) Usa Inc (HQ) | Manufacturer of batteries. The company offers lithium coin cells, nickel cadmium batteries, manganese button cells, and silver oxide button cells. | 650-952-8091 | NA | S San Francisco |
| Farasis Energy Inc (HQ) | Designer and developer of energy storage solutions. The company serves the transportation, consumer electronics, and power distribution markets. | 510-732-6600 | NA | Hayward |
| Fenix International (HQ) | Provider of affordable power generation, smart-storage, and distribution solutions for the 1.6 billion people living off the electricity grid. | 415-754-9222 | NA | San Francisco |
| FreeWire Technologies Inc (HQ) | Provider of mobile distributed power solutions. The company serves the business and industrial sectors. | 415-779-5515 | NA | San Leandro |
| IMC Power Sources (HQ) | Supplier of SLA batteries, power test equipment, and test loads. The company serves the industrial market. | 408-924-0800 | NA | San Jose |
| Imprint Energy (HQ) | Developer of zinc-based rechargeable batteries. The company is engaged in energy management solutions. | 510-748-0233 | NA | Alameda |
| King-Solarman Inc (HQ) | Focuses on the sale of solar panels, power inverters, and related supplies. The company is involved in solar project financing services. | 408-373-8800 | NA | Fremont |
| KULR Technology Group Inc (HQ) | Provider of carbon fiber-based thermal management technology for energy storage, mobile devices, cloud computing, drones, and satellite applications. | | NA | San Diego |
| Mojo Mobility Inc (HQ) | Provider of mobile recharge devices such as batteries and pads for computer peripherals and headsets for medical and commercial sectors. | 650-446-0004 | NA | Santa Clara |
| Nanosys Inc (HQ) | Developer of nanotechnology products for the LCD display and battery markets. The company focuses on display backlighting and energy storage devices. | 408-240-6700 | NA | Milpitas |
| PPBC (HQ) | Engaged in the development of protected lithium metal electrodes. The company's products include lithium-sulfur batteries and protected lithium aondes. | 510-841-7242 | NA | Berkeley |
| Primus Power (HQ) | Provider of energy storage solutions. The company develops EnergyPod, energy storage batteries, and EnergyCell for industrial and consumer applications. | 510-342-7600 | NA | Hayward |
| Safeco Electric Supply Inc (HQ) | Distributor of electrical and lighting products. The company offers wires, cables, cords, fasteners, switch boxes, and accessories. | 415-206-0368 | NA | San Francisco |
| Seeo Inc (HQ) | Developer of rechargeable lithium batteries for the needs of electric vehicles and large-scale renewable energy storage. | 510-782-7336 | NA | Hayward |
| Stem Inc (HQ) | Provider of innovative solutions for efficient electricity grids. The company uses powerful learning software and advanced energy storage. | 415-937-7836 | NA | Millbrae |

| COMPANY NAME | PRODUCT / SERVICE | PHONE | EMP | CITY |
|---|---|---|---|---|
| Syrma Technology (BR) | Provider of entrepreneurial manufacturing services. The company's products include magnetics, memory, and RFID. | 408-404-0500 | NA | San Jose |
| Tenergy Corp (HQ) | Designer and manufacturer of batteries and chargers. The company serves medical, consumer electronics, data management, military, and other sectors. | 510-687-0388 | NA | Fremont |
| Top Microsystems Corp (HQ) | Provider of conversion solutions and integration services. The company offers blade, storage, and rack mount servers, medical equipment, and others. | 408-980-9813 | NA | Santa Clara |
| WAGAN Corp (HQ) | Developer and marketer of automotive accessories to mobile professionals. The company's offerings include warmers, defrosters, and heated cushions. | 510-471-9221 | NA | Hayward |
| Xantrex Technology Inc (BR) | Manufacturer of automotive batteries. The company offers power products for trucks, cars, and recreational vehicles. | 408-987-6030 | NA | Livermore |

## 289 = Circuit Breakers

| COMPANY NAME | PRODUCT / SERVICE | PHONE | EMP | CITY |
|---|---|---|---|---|
| Acronics (HQ) | Provider of engineering services. The company is involved in systems and mechanical design services. | 408-432-0888 | NA | San Jose |
| Barrington Consultants Inc (HQ) | Manufacturer of transformer monitors and temperature monitors for testing high voltage circuit breakers and offers circuit breaker simulators. | 707-527-8254 | NA | Santa Rosa |
| Mektec International Corp (HQ) | Manufacturer of printed circuit boards. The company deals with production, prototyping, and application engineering services. | 408-392-4000 | NA | San Jose |

## 290 = Electric Power Control/Transmission Equipment

| COMPANY NAME | PRODUCT / SERVICE | PHONE | EMP | CITY |
|---|---|---|---|---|
| A TEEM Electrical Engineering (HQ) | Provider of outreach safety training, electrical design and construction management, and control system programming services. | 916-457-8144 | 1-10 | Sacramento |
| Advanced Power Solutions (HQ) | Provider of power supplies. The company is involved in manufacturing, sales, and related support services. | 925-456-9890 | NA | Livermore |
| Alpha Scientific Electronics (HQ) | Designer, manufacturer, and seller of precision power supplies and electronic products. The company's products are used in medical instrumentation. | 510-782-4747 | NA | Hayward |
| Amtec Industries Inc (BR) | Manufacturer of industrial custom control panels. The company is engaged in design, fabrication, and installation services. | 510-887-2289 | NA | Pleasanton |
| Aras Power Technologies (HQ) | Provider of power delivery solutions. The company offers conventional, alternating current solutions, and custom power supply design services. | 408-935-8877 | NA | Milpitas |
| Calcon Systems Inc (HQ) | Provider of process control, instrumentation, and automation solutions specializing in turnkey design-build system integration and support. | 925-277-0665 | NA | San Ramon |
| Capital Machine Corporation (HQ) | Provider of machining, welding, fabrication, and design services. The company also distributes steel & power transmission products. | 916-443-6671 | 1-10 | Sacramento |
| Communications & Power Industries Llc (HQ) | Developer and manufacturer of microwave, radio frequency, power, and control solutions. The company serves medical and critical defense fields. | 650-846-2900 | NA | Palo Alto |
| Eta-Usa (HQ) | Provider of power supplies and manufacturer of battery chargers. The company serves the communication, gaming, and computing industries. | 408-778-2793 | NA | Morgan Hill |
| KG Technologies Inc (HQ) | Designer and developer of switching solutions. The company's applications include welding, brazing, and riveting. | 888-513-1874 | NA | Rohnert Park |
| Megmeet Usa Inc (BR) | Manufacturer of electrical motors, general-used converters, and optional devices. The company offers industry automatic solutions. | 408-260-7211 | NA | San Jose |
| Polarity Inc (HQ) | Designer and manufacturer of power products for commercial and government entities. The company also offers supply solutions. | 916-635-3050 | 11-50 | Rancho Cordova |
| Powertronix Corp (HQ) | Provider of in-house engineering and related services. The company offers services to the industrial sector. | 650-345-6800 | NA | Foster City |
| S&C Electric Co (BR) | Provider of equipment and services for electric power systems. The company is involved in design and installation services. | 510-864-9300 | NA | Alameda |
| Sparkle Power Inc (HQ) | Manufacturer of switching power supply devices. The company serves the PC, industrial PC, and telecommunication industries. | 408-519-8888 | NA | Fremont |
| Total Environmental & Power Systems Inc (HQ) | Provider of HVAC, electrical, and telecommunication services. The company's service areas include generators, radio frequency, and fabrication. | 925-681-2238 | NA | Concord |
| Vantage Data Center Services & Solutions (HQ) | Provider of transformers, switches, generators, chillers, switch gears and security, and communication products. | 855-878-2682 | NA | Santa Clara |
| Varentec Inc (HQ) | Provider of grid control and monitoring solutions. The company also offers asset management and outage detection services. | 408-433-9900 | NA | Santa Clara |
| Versatile Power (HQ) | Designer and manufacturer of electronic subsystems for manufacturers. The company focuses on application of radio frequency, ultrasonics, and lasers. | 408-341-4600 | NA | Campbell |

## 291 = Fuses

| COMPANY NAME | PRODUCT / SERVICE | PHONE | EMP | CITY |
|---|---|---|---|---|
| Bentek Corp (HQ) | Provider of manufacturing and engineering services. The company's offerings include power distribution system design and mechanical manufacturing. | 408-954-9600 | NA | San Jose |
| Solarbos Inc (HQ) | Designer and manufacturer of electrical products. The company exclusively caters to the solar industry. | 925-456-7744 | NA | Livermore |

| COMPANY NAME | PRODUCT / SERVICE | PHONE | EMP | CITY |
|---|---|---|---|---|
| **292 = Generators** | | | | |
| Adtec Technology Inc (HQ) | Manufacturer of RF plasma generators, matching units, and power measurement devices. The company serves semiconductor and solar processing tool needs. | 510-226-5766 | NA | Fremont |
| Allmotion Inc (HQ) | Manufacturer and distributor of stepper drives, stepper controllers, servo drives, and servo controllers. | 510-471-4000 | NA | Union City |
| Empire Magnetics Inc (HQ) | Manufacturer of specialty, cryogenic, dust proof, high temperature, water proof, and radiation hardened motors. | 707-584-2801 | NA | Rohnert Park |
| Enphase Energy Inc (HQ) | Distributor of electronic products. The company offers services to the solar, telecom, networking, and software industries. | 877-797-4743 | NA | Petaluma |
| FreeWire Technologies Inc (HQ) | Provider of mobile distributed power solutions. The company serves the business and industrial sectors. | 415-779-5515 | NA | San Leandro |
| Liberty Test Equipment (HQ) | Provider of refurbished and new test equipment and related accessories. The company deals with sales, lease, and rental services. | 916-625-4228 | 1-10 | Roseville |
| National Vapor Industries Inc (HQ) | Manufacturer of hydrogen generators. The company also offers marketing, installation, and other services. | 925-980-7341 | NA | Livermore |
| Omniyig Inc (HQ) | Manufacturer of microwave devices for the defense industry. The company also offers limiters, drivers, and oscillators. | 408-988-0843 | NA | Santa Clara |
| Top Microsystems Corp (HQ) | Provider of conversion solutions and integration services. The company offers blade, storage, and rack mount servers, medical equipment, and others. | 408-980-9813 | NA | Santa Clara |
| **293 = Power & Distribution Equipment** | | | | |
| Amasco (HQ) | Distributor of products for the telecommunications, commercial, industrial, medical, and military electronics markets. | 408-360-1300 | NA | San Jose |
| Aras Power Technologies (HQ) | Provider of power delivery solutions. The company offers conventional, alternating current solutions, and custom power supply design services. | 408-935-8877 | NA | Milpitas |
| Berkeley Nucleonics Corp (HQ) | Designer and manufacturer of precision test, measurement, and nuclear instrumentation. The company mainly offers generators and analyzers. | 415-453-9955 | NA | San Rafael |
| Bloom Energy Corp (HQ) | Provider of power generation systems. The company focuses on solid oxide fuel cells and mission critical systems. | 408-543-1500 | NA | San Jose |
| Construction Electrical Products (HQ) | Provider of electrical products for the construction sector. The company offers temporary power products, extension cords, and portable lighting. | 925-828-9420 | NA | Livermore |
| Digital Power Corp (HQ) | Designer and manufacturer of switching power supplies. The company serves the industrial, military, and medical markets. | 510-657-2635 | NA | Fremont |
| EnerVault (HQ) | Designer and manufacturer of megawatt-hour scale energy storage systems based on iron-chromium redox flow battery technology. | 408-934-6840 | NA | Sunnyvale |
| Eta-Usa (HQ) | Provider of power supplies and manufacturer of battery chargers. The company serves the communication, gaming, and computing industries. | 408-778-2793 | NA | Morgan Hill |
| International Power Technology Inc (HQ) | Provider of operation and maintenance services for power plants. The company also focuses on engineering and field service. | 408-246-9040 | NA | San Jose |
| Kikusui America Inc (HQ) | Provider of electronic measuring instruments and power supplies. The company's products include electronic loads and power supply controllers. | 408-980-9433 | NA | Santa Clara |
| Knurr Usa (BR) | Provider of custom enclosures, mobile equipment carriers and carts, outdoor cabinets, control room consoles, and technical furniture. | 510-353-0177 | NA | Milpitas |
| Martin Sprocket & Gear Inc (BR) | Manufacturer of industrial hand tools, conveyor pulleys, and other products. The company offers power transmission and material handling products. | 916-441-7172 | 11-50 | Sacramento |
| Mean Well Usa Inc (HQ) | Manufacturer of switching power supplies such as AC to DC converters, DC to DC converters, DC to AC inverters, and battery chargers. | 510-683-8886 | NA | Fremont |
| Moog Animatics (BR) | Provider of motion control devices. The company offers actuators, cables, power supplies, and peripherals. | 650-960-4215 | NA | Mountain View |
| NPI Solutions Inc (HQ) | Provider of design, engineering, and custom manufacturing solutions. The company offers on-site engineering services. | 408-944-9178 | NA | Morgan Hill |
| Polarity Inc (HQ) | Designer and manufacturer of power products for commercial and government entities. The company also offers supply solutions. | 916-635-3050 | 11-50 | Rancho Cordova |
| Power Standards Lab (HQ) | Manufacturer of precision electronic power instruments. The company is involved in testing and calibration services. | 510-522-4400 | NA | Alameda |
| Powertronix Corp (HQ) | Provider of in-house engineering and related services. The company offers services to the industrial sector. | 650-345-6800 | NA | Foster City |
| Quality Transformer & Electronics (HQ) | Manufacturer and seller of transformers. The company also specializes in power supplies and other components. | 408-263-8444 | NA | Milpitas |
| Safeco Electric Supply Inc (HQ) | Distributor of electrical and lighting products. The company offers wires, cables, cords, fasteners, switch boxes, and accessories. | 415-206-0368 | NA | San Francisco |
| Solutions Cubed Llc (HQ) | Provider of engineering solutions. The company is involved in early stage electronic prototyping to full production runs. | 530-891-8045 | 1-10 | Chico |
| Sparkle Power Inc (HQ) | Manufacturer of switching power supply devices. The company serves the PC, industrial PC, and telecommunication industries. | 408-519-8888 | NA | Fremont |

| COMPANY NAME | PRODUCT / SERVICE | PHONE | EMP | CITY |
|---|---|---|---|---|
| Steven Engineering Inc (HQ) | Distributor of industrial controls and components. The company also provides contract manufacturing services. | 800-258-9200 | NA | S San Francisco |
| Sunverge Energy Inc (HQ) | Provider of power and energy services. The company focuses on solar power and combines batteries and power electronics. | 209-931-5677 | 1-10 | Stockton |
| Syrma Technology (BR) | Provider of entrepreneurial manufacturing services. The company's products include magnetics, memory, and RFID. | 408-404-0500 | NA | San Jose |
| Tenergy Corp (HQ) | Designer and manufacturer of batteries and chargers. The company serves medical, consumer electronics, data management, military, and other sectors. | 510-687-0388 | NA | Fremont |
| Top Microsystems Corp (HQ) | Provider of conversion solutions and integration services. The company offers blade, storage, and rack mount servers, medical equipment, and others. | 408-980-9813 | NA | Santa Clara |
| Total Environmental & Power Systems Inc (HQ) | Provider of HVAC, electrical, and telecommunication services. The company's service areas include generators, radio frequency, and fabrication. | 925-681-2238 | NA | Concord |
| Varentec Inc (HQ) | Provider of grid control and monitoring solutions. The company also offers asset management and outage detection services. | 408-433-9900 | NA | Santa Clara |
| Versatile Power (HQ) | Designer and manufacturer of electronic subsystems for manufacturers. The company focuses on application of radio frequency, ultrasonics, and lasers. | 408-341-4600 | NA | Campbell |
| Voltage Multipliers Inc (HQ) | Manufacturer of voltage multipliers, high voltage diodes, rectifiers, opto-couplers, and power supplies. | 559-651-1402 | 1-10 | Visalia |
| Xantrex Technology Inc (BR) | Manufacturer of automotive batteries. The company offers power products for trucks, cars, and recreational vehicles. | 408-987-6030 | NA | Livermore |

## 295 = Switchgears and Switchboard Apparatus

| COMPANY NAME | PRODUCT / SERVICE | PHONE | EMP | CITY |
|---|---|---|---|---|
| Arcus Technology Inc (HQ) | Provider of motor controllers, stepper motors, and related accessories such as cables, encoders, and gearboxes. | 925-373-8800 | NA | Livermore |
| Digital Loggers Inc (HQ) | Manufacturer of recording systems and power switches. The company offers call center recorders, radio logging systems, and recording accessories. | 408-330-5599 | NA | Santa Clara |
| KG Technologies Inc (HQ) | Designer and developer of switching solutions. The company's applications include welding, brazing, and riveting. | 888-513-1874 | NA | Rohnert Park |
| Knurr Usa (BR) | Provider of custom enclosures, mobile equipment carriers and carts, outdoor cabinets, control room consoles, and technical furniture. | 510-353-0177 | NA | Milpitas |
| Martin Sprocket & Gear Inc (BR) | Manufacturer of industrial hand tools, conveyor pulleys, and other products. The company offers power transmission and material handling products. | 916-441-7172 | 11-50 | Sacramento |
| Methode Electronics (BR) | Manufacturer of power management electronic products. The company is engaged in design, engineering, and technical support services. | 408-453-9500 | NA | San Jose |
| Norden Millimeter Inc (HQ) | Developer and manufacturer of amplifier products. The company specializes in millimeter wave amplifier products. | 530-642-9123 | 1-10 | Placerville |
| Praesum Communications Inc (HQ) | Provider of switching communication products. The company offers IP cores, boards, and system level products. | 707-338-0946 | NA | Santa Rosa |
| Safeco Electric Supply Inc (HQ) | Distributor of electrical and lighting products. The company offers wires, cables, cords, fasteners, switch boxes, and accessories. | 415-206-0368 | NA | San Francisco |
| Sparkle Power Inc (HQ) | Manufacturer of switching power supply devices. The company serves the PC, industrial PC, and telecommunication industries. | 408-519-8888 | NA | Fremont |
| Trayer Engineering Corp (HQ) | Manufacturer of electronic distribution switchgears. The company's services include design, maintenance, and installation. | 415-285-7770 | NA | San Francisco |

## 296 = Transformers

| COMPANY NAME | PRODUCT / SERVICE | PHONE | EMP | CITY |
|---|---|---|---|---|
| Delta Star Inc (BR) | Manufacturer of devices for the electrical sector. The company offers devices for the generation, transmission, and distribution of electrical energy. | 800-892-8673 | NA | San Carlos |
| Powertronix Corp (HQ) | Provider of in-house engineering and related services. The company offers services to the industrial sector. | 650-345-6800 | NA | Foster City |
| Quality Transformer & Electronics (HQ) | Manufacturer and seller of transformers. The company also specializes in power supplies and other components. | 408-263-8444 | NA | Milpitas |
| Stangenes Industries Inc (HQ) | Manufacturer of isolation transformers, current monitors, charging inductors, and magnetic components. | 650-493-0814 | NA | Palo Alto |
| Steven Engineering Inc (HQ) | Distributor of industrial controls and components. The company also provides contract manufacturing services. | 800-258-9200 | NA | S San Francisco |
| West Coast Magnetics (HQ) | Provider of electrical products. The company specializes in inductor products, transformers, chokes, and planar magnetic products. | 800-628-1123 | 1-10 | Stockton |

## 297 = Turbines, Turbine Generator Sets

| COMPANY NAME | PRODUCT / SERVICE | PHONE | EMP | CITY |
|---|---|---|---|---|
| Halus Power Systems (HQ) | Manufacturer of renewable energy products specializing in wind turbines and controls. The company offers design and remanufacturing services. | 510-278-2212 | NA | San Leandro |
| International Power Technology Inc (HQ) | Provider of operation and maintenance services for power plants. The company also focuses on engineering and field service. | 408-246-9040 | NA | San Jose |

## 298 = Wire & Wiring devices

| COMPANY NAME | PRODUCT / SERVICE | PHONE | EMP | CITY |
|---|---|---|---|---|
| All Systems Broadband (HQ) | Provider of intelligent connectivity and engineering solutions and a supplier of fiber connectivity products. | 877-272-4984 | NA | Livermore |
| Bentek Corp (HQ) | Provider of manufacturing and engineering services. The company's offerings include power distribution system design and mechanical manufacturing. | 408-954-9600 | NA | San Jose |
| Compatible Cable Inc (HQ) | Manufacturer of custom cable assemblies and off-the shelf cables. The company offers services to the automotive, broadcast, and electronics industries. | 888-415-1115 | NA | Concord |
| Custom Coils Inc (HQ) | Manufacturer of coils, coil assemblies, and solenoids. The company also offers other electro-magnetic devices. | 707-752-8633 | NA | Benicia |
| Dc Electronics (HQ) | Manufacturer of electronic cable assemblies. The company also offers distribution and other services. | 408-947-4500 | NA | San Jose |
| Hbr Industries (HQ) | Provider of electronics manufacturing services. The company offers coil solutions and services for the medical, military, and semiconductor industry. | 408-988-0800 | NA | San Jose |
| Jetronics Co (HQ) | Manufacturer of custom cable assemblies and harnesses, magnetics assemblies, sub-assembly components, front and rear panels, and chassis assemblies. | 707-544-2436 | NA | Santa Rosa |
| Leoco USA Corp (BR) | Manufacturer of interconnects. The company offers wire to board, wire to wire, board to board, and card and telecom connectors. | 510-429-3700 | NA | Fremont |
| Lorom West (HQ) | Manufacturer of PCB assemblies, turnkey OEM/ODM products and custom cable and wire harnesses. The company offers industry solutions. | 510-249-9000 | NA | Fremont |
| Newnex Technology Corp (HQ) | Developer of connecting cables, controllers, and repeaters. The company's services include design, installation, and technical support. | 408-986-9988 | NA | Santa Clara |
| NPI Solutions Inc (HQ) | Provider of design, engineering, and custom manufacturing solutions. The company offers on-site engineering services. | 408-944-9178 | NA | Morgan Hill |
| Precision Contacts Inc (HQ) | Provider of replacement contacts for handler manufacturer. The company's products include sockets, contacts, elements, and custom products. | 916-939-4147 | 1-10 | El Dorado Hills |
| The Okonite Co (BR) | Manufacturer of electrical wire insulators. The company offers high and low voltage, instrumentation, and special purpose cables. | 925-830-0801 | NA | San Ramon |
| Ulbrich Stainless Steels and Special Metals Inc (BR) | The company manufactures and sells specialty strip in stainless steel, and serves the industrial sector. | 559-456-2310 | 11-50 | Fresno |
| Vulcan Inc (HQ) | Focuses on the manufacture and fabrication of aluminum coiled sheets, aluminum sign blanks, and finished traffic control signs. | 510-786-9181 | NA | Hayward |

## 299 = Research, Development & Testing

| | | | | |
|---|---|---|---|---|
| Calchemist (HQ) | Provider of contract research services. The company specializes in chemical, material science and laboratory equipment testing. | 650-551-1495 | NA | San Francisco |

## 300 = Commercial Physical & Biological Research

| | | | | |
|---|---|---|---|---|
| Apollomics Inc (HQ) | Developer of oncology therapeutics. The company focusses on discovering therapeutics for the immune system and molecular pathways to treat cancer. | 650-209-4055 | NA | Foster City |
| Biomedecon Llc (HQ) | Provider of health economics and outcomes research. The company caters to pharmaceutical and medical industries. | 650-563-9475 | NA | Moss Beach |
| Calchemist (HQ) | Provider of contract research services. The company specializes in chemical, material science and laboratory equipment testing. | 650-551-1495 | NA | San Francisco |
| Cell Marque Corp (HQ) | Producer of primary antibodies, buffers and pretreatment, ancillary reagents, and lab equipment for pathology laboratories and research facilities. | 916-746-8900 | 1-10 | Rocklin |
| Celltheon (HQ) | Developer of customized solutions for preclinical studies of the biotechnology and pharmaceutical industries. | 510-306-2355 | NA | Union City |
| Fibrogen Inc (HQ) | Developer of therapeutic products. The company is engaged in commercialization and clinical trial programs. | 415-978-1200 | NA | San Francisco |
| Gilead Palo Alto Inc (BR) | Provider of biopharmaceutical research services. The company discovers and develops medicines to treat life-threatening diseases. | 510-739-8400 | NA | Fremont |
| Hilti Inc (BR) | Developer and manufacturer of construction equipment. The company's services include trainings, engineering, administration, and tools. | 800-879-8000 | NA | San Francisco |
| Human Pheromone Sciences Inc (HQ) | Producer of natural attraction products and is engaged in research in the field of human pheromones in all areas of application. | 408-938-3030 | NA | San Jose |
| Ibm Research - Almaden (BR) | Provider of computer technology services. The company engages in cloud, mobility, and security services. | 408-927-1080 | NA | San Jose |
| InSilixa Inc (HQ) | Manufacturer of CMOS biosensor devices used to identify multiple targets including nucleic acids (DNA or RNA), peptides, or metabolites. | 408-809-3000 | NA | Sunnyvale |
| Marin Biologic Laboratories Inc (HQ) | Provider of client research services. The company serves the pharmaceutical, biotechnology, diagnostic, agricultural, and legal markets. | 415-883-8000 | NA | Novato |
| MedStars Inc (HQ) | Provider of medical devices, healthcare information systems, health related consumer products, and biotechnology for medical and biotech companies. | 650-917-9254 | NA | Los Altos Hills |
| Murigenics (HQ) | Provider of preclinical in-vivo and in-vitro contract drug discovery. The company is also focused on development services. | 707-561-8900 | NA | Vallejo |

| COMPANY NAME | PRODUCT / SERVICE | PHONE | EMP | CITY |
|---|---|---|---|---|
| Ngm Biopharmaceuticals Inc (HQ) | Developer of novel and disease-altering biologics such as protein, peptide, and antibody drug for cancer, cardio-metabolic, and hepatic diseases. | 650-243-5555 | NA | S San Francisco |
| Pro-Form Laboratories (HQ) | Developer and producer of nutritional powders. The company also specializes in contract manufacturing services. | 707-752-9010 | NA | Orinda |
| ProteinSimple (HQ) | Developer of proprietary systems, immunoassay system and consumables for protein analysis and purity of protein-based therapeutics. | 408-510-5500 | NA | San Jose |
| Re Cyte Therapeutics Inc (HQ) | Provider of regenerative medicine. The company focuses on repair of vascular disorders in both age related diseases and injuries. | 510-521-3390 | NA | Alameda |
| Strataglass (HQ) | Manufacturer of thin films. The company offers research and development, pilot production, and outsourced fabrication services. | 650-988-1700 | NA | Mountain View |

## 301 = Consulting/Contracting Services

| COMPANY NAME | PRODUCT / SERVICE | PHONE | EMP | CITY |
|---|---|---|---|---|
| Advanced Integrated Solutions Inc (BR) | Provider of enterprise systems management, call center, and information technology infrastructure library based service management solutions. | 714-572-5600 | 11-50 | El Dorado Hills |
| Bsk Associates (BR) | Provider of geotechnical and environmental testing services. The company also offers materials testing services. | 916-853-9293 | 11-50 | Rancho Cordova |
| Calchemist (HQ) | Provider of contract research services. The company specializes in chemical, material science and laboratory equipment testing. | 650-551-1495 | NA | San Francisco |
| Capital Engineering Consultants Inc (HQ) | Provider of mechanical engineering, sustainable design and green engineering, building commissioning, energy modeling, and other related services. | 916-851-3500 | 11-50 | Rancho Cordova |
| Dynaweb Inc (HQ) | Manufacturer and marketer of web handling and tension control systems. The company's product finds use in packaging, printing, and textile needs. | 925-373-9013 | 1-10 | Sonora |
| Prima Environmental Inc (HQ) | Provider of laboratory testing services. The company specializes in treatability testing, technology evaluation, and scientific consulting services. | 916-939-7300 | 1-10 | El Dorado Hills |
| Quovera (HQ) | Provider of business consulting and technology integration services. The company serves the high-tech and semiconductor industries. | 650-823-0903 | NA | Palo Alto |
| Ray Carlson & Associates Inc (HQ) | Provider of consulting, research, surveying, mapping, video branding, and related services. The company also offers data management products. | 707-528-7649 | NA | Santa Rosa |
| Riga Analytical Lab Inc (HQ) | Provider of laboratory services specializing in electrical failure analysis, circuit extraction, latch up evaluation, and parallel and angel lapping. | 408-496-6944 | NA | Santa Clara |
| Seg Inc (HQ) | Provider of consulting, design, engineering, project management, commissioning, and validation services. | 408-260-8008 | NA | Santa Clara |

## 302 = Dental Laboratories

| COMPANY NAME | PRODUCT / SERVICE | PHONE | EMP | CITY |
|---|---|---|---|---|
| Apollomics Inc (HQ) | Developer of oncology therapeutics. The company focusses on discovering therapeutics for the immune system and molecular pathways to treat cancer. | 650-209-4055 | NA | Foster City |
| Castagnolo Dental Laboratory Inc (HQ) | Provider of custom packed columns, empty synthesis columns, empty synthesis plates, and related supports. | 408-446-1466 | NA | Cupertino |

## 303 = Medical Laboratories

| COMPANY NAME | PRODUCT / SERVICE | PHONE | EMP | CITY |
|---|---|---|---|---|
| Abaxis Inc (HQ) | Provider of on-site patient testing, leading-edge point-of-care technologies for veterinary practices and laboratory services for medical professionals. | 510-675-6500 | NA | Union City |
| AEMTEK Laboratories (HQ) | Provider of testing, research, training and consulting services and sampling products for the food, environmental and pharmaceutical industries. | 510-979-1979 | NA | Fremont |
| Analytical Sciences Llc (HQ) | Provider of laboratory services. The company specializes in environmental testing and analytical chemistry. | 707-769-3128 | NA | Petaluma |
| Associated Pathology Medical Group Inc (HQ) | Provider of medical care services. The company focuses on women's health, dermatopathology, family practice, and urology areas. | 408-399-5050 | NA | Los Gatos |
| BD Biosciences (BR) | Manufacturer of medical devices. The company provides a broad range of medical supplies, devices, laboratory equipment and diagnostic products. | 877-232-8995 | NA | San Jose |
| Borsting Laboratories Inc (HQ) | Provider of histology services. The company specialize in processing skin biopsies and expert second-opinion dermatopathological interpretation. | 415-883-1337 | NA | Novato |
| California Clinical Laboratory Association (HQ) | Provider of an Association for small and large laboratories in California. The company files suits to prevent medicare from denying coverage for lab tests. | 916-446-2646 | 1-10 | Sacramento |
| Cellmax Life (HQ) | Provider of personalized multi-biomarker technologies for non-invasive saliva and blood tests. The company is also involved in drug discovery. | 650-564-3905 | NA | Sunnyvale |
| Climax Laboratories Inc (HQ) | Provider of contract research services. The company offers bioanalytical and analytical testing services. | 408-298-8630 | NA | San Jose |
| CohBar Inc (HQ) | Developer of treatments for metabolic dysfunction that includes NASH, obesity, cancer, neurodegenerative diseases, and more. | 650-446-7888 | NA | Menlo Park |
| Concentric Analgesics Inc (HQ) | Developer of therapeutic solutions. The company focusses on discovery and development of novel, non opioid therapeutics for treating acute and chronic pain. | 415-484-7921 | NA | San Francisco |

| COMPANY NAME | PRODUCT / SERVICE | PHONE | EMP | CITY |
|---|---|---|---|---|
| Diagnostic Pathology Medical Group Inc (HQ) | Specializes in identifying enzymes extracted from extremophiles for molecular biology, diagnostics, and industrial applications. | 916-446-0424 | 1-10 | Sacramento |
| Domino Data Lab Inc (HQ) | Provider of premise and cloud-based enterprise data science platform for analysis applications. The company serves the business sector. | 415-570-2425 | NA | San Francisco |
| Emsl Analytical Inc (BR) | Provider of laboratory analytical testing services. The company specializes in a wide range of environmental, material and forensic testing. | 510-895-3675 | NA | San Leandro |
| Frontier Analytical Laboratory (HQ) | Provider of testing services for analysis of polychlorinated dibenzo dioxins and furans polychlorinated biphenyls and polyaromatic hydrocarbons. | 916-934-0900 | 1-10 | El Dorado Hills |
| Golden Pacific Laboratories LLC (HQ) | Provider of state of the art independent contract research services for agricultural, residential and occupational exposure assessments. | 559-275-9091 | 1-10 | Fresno |
| Hand Biomechanics Lab Inc (HQ) | Provider of Biomechanics treatment devices. The company offers products like Agee Turnkey FCS, WristJack, and Digit Widget. | 916-923-5073 | 1-10 | Sacramento |
| Machaon Diagnostics Inc (HQ) | Provider of laboratory services in diagnosis, treatment and monitoring of hemostatic and thrombotic conditions. | 510-839-5600 | NA | Oakland |
| Quest Diagnostics Inc (BR) | Provider of diagnostic laboratory testing services. The company offers a wide range of test menu for diagnosing medical conditions. | 916-927-9900 | 11-50 | Sacramento |
| Quest Diagnostics Inc (BR) | Provider of diagnostic laboratory testing services. The company offers a wide range of test menu for diagnosing medical conditions. | 510-357-5438 | NA | San Leandro |
| Satori Labs Inc (HQ) | Provider of medical based software services. The company's offerings include FusionForm Desktop and FusionForm Mobile. | 831-457-9100 | 1-10 | Scotts Valley |
| Spectra Laboratories (HQ) | Provider of testing services for a wide range of specialties. The company focuses on chemistry, serology, anemia testing, hematology, and others. | 800-433-3773 | NA | Milpitas |
| Stemexpress (HQ) | Provider of immunophenotyping, DNA quantitation and viability, tissue transplant verification, and related services. | 530-626-7000 | 1-10 | Placerville |
| Transgenomic Inc (BR) | Provider of patient testing and biomarker identification services. The company specializes in high performance products. | 408-432-3230 | NA | San Jose |
| Ultrasound Laboratories Inc (HQ) | Provider of non-invasive ultrasound imaging services. The company focuses on services such as health screening, carotid artery, and kidney screening. | 877-650-0650 | NA | Mountain View |

## 4 = MiscellaneousTechnology-Related Engineering Services

| COMPANY NAME | PRODUCT / SERVICE | PHONE | EMP | CITY |
|---|---|---|---|---|
| 3dtl Inc (HQ) | Provider of authentication technology services. The company develops 3D displays for medical, industrial, and military applications. | 408-541-8550 | NA | Sunnyvale |
| Abbomax Inc (HQ) | Provider of antibody, peptide, and assay products and services. The company offers antibody production, fragmentation, assay development, and other services. | 408-573-1898 | NA | San Jose |
| Acies Engineering (HQ) | Provider of engineering and design development solutions. The company caters to retail, restaurant, residential and commercial sectors. | 408-522-5255 | NA | Santa Clara |
| Acon Builders Construction Inc (HQ) | Provider of scheduling, planning, change management, status reporting, zoning, and code compliance services. | 408-980-1388 | NA | Hayward |
| Actinix (HQ) | Developer of ultraviolet light generation, long-coherence-length pulsed fiber laser systems, high energy laser systems and optical tools/methods. | 831-440-9388 | 1-10 | Felton |
| Adesto Technologies Corporation Inc (HQ) | Provider of power memory solutions. The company's portfolio comprises Fusion Serial Flash, DataFlas, and Mavriq serial memory. | 408-400-0578 | NA | Santa Clara |
| Aditazz (HQ) | Designer, manufacturer, and assembler of building components. The company is engaged in operational modeling. | 650-492-7000 | NA | Brisbane |
| Advantec MFS Inc (HQ) | Producer of filtration media and related scientific products. The company focuses on laboratory instruments and filtration products. | 925-479-0625 | NA | Dublin |
| AerospaceComputing Inc (HQ) | Provider of computer technology application services to aerospace sciences. The company also focuses on business development services. | 650-988-0388 | NA | Mountain View |
| Agra Tech Inc (HQ) | Manufacturer of greenhouses and accessories for commercial, horticultural, and agricultural growers. The company offers heating and cooling equipment. | 925-432-3399 | NA | Pittsburg |
| Alliacense (HQ) | Provider of intellectual property solutions. The company's services include broad spectrum, reverse engineering, and product reports. | 408-446-4222 | NA | Cupertino |
| American Micro Detection Systems Inc (HQ) | Provider of water analysis treatments. The company deals with research, development, and monitoring services. | 209-985-1705 | 11-50 | Stockton |
| Anderson Pacific Engineering Construction Inc (HQ) | Provider of constructing and retrofitting pump stations, lift stations, bridges, reservoirs, treatment plants, and seismic retrofit projects. | 408-970-9900 | NA | Santa Clara |
| Anritsu Co (DH) | Provider of test solutions for telecommunication applications. The company also caters to microwave applications. | 408-778-2000 | NA | Morgan Hill |
| Ansari Structural Engineers Inc (HQ) | Provider of structural consulting services. The company focuses on remodeling, due diligence studies, equipment anchorage, and structural peer review. | 415-348-8948 | NA | San Francisco |
| Applied Engineering (HQ) | Provider of structural analysis and seismic evaluation services. The company is involved in specialty engineering and project management. | 408-263-5900 | NA | Milpitas |
| Applied Materials-Engineering (HQ) | Provider of construction materials consulting services. The company focuses on petrographic and laboratory testing services. | 510-420-8190 | NA | Oakland |
| Ares Corp (HQ) | Provider of engineering, risk assessment, project management, and other services and focuses on nuclear, clean technology, space, and defense fields. | 650-401-7100 | NA | Burlingame |

| COMPANY NAME | PRODUCT / SERVICE | PHONE | EMP | CITY |
|---|---|---|---|---|
| Arx Pax Labs Inc (HQ) | Developer of magnetic field architecture technology for structural isolation, recreation and entertainment, industrial automation, and transportation. | 408-335-7630 | NA | Los Gatos |
| Avp Technology Llc (HQ) | Provider of thin film equipment services. The company provides custom designing, remanufacturing, and field services. | 510-683-0157 | NA | Fremont |
| Azbil North America Inc (BR) | Designer, manufacturer, and supplier of medical devices. The company offers automation products, control products, and industrial automation systems. | 408-245-3121 | NA | Santa Clara |
| Baumbach & Piazza Inc (HQ) | Provider of design, engineering, and boundary and topography surveying, and construction staking services. | 209-368-6618 | 1-10 | Lodi |
| Bess Mti Inc (BR) | Provider of subsurface utility engineering services. The company engages in utility locating and structural concrete scanning services. | 408-988-0101 | 11-50 | Santa Clara |
| Bhatia Associates Inc (HQ) | Provider of design and electrical engineering consulting services to the institutional, commercial, residential, and light industrial buildings. | 415-646-0050 | NA | San Francisco |
| Biomedical Forensics (HQ) | Provider of engineering and applied science. The company specializes in mechanism and causation of trauma and impact biomechanics. | 925-376-1240 | NA | Moraga |
| Bkf Engineers (BR) | Provider of civil engineering consulting, and land surveying services. The company serves business organizations. | 925-940-2200 | NA | Walnut Creek |
| Bkf Engineers (BR) | Provider of civil engineering, design, surveying, design, transportation, and entitlement support services. | 408-467-9100 | NA | San Jose |
| Blankinship & Associates Inc (HQ) | Provider of environmental science and engineering services focusing on biological resources, stormwater & nitrogen management, and other needs. | 530-757-0941 | 1-10 | Davis |
| Blymyer Engineers Inc (HQ) | Provider of solar engineering, facility design, and related services. The company serves the food and beverage and glass manufacturing industries. | 510-521-3773 | NA | Alameda |
| Bureau Veritas Laboratories (BR) | Provider of analytical products and services. The company services customers in the energy, environmental, food, and DNA industries. | 650-576-7765 | NA | San Carlos |
| Carroll Engineering Inc (HQ) | Provider of civil engineering and surveying services focusing on boundary and topographic surveys, civil engineering design, and construction support. | 408-261-9800 | NA | San Jose |
| Chs Consulting Group (HQ) | Provider of transportation planning and traffic signal design services. The company also focuses on traffic safety. | 415-392-9688 | NA | San Francisco |
| Cjs Labs (HQ) | Provider of electronic design, consulting, engineering, and test automation programming assistance services. | 415-923-9535 | NA | San Francisco |
| CKC Engineering LLC (HQ) | Provider of custom equipment solutions for clinical, manufacturing, pharmaceutical, medical device, and drug delivery industries. | 415-494-8225 | NA | Oakland |
| CommWorld of San Francisco (HQ) | Provider of telecommunication services such as computer networking, structured cabling, project management and repair. | 650-358-8700 | NA | Fremont |
| Controlco (HQ) | Provider of automation and solutions to address the Internet of Things for commercial buildings, (BIoT). | 855-371-9511 | NA | Pleasant Hill |
| Cornerstone Environmental Group Llc (BR) | Provider of engineering consulting and field services. The company offers services for the solid waste water industry and agricultural clients. | 877-633-5520 | NA | Dublin |
| Diablo Clinical Research Inc (HQ) | Provider of clinical research services specializing in endocrinology, internal medicine, cardiology, and neurology. | 925-930-7267 | NA | Walnut Creek |
| DigiLens Inc (HQ) | Provider of optical design, software development, electrical engineering, and illumination design services. | 408-734-0219 | NA | Sunnyvale |
| Dst Controls (HQ) | Provider of control systems integration, industrial data management, and related enterprise solutions. The company serves the industrial sector. | 800-251-0773 | NA | Benicia |
| Endpoint Clinical inc (HQ) | Designer of response technology platforms to access data through phones, the web, and mobile devices. The company is engaged in engineering services. | 415-229-1600 | NA | San Francisco |
| Ese Consulting Engineers Inc (HQ) | Provider of structural engineering design, seismic analysis and retrofitting, and peer review services. | 707-747-1755 | NA | Benicia |
| Fall Creek Engineering Inc (HQ) | Provider of civil, environmental, and water resources engineering and consulting services. The company engages in site planning and design services. | 831-426-9054 | 1-10 | Santa Cruz |
| Finjan Holdings Inc (HQ) | Specializes in the research and development of transformative technologies for the securing of information. | 650-282-3228 | NA | East Palo Alto |
| Forell/Elsesser Engineers Inc (HQ) | Provider of structural engineering, design build, earthquake engineering, research and development, and seismic design services. | 415-837-0700 | NA | San Francisco |
| Foundation Constructors Inc (HQ) | Provider of pile solutions and shoring systems. The company also offers pile, H-beams, sheets, and concrete pile types. | 925-754-6633 | NA | Oakley |
| Function Engineering (HQ) | Provider of mechanical design and engineering services for product development. The company serves the consumer electronics and robotics industries. | 650-326-8834 | NA | Palo Alto |
| GDR Engineering Inc (HQ) | Provider of land development and infrastructure engineering services. The company also focuses on land planning and surveying. | 209-538-3360 | 1-10 | Ceres |
| Glenmount Global Solutions (HQ) | Provider of industrial equipment control, energy management, and other systems. The company serves automotive, food, chemical, and other sectors. | 707-258-8400 | NA | Napa |

| COMPANY NAME | PRODUCT / SERVICE | PHONE | EMP | CITY |
|---|---|---|---|---|
| Hammett & Edison Inc (HQ) | Provider of engineering and related services to the wireless telecommunications and broadcasting industries. | 707-996-5200 | NA | Sonoma |
| Heco Pacific Manufacturing Inc (HQ) | Manufacturer and seller of industrial cranes and overhead cranes. The company offers custom engineering, maintenance, testing, and other services. | 510-487-1155 | NA | Union City |
| Hesco (HQ) | Provider of portable x-ray imaging services. The company offer services for power plants, bridges, dams, refineries, and more. | 510-568-1380 | NA | San Leandro |
| Honda Research Institute Usa Inc (HQ) | Manufacturer of engines. The company focuses on material science research, computer science research, and academic outreach activities. | 650-314-0400 | NA | Mountain View |
| Ibm Research - Almaden (BR) | Provider of computer technology services. The company engages in cloud, mobility, and security services. | 408-927-1080 | NA | San Jose |
| Ic Engineering Inc (HQ) | Provider of design and engineering services to industrial & commercial clients. The company serves food, oil, parts manufacturing, and other sectors. | 925-415-0074 | NA | San Ramon |
| Inspection Services Inc (HQ) | Provider of structural steel and welding, wood framing, anchor and dowel installation, roofing, and waterproofing services. | 510-900-2100 | NA | Berkeley |
| Integrated Science Solutions Inc (HQ) | Provider of professional services to federal and state clients. The company offers earth and environmental science and engineering services. | 925-979-1535 | NA | Walnut Creek |
| JON BRODY Structural Engineers (HQ) | Provider of structural engineering services. The company focuses on construction documentation, reports and studies, and seismic retrofitting. | 415-296-9494 | NA | San Francisco |
| Kahler Engineering Inc (HQ) | Designer of instrumentation and power control systems. The company provides engineering services to power plant owners, operators, and constructors. | 415-453-8836 | NA | San Anselmo |
| KEMPF Inc (HQ) | Provider of driving solutions. The company offers digital hand controls and other handicap driving aids for paraplegic drivers. | 408-773-0219 | NA | Sunnyvale |
| Lee & Ro Inc (BR) | Provider of environmental and infrastructure engineering solutions. The company is involved in design-build and construction management. | 925-937-4050 | NA | Walnut Creek |
| Makel Engineering Inc (HQ) | Developer and provider of products and services for aviation, space, military, and commercial applications. | 530-895-2770 | 1-10 | Chico |
| Materials Testing Inc (HQ) | Provider of geotechnical engineering and materials testing services. The company offers geotechnical, environment, special inspection, and material testing services. | 530-222-1116 | 11-50 | Redding |
| Materion Corporation (BR) | Provider of material solutions. The company deals with fabrication, analysis, research and development, and testing services. | 510-623-1500 | NA | Fremont |
| Matriscope (BR) | Provider of geotechnical and environmental engineering services. The company also provides materials testing and special inspection services. | 916-375-6700 | 11-50 | Sacramento |
| Maxeler Technologies Inc (HQ) | Developer of computing solutions. The company offers services to the oil and gas, analytical, and financial sectors. | 650-938-8818 | NA | Mountain View |
| Meridian Surveying Engineering Inc (HQ) | Provider or residential, commercial, and municipal surveys. The company also deals with claims litigation services. | 415-440-4131 | NA | San Francisco |
| Mge Engineering Inc (HQ) | Provider of civil/structural engineering and construction management services. The company focuses on site development and construction inspection. | 916-421-1000 | 11-50 | Sacramento |
| MiNDERA Corp (HQ) | Provider of technology to extract skin biomarkers enabling non-invasive molecular testing for skin cancer and other skin diseases. | 650-491-9643 | NA | S San Francisco |
| Nanometrics Inc (HQ) | Provider of process control metrology and inspection systems for data storage devices and solar photovoltaic applications. | 408-545-6000 | NA | Milpitas |
| Neil O Anderson & Associates Inc (HQ) | Provider of engineering services including geotechnical engineering, foundation, and structural engineering services. | 209-367-3701 | 11-50 | Lodi |
| New Faze Development Inc (HQ) | Provider of construction and management development services. The company also offers project management and property management services. | 916-929-6402 | 1-10 | Sacramento |
| Ngm Biopharmaceuticals Inc (HQ) | Developer of novel and disease-altering biologics such as protein, peptide, and antibody drug for cancer, cardio-metabolic, and hepatic diseases. | 650-243-5555 | NA | S San Francisco |
| Nikon Precision Inc (HQ) | Manufacturer of optical lenses and precision equipment. The company is also the supplier of step-and-repeat and step-and-scan lithography systems. | 650-508-4674 | NA | Belmont |
| Nute Engineering (HQ) | Developer of technologies for the water, wastewater treatment, and environmental protection projects. | 415-453-4480 | NA | San Rafael |
| NV5 (BR) | Provider of technical consulting and certification services. The company serves the infrastructure, construction, and real estate markets. | 916-641-9100 | 11-50 | Sacramento |
| OCAMPO-ESTA Corp (HQ) | Provider of engineering, design, construction management, instrumentation and controls, and project management services. | 707-643-8072 | NA | Vallejo |
| Opac Consulting Engineers Inc (HQ) | Provider of bridge and structural engineering services. The company's services are design, evaluation, and construction engineering. | 415-989-4551 | NA | San Francisco |
| Oscar Larson & Associates (HQ) | Provider of environmental planning, permitting, and related services and it specializes in residential and commercial projects. | 707-445-2043 | 11-50 | Eureka |
| Otsuka America Inc (HQ) | Developer of pharmaceutical products for the treatment of central nervous system, ophthalmology, cardiovascular, and skin conditions. | 415-986-5300 | NA | San Francisco |

| COMPANY NAME | PRODUCT / SERVICE | PHONE | EMP | CITY |
|---|---|---|---|---|
| Paradigm Strucural Engineers (HQ) | Provider of structural engineering and consulting services. The company offers schematic design, planning, and construction documentation services. | 415-362-8944 | NA | San Francisco |
| PAX Scientific Inc (HQ) | Provider of engineering research and product design services. The company is also involved in the design of industrial equipment. | 415-256-9900 | NA | San Rafael |
| Pgh Wong Engineering Inc (HQ) | Provider of engineering, program and construction management, and technology services for transit projects. | 415-566-0800 | NA | San Francisco |
| Presto Engineering Inc (HQ) | Provider of semiconductor test and analysis solutions. The company also offers engineering services to the semiconductor market. | 408-372-9500 | NA | San Jose |
| Procept Biorobotics (HQ) | Provider of healthcare services. The company primarily focuses on personalized image-guided waterjet tissue resection services. | 650-232-7200 | NA | Redwood City |
| Proto Services Inc (HQ) | Provider of process verification, yield analysis, testing design, program management, and functional debugging services. | 408-719-9088 | NA | San Jose |
| QT Ultrasound LLC (HQ) | Developer of ultrasound devices. The company is involved in software development and clinical testing services. | 415-842-7250 | NA | Novato |
| Quest Diagnostics Inc (BR) | Provider of diagnostic laboratory testing services. The company offers a wide range of test menu for diagnosing medical conditions. | 510-357-5438 | NA | San Leandro |
| Quovera (HQ) | Provider of business consulting and technology integration services. The company serves the high-tech and semiconductor industries. | 650-823-0903 | NA | Palo Alto |
| R&A Engineering Solutions Inc (HQ) | Provider of engineering consulting services. The company offers design, analysis, verification, and planning of HVAC, and plumbing system services. | 916-920-5965 | 11-50 | Sacramento |
| Ray Carlson & Associates Inc (HQ) | Provider of consulting, research, surveying, mapping, video branding, and related services. The company also offers data management products. | 707-528-7649 | NA | Santa Rosa |
| Rcb Elevator Consulting Llc (HQ) | Provider of elevator design and structural engineering services to building owners, architects, and elevator companies and offers field surveys. | 415-350-0402 | NA | San Francisco |
| Redline Solutions Inc (HQ) | Provider of produce traceability and bar code solutions, and warehouse and inventory management systems. | 408-562-1700 | NA | Santa Clara |
| Remote Sensing Systems (HQ) | Processor of microwave data. The company collects the data with the help of special satellite microwave sensors. | 707-545-2904 | NA | Santa Rosa |
| Savari Inc (HQ) | Provider of communications technology solutions. The company focuses on connecting cars to traffic lights, pedestrians, and smartphones. | 408-833-6369 | NA | Santa Clara |
| Sc Solutions Inc (HQ) | Provider of control design and implementation services. The company also focuses on structural design and software development. | 408-617-4520 | NA | Sunnyvale |
| Sebastian (HQ) | Provider of structured cabling and electrical contracting services. The company offers services to the residential and commercial sectors. | 559-432-5800 | 11-50 | Fresno |
| Seg Inc (HQ) | Provider of consulting, design, engineering, project management, commissioning, and validation services. | 408-260-8008 | NA | Santa Clara |
| Semifab (HQ) | Supplier of process environment control systems for precise temperature, humidity, air flow, and airborne particulate management. | 408-414-5928 | NA | San Jose |
| Sensor Concepts Inc (HQ) | Developer of portable and integrated measurement systems. The company offers engineering, field measurement and software development services. | 925-443-9001 | NA | Livermore |
| Shen Milsom Wilke Llc (BR) | Provider of technology design and consulting solutions such as acoustics, medical equipment planning, audiovisual, and building security. | 415-391-7610 | NA | San Francisco |
| Sierra Engineering Company Inc (HQ) | Manufacturer of recreational vehicles. The company offers rebuilding, repair, and maintainance services. | 559-855-2659 | 1-10 | Tollhouse |
| Sj Amoroso Construction (HQ) | Provider of construction contracting services. The company focuses on pre-construction consulting, design-build contracting and management. | 650-654-1900 | NA | Redwood City |
| Solar Design & Drafting (HQ) | Designer of solar devices. The company's services include design considerations, flat rate permit packages, and other services. | 415-305-3982 | NA | Petaluma |
| SOMA Environmental Engineering Inc (HQ) | Provider of environmental engineering solutions. The company offers services for remediation and underground storage tanks. | 925-734-6400 | NA | Pleasanton |
| Stantec Inc (BR) | Provider of civil construction services. The company also offers commercial program development and infrastructure management services. | 916-773-8100 | 11-50 | Rocklin |
| Summit Engineering Inc (HQ) | Provider of facility planning, due diligence, design, project management, and other services to wineries, resorts, food, education, and other sectors. | 707-527-0775 | NA | Santa Rosa |
| Tennebaum-Manheim Engineers Inc (HQ) | Developer of engineering services. The company's projects include residential housing, commercial properties, and historical buildings. | 415-772-9891 | NA | San Francisco |
| Turley & Associates Mechanical Engineering Group I (HQ) | Provider of engineering services to health care, education, industrial, public, and retail facilities. | 916-325-1065 | 1-10 | Sacramento |
| Tuv Sud America Inc (BR) | Provider of services for testing, certification, and engineering audits. The company is focused on medical devices and e-mobility. | 510-257-7823 | NA | Fremont |
| Ty Lin International Group (HQ) | Provider of engineering services such as construction management, inspection, design and planning, and surveying. | 415-291-3700 | NA | San Francisco |
| Vantage Data Center Services & Solutions (HQ) | Provider of transformers, switches, generators, chillers, switch gears and security, and communication products. | 855-878-2682 | NA | Santa Clara |

| COMPANY NAME | PRODUCT / SERVICE | PHONE | EMP | CITY |
|---|---|---|---|---|
| Velos LLC (HQ) | Provider of clinical research solutions. The company offers services to hospitals, academic medical centers, and also cancer centers. | 510-739-4010 | NA | Fremont |
| VerTech Engineering Inc (HQ) | Provider of structural engineering services, geotechnical services, and civil engineering services for architects, builders, and developers. | 530-899-8716 | 11-50 | Chico |
| Vlsi Research Inc (HQ) | Provider of chip market research, consultation, semiconductor analysis, and data spreadsheets and reports. | 408-453-8844 | NA | San Jose |
| Walters & Wolf (BR) | Provider of cladding services. The company specializes in design, engineering, fabrication, and delivery and installation. | 510-490-1115 | NA | Fremont |
| Willdan Energy Solutions (BR) | Provider of energy efficiency, water conservation, and renewable energy services. The company serves education, utility, labs, and other sectors. | 916-585-7327 | 11-50 | Elk Grove |
| WNI Global Inc (HQ) | Provider of wireless communications solutions for backhaul infrastructure and ethernet network equipment for voice, data, and video applications. | 408-307-2410 | NA | San Jose |
| Wong Electric Inc (HQ) | Provider of electrical contracting services. The company is involved in industrial and multi-family projects. | 650-813-9999 | NA | Palo Alto |
| X-Z LAB Inc (HQ) | Provider of digital radiation detection services. The company engages in detecting, measuring, and monitoring radiation activities. | 925-355-5199 | NA | San Ramon |
| Zip-Bit Inc (HQ) | Provider of engineering services. The company specializes in 3D printing, 3D modeling, and 3D scanning. | 408-839-4252 | NA | Saratoga |

## 305 = Noncommercial Research Organizations

| COMPANY NAME | PRODUCT / SERVICE | PHONE | EMP | CITY |
|---|---|---|---|---|
| Calchemist (HQ) | Provider of contract research services. The company specializes in chemical, material science and laboratory equipment testing. | 650-551-1495 | NA | San Francisco |
| Crown Bioscience Inc (HQ) | Specializes in drug discovery, clinical trials, and cardiovascular and metabolic disease research programs. | 855-827-6968 | NA | Santa Clara |
| Ets Laboratories (HQ) | Specializes in analytical tools. The company focuses on export analysis, harvest, and fuel ethanol services. | 707-963-4806 | NA | St. Helena |
| Sanbio Inc (HQ) | Developer of regenerative therapies for neurological disorders. The company offers services to the healthcare sector.. | 650-625-8965 | NA | Mountain View |
| Vlsi Research Inc (HQ) | Provider of chip market research, consultation, semiconductor analysis, and data spreadsheets and reports. | 408-453-8844 | NA | San Jose |
| Wiley X Inc (HQ) | Provider of high velocity protection services. The company specializes in climate control frames, light adjusting lenses, and polarized lenses. | 925-243-9810 | NA | Livermore |

## 306 = Testing Laboratories/Services

| COMPANY NAME | PRODUCT / SERVICE | PHONE | EMP | CITY |
|---|---|---|---|---|
| Advantage Pharmaceutics Inc (HQ) | Provider of pharmaceuticals specializing in compounding. The company provides compounded medicines in dosage forms for human and veterinary needs. | 916-630-4960 | 1-10 | Rocklin |
| Advantec MFS Inc (HQ) | Producer of filtration media and related scientific products. The company focuses on laboratory instruments and filtration products. | 925-479-0625 | NA | Dublin |
| AEMTEK Laboratories (HQ) | Provider of testing, research, training and consulting services and sampling products for the food, environmental and pharmaceutical industries. | 510-979-1979 | NA | Fremont |
| Ags Inc (HQ) | Provider of civil, structural, and geotechnical engineering services. The company serves the water and transportation infrastructure markets. | 415-777-2166 | NA | San Francisco |
| Amyris Inc (HQ) | Provider of renewable products. The company delivers cosmetic emollients and fragrances, fuels and lubricants, and even biopharmaceuticals. | 510-450-0761 | NA | Emeryville |
| Analytical Sciences Llc (HQ) | Provider of laboratory services. The company specializes in environmental testing and analytical chemistry. | 707-769-3128 | NA | Petaluma |
| Anamet Inc (HQ) | Provider of materials engineering analysis & lab testing services. The company focuses on product testing, failure analysis, and forensic engineering. | 510-887-8811 | NA | Hayward |
| Anresco Inc (HQ) | Provider of analysis and research to food and food-related industries. The company also offers solutions to support the business and analytical specifications. | 415-822-1100 | NA | San Francisco |
| Antagene Inc (HQ) | Provider of custom antibody and peptide synthesis. The company is engaged in animal and histology services. | 408-588-1998 | NA | Santa Clara |
| Antech Diagnostics (HQ) | Provider of diagnostic and laboratory testing services for chemistry, pathology, endocrinology, serology, hematology, and microbiology. | 800-872-1001 | 11-50 | Fountain Valley |
| Antibodies Inc (HQ) | Manufacturer of monoclonal and polyclonal antibodies, diagnostic reagents, diagnostic kits, and developer of immunoassays. | 530-758-4400 | 1-10 | Davis |
| Apex Testing Labs (HQ) | Provider of testing and inspection services. The company engages in the geotechnical engineering and inspection of construction materials. | 415-550-9800 | NA | San Francisco |
| Apple Inc (HQ) | Provider of analytical testing services. The company specializes in analysis of environmental samples for chemical pollutants. | 559-275-2175 | 1-10 | Clovis |
| Asbestech Laboratory (HQ) | Provider of asbestos and lead testing services. The company also offers transmission electron microscopes. | 916-481-8902 | 1-10 | Carmichael |
| Bay Materials LLC (HQ) | Manufacturer of polymer products. The company offers services for spectroscopy, osmometry, viscosity, and surface measurement. | 650-566-0800 | NA | Fremont |
| Berkeley Analytical Associates Llc (HQ) | Provider of specialized chemical & flame retardant analysis and formaldehyde testing services. The company serves the flooring and textile industries. | 510-236-2325 | NA | Richmond |

| COMPANY NAME | PRODUCT / SERVICE | PHONE | EMP | CITY |
|---|---|---|---|---|
| Bestek Manufacturing Inc (HQ) | Provider of supply chain services. The company engages focuses on systems manufacturing, materials management, and prototype support areas. | 408-321-8834 | NA | San Jose |
| Beta Breakers Software Quality (HQ) | Provider of software and application testing services. The company offers functionality, compatibility, website, and mobile device testing services. | 415-878-2990 | NA | Novato |
| Biocare Medical Llc (HQ) | Developer of automated immunohistochemistry instrumentation, reagents for IHC lab testing. The company also offer tissue diagnostic products for cancer. | 925-603-8000 | NA | Pacheco |
| Biometrix Inc (HQ) | Manufacturer of pathway analysis and variant analysis products. The company specializes in web-analysis. | 415-333-0522 | NA | San Francisco |
| Biovir Laboratories Inc (HQ) | Provider of environmental testing needs, technology, and methodology for quality water, wastewater, and biosolids testing and research services. | 707-747-5906 | NA | Benicia |
| Blue Sky Environmental Inc (HQ) | Provider of air emissions source testing services. The company's services include alternative monitoring and validation testing. | 510-525-1261 | NA | Albany |
| Bolsa Analytical (HQ) | Provider of reliable chemical and microbiological analysis and testing of water, soil, plants and food. | 831-637-4590 | NA | San Jose |
| Brelje & Race Laboratories Inc (HQ) | Provider of water and wastewater testing services. The company analyses process include nitrate, arsenic, and volatile organics compounds. | 707-544-8807 | NA | Santa Rosa |
| Bureau Veritas Laboratories (BR) | Provider of analytical products and services. The company services customers in the energy, environmental, food, and DNA industries. | 650-576-7765 | NA | San Carlos |
| Burlington Safety Laboratory Inc (BR) | Designer and manufacturer of laboratory and electrical safety equipment. The company's customers include electric utilities and contractors. | 925-251-1412 | NA | Pleasanton |
| Calchemist (HQ) | Provider of contract research services. The company specializes in chemical, material science and laboratory equipment testing. | 650-551-1495 | NA | San Francisco |
| Calcoast-Itl (HQ) | Provider of testing services for automotive and roadway lightings. The company offers consultation, assistance, and laboratory installation services. | 510-924-7100 | NA | San Leandro |
| California Laboratory Services (HQ) | Provider of analytical testing services. The company offers a comprehensive range of soil and water testing for government and private agencies. | 800-638-7301 | 1-10 | Rancho Cordova |
| Caltest Analytical Lab (HQ) | Provider of analyses services of wastewater, groundwater, non-radioactive water, and hazardous waste samples. | 707-258-4000 | NA | Napa |
| Ceecon Testing Inc (HQ) | Provider of soil and groundwater remediation services. The company services also include regulatory compliance and remediation equipment. | 650-827-7474 | NA | S San Francisco |
| Cellecta Inc (HQ) | Provider of custom and contract solutions for high-throughput genetic screening needs and also develops therapeutic targets and drugs. | 650-938-3910 | NA | Mountain View |
| Cellmax Life (HQ) | Provider of personalized multi-biomarker technologies for non-invasive saliva and blood tests. The company is also involved in drug discovery. | 650-564-3905 | NA | Sunnyvale |
| Ckc Laboratories Inc (HQ) | Provider of electomagnetic compatibility testing, safety testing, design development and agency certification services for industries. | 209-966-5240 | 11-50 | Mariposa |
| Ckc Laboratories Inc (BR) | Provider of design and testing consultation services. The company offers design consultation, testing, training, and support services. | 510-249-1170 | NA | Fremont |
| Cureline Biopathology LLC (HQ) | Provider of human and animal tissue processing services. The company also focuses on preservation and biospecimen management. | 415-468-6400 | NA | Brisbane |
| Curtis & Tompkins Laboratories (HQ) | Provider of environmental analytical testing services. The company is also engaged in operational management. | 510-486-0900 | NA | Berkeley |
| Daniel B Stephens & Associates Inc (BR) | Provider of services in hydrology, environmental engineering, and science. The company services include water resources and soil testing. | 800-933-3105 | NA | Oakland |
| Datalab (HQ) | Provider of analysis and certification of process tanks and printed circuit board sections. The company also offers chemical process control software. | 408-943-1888 | NA | San Jose |
| Datest Corp (HQ) | Provider of testing and inspection services. The company specializes in engineering testing and counterfeit inspection for industrial products. | 510-490-4600 | NA | Fremont |
| Em Lab P&K (BR) | Provider of indoor air quality testing services. The company offers culturable air fungi, spore trap analysis, and yeast identification services. | 916-374-4483 | 11-50 | West Sacramento |
| Emsl Analytical Inc (BR) | Provider of laboratory analytical testing services. The company specializes in a wide range of environmental, material and forensic testing. | 510-895-3675 | NA | San Leandro |
| Environmental Micro Analysis Inc (HQ) | Provider of food safety consulting services. The company specializes in pesticide residue analysis in agricultural products, processed foods and other matrices. | 530-666-6890 | 1-10 | Woodland |
| Ets Laboratories (HQ) | Specializes in analytical tools. The company focuses on export analysis, harvest, and fuel ethanol services. | 707-963-4806 | NA | St. Helena |
| Exacta Tech Inc (HQ) | Manufacturer of custom machine components and parts and provider of design, inspection and engineering services for industries. | 925-443-8963 | NA | Livermore |
| Excelchem Laboratories Inc (HQ) | Provider of analytical consultation, on-site analysis, custom reporting, and mobile laboratory services. | 916-543-4445 | 1-10 | Rocklin |
| Forensic Analytical Consulting Services Inc (HQ) | Provider of analytical testing services. The company specializes in a wide array of material testing, forensic and environmental testing. | 866-637-9924 | NA | Hayward |

| COMPANY NAME | PRODUCT / SERVICE | PHONE | EMP | CITY |
|---|---|---|---|---|
| Geochemical Research Laboratory (HQ) | The company uses energy dispersive x-ray fluoresence spectrometry to determine the element composition of volcanic rocks. The company specializes in archaelogical geochemistry. | 650-851-1410 | NA | Portola Valley |
| Gigatest Labs (HQ) | Provider of measurement and probing products for the electronics industry. The company offers test equipment and fixtures for modeling and simulation. | 408-524-2700 | NA | Santa Clara |
| Hahnemann Labortories Inc (HQ) | Manufacturer of homeopathic medicines. The company offers dispensing kits, first aid kits, and also professional kits. | 415-451-6978 | NA | San Rafael |
| Harris Industrial Gases (HQ) | Provider of specialty gases welding equipment. The company also offers services for welding supplies and safety equipment. | 916-725-2168 | 11-50 | Citrus Heights |
| Hemostat Laboratories (HQ) | Provider of defibrinated sheep blood and other animal blood products for cell culture, diagnostic and veterinary applications. | 800-572-6888 | NA | Dixon |
| Ieh Jl Analytical Services (HQ) | Provider of laboratory and consulting services for food microbiology, allergens, virology, and parasitology, forensics, and agricultural products. | 209-538-8111 | 1-10 | Modesto |
| iGenix Inc (HQ) | Provider of immunology laboratory services. The company offers service to private practice physicians, hospitals, and clinical reference laboratories. | 650-424-1191 | NA | Milpitas |
| Impax Laboratories Inc (HQ) | Manufacturers and developer of technology-based specialty pharmaceutical drug delivery system. The company's serves physicians and patients. | 510-240-6000 | NA | Hayward |
| InCube Labs (HQ) | Provider of laboratory services. The company offers medical devices and pharmaceuticals to various therapeutic areas. | 408-457-3700 | NA | San Jose |
| Intertek Group PLC (BR) | Provider of advisory, business consulting, risk management, outsourcing, validation, and training services. | 650-463-2900 | NA | Menlo Park |
| Invitae Corp (HQ) | Provider of genetic information. The company offers to bring genetic information into routine medical practice to improve the quality of healthcare. | 415-930-4018 | 501-1000 | San Francisco |
| Iometrix Inc (HQ) | Developer of next generation packet networks and solutions for telecom service providers and equipment manufacturers. | 650-872-4001 | NA | San Francisco |
| Ise Labs Inc (HQ) | Provider of semiconductor services. The company offers services such as production test, test interface, and mechanical testing. | 510-687-2500 | NA | Fremont |
| Kimia Corp (HQ) | Manufacturer of chemicals and custom synthesis services. The company offers amino acids, vitamins, steroids, heptanes, and multifunctional heterocycles. | 408-748-1046 | NA | Santa Clara |
| Machaon Diagnostics Inc (HQ) | Provider of laboratory services in diagnosis, treatment and monitoring of hemostatic and thrombotic conditions. | 510-839-5600 | NA | Oakland |
| Marin Biologic Laboratories Inc (HQ) | Provider of client research services. The company serves the pharmaceutical, biotechnology, diagnostic, agricultural, and legal markets. | 415-883-8000 | NA | Novato |
| Martin Testing Laboratories (HQ) | Provider of product assurance, failure analysis, mechanical, metallurgical, electrical, and paint and coating testing services. | 916-920-4110 | 1-10 | Mcclellan |
| Maselli Measurements Inc (BR) | Provider of liquid measuring solutions. The company manufactures and distributes refractometers and liquid analyzers for several industries. | 209-474-9178 | 11-50 | Stockton |
| Materials Testing Inc (HQ) | Provider of geotechnical engineering and materials testing services. The company offers geotechnical, environment, special inspection, and material testing services. | 530-222-1116 | 11-50 | Redding |
| Mccampbell Analytical Inc (HQ) | Provider of analytical tests on drinking water, effluent, soils, solids, hazardous waste, air, soil vapor, and industrial materials. | 925-252-9262 | NA | Pittsburg |
| Mclab (HQ) | Provider of DNA sequencing services. The company's products include enzymes and biochemical reagents. | 650-871-8771 | NA | S San Francisco |
| Met Labs Inc (BR) | Provider of electrical testing services focusing on product safety, RF testing, and others. The company serves medical, RFID, and other sectors. | 408-748-3585 | NA | Santa Clara |
| Micro Precision Calibration Inc (HQ) | Provider of electrical and mechanical calibration services. The company also offers optical and temperature calibration services. | 530-268-1860 | 1-10 | Grass Valley |
| MicroMed Laboratories (HQ) | Provider of regulatory consulting, microbial identification, environmental monitoring, and sterilization validation services. | 707-782-0792 | NA | Petaluma |
| Nanolab Technologies Inc (HQ) | Provider of cutting edge technology and expertise for failure analysis, advanced microscopy and FIB circuit edit services. | 408-433-3320 | NA | Milpitas |
| Nec Laboratories America Inc (BR) | Provider of technology research services. The company specializes in research departments such as integrated systems, machine learning, and media analytics. | 408-863-6007 | NA | Cupertino |
| Neil O Anderson & Associates Inc (HQ) | Provider of engineering services including geotechnical engineering, foundation, and structural engineering services. | 209-367-3701 | 11-50 | Lodi |
| Ocellus Inc (HQ) | Provider of multidisciplinary technology and services such as nanotechnology-based solutions for aerospace, industrial, and medical applications. | 925-606-6540 | NA | Livermore |
| Peak Laboratories Llc (HQ) | Designer and manufacturer of process gas chromatography systems. The company offers mercuric oxide, pulse discharge, and thermal conductivity detectors. | 650-691-1267 | NA | Mountain View |
| Pegasus Design Inc (HQ) | Provider of machine design and contract manufacturing services. The company serves the pharmaceutical instrument industry. | 925-292-7567 | NA | Livermore |

| COMPANY NAME | PRODUCT / SERVICE | PHONE | EMP | CITY |
|---|---|---|---|---|
| Peninsula Laboratories Inc (HQ) | Manufacturer of immunology products for biomedical research. The company is involved in technical support services. | 650-801-6090 | NA | San Carlos |
| Pharmout Laboratory Inc (HQ) | Provider of analytical laboratory services. The company engages in protein precipitated plasma, liquid-liquid extraction, and solid phase extraction. | 408-481-3090 | NA | Sunnyvale |
| Pickering Laboratories Inc (HQ) | Developer of post-column derivatization technology. The company specializes in manufacturing of cation-exchange columns for amino acid analysis. | 650-694-6700 | NA | Mountain View |
| Prestige Lens Lab (HQ) | Provider of optical laboratory services. The company specializes in prescription safety eyewear programs. | 650-588-5540 | NA | S San Francisco |
| Presto Engineering Inc (HQ) | Provider of semiconductor test and analysis solutions. The company also offers engineering services to the semiconductor market. | 408-372-9500 | NA | San Jose |
| Prima Environmental Inc (HQ) | Provider of laboratory testing services. The company specializes in treatability testing, technology evaluation, and scientific consulting services. | 916-939-7300 | 1-10 | El Dorado Hills |
| Quest Diagnostics Inc (BR) | Provider of diagnostic laboratory testing services. The company offers a wide range of test menu for diagnosing medical conditions. | 510-357-5438 | NA | San Leandro |
| Redwood Toxicology Laboratory (BR) | Provider of drug and alcohol testing laboratories. The company specializes in substance abuse screening products to criminal justice and treatment markets. | 707-577-7959 | NA | Santa Rosa |
| Reliant Labs Inc (HQ) | Provider of environmental testing and reliability services. The company is also engaged in power supply evaluation. | 408-737-7500 | NA | Sunnyvale |
| Riga Analytical Lab Inc (HQ) | Provider of laboratory services specializing in electrical failure analysis, circuit extraction, latch up evaluation, and parallel and angel lapping. | 408-496-6944 | NA | Santa Clara |
| Rod-L Electronics Inc (HQ) | Provider of electrical safety testing equipment. The company also offers hipot test loads, test probes, bond testers, and ground testers. | 650-322-0711 | NA | Mountain View |
| Ryss Lab Inc (HQ) | Provider of biotechnology and pharmaceutical development services. The company offers services to the healthcare sector. | 510-477-9570 | NA | Union City |
| S C Laboratories (HQ) | Provider of medical quality assurance and safety testing services. The company's services include potency testing, pesticide testing, and microbial screening. | 866-435-0709 | 1-10 | Santa Cruz |
| Safebridge Consultants Inc (HQ) | Provider of consulting services and analytical support. The company provides safety, health and environmental services. | 650-961-4820 | NA | Mountain View |
| Samsung Research America (DH) | Provider of commercial, physical, and biological research services. The company is involved in testing and identification solutions. | 650-210-1001 | NA | Mountain View |
| Seatec Lab Repair (HQ) | Provider of services to analytical, biotech, and industrial laboratories. The company also focuses on equipment validation. | 408-828-1815 | NA | Santa Clara |
| Sierra Testing Service (HQ) | Provider of laboratory testing services. The company offers services such as grain testing, silage, and grain samples. | 209-333-3337 | 1-10 | Acampo |
| Simco Electronics (HQ) | Providers of services and software to medical device manufacturers. The company specializes in biotechnology. | 408-734-9750 | NA | Santa Clara |
| Singulex Inc (HQ) | Provider of life science products and cardiovascular monitoring products. The company deals with lab testing services. | 510-995-9000 | NA | Alameda |
| Spectra Laboratories (HQ) | Provider of testing services for a wide range of specialties. The company focuses on chemistry, serology, anemia testing, hematology, and others. | 800-433-3773 | NA | Milpitas |
| Strataglass (HQ) | Manufacturer of thin films. The company offers research and development, pilot production, and outsourced fabrication services. | 650-988-1700 | NA | Mountain View |
| SUNBURST Plant Disease Clinic Inc (HQ) | Provider of solutions for pathological & physiological problems in agriculture. The company focuses on soil & tissue examination and mineral analysis. | 209-667-4442 | 1-10 | Turlock |
| Test O Pac Industries Inc (HQ) | Provider of environmental and package testing services. The company deals with component testing, product reliability, and medical package testing. | 408-436-1117 | NA | San Jose |
| Testamerica Laboratories Inc (BR) | Provider of environmental testing services. The company offers indoor air quality, air testing and emissions, and industrial hygiene services. | 916-373-5600 | 11-50 | West Sacramento |
| Theraject Inc (HQ) | Developer of drug micro-needle technologies. The company is engaged in vaccine and also drug deliveries. | 510-742-5832 | NA | Fremont |
| Thermochem Inc (HQ) | Provider of chemical engineering, laboratory analysis, geochemistry and field testing services and products to a wide range of energy industries. | 707-575-1310 | NA | Santa Rosa |
| Trevi Systems (HQ) | Provider of desalination process services. The company focuses on osmosis system using proprietary membrane and draw solution using thermal heat. | 707-792-2681 | NA | Petaluma |
| Vector Laboratories Inc (HQ) | Provider of labeling and detection services for enzymes, antibodies and antigens, DNA and RNA by using polymer reagents. | 650-697-3600 | NA | Burlingame |
| West Coast Pathology Laboratories (HQ) | Providers of anatomic pathology and cytology services. The company's expertise lies with molecular genetics and diagnostics. | 510-662-5200 | NA | Hercules |
| Westpak Inc (HQ) | Provider of customized product and packaging testing services. The company also deals with packaging, material analysis, and supply chain management. | 408-224-1300 | NA | San Jose |
| Yosemite Pathology Medical Group Inc (HQ) | Provider of anatomic pathology services such as tissue pathology and gynecologic specimens of oncologic and nononcologic diseases. | 209-577-1200 | 1-10 | Modesto |

| COMPANY NAME | PRODUCT / SERVICE | PHONE | EMP | CITY |
|---|---|---|---|---|
| Yy Labs Inc (HQ) | Manufacturer and supplier of optical components. The company provides LN modulators, bias controllers, generators, and accessories. | 510-739-6049 | NA | Fremont |

## 309 = Application-Specific Robotics

| | | | | |
|---|---|---|---|---|
| Genmark Automation Inc (HQ) | Provider of robotics for automated manufacturing applications. The company offers services to the data storage and related industries. | 510-897-3400 | NA | Fremont |
| Kensington Laboratories Llc (HQ) | Provider of automation products for the semiconductor industry. The company is engaged in precision machining, automation, and system integration. | 510-324-0126 | NA | Dublin |
| Kespry Inc (HQ) | Developer of automated drone system and cloud that automatically uploads data in cloud for aggregates, insurance, and construction industries. | 203-434-7988 | NA | Menlo Park |
| MATTERNET (HQ) | Specializes in the creation of integrated delivery solutions. The company's products are used in healthcare, on-campus, and humanitarian applications. | 650-260-2727 | NA | Menlo Park |
| SRI International (RH) | Provider of consulting, research, and development services. The company offers services to the defense, security, and energy sectors. | 650-859-2000 | NA | Menlo Park |

## 310 = Automatic Storage/Retrieval Systems

| | | | | |
|---|---|---|---|---|
| Idec Corp (BR) | Designer and manufacturer of automated machines for various sectors. The company also offers products for environment, safety, and other needs. | 408-747-0550 | NA | Sunnyvale |
| Lexicon Branding Inc (HQ) | Provider of services to develop, select and evaluate brand names. The company services include trademark evaluation, name development, and consumer research. | 415-332-1811 | NA | Sausalito |

## 311 = Automation Manufacturing/R&D Services

| | | | | |
|---|---|---|---|---|
| 3d Robotics Inc (HQ) | Manufacturer of drone systems for exploration and business applications. The company offers autopilot controllers and flight controllers. | 858-225-1414 | NA | Berkeley |
| Adco Manufacturing (HQ) | Provider of consumer packaged goods. The company's solutions include cartoners, top load systems, case packers, sleevers, and robotic packaging. | 559-875-5563 | 1-10 | Sanger |
| CKC Engineering LLC (HQ) | Provider of custom equipment solutions for clinical, manufacturing, pharmaceutical, medical device, and drug delivery industries. | 415-494-8225 | NA | Oakland |
| Distribution Technologies Inc (HQ) | Provider of design, analysis, simulation, automation, and project implementation solutions. The company also deals with technical support. | 415-999-1191 | NA | Tiburon |
| Genmark Automation Inc (HQ) | Provider of robotics for automated manufacturing applications. The company offers services to the data storage and related industries. | 510-897-3400 | NA | Fremont |
| Glenmount Global Solutions (HQ) | Provider of industrial equipment control, energy management, and other systems. The company serves automotive, food, chemical, and other sectors. | 707-258-8400 | NA | Napa |
| Grabit Inc (HQ) | Inventor of electroadhesion technology. The company specializes in parts handling, package handling, and each pick applications. | 408-642-1830 | NA | San Carlos |
| Green Source Automation Llc (HQ) | Provider of redefining solutions for diary industry. The company also offers technology for milking process. | 209-531-9163 | 1-10 | Ceres |
| Hesse Mechatronics Inc (LH) | Developer of equipment for heavy wire and thin wire wedge bonders. The company also focuses on the marketing aspects. | 408-436-9300 | NA | Fremont |
| Kensington Laboratories Llc (HQ) | Provider of automation products for the semiconductor industry. The company is engaged in precision machining, automation, and system integration. | 510-324-0126 | NA | Dublin |
| Ologic (HQ) | Manufacturer of consumer electronics and toy products. The company specializes in defense and educational projects. | 408-663-6638 | NA | Santa Clara |
| Orbotech LT Solar LLC (BR) | Manufacturer of electronic devices. The company offers printed circuit boards, flat panel displays, and touch screens. | 408-226-9900 | NA | San Jose |
| Procept Biorobotics (HQ) | Provider of healthcare services. The company primarily focuses on personalized image-guided waterjet tissue resection services. | 650-232-7200 | NA | Redwood City |
| Quartet Mechanics Inc (HQ) | Provider of LED, MEMS, photovoltaics (PV) solar and medical/lab automation systems. The company also offers wafer sorting and packing products. | 408-564-8901 | NA | Santa Clara |
| Rockwell Automation Inc (BR) | Provider of control systems, sensing devices, security, and other products. The company offers asset management, network, and other services. | 925-242-5700 | NA | San Ramon |
| Rorze Automation Inc (DH) | Manufacturer of automation products. The company's applications include displays, semiconductors, and laboratories. | 510-687-1340 | NA | Fremont |
| Superior Automation (HQ) | Provider of custom automation solutions. The company primarily caters to the semiconductor industry. | 510-413-9790 | NA | Fremont |
| Vantage Robotics LLC (HQ) | Developer and manufacturer of camera drones. The company serves the consumer electronics, automation, and robotics industries. | 510-907-7012 | NA | San Leandro |
| Winslow Automation Inc (HQ) | Provider of lead tinning products and services. The company caters to semiconductor and electrical companies. | 408-262-9004 | NA | Milpitas |

## 12 = Material Dispensing Equipment

| COMPANY NAME | PRODUCT / SERVICE | PHONE | EMP | CITY |
|---|---|---|---|---|
| Jackrabbit Inc (HQ) | Provider of nut harvesting systems including runner, elevator, reservoir cart, conditioner and pruning tower. | 209-599-6118 | 1-10 | Ripon |

## 313 = Programmable Controls for Factory Processes

| COMPANY NAME | PRODUCT / SERVICE | PHONE | EMP | CITY |
|---|---|---|---|---|
| 3d Robotics Inc (HQ) | Manufacturer of drone systems for exploration and business applications. The company offers autopilot controllers and flight controllers. | 858-225-1414 | NA | Berkeley |
| Distribution Technologies Inc (HQ) | Provider of design, analysis, simulation, automation, and project implementation solutions. The company also deals with technical support. | 415-999-1191 | NA | Tiburon |
| Galil Motion Control (HQ) | Manufacturer and supplier of motion controllers and software tools. The company also offers drives and power supplies. | 916-626-0101 | 1-10 | Rocklin |
| Genmark Automation Inc (HQ) | Provider of robotics for automated manufacturing applications. The company offers services to the data storage and related industries. | 510-897-3400 | NA | Fremont |
| Ologic (HQ) | Manufacturer of consumer electronics and toy products. The company specializes in defense and educational projects. | 408-663-6638 | NA | Santa Clara |

## 314 = Robotic Controllers/Manipulators/Feeders

| COMPANY NAME | PRODUCT / SERVICE | PHONE | EMP | CITY |
|---|---|---|---|---|
| 3d Robotics Inc (HQ) | Manufacturer of drone systems for exploration and business applications. The company offers autopilot controllers and flight controllers. | 858-225-1414 | NA | Berkeley |
| Biomicrolab (HQ) | Manufacturer of robotics based sorting and weighing systems sample management automation. The company serves bio-lab purposes. | 925-689-1200 | NA | Concord |
| Distribution Technologies Inc (HQ) | Provider of design, analysis, simulation, automation, and project implementation solutions. The company also deals with technical support. | 415-999-1191 | NA | Tiburon |
| Genmark Automation Inc (HQ) | Provider of robotics for automated manufacturing applications. The company offers services to the data storage and related industries. | 510-897-3400 | NA | Fremont |
| Grabit Inc (HQ) | Inventor of electroadhesion technology. The company specializes in parts handling, package handling, and each pick applications. | 408-642-1830 | NA | San Carlos |
| Idec Corp (BR) | Designer and manufacturer of automated machines for various sectors. The company also offers products for environment, safety, and other needs. | 408-747-0550 | NA | Sunnyvale |
| Intest Ems Products (BR) | Manufacturer of semiconductors to test integrated circuits. The company also focuses on testing wafer products. | 408-678-9167 | NA | Fremont |
| Keri Systems Inc (HQ) | Provider of access control and integrated security systems. The company offers technology support and training solutions. | 408-435-8400 | NA | San Jose |
| Knightscope Inc (HQ) | Provider of security technology. The company specializes in monotonous, computationally heavy, and sometimes dangerous work for security operations. | 650-924-1025 | NA | Mountain View |
| Procept Biorobotics (HQ) | Provider of healthcare services. The company primarily focuses on personalized image-guided waterjet tissue resection services. | 650-232-7200 | NA | Redwood City |
| Vantage Robotics LLC (HQ) | Developer and manufacturer of camera drones. The company serves the consumer electronics, automation, and robotics industries. | 510-907-7012 | NA | San Leandro |
| Willow Garage Inc (HQ) | Developer of hardware and open source software for personal robotics applications. The company also offers robot design and machine learning services. | 650-475-2700 | NA | Menlo Park |

## 315 = Software Development/Services

| | COMPANY NAME | PRODUCT / SERVICE | PHONE | EMP | CITY |
|---|---|---|---|---|---|
| N | Caspio (HQ) | Builds online database applications without coding. | 650-691-0900 | NA | Santa Clara |
| N | CitrusBits (HQ) | Designs and develops impactful mobile apps for businesses of all sizes by using augmented/virtual reality, artificial intelligence, blockchain, and The Internet of Things (IoT). | 925-452-6012 | NA | Pleasanton |
| N | Code-N Technology Inc (HQ) | Leverages advanced semantic web technology to provide software solutions to businesses. | 650-234-8400 | NA | Menlo Park |
| N | CrowdANALYTIX (HQ) | Develops and deploys AI and Data Science solutions. | 866-333-4515 | NA | Sunnyvale |
| N | GitHub Inc (HQ) | Provider of an online platform that allows users to learn, store and share codes with individuals. | 877-448-4820 | NA | San Francisco |
| N | Healthline Networks (HQ) | Provider of health information. | 415-281-3100 | NA | San Francisco |
| N | Import.io (HQ) | Enables organizations to gain intelligence, abilities, and competing advantages from the vast amount of data on the web. | 650-935-4336 | NA | Saratoga |
| N | Informatica Corp (HQ) | Provides data management software and services to help a company to achieve a competitive edge. | 650-385-5000 | NA | Redwood City |
| N | Intellectsoft (HQ) | Provider of impactful digital engineering solutions with latest technologies. | 650-300-4335 | NA | Palo Alto |
| N | Lob.com (HQ) | Builds an API toolkit that allows organizations to innovate, move faster, and better differentiate themselves. | 847-630-9275 | NA | San Francisco |
| N | Paxata Inc (HQ) | Enables business analysts to easily absorb, analyze, and curate numerous raw data sets into consumable information in a self-service manner. | 650-542-7900 | NA | Redwood City |
| N | Practice Fusion Inc (HQ) | Provider of cloud-based electronic health records (EHR) platform in the U.S. | 415-346-7700 | NA | San Francisco |
| N | Quid Inc (HQ) | Developers of artificial intelligence to help organizations make important decisions. | 415-813-5300 | NA | San Francisco |
| N | Splunk Inc (HQ) | Develops software for monitoring, searching, and analyzing machine-generated big data through a web-style interface. | 415-848-8400 | NA | San Francisco |

| | COMPANY NAME | PRODUCT / SERVICE | PHONE | EMP | CITY |
|---|---|---|---|---|---|
| N | Verdafero Inc (HQ) | Offers a wide range of cloud-based software solutions that enable companies to manage their utility data and analytics. | 650-206-2441 | NA | San Jose |
| N | Vidado Inc (HQ) | Designed to help organizations collect and digitize inaccessible data. | 415-237-3676 | NA | Oakland |
| | WSI Smart Solutions (HQ) | Provider of search engine optimization services. The company also deals with internet marketing and web design solutions. | 925-245-0216 | NA | Livermore |
| N | Xignite Inc (HQ) | Provider of financial Data-as-a-Service (DaaS) solution to deliver market data from the AWS public cloud. | 650-655-3700 | NA | San Mateo |

## 316 = CAD/CAM & visualisation

| COMPANY NAME | PRODUCT / SERVICE | PHONE | EMP | CITY |
|---|---|---|---|---|
| 2ndEdison Inc (HQ) | Provider of e-Commerce applications. The company also offers business process consulting and design services. | 844-432-8466 | NA | Orinda |
| Acrylic Art (HQ) | Provider of fabrication and machining services. The company focuses on painting, product finishing, anodizing, and vapor polishing. | 510-654-0953 | NA | Emeryville |
| Ad Art Inc (HQ) | Provider of digital signage solutions. The company also offers graphic designs, animation, commercial lighting, and maintenance services. | 800-675-6353 | NA | San Francisco |
| Advanced Laser & Waterjet Cutting Inc (HQ) | Provider of precision cutting services for all types of materials. The company's services include electronic shielding, fabrivision, and overnight shipping. | 408-486-0700 | NA | Santa Clara |
| Alliance Support Partners Inc (HQ) | Provider of test solutions, instrumentation engineering, test system design, and turn-key outsourcing support services. | 925-363-5382 | NA | Concord |
| American Prototype And Production Inc (HQ) | Manufacturer of industrial laser cutting machines. The company focuses on industries such as CNC milling, CNC turning, and laser engraving. | 650-595-4994 | NA | San Carlos |
| Applied Engineering (HQ) | Provider of structural analysis and seismic evaluation services. The company is involved in specialty engineering and project management. | 408-263-5900 | NA | Milpitas |
| Aquifi Inc (HQ) | Developer of fluid technology solutions. The company is involved in computer vision and machine learning algorithms. | 650-213-8535 | NA | Palo Alto |
| Artwork Conversion Software Inc (HQ) | Developer of CAD translation programs and CAD viewers software. The company also offers plotting software and IC packaging software. | 831-426-6163 | 1-10 | Santa Cruz |
| ASCENX Technologies Inc (HQ) | Provider of engineering services to the semiconductor industry. The company is also engaged in contract manufacturing and repair services. | 408-945-1997 | NA | Fremont |
| Autodesk Inc (BR) | Provider of 3D design, engineering, and entertainment software solutions. The company also offers technical support services. | 415-356-0700 | NA | San Francisco |
| CAD Masters Inc (HQ) | Designer and developer of software and hardware solutions. The company focuses on drafting, engineering, plotting, and on-site project assistance. | 925-939-1378 | NA | Walnut Creek |
| Capital Engineering Consultants Inc (HQ) | Provider of mechanical engineering, sustainable design and green engineering, building commissioning, energy modeling, and other related services. | 916-851-3500 | 11-50 | Rancho Cordova |
| Cyberglove Systems Llc (HQ) | Provider of data glove technology. The company offers system installation and integration and custom software and hardware services. | 408-943-8114 | NA | San Jose |
| Digital Anarchy (HQ) | Provider of photography and video plugins for Photoshop, elements, after effects, and final cut pro. | 415-287-6069 | NA | Brisbane |
| Engineering By Design (HQ) | Provider of engineering and support services. The company's products include laminators, coil and fiber winders, motors, and extrusion pullers. | 408-324-1500 | NA | San Jose |
| Funmobility Inc (HQ) | Provider of solutions for mobile engagement and mobile marketing. The company also offers content marketing, digital strategy, and other services. | 925-598-9700 | NA | San Ramon |
| Geofusion Inc (HQ) | Specializes in virtual reality and 3D visualization services. The company offers software development kits. | 831-458-1418 | 1-10 | Santa Cruz |
| Global Presenter (BR) | Designer and builder of meeting room communication systems. The company is a provider of design, delivery, and system integration solutions. | 408-526-0221 | NA | San Jose |
| GoEngineer (BR) | Provider of solid works engineering and Oracle agile PLM products. The company offers services to the business sector. | 408-213-1580 | NA | Santa Clara |
| Hawk Ridge Systems (BR) | Provider of 3D design software solutions. The company offers CAD, analysis consulting, product data management, and solid works services. | 510-482-6110 | NA | Orinda |
| iCharts Inc (HQ) | Provider of collaborative visual intelligence solutions. The company offers services to business and media companies. | 650-472-0650 | NA | Mountain View |
| Imaging Visions (HQ) | Provider of design, prototyping, and visualization services that include architectural and lighting, exterior and landscape, and furnishing design. | 408-358-6427 | NA | Los Gatos |
| Intergraphics (HQ) | Developer of multi-lingual graphics. The company provides translation, typography, and other services. | 650-359-3087 | NA | Pacifica |
| It Concepts Llc (BR) | Manufacturer of borescopes, videoscopes, fiberscopes, documentation solutions, and accessories for remote visual inspection needs. | 925-401-0010 | NA | Pleasanton |
| Lumina Decision Systems Inc (HQ) | Provider of analytical training and consulting services. The company is engaged in technical support services. | 650-212-1212 | NA | Los Gatos |
| Mckenzie Machining Inc (HQ) | Provider of precision machining services of pre-fabricated components. The company R&D, manufacturing design, and other services. | 408-748-8885 | NA | Santa Clara |
| Moon Valley Circuits (HQ) | Manufacturer of control systems for wineries. The company specializes in tank temperature, barrel-room, and refrigeration control systems. | 707-996-4157 | NA | Glen Ellen |

| COMPANY NAME | PRODUCT / SERVICE | PHONE | EMP | CITY |
|---|---|---|---|---|
| **N** MSC Software (BR) | Developer of simulation software for acoustics, thermal analysis, and other needs. The company also offers software implementation and systems design services. | 714-540-8900 | 11-50 | Newport Beach |
| Netblaze Systems Inc (HQ) | Provider of IT, integration, and network consulting services. The company is also engaged in cloud computing, web hosting, and hosted exchange. | 925-932-1765 | NA | Walnut Creek |
| OCAMPO-ESTA Corp (HQ) | Provider of engineering, design, construction management, instrumentation and controls, and project management services. | 707-643-8072 | NA | Vallejo |
| Opac Consulting Engineers Inc (HQ) | Provider of bridge and structural engineering services. The company's services are design, evaluation, and construction engineering. | 415-989-4551 | NA | San Francisco |
| Parametric Technology Corp (BR) | Provider of product life cycle management solutions to the aerospace, defense, automotive, consumer, and medical device industries. | | NA | San Francisco |
| Performex Machining Co (HQ) | Provider of machining services. The company specializes in computer aided machining, designing, and fabrication. | 650-595-2228 | NA | San Carlos |
| Phasespace Inc (HQ) | Developer of technologies for motion tracking markets. The company focuses on motion capture for industrial research and graphic community. | 510-633-2865 | NA | San Leandro |
| Plastikon Industries (HQ) | Provider of contract manufacturing services for custom designed plastic injection molding, for medical, pharmaceutical and other industries. | 510-400-1010 | NA | Hayward |
| Plethora (HQ) | Focuses on CNC milling with automatic manufacturing analysis. The company is also involved in prototyping services. | 415-726-2256 | NA | San Francisco |
| Shields Harper & Co (HQ) | Provider of design assistance, testing, monitoring, fleet fuel control, and underground solutions to contractors, engineers, and designers. | 510-653-9119 | NA | Martinez |
| Solutionware Corp (HQ) | Provider of design solutions. The company offers computer aided design and computer aided manufacturing services. | 408-249-1529 | NA | San Jose |
| Ssp Data (HQ) | Developer of network solutions. The company also offers design, deployment, and in-house management services. | 510-215-3400 | NA | Richmond |
| Warren & Baerg Manufacturing Inc (HQ) | Manufacturer of agricultural and industrial systems. The company's services include installation, manufacturing, and technical support. | 559-591-6790 | 11-50 | Dinuba |
| Zspace Inc (HQ) | Provider of solutions for viewing, manipulating, and communicating complex ideas through direct interaction with virtual-holographic simulations. | 408-498-4050 | NA | Sunnyvale |

## 317 = Games

| COMPANY NAME | PRODUCT / SERVICE | PHONE | EMP | CITY |
|---|---|---|---|---|
| 2K Games Inc (HQ) | Developer of interactive entertainment for console systems. The company also focuses on handheld gaming systems and personal computers. | 415-479-3634 | NA | Novato |
| Azul Systems Inc (HQ) | Provider of Java applications for real time businesses. The company's Zing is a JVM enterprise application. | 650-230-6500 | NA | Sunnyvale |
| Bandai Namco Entertainment America Inc (HQ) | Provider of gaming solutions. The company is engaged in technical support and it serves the entertainment industry. | 408-235-2000 | NA | Santa Clara |
| Capcom Usa (LH) | Manufacturer and distributor of electronic game machines. The company specializes in resident evil, monster hunter, lost planet, and devroom games. | 650-350-6500 | NA | San Francisco |
| Chess com (HQ) | Provider of unlimited chess games and free tournaments that can be played by challenging friends and meet new players. | 800-318-2827 | NA | Palo Alto |
| Crystal Dynamics Inc (HQ) | Designer and developer of animated videos. The company also specializes in mobile gaming software products. | 650-421-7600 | NA | Redwood City |
| Devicelock Inc (HQ) | Developer of device control software solutions. The company offers contextual and content-based control for data leak prevention. | 925-231-4400 | NA | San Ramon |
| Electronic Arts Inc (HQ) | Developer, publisher, and distributor of software for video game systems, personal computers, wireless devices, and internet. | 650-628-1393 | NA | Redwood City |
| Fingerprint Digital Inc (HQ) | Designer and developer of mobile kids network solutions. The company offers services to kids of all ages. | 855-543-4263 | NA | San Francisco |
| HyTrust Inc (HQ) | Provider of security, compliance, and control software for virtualization of information technology infrastructure. | 650-681-8100 | NA | Mountain View |
| Judobaby Inc (HQ) | Focuses on the establishment of software and hardware products. The company offers services to the gaming industry. | 650-368-3499 | NA | Redwood City |
| Mondo Media Inc (HQ) | Provider of gaming solutions. The company's store features men's and women's T-shirts, smart phone cases, and related supplies. | 415-865-2700 | NA | San Francisco |
| Netxperts Inc (HQ) | Provider of unified communication solutions. The company offers services to the healthcare and transportation markets. | 925-806-0800 | NA | Walnut Creek |
| nWay (HQ) | Specializes in the development and publishing of free-to-play online multiplayer games. The company offers services to individuals. | 415-778-2866 | NA | San Francisco |
| Opinionmeter International (HQ) | Designer and developer of mobile research software. The company serves the healthcare, hospitality, and education sectors. | 510-352-4943 | NA | San Leandro |
| Perfect World Co Ltd (HQ) | Provider of gaming solutions. The company is engaged in technical support and it serves the entertainment industry. | 650-590-7700 | NA | Redwood City |
| Realiteer Corp (HQ) | Focuses on building virtual reality creation platform for playing entertaining games. The company offers services to the recreation industry. | | NA | Belmont |
| ROBLOX Corp (HQ) | Specializes in game development, monetization, and publishing services. The company serves businesses. | 888-858-2569 | NA | San Mateo |

| COMPANY NAME | PRODUCT / SERVICE | PHONE | EMP | CITY |
|---|---|---|---|---|
| Rockyou Inc (HQ) | Provider of gaming solutions. The company's games include Poker, Bingo, Zoo World, and others and serves the entertainment sector. | 415-580-6400 | NA | San Francisco |
| Secret Builders (HQ) | Provider of online games for children. The company also focuses on publishing writings, art, and videos. | 650-204-9098 | NA | San Mateo |
| Silvaco Inc (HQ) | Supplier of TCAD and EDA software for circuit simulation. The company also designs analog, mixed-signal, and RF integrated circuits. | 408-567-1000 | NA | Santa Clara |
| Trion Worlds Inc (HQ) | Publisher and developer of games. The company offers Defiance, RIFT, Archeage, and End of Nations games. | 650-273-9618 | NA | Redwood City |
| Vivid Vision Inc (HQ) | Provider of virtual reality solutions. The company offers services to eye clinics and also kids and adults. | 877-877-0310 | NA | San Francisco |
| XEODesign (HQ) | Provider of computer multimedia software, website design hosting, programming, and technical support services. | 510-658-8077 | NA | Oakland |
| Zynga Inc (HQ) | Provider of social game services with more than 240 million monthly active users. The company's games include CityVille, Draw Something, and Hidden Chronicles. | 800-762-2530 | 1001-5000 | San Francisco |

## 318 = Multimedia/Audio/Video

| COMPANY NAME | PRODUCT / SERVICE | PHONE | EMP | CITY |
|---|---|---|---|---|
| Ad Art Inc (HQ) | Provider of digital signage solutions. The company also offers graphic designs, animation, commercial lighting, and maintenance services. | 800-675-6353 | NA | San Francisco |
| Anvato Inc (HQ) | Provider of video software platform to television broadcasters and offers live and on-demand video management, analytics, and tracking features. | 866-246-6942 | NA | Mountain View |
| Applian Technologies Inc (HQ) | Provider of solutions for the capture and conversion of web video, streaming audio, and song and radio program software for Windows users. | 415-480-1748 | NA | San Anselmo |
| AverLogic Technologies Inc (RH) | Designer and seller of integrated ICs. The company primarily caters to multimedia and video applications. | 408-526-0400 | NA | San Jose |
| Avermedia Technologies Inc (DH) | Designer and manufacturer of multimedia, internet TV, and electronic products. The company provides USB, TV box, streaming server, and accessories. | 510-403-0006 | NA | Fremont |
| Brs Media Inc (HQ) | Provider of multimedia e-commerce services. The company specializes in radio and internet applications. | 415-677-4027 | NA | San Francisco |
| Cinematico Inc (HQ) | Provider of 3D design, animation, and motion capture services. The company is involved in product design and motion graphics. | 415-896-5776 | NA | San Francisco |
| Circle Video Productions (HQ) | Provider of video production and multimedia solutions. The company offers video dispositions, editing, and duplication services. | 650-619-7367 | NA | San Mateo |
| Compandent Inc (HQ) | Developer of customized algorithms. The company offers digital sign processing services to telecommunications and semiconductor companies. | 650-241-9231 | NA | Los Altos Hills |
| D-Tools Inc (HQ) | Developer and marketer of software to streamline processes which accompany the integration and installation of low-voltage systems. | 925-681-2326 | NA | Concord |
| Dolphin Graphics (HQ) | Provider of branding and marketing solutions. The company also offers graphics design and web design services. | 510-881-0154 | NA | Castro Valley |
| EXXIM Computing Corp (HQ) | Manufacturer of cutting-edge radiological imaging technology and equipment designed for dental, medical, and scientific and industrial industries. | 925-416-1900 | NA | Pleasanton |
| Harmonic Inc (HQ) | Provider of production and delivery solutions. The company serves the broadcast, media, service providers, and post production markets. | 408-542-2500 | 201-500 | San Jose |
| HyTrust Inc (HQ) | Provider of security, compliance, and control software for virtualization of information technology infrastructure. | 650-681-8100 | NA | Mountain View |
| Inikosoft Inc (HQ) | Provider of web, graphic, and print design services. The company is also engaged in e-commerce development and social media marketing. | 408-402-9545 | NA | Los Gatos |
| IntelliVision Technologies Corp (HQ) | Provider of software and solutions for security, surveillance, traffic, automotive, robotics, drones, smart home, mobile, and retail analytics solutions. | 408-754-1690 | NA | San Jose |
| It Concepts Llc (BR) | Manufacturer of borescopes, videoscopes, fiberscopes, documentation solutions, and accessories for remote visual inspection needs. | 925-401-0010 | NA | Pleasanton |
| J&C Consulting Services (HQ) | Developer of consulting services. The company offers strategic planning, executive coaching, and leadership and team development solutions. | 415-935-4313 | NA | San Francisco |
| Noble Image Inc (HQ) | Provider of website and graphic design, website development, hosting, programming, and technical support services. | 916-419-3570 | 1-10 | Sacramento |
| OJO Technology Inc (HQ) | Manufacturer of video surveillance systems. The company offers services to the education, transportation, and utility sectors. | 877-306-4656 | NA | Fremont |
| Pass Laboratories Inc (HQ) | Developer of prototypes for amplifier design. The company specializes in manufacturing amplifiers and speakers. | 530-878-5350 | 1-10 | Auburn |
| Phasespace Inc (HQ) | Developer of technologies for motion tracking markets. The company focuses on motion capture for industrial research and graphic community. | 510-633-2865 | NA | San Leandro |
| Qwilt Inc (HQ) | Developer of open caching, video intelligence, fixed, and mobile operators solutions. The company offers media analytics products. | 866-824-8009 | NA | Redwood City |
| Realiteer Corp (HQ) | Focuses on building virtual reality creation platform for playing entertaining games. The company offers services to the recreation industry. | | NA | Belmont |

| | COMPANY NAME | PRODUCT / SERVICE | PHONE | EMP | CITY |
|---|---|---|---|---|---|
| | Rearden LLC (HQ) | Provider of cloud computing, motion picture, video game, consumer electronics, wireless, imaging, communications, and alternative energy technologies. | 415-947-5555 | NA | Mountain View |
| | Rollinson Advertising Design (HQ) | Provider of graphic design, traditional marketing, strategic planning, and e-mail blasting services. | 925-518-6698 | NA | Pleasant Hill |
| | Spectra 7 Microsystems Ltd (HQ) | Manufacturer of analog semiconductor devices. The company focuses on micro-thin interconnects for consumer electronic products. | 408-770-2915 | NA | San Jose |
| | Universal Audio Inc (HQ) | Manufacturer of analog recording equipment. The company's products include audio interfaces, channel strips, plug-ins, and compressors. | 831-440-1176 | 1-10 | Scotts Valley |
| | Video Clarity Inc (HQ) | Provider of real time and broadcast quality monitoring, perceptual analysis, recording, and automating services. | 408-379-6952 | NA | Campbell |

## 319 = Prepackaged Software Development

| | COMPANY NAME | PRODUCT / SERVICE | PHONE | EMP | CITY |
|---|---|---|---|---|---|
| | 500friends Inc (HQ) | Provider of omnichannel loyalty solution. The company offers service and technology to deliver seamless and powerful customer retention solutions. | 415-918-2990 | NA | San Francisco |
| | Acesis Inc (HQ) | Provider of web-based platform for overseeing healthcare quality improvement and compliance documentation, workflow, and analytics. | 650-396-7540 | NA | Mountain View |
| N | Actian Corp (HQ) | Provider of on-premises applications and cloud data management solutions. | 650-587-5500 | NA | Palo Alto |
| N | Adaptive Insights (HQ) | Developers of a cloud business planning framework to enable seamless collaboration across the enterprise. | 650-528-7500 | NA | Palo Alto |
| | Adobe Systems Inc (HQ) | Developer of software solutions for digital media creation and editing, multimedia authoring, and web development. | 408-536-6000 | NA | San Jose |
| | ADPAC Corp (HQ) | Provider of software to improve productivity and value of current application software focusing on business rule extraction, M&A, and documentation. | 415-777-5400 | NA | Livermore |
| | Agiloft Inc (HQ) | Provider of contract, work flow, change, and asset management services. The company offers services to armed forces and universities. | 650-587-8615 | NA | Redwood City |
| | Air Computing Inc (HQ) | Provider of file sync & share service such as transfer large files, share securely, server replacement, and data recovery solutions. | | NA | Palo Alto |
| | Apogee Software Inc (HQ) | Provider of integrated development environment for Java and C. The company offers industrial monitors and controllers. | 408-369-9001 | NA | Campbell |
| N | Applozic Inc (HQ) | Empowers businesses with in-app messaging solutions and all-in-one customer support solution. | 310-909-7458 | NA | Palo Alto |
| N | Apptimize Inc (HQ) | Providers of robust mobile experimentation and optimization solution to improve an user's mobile experience through A/B testing. | 415-926-5398 | NA | San Francisco |
| N | Apttus Corp (HQ) | Developers of AI revenue intelligence software. | 650-445-7700 | NA | San Mateo |
| | Arable Corporation (HQ) | Provider of products and services to health care, pharmaceutical, biotechnology and medical device companies. | 408-825-4755 | NA | Cupertino |
| | Atheer Inc (HQ) | Developer of 3D smart glasses and productivity application for aerospace, insurance, field maintenance, oil & gas, and healthcare. | 650-933-5004 | NA | Santa Clara |
| | Augmentum Inc (HQ) | Provider of software development & solution implementation services. The company focuses on internet applications and product development outsourcing. | 650-578-9221 | NA | Foster City |
| | Avistar Communications Corp (HQ) | Provider of communication solutions. The company provides call controls, conference tools, internet gateway tools, and accessories. | 650-525-3300 | NA | San Mateo |
| | Azul Systems Inc (HQ) | Provider of Java applications for real time businesses. The company's Zing is a JVM enterprise application. | 650-230-6500 | NA | Sunnyvale |
| N | Benevity Inc (BR) | Specializes in corporate social responsibility employee engagement software. | 855-237-7875 | NA | San Mateo |
| | Bitglass (HQ) | Provider of data protection solutions. The company focuses on cloud encryption, mobile security, and discovery solutions. | 408-337-0190 | NA | Campbell |
| N | Branch Metrics (HQ) | Provides deep link solutions that unify user measurement across different devices, platforms, and channels. | 650-209-6461 | NA | Redwood City |
| | Buildera (HQ) | Focuses on structural crack monitoring solutions. The company deals with installation services and serves the industrial sector. | 650-587-6738 | NA | Redwood City |
| | Caseware International Inc (DH) | Supplier of software solutions to accountants and auditors worldwide. The company offers working papers to accounting firms. | 416-867-9504 | NA | Berkeley |
| | Centrify (HQ) | Provider of identity and access management solutions. The company offers services to pharma companies and financial institutions. | 669-444-5200 | NA | Santa Clara |
| | Champ Systems Inc (HQ) | Provider of business management and accounting software. The company offers ERP programming, training, software, and hardware services. | 916-424-4066 | 1-10 | Sacramento |
| | ChannelNet (BR) | Provider of digital solutions to connect brands and customers. The company specializes in strategy development, design, and content optimization. | 415-332-4704 | NA | Sausalito |
| | ChemSoft (HQ) | Provider of software consulting services. The company specializes in custom business solutions, access, excel, PowerPoint, word, and visual basic. | 408-615-1001 | NA | San Jose |

| | COMPANY NAME | PRODUCT / SERVICE | PHONE | EMP | CITY |
|---|---|---|---|---|---|
| N | Clari Inc (HQ) | Developers of an AI-based data capturing software that helps the marketing, sales, and customer success teams. | 650-265-2111 | NA | Sunnyvale |
| | Clean Power Research (HQ) | Provider of program automation, customer engagement, and solar data and intelligence solutions. The company offers services to the solar industry. | 707-258-2765 | NA | Napa |
| | Cloudtc (HQ) | Designer and developer of voice communications platform. The company specializes in business applications. | 650-238-5203 | NA | Palo Alto |
| | Computer Software For Professionals Inc (HQ) | Provider of law office management software and related tools. The company offers services to the legal industry. | 510-547-8085 | NA | Oakland |
| N | Contract Room Inc (HQ) | Provides contract management software. | 800-950-9101 | NA | San Mateo |
| | Contrast Media Labs (HQ) | Provider of graphic design and software development services. The company services include android applications and digital and print media design. | 415-471-1323 | NA | San Francisco |
| | Corona Labs Inc (HQ) | Developer of games, e-books, and other interactive content. The company offers services to the educational sector. | 415-996-6877 | NA | San Francisco |
| N | Corona Labs Inc (HQ) | A cross-platform framework for creating apps and games for mobile devices and desktop systems. | 415-996-6877 | NA | San Francisco |
| N | Coupa Software Inc (HQ) | Global technology platform for Business Spend Management (BSM) to deliver measurable value. | 650-931-3200 | 501-1000 | San Mateo |
| | Cyrun Corp (HQ) | Developer of windows-based integrated software system. The company caters to public safety organizations. | 831-458-0949 | 1-10 | Santa Cruz |
| | Datavision Inc (HQ) | Provider of software solutions for accounting, supply chain, and water and utility applications. The company also offers hosting and support. | 530-387-3575 | 1-10 | Cameron Park |
| | Delta Tao Software (HQ) | Provider of Macintosh and Windows products and solutions. The company is engaged in installation and technical support. | 408-730-9336 | 1-10 | Citrus Heights |
| | Digital Keystone Inc (HQ) | Provider of solutions enabling content distribution to tablets, connected TVs, and other entertainment platforms with suite of software and tools. | 650-938-7300 | NA | Cupertino |
| | Dnn Corp (HQ) | Provider of software solutions for content management. The company also offers marketing & eCommerce and product development services. | 650-288-3150 | NA | San Mateo |
| | Docsend Inc (HQ) | Provider of service that makes documents more effective communication tool with intelligence to track, optimize, and control the business documents sent. | 888-258-5951 | NA | San Francisco |
| | Domico Software (HQ) | Supplier of management and accounting software for managing self storage units, tenants, and accounts. | 510-841-4155 | NA | Walnut Creek |
| | Druva (RH) | Provider of cloud based data protection products. The company offers services to the manufacturing, healthcare, and education industries. | 650-238-6200 | NA | Sunnyvale |
| | Dynamic Graphics Inc (HQ) | Provider of geospatial software solutions such as earth modeling, well planning, and visualization for the petroleum industries. | 510-522-0700 | NA | Alameda |
| | Eda Direct Inc (HQ) | Provider of EDA software products and services. The company's products include Cliosoft, MunEDA, and Mentor Graphics. | 408-496-5890 | NA | Santa Clara |
| N | Elasticsearch Inc (HQ) | A software company that builds self-managed and SaaS offerings that make data usable in real time. | 650-458-2620 | NA | Mountain View |
| N | Engagio Inc (HQ) | B2B Marketing Engagement Software that enables marketers and sellers to work as a team. | 650-487-2050 | NA | San Mateo |
| | enSilo (HQ) | Developer of data protection platforms and provider of exfiltration prevention solutions. The company offers services to the network industry. | 800-413-1782 | NA | San Francisco |
| | ePlus Inc (BR) | Provider of integrated technology solutions and services including lease financing, proprietary software, and project management. | | NA | Milpitas |
| | Equilar Inc (HQ) | Developer of industry-leading data and tools for public and private companies, compensation consultants, attorneys, and corporate governance leaders. | 877-441-6090 | NA | Redwood City |
| | Evernote Corp (HQ) | Provider of note management and digital link services. The company also offers handwriting recognition services. | 650-257-0885 | NA | Redwood City |
| | EverString Ltd (HQ) | Provider of AI SaaS solution for B2B sales and marketing professionals. | 650-425-3937 | NA | San Mateo |
| | Exadel Inc (HQ) | Custom software agency that produces software and mobile solutions. | 925-363-9510 | NA | Walnut Creek |
| | Exxact Corp (HQ) | Supplier of workstation graphic cards and solutions. The company also offers servers, HPC clusters, and computing software. | 510-226-7366 | NA | Fremont |
| | F5 Networks Inc (BR) | Provider of strategic points of control throughout the IT infrastructure for organizations to scale, adapt, and align with changing business demands. | 408-273-4800 | NA | San Jose |
| | Fair Isaac Corp (BR) | Provider of credit scoring, decision management, fraud detection, and credit risk score services offering global business consulting. | 415-472-2211 | NA | San Rafael |
| | Fair Isaac Corp (HQ) | Provider of analytical, software installation, and integration services. The company serves business enterprises. | 408-817-9100 | 51-200 | San Jose |
| | Financial Oxygen Inc (HQ) | Provider of cash management and fixed income products and it serves individual banks and broker-dealers. | 925-465-1225 | NA | San Jose |
| | Flickerbox Inc (HQ) | Provider of marketing, design, and technology support services. The company also deals with lead generation campaigns. | 415-436-9383 | NA | San Francisco |
| | ForgeRock (HQ) | Provider of identity solutions. The company serves the digital health, financial services, communication, and media industries. | 415-599-1100 | NA | San Francisco |

| | COMPANY NAME | PRODUCT / SERVICE | PHONE | EMP | CITY |
|---|---|---|---|---|---|
| | Fortemedia Inc (HQ) | Provider of voice processing integrated circuits. The company also offers related hardware and software components. | 408-861-8088 | NA | Santa Clara |
| N | Full Circle Insights Inc (HQ) | Delivers marketing and sales performance measurement solutions to optimize a company's marketing automation solutions. | 650-641-2766 | NA | San Mateo |
| N | Gong.io (HQ) | Developers of revenue intelligence platform that delivers insights at scale. | 650-276-3068 | NA | San Francisco |
| N | Grio (HQ) | Specializes in web, iOS, and Android development. | 415-395-9525 | NA | San Francisco |
| N | HackerRank (HQ) | Technology recruiting tool that helps tech recruiters and hiring managers to identify and hire talents. | 415-900-4023 | NA | Mountain View |
| | Hawk Ridge Systems (BR) | Provider of 3D design software solutions. The company offers CAD, analysis consulting, product data management, and solid works services. | 510-482-6110 | NA | Orinda |
| | Hawk Ridge Systems (BR) | Provider of parametric 3D product design and analysis services. The company also offers data management tools. | 877-266-4469 | NA | Mountain View |
| N | Hiver (HQ) | A B2B SaaS platform that helps teams collaborate over group inboxes. | | NA | San Jose |
| | HyTrust Inc (HQ) | Provider of security, compliance, and control software for virtualization of information technology infrastructure. | 650-681-8100 | NA | Mountain View |
| | Iar Systems Software Inc (RH) | Provider of software tools and embedded systems. The company's products include state machine tools, starter kits, and compiler and debugger tool suite. | 650-287-4250 | NA | Foster City |
| | Identiv Inc (HQ) | Provider of security technology services. The company's products include desktop readers, terminals, modules, and development kits. | 888-809-8880 | NA | Fremont |
| N | Impekable LLC (HQ) | UI design and mobile development studio that helps organizations to create human-centric mobile experiences. | 650-733-6006 | NA | San Jose |
| | Incentia Design Systems Inc (HQ) | Provider of advanced timing and signal integrity analysis, design closure, and logic synthesis software for nanometer designs. | 408-727-8988 | NA | Santa Clara |
| | Increv Corp (HQ) | Developer of business and information technology solutions. The company is engaged in consulting and product development services. | 408-689-2296 | NA | Los Altos |
| | Individual Software Inc (HQ) | Publisher and developer of education, business, and personal productivity software for consumers, schools, businesses, and government. | 925-734-6767 | NA | Livermore |
| | Inductive Automation (HQ) | Supplier of web-based industrial automation software. The company offers solutions for end-users and integrators. | 916-456-1045 | 1-10 | Folsom |
| | InfinIT Consulting (HQ) | Designer and developer of CNC machining and billet products. The company's products include fire extinguisher brackets, shift knobs, and boat accessories. | 866-364-2007 | NA | Campbell |
| | Infrared Industries Inc (HQ) | Developer of gas analyzer instrumentation for the automotive, oil and gas, industrial, environmental, and utility industries. | 510-782-8100 | NA | Hayward |
| | Inikosoft Inc (HQ) | Provider of web, graphic, and print design services. The company is also engaged in e-commerce development and social media marketing. | 408-402-9545 | NA | Los Gatos |
| | Innosys Inc (HQ) | Provider of data communication solutions. The company serves airlines, travel agencies, and online travel services. | 510-222-7717 | NA | Emeryville |
| N | Intelight ITS LLC (HQ) | Provider of electrical engineering solutions. The company offers expertise on systems, traffic products and software. | 520-795-8808 | 11-50 | Carlsbad |
| | Intelli-Touch Apps Inc (HQ) | Specializes in automating and simplifying the personal and business communications and it serves the legal industry. | 925-884-1802 | NA | San Ramon |
| N | Invoice2go Inc (HQ) | A mobile and web app for micro and small business owners to create invoice, track expenses and track time. | 888-818-7110 | NA | Palo Alto |
| | Itrezzo Inc (HQ) | Provider of unified contact management solutions and it serves schools, agencies, and healthcare organizations. | 408-540-5020 | NA | San Jose |
| | Jeda Technologies Inc (HQ) | Provider of chip based digital designs and semiconductor services. The company focuses on validation and automation solutions. | 408-912-1856 | NA | Santa Clara |
| N | Kanopi Studios (HQ) | A web agency that designs and builds websites for clients. | 888-606-7339 | NA | San Francisco |
| | Kaseya International Ltd (BR) | Provider of software solutions. The company offers cloud and network monitoring, asset management, and backup recovery services. | 415-694-5700 | NA | San Jose |
| | Keri Systems Inc (HQ) | Provider of access control and integrated security systems. The company offers technology support and training solutions. | 408-435-8400 | NA | San Jose |
| N | KitApps Inc (HQ) | Provider of networking and other information-based tools to event organizers and attendees (end-users). | 866-944-8678 | NA | San Jose |
| | Klc Enterprises (HQ) | Provider of accounting software for the construction industry. The company offers services to the commercial and industrial sectors. | 415-485-0555 | NA | San Anselmo |
| | Knightscope Inc (HQ) | Provider of security technology. The company specializes in monotonous, computationally heavy, and sometimes dangerous work for security operations. | 650-924-1025 | NA | Mountain View |
| | Knowme Inc (HQ) | Provider of web based customer relationship management services. The company is also engaged in call routing and web and phone integration. | 800-713-9257 | NA | San Francisco |
| | Kovair Software Inc (HQ) | Provider of web-based document management applications. The company offers product support maintenance services. | 408-262-0200 | NA | San Ramon |
| | Laru Technologies (HQ) | Provider of ACH and Wire transaction monitoring and control tools. The company focuses on risk management and compliance solutions. | 916-458-6149 | 1-10 | Folsom |

| COMPANY NAME | PRODUCT / SERVICE | PHONE | EMP | CITY |
|---|---|---|---|---|
| Lattice Semiconductor Corporation (BR) | Provider of design, development, and marketing services for programmable logic devices. The company also offers related software. | 408-826-6000 | NA | San Jose |
| Lattice Technology Inc (BR) | Developer of 3D and 2D software for design review purposes. The company also focuses on 3D simulation and animation needs. | 720-330-3197 | NA | San Francisco |
| Learning In Motion Inc (HQ) | Provider of educational materials and services. The company offers content development, video production, and marketing collateral services. | 831-600-6606 | 1-10 | Santa Cruz |
| LiveAction (HQ) | Provider of network visibility and performance diagnostics products. The company focuses on network and security forensics. | 888-881-1116 | NA | Palo Alto |
| Logen Solutions USA (HQ) | Provider of truck, container, pallet and carton loading and packaging software. The company offers solutions for cargo load planning. | 408-519-5771 | NA | San Jose |
| Marin Software (HQ) | Developer of software products and provides software design and development for the architecture, engineering, and construction industries. | 415-399-2580 | NA | San Francisco |
| Marklogic Corp (HQ) | Provider of enterprise solutions. The company serves the healthcare, legal, and insurance industries. | 650-655-2300 | NA | San Carlos |
| Matisse Software Inc (HQ) | Provider of database software and services. The company is also engaged in training, consulting, and technical support. | 252-227-7013 | NA | Mountain View |
| Mattermost Inc (HQ) | Delivers open-source messaging tools for security-conscious enterprises and developers. | 650-866-5518 | NA | Palo Alto |
| Mcafee Inc (HQ) | Provider of computer security solutions. The company specializes in database, web, email, network, end-point, and mobile security services. | 800-937-2237 | NA | Santa Clara |
| Mindflash (HQ) | Provider of online training and related solutions. The company offers services to the software industry. | 805-963-8417 | 11-50 | Palo Alto |
| Mobitor Corp (HQ) | Provider of mobility software, connectivity, and information solutions. The company serves the aerospace, aviation, and manufacturing industries. | 925-464-7700 | NA | Walnut Creek |
| Montavista Software LLC (HQ) | Developer of embedded Linux system software, development tools, and related software products. The company's products include CGE and DevRocket. | 408-520-1591 | NA | Santa Clara |
| Multi Metrics Inc (HQ) | Provider of geometric dimensioning and tolerance technology products and services and offers training and corporate implementation services. | 650-328-0200 | NA | Menlo Park |
| Netxperts Inc (HQ) | Provider of unified communication solutions. The company offers services to the healthcare and transportation markets. | 925-806-0800 | NA | Walnut Creek |
| Nexant Inc (HQ) | Developer of software for utility, energy, chemical, and other sectors and also offers power grid consulting and energy advisory, and other services. | 415-369-1000 | NA | San Francisco |
| Nextbus Inc (BR) | Provider of transit management solutions. The company also provides real-time passenger information solutions to organizations. | 925-686-8200 | NA | Concord |
| Nexusguard Ltd (RH) | Provider of monitoring and DNA protection services. The company serves service providers and the entertainment sector. | 415-299-8550 | NA | San Francisco |
| Nuance Communications Inc (BR) | Provider of hosted application systems and mobile solutions. The company offers services to businesses and the healthcare sector. | 408-992-6100 | NA | Sunnyvale |
| Ondavia Inc (HQ) | Provider of water analysis solutions. The company offers OndaVia analysis system that enables laboratory-grade water testing. | 510-576-0476 | NA | Hayward |
| Open Source Initiative (HQ) | Works to raise awareness and adoption of open-source software, and build bridges between open source communities of practice. | | NA | Palo Alto |
| Optumsoft Inc (HQ) | Provider of distributed computing and technology based software development that includes maintenance of structured software systems. | 844-361-8222 | NA | Menlo Park |
| Professional Finishing (HQ) | Provider of liquid & powder coatings and finishing to the scientific and aerospace industries. The company focuses on sandblasting and silk screening. | 510-233-7629 | NA | Richmond |
| Prolific Interactive (BR) | Mobile-focused product agency that engages in creating products and delivering mobile experiences for leading brands. | 415-813-4199 | NA | San Francisco |
| Promptu (HQ) | Provider of voice-activated search and navigation services. The company is also engaged in engineering and product marketing. | 650-859-5800 | NA | Menlo Park |
| Provectus IT Inc (HQ) | Accelerates digital transformation by using Artificial Intelligence. | 877-951-2224 | NA | Palo Alto |
| Pulse Secure LLC (HQ) | Provider of product, hardware, partner, and enterprise solutions. The company offers services to the financial services and healthcare industries. | 408-372-9600 | NA | San Jose |
| Quantum Corporation (HQ) | Provider of software for backup, recovery, and archiving needs. The company serves the healthcare, media, and entertainment industries. | 408-944-4000 | NA | San Jose |
| Quantum3D Inc (HQ) | Developer and manufacturer of real-time visual simulation and computing systems for fast-jet, helicopter, refueling, and other needs. | 408-600-2500 | NA | Milpitas |
| Readytech Corp (HQ) | Provider of virtual labs for training, certification, and also sales demonstrations. The company deals with technology support. | 800-707-1009 | NA | Oakland |
| Red Hat Inc (BR) | Provider of training, certification, consulting, cloud, application, and other technical support services. | 650-567-9039 | NA | Sunnyvale |
| Redbooth (HQ) | A task and project management platform for team collaboration tasks, discussions, and file sharing. | 650-521-5459 | NA | San Francisco |
| Refresh Your Memory Inc (HQ) | Provider of CNC Machine Tool monitoring and data collection products. The company is also involved in preventive maintenance services. | 408-224-9167 | NA | San Jose |
| RethinkDB (HQ) | An open-source distributed document-oriented database. | 650-965-8308 | NA | Mountain View |

| COMPANY NAME | PRODUCT / SERVICE | PHONE | EMP | CITY |
|---|---|---|---|---|
| Robertson Precision Inc (HQ) | Manufacturer of precision metals and plastic products. The company's services include engineering support and process control. | 650-363-2212 | NA | Menlo Park |
| Rolepoint (HQ) | Focuses on talent acquisition services. The company serves small and medium businesses and Fortune 500 companies. | 888-571-2851 | NA | San Francisco |
| SAP America Inc (BR) | Developer of software applications. The company provides data and technology, custom development, and implementation services. | 650-849-4000 | NA | Palo Alto |
| **N** Searchmetrics Inc (HQ) | A Search and Content Marketing Platform that uncovers the opportunities and pitfalls of online marketing. | 866-411 9494 | NA | San Mateo |
| Secugen Corp (HQ) | Manufacturer of fingerprint recognition devices. The company's products serve the purpose of integration into 3rd party hardware products. | 408-727-7787 | NA | Santa Clara |
| Sharpesoft Inc (HQ) | Provider of cost accounting, dispatching, and project management software. The company exclusively serves the construction sector. | 530-671-6499 | 1-10 | Yuba City |
| Silicon Dust (RH) | Provider of network connected TV tuners. The company offers global solutions to Live TV streaming in businesses, hotels, and education facilities. | 925-443-4388 | NA | Livermore |
| Silvaco Inc (HQ) | Supplier of TCAD and EDA software for circuit simulation. The company also designs analog, mixed-signal, and RF integrated circuits. | 408-567-1000 | NA | Santa Clara |
| **N** Simplicant Inc (HQ) | Producer of modern recruitment software that also helps to track applicants. | 650-285-2394 | NA | Palo Alto |
| SL Corp (HQ) | Provider of monitoring and analytics solutions for middleware-powered applications. The company serves the electrical commodity market. | 415-927-8400 | NA | Corte Madera |
| Sst Systems Inc (HQ) | Provider of solutions for piping design and analysis. The company's services include plant design and engineering. | 408-452-8111 | NA | San Jose |
| Stella Technology Inc (HQ) | Provider of integration and collaboration solutions. The company deals with technology design, development, and consulting services. | 844-278-3552 | NA | San Jose |
| Stone Cobra (HQ) | Provider of knowledge management solutions. The company offers solutions for architecture, system configuration, and data migration. | 916-797-6272 | 1-10 | Roseville |
| **N** TalkCycle LLC (HQ) | Providers of innovative sales communication software. | 888-400-2220 | NA | San Mateo |
| Teamf1 Inc (HQ) | Provider of networking and security software for embedded devices. The company also offers technical support services. | 510-505-9931 | NA | Fremont |
| Telemanagement Technologies Inc (HQ) | Provider of telemanagement software products and services. The company is engaged in troubleshooting and maintenance services. | 925-946-9800 | NA | Walnut Creek |
| **N** Thoughtbot Inc (BR) | Provider of web and mobile app design and development. | 877-976-2687 | NA | San Francisco |
| **N** ThoughtSpot Inc (HQ) | A business intelligence platform that helps individuals to explore, analyze, and share real-time business analytics data. | 800-508-7008 | NA | Sunnyvale |
| ThreatMetrix (HQ) | Provider of fraud prevention, threat detection, and authentication solutions. The company serves the gaming, media, and insurance industries. | 408-200-5755 | NA | San Jose |
| TIBCO Software Inc (HQ) | Provider of enterprise application integration software. The company serves the government, healthcare, and insurance industries. | 650-846-1000 | NA | Palo Alto |
| **N** Tivix (BR) | Focuses on the agile development of web, cloud, and mobile applications. | 415-680-1299 | NA | San Francisco |
| Tora Trading Services Ltd (BR) | Provider of products such as Compass, Clearpool, and Crosspoint for buy-side traders to specifically address the trading challenges to Asia. | 650-513-6700 | NA | Burlingame |
| Total Resolution Llc (HQ) | Developer of software for electron microscopy needs. The company provides MacTempasX and CrystalKitX. | 510-527-6393 | NA | Berkeley |
| **N** Treasure Data Inc (HQ) | Empower enterprises by unifying data from multiple sources such as online, offline, IoT and device-generated data. | 866-899-5386 | NA | Mountain View |
| Ultra-X Inc (HQ) | Provider of personal computer diagnostic solutions for developers, manufacturers, system engineers, integrators, and computer professionals. | 408-261-7090 | NA | Santa Clara |
| Untangle (HQ) | Designer and developer of network management software. The company specializes in firewall and Internet management application. | 408-598-4299 | NA | San Jose |
| uSens Inc (HQ) | Creator of 3D human computing interaction software and hardware solutions. The company focuses on artificial intelligence. | 408-564-0227 | NA | San Jose |
| Valin (HQ) | Provider of engineered solutions. The company serves the semiconductor, petrochemical, life sciences, and aerospace industries. | 408-730-9850 | NA | San Jose |
| Verific Design Automation Inc (HQ) | Specializes in electronic design automation solutions. The company offers services to the semiconductor industry. | 510-522-1555 | NA | Alameda |
| **N** Veritas Technologies LLC (HQ) | Empowers business with a multi-cloud data management solution. | 866-837-4827 | NA | Santa Clara |
| Vicom Systems Inc (HQ) | Provider of migration data services. The company is involved in offering transparent wire-speed data services for systems and storage. | 650-241-3302 | NA | Santa Clara |
| Wind River (DH) | Provider of automotive networking solutions. The company's products include operating systems, development tools, and middleware technologies. | 510-748-4100 | NA | Alameda |
| XC2 Software LLC (HQ) | Provider of integrated software suite. The company's products find application in water and wastewater utilities. | 800-761-4999 | NA | Fairfax |
| XEODesign (HQ) | Provider of computer multimedia software, website design hosting, programming, and technical support services. | 510-658-8077 | NA | Oakland |
| Xetus Mortgage Corp (HQ) | Provider of mortgage processing services such as documentation monitoring, data and image capture, and reporting and audit trail. | 650-237-1225 | NA | Burlingame |

| COMPANY NAME | PRODUCT / SERVICE | PHONE | EMP | CITY |
|---|---|---|---|---|
| Zeidman Technologies Inc (HQ) | Developer of hardware and software code design tools. The company focuses on embedded system development. | 408-741-5809 | NA | Cupertino |
| Zetta Inc (HQ) | Provider of information technology solutions. The company provides on-line backup, disaster recovery, and archiving solutions. | 650-590-0967 | NA | Sunnyvale |
| Zmanda - A Carbonite Co (HQ) | Provider of open source backup and recovery software solutions. The company's applications include centralized backup of file systems and applications. | 408-732-3208 | 51-200 | Sunnyvale |
| Zoho Corp (HQ) | Developer and provider of IT management software, business technology solutions, and network management framework. | 615-671-9025 | NA | Pleasanton |

## 320 = Software Publication

| COMPANY NAME | PRODUCT / SERVICE | PHONE | EMP | CITY |
|---|---|---|---|---|
| Asmeix Corp (HQ) | Provider of welding procedure software services such as technical support, installation, maintenance, and demo services. | 877-977-7999 | NA | Concord |
| Atypon Systems LLC (HQ) | Provider of service content delivery software for publishers. The company serves information discovery, e-commerce, and business intelligence needs. | 408-988-1240 | NA | Santa Clara |
| Bayometric (HQ) | Supplier of fingerprint scanners, single sign-on solution and access control systems. The company serves the business and industrial markets. | 408-940-3955 | NA | San Jose |
| Bodhtree Solutions Inc (BR) | Provider of information technology consulting services. The company deals with product engineering, application development, and training. | 408-954-8700 | 11-50 | Fremont |
| BuyerLeverage (HQ) | Provider of technologies and services that allow consumers and businesses to profit and control their communications and information. | 650-320-1608 | NA | Palo Alto |
| Calyx Technology Inc (HQ) | Provider of mortgage solutions for banks and credit unions. The company also serves mortgage bankers and brokers. | 408-997-5525 | NA | San Jose |
| Certain Inc (DH) | Provider of enterprise event management solutions that include e-mail marketing, event reporting, registration, and consulting services. | 415-353-5330 | NA | San Francisco |
| Cirius Group Inc (HQ) | Designer and marketer of financial and medical software. The company serves hospitals and healthcare providers. | 925-685-9300 | NA | Pleasant Hill |
| Devicelock Inc (HQ) | Developer of device control software solutions. The company offers contextual and content-based control for data leak prevention. | 925-231-4400 | NA | San Ramon |
| Digital Element Inc (HQ) | Developer of computer artwork, software, and tools for computer artists and developers. The company offers 3D animation, plug-ins, and art tools. | | NA | Fremont |
| DreamFactory Software Inc (HQ) | Provider of software development services. The company offers hosting, external integration, SQL, and user management services. | 415-993-5877 | NA | Campbell |
| Exatron Inc (HQ) | Manufacturer of automatic test equipment and IC handlers. The company also specializes in open short testers. | 408-629-7600 | NA | San Jose |
| Granite Horizon LLC (HQ) | Provider of content management solutions. The company offers design, development, project management, and user and developer training services. | 916-647-6350 | 1-10 | Elk Grove |
| HyTrust Inc (HQ) | Provider of security, compliance, and control software for virtualization of information technology infrastructure. | 650-681-8100 | NA | Mountain View |
| Icube Information International (HQ) | Publisher of software work flow based management systems, documentation, inventory processing, and revision tracking services. | 510-683-8928 | NA | Fremont |
| Imaja (HQ) | Developer of computer applications. The company specializes in the development of educational tools for Macs. | 510-526-4621 | NA | Berkeley |
| Individual Software Inc (HQ) | Publisher and developer of education, business, and personal productivity software for consumers, schools, businesses, and government. | 925-734-6767 | NA | Livermore |
| Learning In Motion Inc (HQ) | Provider of educational materials and services. The company offers content development, video production, and marketing collateral services. | 831-600-6606 | 1-10 | Santa Cruz |
| Mobileframe Llc (HQ) | Provider of enterprise mobility solutions that include mobile application development, device management, GPS tracking, and integration features. | 408-885-1200 | NA | Los Gatos |
| Netxperts Inc (HQ) | Provider of unified communication solutions. The company offers services to the healthcare and transportation markets. | 925-806-0800 | NA | Walnut Creek |
| Nexenta Systems Inc (HQ) | Provider of enterprise class storage software solutions. The company is engaged in virtualization and business continuity planning. | 408-791-3300 | NA | San Jose |
| Omnicia Inc (HQ) | Provider of electronic submissions for the life science sector. The company offers electronics & desktop publishing and document management services. | 650-588-2188 | NA | S San Francisco |
| Onque Technologies Inc (HQ) | Provider of software tools used for the management of human resources. The company serves business organizations and enterprises. | 707-569-3000 | NA | Sonoma |
| Optumsoft Inc (HQ) | Provider of distributed computing and technology based software development that includes maintenance of structured software systems. | 844-361-8222 | NA | Menlo Park |
| Personal Tex Inc (HQ) | Publisher of PCTeX software that enables mathematicians to publish their formulas, equations, and thoughts. | 415-296-7550 | NA | San Francisco |
| Pictron Inc (HQ) | Provider of solutions for media applications in corporate communications, eLearning, broadcast production, and content based video search fields. | 408-725-8888 | NA | Sunnyvale |
| Reprise Software Inc (HQ) | Provider of license management software solutions. The company's products include Exa, Arxan, LMS, and Pace. | 781-837-0884 | NA | San Jose |

| COMPANY NAME | PRODUCT / SERVICE | PHONE | EMP | CITY |
|---|---|---|---|---|
| Silicon Publishing Inc (HQ) | Provider of digital publishing solutions. The company deals with template designs and personalized communications. | 925-935-3899 | NA | San Francisco |
| Trion Worlds Inc (HQ) | Publisher and developer of games. The company offers Defiance, RIFT, Archeage, and End of Nations games. | 650-273-9618 | NA | Redwood City |
| Zag Technical Services Inc (HQ) | Provider of services for server, email stability, reliability, migration, and security assessment needs. | 408-383-2000 | NA | San Jose |
| Zetta Inc (HQ) | Provider of information technology solutions. The company provides on-line backup, disaster recovery, and archiving solutions. | 650-590-0967 | NA | Sunnyvale |

### 321 = Software - Related Services

| COMPANY NAME | PRODUCT / SERVICE | PHONE | EMP | CITY |
|---|---|---|---|---|
| Crypto Forensics Technologies Inc (HQ) | Provider of cybersecurity solutions to businesses, organizations, and the government. The company focuses on cyberforensics and compliance services. | 510-483-1955 | NA | San Leandro |

### 322 = Application-Specific Software

| COMPANY NAME | PRODUCT / SERVICE | PHONE | EMP | CITY |
|---|---|---|---|---|
| 37 Degrees Inc (HQ) | Provider of technology and management consulting services for publishing, media, software technology, and beverage industries. | 415-315-9380 | NA | San Francisco |
| A9 com Inc (HQ) | Provider of product, visual, and cloud search services. The company also focuses on mobile apps, advertising, and technical operations. | 650-331-2600 | NA | Palo Alto |
| Ablesys Corp (HQ) | Provider of financial trading software and web applications. The company focuses on portfolio and algorithmic trading solutions. | 510-265-1883 | NA | Hayward |
| Accela Inc (HQ) | Provider of licensing, asset and land management, and public health and safety solutions. The company offers technical support services. | 925-659-3200 | NA | San Ramon |
| Accelerate Mobile Apps Inc (HQ) | Provider of design, live training, and performance support tools such as the influencer app that helps assess working style for managers. | 831-438-8500 | 1-10 | Scotts Valley |
| Accenture (BR) | Provider of management consulting and technology services. The company also offers application outsourcing and IT consulting services. | 415-537-5000 | NA | San Francisco |
| Accounting Micro Systems (HQ) | Developer of accounting and business management software products. The company offers MAS500, MAS90 and MAS200, FAS Asset solutions, and SalesLogix. | 415-362-5100 | NA | San Francisco |
| Acionyx (HQ) | Provider of systems development and engineering consulting services. The company also deals with testing and quality assurance. | 408-366-2908 | NA | San Jose |
| Adapt Corp (HQ) | Provider of post-tensioning and reinforced concrete structural analysis software for building design. | 650-306-2400 | NA | Redwood City |
| Adaptive Insights (HQ) | Provider of training, consulting, and related support services. The company serves the healthcare, insurance, and manufacturing industries. | 650-528-7500 | NA | Palo Alto |
| Addepar Inc (HQ) | Provider of investment management solutions and technology platform for data aggregation, powerful analytics, and empowering clients to excel. | 855-464-6268 | NA | Mountain View |
| Advantage for Analysts Inc (HQ) | Developer of structuring and analysis software. The company finds application in originating, trading, and managing complex financial assets. | 415-568-4800 | NA | Sausalito |
| AerospaceComputing Inc (HQ) | Provider of computer technology application services to aerospace sciences. The company also focuses on business development services. | 650-988-0388 | NA | Mountain View |
| Agnitus (HQ) | Developer of touch enabled learning applications for iPad. The company specializes in educational games such as little bo peep and ABC hide n seek. | 877-565-1460 | NA | Palo Alto |
| Air Worldwide Corp (BR) | Provider of software development and consulting services. The company focuses on risk modeling software and risk assessment and management consulting. | 415-912-3111 | NA | San Francisco |
| Algo-Logic Systems (HQ) | Specializes in building networking solutions. The company also offers technological and data handling services to firms. | 408-707-3740 | NA | San Jose |
| AmigoCloud Inc (HQ) | Provider of geospatial platform that helps to collect, manage, analyze, visualize, and publish the location data using smartphone, camera, and sensors. | 415-935-1447 | NA | San Francisco |
| Amind Solutions Llc (HQ) | Provider of technology and services. The company offers enterprise mobility, quoting and ordering, product configuration, and e-Commerce services. | 925-804-6139 | NA | Alamo |
| Amobee Inc (HQ) | Provider of marketing intelligence and cross channel, cross device advertiser, and publisher solutions for marketers, publishers, and operators. | 650-353-4399 | NA | Redwood City |
| Anki Inc (HQ) | Provider of robotic racing products such as drive and expansion cars, starter, bottleneck and crossroad tracks, and accessories for consumers. | 415-670-9488 | NA | San Francisco |
| Apogee Software Inc (HQ) | Provider of integrated development environment for Java and C. The company offers industrial monitors and controllers. | 408-369-9001 | NA | Campbell |
| Apple Inc (HQ) | Designer and marketer of consumer electronics. The company also focuses on computer software and personal computers. | 408-996-1010 | NA | Cupertino |
| Applian Technologies Inc (HQ) | Provider of solutions for the capture and conversion of web video, streaming audio, and song and radio program software for Windows users. | 415-480-1748 | NA | San Anselmo |
| Applied Expert Systems Inc (HQ) | Developer of networking solutions for business service management. The company provides virtualization and cloud computing services. | 650-617-2400 | NA | Palo Alto |

| COMPANY NAME | PRODUCT / SERVICE | PHONE | EMP | CITY |
|---|---|---|---|---|
| Appsec Consulting (HQ) | Provider of services to identify vulnerabilities in applications. The company focuses on penetration testing and PCI compliance. | 408-224-1110 | NA | San Jose |
| Apptology (HQ) | Provider of mobile application development, training, marketing, iPhone application development, and Android application development services. | 877-990-2777 | 11-50 | Folsom |
| Aptible Inc (HQ) | Developer of secure, private cloud deployment platform built to automate HIPAA compliance for digital health. | 866-296-5003 | NA | San Francisco |
| Aragon Consulting Group Inc (HQ) | Provider of software development services. The company also offers authoring, coding, consulting, and technical support solutions. | 415-869-8818 | NA | Cupertino |
| Arasan Chip Systems Inc (RH) | Provider of total IP solutions such as digital IP cores, protocol analyzers, and traffic generators for mobile storage and connectivity applications. | 408-282-1600 | NA | San Jose |
| Arterys Inc (DH) | Developer of medical imaging cloud platform. The company specializes in diagnostic platform to make healthcare more accurate and data driven. | 650-319-7230 | NA | San Francisco |
| Artifex Software Inc (HQ) | Provider of software solutions for host based applications. The company also focuses on embedded printer markets. | 415-492-9861 | NA | Novato |
| Artium Technologies Inc (HQ) | Developer of products for spray diagnostics, particulate monitoring, and cloud research applications. | 408-737-2364 | NA | Sunnyvale |
| Augmentum Inc (HQ) | Provider of software development & solution implementation services. The company focuses on internet applications and product development outsourcing. | 650-578-9221 | NA | Foster City |
| Aurionpro Solutions Inc (DH) | Provider of solutions to streamline corporate banking, treasury, fraud prevention, risk management, governance and compliance needs. | 925-242-0777 | NA | San Ramon |
| Autonet Mobile (HQ) | Provider of internet based telematics and applications service platform for the automotive transportation market. | 415-223-0316 | NA | Santa Rosa |
| Avid Technology Inc (BR) | Manufacturer of computer automated audio mixing consoles. The company offers audio product registration and software activation services. | 800-955-0960 | NA | Santa Clara |
| Aviso Inc (HQ) | Creator of software to change how enterprises make critical revenue decisions and automate sales forecasting process with data science for enterprises. | 650-567-5470 | NA | Redwood City |
| Ayasdi Inc (HQ) | Provider of software applications that discovers critical intelligence in company data for right operational decisions quickly. | 650-704-3395 | NA | Menlo Park |
| Badger Maps Inc (HQ) | Provider of easy to use interface to manage our daily call routes, track visits, and update records. | 415-592-5909 | NA | San Francisco |
| Banks Integration Group (HQ) | Developer and provider of control systems and plant automation software. The company serves biotech, food, brewery, oil & gas, and other sectors. | 707-451-1100 | NA | Vacaville |
| Barracuda Networks Inc (HQ) | Developer of solutions for IT problems primarily focusing on security and storage. The company also focuses on application delivery and productivity. | 408-342-5400 | NA | Campbell |
| Bcl Technologies (HQ) | Developer of document creation, conversion, and extraction solutions. The company offers BCL easyPDF Cloud, a cloud-based PDF conversion platform. | 408-557-2080 | NA | San Jose |
| Berkeley Design Technology Inc (HQ) | Provider of analysis, advice, and engineering solutions for embedded processing technology and applications. | 925-954-1411 | NA | Walnut Creek |
| BetterDoctor Inc (HQ) | Provider of mobile apps for iPhone to find primary care, OBGYN, pediatricians, dentist, eye, and all specialties doctors. | 844-668-2543 | NA | San Francisco |
| Birst Inc (HQ) | Provider of supply chain, marketing, human resources, financial, and sales analytics solutions for businesses. | 415-766-4800 | NA | San Francisco |
| BitTorrent Inc (HQ) | Provider of download software solutions. The company offers design, data and content management, and installation services. | 415-568-9000 | NA | San Francisco |
| Blackstone Technology Group Inc (HQ) | Provider of IT solutions, commercial, and government consulting, staffing services, and trellis natural gas transaction management web solution. | 415-837-1400 | NA | San Francisco |
| Blue Jeans Network Inc (HQ) | Provider of cloud-based video conferencing solutions. The company also offers mobile video collaboration and cloud video bridging solutions. | 408-550-2828 | NA | Mountain View |
| Blunk Microsystems LLC (HQ) | Provider of turnkey packages for embedded development to customers around the world. The company also offers development tools. | 408-323-1758 | 1-10 | Sacramento |
| Border Collie Solutions Inc (HQ) | Provider of security surveillance software products. The company focuses on security panel, energy management, and medical monitoring. | 650-343-2400 | NA | Burlingame |
| Bramasol Inc (BR) | Provider of SAP-based solution for high tech software, life science, industrial machinery & components, and Telco, wireless, and internet services. | 408-831-0046 | NA | Santa Clara |
| California Software Systems (HQ) | Provider of graphics software solutions. The company products include DNC file server for windows and graphics software. | 831-477-6843 | 1-10 | San Juan Bautista |
| Callidus Software Inc (HQ) | Provider of sales performance management software. The company also offers incentive compensation management software and services. | 925-251-2200 | NA | Pleasanton |
| Capitol Digital Document Solutions (HQ) | Provider of litigation support services. The company offers forensic data collection, online document review, and e-discovery processing services. | 916-449-2820 | 1-10 | Sacramento |
| Castle Rock Computing Inc (HQ) | Designer and manufacturer of SNMPC network management software. The company's product caters to a wide range of sectors. | 408-366-6540 | NA | Saratoga |

| COMPANY NAME | PRODUCT / SERVICE | PHONE | EMP | CITY |
|---|---|---|---|---|
| Celestix Networks Inc (HQ) | Provider of security appliances and solutions for healthcare, legal & financial, education, commercial, small business, and public sector industries. | 510-668-0700 | NA | Fremont |
| Centric Software Inc (HQ) | Provider of product lifecycle management solution to apparel, consumer goods, luxury good, and footwear industries. | 408-574-7802 | NA | Los Gatos |
| Centrify (HQ) | Provider of identity and access management solutions. The company offers services to pharma companies and financial institutions. | 669-444-5200 | NA | Santa Clara |
| Certent Inc (HQ) | Provider of equity compensation management, equity compensation reporting, and disclosure management solutions. | 925-730-4300 | NA | Pleasanton |
| Check Point Software Technologies Inc (HQ) | Developer of software technology solutions such as mobile security and next generation firewalls for retail/point of sale and financial services. | 800-429-4391 | NA | San Carlos |
| Chelsio Communications (HQ) | Provider of Ethernet adapters. The company offers storage routers, wire adapters, virtualization and management software, and accessories. | 408-962-3600 | NA | Sunnyvale |
| Chesapeake Technology Inc (HQ) | Provider of sonar mapping software as well as consulting services to the marine, geophysical, and geological survey industries. | 650-967-2045 | NA | Los Altos |
| Chess com (HQ) | Provider of unlimited chess games and free tournaments that can be played by challenging friends and meet new players. | 800-318-2827 | NA | Palo Alto |
| Chiapas Edi Technologies Inc (HQ) | Developer of electronic data interchange software for health insurance exchange brokers, MSOs, HMOs, and healthcare business data analytics services. | 415-298-8166 | 1-10 | Davis |
| Chrometa LLC (HQ) | Provider of time keeping management software and services. The company offers products for PC, Mac, iPhone, and Android platforms. | 916-546-9974 | 1-10 | Sacramento |
| Circleci (HQ) | Provider of continuous integration and delivery solution. The company offers apps for docker, enterprise, and mobiles. | 800-585-7075 | NA | San Francisco |
| Cirius Group Inc (HQ) | Designer and marketer of financial and medical software. The company serves hospitals and healthcare providers. | 925-685-9300 | NA | Pleasant Hill |
| Citrix Systems Inc (BR) | Provider of transition to software-defining the workplace, uniting virtualization, mobility management, networking, and SaaS solutions. | 408-790-8000 | NA | Santa Clara |
| Claresco Corp (HQ) | Provider of design and implementation services for customized business software. The company serves multi-national firms. | 510-528-0238 | NA | Berkeley |
| Clean Power Research (HQ) | Provider of program automation, customer engagement, and solar data and intelligence solutions. The company offers services to the solar industry. | 707-258-2765 | NA | Napa |
| Codeobjects Inc (HQ) | Developer of insurance process management and business intelligence solutions. The company also offers claims management services. | 408-432-1180 | NA | Milpitas |
| Colabo Inc (HQ) | Provider of multi-functional software that enables professionals across all industries to achieve a number of business objectives. | 650-288-6649 | NA | San Carlos |
| Computers & Structures Inc (HQ) | Provider of integrated design, analysis, assessment, drafting of building systems, and related support services. | 510-649-2200 | NA | Walnut Creek |
| Conformiq Inc (HQ) | Provider of automated test designing services. The company focuses on training, project implementation, change management, and executive consulting. | 408-898-2140 | NA | Saratoga |
| Corman Technologies Inc (HQ) | Provider of software development and consulting services for a variety of clients in the software industry. | 707-575-7800 | NA | Santa Rosa |
| Corona Labs Inc (HQ) | Developer of games, e-books, and other interactive content. The company offers services to the educational sector. | 415-996-6877 | NA | San Francisco |
| Crestpoint Solutions Inc (HQ) | Provider of project planning, programming, web hosting, and wireless and records management services. | 925-828-6005 | NA | Pleasanton |
| Crmantra Inc (HQ) | Developer of software for customer relationship management needs. The company also focuses on business intelligence and analysis. | 415-839-9672 | NA | Emeryville |
| Cyberglove Systems Llc (HQ) | Provider of data glove technology. The company offers system installation and integration and custom software and hardware services. | 408-943-8114 | NA | San Jose |
| Cybersoft (BR) | Provider of offshore business and knowledge process outsourcing services. The company specializes in title, financial, and document processing services. | 415-449-7998 | NA | San Francisco |
| Cygna Energy Services Inc (HQ) | Provider of application development, data integration, systems integration, consulting, and web services. | 925-930-8377 | NA | Walnut Creek |
| Data ID Systems (HQ) | Provider of identification management solutions. The company offers passport readers, bar code scanners, and fixed asset tracking products. | 408-371-5764 | NA | Campbell |
| Data Tech (HQ) | Developer of specialized accounting software. The company primarily caters to the agricultural industry. | 800-833-8824 | 1-10 | Fresno |
| Dataglance Inc (HQ) | Provider of data management software that support LIVE data conversion/migration, electronic document generation & processing, and web services. | 510-656-0500 | NA | Fremont |
| Dcm Datasystems (RH) | Provider of managed IT services. The company focuses on system administration, storage, enterprise management, and staffing services. | 510-494-2321 | NA | Fremont |
| Denodo Technologies Inc (HQ) | Provider of enterprise data virtualization, data federation, and cloud data integration middleware solutions. | 650-566-8833 | NA | Palo Alto |

| COMPANY NAME | PRODUCT / SERVICE | PHONE | EMP | CITY |
|---|---|---|---|---|
| Devonway (HQ) | Provider of enterprise software solutions for utilities and process industries. The company specializes in enterprise asset management solutions. | 415-904-4000 | NA | San Francisco |
| Digilabs Inc (HQ) | Provider of online proofing, proof albums, prints, gallery wraps, wedding photographer products, and web galleries for the photographers. | | NA | Palo Alto |
| Digital Keystone Inc (HQ) | Provider of solutions enabling content distribution to tablets, connected TVs, and other entertainment platforms with suite of software and tools. | 650-938-7300 | NA | Cupertino |
| DOCOMO Innovations Inc (HQ) | Provider of products and services for businesses. The company focuses on business development, network solutions, and mobile network technology. | 650-493-9600 | NA | Palo Alto |
| Dogpatch Technology Inc (HQ) | Provider of digital strategy and mobile development solutions for game design and research, global media and communications, and grant writing projects. | 415-663-6488 | NA | San Francisco |
| Dolphin Corp (HQ) | Provider of information life cycle and business process management services for organizations using SAP solutions. | 610-725-9125 | NA | Morgan Hill |
| Domico Software (HQ) | Supplier of management and accounting software for managing self storage units, tenants, and accounts. | 510-841-4155 | NA | Walnut Creek |
| DreamFactory Software Inc (HQ) | Provider of software development services. The company offers hosting, external integration, SQL, and user management services. | 415-993-5877 | NA | Campbell |
| Droisys Inc (HQ) | Provider of business solutions and offers services such as content management, enterprise resource planning, and business efficiency consulting. | 408-874-8333 | NA | Santa Clara |
| Dsp Concepts Inc (HQ) | Provider of embedded audio processing tools and services. The company offers system design, embedded software development, and optimization services. | 408-747-5200 | NA | Santa Clara |
| eASIC Corp (HQ) | Developer of structured ASIC fabric for SoC and platform designs. The company focuses on programming and development services. | | NA | Santa Clara |
| Elementum Scm Inc (HQ) | Provider of apps to manage your global supply chain. The company offers manufacturing operations, mission control, supplier, and logistics management. | 650-318-1491 | NA | Mountain View |
| Ellie Mae Inc (HQ) | Focuses on mortgage compliance services. The company offers services to banks and other financial institutions. | 925-227-7000 | NA | Pleasanton |
| energyOrbit Inc (HQ) | Provider of cloud based platform and solution for streamline demand side management programs, projects, and relationship management for customers. | 866-628-8744 | NA | San Francisco |
| Envestnet (BR) | Provider of application software for financial service firms. The company is involved in practice and portfolio management. | 866-924-8912 | NA | San Jose |
| Errigal Inc (HQ) | Designer and developer of software products and services. The company also deals with configuration management and ticketing. | 415-523-9245 | NA | San Francisco |
| Evernote Corp (HQ) | Provider of note management and digital link services. The company also offers handwriting recognition services. | 650-257-0885 | NA | Redwood City |
| Evolphin Software Inc (HQ) | Provider of digital and media assest management software for video production, game developers, media, television broadcasters, and eLearning groups. | 888-386-4114 | NA | San Ramon |
| Evolveware Inc (HQ) | Developer of products to automate and modernize IT infrastructure focusing on assessment, documentation, impact analysis, and other solutions. | 408-748-8301 | NA | Santa Clara |
| Exadel Inc (HQ) | Provider of software using technologies including mobile, cloud, and web user interfaces. The company also delivers tools and products for users. | 925-363-9510 | NA | Walnut Creek |
| Extractable Inc (HQ) | Provider of websites, applications, social and mobile experiences for transactional, educational, lead generation, and entertainment purposes. | 415-426-3600 | NA | San Francisco |
| Facebook Inc (HQ) | Designer and developer of technologies to communicate with their family, friends, and also coworkers. | 650-543-4800 | NA | Menlo Park |
| Fiduciary Management Technologies Inc (HQ) | Provider of insolvency case, fiduciary case, and estate management solutions. The company offers SEC distribution fund administration services. | 916-930-9900 | 1-10 | Sacramento |
| Five9 Inc (HQ) | Seller of call center software focusing on IVR System, an interactive voice response software, Outbound Call Center software, and Auto Dialer. | 925-201-2000 | NA | San Ramon |
| Foxit Corp (HQ) | Developer of software. The company offers software such as Foxit Reader, Enterprise, and Mobile Reader. | 510-438-9090 | NA | Fremont |
| Future Facilities Inc (BR) | Developer of engineering simulation software for the design and operation of electronics products. The company serves the industrial sector. | 408-436-7701 | NA | San Jose |
| Futuredial Inc (HQ) | Developer of carrier-grade solutions and tools for mobile device recyclers, wireless operators, and mobile device manufacturers. | 408-245-8880 | NA | Sunnyvale |
| G4s Secure Solutions (usa) Inc (BR) | Provider of security management solutions such as compliance and investigations, disaster and emergency, and fraud abatement. | 408-453-4133 | NA | San Jose |
| Game Your Game Inc (HQ) | Developer of digital tracking system such as automatic shot tracking and hands-free game tracking device to get the insights to improve the game. | 888-245-3433 | NA | San Francisco |
| Gatan Inc (HQ) | Manufacturer of instrumentation and software used to enhance and extend the operation and performance of electron microscopes. | 925-463-0200 | NA | Pleasanton |

| COMPANY NAME | PRODUCT / SERVICE | PHONE | EMP | CITY |
|---|---|---|---|---|
| Genmark Automation Inc (HQ) | Provider of robotics for automated manufacturing applications. The company offers services to the data storage and related industries. | 510-897-3400 | NA | Fremont |
| GestureTek Inc (HQ) | Provider of gesture-based user interfaces for mobile devices. The company offer services to the gaming and entertainment industries. | 408-506-2206 | NA | Santa Clara |
| Gigya Inc (HQ) | Provider of widget distribution, content sharing, and advertising platform. The company caters to the needs of social web. | 650-353-7230 | NA | Mountain View |
| Glassbeam Inc (HQ) | Provider of support solutions and it serves the medical, storage, and wireless networking industries. | 408-740-4600 | NA | Santa Clara |
| Global Cybersoft Inc (HQ) | Provider of software development and IT outsourcing services, such as systems integration and maintenance. | 424-247-1226 | NA | Pleasanton |
| Global Infotech Corp (HQ) | Provider of software services. The company's software solutions focuses on staff augmentation, telecom, systems integration, chip design, ERP, and CRM domains. | 408-567-0600 | NA | San Jose |
| GlobalSoft Inc (HQ) | Provider of software consultancy services. The company offers application development, training program management, and engineering services. | 408-564-0307 | NA | San Jose |
| Good Dog Design (HQ) | Provider of digital designing services. The company offers web development & designing and mobile application services. | 415-383-0110 | NA | Mill Valley |
| Google Inc (HQ) | Provider of search engine to make world's information universally accessible. The company specializes in internet-related services and products. | 650-253-0000 | NA | Mountain View |
| Harmon Ie (HQ) | Provider of SharePoint applications for Outlook, mobile, and desktop platforms. The company offers records and knowledge management services. | 408-907-1339 | NA | Milpitas |
| Heirloom Computing Inc (HQ) | Focuses on the transformation of enterprise applications. The company offers services to the industrial sector. | 510-573-3579 | NA | Alamo |
| Highwired Inc (HQ) | Developer of multimedia and supporting products and services. The company focuses on branding, billing, and delivery solutions. | 516-785-6197 | 1-10 | Redwood Valley |
| Hilti Inc (BR) | Developer and manufacturer of construction equipment. The company's services include trainings, engineering, administration, and tools. | 800-879-8000 | NA | San Francisco |
| Hortonworks (HQ) | Specializes in open and connected data platforms. The company offers predictive analysis and data discovery solutions to the oil and gas industry. | 408-675-0983 | NA | Santa Clara |
| Hsq Technology (HQ) | Provider of control system and energy management services, specializing in data and SCADA monitoring. | 510-259-1334 | NA | Hayward |
| HyTrust Inc (HQ) | Provider of security, compliance, and control software for virtualization of information technology infrastructure. | 650-681-8100 | NA | Mountain View |
| Iar Systems Software Inc (RH) | Provider of software tools and embedded systems. The company's products include state machine tools, starter kits, and compiler and debugger tool suite. | 650-287-4250 | NA | Foster City |
| iCharts Inc (HQ) | Provider of collaborative visual intelligence solutions. The company offers services to business and media companies. | 650-472-0650 | NA | Mountain View |
| Ideablade (HQ) | Provider of data base application services. The company's products include DevForce, Coctail, and Breeze. | 510-596-5100 | NA | Orinda |
| Iksanika Llc (HQ) | Provider of custom software development, testing, quality assurance, porting, and re-engineering services. | 408-490-0777 | NA | San Jose |
| Imagine That Inc (HQ) | Developer of simulation software. The company offers services to the retail, healthcare, insurance, and financial services industries. | 408-365-0305 | NA | San Jose |
| Imperva Inc (HQ) | Provider of application and data security solutions. The company's products include database firewalls, management server, and monitoring software. | 650-345-9000 | NA | Redwood Shores |
| Infinera Corp (HQ) | Provider of services and solutions in optical networks. The company serves cable operators and internet content providers. | 408-572-5200 | NA | Sunnyvale |
| Infostretch Corp (HQ) | Provider of mobile application development, quality assurance testing and automation, SaaS solutions, and ERP testing solutions. | 408-727-1100 | NA | Santa Clara |
| Infoyogi LLC (HQ) | Provider of information technology solutions for software application development and systems integration. | 408-850-1700 | NA | Santa Clara |
| Innominds Software Inc (HQ) | Provider of product incubation services for the technology industries. The company focuses on app development, analytics, mobility, and testing. | 408-434-6463 | NA | San Jose |
| Innovative Interfaces Inc (HQ) | Provider of technology solutions and services. The company deals with training and hosting, and technical support. | 510-655-6200 | NA | Emeryville |
| Instart Logic Inc (HQ) | Provider of software-defined application delivery solutions. The company offers services to the travel and hospitality industries. | 650-919-8856 | NA | Palo Alto |
| Intapp Inc (HQ) | Provider of software and services for risk management, time management, and box management. The company's products include Intapp Time and Wall Builder. | 650-852-0400 | NA | Palo Alto |
| Integral Development Corp (HQ) | Provider of customer-branded trading solutions for brokers, dealers, banks, and fund investment managers. | 650-424-4500 | NA | Palo Alto |
| Intellicon Solutions (HQ) | Provider of intelligent consulting solutions for learning and development, performance management systems, and related social media communication. | 925-377-7925 | 11-50 | Moraga |

| COMPANY NAME | PRODUCT / SERVICE | PHONE | EMP | CITY |
|---|---|---|---|---|
| Intresys Inc (BR) | Provider of child support and egovernment solutions. The company serves attorneys, public sector agencies, and governments. | 888-372-1790 | NA | Belmont |
| Ipdialog Inc (HQ) | Developer of hardware and software technology. The company creates SIP stack, user interface, and media stream handling for phones. | 408-830-0800 | NA | Sunnyvale |
| Iron Systems Inc (HQ) | Provider of network storage, hybrid cloud, and big data infrastructure solutions. The company offers OEM/ODM manufacturing services. | 408-943-8000 | NA | Fremont |
| Isomorphic Software (HQ) | Focuses on building web applications. The company is engaged in training, consulting, and technical support services. | 415-222-9902 | NA | San Francisco |
| Itrenew Inc (HQ) | Provider of information technology services. The company focuses on data eradication, server application, logistics management, and configuration. | 408-744-9600 | NA | Newark |
| Ixl Learning (HQ) | Specializes in online maths practice and related lessons. The company serves educational institutions. | 650-372-4040 | NA | San Mateo |
| Jeda Technologies Inc (HQ) | Provider of chip based digital designs and semiconductor services. The company focuses on validation and automation solutions. | 408-912-1856 | NA | Santa Clara |
| Jitterbit Inc (HQ) | Focuses on application integration solutions for aerospace and defense, life sciences, pharmaceuticals, and financial services. | 877-852-3500 | NA | Alameda |
| Jiva Creative Llc (HQ) | Provider of interactive design technology solutions. The company focuses on architecture, website hosting, and enterprise application development. | 510-864-8625 | NA | Alameda |
| Jova Solutions Inc (HQ) | Developer of systems for distributed process control and data management for science and industrial sectors. The company offers USB instruments. | 415-816-4482 | NA | San Francisco |
| Junar Inc (HQ) | Provider of cloud-based open data platform. The company offers collaboration services to business organizations. | 844-695-8627 | NA | San Jose |
| Kaazing Corp (HQ) | Provider of software services. The company's IoT gateway is used by mobile users, marketplaces, and machines to connect and communicate in real-time. | 877-522-9464 | NA | San Jose |
| Key Performance Ideas Inc (HQ) | Provider of enterprise performance management & business intelligence solutions. The company offers Oracle Hyperion and OBIEE software for this need. | 855-457-4462 | NA | San Francisco |
| Kiefer Consulting Inc (HQ) | Provider of mobile application software services. The company also offers SharePoint, Microsoft Dynamics, and Microsfot .Net application services. | 916-932-7220 | 1-10 | Folsom |
| Larson Automation Inc (HQ) | Developer of automated test solutions for telecommunication companies. The company offers board test stations and level shifters. | 408-432-4800 | NA | San Jose |
| Lattice Engines (HQ) | Provider of business to business sales intelligence software. The company is engaged in web design and hosting and programming solutions. | 877-460-0010 | NA | San Mateo |
| Lavante Inc (HQ) | Provider of on-demand strategic profit recovery solutions. The company also offers vendor information management software. | 408-754-1410 | NA | San Jose |
| Ledger Systems Inc (HQ) | Provider of network design and support services. The company also offers accounting and e-Commerce solutions. | 650-592-6211 | NA | San Carlos |
| LibraryWorld Inc (HQ) | Provider of library automation software solutions. The company serves schools, healthcare, law firms, museum, and architectural firms. | 408-993-2140 | NA | San Jose |
| LifeMed ID Inc (HQ) | Provider of patient identification technology solutions. The company offers services to healthcare organizations. | | 1-10 | Roseville |
| Lighthouse Worldwide Solutions (HQ) | Provider of dental supplies such as implants, dentures, partials, implant bars, and related accessories. | 510-438-0500 | NA | Fremont |
| Livevol Inc (BR) | Designer and developer of customized data solutions. The company's services include consulting and technical support. | 415-200-4536 | NA | San Francisco |
| Lynch Marks Llc (HQ) | Provider of software development and technology solutions focused on shipping applications. The company focuses on consulting and package tracking. | 510-559-7200 | NA | Berkeley |
| Lynx Software Technologies (HQ) | Developer of software technologies. The company offers development tools, real-time monitoring systems, and secure virtualization products. | 408-979-3900 | NA | San Jose |
| Magnet Systems Inc (HQ) | Provider of mobile apps with software, infrastructure and tools to build enterprise-grade mobile apps. The company serves enterprises. | 650-329-5904 | NA | Palo Alto |
| Maintenance Connection Inc (HQ) | Provider of enterprise web based maintenance management software, work order software, and facility maintenance software. | 888-567-3434 | 1-10 | Davis |
| Marketo Inc (HQ) | Provider of marketing automation software services. The company offers email and social marketing, marketing software, and digital marketing services. | 650-581-8001 | NA | San Mateo |
| Matisse Software Inc (HQ) | Provider of database software and services. The company is also engaged in training, consulting, and technical support. | 252-227-7013 | NA | Mountain View |
| Media Net Link Inc (HQ) | Provider of web business solutions. The company focuses on application development, systems intergration, website design, and project management. | 866-563-5152 | NA | Oakland |
| Meta Integration Technology Inc (HQ) | Provider of metadata components to data modeling, data integration, business intelligence, and metadata management tool vendors. | 650-273-6382 | NA | Mountain View |
| MetaCert (HQ) | Provider of security API for mobile app developers. The company offers content-based filtering services. | 415-529-2571 | NA | San Francisco |

| COMPANY NAME | PRODUCT / SERVICE | PHONE | EMP | CITY |
|---|---|---|---|---|
| mobiDEOS Inc (HQ) | Manufacturer of video surveillance equipment. The company offers services to government entities and businesses. | 408-716-8347 | NA | Los Gatos |
| Mobileiron Inc (HQ) | Provider of mobile security, device, and application management solutions. The company focuses on technical support services. | 650-919-8100 | NA | Mountain View |
| Motiondsp Inc (HQ) | Provider of software products. The company serves the defense & intelligence, law enforcement, energy, and transportation markets. | 650-288-1164 | NA | Burlingame |
| Mphasis Corp (BR) | Provider of applications, infrastructure, and business process outsourcing services to the banking and healthcare sectors. | 408-327-1240 | NA | San Jose |
| Netpace Inc (HQ) | Provider of consulting, cloud computing, data base management, and proprietary development services. | 925-543-7760 | NA | San Ramon |
| Netpulse Inc (HQ) | Provider of custom branded mobile apps. The company also offers technical support services to its customers. | 877-638-7857 | NA | San Francisco |
| Netscout (BR) | Developer of service assurance and applications, service delivery management, network performance management software, and hardware solutions. | 408-571-5000 | NA | San Jose |
| New Generation Software Inc (HQ) | Supplier of packaged data mart models with analytical presentations and reports for wholesale distribution, healthcare, and financial reporting. | 916-920-2200 | 1-10 | Sacramento |
| Newport-West Data Services Inc (HQ) | Designer and developer of minicomputer based business applications. The company specializes in installation. | 925-855-1131 | NA | San Ramon |
| Nextaxiom Technology Inc (HQ) | Provider of testing, certification, and other professional services. The company offers work management and scheduling solutions. | 415-373-1890 | NA | San Francisco |
| Nextbus Inc (BR) | Provider of transit management solutions. The company also provides real-time passenger information solutions to organizations. | 925-686-8200 | NA | Concord |
| NextInput Inc (HQ) | Provider of MEMS-based force sensing solutions for touch enabled devices in markets such as wearable, automotive, industrial, and medical applications. | 650-963-9310 | NA | Mountain View |
| NextLabs Inc (HQ) | Developer of software products. The company offers information risk management software products for enterprises. | 650-577-9101 | NA | San Mateo |
| Nobix Inc (HQ) | Provider IT management products for job scheduling, problem alerting, and notification as well as provides software engineering services. | 925-659-3500 | NA | San Ramon |
| Nomis Solutions Inc (HQ) | Provider of pricing and profitability management solutions. The company caters to the financial services. | 650-588-9800 | NA | Brisbane |
| Nova Measuring Instruments Inc (BR) | Provider of metrology solutions for semiconductor manufacturing industries. The company offers integrated and stand-alone metrology platforms. | 408-510-7400 | NA | Fremont |
| Nutanix Inc (HQ) | Focuses on the simplification of datacenter infrastructure by integrating server and storage resources into a turnkey hyperconverged platform. | 855-688-2649 | NA | San Jose |
| Nuvel Holdings Inc (HQ) | Provider of data acceleration solutions. The company focuses on data transfers and related communication services. | 408-884-8069 | NA | Los Gatos |
| Okta Inc (HQ) | Provider of identity and automated user management, administration, reporting, and application integration solutions. | 888-722-7871 | NA | San Francisco |
| Opal Soft Inc (HQ) | Provider of communications equipment installation and networking. The company's services include application development, network management, and maintenance. | 408-267-2211 | NA | Sunnyvale |
| Openclovis (HQ) | Provider of system infrastructure software platform. The company mainly serves the communication industry. | 707-981-7120 | NA | Petaluma |
| Openwave Mobility Inc (DH) | Provider of mobile media optimization solutions. The company is engaged in the mediation of encrypted traffic streams. | 650-480-7200 | NA | Redwood City |
| Opinionmeter International (HQ) | Designer and developer of mobile research software. The company serves the healthcare, hospitality, and education sectors. | 510-352-4943 | NA | San Leandro |
| Optimal Synthesis Inc (HQ) | Provider of research, algorithm development, and software design services. The company caters to a variety of engineering and science applications. | 650-559-8585 | NA | Los Altos |
| Oracle Corp (BR) | Developer of hardware and software systems. The company provides Oracle database, engineered systems, and enterprise manager solutions. | 415-402-7200 | NA | San Francisco |
| Orbeon Inc (HQ) | Provider of web form deployment services. The company offers basic, gold, and platinum development support, and validation services. | 650-762-8184 | NA | San Mateo |
| Organic Inc (HQ) | Provider of information technology services. The company develops websites, mobile applications, banner, and digital signage. | 415-581-5300 | NA | San Francisco |
| Originate Inc (DH) | Developer of software to integrate, network, and economically operate energy storage systems. The company is engaged in analysis services. | 800-352-2292 | NA | San Francisco |
| Outside Technology (HQ) | Provider of automated reservation systems. The company mainly caters to the outdoor recreation industry. | 415-488-4909 | NA | San Anselmo |
| Paradromics Inc (HQ) | Developer of next generation brain-machine interfaces. The company specializes in CMOS sensor technology with microwire bundles. | 408-280-0500 | NA | San Jose |
| Pariveda Solutions Inc (BR) | Provider of IT consulting services and technology solutions such as custom application development, portals and enterprise content management. | 844-325-2729 | NA | San Francisco |
| Pdf Solutions Inc (HQ) | Provider of yield improvement technologies and services for the integrated circuit manufacturing process. | 408-280-7900 | NA | San Jose |

| COMPANY NAME | PRODUCT / SERVICE | PHONE | EMP | CITY |
|---|---|---|---|---|
| Pivot Systems Inc (HQ) | Provider of software development services and related solutions for small, large and mid-size companies. | 408-435-1000 | NA | San Jose |
| PlanGrid (HQ) | Developer of construction apps which automatically syncs notes, mark-ups, and photos to all the users' devices. | 800-646-0796 | NA | San Francisco |
| Polycom Inc (HQ) | Manufacturer and seller of teleconferencing equipment and provider of all other communications solutions. | 408-586-3837 | NA | San Jose |
| Posiq Inc (HQ) | Provider of customer relationship management and data solutions. The company offers services to the hospitality sector. | 408-676-7470 | NA | San Jose |
| Powertest Inc (HQ) | Provider of software-related professional services. The company is also involved in load testing and application performance management. | 415-778-0580 | NA | S San Francisco |
| Presentek Inc (HQ) | Designer of websites and web portals. The company also offers content management systems and e-commerce handlers. | 408-354-1264 | NA | Los Gatos |
| Prezi Inc (HQ) | Provider of collaboration solutions. The company offers strategy and technical consulting services. | 844-551-6941 | NA | San Francisco |
| Primarylo (HQ) | Provider of business analytics and transaction processing solutions. The company offers storage acceleration data services for business applications. | 415-601-0061 | NA | San Carlos |
| Prosoft Engineering Inc (HQ) | Developer of data recovery software. The company provides Drive Genius, Data Rescue, and Data Backup software. | 877-477-6763 | NA | Livermore |
| Proxim Diagnostics Corp (HQ) | Manufacturer of diagnostics products and related supplies. The company deals with testing and research related services. | 408-391-6090 | NA | Mountain View |
| Qantel Technologies (HQ) | Manufacturer of software systems. The company provides network connectivity and business software solutions. | 510-731-2080 | NA | Hayward |
| Qarbon Inc (HQ) | Publisher of presentation software and the originator of patented Viewlet technology. The company serves business, government, and education markets. | 408-430-5560 | NA | San Jose |
| Quantum Secure Inc (HQ) | Provider of physical identity and access management solutions. The company focuses on compliance and risk management, and security intelligence. | 408-453-1008 | NA | San Jose |
| Qubop Inc (HQ) | Developer of applications and games for mobile platforms. The company specializes in web applications, localization, IOS, and android development. | 415-891-7788 | NA | San Francisco |
| Quest America Inc (HQ) | Provider of information technology services. The company offers solutions through strategy, consulting, and outsourcing. | 408-492-1650 | NA | San Jose |
| Quicklogic Corp (HQ) | Provider of trading solutions for stock market investors. The company offers online trading platforms for mobiles, smartphones, and tablets. | 408-990-4000 | NA | San Jose |
| Quiq Labs (HQ) | Developer of tools and solutions. The company focuses on influencing consumer behavior and engagement. | 559-745-5511 | 1-10 | Fresno |
| Quisk Inc (HQ) | Specializes in the development of payment solutions. The company offers services to financial institutions. | 408-462-6800 | NA | Sunnyvale |
| Quizlet Inc (BR) | Provider of learning tools for students and teachers. The company offers services to the educational sector. | 510-495-6550 | NA | San Francisco |
| Quorum Technologies (HQ) | Developer of recycling and waste disposal solutions for the automotive, industrial, municipal, hospitality, and food industries. | 916-669-5577 | 1-10 | Sacramento |
| R Systems Inc (RH) | Provider of information technology services and solutions. The company offers application, testing, BPO, and packaged services. | 800-355-5159 | 1-10 | El Dorado Hills |
| Realiteer Corp (HQ) | Focuses on building virtual reality creation platform for playing entertaining games. The company offers services to the recreation industry. | | NA | Belmont |
| Retail Pro International (HQ) | Provider of software solutions. The company's services include automated retail planning and content strategy. | 916-605-7200 | 1-10 | Folsom |
| Rightware Inc (BR) | Provider of user interface technologies serving the mobile, automotive, and other embedded industries. | 877-775-2694 | NA | Palo Alto |
| Rockliffe Systems Inc (HQ) | Provider of mobile communication software for service providers, enterprises, and consumers. The company offers design services. | 408-879-5600 | NA | Campbell |
| Rockwell Automation Inc (BR) | Provider of information and asset management solutions. The company serves the marine, metals, and pulp, and paper industries. | 408-271-3400 | NA | San Jose |
| Rollbar Inc (HQ) | Developer of error tracking software. The company is also engaged in coding and troubleshooting services. | 888-568-3350 | NA | San Francisco |
| Rootdesign Llc (HQ) | Provider of design solutions specializing in brand strategy, user interface design, and database development services. | 415-282-2484 | NA | San Francisco |
| Runtime Design Automation (HQ) | Provider of management system software for the IC design industry. The company is engaged in documentation and technical support. | 408-492-0940 | NA | Santa Clara |
| Sancrosoft USA Inc (RH) | Provider of technology consulting, IT staffing, and recruiting services. The company offers systems integration and application development services. | 916-671-5593 | 11-50 | Fair Oaks |
| SAP America Inc (BR) | Developer of software applications. The company provides data and technology, custom development, and implementation services. | 650-849-4000 | NA | Palo Alto |
| Searchforce (HQ) | Developer of automation software. The company offers software for automation, optimization, campaign management, and tracking. | 650-235-8800 | NA | San Mateo |

| COMPANY NAME | PRODUCT / SERVICE | PHONE | EMP | CITY |
|---|---|---|---|---|
| Simco Electronics (HQ) | Providers of services and software to medical device manufacturers. The company specializes in biotechnology. | 408-734-9750 | NA | Santa Clara |
| Simplion Technologies (HQ) | Provider of consulting solutions. The company offers strategy development, implementation, deployment, and technical support services. | 408-935-8686 | NA | Milpitas |
| SL Corp (HQ) | Provider of monitoring and analytics solutions for middleware-powered applications. The company serves the electrical commodity market. | 415-927-8400 | NA | Corte Madera |
| Smc Ltd (BR) | Provider of custom packing for product sterilization. The company is engaged in supply chain management solutions. | 707-303-3000 | NA | Santa Rosa |
| Software Illustrated (HQ) | Developer of spreadsheet mapping software capable of working inside Microsoft Excel. It's product serves sales, marketing, and business data needs. | | NA | Danville |
| Solution Architects Inc (HQ) | Provider of sophisticated IT solutions for complex systems. The company's services include analysis and product development. | 415-775-1656 | NA | San Francisco |
| Sonasoft Corp (HQ) | Provider of software based solutions to simplify and automate replication, archiving, backup, recovery, and data protection operations. | 408-708-4000 | NA | San Jose |
| SoundHound Inc (HQ) | Developer of a sound and speech responsive search engine. The company's product finds application in mobile and communication devices. | 408-441-3200 | NA | Santa Clara |
| Speedinfo (HQ) | Developer of traffic measurement solutions for broadcast media, government planning, and mobile applications. | 408-446-7660 | NA | San Jose |
| Spirent Communications Inc (LH) | Provider of performance analysis technology services. The company also offers network equipment and data center solutions. | 408-752-7100 | NA | San Jose |
| Splunk Inc (HQ) | Provider of search engine services specializing in IT data. The company serves the government, healthcare, and telecommunication industries. | 415-848-8400 | NA | San Francisco |
| SRI International (RH) | Provider of consulting, research, and development services. The company offers services to the defense, security, and energy sectors. | 650-859-2000 | NA | Menlo Park |
| StarNet Communications Corp (HQ) | Developer of X Windows solutions for connecting computers to Unix and Linux desktops and applications. | 408-739-0881 | NA | Santa Clara |
| Stevens Creek Software (HQ) | Provider of software solutions for the palm computing platform. The company is involved in custom development and technical support. | 408-725-0424 | NA | Cupertino |
| Stonefly Inc (HQ) | Provider of storage optimization and disaster recovery protection for software solutions. The company also offers storage area networks. | 510-265-1616 | NA | Hayward |
| Stratedigm Inc (HQ) | Manufacturer of software products, consumables, and related accessories. The company deals with upgrades and installation. | 408-512-3901 | NA | San Jose |
| Structural Integrity Associates Inc (HQ) | Provider of solutions for prevention and control of structural and mechanical failures and serves nuclear plants, oil and gas, and other sectors. | 408-978-8200 | NA | San Jose |
| Suez Smart Solutions (HQ) | Developer of water utility optimization software. The company offers the Aquadapt software product for water utility companies. | | NA | San Francisco |
| Synapsense Corp (HQ) | Provider of wireless monitoring and cooling control solutions. The company also deals with data center infrastructure management. | 916-294-0110 | 1-10 | Folsom |
| Synaptris Inc (HQ) | Provider of business reporting solutions. The company's products include IntelliVIEW, IntelliPRINT, and Synaptris Widget Viewer. | 914-620-1614 | NA | San Jose |
| Synergex (HQ) | Provider of business application optimization solutions. The company serves the transportation, retail, and manufacturing sectors. | 916-635-7300 | 1-10 | Gold River |
| Synopsys Corporate (HQ) | Developer of synthesis technology solutions. The company is also involved in design flow deployment, physical design assistance, and related services. | 650-584-5000 | NA | Mountain View |
| Tapjoy Inc (HQ) | Provider of advertising and targeting solutions. The company also deals with developer services such as consulting and real-time reporting. | 415-766-6900 | NA | San Francisco |
| Taseon Inc (HQ) | Developer of technology related solutions. The company also offers system engineering and software development services. | 408-240-7800 | NA | San Jose |
| TechExcel Inc (HQ) | Provider of customer relationship management software applications. The company is involved in game development and hybrid agile management solutions. | 925-871-3900 | NA | Lafayette |
| Techvalidate Software Inc (HQ) | Provider of online content management services. The company handles content collection, validation, publishing, and utilization services. | 510-982-6640 | NA | Emeryville |
| TEKEVER Corp (DH) | Developer of technologies for the enterprise, aerospace, defense, and security markets, with subsidiaries in Europe, Asia, and the Americas. | 408-730-2617 | NA | Santa Clara |
| Teleresults Corp (HQ) | Provider of electronic medical record solutions and transplant software. The company's services include data conversion, interfaces, and training. | 415-392-9670 | NA | San Francisco |
| TFD Group/Systems Exchange Inc (BR) | Developer of analytical methods and software tools. The company caters to aerospace and defense sectors. | 831-649-3800 | NA | Monterey |
| Third Pillar Systems (HQ) | Developer of networks and software for the commercial lending industry. The company offers implementation and integration services. | 650-372-1200 | NA | Burlingame |
| Thought Inc (HQ) | Provider of data management solutions. The company uses dynamic mapping and related software for this purpose. | 415-836-9199 | NA | San Francisco |
| Three Palm Software (HQ) | Designer and developer of software products for medical imaging and information. The company also deals with data processing services. | 408-356-3240 | NA | Carmel |
| TokBox Inc (HQ) | Developer of free video chat tools and widgets. The company offers services for the recreation and entertainment industries. | 415-284-4688 | NA | San Francisco |

| COMPANY NAME | PRODUCT / SERVICE | PHONE | EMP | CITY |
|---|---|---|---|---|
| Trackdata Systems Corp (HQ) | Provider of greyhound, thoroughbred, and harness racing information. The company features up-to-date listing of racing schedules. | 408-446-5595 | NA | Cupertino |
| Transend Corp (HQ) | Provider of email migration and conversion solutions that support email systems. The company serves business, education, reselling, and other sectors. | 650-324-5370 | NA | Palo Alto |
| Turbo-Doc Medical Record Systems Inc (HQ) | Provider of electronic medical record systems. The company offers walk-out statements, drug information handouts, and medication rewrites. | 530-877-8650 | 1-10 | Paradise |
| Ultra-X Inc (HQ) | Provider of personal computer diagnostic solutions for developers, manufacturers, system engineers, integrators, and computer professionals. | 408-261-7090 | NA | Santa Clara |
| Untangle (HQ) | Designer and developer of network management software. The company specializes in firewall and Internet management application. | 408-598-4299 | NA | San Jose |
| V-Soft Inc (HQ) | Provider of product development services. The company also specializes in mobile application development. | 408-342-1700 | NA | San Jose |
| ValueLabs Inc (BR) | Provider of technology solutions and services. The company's services include digital solutions, quality assurance, and application development. | 408-475-2445 | NA | Sunnyvale |
| Vayusphere Inc (HQ) | Developer of instant messaging applications. The company's customers include Morgan Stanley, Deutsche Bank, and others. | 650-960-2900 | NA | Mountain View |
| Vertical Systems Inc (HQ) | Provider of centric solutions for the hospitality industry. The company is also engaged in mobile application and custom solutions. | 408-752-8100 | NA | San Jose |
| Viscira Llc (HQ) | Manufacturer of software products. The company deals with the development of animation technology solutions. | 415-848-8010 | NA | San Francisco |
| Visible Energy Inc (HQ) | Provider of products and interactive energy conservation services that take control of electricity consumption. | | NA | Palo Alto |
| Vivotek Usa (BR) | Provider of surveillance solutions. The company specializes in manufacturing network cameras for the network video surveillance industries. | 408-773-8686 | NA | San Jose |
| VMware Inc (HQ) | Provider of storage, data center, application virtualization, and enterprise mobility management products. | 650-427-1000 | NA | Palo Alto |
| Weatherflow Inc (HQ) | Provider of modeling and forecasting technologies for the weather forecast industry. The company also offers wind-based and coastal forecasting. | 800-946-3225 | 1-10 | Scotts Valley |
| Workday Inc (HQ) | Provider of software solutions for human resources management and financial management. The company specializes in SaaS based enterprise solutions. | 925-951-9000 | NA | Pleasanton |
| Wso2 Inc (HQ) | Provider of open source middleware platforms, security and identity gateway solutions, and enterprise integration solutions. | 408-754-7388 | NA | Palo Alto |
| Xactly Corp (HQ) | Provider of web-based sales compensation applications. The company offers services to business organizations and enterprises. | 408-977-3132 | NA | San Jose |
| XC2 Software LLC (HQ) | Provider of integrated software suite. The company's products find application in water and wastewater utilities. | 800-761-4999 | NA | Fairfax |
| Xtime Inc (HQ) | Provider of CRM solutions for automotive service operations. The company offers scheduling and marketing solutions for automotive retailers. | 650-508-4300 | NA | Redwood City |
| Zapty Inc (HQ) | Manufacturer of project monitoring tools. The company is engaged in design services and it serves the business sector. | 415-830-4595 | NA | San Francisco |
| Zendesk Inc (HQ) | Designer and developer of cloud-based customer service software. The company deals with reporting and analytics solutions. | 415-418-7506 | NA | San Francisco |
| Zl Technologies (HQ) | Provider of electronic content archiving software solutions such as consulting and installation, product customization, and software upgrades. | 408-240-8989 | NA | Milpitas |
| Zone24x7 Inc (HQ) | Provider of technology innovation, business consultation, software development, hardware design, and system integration services. | 408-922-9887 | NA | San Jose |

## 823 = Custom Software Development

| | | | | |
|---|---|---|---|---|
| 4d Inc (DH) | Developer of web and internet applications. The company serves universities, corporations, governments, and individuals. | 408-557-4600 | NA | San Jose |
| A10 Networks Inc (HQ) | Provider of networking and security solutions such as cloud computing and virtualization and bandwidth management. | 408-325-8668 | NA | San Jose |
| Abacus Solutions Inc (HQ) | Developer of SATURN, an integrated enterprise ETRM system and focuses on generation optimization, parameters estimation, and credit management. | 650-941-1728 | NA | Los Altos Hills |
| Abbyy Usa (HQ) | Provider of optical character recognition solutions. The company offers scanners, screen-shot readers, document converters, and linguistic solutions. | 408-457-9777 | NA | Milpitas |
| Accel North America Inc (HQ) | Provider of software development and technology services for automotive, healthcare, life science, networking, storage, and enterprise software markets. | 408-514-5199 | NA | Santa Clara |
| Accela Inc (HQ) | Provider of licensing, asset and land management, and public health and safety solutions. The company offers technical support services. | 925-659-3200 | NA | San Ramon |
| Accenture (BR) | Provider of management consulting and technology services. The company also offers application outsourcing and IT consulting services. | 415-537-5000 | NA | San Francisco |
| Accenture (BR) | Provider of management consulting, technology services and outsourcing services. The company serves a wide range of industries. | 408-817-2700 | NA | San Jose |

| COMPANY NAME | PRODUCT / SERVICE | PHONE | EMP | CITY |
|---|---|---|---|---|
| Access Business Technologies Llc (HQ) | Provider of cloud-based software and hosting solutions for government agencies, banks, credit unions, accounting firms, and servicing companies. | 888-636-5426 | 1-10 | Folsom |
| Access Softek Inc (HQ) | Developer of mobile banking software solutions. The company focuses on software and product development, QA testing, user interface, and graphic design. | 510-848-0606 | NA | Berkeley |
| Acrylic Art (HQ) | Provider of fabrication and machining services. The company focuses on painting, product finishing, anodizing, and vapor polishing. | 510-654-0953 | NA | Emeryville |
| Ad Art Inc (HQ) | Provider of digital signage solutions. The company also offers graphic designs, animation, commercial lighting, and maintenance services. | 800-675-6353 | NA | San Francisco |
| Addepar Inc (HQ) | Provider of investment management solutions and technology platform for data aggregation, powerful analytics, and empowering clients to excel. | 855-464-6268 | NA | Mountain View |
| Advantage for Analysts Inc (HQ) | Developer of structuring and analysis software. The company finds application in originating, trading, and managing complex financial assets. | 415-568-4800 | NA | Sausalito |
| Advantech Inc (DH) | Provider of system integration, hardware, software, embedded systems, automation products, and logistics support. | 408-519-3898 | NA | Milpitas |
| Advent Software Inc (HQ) | Provider of data services, portfolio, performance, research, client, margin and finance, and revenue management solutions. | 415-645-1000 | NA | San Francisco |
| Advisor Software Inc (HQ) | Provider of planning, proposal generation, portfolio construction, rebalancing, and investment analytics services. | 925-299-7782 | NA | Walnut Creek |
| Aechelon Technology Inc (HQ) | Developer of real time computer graphics applications in the training, simulation, and entertainment markets. | 415-255-0120 | NA | San Francisco |
| Agile Global Solutions Inc (HQ) | Provider of business and IT solutions such as custom and enterprise application management and mobile business solutions. | 916-655-7745 | 11-50 | Folsom |
| AGTEK Development Company Inc (HQ) | Developer of high tech surveying, analysis, and control solutions for residential, commercial, transportation, water, energy, and government. | 925-606-8197 | NA | Livermore |
| Aktana Inc (HQ) | Provider of decision support engine that pores through multiple data services and delivers insights and suggestions right in the rep's workflow. | 888-707-3125 | NA | San Francisco |
| Alchemic Solutions Group Inc (HQ) | Provider of technology marketing solutions for wireless sectors. The company focuses on product management, software development, and consultation. | 510-919-8105 | NA | San Mateo |
| Aldelo LP (HQ) | Provider of software solutions. The company offers solutions for the hospitality, retail, and payment processing industries. | 925-621-2410 | NA | Pleasanton |
| Alert Technologies Corp (HQ) | Developer of emergency management software. The company offers professional services to assist customers in solving their information management challenges. | 925-461-5934 | NA | Pleasanton |
| Allegro Consultants Inc (HQ) | Provider of operating system technical support for third party maintenance and multi-vendor service community. | 408-252-2330 | NA | Menlo Park |
| Ameritechnology Group (HQ) | Provider of IT consulting, asset tracking, auditing, telecom connectivity logistics, relocation, and data recovery solutions for businesses. | 916-395-6776 | 1-10 | Sacramento |
| AmigoCloud Inc (HQ) | Provider of geospatial platform that helps to collect, manage, analyze, visualize, and publish the location data using smartphone, camera, and sensors. | 415-935-1447 | NA | San Francisco |
| Amind Solutions Llc (HQ) | Provider of technology and services. The company offers enterprise mobility, quoting and ordering, product configuration, and e-Commerce services. | 925-804-6139 | NA | Alamo |
| Amulet Technologies Llc (HQ) | Provider of embedded graphical user interface solutions. The company also specializes in modules and chips. | 408-374-4956 | NA | Campbell |
| Anand Systems Inc (HQ) | Designer of custom software solutions for the hotel industry. The company also offers related hardware, website design, and surveillance systems. | 209-830-1484 | 1-10 | Tracy |
| Anvato Inc (HQ) | Provider of video software platform to television broadcasters and offers live and on-demand video management, analytics, and tracking features. | 866-246-6942 | NA | Mountain View |
| Apogee Software Inc (HQ) | Provider of integrated development environment for Java and C. The company offers industrial monitors and controllers. | 408-369-9001 | NA | Campbell |
| Apple Inc (HQ) | Designer and marketer of consumer electronics. The company also focuses on computer software and personal computers. | 408-996-1010 | NA | Cupertino |
| Apsalar Inc (HQ) | Provider of data-powered mobile advertising solutions. The company offers marketing attribution and in-app analytics services. | 877-590-1854 | NA | San Francisco |
| Apx Power Markets Inc (BR) | Provider of e-commerce services for the electrical sector. The company serves residential, commercial, and industrial properties. | 408-517-2100 | NA | San Jose |
| Aqua Terra Consultants (HQ) | Provider of environmental consulting and water resource engineering services. The company also offers software development and consulting services. | 650-962-1864 | NA | Mountain View |
| Aragon Consulting Group Inc (HQ) | Provider of software development services. The company also offers authoring, coding, consulting, and technical support solutions. | 415-869-8818 | NA | Cupertino |
| Arcsoft Inc (HQ) | Developer of multimedia technologies and applications. The company serves both desktop and embedded platforms. | 510-440-9901 | NA | Fremont |
| Articulate Solutions Inc (HQ) | Provider of branding services such as website development, identity design, social media marketing, and search engine optimization. | 408-842-2275 | NA | Gilroy |

| COMPANY NAME | PRODUCT / SERVICE | PHONE | EMP | CITY |
|---|---|---|---|---|
| Artwork Conversion Software Inc (HQ) | Developer of CAD translation programs and CAD viewers software. The company also offers plotting software and IC packaging software. | 831-426-6163 | 1-10 | Santa Cruz |
| Aspera Inc (HQ) | Developer of file transport technologies. The company provides client and server software, consoles, and mobile uploaders. | 510-849-2386 | NA | Emeryville |
| Atlassian (BR) | Provider of software development and collaboration tools. The company offers software for chats, tracking, repository management, and code hosting. | 415-701-1110 | NA | San Francisco |
| Attention Control Systems Inc (HQ) | Manufacturer of cognitive aids. The company also offers technical assistance solutions and serves the healthcare sector. | 888-224-7328 | NA | Mountain View |
| Augmentum Inc (HQ) | Provider of software development & solution implementation services. The company focuses on internet applications and product development outsourcing. | 650-578-9221 | NA | Foster City |
| Auriga Corp (HQ) | Provider of technology consulting services for electric power, telecommunications, transportation, and information technology systems. | 408-946-5400 | NA | Milpitas |
| Autodesk Inc (BR) | Provider of 3D design, engineering, and entertainment software solutions. The company also offers technical support services. | 415-356-0700 | NA | San Francisco |
| AutoGrid Systems Inc (HQ) | Provider of grid-sensing technologies. The company focuses on energy data platform and optimized demand management services. | 650-461-9038 | NA | Redwood City |
| Avatier Corp (HQ) | Provider of identity management consulting, software development, password management, and user provisioning solutions. | 925-217-5170 | NA | Pleasanton |
| Avontus Software Corp (DH) | Creator of software for formwork, scaffolding, and shoring industries, both custom development for enterprises and packaged software for public. | 800-848-1860 | NA | Berkeley |
| Backshop Inc (HQ) | Provider of commercial real estate software for full deal-stack modeling, loan origination, asset management, and data library for customers. | 415-332-1110 | NA | Sausalito |
| Barco Inc (RH) | Manufacturer of digital scan conversion equipment and radars. The company serves healthcare, defense, media, simulation, and other needs. | 888-414-7226 | 11-50 | Rancho Cordova |
| BCS North America Inc (DH) | Designer and manufacturer of products for baggage handling and security screening systems. The company serves the aviation sector. | | NA | San Jose |
| Beganto Inc (HQ) | Provider of web-based applications and support services. The company specializes in application, component, design, and sales engineering. | 510-280-0554 | NA | Santa Clara |
| Big Switch Networks Inc (HQ) | Provider of hyperscale networking design principles and applying them to fit-for-purpose products for enterprises, cloud, and service providers. | 650-322-6510 | NA | Santa Clara |
| Birst Inc (HQ) | Provider of supply chain, marketing, human resources, financial, and sales analytics solutions for businesses. | 415-766-4800 | NA | San Francisco |
| BlackBag Technologies Inc (HQ) | Provider of Mac-based data forensic and eDiscovery solutions. The company is involved in data processing and related services. | 408-844-8890 | NA | San Jose |
| Border Collie Solutions Inc (HQ) | Provider of security surveillance software products. The company focuses on security panel, energy management, and medical monitoring. | 650-343-2400 | NA | Burlingame |
| Bradford Technologies Inc (HQ) | Developer of appraising software solutions for the real estate sector. The company offers backup and storage and digital signature scanning services. | 408-360-8520 | NA | San Jose |
| Bright Computing Inc (HQ) | Provider of software solutions for provisioning and managing HPC clusters, Hadoop clusters, and openstack private clouds. | 408-300-9448 | NA | San Jose |
| Brightidea Inc (HQ) | Provider of innovative management software solutions. The company's products include WebStorm, Switchboard, and Pipeline modules. | 415-692-1912 | NA | San Francisco |
| Brightsign Llc (HQ) | Provider of digital sign media players, software, and networking solutions for the commercial digital signage industry. | 408-852-9263 | NA | Los Gatos |
| Bromium Inc (HQ) | Provider of enterprise security solutions. The company focuses on security software development, technical support, and task introspection. | 408-213-5668 | NA | Cupertino |
| Burstorm Inc (HQ) | Provider of cloud design tools application. The company specializes in design, collaborate, quote, and implement of cloud architecture. | 650-610-1480 | NA | Danville |
| Busse Design Usa Inc (HQ) | Provider of interface design services. The company's services include website design and application user interface. | 415-689-8090 | NA | Oakland |
| Ca Technologies (BR) | Focuses on technology leadership and category-leading semiconductor and infrastructure software solutions. | 800-225-5224 | NA | Petaluma |
| California Software Systems (HQ) | Provider of graphics software solutions. The company products include DNC file server for windows and graphics software. | 831-477-6843 | 1-10 | San Juan Bautista |
| Calsoft Inc (HQ) | Designer and developer of storage, networking, and operating systems. The company deals with design, delivery, and installation. | 408-834-7086 | NA | San Jose |
| Calypso Technology Inc (HQ) | Provider of front-to-back technology solutions for the financial markets. The company offers technology platform for cross asset trading risk management. | 415-530-4000 | NA | San Francisco |
| Carbon Five Inc (HQ) | Provider of software development services such as lean design and agile development for the web and mobile sectors. | 415-546-0500 | NA | San Francisco |
| Carefree Computing Inc (HQ) | Provider of web hosting, software design, programming, technical support, and network design services. | 866-377-6275 | NA | San Francisco |
| Casetrakker (HQ) | Developer of Windows-based case management software. The company is engaged in programming and hosting solutions. | 916-757-1444 | 1-10 | Roseville |

| COMPANY NAME | PRODUCT / SERVICE | PHONE | EMP | CITY |
|---|---|---|---|---|
| Catalyst Business Solutions (HQ) | Provider of technology consulting services in business applications, data center, and machine-to-machine/internet of things. | 408-281-7100 | NA | San Jose |
| CCS Inc (HQ) | Provider of business accounting software solutions. The company is also engaged in web integration and custom software development. | 949-855-9020 | 1-10 | Lincoln |
| Cdnetworks Inc (RH) | Developer of web and network acceleration solutions. The company serves the travel, tourism, gaming, and technology industries. | 408-228-3700 | NA | Campbell |
| Celigo Inc (HQ) | Provider of cloud computing products and solutions. The company offers NetSuite consulting services that include implementation and optimization. | 650-579-0210 | NA | San Mateo |
| Ceva Inc (HQ) | Provider of digital signal processor technology. The company also specializes in offering consulting services. | 650-417-7900 | NA | Mountain View |
| ChannelNet (BR) | Provider of digital solutions to connect brands and customers. The company specializes in strategy development, design, and content optimization. | 415-332-4704 | NA | Sausalito |
| ChemSoft (HQ) | Provider of software consulting services. The company specializes in custom business solutions, access, excel, PowerPoint, word, and visual basic. | 408-615-1001 | NA | San Jose |
| Ciphercloud Inc (DH) | Provider of comprehensive cloud application discovery and risk assessment, data protection, data loss management, key management, and malware detection. | 855-524-7437 | NA | San Jose |
| Cityspan Technologies Inc (HQ) | Developer of software for social services. The company offers software to manage grants, track clients, and evaluate outcomes. | 510-665-1700 | NA | Berkeley |
| ClearCare Inc (HQ) | Provider of front and back office software solution such as billing, payroll, and marketing management for private duty home care agencies. | 800-449-0645 | NA | San Francisco |
| Clickatell (pty) Ltd (HQ) | Provider of SMS solutions such as SMS alerts, reminders, call centers, reservations and bookings for healthcare, marketing, and IT/software industries. | 650-641-0011 | NA | Redwood City |
| Clinisense Corp (HQ) | Developer of technology for shelf-life monitoring. The company offers applications such as diagnostics, medical supplies, and RFID tags. | 408-348-1495 | NA | Los Gatos |
| Cloudera Inc (HQ) | Provider of professional services that include cluster certification, descriptive analytics pilot, and security integration pilot. | 650-362-0488 | NA | Palo Alto |
| Cloudian (LH) | Provider of cloud storage platform and unstructured data storage. The company offers cloud object storage software and appliances. | 650-227-2380 | NA | Foster City |
| Cloudmark Inc (HQ) | Provider of messaging infrastructure and security solutions. The company delivers scalable messaging platform, security intelligence, and filtering. | 415-946-3800 | NA | San Francisco |
| Coastside Net (HQ) | Provider of internet access and technology solutions. The company also offers website services including website hosting, design, and development. | 650-712-5900 | NA | El Granada |
| Cognex Corp (BR) | Supplier of barcode readers and sensor products. The company offers vision sensors, fixed mount readers, handheld readers, and mobile computers. | 858-481-2469 | NA | Cupertino |
| Cognizant Technology Solutions (BR) | Provider of business consulting, enterprise application development, IT infrastructure, and outsourcing services. | 925-790-2000 | NA | San Ramon |
| Colfax International (HQ) | Provider of workstations, servers, clusters, storage, and personal supercomputing solutions to accelerate business and research outcomes. | 408-730-2275 | NA | Sunnyvale |
| Comprehend Systems Inc (HQ) | Provider of invaluable clinical data insights enabling us to do better science and optimize clinical operations. | 650-521-5449 | NA | Redwood City |
| Computer Deductions Inc (HQ) | Provider of software development services as a subcontractor to corporations. The company also offers management consulting services. | 916-987-3600 | 11-50 | Orangevale |
| Computer Presentation Systems Inc (HQ) | Designer and developer of hardware and software solutions for home builders ranging from local entrepreneurs to regional builders. | 916-635-3487 | 1-10 | Rancho Cordova |
| Computers & Structures Inc (HQ) | Provider of integrated design, analysis, assessment, drafting of building systems, and related support services. | 510-649-2200 | NA | Walnut Creek |
| CompuTrust Software (HQ) | Developer and seller of software for public administrators. The company offers services to businesses and enterprises. | 800-222-7947 | NA | Morgan Hill |
| Contrast Media Labs (HQ) | Provider of graphic design and software development services. The company services include android applications and digital and print media design. | 415-471-1323 | NA | San Francisco |
| Corman Technologies Inc (HQ) | Provider of software development and consulting services for a variety of clients in the software industry. | 707-575-7800 | NA | Santa Rosa |
| Corona Labs Inc (HQ) | Developer of games, e-books, and other interactive content. The company offers services to the educational sector. | 415-996-6877 | NA | San Francisco |
| Couchbase Inc (HQ) | Developer of products and technology to meet the elastic scalability, always-on availability, and data mobility requirements of critical applications. | 650-417-7500 | NA | Santa Clara |
| Csrware Inc (HQ) | Developer of sustainability resource management software. The company specializes in supply chain, enterprise ERP solutions, and consulting services. | 855-277-9273 | NA | Mill Valley |
| Css Corp (HQ) | Provider of enterprise level support solutions for IT products. The company is involved in virtualization, storage, and archiving solutions. | 650-385-3820 | NA | Milpitas |

| COMPANY NAME | PRODUCT / SERVICE | PHONE | EMP | CITY |
|---|---|---|---|---|
| CUneXus Solutions Inc (HQ) | Provider of pre-screening lending strategy that pre-approves entire loan product portfolio for customers. | 877-509-2089 | NA | Santa Rosa |
| Current Controls Inc (HQ) | Designer and manufacturer of control panels for OEMs in many sectors. The company also offers PLC programming, system integration, and other services. | 916-630-5507 | 1-10 | Rocklin |
| Cyberdata Corp (HQ) | Designer and manufacturer of USB cables. The company also offers VoIP and printed circuit board design services. | 831-373-2601 | NA | Monterey |
| D-Tools Inc (HQ) | Developer and marketer of software to streamline processes which accompany the integration and installation of low-voltage systems. | 925-681-2326 | NA | Concord |
| D2s Inc (HQ) | Supplier of a computational design platform to maximize eBeam technology. The company's products include TrueMask MDP and DS. | 408-781-9017 | NA | San Jose |
| Data Path Inc (HQ) | Provider of IT services such as IT management, web design, software development, and education related data services. | 209-521-0055 | 1-10 | Modesto |
| Dataglance Inc (HQ) | Provider of data management software that support LIVE data conversion/migration, electronic document generation & processing, and web services. | 510-656-0500 | NA | Fremont |
| Datameer Inc (BR) | Provider of data analytics solution for business users. The company also focuses on integration, business analytics consulting, and training. | 800-874-0569 | NA | San Francisco |
| Delphix (HQ) | Developer of software, database, and database virtualization. The company focuses on website design and hosting and software application development. | 650-494-1645 | NA | Redwood City |
| Deplabs Inc (HQ) | Provider of eCommerce projects. The company involves in eCommerce co-development, application development, third party integration, and back-end integration. | 855-445-6560 | NA | Petaluma |
| Desaware Inc (HQ) | Developer of tools and components for visual studio programmers. The company offers documentation and professional services. | 408-404-4760 | NA | San Jose |
| DesignMap (HQ) | Provider of web site and application design services. The company also specializes in research, usability studies, and visual design. | 415-357-1875 | NA | San Francisco |
| Dhap Digital Inc (HQ) | Provider of interface that translates a desktop experience to a smartphone and go through Scion vehicle configurations without app download. | 415-962-4900 | NA | San Francisco |
| Dialogic Inc (HQ) | Provider of communications products and media server software. The company serves business enterprises and organizations. | 408-750-9400 | 51-200 | Milpitas |
| Digipede Technologies LLC (HQ) | Provider of distributed computing solutions for academic research, entertainment, financial services, and manufacturing business applications. | 510-834-3645 | NA | Lafayette |
| Digital Anarchy (HQ) | Provider of photography and video plugins for Photoshop, elements, after effects, and final cut pro. | 415-287-6069 | NA | Brisbane |
| Digital Element Inc (HQ) | Developer of computer artwork, software, and tools for computer artists and developers. The company offers 3D animation, plug-ins, and art tools. | | NA | Fremont |
| Digital Mountain Inc (HQ) | Provider of electronic discovery and computer forensic services focusing on reduplication, data management, ESI planning, and cybersecurity. | 866-344-3627 | NA | Santa Clara |
| Direct Technology (HQ) | Provider of software application design and hosting services. The company is engaged in software application development. | 916-787-2200 | 11-50 | Roseville |
| DisplayLink Corp (HQ) | Provider of solutions for virtual graphics connectivity between computers and displays. The company makes use of USB, wireless USB, and ethernet. | 650-838-0481 | NA | Palo Alto |
| Docusign Inc (HQ) | Provider of digital transaction management platform helps to accelerate transactions, reduce costs, and delight customers, suppliers, and employees. | 877-720-2040 | NA | San Francisco |
| Dolcera Corp (BR) | Provider of business research, analytics, collaboration, IP patent licensing, and related support services. | 650-425-6772 | NA | San Mateo |
| Droisys Inc (HQ) | Provider of business solutions and offers services such as content management, enterprise resource planning, and business efficiency consulting. | 408-874-8333 | NA | Santa Clara |
| Dt Research Inc (HQ) | Developer and manufacturer of embedded computing systems. The company serves hospitality, healthcare, and digital signage needs. | 408-934-6220 | NA | San Jose |
| Dynamic Ventures Inc (HQ) | Provider of onsite and offsite custom software development services. The company also focuses on maintenance. | 408-343-0234 | NA | Cupertino |
| DynEd International Inc (HQ) | Provider of computer-based English language teaching solutions. The company offers mobile solutions, analytics, testing, and monitoring tools. | 650-375-7011 | NA | Burlingame |
| Ebusinessdesign (HQ) | Provider of technology consulting services, specializing in business analysis, architecture design, and open source development. | 408-654-7900 | NA | Campbell |
| Ecodomus Inc (HQ) | Provider of information technology software for improved design & construction data collection, facility management, operation, and maintenance. | 571-277-6617 | NA | San Francisco |
| Egain (HQ) | Provider of custom engagement software solutions. The company offers co-browsing, email management, web self-service, and analytics services. | 408-636-4500 | NA | Sunnyvale |
| Electric Cloud Inc (BR) | Provider of software development, information technology consulting, test automation, virtualization, and cloud computing solutions. | 408-419-4300 | NA | San Jose |

| COMPANY NAME | PRODUCT / SERVICE | PHONE | EMP | CITY |
|---|---|---|---|---|
| Elucit (HQ) | Provider of hardware & software development services. The company also offers data recorders and calibratrion services. | 707-961-1016 | 1-10 | Fort Bragg |
| Emanio Inc (HQ) | Developer of products for data management, dashboarding, and reporting & predictive analysis needs. The company focuses on consulting and training. | 510-849-9300 | NA | Berkeley |
| Endicia (HQ) | Provider of electronic postage software solutions and offers shipping and mailing services to online sellers, warehouse shippers, and office mailers. | 650-321-2640 | NA | Mountain View |
| energyOrbit Inc (HQ) | Provider of cloud based platform and solution for streamline demand side management programs, projects, and relationship management for customers. | 866-628-8744 | NA | San Francisco |
| Ensenta Corp (HQ) | Developer of software solutions. The company is involved in development of cloud-based imaging and self-service technology. | 866-219-4321 | NA | Redwood Shores |
| Envestnet (BR) | Provider of application software for financial service firms. The company is involved in practice and portfolio management. | 866-924-8912 | NA | San Jose |
| Enview Inc (HQ) | Specializes in threat prevention systems. The company deals with data analytics and remote sensing services. | 415-483-5680 | NA | San Francisco |
| Epsilon Strategic Systems (HQ) | Provider of management consulting and information technology services. The company offers customization, advisory, and staff development services. | 650-579-5515 | NA | San Mateo |
| Epylon Corp (HQ) | Developer of e-procurement software and services. The company serves the government and education sectors. | 925-407-1020 | NA | Danville |
| Etouch Systems Corp (BR) | Provider of design web engineering services. The company focuses on business process management and enterprise application integration services. | 510-795-4800 | NA | Fremont |
| Excelfore Corp (HQ) | Provider of cloud applications. The company offers infotainment and telematics products for insurance, financing, and logistics sectors. | 510-868-2500 | NA | Fremont |
| Expandable Software Inc (HQ) | Developer of enterprise software for manufacturers. The company is engaged in medical technology and general manufacturing solutions. | 408-261-7880 | NA | Santa Clara |
| Exponent Partners (HQ) | Provider of performance and outcomes management solutions. The company's services include systems integration and custom application development. | 800-918-2917 | NA | San Francisco |
| Extend Inc (HQ) | Developer of business software. The company also provides internet and marketing consulting services. | 925-484-0395 | NA | Pleasanton |
| EXXIM Computing Corp (HQ) | Manufacturer of cutting-edge radiological imaging technology and equipment designed for dental, medical, and scientific and industrial industries. | 925-416-1900 | NA | Pleasanton |
| Eyefinity Inc (HQ) | Provider of software solutions for the eyecare industry. The company focuses on practice & revenue cycle management and electronic health records. | 877-448-0707 | 1-10 | Rancho Cordova |
| Ferrotec Usa Corp (RH) | Manufacturer and distributor of quartz solutions and fluid sealants. The company serves business organizations and enterprises. | 408-964-7700 | NA | Santa Clara |
| Fiduciary Management Technologies Inc (HQ) | Provider of insolvency case, fiduciary case, and estate management solutions. The company offers SEC distribution fund administration services. | 916-930-9900 | 1-10 | Sacramento |
| Filemaker Inc (DH) | Provider of database software which assists organizations in the management, analysis, and sharing of information. | 408-987-7000 | NA | Santa Clara |
| Fileopen Systems Inc (HQ) | Provider of digital rights management and document security solutions for corporations and governments. | 831-706-2170 | 1-10 | Santa Cruz |
| FireEye Inc (HQ) | Focuses on cyber security solutions. The company serves the utilities and pharmaceutical industries. | 408-321-6300 | NA | Milpitas |
| Flexstar Technology (HQ) | Provider of testing and measurement solutions. The company's systems are used to test quality and reliability of storage related devices. | 408-643-7000 | NA | San Jose |
| Forio Corp (HQ) | Provider of software products for simulations, data explorations, and predictive analysis needs. The company caters to universities and corporations. | 415-440-7500 | NA | San Francisco |
| Fortinet Inc (HQ) | Provider of network security appliances and threat management solutions such as network security platform and reporting and authentication. | 408-235-7700 | NA | Sunnyvale |
| Franz Inc (HQ) | Provider of information technology solutions. The company offers web technology and enterprise development tools, and professional services. | 510-452-2000 | NA | Oakland |
| Freshworks Inc (HQ) | Provider of multi-channel support and asset management services. The company serves business organizations. | 650-513-0514 | NA | San Bruno |
| Gallery Systems Inc (BR) | Provider of collection management systems. The company offers procedures consulting, project management, and strategic planning services. | 510-652-8950 | NA | Berkeley |
| Game Your Game Inc (HQ) | Developer of digital tracking system such as automatic shot tracking and hands-free game tracking device to get the insights to improve the game. | 888-245-3433 | NA | San Francisco |
| GestureTek Inc (HQ) | Provider of gesture-based user interfaces for mobile devices. The company offer services to the gaming and entertainment industries. | 408-506-2206 | NA | Santa Clara |
| Gigwalk Inc (HQ) | Provider of analytics and collaboration tools and they are used in the management of mobile work force. | 888-237-5896 | NA | San Francisco |

| COMPANY NAME | PRODUCT / SERVICE | PHONE | EMP | CITY |
|---|---|---|---|---|
| Gilmour Craves (HQ) | Provider of graphic design, advertising, media planning, strategic marketing, and print management services. | 415-431-9955 | NA | San Francisco |
| Glenmount Global Solutions (HQ) | Provider of industrial equipment control, energy management, and other systems. The company serves automotive, food, chemical, and other sectors. | 707-258-8400 | NA | Napa |
| Global Infotech Corp (HQ) | Provider of software services. The company's software solutions focuses on staff augmentation, telecom, systems integration, chip design, ERP, and CRM domains. | 408-567-0600 | NA | San Jose |
| Global Software Resources (HQ) | Provider of application development, business intelligence, testing and mobile computing, and collaboration services. | 925-249-2200 | NA | Pleasanton |
| Globant (BR) | Provider of software products and solutions for cloud computing, mobile, gaming, enterprise consumerization, and data visualization. | 877-215-5230 | NA | San Francisco |
| Glyphic Technology (HQ) | Provider of software design and architecture solutions. The company focuses on internet, server, desktop, mobile, and embedded systems. | 650-964-5311 | NA | Mountain View |
| Gracenote Inc (HQ) | Provider of music, video, and automotive solutions. The company focuses on television businesses and entertainment products. | 510-428-7200 | NA | Emeryville |
| Grandflow Inc (HQ) | Provider of e-cataloging and marketing automation solutions. The company offers print production, warehousing, and document management services. | 925-443-0855 | NA | Livermore |
| Grey San Francisco (BR) | Provider of advertising, planning, sports marketing solutions. The company also focuses on customer relationship management. | 415-403-8000 | NA | San Francisco |
| Greytrix (RH) | Provider of integration and migration solutions. The company deals in analytics, cloud, mobility, and ERP/CRM consulting. | 888-221-6661 | NA | San Francisco |
| Grid Net Inc (HQ) | Developer of products for applications such as advanced metering, distribution monitoring and control, and premise area networking. | 415-872-5097 | NA | San Francisco |
| Growing Energy Labs Inc (HQ) | Developer of software to integrate, network, and economically operate energy storage systems. The company is engaged in analysis services. | 415-857-4354 | NA | San Francisco |
| Hazelcast Inc (HQ) | Provider of training, consulting, and technical support services. The company serves the logistics and healthcare industries. | 650-521-5453 | NA | Palo Alto |
| Hcl America Inc (LH) | Provider of software and IT solutions, infrastructure, engineering, research and development, and outsourcing services. | 408-733-0480 | NA | Sunnyvale |
| Heroku Inc (HQ) | Designer and developer of cloud application platforms. The company offers services to software developers. | 866-278-1349 | NA | San Francisco |
| Highfive (HQ) | Focuses on video conferencing and re-imaging solutions. The company offers services to business organizations. | 844-464-4445 | NA | Redwood City |
| Hyperarts Web Design Development & Maintenance (HQ) | Provider of web design, development, and consulting services. The company performs SEO, SEM services, and web application development. | 510-339-6084 | NA | Oakland |
| Ideablade (HQ) | Provider of data base application services. The company's products include DevForce, Coctail, and Breeze. | 510-596-5100 | NA | Orinda |
| Iksanika Llc (HQ) | Provider of custom software development, testing, quality assurance, porting, and re-engineering services. | 408-490-0777 | NA | San Jose |
| Illumio Inc (HQ) | Developer of security platform and it is also involved in data encryption and technical support services. | 669-800-5000 | NA | Sunnyvale |
| Imaja (HQ) | Developer of computer applications. The company specializes in the development of educational tools for Macs. | 510-526-4621 | NA | Berkeley |
| Impression Technology (HQ) | Provider of automated data capture solutions that meet the business objectives. The company primarily offers scanners. | 925-280-0010 | NA | Walnut Creek |
| Increv Corp (HQ) | Developer of business and information technology solutions. The company is engaged in consulting and product development services. | 408-689-2296 | NA | Los Altos |
| Individual Software Inc (HQ) | Publisher and developer of education, business, and personal productivity software for consumers, schools, businesses, and government. | 925-734-6767 | NA | Livermore |
| Industrial Control Links Inc (HQ) | Designer and manufacturer of SCADA hardware and software solutions. The company focuses on monitoring, alarming, data collection, and other needs. | 530-888-1800 | 1-10 | Auburn |
| Ineda Systems Inc (RH) | Provider of IoT and wearable applications with multiple connectivity options, based on I/O virtualization and hierarchical computing technologies. | 408-400-7375 | NA | Santa Clara |
| Infinite Technologies Inc (HQ) | Provider of information technology, strategic consulting, and engineering services. The company serves government and corporate entities. | 916-987-3261 | 11-50 | El Dorado Hills |
| Infolane Inc (HQ) | Provider of web design and development and support services that includes web content management, application development, and technical improvements. | 510-277-2399 | NA | Emeryville |
| Informatix Inc (HQ) | Provider of information technology and business solutions that include software development, document management, networking, and consulting services. | 916-830-1400 | 1-10 | Sacramento |
| Inikosoft Inc (HQ) | Provider of web, graphic, and print design services. The company is also engaged in e-commerce development and social media marketing. | 408-402-9545 | NA | Los Gatos |
| Inmon Corp (HQ) | Developer of traffic management and monitoring products such as sFlow Trend, sFlow-RT, Hyper-V Agent, and others. | 415-946-8901 | NA | San Francisco |

| COMPANY NAME | PRODUCT / SERVICE | PHONE | EMP | CITY |
|---|---|---|---|---|
| Innominds Software Inc (HQ) | Provider of product incubation services for the technology industries. The company focuses on app development, analytics, mobility, and testing. | 408-434-6463 | NA | San Jose |
| Innovative Interfaces Inc (HQ) | Provider of technology solutions and services. The company deals with training and hosting, and technical support. | 510-655-6200 | NA | Emeryville |
| Input Optics Inc (HQ) | Provider of integration solutions for dental practice. The company also offers complimentary assessments and web services. | 650-969-3108 | NA | Mountain View |
| Inspironix Inc (HQ) | Provider of information technology solutions. The company offers software development, web application development, web design, and network services. | 916-488-3222 | 1-10 | Sacramento |
| Instant Systems Inc (HQ) | Provider of internet based business software and services. The company's services include distribution and technical support. | 415-682-6000 | NA | Fremont |
| InStyle Software Inc (HQ) | Provider of Enterprise Resource Planning Software solutions. The company offers services to the apparel industry. | 314-631-6982 | NA | Santa Rosa |
| Inszoom Inc (HQ) | Focuses on immigration case management and compliance automation solutions. The company offers services to law firms. | 925-244-0600 | NA | San Ramon |
| Integrated Wave Technologies (HQ) | Provider of voice recognition technology services. The company offers printing calculators and electronic camera shutters. | 510-353-0260 | NA | Fremont |
| N Intelight ITS LLC (HQ) | Provider of electrical engineering solutions. The company offers expertise on systems, traffic products and software. | 520-795-8808 | 11-50 | Carlsbad |
| Intelligent Inference Systems Corp (HQ) | Provider of computational intelligence services. The company primarily caters to high-tech companies. | 408-390-1455 | NA | Moffett Field |
| Intelliswift Software Inc (HQ) | Provider of application development services for enterprises. The company also focuses on big data, cloud, web solutions, and staffing services. | 510-490-9240 | NA | Fremont |
| Intercom Inc (HQ) | Designer and developer of communication packages. The company also focuses on user intelligence solutions. | 877-595-5175 | NA | San Francisco |
| Internet Software Sciences (HQ) | Developer of web based applications for IT help desk, customer support, asset tracking, and facilities management needs. | 650-949-0942 | NA | Los Altos Hills |
| Interra Systems Inc (HQ) | Provider of diversified software products and services for digital media and semiconductor industries. | 408-579-2000 | NA | Cupertino |
| Intrinsyx Technologies Corp (BR) | Provider of information technology solutions. The company caters to federal, state, and commercial stakeholders. | 650-210-9219 | NA | Moffett Field |
| Io Informatics Inc (HQ) | Provider of software and services for data integration applications in areas such as life science and medicine. | 510-705-8470 | NA | Berkeley |
| Io Integration Inc (HQ) | Provider of marketing technology and digital media workflow solutions. The company offers marketing automation and cross-media publishing services. | 408-996-3420 | NA | Cupertino |
| iota Computing Inc (HQ) | Specializes in turnkey architecture . The company is engaged in building core technology for tiny edge devices. | 888-440-4004 | NA | Palo Alto |
| Ip Infusion Inc (HQ) | Developer of software for wireless internet products and offers data center networking, carrier ethernet transport, and mobile backhauling services. | 408-400-1900 | NA | Sunnyvale |
| Ipera Technology Inc (HQ) | Provider of multi-format video transcoder solutions for broadcast and IP multi-screen video production. | 650-286-0889 | NA | Cupertino |
| Irislogic Inc (HQ) | Provider of global consulting services and solutions. The company specializes in custom software development, network security, cloud, and testing. | 408-855-8741 | NA | Santa Clara |
| Iron Systems Inc (HQ) | Provider of network storage, hybrid cloud, and big data infrastructure solutions. The company offers OEM/ODM manufacturing services. | 408-943-8000 | NA | Fremont |
| ISSE Services (HQ) | Provider of security solutions principally focusing on supporting system implementation and security testing. | 916-670-1082 | 1-10 | Elk Grove |
| Issio Solutions Inc (HQ) | Provider of workforce management software for surgical facilities. The company also serves ambulatory surgical centers. | 888-994-7746 | NA | Concord |
| It Flux (HQ) | Provider of custom software development services, outsourcing, and outsourced software testing services. | 408-649-5642 | NA | Napa |
| Ivalua Inc (HQ) | Designer and developer of spend management solutions. The company offers services to medium and large sized companies. | 650-930-9710 | NA | Redwood City |
| N JAMIS Software Corp (HQ) | Provider of job-cost, billing, and accounting systems and solutions. The company caters to the government contractors. | 800-655-2647 | 11-50 | San Diego |
| Jasper Technologies Inc (HQ) | Designer and developer of IoT Service Platform. The company serves law enforcement agencies and the security industry. | 669-212-2340 | NA | Santa Clara |
| Jeda Technologies Inc (HQ) | Provider of chip based digital designs and semiconductor services. The company focuses on validation and automation solutions. | 408-912-1856 | NA | Santa Clara |
| Judobaby Inc (HQ) | Focuses on the establishment of software and hardware products. The company offers services to the gaming industry. | 650-368-3499 | NA | Redwood City |
| Juniper Networks Inc (HQ) | Provider of network security solutions. The company serves the government, healthcare, utilities, and manufacturing industries. | 408-745-2000 | NA | Sunnyvale |
| Kaybus Inc (HQ) | Focuses on reshaping content management, sales enablement and a top-down approach to enterprise collaboration. | 800-408-5161 | NA | San Francisco |
| Keen Systems Inc (HQ) | Provider of web-to print solutions. The company offers cloud-based services to small and medium sized printing companies. | 888-506-5336 | NA | San Mateo |

| COMPANY NAME | PRODUCT / SERVICE | PHONE | EMP | CITY |
|---|---|---|---|---|
| Keep IT Simple (HQ) | Provider of virtualization and information technology services. The company focuses on virtualization assessment, cloud computing, and networking. | 510-403-7500 | NA | Fremont |
| Key Solutions Inc (HQ) | Provider of software development and database management services. The company also specializes in business intelligence. | 510-456-4500 | NA | Fremont |
| Kki Corp (HQ) | Provider of web and business services and software solutions. The company is also involved in design and technical support services. | 209-863-8550 | 1-10 | Modesto |
| Klc Enterprises (HQ) | Provider of accounting software for the construction industry. The company offers services to the commercial and industrial sectors. | 415-485-0555 | NA | San Anselmo |
| Kovair Software Inc (HQ) | Provider of web-based document management applications. The company offers product support maintenance services. | 408-262-0200 | NA | San Ramon |
| Kovarus Inc (HQ) | Provider of integrated business IT solutions. The company also deals with leasing, financing, project management, and related services. | 650-392-7848 | NA | San Ramon |
| Ladd Associates Inc (HQ) | Provider of decision support software systems for publishers, subscription businesses, and direct response marketing clients. | 415-921-1001 | NA | San Francisco |
| Langtech (HQ) | Provider of information technology services. The company provides software solutions, cloud services, system integration, and consulting. | 415-364-9600 | NA | San Francisco |
| Language Quest Traveler (HQ) | Retailer of foreign language bibles, software, books, and dictionaries. The company also offers video/audio supplies. | 530-918-9540 | 1-10 | Mount Shasta |
| LeapFILE Inc (HQ) | Provider of on-demand file transfer, delivery, and collaboration solutions for businesses. The company serves the healthcare and advertising sectors. | 650-701-7241 | NA | Cupertino |
| Lenos Software (HQ) | Provider of enterprise resource management, development of motion graphics, and value-added management services. | 415-281-8828 | NA | San Francisco |
| Lightning Bolt Solutions Inc (HQ) | Provider of medical staff scheduling software and solutions. The company's services include scheduling, keeping backups, technical support, and training. | 866-678-3279 | NA | S San Francisco |
| Lightwind Corp (HQ) | Provider of semiconductor manufacturing solutions. The company also deals with chemical analysis, process assessment, and refurbishment services. | 707-981-4301 | NA | Petaluma |
| Lilee Systems (HQ) | Provider of integrated services that include system prediction modeling, project management, and training services for the railroad industry. | 408-988-8672 | NA | San Jose |
| Linden Research Inc (HQ) | Designer and developer of digital entertainment solutions. The company's products include Desura, Patterns, and Versu. | 415-243-9000 | NA | San Francisco |
| Linkbit Inc (HQ) | Manufacturer of network equipment. The company primarily caters to service providers and network operators. | 408-969-9940 | NA | Santa Clara |
| Livermore Software Technology Corp (HQ) | Developer of software for automotive crashworthiness, metal forming, aerospace, and other needs. The company also offers training. | 925-449-2500 | NA | Livermore |
| Lorentz Solution Inc (HQ) | Developer of electronic design automation software services. The company is engaged in modeling and electromagnetic shielding. | 408-922-0765 | NA | Santa Clara |
| Lytrod Software Inc (HQ) | Provider of variable data print software products. The company's products include VisionDP Production and Automate, Proform Designer, and Office Designer. | 707-422-9221 | NA | Fairfield |
| Mailshell Inc (HQ) | Provider of traffic reputation software engines. The company also specializes in anti-spam and anti-phishing software engines. | 415-294-4242 | NA | Santa Clara |
| Marketo Inc (HQ) | Provider of marketing automation software services. The company offers email and social marketing, marketing software, and digital marketing services. | 650-581-8001 | NA | San Mateo |
| Marymonte Systems (HQ) | Provider of bar coding, wireless, time data collection, and RFID technology. The company offers inventory control and material handling solutions. | 408-927-0606 | NA | San Jose |
| Matrix Computer Solutions Inc (HQ) | Provider of computer and technology solutions for residential and business customers. The company also offers data backup, repair, and other services. | 415-331-3600 | NA | Sausalito |
| Matrix Logic Corp (HQ) | Provider of enterprise content management solutions for law firms, businesses, and government agencies. | 415-893-9897 | 11-50 | Chico |
| Meditab Software Inc (HQ) | Developer of physical therapy, urology, cosmetic, and plastic surgery solutions. The company serves the healthcare industry. | 510-201-0130 | 1-10 | Sacramento |
| Medsoftware Inc (HQ) | Provider of practice management software solutions. The company's services include data conversion and repair, training, and implementation. | 916-797-2363 | 1-10 | Granite Bay |
| Meltwater Group (HQ) | Developer of software products such as Meltwater BUZZ, Meltwater NEWS, and Meltwater DRIVE to meet the specific needs of businesses around the world. | 415-236-3144 | NA | San Francisco |
| Memsql Inc (HQ) | Provider of technology solutions and services. The company serves the finance and digital advertising industries. | 855-463-6775 | NA | San Francisco |
| Metabyte Inc (HQ) | Provider of software solutions and related services to the government, healthcare, and retail industries. | 510-494-9700 | NA | Fremont |
| Metaswitch Networks (DH) | Provider of service management solutions. The company offers original equipment manufacturer, multimedia subsystem, and hosted business services. | 415-513-1500 | NA | Los Altos |

| COMPANY NAME | PRODUCT / SERVICE | PHONE | EMP | CITY |
|---|---|---|---|---|
| MetricStream Inc (HQ) | Provider of enterprise risk, compliance, and internal audit management solutions. The company offers training services. | 650-620-2955 | NA | Palo Alto |
| Mg Technologies Inc (HQ) | Provider of software services. The company offers conversion, training, installation, and tuning services. | 408-255-8191 | NA | Cupertino |
| Mirabilis Design Inc (HQ) | Provider of systems engineering solutions for performance analysis and architecture exploration of electronics and real-time software. | 408-844-3234 | NA | Sunnyvale |
| Mistral Solutions Inc (HQ) | Provider of technology design and systems engineering solutions. The company's solutions include hardware board design and embedded software development. | 408-705-2240 | NA | Fremont |
| Mobileiron Inc (HQ) | Provider of mobile security, device, and application management solutions. The company focuses on technical support services. | 650-919-8100 | NA | Mountain View |
| Mobiveil Inc (HQ) | Provider of technology solutions. The company's products include Silicon IP and COTS Modules and offers IC design and embedded software services. | 408-212-9512 | NA | Milpitas |
| Modius Inc (HQ) | Provider of performance management software. The company serves infrastructure monitoring applications. | 415-655-6700 | NA | San Francisco |
| Momentum Design Lab (HQ) | Designer of enterprise-grade software products. The company focuses on design, discovery, and development of software. | 650-452-6290 | NA | San Mateo |
| Mondee Inc (HQ) | Developer of technology for the generation of private fare distribution. The company offers services to the travel industry. | 650-646-3320 | NA | San Mateo |
| Moogsoft Inc (HQ) | Provider of collaborative situation management software solutions for Web-scale information technology (IT) operations. | 415-738-2299 | NA | San Francisco |
| Moonstone Interactive Inc (HQ) | Provider of website design services. The company offers web design and development, content management, and market visibility services. | 866-246-9091 | NA | San Ramon |
| Mountford Group Inc (HQ) | Provider of system development and web application services. The company also focuses on technical communication. | 925-686-6613 | NA | Concord |
| Mozilla Corp (HQ) | Designer and developer of web application tools and browsers. The company serves individuals and businesses. | 650-903-0800 | NA | Mountain View |
| MYCOM OSI Inc (BR) | Provider of performance management, compliance, employer reporting, patient engagement, and satisfaction solutions. | 916-467-1500 | 11-50 | Folsom |
| Nada Technologies Inc (HQ) | Provider of enterprise Oracle applications. The company also offers business intelligence solutions. | 650-678-4666 | NA | Danville |
| Naehas Inc (HQ) | Specializes in the automation of sales and marketing services. The company offers services to finance and insurance companies. | 877-262-3427 | NA | Palo Alto |
| Navis Llc (HQ) | Provider of terminal operating solutions. The company offers solutions for container terminal operations, expert decking, and process automation. | 510-267-5000 | NA | Oakland |
| Nehanet Corp (HQ) | Provider of corporate responsibility management and sales and operation planning solutions to semiconductor and electronics component manufacturers. | 888-552-4470 | NA | Santa Clara |
| Neova Tech Solutions Inc (BR) | Provider of cloud solutions for web and mobile. The company offers mobile development and QA automation services. | 781-640-0588 | NA | Santa Clara |
| Netskope Inc (HQ) | Provider of cloud security brokering services. The company offers services to the healthcare sector. | 800-979-6988 | NA | Los Altos |
| Netwoven Inc (HQ) | Provider of enterprise content management and business intelligence solutions. The company also focuses on process management. | 877-638-9683 | NA | Milpitas |
| Neuron Corp (HQ) | Provider of computer and physical security products and services for the military, government, and corporate sectors. | 408-540-7959 | NA | San Jose |
| Nexenta Systems Inc (HQ) | Provider of enterprise class storage software solutions. The company is engaged in virtualization and business continuity planning. | 408-791-3300 | NA | San Jose |
| Nice Touch Solutions Inc (HQ) | Developer of software for the heavy highway construction industry. The company focuses on products for generating extra work bills. | 925-385-8321 | NA | Alamo |
| Nova Measuring Instruments Inc (BR) | Provider of metrology solutions for semiconductor manufacturing industries. The company offers integrated and stand-alone metrology platforms. | 408-510-7400 | NA | Fremont |
| Numerify Inc (HQ) | Provider of business, service, and asset analytics services. The company offers services to information technology organizations. | 408-822-9611 | NA | San Jose |
| Objectivity Inc (HQ) | Provider of distributed, real-time, SOA-enabled service and offers embedded database management solutions. | 408-992-7100 | NA | San Jose |
| Oea International Inc (HQ) | Developer of signal integrity software. The company serves the electronic design automation industry. | 408-778-6747 | NA | Morgan Hill |
| Ohanae Inc (HQ) | Provider of data and password protection and data compliance solutions. The company offers services to businesses. | 888-617-7288 | NA | Monte Sereno |
| Omnicia Inc (HQ) | Provider of electronic submissions for the life science sector. The company offers electronics & desktop publishing and document management services. | 650-588-2188 | NA | S San Francisco |
| Oomnitza (HQ) | Provider of information technology asset management and related services. The company focuses on third party solutions. | 650-417-3694 | NA | San Francisco |
| Opal Soft Inc (HQ) | Provider of communications equipment installation and networking. The company's services include application development, network management, and maintenance. | 408-267-2211 | NA | Sunnyvale |

| COMPANY NAME | PRODUCT / SERVICE | PHONE | EMP | CITY |
|---|---|---|---|---|
| Openclovis (HQ) | Provider of system infrastructure software platform. The company mainly serves the communication industry. | 707-981-7120 | NA | Petaluma |
| OpensourceCM (HQ) | Designer and developer of contract management software. The company also offers technical support services. | 650-200-0506 | NA | Foster City |
| Openvpn Technologies Inc (HQ) | Specializes in deploying VPN access solutions. The company is engaged in marketing and communication services. | 925-399-1481 | NA | Pleasanton |
| Opswat Inc (HQ) | Provider of end-point software management, compliance, URL filtering, network monitoring, and related solutions. | 415-590-7300 | NA | San Francisco |
| Optimal Synthesis Inc (HQ) | Provider of research, algorithm development, and software design services. The company caters to a variety of engineering and science applications. | 650-559-8585 | NA | Los Altos |
| Orange Enterprises Inc (HQ) | Provider of software solutions. The company mainly focuses on payroll tracking and agriculture management. | 559-229-2195 | 1-10 | Fresno |
| Orion Wine Software (HQ) | Developer of winery management solutions. The company is also engaged in sales and inventory management. | 877-632-3155 | NA | Santa Rosa |
| Osisoft Llc (HQ) | Developer of PI system software. The company offers software such as PI Computing Engine, Batch, Data Access, and Clients. | 510-297-5800 | NA | San Leandro |
| Otrs Inc (BR) | Focuses on business solutions. The company offers services to the hospitality, education, and financial sectors. | 408-549-1717 | NA | Cupertino |
| Outside Technology (HQ) | Provider of automated reservation systems. The company mainly caters to the outdoor recreation industry. | 415-488-4909 | NA | San Anselmo |
| Palantir Technologies Inc (HQ) | Provider of software for anti fraud, cyber security, intelligence, and other needs. The company serves government, commercial, and non-profit sectors. | 650-815-0200 | NA | Palo Alto |
| Palo Alto Networks Inc (HQ) | Provider of network and cyber security solutions. The company offers consulting and support, and solution assurance services. | 408-753-4000 | NA | Santa Clara |
| PanTerra Networks Inc (HQ) | Provider of cloud-based communications software solutions. The company is engaged in unified communication and technical support. | 800-805-0558 | NA | Santa Clara |
| Parametric Technology Corp (BR) | Provider of product life cycle management solutions to the aerospace, defense, automotive, consumer, and medical device industries. | | NA | San Francisco |
| Pariveda Solutions Inc (BR) | Provider of IT consulting services and technology solutions such as custom application development, portals and enterprise content management. | 844-325-2729 | NA | San Francisco |
| Pasco Scientific (HQ) | Provider of technology-based solutions for hands-on science services. The company is engaged in technical support. | 916-786-3800 | 1-10 | Roseville |
| Pc Professional (HQ) | Provider of information technology solutions. The company focuses on cloud computing, application development, networking, and disaster recovery. | 510-874-5871 | NA | Oakland |
| Perforce Software Inc (BR) | Developer of software management tools and technology solutions. The company serves game development, banking, healthcare, and other sectors. | 510-864-7400 | NA | Alameda |
| PFU America Inc (BR) | Provider of technology solutions. The company designs, develops, and sells computer hardware, peripheral products, and systems. | 408-992-2900 | NA | Sunnyvale |
| Pivotal Labs (HQ) | Focuses on software development and related services. The company serves start-ups and Fortune 1000 companies. | 415-777-4868 | NA | San Francisco |
| Planisware (HQ) | Designer of portfolio management software solutions for product development and research and development organizations. | 415-591-0941 | NA | San Francisco |
| Polymath Research Inc (HQ) | Developer of wave propagation and interaction, and photonic devices. The company offers FEMLAB based photonics modeling package and wavelet tools. | 925-417-0609 | NA | Pleasanton |
| Portrait Displays Inc (HQ) | Provider of extensible platforms supporting embedded control of all display technologies and monitors and operating system software. | 925-227-2700 | NA | Pleasanton |
| POS Specialists (HQ) | Provider of digital dining solutions. The company is engaged in business consultation, on-site training, and cloud services. | 925-626-3930 | NA | Concord |
| Posiflex Business Machines Inc (LH) | Provider of point of service hardware and platform technology. The company caters to diverse markets. | 510-429-7097 | NA | Hayward |
| Presentek Inc (HQ) | Designer of websites and web portals. The company also offers content management systems and e-commerce handlers. | 408-354-1264 | NA | Los Gatos |
| Presidio Inc (BR) | Provider of IP telephony and wireless networking services. The company also deals with deployment, integration, and hardware and software development. | 415-501-9020 | NA | Pleasanton |
| ProcessWeaver Inc (BR) | Developer of multi-carrier shipping software and a provider of shipping solutions. The company also offers inbound and desktop shipping solutions. | 888-932-8373 | NA | Santa Clara |
| Progent Corporation (HQ) | Provider of online technical support for small networks, and specializes in remote diagnosis, repair, and consulting services. | 408-240-9400 | NA | San Jose |
| Prolific Minds Inc (HQ) | Provider of software solutions. The company develops software architecture, and offers analysis, technical design, and development services. | 408-777-1211 | NA | Cupertino |
| Prosoft Engineering Inc (HQ) | Developer of data recovery software. The company provides Drive Genius, Data Rescue, and Data Backup software. | 877-477-6763 | NA | Livermore |

| COMPANY NAME | PRODUCT / SERVICE | PHONE | EMP | CITY |
|---|---|---|---|---|
| Provectus IT Inc (HQ) | Provider of software development, wire framing, related design, and cloud and server development services. | 800-679-8721 | NA | Palo Alto |
| Qarbon Inc (HQ) | Publisher of presentation software and the originator of patented Viewlet technology. The company serves business, government, and education markets. | 408-430-5560 | NA | San Jose |
| QSolv Inc (HQ) | Provider of cloud automation services. The company provides network management, gap analysis, tool evaluation, and framework implementation services. | 408-962-3803 | NA | Sunnyvale |
| Quadbase Systems Inc (HQ) | Designer of web-delivered and mobile enabled business intelligence reporting, charting, and dashboard tools. | 408-982-0835 | NA | Santa Clara |
| Quantum3D Inc (HQ) | Developer and manufacturer of real-time visual simulation and computing systems for fast-jet, helicopter, refueling, and other needs. | 408-600-2500 | NA | Milpitas |
| Qubell Inc (HQ) | Specializes in autonomic management solutions. The company focuses on e-commerce and other cloud applications. | 888-855-9440 | NA | Menlo Park |
| Quicklogic Corp (HQ) | Provider of trading solutions for stock market investors. The company offers online trading platforms for mobiles, smartphones, and tablets. | 408-990-4000 | NA | San Jose |
| R-Computer (HQ) | Provider of computer solutions for small and medium-sized companies. The company also offers lifetime product guarantees and sales consultation. | 925-798-4884 | NA | Concord |
| Real Intent Inc (HQ) | Provider of electronic design automation services. The company offers techniques for automatic design verification. | 408-830-0700 | NA | Sunnyvale |
| Redolent Inc (HQ) | Provider of software solution in web, open source, e-commerce applications. The company also focuses on enterprise wide applications. | 650-242-1195 | NA | San Jose |
| Redwhale Software Corp (HQ) | Provider of software tools, technologies, and professional services for the design, development, and run-time management of user interfaces. | 650-312-1500 | NA | Redwood City |
| Reprise Software Inc (HQ) | Provider of license management software solutions. The company's products include Exa, Arxan, LMS, and Pace. | 781-837-0884 | NA | San Jose |
| Resilient Networks Systems Inc (HQ) | Developer of internet software products. The company serves the healthcare, media, information security, and government sectors. | 415-291-9600 | NA | San Francisco |
| Revel Systems Inc (BR) | Provider of POS systems and related services. The company serves customers in the accounting, security, reporting, and other industries. | 415-744-1433 | NA | San Francisco |
| RightITnow (HQ) | Provider of information technology operations management software. The company offers services to government agencies and business organizations. | 415-350-3581 | NA | San Francisco |
| River Rock Software Inc (BR) | Developer of software tools such as graphical user interfaces, client server applications, spool file viewers, and report formatters. | 916-797-6746 | 11-50 | Granite Bay |
| Rocket Communications Inc (HQ) | Developer of user interface, visual, and icon design services for software and related applications. | 415-863-0101 | NA | San Francisco |
| Rocket Software Inc (BR) | Developer and designer of software and mobile solutions. The company offers services for the telecommunications industry. | 781-577-4323 | NA | Emeryville |
| Rockliffe Systems Inc (HQ) | Provider of mobile communication software for service providers, enterprises, and consumers. The company offers design services. | 408-879-5600 | NA | Campbell |
| Rockwell Automation Inc (BR) | Provider of control systems, sensing devices, security, and other products. The company offers asset management, network, and other services. | 925-242-5700 | NA | San Ramon |
| RS Software Inc (BR) | Provider of business payment solutions for the risk prediction, residual management, payment gateway, and merchant boarding areas. | 408-382-1200 | NA | Milpitas |
| S2c Inc (HQ) | Provider of prototyping solutions. The company's customers include chip design and system design companies. | 408-213-8818 | NA | San Jose |
| Saba Software Inc (HQ) | Provider of learning and talent management solutions such as social web meetings and trainings, onboarding, planning, and support services. | 877-722-2101 | NA | Dublin |
| Samsung Research America (DH) | Provider of commercial, physical, and biological research services. The company is involved in testing and identification solutions. | 650-210-1001 | NA | Mountain View |
| Sanah Inc (HQ) | Provider of IT services such as IT strategy consulting, systems integration, and custom application development. | 888-306-1942 | 1-10 | Sacramento |
| SAP America Inc (BR) | Developer of software applications. The company provides data and technology, custom development, and implementation services. | 650-849-4000 | NA | Palo Alto |
| Sendero Group Llc (HQ) | Provider of GPS systems and products to the visually impaired. The company focuses on documentation and technical support services. | 888-757-6810 | 1-10 | Rancho Cordova |
| Sercomm Usa Inc (BR) | Provider of software and firmware for the development of broadband networking. The company also offers solutions for fixed mobile convergence. | 510-870-1598 | NA | Fremont |
| Sharper Technology Inc (HQ) | Provider of network security solutions and services. The company also offers design, implementation, and training services. | 650-964-4600 | NA | Palo Alto |
| N Silex Technology America Inc (HQ) | Manufacturer of print servers for network printers and fingerprint readers. The company serves security applications. | 657-218-5199 | 11-50 | Santa Ana |
| Silicon Publishing Inc (HQ) | Provider of digital publishing solutions. The company deals with template designs and personalized communications. | 925-935-3899 | NA | San Francisco |
| Silver Peak Systems Inc (HQ) | Provider of miscellaneous communication equipment & services. The company focuses on WAN optimization, cloud networking, and replication acceleration. | 408-935-1800 | NA | Santa Clara |

| COMPANY NAME | PRODUCT / SERVICE | PHONE | EMP | CITY |
|---|---|---|---|---|
| Sitepen Inc (HQ) | Developer and provider of software products and services. The company also offers web application development and java support services. | 650-968-8787 | NA | Palo Alto |
| Smart ERP Solutions Inc (HQ) | Developer of enterprise class software. The company provides vendor management software and support services. | 925-271-0200 | NA | Pleasanton |
| Socket Mobile Inc (HQ) | Developer of wireless handheld and hands-free barcode scanners and other products and serves retail, logistics, automotive, and other sectors. | 510-933-3000 | NA | Newark |
| Sonasoft Corp (HQ) | Provider of software based solutions to simplify and automate replication, archiving, backup, recovery, and data protection operations. | 408-708-4000 | NA | San Jose |
| Sono Group Inc (HQ) | Provider of custom software and application development, training, social networking, and IT staffing services. | 925-855-8552 | NA | Danville |
| Space-Time Insight Inc (HQ) | Developer of geospatial and information visualization software. The company also offers visual analytics solutions. | 650-513-8550 | NA | San Mateo |
| Spence Engineering Services Inc (HQ) | Provider of solutions for hardware and software engineering problems. The company offers services to the technical sector. | 650-571-6500 | NA | San Mateo |
| Splunk Inc (HQ) | Provider of search engine services specializing in IT data. The company serves the government, healthcare, and telecommunication industries. | 415-848-8400 | NA | San Francisco |
| SS Papadopulos & Associates Inc (BR) | Provider of web-based applications for customized online communities. The company serves business enterprises. | 415-773-0400 | NA | San Francisco |
| Stanfield Systems Inc (HQ) | Provider of system engineering and data management services. The company also focuses on web development and technical services. | 916-608-8006 | 1-10 | Folsom |
| Stevens Creek Software (HQ) | Provider of software solutions for the palm computing platform. The company is involved in custom development and technical support. | 408-725-0424 | NA | Cupertino |
| Stone Cobra (HQ) | Provider of knowledge management solutions. The company offers solutions for architecture, system configuration, and data migration. | 916-797-6272 | 1-10 | Roseville |
| Stopware Inc (HQ) | Developer of visitor management security software. The company offers hardware, badge stock, and training services. | 408-367-0220 | NA | Pleasanton |
| Stratovan Corp (HQ) | Developer of visual analysis software. It's product finds application in 3D imaging and surgical planning research. | 530-746-7970 | 1-10 | Davis |
| Sts International Inc (HQ) | Provider of information technology solutions that include infrastructure management, software application development, and systems integration. | 925-479-7800 | NA | Pleasanton |
| Subrosasoft.Com Inc (HQ) | Developer of software for Mac operating systems. The company offers software such as FileSalvage, CopyCat, and ParentRemote. | 510-870-7883 | NA | Fremont |
| Succeed.Net (BR) | Provider of internet services. The company specializes in metro Ethernet, wireless broadband, DSL service, national dial-up, and server co-location. | 530-674-4200 | 11-50 | Sacramento |
| Sun-Net Inc (HQ) | Provider of enterprise software solutions supporting outage scheduling, logging, and reporting for power, gas, and water utilities. | 408-323-1318 | NA | San Jose |
| Symplectic Engineering Corp (HQ) | Provider of custom computational mechanics solutions. The company is involved in consulting services and it serves the industrial sector. | 510-528-1251 | NA | Berkeley |
| Synapse Design (HQ) | Provider of embedded software design services. The company also offers test bench analysis and block and chip level verification services. | 408-850-3640 | NA | Santa Clara |
| Synaptics Inc (HQ) | Developer of human interface solutions. The company's products find application in mobile computing and entertainment devices. | 408-904-1100 | NA | San Jose |
| Synchron Networks Inc (HQ) | Developer of application and file distribution software. The company focuses on system management and digital asset delivery services. | 831-461-9735 | 1-10 | Scotts Valley |
| Synergy Business Solutions (HQ) | Provider of technology evaluation, business process improvement, and custom software development services to a wide range of sectors. | 415-263-1843 | NA | San Francisco |
| Syntest Technologies Inc (HQ) | Provider of test solutions for the electronics industry. The company is involved in fault simulation solutions and services. | 408-720-9956 | NA | San Jose |
| SyTech Solutions Inc (HQ) | Provider of document management technology services. The company offers archieve scanning, web-based document management, and data capture services. | 916-381-3010 | 1-10 | Elk Grove |
| Talari Networks (HQ) | Provider of enterprise WANs. The company focuses on the banking, healthcare, manufacturing, and mining industries. | 408-689-0400 | NA | San Jose |
| Talisman Systems Group Inc (HQ) | Provider of document and panel management tools. The company serves insurance companies and managed care organizations. | 727-424-4261 | NA | San Francisco |
| Tangent Inc (HQ) | Provider of computer solutions. The company caters to healthcare, industrial, and military applications. | 650-342-9388 | NA | Burlingame |
| Tech Soft 3d (HQ) | Provider of software solutions. The company offers software for desktop visualization, modeling, cloud and mobile solutions, and data exchange. | 510-883-2180 | NA | Berkeley |
| Tela Innovations Inc (HQ) | Provider of lithography optimized solutions. The company's services include design, implementation, and technical support. | 408-558-6300 | NA | Los Gatos |
| Telosa Software Inc (HQ) | Provider of CRM and fundraising software for nonprofits. The company focuses on gift and grant tracking, donor and volunteer management. | 800-750-6418 | NA | Palo Alto |
| Terrace Consulting Inc (HQ) | Provider of custom software development services. The company focuses on eCommerce, back office, business intelligence, cloud, and other services. | 415-848-7300 | NA | San Francisco |
| TFD Group/Systems Exchange Inc (BR) | Developer of analytical methods and software tools. The company caters to aerospace and defense sectors. | 831-649-3800 | NA | Monterey |

| COMPANY NAME | PRODUCT / SERVICE | PHONE | EMP | CITY |
|---|---|---|---|---|
| The AIS Group (HQ) | Developer and provider of accounting software. The company also specializes in system integration services. | | NA | Napa |
| The Armada Group Inc (HQ) | Provider of information technology and talent consultation services. The company specializes in software engineering and project management. | 800-408-2120 | 11-50 | Santa Cruz |
| Think Connected LLC (HQ) | Provider of data center, consulting, managed, and supplemental information technology services for small and medium-sized businesses. | 877-684-4654 | NA | San Francisco |
| Thinkify (HQ) | Provider of radio frequency identification technology application services. The company provides engineering services as well. | 408-782-7111 | NA | Morgan Hill |
| Third Pillar Systems (HQ) | Developer of networks and software for the commercial lending industry. The company offers implementation and integration services. | 650-372-1200 | NA | Burlingame |
| Thoughtworks Inc (BR) | Provider of system design and e-business consulting services. The company is also involved in software design and delivery and support. | 415-273-1389 | NA | San Francisco |
| Tom Sawyer Software Corp (HQ) | Developer of data relationship visualization and analysis software for application developers. The company offers training and consulting services. | 510-208-4370 | NA | Berkeley |
| Toolwire Inc (HQ) | Designer and developer of experiential learning solutions for higher education and corporate training institutions. | 925-227-8500 | NA | Pleasanton |
| Torian Group Inc (HQ) | Provider of computer, network, and web solutions such as virus removal, home network setup, and email. | 559-733-1940 | 1-10 | Visalia |
| TRAXPayroll (HQ) | Specializes in payroll management solutions. The company also offers wage garnishment, worker's compensation, and tax filing solutions. | 866-872-9123 | NA | Hercules |
| Trinity Consultants Inc (BR) | Provider of environmental consulting services. The company engages in environmental outsourcing and litigation support services. | 510-285-6351 | NA | Oakland |
| Tti Inc (BR) | Distributor of passive, connector, electromechanical, and discrete components for the industrial, military, and aerospace sectors. | 916-987-4600 | 11-50 | Folsom |
| Ultra-X Inc (HQ) | Provider of personal computer diagnostic solutions for developers, manufacturers, system engineers, integrators, and computer professionals. | 408-261-7090 | NA | Santa Clara |
| Unigen Corp (HQ) | Manufacturer and designer of custom enterprise-grade flash storage and DRAM and ARMOUR product applications serving the telecommunications industry. | 510-896-1818 | NA | Newark |
| uSens Inc (HQ) | Creator of 3D human computing interaction software and hardware solutions. The company focuses on artificial intelligence. | 408-564-0227 | NA | San Jose |
| USWired Inc (HQ) | Provider of computer networking solutions that include cloud hosting, network design and installation, and wireless networks. | 408-669-3522 | NA | San Jose |
| V-Soft Inc (HQ) | Provider of product development services. The company also specializes in mobile application development. | 408-342-1700 | NA | San Jose |
| V2plus Technology Inc (HQ) | Provider of technology solutions. The company offers services for voice, data, and video over local wired and wireless communication networks. | 510-226-6006 | NA | Fremont |
| Valiantica Inc (HQ) | Provider of global IT solutions. The company's services include consulting, outsourcing, and mobile, enterprise and business application development. | 408-725-2426 | NA | San Jose |
| Varite Inc (HQ) | Provider of custom software development, integration, deployment, and implementation services in the domains of core networking and virtualization. | 408-977-0700 | NA | San Jose |
| Veeva Systems (HQ) | Provider of cloud-based business solutions such as customer relationship management and content management for the life sciences industry. | 925-452-6500 | NA | Pleasanton |
| Versa Shore Inc (HQ) | Provider of data warehouse implementation, strategic blueprint creation, project management, and testing consulting services. | 408-874-8330 | NA | Campbell |
| Versonix Corp (HQ) | Provider of integrated and customized software solutions. The company serves the travel and leisure industries. | 408-873-3131 | NA | San Jose |
| Vistrian Inc (HQ) | Developer of software products. The company's services include escalation management, problem isolation, and remote access. | 408-719-0500 | NA | Milpitas |
| VisualOn Inc (HQ) | Provider of software applications for the mobile handset market enabling customers to access multimedia content without dedicated hardware. | 408-645-6618 | NA | San Jose |
| Wave Systems Corp (HQ) | Provider of customized software development for the law enforcement, casino, corporate security, and hospitals segments. | 408-524-8630 | NA | Sunnyvale |
| William Stucky & Associates Inc (HQ) | Provider of software products and services. The company mainly caters to the asset-based lending industry. | 415-788-2441 | NA | San Francisco |
| Wilson Research Group Llc (HQ) | Provider of market research products and services. The company serves publishing, embedded systems, and high technology fields. | 530-350-8377 | 1-10 | El Dorado Hills |
| Workday Inc (HQ) | Provider of software solutions for human resources management and financial management. The company specializes in SaaS based enterprise solutions. | 925-951-9000 | NA | Pleasanton |
| Wright Williams & Kelly Inc (HQ) | Provider of software products and consulting services. The company also offers decision tolls for cost management. | 925-399-6246 | NA | Pleasanton |
| X-Z LAB Inc (HQ) | Provider of digital radiation detection services. The company engages in detecting, measuring, and monitoring radiation activities. | 925-355-5199 | NA | San Ramon |
| Xmatters Inc (HQ) | Provider of voice and text alerting system software. The company serves the healthcare, telecommunications, and manufacturing industries. | 925-226-0300 | NA | San Ramon |

| COMPANY NAME | PRODUCT / SERVICE | PHONE | EMP | CITY |
|---|---|---|---|---|
| Xoriant Corp (HQ) | Provider of enterprise applications. The company also offers mobile analytics and web application development services. | 408-743-4400 | NA | Sunnyvale |
| Zmanda - A Carbonite Co (HQ) | Provider of open source backup and recovery software solutions. The company's applications include centralized backup of file systems and applications. | 408-732-3208 | 51-200 | Sunnyvale |
| ZoZo Engineering (HQ) | Manufacturer of RF surgical generators. The company also offers gas analyzers and related equipment. | 415-227-4450 | NA | San Francisco |

## 324 = Data Preparation & Processing Services

| COMPANY NAME | PRODUCT / SERVICE | PHONE | EMP | CITY |
|---|---|---|---|---|
| 314e Corp (HQ) | Provider of IT skills, methodologies, and cost-effective managed services for healthcare application and technical support services. | 510-371-6736 | NA | Fremont |
| 6connect Inc (HQ) | Provider of network resource provisioning and automation products and services such as data normalizer, pro services, and provision jumpstart. | 650-646-2206 | NA | San Francisco |
| 8x8 Inc (HQ) | Provider of cloud communications and computing solutions. The company sells IP phones, IP conference, soft, video and analog phones and accessories. | 408-727-1885 | NA | San Jose |
| Accenture (BR) | Provider of management consulting and technology services. The company also offers application outsourcing and IT consulting services. | 415-537-5000 | NA | San Francisco |
| Accu-Image Inc (HQ) | Supplier of transfer document image processing equipment. The company is engaged in business process consulting and document management. | 408-736-9066 | NA | Santa Clara |
| Active Video Networks (HQ) | Designer and developer of advertising solutions. The company also provides mosaic, guide, and navigation enablement services. | 408-931-9200 | NA | San Jose |
| Acxiom LLC (BR) | Provider of e-mail marketing services for online marketers. The company is engaged in consulting and analytics services. | 888-322-9466 | NA | Redwood City |
| Advance Research Associates (HQ) | Developer of human bio-therapeutic platform technology solutions, drug discovery, and related support services. | 650-810-1190 | NA | Santa Clara |
| Advantrics Llc (HQ) | Designer and developer of internet technologies. The company also specializes in multimedia-based products. | 530-297-3660 | 1-10 | Davis |
| Agrian Inc (HQ) | Provider of agridata tracking and information sharing system for applicator, retail outlets, grower, and crop consultant via computer and mobile devices. | 559-437-5700 | 1-10 | Fresno |
| Airnex Communications Inc (HQ) | Provider of digital wireless telecommunications and internet access services. The company also focuses on web hosting. | 800-708-4884 | NA | Pleasanton |
| Alacrinet Consulting Services Inc (HQ) | Developer of software solutions. The company offers enterprise search, web content management, business intelligence, and analytics services. | 650-646-2670 | NA | Palo Alto |
| Aldo Ventures Inc (HQ) | Provider of studies such as software technology, markets, companies, platforms, products, and investment strategies of the software industry. | 831-662-2536 | 1-10 | Aptos |
| Alten Calsoft Labs (HQ) | Provider of breed consulting, enterprise IT, and product engineering services for enterprises in healthcare, telecom, and high-tech & retail industries. | 408-755-3000 | NA | Santa Clara |
| Altierre Corp (HQ) | Provider of digital retail services. The company offers retail integration, software support, and consulting services. | 408-435-7343 | NA | San Jose |
| Applied Computer Solutions (BR) | Provider of information technology solutions. The company offers solutions for virtualization, storage, security, and networking. | 925-251-1000 | NA | Pleasanton |
| Arc (HQ) | Provider of document management services to the architectural, engineering, and construction industries. | 925-949-5100 | NA | San Ramon |
| Asani Solutions Llc (HQ) | Provider of networking solutions and system integration services. The company also focuses on internet and corporate consulting. | 408-330-0821 | NA | Santa Clara |
| Astreya (HQ) | Provider of staffing services. The company specializes in recruitment of systems administrators, network engineers, system, and network architects. | 800-224-1117 | NA | San Jose |
| Bitglass (HQ) | Provider of data protection solutions. The company focuses on cloud encryption, mobile security, and discovery solutions. | 408-337-0190 | NA | Campbell |
| BMC Software Inc (BR) | Provider of cloud management, workforce automation, and IT service management solutions. The company serves business enterprises and service providers. | 800-793-4262 | NA | Santa Clara |
| Bromium Inc (HQ) | Provider of enterprise security solutions. The company focuses on security software development, technical support, and task introspection. | 408-213-5668 | NA | Cupertino |
| Bunchball Inc (HQ) | Provider of cloud-based software as a service gamification products. The company's products include Nitro, Nitro for Salesforce, and Nitro for Jive. | 408-985-2034 | NA | Redwood City |
| Capital Datacorp (HQ) | Provider of sales, design, installation, and support of networking technologies for businesses and government agencies. | | 1-10 | Sacramento |
| Capitol Digital Document Solutions (HQ) | Provider of litigation support services. The company offers forensic data collection, online document review, and e-discovery processing services. | 916-449-2820 | 1-10 | Sacramento |
| Carefree Computing Inc (HQ) | Provider of web hosting, software design, programming, technical support, and network design services. | 866-377-6275 | NA | San Francisco |
| Certain Inc (DH) | Provider of enterprise event management solutions that include e-mail marketing, event reporting, registration, and consulting services. | 415-353-5330 | NA | San Francisco |

| COMPANY NAME | PRODUCT / SERVICE | PHONE | EMP | CITY |
|---|---|---|---|---|
| ChannelNet (BR) | Provider of digital solutions to connect brands and customers. The company specializes in strategy development, design, and content optimization. | 415-332-4704 | NA | Sausalito |
| Climate Earth (HQ) | Provider of environmental product declarations and supply chain solutions such as supply chain, climate change risk, and natural capital management . | 415-391-2725 | NA | Berkeley |
| Cloudpassage Inc (HQ) | Developer of software solutions. The company also offers account management, configuration security monitoring, and alerting services. | 415-886-3020 | NA | San Francisco |
| Cloverleaf Solutions Inc (HQ) | Provider of data validation and information processing computer solutions. The company caters to businesses. | 916-484-4141 | 1-10 | Sacramento |
| Collaborative Drug Discovery Inc (HQ) | Provider of drug discovery research informatics. The company offers hosted biological and chemical database that securely manages private and external data. | 650-242-5259 | NA | Burlingame |
| Computer Methods (HQ) | Manufacturer of physical therapy testing equipment. The company's products include WebExam, PP004, WinHand, and ActivitySuite. | 510-824-0252 | 1-10 | Tracy |
| Computerland Of Silicon Valley (HQ) | Provider of hardware, software, and networking services. The company serves government and educational institutions. | 408-519-3200 | NA | San Jose |
| Connected Marketing (HQ) | Provider of marketing services. The company also offers web development, branding, and lead generation services. | 408-647-2198 | NA | San Jose |
| Corrigo Inc (BR) | Developer of facilities management platforms. The company offers services to business organizations. | 877-267-7440 | NA | San Mateo |
| CP Media Group Inc (HQ) | Provider of audio visual production, website development and hosting, social media marketing, and related services. | 951-694-4830 | NA | San Ramon |
| Cybersoft (BR) | Provider of offshore business and knowledge process outsourcing services. The company specializes in title, financial, and document processing services. | 415-449-7998 | NA | San Francisco |
| Cypress Digital Media (HQ) | Provider of web design, mobile development, and online marketing for interactive agencies and marketing campaigns. | 650-257-0741 | NA | Mountain View |
| Daniel B Stephens & Associates Inc (BR) | Provider of services in hydrology, environmental engineering, and science. The company services include water resources and soil testing. | 800-933-3105 | NA | Oakland |
| Data Distributing Llc (HQ) | Provider of solutions such as mass storage, peripheral, storage management software, import, archive, and images and data distribution. | 831-457-3537 | 11-50 | Santa Cruz |
| Database Republic (HQ) | Provider of enterprise analysis and strategy modeling services. The company also focuses on DB design and implementation. | 530-692-2500 | 1-10 | Oregon House |
| Dataglance Inc (HQ) | Provider of data management software that support LIVE data conversion/migration, electronic document generation & processing, and web services. | 510-656-0500 | NA | Fremont |
| Dataguise (HQ) | Provider of cloud migration, auditing, and monitoring solutions. The company serves the healthcare, consumer, and retail industries. | 877-632-0522 | NA | Fremont |
| Datasafe (HQ) | Provider of digital solutions. The company's services include records storage, document shredding and imaging, and rotation. | 650-875-3800 | NA | S San Francisco |
| Datastax Inc (RH) | Distributor of database management system for internet enterprise. The company offers training & certification, expert support, and consulting services. | 408-933-3120 | NA | Santa Clara |
| Delphix (HQ) | Developer of software, database, and database virtualization. The company focuses on website design and hosting and software application development. | 650-494-1645 | NA | Redwood City |
| Device Authority Ltd (RH) | Provider of IoT security solutions for industrial, automotive, transportation, healthcare, utilities, and smart cities. | 650-603-0997 | NA | Fremont |
| Devonway (HQ) | Provider of enterprise software solutions for utilities and process industries. The company specializes in enterprise asset management solutions. | 415-904-4000 | NA | San Francisco |
| Digital Mountain Inc (HQ) | Provider of electronic discovery and computer forensic services focusing on reduplication, data management, ESI planning, and cybersecurity. | 866-344-3627 | NA | Santa Clara |
| Direct Mail Center (HQ) | Provider of data processing, fulfillment, digital and offset printing, mail production, and logistics services. | 415-252-1600 | NA | San Francisco |
| Elucit (HQ) | Provider of hardware & software development services. The company also offers data recorders and calibratrion services. | 707-961-1016 | 1-10 | Fort Bragg |
| Emagined Security Inc (HQ) | Provider of professional services for information security solutions. The company also focuses on compliance. | 415-944-2977 | NA | San Carlos |
| enSilo (HQ) | Developer of data protection platforms and provider of exfiltration prevention solutions. The company offers services to the network industry. | 800-413-1782 | NA | San Francisco |
| Equinix (HQ) | Provider of interconnection data center and global colocation services focusing on cloud, business continuity, financial, and digital media. | 866-378-4649 | NA | Redwood City |
| First Class Plus Llc (HQ) | Provider of fundraising and marketing solutions. The company deals with print production, design assistance, and pre-press services. | 650-589-8346 | NA | S San Francisco |
| Funambol Inc (HQ) | Provider of open source mobile application server software. The company offers training and technical support services. | 650-701-1450 | NA | Foster City |
| Gigamon (HQ) | Provider of traffic visibility solutions for enterprises, data centers, and the education, financial, and healthcare industries. | 408-831-4000 | NA | Santa Clara |

| COMPANY NAME | PRODUCT / SERVICE | PHONE | EMP | CITY |
|---|---|---|---|---|
| Grandflow Inc (HQ) | Provider of e-cataloging and marketing automation solutions. The company offers print production, warehousing, and document management services. | 925-443-0855 | NA | Livermore |
| Greytrix (RH) | Provider of integration and migration solutions. The company deals in analytics, cloud, mobility, and ERP/CRM consulting. | 888-221-6661 | NA | San Francisco |
| H M Franklin Associates (HQ) | Provider of data processing consulting and related services. The company serves the government and corporate industries. | 925-735-8848 | NA | San Ramon |
| Health Fidelity Inc (HQ) | Provider of natural language processing technology and inference platform to analyze vast amounts of unstructured data for clinical and financial insights. | 650-727-3300 | NA | San Mateo |
| Hydropoint Data Systems Inc (HQ) | Provider of irrigation solutions. The company specializes in site evaluations, upgrade planning, deployment, and optimization services. | 800-362-8774 | NA | Petaluma |
| Imperva Inc (HQ) | Provider of application and data security solutions. The company's products include database firewalls, management server, and monitoring software. | 650-345-9000 | NA | Redwood Shores |
| Inabyte Inc (HQ) | Manufacturer of developer tools. The company also offers solutions and services for developers and end users of PCs or workstations. | 415-898-7905 | NA | Novato |
| Infoblox Inc (HQ) | Provider of automated network control solutions. The company's services include training, implementation, migration, upgrade, repair, and maintenance. | 408-986-4000 | NA | Santa Clara |
| Infoimage Inc (HQ) | Provider of technology solutions for job tracking and business continuity needs. The company also focuses on data integrity. | 650-473-6388 | NA | Menlo Park |
| Informatica Corp (HQ) | Provider of enterprise data integration and management solutions including data migration, warehousing, identity resolution, and other needs. | 650-385-5000 | NA | Redwood City |
| Integrated Archive Systems Inc (HQ) | Provider of global data management services. The company offers storage, data protection, microsoft exchange, and virtualization services. | 650-390-9995 | NA | Palo Alto |
| IntelinAir Inc (HQ) | Provider of aerial imagery analytics such as image analysis and change detection and deep learning and neural networks for farmers. | 818-445-2339 | NA | San Jose |
| Interface Masters Technologies Inc (HQ) | Developer of technology and networking solutions. The company's products include embedded switches, adapters, and related accessories. | 408-441-9341 | NA | San Jose |
| Intuit Inc (HQ) | Provider of financial management software solutions. The company offers services to small businesses and related organizations. | 800-446-8848 | NA | Mountain View |
| Ionix Internet (HQ) | Provider of web hosting solutions. The company offers network security, research, hi-speed access, and telecommuting services. | 888-884-6649 | NA | San Francisco |
| Irislogic Inc (HQ) | Provider of global consulting services and solutions. The company specializes in custom software development, network security, cloud, and testing. | 408-855-8741 | NA | Santa Clara |
| It Concepts Llc (BR) | Manufacturer of borescopes, videoscopes, fiberscopes, documentation solutions, and accessories for remote visual inspection needs. | 925-401-0010 | NA | Pleasanton |
| JAMIS Software Corp (HQ) | Provider of job-cost, billing, and accounting systems and solutions. The company caters to the government contractors. | 800-655-2647 | 11-50 | San Diego |
| Jiva Creative Llc (HQ) | Provider of interactive design technology solutions. The company focuses on architecture, website hosting, and enterprise application development. | 510-864-8625 | NA | Alameda |
| Kaazing Corp (HQ) | Provider of software services. The company's IoT gateway is used by mobile users, marketplaces, and machines to connect and communicate in real-time. | 877-522-9464 | NA | San Jose |
| Kaliotek Inc (HQ) | Provider of enterprise applications. The company also specializes in technical infrastructure for companies. | 408-550-8000 | NA | Cupertino |
| Kovarus Inc (HQ) | Provider of integrated business IT solutions. The company also deals with leasing, financing, project management, and related services. | 650-392-7848 | NA | San Ramon |
| Litmos Ltd (HQ) | Provider of learning management system solutions. The company serves the energy and engineering industries. | 925-251-2220 | NA | Dublin |
| Medallia Inc (HQ) | Provider of consulting, system configuration, user training, and data warehouse integration services. | 650-321-3000 | NA | Palo Alto |
| Micromega Systems Inc (HQ) | Provider of database systems and e-business website design services. The company also focuses on training and installation. | 415-924-4700 | NA | Corte Madera |
| Modius Inc (HQ) | Provider of performance management software. The company serves infrastructure monitoring applications. | 415-655-6700 | NA | San Francisco |
| Moonstone Interactive Inc (HQ) | Provider of website design services. The company offers web design and development, content management, and market visibility services. | 866-246-9091 | NA | San Ramon |
| Mountford Group Inc (HQ) | Provider of system development and web application services. The company also focuses on technical communication. | 925-686-6613 | NA | Concord |
| Multimedia Consulting Services Inc (HQ) | Provider of multimedia consulting services. The company offers design, implementation, and maintenance of the information technology infrastructure. | 650-578-8591 | NA | Foster City |
| Navlink (LH) | Provider of managed data services, managed hosting services, and managed enterprise networking solutions. | 650-616-4042 | NA | San Bruno |
| Neospeech Inc (HQ) | Provider of text-to-speech software and applications for the mobile, enterprise, entertainment, and education markets. | 408-914-2710 | NA | Santa Clara |

| COMPANY NAME | PRODUCT / SERVICE | PHONE | EMP | CITY |
|---|---|---|---|---|
| NetApp Inc (HQ) | Provider of virtualization, mobile information management, and cloud storage solutions. The company serves the business sector. | 408-822-6000 | NA | Sunnyvale |
| Netwoven Inc (HQ) | Provider of enterprise content management and business intelligence solutions. The company also focuses on process management. | 877-638-9683 | NA | Milpitas |
| New Tech Solutions Inc (HQ) | Provider of technology solutions. The company caters to networking, security, and communication manufacturers. | 510-353-4070 | NA | Fremont |
| Nextier Networks Inc (HQ) | Provider of data security services and solutions for vertical markets and original equipment manufacturers. | 408-282-3561 | NA | Santa Clara |
| Novani Llc (HQ) | Provider of disaster prevention and recovery solutions. The company also offers business continuity and virtualization solutions. | 415-731-1111 | NA | San Francisco |
| Numenta Inc (HQ) | Developer of biotechnology machine intelligence technologies for commercial and scientific applications. | 650-369-8282 | NA | Redwood City |
| Objectivity Inc (HQ) | Provider of distributed, real-time, SOA-enabled service and offers embedded database management solutions. | 408-992-7100 | NA | San Jose |
| Ordinal Technology Corp (HQ) | Provider of sorting services of massive and production data sets such as web logs for high-traffic web sites, phone logs, and government agency data. | 925-253-9204 | NA | Orinda |
| Overland Storage Inc (BR) | Provider of data management and protection solutions. The company offers network attached storage, virtual tape libraries, LTO drives, and software. | 408-283-4700 | NA | San Jose |
| Persistent Systems Inc (BR) | Developer of software & technology products for life science, banking, and other sectors. The company offers big data, security, and cloud solutions. | 408-216-7010 | NA | Santa Clara |
| Planeteria Media (HQ) | Designer and developer of websites, applications, e-commerce, content management systems, video, and offers flash, and internet marketing services. | 707-843-3773 | NA | Santa Rosa |
| Presidio Inc (BR) | Provider of IP telephony and wireless networking services. The company also deals with deployment, integration, and hardware and software development. | 415-501-9020 | NA | Pleasanton |
| Proofpoint (RH) | Manufacturer of threat, email, social media, and information protection products. The company offers security and compliance solutions. | 408-517-4710 | NA | Sunnyvale |
| Quest America Inc (HQ) | Provider of information technology services. The company offers solutions through strategy, consulting, and outsourcing. | 408-492-1650 | NA | San Jose |
| Quisk Inc (HQ) | Specializes in the development of payment solutions. The company offers services to financial institutions. | 408-462-6800 | NA | Sunnyvale |
| R Systems Inc (RH) | Provider of information technology services and solutions. The company offers application, testing, BPO, and packaged services. | 800-355-5159 | 1-10 | El Dorado Hills |
| Radiant Logic Inc (HQ) | Provider of identity and context virtualization solutions. The company caters to identity integration and management needs. | 415-209-6800 | NA | Novato |
| SACC Inc (HQ) | Provider of enterprise resource planning, data warehousing, technology infrastructure, business process outsourcing, and staffing services. | 408-755-3000 | NA | Santa Clara |
| Sasken Technologies Ltd (BR) | Provider of research and development consultation, wireless software products, and software services to automotive and health care sectors. | 408-730-0100 | NA | Sunnyvale |
| Servicesource International Inc (HQ) | Provider of recurring revenue management solutions. The company focuses on process automation and managed services. | 720-889-8500 | NA | San Francisco |
| Sierra Data Systems (HQ) | Provider of data communication systems, internet related services, miscellaneous communications equipment, telephone, and voice equipment. | 916-242-4604 | 1-10 | Grass Valley |
| Single Point Of Contact (HQ) | Provider of IT management, enterprise, and planning services. The company is also engaged in cloud computing, web hosting, and hosted exchange. | 800-791-4300 | NA | Palo Alto |
| Sios Technology Corp (LH) | Provider of cloud virtualization protection solutions. The company also offers managed information technology services. | 650-645-7000 | NA | San Mateo |
| Sumo Logic (RH) | Provider of compliance, security, monitoring, troubleshooting, and delivery solutions. The company serves security, IT, and development teams. | 650-810-8700 | NA | Redwood City |
| SyTech Solutions Inc (HQ) | Provider of document management technology services. The company offers archieve scanning, web-based document management, and data capture services. | 916-381-3010 | 1-10 | Elk Grove |
| Taseon Inc (HQ) | Developer of technology related solutions. The company also offers system engineering and software development services. | 408-240-7800 | NA | San Jose |
| TextDigger Inc (HQ) | Developer of horizontal semantic solutions for search engines. The company focuses on content mining and analytics. | 408-416-3142 | NA | San Jose |
| ThreatMetrix (HQ) | Provider of fraud prevention, threat detection, and authentication solutions. The company serves the gaming, media, and insurance industries. | 408-200-5755 | NA | San Jose |
| Tom Sawyer Software Corp (HQ) | Developer of data relationship visualization and analysis software for application developers. The company offers training and consulting services. | 510-208-4370 | NA | Berkeley |
| Toolwire Inc (HQ) | Designer and developer of experiential learning solutions for higher education and corporate training institutions. | 925-227-8500 | NA | Pleasanton |
| Tvu Networks Corp (HQ) | Provider of wireless electronic news gathering services. The company offers TV broadcast, web streaming, and law enforcement services. | 650-969-6732 | NA | Mountain View |

| COMPANY NAME | PRODUCT / SERVICE | PHONE | EMP | CITY |
|---|---|---|---|---|
| Watchwith Inc (HQ) | Provider of software and data solutions for the film and television content creators and consumer electronics manufacturers. | 415-552-1552 | NA | San Francisco |
| Wilson Research Group Llc (HQ) | Provider of market research products and services. The company serves publishing, embedded systems, and high technology fields. | 530-350-8377 | 1-10 | El Dorado Hills |
| WindSpring Inc (HQ) | Manufacturer of data management tools. The company provides a framework for optimized compressed data management in the storage and embedded fields. | 408-452-7400 | NA | San Jose |
| Xtime Inc (HQ) | Provider of CRM solutions for automotive service operations. The company offers scheduling and marketing solutions for automotive retailers. | 650-508-4300 | NA | Redwood City |
| Zephyr Health Inc (HQ) | Focuses on Service enterprise solutions. The company deals with segment and referral analytics and serves physicians and hospitals. | 415-529-7649 | NA | San Francisco |

## 325 = Internet-Related Services

| COMPANY NAME | PRODUCT / SERVICE | PHONE | EMP | CITY |
|---|---|---|---|---|
| 6WIND USA Inc (RH) | Manufacturer of virtual accelerators, routers, and related accessories. The company offers network security and network appliance solutions. | 408-816-1366 | NA | Santa Clara |
| A A Networks (HQ) | Provider of internet, networks and cabling, computer hardware and software, remote and on-site technical support services. | 650-872-1998 | NA | Burlingame |
| A3 Solutions Inc (HQ) | Developer and marketer of enterprise modeling software. The company is also engaged in unified budgeting and consolidation services. | 415-356-2300 | NA | San Francisco |
| Ablesys Corp (HQ) | Provider of financial trading software and web applications. The company focuses on portfolio and algorithmic trading solutions. | 510-265-1883 | NA | Hayward |
| Accel (HQ) | Provider of investment services specializing in the mobile, retail, energy, and security industries. | 650-614-4800 | NA | Palo Alto |
| Accelerance Inc (HQ) | Provider of software design, development, and deployment services. The company focuses on web hosting and programming solutions. | 650-472-3785 | NA | Redwood City |
| Accellion (HQ) | Provider of web-based file transfer applications. The company also focuses on data management solutions. | 650-485-4300 | NA | Palo Alto |
| Access Softek Inc (HQ) | Developer of mobile banking software solutions. The company focuses on software and product development, QA testing, user interface, and graphic design. | 510-848-0606 | NA | Berkeley |
| Accounting Micro Systems (HQ) | Developer of accounting and business management software products. The company offers MAS500, MAS90 and MAS200, FAS Asset solutions, and SalesLogix. | 415-362-5100 | NA | San Francisco |
| Accu-Image Inc (HQ) | Supplier of transfer document image processing equipment. The company is engaged in business process consulting and document management. | 408-736-9066 | NA | Santa Clara |
| Acrylic Art (HQ) | Provider of fabrication and machining services. The company focuses on painting, product finishing, anodizing, and vapor polishing. | 510-654-0953 | NA | Emeryville |
| Adaptive Insights (HQ) | Provider of training, consulting, and related support services. The company serves the healthcare, insurance, and manufacturing industries. | 650-528-7500 | NA | Palo Alto |
| Adobe Systems Inc (HQ) | Developer of software solutions for digital media creation and editing, multimedia authoring, and web development. | 408-536-6000 | NA | San Jose |
| Advancing Ideas LLC (HQ) | Provider of market research and analysis, application branding, and user interface development services. | 415-625-3338 | NA | San Francisco |
| Advantage for Analysts Inc (HQ) | Developer of structuring and analysis software. The company finds application in originating, trading, and managing complex financial assets. | 415-568-4800 | NA | Sausalito |
| Aerohive Networks Inc (HQ) | Provider of enterprise mobility solutions. The company offers access points, routers, switches, and VPN gateway solutions. | 408-510-6100 | NA | Milpitas |
| Agari Data Inc (HQ) | Provider of email security and social engineering solutions. The company serves the healthcare, financial services, and government industries. | 650-627-7667 | NA | Foster City |
| Air Computing Inc (HQ) | Provider of file sync & share service such as transfer large files, share securely, server replacement, and data recovery solutions. | | NA | Palo Alto |
| Algo-Logic Systems (HQ) | Specializes in building networking solutions. The company also offers technological and data handling services to firms. | 408-707-3740 | NA | San Jose |
| Allied Telesis Inc (BR) | Developer of network solutions for internet protocol surveillance. The company focuses on web hosting and programming solutions. | 408-519-8700 | NA | San Jose |
| AlphaSense Inc (HQ) | Provider of financial search engine. The company offers natural language processing algorithms with advanced semantic indexing and search technology. | 415-738-8090 | 11-50 | San Francisco |
| Amdocs Ltd (BR) | Provider of customer management and billing solutions software. The company offers services to the industrial sector. | 916-934-7000 | 11-50 | El Dorado Hills |
| American International Group Inc (RH) | Provider of international insurance solutions and financial services. The company serves individuals, group, and businesses. | 415-836-2700 | NA | San Francisco |
| American Telesource Inc (HQ) | Provider of voice and data communication applications. The company offers unified communications, wireless, and process automation solutions. | 800-333-8394 | NA | Emeryville |
| Amind Solutions Llc (HQ) | Provider of technology and services. The company offers enterprise mobility, quoting and ordering, product configuration, and e-Commerce services. | 925-804-6139 | NA | Alamo |
| Anand Systems Inc (HQ) | Designer of custom software solutions for the hotel industry. The company also offers related hardware, website design, and surveillance systems. | 209-830-1484 | 1-10 | Tracy |

| COMPANY NAME | PRODUCT / SERVICE | PHONE | EMP | CITY |
|---|---|---|---|---|
| Andover Consulting Group Inc (HQ) | Supplier of network components. The company offers data center liquidation, network security, and network equipment services. | 415-537-6950 | NA | S San Francisco |
| Anomali (RH) | Specializes in the delivery of cyber security solutions. The company services to big and small organizations. | 844-484-7328 | NA | Redwood City |
| Apogee Software Inc (HQ) | Provider of integrated development environment for Java and C. The company offers industrial monitors and controllers. | 408-369-9001 | NA | Campbell |
| Apolent Corp (HQ) | Provider of business process and software technology outsourcing services focusing on niche market segments. | 408-203-6828 | NA | San Jose |
| Applied Expert Systems Inc (HQ) | Developer of networking solutions for business service management. The company provides virtualization and cloud computing services. | 650-617-2400 | NA | Palo Alto |
| Applied Simulation Technology Inc (HQ) | Developer of stimulators and molders in signal integrity, power integrity, and circuit simulation tools. | 408-436-9070 | NA | San Jose |
| Apsalar Inc (HQ) | Provider of data-powered mobile advertising solutions. The company offers marketing attribution and in-app analytics services. | 877-590-1854 | NA | San Francisco |
| Arc (HQ) | Provider of document management services to the architectural, engineering, and construction industries. | 925-949-5100 | NA | San Ramon |
| ARX Networks Corp (HQ) | Provider of IT support and maintenance and cloud services. The company also focuses on unified communications and procurement. | 650-403-4000 | NA | Newark |
| Aryaka Networks Inc (HQ) | Provider of cloud-based WAN optimization services. The company focuses on application performance, data protection, and bandwidth reduction. | 877-727-9252 | NA | Milpitas |
| Asap Systems (HQ) | Developer of inventory management and asset tracking software. The company also offers barcode scanners & printers and RFID tags. | 408-227-2720 | NA | San Jose |
| Aspire Systems Inc (BR) | Provider of product engineering, infrastructure and application support, and testing services. The company serves healthcare and education fields. | 408-260-2076 | NA | San Jose |
| Astreya (HQ) | Provider of staffing services. The company specializes in recruitment of systems administrators, network engineers, system, and network architects. | 800-224-1117 | NA | San Jose |
| Audible Magic Corp (HQ) | Developer of media identification and synchronization, content registration, and copyright compliance solutions. | 408-399-6405 | NA | Los Gatos |
| Augmentum Inc (HQ) | Provider of software development & solution implementation services. The company focuses on internet applications and product development outsourcing. | 650-578-9221 | NA | Foster City |
| Automattic Inc (HQ) | Provider of blogging services. The company specializes in handling non-profit and open source projects. | 877-273-3049 | NA | San Francisco |
| Autonomic Software Inc (HQ) | Developer of software for endpoint & security management, imaging, and other needs. The company serves government, finance, and other sectors. | 925-683-8351 | NA | Danville |
| AvantPage (HQ) | Provider of foreign language translation services for the medical, technical, healthcare, financial industries. | 530-750-2040 | 1-10 | Davis |
| Axsen Llc (HQ) | Developer of web designs and provider of online marketing solutions. The company serves the industrial sector. | 866-462-9736 | NA | Pleasanton |
| Bay Dynamics Inc (HQ) | Provider of IT analytics solutions. The company offers data loss prevention, system management, and security tool implementation services. | 415-912-3130 | 11-50 | San Francisco |
| Bcl Technologies (HQ) | Developer of document creation, conversion, and extraction solutions. The company offers BCL easyPDF Cloud, a cloud-based PDF conversion platform. | 408-557-2080 | NA | San Jose |
| Bct Consulting Inc (HQ) | Provider of computer network support, web design, application programming, and other technology services. | 559-579-1400 | 11-50 | Fresno |
| Bear River Associates Inc (HQ) | Provider of enterprise mobile computing products and services. The company serves business services, government, high-tech, and life science sectors. | 510-834-5300 | NA | Oakland |
| BitPusher LLC (HQ) | Provider of IT infrastructure management services. The company also focuses on consulting and hosted IT services. | 415-751-1055 | NA | San Francisco |
| Bitsculptor (HQ) | Provider of web design, hosting, branding and search engine positioning solutions. The company also offers SEO, photography, and consulting services. | 707-263-5241 | 1-10 | Lakeport |
| BitTorrent Inc (HQ) | Provider of download software solutions. The company offers design, data and content management, and installation services. | 415-568-9000 | NA | San Francisco |
| BizeeBee Inc (HQ) | Provider of lightweight software solution designed to help fitness studios and other membership based businesses. | 650-489-6233 | NA | Palo Alto |
| BlackBag Technologies Inc (HQ) | Provider of Mac-based data forensic and eDiscovery solutions. The company is involved in data processing and related services. | 408-844-8890 | NA | San Jose |
| Blacksquare Llc (HQ) | Provider of location-based, social, m-commerce, game, and video applications. The company serves Fortune 500 companies. | 415-640-6339 | NA | San Francisco |
| Blast Analytics & Marketing (HQ) | Provider of web design, e-commerce, and brand design services. The company is involved in hosting and technical support. | 916-724-6701 | 11-50 | Rocklin |
| Blue Jeans Network Inc (HQ) | Provider of cloud-based video conferencing solutions. The company also offers mobile video collaboration and cloud video bridging solutions. | 408-550-2828 | NA | Mountain View |

| COMPANY NAME | PRODUCT / SERVICE | PHONE | EMP | CITY |
|---|---|---|---|---|
| Blunk Microsystems LLC (HQ) | Provider of turnkey packages for embedded development to customers around the world. The company also offers development tools. | 408-323-1758 | 1-10 | Sacramento |
| Boardwalktech Inc (HQ) | Provider of enterprise collaboration software specializing in tax planning, cash management, and revenue forecasting solutions. | 650-618-6200 | NA | Cupertino |
| Bodhtree Solutions Inc (BR) | Provider of information technology consulting services. The company deals with product engineering, application development, and training. | 408-954-8700 | 11-50 | Fremont |
| Boldfocus Inc (HQ) | Provider of digital communications and technology services focusing on development, content management, and search engine optimization. | 650-212-2653 | NA | San Mateo |
| Brekeke Software Inc (HQ) | Developer of session initiation protocol software products for internet protocol network communication needs. | 650-401-6633 | NA | San Mateo |
| BrightEdge Technologies Inc (HQ) | Developer of mobile web applications, websites, and publishing platforms. The company specializes in SmartPath technology. | 800-578-8023 | NA | Foster City |
| Brighterion Inc (HQ) | Provider of products for fraud prevention, predictive intelligence, risk management, and homeland security. The company focuses on adaptive analytics. | 415-986-5600 | NA | San Francisco |
| Brightsign Llc (HQ) | Provider of digital sign media players, software, and networking solutions for the commercial digital signage industry. | 408-852-9263 | NA | Los Gatos |
| Brs Media Inc (HQ) | Provider of multimedia e-commerce services. The company specializes in radio and internet applications. | 415-677-4027 | NA | San Francisco |
| Bunchball Inc (HQ) | Provider of cloud-based software as a service gamification products. The company's products include Nitro, Nitro for Salesforce, and Nitro for Jive. | 408-985-2034 | NA | Redwood City |
| Busse Design Usa Inc (HQ) | Provider of interface design services. The company's services include website design and application user interface. | 415-689-8090 | NA | Oakland |
| Calsoft Inc (HQ) | Designer and developer of storage, networking, and operating systems. The company deals with design, delivery, and installation. | 408-834-7086 | NA | San Jose |
| Cantaloupe Systems Inc (HQ) | Developer of SQL based encryption solutions for wireless vending services. The company also focuses on dynamic scheduling and remote monitoring. | 415-525-8100 | NA | San Francisco |
| Capital Datacorp (HQ) | Provider of sales, design, installation, and support of networking technologies for businesses and government agencies. | | 1-10 | Sacramento |
| Caseware International Inc (DH) | Supplier of software solutions to accountants and auditors worldwide. The company offers working papers to accounting firms. | 416-867-9504 | NA | Berkeley |
| Castle Rock Computing Inc (HQ) | Designer and manufacturer of SNMPC network management software. The company's product caters to a wide range of sectors. | 408-366-6540 | NA | Saratoga |
| Ccintegration Inc (HQ) | Provider of business engagement models such as OEM and virtual OEM. The company services include design, integration, and logistics. | 408-228-1314 | NA | San Jose |
| Cdnetworks Inc (RH) | Developer of web and network acceleration solutions. The company serves the travel, tourism, gaming, and technology industries. | 408-228-3700 | NA | Campbell |
| Celestix Networks Inc (HQ) | Provider of security appliances and solutions for healthcare, legal & financial, education, commercial, small business, and public sector industries. | 510-668-0700 | NA | Fremont |
| Celigo Inc (HQ) | Provider of cloud computing products and solutions. The company offers NetSuite consulting services that include implementation and optimization. | 650-579-0210 | NA | San Mateo |
| Centrify (HQ) | Provider of identity and access management solutions. The company offers services to pharma companies and financial institutions. | 669-444-5200 | NA | Santa Clara |
| ChemSoft (HQ) | Provider of software consulting services. The company specializes in custom business solutions, access, excel, PowerPoint, word, and visual basic. | 408-615-1001 | NA | San Jose |
| Chesapeake Technology Inc (HQ) | Provider of sonar mapping software as well as consulting services to the marine, geophysical, and geological survey industries. | 650-967-2045 | NA | Los Altos |
| Chouinard & Myhre Inc (HQ) | Provider of IT solutions such as data management, enterprise security management, and private, public, and hybrid cloud solutions and services. | 415-480-3636 | NA | Mill Valley |
| Cisco Systems Inc (BR) | Provider of networking products and services such as routers, switches, and optical and wireless networking devices. | 800-553-6387 | NA | San Francisco |
| Cityspan Technologies Inc (HQ) | Developer of software for social services. The company offers software to manage grants, track clients, and evaluate outcomes. | 510-665-1700 | NA | Berkeley |
| Civil Maps (HQ) | Developer of autonomous vehicles and cognitive perception systems. The company specializes in localization technology and artificial intelligence. | 415-287-9977 | NA | San Francisco |
| Clare Computer Solutions (HQ) | Provider of information technology services. The company offers computer network, software consultation, visualization, and cloud computing solutions. | 925-277-0690 | NA | San Ramon |
| Claresco Corp (HQ) | Provider of design and implementation services for customized business software. The company serves multi-national firms. | 510-528-0238 | NA | Berkeley |
| Clarizen (HQ) | Provider of collaborative online project management software. The company offers work management, time tracking, and project scheduling solutions. | 866-502-9813 | NA | San Mateo |

| COMPANY NAME | PRODUCT / SERVICE | PHONE | EMP | CITY |
|---|---|---|---|---|
| Clearstory Data Inc (HQ) | Provider of data analysis and collaboration solutions for food & beverage, healthcare & life services, media and entertainment, and financial services. | 650-322-2408 | NA | Menlo Park |
| Clicktime Com Inc (HQ) | Provider of web-based tools, software, and IT consulting services. The company serves the aerospace, defense, automotive, and construction industries. | 415-684-1180 | NA | San Francisco |
| CloudFlare Inc (RH) | Provider of load balancers, traffic controllers, and web optimization products. The company is engaged in analytics services. | 650-319-8930 | NA | San Francisco |
| Cloudpassage Inc (HQ) | Developer of software solutions. The company also offers account management, configuration security monitoring, and alerting services. | 415-886-3020 | NA | San Francisco |
| Cloudwords Inc (HQ) | Provider of translation management systems and content localization solutions to manage translation process, vendors, and content systems. | 415-394-8000 | NA | San Francisco |
| Coastside Net (HQ) | Provider of internet access and technology solutions. The company also offers website services including website hosting, design, and development. | 650-712-5900 | NA | El Granada |
| Cohesion Inc (BR) | Provider of software and services. The company offers SAP quality management, batch management, business warehousing, and other services. | 650-591-9122 | NA | San Carlos |
| CommerceNet (HQ) | Provider of internet based research and piloting services such as internet business, open trading networks, and internet-user demographic surveys. | 650-289-4040 | NA | Los Altos |
| Connected Marketing (HQ) | Provider of marketing services. The company also offers web development, branding, and lead generation services. | 408-647-2198 | NA | San Jose |
| ConSol Consulting & Solutions Corp (HQ) | Provider of information technology services. The company offers software, networking, outsourcing, and monitoring solutions. | 925-479-1370 | NA | San Francisco |
| Contrast Security (HQ) | Designer and developer of self-protection software. The company is also engaged in operations support services. | 888-371-1333 | NA | Los Altos |
| Corrigo Inc (BR) | Developer of facilities management platforms. The company offers services to business organizations. | 877-267-7440 | NA | San Mateo |
| CP Media Group Inc (HQ) | Provider of audio visual production, website development and hosting, social media marketing, and related services. | 951-694-4830 | NA | San Ramon |
| Crmantra Inc (HQ) | Developer of software for customer relationship management needs. The company also focuses on business intelligence and analysis. | 415-839-9672 | NA | Emeryville |
| Css Corp (HQ) | Provider of enterprise level support solutions for IT products. The company is involved in virtualization, storage, and archiving solutions. | 650-385-3820 | NA | Milpitas |
| Cumulus Networks Llc (HQ) | Provider of Linux operating system hardware and software solution that offers flexibility for modern data networking designs and operations. | 650-383-6700 | NA | Mountain View |
| Customweather Inc (HQ) | Provider of industry solutions. The company offers hurricane tracking, developer tools, and marine forecasts. | 415-777-3303 | NA | San Francisco |
| Cygna Energy Services Inc (HQ) | Provider of application development, data integration, systems integration, consulting, and web services. | 925-930-8377 | NA | Walnut Creek |
| Cypress Digital Media (HQ) | Provider of web design, mobile development, and online marketing for interactive agencies and marketing campaigns. | 650-257-0741 | NA | Mountain View |
| D-Tools Inc (HQ) | Developer and marketer of software to streamline processes which accompany the integration and installation of low-voltage systems. | 925-681-2326 | NA | Concord |
| d2m Interactive (HQ) | Provider of web development, management, and e-commerce services. The company also focuses on marketing. | 408-315-6802 | 1-10 | Los Gatos |
| Daniel B Stephens & Associates Inc (BR) | Provider of services in hydrology, environmental engineering, and science. The company services include water resources and soil testing. | 800-933-3105 | NA | Oakland |
| Data Distributing Llc (HQ) | Provider of solutions such as mass storage, peripheral, storage management software, import, archive, and images and data distribution. | 831-457-3537 | 11-50 | Santa Cruz |
| Data Path Inc (HQ) | Provider of IT services such as IT management, web design, software development, and education related data services. | 209-521-0055 | 1-10 | Modesto |
| Database International (HQ) | Provider of database application development and database administration services and also offers project management and event coordination services. | 650-965-9102 | NA | Los Altos |
| Datameer Inc (BR) | Provider of data analytics solution for business users. The company also focuses on integration, business analytics consulting, and training. | 800-874-0569 | NA | San Francisco |
| Datasafe (HQ) | Provider of digital solutions. The company's services include records storage, document shredding and imaging, and rotation. | 650-875-3800 | NA | S San Francisco |
| Dcm Datasystems (RH) | Provider of managed IT services. The company focuses on system administration, storage, enterprise management, and staffing services. | 510-494-2321 | NA | Fremont |
| Device Authority Ltd (RH) | Provider of IoT security solutions for industrial, automotive, transportation, healthcare, utilities, and smart cities. | 650-603-0997 | NA | Fremont |
| Digipede Technologies LLC (HQ) | Provider of distributed computing solutions for academic research, entertainment, financial services, and manufacturing business applications. | 510-834-3645 | NA | Lafayette |
| Digital Canvas (HQ) | Provider of web design and web application development services. The company also offers web hosting, security solutions, and services. | 925-706-1700 | NA | Antioch |
| Digital Keystone Inc (HQ) | Provider of solutions enabling content distribution to tablets, connected TVs, and other entertainment platforms with suite of software and tools. | 650-938-7300 | NA | Cupertino |

| COMPANY NAME | PRODUCT / SERVICE | PHONE | EMP | CITY |
|---|---|---|---|---|
| Digital Mountain Inc (HQ) | Provider of electronic discovery and computer forensic services focusing on reduplication, data management, ESI planning, and cybersecurity. | 866-344-3627 | NA | Santa Clara |
| Digite Inc (HQ) | Provider of collaborative enterprise application software. The company's product finds application in process and portfolio management. | 408-418-3834 | NA | Cupertino |
| Direct Mail Center (HQ) | Provider of data processing, fulfillment, digital and offset printing, mail production, and logistics services. | 415-252-1600 | NA | San Francisco |
| Docker Inc (HQ) | Provider of docker platform and docker ecosystem of contributors, partners, and adopters the way distributed applications are built, shipped, and run. | 415-941-0376 | NA | San Francisco |
| DOCOMO Innovations Inc (HQ) | Provider of products and services for businesses. The company focuses on business development, network solutions, and mobile network technology. | 650-493-9600 | NA | Palo Alto |
| Dolcera Corp (BR) | Provider of business research, analytics, collaboration, IP patent licensing, and related support services. | 650-425-6772 | NA | San Mateo |
| Drivesavers Inc (HQ) | Provider of data recovery services for financial institutions, healthcare providers, major film studios, government agencies, and small businesses. | 415-382-2000 | NA | Novato |
| Dropbox Inc (HQ) | Provider of data transfer and sharing services that involves sharing of files, documents, and pictures from anywhere. | 415-857-6800 | NA | San Francisco |
| Druva (RH) | Provider of cloud based data protection products. The company offers services to the manufacturing, healthcare, and education industries. | 650-238-6200 | NA | Sunnyvale |
| Dsp Concepts Inc (HQ) | Provider of embedded audio processing tools and services. The company offers system design, embedded software development, and optimization services. | 408-747-5200 | NA | Santa Clara |
| Dt Research Inc (HQ) | Developer and manufacturer of embedded computing systems. The company serves hospitality, healthcare, and digital signage needs. | 408-934-6220 | NA | San Jose |
| Dubberly Design Office (HQ) | Developer of software related solutions. The company offers user interface and visual design, brand development, and usability testing services. | 415-648-9799 | NA | San Francisco |
| N Duda (HQ) | A web design platform offering web design services to small businesses. | 866-776-1550 | NA | Palo Alto |
| Dynamic Graphics Inc (HQ) | Provider of geospatial software solutions such as earth modeling, well planning, and visualization for the petroleum industries. | 510-522-0700 | NA | Alameda |
| N eClincher Inc (HQ) | Develops social media management platform that helps businesses to manage and organize their social media presence. | 408-718-6203 | NA | Palo Alto |
| Effone Software Inc (HQ) | Provider of IT consulting services including software development, application integration, and staff augmentation. | 408-830-1010 | NA | Santa Clara |
| Egnyte Inc (HQ) | Provider of online storage, cloud computing, and file sharing services. The company serves the financial, banking, and pharmaceutical industries. | 650-968-4018 | NA | Mountain View |
| Elegrity Inc (HQ) | Provider of law business management software, SharePoint, virtualization, and unified communication solutions. | 415-821-0900 | NA | San Francisco |
| Emagined Security Inc (HQ) | Provider of professional services for information security solutions. The company also focuses on compliance. | 415-944-2977 | NA | San Carlos |
| Endicia (HQ) | Provider of electronic postage software solutions and offers shipping and mailing services to online sellers, warehouse shippers, and office mailers. | 650-321-2640 | NA | Mountain View |
| Enfos Inc (HQ) | Provider of business software solutions for environmental management. The company specializes in financial, compliance, and GIS data management. | 650-357-0007 | NA | San Mateo |
| enSilo (HQ) | Developer of data protection platforms and provider of exfiltration prevention solutions. The company offers services to the network industry. | 800-413-1782 | NA | San Francisco |
| Enview Inc (HQ) | Specializes in threat prevention systems. The company deals with data analytics and remote sensing services. | 415-483-5680 | NA | San Francisco |
| Equinix (HQ) | Provider of interconnection data center and global colocation services focusing on cloud, business continuity, financial, and digital media. | 866-378-4649 | NA | Redwood City |
| Errigal Inc (HQ) | Designer and developer of software products and services. The company also deals with configuration management and ticketing. | 415-523-9245 | NA | San Francisco |
| eShares Inc (HQ) | Specializes in capitalization table management and valuation software. | 650-669-8381 | NA | San Francisco |
| Esp Interactive Solutions Inc (HQ) | Provider of web design and development services such as web video creation, content management system, and social networks marketing. | 510-526-2592 | NA | Albany |
| Excelfore Corp (HQ) | Provider of cloud applications. The company offers infotainment and telematics products for insurance, financing, and logistics sectors. | 510-868-2500 | NA | Fremont |
| Exit445 Group (HQ) | Provider of information architecture, e-Commerce, email marketing, search engine optimization, website hosting, and other services. | 415-381-1852 | NA | Mill Valley |
| Extend Inc (HQ) | Developer of business software. The company also provides internet and marketing consulting services. | 925-484-0395 | NA | Pleasanton |
| Extractable Inc (HQ) | Provider of websites, applications, social and mobile experiences for transactional, educational, lead generation, and entertainment purposes. | 415-426-3600 | NA | San Francisco |

| COMPANY NAME | PRODUCT / SERVICE | PHONE | EMP | CITY |
|---|---|---|---|---|
| Eyefinity Inc (HQ) | Provider of software solutions for the eyecare industry. The company focuses on practice & revenue cycle management and electronic health records. | 877-448-0707 | 1-10 | Rancho Cordova |
| Ezb Solutions (HQ) | Provider of software, hardware, and installation services. The company also deals with training, consulting, and technical support. | 408-988-8760 | NA | Santa Clara |
| eze System (HQ) | Provider or monitoring and measuring solutions. The company's products include controllers, controller expansions, and sensors. | 716-393-9330 | 11-50 | Folsom |
| Fab 7 Designs (HQ) | Provider of graphic designing services. The company offers website, multimedia, editorial, and package designing services. | 650-462-9745 | NA | Palo Alto |
| Farallon Geographics Inc (HQ) | Provider of strategic planning, spatial data processing, training, and web application development services. | 415-227-1140 | NA | San Francisco |
| FinancialContent Services Inc (HQ) | Provider of stock market information. The company deals with advertising, newspaper, and consulting services. | 888-688-9880 | NA | San Carlos |
| Financialforce Com (HQ) | Developer of automation software solutions. The company also deals with cloud accounting and resource planning solutions. | 866-743-2220 | NA | San Francisco |
| Finesse Solutions Llc (HQ) | Manufacturer of bioreactor controllers and related supplies. The company offers technical support services. | 408-570-9000 | NA | Santa Clara |
| First Class Plus Llc (HQ) | Provider of fundraising and marketing solutions. The company deals with print production, design assistance, and pre-press services. | 650-589-8346 | NA | S San Francisco |
| Flashtalking (BR) | Provider of online advertising technologies. The company is also engaged in analytics and reporting services. | 628-207-8080 | NA | San Francisco |
| Forecross Corp (HQ) | Provider of automated migration of legacy systems. The company specializes in XML solutions, migration solutions, and integrity solutions. | 415-543-1515 | NA | San Francisco |
| Forescout Technologies Inc (HQ) | Provider of network access control and policy compliance management solutions. The company serves the business sector. | 408-213-3191 | NA | Campbell |
| Forio Corp (HQ) | Provider of software products for simulations, data explorations, and predictive analysis needs. The company caters to universities and corporations. | 415-440-7500 | NA | San Francisco |
| Fortinet Inc (HQ) | Provider of network security appliances and threat management solutions such as network security platform and reporting and authentication. | 408-235-7700 | NA | Sunnyvale |
| Foxit Corp (HQ) | Developer of software. The company offers software such as Foxit Reader, Enterprise, and Mobile Reader. | 510-438-9090 | NA | Fremont |
| FUEL Creative Group (HQ) | Provider of graphic design, branding, and signage services. The company also focuses on packaging and printing. | 916-669-1591 | 1-10 | Sacramento |
| Funambol Inc (HQ) | Provider of open source mobile application server software. The company offers training and technical support services. | 650-701-1450 | NA | Foster City |
| Fusionstorm (BR) | Provider of information technology services. The company specializes in IT consulting, data center, networking, and enterprise content management. | 800-228-8324 | NA | San Francisco |
| Gallery Systems Inc (BR) | Provider of collection management systems. The company offers procedures consulting, project management, and strategic planning services. | 510-652-8950 | NA | Berkeley |
| Gen-9 Inc (HQ) | Provider of personal information management services. The company offers services to the industrial and commercial markets. | 650-903-2235 | NA | Mountain View |
| Genbook Inc (HQ) | Developer of online appointment scheduling software. The company is engaged in social media marketing services. | 415-227-9904 | NA | San Francisco |
| Gilmour Craves (HQ) | Provider of graphic design, advertising, media planning, strategic marketing, and print management services. | 415-431-9955 | NA | San Francisco |
| GiS Planning Inc (HQ) | Provider of geographic information systems. The company is engaged in the building of patent-protected site selection website. | 415-294-4775 | NA | San Francisco |
| Glassbeam Inc (HQ) | Provider of support solutions and it serves the medical, storage, and wireless networking industries. | 408-740-4600 | NA | Santa Clara |
| Global Cybersoft Inc (HQ) | Provider of software development and IT outsourcing services, such as systems integration and maintenance. | 424-247-1226 | NA | Pleasanton |
| GlobalSoft Inc (HQ) | Provider of software consultancy services. The company offers application development, training program management, and engineering services. | 408-564-0307 | NA | San Jose |
| Globant (BR) | Provider of software products and solutions for cloud computing, mobile, gaming, enterprise consumerization, and data visualization. | 877-215-5230 | NA | San Francisco |
| Go Balto (DH) | Provider of solutions for biotechnology and pharma. The company has products include Activate and Analyze. | 650-506-7000 | NA | Redwood Shores |
| Golden Valley Systems Inc (HQ) | Provider of enterprise integration solutions. The company offers technical, IT consulting, and green energy services. | 408-934-5898 | NA | Milpitas |
| Good Dog Design (HQ) | Provider of digital designing services. The company offers web development & designing and mobile application services. | 415-383-0110 | NA | Mill Valley |
| Google Inc (HQ) | Provider of search engine to make world's information universally accessible. The company specializes in internet-related services and products. | 650-253-0000 | NA | Mountain View |
| Granite Horizon LLC (HQ) | Provider of content management solutions. The company offers design, development, project management, and user and developer training services. | 916-647-6350 | 1-10 | Elk Grove |

| COMPANY NAME | PRODUCT / SERVICE | PHONE | EMP | CITY |
|---|---|---|---|---|
| GridGain Systems Inc (HQ) | Developer of a Java and Scala-based cloud computing middleware for a wide range of multimedia applications. | 650-241-2281 | NA | Foster City |
| Gt Nexus Inc (HQ) | Provider of supply chain, transportation, and investment management solutions. The company serves retailers and manufacturers. | 510-808-2222 | NA | Oakland |
| Guardian Analytics (HQ) | Provider of enterprise and community banking solutions. The company is engaged in training and applied fraud analysis services. | 650-383-9200 | NA | Mountain View |
| Harmon Ie (HQ) | Provider of SharePoint applications for Outlook, mobile, and desktop platforms. The company offers records and knowledge management services. | 408-907-1339 | NA | Milpitas |
| Hero Digital (HQ) | Provider of website and mobile design and development services. The company specializes in mobile marketing programs. | 415-409-2400 | NA | San Francisco |
| Hillstone Networks (RH) | Provider of security solutions for enterprises and data center networks. The company serves Fortune 500 companies and educational institutions. | 408-508-6750 | NA | Santa Clara |
| Hurd & Associates Design (HQ) | Provider of print, logo, and web design, branding, marketing, advertising, and identity management services. | 925-930-8580 | NA | Walnut Creek |
| Hyperarts Web Design Development & Maintenance (HQ) | Provider of web design, development, and consulting services. The company performs SEO, SEM services, and web application development. | 510-339-6084 | NA | Oakland |
| iCharts Inc (HQ) | Provider of collaborative visual intelligence solutions. The company offers services to business and media companies. | 650-472-0650 | NA | Mountain View |
| Iconix Inc (HQ) | Provider of business solutions such as email identity software. The company caters to brand and customer security needs. | 408-727-6342 | NA | San Jose |
| Ideablade (HQ) | Provider of data base application services. The company's products include DevForce, Coctail, and Breeze. | 510-596-5100 | NA | Orinda |
| Identiv Inc (HQ) | Provider of security technology services. The company's products include desktop readers, terminals, modules, and development kits. | 888-809-8880 | NA | Fremont |
| Iksanika Llc (HQ) | Provider of custom software development, testing, quality assurance, porting, and re-engineering services. | 408-490-0777 | NA | San Jose |
| Imageteq Technologies Inc (HQ) | Provider of IT consulting and services. The company focuses on consulting, enterprise application, and staff augmentation. | 650-403-4806 | NA | Burlingame |
| Imaja (HQ) | Developer of computer applications. The company specializes in the development of educational tools for Macs. | 510-526-4621 | NA | Berkeley |
| iMiners Inc (HQ) | Provider of investor relations management tools & web-based communication platforms. The company offers website plug-ins and shareholder message boards. | 925-447-6073 | NA | Livermore |
| Imperva Inc (HQ) | Provider of application and data security solutions. The company's products include database firewalls, management server, and monitoring software. | 650-345-9000 | NA | Redwood Shores |
| Inabyte Inc (HQ) | Manufacturer of developer tools. The company also offers solutions and services for developers and end users of PCs or workstations. | 415-898-7905 | NA | Novato |
| Incentia Design Systems Inc (HQ) | Provider of advanced timing and signal integrity analysis, design closure, and logic synthesis software for nanometer designs. | 408-727-8988 | NA | Santa Clara |
| Indec Medical Systems (HQ) | Provider of hardware and software solutions for cardiovascular imaging applications such as intravascular ultrasound and angiography. | 408-986-1600 | NA | Santa Clara |
| Inflection Llc (HQ) | Provider of technology solutions and software products. The company develops search engines, cloud management, and web server applications. | 650-618-9910 | NA | Redwood City |
| Infobahn Softworld Inc (HQ) | Provider of consulting, enterprise application integration, service oriented architecture, and systems integration solutions to fortune 500 companies. | 408-855-9616 | NA | San Jose |
| Infoblox Inc (HQ) | Provider of automated network control solutions. The company's services include training, implementation, migration, upgrade, repair, and maintenance. | 408-986-4000 | NA | Santa Clara |
| Infolane Inc (HQ) | Provider of web design and development and support services that includes web content management, application development, and technical improvements. | 510-277-2399 | NA | Emeryville |
| Infostretch Corp (HQ) | Provider of mobile application development, quality assurance testing and automation, SaaS solutions, and ERP testing solutions. | 408-727-1100 | NA | Santa Clara |
| Innovative Interfaces Inc (HQ) | Provider of technology solutions and services. The company deals with training and hosting, and technical support. | 510-655-6200 | NA | Emeryville |
| Intapp Inc (HQ) | Provider of software and services for risk management, time management, and box management. The company's products include Intapp Time and Wall Builder. | 650-852-0400 | NA | Palo Alto |
| Integrated Archive Systems Inc (HQ) | Provider of global data management services. The company offers storage, data protection, microsoft exchange, and virtualization services. | 650-390-9995 | NA | Palo Alto |
| Intellicon Solutions (HQ) | Provider of intelligent consulting solutions for learning and development, performance management systems, and related social media communication. | 925-377-7925 | 11-50 | Moraga |
| Interface Masters Technologies Inc (HQ) | Developer of technology and networking solutions. The company's products include embedded switches, adapters, and related accessories. | 408-441-9341 | NA | San Jose |

| COMPANY NAME | PRODUCT / SERVICE | PHONE | EMP | CITY |
|---|---|---|---|---|
| Intergraphics (HQ) | Developer of multi-lingual graphics. The company provides translation, typography, and other services. | 650-359-3087 | NA | Pacifica |
| Intermedia Net Inc (HQ) | Provider of cloud services including VoIP telephony, instant messaging, and file management to small and mid-sized businesses. | 800-379-7729 | NA | Mountain View |
| N  Intermedia.net Inc (HQ) | Provider of UCaaS, CCaaS, and cloud business applications that helps businesses and partners with secure solutions for communication and collaboration. | 650-641-4000 | NA | Sunnyvale |
| Internet Software Sciences (HQ) | Developer of web based applications for IT help desk, customer support, asset tracking, and facilities management needs. | 650-949-0942 | NA | Los Altos Hills |
| Intertrust Technologies Corp (HQ) | Provider of security technology services such as content protection, white label video distribution, and software tamper resistance. | 408-616-1600 | NA | Sunnyvale |
| Intresys Inc (BR) | Provider of child support and egovernment solutions. The company serves attorneys, public sector agencies, and governments. | 888-372-1790 | NA | Belmont |
| Intrinsyx Technologies Corp (BR) | Provider of information technology solutions. The company caters to federal, state, and commercial stakeholders. | 650-210-9219 | NA | Moffett Field |
| It Flux (HQ) | Provider of custom software development services, outsourcing, and outsourced software testing services. | 408-649-5642 | NA | Napa |
| It Pro Source (HQ) | Provider of on call plans, managed services, web based monitoring, and communication cabling services. | 925-455-7701 | NA | Livermore |
| IT Systemworks (HQ) | Provider of networking and technological solutions. The company's services include installation, implementation, repair, and maintenance. | 415-507-0123 | NA | San Rafael |
| Ivalua Inc (HQ) | Designer and developer of spend management solutions. The company offers services to medium and large sized companies. | 650-930-9710 | NA | Redwood City |
| N  JAMIS Software Corp (HQ) | Provider of job-cost, billing, and accounting systems and solutions. The company caters to the government contractors. | 800-655-2647 | 11-50 | San Diego |
| Jelli Inc (HQ) | Developer of user-controlled radio used in iPhone and radio stations. The company's products are used in the automation of radio advertising. | 855-790-8275 | NA | San Mateo |
| Joe Kline Aviation Art (HQ) | Provider of military aircraft painting services. The company offers customized prints, helicopter paintings, fixed wing paintings, and other prints. | 408-842-6979 | NA | Gilroy |
| Jolly Technologies Inc (HQ) | Provider of secure identification, visitor management, barcode and asset tracking software services. | 650-594-5955 | NA | San Mateo |
| Jova Solutions Inc (HQ) | Developer of systems for distributed process control and data management for science and industrial sectors. The company offers USB instruments. | 415-816-4482 | NA | San Francisco |
| Joyent Inc (HQ) | Provider of cloud infrastructure services. The company's products include Compute service, Manta storage, and Private Cloud. | 415-400-0600 | NA | San Francisco |
| Juniper Networks Inc (HQ) | Provider of network security solutions. The company serves the government, healthcare, utilities, and manufacturing industries. | 408-745-2000 | NA | Sunnyvale |
| Jway Group Inc (HQ) | Retailer of web consulting and service solutions such as web application development, web design, and mobile programming services. | 408-247-5929 | NA | San Jose |
| Kaazing Corp (HQ) | Provider of software services. The company's IoT gateway is used by mobile users, marketplaces, and machines to connect and communicate in real-time. | 877-522-9464 | NA | San Jose |
| Kaliotek Inc (HQ) | Provider of enterprise applications. The company also specializes in technical infrastructure for companies. | 408-550-8000 | NA | Cupertino |
| Keep IT Simple (HQ) | Provider of virtualization and information technology services. The company focuses on virtualization assessment, cloud computing, and networking. | 510-403-7500 | NA | Fremont |
| Key Performance Ideas Inc (HQ) | Provider of enterprise performance management & business intelligence solutions. The company offers Oracle Hyperion and OBIEE software for this need. | 855-457-4462 | NA | San Francisco |
| Kii Corp (HQ) | Provider of applications to device manufacturers and mobile network operators. The company serves enterprise, cross-platform games, and other needs. | 650-577-2340 | NA | San Mateo |
| Kki Corp (HQ) | Provider of web and business services and software solutions. The company is also involved in design and technical support services. | 209-863-8550 | 1-10 | Modesto |
| Klh Consulting Inc (HQ) | Provider of IT consulting, cloud computing, and related business solutions. The company offers services to business executives and professionals. | 707-575-9986 | NA | Santa Rosa |
| Konicom Inc (HQ) | Provider of computer services to businesses and individuals. The company offers internet related services such as wireless network and hot spot setup. | 916-441-7373 | 1-10 | Sacramento |
| Kovair Software Inc (HQ) | Provider of web-based document management applications. The company offers product support maintenance services. | 408-262-0200 | NA | San Ramon |
| Kovarus Inc (HQ) | Provider of integrated business IT solutions. The company also deals with leasing, financing, project management, and related services. | 650-392-7848 | NA | San Ramon |
| KP LLC (BR) | Provider of marketing and outsourcing solutions offering digital and offset printing and mailing services. | 510-351-5400 | NA | San Leandro |

| COMPANY NAME | PRODUCT / SERVICE | PHONE | EMP | CITY |
|---|---|---|---|---|
| Kreck Design Solutions (HQ) | Provider of graphic design and internet-related services. The company focuses on corporate identity & marketing, web design, SEO, content management. | 707-433-6166 | NA | Santa Rosa |
| Langtech (HQ) | Provider of information technology services. The company provides software solutions, cloud services, system integration, and consulting. | 415-364-9600 | NA | San Francisco |
| Lastline (HQ) | Manufacturer of malware protection products. The company serves schools, restaurants, and the enterprise security industry. | 877-671-3239 | NA | San Mateo |
| Lattice Engines (HQ) | Provider of business to business sales intelligence software. The company is engaged in web design and hosting and programming solutions. | 877-460-0010 | NA | San Mateo |
| Lavante Inc (HQ) | Provider of on-demand strategic profit recovery solutions. The company also offers vendor information management software. | 408-754-1410 | NA | San Jose |
| Leadman Electronics USA Inc (HQ) | Provider of ODM/OEM, hardware engineering expertise, and custom solutions for a wide range of security, storage, server, and network applications. | 408-380-4567 | NA | Santa Clara |
| LekasMiller Design (HQ) | Provider of photography, printing, advertising, graphic design, mailing, and project management services. | 925-934-3971 | NA | Walnut Creek |
| Lenos Software (HQ) | Provider of enterprise resource management, development of motion graphics, and value-added management services. | 415-281-8828 | NA | San Francisco |
| Livevol Inc (BR) | Designer and developer of customized data solutions. The company's services include consulting and technical support. | 415-200-4536 | NA | San Francisco |
| Lmi Net (HQ) | Provider of solar-assisted internet connections. The company offers computer repair, IT services, web site development, and virus removal services. | 510-843-6389 | NA | Berkeley |
| Lucidworks (HQ) | Provider of commercial foundation for architecture, design, development, and deployment of search solutions built with lucid works enterprise. | 415-329-6515 | NA | San Francisco |
| Lunagraphica Inc (HQ) | Provider of internet marketing and consulting solutions. The company offers services in graphic design, website design, and web development. | 408-962-1588 | NA | Sunnyvale |
| Mailshell Inc (HQ) | Provider of traffic reputation software engines. The company also specializes in anti-spam and anti-phishing software engines. | 415-294-4242 | NA | Santa Clara |
| Markmonitor Inc (HQ) | Provider of brand protection, domain management, domain advisory, anti-piracy, and managed services. | 415-278-8400 | NA | San Francisco |
| Maxeler Technologies Inc (HQ) | Developer of computing solutions. The company offers services to the oil and gas, analytical, and financial sectors. | 650-938-8818 | NA | Mountain View |
| Medallia Inc (HQ) | Provider of consulting, system configuration, user training, and data warehouse integration services. | 650-321-3000 | NA | Palo Alto |
| Media Flint (HQ) | Provides internet marketing and advertising solutions to companies. | 888-592-2921 | NA | Mountain View |
| Media Net Link Inc (HQ) | Provider of web business solutions. The company focuses on application development, systems intergration, website design, and project management. | 866-563-5152 | NA | Oakland |
| Megapath (HQ) | Provider of voice, data, networking, cloud, and security services. The company serves healthcare, finance, restaurant, and retail sectors. | 866-300-0749 | NA | Pleasanton |
| Meltwater Group (HQ) | Developer of software products such as Meltwater BUZZ, Meltwater NEWS, and Meltwater DRIVE to meet the specific needs of businesses around the world. | 415-236-3144 | NA | San Francisco |
| Menlo Security (HQ) | Provider of security solutions. The company's offerings include web isolation, document, and phishing isolation services. | 650-614-1705 | NA | Palo Alto |
| Micromega Systems Inc (HQ) | Provider of database systems and e-business website design services. The company also focuses on training and installation. | 415-924-4700 | NA | Corte Madera |
| Milestone Internet Marketing Inc (HQ) | Provider of hotel internet marketing and website development services. The company focuses on website & social media marketing and ROI tracking. | 408-492-9055 | NA | Santa Clara |
| Mirantis Inc (HQ) | Specializes in the development and support of Kubernetes and OpenStack. | 650-963-9828 | NA | Campbell |
| MMC AD Systems (HQ) | Provider of architectural and consulting services. The company focuses on strategic planning, market research, and business and web development. | 925-485-4949 | NA | Pleasanton |
| Moonstone Interactive Inc (HQ) | Provider of website design services. The company offers web design and development, content management, and market visibility services. | 866-246-9091 | NA | San Ramon |
| Motiondsp Inc (HQ) | Provider of software products. The company serves the defense & intelligence, law enforcement, energy, and transportation markets. | 650-288-1164 | NA | Burlingame |
| Mountford Group Inc (HQ) | Provider of system development and web application services. The company also focuses on technical communication. | 925-686-6613 | NA | Concord |
| MTI California Inc (HQ) | Specializes in designing and validating manufacturing controls. The company offers services to biotech companies. | 925-937-1500 | NA | Walnut Creek |
| Multimedia Consulting Services Inc (HQ) | Provider of multimedia consulting services. The company offers design, implementation, and maintenance of the information technology infrastructure. | 650-578-8591 | NA | Foster City |
| Natural Logic (HQ) | Provider of consulting, product development, e-learning, digital content, and product support services. | 510-248-4940 | NA | Berkeley |

| | COMPANY NAME | PRODUCT / SERVICE | PHONE | EMP | CITY |
|---|---|---|---|---|---|
| N | Neo4j Inc (HQ) | Graph database platform that helps companies to access the business value of data connections. | 855-636-4532 | NA | San Mateo |
| | Netease Inc (HQ) | Provider of web hosting services. The company offers domain registration, hosting, and dial-up services. | 800-580-0932 | NA | Forestville |
| | Netronome (HQ) | Provider of flow processing, server virtualization, cyber security, and software-defined networking solutions. | 408-496-0022 | NA | Santa Clara |
| | Netwoven Inc (HQ) | Provider of enterprise content management and business intelligence solutions. The company also focuses on process management. | 877-638-9683 | NA | Milpitas |
| | Nexb Inc (HQ) | Designer and developer of software tools and services. The company offers services to business enterprises and related organizations. | 650-592-2096 | NA | San Carlos |
| | Nextbus Inc (BR) | Provider of transit management solutions. The company also provides real-time passenger information solutions to organizations. | 925-686-8200 | NA | Concord |
| | Noble Image Inc (HQ) | Provider of website and graphic design, website development, hosting, programming, and technical support services. | 916-419-3570 | 1-10 | Sacramento |
| | Nok Nok Labs Inc (HQ) | Focuses on the development on online security solutions. The company is also involved in third party research services. | 650-433-1300 | NA | Palo Alto |
| | Nomis Solutions Inc (HQ) | Provider of pricing and profitability management solutions. The company caters to the financial services. | 650-588-9800 | NA | Brisbane |
| | Obscura Digital Llc (HQ) | Provider of technology-driven creative solutions. The company caters to advertising and marketing needs. | 415-227-9979 | NA | San Francisco |
| | Omnicia Inc (HQ) | Provider of electronic submissions for the life science sector. The company offers electronics & desktop publishing and document management services. | 650-588-2188 | NA | S San Francisco |
| | OneLogin (HQ) | Provider of single sign-on and identity management for cloud-based applications. The company serves the industrial sector. | 415-645-6830 | NA | San Francisco |
| | Onfulfillment Inc (HQ) | Provider of printing solutions. The company offers order fulfillment, online delivery, and print management services. | 510-793-3009 | NA | Newark |
| | Opal Soft Inc (HQ) | Provider of communications equipment installation and networking. The company's services include application development, network management, and maintenance. | 408-267-2211 | NA | Sunnyvale |
| | Opengov Inc (HQ) | Provider of financial transparency and business intelligence solutions. The company offers services to government agencies. | 650-336-7167 | NA | Redwood City |
| | Oracle Corp (BR) | Developer of hardware and software systems. The company provides Oracle database, engineered systems, and enterprise manager solutions. | 415-402-7200 | NA | San Francisco |
| | Orbeon Inc (HQ) | Provider of web form deployment services. The company offers basic, gold, and platinum development support, and validation services. | 650-762-8184 | NA | San Mateo |
| | Ordinal Technology Corp (HQ) | Provider of sorting services of massive and production data sets such as web logs for high-traffic web sites, phone logs, and government agency data. | 925-253-9204 | NA | Orinda |
| | Organic Inc (HQ) | Provider of information technology services. The company develops websites, mobile applications, banner, and digital signage. | 415-581-5300 | NA | San Francisco |
| N | Owler Inc (HQ) | Provider of reliable and up-to-date business information. | 650-242-9253 | NA | San Mateo |
| N | Pearl Lemon (HQ) | Digital marketing agency that offers results-oriented SEO services. | 628-214-1309 | NA | San Francisco |
| | Perforce Software Inc (BR) | Developer of software management tools and technology solutions. The company serves game development, banking, healthcare, and other sectors. | 510-864-7400 | NA | Alameda |
| | Perryman Group Inc (HQ) | Provider of website design and hosting, e-commerce solutions, and networking services. The company serves business and residential customers. | 916-630-7456 | 1-10 | Folsom |
| | Pica8 Inc (HQ) | Manufacturer of white box switches. The company specializes in traditional switches and routing protocols. | 650-614-5838 | NA | Palo Alto |
| | Pierce Washington (HQ) | Provider of systems integration and e-commerce solutions. The company also deals with the development of software tools. | 415-431-8300 | NA | San Francisco |
| | Pinterest (HQ) | Specializes in mobile application tools. The company focuses on pinning items, creating boards, and interacting with other members. | 415-762-7100 | NA | San Francisco |
| | Pipsqueak Productions LLC (HQ) | Provider of graphic design, photography, writing, editing, animation, and website development services. | 415-668-4372 | NA | San Francisco |
| | Pixami Inc (HQ) | Provider of imaging technologies. The company caters to both photo-based and non-photo-based businesses. | 925-465-5167 | NA | Pleasanton |
| | Planeteria Media (HQ) | Designer and developer of websites, applications, e-commerce, content management systems, video, and offers flash, and internet marketing services. | 707-843-3773 | NA | Santa Rosa |
| | Presentek Inc (HQ) | Designer of websites and web portals. The company also offers content management systems and e-commerce handlers. | 408-354-1264 | NA | Los Gatos |
| | Presidio Inc (BR) | Provider of IP telephony and wireless networking services. The company also deals with deployment, integration, and hardware and software development. | 415-501-9020 | NA | Pleasanton |
| | Prosoft Engineering Inc (HQ) | Developer of data recovery software. The company provides Drive Genius, Data Rescue, and Data Backup software. | 877-477-6763 | NA | Livermore |

| COMPANY NAME | PRODUCT / SERVICE | PHONE | EMP | CITY |
|---|---|---|---|---|
| PubMatic Inc (HQ) | Developer of marketing automation software. The company deals with the planning of media campaigns and offers services to publishers. | 650-331-3485 | NA | Redwood City |
| Pulse Secure LLC (HQ) | Provider of product, hardware, partner, and enterprise solutions. The company offers services to the financial services and healthcare industries. | 408-372-9600 | NA | San Jose |
| Punchcut LLC (HQ) | Provider of interface designs. The company offers mid, small, large, micro, and medium screen solutions. | 415-445-8855 | NA | San Francisco |
| Qarbon Inc (HQ) | Publisher of presentation software and the originator of patented Viewlet technology. The company serves business, government, and education markets. | 408-430-5560 | NA | San Jose |
| Qualys Inc (HQ) | Provider of security and compliance solutions. The company also offers asset discovery and threat protection solutions. | 650-801-6100 | NA | Foster City |
| Quantitative Medical Systems Inc (HQ) | Provider of medical systems and dialysis billing software products. The company is engaged in clinical support. | 510-654-9200 | NA | Emeryville |
| Qubop Inc (HQ) | Developer of applications and games for mobile platforms. The company specializes in web applications, localization, IOS, and android development. | 415-891-7788 | NA | San Francisco |
| Quest Business Systems Inc (HQ) | Provider of solutions in police equipment tracking systems. The company also focuses on purchasing management. | 925-634-2670 | NA | Brentwood |
| Quorum Technologies (HQ) | Developer of recycling and waste disposal solutions for the automotive, industrial, municipal, hospitality, and food industries. | 916-669-5577 | 1-10 | Sacramento |
| Range Networks Inc (HQ) | Provider of mobile network solutions. The company is also engaged in software and hardware solutions and services. | 415-778-8700 | NA | Santa Clara |
| Rasteroids Design (HQ) | Provider of web designing, custom programming, implementation, custom software development, and hosting services. | 408-979-9138 | NA | San Jose |
| Real-Time Innovations Inc (HQ) | Provider for real-time infrastructure software solutions. The company also offers engineering and product development services. | 408-990-7400 | NA | Sunnyvale |
| Rearden LLC (HQ) | Provider of cloud computing, motion picture, video game, consumer electronics, wireless, imaging, communications, and alternative energy technologies. | 415-947-5555 | NA | Mountain View |
| Redwhale Software Corp (HQ) | Provider of software tools, technologies, and professional services for the design, development, and run-time management of user interfaces. | 650-312-1500 | NA | Redwood City |
| Relay2 Inc (HQ) | Provider of cloud Wi-Fi Services platform which allows service providers to monetize value added Wi-Fi services. | 408-380-0031 | NA | Milpitas |
| Resilient Networks Systems Inc (HQ) | Developer of internet software products. The company serves the healthcare, media, information security, and government sectors. | 415-291-9600 | NA | San Francisco |
| Resilinc Corp (HQ) | Provider of supply chain and risk management solutions. The company serves the life science and automotive industries. | 408-883-8053 | NA | Milpitas |
| RetailNext (HQ) | Provider of in-store analytics solutions. The company offers services to retail labs, marketing departments, and shopping centers. | 408-884-2162 | NA | San Jose |
| Revstream Inc (HQ) | Provider of enterprise revenue and billing management solutions. The company also offers advisory and technical support services. | 888-738-0206 | NA | Redwood Shores |
| Ridge Communications Inc (HQ) | Provider of network deployment and project management services. The company serves the wireless carrier industry. | 925-498-2340 | NA | San Ramon |
| Rootdesign Llc (HQ) | Provider of design solutions specializing in brand strategy, user interface design, and database development services. | 415-282-2484 | NA | San Francisco |
| Runscope Inc (HQ) | Specializes in automated performance monitoring and testing solutions. The company serves developers. | 888-812-6786 | NA | San Francisco |
| Samsara Networks Inc (HQ) | Manufacturer of flexible sensors. The company is engaged in fleet monitoring, industrial sensing, cold chain monitoring, and fleet telematics. | 415-985-2400 | NA | San Francisco |
| Sasken Technologies Ltd (BR) | Provider of research and development consultation, wireless software products, and software services to automotive and health care sectors. | 408-730-0100 | NA | Sunnyvale |
| SDL USA (BR) | Provider of web content and structured content management, as well as e-commerce solutions, and language technologies. | 408-743-3600 | NA | San Jose |
| SE Ranking (BR) | SEO platform that allows individuals to optimize and promote a website on the web. | 415-704-4387 | NA | Palo Alto |
| Selectiva Systems Inc (HQ) | Provider of solutions for revenue reporting, customer service, and distributor management. The company serves hi-tech, pharma, and other sectors. | 408-297-1336 | NA | San Jose |
| Sensory Inc (HQ) | Provider of speech recognition and voice biometric ICs. The company's products are used in toys and home electronic products. | 408-625-3300 | NA | Santa Clara |
| ShareThis Inc (HQ) | Developers of social sharing solutions for website owners. | 650-323-1783 | NA | Palo Alto |
| Sharper Technology Inc (HQ) | Provider of network security solutions and services. The company also offers design, implementation, and training services. | 650-964-4600 | NA | Palo Alto |
| Single Point Of Contact (HQ) | Provider of IT management, enterprise, and planning services. The company is also engaged in cloud computing, web hosting, and hosted exchange. | 800-791-4300 | NA | Palo Alto |
| Skybox Security Inc (HQ) | Provider of risk analytics for cyber security. The company offers threat management and network security management solutions. | 408-441-8060 | NA | San Jose |

| COMPANY NAME | PRODUCT / SERVICE | PHONE | EMP | CITY |
|---|---|---|---|---|
| Skyhigh Networks Inc (RH) | Developer of cloud security software. The company is engaged in compliance, threat protection, and data security services. | 866-727-8383 | NA | Campbell |
| Sleepless Media (HQ) | Provider of website design and development services. The company focuses on content management, e-commerce, SEO, hosting, and brand identity. | 831-427-1969 | 11-50 | Soquel |
| Smart ERP Solutions Inc (HQ) | Developer of enterprise class software. The company provides vendor management software and support services. | 925-271-0200 | NA | Pleasanton |
| Softsol Inc (HQ) | Provider of software solutions. The company offers software such as Intellicourt Case Management, Corporate Investigations, STIC, and PB Migration. | 510-824-2000 | NA | Fremont |
| Software Ag (BR) | Provider of enterprise management and business solutions that include process intelligence and automation, and enterprise architecture. | 800-823-2212 | NA | Santa Clara |
| Soliton Systems Inc (BR) | Provider of information technology solutions. The company offers IT security, network infrastructure, cloud computing, and IT management services. | 408-434-1923 | NA | San Jose |
| Solution Architects Inc (HQ) | Provider of sophisticated IT solutions for complex systems. The company's services include analysis and product development. | 415-775-1656 | NA | San Francisco |
| Spence Engineering Services Inc (HQ) | Provider of solutions for hardware and software engineering problems. The company offers services to the technical sector. | 650-571-6500 | NA | San Mateo |
| Spiralinks Corporation (HQ) | Provider of compensation management software products. The company offers compensation management, HR analytics, and payroll integration services. | 408-608-6900 | NA | Campbell |
| Splunk Inc (HQ) | Provider of search engine services specializing in IT data. The company serves the government, healthcare, and telecommunication industries. | 415-848-8400 | NA | San Francisco |
| SPYRUS (HQ) | Developer and marketer of hardware encryption, authentication, and digital content security products. | 408-392-9131 | NA | San Jose |
| Stanfield Systems Inc (HQ) | Provider of system engineering and data management services. The company also focuses on web development and technical services. | 916-608-8006 | 1-10 | Folsom |
| StarNet Communications Corp (HQ) | Developer of X Windows solutions for connecting computers to Unix and Linux desktops and applications. | 408-739-0881 | NA | Santa Clara |
| Stevens Creek Software (HQ) | Provider of software solutions for the palm computing platform. The company is involved in custom development and technical support. | 408-725-0424 | NA | Cupertino |
| Subrosasoft.Com Inc (HQ) | Developer of software for Mac operating systems. The company offers software such as FileSalvage, CopyCat, and ParentRemote. | 510-870-7883 | NA | Fremont |
| Succeed.Net (BR) | Provider of internet services. The company specializes in metro Ethernet, wireless broadband, DSL service, national dial-up, and server co-location. | 530-674-4200 | 11-50 | Sacramento |
| Sumo Logic (RH) | Provider of compliance, security, monitoring, troubleshooting, and delivery solutions. The company serves security, IT, and development teams. | 650-810-8700 | NA | Redwood City |
| Sun-Net Inc (HQ) | Provider of enterprise software solutions supporting outage scheduling, logging, and reporting for power, gas, and water utilities. | 408-323-1318 | NA | San Jose |
| **N** SurveyMonkey (HQ) | Provider of a cloud-based people-powered data platform. | 650-543-8400 | NA | San Mateo |
| Switchfly (HQ) | Provider of software solutions such as travel commerce platforms, payments engines, mobile platforms, and social media solutions. | 415-541-9100 | NA | San Francisco |
| Symantec Corp (HQ) | Developer of storage management and disaster recovery software. The company is engaged in consulting, archiving, and clustering. | 650-527-8000 | NA | Mountain View |
| Synack (HQ) | Provider of security intelligence solutions. The company offers services to the commercial, industrial, and business sectors. | 855-796-2251 | NA | Redwood City |
| Synaptris Inc (HQ) | Provider of business reporting solutions. The company's products include IntelliVIEW, IntelliPRINT, and Synaptris Widget Viewer. | 914-620-1614 | NA | San Jose |
| Syncplicity Llc (HQ) | Provider of cloud-based file management solutions such as access, sync, backup and share of files from anywhere for businesses and individuals. | 888-997-9627 | NA | Santa Clara |
| Synergy Business Solutions (HQ) | Provider of technology evaluation, business process improvement, and custom software development services to a wide range of sectors. | 415-263-1843 | NA | San Francisco |
| Tech Soft 3d (HQ) | Provider of software solutions. The company offers software for desktop visualization, modeling, cloud and mobile solutions, and data exchange. | 510-883-2180 | NA | Berkeley |
| Techvalidate Software Inc (HQ) | Provider of online content management services. The company handles content collection, validation, publishing, and utilization services. | 510-982-6640 | NA | Emeryville |
| Telemanagement Technologies Inc (HQ) | Provider of telemanagement software products and services. The company is engaged in troubleshooting and maintenance services. | 925-946-9800 | NA | Walnut Creek |
| Telosa Software Inc (HQ) | Provider of CRM and fundraising software for nonprofits. The company focuses on gift and grant tracking, donor and volunteer management. | 800-750-6418 | NA | Palo Alto |
| Terrace Consulting Inc (HQ) | Provider of custom software development services. The company focuses on eCommerce, back office, business intelligence, cloud, and other services. | 415-848-7300 | NA | San Francisco |
| Text Analysis International Inc (HQ) | Provider of software development services for text analysis. The company focuses on project management, testing and implementation, and deployment. | 650-308-9323 | NA | Cupertino |

| COMPANY NAME | PRODUCT / SERVICE | PHONE | EMP | CITY |
|---|---|---|---|---|
| TextDigger Inc (HQ) | Developer of horizontal semantic solutions for search engines. The company focuses on content mining and analytics. | 408-416-3142 | NA | San Jose |
| The AIS Group (HQ) | Developer and provider of accounting software. The company also specializes in system integration services. | | NA | Napa |
| The Igneous Group Inc (HQ) | Provider of technology consulting services. The company focuses on web content, application development, and e-commerce. | 831-469-7625 | 1-10 | Santa Cruz |
| The Wecker Group (HQ) | Provider of design studio and ad agency services. The company specializes in corporate identity, collateral, TV advertising, and event promotion. | 831-372-8377 | NA | Monterey |
| Thrasys Inc (HQ) | Provider of health networking solutions. The company serves patients, service centers, payers, and public health administrators. | 650-449-1000 | NA | San Francisco |
| ThreatMetrix (HQ) | Provider of fraud prevention, threat detection, and authentication solutions. The company serves the gaming, media, and insurance industries. | 408-200-5755 | NA | San Jose |
| TokBox Inc (HQ) | Developer of free video chat tools and widgets. The company offers services for the recreation and entertainment industries. | 415-284-4688 | NA | San Francisco |
| Toolwire Inc (HQ) | Designer and developer of experiential learning solutions for higher education and corporate training institutions. | 925-227-8500 | NA | Pleasanton |
| Totango Inc (HQ) | A customer success software helps to connect customer data, monitor health changes, and proactively engage the customers by using an integrated platform. | 800-634-1990 | NA | San Mateo |
| Trackdata Systems Corp (HQ) | Provider of greyhound, thoroughbred, and harness racing information. The company features up-to-date listing of racing schedules. | 408-446-5595 | NA | Cupertino |
| Transend Corp (HQ) | Provider of email migration and conversion solutions that support email systems. The company serves business, education, reselling, and other sectors. | 650-324-5370 | NA | Palo Alto |
| Twilio Inc (HQ) | Provider of infrastructure APIs for businesses to build scalable, reliable voice, and text messaging apps. | 415-390-2337 | NA | San Francisco |
| Unisoft Corp (HQ) | Provider of broadcast, development, and testing tools specific to interactive TV standards. The company focuses on US cable and broadcast industries. | 650-259-1290 | NA | Millbrae |
| Unitedlayer Llc (HQ) | Provider of cloud hosting solutions. The company offers server clusters and routers, disaster recovery, infrastructure, and colocation services. | 415-349-2100 | NA | San Francisco |
| Untangle (HQ) | Designer and developer of network management software. The company specializes in firewall and Internet management application. | 408-598-4299 | NA | San Jose |
| UpGuard Inc (HQ) | Provider of integrity monitoring, vulnerability analysis, vendor risk assessment, and configuration differencing solutions. | 888-882-3223 | NA | Mountain View |
| Upwork Global Inc (HQ) | Web based platform for remote work. | 650-316-7500 | NA | Santa Clara |
| UserTesting (HQ) | Deliver a human insight platform powered by customer experience for product teams, marketers, and advertising companies. | 888-877-1882 | NA | San Francisco |
| vArmour Inc (HQ) | Provider of cloud security, segmentation, monitoring, and deception solutions. The company serves banks and healthcare organizations. | 650-564-5100 | NA | Los Altos |
| Veeva Systems (HQ) | Provider of cloud-based business solutions such as customer relationship management and content management for the life sciences industry. | 925-452-6500 | NA | Pleasanton |
| Verient Inc (HQ) | Provider of cloud based financial products. The company's offerings convert non revenue producing payments to credit card transactions. | 408-521-1660 | NA | San Jose |
| Verix Inc (HQ) | Designer and developer of precision tooling and equipment for performance engine builders and mechanists. | 650-949-2700 | NA | San Jose |
| Victorious (HQ) | Search engine optimization agency that leverages a wealth of performance data and market research to create scientifically-driven SEO strategies. | 415-621-9830 | NA | San Francisco |
| Video Clarity Inc (HQ) | Provider of real time and broadcast quality monitoring, perceptual analysis, recording, and automating services. | 408-379-6952 | NA | Campbell |
| Vindicia Inc (HQ) | Developer of marketing and analytics solutions. The company offers customer acquisition and retention and customer relationship management services. | 650-264-4700 | NA | Redwood City |
| Vintara Inc (HQ) | Provider of web-based enterprise process management solutions and services. The company caters to a number of industries. | 877-846-8272 | NA | Oakland |
| VipeCloud (HQ) | Developers of marketing CRM that helps small- and mid-sized businesses accelerate the growth. | 650-308-8473 | NA | Palo Alto |
| Visible Energy Inc (HQ) | Provider of products and interactive energy conservation services that take control of electricity consumption. | | NA | Palo Alto |
| Visualware Inc (HQ) | Provider of solutions to measure broadband connection performance for enterprises, homes, and offices. The company offers both hardware and software. | 209-262-3491 | 11-50 | Turlock |
| Vivante Corp (HQ) | Provider of semiconductors for graphics and multimedia. The company focuses on image and video processing services. | 408-844-8560 | NA | San Jose |
| Webenertia (HQ) | Provider of web applications and e-commerce services. The company also focuses on motion graphics and internet marketing solutions. | 408-246-0000 | NA | San Jose |
| Webvanta Inc (HQ) | Provider of hosted content management and database system services. The company is involved in website and mobile application development. | 888-670-6793 | NA | Sausalito |

| COMPANY NAME | PRODUCT / SERVICE | PHONE | EMP | CITY |
|---|---|---|---|---|
| WellnessFX Inc (HQ) | Specializes in web-based services. The company focuses on diagnostic testing and it serves medical practitioners. | 415-796-3373 | NA | San Francisco |
| Whitehat Security (HQ) | Provider of web application security solutions such as vulnerability management, threat modeling, and risk profiling. | 408-343-8300 | NA | San Jose |
| William Stucky & Associates Inc (HQ) | Provider of software products and services. The company mainly caters to the asset-based lending industry. | 415-788-2441 | NA | San Francisco |
| WindSpring Inc (HQ) | Manufacturer of data management tools. The company provides a framework for optimized compressed data management in the storage and embedded fields. | 408-452-7400 | NA | San Jose |
| Wipro Technologies (BR) | Provider of analytics and information management, business process outsourcing, consulting, and managed and cloud services. | 650-316-3555 | NA | Mountain View |
| Xactly Corp (HQ) | Provider of web-based sales compensation applications. The company offers services to business organizations and enterprises. | 408-977-3132 | NA | San Jose |
| Xtelesis Corp (HQ) | Provider of voice and data solutions. The company is engaged in data networking, audio web conferencing, and managed IT services. | 650-239-1400 | NA | Burlingame |
| Yola Inc (HQ) | Provider of digital marketing services. The company offers mobile, facebook, and web publishing, domain names, and reliable hosting services. | 866-764-0701 | NA | San Francisco |
| Zag Technical Services Inc (HQ) | Provider of services for server, email stability, reliability, migration, and security assessment needs. | 408-383-2000 | NA | San Jose |
| N  Zapier Inc (HQ) | Developers of an integrated app that shares information within a user's collective web app automatically. | 877-381-8743 | NA | San Francisco |
| Zscaler Inc (HQ) | Provider of SaaS security solutions. The company offers cloud security solutions for mobile enterprises. | 408-533-0288 | NA | San Jose |
| Zynga Inc (HQ) | Provider of social game services with more than 240 million monthly active users. The company's games include CityVille, Draw Something, and Hidden Chronicles. | 800-762-2530 | 1001-5000 | San Francisco |

## 326 = Miscellaneous Software-Related Services

| COMPANY NAME | PRODUCT / SERVICE | PHONE | EMP | CITY |
|---|---|---|---|---|
| 15five Inc (HQ) | Provider of services that allow you to question and start conversations that matters to elevate performance of employees, managers, and entire organizations. | 415-967-3483 | NA | San Francisco |
| 21Tech LLC (BR) | Provider of business and technology solutions such as technology consultancy, strategic sourcing/placement, and branding and creative services practice. | 415-355-9090 | NA | Oakland |
| 314e Corp (HQ) | Provider of IT skills, methodologies, and cost-effective managed services for healthcare application and technical support services. | 510-371-6736 | NA | Fremont |
| 500friends Inc (HQ) | Provider of omnichannel loyalty solution. The company offers service and technology to deliver seamless and powerful customer retention solutions. | 415-918-2990 | NA | San Francisco |
| 6connex (HQ) | Provider of virtual environment space and powering virtual destinations for career fairs, corporate universities, product launches, and user conferences. | 800-395-4702 | NA | Pleasanton |
| 6WIND USA Inc (RH) | Manufacturer of virtual accelerators, routers, and related accessories. The company offers network security and network appliance solutions. | 408-816-1366 | NA | Santa Clara |
| A A Networks (HQ) | Provider of internet, networks and cabling, computer hardware and software, remote and on-site technical support services. | 650-872-1998 | NA | Burlingame |
| A9 com Inc (HQ) | Provider of product, visual, and cloud search services. The company also focuses on mobile apps, advertising, and technical operations. | 650-331-2600 | NA | Palo Alto |
| Abacus Solutions Inc (HQ) | Developer of SATURN, an integrated enterprise ETRM system and focuses on generation optimization, parameters estimation, and credit management. | 650-941-1728 | NA | Los Altos Hills |
| Ablesys Corp (HQ) | Provider of financial trading software and web applications. The company focuses on portfolio and algorithmic trading solutions. | 510-265-1883 | NA | Hayward |
| Accel North America Inc (HQ) | Provider of software development and technology services for automotive, healthcare, life science, networking, storage, and enterprise software markets. | 408-514-5199 | NA | Santa Clara |
| Accelerance Inc (HQ) | Provider of software design, development, and deployment services. The company focuses on web hosting and programming solutions. | 650-472-3785 | NA | Redwood City |
| Accellion (HQ) | Provider of web-based file transfer applications. The company also focuses on data management solutions. | 650-485-4300 | NA | Palo Alto |
| Accenture (BR) | Provider of management consulting and technology services. The company also offers application outsourcing and IT consulting services. | 415-537-5000 | NA | San Francisco |
| Accenture (BR) | Provider of management consulting, technology services and outsourcing services. The company serves a wide range of industries. | 408-817-2700 | NA | San Jose |
| Access Business Technologies Llc (HQ) | Provider of cloud-based software and hosting solutions for government agencies, banks, credit unions, accounting firms, and servicing companies. | 888-636-5426 | 1-10 | Folsom |
| Access Softek Inc (HQ) | Developer of mobile banking software solutions. The company focuses on software and product development, QA testing, user interface, and graphic design. | 510-848-0606 | NA | Berkeley |

| COMPANY NAME | PRODUCT / SERVICE | PHONE | EMP | CITY |
|---|---|---|---|---|
| Access Video Productions (HQ) | Provider of production, editing, and duplication services for small and large companies, and individuals. | 510-528-6044 | NA | Berkeley |
| Acrylic Art (HQ) | Provider of fabrication and machining services. The company focuses on painting, product finishing, anodizing, and vapor polishing. | 510-654-0953 | NA | Emeryville |
| Actiance Inc (BR) | Provider of real-time internet communications solutions. The company serves the energy, healthcare, and utilities industries. | 650-631-6300 | NA | Redwood City |
| Active Video Networks (HQ) | Designer and developer of advertising solutions. The company also provides mosaic, guide, and navigation enablement services. | 408-931-9200 | NA | San Jose |
| Acxiom LLC (BR) | Provider of e-mail marketing services for online marketers. The company is engaged in consulting and analytics services. | 888-322-9466 | NA | Redwood City |
| Adapt Corp (HQ) | Provider of post-tensioning and reinforced concrete structural analysis software for building design. | 650-306-2400 | NA | Redwood City |
| Advanced Software Design Inc (HQ) | Provider of knowledge based engineering software and industry focused business solutions. The company offers services to the public sector. | 925-975-0694 | NA | Walnut Creek |
| Advancing Ideas LLC (HQ) | Provider of market research and analysis, application branding, and user interface development services. | 415-625-3338 | NA | San Francisco |
| Aechelon Technology Inc (HQ) | Developer of real time computer graphics applications in the training, simulation, and entertainment markets. | 415-255-0120 | NA | San Francisco |
| AerospaceComputing Inc (HQ) | Provider of computer technology application services to aerospace sciences. The company also focuses on business development services. | 650-988-0388 | NA | Mountain View |
| Agari Data Inc (HQ) | Provider of email security and social engineering solutions. The company serves the healthcare, financial services, and government industries. | 650-627-7667 | NA | Foster City |
| Agile Global Solutions Inc (HQ) | Provider of business and IT solutions such as custom and enterprise application management and mobile business solutions. | 916-655-7745 | 11-50 | Folsom |
| Agilis Software Llc (HQ) | Developer of software licensing and software license management solution for enterprise software, embedded systems, and cloud software industries. | 415-458-2614 | NA | San Francisco |
| Air Worldwide Corp (BR) | Provider of software development and consulting services. The company focuses on risk modeling software and risk assessment and management consulting. | 415-912-3111 | NA | San Francisco |
| Aktana Inc (HQ) | Provider of decision support engine that pores through multiple data services and delivers insights and suggestions right in the rep's workflow. | 888-707-3125 | NA | San Francisco |
| Alacrinet Consulting Services Inc (HQ) | Developer of software solutions. The company offers enterprise search, web content management, business intelligence, and analytics services. | 650-646-2670 | NA | Palo Alto |
| Alten Calsoft Labs (HQ) | Provider of breed consulting, enterprise IT, and product engineering services for enterprises in healthcare, telecom, and high-tech & retail industries. | 408-755-3000 | NA | Santa Clara |
| Altierre Corp (HQ) | Provider of digital retail services. The company offers retail integration, software support, and consulting services. | 408-435-7343 | NA | San Jose |
| Altigen Communications Inc (HQ) | Manufacturer of voice and data telecommunication equipment. The company specializes in hosted business communication solutions. | 408-597-9000 | NA | San Jose |
| American International Group Inc (RH) | Provider of international insurance solutions and financial services. The company serves individuals, group, and businesses. | 415-836-2700 | NA | San Francisco |
| American Telesource Inc (HQ) | Provider of voice and data communication applications. The company offers unified communications, wireless, and process automation solutions. | 800-333-8394 | NA | Emeryville |
| AmigoCloud Inc (HQ) | Provider of geospatial platform that helps to collect, manage, analyze, visualize, and publish the location data using smartphone, camera, and sensors. | 415-935-1447 | NA | San Francisco |
| Andes Technology USA Corporation (RH) | Provider of infrastructural solutions for embedded system applications. The company serves the semiconductor industry. | 408-809-2929 | NA | San Jose |
| Anomali (RH) | Specializes in the delivery of cyber security solutions. The company services to big and small organizations. | 844-484-7328 | NA | Redwood City |
| Ansys Inc (BR) | Provider of engineering solutions. The company serves the aerospace, defense, and construction industries. | 844-462-6797 | NA | Berkeley |
| Apex Technology Management Inc (HQ) | Provider of information technology services such as business continuity planning, virtualization, and email protection. | 800-310-2739 | 1-10 | Redding |
| Apolent Corp (HQ) | Provider of business process and software technology outsourcing services focusing on niche market segments. | 408-203-6828 | NA | San Jose |
| AppEnsure Inc (HQ) | Provider of cloud application performance and infrastructure management such as application-aware infrastructure performance management solution. | 408-418-4602 | NA | San Jose |
| Applied Computer Solutions (BR) | Provider of information technology solutions. The company offers solutions for virtualization, storage, security, and networking. | 925-251-1000 | NA | Pleasanton |
| Apsalar Inc (HQ) | Provider of data-powered mobile advertising solutions. The company offers marketing attribution and in-app analytics services. | 877-590-1854 | NA | San Francisco |
| Aptible Inc (HQ) | Developer of secure, private cloud deployment platform built to automate HIPAA compliance for digital health. | 866-296-5003 | NA | San Francisco |
| Aravo Solutions Inc (HQ) | Provider of risk and performance management, Supplier Information Management (SIM), and related services. | 415-835-7600 | NA | San Francisco |

| COMPANY NAME | PRODUCT / SERVICE | PHONE | EMP | CITY |
|---|---|---|---|---|
| Arc (HQ) | Provider of document management services to the architectural, engineering, and construction industries. | 925-949-5100 | NA | San Ramon |
| Artec Group Inc (BR) | Developer and distributor of 3D scanners and 3D cameras. The company's products include Artec iD, Artec 3D, Viewshape, and Shapify. | 669-292-5611 | NA | Santa Clara |
| Artifex Software Inc (HQ) | Provider of software solutions for host based applications. The company also focuses on embedded printer markets. | 415-492-9861 | NA | Novato |
| Aryaka Networks Inc (HQ) | Provider of cloud-based WAN optimization services. The company focuses on application performance, data protection, and bandwidth reduction. | 877-727-9252 | NA | Milpitas |
| Asap Systems (HQ) | Developer of inventory management and asset tracking software. The company also offers barcode scanners & printers and RFID tags. | 408-227-2720 | NA | San Jose |
| Asi Controls (HQ) | Manufacturer of direct digital controls for HVAC and light industrial marketplace. The company also offers networking products and unitary controls. | 925-866-8808 | NA | San Ramon |
| Asmeix Corp (HQ) | Provider of welding procedure software services such as technical support, installation, maintenance, and demo services. | 877-977-7999 | NA | Concord |
| Aspera Inc (HQ) | Developer of file transport technologies. The company provides client and server software, consoles, and mobile uploaders. | 510-849-2386 | NA | Emeryville |
| Aspire Systems Inc (BR) | Provider of product engineering, infrastructure and application support, and testing services. The company serves healthcare and education fields. | 408-260-2076 | NA | San Jose |
| Assia Inc (HQ) | Provider of broadband solution such as cloudcheck, technology licensing, DSL expresse, and expresse products and solution. | 650-654-3400 | NA | Redwood City |
| Assurx Inc (HQ) | Provider of quality management and regulatory compliance software solutions for biotechnology, medical devices, pharmaceutical, and energy industries. | 408-778-1376 | NA | Morgan Hill |
| AsTech Consulting (HQ) | Provider of source code security assessment, penetration testing, continuous monitoring, and secure development lifecycle consulting services. | | NA | Larkspur |
| Attention Control Systems Inc (HQ) | Manufacturer of cognitive aids. The company also offers technical assistance solutions and serves the healthcare sector. | 888-224-7328 | NA | Mountain View |
| Aurionpro Solutions Inc (DH) | Provider of solutions to streamline corporate banking, treasury, fraud prevention, risk management, governance and compliance needs. | 925-242-0777 | NA | San Ramon |
| AutoGrid Systems Inc (HQ) | Provider of grid-sensing technologies. The company focuses on energy data platform and optimized demand management services. | 650-461-9038 | NA | Redwood City |
| Automattic Inc (HQ) | Provider of blogging services. The company specializes in handling non-profit and open source projects. | 877-273-3049 | NA | San Francisco |
| Autonomic Software Inc (HQ) | Developer of software for endpoint & security management, imaging, and other needs. The company serves government, finance, and other sectors. | 925-683-8351 | NA | Danville |
| Aviso Inc (HQ) | Creator of software to change how enterprises make critical revenue decisions and automate sales forecasting process with data science for enterprises. | 650-567-5470 | NA | Redwood City |
| Avontus Software Corp (DH) | Creator of software for formwork, scaffolding, and shoring industries, both custom development for enterprises and packaged software for public. | 800-848-1860 | NA | Berkeley |
| Axcient Inc (HQ) | Provider of single integrated cloud platform that makes it simple to restore data, failover applications, and virtualize servers or an entire office. | 800-715-2339 | NA | Mountain View |
| Ayasdi Inc (HQ) | Provider of software applications that discovers critical intelligence in company data for right operational decisions quickly. | 650-704-3395 | NA | Menlo Park |
| Ayla Networks Inc (HQ) | Provider of Ayla's IoT cloud platform that brings connected products to market quickly and securely for manufacturers and service providers. | 408-830-9844 | NA | Santa Clara |
| Backshop Inc (HQ) | Provider of commercial real estate software for full deal-stack modeling, loan origination, asset management, and data library for customers. | 415-332-1110 | NA | Sausalito |
| Badger Maps Inc (HQ) | Provider of easy to use interface to manage our daily call routes, track visits, and update records. | 415-592-5909 | NA | San Francisco |
| Bay Microsystems Inc (HQ) | Provider of secure networking solution for commercial market such as life sciences/healthcare, oil and gas, digital media, and financial services. | 408-841-4700 | NA | San Jose |
| BayNODE LLC (HQ) | Provider of data network solutions, outsourcing, and network security services. The company caters to the IT sector. | 415-274-3100 | NA | San Francisco |
| Bcg Management Resources Inc (HQ) | Provider of enterprise software solutions and professional services such as dynamics NAV and bc solutions for food and manufacturing industry. | 800-456-8474 | NA | Concord |
| Bcl Technologies (HQ) | Developer of document creation, conversion, and extraction solutions. The company offers BCL easyPDF Cloud, a cloud-based PDF conversion platform. | 408-557-2080 | NA | San Jose |
| BCS North America Inc (DH) | Designer and manufacturer of products for baggage handling and security screening systems. The company serves the aviation sector. | | NA | San Jose |
| Bct Consulting Inc (HQ) | Provider of computer network support, web design, application programming, and other technology services. | 559-579-1400 | 11-50 | Fresno |
| Bear River Associates Inc (HQ) | Provider of enterprise mobile computing products and services. The company serves business services, government, high-tech, and life science sectors. | 510-834-5300 | NA | Oakland |

| COMPANY NAME | PRODUCT / SERVICE | PHONE | EMP | CITY |
|---|---|---|---|---|
| Bestek Manufacturing Inc (HQ) | Provider of supply chain services. The company engages focuses on systems manufacturing, materials management, and prototype support areas. | 408-321-8834 | NA | San Jose |
| Beta Breakers Software Quality (HQ) | Provider of software and application testing services. The company offers functionality, compatibility, website, and mobile device testing services. | 415-878-2990 | NA | Novato |
| Bitglass (HQ) | Provider of data protection solutions. The company focuses on cloud encryption, mobile security, and discovery solutions. | 408-337-0190 | NA | Campbell |
| Blast Analytics & Marketing (HQ) | Provider of web design, e-commerce, and brand design services. The company is involved in hosting and technical support. | 916-724-6701 | 11-50 | Rocklin |
| Blue Chip Tek Inc (HQ) | Provider of data management and protection, information life cycle management, networking, security, and data center solutions. | 408-731-7700 | NA | Santa Clara |
| Blue Jeans Network Inc (HQ) | Provider of cloud-based video conferencing solutions. The company also offers mobile video collaboration and cloud video bridging solutions. | 408-550-2828 | NA | Mountain View |
| BMC Software Inc (BR) | Provider of cloud management, workforce automation, and IT service management solutions. The company serves business enterprises and service providers. | 800-793-4262 | NA | Santa Clara |
| Bodhtree Solutions Inc (BR) | Provider of information technology consulting services. The company deals with product engineering, application development, and training. | 408-954-8700 | 11-50 | Fremont |
| Bramasol Inc (BR) | Provider of SAP-based solution for high tech software, life science, industrial machinery & components, and Telco, wireless, and internet services. | 408-831-0046 | NA | Santa Clara |
| Brekeke Software Inc (HQ) | Developer of session initiation protocol software products for internet protocol network communication needs. | 650-401-6633 | NA | San Mateo |
| Bright Computing Inc (HQ) | Provider of software solutions for provisioning and managing HPC clusters, Hadoop clusters, and openstack private clouds. | 408-300-9448 | NA | San Jose |
| Bright Pattern Inc (HQ) | Provider of enterprise contact center application for blended multi-channel interactions. The company offers products based on modern technology. | 650-529-4099 | NA | San Bruno |
| Brighterion Inc (HQ) | Provider of products for fraud prevention, predictive intelligence, risk management, and homeland security. The company focuses on adaptive analytics. | 415-986-5600 | NA | San Francisco |
| Brightidea Inc (HQ) | Provider of innovative management software solutions. The company's products include WebStorm, Switchboard, and Pipeline modules. | 415-692-1912 | NA | San Francisco |
| Brightsign Llc (HQ) | Provider of digital sign media players, software, and networking solutions for the commercial digital signage industry. | 408-852-9263 | NA | Los Gatos |
| Bugcrowd (HQ) | Provider of security solutions. The company is engaged in pre-launch consulting, research, and testing services. | 888-361-9734 | NA | San Francisco |
| BuildingIQ Inc (HQ) | Provider of software-as-a-service solution to optimize energy use in commercial buildings such as hospitality, healthcare facilities, and utilities. | 888-260-4080 | NA | San Mateo |
| Burstorm Inc (HQ) | Provider of cloud design tools application. The company specializes in design, collaborate, quote, and implement of cloud architecture. | 650-610-1480 | NA | Danville |
| Ca Technologies (BR) | Focuses on technology leadership and category-leading semiconductor and infrastructure software solutions. | 800-225-5224 | NA | Petaluma |
| CAD Masters Inc (HQ) | Designer and developer of software and hardware solutions. The company focuses on drafting, engineering, plotting, and on-site project assistance. | 925-939-1378 | NA | Walnut Creek |
| Cadence Design Systems Inc (HQ) | Provider of semiconductor IP and electronic design automation services. The company offers tools for logic & RF design, IC packaging, and other needs. | 408-943-1234 | NA | San Jose |
| Calypso Technology Inc (HQ) | Provider of front-to-back technology solutions for the financial markets. The company offers technology platform for cross asset trading risk management. | 415-530-4000 | NA | San Francisco |
| Calyx Technology Inc (HQ) | Provider of mortgage solutions for banks and credit unions. The company also serves mortgage bankers and brokers. | 408-997-5525 | NA | San Jose |
| Capital Network Solutions Inc (HQ) | Provider of internet security systems, phone systems, and off-site encrypted backup for small and medium sized businesses. | 916-366-6566 | 1-10 | Sacramento |
| Capitol Digital Document Solutions (HQ) | Provider of litigation support services. The company offers forensic data collection, online document review, and e-discovery processing services. | 916-449-2820 | 1-10 | Sacramento |
| Capriza Inc (HQ) | Provider of codeless enterprise mobility platform. The company offers mobile-enabling business applications such as design, zaaps, manage, and security. | 650-600-3661 | NA | Palo Alto |
| Carefree Computing Inc (HQ) | Provider of web hosting, software design, programming, technical support, and network design services. | 866-377-6275 | NA | San Francisco |
| Casahl Technology Inc (HQ) | Provider of collaboration and content environment optimization services. The company focuses on cloud integration and content management. | 925-328-2828 | NA | San Ramon |
| Caseware International Inc (DH) | Supplier of software solutions to accountants and auditors worldwide. The company offers working papers to accounting firms. | 416-867-9504 | NA | Berkeley |
| Catalyst Business Solutions (HQ) | Provider of technology consulting services in business applications, data center, and machine-to-machine/internet of things. | 408-281-7100 | NA | San Jose |

| COMPANY NAME | PRODUCT / SERVICE | PHONE | EMP | CITY |
|---|---|---|---|---|
| Ccintegration Inc (HQ) | Provider of business engagement models such as OEM and virtual OEM. The company services include design, integration, and logistics. | 408-228-1314 | NA | San Jose |
| Cdnetworks Inc (RH) | Developer of web and network acceleration solutions. The company serves the travel, tourism, gaming, and technology industries. | 408-228-3700 | NA | Campbell |
| Celigo Inc (HQ) | Provider of cloud computing products and solutions. The company offers NetSuite consulting services that include implementation and optimization. | 650-579-0210 | NA | San Mateo |
| CellarStone Inc (HQ) | Provider of sales commissions and incentive compensation software and solutions. The company offers version upgrades and re-engineering services. | 650-242-0008 | NA | Half Moon Bay |
| Centrify (HQ) | Provider of identity and access management solutions. The company offers services to pharma companies and financial institutions. | 669-444-5200 | NA | Santa Clara |
| Certain Inc (DH) | Provider of enterprise event management solutions that include e-mail marketing, event reporting, registration, and consulting services. | 415-353-5330 | NA | San Francisco |
| Certent Inc (HQ) | Provider of equity compensation management, equity compensation reporting, and disclosure management solutions. | 925-730-4300 | NA | Pleasanton |
| ChannelNet (BR) | Provider of digital solutions to connect brands and customers. The company specializes in strategy development, design, and content optimization. | 415-332-4704 | NA | Sausalito |
| Check Point Software Technologies Inc (HQ) | Developer of software technology solutions such as mobile security and next generation firewalls for retail/point of sale and financial services. | 800-429-4391 | NA | San Carlos |
| Chiapas Edi Technologies Inc (HQ) | Developer of electronic data interchange software for health insurance exchange brokers, MSOs, HMOs, and healthcare business data analytics services. | 415-298-8166 | 1-10 | Davis |
| Chouinard & Myhre Inc (HQ) | Provider of IT solutions such as data management, enterprise security management, and private, public, and hybrid cloud solutions and services. | 415-480-3636 | NA | Mill Valley |
| Chrometa LLC (HQ) | Provider of time keeping management software and services. The company offers products for PC, Mac, iPhone, and Android platforms. | 916-546-9974 | 1-10 | Sacramento |
| Ciena Corp (BR) | Provider of cloud networking, network transformation, and packet network solutions for multi-data center environments. | 408-904-2100 | NA | San Jose |
| Ciphercloud Inc (DH) | Provider of comprehensive cloud application discovery and risk assessment, data protection, data loss management, key management, and malware detection. | 855-524-7437 | NA | San Jose |
| Circleci (HQ) | Provider of continuous integration and delivery solution. The company offers apps for docker, enterprise, and mobiles. | 800-585-7075 | NA | San Francisco |
| Citrix Systems Inc (BR) | Provider of transition to software-defining the workplace, uniting virtualization, mobility management, networking, and SaaS solutions. | 408-790-8000 | NA | Santa Clara |
| Clare Computer Solutions (HQ) | Provider of information technology services. The company offers computer network, software consultation, visualization, and cloud computing solutions. | 925-277-0690 | NA | San Ramon |
| Claresco Corp (HQ) | Provider of design and implementation services for customized business software. The company serves multi-national firms. | 510-528-0238 | NA | Berkeley |
| Clarizen (HQ) | Provider of collaborative online project management software. The company offers work management, time tracking, and project scheduling solutions. | 866-502-9813 | NA | San Mateo |
| ClearCare Inc (HQ) | Provider of front and back office software solution such as billing, payroll, and marketing management for private duty home care agencies. | 800-449-0645 | NA | San Francisco |
| Clickatell (pty) Ltd (HQ) | Provider of SMS solutions such as SMS alerts, reminders, call centers, reservations and bookings for healthcare, marketing, and IT/software industries. | 650-641-0011 | NA | Redwood City |
| Climate Earth (HQ) | Provider of environmental product declarations and supply chain solutions such as supply chain, climate change risk, and natural capital management . | 415-391-2725 | NA | Berkeley |
| Cloudera Inc (HQ) | Provider of professional services that include cluster certification, descriptive analytics pilot, and security integration pilot. | 650-362-0488 | NA | Palo Alto |
| Cloudian (LH) | Provider of cloud storage platform and unstructured data storage. The company offers cloud object storage software and appliances. | 650-227-2380 | NA | Foster City |
| Cloudmark Inc (HQ) | Provider of messaging infrastructure and security solutions. The company delivers scalable messaging platform, security intelligence, and filtering. | 415-946-3800 | NA | San Francisco |
| Cloudshare Inc (HQ) | Provider of flexible and cloud-computing platform for developing and testing IT applications, software, and systems. | 888-609-4440 | NA | San Francisco |
| Cloudwords Inc (HQ) | Provider of translation management systems and content localization solutions to manage translation process, vendors, and content systems. | 415-394-8000 | NA | San Francisco |
| Clustrix Inc (HQ) | Provider of a SQL database with no limits to database size, table size, query complexity, and performance. | 415-501-9560 | NA | San Francisco |
| Cognex Corp (BR) | Supplier of barcode readers and sensor products. The company offers vision sensors, fixed mount readers, handheld readers, and mobile computers. | 858-481-2469 | NA | Cupertino |

| COMPANY NAME | PRODUCT / SERVICE | PHONE | EMP | CITY |
|---|---|---|---|---|
| Cognizant Technology Solutions (BR) | Provider of business consulting, enterprise application development, IT infrastructure, and outsourcing services. | 925-790-2000 | NA | San Ramon |
| Cohesion Inc (BR) | Provider of software and services. The company offers SAP quality management, batch management, business warehousing, and other services. | 650-591-9122 | NA | San Carlos |
| Collaborative Drug Discovery Inc (HQ) | Provider of drug discovery research informatics. The company offers hosted biological and chemical database that securely manages private and external data. | 650-242-5259 | NA | Burlingame |
| CommerceNet (HQ) | Provider of internet based research and piloting services such as internet business, open trading networks, and internet-user demographic surveys. | 650-289-4040 | NA | Los Altos |
| ComplianceEase (HQ) | Provider of intelligent business solutions to financial service institutions. The company offers automated compliance and risk management solutions. | 650-373-1111 | NA | Burlingame |
| Comprehend Systems Inc (HQ) | Provider of invaluable clinical data insights enabling us to do better science and optimize clinical operations. | 650-521-5449 | NA | Redwood City |
| Computer Logistics Corp (HQ) | Provider of system and internet integration, system design, custom programming, web design, and hosting services. | 530-241-3131 | 1-10 | Redding |
| CompuTrust Software (HQ) | Developer and seller of software for public administrators. The company offers services to businesses and enterprises. | 800-222-7947 | NA | Morgan Hill |
| Conformiq Inc (HQ) | Provider of automated test designing services. The company focuses on training, project implementation, change management, and executive consulting. | 408-898-2140 | NA | Saratoga |
| Corecess Global Inc (BR) | Designer, developer, and manufacturer of telecommunication equipment for the broadband access network. | 408-567-5300 | NA | Santa Clara |
| Corona Labs Inc (HQ) | Developer of games, e-books, and other interactive content. The company offers services to the educational sector. | 415-996-6877 | NA | San Francisco |
| Corrigo Inc (BR) | Developer of facilities management platforms. The company offers services to business organizations. | 877-267-7440 | NA | San Mateo |
| Couchbase Inc (HQ) | Developer of products and technology to meet the elastic scalability, always-on availability, and data mobility requirements of critical applications. | 650-417-7500 | NA | Santa Clara |
| Cp Software Group Inc (HQ) | Provider of capital formation, fund raising, management consulting, technical and marketing, and incubator services for startup and established companies. | 916-985-4445 | 1-10 | Folsom |
| Cpacket Networks (HQ) | Provider of solutions for network traffic monitoring and data center performance management. The company specializes in traffic monitoring switches. | 650-969-9500 | NA | San Jose |
| Crmantra Inc (HQ) | Developer of software for customer relationship management needs. The company also focuses on business intelligence and analysis. | 415-839-9672 | NA | Emeryville |
| CRMIT Solutions Pvt Ltd (HQ) | Provider of customer experience cloud solutions for banking, insurance education, retail, life science, energy, telecom, and financial services. | 408-722-0634 | NA | Milpitas |
| Cross-Circuit Networks Inc (HQ) | Provider of networking solutions specializing in information technology infrastructure design, systems virtual environment and consolidation. | 408-654-9637 | NA | San Jose |
| Crypto Forensics Technologies Inc (HQ) | Provider of cybersecurity solutions to businesses, organizations, and the government. The company focuses on cyberforensics and compliance services. | 510-483-1955 | NA | San Leandro |
| Css Corp (HQ) | Provider of enterprise level support solutions for IT products. The company is involved in virtualization, storage, and archiving solutions. | 650-385-3820 | NA | Milpitas |
| Cubus Solutions Inc (HQ) | Provider of online banking solutions to seamlessly integrate with core system while delivering real-time, and secure, banking services to members. | 925-606-8708 | NA | Livermore |
| Cultivate Systems (HQ) | Provider of construction services. The company offers civil site work, construction, demolition, and general contracting services. | 707-690-9425 | NA | Napa |
| Cumulus Networks Llc (HQ) | Provider of Linux operating system hardware and software solution that offers flexibility for modern data networking designs and operations. | 650-383-6700 | NA | Mountain View |
| CUneXus Solutions Inc (HQ) | Provider of pre-screening lending strategy that pre-approves entire loan product portfolio for customers. | 877-509-2089 | NA | Santa Rosa |
| Cyberglove Systems Llc (HQ) | Provider of data glove technology. The company offers system installation and integration and custom software and hardware services. | 408-943-8114 | NA | San Jose |
| Cybersoft (BR) | Provider of offshore business and knowledge process outsourcing services. The company specializes in title, financial, and document processing services. | 415-449-7998 | NA | San Francisco |
| Database International (HQ) | Provider of database application development and database administration services and also offers project management and event coordination services. | 650-965-9102 | NA | Los Altos |
| Databricks Inc (HQ) | Provider of platform for big data processing solutions. The company offers exploration and visualization, production pipelines, and third party apps. | 866-330-0121 | NA | San Francisco |
| DataDirect Networks Inc (BR) | Provider of storage array, file system, and object storage appliances to broadcast, biopharma, supercomputing, and financial service sectors. | 408-419-2800 | NA | Santa Clara |

| COMPANY NAME | PRODUCT / SERVICE | PHONE | EMP | CITY |
|---|---|---|---|---|
| Dataglance Inc (HQ) | Provider of data management software that support LIVE data conversion/migration, electronic document generation & processing, and web services. | 510-656-0500 | NA | Fremont |
| Dataguise (HQ) | Provider of cloud migration, auditing, and monitoring solutions. The company serves the healthcare, consumer, and retail industries. | 877-632-0522 | NA | Fremont |
| Datastax Inc (RH) | Distributor of database management system for internet enterprise. The company offers training & certification, expert support, and consulting services. | 408-933-3120 | NA | Santa Clara |
| Datest Corp (HQ) | Provider of testing and inspection services. The company specializes in engineering testing and counterfeit inspection for industrial products. | 510-490-4600 | NA | Fremont |
| Dcl (HQ) | Provider of fulfillment and supply chain management services. The company offers e-Commerce, retail fulfillment, and reverse logistics services. | 510-330-1938 | NA | Fremont |
| Delphix (HQ) | Developer of software, database, and database virtualization. The company focuses on website design and hosting and software application development. | 650-494-1645 | NA | Redwood City |
| Desaware Inc (HQ) | Developer of tools and components for visual studio programmers. The company offers documentation and professional services. | 408-404-4760 | NA | San Jose |
| DesignMap (HQ) | Provider of web site and application design services. The company also specializes in research, usability studies, and visual design. | 415-357-1875 | NA | San Francisco |
| Device Authority Ltd (RH) | Provider of IoT security solutions for industrial, automotive, transportation, healthcare, utilities, and smart cities. | 650-603-0997 | NA | Fremont |
| Digital Anarchy (HQ) | Provider of photography and video plugins for Photoshop, elements, after effects, and final cut pro. | 415-287-6069 | NA | Brisbane |
| Digital Canvas (HQ) | Provider of web design and web application development services. The company also offers web hosting, security solutions, and services. | 925-706-1700 | NA | Antioch |
| Digital Element Inc (HQ) | Developer of computer artwork, software, and tools for computer artists and developers. The company offers 3D animation, plug-ins, and art tools. | | NA | Fremont |
| Dnn Corp (HQ) | Provider of software solutions for content management. The company also offers marketing & eCommerce and product development services. | 650-288-3150 | NA | San Mateo |
| Docker Inc (HQ) | Provider of docker platform and docker ecosystem of contributors, partners, and adopters the way distributed applications are built, shipped, and run. | 415-941-0376 | NA | San Francisco |
| Docusign Inc (HQ) | Provider of digital transaction management platform helps to accelerate transactions, reduce costs, and delight customers, suppliers, and employees. | 877-720-2040 | NA | San Francisco |
| Drivesavers Inc (HQ) | Provider of data recovery services for financial institutions, healthcare providers, major film studios, government agencies, and small businesses. | 415-382-2000 | NA | Novato |
| Droisys Inc (HQ) | Provider of business solutions and offers services such as content management, enterprise resource planning, and business efficiency consulting. | 408-874-8333 | NA | Santa Clara |
| Dropbox Inc (HQ) | Provider of data transfer and sharing services that involves sharing of files, documents, and pictures from anywhere. | 415-857-6800 | NA | San Francisco |
| Druva (RH) | Provider of cloud based data protection products. The company offers services to the manufacturing, healthcare, and education industries. | 650-238-6200 | NA | Sunnyvale |
| Dt Research Inc (HQ) | Developer and manufacturer of embedded computing systems. The company serves hospitality, healthcare, and digital signage needs. | 408-934-6220 | NA | San Jose |
| DynEd International Inc (HQ) | Provider of computer-based English language teaching solutions. The company offers mobile solutions, analytics, testing, and monitoring tools. | 650-375-7011 | NA | Burlingame |
| E la Carte Inc (HQ) | Provider of digital restaurant services. The company specializes in operations, engineering, business development, and marketing. | 650-468-0680 | NA | Redwood City |
| Ecodomus Inc (HQ) | Provider of information technology software for improved design & construction data collection, facility management, operation, and maintenance. | 571-277-6617 | NA | San Francisco |
| Ecrio Inc (HQ) | Provider of wireless messaging applications. The company offers video telephony, content sharing, social communications, and enterprise solutions. | 408-973-7290 | NA | Cupertino |
| Eda Direct Inc (HQ) | Provider of EDA software products and services. The company's products include Cliosoft, MunEDA, and Mentor Graphics. | 408-496-5890 | NA | Santa Clara |
| Edgewater Networks Inc (HQ) | Provider of enterprise session controllers for business purposes. The company also offers security and policy management services. | 408-351-7200 | NA | San Jose |
| Electric Cloud Inc (BR) | Provider of software development, information technology consulting, test automation, virtualization, and cloud computing solutions. | 408-419-4300 | NA | San Jose |
| Elegrity Inc (HQ) | Provider of law business management software, SharePoint, virtualization, and unified communication solutions. | 415-821-0900 | NA | San Francisco |
| Elementum Scm Inc (HQ) | Provider of apps to manage your global supply chain. The company offers manufacturing operations, mission control, supplier, and logistics management. | 650-318-1491 | NA | Mountain View |
| Ellie Mae Inc (HQ) | Focuses on mortgage compliance services. The company offers services to banks and other financial institutions. | 925-227-7000 | NA | Pleasanton |

| COMPANY NAME | PRODUCT / SERVICE | PHONE | EMP | CITY |
|---|---|---|---|---|
| Emanio Inc (HQ) | Developer of products for data management, dashboarding, and reporting & predictive analysis needs. The company focuses on consulting and training. | 510-849-9300 | NA | Berkeley |
| Emlinux (HQ) | Developer of embedded Linux designs. The company provides marketing level definition and system architecture services. | 408-249-5574 | NA | San Jose |
| Emtrain (HQ) | Provider of learning management system such as online training platform for all levels of HR professionals, trainers, and administrators. | 800-242-6099 | NA | San Francisco |
| Endicia (HQ) | Provider of electronic postage software solutions and offers shipping and mailing services to online sellers, warehouse shippers, and office mailers. | 650-321-2640 | NA | Mountain View |
| Enlighta (HQ) | Provider of software solutions to service organizations grappling with governance and management of global services delivery. | 510-279-5820 | NA | San Ramon |
| Ensenta Corp (HQ) | Developer of software solutions. The company is involved in development of cloud-based imaging and self-service technology. | 866-219-4321 | NA | Redwood Shores |
| enSilo (HQ) | Developer of data protection platforms and provider of exfiltration prevention solutions. The company offers services to the network industry. | 800-413-1782 | NA | San Francisco |
| Ent Networks Inc (HQ) | Provider of custom system manufacturing, database management, hardware sales, business consulting, and repair services. | 925-462-7125 | NA | Pleasanton |
| Enview Inc (HQ) | Specializes in threat prevention systems. The company deals with data analytics and remote sensing services. | 415-483-5680 | NA | San Francisco |
| Eonite Perception Inc (HQ) | Focuses on building 3D mapping and ego-tracking systems. The company serves the entertainment, robotics, and construction industries. | 650-681-9257 | NA | Los Altos |
| ePlus Inc (BR) | Provider of integrated technology solutions and services including lease financing, proprietary software, and project management. | | NA | Milpitas |
| Errigal Inc (HQ) | Designer and developer of software products and services. The company also deals with configuration management and ticketing. | 415-523-9245 | NA | San Francisco |
| Esp Interactive Solutions Inc (HQ) | Provider of web design and development services such as web video creation, content management system, and social networks marketing. | 510-526-2592 | NA | Albany |
| Etouch Systems Corp (BR) | Provider of design web engineering services. The company focuses on business process management and enterprise application integration services. | 510-795-4800 | NA | Fremont |
| Etrigue Corp (HQ) | Provider of marketing automation solutions such as email marketing, event management, derived data, 3-D leading scoring, and marketing database management. | 408-490-2900 | NA | San Jose |
| Evolveware Inc (HQ) | Developer of products to automate and modernize IT infrastructure focusing on assessment, documentation, impact analysis, and other solutions. | 408-748-8301 | NA | Santa Clara |
| Exabeam Inc (HQ) | Provider of software to discover attackers impersonating users and to protect against cyber attacks. | 844-392-2326 | NA | San Mateo |
| Excelfore Corp (HQ) | Provider of cloud applications. The company offers infotainment and telematics products for insurance, financing, and logistics sectors. | 510-868-2500 | NA | Fremont |
| Exit445 Group (HQ) | Provider of information architecture, e-Commerce, email marketing, search engine optimization, website hosting, and other services. | 415-381-1852 | NA | Mill Valley |
| Experexchange Inc (HQ) | Provider of software and professional IT solutions such as web based applications, software life cycle service, embedded systems, and software testing. | 510-623-7071 | NA | Fremont |
| Ezb Solutions (HQ) | Provider of software, hardware, and installation services. The company also deals with training, consulting, and technical support. | 408-988-8760 | NA | Santa Clara |
| eze System (HQ) | Provider or monitoring and measuring solutions. The company's products include controllers, controller expansions, and sensors. | 716-393-9330 | 11-50 | Folsom |
| F5 Networks Inc (BR) | Provider of strategic points of control throughout the IT infrastructure for organizations to scale, adapt, and align with changing business demands. | 408-273-4800 | NA | San Jose |
| Fair Isaac Corp (HQ) | Provider of analytical, software installation, and integration services. The company serves business enterprises. | 408-817-9100 | 51-200 | San Jose |
| Famsoft (HQ) | Provider of ERP consulting and infrastructure management services such as managed support, IBM products, enterprise solution, and migration services. | 408-452-1550 | NA | San Jose |
| Farallon Geographics Inc (HQ) | Provider of strategic planning, spatial data processing, training, and web application development services. | 415-227-1140 | NA | San Francisco |
| FCS Software Solutions (HQ) | Provider of consulting, product development, e-learning, digital content, and product support services. | 408-324-1203 | NA | San Jose |
| Fidus Systems Inc (BR) | Specializes in electronic product development and consulting services. The company also deals with hardware design. | 408-217-1928 | NA | Fremont |
| Filemaker Inc (DH) | Provider of database software which assists organizations in the management, analysis, and sharing of information. | 408-987-7000 | NA | Santa Clara |
| Fileopen Systems Inc (HQ) | Provider of digital rights management and document security solutions for corporations and governments. | 831-706-2170 | 1-10 | Santa Cruz |
| Filetrail Inc (HQ) | Provider of digital and physical management software and it serves the energy, pharmaceutical, and other industries. | 408-289-1300 | NA | San Jose |

| COMPANY NAME | PRODUCT / SERVICE | PHONE | EMP | CITY |
|---|---|---|---|---|
| Finjan Holdings Inc (HQ) | Specializes in the research and development of transformative technologies for the securing of information. | 650-282-3228 | NA | East Palo Alto |
| FireEye Inc (HQ) | Focuses on cyber security solutions. The company serves the utilities and pharmaceutical industries. | 408-321-6300 | NA | Milpitas |
| First Databank Inc (HQ) | Provider of healthcare solutions to hospitals, retail pharmacies, payers, drug manufacturers, and healthcare providers. | 650-588-5454 | NA | S San Francisco |
| Flexstar Technology (HQ) | Provider of testing and measurement solutions. The company's systems are used to test quality and reliability of storage related devices. | 408-643-7000 | NA | San Jose |
| Fluid Inc (HQ) | Provider of software solutions. The company's services include automated retail planning and content strategy. | 877-343-3240 | NA | Oakland |
| Forecross Corp (HQ) | Provider of automated migration of legacy systems. The company specializes in XML solutions, migration solutions, and integrity solutions. | 415-543-1515 | NA | San Francisco |
| Forensic Logic Inc (HQ) | Provider of software-as-a-service information technology to local, state and federal government workers and private sector organizations. | 833-267-5465 | NA | Walnut Creek |
| Forescout Technologies Inc (HQ) | Provider of network access control and policy compliance management solutions. The company serves the business sector. | 408-213-3191 | NA | Campbell |
| Fortinet Inc (HQ) | Provider of network security appliances and threat management solutions such as network security platform and reporting and authentication. | 408-235-7700 | NA | Sunnyvale |
| Franz Inc (HQ) | Provider of information technology solutions. The company offers web technology and enterprise development tools, and professional services. | 510-452-2000 | NA | Oakland |
| Frequentz LLC (HQ) | Designer and developer of product tracking software. The company serves the life sciences and industrial sectors. | 925-824-0300 | NA | San Ramon |
| Freshworks Inc (HQ) | Provider of multi-channel support and asset management services. The company serves business organizations. | 650-513-0514 | NA | San Bruno |
| Full Circle Crm Inc (HQ) | Specializes in response management and it offers management products. The company serves businesses. | 650-641-2766 | NA | San Mateo |
| Funmobility Inc (HQ) | Provider of solutions for mobile engagement and mobile marketing. The company also offers content marketing, digital strategy, and other services. | 925-598-9700 | NA | San Ramon |
| Fusionstorm (BR) | Provider of information technology services. The company specializes in IT consulting, data center, networking, and enterprise content management. | 800-228-8324 | NA | San Francisco |
| Futuredial Inc (HQ) | Developer of carrier-grade solutions and tools for mobile device recyclers, wireless operators, and mobile device manufacturers. | 408-245-8880 | NA | Sunnyvale |
| Gauss Surgical Inc (HQ) | Manufacturer of mobile devices. The company is engaged in research and development services and it serves the healthcare sector. | 650-949-4153 | NA | Los Altos |
| Genbook Inc (HQ) | Developer of online appointment scheduling software. The company is engaged in social media marketing services. | 415-227-9904 | NA | San Francisco |
| GestureTek Inc (HQ) | Provider of gesture-based user interfaces for mobile devices. The company offer services to the gaming and entertainment industries. | 408-506-2206 | NA | Santa Clara |
| Gigamon (HQ) | Provider of traffic visibility solutions for enterprises, data centers, and the education, financial, and healthcare industries. | 408-831-4000 | NA | Santa Clara |
| Gigwalk Inc (HQ) | Provider of analytics and collaboration tools and they are used in the management of mobile work force. | 888-237-5896 | NA | San Francisco |
| Gigya Inc (HQ) | Provider of widget distribution, content sharing, and advertising platform. The company caters to the needs of social web. | 650-353-7230 | NA | Mountain View |
| Gilmour Craves (HQ) | Provider of graphic design, advertising, media planning, strategic marketing, and print management services. | 415-431-9955 | NA | San Francisco |
| Glenmount Global Solutions (HQ) | Provider of industrial equipment control, energy management, and other systems. The company serves automotive, food, chemical, and other sectors. | 707-258-8400 | NA | Napa |
| Global Touchpoints Inc (DH) | Provider of application development, big data engineering, and analytics solutions and it serves the public and commercial sectors. | 916-878-5940 | 11-50 | Roseville |
| GlobalSoft Inc (HQ) | Provider of software consultancy services. The company offers application development, training program management, and engineering services. | 408-564-0307 | NA | San Jose |
| Glyphic Technology (HQ) | Provider of software design and architecture solutions. The company focuses on internet, server, desktop, mobile, and embedded systems. | 650-964-5311 | NA | Mountain View |
| Go Balto (DH) | Provider of solutions for biotechnology and pharma. The company has products include Activate and Analyze. | 650-506-7000 | NA | Redwood Shores |
| Google Inc (HQ) | Provider of search engine to make world's information universally accessible. The company specializes in internet-related services and products. | 650-253-0000 | NA | Mountain View |
| Grandflow Inc (HQ) | Provider of e-cataloging and marketing automation solutions. The company offers print production, warehousing, and document management services. | 925-443-0855 | NA | Livermore |
| Greytrix (RH) | Provider of integration and migration solutions. The company deals in analytics, cloud, mobility, and ERP/CRM consulting. | 888-221-6661 | NA | San Francisco |
| Gt Nexus Inc (HQ) | Provider of supply chain, transportation, and investment management solutions. The company serves retailers and manufacturers. | 510-808-2222 | NA | Oakland |

| COMPANY NAME | PRODUCT / SERVICE | PHONE | EMP | CITY |
|---|---|---|---|---|
| Guardian Analytics (HQ) | Provider of enterprise and community banking solutions. The company is engaged in training and applied fraud analysis services. | 650-383-9200 | NA | Mountain View |
| Guzik Technical Enterprises (HQ) | Manufacturer of test equipment for the computer industry. The company is involved in sales, training, and software downloads. | 650-625-8000 | NA | Mountain View |
| Hazelcast Inc (HQ) | Provider of training, consulting, and technical support services. The company serves the logistics and healthcare industries. | 650-521-5453 | NA | Palo Alto |
| Health Gorilla Inc (DH) | Focuses on diagnostic tests. The company offers services to clinics, patients and healthcare organizations. | 844-446-7455 | NA | Sunnyvale |
| Healthcare Systems & Technologies LLC (HQ) | Designer and developer of AC surgery software. The company offers services to corporate management companies. | 800-290-4078 | NA | Lafayette |
| Highwired Inc (HQ) | Developer of multimedia and supporting products and services. The company focuses on branding, billing, and delivery solutions. | 516-785-6197 | 1-10 | Redwood Valley |
| Hillstone Networks (RH) | Provider of security solutions for enterprises and data center networks. The company serves Fortune 500 companies and educational institutions. | 408-508-6750 | NA | Santa Clara |
| Hortonworks (HQ) | Specializes in open and connected data platforms. The company offers predictive analysis and data discovery solutions to the oil and gas industry. | 408-675-0983 | NA | Santa Clara |
| HumanAPI (HQ) | Focuses on the integration of health data and it specializes in retrieval of health data and other healthcare applications. | 650-241-8242 | NA | San Mateo |
| Hydropoint Data Systems Inc (HQ) | Provider of irrigation solutions. The company specializes in site evaluations, upgrade planning, deployment, and optimization services. | 800-362-8774 | NA | Petaluma |
| Illumio Inc (HQ) | Developer of security platform and it is also involved in data encryption and technical support services. | 669-800-5000 | NA | Sunnyvale |
| Imageteq Technologies Inc (HQ) | Provider of IT consulting and services. The company focuses on consulting, enterprise application, and staff augmentation. | 650-403-4806 | NA | Burlingame |
| Imagine That Inc (HQ) | Developer of simulation software. The company offers services to the retail, healthcare, insurance, and financial services industries. | 408-365-0305 | NA | San Jose |
| iMaxsoft Corporation (HQ) | Provider of database and application migration services. The company offers services to government agencies. | 408-253-1987 | NA | Cupertino |
| iMiners Inc (HQ) | Provider of investor relations management tools & web-based communication platforms. The company offers website plug-ins and shareholder message boards. | 925-447-6073 | NA | Livermore |
| Imperva Inc (HQ) | Provider of application and data security solutions. The company's products include database firewalls, management server, and monitoring software. | 650-345-9000 | NA | Redwood Shores |
| Increv Corp (HQ) | Developer of business and information technology solutions. The company is engaged in consulting and product development services. | 408-689-2296 | NA | Los Altos |
| Indec Medical Systems (HQ) | Provider of hardware and software solutions for cardiovascular imaging applications such as intravascular ultrasound and angiography. | 408-986-1600 | NA | Santa Clara |
| InfinIT Consulting (HQ) | Designer and developer of CNC machining and billet products. The company's products include fire extinguisher brackets, shift knobs, and boat accessories. | 866-364-2007 | NA | Campbell |
| Infinite Technologies Inc (HQ) | Provider of information technology, strategic consulting, and engineering services. The company serves government and corporate entities. | 916-987-3261 | 11-50 | El Dorado Hills |
| Infobahn Softworld Inc (HQ) | Provider of consulting, enterprise application integration, service oriented architecture, and systems integration solutions to fortune 500 companies. | 408-855-9616 | NA | San Jose |
| Infostat Systems Inc (HQ) | Provider of reporting, database, and data distribution solutions. The company serves drilling contractors and well operating companies. | 916-649-3244 | 1-10 | Sacramento |
| InfoTech Spectrum Inc (HQ) | Provider of integrated creative IT services including IT consulting, advanced technology deployment, and product development. | 408-705-2237 | NA | Santa Clara |
| Ingenuus Software Inc (HQ) | Provider of enterprise process orchestration solutions. The company develops business process management and process optimization software. | 510-824-5653 | NA | Fremont |
| Inikosoft Inc (HQ) | Provider of web, graphic, and print design services. The company is also engaged in e-commerce development and social media marketing. | 408-402-9545 | NA | Los Gatos |
| Input Optics Inc (HQ) | Provider of integration solutions for dental practice. The company also offers complimentary assessments and web services. | 650-969-3108 | NA | Mountain View |
| Insight Solutions Inc (BR) | Provider of mobility, network, and security solutions. The company is engaged in design, integration, and implementation services. | 877-776-0610 | NA | Cupertino |
| Instart Logic Inc (HQ) | Provider of software-defined application delivery solutions. The company offers services to the travel and hospitality industries. | 650-919-8856 | NA | Palo Alto |
| Inszoom Inc (HQ) | Focuses on immigration case management and compliance automation solutions. The company offers services to law firms. | 925-244-0600 | NA | San Ramon |
| Interloc Solutions (HQ) | Provider of consulting services and mobile solutions. The company serves the oil and gas and transportation industries. | 916-817-4590 | 11-50 | Folsom |
| Intermolecular Inc (HQ) | Provider of high productivity combinatorial technologies. The company serves solar device manufacturers. | 408-582-5700 | NA | San Jose |

| COMPANY NAME | PRODUCT / SERVICE | PHONE | EMP | CITY |
|---|---|---|---|---|
| Intertrust Technologies Corp (HQ) | Provider of security technology services such as content protection, white label video distribution, and software tamper resistance. | 408-616-1600 | NA | Sunnyvale |
| Intresys Inc (BR) | Provider of child support and egovernment solutions. The company serves attorneys, public sector agencies, and governments. | 888-372-1790 | NA | Belmont |
| Intuit Inc (HQ) | Provider of financial management software solutions. The company offers services to small businesses and related organizations. | 800-446-8848 | NA | Mountain View |
| Io Informatics Inc (HQ) | Provider of software and services for data integration applications in areas such as life science and medicine. | 510-705-8470 | NA | Berkeley |
| Io Integration Inc (HQ) | Provider of marketing technology and digital media workflow solutions. The company offers marketing automation and cross-media publishing services. | 408-996-3420 | NA | Cupertino |
| Ip Infusion Inc (HQ) | Developer of software for wireless internet products and offers data center networking, carrier ethernet transport, and mobile backhauling services. | 408-400-1900 | NA | Sunnyvale |
| Irislogic Inc (HQ) | Provider of global consulting services and solutions. The company specializes in custom software development, network security, cloud, and testing. | 408-855-8741 | NA | Santa Clara |
| iSOA Group Inc (BR) | Provider of business process management, service oriented architecture, and business analytics services to finance, energy, retail, and other sectors. | 925-465-7400 | NA | Walnut Creek |
| Issio Solutions Inc (HQ) | Provider of workforce management software for surgical facilities. The company also serves ambulatory surgical centers. | 888-994-7746 | NA | Concord |
| It Pro Source (HQ) | Provider of on call plans, managed services, web based monitoring, and communication cabling services. | 925-455-7701 | NA | Livermore |
| Itradenetwork Inc (HQ) | Provider of supply chain management and intelligence solutions for procurement, order management, and data services. | 925-660-1100 | NA | Dublin |
| Itrezzo Inc (HQ) | Provider of unified contact management solutions and it serves schools, agencies, and healthcare organizations. | 408-540-5020 | NA | San Jose |
| Jolly Technologies Inc (HQ) | Provider of secure identification, visitor management, barcode and asset tracking software services. | 650-594-5955 | NA | San Mateo |
| Joyent Inc (HQ) | Provider of cloud infrastructure services. The company's products include Compute service, Manta storage, and Private Cloud. | 415-400-0600 | NA | San Francisco |
| Junar Inc (HQ) | Provider of cloud-based open data platform. The company offers collaboration services to business organizations. | 844-695-8627 | NA | San Jose |
| Keen Systems Inc (HQ) | Provider of web-to print solutions. The company offers cloud-based services to small and medium sized printing companies. | 888-506-5336 | NA | San Mateo |
| Keep IT Simple (HQ) | Provider of virtualization and information technology services. The company focuses on virtualization assessment, cloud computing, and networking. | 510-403-7500 | NA | Fremont |
| Kespry Inc (HQ) | Developer of automated drone system and cloud that automatically uploads data in cloud for aggregates, insurance, and construction industries. | 203-434-7988 | NA | Menlo Park |
| Key Solutions Inc (HQ) | Provider of software development and database management services. The company also specializes in business intelligence. | 510-456-4500 | NA | Fremont |
| Key Source International Inc (HQ) | Provider of disinfect and germicidal wipes for keyboards. The company focuses on infection control and cross contamination. | 510-562-5000 | NA | Oakland |
| Kidaptive Inc (HQ) | Provider of learning and integration solutions. The company offers services to learners and the educational sector. | 650-265-2485 | NA | Redwood City |
| Klh Consulting Inc (HQ) | Provider of IT consulting, cloud computing, and related business solutions. The company offers services to business executives and professionals. | 707-575-9986 | NA | Santa Rosa |
| Ladd Associates Inc (HQ) | Provider of decision support software systems for publishers, subscription businesses, and direct response marketing clients. | 415-921-1001 | NA | San Francisco |
| Lanlogic (HQ) | Provider of information technology services. The company offers network management and support services. | 925-273-2300 | NA | Livermore |
| Lastline (HQ) | Manufacturer of malware protection products. The company serves schools, restaurants, and the enterprise security industry. | 877-671-3239 | NA | San Mateo |
| Lattice Engines (HQ) | Provider of business to business sales intelligence software. The company is engaged in web design and hosting and programming solutions. | 877-460-0010 | NA | San Mateo |
| LCS Technologies Inc (HQ) | Provider of information services for customers with Oracle software and service needs using resources such as people, hardware, and software. | 855-277-5527 | 1-10 | Gold River |
| LeapFILE Inc (HQ) | Provider of on-demand file transfer, delivery, and collaboration solutions for businesses. The company serves the healthcare and advertising sectors. | 650-701-7241 | NA | Cupertino |
| Ledger Systems Inc (HQ) | Provider of network design and support services. The company also offers accounting and e-Commerce solutions. | 650-592-6211 | NA | San Carlos |
| Leica Geosystems HDS LLC (RH) | Manufacturer of surveying hardware and software solutions for measuring and modeling sites and structures with high accuracy, detail, speed, and safety. | 925-790-2300 | NA | San Ramon |
| Linden Research Inc (HQ) | Designer and developer of digital entertainment solutions. The company's products include Desura, Patterns, and Versu. | 415-243-9000 | NA | San Francisco |

| COMPANY NAME | PRODUCT / SERVICE | PHONE | EMP | CITY |
|---|---|---|---|---|
| Linguastat Inc (HQ) | Provider of web based services to corporations and government agencies. The company offers optimized product descriptions for millions of landing pages. | 415-814-2999 | NA | San Francisco |
| LiveVox Inc (HQ) | Specializes in business analytics and related services. The company serves the telecom and healthcare industries. | 415-671-6000 | NA | San Francisco |
| Locus Technologies (HQ) | Provider of web based environmental information management systems. The company's services include field installation, training, and technical support. | 650-960-1640 | NA | Mountain View |
| Logen Solutions USA (HQ) | Provider of truck, container, pallet and carton loading and packaging software. The company offers solutions for cargo load planning. | 408-519-5771 | NA | San Jose |
| Lucidworks (HQ) | Provider of commercial foundation for architecture, design, development, and deployment of search solutions built with lucid works enterprise. | 415-329-6515 | NA | San Francisco |
| Lynx Software Technologies (HQ) | Developer of software technologies. The company offers development tools, real-time monitoring systems, and secure virtualization products. | 408-979-3900 | NA | San Jose |
| Marklogic Corp (HQ) | Provider of enterprise solutions. The company serves the healthcare, legal, and insurance industries. | 650-655-2300 | NA | San Carlos |
| Markmonitor Inc (HQ) | Provider of brand protection, domain management, domain advisory, anti-piracy, and managed services. | 415-278-8400 | NA | San Francisco |
| Maxta Inc (HQ) | Provider of software-defined storage, disaster recovery, and also testing and development solutions. | 669-228-2800 | NA | Santa Clara |
| Meditab Software Inc (HQ) | Developer of physical therapy, urology, cosmetic, and plastic surgery solutions. The company serves the healthcare industry. | 510-201-0130 | 1-10 | Sacramento |
| Menlo Security (HQ) | Provider of security solutions. The company's offerings include web isolation, document, and phishing isolation services. | 650-614-1705 | NA | Palo Alto |
| Mentor Graphics (RH) | Provider of electronic design automation software. The company focuses on mechanical analysis, system modeling, manufacturing, and verification. | 510-354-7400 | NA | Fremont |
| MeshDynamics Inc (HQ) | Provider of wireless mesh networking solutions focusing on wireless video surveillance, emergency response networks, and smart-grid multiuse products. | 408-373-7700 | NA | Santa Clara |
| Messagesolution Inc (HQ) | Provider of enterprise archiving, e-discovery, and migration solutions. The company deals with storage management solutions. | 408-383-0100 | NA | Milpitas |
| Metis Technology Solutions Inc (HQ) | Provider of technical services. The company engages in engineering, IT, aviation, space, and earth sciences fields. | 650-967-3051 | 11-50 | Sunnyvale |
| Michael Patrick Partners (HQ) | Provider of branding solutions. The company also offers logo design, portfolio creation, web content, and marketing services. | 650-327-3185 | NA | San Francisco |
| Mirabilis Design Inc (HQ) | Provider of systems engineering solutions for performance analysis and architecture exploration of electronics and real-time software. | 408-844-3234 | NA | Sunnyvale |
| Mixbook (HQ) | Provider of customizable photo books, cards and calendars, as well as creation of online scrapbooks on the web using design software. | 855-649-2665 | NA | Redwood City |
| mobiDEOS Inc (HQ) | Manufacturer of video surveillance equipment. The company offers services to government entities and businesses. | 408-716-8347 | NA | Los Gatos |
| Mobileiron Inc (HQ) | Provider of mobile security, device, and application management solutions. The company focuses on technical support services. | 650-919-8100 | NA | Mountain View |
| Moogsoft Inc (HQ) | Provider of collaborative situation management software solutions for Web-scale information technology (IT) operations. | 415-738-2299 | NA | San Francisco |
| Motiondsp Inc (HQ) | Provider of software products. The company serves the defense & intelligence, law enforcement, energy, and transportation markets. | 650-288-1164 | NA | Burlingame |
| Mphasis Corp (BR) | Provider of applications, infrastructure, and business process outsourcing services to the banking and healthcare sectors. | 408-327-1240 | NA | San Jose |
| MYCOM OSI Inc (BR) | Provider of performance management, compliance, employer reporting, patient engagement, and satisfaction solutions. | 916-467-1500 | 11-50 | Folsom |
| Myvest Corp (HQ) | Provider of enterprise wealth management solutions. The company offers services to business organizations. | 415-369-9511 | NA | San Francisco |
| Nada Technologies Inc (HQ) | Provider of enterprise Oracle applications. The company also offers business intelligence solutions. | 650-678-4666 | NA | Danville |
| Naehas Inc (HQ) | Specializes in the automation of sales and marketing services. The company offers services to finance and insurance companies. | 877-262-3427 | NA | Palo Alto |
| Natero (HQ) | Developer of data science techniques for the analysis and prediction of human behavior. The company is also engaged in honing marketing skills. | 650-727-0770 | NA | San Mateo |
| Natural Logic (HQ) | Provider of consulting, product development, e-learning, digital content, and product support services. | 510-248-4940 | NA | Berkeley |
| Nehanet Corp (HQ) | Provider of corporate responsibility management and sales and operation planning solutions to semiconductor and electronics component manufacturers. | 888-552-4470 | NA | Santa Clara |
| Neo Technology Inc (HQ) | Developer of enterprise applications. The company focuses on technical support and related services. | 855-636-4532 | NA | San Mateo |
| Neospeech Inc (HQ) | Provider of text-to-speech software and applications for the mobile, enterprise, entertainment, and education markets. | 408-914-2710 | NA | Santa Clara |

| COMPANY NAME | PRODUCT / SERVICE | PHONE | EMP | CITY |
|---|---|---|---|---|
| Net4site Llc (HQ) | Provider of SAP solutions. The company serves customers in the enterprise mobility, business intelligence, and ERP arenas. | 408-427-3004 | NA | Santa Clara |
| NetApp Inc (HQ) | Provider of virtualization, mobile information management, and cloud storage solutions. The company serves the business sector. | 408-822-6000 | NA | Sunnyvale |
| Netformx Inc (HQ) | Designer and builder of solutions for the networking and service providers. The company specializes in desktop and cloud applications. | 408-423-6600 | NA | San Jose |
| Netpulse Inc (HQ) | Provider of custom branded mobile apps. The company also offers technical support services to its customers. | 877-638-7857 | NA | San Francisco |
| Netronome (HQ) | Provider of flow processing, server virtualization, cyber security, and software-defined networking solutions. | 408-496-0022 | NA | Santa Clara |
| Netscout (BR) | Developer of service assurance and applications, service delivery management, network performance management software, and hardware solutions. | 408-571-5000 | NA | San Jose |
| Netskope Inc (HQ) | Provider of cloud security brokering services. The company offers services to the healthcare sector. | 800-979-6988 | NA | Los Altos |
| Network Design Associates Inc (HQ) | Provider of engineering services for computer systems. The company's services include network design, implementation, support, and maintenance. | 916-853-1632 | 1-10 | Citrus Heights |
| Netxperts Inc (HQ) | Provider of unified communication solutions. The company offers services to the healthcare and transportation markets. | 925-806-0800 | NA | Walnut Creek |
| Neudesic LLC (BR) | Provider of technology services. The company focuses on social software, integration platform, and CRM solutions and offers cloud computing services. | 303-248-8300 | 11-50 | Irvine |
| Nevtec Inc (HQ) | Provider of networks implementation and maintenance services. The company also focuses on workstations and the internet. | 408-292-8600 | NA | San Jose |
| New Tech Solutions Inc (HQ) | Provider of technology solutions. The company caters to networking, security, and communication manufacturers. | 510-353-4070 | NA | Fremont |
| Nexb Inc (HQ) | Designer and developer of software tools and services. The company offers services to business enterprises and related organizations. | 650-592-2096 | NA | San Carlos |
| Nextbus Inc (BR) | Provider of transit management solutions. The company also provides real-time passenger information solutions to organizations. | 925-686-8200 | NA | Concord |
| Nextier Networks Inc (HQ) | Provider of data security services and solutions for vertical markets and original equipment manufacturers. | 408-282-3561 | NA | Santa Clara |
| NextLabs Inc (HQ) | Developer of software products. The company offers information risk management software products for enterprises. | 650-577-9101 | NA | San Mateo |
| Nextrials Inc (HQ) | Provider of e-clinical and electronic health record tools. The company is engaged in clinical research and related services. | 925-355-3000 | NA | San Ramon |
| Nexusguard Ltd (RH) | Provider of monitoring and DNA protection services. The company serves service providers and the entertainment sector. | 415-299-8550 | NA | San Francisco |
| Nice Touch Solutions Inc (HQ) | Developer of software for the heavy highway construction industry. The company focuses on products for generating extra work bills. | 925-385-8321 | NA | Alamo |
| Nimbus Design (HQ) | Provider of design services. The company specializes in website design, content management, and e-commerce tools. | 650-365-7568 | NA | Redwood City |
| Nok Nok Labs Inc (HQ) | Focuses on the development on online security solutions. The company is also involved in third party research services. | 650-433-1300 | NA | Palo Alto |
| Nokia Corp (BR) | Specializes in mobile network infrastructure structure and services. The company is engaged in technology development. | 408-737-0900 | NA | Sunnyvale |
| Nuance Communications Inc (BR) | Provider of hosted application systems and mobile solutions. The company offers services to businesses and the healthcare sector. | 408-992-6100 | NA | Sunnyvale |
| Nuvel Holdings Inc (HQ) | Provider of data acceleration solutions. The company focuses on data transfers and related communication services. | 408-884-8069 | NA | Los Gatos |
| Oea International Inc (HQ) | Developer of signal integrity software. The company serves the electronic design automation industry. | 408-778-6747 | NA | Morgan Hill |
| One Touch Systems (HQ) | Provider of virtual distance learning, training and communication systems. The company offers services to the educational sector. | 408-660-8435 | NA | San Jose |
| OneLogin (HQ) | Provider of single sign-on and identity management for cloud-based applications. The company serves the industrial sector. | 415-645-6830 | NA | San Francisco |
| Onfulfillment Inc (HQ) | Provider of printing solutions. The company offers order fulfillment, online delivery, and print management services. | 510-793-3009 | NA | Newark |
| Openclovis (HQ) | Provider of system infrastructure software platform. The company mainly serves the communication industry. | 707-981-7120 | NA | Petaluma |
| Opengov Inc (HQ) | Provider of financial transparency and business intelligence solutions. The company offers services to government agencies. | 650-336-7167 | NA | Redwood City |
| OpensourceCM (HQ) | Designer and developer of contract management software. The company also offers technical support services. | 650-200-0506 | NA | Foster City |
| Opsol Integrators Inc (HQ) | Provider of universal messaging, data integration, and encryption products. The company serves banks, retail, telecom, and other sectors. | 408-364-9915 | NA | Campbell |
| Optumsoft Inc (HQ) | Provider of distributed computing and technology based software development that includes maintenance of structured software systems. | 844-361-8222 | NA | Menlo Park |

N

| COMPANY NAME | PRODUCT / SERVICE | PHONE | EMP | CITY |
|---|---|---|---|---|
| Oracle Corp (BR) | Developer of hardware and software systems. The company provides Oracle database, engineered systems, and enterprise manager solutions. | 415-402-7200 | NA | San Francisco |
| Orbeon Inc (HQ) | Provider of web form deployment services. The company offers basic, gold, and platinum development support, and validation services. | 650-762-8184 | NA | San Mateo |
| Outformations Inc (HQ) | Provider of consulting, application development, programming, technical support, and design services. | 510-655-7122 | NA | Oakland |
| Overland Storage Inc (BR) | Provider of data management and protection solutions. The company offers network attached storage, virtual tape libraries, LTO drives, and software. | 408-283-4700 | NA | San Jose |
| PanTerra Networks Inc (HQ) | Provider of cloud-based communications software solutions. The company is engaged in unified communication and technical support. | 800-805-0558 | NA | Santa Clara |
| Paradromics Inc (HQ) | Developer of next generation brain-machine interfaces. The company specializes in CMOS sensor technology with microwire bundles. | 408-280-0500 | NA | San Jose |
| Parametric Technology Corp (BR) | Provider of product life cycle management solutions to the aerospace, defense, automotive, consumer, and medical device industries. | | NA | San Francisco |
| Park Computer Systems Inc (HQ) | Provider of mobile products and services. The company also offers sales content automation and staff augmentation services. | 510-353-1700 | NA | Newark |
| Perforce Software Inc (BR) | Developer of software management tools and technology solutions. The company serves game development, banking, healthcare, and other sectors. | 510-864-7400 | NA | Alameda |
| Persistent Systems Inc (BR) | Developer of software & technology products for life science, banking, and other sectors. The company offers big data, security, and cloud solutions. | 408-216-7010 | NA | Santa Clara |
| Pictron Inc (HQ) | Provider of solutions for media applications in corporate communications, eLearning, broadcast production, and content based video search fields. | 408-725-8888 | NA | Sunnyvale |
| Pivotal Labs (HQ) | Focuses on software development and related services. The company serves start-ups and Fortune 1000 companies. | 415-777-4868 | NA | San Francisco |
| Pixami Inc (HQ) | Provider of imaging technologies. The company caters to both photo-based and non-photo-based businesses. | 925-465-5167 | NA | Pleasanton |
| Planeteria Media (HQ) | Designer and developer of websites, applications, e-commerce, content management systems, video, and offers flash, and internet marketing services. | 707-843-3773 | NA | Santa Rosa |
| Powertest Inc (HQ) | Provider of software-related professional services. The company is also involved in load testing and application performance management. | 415-778-0580 | NA | S San Francisco |
| Primarylo (HQ) | Provider of business analytics and transaction processing solutions. The company offers storage acceleration data services for business applications. | 415-601-0061 | NA | San Carlos |
| ProcessWeaver Inc (BR) | Developer of multi-carrier shipping software and a provider of shipping solutions. The company also offers inbound and desktop shipping solutions. | 888-932-8373 | NA | Santa Clara |
| Progent Corporation (HQ) | Provider of online technical support for small networks, and specializes in remote diagnosis, repair, and consulting services. | 408-240-9400 | NA | San Jose |
| Project Partners Llc (HQ) | Provider of business solutions and information technology systems. The company offers NetSuite, Oracle Fusion Applications, and Primavera. | 650-712-6200 | NA | Half Moon Bay |
| Prolific Minds Inc (HQ) | Provider of software solutions. The company develops software architecture, and offers analysis, technical design, and development services. | 408-777-1211 | NA | Cupertino |
| Proofpoint (RH) | Manufacturer of threat, email, social media, and information protection products. The company offers security and compliance solutions. | 408-517-4710 | NA | Sunnyvale |
| Proplus Design Solutions Inc (HQ) | Provider of electronic design automation solutions. The company's products include NoisePro, NanoSpice, and NanoYield. | 408-459-6128 | NA | San Jose |
| Proxio Inc (HQ) | Provider of digital real estate marketing solutions for agents, brokers and developers. The company serves businesses. | 415-723-1691 | NA | Santa Clara |
| Pulse Secure LLC (HQ) | Provider of product, hardware, partner, and enterprise solutions. The company offers services to the financial services and healthcare industries. | 408-372-9600 | NA | San Jose |
| Q Analysts Llc (HQ) | Provider of consulting, strategic advisory, and related compliance services. The company is also involved in mobile testing. | 408-907-8500 | NA | San Jose |
| Quadbase Systems Inc (HQ) | Designer of web-delivered and mobile enabled business intelligence reporting, charting, and dashboard tools. | 408-982-0835 | NA | Santa Clara |
| Quanergy Systems Inc (HQ) | Developer of smart sensing solutions. The company offers solutions for real-time 3D mapping, object detection, and tracking. | 408-245-9500 | NA | Sunnyvale |
| Quantum Corporation (HQ) | Provider of software for backup, recovery, and archiving needs. The company serves the healthcare, media, and entertainment industries. | 408-944-4000 | NA | San Jose |
| Qubell Inc (HQ) | Specializes in autonomic management solutions. The company focuses on e-commerce and other cloud applications. | 888-855-9440 | NA | Menlo Park |
| Quesgen Systems Inc (HQ) | Provider of data management solutions. The company is involved in clinical research and related support services. | 415-738-8452 | NA | Burlingame |
| Quest Business Systems Inc (HQ) | Provider of solutions in police equipment tracking systems. The company also focuses on purchasing management. | 925-634-2670 | NA | Brentwood |

| COMPANY NAME | PRODUCT / SERVICE | PHONE | EMP | CITY |
|---|---|---|---|---|
| Quest Inc (HQ) | Provider of technology and infrastructure management services. The company caters to a wide range of businesses. | 800-326-4220 | 1-10 | Roseville |
| Quiq Labs (HQ) | Developer of tools and solutions. The company focuses on influencing consumer behavior and engagement. | 559-745-5511 | 1-10 | Fresno |
| Quisk Inc (HQ) | Specializes in the development of payment solutions. The company offers services to financial institutions. | 408-462-6800 | NA | Sunnyvale |
| Qumu Inc (BR) | Provider of web casting, marketing, event, and other professional services. The company offers enterprise video solutions. | 650-396-8530 | NA | San Bruno |
| Quorum Technologies (HQ) | Developer of recycling and waste disposal solutions for the automotive, industrial, municipal, hospitality, and food industries. | 916-669-5577 | 1-10 | Sacramento |
| R&D Logic Inc (HQ) | Developer of performance management software for R&D focused companies. The company offers implementation and training services. | 650-356-9207 | NA | San Mateo |
| RackWare Inc (HQ) | Provider of disaster prevention and recovery solutions. The company also offers business continuity and virtualization solutions. | 408-430-5821 | NA | San Jose |
| Radiant Logic Inc (HQ) | Provider of identity and context virtualization solutions. The company caters to identity integration and management needs. | 415-209-6800 | NA | Novato |
| Reach Analytics Llc (HQ) | Provider of hosted training solutions. The company serves the healthcare, retail, and insurance industries. | 650-948-4993 | NA | Redwood City |
| Readytech Corp (HQ) | Provider of virtual labs for training, certification, and also sales demonstrations. The company deals with technology support. | 800-707-1009 | NA | Oakland |
| Real-Time Innovations Inc (HQ) | Provider for real-time infrastructure software solutions. The company also offers engineering and product development services. | 408-990-7400 | NA | Sunnyvale |
| Redis Labs Inc (HQ) | Provider of zero management, infinite scalability, and other solutions for start-ups and business enterprises. | 415-930-9666 | NA | Mountain View |
| Redline Solutions Inc (HQ) | Provider of produce traceability and bar code solutions, and warehouse and inventory management systems. | 408-562-1700 | NA | Santa Clara |
| Reflektion Inc (HQ) | Focuses on personalized site search, marketing, analytics, and predictive product recommendation solutions. | 650-293-0800 | NA | San Mateo |
| Refresh Your Memory Inc (HQ) | Provider of CNC Machine Tool monitoring and data collection products. The company is also involved in preventive maintenance services. | 408-224-9167 | NA | San Jose |
| Relay2 Inc (HQ) | Provider of cloud Wi-Fi Services platform which allows service providers to monetize value added Wi-Fi services. | 408-380-0031 | NA | Milpitas |
| Resilinc Corp (HQ) | Provider of supply chain and risk management solutions. The company serves the life science and automotive industries. | 408-883-8053 | NA | Milpitas |
| Retail Pro International (HQ) | Provider of software solutions. The company's services include automated retail planning and content strategy. | 916-605-7200 | 1-10 | Folsom |
| RetailNext (HQ) | Provider of in-store analytics solutions. The company offers services to retail labs, marketing departments, and shopping centers. | 408-884-2162 | NA | San Jose |
| Revel Systems Inc (BR) | Provider of POS systems and related services. The company serves customers in the accounting, security, reporting, and other industries. | 415-744-1433 | NA | San Francisco |
| RightITnow (HQ) | Provider of information technology operations management software. The company offers services to government agencies and business organizations. | 415-350-3581 | NA | San Francisco |
| River Rock Software Inc (BR) | Developer of software tools such as graphical user interfaces, client server applications, spool file viewers, and report formatters. | 916-797-6746 | 11-50 | Granite Bay |
| Rocket Communications Inc (HQ) | Developer of user interface, visual, and icon design services for software and related applications. | 415-863-0101 | NA | San Francisco |
| Rockyou Inc (HQ) | Provider of gaming solutions. The company's games include Poker, Bingo, Zoo World, and others and serves the entertainment sector. | 415-580-6400 | NA | San Francisco |
| Rollbar Inc (HQ) | Developer of error tracking software. The company is also engaged in coding and troubleshooting services. | 888-568-3350 | NA | San Francisco |
| RS Software Inc (BR) | Provider of business payment solutions for the risk prediction, residual management, payment gateway, and merchant boarding areas. | 408-382-1200 | NA | Milpitas |
| Runscope Inc (HQ) | Specializes in automated performance monitoring and testing solutions. The company serves developers. | 888-812-6786 | NA | San Francisco |
| Runtime Design Automation (HQ) | Provider of management system software for the IC design industry. The company is engaged in documentation and technical support. | 408-492-0940 | NA | Santa Clara |
| S2c Inc (HQ) | Provider of prototyping solutions. The company's customers include chip design and system design companies. | 408-213-8818 | NA | San Jose |
| Sainergy Inc (HQ) | Provider of SAP consulting services such as business intelligence to clients in the technical and functional areas. | 408-532-9800 | NA | Campbell |
| Selectiva Systems Inc (HQ) | Provider of solutions for revenue reporting, customer service, and distributor management. The company serves hi-tech, pharma, and other sectors. | 408-297-1336 | NA | San Jose |
| Sentient Energy Inc (HQ) | Provider of sensor devices for operational practices and engineering applications. The company also offers communication software. | 650-523-6680 | NA | Burlingame |
| SentinelOne (HQ) | Developer of end-point protection software. The company serves the healthcare, oil and gas, and financial services industries. | 855-868-3733 | NA | Mountain View |
| Sercomm Usa Inc (BR) | Provider of software and firmware for the development of broadband networking. The company also offers solutions for fixed mobile convergence. | 510-870-1598 | NA | Fremont |

| COMPANY NAME | PRODUCT / SERVICE | PHONE | EMP | CITY |
|---|---|---|---|---|
| Servicesource International Inc (HQ) | Provider of recurring revenue management solutions. The company focuses on process automation and managed services. | 720-889-8500 | NA | San Francisco |
| Shape Security (HQ) | Provider of defense solutions against malicious automated cyber-attacks on web and mobile applications. | 650-399-0400 | NA | Santra Clara |
| Sharper Technology Inc (HQ) | Provider of network security solutions and services. The company also offers design, implementation, and training services. | 650-964-4600 | NA | Palo Alto |
| Sierra Data Systems (HQ) | Provider of data communication systems, internet related services, miscellaneous communications equipment, telephone, and voice equipment. | 916-242-4604 | 1-10 | Grass Valley |
| Silicon Laboratories (BR) | Provider of silicon, software, and system solutions. The company focuses on internet infrastructure, industrial control, and consumer markets. | 408-702-1400 | NA | San Jose |
| Silicon Publishing Inc (HQ) | Provider of digital publishing solutions. The company deals with template designs and personalized communications. | 925-935-3899 | NA | San Francisco |
| Silvaco Inc (HQ) | Supplier of TCAD and EDA software for circuit simulation. The company also designs analog, mixed-signal, and RF integrated circuits. | 408-567-1000 | NA | Santa Clara |
| Silver Peak Systems Inc (HQ) | Provider of miscellaneous communication equipment & services. The company focuses on WAN optimization, cloud networking, and replication acceleration. | 408-935-1800 | NA | Santa Clara |
| Simplion Technologies (HQ) | Provider of consulting solutions. The company offers strategy development, implementation, deployment, and technical support services. | 408-935-8686 | NA | Milpitas |
| Single Point Of Contact (HQ) | Provider of IT management, enterprise, and planning services. The company is also engaged in cloud computing, web hosting, and hosted exchange. | 800-791-4300 | NA | Palo Alto |
| Sitepen Inc (HQ) | Developer and provider of software products and services. The company also offers web application development and java support services. | 650-968-8787 | NA | Palo Alto |
| Skyhigh Networks Inc (RH) | Developer of cloud security software. The company is engaged in compliance, threat protection, and data security services. | 866-727-8383 | NA | Campbell |
| SL Corp (HQ) | Provider of monitoring and analytics solutions for middleware-powered applications. The company serves the electrical commodity market. | 415-927-8400 | NA | Corte Madera |
| Smart ERP Solutions Inc (HQ) | Developer of enterprise class software. The company provides vendor management software and support services. | 925-271-0200 | NA | Pleasanton |
| Softjourn Inc (HQ) | Provider of outsource software development services and focuses on offshore assessments, application development, and quality assurance testing. | 510-744-1528 | NA | Fremont |
| Softnet Solutions Inc (HQ) | Provider of enterprise solutions for high performance computing and network security. The company specializes in IT consulting and cloud services. | 408-542-0888 | NA | Sunnyvale |
| Softsol Inc (HQ) | Provider of software solutions. The company offers software such as Intellicourt Case Management, Corporate Investigations, STIC, and PB Migration. | 510-824-2000 | NA | Fremont |
| Software Illustrated (HQ) | Developer of spreadsheet mapping software capable of working inside Microsoft Excel. It's product serves sales, marketing, and business data needs. | | NA | Danville |
| Solarius Development Inc (HQ) | Manufacturer of 3D metrology surface measurement systems. The company offers metrology services for surface form. | 408-435-2777 | NA | San Jose |
| Sonasoft Corp (HQ) | Provider of software based solutions to simplify and automate replication, archiving, backup, recovery, and data protection operations. | 408-708-4000 | NA | San Jose |
| SoundHound Inc (HQ) | Developer of a sound and speech responsive search engine. The company's product finds application in mobile and communication devices. | 408-441-3200 | NA | Santa Clara |
| Space-Time Insight Inc (HQ) | Developer of geospatial and information visualization software. The company also offers visual analytics solutions. | 650-513-8550 | NA | San Mateo |
| Spiralinks Corporation (HQ) | Provider of compensation management software products. The company offers compensation management, HR analytics, and payroll integration services. | 408-608-6900 | NA | Campbell |
| Stopware Inc (HQ) | Developer of visitor management security software. The company offers hardware, badge stock, and training services. | 408-367-0220 | NA | Pleasanton |
| Stratogent Corp (HQ) | Provider of hosting and critical software systems operations. The company is engaged in design and programming solutions. | 650-577-2332 | NA | San Mateo |
| Stratovan Corp (HQ) | Developer of visual analysis software. It's product finds application in 3D imaging and surgical planning research. | 530-746-7970 | 1-10 | Davis |
| StrongKey (HQ) | Provider of enterprise key management solutions. The company serves the cloud computing, e-commerce, healthcare, finance, and other sectors. | 408-331-2000 | NA | Cupertino |
| Subrosasoft.Com Inc (HQ) | Developer of software for Mac operating systems. The company offers software such as FileSalvage, CopyCat, and ParentRemote. | 510-870-7883 | NA | Fremont |
| Sumo Logic (RH) | Provider of compliance, security, monitoring, troubleshooting, and delivery solutions. The company serves security, IT, and development teams. | 650-810-8700 | NA | Redwood City |
| Switchfly (HQ) | Provider of software solutions such as travel commerce platforms, payments engines, mobile platforms, and social media solutions. | 415-541-9100 | NA | San Francisco |
| Symantec Corp (HQ) | Developer of storage management and disaster recovery software. The company is engaged in consulting, archiving, and clustering. | 650-527-8000 | NA | Mountain View |

| COMPANY NAME | PRODUCT / SERVICE | PHONE | EMP | CITY |
|---|---|---|---|---|
| Synack (HQ) | Provider of security intelligence solutions. The company offers services to the commercial, industrial, and business sectors. | 855-796-2251 | NA | Redwood City |
| Synapse Design (HQ) | Provider of embedded software design services. The company also offers test bench analysis and block and chip level verification services. | 408-850-3640 | NA | Santa Clara |
| Synopsys Corporate (HQ) | Developer of synthesis technology solutions. The company is also involved in design flow deployment, physical design assistance, and related services. | 650-584-5000 | NA | Mountain View |
| Syntest Technologies Inc (HQ) | Provider of test solutions for the electronics industry. The company is involved in fault simulation solutions and services. | 408-720-9956 | NA | San Jose |
| Tamalpais Group Inc (HQ) | Provider of information technology solutions. The company offers data-centric delivery, infrastructure assessment, and IT performance services. | 415-455-5770 | NA | San Anselmo |
| Tapjoy Inc (HQ) | Provider of advertising and targeting solutions. The company also deals with developer services such as consulting and real-time reporting. | 415-766-6900 | NA | San Francisco |
| Taseon Inc (HQ) | Developer of technology related solutions. The company also offers system engineering and software development services. | 408-240-7800 | NA | San Jose |
| Teamf1 Inc (HQ) | Provider of networking and security software for embedded devices. The company also offers technical support services. | 510-505-9931 | NA | Fremont |
| Teleresults Corp (HQ) | Provider of electronic medical record solutions and transplant software. The company's services include data conversion, interfaces, and training. | 415-392-9670 | NA | San Francisco |
| Telosa Software Inc (HQ) | Provider of CRM and fundraising software for nonprofits. The company focuses on gift and grant tracking, donor and volunteer management. | 800-750-6418 | NA | Palo Alto |
| Tg Service Inc (HQ) | Producer of multimedia and internet solutions. The company engages in microarray analysis on machines. | 510-243-9931 | NA | El Sobrante |
| The Armada Group Inc (HQ) | Provider of information technology and talent consultation services. The company specializes in software engineering and project management. | 800-408-2120 | 11-50 | Santa Cruz |
| Thought Inc (HQ) | Provider of data management solutions. The company uses dynamic mapping and related software for this purpose. | 415-836-9199 | NA | San Francisco |
| ThreatMetrix (HQ) | Provider of fraud prevention, threat detection, and authentication solutions. The company serves the gaming, media, and insurance industries. | 408-200-5755 | NA | San Jose |
| Trion Worlds Inc (HQ) | Publisher and developer of games. The company offers Defiance, RIFT, Archeage, and End of Nations games. | 650-273-9618 | NA | Redwood City |
| Trofholz Technologies Inc (HQ) | Developer of IT information and security systems. The company also specializes in communication solutions. | 916-577-1903 | 11-50 | Rocklin |
| Turbo-Doc Medical Record Systems Inc (HQ) | Provider of electronic medical record systems. The company offers walk-out statements, drug information handouts, and medication rewrites. | 530-877-8650 | 1-10 | Paradise |
| Twilio Inc (HQ) | Provider of infrastructure APIs for businesses to build scalable, reliable voice, and text messaging apps. | 415-390-2337 | NA | San Francisco |
| Ultra-X Inc (HQ) | Provider of personal computer diagnostic solutions for developers, manufacturers, system engineers, integrators, and computer professionals. | 408-261-7090 | NA | Santa Clara |
| Unigen Corp (HQ) | Manufacturer and designer of custom enterprise-grade flash storage and DRAM and ARMOUR product applications serving the telecommunications industry. | 510-896-1818 | NA | Newark |
| Unisoft Corp (HQ) | Provider of broadcast, development, and testing tools specific to interactive TV standards. The company focuses on US cable and broadcast industries. | 650-259-1290 | NA | Millbrae |
| Untangle (HQ) | Designer and developer of network management software. The company specializes in firewall and Internet management application. | 408-598-4299 | NA | San Jose |
| UpGuard Inc (HQ) | Provider of integrity monitoring, vulnerability analysis, vendor risk assessment, and configuration differencing solutions. | 888-882-3223 | NA | Mountain View |
| USWired Inc (HQ) | Provider of computer networking solutions that include cloud hosting, network design and installation, and wireless networks. | 408-669-3522 | NA | San Jose |
| Valiantica Inc (HQ) | Provider of global IT solutions. The company's services include consulting, outsourcing, and mobile, enterprise and business application development. | 408-725-2426 | NA | San Jose |
| Vantage Data Center Services & Solutions (HQ) | Provider of transformers, switches, generators, chillers, switch gears and security, and communication products. | 855-878-2682 | NA | Santa Clara |
| Varite Inc (HQ) | Provider of custom software development, integration, deployment, and implementation services in the domains of core networking and virtualization. | 408-977-0700 | NA | San Jose |
| vArmour Inc (HQ) | Provider of cloud security, segmentation, monitoring, and deception solutions. The company serves banks and healthcare organizations. | 650-564-5100 | NA | Los Altos |
| Vayusphere Inc (HQ) | Developer of instant messaging applications. The company's customers include Morgan Stanley, Deutsche Bank, and others. | 650-960-2900 | NA | Mountain View |
| Veeva Systems (HQ) | Provider of cloud-based business solutions such as customer relationship management and content management for the life sciences industry. | 925-452-6500 | NA | Pleasanton |
| Veracentra (HQ) | Provider of data leveraging services to brands for marketing needs and also focuses on customer intelligence, marketing execution, and consultation. | 707-224-6161 | NA | Napa |

| COMPANY NAME | PRODUCT / SERVICE | PHONE | EMP | CITY |
|---|---|---|---|---|
| Verient Inc (HQ) | Provider of cloud based financial products. The company's offerings convert non revenue producing payments to credit card transactions. | 408-521-1660 | NA | San Jose |
| VinSuite (HQ) | Developer of wine software and serves the consumer sector. The company offers support services to wineries and tasting rooms. | 707-253-7400 | NA | Napa |
| Vintara Inc (HQ) | Provider of web-based enterprise process management solutions and services. The company caters to a number of industries. | 877-846-8272 | NA | Oakland |
| Viscira Llc (HQ) | Manufacturer of software products. The company deals with the development of animation technology solutions. | 415-848-8010 | NA | San Francisco |
| Vistrian Inc (HQ) | Developer of software products. The company's services include escalation management, problem isolation, and remote access. | 408-719-0500 | NA | Milpitas |
| VMware Inc (HQ) | Provider of storage, data center, application virtualization, and enterprise mobility management products. | 650-427-1000 | NA | Palo Alto |
| Watchwith Inc (HQ) | Provider of software and data solutions for the film and television content creators and consumer electronics manufacturers. | 415-552-1552 | NA | San Francisco |
| Whitehat Security (HQ) | Provider of web application security solutions such as vulnerability management, threat modeling, and risk profiling. | 408-343-8300 | NA | San Jose |
| Whizz Systems (HQ) | Provider of electronics design and manufacturing services for the semiconductor, defense, computing, and industrial equipment markets. | 408-980-0400 | NA | Santa Clara |
| Willow Garage Inc (HQ) | Developer of hardware and open source software for personal robotics applications. The company also offers robot design and machine learning services. | 650-475-2700 | NA | Menlo Park |
| Wind River (DH) | Provider of automotive networking solutions. The company's products include operating systems, development tools, and middleware technologies. | 510-748-4100 | NA | Alameda |
| Winedirect (HQ) | Provider of DTC services such as commerce, compliance, fulfillment, marketing, and enterprise services for wineries. | 800-819-0325 | NA | American Canyon |
| Wipro Technologies (BR) | Provider of analytics and information management, business process outsourcing, consulting, and managed and cloud services. | 650-316-3555 | NA | Mountain View |
| Xmatters Inc (HQ) | Provider of voice and text alerting system software. The company serves the healthcare, telecommunications, and manufacturing industries. | 925-226-0300 | NA | San Ramon |
| Xoriant Corp (HQ) | Provider of enterprise applications. The company also offers mobile analytics and web application development services. | 408-743-4400 | NA | Sunnyvale |
| Yola Inc (HQ) | Provider of digital marketing services. The company offers mobile, facebook, and web publishing, domain names, and reliable hosting services. | 866-764-0701 | NA | San Francisco |
| Zapty Inc (HQ) | Manufacturer of project monitoring tools. The company is engaged in design services and it serves the business sector. | 415-830-4595 | NA | San Francisco |
| Zl Technologies (HQ) | Provider of electronic content archiving software solutions such as consulting and installation, product customization, and software upgrades. | 408-240-8989 | NA | Milpitas |
| Zscaler Inc (HQ) | Provider of SaaS security solutions. The company offers cloud security solutions for mobile enterprises. | 408-533-0288 | NA | San Jose |

## 327 = Programming Services

| COMPANY NAME | PRODUCT / SERVICE | PHONE | EMP | CITY |
|---|---|---|---|---|
| 4d Inc (DH) | Developer of web and internet applications. The company serves universities, corporations, governments, and individuals. | 408-557-4600 | NA | San Jose |
| Acrylic Art (HQ) | Provider of fabrication and machining services. The company focuses on painting, product finishing, anodizing, and vapor polishing. | 510-654-0953 | NA | Emeryville |
| Advanced Laser & Waterjet Cutting Inc (HQ) | Provider of precision cutting services for all types of materials. The company's services include electronic shielding, fabrivision, and overnight shipping. | 408-486-0700 | NA | Santa Clara |
| Agrian Inc (HQ) | Provider of agridata tracking and information sharing system for applicator, retail outlets, grower, and crop consultant via computer and mobile devices. | 559-437-5700 | 1-10 | Fresno |
| Alchemic Solutions Group Inc (HQ) | Provider of technology marketing solutions for wireless sectors. The company focuses on product management, software development, and consultation. | 510-919-8105 | NA | San Mateo |
| Alertenterprise Inc (HQ) | Developer of information and operational technology solutions such as identity intelligence, and enterprise access, and incident management. | 510-440-0840 | NA | Fremont |
| Alpha Research & Technology Inc (HQ) | Designer and manufacturer of airborne systems for command, communications, intelligence, surveillance, and other needs and focuses on installation. | 916-431-9340 | 1-10 | El Dorado Hills |
| American International Group Inc (RH) | Provider of international insurance solutions and financial services. The company serves individuals, group, and businesses. | 415-836-2700 | NA | San Francisco |
| Andover Consulting Group Inc (HQ) | Supplier of network components. The company offers data center liquidation, network security, and network equipment services. | 415-537-6950 | NA | S San Francisco |
| Ansys Inc (BR) | Provider of engineering solutions. The company serves the aerospace, defense, and construction industries. | 844-462-6797 | NA | Berkeley |
| Applied Simulation Technology Inc (HQ) | Developer of stimulators and molders in signal integrity, power integrity, and circuit simulation tools. | 408-436-9070 | NA | San Jose |
| Beachhead Solutions Inc (HQ) | Provider of web-based console to enforce encryption, manage security, and give providers the ability to change policy on iPhones and android devices. | 408-496-6936 | NA | San Jose |

| COMPANY NAME | PRODUCT / SERVICE | PHONE | EMP | CITY |
|---|---|---|---|---|
| Blue Chip Tek Inc (HQ) | Provider of data management and protection, information life cycle management, networking, security, and data center solutions. | 408-731-7700 | NA | Santa Clara |
| Boardwalktech Inc (HQ) | Provider of enterprise collaboration software specializing in tax planning, cash management, and revenue forecasting solutions. | 650-618-6200 | NA | Cupertino |
| Bugcrowd (HQ) | Provider of security solutions. The company is engaged in pre-launch consulting, research, and testing services. | 888-361-9734 | NA | San Francisco |
| Busse Design Usa Inc (HQ) | Provider of interface design services. The company's services include website design and application user interface. | 415-689-8090 | NA | Oakland |
| Carbon Five Inc (HQ) | Provider of software development services such as lean design and agile development for the web and mobile sectors. | 415-546-0500 | NA | San Francisco |
| Casahl Technology Inc (HQ) | Provider of collaboration and content environment optimization services. The company focuses on cloud integration and content management. | 925-328-2828 | NA | San Ramon |
| Clustrix Inc (HQ) | Provider of a SQL database with no limits to database size, table size, query complexity, and performance. | 415-501-9560 | NA | San Francisco |
| Cognizant Technology Solutions (BR) | Provider of business consulting, enterprise application development, IT infrastructure, and outsourcing services. | 925-790-2000 | NA | San Ramon |
| Connected Marketing (HQ) | Provider of marketing services. The company also offers web development, branding, and lead generation services. | 408-647-2198 | NA | San Jose |
| Contrast Security (HQ) | Designer and developer of self-protection software. The company is also engaged in operations support services. | 888-371-1333 | NA | Los Altos |
| Csrware Inc (HQ) | Developer of sustainability resource management software. The company specializes in supply chain, enterprise ERP solutions, and consulting services. | 855-277-9273 | NA | Mill Valley |
| Dogpatch Technology Inc (HQ) | Provider of digital strategy and mobile development solutions for game design and research, global media and communications, and grant writing projects. | 415-663-6488 | NA | San Francisco |
| Dynaweb Inc (HQ) | Manufacturer and marketer of web handling and tension control systems. The company's product finds use in packaging, printing, and textile needs. | 925-373-9013 | 1-10 | Sonora |
| Egnyte Inc (HQ) | Provider of online storage, cloud computing, and file sharing services. The company serves the financial, banking, and pharmaceutical industries. | 650-968-4018 | NA | Mountain View |
| Eonite Perception Inc (HQ) | Focuses on building 3D mapping and ego-tracking systems. The company serves the entertainment, robotics, and construction industries. | 650-681-9257 | NA | Los Altos |
| Epylon Corp (HQ) | Developer of e-procurement software and services. The company serves the government and education sectors. | 925-407-1020 | NA | Danville |
| Exxact Corp (HQ) | Supplier of workstation graphic cards and solutions. The company also offers servers, HPC clusters, and computing software. | 510-226-7366 | NA | Fremont |
| Fidus Systems Inc (BR) | Specializes in electronic product development and consulting services. The company also deals with hardware design. | 408-217-1928 | NA | Fremont |
| Icube Information International (HQ) | Publisher of software work flow based management systems, documentation, inventory processing, and revision tracking services. | 510-683-8928 | NA | Fremont |
| Inabyte Inc (HQ) | Manufacturer of developer tools. The company also offers solutions and services for developers and end users of PCs or workstations. | 415-898-7905 | NA | Novato |
| Issio Solutions Inc (HQ) | Provider of workforce management software for surgical facilities. The company also serves ambulatory surgical centers. | 888-994-7746 | NA | Concord |
| It Pro Source (HQ) | Provider of on call plans, managed services, web based monitoring, and communication cabling services. | 925-455-7701 | NA | Livermore |
| N JAMIS Software Corp (HQ) | Provider of job-cost, billing, and accounting systems and solutions. The company caters to the government contractors. | 800-655-2647 | 11-50 | San Diego |
| Lytrod Software Inc (HQ) | Provider of variable data print software products. The company's products include VisionDP Production and Automate, Proform Designer, and Office Designer. | 707-422-9221 | NA | Fairfield |
| Medallia Inc (HQ) | Provider of consulting, system configuration, user training, and data warehouse integration services. | 650-321-3000 | NA | Palo Alto |
| Metaswitch Networks (DH) | Provider of service management solutions. The company offers original equipment manufacturer, multimedia subsystem, and hosted business services. | 415-513-1500 | NA | Los Altos |
| Myers Network Solutions (HQ) | Provider of network solutions. The company focuses on IT consulting, disaster recovery, network assessment, and cloud computing. | 408-483-1881 | NA | San Jose |
| Nearsoft Inc (HQ) | Provider of services to grow development team in companies. The company exclusively caters to software product sectors. | 408-691-1034 | NA | San Jose |
| Nsymbio (HQ) | Provider of printing services. The company is engaged in project management, graphic design, print, and online ordering system services. | 650-968-2058 | NA | Mountain View |
| Nuvation Engineering (HQ) | Provider of electronic engineering services. The company focuses on product design, embedded software development, and single integrity analysis. | 408-228-5580 | NA | Sunnyvale |
| Opal Soft Inc (HQ) | Provider of communications equipment installation and networking. The company's services include application development, network management, and maintenance. | 408-267-2211 | NA | Sunnyvale |

| COMPANY NAME | PRODUCT / SERVICE | PHONE | EMP | CITY |
|---|---|---|---|---|
| Openclovis (HQ) | Provider of system infrastructure software platform. The company mainly serves the communication industry. | 707-981-7120 | NA | Petaluma |
| Pc Professional (HQ) | Provider of information technology solutions. The company focuses on cloud computing, application development, networking, and disaster recovery. | 510-874-5871 | NA | Oakland |
| PeerNova inc (HQ) | Provider of silicon valley-based technology such as distributed systems, networking solutions, big data, compiler technology, and financial services. | 669-400-7800 | NA | San Jose |
| Penguin Computing Inc (HQ) | Provider of Linux-based cloud and HPC solutions. The company's products include servers, network switches, and integrated rack solutions. | 415-954-2800 | NA | Fremont |
| Proxio Inc (HQ) | Provider of digital real estate marketing solutions for agents, brokers and developers. The company serves businesses. | 415-723-1691 | NA | Santa Clara |
| Qualys Inc (HQ) | Provider of security and compliance solutions. The company also offers asset discovery and threat protection solutions. | 650-801-6100 | NA | Foster City |
| Quanergy Systems Inc (HQ) | Developer of smart sensing solutions. The company offers solutions for real-time 3D mapping, object detection, and tracking. | 408-245-9500 | NA | Sunnyvale |
| Qumu Inc (BR) | Provider of web casting, marketing, event, and other professional services. The company offers enterprise video solutions. | 650-396-8530 | NA | San Bruno |
| R-Computer (HQ) | Provider of computer solutions for small and medium-sized companies. The company also offers lifetime product guarantees and sales consultation. | 925-798-4884 | NA | Concord |
| RackWare Inc (HQ) | Provider of disaster prevention and recovery solutions. The company also offers business continuity and virtualization solutions. | 408-430-5821 | NA | San Jose |
| RetailNext (HQ) | Provider of in-store analytics solutions. The company offers services to retail labs, marketing departments, and shopping centers. | 408-884-2162 | NA | San Jose |
| SACC Inc (HQ) | Provider of enterprise resource planning, data warehousing, technology infrastructure, business process outsourcing, and staffing services. | 408-755-3000 | NA | Santa Clara |
| SAP America Inc (BR) | Developer of software applications. The company provides data and technology, custom development, and implementation services. | 650-849-4000 | NA | Palo Alto |
| Servicesource International Inc (HQ) | Provider of recurring revenue management solutions. The company focuses on process automation and managed services. | 720-889-8500 | NA | San Francisco |
| Softjourn Inc (HQ) | Provider of outsource software development services and focuses on offshore assessments, application development, and quality assurance testing. | 510-744-1528 | NA | Fremont |
| Stopware Inc (HQ) | Developer of visitor management security software. The company offers hardware, badge stock, and training services. | 408-367-0220 | NA | Pleasanton |
| StrongKey (HQ) | Provider of enterprise key management solutions. The company serves the cloud computing, e-commerce, healthcare, finance, and other sectors. | 408-331-2000 | NA | Cupertino |
| Tanium Inc (HQ) | Provider of IT operations management, asset visibility, and security hygiene solutions. The company serves the healthcare and retail industries. | 510-704-0202 | NA | Emeryville |
| Tech Soft 3d (HQ) | Provider of software solutions. The company offers software for desktop visualization, modeling, cloud and mobile solutions, and data exchange. | 510-883-2180 | NA | Berkeley |
| The Armada Group Inc (HQ) | Provider of information technology and talent consultation services. The company specializes in software engineering and project management. | 800-408-2120 | 11-50 | Santa Cruz |
| Think Connected LLC (HQ) | Provider of data center, consulting, managed, and supplemental information technology services for small and medium-sized businesses. | 877-684-4654 | NA | San Francisco |
| uSens Inc (HQ) | Creator of 3D human computing interaction software and hardware solutions. The company focuses on artificial intelligence. | 408-564-0227 | NA | San Jose |
| V5 Systems (HQ) | Provider of outdoor security and computing platforms. The company offers services to the government, military, and law enforcement industries. | 844-604-7350 | NA | Fremont |
| Webvanta Inc (HQ) | Provider of hosted content management and database system services. The company is involved in website and mobile application development. | 888-670-6793 | NA | Sausalito |
| Wipro Technologies (BR) | Provider of analytics and information management, business process outsourcing, consulting, and managed and cloud services. | 650-316-3555 | NA | Mountain View |
| Workday Inc (HQ) | Provider of software solutions for human resources management and financial management. The company specializes in SaaS based enterprise solutions. | 925-951-9000 | NA | Pleasanton |

## 28 = Software Consulting & R&D

| COMPANY NAME | PRODUCT / SERVICE | PHONE | EMP | CITY |
|---|---|---|---|---|
| Accel (HQ) | Provider of investment services specializing in the mobile, retail, energy, and security industries. | 650-614-4800 | NA | Palo Alto |
| Accenture (BR) | Provider of management consulting, technology services and outsourcing services. The company serves a wide range of industries. | 408-817-2700 | NA | San Jose |
| Algo-Logic Systems (HQ) | Specializes in building networking solutions. The company also offers technological and data handling services to firms. | 408-707-3740 | NA | San Jose |
| Applied Computer Solutions (BR) | Provider of information technology solutions. The company offers solutions for virtualization, storage, security, and networking. | 925-251-1000 | NA | Pleasanton |
| Appsec Consulting (HQ) | Provider of services to identify vulnerabilities in applications. The company focuses on penetration testing and PCI compliance. | 408-224-1110 | NA | San Jose |

| COMPANY NAME | PRODUCT / SERVICE | PHONE | EMP | CITY |
|---|---|---|---|---|
| Aspera Inc (HQ) | Developer of file transport technologies. The company provides client and server software, consoles, and mobile uploaders. | 510-849-2386 | NA | Emeryville |
| Assia Inc (HQ) | Provider of broadband solution such as cloudcheck, technology licensing, DSL expresse, and expresse products and solution. | 650-654-3400 | NA | Redwood City |
| AsTech Consulting (HQ) | Provider of source code security assessment, penetration testing, continuous monitoring, and secure development lifecycle consulting services. | | NA | Larkspur |
| Beachhead Solutions Inc (HQ) | Provider of web-based console to enforce encryption, manage security, and give providers the ability to change policy on iPhones and android devices. | 408-496-6936 | NA | San Jose |
| Beyond Lucid Technologies Inc (HQ) | Developer of cloud-based software platform. The company offers services to the emergency medical, disaster management, and first response industries. | 650-648-3727 | NA | Concord |
| Blue Chip Tek Inc (HQ) | Provider of data management and protection, information life cycle management, networking, security, and data center solutions. | 408-731-7700 | NA | Santa Clara |
| Blue Harbors (HQ) | Provider of warehouse and transportation management, and shipping solutions. The company serves the industrial sector. | 415-799-7769 | NA | San Francisco |
| BuyerLeverage (HQ) | Provider of technologies and services that allow consumers and businesses to profit and control their communications and information. | 650-320-1608 | NA | Palo Alto |
| C&P Microsystems Llc (HQ) | Manufacturer and seller of paper cutter control systems. The company offers microcip, cutternet, and microfacts. | 707-776-4500 | NA | Petaluma |
| Capriza Inc (HQ) | Provider of codeless enterprise mobility platform. The company offers mobile-enabling business applications such as design, zaaps, manage, and security. | 650-600-3661 | NA | Palo Alto |
| Casahl Technology Inc (HQ) | Provider of collaboration and content environment optimization services. The company focuses on cloud integration and content management. | 925-328-2828 | NA | San Ramon |
| Certain Inc (DH) | Provider of enterprise event management solutions that include e-mail marketing, event reporting, registration, and consulting services. | 415-353-5330 | NA | San Francisco |
| Chesapeake Technology Inc (HQ) | Provider of sonar mapping software as well as consulting services to the marine, geophysical, and geological survey industries. | 650-967-2045 | NA | Los Altos |
| Clare Computer Solutions (HQ) | Provider of information technology services. The company offers computer network, software consultation, visualization, and cloud computing solutions. | 925-277-0690 | NA | San Ramon |
| Clean Power Research (HQ) | Provider of program automation, customer engagement, and solar data and intelligence solutions. The company offers services to the solar industry. | 707-258-2765 | NA | Napa |
| Crestpoint Solutions Inc (HQ) | Provider of project planning, programming, web hosting, and wireless and records management services. | 925-828-6005 | NA | Pleasanton |
| Cygna Energy Services Inc (HQ) | Provider of application development, data integration, systems integration, consulting, and web services. | 925-930-8377 | NA | Walnut Creek |
| Database Republic (HQ) | Provider of enterprise analysis and strategy modeling services. The company also focuses on DB design and implementation. | 530-692-2500 | 1-10 | Oregon House |
| Exponent Partners (HQ) | Provider of performance and outcomes management solutions. The company's services include systems integration and custom application development. | 800-918-2917 | NA | San Francisco |
| Fusionstorm (BR) | Provider of information technology services. The company specializes in IT consulting, data center, networking, and enterprise content management. | 800-228-8324 | NA | San Francisco |
| Global Software Resources (HQ) | Provider of application development, business intelligence, testing and mobile computing, and collaboration services. | 925-249-2200 | NA | Pleasanton |
| Glyphic Technology (HQ) | Provider of software design and architecture solutions. The company focuses on internet, server, desktop, mobile, and embedded systems. | 650-964-5311 | NA | Mountain View |
| Health Fidelity Inc (HQ) | Provider of natural language processing technology and inference platform to analyze vast amounts of unstructured data for clinical and financial insights. | 650-727-3300 | NA | San Mateo |
| Hitachi Consulting Corp (BR) | Provider of business application implementation, integration, upgrade, and support solutions for application management needs. | | NA | Newark |
| Ibm Research - Almaden (BR) | Provider of computer technology services. The company engages in cloud, mobility, and security services. | 408-927-1080 | NA | San Jose |
| Individual Software Inc (HQ) | Publisher and developer of education, business, and personal productivity software for consumers, schools, businesses, and government. | 925-734-6767 | NA | Livermore |
| Inductive Automation (HQ) | Supplier of web-based industrial automation software. The company offers solutions for end-users and integrators. | 916-456-1045 | 1-10 | Folsom |
| Ineda Systems Inc (RH) | Provider of IoT and wearable applications with multiple connectivity options, based on I/O virtualization and hierarchical computing technologies. | 408-400-7375 | NA | Santa Clara |
| InfinIT Consulting (HQ) | Designer and developer of CNC machining and billet products. The company's products include fire extinguisher brackets, shift knobs, and boat accessories. | 866-364-2007 | NA | Campbell |
| InfoTech Spectrum Inc (HQ) | Provider of integrated creative IT services including IT consulting, advanced technology deployment, and product development. | 408-705-2237 | NA | Santa Clara |

| COMPANY NAME | PRODUCT / SERVICE | PHONE | EMP | CITY |
|---|---|---|---|---|
| iSOA Group Inc (BR) | Provider of business process management, service oriented architecture, and business analytics services to finance, energy, retail, and other sectors. | 925-465-7400 | NA | Walnut Creek |
| ISSE Services (HQ) | Provider of security solutions principally focusing on supporting system implementation and security testing. | 916-670-1082 | 1-10 | Elk Grove |
| Key Business Solutions Inc (HQ) | Provider of software development and database management services. The company also specializes in business intelligence. | 916-646-2080 | 11-50 | Sacramento |
| Klh Consulting Inc (HQ) | Provider of IT consulting, cloud computing, and related business solutions. The company offers services to business executives and professionals. | 707-575-9986 | NA | Santa Rosa |
| Kovarus Inc (HQ) | Provider of integrated business IT solutions. The company also deals with leasing, financing, project management, and related services. | 650-392-7848 | NA | San Ramon |
| Lanlogic (HQ) | Provider of information technology services. The company offers network management and support services. | 925-273-2300 | NA | Livermore |
| LCS Technologies Inc (HQ) | Provider of information services for customers with Oracle software and service needs using resources such as people, hardware, and software. | 855-277-5527 | 1-10 | Gold River |
| Linden Research Inc (HQ) | Designer and developer of digital entertainment solutions. The company's products include Desura, Patterns, and Versu. | 415-243-9000 | NA | San Francisco |
| Metabiota Inc (HQ) | Provider of risk analytics that help protect global health for governments and multinationals, food risk, and financial risk insights. | 415-398-4712 | NA | San Francisco |
| Modius Inc (HQ) | Provider of performance management software. The company serves infrastructure monitoring applications. | 415-655-6700 | NA | San Francisco |
| Monterey Computer Corp (HQ) | Provider of technology and integrated network services. The company offers networking, wireless internet, server hosting, and surveillance services. | 831-646-1147 | NA | Monterey |
| **N** Neudesic LLC (BR) | Provider of technology services. The company focuses on social software, integration platform, and CRM solutions and offers cloud computing services. | 303-248-8300 | 11-50 | Irvine |
| Panasas Inc (HQ) | Provider of scale-out NAS storage system for most demanding workloads in life sciences, media and entertainment, energy, and education environments. | 408-215-6800 | NA | Sunnyvale |
| PeerNova inc (HQ) | Provider of silicon valley-based technology such as distributed systems, networking solutions, big data, compiler technology, and financial services. | 669-400-7800 | NA | San Jose |
| Pierce Washington (HQ) | Provider of systems integration and e-commerce solutions. The company also deals with the development of software tools. | 415-431-8300 | NA | San Francisco |
| Planisware (HQ) | Designer of portfolio management software solutions for product development and research and development organizations. | 415-591-0941 | NA | San Francisco |
| POS Specialists (HQ) | Provider of digital dining solutions. The company is engaged in business consultation, on-site training, and cloud services. | 925-626-3930 | NA | Concord |
| Project Partners Llc (HQ) | Provider of business solutions and information technology systems. The company offers NetSuite, Oracle Fusion Applications, and Primavera. | 650-712-6200 | NA | Half Moon Bay |
| Proxio Inc (HQ) | Provider of digital real estate marketing solutions for agents, brokers and developers. The company serves businesses. | 415-723-1691 | NA | Santa Clara |
| Pulse Secure LLC (HQ) | Provider of product, hardware, partner, and enterprise solutions. The company offers services to the financial services and healthcare industries. | 408-372-9600 | NA | San Jose |
| Quest America Inc (HQ) | Provider of information technology services. The company offers solutions through strategy, consulting, and outsourcing. | 408-492-1650 | NA | San Jose |
| RackWare Inc (HQ) | Provider of disaster prevention and recovery solutions. The company also offers business continuity and virtualization solutions. | 408-430-5821 | NA | San Jose |
| Refresh Your Memory Inc (HQ) | Provider of CNC Machine Tool monitoring and data collection products. The company is also involved in preventive maintenance services. | 408-224-9167 | NA | San Jose |
| Rocket Software Inc (BR) | Developer and designer of software and mobile solutions. The company offers services for the telecommunications industry. | 781-577-4323 | NA | Emeryville |
| SL Corp (HQ) | Provider of monitoring and analytics solutions for middleware-powered applications. The company serves the electrical commodity market. | 415-927-8400 | NA | Corte Madera |
| Software Ag (BR) | Provider of enterprise management and business solutions that include process intelligence and automation, and enterprise architecture. | 800-823-2212 | NA | Santa Clara |
| Space Machine Inc (HQ) | Specializes in academic research. The company focuses on the development of custom models and trading strategies. | 650-669-8629 | NA | Redwood Shores |
| Spreadsheetworld Inc (HQ) | Provider of services for application of MS Excel and VBA tools in various fields. The company focuses on science, engineering, and management. | 818-995-3931 | 1-10 | June Lake |
| Synack (HQ) | Provider of security intelligence solutions. The company offers services to the commercial, industrial, and business sectors. | 855-796-2251 | NA | Redwood City |
| Synergy Business Solutions (HQ) | Provider of technology evaluation, business process improvement, and custom software development services to a wide range of sectors. | 415-263-1843 | NA | San Francisco |
| Tanium Inc (HQ) | Provider of IT operations management, asset visibility, and security hygiene solutions. The company serves the healthcare and retail industries. | 510-704-0202 | NA | Emeryville |

| COMPANY NAME | PRODUCT / SERVICE | PHONE | EMP | CITY |
|---|---|---|---|---|
| The Igneous Group Inc (HQ) | Provider of technology consulting services. The company focuses on web content, application development, and e-commerce. | 831-469-7625 | 1-10 | Santa Cruz |
| Think Connected LLC (HQ) | Provider of data center, consulting, managed, and supplemental information technology services for small and medium-sized businesses. | 877-684-4654 | NA | San Francisco |
| ThreatMetrix (HQ) | Provider of fraud prevention, threat detection, and authentication solutions. The company serves the gaming, media, and insurance industries. | 408-200-5755 | NA | San Jose |
| Untangle (HQ) | Designer and developer of network management software. The company specializes in firewall and Internet management application. | 408-598-4299 | NA | San Jose |
| USWired Inc (HQ) | Provider of computer networking solutions that include cloud hosting, network design and installation, and wireless networks. | 408-669-3522 | NA | San Jose |
| Versa Shore Inc (HQ) | Provider of data warehouse implementation, strategic blueprint creation, project management, and testing consulting services. | 408-874-8330 | NA | Campbell |
| Via Licensing Corp (HQ) | Provider of intellectual property programs and business solutions. The company serves technology companies, entertainment companies, and universities. | 415-645-4700 | NA | San Francisco |
| VinSuite (HQ) | Developer of wine software and serves the consumer sector. The company offers support services to wineries and tasting rooms. | 707-253-7400 | NA | Napa |

## 329 = Systems Design & Integration

| COMPANY NAME | PRODUCT / SERVICE | PHONE | EMP | CITY |
|---|---|---|---|---|
| 2ndEdison Inc (HQ) | Provider of e-Commerce applications. The company also offers business process consulting and design services. | 844-432-8466 | NA | Orinda |
| Advantech Inc (DH) | Provider of system integration, hardware, software, embedded systems, automation products, and logistics support. | 408-519-3898 | NA | Milpitas |
| Agile Global Solutions Inc (HQ) | Provider of business and IT solutions such as custom and enterprise application management and mobile business solutions. | 916-655-7745 | 11-50 | Folsom |
| AGTEK Development Company Inc (HQ) | Developer of high tech surveying, analysis, and control solutions for residential, commercial, transportation, water, energy, and government. | 925-606-8197 | NA | Livermore |
| Alten Calsoft Labs (HQ) | Provider of breed consulting, enterprise IT, and product engineering services for enterprises in healthcare, telecom, and high-tech & retail industries. | 408-755-3000 | NA | Santa Clara |
| Altigen Communications Inc (HQ) | Manufacturer of voice and data telecommunication equipment. The company specializes in hosted business communication solutions. | 408-597-9000 | NA | San Jose |
| Amdocs Ltd (BR) | Provider of customer management and billing solutions software. The company offers services to the industrial sector. | 916-934-7000 | 11-50 | El Dorado Hills |
| Arbor Solution Inc (HQ) | Provider of embedded computing and networking solutions for the transportation, medical, automation, and military segments. | 408-452-8900 | NA | Fremont |
| Arterys Inc (DH) | Developer of medical imaging cloud platform. The company specializes in diagnostic platform to make healthcare more accurate and data driven. | 650-319-7230 | NA | San Francisco |
| Artifex Software Inc (HQ) | Provider of software solutions for host based applications. The company also focuses on embedded printer markets. | 415-492-9861 | NA | Novato |
| Asi Controls (HQ) | Manufacturer of direct digital controls for HVAC and light industrial marketplace. The company also offers networking products and unitary controls. | 925-866-8808 | NA | San Ramon |
| Asteelflash (BR) | Provider of electronic manufacturing services. The company offers engineering design, contract manufacturing, and delivery services. | 510-440-2840 | NA | Fremont |
| Audible Magic Corp (HQ) | Developer of media identification and synchronization, content registration, and copyright compliance solutions. | 408-399-6405 | NA | Los Gatos |
| Auriga Corp (HQ) | Provider of technology consulting services for electric power, telecommunications, transportation, and information technology systems. | 408-946-5400 | NA | Milpitas |
| BBI Engineering Inc (HQ) | Designer and installer of audiovisual, multimedia, teleconferencing and data systems for museums, aquariums, zoos, schools, and universities. | 415-695-9555 | NA | San Francisco |
| Beganto Inc (HQ) | Provider of web-based applications and support services. The company specializes in application, component, design, and sales engineering. | 510-280-0554 | NA | Santa Clara |
| Bkf Engineers (BR) | Provider of civil engineering consulting, and land surveying services. The company serves business organizations. | 925-940-2200 | NA | Walnut Creek |
| Bkf Engineers (BR) | Provider of civil engineering, design, surveying, design, transportation, and entitlement support services. | 408-467-9100 | NA | San Jose |
| Blackstone Technology Group Inc (HQ) | Provider of IT solutions, commercial, and government consulting, staffing services, and trellis natural gas transaction management web solution. | 415-837-1400 | NA | San Francisco |
| Brekeke Software Inc (HQ) | Developer of session initiation protocol software products for internet protocol network communication needs. | 650-401-6633 | NA | San Mateo |
| Bright Pattern Inc (HQ) | Provider of enterprise contact center application for blended multi-channel interactions. The company offers products based on modern technology. | 650-529-4099 | NA | San Bruno |
| Busse Design Usa Inc (HQ) | Provider of interface design services. The company's services include website design and application user interface. | 415-689-8090 | NA | Oakland |
| Cjs Labs (HQ) | Provider of electronic design, consulting, engineering, and test automation programming assistance services. | 415-923-9535 | NA | San Francisco |
| Claresco Corp (HQ) | Provider of design and implementation services for customized business software. The company serves multi-national firms. | 510-528-0238 | NA | Berkeley |

| COMPANY NAME | PRODUCT / SERVICE | PHONE | EMP | CITY |
|---|---|---|---|---|
| Coastside Net (HQ) | Provider of internet access and technology solutions. The company also offers website services including website hosting, design, and development. | 650-712-5900 | NA | El Granada |
| Compudata Inc (HQ) | Provider of sales, accounting, and manufacturing software. The company especially caters to businesses. | 415-495-3422 | NA | San Francisco |
| Computers & Structures Inc (HQ) | Provider of integrated design, analysis, assessment, drafting of building systems, and related support services. | 510-649-2200 | NA | Walnut Creek |
| Configure Inc (HQ) | Provider of communication consulting services. The company specializes in network design, transport service implementation, and project management. | 877-408-2636 | NA | San Jose |
| Cooper (HQ) | Designer of kiosks, medical devices and software, smartphone, IT tools, websites, irrigation, supply chain management, and financial services system. | 415-267-3500 | NA | San Francisco |
| Criterion Network Services Inc (HQ) | Provider of network design, system integration, configuration, and remote network management services. | 650-947-7755 | NA | Los Altos |
| Current Controls Inc (HQ) | Designer and manufacturer of control panels for OEMs in many sectors. The company also offers PLC programming, system integration, and other services. | 916-630-5507 | 1-10 | Rocklin |
| Customweather Inc (HQ) | Provider of industry solutions. The company offers hurricane tracking, developer tools, and marine forecasts. | 415-777-3303 | NA | San Francisco |
| Cybermanor (HQ) | Designer of internet connected home electronic and networking solutions. The company also offers installation services. | 408-399-3331 | NA | Los Gatos |
| D-Tools Inc (HQ) | Developer and marketer of software to streamline processes which accompany the integration and installation of low-voltage systems. | 925-681-2326 | NA | Concord |
| d2m Interactive (HQ) | Provider of web development, management, and e-commerce services. The company also focuses on marketing. | 408-315-6802 | 1-10 | Los Gatos |
| Diamond Systems Corp (HQ) | Supplier of SBCs, embedded-ready subsystems, and system expansion modules targeting real-world applications. | 650-810-2500 | NA | Sunnyvale |
| Dorado Software Inc (HQ) | Provider of inventory, monitoring, storage management, network configuration, and mobile back hauling solutions. | 916-673-1100 | 1-10 | El Dorado Hills |
| Douglas Electronics Inc (HQ) | Provider of CAD/CAM tools for personal computers. The company specializes in custom board manufacturing and electronic design software products. | 510-483-8770 | NA | San Leandro |
| Exxact Corp (HQ) | Supplier of workstation graphic cards and solutions. The company also offers servers, HPC clusters, and computing software. | 510-226-7366 | NA | Fremont |
| Game Your Game Inc (HQ) | Developer of digital tracking system such as automatic shot tracking and hands-free game tracking device to get the insights to improve the game. | 888-245-3433 | NA | San Francisco |
| Global Presenter (BR) | Designer and builder of meeting room communication systems. The company is a provider of design, delivery, and system integration solutions. | 408-526-0221 | NA | San Jose |
| Golden Valley Systems Inc (HQ) | Provider of enterprise integration solutions. The company offers technical, IT consulting, and green energy services. | 408-934-5898 | NA | Milpitas |
| Good Dog Design (HQ) | Provider of digital designing services. The company offers web development & designing and mobile application services. | 415-383-0110 | NA | Mill Valley |
| Ibus Corp (HQ) | Manufacturer and provider of industrial computers. The company also specializes in prototyping and quality control. | 408-450-7880 | NA | Santa Clara |
| Icube Information International (HQ) | Publisher of software work flow based management systems, documentation, inventory processing, and revision tracking services. | 510-683-8928 | NA | Fremont |
| Infoyogi LLC (HQ) | Provider of information technology solutions for software application development and systems integration. | 408-850-1700 | NA | Santa Clara |
| Input Optics Inc (HQ) | Provider of integration solutions for dental practice. The company also offers complimentary assessments and web services. | 650-969-3108 | NA | Mountain View |
| IntelinAir Inc (HQ) | Provider of aerial imagery analytics such as image analysis and change detection and deep learning and neural networks for farmers. | 818-445-2339 | NA | San Jose |
| JAMIS Software Corp (HQ) | Provider of job-cost, billing, and accounting systems and solutions. The company caters to the government contractors. | 800-655-2647 | 11-50 | San Diego |
| Jitterbit Inc (HQ) | Focuses on application integration solutions for aerospace and defense, life sciences, pharmaceuticals, and financial services. | 877-852-3500 | NA | Alameda |
| Kaazing Corp (HQ) | Provider of software services. The company's IoT gateway is used by mobile users, marketplaces, and machines to connect and communicate in real-time. | 877-522-9464 | NA | San Jose |
| Kovarus Inc (HQ) | Provider of integrated business IT solutions. The company also deals with leasing, financing, project management, and related services. | 650-392-7848 | NA | San Ramon |
| Matrix Computer Solutions Inc (HQ) | Provider of computer and technology solutions for residential and business customers. The company also offers data backup, repair, and other services. | 415-331-3600 | NA | Sausalito |
| Media Net Link Inc (HQ) | Provider of web business solutions. The company focuses on application development, systems intergration, website design, and project management. | 866-563-5152 | NA | Oakland |
| Michael Patrick Partners (HQ) | Provider of branding solutions. The company also offers logo design, portfolio creation, web content, and marketing services. | 650-327-3185 | NA | San Francisco |

| COMPANY NAME | PRODUCT / SERVICE | PHONE | EMP | CITY |
|---|---|---|---|---|
| Mirabilis Design Inc (HQ) | Provider of systems engineering solutions for performance analysis and architecture exploration of electronics and real-time software. | 408-844-3234 | NA | Sunnyvale |
| Mistral Solutions Inc (HQ) | Provider of technology design and systems engineering solutions. The company's solutions include hardware board design and embedded software development. | 408-705-2240 | NA | Fremont |
| Mobitor Corp (HQ) | Provider of mobility software, connectivity, and information solutions. The company serves the aerospace, aviation, and manufacturing industries. | 925-464-7700 | NA | Walnut Creek |
| Mobiveil Inc (HQ) | Provider of technology solutions. The company's products include Silicon IP and COTS Modules and offers IC design and embedded software services. | 408-212-9512 | NA | Milpitas |
| Mondo Media Inc (HQ) | Provider of gaming solutions. The company's store features men's and women's T-shirts, smart phone cases, and related supplies. | 415-865-2700 | NA | San Francisco |
| Monterey Computer Corp (HQ) | Provider of technology and integrated network services. The company offers networking, wireless internet, server hosting, and surveillance services. | 831-646-1147 | NA | Monterey |
| **N** MSC Software (BR) | Developer of simulation software for acoustics, thermal analysis, and other needs. The company also offers software implementation and systems design services. | 714-540-8900 | 11-50 | Newport Beach |
| Nada Technologies Inc (HQ) | Provider of enterprise Oracle applications. The company also offers business intelligence solutions. | 650-678-4666 | NA | Danville |
| Netformx Inc (HQ) | Designer and builder of solutions for the networking and service providers. The company specializes in desktop and cloud applications. | 408-423-6600 | NA | San Jose |
| Netpace Inc (HQ) | Provider of consulting, cloud computing, data base management, and proprietary development services. | 925-543-7760 | NA | San Ramon |
| Network Design Associates Inc (HQ) | Provider of engineering services for computer systems. The company's services include network design, implementation, support, and maintenance. | 916-853-1632 | 1-10 | Citrus Heights |
| New Tech Solutions Inc (HQ) | Provider of technology solutions. The company caters to networking, security, and communication manufacturers. | 510-353-4070 | NA | Fremont |
| Nextaxiom Technology Inc (HQ) | Provider of testing, certification, and other professional services. The company offers work management and scheduling solutions. | 415-373-1890 | NA | San Francisco |
| Novani Llc (HQ) | Provider of disaster prevention and recovery solutions. The company also offers business continuity and virtualization solutions. | 415-731-1111 | NA | San Francisco |
| Nuvation Engineering (HQ) | Provider of electronic engineering services. The company focuses on product design, embedded software development, and single integrity analysis. | 408-228-5580 | NA | Sunnyvale |
| Office Information Systems (HQ) | Provider of computer network design and consulting services. The company serves small and medium sized organizations and law firms. | 510-568-7900 | NA | Oakland |
| Opal Soft Inc (HQ) | Provider of communications equipment installation and networking. The company's services include application development, network management, and maintenance. | 408-267-2211 | NA | Sunnyvale |
| Opsol Integrators Inc (HQ) | Provider of universal messaging, data integration, and encryption products. The company serves banks, retail, telecom, and other sectors. | 408-364-9915 | NA | Campbell |
| Outside Technology (HQ) | Provider of automated reservation systems. The company mainly caters to the outdoor recreation industry. | 415-488-4909 | NA | San Anselmo |
| Park Computer Systems Inc (HQ) | Provider of mobile products and services. The company also offers sales content automation and staff augmentation services. | 510-353-1700 | NA | Newark |
| Portola Systems (HQ) | Provider of computer network engineering and integration services. The company also specializes in IT consultation. | 707-824-8800 | NA | Sebastopol |
| POS Specialists (HQ) | Provider of digital dining solutions. The company is engaged in business consultation, on-site training, and cloud services. | 925-626-3930 | NA | Concord |
| PubMatic Inc (HQ) | Developer of marketing automation software. The company deals with the planning of media campaigns and offers services to publishers. | 650-331-3485 | NA | Redwood City |
| Punchcut LLC (HQ) | Provider of interface designs. The company offers mid, small, large, micro, and medium screen solutions. | 415-445-8855 | NA | San Francisco |
| Qumu Inc (BR) | Provider of web casting, marketing, event, and other professional services. The company offers enterprise video solutions. | 650-396-8530 | NA | San Bruno |
| R&D Logic Inc (HQ) | Developer of performance management software for R&D focused companies. The company offers implementation and training services. | 650-356-9207 | NA | San Mateo |
| R-Computer (HQ) | Provider of computer solutions for small and medium-sized companies. The company also offers lifetime product guarantees and sales consultation. | 925-798-4884 | NA | Concord |
| RackWare Inc (HQ) | Provider of disaster prevention and recovery solutions. The company also offers business continuity and virtualization solutions. | 408-430-5821 | NA | San Jose |
| Rocket Communications Inc (HQ) | Developer of user interface, visual, and icon design services for software and related applications. | 415-863-0101 | NA | San Francisco |
| Sanah Inc (HQ) | Provider of IT services such as IT strategy consulting, systems integration, and custom application development. | 888-306-1942 | 1-10 | Sacramento |
| Savari Inc (HQ) | Provider of communications technology solutions. The company focuses on connecting cars to traffic lights, pedestrians, and smartphones. | 408-833-6369 | NA | Santa Clara |

| COMPANY NAME | PRODUCT / SERVICE | PHONE | EMP | CITY |
|---|---|---|---|---|
| Silver Spring Networks Inc (HQ) | Provider of earthwork optimization solutions principally focusing on stress and property measurements for geotechnics. | 669-770-4000 | NA | San Jose |
| Spreadsheetworld Inc (HQ) | Provider of services for application of MS Excel and VBA tools in various fields. The company focuses on science, engineering, and management. | 818-995-3931 | 1-10 | June Lake |
| SS Papadopulos & Associates Inc (BR) | Provider of web-based applications for customized online communities. The company serves business enterprises. | 415-773-0400 | NA | San Francisco |
| Symplectic Engineering Corp (HQ) | Provider of custom computational mechanics solutions. The company is involved in consulting services and it serves the industrial sector. | 510-528-1251 | NA | Berkeley |
| Synapse Design (HQ) | Provider of embedded software design services. The company also offers test bench analysis and block and chip level verification services. | 408-850-3640 | NA | Santa Clara |
| Systemacs (HQ) | Provider of solutions for upgrading or setting up networks which include hardware, software, and routers. | 650-329-9745 | NA | Palo Alto |
| Tanium Inc (HQ) | Provider of IT operations management, asset visibility, and security hygiene solutions. The company serves the healthcare and retail industries. | 510-704-0202 | NA | Emeryville |
| Tesco Controls Inc (HQ) | Manufacturer of instrumentation, control systems, and service pedestals for water and traffic sectors. The company offers system integration services. | 916-395-8800 | 11-50 | Sacramento |
| The AIS Group (HQ) | Developer and provider of accounting software. The company also specializes in system integration services. | | NA | Napa |
| V5 Systems (HQ) | Provider of outdoor security and computing platforms. The company offers services to the government, military, and law enforcement industries. | 844-604-7350 | NA | Fremont |
| Virtual Driver Interactive (HQ) | Manufacturer of virtual training simulators. The company serves schools, corporations, schools, and hospitals. | 877-746-8332 | 1-10 | El Dorado Hills |
| Virtual Instruments (HQ) | Developer of storage area network and virtual infrastructure solutions. The company serves healthcare, federal, and outsourcing & hosting sectors. | 408-579-4000 | NA | San Jose |
| Xerox Corp (BR) | Provider of color printers and copiers. The company also specializes in document management solutions. | 510-460-4161 | NA | Walnut Creek |
| Zmanda - A Carbonite Co (HQ) | Provider of open source backup and recovery software solutions. The company's applications include centralized backup of file systems and applications. | 408-732-3208 | 51-200 | Sunnyvale |

## 330 = Biomaterials

| COMPANY NAME | PRODUCT / SERVICE | PHONE | EMP | CITY |
|---|---|---|---|---|
| Aduro Biotech Inc (HQ) | Provider of engineered immunotherapy for the treatment of cancer. The company is engaged in clinical trials. | 510-848-4400 | NA | Berkeley |
| Antibody Solutions (HQ) | Provider of antibody products and services. The company serves biotechnology, diagnostic and pharmaceutical companies. | 650-938-4300 | NA | Sunnyvale |
| Bell Biosystems Inc (HQ) | Provider of biotechnology services. The company develops proteins targeted to kill specific bacteria but cause minimal collateral damage. | 877-420-3621 | NA | Berkeley |
| Biocheck Inc (HQ) | Provider of custom immunoassay development, antibody conjugation and purification, and contract manufacturing services. | 650-573-1968 | NA | S San Francisco |
| Biocision Llc (HQ) | Provider of cell freezing and cell thawing systems, and related supplies. The company's products are used in research applications. | 800-367-4887 | NA | San Rafael |
| MTI California Inc (HQ) | Specializes in designing and validating manufacturing controls. The company offers services to biotech companies. | 925-937-1500 | NA | Walnut Creek |
| Novozymes Inc (BR) | Provider of industrial biotechnology solutions for the food and beverage, agriculture, textile, and pulp and paper industries. | 530-757-8100 | 11-50 | Davis |

## 331 = Sensors

| COMPANY NAME | PRODUCT / SERVICE | PHONE | EMP | CITY |
|---|---|---|---|---|
| Allied Fire Protection (HQ) | Designer and manufacturer of fire protection sprinkler systems. The company also offers installation services. | 510-533-5516 | NA | Oakland |
| Cellecta Inc (HQ) | Provider of custom and contract solutions for high-throughput genetic screening needs and also develops therapeutic targets and drugs. | 650-938-3910 | NA | Mountain View |
| G4s Secure Solutions (usa) Inc (BR) | Provider of security management solutions such as compliance and investigations, disaster and emergency, and fraud abatement. | 408-453-4133 | NA | San Jose |
| MTI California Inc (HQ) | Specializes in designing and validating manufacturing controls. The company offers services to biotech companies. | 925-937-1500 | NA | Walnut Creek |

## 332 = Hybrids

| COMPANY NAME | PRODUCT / SERVICE | PHONE | EMP | CITY |
|---|---|---|---|---|
| 4d Molecular Therapeutics Llc (HQ) | Provider of gene therapy product research & development for the treatment of genetic diseases such as diabetes, arthritis, and heart failure. | 510-505-2680 | NA | Emeryville |
| Bell Biosystems Inc (HQ) | Provider of biotechnology services. The company develops proteins targeted to kill specific bacteria but cause minimal collateral damage. | 877-420-3621 | NA | Berkeley |
| Bioneer Inc (BR) | Developer of molecular biology products and technologies for life science researchers in academia, biotech, and pharmaceutical companies. | 877-264-4300 | NA | Oakland |
| Centrillion Technology Holdings Ltd (HQ) | Developer of genomics solutions for the researchers, physicians, and consumers. The company also offers clinical testing and consumer genomics services. | 650-618-0111 | NA | Palo Alto |
| Dnamito Inc (HQ) | Provider of DNA technology and cloud platform to enable cancer treatment and early prediction of chronic disease thus vastly improving patient care. | 650-687-0899 | NA | Palo Alto |

| COMPANY NAME | PRODUCT / SERVICE | PHONE | EMP | CITY |
|---|---|---|---|---|
| Genapsys Inc (HQ) | Developer of DNA sequencing to enable a paradigm shift in genomic diagnostics. The company specializes in GENIUS system that has footprint of Apple iPad. | 650-330-1096 | NA | Redwood City |
| Karius Inc (HQ) | Provider of microbial genomics diagnostics. The company focusses on transforming infectious disease diagnostics with genomics. | 866-452-7487 | NA | Redwood City |
| MTI California Inc (HQ) | Specializes in designing and validating manufacturing controls. The company offers services to biotech companies. | 925-937-1500 | NA | Walnut Creek |
| Natera Inc (HQ) | Provider of prenatal testing services. The company specializes in non-invasive prenatal testing, genetic carrier screening and paternity testing. | 650-249-9090 | 501-1000 | San Carlos |
| SwitchGear Genomics Inc (HQ) | Focuses on custom cloning, pathway screening, target validation, sequence variant assay, and custom mutagenesis services. | 760-431-1263 | 11-50 | Carlsbad |

### 333 = Antihistamine

| COMPANY NAME | PRODUCT / SERVICE | PHONE | EMP | CITY |
|---|---|---|---|---|
| Acelrx Pharmaceuticals Inc (HQ) | Manufacturer of pharmaceuticals. The company provides therapies for treatment of acute and breakthrough pain. | 650-216-3500 | NA | Redwood City |
| Aridis Pharmaceuticals Llc (HQ) | Focuses on anti-infective alternatives to conventional antibiotics. The company offers services to the pharmaceutical sector. | 408-385-1742 | NA | San Jose |
| Coherus Biosciences (HQ) | Developer of biosimilars and it serves the global marketplace. The company is engaged in delivery services. | 800-794-5434 | NA | Redwood City |
| Credence MedSystems Inc (HQ) | Provider of pharmaceutical products. The company specializes in single-dose injectable medications in pre-filled syringes. | 844-263-3797 | NA | Menlo Park |
| Emsl Analytical Inc (BR) | Provider of laboratory analytical testing services. The company specializes in a wide range of environmental, material and forensic testing. | 510-895-3675 | NA | San Leandro |
| Gliamed Inc (HQ) | Provider of drugs for the regeneration of skin, cardiac muscle, cartilage, bone, brain and other tissues. | 408-457-8828 | NA | San Jose |

### 334 = Laser

| COMPANY NAME | PRODUCT / SERVICE | PHONE | EMP | CITY |
|---|---|---|---|---|
| Peridot Corp (HQ) | Provider of design for manufacturing and packaging. The company also manufacturers of medical components, miniature component and general product prototypes. | 925-461-8830 | NA | Pleasanton |
| PinPointe (HQ) | Developer of laser light-based therapies for treating nail fungus. The company serves patients in patients in Australia and other countries. | 530-809-1970 | 1-10 | Chico |
| Relucent Solutions Llc (HQ) | Manufacturer of medical devices. The company is involved in laser cutting, precision manufacturing, wire crimping, and related services. | 800-630-7704 | NA | Santa Rosa |
| Sciton Inc (HQ) | Provider of laser and light source solutions. The company's products include JOULE, BBL, ClearSense, Halo, and more. | 650-493-9155 | NA | Palo Alto |